Symbols of plenty – bread and wine, meat and eggs (*Phot. Nicolas*)

New Larousse Gastronomique

The World's Greatest Cookery Reference Book

New Larousse Gastronomique

The World's Greateșt Cookery Reference Book

by
Prosper Montagné

Preface by
Robert J. Courtine

Text translated from the French by
Nina Froud, Patience Gray,
Maud Murdoch and Barbara Macrae Taylor

Additional material for this edition
translated by Marion Hunter

Edited by Janet Dunbar

HAMLYN
LONDON · NEW YORK · SYDNEY · TORONTO

Originally published under the title
Nouveau Larousse Gastronomique
by Prosper Montagné

Seventh impression 1983
Published by The Hamlyn Publishing Group Limited
London - New York - Sydney - Toronto
Astronaut House, Feltham, Middlesex, England

ISBN 0 600 36545 X

Filmset by Keyspools Limited, Golborne, Lancashire
Printed in Italy by New Interlitho S.p.A. - Milan

Preface

In his preface to the first edition of *Larousse Gastronomique* Escoffier wrote:

'The history of a nation's table is a reflection of the civilisation of that nation. To show the changes in the order and serving of meals from century to century, to describe and comment on the progress of the French cuisine, is to paint a picture of the many stages through which a nation has evolved since the distant times when, as a weak tribe, men lived in dark caves, eating wild roots, raw fish and the still pulsating flesh of animals killed with the spear.

'It is this history that is the subject of *Larousse Gastronomique*, in which Prosper Montagné has outlined in some thousand pages all the improvements brought to the culinary art from prehistoric times to the present day. Presented in the form of a dictionary, it sums up all that has been achieved by the science of alimentation, and everything in it has been minutely studied and described.

'Those who make a profession of gastronomy will find in this book matter for comparison between what used to be the art of good eating and what it is today. Housewives will be particularly interested in the evolution of the table through the ages, its refinements modified in each epoch – to a certain extent by the exigencies of reigning fashions. Professional cooks, both men and women, will be able to draw inspiration from the principles of a culinary technique founded on the universally recognised knowledge and authority of the author. The rest of the book and the recipes are enlivened by attractive anecdotes and legendary tales.'

The work of Prosper Montagné (and of Dr. Gottschalk, who helped him notably with the historical, scientific and medical material) is an historic work which it is proper to revive today, adding new gastronomic treats while retaining its style and balance. Indeed, if the history of cooking, which is inseparable from the domestic history of the people, hasn't changed and if the great recipes remain the same despite the tremendous simplification of modern cooking, on the other hand dietetics is a new science which has rediscovered – in order to endorse them – the broad outlines of ancient practice, somewhat forgotten since the beginning of this century. It is essential to incorporate into this work the lessons learnt from a combination of ancient wisdom and modern research.

Legislation, as well, has modified the basic nutrition of twentieth-century man, and if the gourmet can still, with justification, reject certain forms of progress, he must nevertheless take note of them. Moreover, taking his pleasures of the table where he can find them, he has to recognise, for instance, that deep freezing or freeze-drying (words which were unknown to Prosper Montagné and his contemporaries) offer to the appetite as well as to the greed of man many satisfying solutions.

The laws pertaining to wine and vines have considerably altered the wine scene in France. Chefs in general are little interested in wine, and this is doubtless why hitherto *Larousse Gastronomique* has neglected the cellar. My friends and I have made a better selection from French wines and those from other countries, bearing in mind the latest rules and regulations.

Jean Desmur, who may deserve the title 'Pic de La Mirandole de la gastronomie', took upon himself the duty of recounting the details of domestic history and gastronomical folklore, and because one must be up to date with what one loves, we list the food and wine associations which have multiplied since the last war.

All this rounds out the original work without either changing the direction or the balance. This is at least our profound wish.

It remains for me to introduce and thank the contributors of this new edition:

Madeleine Decure, director of the publication *Cuisine et vins de France*
Jean D. Arnaboldi, chief editor of the publication *Bien Vivre*
François d'Athis, general secretary of the *Revue du vin de France*
Henry Clos-Jouve, of l'Académie Rabelais
Jean Desmur
Pierre Neuville

Robert J. Courtine

Useful Facts and Figures

Throughout this work quantities have been given in metric measures, followed by the Imperial and American measures in brackets. Exact conversion from Imperial to metric measures does not usually give very convenient working quantities so the metric measures have been rounded off into units of 25 grams. The table below shows recommended equivalents.

Ounces/fluid ounces	Approx. g. and ml. to nearest whole figure	Recommended conversion to nearest unit of 25
1	28	25
2	57	50
3	85	75
4	113	100
5 (¼ pint)	142	150
6	170	175
7	198	200
8	226	225
9	255	250
10 (½ pint)	283	275
11	311	300
12	340	350
13	368	375
14	396	400
15 (¾ pint)	428	425
16 (1 lb.)	456	450
17	486	475
18	512	500
19	541	550
20 (1 pint)	569	575

Note: The British pint measures 20 fluid ounces whereas the American pint equals 16 fluid ounces.

When converting quantities over 20 oz. first add the appropriate figures in the centre column, then adjust to the nearest unit of 25. This method of conversion gives good results in nearly all cases, but in certain pastry and cake recipes a more accurate conversion is necessary to produce a balanced recipe. Quantities for such ingredients as vegetables, fruit, meat and fish which are not critical are rounded off to the nearest quarter of a kg. as this is how they are likely to be purchased.

Liquid measures The millilitre being a very small unit of measurement, decilitres (units of 100 ml.) have been used for liquid measures. For quantities of 1¾ pints or over, litres and fractions of a litre have been used.

Linear measures The metric unit of length is the metre which is roughly equal to 3 feet 3 inches. There are 100 centimetres (cm.) to the metre, 10 millimetres to the centimetre and 1 inch is 2.54 cm. Measurements have been rounded up or down to the nearest whole centimetre, so a 9-inch cake tin has been converted to a 23-cm. tin (exactly 22.86 cm.).

Oven temperatures The following chart shows recommended oven temperatures in degrees Celsius, and Fahrenheit, together with the Gas Mark.

	°C	°F	Gas Mark
Very cool	110	225	¼
	120	250	½
Cool	140	275	1
	150	300	2
Moderate	160	325	3
	180	350	4
Moderately hot	190	375	5
	200	400	6
Hot	220	425	7
	230	450	8
Very hot	240	475	9

Reading List

Compiled by Janet Dunbar

Cordon Bleu Cookbook *HUME, Rosemary, and DOWNES, Muriel*
Hamlyn/Phoebus £2.95
The authors are principals of a noted school of cookery; this title is a sound book for the hostess incorporating recipes for freezing and entertaining.

Recipes for Boulestin *BOULESTIN, Marcel*
Heinemann £2.50
Haute cuisine recipes as served in his famous restaurant, by a master-chef in the great French tradition.

Dinner Parties *HUME, Rosemary, and DOWNES, Muriel*
Macdonald £2.50
Few people give formal dinner parties nowadays, but this book may well set a trend – the recipes and illustrations make one dream of gracious living.

The Hamlyn Encyclopedia of Freezing *ELLIS, Audrey*
Hamlyn £4.95
An up-to-date comprehensive book, written by a leading authority on food freezing.

Freezer and Fridge Cookery *NORWAK, Mary*
Ward Lock 90p
Clearly set out instructions for packaging, labelling and cooking for the freezer, and using the refrigerator to the best advantage.

The Constance Spry Cookery Book *SPRY, Constance, and HUME, Rosemary*
Pan paperback (in a case) £2.95
Two well-known personalities in *haute cuisine* combine in an outstanding book of good cookery, with special emphasis on herbs and vegetables.

500 Recipes for Vegetarian Cookery *FISHER, Patty*
Hamlyn paperback 50p
Vegetarian cookery is often thought of as tasteless and unimaginative. This book shows that meatless cookery can be varied and interesting.

Vegetarian Cookery Made Easy *VEZZA, Veronica*
Clifton £1.25
An excellent introduction to vegetarian cookery.

Hamlyn's Fondue Cookbook *SPENCER, Jill*
Hamlyn £2.95
Suggestions for a pleasantly informal way of entertaining friends, with 'audience participation'.

Tante Heidi's Swiss Kitchen *BORAR, Eve Marie* (adapted Sheila Watson)
Kaye and Ward £2.25
Real Swiss cooking is unusual and delicious. While borrowing ideas from its French and German-speaking cantons, Switzerland has a cuisine of its own which visitors find memorable.

New Casserole Treasury *BRUNNER, Lousene Rousseau*
Pan paperback 60p
A good range of practical recipes for casserole cookery, including suggestions for using frozen foods.

All About Good Cooking *STREET, Myra, and TODD, Jane*
Hamlyn £1.95
Practical advice on modern appliances and how to use them. Attractive colour plates and helpful information about foods suitable for freezing. An admirable present for a bride.

Leave It To Cook *ATTERBURY, Stella*
Penguin paperback 60p
An excellent book – unless you are the forgetful type, who leaves it to cook until tomorrow's supper. Recommended for the busy bee and the harassed housewife.

Fish Cookery *GRIGSON, Jane*
Penguin paperback 80p
Comprehensive selection of the various ways of cooking many kinds of fish.

International Fish Dishes *FROUD, Nina, and LO, Tamara*
Sphere paperback 65p
Basic recipes that can be adapted to the fish available from our own shores. Also useful for recognising foreign fish dishes when you are abroad.

The Adventurous Fish Cook *LASSALLE, George*
Macmillan £3.95
Adventurous is the right word: these fish and shellfish recipes are challenging and exciting, a world away from the fried-fish-and-chips school. The information about shellfish is especially good, enticing you to branch out further than supermarket packets of frozen prawns.

Recipes from Country Inns and Restaurants *SMITH, Delia*
Ebury Press £3.50
Delectable dishes collected by the TV and radio cook when she ate her way round some of the best inns and restaurants in the English countryside. Full of photographs of the places visited; an enchanting book.

Use Your Loaf *NORMAN, Ursel*
Collins paperback £1.50
First-rate guide to breadmaking, including methods in other lands.

Cake Decorating and Sugarcraft *WALLACE, Evelyn*
Hamlyn £3.75
The delightful cover is a fitting introduction to a book that explores a vast field of artistic sugar decoration, from buns to wedding cakes. The step-by-step directions and colour

Herbs and spices: from left to right – juniper berries, cinnamon, basil, paprika; aniseed, cayenne, *ajoujoli*, coriander; curry, caraway, *raz el hamout*, rosemary; pepper, ginger, fennel, sweet pepper; celery, saffron, cloves, sage (*Hédiard. Phot. Larousse*)

photographs encourage you to experiment beyond icing little fairy cakes and sticking a glacé cherry on top.

Larousse Dictionary of Wines of the World
Hamlyn £5.95
The most authoritative and wide-ranging book on wines, with descriptions of the vineyards, the process of making wine, and the all-important subject of vintages. A guide for the novice no less than a bible for the connoisseur.

500 Recipes for Cocktails and Mixed Drinks *BRENNER, Felix*
Hamlyn paperback 60p
Good collection, with unusual as well as familiar combinations of drinks. A direct incentive to mix your drinks!

Cooking with Wine *McDOUALL, Robin*
Penguin paperback 60p
Suggestions from a much-travelled gourmet who has a special knowledge of Mediterranean cookery.

Ices Galore *BUSH and RUBENSTEIN*
André Deutsch £2.95
The first and last word on this delicious subject, by two practitioners who are as expert on their own kind of ice as John Currie is on his.

Mixer and Blender Cookbook *STREET, Myra*
Hamlyn £1.50
Mixing and blending it smoothly, and saving time and energy in the process. A sensible guide to making established favourites more appetising by using modern techniques.

The Best of Eliza Acton *ed. RAY, Elizabeth*
Pan paperback 75p
Selected recipes from the famous Victorian's classic cookbook, 'modern' in her day and equally modern in ours.

The Hamlyn Pressure Cookbook *TODD, Jane*
Hamlyn £1.75
A clear and comprehensive guide to pressure cooking, the method that conserves the vital element in food. Vegetables take a very few minutes to cook and no vitamins are lost. Meat is pot-roasted in its own juices, which means real flavour – and a spectacular saving in fuel costs.

Great Dishes of the World in Colour *ed. FELLER, Jennifer*
Hamlyn £3.95
A treasure house of classic world cookery: American, European, Chinese, Far Eastern, etc. Each section has been contributed by an expert in the area, and the exotic is balanced by traditional cuisine. An encouragement for perfection in cooking.

The Times Calendar Cookbook *STEWART, Katie*
Hamlyn £5.95
Beautifully illustrated and presented, this book has been devised by one of the best known cookery writers. A perfect kitchen companion throughout the year, full of imaginative ideas.

Everyday Cookbook *PATTEN, Marguerite*
Hamlyn £2.50
An ideal cookbook for the busy housewife or bachelor cook. Over 1,000 recipes and 100 colour pictures so you can *see* just how the finished dish should look.

Cooking for You *CARRIER, Robert*
Hamlyn £3.50
A book by a master of his craft covering recipes for appetisers through to cooking with wine. Every dish is illustrated in colour.

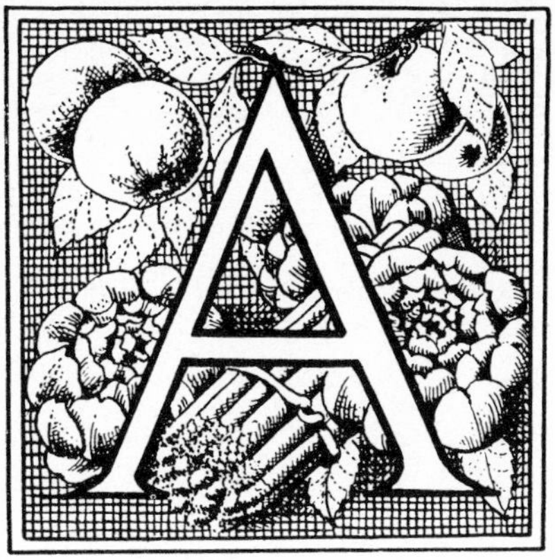

ABAISSE – A term used in French pastry-making to describe a piece (or sheet) of rolled-out pastry. It is also used to describe a layer of sponge cake or biscuit.

An abaisse of pastry

ABAT-FAIM (Hunger-killer) – A substantial dish served early in the meal.

ABATTE (Beater) – A popular corruption of the French word *battre* (to beat). An *abatte* is a rather thick, broad, double-edged knife used for flattening meat.

ABEL-MUSK. AMBRETTE – An aromatic plant grown in Martinique, the seeds of which have a very strong, musty smell. In India these seeds are mixed with coffee to give it a special aroma, and to heighten its stimulating properties.

Ambrette is also the name of an ambergris-scented variety of pear.

ABLUTIONS, TABLE. ABLUTIONS DE TABLE – The custom of passing bowls of water to guests at table, to rinse their fingers at the end of a meal, or after eating certain dishes with the fingers, goes back to earliest antiquity. It was a common practice with the ancient Egyptians, the Greeks and the Romans, who not only washed their hands before the meal but also between the courses.

'This practice, common to all ancient people, is explained by the fact that in those days food was taken with the fingers. A servant poured the contents of a vessel (usually scented water) over the fingers of the guest. In other circumstances, hands were simply washed in a basin.' (*Vie privée des anciens*, by Louis Nicolas Menard)

Recipe for finger-bowl water. RECETTE POUR UNE EAU D'ABLUTION – 'Boil a handful of sage in water. Pour off the resulting liquid and cool until tepid. Camomile or marjoram may be substituted for the sage or, better still, a handful of rosemary boiled with the skin of an orange. Bay leaves are also good.' (*le Ménagier de Paris*, fourteenth century)

ABOMASUM. CAILLETTE – Fourth stomach of the ruminants. Dried *caillette* (solid rennet) or its extract, liquid rennet (obtained by infusion) is used in the cheese-making industry for coagulating milk.

Caillette is also the name given in the Ardèche and La Drôme to a large sausage stuffed with a mixture of minced pig's liver and chard leaves.

ABONDANCE – Wine diluted with water.

This word ironically describes the drink which in days gone by used to be served in schools or colleges, where wine was scarce and water abundant. The term is used, deprecatingly, of watered-down wine.

ABROTONITE – Herb-flavoured wine. The ancients used to macerate a sort of mugwort called *abrotanum* in this wine to enhance its flavour.

ABSINTH. ABSINTHE – Liqueur made by macerating and distilling the leaves of wormwood (*Artemisia absinthium*) then adding other aromatic plants (fennel, Chinese anise, hyssop, etc.).

Absinth (colloquially known as *la verte*) was the apéritif in vogue before the 1914 war.

Absinth wine. VIN D'ABSINTHE – Wine spiced by infusion of wormwood leaves.

Wormwood
a. Branch
b. Inflorescence
c. Flower

ABSORPTION (Whimsical gastronomy) – This was the meal offered in bygone times to the senior students of *l'École polytechnique* by the new arrivals. 'Enough is absorbed there to justify the name of the ceremony.' (Lorédan Larchey)

ABSTINENCE – Days of abstinence are those on which one should abstain from eating meat, although one is not obliged to fast. Meat abstinence does not prevent one from living a perfectly normal life. In fact, the total exclusion of certain foods and condiments is indispensable in a number of dietary regimes. A few days' fasting is also prescribed for those who have over-indulged at table.

ABUTILON – There are more than sixty varieties of this plant scattered throughout the world. An edible species known as *Abutilon esculentum* grows in Brazil. The Brazilians call it *bençàs de deos* and cook its flowers with meat.

In Europe, abutilon is cultivated as a garden plant for the beauty of its flowers, but only rarely for use as food. In some countries, particularly in Asia and in the West Indies, its leaves are cooked and eaten in the manner of sorrel or spinach. In India the natives are very fond of the species known as *Abutilon indicum*.

ACACIA – Acacia blossoms are used for making fritters and a home-made liqueur.

Acacia blossom fritters – See FRITTERS.

Acacia liqueur or ratafia – See LIQUEUR.

ACANTHUS (Brank-ursine). ACANTHE – This most decorative plant is commonly found in southern France where its elegant, denticulated leaves are eaten, when young, as a salad. It has emollient qualities.

ACARNE – Name given to the European fish commonly known as sea bream.

ACAVUS. ACAVE – A variety of snail common in French vineyards and gardens.

ACCOLADE, IN – A manner of arranging pieces of the same nature – meat, poultry, fish – back to back on one dish. This method of presentation was much in vogue in the olden days.

Chickens served en accolade

ACELINE – French name for a European fish a little resembling the perch. Its flesh is quite good and it is prepared like perch (q.v.).

ACETABULUM. ACÉTABULE – The ancient Romans used the word *acetabulum* to describe the vessel that held the vinegar. It was also used as a measure in medicine.

ACETIC ACID. ACÉTIQUE – The acid which forms the basis of vinegar. It is used in cooking sugar in confectionery.

ACETIFICATION. ACÉTIFICATION – The chemical reaction caused by a yeast (*Mycoderma aceti*). Aided by various industrial processes (see VINEGAR), it transforms wine alcohol (or other alcoholic liquid) into acetic acid.

ACETIMETER. ACÉTIMÈTRE – Instrument for assessing the degree of concentration of vinegar.

ACETO-DOLCE ('Sour-sweet') – An Italian commercial product consisting of a mixture of vegetables and fruit, first pickled in vinegar, then preserved in a syrup of Muscat grape must, honey and mustard. It is usually served as an *hors-d'œuvre*.

ACETOMEL. ACÉTOMEL – Sour-sweet syrup made of honey and vinegar used in the preservation of fruit. Quinces, pears and grapes thus preserved take the name of *aceto-dolce*, i.e. sour-sweet fruit.

ACETONE. ACÉTONE – A colourless, inflammable liquid with an acrid burning taste and a quince-like smell. Acetone appears in the body when the process of decomposition of fatty matter is deficient and particularly when the diet is lacking in carbohydrates (sugar). This frequently arises in severe cases of diabetes and starvation.

ACHAR. ACHARD – This word, derived from the Persian word *atchar*, describes a strongly spiced pickle (usually saffron-coloured) made from fruit, or vegetables, or very young, tender buds of palm cabbage (palmetto) or bamboo sprouts. It is highly regarded throughout the Indian Archipelago, in Mauritius, and Réunion Island.

Lemon achar (Creole cookery). ACHARDS DE CITRONS – Choose thin-skinned lemons and quarter them. Extract the juice, discard the pips, and macerate the lemons in layers of kitchen salt.

Remove the lemons from the salt and soak them in cold water for 24 hours, changing the water several times. Boil in fresh water until the lemons become soft. Strain off the water. Dry the lemons and put them to marinate in the following sauce:

Pound a large onion, a pimento, and a large piece of ginger to a fine paste in a mortar. (Ginger, as well as allspice, Bourbon saffron and Indian curry powder can be bought in delicatessen shops.) Add vinegar and a teaspoon of Bourbon saffron. Blend with sufficient best quality olive oil to ensure that the lemons, when packed into jars, will be completely covered.

Palmetto achar (Creole cookery). ACHARDS DE PALMISTES – Palmettos (palm cabbage) can be bought in delicatessen shops. Remove carefully from the can, discard the oil in which they were packed, and dress with good quality olive oil.

Vegetable achar (Creole cookery). ACHARDS DE LÉGUMES – Remove the seeds and pulp from 1 or 2 cucumbers, and the insides from 2 large pimentos. Cut cucumbers, pimentos, and several carrots and French beans into thin strips about 4 cm. ($1\frac{1}{2}$ inches) long. Mix with florets of cauliflower and roughly chopped cabbage leaves.

Macerate these vegetables for 36 hours. Drain thoroughly, dry, and season with sauce described in the recipe for *Lemon achar* above.

To preserve the achar, spoon into glass preserving jars, cover completely with good quality olive oil, and seal the jars hermetically.

ACHILLEA (Milfoil). ACHILLÉE – Plant, of which one species, *Achillea ptarmica*, which grows in woods, is edible. Its tender young leaves are added to salads.

ACID. ACIDE – A chemical hydrogen compound recognisable by its property of causing litmus solution to turn red.

The acids most commonly used in cooking are vinegar, lemon juice and verjuice.

ACIDIFIERS (Edible). ACIDIFIANTS – Foods that build up an excess of acid in the system, leading to acidification of the body fluids.

Acid-tasting fruits are not necessarily acidifiers; nor do

the latter necessarily possess an acid taste; lemons, for example, are not acidifiers.

Meat, game, sea fish, offal, cereals, flour, pasta and bread are powerful acidifiers; ham, freshwater fish, eggs, butter, fats, chocolate, asparagus, hop shoots, Brussels sprouts, artichokes, onions, chestnuts, peanuts, walnuts, hazelnuts and almonds less seriously so.

ACIDIFY. ACIDIFIER – To add acid (lemon juice, vinegar or verjuice) to a culinary preparation.

ACIDITY. ACIDITÉ – Acid taste. It exists naturally in certain vegetables and fruit and disappears or diminishes as a result of a 'blanching' operation (see BLANCHING).

Nowadays, the acidity of a liquid is measured in pH units; these range from zero, for pure acid (such as hydrochloric acid), to 7, which indicates a completely neutral substance. The scale continues above 7 to indicate degrees of alkalinity (opposite of acidity).

The acidity scale shows the degree of acidity of certain foods.

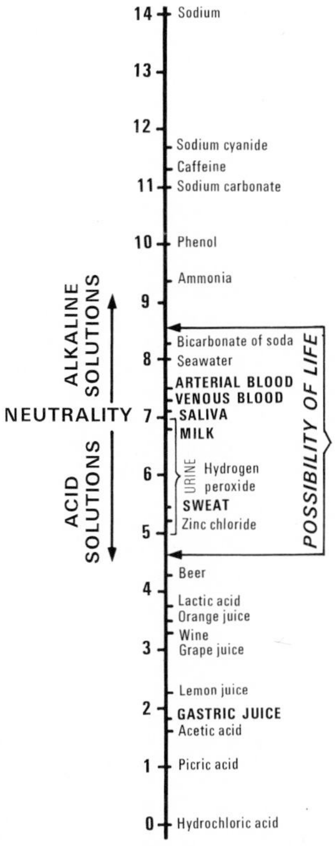

Acidity scale

ACIDULATE. ACIDULER – To render a dish slightly acid, sour or piquant by the addition of lemon, vinegar, etc.

ACIDULATED. ACIDULÉ – Term which is only used to describe mineral waters charged with carbonic acid.

ACON – An implement used by French mussel farmers to gather the mussels from the mussel beds in the cove of Aiguillon; near La Rochelle.

The use of this tool dates back to antiquity. It is mentioned in Charlemagne's *Capitularies*.

ACORN. GLAND – Fruit of the oak tree. Some types are edible and were eaten by certain Asian peoples before they discovered cereals. In some countries, such as Spain, acorns are eaten raw or roasted. Acorn flour (which unlike chicory has costive properties) is used as a substitute for coffee. For this purpose the roasted acorns of the ballota oak are most commonly used.

ACORN BARNACLE. BALANE – A small shellfish with a conical irregular shell which is found in all seas, attached to rocks. It is also commonly called *acorn shell* and *turban shell*. Its flesh is quite delicate and is prepared like crab (q.v.).

Acorn barnacles stuck to a piece of shell

ACQUETTE – An old, spirituous and very aromatic liquor, much prized in Italy and throughout the south of France. Its appearance resembles that of *Danziger Goldwasser* (Danzig *eau de vie*). There are two varieties: *silver acquette* (in Italian *aqua bianca*), and *gold acquette* (*aqua d'oro*).

Silver acquette is made as follows:

Ceylon cinnamon	225 g. (8 oz.)
Cloves	25 g. (1 oz.)
Nutmeg	25 g. (1 oz.)
85° alcohol	20 litres ($4\frac{1}{2}$ gallons, $5\frac{1}{2}$ gallons)

Steep these various ingredients in the alcohol for 24 hours, then distil without rectifying; you will obtain 20 litres ($4\frac{1}{2}$ gallons, $5\frac{1}{2}$ gallons) liqueur. Dissolve 25 kg. (55 lb.) sugar in 11 litres ($2\frac{1}{2}$ gallons, 3 gallons) water and add the syrup obtained as a result of the distillation. Leave to rest for the time required, filter and put a crushed silver leaf into each bottle.

To prepare gold acquette take:

Ceylon cinnamon	225 g. (8 oz.)
Cloves	15 g. ($\frac{1}{2}$ oz.)
Angelica roots	75 g. (3 oz.)
Daucus of Crete	75 g. (3 oz.)
Fresh lemon (peel of)	40 g. ($1\frac{1}{2}$ oz.)
85° alcohol	20 litres ($4\frac{1}{2}$ gallons, $5\frac{1}{2}$ gallons)

Proceed as for preparing silver acquette, with just one difference, that you put a crushed gold leaf into each bottle.

ACRIDOPHAGE – One who feeds on locusts. This food may seem extraordinary to the epicures of Europe, but it is quite acceptable to African gastronomes. It appears that the taste of locusts resembles, if somewhat remotely, that of raw shrimps.

ACROAMA – A Greek word, adopted by the Romans, meaning 'that to which one listens', further extended to mean 'that to which one pays attention'.

To better entertain their guests, the patricians made a habit of summoning musicians, poets, actors (who enacted, at times, very licentious scenes), men and women dancers, jugglers, acrobats, tumblers, dwarfs and even gladiators and savage beasts to perform while the meal was in progress.

To the Romans this word *acroama* meant not only these various types of entertainment, but also the performers themselves.

The custom of the *acroama* continued through the centuries but was renamed *entremets* ('between courses'). These *entremets* had nothing in common with what today describes a course of vegetables or a sweet course served towards the end of a meal. *Acroama*, and the 'spectacular *entremets*' that succeeded it, were enacted all through the meal.

ACTINIA (Sea anemone). ACTINIE – Although actiniae are urticating (stinging) animals, they are used as food in certain localities. The inhabitants of southern coasts of France relish a species of actinia which they call *rastègne* and maintain that their taste resembles that of crabs.

Actiniae have to be thoroughly beaten before cooking to tenderise them. They can then be fried, made into fritters, omelettes, etc.

ADOC – Name sometimes given to sour milk.

ADULTERATION. FALSIFICATION – A deliberate lowering of the quality of foodstuffs for the purpose of illicit gain.

ÆGINETIA. ÆGINETIE – The type genus of this plant, *Æginetia indica*, is indigenous to the East Indies. The natives of the coast of Malabar call it *tsiem-cumulu* and blend it with nutmeg and sugar to form an excellent mascatory (chewing-gum) used for strengthening the teeth and combating bad breath.

AEGIS OF RHODES. AEGIS DE RHODES – One of the seven great masters of ancient Greek *cuisine* (third century B.C.). He excelled in the art of cooking fish.

AFFINAGE – Word used in the French cheese industry to describe the process of ripening or maturing cheese in temperature-controlled cellars.

AFFRIANDER – French culinary term which means to tempt; to attract by the pleasant appearance of a dish.

AFTER-TASTE. ARRIÈRE-GOÛT – Taste that returns to the mouth after ingestion of certain foods and beverages.

AGAMI (Trumpeter) – A bird of the wader family of which the *Guiana agami* is typical. Its flesh has appreciable merit. The agami is used in cookery mainly in South America, boiled in consommé or braised with rice.

Its flesh has a pleasant flavour but is rather dry, although less so in the domesticated bird.

Agami

Agami à la chilienne – Choose as tender an agami as possible. Pluck, draw, singe and clean it. Prepare a garnish of rice cooked in fat stock with pimentos. Bard it and put to braise in a braising pan with the usual accompaniments of vegetables and spices, and some dry white wine.

Separately, braise in veal jelly stock 12 medium-sized onions stuffed with a *salpicon* (q.v.) of sweet pimentos blended with a few tablespoons of reduced *velouté* (q.v.). Prepare also 450 g. (1 lb.) *Okra in tomato sauce* (see OKRA).

As soon as the agami is cooked, remove from the braising pan. Glaze it in the oven.

Strain the pan juices, remove excess fat and reduce to the desired consistency.

Place the agami on a serving dish surrounded by the garnishes. Coat with the sauce.

AGAPE (Love feast) – This was the name of the meal which the early Christians held together in church, in memory of the Last Supper. The Council of Carthage abolished the agapes in A.D. 397 in order to put an end to the calumnies of which they were the object.

The meals held by the early Christians in the catacombs in memory of the martyrs were also called *agapes*.

This word nowadays is used to define an important family meal.

AGAR-AGAR (Bengal isinglass) – A product obtained from various seaweeds, known also as *Japanese moss*, *Ceylon moss*.

Agar-agar is collected in the form of thin, crinkly, whitish, transparent strips. It swells slightly in cold water and considerably so in boiling water, in which it finally dissolves. A fairly stiff jelly can be obtained from it, which is used in bacteriology.

Its neutral taste makes it suitable for use in cooking and confectionery, and for making jellies.

It is by regurgitating seaweed of this type that the salangane (Chinese swallow) builds its nest, so much prized by the Chinese under the name of 'bird's nest', for which factory-made agar-agar is often passed-off in the West.

Agar-agar always contains the carapaces of diatoms (microscopic unicellular algae) easily identifiable under the microscope. This factor makes possible the rapid detection of any fraudulent use of the product.

AGARIC – A family of fungi with a compact cap and radiating gills, that grows profusely in damp and shaded places, and is also found in fields, on tree trunks, in caves and on decayed wood. There are about 2000 known species of agarics and quite a large number of them are edible. The poisonous species are chiefly found among the genus called *Amanita*.

Among the edible agarics are the following:

Edible agaric or *cultivated mushrooms*, grown in the quarries around Paris – the classic type of mushroom. This is often described under the term *champignon* without any other qualification.

A type of agaric which has very distinctive ridges on the underside of the cap

Royal agaric, agaric odorain or *St. George's agaric* and the *cultivated agaric* are also found in the Paris region.

Among the poisonous species are *Amanita phalloides* (death cap) and *Amanita verna* (gill) (see MUSHROOMS).

To prepare edible agarics, sauté in a shallow pan in oil or butter; dress with herbs, *Cream sauce* (see SAUCE), *à la provençale*, *à la bordelaise* (see GARNISHES). They can also be used as a garnish for a large number of dishes.

AGATHON – Poet, born in Athens, and not in Samos, as certain authors maintain.

His sumptuous repasts gave rise to a great deal of jesting on the part of Aristophanes and other dramatists. Some people claim that Plato's *Banquet* was composed at his table.

AGAVE – A genus of South American plants belonging to the family *Agavaceae* – a native of Mexico. In Cuba and Mexico its pulp is fermented to make an alcoholic beverage called *pulque*.

AGNOLOTTI. Agnolotti à la piémontaise (Italian cookery) – Prepare a noodle paste in the following manner: put 450 g. (1 lb., 4 cups) flour in a circle or 'fountain' on a table. In the middle of this circle put 4 egg yolks, 20 g. (a generous tablespoon) butter, a pinch of salt and 1 dl. (6 tablespoons, scant $\frac{1}{2}$ cup) water.

Knead for 10 minutes but avoid giving too much body to the paste. Allow to rest for 10 minutes.

Roll out the paste with a rolling-pin as thinly as possible. Place walnut-sized pieces of forcemeat (see FORCEMEAT, *Beef forcemeat*) along it in a horizontal line, spacing them 5 cm. (2 inches) from the edge of the paste and 5 cm. (2 inches) from each other.

Fold the overlapping edge of the paste over this row of agnolotti. Press down around each heap of forcemeat, to make the paste stick well. Cut out the agnolotti with a crescent-shaped, fluted-edged pastry-cutter, thus obtaining little turnovers.

Poach them in boiling water for 10 minutes, allowing 2 teaspoons salt per litre ($1\frac{3}{4}$ pints, generous quart) water. Drain, and place in a dish.

Make a sauce from the braised beef left over from the forcemeat. Serve this and grated Parmesan cheese with the agnolotti.

AGONE D'ISTRIA (Smaris graerlis). AGON – In Italy it is known under the name of *sardina* and indeed it has much the same flavour and is similar in size to the sardine. All the recipes given for sardines (q.v.) can be applied to it. Like sardines, *agone* can be salted.

AGORANOME – Inspector of markets in ancient Greece. He controlled the price of produce and was responsible for the implementation of the laws relating to its markets. The *agoranome* of the Greeks corresponds to the *aedile* of the Romans.

AGOU – *Agou* or *negroes' sago* resembles small-grain millet. This grain is of brownish-grey colour with a yellow spot where it joins the stem. It is cooked like rice. Flour made from it is used to make cakes and porridge.

AGOUTI – Rodent the size of a hare found in Brazil (where it is called *cotia*), Guiana, the Dominican Republic, and generally throughout the West Indies. The agouti can live in Europe if it is protected from the cold.

The flesh is good to eat, even though the flavour is rather strong. It is prepared like sucking pig (see PORK, *Piglet*).

AGRAS – Agras is an Algerian iced beverage; to be more precise, a *granité*. Its main ingredients are almonds and verjuice.

Ingredients. 150 g. (5 oz., 1 cup) sweet almonds, 1 litre ($1\frac{3}{4}$ pints, generous quart) verjuice, $\frac{1}{2}$ litre (scant pint, $2\frac{1}{4}$ cups) water and 150 g. (5 oz., $\frac{2}{3}$ cup) brown or granulated sugar.

Method of preparation. Blanch the almonds after having scalded them with boiling water. Pound them in a mortar as finely as possible, moistening them with a little of the water. When they form a paste, dilute with the rest of the water and verjuice and strain through a napkin, then put under a press to extract all the liquid. $1\frac{1}{2}$ dl. ($\frac{1}{4}$ pint, $\frac{2}{3}$ cup) white vinegar combined with 1 litre ($1\frac{3}{4}$ pints, generous quart) water may be substituted for the verjuice and water.

Sweeten the liquid with the brown sugar, or, if this is not available, granulated sugar, and strain through a napkin once again, but this time without pressing.

Stand this mixture in an ice bucket, surrounded by a mixture of crushed ice and sea salt (coarse salt), allowing 10 per cent of salt, and leave to chill. Loosen the parts which get stuck to the sides of the ice bucket about every 15 minutes. When the whole mixture acquires a granulated texture, serve it in sherbet glasses, adding half a coffeespoon of kirsch to each glass.

AGUAXIMA – A species of Brazilian pepper not very different from ordinary pepper.

AGUNCATE. AGUNCATÉ – A fruit grown in Peru, called *palta* in Lima. It is shaped like a calabash (gourd), is green in colour and has a varnished appearance. Its skin comes away from the flesh easily when the fruit is ripe. This flesh, somewhat insipid, is eaten with salt. It has something in common with the flesh of avocado pear (q.v.).

AIGRE DE CÈDRE (French name for Citrus medica) – Fruit of a citron tree cultivated in Provence, around Grasse and Nice, also at San Remo and near Genoa in Italy. It makes a very refreshing summer drink.

AIGUILLETTE – An *aiguillette* means a thin slice cut lengthways on the breast of poultry and winged game.

Strictly speaking, the word should only be used to describe thin slices of fowl, but it is often used when referring to thin slices of meat, e.g., 'cut a fillet of beef into *aiguillettes*'. *Aiguillette* is also used to describe the top rump (see BEEF).

Agouti

AILLADE – Definition used in the south of France, which applies, according to the district (Languedoc or Provence) to preparations which differ somewhat but are all garlic based.

Firstly, *aillade sauce*, a sort of garlic *vinaigrette* (q.v.), sometimes including shallots, chives and other garnishes.

Aillade sauce is served with cold meat and fish, with potatoes and, generally, with all dishes served *à la vinaigrette*.

Secondly, bread *à l'aillade*, a slice of toasted bread, thoroughly rubbed with garlic and sprinkled with olive oil. This provençal *aillade* is the equivalent of the Languedocian *chapon* (garlic-rubbed bread).

Certain authors also mention other regional preparations known under the name of *aillade*. Among these are:

Aillade albigeoise which is nothing more than an *aïoli* (q.v.).

Aillade à la toulousaine which is also an *aïoli* with blanched and pounded walnuts added.

All these preparations are very appetising but something of an acquired taste, garlic being their outstanding characteristic. They are excellent for seasoning salads.

AÏOLI or AILLOLI – Peel 4 large cloves of garlic, and pound to a fine paste in a mortar with 1 egg yolk. Season with a pinch of salt, and continue to pound, adding 2½ dl. (scant ½ pint, generous cup) olive oil little by little, as for mayonnaise. Stir this mixture vigorously. When finished, it should have the appearance of a thick smooth mayonnaise.

Aïoli is served mainly with boiled fish, hot or cold, but can also be served with cold meat, or used as a seasoning for salads and cooked vegetables.

Garnished aïoli. AÏOLI GARNI – This dish, very popular in Provence, is composed of a variety of ingredients, such as boiled cod, snails cooked in salt water, fennel, onions stuck with cloves, boiled carrots, french beans, artichokes cooked in salt water, unskinned potatoes, hard-boiled eggs, etc. Small octopi, boiled in salted water with herbs, are sometimes added. All these are arranged on a large dish and served with *aïoli*.

The preparation of this dish, says J. B. Reboul, one of the *maîtres de la cuisine provençale*, demands a great deal of artistic arrangement. Not all the ingredients which we have enumerated, however, are absolutely essential. There is no set rule on this point. One should proceed according to one's tastes and the means at one's disposal.

Aïoli à la grecque – A kind of *vinaigrette sauce* which is prepared as follows: combine pounded walnuts, almonds and hazelnuts with fresh breadcrumbs sieved and soaked in milk, and pounded garlic. Blend with oil, vinegar and lemon juice. Serve with fried and boiled fish.

AISY – Name given to the (soured) whey left over from the scalding of milk used in the production of Gruyère. This whey is used to make cheeses of an inferior quality called *serai*. The *aisy* is stored in barrels and added to daily as more whey becomes available.

ALARIA – A genus of seaweed of which five species are found in the seas of northern Europe.

One variety, known as badderlocks in Scotland and murlins in Ireland, flourishes along the Atlantic coast of the British Isles. It is eaten in Scotland, in Ireland, and in the Faroe Islands. Only the slightly sweet central cartilaginous vein is consumed.

ALBACORE (Yellowfin tuna) – A large species of tunny (tuna) fish. This is also the Portuguese word for the swordfish (q.v.).

ALBARELLE – A genus of edible fungi which grows on chestnut trees and white poplars.

ALBATROSS. ALBATROS – Sea bird with very tough flesh. That of the young bird is eaten, nevertheless, and is prepared like *Wild duck* (see DUCK).

ALBIGEOISE – Garnish for large and small cuts of meat. It consists of stuffed tomatoes and potato croquettes.

Albatross

ALBUFÉRA (D') – Definition applying to various kinds of dishes chiefly characterised by the sauce which goes with them.

The term *d'Albuféra* was probably first used either by Carême or by his successor Plumerey, so the recipe for *Duckling à la d'Albuféra* is almost certainly the authentic one. It differs slightly from the modern version.

Marshal Suchet was made Duke of Albuféra in 1812 after the victories of Oropéza, Murviedro and Valencia in Spain. The lake of Albuféra is near Valencia. (See DUCK, CHICKEN.)

ALBUMEN – A constituent of seeds containing food reserves for the plant in germination. Albumen is sometimes farinaceous, as in cereals such as maize, barley, corn and rye; sometimes oily or fleshy as in coconut palm and in black poppy. In certain palms it acquires the hardness of ivory.

The albumen contained in coconuts is in the form of an outer layer surrounding the inner cavity that contains the liquid commonly known as coconut milk.

Section of a grain of corn showing the albumen

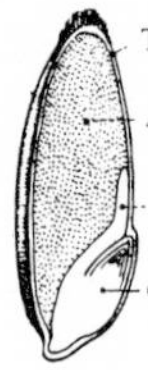

Many types of grain are used for their albumen in domestic economy, in medicine and in the arts. Thus cereals provide us with flour; the coffee shrub with an alkaloid known as caffeine; the black poppy with poppyseed oil, used almost universally as a food. The seeds of certain species of water-lilies, very pleasant to the palate, are much used in China and Vietnam as food. The kernels of a species of pine that grows in Provence and Italy contain an oily, delicately flavoured albumen, which makes them much valued in confectionery, particularly in the manufacture of sugared pine nuts. Several species of palm tree provide both edible oil and oil for lighting. Linseed oil comes from the seeds of flax.

A species of dwarf palm, found in Peru, produces a large fruit which the natives call *cana* or *cabezo de negro*. When the fruit is green, the albumen of its seeds is a pleasant-tasting liquid which, when fermented, yields a wine that is much appreciated by the Peruvians. The fruit, when ripe, becomes very hard and can be put to the same uses as ivory; in fact it is exported under the name of raw ivory or vegetable ivory. When burned, the product obtained compares favourably with ivory black, which is obtained from elephants' teeth and tusks.

ALBUMIN. ALBUMINE – Viscous whitish matter with a slightly salty taste. An example is white of egg, which contains albumin up to 59 per cent of its total weight (see EGGS).

Albumin is also found in blood serum, in milk and in plants, particularly in the seeds of dried vegetables. It is for this reason that the water in which peas, beans and lentils are cooked becomes viscous when cooled. Albumin is soluble in water in its raw state but coagulates at a temperature of 78–80°C. (172–176°F.) and then becomes insoluble.

Albumin in the form of a thin yellowish transparent sediment can be obtained by evaporating the white of egg at a temperature of about 50°C. (122°F.).

Albumin is used in the confectionery industry as a substitute for white of egg in the manufacture of certain kinds of whisked pastes such as marshmallow, liquorice, Montélimar nougat and various meringue products.

It is also used as an egg substitute in the manufacture of cheap biscuits and almond paste. Before use it has to be dissolved in about seven times its weight of cold water.

Albumin in the form of beaten whites of egg is used in the clearing of wine.

ALBUMINOIDS. ALBUMINOÏDES – Substances possessing properties akin to those of albumin (coagulable by heat), also called nitrogenous, quaternary or proteinic substances. They exist in all living organisms, whether animal or vegetable.

Chemical analysis reveals the same four basic elements: carbon, hydrogen, oxygen and nitrogen associated in varying quantities with other elements.

Albuminoids constitute one of the essential elements of our diet. Of all the substances we generally eat, the only ones lacking in albuminoids are those which have undergone an industrial purifying process such as oil and sugar.

In dietetics, an increased ration of albuminoids is occasionally prescribed (in cases of malnutrition, etc.) but more frequently the amount of albuminoids in the diet is reduced when, for example, the kidneys fail to eliminate waste products or the liver is unable to transform them.

Without going to the extent of reproducing specialist tables of analyses, it is possible to divide albuminoid or nitrogenous food into four categories:

Very poor in albumins (less than 1 per cent): green vegetables, pulpy fruit, potatoes, rice, cream, butter, honey, sugar, oils.

Poor (up to 6 per cent): spinach, artichokes, green cabbages, Brussels sprouts, chestnuts, green peas, cocoa, chocolate.

Rich (6 to 12 per cent): bread, flours, cereals, noodles, eggs.

Very rich (12 to 30 per cent): walnuts, almonds, hazelnuts, various meats, fish, dried beans, dried peas, lentils, beans, chick peas, cheeses.

ALBUNDIGAS (Mexican cookery) – The origin of *albundigas* appears to be Spanish or Mexican. In Mexico it is almost a national dish.

Combine 450 g. (1 lb.) finely chopped fillet of beef and 100 g. (4 oz.) fairly coarsely chopped fat bacon. Season with salt and pepper. Add a little crushed garlic and a teaspoon of chopped parsley, and bind with an egg. Shape into thickish cakes. Fry in clarified butter. Put into an ovenproof dish and cover with tomato sauce. Cook in the oven for 20 minutes. Serve with *Rice à la créole* (see RICE).

Albundigas can also be made from a mixture of veal and pork.

The Mexicans also have a soup called by this name:

Ingredients. For 3 litres ($5\frac{1}{4}$ pints, $6\frac{1}{2}$ pints) light stock or water, take 225 g. (8 oz.) fillet of pork, veal or beef, 5 medium-sized onions, a clove of garlic, 4 green pimentos, 3 peeled and deseeded tomatoes, 50 g. (2 oz., $\frac{1}{4}$ cup) butter, 2 tablespoons (3 tablespoons) wheat flour, the same amount of sieved breadcrumbs, $\frac{1}{2}$ teaspoon coriander or thyme, or, better still, marjoram, which has a more delicate flavour, 1 egg and 1 tablespoon salt.

Method. Slice the onions and pimentos and brown them in butter. Add slightly crushed garlic. Sprinkle with flour, stir, allow to brown lightly, and add the meat (which has been minced), breadcrumbs, and seasoning. Add the egg and blend well. Moisten with a little of the stock or boiling water, and leave to simmer for a quarter of an hour.

Put this forecemeat mixture, while still hot, into a pastry forcing-bag fitted with a ring. Hold the bag over a saucepan of boiling stock and squeeze; cut off small slices of the sausage as it comes out of the bag. Simmer these quenelles in the boiling stock leaving the lid off the pan.

Chop the tomatoes, soften them in butter, and add them to the soup just before it is served.

Alcarazza

ALCARRAZA (Water cooler). ALCARAZAS – The French have borrowed this word from the Spanish, who in turn borrowed it from the Arabic *alkourraz* (pitcher). In Egypt, the *alcarraza* is called *bardak*; this has become the French *bardague* and *balasse*. *Bardak* is a Turkish word probably stemming from the Arabic root *bara*, meaning to cool, and from which is derived *barrada* (meaning, like *alcarraza*, a vessel for cooling liquids) and the Spanish word *albarrada*.

These porous, unglazed jugs of various shapes are filled with water and hung in the shade in a draught. The water oozes through the pores of the jug and evaporates. The hotter the outside temperature and the drier the air, the quicker the evaporation. The heat necessary for evaporation is extracted from the liquid inside the jug, which is thus cooled.

ALCAZAR (Pâtisserie) – Line a sponge tin with *Lining paste* (see DOUGH). Prick the bottom and spread with 2 tablespoons (3 tablespoons) apricot jam. Fill three-quarters of the tin with the following mixture:

Ingredients. 125 g. (4 oz., 1 cup) icing sugar, 4 egg whites, 60 g. (2 oz., $\frac{1}{2}$ cup) ground almonds, 60 g. (2 oz., $\frac{1}{2}$ cup) flour, 25 g. (1 oz., 2 tablespoons) melted butter, kirsch.

Method of preparation. Beat the sugar and the egg whites over gentle heat to obtain a firm meringue, then add ground almonds, flour and, finally, melted butter mixed with half a wine glass of kirsch. Spread on a buttered and floured baking sheet. Bake in the oven at 180°C. (350°F., Gas Mark 4) for 50 to 60 minutes and turn out onto a wire tray.

Fit a cloth piping-bag with a fluted pipe, and fill with uncooked almond paste in the proportion of 450 g. (1 lb.) to 450 g. (1 lb.) (see ALMOND, *Almond paste I*). Pipe a lattice-work over the pastry, then pipe a border. Place in a hot oven to colour the almond paste. Cover with thick apricot jam and put half a pistachio nut in the centre of each lozenge.

As an alternative to an almond paste border use apricot jam sprinkled with chopped roasted almonds.

ALCOHOL. ALCOOL – Liquid obtained by distilling fermented liquors.

In chemistry, all organic substances composed of carbon, hydrogen and oxygen, capable of being combined into an acid to form an ether, are defined as alcohol. We shall deal only with ethyl alcohol or wine alcohol, also called wine spirit. It is the principal product of the fermentation of sweet liquids formed by the double decomposition of glucose under the action of yeast. This microscopic vegetable cell reproduces itself by splitting glucose into carbonic acid and alcohol and a few palatable and sweet-smelling by-products. (See BEER, WINE.)

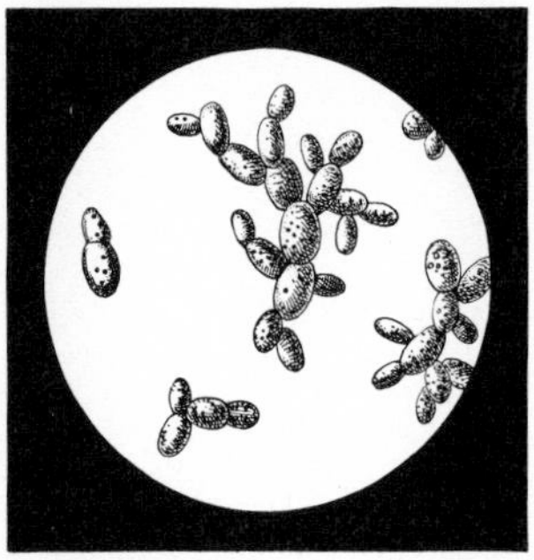

Microscopic cells inducing alcoholic fermentation

Alcohol is produced by fermenting natural sweet juices (grapes, apples, sugar cane, beetroot, etc.) or amyloide musts, which have been subjected to preliminary fermentation which transforms the starch into glucose. Wort of cereals (beer), potatoes, etc. are used.

The distillation of these musts and worts produces spirits (q.v.); the concentration and rectification of these spirits produces industrial alcohols.

Absolute 100 per cent alcohol is a laboratory product; it is a caustic liquid, which boils at 78·3°C. Because of its high water absorption potentiality it must be treated with great caution.

Officinal (medicinal) 95° alcohol is a colourless, mobile, non-residual liquid, volatile, with a pleasant odour and a burning taste; it boils at 79·9°C. It can be mixed with water in all proportions, with contraction (that is to say, the total volume of the mixture is lower than that of the components) and with emission of heat.

85° alcohol is commonly called 'three-six' (*trois-six*) because three parts of this alcohol, mixed with an equal quantity of pure water, produce six parts of ordinary *eau-de-vie*.

Alcohol possesses antiseptic properties; it is a diffusible stimulant which has numerous uses in therapeutics.

In its chemical composition alcohol approaches sugars (1 molecule of glucose is split, by fermentation, into 2 molecules of alcohol). It possesses definite but moderate alimentary properties, because it decomposes too quickly in the organism, and the energy released can only be used to a small degree, mainly because it becomes a toxic substance when taken in large doses (see ALCOHOLISM).

ALCOHOLISM. ALCOOLISME – Intoxication produced by the abuse of liquids containing alcohol. There are three distinct forms:

1. Inebriety – Occurring when alcohol reaches a certain degree, variable with individuals, manifesting itself in the following manner: *First degree:* Sensation of well-being, stimulation of the intellectual faculties and the imagination, slight swelling of the face; *Second degree:* Mental incoherence, diminution of muscular strength, lack of movement co-ordination, congestion of the face, overpowering drowsiness; *Third degree:* Loss of mobility, sensitiveness and will.

2. Acute intoxication – Early symptoms the same as in inebriety, but the period of excitation is very short, resulting quickly in somnolence, which can develop into a coma and even death through cerebral or pulmonary congestion.

3. Chronic alcoholism – Repeated abuse of alcoholic liquids produces lesions of the stomach (gastritis), of the liver (cirrhosis), of the kidneys (nephritis), and of the nervous system (delirium, neuritis).

ALE – English beer, lightly hopped and slightly bitter. It is used in cooking for making various cheese dishes, notably for Welsh rarebit (q.v.).

Ale is obtained by rapid fermentation and acquires strength on maturing; fermented small beer, on the other hand, has only a short life. Stout and porter are brewed from roasted grain; ale is made from grain in its natural state.

It used to be a tradition in wealthy English families to celebrate the birth of a son by filling one or more barrels of ale, specially brewed for the occasion. The barrels were hermetically sealed and not opened until the son and heir reached his majority. On this memorable day – called the 'coming of age' – friends, tenants and servants were invited to a great repast, which concluded with the passing round of the splendid twenty-one-year-old ale.

Ale posset – Heat 1 litre ($1\frac{3}{4}$ pints, generous quart) ale with a little sugar, a pinch of powdered ginger and grated nutmeg. Boil 1 litre ($1\frac{3}{4}$ pints, generous quart) unskimmed milk and mix it, while still boiling, with the ale.

Toast and ale – An English beverage which used to be served in winter, after the dinner, at the same time as the cheese.

Method. Bring 1 litre ($1\frac{3}{4}$ pints, generous quart) old ale, to which a coffeespoon of ginger has been added, to the boil. Pour it, whilst almost boiling, into a jug with a metal lid containing a thick slice of bread toasted on both sides. Leave the ale to stand for a short time before serving.

ALECTRYON – A large tree of which the best-known species is found in New Zealand.

Its red berries, much prized for their pleasant acid flavour, are used in the manufacture of refreshing beverages. An excellent oil is extracted from its seeds (and exported).

ALEMBIC. ALAMBIC – Apparatus used for distilling. It comprises a cucurbit, or tinned copper boiler, with or without a *bain-marie*, surmounted by a cap with a serpentine, i.e., a tin, or tinned copper, spiral coil leading from it.

Old-fashioned alembic

The liquid to be distilled is put directly into the boiler (in the case of a naked-flame alembic), or on top of the *bain-marie* that forms part of it. The alembic is then heated. The action of the heat releases alcoholic vapours. These pass into the serpentine (which is cooled by flowing water), and condense. The traditional Charente method was to heat the alembics directly over wood fires. The first liquid obtained, *le brouillis* – murk – had to be redistilled by passing it through the alembic once more.

A number of improvements have been incorporated in the old-fashioned alembic to enable alcohol to be obtained at the first attempt, and to ensure continuous feeding of the apparatus.

Traditionalists insist, however, that these improvements have only increased the 'boiler taste' and yield inferior results.

In industry, more complicated apparatus, such as distilling towers with rectifiers, etc., are used.

ALGAE. ALGUE – Plants which live in water. The nutritive value of algae is indubitable, and has generally been more conclusively proved than that of fungi. During the 1914 war, these plants were used as fodder for horses.

Recent research has confirmed the dietetic value of algae. As far as feeding human beings is concerned, it seems that certain small primitive tribes in the extreme North use algae as emergency nourishment when food is scarce. Several varieties of algae are eaten in Scotland.

Algae are highly esteemed in the Far East and are used as a basis for a large number of widely marketed foodstuffs. It is from certain laminaria species (sea tangle) that the Japanese prepare *kombu*, or *kombus*, for there are several seaweed-based dishes so called.

The algae are soaked in vinegar for hours until thoroughly saturated, and dried in the open air. The skin of the leaves is then shredded off, using a sharp knife, and the white underlying pulp scraped. This pulp is then dried and crushed into a powder, or cut into small geometrical shapes according to requirements. A condiment, rather like anchovy essence, and very popular with the Japanese, is made from fragments of this same pulp, boiled in soy sauce.

The central part of these algae is cooked with fish, vegetables and soups to enhance their flavour. A beverage made from pulverised *kombu* is drunk like tea. *Kombu* is added to stews and used as a condiment for rice. It is often cut into pieces and dried by a fire, and either consumed thus, or after soaking it for a few moments in boiling water.

The Japanese eat another variety of algae, one which they cultivate artificially. After being washed, these are dried in the sun, lightly roasted, crumbled into small pieces, and used to flavour soups and sauces.

Another algae product often used in Japan is *kantus*, a sort of glue or gelatine in the form of white, shiny, half-transparent shavings or flakes. *Kantus* is used like tapioca for preparing jellies, soups and sauces.

Algae in dietetics – Dieticians have great faith in the nutritional value of algae. And, in fact, man has long included certain varieties of algae in his diet.

It was the Japanese who were the first to recognise the dietetic value of algae and to exploit them systematically. Red algae of the *porphyry* genus are cultivated in the bays of Tokyo and Hiroshima. Thousands of algae beds have sprung up on the edge of the ocean, 1 to 2 m. (1 to 2 yards) below the surface. Cultivation presents no particular problem and the harvest continues right through the year.

The Japanese consume algae in a wide variety of ways: in soups, in salads, in the preparation of various dishes. The algae are often sliced thinly, hardened over a fierce heat, and chopped. This makes them easier to use. Various species of laminaria are used as a base in the manufacture of *kombu*, which is then used as a vegetable for soup or mixed with rice seasoned with soy sauce. Other species, *kanten* for example, are used in *pâtisserie* and confectionery.

But algae are not simply a culinary expedient, and interest in them is not confined to Far Eastern countries; in the opinion of the experts, they constitute a valuable food resource for the future.

It is in this way that *chlorella*, microscopic freshwater algae which, under favourable conditions, reproduce themselves with astonishing rapidity, may one day save our planet from famine. E. and A. Naegele have good reason to write: 'Experimental feeding of laboratory animals has proved beyond any doubt the food and energy value of chlorellae. It is apparent that chlorellae are rich in proteinic, lipic and vitaminised substances, and that accelerated cultivation will provide man with an important nutritional supplement. It is not a question of replacing traditional cultivation with that of algae, but the latter may come in useful in the exploitation of solar energy in arid or semi-arid zones.'

This means that the underprivileged peoples of the globe could receive their quota of vitamins and trace elements which at present they entirely lack.

ALGERIA. ALGÉRIE – Algeria is an essentially agricultural country, especially in the Tell region where cereal cultivation predominates. Pasture lands extend to the high plains, while the mountains and land unsuitable for agriculture are covered with forest. It is a country, therefore, of considerable resources. In ancient times it was one of Rome's granaries.

Algeria has every form of cereal: wheat, barley, oats, maize, millet, etc. Wheat is especially valued for the manufacture of pasta and semolina products, since it produces a pasta which, while swelling in the process of cooking, does not lose its shape.

The Algerian vineyards, work of the French colonists, are situated mainly around Oran and Algiers. They are gradually diminishing in number. The wines of Mascara, Mostaganem and Médéa are among the best known. Since the time of the French administration they have been classified V.D.Q.S. (q.v.). They are generally of high alcohol content and have good keeping qualities, which make them the providence of wine dealers who specialise in blending. Early dessert grapes are exported in June.

Plums, greengages and almonds are other equally early fruits. Then there are the specifically Algerian fruits such as oranges, tangerines, dates and figs. The last two are dried and exported in considerable quantities. A large proportion of the oranges and tangerines are used locally in the manufacture of liqueurs.

Vegetable farming produces excellent quality potatoes, beans, artichokes, tomatoes, peas, carrots, melons, watermelons and aubergines (eggplants). Olives are cultivated in the littoral regions and in a few higher regions – up to 900 m. (over 3000 feet) in altitude. Refineries situated on the spot produce a very good quality oil, easy-flowing, fruity, golden.

The coasts furnish all the fish and crustaceans of the Mediterranean, as well as *fruits de mer* very similar to those found on the coast of Provence.

Large herds of livestock feed on the pasture lands of the interior. There are about ten times as many sheep as cattle, which explains why there are so many more recipes for mutton than for beef. Indigenous Algerian animals, such as camels and gazelles, appear on the menu more as a gastronomical curiosity than anything else, and are treated in an exceptional manner.

Algerian cooking is not so very different from that of

Tunisia and Morocco. All three come under the heading of Arab *cuisine*.

Spices abound: absinth, verbena, basil, citron, gum resin, mint, sesame, pimentos, etc. Dishes are flavoured with *ras el-hanout*, a blend of twenty-seven different spices inseparably linked with the feast of *Aïd-el-Kébir*.

Arab cuisine or 'tent cookery'. CUISINE ARABE – This type of food is simple and healthy; the milk, oil, semolina, rice, dates, vegetables, pasta products, condiments and meats which go into its composition are all excellent and produce easily digestible dishes.

The method of slaughter used by the Arabs, consisting of severing the neck, the windpipe and the two jugular veins, without lifting the knife off until severance is complete, is particularly to be recommended.

The Arabs eat only the flesh of animals; the blood is forbidden. The Koran lays down which foods the Arabs are permitted to eat. This includes aquatic animals, all the poultry and all birds, except birds of prey – day or nocturnal – all livestock animals, camels, oxen, sheep, etc., with the exception of pig and wild boar.

The lawgiver advises his faithful: 'Do not eat in a crouching or huddled position, as this position inclines one to eat too much, but sit at the table in such a manner as to appear always ready to get up.'

Arabs generally drink only once, after a meal, when a communal vessel (*guerba*), containing spring water or milk, makes the round of those participating in the meal.

The person drinking should not breathe into the bowl containing the liquid; he must remove it from his lips before beginning to breathe again. Then he may resume drinking. A cup of coffee and a pipe of tobacco always conclude the meal of the true Arab.

Coffee, a Moslem beverage, is the inseparable companion of tobacco (they constitute the two great pleasures of the Arab). It is very rich in tonic substances and therefore very beneficial in a country where the summer temperature varies between 25°C. and 50°C. (77°F. and 122°F.).

The tea hour is a ritual. There is mint tea, absinth and sage tea laced with marjoram, basil and ambergris (an aromatic infusion served with ambergris balls mounted in silver is the ultimate refinement).

Arabs drink no wine; the Koran forbids it.

One of the authors of the commentaries to the Koran, Sidi Dylaleddine, thinks, however, that the Prophet simply wanted to forbid excessive wine drinking, and that wine is permitted provided one does not get drunk.

Another, going one better, said: 'Eat and drink, but without excess, for God loves not him who commits excess.'

Arab gastronomical customs – 'When the food is served,' says El Syauté, 'help yourself from around the edge of the dish, leaving the middle, as the blessing of heaven will descend upon it.'

The laws of hospitality are rigorously observed by the Moslems. If a stranger, be he well or poorly dressed, appears at the entrance to a tent, or at the door of a house, and asks for hospitality, the master of the household immediately answers: 'Be welcome,' and bids him enter, indicating a place on the carpet or mat which covers the floor. Immediately, the visit is treated as a festive occasion and the guest is offered a cup of coffee or tea and whatever there is ready to eat.

Hospitality is the duty of every good Moslem.

When a Moslem family offers you some *messelmen* or some *sebaas-el aarroussa* (cakes in the form of tapering fingers or biscuits shaped like small hands) it is a sign that you are welcome.

The pattern of the hand seen on the cakes, on the tents, on the walls, windows and doors of Moslem houses, is a symbol of power and has an historical significance.

Moses, having changed his rod into a serpent, showed his hand to Pharaoh, as if to bear witness to his power. The faithful thus adopted the symbol of the hand of Moses as a protection from the evil eye.

A very rigid period of fasting, the Ramadan, is prescribed for all Moslems during all daylight hours of the entire month of Ramadan, which is the ninth month of the Mohammedan year.

The word Ramadan comes from a verb meaning to rain, because it washes away the sins of the flesh and cleanses the heart of its impurities.

The period of fasting was laid down by Mohammed, during the second year of the Hegira, to sanctify by religious observance the memory of what happened to the first man when he ate the forbidden fruit. Adam, banished from the Garden of Eden, cried bitterly, but his repentance was not accepted by God until thirty days after his fall, when his body had been cleansed of the impurities with which his disobedience had tainted him, and posterity was thus condemned to a consecutive fast of thirty days a year.

During the month of Ramadan the Moslems must abstain from food, drink and tobacco from sunrise to sunset.

In North Africa, where Islam is the predominating religion, a burst of artillery fire announces to the faithful that Ramadan has commenced. During the ensuing thirty days a single cannon shot fired each evening at sunset signals the end of fasting for that day.

Ramadan ends with pantagruelian feasts, called *Aïd-el-Kébir*, which somewhat resemble the Christian Christmas dinner. Moslems who cannot celebrate this feast at home gather together in Moorish cafés.

Culinary specialities of North Africa –

Aâssida. Flour boiled in water, then mixed with butter.

Bascoutou. Spanish loaf made of egg yolks, flour and orange blossoms.

Bissar. Dried beans cooked in water and oil until they form a sort of jelly; eaten hot or cold.

Bouzellouf. Sheep's head singed on a brisk fire to remove all hairs; boiled, then seasoned with oil, vinegar, salt, pepper and garlic.

Breyes beylicales. Little squares of cooked semolina mixed with pistachio nuts, walnuts and almonds.

Brik. Eggs in puff pastry fried in oil.

Cacao. Little reddish-brown lozenges made from sugar, pistachio nuts, almonds and lemon essence.

Chekchuka. A dish made of sweet or strong peppers, tomatoes, baby marrows (zucchini) or aubergines (eggplants), cut in pieces and fried in olive oil with garlic and onion, the whole either mixed with beaten eggs, or not, and cooked for a few minutes on a slow fire.

Cherba-bel-frik. Green corn soup.

Djendjelem. A whitish, soft paste, made of sugar, ginger, starch and a pinch of pepper. It is bought ready-made.

Dolma. Highly seasoned mixture of rice, chopped meat and onions wrapped in cabbage leaves, covered with water and cooked in a casserole with fire below and above. Similar to Turkish dolma.

Douara. Boiled pluck and tripe seasoned with cumin and spices.

Guizada. A kind of scalloped little cookie made from semolina and eggs, baked in the oven.

Homse. Little balls of paste fried and coated with honey.

Kabab. Mutton cut into squares, braised in butter, seasoned with salt and pepper and served liberally garnished with sliced onions and parsley.

Kefta. Chopped and spiced mutton, shaped into rissoles

and grilled over a wood fire.

Khali'. Dried mutton cooked in oil and fat and thus preserved.

Liani. Lamb stew with chick peas, seasoned with wild parsley.

Makrouda. Pastry lozenges stuffed with dates.

M'darbel. Mixture of fried baby marrows (zucchini) and little pieces of beef fried in oil seasoned with hot pimento and a dash of vinegar.

Mekechter. Chicken *fricassée* with chick peas.

Merga. Strongly spiced stock made of mutton or chicken, or both, which the Arabs drink only when it is very cold or in cases of illness.

M'habia. Cake made from milk, semolina, pistachio nuts, walnuts and pine nuts.

M'hamsa. Soup with pasta and tomatoes.

Mokh. Sheep's brain and tongue, seasoned with garlic, cayenne pepper and wild parsley.

Osbane. Forcemeat made from chopped sheep's pluck and meat, mixed with rice, seasoned with red pepper and spices. Used for stuffing sheep's intestines.

Rim-bel-terfass. A stew made of gazelle meat and Saharan truffles (Saharan dish).

Sferia. Mixture of chopped mutton and onions seasoned with salt, pepper and cumin. These are shaped into little balls, dipped in egg and fried in butter.

Tadjin helou. Very delicate stew made of mutton or beef, vegetables in season, prunes or raisins and a few quinces. This is covered with pie pastry and cooked in the oven.

Terbia-bel-hebar. *Macédoine* of vegetables served with a roast bustard (little bustard or field duck).

Tleitli. Macaroni garnished with chopped meat and baked eggs.

Tomina. Coarse semolina cooked in an earthenware casserole and plunged into butter and boiling honey.

Yubbo. Cake made from honey, olive oil, rose petals, flour and dandelions.

Other specialities include *lagni*, much-valued palm milk; *leben*, which is nothing but whey; and *kéfir* made from cow's, goat's or sheep's milk; *chreyba*, *rahatloucoum*, *sahleb*, *rogagues*, *messelmen*, *makroutes*, *stuffed dates*, etc.

And when we add to this list *tadjins* (in its several forms), *méchoui* and *couscous* with its various accompaniments (see COUSCOUS) and the delicacies of Tunisian and Israeli *cuisine*, we realise that African regional cookery need not fear comparison with more sophisticated metropolitan cusine.

ALGÉRIENNE (À L') – This is the name of a garnish, applicable principally to meat. It consists of small tomatoes braised in oil accompanied by sweet potato croquettes, or sweet potatoes cooked in butter.

ALICA – A sort of porridge of which the Romans were very fond. It was prepared with spelt (hard or durum wheat, what today is known as German wheat) mixed with a sort of clay (*creta*) found between Pozzuoli and Naples on the hill of Leucogee (Pliny). A drink was also made from Alica.

It is said that Augustus paid a rent of 20,000 sesterces to the Neapolitans for the exclusive right to this clay. (*Creta* in Latin means both 'clay' and 'chalk'.)

ALICANTE WINE. ALICANTE (VIN D') – A very well-known dessert wine from the Spanish province of Alicante. This is also the name given in the *midi* of France to a variety of red grape (known, too, as Grenache).

ALICUIT (Languedoc cookery) – *Ragoût* of giblets (principally turkey gizzards and wings) prepared as described in the recipe for *Turkey giblets bonne-femme* (see GIBLETS).

This *ragoût* is a country dish called *alicot* in dialect. The etymological root is retained in all its various forms: *ali*, wings; *cuit*, cooked.

ALIMENT – Derived from the Latin word *alere*: to nourish, to cause to grow. The Celtic root *alt* means nourishment. The word 'aliment' indicates an object, while the word 'nourishment' indicates an action, although the latter is often employed as a synonym of 'aliment'.

Any substance which upon entering the body is capable of supplying it with materials for growth or repair and with fuel for its energy requirements is an aliment.

Simple aliments are those that the organism consumes and absorbs without first submitting them to modification; water, which is of considerable alimentary importance (see WATER), and sea salt are about the only substances in this category.

To study the aliments we must begin by selecting the genuinely alible elements of each one and proceed to examine them individually. Today we consider as elementary aliments, *ternary* substances (that is substances of carbon, hydrogen and oxygen). These ternary substances are always associated with other mineral elements, namely the carbohydrates, fats and *quaternary* substances (also called *nitrogenous* substances because nitrogen combines with the carbon, hydrogen and oxygen). *Quaternary* substances are *proteids* or *proteins* (formerly called albuminoids). To these three broad classes of aliments (simple, ternary and quaternary) we must add *mineral substances* and *vitamins*.

Carbohydrates are represented by the starches and sugars. Apart from small quantities present in some animal tissues, these are all of vegetable origin. The action of the digestive ferments transforms them into glucose which is absorbed by the blood, then condensed by the liver into *glycogen* or animal starch. This is broken down little by little to meet the body's requirements. The final stage of this decomposition yields water and carbonic acid. In certain illnesses the process of decomposition is arrested and intermediary products form (acids) which remain in the blood. When the quantity of glucose circulating in the blood reaches too high a level as a result of inadequate transformation, part of it is eliminated in the urine (which normally does not contain any). Such is the case in diabetes.

The body can transform carbohydrates into fats. These two aliments are therefore to an extent interchangeable.

The fats or fatty bodies are *esters*: compounds of glycerine and fatty acids. Alimentary fatty bodies are present in both the animal and vegetable kingdoms. The digestive ferments decompose the fats, which then reconstitute themselves to form organic fats. The fat is then laid down in the tissues and especially in the cellular tissue, and is utilised by the body according to its needs. When the fat thus laid in reserve is not used in sufficient quantity by the body, it accumulates in the organs and tissues and results in obesity.

Fats may be partially replaced in the diet by carbohydrates, but these are not absolute equivalents and the diet of an adult must contain a minimum of 70 g. ($2\frac{1}{2}$ oz.) fats daily. This amount may be decreased in summer but it must never fall below 40 g. ($1\frac{1}{2}$ oz.) per day, of which 25 g. (1 oz.) should be animal fat.

Although fat forms a normal part of certain organs, and although carbohydrates, too, are constitutive elements of certain tissues, the principal function of these two elements is to provide energy. It is thanks to them that the body is capable of physical exertion and of maintaining its temperature. They are considered, therefore, mainly as combustives, or as respiratory aliments, since it is through the oxygen in the air that this combustion is effected.

Theoretically, fats decompose into carbonic acid and water (like the carbohydrates); but in certain illnesses this decomposition stops at one of several intermediate stages and the resulting excess of fatty acids found in the blood constitutes one of the factors of acidosis.

The albuminoids (*proteinic* or *quaternary substances*) contain carbon, hydrogen, oxygen as their principal elements, and a fourth – nitrogen. Their chemical composition is extremely complex (see ALBUMINOIDS). Under the influence of digestive elements they are subjected to a series of modifications which terminate in the production of albumins; these are used in the constitution of our tissues.

The organism uses the albuminoids partly as energy factors, but principally to aid growth and in the reparation of our tissues.

Unlike carbohydrates and fats, albuminoids do not undergo total decomposition; in eight cases out of ten this stops at the *urea* stage, the remainder being eliminated in the form of various nitrogenous substances, some of which have still not been determined.

Deficiencies of the liver (the great transformer of nitrogenous substances) or of the kidneys (the great eliminators of the same) cause proteins, or their products of disintegration, to accumulate in the blood and a serious disorder called *azotaemia* results (of which uraemia is a modification). In other instances, the urine is found to contain substances it ought not to contain such as aminic acids or even albumins (*albuminuria*).

The albuminoid group also comprises closely related substances known as *proteidae* which are albumins combined with a carbohydrate to form a *paranucleine* (*paranucleoproteides*).

Finally, classed as 'albuminoids' are non-proteic nitrogenous substances like gelatine, keratin, etc.

Minerals, too, are indispensable elements of our alimentation. Sodium chloride (sea salt) is the only mineral used alone in its natural state; the others occur as elements of various compounds (probably the only form in which they are assimilable) combined with the albuminoids, carbohydrates and fats of our natural foods.

We know the approximate needs of the organism as regards certain chemical substances that are eliminated daily in ponderable quantities. The *excreta*, for example, remove from the body each day on average 7 g. soda, 4·75 g. potassium, 1·25 g. calcium, 1·63 g. phosphorus, 0·5 g. magnesia, 0·05 g. iron, 0·05 g. sulphur, as well as a small quantity of chloride and traces of manganese, bromine, iodine, silica and fluorine. Other elements enter into alimentation in imponderable quantity, which does not mean to say that their rôle is insignificant; in fact there is a probability that we may find among these imponderables an explanation for the part vitamins play in the diet. For example, recent research has revealed that vitamins act as coenzymes (or codiastases) and are therefore involved in the degradation or resynthesis of the various nutriments.

Remineralisation experiments have been carried out with animals. That is to say, the principal minerals have been removed from their alimentation and replaced by complex mineral mixtures. These experiments invariably failed when chemically pure salts were used; positive results were obtained using less-well-purified salts, which shows the important rôle impurities (i.e., the imponderable traces of certain elements) play in the diet.

Most of the chemists who have analysed the aliments have determined their total mineralisation by reducing them to the form of ash. This calls for complicated calculations and gives far from accurate results when the final figure is applied to fresh foods, such as those we consume daily. This is explained not only by the diversity of the methods employed, but also (in the animal) by the differences arising from the race, feeding and cuts considered; in the vegetable, the variety, the soil in which it has been cultivated, the fertiliser used, the part analysed.

M. R. Berg has calculated the figures for cabbages in the accompanying table.

	CABBAGES GATHERED	
	in March	*in December*
Oxide of potassium	0·5067	0·6748
Oxide of sodium	0·0330	0·0640
Oxide of lime	0·1730	0·1596
Oxide of iron	0·2216	0·2870
Phosphoric anhydride	0·5833	0·0287
Sulphuric anhydride	0·5833	0·2569
Chlorine	0·6550	0·4445

Per cent of fresh substances

Figures vary according to whether analysis is made of the exterior leaves, the interior leaves or the buds of the vegetable. Basic elements predominate in the exterior, whereas the interior leaves and, in particular, the buds, are distinctly acid.

Cooking procedures modify the ratio and proportion of mineral salts primarily by dissolving the alkaline elements, so that if a piece of beef in which the acid elements predominate is boiled an alkaline stock can be obtained.

The effect of cooking is even more marked with vegetables. Blanching (prerequisite in the manufacture of tinned food) reduces the mineral content of vegetables and destroys the basic minerals. Prolonged boiling has an even more damaging effect. The effects of other methods of cooking are less drastic since the juices released by the vegetable are usually consumed with it.

TOTAL MINERAL LOSS DURING COOKING IN:

	Water *per cent*	*Oil* *per cent*	*Fat* *per cent*	*Butter* *per cent*
Carrots	49·95	30·59	20·91	19·65
Potatoes	66·74	31·33	52·38	42·85
Onions	66·67	47·25	60	53·44
	LOSS OF POTASSIUM SALTS			
Carrots	52·05	23·97	14·38	22·60
Potatoes	57·61	20·46	11·51	11·97
Onions	66·67	13·33	19·16	26·67

Some experiments have shown how the total loss of minerals and potassium salts varies according to different cooking procedures.

Artificial aliments – Natural foods that have been prepared industrially are not included under this heading (they will be dealt with later). Here we are referring to aliments that have been chemically treated in order to make them more digestible or more easily assimilated: there are many of them. Among the nitrogenous substances are purified albumins, legumin, albumoses and peptones. All these products can be prescribed therapeutically but their prolonged use inevitably leads to disorders; they have never succeeded in supplementing natural foods in the adult diet. As far as children are concerned, modified artificial foods are those most frequently used, dextrined and malted flours, etc.

Chemical aliments – We must not forget that even if albuminoids, carbohydrates and fatty bodies are elements of our alimentation, they are not aliments. Aliments have a traditional form and are borrowed (apart from a few minerals) from the animal or vegetable kingdoms; the three elements listed are merely constituents of aliments (along with a few indigestible substances such as cellulose). The presence of cellulose besides providing bulk has been proved after exhaustive research to be indispensable in the accomplishment of digestive phenomena.

Complete aliment – An aliment that contains, or is reputed to contain, the various alimentary substances in the right proportions. Milk is the only practically complete food (as far as babies are concerned) and even it is deficient in Vitamin C.

Economy aliments – Some of the substances we occasionally describe in this way have, like cocoa and chocolate, real food value; others, such as tea, coffee, coca-cola, only act through the nervous excitation they provoke.

It is arguable whether or not the ingestion of these substances can increase the energy output of a diet, but they can, under certain conditions, calm or falsely appease, the sensation of hunger and impart a feeling of well-being.

Nutritive value of certain elements – Bearing in mind the importance of the various elements in the normal diet (albumins, carbohydrates, fats, etc.) an aliment will be more nourishing the more fatty bodies it contains, for these are richest, volume for volume, in calories.

The mutual substitution tables of various groups of aliments (see below) give some indication of the relative values of certain aliments of animal and vegetable origin. We have to thank Mme. Lucie Randoin, MM. Legallic, Causerets and G. Duchêne for them.

Meat, milk, butter and bread have been taken as basic elements in these substitution tables. The compilers have then calculated the quantities of other aliments (closely related in nutritive value) required to replace a given weight of each of these basic elements.

In establishing these quantities, they have naturally taken into account that the aliments mentioned in each group are not of precisely the same composition and may even differ profoundly on certain points. We can nevertheless see the advantage of comparing aliments which, practically speaking, are interchangeable. If the alimentation is sufficiently varied the organism can only benefit from their different nutritional values.

Volume of aliments – Nothing is more variable than the capacity of that elastic organ the stomach; although 1200 $cm.^3$ is the recognised average capacity, this may fall to 600 $cm.^3$ or rise to 2000 $cm.^3$ according to the individual.

We must not forget that ingested liquids leave the stomach very rapidly and enter only minimally into calculations involving the volume of aliments.

Classification of the aliments – Any attempt to draw up a set of guiding principles for sensible eating must be based upon quite a simple classification of the aliments.

There is little to choose between the various classifications suggested by nutritionists, but like Mme. Randoin we prefer the following:

1. Milk and its derivatives (with the exception of butter).
2. Various meats and fish, eggs.
3. Fatty substances.
4. Starchy foods (flour, bread, noodles, rice, dried vegetables, potatoes) and sweetened foods (dried fruit, sugar, jam, chocolate, etc.).
5. Fresh vegetables and fruit:
   (a) eaten raw (*crudités*)
   (b) eaten cooked.
6. Beverages:
   (a) water
   (b) fruit juices
   (c) alcoholic drinks
   (d) aromatic drinks.

Weight of aliments – Normally the stomach is more sensitive to the weight of aliments than to their volume. The weight of the total diet (beverages excluded) ranges from 1500 to 1800 g. for a man, a little less for a woman; the weight becomes excessive above 2500 g.

The average weight of a meal must not exceed 800 to 1000 g. for a man and 600 to 800 g. for a woman. Generally a feeling of satiety occurs before these limits are reached.

MUTUAL SUBSTITUTION OF ANIMAL FOODS

100 G. MEAT (net weight) can be replaced as a source of protein by:
- 100 g. offal or variety meats
- 100 g. fish (net weight)
- 2½ eggs
- ½ litre milk or the equivalent in milk derivatives (see table below)

MUTUAL SUBSTITUTION OF DAIRY FOODS

¼ LITRE MILK can be replaced by:
- 120 g. unsweetened concentrated milk
- 80 g. sweetened concentrated milk
- 30 g. powdered milk
- 125 g. curdled milk (cream cheese)
- 2 small cartons yoghurt (about 250 g.)
- 4 *petits suisses* (about 120 g.)
- 1 *demi-sel* (about 60 g.)
- 40–50 g. fermented soft cheese (*Brie*, *Camembert*, *Coulommiers*, *Livarot*, *Munster*, etc.)
- 30–40 g. fermented hard cheeses (*Gruyère*, *Dutch cheese*, *Saint-Paulin*, *Cantal*, etc.)
- 60 g. *Gruyère* cream cheese
- 25 g. goat cheese

MUTUAL SUBSTITUTION OF FARINACEOUS FOODS

100 G. BREAD can be replaced as a source of calories by:
- 70 g. cereal flour
- 70 g. rusks or dry sponge fingers
- 50 g. biscuits
- 80 g. gingerbread
- 70 g. porridge oats
- 70 g. pasta or noodles
- 70 g. rice
- 75 g. dried vegetables (haricot beans, lentils, peas, etc.)
- 350 g. potatoes (gross weight)
- 150 g. chestnuts (gross weight)
- 90 g. dried fruit (dates, figs, prunes, etc.)

MUTUAL SUBSTITUTION OF FATTY SUBSTANCES

100 G. BUTTER can be replaced as a source of lipids by:
- 100 g. animal fat (lard, mutton fat, etc.)
- 85 g. oil
- 100 g. margarine
- 120 g. unsmoked bacon

Consistency of the aliments – The consistency of foods is of far greater importance (as regards their digestion) than their volume or weight. As a rule, whatever their initial consistency, aliments ought to reach the stomach reduced to a pulp (or pap) through mastication and insalivation (for the gastric musculature is too feeble in the human species to break down large fragments; the latter lie too long in the stomach and can cause dyspepsia). The bad habit of not chewing food properly, of swallowing too quickly (tachyphagia) has the worst possible effects.

X-ray examination reveals, for example, that a hard-boiled egg, considered to be one of the most indigestible of foods, leaves the stomach just as quickly as a soft-boiled egg if it is grated finely (or chewed very thoroughly) to give it a similar consistency.

We must not conclude from this that the ideal way of ingesting food is in the form of a purée; on the contrary, puréed foods are a last resort, to have recourse to in cases of infection of the mouth and teeth, or as a temporary measure in some forms of dyspepsia, or in the early stages of convalescence. The importance of mastication, insalivation, and digestion cannot be over emphasised; a diet consisting solely of puréed foods would not stimulate the stomach muscles sufficiently and could cause gastric atony; it could also lead to dental caries owing to the enforced idleness imposed on the teeth. So one must encourage the culinary habit of adding some hard substances (fried croûtons, for example) to foods presented in puréed form.

Temperature of the aliments – Hot foods are more stimulating than cold and man always looks for such stimulation in his food, for unlike other animal species he is not content simply to have his hunger appeased.

Only extreme temperatures are harmful to the organism. If food is too hot it can cause burns to the mouth, the tongue, and the œsophagus, especially when hot liquids are gulped down. The latter can also cause irritation to the stomach which may even develop into gastritis.

Foods which are too cold induce constriction of the capillary blood vessels of the stomach, causing subsequent dilatation. The side effects are even worse than those produced by foods which are too hot.

The nature and consistency of the aliments have a strong bearing on how their temperature is withstood; one can, if need be, sip broth or coffee at 60°C. (140°F.); porridge taken at the same temperature would have serious effects. The particular moment at which these foods are quickly swallowed is also significant; an iced substance taken on an empty stomach can be harmful, whereas the effect of an ice cream taken immediately after a meal and received by an already full stomach would not be nearly so serious.

Too swift a transition from hot to cold, for example, a hot food followed immediately by an iced drink, is extremely harmful to the enamel of the teeth.

Soups rapidly become cold in the plate, so they are usually served very hot; it is hardly possible to drink a clear soup heated above 60°C. (140°F.) – even above 58°C. (136°F.). Most people wait until it cools to 37° to 45°C (99° to 103°F.) to taste the flavour.

Thick soups, porridges, vegetable purées must not be drunk above 38° to 42°C. (100° to 107°F.).

Roast meat is usually served between 40° and 45°C. (104° and 113°F). Its temperature must not fall below 40°C. (104°F.) otherwise the fat begins to congeal (this is especially true of roast mutton). This is why plates are heated (particularly meat plates).

Hot bread of 38°C. (100°F.) and above is much more indigestible than cold bread; this depends less on the temperature itself than on the physical condition of the crumb. It is a widespread belief, however, that slow digestion of cold foods is beneficial. Ninon de Lenclos attributes his sprightly old age to having all his life eaten cold food.

Psychological effects of the aliments – For its curiosity value, here, according to a learned Swedish doctor, are the effects produced on man by the different foods he eats:

– By eating beef (especially roast beef) for months on end, one is certain to acquire self-confidence and audacity . . .

– Mutton makes one melancholy . . .

– Pork makes one pessimistic. Could it be that pork butchers only see the black side of things?

– Duck flesh makes man bad-tempered . . .

– For wit and beauty eggs are supreme . . .

– Walnuts, hazelnuts, almonds, dried figs develop the mind . . .

– Tomatoes, oranges and lemons considerably improve the quality of the voice . . .

– Finally, doughy English-type bread slows the mental processes; light-textured bread assures a buoyant morale. Rye bread and buckwheat pancake make one melancholy . . .

ALIMENTATION – Alimentation varies according to age, climate, profession, and state of health.

Alimentation must be adequate. It must provide (with a small excess) the wherewithal for growth (in the young person), for the repair and upkeep of the tissues and organs, and for the expenditure of energy.

To determine the energy value of an aliment or diet, we employ as a measure the calorie (q.v.), going on the principle that all forms of energy can be transformed into heat.

Various methods are used to determine the requirements of the human body. One way is by calculating the average from the global alimentation of a population. Another method is by analysing the *ingesta* (aliments and oxygen consumed), and the *excreta* (excretions, secretions, carbonic acid exhaled) and the quantity of heat discharged.

Modern dieticians are agreed that the normal alimentation for an adult of average weight (65 kg. or 143 lb.) in repose or engaged in only light duties must correspond to 2350 calories, that is approximately 36 calories for every kg. of weight (2·2 lb.). Previously a much higher calorie intake was considered necessary.

We usually allow that:

1 g. albuminoids gives out	4·44 calories
1 g. carbohydrates gives out	4·23 calories
1 g. fat gives out	9·40 calories

The figures of the physiologist M. Atwater are slightly lower because he incorporated losses and waste products in them. His table reads as follows:

Albuminoids	3·68 calories per g.
Carbohydrates	3·00 calories per g.
Fats	8·65 calories per g.

He also distinguished between substances of animal origin (best utilised) and substances of vegetable origin. To obtain 100 calories one must consume, according to him:

Animal proteins	23·50 g.
Vegetable proteins	28·19 g.
Amyloide substances	25·00 g.
Animal fats	11·18 g.
Vegetable fats	11·97 g.

We must not lose sight of the fact that these figures are merely averages, and while of great interest in alimentary studies of collectivities they lose their precision when reduced to the level of individuals.

The food requirements of the child are (in proportion to its weight) slightly higher than those of an adult since it must satisfy its growing needs. Those of the aged are less because of the reduced expenditure of energy. Food requirements increase with the lowering of exterior temperatures and with the work done.

The daily diet must be balanced. It must contain a minimum amount of albuminoids and fats, and enough carbohydrates to ensure that the two preceding elements are thoroughly utilised.

The normal diet must comprise:

80 g. albuminoids
70 g. fats
350 g. carbohydrates

The proportion of fats in an infant's diet must be higher in relation to carbohydrates.

The daily diet must be varied. The impossibility of measuring the imponderables of alimentation (very minute mineral substances and vitamins) obliges us to procure our alimentary elements from a wide variety of nutrients (something, in fact, that man has always done instinctively).

It is probable that the disorders arising from following too uniform a diet are caused by the absence or deficiency of these imponderables.

The daily diet must be pleasant. Although it is possible to feed like animals simply upon what nature provides (as members of certain sects do) man has always tried to increase the savouriness of his food by adding palatable condiments and by applying heat. The culinary art, which is derived from these two operations, has the effect of adding to the psychological need and satisfaction of taking nourishment, a gustative, olfactory satisfaction, and in so doing has exerted an influence on the development of the human species.

Natural alimentation – Without either denigrating culinary qualities or betraying gastronomic traditions, dieticians encourage us to use natural foods in the composition of menus.

This means that we ought not to consume food products that have been subjected to any form of chemical adulteration. Mme. Randoin defined the problem perfectly when she wrote: 'Nourishing ourselves is a serious business upon which much, good and bad, depends. It is incumbent, therefore, upon each one of us to realise that we make or break our health by a judicious or injudicious choice of the elements that constitute our daily diet.'

The fact remains that every individual case is different, and that although we have a few general lines to go on, there are no truly standard régimes in alimentation.

Besides using natural products wherever possible, the best one can do is to follow the precepts of quantity, of preparation, and of cooking methods laid down by the dieticians.

Forced feeding – The introduction of aliments directly into the stomach.

Artificial feeding – Alimentary substances can be made to penetrate the organism by channels other than the gastric one. These procedures are confined to the medical domain.

ALKALESCENTS (Food). ALCALINISANTS (Aliments) – Foods that contain an excess of basic elements (lime, soda, potassium, magnesium).

Milk and blood are the only alkalescents of animal origin. On the other hand, most foods of vegetable origin are alkalescents with the exception of cereals, cereal products and a number of vegetables of which we consume the flowers (artichoke) or buds (asparagus, Brussels sprouts). All acid-tasting fruit such as lemons, redcurrants, etc., are alkalescents.

Celery, Jerusalem artichokes, turnips, carrots, beetroot, cucumber, cabbage, dandelions, endive, lettuce, tomatoes, spinach, oranges, tangerines and lemons are very strong alkalescents; other fruits, milk, potatoes and cauliflower, less so.

ALKALI VOLATILE. ALCALI VOLATIL – Commonly known as liquid ammonia. It is a colourless liquid, lighter than water, with an extremely strong pungent odour reminiscent of urine. Its fumes can be asphyxiating. It is used in confectionery as a solvent for cochineal carmines.

ALKALOIDS. ALCALOÏDES – Substances of vegetable origin that have a powerful effect on the organism, even when absorbed in minute quantities. (The stimulants in coffee, tea and chocolate are alkaloids.)

ALKERMES. ALKERMÈS – An old-fashioned red cordial, once very popular, produced by distilling a sweetened infusion of nutmeg, cinnamon, bay leaf and cloves. Its colour is derived from kermes, hence its name.

ALLARIA (Jack-by-the-hedge). ALLIAIRE – This plant has a very pronounced garlic flavour, and can be used as a condiment for salads.

ALLEMANDE SAUCE – The name given to a classic white sauce made by adding egg yolks and cream to a *velouté* (q.v.).

A more modern version of the recipe for this sauce (one of the best in the French culinary repertoire) is given in the section devoted to sauces.

Despite its name, this sauce is not of German origin. According to Carême it is so called because of its light colour, and to distinguish it from *espagnole sauce*, which is dark. (The latter does not seem to have originated in Spain, either.)

In the French culinary repertoire, there is an enormous number of designations borrowed from other countries, most of them describing dishes of entirely French origin. Modern authors also refer to the *allemande* as *Sauce parisienne* (see SAUCE).

Carême's recipe – Carême begins by giving the recipe for *Velouté sauce* (see SAUCE), then describes the preparation of *allemande sauce* as follows:

'Pour half the *velouté* into a saucepan. Add an equal quantity of good chicken consommé, to which has been added a few mushrooms (stalks and peel), and as much salt as can be held on the point of a knife.

Place the sauce over a brisk heat and stir with a wooden spoon until it comes to the boil. Draw it away from the flame, cover, and leave to simmer for about an hour. Skim off the fat and replace on a high flame, stirring with the wooden spoon to prevent it sticking to the bottom of the pan. When perfectly cooked, the sauce should coat the surface of a spoon quite thickly; and when poured, it should be of the same consistency as redcurrant jelly.

Remove the saucepan from the heat and prepare a liaison using 4 egg yolks mixed with 2 tablespoons (3 tablespoons) cream. Pass this through a sieve, adding a piece of best butter the size of an egg, cut into small pieces. Pour the liaison, little by little, into the *velouté*, stirring carefully with the wooden spoon to make sure that it is blended in smoothly. When it is all perfectly incorporated, replace the sauce on a moderate heat and continue stirring.

As soon as a few bubbles start to rise, remove from the heat and add as much grated nutmeg as can be held on the point of a knife. When well blended, pass through a sieve.'

ALLIGATOR – A species of American crocodile commonly called *cayman.*

The alligator has already become a part of the gastronomic world. Not only is its rather too musky flesh eaten by the natives who capture it, but slices of alligator are occasionally served in London and Paris.

The most valued parts of the reptile are the feet or flippers, since the alligator, although less aquatic than most crocodiles, also lives in water. These flippers are prepared *à l'américaine*, *à l'indienne* or in any similar manner. (See TURTLE.)

ALLSPICE. TOUTE ÉPICE – Common name for the myrtle seed (Jamaica pepper) and for cultivated nigella (fennel flower).

ALLUMETTES – Strips of puff pastry variously garnished and baked in the oven.

Little cakes made of puff pastry and filled or garnished with various mixtures are also called *allumettes*.

Allumettes (hot hors-d'œuvre) – Roll out a strip of puff pastry to a thickness of ½ cm. (¼ inch) and about 7 to 8 cm. (3 inches) wide. Cover the surface with *Fish forcemeat*, or any other suggested mixture (see FORCEMEATS or STUFFINGS). Cut into rectangles, place on a baking tray, and bake in the oven at 200°C. (400°F., Gas Mark 6) for about 15 minutes.

Allumettes à la périgourdine – Coat the puff pastry with a purée of chicken livers (see FORCEMEATS or STUFFINGS) mixed with finely chopped truffles. Bake in the oven.

Allumettes à la reine – Coat the puff pastry with a very fine mixture of minced breast of chicken and truffles, blended with thick *Velouté sauce* (see SAUCE). Bake in the oven.

Allumettes à la toscane – Sprinkle the sheet of puff pastry with grated Parmesan. Cut into strips and bake in the oven.

Ox palate allumettes. ALLUMETTES DE PALAIS DE BŒUF – 'Remove the skin from 2 ox palates previously cooked in water. Cut into strips the size of matchsticks and marinate in lemon juice or vinegar seasoned with a little salt, sprigs of parsley, and whole spring onions. When they are thoroughly macerated drain them, and dip them in a batter made as follows:

'Place 2 good handfuls of flour, 1 tablespoon fine oil, and a little finely ground salt, into a basin. Dilute this gradually with beer until the batter reaches the consistency of thick cream. Dip the palate strips into it and fry until golden brown. Serve as hot as possible.' (*La Cuisine bourgeoise*, 1769, Paris)

Allumettes (cakes)

Allumettes (cakes) – These sweet pastry cakes are said to have been created a century ago by a Swiss pastry-cook who lived in Dinard (Ille-et-Vilaine). M. Lacam, who wrote a history of pastry-making, describes the invention as follows: 'One day Planta, the above-mentioned pastry-cook, had some icing left over and did not know what to do with it. Having softened it, he added a pinch of flour to it in order to prevent the sugar from running in the heat of the oven, and spread it on a sheet of puff pastry. This he cut into little sticks and baked in the oven.'

Thus *allumettes*, a sort of dry *petit four* which are now so popular, were invented.

Method. Roll out some puff pastry to the thickness of 4 mm. (⅛ inch) and cut it into strips 8 cm. (3 inches) wide. Spread a thin layer of *Royal icing* (see ICING) on these strips, cut them into pieces 2 to 3 cm. (1 inch) wide, and bake in the oven at 200°C. (400°F., Gas Mark 6) for 12 minutes.

ALMOND. AMANDE – Kernel of a stone fruit, particularly of the almond tree. There are two varieties, *sweet almond* and *bitter almond*. They come mostly from North Africa, Provence, Italy and Languedoc, and from California, U.S.A.

More than half their weight is oil. There are two varieties of this; one is used principally in perfumery, the other in pharmaceutics, in the manufacture of soothing emulsions. The almond tree is mentioned in Genesis, and almonds were among the fruit offered to Joseph (see ALMOND, *Country almond*).

Almond

Aboukir almonds (confectionery). AMANDES D'ABOUKIR – *Petits fours*, made of kirsch-flavoured, green-coloured almond paste, shaped in the form of an almond, and stuffed with a blanched almond. Aboukirs are coated with gum, or iced with sugar cooked to hard crack stage (see SUGAR).

Almond and puff pastry gâteau. GÂTEAU FEUILLETÉ AUX AMANDES – This gâteau is known under the name of *Pithiviers* (q.v.).

Almond butter. BEURRE D'AMANDES – Pound 150 g. (5 oz., 1 cup) freshly blanched almonds in a mortar until they are reduced to a paste, adding a few drops of cold water to prevent them from turning into oil. Pound in 225 g. (8 oz., 1 cup) fresh butter. Pass through a very fine sieve.

This butter is used for flavouring certain sauces and cream soups; it is also used in the preparation of cold *hors d'œuvre*.

Almond cookies. PAINS ANGLAIS – Small dry cookies prepared in the following manner.

Ingredients. 225 g. (8 oz., 2 cups) sieved flour, 225 g. (8 oz., 2 cups) ground almonds, 225 g. (8 oz., 1 cup) castor (fine) sugar, 100 g. (4 oz., ½ cup) butter, 4 eggs, half a liqueur glass of rum.

Method. Sieve the flour onto the table. Make a well in the centre and add the almonds, the sugar and the well-softened butter. Break the eggs into these ingredients and pour in the rum. To prevent burning, mix the paste without kneading it (if too firm, add an egg yolk).

Roll the paste into long sausages on the lightly floured table. Cut them into small pieces and roll these into balls.

Space the balls out on buttered trays (use two). Coat each ball twice with beaten egg and score with the blade of a wet knife. Bake for 20 minutes in a slow oven.

Almond cookies (lemon-flavoured). PAINS ANGLAIS AU CITRON – Pound 225 g. (8 oz., 1½ cups) blanched almonds finely with 225 g. (8 oz., 1 cup) castor (fine) sugar and 2 whole eggs.

Sieve 225 g. (8 oz., 2 cups) flour onto the table. Make a well in the centre and place the pounded mixture in it. Add 175 g. (6 oz., $\frac{3}{4}$ cup) butter and the grated rind of 1 lemon (or orange). Knead well together.

Divide the paste into walnut-sized pieces. Sprinkle the table lightly with flour and form these into little cigars, pointed at each end. Place them on a buttered baking sheet, brush with beaten egg and score in the centre. Bake in a hot oven for 8 to 10 minutes.

Almond cream. CRÈME D'AMANDES – Prepare $\frac{1}{2}$ litre (scant pint, $2\frac{1}{4}$ cups) *crème pâtissière* in the usual manner, cool it and add to it 250 g. (9 oz., $1\frac{2}{3}$ cups) freshly blanched almonds pounded to a smooth paste with 250 g. (9 oz., generous cup) sugar and 250 g. (9 oz., generous cup) butter.

This cream is used for filling sweet dishes. For *crème pâtissière* see CREAMS, *French pastry cream*.

Almond loaf. PAIN COMPLET – A cake made of almond paste shaped like a loaf.

Almond milk. LAIT D'AMANDES – The codex gives the following recipe for almond milk:

Ingredients. 50 g. (2 oz., scant $\frac{1}{2}$ cup) blanched sweet almonds, 50 g. (2 oz., $\frac{1}{4}$ cup) white sugar, 1 dl. (6 tablespoons, scant $\frac{1}{2}$ cup) distilled water.

Method. Place the almonds, sugar and water in a marble mortar and pound to a very smooth paste. Press through a fine sieve.

Almond nougat. NOUGAT AUX AMANDES – Dry 500 g. (18 oz., $4\frac{1}{2}$ cups) blanched, chopped almonds in the oven. Place them in a copper bowl in which 400 g. (14 oz., $1\frac{3}{4}$ cups) sugar, flavoured with a squeeze of lemon juice, has been boiled to a pale caramel. Stir this mixture with a spatula.

While the mixture is still hot, pour it into variously shaped greased moulds. Alternatively, the nougat may be spread thinly on an oiled marble slab and cut into different shapes.

Nougat prepared in this way may be shaped into bowls, baskets, clogs and other objects.

Almond paste I. PÂTE D'AMANDES – Crush 450 g. (1 lb., 3 cups) blanched almonds and place them in a mortar with the selected flavouring (vanilla sugar or liqueur). Cook 900 g. (2 lb., 4 cups) sugar to hard crack stage (see SUGAR). Add this gradually to the almonds, pounding vigorously until well mixed.

Almond paste II. PÂTE D'AMANDES – *Ingredients.* 475 g. (17 oz., $3\frac{1}{2}$ cups) sweet almonds, 25 g. (1 oz., 3 tablespoons) bitter almonds, 5 g. (1 teaspoon) gum arabic, 100 g. (4 oz., scant cup) icing sugar, 1 egg white, juice of 1 lemon.

Method. Pound the almonds with the lemon juice and pass through a fine strainer. Put into a copper pan with the icing sugar and egg white. Dry this mixture gently over heat, stirring all the time. Add the gum arabic dissolved in a little water.

To be perfect this paste must not be sticky. It is used as an *abaisse* (q.v.) in various sweet dishes and *petits fours*.

Almond praline. PRALIN AUX AMANDES – Melt 450 g. (1 lb., 2 cups) castor (fine) sugar slowly in a copper pan. Cook it until it reaches the degree of light caramel, 160°C. (320°F.). Add to this sugar 450 g. (1 lb., 3 cups) raw unblanched well-dried almonds.

Tip all this mixture onto an oiled marble slab. Allow to cool. Pound the mixture in a mortar. Pass it through a fine sieve. Keep this dry almond powder in tins with well-fitting lids.

Almond tartlets. TARTELETTES AMANDINES – The recipe for these very delicate tartlets was set to rhyme by Edmond Rostand in *Cyrano de Bergerac*. The recipe itself is attributed to Ragueneau, the famous seventeenth-century pastry-cook.

Here it is in verse:

Comment on fait les tartelettes amandines

Battez, pour qu'ils soient mousseux,
Quelques œufs;
Incorporez à leur mousse
Un jus de cédrat choisi;
Versez-y
Un bon lait d'amande douce;
Mettez de la pâte à flan
Dans le flanc
De moules à tartelette;
D'un doigt preste abricotez
Les côtés;
Versez goutte à gouttelette
Votre mousse en ces puits, puis
Que ces puits
Passent au four, et, blondines,
Sortant en gais troupelets,
Ce sont les
Tartelettes amandines.

Beat your eggs, the yolk and white
Very light;
Mingle with their creamy fluff
Drops of lime juice, cool and green;
Then pour in
Milk of almonds, just enough.
Dainty patty pans, embraced
In puff-paste –
Have these ready within reach;
With your thumb and finger, pinch
Half an inch
Up around the edge of each –
Into these, a score or more,
Slowly pour
All your store of custard; so
Take them, bake them golden-brown –
Now sit down! . . .
Almond tartlets!*

* *From Brian Hooker's translation of* Cyrano de Bergerac *by Edmond Rostand. Published by Heinemann in association with Allen & Unwin.*

Bitter almonds. AMANDES AMÈRES – Bitter almonds owe their bitterness to the relatively high amount of prussic acid they contain. They should therefore be used in moderation.

These almonds are employed in *pâtisserie* for flavouring icings and fillings; and in confectionery. They are not used as dessert fruit.

The oil obtained from them is poisonous.

Blanched almonds. AMANDES MONDÉES – Dried almonds from which the skin has been removed. Proceed in the following manner. Put the almonds into a sieve; plunge into a saucepan of boiling water and immediately draw the saucepan to the side of the stove.

Drain the almonds, a few at a time, and skin them as soon as you see that the skin comes off when pressed with the fingers. Drop them into cold water, drain and pat dry. If they are to be kept, scatter on a sieve or fine grill and dry thoroughly in a slow oven. Store in a tin or jar with a well-fitting lid. Keep in a dry place.

Chopped almonds. AMANDES HACHÉES – These are blanched almonds roughly or finely chopped depending upon how they are to be employed.

Coloured almonds. AMANDES COLORÉES – Variously coloured shredded and ground almonds are used for colouring nougat and for sprinkling on iced *petits fours*, cakes, biscuits (cookies) and sweet dishes.

Flavouring appropriate to the colour may be added: thus pink may be scented with raspberry essence; mauve flavoured with essence of violets.

Country almond (Indian almond tree). BADAMIER – This tree, which is also called *catappa*, grows generally in Asia. The fruit is an almond, of pleasant taste, from which an oil somewhat similar to olive oil is extracted.

Another species of country almond produces resinous and aromatic matter, a kind of gum benzoin, which is used in confectionery.

Diced almonds. AMANDES EN DÉS – Blanched, halved almonds cut into large or small dice as required. They are used for sweet dishes and in *pâtisserie*.

Raw almonds. AMANDES BRUTES – This is the name given in *pâtisserie* and confectionery to almonds which have simply been taken out of their hard shells but are left unskinned.

The hard-shelled Provençal almonds are the most sought after for *pâtisserie*. But medium-sized almonds grown in the plains are also in great demand. These often contain quite a high proportion of bitter almonds and are the ones preferred for making almond paste.

The broad and fleshy *béraude almonds* comprise a smaller percentage of bitter almonds and are generally shredded or ground and used for sprinkling on *petits fours*, biscuits and sweet dishes.

Tournefort almonds are irregular in shape and very small. Because of their excellent flavour, they are much in demand for the confection of almond paste.

Roasted almonds. AMANDES GRILLÉES – Shred the almonds and dry them in the oven until they turn pale golden.

Salted almonds. AMANDES SALÉES – Toast sweet blanched almonds in the oven until their colour changes to pale yellow, turning once. Sprinkle with a pinch of saffron, red pepper and ginger then fry in butter until golden brown. Drain on a cloth and cool. Finally, coat the almonds with a clear solution of gum arabic and sprinkle with fine salt.

Shredded almonds. AMANDES EFFILÉES – These are used a great deal in *pâtisserie* and in confectionery. Shredded and roasted almonds are used for coating and garnishing sweet dishes; shredded, unroasted (white) almonds are used for coating *petits fours*, and in the confection of cooked nougat, Montélimar nougat, *petits fours*, meringues, almond slices, etc.

There are several very efficient implements for shredding almonds, although the operation can be performed equally well by hand. The almonds should be cut lengthwise and each one shredded into twelve to fifteen pieces. This should be done immediately after blanching and before the almonds are dried. After shredding they should be laid on a metal sheet and dried in a very slow oven or in a warming cupboard. During the drying process they should be turned three times a day. Store in hermetically sealed tins.

Sugared almonds. DRAGÉES – Almonds coated with hard sugar. Sugared almonds (not, strictly speaking, exactly as we know them today, but nevertheless coated with sugar or honey) have a long history. It is said that around the year 177 B.C. a patrician Roman family, the illustrious Fabius family, had the habit of distributing sugared almonds to the populace as a token of rejoicing on the occasion of a birth or marriage in the family. So it is evident that the custom of presenting sugared almonds at the celebration of a birth goes back a very long way.

It is difficult to make sugared almonds at home, and hardly necessary, considering the excellent sugared almonds manufactured commercially. Some are made from windfall almonds; others with hazelnuts or pistachios; others again filled with a few drops of liqueur, chocolate, almond or filbert paste, etc. Verdun sugared almonds are particularly esteemed.

Sweet almonds. AMANDES DOUCES – Sweet almonds are in great demand for *pâtisserie* and confectionery; all Spanish and Italian almonds are sweet.

Green sweet almonds are greatly esteemed as dessert fruit and are consumed in great quantities. They are less oily and for that reason easier to digest than dry almonds.

Whole almonds. AMANDES ENTIÈRES – When a recipe in *pâtisserie* and confectionery calls for a certain amount of whole almonds, this means blanched almonds and not raw almonds, which are always referred to as raw, meaning with the thin brown skin left on.

ALMONDS, EARTH. AMANDES DE TERRE – These are *cyperus* tubers, which grow in marshy ground in countries with hot and temperate climates.

These almond-shaped tubers are brown outside, very white inside and extremely starchy. They can either be eaten raw (like hazelnuts) or cooked (like chestnuts). A kind of flour is made from them.

ALOCASIA – Plant indigenous to the Indies of which there are about fifteen known species. The most important of these, a native of Ceylon, has spread throughout most of the Indian subcontinent. There its voluminous roots serve as a food, but only after a prolonged period of cooking.

ALOE. ALOÈS – A genus of plants belonging to the family *Liliaceae*. From the leaves of this plant a purgative gum resin is extracted. Certain species found in Vietnam produce an edible starch.

ALPHEUS. ALPHÉE – A kind of shellfish with a slightly compressed body resembling that of the crayfish. Some species are found in all French coastal waters; others are peculiar to the Mediterranean. Some varieties are confined to the seas of Asia, Australia and America.

Although inferior in quality to the spiny lobster, this shellfish is quite highly esteemed. All methods of preparation given for lobster are applicable to it.

ALSACE – The Alsatian larder is well stocked with numerous and excellent foods. Alsace has a long tradition of good fare so it is not surprising that its gastronomic repertoire is a lengthy one, full of succulent dishes.

From Strasbourg and Colmar come that source of unending delight to gourmands, the magnificent *terrines* and *pâtés de foies gras truffés*, which rival in their delicacy even those of the south-west of France (see PÂTÉS, TERRINES).

The most delectable *charcuteries* in France are also found in Alsace, and thanks to the quality of the pork shoulder, smoked bacon, *saveloy* and sausages, the *choucroute* prepared *à la mode strasbourgeoise* is more delicious than any others.

But *choucroute* and *foies gras truffés*, excellent though they be, are not the only specialities.

Meat in this region is of good quality. Pork is particularly tasty. *Seigneur cochon* ('the noble pig') holds a place of high honour in Alsace. The Benedictine monks were the first to recognise the advantages of pig breeding.

'The Benedictine monks, who were the first to keep fish ponds, thus laying the basis of pisciculture, were also the first to recognise the advantages of pig breeding,' writes Paul Bouillard in an essay on the cookery of Alsace. In fact, the region produces firm-textured, delicately flavoured, admirable pork. The Strasbourg pork butchers, masters of their art, transform it into a number of preparations which are not only enjoyed by the gourmets of Alsace but in all the best Paris restaurants.

Gastronomic map of Alsace

Alsatian geese are famous for the delicacy of their flesh. It is from these specially fattened geese that the magnificent liver is obtained which the *maîtres de cuisine* in Alsace transform so skilfully into the celebrated *pâtés* and *terrines*.

The vegetables of Alsace look good and taste good. And the orchards of Alsace produce delectable fruit of which some, such as quetsches (Alsace plums) and mirabelle plums, are not only delicious to eat fresh but are also used to make noted *eaux-de-vie* (see SPIRITS). The list would not be complete without mentioning the cherries and the raspberries, which are distilled to make well-known liqueurs. The freshwater fish are renowned, too. Who does not know the succulence of the Rhine salmon, the river trout, the crayfish from the streams of the Vosges; the eels, tench and bream from which delicious *matelotes au vin d'Alsace* are prepared?

With such raw materials – and we have by no means mentioned all of them – the *maîtres de cuisine* and *cordon bleu* chefs of Alsace cannot help but cook well. In fact the Alsace meal is a perfect epicurean symphony.

Besides the magnificent *choucroute de Strasbourg* and *pâté de foie gras aux truffes* the following are the principal dishes of Alsace, dishes truly representative of the region's superb cuisine:

Culinary specialities – Alsatian *potée: matelote of fish de l'Ill; crayfish 'cardinalised in Alsatian wine'; stuffed carp à l'alsacienne; crayfish flan; stuffed breast of veal; hot meat pâté; onion flan* or *zewelewaï; civet of hare with noodles; saddle of hare à la crème; beckenoffe,* a kind of *estouffade* made with mutton, pork and potatoes, which must be cooked in a baker's oven to justify its name; *fat geese à l'alsacienne;* the *schifela,* i.e., shoulder of pork with pickled turnips; *ham cooked in pastry; fricassée of chicken à l'alsacienne; salmis of goose; turkey with chestnuts; calf's liver fritters; chartreuse of partridges; kalereï,* a kind of pork brawn; Strasbourg *black puddings, saveloys* and *sausages; stuffed sucking pig 'à la peau de goret'; red cabbage with chestnuts; potatoes à l'alsacienne; kohl rabi à la crème;*

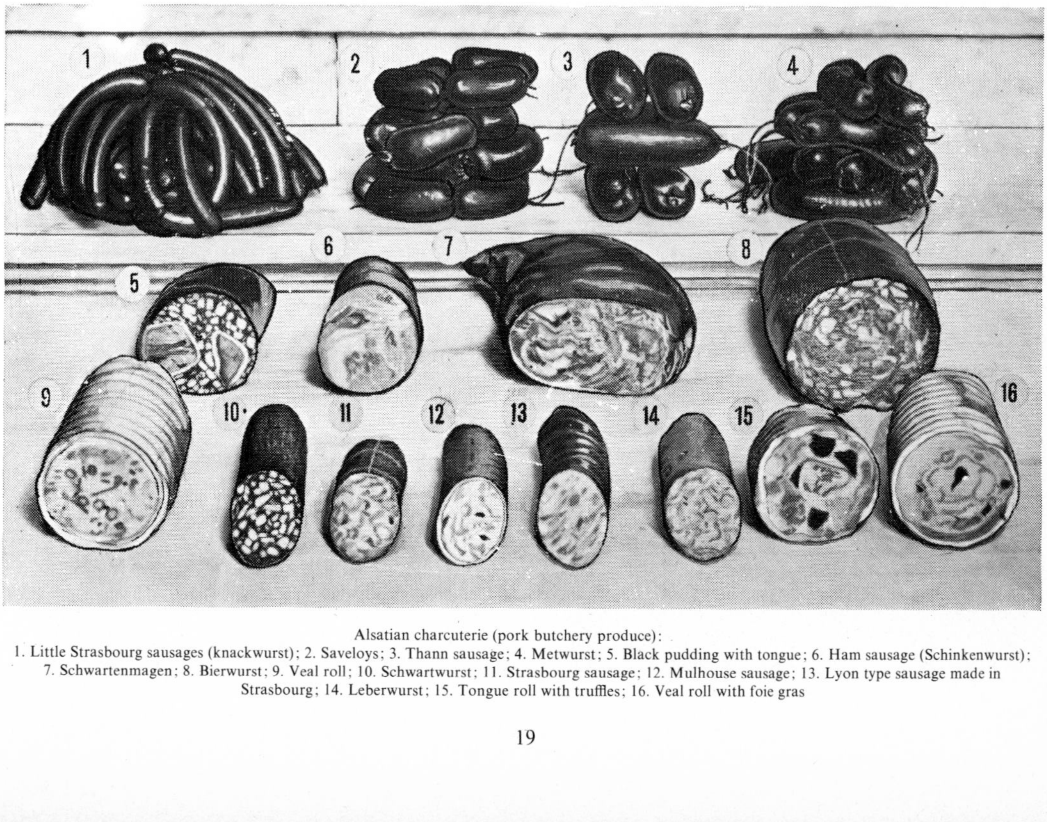

Alsatian charcuterie (pork butchery produce):
1. Little Strasbourg sausages (knackwurst); 2. Saveloys; 3. Thann sausage; 4. Metwurst; 5. Black pudding with tongue; 6. Ham sausage (Schinkenwurst); 7. Schwartenmagen; 8. Bierwurst; 9. Veal roll; 10. Schwartwurst; 11. Strasbourg sausage; 12. Mulhouse sausage; 13. Lyon type sausage made in Strasbourg; 14. Leberwurst; 15. Tongue roll with truffles; 16. Veal roll with foie gras

Alsatian kugelhopf

noodles à l'alsacienne; knepfle, a kind of fritter; *milchstriwle; bretzel; schenkele; beignets de carnaval* (carnival fritters); various types of Alsatian tarts; *kougloff* or *kugelhopf;* Jewish *kouguel; bilberry flan; kaffeekrantz,* etc.

Wines – To accompany all these good things, Alsace produces, in addition to a delicious beer, some rare and exceptional wines, which are mostly white.

The decree of 3 October 1962 created the *appellation* 'Alsace' or 'vin d'Alsace'. This *appellation* can include the variety of grape. In fact, Alsace wine does not usually bear the name of the locality from which it comes, but of the variety of grape used in its production.

Cépages nobles. Sylvaner. A fresh, fruity wine, best drunk young. Excellent accompaniment for *sauerkraut* and *charcuterie.*

Muscat. A wine with a distinct aromatic flavour that is generally served as an apéritif or dessert wine.

Pinot gris (or 'Alsace Tokay'): Quite a full-bodied wine with a delicate bouquet.

Pinot blanc (or Clevner): A fresh, rather sharp wine, often used for blending.

Gewürztraminer and Traminer. The wine from this grape is very fruity, with a distinctive flavour, and is often drunk well matured.

Riesling. A dry, very elegant wine, full of vigour. Perfect for fish, shellfish and seafood. It also goes well with *sauerkraut.*

Vines in Alsace (*French Government Tourist Office*)

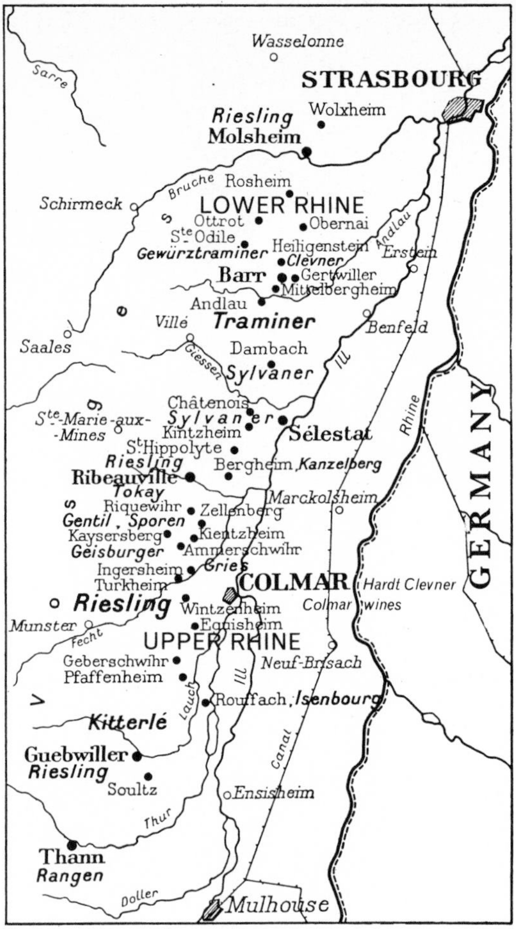

Wine map of Alsace

Cépages courants. Chasselas and Kniperlé. Carafe wines. The wine resulting from the blending of *cépages nobles* and *cépages courants* is called Zwicker. Edelzwicker is the name given to a blend of *cépages nobles.*

Red wines and *Rosés.* The red wines are made from the black Pinot grape, rosé from the grey Pinot grape. Production is poor compared to that of white wine. The name of the locality often accompanies that of the grape. Among the best known are Ammerschwihr, Barr, Eguisheim, Kaysersberg, Kientzheim, Mittelwihr, Ribeauvillé, Riquewihr.

ALSACIENNE (À L') – Definition applying to an enormous number of preparations. The predominating ingredients of dishes thus prepared are *sauerkraut,* ham and Strasbourg sausage.

ALUM. ALUN – A double sulphate of aluminium and potassium or ammonium; an astringent-tasting salt.

Alum was once used in confectionery to set the colour of crystallised fruits, and in *pâtisserie* to prevent egg whites from curdling while being whisked. This is now forbidden by law.

ALUMINITE – A kind of alumina-based fireproof porcelain. All porcelains, in fact, are based on alumina silicates, but aluminite has a higher content of alumina (oxide of aluminium) and is consequently much tougher than other porcelains and possesses a far greater resistance to heat.

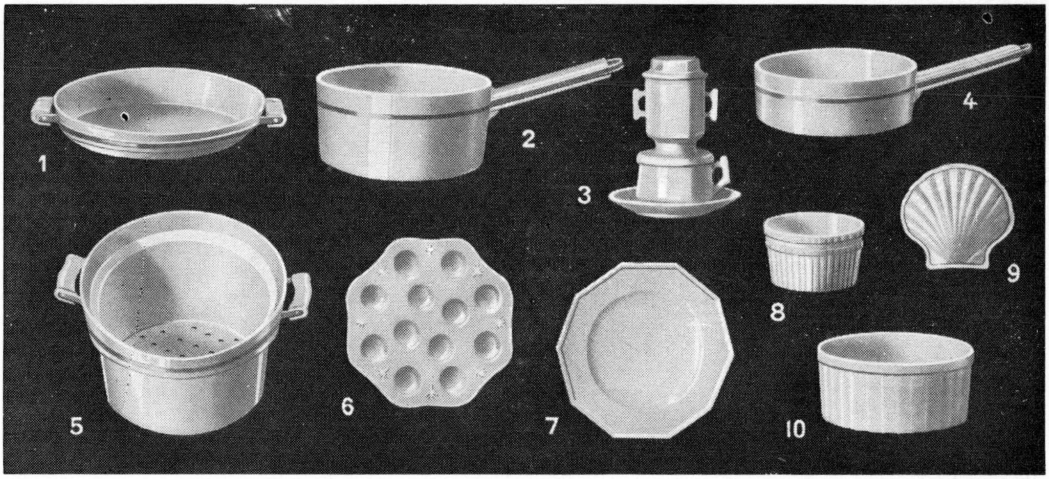

Aluminite kitchen utensils:
1. Gratin dish; 2. Saucepan; 3. Coffee filter; 4. Sauté pan; 5. Vegetable steamer; 6. Snail dish; 7. Plate; 8. Ramekin; 9. Shell; 10. Soufflé dish

ALUMINIUM – Ductile, resistant metal that looks like silver, its principal characteristic being its extreme lightness.

The numerous properties of aluminium have led to its use in the manufacture of kitchen utensils: saucepans, *marmites*, stewpans, etc. Conclusive experiments were previously carried out to determine the action various liquids used in the preparation of food had on aluminium.

It has been proved that there is little or no reaction with red or white wine, brandy, pure alcohol, coffee or tea poured in hot, beer, 5 per cent solution of tartaric, acetic, citric, lactic or phenic acids, 3 per cent solution of butyric acid, 0·2 per cent solution of salicylic acid. Nitric acid, on the other hand, attacks the metal vigorously.

AMANITA. AMANITE – A genus of fungi of the agaric group. There are numerous species of *amanitae*, some edible, others dangerous and even deadly. It is, therefore, very important to learn to recognise them. (See MUSHROOMS.)

AMARANTH. AMARANTE – This plant is cultivated in France mainly for the beauty of its flowers. In Italy, however, the tender leaves of one variety of amaranth are eaten, prepared rather like spinach.

AMBERGRIS. AMBRE GRIS – An intestinal concretion of the sperm whale found floating on the surface of Far Eastern seas. It is a wax-like substance, dotted with yellow and black spots, and possessing a strong and pleasant smell. Used in ancient pharmacopoeia as an antispasmodic, it was also credited with aphrodisiac and restorative properties. Brillat-Savarin, in a positively ecstatic outpouring, sings the praises of the restorative powers of ambergris chocolate.

This product, which was formerly used in confectionery and in cookery, is today used as a fixative in perfumery.

In *Méditation VI* Brillat-Savarin refers to ambergris chocolate as the 'chocolate of the afflicted': 'I know that Marshal Richelieu, of glorious memory, constantly chewed ambergris lozenges; as for myself, when I get one of those days when the weight of age makes itself felt, or when one's mind is sluggish, I add a knob of ambergris the size of a bean, pounded with sugar, to a strong cup of chocolate, and I always find my condition improves marvellously. The burden of life becomes lighter, thoughts flow with ease, and I do not suffer from insomnia, which would have been the invariable result of a cup of coffee taken for the same purpose.'

Brillat-Savarin also highly praises the power of ambergris in his *Magistères Restaurants*.

AMBIGU (Cold collation) – *Trévoux Dictionary* gives the following definition: 'A mixed collation at which meat and fruit are served together in such a manner as to make one wonder whether it is a simple collation or a supper.'

In other dictionaries the same definition, or nearly the same, is given with the proviso that the dishes served at this kind of meal must be cold.

In his *Dictionnaire universel de cuisine*, Joseph Favre says that the word *ambigu* is applicable to a meal which is taken between luncheon and dinner, or between dinner and lun-

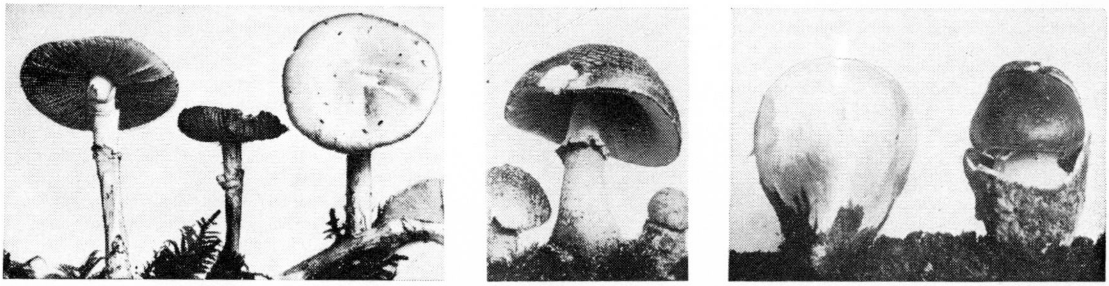

Amanitae

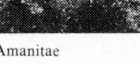

cheon, and at which all the dishes, the sweets and the dessert, are served at the same time.

This name should apply specifically to an evening meal, or supper served between midnight and two o'clock in the morning, in the course of a *soirée* (evening party).

AMBROSIA. AMBROSIE – A kind of tea made from the *ambrosier*, a bush with sweet-smelling flowers and leaves. It is said to have restorative powers, especially for stomachic complaints.

AMÉLÉON – A French word used in Normandy for a particular kind of cider.

AMERICA – Wines and *cuisine*. (See WINES, INTERNATIONAL COOKERY.)

AMÉRICAINE (À L') – Name given to various methods of preparing meat, fish, eggs, vegetables. Among these preparations the best-known is *Lobster à l'américaine* (see LOBSTER).

AMERICAN PARTRIDGE. COLIN – Bird of the partridge family, a little larger than quail, very common in America.

The *colin loui*, also called *American quail* (*bob-white, Virginian colin*) is highly esteemed in the United States, and is now established in England. (For its culinary preparation, see QUAIL, PARTRIDGE.)

AMIENS – This town in Picardy is famous, gastronomically speaking, for its duck pie, its *andouillettes* and its macaroons.

AMIRAL (À L') – Name given to fish dishes. The characteristic feature of these dishes is their garnish, composed of fried mussels and oysters, crayfish tails and truffles, to which peeled mushrooms are added. The sauce is a *Normandy sauce* (see SAUCE) flavoured with *Crayfish butter* (see BUTTER).

AMMAPERDRIX – A variety of the European partridge found in Algeria, Egypt, Israel, India and Persia. It only differs from the red-legged partridge in its size (it is smaller) and in the absence of a tarsal spur. The ammaperdrix likes hiding in rocky places and, like the French partridge, feeds on plants resembling thyme and wild thyme. They are sometimes found wandering about the fields on the Mediterranean coast of France. All methods of preparation given for partridge (q.v.) can be applied to this bird.

AMMOCOETE. AMMOCÈTE – A fish resembling the lamprey, found in the mouth of the Seine.

The methods of preparation given for eel (q.v.) and lamprey (q.v.) are applicable to this fish.

AMMONIA. AMMONIAC – A gaseous compound of nitrogen and hydrogen possessing strong alkaline and caustic properties. This gas affects the breathing and causes sneezing, watering of the eyes, and coughing. It is easily soluble in water, and then constitutes liquid ammonia or volatile alkali (the aqueous solution of ammonia). A few drops of it are recommended in cases of inebriety to induce vomiting.

AMMONIA, CARBONATE OF. AMMONIAQUE, CARBONATE D' – A salt that decomposes under the action of heat into ammonia and carbonic acid (both gaseous) without leaving any residue. It is used in certain preparations under the names of baking powder or Alsatian yeast to render non-fermented dough spongy and porous. The gases, in escaping, occupy a greater volume than the grains of flour, and form vacuoles in the dough. These then disappear completely if the heat of the oven is sufficiently strong.

AMOMUM. AMOME – Perennial herb of the ginger family found in Asia and Africa. The species known under the scientific name of *Amomum cardamon* produces capsular fruit often called cardamom, which are used as a substitute for real cardamom.

Considerable quantities of amomum are exported from Siam, Singapore and Saigon. In France the seeds are variously known as grains of paradise, Malaguetta pepper, Guinea grains, and are occasionally used as a substitute for pepper.

AMOU – Béarnaise cheese consumed from October to May.

AMOURETTES – Culinary name for the spinal marrow of oxen and calves. Calves' amourettes, very delicate in flavour, are used as a filling for patties, hot *timbales*, pies, *vol-au-vent*, etc.

Amourettes can also be prepared as an independent dish, made into croquettes, and various fried dishes, etc.

Most of the recipes given for calves' and lambs' brains – which amourettes rather resemble – can be applied to them.

No matter how amourettes are prepared, they should first be boiled in *court-bouillon* (q.v.) in the same way as calves' and lambs' brains (see OFFAL or VARIETY MEATS).

AMPHICLES – Celebrated cook of ancient Greece. More than any of his colleagues of that distant epoch, Amphicles deserves to be rescued from oblivion. He alone recognised all that was barbarous and foolishly ostentatious in the culinary methods of his time, and in his teachings, and in practice, he devoted himself to the task of bringing to them a saner logic. 'Amphicles liked to prepare nature's products simply. He had a hare cooked on a spit and served underdone with nothing but a sprinkling of coriander and fennel. He maintained that a sucking pig should simply be boiled and placed on a bed of sage. He wrapped larks in vine leaves and red mullet in fig leaves and cooked them among the cinders. No-one knew better than he how to harmonise a piece of flesh and an aromatic. No-one disapproved more than he did of the practice of disguising the flavour of a meat or vegetable. This friend of Theotime even used spices sparingly in his sauces. Where his predecessors indiscriminately mixed the most ill-assorted condiments together, where his emulators, whimsical to excess, lavished twenty ingredients on a single dish, Amphicles confined himself to two or three.'

Our reason for dwelling on this ancient *maître de cuisine* is simply to remind more modern practitioners of the art that culinary merit does not necessarily lie in the extravagance of the trimmings.

AMPHITRYON (Host) – Authors of gastronomical books (such as Brillat-Savarin, Grimod de la Reynière, Berchoux, Monselet and Chavette) and most dictionaries define the word as 'the one with whom we dine'. According to Molière:

> 'The real Amphitryon
> Is mine host with whom I dine.'

All the gastronomical writers have laid down precepts on the relationships of hosts and guests. The most famous of these works is the *Manuel des amphitryons* by Grimod de la Reynière.

In more recent times Auguste Michel has devoted a whole book full of useful hints to 'the man who receives at his table' concerning his rôle of host, entitled *Manuel des amphitryons au debut du XXe siècle*.

Strictly speaking, the word amphitryon only means host, and applies, and should only apply, to the person who entertains someone at his table.

We find it difficult to imagine what a host was like in ancient times. One of the most celebrated amphitryons,

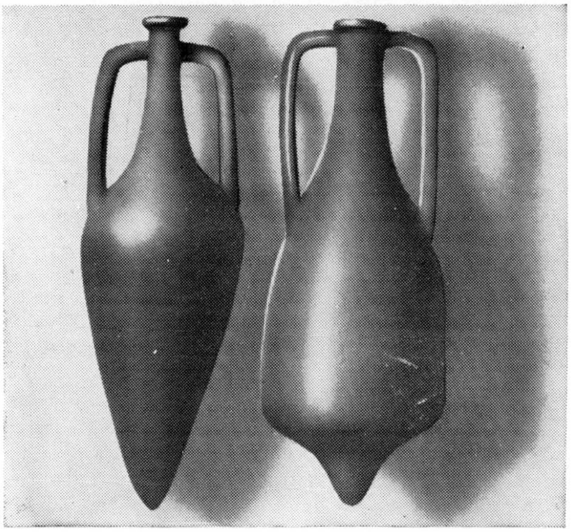

Terracotta amphorae for storing oil or wine

Decorated Greek amphora

historical or legendary, was Lucullus. He can be taken as a model of amphitryons, for he offered his guests truly magnificent feasts.

Historians have given us accounts of the lavishness of Maecenas' table; he, too, is described as a great master of the art of entertaining. Heliogabulus was another renowned for the extraordinary luxury of his table. Then there were the three men of the name Apicius in ancient Rome (see APICIUS).

Let us not forget Assurbanipal, even though he belongs to legend rather than to history. He was one of the most ostentatious of the Assyrian kings – none other than the legendary Sardanapalus.

Belshazzar, too, must have been an amphitryon on a grand scale, because even today, when describing a truly magnificent banquet, we still say that it was 'a veritable Belshazzar's feast'.

'For a rich man,' writes Grimod de la Reynière, 'the best rôle in the world is that of host.'

Berchoux, for his part, says:

'S'il est un rôle noble et bien digne d'envie,
C'est celui d'un mortel qui fait en sa maison,
Les honneurs de sa table en digne amphitryon.'

'If there is a noble rôle, a truly enviable one,
It is that of a mortal who in his house does
The honours of his table like a true amphitryon.'

Barras, Cambacérès and Talleyrand were distinguished amphitryons. Napoleon said of Cambacérès: 'If you wish to eat really well, go and visit my arch-chancellor.' Other tables were renowned for the quality of their food, although some, like that of Princess Mathilde, for their mediocrity. The disappearance of great wealth, the servant problem, the habit of entertaining in restaurants, have pushed amphitryonism to the background. But there are still houses where great pains are taken to ensure the *bonheur gourmand* of the guests.

AMPHORA. AMPHORE – A terracotta vase used in ancient times for measuring liquids. The capacity of the Italic amphora, that of the Romans, was 25·89 litres. An amphora kept in the Capitol served as a standard measure. The Attic amphora, that of the Greeks, was a third larger. Amphorae were used to store oil, wine, olives and raisins.

The amphora was *sessilis* or *non sessilis* according to whether it stood upright on its base or terminated in a rounded point. In the latter case it was placed in a hole in the ground or on a specially constructed pierced shelf.

AMYGDALINE – Chemical name for the substance that makes the oil of bitter almonds noxious. *Amygdalin* is the term applied to all substances, cakes or sweets, that contain almonds.

ANAEMIA. ANÉMIE – Anaemia is characterised by a diminution of the red corpuscles of the blood. Persons suffering from anaemia are said to be anaemic.

Diet for anaemics – Iron being the principal medicine for anaemic conditions, dieticians introduce as many iron-rich foods into the diet as possible. These are yolk of egg, meat, pig's blood, etc. (animal origin); green cabbage, spinach, chicory, oats, lentils, white haricot beans, carrots, etc. (vegetable origin); also red wine. It is naturally advisable, before following such a diet, to take into account the condition of the digestive organs, since they are usually deficient. This is the reason why, for example, pig's blood, although rich in iron, can rarely be used. This diet has recently been modified following research carried out by an American scholar, Dr. Whipple, who has proved both experimentally and in practice that calf's liver is the food that best assures the regeneration of the blood; kidneys, hearts and meat also react well, but less effectively. The efficacy of preparations based on dehydrated stomach, usually prescribed in pharmaceutical form, has also been recognised.

Whipple's diet consists of a daily ration of 150–250 g. (5–9 oz.) calf's liver eaten for breakfast or lunch, a little meat, fresh vegetables chosen from those rich in iron, fruit (peaches, apples, etc.). Bread, starch products, eggs and sugar are restricted; oils and fats are forbidden apart from a little fresh butter; skimmed milk is generally allowed. The liver has preferably to be eaten raw, especially for grave forms of pernicious anaemia.

There are various recipes for the preparation of raw or cooked liver.

Raw liver. Slice the liver, then mince it. The resulting pulp should be free from all stringy tissues.

Serve it in sandwiches, or mixed with preserves, or with warm beef tea to form a purée.

There is even a recipe for liver cocktail. Pound about 100 g. (4 oz.) lightly cooked liver. Place on lettuce leaves, and season with salt and pepper. Add a slice of raw tomato, chopped parsley and a little mustard. Prepare $\frac{1}{2}$ cup tomato sauce, $\frac{1}{4}$ cup lemon juice, 2 coffeespoons Worcestershire sauce, $\frac{1}{2}$ coffeespoon finely chopped shallots, salt and pepper.

Mix 1 part of minced or grated liver to $2\frac{1}{2}$ parts of this mixture, shake and chill.

Calf's liver au gratin. Blanch and dice 450 g. (1 lb.) calf's liver, and place it on a buttered plate. Cover with breadcrumbs, white sauce and pulped tomatoes. Season with salt and pepper and brown in the oven. A little ham and chopped parsley may be added.

Liver balls. Blanch and pound 450 g. (1 lb.) liver with 2 rashers of fat bacon. Add 2 tablespoons (3 tablespoons) cream, 1 chopped onion, 2 eggs (or the yolks only), and stale or fresh breadcrumbs until of a consistency to form into rather large balls. Bake these in the oven.

Liver cream. Mix $\frac{1}{4}$ cup pounded liver with 1 egg, well beaten, and season with salt and pepper. Thin with milk, pour into a *bain-marie*, and place in the oven until set.

Raw liver vinaigrette. Cut raw liver into small pieces and season with vinegar, onion, parsley and chervil.

ANAGNOST. ANAGNOSTE – Name given by the Romans to the slave whose job it was to read during meals.

The custom dates from the time of the Emperor Claudius, although nowadays it hardly exists, except in some nunneries and monasteries.

Not so long ago, however, there was an *anagnoste* in each of the French educational establishments run by the Church. He was considered a privileged person. His meals were served to him after his companions had left the table, and he was usually given a wider choice and more copious portions of food. The post was much sought after by the pupils.

ANALECT. ANALECTE – Name given to the slave whose duty it was to collect the remains of a Roman meal. History does not relate what happened to these left-overs; they were probably neatened into acceptable portions, artistically arranged, and sold in special markets. (See ARLEQUINS.)

ANALEPTIC. ANALEPTIQUE – Whatever builds up and restores exhausted forces. Term applied to light foods which are easy to digest and which quickly produce a sensation of well-being. Full-bodied wines, beef tea, meat jellies, tapioca and chocolate are all analeptics.

ANALYSIS. ANALYSE – Scientific term for the separation of the whole into its component parts. The various constituents of food have often been scientifically analysed.

ANAPHYLAXIS. ANAPHYLAXIE – Word created by Professor C. Richet to define the curious phenomenon discovered by him: that certain poisons increase rather than diminish the sensitiveness of an organism to their action.

A minimal dose of poison given to a non-sensitised animal has no serious effects, while alarming effects are produced in an animal that has previously been given a non-fatal dose of the same poison.

This is especially true after internal injections. It also explains the disorders that occur after the ingestion of certain foods.

Food anaphylaxis – Some people, following the ingestion of certain foods such as bread, eggs, milk, honey, chocolate, etc., are subject either to skin eruptions, often of the nettle-rash kind, or to a respiratory disorder akin to asthma, or to severe headaches.

The desensitisation treatment is a delicate one and belongs entirely to the realm of medicine.

ANCHOVY. ANCHOIS – Small sea fish, 15 cm. (6 inches) long. Its back is a beautiful green colour which later turns a dark greenish blue, then almost black, all of which helps the buyer to determine its freshness. It can be distinguished from the sardine by its projecting snout, and large mouth, which

Preparation of anchovies (after a drawing by J Houel)

stretches almost to the gills.

The anchovy has long been appreciated as a food. It is mentioned in the works of Elien and Aristotle, and its viscera are used in the making of garum (q.v.), which the Greeks and Romans called 'the most precious sauce'.

Anchovies have a very delicate flavour when fresh, but can only be eaten fresh in the countries where they are caught. When fried they are much tastier than gudgeon or smelt. The best anchovies come from the Mediterranean coast from Nice to Catalonia, and are very large in that region.

Anchovy fillets, prepared at home or industrially, are used in many dishes, hot and cold; in pizza, for example.

Method of preparation. Cut the head off and clean out the inside. Wipe the fish without pressing too hard, as the flesh is very delicate.

Perhaps the best and most popular method of cooking fresh anchovies is frying them in olive oil. When they are large, all the recipes given for cooking fresh sardines (q.v.) can be applied to anchovies.

Anchovy is mostly prepared in brine, and is found in this form in all the markets of Europe. It can also be preserved in oil, or pickled.

Anchovies à la silésienne. ANCHOIS À LA SILÉSIENNE – Fillet 6 fresh anchovies and leave them to soak for half-an-hour in white wine.

Soak the soft roes of 2 salted herring in water, and rub them through a fine sieve. Add 2 teaspoons finely chopped shallot mixed with chopped parsley. Thin down this purée with the white wine in which the anchovies were soaked.

Spread the mixture in an *hors-d'œuvre* dish, and arrange the anchovy fillets on it in a criss-cross pattern. Surround the fillets with a border of mixed salad composed of boiled potatoes and tart apples, cut into small dice and well seasoned. Garnish with sprigs of parsley and thin slices of lemon and beetroot. Just before serving, sprinkle with olive oil.

Anchovy canapés. CANAPÉS AUX ANCHOIS – Cut anchovy fillets in small pieces and arrange them on long slices of bread which have had the crusts removed and been spread with a light coating of *Maître d'hôtel butter* (see BUTTER). Chop (separately) the yolks and whites of hard-boiled eggs, and some parsley; arrange little heaps of these between the pieces of anchovy. Garnish with curly parsley.

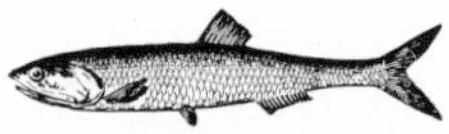

Anchovy

Anchovy canapés

Anchovy fillets. FILETS D'ANCHOIS – Desalt the anchovies and trim them (that is, remove bones and skin). Wipe these fillets with a cloth and cut into 2 or 3 strips lengthwise. (Canned fillets may be used.)

Arrange the fillet strips decoratively in an *hors-d'œuvre* dish. Garnish with yolks and whites of hard-boiled eggs, chopped separately, and chopped parsley and capers. Sprinkle the fillets with a few tablespoons of olive oil.

The arrangement of anchovy fillets in porcelain, cut-glass or silver *hors-d'œuvre* dishes lends itself to a variety of artistic expression. Slices of lemon, quartered lettuce hearts, small gherkins cut in various shapes, beetroot cut in rounds or crescents, etc., can also be added to the ingredients mentioned above.

Anchovy fillets à la suédoise. FILETS D'ANCHOIS À LA SUÉDOISE – Arrange the anchovy fillets, prepared in the usual manner, on a foundation of salad composed of tart red apples and cooked beetroot, cut in small dice, seasoned with oil, vinegar, salt and pepper.

Surround this salad with a garnish of little bunches of parsley, yolks and whites of hard-boiled eggs, and cooked truffles, all chopped separately and arranged in individual groups. Sprinkle with a few tablespoons of oil.

Anchovy toast. TOASTS AUX ANCHOIS – Garnish lightly toasted pieces of bread with fillets of anchovies. Sprinkle them with breadcrumbs which have been fried in butter, and brown in the oven for a few minutes.

Fried anchovies. ANCHOIS FRITS – Clean and prepare fresh anchovies. Dip them in milk, drain them, and roll them in flour, keeping the fish separate as far as possible.

Fry them in very hot fat. Drain, and sprinkle with fine, dry salt. Pile them on a heated plate and garnish with fried parsley and lemon quarters.

Medallions of anchovy à la niçoise. MEDAILLONS D'ANCHOIS À LA NIÇOISE – Spread slices of crustless bread with butter that has been mixed with thick tomato purée. Put a slice of hard-boiled egg on each slice, and a rolled fillet of anchovy on the egg.

Garnish these medallions with stoned black olives, and sprinkle with a little chopped parsley. Arrange them on a paper doyley, and add a further garnish of curly parsley.

Portuguese anchovy fillets. FILETS D'ANCHOIS PORTUGAISE – Prepare desalted anchovies in fillets, and cut them into thin strips. Canned fillets may be used.

Prepare a *fondue* of tomatoes (see TOMATO), cooked lightly in oil, and put it in an *hors-d'œuvre* dish. Arrange the fillets in a criss-cross pattern on top of the *fondue*. Decorate with capers, chopped parsley, slices of peeled lemon, and sprinkle with a few tablespoons of olive oil.

Preserved anchovies. CONSERVE D'ANCHOIS – This must be made with freshly caught anchovies. Remove the heads, the gall-bladders and intestines by pressing with the thumb. Put the anchovies in layers into a small barrel with salt mixed with red ochre or powdered brick; the proportions are 6 kg. (12 lb.) salt to 500 g. (1 lb.) powdered brick. The layers of anchovies should be 6 cm. ($2\frac{1}{2}$ inches) thick, each layer separated from the next by a 2-cm. ($\frac{3}{4}$-inch) layer of the mixed salt and brick dust.

When the barrel is full, put on the lid, which must have a hole pierced in the middle. Pour a concentrated solution of sea salt on the anchovies through this hole. Leave the barrel in the sun, with a brick over the hole in the lid. The heat of the sun produces fermentation which preserves the fish and ensures their keeping quality, and the brick over the hole prevents the brine from evaporating.

When the degree of fermentation is considered sufficient, remove the brick and put a cork in the hole in the lid.

Anchovies preserved in brine can be used as *hors-d'œuvre* and for other preparations.

Rolled anchovies à la Talleyrand. PAUPIETTES D'ANCHOIS À LA TALLEYRAND – Trim and flatten the fillets. Stuff them with a purée made of pickled tunny (tuna fish) mixed with finely chopped truffles and bound with a tablespoon of mayonnaise.

Arrange the stuffed and rolled anchovies on thick slices of hard-boiled egg. Put them on an *hors-d'œuvre* dish and surround them with a *chiffonade* (q.v.) of finely shredded lettuce. Decorate with slices of lemon and beetroot, and sprinkle with olive oil.

Rolled anchovies à la tartare. PAUPIETTES D'ANCHOIS À LA TARTARE – Trim and flatten anchovy fillets. Stuff them with a purée of grated horseradish which has been kneaded with butter. Put the rolled anchovies on rather thick slices of cooked beetroot (cut with fluted cutters) and arrange them on an *hors-d'œuvre* dish. Decorate with chopped hard-boiled eggs and capers, and sprinkle with olive oil.

Rolled anchovies with hard-boiled eggs. PAUPIETTES D'ANCHOIS AUX OEUFS DURS – Trim the anchovy fillets and shape them into rolls (canned or bottled anchovies may be used).

Arrange them in an *hors-d'œuvre* dish, decorate with chopped hard-boiled eggs, parsley and capers, and sprinkle with olive oil.

Soused anchovies. ANCHOIS MARINÉS – Clean 450 g. (1 lb.) fresh anchovies. Lay them on a plate, sprinkle with salt, and leave to souse for 2 hours.

Dry the anchovies, and fry them in smoking hot oil just long enough to stiffen them. Drain, put them into an earthenware dish, and cover with a marinade prepared in the following manner:

Heat the oil in which the anchovies were cooked (adding 5 or 6 tablespoons of fresh oil). Fry a finely sliced medium-

Medallions of anchovy à la niçoise

sized onion and a sliced carrot in the oil. Add 3 unpeeled cloves of garlic, 1 dl. (6 tablespoons, scant $\frac{1}{2}$ cup) vinegar, and 1 dl. (6 tablespoons, scant $\frac{1}{2}$ cup) water. Season with fine salt, and add a sprig of thyme, 3 sprigs parsley, $\frac{1}{2}$ bay leaf and $\frac{1}{2}$ teaspoon crushed peppercorns.

Boil for 10 minutes. Pour the mixture, still boiling, on the anchovies. Leave to souse for 24 hours.

Serve in an *hors-d'œuvre* dish garnished with slices of lemon.

ANCHOYADE (Provençal cookery) – A preparation based on anchovy paste. Pound the anchovies in a mortar, add olive oil and a few drops of vinegar. Spread this paste on slices of home-made bread, and sprinkle with finely chopped onion, chopped hard-boiled egg, and a little olive oil. Brown in the oven.

Anchoyade à la niçoise – Add chopped shallot and parsley to anchovy paste, moisten with olive oil, and spread this mixture on slices of toast, or bread fried in oil until golden brown. Sprinkle with breadcrumbs mixed with chopped parsley and garlic, and then with olive oil. Brown in the oven.

ANCIENNE (À L') – Name given to preparations treated according to the precepts of the old school. These dishes were usually mixed garnishes, and braised beef slowly simmered for a long time. The most characteristic type is *Rump of beef à l'ancienne* (see BEEF).

The term also applies to dishes such as pastry shells baked blind (empty) and filled with *ragoûts* of cocks' combs and kidneys, or quenelles of truffles and mushrooms. (For *Chicken à l'ancienne mode* see CHICKEN, and for *Escalopes of calves' sweetbreads à l'ancienne* see OFFAL or VARIETY MEATS.)

The term *à l'ancienne* also applies to *blanquettes* (q.v.) and *fricassées* (q.v.) of lamb, veal and chicken treated in a special way.

ANDALOUSE (À L') – Name given to different preparations characterised mainly by tomatoes, sweet pimentos and sometimes chipolata sausages, aubergines and rice pilaf. (See EGGS, *Eggs à l'andalouse*; CHICKEN, *Chicken à l'andalouse*.)

ANDOUILLE – A large pig intestine filled with strips of chitterlings and stomach of the same animal. These popular sausages are generally served cold, as an *hors-d'œuvre*. (See PORK.)

Large smoked *andouilles* such as those of Vire and Guéméné are sold ready-cooked, and should be served thinly sliced.

Vire and Guéméné andouille (*Larousse*)

ANDOUILLETTES (Chitterlings) – *Andouillettes* are prepared like *andouilles*, but smaller intestines are used. There are many varieties, differing for the most part in the spices used in their composition. Some are made *à la ficelle* (old method); the tripe is cut lengthwise into strips. Others are stuffed with diced or minced tripe.

One of the most exclusive of gastronomic societies, comprising only five branches, is the *Association amicale des amateurs d'authentiques andouillettes* (A.A.A.A.A.) – 'Society of lovers of authentic *andouillettes*'. A diploma from this society is much sought after. Its members have opportunities to discuss at length the comparative merits of the *andouillettes* of Troyes, Arras, Cambrai, Paris, Fleurie in Beaujolais, Aubagne, Lourdes, etc.

Andouillettes, like *andouilles*, are sold ready poached and cooled. All that needs to be done is to slit the skin and grill them gently.

It is a mistake to serve fried vegetables with *andouillettes*. The A.A.A.A.A. has experimented with creamed potatoes, fried onions, raw red cabbage, creamed celery, lentils, red beans, vegetables *au gratin*, stewed apples, etc., but total agreement has been reached on only one point: *andouillettes* require a good strong mustard.

Andouillettes à la lyonnaise – Slit the *andouillettes* and cook them in lard or butter. When two-thirds done, add a finely chopped onion previously lightly cooked in lard or butter. Simmer until done. When ready to serve, add a tablespoon of chopped parsley and a tablespoon of vinegar.

ANDROPOGON (Vlue grass) – A genus of plant of the *Gramineae* family. Numerous species of it are known, one of which is the sugar cane. Several of the plants are used for infusion, like tea.

ANECDOTES (Historic, gastronomic and culinary) – A convalescent Pompey was advised by his physician that his recovery would be hastened by following a diet of thrushes. When his servants returned with the news that it was impossible to find any in the height of summer except at the home of Lucullus, the invalid turned to his physician and remarked, 'What's this? Does Pompey's survival depend upon the fact that Lucullus is a glutton?' (*Les Classiques de la table*)

Le duc de Duras, seeing Descartes tucking into a good meal one day, remarked jestingly, 'What ho! Do philosophers have a use for such delicacies?'

'Why not?' retorted Descartes. 'Do you imagine that Nature produced the good things of the earth simply for the ignorant?' (Panckoucke)

It is well known that Mme. de Maintenon was extremely poor at the time of her first marriage. One evening while she was entertaining some people to supper and had no roast to offer, her lackey, a witty fellow of some spirit, sidled up to his mistress, who was entertaining the company with her charmingly witty conversation, and whispered, 'Madame, one more story, and no-one will notice that you have no roast for supper.' (La Beaumelle)

The food was very bad at Mme. d'Aligre's house and much discussed. 'Really,' remarked M. de Lauraguais, 'if one did not eat one's own bread as well as one's neighbour's, here one would die of hunger.' (Grimm, *Correspondance*)

One day Admiral Russel invited the officers and crews of his fleet to drink punch with him. He had a marble basin specially constructed for the occasion in the middle of a magnificent garden, into which he ordered to be poured six hundred bottles of Cognac (brandy), six hundred bottles of rum, twelve hundred bottles of Málaga, four tons of boiling water, the juice of two thousand six hundred lemons, six hundred pounds of the best Lisbon sugar and two hundred grated nutmegs. A young man representing Hebe rowed round the basin in a small mahogany boat, filling the cups of more than six thousand drinkers seated in an amphitheatre of benches round the basin. (*Ivrogniana*)

Heliogabalus used to entertain his parasites to meals of grass, and was wont to cover his table with embroidered or tapestry tablecloths upon which were worked all the dishes that ought to have appeared at the different courses. At other times he tantalised their gaze with paintings of various foods, seemingly offering them everything they could wish for, yet leaving them ravenously hungry. (Lampride)

M. le president B. gave a regular weekly dinner; splendid table, fine wines, *cuisine* worthy of an archbishop, and wit worthy of a member of *l'Académie française* 'of the forty-first chair'. An old and faithful servant was put in charge of the cellar, and was also commissioned to offer the various wines to the guests. He acquitted himself of this task with a discreet and dignified air; though intonations of an amorous tabby-cat crept into his voice each time he announced the name and the patent of nobility of these great wines – the glory of France. He announced with particular fervour a certain *vin de fond*. When he said '*Vin de fond*' he gave the impression that he was rolling it around in his mouth, so that even the least enthusiastic of the gourmets allowed his glass to be filled. However, this wine, so brilliantly presented, gave little pleasure to those who tasted it. As a rule they pulled wry faces while drinking *vin de fond*.

'Tell me, what *is* this *vin de fond*?' Mme. la presidente B. asked her *sommelier* one day. 'Is there much of it in the cellar?'

'Madame,' replied the servant with an air of mystery, 'there is enough to last for ever.'

'Ah!' said Mme. de B., still looking perplexed.

'It is quite simple,' continued the *sommelier*. 'I make it myself from the dregs of the bottles. It is quite good enough for people who are prepared to drink without knowing what they are drinking and who cannot tell the difference between a Clos-Vougeot and a Bordeaux-Lafitte.'

From that day onwards the *vin de fond* disappeared from the table of M. le president B. (J. Richard, *l'Époque*)

The man with the most voracious appetite in history was the Emperor Maximin, successor of Alexander Severus (Marcus Aurelius). He went to the extent of consuming (at an ordinary meal) forty pounds of meat and an amphora of wine; that is to say, according to some, twenty-eight French pints; according to others, thirty-six. (*Encyclopédie méthodique*)

Note. A pint in Paris was 0·93 of a litre.

The landlord of a village inn had the honour of serving George II with an egg on an occasion that he broke his journey there, and asked one guinea in payment.

His Majesty smilingly remarked:

'It seems eggs are rather scarce hereabouts.'

'Oh no, sire,' replied the innkeeper, 'not the eggs – the kings.'

Oh, happy and unhappy cooks! A most factious and detestable race, according to Hegesender.

The Athenian government gave the freedom of the city to a certain Cherips because his father had invented an excellent truffled *ragoût*.

Anthony, well pleased with a dinner, presented a town to his cook.

President Henault made the following remark about Mme. du Deffand's cook whose *cuisine* was far too unrefined and uninspired for a gastronome of his calibre: 'The difference between her and la Brinvilliers is in their intention.'

By skilful grafting a gardener from Montreuil succeeded in propagating a most exquisite variety of peach. He desired to present the fruit in homage to Louis XVIII, but before exposing himself to a test upon which his reputation so much depended, he decided to visit M.P.R. The latter, stretched out in his armchair, legs crossed and hands clasped, prepared himself in gentle contemplation to deliver the important verdict that was expected of him. The gardener requested a plate with a silver knife. He cut the precious peach in quarters, speared one of these with the point of the knife and gravely pushed it into M.P.R.'s mouth, saying, 'Taste the juice!' His eyes closed, M.P.R. tasted the juice without uttering a word. The gardener observed him, his eyes clouded with anxiety. After an interval of two or three minutes, those of his mentor opened. 'Good, very good, my friend,' were the only words he had time to utter. Immediately, the second quarter was advanced like the first, and the gardener, in a firmer, more confident tone, commanded, 'Taste the flesh'. There followed the same silence, the same gravity on the part of the learned gourmet. This time the movement of his mouth was more pronounced, for he was chewing. At last he nodded his head. 'Ah, very good, very good!' You are going to think that the superiority of the peach had been judged and that no more remained to be said? Not at all! The third slice followed in its turn. 'Savour the aroma!' continued the gardener. The aroma was found to be worthy of the juice and the flesh. Whereupon the gardener drew himself up to his full height to present the last quarter. His face, slightly flushed, glowed with pride and satisfaction: 'Taste the whole!' His triumph was complete. M.P.R. tasted it, and came towards him moist-eyed and smiling. He grasped his hand effusively. 'Ah, my friend, it is perfect! I offer you my heartfelt compliments.'

Fontenelle dined each night at one of a number of elegant houses, a fact that caused Piron to remark upon seeing the doyen of the *Académie* passing his window one day accompanied by his retinue: 'That is the first time I have seen M. de Fontenelle leave home without intending to dine out!'

Artaxerxes, king of Persia, having been defeated in battle, was constrained to eat dried figs and barley bread during the retreat. He found this rough fare excellent. 'O ye gods,' he exclaimed, 'what pleasure I have denied myself up to now by being over-fastidious in my tastes!'

Montmaur was eating one day with a large, noisy company of coughing and singing friends. 'Hey there, gentlemen!' he called out, 'A little silence, pray, else how are we to know what we are eating.' (*Menagiana*)

Marshal Albert immediately felt ill if wild boar or sucking pig appeared on the table.

Erasmus had only to smell fish to become feverish.

When anyone placed apples near Duchesne, secretary to François I, blood poured from his nose.

According to Furetière, in the chapter devoted to large appetites:

'I have seen one man eat a loin of veal, a capon, a brace of woodcock and a mountain of bread without any help.

'The ballet dancer Aglaïs, who lived two hundred or so years before Christ, was so greedy that for supper she would eat ten pounds of meat, and a dozen loaves of bread, and drink the equivalent of six pints of wine.

'The Emperor Claudius Albinus one day ate for lunch five hundred figs, a hundred peaches, ten melons, a hundred *beccaficchi*, forty-eight oysters and many grapes.

'The athlete Milon of Crotonia ate a whole ox after having carried it for a considerable length of time on his shoulders.

'The Emperor Maximin became so fat through over-eating that he used his wife's bracelets as rings.

'An actor by the name of Phagon ate, in the presence of the Emperor Aurelius: a wild boar, a sheep, a hundred round loaves of bread, and a sucking pig. He washed it down with twenty-four measures of wine.' (*Les Classiques de la table*)

A FEW GOURMANDS. QUELQUES GOURMANDS –

Louis XIII – He was excellent at preparing eggs and did so in a variety of ways: *perdus*, poached in black butter, hard-boiled and chopped up with bacon (one of his inventions), etc. He also larded loins of beef magnificently, using his own vermeil larding needle.

Mme. de Maintenon – She was adept at preparing dainty dishes for the king (still of good appetite despite his advancing years). Her particular speciality was dressed cutlets seasoned with parsley, which she wrapped in buttered paper and grilled. In other words cutlets *en papillote*.

Mme. de Conti – She invented the method of preparing loin of mutton that bears her name, while Mme. de Sévigné had a talent for preparing waffles.

Louis XV – He loved to make his own coffee, and invented an omelette of asparagus tips for Mme. du Barry.

Louis XVI – Like his grandfather, Louis XIV, he had the sort of appetite nothing could upset; the very evening before the opening of his trial he ate six cutlets, a chicken and several eggs.

Balzac (Honoré de) – Even if he did not always eat his fill (because he happened to be working) Balzac had by nature an astonishing capacity of absorption. And the menu he ordered for himself alone at Very's one day was not exceptional:

Hors-d'œuvre
Eight dozen Ostend oysters
Twleve *pré-salé* mutton cutlets *au naturel*
A duckling with turnips
A brace of roast partridges
A Normandy sole
Sweet
Fruit
Coffee and liqueurs

Whereupon he slept for two hours, drank some coffee and worked the whole night until seven or eight o'clock in the morning.

Victor Hugo – The great poet was a real guzzler, especially late in life: he not only ate a cutlet, but the bone as well, crunching it loudly between his powerful jaws. Sometimes, to amuse his grandchildren after a meal, he would have all the left-overs brought in: *ragoût*, fish, vegetables and dessert. These he put with seasoning into a large salad bowl and ate, sharing the dish with the enraptured children. He called the concoction 'daubs'.

Lamartine – A thin man who only liked ice cream.

Stendhal – A fat man with a penchant for macaroni.

Théophile Gautier – A delicate palate who did not allow himself to be deceived. It was he who, at the Russian court, observed to the chef that his almond gâteau (which everyone else adored) was nothing more nor less than pounded macaroons.

Zola – He had a fondness for shellfish although he called them 'filth'.

Renan – Invited one day to a house where the hostess desired that each guest in turn should contribute to the conversation, Renan persistently tried to intervene during the course of the meal. At last the mistress of the house turned to him and said, 'Now, Master Renan, it's your turn.'

'Oh Madame,' said Renan, 'all I wanted was a second helping of peas.'

ANETHOLE. ANÉTHOL – Compound of a hydro-carbon (resembling oil of turpentine) and a certain crystallisable substance possessing a strong anise-like odour.

The essences of anise, fennel, Chinese anise and tarragon are mainly formed of anethole.

It is used for flavouring sweets, sweet dishes, and various liqueurs.

ANETHUM. ANETH – See FENNEL.

ANGEL CAKE – See CAKE.

ANGEL FISH (Squatina squatina). ANGE DE MER – A kind of dog fish, with a large, flattened body; the pectoral and ventral fins seeming to continue the lateral line of the body in all its thickness. The tail is big and rounded, while the back is covered with a rough brownish-green skin marked with small whitish and grey spots. The belly is whitish. Angel fish is the intermediary type between the family of sharks and that of ray and skates. On the French coasts, where it abounds, the fishermen call this fish *angelot* or *angel*.

The flesh of the angel fish is quite delicate and recalls that of the ray. All methods of preparation given for the latter are applicable to angel fish.

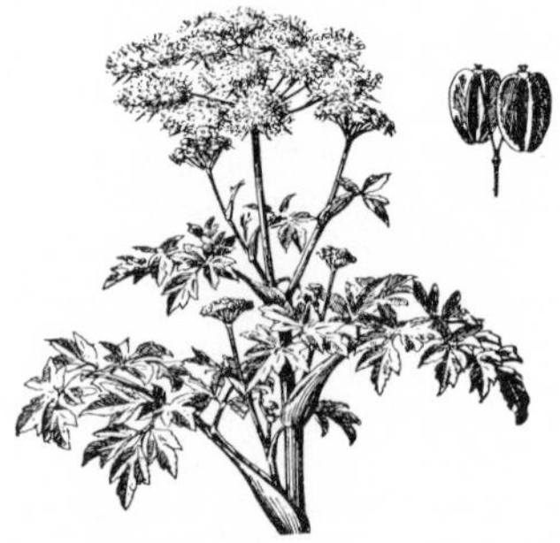

Angelica

ANGELICA. ANGÉLIQUE – A genus of plants of the family *Umbelliferae*, of which the prototype is generally known under the common name of angelica, angelic herb. It is a large perennial herb usually grown as a biennial. In appearance it closely resembles cow parsley.

Angelica archangelica grows wild in the Alps, in the Pyrenees and in northern Europe. It has long been valued as a stomachic, carminative and anti-spasmodic stimulant. Today it is cultivated mostly for the sake of its roots and stalks.

The fresh stalks, candied in sugar, make a pleasant preserve called Niort angelica, or Nevers angelica, or Châteaubriand angelica. It is used by confectioners and wine and spirit merchants.

The roots, which come principally from Bohemia, are wrinkled, grey outside and white inside. They are deceptive to the palate: sweet at first, producing an acrid and bitter after-taste.

The roots also contain a volatile oil, angelicine, angelic acid, tannin, malic acid, pectic acid, the malates, etc. They possess very strong digestive and anti-dyspeptic properties. It is for this reason that they are used in the production of meliss cordials and other liqueurs such as chartreuse, vespetro, gin and English bitters.

Angelica liqueur. LIQUEUR ANGÉLIQUE – Put 1 kg. ($2\frac{1}{4}$ lb.) angelica stalks, cut into small pieces, and 1 litre ($1\frac{3}{4}$ pints, generous quart) brandy, in a bottling jar. Macerate for a month. See that the jar is hermetically sealed. Expose it to the sun whenever possible.

Add from 600 to 800 g. ($1\frac{1}{4}$ to $1\frac{3}{4}$ lb.) lump sugar dissolved in very little water. Press the whole through a silk or fine muslin sieve. Leave to stand for a few hours, then filter the liqueur through soft paper.

Decant into bottles, cork and seal.

Candied angelica. ANGÉLIQUE CONFITE – Cut the angelica stalks into 15- to 20-cm. (6- to 8-inch) pieces and soak in cold water.

Plunge them into a pan of boiling water until the pulp begins to give slightly when pressed with the fingers. Cool under a cold tap, drain and peel, taking care to remove all stringy parts.

Macerate in a syrup of 1 cup sugar to 1 cup water for 24 hours.

Drain. Boil the syrup to 102°C. (215°F.) and pour it over the pieces of angelica.

Repeat this operation three days running. On the fourth day cook the syrup to small pearl, i.e. 105°C. (221°F.). Put angelica into this syrup and bring it to the boil several times.

Remove the pan from the fire and let it stand.

Drain the pieces of angelica on a sieve. Lay them on a marble slab, sprinkle with fine sugar and put them to dry in a very slow oven. Store in tins.

Niort angelica à la sybarite. ANGÉLIQUE DE NIORT À LA SYBARITE – Have ready a dozen or so best quality butter brioches (kept hot), a fruit dish filled with sticks of candied angelica, a bottle of angelica cream, a carafe of iced water, a packet of Egyptian cigarettes.

Light a cigarette, sip a mouthful of iced water, crunch a piece of Niort angelica with a piping hot bite of brioche, sip, breathe and savour a few drops of angelica liqueur, and then repeat the whole process.

If, according to Austin de Croze, to whom we owe this recipe, the room is sprayed with a fresh, light perfume (verbena or southernwood) one can have an idea of the blessed joys of sybaritism.

ANGELS ON HORSEBACK (English cookery). ANGES À CHEVAL – This hot *hors-d'œuvre* is prepared in the following manner. Take plump oysters out of their shells, drain their liquor and remove their beards, and wrap each one in a very thin rasher of bacon. Thread them on little metal skewers, season with salt and pepper, and grill. Arrange on fingers of toast.

Just before serving, sprinkle with breadcrumbs which have been fried in butter.

ANGLAISE – In cookery, the term *anglaise* is applied to a mixture composed of eggs, oil ($\frac{1}{2}$ teaspoon per egg), salt and pepper.

Various ingredients which have to be dipped in breadcrumbs are first coated with this mixture, and are said to be '*à l'anglaise*'. They are then sautéed in butter or oil, or deep-fried.

ANGLAISE (À L') – Name given to various preparations usually cooked in water (see MUTTON, *Leg of mutton*) or in white stock (see CHICKEN, *English boiled chicken*).

This term also applies to the following fish: fish poached in *court-bouillon* (q.v.); fish grilled or fried in breadcrumbs; vegetables, mainly potatoes, boiled in water or steamed (see POTATOES, *Potatoes à l'anglaise*).

Grilled fish à l'anglaise. POISSONS GRILLÉS À L'ANGLAISE – This method can be applied to all fish. The large fish are cut into slices or steaks, the small ones are cooked whole, after having a few slits cut in them. The fish, whole or sliced, is coated with oil or melted butter and seasoned with salt and pepper before being put under a grill. It must be cooked on a low flame.

When fish with a delicate flesh is being grilled, such as whiting, fresh sliced cod, etc., it should be dusted with flour and sprinkled with melted butter or oil before putting it under the grill.

Grilled fish à l'anglaise is served simply with melted butter or *Maître d'hôtel butter* (see BUTTER) and (optionally) potatoes, either steamed or boiled.

ANGLAISE (Custard) – Variously flavoured custard made of yolks of egg, sugar and milk (see CREAM, *Custard cream*).

ANGLER (U.S. ANGLERFISH). LOTTE DE MER, BAUDROIE – This fish is extremely ugly. Its foreparts are very broad while its hind-quarters are exceedingly narrow. Its head, which is enormous, is very flat and spiky. Along its back it has three very mobile filaments. The first and largest ends in a sort of flail, shaped like a spearhead, which can lash out in all directions. It is believed that the angler uses this as bait to attract its prey.

The skin of the angler is olive brown along the back and grey on the belly. It is flabby and sticky and entirely without scales. Instead it is covered with bony filaments similar to the spikes on its head.

The angler is used mainly as an ingredient of *bouillabaisse* (q.v.) and other fish soups, but it can be cooked in the same way as cod or other large sea fish.

In whatever manner it is prepared, angler should be rather highly seasoned, since it is a somewhat tasteless fish. In the U.S.A. the anglerfish, while plentiful, is not widely marketed. White fish fillets or steaks can be used in the following recipes.

Angler à l'anglaise. LOTTE DE MER À L'ANGLAISE – Fillet a medium-sized raw angler, and trim the fillets. Flatten them and season with salt and pepper. Dip them in egg and breadcrumbs and fry them in butter, browning on both sides. Serve on a long dish, covering the fish with *Maître d'hôtel butter* (see BUTTER).

Boiled angler with various sauces. LOTTE DE MER BOUILLIE – Skin the angler and cut it into thick steaks. Cook in a *court-bouillon* (q.v.) as for *Boiled cod* (see COD). Serve with any sauce suitable for boiled fish.

Cold angler pâté. PÂTÉ FROID DE LOTTE DE MER – Proceed as for *Cold eel pie* (see EEL).

Fillets of angler braised in white wine. FILETS DE LOTTE DE MER BRAISÉS AU VIN BLANC – Trim and flatten the fillets. Season with salt and pepper. Lay them in a buttered baking tin and moisten with *Fish fumet* (see FUMET) with white wine. Cook in a moderate oven.

Drain the fillets. Serve on a long dish with a white wine sauce made from the cooking stock (see SAUCE, *White sauces*).

Fried angler. LOTTE DE MER FRITE – Cut the fillets of angler into strips. Dip them in milk, flour lightly, and deep-fry in boiling fat.

Drain and season. Serve on a napkin, garnished with fried parsley and lemon.

Hot angler pâté. PÂTÉ CHAUD DE LOTTE DE MER – This pie is made from fillets of angler, with pike or whiting stuffing, in the same way as *Hot eel pie* (see EEL).

Matelot of angler. MATELOTE DE LOTTE DE MER – Cut the fillets of angler into squares. Cook them *en matelote* in white or red wine, as for *Eel en matelote* (see EEL).

ANGLET – Town situated 4 km. ($2\frac{1}{2}$ miles) from Bayonne, near the sea. A famous white wine is produced here, dry and heady, which is called Vin de sable.

Rock salt also comes from Anglet.

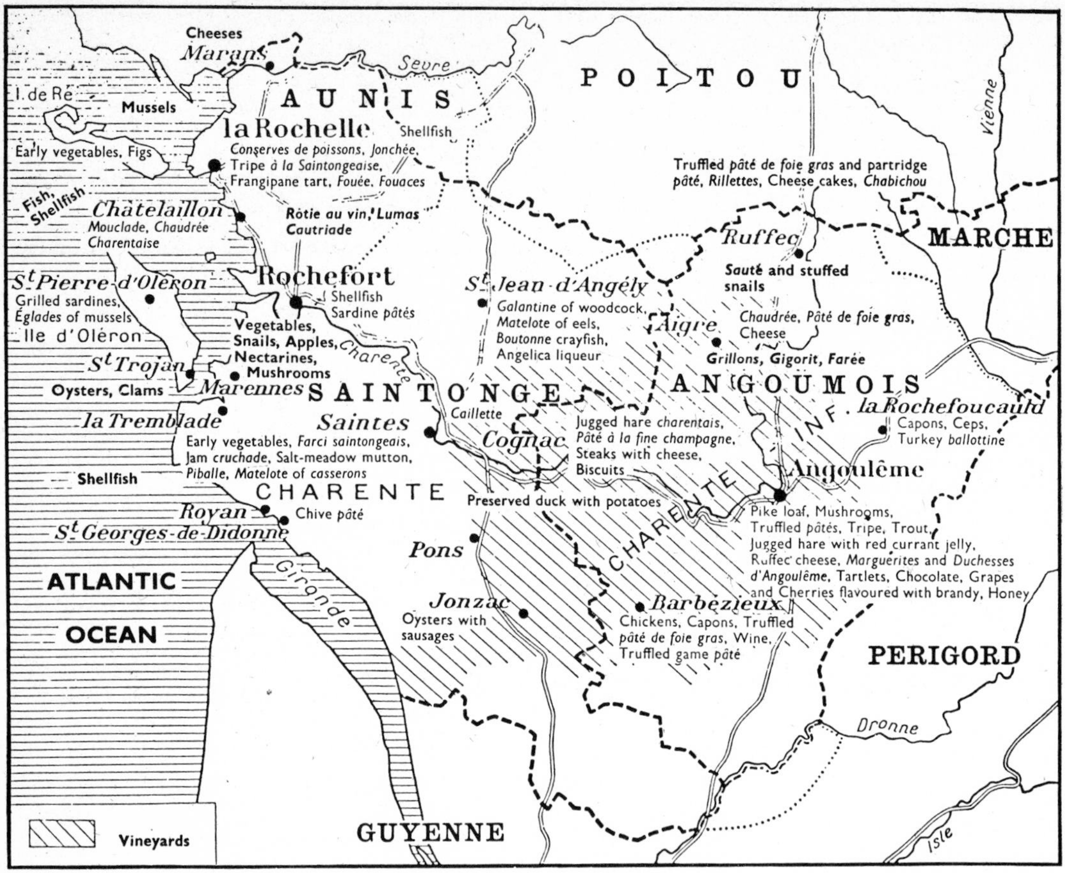

Gastronomic map of Angoumois, Aunis and Saintonge

ANGOULÊME – A town in the Charente where famous brandies are distilled. A noted partridge *pâté* is made at Angoulême.

ANGOUMOIS – This area is situated between Poitou and Périgord, Limousin and Saintonge. Such a neighbourhood could not help but turn the inhabitants into gastronomes, considering the excellence of its food products.

Ground and feathered game abound in Angoumois. Freshwater fish of all kinds are to be found in its rivers; the Touvre, which flows past Angoulême, is still, as Clement Marot said, 'paved with trout, edged with eels and crayfish,' and these delicious fish and shellfish are made into mouth-watering *matelotes*.

Various species of mushrooms are gathered in Angoumois. In the quarries around Angoulême cultivated mushrooms are grown; the delicacy of their flavour rivals the famous mushrooms cultivated in the quarries around Paris.

Cattle bred in this region produce excellent beef. First-class poultry is raised there, Barbezieux chickens being particularly esteemed.

Culinary specialities – *Friture charentaise* composed of various small fish; *cagouilles*, stuffed or in *ragoût*. (By *cagouilles* we mean snails. The inhabitants of Charente are so fond of them that they, themselves, are nicknamed *cagouillards*.)

Tourtière (raised pie containing chicken and salsify); *jugged hare*, to which is added redcurrant jelly; *preserved duck*, which is served with potatoes sautéed in goose fat, or with *cèpes* sautéed *à la bordelaise*; *gigorit* or lamb's pluck; stuffed cabbage called *farée*; a selection of various *pâtés* such as *pâté de foie gras truffé* of Barbezieux and Angoulême, *partridge pâté* of Ruffec, *lark pâtés* of Exideuil. *Sausages, saveloys, black puddings, chitterlings* and other *charcuterie* are all excellent.

Among the sweet dishes and cakes there are *marvels*, a kind of fritter; *cheesecake* made of Ruffec cheese; *chocolate tartlets* flavoured with brandy.

Wines – The wines of the Angoumois region are mediocre and are rarely drunk outside the province. They are excellent for distilling purposes, however. Charente cognac is made from these wines (see COGNAC).

ANGREC – A group of plants, some of the best known of which grow in Réunion Island and Madagascar, others on the Cape of Good Hope and on the west coast of Africa. The most important species is the *Angraecum fragrans*; its leaves furnish the *faham*, or tea of Réunion Island, which is widely used in the same way as China tea.

ANIMELLES – This is a culinary term for the testicles of male animals, in particular those of rams. In the past, *animelles* were very much in vogue in France, Spain and Italy. For recipes see OFFAL or VARIETY MEATS, *Animelles*.

ANISEED (Sweet cumin). ANIS VERT – Plants with ovoid seeds, slightly contracted at the top, with a ribbed surface and short stiff greyish-green hairs.

Aniseed
a. Fruit
b. Flower

The seeds sold in the shops must be cleansed of the soil which often sticks to them. Parsley seed, with the hairs removed, is sometimes fraudulently sold as *pâtisserie* aniseed. Aniseed is used in confectionery and distilling.

Aniseed cookies (Alsatian pastry). PAINS À L'ANIS – Mix 500 g. (18 oz., $2\frac{1}{4}$ cups) fine castor sugar and 12 eggs in a copper basin. Beat the mixture with a whisk as for an ordinary sponge cake.

When the mixture is well whisked, add 500 g. (18 oz., $4\frac{1}{2}$ cups) sieved flour, 200 g. (7 oz., scant 2 cups) cornflour and 50 g. (2 oz., $\frac{1}{3}$ cup) aniseed (in grains). Mix well.

Drop tablespoons of the mixture onto a wetted baking sheet. Place in a warm place to dry. When the cookies begin to rise slightly, bake in a cool oven.

Aniseed-flavoured sugar. SUCRE ANISÉ – Aniseed-flavoured sugar is used for several preparations. The proportion of aniseed varies. When it is intended for the preparation of aniseed cake, 25 g. (1 oz., 3 tablespoons) aniseed are added to 500 g. (18 oz., $2\frac{1}{4}$ cups) castor sugar. If, on the other hand, it is to be used to flavour sponge cakes, biscuits, custards or creams, the proportion of aniseed can go up to 100 grams (4 oz., $\frac{3}{4}$ cup) per 500 g. (18 oz., $2\frac{1}{4}$ cups) sugar.

Method. Pick over the aniseed carefully and rub on a fine sieve to remove the stalks. Dry in a slow oven for 12 hours. Pound with lump sugar, and sift through a fine sieve to obtain a very fine powder. Pound whatever remains in the sieve until the whole has been sifted.

Keep this sugar in a hermetically sealed jar or tin, and store in a dry place.

Aniseed-flavoured sugar is a more satisfactory flavouring agent than aniseed essence, which is rather strong and inclined to have more of an aniseed smell than flavour.

ANISETTE – Aniseed-based liqueur. The best aniseed liqueur in France is made in Bordeaux. Dutch anisette is also held in high repute.

(For the preparation of the liqueur see LIQUEURS, *Anise or anisette liqueur.*)

ANJOU – Land of sweetness and harmony where the *cuisine* and wines match its natural beauty.

Henry Coutant, a great gastronome and a native of Anjou, wrote: 'Its *cuisine* is as mellow as its skies, harmonious as its horizons. Did not one of Anjou's wittiest sons and a great gourmet, the humourist Curnonsky, say that Anjou is to gastronomy what Racine is to literature?' And Coutant went on:

'As to its wines, they are like the humour of its inhabitants:

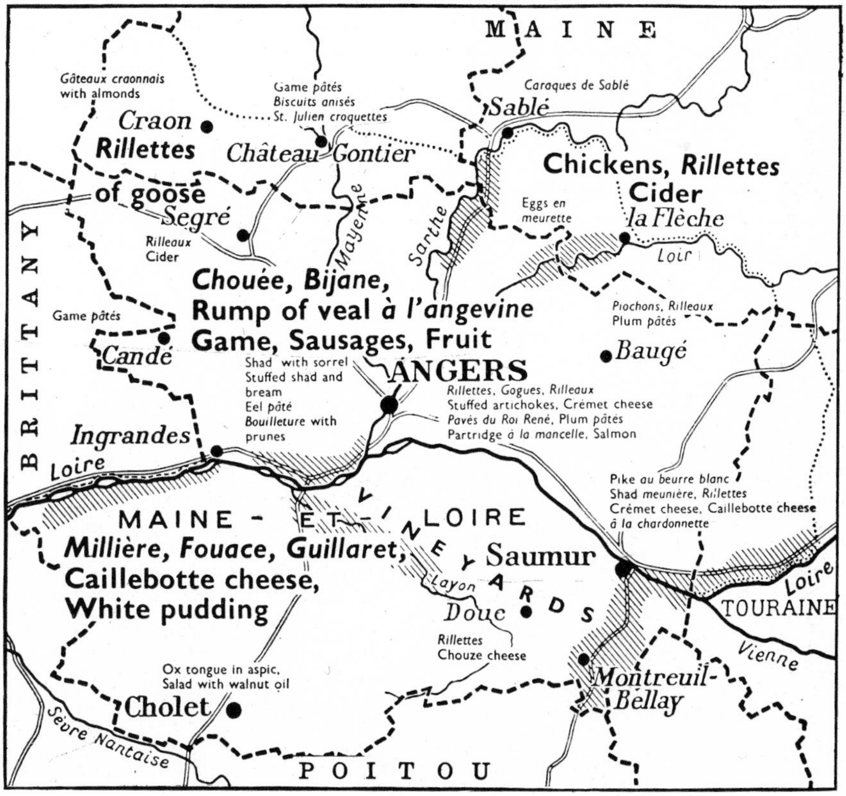

Gastronomic map of Anjou

light and sparkling, of incomparable taste, but at times also malicious and treacherous towards those who have no idea how to face up to their caprices with adequate preparation. Admirable wines, however, which merit one of the first places among the great wines of France.'

Anjou cattle, bred for food, give meat of excellent quality. The Maine region cattle are famous for the quality of their meat, and so are the Cholet cattle.

Anjou pork is of the greatest delicacy, and various locally made *charcuterie – rillettes, potted pork mince, andouilles, sausages, black* (U.S. blood) *puddings* – are admirable 'bacchic spurs', as Rabelais called them, just the thing to make one appreciate the fragrant wines of the Anjou vineyards.

Anjou chickens are tender and plump, and make excellent *fricassées.*

'The fish which the Loire so generously offers us between Saumur and Champtoceaux is more delicate than anywhere else,' declares an Anjou gourmand.

Its pike are among the finest; its shad, its tench and its bream know no rivals. For pike and shad, the cooks of Anjou have passed on from generation to generation the recipe for a succulent sauce, *beurre blanc* (white butter), the creamy taste of which is a fragrant delight. Tench and bream, particularly bream, are cooked chiefly with a sorrel stuffing which makes a savoury foundation for their flesh.

The Loire salmon are famous; they are considered the best of all French river salmon.

Poultry is excellent in Anjou. The whole world knows of *capon de la flèche* and *chicken du Mans.* First-class game is also found here.

Anjou vegetable produce is superb. The green cabbages of this region, the *piochous,* as they are called, are well known and are made into those *fricassées* which delight the lovers of country dishes.

The Anjou orchards produce excellent fruit; pears, dessert and cider apples, plums and strawberries. 'We must pay homage to the fruits of Anjou, which form a vegetable aristocracy of this province of France,' said gastronome Henry Coutant.

Anjou cheeses are renowned. The famous Angers *crémets* (soft fresh cream cheeses) should really be classed among the sweet courses rather than the cheeses. These *crémets,* which are generally eaten with sugar, can also be sprinkled with salt and flavoured with chives.

The Loire near Saumur (*French Government Tourist Office*)

With food of such quality available the master cooks and *cordons bleus* of Anjou are naturally noted for their *cuisine.*

Culinary specialities – Saumur *rillettes; rillons* (greaves); *potted pork mince; white puddings* and other *charcuterie* made from the fine pork of the region.

Bouilleture, a kind of *matelote* of various fishes, principally eels; *stuffed shad; bream in butter; pike* or *shad au beurre blanc* (white butter); *matelotes of freshwater fish; perch with prunes; fish stews; eel pâté.*

Rump of veal à l'angevine; pig's fry; gogue; fricassée of chicken; partridge à la mancelle; chouée (boiled green cabbage sprinkled with butter); *fricassée of green cabbage; fricassée of cauliflower; green salads with walnut oil.*

Well-known cheeses include the Saumur *chouzé; caillebotte à la chardonette,* and the Saumur and Angers *crémets.*

Other famous dishes are *bijane* or 'magpie soup' (similar to the Saintonge broth) – bread crumbled into sweetened red wine; *roast meat with hot wine; millière* (maize meal and rice porridge); *fouée* (a sort of flat girdle cake made of bread dough, spread with butter); *fouace* (flat cakes baked in the

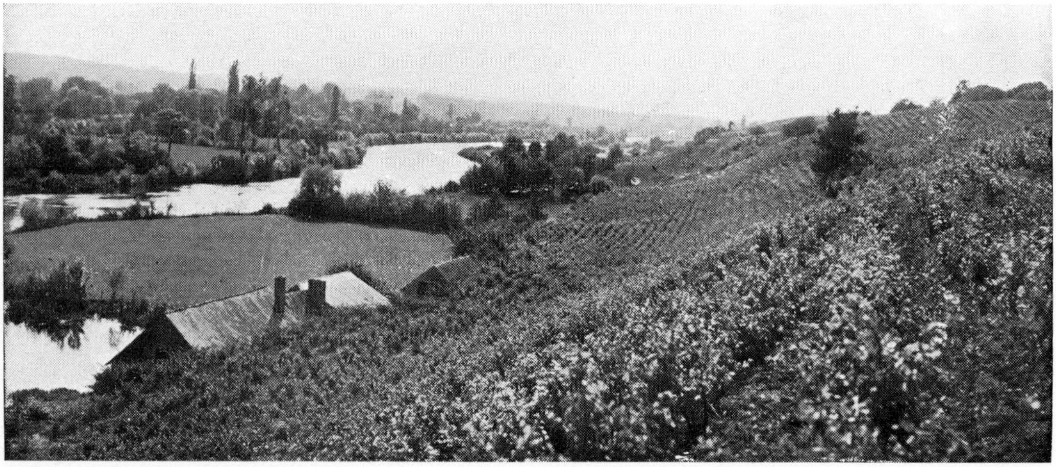

A vineyard on the bank of the Loire at Huillé

Map of the principal vineyards in Anjou

Bottles and a glass for Anjou wine

hearth). Rabelais speaks of '*fouaciers* of Lerné (or Lernay), of Maine-et-Loire,' which shows how long these cakes have been known. There are also *guillaret* or *échaudé*; Angers *aniseed biscuits; prune pie*. The *fouace* and the *guillaret* are not delicate pastries; in the past they used to be sold in the markets and at fairs in western France. Their main quality was to provoke thirst.

Wines – The Anjou wines include those of the Angers and Saumur regions (which have a right to the *appellations* 'Anjou' and 'Saumur').

White wines. These are made from the Chénin grape.

Saumur. Very dry white wines with a strong bouquet. They stand up very well to the fermenting process of the *méthode champenoise* to give very pleasant semi-sparkling and sparkling wines. The grapes are grown on the banks of the Loire and on those of its tributary, the Thouet. Brézé, Parnay and Montsoreau are three of the principal vineyards.

Coteaux de la Loire. Fine, elegant white wines with a strong bouquet are produced here; these get dryer every year. The best-known vineyards are those of Epiré, Savennières (which has a right to a special *appellation*), la Roche-aux-Moines and la Coulée de Serrant, both on the right bank.

La Coulée de Serrant is a walled vineyard that was presented by Louis XI to his chamberlain Perthus de Brie along with a château which has since disappeared.

It was at la Roche-aux-Moines, on 27 July 1214, that John Lackland was defeated by Louis XI, son of Philippe Auguste. The vineyard, planted by the monks of Saint-Nicolas of Angers, dates back to the eleventh century A.D.

Coteaux du Layon. Liqueur-like aromatic white wines made from over-ripe grapes ('*la pourriture noble*' or 'noble rot', *Botrytis cenerea*).

The great liqueur-like Anjou wines are at their best in the Bonnezeaux and Quarts-de-Chaume *appellations.* The *Coteaux de l'Aubance* are also worth mentioning – excellent white wines from the banks of the River Aubance.

Red wines. The red wines of Anjou and Saumur come from the Cabernet grape. The best known of them (and for good reason) is Saumur-Champigny with its exquisite strawberry bouquet and deep ruby colour. It was Curnonsky's favourite wine.

Rosé wines. The rosés of Anjou and Saumur, velvety or dry, are well known and much in demand. They are made from the Gamay, Côt and Groslot grapes. The Cabernet rosé is (as its name indicates) produced exclusively from the Cabernet grape.

The Angevin poet Marc Leclerc has put it all into verse:

Voici les vins du Layon,
Beaulieu, Rablay, Touarcé, Faye,
Doux coum' le miel au rayon,
Chauds coum' le soleil qui raye,
Voilà la Coulée d' Serrant,
Saint-Barthélemy, Savennières,
Qui tiennent ben aussi leu rang
Avec ceuss d' La Possonnière,
Ceux de Saumur et d'alentour,
Varrains ou Saint-Cyr-en-Bourg,
Montsoreau, Parnay, Dampierre,
Et leu si plaisant goût d' pierre,
L' champigny qu'à la couleur
Et la senteur des framboèses
Et l'on n' sait quel est l' meilleur
Vin de tuffeau ou vin d'ardoèse.

Here are the wines of Layon,
Beaulieu, Rablay, Touarcé, Faye,
Sweet as honey in the comb,
Glowing like the sun's ray,
There is the Coulée de Serrant,
Saint-Barthélemy, Savennières,
That are every bit as good
As those of La Possonnière
Of Saumur and its neighbours
Varrains or Saint-Cyr-en-Bourg,
Montsoreau, Parnay, Dampierre,
And the raspberry-scented Champigny
The colour of rubies
Laced with the tang of the soil
Chalk or slate
Who can say which is best.

Good quality marc brandies (distilled from the husks of grapes after the wine has been made) and some highly esteemed liqueurs such as Guignolet d'Angers are also produced in this region.

Finally, there is Segré cider, which is excellent.

Casserole for Anna potatoes

ANNA POTATOES. POMMES DE TERRE ANNA – A method of preparing potatoes cut in thin round slices, cooked in butter in a special utensil or a covered *terrine*. (See POTATOES.)

ANNETTE POTATOES. POMMES DE TERRE ANNETTE – Prepared like *Anna potatoes*, but the potatoes should be shredded into fine *julienne* strips (q.v.). (See POTATOES.)

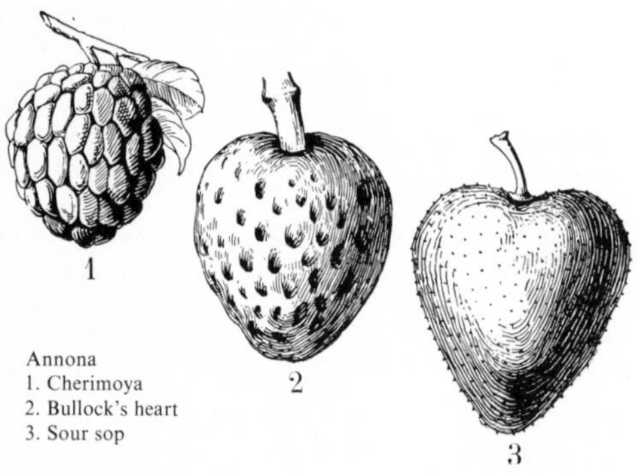

Annona
1. Cherimoya
2. Bullock's heart
3. Sour sop

ANNONA. ANONE – The annona or custard apple is the fruit of a family of trees (*Annonaceae*) native to tropical America but cultivated in southern California and tropical Asia. The cherimoya (*Annona cherimolia*), one of the most popular varieties, resembles a globe artichoke in both colour and shape, with the difference that its skin is shiny. It has cream coloured flesh, less white than that of the sour sop (*Annona muricata*), which is larger and more acid in flavour. The sweet sop (*Annona squamosa*), which some people say is the true custard apple, is particularly popular in the West Indies and has a sweet, custard-like flavour and a strong scent. Annonas are only eaten raw.

ANON – This fish, one of the varieties of haddock, abounds in vast numbers in the English Channel. Its flesh is very white, and layered.

The fishing season for it is mainly January and February. In the U.S.A. hake and cusk (usually sold in fillets) are very similar to this fish.

For cookery purposes it is treated as whiting (q.v.).

ANTHRACITE – Coal remarkable for its great purity; one of the fuels which is used, in preference to others, for heating and cooking.

ANTIDOTE. CONTRE-POISON – Substance capable of neutralising the toxic properties of another substance, by forming with it an insoluble non-toxic combination.

ANTISEPSIS. ANTISEPSIE – Method which aims at the prevention of putrefaction or infection by use of chemical substances. The salting and smoking of meat actually constitutes an application of antiseptic treatment. The use of vinegar in marinades, and of salt or alcohol for preserving fruit, also achieves this purpose. With exceptions, the use of antiseptics as preservatives for food substances is generally condemned. The practice can be dangerous, except in the hands of qualified food chemists, who use, when required, selected substances which are strictly controlled by appropriate laws.

ANTISEPTICS. ANTISEPTIQUES – Substances which counteract putrefaction, fermentation and infection. (See PRESERVATION.)

ANVERSOISE (À L') – Method of preparing large and small pieces of meat, calves' sweetbreads and eggs. These are garnished with hop stalks in butter or cream and potatoes fried in butter.

AOUDZÉ – Name given in Ethiopia to a strongly spiced sauce which is made of pimento, ginger, cloves and an aromatic plant somewhat similar to thyme, known as *zégakelie*.

The Ethiopians serve this sauce with a dish which they call *brondo*, of which they are very fond.

APÉRITIF – The old pharmacopoeia recognised major bitters (roots of parsley, fennel, asparagus and butcher's broom) and minor bitters (roots of maidenhair fern, couch-grass, thistle, rest-harrow and strawberry-plant). The term as used today only applies to stimulants of appetite.

Apéritifs served in cafés are drinks of a greater or lesser degree of bitterness, variously flavoured, which are drunk neat or diluted with water. They generally have a strong alcoholic content, because the essences of which they are composed are not soluble except in strong alcohol (which is why they go cloudy when mixed with water) and this alcohol content to a great extent nullifies the beneficial action of the bitters.

But, through sheer force of habit (or perhaps through imagination), some people think that they have no appetite unless they have their daily apéritif (or apéritifs). It is this fact which has led to the coining of the phrase that if an apéritif can open the appetite, it does so with a skeleton key. Be this as it may, the apéritif was, and still is, a traditional rite in certain circles.

La Partie de Plaisir, an engraving by de Moitte after a painting by Lancret

The traditional apéritif 'rite' is tending to disappear. Those who used to look upon it as an occasion to meet their friends or simply as a form of relaxation are beginning to substitute for this 'agreeable *faux pas* of the palate' perhaps a fruit juice, or a glass of mineral water, or – better still – simply a glass of wine.

Doctor Ramain, who calls himself an 'independent gastronome', has selected what he considers to be the best apéritifs and lists them in the following order:

1. The best vintage *brut* Champagne, served well chilled and sparkling with tiny bubbles.

2. The still Champagne Blanc de Blancs.

3. A glass of genuine old sherry; or, better still, an authentic Château-Châlon yellow wine from the Jura.

4. An 'Aligoté' white Burgundy (Aligoté is the name of the grape) blended with a little fine Cassis. 'Kir,' as this mixture is called, is a misnomer, since it was already being drunk in Burgundy in 1912, long before the Alsatian Canon Kir held office as deputy mayor of Dijon.

5. A good quality Scotch whisky served neat or with a splash of soda.

6. Certain authentic Italian vermouths, alone, or with ice, or with chilled sparkling mineral water.

7. One of a small number of good dry French vermouths such as Noilly, drunk neat, or with sparkling mineral water – or (wait for it!) blended with Casis. Even the ancient (but reborn!) Savoyard Chambéry vermouths are recommended.

8. As a last resort, during the long hot summer days (especially if you happen to live in the south of France) a splendid light '*pastis*' simply because its tart aniseed flavour refreshes the palate without spoiling the appetite.

APHORISMS AND AXIOMS. APHORISMES ET AXIOMES – Short pithy maxims, expressing rules and precepts of gastronomy, hygiene and everything pertaining to the table, the most celebrated of which are those of Brillat-Savarin, given by this master of gastronomical sciences as a preface to *Physiologie du goût*. Here they are:

1. The universe is nothing except for life, and everything that lives has to feed itself.

2. Animals feed; man eats; only a man of wit knows how to eat.

3. The destiny of nations depends on their manner of eating.

4. Tell me what you eat, and I shall tell you what you are.

5. The Creator, by making man eat to live, invites him to do so with appetite and rewards him with pleasure.

6. Gourmandism is an act of judgement, by which we prefer things which have a pleasant taste to those which lack this quality.

7. The pleasures of the table belong to all ages, to all conditions, to all countries and to every day; they can be associated with all the other pleasures and remain the longest to console us for the loss of the rest.

8. The table is the only place where one is never bored during the first hour.

9. The discovery of a new dish does more for the happiness of mankind than the discovery of a star.

10. Those who give themselves indigestion or get drunk, do not know how to eat or drink.

11. The correct order of foods is starting with the heaviest and ending with the lightest.

12. The correct order of beverages is starting with the most temperate and ending with the most heady.

13. To claim that wines should not be changed is a heresy; the palate becomes saturated and after the third glass the best of wines arouses nothing but an obscure sensation.

14. A dessert without cheese is like a beautiful woman with one eye.

15. One can learn to cook, but a restaurateur is born.

16. The most indispensable quality of a cook is punctuality; it should also be that of a guest.

17. To wait too long for a late-comer is to show a lack of consideration for all those present.

18. He who receives his friends and gives no personal attention to the meal which is being prepared for them, is not worthy of having friends.

19. The mistress of the house must always make sure that her coffee is excellent, and the master of the house that his wines are choice.

20. To invite someone is to take charge of his happiness during the time he spends under your roof.

Some of Brillat-Savarin's aphorisms, notably the one which claims that 'One can learn to cook, but a restaurateur is born' are rather disputable!

There are many other gastronomic aphorisms. We quote some which are attributed to the actor Des Essarts, who, according to a contemporary author, had an appetite proportionate to his corpulence (Des Essarts was very fat) and was as much a gastronome as a man of wit – qualities which often go together.

Some people claim that he was the precursor of Brillat-Savarin. A good dinner would put him into good spirits. He would eloquently analyse the qualities of each dish and create amusingly bizarre combinations of words:

'Good cookery is the food of a clear conscience.'

'Let the leg of mutton be awaited as the first lovers' meeting, mortified as a liar caught in the act, golden as a young German girl, and bloody as a Carib.'

'Take advantage of the gracious condescension of the elegant calf's kidney, multiply its metamorphoses; you can, without giving it offence, call it the chameleon of *cuisine*.'

'Make of an egg an amiable intermediary which comes between the various parts of food to bring about difficult reconciliations.'

'Mutton is to lamb what a millionaire uncle is to his poverty-stricken nephew.'

'A vine-leaf wrapped round a partridge brings out its quality, just as the barrel of Diogenes brought forth the qualities of the great thinker.'

'Never forget that the pheasant must be awaited like the pension of a man of letters who has never written epistles to the ministers or madrigals to their mistresses.'

Des Essarts, born at Langres in 1740, was one of the best actors of the Comédie-Française. He died suddenly in 1793, on hearing of the arrest of one of his best friends.

The poets and prose writers of the past have also formulated gastronomical aphorisms and axioms.

Horace, who set great store by the cleanliness of the table, and above all insisted that one should be able to see one's reflection mirrored in the plates and glasses, wrote as follows:

'The stomach heaves when one receives from a valet a goblet bearing the greasy imprint of his sauce-stained fingers, and when one sees at the bottom the filthy dregs collected there.'

Plutarch makes this statement – which he attributes to Aemilius Paulus, the conqueror of Persia: 'The same intelligence is required to marshal an army in battle as to order a good dinner. The first must be as formidable as possible, the second as pleasant as possible, to the participants.'

In these words Plutarch gives a valuable lesson to all would-be gastronomes, to those who frequently compose menus which would give no pleasure to a true gastronome.

Rabelais categorically declares that only 'candle-lit'

dinners and suppers are pleasing. He goes on to say: 'There is no good cheer except at night when the lanterns are in place with their gentle flickering lights.'

Nearer to our own time, other writers and gastronomes have formulated many aphorisms which may be taken as sound gastronomical rules.

Thus Carême gives the following advice to ministers and diplomats: 'The culinary art follows diplomacy, and every prime minister should pay it tribute.'

Talleyrand knew this only too well. He used to advise French ambassadors at the courts of foreign sovereigns to rely more on their casseroles than on their secretaries.

Carême also says: 'To preside over a political chamber, or to hold a post in an embassy, is to take a course in gastronomy.'

Another of Carême's aphorisms stresses how very important is the part played by cookery: 'When there is no more cookery in the world there will be no more letters, no quick and lofty intelligence, no pleasant easy relationships, no more social unity.' (*Pâtissier pittoresque*)

Saint-Beuve is responsible for this aphorism: 'Intellectual men who quickly wolf down whatever nourishment is necessary for their bodies with a kind of disdain, may be very rational and have a lofty intelligence, but they are not men of taste.'

Monselet, who was a gastronome and extremely witty, formulated many aphorisms in his writings. This one shows the social importance of good dinners:

'*Tout se fait en dînant dans le siècle où nous sommes*
Et c'est par des dîners qu'on gouverne les hommes.'

'Everything is done at dinner in the century in which we live, and it is by dinners that men are governed.'

Monselet also wrote:

'Gastronomy is the joy of every condition and every age. It adds beauty to wit.'

'A gourmet is a being pleasing to Heaven.'

'All passions, rationalised and controlled, become an art. Gastronomy, more than any other passion, is sensitive to reasoning and direction.'

'Ponder well on this point: the pleasant hours of our life are all connected, by a more or less intangible link, with some memory of the table.'

'There are many flowers which serve only to produce essences, of which one could have made savoury dishes.'

And in his *Lettres à Emilie* he gives the following advice to all women: 'Enchant, stay beautiful and gracious; but to do this, eat well. Bring the same consideration to the preparation of your food as you devote to your appearance. Let your dinner be a poem, like your dress.'

Lucien Tendret, the great-nephew of Brillat-Savarin, created a few gastronomical aphorisms in his book *La Table au pays de Brillat-Savarin*. They are, no doubt, less famous than those of the author of *Physiologie du goût*, but a few of them deserve to be quoted here:

'*Cuisine* is both an art and a science. It is an art when it strives to bring about the realisation of the true and the beautiful, called *le bon* (the good) in the order of culinary ideas. As a science, it is analagous to chemistry, physics and natural history. Its axioms are called aphorisms, its theorems recipes, and its philosophy gastronomy.'

'The beautiful and the good are identical, but the fleeting impressions created by the work of a cook or a musician disperse even as they are being experienced. Raphael's painting *The Transfiguration* is immortal, but Carême's *Ragoût de truffes à la parisienne* lasts only while it is being eaten, just as roses last as long as their fragrance can be enjoyed.'

'The cook is no less than an artist, and even if he may not be on the level of Polygnotus and Phidias, he has his part and his place in civilisation as a whole.'

'Skilful and refined cookery has always made its appearance during the most glorious epochs in history.'

'Vatel is not less famous than his master, the conqueror of Rocroi, and if glory is nothing but smoke, then Antonin Carême has made as much of it as Napoleon.'

'To give life to beauty, the painter uses a whole range of colours, the musician of sounds, the cook of tastes – and it is indeed remarkable that there are seven colours, seven musical notes and seven tastes.'

Lucien Tendret also made the following remarks illustrating the importance of good *cuisine* in diplomatic affairs:

'Political issues are decided at table. Talleyrand often owed his successes to the skilful creations of Antonin Carême.'

'At the time of the Congress of Vienna, the ambassador (Talleyrand), taking leave of Louis XVIII, said to him: "Please believe me, your Majesty, I need saucepans more than written questions."'

'Monsieur Guizot assures us that while he was ambassador in London, his cook was more useful to him politically than his secretaries.'

He also gave the following advice, in the form of axioms, to his hosts and guests:

'To order and conduct a dinner is given only to fine gastronomes, of delicate and cultivated tastes. A skilful host is as rare as a good cook.'

'One only dines well at the homes of true gastronomes who feel all the nuances. The least puffiness spoils the loveliest of faces, and attention to detail creates perfection.'

'With money, anyone can offer succulent dishes and famous wines, but courtesy and kindness cannot be bought.'

'To make people who have no appetite eat, to make the wit of those who have it sparkle, to enable those who lack these qualities to find them – this is the supreme science of a gastronome-host.'

'The gourmets, if they are not seated comfortably and have no elbow room, count both the wines and the food for nothing.'

And to sum up his philosophy Lucien Tendret says:

'French conversation was born in the salons of the eighteenth century. From the dining-rooms of the Regent, from those of President Hénault, Baron Holbach and Mme. Geoffrin, there emerged a society, certainly sceptical and impious, but permeated with suave urbanity and that ingenious and enlightened courtesy which has since spread throughout Europe, and has become one of the salient characteristics of modern civilisation.'

Jean Richepin makes a practical point in his poem, *À Table*:

Est-on dix, y compris la famille, on se serre!
Mais pas trop cependant, et sans être à l'étroit
Il faut qu'on ait de l'air aux coudes, et le droit
De faire en bavardant, si l'on veut, de grands gestes;
Grignotés de profil, les mets sont indigestes.

'We are ten, with the family; sit closer together!
But not too closely: we don't want to be cramped,
We must have elbow room, and be able
To talk and make gestures, if we feel so inclined;
Sitting sideways and picking at food is courting
indigestion.'

To return to Lucien Tendret, he has something to say to reassure people who think they are doing wrong in giving themselves up to the pleasures of the table:

'The casuists have classed gluttony as one of the seven deadly sins, but if it is not tainted by the vice of drinking to

The Five Senses, a painting by D Téniers

inebriation or eating to excess, it deserves to be ranked with the theological virtues.' And –

'Those who have a profound indifference to the pleasures of the table are generally gloomy, charmless and unamiable.'

Apothegms. APOPHTEGMES GOURMANDS – The aphorisms of Brillat-Savarin are known throughout the world. Much less known are the gastronomical apothegms which the author of *Physiologie du goût* has set forth on the philosophy of the table:

Cookery. 'Cooking is one of the oldest arts, and one which has rendered us the most important service in civil life.'

'The science which feeds men is worth at least as much as the one which teaches how to kill them.'

'Once fire was discovered, the instinct for improvement made men bring food to it, in the first place to dry it, and afterwards to put on the fire to cook.'

'Cookery made great progress when fire-resisting vessels in bronze or clay appeared.'

'Meals, in the sense in which we understand the word, began with the second age of the human species.'

'In the state of society in which we now find ourselves, it is difficult to imagine a nation which lived solely on bread and vegetables.'

Gourmandism and Gourmands. 'Gourmandism is an ardent, rational and habitual preference for things which flatter the taste.'

'From whatever point of view you look at gourmandism, it deserves nothing but praise and encouragement.'

'Gourmandism is one of the main links uniting society.'

'If there are gastronomes by predestination, then there are also some by circumstance.'

Taste. 'Taste is simple in its action, that is to say, it cannot react to two flavours at once.'

'Man's palate, by the delicacy of its texture and of the various membranes that surround it, gives sufficient proof of the sublimity of functions for which it was intended.'

Appetite and digestion. 'Appetite proclaims itself by a slight sensation of languor in the stomach, and a feeling of tiredness.'

'Digestion is an absolutely mechanical function, and the digestive organs can be thought of as a mill equipped with sieves.'

'To understand digestion as a whole, it must be linked with food and its consequences.'

'Digestion, of all the bodily functions, is the one which exercises the greatest influence on the mental state of an individual.'

'Some people are in a bad temper while digestion is in progress; it is therefore not the time either to suggest projects or to ask favours of them.'

'Theory and experience both prove that the quality and quantity of food have a powerful influence on work.'

'A badly nourished man cannot adequately cope with the effort of continuous work for any length of time.'

Obesity and Thinness. 'Obesity is never found among the savages or among the classes of society where the people have to work to eat, and where they only eat to live.'

'Thinness is not a great drawback for men, but it is a dreadful misfortune for women.'

Foods. 'By foods one means substances which, introduced into the stomach, can be assimilated by digestion, and restore the energy lost by the human body.'

'We were not satisfied with the qualities nature gave to poultry; art stepped in, and under the pretext of improving fowls, made martyrs of them.'

'Poultry is for cookery what canvas is for painting, and the cap of Fortunatus for charlatans. It is served to us boiled, roast, hot or cold, whole or in portions, with or without sauce, and always with equal success.'

'Three lands of ancient France contest the honour of producing the best poultry: Caux, Le Mans and Bresse.'

'Turkey is undoubtedly one of the best gifts that the New

World has made to the Old.'

'Game provides the delights of our table; it is healthy, rich, savoury food, excellent in taste and easy to digest, especially when young.'

'Under the direction of an able chef, game goes through many skilful modifications and transformations, and provides most of the full-flavoured dishes which constitute superlative *cuisine*.'

'The taste of a Périgord partridge is not the same as that of a Sologne partridge.'

'If the garden warbler were the size of a pheasant, it would most certainly cost as much as an acre of land.'

'The quail is the sweetest and the nicest of game birds. It is an act of ignorance to serve it in any way except roasted.'

'A woodcock is in its full glory only when roasted actually before the eyes of the hunter; above all, the hunter who shot it.'

'In the hands of an able cook, fish can become an inexhaustable source of delight.'

'The smelt is the garden warbler of the water; the same smallness, the same high flavour, the same superiority.'

APHTONITUS – One of the seven great chefs of Ancient Greece. He invented the pudding.

APICIUS – There were three Romans by the name of Apicius. All three were famous, not for their genius, their virtues, or their great qualities, but for their gluttony and achievements in the gastronomical art.

The first lived under Sulla, the second under Augustus and Tiberius, and the third under Trajan. It is the second Apicius who is the most famous, and it is of him that Seneca, Pliny, Juvenal and Martial have spoken so much. Athenaeus says that he spent immense sums to satisfy his gluttony and that he invented several kinds of cakes which bear his name. Seneca, who was his contemporary, tells us that he ran a sort of school of 'good fare'. He adds that Apicius, having got into heavy debt, was at last forced to examine the state of his affairs, and that, seeing he had only 250,000 Roman pounds left (some authors say forty million sesterces, about an income of £80,000), he poisoned himself, fearing that such a sum would not be enough for him to live on.

Pliny often speaks of the *ragoûts* which Apicius invented, and calls them *nepotum omnium altissimus gurges*.

The third Apicius lived under Trajan. Having invented a secret method of preserving oysters, he managed to deliver some very fresh ones to the Emperor, who was busy fighting the Parthians at the time.

The name Apicius was not only given to cakes but to several kind of sauces.

There exists, under the name of Coelius Apicius, a treatise *De re culinaria*, printed for the first time in Milan (1498); the critics do not think, however, that it was written by any of the three men named Apicius. Martin Lister produced a magnificent edition of this book entitled *De obsonus et condimentis, sive de arte coquinaria* (London 1705), of which 125 copies were printed.

However, the first edition, which is undated, seems to be older than the Milan edition. It was printed in Venice by Bernardus de Vitalibus, and comprises forty quarto pages, the first thirty-two of which constitute Apicius's book.

But the latest edition, a remarkable summary of the *Dix livres de cuisine d'Apicius* is that of Bertrand Guégan (published by René Bonnel, Paris, 1933).

To return to Marcus Gavius Apicius, it is interesting to note some of his discoveries. To improve sows' livers, he fattened them with dried figs, gave them honeyed wine to drink, then suddenly slaughtered them without warning. When camel was on the menu he only had the most delicate part served up – the heel.

Did Imperial Rome have her gastronomes in the strictest sense of this word, and were the illustrious personages, whose prowess at table has been described in history or legend, real connoisseurs of culinary matters? On this point Carême, who made a profound study of the history of ancient Rome, says that Roman cookery was 'fundamentally barbaric'.

What the historians tell us of the three men named Apicius leads us to agree with Carême. The Roman table was certainly sumptuous and magnificent, in the spectacular sense, but it was not at all refined.

Rome, at the time of the Apicius family, governed the whole world, at any rate the world as it was then known. She dictated her laws to distant provinces. From these subjugated provinces she received great quantities of various food products. Gallia Narbonensis sent her pork. Africa and Asia sent delectable foods which the Roman cooks, trained by the Greeks, prepared in lavish manner.

APONOGETONACEAE. APONOGETONS – Flowering rush family, represented by one genus, *Aponogeton*. Their leaves float on the surface of the water, rather like waterlilies.

The *Aponogeton distachyus* is widely cultivated in the temperate parts of Europe. For some years now it has become completely naturalised at Montpellier, where its young shoots are eaten and called *Cape asparagus*. The common names for this plant are *Cape pond weed* and *water hawthorn*.

APOPHORETA – Name given by the ancient Romans to the gifts which the host made to his guests for members of their families. These gifts were often of great value. They were mostly precious dishes or vases which had been used at the feast. Sometimes the slaves who served at table were also presented to the guests.

APOTHECA. APOTHÉCA – Roman name of a room, situated under the roof of a house, so arranged that the smoke of various fireplaces passed through it, with the sole purpose of boiling down the famous Caecubum wine to the desired syrupy consistency.

This wine took at least fifteen years to mature.

APPAREIL – In French culinary terminology this word is used to describe mixed preparations that go into the making of dishes. For example, the following terms are used: *appareil à soufflé* (soufflé mixture); *appareil à biscuit* (sponge mixture); *appareil à crème renversée* (custard mixture), etc.

APPELLATIONS D'ORIGINE – According to French legislation the label of a controlled wine must bear an *appellation d'origine*; that is to say the name of the viticultural area to which it belongs.

Appellations d'origine are divided into two categories: *appellation d'origine contrôlée* (A.O.C.) and *vins délimités de qualité supérieure* (V.D.Q.S.). The first and superior group consists of wines belonging to the viticultural areas that produce wines of great quality and individuality, following traditional methods. The latter is a secondary group of controlled wines belonging to viticultural areas that have earned a reputation for their general quality while not producing wines of such individual characteristics as those of the first group.

Nicolas Appert

APPERT – It is impossible to explain how so many people (including the authors of the first edition of this dictionary) committed the error of naming François Appert in this context, when it ought to be Nicolas – at least according to a short report in *l'Encyclopédie universelle du XIXe siècle* (1858 edition, published eighteen years after the death of Charles-Nicolas Appert).

His biography is so vague that we prefer to repeat what the canners themselves have to say about him.

About a hundred and sixty years ago, the Frenchman Nicolas Appert discovered how to preserve food products by the action of heat.

The only document that has been found relating to Appert's civil state is his death certificate, although we do know that he was born in Châlons, in the Marne, in 1750. Whether it was Châlons-sur-Marne or Châlons-sur-Vesle remains a mystery.

His father was a wine merchant in the Champagne region, and Nicolas began work with him, corking bottles.

Then he moved on to learn the culinary art as a cook at the court of Christian IV. He also worked in several brasseries and private households. Finally when he was about thirty years old (about 1780) he set up as a confectioner in rue des Lombards, Paris.

Appert became deeply interested in the preparation of food products. He soon realised the inadequacy and disadvantages of contemporary methods of preservation, and set himself the task of investigating new ones.

In 1810, in order to bring his invention to the notice of the public, Appert published *le Livre de tous les ménages ou l'Art de conserver pendant plusieurs années toutes les substances animales et végétales* ('The Manual for Every Household or the Art of Preserving all Varieties of Animal and Vegetable Substances for Several Years').

He wrote: 'My method is not a vain theory; it is the fruit of late nights, much deep thinking and research, and innumerable experiments.'

Most probably Appert intuitively recognised the destructive action of heat on the 'ferments' that alter animal and vegetable substances. He realised that if it were possible to destroy or attenuate the effect of these 'ferments' by heating them sufficiently, and afterwards succeed in preventing other 'ferments' from being introduced into the substance, the conservation of the latter would be prolonged, if not indefinitely, at least for a very long period. Although this discovery was not based upon scientific theory, Appert managed through empirical (rule-of-thumb) methods to perfect a system of food preservation which in principle is little different from that employed in manufacturing processes today.

Encouraged by official approval, Appert gave up his confectionery business and occupied himself exclusively with experiments; these at length proved the validity of his theories.

In 1794 he settled in Ivry-sur-Seine. In 1804, with the help of some financial backing, he acquired a piece of land of 4 hectares (10 acres) at Massy in Seine-et-Oise, and built a factory. This he equipped with what to us would seem rather primitive machinery. He employed about fifty workers.

Scientific controversies arose over Appert's discovery, and it was not until Pasteur arrived on the scene that a satisfactory explanation was reached.

Massy was destroyed by the Allies in 1814.

Although old and practically penniless, Appert did not give up. In 1817 he settled in rue Cassette, in Paris, and managed to obtain premises in rue Moreau from the government. There he resumed the application of his manufacturing processes on a large scale.

The last years of his life, like his early years, are something of a mystery. He died in extreme poverty on 1 June 1840. In 1852, Chevallier-Appert took up where the other had left off.

He was Appert's successor and he perfected Appert's ideas. He had the idea of putting canned foods in the autoclave (q.v.), which up to then had been used for entirely different purposes. He raised the temperature to a high level. Since it was necessary to know the temperature inside the autoclave during the operation in order to preserve the quality of the canned foods, Chevallier-Appert devised a pressure gauge as well.

Calville Blanc apple

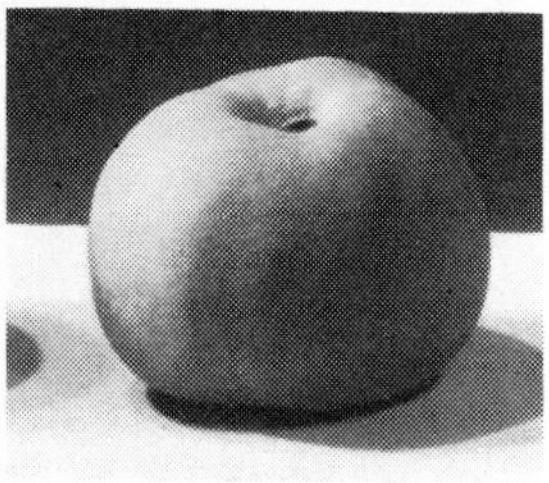

Reinette du Canada apple

Richared apple (*Pomona*)

Stark Jaugrines apple (*Pomona*)

APPETENCE. APPÉTENCE – A feeling which brings desire for food; this is the first stage for appetite.

APPÉTIT – Common name for chives in French. (See CHIVES.)

APPETITE. APPÉTIT – Psychologists define under the term natural appetite the tendencies which instinctively cause us to satisfy the needs of the body.

In physiology appetite is defined as something rather different from hunger. Hunger in reality is nothing more than the need to eat, whereas appetite is the lure of pleasure which one experiences whilst eating, brought about by a particular condition of the organism.

The sensation of hunger, which develops at regular mealtimes in civilised people, sometimes disappears if it is not satisfied at the usual hour. The appetite is stimulated by the sight and smell of food; bitter substances frequently awaken lost appetite by releasing digestive secretions.

In certain psychic and mental cases, appetite can degenerate into a craving for offensive and non-edible substances.

The opposite of appetite is *anorexia*, which means distaste for food.

APPIGRET – An old French word which Rabelais used to define gravy, juice, seasoning.

APPLE. POMME – Apples are the fruit of a tree belonging to the family *Rosaceae*.

The numerous varieties of apples are divided into cooking and eating apples.

The best dessert apples among the American varieties are: *Golden Delicious*, golden yellow in colour, truncated in shape, with a delicate juice, very tasty flesh, eaten between October and April; *Red Delicious*, *Starking Delicious* and *Richared*, truncated in shape, in varying shades of dark red, keeping well until March. Among the varieties of French origin are: *Reine des reinettes*, early variety, yellow streaked with russet; *Reinette du Canada*, rough-skinned, yellowish-green with brown spots, mid-season variety keeps well if it has been grown at a high altitude; *Reinette du Mans* and *Reinette Clochard*, late varieties both cultivated in the Loire valley.

Calville, in particular *Calville Blanc*, irregular in shape with more or less prominent sides and pronounced 'shoulders', is gradually disappearing, but still has some adherents on account of its very delicate flavour. These different varieties of apples keep the market well supplied from September to April or May. French production is important both quantitatively and qualitatively, and is complemented by apples imported from Italy and Holland. During the season France exports her excess (the golden varieties especially) to Germany and Great Britain. Imports are also received from the southern hemisphere in April, May and June, when stocks of French apples are exhausted.

The apple, like the grape, is one of our choicest dessert fruits. It is rich in assimilable minerals – calcium, copper, iron, magnesium and potassium – and contains Vitamins B and C, and tannin. Apples are used in the preparation of numerous sweet dishes, preserves, etc., and in the manufacture of pastries and apple sugar in confectionery. They are also pressed and used in the alembic to give cider, from which is derived Calvados.

Baked apples in pastry or douillon normand. RABOTTES DE POMMES OU DOUILLON NORMAND – Choose big sound baking apples and core them, to remove the central part containing the pips. Make a circular incision round the middle, to pre-

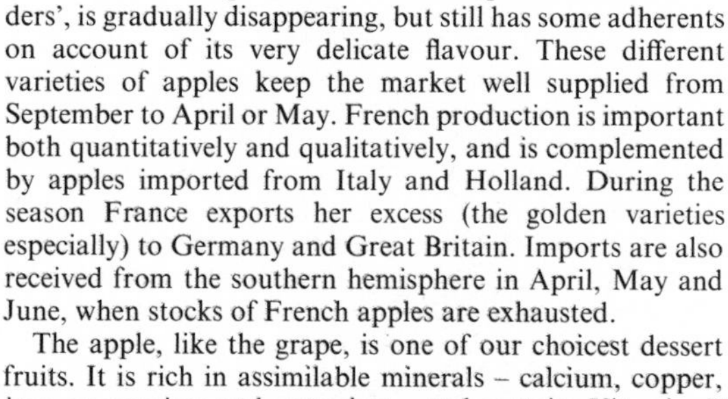

Baked apples in pastry

vent their bursting. Fill the middle, hollowed out by the corer, with butter kneaded with sugar (and with a pinch of cinnamon, if desired).

Enclose each apple in a piece of *Lining paste* (see DOUGH), rolled out not too thick. Put a little circlet of paste (cut out with a fluted-edged cutter) on top of each apple. Brush with beaten egg and score the outside of the apples lightly with a knife.

Bake in a moderate oven from 25 to 30 minutes. Serve piping hot.

Note. The apples can be peeled before being put into pastry. They can also be cooked first as for *Apples bonne femme* (see below). In that case the baking will only take 15 minutes. Lining paste can be replaced by left-over pieces of puff pastry.

Apples bonne femme. POMMES BONNE FEMME – Make a light circular incision round the middle of some baking apples, and core them.

Put them in a buttered ovenproof dish. Fill the middle of each apple with a little butter mixed with fine castor sugar. Pour a few tablespoons of water into the dish, bake gently in the oven and serve in the same dish.

Apples Bourdaloue. POMMES BOURDALOUE – Poach apples, whole, halved or quartered, in syrup, as described in the recipe for *Apricots Bourdaloue* (see APRICOT).

Apple butter, marmalade – See JAM, *Apple jelly*; MARMALADE, *Apple marmalade*.

Buttered apples. POMMES AU BEURRE – Peel and core some baking apples and parboil for 2 minutes in boiling water with a dash of lemon juice added to it. Drain the apples, put them in a buttered ovenproof dish, sprinkle with fine sugar, moisten with a few tablespoons of water (or light syrup) and cook gently in the oven.

Serve each apple on a round croûton of bread which has been fried in butter. Dilute the pan juices with a few tablespoons of water, add a little butter and pour over the apples.

Apples au chambertin. POMMES AU CHAMBERTIN – Peel and core several apples. Poach them in sweetened Chambertin wine, allowing 300 g. sugar per litre (6 oz. per pint, $1\frac{1}{4}$ cups per quart) of wine. Leave the apples to cool in this syrup. Arrange in a fruit dish or a *timbale*. Boil down the syrup by half, leave until cold, then pour over the apples.

Apple charlotte – See CHARLOTTE.

Apple compote – See COMPOTE.

Apples Condé. POMMES CONDÉ – Prepare as described in the recipe for *Apricots Condé* (see APRICOT).

Apples à la crème au kirsch. POMMES À LA CRÈME AU KIRSCH – Peel, core and cook the apples in a vanilla-flavoured syrup. Leave to cool in the syrup. Drain, dry and arrange them individually in glass goblets (or on a fruit dish). At the last moment top with half-whipped fresh cream, sweetened with sugar and flavoured with kirsch.

Note. Apples, prepared as described above, can be topped with cream flavoured with various liqueurs, such as anisette, bénédictine, cassis, chartreuse, raspberry liqueur, rum, etc.

Crêpes stuffed with apples (apple pancakes). CRÊPES FOURRÉES AUX POMMES – Prepare the *crêpes* (q.v.) in the usual manner and coat them with concentrated *Apple sauce* (see below).

Roll the pancakes or fold them in four. Put them on a baking sheet, sprinkle with icing sugar and glaze quickly in the oven. Serve on a folded napkin.

Note. Stuffed *crêpes* are usually called *pannequets* in French.

Apple croûte. CROÛTE AUX POMMES – Poach halved or quartered apples in vanilla-flavoured syrup, and prepare as described in the recipe for *Apricot croûte* (see APRICOT).

Apples Figaro. POMMES FIGARO – Philéas Gilbert gives the following recipe: 'Scald 650 g. ($1\frac{1}{2}$ lb.) chestnuts, remove the shells and the inner grey skin, put them into a pan with a vanilla bean and enough milk (previously boiled) to cover them completely. Simmer gently for 45 to 50 minutes.

'Core and peel 10 medium-sized apples. Cook them in a light syrup, strongly flavoured with vanilla; it is enough for the pulp just to be softened.

'Shred about 15 almonds and roast them until they go slightly yellow (not brown). Add to them 50 g. (2 oz., 3 tablespoons) coarsely crumbled *marrons glacés*.

'Make a cream with 150 g. (5 oz., $\frac{2}{3}$ cup) castor sugar, 4 egg yolks, $1\frac{1}{2}$ tablespoons (2 tablespoons) flour and 4 dl. ($\frac{3}{4}$ pint, scant 2 cups) vanilla-flavoured, boiled milk. After boiling this cream for 1 minute, remove from the heat and incorporate 2 tablespoons (3 tablespoons) butter. Do not allow to boil again. Rub the chestnuts through a sieve, put this purée into a sauté pan, and add 125 g. (4 oz., $\frac{1}{2}$ cup) castor sugar and $1\frac{1}{2}$ dl. ($\frac{1}{4}$ pint, $\frac{2}{3}$ cup) cream. Stir on the fire for 2 minutes, and spread on a dish.

'Place the well-drained apples on this chestnut purée, pour the cream over them, and sprinkle with the almond and chestnut mixture.'

Apples flambé au kirsch (or other liqueurs). POMMES FLAMBÉES AU KIRSCH – There are two ways of preparing this dish.

1. Core cooking apples, peel them and poach in a light, vanilla-flavoured syrup. Drain them, put into a silver *timbale* or an ovenproof china or glass dish. Sprinkle with kirsch, heat, and set alight just before serving.

2. Put the peeled and cored apples into a buttered dish. Sprinkle with sugar and melted butter, and bake slowly in the oven.

Transfer the apples to a silver *timbale* or an ovenproof china or glass dish, sprinkle with kirsch, and set alight just before serving.

Note. Apple flambé can also be set alight with brandy, raspberry *eau-de-vie*, Calvados, quetsche, rum, or any other liqueur with a high-degree alcohol content.

Apple flan – See TART, FLAN.

Apple fritters – See FRITTERS, *Dessert (sweet) fritters*.

Apples glacé à l'impératrice. POMMES GLACÉES À L'IMPÉRATRICE – Using dessert apples, poached in syrup and well drained, prepare as described in the recipe for *Peaches à l'impératrice* (see PEACHES).

Apple gratiné. POMMES GRATINÉES – Peel tart apples, cut into quarters, and cook in vanilla-flavoured syrup, keeping them fairly firm. Drain and dry.

Arrange in an ovenproof dish on a layer of apple sauce prepared as for a charlotte (see CHARLOTTE, *Apple charlotte*). Scatter some crushed macaroons on top, sprinkle with a little melted butter, and brown the top in a slow oven.

Note. For this dish apples can also be cut into quarters and cooked in butter, instead of being poached in syrup.

Apple jelly – See JAMS AND JELLIES.

Apple mousse à la Chantilly. MOUSSE AUX POMMES À LA CHANTILLY – Prepare a very fine, thick, vanilla-flavoured *Apple sauce* (see below). Cool the sauce and whisk it on ice, adding to it a few tablespoons fresh thick cream, making sure that the mixture does not lose its consistency. Pour into glass goblets or a fruit dish, piling it up in a dome.

Top with vanilla-flavoured whipped cream, whisked stiff.

Apple omelette à la normande. OMELETTE FOURRÉE AUX POMMES DITE À LA NORMANDE – Make the omelette in the usual manner, using eggs sweetened with sugar. Just before folding, fill the omelette with concentrated *Apple sauce* (see below) or with tart apples, peeled, diced, cooked in butter and sugar, and mixed with a little apple sauce, or with thick fresh cream.

Arrange the omelette on a long dish. Sprinkle with sugar and glaze with a glazing iron or with a salamander.

Apple pectin. JUS DE POMMES – This juice, which has a strongly viscous consistency, is used for preparing *Apple jelly* (see JAMS AND JELLIES).

It is also used for preparing many other jellies made of fruit with too high a water content; without such an addition these jellies would not have the desired consistency, and would run the risk of fermenting.

Added in the right proportions, apple juice does not alter the flavour of other fruit.

To obtain about $2\frac{1}{2}$ litres ($4\frac{1}{2}$ pints, $5\frac{1}{2}$ pints) apple juice, cut 36 sound apples in quarters, without peeling or coring them, as both the peel and the pips provide a great deal of mucilaginous matter. Put them in a copper pan with 2 litres ($3\frac{1}{2}$ pints, $4\frac{1}{2}$ pints) water. Seal the pan closely (hermetically, if possible) and cook on sustained heat (not too brisk) until the apple quarters become soft enough to 'give' easily when pressed with a finger.

Pour the fruit into a muslin cloth fixed over a bowl and leave for some time; the juice will drip through. Do not press the fruit itself in order to hurry the process. The juice can be used as indicated in various recipes.

The residue, i.e., the apple pulp left behind, can be used for preparing *Apple sauce* (see below) or paste, and for various sweet flans, loaves and soufflés.

Apple pie – See PIE.

Apple pudding – See PUDDING.

Apples with rice. POMMES GRATINÉES AU RIZ – Prepare 125 g. (4 oz., $\frac{2}{3}$ cup) rice as for *Dessert rice* (see RICE). Put it into an ovenproof dish in layers, alternating with 225 g. (8 oz.) apples, sliced and cooked in butter. Smooth the surface of the top rice layer, and cover with 10 apple quarters, cooked in butter. Sprinkle with crushed macaroons and a tablespoon of melted butter, and brown the top. Serve in the same dish, with kirsch-flavoured *Apricot sauce* (see SAUCE), served separately.

Apples with rice and meringue. POMMES MERINGUÉES AU RIZ – Poach apple quarters in vanilla-flavoured syrup, or cook them in butter. Proceed as described for *Apricots with rice and meringue* (see APRICOT).

Apple ring à la normande. BORDURE DE POMMES À LA NORMANDE – Peel, core and halve the apples, and cook them in vanilla-flavoured syrup. Leave to cool in the syrup, then drain on a flat sieve until they are dry.

Prepare a *crème moulée* (see CUSTARD, *Vanilla custard*), flavouring with 1 to 2 tablespoons Calvados (applejack), and cook it in a *bain-marie* (q.v.) in a plain ring mould. When it is cold, turn out the mould onto a dish. Fill the middle with the dry apple halves, piling them up into a dome. Decorate with firmly whipped cream piped through a forcing-bag with a fluted nozzle. Serve with Calvados-flavoured *Apricot sauce* (see SAUCE).

Apple ring Brillat-Savarin. BORDURE DE POMMES BRILLAT-SAVARIN – Fill a *savarin* (q.v.), steeped in syrup and flavoured with rum, with stewed apples which have been mixed with rum-flavoured confectioner's custard (see CREAMS, *French pastry cream*).

Poach apple halves in vanilla-flavoured syrup, drain well, and coat with reduced apricot pulp. Place these on top of the *savarin* and decorate with halves of fresh walnuts, crystallised cherries and lozenges of angelica. Serve with rum-flavoured custard.

Apple rissoles. RISSOLES DE POMMES – Roll out a piece of *Puff pastry* (see DOUGH) and cut into little circles 8 to 10 cm. (3 to 4 inches) in diameter. Put a tablespoon of highly concentrated *Apple sauce* (see below), flavoured with kirsch (or any other liqueur), in the middle of each circle. Fold the pastry to enclose the filling completely, and seal the edges, moistening them with water.

Just before serving, fry in smoking-hot deep fat. Drain the rissoles and arrange them on folded napkins. Serve kirsch-flavoured *Apricot sauce* separately (see SAUCE).

Apple (or other fruit) rissoles can also be prepared using lining paste, or ordinary brioche dough, and can be made in various shapes.

Apple sauce. MARMELADE DE POMMES – Cook quartered apples in a little water until soft. Pass through a strainer. Add a pinch of salt and enough sugar to sweeten. Boil down until thick. A squeeze of lemon juice improves the flavour.

Apple soufflé. SOUFFLÉ AUX POMMES – Prepare as described in the recipe for fruit soufflés, using apple pulp and cream. (See SOUFFLÉS, *Sweet soufflés*.)

APPLE-CORER. VIDE-POMMES – Tube-shaped implement for taking the cores out of apples.

APPRÊT – In French cookery this word means a finished culinary preparation.

APRICOT. ABRICOT – Fruit of the apricot tree, brought from Armenia into Italy but not widely known in Europe until the fifteenth century.

The *musk apricot*, justly famous for its succulent flesh, is found in the south of France, Algeria and Spain.

In Auvergne, another much prized variety of apricot is cultivated for the high quality of jam which is produced from it.

Among the best varieties of apricot is *clingstone*, a species of apricot with white flesh which adheres to the stone. It has a somewhat tart flavour. *Peach apricot*, a choice fruit, is much sought after for the delicacy of its flesh; it is fragrant, juicy and sweet.

Apricots are one of the fruits most used in *pâtisserie*. They are used in a number of preparations, including sweet courses and confectionery. They also make excellent tarts, as well as delicious compotes and jellies.

Compotes can be made from green preserved apricots, which should be peeled before being bottled.

Varieties of apricots
(*Pépinière G Delbard*)

The early Boulbon apricot

Luizet apricots

Nancy peach apricot

Apricots à l'ancienne. ABRICOTS À L'ANCIENNE – Halve large apricots, remove the stones, and poach in vanilla-flavoured syrup. Arrange on a layer of sponge cake soaked in rum and coated with a layer of apple sauce. Sprinkle with chopped almonds, sugar and a little melted butter. Put in the oven to set. Serve with apricot jam diluted in a little water, strained and laced with rum.

Apricot barquettes – See BARQUETTES.

Apricot bombe. BOMBE ABRICOTINE – Line a mould with chocolate ice cream. Fill with *Mousse* (*bombe*) *mixture* (see ICE CREAMS AND ICES), flavoured with apricot brandy or apricot purée.

Apricot bouchées. BOUCHÉES À L'ABRICOT – These cakes can be made with either Genoese or sponge batter, and are filled and coated with apricot jam.

Ingredients. 250 g. (9 oz., generous cup) fine sugar, 8 whole eggs, 200 g. (7 oz., 1¾ cups) sieved flour, 200 g. (7 oz., ¾ cup plus 2 tablespoons) best butter, a small glass of kirsch or rum.

Method. Beat the sugar and the eggs in a copper bowl on a low heat, or over hot water. When the mixture becomes pale, light and frothy, blend in carefully the sieved flour and the melted butter (to which the chosen flavouring has been added).

Pour the mixture into shallow round moulds (cake or muffin tins) filling up to three-quarters. Cook for about 20 minutes in a slow oven. Turn out and allow to cool. When quite cold, cut each *bouchée* in half with a thin sharp knife, to avoid crumbling the sponge. Spread with kirsch-flavoured apricot jam, then sandwich the *bouchées* together again. Brush with concentrated apricot jam and coat the sides all round with chopped roasted almonds. Decorate the tops with half a glacé cherry.

Apricots Bourdaloue I. ABRICOTS BOURDALOUE – Cook 16 apricot halves in a light vanilla-flavoured syrup. Remove, drain and arrange in a shallow ovenproof dish two-thirds filled with semolina cooked in milk and bound with 2 egg yolks (see SEMOLINA, *English semolina pudding*).

Cover the apricots with a light layer of semolina, sprinkle with the crumbs of 2 crushed macaroons and a teaspoon of fine powdered sugar. Put in a very hot oven for a few minutes to glaze the top.

Serve with an apricot and kirsch sauce (apricot jam thinned down with the syrup in which the apricots were cooked, strained and laced with a tablespoon of kirsch).

Apricots Bourdaloue II. ABRICOTS BOURDALOUE – Cook apricots lightly in syrup, halve them, and place on a layer of *Frangipane cream* (see FRANGIPANE) in an ovenproof dish or on a flan shell.

Sprinkle with crushed macaroons and melted butter, and glaze in the oven. Serve with an apricot and kirsch sauce as above.

Candied or crystallised apricots (apricot comfits). ABRICOTS CONFITS – Choose very firm white apricots, of uniform size. Make a light incision at the opposite end to the stalk.

Put them, a few at a time, in a copper pan full of cold water, so that they are completely covered. Place the pan over a low flame. As soon as the apricots rise to the surface, take them out of the water with a perforated spoon and feel them to see if they are thoroughly softened; this is the blanching operation.

Soak the apricots for 12 hours in cold water, which should be changed every 2 hours.

Prepare the following syrup: 1 cup sugar to 1¾ cups water, boiled to 18° by a syrup gauge (see SUGAR). Pour this boiling syrup over the drained apricots, which have been put back in the copper pan. Bring to the boil over a high flame. Decant the apricots and syrup into an earthenware bowl and leave overnight.

Next day, drain the apricots and boil the syrup (it should not be above 12° on the syrup gauge). Add ¼ cup sugar, and bring up to 18° on the syrup gauge. When it is boiling, add the apricots, bring again to the boil, and return to the earthenware bowl. (This operation is called 'giving a dressing'.) Continue to give a dressing in this manner every other day. When boiling, bring the syrup up by 6° each time. Add sugar and boil down when there is too much syrup, which must, however, completely cover the fruit each time.

When it comes up to 30° (average syrup density) – that is, after the third dressing – do not bring it up by more than 4°, and give the dressings only every 3 days. Proceed in this manner until the syrup reaches 36° (moderately thick).

Stone the apricots by inserting a copper needle at the stalk end and pushing the stone towards the incision made at the beginning of the operation. Some of the apricots may not look as good as the rest, perhaps by being slightly damaged during the stoning process. Cut these into small pieces and stuff them into the rest of the apricots to keep them in a round shape. Lay them in an earthenware bowl.

Bring the syrup to the boil, check the degree (36°), and pour it, still boiling, over the apricots. Leave to cool. Spoon the apricots and syrup into jars and cover with greaseproof paper, as you would jam. Keep the jars in a cool, dry place.

Candied apricots or apricot comfits in brandy. ABRICOTS CONFITS À L'EAU-DE-VIE – Choose very small, firm apricots of uniform size. Blanch them as described in the recipe for candied apricots above. Soak them in cold water for an hour, drain, and put them in syrup, which should be brought up to 25° (see SUGAR). Leave them in the syrup at this degree for 4 days, then drain, and put them into preserving jars. Fill with the following mixture:

Syrup in which the fruit was candied, 1 litre (1¾ pints, generous quart).

Neutral alcohol, tasteless, of 90°, 1 litre (1¾ pints, generous quart).

Add a piece of vanilla pod, or 1 teaspoon vanilla essence or 1 dl. (6 tablespoons, scant ½ cup) rum or kirsch per 2 litres (3½ pints, generous 2 quarts) liquid. Mix well. When the jars have been filled, seal them with their special tops, or with cork lids.

Keep in a cool place, protected both from heat and humidity. At the end of one month the fruit will be ready for use.

Caramel apricots in brandy (petit fours). ABRICOTS (À L'EAU-DE-VIE) AU CARAMEL – Drain the preserved apricots as described in the recipe for *Crystallised apricots* (see below). Roll them in powdered gum arabic, then dip them, one by one, in sugar cooked to crack stage (see SUGAR).

Space them carefully on a slightly oiled marble slab, and when they are quite dry, put them into fluted paper cases.

Apricot charlotte – See CHARLOTTE, *Fruit charlottes*.

Colbert apricots. ABRICOTS COLBERT – Halve the apricots, remove the stones, and poach the fruit in a light syrup (flavoured with vanilla, if desired). Simmer gently from 8 to 10 minutes, depending on the ripeness of the fruit. Cool.

To serve, arrange the apricots in a fruit dish; add a few drops of kirsch to the syrup and pour it over the fruit.

For this compote the halved apricots can be peeled. To make the operation easier, dip the apricot halves for a few seconds into boiling water. Flavour the compote by adding to it a few of the kernels which have been extracted from the apricot stones, and blanched.

Apricot compote – See COMPOTE.

Apricots Conde (old recipe). ABRICOTS CONDÉ – Cook halved apricots in syrup. Drain, arrange on a *savarin* (q.v.) and top with apricot syrup flavoured with kirsch.

Garnish the middle of the *savarin* with a mixture of 25 g. (1 oz., $\frac{1}{4}$ cup) cornmeal or maize flour cooked in a double boiler with scant litre ($1\frac{1}{2}$ pints, 4 cups) scalded, sweetened, vanilla-flavoured milk, until thick. Dilute the mixture with cream. Make little cork-shaped croquettes from the corn meal or maize flour mixture, and place them round the *savarin*.

Apricots Condé I. ABRICOTS CONDÉ – Fill three-quarters of a shallow fireproof dish with *Dessert rice* (see RICE). Cook apricot halves in syrup, drain, and arrange them on the rice. Decorate with glacé cherries and angelica cut into lozenges. Heat thoroughly in the oven, and serve with *Apricot and kirsch sauce* (see SAUCE).

Apricots Condé (*Scarnati*)

Apricots Condé II. ABRICOTS CONDÉ – Arrange the apricot halves on a ring of *Dessert rice* (see RICE). Stud the apricots with halved, blanched almonds, and decorate with glacé cherries and lozenges of angelica. Heat through in the oven and serve with *Apricot and kirsch sauce* (see SAUCE).

Apricot coupe – See ICE CREAMS AND ICES.

Apricot croûte. CROÛTE AUX ABRICOTS – Arrange a dozen or so slices of *savarin* in a circle on a dish, as described in the recipe for *Fruit croûtes* (see CROÛTES) replacing the pineapple slices by a layer of apricot jam spread evenly on the *savarin* slices.

Cook halved apricots in syrup, drain them, and lay them on the *savarin* slices. Decorate with crystallised fruit. Heat in the oven and serve with *Apricot and kirsch sauce* or *Madeira sauce* (see SAUCE).

Crystallised apricots in brandy (petits fours). ABRICOTS (À L'EAU-DE-VIE) CRISTALLISÉS – Use apricots which have been preserved in brandy (see *Candied apricots in brandy*). Lay the apricots on a flat sieve and drain for 2 hours. Melt a little gum arabic in water. Put the apricots in a bowl and pour the gum arabic over them, a little at a time, gently shaking the bowl until all the apricots are coated.

Remove them, one at a time, with cooking tongs, and roll them in crystallised sugar. Leave for an hour on a wire cake sieve, and when they are quite dry arrange them in paper cases.

Apricots à la diable. ABRICOTS À LA DIABLE – Spread the flat sides of 8 large macaroons with a layer of apricot jam flavoured with kirsch. Place them on a fireproof dish in a circle.

Cook the same number of apricots in syrup, drain, halve them, and place 2 halves on each macaroon. Spread over them a few teaspoons of *Praline custard cream* (see CREAMS). Sprinkle the apricots with fine sugar and glaze in a very hot oven.

When ready to serve, add to the dish a few tablespoons of apricot sauce laced with kirsch.

Apricots flambé in kirsch. ABRICOTS FLAMBÉS AU KIRSCH – Cook apricots in syrup, drain, halve them, and put 2 or 3 halves into individual fireproof dishes. Add to each dish 2 tablespoons (3 tablespoons) of the syrup in which the apricots were cooked, blended with some cornflour or arrowroot. Heat to boiling point.

When ready to serve, pour into each dish a teaspoon of kirsch and set it alight.

Apricot flan – See TART.

Apricot fritters – See FRITTERS.

Apricot ice cream – See ICE CREAMS AND ICES.

Apricots à l'impératrice I. ABRICOTS À L'IMPÉRATRICE – Three-quarters fill a dessert dish with *Rice à l'impératrice* (see RICE). Set in a cold place, on ice, if possible. Cook a dozen apricots in a sugar syrup flavoured with vanilla, drain well, halve the apricots, and arrange them in a circle on the rice. Top them with a coating of redcurrant jelly (see JAMS AND JELLIES, *Currant jelly*). Decorate with cherries and lozenges of angelica. Keep on ice until ready to serve, then put the dish on a larger one covered with a napkin, and surround with crushed ice.

Apricots à l'impératrice II

Apricots à l'impératrice II. ABRICOTS À L'IMPÉRATRICE – Prepare *Rice à l'impératrice* (see RICE) in a charlotte mould. Turn it out into a shallow fruit bowl and arrange on it a circle of halved apricots, cooked in syrup and drained. Decorate with glacé cherries and lozenges of angelica. This method of presentation may be applied to all fruit desserts *à l'impératrice*.

The rice can also be served in a *savarin* mould, turned out onto a dish, the centre filled with cooked, drained half apricots.

Apricot jam – See JAMS AND JELLIES.

Apricot omelette. OMELETTE AUX ABRICOTS – See EGG, *Omelette*: *Jam and fruit omelette*.

Apricot oreillons. OREILLONS D'ABRICOTS – Halved apricots are called *Apricot oreillons*. They are bottled in water or a sugar syrup.

Apricot pudding. POUDING AUX ABRICOTS – See PUDDING, *Fruit pudding*.

Chicken in aspic (*Robert Carrier*)

Aspic of frogs' legs à l'ancienne. ASPIC DE GRENOUILLES À L'ANCIENNE – Poach trimmed frogs' legs in white wine flavoured with a sprig of thyme and a bay leaf. Leave to cool in the liquor.

Drain, dry, and coat half of them completely with a white *Chaud-froid sauce* based on meatless stock, and the other half with a *Chaud-froid sauce* coloured with crayfish butter (see SAUCE, *Compound sauces*).

Lay the frogs' legs on a wire tray, one by one, and leave them to get quite cold. Decorate with truffles cut in thin slices. Coat with aspic jelly.

Arrange the frogs' legs round the sides of a mould which has been coated with jelly, alternating them with peeled crayfish tails. Fill the middle of the mould with a *Parisian salad* (see SALAD), dressed with mayonnaise which has been thickened with gelatine. Pour a thin layer of aspic jelly over the whole, and chill on ice.

To serve, turn out onto a dish and decorate with a border of jelly croûtons (q.v.).

Little chicken aspics

Aspic of poultry and feathered game. ASPIC DE VOLAILLES – Coat slices of chicken or game with white or brown *Chaud-froid sauce* (see SAUCE) and put them in a mould which has been coated with aspic jelly. Fill the mould with either a chicken or game mousse, or with some other mixture used for cold dishes.

Aspic of shrimps or other shellfish. ASPIC DE CREVETTES – Coat an aspic mould with clear fish jelly. Decorate the sides with peeled shrimp tails and small pieces of truffle. Fill the middle of the mould with a cold shrimp mousse mixed with shrimp tails and truffles cut into large dice. Fill the mould with jelly, and leave on ice to set.

Crayfish aspics can be prepared in the same way, using trimmed crayfish tails and crayfish mousse. Spiny lobster or lobster aspics are made by using slices of one or other of these shellfish, together with the appropriate mousse.

ASSIETTE – See PLATE.

Assiette anglaise – Assortment of cold meats arranged on a plate or a dish.

The assortment usually consists of York ham, salt beef, tongue, rib of beef or roast beef. Mortadella, galantine, etc., are sometimes added to it.

The meat is garnished with chopped jelly, cress and gherkins. The *assiette anglaise* is served chiefly at lunch.

The term *assiettes assorties* describes various preparations served as *hors-d'œuvre*, though *hors-d'œuvre* are usually served nowadays in special *hors-d'œuvre* dishes.

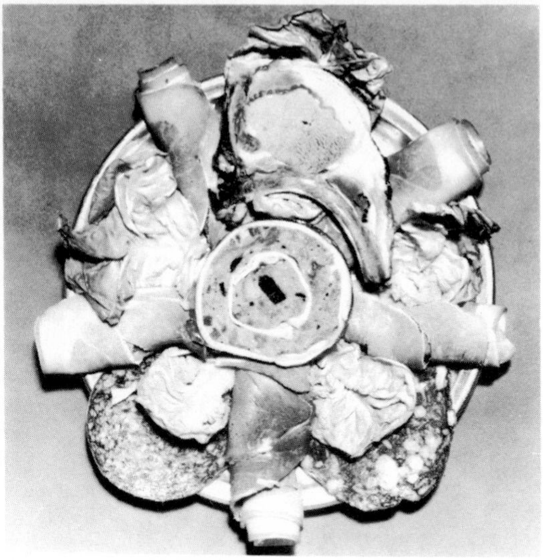

Plate of cold meats (*Larousse*)

Assiettes volantes – This term describes a selection of several items of food on one plate, in the manner of an *hors-d'œuvre*, particularly various kinds of salty foods cut in thin slices.

Assiettes garnies – At the beginning of the nineteenth century, this term also applied to a dish.

Carême says: 'Lunch consisted of six *assiettes* on which veal cutlets, fish, chicken, game, a side-dish of vegetables, and soft-boiled eggs were served.'

ASTI – Italian town situated 40 km. (about 25 miles) from Turin. It is the ancient *Asta Colonia* or *Asta Pompeia* of the Romans, and is famous for its sparkling wine, made from Moscato grapes, called *Asti Spumante* (see WINE).

ASTRAGAL (Milk vetch). ASTRAGALE – Many varieties of astragal grow in Asia; it is also found in the temperate regions of the Lebanon. One variety of milk vetch produces gum tragacanth, which is used in confectionery and pastry-making.

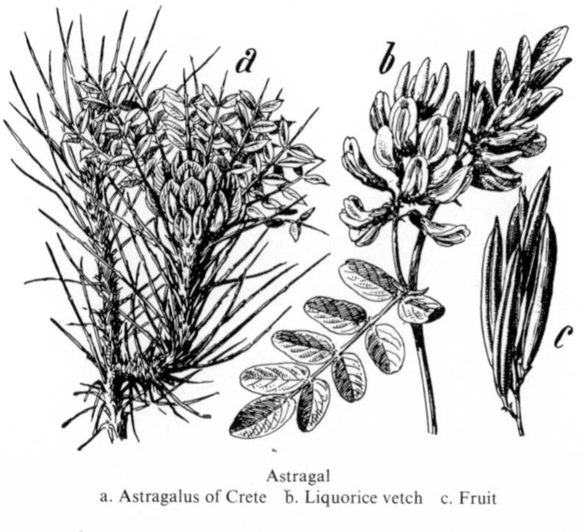

Astragal
a. Astragalus of Crete b. Liquorice vetch c. Fruit

Another variety produces fruit in the form of pods, which, before the seeds contained in them are formed, resemble worms. In the past these pods used to be added to salads (to mystify the guests!). Astragalus pods are also pickled in vinegar, like capers.

There is yet another variety of astragalus, the seeds of which, when ripe, are used in cookery.

ASTRINGENT – Binding, contracting. The vegetable astringents owe their properties to tannin. Among them are cutch, bark of oak, quinquina, leaves of walnut tree, arbutus tree and bramble, lemon juice, quinces, etc.

ASTRODERME – Sea fish of an unusual appearance, yellowish pink on the back and sides with black round spots, alternating with silvery spots on the belly. Young astrodermes have purplish-blue bodies and silvery bellies. This fish, called *feï d'America* by Nice fishermen, is well known along the whole of the Mediterranean coast of France (Côte d'Azur).

It is chiefly used as an ingredient for *bouillabaise*.

ATHENAEUS – Greek writer, born in Naucratis, in Egypt, in the reign of Marcus Aurelius. He was still alive in the reign of Alexander Severus, about the year A.D. 228.

Only one of his works has survived, entitled *Deipnosophistai* or *Specialists in Dining*, which is a gem of erudition, giving much information on ancient history which we would otherwise lack.

In *Specialists in Dining*, there are several passages relating to flowers and fruit and their various uses, both practical and pleasurable.

ATHÉNIENNE (À L') – Name applying to various dishes which are usually flavoured with lightly fried onion, and garnished with aubergines, tomatoes and sweet pimentos.

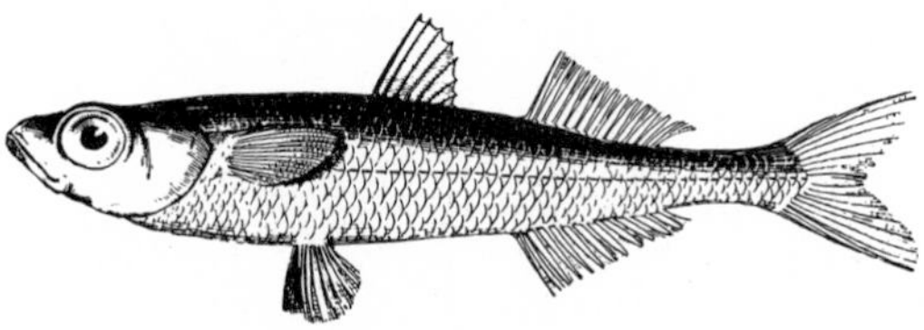

Athérine

ATHÉRINE – Little fish, with a long, spindle-shaped body, covered with rounded scales at the posterior end. The sides have a silvery stripe, the head is flattened on the top, the upper jaw is shorter than the lower, and the teeth are very small.

Two species of this fish are known on the coasts of France, where they are called *prêtre* and *faux éperlan*.

Common names in English are *silverside* and *sand-smelt*, and the fishermen take enormous catches. Other species are found in the estuaries and Mediterranean coast lakes.

In the U.S.A., smelts correspond to this fish. Its flesh is delicate in flavour. *Athérines* are usually fried in deep fat, but all recipes suitable for small bass can be applied to this fish.

ÂTRE (Hearth stone) – This word is no longer used today, except to describe the central part of the baker's or pastry-cook's oven.

In the past, when a great number of dishes were cooked in the fireplace, the part where the fire was actually burning was called the *âtre* (hearth). It was in the hearth that stews and other preparations which take a long time were slowly cooked, surrounded by hot coals.

All these dishes are today cooked in ovens heated by gas, electricity, coal or oil. Quite a few gastronomes protest against these methods of cooking, maintaining that dishes cannot taste so good prepared in this way as when cooked by the old methods.

Experience shows that there is nothing in the claim. When well-made utensils are used (and kitchen utensils have today reached a high point of perfection), food can be cooked successfully, whatever the product and whatever the method.

ATRIPLEX – Herbaceous plant of the same family as spinach and the goosefoot genus *Chenopodium*.

The atriplex is commonly known as garden orach; it is cultivated and grown all over France. It is prepared like spinach. (See ORACH.)

Antique attelets (*Collection of Dr Gottschalk. Phot. Larousse*)

ATTELET – This word comes from the Latin *hasta*, meaning staff or rod, and in the past was spelt *hatelet*. It is often used, incorrectly, to describe little metal skewers on which various pieces of meat, sheeps' kidneys, lambs' sweetbreads, larks, etc., are threaded.

To be precise, an *attelet* is a little utensil in the shape of a pin or skewer, but with an ornamental top. These, with truffles, cocks' combs, crayfish and other items of food threaded on them, are used solely for decorating hot or cold dishes served in the grand style.

For arranging these grand *entrées*, Carême advocated the use of a great number of *attelets*. In modern cookery practice this decoration has been practically abandoned. Modern cooks disdain, as a rule, the use of any decoration which is not actually edible.

It is probable that the *attelets* decorating Carême's *entrées* and *removes* were, in fact, edible and the effects obtained were certainly beautiful.

ATTENDU – French culinary term applied to a dish or beverage the consumption of which is intentionally postponed in order to improve it. Thus a pheasant should be *attendu*, that is, kept hung, before being cooked and eaten.

ATTEREAU (Skewer) – In his *Dictionnaire de cuisine et d'économie* (Paris 1836), Burnet, one-time steward of the royal household, gives the following definition of *attereau*: 'Name which keepers of eating-houses attribute to a kind of *ragoût* made of fillet of veal, cut in very thin slices. They are studded with lardoons and cooked in a pie dish with a little stock poured over them.'

Carême, however, in his works published before Burnet's dictionary, describes a method of preparation of *attereaux* which indicates that this dish is in no way a *ragoût*. In modern cookery, *attereau* describes both the metal skewer on which various ingredients are threaded, and the dish itself. This is usually served as an *hors-d'œuvre*, but can also be served as a small *entrée* if supplemented by a garnish.

Attereaux differ from *brochettes* in being dipped in a sauce to give them a firm coating, rolled in breadcrumbs, and usually deep-fried.

The ingredients which make up the *attereaux* can be cooked on wooden skewers, and then transferred to silver *attelets*. The *attereaux* can also be served without the skewers on which they were cooked.

Sweet courses can be prepared *en attereau*, the method being the same as that given for savoury *attereaux*.

Attereaux à la chalonaise – Thread the *attereaux* with cocks' combs and kidneys cooked in a white *court-bouillon* (q.v.), and drained. Add mushrooms and truffles.

Dip the *attereaux* in *Villeroi sauce* (see SAUCE). Roll them in breadcrumbs and fry in smoking hot deep fat. Drain, season with fine salt, and arrange on a napkin or paper doyley, garnished with fried parsley.

Attereaux à la duchesse (dessert) – Prepare a mixture of *crème frite* (see CUSTARD, *Fried custard*) to which have been added 2 crushed macaroons and 1 tablespoon crystallised fruit, cut in very small dice and steeped in rum. When firm, thread slices of this mixture on the *attereau*. Roll in very fine breadcrumbs and deep-fry in smoking hot fat.

Attereaux à l'écossaise – Make up the *attereaux* using pieces of *Pickled ox tongue* (see OFFAL or VARIETY MEATS), mushrooms, and rather thick slices of truffles. Finish as described in the recipe for *Attereaux à la chalonaise*.

Attereaux à la maraîchère – Use pieces of turnip-rooted celery (celeriac) previously simmered in butter; mushrooms, and pieces of cooked ham for the *attereaux*. Finish as described in the recipe for *Attereaux à la chalonaise*.

Attereaux à la niçoise – Make up the *attereaux* with large stoned olives stuffed with a purée of anchovies, mushrooms, and pieces of pickled tunny. Dip them in *Villeroi sauce* (see SAUCE), with a tablespoon of concentrated tomato purée, and add chopped tarragon. Finish as described in the recipe for *Attereaux à la chalonaise*.

Attereaux à la normande – Make up the *attereaux* by threading on plump mussels cooked *à la marinière*, drained, and stuffed with finely pounded fish forcemeat. Add mushrooms cut in round slices. Finish as described in the recipe for *Attereaux à la chalonaise*.

Attereaux à la piémontaise – Make up the *attereaux* with slices of polenta (q.v.) cooked in butter, and thick slices of truffles. Dip them in egg and breadcrumbs and deep-fry in sizzling fat.

Attereaux à la Saint-Hubert – Make up the *attereaux* by threading on slices of pheasant, grouse, or any other winged game. Add sliced mushrooms and pieces of cooked lean ham. Dip the *attereaux* in *Villeroi sauce* (see SAUCE) to which has been added concentrated game stock reduced to a *fumet* (q.v.). Finish as described in the recipe for *Attereaux à la chalonaise*.

Attereaux au parmesan (Parma style) – Cook semolina (q.v.) in butter, and when firm, thread slices on the *attereaux*. Add slices of Gruyère cheese.

Dip the *attereaux* in egg and breadcrumbs and deep-fry.

Attereaux of calves' sweetbreads Villeroi. ATTEREAUX DE RIS DE VEAU VILLEROI – Braise uniform pieces of calves' sweetbreads in a white *court-bouillon* (q.v.) and thread them on the *attereaux*. Finish as described in the recipe for *Attereaux à la chalonaise*.

Attereaux of chicken livers à la mirepoix. ATTEREAUX DE FOIES DE VOLAILLE À LA MIREPOIX – Fry chicken livers in butter, drain and cool. Thread them on the *attereaux*, together with pieces of lean cooked ham, and sliced mushrooms. Coat the *attereaux* with a *fondue* (q.v.) of root vegetables cut into very small pieces, roll in breadcrumbs, and finish as described in the recipe for *Attereaux à la chalonaise*.

Attereaux of lambs' brains Villeroi. ATTEREAUX DE CERVELLE D'AGNEAU VILLEROI – Cut up lambs' brains and cook them in a white *court-bouillon* (q.v.). Cool and drain, and season with salt, pepper, oil, a few drops of lemon juice, and a little chopped parsley. Thread on the *attereaux*, and finish as described in the recipe for *Attereaux à la chalonaise*.

Attereaux of calves' brains are prepared in the same manner.

Attereaux of lambs' sweetbreads Villeroi

Attereaux of lambs' sweetbreads Villeroi. ATTEREAUX DE RIS D'AGNEAU VILLEROI – Braise lambs' sweetbreads in a white *court-bouillon* (q.v.) and thread them on the *attereaux*. Finish off as described in the recipe for *Attereaux à la chalonaise*.

Attereaux à la Villeroi can, in addition to the basic element, also contain mushrooms cooked in white mushroom *court-bouillon* and cut in slices.

Attereaux of ox palate. ATTEREAUX DE PALAIS DE BOEUF – Cut the ox palate (cooked as described under OFFAL or VARIETY MEATS, *Ox palate*), into round slices. Put them on *attereaux* with alternate rows of fried mushroom heads

Apricot omelette

Apricot sauce – See SAUCE, *Dessert sauces.*

Apricot soufflé – See SOUFFLÉS, *Sweet soufflés.*

Apricots preserved in syrup. CONSERVE D'ABRICOTS AU SIROP – The procedure is exactly the same as for *Compote of apricots in syrup* (see COMPOTE, *Preserved fruit in compote*).

Apricots preserved au naturel. CONSERVE D'ABRICOTS AU NATUREL – Pack the apricots into preserving jars without adding either water or sugar. Screw on the lids and sterilise for 15 to 20 minutes at 90°C. (194°F.).

Apricots with rice. ABRICOTS AU RIZ – Cook 1 cup rice in 2 cups sweetened milk which has been flavoured with vanilla. Place in a fruit dish. Cook halved apricots in a sugar syrup, stone them, and arrange on the bed of rice. Add a few tablespoons of apricot sauce, if desired. Serve hot or cold.

Apricots with rice and meringue. ABRICOTS MERINGUÉS AU RIZ – Cook 125 g. (4 oz., $\frac{2}{3}$ cup) rice as for *Dessert rice* (see RICE) and arrange it in a thick layer on an ovenproof dish. Cook a dozen or so apricots in a sugar syrup flavoured with vanilla, halve and stone them. Arrange the halves in a circle on the rice. Cover with meringue (q.v.), smoothing the surface. Decorate with meringue piped round the edge.

Sprinkle with icing sugar and bake in a moderate oven, raising the temperature to very hot at the last moment to make the meringue golden brown. When baked, decorate the piped edge further with a little apricot and redcurrant jelly, alternating the colours. This dessert is usually served hot, but it can also be served cold.

Pineapple, bananas, cherries, peaches, pears and apples can be prepared in the same manner. The fruit should previously be poached in vanilla-flavoured syrup or stewed in butter; it can be used whole, halved, in slices, or diced.

Apricot tarts and tartlets – See TART, TARTLET.

APRICOTING. ABRICOTER – This is the term used in *pâtisserie* to define the operation which consists in covering a cake or sweet with a thin layer of apricot jam which has been boiled down to a thick consistency, flavoured with liqueur, and passed through a fine strainer.

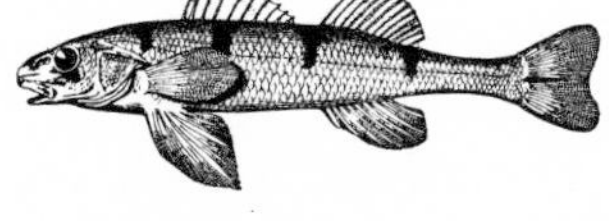

Apron

APRON – A small fish, with a rounded, elongated body covered with very rough scales. Its head is flattened, the snout protrudes above its mouth, its dorsal fins are placed at a distance from each other, its gill slits are large.

Only two species of apron are known, one which is found in the Danube, and the common apron, which abounds in the Rhône and all its tributaries.

The apron rarely exceeds 18 cm. (7 inches) in length. The upper part of its body is yellowish brown streaked with darkish bands or stripes, which extend obliquely down its sides. Its belly is a greyish white, its fins are yellow spotted with grey. Its flesh is very succulent and resembles that of perch, and it is much appreciated by gastronomes. For culinary preparation see PERCH.

ARAB COOKERY – See ALGERIA.

ARAPEDE – French name for a univalve shellfish commonly found in Provence. It is prepared in the same way as cockles.

ARBOIS – A small town in the Jura (Franche-Comté) which has given its name to highly esteemed white, red and rosé wines. (See FRANCHE-COMTÉ.)

ARBOLADE – Once a most popular dessert. Here is La Varenne's recipe for it: 'Melt a little butter in a pan and add yolks of egg, pear juice, sugar and a pinch of salt. Cook together, then sweeten with flower water. Colour a pale green and serve.'

ARBUTUS BERRY. ARBOUSE – Fruit of the cane apple, a shrub which is found in profusion in the southern parts of North America, Mexico, southern Europe and the Canary Islands.

This shrub, which is grown in some parts of southern France, mainly in the Languedoc, is also known as strawberry tree. It owes this name to the shape and colour of its fruit, which resembles the strawberry but has neither its scent nor its melting flesh.

Italy, Spain and Algeria are the main suppliers of wine and spirits distilled from the arbutus berry.

Besides wine and spirits, the fruit of this berry also yields a liqueur called *crème d'arbouse*, which has the reputation of being helpful to digestion.

The berries are very fleshy when ripe; they are sweet, and have a faintly acid after-taste. They are reputed to be astringent and diuretic.

ARCA – A bivalve mollusc commonly known as *arch.* Its shells, which are of rather a dark colour, are found on all the coasts of France.

This mollusc is eaten raw or prepared in the same way as mussels.

ARCACHON – This town, situated on the southern shores of the Bassin d'Arcachon (an inlet of the Bay of Biscay), is dear to the heart of gastronomes and lovers of oysters, for Arcachon is famous for its magnificent oyster beds (and for its *gravettes* in particular).

ARCANETTE – Name given in Lorraine to a species of small local teal. It differs from an ordinary teal and from garganey in that it does not migrate, and is found in its native land all the year round. Its flight is short but swift. Arcanette shooting is like duck shooting, the two species being of similar behaviour.

The flesh of this species of teal is excellent and much appreciated by gastronomes. In taste it can be compared with that of wild duck. For culinary preparation see DUCK.

ARCH – See ARCA.

ARCHANGELICA. ARCHANGÉLIQUE – See ANGELICA.

ARCHESTRATUS – Greek poet of about 350 B.C., who was a very great gastronome, it is said. He was the author of a work in verse, *Gastronomy*, of which only a few short fragments have survived.

Archestratus was born, it is believed, in Athens, although some say in Gela, an ancient town in southern Sicily; and he lived for a long time in Syracuse. He was chiefly renowned for the numerous voyages he made to collect notes on culinary methods and the eating habits of different nations.

Archestratus is sometimes referred to as a cook. From the writings of authors of the time it is apparent that he was more of a gastronome and an able writer, not a cookery technician. He can be described as the Brillat-Savarin of his time.

The most reliable data we have concerning this poet–gastronome comes from *Deipnosophistai* or *Specialists in Dining* by Athenaeus, a work translated into French from the Latin text by Michel de Marolles in 1680. There we find all that pertains to gastronomy, food production, cookery and ceremonial banquets.

Here is what Barthélemy, inspired by Athenaeus, says of Archestratus:

'This author was a friend of one of Pericles' sons. He crossed many lands and seas to find out for himself what was the best they had to offer. In his voyages he did not study the customs and manners of peoples, which it is useless to study since it is impossible to change them, but went into the places where the delights of the table were manufactured, and had no dealings except with people who catered for these pleasures. His poem is a shining treasure, and does not contain a single verse which is not a plea for gastronomy.'

ARCHIDUC (À L') – A term applying to a great number of preparations. Dishes *à l'archiduc* are usually seasoned with paprika and blended with cream. (See *EGGS; CHICKEN, Chicken sauté Archduke*.)

ARCHIL (Orchil, Dyer's moss). ORSEILLE – Purplish-red paste made from lichen, used as colouring matter. It is mainly used for tinting pickled tongue – *langue à l'écarlate*.

ARDENNAISE (À L') – A term applying mostly to dishes of small birds cooked in a *cocotte* with juniper berries. (See THRUSH.)

The same name also applies to a method of preparing crayfish (q.v.).

ARDOISE (Slate) – Slang name given to the bills for meals taken in cheap restaurants; in days gone by, these bills were written on a slate.

ARENGA (Sugar palm) – A genus of palm tree. Its trunk contains abundant pith, which produces a large quantity of starchy matter, obtained by making an incision on the trunk, from which sago (q.v.) is prepared.

From the clusters, which develop all the year round between the lower leaves, there is a flow of sweet sap which, by simple evaporation, furnishes a kind of sugar of a brownish colour, and, by a process of fermentation, a palm wine.

In England and in some parts of France, where imported sago is to be had, fruit of the sugar palm, gathered green, is candied, and is much valued as a stomach remedy.

ARGENTEUIL – Asparagus cultivated in the Argenteuil region, in Seine-et-Oise, enjoys a world-wide reputation.

Nowadays, Argenteuil exports its 'cuttings' and spreads the renown of its asparagus with the help of the 'Confraternity of the Argenteuil asparagus'. (See ASPARAGUS.)

Argenteuil wine once rivalled that of Suresnes. A few casks of it are still produced annually.

ARGUS PHEASANT – Bird thus called because of the great number of 'eyes' on its magnificent plumage. It bears some resemblance to the peacock, and is found in Java and Sumatra.

The flesh of argus pheasant is very delicate. All the methods of preparation given for pheasant (q.v.) are also applicable to argus pheasant.

ARIÈGE – The Ariège *département* of France, situated on the Spanish frontier between Haute-Garonne in the west and Pyrénées-Orientales in the east, is chiefly famous for the mineral waters of the thermal springs at the spas of Ax and Aulus.

Among Ariège culinary specialities there are many good dishes; above all, those rich in fat meat.

Excellent *Confits d'oie* (see CONFIT) are made in this region. The Ariège geese have a very fine flesh. Ariège pork is also of high quality, and is made into good *charcuterie*; Ariège hams and sausages are famous. (See LANGUEDOC.)

ARIÉGEOISE (À L') – Name given to various dishes almost all of which include the following ingredients as garnish: green cabbage and pickled pork, and sometimes kidney beans. (See CHICKEN, *Stuffed chicken à l'ariégeoise*; MUTTON, *Stuffed breast of mutton à l'ariégeoise*.)

ARLEQUIN (Harlequin) – The *arlequin* is (or rather was, for it is almost a thing of the past) an assortment of scraps of food, bought from bottle washers or washers-up in restaurants.

The scraps were made to look palatable and sold to people of small means, who could, for a few sous, have the illusion of eating a good meal.

These bits and pieces were also called *bijoux* – jewels.

Privat d'Anglemont says: 'Arlequin is so called because these dishes are composed of bits and pieces, thrown together in a haphazard fashion, just like the parti-coloured tights of the citizen of Bergamo. A bucket of pieces costs 3 francs; there you can find everything, from truffled chicken and game to beef and cabbage.'

ARLES – Many famous gastronomic products originate in this city and its neighbourhood, situated in the south of France.

Chief among them is the celebrated *saucisson d'Arles* (Arles sausage), but the region also produces excellent oil. (See PROVENCE.)

ARLÉSIENNE (À L') – The name applies to dishes some of which have a garnish of aubergines fried in oil, sautéed tomatoes, and onion rings dredged in flour and fried.

Another garnish consists of whole small tomatoes peeled and cooked in butter, and very tender pickled endive hearts fried in oil.

Yet another garnish consists of small tomatoes stuffed with pilaf and browned on top, large olives stuffed with chicken forcemeat, and new potatoes.

ARMADILLO. TATOU – Small toothless mammal covered with scales, found in South America. It is about the size of a guinea-pig, but more highly esteemed as meat.

ARMAGNAC – Region in the old province of Gascony, now almost entirely included in the *département* of Gers. The Armagnac brandies are famous. Armagnac (which is even shaped like a vine leaf) is divided into three zones: lower Armagnac, upper Armagnac, and Ténarèze. (See SPIRITS.)

ARMORICAINE – Armorica (older Aremorica) was the ancient name for a region in north-west France comprising the coast of Gaul, between the Seine and Loire rivers.

Armoricaine nowadays is the name given to a very choice variety of oysters (q.v.).

ARMORICAINE (À L') – Corruption by certain authors of the name of dishes called *à l'américaine*, particularly lobster. As a result of this corruption, the dish, so typically Provençal, has been placed under the patronage of legendary Armorica.

AROMA. AROME – Gastronomically speaking, this word describes the characteristic fragrance of various dishes. The word aroma is stronger than either odour or smell. The word perfume, on the other hand, is more specifically reserved for essences and other non-edible substances. It is right and proper that gastronomical literature should have a terminology of its own. We say, the aroma of this consommé, the aroma of this *fumet* (q.v.), the aroma of this coffee.

AROMATIC PLANTS. PLANTES AROMATIQUES – A great number of aromatic plants, with either a bland or pungent aroma, are used as flavourings in cookery.

The following are among the herbs most commonly used in the kitchen: parsley, chervil, tarragon, rosemary, thyme, bay leaf, wild thyme, sage, savoury; and the following are the most common aromatics: garlic, shallots, spring onions, chives and onions.

AROMATICS. AROMATES – Taken in its general sense, this word describes all substances which give out an odour of varying degrees of sweetness. The greatest number of aromatics is provided by plants of hot countries, notably Arabia. We are only concerned here with aromatics used in cookery, *pâtisserie* and confectionery.

Without indulging in the excesses of ancient practice, when scents like rose water and benzoin were used on every possible occasion, present-day cookery has at its disposal a great number of aromatics. The following are among those most widely used as condiments: dill, betel pepper, cinnamon, cloves, coriander, bay leaf, mace, mustard, nutmeg, pepper and thyme. Next come the aromatics used mostly for flavouring food: ambergris, anise, star anise, basil, cumin, fennel, juniper, ginger, horseradish, rosemary, sage, etc.

Some aromatic plants are frequently used fresh, for instance: chervil, tarragon, parsley, etc. The essence extracted from the peel of oranges, lemons and tangerines is also used. *Pâtisserie* and confectionery, in addition to the aromatics mentioned, also use vanilla, tea, chocolate and coffee.

Garlic, spring onions, shallots and onions are dealt with under separate entries in their alphabetical order, as well as the aromatic roots of carrot, celery and parsnip, which are really more vegetables than aromatics.

Cellar at Condom, Gers, a leading centre of Armagnac distillation
(*French Government Tourist Office*)

Medical opinion concerning the use of aromatics in cookery varies. Some doctors denounce it, others tolerate it, and yet others insist upon it. Formerly the use of aromatics and strong seasoning was abused. Modern cookery has, in large measure, done away with these excesses.

Aromatherapia (treatment for maladies by the use of plants) is now being successfully practised, often simply incorporated in the daily diet. (See SEASONING, CONDIMENTS.)

AROMATISE. AROMATISER – To impart some aroma to a culinary preparation or a pastry. Pastries are also aromatised with liqueurs.

ARPENTEUR – Common French name for plover.

ARQUEBUSE – An old liqueur made of various aromatic plants.

Eau d'arquebuse – Also known under the name of *eau d'arquebusade*. This beverage is obtained by infusion or maceration of vulnerary plants (kidney vetch, lady's finger, wound-wort).

ARRACACHA or ARRACACIA – Plant, native of Columbia, which grows in the Andes and in North America.

Its roots, which are farinaceous, produce a flour which is eaten in its country of origin. The roots can also be cooked like yams and sweet potatoes (q.v.).

The starch which is extracted from the roots of the arracacha is similar to arrowroot.

ARRACK. ARACK – Name given to a spirit distilled from fermented rice. Arrack is also distilled either from sugar and coconut milk left to ferment, or from the juice which seeps through incisions made on the coconut palm. In Réunion Island, in Madagascar and in most parts of the South African sub-continent, where sugar cane is cultivated, the name of arrack is also given to a spirit distilled from fermented cane juice (sugar cane juice squeezed out under a press).

ARROWROOT – Name given to starchy extracts obtained from the roots of various plants of the tropical regions.

There is a legend that this name originated because the Indians considered the sap obtained from the roots capable of healing wounds caused by arrows. Hence the name in English, 'arrow-root'. The fact is, however, that arrowroot takes its name from the American Indian word for flour-root, *araruta*.

The chief of these starches is the West Indian arrowroot (*Maranta arundinacea*), thus called because the plant from which the flour is produced originated in the West Indies. The English introduced it into India and it is also called West Indian salep.

The plant also grows in Madagascar.

Arrowroot is eminently edible and is imported into Europe in great quantities. This very delicate starch is used in thickening soups and gravies, as well as in the preparation of blancmanges, milk puddings and numerous sweet dishes.

Easily digestible, arrowroot is especially valued as a food for young children, invalids and the aged.

Arrowroot liaison. LIAISON À L'ARROWROOT – Pour into 1 litre ($1\frac{3}{4}$ pints, generous quart) boiling veal (or other) stock, 1 tablespoon arrowroot, well blended with a little cold stock or water. Mix, bring to the boil and strain.

Arrowroot porridge. BOUILLIE À L'ARROWROOT – Mix 3 tablespoons ($\frac{1}{4}$ cup) arrowroot with 3 tablespoons ($\frac{1}{4}$ cup) cold milk taken from 6 dl. (1 pint, $2\frac{1}{2}$ cups). Bring the remainder of the milk to the boil, adding either 1 teaspoon salt or 75 g. (3 oz., 6 tablespoons) sugar. Pour some of the hot milk onto the arrowroot, then return to the pan and cook gently from 8 to 10 minutes, stirring from time to time. Stock can be used instead of milk.

Arrowroot pudding. POUDING À L'ARROWROOT – See PUDDING, *Semolina pudding*.

ARSENIC – An element which is normally present in minute quantities in the tissues of the human body (thyroid gland, thymus gland, mammary gland, head and body hair). Certain vegetables (kohlrabi, turnips, certain cereals), sea fish, sea salt, milk and egg yolk contain small quantities of it, sufficient for the requirements of the organism.

ARTAGNAN (À LA D') – Name of a garnish composed of *cèpes* prepared *à la béarnaise* (see SAUCE), little stuffed tomatoes and cork-shaped potato croquettes.

This garnish is served with large or small pieces of meat and with poultry.

Artichoke showing inflorescence
a. Large green from Laon b. Camus from Brittany c. Artichoke bud

ARTICHOKE. ARTICHAUT – Vegetable derived from the cardoon, vastly improved by scientific methods.

This plant has been cultivated in France since the beginning of the sixteenth century and is mentioned by Rabelais. It originated in Sicily, and was brought to France by Catherine de Medici, who ate so many of them that she '*cuyda crever*' ('almost burst'). (*Journal* of P. de l'Estoile)

The principal regions of French production are in the west (Brittany and Anjou); the south-east (Provence and the Hyères region); the Garonne valley; the Paris region; and Roussillon. The most sought after are the large green artichokes of Laon, the *camus* of Brittany, the violet artichoke of Provence, the green (or 'white') variety of the same region, and the large *macau*.

The green and the violet Provençal artichokes are also cultivated in North Africa and exported to France at the beginning of the season. The bulk of French production takes place in the months of May and June.

The artichoke is a health-giving food, and lends itself to numerous delicious dishes. When it is young, and therefore very tender, it is eaten raw, *à la croque-au-sel* which means with 'nought but a grain of salt', *à la poivrade*, and *à la vinaigrette* (see HORS-D'ŒUVRE).

Artichoke hearts, cooked and chilled, make one of the best garnishes for cold dishes. They can be stuffed with various ingredients. They are also served as an *hors-d'œuvre*. (See also JERUSALEM ARTICHOKE.)

WHOLE ARTICHOKES. ARCTICHAUTS ENTIERS

Artichokes barigoule. ARTICHAUTS BARIGOULE – Prepare the artichokes as described in *Whole boiled artichokes* below.

Fill the insides with a *duxelles* (q.v.) mixture, adding to it a quarter of its volume in finely shredded fat bacon, the same amount of chopped lean ham, and some chopped parsley.

Surround the artichokes with rashers or strips of fat bacon, and braise them as described in the recipe for *Large braised artichokes stuffed au gras* (see below). Finish as described in that recipe.

Note. A variant of this recipe consists of cooking the stuffed artichokes in oil with a little white wine.

In home cookery, in the absence of *Demi-glace* (see SAUCE), the braising liquor can be thickened with *Kneaded butter* (see BUTTER).

Whole boiled artichokes. ARTICHAUTS ENTIERS BOUILLIS – Cut off the stalks, pull off the hard outer leaves and trim them. Shorten them evenly, cutting off the tops to two-thirds of their height. Wash, tie with string round the largest circumference, and put them, bases downwards, into a saucepan of boiling salted water.

Cook, keeping the water boiling, until done; the time depends on the size and freshness of the artichokes. Drain, dry on a cloth, remove the string. Serve as indicated in the recipe chosen.

The artichokes must not be overcooked. To ensure this, test the bottom of the vegetable, which should 'give' under very light pressure when cooked sufficiently. If the artichokes are to be served cold, put them in cold water as soon as they are cooked.

Boiled artichokes with various cold sauces. ARTICHAUTS BOUILLIS – Boil, cool and serve with one of the following sauces: *Mayonnaise, Mustard, Tartare, Vinaigrette* (see SAUCE).

To serve artichokes cold, cook them, scoop out the choke, and remove the leaves which surround it. Replace them in the cavity left by the removal of the choke. Season these leaves with a pinch of chopped chervil and parsley.

Boiled artichokes with various hot sauces. ARTICHAUTS BOUILLIS – Boil as described in the recipe for *Whole boiled artichokes*, and serve with one of the following sauces: *White, Butter, Cream, Hollandaise, Mousseline* (see SAUCE).

Large braised artichokes stuffed au gras (with meat). GROS ARTICHAUTS BRAISÉS FARCIS AU GRAS – Pare and trim the artichokes. Blanch for 5 minutes in boiling salted water. Plunge into cold water or leave under a running tap to cool; drain and remove the choke.

Season, stuff as desired, wrap them in a thin rasher, or slice, of fat bacon, and tie with string. Melt some butter in a sauté pan, put in finely shredded bacon, onions and carrots, and place the artichokes on this foundation. Season and add a *bouquet garni* (q.v.).

Simmer in butter and a small quantity of white wine until the liquor is almost completely boiled down; then add a few tablespoons of veal stock and cook in a moderate oven 180°C. (350°F., Gas Mark 4), with the lid on the pan for 55 to 60 minutes. Baste frequently during cooking.

Drain the artichokes, remove string and bacon, and place the artichokes on a dish. Strain the liquor in which they were cooked and skim off surplus fat. Strain again, add *Demi-glace* (see SAUCE), veal stock or any other sauce, according to the recipe. Boil down the liquor and pour over the artichokes.

Large braised artichokes stuffed au maigre (without meat). GROS ARTICHAUTS BRAISÉS FARCIS AU MAIGRE – Proceed as described above, leaving out the bacon and replacing veal stock by vegetable stock.

Small braised artichokes. PETITS ARTICHAUTS BRAISÉS – These are served as a garnish and as a vegetable. Choose very young small artichokes; pare them, trim off the stalks evenly and rub the bottoms with lemon; blanch in boiling water to which has been added salt and vinegar. Dip in cold water to cool, and drain. Place them, bases downwards, in a buttered sauté pan, or heavy frying pan, on a foundation of vegetables, as described in the recipe for *Large braised artichokes*. Cook over a low heat with the lid on for about 10 minutes, and finish cooking as described above.

Drain the artichokes, and use as indicated. Strain the braising liquor, reduce, skim off surplus fat, and pour this sauce over the artichokes.

Note. Small braised artichokes can also be prepared *au maigre* (without meat) by following the instructions given for large braised artichokes *au maigre*.

One can put the artichokes into a buttered sauté pan without blanching, provided one works quickly enough to prevent their going black.

Artichokes Clamart. ARTICHAUTS CLAMART – Choose 12 very small young artichokes; trim them and put them in a sauté pan, or heavy frying pan, with plenty of butter.

Add 225 g. (8 oz., 2 cups) shelled fresh garden peas and 2 shredded lettuce hearts. Season with salt and sugar. Moisten with 3 tablespoons (scant $\frac{1}{4}$ cup) water. Cook with the lid on, simmering gently. At the last moment, add a tablespoon of fresh butter.

This vegetable, being delicate and fragile, can be prepared in a bi-metal or aluminium sauté pan, or in an earthenware or enamelware *cocotte*, and served in the same dish (to avoid damage when transferring the artichokes to a dish for table).

Artichokes Crécy. ARTICHAUTS CRÉCY – Proceed as described in the preceding recipe, replacing peas and lettuce by an equal quantity of young peeled carrots.

Artichokes à la diable or Carciofo à l'inferno (Italian cookery). ARTICHAUTS À LA DIABLE – Lightly trim the tips of very tender, medium-sized artichokes. Remove the choke, blanch and drain. Fill the artichokes with a mixture of breadcrumbs, chopped garlic, capers and parsley, and season with salt and pepper.

Put into a sauté pan with oil, packing them in closely. Sprinkle generously with olive oil and season again. Cook in the oven, uncovered, basting frequently. When cooked, the artichokes should be crisp at the tips.

Arrange on a dish and sprinkle with the oil in which they were cooked.

Dried artichokes. CONSERVE D'ARTICHAUTS SÉCHÉS – Trim the artichokes and blanch them for 5 minutes in water to which lemon juice has been added.

Drain them, and put to dry on trays in the sun, or in a slow oven. (They can also be threaded on a string and dried in the open air.)

For this method of preserving artichokes, the blanching water must not be salted, otherwise saline particles would impregnate the artichokes, drawing humidity and thereby preventing desiccation.

Fried artichokes – See below *Artichoke hearts fried in batter*.

Artichoke fritters. BEIGNETS D'ARTICHAUTS – These can be served as *hors-d'œuvre* or as a vegetable. (See HORS-D'ŒUVRE, *Fritters*.)

Artichokes à la lyonnaise. ARTICHAUTS À LA LYONNAISE – Proceed as described in the recipe for *Artichokes barigoule*, replacing the *duxelles* mixture by sausage meat with a quarter of its weight of chopped, lightly fried onion and chopped parsley added to it.

Artichokes à la ménagère. ARTICHAUTS À LA MÉNAGÈRE – Proceed as described in the recipe for *Artichokes barigoule*, replacing the *duxelles* mixture by chopped boiled beef mixed with finely shredded fresh bacon and chopped parsley.

Artichokes mirepoix. ARTICHAUTS MIREPOIX – Put 12 small artichokes, prepared as described in the recipe for *Artichokes Clamart*, into a sauté pan on a foundation of 2 dl. ($\frac{1}{3}$ pint, scant cup) *Vegetable mirepoix* (see MIREPOIX), mixed with 2 tablespoons (3 tablespoons) lean ham cut into tiny dice.

Simmer for 5 minutes over a low flame, keeping the pan uncovered. Moisten with 4 tablespoons ($\frac{1}{3}$ cup) white wine. Simmer for 5 minutes, add 1 dl. (6 tablespoons, scant $\frac{1}{2}$ cup) veal stock, cover with a lid and simmer for 35 minutes.

Serve in a vegetable dish. Pour the *mirepoix* over the artichokes, and sprinkle with chopped parsley.

Pickled artichokes. CONSERVE D'ARTICHAUTS – Trim freshly gathered artichokes. Put them, whole or in quarters, in water to which lemon juice has been added. Blanch them in salted water, allowing 10 per cent of salt. Allow 10 minutes for whole artichokes and 5 minutes for quarters. Drain and refresh in cold water.

Drain them again, put into cans, and pour in the following pickling brine:

For 20 litres (4 gallons, 5 gallons) water, 1 kg. (2 lb.) well-refined salt and 2 tablespoons (3 tablespoons) lemon juice.

Weight of cans	*Cooking time with 110°C. (230°F.) pressure steriliser*	*Cooking time in a bain-marie or canning kettle*
500 g. (1 lb.)	30 minutes	1 hour
1 kg. ($2\frac{1}{4}$ lb.)	40 minutes	$1\frac{1}{2}$ hours
2 kg. ($4\frac{1}{2}$ lb.)	60 minutes	2 hours

Pickled artichokes à la grecque. CONSERVE D'ARTICHAUTS À LA GRECQUE – This is a pickle for which only small artichokes are used. Large artichokes have to be cut into quarters, which changes the aspect of this *hors-d'œuvre*.

Method. Pare and trim 100 small artichokes of the same size. As they are trimmed, plunge them into the following previously prepared mixture:

5 litres ($4\frac{1}{2}$ quarts, $5\frac{1}{2}$ quarts) water; 5 dl. (scant pint, $2\frac{1}{4}$ cups) olive oil; $1\frac{1}{2}$ tablespoons coriander; 1 teaspoon peppercorns; $1\frac{1}{2}$ tablespoons salt; a large *bouquet garni* composed of thyme, bay leaf, fennel and a stalk of celery; and the juice of 10 lemons strained through a muslin bag. Bring the artichokes to the boil and continue boiling for 8 to 10 minutes.

For a smaller quantity (20 artichoke hearts or quarters), see *Artichokes à la grecque* (HORS-D'ŒUVRE, *Cold hors-d'œuvre*). Cook for 8 to 10 minutes.

Transfer them, with their liquor, to a large earthenware crock and allow to cool. Put into 1- or $\frac{1}{2}$-litre (2- or 1-lb.) cans. Fill with the liquor to within the width of a finger from the top. Seal hermetically.

Place in a boiler, and boil 20 minutes for the $\frac{1}{2}$-litre (1-lb.) cans and 30 minutes for the 1-litre (2-lb.) cans.

Artichokes à la poivrade – See HORS-D'ŒUVRE.

Purée of artichokes for garnish. PURÉE D'ARTICHAUTS – Half-cook artichoke hearts in a white vegetable *court-bouillon* (q.v.), and simmer in butter. Rub through a fine

Preparing artichoke hearts (*Scarnati*)

sieve. Heat the purée and add butter or cream, as directed in the recipe. If required, thicken its consistency by adding an equal amount of potato purée.

Purée of artichokes soubisée for garnishes. PURÉE D'ARTICHAUTS SOUBISÉE – Proceed as described in the preceding recipe. Add to the artichoke purée one third of its volume of *Onion soubise* (see PURÉE).

Artichoke salad – See SALAD, *Mixed salads.*

Artichoke soufflé – See SOUFFLÉS, *Soufflé of various vegetables.*

Artichoke stalks. MOELLE D'ARTICHAUT – Peel the stalks of large artichokes, taking care to remove all the woody casing. Cut them into sticks 5 cm. (2 inches) long. Blanch in salt water flavoured with lemon.

When they are blanched, artichoke stalks can be prepared in various ways; simmered in butter or cream in a covered pan; in *fritots* (q.v.); *à la grecque* (q.v.); curried; with gravy.

ARTICHOKE HEARTS. FONDS D'ARTICHAUTS – Artichoke hearts prepared as described below can be served as a vegetable or as a garnish. When sliced and blended with a sauce, white or brown, they should be served in a vegetable dish, in a *gratin* dish, or in a *croustade* (q.v.), *timbale*, or *vol-au-vent* cases. For preparation of the hearts see *Artichoke hearts in court-bouillon* below.

Artichoke hearts à l'allemande. FONDS D'ARTICHAUTS À L'ALLEMANDE – Blanch the artichokes lightly and stew in butter. Transfer into a vegetable dish and cover with *Allemande sauce* (see SAUCE).

If the artichoke hearts are too big, cut them into slices.

Artichoke hearts à la béchamel. FONDS D'ARTICHAUTS À LA BÉCHAMEL – Proceed as above, using *Béchamel sauce* (see SAUCE).

Artichoke hearts cooked in butter – FONDS D'ARTICHAUTS ÉTUVÉS AU BEURRE – Pare and trim the artichokes as described in the next recipe. Rub them with lemon, and blanch for 10 minutes in boiling salt water to which a few drops of lemon juice have been added.

Drain, put the artichokes in a well-buttered sauté pan, season, sprinkle with melted butter, and cook with the lid on the pan for 18 to 25 minutes, according to their size. Use as indicated in the recipe chosen.

Artichoke hearts in court-bouillon. FONDS D'ARTICHAUTS AU BLANC – Strip off the outside leaves on medium-sized artichokes. Trim them as evenly as possible, leaving only the fleshy middle part. Remove the choke, trim the hearts and rub them with lemon. Put into cold water as each one is trimmed.

Cook the hearts in boiling white vegetable *court-bouillon* (q.v.). They can be blanched or cooked until soft, according to the final dish chosen. Drain well.

Artichoke hearts à la crème. FONDS D'ARTICHAUTS À LA CRÈME – Proceed as above. As soon as the artichoke hearts are cooked, pour boiling cream over them. Simmer down by half. Transfer the artichoke hearts to a vegetable dish. Add butter to the sauce, strain it, and pour over the artichokes.

A prepared cream sauce can also be used for pouring over the hearts (see SAUCE, *Cream sauce*).

Artichoke hearts fines herbes. FONDS D'ARTICHAUTS FINES HERBES – Blanch lightly, slice, and fry in butter in a shallow pan. Transfer to a vegetable dish, and sprinkle with chopped chervil and parsley.

If the artichokes are very young and tender, slice them raw and fry in butter before sprinkling with the chervil and parsley.

Artichoke hearts fried in batter. FONDS D'ARTICHAUTS EN FRITOT – Blanch the artichoke hearts, slice them, and marinate in oil, lemon juice, salt, pepper and *fines herbes* (q.v.). When required, dip them in batter and deep-fry.

Drain, season with fine salt, arrange them in a heap on a folded napkin, and garnish with fried parsley.

Garnished artichoke hearts. FONDS D'ARTICHAUTS GARNIS – Artichoke hearts used principally as a garnish for hot and cold dishes can be filled with various mixtures. Here are the main ingredients which can be added to them: for hot dishes, the artichoke hearts, cooked in white vegetable *court-bouillon* (q.v.) and simmered in butter, are filled at the last moment with vegetables or other ingredients, but are not put in the oven to brown the tops as recommended for stuffed artichoke hearts.

Artichoke hearts intended as a garnish for cold dishes are cooked in this *court-bouillon*, drained, dried, and filled with various vegetables which have been set in a jelly. Or they can be seasoned with *vinaigrette*, mayonnaise or other *salpicons* (q.v.).

Artichoke hearts can also be covered with aspic jelly or *Chaud-froid sauce* (see SAUCE).

Filled artichoke hearts as garnish for cold dishes – Fill the hearts with various butters which have been pounded with any of the following: caviare, shrimps, crayfish and other shellfish, hard-boiled eggs, fish and shellfish purées, various *salpicons*, etc.

Filled artichoke hearts as garnish for hot dishes – *Anversoise:* hop shoots in cream; *argenteuil:* purée of white asparagus; *bretonne:* purée of kidney beans; *Compoint:* purée of green asparagus; *Conti:* lentil purée; *écossaise:* *brunoise* (q.v.) of carrots, celery, French beans and onions; *macédoine of vegetables* in butter; *princess:* asparagus tips and diced truffles; *Saint-Germain:* purée of fresh garden peas; thick sauces such as *béarnaise, Choron, Henri IV, paloise; Vichy:* carrots à la Vichy. (For sauces see SAUCE.)

Artichoke hearts à la hollandaise. FONDS D'ARTICHAUTS À LA HOLLANDAISE – Cook in *Court-bouillon IV* (see COURT-BOUILLON), drain, put in a vegetable dish and cover with *Hollandaise sauce* (see SAUCE).

Artichoke hearts Mornay. FONDS D'ARTICHAUTS MORNAY – Simmer in butter in a covered pan. Put in a fireproof dish which has been coated with *Mornay sauce* (see SAUCE). Cover the artichoke hearts with the same sauce, sprinkle with grated Parmesan cheese and melted butter, and brown the top.

Pickled artichoke hearts. CONSERVE DE FONDS D'ARTICHAUTS – Choose small, tender artichokes. Trim them with a special peeler or by hand and put them as they are trimmed into water with lemon juice added. Blanch them for 5 minutes in salted water (8 per cent solution). Drain, and refresh in cold water.

Drain again, put into cans, and pour over the same pickling brine as for *Pickled artichokes* (see above).

Weight of cans	*Cooking time with 110°C. (230°F.) pressure steriliser*	*Cooking time in a bain-marie or canning kettle*
500 g. (1 lb.)	20 minutes	40 minutes
1 kg. (2¼ lb.)	30 minutes	60 minutes

Artichoke hearts stuffed à la cévenole. FONDS D'ARTICHAUTS FARCIS À LA CÉVENOLE – Blanch the artichoke hearts, drain, and simmer in butter. Garnish with a *Chestnut purée* flavoured with *Onion soubise* (see PURÉE). Sprinkle with grated Parmesan cheese and melted butter, and brown the top.

Artichoke hearts stuffed à la chalonnaise. FONDS D'ARTICHAUTS FARCIS À LA CHALONNAISE – As above, with *Salpicon à la chalonnaise* (see SALPICON).

Artichoke hearts stuffed à la duxelles. FONDS D'ARTICHAUTS FARCIS À LA DUXELLES – As above, with very thick *duxelles* (q.v.).

Artichoke hearts stuffed à la florentine. FONDS D'ARTICHAUTS FARCIS À LA FLORENTINE – Simmer the artichoke hearts in butter, and fill them with spinach that has also been simmered in butter. Pour *Mornay sauce* (see SAUCE) over the artichokes, sprinkle with grated cheese, and brown the top.

Artichoke hearts stuffed à la lyonnaise. FONDS D'ARTICHAUTS FARCIS À LA LYONNAISE – As above. Stuff the artichokes with sausage meat and chopped onion which have been lightly fried in butter.

Artichoke hearts stuffed à la niçoise. FONDS D'ARTICHAUTS FARCIS À LA NIÇOISE – Blanch the artichoke hearts, fry them in oil, and fill with *Tomato fondue* (see TOMATO). Sprinkle with breadcrumbs and melted butter, and brown the top.

Artichoke hearts stuffed Piémontaise. FONDS D'ARTICHAUTS PIÉMONTAISE – Simmer in butter in a covered pan.

Fill with *Risotto à la Piémontaise* (see RICE), sprinkle with grated Parmesan cheese, and brown the top.

Artichoke hearts stuffed Soubise. FONDS D'ARTICHAUTS FARCIS SOUBISE – As above, with a thick *Onion soubise* (see PURÉE).

ARTICHOKE QUARTERS. QUARTIERS D'ARTICHAUTS – Pare and trim medium-sized artichokes and cut them into quarters. Trim them carefully, rub with lemon, and blanch for 6 minutes in boiling water to which salt and lemon juice have been added. Cool under a cold running tap and drain until quite dry.

In addition to the specific recipes given in this section, most of those given for small artichokes, and some of those given for artichoke hearts, can be applied to artichoke quarters.

Artichoke quarters in butter. QUARTIERS D'ARTICHAUTS AU BEURRE – Blanch quarters of 6 artichokes and put them in a well-buttered heavy pan. Season, and moisten with 3 tablespoons (scant ¼ cup) water. Sprinkle with a tablespoon of melted butter, bring to the boil, cover with a lid and simmer gently for 30 to 35 minutes. Serve in a vegetable dish, pouring the juices from the pan over the artichokes.

Artichoke quarters aux fines herbes – QUARTIERS D'ARTICHAUTS AUX FINES HERBES – Prepare as in the recipe for *Artichoke quarters in butter*. Put in a vegetable dish. Dilute the pan juices with 1 dl. (6 tablespoons, scant ½ cup) white wine, and boil down. Add 3 tablespoons (scant ¼ cup) thickened veal stock and boil for a few moments. Strain this sauce, and add to it 1 tablespoon melted butter, a few drops of lemon juice and 1 tablespoon chopped *fines herbs* (q.v.). Pour the sauce over the artichoke quarters.

Note. This recipe can also be prepared *au maigre* (without stock). Proceed as described in the recipe for artichoke quarters in butter, but finish off with lemon juice and chopped *fines herbes*.

Artichoke quarters fried in batter. QUARTIERS D'ARTICHAUTS EN FRITOT – Trim, blanch and marinate artichoke quarters. Proceed as described in the recipe for *Artichoke hearts fried in batter*.

Artichoke quarters à la grecque. QUARTIERS D'ARTICHAUTS À LA GRECQUE – Trim artichoke quarters, and proceed as described in the recipe for *Pickled artichokes à la grecque*. These are served as cold *hors-d'œuvre*.

Artichoke quarters à l'italienne. QUARTIERS D'ARTICHAUTS À L'ITALIENNE – Proceed as described in the recipe for *Artichoke quarters aux fines herbes*. Finish off with *Italian sauce* (see SAUCE).

Artichoke quarters au jus. QUARTIERS D'ARTICHAUTS AU JUS – Proceed as described in the recipe for *Artichoke quarters aux fines herbes*, but omit the herbs.

Artichoke quarters à la lyonnaise. QUARTIERS D'ARTICHAUTS À LA LYONNAISE – Proceed as described for *Artichoke quarters aux fines herbes*. Finish off with *Lyonnaise sauce* (see SAUCE).

Artichoke quarters à la moelle. QUARTIERS D'ARTICHAUTS À LA MOELLE – Cook the artichoke quarters as described for those *au jus*. Finish off with *Marrow sauce* (see SAUCE), and garnish with thin slices of bone-marrow which have been poached and drained.

Artichoke quarters à la portugaise. QUARTIERS D'ARTICHAUTS À LA PORTUGAISE – Simmer the quarters in 4 tablespoons (⅓ cup) oil, together with 3 tablespoons (scant ¼ cup) chopped onions. Add 2 peeled and pounded tomatoes, and a little grated garlic and chopped parsley. Cook in an uncovered pan, simmering gently. Serve in a vegetable dish and sprinkle with chopped parsley.

ARTICHOKE, WINTER. ARTICHAUT D'HIVER – Another name for Jerusalem artichoke (q.v.).

ARTOCARPUS. ARTOCARPE – See BREADFRUIT TREE.

ARTOIS AND BOULONNAIS – The principal food resources of this ancient province of France come from the sea.

Boulogne is the most important fishing port in France, with the best supply of herring and mackerel. Whole convoys of lorries carrying mackerel, herring, gurnet (gurnard) and other fish leave this seaport every day with supplies of fish for all parts of France.

The climate of this region, rather variable, is damp and not suitable for fruit growing, so not much fruit is found there, except cider apples. Cider, together with beer, is the main beverage of the region.

Artois market gardens produce very good vegetables. Those from around Saint-Omar are particularly fine. Good quality beef and mutton are produced in Artois; but poultry and game are only of average quality.

Rivers and ponds abound in fish of all kinds. Magnificent salmon is found in the estuaries of the small coastal rivers, and, in the Canche, trout with flesh of great delicacy.

Culinary specialities – These are not very numerous. Almost all of them are based on seafood – fish and shellfish. The principal specialities of the region are: *andouilles* (q.v.) *d'Arras* and various *charcuterie* such as *saucisses de campagne* (country sausages); *black* (blood) *puddings*; Valenciennes *tongue*.

Beer soup and *leek soup*, the latter very popular in Artois and in Flanders; *hotch-potch*, a dish of Flemish origin and *woodcock pâté* of Montreuil-sur-Mer – excellent dishes which are not often made nowadays; *wild rabbit with prunes or raisins*, a speciality of Valenciennes; *goose à la flamande;*

Port of Boulogne. On the left: trawler harbour. On the right: harbour for smaller fishing vessels (*Perceval*)

jellied eel; the *caudière de Berck*, a kind of *matelote* similar to the *chaudrée* of Aunis.

There is naturally a whole range of fish dishes, from *mackerel à la boulonnaise* to more complicated dishes made of various kinds of sea fish: burbot, turbot, striped mullet, smelt, coal-fish (green pollack), bass, sole, red mullet, skate.

But Boulogne is, above all, the town of herring and mackerel – this can be traced back to the ninth century. The herring industry – herring dried, smoked, pickled or sold ready for serving – has assumed enormous proportions.

Herring are prepared in a variety of ways. There are *bloaters*, slightly salted herring which have been smoked; *salted herring* proper; smoked herring called *gendarmes; kippers*, cured and split; *herring pickled in white wine; cured herring fillets in oil*; canned herring and other preparations of this fish which are eaten as *hors-d'œuvre*.

Canned mackerel also come from Boulogne, and are often eaten as *hors-d'œuvre*.

Among the pastries and confectionery products of the region are the Arras *hearts* and *caramels*, the Lille *délices*, the Cambrai *bêtises*, and the Berck *chiques*.

ARUM MACULATUM – This plant is also known under the names of *lords and ladies, cuckoo-pint, calf's foot* and *wake-robin*. In French it is known as *chou-poivre* (pepper-cabbage) because of the acridity of its leaves and roots. In the U.S.A. it is sometimes called *wild ginger* for the same reason.

The roots are much valued by the Arabs, who cook them on hot cinders.

ASAFOETIDA – Resinous gum of a species of oriental palm. In spite of its offensive smell, some people in the East

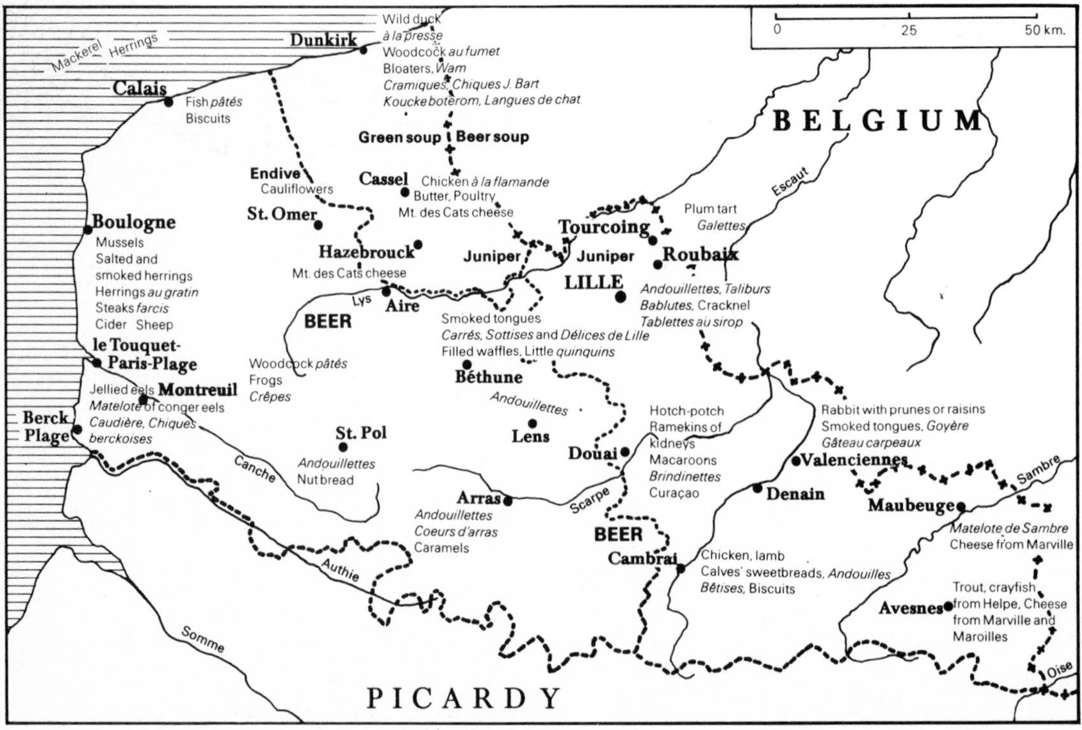

Gastronomic map of Artois and Boulonnais

and Far East use it as a condiment. The Romans added it to many dishes under the name of *sylphium* or *silphion*.

ASBESTOS. AMIANTE – Fibrous mineral substance which is found in eruptive rocks. Asbestos fibres are sufficiently flexible to be plaited and woven. The principal characteristic of asbestos is its incombustibility; a piece of asbestic material put into a blazing fire will not burn.

The properties of asbestos are exploited nowadays for the interiors of kitchen stoves. Asbestos, being a bad conductor, does not absorb heat. Unlike metal, it reflects by radiation, and the maximum of heat is obtained with the minimum of fuel, which results in a considerable saving of expense.

ASCALAPHUS – He was Pluto's cook and the guardian of Proserpine, according to legend. This position of confidence brought him misfortune, for he incurred the enmity of Ceres. Jupiter had agreed to return Proserpine to Ceres, her mother, on condition that the girl had eaten nothing during her sojourn in the infernal regions. Ascalaphus revealed that Proserpine had eaten six grains of pomegranate while she was there, and Ceres turned him into an owl because of this indiscreet revelation. Minerva, to console him in his misfortune, took him under her protection.

ASH. FRÊNE – The young shoots of this tree can be eaten in a salad. The seeds are sometimes preserved.

ASHDRINK. FRÉNETTE – An economical drink which is said to be health-giving. Its basis is ash leaves, and the recipe is as follows:

Boil 75 g. (3 oz., 3 cups) ash leaves and 55 g. (1¾ oz.) roasted chicory in 3 litres (5¼ pints, 6½ pints) water. In another vessel dissolve 2½ kg. (5½ lb.) sugar and 40 g. (1½ oz.) citric acid in 2 litres (3½ pints, 4½ pints) water.

Mix the two liquids, leave to cool; then add 25 g. (1 oz.) yeast dissolved in water. Pour the whole into a barrel. Add enough water to make 50 litres (11 gallons, 14 gallons) and leave to ferment for 12 days.

Bottle the liquid, corking the bottles tightly, and store in a cool place.

The drink is a kind of lemonade with a certain amount of alcoholic content.

ASHES. CENDRES – Residue after combustion. Various foods are cooked in the ashes of a wood fire, notably chestnuts, potatoes and truffles.

ASIALIA. ASIALIE – A deficiency of saliva. It occurs in certain diseases and in certain nervous conditions.

ASITIA. ASITIE – Forced abstinence. Loss of desire for food.

ASPARAGUS. ASPERGE – A genus of *Liliaceae*, containing more than a hundred species, found in temperate and warm regions of Europe and America.

Asparagus grows wild in meadows and bushy places, especially in sandy soil, over a great part of France, as well as on sandy coasts on the Atlantic and the Mediterranean sides.

In France, asparagus came into vogue during the reign of Louis XIV, thanks to Quintinie, who was the first to grow asparagus for Le Roi Soleil. He was able to supply the royal kitchen with asparagus all the year round.

Asparagus officinalis (common asparagus), has been widely cultivated since time immemorial as a garden vegetable. Its young sprouts, or shoots, are eaten either whole or just the tips, i.e., the terminal buds. In Spain, young shoots of a certain species, which have long, sharp thorns on the stems, are also eaten.

A great number of asparagus varieties exist, but for cooking purposes these fall into several main types: *French asparagus*, of which the best known and most delicious is *Argenteuil asparagus; Italian asparagus* or *purple Genoa asparagus; white Belgian asparagus; white German asparagus.* There is also *green asparagus*, which is sub-divided into two types: small, used for garnishes and known as *asparagus tips*, and large, which is prepared like *Argenteuil asparagus*.

Early asparagus can be found in France from February onwards, and is usually sold at high prices.

Method of preparation. This is simple. Scrape, or better still, peel the asparagus, wash and tie into medium-sized bundles, and cook in a fairly full pan of boiling salted water; allow 1½ teaspoons salt per litre (1¾ pints, generous quart) water. When it is cooked, drain the asparagus thoroughly and arrange on a dish covered with a napkin, or on a special asparagus dish which is equipped with a flat strainer.

The cooking period varies from 18 to 20 minutes, depending on the size and nature of the asparagus. It should not be overcooked, as this renders it watery and tasteless.

Note. At the end of the season asparagus becomes a little bitter, and should be put into fresh water for a short time after it has been cooked. Drain thoroughly.

Hot or cold asparagus is served with various sauces. When it is to be served cold, it should be left under a running tap to cool.

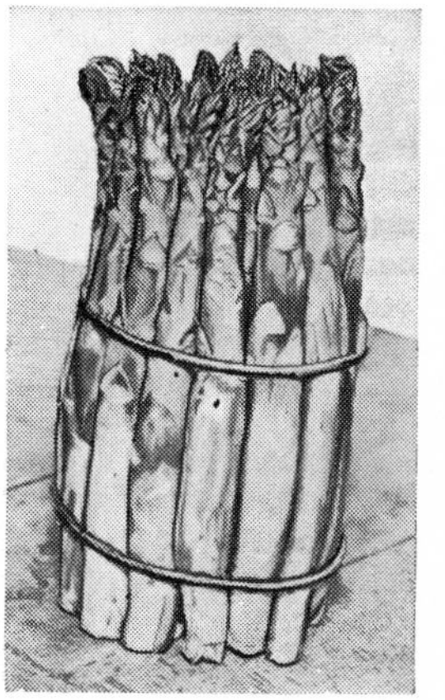
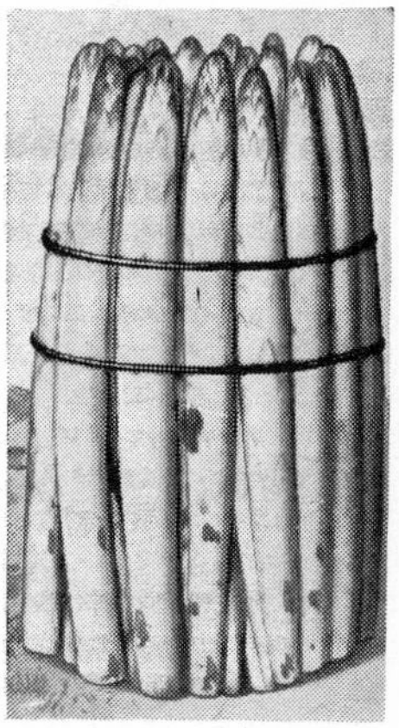

Lauris asparagus/Argenteuil asparagus

Generally speaking, allow about 600 g. (1¼ lb.) asparagus per person, served with sauce (see SAUCE).

Canned asparagus. CONSERVE D'ASPERGES – This should not be attempted except with freshly gathered asparagus.

Scrape off the skin and dry carefully, but do not wash the asparagus. Cut off the ends evenly so as to have them all the same length, and tie into small bundles, choosing stalks of the same thickness to ensure even cooking.

Special boilers for asparagus can be obtained for preserving; these are equipped with devices for controlling the movement of the boiling basket provided. Fill the boiler, according to the instructions given, with water to which 8 per cent salt has been added, and bring to the boil. Put the asparagus bundles into the basket, standing them up and not packing them too closely. Lower the basket into the boiler so that the asparagus bundles are immersed up to one-third of their length and boil for 3 minutes.

Disengage the basket and drop it down lower into the boiler, so that two-thirds of the asparagus tips are immersed, and boil for another 3 minutes.

Remove the basket and plunge it into a tub of cold running water, taking care that the jets of water cannot damage the asparagus tips. Leave in this water for about an hour. Drain with great care.

Put the asparagus into cans or preserving jars, placing some with heads up and others with heads down. Cover with water which has been salted in the proportion of 300 g. (11 oz. $1\frac{1}{4}$ cups) refined salt to 10 litres (9 quarts, 11 quarts) water.

Weight of cans	*Cooking time in a 115°C. (238°F.) steriliser*	*Cooking time in a bain-marie*
500 g. (1 lb.)	10 minutes	20 minutes
1 kg. ($2\frac{1}{4}$ lb.)	15 minutes	30 minutes
2 kg. ($4\frac{1}{2}$ lb.)	20 minutes	40 minutes

Canned green asparagus tips. CONSERVE DE POINTES D'ASPERGES VERTES – Divide the asparagus stalks into three parts: the base, the middle and the tips.

First put the bases (the toughest parts) into a saucepan of salted boiling water and boil them for 2 minutes. Add the middle sections and boil for another 2 minutes. Add the tips and boil for a third 2 minutes. Drain very carefully.

Put them into cans or preserving jars and cover with the same brine as in the preceding recipe.

Weight of cans	*Cooking time in a 110°C. (230°F.) steriliser*	*Cooking time in a bain-marie*
500 g. (1 lb.)	10 minutes	20 minutes
1 kg. ($2\frac{1}{4}$ lb.)	15 minutes	30 minutes
2 kg. ($4\frac{1}{2}$ lb.)	—	40 minutes

Cream of asparagus soup – See SOUP, *Cream soups*.

Asparagus heaped in a croustade à la Carême. BUISSON D'ASPERGES EN CROUSTADE À LA CARÊME – Cook the tips of thick white asparagus in salted water, keeping them a little underdone. Drain and dry on a napkin. Coat each one in aspic mayonnaise. Chill thoroughly in a refrigerator.

Arrange in a low flan shell, made of pie pastry and baked blind, and half-filled with a salad of green asparagus tips and truffles, seasoned with oil and lemon juice.

Asparagus heaped in a croustade à la Carême

Asparagus à la flamande. ASPERGES À LA FLAMANDE – Serve hot, with melted butter. Halves of hot, hard-boiled eggs are served separately. The guests mash the eggs on their plates and mix them with the melted butter.

Asparagus fried in batter. FRITOT D'ASPERGES – Cook the tips of large white or green asparagus in salted boiling water for 5 minutes. Drain, dry, and marinate for 30 minutes in oil, lemon juice or vinegar, salt and pepper. When nearly ready to serve, dip the asparagus tips into a light batter and fry in smoking-hot deep fat. Drain, dry, season with fine salt, and arrange in a heap on a napkin.

Asparagus à la Fontanelle. ASPERGES À LA FONTANELLE – Boil the asparagus in salted water and drain. Serve with melted butter.

Soft-boiled eggs are served with this dish, the guests dipping the asparagus in the melted butter and then in the egg.

Asparagus au gratin

Asparagus au gratin. ASPERGES AU GRATIN – Cook in salted water and drain thoroughly. Arrange the asparagus in tiers in a fireproof dish.

Pour *Mornay sauce* (see SAUCE) over the tips only. Cover the rest of the asparagus with greaseproof paper. Sprinkle the sauce with grated Parmesan cheese and melted butter, and brown the tips. Remove the paper before serving.

Asparagus à la milanaise. ASPERGES À LA MILANAISE – Proceed as described in the recipe for *Asparagus au gratin*, but omit the *Mornay sauce*.

Asparagus à la Mornay. ASPERGES À LA MORNAY – Another name for *Asparagus au gratin*.

Asparagus with noisette butter. ASPERGES AU BEURRE NOISETTE – Cook the asparagus by the usual method. Serve *Noisette butter* (see BUTTER) separately.

Alternatively, arrange cooked and well-drained asparagus in a dish, and keep it warm in the oven. Just before serving, sprinkle it with sizzling *noisette butter*.

Asparagus à la polonaise. ASPERGES À LA POLONAISE – Proceed as described in the recipe for *Asparagus au gratin*. Cover the tips with chopped yolks of hard-boiled eggs and parsley.

When ready to serve, pour on sizzling *Noisette butter* (see BUTTER) in which freshly grated white breadcrumbs have been fried until light golden brown.

Alternatively, arrange the asparagus on a serving dish and serve the butter and breadcrumbs separately.

Asparagus soufflé. See SOUFFLÉS, *Soufflé of various vegetables*.

Asparagus tips for garnishes. POINTES D'ASPERGES – Scrape, if necessary, and cut the tips into 5-cm. (2-inch) lengths; tie into bundles. Cook as described in the recipe for *Green asparagus tips*. (see below).

If this garnish is used for hot dishes, the asparagus tips should be added at the very last moment; cook them first in water, drain, and dress with melted butter or cream.

Asparagus makes an excellent garnish for eggs which have been scrambled, lightly boiled, *au plat*, poached or in an omelette. Also for some fish dishes, and for meat served in small portions – cutlets, escalopes, *noisettes*, small fillets, *tournedos*, etc., for calves' sweetbreads, and for fowls and chickens.

When asparagus tips are intended for garnishing or for cold salads, they must be dipped in cold water as soon as they are cooked, and well drained. Season with *vinaigrette*, or mayonnaise, or bind with meat jelly.

Asparagus tips with cream. POINTES D'ASPERGES À LA CRÈME – Cook asparagus tips and add a few tablespoons of fresh double cream which has previously been scalded. Blend in lightly and season. Arrange in a vegetable dish with tips uppermost.

Asparagus tips in butter. POINTES D'ASPERGES AU BEURRE – Remove the tips from a bundle of asparagus; scrape and dice the rest. Cook the diced pieces, drain well, and dry in a pan over heat. Add small pieces of butter in the proportion of 75 g. (3 oz., 6 tablespoons) butter to 250 g. (9 oz.) asparagus, and stir gently. Heap into a dish, and garnish with the tips, which have been lightly cooked in salted water.

Green asparagus tips. POINTES D'ASPERGES VERTES – Cut off the tough stalks, keeping the tender parts of green asparagus. Tie these into bundles of 8 to 10 shoots. Cut the lower part of these bundles into dice, keeping the actual tips tied together.

Cook the diced asparagus in boiling salted water for 4 minutes, then add the bundles of tips. Boil briskly, with the saucepan uncovered, for 7 or 8 minutes. Drain the bundles and the diced asparagus. Dip in cold water and cool. Proceed as indicated in the chosen recipe.

Purée of green asparagus. PÚREE D'ASPERGES VERTES – Cook asparagus tips in fast-boiling, salted water, drain, and rub through a fine sieve. Heat the purée, and add butter and cream.

This purée is used as a garnish.

White asparagus with fried bread. CROÛTE GRATINÉE AUX ASPERGES BLANCHES – Blanch 500 g. (1 lb.) of white asparagus tips in salted water for 8 minutes, drain, and simmer in butter until cooked. Cut decrusted bread into slices 10 cm. (4 inches) long and 6 cm. ($2\frac{1}{2}$ inches) wide, and fry in butter. Put 7 or 8 asparagus tips on each slice of fried bread, sprinkle with grated Parmesan cheese, pour on the butter in which the asparagus was cooked, and brown the top lightly.

White asparagus with melted butter. ASPERGES BLANCHES AU BEURRE FONDU – Cook the asparagus in salted water, drain and serve, piping hot, with warm melted butter. The butter should be melted over a gentle heat and seasoned with salt, pepper and a dash of lemon juice.

Purée of white asparagus. PURÉE D'ASPERGES BLANCHES – Blanch 500 g. (1 lb.) white asparagus tips for 8 minutes, drain, and simmer lightly in butter. Season with salt and pepper.

Moisten with $2\frac{1}{2}$ dl. (scant $\frac{1}{2}$ pint, generous cup) thick *Béchamel sauce* (see SAUCE). Boil for 15 minutes. Rub through a fine sieve. Heat the purée and add butter.

This purée is used as a garnish for poached or lightly boiled eggs, for small pieces of meat, for chicken, for filling patties and tartlets.

White asparagus salad. SALADE D'ASPERGES BLANCHES – Cook the asparagus tips in salted water. Drain, dip in cold water, drain again and dry in a napkin.

Arrange in a salad bowl or an *hors-d'œuvre* dish. Pour on well-whisked *vinaigrette*, or a mixture of oil, lemon juice, salt and pepper. This must be well whisked, so that the sauce covers the asparagus in a layer. Serve chilled.

White asparagus with cold sauces. ASPERGES BLANCHES AVEC SAUCES FROIDES – Cook the asparagus and drain. Arrange on a dish and serve with one of the following sauces: *Mayonnaise, Mustard, Tartare, Vinaigrette* (see SAUCE).

White asparagus with hot sauces. ASPERGES BLANCHES AVEC SAUCES CHAUDES – Cook the asparagus in salted water and drain. Serve separately one of the following sauces: *Butter, Bâtarde, Chantilly, Cream, Hollandaise, Maltaise, Mousseuse, Noisette* (see SAUCE).

ASPERULA. ASPÉRULE – Plant which is both useful and pleasant. It is also called *sweet woodruff, mugwort, sweet grass* and *quinsy wort*. Its white flowers are used as an infusion, and for distilling liqueurs.

In some northern countries it is also used for flavouring sausages.

ASPIC – Term which applies to a way of arranging cold dishes. It consists of putting slices or fillets of chicken, game, various meats, fish, vegetables, fruit, etc., into moulded jelly.

Many authors believe that this name comes from the serpent called asp, 'whose icy coldness recalls that of the jelly', but it is more probably derived from the Greek word *aspis*, which means buckler or shield. It was, in fact, in this form that the first moulds were made; others were made in the shape of a coiled snake, doubtless to justify the name 'aspic'.

Whatever its origin, the word aspic is applied to very different preparations: *foie gras in aspic, chicken in aspic, partridge in aspic, lobster in aspic, fillets of sole in aspic.*

For methods of aspic preparations of meat, chicken, game, shellfish and fish, see the following entries in their alphabetical order: CHICKEN, LOBSTER, PHEASANT, SHRIMP, SOLE.

Sweet dishes made of fruit and set in jelly moulds are also called aspics. The word aspic is used, too, for the actual jelly.

In his book devoted to cold *entrées*, Carême describes the method of preparing aspic jelly as follows:

'Clean and singe 2 chickens, wash them thoroughly, truss them, and place in a small *marmite* (q.v.) with a round of veal, other veal trimmings and a little ham. Add 6 boned and blanched calves' feet, fill the *marmite* with water, and leave to cook on a hot stove, but away from the flame. A much lighter aspic, easy to clarify, is obtained by this process. Skim thoroughly, and add half a bay leaf, a little thyme and basil, a bunch of parsley and spring onions, 2 carrots and 2 onions. Keep the jelly simmering gently for 4 hours.

'Whisk 4 egg whites with a glass of white wine or Madeira, and the same amount of veal stock if you wish to give it some colour; if not, omit the stock. Add to the jelly, place on a high flame, and whisk until the mixture is boiling. Turn heat to very low. Taste, in case a little salt is needed.

Cover the pan and leave to simmer for about 2 minutes, when the mixture should be clear.

Rinse a napkin in water, wring out well, and tie the corners to an upturned chair. Strain the aspic through the napkin.'

Carême also describes how aspic should be coloured: 'One of the principal presentations of cold dishes consists of these clarified, transparent jellies of 2 colours only – one should be white and the other of a good strong colour.'

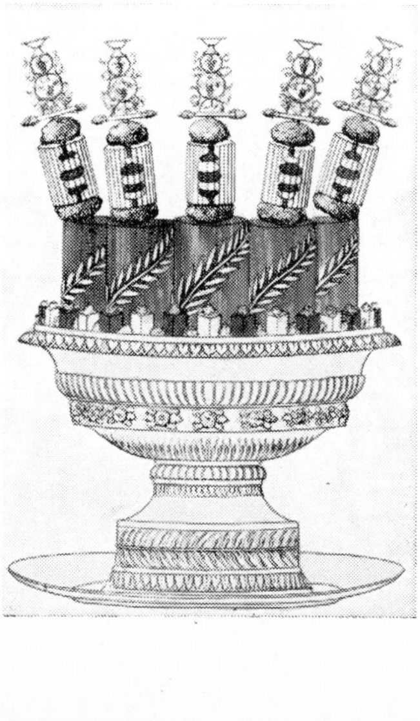

Arrangement of aspic, after Carême

Aspic moulds

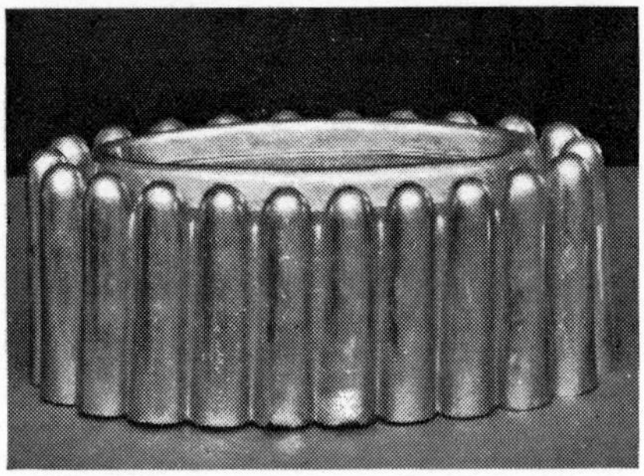

He tells how the great Laguipière achieved perfect colourings for his jellies: 'Melt granulated sugar and, without moistening it, let it colour little by little on red-hot cinders, which should take about a quarter of an hour. When it becomes amber-red caramel, moisten with half a glass of water and place the pan over a hotter flame. After several minutes of boiling it becomes a clear amber-red, totally unlike the bitter caramel which is allowed to get black on a high flame and which is commonly called "monkey's blood."'

The modern method of the clarifying process is given under the entry entitled JELLIES, and in the one below.

Clarification of aspic jelly – To clarify 5 litres ($4\frac{1}{2}$ quarts, $5\frac{1}{2}$ quarts) jelly stock, add 3 egg whites and 500 g. (1 lb.) lean minced beef. Add a tablespoon of tarragon and a tablespoon of chervil, roughly chopped. Whisk lightly. Heat the stock a little until it is tepid, skimming off all the fat: this is important. Bring to the boil, whisking all the time. Lower the heat and simmer gently for 35 minutes.

Rinse a napkin in water, wring out thoroughly, and strain the aspic through the napkin.

Aspic jelly can be flavoured with various dessert wines: Frontignan, port, sherry, Marsala, Madeira, Malvasia (Malvoisie). These wines, which are only added to the jelly when it is tepid, are used in the proportion of 1 dl. per litre (3 tablespoons per pint) of jelly in the case of dessert wines, and 2 dl. in the case of Champagne, Sauternes, Alsatian, or other white wines.

Instructions for making various aspic jellies will be found under JELLIES, *Meat jellies*.

Aspics in moulds – Aspics are set in plain moulds, charlotte-type moulds or moulds with a hole in the middle.

Coat the mould with a thin layer of jelly, as indicated in the recipes. Decorate by pressing into the jelly small pieces of truffle, cooked lean ham or tongue, and white of hard-boiled egg for meat, chicken or game aspics. For fish or shellfish aspics use pieces of truffle, white of hard-boiled egg, the coral of shellfish or slivers of smoked salmon.

Aspic croûtons. CROÛTONS DE GELÉE – Aspics cut into shapes – triangles, rectangles, crescents, etc. The jelly must be clear and solid.

When a number of croûtons have to be made, pour the jelly into a large baking dish to set. When it is quite firm, turn out onto a damp cloth which has been stretched and fastened to a table. Cut up with a knife if the croûtons are rectilinear in shape, or with a pastry-cutter if they are round.

The technical term *croûtonner de gelée* means to surround some cold food with croûtons of jelly cut into shapes.

Aspic of freshwater crayfish tails. ASPIC DE QUEUES D'ÉCREVISSES – Cook the crayfish *à la mirepoix* (see MIREPOIX). Shell the tails and arrange them in a plain round mould which has been coated with jelly. Fill the mould either with a *Crayfish mousse* (see CRAYFISH) or a *Russian salad* (see SALAD). Chill on ice.

Aspic of fish. ASPIC DE POISSONS – This can be made with fish of various kinds, cut in fillets, slices or medallions. Fill the middle of the aspic dish with a fish mousse appropriate to the particular recipe; with Russian salad; or with any mixture normally used for cold dishes.

Aspic of foie gras I. ASPIC DE FOIE GRAS – Coat a plain mould with jelly and fill it with uniform slices of *foie gras*, garnished with large slivers of truffles. Fill the mould with half-set jelly. Leave on ice to set. Serve on a plate or in a glass dish.

Aspic of foie gras II. ASPIC DE FOIE GRAS – Coat a mould with port-flavoured jelly (or jelly flavoured with any other heavy wine). Fill with truffles cut into neat round slices, round pieces of ham or pickled tongue, and, if desired, the whites of hard-boiled eggs cut in rings.

Fill the mould with jelly. Chill on ice or in the refrigerator. To serve, turn the aspic onto a flat dish, or onto slices of buttered bread. If served on a dish, decorate with chopped jelly and jelly triangles.

This aspic can also be made by filling the mould with slices of *foie gras* cut out with a shell-shaped scoop.

Lobster in aspic (*Battendier. Phot. Larousse*)

Sole in aspic (*Battendier. Phot. Larousse*)

and slivers of truffles. Coat in *Villeroi sauce* (see SAUCE) and allow to cool. Dip them in egg and breadcrumbs and roll into cylindrical shape.

Deep-fry in sizzling fat and arrange on a napkin garnished with fried parsley. Serve with *Périgueux sauce* (see SAUCE).

Attereaux of oysters Monselet. ATTEREAUX D'HUÎTRES MONSELET – Poach and drain oysters. Thread them on *attereaux*, together with cooked mushrooms cut in slices, and thick slices of truffles. Finish as described in the recipe for *Attereaux of brains*, using *Villeroi sauce* (see SAUCE) based on fish stock boiled down to a *fumet* (q.v.).

Attereaux of pineapple (dessert). ATTEREAUX D'ANANAS – Thread pieces of pineapple on the *attereaux*. Dip them in a *crème frite* (see CUSTARD, *Fried custard*) and breadcrumbs. Fry in smoking hot deep fat, drain, and sprinkle with fine sugar.

Serve with *Apricot sauce* (see SAUCE) laced with kirsch.

Attereaux of salmon – See SALMON.

Attereaux Pompadour (dessert) – Make up the *attereaux* by threading on slices of stale brioches, alternating with halved apricots which have been cooked in syrup and drained. Dip them in a *crème frite* (see CUSTARD, *Fried custard*) flavoured with kirsch. Roll in breadcrumbs and fry in smoking hot fat. Drain, and sprinkle with sugar.

Attereaux Victoria (dessert) – Thread slices of plum pudding on the *attereaux*, alternating them with slices of cooking apples which have been steeped in rum. Dip in egg and breadcrumbs and fry in smoking hot fat. Drain, and dredge with fine sugar.

AUBENAS – Small town in the Ardèche *département*, where truffles are found. These, though they may not rival the flavour of Périgord truffles, are nevertheless excellent.

Marrons glacés are much-prized preserves which are made at Aubenas.

Varieties of aubergines
1. Long purple 2. Very early Barbentane
3. Very large round purple 4. Very early dwarf purple

AUBERGINE or EGGPLANT – Fruit of a plant originating in India, known also in France under the names of *melongena* and *morelle*. It has been cultivated in France since the beginning of the seventeenth century. In the U.S.A. it is called eggplant.

There are many varieties of this plant. The most used in cookery is the *long purple*, which is used as a vegetable and as a garnish. Among other edible varieties are: the *Barbentane aubergine*; the *round purple aubergine*, the *giant New York aubergine*, and the *round Valencia aubergine*.

Methods of preparation. There are many recipes for cooking aubergines, and the initial preparation varies greatly. When this vegetable is to be stewed, baked in the oven or fried, it must be steeped in salt for 30 minutes to make its excess water ooze out. The aubergines are then thoroughly dried and cooked as indicated in the recipes.

Various uses. Aubergines, cut in dice and fried in butter or oil, can be used as a garnish for the following: eggs (*sur le plat*, scrambled, poached, fried, or cooked in an omelette); fish *meunière*; lamb or mutton chops, cutlets or *noisettes*; *tournedos*; and chicken fried or *en cocotte* (see CHICKEN).

Sliced in half lengthways, fried or grilled, aubergines can be used in the arrangement of poached eggs, or fillets of fish. Peeled, cut in thick slices and fried or grilled, they can be used as a foundation for escalopes, *noisettes*, *tournedos* and other small pieces of meat.

Aubergines à la crème – Peel 2 firm aubergines. Cut them in round slices $\frac{1}{2}$ cm. ($\frac{1}{4}$ inch) thick, and steep in salt for 30 minutes. Dry, and simmer in butter in a sauté pan or heavy frying pan.

Just before serving, add $1\frac{1}{2}$ dl. ($\frac{1}{4}$ pint, $\frac{2}{3}$ cup) *Cream sauce* (see SAUCE). Stir, taking care not to damage the aubergines. Arrange in a vegetable dish.

Dilute the pan juice with 3 dl. ($\frac{1}{2}$ pint, $1\frac{1}{4}$ cups) cream. Boil down by half, remove from the heat, and add 50 g. (2 oz., $\frac{1}{4}$ cup) fresh butter. Strain and pour over the aubergines.

Fried aubergines. AUBERGINES FRITES – Cut the aubergines in thin slices, dredge with flour, and plunge into a deep pan of sizzling oil. Drain, season with fine salt, and arrange on a napkin.

Aubergines intended for deep-frying can also be cut into thick square pieces, or cut fan-wise.

Aubergines au gratin – Cut the aubergines lengthwise in half. Make a few shallow incisions and leave in a dish, sprinkling thickly with salt. Dry, then fry in sizzling hot oil. Drain, and with a spoon carefully scoop out the pulp without damaging the outside skin. Chop the pulp, and add to it an equal quantity of *duxelles* (q.v.) mixture and a tablespoon of chopped parsley.

Fill the aubergine skins with this mixture, and put them into a buttered or oiled fireproof dish. Sprinkle with finely grated breadcrumbs, fresh or toasted, add melted butter or a few drops of oil, and brown the top.

When cooked, pipe a border of *Demi-glace* (see SAUCE) around the aubergines.

Aubergines au gratin à la catalane – Halve aubergines, scoop out the pulp, chop it, and mix it with 1 hard-boiled egg chopped up finely. Add a tablespoon of chopped onion which has been lightly fried in oil, a tablespoon of finely grated breadcrumbs, some chopped parsley and garlic. Finish cooking as above.

Aubergines au gratin à l'italienne – Halve aubergines, as above, and mix the chopped pulp with an equal quantity of risotto and a little chopped parsley and garlic. Finish cooking as above.

Aubergines au gratin à la languedocienne – Method as above, filling the aubergine halves with sausage meat. Finish cooking as above.

Aubergines Imam Baaldi (*Robert Carrier*)

Aubergines au gratin à la portugaise – Method as above. Fill the aubergine halves with their chopped pulp to which has been added an equal quantity of chopped tomatoes lightly fried in butter, chopped onion, parsley and garlic. Finish cooking as above.

Aubergines au gratin à la reine – Method as above. Fill the aubergine halves with their chopped pulp mixed with an equal quantity of *salpicon* (q.v.) of chicken bound with 2 tablespoons (3 tablespoons) thick *Velouté sauce* (see SAUCE). Finish cooking as above.

Aubergines au gratin à la toulousaine – Peel the aubergines, cut into thick slices, across or lengthways, and leave in a dish sprinkled with salt. Dry, and toss in a pan of hot oil.

Arrange in layers in a fireproof dish in rows, alternating with an equal quantity of tomatoes cut in half and also tossed in oil.

Sprinkle generously with freshly grated breadcrumbs mixed with chopped garlic and parsley. Pour on a little oil and brown in the oven.

This dish is sometimes called *aubergines à la languedocienne*.

Aubergines au gratin à la turque – Fill aubergine halves with their chopped pulp mixed with an equal quantity of braised chopped mutton, and rice cooked in water (taking these ingredients in equal proportions). Add chopped garlic and parsley, and a small pinch of cayenne. Brown the top. When cooked, pipe a border of tomato sauce round the aubergines.

Aubergines in gravy. AUBERGINES AU JUS – Proceed as described in the recipe given for *Aubergines à la crème*, but substitute thickened veal stock.

Aubergines à la grecque (hors-d'œuvre) – Peel 2 large aubergines; cut them in dice or thick square pieces. Throw them, a few at a time, into a *court-bouillon* prepared as described in the recipe for *Artichokes à la grecque* (see ARTICHOKE). Bring to a full boil, and cook for 12 to 15 minutes. Transfer into a *terrine* with the liquor, and serve as an *hors-d'œuvre*.

Grilled aubergines. AUBERGINES GRILLÉES – Peel the aubergines, cut them into thick slices, and leave to stand in a dish well sprinkled with salt. Dry them, brush with oil, and grill on a gentle heat.

For serving as a vegetable, arrange the aubergines in a crown shape on a dish, and dab with a few tablespoons of *Maître d'hôtel butter* (see BUTTER).

Aubergines Imam Baaldi (Turkish cookery) – 'Take good sound aubergines, slit them along their entire length without peeling, and scoop out some of the pulp. Prepare a stuffing composed of aubergine pulp, tomatoes, onions and currants. Fry this mixture in oil, and fill the aubergines with it. Put them into an earthenware dish and pour in sufficient oil to cover them completely. Add a little thyme and a bay leaf. Cook for 3 hours on low heat until the aubergines are quite soft. Leave to cool.

'This dish should be served very cold. If possible, prepare it the day before it is required, to allow the aubergines to be well saturated in the oil.'

Imam Baaldi in Turkish means 'the priest has fainted'. The legend goes that when aubergines prepared in this way were offered to a certain *imam* (priest), he was so moved by the fragrant odour of the dish that he fainted from sheer gastronomical joy.

Aubergine purée (garnish). PURÉE D'AUBERGINES – Peel the aubergines, cut them in slices, and leave in a dish with salt. Dry them, and cook in a covered casserole with a little butter and salt. Rub through a sieve. Heat this purée, add 2 tablespoons (3 tablespoons) butter, and serve.

A few tablespoons of thick *Béchamel sauce* (see SAUCE) added to the aubergines before rubbing them through the sieve will give the purée a more substantial consistency, and will make it whiter.

Aubergine salad. SALADE D'AUBERGINES – Peel the aubergines, cut into thin slices, and leave to stand in a dish with salt. Dry, season *à la vinaigrette* (see SAUCE, *Cold Sauces*), and add chopped chervil and tarragon.

Note. This salad can also be prepared with aubergines which have been cooked in salted water, drained and dried.

Sautéed aubergines. AUBERGINES SAUTÉES – Peel the aubergines and cut them into 4-cm. ($1\frac{1}{2}$-inch) square pieces. Leave to stand in a dish with salt. Dry, dredge with flour, and sauté the pieces in oil, butter or other fat over brisk heat. Serve sprinkled with chopped parsley.

Aubergine soufflés. AUBERGINES SOUFFLÉES – Prepare the aubergines as described in the recipe for *Aubergines au gratin.* Rub the scooped-out pulp through a sieve. Add an equal quantity of thick *Béchamel sauce* (see SAUCE). Bind with yolks of egg and season with salt, pepper and a little grated nutmeg. At the last moment fold in whites of egg whisked to a stiff froth.

Fill the aubergine skins with the mixture, put them into a fireproof dish, and cook in a moderate oven for 8 to 10 minutes. Serve at once.

Aubergine soufflés à la hongroise. AUBERGINES SOUFFLÉES À LA HONGROISE – Proceed as above, adding 2 tablespoons (3 tablespoons) chopped onion lightly fried in butter, and seasoned with paprika.

Aubergine soufflés au parmesan. AUBERGINES SOUFFLÉES AU PARMESAN – As above, adding 2 tablespoons (3 tablespoons) grated Parmesan cheese to the filling.

AUDE – This *département* is formed of the lower part of Languedoc, a region where good cookery has always been held in respect. Among the specialities (which will be found in their alphabetical order) is the well-known *cassoulet*. There are two kinds in Aude – the *cassoulet* of Castelnaudary and the *cassoulet* of Carcassonne. Another is the *cassoulet* of Toulouse.

According to reliable historians, white beans, introduced by the Arabs, were cultivated in Gallia Narbonensis long before beans were brought from America. The Arabs taught the inhabitants to prepare a mutton *ragoût* with white beans which is the ancestor of the present-day *cassoulet*. (See CASSOULET for further details of this dish, of which the region is understandably proud.)

Wines – Aude has a large production of *vins ordinaires* and *vins d'appellation d'origine*. (See LANGUEDOC.)

AUDIGER – Head of the household to la comtesse de Soissons, and later to Colbert. Audiger is the author of a book published in 1692 of which the translated title is *The Well-Ordered Residence and the Art of Governing a Nobleman's House and Other Gentlemen's Town and Country Residences, and the Duties of Senior Staff and Domestics in General.* In it he describes the composition of a lord's 'household'.

Travelling in Italy in 1660, he came across *petits pois* growing in January. He filled a crate with them and presented it to the French court, who marvelled at the sight of such an early vegetable. That was how *petits pois* became so fashionable, and why even today every effort is made to produce them as early as possible.

AUK. ALQUE – Sea birds of the *Alcidae* family. The *little auk* measures 38 cm. (16 inches) when fully grown. Its wings are equipped for flying, which enables the bird to escape from the pursuit of fishermen hunting it.

Although originating in Arctic regions, it is frequently to

be seen in autumn and winter on the coasts of England, Scotland, Belgium and France. It migrates as far as Spain, Portugal, Italy and Algeria. Not infrequently it breeds on the French ocean coasts. The Icelanders call it *alka* (*aalga*) or *klumba*. The flesh and fat of these birds are greatly valued by fishermen, who snare them among the rocks where they nest.

AUNIS AND SAINTONGE – The region of Aunis has fertile, well-cultivated lands, where crops of cereals, vegetables and fruit of the first quality are grown. Animals raised for food produce meat of excellent quality, including some very good lamb; and from the neighbouring sea and lakes of the region come fish and shellfish acceptable to gastronomes.

Among the specialities are the oysters of Marennes, La Tremblade, and Château d'Oléron; they are white, or stained with the fine green weed from the fattening ponds, and are considered the best in the world. The *Portuguese oysters* which are bred here have a specially delicate flavour. Other shellfish include mussels and clams of Cléron and La Rochelle, cockles which are found in the Marennes fattening ponds, prawns (*salicoques*) which are locally called *chevrettes*, and shrimps, which are called *boucs*.

La Rochelle, after Boulogne, is the greatest fishing port in France, and among fish found in the region are hake, coalfish (U.S. pollock), and sole, which are sold immediately after being caught. Fresh sardines, known as Royan sardines, enjoy a wide reputation, and there are also grey mullet (called *meuils* locally) and brill (U.S. sea perch). In the Charente and Sèvre Niortaise and their tributaries there are eels which are delicious stewed or *en matelote*.

Fruit and vegetables are particularly good. The garden peas are sweet and tender; it is this variety that is canned at Bordeaux and La Roche-sur-Yon.

Broad beans from Marennes and the island of Oléron are considered the best in the world. Kidney beans and red beans (*mogettes*) are excellent.

Orchard and vegetable garden produce include Saintonge *brugnons* (nectarines); the apples of Saint-Porchaire (*reinettes grises* and *clochard*) which are exported to England; white Chasselas grapes; mushrooms such as *cèpes* and oyster mushrooms; Saintonge oranges; *brunettes; pleurote du panicot*.

The game of this region is of excellent quality. The finest butter, which can compare with the best Normandy butter, is made in Aunis.

Culinary specialities – *Mouclade* (mussels à la crème); *mussel soup; roast mussels* (cooked on cinders); *oysters with sausages; razor-fish soup* (solen); *razor-fish* stuffed with breadcrumbs which have been mixed with chopped garlic and parsley and browned on top; *scallops aux fines herbes; ragoût of lavagnons; small cuttlefish fried in deep fat; deep-fried crameou* (crabs that have shed their shells); *hake soup* (made with the fish head); *chaudrée* (fish soup rather like the Breton *cotriade*); *roast eel; fried eels du Mignon*.

Special meat and poultry dishes include *chicken fricassée* with onions and potatoes; Aunis *civet*, which is made of pig's fry; a *salmi of sea birds*; various *charcuterie; rillettes* (potted pork); *pâtés* and *terrines; black* and *white puddings*. Other special dishes of this region include *roast garlic*, cooked on hot cinders, which is eaten with butter; *curds à la chardonnette; jonchée* (a kind of cream cheese made with ewe's or goat's milk); various *fouaces* (scones) and *coireaux* (made of maize flour); *la fouée* (oil seed cake); *gâteau d'Assemblée; Easter gâteau; Taillebourg brioches; grape jelly; Pons rusks; Frangipane tart*.

Wines – Saintonge produces mediocre table wines, most of which are used for distilling purposes (see COGNAC).

The vineyard proprietors of this region make a liqueur wine for themselves and their friends, white or sometimes red, locally called *pineau*. It is made by pouring local brandy on the must during fermentation, which is thus arrested, preserving all the fruit.

AURILLAC – Town in the Auvergne region, which is the centre of the production of Cantal cheese.

AURIOL – Name for mackerel in Marseille.

AUROCHS – Wild ox, ox of the plains. This animal, which in the past used to be found in the forests of temperate Europe, is now only found, and in very small numbers, in Lithuania, in the Carpathians and in the Caucasus.

The meat of aurochs is prepared as ordinary beef.

AURORE (À L') – Name applied principally to a sauce, the recipe for which is given in the section on sauces; and to all the dishes cooked with this sauce.

This name is also given to a dish of stuffed hard-boiled eggs (see EGGS, *Aurora eggs*).

The name also applies to a cheese made in Normandy.

AUSTRALIA. AUSTRALIE – Australian vineyards and wines (see WINE).

AUSTRIA. AUTRICHE – Austrian wine and *cuisine* (see WINE, INTERNATIONAL COOKERY).

Papin marmite or autoclave (*Conservatoire des Arts et Métiers. Phot. J Boyer*)

AUTOCLAVE (Pressure cooker) – High-pressure steam vessel. A sort of boiler, with very strong walls, which can be closed hermetically. It is provided with a safety valve, and is capable of raising the temperature of the water above boiling point.

No living bacteria can survive the temperature of 120°C. (248°F.) in a liquid medium over a certain period of time. Thus the autoclave is used in the canning industry to sterilise food products contained in hermetically sealed cans. (See PRESERVATION OF FOOD.)

This instrument was invented by Denis Papin, and the original Papin *marmite* has become popular once again in the form of the pressure cooker, which, by bringing food to a temperature often reaching 140°C. (284°F.), makes it possible to cook in a very short time dishes which would take much longer cooked by the ordinary method.

The results, though acceptable in a good many cases, are, however, far from being as good as those obtained by the traditional methods. The decomposition of certain foods,

meat in particular, is taken much further than in ordinary cooking. Furthermore, vitamins can be entirely destroyed.

AUTO-INTOXICATION, DIGESTIVE – This form of intoxication, due to healthy foods ingested in excessive quantity and subjected to bacterial putrefaction in the intestines, should not be confused with alimentary intoxication due to ingestion of toxic foods or foods which have gone bad.

AUTRICHIENNE (À L') – This expression is applied to various preparations characterised, as in the case of those called *à la hongroise*, by being seasoned with paprika, or Hungarian pepper, and sometimes by the addition of onion, lightly fried, of fennel or sour cream.

Auvergne
(*French Government Tourist Office*)

AUVERGNE – There is a belief that the cookery of this region consists entirely of cabbage soup or *potée*, made of fresh and salt pork.

In fact, *potée* is not a specifically Auvergnat dish. Each region of France, including the Ile de France, has its *potée*. There is the Bourguignonne *potée*, a wonderful dish; the Alsatian *potée* which, too, is succulent, as is that of Cantal; the Languedoc *potée*, which is very savoury, and the Parisian *potée*, which figures daily on the bills of fare of the capital's restaurants. There are, besides, many other *potées* in France, recipes for which will be found in their alphabetical order, under SOUP. All of them are made of fresh or salt pork as a basic element, with cabbage, carrots, onions, leeks and potatoes completing the dish.

Auvergne and Velay (for these two charmingly picturesque regions are inseparable) are rural areas offering gastronomes wholesome, unpretentious country cooking 'with a straightforward, honest flavour' (to quote Curnonsky).

Besides the cabbage soup, there are peasant soups like *mourtayrol*, the great Auvergnat *pot-au-feu* (beef, ham, chicken, saffron); *cousinat* (chestnut soup); and the cheese soup of Cantal.

Excellent vegetables are grown in Auvergne. The orchards

Pewter sugar dredger, ewer and porringer from old Auvergne

of Limagne produce choice dessert fruit (apricots, peaches, apples, pears, cherries) and also supply the important crystallised fruit industry of Clermont-Ferrand. Auvergne walnuts and chestnuts are well known.

In the mountainous pasture lands, oxen are raised which give meat of excellent flavour. Mutton is greatly valued, particularly that from sheep raised in Vassivières and Chaudesaigues.

The pork of Auvergne is known for the delicacy of its flesh. This is made into many kinds of *charcuterie* which can be found in the shops of Paris and other big cities.

The poultry of the region may not have the quality of that raised at Bresse, but it is nevertheless good, as is the game of Auvergne, both ground and winged.

The freshwater fish is excellent. Carp, perch, tench, pike and eels abound in the rivers and lakes, and provide ingredients for succulent *matelotes*. The trout found in the Massiac, Aurillac, Murols and Marsenac rivers are delicious prepared *au bleu* or *à la meunière*. The flesh of Brioude salmon is comparable with that of Loire salmon.

In the spring, succulent mushrooms, particularly morels, are gathered in the woods and forests of Auvergne.

Culinary specialities – The culinary specialities of this region are not very numerous. There is the succulent *potée*, which is made of salt pork as a basic ingredient, with cabbage, carrots, turnips, onions, leeks and potatoes as accompaniments, and with garlic as a local touch. The *soupe au farci* is a kind of rustic *pot-au-feu*, in which a cabbage stuffed with sausage meat and flavoured with chopped garlic and parsley is cooked.

The *charcuterie* are delicious: *hams; large and small country sausages; black puddings* (blood sausage); *greaves* (cracklings); and *fricandeau* (q.v.), made of a kind of pork *pâté* cooked in a thin piece of salt pork.

Among local specialities are *tourte à la viande*, a pie made in a shallow dish, lined with puff pastry and filled with pork and veal forcemeat; *omelette brayaude*, an omelette made of beaten egg mixed with diced potatoes and diced lean ham which, before it is turned over in the frying pan, is filled with grated cheese and thick cream; *friands de Saint-Flour*, which are like those found in the Parisian shops selling *charcuterie*; *leg of lamb brayaude*, which is studded with garlic, braised with the usual vegetables and aromatics in white wine, and served with red beans, with onions, and sometimes with braised cabbage; *truffade*, potatoes cooked in a shallow pan with lean rashers of bacon, flavoured with garlic, and – added at the last minute – fresh diced Tomme cheese; *potatoes with bacon*; Murat *pickled pork; coq au vin*, a dish for which one of the inns at the top of the Puy-de-Dôme is well known; the *tripoux* of Saint-Flour.

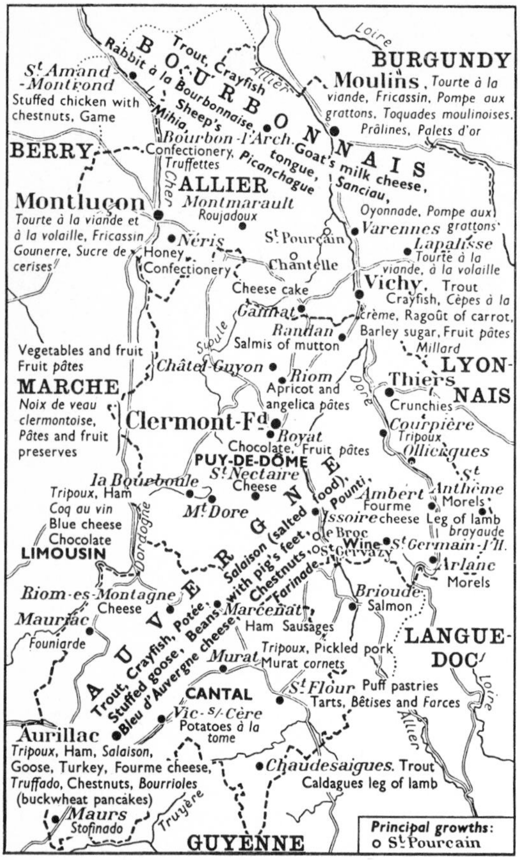

Gastronomic map of Auvergne

Among the fish dishes, Ussel *jellied eel* is notable, and among the game dishes, Brioude *thrush cutlets*. The pasta products of Clermont-Ferrand are excellent. Sweet dishes and confectionery include *flagnarde; millards de cerise*; Clermont-Ferrand *angelica*; Thiers *crunchies*; Riom *échaudé*; Murat *cornets*; Saint-Flour *bêtises* and *farces*; Aurillac *chestnut tart* and *buckwheat pancakes*.

Cheeses of Auvergne include the famous Cantal cheese; the Bleu d'Auvergne, the small Riommois cheeses; goat's milk cheese.

Wines – The vineyards of this region do not produce any great red or white wines, but some very good table wines. The wines of Auvergne are classed among the V.D.Q.S. They are the *appellations* Côtes d'Auvergne and Vins d'Auvergne, from the Gamay and white and black Pinot grapes. Chanturgue is the best known of the local vineyards.

AUVERGNAT – Variety of vine, native of Auvergne and cultivated in the country around Orléans. It is best known because of the poet Boileau, and does indeed produce wine which, as he says, is heady and of a strong colour. As far back as the days of Louis XIV, inn-keepers were in the habit of mixing it with lighter and less-coloured wines, such as the *lignage*, to obtain pale or rosé wines, which were sold under the name of Ermitage, and which are now known under different names.

AVICE – French pastry-cook, contemporary of Antonin Carême. In his books, Carême speaks of him with great respect and gives him first place among the pastry-cooks of that brilliant epoch.

AVINER – French word meaning to season, or impregnate a new wine cask to make it lose the taste of wood.

To season a vat also means to press the grapes as the vat is being filled.

Avocado pear

AVOCADO PEAR. AVOCAT – The fruit of the avocado tree, native of tropical and sub-tropical America.

The kernel, in the middle of the pulp, is about the size of a walnut. The flesh of the avocado is much prized by the Americans. It is thick, buttery, spreads like butter, and is nutty in taste.

The avocado pear is slightly acid. It is eaten *au naturel* or seasoned with *Vinaigrette sauce* (see SAUCE) or stuffed with crab salad.

For some years now chefs have been testing their ingenuity in the creation of new recipes for this fruit (avocado soup, creamed avocados, avocados as dessert, etc.). The best variety of avocado pear comes from Brazil.

Avocet

AVOCET. AVOCETTE – A genus of wading birds. It is found in countries with cold or temperate climates, particularly along the coasts of Europe and America.

The flesh of the avocet, although quite delicate, savours of the food it lives on, which consists almost entirely of fresh fish, worms and aquatic insects.

The European avocet is about the size of a pigeon, and is recognisable by its pied plumage. Avocet shooting is practised in Poitou.

All the culinary methods given for teal (q.v.) can be applied to avocet.

AY – Village in Champagne, cradle of Champagne wine (which was famous even before it became a sparkling wine). Leon X, Charles Quint, Henry VIII and François I had officers permanently stationed at Ay to look after the precious vineyard and ensure that the court had regular supplies of the wine. Henri IV willingly accepted the title of 'Sire of Ay'.

AYAPANA – Plant originating in South America. Its leaves, exuding a pleasant aroma, are used as infusions, aperients and soporifics.

The infusion is made in the same way as tea, but as the smell of the ayapana is very strong, 12 or 13 leaves are enough for a six-cup teapot.

Ayapana blends perfectly with egg yolks, and with cream.

AZAROLE – Fruit of the Neapolitan medlar; common name of a shrub known as *Crataegus azarolus* which is of the same species as hawthorn. It is also called *épine d'Espagne* in France. This shrub is similar to a service tree.

The Neapolitan medlar is indigenous to the whole of the Mediterranean area, and it is also cultivated in the Paris region. The medlar berry is oval, reddish or yellowish in colour, acid and slightly sweet in taste. It is used for compotes, confectionery and a much-prized liqueur.

In Provence, in Italy and in Spain, as well as throughout the whole of Algeria, it is used for jam, which is a very popular preserve.

AZI or AZY – French term for rennet, which is made from whey to which a certain amount of vinegar is added.

AZYMOUS (Bread). AZYME – Etymologically, the word azymous means unleavened.

The Jews had two ways of making their unleavened bread; either by previously grilling the flour, or by using ordinary flour kneaded with warm water and salted, allowing $1\frac{1}{2}$ teaspoons of salt per 450 g. (1 lb.) flour. The paste was rolled out to a thickness of 1 cm. ($\frac{1}{2}$ inch) and placed on a metal sheet. The rolled-out pastry was then pricked and baked in a slow oven.

Unleavened bread made from grilled oatmeal flour is prepared in the same manner.

Azarole

BABA – Cake made of leavened dough, mixed with raisins and steeped in kirsch or rum after cooking.

The invention of this cake is said to be due to King Stanislas Leczinski. Some authors state that the royal gastronome did not invent the baba we know, but found a new way of eating a *kugelhopf*, which had been made in Lemberg (Lvov) since 1609. He sprinkled the cake with rum and set it alight as one does a plum pudding.

The *kugelhopf*, done in this way, had a great success at the court of Lorraine, where it was served accompanied by a sweetened and spiced Malaga wine. King Stanislas was an avid reader of the *Thousand and One Nights*, and named his favourite sweet after one of its heroes, Ali Baba.

The cake was introduced in Paris at the beginning of the nineteenth century by a pastry-cook, Sthorer, who had seen it in Lunéville, where the court of Poland was transferred. He made it a speciality of his establishment in rue Montorgueil, and called it simply 'baba'. Sthorer made the babas in advance, moistening them with a brush dipped in wine just before selling them. Later, the process was to immerse them in rum-flavoured syrup.

In the 1840s, a cake of similar nature, called *fribourg*, was made at Bordeaux. At the same time a Parisian *maître pâtissier*, omitting raisins from the dough, gave the cake another shape, and steeping it in a syrup of his own creation, produced the *brillat-savarin*, which later became *savarin*.

Says Lacam: 'He gave to his friend Bourbonneux, with whom he worked at Chiboust's, the idea of using the same dough baked in a hexagonal mould, and creating a cake which was called *gorenflot*, after one of the heroes of *la Dame de Montsoreau*.'

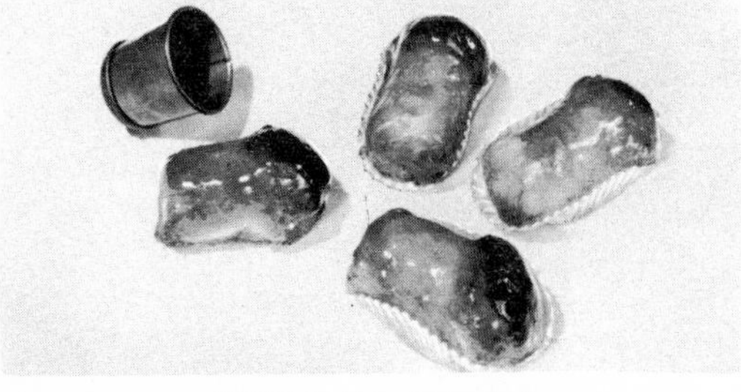

Rum babas and mould (*Larousse*)

Large baba mould (*Larousse*)

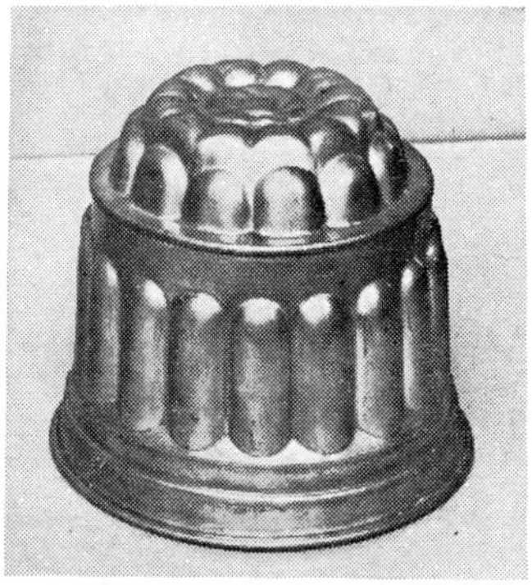

Baba

Recipe used by the pastry-cooks for babas:

Sift 500 g. (18 oz., $4\frac{1}{2}$ cups) flour into a large wooden bowl, make a well in the middle, put into this well $1\frac{1}{2}$ teaspoons salt and 20 g. ($\frac{2}{3}$ oz., 1 cake) yeast which has been dissolved in 1 dl. (6 tablespoons, scant $\frac{1}{2}$ cup) warm milk. Add 7 whole eggs, and work the paste with the hands to mix well. Distribute 300 g. (11 oz., $1\frac{1}{3}$ cups) butter, which has been softened, in small pieces over the paste. Cover, and keep the paste in a warm place until the yeast has risen to double its original size.

Add 25 g. (1 oz., 2 tablespoons) fine sugar, and knead the paste well so that it absorbs the butter. Add 50 g. (2 oz., scant $\frac{1}{2}$ cup) currants and 50 g. (2 oz., scant $\frac{1}{2}$ cup) golden sultanas.

Mix well. Put the paste into well-buttered baba moulds, filling up to one-third of their height.

Bake in a hot oven and allow to cool before turning the babas out of the moulds. Sprinkle with rum or kirsch.

Syrup for babas. SIROP À BABA – Add 2½ dl. (scant ½ pint, generous cup) rum to 1½ litres (2¾ pints, 3¼ pints) syrup cooked to 104°C. (219°F.). A small quantity of coriander is sometimes used to flavour the syrup.

BABIROUSSA – This mammal, allied to the wild boar, differs from the latter in the curious development of the canines. Its general appearance and squat shape give it a certain similarity to the rhinoceros. Like the latter, it lives in the swampy forests of the Malay Archipelago, and is fairly easily tamed. Its flesh, which is prepared in the same way as that of wild boar (q.v.), is much prized.

BACCHANALIA. BACCHANALES – Festivals celebrated in honour of Bacchus. These festivals began in Egypt, spread to Phoenicia, and then to Greece and Italy.

BACCHANTE – Priestess, votary of Bacchus.

Bacchus on a barrel of wine. Faïence. (*Larousse*)

BACCHUS – Roman god of wine, the Dionysus of the Greeks. He was born, according to legend, in Thebes in Boeotia. Jupiter was his father. Semele, his mother, was one of the daughters of Cadmus and Hermione.

When Semele lay dead (struck down by the fiery bolts of her lover), Bacchus, too, would have perished had not Jupiter made Vulcan draw out the young fruit of love from Semele's body, lying at his feet. Macris, the daughter of Aristaeus, received the child into her arms and Sabazius put him in the god's thigh to complete the nine months of his gestation.

His three aunts, Inno, Agave and Antonöe nursed the child in his early years, and cared for him with maternal devotion. From the hands of the Nymphs, Bacchus passed into those of the Muses, and Silenus. The Muses initiated him into the knowledge of harmony and dance; Silenus taught him viniculture and the making of wine.

The nature of his birth makes Bacchus a hero rather than a god; but he is the love-child of a god and a mortal, and we cannot deny his divinity in the pagan sense of the word. He is the lord of wine, as Ceres was the goddess of corn-bearing and agriculture. The ancients thought that they were the sacred couple presiding over the solid and the liquid, which sustain and animate life.

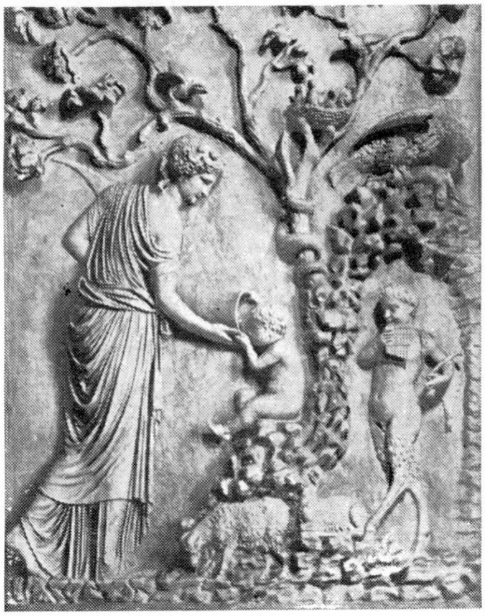

The nymph Leucothea and the infant Bacchus

BACON. LARD MAIGRE FUMÉ – Once used to mean pork in general, particularly salt pork.

'A big hog (bacon) had been killed,' we read in Segretain Moine's medieval tale. And in the fable of Cockayne we read:

Si païs si a non Coquaigne
Qui plus i dort, plus i gaigne.
De bars, de saumons et d'aloses
Sont toutes les maisons encloses;
Si chevron i sont d'esturgeon;
Les couvertures de bacons
Et les lates sont de saucisses.

In this land, the land of Cockayne,
The more one sleeps, the more one would gain by it.
With bass, salmon and shad
All the houses are enclosed;
Their rafters are made of sturgeon;
The roof of bacon
And the slates are sausages.

BACONIQUE – Adjective once applied in France to meals which consisted exclusively of pork, fresh or salt, prepared in various ways.

Badian anise

BADIAN ANISE. BADIANE – Fruit of a tree of the same name tasting of anise. It is better known under the name of *star anise*, and is also called *Chinese anise*. It is used as a carminative in the form of an infusion (50 to 60 g. per litre, 2 to 2½ oz. per scant quart, generous quart) and in the preparation of certain liqueurs. Its taste is more pungent than that of green anise, and the essence to which this fruit owes its aroma is toxic if taken in heavy doses. Cases of poisoning as a result of taking too strong an infusion have been known.

In India, China and Japan, this plant is burnt to scent the houses; it is eaten after a meal to freshen the mouth, and it is also mixed with tea and liqueurs.

Badian anise, which was brought into Europe by an English sailor at the end of the sixteenth century, is used in the manufacture of Bordeaux *anisette*. The seeds of badian anise are used in confectionery and pastry-making. In some northern countries it is used for flavouring bread.

BAGRATION – The name of a Russian general who fought against Napoleon. It is given to various dishes: *Bagration soup, Bagration salad* (see SOUP, SALAD).

BAIN-DE-PIED (Footbath) – Colloquial French for an excess of liquid, principally coffee, if it overflows and spills from the cup into the saucer.

Bain-marie

BAIN-MARIE – In cookery and confectionery, this is a vessel half-filled with hot water, in which sauces and other delicate dishes can be kept hot until required.

Cooking in a bain-marie – Certain dishes, such as scrambled eggs, butter sauces, custard creams, mousses, meat and fish loaves, which may turn 'oily' or disintegrate if they are cooked on direct heat, can be cooked in their own utensils, which are lowered into the hot water. In U.S.A. a utensil called the double-boiler is used for this purpose.

In France, the name *bain-marie* is also applied to a utensil for sterilising babies' bottles.

BAISER – In some regions of France, this is the name given to two small meringues joined together with thick cream or other sweet mixture.

BAJET – A species of oyster commonly found on the coast of west Africa. The shell is flat, round, and thicker than that of ordinary oysters. The flesh is edible but not very delicate.

BAKERY. BOULANGERIE – Shop where bread baked by the baker himself is sold.

The first bakers in Italy were those the Romans brought from Greece, following their campaign against Philip, Hannibal's ally. Later, together with the freed slaves, bakers formed an organisation which enjoyed considerable privileges.

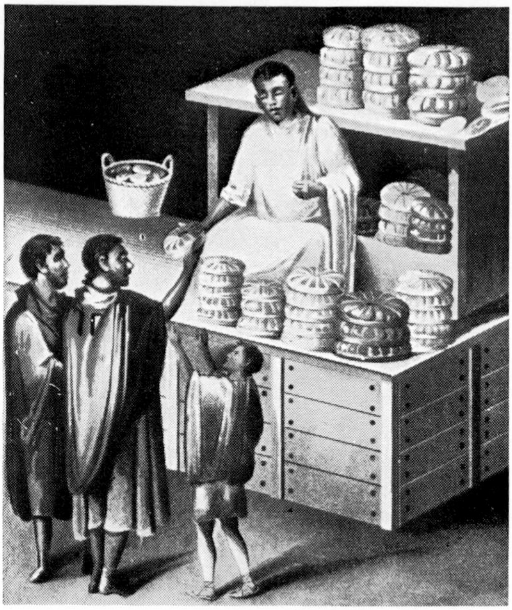

A Roman baker, after a Pompeii fresco

In France, the bakers' corporation was a confraternity, or religious society, under the name of *talemeliers*. Their statutes can be traced back to the time of Saint Louis, and the oldest complete set of regulations in existence is that preserved for us by Estienne Boileau at the beginning of the *Registres des métiers* (Register of Trades), collected about 1260.

The first clause decrees: 'No-one can become a *talemelier* in the suburbs of Paris who does not buy the right to trade from the King'.

One of their privileges was the buying and reselling of pigs without paying for this right, because they needed pigs to eat the bran which was not yet, in those days, separated from the flour. To become a master baker, and to have the right to practise his trade, a baker had to serve a four-year apprenticeship, and to buy the master's certificate from the king or from the king's pantler. From the time he received this, a right of inspection was established. Bread of insufficient weight was confiscated and distributed to the poor, penalties for the violation of the law being left to the discretion of the head of the community.

Appeals were brought before the grand pantler, whose judgement was final. The penalty was simple: a fine of 6 *deniers* (pennies) for any violation of the law.

Ancient bakers' arms

Philip the Fair, who introduced reforms into this legislation, decreed that the fines should be discretionary and proportionate to the offence. He appointed the Provost of Paris to be the bakers' judge, and, at the same time, considerably reduced their privileges. The trade of bakery was to be free; he forbade the buying of grain in the markets for resale, and permitted private persons to buy in the same way as wholesale merchants.

In 1366, Charles V ordered that the bakers, both in Paris and outside, should bring their bread to the market on market days. They must all make bread of the same flour and content, the same weight, and sell it at the same price; and they should make two sizes of loaf, one which cost 4 *deniers* and one which cost 2 *deniers*, the price being determined by the weight.

In 1372, the king decided that the price of bread in Paris should be fixed in accordance with the varying price of grain. When grain cost 8 *sous*, white bread or *pain de chailli* costing 2 *deniers* a loaf should weigh 25½ oz. when baked. The *bourgeois* loaf at the same price should weigh 37½ oz. when baked. Inferior quality *pain de brode*, costing 1 *denier*, should weigh 36 oz. baked.

At the beginning of the fourteenth century Charles VI decreed:

'That the bakers may not buy or cause to be bought either grain or flour on the Paris markets if the market has not been open at least one hour.

'That no baker can at the same time be a miller or a measurer of grain.

'That the bakers may not buy grain except through the intermediary of a sworn-in measurer.'

In the reign of Charles VI, the rigours of an interminable war, the scarcity and high prices of cereals, the sale of bread against uncertain payment and other causes forced many of the bakers to give up their trade and to destroy their ovens. A written decree was issued in 1415 ordering them to rebuild the ovens without delay, on pain of banishment.

Further regulations were issued from time to time. In 1439, Charles VII introduced new measures, one being that the price of bread should be posted up in the markets. In addition, 'The bakers shall not buy grain before noon.' The bourgeois classes were baking their own bread, and this regulation aimed at preventing the bakers from bulk buying, and maintaining their monopoly.

There were other decrees. All guilds, including the bakers', were to have their own banners and insignia. In 1569, a curious regulation laid down what bakers were to wear: shirt, drawers without trunk hose, a cap. They were forbidden to go out, except on Sundays and official closing days, forbidden 'to gather together', to set up monopolies, or to wear daggers, swords or other weapons.

The seventeenth century marks a milestone in the history of the Paris bakery trade. There were improvements in manufacture, permission to sell flour without bran, a regulation forbidding the use of brewer's yeast, and the new *pain mollet* (bread roll) process.

The Chapter of the Cathedral of Notre-Dame baked bread which was called *pain de chapitre*, which had a vogue before it was superseded by the favourite bread of Queen Marie de Medici: a salted bread prepared with brewer's yeast and called *pain à la reine*. Then came bread known as *pains à la Montauron*, which was kneaded with milk. *Pain de Gentilly* was made with butter. Besides *pain mollet*, there was *pain blême* (pale bread) and *pain à la citrouille* (pumpkin loaves), made by the bakers of small loaves.

Richelieu did away with many out-of-date measures and introduced bold reforms, legislation which is in force to this day. He laid down:

'Grain merchants shall not make their purchases except outside the ten-league (40-km., 25-mile) limit around Paris. Bakers of small loaves and pastry-cooks shall not buy grain before 11 o'clock in summer and noon in winter; large-loaf bakers shall not buy grain before 2 o'clock, to enable the needs of the bourgeois to be supplied first. Bakers shall put their distinctive trade-mark on their loaves, and keep scales and weights in their shops, on pain of being deprived of licence or even more severe punishment.'

They were likewise forbidden to store away unsold bread; they had to dispose of it at a reduced price if still unsold within three days of baking.

In 1650, sifted flour began to make its appearance, and enabled a great quantity to be transported at a time, bran no longer being part of the flour. From that time onwards bakers were not allowed to raise pigs. In 1666, in the reign of Louis XIV, a curious case was recorded by Fournier, *Molière et le procès du pain mollet* (Molière and the bread roll), in the *Revue Française*. (A man called Poquelin, a relative of Molière, was involved in the case, which concerned a claim that brewers' yeast had caused illness). The verdict declared that the use of brewer's yeast in bread was detrimental to health, and was therefore forbidden.

By the beginning of the eighteenth century the number of bread markets had risen to 15, to which between 500 and 600 bakers came from the city and the outlying suburbs; a further 1,000 came from Gonesse, Corbeil and Saint-Germain-en-Laye. They traded in the main markets, but there were many bakers who plied their trade without holding master bakers' certificates. These unauthorised bakers lived around the Temple, Saint-Jean-de-Latran, Saint-Denis, la Châtre and Quinze-Vingts. They enjoyed the same rights in the city as the people from outside, except for the master bakers, who had all the privileges conferred by the licence.

Boulanger-cabaretier (Miniature from the Bibliothèque de l'Arsenal)

Bakers at work, after a lithograph of 1830

Louis XIV abolished the jurisdiction of the royal pantler. Artisans and suburban merchants were now on the same footing as those of the town, and newly qualified master bakers were enabled to practise on the same conditions as their established colleagues by paying the same taxes. The principal aim of this concession was no doubt due to the fact that after several years of great poverty among the people, the Treasury was depleted, and the State was able to increase taxation by imposing it on suburban bakers as well as on those in the city.

There followed additional laws compelling each baker to bring a certain quantity of bread to market (Abbé Jaubert, *Dictionnaire Universel des Arts et Métiers*, 1773) – a great hardship, as they had to get rid of all the bread after a certain hour, and so must sell any surplus very cheaply.

At this period, the latter part of the eighteenth century, apprenticeship lasted five years, followed by four years working for the bakers' guild. At the end of the nine years the apprentice, unless he was the master baker's son, had to present his *chef-d'œuvre*, and on paying for a certificate, might at last practise as a master baker. Thus matters continued until the French Revolution, but even after 1789 the breadmaking industry remained under strict control. It was only in 1863 that it became free.

Baker's assistant. MITRON – The term comes from the paper head-dress or *mitre* which bakers wore at work.

Bakery equipment – This changed very slowly. Kneading was done by hand for many centuries in a huge wooden trough, longer than it was wide, which stood on four legs. It had a flat cover called the *tour*. Modern bakeries have mechanical metal kneading machines.

The ovens remained as they are shown in Diderot's *Encylopédie* from the days of the Romans until the nineteenth century: a block of masonry with the actual baking-oven inside, square in shape, the inside edges rounded off, surmounted by a dome called the *chapelle*. The walls were at least 50 cm. (20 inches) thick and the oven was heated by wood. Coal, burnt in a special fireplace below the opening of the oven, replaced wood; then came gas, oil heating, and electricity. Today, pipes containing a liquid which is first heated in a coal-fired chamber circulate round the oven; a system that has the advantage of being clean, uniform and economical.

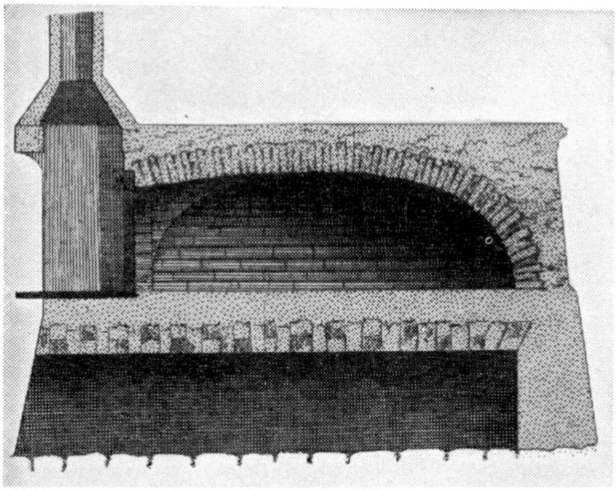

Bakers' ovens, reproduced from Diderot's *Encyclopédie*

In France, breadmaking is still mainly carried on in small-scale establishments, producing a few hundred kg. of bread a day, but the trend is towards mass production in large factories, with skilled technical organisation and highly developed mechanisation.

The work involved in transforming flour into bread is described under the entry BREAD.

BALACHAN – Seasoning much used in Siam. In Tonkin it is known as *nukemum*. It is made of small shrimps, pounded with salt into thick brine, which is dried in the sun. Balachan, it is said, stimulates the appetite and fortifies the stomach.

BALAINE or BALEINE – Name of a restaurant-keeper who ran *le Rocher de Cancale* in rue Montorgueil. Grimod de la Reynière, who gave parties at this restaurant, spoke very highly of him. Carême considered him to be a second-rate caterer. (See RESTAURANTS OF BYGONE DAYS.)

BALANUS – Fruit of the balanite, a shrub indigenous to upper Egypt. It is about the size of a hazelnut, and when pressed yields an oil used in the perfumery industry. When fresh and very ripe, the fruit is edible and known as the desert date; its flavour is enhanced if served along with other foods.

BALAOU – French name for a small fish, similar to the sardine, which abounds in Martinique. Its flesh is delicate and easily digestible.

All methods of cooking sardines can be applied to *balaou*.

BALLOTTINE – Galantine normally served as a hot *entrée*; it can also be served cold. The ballottine is made of a piece of meat, fowl, game or fish which is boned, stuffed, and rolled into the shape of a bundle. The term *ballottine* should strictly apply only to meat, boned and rolled, but not stuffed. It is, however, also applied to dishes which are actually galantines.

Ballottine of lamb à la boulangère. BALLOTTINE D'AGNEAU À LA BOULANGÈRE – Prepare like *Shoulder of lamb à la boulangère* (see LAMB).

Ballottine of lamb à la bourgeoise. BALLOTTINE D'AGNEAU À LA BOURGEOISE – Prepare like *Ballottine of lamb à la bonne femme* (see below), replacing the garnish indicated in that recipe by garnish *à la bourgeoise* (see GARNISHES) which should be cooked with the meat.

Ballottine of lamb braised à la bonne femme. BALLOTTINE D'AGNEAU BRAISÉE À LA BONNE FEMME – Stuff a boned shoulder of lamb with sausage meat mixed with chopped onion which has been lightly fried in butter or lard, and chopped parsley.

Roll the shoulder into a ballottine, tie with string, and brown in the oven. Put into an earthenware *cocotte* (deep dish). Slice and fry 12 medium-sized onions in butter, together with about 100 g. (4 oz.) lean bacon which has been blanched and diced. Moisten with 2 dl. (⅓ pint, scant cup) dry white wine which has been boiled down a little. Add a *bouquet garni* (q.v.) and enough thickened meat stock just to cover the ballottine. Bring to the boil.

Cover the *cocotte* and put it in a hot oven for 45 minutes. Add 500 g. (generous 1 lb.) potato balls and cook at a lower heat for 35 minutes. Drain the ballottine, remove string, put back in the *cocotte*, and serve.

Ballottine of lamb, braised, with various garnishes. BALLOTTINE D'AGNEAU BRAISÉE – Prepare the ballottine and braise it in a deep earthenware dish, as described in the preceding recipe, but without adding bacon, potatoes or onions.

When the ballottine is cooked, drain, and remove string. Arrange on a serving dish, surround with a garnish, or serve the garnish separately. Boil down the braising liquor, remove the surplus fat, strain, and pour it over the ballottine.

Garnishes which are suitable for this dish (see GARNISHES) are as follows: *bouquetière, bretonne, bruxelloise,* chipolata, *flamande, jardinière, macédoine, milanaise, nivernaise*. The dish may be served with noodles, rice, pilaf, risotto, also with fresh vegetables dressed with butter or cream, braised or glazed vegetables, and potatoes prepared in various ways.

Ballottine of lamb, cold, with various garnishes. BALLOTTINE D'AGNEAU FROIDE – When the ballottine is quite cold, pour over it a little liquid aspic jelly, and leave until set. Arrange on a serving dish, or on a decrusted buttered croûton. Garnish, and decorate with chopped jelly.

All the garnishes recommended for cold meat and poultry are suitable for cold ballottine.

Ballottine of lamb in jelly. BALLOTTINE D'AGNEAU À LA GELÉE – Stuff a boned and flattened shoulder of lamb with *Galantine forcemeat* (see FORCEMEAT) mixed with a *salpicon* (q.v.) composed of pickled tongue, ham and truffles. Roll, wrap in a piece of muslin, and tie with string. Cook in jelly stock as described in the recipe for galantine (q.v.).

Drain the ballottine, unwrap, and tie it up again tightly in a cloth, securing each end with string and tying it also in the middle. Cool under a press. Unwrap the ballottine and glaze it with cold aspic jelly made from the stock in which it was cooked, clarified and reinforced with gelatine, if necessary.

Arrange on a serving dish and garnish with chopped jelly.

Ballottine of lamb in jelly

Ballottine of mutton. BALLOTTINE DE MOUTON – Proceed as described for *Ballottine of lamb*.

Ballottine of pork, braised, with various garnishes. BALLOTTINE DE PORC BRAISÉE – Bone a shoulder of pork and prepare as *Ballottine of lamb*. When the ballottine is braised, drain, remove string, glaze with jelly, and serve with one of the garnishes normally used for meat (see GARNISHES). Boil down the braising liquor, remove fat, strain, and pour over the ballottine.

Ballottine of pork in jelly. BALLOTTINE DE PORC À LA GELÉE – Bone a shoulder of pork and prepare as *Ballottine of lamb in jelly*. Garnish and serve as described in the recipe for *Ballottine of lamb*.

Ballottine of veal. BALLOTTINE DE VEAU – Take a boned shoulder or a thin slice of chump end of loin (U.S. sirloin steak or cutlet), and proceed as described in the recipe for *Ballottine of lamb*.

Ballottine of veal, either hot or cold, can be served with one of the garnishes recommended for meat (see GARNISHES).

Ballottine of chicken with dark sauce, served with various garnishes. BALLOTTINE DE POULARDE À BRUN – Bone a medium-sized fowl (see GALANTINE). Stuff it with a quenelle of finely pounded *Pork forcemeat* (see FORCEMEAT).

Boil the ballottine in a cloth which has been previously soaked in hot water and wrung out, and tie it with string. Cook in a braising pan with just enough chicken stock to cover the fowl. Bring to the boil, put on the lid, and simmer for 50 minutes.

Drain the ballottine and keep it hot for 10 minutes in the oven, to ensure that the forcemeat settles properly. Remove fat from the braising liquor, strain through muslin, and boil down by two-thirds. Blend with 2 dl. (⅓ pint, scant cup) thickened veal stock, and strain through a fine sieve.

Unwrap the ballottine and glaze it in the oven, basting with the thickened gravy. Arrange on a dish, surround with garnish, and pour over it a few tablespoons of the gravy; serve the rest of the gravy in a sauceboat.

The following garnishes are recommended: noodles, celery, mushrooms or chipolata, *bouquetière, Demidoff, espagnole, Godard, milanaise, niçoise, orientale, périgourdine, piémontaise, portugaise, Rossini,* and with all other garnishes recommended for chicken or fowl served in small pieces with a dark sauce.

Ballottine of chicken, with light sauce, served with various garnishes. BALLOTTINE DE POULARDE À BLANC – Prepare and cook the ballottine as described above, and glaze it lightly.

Arrange on a fried croûton, or on a foundation of rice or semolina. Surround with a garnish and serve with *Velouté* or *Suprême sauce* (see SAUCE), using the liquor in which the ballottine was cooked.

Recommended garnishes: celery, mushrooms, noodles, rice, *Albuféra*, *anversoise*, *banquière*, *Chivry*, *demi-deuil*, *ivoire*, *princesse*, *régence*, *Toulouse*, and, generally, with garnishes recommended for poultry prepared with light sauce.

Small ballottines of chicken. PETITES BALLOTTINES DE VOLAILLE – Ballottines made of chickens' legs, when the wings and breast are used for some other dish.

The legs are boned and stuffed as described in the first recipe for *Ballottine of chicken*. They are braised *à brun* or *à blanc*, and garnished and served as described in the directions for *Ballottine of chicken*.

Sometimes this dish is given the shape of a ham knuckle, in which case it is served under the name of *Jambonneaux de volaille*.

Ballottine of chicken in jelly (chaud-froid) I. BALLOTTINE DE POULARDE À LA GELÉE (EN CHAUD-FROID) – Prepare and cook as described in preceding recipes. Finish as indicated in one of the recipes for cold chicken – *Chicken mayonnaise*, *Néva*, *parisienne* (see CHICKEN).

Ballottine of chicken in jelly II. BALLOTTINE DE POULET À LA GELÈE – Prepare and cook the ballottine as described in preceding recipes. Unwrap, and allow to cool in its liquor, which has been strained and the fat removed.

Arrange the chicken on a serving dish, glaze, and decorate with jelly made from the stock in which it was cooked.

Ballottine of glazed chicken (chaud-froid). BALLOTTINE DE POULET GLACÉE (EN CHAUD-FROID) – Cook the ballottine as described in preceding recipes, chill, and prepare as in the recipe for *Chaud-froid of chicken* (see CHICKEN).

Ballottines of various poultry. BALLOTTINES DE VOLAILLES DIVERSES – Proceed with ducks, turkeys, pigeons or guinea-fowl as described in the recipe for *Ballottine of chicken*. Forcemeat for stuffing ducks or guinea-fowl can be mixed with one-third of its volume of *foie gras*, and chopped truffles.

These ballottines are served hot or cold, with garnishes recommended for chicken.

BALM. BAUME – Name applied to various aromatic plants of the mint type.

BAMBOCHER – Slang term in French meaning 'to live it up'. The word comes from the nickname of a Dutch painter, Pierre van Laer, called 'Le Bamboche', who specialised in depicting rustic scenes (*bambochades*).

BAMBOO. BAMBOU – Arborescent reeds (a genus of woody-stemmed grasses) grown in tropical countries. Its young shoots are edible, and are pickled in vinegar and sold canned, as a luxury product. The shoots, which are spiky, are eaten raw in China, Indo-China, India, Japan etc.

The Japanese pickle tender bamboo shoots in saké vinegar (saké is a spirit distilled from rice). In the Sunda Isles, bamboo stems are pickled in palm vinegar.

The pith of various species of bamboo is very sweet, and a kind of spirit oozes from it. The fruit of the bamboo is the size of a pear, and is formed of a great number of edible seeds resembling ripe ears of maize or Indian corn. Young bamboo shoots are covered with fine but sharp hairs, which must be removed before cooking, otherwise perforation of the intestines may result.

BAMBOO MUSHROOM. CHAMPIGNON DE BAMBOU – A mushroom much valued in Chinese *cuisine*. It is available in Europe only in its dried form.

BANANA. BANANE – Fruit of the banana tree, which grows in tropical regions. About 30 species of it are known.

In the Hindu religion there is a legend in which the banana was the fruit forbidden to Adam and Eve in the terrestrial paradise, which, according to the legend, was on the island of Ceylon, where the parents of the human race covered their nakedness with banana leaves. This explains the names of *Adam's fig-tree* and *Paradise banana*, which the Indians have given to two species of banana tree.

The dietetic qualities of the banana are undisputed. It provides 100 calories per 100 g. (250 calories per 100 g. in its dried form) and a sufficient quantity of all the mineral salts necessary for the body's maintenance.

It is rich in starch, which is transformed into extremely energising sugar when the fruit is fully ripe. It also contains a wide variety of vitamins: A, B, B_1, B_2, B_{12}, D and E.

When ripe, the banana is full of nourishing constituents. It contains 74 per cent water and 22 per cent carbohydrates. These carbohydrates are only assimilable when the fruit is fully ripe; in green bananas it remains a non-assimilable starch.

Bananas destined for export are harvested when they are still green, at a stage when their flesh is white and without flavour. They have to be transported in conditions of a steady temperature of 12·5° to 13°C. (54·5° to 55·5°F.) in ships specially equipped for this purpose. They are shipped in complete stems of from 15 to 40 kg. (33 to 88 lb.) wrapped in special paper or polythene bags, or in 'hands' of from 8 to 12 bananas packed in cartons or crates.

On arrival, the bananas (which should be at the same stage of maturity as they were at the port of embarkation) are ripened either in converted cellars heated to a temperature of from 16·5° to 20°C. (61·5° to 68°F.) with a humidity value of 90 per cent to 95 per cent, or in specially equipped depôts. The ripening period is carried out according to requirements, and varies from 3 to 8 days.

When bananas are to be eaten raw, preference should be given to those which are a uniform golden-yellow colour, or lightly spotted.

There are some two hundred species of bananas in cultivation throughout the world. Of these, three varieties are commonly found on the French market: *sinensis* and *poyo*, similar to each other, both slightly curved, with fragrant, tasty flesh, and *gros-Michel*, larger, straighter, less fragile (and therefore more resistant to handling) but less fragrant.

Ripening place for bananas (*Pomona*)

Sinensis and *poyo* come from Martinique, Guadeloupe, the Ivory Coast and the Canaries. The *gros-Michel* is grown in Central America, South America and Cameroun. The latter is gradually being replaced by *poyo*.

In France, the *gros-Michel* of Cameroun is marketed principally in the east of the country, the *poyo* of the Ivory Coast and Canary bananas in the south, Antilles bananas in the Paris region and the west.

Curved banana from the Canaries and straight banana from America

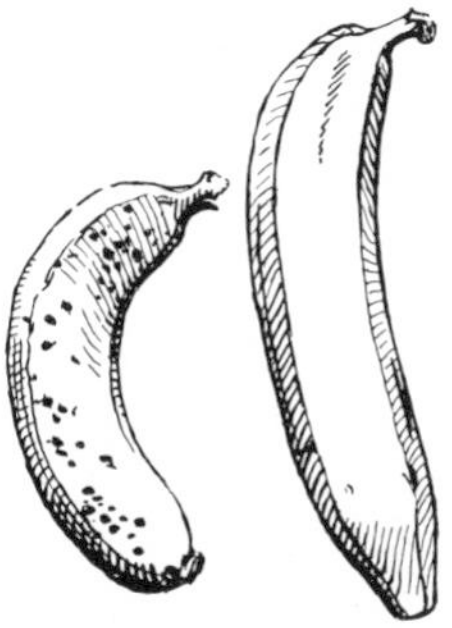

Bananas are sometimes dried in their country of origin and exported in this form. Their calorific value then rises to about 285 calories per 100 g. – twice that of meat. The banana can also be reduced to 'flour'. It takes this form in a number of industrial preparations, usually flavoured with cocoa.

A stem of bananas may consist of as many as 200, and weighs from 35 to 40 kg. (77 to 88 lb.).

Baked bananas. BANANES AU FOUR – Bake the bananas in the oven without peeling them. Serve with melted butter and fine sugar. Serve with a red fruit jelly, if desired.

Bananas Beauharnais. BANANES BEAUHARNAIS – Put 6 peeled bananas into a buttered fireproof dish. Dust with fine sugar, sprinkle with 4 tablespoons (5 tablespoons) white rum, and heat on the stove. Cook in the oven for 5 minutes. Pour thick cream over them, sprinkle with crushed macaroons and a little melted butter, and glaze in a hot oven. Serve in the same dish.

Bananas Bourdaloue. BANANES BOURDALOUE – Peel and poach the bananas in syrup, and proceed as described in the recipe for *Apricots bourdaloue* (see APRICOTS).

Bananas in butter. BANANES AU BEURRE – Peel bananas, put them in a buttered fireproof dish, and sprinkle with sugar. Cook slowly in the oven (180°C., 350°F., Gas Mark 4) for 20 to 30 minutes.

Banana compote – See COMPOTE.

Bananas Condé. BANANES CONDÉ – Peel and poach the bananas and proceed as described in the recipe for *Apricots Condé* (see APRICOT).

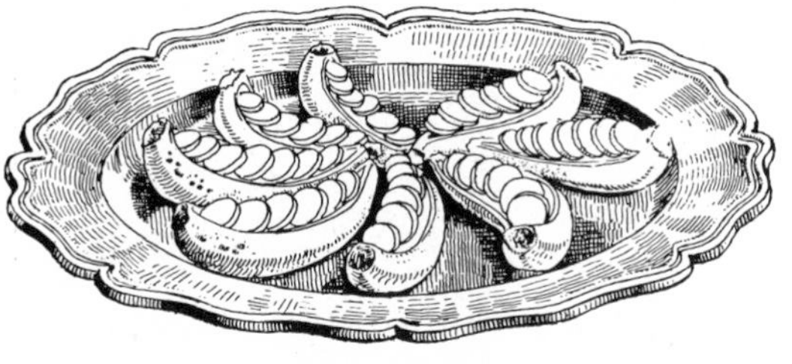

Bananas à la créole

Bananas à la créole. BANANES GRATINÉES À LA CRÉOLE – Choose firm bananas and cut them lengthwise. Remove the fruit and soak the skins for 2 minutes in boiling water. Drain, and dip them in cold water to cool.

Cut the banana halves into slices, and steep them in sugar and rum for 30 minutes. Partly fill the banana skins with *Dessert rice* (see RICE) mixed with a *salpicon* (q.v.) of crystallised fruit, and flavoured with rum. Arrange the banana slices on top, put the fruit on a baking tray, sprinkle with melted butter and finely ground macaroons, and brown in a hot oven.

Serve with rum-flavoured *Apricot sauce* (see SAUCE).

Banana croûtes à la Bauvilliers. CROÛTES AUX BANANES À LA BAUVILLIERS – Cut a stale brioche into a dozen rectangular slices 6 cm. (2½ inches) long and a little wider than a banana. Put the slices on a baking tray, sprinkle with fine sugar, and glaze in the oven.

Peel 6 bananas and halve lengthways. Put them on a buttered baking tray, sprinkle with fine sugar and cook in the oven for 5 minutes. Arrange the bananas, alternating with slices of brioche, in a circle in a fireproof dish. Fill the centre with semolina cooked with milk, sugar and vanilla, and bound with egg yolks (see SEMOLINA. *English semolina pudding*). Mix with a *salpicon* (q.v.) of preserved fruit steeped in maraschino.

Sprinkle the whole dish with finely crushed macaroons and melted butter, and brown in the oven. Before serving, surround with *Apricot sauce* (see SAUCE) flavoured with maraschino.

Banana croûtes à la maltaise. CROÛTES AUX BANANES À LA MALTAISE – Prepare as described in the recipe for *Banana croûtes à la Bauvilliers*, replacing semolina by thick *French pastry cream* (see CREAMS), flavoured with grated orange peel.

Decorate the circle of bananas with candied orange peel and halved almonds.

Bananas flambé. BANANES FLAMBÉES – Peel bananas and cook them in vanilla-flavoured syrup. Drain, and put into a *timbale* or a shallow ovenproof dish. Sprinkle with liqueur, and set alight when serving.

Banana flan or tart à la crème. FLAN DE BANANES À LA CRÈME – Peel bananas and halve them lengthways. Put them in a buttered dish, sprinkle with fine sugar, and cook in the oven. Arrange them in a flan made of short pastry, and fill with *French pastry cream* (see CREAMS). Sprinkle with crushed macaroons, and brown in the oven.

Fried bananas (garnish for meat). BANANES FRITES – Peel and halve the bananas lengthways. Marinate for 30 minutes in oil, lemon juice, salt and pepper. Dip the halves in a light batter and fry, when required.

As a dessert or sweet course, these are the same as *Banana fritters* (see below).

Fried bananas with cream

Ashurbanipal (669–626 B.C.) feasting with his queen (*British Museum*)

Banana fritters. BEIGNETS DE BANANES – Halve the bananas lengthways and steep them for an hour in rum or kirsch and sugar. When required, dip them in batter and deep-fry in sizzling fat. Drain, dry, and sprinkle with fine sugar before serving.

Batter. Make a smooth thick paste with 3 tablespoons (scant $\frac{1}{4}$ cup) flour and warm water. Add a tablespoon olive oil, and leave to stand for 2 to 3 hours, stirring from time to time.

Just before using, fold 2 stiffly whisked egg whites into the batter.

Banana mousse glacé – See ICE CREAMS AND ICES, *Fruit mousse*.

Banana soufflé. SOUFFLÉ AUX BANANES – Blend a tablespoon flour and a small pinch of salt into a smooth paste with 1 dl. (6 tablespoons, scant $\frac{1}{2}$ cup) milk which has been boiled with 35 g. (2 tablespoons, 3 tablespoons) sugar and allowed to cool. Add half a vanilla bean (or $\frac{1}{2}$ teaspoon vanilla essence) and stir well. Bring slowly to just under the boil, stirring all the time; remove from the heat. The texture should be that of thick cream.

Rub the pulp of 4 bananas through a fine sieve, mix with 2 egg yolks and a heaped tablespoon butter, and add this mixture to the cream in the saucepan. Add the stiffly whisked egg whites.

Butter a soufflé dish, sprinkle with fine sugar, and pour in the mixture. Bake in a slow oven (160°C., 325°F., Gas Mark 3) for 12 to 15 minutes.

BANDOL – Charming fishing port in the *département* of Var which has given its name to excellent white, red and rosé wines produced in the locality. (See PROVENCE.)

BANGI – Small tree which grows in the Philippines. It is lactescent and produces a pleasant, green coloured fruit, the size of an orange.

BANILLES – Long, tapering small pods which have some similarity to the vanilla bean. They contain a fragrant, sugary juice which is often used instead of vanilla in the manufacture of chocolate.

BANQUET – The word possibly comes from *banc* (bench). It may have been on benches that the first Christians sat as they celebrated their *agapes* in the catacombs.

Whatever the origin of the word, banquet signifies a sumptuous meal given to a large number of guests on festal or ceremonial occasions. Or it is given to bring together people of the same literary or artistic tastes, or religious or political ideas, or of the same social status, profession, or ethnic origin, and so on.

The mystic character of a banquet is to be found in prehistory. In the origins of all human activity there was magic, the need of man to make the mysterious forces of nature favourable to him. On the walls of the *Trois Frères* caves in Ariège, there is a primitive painting of a sorcerer in ceremonial robes, performing a sacred dance in the middle of an immense herd of cattle; apparently some kind of incantation to make the tribe's hunting successful.

When a slaughtered animal lay on the ground, it was divided into two parts, the first for the benevolent deities, the other for the tribe, clan or family. In this way men got used to meeting together, to divide amongst themselves the chosen parts of the animal. They continued to do this on the occasion of the two great events of their lives, birth and death. These were the first banquets.

When large gatherings at table became possible, the era of banquets began. The most magnificent were those that took place in the fertile fields of the orient, especially rich in spices and flavourings.

The banquets of the Egyptians – The Egyptians were very careful in their cooking, because they believed that illnesses were caused by the wrong choice and cooking of food. Contrary to the customs of most Eastern countries, the women took charge of the organisation of banquets in Egypt, directing the service and presiding at table. The guests were ushered into an ante-room on their arrival, where they washed their hands and feet. They then disported themselves in various games before the feast.

At the entrance to the banqueting hall, servants crowned them with wreaths of flowers. The first drinks were served, prayers were said, and the meal began. The guests sat on the floor, and the various dishes were placed near them, in baskets. Young musicians provided music on the harp, lyre and tambourine; sometimes there were performances by acrobats and mimes.

Herodotus, Athanaeus and Plutarch have recorded that in order to stimulate the guests to enjoy earthly pleasures to the full, a coffin was sometimes brought in at the end of the meal, with an imitation skeleton in it, so that they should appreciate more highly the good things of life, especially those of the table.

The banquets of the Assyrians and the Chaldeans – Strabo tells us that the epitaph inscribed on the tomb of Sardana-

Fresco showing a meal in Greek times

palus reads: 'Sardanapalus, the son of Anacyndara, had the towns of Anchiale and Tarsus built in a day. Passer-by, eat, drink and be merry, for nothing else matters!'

The Assyrians celebrated the victories of their armies with banquets. In an Assyrian bas-relief, we can see the king reclining on a sumptuous couch, the queen sitting at his feet, the table richly decked, slaves playing on stringed instruments. The vessels on the table have no feet; they were designed to be quaffed in one copious draught.

Maspéro, in his *Lectures Historiques*, gives a description of one of these banquets ordered by Ashur-bani-pal, the king under whom Nineveh reached the height of its power:

'The doors of the palace remained open to all comers for seven days. Multi-coloured draperies hung on the walls, transforming the courtyards into immense banqueting halls. People crowded into them from morning till night, stretching out on couches and ordering whatever they liked. Women and children, as well as men, were admitted to this largesse. Nor were soldiers, whose duties prevented them leaving the barracks, forgotten; the king sent food and drink to those who could not come.'

In Babylon, there were orchards and gardens capable of supplying the town with food during a long siege. The sumptuousness of the banquets there equalled those of the Assyrians.

The banquets of the Hebrews – The Hebrews were nomads for a long period, having come out of Chaldea to occupy the land of Canaan. Prosperity and peace on the banks of the Jordan enabled them to partake of the pleasures of the table. At first they were simple pleasures, but when luxury and refinement were introduced their banquets became very elaborate. At the time of the kings they sat down to table, but later adopted the habit of reclining on couches to eat. They perfumed their wine with essences, and when guests arrived for a banquet, holy water and perfume was poured over them, they were crowned with flowers, and took their places according to their rank.

Music was made 'with the harp, the tabret and pipe.' Women were not at first admitted to the feasts, but they were accepted in time, and were handsomely entertained, the Sabeans from the desert putting bracelets on their wrists and crowns on their heads.

The banquets of the Persians – Athenaeus says: 'One thousand animals are slaughtered daily for the king's table; horses, camels, oxen, asses, deer and most of the smaller animals. Many birds are also consumed, such as Arabian ostriches, geese and cocks.'

The Book of Esther describes a banquet given by Ahasuerus, when Queen Vashti's fall from favour was proclaimed after she had refused to appear, at the king's orders. This magnificent banquet, served in the palace gardens, lasted seven days. The couches were of silver and gold, and an abundance of wine was poured into gold cups.

The banquets of the Greeks – City Feasts were organised by the ancient Greeks on social or religious occasions. In addition to these banquets for special occasions, citizens were required to eat a sacred meal together every day, within the *prytaneum*, in the presence of the sacred fire and the protecting gods. The Greeks believed that if this custom was missed by a single day, they would lose the favour of their gods.

In Athens, men were selected by lot to attend the meal, and were severely punished if they refused to perform this duty. Those who sat at the sacred table wore white robes and crowns of flowers. They were called *parasites*, then a sacred title, but later destined to become a term of contempt. The parasites had disappeared by the time of Demosthenes, but the *prytanes* were still required to eat together in the *prytaneum*.

Women were never invited to a Greek banquet. The guests took their shoes off before entering the banqueting hall, rested on couches for a time, washed, and invoked the gods of home and country before sitting down to the feast. Young girls played upon the harp and lute, and there were dancing girls.

Dancing and music at a Greek banquet

The banquets of the Romans – The splendours of Imperial Rome were reflected in their banquets. The Romans often sacrificed the dishes themselves to presentation and ostentation. At one meal Heliogabalus served to his guests 600 ostrich brains, peas with grains of gold, lentils with precious stones, and other dishes with pearls and amber.

The room where the Romans took their meals was called the *triclinium*; it was the custom to put only three couches round a table. Each guest brought his own napkin. On arrival, the guests changed into white robes and sandals, and took their places at table according to their status. After invoking the Penates, Lares and Jupiter, they began the feast, eating with their fingers.

A Roman banquet

The first course was the *hors-d'œuvre*, served with a light wine. The second was the *coena*, which was the main course, after which sacrifices were made to the Lares amid silence. The third course was the dessert, fresh or dried fruit or fruit baked in pastries, but there was sometimes a more solid course instead of dessert. In a menu found in the ruins of Pompeii, this course included sows' udders, wild boar's head, *fricassée* of wild duck, and a cream made of flour and Vicence cakes.

Musicians, poets and dancers appeared at important banquets, and sometimes there were gladiator fights, acrobats and clowns.

There are many accounts of the grandiose luxury of the barbaric feasts given by the Romans. Petronius gives us some idea of what they were like in this extract from a description of one of these, *Trimalchio's feast*:

'On a tray of relishes stood a small bronze ass, carrying twin baskets, one containing green and the other black olives. Salvers, moulded like bridges, contained dormice, seasoned with honey and poppy seeds. There were sizzling sausages on a silver gridiron, with Syrian plums and pomegranate seeds placed beneath it... A basket was placed before us containing a hen, wings spread out as if she were hatching. We broke the egg, which was made of light pastry looking exactly like the shell . . . and found in it a plump *beccafico* (garden warbler), deliciously spiced, hidden inside the yolk.

Crystal flagons, carefully sealed, were brought in. Around the neck of each bottle hung a label: *Falernian opimian wine 100 years old.*'

The long account goes on to list the fantastic manner in which dishes were served; a tray with the twelve signs of the zodiac reproduced on it in a circle, on which the chef had placed dishes analogous to the particular constellation – a piece of beef over Taurus (the Bull), kidneys and testicles over Cancer (the Crab), the uterus of a sow over Virgo (the Virgin), a hare over Sagittarius (the Archer), two mullets over Pisces (the Fish), and so on. An enormous wild boar was served on a platter, with little pastry sucking pigs pressing on the teats . . . A slave gave the boar a stab in the belly and out flew a cloud of thrushes, trying to escape. Bird catchers caught them with fowlers' rods, and offered them to the guests.

The banquets of the Gauls (100 B.C.) – The food of the early Gauls consisted mainly of fresh or salted pork, the animals they raised in the forests, and milk. Their meals together were long, served by young people. A brazier with spits and cauldrons was placed near the tables, and food was cooked in them.

The guests sat on bundles of straw round low tables. Great quantities of meat, boiled, roasted on the spit or grilled, with a little bread, constituted the meal.

Posidonious, the Greek stoic philosopher, has left a description of the meal:

'The food is served in a clean way: on silver or copper dishes in rich houses, on earthenware or wooden ones in the homes of the poor. Each man takes a whole joint and bites; should the piece be too tough or too big, he cuts it with a small knife, the scabbard of which is attached to his sword. A single drinking vessel of earthenware or metal is handed round by slaves and makes many rounds, but one drinks little at a time.'

The Gauls drank various wines from the horns of wild oxen, ornamented with gold or silver rings; and sometimes from the skulls of their enemies killed in battle, or of their own dead parents, whose memory they thus wished to honour, out of filial piety.

The wines of Bezier and Vienna, and Italian and Greek wines, were seen on the tables of the rich. They were taken in small quantities, and diluted with water. The poor drank beer, and *hydromel* – herb and spice-flavoured honey, diluted with water.

Fish was eaten in areas near the sea, and mainly grilled, seasoned with salt and cumin and sprinkled with vinegar.

On special occasions, the guests sat at a round table, a prominent place being given to the most distinguished or the most valiant. There was a custom that the legs of the animals served should be allotted to the bravest. This was a source of quarrels, and often a fight to the death.

The banquets of the Gallo-Romans – The wealthy Gallo-Romans adopted Latin customs, and their banquets were modelled on the Roman, though they discarded the custom of reclining on couches.

De la Bédolière, in his *Moeurs et vie privée des Français*, describes the banquets of the Gallo-Romans; here are extracts:

'Some Gauls, disdaining the indolence of the Romans, use benches, stools and other wooden seats covered with a carpet instead of couches . . . The guests put on special robes and sandals and take their places around the table . . . Slaves bring in a great quantity of meat, roast or boiled, which is carved with great skill and dexterity by servants. The meal starts with a tasting of *mulsum* or *medum*, mulled wine mixed with honey . . . A salver is placed in the centre of the table and various dishes are put on it one after the other: fresh eggs, quarters of beef, mutton, pork, goat, all seasoned with yolks of egg, black pepper, brine, cumin, salt . . .

As a dessert, the guests are served with hot or cold tarts, honey cakes, soft cheese, grilled *escargots*, medlars, chestnuts, figs, Gaul peaches and grapes. At the end of the meal hot *mulsum* is brought in once again, and slaves distribute toothpicks made of feathers, wood and silver.'

The banquets of the Franks – Caius Sollius Apollinaris Sidonius states that one could find in the banquets of the Franks 'the elegance of Greece, the abundance of Gaul, the dispatch of Italy, the pomp of public ceremonial allied to the fastidiousness of a private table, of the order befitting a king's palace.'

Writers of the period mention silver tables, gold and silver utensils, tablecloths fashioned from fresh roses. The Franks were very hospitable, and had a strict code of table manners. Wine was passed round the table and the guests drank from the same cup. Lamps were considered to desecrate the table at a banquet; the room was lit by torches held aloft by slaves.

French banquets from the Middle Ages to the fifteenth century – The beginning of a banquet was announced by the sound of a horn, a privilege reserved for the highest personages in the kingdom. Guests washed their hands with perfumed water before sitting down, and after each course; forks had not been invented; food was eaten with fingers.

Meal served to Grandgousier, Gargantua's father, from an old edition of the works of Rabelais

Goblets and tankards were placed on a side table, and filled by pages who brought them to the guests. This manner of serving wine during meals survived until the end of the eighteenth century. In royal courts, the dishes were tasted by a special servant, or touched with a talisman, to assure the royal personages that the food was not poisoned. The menus were exotic, and included roast peacocks with gilded bills and claws, swans and pheasants dressed in their plumage, calves and pigs ornately presented. The dessert, of fruit and creams, was followed by dried fruit preserves, pastry and *hippocras* (spiced wine).

French banquets of the sixteenth century – The great banquets given during this century show a love of opulence; richly wrought and engraved gold and silver dinner plate, Faïence and Nevers porcelain, Venetian glass. Forks and long-handled spoons had come into use, and cooking had become more refined. Belon, in his *Traité des Oyseaux* writes of 'a thousand little disguises of flesh, made into soups, *fricassées*, hashes, salads.' After roast and boiled joints and game, there were cold desserts 'such as fruits, milk products, sweetmeats, cakes, cheese, chestnuts, Capendy apples, a salad of lemons or pomegranates.'

French banquets of the seventeenth century – In the reign of Louis XIII, there was less display at banquets and more emphasis on harmony and simplicity. Under Louis XIV, however, there were usually four substantial dishes – roast

A Royal banquet during the reign of Louis XIV

Kings at table (woodcut, Lyon, 1508)

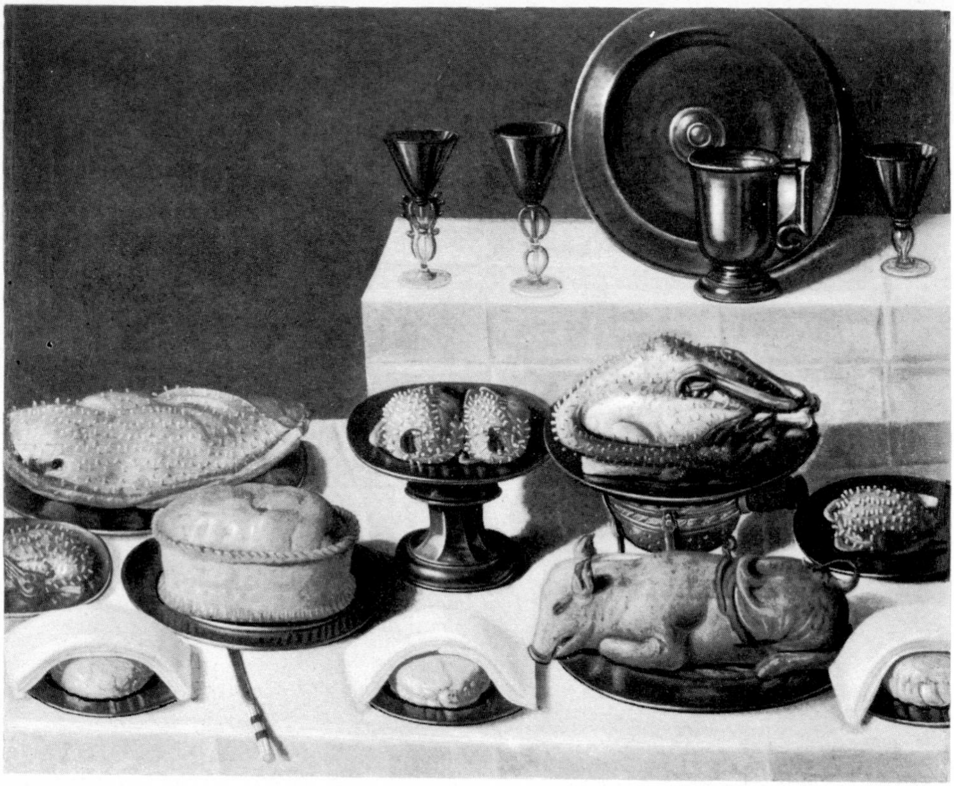

Seventeenth century French banquet fare (*Giraudon*)

meat, poultry and game as well as tureens of soup. These were followed by melons, various salads in bowls 'or in little plates to make serving them easier,' comments Nicolas de Bonnefons (*Délices de la campagne*), and goes on to describe what he considers to be an ideal banquet for a company of thirty people. Among other dishes there should be a *potage de la Reine*, made of minced partridge or pheasant, in the first course; roast venison haunches baked in pastry in the second; woodcock, turkeys, chickens and whole lambs in the third; snipe, thrushes, larks and 'all sorts of small fried things' in the fourth; whole salmon, trout, carp, pike, with *fricassées* of turtle in the fifth; and three finishing courses which would include blancmanges, fruit, almonds and green walnuts, preserves in syrup, or dried marzipans and sugar almonds.

French banquets of the eighteenth century – Great pomp accompanied banquets in the reign of Louis XV. On the occasion of the anointing of the king in 1772, a royal banquet was held in the archiepiscopal palace at Rheims.

After gorgeous processions headed by musicians playing oboes, trumpets and flutes, the king was led to a table on a dais and joined by high officers of state.

The company comprised the noblest in the land, but ladies and princelings were not seated with the gentlemen, and had to wait until the king had retired. According to the old document from which the above descriptions are taken: 'During this sumptuous banquet the Duchess of Lorraine, who, from her tribune, could see all the succulent dishes filing past without being able to touch them, quietly nibbled biscuits, with which she was fortunately provided . . . After the dinner, the Archbishop of Rheims said grace – the Duchess of Lorraine by this time had reached her reserves of dried plums – and the king was re-conducted to his apartments in the same order and with the same ceremony with which he had been ushered in.'

Madame Vigée-Lebrun's Greek supper. Among legendary eighteenth century meals was a supper given by the artist, Vigée-Lebrun. In her memoirs she describes 'the most brilliant supper I ever gave,' which was, in fact, a miniature banquet. Her brother was reading a book of travels to her one afternoon while she was resting, and came to a passage describing a Greek dinner and the manner of preparing

Cutlery belonging to Louis XIV

several sauces. Madame Lebrun immediately decided to have certain of these sauces for a supper party she was giving that evening and summoned her cook, ordering that Greek sauces should be served with chickens and eels on the evening's menu.

A friend who had a collection of Greek urns and vases lent her several of his best pieces, and the room was decorated in classical style.

Two guests, Monsieur Vaudreuil and Monsieur Boutin, were not able to come until ten o'clock, but the other guests arrived soon after half-past nine. Madame Lebrun dressed the women in Grecian fashion from draperies she had in her studio workroom, and found cloaks and other picturesque garments for the men.

While they waited for the two late guests, her brother recited several odes of Anacreon, and when the others arrived, they found the company singing Gluck's chorus from *Le Dieu de Paphos et de Cnide*, with M. de Cubières accompanying them on a lyre which he had improvised from a guitar.

'In all my life I have never seen two faces more astonished than those of Monsieur de Vaudreuil and his companion,' continues Madame Lebrun in her recital of the event. 'They were astounded and charmed.'

At supper, dishes were served with the Greek sauces, as well as a sweet made from honey and currants. They drank a bottle of old Cyprus wine which had been a present to the artist. 'That was all the excess,' she remarks.

Rumour quickly ran round Versailles about this famous supper. It was said to have cost 20,000 francs. In Rome the whispered figure was raised to 40,000 francs, in Vienna to 60,000 francs, in Petersburg to 80,000. In fact, it cost Madame Lebrun, according to her memoirs, 15 francs.

French banquets in the nineteenth century – The beginning of this century saw the publication of Brillat-Savarin's *la Physiologie du goût*, in which he established the rules of

Banquet given by the Duke of Alba to celebrate the birth of the Prince of Asturias in 1707

Banquet given in honour of Louis XVI and Queen Marie Antoinette on the occasion of the birth of the Dauphin in 1785 (engraving on metal, *Louvre*)

Dinner given on 7 March 1806 by the Paris print dealers to their fellow dealer Le Confrère. The legend on the print bears the following inscription: 'They beg him to accept this light sketch as a token of their esteem and friendship. May he remember them sometimes in his retirement and for a long time enjoy the happiness he deserves for his kindness of heart and probity'

dining harmoniously. For a great gala dinner he laid down:

'That the dining-room be luxuriously lit, the cloth be of the utmost cleanliness, and the temperature from 13 to 16 degrees by the Réaumur thermometer (61° to 66°F.).

'That the men be witty without pretensions and the women charming without being too coquettish.

'That the choice of dishes be exquisite but restrained in number, and the wines of the first quality, each the best of its kind.

'That the order for the former should be from the most substantial to the lightest, and for the latter from the lightest to those with the greatest bouquet.

'That the speed of eating should be moderate, dinner being the last affair of the day; and that the guests behave like travellers who aim to arrive at the same destination together.

'That the coffee be scalding hot, and the liqueurs specially chosen by the master of the house.'

He added rules for the guests' entertainment after dinner:

'That the salon be sufficiently spacious to organise a game of cards for those who cannot do without, and to leave enough room to enable the rest to enjoy conversation.

'That the guests be held by the pleasure of the company, and stirred by the hope that the evening will not pass without some further entertainment.'

In the same epoch, the gastronome Grimod de la Reynière also established a *Charte de bon manger*. In his *Manuel des amphitryons* are decreed laws governing banquets. He himself gave grand dinners, some of them eccentric; he once sent out invitations for a dinner in the form of obituary notices, bidding his guests 'attend the funeral and obsequies of a big feed.'

Fashionable restaurants. During the nineteenth century, there was a vogue for magnificent banquets in certain restaurants. At one such dinner, given at *Rocher de Cancale* by a certain English Lord W., Marennes oysters, a ham roasted on a spit, grouse brought specially from Scotland, salads, special sweet dishes and several kinds of cheese, figure on the menu. The wine was Clos-Vougeot, and the company did not depart until three o'clock in the morning.

Banquets under the Second Empire – There was a number of magnificent gastronomical galas, and in the sections headed COOKING and MENUS, examples are given of what these state dinners were like.

The coronation dinner of Charles X at Reims

Banquet held in la Galerie des Machines in Paris, 5 November 1905

Later banquets – Things were quite different in the later banquets and at the celebrated 'mayors' banquet' (22 September 1900), 22,295 guests of the President of the Republic, attired in frock coats and crush hats, were served with an identical menu:

Hors-d'œuvre
Filet de boeuf en Bellevue
Pains de canetons de Rouen
Poularde de Bresse rôtie
Ballottine de faisan Saint-Hubert
Salade Potel
Glace succès Condé
Desserts

Never before had such a large number of guests sat down together at a single meal, recounts M. Christian Guy in his *Histoire de la cuisine française*; this was successfully achieved by the excellent organisation of *Maison Potel et Chabot*.

It is interesting to note that the menus of official banquets never mention the cheeses served. This may have been because cheese formed part of the dessert and so needed no special mention.

BANQUIÈRE (À LA) – Garnish used for chicken, calves' sweetbreads, *vol-au-vent*. It is made of quenelles, mushrooms, thin slivers of truffles and *banquière sauce*. (See GARNISHES.)

BANTAM – A variety of Java chickens, named after the town where they originated. These birds have a very delicate flesh, and are prepared in the same way as ordinary chickens.

BANVIN – French word for the feudal right which allowed the seigneur to sell the wine from his estate for a certain time, before anyone else. The word is also used for the proclamation announcing the day after which private persons could sell new wine.

BANYULS – Commune in the eastern Pyrenees, which has given its name to a well-known *appellation controlée* dessert wine – Banyuls and Banyuls *grand cru*, which is produced from the slaty mountainous terrain in a restricted zone comprising the communes of Banyuls, Port-Vendres, Cerbère and Collioure. This wine is made almost exclusively from the black Grenache grape. The Banyuls *grand cru* have to undergo an obligatory maturing period of thirty months in wood before being released for consumption.

BAOBAB – The largest known tropical African tree. Its fruit is called *monkey-bread*, because monkeys eat it. Its pulp, which is very sweet with a slight acid flavour, is made into a refreshing drink much liked by the local inhabitants of the region where this magnificent tree grows, and is drunk a great deal in Morocco and Egypt.

The Africans dry the leaves of the baobab in the shade, reduce them to powder which they call *lalo*, and mix it with their food.

Baobab

BARAQUILLES – A hot *hors-d'œuvre*; triangular patties, filled with a *salpicon* (q.v.) of winged game fillets, calves' sweetbreads, *foie gras*, truffles and mushrooms, bound with Madeira-flavoured *Allemande sauce* (see SAUCE). *Baraquilles* are also prepared as rissoles.

BARASHEK IZ MASLA (Butter lamb) (Russian cookery) – Make a model of a lamb with butter which has been rendered firm by being left in ice water. Cover the model with a thin coating of butter, pressing down with a coarse-weave cloth or canvas to give the appearance of fleece. Mark the eyes with two little circles of truffles, or two raisins. Put a small green branch in the lamb's mouth.

This symbolic lamb is a feature of the traditional table laid for the ritual Easter meal in Russia.

BARBADOS CREAM. CRÈME DES BARBADES – Liqueur made of lemon, orange and citron peel, mace, cinnamon, cloves, sugar and *eau-de-vie*, which was once a fashionable drink.

BARBAREA. BARBARÉE – This plant – also called *herb of St Barbara, yarrow,* and *yellow rocket* – has a piquant, rather bitter flavour not unlike that of cress, and has the same anti-scorbutic properties. It grows wild in damp and sandy places.

A variety of barbarea, called *land cress* or *American cress* (U.S. *winter cress*) is cultivated and eaten in salads.

Barbarea can be prepared in all the ways recommended for cress. In certain regions it is mixed with spinach.

BARBARIN – French name for a fish of the mullet family.

BARBARINE – A variety of marrow (U.S. squash) of various shapes and sizes. It has an elongated shape, rather like a cucumber, plain yellow or parti-coloured, sometimes striped with green. The best barbarines are pale yellow, and can be prepared according to the recipes given for marrows and cucumbers.

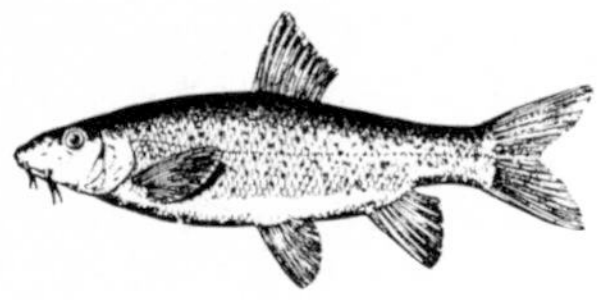

Barbel

BARBEL. BARBEAU, BARBILLON – River fish recognisable by the barbels at the end of the snout, and at the corners of the jaws.

In France, the *common barbel* is found in all the rivers. The *southern barbel* is found in the south of France, in the Alpes-Maritimes and in the Pyrénées-Orientales.

The flesh of the barbel is insipid, and it has too many bones to be pleasant. The fish feeds on the river bed and nibbles at the fishermen's bait, especially those of animal origin, which are very much to its taste. It is fond of crickets and grass-hoppers, and in the autumn rises to the surface in their pursuit.

Large barbel, found in the Loire, are considered the best, and may be poached, braised, baked or roast. The small ones, usually called *barbillons*, are grilled or fried. Recipes for barbel can be applied to the catfish of U.S.A. The soft roes of barbel are delicate, but the hard roes are reputed to be poisonous.

Boiled barbel with various sauces. BARBEAU BOUILLI – Poach the barbel in *Court-bouillon IV* (see COURT-BOUILLON). Drain thoroughly. Garnish with boiled potatoes and fresh parsley. Serve, as recommended in individual recipes, with melted butter or *White sauce, Butter sauce, Hollandaise sauce* or *Caper sauce* (see SAUCE).

Barbel à la bourguignonne. BARBEAU À LA BOURGUIGNONNE – Proceed as described in the recipe for *Brill à la bourguignonne* (see BRILL).

Fried barbel. BARBILLON FRIT – Proceed as described in the recipe for *Fried bass* (see BASS).

Grilled barbel. BARBILLON GRILLÉ – Proceed as described in the recipe for *Grilled bass* (see BASS).

Barbel à la meunière. BARBILLON À LA MEUNIÈRE – Proceed as described in the recipe for *Bass à la meunière* (see BASS).

Barbel à la mode des mariniers. BARBEAU À LA MODE DES MARINIERS – Clean and scale a 1-kg. (2-lb.) barbel and cut off the wattles and fins. Put the roe, if any, back into the fish, seasoned with salt and pepper.

Fry 2 chopped onions and 4 shallots lightly in butter without browning, and place in an earthenware dish, together with 7 or 8 chopped dried walnuts and 100 g. (4 oz.) chopped mushrooms.

Make a few slits in the fish, season with salt and pepper, and place on the above ingredients in the dish. Add 2 glasses red wine, and 100 g. (4 oz., $\frac{1}{2}$ cup) butter divided into small pieces. Bring slowly to the boil on top of the stove, then cook in a hot oven for 35 minutes, basting frequently. Ten minutes before the end of cooking, sprinkle with breadcrumbs and melted butter and replace in the oven. By the end of the 35 minutes the wine should have boiled away.

Sprinkle with chopped parsley before serving.

Roast barbel. BARBEAU RÔTI – Make slits in a medium-sized barbel, insert fillets of anchovy in the slits, sprinkle with oil or melted butter, season, and roast in the oven or on a spit. Baste frequently during cooking.

When the fish is cooked and placed on a dish, dilute the pan juices with white wine, boil down, add 1 tablespoon butter and a dash of lemon juice, stir well, and serve with the fish.

Anchovy butter or *Maître d'hôtel butter* (see BUTTER) can be served at the same time.

BARBERON – Name used in some parts of the south of France for salsify.

BARBERRY. ÉPINE-VINETTE – A common prickly shrub. Its green berries can be pickled in vinegar, like capers. The berries, which ripen to a red colour in November, contain a great deal of malic and citric acid, and are used to make syrup, jam, and a kind of wine.

Barberries are also used to make a refreshing drink for feverish conditions. A tisane brewed from the roots is used as a diuretic, especially in cases of jaundice.

Dried candied barberries. ÉPINE-VINETTE CONFITE AU SEC – An old recipe says: 'Take large ripe barberries of a fine red colour. Leave them in clusters. For 1 kg. (2 lb.) berries, cook $1\frac{1}{4}$ kg. ($2\frac{1}{2}$ lb.) sugar to a large feather (see SUGAR). Put in the barberries and boil on a high flame until bubbles appear.

'Take off the stove. When the fruit is beginning to cool, put it in a hot cupboard, leaving it to drain on a thick cloth until next day. Transfer to sheets of clean white paper to finish draining. Dust the clusters of berries with sugar which has been rubbed through a very fine sieve, and return them to the hot cupboard to dry off completely.'

BARBOTEUR ('Paddler') – Common French name for the domestic duck. (See DUCK.)

BARD. BARDER – To bard means to cover a piece of meat, poultry, game or, more rarely, a large fish before braising it, with thin slices of bacon or salt or fresh pork, tied with string.

After cooking, the barding fat is removed. Its main purpose is to protect delicate parts of the meat, or breast of poultry. It is, however, customary to serve roast game – woodcock, quail, pheasant, partridge, etc. – with the fat or bacon which was used for barding.

BARDING FAT. BARDE – Slices of fat bacon, or pork fat (fresh or salted) for enveloping poultry and game, as well as various cuts of meat, before they are braised, poached or roasted. It is also used for lining *pâtés* cooked in pie-crust and *terrines*.

BARIGOULE – Name for a mushroom which is also called *brigoule* and *bourigoule* in the south of France. It is very good to eat.

BARIGOULE (À LA) – Some authors of cookery books say that the term *à la barigoule*, given to stuffed artichokes, is derived from the name of the mushroom which is used in the south-east of France for filling artichokes.

BAR-LE-DUC – Town in Lorraine which is famous for its redcurrant jams.

BARLEY. ORGE – One of the most ancient cultivated cereals, which still exists in its original form on the shores of the Red and Caspian Seas.

Barley grain is poorer in gluten than wheat, and its flour does not form an elastic paste when formed with water. It is therefore not suitable as an ingredient for bread. Barley bread, which is generally mixed with wheat (once a staple food for agricultural labourers), is rarely made nowadays. It has good keeping qualities but is difficult to digest.

A barley infusion (barley water) was one of the most popular medicines prescribed by Hippocrates. Barley water is refreshing and emollient. To prepare it, wash 20 g. ($1\frac{1}{2}$ tablespoons, 2 tablespoons) pearl barley, and boil in 1 litre ($1\frac{3}{4}$ pints, generous quart) water until cooked. Leave to stand for a short time, strain, and press well with the back of a wooden spoon.

A tisane, which is slightly laxative, is made in the proportion of 1 to 2 tablespoons barley water to 1 litre (scant quart, generous quart) water. This tisane is beneficial in feverish conditions.

Barley is used in cookery in the form of hulled barley and pearl barley, mainly used for soups, creams, porridge (*bouillie*), and as garnish for *ragoûts* (see MUTTON, *Ragoût of mutton with barley*).

Barley flakes and barley flour are used to lighten cereal diets. Artificially germinated barley produces malt (q.v.).

Barley sugar (confection). SUCRE D'ORGE – Cook 250 g. (9 oz., $1\frac{1}{4}$ cups) hulled barley in 5 litres ($4\frac{1}{2}$ quarts, $5\frac{1}{2}$ quarts) water for 5 hours. Strain the liquid (which resembles white jelly) and decant. Add some sugar, previously cooked to soufflé degree (110°C., 230°F.) to this liquid, and cook until sugar reaches crack degree (150°C., 302°F.). Pour onto an oiled marble slab (or oiled metal sheet) and when it begins to cool, cut into long strips and twist.

This is the original method of making barley sugar sticks. They are now made from drawn sugar.

Consommé with pearl barley. CONSOMMÉ À L'ORGE PERLÉ – Wash 100 g. (4 oz., generous $\frac{1}{2}$ cup) pearl barley in warm water and add it to $2\frac{1}{2}$ litres ($4\frac{1}{2}$ pints, $5\frac{1}{2}$ pints) consommé (meat stock). Add a stalk of celery, and simmer slowly for 2 hours.

Cream of barley soup – See SOUPS AND BROTHS.

Hulled barley broth. DÉCOCTION D'ORGE MONDÉ – Wash 100 g. (4 oz., generous $\frac{1}{2}$ cup) hulled barley in warm water, and soak in $3\frac{1}{2}$ litres (3 quarts, $7\frac{1}{2}$ pints) cold water for an hour. Add 25 g. (4 teaspoons) salt, 2 carrots, 1 onion studded with a clove, 4 leeks and 2 stalks celery.

Simmer very slowly for 3 hours, and strain. This barley broth is most refreshing.

Mutton broth with barley – See SOUPS AND BROTHS, *Mutton broth*.

BARNACLE. BERNICLE – Common name for the limpet, the mollusc with the conical shell that attaches itself to rocks on the seashore. It is known by various names in different regions of France, for example, *flie*, *bassin*, *jamble* and *arapède*.

Barnacles

Its flesh is rather tough and is eaten raw, or with *vinaigrette dressing*. Small limpets can be prepared like mussels, while the large ones are often brushed with butter and grilled, or prepared *à l'américaine*, *en matelote*, etc.

BARNACLE GOOSE. BARNACHE, BERNACLE – Bird of passage resembling the greyleg goose. It is also called *oie-marine* (sea goose) in France.

Barnacle geese winter on the coasts of Europe. Their flesh is edible but indigestible. Preparation is the same as for bustard (q.v.).

BARON – This is the French name of a large joint of mutton comprising the saddle and the two legs. The term is also applied to lamb.

In England, it is only used for a large piece of beef: a baron of beef, or double sirloin. In U.S.A. the term is used mostly for the hindquarters (both legs and both loins) of lamb.

The following anecdote is told about baron or sirloin of beef. King Henry VIII, who was a hearty eater, was fond of roast beef. One day, delighted by the sight of a double loin set before him, he conferred knighthood upon it. The noble title bestowed on this piece of beef has been sanctioned by custom, and the cut is known to this day as *sirloin* or *baron* of beef.

The sirloin is generally prepared as a roast, and sometimes cooked on a spit. In England, where the dish is much esteemed, it is served with Yorkshire pudding, which is made from batter cooked in the dripping pan under the roasting joint.

Barons of mutton or lamb are also roasted, garnished with vegetables; or they can be served with their own gravy, and garnished with watercress.

BARQUETTES – Oval tartlet shells filled with various compositions before cooking. They can be baked blind (empty) and then filled.

Barquettes are also used for a small *hors-d'œuvre* (q.v.) or a small *entrée*. (For more sweet *barquettes*, see TARTLETS.)

Apricot barquettes I. BARQUETTES AUX ABRICOTS – Make *Flaky pastry* (see DOUGH) with 250 g. (9 oz., $2\frac{1}{4}$ cups) sieved flour, scant teaspoon salt, $2\frac{1}{2}$ teaspoons sugar, 1 egg yolk, 150 g. (5 oz., generous $\frac{1}{2}$ cup) butter and 1 dl. (6 tablespoons, scant $\frac{1}{2}$ cup) water.

Roll out the paste to a thickness of 3 to 4 mm. ($\frac{1}{8}$ inch) cut out with a fluted oval pastry-cutter and line boat-shaped tartlet tins with the ovals. Prick the bottom of the paste to prevent it rising during baking. Sprinkle with fine sugar.

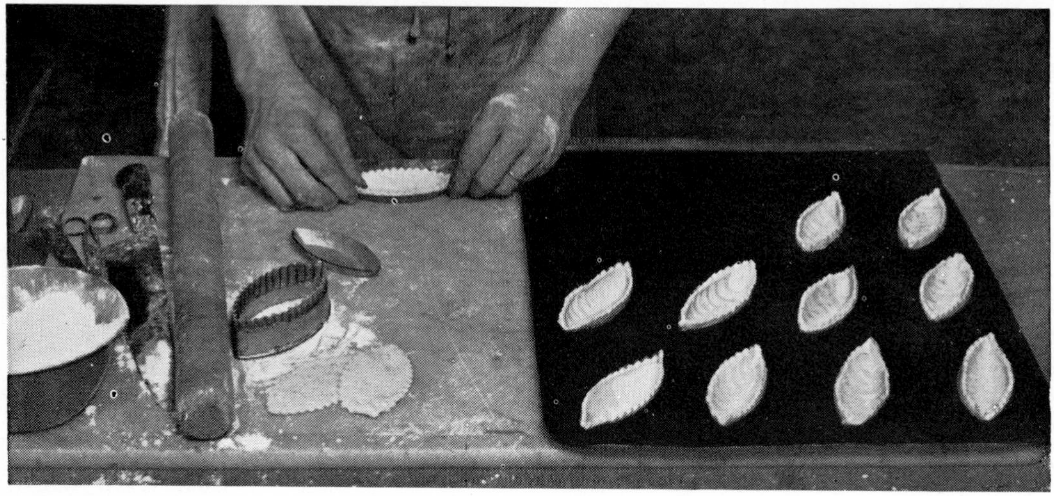

Making barquettes (*Larousse*)

Stone and quarter fresh apricots, and arrange in the tartlets, skin side down. Bake in a moderate oven (180°C., 350°F., Gas Mark 4) for about 20 minutes. Take the tartlets out of the tins and cool them on a wire cake tray. Spoon apricot jam into them. Break the apricot stones, blanch the kernels, and put two halves on each tartlet.

Apricot barquettes II. BARQUETTES AUX ABRICOTS – As in preceding recipe, using puff pastry instead of flaky pastry.

Apricot barquettes à l'ancienne. BARQUETTES AUX ABRICOTS À L'ANCIENNE – Fill flaky pastry tartlets with vanilla-flavoured *Butter cream* (see CREAMS). Decorate with halves of blanched almonds and crystallised cherries.

Savoury barquettes

BARREL. BARIL – Small cask of variable capacity, usually 72 litres (15¾ gallons, 19¾ gallons) used as a container for brandy, vinegar, oil, anchovies, herrings or other fish, olives, etc. A barrel of wine in Britain amounts to 115 litres (25 gallons, 31 gallons), in Tuscany 20 litres (4½ gallons, 5½ gallons).

BARRIQUE – Large cask or barrel used for transporting liquids in France. Its capacity varies in different regions. In Bordeaux and in the south of France it is about 225 litres (49½ gallons, 62 gallons), in Cognac about 205 litres (45 gallons, 56 gallons), in Mâcon about 213 litres (47 gallons, 58½ gallons), and in Nantes, 210 litres (46 gallons, 57½ gallons).

BARROT – French word for a small barrel containing anchovies; the term applies only to anchovy barrels.

BARSAC – Commune in the Gironde that has given its name to a fine white Bordeaux wine. Barsac has the right to the *appellation* Sauternes. (See BORDEAUX.)

BASELLA (Indian spinach). BASELLE – Edible plant, native of tropical countries, cultivated in some parts of France. It is prepared in the same way as spinach.

BASIL. BASILIC – Plant cultivated in gardens for the sake of its fragrance. There are several varieties: *sweet basil*, the leaves of which are dried and used as a condiment in cookery; *monk's basil*, which can be similarly preserved; and *bush basil*, which is often grown as a pot herb. It is used in Provence, together with garlic, for flavouring *pistou*, a popular soup in this region.

Basil was once considered a royal plant; only the sovereign (*basileus*) could cut it, and even then only with a golden sickle. The plant has now come into common use.

Basil

BASQUAISE (À LA) – Garnish for large cuts of meat composed of fried *cèpes* and Anna potatoes in *dariole* moulds sprinkled with chopped Bayonne ham.

BAS-ROND – Term incorrectly used in some cookery books instead of baron (q.v.).

BASS. BAR – This fish, which is also called *sea dace*, *sea wolf* or *sea perch* abounds in the Mediterranean. It is also found, in smaller numbers, in the Atlantic Ocean. Bass does not normally go beyond the English Channel, and rarely penetrates into the Baltic.

Two species are known: the *common bass* (*sea wolf*) on the Mediterranean coast, and *striped bass*. The *common bass* is seen a great deal in French markets, and is recognisable by its silvery, grey-blue back and white belly. The bass of the U.S.A., while not exactly the same, is prepared in the same way. Some gastronomes do not admit that the flesh of the bass has any particular delicacy, but many people like it.

To prepare. Clean the fish through the gills and through a light incision made on the belly. Do not scale the bass if it is to be poached, but scale it, without breaking the skin, if it is to be braised, fried or grilled. Wash and dry the fish.

Make a few light incisions on the fleshy part of the back, slit it along the backbone, or cut into uniform-sized pieces; proceed according to the recipe chosen.

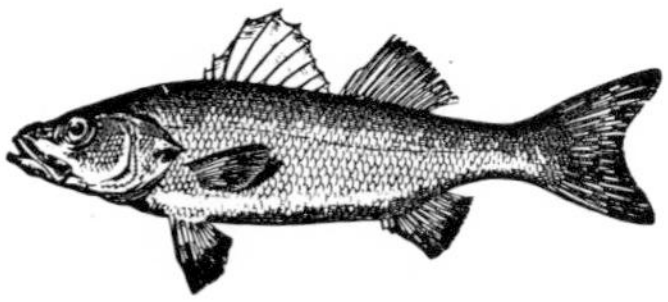

Bass

Boiled or poached bass with various sauces. BAR BOUILLI OU POCHÉ – Put the bass into *Court-bouillon III* (see COURT-BOUILLON). As soon as it boils, draw the pan to the edge of the burner, and poach, simmering lightly. Drain the bass, and garnish with fresh parsley.

Serve with melted butter, or with *Hollandaise sauce* or any other sauce recommended for boiled fish (see SAUCE).

Boiled bass, like all poached fish, is served with steamed or boiled potatoes.

Braised bass with various sauces and garnishes. BAR BRAISÉ – Clean the bass, and spread the inside with a large piece of butter which has been kneaded with chopped parsley and seasoned with salt and pepper. Season the outside. Put it in a fish kettle on a foundation of shredded carrots and onions lightly fried in butter. Add a *bouquet garni* (q.v.). Moisten with dry white wine; for a bass weighing 1 kg. ($2\frac{1}{4}$ lb.) use 3 dl. ($\frac{1}{2}$ pint, $1\frac{1}{4}$ cups) wine. Sprinkle with 2 tablespoons (3 tablespoons) melted butter. Bring to the boil, then transfer the fish kettle to the oven and cook, uncovered, for 25 to 30 minutes, basting frequently.

Drain the bass and arrange on a dish. Reduce the braising liquor, add butter, and pour over the fish. Add the garnish.

Serve with *Espagnole sauce* (made with fish stock) or with *Velouté* (see SAUCE). All garnishes recommended for large braised fish are suitable for bass (see BRILL, TURBOT, SALMON).

Cold bass with various sauces. BAR FROID – Cook the fish, whole or in large pieces, in *Court-bouillon III* (see COURT-BOUILLON). Allow to cool in the liquor. Drain, and garnish with fresh parsley. Serve with a cold sauce.

Cold bass can also be prepared by following one of the recipes given for salmon and salmon trout. Cooked in *court-bouillon*, it can also be served with the garnishes used for large cold fish, such as hard-boiled eggs, stuffed artichoke hearts, lettuce hearts, *macédoines* of vegetables, etc.

Curried bass à l'indienne. BAR AU CURRIE, À L'INDIENNE – Cut the bass into uniform pieces. Cook as described in the recipe for *Curried fillets of brill* (see BRILL).

Bass Dugléré. BAR DUGLÉRÉ – Scale a bass weighing about 750 g. ($1\frac{3}{4}$ lb.). Cut into pieces of equal size. Melt some butter in a sauté pan, and add 1 tablespoon chopped onion, 4 peeled, seeded and chopped tomatoes, 1 tablespoon coarsely chopped parsley, a sprig of thyme, quarter of a bay leaf, and a pinch of grated garlic. Put the bass on this foundation, season, and moisten with $1\frac{1}{2}$ dl. ($\frac{1}{4}$ pint, $\frac{2}{3}$ cup) dry white wine. Bring to the boil, cover the pan, and transfer it to the oven, cooking for 12 to 15 minutes. Drain the pieces of bass and arrange them on a dish in the shape of the fish.

Remove the thyme and bay leaf from the pan, add 60 g. ($2\frac{1}{2}$ oz., $\frac{1}{3}$ cup) butter and 2 tablespoons (3 tablespoons) *Velouté sauce* (see SAUCE) made of fish stock. Pour the sauce over the fish and sprinkle with chopped parsley.

Alternatively, instead of using *velouté sauce*, thicken with a tablespoon of kneaded butter, or with $\frac{1}{2}$ tablespoon flour mixed with 2 tablespoons (3 tablespoons) water; this last is called *à la meunière*.

Fillets of bass. FILETS DE BAR – Bass is not often prepared in fillets, but when this method is adopted, the fillets should be skinned and well trimmed. All the recipes given for whole bass, as well as those given for bream (U.S. porgy or scup), mullet or river trout, can be applied to fillets of bass. So can recipes given for fresh cod, whiting, mackerel and, generally, for all sea fish.

Fried bass. BAR FRIT – This method is suitable for small-size bass. Scale the fish, make a few slits, and soak it in salted milk which has been boiled and allowed to get cold. Dredge with flour and deep-fry in sizzling oil.

Drain, dry, sprinkle with fine salt, and garnish with fried parsley and slices of lemon.

When no small bass are available, large fish, cut into slices or steaks, can be prepared in the same way.

Bass au gratin. BAR AU GRATIN – This method is mostly applied to fillets of bass. Proceed as described in the recipe for *Sole au gratin* (see SOLE).

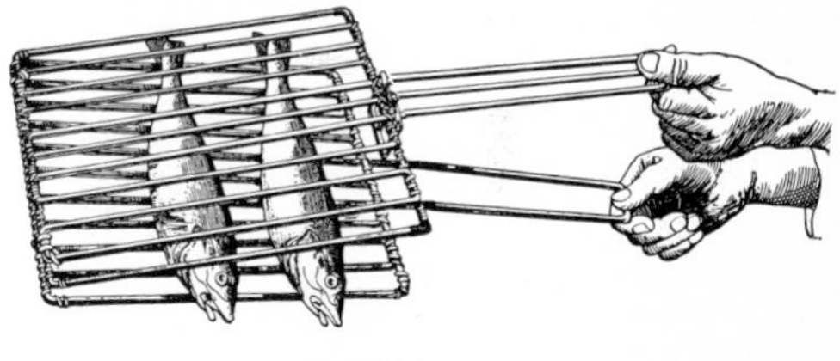

Double grill for small fish

Grilled bass with various sauces. BAR GRILLÉ – This method is applied to bass of medium size. Scale the fish, make a few shallow incisions, season, dredge with flour, brush with oil or melted butter, and grill on a moderate heat.

Turn the bass once during cooking, and baste with oil or melted butter from time to time.

Garnish with fresh parsley, and surround with slices of decoratively cut lemon. Serve with *Maître d'hôtel butter*, *Anchovy butter*, *Ravigote butter* (see BUTTER), or one of the special sauces recommended for grilled fish.

Bass à la livornaise. BAR À LA LIVORNAISE – This method is suitable for small-size bass. Scale 4 bass, season, and put them in a well-buttered or oiled fireproof dish on a foundation consisting of 2 dl. ($\frac{1}{3}$ pint, scant cup) *Tomato fondue* (see FONDUE) mixed with plenty of chopped onion, and flavoured with a pinch of pounded garlic.

Scatter breadcrumbs on top, sprinkle with oil, and cook in the oven for about 15 minutes. Sprinkle with chopped parsley before serving.

Bass à la meunière. BAR À LA MEUNIÈRE – Suitable for small-size bass. Scale them, make a few incisions, sprinkle with flour, and cook in a frying pan in butter. Use an oval-shaped pan, if possible.

When the fish is cooked and golden on both sides, place on a dish and sprinkle with chopped parsley and a few drops of lemon juice.

Heat the butter left in the pan until it browns, adding more if necessary, and pour it over the fish. Bass prepared in this way may be served with various garnishes (see SOLE, *Sole meunière*).

Bass à la portugaise I. BAR À LA PORTUGAISE – Scale a bass weighing about 300–400 g. (¾ lb.). Slit lightly along the back, season, and put into a buttered pan.

Boil equal quantities of white wine and concentrated fish stock down to a *fumet* (q.v.), pour over the fish, and cook in the covered pan for 15 minutes. Drain the bass, put in a fireproof dish, and surround with a border of thick *Tomato fondue* (see FONDUE). Boil down the pan juices, add 3 tablespoons (scant ¼ cup) *Velouté sauce* (see SAUCE) based on fish stock and some butter, and pour it over the bass.

Glaze in a very hot oven, and sprinkle with chopped parsley before serving.

Bass à la portugaise II. BAR À LA PORTUGAISE – Proceed as described for *Bass Dugléré* (but leaving the fish whole). Place in a fireproof dish. Boil down the pan juices, to which some butter has been added, pour over the fish, sprinkle with breadcrumbs, and glaze in a very hot oven.

Bass à la provençale. BAR À LA PROVENÇALE – Scale the bass, make a few shallow slits, dredge with flour, and fry briskly in oil.

When cooked and golden brown on both sides, put the fish in a fireproof dish, cover with *Provençale sauce* (see SAUCE), sprinkle with breadcrumbs and oil, and brown in a hot oven for a few minutes.

Sprinkle with chopped parsley before serving.

Stuffed braised bass with various garnishes. BAR BRAISÉ FARCI – Stuff a bass with one of the special forcemeats recommended for large fish. Braise it as described above.

BASTE. JUTER – To pour roasting or braising stock over a joint in order to keep it moist during cooking.

BAT – French culinary term for tail of fish. The length of fish is measured from eye to tail.

BAT. CHAUVE-SOURIS – Small mammal provided with membranous wings which enable it to fly. The meat is esteemed in certain oriental countries, notably in China.

BA-TA-CLAN – Pastry dessert said to have been invented by Lacam, the celebrated Parisian pastry-cook. It is still made in high-class Paris cake shops.

Pound 250 g. (9 oz., 1¾ cups) freshly blanched almonds in a mortar. Turn into a bowl, and add 9 eggs, one by one; mix well. Add 375 g. (13 oz., 1½ cups) fine sugar flavoured with vanilla, 1 dl. (6 tablespoons, scant ½ cup) rum, 125 g. (4 oz., 1 cup) sieved flour, and mix thoroughly until quite smooth.

Pour into a shallow tin with fluted edges and bake in a moderate oven. When cooked, leave to cool, and cover with vanilla icing.

BÂTARDE – Name given to *Butter sauce I* (see SAUCE).

BATAVIA – Variety of hearted lettuce in season in summer or winter.

BATEAUX – French name for china, glass or metal containers used for serving cold *hors-d'œuvre*. They are usually boat-shaped, hence their name.

BÂTONNETS or BÂTONS – Various preparations shaped in the form of little sticks.

Almond bâtonnets. BÂTONNETS AUX AMANDES – Fancy biscuits (cookies), which come into the category of *petits fours*.

Pound 250 g. (9 oz., 1¾ cups) blanched almonds in a mortar with 250 g. (9 oz., generous cup) fine sugar. Turn into a bowl and mix with 3 egg whites and 1 dl. (6 tablespoons, scant ½ cup) rum. Blend thoroughly into a smooth paste and roll out 2 cm. (¾ inch) thick on a marble slab lightly dusted with flour.

Cut the paste into strips 8 cm. (3 inches) wide, and cut the strips into *bâtonnets*, 2 cm. (¾ inch) wide. Dip them into lightly beaten egg white then into crystallised sugar. Brush baking trays with butter, sprinkle with flour, and bake the *bâtonnets* in a moderate oven (180°C., 350°F., Gas Mark 4).

Bâtons with vanilla icing. BÂTONS GLACÉS À LA VANILLE – Pound 250 g. (9 oz., 1¾ cups) blanched almonds with 250 g. (9 oz., generous cup) fine sugar in a mortar. Turn into a basin and add 3 egg whites and ½ teaspoon vanilla extract. Blend the mixture thoroughly and roll out on a lightly floured marble slab until the paste is 1 cm. (½ nch) thick and about 15 cm. (6 inches) wide. Coat with a layer of vanilla-flavoured *Royal icing* (see ICING). Cut into sticks 2 cm. (¾ inch) wide. Brush a baking tray with melted butter, sprinkle with flour, and bake the *bâtons* in a moderate oven (180°C., 350°F., Gas Mark 4).

Chocolate bâtonnets. BÂTONNETS AU CHOCOLAT – Proceed as in the recipe for *Almond bâtonnets*, using 250 g. (9 oz., 1¾ cups) almonds, 250 g. (9 oz., generous cup) fine sugar, 200 g. (7 oz., 1¾ cups) cocoa, 25 g., (1 oz., 2 tablespoons) vanilla-flavoured sugar, 3 egg whites.

Cumin bâtonnets. BÂTONNETS AU CUMIN – Add cumin to *Short pastry II* (see DOUGH), when rolling it out. Cut into small sticks, roll them, place on a buttered baking tray, brush with egg, and bake in a moderately hot oven (200°C., 400°F., Gas Mark 6).

Hazelnut bâtonnets. BÂTONNETS AUX AVELINES – These are made in the same way as *Almond bâtonnets*, replacing almonds with hazelnuts which have been blanched and dried in the oven. Flavour the mixture with kirsch.

Jacob's bâtons. BÂTONS DE JACOB – Cakes made from *Chou paste* (see DOUGH) in the shape of little hollow sticks filled with French pastry cream, and coated on top with sugar cooked to crack degree (150°C., 302°F.). (See ÉCLAIR.)

Royal bâtons (hot hors-d'oeuvre). BÂTONS ROYAUX – Roll out a piece of shortcrust paste and cut into small rectangles. Fill the middle of each with *Chicken and partridge forcemeat* (see FORCEMEAT). Roll each piece, sealing the ends well. Deep-fry in smoking hot fat. Garnish with fried parsley.

BATTERS FOR FRYING. PÂTE À FRIRE – **Frying batter I (Carême's recipe)** – 'Sift 350 g. (12 oz., 3 cups) flour into a bowl, mix with slightly warmed water in which 50 g. (2 oz., ¼ cup) butter has been melted. Stir to a soft paste, free from lumps. Add a pinch of salt and 2 tablespoons (3 tablespoons) brandy, stir well, and fold in 2 stiffly whisked egg whites. Use at once.'

Frying batter II – Mix 250 g. (9 oz., 2¼ cups) sifted flour, 1 tablespoon oil, 1½ dl. (¼ pint, ⅔ cup) beer, 2 dl. (⅓ pint, scant cup) warm water and a tablespoon brandy into a smooth batter, adding a pinch of fine salt. Just before using, fold in 2 stiffly whisked egg whites.

Frying batter (for fruit fritters glazed in the oven) – Mix the batter as described in the previous recipe, using 250 g. (9 oz., 2¼ cups) sifted flour, 2 tablespoons (3 tablespoons) melted butter, 1½ dl. (¼ pint, ⅔ cup) beer, 2 dl. (⅓ pint, scant cup) water, one whole egg, 1 tablespoon brandy, a pinch of sugar and a pinch of salt.

After mixing, keep in a warm place to ferment. Just before using, whisk the batter.

To glaze fruit fritters, drain after frying, place on a metal sheet which has been lightly sprinkled with icing sugar, and set in a hot oven.

Frying batter (for vegetable fritters) – The batter should be prepared at least an hour before use.

Mix 250 g. (9 oz., $2\frac{1}{4}$ cups) sifted flour with 4 tablespoons (5 tablespoons) melted butter, 2 whole eggs, a good pinch of salt, and enough water to make not too thick a batter.

Frying batter (for meat and fish fritters) – Put 250 g. (9 oz., $2\frac{1}{4}$ cups) sifted flour into a bowl. Make a well in the centre and put into it 4 tablespoons (5 tablespoons) oil or melted butter, 4 dl. ($\frac{3}{4}$ pint, scant 2 cups) slightly warmed water, and a good pinch of salt. Mix well with a wooden spoon.

Just before using, fold in 4 stiffly whisked egg whites.

Frying batter (à la provençale) – 'Mix 350 g. (12oz., 3 cups) sieved flour, 2 egg yolks, 4 tablespoons (5 tablespoons) Aix oil, and enough cold water to make a soft paste. Add a small pinch of salt, and fold in 2 stiffly whisked egg whites. Use at once.' (Carême's recipe).

Batters (sweet) – See DOUGH.

BAVARIAN CREAM. BAVAROIS – Cold sweet once known as *fromage bavarois*, the name Carême gives it in his *Traité des entremets de douceur*.

The name *bavarois* was given to it by a French chef who practised his art in a stately home in Bavaria.

This dish, of solid consistency, should not be confused with the liquid preparation known as the *bavaroise* (q.v.), which used to be called *crème bavaroise*, and, according to culinary historians, was invented in Bavaria towards the end of the seventeenth century.

The *bavarois* in past days was prepared quite differently from present-day methods; the mixture was bound only with clarified isinglass, not with egg yolks, as used in some modern recipes.

Bavarian cream mould

The following include several of Carême's recipes.

Basic Bavarian cream. BAVAROIS À LA CRÈME – Blend 500 g. (18 oz., $2\frac{1}{4}$ cups) fine sugar and 16 egg yolks in a small saucepan over low heat, adding a pinch of salt. When the mixture is quite smooth moisten with 1 litre ($1\frac{3}{4}$ pints, generous quart) milk which has been previously boiled and flavoured with a vanilla bean. Add 25 g. (1 oz.) gelatine which has been dissolved in cold water. Keep stirring until the mixture is thick enough to coat the spoon; do not boil. Transfer to a bowl and leave to cool, frequently fanning it to help the process.

As soon as the mixture begins to set, fold in 1 litre ($1\frac{3}{4}$ pints, generous quart) stiffly whipped cream and 100 g. (4 oz., $\frac{1}{2}$ cup) fine sugar.

Pour the *bavarois* into a mould which has been rinsed with iced water, cover with white paper, and chill for 2 hours in the refrigerator, or on crushed ice.

To loosen the *bavarois*, dip the mould in hot water, wipe it dry, and turn into a dish.

The same recipe may be used for *bavarois* flavoured with coffee, chocolate, tea, brandies and various liqueurs (anisette, Armagnac, Calvados, Curaçao, fine Champagne brandy, kirsch, kummel, rum, etc.), lemon, tangerine, orange, praline of burnt almond, hazelnuts, etc.

Bavarian cream à la cévenole. BAVAROIS À LA CÉVENOLE – Coat a mould with a layer of *Basic Bavarian cream*. Fill with a mixture of this cream and a purée of *marrons glacés*, flavoured with kirsch. Chill in the refrigerator.

Turn out the *bavarois* onto a dish, and decorate with *Chantilly cream* (see CREAMS). Surround with *marrons glacés*.

Bavarian cream à la créole. BAVAROIS À LA CRÉOLE – Coat a mould with sweet almond oil and fill it with alternate layers of rum-flavoured and pineapple-flavoured *Basic Bavarian cream*, mixed with a *salpicon* (q.v.) of bananas steeped in rum. Turn out onto a dish, decorate with *Chantilly cream* (see CREAMS) piped through a pastry-bag, and sprinkle with blanched, shredded pistachio nuts.

Bavarian cream à la normande. BAVAROIS À LA NORMANDE – Line a mould with a layer of Calvados-flavoured *Basic Bavarian cream*, fill with thick *Apple sauce* (see SAUCE) whisked with gelatine which has been dissolved in water.

Turn out on a dish and surround with apple quarters peeled, cooked in syrup, and well drained. Top with whipped cream.

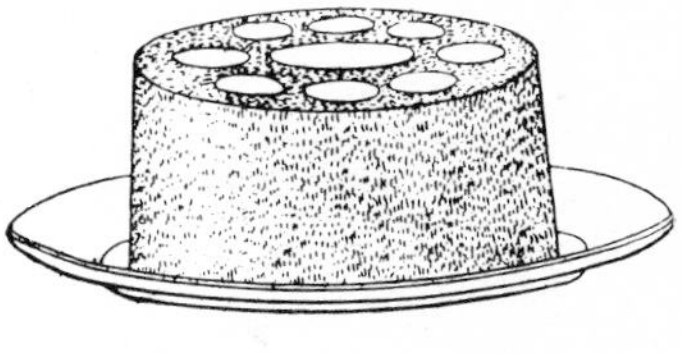

Bavarian cream, after Carême

Bavarian cream au parfait amour (Carême). FROMAGE BAVAROIS AU PARFAIT AMOUR – 'Shred half the peel of a lemon very finely. Boil 2 cups milk, add the shredded lemon, 6 crushed cloves and 225 g. (8 oz., 1 cup) sugar. Leave to infuse for an hour, and strain through a muslin cloth into a basin. Add 25 g. (1 oz.) slightly warmed and clarified isinglass, and a few drops of cochineal essence. Put the basin into a bowl of ice. As soon as the mixture begins to set, fold in whipped cream.'

Bavarian cream with pistachio nuts (Carême). FROMAGE BAVAROIS AUX NOIX VERTES – 'Shell about 100 choice pistachio nuts, pound them in a mortar, and moisten with a little water from time to time to prevent them turning oily. Dissolve 225 g. (8 oz., 1 cup) sugar in 2 cups cream. Put the pounded nuts into a bowl, and add the cream, a little at a time, stirring well. Leave for an hour, and strain through a fine sieve.

Add 25 g. (1 oz.) slightly warm clarified isinglass which has been dissolved in a little water. Pour the mixture into a mould or a medium-sized *terrine*, and place on crushed ice for 15 minutes. Stir well, (with a large silver spoon, if possible) and stir again from time to time. As soon as it begins to set, stir all the time until a smooth-flowing mixture is achieved. Add whipped cream, a little at a time, until the *bavarois* has a velvety texture.

Keep on crushed ice for an hour and a half before turning out onto a dish.

Bavarian cream made with fruit (*Robert Carrier*)

Bavarian cream aux roses (Carême). FROMAGE BAVAROIS AUX ROSES – 'Strip the petals off about 30 freshly picked roses, and put them, with a pinch of cochineal grains, into 225 g. (8 oz., 1 cup) clarified boiling sugar syrup. Cover, and when it has become just warm, add 25 g. (1 oz.) isinglass. Strain the mixture through muslin into a bowl, and when it begins to set, fold in whipped cream.'

Bavarian fruit cream. BAVAROIS AUX FRUITS – Put into a bowl 5 dl. (scant pint, $2\frac{1}{4}$ cups) fruit purée, 5 dl. (scant pint, $2\frac{1}{4}$ cups) heavy (30°) syrup, the juice of 3 lemons, and 25 g. (1 oz.) gelatine which has been dissolved in a little water and strained through muslin.

Blend well, and add $\frac{1}{2}$ litre (scant pint, $2\frac{1}{4}$ cups) whipped cream. Pour into a mould which has been coated with sweet almond oil (or rinsed in ice water) and leave to set for about $1\frac{1}{2}$ hours.

Mocha coffee Bavarian cream (Carême). FROMAGE BAVAROIS AU CAFÉ MOKA – 'Put 175 g. (6 oz., $1\frac{1}{2}$ cups) mocha coffee beans into a small saucepan, and heat on a moderate fire, stirring constantly until they acquire a reddish-yellow colour. Roasting is complete as soon as the beans become oily.

'Drop them into a basin containing 3 cups boiling milk, cover, and leave until the milk is just warm. Strain through a fine cloth. Add 225 g. (8 oz., 1 cup) sieved sugar and 25 g. (1 oz.) isinglass. Blend until quite smooth, and strain again.

'When the mixture begins to set, add whipped cream, and pour into a mould. Place on crushed ice until fully set.'

Strawberry Bavarian cream. BAVAROIS AUX FRAISES – Rub $2\frac{1}{2}$ dl. (scant $\frac{1}{2}$ pint, generous cup) strawberry pulp through a fine sieve, and add $2\frac{1}{2}$ dl. (scant $\frac{1}{2}$ pint, generous cup) heavy syrup (30°), the juice of a lemon, and 15 g. ($\frac{1}{2}$ oz.) gelatine which has been dissolved in a little water and strained through muslin. Add $2\frac{1}{2}$ dl. (scant $\frac{1}{2}$ pint, generous cup) whipped cream to the mixture.

Pour into a mould and chill on crushed ice, or in a refrigerator. Turn out onto a dish and surround with large hulled strawberries, sprinkled with fine sugar.

Apricot, peach, pineapple, pear, raspberry and other fruit *bavarois* can be prepared in the same way.

Striped chocolate and vanilla Bavarian cream. BAVAROIS RUBANÉ AU CHOCOLAT ET À LA VANILLE – Sift 250 g. (9 oz., generous cup) fine sugar into a saucepan, add 8 egg yolks and a pinch of salt. Stir over very low heat until the mixture is perfectly blended. Boil 5 dl. (scant pint, $2\frac{1}{4}$ cups) milk separately, add 1 vanilla bean. Add slowly to the other mixture, and stir constantly over low heat. When the resulting custard thickens sufficiently to coat a spoon, remove from the heat.

Strain the custard and divide in two parts. Add 50 g. (2 oz., 2 squares) melted chocolate to one part, and blend in whipped cream when it begins to set. Blend whipped cream similarly into the remaining custard mixture.

Rinse a mould in ice water, or brush with sweet almond oil. Fill with alternate layers of the two mixtures, taking care not to add a new layer until the preceding one has set properly. Place the mould on crushed ice, or in the refrigerator, and leave to set $1\frac{1}{2}$ to 2 hours. To loosen the *bavarois*, dip the mould in warm water, dry it, and turn the *bavarois* into a glass dish.

Striped Bavarian cream (various flavours). BAVAROIS RUBANÉS AUX PARFUMS DIVERS – Proceed as described in the previous recipe. Variegated Bavarian cream can be made by using alternate layers of vanilla and strawberry mixture (or any other red fruit), vanilla and coffee, vanilla and apricot, vanilla and pistachio nuts, etc.

Vanilla Bavarian cream (Carême). FROMAGE BAVAROIS À LA VANILLE – Add a vanilla bean to 3 cups cream and bring to the boil. Lower the heat and reduce the cream by one-third. Add 225 g. (8 oz., 1 cup) sieved sugar and 25 g. (1 oz.) isinglass. Blend thoroughly, strain through muslin into a basin, and place on crushed ice. When the mixture begins to set, fold in whipped cream.

Striped Bavarian cream

BAVAROISE – Pleasant beverage prepared in several ways from tea, syrup, milk, etc.

In the early part of the eighteenth century several Bavarian princes sojourning in Paris were in the habit of taking tea together at the *Café Procope*, rue des Fossés-Saint-Germain-des-Prés (today rue de l'Ancienne-Comédie): but they insisted that it should be served to them from crystal decanters, and preferred it sweetened with capillary syrup rather than sugar. Thence the name *bavaroise* was given to the new beverage. Other cafés began to serve it, simply by replacing the capillary syrup with clarified sugar cooked to the consistency of a syrup, and adding milk.

Bavaroise I – Mix together 2 dl. ($\frac{1}{3}$ pint, scant cup) very strong tea, 1 tablespoon fine sugar, 1 tablespoon sugar syrup (104°C., 220°F.) and an egg yolk. Whisk until the mixture becomes frothy. Add a little boiled milk and 5 teaspoons kirsch.

Flavourings can be rum, maraschino, or any other liqueur.

Bavaroise II – Whisk 4 egg yolks with 125 g. (4 oz., $\frac{1}{2}$ cup) fine sugar until thick. Add $\frac{1}{2}$ dl. (3 tablespoons, scant $\frac{1}{4}$ cup) syrup (104°C., 220°F.), $2\frac{1}{2}$ dl. (scant $\frac{1}{2}$ pint, generous cup) freshly made hot tea, and the same amount boiling milk. Whisk until the mixture is very frothy. Add 1 dl. (6 tablespoons, scant $\frac{1}{2}$ cup) rum, kirsch or Calvados.

The *bavaroise* can also be flavoured with orange, lemon or vanilla, which should first be infused in boiling milk.

BAVAROISE AUX CHOUX – French slang expression describing a mixture of absinth and orgeat.

BAY. LAURIER-SAUCE – Bay leaves are a traditional ingredient of the *bouquet-garni* (q.v.). The berries of the bay tree are used in a distillation of aromatic herbs called *Fioravanti*.

BAYONNE – Town in the Basses-Pyrénées where the egg and oil sauce called mayonnaise is said to have been invented. It is also known for Bayonne hams which are, in fact, made in a neighbouring town, Orthez.

The ham is usually eaten raw. It is also used to improve the flavour of *ragoûts* and sauces, and cooked as a garnish for eggs prepared in various ways.

Bayonne and the neighbouring region produce excellent local dishes. There are *garbures* (q.v.) (a mixture of cabbage, bacon, goose fat and rye bread, popular in the Pyrénées district), preserved goose, preserved pork, locally called *methode*. All the *charcuterie* of the Bayonne region is good, especially the black (blood) puddings.

Among the sweets, *pâté de cédrat* (a citron preserve), is delicious, and Bayonne chocolate is noted.

BEAN. HARICOT – A pulse of which there are many varieties, some edible, others ornamental. Among edible varieties are climbing beans, which grow to a height of 2 to 3 m. (6 to 10 feet), and are trained on bean poles. The dwarf varieties need no support. In most varieties the pod is tender and edible when young.

Edible bean pods fall under the general heading of green beans. In some varieties the pod remains tender and good to eat even when fully grown, but in the case of parchment-skinned beans, it becomes tough and leathery.

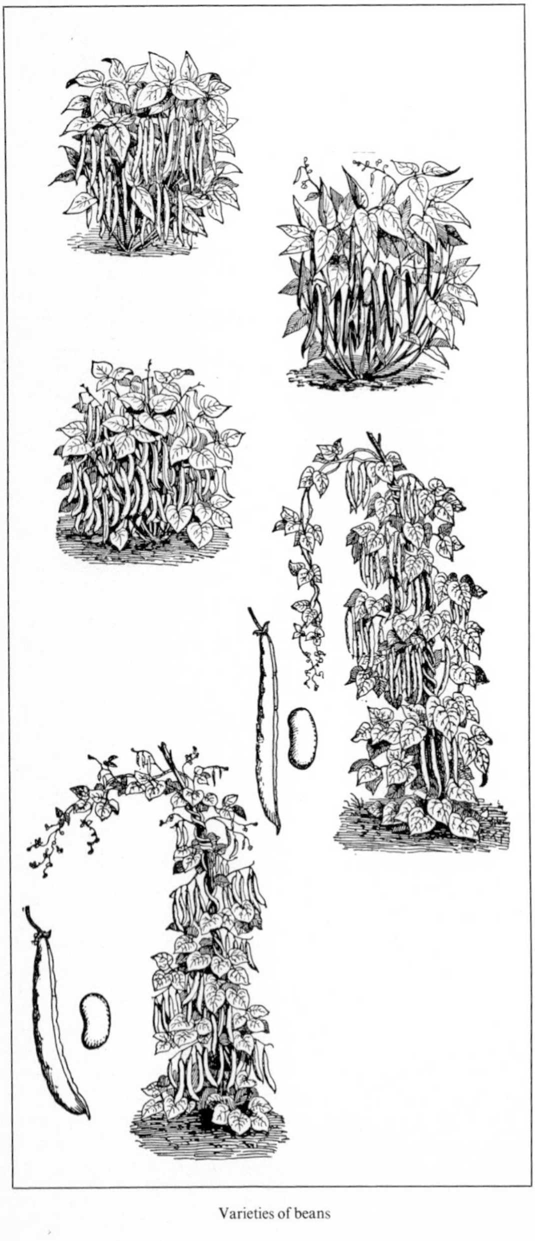

Varieties of beans

BROAD BEANS (U.S. Shell beans). FÈVES – Annual plant of the *Leguminosae* family, cultivated for its seeds, which serve as food for man and for animals. The broad bean, of which the *Windsor* is best known, is the common bean of Europe. Other well-known broad beans are the *lima bean*, a species originating in South America and cultivated extensively in California; the *soya bean* of China, Japan and India, now very widely cultivated. Some beans, such as the *horse bean* of Scotland and the *cow pea* of southern U.S.A. are chiefly used for forage.

The fresh broad beans that are commonly used in Europe do not have a very high food value. Dried beans, on the other hand, are rich in amino acids and potassium salts; they also contain large quantities of nitrogenous substances and Vitamins B and E. Their nutritive value is therefore greater than fresh beans. However, eaten in excess they can cause serious blood disorders (favism).

100 g. (4 oz.) unpodded beans yield approximately 50 g. (2 oz.) comestible beans.

To cook fresh broad beans. Shell the beans. Remove the tough outer skin and cook in boiling salted water with a bunch of savory. Drain, and proceed according to the selected recipe.

Fresh broad beans à l'anglaise. FÈVES FRAÎCHES À L'ANGLAISE – Cook the beans as indicated above, but leave in their skins. Drain, and serve with fresh butter.

Fresh broad beans in butter. FÈVES FRAÎCHES AU BEURRE – Proceed as for *Peas in butter* (see PEAS), and add chopped savory.

Broad beans in cream. FÈVES À LA CRÈME – Proceed as for *Peas in butter* (see PEAS). Moisten with thick fresh cream, and simmer for a minute or two.

Broad beans à la croque-au-sel. FÈVES À LA CROQUE-AU-SEL – Fresh broad beans served raw as an *hors-d'œuvre.* The guests shell the beans themselves, seasoning them with coarse salt. This *hors-d'œuvre* is popular all over the south of France.

Fresh broad beans à la française. FÈVES FRAÎCHES À LA FRANÇAISE – Shell and skin the beans, and cook as for *Peas à la française* (see PEAS), together with a bunch of savory.

Purée of fresh broad beans for garnishing. PURÉE DE FÈVES FRAÎCHES – Proceed as for *Purée of fresh garden peas* (see PEAS).

Purée of bean soup – See SOUPS AND BROTHS.

Fresh broad beans with savory. FÈVES FRAÎCHES À LA SARRIETTE – Shell and skin the beans, and cook in boiling salted water with a bunch of savory. Drain, return them to the pan, and shake over heat for a few seconds to get rid of any moisture left. Add fresh butter cut into small pieces. Mix carefully so as not to damage the beans.

FIELD BEANS. FÉVEROLES – European broad bean, smaller than the ordinary kind, cooked in the same way. These beans usually remain white. Field bean flour is sometimes added to wheaten flour for the manufacture of bread.

FLAGEOLET BEANS. HARICOTS FLAGEOLETS – Used mainly as a garnish (whether fresh or dried) for meat dishes. They are excellent with cuts of mutton or lamb, and make delicately flavoured purées. They are not common in U.S.A.

Fresh flageolets. HARICOTS FLAGEOLETS FRAIS – Small beans of a greenish colour. They are cooked in the same way as *Fresh white haricot beans* (see below). All recipes for haricot beans are suitable for flageolets.

FRENCH BEANS (U.S. String beans). HARICOTS VERTS – A delicately flavoured vegetable, which should be freshly picked, when they only need to be topped and tailed. With older beans, it is necessary to cut away the stringy edges.

Wash the beans in cold water, drain, and put them in a large saucepan full of boiling salted water ($1\frac{1}{2}$ teaspoons salt per litre, scant quart, generous quart water). Leave the saucepan uncovered and cook over a high flame. The beans are ready when they are tender but still firm in texture. Do not overcook. Drain thoroughly.

If the beans are to be kept for later use, or are to be dressed with oil and vinegar as a salad, they should be put in a colander under running water. If they are to be served at once in butter, cream or some other way, they should not be cooled after being boiled, but should be well drained.

French beans à l'anglaise. HARICOTS VERTS À L'ANGLAISE – Boil the beans in salted water, drain, and dry in a cloth. Serve with fresh butter.

French beans à la bonne femme. HARICOTS VERTS À LA BONNE FEMME – Boil the beans in salted water until they are three-parts cooked. Drain, and dry in a cloth.

Blanch about 200 g. (6 oz.) lean bacon, and cut into small dice. Fry in butter. Add 500 g. (1 lb.) of the nearly cooked beans, moisten with thickened brown veal stock, cover the pan, and simmer slowly until the beans are completely cooked.

When ready to serve, add a little butter and sprinkle with chopped parsley.

French beans in brown butter. HARICOTS VERTS AU BEURRE NOISETTE – Boil the beans in salted water as indicated above. Drain, and dry in a cloth. Brown 25 g. (1 oz., 2 tablespoons) butter in a pan, add the beans, season, and toss them well until they have absorbed the butter. Sprinkle with chopped parsley before serving.

French beans in butter à la maître d'hôtel. HARICOTS VERTS AU BEURRE À LA MAÎTRE D'HÔTEL – Boil the beans as indicated above, and drain thoroughly. Toss them in a pan over heat for a few moments to ensure that all moisture left in them has evaporated.

Season, and add butter cut into very small pieces – 90 to 100 g. butter to 500 g. beans (3 to 4 oz., scant $\frac{1}{2}$ cup butter per 1 lb. beans). Mix the beans in the butter so that they are all evenly coated. Sprinkle with parsley before serving.

French beans in cream I. HARICOTS VERTS À LA CRÈME – Boil the beans in salted water until they are three-parts cooked.

Drain, and dry in a cloth. Toss in melted butter, and cover with fresh thick cream. Simmer until the sauce has been reduced to half its original volume. Season.

French beans in cream II. HARICOTS VERTS À LA CRÈME – Follow the preceding recipe, but simmer the beans in a rather thin *Béchamel sauce* (see SAUCE) instead of cream. Add butter just before serving.

French beans prepared in this way and sprinkled with chopped parsley are called *haricots verts à la tourangelle*.

Dried French beans. HARICOTS VERTS SECS – Soak for a long time in cold water and cook like fresh French beans.

French beans à la française. HARICOTS VERTS À LA FRANÇAISE – Slice the beans in pieces about 3 cm. (1 inch) long. Proceed as for *Peas à la française* (see PEAS).

French beans au gratin. HARICOTS VERTS AU GRATIN – Proceed as for *French beans in cream*. Put the beans in an ovenware dish with grated cheese. Pour melted butter over them and sprinkle with more grated cheese. Brown slowly in the oven.

French beans in gravy. HARICOTS VERTS AU JUS – Boil the beans in salted water until they are three-parts cooked. Drain, and stew them slowly in butter. Moisten with thickened brown stock.

French beans à la lyonnaise. HARICOTS VERTS À LA LYONNAISE – Boil 500 g. (1 lb.) French beans in salted water. Drain and dry in a cloth.

Brown 100 g. (4 oz., 1 cup) chopped onions in butter and add the beans. Sauté all together; the beans should be very slightly browned. Sprinkle with chopped parsley and add a little vinegar.

Mixed beans. HARICOTS VERTS PANACHÉS – Boil separately, in salted water, equal quantities of French beans and small fresh kidney beans (flageolets). Drain thoroughly. Blend the two in butter or cream.

French beans à la normande. HARICOTS VERTS À LA NORMANDE – Proceed as for *French beans in cream*. After the beans are cooked, blend in yolks of eggs. Just before serving add butter.

French bean salad

French bean salad. SALADE DE HARICOTS VERTS – Boil the beans in salted water. Drain and dry in a cloth. Serve with a French dressing.

The salad can be seasoned while the beans are still hot, flavoured with finely chopped mixed herbs or with thinly sliced onion rings.

French beans sautéed in butter. HARICOTS VERTS SAUTÉS AU BEURRE – Boil the beans in salted water. Drain and dry in a cloth. Sauté in a heavy iron pan in butter, slightly browning the beans. Sprinkle with chopped parsley.

French beans sautéed à la provençale. HARICOTS VERTS SAUTÉS À LA PROVENÇALE – Proceed as for *French beans sautéed in butter*, substituting oil for the butter. Just before serving, add a little grated garlic and chopped parsley.

Preserved French beans – See PRESERVATION OF FOODS.

Purée of French beans. PURÉE DE HARICOTS VERTS – Boil the beans in salted water. Drain and dry in a cloth. Stew for a few minutes in butter, and rub them through a fine sieve. Add to this purée half its volume of mashed potato, and heat up the mixture. Add butter just before serving.

French beans in tomato sauce. HARICOTS VERTS À LA TOMATE – Boil the beans in salted water until they are three-parts cooked. Drain, and dry in a cloth. Stew for a few minutes in butter, and add several tablespoons *Tomato sauce* (see SAUCE). Simmer. Sprinkle with chopped parsley.

LIMA BEANS. HARICOTS DE LIMA – Lima beans, sometimes called *Cape peas*, are popular in America. They are green, like flageolets, and about the size of broad beans.

All recipes for *Fresh white haricot beans* (see below) are suitable for lima beans.

RED BEANS. HARICOTS ROUGES –

Fresh red beans (U.S. kidney beans). HARICOTS ROUGES FRAIS – Cook in the same way as *Fresh white haricot beans* (see below). All recipes for white beans are suitable for red beans.

Dried red beans. HARICOTS ROUGES SECS – Cook in the same way as *Dried white haricot beans* (see below). All recipes for dried white beans are suitable for dried red beans.

Red beans in red wine à la bourguignonne. HARICOTS ROUGES AU VIN ROUGE À LA BOURGUIGNONNE – Cook the beans in equal parts of water and red wine, with herbs and a piece of blanched lean bacon, or lean smoked bacon.

When the beans are soft, drain and fry them, together with some coarsely chopped bacon, in butter. Serve with creamed butter.

TONKA BEANS – The seed of a pulse rich in coumarin, a fragrant crystalline substance, analogous to volatile oils and camphor, used in the manufacture of some liqueurs.

FRESH WHITE HARICOT BEANS. HARICOTS BLANCS FRAIS – Cook in boiling salted water to which has been added aromatic vegetables and a *bouquet garni* (q.v.). They can also be cooked as follows:

Cut a carrot and an onion into quarters and brown them lightly in butter. Add the beans, a *bouquet garni* and 300 g. (11 oz.) blanched lean bacon. Cover with 3 litres (5¼ pints, 6½ pints) water, seasoned with salt.

Bring to the boil, and after 25 minutes add the beans. Simmer slowly. This method of cooking greatly improves the flavour of the beans, which can be dressed in a number of different ways.

(Dry white haricot beans must be soaked in cold water for a time before cooking.)

Fresh white beans à la bretonne. HARICOTS BLANCS FRAIS À LA BRETONNE – Cook the beans as indicated in the previous recipe. Drain, and put them in a pan. Blend in *Bretonne sauce* (see SAUCE) in the proportion of 2½ dl. (scant ½ pint, generous cup) sauce to 1 litre (scant quart, generous quart) cooked beans. Simmer for a few minutes, and sprinkle with chopped parsley.

Fresh white beans in butter. HARICOTS BLANCS FRAIS AU BEURRE – Cook the beans as indicated in the previous recipes. Drain, and put in a saucepan. Toss them over a flame for a few seconds to dry them. Blend in 75 g. (3 oz., 6 tablespoons) butter to every litre (scant quart, generous quart) cooked beans.

Fresh white beans en cassoulet. HARICOTS BLANCS FRAIS EN CASSOULET – The *cassoulet* of Languedoc is made from dried white haricot beans, but it may also be made from fresh beans. (See CASSOULET.)

Fresh white beans in cream. HARICOTS BLANCS FRAIS À LA CRÈME – Cook the beans as indicated in *Fresh white haricot beans*. Drain, and cover with thick fresh cream. Return to the pan, simmer until the cream has been reduced to half its volume, and add fresh cream. Mix well.

Estouffat of fresh white beans à l'occitane. ESTOUFFAT DE HARICOTS BLANCS FRAIS À L'OCCITANE – Brown 250 g. (½ lb.) belly of pork, or salt pork, diced and blanched, in butter or goose fat. Add 1 chopped onion, 2 peeled, chopped tomatoes, and a little crushed garlic. Cook for 10 minutes. Add 1½ litres (2¾ pints, 3¼ pints) white haricot beans which have been three parts cooked, and then drained. Cover, and finish cooking.

Fresh white beans à la lyonnaise. HARICOTS BLANCS FRAIS À LA LYONNAISE – Cook and drain the beans. To each litre (scant quart, generous quart) beans add 2 onions thinly sliced and cooked in butter until tender. Simmer for a few minutes in a casserole. Sprinkle with 2 tablespoons (3 tablespoons) chopped parsley.

Fresh white beans with parsley. HARICOTS BLANCS FRAIS AUX FINES HERBES – Proceed as for *Fresh white beans in butter*, with chopped parsley added.

Purée of fresh white beans. PURÉE DE HARICOTS BLANCS FRAIS – Cook the beans, drain, and rub through a fine sieve. Warm this purée, stirring with a wooden spoon until it is smooth. Before serving, add fresh butter in the proportion

Haricot beans (*Nicolas*)

of 100 g. (4 oz., $\frac{1}{2}$ cup) butter to 500 g. (generous 1 lb., 2 cups) purée.

If the bean purée is to be served as a vegetable or a garnish it should be fairly thick.

Fresh white bean salad. SALADE DE HARICOTS BLANCS FRAIS – Cook and drain the beans. Put them in a salad bowl and dress with oil and vinegar, season with salt, pepper and chopped mixed herbs (parsley, chervil and chives). Mix well.

This salad needs a lot of seasoning. Onion rings or chopped onion may be added to it.

DRIED WHITE HARICOT BEANS (U.S. Horticultural beans). HARICOTS BLANCS SECS – Dried white haricot beans are usually soaked for a long time in water, but this traditional practice is a bad one. If dried beans or other dried vegetables have to be soaked they should be left for a short time only. Some recipes recommend 12 or even 24 hours of soaking, whereas soaking, even for a few hours, may cause slight fermentation which noticeably spoils the flavour of the beans and can also make them slightly poisonous. To swell the beans, $1\frac{1}{2}$ to 2 hours soaking is sufficient.

If the beans are of good quality and have been dried within the year, they can be cooked without soaking.

Pick through the beans and wash them. Put them in a deep saucepan with plenty of cold water, and bring slowly to the boil. Skim. Season. Flavour with aromatic vegetables (onions stuck with cloves, quartered carrots, a *bouquet garni* (q.v.) and a small clove of garlic). Cover the pan and simmer very slowly.

In some cases, especially for *cassoulet* (q.v.) and *estouffat* (q.v.) it is advisable to cook the dried beans with fat. This is done by adding to the stock salted bacon, chine of salt pork or knuckle of pork, and fresh pork skin. This adds flavour to the beans.

Once cooked, dried white beans can be used in the same ways as fresh white beans: in butter, *à la bretonne*, *en cassoulet*, *en estouffat*, *à la lyonnaise*, in cream, with herbs, as a purée, in salad, etc.

Dried white beans à l'américaine. HARICOTS BLANCS SECS À L'AMÉRICAINE – Cook the beans in the usual way, adding 500 g. (generous 1 lb.) lean bacon to a litre ($1\frac{3}{4}$ pints, generous quart) dried haricot beans. Drain, trim and dice the bacon.

Mix the beans with tomato sauce, add the bacon and simmer until the bacon is well cooked.

Dried white beans à l'anglaise. HARICOTS BLANCS SECS À L'ANGLAISE – Boil the beans in water with seasoning and herbs, and drain. Serve with fresh butter.

Dried white beans à la berrichonne. HARICOTS BLANCS SECS À LA BERRICHONNE – Proceed as for *Dried white beans au gratin* (see below). Alternate layers of beans and thick mutton hash in an ovenware dish. Sprinkle with breadcrumbs, pour melted butter over, and brown in the oven.

Dried white beans à la charcutière. HARICOTS BLANCS SECS À LA CHARCUTIÈRE – Cook the beans with a piece of desalted lean raw ham, and herbs. When the ham is cooked, drain it and cut into coarse dice. Drain the beans thoroughly. Brown 150 g. (5 oz., $1\frac{1}{4}$ cups) chopped onion in butter. Add the beans and simmer, presently adding the diced ham.

Transfer to a buttered ovenware dish. Cook 6 small pork sausages (*crépinettes*) in butter, and press them down on the beans. Sprinkle with breadcrumbs, and add the butter in which the sausages were cooked. Brown slowly.

Dried white beans au gratin. HARICOTS BLANCS SECS AU GRATIN – Cook and drain the beans, and add some concentrated veal stock. Pour into a buttered ovenware dish, sprinkle with toasted breadcrumbs, and add melted butter. Brown slowly in the oven.

Dried white beans in tomato sauce. HARICOTS BLANCS SECS AU TOMATES – Cook and drain the beans. To each litre (scant quart, generous quart) beans add 3 dl. ($\frac{1}{2}$ pint, $1\frac{1}{4}$ cups) *Tomato fondue* (see FONDUE) flavoured with a little garlic and a tablespoon chopped parsley. Simmer all together in a pan for a few minutes, and serve.

BEAR. OURS – Bear meat can only be used after it has been marinated for a long time. It is not particularly tasty and is often tough. Prepare in any way suitable for wild boar or venison. Some gastronomes consider bear's paws to be a great delicacy.

Bear ham. JAMBON D'OURS – This ham, common in Russia and some European countries, is cured in the same way as pork ham. It is eaten cooked or raw. All recipes for pork ham are suitable for bear ham.

Bear's paw. PATTE DE L'OURS – The earliest delicacy known to the Chinese. Mencius, who lived about a hundred years after Confucius, said: 'Fish is what I like, so are bear's paws; but if I cannot have both, I will forego the fish and choose the bear's paw.'

The supply of this delicacy is now very limited, and is to be had, if at all, in north China. Its taste is unique. Mr. Cheng, one-time ambassador to the Court of St. James', said: 'The nearest comparison is that it is like the fat part of the best ham, or rather much better, for it has not the greasiness of the latter. It is so smooth and delicious that it simply melts in the mouth.'

To cook. Wrap the paw in clean mud and bake in the oven. When the mud becomes firm like clay, take the paw out of the oven, leave to cool, and peel off the mud – this will automatically tear off the hairy skin of the paw. Simmer in water, changing the water frequently to get rid of its gamey smell and taste.

When the paw has become very soft and 'tasteless', cook over low heat with shredded chicken meat, lean ham, sherry and just enough water to enable the ingredients to yield a thick gravy. Cut in slices, like ham.

BEARBERRY. RAISIN D'OURS – See ARBUTUS.

BÉARN, PAYS BASQUE, BIGORRE – The art of cookery is highly esteemed in these three picturesque provinces of the Pyrenees.

Culinary specialities – Among the many notable dishes are *garbure*, a substantial soup; *lou trebuc*, preserved goose or pork; *toulia* in Bigorre and *ouliat* in Béarn, onion soup to which a dash of vinegar is sometimes added, and which is also made of cheese, tomatoes, leeks and garlic, when it takes the name of *soupe du berger*.

Poule au pot d'Henri IV is a historic dish; tender lamb is to be had in the Ossau valley in Béarn, mutton cutlets in Barèges; there are also *daube à la béarnaise*, or *estouffat*; preserved goose, pork, turkey and duck.

Wines – Béarn produces excellent local wines. The *département* of the Basses-Pyrénées produces several wines that come under the categories of the *appellations d'origine* and V.D.Q.S.

The Jurançon is the best known of the *appelations d'origine* wines. It was with this wine that the King of Navarre moistened the lips of his nephew, the future Henry IV. It is a robust, rosy-tinged wine with an unusual, mellow bouquet, and comes from the so-called 'Manseng' vine. This vine, together with the Sémillon and Sauvignon, also gives the Pacherenc de Vicbilh, a white wine produced in the north of the province.

The Madiran is a very strong wine, the perfect accompaniment to the *cuisine* of the region. Among the V.D.Q.S.

Buffet set out for a formal occasion (*Potel and Chabot. Phot. Nicolas*)

Sauveterre de Béarn, Béarn (*French Government Tourist Office*)

there is the Irouléguy, the red wine of the Basque country, the white and red wines of Béarn, the Rousselet, and the very dry rosés of Béarn – which are beginning seriously to rival those of Provence.

Paul de Cassagnac, a great gourmet, who studied the wines of the Adour basin, quotes among the remarkable vintages of the Madiran those of 1870, 1886, 1898, 1904 and 1916. He had also occasion to drink a Madiran of 1848 which was still 'at the height of its form'.

'The Portet is a white wine, gathered late, towards the end of November. It is sweet and soft, or dry, depending on the year.

'The characteristic feature of the Jurançon is its sweetness, which does not destroy its bouquet or turn it into a syrup. The vintage years are mostly irregular; often the good qualities of Jurançon are swamped in the excess of sugar. 1886, 1905 and 1916 produced splendid results.'

A red Jurançon (Bouchy) is also made in Béarn and is greatly esteemed as a table wine, but it cannot compare with white Jurançon.

Map of Béarn

BÉARNAISE SAUCE – This famous sauce is said to have originated in Béarn, though some culinary writers assert that it originated at Saint-Germain-en-Laye and was named in honour of Henry IV, the *Great Béarnais*. But in fact the Henry IV pavilion dates as a restaurant from the year 1836 and the recipe for *Béarnaise sauce* first appeared in 1818 in *la Cuisinière des villes et des campagnes*.

BEAST. BÊTE – Animals intended for slaughter, which come under the general term of livestock, are enumerated under that heading. In addition, some beasts of burden, such as horse, mule, donkey and camel, are edible.

Among the wild animals, i.e. ground game, all of which are edible, are deer, chamois, fallow-deer, red deer, wild boar.

BÉATILLES (Titbits) – Cocks' combs and kidneys, lambs' sweetbreads, mushrooms, used as a garnish for *vol-au-vent*, *bouchées* and *tourtes* (q.v.), bound with a *Velouté sauce* or *Suprême sauce* (see SAUCE).

Ragoût of béatilles (titbits) – Here is an old recipe:

'Gently cook in butter 250 g. (9 oz.) lambs' sweetbreads (which have previously been soaked in cold water and blanched). Skin and soak in cold water 125 g. (4 oz.) cocks' combs, and cook in a *court-bouillon* (q.v.). Add 25 g. (1 oz.) cocks' kidneys, cooked in 1 dl. (6 tablespoons, scant $\frac{1}{2}$ cup) Madeira and a tablespoon butter. Sauté briskly in butter 250 g. (9 oz.) sliced and seasoned chicken livers. Cook 250 g. (9 oz.) trimmed and washed mushrooms in butter. Put the lambs' sweetbreads, chicken livers, cocks' combs and kidneys and the mushrooms in a saucepan. Add 125 g. (4 oz.) sliced truffles and $1\frac{1}{2}$ dl. ($\frac{1}{4}$ pint, $\frac{2}{3}$ cup) Madeira. Simmer with a lid on.

'Make a *Velouté* (q.v.) using concentrated chicken stock. Add to it half its volume of fresh cream. Boil down by half. Lace with a little Madeira, add some butter, strain, and pour over the *ragoût*.'

BEAUGENCY – Small town in Loiret, producing wine which resembles the Basse-Bourgogne (Lower Burgundy) wines.

BEAUHARNAIS (À LA) – Method of preparing small cuts of meat, mainly *tournedos*.

Garnish with small artichoke hearts and *Béarnaise sauce* (see SAUCE), with a purée of tarragon added to it; and little potato balls.

BEAUJOLAIS – Ancient French region that has given its name to a 'gulping' wine with a very strong bouquet which must be drunk when it is young and fresh. Léon Daudet said that Lyon was watered by three rivers: the Rhône, the Saône and the Beaujolais. The *appellation* 'Beaujolais' is linked with the viticultural region of Burgundy (q.v.).

BEAUMONT – Savoy cheese in season from October to June.

BEAUNE – Sub-prefecture of the Côte-d'Or. Famous since the Middle Ages for the excellence of its wines. It has given its name to an *appellation contrôlée*.

The white and red wines of the southern part of the Côte-d'Or are classed under the name of 'Côte de Beaune'. They are among the finest of the Burgundy wines (see BURGUNDY).

The annual wine auction of the *Hospices de Beaune* attracts buyers from all over the world.

BEAUVILLIERS – Beauvilliers was a great *cuisinier*. He served as Steward of the Household to the Count of Provence and Attaché Extraordinary of the Royal Household.

The restaurant which he founded (in 1782, according to Brillat-Savarin, in 1786 according to others) was situated at 26 rue de Richelieu and was called *la Grande Taverne de Londres*. It can be considered the first real restaurant to be opened in Paris. Rivarol, Pelletier, Champcenetz, etc. were

A Beaujolais wine-cellar (*French Government Tourist Office*)

habitués and more than one issue of the *Journal des Apôtres* was composed after a good dinner in another restaurant that Beauvilliers owned in rue de Valois. He bought three arcades of the Palais-Royal in 1790 for 157,000 francs.

During the turmoil of the Revolution *la Grande Taverne de Londres* had to close its doors. Towards the end of the *Directoire*, Beauvilliers reopened it. In 1824 he wrote his book *l'Art du cuisinier*, which for a long time remained an authoritative standard work. Brillat-Savarin wrote:

'Beauvilliers had a prodigious memory. He recognised and welcomed people whom he had not seen for twenty years, people who may only have eaten at his restaurant once or twice.

'He would advise which dish not to take, which to snap up, and would then order a third one which no one else would have thought of; he would have wine brought up from the vaults, to which only he had the key... But this rôle of a host lasted but a moment and having accomplished it he would vanish. And a little while later the amount of the dinner bill and the bitterness of paying it showed clearly that one had dined with a great restaurateur. Beauvilliers made his fortune, lost it and made it again several times.'

BEAUVILLIERS – Garnish for braised meat consisting of spinach kromeskies, tomatoes stuffed with a purée of brains, and salsify sautéed in butter.

BEAUVILLIERS AND BONVALET – These two cakes, the recipes for which are almost identical, were created towards the middle of the nineteenth century.

One of Beauvilliers' old pupils. Monnier, set up a cake shop in rue Monsieur-le-Prince and, as homage to his teacher, named his creation after him. This was the first cake intended for travel, wrapped in tinfoil.

The Bonvalet cake was created by Jules Leroy, head pastry-cook at Machin's, 99 rue de Turenne, and he dedicated it to a Monsieur Bonvalet in 1869. Here is the recipe for these cakes, as given by Philéas Gilbert:

'Pound 200 g. (7 oz., scant 1½ cups) almonds with an equal amount of sugar, add 5 egg whites little by little. Rub this mixture through a sieve.

'Blend 500 g. (18 oz., 2¼ cups) sugar with 350 g. (12 oz., 1½ cups) butter and 4 whole eggs in a bowl. When quite smooth, add the almond mixture, 175 g. (6 oz., 1¾ cups) fine cake flour, the same amount of rice flour and potato flour. Add 7 egg whites whisked to a stiff froth. Cook in a moderate oven (160°C., 325°F., Gas Mark 3) in a special cake-baking tin (with a hole in the middle) called *à trois frères*, sprinkled with potato flour.

'When the cake is cold, ice it with kirsch icing and fill the centre with *Chantilly cream* (see CREAMS) or *Plombière ice cream*' (see ICE CREAMS AND ICES).

BEAVER. CASTOR – A mammal rare in Europe but common in U.S.A. Its meat is sometimes eaten, but has a rather disagreeable musky flavour.

BEC (Beak) – Word often used in French colloquial expressions, such as *rincer le bec* (to wet one's whistle), which means to drink; *tortiller du bec* (to wolf down, to make short work of food), which means to eat; *fin bec*, which means a gourmet.

BEC-PLAT ('Flat-beak', i.e. Shoveller) – Common French name for spoon-bill duck, called so because of its flat beak. It can be prepared in all the ways suitable for *Wild duck* (see DUCK).

BEC-POINTU – French name for white skate. They call it 'sharp beak' because its head is elongated and the body oval. It can be prepared as ordinary skate (q.v.).

BÉCARD (Hooked nose) – French term for old male salmon. Its snout begins to protrude like a hooked beak, hence the name. (See SALMON.)

BÉCASSEAU – French name for the young woodcock, until its seventh month.

All the methods of preparation given for woodcock are applicable, but *becasseau* are mostly cooked on a spit.

Woodcock

BÉCHAMEIL (Louis de) – Marquis de Nointel, a financier who made his fortune during the Fronde (the rising of the aristocracy and the Parliament against Mazarin in 1648–53) and got himself the post of Lord Steward of the Royal Household to Louis XIV. The invention of *béchamel sauce* is attributed to him but is more likely to have been the invention of a court chef who dedicated it to Béchameil as a compliment.

The old Duc d'Escars said: 'That fellow Béchameil has all the luck. I was serving breast of chicken *à la crème* twenty years before he was born, but I have never had the chance of giving my name to the most insignificant of sauces!'

BÉCHAMEL SAUCE – Was *béchamel sauce* really invented by Marquis Louis de Béchameil? Was this financier a gastronome and a gourmet, and was he in any way competent in the culinary art? We do not know, but everything seems to indicate that, in fact, *béchamel sauce*, being a major sauce, must have been perfected by one of the *queux de semestre* – cooks in the service of the royal kitchen.

Originally, *béchamel* was made by adding a liberal amount of fresh cream to a thick *velouté sauce*. Nowadays *béchamel* is made by pouring boiling milk on white *roux* (blend of butter and flour). When a meat *béchamel* is wanted, lean veal, diced and simmered in butter with a minced onion, is added. (See SAUCE.)

Béchamel sauce (Carême's recipe) – 'When the *velouté* is thick, bind it with egg yolks and thick cream. Stir with a wooden spoon to make sure the sauce does not stick to the pan. Remove it from the heat, add a piece of butter the size of a walnut and a few tablespoons of thick double cream. Add a pinch of grated nutmeg, sieve through a white cloth and keep hot in a *bain-marie*.'

BECQUETER – French slang word which means 'to peck at food'.

BEDSTRAW. GAILLET – Plant of the *Rubiaceae* family. The flowering tops of the yellow bedstraw or cheese-rennet contain a substance which is used in the curdling of milk. It is used in the preparation of Cheshire cheese.

BEECH. HÊTRE – Handsome tree found in upland groves. Beech nut is good to eat. Beech oil is extracted from these nuts, and is second only to olive oil in quality.

Beech nut. FAINE – (See above.) Its flavour is midway between that of the hazelnut and the chestnut, with a slightly astringent taste which disappears when roasted, as in the case of chestnuts.

Cattle market at Bordeaux (*French Government Tourist Office*)

BEEF. BOEUF – Beef is the most fortifying and most nourishing of all red meat.

In France, there are three qualities of beef, graded according to breed, age, state of fattening, work done and sex of the animal (for beef includes the meat of bullocks, heifers, cows and bulls).

The English have long specialised in rearing and feeding cattle for beef. County Durham Shorthorns were imported into France to improve the strain of beef-producing stock. The Durham-Manceau crossbreeds, Charolais, Limousin, Garonne, Normandy and Salers are also good for fattening.

Charolais cattle

Prime beef is bright red in colour, firm and elastic to the touch. It has a fresh smell; the fat intermingles with the lean, peppering it with white or slightly yellowish grains of fat. Blotting paper applied to the surface should never be covered with greasy spots, as in the case of horse meat.

In France beef is classified in three categories according to its market value, which depends on how firm and fine-grained the texture is, as well as on the proportion of sinews and fat:

First category. Fillet, porterhouse steak, sirloin, top rump, rump steak, silverside and inner parts of the flank and round.

Second category. Top of sirloin, plate, top ribs, fore-rib and three-rib, shoulder of beef, chuck end of clod, and clod.

Third category. Flank, brisket, leg of beef, neck, ox-cheek, shin, ox-knees, shin of beef, knuckle.

Cows' meat is inferior to that of bullocks, generally speaking, although the flesh of young heifers and sterile cows can often be extremely good. Bull's meat is tough; it swells a great deal in cooking, but is not suitable for anything except the stockpot. The meat of a young bullock is usually the best.

Good quality beef is 97 per cent assimilable (provided it is not eaten to excess) and, since it leaves little residue, is easily digested. Eating beef to excess, that is to say, in larger quantities than the digestive juices can cope with (saturation point varies from individual to individual) leads to intestinal disorders. The fattier the piece of beef, the more calories it provides. However, an excessive amount of meat fat is difficult to digest, which explains why so many people eat the meat and leave the fat.

Aiguillette de boeuf – French term for the part which is also called *pointe de culotte* and *pièce de boeuf*. This is the top part of the rump and is usually braised or poached.

Baron of beef. BARON DE BOEUF – Joint served in England at Christmas time. It comprises the two sirloins and a part of the ribs.

This large joint is treated as *Roast sirloin à l'anglaise* (see below).

Beefsteak. BIFTECK – This word, of English origin, defines a slice of beef taken from the fillet and grilled. The name is also given to a slice of beef taken from the sirloin, or *contre-filet*.

Instead of grilling beefsteak, it may also be fried in butter or lard. For recipes see *Entrecôte, Chateaubriand, Contre-filet*, etc. In France, minced beef, served raw or cooked, is also called *bifteck*.

Beefsteak à l'américaine. BIFTECK À L'AMÉRICAINE – Trim 400 g. (14 oz.) fillet of beef, cut off fat, mince the meat finely, and shape into flat cakes. Make a little nest in the centre of each 'steak' and slip a raw yolk of egg into it.

Serve with the beef cakes chopped onion and parsley, and capers pickled in vinegar.

This dish is often prescribed in a building-up diet.

Beefsteak à l'andalouse. BIFTECK À L'ANDALOUSE – Mince 400 g. (14 oz.) beef finely, add to it 50 g. (2 oz., $\frac{1}{2}$ cup) chopped onion lightly fried in butter, with a pinch of pounded garlic. Season and shape into flat cakes. Dredge with flour and fry in oil.

Arrange the beef cakes on half tomatoes which have been sautéed in oil. Fill the centre of the dish with rice pilaf. Dilute the pan juices left over from frying the meat with 1 dl. (6 tablespoons, scant $\frac{1}{2}$ cup) sherry; boil down, add butter and pour over the beef cakes.

Beefsteak à cheval. BIFTECK À CHEVAL – Season the steak with salt and pepper and sauté quickly in hot butter. Arrange on a plate with one or two fried eggs on top. Pour butter and the cooking juices over the beef.

Beefsteak pie (English cookery). PÂTÉ CHAUD DE BOEUF À L'ANGLAISE – Cut $1\frac{1}{2}$ kg. ($3\frac{1}{4}$ lb.) best quality lean beef into slices 1 cm. ($\frac{1}{2}$ inch) thick. Season with salt, pepper and grated nutmeg, and sprinkle with chopped onion and parsley. Put the slices into a pie dish. Add stock or water.

rib

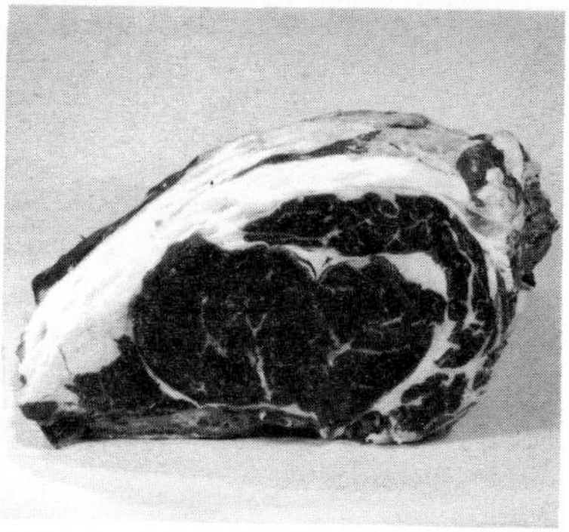

entrecôte

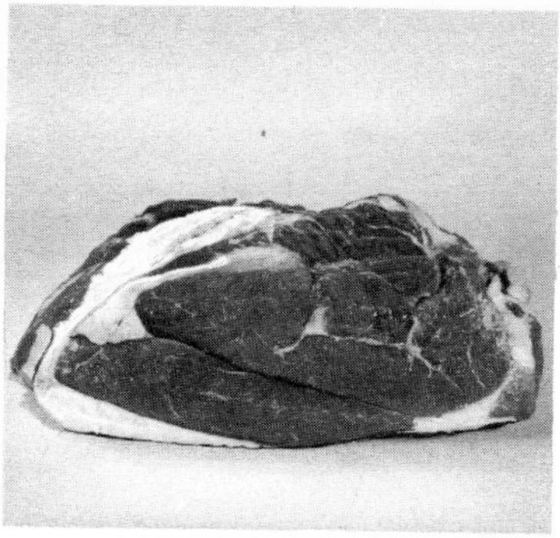

rump steak

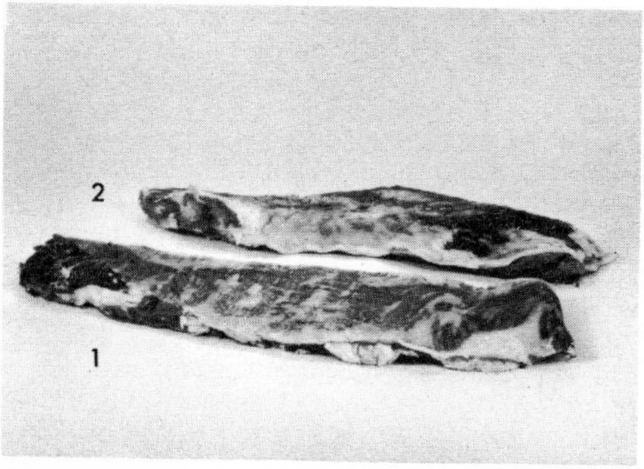

1, flank; 2. skirt

brisket

top rump

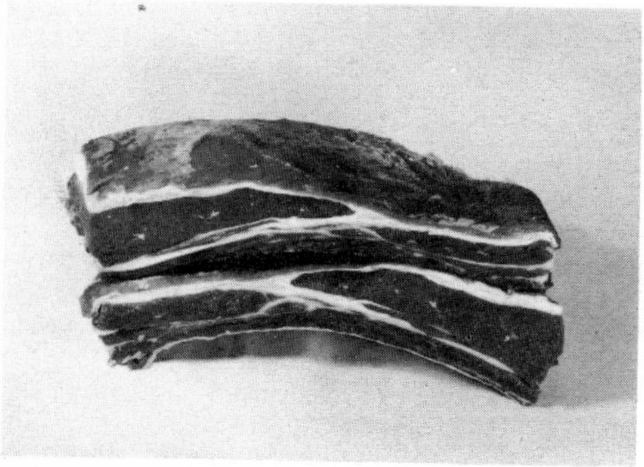

top rib

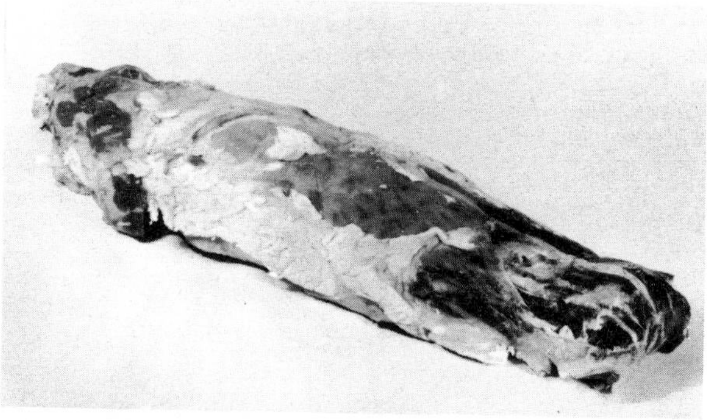

fillet

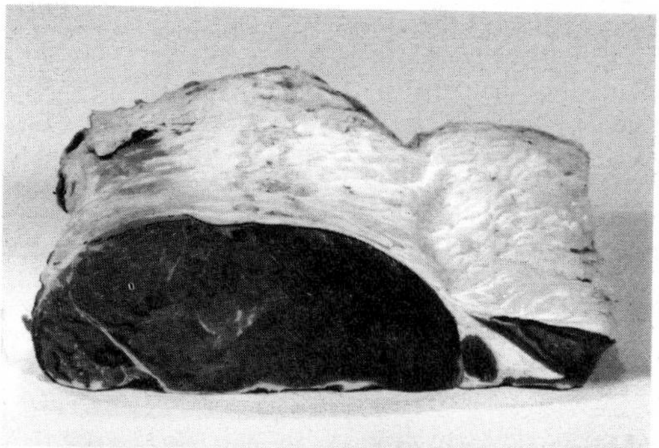

contre-filet

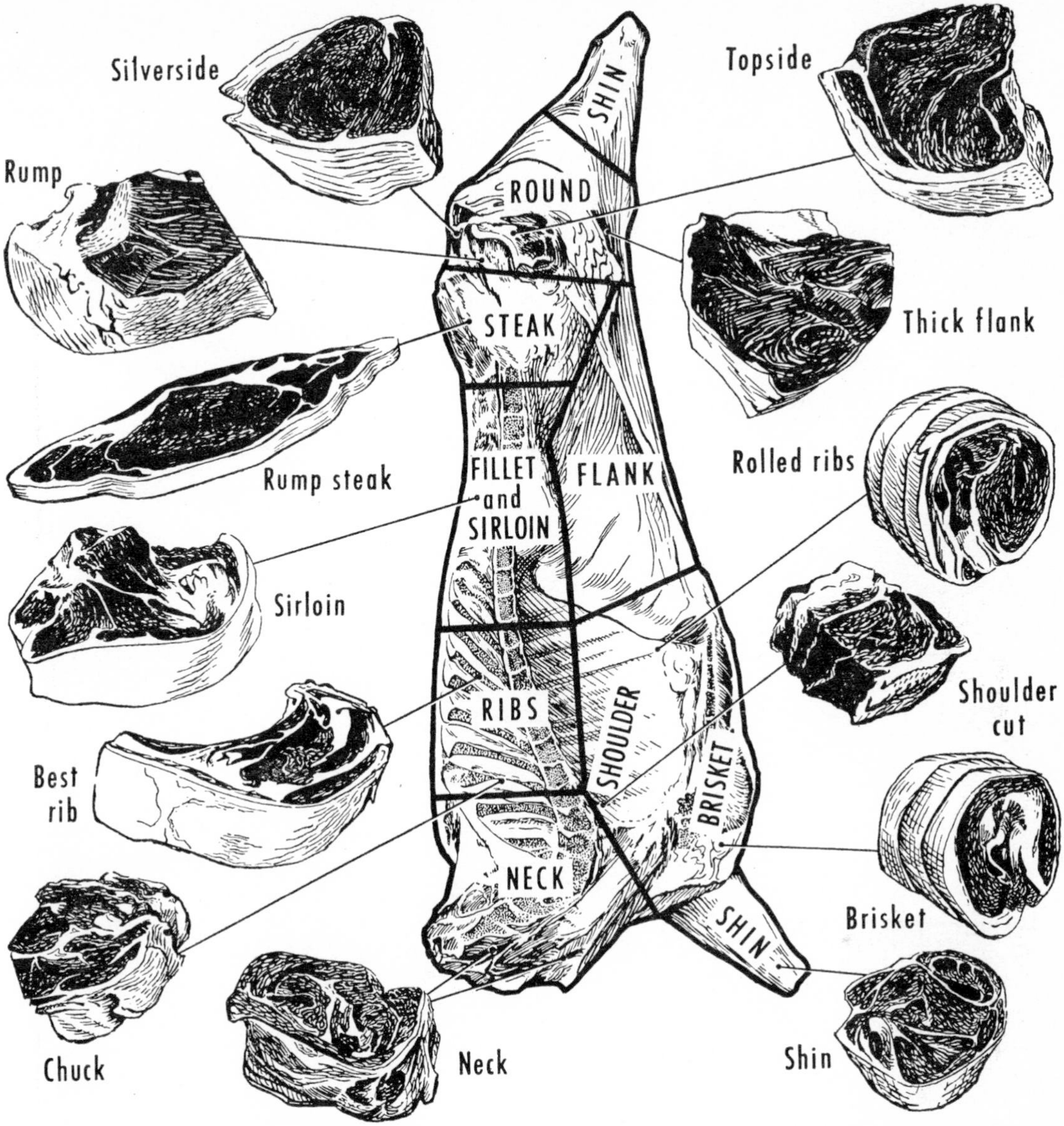

English cuts of beef

Bifteck à cheval

Beefsteak pie

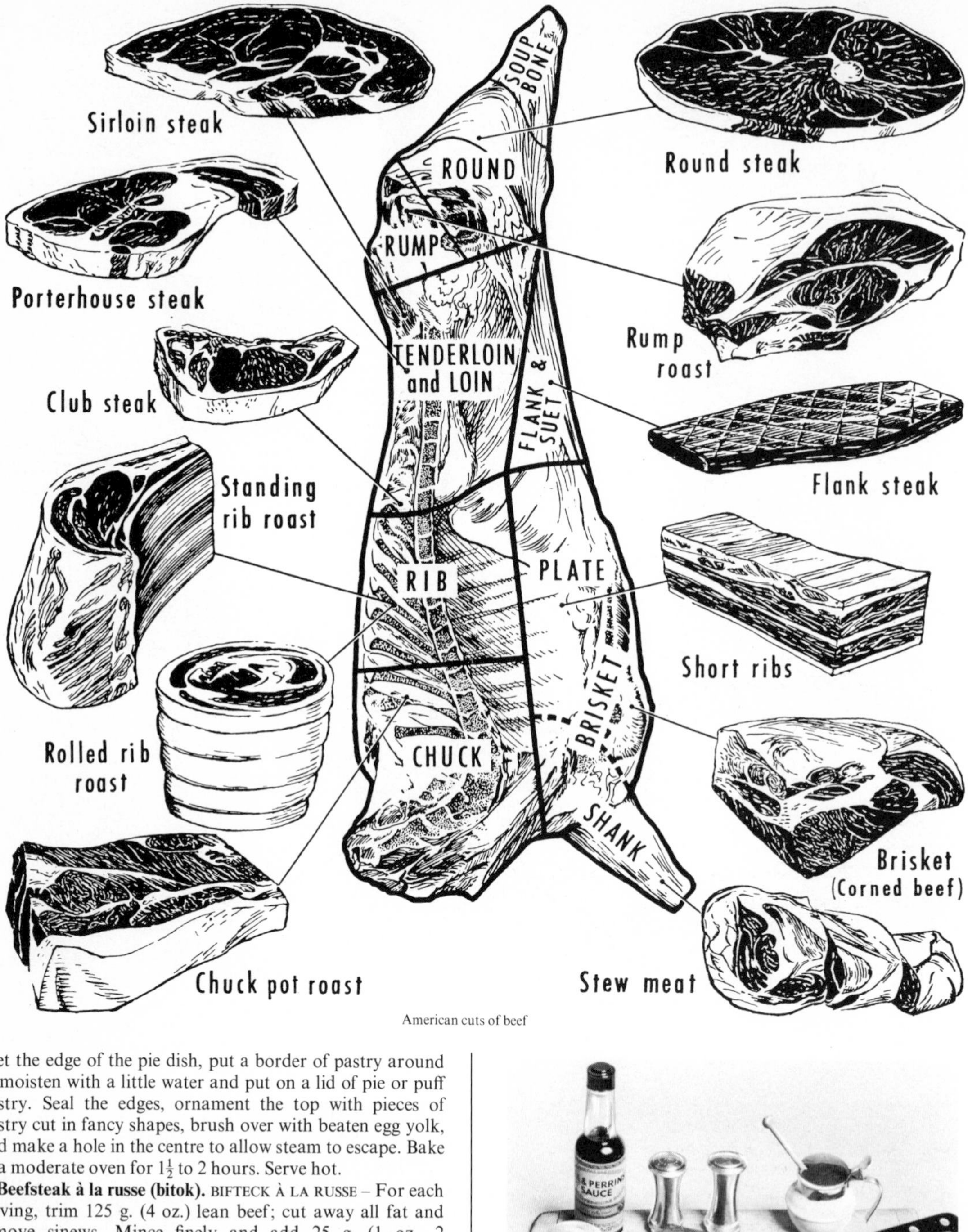

American cuts of beef

Wet the edge of the pie dish, put a border of pastry around it, moisten with a little water and put on a lid of pie or puff pastry. Seal the edges, ornament the top with pieces of pastry cut in fancy shapes, brush over with beaten egg yolk, and make a hole in the centre to allow steam to escape. Bake in a moderate oven for $1\frac{1}{2}$ to 2 hours. Serve hot.

Beefsteak à la russe (bitok). BIFTECK À LA RUSSE – For each serving, trim 125 g. (4 oz.) lean beef; cut away all fat and remove sinews. Mince finely and add 25 g. (1 oz., 2 tablespoons) butter. Season with salt, pepper and nutmeg. Shape into flat cakes, dip in flour and fry in clarified butter. Add 2 tablespoons (3 tablespoons) cream (sour cream, for preference) and 1 tablespoon *demi-glace* (q.v.) to the butter left in the pan. Put 1 tablespoon chopped onion, lightly fried in butter, on each meat cake, and garnish with sautéed potatoes.

Beefsteak tartare. BIFTECK À LA TARTARE – Proceed as described in the recipe for *Beefsteak à l'américaine* but omit the raw egg yolk. Serve *Tartare sauce* separately (see SAUCE).

Bifteck à la tartare (*Ledoyen. Phot. Nicolas*)

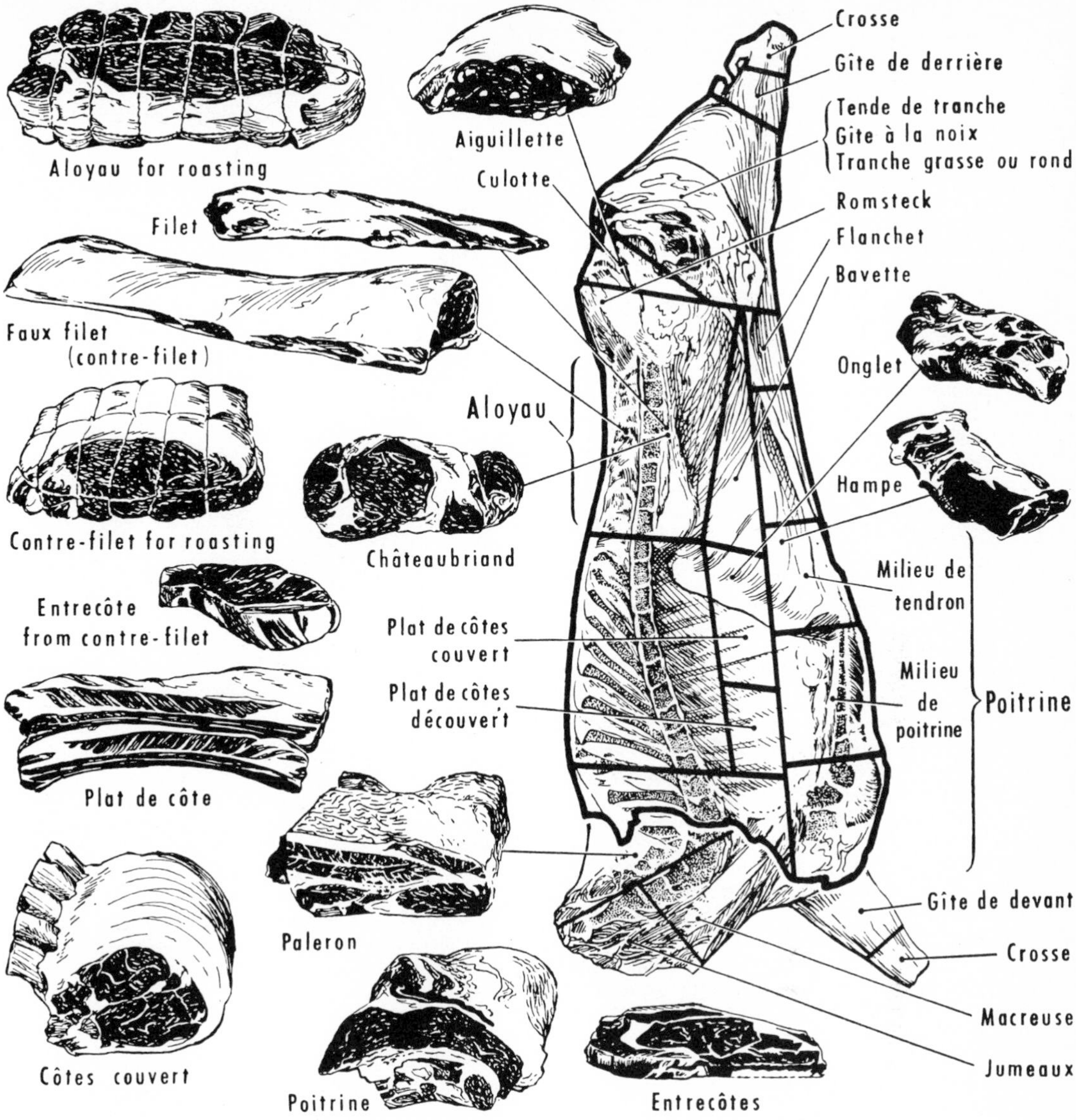

French cuts of beef

Cold boiled beef. BOEUF BOUILLI DE DESSERTE – Left-over pieces of boiled beef, cut in thick slices, served with various sauces.

Cold boiled beef à la parisienne. BOEUF BOUILLI FROID À LA PARISIENNE – Cut the boiled beef into thin slices. Arrange on a long dish in a straight row. Garnish with boiled potatoes (peeled and cut in slices), sliced tomatoes, French beans, quarters of hard-boiled eggs, watercress and any other vegetables in season. Decorate the meat with thin onion rings, and sprinkle with *Vinaigrette sauce* (see SAUCE) and chopped parsley, chervil and tarragon. Serve cold.

Left-over pieces of boiled beef can be prepared in various ways, including: *boulettes, croquettes, kromeskies, en fritot* (i.e. fried in deep fat), *en miroton.*

Boiled beef à la diable. BOEUF BOUILLI À LA DIABLE – Cut boiled beef into thick slices. Spread with mustard, sprinkle with melted butter or oil, and coat with white breadcrumbs. Grill on a low heat, making both sides golden. Serve with *Diable sauce* (see SAUCE).

Boiled beef à la hongroise. BOEUF BOUILLI À LA HONGROISE – Cut the beef into large dice, and sauté in oil or butter in which 100 g. (4 oz., 1 cup) chopped onion has been lightly fried. Season with paprika. Add *Cream sauce* (see SAUCE).

Boiled beef with horseradish sauce. BOEUF BOUILLI SAUCE RAIFORT – Beef from the stockpot with *Horseradish sauce* (see SAUCE) served separately.

Boiled beef à l'indienne. BOEUF BOUILLI À L'INDIENNE – Like *Boiled beef à la hongroise*, substituting curry powder for paprika. Serve *Rice à l'indienne* separately (see RICE).

Boiled beef au pauvre homme (old recipe). BOEUF BOUILLI AU PAUVRE HOMME – Left-over boiled beef, cut into slices, sprinkled with salt, pepper, chopped spring onions and parsley. Add a little dripping or fat skimmed off the stockpot, a pinch of garlic, a glass of stock or water, and breadcrumbs. Leave to simmer for quarter of an hour on hot ashes. (This dish, it is said, was considered a great treat by Louis XV.)

Boiled beef with piquante sauce. BOEUF BOUILLI SAUCE

PIQUANTE – Beef from the stockpot, with *Piquante sauce* (see SAUCE) served separately.

Boiled beef à la provençale. BOEUF BOUILLI À LA PROVENÇALE – Prepare as *Boiled beef à la hongroise*, substituting for the cream sauce an equal quantity of *Tomato fondue* (see FONDUE) flavoured with garlic. Sprinkle with chopped parsley.

Boiled beef with root vegetables. BOEUF BOUILLI AUX RACINES – Boiled beef served with various stockpot vegetables, such as carrots, turnips, leeks.

Sea salt, gherkins, pickles, etc., are served at the same time.

Boiled beef sautéed à la lyonnaise. BOEUF BOUILLI SAUTÉ À LA LYONNAISE – Cut 500 g. (generous 1 lb.) boiled beef into small slices and fry in cooking fat or butter. Add 225 g. (8 oz., 2 cups) chopped onions, previously fried in butter. Cook together, season with salt and pepper. Sprinkle with chopped parsley and 2 tablespoons (3 tablespoons) vinegar, heated in the pan in which the beef was cooked.

Boiled beef sautéed Parmentier. BOEUF BOUILLI SAUTÉ PARMENTIER – Cut 2 medium-sized potatoes into large dice and fry in butter. When nearly done, remove from the pan. In the same butter brown 500 g. (generous 1 lb.) cut-up pieces of boiled beef. Add the potatoes and fry everything together. Sprinkle with chopped parsley.

Boiled beef with tomato sauce. BOEUF BOUILLI SAUCE TOMATE – Beef from the stockpot with *Tomato sauce* (see SAUCE) served separately.

Beef bouillon. BOUILLON DE BOEUF – This stock, which constitutes the basis of clear soups, is also used for moistening sauces.

Beef stock is obtained by cooking lean beef with carrots, onions, leeks, celery and parsnips in water for about 4 hours. When the stock is to be served as soup, turnips are added.

For the method of preparation of beef stock, see SOUP, *Clear soup*.

Braised beef. ESTOUFFADE DE BOEUF – Fry lightly 300 g. (11 oz.) lean, blanched, diced bacon in butter. Drain, and in the same butter fry 1½ kg. (3¼ lb.) beef, cut into pieces, each weighing about 100 g. (4 oz.). Add 3 medium-sized onions cut into quarters. Season with salt and pepper, add pounded thyme, bay leaf and a crushed clove of garlic.

When all these ingredients are well browned, sprinkle in 2 tablespoons (3 tablespoons) flour. Let the flour colour slightly, stirring all the time. Moisten with 1 litre (1¾ pints, generous quart) red wine and the same amount of stock. Blend well, add a *bouquet garni* (q.v.) and bring to the boil. Cover the pan and cook in a slow oven for 2½ to 3 hours.

Drain on a sieve placed over a bowl. Put the pieces of beef and bacon into a pan, add to them 300 g. (11 oz.) mushrooms, sliced and sautéed in butter. Skim surplus fat off the sauce; boil it down, strain, and pour over the meat. Simmer gently for 25 minutes.

Brisket. POITRINE DE BOEUF – This part of beef is used for the stockpot. It can also be cooked as *Forequarter flank*.

Carbonades of beef à la flamande. CARBONADES DE BOEUF À LA FLAMANDE – Cut 750 g. (1¾ lb.) lean beef (thick skirt, or chuck) into thin slices. Season with salt and pepper, brown quickly on both sides in sizzling fat (lard or clarified stock fat).

Remove from the pan and in the same fat fry 4 medium-sized chopped onions until golden. Put the beef and onions into a casserole in alternate layers and add a *bouquet garni* (q.v.).

Dilute the pan juices with 6 dl. (1 pint, 2½ cups) beer and a few tablespoons stock. Thicken with 3 tablespoons (scant ¼ cup) *Brown roux* (see ROUX), add a tablespoon brown sugar, stir, cook for a few moments and strain through a fine sieve onto the meat.

Bring to the boil, cover with a lid, and cook in the oven 2½ hours.

Carbonades of beef with lambic (Belgian cookery). CARBONADES DE BOEUF AU LAMBIC – Cut the beef into slices and fry as described above in the recipe for *Carbonades of beef à la flamande*.

Remove from the pan and in the same fat fry the onions. Brown lightly, sprinkle in a good tablespoon of flour and cook for a few moments.

Put the beef slices into a casserole, season, add a *bouquet garni* (q.v.), moisten with lambic (strong Belgian beer), and bring to the boil. Cover the casserole with a lid and cook in a hot oven for 2½ hours.

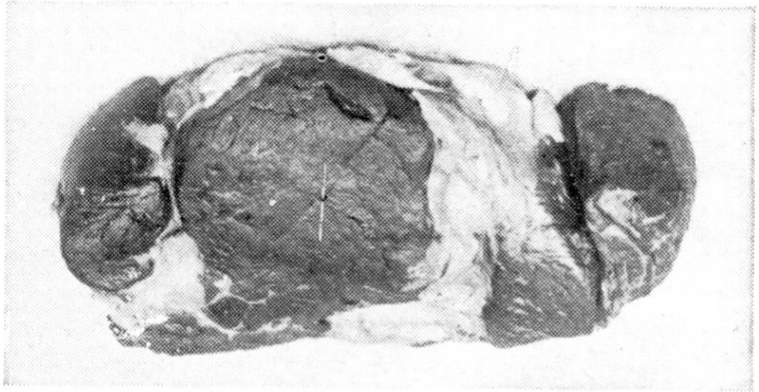

Chateaubriand

Chateaubriand – Thick slice of beef fillet taken from the middle of the fillet, weighing between 400 and 800 g. (14 oz. and 1¾ lb.). It is usually grilled, garnished with *Château potatoes* (see POTATOES) and served with *Colbert sauce* (see SAUCE) or *Maître d'hôtel butter* (see BUTTER). *Chateaubriand* can either be fried, or cooked in any way suitable for T-bone steak, fillets and rump steak.

Grilled. Brush the *chateaubriand* with butter, and season. First place under a hot grill to seal the juices, then lower the heat and continue cooking, keeping it a little underdone.

Fried. Season the *chateaubriand*, and sauté in hot butter. Fry briskly but on a medium flame, to avoid the meat becoming dry. Keep underdone. Garnish and serve with a sauce made from the diluted pan juices.

The garnishes recommended for T-bone, rump steaks, *tournedos* and small fillet steaks are applicable to *chateaubriands*.

Contre-filet – Cut of meat located above the loins and chine of the animal, classed in the first category of beef. It can be grilled or, after being boned, trimmed and dressed, it can be roasted or braised.

Grilled. Cut into thick slices and grill as T-bone or rump steaks.

Roast. See CULINARY METHODS, *Average cooking times for roasts.*

Braised. Proceed as described in the recipe for *Braised beef.* Served as a remove, the *contre-filet*, braised or roasted, is accompanied by vegetables. It is very good served cold.

Contre-filet braised à l'ancienne. CONTRE-FILET BRAISÉ À L'ANCIENNE – Proceed as described in the recipe for *Top rump braised à l'ancienne* (see below).

Contre-filet braised à la bourgeoise. CONTRE-FILET BRAISÉ À LA BOURGEOISE – Proceed as described in the recipe for *Top of rump à la bourgeoise* (see below).

Contre-filet cold, with various salads. CONTRE-FILET FROID GARNI – Arrange as described for *Contre-filet jellied* (see

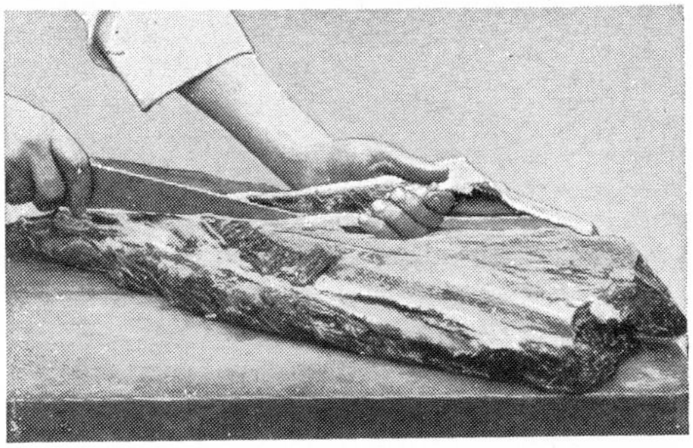

Preparation of contre-filet (*Larousse*)

below). Serve with a salad, stuffed artichoke hearts, hard-boiled eggs, lettuce hearts, etc.

Contre-filet jellied. CONTRE-FILET À LA GELÉE – Useful for serving left-over pieces of roast *contre-filet*. Trim the piece, coat with slightly coloured strong aspic jelly, garnish with chopped jelly and watercress, and put jelly croûtons round the border of the serving dish.

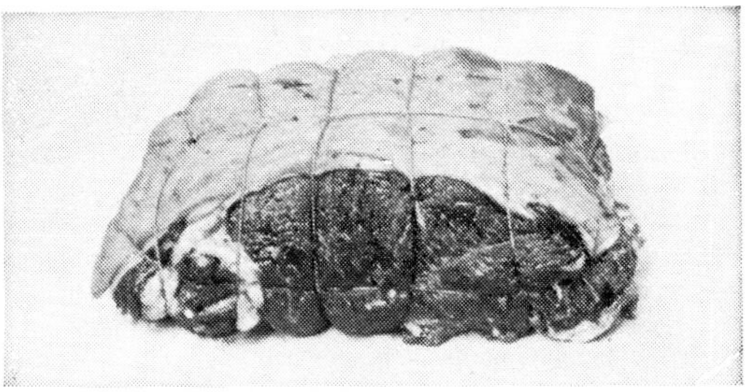

Contre-filet

Contre-filet with garnishes. CONTRE-FILET GARNI – The following are suitable for this meat. For their method of preparation see GARNISHES. (Those followed by the letter (b) are suitable for *Braised contre-filet*.

Algérienne, alsacienne (*b*), *anversoise, Béatrix, bouquetière, bourguignonne* (*b*), *Brillat-Savarin, bruxelloise, châtelaine,* chipolata sausages (b), *Clamart, dauphine, duchesse, favorite, flamande* (*b*), *française, hongroise, jardinière, languedocienne, lorraine* (*b*), *lyonnaise* (*b*), *macédoine, maraîchère, mentonnaise, moderne, niçoise, nivernaise, orientale, piémontaise, portugaise, pritanière, provençale, Richelieu, romaine, sarde.*

The *contre-filet* can also be served with buttered or braised green vegetables, potatoes, macaroni and other pasta products, rich pilaf, risotto, and purée of dried vegetables.

Coquilles (scallop shells) au gratin. COQUILLES DE BOEUF AU GRATIN – Line scallop shells with half-slices of boiled potatoes which have been coated with *Italian sauce* (see SAUCE), and fill with thin slices of cold boiled beef cut up small. Cover with more sauce, sprinkle with cheese and breadcrumbs and brown in the oven.

A number of recipes for preparing hot and cold *coquilles* will be found under HORS-D'ŒUVRE, *Scallop shells*.

Beef à la Créole (Créole cookery). BOEUF À LA CRÉOLE – Put some fat and a tablespoon of olive oil into a casserole, and add 2 sliced onions. Cut the beef in large pieces as for *Beef ragoûts* (see below), and put them on this bed of onions. Add a tablespoon tomato sauce, a clove of garlic, a sprig of thyme and parsley and a few pinches of saffron. Cook gently for 3 hours with the lid on. The beef and the onions give out juice, but if at the end of cooking the juice becomes too concentrated, add a few drops of water or stock. If there is too much sauce, boil it down.

Daube of beef. DAUBE DE BOEUF – This old dish is prepared in different ways in different regions. Basically, it consists of a piece of beef, cooked in a *daubière* (q.v.) in braising liquor, with white or red wine added to it. In some provinces the meat (usually taken from the rump) is cooked whole, in others it is cut into square pieces or thick escalopes.

Prepared in this way, the *daubes* are very similar to *Braised beef.*

Daube of beef à l'ancienne. DAUBE DE BOEUF À L'ANCIENNE – Lard a piece of rump with thick lardoons (strips of salt pork) and marinate for a few hours in white wine and brandy, together with sliced carrots and onions, parsley, thyme, bay leaf and pounded garlic. Proceed as for *Top rump* (see below).

Daube of beef à la béarnaise. DAUBE DE BOEUF À LA BÉARNAISE – Cut 2 kg. ($4\frac{1}{2}$ lb.) beef, taken from rump or shoulder of beef, into 5-cm. (2-inch) square pieces. Lard each of these pieces with a thick lardoon (strip of salt pork), which has been rolled in chopped parsley and garlic, seasoned with powdered thyme and bay leaf, and sprinkled with brandy. Leave to marinate for 2 hours in red wine and brandy, with sliced carrots and onions, a sprig of parsley and thyme, and a bay leaf. Line a *daubière* (q.v.) with slices of Bayonne ham, alternating with layers of carrots and sliced onions which have been lightly fried in lard or goose fat. Dry the pieces of beef, dredge with flour, and put them in layers in the *daubière*. Add a *bouquet garni* (q.v.). Bring the stock in which the meat was marinated to the boil, add 2 crushed cloves of garlic, and simmer for 25 minutes. Strain and pour over the meat. There should be enough liquor to cover the meat completely; if not, add a few tablespoons meat stock.

Cover the *daubière* with a lid, sealing it with a strip of flour-and-water paste. Bring to the boil on top of the stove, then cook in the oven, maintaining an even heat, for 4 hours. Serve in the *daubière*, having first removed the *bouquet garni* and skimmed off surplus fat.

In Béarn, this *daube* is served with *broyo* instead of bread.

Daube à la provençale

Daube of beef à la provençale. DAUBE DE BOEUF À LA PROVENÇALE – Cut the beef into pieces, lard them and marinate for 2 hours as described above, but using white wine instead of red and adding 3 tablespoons (scant ¼ cup) oil to it. Drain the pieces of beef and put them into a *daubière* which should be large enough to take all the ingredients. Spread in layers, alternating with fresh bacon rinds cut into small dice, blanched, diced bacon, sliced carrots, chopped onions, raw chopped mushrooms, peeled and chopped tomatoes, pounded cloves of garlic and stoned black olives. Put a *bouquet garni* (q.v.) in the middle of all these ingredients and, besides the usual aromatic herbs, add a small piece of bitter orange peel.

Pour the marinating liquor over the whole, add some veal stock, and cover, sealing the lid with a strip of flour-and-water paste. Cook in a moderate oven for 5 or 6 hours.

Serve in the *daubière*, having first removed the *bouquet garni* and skimmed off surplus fat.

Entrecôte or Steak – *Entrecôte* is the part of the meat between the bones of the ribs of beef. A slice taken from the *contre-filet* or from the rump is often served under this name.

The real *entrecôte* is usually grilled; a slice of *contre-filet*, often called rump steak in France, is sometimes fried in butter.

These steaks are generally boned before being grilled. When the pieces are thick, however, rib bones are left on.

Grilled. Trim and flatten the steak, brush with butter or oil, season and cook under a grill, first on a brisk and then on a lowered heat. Arrange and serve as indicated in the recipe.

Sautéed. Trim and flatten the steak, season it and sauté briskly in butter. Arrange and garnish as indicated in the recipe. Pour over it the pan juices left over from frying, having diluted them and finished off as described in the recipe.

In France, a steak taken from ribs of beef, or *contre-filet*, of 400 to 500 g. (about 1 lb.) is considered sufficient for four persons.

Entrecôte or Steak à la béarnaise – Grill the steak, and garnish with *Château potatoes* (see POTATOES) and watercress. Serve *Béarnaise sauce* (see SAUCE) separately.

Entrecôte or Steak à la Bercy – Grill the steak and cover with *Bercy butter* (see BUTTER, *Compound butters*).

Entrecôte or Steak à la bonne femme, or 'Grand-mère' – Sauté the steak in butter, browning on both sides. Surround it in the pan wtih 12 small glazed onions, 2 blanched potatoes cut small, and 50 g. (2 oz.) diced and blanched salt pork or bacon. Cook all together. Arrange in an earthenware dish, with the garnish surrounding it. Dilute the butter left in the pan with ½ dl. (3 tablespoons, scant ¼ cup) stock or water and pour over the dish. Sprinkle with chopped parsley.

Entrecôte or Steak à la bordelaise – Grill the steak. Arrange on a dish and place 10 slices of poached and drained bone marrow on top. Serve with *Bordelaise sauce* (see SAUCE).

The steak can also be served sautéed, with the pan juices added to the sauce.

Entrecôte or Steak à la bourguignonne – Sauté the *entrecôte* in butter, and garnish *à la bourguignonne* (see GARNISHES). Dilute the pan juices with 1 dl. (6 tablespoons, scant ½ cup) red wine, add 1 dl. (6 tablespoons, scant ½ cup) *demi-glace* (q.v.), boil down, strain and pour over the dish.

Entrecôte or Steak Dumas – Season and cook *contre-filet* steaks over a high heat. Lay them on a heated meat plate and place 3 slices of previously cooked beef marrow on each.

Make a sauce with the residue left in the pan by adding 1 dl. (6 tablespoons, scant ½ cup) dry white wine and 2 tablespoons (3 tablespoons) chopped shallots. Boil down by three-quarters. Pour in 1 dl. (6 tablespoons, scant ½ cup) veal stock and bring to the boil. Boil for one minute. Add 100 g. (4 oz., ½ cup) butter and season to taste.

Sprinkle the steaks with pepper and chopped parsley. Coat with the sauce and serve. (Recipe from the *Restaurant Lasserre.*)

Entrecôte or Steak à la fermière – Prepare *Steak à la bonne femme,* replacing the garnish indicated for that recipe by 1½ dl. (¼ pint, ⅔ cup) *Vegetable fondue* (see FONDUE). Pour over it the pan juices, diluted with white wine and thickened veal stock.

Entrecôte or Steak à la forestière – Prepare *Steak with mushrooms I* or *II* (see below), replacing the mushrooms by the garnish called *à la forestière* (see GARNISHES).

Entrecôte or Steak à la hongroise – Season the steak with paprika, and sauté it in butter. When three-quarters done, add a tablespoon chopped onion, lightly fried in butter and seasoned with salt and paprika. Dilute the pan juices with 1 dl. (6 tablespoons, scant ½ cup) white wine, add 1 dl. (6 tablespoons, scant ½ cup) thin *Velouté sauce* (see SAUCE). Cook for a few moments and pour over the steak. Serve with boiled potatoes.

Entrecôte or Steak à la lyonnaise I – Sauté the steak in butter. When three-quarters done, add 2 tablespoons (3 tablespoons) chopped onion lightly fried in butter. Dilute the pan juices with 1 tablespoon vinegar and 2 tablespoons (3 tablespoons) white wine, add 1 dl. (6 tablespoons, scant ½ cup) *demi-glace* (q.v.); boil down, add a tablespoon chopped parsley and pour over the steak.

Entrecôte or Steak à la lyonnaise II – Cook as above. Dilute the pan juices with vinegar and white wine. Add stock, and thicken the sauce with *Kneaded butter* (see BUTTER, *Compound butters*).

Entrecôte or Steak maître d'hôtel – Grill the steak. Serve with *Maître d'hôtel butter* (see BUTTER, *Compound butters*).

Entrecôte or Steak marchand de vin – Grill the steak. Serve with *Marchand de vin butter* (see BUTTER, *Compound butters*).

Entrecôte or Steak à la ménagère – Prepare as *Entrecôte à la bonne femme.* Replace the garnish in that recipe by an equal quantity of small glazed onions, mushrooms and cooked carrots. Pour the pan juices, diluted with white wine and thickened veal stock, over the dish.

Entrecôte or Steak à la minute – Flatten the steak to make it as thin as possible. Season and sauté in butter. Add a few drops of lemon juice and half a tablespoon of chopped parsley to the butter in which it was cooked and pour over the steak.

Entrecôte or Steak Mirabeau – Grill the steak. Arrange on a dish, decorate with anchovy fillets and tarragon leaves, garnish with stoned, blanched olives and serve with *Anchovy butter* (see BUTTER. *Compound butters*).

Entrecôte or Steak with mushrooms I. ENTRECÔTE AUX CHAMPIGNONS – Sauté the steak in butter. When three-quarters done, add 8 mushroom caps, and finish cooking. Arrange the mushrooms around the meat on a dish.

Dilute the butter left in the pan with 1 dl. (6 tablespoons, scant ½ cup) white wine, add 1 dl. (6 tablespoons, scant ½ cup) *demi-glace* (q.v.), boil down, strain, add a teaspoon fresh butter, and pour over the meat.

Entrecôte or Steak with mushrooms II. ENTRECÔTE AUX CHAMPIGNONS – Proceed as above. Dilute the pan juices with white wine, add stock and thicken with *Kneaded butter* (see BUTTER, *Compound butters*).

Entrecôte or Steak à la niçoise – Sauté the steak in butter or oil. Arrange on a dish, garnish with *Tomato fondue à la niçoise* (see TOMATO), new potatoes cooked in butter, and

Entrecôte Mirabeau (*Robert Carrier*)

black olives. Dilute the pan juices with white wine and tomato-flavoured veal stock, and pour over the steak.

Entrecôte or Steak à la tyrolienne – Grill the steak, top with onion rings fried in butter, surround with a border of *Tomato fondue* (see FONDUE), and sprinkle with chopped parsley.

Entrecôte or Steak au vert-pré – Grill the steak, garnish with straw potatoes alternating with bunches of water-cress, and serve with *Maître d'hôtel butter* (see BUTTER, *Compound butters*).

Entrecôte or Steak à la viennoise (Austrian cookery) – Beat the steak to flatten thoroughly, season with salt and paprika, dredge with flour, and sauté briskly in lard. Cover with onion rings which have been fried in lard, drained, and dressed with butter and vinegar.

Serve boiled potatoes separately.

Beef essence. ESSENCE DE BOEUF – Concentrated meat juice prepared as described under *Beef-tea* (see below).

Filets mignons – These cuts are taken from the end of the fillet. The *filet mignon* is trimmed into the shape of a triangle; its weight varies according to the size of the fillet. If it is too big, it can be divided in two and thus provide two *filets mignons*.

This part of the fillet of beef can also be used for the preparation of steak on skewers, *bitki*, *pilafs* and quick sautés.

Grilled. Flatten the *filet mignon* slightly, season it, dip into melted butter and cover with breadcrumbs, pressing with the flat part of the knife to make the breadcrumbs adhere properly. Sprinkle with melted butter and cook under a low grill. Serve with the garnish and sauce recommended in the recipe. As the fillet is cooked in breadcrumbs, the sauce accompanying it should be served separately.

Sautéed. Flatten the *filet mignon*, season, and sauté briskly in butter. Serve with a garnish and the sauce recommended in the recipe.

Filet mignon can be prepared in ways suitable for *entrecôtes*, rump steaks and other cuts, for escalopes of veal, *noisettes* and *tournedos*.

Filets mignons en chevreuil – Trim, flatten slightly, and lard the fillets with strips of bacon, inserting them in a rosette pattern. Leave to marinate for 24 to 28 hours in the summer, from 3 to 4 days in the winter (see MARINADES).

Take the fillets out of the marinade and dry them in a cloth. Sauté as quickly as possible in clarified butter or oil. Serve with the garnish and sauce recommended in the recipe.

The following are the most appropriate garnishes for *filet en chevreuil*: celeriac, lentils, chestnuts, onions. They can also be served with fresh or dried noodles, rice pilaf, risotto, etc.

Filets en chevreuil can also be prepared *au chausseur, à la hongroise, à la poivrade, à la romaine, en venison*, etc.

Fillet of beef. FILET DE BOEUF – The fillet is the undercut of sirloin. The end of the fillet is used for making *tournedos* and *filets mignons*. The middle of the fillet, after the fat and sinews have been removed, makes tender and delicate roasts, or, cut into slices, delicious grills. The top of the fillet, less delicate in taste, more sinewy than the middle, is roasted or grilled.

Trim the fillet, removing skin and sinews. Cut into thick slices if it is to be served as a *chateaubriand*, as grilled fillet, *tournedos*, or *filet mignon*.

If it is to be served whole, trim the fillet and lard it with thin strips of bacon; or bard with rashers and secure with string. Roast it in the oven or on a spit, fry or braise it, accord-

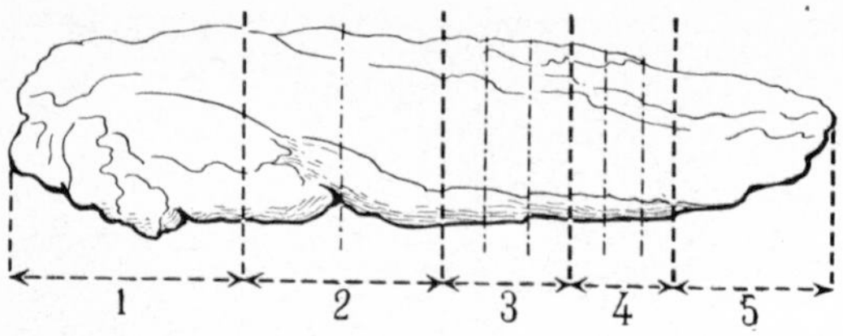

Division of a fillet of beef:
1. Beefsteak; 2. Chateaubriand; 3. Fillet steaks;
4. Tournedos; 5. Filets mignons

ing to the recipe chosen. Follow the special instructions for braising, frying, roasting, under CULINARY METHODS.

When the fillet is cooked, untie the string and remove the barding. Arrange on a heated dish, surround with the garnish indicated, and serve with its own juice or the sauce recommended.

Fillet of beef with garnish. FILET DE BOEUF GARNI – For various garnishes suitable for fillet of beef, fried or roast, see GARNISHES. In the following list of recommended garnishes, those followed by the letter (f) are intended for fried fillets; the others are suitable both for fried and roast fillets.

Anversoise, Béatrix, bouquetière, Brillat-Savarin, bruxelloise, châtelaine (f), *Clamart, dauphine, duchesse, favorite, financière* (f), *forestière, française* (f), *Frascati* (f), *Godard* (f), *hongroise, jardinière, italienne* (f), *languedocienne, macédoine, massenet* (f), *mentonnaise* (f), *milanaise* (f), *moderne* (f), *niçoise* (f), *nivernaise* (f), *orientale, parisienne, piémontaise* (f), *portugaise, printanière, provençale* (f), *renaissance* (f), *Richelieu, romaine* (f), *Romanov* (f), *sarde* (f), *Saint-Germain, viennoise* (f).

Fried or roast fillet of beef can also be accompanied by buttered or braised vegetables, potatoes and purées of various vegetables. These purées should be served separately.

Fillet of beef London House. FILET DE BOEUF LONDON HOUSE – This is the same as *Fillet Prince Albert* (see below).

Fillet of beef Matignon. FILET DE BOEUF MATIGNON – Lard a fillet with pieces of *tongue à l'écarlate* (salt beef tongue) (see OFFAL or VARIETY MEATS), and truffles cut into strips. Cover with a layer of *matignon* (q.v.), wrap in wide, thin rashers of bacon, and secure with string.

Put into a braising pan (see CULINARY METHODS). Moisten with Madeira, and cook with the lid on for 1 hour. Drain the fillet, remove the bacon rashers and *matignon*. Glaze the fillet in the oven, arrange on a dish on a croûton of fried bread.

Surround with garnish *à la matignon*. Strain the braising liquor, skim off surplus fat, pour a little of the sauce around the fillet and serve the rest separately.

Fillet of beef à la périgourdine. FILET DE BOEUF À LA PÉRIGOURDINE – Insert slivers of truffle into the fillet, bard it, tie with string and braise in Madeira-flavoured braising stock. Drain, remove barding bacon and glaze. Surround with slices of *foie gras* tossed in butter, and tartlets filled with a *salpicon* (q.v.) of truffles. Boil down the braising liquor, strain, and pour over the fillet.

Fillet of beef Prince Albert. FILET DE BOEUF PRINCE ALBERT – Lard a trimmed fillet of beef with thin strips of bacon. Slit the fillet open without completely separating the two halves.

Fill the inside with pieces of uncooked *foie gras*, seasoned and studded with pieces of truffles. Close the fillet, tie with string, and brown in a hot oven. Put into a braising pan with the ingredients given in the recipe for *Fillet of beef Matignon*. Moisten with port, cook in the oven, and complete as described in the above-mentioned recipe. Surround with Prince Albert garnish (large truffles cooked in Madeira) and mushroom caps cooked in butter.

This fillet of beef is also known as Prince of Wales.

Fillet of beef on skewers. BROCHETTES DE FILET DE BOEUF – Prepared in the same way as *Fillets of mutton on skewers* (see MUTTON), using squares of fillet beef, pieces of blanched and fried lean bacon, and mushrooms.

Cold fillet of beef. FILET DE BOEUF FROID – Cold beef fillets can be garnished with various vegetables, boiled, drained, allowed to cool and mixed with half-set aspic jelly. They can also be garnished with various mousses.

Full instructions for these preparations, as well as a list of appropriate garnishes, will be found under the entry COLD FOODSTUFFS.

Jellied cold fillet of beef. FILET DE BOEUF FROID À LA GELÉE – This method is mostly applied to left-over pot-roasted or roasted fillet. If the piece is big enough to be served whole, cover it with aspic jelly and decorate with chopped jelly and watercress. Or cut it into thin slices and garnish with chopped jelly and watercress.

The fillet can also be trimmed and placed whole in a shallow serving dish, and covered completely with meat aspic jelly flavoured with Madeira, port or sherry.

Serve a green or a vegetable salad with the fillet, as well as a cold sauce: *Mayonnaise, Rémoulade, Tartare*, etc. (see SAUCE).

Cold fillet of beef à la niçoise. FILET DE BOEUF FROID À LA NIÇOISE – Roast or pot-roast the fillet, keeping it a little underdone. Leave to get quite cold. Line a mould with tarragon-flavoured jelly, decorated with truffles, pieces of hard-boiled egg white, and tarragon leaves which have been blanched, dipped in cold water and dried. Put in the fillet, fill the mould with jelly, and leave to set on ice, or in the refrigerator. Turn out onto a dish, on a foundation of tarragon-flavoured jelly.

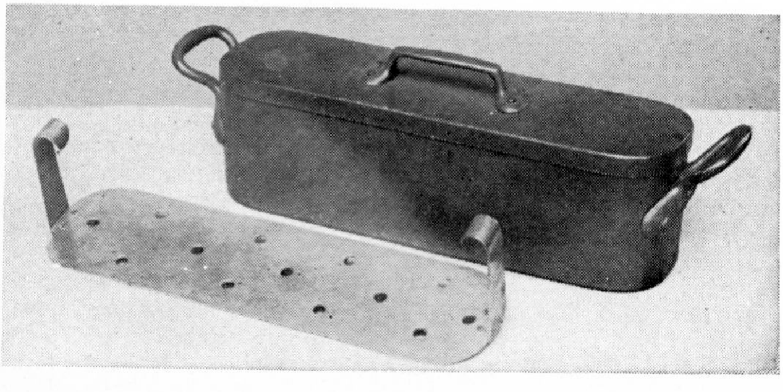

Special braising pan for fillets (*Dehillerin. Phot. Larousse*)

Marinate 12 small tomatoes in oil, vinegar, salt and pepper, remove the insides, and stuff with a *salpicon* (q.v.) of truffles. Stuff 12 artichoke hearts with green asparagus tips; place these round the beef. Garnish further with stoned olives stuffed with *Anchovy butter* (see BUTTER, *Compound butters*).

Put a little chopped jelly between each group of garnish and decorate the edge of the dish with jelly croûtons.

Cold fillet of beef à la parisienne. FILET DE BOEUF FROID À LA PARISIENNE – Pot-roast or roast the fillet and leave to cool. Trim, dry, and coat with jelly. Arrange on a dish, or on a buttered croûton of bread, or on a foundation of cooked rice. Surround with small *timbales* of *Macédoine of vegetables* (see MACÉDOINE). Decorate the dish with jelly croûtons. Serve with *Mayonnaise sauce* (see SAUCE).

Cold fillet of beef à la russe. FILET DE BOEUF À LA RUSSE – Cook the fillet as described in the recipe for *Cold fillet of beef à la parisienne* and leave to get cold. Cut out the central part, leaving only a 'frame', with a narrow strip of about 4 to 5 cm. (2 inches) at each end. Cut the cut-out meat into thin slices, and put them back in the hollowed-out meat case, pressing them in tightly. Cover with Madeira-flavoured aspic jelly which has had chopped truffles added.

Arrange the fillet on a bread croûton or a foundation of cooked rice, and garnish with hard-boiled eggs, halved and covered with jelly, artichoke hearts stuffed with vegetables dressed with mayonnaise, and lettuce hearts cut in quarters.

Cold fillet of beef à la strasbourgeoise. FILET DE BOEUF FROID À LA STRASBOURGEOISE – Prepare and cook the fillet as described in the recipe for *Fillet of beef Prince Albert*, studding it with truffles instead of strips of larding bacon. Leave to get cold.

Trim the fillet and cover with port-flavoured jelly. Arrange on a buttered croûton of bread, or on a foundation of cooked rice. Garnish with truffles cooked in port, cooled and dipped in jelly, and with chopped jelly and bunches of parsley. Decorate with jelly croûtons.

Fillet of beef steaks. FILETS DE BOEUF DE DÉTAIL – Slices cut off fillet of beef can be prepared in any way suitable for steaks, rump steak and *tournedos*.

Grilled. Trim and slightly flatten the fillet, brush with butter or other fat, season and grill under a brisk heat.

Sautéed. Season the fillet and cook in a sauté pan in butter. Keep slightly underdone.

Small fillets of beef. PETITS FILETS DE BOEUF – Small slices of fillets cut a little bigger than *tournedos*. All the methods

Grilled small fillets

Small fillets à la niçoise (*Larousse*)

of cooking given for *tournedos* are applicable to small fillets.

Small fillets of beef à la niçoise. PETITS FILETS DE BOEUF À LA NIÇOISE – Sauté the fillets in butter, drain them and place each on a croûton of bread fried in butter. Fill the middle of the dish with cooked French beans dressed with butter, and place between each fillet a little heap of small potatoes (or potato balls) cooked in butter.

Dilute the pan juices with white wine, add *Tomato fondue* (see FONDUE) flavoured with garlic and chopped tarragon, and pour the sauce over the fillets. Top with rolled anchovy fillets and sprinkle with chopped parsley.

Beef forcemeat for agnolotti – See FORCEMEAT.

Forequarter flank. PLAT-DE-CÔTE – Top part of the rib, generally used for the stockpot.

After pickling in brine for several days, it can be poached in water with vegetables and aromatics, and served hot with a garnish: braised red cabbage, braised green cabbage, butter beans, and purées of fresh or dried vegetables.

This cut can also be used for making stews, and can be prepared as *Pressed beef* (see below).

Fricadelles of cooked beef. FRICADELLES DE BOEUF AVEC VIANDE CUITE – Mince 750 g. ($1\frac{3}{4}$ lb.) cooked beef (remains of a piece of boiled or braised beef) and mix with 350 g. (12 oz., $1\frac{1}{2}$ cups) thick potato purée. Add 150 g. (5 oz., $1\frac{1}{4}$ cups) chopped onion, and bind with 2 whole eggs. Season with salt, pepper and grated nutmeg, and mix well.

Divide into pieces of about 100 g. (4 oz.) each. Roll them on a board sprinkled with flour, and shape into thick, flat cakes. Brown them on both sides in butter and finish cooking in the oven.

Serve with a well-spiced sauce: *Piquante* or *Robert sauce* (see SAUCE), or with a vegetable purée.

Fricadelles of raw beef. FRICADELLES DE BOEUF AVEC VIANDE CRUE – Chop together 750 g. ($1\frac{3}{4}$ lb.) lean beef, 250 g. (9 oz.) decrusted bread, soaked and squeezed out, and add 350 g. (12 oz., $1\frac{1}{2}$ cups) butter, 125 g. (4 oz., 1 cup) onion chopped and lightly fried in butter, and a tablespoon chopped parsley. Bind with 3 whole eggs, season with salt, pepper and a pinch of grated nutmeg, and mix well.

Prepare and cook the *fricadelles* as described in the preceding recipe.

Beef glaze. GLACE DE BOEUF – Boil down concentrated beef stock to a syrupy consistency.

This glaze is used for flavouring sauces, gravies and stews. (See EXTRACTS, *Meat extract*.)

Goulash (Hungarian cookery). GULYAS DE BOEUF – A way of stewing beef (or other meat), spiced with paprika, or Hungarian red pepper.

These stews, in Hungary as in France, are prepared in different ways. Two popular methods are given below.

Goulash

Hungarian goulash I. GULYAS DE BOEUF À LA HONGROISE – Fry 1½ kg. (3½ lb.) lean beef cut into pieces, and 2 medium onions, cut into large dice, in 125 g. (4 oz., ½ cup) lard. Season with salt and a teaspoon of paprika.

When all the ingredients are well browned, add 500 g. (generous lb.) tomatoes, peeled, seeded and diced. Moisten with 2 dl. (⅓ pint, scant cup) water, bring to the boil, cover with a lid, and simmer for 1½ hours. Add 2 dl. (⅓ pint, scant cup) water and 4 quartered potatoes, and continue to cook for about another hour.

Hungarian goulash II. GULYAS DE BOEUF À LA HONGROISE – Brown pieces of beef and chopped onion in lard. Season with salt and paprika. Sprinkle 2 tablespoons (3 tablespoons) flour into the pan and cook for a few moments. Add enough clear brown stock to cover the meat, 2 dl. (⅓ pint, scant cup) tomato purée, and a *bouquet garni* (q.v.). Stir, bring to the boil, cover, and cook in the oven for 2½ hours. Serve with boiled potatoes.

Beef au gros sel. BOEUF AU GROS SEL – Boiled meat, served hot, garnished with the vegetables with which it was cooked, and sea salt. (See BOUILLON, SOUP.)

Hamburger steak (also called steak à l'allemande). BIFTECK À LA HAMBOURGEOISE – Mince finely 400 g. (14 oz.) beef, taken from *contre-filet* or fillet. Add 50 g. (2 oz., ½ cup) chopped, lightly fried onion, and 2 raw eggs. Season well with salt, pepper and grated nutmeg, and shape into 4 flat cakes.

Dredge with flour and fry in clarified butter, keeping them a little underdone inside (they are just right when little beads of blood form on the surface). Put a tablespoon of sliced onion, fried in butter, on each steak.

Beef hash. HACHIS DE BOEUF – This is made out of boiled or braised left-over meat.

Recipes for beef hashes will be found under the section HASHES. They can be made in scallop shells, as kromeskies, croquettes, *aux fines herbes, à la hongroise, à l'italienne, à la lyonnaise, Parmentier, à la polonaise, à la portugaise.*

Beef juices. JUS DE BOEUF – These juices, usually called *jus de viande*, are used in building-up diets, and are obtained by pressing grilled lean slices of beef in a special apparatus.

Keftedes of beef (German cookery). KEFTEDES DE BOEUF – Prepare *Hamburger steaks* omitting the onion garnish.

This method of preparation can also be applied to other meat. It is similar to *bitki* or *cutlets à la Pozharsky*, which can be made of veal, chicken or game, and fish.

Ox (beef) liver. FOIE DE BOEUF – This is less delicate than calf's liver. All recipes for calf's liver are suitable for ox (beef) liver. (See OFFAL or VARIETY MEATS.)

Beef marrow on croûtes. CROÛTES À LA MOELLE – Poach slices of marrow in salted water, and drain thoroughly. Fry slices of bread in butter. Chop a slice of the marrow in small pieces and mix with concentrated veal stock and a chopped shallot which has been simmered in a little white wine. Put this mixture on the croûtes. Place the remaining marrow slices on the mixture, cover with fine breadcrumbs, season with freshly ground pepper, and brown in a hot oven.

Medallions of beef fillet. MÉDAILLONS DE FILET DE BOEUF – Round slices of fillet, rather smaller than *tournedos.* Their weight varies between 80 and 100 g. (3 to 4 oz.) and they can be prepared in any way suitable for *tournedos* or *noisettes.* They are sometimes called *coeur de filet de boeuf.*

Miroton of beef. MIROTON DE BOEUF – Arrange thin slices of boiled beef, overlapping slightly, in a fireproof dish on a thick foundation of *Lyonnaise sauce* (see SAUCE) mixed with sliced onions which have been lightly fried in butter. Pour *Lyonnaise sauce* over the meat, sprinkle with melted butter or dripping, and brown the top in the oven. Sprinkle with chopped parsley.

Paupiettes of beef. PAUPIETTES DE BOEUF – *Paupiettes* are ballottines (q.v.) made of thin slices of various meats, stuffed and rolled.

Flatten thin slices of beef, season with salt and pepper and cover with a layer of pork sausage or well-spiced forcemeat. Roll into the shape of large corks, wrap in thin rashers of bacon, and tie with string.

Braise the *paupiettes,* and moisten with white wine or Madeira (see CULINARY METHODS, *Braising*).

Remove bacon. Boil down, strain the braising liquor and pour it over the *paupiettes.* Garnish. All garnishes for braised beef can be served with *paupiettes.* Certain types of garnish, such as *bourgeoise,* chipolata sausages or small onions, should be added when the *paupiettes* are half cooked, covered with the strained braising liquor, and left to finish cooking with the *paupiettes.*

Paupiettes of beef can be prepared *à la bourguignonne* (braised in red wine). The garnish – small onions, lardoons (strips of salt pork) and mushrooms – must be cooked with the *paupiettes.*

Paupiettes of beef à la hongroise. PAUPIETTES DE BOEUF À LA HONGROISE – Stuff the *paupiettes* with veal forcemeat mixed with chopped onion fried in butter. Place in a pan on a foundation of more fried onion, and season with salt and paprika. Put the lid on the pan and simmer for 10 minutes. Moisten with dry white wine, allowing 2 dl. (⅓ pint, scant cup) for 10 *paupiettes.* Boil down, then add about 4 dl. (¾ pint, scant 2 cups) light *Velouté sauce* (see SAUCE). Put a *bouquet garni* (q.v.) in the middle of the dish. Bring to the boil, cover the pan, and cook in the oven, basting frequently.

When the *paupiettes* are nearly done, drain them, remove barding, put back into the pan and add 20 small mushrooms lightly tossed in butter. Add cream to the sauce, boil down a little, strain, and pour over the *paupiettes.* Cook until they are done.

Serve on croûtons fried in butter, covering them with sauce and mushrooms.

Paupiettes of beef with pilaf. PAUPIETTES DE BOEUF AU RIZ PILAF – Prepare as for *Paupiettes of beef with risotto* (see below), replacing the risotto with pilaf rice.

Paupiettes of beef with risotto. PAUPIETTES DE BOEUF AU RISOTTO – Cook the *paupiettes,* glaze them, and serve with *Risotto* (see RICE). Simmer down the liquor in which the *paupiettes* were braised, strain, and pour over them.

Paupiettes of beef Sainte-Menehould. PAUPIETTES DE BOEUF SAINTE-MENEHOULD – Braise the *paupiettes* until three-quarters done. Allow to cool in the strained braising liquor. Drain, dry, and spread with mustard flavoured with a pinch of cayenne pepper. Sprinkle with melted butter, roll in fresh breadcrumbs, and cook under a moderate grill.

Garnish with watercress, and serve with the braising liquor boiled down and strained.

Ragoût of beef (*Robert Carrier*)

Paupiettes of beef with vegetables. PAUPIETTES DE BOEUF AUX LÉGUMES – Braise the *paupiettes* and serve garnished with vegetables: buttered French beans, broad beans, green peas, etc., braised celery, endive, lettuce, glazed carrots, turnips, small onions, etc., potatoes prepared in various ways, purées of dried or fresh vegetables.

Porterhouse steak – Cut from the chump end of the sirloin.

Pressed beef. BOEUF PRESSÉ – Pressed beef, which is served as an *hors-d'œuvre*, is usually bought ready-cooked in the shops, but it can be made at home.

Take 3 kg. ($6\frac{1}{2}$ lb.) brisket, prick with a thick trussing needle, and pickle in brine for 8 to 10 days. The process is completed more quickly in summer than in winter.

The pickling brine is the same as that used for *Pickled (scarlet) beef or ox tongue* (see OFFAL). Care must be taken that the beef is completely submerged in the liquid; cover with a wooden board and put a weight on top.

Wash the beef in cold water and cut into pieces to fit the moulds in which they will later be placed. Cook in water with a carrot cut in quarters and a bunch of leeks. After thorough cooking, drain, put into square moulds, cover with a wooden board and put a weight on top.

When the meat is quite cold, take out of the moulds. Coat with gelatine which has been diluted and mixed with burnt sugar and a little carmine. When one layer is set, add another, then another. These make a protective covering for the meat, enabling it to keep for some time.

To serve, cut into thin slices and decorate with fresh parsley.

Beef ragoûts. RAGOÛTS DE BOEUF – Pieces of rump, shoulder or rib are used for these *ragoûts*. Bone the meat and cut into pieces of about 100 g. (4 oz.). Brown in dripping or butter, together with onions and carrots cut into quarters. Season with salt and pepper.

When the meat and the vegetables acquire a good colour, sprinkle in some flour, moisten with clear brown stock and mix. Add a *bouquet garni* (q.v.) and a crushed garlic clove. Simmer, with the lid on, for $1\frac{1}{2}$ hours. Drain, and place the pieces of meat in a large ovenware dish.

Put a garnish on top of the meat. Boil down the sauce, strain and pour over the *ragoût*. Complete the cooking in the oven for $1\frac{1}{2}$ hours, with the dish uncovered.

Garnishes suitable for beef *ragoûts*: *Bourgeoise, bourguignonne,* chipolata sausages, mushrooms, chestnuts, salsify.

Beef *ragoûts* can be moistened with red wine, and are then called *beef à la bourguignonne*. It is a popular dish not only in Burgundy, where it originates, but also in Paris, where it figures almost daily on the menus of small restaurants, especially those kept by wine merchants. On these menus the dish is described as *Bourguignon*.

The garnish for *beef à la bourguignonne* consists of lean rashers of bacon, scalded and browned, small glazed onions and mushrooms.

Rib of beef. CÔTE DE BOEUF – This cut is also called *train de côtes*. It is divided into *train de côtes découvert* and *train de côtes couvert*.

When boned, the rib is cut in slices or *entrecôtes*, which are then grilled (see *Entrecôte*).

Roasted or braised whole, ribs of beef are excellent.

In big restaurants roast rib of beef is served on a mobile hotplate, and is carved in front of the guests. The garnish or gravy and sauce are also kept on the same trolley in *bains-marie*.

Roast rib of beef is treated like all red meats and must be underdone on the inside (see CULINARY METHODS, *Average cooking times for roasts*).

Braised rib of beef is prepared in the same way as *Top rump*.

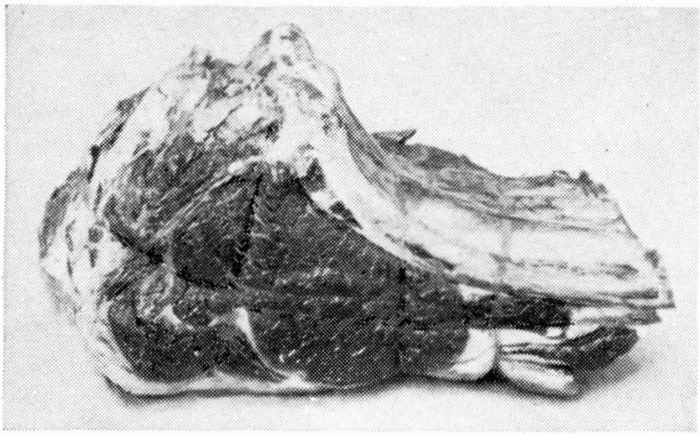

Rib of beef

Rib of beef (roast or braised) is served with all the garnishes recommended for *contre-filet* and fillet. When roasted, it is usually served with its own juices, clear and strong; when braised, with the braising liquor boiled down. The left-overs of rib of beef can be made into various dishes, recipes for which are given under ÉMINCÉ, HASH, SALPICON.

Roast in the oven. Trim the ribs. Cover with pieces of fat beaten flat, and tie with string. Brush with dripping, sprinkle with salt, put in a roasting pan and cook in the oven, uncovered. When cooked, remove string, trim, and keep hot until ready to serve. Garnish and serve as indicated in the recipe.

Roast rib of beef (boned and rolled)

Roasting on a spit. Trim the rib. Tie with string as described above. Brush with dripping, season with salt, and cook in front of a hot fire to seal the juices. Reduce to a more moderate heat to ensure that the meat cooks through. Take off the spit and proceed as described above.

Rib of beef roasted on a spit should be taken off the spit and kept in a slow oven 30 minutes to 1 hour, depending on size (this applies to whole roast rib). The cooking is thus completed and the meat settles in the gentle heat and becomes more tender.

Rib of beef à la bouquetière. CÔTE DE BOEUF À LA BOUQUETIÈRE – Cut a thick slice (containing two bones) off a trimmed rib of beef. Season this slice of rib and cook in a sauté pan in clarified butter.

Drain, and garnish with carrots and turnips cut to a uniform size, French beans, artichoke hearts stuffed with garden peas, new potatoes cooked in butter, florets of cauliflower.

Dilute the pan juices with Madeira, add a little *demi-glace* (q.v.) and pour over the rib of beef.

Decorating a roast (*French Government Tourist Office*)

Braised rib of beef. CÔTE DE BOEUF BRAISÉE – Proceed as described in the recipe for *Braised beef*.

Note. To braise, use pieces of rib, cut in thick slices weighing from 2 to 3 kg. ($4\frac{1}{2}$ to $6\frac{1}{2}$ lb.).

Cold rib of beef à la mode. CÔTE DE BOEUF FROIDE À LA MODE – Proceed as for *Top rump à la mode* (see below).

Rib of beef with garnish. CÔTE DE BOEUF GARNIE – For garnishes suitable for roast or braised ribs of beef, see GARNISHES. The following are the principal garnishes: letter (b) following the name of the garnish indicates that it is intended for braised rib of beef:

Bourgeoise (b), *bourguignonne* (b), *bruxelloise*, chipolata sausages (b), *dauphine*, *duchesse*, *flamande*, *hongroise*, *jardinière*, *lorraine*, *lyonnaise*, *macédoine*, *maraîchère*, *milanaise*, *moderne*, *nivernaise*, *parisienne*, *piémontaise*, potatoes cooked in various ways, *portugaise*, *Richelieu*.

In addition to these garnishes, roast ribs of beef can be served with buttered or braised vegetables, and purées of vegetables.

Jellied rib of beef. CÔTE DE BOEUF À LA GELÉE – Trim left-over rib of beef, cover with slightly coloured aspic jelly, garnish with chopped jelly and watercress, and decorate the border of the dish with jelly croûtons.

Jellied rib of beef can be accompanied by various plain or mixed salads.

Roast rib of beef à l'anglaise. CÔTE DE BOEUF RÔTIE À L'ANGLAISE – Roast the rib as described in the preceding recipes but allow a little more cooking time.

Serve with Yorkshire pudding, baked in the dripping-pan if the joint is cooked on a spit, or in an ordinary pan, using beef drippings for fat, if the joint is cooked in the oven.

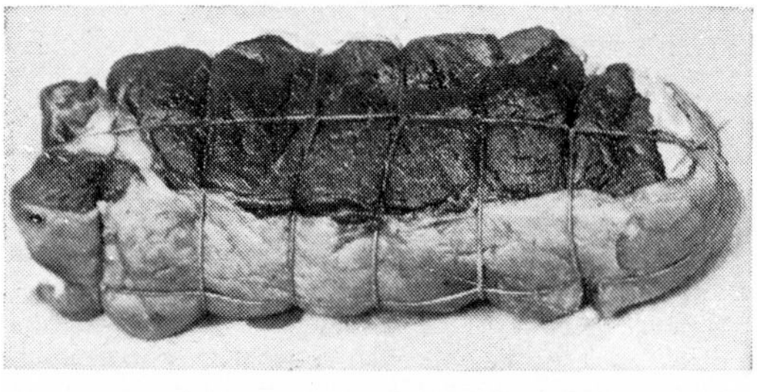

Sirloin joint ready for roasting

Roast beef. ROSBIF – Rib roasts, fillets (U.S. tenderloin) sirloin and rump make excellent roasts. The meat should be covered with dripping or other fat and roasted in a moderately hot oven (see CULINARY METHODS, *Average cooking times for roasts*).

Rump of beef. CULOTTE DE BOEUF – This cut represents what is left of the hindquarter after the sirloin has been cut off. It is first category beef and is braised and used for stocks.

The top of the rump, commonly known as *pièce de boeuf*, is served as a remove. All the recipes applicable to it will be found under *Top rump* (see below).

Rump steak. ROMSTECK – Rump steak is a slice of beef, varying in thickness, taken from the top of sirloin (U.S. face of the rump), or the lower part of the sirloin, formed by the thick, fleshy parts which cover the pelvic girdle. This cut is used for roasts and is also excellent when braised, but is chiefly preferred grilled.

Rump steak can be cooked in any way suitable for beefsteaks and fillets.

Grilled. Proceed as described for *Entrecôte, grilled.*

Sautéed. Proceed as described for *Entrecôte, sautéed.*

Salt and smoked beef. BOEUF SALÉ ET FUMÉ – Suitable principally for brisket, but top rump and shoulder of beef (chuck) can also be prepared in this manner.

After having been kept in brine (in the same way as ox tongue) for a period of time according to season, these cuts are desalted and cooked in water, allowing 15 minutes per 500 g. (1 lb.).

Salt beef is served hot, accompanied by various vegetables (braised red or green cabbage, *sauerkraut*) and, in general, with all vegetables normally served with poached beef. It is also used in *potée*. To serve cold, cool under a press, as described in the earlier recipe for *Pressed beef*.

Smoked beef, which must be pickled in brine before being smoked, is prepared in the same way as salt beef. It is served hot or cold.

Sautés of beef. SAUTÉS DE BOEUF – These are prepared from parts of rump and centre fillet cut in pieces. Season with salt and pepper. Sauté briskly in butter, keeping underdone on the inside. Remove from the pan as soon as the meat is browned, and keep hot. Dilute the pan juices with wine, add thickened brown veal stock or *demi-glace* (q.v.), boil down, and strain. Put the pieces of beef back into the pan, pour the sauce over them, and reheat without boiling.

Sautés of fillet of beef can be cooked with various garnishes; mushrooms cooked in the same butter as the beef; truffles, cut in thick slices, lightly tossed in the same butter; potatoes, cut in dice and fried in butter, added to the beef after it has been transferred into a *timbale*; fresh buttered or glazed vegetables.

The following methods are also suitable for preparing sautés of beef; *à la crème*, the pan juices being diluted with Madeira and moistened with fresh cream; *à la bourguignonne*, pan juices diluted with red wine, with a garnish of lean rashers of bacon, blanched and fried, and small glazed onions and mushrooms sautéed in butter; *à la provençale*, the pan juices diluted with white wine and moistened with *Tomato fondue* (see TOMATO).

Sauté of beef can also be served surrounded with a border of rice pilaf or risotto.

Shoulder of beef. PALERON DE BOEUF – Fleshy part of the shoulder. It is mainly used for making stock, but it can also be braised, as top rump, and made into stews.

Sirloin. ALOYAU DE BOEUF – This cut, which is classed in the first category of beef, is the part of the animal from the hook to the first ribs. It includes the *contre-filet* or *faux-filet* (U.S. sirloin) and the beef fillet (U.S. tenderloin). It is only called *aloyau* (sirloin) when it includes these two cuts, which should be cooked together, without boning. It is not found in retail markets in U.S., but a *sirloin roast* can substitute in the following recipes.

When the sirloin is cooked whole, the top has to be trimmed off slightly and the ligament all along the chine has to be severed in several places. The fillet, which is just inside this cut, should have quite a lot of fat left on it; some of the fat surrounding it should be cut off. After having been thus trimmed, the joint is seasoned with salt and pepper and tied with string.

The sirloin, served as a meat remove, is generally roasted. It is cooked either on a spit or in the oven and kept a little underdone inside. It can also be braised, cut into pieces 2 to 3 kg. ($4\frac{1}{2}$ to $6\frac{1}{2}$ lb.), in the usual manner (see CULINARY METHODS, *Braising*).

Sirloin à la d'Albuféra (Carême's recipe). ALOYAU À LA D'ALBUFÉRA – 'Prepare, braise and glaze a sirloin. Pour round it a *ragoût* made in the following manner: Put some of the pan juices and a little fresh butter into *Tortue sauce* (see SAUCE), add to it a plateful each of lightly fried calves' sweetbreads, salt beef tongue and mushrooms. Bring the *ragoût* to the boil once. Garnish with sliced fillets of young *rabbits à la Orly*. Decorate with *attelets* (q.v.); put on the *attelet* first a plump double cock's comb, then a slice of *rabbit à la Orly*, then another cock's comb and a glazed black truffle.'

Braised sirloin. ALOYAU BRAISÉ – Trim a piece of sirloin, cutting across the joint, with the grain of the meat. Lard it with thick lardoons, which have been seasoned with salt, pepper and spices, sprinkled with chopped parsley and steeped for an hour in a sprinkling of brandy with carrots and onions. Tie with string and braise.

Reduce pan juices, skim off fat, strain, and pour over the sirloin before serving.

Braised sirloin with various garnishes. ALOYAU BRAISÉ AVEC GARNITURES DIVERSES – Braise the sirloin as described above. Serve with one of the following garnishes, disposed around the meat or served separately: *Bourgeoise*, *bruxelloise*, celery, chipolata sausages, *sauerkraut*, kohlrabi, *Dubarry*, *duchesse*, *flamande*, *jardinière*, *milanaise*, *napolitaine*, noodles, *piémontaise*, various potatoes, *provençale*, *Richelieu*, *risotto* (see GARNISHES).

Sirloin, left-over pieces braised or roast. DESSERTE DE L'ALOYAU – All the recipes given for the preparation of *Rib of beef* or *Contre-filet* are applicable to sirloin.

Bones which remain after the meat has been completely used up can be used for making *Beef stock* (see STOCKS).

Roast sirloin. ALOYAU RÔTI – This can be cooked whole or in pieces. Cut off the top and trim the sirloin, leaving a light layer of fat on the fillet, to prevent it from drying during cooking. Tie with string.

Roast it, on a spit or in the oven, by following the instructions given for the cooking of red meats (see CULINARY METHODS). Garnish with watercress and serve its own juices separately.

Roast sirloin à l'anglaise. ALOYAU RÔTI À L'ANGLAISE – Trim and tie the joint, enclose in paste made of flour and hot water, with one quarter of its weight of chopped and salted beef fat added to it. When nearly cooked, remove the crust and brown the joint.

Serve with Yorkshire pudding (q.v.) cooked in the roasting pan, and the joint's own juices.

Roast sirloin with various garnishes. ALOYAU RÔTI – Roast the joint as described above. Serve with one of the garnishes recommended for *Braised sirloin*. The sirloin, braised or roasted, can also be accompanied by the garnishes recommended for *Contre-filet* (U.S. sirloin), *Rib* and *Fillet of beef* (U.S. tenderloin).

Sliced beef with various sauces. ÉMINCÉS DE BOEUF – Left-over poached, braised or roast meat is usually used for this dish. Cut the piece of meat into thin slices, and pour over them one of the following sauces: *Bordelaise, bourguignonne, charcutière, chasseur, duxelles, fines herbes, italienne, lyonnaise,* Madeira, *piquante, poivrade.*

Steak – See *Beefsteak, Chateaubriand, Contre-filet, Entrecôte,* etc.

Ox tail – See OFFAL or VARIETY MEATS.

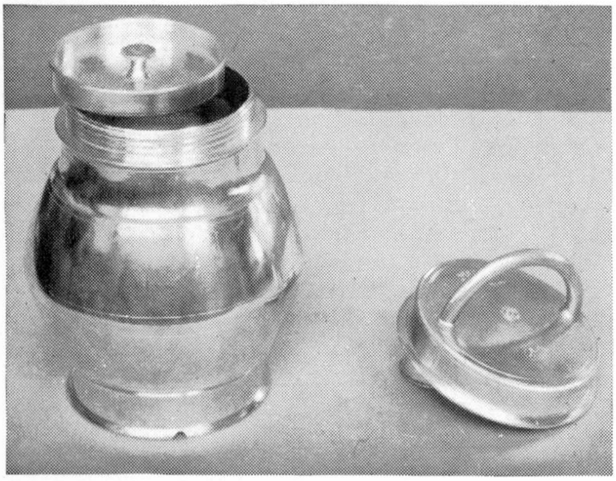

American marmite for beef-tea

Beef-tea – Concentrated consommé or meat juice, obtained by cutting lean beef into small dice and sealing them hermetically in a wide-necked bottle, or in a special screw-top pewter receptacle (American marmite). Put into a pan of boiling water for 40 to 50 minutes.

500 g. (1 lb.) meat will give about 150 g. (4 to 5 oz.) liquid.

Beef-tea has a greater nutritive value than ordinary meat-stock but it is chiefly given, in small doses, to convalescents, for stimulating the secretion of digestive glands and awakening the appetite.

Tongue – See OFFAL or VARIETY MEATS, *Beef or Ox tongue.*

Top rump. PIÈCE DE BOEUF (POINTE DE CULOTTE) – (See *Rump of beef.*) Top rump is sometimes called *pointe de culotte*, but is more frequently described on menus as *pièce de boeuf.*

Braised. Lard a 3-kg. ($6\frac{1}{2}$-lb.) piece of top rump with strips of salt pork, well seasoned and sprinkled with brandy. Season the meat with fine salt, pepper and spices, and tie with string.

Marinate for 5 hours in wine with thyme, bay leaf, parsley and a crushed clove of garlic.

Drain and dry the meat with a cloth. Brown in butter or other fat. Fry 2 sliced onions and 2 sliced carrots in butter, put them into a braising pan with $1\frac{1}{2}$ kg. ($3\frac{1}{4}$ lb.) fleshy bones, a calf's knuckle chopped into small pieces and browned in the oven, 2 calf's feet, boned, scalded, dipped in cold water and tied with string, and a *bouquet garni* (q.v.). Lay the meat on this foundation. Add the marinating liquor, cover the pan, and cook a little away from direct heat until the liquor is almost completely reduced. Add slightly thickened veal stock mixed with 3 tablespoons (scant $\frac{1}{4}$ cup) tomato sauce to cover the meat.

Bring to the boil. Cover the pan and put in a slow oven for about 4 hours. Drain the meat, untie, and glaze it in the oven, basting with its own gravy.

Arrange on a large dish, surround with the garnish recommended, disposed in separate groups. Boil down the braising liquor, skim off the fat, and pour over the meat.

Poached. Tie with string and cook, with the usual garnish, in a large stockpot, as indicated for *Pot-au-feu* (see SOUPS). Bring to the boil, remove scum, season, and leave to simmer for 4 to 5 hours. Drain the meat, remove string, and serve with its own strained liquor, grated horseradish, and rock salt.

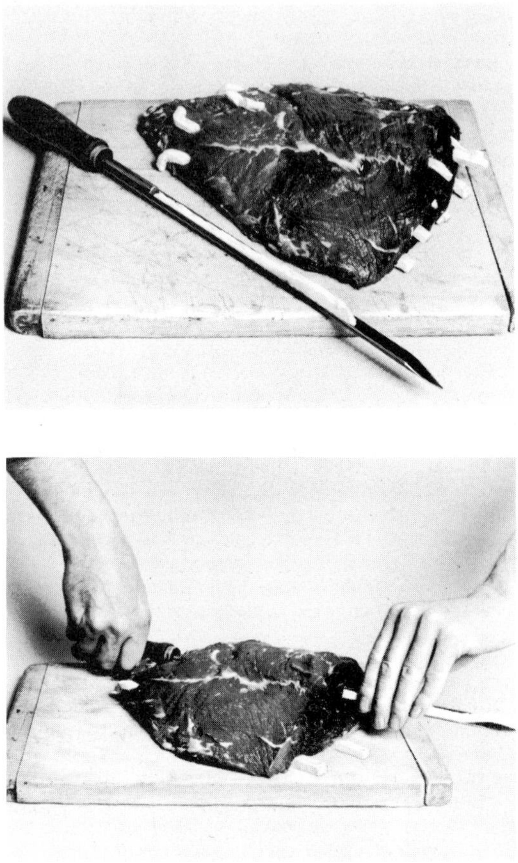

How to lard top rump (*Nicolas*)

Top rump à la bourgeoise. PIÈCE DE BOEUF À LA BOURGEOISE – Steep lardoons in brandy and spices and insert in a large piece of rump. Season and marinate in 5 dl. (scant pint, $2\frac{1}{4}$ cups) white wine for 6 hours.

Cook in a braising pan with vegetables and other garnish as indicated for *Braising meat* (see CULINARY METHODS).

When three-quarters cooked, drain the meat and put it in a casserole with 4 carrots which have been cut into small pieces and two-thirds cooked in stock, and small glazed onions. Add calf's feet, braised with the meat, boned and cut into pieces. Strain the braising liquor, skim off fat, and pour over the meat. Cook with a lid on for $1\frac{1}{4}$ hours.

Drain the meat and serve with the liquor.

Top rump à la bourguignonne. PIÈCE DE BOEUF À LA BOURGUIGNONNE – Insert large lardoons into a piece of rump and marinate in brandy for 6 hours. Braise in red wine, following the recipe for *Braising meat* (see CULINARY METHODS).

When three-quarters cooked, drain the meat and put into a *daubière* (q.v.) with garnish *à la bourguignonne* (see GARNISHES) and its braising liquor, strained and with fat skimmed off. Simmer slowly.

Top rump braised à l'ancienne. PIÈCE DE BOEUF BRAISÉE À L'ANCIENNE – Trim top rump, and tie with string. Braise, and when the meat is still a little firm, drain, put under a press, or in a pan with a weight on top. Leave to cool.

Cut out the centre part, leaving a meat ring about 1½ cm. (¾ inch) thick. Brush with beaten egg and cover with white breadcrumbs mixed with grated Parmesan cheese. Press well to make the breadcrumbs adhere, sprinkle with melted butter, and brown in the oven.

Cut the meat taken out of the centre part into very thin slices, put them into a sauté pan, added thin slices of *tongue à l'écarlate* (salt beef tongue) and some sliced mushrooms, lightly fried in butter. Moisten with a few tablespoons concentrated braising liquor, strained and with the fat skimmed off. Add ½ dl. (3 tablespoons, scant ¼ cup) Madeira and leave to stew slowly but do not boil.

Place these slices in the meat ring, and serve with the remainder of the sauce.

Top rump à la mode. PIÈCE DE BOEUF À LA MODE – Cook as described in the recipe for *Top rump à la bourgeoise*, replacing white wine by red.

Top skirt. ONGLET DE BOEUF – This juicy cut can be prepared in any way suitable for *Beefsteak*. It is also used for *carbonades*, for extracting meat juice, and for beef sautées. Grill or sauté.

Tournedos (medallions of fillet of beef) – Small slices of fillet of beef, usually fried in butter, or in a mixture of butter and oil, or in oil. Their preparation is similar to that of *Noisettes of mutton* (see MUTTON). They should be cooked very quickly, to make sure that they remain pink inside.

Tournedos can also be grilled (see *Filets mignons, grilled*). Before garnishing, they are sometimes placed on grilled or fried croûtons, potato cakes, artichoke hearts, small mounds of rice, etc. Garnishes and sauces for *tournedos* will be found in alphabetical order under GARNISHES and SAUCE.

Tournedos Abrantès – Season the *tournedos* with salt and paprika and sauté them in oil. Place them on grilled slices of aubergines. Fry 1 tablespoon chopped onion in the oil, add a *salpicon* (q.v.) of peeled pimentos and a few tablespoons tomato sauce, and pour over the *tournedos*. Serve with potatoes which have been cut small and cooked in butter.

Tournedos à l'algérienne – Season the *tournedos* with salt and paprika and sauté in butter. Place on fried croûtons and surround with *Garnish algérienne* (see GARNISHES). Dilute the pan juices with white wine to which has been added tomato-flavoured veal stock, and pour over the *tournedos*.

Tournedos archiduc – Sauté the *tournedos* in butter and place them on potato cakes, garnishing with small croquettes of calves' brains. Toss slivers of truffle in butter and place 2 on each garnished *tournedo*. Dilute the pan juices with sherry, add fresh cream and veal stock in equal proportions, boil down a little, season with paprika, strain, and pour over the *tournedos*.

Tournedos à la béarnaise – Garnish grilled *tournedos* with small *Château potatoes* (see POTATOES). Serve with *Béarnaise sauce* (see SAUCE).

Tournedos à la bordelaise – Place thin slices of poached and drained marrow on grilled *tournedos*. Sprinkle with chopped parsley and serve with *Bordelaise sauce* (see SAUCE).

Tournedos chasseur – Sauté the *tournedos* in butter, and place on a dish. Sauté sliced mushrooms in the same pan, adding a spoonful of chopped shallots. Season, brown for a few minutes, and add a little dry wine and a few tablespoons *demi-glace* (q.v.) (or thickened veal stock). Boil for 2 minutes. Add 2 teaspoons chopped parsley, chervil and tarragon, and a little butter to the sauce. Stir well and pour over the *tournedos*.

Tournedos Choron – Sauté the *tournedos* in butter, and place them on fried croûtons. Garnish with artichoke hearts which have been stewed in butter and filled with garden peas or asparagus tips dressed in butter. Pour on each *tournedo* a ring of thick *Choron sauce* (see SAUCE). Dilute the pan juices with white wine and thickened veal stock, and pour a few tablespoons over the *tournedos*.

Tournedos à la Clamart – Sauté the *tournedos* in butter. Simmer artichoke hearts in butter, and fill with a purée of fresh peas and small new potatoes which have been cooked in butter. Dilute the pan juices with white wine and thickened veal stock, and pour over the *tournedos*.

Tournedos Helder – Sauté the *tournedos* in butter, place them on fried croûtons, and top each one with a ring of *Béarnaise sauce* (see SAUCE), further decorated with a teaspoon of thick *Tomato fondue* (see FONDUE). Garnish with potatoes fried in butter, Dilute the pan juices with white wine and thickened veal stock, and pour over the *tournedos*.

Tournedos Henri IV – Sauté the *tournedos* in butter and place on fried croûtons. Top each *tournedo* with a small artichoke heart filled with thick *Béarnaise sauce* (see SAUCE), decorated with a sliver of truffle. Garnish with small potatoes. Dilute the pan juices with Madeira and *demi-glace* (q.v.) and pour over the *tournedos*.

Tournedos Marguery

Tournedos Marguery – Sauté the *tournedos* in butter, and top each with an artichoke heart filled with a *salpicon* (q.v.) of truffles *à la crème*. Fill the centre of the dish with morels fried in butter, and place a few cocks' combs and kidneys between the *tournedos*. Dilute the pan juices with port, add fresh cream, boil down a little, and pour over the *tournedos*.

Tournedos Massena – Grill the *tournedos* and arrange them on artichokes which have been simmered in butter. Add a slice of poached bone-marrow to each *tournedo*. Cover with *Marrow sauce I* (see SAUCE), and put a pinch of chopped parsley on each slice of marrow.

Tournedos with mushrooms – Sauté the *tournedos* in butter. When half cooked, add small mushrooms which have been lightly fried in butter, and complete cooking. Arrange the *tournedos* in a crown on a dish, and surround with the mushrooms. Dilute the pan juices with Madeira, moisten with *demi-glace* (q.v.) or thickened veal stock, and pour over the *tournedos*.

Tournedos à la perigourdine – Sauté the *tournedos* in butter, place on fried croûtons, and top each with slices of truffle which have been tossed in the cooking butter. Dilute the pan juices with Madeira and *demi-glace* (q.v.) and pour over the *tournedos*.

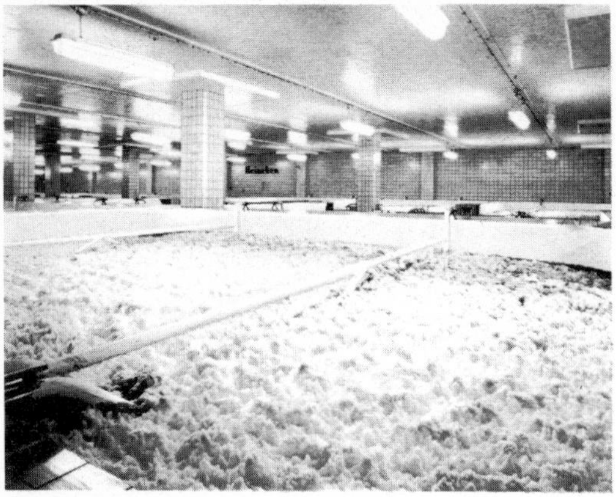
Beer: fermentation room (Heineken) (*Adwindig*)

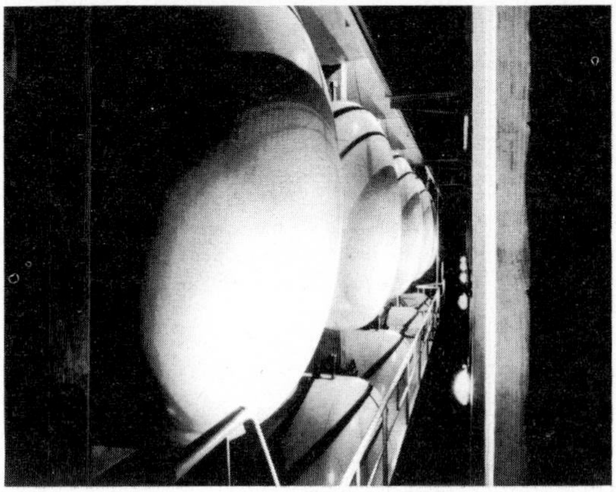
Beer: tank cellar (Heineken) (*Adwindig*)

Tornedos à la portugaise – Sauté the *tournedos* in butter and oil, and garnish with small stuffed tomatoes and *Château potatoes* (see POTATOES). Dilute the pan juices with white wine and tomato-flavoured veal stock and pour over the *tournedos*.

Tournedos Rossini – Sauté the *tournedos* in butter and arrange on croûtons. Put a slice of *foie gras* tossed in butter on each, and top with slices of truffles, heated in the same butter in which the *tournedos* were cooked.

Dilute the pan juices with Madeira and *demi-glace* (q.v.) and pour over the *tournedos*.

Tournedos Saint-Germain – Sauté the *tournedos* in butter, place on fried croûtons, and garnish with a thick purée of fresh peas.

Dilute the pan juices with thickened veal stock and pour over the *tournedos*. Garnish with young glazed carrots and small new potatoes cooked in butter, alternating these vegetables round the dish. Serve with *Béarnaise sauce* (see SAUCE).

Tournedos can be cooked in any way suitable for small cuts of meat, especially as described in recipes for *Noisettes of mutton* (see MUTTON). Sautéed or grilled *tournedos* can also be dressed with butter or fresh cream, and served with French beans, kidney beans, peas, asparagus tips. They can also be garnished with fresh vegetables cooked in butter or braised, such as cucumbers, chicory, lettuce, small marrows, aubergines, celeriac, celery, spinach; as well as with potatoes cooked in various ways; and with purées of fresh or dried vegetables, rice pilaf, risotto, pasta products and cereals.

Beef à la vinaigrette. BOEUF À LA VINAIGRETTE – Boiled beef, diced or cut in thin slices, seasoned with salt, pepper, oil, vinegar, onion and chopped parsley. Serve with sliced boiled potatoes.

BEEF-EATERS – Nickname given to the Yeoman of the Guard on duty at the Tower of London. The name may have been derived from the French *beaufaitier* – one who attends the buffet. It is more likely that these yeomen were called beef-eaters in the seventeenth century, from their receiving a large daily ration of beef.

BEER. BIÈRE – A generic term used for all fermented malt beverages, and includes porter, ale and stout. The beverage is obtained through the action of yeast on an infusion of malted cereals. It is a refreshing and slightly stimulating drink which has some food value.

The invention of fermented beverages from grain is attributed to the Egyptians, who practised the manufacture of alcoholic liquor from grain at least 5,000 years ago. *Papyri* of the period 1300 B.C. refer to the regulation of beer shops to prevent people over indulging in beer. The Egyptians made several kinds of beer, and they also made a wine from barley which they called *xithum*.

The Pannonians, who lived along the Danube, made a potent drink out of barley and millet. A similar beverage existed in Illyria. Teutons made a kind of wine from fermented barley and wheat. 'The people of the west,' said Pliny, 'get drunk on mouldy grain.'

The beer made by all these people was not intended to be kept. Hops were later introduced in the brewing of beer in the Netherlands, and in the fifteenth century in England.

Hop field (*J. Boyer*)

In all regions and at all latitudes, beer is brewed from

Beer: filtering and refrigeration (Gruber, Melun) (*Larousse*)

Beer: bottle assembly line (Heineken) (*Adwindig*)

various cereals: wheat, oats, rice (the Japanese saké), millet, maize (U.S. corn), sorghum, etc; and even from starchy roots (sweet potatoes, cassava), when cereals are not available.

Industrial brewing. In Europe, beer is generally produced by the alcoholic fermentation of a sweetened juice, the wort, flavoured with hops and fermented by a micro-organism, yeast. The wort is the product of the maceration of malt flour or sprouted barley in water at suitably controlled temperatures. Cereal starch is not directly fermentable. The purpose of germinating the barley in the malting process is to breed enzymes in the grain; these induce the transformation of the starch into malt sugar or maltose during the mashing process.

After having been cleaned and picked over, the barley grains are set to soak in tuns, and dispatched to the malt houses. The sprouted barley is then dried in malt kilns, thus arresting germination. This operation is regulated according to the quality of malt desired: pale malt for the manufacture of pale ale; coloured, flavoured malt for the manufacture of brown ale. The malt is then degermed; that is to say, the rootlets or malt combs are removed. These have a high protein and nitrogen content which makes them ideal cattle feed.

During the mashing process the crushed malt is put to macerate in water and the mixture heated to a temperature of 75°C. (167°F.). In the course of this operation, which is done by decoction or infusion, the starch is transformed by enzymes into sugar: this is the process of saccharification. The wort is separated by filtration from the residue, called the draff; this is also used as cattle food. The filtered wort is cooked and hops are added in the proportion of 150 to 500 g. per hectolitre (5 oz. to 18 oz. per 22 gallons, 28 gallons).

The cooled wort is then sent to fermentation tuns. The addition of culture yeast completes the process and the beer is placed in maturing cellars cooled to 0° or 2°C. (32° or 36°F.), where it remains for a variable length of time depending upon its type and quality.

There are two principal types of beer: low fermentation beers and high fermentation beers. They differ in the type of leavening used, in the speed of fermentation and in the method of mashing the wort. In the former, the temperature of fermentation is maintained artificially above 10°C. (50°F.). After a period of six to twelve days most of the leavening is precipitated and forms a deposit at the bottom of the tun, from which comes the term 'low bottom fermentation yeast'. In the second case, the temperature rises to 15° or 20°C. (59° or 68°F.). Fermentation lasts from two to four days, and the yeast gathers at the top of the liquid, hence the term 'top fermentation yeast'.

Top fermentation, which used to be the most universally popular method, is still employed in Britain, Belgium and northern France. Bottom fermentation has developed since the introduction of refrigeration. It makes possible the production of a more consistent quality of beer.

Also manufactured, mostly in Belgium, is a yeastless beer called *lambic* and *faro*.

After a period in the maturing cellars the beer is filtered, then conditioned in casks or bottles. This liquid, so easily spoiled, requires the most careful handling. The premises and receptacles must be perfectly clean and regularly sterilised. The beer conditioned in bottles is generally pasteurised – heated to a temperature of 60° to 65°C. (140° to 149°F.).

Bottled beer is charged under pressure with carbonic acid which enables all its freshness and flavour to be preserved, provided that it is consumed immediately it is opened.

Low (bottom) fermentation beers used to be classed in three types: *pilsen*, a light blend beer; *munich*, a strong brown beer; *vienne*, a sweet, amber-coloured beer rapidly decreasing in popularity.

Among the top fermentation beers are the English brews: *pale ale*, a blend beer; *porter* and *stout*, brown beers. There are also special beers: the white beers of Louvain and Berlin, the *lambic* and *faro* of Belgium. The various beers belong to these types. The most widely distributed is the pilsen-type of pale ale. It is true, however, to say that there are as many varieties of beer as there are breweries.

The legal densimetric unit of beer is not the same in every country. In France it is the '*Régie*' degree. There is a tendency to refer back to the original extract – that is, the extract contained by the wort before fermentation. This density is never expressed in alcoholic degrees, for the alcoholic content of beer depends on its attenuation – on the diminution of the extract in the course of fermentation. The alcohol content of beers made from the original extract fluctuates according to the degree of attenuation.

The chemical composition of beers varies according to the type and density of the original wort. The volume of alcohol it contains ranges from 3 per cent to 6 per cent, sometimes greater, depending upon the beer. English beers in particular can exceed this amount.

The extract is formed by dextrines, the maltose not transformed into alcohol, and by soluble nitrogenous substances. It is present in the proportion of from 4 to 9 per cent. This extract is what gives a sensation of fullness to the palate which the tasters call the *mash*. It is also due to this extract that the carbonic acid forms the substantial froth or head which indicates careful drawing and skilful brewing.

Beer contains amyloïdes, protides, alcohol, minerals, vitamins, etc. It is an excellent beverage easily assimilated by the body. The alcohol and the hops' extract have a stimulating effect. It can be used in a considerable number of dishes. A Belgian culinary school strongly recommends the beer dishes conceived by the late chef Raoul Morleghem.

In France, a special governmental body makes a regular check on beers, and severely punishes any infractions of the manufacturing regulations.

Besides the basic elements used in its manufacture (barley, hops, yeast), beer is rich in mineral salts and vitamins (B_1, B_2, B_{12}, PP). Its consumption must be controlled, or rather drastically reduced, in the case of overweight, gout, and diabetes, as well as in certain types of dyspepsia. It is recommended in diets for increasing weight, and for nursing mothers, so long as it does not have too strong an alcoholic content.

Ale, stout and porter are consumed in much greater quantities in Europe than in U.S.A. Some ale is manufactured in the United States, but most American breweries produce a lager beer which is lighter bodied than the European varieties. There is a large volume of importing and exporting of beers between Europe and the United States.

Barley beer. CERVOISE – Decoction of barley, fermented with yeast – perhaps derived from fermenting grapes, which produces a kind of barley wine rather than a beer. This was a drink of the ancient Gauls.

Ginger beer. BIÈRE DE GINGEMBRE – Boil 2¼ kg. (5 lb.) loaf sugar, 75 g. (3 oz., ¾ cup) ground ginger and 14 litres (3 gallons, 3¾ gallons) water for 1 hour. When cold, add the juice and thinly peeled rind of 5 lemons. Add ¼ cup brewer's yeast smeared on a piece of toast. Keep in a wooden tub, covered with a thick cloth, for 2 or 3 days. Strain through a cloth, bottle, and cork securely, tying the corks down.

The beer will be ready for drinking in 4 or 5 days. If a stronger brew is desired, add more ginger.

Home-made beer I. BIÈRE DE MÉNAGE – Boil 2 litres (3½ pints, 4½ pints) ordinary barley in 22 litres (4¾ gallons, 6 gallons) water for 2 hours. Add 125 g. (4 oz.) hops and 10 g. (⅓ oz.) chicory, and leave to infuse. Strain, and pour into a 30-litre (6½-gallon, 8-gallon) tun. Add 1¼ kg. (2½ lb.) sugar which has been dissolved in 10 litres (9 quarts, 11 quarts) water. Mix well. Leave the tun uncovered until the following day.

Add 50 g. (2 oz.) brewer's yeast which has been dissolved in a little hot water. Stir with a stick. Leave the tun open for 6 days. Add more liquid every morning and evening to replace that lost through fermentation. On the seventh day, bung the barrel, and on the eighth day, bottle the beer. Boil the corks in water for 5 minutes, and cork the bottles tightly.

Home-made beer II. BIÈRE DE MÉNAGE – Boil 100 g. (4 oz.) hulled barley, 500 g. (18 oz., 2¼ cups) sugar and a handful of hops in 4 litres (3½ quarts, 4½ quarts) water; keep boiling for ½ hour. Remove from heat, add 10 g. (⅓ oz.) yeast and 10 litres (9 quarts, 11 quarts) water.

Leave to ferment for 4 days, then bottle and cork. (A little burnt sugar may be added to this beer to give it colour.)

Malt beer. BIÈRE DE MALT – This beer is obtained by adding concentrated malt extract to the wort and letting it ferment slightly. It has much greater nutritive properties than ordinary beer and is used as a tonic, or for nursing mothers.

Beer soup (German cookery). SOUPE À LA BIÈRE – Dilute 150 g. (5 oz.) light *roux* (q.v.) made of butter and flour with 1½ litres (2¾ pints, 3¼ pints) light beer. Mix well. Season with salt and pepper and add 2 teaspoons fine sugar and a small pinch powdered cinnamon. Bring to the boil, and simmer for 25 minutes.

Before serving, thicken with 2 dl. (⅓ pint, scant cup) double cream. Pour over thin slices of toast into a soup tureen while it is still boiling.

BEESTINGS. AMOUILLE – Name commonly given to the first milk of a cow after parturition.

BEESWAX. CIRE – Product transformed from the honey absorbed by the working bee, which it uses to construct the cells in honeycombs and in the interior of the hive.

The name *cires végétales* is given to substances extracted from certain vegetables, in particular from certain palms.

BEET – See BEETROOT.

BEETROOT (U.S. Beet). BETTERAVE – There are many varieties of this plant, some cultivated solely for distillery purposes, some as animal foodstuff and some, as in the case of garden beet, as vegetable.

Among the best varieties of garden beetroot are: red stump-rooted, dark red Massy, large red, early red globe, dark red turnip-rooted Egyptian, red globe summer beet, dark red globe early beet.

Five varieties of beetroot

The Romans used beetroot leaves as a vegetable.

In Russian cookery both the roots and the leaves of beets are used, notably for various soups (see SOUPS AND BROTHS, *Beetroot soup à la Russe*).

Beetroot in *hors-d'œuvre* is refreshing and increases the appetite but is not recommended for sufferers of dyspepsia and colitis, since it is inclined to be indigestible and its cellulose fibres can cause flatulence.

For information on sugar beet, see SUGAR.

Beetroot leaves are perfectly edible, and are used in many recipes. In France the roots, boiled or baked, are used as garnish for salads, *hors-d'œuvre* and various game *entrées*.

Wash and scrub the beets with a brush. Dry them and bake in the oven. They are ready when they begin to 'give' a little, if pressed with a finger. Keep in a cool place.

Beet à l'anglaise. BETTERAVES À L'ANGLAISE – Choose tender beets, peel, cut into slices and boil in salted water. Drain, dry and serve with fresh butter.

Beetroot à la béchamel. BETTERAVES À LA BÉCHAMEL – Bake 2 beets in the oven, peel, and cut into fairly thick slices. Simmer gently in a sauté pan with 2 tablespoons (3 tablespoons) butter and a pinch of salt.

To serve, cover with not too thick *Béchamel sauce* (see SAUCE), to which butter has been added.

Beetroot in cream. BETTERAVES À LA CRÈME – Stew slices of beet in butter. Dilute the pan juices with 4 dl. (¾ pint, scant 2 cups) pre-boiled cream. Cook down by half, season, remove from heat, blend in 50 g. (2 oz., ¼ cup) butter, and pour over the beets.

Beetroot for garnish. BETTERAVES POUR GARNITURES – Choose well-shaped, uniformly sized beetroot. Bake them in the oven, allow to become quite cold, and peel. Cut into slices or dice, or shred into a *julienne*.

Prepared in this way beetroot can be served as a garnish for *hors-d'œuvre* or for salads.

Beetroot in gravy. BETTERAVES AU JUS – Proceed as described in the recipe for *Beetroot in cream*, replacing the latter by 2 dl. (⅓ pint, scant cup) thickened brown veal stock. Boil the beets in the stock for a few moments.

Beetroot à la lyonnaise. BETTERAVES À LA LYONNAISE – Melt 50 g. (2 oz., ¼ cup) butter in a pan, add 4 tablespoons (5 tablespoons) finely chopped onion, cook slowly without allowing it to colour, add sliced beetroot and simmer together.

Before serving, moisten with 2 dl. (⅓ pint, scant cup) thickened brown veal stock.

Beetroot à la poitevine. BETTERAVES À LA POITEVINE – Stew sliced beetroot for a few moments in 2 dl. (⅓ pint, scant cup) *Lyonnaise sauce* (see SAUCE). Add a tablespoon vinegar before serving.

Stuffed beetroot cassolettes. CASSOLETTES DE BETTERAVES GARNIES – These are served as *hors-d'œuvre*. Bake large beets in the oven and cut them into thick slices. Trim these to look like *cassolettes* and fill with cold *hors-d'œuvre* composition: *salpicons* (q.v.) of hard-boiled eggs, fish, vegetables, dressed with mayonnaise, various purées, etc.

BÉGUINETTE – Name used in some parts of France for the garden warbler.

BEIGNETS – See FRITTERS.

Beignets (petits fours) I – Pound 500 g. (18 oz., 3½ cups) blanched almonds with 500 g. (18 oz., 2¼ cups) sugar and 5 egg whites.

Add 2 whole eggs, and flavour with vanilla, orange or lemon peel, or shredded crystallised pineapple. Colour with carmine or green vegetable colouring agent. Fold in 16 stiffly whisked egg whites, and spoon into buttered and floured *petits fours* moulds. Decorate with pieces of candied orange or pineapple. Sprinkle with icing sugar and bake in a slow oven.

Beignets II – Pound together 250 g. (9 oz., 1¾ cups) blanched almonds and 250 g. (9 oz., generous cup) sugar. Add one egg white to the mixture and blend in one whole egg. Flavour with vanilla.

Whisk 8 egg whites into a very stiff froth and fold them into the mixture. Spoon into small biscuit moulds, sprinkle with icing sugar, and bake in a slow oven.

BEILCHE – A dish that goes far back in the history of German *cuisine*.

Trim and remove the fat from a round of beef. Make surface incisions cross-wise all over it (these cuts must not be too deep). Season inside the incisions with salt, pepper and spices.

Place the beef in a large *terrine* or cast-iron pan. (In Germany, a special silver receptable used to be employed for this dish.) Cover it with very large floury potatoes. Season these and sprinkle with fat or butter. Place a lid on top, sealing it with a flour-and-water paste. Bake in cinders mixed with glowing charcoal for 4 to 5 hours. Serve in the receptacle in which it has been cooked.

BELGIUM – See INTERNATIONAL COOKERY.

BELLE-ALLIANCE – An excellent winter dessert pear (December and January). The skin is yellowish on one side and red on the other.

BELLE-ANGEVINE – Variety of large winter pear. Its skin is green at first, then becomes bright yellow, flushed with red and pitted with brown.

This pear, in season in February and March, is better to look at than to eat, and is used mostly for filling decorative baskets of fruit.

BELLE-CHEVREUSE – Variety of peach, with bright red skin. It should be eaten when it is just ripe; when it is too ripe, its flesh becomes 'sleepy'.

BELLE-DE-BERRY – Another name for a variety of pear called *poire de curé*.

BELLE-ET-BONNE – Pear with mediocre flesh, usually cooked in syrup or red wine.

BELLE-GARDE – Peach which ripens in September and October. Its flesh is on the firm side, and it is mostly used for compotes and in pastry-making.

BELLONE – A variety of very large fig, which grows in Provence. These figs are used for preserves.

BELON – River in Brittany. The oysters of the beds there bear the same name.

BELSHAZZAR. BALTHAZAR – Colloquial usage for copious meals; an allusion to the famous feasts mentioned in the Bible.

BÉLUGA (Huso Huso) – The white sturgeon of the Black Sea, Caspian Sea and other waters. It is the largest of the sturgeon family, producing the best caviare.

BÉNARI – Local name for a variety of ortolan found in the Languedoc district. They are fattened in the same way as the Landes district ortolans. For methods of preparation see ORTOLAN.

BÉNÉDICTIN (Cake) – Cream in a bowl 250 g. (9 oz., 2¼ cups) ground almonds, 250 g. (9 oz., generous cup) fine sugar, 2 whole eggs and 12 egg yolks. When the mixture is smooth, add 2 more eggs, one by one. Mix well, and add 1 tablespoon Benedictine liqueur; and 100 g. (4 oz., 1 cup) sieved flour, and 100 g. (4 oz., ⅔ cup) potato flour which have been first sieved together.

Butter baking tins, sprinkle with flour, and fill two-thirds full with the cake mixture. Bake in an oven at 180°C. (350°F., Gas Mark 4). Remove cakes from the tins as soon as they are baked and cool on a flat wire rack. Sprinkle each cake with Benedictine, and when this is absorbed, cover the tops and sides of the cakes with thick apricot jam. Decorate the sides with chopped roasted almonds.

Ice the top of the cakes with pale yellow fondant icing which has been flavoured with Benedictine, and when it is set make a pattern of squares on it with mauve fondant icing, using a forcing-bag. Decorate the centre of each square with half a pistachio nut.

The same mixture can be used for small iced *petits fours*. The cake is made as described above, but is steeped in liqueur and cut into uniform squares before icing. Decorate each *petit four* with a mauve fondant spiral.

BENEDICTINE. BÉNÉDICTINE – Renowned French liqueur invented by the Benedictine monks at the Abbey of Fécamp, and still produced there.

BÉNÉDICTINE (À LA) – Garnish suitable for poached fish or eggs, composed of a *brandade* (q.v.) of cod and truffles.

Salt cod à la bénédictine. MORUE À LA BÉNÉDICTINE – The cod is pounded as for *brandade*, but mixed with potatoes prepared as for purée. (See SALT COD.)

Joseph Berchoux (1765–1839)

BERCHOUX (Joseph) – French poet, born at Saint-Symphorien-de-Lay (Loire) in 1765, who made a name for himself in gastronomical literature with a poem entitled *la Gastronomie*, published in 1800. Berchoux was not a gastronome, but his poem was valued for its zest and light-hearted, witty tone, and was included in a volume of gastronomic writers of the quality of Grimod de la Reynière and Brillat-Savarin, published by Charpentier in 1829 under the title *les Classiques de la table*.

Bergamot

BERGAMOT ORANGE. BERGAMOTE – Fruit of the bergamot tree, a kind of orange with a very acid but pleasant taste. The highly scented oil extracted from its rind is used in perfumery, pharmaceutics and confectionery. Candied bergamot peel is used in *pâtisserie*.

The bergamots of Nancy are the most sought after in confectionery.

BERGAMOT PEAR. BERGAMOTE – Name applied to several varieties of pear. The *bergamote d'automne* is the best.

BERLINGOT – A hard, sweet candy variously flavoured, but usually with peppermint. Several regions of France have their own special variety of *berlingots*; those of Carpentras are renowned.

BERNARD (Émile) – Famous nineteenth century chef employed by Wilhelm I, King of Prussia. In collaboration with Urbain Dubois he wrote one of the best cookery books of the period: *Cuisine classique*.

BERRICHONNE (À LA) – Garnish used for large cuts of meat and especially for mutton. It is composed of braised cabbage, small onions, chestnuts and rashers of streaky bacon.

BERRY – The richest sheep producing region of France. But lamb and mutton are not the only gastronomic assets of Berry. The province has always had a reputation for *bonne chère* and produces many other delicacies, solid and liquid.

The *cuisine* of the Berry region has an agreeable simplicity. There is the fine poultry of Bourges, good ground and winged game, a great variety of freshwater fish, including Vierzon lamprey, and excellent fruit and vegetables.

Argenton-sur-Creuse (*French Government Tourist Office*)

Culinary specialities – These include soups with *truches* or *tartouffes* (potatoes), with *reuves* and salt pork; *sanguine*, a kind of pancake made with chicken's blood; various *matelotes*; *citrouillat* (pumpkin pie); *sauciaux*, a peasant pancake; *truffiat*, home-made potato scone; *grignaudes*, flat cakes made of pork greaves or cracklings; *poulet en barbouille*, chicken coated with its own blood; *matafan*, pancake; *potato gouère* or *gouéron*.

Wines – Wine connoisseurs have a high regard for the wines of this region. And, indeed, the very dry white wines of Berry have every right to be acclaimed for their delicacy and bouquet. They all come from the Sauvignon grape.

Then there are the Sancerre wines from the vineyards surrounding the town of that name (immortalised by Balzac) and those in the neighbouring communes, particularly Bué, Verdigny, Champtin, Saint-Satur, Ménétrol, Reigny, Sury-en-Vaux.

The hamlet of Chavignol, near Sancerre, produces famous wine which the poet Hugues Lapaire, a native of Berry, placed far above the rest. Chavignol was also highly esteemed by Balzac and by the '*bonne dame*' of Nohant – George Sand.

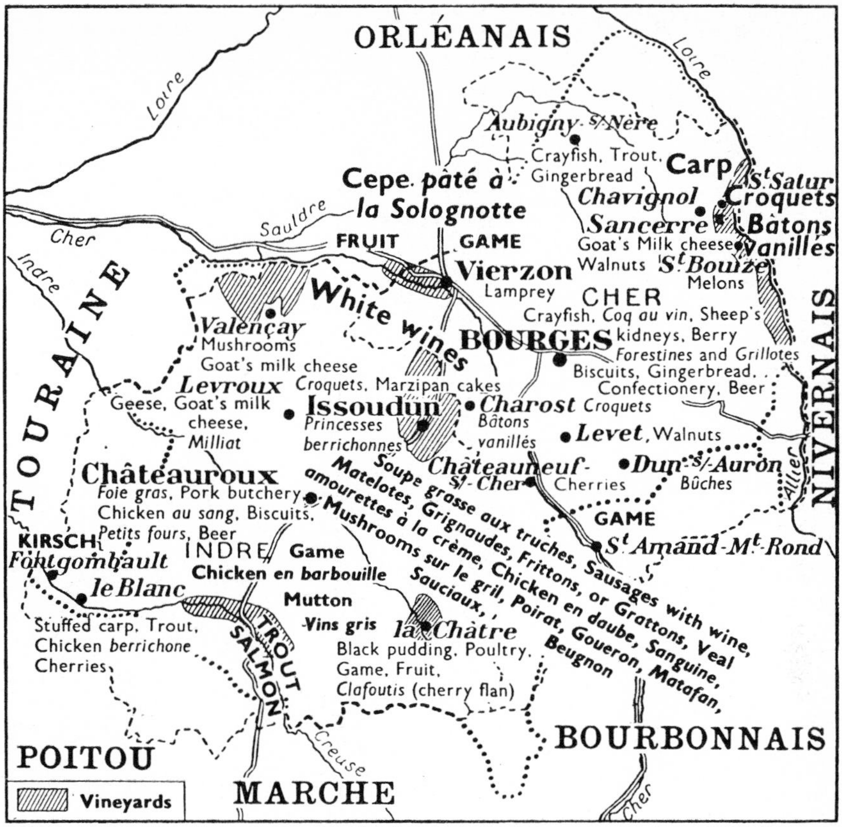

Gastronomic map of Berry

These wines are perfect with seafood, fish and with the celebrated goat cheese of the region. They are best drunk slightly chilled.

An excellent dry and fruity rosé is also produced in Sancerre from the black Pinot grape. In a good vintage year a very good red wine comes from the same source. Then there is Menetou-Salon, near Sancerre, which gives white wines similar to those already mentioned. Still in the *département* of Cher, at Quincy, some white wines of almost equally fine quality are produced.

BESAIGRE – Term indicating that a wine is beginning to turn sour.

BESI – Name in the Jura and Franche-Comté for salted and dried cow's meat. It is also a generic term for a variety of pear.

Besi de Caissoy – Winter pear, also called *rousette d'Anjou.*

Besi d'Héry – Winter pear, which takes its name from a forest in Brittany where it originated.

Besi de la Motte – Autumn pear with white, succulent flesh.

BÊTE ROUSSE – Term used in France to describe a wild boar six months to one year old.

BEURRÉ – Juicy dessert pear. There are many varieties, among which are *beurré gris* and *beurré d'hiver nouveau,* which reach maturity in January and February; *beurré Cappiannont,* October and November; *beurré Giffard,* ripe at the end of July, and *beurré Diel.*

BEVERAGE. BOISSON – Liquid taken by the mouth to maintain or re-establish normal proportion of water in the organism.

Our bodies contain approximately 70 per cent water, eliminating daily an average of 3 litres ($5\frac{1}{4}$ pints, $6\frac{1}{2}$ pints). When the water content is lowered to a considerable degree, the sensation of thirst results. We therefore have to replace the water eliminated, partly by solid foods which contain a considerable proportion of water, partly by liquids.

Numerous beverages have been invented. Apart from milk (q.v.) which is considered a liquid food, beverages are classified in five categories:

1. Pure water and mineral waters (see WATER).
2. Aromatic and stimulating infusions (see INFUSIONS, HERBAL TEAS, COFFEE, CHOCOLATE, MATÉ, TEA) as well as various preparations based on these: Bavarian creams, iced coffee, bishop, etc. (dealt with in alphabetical order).
3. Fruit juices, freshly extracted and not modified by fermentation, which are drunk either in their pure state (grape juice), or mixed with water and sugar (lemonade, orangeade, etc.).
4. Fermented beverages, the principal of which is wine; then beer, cider, perry, hydromel and various fruit liqueurs (dealt with in alphabetical order). There is another large group of fermented or compound beverages, referred to as economical or medicinal, which will be found in this section.
5. Fermented and distilled beverages or mixtures, and preparations based on alcoholic drinks (dealt with in alphabetical order).

Quantity and temperature of beverages – The normal intake of beverages varies according to their nature, the requirements of the organism, outside temperature and state of health. Excessive intake of liquids diminishes appetite and impedes digestion. In some cases it is advisable to increase the intake of liquids in order to improve elimination and cleanse the organism. In others, it is advisable to reduce the intake of liquids.

Should beverages be taken with meals or in between meals? Man alone drinks while eating; other animals separate their solid feeding from absorption of liquids. Half a litre (scant pint, $2\frac{1}{4}$ cups) water drunk on an empty stomach leaves it in less than half an hour. The water would remain in the stomach much longer if accompanied by other food. A meal eaten without drinking is digested quicker and better. It is advisable, therefore, in diets for people suffering from dyspepsia and enteritis to separate the intake of solids and liquids. They should drink an hour or so before the meal, so as to ensure that the stomach is empty in time for solid food. The result will not be the same if the liquid is taken after the meal; the stomach will be full, and the conditions will be the same as when drinking during a meal. With perfectly healthy people, however, provided the amount of drink taken is not so excessive as to impede digestion, the above does not apply.

Too much meat, highly spiced dishes and the excessive use of salt, considerably increases the sensation of thirst. Diet consisting mainly of vegetables, containing little salt, does not provoke thirst so much.

Moderately warm beverages dilate the blood vessels of the stomach, are better absorbed, and quench thirst efficiently. If too cold, they cause the contraction of the abdominal capillary system, and may lead to disorders, at times of a serious nature: colic, precordial anxiety, and even syncopes (loss of consciousness from fall of blood pressure). These disorders are more likely to occur if one drinks a quantity of cold liquid quickly. To prevent such occurrences, sportsmen are advised to drink hot beverages after violent exercise. Such accidents occur less frequently with iced drinks, because these can only be swallowed in small sips.

The palate's reaction to various temperatures of beverages varies according to their nature. Below 6° to 8°C. (43° to 47°F.) water gives the impression of being ice-cold; it is pleasantly cool at 12°C. (54°F.), it becomes warm and unpleasant at 16°C. (61°F.), and at 25°C. (77°F.) it is too hot for most people. Aerated water seems colder than ordinary water at 6°C. (43°F.) owing to the release of carbon dioxide, and remains cold up to 10°C. (50°F.), becoming pleasantly cool up to 17°C. (62°F.).

The temperature of milk at the farm immediately after milking varies between 33° and 34°C. (91° and 93°F.). When heated to 55° to 56°C. (131° to 133°F.) it seems very hot and causes perspiration.

Wines. The best temperature for an average white wine is about 10°C. (50°F.). Some wines, such as Sauternes, can be chilled (*frappés*).

Sparkling wines should only be cooled by ice, without adding salt (often an expedient in a restaurant for clients who are in a hurry). These wines lose a great deal of their quality at a temperature below 6°C. (43°F.). Red wines, especially the great wines of Bordeaux, are served *chambrés* – brought slowly to room temperature (16° to 18°C., 61° to 64°F.). Burgundy wines are drunk at a cooler temperature, and light white wines are served cold.

BEVERAGES IN DIETETICS. BOISSON EN DIÉTÉTIQUE – Beverages are of supreme importance in dietetics. Water, man's natural beverage, is essential to him. It is possible to go up to forty days, and even more, without eating if one drinks large quantities of water; being deprived of it leads to death.

Generally speaking, a man absorbs in twenty-four hours as many cubic cm. of water as he ingests calories. The need for water is related to the chemical composition of the diet. A protein-rich diet requires a considerable hydrous intake.

FERMENTED BEVERAGES. BOISSONS FERMENTÉES – The manufacture of fermented drinks demands a series of operations, often complicated. Spontaneous fermentation of grapes, apples, oranges, pineapples may have produced a pleasant drink by chance; but chance does not account for the alcoholic fermentation of cows', mares' and she-camels' milk, which does not take place of its own accord. Still more curious, historically speaking, is the transformation of cereal crops into fermented liquor. Small tribes in the far past, having neither fruit nor milk nor cereals at their disposal, managed to produce an intoxicating beverage from the tubers of cassava or sweet potatoes. The use of fermented liquors appears to be a need peculiar to mankind.

Cabaretier selling drinks
in the seventeenth century (*Guérard*)

Barley cordial. BOISSON D'ORGE – Put 500 g. (18 oz.) ordinary barley and 200 g. (7 oz.) couch grass into 20 litres ($4\frac{1}{2}$ gallons, $5\frac{1}{2}$ gallons) water. Boil. Add 100 g. (4 oz.) liquorice cut into small pieces. Leave to get cold, strain, and bottle.

Barley water. EAU D'ORGE – Pour boiling water on a handful of barley and bring to the boil again. Pour off the water and replace with boiling water, this time boiling for 15 to 20 minutes.

If pearl or hulled barley is used, 1 tablespoon per litre (scant quart, generous quart) water, there is no need to boil it in two waters. Cook the barley until the grains split.

Cider type drink. BOISSON FAÇON CIDRE – Blend 11 litres ($2\frac{1}{2}$ gallons, 3 gallons) water, 1 litre ($1\frac{3}{4}$ pints, generous quart) double beer, 10 g. ($\frac{1}{3}$ oz.) citric acid and a large glass brandy. Stir well. Decant into bottles and tie down the corks. This drink will be ready for use in 5 to 6 days' time.

Clairet – Boil $6\frac{1}{2}$ kg. ($14\frac{1}{2}$ lb.) carrots and 125 g. (4 oz.) liquorice roots in 10 litres (9 quarts, 11 quarts) water. Strain, pressing the ingredients so as to extract as much liquid as possible.

Add 250 g. (9 oz.) tartaric acid, 250 g. (9 oz, $2\frac{1}{4}$ cups) ground ginger, 2 kg. ($4\frac{1}{2}$ lb., 9 cups) brown sugar and 2 litres ($3\frac{1}{2}$ pints, $4\frac{1}{2}$ pints) brandy to the liquid.

Pour into a barrel of 100 litres (22 gallons, 28 gallons) capacity. Fill with water, and leave for 8 days. Bottle and cork, tying down the corks.

Economical drink I. BOISSON ÉCONOMIQUE – To make 60 litres (13 gallons, $16\frac{1}{2}$ gallons), put 4 litres ($3\frac{1}{2}$ quarts, $4\frac{1}{2}$ quarts) red or white wine into a tun, add 56 litres ($12\frac{1}{4}$ gallons, $15\frac{1}{4}$ gallons) water, 2 kg. ($4\frac{1}{2}$ lb., 9 cups) sugar (having dissolved it before putting it into the tun), a small lemon cut into pieces and tied in a muslin bag. Leave for 5 to 6 days, stirring once a day, decant into bottles, storing them upright.

Economical drink II. BOISSON ÉCONOMIQUE – Put into a receptacle 20 litres ($4\frac{1}{2}$ gallons, $5\frac{1}{2}$ gallons) water, 1 litre ($1\frac{3}{4}$ pints, generous quart) wine, 1 kg. ($2\frac{1}{4}$ lb., $4\frac{1}{2}$ cups) sugar and 1 lemon cut into slices. Leave to macerate for 4 days, stirring once a day. Bottle and tie down the corks. This drink will be ready for use in 4 to 6 days' time.

Elderblossom cordial. BOISSON DE SUREAU – Take a barrel of about 60 litres (13 gallons, $16\frac{1}{2}$ gallons) capacity, enlarge the bung hole and fill the barrel with water. Put the following ingredients into a muslin bag: 2 kg. ($4\frac{1}{2}$ lb., 9 cups) refined sugar or, if that is not available, ordinary granulated sugar, 100 g. (4 oz.) dried elderblossom, 50 g. (2 oz.) hops, 1 lemon cut into pieces and the juice squeezed into the water, and $2\frac{1}{2}$ dl. (scant $\frac{1}{2}$ pint, generous cup) vinegar. Leave to infuse for 5 days, stirring with a stick once a day. Leave to rest on the sixth day and bottle on the seventh (decanting into champagne bottles, if possible). Tie down the corks. This beverage will be ready for use in 5 days' time. Keep the bottles upright in the cellar.

Elder and lime cordial. BOISSON DE SUREAU ET TILLEUL – Mix a handful each of elder and lime-tree leaves with 7 litres (6 quarts, $7\frac{1}{2}$ quarts) water. Add 250 g. (9 oz., generous cup) sugar, 2 lemons and 1 glass vinegar.

Leave to macerate for 3 days, stirring once a day. Strain, bottle and tie down corks. This beverage will be ready for use in 5 days' time.

Hippocras. HYPOCRAS – Spiced wine, tonic and stomachic. There are beer hippocras, cider hippocras, red wine hippocras, etc.

The beverage can be flavoured with any stone fruit, oranges, vanilla, wormwood, violets, etc.

Angelica hippocras. HYPOCRAS À L'ANGÉLIQUE – Leave 8 g. ($\frac{1}{4}$ oz.) fresh angelica and a pinch of ground nutmeg to infuse in 1 litre ($1\frac{3}{4}$ pints, generous quart) cold wine (red or white) for 2 days. Add sugar and a little brandy to taste. Filter.

Juniper hippocras. HYPOCRAS AU GENIÈVRE – Leave 25 g. (1 oz.) crushed juniper berries to infuse in 1 litre ($1\frac{3}{4}$ pints, generous quart) cold wine, mixed with 50 g. (2 oz.) alcohol, for 24 hours. Add a little vanilla and 75 g. (3 oz., 6 tablespoons) fine sugar, and filter.

Raspberry hippocras. HYPOCRAS À LA FRAMBOISE – Strain 500 g. (18 oz., $3\frac{1}{2}$ cups) freshly gathered raspberries over a bowl, pour in 1 litre ($1\frac{3}{4}$ pints, generous quart) red wine, sweeten with sugar, add 50 g. (2 oz.) wine alcohol, and filter.

Hippocras with spices. HYPOCRAS AUX ÉPICES – Infuse 2 teaspoons cinnamon, 15 g. ($\frac{1}{2}$ oz., 2 tablespoons) nutmeg, a pinch of mace and 3 cloves (all ground into powder) in 50 g. (2 oz.) alcohol. Leave for 2 days. Add 1 litre ($1\frac{3}{4}$ pints, generous quart) white or red wine, 3 drops amber essence and 75 g. (3 oz., 6 tablespoons) fine sugar, and stir well. Leave to stand for 24 hours, then filter.

Honey water. EAU MIELLÉE – Dissolve some pure honey in hot water, add a little rum or brandy and a dash of vinegar. It is a refreshing drink but does not keep.

Hop drink. BOISSON AU HOUBLON – Put into a 20-litre ($4\frac{1}{2}$-gallon, $5\frac{1}{2}$-gallon) crock 1 kg. ($2\frac{1}{4}$ lb., $4\frac{1}{2}$ cups) sugar, 2 handfuls hop flowers, 8 to 10 orange leaves and a glass vinegar. Fill with water. Leave to macerate for 2 days, stirring frequently. Strain through a cloth, decant into bottles, and cork, tying down the corks.

Hydromel (Codex recipe) – Dilute 100 g. (4 oz., $\frac{1}{3}$ cup) pure white honey in 1 litre ($1\frac{3}{4}$ pints, generous quart) warm water, and strain.

Vinous hydromel is made from one part honey and three parts water.

Hygienic and refreshing drink. BOISSON HYGIÉNIQUE ET RAFRAÎCHISSANTE – Mix 50 litres (11 gallons, 14 gallons) water, 1 litre ($1\frac{3}{4}$ pints, generous quart) brandy, $\frac{1}{2}$ litre (scant pint, $2\frac{1}{4}$ cups) coffee and 1 kg. ($2\frac{1}{4}$ lb., $4\frac{1}{2}$ cups) brown sugar together. Stir well.

Kefir. KÉFIR – This beverage, made from fermented cows' milk, is used in countries bordering on the Caucasus. The fermented kefir is dried, preserved, and transported in the form of grains called *pousse toujours*. They multiply indefinitely by fermentation, so that a minute quantity is enough to produce any amount of kefir.

Allow 40 g. ($1\frac{1}{2}$ oz.) kefir to 1 litre (scant quart, generous quart) water. Put the kefir into a stone jug, dilute with water, sweeten slightly, stir, and leave for 24 hours. Stir again, leave for 4 days, and bottle. Ready for use in 6 or 7 days' time after bottling.

Lemonade – See LEMONADE.

Fizzy lemonade. LIMONADE GAZEUSE – Ordinary lemonade aerated with carbon dioxide by means of aerating apparatus.

Lemonade with pomegranate juice. LIMONADE AU SUC DE GRENADE – Extract the juice from 6 ripe red pomegranates either by pressing in a fruit squeezer or by rubbing through a sieve. Add the juice of 2 lemons and 2 oranges, and the zest of 1 lemon and 1 orange. Add twice as much water as there is juice, sugar to taste, strain through a fine sieve and chill the lemonade.

Liquorice and orange water. EAU DE RÉGLISSE À L'ORANGE – Put 80 to 100 g. ($3\frac{1}{2}$ to 4 oz.) well-washed liquorice roots, cut into small pieces, in a pan. Add 10 g. ($\frac{1}{3}$ oz.) orange zest.

Cover with 4 litres ($3\frac{1}{2}$ quarts, $4\frac{1}{2}$ quarts) water, boil for 5 minutes, and strain through a cloth.

Oatmeal water. EAU DE GRUAU – Using oatmeal, proceed as described in the recipe for *Barley water*.

Orangette or Frénette cordial. BOISSON ORANGETTE OU FRÉNETTE – Take 50 g. (2 oz.) ash tree leaves, peel of 10 oranges, 3 kg. ($6\frac{1}{2}$ lb., 13 cups) granulated sugar, 50 g. (2 oz.) citric acid, 25 g. (1 oz.) brewer's yeast, burnt sugar.

Boil the ash tree leaves with the orange peel for 25 or 30 minutes in 2 litres ($3\frac{1}{2}$ pints, $4\frac{1}{2}$ pints) water. Strain through a cloth.

Dissolve 3 kg. ($6\frac{1}{2}$ lb., 13 cups) granulated sugar in the above liquid. Add 50 g. (2 oz.) citric acid. Put into a barrel of about 50 litres (11 gallons, 14 gallons) capacity.

Dilute 25 g. (1 oz.) yeast in cold water, mix with 2 tablespoons (3 tablespoons) burnt sugar and add to the barrel. Fill with water, leave to ferment for 8 days, bottle and cork.

Beverage made out of pea-pods. BOISSON DE COSSES DE POIS-VERTS – Put pods of green peas into a stockpot and add plenty of water. Boil for 3 hours, and leave to get cold. Add a handful of sage to 10 litres (9 quarts, 11 quarts) liquid.

Leave to ferment in a barrel. Draw off and bottle.

Golden rhubarb cordial. EAU DORÉE DE RHUBARBE – Tonic

and apéritif obtained by macerating a piece of rhubarb in a jug of water.

Rice water. EAU DE RIZ – Proceed as described in the recipe for *Barley water*.

Three flowers cordial. BOISSON DES TROIS FLEURS – Put 50 g. (2 oz.) hop flowers, 50 g. (2 oz.) violet flowers and 35 g. ($1\frac{1}{2}$ oz.) elder blossom into 20 litres ($4\frac{1}{2}$ gallons, $5\frac{1}{2}$ gallons) boiling water. Boil for 5 minutes and strain through a fine cloth.

Pour into a barrel with $4\frac{1}{2}$ kg. (10 lb., 20 cups) brown sugar. Add $\frac{1}{2}$ litre (scant pint, $2\frac{1}{4}$ cups) vinegar and 12 g. ($\frac{1}{2}$ oz.) brewer's yeast, broken up into pieces. Mix well. Fill the barrel with 80 litres ($17\frac{1}{2}$ gallons, 22 gallons) water, stir vigorously, bung the barrel, and leave to ferment.

Wine-flavoured water. EAU VINEUSE – Beverage for convalescents, made by adding a small quantity of Bordeaux or Burgundy wine to water or soda water. A little sugar and lemon essence is sometimes added.

Blackcurrant wine. VIN DE CASSIS – Press ripe blackcurrants in a tub, and leave for 24 hours.

Rub through a sieve or a coarse cloth and separate the juice. Cover the remaining *marc* with water, equalling in volume the amount of juice extracted, and leave to macerate for 12 hours. Press through the sieve again. Mix the two juices, and add 50 g. (2 oz., $\frac{1}{4}$ cup) sugar per litre (scant quart, generous quart) liquid.

Pour the liquid into a barrel or some other receptacle and leave to ferment. When fermentation begins to be established, bung the barrel, leaving an opening the size of a vent-peg. After a few days, remove bung, to allow carbon dioxide to escape. Repeat this operation from time to time until there is no longer any risk of too great an expansion of gas, then bung the barrel. Draw off at the end of six months.

Cherry wine. VIN DE CERISES – Proceed as described in the recipe for *Blackcurrant wine*.

Fig wine or figuette. VIN DE FIGUES (FIGUETTE) – Put 1 kg. ($2\frac{1}{4}$ lb.) dried figs and 10 juniper berries into a small barrel. Add 10 litres (9 quarts, 11 quarts) water and leave to macerate for 6 to 8 days. Strain the liquid, bottle, and leave for 4 or 5 days before using.

Ginger wine. VIN DE GINGEMBRE – Put 9 kg. (20 lb., 40 cups) sugar into 40 litres ($8\frac{3}{4}$ gallons, 11 gallons) boiling water. When the sugar dissolves, add 300 g. (11 oz., $2\frac{3}{4}$ cups) pounded ginger roots. Boil for a quarter of an hour, and remove from heat.

When the liquid is nearly cold, add 250 g. (9 oz.) brewer's yeast. Leave to ferment in a barrel. Draw off after fermentation, and when the wine is quite clear, decant into bottles.

Juniper wine. VIN DE GENIÈVRE – Mix 5 kg. (11 lb.) honey (or brown sugar) with 2 kg. ($4\frac{1}{2}$ lb.) brewer's yeast and 50 kg. (110 lb.) crushed juniper berries.

Add 100 litres (22 gallons, 28 gallons) hot water and a little crushed coriander. Pour this mixture into a cask and stir vigorously for 5 minutes. Cover with boards, sealing the cask hermetically if possible.

Leave to ferment in a place with a temperature of 25°C. (77°F.). When fermentation is complete and the wine has become clear, draw off into a keg and put in a place with a temperature not exceeding 15°C. (59°F.). At the end of one month, draw off again and keep in a cellar in a full, well-bunged keg. After one year, decant into bottles.

Juniper wine (genevrette). VIN DE GENIÈVRE (GENEVRETTE) – Put 50 litres (11 gallons, 14 gallons) juniper berries into 100 litres (22 gallons, 28 gallons) water, add 2 handfuls of wormwood and leave to ferment in a cool place for one month. Filter and bottle.

The supply of this beverage may be prolonged by leaving the berries in the receptacle and adding water to replace the liquid drawn off. This is a bitter, aromatic, stimulating beverage.

Raisin wine. VIN DE RAISINS SECS – Put 1 litre ($1\frac{3}{4}$ pints, generous quart) raisins, 300 g. (11 oz., $1\frac{1}{2}$ cups) granulated sugar and $\frac{1}{2}$ dl. (3 tablespoons, scant $\frac{1}{4}$ cup) wine vinegar into a small barrel. Add water. Leave to macerate for 8 days, then bottle. The wine will be ready for use 8 days after bottling in the winter, and after 4 days in the summer.

BÉZIERS – Town of the Hérault *département* which produces a great deal of red table wines. The culinary specialities of the region are the same as those found in all towns of Languedoc. They include *escargots à la lodévoise*; *cabassols*; *manouls*; small Béziers *pâtés* called *pâtés des Pézenas*; *flaunes* or *flauzonnes de Lodève*; *fouaces aux frittons*; and *oreilletes*.

BEZIEU SOEP or REDCURRANT SOUP (Belgian cookery). SOUPE AUX GROSEILLES – Cook vermicelli in water; when ready, add salt and potato flour diluted in a little cold water. Add redcurrant juice and sugar.

BIARROTTE (À LA) – Garnish for small cuts of meat composed of *cèpes* and *galettes*; the latter, prepared as for *Duchesse potatoes* (see POTATOES), form the base.

BICARBONATE OF SODA. BICARBONATE DE SOUDE – In medicine, this is used as an alkali and antacid. In cooking, it is added to soften the water used for certain vegetables. It is sometimes added to the water for the carrots prepared *à la Vichy*.

BICHIQUES – Very small fish. (See CURRY, *Bichique curry*.)

BIGARADE SAUCE – See SAUCE.

BIGARREAU – Variety of hard-fleshed cherry, red and white. (See CHERRY.)

BIGNON (Louis) – Nineteenth century restaurateur. After a good training and much experience in well-known Paris restaurants, he took over the management of *Café Riche*, which soon became famous; *sole à la Riche* and *woodcock à la Riche* were among many noted specialities. The restaurant was frequented by most of the men of letters of the period.

Bignon was a remarkably intelligent man who took an interest in viniculture and agriculture. He received the highest awards at world exhibitions of agricultural produce, and became the first French restaurateur to be awarded the Legion of Honour, in 1867.

BIGOS (Polish cookery) – Wash 4 kg. (9 lb.) *sauerkraut* in several waters before boiling it in water. Drain, and add 2 pounded onions and 4 peeled and diced cooking apples. Mix well. Put in a casserole in layers with cooked meats such as venison, chicken, mutton, duck, ham, sausages or pickled pork. Add butter to each layer, pour in a little stock, and cook in a slow oven for 2 hours.

About 25 minutes before serving, add a butter-and-flour *roux* (q.v.) made with a little of the liquor in which the *sauerkraut* was cooked, and serve in this sauce.

BIJANE – Cold soup popular in the Anjou region made by crumbling bread into sweetened red wine.

BILBERRY. MYRTILLE – Small plant common in upland woods (naturalised in U.S.A.). The tart purple berries can be stewed, and they are also used in jam, syrups and liqueurs.

BILE – Thick, greenish-yellow, bitter fluid secreted by the liver. It is called 'gall' in cookery and in industry.

BIRD. OISEAU – Many wild and domestic birds are edible.

Biscuits (*Nicolas*)

In classic French cookery the term covers various small birds of the sparrow type, which are generally roasted or cooked on skewers like larks.

BIRD'S-FOOT TREFOIL (U.S. Lotus). LOTIER – Leguminous plant which grows abundantly in meadows, along the highways, and in fields of cereal crops. The leaves, stems and flowers have a pleasant fragrance, especially when dried, and can be used to flavour marinades.

In some districts the leaves and flowers of this plant are used to impart the flavour of wild rabbit to hutch rabbits when cooked. The rabbit is stuffed with a handful of bird's-foot trefoil after being drawn.

BISCOTTE – See RUSK.

BISCUIT – Term applied to many kinds of biscuit, and, in French, to an iced sweet, made of ice cream mixture, cut to look like biscuits (See ICE CREAMS AND ICES, *Neapolitan ice cream*).

Army biscuits. BISCUITS DE GUERRE – These used to be made of a fairly substantial paste (6 parts flour to 1 part water), baked for 20 to 25 minutes, and cooled off until completely dry. Sometimes a little leaven was added to the paste, and invariably some seasoning to give the dough some taste, as it had no salt in it. The biscuits were difficult to chew, and were not much good in soups, as they did not absorb enough liquid when soaked.

After 1894, as a result of the work of the Army food chemist, Balland, biscuit was replaced by *army bread*, which was porous and absorbant, though still not popular with soldiers.

SWEET BISCUITS (U.S. cookies). BISCUITS DE PÂTISSERIE –

Apricot biscuits (petits fours). BISCUITS À L'ABRICOT – Cream 500 g. (18 oz., 2¼ cups) fine sugar and 16 egg yolks in a bowl. Add 625 g. (1 lb. 6 oz., 5½ cups) sieved flour. Whisk the egg whites into a stiff froth, and fold carefully into the paste.

Half-fill greased and flour-sprinkled baking tins with the biscuit mixture, piped through a forcing-bag. Add a little apricot jam, and cover with the remaining mixture, sifting fine sugar over the top. Bake in a moderate oven for 20 minutes. When cool, store in airtight tins.

Chocolate soufflé biscuits (cookies). BISCUITS SOUFFLÉS AU CHOCOLAT – Whisk 500 g. (18 oz., 2¼ cups) fine sugar and 10 egg whites over low heat. When the mixture is firm, add 300 g. (11 oz., 11 squares) softened chocolate which has been blended with 2 egg whites.

Pipe through a forcing-bag onto a buttered baking sheet which has been dusted with flour, or spoon the mixture into small paper cases. Bake in a moderate oven (180°C., 350°F., Gas Mark 4).

Genoa biscuits (cookies). BISCUITS GENEVOIS – Mix together 125 g. (4 oz., ½ cup) fine sugar, 3 egg yolks, 1 whole egg, a little grated lemon rind and a pinch of salt. Stir with a wooden spoon for 2 minutes. Add 50 g. (2 oz., ¼ cup) melted butter, 35 g. (1½ oz., 6 tablespoons) ground almonds, 125 g. (4 oz., 1 cup) sieved flour, and mix. Lastly fold in 3 egg whites whisked to a stiff froth.

Pour the mixture into finger-shaped moulds which have been buttered and dusted with a mixture of fine sugar and cornflour (cornstarch). Bake in a very slow oven. Dry the biscuits on a sieve and store in airtight tins.

Ginger biscuits (cookies). BISCUITS AU GINGEMBRE – Mix 125 g. (4 oz., ½ cup) fine sugar, 2 teaspoons ground ginger and 4 egg yolks, stirring with a wooden spoon until quite smooth. Add 50 g. (2 oz., ⅓ cup) rice flour and 25 g. (1 oz., 3 tablespoons) potato flour and stir well. Fold in 4 egg whites whisked to a stiff froth.

Pipe the mixture onto greased paper through a forcing-bag, shaping it into small sticks. Sprinkle with sugar, and place on a baking sheet. Bake in the oven at 180°C. (350°F., Gas Mark 4) for 8 to 10 minutes. Dry on a rack, and store in an airtight tin.

Lemon biscuits (cookies). BISCUITS AU CITRON – Cream 50 g. (2 oz., ¼ cup) fine sugar with 2 egg yolks until the mixture is firm. Add grated rind of 1 lemon, 25 g. (1 oz., ¼ cup) sifted flour, 15 g. (½ oz., 4 teaspoons) potato flour, 1 teaspoon ground almonds, and 2 egg whites whisked to a stiff froth.

Pipe through a forcing-bag into biscuits on wafer paper. Sprinkle with powdered sugar, and bake at 160°C. (325°F., Gas Mark 3). Dry and store the biscuits as in preceding recipes.

Italian biscuits. BISCUITS À L'ITALIENNE – Cream 500 g. (18 oz., 2¼ cups) fine sugar with 10 egg yolks until smooth. Whisk the egg whites to a stiff froth and fold into the mixture. Add 100 g. (4 oz., ⅔ cup) potato flour and 100 g. (4 oz., 1 cup) sifted flour. Mix well.

Butter biscuit baking tins, using very hot melted butter, sprinkle the entire surface with icing sugar, and fill the tins with the biscuit mixture. Sprinkle with more icing sugar and bake in a hot oven.

Turn out the biscuits, ice with Curaçao-flavoured icing, and decorate the tops with candied orange peel.

Small unleavened biscuits. PETITS PAINS AZYME – Mix 500 g. (18 oz., 4½ cups) sieved flour and 500 g. (18 oz., 2¼ cups) fine sugar. Spread on the table, make a well in the centre, put in a pinch of salt dissolved in water and 8 eggs. Mix to a firm dough, adding a little water of necessary.

Leave the dough in a cool place. Roll out and cut into circles with a pastry-cutter. Place on a lightly buttered baking sheet, prick the biscuits all over, and bake in a slow oven.

BISHOP (Mulled wine). BISCHOF – Hot beverage popular in northern European countries.

The *bischof* (the word can also be spelt *bishop* in this connection) is heated wine spiced with orange and lemon peel, cinnamon, cloves, and sometimes star anise. It is served mostly at evening parties.

Iced bishop. BISCHOF GLACÉ – Pour a bottle of Champagne and 5 dl. (scant pint, 2¼ cups) lime-blossom tea into a bowl, add an orange and half a lemon cut into thin slices, and a sufficient quantity of heavy (32°) sugar syrup to bring the mixture to a light syrup consistency (18°). Leave in a cool place for 1 hour. Strain through a fine strainer.

Ice as for a *granité*. Add 4 small glasses fine Champagne brandy and serve in punch glasses.

Rhine wine bishop. BISCHOF AU VIN DU RHIN – Melt 250 g. (9 oz., generous cup) sugar and mix with grated rind of 1 orange and 1 lemon, 2 cloves and a small stick of cinnamon dissolved in 3 dl. (½ pint, 1¼ cups) water. Cook for 5 minutes.

Add 1 bottle of Rhine wine. Heat until a light white foam is formed on the surface. Sieve through a fine strainer. Serve in a jug or in a large silver punch bowl.

Bishop can also be prepared with Champagne or any other wine. To make it more stimulating, a little Madeira, sherry or Marsala is sometimes added.

BISON – Genus of wild cattle, allied to the ox and yak. It differs from the ox by its shorter, wider skull, the way in which the line of the back falls away from the rounded humped shoulders, by the thick woolly coat covering head and forequarters, and by its beard.

Bison

The American is different from the European bison, which is found in some parts of Russia.

All methods of preparation indicated for beef are applicable to bison, but only after marinating the meat for several hours.

BISQUE – Name of a preparation in the form of a purée, more particularly a purée of crayfish, or other shellfish, served as a thick soup.

Bisque soups in the eighteenth century were made of poultry and game without any shellfish, and were not purées, but a presentation of boiled poultry or game, sometimes served with a garnish of cocks' combs and kidneys.

In 1758, in the last edition of *Dons de Comus*, there is a recipe for a quail soup with crayfish, which really was a bisque soup, made of quails, topped with crayfish purée. Bisque, therefore, probably meant a soup, with some kind of meat and breadcrumbs.

What could have given the crayfish purée the name of bisque soup was the addition of crayfish meat to various soups, which were then called bisques.

Bisques, whether made of shellfish, poultry or game, are considered high style preparations, and have always been excessively spiced.

For *Crab bisque*, *Crayfish bisque*, *Lobster bisque* and *Spiny lobster bisque*, see SOUP.

BISTORT. BISTORTE – A farinaceous plant, the roots of which are twisted in an S-shape, baked on hot coals and eaten by the Samoyeds instead of bread.

The tender leaves of this plant, found in some high Alpine regions, are eaten like spinach.

BITOK (Russian cookery). BITOKE – *Bitok* can be made of any kind of meat; beef, mutton, pork, veal, chicken, rabbit, etc.

Mince the meat, add bread soaked in milk and finely chopped onion (either raw or lightly fried), season, and put through a mincer again to ensure perfect smoothness. Shape into cakes about 4 cm. (1½ inches) in diameter, dredge in flour, fry in butter, cover with sour cream, and simmer for 5 to 7 minutes.

BITTER. AMER – Having an unpleasant, wormwood taste. Among the bitter plants which are used for making infusions or decoctions are: *wormwood, camomile, endive, fumitory, gentian, germander, hops, lichen, wild pansy, lesser centaury, quassia amara* (bitter ash), *cinchona, rhubarb*.

According to Foussagrives, infusions or liqueurs made of bitter plants may be divided into five classes (i) *purgative bitters*, based on rhubarb, aloes, etc.; (ii) *nauseous bitters*, based on camomile; (iii) *astringent bitters*, which, with the bitter substance content of tannin, include cinchona, knapweed, bark of chestnut tree, etc.; (iv) *stimulating bitters* (apéritifs) based on wormwood, peel of bitter oranges, gentian, germander, hops, etc.; (v) *convulsing* or *toxic bitters* belong in the province of medicine.

BITTER ASH. BOIS-AMER – *Quassia amara* (q.v.), used in the preparation of apéritifs.

BLACKBIRD. MERLE – Bird of the thrush family, with black plumage and yellow beak. Its flesh is aromatic in flavour and slightly bitter, and is most fragrant in autumn. Corsican blackbirds enjoy a great reputation. (See THRUSH.)

BLACK CUMIN. NIGELLE – Plant of the *Ranunculus* family, the pungent seeds of which are used as a spice in India and the Mediterranean region. The seeds can be used instead of pepper.

BLACKCURRANT. CASSIS – Fruit of the blackcurrant bush used to make a liqueur (see RATAFIA) and preserves.

BLADDER. VESSIE – Membraneous bag in animals, used after butchering in *charcuterie* to prepare certain dishes, for example *Rouen duckling en chemise* (see DUCK).

BLAISOIS or BLÉSOIS – Region of France bordering on the Loire.

Culinary specialities – The specialities of Blaisois are similar to those of nearby Orléanais.

Blois *rillettes* and *rillons* are well known for their quality. All the *charcuterie* of this region is excellent, particularly the *sausages*, *andouillettes* and *black* (blood) *puddings* (see PORK); *game pâtés*; *lark pâtés* which are made in the same shape as the famous Pithiviers *pâtés*; and Chartres *pâté*, made of partridges.

Also excellent are the pike, carp and other freshwater fish, prepared *en matelote* (q.v.), stewed, or *au beurre blanc* (see PIKE). Meat in Blaisois is of good quality. The following specialities are esteemed by gastronomes: *lapereau à la solognote* (young rabbit cooked in the Sologne style); *gâteau Pithiviers* (see PITHIVIERS); *tarte des demoiselles Tatin* (see TART); *Lamotte-Beuvron* (tart) and Orléans *cotignacs* (q.v.).

Wines – Wines of Blaisois and Orléanais include Saint-Jean-de-Braye, Meung and Beaugency among the Orléans wines, and Côte-des-Grouets of the Blois wines.

These wines often suffer from a lack of sun and tend to set one's teeth on edge, but they go perfectly with the local dishes of the region.

BLANC – A French culinary term usually used to describe a *court-bouillon* made from a mixture of water and flour in which various substances, such as white offal and certain vegetables, are cooked. A *court-bouillon* in which cultivated mushrooms are cooked is also called *blanc* (see COURT-BOUILLON).

This name is also applied to white stock, based either on veal or chicken (see STOCKS, *White Stocks*).

The term *blanc* is used to define breast of chicken or other poultry which are described on menus as *blancs de volaille*, etc.

BLANC DE BLANCS – Name given to Champagne obtained from the Pinot-Chardonnay white grapes, as distinct from the Champagne obtained from black grapes, the 'Blanc de Noirs'.

BLANCHING. BLANCHIR – Operation consisting of boiling various ingredients in salted water either to harden them, or, as in the case of some green vegetables, to cook them.

Some ingredients, previously soaked in cold water, are blanched in water (gradually brought to the boil), as in the case of calves' heads and trotters, calves' and lambs' sweetbreads, etc., both to cleanse them and to harden the skin. Bacon (pork) fat, generally cut in large dice, is blanched to extract surplus salt, before frying it. Certain green vegetables, such as green cabbages, onions, etc., are blanched to reduce their pungency. Other vegetables and fruit, such as tomatoes, peaches, etc., are blanched to render them easier to peel.

BLANCHING (Nuts). MONDER – To remove skin, husk, etc. of almonds, walnuts, pistachios and hazelnuts.

Pour boiling water over the shelled nuts to soften the skin.

BLANCMANGE. BLANC-MANGER – 'These delicious sweets,' said Carême in his *Traité des entremets de douceur*, 'are greatly esteemed by gastronomes, but, to be enjoyed, they must be extremely smooth and very white. Given these two qualities (so rarely found together), they will always be preferred to other creams, even to transparent jellies. This is because almond is very nourishing and contains creamy, balsamic properties which are just right for sweetening the bitterness of humours.'

Blancmange (Carême's recipe). BLANC-MANGER – 'Blanch 450 g. (1 lb., generous 3 cups) sweet almonds and about twenty bitter almonds. Leave them to soak in a bowl of cold water, which renders them singularly white. Drain on a sieve and rub in a napkin. Pound in a mortar, moistening them, little by little, with ½ tablespoon water at a time, to prevent them turning into oil. When they are pounded into a fine paste, put into a bowl and dilute with 5 glasses filtered water, added a little at a time. Spread a clean napkin over a dish, pour the blancmange into it and, with 2 people twisting the napkin, press out all the almond milk. Put in 350 g. (12 oz., 1½ cups) granulated sugar and rub through a fine sieve. Strain through a napkin once again, add 30 g. (1 oz. plus 4 grains) clarified isinglass a little warmer than tepid. Blend with the blancmange. Pour into a mould and place in a container with crushed ice.

'To make rum blancmange, add ½ glass rum to the mixture described above. To make a maraschino blancmange, add ½ glass maraschino.

'To serve this sweet in small pots, prepare two-thirds of the quantity given in the preceding recipe; you will, however, need a little less isinglass, as blancmange served in small pots has to be more delicate than when it is to be turned out.

Blancmanges can be flavoured with lemon, vanilla, coffee, chocolate, pistachio nuts, hazelnuts and strawberries. Whipped cream can also be incorporated.'

Blancmange (modern method). BLANC-MANGER – Blanch and skin 250 g. (9 oz., 1¾ cups) sweet almonds and 15 g. (½ oz., 5 teaspoons) bitter almonds and pound in a mortar with a little water. Dilute with ½ litre (scant pint, 2¼ cups) cold water. Turn this paste on to a coarse linen cloth over a bowl and squeeze out all the almond milk. Return the paste to the mortar and pound again, adding enough fresh water to extract ½ litre (scant pint, 2¼ cups) almond milk.

Heat 200 g. (7 oz.) lump sugar, 15 g. (½ oz.) softened gelatine and the almond milk, and stir with a wooden spoon until it boils. Strain and leave to cool. When it is tepid, add 1 dl. (6 tablespoons, scant ½ cup) rum or kirsch.

When the mixture is cold, pour into a *bavarois* mould greased with sweet almond oil, and place on crushed ice. The blancmange can be turned out and served after an hour.

BLANQUET – French pear which ripens in July or August.

There are two kinds: the *large* and the *small blanquet*. They are mediocre in flavour, and used mostly for compotes.

BLANQUETTE – White *ragoût*, based on lamb, veal or chicken meat, bound with egg yolks and cream, and accompanied by a garnish of small onions cooked in *court-bouillon* (q.v.), and mushrooms. Other ingredients are sometimes added to the garnish.

Cut the meat into pieces. Cover with white stock or water, season and bring to the boil. Remove scum.

Add an onion studded with a clove, a carrot and a *bouquet garni* (q.v.). Simmer gently for 45 minutes for lamb or chicken, and 1¼ hours for veal. Drain the pieces and return them to the pan with small onions and mushrooms which have been cooked in white *court-bouillon* (q.v.).

Prepare a *velouté* (q.v.) by thickening the liquor with white *roux* (q.v.) and binding with egg yolks and cream. Add a little lemon juice, sprinkle with chopped parsley, and garnish with heart-shaped croûtons fried in butter.

Blanquette à la ménagère, also called Fricassée – Fry pieces of meat, as described above, in butter, without allowing them to brown. Sprinkle with flour, stir, moisten with white stock or water, bring to the boil, season, and add an onion stuck with a clove, a carrot and a *bouquet garni* (q.v.).

Bind with egg yolks and cream, as described in the recipe for *Blanquette*. For further recipes for various *blanquettes*, see LAMB, VEAL, CHICKEN.

BLANQUETTE DE LIMOUX – Sparkling white wine made by the 'natural' method; the sparkle is derived from gas generated by natural fermentation. A second fermentation takes place in the bottle without the addition of sugar. (In other words, through the transformation of natural grape sugar remaining in the parent wine after the first fermentation.) It is produced from the Mauzac and Clairette grapes, and gets its name from the commune of Limoux in the Aude.

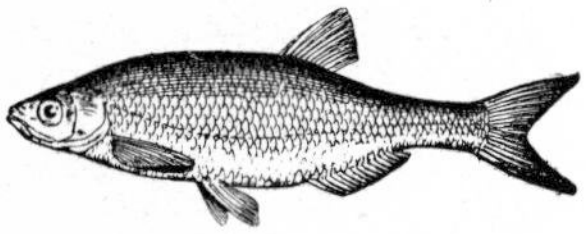

Bleak

BLEAK (Ablet). ABLETTE – Small European freshwater fish, with white, rather insipid flesh. It is used mostly for frying.

BLENNY. BLENNIE CAGNETTE – A genus of European freshwater fish. All the other members of the blenny family are sea fish. A characteristic which is common to all blennies is the absence of scales, the body being covered with a layer of viscous mucus of exceptional thickness. It varies in size from 10 to 15 cm. (4 to 6 inches) and is fawn-coloured, speckled with brown, with brown transversal strips along the back.

The blenny abounds in the waterways of the Hérault *département*. It is particularly plentiful in Agde, where it is called *lièvre* (hare), because the shape of its head resembles that of the hare. It is also found in the lake of Bourget and the fishermen of this region call it *chasseur* (hunter). In other regions it is known as *bavecca*.

The blenny's flesh, white and good in flavour, is mainly fried, but can also be used as an ingredient for *matelotes* (q.v.).

BLETTE – Name given in some parts of France to white beet or chard.

BLEU (To cook au bleu) – Method applied to freshwater fish, mainly to trout. This consists of plunging the fish into a boiling *court-bouillon* (q.v.), generally a mixture of water and vinegar, seasoned with salt and sometimes spiced with thyme and bay leaf.

Cooked in this way, the skin of the fish, especially that of trout, takes on a slightly bluish colour. To accentuate the blueing, the fish can be sprinkled with pure vinegar, before immersing it in *court-bouillon*.

All fish cooked *au bleu* are generally served with melted butter, handed separately; or with *Hollandaise sauce* (see SAUCE), or any other white sauce specially recommended for poached fish.

BLEU D'AUVERGNE – Cheese that is still sometimes called *Bleu de Salers*, eaten from November to May.

BLEU DE BASSILLAC – Limousin cheese eaten from November to May.

BLEU DE BRESSE – Round blue cheese from the co-operative of Servaz in the Ain.

BLIND (To bake). CUIRE À BLANC – Flan (pie shell) baked 'blind', i.e. empty. Some tart and flan cases are baked in the oven, and filled with dried vegetables, which are removed once the cases are cooked. They are then filled with the ingredients indicated in the recipe.

Cuire au blanc also describes the cooking of certain substances (mostly white offal or variety meats) in a special *court-bouillon* (q.v.).

Frying pan for blini

BLINI (Russian cookery) – *Blini* are pancakes which have been made in Russia from time immemorial, especially during Shrovetide. Recipes for *blini* and various fillings are given under HORS-D'ŒUVRE.

A. Petit, in his *Traité de la cuisine russe*, says that during Shrovetide, 'from the humblest cottage to the richest palace, they all have their *blini*, twice a day, the whole of that week'.

Batter for blini. PÂTE À BLINIS – Prepare a light batter of 20 g. (⅔ oz., 1 cake) yeast diluted in ½ litre (scant pint, 2¼ cups) warm milk and 50 g. (2 oz., ½ cup) sieved flour. Leave to ferment in a warm place for 2 hours.

Add 250 g. (9 oz., 2¼ cups) sieved flour, 4 egg yolks, 3 dl. (½ pint, 1¼ cups) warm milk and a pinch of salt. Mix thoroughly. Add 4 egg whites whisked to a stiff froth, and 1 dl. (6 tablespoons, scant ½ cup) whipped cream. Leave the batter to rise for 35 minutes. Make small pancakes, frying them in butter.

BLOATER. CRAQUELOT – Slightly salted, smoked herring served mainly in England for breakfast and for high tea.

The bloater is grilled on a low fire and served with melted butter or *Maître d'hôtel butter* (see BUTTER, *Compound butters*).

BLOCK. BILLOT – Thick, short piece of tree trunk, placed on three legs, which serves for chopping-up meat.

A butcher's block is usually a wooden table enclosed in a wooden frame.

BLOND DE VEAU – Old French culinary term which describes white veal stock. Carême, in his *Traité des sauces*, uses this term.

White veal stock is used in the preparation of some brown sauces (see SAUCE) or for glazing certain substances.

BLOND DE VOLAILLE – A synonym of *fond blond*, clear or thickened chicken stock (see SAUCE, *Brown sauces*).

Rich veal or chicken stocks are used for braising certain vegetables, such as celery, artichoke hearts, lettuces, etc.

BLONDIR – The operation of lightly cooking any substance in butter, oil, or other fat.

The term *faire blondir* also describes the cooking of a flour and butter mixture which constitutes a light *roux* (q.v.).

BLOOD. SANG – The blood of butchered animals has no part in nutrition but it has a number of industrial uses (the treatment of wines, clarification of sugar, the manufacture of coal products, fertilisers, etc.).

The blood of the pig (often mixed with other blood) is used to make *boudin* (black pudding), and the blood of rabbit, hare and chicken is used to thicken the dishes called *civets*, which – after the blood has been added – must not be heated above 70°C. (158°F.), the temperature above which blood coagulates and the mixture curdles.

Blood soups are made in Sweden (*svartsoppe*) and Poland (*tchernina*).

BLOOD PUDDING – See PORK.

BLUE GAZELLE. GAZELLE BLEUE – Edible goat found mainly at the Cape. Its meat, which is very delicate, is cooked like roebuck.

BOAR – See WILD BOAR.

BOCAL – Wide-mouthed, short-necked glass bottle or jar for bottling or pickling vegetables and fruit (gherkins, capers, small onions, mixed vegetables, cherries, small melons, etc.) or for preserving fruit in brandy.

BODY (To have). CORPS (AVOIR DU) – One says a wine has body when it produces a sensation of plenitude in the mouth resulting from a harmonious combination of strength and flavour.

BOILING. ÉBULLITION – The movement of a liquid in the process of vaporisation. Boiling takes place when, as a result of heating, the steam pressure is at least equal to that of the liquid.

While a liquid is boiling its temperature remains constant. The boiling point of water has been taken as the norm for comparative purposes, and stands at 100°C. (212°F.). This temperature decreases by about a third of a degree per 100 m. (108 yards) of altitude.

BOIS DE SAINTE-LUCIE – Variety of fragrant cherry tree.

BOLÉE – Receptacle, usually brown earthenware, used for drinking cider in Normandy and Brittany. This term also applies to the cider contained in the receptacle. Thus it is said: '*Boire une bolée de cidre*' – 'To drink a bowlful of cider'.

BOLETUS (Cèpe). BOLET – Genus of fungi of which about 70 species are known in France. Unless one is an expert, the only boletus mushroom which can safely be gathered is the *boletus edulis*, known in France as *cèpe de Bordeaux* and *tête de nègre* when it is young. It has a bronze-coloured cap, white underneath, on a white and swollen stem. As it grows, the cap becomes a lighter brown, begins to overlap the stem, the underneath becomes yellow. Later the tubes turn green, and can be removed like a choke of a cooked artichoke.

This mushroom is found in woods, under oak, chestnut and beech trees and sometimes under pines. In the Paris region it appears in April and is sometimes very plentiful in the autumn. The underneath may be white, yellow or greenish but never red. The stem is white, yellow or brown; it should never have any red spots. The flesh which is exposed to the air remains white and never becomes green; its taste is very pleasant, never bitter.

Very old *cèpes*, with green tubes and damaged by slugs, should be avoided.

The *cèpe* is a highly prized mushroom; it is, however, a little indigestible. According to some authorities, its nutritive value, like that of other fungi, is insignificant. (See MUSHROOMS.)

Bombe moulds:
left, modern conical mould; *right*, old-fashioned round mould

BOMBE (Ice cream). BOMBE GLACÉE – Ice cream made in a spherical mould, hence its name. In modern cookery it is made in a conical mould. (See ICE CREAMS, *Bombes*.)

BONBON (Sweet, candy) – Sweets could not have been made in Europe until sugar was brought from the Orient by the returning crusaders in the thirteenth century. It is known that the first experiments with sugar-cane juices were carried out by the Jews in Sicily about A.D. 1230. Before that time, *bonbons* were made in France with fruit juice and honey, flavoured with amber or cinnamon.

The art of making sweets spread very rapidly. In order to appeal to the ladies at court, as well as to the great gentlemen who also had a liking for sweetmeats, confectionery methods were improved and the variety of sweets increased. During the brilliant epoch of the Renaissance this art was carried even further. All the great gentlemen carried *bonbonnières* of sweets, which they offered to the ladies. These *bonbonnières* were often works of art, some of them set with precious stones.

The making of confectionery continued, and a great variety of sweets is available today.

Sweets can be classified in four principal groups as follows: *dragées* (sugar-coated almonds) and *pralines*; *bonbons fondants*; *boiled sweets* and *pastilles*.

Other confectionery preparations, now factory-made, are also classed in the category of *bonbons*, such as caramels, butterscotch, toffee, fruit paste, a certain number of marzipan preparations, crystallised fruit and walnuts, almonds and hazelnuts dipped into sugar cooked to crack degree.

BON-CHRÉTIEN – A pear of which two varieties are known; one ripens in summer, the other in winter.

The flesh of this pear is quite sweet but a little gritty. It is usually eaten cooked.

BONDON – Type of cheese manufactured in Neufchâtel in Normandy. (See CHEESE.)

BONE. OS – Any of the separate parts of a vertebrate skeleton, forming its framework. Bones are composed of a cartilaginous substance impregnated with calcareous salts. By boiling in water, especially under pressure, they produce gelatine. Bones, added to stock, give it a gelatinous consistency.

Uses of bones and meat parings – After prolonged cooking, bones retain a considerable quantity of juices and gelatine which can be extracted, flavoured with vegetables, seasoned, and used for soup.

Boil down this stock until it is transformed into meat jelly which keeps well and can be used for strengthening soups and sauces.

To extract all the juices, the bones should then be broken up as small as possible. This second stock is not an economical proposition, unless it can be done without using any further fuel, for instance, if one has a permanent fire at one's disposal.

BONE-MARROW. MOELLE – A soft, fatty substance contained in marrow-bones.

Spinal marrow is that part of the central nervous system contained in the spinal cord. The spinal marrow of meat sold in sections is called *amourette* (see OFFAL or VARIETY MEATS).

Beef bone-marrow. MOELLE DE BOEUF – Cut the marrow in thick slices (using a knife dipped in boiling water). Poach without boiling in salt water, and drain. This is used to garnish steaks.

Beef bone-marrow, diced, poached and drained, is also used in various brown sauces.

Bone-marrow canapés. CANAPÉS À LA MOELLE – Made from the marrow of the large marrow-bone cooked in the *pot-au-feu* or *petite marmite* (see SOUPS AND BROTHS).

These *canapés* can be served in two ways:

1. Spread the marrow on slices of toast. Season with salt and freshly ground pepper.

2. Spread a *salpicon* (q.v.) of marrow (poached and well drained) on slices of toast. Decorate with strips of marrow, poached in salt water and drained, or seasoned with peppercorns ground in a mill. Sprinkle with fresh breadcrumbs tossed in butter and drained. Put the *canapés* in the oven for a few moments.

Bone-marrow fritots. FRITOTS À LA MOELLE – Cut into thick slices. Stick them together in pairs with forcemeat (preferably *à gratin*), and steep for 20 minutes in oil, lemon juice, salt, pepper and chopped parsley.

Dip them in a light batter, deep-fry in very hot fat. Drain, dry in a cloth, and garnish with fried parsley.

Salpicon of bone-marrow. SALPICON DE MOELLE – Dice the marrow and poach without bringing to the boil. Blend with *Demi-glace sauce* (see SAUCE), flavoured with shallot which has been cooked in white wine until all the liquid has evaporated.

This is used as a filling or garnish for flaky pastry *vol-au-vent* and *canapés*, fried bread (in fancy shapes), coddled or poached eggs, artichoke hearts, large mushrooms, etc.

Bone-marrow sauce. SAUCE À LA MOELLE – Sauce served with meat, grilled or sautéed fish, and poached or coddled eggs. (See SAUCE.)

Small vol-au-vent with bone-marrow. BOUCHÉES À LA MOELLE – Flaky pastry *vol-au-vent* filled while hot with a *salpicon* (q.v.) of beef bone-marrow blended with *Demi-glace sauce* (see SAUCE), or very concentrated veal stock. Flavour, if desired, with a little shallot cooked in white wine until all the liquid has evaporated.

BONING. DÉSOSSER – The process of removing the bones from a joint of meat, poultry or other food, whether cooked or raw, which contains bones.

The boning of raw meat or poultry requires skill, since the bones should be taken out without damaging the meat.

BONITO. BONITE – Small species of tunny, commonly found in the Mediterranean and on the Atlantic coast, where French fishermen also call it *germon*. It is an important fish on the North American Pacific coast and is prepared in the same way as tunny (tuna).

BONNE-DAME – Common name for orach in France.

BONNES-MARES – Vineyard of the Côte de Nuits that produces noted red wines. It is situated partly in the commune of Morey-Saint-Denis and partly in that of Chambolle-Musigny (Côte-d'Or), and has the legal right to a special *appellation*. (See BURGUNDY.)

BONNET-TURC – Variety of pumpkin.

BONVALET – This cake, almost identical with the one called *Beauvilliers* was created in 1869 by a pastry-cook, Jules Leroy, who was in charge of the *Maison Machin*. (See BEAUVILLIERS.)

BOOPS. BOGUE – Mediterranean fish of which two species are known: the *common boops* which reaches 35 cm. (14 inches) in length, and the *bogue saupe*.

This fish, which can be served fried, *à la meunière*, and poached, and which is also used in *bouillabaisse*, is remarkable for the brightness of its colour – olive-yellow on the back and silver on the belly.

BORAGE. BOURRACHE – Herbaceous perennial plant. Its flowers are cooked in some regions of France as fritters. The young leaves are used for flavouring salads, iced drinks, herbal tea and vegetables, and also for flavouring claret cup.

BORAX or SODIUM PERBORATE. BORATE DE SOUDE – This was sometimes fraudulently used, under various names such as 'preservative powder', 'antiferment', etc., for preserving meat, fish, butter, wine, etc.

Its use was forbidden in France by an order of 14 July, 1891.

BORD-DE-PLAT – Small utensil used in the kitchen to protect the border of a dish on which food in sauce is being served.

BORDEAUX – *Gourmands*, connoisseurs of good things to eat, and *gourmets*, experts in the subtle art of wine tasting, hold this town in particular regard.

Bordeaux, whose wines and food were being sung long ago by the poet Decimus Magnus Ausonius, born in A.D. 310, is the birthplace of one of the greatest men in French classical cookery, Dugléré. He had for long been in charge of the kitchens at the *Café Anglais* in Paris, which at that time was frequented by kings, princes and all the most illustrious gastronomes of Europe.

Culinary specialities – *Crayfish à la bordelaise*; *lamprey with leeks*; *mussels à la bordelaise*; *escargots à la Caudéran*; *fried whitebait*; *sausages with oysters*; *entrecôte à la bordelaise*; *leg of lamb à la ficelle*; *chicken sauté à la bordelaise*; *Pauillac lamb à la persillade*; *foie gras with grapes*; *terrine de Nérac*; *pâté de foie gras au truffes*; *cèpes*

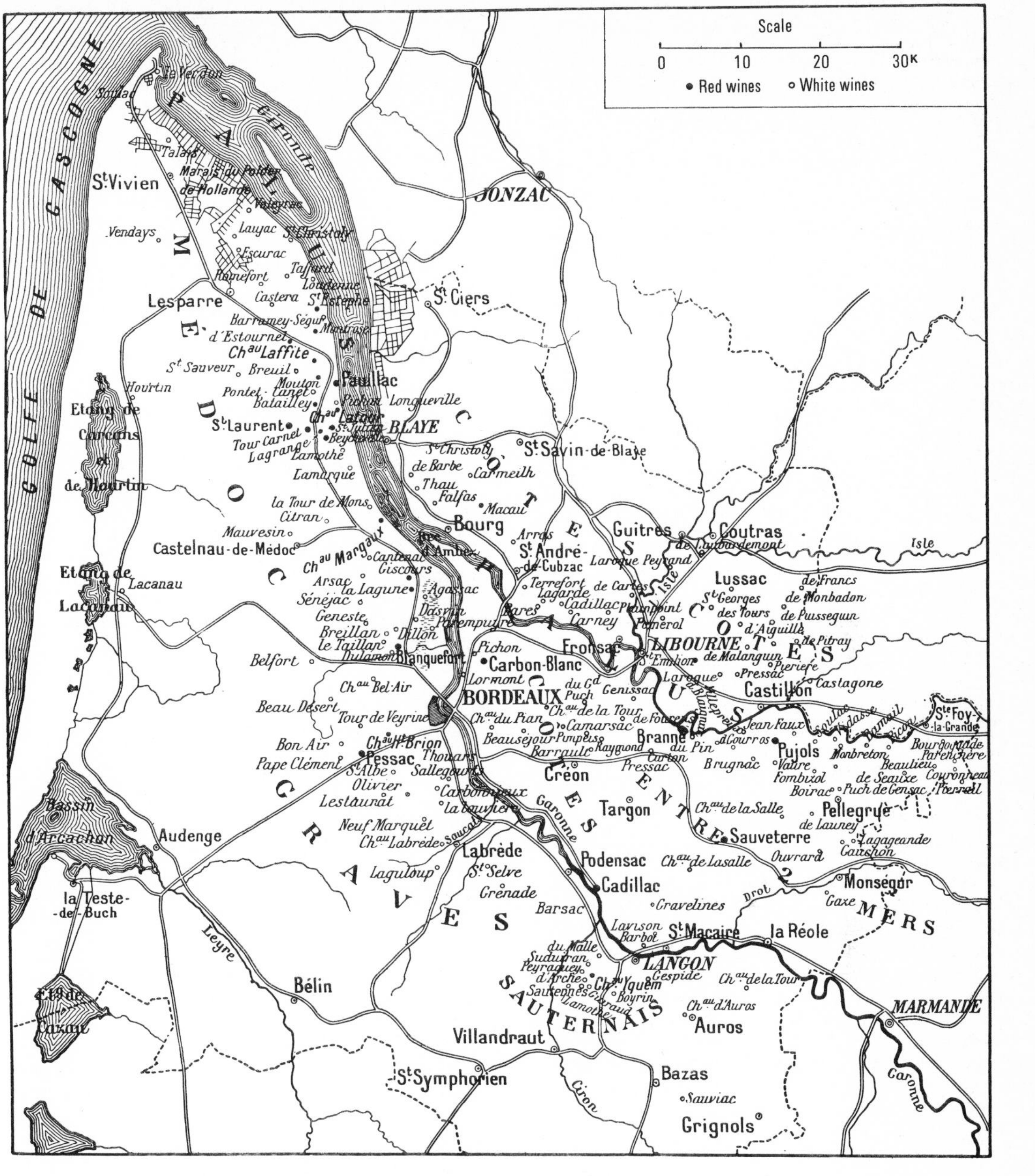

Map of the Bordeaux wine-growing district

à la bordelaise; *aubergine sauté with garlic*; *pancakes à la bordelaise*; and famous cakes made by the pastry-cooks of Bordeaux.

Excellent cheeses are produced throughout the region.

Wines – Bordeaux is one of the great viticultural regions of France, producing some of the world's best wines. The wine district of Bordeaux is completely contained within the borders of the Gironde *département*, mainly in the parts lying along the course of the rivers Gironde, Garonne and Dordogne. It has been known and esteemed for more than two thousand years. Even the Latin poet Ausone sang the praises of these wines.

Bordeaux has a very comprehensive range of wines: white, from the driest to the most liqueur-like; red, from the lightest (the Englishman's 'claret') to the most full-bodied.

Besides the so-called 'generic' *appellations* of white and red Bordeaux, Bordeaux supérieur, Bordeaux clairet and Bordeaux rosé, which are produced all over the region, the great divisions are sub-divided into regions, which in their turn are divided into vineyards and *appellations*.

Médoc. A long strip of land approximately 15 km. (9 miles) broad, situated on the left banks of the Garonne and the Gironde, extending from Blanquefort in the south to Pointe de Graves in the north. There are two distinct

A Bordeaux vineyard (*French Government Tourist Office*)

divisions within the region: Bas-Médoc in the north; Haut-Médoc in the south where the communes of the great *appellations* of Margaux, Saint-Julien, Pauillac, Saint-Estèphe, Moulis and Listrac are situated.

Médoc wines are tannic and generous, and mature admirably. They are superbly elegant wines with a fine bouquet and aroma, and make excellent accompaniments to all types of roast and grilled meats. Those of Moulis, Listrac and Saint-Estèphe are best drunk with red meat and game; those of Margaux, Saint-Julien and Pauillac with white meat and lamb. (See accompanying table for the classification of these wines.)

The Château-Haut-Brion in the commune of Pessac is not actually in Médoc but in Graves, and is the only exception in the *first growth* category.

Graves. The Graves region lies to the south of Médoc, encircling the town of Bordeaux and extending along the left bank of the Garonne to the region of Sauternes. It produces red 'sappy' wines closely related to those of Médoc, of good lasting quality and with a bouquet reminiscent of the resin and undergrowth of the nearby pine forests; aristocratic dry white wines, also sappy, with a superbly elegant bouquet and taste, pleasant when drunk young in the not-so-good years but capable of maturing to perfection in the great vintage years. White liqueur-like wines, very similar to Sauternes, are produced in the south of the region.

The dry white wines of Graves make worthy companions to oysters, seafood, fish and shellfish, poached or grilled or in delicate sauces. The red wines serve the same purpose as those of Médoc. They, too, age magnificently. (See classification GRAVES.)

Sauternes-Barsac and Cérons. These wine districts form a sort of enclave in the Graves region north and west of Langon. They produce white, liqueur-like wines the colour and taste of honey, and have a flowery bouquet, greatly esteemed by connoisseurs. These wines are the product of the vinification of over-ripe grapes which are almost in a crystallised state when picked, owing to the action of a microscopic fungus called 'botrytis', which encourages the sugar to concentrate in the grape. Sauternes wines are usually consumed as dessert wines, but real connoisseurs like to drink them with *foie gras*, fish in sweet sauces and certain parslied cheeses.

Loupiac and Saint-Croix-du-Mont, situated on the opposite side of the Garonne on picturesque slopes overlooking the river, produce white wines similar to those of Sauternes. (See classification tables.)

Saint-Émilion. This wine district is situated on the right bank of the Dordogne east of the town of Libourne, and extends into the commune of the same name and several neighbouring areas.

Also worth mentioning are the 'satellite' *appellations* such as Saint-Georges-Saint-Émilion, which have the right to affix the *appellation* 'Saint-Émilion' to their own. Two types of wine can be singled out: those of the 'slopes' which are rounder and more full-bodied, and those of the 'gravel', which are sappy and more tannic. Both have the same rubiness and fullness which make them ideal with red meat, game, meat and sauce dishes, and the cheeses.

The *appellations contrôlées* of Saint-Émilion are: Saint-Émilion-Premier-Grand-Cru-Classé, Saint-Émilion-Grand-Cru-Classé, Saint-Émilion-Grand-Cru, Saint Émilion.

'Satellite' *appellations*: Lussac-Saint-Émilion, Montagne-Saint-Émilion, Parsac-Saint-Émilion, Puisseguin-Saint-Émilion, Saint-Georges-Saint-Émilion, Sablés-Saint-Émilion.

Pomerol. This wine district begins at the very gates of Libourne. A ferruginous subsoil with a pebbly topsoil gives rich, sappy, full-bodied wines with a pronounced personality and a powerful bouquet – perfect companions for red meat, meat in sauce, game (even big game) and cheese.

Dordogne River and vineyards of Saint-André-de-Cubzac

Pressing grapes at Saint-Emilion
(*French Government Tourist Office*)

There is no official classification of the Pomerol wines; Château-Pétrus is usually given first place.

'Satellite' *appellations* of Pomerol: Lalande de Pomerol, and Néac (which has the right to the *appellation* 'Lalande de Pomerol'); all of these are red wines.

Other appellations. The wine district of Bordeaux is rich in other *appellation* wines, which include the strong glowing wines of the Côtes de Fronsac and Canon-Fronsac, west of Libourne on the right bank of the Garonne; and the Bourgeois and the Blayais on the right bank of the Gironde, opposite Médo .

Between the Garonne and the Dordogne, in the triangle formed by the confluence of the two rivers, is situated the region 'Entre-deux-Mers'. The *appellation* covers a large production of white wine which used to be mellow, but which is vinified drier and drier to meet the current demands of today. There are some very good red wines which have the right to the *appellations* Bordeaux and Bordeaux supérieur. In the same geographical region there are the Premières, Côtes de Bordeaux, the Graves de Vayres, Bordeaux-Saint-Macaire and, on the border of the Dordogne *département*, Saint-Foy-La-Grande.

CLASSIFICATION OF THE GREAT MÉDOC WINES

First growth	COMMUNE
Château-Lafite	Pauillac
Château-Margaux	Margaux
Château-Latour	Pauillac
Château-Haut-Brion	Pessac (Graves)

Second growth	
Mouton-Rothschild	Pauillac
Rauzan-Ségla	Margaux
Rauzan-Gassies	Margaux
Léoville-Lascases	Saint-Julien
Léoville-Poyferré	Saint-Julien
Léoville-Barton	Saint-Julien
Durfort-Vivens	Margaux
Lascombes	Margaux
Gruaud-Larose-Sarget	Saint-Julien
Gruaud-Larose	Saint-Julien
Brane-Cantenac	Cantenac
Pichon-Longueville	Pauillac
Pichon-Longueville-Lalande	Pauillac
Ducru-Beaucaillou	Saint-Julien
Cos d'Estournel	Saint-Estèphe
Montrose	Saint-Estèphe

Third growth	
Kirwan	Cantenac
Issan	Cantenac
Lagrange	Saint-Julien
Langoa-Barton	Saint-Julien
Giscours	Labarde
Malescot Saint-Exupéry	Margaux
Cantenac-Brown	Cantenac
Boyd	Cantenac
Palmer	Cantenac
La Lagune	Ludon
Desmirail	Margaux
Calon-Ségur	Saint-Estèphe
Ferrière	Margaux
Marquis d'Alesme-Becker	Margaux

Fourth growth	
Saint-Pierre-Sevaistre	Saint-Julien
Saint-Pierre-Bontemps	Saint-Julien
Branaire-Ducru	Saint-Julien
Talbot	Saint-Julien
Duhart-Milon	Pauillac
Poujet	Cantenac
La Tour Carnet	Saint-Laurent
Lafon Rochet	Saint-Estèphe
Beychevelle	Saint-Julien
Le Prieuré	Cantenac
Marquis de Terme	Margaux

Fifth growth	
Pontet-Canet	Pauillac
Batailley	Pauillac
Grand-Puy-Lacoste	Pauillac
Grand-Puy-Ducasse	Pauillac
Lynch Bages	Pauillac
Lynch Moussas	Pauillac
Dauzac	Labarde
Mouton-Baron Philippe	Pauillac
Le Tertre	Arsac
Haut-Bages	Pauillac
Pédesclaux	Pauillac
Belgrave	Saint-Laurent
Camensac	Saint-Laurent
Cos-Labory	Saint-Estèphe
Clerc Milon	Pauillac
Croizet Bages	Pauillac
Cantemerle	Macau

CLASSIFICATION OF THE SAUTERNES WINES

First great growth	COMMUNE
Château d'Yquem	Sauternes
First growth	
Château-La Tour Blanche	Bommes
Château-Peraguey	Bommes
Château-Rayne-Vigneau	Bommes
Château-Suduiraut	Preignac
Château-Coutet	Barsac
Château-Climens	Barsac
Château-Guiraud	Sauternes
Château-Rieussec	Fargues
Château-Rabaud-Sigalas	Bommes
Château-Rabaud-Promis	Bommes
Second growth	
Château-Myrat	Barsac
Château-Doisy-Dubroca	Barsac
Château-Doisy-Daëne	Barsac
Château-Doisy-Védrines	Barsac
Château-Arche	Sauternes
Château-Arche-Lafaurie	Sauternes
Château-Filhot	Sauternes
Château-Broustet	Barsac
Château-Nairac	Barsac
Château-Caillou	Barsac
Château-Suau	Barsac
Château-de Malle	Preignac
Château-Romer-Lafon	Fargues
Château-Lamothe-Bergèy	Sauternes
Château-Lamothe-Espagnet	Sauternes

BORDELAISE (À LA) – Culinary term which applies to different dishes in four categories. The first is characterised by the *sauce bordelaise*, with white or red wine and marrow-bone fat; the second by the addition of *cèpes*; the third by *mirepoix*; and the fourth by a garnish of artichokes and potatoes. Other ingredients can be added.

This term also applies to various sweet courses (desserts), cakes, etc. (See MUSHROOMS, *Cèpes à la bordelaise*; CRAYFISH, MIREPOIX, SAUCE.)

BORDER (Ring). BORDURE – Dishes that are served in the form of a ring, which can be made of quenelle or other forcemeat, rice, semolina and duchess potatoes for hot dishes; jelly, custards and creams, *rice à l'impératrice*, etc. for cold and sweet dishes.

Borders can be made of small croûtons of bread, cut into various shapes and fried in butter, fixed to the inside edge of the serving dish with a mixture of flour and egg white. Fancy jelly shapes can be similarly used for cold dishes, and vegetable borders for hot dishes.

Ring (border) of béatilles à l'ancienne. BORDURE DE BÉATILLES À L'ANCIENNE – Fill a buttered ring mould with a veal or chicken *Mousseline forcemeat* (see FORCEMEATS) and poach slowly in the oven in a *bain-marie* (q.v.). When cooked, allow to stand for a few minutes for the forcemeat to settle.

Turn the ring out onto a dish, and fill the centre with a *ragoût* of lambs' sweetbreads, cocks' combs and kidneys, truffles and mushrooms, mixed in a *Velouté sauce* (see SAUCE) flavoured with Madeira-laced *Truffle fumet* (see FUMET). Garnish with slivers of truffle heated in concentrated meat stock.

Ring for brains à la piémontaise. BORDURE DE CERVELLE À LA PIÉMONTAISE – Butter a ring mould and fill it with *Risotto à la piémontaise* (see RICE). Put the mould in the oven for a few minutes to heat it thoroughly.

Turn out and fill the centre with escalopes of *Calves' brains à la poulette* (see OFFAL or VARIETY MEATS) mixed with sliced mushrooms. Decorate the brains with thin slices of truffles heated in concentrated meat stock.

Egg ring Brillat-Savarin. BORDURE D'OEUFS BRILLAT-SAVARIN – Fill a mould with *Veal forcemeat* (see FORCEMEATS) and poach in the oven in a *bain-marie* (q.v.). Turn out and fill the centre with eggs which have been scrambled with Parmesan cheese and diced truffles. Sprinkle with grated Parmesan, pour a little melted butter over, and brown the top in a very hot oven.

Egg ring à la princesse. BORDURE D'OEUFS PRINCESSE – Prepare as *Egg ring Brillat-Savarin*, using scrambled eggs with asparagus tips and truffles. Scrambled eggs with crayfish, shrimps, *fruits de mer*, mushrooms, truffles, tomatoes, etc. can be prepared in the same way.

Cream fish forcemeat (see FORCEMEATS) is used for Lenten *entrées*.

Fish forcemeat ring with various garnishes. BORDURE DE FARCE DE POISSONS – These rings, also Lenten fare, are made of *Cream fish forcemeat* (see FORCEMEATS) of pike, whiting or other fish, moulded and baked as described above.

They are filled with a *ragoût* of fish or shellfish, the following being particularly suitable for the purpose: *Ragoût of fruits de mer in shrimp, nantua or normande sauce*; *oysters and mushrooms in velouté sauce*; *mussels à la poulette*; *shrimps*; *slices of lobster or spiny lobster à la crème or à l'américaine*; *fish purées or salpicons with truffles and mushrooms.*

Ring of frogs' legs vert-pré – BORDURE DE GRENOUILLES VERT-PRÉ – Prepare the frogs' legs as described in the recipe for *Aspic of frogs' legs à l'ancienne* (see ASPIC), coating them only with *White chaud-froid sauce* (see SAUCE). Cover with jelly.

Prepare a jelly ring decorated with circlets of truffles. Season cooked, well-drained asparagus tips with oil, vinegar, salt and pepper. Turn the ring out, and put the frogs' legs on it, overlapping them slightly. Fill the centre with the asparagus tips blended with concentrated aspic jelly. Decorate with truffle dipped in jelly.

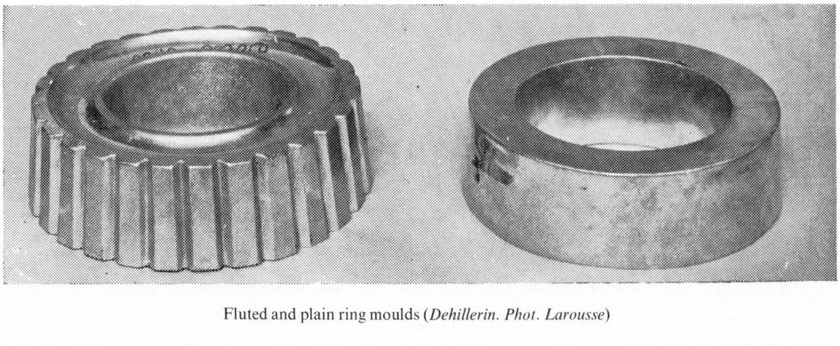

Fluted and plain ring moulds (*Dehillerin. Phot. Larousse*)

Piping a border of duchess potatoes (*Larousse*)

Border of duchess potatoes (*Larousse*)

Game forcemeat ring with various garnishes. BORDURE DE FARCE DE GIBIERS – These are made of *Game forcemeat* (see FORCEMEATS). The rings are filled with purées or *salpicons* of game in *White* or *Brown sauce* (see SAUCE).

Potato ring. BORDURE DE POMMES DE TERRE – *Duchess potato mixture* (see POTATOES) piped through a forcing-bag onto a buttered dish, or moulded by hand into a ring.

Fill the centre with slices of cooked fish covered with *Mornay sauce*; slices of various shellfish; hashes of various kinds of meat; vegetables cooked in butter, etc.

Brush the ring with beaten egg, sprinkle with grated Parmesan, and brown in the oven or under the grill.

Rice ring with various garnishes. BORDURES DE RIZ – These rings (borders) are usually prepared from rice pilaf, risotto, or rice cooked in consommé and bound with egg.

Press the rice well into the mould and set it in the oven for a few minutes.

When turned out onto a serving dish, fill the centre with various ingredients, such as mixed *ragoûts* in white or brown sauce, various *salpicons*, etc.

Semolina ring with various garnishes. BORDURE DE SEMOULE – Prepare like *Rice ring*, using semolina cooked in consommé and bound with egg.

Ring (border) of sole à la normande

Ring of sole à la normande. BORDURE DE SOLES À LA NORMANDE – Prepare a *Cream fish forcemeat* (see FORCEMEAT), bake and turn it out on a dish. Fill the centre with a *ragoût* of mussels, shrimps and mushrooms, bound with *Normande sauce* (see SAUCE).

Roll up small sole fillets and cook in white wine. Place a poached, debearded oyster on each fillet, cover with *normande sauce* and decorate with thin strips of truffle. Garnish with crayfish cooked in *court-bouillon* (q.v.).

Veal or chicken forecemeat ring with various garnishes. BORDURE DE FARCE DE VEAU, DE VOLAILLE – Prepare as indicated in the recipe for *Ring of béatilles à l'ancienne*.

Turn the ring out onto a dish. Fill the centre with a garnish: *veal amourettes à la poulette, cocks' combs and kidneys à la crème*, slices of *chicken in velouté sauce, lambs' or calves' brains à la poulette, veal or chicken hash à la crème*, simple or mixed *salpicons in white or brown sauce, purée of chicken in velouté sauce*, eggs scrambled with various ingredients, fresh vegetables dressed with butter or cream, *macédoine of vegetables* blended with butter or cream, *mushrooms à la crème*.

Fancy jelly shapes arranged in a border round a dish (*Larousse*)

Cold rings for entrées or sweet dishes. BORDURES FROIDES D'ENTRÉES, D'ENTREMETS – These borders are usually made of aspic or fruit jelly. Cold *entrée* borders can also be made from *foie gras*, ham, game, chicken or fish mousses.

RINGS FOR DESSERTS. BORDURES D'ENTREMETS – For cold sweets, custards (see CREAMS, *Custard creams*) are made in a mould that has been caramelised. When turned out, the centre is filled with *macédoines* or purées of fruit, etc.

Rings can be made of *Dessert rice* (see RICE) and semolina (q.v.), and filled with *macédoines* of fruit or any other mixture suitable for a hot sweet.

Custard ring with mirabelles à la vosgienne. BORDURE DE MIRABELLES À LA VOSGIENNE – Prepare a kirsch-flavoured *Custard cream* (see CREAMS).

Fill a caramel-coated ring mould with the cream, and cook in a *bain-marie* (q.v.). Allow to cool completely before turning out.

Cook the mirabelles in syrup. Prepare whipped cream or *Chantilly cream* (see CREAMS). Turn out the ring onto a dish, and fill the centre with well-drained mirabelles. Top with whipped cream. Serve with mirabelle sauce laced with kirsch.

Rice ring with cherries. BORDURE DE RIZ AUX CERISES – Fill a buttered ring mould with *Dessert rice* (see RICE). Heat the mould for a few minutes in the oven, and turn it out onto a dish. Fill the centre with stoned cherries which have been simmered in syrup and combined with a little gooseberry jelly.

Rice ring à la créole. BORDURE DE RIZ À LA CRÉOLE – Butter a *savarin* ring mould and fill with sweetened dessert rice. Turn out, and fill the middle with half-slices of pineapple which have been poached in vanilla-flavoured syrup. Decorate with preserved cherries and angelica lozenges.

Heat in the oven, and serve with rum-flavoured *Apricot sauce* (see SAUCE).

Rice ring Montmorency. BORDURE DE RIZ MONTMORENCY – Fill a buttered ring mould with sweetened dessert rice, pressing it on well to ensure that there are no holes. Cover, and cook in the oven for a few minutes. Remove, and turn onto a dish.

Fill the middle with stoned cherries which have been cooked in syrup and well drained, alternating them with layers of hot *French pastry cream* (see CREAMS). Finish with a layer of cherries, piling them slightly into a dome shape. Sprinkle with crushed macaroons, pour on some melted butter, and glaze in a very hot oven.

Serve with *Cherry sauce* (see SAUCE) which has been laced with kirsch.

Semolina ring filled with various fruit. BORDURE DE SEMOULE GARNIE DE FRUITS – Fill a buttered ring mould with sweetened dessert semolina, pressing it well into the mould. Heat for a few moments in a low oven.

Turn onto a dish, and fill with fruit cooked in vanilla-flavoured syrup: halved apricots, sliced pineapple, cherries, pears, quartered apples, etc.

Heat in the oven for a few minutes, and when ready to serve, pour over it a few tablespoons of liqueur-flavoured apricot sauce, or other fruit sauce which goes with the filling.

BORIC (Acid). BORIQUE – Sometimes used as a preservative agent (see BORAX).

BORSCH – See SOUPS.

BOTER MELK or BUTTERMILK (Belgian cookery) – Boil pearl barley in buttermilk, sweetened with brown sugar, for 1½ to 2 hours. Before serving, blend in a little cornflour (cornstarch) diluted in cold water. Treacle (molasses) is sometimes added.

Vermicelli, rice, semolina, and tapioca can also be cooked in buttermilk, with currants, sultanas and cooked apples added.

BOTHEREL (Vicomte de) – Famous financier who was born in Dinan in 1784 and who died there in 1859. His name deserves to be mentioned in a dictionary of cookery for it was he who, under the Restoration, created 'omnibus-restaurants'.

BOTTLE. BOUTEILLE – Oenology, the science which deals with wine, gives the following definition to the word bottle:

'A glass phial of various shapes and colours according to the nature of the wine it is intended to contain.' This means

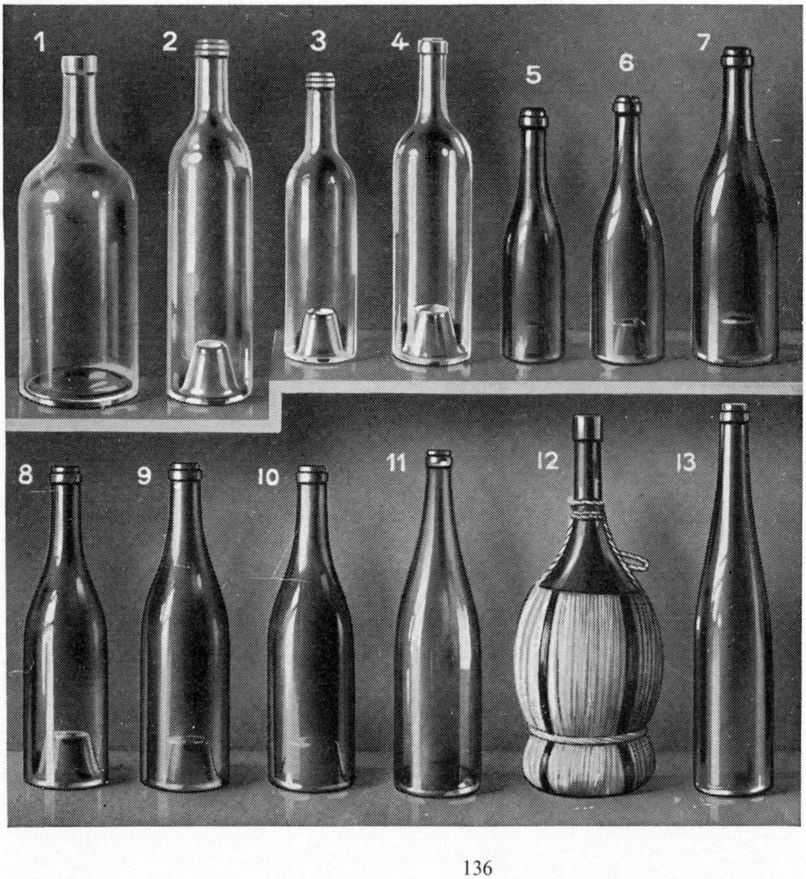

Bottles:
1. Double litre;
2. Litre;
3. Demi-litre;
4. Bordeaux bottle;
5. Fillette d'Anjou;
6. Demi-Anjou;
7. Anjou;
8. Mâconnaise;
9. Champagne;
10. Bourgogne;
11. Saint-Galmier;
12. Fiasco de Chianti;
13. Flûte à vin d'Alsace

that Bordeaux wines should not be bottled in Burgundy wine bottles, and vice versa. No doubt this law can be digressed when it is a case of ordinary table wines; in fact, most of these wines are sold in so-called Saint-Galmier bottles. The practice of serving very old wines and wines of great growths out of wicker cradles is not approved by gastronomes; these should be decanted into carafes for serving.

Contents of bottles in France – The law of January 1930, states:

Article 1. Under the conditions of Article 2 given below, it is forbidden to put on sale or to sell wines other than sparkling wines, wines imported in bottles and wines intended for export, wines imported in bottles and wines intended for export, in bottles other than:

1. Bottles known as *bordelaise*, *bourguignonne* and *mâconnaise*, the type and capacity of which are indicated in the table appended in the law passed on 13 June 1866, concerning trade usages;

2. Bottles which correspond to the following characteristics:

Type	*Capacity* (*cl.*)
Double litre	200
Litre	100
Demi-litre	50
Saint-Galmier	90
Anjou	75
Demi-Anjou	37·5
Fillette d'Anjou or Fillette de Touraine	35
Rhine wine	72

The capacity indicated above is that of a receptacle measured at neck rim at a temperature of 15°C. (59°F.). This capacity has a tolerance of 2 per cent.

Article 2. It will not be permitted to use bottles the appearance of which answers the description given in Article 1 which have not the minimum legal capacity, unless these bottles bear a label indicating their capacity.

In the case where, in accordance with the preceding paragraph, a label is used, this should bear, in addition to the indication of the minimum capacity, the indication of the degree of alcohol contained in the wine, where such indication is compulsory.

Article 3. The conditions laid down in this decree are not applicable to:

1. Bottles containing wines made before the publication of this decree and put into the above-ementioned bottles before the said publication;

2. Receptacles other than bottles, such as carafes, cellar-jugs, pitchers, etc., in which wines are served for consumption on the premises.

BOTULISM. BOTULISME – Serious infection caused by anaerobic bacteria (the organism involved is *Clostridium botulinum*) which develop in canned meat, fish or vegetables; both home and factory canned. It differs from ptomaine poisoning in that the substances affected by the botulism bacillus (ham, pork produce and other canned food) show no signs of putrefaction, although at times they do have a peculiar sour smell.

To avoid the occurrence of botulism only properly sterilised canned foods must be used. Vacuum, even a perfect one, is not a sufficient guarantee, because anaerobes develop even in the absence of oxygen. Food pickled in chlorine should contain at least 10 per cent of sodium chloride. If vinegar is used for pickling, its acetic acid content should be more than 2 per cent.

All suspect canned foods and those having a rancid smell should be avoided, as should foods showing signs of fermentation (bubbles of gas, bulging lids).

BOUCANADE – Spanish term derived from times when wine was placed in goatskin bottles. In slang it means quaffing straight from the bottle.

BOUCHE DU ROI – Term used under the old régime to describe the service which dealt with the kitchens of the royal household. These services, under certain kings, at times employed over 500 people (most of whom worked for only six months in the year). They were exclusively concerned with the king's table and were distinct from the common service, which catered for the officers and certain members of the royal household.

Bouche du roi included dealing with food supplies, the pantler's office and the royal butler's office. The pantler's office had charge of everything concerned with the king's tableware, bread, and accessories of the table. There were thirteen heads of service, four assistants, one keeper of table-service, one *sommier*, one washer-up, and several boys who assisted the officials in charge of these various posts.

The butler's office was mainly concerned with the beverages served to the king, and consisted of thirteen heads of service, five assistants and four *sommiers*, who directed the convoys of pack animals carrying baggage whenever the king travelled, or was at war. The butler carried a loaf of bread, two bottles of wine, two bottles of water, two napkins and some ice for the king's canteen, to His Majesty's closet early every morning. The canteen contained an emergency stock of beverages should the king require a drink while he was in his closet. These beverages were tasted first by an officer of the royal butler's office.

The staff for the royal kitchens included equerries, master cooks, cooks in charge of roasting, soup-cooks, pastry-cooks, and three *galopins* or kitchen errand boys, who were the *commis* of the kitchens of those days.

There were also water-carriers, fuel-carriers, armchair-carriers, ushers, *sommiers*, heralds, valets of *sert-d'eau*, and four washers-up.

The queen, the dauphin and the dauphine all had their separate kitchen services, bringing the total of servants to a very great number. The officials of the royal household were all members of the aristocracy until the end of the reign of Louis XIV, and supplies for the royal service were bought by these gentlemen. But the severe fiscal laws which came in made supplies prohibitively expensive, and aristocrats no longer sought these positions of high office. Instead, the duties were passed on to rich burghers, who paid a high price to obtain them.

Members of the Bouche du roi

BOUCHÉES – Name given to little patties made of puff pastry baked blind (empty) and filled with various mixtures.

It is said that these *bouchées* were invented by Marie Leczinska, who, being very fond of her food, 'adored' the *vol-au-vent*, and decided to eat it regularly. So the small, individual *vol-au-vent* was created – the '*bouchée à la reine*'.

Recipes for the preparation of puff pastry *bouchées* will be found under HORS-D'ŒUVRE.

BOUDY – Good-looking apples which are rather mediocre in taste. They are used mainly for decorating fruit baskets, but they can also be cooked.

BOUFFOIR – Bellows which butchers use to force air under the skin and into the cellular tissues of carcases.

BOUGRAS (Périgord cookery) – Soup prepared from cabbage, leeks, onions and potatoes, using water in which black puddings were cooked for stock. This soup, much appreciated in Périgord, is made at Shrovetide, when pigs are slaughtered and the delicious Périgord black puddings are made. Here is the recipe:

Bring about 2 litres ($3\frac{1}{2}$ pints, $4\frac{1}{2}$ pints) water to the boil and put into it the sliced, blanched heart of a curly green cabbage, carrots, turnips, leeks, celery and quartered onions. Simmer slowly for 40 minutes. Add 2 large sliced potatoes, and continue cooking for a further 35 minutes.

About 15 minutes before serving, drain some of the vegetables, cut into slices, and fry lightly. Sprinkle with flour and a little stock, and add to the soup. (This is called *fricassée* in Périgord and is added to most soups.) Bring to the boil and pour into a tureen over thin slices of bread.

BOUILLABAISSE – This Mediterranean speciality is prepared all along the south coast of France from Cap Cebère to Menton, each having its special flavour and recipe. Connoisseurs consider that the only authentic *bouillabaisse* is to be found in the region between Marseilles and Toulon, though the varieties at Nice and Menton come a close second.

Legend attributes the invention of this dish to Venus, who, it is said, prepared it for her husband, Vulcan. Méry, however, gives the credit to the abbess of a Marseilles convent:

'*Pour le vendredi maigre, un jour, certaine abbesse*
D'un couvent marseillais créa la bouille-abaisse.'

'For a Friday abstinence meal, one day, a certain abbess
Of a Marseilles nunnery created the *bouillabaisse*.'

He then goes on to say what a real *bouillabaisse* is like, and what fish should go into the making of it:

Ecoutez bien ceci, vieux cuisiniers novices,
Qui faites des homards avec des écrevisses,
Et qui croyez qu'on peut, chez Potel ou Chabot,
Traduire mon plat grec en tranches de turbot.
L'heure est enfin venue où notre capitale
Peut joindre à ses banquets la table orientale,
Et donner aux gourmands, chez le restaurateur,
Un ragoût marseillais et non un plat menteur.

À ce plat phocéen, accompli sans défaut,
Indispensablement, même avant tout, il faut
La rascasse, poisson, certes, des plus vulgaires.
Isolé sur un gril, on ne l'estime guère,
Mais dans la bouillabaisse aussitôt il répand
De merveilleux parfums d'où le succès dépend.
La rascasse, nourrie aux crevasses des syrtes,
Dans les golfes couverts de lauriers et de myrtes,
Ou devant un rocher garni de fleurs de thym.
Puis les poissons nourris assez loin de la rade,
Dans le creux des récifs: le beau rouget, l'orade,
Le pagel délicat, le saint-pierre odorant,
Gibier de mer suivi par le loup dévorant,
Enfin, la galinette, avec ses yeux de bogues,
Et d'autres, oubliés par les ichthyologues
Fins poissons que Neptune, aux feux d'un ciel ardent,
Choisit à la fourchette et jamais au trident.

Hearken to me, old cooks and new
All those who make lobsters out of prawns
And think that one can, Chez Potel or Chabot,
Translate my dish into slices of turbot.
The hour has come at last, when our capital
Can add oriental dishes to her banquets
And give the gourmands in a restaurant
A real Marseilles *ragoût*, and not a lying dish.

For this Phocaean dish, accomplished without fault,
Above all, is indispensable the rascasse,
'Tis true, a very common fish.
Served on a grill alone, it does not find favour,
But in a *bouillabaisse* it does exude
A marvellous aroma on which success depends.
The rascasse feeds in crevasses, in quicksands,
In bays shaded with laurel and myrtle bushes
Or around rocks covered with flowering thyme.

Then the fish which feed away from the roads,
Among the reefs: the beautiful red mullet and orades,
The delicate sea bream, the sweet-smelling saint-pierre,
Sea game escaping from the devouring sea perch,
And finally, the galinette, with its boops' eyes,
And others, forgotten by the ichthyologists,
Fine fish, that Neptune, in the fire of a blazing sky,
Spikes on a fork, and never on a trident.

In some regions, notably in Perpignan, potatoes are added to *bouillabaisse*, and often the saffron is omitted, which brings this soup nearer to the *chaudrée* (q.v.) or the *cotriade* (q.v.). At Sète a garlic-flavoured fish soup is made which is somewhat similar to the Flemish *waterzootje* (q.v.).

Ingredients for bouillabaisse – The Provence *bouillabaisse*, or, more correctly, the Marseilles *bouillabaisse*, is made of the following fish: rascasse, chapon, saint-pierre, conger eel, lophius (angler fish), red mullet, rouquier, whiting, sea perch, spiny lobster, crabs and other shellfish. (Many of the fish used for *bouillabaisse*, such as the traditional rascasse, are not found except in the Mediterranean. These are virtually unknown in England and America but gurnet, mackerel, small turbot, fresh tunny, perch, pike, grayling, trout, eel-pout and various rock fish can be substituted if necessary.)

All these fish should be cut into uniform-sized pieces. To make enough *bouillabaisse* for 8 to 10 persons you will need about 3 kg. ($6\frac{1}{2}$ lb.) fish and shellfish.

Put 200 g. (7 oz., $1\frac{3}{4}$ cups) chopped onions, 3 large seeded and chopped tomatoes, 4 pounded garlic cloves, a sprig of fennel and 3 sprigs of bruised parsley, a sprig of thyme, a bay leaf and a piece of dry orange peel into a large casserole. Add the shellfish, then the firm-fleshed fish.

Sprinkle with 2 dl. ($\frac{1}{3}$ pint, scant cup) olive oil and season with salt and freshly ground pepper. Add a good pinch of powdered saffron and enough water to cover the fish completely.

Boil briskly, with a lid on, for 7 to 8 minutes. Then add the fish with delicate flesh, such as whiting and red mullet, and cook together. Total cooking time of *bouillabaisse* does not exceed 14 to 15 minutes.

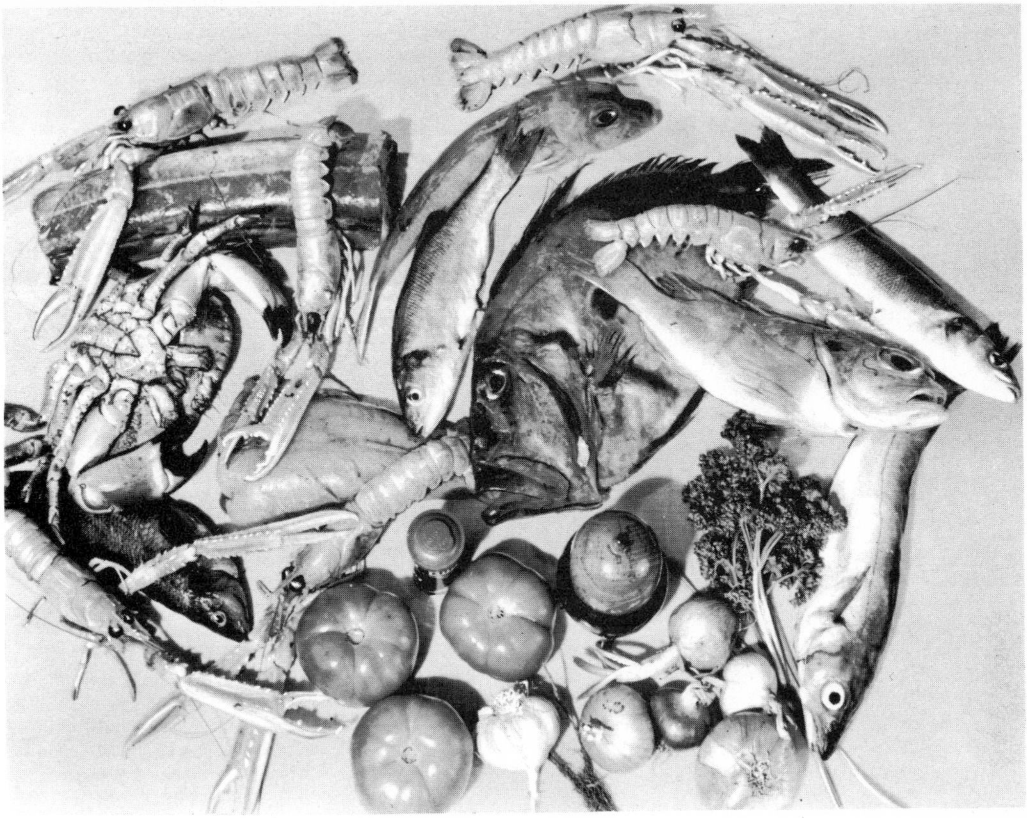

Ingredients for bouillabaisse (*Scarnati*)

Strain the soup over slices of bread, and serve with the fish and shellfish. Sprinkle soup and fish with chopped parsley. In Marseilles, special bread, called *marette*, is used for this purpose.

To make good *bouillabaisse*, one of the essential points is to cook it as quickly as possible, which results in the soup having the right consistency.

Originally a fisherman's dish, *bouillabaisse* ought not to contain lobster, only the cheaper cuts of fish.

Bouillabaisse borgne (Provençal cookery) – This *bouillabaisse* is called *l'aigo-sau-d'iou* in Provence.

Cook sliced potatoes slowly in fish stock prepared as described in the recipe for *Bouillabaisse à la parisienne* (see below). When the potatoes are done, poach fresh eggs, one by one, in the stock, taking care not to break them.

Pour the soup into a tureen over slices of bread, and arrange the potatoes and the poached eggs on another dish. Sprinkle with parsley and serve the two dishes at the same time.

Cod bouillabaisse. BOUILLABAISSE DE MORUE – Prepared as *Bouillabaisse à la parisienne* (see below), this is a stew rather than a soup. For method of preparation, see COD.

Ocean bouillabaisse. BOUILLABAISSE DE L'OCÉAN – Although the *bouillabaisse* is essentially a Mediterranean dish, a kind of *bouillabaisse* is made on the Atlantic coast.

Fry 5 big chopped onions, 500 g. (generous 1 lb.) potatoes cut into slices, and 4 chopped leeks in 6 tablespoons ($\frac{1}{2}$ cup) oil and 3 tablespoons (scant $\frac{1}{4}$ cup) butter. Add a little thyme, savory and fennel, a bay leaf, 4 cloves, 4 garlic cloves, 2 celery stalks, 4 peeled and chopped tomatoes and a pinch of saffron.

Cut into slices 4 whitings, 1 conger eel, 3 red mullets, 3 mackerels, a few fresh sardines, 2 small lobsters or 2 crabs, and some Dublin Bay prawns, cut into chunks. Season with salt, pepper and a little cayenne pepper and add enough dry white wine and water to cover the fish.

Separately, cook 1 litre ($1\frac{3}{4}$ pints, generous quart) mussels and, when done, discard the shells and add the mussels, and the liquor they were cooked in, to the fish. Bring to the boil and simmer gently for 30 minutes.

Fry slices of bread until golden brown. Strain the fish and pour the liquor over the fried bread. Arrange the fish on a separate dish and serve at the same time as the soup.

Bouillabaisse à la parisienne – Fry briskly 150 g. (5 oz., $1\frac{1}{4}$ cups) chopped onion and 75 g. (3 oz., $\frac{3}{4}$ cup) chopped leeks (using only the white parts) in $1\frac{1}{2}$ dl. ($\frac{1}{4}$ pint, $\frac{2}{3}$ cup) oil, without allowing them to colour. Moisten with 6 dl. (1 pint, $2\frac{1}{2}$ cups) white wine, and add 1 litre ($1\frac{3}{4}$ pints, generous quart) water. Add to this stock 4 peeled, seeded and chopped tomatoes, 4 crushed garlic cloves, a sprig of thyme and a bay leaf. Season with salt, pepper and a good pinch of powdered saffron. Add to this stock any heads and trimmings of fish intended for another dish. Cook briskly for 20 minutes and pass through a fine strainer.

Cut up gurnet, red mullet, whiting, conger eel, weever, and spiny lobster into chunks, and lay them flat in a deep pan. Place mussels, well washed, on top, season with salt and pepper and sprinkle with chopped parsley and oil.

Cook briskly for 15 minutes. Add 3 tablespoons (scant $\frac{1}{4}$ cup) kneaded butter.

Arrange the fish in a *timbale* (q.v.). Pour the soup into another *timbale* over grilled slices of bread.

Sardine bouillabaisse. BOUILLABAISSE DE SARDINES – Fry 1 chopped onion and 2 leeks in oil. Add a peeled, seeded and chopped tomato, 2 pounded garlic cloves, 1 bay leaf, 1 sprig of fennel and a small piece of orange peel. Moisten with $\frac{3}{4}$ litre ($1\frac{1}{3}$ pints, $1\frac{3}{4}$ pints) water. Season with salt, pepper and a pinch of saffron. Add 6 sliced potatoes, and cook with the lid on the pan.

When the potatoes are nearly done, arrange 1 kg. ($2\frac{1}{4}$ lb.) cleaned, scaled and washed fresh sardines on them, and cook for 8 minutes. Sprinkle with parsley and serve separately. Strain the *bouillabaisse* over slices of bread laid in a deep dish.

Spinach bouillabaisse (Provençal cookery). BOUILLABAISSE D'ÉPINARDS – Here is a recipe contributed by the great master of Provençal cuisine, J. B. Reboul:

'Pick over and wash 1 kg. ($2\frac{1}{4}$ lb.) spinach, cook for 5 minutes in boiling water, then dip into cold water and drain. Press with the hands to extract all water, and chop the spinach.

'Put $\frac{1}{2}$ dl. (3 tablespoons, scant $\frac{1}{4}$ cup) oil into an earthenware casserole, add a chopped onion, previously fried lightly without browning, and the spinach. Cook on a low fire for 5 minutes, stirring all the time.

'When the spinach is seared, add 5 sliced waxy potatoes. Season with salt, pepper and a little saffron. Moisten with 1 litre ($1\frac{3}{4}$ pints, generous quart) boiling water, add 2 chopped garlic cloves and a sprig of fennel, and cook, covered with a lid, on a low flame.

When the potatoes are cooked, poach 4 eggs in the pan.'

BOUILLANT – Small puff pastry patty, filled with a *salpicon* (q.v.) of chicken, served very hot as an *hors-d'œuvre*. (See HORS-D'ŒUVRE, *Small patties and rissoles*.)

BOUILLE – Vessel used for transporting milk.

BOUILLETURE or BOUILLITURE (Anjou cookery) – *Matelote* (q.v.), made mainly of eel, moistened with red wine, thickened with kneaded butter, garnished with mushrooms, little onions and – a local touch – with prunes.

This *matelote* is served garnished with slices of toast.

BOUILLI – Abbreviation of *boeuf bouilli*, i.e. boiled beef.

For recipes, see BEEF, *Boiled beef*.

BOUILLON – Stock or broth.

Plain white stock serves as a basis for all soups, clear and thickened. It is also used for making white or brown sauces. Stock is a basic liquid obtained by prolonged boiling of meat and vegetables in slightly salted water.

Bouillon is one of the basic elements of French cookery, both in home kitchens and in the most sumptuous establishments.

Clear soup is a food of mediocre nutritive value (which can, however, be increased by the addition of pasta products, bread and various substances), but an excellent 'quickener' of digestion, and a stimulant which tones up the heart and slightly raises the blood pressure.

Clarification of bouillon. CONSOMMÉ BLANC SIMPLE – The object of clarifying *bouillon* is to make ordinary *bouillon* more limpid; it also improves the taste. It is done with white of egg and lean beef and vegetables cut into small dice. *Bouillon* clarified in this way is called *consommé*.

In domestic cookery, stock is served without clarification. Served as a soup after adding various garnishes (principally some form of pasta), it is made with beef and fowl, carrots, turnips, leeks, parsnips, onion, celery, garlic, cloves.

To clarify *bouillon*, whisk 750 g. ($1\frac{3}{4}$ lb.) lean meat, 2 leeks cut up into small dice, and a fresh egg white in a deep pan. Add $2\frac{1}{2}$ litres ($4\frac{1}{2}$ pints, $5\frac{1}{2}$ pints) lukewarm *bouillon*. Continue to whisk the contents of the pan until it boils. Lower the heat and simmer for $1\frac{1}{2}$ hours. Strain through a cloth.

Bouillon de noce (wedding soup) (Périgord cookery) – This Périgord clear soup is really a version of *ollapodrida* (q.v.). Four kinds of meat are used: beef, a veal knuckle, a stuffed chicken and a turkey.

All these are cooked in stock flavoured with vegetables, together with Swiss chard. Add onion, fried in lard until golden, and vermicelli.

Cereal bouillons. BOUILLONS DE CÉRÉALES – These are rich in assimilable mineral substances and soluble nutritive matter which, being responsible for giving vegetable embryo the nutriment necessary for growth, have a beneficial effect on growing children. Boil 1 tablespoon each of wheat, oats, barley, rye, maize and bran for a long time in 3 litres ($5\frac{1}{4}$ pints, $6\frac{1}{2}$ pints) water until the liquid has boiled down to 1 litre ($1\frac{3}{4}$ pints, generous quart). Strain, and add salt and sugar.

Herb bouillon (stock). BOUILLON AUX HERBES – Wash 40 g. ($1\frac{3}{4}$ oz.) fresh sorrel leaves, 20 g. ($\frac{3}{4}$ oz.) fresh lettuce leaves, 10 g. ($\frac{1}{3}$ oz.) fresh chervil leaves and cook in 1 litre ($1\frac{3}{4}$ pints, generous quart) water until done. Add a pinch of sea salt and 1 teaspoon fresh butter. Cook a little longer, and strain.

Vegetable bouillon (stock). BOUILLON DE LÉGUMES – Vegetarian cookery books give many recipes for these. Clear vegetable soups can be used in children's diets, partially replacing milk; and in diets for invalids. With tapioca or vermicelli added, these soups acquire more nutritive value.

Dr. Leclerc gives a vegetable stock for children: Boil 50 g. (2 oz.) carrots, 60 g. ($2\frac{1}{2}$ oz.) potatoes, 15 g. ($\frac{1}{2}$ oz.) turnips, 6 g. ($\frac{1}{4}$ oz.) dried peas and 6 g. ($\frac{1}{4}$ oz.) dried beans in 3 litres ($5\frac{1}{4}$ pints, $6\frac{1}{2}$ pints) water in a covered stockpot for 4 hours. Boil down to 1 litre ($1\frac{3}{4}$ pints, generous quart) and add scant teaspoon salt.

Rice flour or other cereals can be added to this stock, or it can be used as a basis for other soups.

BOUILLON – Little restaurants which serve meals at a fixed price; the menu is usually limited.

BOUILLON AVEUGLE – Colloquial expression applied to mediocre clear soup when small spots of fat, called *eyes*, cannot be seen on the surface. Many of these soups, however, have the spots of fat carefully skimmed off before serving.

BOULE-DE-NEIGE – Name given to edible agaric.

BOULE-DE-NEIGE (Pâtisserie) – Cakes in the shape of balls, dipped in whipped cream. They are usually made of layers of fine sponge coated with butter cream.

The term is also applied to an iced sweet, made of bombe ice-cream mixture set in a round mould, and covered with whipped cream before serving (see SNOWBALL).

BOULE DE SON ('Bran Ball') – Slang term used to describe ration bread, called so because of the relatively high proportion of bran which went into its preparation.

BOULETTE – Dish prepared from some mixture (forcemeat, hash or purée) which is given a spherical form. *Boulettes* are often made from pieces of left-over meat or fish. They are dipped in egg and breadcrumbs and fried in deep fat. Or they are brushed with butter or lard and cooked in the oven.

BOUQUET. BOUQUET DE VIN – Wine bouquet is due to

ethers and essences or essential oils, which are extremely volatile. In the process of evaporation these essences release the multiple aromas pertaining to each wine.

The four elements which determine the quality of a wine are the colour, the bouquet, fruitiness and vinosity (the flavour and strength of the wine). Its quality lies in the right proportion of these elements.

BOUQUET GARNI – Aromatic herbs or plants tied together in a little faggot. The usual herbs are parsley, thyme and bay leaf, and their proportions are adjusted according to the nature of the dish. The strength of thyme and bay leaf must be taken into account and these aromatics used sparingly. *Bouquets garnis* can be small, medium or large, and for certain kinds of dishes they can include basil, celery, chervil, tarragon, burnet, rosemary, savory, etc. They are removed from stews and sauces before serving.

BOUQUETIÈRE (À LA) – Garnish used for meat dishes, composed of various vegetables disposed in bouquets. (See GARNISHES.)

BOURBONNAIS – Bourbonnais, ancient province of France, forms the whole of the *département* of Allier and a small part of Puy-de-Dôme, Creuse and Cher.

The 'Bourbonnichons' (i.e. natives of the district) are generally hearty eaters and enjoy good country dishes. Highest quality beef, mutton and pork are produced here. The rivers and ponds abound in succulent fish: carp, pike, eel, which are cooked *en matelote* (q.v.) or *au bleu* (q.v.). The streams are full of trout and crayfish. Very good game, both ground and winged, and excellent poultry, particularly geese, are also found in this district. The vegetable gardens and the orchards produce choice vegetables and fruit.

Beverages – The wines of Bourbonnais have an interesting bouquet. The white, red and rosé wines of Saint-Pourçain-sur-Sioule are classified as V.D.Q.S.

The mineral waters of Bourbonnais are famous. From time immemorial Vichy has been a famous watering-place. Its hot mineral waters were well known to the Romans. In the Middle Ages, Vichy was the seat of a castellany, which was acquired in 1344 by Pierre I of the house of Bourbon. His son, Louis II, in 1411 founded a Celestine monastery and it is to these monks, who propagated the virtue of its waters, that Vichy partly owes its fame. The religious wars, from which this town suffered a great deal, arrested its progress, but in the reign of Henri IV its fame began to spread. In 1605 a general administration of mineral and medicinal waters was created in France, and Vichy became its headquarters in 1648.

The popularity of Vichy water grew during the seventeenth and eighteenth centuries. Louis XIV protected its early fortune, and the letters of Madame de Sévigné, who went there for a cure in 1676 and 1677, completed its rise to success. In 1716 Louis XV endowed the Vichy hospital. Louis XVI's aunts, Adelaide and Victoire, having undergone successful treatment, built a new establishment to replace the existing modest 'Maison du Roi'. In 1853, the mineral waters concession was granted to a company.

Culinary specialities – *Freshwater matelotes and stews*; *pike à la crème*; Montluçon and Moulin *meat pies*; *sheeps' tongues with turnips*; *goose stew* called *oyonnade* locally; *pompe aux grattons*; *potato pie*; *mihior* or *millias*, rather similar to the one made in Languedoc; *cherry tarts*; *pancakes* which are called *sauciaux* locally; *pear gâteaux*; *gounerre*, a kind of potato pie; Gannat *brioche*; and *tarte bourbonnaise*, a pleasant country cheesecake for which the recipe is as follows: Pound fresh cream cheese in a bowl with fine salt, 4 eggs, 50 g. (2 oz., ¼ cup) fresh butter and 4 tablespoons (⅓ cup) flour. When the paste is smooth, spread it in a buttered pie dish, indent 7 or 8 holes with a finger and put a piece of fresh butter in each. Bake in a slow oven for 30 minutes. Sprinkle with sugar before serving.

BOURGEOISE (À LA) – Name which is applied to various dishes, mainly to large pieces of braised meat, prepared *à la mode bourgeoise*. These dishes always include a garnish composed of carrots, small onions and large dice of lean bacon. (See GARNISHES; BEEF, *Top rump à la bourgeoise*.)

BOURGUEIL – Wine produced from the Cabernet franc grape (nicknamed 'Breton' in the region). It has a delicious raspberry flavour and, generally speaking, is best drunk young. It is an excellent accompaniment to the regional dishes and to the goat cheeses.

The neighbouring *appellation*, Saint-Nicolas-de-Borgueil, produces wines of a similar character, but usually more robust and with a distinct tang.

BOURGUIGNONNE (À LA) – See the beginning of the article on BURGUNDY.

BOURRICHE – Type of long, handleless basket used to transport fruit, game, oysters, etc.

BOURRIDE (Provençal cookery) – Put 1 kg. (2¼ lb.) various small fish in a large pan with 2 litres (3½ pints, 4½ pints) water, 2 onions, 2 tomatoes, 2 garlic cloves – all finely chopped – and a *bouquet garni* (q.v.). Add a little bitter orange peel, seasoning, 2 tablespoons (3 tablespoons) olive oil and some saffron. Boil fast for 15 minutes.

Strain the stock through a sieve, pressing the vegetables through. Bind the stock with 2 egg yolks mixed with *ailloli* (q.v.). Simmer lightly and pour into a soup tureen on slices of bread. Serve with the fish.

BOURRU (Wine) – Name given in the past to spiced wine. For a hogshead of the wine, it was prepared by mixing white wine with 1 litre (1¾ pints, generous quart) of a very strong concoction of wheat and elder flowers.

Nowadays new wine is often called *vin bourru*.

BOUTARGUE – Preparation of dried, pressed mullet roe that can be bought ready-made. It is a speciality of Provençe. For instructions on how to make it see HORS-D'ŒUVRE.

BOUTEILLER (Charge de) – This title in the olden days was given to the man in charge of the wine cellar of the king, of a prince, or some other great aristocrat. At the court of the kings of France the post was always held by high-ranking gentlemen. Today the word *bouteiller* – which in fact is hardly ever used – is synonymous with *sommelier* (wine waiter).

BOUTER – French term for wine that has turned sour.

BOUT-SAIGNEUX – The neck of a calf or a sheep.

BOUVILLON – The word *bouvillon* is applied to a young steer until it loses its first milk-tooth.

BOUZY – One of the greatest and most highly regarded vineyards of Champagne. Its black Pinot grapes made into white wine contribute to the best Champagne. Made into red wine, this grape gives a delicious, natural fruity wine, much esteemed by gourmets. It is best drunk young, but in a good year it matures admirably; the wine growers of Champagne have some splendid bottles in their cellars.

BOWELS. BOYAUX – Intestines of slaughtered animals. Pigs' intestines are mainly used for making *andouilles* (q.v.) and *andouillettes* (q.v.). The smallest ones are used as

Bowls (*Nicolas*)

casings for sausages. Fat intestines are used in the preparation of Lyons sausages.

Pigs' intestines are divided into two categories: the big and the small. Before being used pigs' intestines should be prepared and cleaned with minute care.

BOWL. BOL – Term used for basins of varying capacity, made of porcelain, earthenware, glass or metal. They are sometimes used in France for hot drinks (coffee, chocolate or tea with milk) served at breakfast.

The term 'punch bowl' is applied to a bigger receptacle usually made of silver, in which punch and mulled wine are prepared. In French the word *bol* also applies to china, glass or metal finger bowls put before guests after serving fish, or at the end of a meal. In the past, porcelain, pottery, silver and even gold basins were used for this purpose. They were sometimes set in stands, which can still be found in antique shops. It must be remembered that until the middle of the sixteenth century, forks were not used at table, and that it was customary for two people to eat out of one bowl. It was therefore essential to have washing arrangements for the guests in the room where the meals were served.

BRABANÇONNE (À LA) – Garnish of chicory and potato croquettes for large pieces of meat. The garnish is often supplemented by hop shoots cooked in butter or cream.

BRAIN. CERVELLE – Culinary term for the brain substance of edible animals. The brain is rich in vitamins and phosphorus, and provides a great deal of nourishment in proportion to its volume.

Water	69·10	per cent
Nitrogenous substances	13·26	per cent
Fatty substances	16·23	per cent
Extractive substances	0·12	per cent
Ash	0·19	per cent

It also contains phosphorated fats similar to the lecithin of egg yolk.

The weight of an ox brain varies from 450 g. to 700 g. (1 lb. to $1\frac{1}{2}$ lb.); that of a calf's brain from 250 g. to 300 g. (9 oz. to 11 oz.); that of lamb's or sheep's brain about 100 g. (4 oz.); the weight of a pig's brain is about 150 g. (5 oz.). (The last is rarely used in cooking.)

Whatever the recipe, brains must be well purged and cooked in a *court-bouillon* (q.v.). For the various methods of preparation see OFFAL or VARIETY MEATS.

BRAISE. BRAISER – To cook various foods by braising in a special utensil called a *daubière* (q.v.), or a braising pan.

BRAISING. BRAISAGE – Method which can be applied to most food substances, cooked in an airtight pan, adding very little liquid. Instructions relevant to braising will be found in the section entitled CULINARY METHODS.

BRAISING PAN. BRAISIÈRE – Utensil made of tinned copper, nickel, aluminium, enamelled cast-iron, earthenware and fireproof porcelain.

In restaurant terminology, the word *braisière* is applied to any kind of a stock, made out of various meat trimmings and bones, used for the preparation of basic sauces. This stock is used instead of *estouffade* (q.v.) and clear beef or veal stock, which should properly be used for the moistening of *roux* (q.v.), as is white consommé.

Braising pan (*Dehillerin. Phot. Larousse*)

BRAMBLE (Blackberry). RONCE – Prickly bush whose berries can be used to make syrup and jam. The young shoots can be eaten like asparagus.

BRAN. SON – Outer casing of the grain, which is separated from the flour by milling.

BRANDADE – Method of preparing pounded salt cod, which is very popular in Languedoc and Provence. It is flavoured with garlic, and is prepared by cooking slowly over moderate heat and stirring vigorously and constantly with a wooden spoon, maintaining the same heat throughout the operation. Add oil, little by little. (See COD, *Brandade of salt cod.*)

BRANDEVIN – Spirit distilled from wine. (See SPIRITS.)

BRANDEVINIER – Man who goes about the countryside with his still for distilling spirit from wine, marc or fruit.

BRASSERIE – Establishment where beer and cider are made or sold. Breweries, of which there are a great many in Germany and in the eastern regions, were not established in Paris and other parts of France until the middle of the nineteenth century. Brasseries in modern times are cafés or restaurants where food and drink are served.

Certain types of brasseries used to serve as a meeting-place for politicians, artists, men of letters and bohemians. Among the brasseries which have either become converted into something else or have disappeared altogether, are those in rue des Martyrs, associated with Nadar, Pelloquet, Privat d'Anglemont, Villiers de l'Isle-Adam, Baudelaire, Courbet and Carjat.

Brasserie Pousset, which at one time was a centre for literary men and journalists, became the meeting-place of government and colonial officials. Other famous brasseries were the Brasserie du Petit-Poucet, where one could meet Ponchon and Grenet-Dancourt; and Brasserie Steinbach in the Quartier Latin where Jean Moréas used to call for a chat with Maurice Maindron or Paul Mounet.

The brasserie style survives in Paris today in Lipp, Bofinger, and the charming Brasserie Flo in the Passage des Petites-Ecuries.

BRAZIL NUT. NOIX DU BRÉSIL – Fruit of the bertholettia, a tree which grows in Paraguay and Brazil, sometimes to 35 m. (114 feet) in height. The nut is also known as American chestnut. In South America it is called *juvia*; the Portuguese call it *castenas de maranon*.

Its shell, which has three sharp edges, is brown and hard; the white kernel is similar in flavour to coconut and hazelnut.

BREAD. PAIN – Dough made of flour and water, fermented and baked.

Cereals were first used in the form of meal, then as a cake made from a mixture of meal or flour with honey, oil, sweet wine, various grains, fruit and meat.

The Hebrews, the Egyptians and the Chinese introduced flat cakes made of flour and water dough, baked without leaven. The discovery of fermented bread, no doubt an accidental one, is attributed to the Egyptians, who used the leaven of sour dough, left over from the previous bread-making, and the must of grapes, kneaded with flour and dried in the sun.

The use of fermented bread spread quickly but did not supersede the old method of making unleavened flat cakes, the only bread known to the Roman soldiers. In the middle ages, under the name of *trenchers*, these flat cakes were used instead of plates for cutting up meat; they were then eaten or thrown to the poor.

Making bread commercially – The flour, which must be kept for at least 15 days after milling, goes through a kneading operation, which consists of mixing it with yeast and moistening it with water.

The leaven, which gives the dough the ferments (alcohol barm and associated fungus) necessary for transforming sugar into alcohol and carbon dioxide, is taken from a previous kneading, or is a mixture of yeasts.

Kneading with yeast is the usual method. The flour is put in a bowl, a well made in the centre, yeast and warm water added, and the mixture left to ferment for 4 or 5 hours, to form the 'main leaven'. It is then 'refreshed' by adding an equal weight of flour to obtain the 'first leaven'. More flour is added later to obtain the 'second leaven' or *tout point*, which represents half or a third of the batch of loaves.

During the final kneading, the remaining flour is added, and the dough is moistened with warm, salted water. This operation is called *frase* (kneading) and is followed by *contre-frase* (second kneading), which is very hard work when done by hand. It consists of moulding the dough into one lump, leaving it to rise, allowing it to subside, dividing, stretching and kneading it into one lot again – and all these operations have to be done very quickly. In modern establishments they are done in mechanical kneaders.

When the kneading is completed, it is left to stand in a kneading trough covered with a cloth.

Bread kneaded with leaven is whiter and has more taste than bread kneaded only with diluted yeast.

Through the action of leaven, the released carbon dioxide puffs up the dough. When it reaches double its original volume, it is divided into loaves, the underside is sprinkled with wholemeal flour, rice flour or finely ground maize (corn meal) and the loaves put in the oven.

The oven is heated to between 220° and 300°C. (425° and 575°F.), in such a way as to sear the whole surface of the loaf immediately, while the interior continues to ferment. Carbon dioxide swells the dough, forms holes in the bread and causes the surface to bulge. When the inside temperature reaches 60°C. (140°F.), the starch is transformed into starch-paste. Fermentation ceases when the temperature goes up to 80°C. (176°F.). When the inside temperature reaches 100°C. (212°F.), the crust loses a large proportion of water by evaporation.

When the temperature of the oven (which will have gone down while the bread was being put into it) reaches 200°C. (400°F.) the starch is roasted. Water steam is then injected (or the oven is sprayed with water) to prevent the formation of too thick a crust. The baking time varies according to the size of the loaves.

The total loss of water is proportional to the size of the loaf; to obtain 1000 g. (2·2 lb.) bread, 1140 g. (2·5 lb.) dough will be needed for loaves of 4 kg. (8·8 lb.) and 1670 g. (3·7 lb.) for loaves of 1 kg. (2·2 lb.).

If the fermentation of the dough is excessive, carbon dioxide is released before the loaves are placed in the oven, and the bread will be heavy and compact, with a cavity between the crumb and the crust.

Alcohol, which forms during fermentation, evaporates during baking as well as carbon dioxide, which continues to be released during cooling. A condensation of steam takes place during this cooling-off period in newly baked bread, which then begins to look greasy and shiny.

Qualities of bread – A good quality loaf should have a pale yellow or light brown bottom crust and a golden yellow or light brown top crust, which should be thick, domed, and resonant when tapped. Both the crusts should adhere to the crumb, and together equal one-fifth of the weight of the loaf (the thicker the crust, the less water there is in a loaf). If the crusts of a slice of bread are pressed together the slice should quickly regain its original shape.

The crumb should be homogenous, without any white or yellowish lumps, without grey, red or black spots; it should not stick to the fingers; the holes in it should be uneven, not too big (which is a sign of badly kneaded dough), nor too small (which is a sign of insufficient fermentation); the smell should be sweet, the taste clean and pleasant.

Too white a crumb is a sign of rice flour having been added; greyish-brown crumb shows that rye or buckwheat flour has been added.

If kept for a long time, bread becomes stale, the crumb dries up and the crust grows soft. This is not due solely to the loss of water (stale bread contains only about 1 per cent less water than fresh bread), but to a partial transformation of starch into dextrine. By heating stale bread (which causes it to lose 3 per cent of its water content) a distillation process is achieved; moisture from the crust penetrates the crumb, giving it, for a short time, the appearance of fresh bread.

Varieties of bread – In France, ordinary or household bread (*pain ordinaire*, or *pain de ménage*) is long and cylindrical in shape, flattened on the top, and slashed with slanting or parallel markings, The *boulot* or *bouleau loaf* is the same shape, but floured on top. The *polka loaf* is long or round, with a hard crust, slashed with lozenge-shaped decorations. A *split loaf* is made by joining two long loaves together; it is thicker and has less crust. The *round loaf* is of the traditional round shape, the upper crust having a domed top; the *crown loaf*, as its name implies, is circular in form.

Fancy loaves, sold by the piece and not by weight, are made out of highest quality flour and shaped either into batons, with a golden brown or floured surface, or into flat loaves or small rolls of various shapes.

The *Vienna loaf* is kneaded with a certain quantity of milk. The *tin* or *pan loaf*, square-shaped with a very thin crust, is used in France mainly for toast, *canapés*, garnish croûtons and sandwiches.

On the borderline between the domains of bakery and pastry-making we have brioche dough loaves and puff pastry croissants.

Bread containing some or all of the bran and germ of the grain and endosperm is theoretically more nutritive, but being less easily assimilated by the intestines, the advantages are rather problematical.

Wholemeal bread is made from meal containing the the entire wheat grain. In some parts of Germany very dark bread (pumpernickel) is made of coarse unbolted rye.

Bread wedges (*Nicolas*)

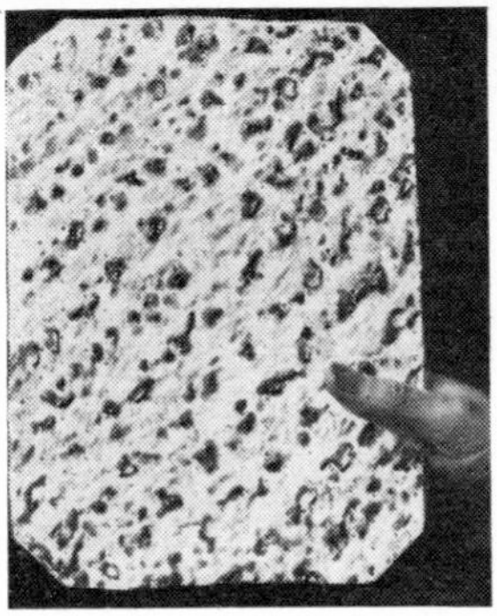

Unleavened bread (*Larousse*)

Eight varieties of French ordinary bread (*Maison Syda. Phot. Larousse*)

Wheaten flour is used for fine bread, but in many countries rye is the principal bread grain. Barley bread, bread made from a mixture of barley and wheat, used to be made and kept fresh for a long time, but it was very coarse, as can be judged from the saying 'as coarse as barley bread', because it is difficult to hull barley.

Rye bread, made of 15 per cent bolted whole rye, has a heavy, compact texture; bread made out of a mixture of rye and wheat (one part rye to three parts wheat) keeps well and is sold as quality bread.

Gluten bread, manufactured for diabetics, has gluten added to the dough; it contains up to 40 per cent starch.

Unleavened bread is much less used than ordinary bread, though in some countries, Sweden for example, it is served with *hors-d'œuvre*.

Adulteration of bread – The most prevalent method is to retain as great a proportion of water in the bread as possible, but there are other fraudulent practices, involving the use of grain poor in gluten content, and adding various 'improving agents' – chemical products – to the flour, thus rendering bread-making easier. This process, condemned by all nutritionists, has contributed not a little to the disfavour in which bread is held by dieticians.

Digestibility of bread – Bread is a food which is used, and abused, more than any other, especially in France. For many, it is the staple food, which children are taught – and forced – to eat with all other food; in many circles the quantity of bread consumed exceeds in volume that of all other foods put together.

Good bread taken in moderate quantities is an excellent food, but it should not be consumed in excessive quantities. The crust is more digestible than the crumb, both because being hard it has to be chewed with greater care, and because one eats less of it. For the same reason, toasted bread is better for dyspeptics, who will thus be forced to chew it more thoroughly and will be less tempted to over-eat.

The difference in the composition of the crust and the crumb lies mainly in the latter's greater water content.

There are various prejudices concerning bread, the worst being the preference for white bread. This, having been reserved for the richer classes in times gone by, was always coveted by the less favoured classes. To satisfy them, the use of higher extracted flour was resorted to for the manufacture of 'rich' bread and artificially-bleached flour for the other kinds.

The principal drawback of excessively white bread, so popular at present, is that it is practically uneatable if stored for more than a few hours. Besides, its dietetic qualities are nil and undoubtedly it is harmful to people with delicate digestions.

Fortunately there is natural or dietary bread made with yeast and baked on stone over a wood fire by which means the goodness of this staple food is retained.

BREAD IN DIETETICS. PAIN EN DIÉTÉTIQUE –

Wholemeal bread – Dieticians are not wholly in agreement concerning the nutritive value of wholemeal bread, but they are unanimous in recognising that the white bread at present on sale commercially is no longer the ideal food it was when made with wheat flours stone-ground (and not by rollers), prepared with natural leavenings (and not with chemical ones), and cooked in a wood-fired oven (not an oil-fired one).

Wholemeal bread, on the other hand, is still this ideal food. But the consumer must ensure that it is really wholemeal bread and not bread made with ordinary flour mixed with bran, or even bread 'enriched' with wheatgerm or some such ingredient.

The only proper bread is that made with pure wheat flour, preferably bolted (between 90 per cent and 95 per cent, at best 80 per cent), leavened with natural yeast and baked on stone over a wood fire.

However, not all stomachs or digestive systems tolerate wholemeal bread, excellent though it may be. It is important to note that since wholemeal bread does more for the organism than ordinary bread, the usual daily ration can be reduced by a third or more. Also that wholemeal bread does not go very well with meats, highly spiced dishes, or alcoholic beverages.

According to the dieticians, wholemeal bread and a basically vegetarian diet is the ideal.

METHODS FOR MAKING GOOD BREAD – We give, quoting from Carême, three Edlin recipes.

'Cooks,' he writes, 'who travel with their gastronomicallyminded masters can, from now on, by following this method, procure fresh bread every day.'

Ordinary method. MÉTHODE ORDINAIRE – 'Put 2¼ kg. (5 lb., 20 cups) flour in the mixing trough. Make a well in the middle and put in 50 g. (2 oz.) yeast. Moisten with warm water and mix until the consistency of brioche dough is reached, kneading well and adding 50 g. (2 oz., 3 tablespoons) fine salt, diluted in a little warm water. Cover and put in a warm place to ferment and rise.

'After having left the dough in this condition for an hour or two, knead it again, then cover and leave for another 2 hours.

'Divide the dough into 8 equal parts and shape into loaves. Put them in a hot oven as quickly as possible. When baked, rub the crust with a little butter, to make it golden.'

French rolled loaf. PAIN FRANÇAIS EN ROULEAU – 'Put 2¼ kg. (5 lb., 20 cups) sieved flour into a kneading trough. Knead it with generous litre (2 pints, 2½ pints) milk, 250 g. (8 oz., 1 cup) warm butter, 60 g. (2½ oz.) yeast and 50 g. (2 oz., 3 tablespoons) salt. When all the ingredients have been mixed, knead with a sufficient quantity of hot water. Mix well, cover, and leave for 2 hours. Shape into rolls, put them on baking trays and leave in a warm place to rise for an hour. Bake in a very hot oven for 20 minutes.'

Loaf à la terrine or à la grecque. PAIN À LA TERRINE, À LA GRECQUE – 'Put 2¼ kg. (5 lb., 20 cups) slightly warm fine flour into a big mixing bowl, also warm. Add 50 g. (2 oz.) yeast, 50 g. (2 oz., 3 tablespoons) salt and a sufficient quantity of water or milk to make the dough rather soft.

'Knead thoroughly, cover, and keep in a warm place for 3 hours. Divide into 8 loaves and put these into buttered *terrines*.

'Bake in a very hot oven. When nearly baked, remove from the *terrines* and put on baking trays for a few minutes to let them brown a little.'

Choine bread. PAIN DE CHOINE – A fine-textured white bread. It was once a salted bread, therefore a luxury, salt being extremely expensive in the sixteenth century.

Consecrated bread. PAIN BÉNIT – Consecrated bread, which is distributed in churches of big towns, is most frequently made of fine brioche dough.

In the country the dough for consecrated bread is made like brioche dough, using the following ingredients: 1 kg. (2¼ lb., 9 cups) sieved flour, 500 g. (18 oz., 2¼ cups) butter, 20 g. (⅔ oz.) brewer's yeast, ½ litre (scant pint, 2¼ cups) boiled milk and a pinch of salt.

English or tin loaf. PAIN ANGLAIS, DIT AUSSI PAIN DE MIE – Used for croûtons, white breadcrumbs, etc., or for making sandwiches, toast, or *canapés* served as *hors-d'œuvre*.

English loaves are baked in rectangular tins, and are used for making hollowed-out *croustades* (q.v.) in which various *ragoûts*, purées, etc. are served.

Finger rolls with milk. PETITS PAINS AU LAIT – Spread 1 kg. (2¼ lb., 9 cups) sieved flour on the table in a circle. Make a well in the centre, and put into it 250 g. (9 oz., generous cup) butter, 25 g. (1 oz., 2 tablespoons) fine sugar, and a pinch of salt. Moisten with 5 dl. (scant pint, 2¼ cups) boiled milk and add a little warm water. Knead with 40 g. (1½ oz., 2 cakes) baker's yeast and leave until the next morning.

Divide the dough into small 60-g. or 80-g. (2½-oz. or 3-oz.) pieces and shape into slightly oval rolls. Split the rolls slightly in the centre, brush with beaten egg and bake in a hot oven.

Finger rolls with eggs. PETITS PAINS AUX OEUFS – These are made like *Finger rolls with milk*, adding 3 egg yolks.

Gonesse Bread. PAIN DE GONESSE – This was renowned for its whiteness and taste. Gonesse was once a village on the outskirts of Paris. Olivier de Serres said that the bakers of Gonesse, having been questioned juridically on the reasons for the superior quality of their bread, attributed it to the water they used in its preparation.

Plaited bread. NATTE – Bread baked in the form of a plait.

Bread for soups. PAIN POUR POTAGES – This bread, which is made in the shape of a long thin roll and is sold only in big Paris bakeries, is prepared of dough very rich in gluten. These rolls are cut into thin slices and dried in the oven, or they can be cut and hollowed out in various shapes. (See CROÛTES.)

Unleavened bread. PAIN AZYME – The Book of Exodus tells us that in their haste to leave Egypt the Jews forgot to bring yeast with them, and that for a long time after that they had to eat unleavened bread.

The Israelites perpetuated the memory of this privation by eating only unleavened bread during Pesach. This is how this bread is made:

Knead some sieved wheaten flour with salt and water into a slightly softish paste. Roll out into round or square pieces 1 cm. (½ inch) thick. Prick them all over and bake in a low oven.

Unleavened or offering bread. PAIN AZYME, À HOSTIE – Strain the flour through a silk sieve. Dilute with enough slightly salted water to obtain a softish paste, as for wafers, called *oublies*.

Pour into special moderately hot iron moulds in such a way as to dry the paste without allowing it to colour. Leave to dry on wicker trays in the oven. Store in a dry place in wooden boxes with well-fitting lids.

Viennese bread. PAIN VIENNOIS – Viennese bread was brought to Paris in 1840 by Count Zang, First Secretary of the Austrian Embassy, who founded the first Parisian bakery, in rue Richelieu, using Viennese methods. Zang made such a success of the venture that he became over confident, enlarged the bakery beyond his means, and ruined himself installing equipment. He was obliged to leave Paris following the events of 1848, but his Viennese bread remained.

BREADCRUMBS. CHAPELURE – The French word *chapelure* comes from *chapeler*, which meant to crush bread that had been dried very slowly in the oven.

White breadcrumbs are obtained by sieving stale white bread through a metal sieve with a fairly large mesh, and are used for crumbing objects destined for frying. Loaf bread, called 'English bread' in France, is generally used for this purpose. When French bread is used, the operation is easier if, after the removal of the crust, the bread is rolled in a lightly floured cloth. Then this bread passes much more easily through the meshes of a sieve.

White breadcrumbs can be kept for two or three days. If one takes the precaution of drying the breadcrumbs gently above the stove, without allowing them to brown, they keep much longer.

Golden breadcrumbs are prepared by drying bread crusts in a very slow oven. Once dry and slightly coloured, these crusts are pounded in a mortar (or crushed with a rolling-pin) and passed through a wire-mesh sieve. This type of breadcrumb will keep indefinitely in a covered glass jar in a dry atmosphere.

Golden breadcrumbs (if white breadcrumbs are not available) can be used for coating meat and fish with egg and breadcrumbs before frying, but they are mainly used for sprinkling over preparations which are cooked *au gratin*.

BREADCRUMB (To). PANER – To coat an object with breadcrumbs before frying it in clarified butter.

Coat with butter and breadcrumbs. PANER AU BEURRE – To brush various meats, before grilling them, with plenty of melted butter, and roll them in freshly grated breadcrumbs.

Coat with breadcrumbs à la milanaise. PANER À LA MILANAISE – As *à l'anglaise* (see below), but adding one-third of their volume of grated Parmesan cheese to the breadcrumbs.

Coat with egg and breadcrumbs. PANER À L'ANGLAISE – To dip various foods – escalopes, fillets of fish, cutlets, etc. – in a mixture of beaten egg, seasoned with a little oil, salt and pepper, and white breadcrumbs. The items of food are then fried in clarified butter.

Breadfruit tree

BREADFRUIT TREE. ARBRE À PAIN – Genus of plants which includes the sago palm and the raffia palm. It is a beautiful tree, with soft timber and deeply divided leaves. The tree is a native of tropical regions and is cultivated throughout the islands of the Asiatic archipelago and in the Pacific islands close to the equatorial regions. It attains a height of 15 to 20 m. (50 to 65 feet) and contains a thick, viscous, milky juice which is made into a kind of glue. The juice, which hardens on exposure to the air, is used by the natives of the South Seas to waterproof their canoes. The timber, in spite of not being very hard, is used in the building of huts and canoes. The fibrous inner bark is beaten out and made into a kind of cloth. The leaves, which reach enormous dimensions, serve as wrapping for food and roofing for dwellings. The dried spikes of the male flowers are used as tinderwood.

The fruit itself is large and round and of a greenish-yellow colour; it is an important item of food for the islanders. When fully ripe it has a sweetish taste, is laxative and indigestible, and goes bad quickly. It is gathered before it is fully ripe, when the flesh is firm and white, mealy and rich in starch, and has almost all the nutritive qualities of wheaten bread.

It is cut in slices and baked or toasted on hot coals, or baked in the oven until the outside skin becomes rather dark.

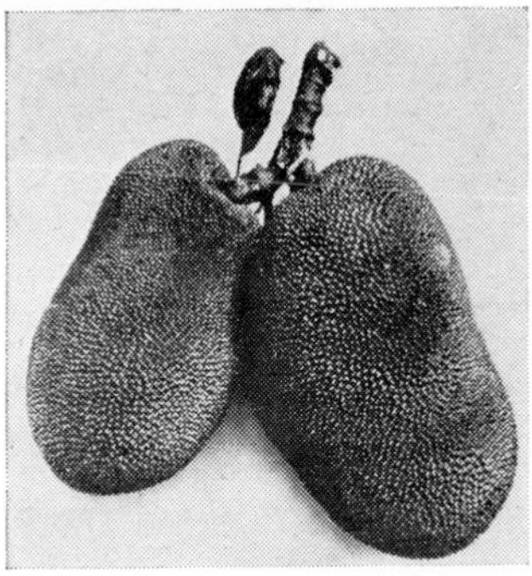

Breadfruit

Prepared in this way it is a valuable food, very nutritious, its taste recalling that of freshly baked bread, with a slight hint of artichoke and Jerusalem artichoke.

Two or three of these trees, it is claimed, provide sufficient food for one man for a whole year. The seeds are also edible, and are roasted in the cinders or cooked in water like chestnuts, which they resemble a little in size and taste.

Another species of the breadfruit tree called the *jack tree* has fruit structurally resembling the breadfruit, and is eaten on a vast scale, but it is greatly inferior to the real breadfruit in taste. Its ocrea is eaten like chestnuts. A small quantity of fruit and the green ocrea of the genuine breadfruit tree are exported.

BREAD SAUCE (English cookery) – Sauce made of milk and breadcrumbs. It is served with roast game. In England fried breadcrumbs are usually served at the same time as this sauce. (See SAUCE.)

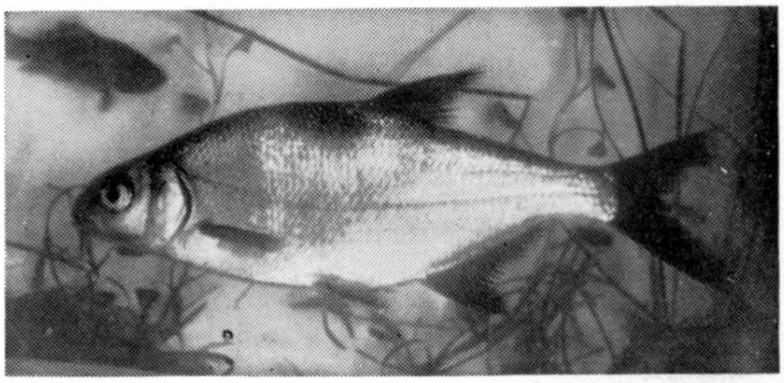

Bream

BREAM. BRÈME – European freshwater fish, in appearance resembling the carp. All the recipes given for carp (q.v.) can be applied to bream. It is mostly used for *matelotes* (q.v.) and fish stews.

BRÉBANT – Famous Parisian restaurateur. (See RESTAURANTS OF BYGONE DAYS.)

BRÈDES (Créole cookery) – Name given in some of the old French colonies to a dish made from leaves of different plants: watercress, tips of pumpkin shoots, cabbage, spinach, lettuce. This dish is a speciality of Réunion Island; it is very refreshing and is served with *Rice à la créole* (see RICE).

Cabbage brèdes. BRÈDES DE CHOU – Trim the leaves of a white cabbage and remove the tough centre veins. Shred finely as for *sauerkraut*.

Cut some bacon into strips and fry until it is light golden. Add a pinch of pounded ginger and a chopped tomato.

Moisten with a little water, simmer for 20 minutes. Put the shredded cabbage into this sauce and cook for about 1½ hours. Serve *Rice à la créole* (see RICE) separately.

Lettuce brèdes. BRÈDES DE LAITUES – Wash the leaves of cabbage lettuce and cut them lengthways. Soak in cold water. Prepare in the same manner as *Watercress brèdes* (see below) but use less sauce and allow shorter cooking time.

Pumpkin brèdes. BRÈDES DE CITROUILLE – Detach the leaves of pumpkin shoot tips, leaving a piece of stalk 1 cm. (½ inch) long on each leaf. Peel off all skin and stringy parts, and scrape off all green knots. Wash carefully and leave to soak in cold water. Drain. Put some good fat in a casserole, add some diced bacon, and brown a chopped onion in this mixture. Add a large, skinned, seeded and quartered tomato, and some salt, garlic and ginger, which have been pounded in a mortar. Simmer for a few moments. Add the prepared pumpkin shoots and simmer without adding water.

Spinach brèdes. BRÈDES D'ÉPINARDS – Prepare as above, blanching the spinach before putting it into the sauce.

Watercress brèdes. BRÈDES DE CRESSON – Wash and pick over the cress as for a salad. Fry 150 g. (5 oz.) thickly sliced bacon and a chopped onion until golden. Pound 2 garlic cloves, a pinch of ginger and salt in a mortar, and add to the mixture, together with a peeled, seeded and sliced tomato. Allow to brown for a few moments, then add 1½ large glasses of water. Boil down the sauce slightly, and put in the cress to simmer until it is done. Serve with plenty of sauce and hand *Rice à la créole* (see RICE) separately.

BRESOLLES – This dish was said to have been invented by the chef in charge of Marquis de Bresolles' kitchen who called it after his master.

'Chop finely 250 g. (generous ½ lb.) lean ham with onions, a few spring onions, some mushrooms and a garlic clove. Season with salt, pepper and a little grated nutmeg, and add a little olive oil.

'Put a layer of this forcemeat into a buttered earthenware casserole. Lay thin slices of veal, beef or mutton on top, and continue alternating layers of forcemeat and slices of meat until the casserole is filled up to ½ cm. (¼ inch) from the top. Cover with a lid and cook in the oven.

'Garnish with braised chestnuts, and pour over some *Demi-glace sauce* (q.v.) flavoured with Madeira.'

BRESSE – The name of this ancient part of France is known throughout the world for the excellence of Bresse chickens and capons.

BRESTOIS – Cake which used to be made in Brest:

Whisk 12 eggs and 500 g. (18 oz., 2¼ cups) fine sugar over a low heat (as for Genoese pastry).

Add 125 g. (4 oz., ¾ cup) sweet blanched almonds pounded in a mortar with 3 whole eggs. Flavour with a few drops of lemon essence, a little bitter almond essence, and a small glass of Curaçao. Whisk the mixture thoroughly and add 375 g. (13 oz., generous 1½ cups) melted butter and 375 g. (13 oz., 3¼ cups) sieved cake flour. Blend well.

Put the mixture into buttered brioche moulds. Bake in a slow oven. This type of cake, if wrapped in foil, will keep in perfect condition for a long time. It is a kind of 'travelling cake' (*gâteau de voyage*).

BRETON (Gâteau) – This gâteau was created by Monsieur Dubusc, chief of the Seugnot laboratories.

The *Breton*, made from almond biscuit paste, is assembled by placing different cakes on top of one another, icing each with a different colour fondant icing and then decorating it.

BRETON FAR. FAR BRETON – Cream flan, a Breton speciality, made commercially.

BRETONNE (À LA) – Most dishes prepared *à la bretonne* include a garnish of beans cooked *à la bretonne* (see BEAN, *Fresh white haricot beans*). Thus *Leg* or *Shoulder of mutton à la bretonne* (see MUTTON) is roasted or pot-roasted (sometimes braised), and served with beans.

Purée bretonne is made of beans cooked *à la bretonne* and served, clarified, as a soup; or if a thicker consistency is retained, as a vegetable or a garnish for meat.

Sauce bretonne is poured over poached or soft-boiled eggs and braised fillets of fish. This does not contain any beans but is made by adding finely shredded carrots, celery and leeks, lightly tossed in butter, to thick *velouté sauce* with cream, or to white wine sauce. (See SAUCE; SOLE, *Sole à la bretonne*.)

BRETONNEAU – An old Norman name for turbot.

BRIE – Name of an ancient province of France, situated to the east of Paris, with the town of Meaux as capital. The province was once divided into three regions: Brie champenoise (Meaux), Brie française (Brie-Comte-Robert) and Brie pouilleuse (Château-Thierry). These regions were part of the government of Champagne.

The name of Brie is known for the excellent cheeses produced there. There are no other gastronomical specialities. The *cuisine* is the same as that of the Ile-de-France and, therefore, similar to the one which constitutes the basis of Parisian cookery.

Brie cheeses. FROMAGES DE BRIE – In a research dedicated to Brie cheeses one reads the following: Every year 12 million cheeses are sold in the *département* of Seine-et-Marne. In Meaux alone 4,420,000 francs' worth of cheese is sold annually; in Crécy 1,300,000 francs' worth.

There are two distinct qualities of Brie cheeses: skim-milk cheeses made, as their name states, from skimmed milk, and cream cheese made from whole cows' milk. The latter (especially the cheeses made in the region of Nangis with pure whole milk drawn twice daily, morning and evening) are extremely delicate. According to M. Teyssier des Forges, it was these cheeses that were served at the Congress of Vienna and proclaimed 'the best in the world'.

It seems that this estimation of Brie cheeses, made in 1863, still holds good. The quality continues to be excellent especially where farm cheeses are concerned, although these, unfortunately, are becoming more and more difficult to find.

The *Brie de Meaux* and *Brie de Coulommiers* are best eaten from October to May. The *Brie de Melun* can be consumed throughout the year. (See CHEESE.)

BRIGNOLE – Dried plum which gets its name from the town of Brignoles in the *département* of Var. It is used in compotes in the same way as dried apricots and prunes.

BRILL. BARBUE – Flat sea fish, possessing a certain similarity to turbot, from which it differs by its smaller size, slightly more elongated shape, and by the tiny scales which cover its skin. Its flesh is light and delicate.

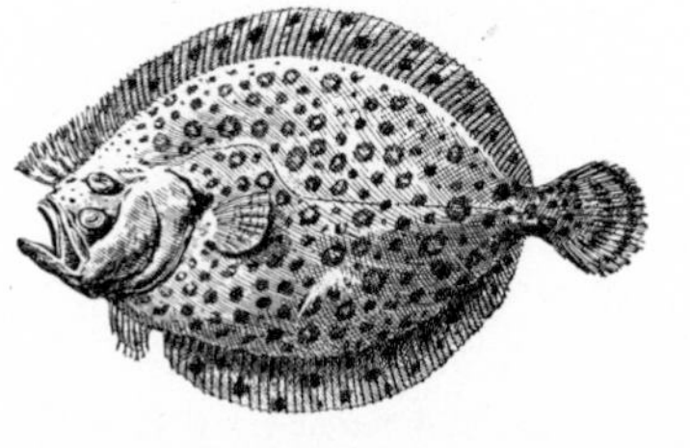

Brill

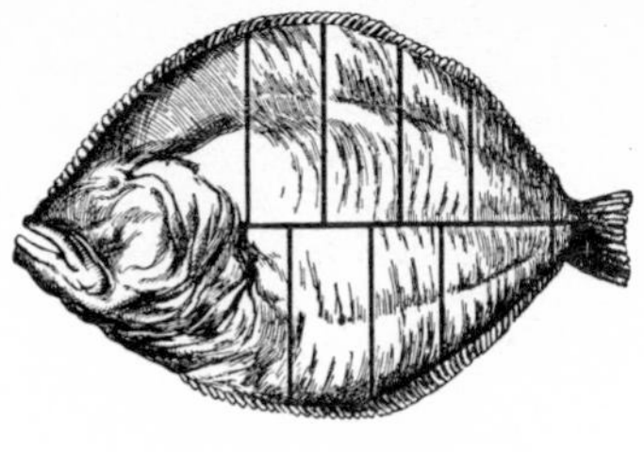

How to divide a brill

This fish abounds in all the seas of Europe, but the brill caught in the Atlantic Ocean is of the greatest gastronomical value. Grey sole, a species of flounder, resembles brill. Winter flounder, dab and lemon sole can be prepared in the same way as brill.

Clean the fish by making a transverse incision under the head on the dark-skinned side. Scale and trim, shortening the tail a little. Wash the fish, and cut in half, or in slices or fillets.

Brill à l'américaine. BARBUE À L'AMÉRICAINE – Cook a medium-sized brill as described in the recipe for *Brill in white wine* (see below). Drain, and garnish with slices of small lobster or *Lobster à l'américaine* (see LOBSTER).

Boil down the liquor in which the fish was cooked, and add to it *American sauce* (see SAUCE). Pour over the brill.

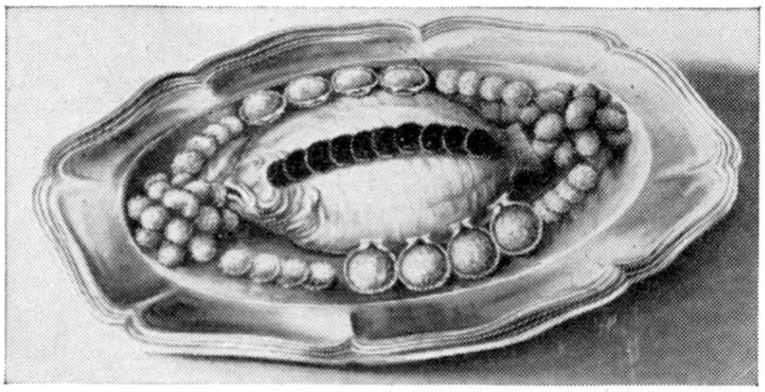

Brill à l'amiral

Brill à l'amiral. BARBUE À L'AMIRAL – Scale and slit lengthwise, on the dark-skinned side, a 1-kg. ($2\frac{1}{4}$-lb.) brill. Place it in a buttered shallow pan. Season, and pour in white wine fish stock which has been boiled down to a *fumet* (q.v.), enough to reach the level of the fish. Season.

Bring to the boil, cover, and place in a hot oven for 25 to 30 minutes. After the fish has been partly cooked, baste from time to time with its own liquor; if basted earlier there is a risk of the fish splitting. When cooked, drain and remove all the dark skin. Trim off the side bones.

Place on a serving dish, taking care to wipe away all liquid. Heat for a moment or two in the oven. Make *Normande sauce* (see SAUCE) from the liquor in the pan, which has been strained, boiled down, and had a little *Crayfish butter* (see BUTTER) added to it.

Garnish with oysters coated in egg and breadcrumbs and fried, mussels *à la Villeroi*, scallop shells filled with crayfish tails *à la Nantua* with the tops slightly browned under the grill, and mushrooms cooked in *court-bouillon* (q.v.). Decorate the brill with thin slices of truffle which have been heated in butter and seasoned with salt and pepper.

The method of cooking *Brill à l'amiral* applies to all flat fish which are braised; braise in very little *court-bouillon*, and flavour the stock or *fumet* very well.

Sometimes the fish is glazed by dotting it with crayfish butter and heating it in the oven, surrounded by the above garnish, with the sauce served separately.

Brill à la Bercy. BARBUE À LA BERCY – Make a few incisions on the dark-skinned side of a brill, lifting the fillets lightly and seasoning the fish inside and out. Butter a fireproof dish long enough to take the brill whole, sprinkle it with a tablespoon chopped shallots and parsley, and put in the fish. Add 1 dl. (6 tablespoons, scant $\frac{1}{2}$ cup) white wine and 1 dl. (6 tablespoons, scant $\frac{1}{2}$ cup) concentrated fish stock which has been boiled down to the consistency of a *fumet* (q.v.). Cut 50 g. (2 oz., $\frac{1}{4}$ cup) butter into very small pieces and scatter over the fish. Bring to the boil, and put in the oven to cook for 12 to 15 minutes, basting frequently.

When the brill is nearly cooked, glaze it by putting the dish into the hottest part of the oven.

Boiled or poached brill with various sauces. BARBUE BOUILLIE, POCHÉE – Make a *court-bouillon* (q.v.) of water and salted boiled milk in equal proportions. Put the brill on a wire grill in a shallow pan, and pour the *court-bouillon* over it. Heat slowly. When it boils, skim off the impurities which rise to the surface of the liquid, cover the brill with a napkin and leave to simmer very slowly, allowing 12 minutes cooking time per 500 g. (1 lb.) of fish.

When cooked, drain the brill thoroughly, and brush over with melted butter before serving. Garnish with boiled potatoes and fresh parsley, and serve with one of the sauces recommended for boiled fish (see SAUCE).

Brill à la bonne femme. BARBUE À LA BONNE FEMME – Prepare as for *Brill à la Bercy*, adding 125 g. (4 oz.) thinly sliced mushrooms, and moistening with white wine and a few tablespoons *Velouté sauce* (see SAUCE) based on fish stock. Bring to the boil on the stove, and finish cooking in the oven. Glaze.

Brill à la bourguignonne. BARBUE À LA BOURGUIGNONNE – Season a brill with salt and pepper, put in a buttered pan and surround with small glazed onions and small mushrooms. Add a *bouquet garni* (q.v.) and 4 dl. ($\frac{3}{4}$ pint, scant 2 cups) red wine, preferably Burgundy. Cover the pan and cook in the oven.

Remove the brill when cooked, and garnish. Boil down the liquor until it reaches the consistency of a *fumet* (q.v.). Blend in 2 tablespoons (3 tablespoons) *Kneaded butter* (see BUTTER), boil for a minute or two, add 75 g. (3 oz., 6 tablespoons) butter, blend thoroughly, and strain. Pour this sauce over the brill.

Braised brill with various garnishes. BARBUE BRAISÉE – Season the brill and put it in a shallow pan on a foundation of sliced carrots and onions which have been lightly fried in butter. Add concentrated fish stock, thyme, parsley and a bay leaf. Bring to the boil, and cook in a slow oven, basting frequently.

Drain the brill and remove the backbone. This is most easily done by placing the fish, dark side up, on a well-buttered long plate or dish, removing the fillets with a very sharp knife, taking out the bone, and replacing the fillets.

Garnish as indicated in the recipe you are using, and cover with a sauce to which has been added the braising liquor, boiled down and strained. Braised brill moistened with red wine fish stock reduced to the consistency of a *fumet* (q.v.), can be served with the following garnishes: *bourguignonne* (see above), *Chambertin*, *mâconnaise*, etc. (see below). Brill braised in white wine can be served with one of the garnishes used for fish cooked in white wine, especially those recommended for soles.

Brill Brancas. BARBUE BRANCAS – Scale and trim a brill weighing about 750 g. ($1\frac{3}{4}$ lb.), and cut into uniform pieces. Put an onion, leek and half a heart of celery shredded to a fine *julienne* (q.v.) into a pan with 25 g. (1 oz., 2 tablespoons) butter and a pinch of salt. Cook very slowly. When the vegetables are about three-quarters done, add 125 g. (4 oz.) finely shredded mushrooms, and finish cooking. This *julienne* is called *bretonne*.

Sauté a tablespoon chopped onion in butter, and add 4 peeled, seeded and chopped tomatoes, together with a little chopped garlic, salt and pepper. Simmer slowly, stirring from time to time, until you get a tomato *fondue*. Add a small spoon chopped parsley.

Butter an ovenware dish, sprinkle with salt and freshly ground pepper, and pour in half the vegetable *julienne*. Put a *bouquet garni* (q.v.) in a corner of the dish so that it can be easily removed at the end of cooking. Place the pieces of brill on the dish in the shape of the original fish, season with salt and pepper, and cover with the rest of the *julienne*. Sprinkle with a few drops of lemon juice and add 2 dl. ($\frac{1}{3}$ pint, scant cup) white wine. Scatter a few dabs of butter on the surface of the fish.

Bring slowly to the boil on the stove, then place the dish in a slow oven for 15 to 18 minutes, basting frequently. A few minutes before the end of cooking, put a border of the tomato *fondue* round the brill. Return the dish to a much hotter oven to glaze the fish. Before serving, sprinkle with chopped parsley.

This way of cooking, evolved from the Dugléré method of preparation, can be used for fish such as young turbot, sole, whiting, fresh cod, plaice (U.S. flounder).

Brill à la cancalaise. BARBUE À LA CANCALAISE – Cook the brill in white wine as described in the recipe for *Brill à l'amiral*. Drain thoroughly. Garnish with oysters poached in their own liquor, drained, and with their beards removed.

Boil down the liquor in which the fish was cooked, and add to *Normande sauce* (see SAUCE), which is suitable for brill.

Brill cardinal. BARBUE CARDINAL – Remove the backbone, as described for *Braised brill with various garnishes*. Season the brill, and stuff it with finely pounded *Pike forcemeat* (see FORCEMEAT), to which has been added *Lobster butter* or *Crayfish butter* (see BUTTER).

Poach the brill in white wine, drain, and garnish with slices of lobster or crayfish. Cover with *Cardinal sauce I* (see SAUCE, *White sauces*). Sprinkle with chopped coral.

Brill au Chambertin. BARBUE AU CHAMBERTIN – Cook the brill in concentrated fish stock made with Chambertin wine, as described for *Brill à la bourguignonne*, making the sauce with Chambertin instead of Burgundy.

Brill au Chambertin is garnished with mushrooms which have been cooked with the fish; brill prepared *à la bourguignonne* is garnished with mushrooms and small glazed onions.

Brill in Champagne: à la champenoise. BARBUE AU CHAMPAGNE: À LA CHAMPENOISE – Bone and stuff the brill with *Pike forcemeat* (see FORCEMEAT). Season with salt and pepper, and place in a fireproof dish on a foundation of *julienne* (q.v.) of mushrooms which have been lightly tossed in butter.

Add dry Champagne, scatter small pieces of butter on the fish, bring slowly to the boil, and place in the oven to complete cooking, basting frequently.

Drain the fish, and add to the liquor in the dish 3 tablespoons (scant $\frac{1}{4}$ cup) *Velouté sauce* (see SAUCE) based on fish stock, and 5 tablespoons (6 tablespoons) cream. Add butter to the sauce, strain, pour over the brill, and glaze in a very hot oven for a few minutes.

Brill Chérubin. BARBUE CHÉRUBIN – Season the brill with paprika, place in a buttered pan on a foundation of a fine *salpicon* (q.v.) of carrots, leeks and celery, add concentrated fish stock, and cook in the oven, basting frequently.

Drain the brill, and surround with small heaps of very thick *Tomato fondue* (see FONDUE) alternating with truffles cut into large dice.

Boil down the liquor in which the fish was cooked to a *fumet* (q.v.), strain, and add a *julienne* (q.v.) of sweet (red) pimentos which have been lightly fried in butter. Mix with *Hollandaise sauce* (see SAUCE) and pour it over the brill. Glaze in a very hot oven.

Cold brill with various sauces. BARBUE FROID – Cook the fish as described in the recipe for *Boiled brill*, and leave to cool in the liquor. Drain the brill well, garnish with fresh parsley or lettuce hearts, and serve with mayonnaise or any other sauce recommended for cold fish.

Brill with crayfish: à la Nantua. BARBUE AUX ÉCRIVISSES: À LA NANTUA – Prepare as *Brill with shrimps* (see below), replacing shrimps by crayfish tails, and covering with *Nantua sauce* (see SAUCE, *Compound sauces*). Boil down the liquor and add to the sauce before serving.

Brill in cream au gratin. BARBUE À LA CRÈME AU GRATIN – Prepare as *Creamed cod au gratin* (see COD), using brill cut into pieces.

Brill à la dieppoise. BARBUE À LA DIEPPOISE – Cook whole or filleted brill in white wine. Drain well. Garnish with mussels *à la dieppoise* (cooked in white wine) and peeled shrimps. Pour over the fish *White wine sauce I* (see SAUCE, *White sauces*) to which the concentrated pan juices have been added. Glaze in a very hot oven.

Brill Dugléré. BARBUE DUGLÉRÉ – Cut the brill into pieces and prepare as described in the recipe for *Bass Dugléré* (see BASS).

Brill à la fermière. BARBUE À LA FERMIÈRE – Season the brill with salt and pepper and place in a buttered dish on a foundation of a *fondue* (q.v.) made from carrots, onions, leeks and celery, shredded and lightly cooked in butter. Cover the brill with more *fondue*. Add a few tablespoons of dry white wine, or concentrated fish stock based on white wine (see STOCK, *Fish stock*). Scatter a few dabs of butter on the fish and cook in a slow oven, basting frequently. When the fish is done, add 3 tablespoons (scant $\frac{1}{4}$ cup) cream. Glaze in the oven.

Another method is to put the fish in a buttered oven-proof dish on a foundation of chopped onion which has been lightly fried in butter. Cover with sliced mushrooms, moisten with red wine, and add a few small pieces of butter. Cook in the oven.

Strain the pan juices, bring to the boil, and thicken with kneaded butter. Add a little fresh butter, stir well, and pour this sauce over the fish. Glaze in the oven.

Fillets of brill. FILETS DE BARBUE – Clean, scale and wash the fish, and fillet by slitting it down the middle from head to tail. Slide a sharp knife under the fillets to lift them, taking care to sever them completely from the body of the fish. Put the fillets flat on the table, skin side down, and slide the knife blade between the fish and the skin, holding the fillet at one end so as to remove the skin in one piece.

All methods of preparation for whole brill can be applied to fillets.

Fillets of brill à l'anglaise. FILETS DE BARBUE À L'ANGLAISE – Flatten the fillets a little, dip in egg and breadcrumbs, and fry in clarified butter until both sides are golden. Put softened *Maître d'hôtel butter* (see BUTTER, *Compound butters*) on each fillet. Decorate with half-slices of lemon placed round the border of the dish.

Fillets of fish grilled and accompanied by melted butter and boiled potatoes are often served under the name of fillets of fish *à l'anglaise*.

Fillets of brill à la créole. FILETS DE BARBUE À LA CRÉOLE – Season the fillets with salt and paprika, lightly dredge with

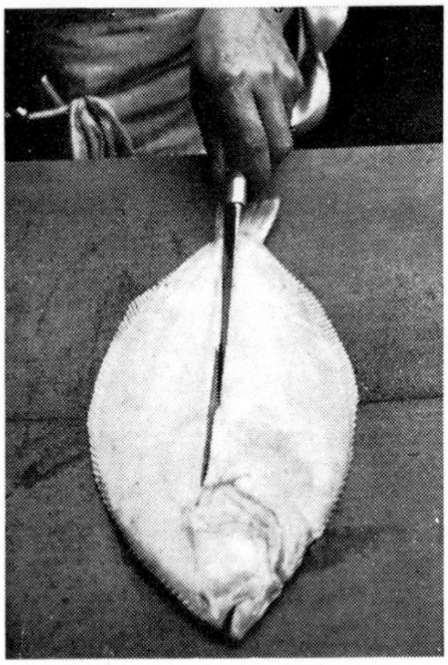

How to fillet brill.

First cut the fish lengthwise, then slide the knife along the backbone to detach the fillet (*Larousse*)

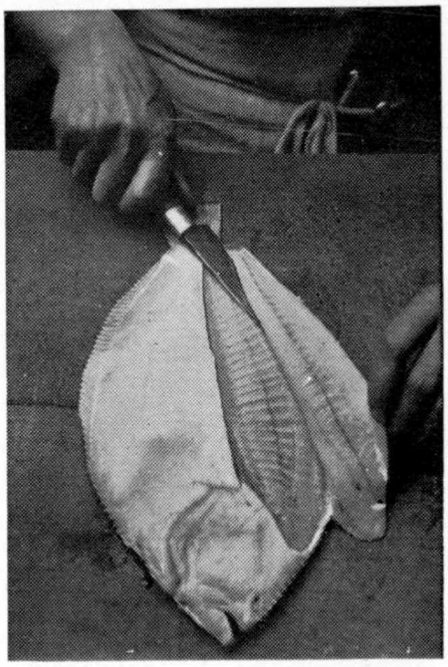

flour and fry in butter or oil. Garnish with halved tomatoes cooked in oil. Scoop out the centre of each half-tomato and fill with a spoonful of *Rice pilaf* (see PILAF). Add to this garnish peeled and diced sweet pimentos which have been cooked in oil.

Add a tablespoon chopped garlic and parsley to the hot oil in the pan, sprinkle the fillets with lemon juice, and pour the oil over them just before serving.

Fillets of brill curried. FILETS DE BARBUE À L'INDIENNE – Season the fillets with salt and pepper and put them into an ovenproof dish on a foundation of 100 g. (4 oz., 1 cup) chopped onion which has been fried in butter, and seasoned with curry powder and a pinch of pounded garlic. Place 4 peeled, seeded and chopped tomatoes on the fish, and moisten with $1\frac{1}{2}$ dl. ($\frac{1}{4}$ pint, $\frac{2}{3}$ cup) white wine. Add a few small pieces of butter.

Cook in the oven for 10 minutes, basting frequently. Add 2 dl. ($\frac{1}{3}$ pint, scant cup) thick cream. Finish cooking in the oven, still basting frequently. Serve with *Rice à l'indienne* (see RICE).

Fillets of brill à la Duxelles. FILETS DE BARBUE À LA DUXELLES – Season the fillets with salt and pepper, lightly dredge with flour and fry in a mixture of oil and butter.

Place on a serving dish on a foundation of a *duxelles* (q.v.) bound with *Tomato sauce* (see SAUCE). Garnish with slices of peeled lemon, sprinkle with chopped parsley, and pour the hot butter left from frying over the fish.

Fillets of brill Richelieu. FILETS DE BARBUE RICHELIEU – Dip the fillets in egg and breadcrumbs and fry in butter until both sides are golden. Garnish with thin slices of truffles heated in butter. Put dabs of *Maître d'hôtel butter* on top (see BUTTER, *Compound butters*).

Fillets of brill à la toulonnaise. FILETS DE BARBUE À LA TOULONNAISE – Season the fillets with salt and pepper and dip them in egg and breadcrumbs. Fry in oil until both sides are golden. Arrange on a bed of thick *Tomato fondue* (see FONDUE) which, together with chopped onion, has been cooked in oil; add a pinch of pounded garlic. Surround with diced aubergines fried in oil, and put thin slices of lemon on the fillets. Sprinkle with a few tablespoons of the hot oil.

Fillets of brill à la tyrolienne. FILETS DE BARBUE À LA TYROLIENNE – Season the fillets with salt and paprika, brush with oil and grill on low heat. Arrange on a bed of *Tomato fondue* (see FONDUE) and cover with onion rings which have been fried in oil.

Fillets of brill Véron. FILETS DE BARBUE VÉRON – Cut the fillets in half lengthways, season with salt and pepper, dip in melted butter and breadcrumbs, sprinkle with more melted butter and cook under a low grill. Arrange on a layer of *Véron sauce* (see SAUCE) when serving.

Brill à la florentine. BARBUE À LA FLORENTINE – Cook in a little concentrated white wine stock. Drain, and arrange on a foundation of leaf spinach which has been cooked in butter. Cover with *Mornay sauce* (see SAUCE), sprinkle with grated cheese and melted butter, and glaze.

This method is used for fillets cooked in white wine; very little liquid should be used. When cooking whole fish, remove the central bone after cooking, and trim all round before arranging it on the spinach.

Fried brill. BARBUE FRITE – Clean small brill, soak in milk, lightly dredge with flour, and deep-fry in very hot oil. Drain, dry in a cloth, season with fine salt, and garnish with fried parsley and slices of lemon.

Brill au gratin. BARBUE AU GRATIN – Proceed as described in the recipe for *Sole au gratin* (see SOLE), using small brill.

Grilled brill. BARBUE GRILLÉE – Make a few shallow incisions on the brill, season with salt and pepper, brush with oil or butter and grill on low heat. Garnish with fresh parsley and slices of lemon, and serve with *Maître d'hôtel butter* (see BUTTER, *Compound butters*) or any sauce recommended for grilled fish.

Jellied brill with various garnishes. BARBUE GLACÉE À LA GELÉE – Cook the brill in a little concentrated stock, based either on red or white wine, depending on the nature of the dish. Allow it to cool in its own strained liquor. Dry and trim the brill, and coat it with clarified jelly (see JELLY).

All garnishes recommended for *Cold salmon* (see SALMON) can be applied to brill.

Brill à la mâconnaise. BARBUE À LA MÂCONNAISE – Bone a medium-sized brill, taking care not to tear the white skin. Season, and stuff with fish forcemeat mixed with dry *duxelles* (q.v.) and chopped parsley.

Cook in concentrated fish stock based on red (Mâcon) wine, as described in the recipe for *Brill à la bourguignonne*. Drain the brill thoroughly and arrange on a dish. Surround with small white *cèpes* which have been fried in butter and seasoned with small shallots. Cover with a sauce as described in the recipe for *Brill à la bourguignonne*. Simmer small artichokes in butter, fill with a *salpicon* (q.v.) of truffles *à la crème*, brown the top, and place round the fish.

Brill à la marinière. BARBUE À LA MARINIÈRE – Prepare like *Brill in white wine* (see below). Garnish *à la marinière* (see GARNISHES) and cover with *Marinière sauce* (see SAUCE).

Brill à la ménagère. BARBUE À LA MÉNAGÈRE – Season the fish with salt and pepper, and place in an ovenproof dish on a foundation of chopped onions, lightly fried in butter and seasoned with pounded thyme and bay leaf. Moisten with red wine and cook in a covered pan.

When the brill is ready, arrange on a dish and thicken the pan juices with kneaded butter. Bring to the boil, add a little fresh butter, and pour over the fish.

Brill Mornay. BARBUE MORNAY – Cook fillets of brill in concentrated fish stock and arrange on a dish lined with *Mornay sauce* (see SAUCE). Cover with some of the same sauce, sprinkle with a mixture of grated Gruyère and Parmesan cheese, add melted butter, and brown the top.

Brill with mushrooms. BARBUE AUX CHAMPIGNONS – Cook the brill – whole, in fillets or cut in pieces – in a concentrated white wine fish stock. Drain thoroughly, arrange on a dish, and garnish with mushrooms. Serve with *White wine sauce I* (see SAUCE), incorporating the liquor in which the fish was cooked.

Brill with mussels. BARBUE AUX MOULES – Cook the brill in a little concentrated fish stock. Drain, arrange on a dish, and surround with mussels which have been cooked in white wine. Cover with white wine sauce, or *Normande sauce* (see SAUCE) which has incorporated the liquor in which the fish and the mussels were cooked.

Brill à la normande. BARBUE À LA NORMANDE – Cook the brill in a little concentrated fish stock. Drain, arrange on a dish, and surround with garnish *à la normande* (see GARNISHES). Cover with *Normande sauce* (see SAUCE), to which has been added the boiled-down liquor in which the fish was cooked.

The method of preparation known as *à la normande* is also applied to turbot, plaice and sole.

Brill with oysters. BARBUE AUX HUÎTRES – Cook the brill in a little concentrated white wine fish stock. Drain, and garnish with poached oysters. Add a white wine sauce to the liquor in which the brill and the oysters were cooked, and pour over the fish.

Brill sur le plat. BARBUE SUR LE PLAT – Proceed as described in the recipe for *Sole sur le plat* (see SOLE), using small brill.

Brill à la portugaise. BARBUE À LA PORTUGAISE – Proceed as described in the recipe for *Bass à la portugaise* (see BASS).

Brill à la provençale. BARBUE À LA PROVENÇALE – As *Bass à la provençale* (see BASS).

Brill in red wine. BARBUE AU VIN ROUGE – Cook the brill in a little concentrated fish stock based on red wine. Drain, and arrange on a dish.

Make a red wine sauce, incorporating the liquor in which the fish was cooked. Thicken with kneaded butter, or blend with *Espagnole sauce* based on fish stock (see SAUCE). Add a little butter, strain, and pour over the brill.

Brill à la russe. BARBUE À LA RUSSE – As described in the recipe for *Sole à la russe* (see SOLE), using medium brill.

Brill in scallop shells. COQUILLES DE BARBUE – Pipe a border of *Duchess potato mixture* (see POTATOES) round the edges of scallop shells. Cover the centre of the shells with *Mornay sauce* (see SAUCE), add small slices of hot brill, and cover with more *Mornay sauce*. Scatter grated cheese on top, sprinkle with melted butter and brown the top.

Brill with shrimps. BARBUE AUX CREVETTES – Cook the brill in a little white wine fish *fumet* (q.v.). Drain, and garnish the sides with peeled shrimps. Boil down the liquor in which the brill was cooked, add *Shrimp sauce* (see SAUCE) and pour over the fish.

Brill stuffed with salmon, with various sauces and garnishes. BARBUE SAUMONÉE – Clean a brill weighing about 2 kg. ($4\frac{1}{2}$ lb.) and slit it lengthwise down the middle on the dark side. Remove the central bone through this opening, taking care not to tear the white skin.

Season, and stuff the brill with a cream forcemeat made of salmon and truffles. Lay the fish in a buttered ovenproof dish, season, moisten with 4 dl. ($\frac{3}{4}$ pint, scant 2 cups) white wine fish *fumet* (q.v.) and poach gently in the oven with the lid on the dish.

When the brill is cooked, drain, dry in a cloth, and arrange on a dish. Boil down the juices, add to *normande sauce*, and pour over the fish.

All methods of preparation given for brill and sole poached in white wine can be applied to this dish, for which the following garnishes are suitable: *amiral, cancalaise, cardinal, champenoise, diplomate, Nantua, normande, Polignac, Victoria*.

Stuffed brill with various garnishes. BARBUE FARCIE – Bone the brill as described in the recipe for *Brill stuffed with salmon*. Stuff with *Fish forcemeat* (see FORCEMEAT). Poach in a little concentrated fish stock.

Drain the fish, arrange on a dish, surround with the chosen garnish, and pour over it a sauce that goes well with the garnish.

All the methods given for *Braised brill in red or white wine* can be applied to stuffed brill.

Brill à vénitienne. BARBUE À LA VÉNITIENNE – As *Sole à la vénitienne* (see SOLE).

Brill à la Victoria. BARBUE À LA VICTORIA – Cook the brill as described for *Brill in white wine* (see below). Drain, arrange on a dish, and garnish with a *salpicon* (q.v.) of the flesh of spiny lobster (U.S. crayfish) and truffles. Cover with *Victoria sauce* (see SAUCE). Glaze in the oven.

Brill in white wine. BARBUE AU VIN BLANC – Season the brill and place in a buttered pan with a thinly sliced onion and a *bouquet garni* (q.v.). Moisten with a few tablespoons white wine, or with concentrated fish stock based on white wine and boiled down to the consistency of a *fumet* (q.v.). Cook on low heat with the lid on the pan.

Drain the brill, arrange on a dish, and cover with *White wine sauce* (see SAUCE), using as a basis the liquor in which the fish was cooked. The brill can be served as it is, or glazed quickly in a very hot oven or under a hot grill.

Jean Anthelme Brillat-Savarin

BRILLAT-SAVARIN (Jean Anthelme) – French magistrate, politician and gastronome, born at Belley in 1755, died in Paris in 1826.

He started his career as a lawyer at the Court of Belley, became deputy of the National Assembly in 1789, was made mayor and commander of the National Guard of Belley in

1793, was banished during the Reign of Terror, fled to Switzerland, then spent three years as a refugee in America.

He returned to France in September, 1797, had his name removed from the list of *émigrés*, became first a commissioner to the army in Germany under Augereau, then commissioner at the court of the *département* of Seine-et-Oise, then member of the Supreme Court of Appeal.

He published various pamphlets, political and on subjects of law, but his lasting fame rests on a gastronomical work on which he had long been engaged, and which was published shortly before his death, *la Physiologie du goût*.

BRILLAT-SAVARIN (Method of preparing meat) – Lamb and mutton *noisettes*, with a garnish of duchess potato *cassolettes* (q.v.), filled with a *salpicon* (q.v.) of *foie gras*, truffles, and green asparagus tips in butter.

BRINDE – Old French word for a two-handled cup used for wine.

BRINE. SAUMURE – Solution of sea salt, to which is often added sugar, saltpetre and aromatics. Preserving mixture for foodstuffs.

Liquid brine. SAUMURE LIQUIDE – For pickled tongues and pressed beef. Boil in a large pan 5 litres (4½ quarts, 5½ quarts) water, 2¼ kg. (5 lb.) rock salt, 300 g. (11 oz., 1½ cups) brown sugar, 150 g. (5 oz.) saltpetre, 15 peppercorns, 15 juniper berries, a sprig of thyme and a bay leaf. Boil for 25 minutes and leave to cool.

Prick the tongues, rub with salt and saltpetre, and place in a receptacle. Pour in the brine, and cover the receptacle with a piece of smooth wood, pressing it well down on the tongues. Keep in a cool place for six days in summer, eight in winter.

Full brine pickle for various meats. GRANDE SAUMURE – Pour 25 litres (5½ gallons, 7 gallons) water into a large copper vessel and add 12½ kg. (27½ lb.) rock salt, 1⅓ kg. (3 lb.) saltpetre and 800 g. (1¾ lb., 3½ cups) brown sugar. Bring to the boil on a strong heat.

To test the density of the brine, put a peeled potato into it. If the potato floats, the proportion of salt is too high and more water should be added; if the potato sinks to the bottom, the liquid should be boiled down until the potato is suspended in the middle. When this is achieved, remove the brine from the heat and leave to cool.

Prick the meat to be preserved with a long needle which has been rubbed in salt mixed with saltpetre and place in a brine tub, which should have a grille at the bottom for the meat to stand on. Pour in the brine when it is quite cold. Leave to pickle for at least 8 days if the meat weighs 4 to 5 kg. (8½ to 11 lb.). If larger cuts are used, inject brine into the meat with a special pump.

BRIOCHE – Cake made from yeast dough, usually in the shape of a ball with a smaller ball pressed into the top as a 'head'.

Brioches were made in Paris with baker's yeast until the middle of the eighteenth century. Brewer's yeast, which had been in use for a long time in Poland and Austria, was introduced into Alsace and Lorraine when the court of King Stanislas was transferred to Lunéville. The brioches of Gisors and Gournay, great butter marketing centres, were famous. Sansvoisin gives a recipe for Gisors brioches:

'The dough is made the night before baking. Make a dough of 750 g. (1¾ lb., 7 cups) flour and 7 eggs. Mix 250 g. (9 oz., 2¼ cups) flour with 10 g. (⅓ oz.) yeast. Mix with the dough, together with 750 g. (1¾ lb., 3½ cups) butter. Keep the dough in a bowl.

'When ready for baking, shape into brioches just before putting them in the oven.'

Various brioche doughs are given under the heading

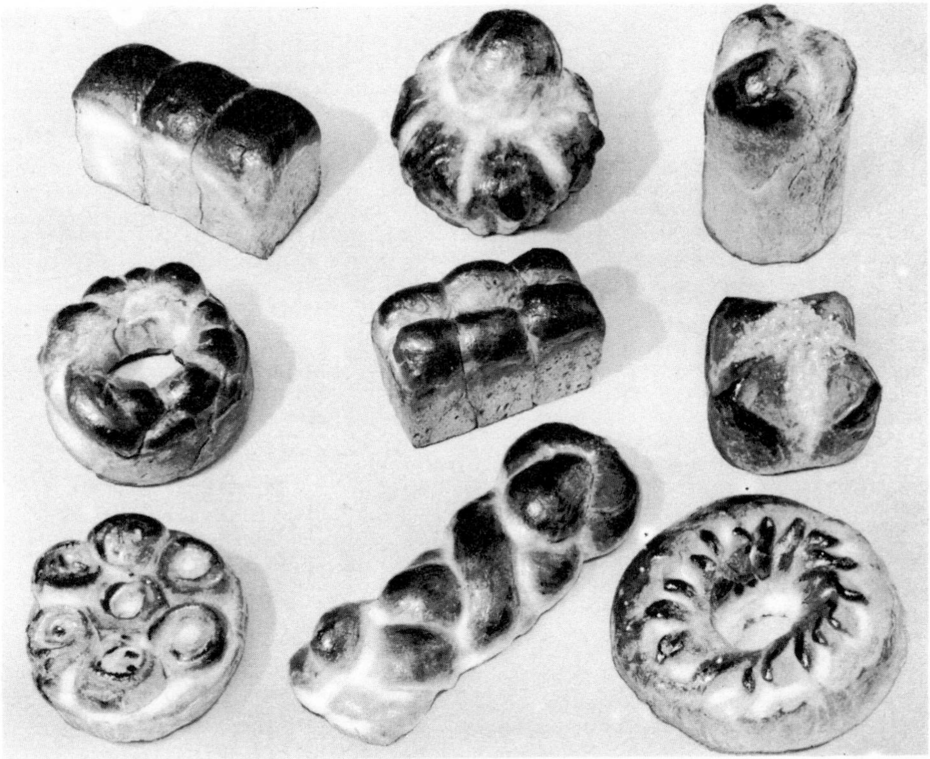

Brioches (*Scarnati*)

DOUGH. For the preparation of various *hors-d'œuvre* and small hot *entrée* dishes, a standard brioche is made.

Standard brioche dough. PÂTE À BRIOCHE COMMUNE – Proceed as described in the recipe for *Brioche dough* (see DOUGH).

Dough for brioche mousseline. PÂTE À BRIOCHE MOUSSELINE – Make a *Brioche dough* (see DOUGH), using 400 g. (14 oz., 1¾ cups) butter and 500 g. (18 oz., 4½ cups) flour. Add 60 g. (2½ oz., 5 tablespoons) softened butter to each 500 g. (1 lb.) dough.

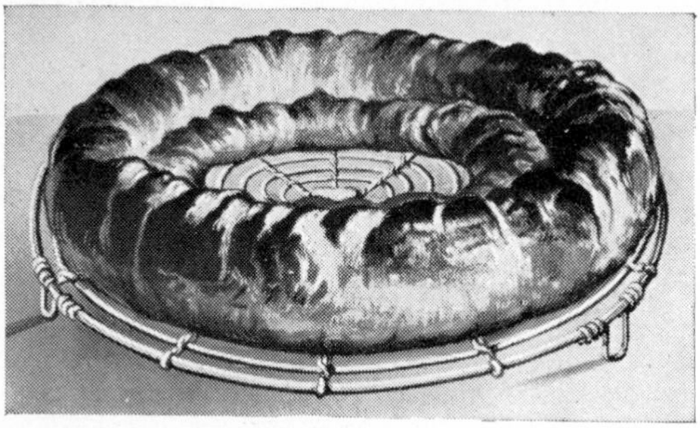

Brioche en couronne

Brioche en couronne – Roll brioche dough into a round loaf, place on a baking sheet in the shape of a crown, and make a few light incisions on the surface. Brush with beaten egg and bake in a moderate oven.

Brioche Goubard

Brioche Goubaud – Line a buttered cake tin with brioche dough. Roll out another piece of dough, cut into pieces, moulding them into little pies. Stuff them with a *salpicon* (q.v.) of preserved fruit which has been steeped in rum or liqueur. Fill the cake tin with the pies, leave to rise in a warm place, brush with beaten egg and bake. When removed from the oven, brush the pie-tops with diluted apricot jam.

Brioche mousseline – This is baked in a tall mould, further heightened by buttered greaseproof paper tied round the top.

Butter the mould and three-parts fill it with *Mousseline brioche dough* (see DOUGH). Leave to rise and bake in a moderate oven.

Cheese brioche. BRIOCHE AU FROMAGE – Dice or grate 250 g. (9 oz.) Gruyère cheese, and knead into 2 kg. (4½ lb.) ordinary dough. Leave to rise, and bake in a buttered mould.

Filled brioches à la bohémienne. BRIOCHES GARNIES À LA BOHÉMIENNE – Small brioches, three-quarters scooped out and filled with various mixtures: mousses, purées, *salpicons*, etc.

Brioche mousseline

Fruit briochin. BRIOCHIN AUX FRUITS – Line a flan ring with firm brioche dough, adding a layer of frangipane (q.v.). Steep sliced or diced fruit in liqueur, place on the frangipane, and cover with brioche dough. Leave to rise for an hour, brush with beaten egg, and bake in a fairly hot oven.

Brioche à tête

Large brioche à tête. GROSSE BRIOCHE À TÊTE – Roll a piece of brioche dough into a ball and place in a buttered mould. Make a hole in the dough and put into it a small ball of the dough, tapered to a point. Make a few light incisions on the surface of the dough, brush with beaten egg and bake in a hot oven.

Small brioches. PETITES BRIOCHES – Bake in small fluted moulds in the same way as *Large brioche à tête*.

BRIOLET – Slang word synonymous with another slang word, *piquette* (i.e., wine of poor quality). An allusion to a Brie wine which is rather mediocre.

BRIOLI (Corsican cookery) – Chestnut meal, prepared in the same way as polenta, with the addition of milk or cream.

BRIONNE – Name for chayote, a vegetable of the *Cucurbitaceae* family. (See CHAYOTE.)

BRISSE (Baron) – Author of culinary works which were not always accurate. His books include *la Cuisine à l'usage des ménages bourgeois et des petits ménages, la Petite cuisine du baron Brisse* and *366 menus*, all published in the latter part of the nineteenth century. He had a high-flown romantic style, speaking of turkeys 'in blossom', and is remembered for his curiosity value rather than for gastronomy.

BRITAIN – See INTERNATIONAL COOKERY.

A Breton farmhouse (*French Government Tourist Office*)

Sampling the culinary specialities of Brittany (*French Government Tourist Office*)

BRITTANY. BRETAGNE – Choice food products are found in abundance in Brittany, whether they originate in the sea or on land. Excellent sheep (notably 'salt-meadow' sheep) and cattle are raised.

The Breton larder is well stocked with all sorts of foods and all of first-class quality. Let us give a rapid survey of these.

Among the seafoods are Cancale and Morbihan oysters, and oysters found in the rivers Auray and Belon; clams, cockles, scallops, winkles, ormers, haliotes, spiny lobsters, crabs, shrimps, Lorient sardines, conger eels (which are made into *cotriade*, so popular with the Breton fishermen), soles, turbot, brill, plaice, mackerel, herrings, tunny.

The rivers produce pike, carp, trout, eels, shad; the Odet and Aulne salmon are famous. Meat is of good quality; mutton and pork are excellent.

Among the poultry particular mention should be made of the Nantes ducklings and succulent young turkeys. Ground and winged game are famous.

Roscoff cauliflowers and artichokes are sent to the markets of London and Paris. Breton potatoes must be mentioned, and Plougastel strawberries and apples are noteworthy.

Beverages – Cider is the usual drink of the Bretons. Among the famous growths are those of Pleudihen, Fouesnant, Clohars and Saint-Féréou.

The Loire-Atlantique produces an excellent dry white wine, best drunk young: the Muscadet. The name 'Muscadet' is the local *appellation* for a variety of vine, the 'melon', that was introduced into Brittany from Burgundy in the seventeenth century. There are two Muscadets, that of Sèvres-et-Maine and that of the banks of the Loire.

Gastronomic map of Brittany

The region of Nantes also produces a V.D.Q.S., the best of the wines, very dry with a hint of acidity which is much appreciated by connoisseurs. It is an excellent accompaniment for fish and shellfish.

Culinary specialities – The best known are Cornouaille *buckwheat and bacon soup*; *cotriade* – the soup of the Breton fishermen similar to the *chaudrée* (q.v.) of the Aunis sailors; Morlaix *hams*; Ancenis *andouilles* and *sausages*, large *andouilles de Bretagne*; excellent *black puddings*; Quimperlé *andouilletes*; *pike au beurre blanc*; *shad à la crème*; Nantes *bacon*; *roast leg of salt-meadow lamb with beans* called *'à la bretonne'*; *buckwheat girdlecakes* and *pancakes*; Quimperlé *oat loaf à la crème*; Quimper *pancakes*; Morlaix *brioches*; Lorient and Quimper *cakes*; Rennes *mingaux* (a kind of cream cheese similar to the Saumur *crémets*); Nantes *flat cakes and guillarets*; *biscuits*.

BROCCIO – See CHEESE.

BROCCOLI. CHOUX BROCOLIS – The flower heads which develop in the leaf axils are eaten before they are fully grown. They are also called broccoli tips. All methods of preparation given for cauliflower apply to broccoli.

The flower in this type of cabbage is generally very small. Broccoli is also eaten for its leaves as well as its flowers.

BROCKET. DAGUET – The name given to a young stag, between one year and eighteen months old. The French name *daguet* comes from *dague*, dagger, and refers to the shape of the young stag's horns.

In cookery, all recipes for roebuck (q.v.) are suitable for brocket.

BROOKLIME. BECCABUNGA – This plant is also called *water pimpernel*. It is a kind of European cress which grows wild on the banks of streams and ponds.

It is eaten in salads like watercress and can be prepared in all the ways suitable for the latter (see CRESS).

It is ordinarily used as a condiment for salad.

BROUILLY – Famous red Beaujolais wine.

BROUTES or BROUTONS (Béarn cookery) – Old cabbage shoots, served mainly during Lent.

Trim and wash the cabbage and cook in salted water. Drain and dry. Season with oil and vinegar.

In some villages in the Basses-Pyrénées a mixture of leeks and white cabbage, cooked together, drained, pressed and cut into pieces, is also called *broutes*.

BROYE (Béarn cookery) – Meal prepared from white or roasted maize (corn) flour.

'If white, that is to say unroasted, flour is used, make the *broye* as an ordinary *bouilli*. Bring some vegetable stock or simply salted water to the boil and little by little add the flour until a paste of a fairly firm consistency is obtained.

'When the *bouilli* is cooked, and it should be stirred all the time during cooking, it is served with a ladle, which should be dipped in fat to prevent the *bouilli* sticking to it.

'If roasted flour is used (*troustado* or *tourrado*, as they say in Béarn), you make a well out of it, moisten with the liquid indicated, blend well and proceed to cook.

'Cold *broye* can be cut into slices and fried in sizzling fat until golden.' (From *la Cuisine en Béarn*, by Simin Palay.)

BRUGNON – A French name for nectarine or smooth-skinned peach. For methods of preparation, see PEACH.

BRUNOISE – This word has the following meanings:

1. A method of shredding vegetables very finely. (Thus, people speak of shredding carrots, leeks, celery, into a *brunoise*.) All these ingredients are then cooked in butter or some other fat.

2. A mixture of vegetables, such as carrots, onions, leeks, celery and sometimes turnips slowly cooked in butter. This sort of *brunoise* is used for making soups or as a supplementary element for certain forcemeats, sauces and *salpicons* (q.v.).

3. A mixture of vegetables cut into small dice which is used as an aromatic element for crayfish and other dishes. (See CRAYFISH, TRUFFLES.)

Vegetable brunoise for soups. BRUNOISE DE LÉGUMES POUR POTAGES – Cut the following into dice about 3 mm. ($\frac{1}{8}$ inch) across: 3 small carrots (150 g., 5 oz.), $\frac{1}{2}$ small turnip (100 g., 4 oz.), 2 leeks (75 g., 3 oz.), 1 very small onion (25 g., 1 oz.) and 2 stalks white celery (50 g., 2 oz.). Season these vegetables with salt and a pinch of fine sugar and simmer them in a covered pan on a low heat with 50 g. (2 oz., $\frac{1}{4}$ cup) butter. When they are nicely softened add 2 dl. ($\frac{1}{3}$ pint, scant cup) stock and leave to cook for 15 minutes. At the last moment, add a tablespoon cooked garden peas and a tablespoon diced French string beans.

Add 2 or 3 tablespoons of this mixture to every litre (scant quart, generous quart) soup.

BRUSH. PINCEAU – Kitchen tool consisting of hair or bristle attached to a handle used for brushing with melted butter or oil various articles intended for grilling.

The brush is also used in pastry-making, for buttering baking tins and other utensils, and for brushing the tops of pastries with beaten egg.

BRUSSELS SPROUTS. CHOUX DE BRUXELLES – The buds which develop in the leaf axils are eaten between October and the end of March.

Boiled Brussels sprouts. CHOUX DE BRUXELLES À L'ANGLAISE – Trim the sprouts, which means removing outer leaves which are either too hard or too withered, and cutting the base of each sprout. Wash them well.

Cook the sprouts in boiling salted water and drain. Serve fresh butter separately.

Brussels sprouts with cream. CHOUX DE BRUXELLES À LA CRÈME – Half cook the sprouts in salted boiling water, drain well, and simmer in butter. Cover with boiling fresh cream to which butter has been added. The sprouts can also be moistened with a *Cream sauce* (see SAUCE) instead of cream.

Brussels sprouts à l'indienne. CHOUX DE BRUXELLES À L'INDIENNE – Simmer the sprouts in butter and moisten with a curry sauce. Surround with a border of rice cooked the Indian way (see RICE).

Brussels sprouts in gravy. CHOUX DE BRUXELLES AU JUS – Simmer the sprouts in butter until cooked, then add a few tablespoons rich veal stock. Cook a little longer so that the sprouts can get well soaked in the gravy.

Brussels sprouts à la milanaise. CHOUX DE BRUXELLES À LA MILANAISE – Boil the sprouts and drain them well. Heap them on a buttered dish which has been sprinkled with grated cheese. Sprinkle with more grated cheese, pour melted butter over the sprouts, and brown in the oven. Serve with *Noisette butter* (see BUTTER, *Compound butters*).

Brussels sprouts Mornay. CHOUX DE BRUXELLES MORNAY – This is prepared in the same way as *Cauliflower Mornay* (see CAULIFLOWER) with the sprouts heaped on a *gratin* dish.

Brussels sprouts à la polonaise. CHOUX DE BRUXELLES À LA POLONAISE – Prepare like *Cauliflower a la polonaise* (see CAULIFLOWER).

Brussels sprouts purée. PURÉE DE CHOUX DE BRUXELLES – Prepare with blanched Brussels sprouts simmered in butter, in the same way as *Cauliflower purée* (see CAULIFLOWER).

Brussels sprouts salad. SALADE DE CHOUX DE BRUXELLES –

Festive buffet, 1785

Boil the sprouts, drain well, and arrange in a salad bowl. Season with oil, vinegar, salt and pepper. Sprinkle with chopped chervil or with salad herbs.

Brussels sprouts sautéed in butter. CHOUX DE BRUXELLES SAUTÉS AU BEURRE – Boil and drain the sprouts. Sauté lightly in butter until they are brown. Sprinkle with chopped parsley.

BRUXELLOISE (À LA) – Garnish for pieces of meat, small or large, composed of Brussels sprouts and *pommes château*.

BUCCAN. BOUCAN – Place where Indians cured their meat. The word also applies to the actual grid on which the smoking was done.

BUCKWHEAT. BLÉ NOIR – Variety of Saracen corn.

Buckwheat (Russian soup garnish). GRUAU DE SARRASIN, BLÉ NOIR – Add 1 kg. ($2\frac{1}{4}$ lb.) buckwheat to 7 or 8 dl. ($1\frac{1}{4}$ pints, $1\frac{1}{2}$ pints) salted warm water and work to a smooth paste. Press into a deep pan; bake in hot oven for 2 hours.

Remove the crust which has formed on the surface, and turn out the buckwheat mixture into a pan without touching the crust which has formed at the bottom and on the sides of the dish.

Work the dough with 100 g. (4 oz., $\frac{1}{2}$ cup) butter, and spread out on a slab until it is 2 cm. ($\frac{3}{4}$ inch) thick. Leave to cool under a weight.

Cut into biscuits with a pastry-cutter and brown these with butter. Serve with broth. No use is made of the crusts left in the dish.

Buckwheat kasha – See KASHA.

BUFFALO. BUFFLE – Member of the ox family which is found in hot, swampy countries of the Old World. Buffaloes are domesticated in Italy and Asia. The American buffalo, more properly called bison, is much larger than the Asiatic buffalo. This animal is fast becoming extinct. The flesh of Asiatic and Italian buffaloes can be prepared in any manner suitable for beef (q.v.).

BUFFET (Restaurant) – The word *buffet* means a large tiered table often set near the entrance of a restaurant, on which dishes of meats, poultry, fish, cold sweets and pastries are arranged in a decorative manner. The buffet of a large restaurant is, in fact, a show of choice edibles.

Large tables with a display of foods set in or near a ballroom are also called buffets. The food is dispensed by a butler and the guests come to the table to be served with sandwiches, cold meats, pastries, and various drinks; or to have consommé served in cups. Buffets of this type are also arranged for wedding lunches.

Buffet at Marly, 1859 (*Arts décoratifs*)

The buffet
Anonymous painting of the 18th century exhibited at the Pavillon de Marsan (1936) (*M. Léon Helft*)

General view of Nantua

BUFFET (Station). BUFFET DE GARE – A few years ago the S.N.C.F. (National French Railways) initiated a series of '*buffets gastronomiques*'. Those of Lille, Épernay and Avignon have an especially high reputation.

BUFFETER – Action of drawing-off wine from a barrel and replacing it with water. '*Servir à buffet*' used to mean serving guests with wine which had been liberally watered down.

BUGEY – Includes the part of Savoy which is today the *département* of Ain. Brillat-Savarin was born in Belley, which was the chief town of the old *département* of Bugey. The *cuisine* of this area is said to be among the best in France. Nantua, in particular, is celebrated for its crayfish, and all the famous cheeses of Burgundy are to be found there. The markets are full of choice plump capons, chickens, ducks and the best salt-meadow lamb. Trout and pike abound in the rivers, and the Bourget lake supplies lavaret, perch and char. The country hams are noted, and the hillsides and the plains provide succulent game. This fertile region also produces truffles, morels, and a great variety of other mushrooms.

Culinary specialities – *Salt ham*; Belley *sausage*; Belley *fondue*; Bugey *rissoles*; *'cardinalised crayfish'*; *crayfish croquettes*; *timbale of crayfish tails à la Nantua*; *char à la façon du lac du Bourget*; *quenelles and lavaret gâteaux*; *crayfish tails au gratin*; *pike à la crème*; *fillet of beef studded with black truffles*; *braised leg of mutton with onions*; *round of veal with* Valromey *black morels*; *calves' sweetbreads and black truffles*; *stuffed calves' ears*; *truffled turkey*; *truffled giblets with chestnuts*; Bresse *truffled chicken*; *chicken fricassée*; *chicken Célestine*; *gâteau de foies blondes*; *jugged hare de Diane de Châteaumorand*; *Bernardini salmis of woodcock*. The *salé* of Bugey is the national dish of the region, just as *anguries*, a watermelon salad, is associated with Belley. The well-known Bugey *rissole* is a hot *hors-d'œuvre* eaten at Christmas; the following proportions will make a dozen rissoles.

Bugey crayfish

Cut 250 g. (9 oz.) roast turkey into small pieces. Clean 150 g. (5 oz.) tripe thoroughly, cut up, and cook for 3 hours in a *court-bouillon* (q.v.) of white wine and beef stock, seasoned with salt, pepper, onions and a small *bouquet* of thyme and chervil. Cook a chopped onion in butter without allowing it to brown, add the meats, season with salt and pepper, moisten with a small quantity of roast turkey juices, and sauté for 5 or 6 minutes. Simmer until the liquor has boiled down by half, and add 50 g. (2 oz., $\frac{1}{3}$ cup) large currants. Leave to cool.

Make some puff pastry, roll out about 5 mm. ($\frac{1}{4}$ inch) thick, cut into small rectangles. Spoon some filling onto these, fold over, brush with beaten egg, and bake in the oven.

BUGLOSS. BUGLOSSE – Common name for *anchusa*, a plant also known as *alkanet*. Its flowers are eaten as a salad, considered to be a tonic, and said to have been a great favourite of Louis XIII. In some regions the leaves are eaten prepared the same way as spinach.

BUGNES – A kind of fritter, made from rolled-out dough which is cut up and fried in oil. Lyons is the 'capital' of the *bugnes*.

BULBOUS CHERVIL. CERFEUIL BULBEUX – Biennial plant cultivated for its tuberous roots, which are rich in fecula and have a strong aromatic flavour. The roots are prepared like Chinese artichokes.

BULL. TAUREAU – Flesh of young bulls is tougher than that of beef, but of good quality. The flesh of old animals is very tough, and often musky in taste.

BULLY-BEEF. ENDAUBAGE – Slang term for tinned meat supplied to the armed forces.

BUNDENFLEISCH – German word meaning Grisons salt beef.

Pickle a lean piece of meat for 6 days, take out of the brine and hang for 5 or 6 months. This pickling is done in the Swiss canton of Grisons in November, and the salted meat sold to the public the following April. When taken out of the brine it is put in a smoke-curing house for one day, except in the Engadine, where pickling is done commercially on a large scale, and the beef is not smoke-cured.

BUNG. BONDE – Wooden stopper for barrel bung-holes.

BUNTING. BRUANT – Genus of aquatic, web-footed birds, found in the marches of Bresse and Dauphiné. It is prepared in the same way as wild duck (see DUCK, *Wild duck*).

BURBOT. LOTTE DE RIVIÈRE – Species of freshwater fish with long dorsal fins, a long tail fin, and drooping barbels on the chin.

Burbot liver. FOIE DE LOTTE DE RIVIÈRE – Prepared in the same way as the soft roes of various fish, though it requires longer poaching than soft roes.

The liver is highly prized by connoisseurs. It is poached in white wine and used for various Lenten garnishes. It is also made into *pâté* (q.v.).

BURDOCK (Butter-bur, Beggar's buttons). BARDANE – Hardy perennial plant which grows along paths on the roadside and in the hedgerows. It is also called *herbe aux teigneux* (scurvy grass) because in the past its leaves were used as poultices for certain kinds of sores. The fresh spring root is well known as a depurative and is particularly useful in the treatment of furunculosis.

The tea made from its leaves is refreshing and stimulates the digestion. It soothes inflammations of the stomach and is an excellent remedy for stomach ulcers.

In Scotland young shoots and peeled roots of burdock are used in cooking; they are prepared as salsify.

BURGUNDY. BOURGOGNE – Burgundy is the region of France where the best food is to be had, and it enjoys the esteem of gastronomes for the quality and variety of its wines.

We are beholden to its excellent *cuisine* for a method of preparation called *à la bourguignonne*, used mainly for large cuts of braised meat, also for eggs, fish and poultry; a red wine sauce with a garnish of mushrooms and small onions.

Ain is the district where the best poultry is raised, and where the town of Belley, associated with Brillat-Savarin, is situated. Nantua evokes visions of crayfish *à la crème*; Saône-et-Loire has the town of Mâcon, which has given its name to one of our best wines; the Côte-d'Or, with Dijon, may be said to be one of the capitals of gastronomy; the Yonne produces Chablis wines, esteemed by gourmets.

The Burgundy larder is abundantly rich. In the pasture lands of Charolais the cattle give succulent beef. The poultry of Bresse is considered among the best in France. In Morvan, ground and winged game abounds. The woodcock of the Dombes marshes is unrivalled.

In the ponds, rivers and streams, pike, char, trout, salmon trout and crayfish are found. The *escargots* of Burgundy are most succulent. Among other excellent products are Courtivron and Oyonnax morels, St George's agaric, *cèpes* and other mushrooms, found in abundance in the woods and fields, and the choice vegetables cultivated in Auxonne and around Dijon.

The fruit of the Burgundy orchards is famous: Saint-Bris cherries; and blackcurrants used not only to prepare the famous Cassis liqueur made in Dijon, but also for a vast number of sweetmeats. Dijon mustard is considered the best; condiments seasoned with vinegar, such as pickled gherkins, are also made in Dijon.

The region which, with Bordeaux and Champagne, produces magnificent wines, produces excellent cheeses to

Spring in Burgundy

Cauliflower *à la polonaise* (*Phot. Nicolas*)

Display of grapes and apples from Dijon

accompany them. Among those highly esteemed by gastronomes are Gex blue-veined cheese which has a certain similarity to Roquefort; Soumaintrain, Cîteaux, Beugnon, Butteaux, Germigny, Pougny, the famous Époisses cheeses (which are made in the Yonne), Saint-Florentin, Passin which, according to some experts, is as good as the best Gruyère, various Morvan goat cheeses and the Saône-et-Loire cream cheeses.

For centuries Burgundy has been the land of great gastronomical feasts. The most characteristic were given at the time of grape-harvesting. Philéas Gilbert wrote a description of these feasts: 'From the moment the village crier had sounded the call (the roll of the drum before the proclamation), when only the *père de la vigne* and the masters of wine layering had the word, until the evening, when the last cask of grapes crushed by the wine press was poured into the vats, all was joy and song.

'And as a compensation for the mid-day meal, the supper menu promised a veritable feast, with the traditional *potée* – its robust fragrance teasing the men and women wine harvesters long before it was ready. *La tisane de choux sucrée avec de lard*, as Henri II used to say. Then there was *goose à la taribaude*, and a sheep, sacrificed for the occasion and transformed into strange yet exquisite *ragoûts*. The

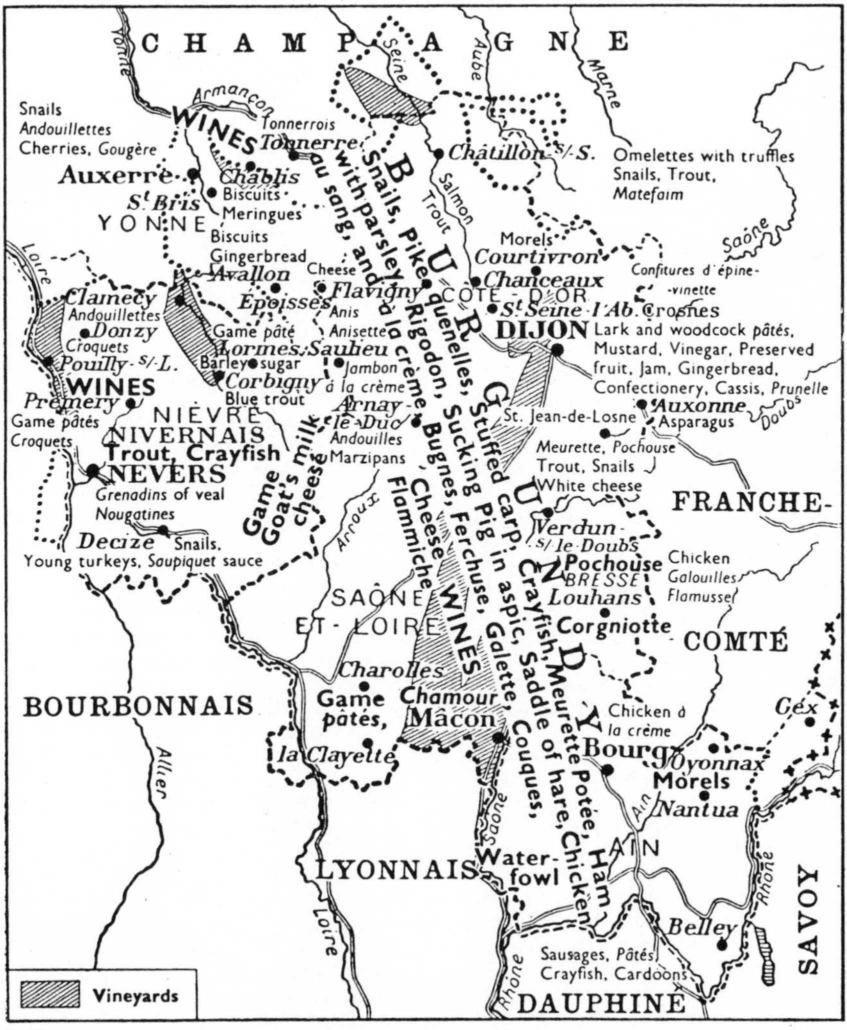

Gastronomic map of Burgundy

flesh of this sheep, the grandam of the flock, at times tasted of wool grease (to say nothing of its toughness!) but, to make it go down, the pot-bellied jugs poured forth cool wine; it was 'plenty of grub' and carousing to one's heart's content . . ..

'Ah! Those admirable Burgundian meals, when a great profusion of delectable dishes is served, such as *escargots – à la bourguignonne*, naturally! – *meurette* (q.v.) of various fish; *andouillettes* (q.v.) with beans; a succulent *daube* (q.v.) of beef; the traditional *ferchuse à la ménagère, flammiche aux poireaux, fouée au lard*, and the Burgundy *rigodon*!'

Culinary specialities – To Philéas Gilbert, the *escargot*, prepared in accordance with Burgundian rites, eaten scalding hot as it is taken out of its garlic-scented butter bath, symbolises the gastronomy of Burgundy. But there is an infinite variety of other dishes, recipes for which will be found in alphabetical order.

Potée bourguignonne, which is similar to various French *potées*, for each region of France has its *potée*; *pochouse* (q.v.) and various freshwater fish *matelotes* (q.v.); *beef à la bourguignonne*, which must be made with red wine; *round of veal à la crème*; *andouille with white beans*; *ferchuse* (a corruption of the word *fressure*, i.e. pluck); *daube bourguignonne*; *flammiche with leeks*; *fouée*, which is a cream flan filled with slices of bacon and sprinkled with walnut oil; *poulet au sang*; *young pigeons à la gobinette*; *canard au laurier*; *jugged hare à la bourguignonne*; *saddle of hare à la Piron*; *omelette au sang*.

There are *pike à la crème*; Arnay-le-Duc *andouille*; Sens *andouillette*; Dijon *ham with parsley*; the *sausages* of Belley (Brillat-Savarin's native place); *crayfish tails à la Nantua*; *pike quenelles with crayfish*; Pernollet *chicken à la crème*; *coq au chambertin*; *sucking-pig à la bourguignonne*; *ham rigodon*, and a whole range of *charcuterie*: large and small *sausages*; *black pudding* and *pork pies*, which are made in the Côte-d'Or, Ain, Saône-et-Loire and in Yonne.

Among the cakes, sweets and pastries of the Burgundy region are the *rigodon* (q.v.) (which can also be made as a dessert or sweet course); Lower Burgundy *girdle cakes*; Upper Burgundy girdle cakes known as *pognon*; *pancakes*, called *matefaims* in Upper Burgundy; *bugnes* or *couques*; Sens and Auxerre *gougère*; Louhans *corgniottes*; *chamoure* – a kind of marrow flan which is mainly made in Lower Mâconnais; *fruit tartouillat*; *tarte aux boulettes*; *flamusse bressane*; and *gaudes*.

Among local pastry and confectionery specialities are Dijon *nonnettes* and *pain d'épice*; Avallon and Chablis *biscuits*; Sens *macaroons*; Chablis *meringues*; Arnay-le-Duc *marzipans*; *nougatines*; *blackcurrant fondants*; *sugar-coated cherries* (cherries in petticoats); excellent jams, among which the best known are Chanceaux *raisiné*, *confiture d'épine-vinette*; and Flavigny *aniseed sweets*.

To conclude the list of local produce are the esteemed *cassis* liqueurs made at Dijon; and *prunelle*, made at Flavigny.

Wines – The quality and variety of Burgundy wines assure them a leading place not only in France but in the world.

Viticultural Burgundy goes beyond the frontiers of historic Burgundy. It extends across four *départements*: Yonne, Côte-d'Or, Saône-et-Loire and Rhône, embracing the great regions of Chablis, Côte de Nuits, Côte de Beaune, Côte chalonnaise, Mâconnais, Beaujolais. Each of these regions comprises several *appellations*, some communes, some vineyards, besides regional or 'generic' *appellations* (see accompanying table).

Chablis. The little town of Chablis in Yonne has given its name to this excellent dry wine with its greeny-gold hue and delicate bouquet. It is a wine that matures beautifully in

Map of the Burgundy wine-growing district

good vintage years. Connoisseurs enjoy drinking it with oysters, seafood, fish and shellfish.

Côte de Nuits. This is the name given to the northern part of the Côte-d'Or, which begins south of Dijon with the commune of Fixin and ends south of Nuits-Saint-Georges. The vineyards climb halfway up a line of hills situated west of the autoroute Dijon-Mâcon.

The Côte de Nuits produces mostly red wines. These strong, full-bodied, glowing, fragrant wines enjoy an excellent reputation and accompany roast or grilled meat, game (even when it is high), piquant dishes and cheeses to perfection.

Côte de Beaune. This comes immediately after the Côte de Nuits and gets its name from the village of Beaune. Côte de Beaune extends from Ladoix-Serrigny in the north to Santenay, on the borders of the *département* of Saône-et-Loire in the south. Apart from some great red wines, Côte de Beaune produces some very fine dry white wines, the most famous being Montrachet, with its delicious fragrance of fresh almonds. Puligny-Montrachet often equals it; the Chassagne-Montrachet and Bâtarde-Montrachet have better lasting qualities. The powerful Corton-Charlemagne, the fragrant, full-bodied Meursault are, like all the wines of this region, wines to serve with fish and shellfish; they also make fitting companions to the richest of sauces.

The red wines are as good as those of the Côte de Nuits. They can be drunk with meat, but it is preferable (apart from

The manufacture of Burgundy wines, 1470 (from contemporary tapestries)

Corton or Pommard) to keep them for less rich dishes than those that Côte de Nuits wines usually accompany.

Côte chalonnaise. This is the continuation of the line of sun-drenched hill slopes that begin south of Dijon. The red Mercurey, the white Rully, are worthy of their famous brothers of the Côte-d'Or. (There is also a white Mercurey and a red Rully.) We must not forget the Montagny (white) and the Givry (both red and white).

Mâconnais. Under the *appellations* Mâcon, Mâcon supérieur and Mâcon-Villages (white only) we find red, rosé and white wines which, when well vinified, make good carafe wines.

Also among the Mâconnais wines there is a superb dry white wine known all over the world: Pouilly-Fuissé which, gastronomically speaking, is interchangeable with Chablis wines or those of the Côte de Beaune. Two communal *appellations*, Pouilly-Vinzelles and Pouilly-Loché are in the same class.

Beaujolais. Although classed among the Burgundy wines, Beaujolais is a wine with a strong personality. Its name evokes light, fruity wines, the kind that are pleasant to drink when they are young and fresh – 'gulping' wines, the growers call them. It belongs to the Gamay kingdom, whereas the great wines of the Côte-d'Or come from the black Pinot.

The wine-growing district of Beaujolais begins in the *département* of Saône-et-Loire in the north and extends southwards to the environs of Lyons. The 'generic' *appellations* are 'Beaujolais', 'Beaujolais supérieur' and 'Beaujolais-Villages'; they are the lightest varieties and very drinkable.

Nine growths merit a special *appellation*, each of them with its own individual character (see accompanying table).

It is worth noting that contrary to most Beaujolais, which must be drunk young, the Morgon, Fleurie and Moulin-à-Vent can – in a good year – be laid down.

LIST OF APPELLATIONS CONTRÔLÉES OF BURGUNDY

White (W) and red (R) wines

Appellations régionales	
Bourgogne	W, R
Bourgogne clairet ou rosé	R
Bourgogne aligoté	W
Bourgogne passe-tout-grain	R
Bourgogne grand ordinaire	W, R

Région de Chablis

Chablis grand cru	W
Chablis premier cru	W
Chablis	W
Petit Chablis	W

Côte de Nuits

Chambolle-Musigny	R
Fixin	R
Gevrey-Chambertin	R
Morey-Saint-Denis	W, R
Nuits-Saint-Georges	W, R
Vougeot	W, R
Vosne-Romanée	R
Côte de Nuits-Villages	R
Bourgogne-Marsannay-la-Côte	R
Bourgogne-Vins fins des Hautes Côtes de Nuits	R

Great wines of Côte de Nuits

Bonnes Mares	R
Chambertin	R
Chambertin-Clos de Bèze	R
Chapelle-Chambertin	R
Charmes or Mazoyères-Chambertin	R
Clos de la Roche	R
Clos Saint-Denis	R
Clos de Tart	R
Clos de Vougeot	R
Echézeaux	R
Grands-Echézeaux	R
Griottes-Chambertin	R
La Tâche	R
Latricières-Chambertin	R
Mazis-Chambertin	R
Musigny	W, R
Richebourg	R
La Romanée	R
Romanée-Conti	R
Romanée-Saint-Vivant	R
Ruchottes-Chambertin	R

Côte chalonnaise

Givry	W, R
Mercurey	W, R
Montagny	W
Rully	W, R

Côte de Beaune

Aloxe-Corton	W, R
Auxey-Duresses	W, R
Beaune	W, R
Blagny	W, R
Chassagne-Montrachet	W, R
Chorey-lès-Beaune	R
Côtes de Beaune	W, R
Côtes de Beaune-Villages	R
Ladoix	W, R
Meursault	W, R
Monthélie	W, R
Pernand-Vergelesses	W, R
Pommard	R
Puligny-Montrachet	W, R
Saint-Aubin	W, R
Santenay	W, R
Savigny-lès-Beaune	W, R
Volnay	R
Cheilly-lès-Maranges	W, R
Dezize-lès-Maranges	W
Sampigny-lès-Maranges	R
Saint-Romain	W, R
Bourgogne-Hautes Côtes de Beaune	R

Great wines of Côte de Beaune

Corton	W, R
Corton-Charlemagne	W
Bâtard-Montrachet	W
Bienvenue-Bâtard-Montrachet	W
Criots-Bâtard-Montrachet	W
Chevalier-Montrachet	W
Montrachet	W

Beaujolais

Beaujolais	W, R
Beaujolais supérieur	W, R
Beaujolais-Villages	R
Brouilly	R
Chénas	R
Chiroubles	R
Côtes de Brouilly	R
Fleurie	R
Juliénas	R
Morgon	R
Moulin-à-Vent	R
Saint-Amour	R

Mâconnais

Mâcon	W, R
Mâcon supérieur	W, R
Mâcon-Villages	W
Pouilly-Fuissé	W
Pouilly-Vinzelles	W
Pouilly-Loché	W

BUSH (In a). BUISSON (EN) – Method of arranging various ingredients, particularly shellfish: *crayfish en buisson, lobsters en buisson, spiny lobsters en buisson.* Smelts and other small fish are also fried and arranged 'in a bush'.

BUSTARD. OUTARDE – Genus of bird of the family *Otidiae*, found in both hot and temperate regions of the Old World. The *great bustard* is the largest land bird in Europe, where it comes in December and stays until March. It is known for the delicacy of its flesh.

The *little bustard* is more highly prized. It comes to Beauce and Berry in April, but is non-migrant in Spain, Italy, Greece and Sardinia. The special feather structure on the head of the great bustard male is absent from the head of the little bustard male.

The principal method of cooking bustard is roasting. All the recipes indicated for the preparation of the domestic goose and the Nantes duckling can be applied to bustard.

BUTCHER'S SHOP. BOUCHERIE – Shop for the retail sale of meat for human consumption. The meat trade has a long history. The Jewish High Priest in Biblical times, performing the sacrificial offering, was the real precursor of the butcher.

In Egypt, a fire was lit in front of the altar where a sacrifice was to be made, wine was offered and a god invoked. The throat of the animal was slit, the head severed and the carcase skinned. The head was taken to market; it was sold to a Greek if one could be found, if not, the head was thrown into the river.

The Romans made similar sacrifices, but created a special body of men to carry out the actual butchery of the animals, giving these men special privileges to compensate for the fact that their occupation was held in contempt by the higher classes. Under Nero, the Roman butcher's shop was an

Butcher's shop until end of seventeenth century which included the slaughtering of animals (*l'Encyclopédie*)

imposing establishment, and they established a guild, which was subject to official regulations. Butchers specialising in the buying and selling of pigs were called *suarii*.

In France, a butchers' guild had been established by the eighth century; a man had to serve a three years' apprenticeship and buy, dress, cut and sell meat for a further three years before he could become a master butcher and buy an official diploma; both privileges cost a great deal of money. The guild was directed by a master of master butchers, and became extremely powerful, arrogating to themselves not only the monopoly of selling beef, veal, mutton, pork and sucking-pig, but also sea and river fish.

Arms of the butchers' guild

Charles VI revoked some of their privileges, and their power declined for a time, but in the sixteenth century they were raised to the status of tradesmen, and were subject to statutes, among which were ordinances which forbade them to open new stalls without authority; keep open after a certain time; exhibit meat on days of abstinence or during Lent in more than one stall out of ten, and that only for the sick; solicit custom or abuse customers; slaughter animals without informing the authorities; sell cooked meat; or pursue any other trade but that of a butcher.

They were expected to sell meat from healthy animals which had been properly slaughtered and had not died from disease or suffocation, to prepare it in a clean way and to sell it at the right time, not too fresh or kept for too long, i.e., more than 2 days in winter and 1½ days in summer – it being reckoned that the meat became unfit for human consumption after these periods.

The sale of meat measured out by hand, a method of approximate estimation, caused continual arguments, and was replaced by the system of scales, which offered the greatest fairness. Fines, confiscations and penalties involving the loss of civil rights were inflicted on the lawbreakers. It was the duty of the provost of Paris to see that these statutes were carried out.

The royal regulations were maintained until the end of absolute monarchy. Napoleon succeeded in doing away with privately owned slaughter houses, and created the public slaughter house. As soon as butchers were forced to take animals there, two branches of the industry developed: the wholesale trade and the retail trade. The first covered the purchase of livestock, transport to the slaughter house, and the work of the scalding room. The second consisted of retailing the carcases of meat to the consumer.

Cattle markets were created in the nineteenth century, among them those at Sceaux, Pontoise and Passy for the Paris area. A fund was also set up from which butchers could obtain the necessary money for purchases, with a charge of 5 per cent interest, and a proviso that the loan be repaid within a fortnight. Thus the butchers retained one of their ancient privileges. Their creditors could not press claims on the eve of, or on, market day, nor seize the meat in the shop. These conditions were essential to safeguard the town's meat supplies.

During the nineteenth century the meat trade became free, but there was a transition period during which it was necessary to pay a fee of 3,000 francs to prove that an apprenticeship had been served and that one possessed the necessary knowledge to retail meat, to present a certificate of good conduct and character, and to undertake not to leave the business without giving the prefecture three months' notice.

Towards the middle of the century there were only 500 retail butcher shops left. Police regulations laid down the details relating to the running of shops; they had to be tiled, well ventilated and well positioned. No butcher could set up business before the police commissioner of his area had visited his premises and given his approval. Any butcher who displayed meat outside his premises was fined. A shop that did not display meat for three consecutive days was closed for six months.

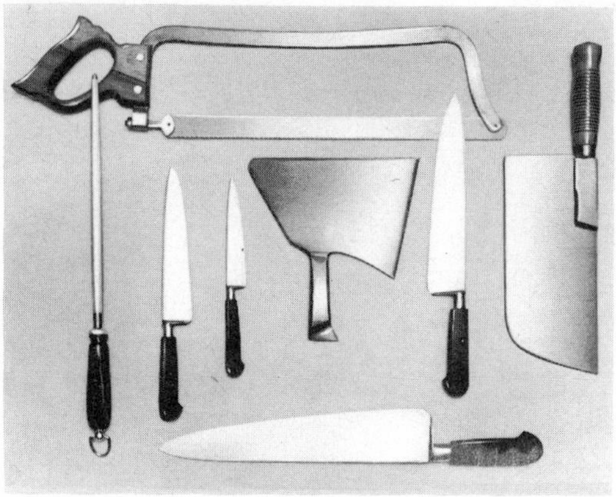

Butcher's tools (*Nicolas*)

Since 1863 the number of shops has considerably increased. They are still controlled by police regulations, but the butchers' guild no longer has the prerogatives it enjoyed under the old régime. The work of slaughtering animals is now carried out in recognised slaughter houses, except in a very few localities where the butcher does the slaughtering himself. The bulk of a butcher's work is the preparation of cuts of meat for cooking, and the butcher often stuffs and dresses the joints himself.

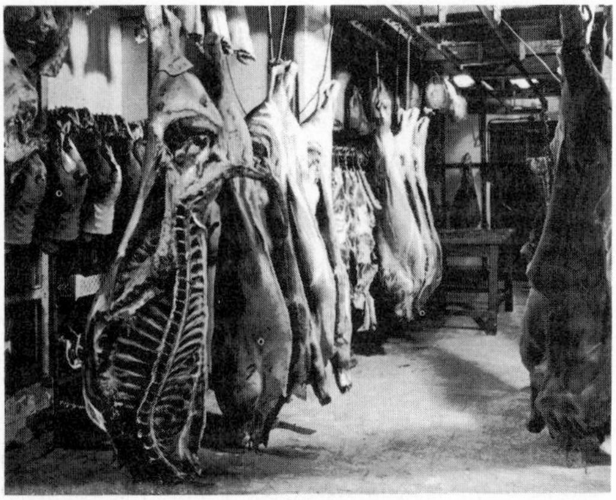

Butcher's cold room (*Nicolas*)

The preparatory work is carried out on a chopping block: a section of a tree trunk, usually elm, mounted on three legs. The slab, also used as a bench, has a cross-grained wooden working surface with fittings for tools, and large drawers. The tools include choppers, saws and knives of various sizes; the latter are sometimes placed in a wooden case, called a *boutique*. These tools are often seen in the kitchens of large catering establishments which buy complete carcases or large cuts wholesale, or direct from the slaughter house, for their own cooks to carve and prepare.

Butchers' shops also have scales which must be kept very clean, marble tables and ceramic plates to display the meat. Modern rules of hygiene being made to protect food from dust, many butchers' shops are provided with display counters enclosed with glass, and often with means of refrigeration. Uncut carcases are hung from rails on hooks, and enclosed in a refrigerated chamber or in a large refrigerator. The walls and floors of a butcher's shop are usually tiled, and kept scrupulously clean. Employees are dressed in light-coloured clothes and wear white aprons.

BUTTER. BEURRE – Fatty substances extracted from the milk of mammals, known and used as food by man. The origin of butter goes back to the early nomadic people who used the milk of goats, cows, ewes, mares, she-asses and she-camels to prepare it.

The Aryans brought butter to the inhabitants of India, who soon considered it a sacred food.

The Hebrews used butter as a medicine as well as a food. Abraham offered butter, a symbolic food, to three men who came to his tent in the plains of Mamre. In his proverbs Solomon says: 'Surely, the churning of milk bringeth forth butter . . .'.

The Scythians also had butter, and brought it to the Greeks, and its use spread throughout the civilised world.

People living in some southern countries, like the Romans, used oil much more than butter in their cooking. This preference still persists in certain parts of the south of France, mainly in Provence, where oil plays a principal part in all the dishes.

Old way of making butter

Preparation of butter – In their emulsive state, the fatty globules of milk are relatively stable, but when the liquid is left to stand, they rise to the surface in the form of cream. Cream is generally obtained by the centrifugation of milk in separators. Once agitated (in what constitutes the churning operation) the fatty globules agglutinate into a compact mass called butter.

Modern butter factory (*Rayot*)

This mass in the churn exudes a quantity of watery liquid called buttermilk, which is drawn off. The remaining solid is rinsed in pure water while still in the churn, then worked until a homogenous butter is obtained.

The cream may be churned fresh from the cow, but the quality and yield of the butter are definitely improved by allowing the cream to mature. During this period of maturation the cream turns slightly sour under the influence of lactic ferments. This farm production method of maturing the cream before use is still observed in the industrial manufacture of butter but, in the latter case, maturation is preceded by heat treatment called pasteurisation, which ensures the destruction of possible microbes. Very high and consistent quality is obtained by subsequently sowing yeasts containing acidifying and flavouring elements in the butter.

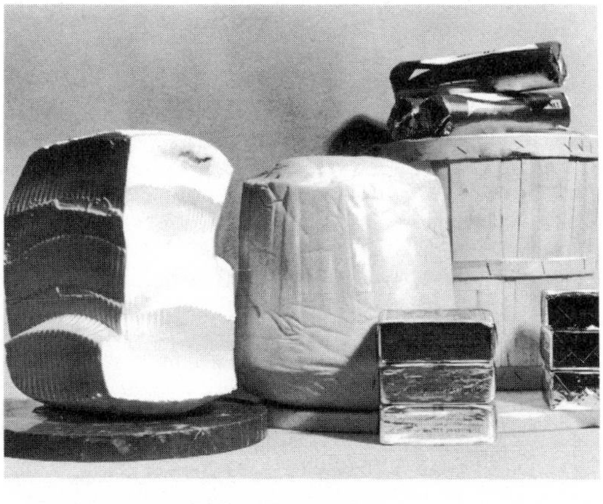

Blocks and packets of butter
(*Rayot. Phot. Nicolas*)

For retail distribution, butter is usually machine packed in blocks and to satisfy trade regulations, it has to be protected from contamination by greaseproof paper or tinfoil. Salted and *demi-sel* butters are often packed in waxed cardboard cartons.

Quality of butter – A good butter should have a semi-soft consistency at room temperature and ought not to 'sweat' (an indication that it contains too high a proportion of water). It should have a slightly aromatic smell and a sweet, pleasant flavour. When placed on the tongue it should melt without leaving any deposit.

The colour varies according to the time of year it was produced and the type of animal feeding chosen by the farmers. It can be almost white. The content of substances other than fat (milk constituents remaining in the butter after churning and washing) must not exceed 18 per cent, of which 16 per cent should be water.

Butter is a valuable energy food (750 calories per 100 g., 4 oz.). It contains a large amount of Vitamin A (the vitamin that promotes growth) and Vitamin D (the anti-rachitic vitamin), but the quantities of these vary according to the quality of the butter, animal feeding methods, and the season. Unadulterated, it is the most digestible of the animal fats, provided that it is eaten raw.

Adulteration of butter – Like many other quality foods, butter used to lend itself to fraudulent falsification. Now that industrial manufacture (subject to strict controls) has replaced farm production, the only danger is insufficient working of the butter mass, leaving a residue of buttermilk and water in excess of 18 per cent; or, in the case of farm butters, the addition of preservatives, such as boric acid. The effects of prolonged storage at too high a temperature, possibly near other foodstuffs, is also a factor that cannot be ignored. Finally, cattle-food may, at certain periods of the year, produce peculiar odours and taste; these, however, can be eliminated by industrial processes.

The most frequent type of adulteration is that which gives rise to a greasy, rancid or poisonous taste, the consequences of careless production, or (more frequently) prolonged storage. These drawbacks can be eliminated by choosing a reliable retailer and a good brand of butter.

Preservation of butter – There are various methods of preserving butter, two of the most common being salting and amalgamation.

Salted butter is done by working a quantity of fine salt into the butter. There are two types: *demi-sel* butters (3 to 5 per cent salt) and salted butters (8 to 10 per cent salt). *Demi-sel* or salted are the most suitable for cooking.

Amalgamated butter is effected by amalgamation in a *bain-marie*, or processed over intense heat. The second method gives a product that has superior keeping qualities, but the process is detrimental to the flavour.

Butter is frequently clarified for cooking purposes; the water is evaporated, precipitating the casein contained in the butter. By using clarified butter, food can be lightly fried or sautéed without overbrowning and, the butter having been dehydrated, without causing spitting and splutterings of fat.

Clarification of butter – See CLARIFICATION.

VEGETABLE BUTTERS. BEURRES VÉGÉTAUX – These must not be sold under the name of butter, but should be labelled 'vegetable fat' or given a trade name.

It is possible to give a solid or semi-solid consistency to certain vegetable oils. For example, the hydrogenation of cottonseed oil, using nickel mousse as a catalyst, produces a kind of artificial butter or lard – in imitation of American lard.

Cocoa butter. BEURRE DE CACAO – Fatty substance obtained from roasted cocoa beans. It is sold in the form of rectangular blocks, with a sweet and pleasant taste, like that of chocolate. It melts at a temperature between 30°C. (86°F.) and 33°C. (91°F.) and stays liquid by cooling at a lower temperature, solidifying at 23°C. (73°F.).

This product, of which there are several brands, is sterilised and keeps very well. It contains no water and is easily digestible, perhaps more so than ordinary butter. Its taste is neutral and can in no way be compared to that of butter.

Coconut butter. BEURRE DE COCO – A vegetable butter frequently used in France. The copra (albuminous lining of the interior of the coconut), dried and put under pressure, yields an oil used in soap-making. After bleaching and various other processes the oil is transformed into an edible product of firm consistency, which looks like butter.

Nutmeg butter. BEURRE DE MUSCADE – Fatty substance obtained from nutmegs, sold in the form of rectangular loaves covered with palm leaves.

Walnut butter, hazelnut butter, peanut butter. BEURRE DE NOIX, NOISETTES, ARACHIDES – Factory-made products, high in nutritive value.

COMPOUND BUTTERS. BEURRES COMPOSÉS – (1) Butters mixed with one or more substances, generally reduced to a purée or chopped. (2) Butters cooked to various degrees, or melted, seasoned and served spiced; as accompaniment to various fish, meat and vegetable dishes.

Compound butters of the first category are used either in sauces and various dishes, or as garnish for cold *hors-d'œuvre.*

Almond butter. BEURRE D'AMANDES – Pound 75 g. (3 oz., ⅔ cup) sweet blanched and washed almonds to a fine paste, adding a few drops of cold water to prevent them turning oily. Add 150 g. (5 oz., 10 tablespoons) butter. Rub through a fine sieve.

Uses. As garnish for cold *hors-d'œuvre*, and as an addition to soups and some white sauces.

Anchovy butter. BEURRE D'ANCHOIS – Desalt and dry 75 g. (3 oz.) anchovy fillets and pound them in a mortar with 200 g (7 oz., scant cup) butter. Rub through a fine sieve.

Uses. As indicated for *Garlic butter* (see below). Anchovy butter is also a good accompaniment for grilled fish and meat.

Bercy butter. BEURRE BERCY – Add 1½ tablespoons finely chopped shallots to 2 dl. (⅓ pint, scant cup) white wine and boil down by half. When the liquor is almost cold, add 200 g. (7 oz., scant cup) softened butter and 500 g. (18 oz.) beef bone-marrow which has been cut in dice, poached in salted water and drained. Add 1 tablespoon chopped parsley and the juice of half a lemon. Season with 1 teaspoon fine salt and a pinch of freshly ground pepper.

Uses. Accompaniment for grilled fish and meat.

Brown butter. BEURRE NOIR – Cook 150 g. (5 oz., 10 tablespoons) butter to a dark brown colour. Add 2 tablespoons (3 tablespoons) washed and dried parsley leaves and 1 tablespoon capers. Pour the butter into a sauceboat or over the food with which it is to be served, and add a tablespoon vinegar heated in the same pan.

Uses. Brown butter is served with eggs; various fish; vegetables boiled in salted water; brains; and a number of other dishes.

For *eggs with browned butter* omit the parsley and the capers.

Caviare butter. BEURRE DE CAVIAR – Pound 75 g. (3 oz.) pressed caviare in a mortar. Add 150 g. (5 oz., 10 tablespoons) butter, and blend well. Rub through a fine sieve.

Uses. As a garnish for *canapés à la russe* and for various cold *hors-d'œuvre*, and for certain fish forcemeat.

Chive butter. BEURRE DE CIBOULETTE – Prepare and use as *Shallot butter* (see below), using green chives.

Chivry butter. BEURRE CHIVRY – Blanch 15 g. (½ oz.) each of parsley, tarragon and chervil leaves, fresh burnet and chives for 3 minutes in salted water. Drain, dip in cold water, and dry. Pound in a mortar with 25 g. (1 oz., ¼ cup) chopped, blanched shallots. Add 150 g. (5 oz., 10 tablespoons) butter. Rub through a fine sieve.

Uses. In white sauces and as a garnish for cold *hors-d'œuvre*. It is sometimes called *beurre ravigote*.

Colbert butter. BEURRE COLBERT – Prepare *Maître d'hôtel butter* (see below). Add 1 teaspoon chopped tarragon and 1 tablespoon dissolved meat jelly for 100 g. (4 oz., ½ cup) butter.

Uses. Accompaniment for fried fish *à la Colbert* and for grilled meat and fish.

Crab butter. BEURRE DE CRABES – Prepare and use as *Shrimp butter* (see below), using small crabs which have been cooked in *court-bouillon* (q.v.) and drained.

Crayfish butter (cold). BEURRE D'ÉCREVISSES (À FROID) – Prepare and use as *Shrimp butter (cold)* (see below), using shells and trimmings of crayfish cooked *à la mirepoix*.

Crayfish butter (hot). BEURRE D'ÉCREVISSES (À CHAUD) – Pound in a mortar the shells and trimmings of crayfish cooked *à la mirepoix* (the tails being used for some other dish). Add the same amount of fresh butter and blend well. Put the mixture in a small saucepan standing in a larger pan of hot water, allowing the crayfish butter to melt slowly.

When it is completely melted, pour it through a cloth secured over a bowl of iced water. Twist the cloth to squeeze out all the butter. This will solidify in the icy water, when it can be spooned out of the bowl and dried on a muslin cloth.

Uses. Add to sauces, gravies, thick shellfish soups, fish forcemeats and shellfish *ragoûts*. Crayfish butters form the basis for the sauce called *à la Nantua*.

Filbert butter. BEURRE D'AVELINES – Prepare in the same way as *Almond butter*. It has the same uses.

Garlic butter. BEURRE D'AIL – Peel, blanch, drain and dry 8 large cloves garlic, and pound in a mortar with 200 g. (7 oz., scant cup) fresh butter. Rub through a sieve.

Uses. For certain sauces, and as garnish for cold *hors-d'œuvre*.

Gascogne butter. BEURRE DE GASCOGNE – Prepare with garlic, which is first cooked for a few minutes in salted water, drained, pounded with a little butter, and seasoned.

Uses. For seasoning kidney beans and for sprinkling over grilled mushrooms.

Green butter. BEURRE VERT – Wash and dry spinach leaves and pound them in a mortar. Put into a strong cloth, twist to extract all the juice; pour this into a double saucepan to thicken. Turn out onto a muslin cloth stretched over a bowl, and filter. Scrape off the green residue which remains on the cloth; this is called *vert d'épinard* (spinach green). Add double its weight of softened butter which has been rubbed through a sieve.

Uses. As for *Chivry butter* and *Montpellier butter* (see below).

Hazelnut butter. BEURRE DE NOISETTE – Prepare and use like *Almond butter*, using lightly roasted hazelnuts or filbert nuts.

Herring butter. BEURRE DE HARENG – Made of fillets of pickled herrings, as *Anchovy butter* and used in the same ways.

Horseradish butter. BEURRE DE RAIFORT – Pound in a mortar 75 g. (3 oz., ½ cup) grated horseradish. Add 200 g. (7 oz., scant cup) butter. Rub through a sieve.

Uses. As for *Garlic butter*.

Kneaded butter. BEURRE MANIÉ – Blend 75 g. (3 oz., 6 tablespoons) butter and 100 g. (4 oz., 1 cup) flour into a smooth paste.

Uses. To bind some sauces, notably those called *à la matelote*.

Lemon butter. BEURRE DE CITRON – Add finely grated rind of 1 lemon to 200 g. (7 oz., scant cup) butter. Season with salt and white pepper. Blend well.

Uses. This is a garnish for cold *hors-d'œuvre.*

Lobster butter (cold). BEURRE DE HOMARD (À FROID) – Using the creamy parts, the eggs and the coral of the lobster cooked in *court-bouillon* (q.v.), proceed as described in recipe for *Shrimp butter (cold)* (see below). Use in the same ways.

Lobster butter (hot). BEURRE D'HOMARD (À CHAUD) – Using shells and trimmings of lobster, which have been cooked in *court-bouillon* (q.v.) or *à la mirepoix* (q.v.), prepare and use as for *Crayfish butter* (*hot*).

This butter is often called red colouring butter, which is prepared by pounding together in a mortar the coral, or eggs, of various shellfish which have been cooked in *court-bouillon* with an equal quantity of butter.

Maître d'hôtel butter. BEURRE À LA MAÎTRE D'HÔTEL – Mix 200 g. (7 oz., scant cup) fresh butter with 1½ tablespoons chopped parsley, ¾ teaspoon fine salt, a small pinch of freshly ground pepper and a dash of lemon juice. Stir with a spoon until it forms a smooth paste.

Uses. Accompaniment for grilled meat and fish, fish fried in egg and breadcrumbs, and various boiled vegetables.

Melted *maître d'hôtel butter* may be served separately or put on or under the ingredients which it accompanies.

Marchand de vins butter. BEURRE MARCHAND DE VINS – Add 25 g. (1 oz., ¼ cup) finely chopped shallots to 3 dl. (½ pint, 1¼ cups) red wine and boil slowly down to half. Add a tablespoon dissolved meat jelly or 2 tablespoons (3 tablespoons) rich brown veal stock, 150 g. (5 oz., 10 tablespoons) butter softened to a paste, 1 tablespoon chopped parsley, and the juice of quarter of a lemon. Season with salt and pepper, and blend well.

Uses. Accompaniment for grilled rump steak *à la marchand de vins.*

Marseille butter. BEURRE DE MARSEILLE – Name ironically used for oil, in the same way as garlic is referred to as *Marseille vanilla.*

Melted butter. BEURRE FONDU – Melt butter slowly, season with salt and a pinch of white pepper, and add a few drops of lemon juice.

Uses. Accompaniment for poached fish and boiled vegetables.

Meunière butter. BEURRE À LA MEUNIÈRE – Heat butter in a pan until it acquires a light brown colour. Add a dash of lemon juice and salt and pepper.

Uses. Accompaniment for fish prepared *à la meunière* (see BASS, *Bass à la meunière*) and for certain vegetables, poached or simmered in butter.

Montpellier butter. BEURRE DE MONTPELLIER – Blanch in salted water the following herbs, picked over and washed: 20 g. (¾ oz.) each parsley, chervil, cress, tarragon, chives, 25 g. (1 oz.) spinach leaves, and 40 g. (1½ oz., 6 tablespoons) chopped shallot.

Drain, dip in cold water, and press well to extract all the water. Pound in a mortar, adding 3 medium-sized gherkins, 1 tablespoon well-pressed capers, 4 desalted anchovy fillets, and 1 small garlic clove.

When all the ingredients have been reduced to a smooth paste, add to them 750 g. (1¾ lb., 3½ cups) butter, 3 hard-boiled egg yolks and 2 raw egg yolks.

Still pounding with a pestle, add little by little 2 dl. (⅓ pint, scant cup) olive oil. Season with salt and a pinch of cayenne pepper. Rub through a fine sieve. Whisk until quite smooth.

Uses. Mainly for dressing cold dishes particularly fish. However, when *Montpellier butter* is prepared specially for decorating cold dishes and for spreading on croûtons, raw egg yolks and oil are omitted.

Mushroom butter. BEURRE DE CHAMPIGNONS – Slice 150 g. (5 oz., 1½ cups) cultivated mushrooms; toss briskly in butter, season with salt and pepper, and pound in a mortar. Add 150 g. (5 oz., 10 tablespoons) fresh butter, blend and rub through a fine sieve.

Uses. Addition to white sauce and garnish for cold *hors-d'œuvre.*

Mustard butter. BEURRE DE MOUTARDE – Add 2 tablespoons (3 tablespoons) mustard to 200 g. (7 oz., scant cup) butter softened to a paste. Blend well.

Uses. The same as those for *Anchovy butter.*

Noisette butter. BEURRE NOISETTE – Cook butter to a light hazelnut colour.

Uses. Poured over eggs, lambs' or calves' brains, skate cooked in *court-bouillon* (q.v.), soft roes, and vegetables cooked in water and well drained. The juice of a lemon is squeezed into it if served separately.

Paprika butter. BEURRE DE PAPRIKA – Blend into a smooth paste 200 g. (7 oz., scant cup) butter, seasoned with 1 tablespoon paprika.

Uses. Garnish for *canapés* and other cold *hors-d'œuvre.*

Pistachio butter. BEURRE DE PISTACHES – Prepared like *Almond butter*, using blanched pistachio nuts.

Uses. The same as *Almond butter.*

Printanier butter. BEURRE PRINTANIER – Pound in a mortar an equal quantity of butter and green vegetables (green peas, asparagus tips, French beans, etc.) which have been cooked in water, drained and dried. Blend, and rub through a fine sieve.

Uses. Garnish for cold *hors-d'œuvre*; addition to thickened soups and some white sauces.

Ravigote butter. BEURRE RAVIGOTE – Name for *Chivry butter.*

Red butter. BEURRE ROUGE – Name given to *Lobster butter* and butter mixed with other shellfish.

Salmon butter. BEURRE DE SAUMON – Using fresh or smoked salmon, proceed as described in the recipe for *Anchovy butter.* Use in the same ways.

Sardine butter. BEURRE DE SARDINES – Prepared and used like *Anchovy butter*, using fillets of sardines in oil.

Shallot butter. BEURRE D'ÉCHALOTE – Shred, blanch, drain and dry 8 shallots and pound them in a mortar. Add the same weight of butter and rub through a fine sieve.

Uses. Accompaniment to grilled meat and fish.

Shrimp butter (cold). BEURRE DE CREVETTES (À FROID) – Pound 150 g. (5 oz.) cooked shrimps in a mortar with an equal amount of butter. Rub through a fine sieve.

Uses. Addition to fish sauces, and garnish for cold *hors-d'œuvre* and cold fish.

Shrimp butter (hot). BEURRE DE CREVETTES (À CHAUD) – Using cooked shrimps, prepare in the same way as *Crayfish butter (hot).*

Uses. The same as for *Crayfish butter (hot).*

Shrimp butter, as in the case of other shellfish, may be made using only the shells, if the flesh is needed for some other dish.

Butter for snails, à la bourguignonne. BEURRE POUR ESCARGOTS, À LA BOURGUIGNONNE – Add the following ingredients to 700 g. (1½ lb., 3 cups) best unsalted butter: 75 g. (3 oz., ¾ cup) finely chopped shallots, 2 garlic cloves pounded into paste, 2 tablespoons (3 tablespoons) chopped parsley. Season with 4 teaspoons salt and ½ teaspoon pepper. Blend well.

Uses. For filling *escargot* shells cooked *à la bourguignonne.*

Soft roe butter. BEURRE DE LAITANCES – This butter is prepared by pounding together in a mortar equal quantities of soft roes of pickled herrings and butter, rubbed through a sieve.

It can also be prepared by pounding in a mortar 125 g. (4 oz.) soft roes of various fish (especially those of carp), poached, cooled and well dried, with 200 g. (7 oz., scant cup) butter.

Uses. It is added to some fish sauces and used as a garnish for cold *hors-d'œuvre*.

Spiny lobster butter. BEURRE DE LANGOUSTE – Prepare, using shells and trimmings of the spiny lobster (U.S. crayfish) as for *Lobster butter*. Use in the same ways.

Sweet pimento butter. BEURRE DE POIVRONS DOUX – Pound finely in a mortar 150 g. (5 oz.) sweet pimentos (red or green) previously stewed in butter. Add 200 g. (7 oz., scant cup) butter and rub through a fine sieve.

Uses. The same as for *Garlic butter*.

Tarragon butter. BEURRE D'ESTRAGON – Blanch 125 g. (4 oz.) fresh tarragon leaves for 2 minutes in salted boiling water. Drain, dip in cold water, dry, and pound in a mortar with 200 g. (7 oz., scant cup) fresh butter. Rub through a fine sieve.

Uses. Addition to various sauces, and garnish for cold *hors-d'œuvre*, especially *Canapés à la russe* (see HORS-D'ŒUVRE, *Cold hors-d'œuvre*).

Tomato butter. BEURRE DE TOMATES – Soften 200 g. (7 oz., scant cup) butter, add 2 dl. ($\frac{1}{3}$ pint, scant cup) concentrated tomato juice, and blend well.

Uses. The same as for *Anchovy butter*. It is also used for thickening soups and white sauces.

Truffle butter. BEURRE DE TRUFFES – Pound in a mortar 100 g. (4 oz.) fresh truffles with 150 g. (5 oz., 10 tablespoons) butter. Rub through a fine sieve.

Uses. Garnish for *canapés* and other cold *hors-d'œuvre*.

Tunny (tuna fish) butter. BEURRE DE THON – Prepare as *Anchovy butter*, using tunny in oil.

Uses. The same as for *Anchovy butter*.

Walnut butter. BEURRE DE NOIX – Prepare as *Almond butter*, using dried, blanched walnuts.

Uses. The same as for *Almond butter*.

White butter. BEURRE BLANC – See PIKE, *Pike au beurre blanc*.

BUTTER CREAMS – See CREAMS.

BUTTER DISH. BEURRIER – Small dish used for serving butter on the table. Some butter dishes are made in such a way that the butter is always kept under salted water. Thus enclosed, the butter can be kept fresh for a longer period. There are more modern types consisting of a double-walled, bell-shaped cover in porous earthenware filled with water, which is changed every day. This cover is placed over the butter contained in a glass dish.

BUTTERMILK. BABEURRE – Milk which is left after churning butter. This product differs, depending on whether fresh or sour milk is being churned, and on whether the cream is taken off by centrifugal machinery.

Buttermilk contains all the casein of milk. This casein, following acidification, undergoes changes which render it more soluble and more digestible. It contains all the mineral salts found in milk and a proportion of lactose which has not yet been transformed into lactic acid.

Buttermilk soup. SOUPE DE BABEURRE – Mix a little flour (wheat, barley, rice, etc.) allowing one tablespoon per litre (scant quart, generous quart) in a small quantity of cold buttermilk, blending to avoid lumps. Add to heated buttermilk, and bring slowly to the boil. Boil down by one quarter, and sweeten with sugar, allowing 70 to 90 g. ($2\frac{1}{2}$ to $3\frac{1}{2}$ oz.) sugar per litre (scant quart, generous quart).

The object of adding flour is to break up the globules of casein and thus make it more digestible. Prepared in this way, buttermilk soup has a nutritive value to a considerable extent approaching that of human milk.

BUTYRIC ACID. BUTYRIQUE – Acid which develops in butter by oxidation, and which causes it to become rancid.

BUTYROMETER. BUTYROMÈTRE – Instrument consisting of a calibrated glass tube for measuring the butter content of milk.

The milk is mixed with a certain volume of ether which dissolves the butter. Then an equal volume of alcohol is added. The butter floats on the surface in the form of an oily layer and its thickness, measured by the graduation of the tube, clearly shows the proportion of butter.

BUTYROUS. BUTYREUX – Having the consistency and appearance of butter.

BUVETTE – This was the name given to the small refreshment bars that existed under the *Ancien Régime* in the judicial high courts. They were necessary at a time when the judges assembled very early in the morning and sat often until mid-day without intermission. Later, *buvettes* became objects of ridicule and provoked epigrams such as the following:

Themis inspires the magistrates in the *buvette*
With the strictest equity;
During the hearing can be observed
Arrest after arrest by Bacchus served.

The Revolution put an end to the *buvettes* along with the judicial high courts; but they reappeared with the legislative assemblies.

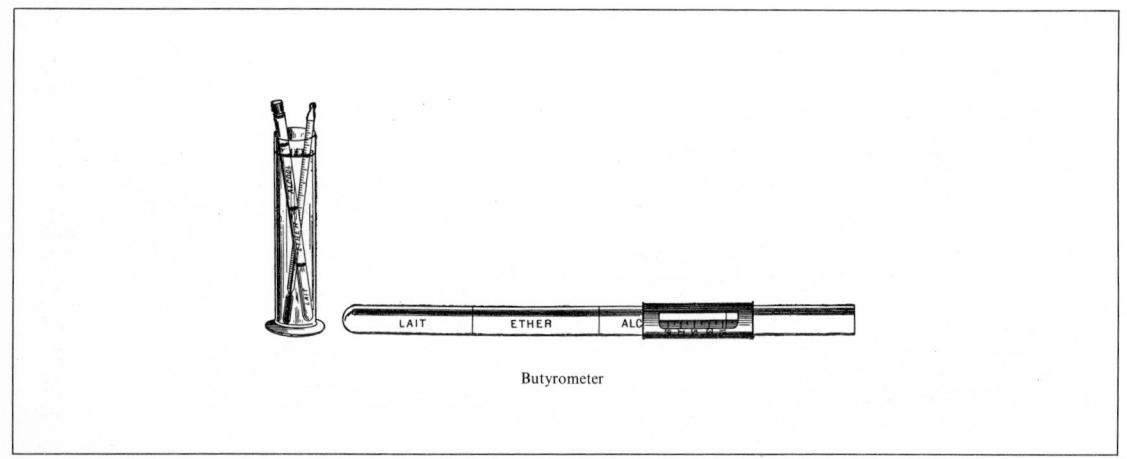

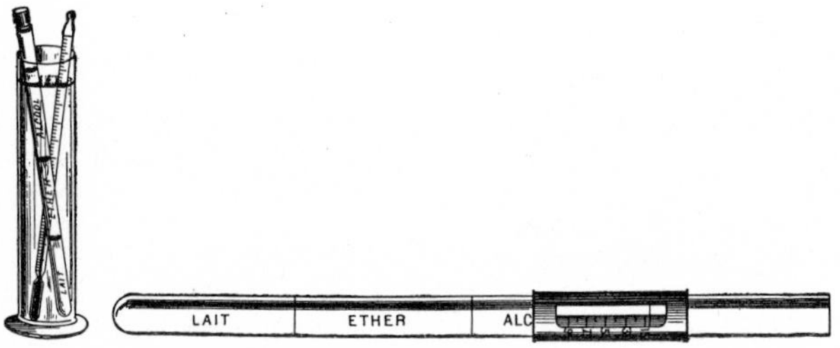

Butyrometer

CABARET – There are various opinions on the origin of this term, ranging from the ancient Hebrew *cabar* (to assemble) to the mediaeval Latin verb *cabare* (to dig or make a cave). In a general sense the term means a tavern where drinks can be consumed on the premises, and where food is sometimes served.

The name is linked to the original *courtille*, a rustic tavern situated near vineyards, 'a green oasis which became alive on holidays with a joyous throng of people who flocked there to find in pleasure a revenge against boredom.' The *courtilles* were reserved for carousing on feast days; some of them can be traced by streets which still exist, identified by the names of the vineyards round the *courtilles*. Thus the *clos Georgeot*, which spread its vineyards on the southern slopes of the butte Saint-Roch has given its name to a little street close to the Palais Royal; the *clos des Posteries*, traversed by the *rue des Postes*, is also represented by the *impasse des Vignes*.

These *clos*, or vineyards, the approaches to which were enlivened by the *courtilles*, were sometimes part of a nobleman's domain, and then the vineyards were well guarded – vines were forbidden fruit. Sometimes the crowd grew angry, and took revenge by rioting. The provost of merchants had his country seat, *courtille Barbette*, burnt down, together with his vineyards. 'And when they got to the *clos de la Ville-l'Evêque*, a famous episcopal *courtille*, it was not only caustic jibes that they aimed at the fat canons hiding under heavily laden climbing vines, who had gathered for a "theological banquet".

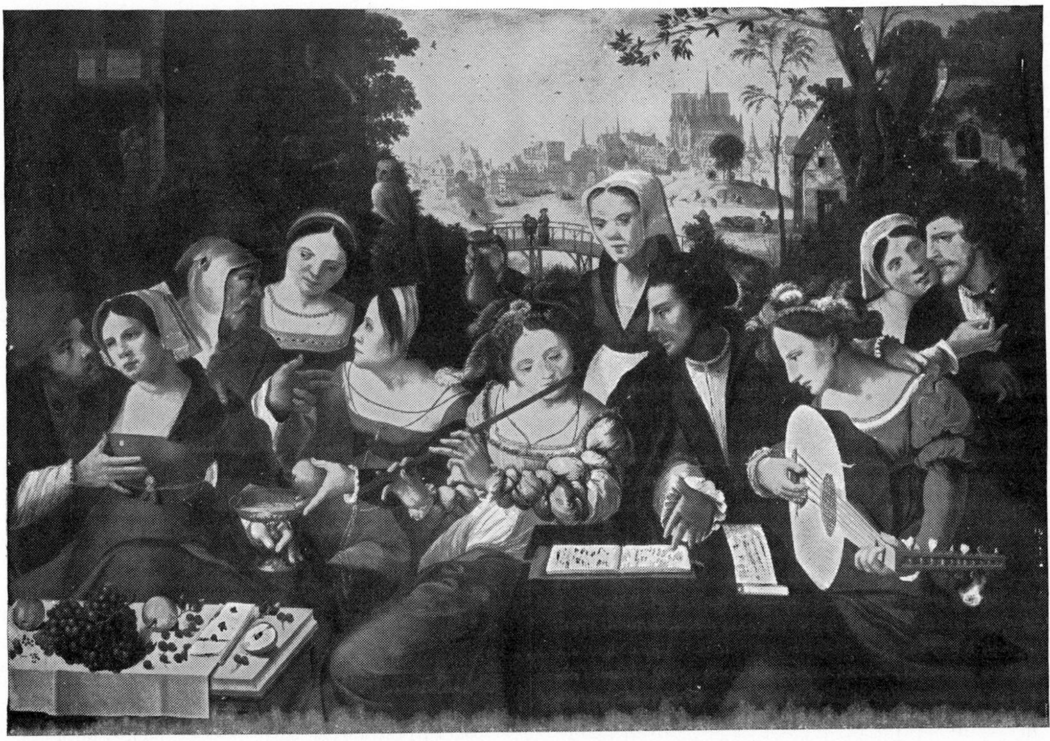

A cabaret during the reign of François I (*Flemish school*)

'When the holidays came the people felt they were free for a few days. They were not afraid to forget themselves beside a jug of wine, and when the hot sun rays invited them to leave their damp and smoky dwelling-places they would venture into the country, in groups, as far as the most distant *courtilles*.

'But, as we know, not every day is a holiday. Whilst fully conscious of the truth of this old axiom, the people did not feel any the less the need to satisfy their daily thirst during the week. On Sundays they could regard it as a duty.

'They needed therefore, in the absence of the *courtilles* reserved for carousing on good feast days, some place not far from their homes where they could minister to the caprices of this daily thirst. These places were the first *cabarets*.

'A drinker worthy of the name never mistook a *cabaret* for a tavern. In a tavern he could sit down at a table and drink but he could not do so in a *cabaret*; he had to drink outside.

'A stout wooden trellis-work guarded the entry to the houses of *cabaret* keepers. Through an opening cut in the trellis-work the publican handed the wine to the customer. He had to hold the jug, which he used as a measure, upside down to show that there was no possible way of drinking on his premises. Such were the official orders of the provost, and the inn-keeper had to abide by this method of selling "by means of a cut door and an overturned jug"!'

In the centuries which followed, the *cabarets* became identified with taverns, and the two words became synonymous.

Some *cabarets* which were frequented by writers, especially in the seventeenth century, acquired lasting fame. Among them were *le Mouton blanc* (in rue du Vieux-Colombier) where Racine, La Fontaine and Boileau used to meet; *le Sabot* (rue du Pot-de-Fer) where Ronsard would come in for a drink and which Chapelain also visited; *l'Ecu d'Argent*; *la Pomme de Pin* (rue de la Licorne), the meeting-place of the *scholars* mentioned by Rabelais. Notable among eighteenth century inns were *le Caveau* (on the Buci crossroads) where Collé, Piron and many other epicureans used to gather to sing their bawdy songs and where in 1737 the Caveau Society was formed; and *le Chat blanc* (rue de la Vieille-Lanterne).

CABARET (Liqueur stand) – A liqueur set, including glasses and decanters, presented either on a tray or in a special cabinet.

CABBAGE. CHOU – Highly esteemed by the Greeks and particularly by the Romans, the cabbage seems to have been unknown to the Hebrews. It is not mentioned in the Bible.

Apart from *seakale*, no species of cabbage survives in a wild state.

A great many new varieties have been developed through cultivation.

The three main classes of full-hearted cabbages are: the 'headed' smooth-leafed green cabbage, the Milan curly-leafed cabbage, and the red cabbage.

The spring 'headed' cabbage is usually conical and commonly known as 'pointed' cabbage. The summer or autumn 'headed' cabbage is rounder in shape and includes the varieties *de Boston* or *de Brunswick* and *quintal d'Alsace* which are often used in the manufacture of *sauerkraut*. Best known of the winter cabbages are *de Noël* and *de Vaugirard d'hiver*.

Milan cabbages have curly (occasionally crinkled) leaves. There are no less than twenty-five varieties.

Five varieties of red cabbage are cultivated in France. These are common to all regions and are in season throughout the year.

The cabbage is a particularly interesting vegetable from a nutritional point of view. It is rich in Vitamins B1 and B2 (essential for the assimilation of sugars and fats), in Vitamin C (it contains as much as a lemon), and in Vitamin K. Moreover, it contains large quantities of mineral salts: calcium, magnesium, potassium, sulphur, etc. Unfortunately, owing to its indigestibility, it requires prolonged cooking during which much of its nutritional value is lost. (This disadvantage can be partly overcome by shredding the cabbage finely and cooking it rapidly in a cupful of boiling water.) Dietetically speaking, it is best eaten raw.

GREEN CABBAGE. CHOUX VERTS –

Boiled cabbage. CHOU VERT À L'ANGLAISE – Cut a cabbage into quarters. Remove the fibrous part of the stem and the coarse outer leaves, cook in salt water until tender. Drain, press between two plates to extract the moisture, slice cabbage into rectangles.

Green cabbage prepared in this way is used as a vegetable served with melted butter, or as a garnish.

Braised cabbage. CHOU VERT BRAISÉ – Divide a cabbage into quarters, blanch, put under the cold tap, and then drain. Break up the cabbage and remove the thick portions of the stem. Season with salt, pepper and grated nutmeg. Line a deep casserole with strips of larding bacon, add the cabbage, an onion stuck with a clove, a large carrot cut into quarters, and a *bouquet garni* (q.v.). Moisten with stock which has not been skimmed of its fat (if there is no fat, add 3 tablespoons (scant ¼ cup) clarified fat to it). Cover with strips of fat bacon. Start cooking on top of the stove then cover the pan and put it in a moderate oven for about 1½ hours.

A piece of blanched lean pork can be added. Braised cabbage may be used as a vegetable but, more often, appears in a garnish.

Cabbage in marinade. CHOU VERT MARINÉ – Prepared like *Red cabbage in marinade* (see below).

Cabbage salad. SALADE DE CHOU VERT – Slice the cabbage finely, blanch for 15 minutes in salted water. Put under the cold tap, drain and dry. Season with oil, vinegar, salt and pepper like an ordinary green salad.

Little stuffed cabbage balls (*Larousse*)

Little stuffed cabbage balls. PETITS CHOUX POUR GARNITURE – Divide a large cabbage into quarters, wash, blanch for 8 to 10 minutes in salt water, rinse, and drain.

Remove all the leaves and trim them by paring the ribbed stalks. Make a stuffing with the tender inner leaves and an equal quantity of forcemeat. Put a round of stuffing on each leaf and roll into tight balls. Braise in the usual way.

Stuffed cabbage balls are used to garnish large braised joints. The cabbage leaves can be stuffed with all kinds of hashes or purées.

Stuffed cabbage a la provençale (*Robert Carrier*)

Stuffed cabbage (*Larousse*)

Stuffed cabbage. CHOU VERT FARCI – Blanch a whole cabbage in salted water, put it under the cold tap, drain, and remove the stem.

Spread out the cabbage on a damp cloth. Stuff the heart with a ball of fine pork stuffing. Close the leaves round this, and fill the outer leaves, closing them in to reform the shape of the cabbage. Wrap in thin strips of bacon fat and tie in the cloth. Put the cabbage in a braising pan lined with bacon rinds and slices of onion and carrot.

Cover with a fat stock and braise for about 1½ hours. Drain the cabbage and remove the bards. Serve with a sauce made of the cooking liquor boiled down and enriched with a little brown sauce. This stuffed cabbage, cut into thick slices, is served as a garnish for large joints.

The cabbage can be prepared in another way. Remove the heart, chop the tender leaves, mix with the stuffing and fill the cabbage with this mixture and braise it.

Stuffed cabbage à la provençale (Niçoise cookery). CHOU FARCI – Blanch a large cabbage for 8 minutes in salted water, rinse in cold water, and drain. Remove the large outer leaves and the ribbed stems. Spread these leaves out flat on a thin damp cloth stretched on the table and chop the inside leaves. Stuff the outer leaves with the chopped-up leaves and the following ingredients, arranged in layers: 250 g. (9 oz.) blanched best leaves; 200 g. (7 oz.) diced and browned lean pork; 1 medium-sized onion, chopped and lightly fried in butter; 2 large tomatoes, peeled, seeded and chopped; 100 g. (4 oz., ¾ cup) blanched rice; 100 g. (4 oz., ¾ cup) fresh green peas; 750 g. (1¾ lb.) sausage meat seasoned with a crushed garlic clove.

Fold the cabbage leaves round the stuffing in the form of a ball, tie up the cloth and put into a *pot-au-feu* prepared in the usual way but using mutton instead of beef. Cook slowly for about 3½ hours.

Drain the cabbage and pour a few tablespoons of the cooking liquor over it.

This dish, which is fundamental to the *cuisine niçoise*, can be served with the soup from the *pot-au-feu* in which it was cooked.

Stuffed cabbage rolls. CHOU VERT FARCI EN BALLOTTINE – Lay out slices of larding bacon on a damp cloth and place on top of them cabbage leaves which have been blanched, rinsed and dried, the leaves overlapping to form a rectangle. Put rolls of stuffing in the centre of the leaves, wrap them round the stuffing, and tie up in the cloth. Braise in the manner indicated above.

RED CABBAGE. CHOUX ROUGES –

Red cabbage à la flamande. CHOU ROUGE À LA FLAMANDE – Wash, quarter and shred the cabbage, removing the hard core and stem. Season with salt and pepper, and sprinkle with a few drops of vinegar. Cook slowly in butter. When three-quarters cooked add 3 peeled, quartered tart apples and 1 tablespoon brown sugar. Finish cooking on a low heat, the overall time being about 2 hours.

Red cabbage à la limousine. CHOU ROUGE À LA LIMOUSINE – Shred the cabbage and put it into an earthenware casserole. Moisten with bouillon and add 4 tablespoons (⅓ cup) pork fat, and chopped peeled chestnuts. Season with salt and pepper. Cook with the lid on for about 2 hours.

Red cabbage in marinade. CHOU ROUGE MARINÉ – Shred the cabbage after removing the hard core and ribs. Sprinkle with fine salt and leave for 48 hours, stirring from time to time.

Drain the cabbage and put it in an earthenware bowl with peppercorns, fragments of bay leaf, and a garlic clove. Cover with vinegar which has been boiled and allowed to cool. Marinate for 24 to 48 hours.

Red cabbage in marinade is used as an *hors-d'œuvre*. It is also served with boiled beef.

Stalks and stumps of red and green cabbage. MOELLE DE CHOU ROUGE ET CHOU VERT – The core of these vegetables is usually discarded, but it can be very tasty and can, if well cooked, provide very good dishes.

Remove all the woody outer casing. Blanch whole if it is to be served with the vegetable. If it is to be cooked separately, cut into rounds. After blanching, these stalks and stumps can be prepared in the same way as artichoke stalks or endive stumps.

CABBAGE PALM. PALMISTE – Terminal bud of several species of palm.

Cabbage palm en daube (Creole cookery). PALMISTE EN DAUBE – Parboil pieces of cabbage palm shoots cut lengthways into strips and tied in bundles to keep them together.

Brown in fat on a low heat for about 30 minutes. Add 1 tablespoon flour and blend it in, frying it lightly. Add ½ teaspoon tomato purée and moisten with concentrated chicken stock prepared in advance from chicken giblets.

Cook for several minutes, put in the oven for a while without allowing the top to brown, and serve in a little sauce.

CABERNET – Variety of vine grown extensively in the Bordeaux vineyards. There are two species: *cabernet-franc* and *cabernet-sauvignon*.

The red wines of Chinon, Bourgueil and Saumur-Champigny are also made from this grape. A well-known Anjou rosé bears the same name.

CACHALOT (Sperm-whale) – Sea mammal, the flesh of which is sometimes used as food.

Stuffed cabbage rolls

CACHOU. CACHUNDÉ – Aromatic tablets used in the Far East, to which stomachic properties are attributed. They are mainly used to freshen and sweeten breath and are made of amber, musk, sandalwood, sweet calamus, galingale, cinnamon, bole, etc.

Cadenas for the royal cutlery

CADENAS – Container, with grooves, which closed like a drawer. It was used in the royal households for the same purpose as the *nef*, a basket containing royal cutlery, napkins, etc. It held fork, knife and spoon, and bread was placed on the dish. Under Louis XIV it became a hexagonal tray on which napkin, fork, knife and spoon were placed. The grand pantler had the *nef* and the *cadenas* conjoined on his coat-of-arms.

CAFÉS – Establishments where, in principle, only liquid refreshments are served, originally only wine and coffee.

Suleiman Aga first brought coffee in large quantities to France in 1669. Later, an Armenian called Pascal opened a coffee shop at the Saint-Germain fair, and did a roaring trade. After the fair, he went to quai de l'École and opened a new shop but did not have the same success as at the Saint-Germain fair. He then went to London, where coffee had been known since 1652. After Pascal, another Armenian, Maliban, opened a café, but a little while later went to Holland, leaving his house to a man called Gregoire who moved his establishment to rue Mazarine to be near the Comédie which was then in that street, opposite rue Guénégaud.

At the same period in Paris a man called Candiol went about carrying a hawker's tray with domestic utensils. He also sold coffee, which could be taken home at the price of two *sous* a cup, including sugar. His associate, Joseph, opened a café at the end of Notre-Dame bridge, and Etienne, a Levantine from Aleppo, opened another in rue Saint-André-des-Arts, facing the Saint-Michel bridge. These cafés were really no more than dirty little smoking-saloons frequented by confirmed smokers, travellers from the Lebanon and by several Knights of Malta. The coffee sold in these shops was mediocre and badly served. By 1754 there were 56 cafés in Paris; by the end of the eighteenth century their numbers had risen to 600, of a much higher quality.

The cafés very soon replaced the *cabarets* as meeting-places for men of letters. Among literary cafés the first was the *Café du Parnasse* at the end of the Pont-Neuf, near the Samaritaine; then the *Veuve Laurent*, in rue Dauphine; and the *Café Procope* whose fame goes back to the eighteenth century when it counted among its regulars Buffon, Gilbert, Marmontel, Voltaire, d'Holbach, Diderot, d'Alembert and others.

The widow Fournier, whose café in rue Saint-Antoine was founded by Baptiste in 1690, was the first to think of the idea of providing her regular customers with newspapers. She subscribed to *Gazette de France, Mercure* and *Journal des Savants*. The *Café des Grâces*, in rue de l'Arbre-Sec, was the first establishment in Paris to have public billiards. The *Café de la Régence* became the meeting-place of chess-players, and Jean-Jacques Rousseau tried his skill there against the celebrated Philidor. During the Revolution the cafés played an important rôle as meeting-places of secret committees of members of the National Convention and as tribunes for orators.

The Palais-Royal cafés, too, have had their hour of fame: *Café de Foy*, *Café de la Rotonde*, *Café Corazza* and *Café Lamblin* were the meeting-places of Bonapartist officers on half-pay.

Under the Second Empire the Boulevard cafés, *Café Riche* and, above all, *Café Frascati*, were the meeting-places of writers, dramatists and journalists. When *Frascati's* disappeared, it was replaced by *Café Napolitain*. In the Latin Quarter, Jean Moréas held court at *Café Vachette*.

Today the cafés, although more numerous and more luxurious than ever, have not the same political and literary influence, with the exception perhaps of a few Left Bank

A café in 1830 (*Schaal*)

establishments, which still serve as meeting-places for young literary and artistic movements. (See RESTAURANTS OF BYGONE DAYS.)

CAFFEINE. CAFÉINE – Alkaloid substance contained in coffee, which acts on the nervous system. A moderate amount of coffee soothes, eliminates the feeling of tiredness and exhaustion, makes mental work easier, dispels drowsiness. A bigger dose can bring on nervous excitation, trembling, insomnia.

Coffee has a stimulating effect on the heart if taken in moderation; excessive coffee drinking causes palpitations and irregularity of the heartbeat.

Coffee also acts as a digestive stimulant, speeding the passage of food through the body (and often causing diarrhoea). It can have a diuretic effect. On the other hand, cases of articular deformation, cited by Brillat-Savarin, are not caused by excessive intake of coffee.

Coffee (especially strong black coffee) must not be given to children, adolescents, people of nervous disposition or those suffering from heart conditions; nor should it be given to certain dyspeptics.

Although Voltaire, who drank six cups of coffee daily, was loud in its praise, his over-indulgence could have had a bearing on the enterocolitis from which he suffered to the end of his life.

Finally, black coffee ought never to be drunk on an empty stomach and white coffee is even worse for the system than black.

CAILLEBOTTE (Curds) – Name given in certain regions of France to curdled milk, drained in a muslin bag and eaten fresh.

CAILLETOT – Name commonly used in Normandy for young turbot.

CAILLIER – Wooden vessel used in the Middle Ages and until the end of the sixteenth century as a drinking cup. It was made in the shape of a bowl of average size supported by a leg, the whole carved out of one piece of wood. There were also bowls made in a larger size which served as containers for wine, the bowl-shaped lids being used as drinking vessels.

CAISSETTES – Small garnished cases offered as hot *hors-d'œuvre* or as a small *entrée.* (See HORS-D'ŒUVRE, *Hot hors-d'œuvre*.)

CAKE. GÂTEAU – The word *gâteau* is said to come from the word *gasteau*, which itself derives from the old term *gastel*, a delicate food that quickly deteriorates (*gâter* – to spoil).

The generic term *gâteau* or cake designates all types of pastry and cakes in the strict sense of the term, while the word *entremets* or sweet (U.S. dessert) applies more especially to sweet preparations such as creams, fritters, charlottes, tarts, flans and pies, puddings, soufflés and all kinds of ices, which belong to the domain of the cook rather than that of the confectioner.

Cakes are made from any of eight doughs in French confectionery: flake pastry (*feuilletage*), short pastry (*pâte brisée*), sweet pastry (*pâte sucrée*), brioche, *savarin*, baba, *génoise*, *chou pastry*.

To these may be added a large number of mixtures of additional ingredients such as almond paste, various kinds of sugar icing, fondant, French pastry cream (*crème pâtissière*), frangipane cream and other creams, praline (q.v.), etc.

In France, as well as in many other countries, there are symbolic cakes which, in some cases, have been being made for centuries, and are eaten on certain feast days. One such is the Twelfth-Night cake, which symbolises the great feast of the Epiphany.

Ancient gâteaux or centre-pieces, after Carême: Turkish pavilion; Ruins of a rotunda; Large fountain

Large cakes: Dijon; Madasgar; St James (*Larousse*)

In France, from the very earliest times, a large number of provinces have produced pastries for which they are noted.

Thus Artois had *gâteaux razis*, and Bourbonnais the ancient *tartes de fromage broyé, de crème et de moyeux d'oeulz*. Flat-cakes are still made in Normandy, Picardy, Poitou and in some provinces of the south of France. They are called variously *fouaces, fouaches, fouées* or *fouyasses*, according to the district. (See HEARTH-CAKE.)

Until the seventeenth century it was usual at Whitsuntide in Paris to throw down *nieules* and *oublies* (wafers), local Parisian confections, upon the heads of the worshippers gathered under the vaulted roofs of the Cathedral of Notre-Dame. At the same time blazing wicks were showered on the congregation.

Among the many pastries which were in high favour from the twelfth to the fifteenth centuries in Paris and other cities were: *échaudés* of which two variants, the *flageols* and the *gobets*, were especially prized by the people of Paris; and *darioles* (q.v.), small tartlets covered with narrow strips of pastry. Two kinds of *darioles* were made, one filled with cream cheese, the other with frangipane cream. *Talemouses* which are known today as *talmouses* (cheese turnovers) were also much appreciated. (See HORS-D'ŒUVRES, *Hot hors-d'œuvre*.)

Casse-museau (q.v.) is a dry, hard pastry still made today; *ratons, petits choux* and *gâteaux feuilletés* are mentioned in a charter by Robert, Bishop of Amiens in 1311, which proves that flaky pastry was known in France before the seventeenth century, when, some writers claim, the process of making flaky pastry was invented by Claude Gelée, the painter.

In the following centuries, pastry-cooks, organised into guilds, produced not only the pastries listed above, but also *gâteaux bavueuls, gâteaux joyeux, brioches, bridaneaux, pains d'épices*, waffles of various kinds, marzipan biscuits, tarts and flans garnished in various ways; *pâtes royales* which were a kind of meringue; almond cakes, dough cakes, *gâteaux de Beauce*; *gâteaux de Milan*, cracknels and *flamiches*. (See FESTIVE COOKERY.)

CAKES AND SMALL CAKES – We list below some of the best known gâteaux and small cakes. Recipes for many of them will be found in this section or in alphabetical order throughout the book.

Alcazar, Allumettes, Almond cake, Amandines, Angel cake, Apple cake.

Baba, Bâton de Jacob, Biscuits de Bruxelles, Biscuits à la cuiller, Biscuits de Savoie, Bouchées à l'abricot, Boule de neige, Brestois, Breton, Brioche, Brioche Goubaud, Briochin.

Chausson aux pommes, Cornets à la crème, Conversation, Croquembouche.

Dampfnudeln, Darioles, Dartois, Dijon, Duchesse, Dumpling.

Échaudés, Éclairs.

Feuilleté aux amandes, Flan aux abricots, Flan aux abricots à l'alsacienne, Flan aux cerises, Flan aux fruits, Flan meringué, Flan aux mirabelles, Flan aux pêches, Flan aux poires, Flan aux pommes, Flan aux pommes grillé, Flan aux prunes.

Galette feuilletée, Galette à l'orange, Gâteau de citrouille, Gâteau de voyage, Génoise à l'abricot, Génoise au chocolat, Génoise au moka, Génoise à la normande, Gimblette, Gorenflot, Gougère.

Jalousie, Kiche, Koulitsche, Kouglof, Langues de chat.

Macaroons, Madasgar, Madeira cake, Madeleines, Malgache, Manchons, Mandarine, Manqué, Marignan, Mascotte, Massepain, Massillon, Mazarin, Meringues, Merveilles, Milanais, Millefeuilles, Millasous, Mirliton de Rouen, Moka, Mokatine, Moques, Monte-Cristo, Montmorency, Mousseline.

Small cakes (*Desmeuzes. Phot. Larousse*)

Buns (*Claire*)

Nantais, Napolitain, Nemours, Néroli, Norvégien, Nougat, Nougatine.

Oublies, Pain anglais, Pain à l'anis, Pain azyme, Pain complet, Pain de maïs, Pain de la Mecque, Palais de dames, Palmiers, Paneton, Parisien, Pastis du Béarn, Pavé au chocolat, Pavé aux fruits, Pavé au moka, Pavé aux noisettes, Pithiviers, Plum cake, Pogne de Romans, Pont-neuf, Poupelin, Profiteroles, Punch cake, Puits d'amour.

Quatre-quarts, Quiche, Quillet.

Rabotte, Ramequin, Religieuse, Richelieu, Rigodon.

Gâteau Saint-Honoré (*Larousse*)

Sablés, Sacristains, Saint-Honoré, Saint-James, Saint-Michel, Savarin, Savarin à la crème, Savarin aux cerises, Schaleth à la juive, Shortbread, Solilème, Souvarov, Spéculos, Strizel, Strudel, Sultane.

Tarte alsacienne, Tarte aux fruits à l'allemande, Tarte aux fruits à l'anglaise, Tarte aux fruits, Tarte des demoiselles Tatin, Tarte au riz, Tarte à la rhubarbe, Tartelettes, Tôt-fait, Trois-frères.

Vacherin, Victoria cake.

Almond cake – See ALMOND.

Angel cake (American pastry) – Whisk 8 egg whites stiffly, add 1 teaspoon cream of tartar dissolved in a little water, and 275 g. (10 oz., 1¼ cups) sugar.

Fold in 100 g. (4 oz., 1 cup) sifted flour and a few drops vanilla essence or 1½ teaspoons vanilla-flavoured sugar. Whisk lightly, and pour into a large, unbuttered angel cake pan with a centre tube.

Bake in a moderate oven (160°C., 325°F., Gas Mark 3) for 45 minutes to 1 hour. Invert the tin on a cake rack and cool before taking the cake out of the mould.

Apple cake – See APPLE.

Christmas yule log. BÛCHE DE NOËL – Symbolic cake sold by French confectioners at Christmas time. It is made of *Genoese cake* (see GENOESE) spread with various creams, usually a butter cream. It is rolled into the shape of a log and decorated by icing the cake with lengthwise strips of chocolate or coffee butter cream to represent the bark of the log.

At Christmas another symbolic cake is made in France. It is shaped like a wooden shoe, made of nougat and decorated with *petits fours* (q.v.).

Easter cake, German (Ostertorte) – Make a sponge cake dough of 125 g. (4½ oz., generous cup) sifted flour, 100 g. (4 oz., ½ cup) sugar, 5 eggs (yolks and whites separated) and 100 g. (4 oz., ½ cup) butter.

Bake in a moderately hot oven (190°C., 375°F., Gas Mark 5) for 40 to 45 minutes. Turn the cake out of the mould, allow to cool, and cut it across into halves. Spread one half with coffee-flavoured butter cream. Place the halves together and ice the cake with *Fondant icing* (see ICING). Decorate with a border of butter cream piped through a forcing-bag and with chocolate eggs, each sitting on a nest of the same cream. In the centre of the cake place a chick made

German Easter cake (Ostertorte)

of sugar surrounded by 4 small chocolate eggs, each in its nest of butter cream.

Fruit loaf or Bireweck (Alsation pastry). PAIN DE FRUITS – *Ingredients.* 1 kg. (2¼ lb., 9 cups) sieved flour, 25 g. (1 oz., 1 cake) yeast, 500 g. (generous 1 lb.) fresh or dried pears, 250 g. (9 oz.) fresh or dried apples, 250 g. (9 oz.) prunes, 250 g. (9 oz.) dried figs, 250 g. (9 oz.) peaches, 125 g. (4½ oz., ¾ cup) stoned (U.S. pitted) dates, 250 g. (9 oz., 1½ cups) seedless raisins, 100 g. (4 oz., ⅔ cup) chopped citron candied peel, 50 g. (2 oz., ⅓ cup) chopped angelica, 100 g. (4 oz., ⅔ cup) whole almonds, 100 g. (4 oz., ¾ cup) hazelnuts, 100 g. (4 oz., 1 cup) shelled walnuts, 50 g. (2 oz., ⅓ cup) each of lemon and orange rind cut into *julienne* strips, 50 g. (2 oz.) star anise, a pinch of spices, and 2 tablespoons (3 tablespoons) kirsch.

Method. Cook the pears, apples, prunes, peaches and figs in water, keeping them rather firm. Make the dough, using the flour and yeast and moistening with the juice in which the fruit was cooked. Leave the dough to rise for 2 hours.

Add the well-drained fruit to the risen dough and mix well. Add the raisins, almonds, hazelnuts, walnuts, dates, citron candied peel, angelica, orange and lemon peel, anise and spices. Moisten with kirsch and blend well.

Divide the paste into 200-g. (7-oz.) pieces, shape them into small loaves, brush with water and bake in a slow oven for 1¾ hours.

Genoa cake. PAIN DE GÊNES – Pound 500 g. (18 oz., 3½ cups) blanched almonds to a powder and add 325 g. (12 oz., 1½ cups) sugar. Stir with a wooden spoon and add 5 eggs one by one. Stir the mixture for 10 minutes and add 100 g. (4 oz., scant cup) cornflour, a little powdered vanilla, 1 tablespoon Curaçao and 150 g. (5 oz., 10 tablespoons) melted butter, lifting the batter to aerate it. Pour the mixture into buttered cake tins lined with buttered paper. Bake in a moderate oven.

Genoa cake will keep well for 5 or 6 days.

Another method is to pound 375 g. (13 oz., generous 1½ cups) fine sugar in a mortar with 6 eggs and 2 drops bitter almond essence. When the mixture is frothy, add 65 g. (2½ oz., 10 tablespoons) sieved flour and 125 g. (4½ oz., 9 tablespoons) melted butter. Blend well. Pour the mixture into lined and buttered cake tins and bake in a moderate oven.

Kulich (Russian Easter cake) – Place 1½ kg. (3¼ lb., 13 cups) flour in a warm bowl and make a well in the centre. Into this pour 25 g. (1 oz., 1 cake) yeast dissolved in a little warm milk and mixed with a little flour to make a leaven. Work the yeast mixture into the flour, cover the bowl and stand the dough to rise in a warm place for 1¼ hours.

Add 500 g. (18 oz., 2¼ cups) half-melted butter, 10 eggs, 250 g. (9 oz., generous cup) fine sugar and a pinch of salt. Beat the mixture until it is no longer sticky and comes away cleanly from the bowl.

Gradually work in 1 kg. (2¼ lb., 9 cups) flour, beating the dough lightly until it is thoroughly mixed. Add 250 g. (9 oz., 1½ cups) each of cleaned sultanas, currants and raisins. Leave the dough to rise again in a warm place. When well risen, turn it onto a floured table, keeping a small piece to decorate the cake. Make the rest of the dough into a large ball and place in a large, well-buttered baking tin.

Roll out the reserved dough and cut it into long, wide strips. Twist the strips and decorate the cake with them. Allow the cake to rise again for 30 minutes. Brush with a mixture of egg yolk and sugar, sprinkle chopped almonds on top, and bake in a hot oven.

It is customary in Russia to ice and decorate the top of the cake.

Maids of honour. DEMOISELLES D'HONNEUR – The recipe for these cakes, which enjoyed a great reputation in England, was for a long time kept secret. History relates that Anne Boleyn, then a maid of honour at the English Court, first made these cakes in the hope of pleasing King Henry VIII who was fond of his food. King Henry, finding them excellent, called them 'maids of honour', which has been their name ever since.

The secret recipe for the cakes was said to have been bought for £1000. Maids of honour were the speciality of Richmond (Surrey), where a confectioner claimed to have the secret recipe, and to make the only true maids of honour, which he sent out daily to all parts of the country.

The cakes are little tarts of light puff pastry, with a filling made of egg, ground almonds and lemon.

Mecca cakes. PAINS DE LA MECQUE – The paste for these is the same as *Chou paste* (see CHOU).

Force the paste through a pastry-bag in the shape of little eggs onto a metal baking sheet. Brush with beaten egg, sprinkle with granulated sugar and bake in a hot oven.

Plum cake – English cake which is prepared as follows:

Soften 500 g. (18 oz., 2¼ cups) butter until creamy, and whisk until it turns white. Add 500 g. (18 oz., 2¼ cups) sugar. Whisk again for a few minutes, and add, one by one, 8 or 9 eggs, whisking all the time. Add 250 g. (9 oz., 1½ cups) chopped candied peel (lemon and orange), 200 g. (7 oz., 1¼ cups) stoned (U.S. pitted) raisins, 150 g. (5 oz., 1 cup) best sultanas and 150 g. (5 oz., 1 cup) currants.

Add 500 g. (18 oz., 4½ cups) sifted flour mixed with 1½ teaspoons baking powder; the grated rind of 2 lemons and ½ dl. (3 tablespoons, scant ¼ cup) rum.

Line a cake-tin with greased paper, so that it extends 4 cm. (1½ inches) above the rim of the tin. Pour the mixture into the tin, taking care not to fill it over two-thirds. Bake in a moderate oven for 3 to 4 hours, reducing heat after 1 hour.

Punch cake – Fill a charlotte mould with *Savoy sponge-cake mixture* (see SPONGE CAKES). Bake the cake, turn out, and leave for two days.

Cut the cake into three horizontal slices of equal thickness, soak them in rum and cover with apricot jam. Decorate with meringue and finish in the oven.

Meringue for the punch cake. Mix 100 g. (4 oz., ⅓ cup) finely sieved apricot jam, ½ dl. (3 tablespoons, scant ¼ cup) rum, 1 tablespoon Curaçao, 100 g. (4 oz., ½ cup) fine sugar. Fold in 6 stiffly beaten egg whites.

Spice cake. PAIN D'ÉPICE – Rye flour should be used for spiced loaf, but ordinary wheat flour can be used. It is not necessary to use best quality honey for this cake.

Heat 500 g. (18 oz., 1½ cups) honey nearly to boiling point and remove the scum. Put 500 g. (18 oz., 4½ cups) sieved bread flour into a bowl, pour the honey into a well in the centre and stir. It may be necessary to add more flour to make a firm paste. Form the paste into a ball, wrap in a cloth and leave to prove. After 1 hour add 12 g. (½ oz.) powdered yeast (dried chemical yeast which is used without moistening) and knead vigorously.

Another method is to mix 500 g. (18 oz., 4½ cups) sieved bread flour and 500 g. (18 oz., 1½ cups) honey, leave to stand, and knead as described above, adding 100 g. (4 oz., ½ cup) fine sugar, 12 g. (½ oz.) dried yeast, used as indicated above, 1¼ teaspoons baking powder, 50 g. (2 oz., ½ cup) blanched, dried and chopped almonds, 25 g. (1 oz., 1½ tablespoons) each of chopped candied orange and lemon peel.

The following can also be added to this dough: 10 g. (½ oz.) aniseed, a pinch of cinnamon, a pinch of powdered cloves, and ½ tablespoon grated or chopped lemon or orange peel.

Roll out either dough to the desired thickness and put it on a buttered baking sheet, or into baking tins. Bake in a moderate oven. As soon as the cake is cooked brush the surface with milk sweetened with sugar (it should be like a thick syrup) and leave for a few seconds in the oven. The milk can be replaced by sugar syrup, cooked to a thread (see SUGAR).

Twelfth-Night cakes. GÂTEAUX DES ROIS – The custom of baking Twelfth-Night cakes is still observed and the celebration that takes place in most French homes when the Twelfth-Night cake is eaten, is a relic of the pagan feast called the *Basilinda.* The name *phoebe* which is given to the bean or symbolic favour baked in the cake, is believed to be a corruption of the word *éphèbe* 'a son of the house' given by the Romans to the child who, hidden under the table, pointed out the guest chosen to receive the piece which held the *phoebe.*

In the seventeenth century the ceremonial was vigorously attacked by the priests of Saint-Germain, but attention had been drawn much earlier to the excesses to which this custom could give rise. Pasquier quotes a passage from a manuscript by Thomas Neargorgus, which refers to the festival:

'Many come together to dine then, and elect a king by lot or vote. This king chooses ministers for himself. Next, he opens the feast which lasts for several days, the celebrations continuing until there are only empty purses left, and the creditors come to be paid.

'Their sons then make haste to follow their example. They, too, elect a king and hold sumptuous banquets either with stolen money, or at their parents' expense, thereby learning luxury and larceny at one and the same time.

'Finally, on the same day, the head of the family, the good master, causes to be brought forth, according to his means and the number of his guests, a cake in which has been hidden a silver coin which must serve as a token. He cuts the cake into as many pieces as there are members of his family present and gives each one his piece. At the same time, he keeps back one for the infant Jesus, one for the Virgin and one for the Magi, in whose names he then gives these to the poor. Whosoever receives the piece containing the silver coin is recognised as king, and all the guests shout for joy.'

Although the ceremonial attending the distribution of the cake is now shorter and rather different from what it used to be, custom still demands that the king or queen chosen at the feast should in turn give a dinner-party at which the symbolic cake is served.

The cake varies in different regions of France. In Paris and the Île-de-France the cake is a flaky pastry *galette* (q.v.). In the south the cake is made from yeast dough, similar to brioche dough, and shaped like a crown.

Bordeaux Twelfth-Night cake. Place 500 g. (18 oz., 4½ cups) flour in a ring on the table with 20 g. (¾ oz.) yeast and

1½ teaspoons salt in the middle. Knead the dough, adding 8 whole eggs, one by one, grated rind of 1 lemon, 200 g. (7 oz., scant cup) sugar, and 200 g. (7 oz., scant cup) softened butter. Mix these ingredients thoroughly. Leave the dough, which should be limp, to rise in a warm place overnight.

Next day, knock down the dough as for *Brioche dough* (see DOUGH), divide into equal parts each shaped into a crown, place on buttered paper and leave to rise in a warm cupboard. Leave the crowns to cool and brush with beaten egg. Decorate with slices of citron and crystallised sugar, and bake in a moderate oven.

Another method is to make a yeast dough of 250 g. (9 oz., 2¼ cups) sieved flour and 20 g. (¾ oz.) yeast. Add water, to make the dough limp, and leave it to rise in a warm place.

Make a well in the centre of 1 kg. (2¼ lb., 9 cups) sieved flour, and add 8 whole eggs and a pinch of salt. Make a lukewarm syrup with 250 g. (9 oz., generous cup) sugar, the grated rinds of 2 lemons and 2 oranges, a 3-dl. (½-pint, 1¼-cup) mixture of orange-flower water, water and rum, and stir gently. Add to the other ingredients in the well, mix gradually with the flour and when well blended add the yeast dough. Mix thoroughly.

Place the dough in a floured bowl, leaving it in a warm place to rise. Knock down the dough and then shape it into a crown on a floured table. Place the crown on a baking sheet covered with buttered paper and decorate the top with pieces of citron. Leave to rise. Brush the cake with egg yolk and bake in a cool oven (150°C., 300°F., Gas Mark 2) for 1¼ hours.

Limoux Twelfth-Night cake. This cake, also in the shape of a crown, is made from dough similar to that used for the *Bordeaux Twelfth-Night cake*, but is richly decorated with candied citron.

Wedding cake. GÂTEAU DE NOCE – In England the centrepiece of the wedding reception is the wedding cake. This cake, made in 2 or 3 tiers, is a symbol rather than a delicacy; a tradition handed down from one century to the next. The cake must be large as each wedding guest is given a slice and pieces are sent in decorated boxes to absent relations and friends.

The ingredients are: 1 kg. (2¼ lb., 4½ cups) butter, 1 kg. (2¼ lb., 4½ cups) sugar, 500 g. (18 oz., 4½ cups) ground almonds or pounded almonds, 500 g. (18 oz., 3⅓ cups) chopped candied peel, 500 g. (18 oz., 3⅓ cups) each of stoned (U.S. pitted) raisins, sultanas and currants, 1¼ kg. (2¾ lb., 11 cups) flour sieved with 2 teaspoons baking powder, 16 to 18 whole eggs, according to size, 15 g. (½ oz., 2 tablespoons) allspice, 1 dl. (6 tablespoons, scant ½ cup) rum. Line the bottom and sides of three graduated round cake tins with buttered paper and fill with the mixture. Bake in a cool oven (150°C., 300°F., Gas Mark 2). Test with a skewer after 3 hours, and then at half-hourly intervals until cooked.

The cake should be made several days before decorating it, to give the mixture time to settle. Trim each tier so that it is flat and round, then spread with apricot jam and cover completely with a layer of almond paste, ½ cm. (¼ inch) thick. Level the tops of the tiers with a rolling-pin. After 24 hours, ice each tier, covering all parts which will be visible when they are put on top of one another. Arrange the tiers on a low stand.

Decorate the cake with motifs made by forcing *Royal icing* (see ICING) through a piping-bag, and place an ornamental motif or spray of flowers on the top tier.

CAKE RACK or TRAY. GRILLE – Flat tray, made from wire-mesh, on which cakes are put to cool when they are taken from the oven.

CALABASH GOURD or BOTTLE GOURD. CALEBASSE – Fruit of the calabash tree of which several species are known. One species has long leaves and a hard green shell with acid white pulp inside, which is made into a syrup in tropical America and the West Indies. The gourds are made into Calabash pipes (imported from South Africa), drinking vessels and other articles.

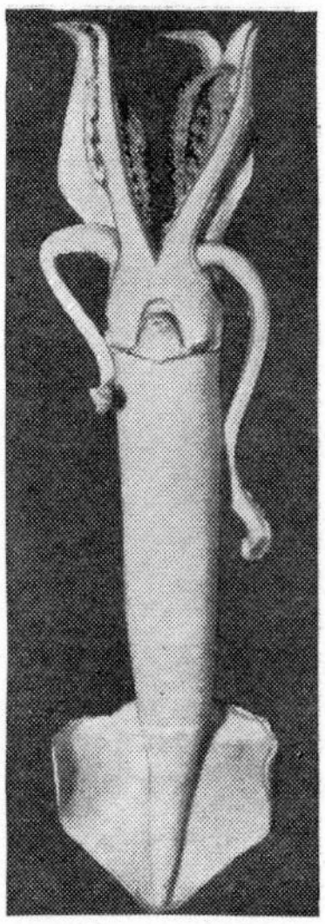

Calamary

Calappa

CALAMARY (Squid). CALMAR – Common name for certain varieties of *cephalopoda*, which have elongated bodies, and arms or tentacles with suckers on the tips. They are found mainly in mid-ocean depths or far out to sea, but come to spawn near the coasts.

Like cuttlefish, calamary have a bag situated near the heart which contains a dark inky liquid used in painting under the name of sepia.

This mollusc is considered a great delicacy in the Mediterranean region. Calamaries *in su tinta* (in their ink) is a Spanish speciality.

Stuffed calamary (squid) à la marseillaise. CALMAR FARCI À LA MARSEILLAISE – Take 4 calamaries, remove the black ink bag, the cranial cartilage and the tentacles. Wash the body sacs and place them flat on a cloth.

Fry a finely chopped onion in a few tablespoons oil, add the finely chopped tentacles and 2 or 3 chopped tomatoes. Season and fry together. Soak a piece of French bread in milk, squeeze it out and add it to the pan with 2 garlic cloves chopped with parsley. Blend well, moisten with 2 tablespoons (3 tablespoons) hot water, add 2 or 3 egg yolks and remove from the heat. Fill the calamaries three-quarters full with the resulting forcemeat, which should be fairly thick. Sew them up and put them one by one into a pan with some oil.

Fry separately a finely chopped onion and add a bay leaf and a crushed clove of garlic. Blend in 1 tablespoon flour and moisten with 1 glass each of white wine and hot water. Season with salt and pepper and simmer for 15 minutes. Strain this sauce over the calamaries, sprinkle with breadcrumbs and oil and gently brown the top.

CALAPPA (Box crab). CALAPPE (COQ DE MER) – Shellfish which has a certain similarity to the crab.

CALEFACTION. CALÉFACTION – Action of warming. Phenomenon whereby a drop of water hitting a very hot surface takes on a spheroid shape and does not dissipate immediately because of the layer of steam which seals it off.

CALF. VEAU – See also VEAL.

Calves' brains – See OFFAL or VARIETY MEATS.

Calf's crow. FRAISE DE VEAU – Membrane which covers the intestines of the calf. This may be cooked in various ways (see OFFAL or VARIETY MEATS *Calf's mesentery*.)

However the crow is to be prepared, it must first be cooked in a flour-and-water stock, as for *Calf's head* (see below).

Calf's ears. OREILLES DE VEAU – Calf's ears must be well cleaned and blanched before use. (See OFFAL or VARIETY MEATS.)

Calf's feet. PIEDS DE VEAU – Blanch and cook the feet in a flour-and-water stock, like *Calf's head.* (See OFFAL or VARIETY MEATS.)

Calf's head. TÊTE DE VEAU – Calf's head is blanched, cooked in a flour-and-water stock and served *à la vinaigrette*. (See OFFAL or VARIETY MEATS.)

Calf's heart. COEUR DE VEAU – All the recipes for calf's kidneys are suitable for calf's heart, which may be cooked whole, braised, pot roasted or roasted. (See OFFAL or VARIETY MEATS.)

Calf's kidneys – See OFFAL or VARIETY MEATS.

Calf's liver – See OFFAL or VARIETY MEATS.

Calves' sweetbreads. RIS DE VEAU – Considered the most delicate of the white offal meats. They can be cooked whole, sliced in *médaillons*, or in various other ways. (See OFFAL or VARIETY MEATS.)

Calf's udder. TÉTINE DE VEAU – Mostly used in Jewish cookery, taking the place of bacon fat. After being soaked in cold water and blanched, the udder can be braised.

CALORIE – Unit of heat. The *small calorie* is the amount of heat necessary to raise 1 g. of water by 1°C. The *large calorie* is equal to 1000 small calories. The calorie is used as a unit in expressing the heat and energy-producing qualities of food.

Food substances are the combination of results produced by the energy borrowed from solar radiations – the source of all energy on earth. On decomposition, which is effected first by digestion and then by the transformations which they undergo in our organism, these substances restore lost energy which can be measured by the heat released.

Experiments have enabled scientists to establish the coefficients of calories released by albuminoids, fats and carbohydrates. Knowledge of the composition of a food product makes it possible to calculate its value in energy, measured in calories. These figures are only approximate and average, and too rigid conclusions should not be drawn from them.

Nutritional experts have devised slimming diets called 'low-calorie diets' based entirely on the calorie content of foods.

CALVADOS – Famous apple brandy from the Normandy region of the same name.

CAMBACÉRÈS (Jean-Jacques, duc de) – Cambacérès who was born at Montpellier in 1753 and died at Paris in 1824 was the second consul appointed by Bonaparte after the *coup d'état*. Marco de Saint-Hilaire wrote in his diary, 'Yesterday I had the honour of being admitted to the table of Consul Cambacérès and I must confess that out of the four courses – each of which consisted of at least sixteen or eighteen dishes, and about a quarter of which I had no chance of tasting – every single one would have been approved by Lucullus or Apicius, of gastronomical memory. Under the Republic, *cuisine* in France has made enormous steps forward, and I proclaim it to be the best in the world.'

Cambacérès (1753–1824)

Cambacérès prepared his dinners (himself compiling the menus) with meticulous care and good taste. In his *Mémoires* Bourienne tells us: 'During the Congress of Lunéville, the first consul, on being informed that mail coaches were carrying a lot of goods, in particular delicacies for the table of prominent persons, gave an order that henceforward postal services were to carry nothing but despatches. That evening, Cambacérès came into the salon, where I was alone with the first consul, who was already laughing at the embarrassment caused to his colleague. "Well, what can you want at this hour, Cambacérès?" "I have come to ask you to make one exception in the order you have given the director of post. How do you expect us to make friends with people if we can't give them elegant dishes? You know yourself that, to a great extent, it is at one's table that one governs." The first consul laughed a great deal, called him a glutton and finished by slapping him on the shoulder and saying, "Console yourself, my poor Cambacérès, and don't be angry. The mail coaches will continue to carry your truffled turkeys, your Strasbourg *pâtés*, your Mayence hams and your partridges."'

CAMBRAI (Boulette de) – See CHEESE.

CAMEL. CHAMEAU – Large mammals with one or two humps. The former are known as dromedaries and the latter as bactrians. Moses forbade the Israelites to eat camel's meat. The Arabs are not bound by this edict, but only eat camels when they are young and the meat is tender.

From the time of Gallien, camel's meat was regarded with favour. Aristophanes maintains that it was served to royalty, and Aristotle praises it.

The hump, the feet and the stomach are the parts most appreciated by connoisseurs. Camel's milk is excellent.

Camel couscous (Arab cooking). COUSCOUS AU CHAMEAU – Prepare the couscous in the usual way, but substitute young camel's meat for the mutton (see COUSCOUS).

Camel escalopes with pimentos and aubergines. TRANCHES DE CHAMEAU AUX POIVRONS ET AUBERGINES – Sauté in butter slices of camel meat taken from the sirloin, which have been marinated in oil, lemon juice, salt, pepper and spices.

Drain the slices and set them on a dish. Put on each slice two rounds of aubergines sautéed in oil. Pour over them the juices of the meat to which have been added 2 sweet pimentos, peeled, cut into strips and cooked in oil; $1\frac{1}{2}$ dl. ($\frac{1}{4}$ pint, $\frac{2}{3}$ cup) white wine; 3 dl. ($\frac{1}{2}$ pint, $1\frac{1}{4}$ cups) tomato purée; and a little garlic. Sprinkle with chopped parsley.

Camel's feet à la vinaigrette. PIEDS DE CHAMEAU À LA VINAIGRETTE – Soak the feet of a young camel and cook in a white *court-bouillon* in the same way as for *Calf's feet* (see OFFAL or VARIETY MEATS). Drain, and serve with *Vinaigrette sauce* (see SAUCE).

Roast camel's fillet. FILET DE CHAMEAU RÔTI – Marinate the fillet with oil, lemon juice, salt, pepper and spices. It can be larded with strips of larding bacon. Roast on a spit in the same way as for a beef fillet.

Roast camel's hump. BOSSE DE CHAMEAU RÔTIE – Only the hump of a very young camel is prepared in this way.

Marinate with oil, lemon juice, salt, pepper and spices. Roast in the same way as for roast sirloin of beef. (See BEEF, *Roast sirloin*.) Serve with its own gravy, and watercress.

Camel's paunch à la marocaine. VENTRE DE CHAMEAU À LA MAROCAINE – Marinate a 2-kg. (4½-lb.) piece of camel's paunch, trimmed and tied with string, in oil, lemon juice, spices and vegetables. Brown in oil in an earthenware casserole and remove when it is browned all over. Put 2 sliced onions into the casserole and cook slowly until soft. Add 4 peeled, seeded and chopped tomatoes, 4 peeled, seeded and diced sweet pimentos, 4 crushed cloves of garlic, and the quartered core of a root of fennel. Season with salt and pepper. Cook for 15 minutes.

Return the camel's paunch to the casserole. Pour over it 4 dl. (¾ pint, scant 2 cups) good stock. Add the liquor from the marinade, and a *bouquet garni* of parsley, thyme, bay and zest of orange. Simmer for 2½ hours. Add 250 g. (9 oz., generous cup) rice after removing the *bouquet garni*. Cook for a further 25 minutes.

Take out the meat, set it on a large dish and arrange the rice around it.

Camel pilaf. PILAF DE CHAMEAU – Prepare with lean camel's meat taken from the fillet or sirloin in the same way as *Mutton pilaf* (see PILAF).

Ragoût of camel with tomato sauce. RAGOÛT DE CHAMEAU À LA TOMATE – Prepare with camel meat cut into pieces and marinated in oil, lemon juice, salt, pepper and spices, in the same way as *Ragoût of mutton with tomato sauce* (see MUTTON).

Camel's ribs with rice. CÔTES DE CHAMEAU AU RIZ – Trim the camel's ribs and marinate them in oil, lemon juice, salt, pepper and spices.

Sauté in butter, lard or oil, drain them of fat, and garnish with *Rice pilaf* (see PILAF). Serve with a sauce made with the juices to which a few tablespoons stock and a little tomato sauce seasoned with garlic have been added.

All methods of preparation applying to ribs of veal or pork can be applied to camel's ribs.

CAMEMBERT – See CHEESE.

CAMOMILE. CAMOMILLE – Common name for a genus of herbs of the *Compositae* family, two varieties of which are the *Roman* or *noble camomile* and the *German* or *common camomile*.

Camomile oil, obtained by gently simmering 65 g. (2½ oz.) camomile flower heads in 500 g. (18 oz.) olive oil (camphorated or not) for 2 days in a *bain-marie*, is a popular remedy.

CAMPANULA. CAMPANULE – Common field plant. It has a purplish-violet flower and one variety is edible. The leaves and roots can be eaten in salad if picked before the plant develops its stalk.

CAMPEACHY WOOD (Logwood). BOIS DE CAMPÊCHE – Tree which grows in Mexico, chiefly around Campeachy Bay. Its wood, if boiled, produces colouring matter – red on contact with acids, turning violet on contact with alkali. Deprived of its toxic properties, it is used in the manufacture of liqueurs and for improving the colour of wine.

CAN, DRUM. BIDON – Originally a wooden jug of 5 litres (4½ quarts, 5½ quarts) capacity; nowadays a metal container for liquids.

As a slang expression in French this word has taken the same meaning as *bedon* (belly).

CANADA – See INTERNATIONAL COOKERY, *American cookery*.

CANAPÉS – The primary meaning of this word is a slice of crustless bread, cut in rectangular shapes, the size and thickness of which varies depending on the nature of ingredients to be put on them.

Canapés, which are also called croûtons, are made of toasted or fried bread and can either be spread with various mixtures or left plain, depending on the nature of the dishes for which they are to serve as an accompaniment.

Canapés, used to accompany winged game, are spread with *à gratin forcemeat* or some other forcemeat.

Canapés (hors-d'œuvres) – These *canapés* are made from crustless bread, home-made bread or brioche dough, and are garnished with various mixtures.

Recipes for this type of *canapé*, some of which are referred to as *canapés à la russe*, will be found in the section entitled HORS-D'ŒUVRE, *Cold hors-d'œuvre*.

Canapés for various dishes – These *canapés* are cut in rectangles, and browned. They are mostly described as croûtons and are used as foundations for fried or grilled escalopes, *noisettes, tournedos*, kidneys, etc.

Canary grass

CANARY GRASS. ALPISTE – Genus of plants of the *Graminaceae* family, one species of which is cultivated in the Canary Islands for its seed which is rich in edible starch and is used as food by the local inhabitants. It was first introduced into Spain; from there it was taken to the south of France where it quickly became naturalised. In some parts of France it is called *canary grain, bird grain* or *spike grain*.

The other species of this plant are suitable only for forage.

CANCALAISE (À LA) – Lenten garnish composed of oysters and shrimps in *Normandy sauce* (see SAUCE).

CANCALE – Small fishing port situated near the English Channel and famous for its 'blonde' plump oysters.

CANCOILLOTTE – See CHEESE.

CANDLEMAS – See FESTIVE COOKERY.

CANDY (Sugar). CANDI (SUCRE) – Purified, crystallised sugar.

CANE. CANNE – Name commonly given to different species of reeds. *Sweet calamus* was used in the past as an infusion. The roots of *giant* or *bamboo reed* are still used in popular medicine as an infusion against lacteal disorders. *Sugar cane* produces sugar.

Cane juice. VESOU – Liquid juice which comes out of sugar cane crushed by the mill. It is also called *vin de canne* (cane wine).

CANNELONI. CANNELONS GARNIS – Pasta dish served as an *hors-d'œuvre* or a small *entrée.* (See HORS-D'ŒUVRE, *Hot hors-d'œuvre.*)

CANNING – See PRESERVATION OF FOOD.

CANON – Old French wine measure of $\frac{1}{16}$ litre. Slang term for a unit of liquid measure used by wine merchants. The word comes from *canon* which means a glass in masonic terminology.

CANTAL – See CHEESE.

CANTALOUP – Melon, thus called because originally it was mainly grown at Cantalupo, near Rome. (See MELON.)

CANTEEN. CANTINE – Camp or barrack shop for liquor and provisions, etc. Refreshment room at work.

The name also applies to a small box containing cooking equipment for officers, and to a vessel for carrying liquids.

CANTON – Former capital of South China. The best of all Chinese *cuisine* is Cantonese.

CAPELIN or CAPLIN. CAPELAN, CAPEL – Small Mediterranean fish which is prepared as whiting (q.v.).

CAPENDU – Variety of red apple with a very short stalk.

CAPER. CÂPRE – Floral bud of the caper bush, which grows wild in the south of France, Algeria, Turkey, Asia Minor, etc. Capers are pickled in vinegar and used as a seasoning and condiment. The best are the round (*nonesuch*) capers from the *départements* of Var and Bouches-du-Rhône. They are firmer and smaller than the English capers, and should not be confused with pickled nasturtium seeds.

CAPITAINE – French name for a sea fish which resembles carp (q.v.) and is cooked in the same manner.

CAPON. CHAPON – Young cock which has been castrated and fattened to improve its flavour. Capons are prepared in the same way as chickens (see CHICKEN).

Capon in a pastry crust (belle aurore). CHAPON EN PÂTE BELLE AURORE – Bone a capon. Spread it out on a table, season with salt and spices. Prepare two stuffings separately. The first is made with the minced meat of a chicken, lean pork, pork fat and ham, seasoned, and combined with egg. The second is made with *à gratin forcemeat* (prepared with chicken livers, beef marrow, truffles and chopped mushrooms), well seasoned and combined with egg. Stuff the capon with these two stuffings in alternate layers. Marinate thin strips of veal fillet, lean pork, breast of chicken, wings of red partridge, saddle of hare, and blanched veal sweetbreads in oil, Cognac, lemon juice and spices, and lay between the two stuffings, adding quartered truffles. Roll up the stuffed capon and tie in a cloth, secured with string. Cook in a *daubière* (q.v.) on a foundation of onion, carrots and celery moistened with a very little stock and flavoured with Madeira wine, for 45 minutes. Drain the capon and cool quickly. Remove the cloth in which it is wrapped, lay the capon on fine pastry, cover with more pastry, and join the edges. Make a hole in the top so that the steam can escape, and decorate with pastry leaves. Brush with egg yolk and bake in a moderate oven. As soon as the pastry is cooked pour in a few tablespoons concentrated chicken stock to which Madeira has been added. Serve with a *ragoût* of mushrooms and truffles sautéed in butter, and with *Suprême sauce* (see SAUCE) which has a little Madeira added.

CAPONATA (Sicilian cookery) – Peel and dice 4 aubergines. Sprinkle with salt and when they have yielded their juice, fry them in oil.

Shred 50 g. (2 oz., $\frac{1}{3}$ cup) capers, 100 g. (4 oz., $\frac{2}{3}$ cup) black olives, 1 heart blanched celery, 4 desalted anchovies into *julienne* (q.v.) strips.

Fry a thinly sliced onion lightly in oil. Add 50 g. (2 oz., $\frac{1}{4}$ cup) sugar and 2 dl. ($\frac{1}{3}$ pint, scant cup) tomato purée. Boil down until it takes on a dark colour, after which add 1 dl. (6 tablespoons, scant $\frac{1}{2}$ cup) vinegar. Leave to simmer for a few minutes, season generously, add some chopped parsley and mix with the aubergines and the other ingredients. Decorate the top with slices of spiny lobster, tuna (tunny) fish in oil, and *poutargue* (salted and dried grey mullet roes).

This dish is served both in summer and winter. It is advisable to prepare it well in advance to allow all the ingredients to be permeated by the sweet-sour taste of the tomato sauce.

CAPSICUM – See PEPPER.

CAPUA. CAPOUE – Italian town situated near Naples, once renowned for its wines which, along with other 'delights', corrupted Hannibal's soldiers after the battle of Cannae.

CAPUCIN – Name by which French hunters call the hare. (See HARE.)

CARAFE – Large-based glass or crystal bottle or flagon used for water or wine. A *carafon* is a small carafe.

CARAMEL (Burnt sugar) – Used in cookery for colouring clear soups, stews, gravies, sauces, brown stocks, jellies, etc. It is also used in pastry-making.

Keep in small bottles with longitudinally-incised corks, which allow the caramel to be poured drop by drop.

Caramels (confectionery). CARAMELS MOUS – 375 g. (13 oz., 3 cups) loaf sugar, $\frac{3}{4}$ litre ($1\frac{1}{3}$ pints, $1\frac{3}{4}$ pints) double cream, 100 g. (4 oz., $\frac{1}{2}$ cup) finest butter, 100 g. (4 oz., 1 cup) glucose, 1 vanilla bean.

Put the sugar, cream, glucose, and vanilla into a pan and boil on a high flame, stirring all the time with a wooden spoon. As the sugar begins to boil, scrape the sides of the basin with the spoon to detach the sugar which is beginning to crystallise. When the sugar has reached the degree of cooking known as thread, add the butter in small pieces, stirring all the time. Cook until ball degree is reached. Remove the pan from heat. Pour the sugar onto a slightly oiled marble slab, keeping it in a frame made with oiled rulers. The sugar layer should be 5 to 6 mm. ($\frac{1}{4}$ inch) thick. The bottom of the pan must on no account be scraped, as this would cause the mixture to go gritty. Remove the vanilla bean, leave the caramel until completely cold, and cut into small squares.

Chocolate caramels. CARAMELS MOUS AU CHOCOLAT – Follow basic recipe. Add 200 g. (7 oz.) slab chocolate that has been previously melted in 1 dl. (6 tablespoons, scant $\frac{1}{2}$ cup) water.

Coffee caramels. CARAMELS MOUS AU CAFÉ – Basic method as above. Flavour with 1 dl. (6 tablespoons, scant $\frac{1}{2}$ cup) triple strength coffee essence.

Caramels with hazelnuts. CARAMELS MOUS AUX AVELINES – Pound finely 75 g. (3 oz., $\frac{2}{3}$ cup) blanched hazelnuts in a mortar or by machine. Put into a bowl, moisten with $\frac{1}{2}$ litre (scant pint, $2\frac{1}{4}$ cups) boiling milk and strain through a cloth, pressing out thoroughly. Add sugar and cream and proceed as for basic recipe.

Pistachio-nut caramels. CARAMELS MOUS AUX PISTACHES – Follow basic method. Add 150 g. (5 oz., 1¼ cups) blanched, finely chopped pistachio nuts.

Vanilla flavouring may be added to all these different preparations.

CARAMELISE. CARAMÉLISER – To caramelise a mould in which a cream or some other mixture is to be poured for cooking in a *bain-marie* (q.v.), coat it with sugar cooked to caramel degree. To do this, heat in the mould several pieces of sugar moistened with a little water, until the sugar acquires a brown colour (see SUGAR, *Sugar boiling*). The mould should then be rotated so as to coat the interior completely with the caramel. The mould can also be caramelised by brushing on sugar cooked to caramel degree. Creams, custards, and other mixtures are caramelised by adding to them some sugar cooked to caramel degree.

Caraway

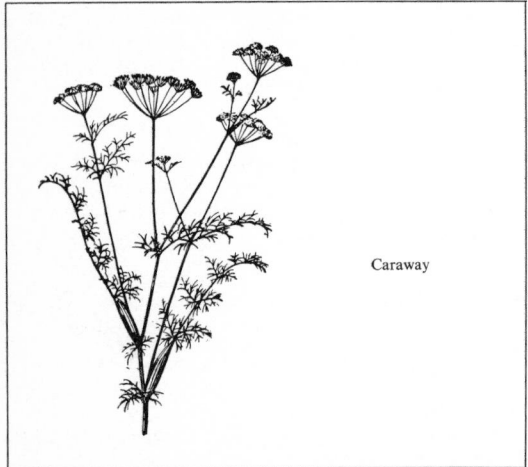

CARAWAY. CARVI – Umbelliferous plant producing black seeds, whose odour and taste is halfway between that of aniseed and fennel. Caraway seeds are used to flavour certain cheeses and cakes. The seeds, which have a carminative effect, were included in the carminative compounds of the old pharmacopoeia. The leaves, and the white shoots in its first season, gathered before the flower stalks have begun to shoot, have a sharp and aromatic taste. They can be eaten in salads, as a vegetable, or in soup. They are also used for flavouring a marinade.

CARBOHYDRATE. CARBONE. HYDRATE DE – See ALIMENT, ALIMENTATION.

CARBON DIOXIDE. CARBONIQUE – Gaseous body formed by the union of one atom of carbon and two atoms of oxygen. This gas is found in the atmosphere, from which it is absorbed by plants. These, under the influence of solar radiation, combine it with hydrogen, obtaining complex hydrocarbon and fat syntheses.

Soluble in cold water, it forms carbonic acid which is found in many mineral waters. When introduced under pressure into ordinary water it forms artificial soda water.

Carbon dioxide is released in large quantities during alcoholic fermentation; it is this gas which forms froth on sparkling wines, beer, cider, etc.

Highly compressed carbon dioxide is used in many industrial processes; in particular, it is used for drawing beer, 'draught beer'.

This gas has no liquid state. When it is cooled or decompressed and projected onto a cold surface, it solidifies in the form of snow which, in turn, vaporises without becoming a liquid. This property has been successfully exploited in the refrigerating industry, where blocks of solid carbon dioxide (U.S. dry ice) are used instead of ice for the cold storage of perishable goods, for air conditioning, etc. The substitution of ice by solid carbon dioxide results in a great saving of space and completely avoids humidity.

Carbon dioxide may cause asphyxia when it is found in large concentration in confined spaces, in vats for harvested grapes, etc. In small doses, however, it is a stimulant.

CARCASE. CARCASSE – Bone structure of an animal. In butcher's parlance, the body of a slaughtered animal, drawn and trimmed.

CARDAMINE or LADY'S SMOCK. CRESSON DES PRÉS – Common plant of American origin. It is eaten as salad, and has the same taste as watercress, but is less strong. It contains vitamins, and is recommended for scorbutic complaints.

CARDAMOM. CARDAMOME – Common name for *Elettaria cardamomum*, a species belonging to the ginger family, whose aromatic seeds are used as a spice.

CARDINAL (À LA) – Fish garnish composed of *coquilles cardinal*, mushrooms and slivers of truffle.

CARDINAL FISH. APOGON – One of the varieties of red mullet, found in the Mediterranean. (See MULLET.) In U.S.A., redfish, which is found from New Jersey to Texas, is very similar.

CARDINALISER – French kitchen term for shellfish which are made to turn red by plunging them into boiling *court-bouillon*.

CARDOON. CARDON – Plant of the same genus as the artichoke, of which the stems are eaten. The principal varieties are the *cardon de Tours, plein inerme* and *improved white*. The *cardon de Tours* is best, though the stems are rather spiny.

Cardoons must always first be cooked in white vegetable *court-bouillon*. They are then simmered in the required sauce.

Cardoons, to cook. Discard the hard stems and those that are wilted. Remove the tender stalks, one by one, and divide them into 8-cm. (3-inch) long slices. Remove all the stringy parts and rub every piece with half a lemon, to prevent them from turning black. Put them in a white vegetable *court-bouillon* which is already boiling. Add the heart of the cardoon, carefully trimmed.

Boil, stirring so as to prevent the cardoon sticking to the bottom of the pan. Put on the lid and simmer for about 2 hours.

Cardoons in béchamel sauce. CARDONS À LA BÉCHAMEL – Drain and dry the cardoons after they have been cooked as above. Simmer in butter, with the lid on the pan, for about 15 minutes. Add 2 dl. (⅓ pint, scant cup) *Béchamel sauce* (see SAUCE). Simmer for 5 minutes.

Cardoons in butter. CARDONS AU BEURRE – Drain the cooked cardoons and cook them in butter for 20 minutes, with the lid on the pan.

Cardoons with cream I. CARDONS À LA CRÈME – Simmer the cooked cardoons in butter. Moisten with 2 dl. (⅓ pint, scant cup) *Cream sauce* (see SAUCE). Simmer for 5 minutes.

Cardoons with cream II. CARDONS À LA CRÈME – Simmer the cooked cardoons in butter. Remove them, and pour 3 dl. (½ pint, 1¼ cups) fresh cream into the pan. Boil down by half. Take off the heat, add 50 g. (2 oz., ¼ cup) butter, and strain through a sieve onto the cardoons.

Cardoons aux fines herbes I. CARDONS AUX FINES HERBES – Cook the cooked cardoons in butter, and drain. Moisten with a few tablespoons *Fines herbes sauce* (see SAUCE). Simmer for 10 minutes.

Cardoons aux fines herbes II. CARDONS AUX FINES HERBES – Proceed in the same way as for *Cardoons in butter*. Add chopped parsley and chervil.

Fried cardoons. CARDONS FRITS – Drain the cooked cardoons, dry, and marinate for 30 minutes in oil, lemon juice and chopped parsley. Dip in light batter and fry in smoking hot oil. Drain again and season with fine salt.

Cardoons à la grecque. CARDONS À LA GRECQUE – Trim and slice the cardoons, rub with lemon juice, and cook in a *court-bouillon* made in the same way as for *Artichokes à la grecque* (see ARTICHOKE). Finish as described in that recipe. They are served as *hors-d'œuvre*.

Cardoons à l'italienne. CARDONS À L'ITALIENNE – Proceed in the same way as for *Cardoons aux fines herbes*. Moisten with *Italian sauce* (see SAUCE).

Cardoons à l'italienne gratinés. CARDONS À L'ITALIENNE GRATINÉS – Prepare the cardoons as described in the previous recipe. Put the cardoons in a *gratin* dish. Cover them with the sauce, sprinkle with fine breadcrumbs and pour over some melted butter. Brown quickly in the oven.

Cardoons à la lyonnaise. CARDONS À LA LYONNAISE – Proceed in the same way as for *Cardoons à l'italienne*. Moisten with *Lyonnaise sauce* (see SAUCE).

Cardoons with marrow I. CARDONS À LA MOELLE – Drain the cardoons after cooking them in *court-bouillon* (q.v.). When serving, lay sliced hearts of the cardoons on top, alternating with slices of marrow poached in salt water and well drained.

Cover the dish with a few tablespoons *Marrow sauce* (see SAUCE). Sprinkle with chopped parsley.

Cardoons with marrow II. CARDONS À LA MOELLE – Arrange the cardoons in a pyramid on a dish, and cover them with sliced cardoon hearts. Pour *Marrow sauce* (see SAUCE) over them and sprinkle with chopped parsley.

Arrange round the edge of the dish, hollowed-out croûtes of bread, buttered and filled with poached diced marrow.

The hollowed-out croûtes can be replaced by puff pastry *bouchées*.

The marrow can have chopped shallot and chopped parsley added, combined with concentrated veal sauce or with dissolved meat glaze.

Cardoons à la milanaise. CARDONS À LA MILANAISE – Cook cardoons in *court-bouillon* (q.v.), drain and dry them. Arrange on a fireproof dish in layers, sprinkling each layer with grated Parmesan. Sprinkle with melted butter and brown in the oven. When removed from the oven, sprinkle with brown butter.

Cardoons Mornay. CARDONS MORNAY – Arrange cooked and drained cardoons in a buttered *gratin* dish. Cover with *Mornay sauce* (see SAUCE) and sprinkle with grated Parmesan. Pour a little melted butter over and brown in a very hot oven.

Cardoons with Parmesan (à blanc). CARDONS AU PARMESAN (À BLANC) – Proceed in the same way as for *Cardons Mornay*.

Cardoons with Parmesan (à brun). CARDONS AU PARMESAN (À BRUN) – Arrange cardoons, cooked and drained, in a buttered *gratin* dish; cover with a *Demi-glace sauce* (see SAUCE). Sprinkle with Parmesan and brown in the oven.

Raw cardoons à la piémontaise or Cardiella Piemontese (Italian cookery). CARDONS CRUS À LA PIÉMONTAISE – Clean white cardoons. Remove the fibres and the thin skin on the inside of the stalks, and place the cardoons in fresh water. Divide the stalks into pieces about 4 to 5 cm. (2 inches) long. Serve them as they are, arranged in an *hors-d'œuvre* dish, with the following sauce:

Put 200 g. (7 oz., scant cup) butter in a pan with 2 dl. (⅓ pint, scant cup) olive oil, 4 shredded cloves of garlic and 6 desalted, diced anchovy fillets. Cook slowly; do not allow the garlic to brown.

Add to this sauce one or two white truffles, peeled and sliced into thin strips. Mix, and serve hot.

Cardoon purée. PURÉE DE CARDONS – Prepare cardoons as for *Cardoons in butter*. Pass through a fine sieve, heat the purée and add butter.

One-third of its volume of potato purée can be added to the cardoon purée. A few tablespoons thick *Béchamel sauce* (see SAUCE) can also be added.

Cardoon salad. SALADE DE CARDONS – Cook cardoons in a *court-bouillon* (q.v.), drain and dry.

Season with oil, vinegar, salt and pepper, and sprinkle with chopped parsley and chervil.

Cardoons with various sauces. CARDONS AVEC SAUCES DIVERSES – Cook and drain cardoons, and serve with any of the following sauces: *Butter, Cream, Hollandaise, Hungarian* or *Mousseline* (see SAUCE).

Antonin Carême (1784–1833)

CARÊME – Marie-Antoine Carême, known as Antonïn, was born in Paris on 8 June 1784, and died there on 12 January 1833.

His father was a poor working man who had so much difficulty in feeding his large family that he found it simplest to abandon little Antoine after a farewell meal in a tavern at the city gate, leaving him provided with this piece of advice: 'Go, little one. In this world there are excellent callings. Leave us to languish; misery is our lot and we must die of misery. This is the time of fine fortunes, it only needs wit to make one, and wit you have. Go, little one, and perhaps this evening or tomorrow some fine house will open its doors to you. Go with what God has given you.'

The boy, thus abandoned, could have knocked on the door of a carpenter or a locksmith. Destiny led him to a humble cookshop, the owner of which gave him his first lesson in cooking. The man who has been called the *Cuisinier des rois et le Roi des cuisiniers* (the Cook of kings and the King of cooks) made his début in the meanest of cookshops. A precarious beginning! But, by a lucky chance, Carême was set to work in a craft for which he had magnificent gifts. The speed with which he rose – starting from such a modest beginning – showed him to be something of a prodigy.

He began work in a restaurant as a kitchen help when he was fifteen years old. His great desire to work, his wise intuition for the secrets and resources of his art, and his serene authority revealed him as a person of exceptional quality. Very soon he moved to the celebrated *pâtissier* Bailly in rue Vivienne, who had as a client M. de Talleyrand, an extremely clever diplomat who made gastronomy serve his political ambitions. On leaving for the Congress of Vienna, where he was able to obtain important advantages for France, Talleyrand declared to Louis XVIII, the gourmet king, who was well able to understand the words: 'Sire, I have more need of casseroles than of written instructions.'

Carême has left us an account of the time he spent with the famous Bailly: 'At seventeen,' he writes, 'I was with M. Bailly as his first *tourtier*. This good master showed a lively interest in me. He allowed me to leave work in order to draw in the print room. When I had shown him that I had a particular vocation for his art he confided to me the task of creating *pièces montées* for the Consul's (Napoleon's) table. At that time, the illustrious Avice flourished in the realm of *pâtisserie*; his work served as my instruction. The knowledge of his procedures gave me courage and I did all I could to follow him, but not to imitate him.'

In brief, Carême created extraordinary decorative pieces which provoked general admiration. This young pastry-cook based his set pieces on the engravings in great French collections which he studied even in his tenderest years. He associated confectionery with architecture and wrote the following sentence, quoted by Anatole France: 'The fine arts are five in number, to wit: painting, sculpture, poetry, music, architecture – whose main branch is confectionery.'

Carême entered the service of M. de Lavalette who kept a famous table and entertained the most distinguished men in politics, the army, the arts and sciences. Here Carême worked, as he puts it, to further the union of delicacy, order and economy! He next stayed twelve years with Prince Talleyrand whose table, he declared, was furnished with grandeur and wisdom. Later, he became chief cook to the Prince Regent in England. Here he stayed for two years. Every morning he explained the properties of each individual dish to the Prince. 'Carême,' said his royal master one day, 'you will kill me with a surfeit of food. I have a fancy for everything you put before me. The temptation is really too great.' 'Your Highness,' replied Carême (who relates this conversation in the preamble to his *Cuisinier parisien*), 'my great concern is to stimulate your appetite by the variety of my dishes. It is no concern of mine to curb it.'

The English fogs depressed him, and he returned to France. The Prince Regent, later King George IV, asked him to return, and offered munificent terms which would assure his present and future prosperity, but Carême refused.

We find him at Saint Petersburg with the Czar Alexander, at the Court of Vienna, at the British Embassy in Paris, at the Congress of Aix-la-Chapelle, in the households of the Princess Bagration and Lord Stewart, and finally with Baron de Rothschild, where he remained for seven years. While he was with this prince of finance, the Rothschild table was considered the best in Europe. M. de Rothschild, having just bought the Ferrières estate, offered him the opportunity of directing the kitchens of the château, and added that he could, if he wished, retire there. Carême declined this offer. His strength was exhausted by the unremitting labours of thirty years.

'My prayer,' he added, 'is not to end my days in a château but in humble lodgings in Paris, and to publish a comprehensive survey of the state of my profession at the present time.' He fell gravely ill and was forced to take to his bed. His great anxiety was his fear of not being able to complete books which he regarded as essential to the future of his art. He died, still under the age of fifty years, on 12 January 1833, burnt out, according to Laurent Tailhade, by the flame of his genius and the fuel of his ovens. His last moments of life were spent in dictating notes to his daughter.

Carême's life is a model of probity and nobility. Money meant nothing to him. His art alone was important. His very conception of culinary art is in tune with the grandeur of his character. It was always Carême's ideal to present sumptuously the culinary marvels with which he enriched the tables of kings. Nothing could be more meticulous than the drawings he made for set pieces, aspics, galantines, baskets of fruit, etc., or even simple borders.

Nowadays, we no longer approve of this ostentatious manner of setting out cooked dishes. We have banished display from our tables, as much for the sake of hygiene as for reasons of expediency. But it must be remembered that Carême worked for the great ones of the earth and wanted his art to 'serve as a foil to European diplomacy'. Nevertheless, while he considered that cooking must be decorative, he was equally emphatic that it must be hygienic. He himself was extremely sober and considered that 'good cooking should strengthen the life of old societies'.

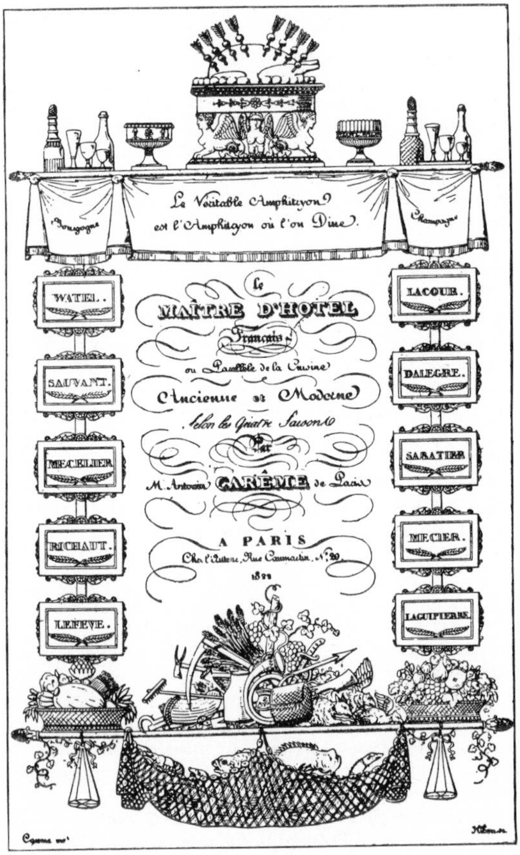

Title page of one of Carême's works

He died poor, leaving only his works, listed below:

Le Maître d'hôtel français. Comparisons of ancient and modern cookery considered from the point of view of the plan and the arrangement of menus according to the four seasons, in Paris, St Petersburg, London and Vienna, 2 volumes.

Le Pâtissier royal parisien. Elementary and practical treatise, 2 volumes. Later edition, ornamented with 41 plates by the author, 2 volumes.

Le Cuisinier parisien. 1 volume.

L'Art de la cuisine au dix-neuvième siècle. 5 volumes.

Le Pâtissier pittoresque. Ornamented with 128 plates by the author.

There is unusual erudition in Carême's works. He prefaced his formulation of modern menus with a treatise on ancient cookery which required a great deal of research, and which bears witness to a devoted passion for his profession.

Le Pâtissier royal parisien is filled with the sentiment which earned his immortality: indignation. Carême was unable to view without disgust that men totally ignorant of the art of cooking published cookery books.

The plan of this book is extremely methodical. The subjects with which he deals are provisions (with observations on their freshness, quality and season), details and organisation of the larder, major and minor sauces, consommés, *hors-d'œuvre*, frying, sweets, the cold buffet; in short, all the details relating to the direction of the kitchen. Carême added to this treatise a vocabulary where he establishes the spelling of the names of dishes which had been travestied by so many.

Carême should be regarded as the founder of '*la grande cuisine*', classic French cookery. His theoretical work, his practical work as an inventor of sauces, as pastry-maker, designer and author of works devoted to cooking, place him at a much higher level than those who preceded him.

CARIBBEAN CABBAGE. CHOU CARAÏBE – Root of *Arum esculentum.* Used in Asia and Africa and also cultivated in the south of France. Prepared as swedes (q.v.).

CARINA. BRÉCHET – Breast bone of poultry and feathered game. If this bone is supple when gently bent to the right and to the left the bird is young and its flesh will be tender.

CARLINE THISTLE. CARLINE – Plant which grows in the mountains, particularly in the Cévennes. The root of the *great carline thistle* is sometimes used as a drug. The young flower-heads, eaten in salads, have a nutty taste, while the roots have a flavour similar to that of fennel.

CARMINATIVE. CARMINATIF – Medicament which prevents the formation, or provokes the expulsion, of gases contained in the intestines. The kind of carminative which featured in the old pharmacopoeia consisted of grains of aniseed, coriander, fennel and caraway in equal parts.

CARMINE. CARMIN – Substance derived from cochineal, of a vivid scarlet red colour, non-toxic, used to colour a variety of food substances.

CARNATION. OEILLET – The petals of the carnation flower are used to make a syrup and a ratafia.

CARNIVAL. CARNAVAL – The period between Epiphany and Ash Wednesday, given up to all kinds of rejoicing especially in the pleasures of the table.

CAROLINA. CAROLINE – Commercial name for a type of rice. (See RICE.)

CAROLINE – Name given in pastry-making to small éclairs served as *hors-d'œuvre.*

CAROTENE. CAROTÈNE – Yellow colouring matter, widespread in the vegetable kingdom. Besides carrots, it is also found in spinach, lettuce, peas, pumpkins, cabbages, oranges, etc. It is also found in butter and egg yolks. This substance plays an important rôle in the growth of animals, and is transformed into vitamins in the animal organism. Its properties emphasise the importance of fresh vegetables in the diet.

CARP. CARPE – Freshwater fish. It probably originated in China, and was imported into England in 1614 and into Holland and Scandinavia about 1660. In 1876 it was taken to U.S.A., put in fish ponds in Washington, D.C., and in 1879 distributed to twenty-five states and territories. It is abundant in the Middle West, and sold in the principal eastern cities of U.S.A.

The carp has a small mouth with four fleshy appendages called barbules, but has no teeth. The river carp has brownish scales on the back, golden-yellow scales on its flanks, greenish-white scales on the stomach. The carp which inhabits lakes and ponds often has a muddy smell, and is darker in colour. Carp can grow to an enormous size. The best season for eating them is between November and the end of March.

Mirror carp

There are several species of carp, of which the chief are the *mirror carp, leather carp, Kollar carp,* and *Bohemian carp.* The mirror carp was called the queen of carp in the old days on account of the great delicacy of its flesh. It is more hardy than the common carp, grows more rapidly, and attains a larger size. The Kollar carp is seldom found in France, but is abundant in Belgium, in Germany and in Hungary.

All these species of carp are prepared in the same way as common carp.

In France, carp are bred in Sologne and in the Dombes, from where they are transported alive to Germany in aquarium trucks for the manufacture of Hamburg carp *pâté.* They are also bred on the shores of the Dead Sea.

Carp à l'alsacienne. CARPE À L'ALSACIENNE – Fill a carp of medium size with a fish cream stuffing (see FORCEMEAT, *Fish forcemeat*). Poach in a little white wine. Garnish with *Sauerkraut garnish* (see GARNISHES), and boiled potatoes. Serve with the boiled-down liquor in which it was cooked, thickened with *Kneaded butter* (see BUTTER) and with a little fresh butter added.

Carp cooked in beer (German cookery). CARPE À LA BIÈRE – Season a carp of moderate size which can be stuffed or not, according to taste. Put it in a fish kettle on a foundation of 150 g. (5 oz., $1\frac{1}{4}$ cups) chopped onion lightly fried in butter, together with 25 g. (1 oz.) gingerbread cut into small squares, and 2 stalks finely sliced celery. Add a *bouquet garni.*

Pour light beer over the fish; sufficient to almost cover it. Poach in a slow oven. When cooked, put the fish on a long platter and garnish with the roes, which have been sliced and poached. Boil down by one third the liquor in which

Leather carp

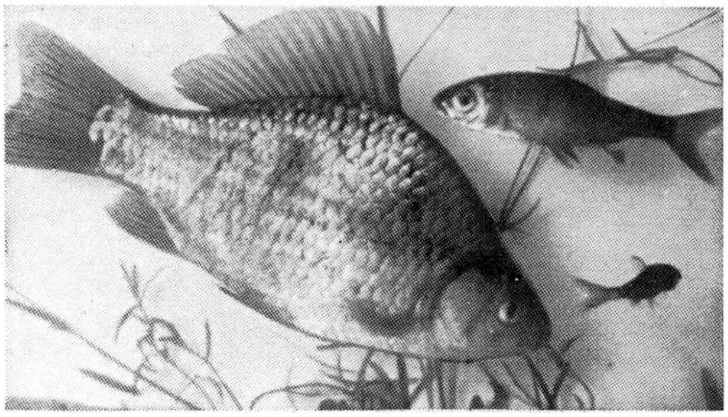

Bohemian carp

the carp was cooked, sieve, add a little fresh butter, and serve with the fish.

Carp au bleu. CARPE AU BLEU – Small carp are used for this preparation. Proceed in the same way as for *Blue trout* (see TROUT).

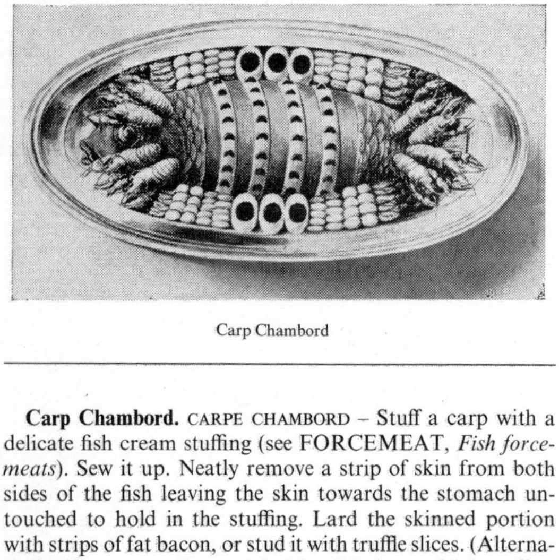

Carp Chambord

Carp Chambord. CARPE CHAMBORD – Stuff a carp with a delicate fish cream stuffing (see FORCEMEAT, *Fish forcemeats*). Sew it up. Neatly remove a strip of skin from both sides of the fish leaving the skin towards the stomach untouched to hold in the stuffing. Lard the skinned portion with strips of fat bacon, or stud it with truffle slices. (Alternatively this part can be spread with a thin layer of fish stuffing garnished with slices of truffle cut in crescent shapes.)

Put the carp on the drainer of the fish kettle on a base of herbs and vegetables which, with some mushroom peelings, have been lightly fried in butter. Add a *bouquet garni* (q.v.).

Pour on some *Fish stock with red wine* (see STOCK) to reach two-thirds up the sides of the fish. Braise in a moderate oven (160°C., 325°F., Gas Mark 3).

Drain the fish, glaze it, and surround with a *Chambord garnish* (see GARNISHES) arranging the different parts of the garnish in separate groups. Put a little *Genevoise sauce* (see SAUCE) in the bottom of the dish, using the liquor from the braised carp. Serve the rest of the sauce separately.

Cold carp. CARPE FROIDE – All methods of preparation given for *Cold salmon* (see SALMON) and *Salmon trout* (see TROUT) apply to carp.

Carp au court-bouillon. CARPE AU COURT-BOUILLON – Poach the fish in a *court-bouillon* (prepared with red or white wine) containing aromatic vegetables and seasoning. Drain the carp, and garnish with fresh parsley. Serve with melted butter or with a sauce used with poached fish.

Fillets of carp. FILETS DE CARPE – Lift the fillets from a medium-sized carp. Trim and season them, and poach in a little concentrated fish stock. Drain the fillets, and cover with one of the following sauces: *Cream, Fines herbes, Hollandaise, Marinière, Normande, White wine,* or any sauce suitable for poached fish (see SAUCE).

Fillets of carp can be accompanied by any of the garnishes appropriate to poached fish, and particularly those given for sole, or fillets of sole (see SOLE).

Fried carp. CARPE FRITE – Deep-fry small carp in hot oil. Drain, and wipe with a cloth. Season with fine salt and garnish with fried parsley and quarters of lemon.

Grilled carp à la maître d'hôtel. CARPE GRILLÉE À LA MAÎTRE D'HÔTEL – Small carp are prepared in this way. Follow the instructions for *Grilled bass* (see BASS).

Carp à la juive. CARPE À LA JUIVE – Cut a medium-sized carp into slices, and cook with 1 chopped onion and 3 chopped shallots which have been cooked in 2 dl. ($\frac{1}{3}$ pint, scant cup) oil without browning. Sprinkle with 35 g. ($1\frac{1}{4}$ oz., 6 tablespoons) flour. Almost cover the fish with white wine and fish stock (or water). Season with salt and a touch of cayenne. Add 2 crushed garlic cloves and a *bouquet garni* (q.v.). Sprinkle with a few tablespoons oil. Bring to the boil, and simmer slowly with the lid on for 20 minutes.

Drain the carp slices and set them on a dish, reforming the shape of the carp.

Boil down the liquor by two-thirds, remove from the heat, and beat in 2 dl. ($\frac{1}{3}$ pint, scant cup) oil. Pour over the carp and leave to cool. Sprinkle with chopped parsley.

Carpe à la juive à l'orientale. CARPE À LA JUIVE À L'ORIENTALE – Prepared in the same way as *Carp à la juive* but after the sauce has been boiled down and the oil incorporated add a pinch of saffron and 25 g. (1 oz., $\frac{1}{4}$ cup) peeled, blanched and chopped almonds.

Carp à la juive with parsley. CARPE À LA JUIVE AU PERSIL – Prepared in the same way as *Carpe à la juive* with the addition of several sprigs fresh parsley to the cooking liquor. Add more chopped parsley when ready to serve.

Carpe à la juive with raisins. CARPE À LA JUIVE AUX RAISINS – Prepared in the same way as *Carp à la juive*. Add to the boiled-down liquor, in which the oil has been incorporated, 15 g. ($\frac{1}{2}$ oz., 2 tablespoons) powdered sugar, 2 tablespoons wine vinegar, 50 g. (2 oz., $\frac{1}{3}$ cup) seeded raisins, and 50 g. (2 oz., $\frac{1}{3}$ cup) currants and sultanas (mixed) which have been allowed to swell in lukewarm water and drained.

Carp en matelote. CARPE EN MATELOTE – Prepared with the carp cut into slices in the same way as *Eel en matelote* (see EEL).

Carp à la polonaise. CARPE À LA POLONAISE – Stuff a medium-sized carp with fish stuffing and place on a foundation of 50 g. (2 oz., $\frac{1}{2}$ cup) chopped onion and 25 g. (1 oz., $\frac{1}{4}$ cup) chopped shallot in a fish kettle or large pan. Add a *bouquet garni* (q.v.) and season. Almost cover the carp with liquor consisting of half red wine and half fish stock. Add 100 g. (4 oz.) gingerbread cut into large squares.

Braise slowly on top of the stove or in the oven.

Drain the carp and cover with the following sauce:

Prepare a pale caramel syrup with 50 g. (2 oz., $\frac{1}{4}$ cup) sugar and 1 dl. (6 tablespoons, scant $\frac{1}{2}$ cup) vinegar. Add the sieved liquor in which the fish was cooked, mixed with 100 g. (4 oz., $\frac{1}{2}$ cup) butter and 50 g. (2 oz., $\frac{1}{2}$ cup) flaked almonds which have been lightly grilled.

Carp quenelles. QUENELLES DE CARPE – Prepare with carp meat in the same way as *Pike quenelles* (see PIKE).

Poach the carp quenelles and serve on *croustades feuilletées* (see CROUSTADE) or on croûtons fried in butter. They are accompanied by various garnishes and are covered with a sauce suitable for the garnish used. (See QUENELLE, *Fish quenelles*.)

Carp quenelles are also used as part of the garnish for large braised fish, and fish pies.

Roast carp. CARPE RÔTIE – Prepare in the same way as *Roast pike* (see PIKE).

Carps' roes. LAITANCES DE CARPE – Often used as part of a garnish for large braised fish. They can also be served as a hot *hors-d'œuvre* or as an *entrée*.

Carps' roes, and those of other fish, should first be poached in a little *court-bouillon*, or cooked in butter with lemon juice added, in a covered pan. Prepare according to the instructions given under the different recipes for soft roes (q.v.).

Stuffed carp à l'ancienne. CARPE FARCIE À L'ANCIENNE – Scale a large, soft-roed carp. Remove the flesh and add it to that of a small eel, and 8 desalted anchovies. Make a *Quenelle forcemeat* (see FORCEMEAT) but without adding any sauce. Keep it rather firm. Be careful, when removing the carp's flesh, to leave the backbone intact, complete with head and tail.

Blanch the roes, cut them into pieces, and sauté them in butter with a little lemon juice. Add truffles and mushrooms and a few tablespoons thick *Allemande sauce* (see SAUCE).

Thickly butter a tin tray of the same length as the carp. Lay forcemeat on this, about 5 cm. (2 inches) deep, in the shape of the carp, and set the backbone, to which the head and tail are still adhering, in place. Cover the bone with a little more forcemeat and add the *ragoût* of truffles, mushrooms and carp's roes. On top of this lay about $2\frac{1}{2}$ cm. (1 inch) forcemeat, keeping carefully to the shape of the carp. Smooth the surface with the blade of a knife dipped in hot water. Butter a large baking sheet and sprinkle breadcrumbs on the butter. Put the tin tray on which the carp has been prepared over heat for a few minutes so that the butter melts. It is then possible to slide the fish onto the baking sheet.

Cover the fish with beaten egg, then with fine dry breadcrumbs, pressing them on with a knife. Pour on melted butter. With the tip of a small spoon press in a pattern of scales, beginning at the head.

Cook the carp in the oven for 45 minutes, basting frequently with clarified butter so that it acquires a golden colour. Remove from the baking sheet with a long fish slice, and slide it onto the serving dish, together with a little *Sauce financière* (see SAUCE), based on fish essence. Serve with more sauce. (*L'art de la cuisine française de Carême*, by Plumerey.)

CARPILLON or CARPEAU – Very small carp. Also a species of small mullet which does not spawn. This fish, which is found in the Rhône, the Saône and other European rivers, is treated in the same way as carp. Its flesh is tender and delicate.

CARPION – Variety of trout, principally found in alpine streams. All methods of preparation indicated for river trout can be applied to it (see TROUT).

CARRÉ DE BONNEVILLE – See CHEESE.

CARRIER PIGEON. BISET – Wild pigeon which is also called *rock pigeon*. It is smaller than the ring dove (or wood pigeon). Its plumage is slate-grey.

It can be prepared in any way suitable for the domestic pigeon (see PIGEON).

In France, this name is also given to a marsh bird similar to the wild duck, which is cooked in the same way as wild duck (see DUCK, *Wild duck*).

CARROTS. CAROTTES – Root vegetables which are used in many dishes, either as an aromatic base or alone as a garnish.

The carrot contains a notable amount of sugar, which adds to its nutritive properties. The following recipes are intended for new carrots. If old ones are used, they should be blanched first.

Carrots in béchamel sauce. CAROTTES À LA BÉCHAMEL – Cook the carrots in salted boiling water or prepare them in the same way as *Glazed carrots* (see below). Before serving, add a few tablespoons *Béchamel sauce* (see SAUCE).

Boiled carrots. CAROTTES À L'ANGLAISE – Cook tender carrots in boiling water. Drain them, and serve fresh butter separately.

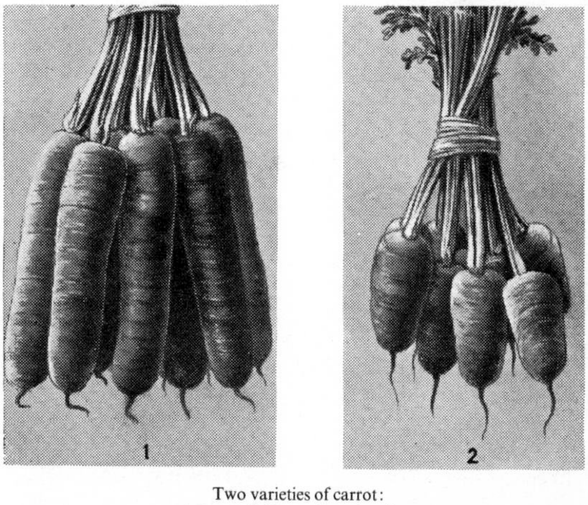

Two varieties of carrot:
1. Long; 2. Short, forced variety

Buttered carrots. CAROTTES AU BEURRE – Boil the carrots, drain, return them to the pan, add a little butter, and shake so that each carrot receives a coating of butter.

Carrots en cheveux d'ange (angel's hair). CAROTTES EN CHEVEUX D'ANGE – Carrot jam which used to be prepared in the south-west of France. (See CHEVEUX D'ANGE.)

Carrots à la crème I. CAROTTES À LA CRÈME – Boil the carrots, drain, return to the pan and cover with boiling cream. Boil down by two-thirds.

Carrots à la crème II. CAROTTES À LA CRÈME – Blanch 500 g. (generous 1 lb.) carrots, rinse in cold water, and drain. Cover with more cold water and add a pinch of salt, 1 tablespoon fine sugar and 50 g. (2 oz., ¼ cup) butter. Bring to boiling point, then reduce the heat and leave to cook until the liquid is syrupy. Test the carrots to make sure they are cooked. If they are still hard, add a few tablespoons hot water and boil down until the liquid again becomes syrupy.

Pour boiling cream over the carrots. Bring to the boil, then lower the heat and simmer until the cream has boiled down a little. Add 1 tablespoon butter, gently mixing it in.

Garnish according to the instructions of the particular recipe.

Carrots aux fines herbes I. CAROTTES AUX FINES HERBES – Proceed in the same way as for *Glazed carrots* (see below). Sprinkle with chopped parsley and chervil.

Carrots aux fines herbes II. CAROTTES AUX FINES HERBES – Pare and slice some tender carrots. Blanch for 5 minutes, drain, and cook in a little butter. Season with salt and a pinch of sugar, and sprinkle with chopped parsley and chervil.

Carrot flan or tart. FLAN AUX CAROTTES – Partly fill the bottom of a baked pastry shell with a slightly sweetened purée of carrots. Cover with finely sliced carrots which have already been cooked according to instructions for *Glazed carrots* (see below). Boil down the liquor in which the carrots have been cooked and pour it over the flan. Set in a hot oven for a few minutes.

This flan can be prepared with a greater quantity of sugar as a sweet.

Glazed carrots. CAROTTES GLACÉES – Pare some young carrots. Put them in a pan and cover with cold water. Bring to the boil with 1 teaspoon salt, 25 g. (1 oz., 2 tablespoons) sugar, and 50 g. (2 oz., ¼ cup) butter, allowing these quantities for each ½ litre (scant pint, 2¼ cups) water.

As soon as it is boiling lower the heat, cover the pan, and simmer until the liquid has practically evaporated. Shake the pan so that the carrots are properly covered with the syrupy liquid and use them according to instructions.

If old carrots are used, cut them in quarters, blanch in boiling salted water, and slice.

Glazed young carrots. CAROTTES NOUVELLES GLACÉES – Pare 500 g. (generous 1 lb.) new carrots of the same size, cover with stock, and cook slowly in a covered pan with 50 g. (2 oz., ¼ cup) butter, a pinch of salt and 1 teaspoon sugar until the liquid is entirely boiled down. When the carrots are cooked and the liquid has become a syrup, roll the carrots in this so that each one is coated.

Carrots au jus. CAROTTES AU JUS – Proceed in the same way as for *Glazed carrots*, but at the last moment add a few tablespoons rich brown veal stock. Simmer for a few minutes and serve.

Carrot purée I. PURÉE DE CAROTTES – Cook 500 g. (generous 1 lb.) sliced new carrots in salted water, with the addition of 1 teaspoon sugar and 1 tablespoon butter. Drain the carrots as soon as they are cooked and put them through a fine sieve.

Heat the purée. Add a little of the cooking liquor if the purée is too thick, and incorporate 50 g. (2 oz., ¼ cup) fresh butter. Mix well and serve. One can use the carrots from *pot-au-feu* (q.v.) in this way.

Carrot purée II. PURÉE DE CAROTTES – Proceed in the same way as for *Carrot purée I*, but 10 minutes after setting the carrots on the stove add a quarter of their volume of sliced potatoes.

Carrot purée with cream. PURÉE DE CAROTTES À LA CRÈME – Proceed in the same way as for *Carrot purée I*. Finish the purée with 4 tablespoons (⅓ cup) boiled cream and 1 tablespoon fresh butter.

Carrot purée with rice. PURÉE DE CAROTTES AU RIZ – The same method as *Carrot purée I*, but with the addition of a quarter of the carrots' weight in rice when putting the carrots on to cook.

The addition of potatoes or rice in carrot purées helps to improve their consistency. They are prepared in this way when used for garnishes.

Carrot soufflé. SOUFFLÉ AUX CAROTTES – Press 250 g. (generous ½ lb.) carrots, prepared as for a purée, through a fine sieve. Remove the moisture from the purée by allowing it to boil rapidly for a few moments.

Take the pan off the heat and add 3 egg yolks. Cool slightly and add 3 stiffly whisked egg whites. Turn into a buttered soufflé dish and cook in the oven (200°C., 400°F., Gas Mark 6) for about 15 minutes. Serve at once.

Small carrot soufflés. PETITS SOUFFLÉS AUX CAROTTES – Proceed in the same way as for *Carrot soufflé*. Put the soufflé mixture in small fireproof dishes and cook for 6 to 8 minutes.

Carrot timbale. PAIN DE CAROTTES – Sieve 250 g. (generous ½ lb.) carrots cooked as for a purée, and place in a pan over heat to dry out for a few minutes. Add 3 whole eggs, mix well, and turn into a buttered charlotte mould decorated with sliced cooked carrots.

Cook in a pan of hot water or *bain-marie* in a moderate oven (180°C., 350°F., Gas Mark 4) for 30 minutes. Allow to stand a few minutes before turning out the mould.

Serve with *béchamel sauce*, cream, or *hollandaise sauce*.

Carrots à la Vichy. CAROTTES À LA VICHY – Pare and slice new carrots, and cook as for *Glazed carrots*, adding for each ½ litre (scant pint, 2¼ cups) water, 1 teaspoon salt, 25 g. (1 oz., 2 tablespoons) sugar and 50 g. (2 oz., ¼ cup) butter.

When the liquid is very concentrated and the carrots are glazed, arrange them in a dish and sprinkle with chopped parsley.

Old carrots can be used for this preparation but cut them into strips, and blanch in salted boiling water before cooking them with the other ingredients.

Sometimes Vichy water is used as the cooking liquor, or a light pinch of bicarbonate of soda is added to plain water.

CARVING. DÉCOUPAGE – The action of cutting up meat, poultry, game, etc. to serve at table. In former times, the carving of meat was considered a noble art, carried out solely by high officials of royal or princely households who were known as *écuyers* (esquires) *tranchants*.

In royal households, the *écuyer tranchant* was usually a nobleman and he always carried out his duties with his sword at his side.

The art of skilful carving was considered essential by our forefathers and was taught to well-born young men as an indispensable part of good education. The last tutor provided for young noblemen was a master of carving.

For a long time in French society the carving and serving of food was carried out by the head of the household, who regarded it as a matter of honour to carve skilfully.

The introduction in France of the *service à la Russe*, which consists of presenting the diners with the food already carved, has caused the decline at the French table of this gracious custom.

The carving of meat is now done, at least in large restaurants, by a specialist known as the 'carver'. He may not have the glamour of the *écuyer tranchant* but he has the status of *maître d'hôtel*, and must know his job inside out. In addition to a complete knowledge of anatomy, he must have great manual skill and physical strength, so as to be able to sever the joints of the animals he has to carve. He must also have an intimate knowledge of the grain and texture of every piece of meat which he has to carve, and he must work with elegance and delicacy.

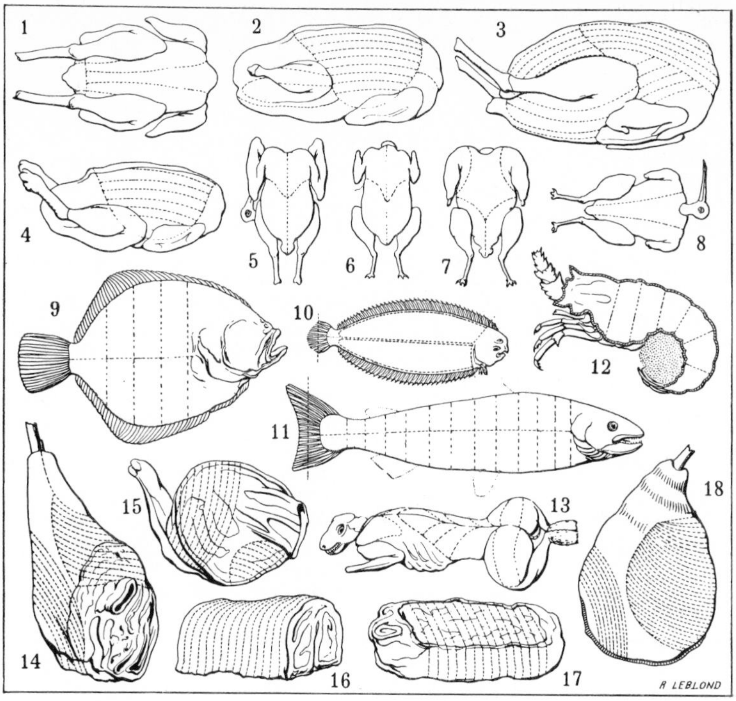

Ways of carving poultry, game, fish, meat.
1. Chicken; 2. Goose; 3. Turkey; 4. Duck; 5. Pigeon; 6. Teal; 7. Partridge; 8. Woodcock; 9. Turbot; 10. Sole; 11. Salmon; 12. Lobster; 13. Hare; 14. Leg of lamb; 15. Shoulder of lamb; 16. Loin of veal; 17. Fillet of beef; 18. Ham

A number of restaurant carvers have won a world-wide reputation. The famous Joseph Dugnol, who founded the Taverne Joseph, was a master in the art of carving. One of his contemporaries thus describes one of the feats accomplished by this most able man:

'It was at a dinner held by M. Paillard for a few important members of the Paris press. In front of the spellbound guests, Joseph Dugnol, who was in charge of the dining-room of this famous establishment, carved a Rouen duckling while holding it up impaled on the prongs of a fork, so that there was nothing to support it. He carved this duck into very thin fillets all of which fell, in perfect order, onto the dish underneath. And that,' adds the narrator, 'with admirable despatch and in less time than it takes to tell.'

Another such was the celebrated Frédéric Delair, the great Frederick of the Tour d'Argent, who was also a master in the complex art of jointing and carving poultry, especially Rouen duckling which was the great speciality of his restaurant.

Principles of carving – As a general principle, all meat should be carved vertically, across the grain of the meat. The slices must be as large and as even as possible.

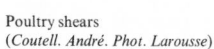

Poultry shears
(*Coutell. André. Phot. Larousse*)

Only leg of lamb or mutton is an exception to this rule. It can be carved in two ways, either parallel to or at right angles to the bone. Ham, whether boned or not, is always carved vertically, towards the bone if it is there.

To carve a chicken, begin with the leg. Insert the fork into the thigh and press down on it, using it as a lever on the leg as the knife slides along the carcase to sever the sinews. Sever the cartilage of the joint. Next, remove the wing. For this purpose, insert the fork under the wing and feel for the joint with the knife. To cut up the carcase, lay the chicken on its back. Hold it firm by wedging the fork high up in the breast. Divide the carcase lengthwise along the breastbone.

Nantes duck is jointed in the same way as chicken. To joint a Rouen duck, begin by detaching the two legs, as for chicken. Lay the duck on its back and shave off the two halves of the breast on either side of the breastbone. Pressing firmly down with the fork, cut the breast horizontally into very thin slices. The wings are removed last of all.

CASEIN. CASÉINE – Albumenoid substance in milk which is coagulated by rennet, the fermentation of which is the origin of all cheeses.

CASHEW. ACAJOU – There are different varieties of these trees. The type commonly known as *pear cashew* is cultivated in the tropical regions. Its fruit, the so-called cashew-nut, is kidney-shaped and contains an edible white nut with a sweet flavour. The fleshy part around this nut is called the cashew-pear, which is eaten raw throughout the whole of South America and in some European countries. It has a pleasant, slightly tart taste. Mixed with sugar, it can be made into excellent preserves, as well as a refreshing beverage.

Fermented, the cashew-nut fruit produces a kind of wine which is popular in Brazil, and a vinegar known as *anacard* or *cashew-nut vinegar*.

CASKING. ENTONNER – Pouring liquid into a cask.

Sauerkraut with breast of veal and a selection of sausages (*Pou. Phot. Nicolas*)

CASSATA. CASSATE – The cassata is an ice cream block or mould consisting of two differently flavoured ice creams with a filling of Chantilly cream and crystallised fruits (previously soaked in brandy or liqueur). It varies greatly in quality and delicacy.

CASSAVA. MANIOC – Plant native to the West Indies, Equatorial America, and Florida, U.S.A. The root, which is a fleshy tuber, contains edible starch. The sap, containing hydrocyanic acid, is poisonous. The poison, however, can be eliminated by fermentation and cooking. Some varieties are sweet and do not contain poison; they can be roasted on embers and eaten.

In South America, cassava is used in the manufacture of tapioca. The roots are grated, left to ferment and then pressed. The residue, baked into a flat cake and powdered, forms a *farinha* (Portuguese for meal). The starch of cassava, dried quickly by heat when in a moist condition, agglomerates into small masses known as tapioca.

In Florida, cassava is used as food for man and beast, and is used to make starch and glucose.

CASSE-MUSEAU (Jawbreaker) – Very hard cake, much in vogue in former times, but hardly ever made today. Here is a recipe for this cake, which dates from 1730:

'Take some cream cheese, 4 eggs, 100 g. (4 oz., ½ cup) butter, juice of ½ lemon, 300 g. (11 oz., 2¾ cups) flour and a pinch of salt. Mix these ingredients into a soft paste and leave for a few hours.

'Make the *casse-museaux* in the form of very small buns. Bake for 15 minutes at a low temperature. Split them open and put them back in the oven to finish baking.'

CASSEROLE – Cooking utensil made in copper, aluminium, stainless steel, nickel, or other metals; and also in terracotta, fireproof porcelain, tempered glass, and enamelled cast-iron. Many are decorative enough to use as serving dishes.

Casseroles are usually made in a rounded form, with one or two handles. When deep-sided, as is most common in U.S.A., they are used in the oven; when shallow-sided, they are normally called *sautoirs, sauteuses, plats à sauter* (sauté pan or frying pan).

CASSEROLE – In French cooking the term casserole also denotes a preparation generally made with rice, which, after cooking, is fashioned in the shape of a casserole, or a *timbale*. Casseroles are also made with a preparation of duchess potatoes.

In U.S.A. a casserole is a dish made of two or more parts, the basis of which can be, besides rice, any pasta (macaroni, spaghetti, etc.) with meat or fish plus a sauce or gravy, and vegetables. This one-dish meal can be prepared in advance and served in a decorative casserole.

Fillings for rice casseroles. GARNITURES POUR CASSEROLES AU RIZ – All the fillings indicated elsewhere for *timbales*, small patty shells or *vol-au-vent* can be used for this *entrée*. Casseroles can also be filled with various minced meats (poultry, game, etc.), *fricassées* of fowl with truffles, various preparations of lambs' sweetbreads, truffled *foie gras* escalopes, and with all kinds of *ragoûts* and *salpicons*.

Rice casserole à l'ancienne (Carême's recipe). CASSEROLE AU RIZ À L'ANCIENNE – 'The rice casserole is as elegant as it is rich; its shape and appetising appearance give it a distinct character; it is certainly the most arresting *entrée* cooked in the oven.

'For a dinner which includes eight *entrées*, one prefers to serve a handsome casserole of rice rather than a hot *pâté* or *vol-au-vent*, and such a preference is right for the casserole is the most attractive of the coloured *entrées*.

Method of preparation. 'Wash 1 kg. (2¼ lb., 4½ cups) Carolina rice in lukewarm water several times and put it in a large casserole. Cover with cold water, bring to the boil, allow to boil for a few seconds, and drain.

'Then cover the rice with good beef stock to about double its volume, and add some fat-skimmings from a chicken broth.

'Bring to the boil and then draw off the heat, in order to remove more easily the small amount of scum that will appear.

'Simmer for about 1 hour, and stir so that the grains burst evenly. Let it simmer for another 20 to 25 minutes, and stir it again. When you find it is soft and easy to crush between the fingers, take it off the heat. If still hard, add a little more stock and leave to cook until perfectly done. Stir it for a few minutes.

'When the rice is cool, work it well for a time with a wooden spoon so that every grain is crushed. It must be firm though malleable.

'Pour out the rice into a baking tin and form it into a casserole-shape 12 cm. (4 to 5 inches) high, making it smooth with the fingers. To decorate it, use the point of a knife and slices of carrot to emphasise the shape of the casserole.

'Cover the rice with clarified butter, and put in a hot oven for about 1½ hours. The colour should be a vivid yellow. When it is cooked, remove the cover which you outlined when forming the casserole, taking care to remove all the rice inside which does not adhere to the crust, which should be quite thin.

'Mix 1 tablespoon rice from the interior with a little *béchamel sauce* (if the filling is to use this sauce), or *Spanish sauce* (if the casserole is to be filled with a *ragoût* containing this), or any other sauce, and use to garnish the crust which is filled with whatever preparation is indicated. Before serving, lightly glaze the projections of the casserole.' (Carême, *Le Pâtissier royal.*)

Small casseroles of rice (Carême's recipe). CASSEROLETTES DE RIZ – 'These are made in the same way as casserole of rice. Place them in a hot oven on a metal sheet 7 cm. (3 inches) apart. Take them out when they are all a good golden colour.

'To serve, fill them with the appropriate *ragoût*.'

CASSIA. CASSE – Pod of a leguminous plant divided into compartments, each enclosing a fairly large seed, surrounded by a brownish pulp, which is sweet, slightly acid, with a flavour resembling that of the prune.

This pulp has laxative properties. When sieved it forms the *casse mondée* of the past.

CASSIS – Picturesque fishing port and commune of Bouches-du-Rhône, which has given its name to highly esteemed red, white and rosé wines. (See PROVENCE.)

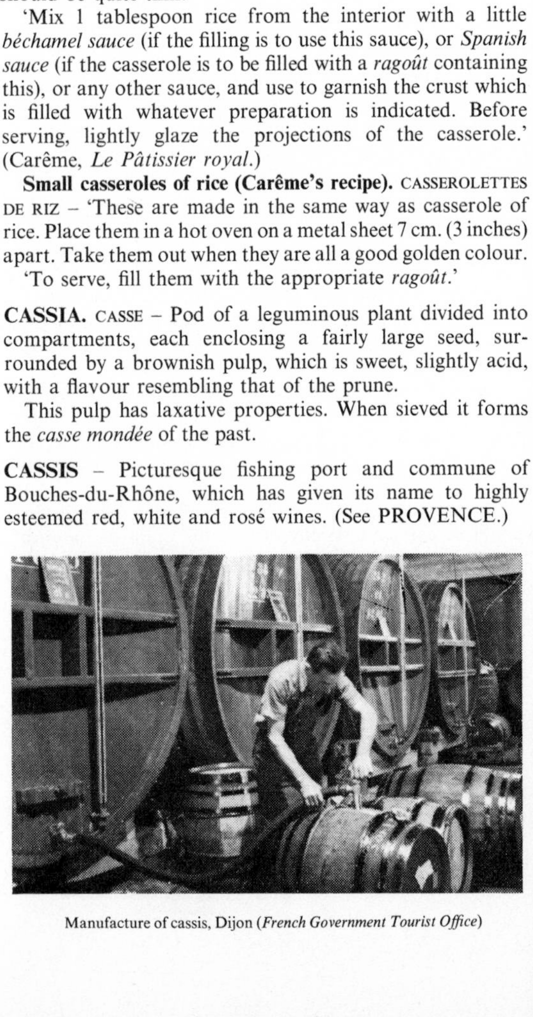

Manufacture of cassis, Dijon (*French Government Tourist Office*)

CHO

CASSOLETTE – Small dish in fireproof porcelain, metal or fireproof glass, used for presenting *hors-d'œuvre*, hot or cold, little *entrées*, and also some desserts.

Duchess potatoes, deep fried, hollowed out and stuffed with various fillings, are also called *cassolettes*. Filled with *salpicons* or *ragoûts* mixed with brown or white sauce, they can be served as *hors-d'œuvre* or *entrées*.

Cassolettes served as sweets are filled with creams, various sweetened pastes, or fruits poached in syrup.

CASSONADE – French term for semirefined sugar. The yellow cane *cassonade* has a slight flavour of rum and is used in *pâtisserie* for this reason. The beet *cassonade* has rather an unpleasant taste.

CASSOULET – Haricot bean stew which originates in Languedoc. It is prepared with pork and mutton, or with goose or duck, in an earthenware dish which used to be known as the *cassolle d'Issel*, from whence derives its name.

Franc-Nohain, humorous poet, sang the praises of Languedoc *cassoulet* in his *Nouvelle cuisinière bourgeoise*. He even gives a recipe in verse for *cassoulet*, the substance of which is here:

'On a moderate fire I see two casseroles. In one, a leg of *confit d'oie* or *confit de canard* (preserved goose or duck) as well as little sausages, ribs of pork and loin of mutton, are browning. Do not forget the flavouring, 2 tomatoes and 2 onions cut in four. Meanwhile the white Soissons haricots are cooking gently in the other utensil. Let the cooking proceed for 2 hours, and then arrange the beans and meat in the same earthenware vessel, in such a way that the goose or duck, mutton and pork are distributed between layers of haricot beans. After which put the *cassoulet* in the oven. Then on the surface of the dish a golden crust forms, thick and fat. Break it, because it must be incorporated with the rest of the ingredients. Put it back in the oven, wait until another crust forms, which again must be broken: and this must be done six times. Serve after breaking the crust seven times. A royal feast; in Languedoc this is called a haricot cream or *cassoulet*.'

Anatole France loved the *cassoulet*. In *Histoire comique* he wrote:

'I am going to lead you to a little tavern in the rue Vavin, *chez Clémence*, who only makes one dish, but a stupendous one: *le cassoulet de Castelnaudary*, which contains legs of *confit d'oie* (preserved goose), haricot beans previously blanched, pork fat, and little sausages. To be good it must have cooked very slowly for a long time. Clémence's *cassoulet* has been cooking for twenty years. She replenishes the pot sometimes with goose, sometimes with pork fat, sometimes she puts in a sausage or some haricots, but it is always the same *cassoulet*. The basis remains, and this ancient and precious substance gives it a savour, which one finds in the paintings of the old Venetian masters, in the amber flesh tints of their women. Come, I wish you to taste Clémence's *cassoulet*.'

There are three kinds of *cassoulets*; that of Castelnaudary, of Carcassonne, and of Toulouse.

The three types should have the following differences: that of Castelnaudary is prepared with fresh pork, ham, knuckle of pork, and fresh bacon skins; that of Carcassonne with the addition to the above of a shortened leg of mutton, and partridges in season; that of Toulouse has added breast of pork, Toulouse sausage, mutton and *confit d'oie* or *confit de canard*.

In Languedoc the way in which the *cassoulet* is made varies according to whoever is preparing it. Some cook the haricots, pork, mutton, bacon skins and sausages together, and then arrange these in alternate layers in the *terrine*, covering the surface with a thick sprinkling of breadcrumbs, and take it to the baker's oven to cook gently for some hours.

Cassoulet de Castelnaudary I – Simmer white haricot

Cassoulet (*Robert Carrier*)

beans and bacon skins in a glazed earthenware pot with the usual seasoning, meats, aromatic vegetables and a pinch of garlic.

Drain and place them in an earthenware pot which has been lined with the fresh bacon skins, knuckle of pork, breast of pork, sausage, and a leg of *confit d'oie*.

Sprinkle with a layer of coarse breadcrumbs and add goose fat. Cook gently in the oven for several hours.

When a good golden crust has formed on the surface of the *cassoulet* stir it in with a spoon and repeat this 2 or 3 times.

Gourmets like this served with either a fine red Aquitaine wine or with an old Minervois wine.

Cassoulet de Castelnaudary II – For eight people soak 1 litre (1¾ pints, generous quart) dried white haricot beans for several hours, but not for too long or they may begin to ferment. Simmer in an earthenware pot with 300 g. (11 oz.) salt breast of pork, 200 g. (7 oz.) desalted rolled-up bacon skins, a carrot, an onion stuck with cloves, and a *bouquet garni* containing 3 cloves of garlic. Season with a very little salt.

In another pan, brown in lard or goose fat, 750 g. (1¾ lb.) loin of pork and 500 g. (generous 1 lb.) boned loin of mutton, well seasoned with salt and pepper. Add 2 medium-sized chopped onions, a *bouquet garni* and 2 crushed cloves of garlic. Continue cooking with the lid on and add gravy or beef stock from time to time.

When the haricots are nearly cooked, remove the carrot, onion, and *bouquet garni*, and put in the pork, mutton, a garlic sausage, a leg of *confit d'oie* or *confit de canard*, and a home-made sausage. Simmer gently for 1 hour.

Remove the pieces of meat from the haricot beans. Cut the pork, mutton and goose into slices of equal size, cut the bacon skins into rectangular pieces, the skinned garlic sausage and the sausage into slices.

Put into a large earthenware pot lined with bacon skins, a layer of haricot beans and then a layer of the various meats with some of their sauce. Fill the pot with alternate layers, seasoning each one with a little freshly ground pepper. On the last layer of haricots lay slices of salt pork, bacon skins, and slices of garlic sausage.

Sprinkle with white breadcrumbs, and pour over them a little goose fat. Cook gently in the oven for about 1½ hours. Serve the cassoulet in the pot in which it has cooked.

There are other Languedocian *cassoulets*, that of Luchon, for example, which is called *pistache*.

CASTAGNACI (Corsican cookery) – Thick fritters or waffles made with chestnut flour.

CASTIGLIONE (À LA) – Preparation of small pieces of meat. The *Castiglione garnish* consists of large mushrooms stuffed with rice and browned in the oven, aubergines sautéed in butter, and slices of poached beef marrow (see GARNISHES).

CASTRATE. CHÂTRER – Castration of animals destined for the butcher, to hasten their fattening.

The word *châtrer* is also applied to the removal of the intestines of crayfish (U.S. crawfish) before cooking. In order to do this the central part of the tail is pinched and the intestines emerge.

CAT. CHAT – Domestic cat whose edible meat has a flavour halfway between that of rabbit and hare. Cat's meat has often been eaten in periods of famine or siege. Legend has it that in the cook-shops the cat is often used in the making of rabbit *fricassées*. Examination of the bones would easily enable one, in case of doubt, to distinguish between the two animals.

CATALANE (À LA) – Garnish for large pieces of meat composed of aubergines sautéed in oil, and pilaf of rice. (See GARNISHES.)

CATECHU. CACHOU – Thick sap which comes from a variety of Indian acacia. *Areca catechu* (betel nut). The catechu is found in compact, crumbly, irregular masses which are brownish on the outside and reddish-brown on the inside. It should neither stick to the tongue nor tint the saliva red.

Its taste, at first bitter and astringent, becomes sweet and clean without any smell. The most highly prized varieties come from Sri Lanka and Burma, the latter having medicinal properties.

The catechu contains a strong proportion of tannin, which gives it astringent properties.

Catfish

CATFISH. POISSON-CHAT – American river fish found principally in the Mississippi basin. It has six barbels or feelers around the mouth reaching from 30 to 60 cm. (12 to 24 inches) in length. The flesh is delicate and there are not too many bones.

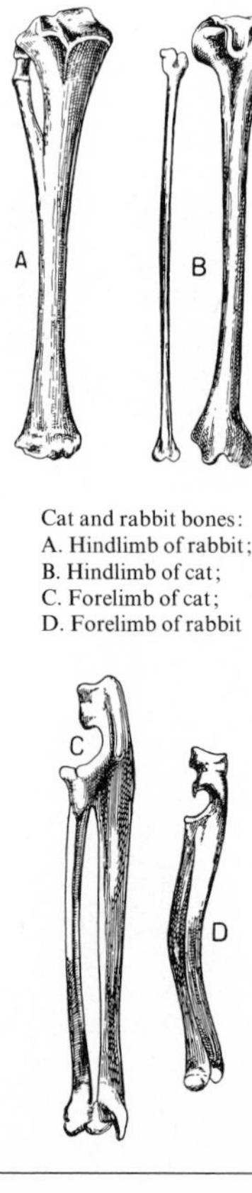

Cat and rabbit bones:
A. Hindlimb of rabbit;
B. Hindlimb of cat;
C. Forelimb of cat;
D. Forelimb of rabbit

CATSUP or KETCHUP – Condiment of English origin, widely used both in England and U.S.A. It has a tomato base and is highly spiced.

CAUF. BANNETON – Receptacle with holes which permits fish to be kept alive in water. This term is also used to describe a baker's bread basket.

CAUL. CRÉPINE – Membrane enclosing the paunch of animals, applied particularly to that of pork and mutton. In French, this is also called *toilette*.

CAULIFLOWER. CHOU-FLEUR – Vegetable of oriental origin, known in Italy since the sixteenth century. A delicate food which must always be bought when its leaves are green. This is an indication of freshness. The leaves are edible.

Boiled cauliflower. CHOU-FLEUR À L'ANGLAISE – Boil a cauliflower in salted water, drain and serve with melted butter.

According to the English method a cauliflower served in this way must be cooked whole, with two rows of tender leaves enveloping the flower-head.

The leaves, ribs, and stems should not be wasted. They are excellent trimmed and cooked with the white part. They can also be used for soup, *hors-d'œuvre*, etc.

Cauliflower, whole and with flower head detached (right), which is the only part generally used for consumption

Boiled cauliflower with various sauces (cold). CHOU-FLEUR BOUILLI – Divide the cauliflower into florets, cook them in salted water, drain, and put them under the cold tap. Arrange the florets in their original form. Serve with *Vinaigrette sauce, Mayonnaise* or some other cold sauce (see SAUCE).

Boiled cauliflower with various sauces (hot). CHOU-FLEUR BOUILLI – Divide the cauliflower into florets, trim, and boil them in salted water. Drain, and arrange them in their original form. Garnish with fresh parsley.

Serve with melted butter or one of the usual sauces for boiled vegetables: *Cream, Hollandaise, White sauce*, etc. (see SAUCE).

Cauliflower with brown butter or noisette butter. CHOU-FLEUR AU BEURRE NOIR – Boil the cauliflower florets in salted water and arrange them on a dish in the shape of a dome. Sprinkle with chopped parsley and lemon juice. Cover with *Brown butter* or with *Noisette butter* (see BUTTER, *Compound butters*.)

Cauliflower with cream. CHOU-FLEUR À LA CRÈME – Cook the cauliflower in the way described above, drain, and toss in butter. Rearrange the florets in their original form. Cover with a *Cream sauce* (see SAUCE).

Cauliflower fritters. CHOU-FLEUR EN FRITOTS – Cook the cauliflower florets in salted water, keeping them rather firm. Drain, and soak them for 30 minutes in oil, lemon juice, chopped parsley, salt and pepper.

Dip the florets in a light batter (see BATTER). Fry in deep fat and sprinkle with fried parsley. Serve with tomato sauce.

Cauliflower au gratin

Cauliflower au gratin. CHOU-FLEUR AU GRATIN – Cook the cauliflower florets in boiling salted water, drain them, and toss gently in butter. Arrange on a buttered *gratin* dish and cover with *Mornay sauce* (see SAUCE). Sprinkle with grated cheese and melted butter, and brown in the oven.

Cauliflower à la milanaise. CHOU-FLEUR À LA MILANAISE – Cook the cauliflower florets in boiling salted water, drain and toss them gently in butter. Sprinkle with grated Parmesan cheese and melted butter. Brown in the oven. When serving, pour on a little *Noisette butter* (see BUTTER, *Compound butters*).

Cauliflower Mornay. CHOU-FLEUR MORNAY – Prepared in the same way as *Cauliflower au gratin*.

Cauliflower mould. PAIN DE CHOU-FLEUR – Made in the same way as *Endive loaf* (see ENDIVE) but with a purée of cauliflower.

Cauliflower à la polonaise. CHOU-FLEUR À LA POLONAISE – Arrange cooked cauliflower on a buttered dish and sprinkle with chopped hard-boiled egg yolks mixed with chopped parsley. Pour over the cauliflower *Noisette butter* (see BUTTER, *Compound butters*) in which have been fried 25 g. (1 oz., $\frac{1}{2}$ cup) fresh breadcrumbs per 100 g. (4 oz., $\frac{1}{2}$ cup) butter. Serve at once; the butter should be frothy.

Cauliflower purée. PURÉE DE CHOU-FLEUR – Cook and drain a cauliflower, dry it for a moment in the oven, and pass it through a sieve. Add one-quarter of its weight of potato purée, and heat. Mix in fresh cream, butter and seasoning.

Cauliflower salad. SALADE DE CHOU-FLEUR – Boil a cauliflower in salted water, and drain. Season with oil, vinegar, lemon juice, salt and pepper. Sprinkle with chopped chervil.

Cauliflower sautéed in butter. CHOU-FLEUR SAUTÉ AU BEURRE – Blanch cauliflower florets, drain, and cook in butter until lightly browned. Arrange in a dish and pour the butter over.

Cauliflower soufflé. SOUFFLÉ DE CHOU-FLEUR – Prepare with cauliflower boiled in salt water. Pass it through a fine sieve, in the same way as for *Chicory soufflé* (see CHICORY, ENDIVE).

Stalks and stumps of cauliflower. MOELLE DE CHOU-FLEUR – Trim the stalks or stumps, removing the woody outer casing. Blanch whole if they are to be served with the vegetable. If they are to be cooked separately, cut into pieces. After blanching, these stalks and stumps can be prepared in the same way as artichoke stalks or endive stumps.

CAVAILLON – Little town in the Vaucluse district which has given its name to a variety of melon (see MELON).

CAVEAU – Small cellar, sometimes reserved for fine wines.

CAVEAU (LE) – Literary society, bacchic and gastronomic. Founded in 1729 by Piron, Collé, Gallet and Crébillon *fils*.

CAVIARE. CAVIAR – The roe of the sturgeon family, lightly salted or marinated.

Caviare is the 'fruit' of the sturgeon, a migratory fish, of which there are a dozen or so different varieties, each belonging to one of two species. That found in the Gironde is *Acipenser sturio*.

The sturgeon lives in coastal waters and in the spring, when fully grown, it swims up the rivers to spawn. The time of this migratory movement depends upon the temperature of the water, which itself depends upon the severity of the preceding winter and the melting snows. It usually takes place sometime between March and July.

The females (then in their eighth or ninth year) search for a deep sandy pool in the upper reaches of the river where the water is fresh; while the males (from six to seven years onwards) engage in a kind of love pursuit, escorting the females to the spawning grounds.

Caviare (*Petrossian. Phot. Nicolas*)

The baby sturgeons rapidly struggle free from the fertile eggs and, after a three-month period in the place of their birth, descend to the mouth of the river where they remain for several years. They then move to the sea and live there until fully grown, returning to the river only when they reach the age of reproduction.

At one time, the Cossacks of the Ural River harpooned the fish through holes in the ice, thus obtaining the first caviare of the year. This yellowy-gold caviare was superior to all the rest, a gift worthy of the Tsar, to whom they presented it.

Extracting the caviare is a knack acquired only through experience. Immediately the fish is caught, it is gutted (while still alive, and after having let its blood through an incision under the caudal fin so as to diminish its reactions). The eggs are immediately extracted and placed on a special sieve to be washed, drained, and salted.

Soviet scientists have perfected a type of Caesarian operation for sturgeons that makes it possible for them to be thrown back into the river alive and recommence the reproduction cycle.

Whatever the process, Iran and Russia, the biggest producers, offer three types of caviare:

Caviare malossol – A fresh caviare with firm, plump, sparkling eggs packed in specially treated tins. *Malossol* means 'slightly salted' in Russia.

Fresh salted caviare – From both Russia and Iran. It is prepared using eggs collected during the hot season. Packed in casks which contain approximately 60 kg. (132 lb.) caviare. It is difficult to find in Europe.

Pressed caviare – Prepared at the end of the fishing season. It consists of a dense mass of crushed black eggs which are packed in small glass jars.

French annual production of caviare does not amount to more than 3 tons, and the sturgeon (which at one time was even caught in the Seine) is becoming more and more rare.

Depending upon its age and size, a female sturgeon yields anything from 4 to 16 kg. (9 to 35 lb.) eggs. The average yield per fish caught in the Gironde is 6 kg. (13 lb.) Eaten lightly salted a few days after being fished, French caviare is delicious.

Gourmets eat caviare as it is, without toast or butter, simply adding a sprinkling of lemon juice.

There are different qualities of caviare and many other fishes' eggs are sold commercially under the name of 'caviare' ('salmon caviare', for example), but the term 'caviare' on its own can only be used to designate products based on sturgeon roe.

CAVOUR (À LA) – Method of preparing small pieces of meat, especially veal escalopes and calves' sweetbreads. These are served on circles of polenta, garnished with grilled mushrooms and filled with a purée of chicken livers and slices of truffle.

CAYENNE PEPPER – See PEPPER, *Red pepper or pimento*.

CELERIAC or CELERY ROOTS. CÉLERI-RAVE – Celeriac is a variety of celery which has a large edible root. Wash and pare the celeriac. Divide into quarters and cut into pieces or large slices. Blanch them for 5 minutes in boiling salted water, plunge into cold water, drain, and wipe dry. Cook them in butter, adding a little white stock or water. All the recipes for branch celery are applicable to celeriac.

The following recipes can also be applied to this vegetable.

Celeriac julienne. JULIENNE DE CÉLERI-RAVE – Used as a garnish. Pare a root of celeriac, wash and cut it into matchstick or *julienne* strips. Put them into a sauté pan in which

1 tablespoon butter has been heated. Add salt and a little powdered sugar, and cook slowly.

Celeriac purée. PURÉE DE CÉLERI-RAVE – Garnish for large or small pieces of meat. The purée is prepared in the same way as for *Cardoon purée* (see CARDOON).

Salpicon of celeriac. SALPICON DE CÉLERI-RAVE – Cut the celeriac into squares, blanch in salted water, drain, and cook in butter.

Stuffed celeriac à la paysanne. CÉLERI-RAVE À LA PAYSANNE – Used as a garnish. Pare and slice 2 celeriac roots into rounds 3 cm. (1 inch) thick. Blanch for 5 minutes in salted water, plunge into cold water, drain, and dry in a cloth. Scoop a hollow in each slice to half its depth.

Dice the pulp which has been hollowed out, and add double the quantity of carrot and onion *brunoise* (q.v.) sautéed in butter and seasoned with salt and pepper.

Stuff the celeriac slices with this mixture. Put them in a buttered ovenware dish, dust them with grated cheese, sprinkle with melted butter, and brown in a moderate oven.

All the stuffings used for tomatoes and artichoke hearts can also be applied to celeriac.

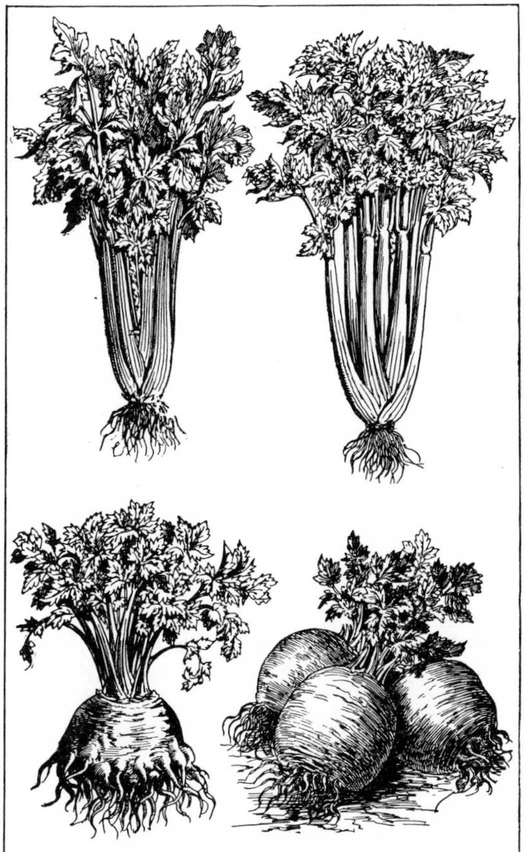

Varieties of celery and celeriac

CELERY. CÉLERI – Cultivated form of wild celery. Used a great deal by the Romans, celery did not come into wider cultivation until the sixteenth century. Growers have tried to develop the leaves as well as the root.

Celery contains an essential oil, which is highly aromatic. According to the different varieties, either the stems, elongated by trussing or culture in the dark, or the roots (celeriac) are eaten. Both are eaten raw in salad, or cooked.

The Loire Valley is the principal region of French production.

Celery has diuretic and appetite-stimulating properties. Celery juice is rich in Vitamins A and C.

BRANCH (FORCED) CELERY. CÉLERI EN BRANCHES – Trim off the upper branches of the celery, keeping only the tender parts. Remove the green outer stems and trim the root. Wash the base of the celery, allowing water to run between the stems so that all earth or other foreign matter is washed away. Pare the outer stems to remove the fibres. Blanch the celery in boiling salted water for 10 minutes. Plunge into cold water, drain, and wipe dry.

Spread out on a cloth, open the stems slightly and season inside. Tie them together, 2 or 3 at a time, and put them in a deep casserole which is already buttered and lined with bacon rinds, chopped onions and sliced carrots. Cover with white stock from which not all the fat has been skimmed, or with beef stock.

Begin cooking on the stove, then remove the pan to the oven and cook for 1½ hours at a low temperature.

Celery can be cooked *au maigre* (without meat) by omitting the bacon rinds and replacing the stock with water.

Celery with béchamel sauce. CÉLERIS À LA BÉCHAMEL – Braise the celery, drain, and halve it lengthways. Fold each portion in half, put in a buttered pan and simmer for 10 minutes. Cover with *Béchamel sauce* – not too thick (see SAUCE). Simmer again for a few minutes.

Celery in butter. CÉLERIS AU BEURRE – Trim, wash, and blanch celery heads for 10 minutes in salted water. Halve them lengthways and bend each portion in two. Place in a well-buttered pan, season, and moisten with a few tablespoons white stock or water. Cook, covered, for 45 minutes or 1 hour.

Celery with cream. CÉLERIS À LA CRÈME – Pare and shorten heads of celery. Wash them and remove the fibres from the outside stems. Blanch in salted boiling water, plunge into cold water, drain, and dry.

Halve the heads lengthways, arrange them in a well-buttered pan, season, and cover with a light *bouillon* (or with water if you want to serve them *au maigre*).

Bring to the boil. Cover the pan and put it in the oven for about 1 hour. Drain the celery, bend the pieces in half, and place on a dish. Strain the liquor, skim, and boil it down. Add to it ½ dl. (3 tablespoons, scant ¼ cup) *Béchamel sauce* (see SAUCE).

Moisten with 2 dl. (⅓ pint, scant cup) thick fresh cream. Boil down by half and add 1 tablespoon butter. Mix, strain, and pour this sauce over the celery.

Celery à la grecque (cold hors d'œuvre). CÉLERIS À LA GRECQUE – Trim celery heads, wash well, divide into quarters and prepare them in the manner described for *Artichokes à la grecque* (see ARTICHOKE).

Celery à l'italienne. CÉLERIS À L'ITALIENNE – The same as for *Cardoons à l'italienne* (see CARDOON).

Celery au jus. CÉLERIS AU JUS – The same as for *Cardoons au jus* (see CARDOON).

Celery with marrow. CÉLERIS À LA MOELLE – The same as for *Cardoons with marrow* (see CARDOON).

Celery Mornay. CÉLERIS MORNAY – The same as for *Cardoons Mornay* (see CARDOON).

Celery with Parmesan. CÉLERIS AU PARMESAN – The same as for *Cardoons with Parmesan* (see CARDOON).

Celery purée. PURÉE DE CÉLERIS – Prepare the purée in the same way as for *Cardoon purée* (see CARDOON), using braised celery, cooked with beef *bouillon* or water. Add potatoes in the proportion of a third of the volume of the celery; this improves the consistency.

Celery with various sauces. CÉLERIS AUX SAUCES DIVERSES – Pare, wash, and blanch celery. Cook in salted water, drain, and serve like asparagus, with sauces handed separately.

Celery vinaigrette. CÉLERIS À LA VINAIGRETTE – Scrape and wash the celery. Arrange the sticks in a crystal glass. Serve with *Vinaigrette sauce* (see SAUCE) handed separately.

CELLAR. CAVE – Underground room with or without an arched ceiling, in which wine is kept. A good cellar must be cool (10° to 12°C., 50° to 54°F.), slightly damp, and the air must circulate a little.

Liqueur cellar. CAVE À LIQUEURS – Chest, made by a cabinet maker or goldsmith, used to lock up precious flagons and sometimes liqueur glasses.

CELLULOSE – A substance of varying degrees of hardness which forms the tissue of vegetable matter.

CENTRAL AMERICA – See INTERNATIONAL COOKERY, *American cookery*.

CENTRAL EUROPE AND THE BALKANS – See INTERNATIONAL COOKERY.

CÉPAGE – Plant, variety of vine. French vines, restocked with American vines, have been grafted onto the ancient vine stocks which are recognised as the best in each region. The number of vine varieties is considerable. Among the principal stocks there are:

In Bordeaux the *Cabernet franc*, the *Cabernet sauvignon*, the *Merlot*, the *Malbec*, and the *Verdot* for red wines; the *Sauvignon*, the *Sémillon*, and the *Muscadelle* for white wines.

In Burgundy, the *Pinot noir* is the principal wine stock for the red wines; the *Chardonnay* for the white. The same in Champagne except that the *Pinot noir* is made into white wine. *Gamay* is the vine *par excellence* in Beaujolais. It is also grown all over central France and in the west. The *Syrah* and the *Viognier* are found mainly in the northern Côtes du Rhône; the *Grenache, Carignon, Cinsault, Mourvèdre, Clairette,* and *Ugni blanc* are the vines common to the south of France and the southern Côtes du Rhône. In Alsace the principal vines are the *Sylvaner, Riesling, Traminer, Pinot gris* (*Tokay*), and *Muscat*.

The white wines of the Loire come from either the *Sauvignon* (Pouilly-sur-Loire, Sancerre, etc:), from the *Chénin* (Vouvray, Saumur, Anjou), or from the *Muscadet*.

The Jura wines come principally from the *Pinot blanc* and the *Poulsart*; the Muscat wines from Roussillon are derived from the *Alicante*; the *Grenache*, the *Aramon*, and the *Carigane* are the vine stocks with a high yield, cultivated in the *départements* of Aude, Hérault and Gard.

Among the notable vine stocks producing table wines are the various *Chasselas*, the *Muscats* (white and red), the *Oeillade*, etc.

CÈPE – French name for boletus or edible mushroom. Recipes will be found under MUSHROOM.

CEREALS. CÉRÉALES – Farinaceous foodstuffs which are the basis of human diet.

Oats, wheat, maize, millet, barley, rice, rye and Indian millet are the gramineous crops; only buckwheat belongs to the polygonaceous group. All cereals can be made into bread, but wheat and rye are particularly suitable for this purpose.

Cereals are indispensable elements of man's diet, providing him with the energy necessary for his physical work, as well as valuable glucosides and Vitamin B.

Flour-refining processes too often deprive the cereal of its husk and germ, both of which contain these vital nutritive elements. It is for this reason that dieticians advocate the consumption of wholemeal bread, sprouted wheat and whole rice.

CERVELAS – Sausage made of pork meat and pork fat, seasoned with garlic. This type of *charcuterie* is so-called because brains (*cervelle*), particularly pigs' brains, once formed part of its composition. It is also called *Saucisson de Paris* (see SAUCISSON, *Parisian saucisson*).

CHABICHOU – See CHEESE.

CHABISSOUS or CABECOUS – See CHEESE.

CHABLIS – Town in the district of Yonne famous for its white wines (see WINE).

CHABOISSEAU – Freshwater fish of the *Cottus* family which has delicate flesh.

CHABOT – Mediterranean fish which locally is called 'scorpion', 'sea-devil', and 'toad', on account of its strange appearance. It is also known as 'tadpole' because of its large head, and 'grumbler' and 'sea-cock' because of the rumbling sound it makes when held in the hand. The flesh of this fish is delicate and is used in *bouillabaisse* and fish soups. It should not be eaten during the spawning season from November to May. In France, chub are sometimes called *chabot*.

CHAINGY – See CHEESE.

CHALK. CHAUX – Calcium oxide, found in various combinations and in different forms in organic tissue. Drinking water often contains too high a proportion of calcium salt and is called 'hard'. This water prevents the satisfactory cooking of vegetables. One can remove the calcium salts from drinking water by decanting it after prolonged boiling and subsequent cooling, but it must then be aerated by beating.

CHAMBERTIN – Vineyard on the Côte d'Or in the commune of Gevrey-Chambertin.

CHAMBORD (À LA) – Method of preparing large braised fish which includes a very complex garnish. (See CARP, *Carp Chambord*; GARNISHES).

CHAMBRER – Said of wines that are brought up from the cellar several hours before they are due to be served, so that they can be slowly raised to room temperature. All red Bordeaux should be *chambré*.

The expression goes back to a time when the word *chambre* could apply to almost any room in the house. The pantry was the *chambre* where the wine was usually kept before being drunk. The cold dishes were kept in the pantry and its temperature was therefore not very high.

Gastronomes are more or less in agreement that the various wines should be served at the following temperatures:

Dry white wines, between 5° and 8°C. (41° and 46°F.)

Dessert white wines, between 2° and 5°C. (36° and 41°F.)

Rosé wines, between 8° and 10°C. (46° and 50°F.)

Light red wines, between 10° and 12°C. (50° and 53°F.)

The great Burgundies, between 15° and 17°C. (59° and 63°F.)

The great Bordeaux, between 16° and 18°C. (61° and 64°F.)

It is also a question of taste. A connoisseur who wishes to have his Burgundy at 18°C. (64°F.) and his Bordeaux at

20°C. (68°F.) does not have to uncork the bottles and leave them in the dining-room, as he would have done in the old days. With central heating, our dining-rooms have a temperature often as high as 22°C. (71°F.) or 24°C. (75°F.). It is therefore necessary to gauge the proper rate of temperature-raising to avoid offering guests overheated wine. The process must be slow. A bottle of wine should never be plunged into hot water or left near a fire or radiator to hasten the process.

CHAMOIS – Wild mammal, bearing some resemblance to the goat, found in the high Alps and in the Pyrenees, where it is called *Isard*.

Chamois meat is considered excellent venison, especially when the animal is young. It is tougher when the chamois is older, and should be properly marinated before cooking. It is prepared in the same way as roebuck (q.v.).

CHAMPAGNE – This province, which comprises approximately the four *départements* of Marne, Ardennes, Haute-Marne and Aube, has a world-wide reputation for its great sparkling white wines.

The cooking in the province is rather limited but excellent. The local *charcuterie* is in the first rank of gastronomic specialities, especially the delicious *andouillettes* of Bar-sur-Aube and Bar-sur-Seine; the *andouillettes de mouton* and the *langues fourrées* of Troyes; the famous *pigs' trotters à la Sainte-Menehould*; Reims hams and knuckles; and many other dishes.

Meat, particularly mutton, is good, and poultry is fairly good. Fruit and vegetables are excellent. Freshwater fish include trout, carp, pike and salmon. Good furred and feathered game is to be found, and the Ardennes thrushes are especially prized by connoisseurs.

Culinary specialities – Among the dishes of Champagne are *matelotes* (q.v.), using champagne; *la potée champenoise*; *quartier de mouton à la champenoise*; *boudin de lapin à la Sainte-Menehould*; *thrushes à l'ardennaise*, *poulet à la peau de goret*; *gougère de l'Aube*; *salade de pissenlit au lard*; and,

Gastronomic map of Champagne

Grape harvest in Champagne (*Laurent-Perrier*)

as a sweet, *beignets au fromage blanc*.

Vineyards – The cellars of Champagne are famous. One single wine embellishes them – Champagne.

The vine-growing district of Champagne is divided into three great regions:

Montagne de Reims. South of Reims, of which the principal vineyards are Villiers-Marmery, Verzy, Verzenay, Beaumont-sur-Vesle, Mailly, Sillery, Puisieulx, Ludes, Rilly-la-Montagne, Chigny, Trois-Puits, Montbré, Villers-Allerand, Sermiers, Charmery, Ecueil, Sacy, Villedomange, Jouy, Vrigny. Linked with the Montagne de Reims is the Petite Montagne with the vineyards of Hermonville, Saint-Thierry, Trigny and Pévy; and the Côte de Bouzy with the vineyards of Trépail, Louvois, Tauxières, Ambonnay and Bouzy.

Vallée de la Marne. Its principal vineyards are: Ay, Mareuil-sur-Ay, Mutigny, Avenay, Dizy, Cumières, Hautvilliers, Damery, Tours, Bisseuil, Venteuil, Fleury-la-Rivière, Reuil, Vandières, Verneuil, and Vincelles on the right bank; Nardeuil, Boursault, Leuvrigny, Festigny, Troissy, and Dormans on the left bank; Epernay, Pierry, Moussy, Vinay, and Saint-Martin on the Côte d'Epernay.

Côte des blancs. South-east of Epernay of which the principal vineyards are: Cuis, Cramant, Avize, Grauves, Oger, Le Mesnil-sur-Oger, Vertus, Bergères-les-Vertus, Mancy, Oiry, Monthelon.

The wine of Champagne – Apart from the 'still' white and red wines which are called *nature* wines, Champagne wine must be made effervescent according to the so-called *Méthode champenoise* with the second fermentation taking place in the bottle. This method (perfected by Dom Pérignon) comprises a series of processes that can be summarised as follows:

1. Usual alcoholic fermentation followed by all the processes employed in the production of white wine. (It should be remembered that in Champagne the black grapes are used *en blanc* which means that only the juice of the grape is fermented.)

2. Constitution of the *cuvée* (or special blend) by combining wines selected from a variety of Champagne growths.

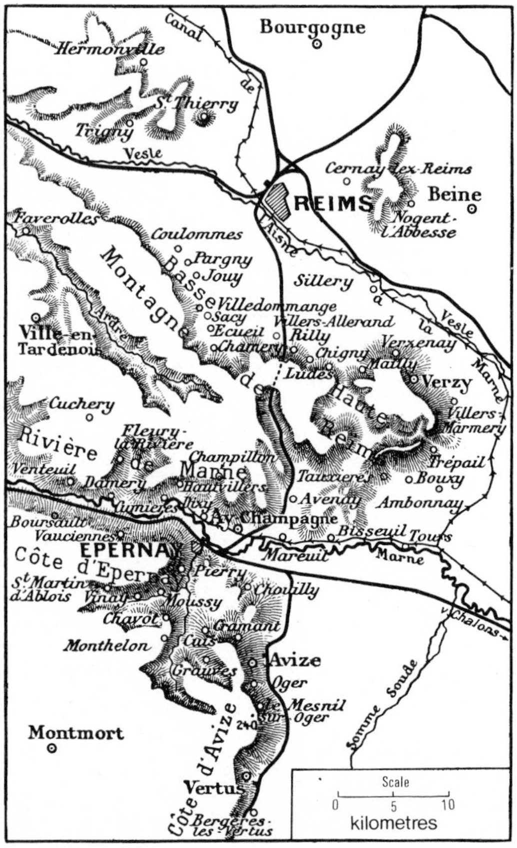

Map of Champagne vineyards

Champagne production

Fermentation chambers
(*Laurent-Perrier*)

Modern bottling plant
(*Yvon*)

'Champagnisation' in the cellars
(*Laurent Perrier*)

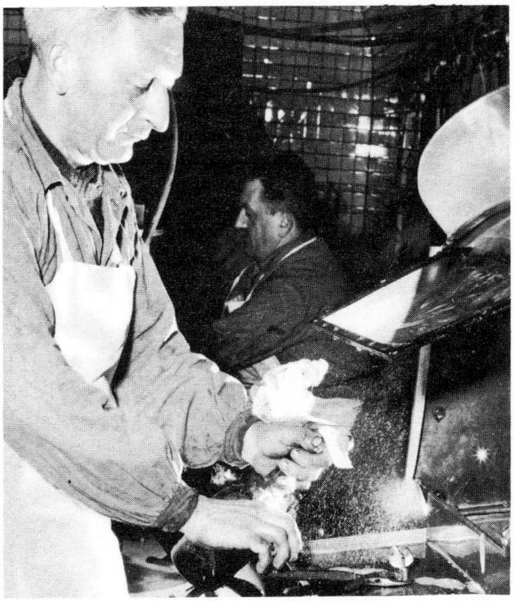

Extraction of sediment-coated cork
(*Laurent-Perrier*)

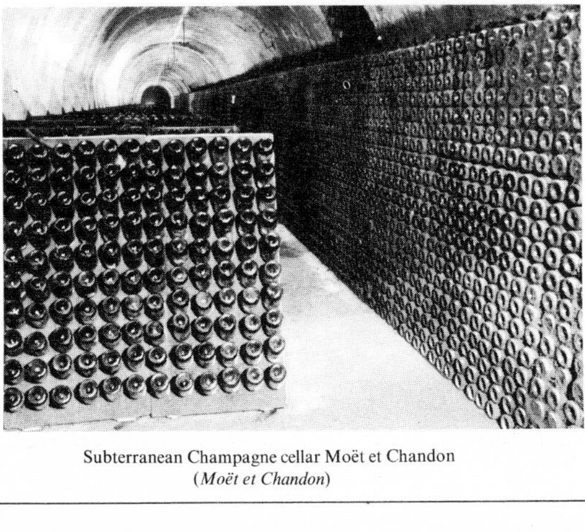

Subterranean Champagne cellar Moët et Chandon
(*Moët et Chandon*)

Modern equipment for labelling bottles
(*Delavaud*)

Old champagne bottles

3. After a 'dosage' of cane sugar, the wine is poured into hermetically sealed bottles. The sugar provokes a second fermentation by releasing carbonic acid gas; this is called the *prise de mousse* (sparkling process).

4. Working of the deposit. The bottles are placed on wooden frames (each bottle having a cage of its own) and slowly raised from a horizontal to a vertical position, to enable the deposit left by fermentation to slide down towards the cork.

5. Disgorging. Removal of the deposit.

6. Topping up the bottles with a '*liqueur*' after the deposit has been removed. This *liqueur* consists of cane sugar solution of varying strengths, depending on whether the client requires an extra dry, dry, *demi-sec* or sweet Champagne.

7. Cellarage. The bottles are matured for a period which varies according to whether the wine is vintage or non-vintage.

CHAMPAGNE (Fine) – Name given to certain brandies made in the Charentes area. The famous name given to the locality which produces these famous brandies is due, it is said, to a resemblance between the soil and the chalky subsoil with that of the Champagne region of north-west France. (See CHARENTE, *Eaux-de-vie*.)

CHAMPAGNISER – To produce the sparkling quality or to treat wines according to the Champagne method.

CHAMPIGNY (Pastry) – Use puff pastry (*pâte feuilletée*) which has been rolled out six times (see DOUGH). Roll it out to a thickness of not more than 3 mm. ($\frac{1}{8}$ inch) in a square shape. Fill the centre with a layer of apricot jam flavoured with a little kirsch and containing a few apricot kernels. Moisten the edge of the pastry, cover with a layer of pastry 1 cm. ($\frac{1}{2}$ inch) thick, and seal the edges, indenting them with a fork. To prevent the jam from seeping out during the baking, press a ribbon of pastry round the edges. Brush with beaten egg and bake in a moderate oven for 25 to 30 minutes. Sprinkle with icing sugar and glaze.

CHAMPOREAU – Black coffee with the addition of *eau-de-vie*, Cognac, Armagnac, rum or kirsch. In slang language one says *faire champoreau*.

CHANFAINA (Spanish cookery) – Cook a lamb's or pig's liver in salt water. Fry 2 large chopped onions in oil. When almost cooked, add diced pimentos, chopped parsley, and chopped fresh mint. Season with salt, pepper, cinnamon, and cumin, and cook for a few minutes. Add the cooked liver, cut up into large dice.

Cook on a fairly strong heat for a few minutes. Add a few tablespoons of the liquor in which the liver has been cooked. Boil for 5 minutes. Add a small quantity of breadcrumbs cooked in water in the manner of a bread *panada* (q.v.) to bind the sauce. Season highly.

CHANTERELLE (Cantharellus cibarius) – Edible mushroom, also known in France as *girolle*. (See MUSHROOMS.)

CHANTILLY – Name given to fresh cream beaten to the consistency of a mousse, sweetened and flavoured with vanilla or other flavours. It can also mean a *hollandaise sauce* to which whipped cream has been added; also a cold sauce composed of mayonnaise and whipped cream. These last two sauces are also known under the name of *mousseline*. The name can be applied to various preparations and pastry confections. (See CHICKEN, *Chicken à la chantilly*; CHARLOTTE, *Charlotte à la chantilly*.)

CHAP. BAJOUE – The lower jaw, or half cheek (especially of pig).

CHAPELER – The preparation of breadcrumbs by drying them in the oven and sieving them. In the old days grilled bread was called *pain cappelé*. (See BREADCRUMBS.)

CHAPON (Mediterranean cookery) – Slice of French bread rubbed with garlic and seasoned with oil and vinegar. In the south of France, and especially in Languedoc, bread treated in this way is added to salads, especially to chicory salad.

CHAR or CHARR. OMBLE CHEVALIER – Fish of the salmon genus, found in the deep lakes and rivers of Switzerland, Savoy and Auvergne. It resembles trout, but has finer scales and teeth; and black spots on the sides. The flesh is very delicate. It is prepared like *Salmon trout* (see TROUT).

CHARCUTERIE (Pork butchery) – The art of preparing meats (especially pork) in order to present them in various ways.

'The pig, whose meat prepared by pork butchers is the delight of gourmets, was despised by the Egyptians, and Moses included it among the impure meats which he forbade the Hebrews to eat.

Inside a pork butcher's shop (*Nicolas*)

'The Greeks raised the status of the animal so far as to make it the favourite victim in sacrifices offered to the gods. They also used pork fat in cooking. The Romans probably learned how to prepare pork from them. The Roman *porcella* law determined the manner of raising, feeding, killing and

Some charcuterie products:
1. Paris ham; 2. Rolled shoulder; 3. Galantine of boar's head; 4. Pain de rillettes; 5. Rillon de Tours; 6. Black pudding; 7. Foie gras sausage; 8. Filet de Saxe; 9. Liver pâté; 10. Rabbit galantine; 11. Poultry galantine; 12. Brawn; 13. Truffled poultry galantine; 14. Truffled foie gras galantine (*Larousse*)

preparing pigs, and controlled pork butchery. Pork meat was prepared in several ways in the time of the Roman empire, and was preserved by mixing it with salt, spices and aromatics. *Mortadellas, salamis* and all the Italian specialities were probably made under other names at that time, but more or less in the same way as they are made today. Particularly appreciated were the uterus and the udder before the animal began to breed. Varieties of small and large sausages called *farcimina, tobelli, tomacula,* and *tomacina* also appeared on Roman tables.

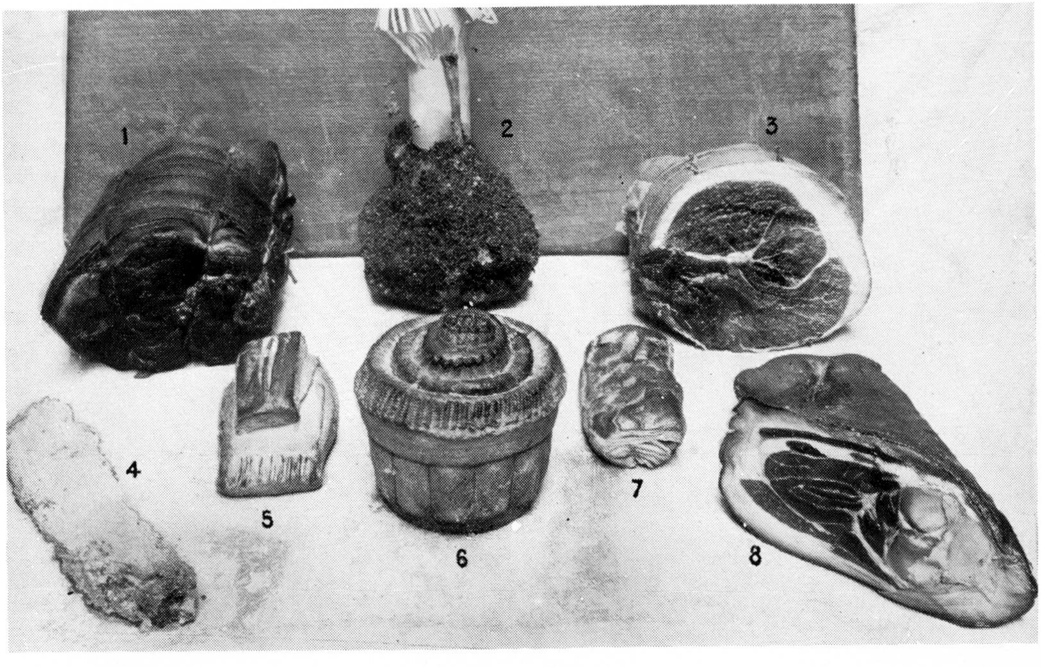

More charcuterie products:
1. Rolled smoked ham; 2. Knuckle of ham; 3. Rolled ham; 4. Trotters Sainte-Menehoud; 5. Parisian pâté; 6. Veal and ham pâté; 7. Small meat pie; 8. Bayonne knuckle of ham (*Larousse*)

'This art of *charcuterie* was preserved during the Middle Ages in France, but the *métier* of pork butchery was for a long time confused with that of *cuisinier-oyer* which, in the fourteenth century, comprised two categories: that of the *chaircutiers* and that of the *rostisseurs* (roasting chefs). In 1476, the *chaircutiers* obtained the monopoly of selling pork meat, cooked or raw (only fat pork in the latter case), but they were not allowed to kill the pigs themselves and had to buy pork meat from the butcher.

'The statutes of 17 January 1475 recognised the sole rights of the *chaircutiers-saucissiers boudiniers* to sell pork meat either cooked or prepared in the form of *cervelas*, sausages, black (U.S. blood) puddings etc.' (Franklin). In the sixteenth century they finally obtained the right to kill the pigs themselves. An order of 26 March 1664 forced them to buy their pigs at a distance of 21 leagues from Paris, a decree which has not been in force since the creation of the stockyards in the city itself.

All Parisians know the famous *foire aux jambons* (ham fair) which is held on the boulevard Richard-Lenoir before Holy Week. The little stalls are laden for days with all the *charcuterie* specialities from the French provinces, and even from abroad. Auvergne and Lorraine dominate with their concentration of sausages, hams, puddings, *pâtés*, etc. This fair dates from the remote past, and is said to have begun in front of Notre-Dame.

Dietetically speaking, opinion is divided about *charcuterie*. Some things – *rillettes*, brawn, *andouilles*, black pudding, etc. – are inclined to be indigestible, and even toxic if of poor quality. On the other hand, lean *charcuterie* such as cooked or raw ham, dried sausage, etc. have definite nutritional value. The virtue of *charcuterie* is that it excites the appetite since the spices that it contains encourage the secretion of saliva and gastric juices. It has no harmful effects if eaten in moderation.

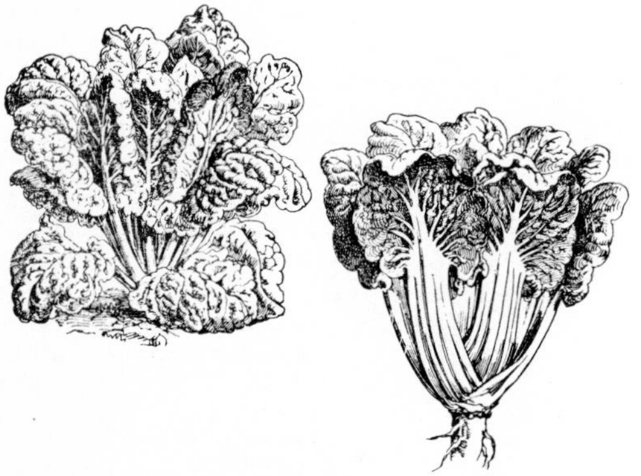

Chard

CHARD. CARDE – Old name for white beet. (See BEETROOT.)

CHARENTE – Name famous for its magnificent brandies known as *Cognac*. They are made from the wines produced in the *département* of Charente-Maritime.

Eaux-de-vie of Charente. EAUX-DE-VIE DES CHARENTES – The general classification of the wines of the Charente region is arranged in the following order:

Grande champagne, Petite champagne, Borderies, Fins-bois, Bons-bois, Bois ordinaires, and Bois du terroir.

'Grande champagne includes the whole of the canton of Segonzac, and part of the Cognac canton south of the Charente river.

'The brandy of this region is the prototype of the brandies of Charente; it is characterised by a very delicate aroma, recalling the gentle perfume of the vine in flower, and by a vigorous and full savour which creates prolonged and pleasurable sensations when tasted. This brandy is warm without burning the palate, and its colour, if it has aged in an ideal situation, is a very pale gold.

'Petite champagne encloses the Grande champagne in a half-circle. It is bounded on the north by the course of the Charente, between Mosnac and Merpins; to the east by a line running from Mosnac to Barbezieux; on the south by the road running from Barbezieux to Jonzac; and on the west by the course of the river Seugne, from Jonzac to Beillant.

'The brandies of this region, without having the great finesse of those of Grande champagne, approach them to a certain degree, particularly in the bordering vineyards.

'The Borderies, as the name implies, form a series of little hills along the banks of the Charente, from Cognac to Chérac, and stretch northwards as far as the heights of Saint-Sulpice and Menac. This borders on the vast plain of the Pays-Bas.

'The Borderies produce good brandies with aroma, a certain finesse and a full body. They are less mellow than the Champagne brandies, but have more body.

The Fin-bois and Bons-bois surround the three preceding areas in the form of a pentagon whose upper angle touches Saint-Jean-d'Angély, and whose limits are the road from Saint-Jean-d'Angély to Angoulême; the line of the railroad from Angoulême to Chalais; a line drawn from Chalais to Montendre; the road from Montendre to Saujon; and a line running from Saujon to Saint-Jean-d'Angély.

'The Bois brandies have a smooth quality, but compared with those of Champagne they are soft, with less finesse, and offer briefer pleasures to the palate.

'All the other vineyards of Charente and the islands produce ordinary brandies, but worthy of imbibing.' (From *les Dissertations gastronomiques* by Ernest Verdier.)

Not only must the brandies of the Charente area come from the areas defined in the accompanying map in order to have the right to a Cognac label, but the wines on which they are based must derive from the following vine-stocks: Sémillon, Folle-blanche, Colombac, Blanc rainé, Jurançon blanc, Montils and Sauvignon.

CHARLEMAGNE (Saint) – See FESTIVE COOKERY.

Charlotte mould (*Dehillerin. Phot. Larousse*)

CHARLOTTE – Two kinds of dessert are known by the name of charlotte. One, *charlotte russe*, is prepared with *Bavarian cream* (q.v.) which is set in a plain mould lined round the side and at the bottom with sponge fingers, and served cold. The other, *fruit charlotte* (and particularly *apple charlotte*, which seems to have been the first of its kind) is made with a confection of fruit in a mould lined with thin slices of buttered bread, usually served hot.

Carême invented the *charlotte russe* at his own establishment in Paris.

COLD CHARLOTTES. CHARLOTTES FROIDES –

Charlotte à la Chantilly – Use a straight-sided mould. Cut several sponge fingers into triangles and line the bottom of the mould in a rosette formation with a sponge finger cut into a circle in the centre. Trim the ends and sides of more sponge fingers and set them in the mould, upright, well pressed together one against the other. Whisk 6 dl. (1 pint, 2½ cups) thick fresh cream (kept on ice or in a cold place until the moment of beating). The cream must be so firm that it has the consistency of whisked egg whites.

Mix 125 g. (4½ oz., 1 cup) fine sugar with the cream and 1 tablespoon vanilla sugar or a few drops vanilla extract. Spoon the cream into the mould, and turn out at once.

Charlotte à la parisienne (Carême's recipe) – 'Take 175 g. (6 oz.) sponge fingers which are frosted on one side, and a packet of green pistachio biscuits. Cut the latter into thin slices and then into diamond shapes, 3½ cm. (1½ inches) long. Make a double star with them in the bottom of a plain octagonal mould. Then, using the sponge fingers cut into suitable shapes, fill the bottom of the mould. With the rest of the sponge fingers line the sides of the mould, setting them upright and close together. Take care to place the frosted side against the mould.

'Fill the charlotte with *Vanilla Bavarian cream* (see BAVARIAN CREAM) and cover the cream with sponge fingers. Surround it with broken ice, and 40 minutes later turn it out onto a silver dish.'

Charlotte plombières – Prepared in the same way as *Vanilla ice cream charlotte* (see below), with a filling of *Plombières ice cream* (see ICE CREAM AND ICES).

Charlotte russe – Line the bottom of a mould with sponge fingers cut into the form of hearts, and the sides with sponge fingers which have been trimmed at the ends and sides. Place these upright round the inside of the mould, pressed well together, and projecting about 2½ cm. (1 inch) above the top.

Fill the charlotte with *Bavarian cream* (q.v.). Place in the refrigerator until ready to be turned out.

Charlotte russe can be filled with *Bavarian cream* of different flavours.

Vanilla ice cream charlotte. CHARLOTTE GLACÉE À LA VANILLE – Line the charlotte mould with sponge fingers as described in the preceding recipe.

Just before serving fill the mould with vanilla ice or with a vanilla filling for a *Bombe* (see ICE CREAM AND ICES).

Iced charlottes filled with ice cream of various flavourings can be prepared in the same way.

FRUIT CHARLOTTES. CHARLOTTES DE FRUIT –

Apple charlotte. CHARLOTTE DE POMMES – Line the bottom of a charlotte mould with slices of bread cut in the form of hearts, and dipped in melted butter. Line the sides with slices of bread cut in rectangles the same height as the mould, and also dipped in melted butter. Slice 12 quartered apples and cook in 50 g. (2 oz., ¼ cup) butter to which has been added 2 tablespoons (3 tablespoons) powdered sugar, a pinch of cinnamon, and a little lemon rind or vanilla. Stir continuously with a wooden spoon or spatula. When the apple mixture is considerably thickened, add 3 or 4 tablespoons apricot jam.

Fill the mould with the mixture and cover with a round of bread dipped in melted butter. Cook in the oven at 180°C. (350°F., Gas Mark 4) for 35 to 40 minutes. Leave the charlotte for a few minutes before turning it out, so that the apple settles. Serve with apricot sauce.

Charlottes can be prepared in the same way with pears, quinces, apricots, peaches, plums. The consistency of the fruit must be kept very stiff; if too liquid, it would soften the bread and the dessert would disintegrate when turned out of the mould.

Charlottes can also be filled with a fruit filling and with *French pastry cream* or with *Frangipane pastry cream* (see CREAM).

Schaleth à la juive is also a kind of charlotte. Line a cast-iron *cocotte* with noodle paste, and fill with cooked apple, sultanas, currants and raisins. Moisten with Malaga wine, and bind with eggs. (See SCHALETH.)

Apple charlotte with rice. CHARLOTTE DE POMMES AU RIZ – Sprinkle a thickly buttered charlotte mould with dried breadcrumbs, add a layer of *Dessert rice* (see RICE), 1 cm. (½ inch) thick. Fill the mould to within 1 cm. (½ inch) of the top with stiff apple filling. Cover with dessert rice and put in a moderate oven (160°C., 325°F., Gas Mark 3) for 30 minutes. Serve with a fruit sauce or *zabaglione* (q.v.).

CHARQUICAN-CHILENO (Chilean cookery) – This is the national dish of Chile. Sauté the *charqui* (lean beef cut into pieces) in oil with garlic and coarsely chopped onion, and then moisten with brown stock. Add carrots, turnips, tomatoes, peas in their pods, pumpkin, celery, green haricots, and pimentos cut into pieces. Braise, and serve in deep soup plates. Fried potatoes can be added.

CHARTREUSE – Liqueur made by the monks of Chartreux. The approximate composition of this liqueur is as follows:

640 g. (1 lb. 7 oz.) balm, 640 g. (1 lb. 7 oz.) hyssop, 320 g. (11 oz.) angelica leaves, 100 g. (4 oz.) cinnamon bark, 40 g. (1½ oz.) mace, 40 g. (1½ oz.) saffron.

Infuse for 10 days in 10 litres (9 quarts, 11 quarts) distilled alcohol, then add 1200 g. (2 lb. 11 oz.) white sugar.

CHARTREUSE – Preparation of partridges and cabbage. In the old days the word applied to a variety of preparations which included neither feathered game nor cabbage.

'The *chartreuse* is undoubtedly the queen of *entrées* which one can serve; it is composed of roots and vegetables, but is only perfect in May, June, July and August, that smiling and propitious season, when everything is renewed in nature, and seems to invite us to take fresh trouble in our preparations on account of the delicacy of these excellent products.' (Carême, *Traité des entrées chaudes*.)

Chartreuse à la parisienne, en surprise (Carême's recipe) – 'Cook 8 truffles in Champagne. When they are cold, pare and cut them in the direction of the greatest length. Peel 100 crayfish tails – these can be replaced by carrots prepared in the same way as for *Chartreuse of partridge* (see PARTRIDGE) – and begin to form a crown on the bottom of a buttered mould. Trim the truffles and place them on the crayfish tails in such a way as to make a Greek border. Add chicken fillets previously stiffened with butter and trimmed. Set on top of this border a crown of crayfish tails to form a parallel with the crayfish border underneath, so that the Greek border is framed with crayfish tails.

'Chop the trimmings of the truffles very finely and scatter them on the bottom of the mould. Cover these with a layer of chicken quenelle forcemeat 2½ cm. (1 inch) thick. Cover the Greek border too. Fill the middle with a *Blanquette of chicken* (see BLANQUETTE); veal or lamb sweetbreads; slices of game fillets; or with a *ragoût à la financière* or *à la Toulouse*. The mould should not be quite filled.

'Make a cover of forcemeat 13 cm. (5 inches) in diameter and 1 cm. (½ inch) thick on a round of buttered paper. Place this on top of the filling (stuffing side down). To remove the paper, put on it, for a second only, a hot lid which melts the butter. Join the forcemeat lid to the forcemeat surround with the point of a knife.

'The *chartreuse* being completed, cover the top with a circle of buttered paper, and put it in a *bain-marie* (q.v.) for an hour and a half.

'To decorate, place a ring of small white mushrooms on the *chartreuse*, and in the centre put a rosette of 8 *filets mignons à la Conti* (fowl or game, according to the nature of the basic ragoût) in the form of a crescent, topped by a mushroom.'

Chartreuse of partridge, or pheasant – See PARTRIDGE, PHEASANT.

Little chartreuses of larks à la française. PETITES CHARTREUSES DE MAUVIETTES À LA FRANÇAISE – Prepare in *dariole* moulds (individual custard moulds) in the same way as *Chartreuse of partridge* (see PARTRIDGE).

The larks, boned and stuffed with *à gratin forcemeat* (see FORCEMEAT), and with *foie gras* and truffles, are rolled into a neat shape and set to cook in cabbage.

The *dariole* moulds are lined with glazed carrots and turnips cut into small balls, with peas and diced green haricot beans cooked in salted water. These vegetables are disposed in alternate layers and kept in place by a layer of quenelle forcemeat. The larks, individually wrapped in braised cabbage, are placed one in each mould. Cover them with a quenelle forcemeat. Cook in a pan of hot water or *bain-marie*, in the oven for 30 minutes.

To serve, pour game sauce, made with rich game stock, over the birds.

CHASSELAS – Species of vine stock considered to provide the best dessert grapes.

The fame of the Fontainebleau Chasselas is established everywhere. It is believed that it was originally imported into the area around Thomery from Switzerland in the sixteenth century. The introduction of Chasselas into Switzerland itself goes back to the Roman conquest by Julius Caesar. The Chasselas vines have always been grown in Turkey.

Only the white variety, or the rosé or violet varieties (obtained by careful selection and budding), are known, despite the fact that in their wild state all vines have black grapes. The Chasselas vine stock is found in Switzerland, Savoy and Pouilly-sur-Loire in the Nièvre. (The *appellation* Pouilly Fumé is reserved for Sauvignon wines.) The wine produced from the Chasselas grape is light and fruity, best drunk young and slightly chilled.

CHASSEUR (À LA) – Method of preparation applied to small pieces of meat, fowl or eggs which is characterised by a garnish of sliced, sautéed mushrooms, flavoured with shallots and moistened with white wine. (See BEEF, *Tournedos chasseur.*)

CHASSE ROYALE – Roast composed of various game arranged in a pyramid on a large dish.

CHÂTEAU (Steak, potatoes, sauce) – Name given to a rather thick slice of porterhouse steak (sirloin uppercut), weighing 800 g. to 1 kg. ($1\frac{3}{4}$ to $2\frac{1}{4}$ lb.), or a slice cut from a rib of beef.

This piece of meat, which in restaurants is called *entrecôte château*, is generally grilled.

The name also applies to potatoes cut into long strips and cooked in butter (see POTATOES) and in restaurants *Chateaubriand sauce* is sometimes abbreviated to *Château sauce*.

CHATEAUBRIAND – Method of preparing a beef fillet invented by Montmireil, chef to Chateaubriand.

The *chateaubriand* is a thick slice taken from the middle of the fillet, grilled and served garnished with *château potatoes* (q.v.) and accompanied by *château sauce* or *béarnaise sauce*.

More rarely the *chateaubriand* is sautéed in butter. (See BEEF, *Chateaubriand.*)

CHÂTEAUNEUF-DU-PAPE – The red wines of Châteauneuf-du-Pape, a small commune in Vaucluse, enjoy a worldwide reputation. They are derived principally from the vine stocks Grenache, Clairette, Syrah and Mourvèdre. They are powerful, full-bodied tannic, aromatic wines that age well. Some producers offer a full-bodied, aromatic, white Châteauneuf-du-Pape which is not without merit.

These wines have been famous for a long time. When Pope Urban X wished to transfer the papal chair from Avignon to Rome he met with a great deal of opposition from a number of Cardinals who did not wish to leave a part of the country producing such exquisite wines.

CHATOUILLARD – Name given to potatoes which are cut with a special implement into long ribbons and deep fried. (See POTATOES.)

Chatouillard was also the nickname given to an expert chef or an excellent *rôtissier* or *friturier*.

CHAOURCE – See CHEESE.

CHAUD-FROID – Preparation of fowl or game which is cooked as a hot dish, but served cold.

Philéas Gilbert says that the *chaud-froid* originated at the Château Montmorency in 1759, and that it was given its name by the maréchal de Luxembourg himself.

'The maréchal de Luxembourg had invited a large and brilliant assembly to his castle at Montmorency that evening. His table was famous as one of the best in the French kingdom. While waiting for grace to be said, a valet announced the arrival of a royal courier, bearer of a message to the maréchal requiring his immediate presence at the king's council.

'There was instant dismay; disappointment showed itself on every face. But the maréchal commanded that his absence should in no way delay the serving of the banquet, and left.

'The guests took their places at the table in an atmosphere of constraint, uneasy in the absence of their host, and only paying distracted attention to the dishes served with unaccustomed haste.

'The maréchal returned very late and imperiously demanded to be served, but he only wanted a single dish, a *fricassée* of chicken embalmed in its ivory-coloured sauce which the famished maréchal tasted with pleasure. Nothing remains so firmly in the mind as a dish which has been enjoyed, and some days afterwards the maréchal expressed the wish for the succulent cold *fricassée* to be served again.

'The dish was presented under the name *refroidi*, but this name displeased the maréchal who insisted that it should appear on the menu under the name of *chaud-froid*.'

Chauds-froids – (*Chaufroids* is also written but it is incorrect) are in fact chicken *fricassées* or *salmis* of game served cold, covered with their gravy and glazed with aspic.

They are served with the appropriate *chaud-froid* sauce and glazed with a clear aspic jelly.

Recipes for *chauds-froids* of chicken, pheasant, partridge, quails, thrushes, will be found under these headings.

Here is Carême's recipe for *chaud-froid of chicken in aspic*.

Chaud-froid of chicken in aspic (Carême's recipe). CHAUD-

Chaud-froid of poultry presented on a dish; behind, the three-tiered plinth made of breadcrumb on which it is mounted

FROID DE POULET À LA GELÉE – 'After having lightly singed 5 fine farmyard chickens, cut them up and soak them for 2 hours in lukewarm water. Drain them, plunge them into cold water, and put them in a pan with enough stock to cover them completely. Boil for a few minutes, then drain and put them in cold water again. Trim the pieces of chicken and sauté them in butter over a moderate heat. Sprinkle with a little flour, continue to sauté, then pour in the strained stock. Stir, season with salt, a little nutmeg, a bouquet of parsley, spring onions, thyme, bay, basil, 2 onions stuck with 2 cloves, and 12 peeled mushrooms. Bring to the boil and simmer for 30 minutes. Skim carefully. Remove the pieces of chicken with a perforated spoon, draining them, and place in a covered casserole.

'Boil down the sauce to a good consistency, remove from the heat, and 2 minutes later add 5 egg yolks. Return the pan to the heat, stirring all the time, until the sauce almost reaches the boil, then sieve it. As soon as it is cold pour one-third into the *fricassée*, which you shake once or twice and set for 30 minutes on crushed ice. Arrange the dish in the following manner:

'Place the legs of the chickens in the form of a crown on the *entrée* dish. In the middle, place the wings, and above the legs put the parsons' noses and the breasts. On top of these put the fillets, as close together as possible.

'As much height as possible should be given to this *entrée*, which should be crowned with a fine truffle cooked in Champagne, and topped with a white double cock's comb.

'Work the sauce with 4 tablespoons ($\frac{1}{3}$ cup) lukewarm *Aspic jelly* (see ASPIC) which should make it very smooth and thick. Cover the surface of the *fricassée* (removing the truffle which is later replaced). Surround the piece with chopped aspic and a border of aspic in two colours cut in decorative shapes. Then serve the dish.' (Carême, *le Pâtissier parisien*.)

CHAUDRÉE DE FOURAS – Fish soup. Prepare a *court-bouillon* with herbs, white wine, a piece of butter and seasoning.

Cut various fish – conger eel, whiting, sole, plaice, *raiteau*, etc. – into pieces.

First put into the *court-bouillon* the firm fish such as conger eel. A few minutes later add the less firm fish. Boil for 15 minutes. Add butter. Serve the soup and the fish separately.

CHAUDRON (Cauldron) – Small copper cauldron, used for cooking.

Confit d'oie and *confit de porc* (preserved goose and pork) are cooked in this utensil. Untinned copper cauldrons may also be used for home-made jams and preserves.

CHAUMONT – See CHEESE.

CHAYOTE – See CUSTARD MARROW.

Making cheese at Beaufortin
(*French Government Tourist Office*)

CHEESE. FROMAGE – Cheese is a product of curds, drained and, more often than not, fermented. From the earliest times cheese has been made in stock-rearing countries to use up surplus milk. Nowadays, there are so many different kinds of cheese that no list, however long, could claim to be complete. Every country, every district, has its own special cheese. Many local cheeses have a deservedly high reputation. Switzerland produces Gruyère and Emmenthal; England, Cheshire, Cheddar and Stilton; Italy, Parmesan and Gorgonzola; Holland, Gouda and Edam, and so on. It may justly be claimed, however, that no country has so great a variety and range of cheeses as France, where almost every rural district has its own local cheese.

The history of cheese is a very ancient one. We know from the *Manuel de l'Antiquité celtique* that the remains of enormous cheese draining racks can be found on Mont Beuvray.

The art of making *fromage persillé*, herb-injected cheese, goes back to the Romans who mixed their cheese with powdered thyme. Le Grand d'Aussy in his book *Histoire de la vie privée des Français* (1783) says: 'Even today in certain regions of Lorraine they make a cheese impregnated with fennel seeds'.

Draining curds

We also know that Blanche de Navarre sent 200 cheeses to Philippe Auguste every year, and that the poet François Villon bequeathed in his famous will a *talmouze*, a kind of cheese soufflé, to his friend Jehan Ragnier.

It was the custom at the beginning of the fifteenth century to send a gift of cheeses to persons one admired. For example, Charles d'Orléans, in the year 1407, sent several to 'ladies to whom he was attached'. In the sixteenth century Brie cheese was considered the best of all. The cheeses of Dauphiné, Vexin, Auvergne, Switzerland, Holland, and Italy were also very much in demand.

Madame de Montespan invented 100 sauces using cheese. When Louis XVI stopped at Varennes in need of refreshment he asked for wine and cheese.

In 1777 there were about thirty varieties that had made a name for themselves. Later Metternich gave a reception at which he served all the French cheeses, and invited his guests to take part in competitions for choosing the best.

Fresh cheeses are distinct from other cheeses in not being fermented. They are produced by spontaneous coagulation (*Fromage à la pie*) or coagulation with rennet (*Petit-suisse*).

Fermented cheeses made from raw curds are of two kinds: soft cheeses (Brie, Coulommiers, Camembert, Livarot, Pont-l'Evêque, etc.), and hard cheeses (Dutch, Cantal, Cheshire, Roquefort, Gorgonzola, etc.). There are also *cheeses made from scalded curds* (Gruyère, Emmenthal, Parmesan, Port-Salut, etc.).

Cheese cellar
(*Maison Androuët. Phot. Larousse*)

The milk of cows, goats, ewes, and sometimes other mammals, can be used skimmed, partly skimmed, whole, or enriched with added cream. Coagulation can take place spontaneously, that is to say by the natural fermentation of the milk, or it can be induced by the addition of certain vegetable juices. Most often it is brought about by the action of rennet, a curdling agent extracted from the stomachs of young mammals. Rennet may be used in solid form (dried or fresh) or in liquid form (plain or seasoned with herbs).

Curdling with rennet is carried out in different ways. The milk may be left to curdle in cold surroundings, when very little rennet is used. It may be curdled at a higher temperature (38° to 40°C., 100° to 104°F.) in which case more rennet is required.

The moulding of the cheese, which is the last stage in the drainage of the curds, is carried out in osier baskets, or in earthenware, pottery, wood or tinplate moulds. These are usually covered with a cloth. For soft cheeses, the curds are carefully broken up before being put in the moulds. For hard cheeses, all moisture is expelled by putting the curds through a press, or by draining them between two boards with weights on top.

At this stage, the process of fermentation begins. Theoretically this process is divided into three stages which, in practice, tend more or less to overlap:

1. The action of the ferments in the milk which attack the lactose (sugar of milk) and turn it into lactic acid.

2. The culture of fungi which appear on the surface of the curds and quickly form a thick, furry fungoid skin (known in the cheese trade as the 'white'). These fungi feed on the lactic acid as soon as it is formed, up to the time when all the lactose has been used. They also play a part in the maturing of the curds. In particular, it is these fungi which give to certain cheeses their characteristic and much-prized bitter flavour; but their action must not be allowed to proceed unchecked.

3. The culture of secondary microbes. These are organisms of various kinds, microbes, fungi, mildew, mainly red or orange in colour (known in the cheese trade as the 'red'). Their function is to inhibit, by co-existence, the too-rapid breeding of the fungi of the second phase. Once the 'red' has been formed, the cheeses settle down and mature more or less quickly according to their nature.

Cheese shop (*Nicolas*)

Cheese platter (*Ledoyen. Phot. Nicolas*)

Dietetically speaking, cheese is a first-class protein capable of replacing meat in vegetarian diets. It is rich in proteins, fats, Vitamins A, B1, B2, and C, and in mineral salts. It is very digestible and, apart from some fatty or fermented varieties, is suitable for all constitutions.

Much has been written about which wine goes with which particular cheese. It is entirely a matter of taste. Saint-Amand described cheese as a drinking spur, but this opinion is debatable, for cheese can over-emphasise the value of the wine and give a false impression of its true quality. The great wines do not require cheese to throw them into relief.

Red wines are generally best. White wines suit goats' milk cheeses and cooked cheese dishes; Comte cheese and Château-Chalon wine go very well together. Never serve the great wines with cheese.

The serving of cheese – In France, cheeses of whatever kind, are always served before the sweet (dessert). Thus they would normally follow the main course, or the salad if this should be served separately after the meat and vegetables.

Each cheese is usually served alone on a separate plate, but cheeses may also be served on a cheese board.

It is desirable to serve fresh butter at the same time as the cheese. In this way, diners may take butter or not, as they please. Generally, connoisseurs prefer not to take butter with their cheese.

Savoury biscuits (U.S. crackers) of various kinds and slices of black bread may also be served with cheese. With certain cheeses, notably Munster, it is usual to serve cumin. Fresh heads of celery or bulb fennel also provide a suitable accompaniment for cheese.

It is the custom in France to offer the cheese first to the master of the house. He examines it and drives the knife into it before it is handed round to the guests. This applies especially to whole cheeses, for there are always shy guests who are reluctant to start, say, an uncut Camembert.

Various laws, decrees and judicial precedents regulate the legal use of the names given to various French cheeses. The name Roquefort, for instance, is strictly reserved for cheeses coming from an area whose boundaries are clearly laid down. In the case of other cheeses, such as Camembert, Brie, and Port-Salut, the name must be followed by a clear indication of the *département* or district in which the cheese has been made.

There are at least 400 different cheeses made in France alone. This section lists the most appreciated French cheeses as well as many foreign cheeses which are obtainable in France and elsewhere.

Aettekees – Belgian cheese which is in season from November to May.

Amou – Cheese made in Béarn which is in season from November to May.

Arrigny – A Champagne cheese in season from November to May.

Asco – Corsican cheese which is in season from November to May.

Aurore – Normandy cheese eaten throughout the year.

Autun – This is called 'cow cheese' and can be eaten all the year round.

(Les) Aydes – This cheese from the Orléanais district is in season between October and June.

Banon – Made in Provence, in the foothills of the Alps. In season from May to November.

Beaufort – Savoy cheese eaten all the year round.

Beaumont – Savoy cheese which is in season from October to June.

Beaupré de Roybon – Cheese made in the Dauphiné which is in season from November to April.

Bleu d'Auvergne – A blue mould cheese which is also known under the name of *Bleu de Salers* and is in season from November to May. It is usually made of a mixture of goats', ewes' and cows' milk.

Bleu de Basillac – Cheese made in the Limousin *département.* It resembles Roquefort, and is at its best between November and May.

Bleus français (French blue cheeses) – In France there are a number of these cheeses, which have something in common with *Roquefort* but are less delicate in flavour. Among the best of these are *Bleu d'Auvergne*, made chiefly in the Mont-Dore district; *Fourme d'Ambert*, *Grand bornant*, and *Thônes* of the Haute-Savoie; the Blue cheese *Gex*, made from cows' milk in the Ain *département*; *Champoléon* from the Queyras (in the High Alps); *Saint-Marcellin* and *Sassenage*, made in the Isère district; *Septmoncel*, made in the Jura mountains.

According to the producers of Roquefort, cows' milk cheeses and Roquefort are two distinct categories of cheeses. *Persillé* is the term used for Roquefort and *bleu* the term used for other veined cheeses. However, the '*persillé*' of the Aravis is allowed.

Blue cheeses from other lands – A great many blue cheeses are made outside France. They include blue *Tyrolean* from Rastadt; *Cabrales* from the Asturias; Portuguese *Castello-branco*; *Sarrazin* from Sarraz in Switzerland; *Stilton* from England; the Italian *Stracchino* which has something in common with *Gorgonzola.*

Bondon – Variety of cheese which is made in Normandy, mostly around Rouen. It is a whole-milk, small, loaf-shaped cheese, rather like Gournay in texture, but with 2 per cent sugar added. It is about 7½ cm. (3 inches) high and 4 to 5 cm. (1½ to 2 inches) in diameter.

Bosson macéré – French cheese made in Provence, which is in season from December to March.

(La) Bouille – Cheese made in Normandy, which is in season between October and May.

Boule de Lille – Dutch cheese, known in Holland under the name of *Oude Kaas*, which can be eaten all the year round.

Boulette d'Avesnes, or Boulette de Cambrai – Cheese made in Flanders, in season from November to May.

Brie – This cheese has a claim to nobility. As long ago as the fifteenth century, Charles d'Orléans, father of Louis XII, ordered Bries by the dozen to give as New Year presents to his friends. Two centuries later, Saint Amant, the poet of good living, devoted a much-quoted ode to 'this gentle jam of Bacchus':

Sus ! qu'à plein gosier on s'écrie:
Bény soit le territoire de Brie,
Pont-l'Evêque, arrière de nous!
Auvergne et Milan, cachez-vous.
C'est luy seulement qui mérite
Qu'en or sa gloire soit escrite;
Je dis en or avec raison,
Puisqu'il feroit comparaison
De ce fromage que j'honore
A ce métal que l'homme adore:
Il est aussi jaune que luy;
Toutefois ce n'est pas d'ennuy,
Car, si tost que le doigt le presse,
Il rit et se crève de gresse . . .
Hé! pourquoy n'est-il infiny
Tout aussi bien en sa matière
Qu'il l'estoit en sa forme entière?
Pourquoy tousjours s'apetissant,
De lune devient-il croissant? . . .

Now then, let us shout with all our might:
Blessed be the land of Brie.
Pont-l'Evêque, get thee behind us!
Auvergne and Milan, out of our sight.
Brie alone deserves that we
Should record her praises in letters of gold.
Gold, I say, and with good reason,
Since it is with gold that one must compare
This cheese to which I now pay homage.
It is as yellow as the gold worshipped by man,
But without its anxiety
For one has only to press it with one's fingers
For it to split its sides with laughter
And run over with fat.
Why then, is it not endless
As indeed its circular form is endless?
Why must its full moon, eternally appetising,
Wane to a crescent? . . .

The cheese of Brie has not deteriorated since that time. On the contrary, it has actually improved in quality and is now more uniformly good, since the local farmers, abandoning the old methods, use the ferments tested and recommended by the laboratory at La Ferté-sous-Jouarre.

Brie is fully ripe when the cheese is all of the same texture. When pressure is exerted on the surface of a section the cheese should bulge but not run. Brie is made in various sizes. A large Brie may be up to 54 cm. (22 inches) in diameter, a medium Brie up to 42 cm. (16 inches), a small one not more than 33 cm. (13 inches). There are different kinds of Brie known as Bries *fermiers, laitiers* and *façon Coulommiers.*

It takes from 13 litres (2¾ gallons, 3½ gallons) to 20 litres (4½ gallons, 5½ gallons) milk to make a cheese, according to size. Although whole milk is always used, some experts advise a little skimming – bringing the percentage of cream down to 25 or 27 per cent – because, they maintain, a higher cream content makes the cheese bitter.

A good Brie must be creamy but not runny, and should be pale yellow in colour.

Brie de Meaux. At its best from November to May.

Brie de Coulommiers. Smaller than Brie de Meaux – approximately 26 cm. (10 inches) in diameter. At its best from November to May.

Brie de Melun. This is made in thicker and smaller rounds than Brie de Meaux. It is a special cheese with a much more pronounced aroma, being saltier and more piquant. It is good all the year round.

Brie de Montereau. Made in the same way as Brie de Meaux but is a smaller and deeper cheese.

Brillat-Savarin – Cheese made in Normandy which can be eaten all the year round.

Brinzen – Hungarian cheese made from fresh ewes' milk, mixed with rennet. It is dried for 10 to 12 days, kneaded with 3 per cent salt, then put into drums and pressed.

Broccio – Corsican cheese, made from goats' milk or sour ewes' milk, very delicate, and similar in appearance to Petit-suisse. A large proportion of this cheese is exported.

It is eaten plain, in fritters or in ravioli and is in season between May and November. It is also used as a stuffing for vegetables. A special cake called *Fiadene* is made with it.

Caccio-cavallo – Italian cheese made in the region of Naples from skimmed cows' milk, moulded in the shape of gourds and left to dry straddled on sticks. Some Caccio-cavallo addicts are not satisfied with merely having the cheese dried, but insist on its being smoke-cured as well, as was done in the time of the Romans.

Camembert – A soft cheese, invented, or rather perfected, in about the year 1790 by a local farmer's wife, Mme Harel, to whom, in grateful memory, a statue has been erected.

Good quality Camembert is made from whole unskimmed milk. The cheese is made mainly in the winter by a process similar to that used in the manufacture of Brie, but the micro-organisms are different and give to the cheese a slight characteristic bitterness which the makers attribute to the oat-straw of the wicker trays.

Camembert, which is chiefly made in the regions of Vimoutiers and Livarot, is disc-shaped, thicker and much smaller than Brie. The cheese must be pale yellow, smooth, without holes, and firm.

It is made today all over France and even in other countries, but by law its place of origin must be indicated. The Camembert season lasts from November to May.

Monument to Mme Harel, the creator of Camembert cheese

Cancoillotte – Very strong cheese mixture made in Franche-Comté, which has to be melted before serving. It is in season from September to June.

Cantal – Hard, strong cheese made in Auvergne. It can be eaten the whole year round but is particularly good from November to May.

Carré de Bonneville – Normandy cheese, in season between September and June.

Chabichou – Poitou cheese, in season from April to December. It is made from goats' milk and is soft and sweet.

Chaingy – Cheese made in Orléans which has its season from September to June.

Champenois – Cheese still called Riceys-Cendré which is in season between September and June.

Chaource – This cheese, made in the Champagne district, is somewhat similar to Soumaintrain. It is in season from November to May.

Chaumont – Cheese made in the Champagne region which is in season from November to May.

Cheddar cheese

Cheddar – English cheese eaten all the year round.

Cheshire – Hard, cows' milk English cheese made in two colours: red and white. It can be eaten all the year round.

Chester – Name by which Cheshire cheese is known in France.

Chevret – Bresse cheese made from goats' milk which is in season from December to April.

Chevrotin – Cheese produced in Savoy. It is made of dried goats' milk and is in season from March to December. The *Chevrotins de Moulins* are little cheeses made in Bourbonnais.

Chevrotton de Mâcon – Cheese, also called *Mâconnais*, that is in season from May to September.

Cierp de Luchon – Cheese made in the Comté de Foix which is in season from November to May.

Comté – Jura cheese which can be eaten all the year round.

Coulommiers – This comes into the category of soft cream cheeses. It is made in the Brie district in the neighbourhood of Coulommiers (Seine-et-Marne), and is at its best between November and May.

Coulommiers cheeses are usually eaten fresh, after salting. They may also be processed like Brie, that is to say, kept until they are covered with white mould.

A good Coulommiers must have a white crust with a slight greyish tinge, be creamy to the touch, and slightly yellowish inside.

Cream cheese. FROMAGE À LA CRÈME – There are several ways of making this cheese. One is to add some cream to the milk before introducing the rennet, another is to make it from skimmed milk worked with fresh cream after draining and put into moulds to complete the drainage.

Crème des Vosges – Alsatian soft cream cheese in season between November and April.

Crottin de Chavignol – Semi-hard goats' milk cheese made in Berry, which is in season from May to December.

Curé – See *Nantais cheese* below.

Dauphin – Cheese made in northern France, good between November and May.

Decize – Nivernais cheese which can be eaten all the year round. It resembles Brie.

Demi-sel – Small whole-milk soft cheese somewhat similar to double-cream. The curd, after being drained, sieved and put in moulds, has 1 to 1½ per cent salt added to it.

Double-cream. DOUBLE-CRÈME – French soft cream cheese in which the milk is enriched with added cream, increasing the weight by one-sixth. A small quantity of rennet is mixed with it so that the slow process of coagulation lasts about 24 hours. The curd, wrapped in a cloth, is put under weights to drain. Next, cream is worked into it. The curds are moulded and wrapped in waxed paper.

Dunlop – Scottish cheese somewhat similar to Cheshire and Double Gloucester, but which, in the opinion of English gastronomes, is much superior to both. Sir Walter Scott was enthusiastic about this cheese.

Dutch cheeses – There are a great many of these. The best-known, *Edam*, is made in a number of European countries and in America. Partly skimmed milk, curdled in 15 to 20 minutes, is mixed with rennet. Fermentation is very slow, and allowed to continue until a hard, non-porous rind is formed. As soon as the cheese is fully fermented, the cheese is painted over with a coating of linseed oil. Sometimes it is given a further coating of paraffin, before being coloured with annatto (dye).

Edam cheese is yellow-red when stove-dried, softish and free from holes.

Emmenthal – Swiss hard cheese named after the high Emme valley (in the Berne Canton), but made in Switzerland wherever there is highland pasture. As the transport of butter from these mountain districts would be uneconomic, Emmenthal cheese is usually made from whole milk. However, in some parts a semi-fat Emmenthal is made.

The cheese is manufactured in the same way as Gruyère. The round Emmenthal cheeses are larger than Gruyères, weighing from 60 to 100 kg. (132 to 220 lb.). Their rind is straw coloured.

The cheese is creamier than Gruyère, less pungent and usually less salty. It has a good many holes called 'eyes', usually three to every bore-hole made.

There is also a French Emmenthal cheese.

Epoisses – Whole-milk, mould inoculated, soft French cheese made in almost every part of Burgundy and in central France. Its name comes from a village on the Côte d'Or. The milk is curdled with a special rennet, flavoured with black pepper, clove, fennel, salt, and brandy. It is eaten either fresh or ripened.

The cheese is left in cellars to ripen for a longer or shorter time according to whether it is to be eaten *passé* (over-ripe) or *coulant* (runny).

The fresh cheese is eaten in summer; the ripe cheese in winter or spring (November to June).

Ercé – Cheese made in the Ariège district, in season between November and May.

Ervy – Cheese from Champagne which is at its best between November and May.

Étuvé – Semi-hard Dutch cheese which is good to eat all the year round.

Excelsior – Normandy cheese, eaten all the year round.

Feuille de Dreux – Cheese made in the Ile-de-France. It is good to eat between November and May.

Fin de siècle – Normandy cheese which is good to eat all the year round.

Fleur de Decauville – Cheese made in the Ile-de-France. It is good to eat between December and May.

Fontine – Cheese made in Franche-Comté all the year round.

Fourme – Cheese from the Limagne. There are the cheeses of Ambert, of Montbrisson, of Salers, etc., known as *Fourme d'Ambert, Fourme de Montbrisson, Fourme de Salers*. The latter is sometimes sold under the name of *Cantal*. These cheeses are generally at their best from November to May.

Foutina – Italian soft, creamy cheese used in making fondues in the Val d'Aosta.

Friesche Kaas – Soft Dutch cheese in season between November and May.

Frinot – Cheese made in the region of Orléans, which is in season between November and June.

Fromage à la pie (fresh unfermented cheese) – Usually made from skimmed milk on farms and is for immediate consumption. It can also be made in the home from whole milk. The milk is left to stand in a cool place (12° to 15°C., 53° to 59°F.). Curdling takes place at the end of 24 to 36 hours, through the action of the lactic ferment. It can also be made with rennet.

Fromage à la pie is eaten fresh, with fresh cream added. It may be seasoned with sugar, or salt and pepper according to taste, and a little chopped chives for added flavour.

Gammelöst – Norwegian all-the-year-round cheese.

Gérômé – Cheese made in the Vosges. Its name is a corruption of Gérardmer.

It is made from whole milk and rennet, and is ripened in cellars for 4 months, until the crust has taken on a tawny colour. Sometimes aniseed, fennel or caraway seeds are added. Gérômé is a winter cheese, eaten between November and April.

Gervais – Well-known make of *Petit-suisse*. (See *Petit-suisse*.)

Gex – French blue-veined cheese manufactured at Gex, principal town of the Ain *département*, between November and May, from unskimmed whole milk, coagulated in 2 hours at 25° to 27°C. (77° to 81°F.).

Before it is offered for sale, it is stored for 2 weeks in ripening cellars where its special qualities develop.

The 'blue' which is due to the *penicillum glaucum*, is self-generating and appears during processing without the aid of any foreign body.

The chief characteristic of Gex cheese, which distinguishes it from all others, is that (except for the blue streaks) it remains pure white. It takes from 2 to 4 months to ripen completely.

Gjetöst – Brown-coloured Norwegian cheese which can be eaten all the year round. It is made of goats' milk.

Gloucester – There are two English cheeses of this name: the famous *Double Gloucester* and *Single Gloucester*.

Double Gloucester. The shape and size of a large grindstone, it is crumbly in texture and has a strong but mellow and delicate flavour. It ripens slowly (this process takes about 6 months) and keeps well.

Single Gloucester. Made during spring and summer, ripens in about 2 months. It is flat and round, similar to Double Gloucester in shape, and has a soft and open texture. It is excellent for toasting.

Glux – Nivernais cheese which can be eaten all the year round.

Goats' milk cheeses. FROMAGE DE CHÈVRE – A wide variety of goats' milk cheeses are manufactured throughout France. Occasionally a little cows' milk is added due to the growing scarcity of goats' milk. Goats' milk cheese is usually strongly salted to make it more closely resemble cows' milk cheese (and to preserve it). In fact, many goats' milk cheeses are far too salty.

Although this cheese is usually eaten fresh it can be preserved in various ways and eaten when very mature. (In the Ardèche it is wrapped in walnut leaves or placed in earthenware pots.)

Among the best known of the goats' milk cheeses are the *Banon* of Provence, the *Cabécou* of Quercy, the *Chabichou* of

Poitou, the *Chavignol* of Berry (*'crottins'*), *la Mothe-Saint-Héraye*, the *Levroux*, small *Mâcons* of Burgundy, the Corsican *Niolo*, the *Rigottes* of Condrieu, the *Rocamadour* and *Saint-Marcellin* of Dauphiné, the *Valençay*, the *Sainte-Maure*.

Gorgonzola – Semi-hard cheese which takes its name from a little village near Milan. It is made by a rather complex process. Good Gorgonzola, which is a spring and summer cheese, has a thin rind. The cheese should be streaked with blue, but not excessively, and should be yellowish white in colour.

Gouda – Dutch cheese made from whole milk, very similar to Cantal but there is no preliminary fermentation.

Gournay – French whole-milk, soft cheese made at Gournay, in Normandy, and in neighbouring districts. At its best between September and June.

Gruyère – The Gruyère valley is situated in the Fribourg Canton, dominated by the Moléson. It has given its name to a cheese which is also made in the Cantons of Vaud and Neuchâtel. True Gruyère is only made in French Switzerland.

Formerly, only semi-fat cheeses or cheeses made from skimmed milk were manufactured, the cream being used for butter, which could be economically exported. Nowadays whole milk Gruyères are also made, especially for export.

This cheese is often confused with Emmenthal. Sometimes cheesemongers advertise 'a genuine Gruyère from Emmenthal' which is like saying 'genuine Brie from Camembert'! It is made in rounds of 50 to 60 kg. (110 to 130 lb.). The rind is golden brown. The cheese is waxy, more or less dry according to age. It is scored with cracks underneath through which drops of serum ooze out. To satisfy the demands of the French market which expects 'eyes' in the cheese, it is processed in such a way for export that little holes appear. These are always smaller than the holes in Emmenthal. The export cheeses are also less salty than those made for local consumption. To enhance the pungent flavour of this excellent cheese, it is usual in Switzerland to preserve the pieces in a cloth soaked in salted water or white wine.

Gruyère is manufactured in cheese factories in the mountains, close to the pastures. It keeps for a very long time uncut. Some connoisseurs demand a very ripe cheese, others prefer it fairly fresh. For *fondue* (q.v.) a mixture of the two kinds is normally required.

Gruyère, Crème de. For some years now, little triangles of processed cheese have been sold, wrapped in silver paper. This cheese is made from Comté and sometimes even from Gruyère.

At first, this cheese was produced mainly as a means of using up defective cheeses, but it has gained so much in popularity that it is now manufactured from cheese made especially for the purpose. There are now a great number of processed and packaged cheeses (called creams) made from a variety of basic cheeses.

Their indeterminate flavour does not always appeal to the connoisseur, but their success is easily explained. They are processed and packaged in a convenient and hygienic form, having no rind and leaving no waste.

Gruyère de Comté. A number of Gruyère-type cheeses are made today in countries all over Europe and in America. For a long time a type of Gruyère has been manufactured in the Jura, but Gruyère de Comté manufacturers themselves now insist that the *appellation* Gruyère de Comté be replaced simply by Comté.

Guerbigny – Cheese from Picardy, which is in season between October and May.

Guéret – Cheese made in Guéret, a city of the *département* of Creuse. It is sometimes called *Creusois*, and is at its best between September and June.

Hervé – Soft, fermented cheese. Made in Belgium, from cows' milk, it is curdled with rennet, and drained under great pressure in square moulds.

Ripening takes place in dark cellars where the cheeses are placed on their sides, one against the other, covered with cloths steeped in beer.

There is a strong and a mild variety of Hervé cheese. Best eaten between November and May.

Huppemeau – Cheese made at Huppemeau in the Loire-et-Cher region. It is somewhat similar to Brie.

Incheville – Normandy cheese which is in season from November to May.

Jonchée – Cheese made from ewes' or goats' milk. Half the milk is boiled with a few bay leaves. This is mixed with the remainder of the raw milk. It is curdled with rennet and decanted into little pots.

Kaunas – Lithuanian cheese which can be eaten all the year round.

Kummel – Dutch cheese with caraway seeds, which can be eaten all the year round. It is also called *Leidsche Kaas*.

(Les) Laumes – This cheese from Burgundy is good between October and July.

Levroux – Goats' cheese made in and around Berry, in season between May and December.

Leyden – Leyden cheese is made in the same way as Edam. It is often flavoured with cumin, cloves or cinnamon. Some connoisseurs prefer Dutch cheese stove-dried. This makes it less creamy but improves its flavour. Leyden is also known as *Leidsche Kaas* and *Kummel*.

Limbourger – Semi-hard, fermented cheese made in Belgium, Alsace and Germany. The whole-milk curds are kneaded with chives, parsley and tarragon, put in moulds and dried in the sun. The surface is made non-porous by salting and brushing.

Livarot – A small town in the Calvados region has given its name to a soft paste cheese (usually coloured annatto brown or deep red). This is an autumn and winter cheese.

Manicamp – Picardy cheese which is in season between October and July.

Maroilles – Semi-hard, full-flavoured cheese which is square in shape and which takes its name from a village in the Avesnes district. It is manufactured in Thiérache and all over Picardy.

The whole-milk curds are salted, quickly dried and stored in a cellar where, at frequent intervals, the cheese is turned over, brushed, and washed with beer. It is at its best between November and June. It is also called *Marolles* or *Marole*.

Metton – Cheese from the Jura mountains which is in season from October to June.

Monsieur – Cheese made in Normandy, good between November and June.

Mont Cenis – A large, round, semi-hard, blue-veined, whole-milk cheese somewhere between a Roquefort and a Gorgonzola. It ripens in cellars where it acquires its characteristic blue streaks.

Mont d'Or – This cheese, which once had a great reputation, used to be made along the banks of the Saône, round Lyons. Only the milk of stable-fed goats was used. The cheese was ripened in cellars for 5 to 6 weeks.

The cheese which now bears its name is made all over France, is manufactured from cows' milk and bears very little resemblance to the original cheese. The best is made at Mont d'Or. Its season lasts from December to April.

Morbier – Lightly veined goats' milk cheese from Franche-Comté. Good between October and June.

(La) Mothe-Bougon – Poitou cheese in season between May and December.

(La) Mothe-Saint-Héraye – Goats' cheese from Poitou which is in season between May and November. Also called *Lamothe-Bougon*.

Munster – Semi-hard, fermented, whole-milk cheese, usually flavoured with caraway or aniseed. Made in Alsace, in the Munster valley (Upper Rhine), it is much prized by lovers of cheese and is good between November and April.

Murol – Cows' milk cheese from Auvergne shaped like a small wheel with a hole in the centre. Good between October and June.

Mysöst – Norwegian cheese which can be eaten all the year round.

Nantais – This Breton cheese, sometimes called *Fromage du curé*, is good to eat all the year round.

Neufchâtel or Bondon – Small French, loaf-shaped cheese made from skimmed milk, whole milk or with added cream. It is ripened on straw bundles in a drying room until a skin, white at first and later bluish, forms on the surface (first skin). The ripening is then completed in cool, well-aired store rooms until a second skin forms, this time red in colour. The cheese is a rather dark yellow and is at its best between October and June.

Niolo – Corsican cheese, which is particularly good from November to May.

Noekkelöst – Norwegian cheese which can be eaten all the yeard round.

Olivet – Whole-milk, mould-inoculated cheese, made in the small town of Olivet, in the Loiret. It is made of ewes' milk, in discs about 2½ cm. (1 inch) thick and 15 cm. (6 inches) in diameter. The curd is white and rather salty. This cheese has its season from October to June.

There is another type of Olivet cheese, called *Olivet Cendré*, which is good to eat from October to June. Fresh creamy Olivet cheese is sold in the summer months.

Oloron – Cheese from Béarn also called *Fromage de la Vallée d'Ossau*, which should be eaten from October to May.

Paladru – Cheese made in Savoy, in season from November to May.

Parmesan – This famous cheese, which keeps for a very long time, is made in Lombardy and in the Romagna under various names. The name 'Parmesan' is used abroad for export cheeses of this type. It is made with skimmed milk.

During the ripening process, which is very slow, harmful microbes can cause liquid patches in the cheese, which are dealt with by Italian cheese-makers. They test the cheese by tapping it with a hammer. When they detect a soft patch, they open up the cheese, cut out the diseased section and cauterise the 'wound' with a red-hot iron. The ripening period lasts for nearly 4 years. At the end of this process the cheese may be kept for a very long time, 20 years or even longer.

Parmesan is a hard cheese which can be eaten all the year round. It is golden yellow in colour and should sweat very slightly.

Pavé de Moyaux – Normandy cheese which is in season from November to June.

Pelardon de Ruoms – Goats' cheese made in Ardèche, which is in season from May to November.

Petit-suisse – Very creamy, unsalted French cheese of the double-cream type, small and cylindrical in shape. It is made from whole milk, with 20 per cent proportion of fresh cream added. In spite of its name, it was first made not in Switzerland but in Gournay in Normandy (Seine-Inférieure). The Gervais Petit-suisse is the best-known make. Manufacturing this cheese is a delicate process, to which the most up-to-date scientific methods of production and supervision are applied.

Picodon de Dieulefit – Cheese made in the Dauphiné which is in season from May to December.

Pithiviers au foin – Cheese made in the Orléans region and ripened on hay. In season from October to May.

Pontgibaud (Puy-de-Dôme) – Made in the same way as Roquefort, but from cows' milk. Eaten all the year round, except in mid-summer.

Pont-l'Evêque – French semi-hard, fermented cheese, made from whole or skimmed milk. It is shaped in square moulds, salted and processed like the Bondon or Neufchâtel. It is ripened in cellars. This takes from 3 to 4 months, or less if the cheese is very rich in cream. Pont-l'Evêque can be eaten the whole year round except in August but is at its best between October and June. It should have a wrinkled, greyish-yellow crust. The cheese is softish and pale yellow in colour.

Port-Salut – A superb creamy, yellow, whole-milk cheese. It was first made at the Trappist Monastery of Port du Salut, near Laval. The name of Port-Salut was given to it by a company established at Entrammes (Mayenne *département*) where it is still made, as well as in Trappist monasteries all over the world, according to a secret formula. It is good throughout the year.

Pouligny-Saint-Pierre – Famous cheese made from May to December in Berry.

Puant Macéré – Cheese from Flanders, in season from November till June.

Pultöst – Norwegian mountain farm cheese which can be eaten all the year round.

Reblochon – Soft cheese made in Savoy. It is made of cows' milk and is in season from October to June.

Récollet de Gérardmer – Cheese from the Vosges, in season from October to April.

Remondou – Belgian cheese called *Fromage piquant* in season from November to June.

Riceys cendré – Cheese sometimes called *Champenois* which is in season from September to June.

Rigotte de Condrieu – Semi-hard, creamy goats' cheese of the Lyon district which is in season from May to November.

Rocamadour – This community in the Lot, celebrated for its picturesque setting and its places of pilgrimage, has given its name to a very small ewes' milk cheese which is in season from November to May.

Rollot – Cheese in the form of a disc resembling Brie and Camembert, although smaller. It is also called *Bigolot*, and comes from Picardy. It is in season from October to May.

Romalour – Cheese from the Loire district which can be eaten all the year round.

Roquefort – The true Roquefort cheese, made in the little town of that name in the Saint-Affrique district (Aveyron), is manufactured exclusively from ewes' milk, sheep being the only animals which can subsist on the arid pastures of the Causses. Corsica exports a large number of cheeses to the Causses to be 'treated' in the caves there.

The unique feature of this cheese is that the curds are mixed with a special type of breadcrumb. The bread is dried and then ground to a fine dust, in which a special greenish mould is allowed to develop. To ensure the right conditions for ripening, the cheeses are stored in damp, cool caves (4° to 8°C., 40° to 47°F.), such as the natural caves which are to be found in the Causses region.

After 30 or 40 days, the cheese is ready for sale, but before it takes on the pungent flavour which makes it so sought-after by the connoisseur, it must be left to ripen for a much longer period. In fact, in the view of the experts, it should be kept for a year.

A good Roquefort has a grey rind. The cheese is yellowish, very fatty and evenly veined with blue. If it is too white in appearance and chalky in texture, it is not completely fermented.

The Roquefort season lasts from May to September but it is eaten all the year round. A number of different districts in France produce a Roquefort-type cheese but these may not be sold under the name of Roquefort.

Rouennais – Normandy cheese which is in season from October to May.

Rougeret – Small goats' cheese made near Mâcon. Is also known under the name of *Maconnet*.

Saint-Agathon – Breton cheese that is in season from October to July.

Saint-Florentin – Burgundian cheese, in season from November to July. It is soft and salty.

Saint-Marcellin – This cheese, manufactured chiefly at Saint-Marcellin, principal town of the Isère district, was formerly made exclusively from goats' milk. Today, both cows' milk and ewes' milk are added or are used as a substitute for goats' milk. It is in season between May and December.

Saint-Maure – Touraine cheese, in season from May to November. It is a soft, creamy, goats' milk cheese.

Saint-Rémi – Square cheese made in Franche-Comté and Haute-Savoie. It is soft and resembles Pont-l'Evêque.

Sassenage – Semi-hard, blue-veined cheese made in the Isère; in season from November to May.

Septmoncel – Small village in the Jura *département* which has given its name to a Roquefort-type cheese which comes from Saint-Claude. It is made in the same way as Gex cheese and is at its best between November and May. Curds from two milkings are sometimes put together, without mixing, to produce a cheese known as 'bastard Septmoncel'.

Serré or Seray – The whey, which is the residue in the manufacture of cheese, sometimes still contains a certain proportion of butter and a considerable quantity of casein and soluble albumen. This is particularly the case where curdling takes place quickly (by scalding). The butter can be extracted from this whey, and if it is first allowed to become acid, it can be curdled a second time with rennet. By this means it is possible to precipitate the serum containing the soluble albumen, and separate it from the lactose and mineral salts. This substance is called *serré* and is used both as human and animal food.

In some regions, notably in the Glaris district, the *serré* (called *ligger* in German) is pounded with herbs, wild celery in particular. This mixture is dried and made into slabs which are called *schabzigger*. Grated and mixed with butter, this cheese, which has a strongly aromatic flavour, is held in high esteem by some connoissuers. For some years, under the name of *Crème de Glaris*, it has been mixed with butter, and sold wrapped in silver paper.

Soumaintrin, also called Saint-Florentin – Burgundian cheese regarded as the prime vintage among all those made in the Armance valley in Burgundy.

It weighs approximately 500 g. (1 lb.), is yellow in colour, with a yellowish-orange rind, and is in season from November to July.

Soya – Cheese made in China from time immemorial. It is the result of fermentation in the juices extracted from soya beans.

The beans, softened and swollen by soaking, are put through a press. The liquid thus extracted is mixed with a little sulphate of lime or magnesium. It coagulates into a grey mass which is left to ferment like curds.

Stilton – English cheese made from whole milk with cream added, which takes a very long time to ripen. The cheese is marked with grey and green streaks. It should not be cut but scooped out of the centre. A little sherry or port should be poured onto it and left to soak into the cheese.

Stracchino – Italian soft goats' cheese.

Stilton cheese

Strong cheese. FROMAGE FORT – This preparation, exceedingly savoury and strong-smelling, is especially well liked in the Morvan and Lyons districts and in Corsica.

Successive layers of grated or thinly sliced milk cheese, salt and mixed herbs, and sometimes a little cream, are put in glazed stoneware jars, which are filled to the top with white wine laced with brandy. They are hermetically sealed and left in a warm place for 2 or 3 weeks to ferment.

Tête de mort – Name sometimes given in France to Dutch Edam cheese. Good all the year round.

Tomme – Cheese of the Savoy, of which several varieties exist. *Tomme de Beauges* and *Tomme au fenouil* are in season from September to June, *Tomme de Boudave* from October to July.

Trappistes – Cheeses of which the most popular variety is known as *Port-Salut*, because it is made by the Trappist monks of Port-du-Salut in the Mayenne. There are several other types in various regions of France: *Trappiste de Citeaux* (Burgundy), *Trappiste de Bricquebec* (Normandy), *Trappiste de Mont-des-Cats* (Picardy), *Trappiste de Sainte-Anne-d'Auray* (Brittany) and *Trappiste de Tamie* (Savoy). These cheeses may be eaten all the year round.

White cheese garnished with radish, anchovy and chives

Troô – Touraine cheese in season from May to January.

Troyes – This creamy soft cheese, resembling Camembert, is in season from November to May. It is also known as *Barberey*.

Vacherin – Soft cheese made in the Jura, in Switzerland and in Franche-Comté. It is in season from November to May.

Valençay – Soft goats' milk cheese from the Berry district. In season from May to December.

Vendôme – There is a soft Vendôme cheese, made in Orléans, which is good from October to June. There is also a hard ewes' milk cheese ripened under ashes, which is good in the same months, and is also called Vendôme.

Vestgötaöst – Swedish cheese which can be eaten all the year round.

Vic-en-Bigorre – Béarnaise winter cheese.

Villedieu – Normandy cheese at its best between November and May.

White cheese. FROMAGE BLANC – Made from whole milk, treated with rennet, and eaten fresh in summer.

CHEESE-RENNET. CAILLE-LAIT – Name given to various plants, the flowers and leaves of which have the property of curdling milk. Yellow bedstraw (*Galium verum*) is most commonly used for this purpose.

CHEF DE CUISINE – Director responsible for a kitchen team (see COOKING).

The rôle of the present-day *chef de cuisine* corresponds to that of *officier de bouche* in great houses in the old days, and in even earlier times to that of *maître des garnisons des cuisines royales* or *grand-queux*.

CHEMISER – To coat a substance, or a mould, with a thin layer of aspic jelly.

CHEMIST'S JAR. CHEVRETTE – Oblong faience vase, with a large mouth, projecting spout, and handle. In the old days only chemists (U.S. druggists) had the right to possess and exhibit this kind of vase in the windows of their shops. These jars have been replaced by glass jars filled with red or green coloured water which chemists stand in their windows, but these ornaments are now tending to disappear too.

The word *chevrette* also denotes a kind of iron tripod on which casseroles and *marmites* are stood.

CHENU – Colloquial term applied to a wine mellowed by old age.

CHÈRE – Word which used to be employed mostly in an expression La Fontaine used, '*faire chère lie*', meaning 'to smile broadly', 'to welcome warmly'. The expression is now restricted to the sense of 'offering a good meal', an integral part of any welcome. Nowadays *chère* in French is a synonym of food.

CHERRY. CERISE – Fruit of a tree of the *Rosaceae* family of which the numerous varieties stem from two primitive species.

The *wild cherry* or *bird cherry*, originating in Persia and Armenia, from which derive the two sweet cherries, the *heart cherry* with soft flesh and coloured juice, and the *whiteheart cherry* with hard flesh and colourless juice.

There are numerous cultivated varieties, some early-fruiting, which ripen in May; others late-fruiting, which ripen in August or September. The whiteheart cherries are usually considered the best dessert fruits. The slightly bitter early English variety of cherry is also served as a dessert fruit. The very bitter *morello cherries* are used industrially.

French cherries are marketed between May and July.

Cherries are one of the most refreshing fruits. They can be preserved by drying in the sun or over heat, or by preserving in sugar or in brandy. Jams, jellies, and syrups are made from them (see JAMS, SYRUPS). They are used for distilling (see KIRSCH), and liqueurs are made with them (see MARASCHINO).

Their stalks, used in infusions, are a popular diuretic.

Cherries à l'allemande I. CERISES À L'ALLEMANDE – Cold *hors-d'œuvre* which is usually made commercially, but it can be prepared in the following way:

Destalk morello cherries which are only just ripe, and put them in a jar, in the same way as for gherkins (q.v.).

Cover with aromatic vinegar prepared in the following way: Put 200 g. (7 oz., 1 cup) brown sugar, a fragment of stick cinnamon, a little grated nutmeg, and 3 cloves into 1 litre ($1\frac{3}{4}$ pints, generous quart) vinegar. Boil, allow to cool and pour over the cherries. Leave the cherries in this for 15 days.

Cherries à l'allemande II. CERISES À L'ALLEMANDE – Put the destalked cherries in a dish and cover with brown sugar. Cook in a very slow oven until the cherries are slightly softened. When they have cooled, put them in a glass jar and cover with aromatic vinegar, prepared as above, but using less brown sugar. Leave for 15 days before use.

With either method, one can add thyme, bay and tarragon to taste.

Cherries prepared *à l'allemande*, served also under the name of *sweet-sour cherries*, are used to accompany boiled meats and cold meats in the same way as gherkins.

Cherries in brandy. CERISES À L'EAU-DE-VIE – Choose well-formed cherries not yet quite ripe. Cut stalks in half and arrange the cherries in a glass jar. Cover with good brandy in which some sugar has been dissolved in the proportion of 225 g. (8 oz., 1 cup) sugar to 1 litre (scant quart, generous quart) brandy. Hermetically seal the jar. To obtain cherries less penetrated with alcohol, use the following method:

Shorten the stalks, and pierce each cherry with the point of a needle at the opposite end from the stalk. Dip in cold water, drain, and put them in a *terrine*, covering them with a syrup made with sugar and water in the proportion of 2 kg. ($4\frac{1}{2}$ lb., 9 cups) sugar to 1 litre (scant quart, generous quart) water. Cover the *terrine* and leave the cherries to absorb the syrup for 24 hours. Drain, put them in a glass jar and cover with the syrup, which has been boiled down. After cooling, add 2 parts brandy for 1 part syrup. Seal the jar hermetically.

Cherries with claret. CERISES AU CLARET – Put 500 g. (generous 1 lb.) destalked cherries in a pan. Cover with red Bordeaux wine, add sugar, and flavour with a little cinnamon. Cook, covered, for 10 to 12 minutes on a gentle heat. Leave the cherries to cool in their syrup. Pour off the wine and boil it down by a third. Add 3 tablespoons (scant $\frac{1}{4}$ cup) gooseberry jelly, and mix well. Pour this syrup over the cherries. Serve cold with sponge fingers.

This dish is also called *Cherry soup à l'anglaise*.

Cherry compote. COMPOTE DE CERISES – Prepare with stoned cherries in the same way as *Apricot compote* (see COMPOTE).

Cherry Condé. CERISES CONDÉ – Prepare with stoned cherries cooked in a vanilla syrup, like *Apricots Condé* (see APRICOT).

Cherry coupe – See ICE CREAMS AND ICES.

Cherry croûtes. CROÛTES AUX CERISES – Prepare with stoned cherries cooked in syrup, like *Apricot croûte* (see APRICOT).

Cherry flan. FLAN DE CERISES – Pastry shell or flan case made with sweetened pastry, filled with raw stoned cherries, and baked in the oven. Cherry tarts or flans are also prepared with *crème à l'alsacienne* or *à la flamande* (see TARTS).

Cherry fritters. BEIGNETS AUX CERISES – Stone the cherries, soak with liqueur and sugar, dip in light batter and fry. (See FRITTERS.)

Cherry ice. GLACE AUX CERISES – Pound 1 litre ($1\frac{3}{4}$ pints, generous quart) stoned cherries or crush in a mortar or blender. Add the pounded cherry kernels to this pulp. Soak the mixture for 1 hour in 1 litre ($1\frac{3}{4}$ pints, generous quart) syrup – 450 g. (1 lb., 2 cups) sugar to 1 litre ($1\frac{3}{4}$ pints, generous quart) water – flavoured with kirsch. Pass through a fine sieve and add the juice of 1 lemon. This preparation should measure 21° on the syrup gauge.

Freeze the mixture in the usual way (see ICE CREAMS AND ICES).

Cherry jam. CONFITURE DE CERISES – Prepared with 750 g. ($1\frac{3}{4}$ lb., 6 cups) lump sugar for each 1 kg. ($2\frac{1}{4}$ lb.) fruit. If the fruit is not very sweet the jam is made with an equal weight of sugar and fruit. (See JAM.)

Cherries jubilee. CERISES JUBILÉ – Simmer stoned cherries in syrup. Drain and put them into ovenproof dishes. Boil down the syrup in which they have cooked, add a little cornflour or arrowroot diluted with cold water, and pour over the cherries.

Add 1 tablespoon warmed kirsch to each dish and flame it at the moment of serving.

Cherry meringue tart or flan with rice. FLAN DE CERISES MERINGUÉES AU RIZ – Put a layer of *Dessert rice* (see RICE) in a *gratin* dish, and add a thick layer of stoned cooked cherries. Sprinkle with sugar and top with meringue. Decorate the top with arabesques in meringue and proceed in the same way as for *Apricots with rice and meringue* (see APRICOT).

Cherry mousse – See ICE CREAMS AND ICES.

Cherry sauce – See SAUCE, *Dessert sauces*.

Cherry soufflé fritters – See FRITTERS.

Cherry soufflé Montmorency. SOUFFLÉ AUX CERISES, DIT MONTMORENCY – Add 400 g. (14 oz., $1\frac{3}{4}$ cups) cherry purée to 500 g. (18 oz., $2\frac{1}{4}$ cups) sugar boiled in 1 litre ($1\frac{3}{4}$ pints, generous quart) water to the crack stage. Fold in 10 stiffly whisked egg whites.

Make the soufflé in the usual way (see SOUFFLÉ).

The soufflé can also be prepared with cream (see SOUFFLÉ, *Cream soufflés*).

Cold cherry soufflé. SOUFFLÉ GLACÉ AUX CERISES – Use the preparation for *Iced cherry mousse* (see ICE CREAMS AND ICES). Tie a fold of white paper round the top of a soufflé dish to reach $2\frac{1}{2}$ cm. (1 inch) above it, and fill with this mixture.

Once the soufflé has set in the refrigerator remove the paper.

Danish cherry tart or flan. FLAN DE CERISES À LA DANOISE – Fill a flaky pastry shell or flan case with stoned cherries soaked in sugar and sprinkled with a pinch of cinnamon.

Cover the cherries with a mixture of 100 g. (4 oz., $\frac{1}{2}$ cup) softened butter, 100 g. (4 oz., $\frac{1}{2}$ cup) sugar, 100 g. (4 oz., 1 cup) ground almonds and 2 eggs.

Bake the tart or flan in the oven at a moderate temperature. Leave to cool, cover with gooseberry jelly, and glaze with rum.

Cherries in vinegar. CERISES AU VINAIGRE – Remove the stalks from ripe cherries. Put them in a glass jar, alternating layers of cherries with powdered sugar, a few cloves, and fragments of cinnamon. Fill the jar with these layers. Boil white wine vinegar with lemon rinds, cool, and pour into the jar.

Seal the jar with a cork covered with linen.

CHERRY BAY (U.S. CHERRY LAUREL). LAURIER-CERISE – The leaves of this shrub emit a smell of bitter almonds when they are rubbed between the fingers. They are used to flavour creams of various kinds, but must be used sparingly as they contain an appreciable amount of poisonous hydrocyanic acid.

CHERVIL. CERFEUIL – Pot-herb with stiff stems and curly leaves, originating in Russia and western Asia and cultivated from the beginning of the Christian era. It is used chopped for seasoning.

Wild chervil which is called *sweet Cecily* has darker, less denticulated, leaves and a more bitter flavour. Chervil, like parsley, is rich in Vitamin C.

CHERVIS – Plant originating in China. The very sweet and aromatic root was greatly sought after in the old days, but it is no longer much esteemed.

CHESTNUTS. CHÂTAIGNES – Chestnuts grow two or three together in a prickly shell. A number of chestnut varieties exist, improved by cultivation. The species of which the fruit contains only a single large nut are called *marrons*.

According to an analysis carried out by M. Baland, roast chestnuts (that is chestnuts cooked dry) retain 40 per cent of their moisture; boiled, they retain 70 per cent.

Dried chestnuts only retain 12 to 15 per cent of their moisture and contain as much nitrogen as wheat.

Chestnuts have considerable food value. $1\frac{1}{2}$ kg. ($3\frac{1}{4}$ lb.) supply sufficient calories to satisfy the needs of an average person. Unfortunately chestnuts also contain a high percentage of starch, which is difficult to assimilate and makes them indigestible for many people. Moreover, the small quantities of Vitamins B1 and C they contain are destroyed during cooking. On the other hand their richness in mineral salts (particularly calcium and potassium) makes them an excellent food for growing children.

Chestnuts are preserved by drying, and flour is made from them. This flour, which is white with red particles here and there (debris of the outer skin) in inferior types, has a sweet flavour, an agreeable smell, and makes a non-elastic paste when combined with water. It is used to make various dishes.

Briloli. A kind of porridge made with chestnut flour to which milk or cream is added.

Castagnacci. Thick fritters, using chestnut flour.

Ferinana. This is *briloli* with oil added.

Pislicine. Cake prepared with chestnut porridge fermented with yeast and flavoured with aniseed.

Polenta. This is obtained by throwing sieved chestnut flour into lightly salted boiling water and mixing with a spatula until the paste no longer adheres to the sides of the cooking dish. Pour onto a floured cloth and cut into slices. These are either eaten as they are, with Broccio (Corsican cheese), grilled, or fried. (See POLENTA.)

Peeling chestnuts on domed face
(*Claire*)

Tourte. This is a porridge to which aniseed with pine kernels and dried raisins have been added. It is poured into a baking dish and cooked in the oven.

To peel chestnuts, slit the surface of the chestnuts on the domed face. Put them in a baking tin with a little water. Roast in the oven for 8 minutes. Peel them while they are still hot.

Another method is to slit the chestnuts as indicated above. Put them, a few at a time, into boiling fat and deep-fry for 2 minutes. Drain. Peel them while they are still hot.

Chestnut barquettes. BARQUETTES AUX MARRONS – Line *barquette* tins with *Fine pastry dough I* (see DOUGH). Bake blind. When they are ready, fill them with a purée of *marrons glacés* (or purée of chestnuts cooked in milk) flavoured with kirsch. Ice the *barquettes* with kirsch-flavoured *Fondant icing* (see ICING).

Boiled chestnuts. MARRONS BOUILLIS – Put the chestnuts in a saucepan and cover with cold water. Season with a pinch of salt and flavour with a little celery, star anise, Chinese anise or any other spice.

Bring to the boil. Cover and simmer gently for 45 minutes to 1 hour. Drain the chestnuts and serve wrapped in a folded napkin, or in a wooden bowl covered with a napkin.

Braised chestnuts. MARRONS BRAISÉS – Peel the chestnuts. Lay them flat in a buttered dish. Put into the middle of the dish a *bouquet garni* with plenty of celery. Season. Pour in a thin layer of concentrated veal stock. Cover the pan and cook in the oven without stirring, so as not to break the chestnuts.

Chestnuts prepared in this way are used as a garnish for various main dishes.

Chestnut compote. COMPOTE DE MARRONS – Cook the chestnuts in a light syrup flavoured with vanilla. To serve, pour the cooking syrup (boiled down if necessary) over the chestnuts.

They can be served either hot or cold, and may be flavoured with liqueur.

Chestnut confection. PÂTÉ DE MARRONS – 'Shell the chestnuts, blanch, peel off the skin, pound in a stone mortar and weigh. Separately, clarify the same amount of sugar, cooked to ball degree. Take off the heat and mix with half its weight of apricot jam or apple jelly. Stir, combine all the ingredients, spread on a slate slab or a metal sheet to a thickness of 2 or 3 lines (see WEIGHTS AND MEASURES) and put into a slow oven until dry. On the following day, cut into squares, lay out on a sieve, turning them from time to time. When they are quite dry store in boxes.' (*le Confiseur moderne*.)

Chestnut croquettes. CROQUETTES DE MARRONS – Chop *marrons glacés* very finely. Chestnuts boiled in milk sweetened with vanilla sugar may also be used. Blend with thick *French pastry cream* (see CREAMS). Spread the mixture on a baking sheet. Leave to cool.

Divide the mixture into small portions. Flour each piece and dip in egg and freshly made breadcrumbs. Deep-fry in clarified butter. Serve with *Apricot sauce* (see SAUCE) flavoured with kirsch.

Chestnut jam. CONFITURE DE MARRONS – Make a chestnut purée with milk or water. Put it in a bowl with an equal weight of sugar, a vanilla pod and 1 dl. (6 tablespoons, scant ½ cup) water to every 1 kg. (2¼ lb.) of the mixture. Warm gently, stirring constantly. The jam is ready if it comes away from the bottom of the pan when stirred.

To ensure longer preservation, put the jam in special jars and sterilise as for bottled fruit.

Marrons glacés – *Marrons glacés* are first preserved and then glazed. This is a long and intricate process and is therefore seldom undertaken in the home.

Chestnut Mont-Blanc (sweet dessert). MONT-BLANC AUX MARRONS – Shell the chestnuts, leaving the inner skin. Cover with water and bring to the boil. Remove the inner skin.

Simmer the chestnuts until soft in milk, with sugar and vanilla. Drain and rub them through a wire sieve over a large ring baking tin, so that the sides of the tin are lined with the sieved purée, which will look like vermicelli.

Turn this border out onto a dish. When it is quite cold, fill the centre with *Chantilly cream* (see CREAMS) flavoured with vanilla. Shape the cream into a dome.

Chestnut purée. PURÉE DE MARRONS – Shell the chestnuts, leaving the inner skin intact. Plunge them into boiling water, drain, and skin. Cook in white stock seasoned with a little celery. Drain, and rub through a fine sieve. Warm this purée in a saucepan, stirring constantly. Just before serving, add fresh butter and a few tablespoons fresh cream.

Chestnut purée soup or cream – see SOUPS AND BROTHS, *Purée soups*.

Chestnuts and rice. BORDURE DE MARRONS AU RIZ – Peel the chestnuts and cook in a light syrup flavoured with vanilla. Drain, and arrange them in a pyramid surrounded by a border of rice prepared as for *Apricots Condé* (see APRICOT). Decorate the top of the border with crystallised fruit and halved almonds. Serve with *Apricot sauce* (see SAUCE) flavoured with kirsch.

Roast chestnuts. MARRONS GRILLÉS – Lightly cut a ring round the chestnuts. Roast them in a pan on hot embers or on the stove, tossing them frequently so that all are thoroughly cooked.

Chestnut soufflé. SOUFFLÉ DE MARRONS – Make a chestnut purée with stock or milk, and use for a soufflé, proceeding as for *Potato soufflé* (see SOUFFLÉ).

Sweet chestnut soufflé. POUDING SOUFFLÉ AUX MARRONS – Peel 1 kg. (2¼ lb.) chestnuts and cook them in a light syrup, flavoured with vanilla. Add to this purée, while stirring it on the stove to evaporate the moisture, 150 g. (5 oz., generous ½ cup) fine sugar and 100 g. (4 oz., ½ cup) butter.

Remove the pan from the stove and blend in 8 egg yolks. Whisk 6 egg whites until they are very stiff. Blend them in at the last minute.

Pour the mixture into a buttered mould. Put the mould in a pan of water and bake in the oven. Serve with custard (q.v.) or *zabaglione* (q.v.).

Stewed chestnuts as a garnish. MARRONS ÉTUVÉS POUR GARNITURE – Peel the chestnuts. Put them in a buttered pan. Cover with clear white stock (or, for fish or vegetable dishes, with water). Add a pinch of salt, 1 teaspoon fine sugar and a stick of celery.

Bring rapidly to the boil. Cover and leave to simmer very slowly for 45 minutes.

Serve as indicated in the recipe for the main dish.

CHEVALER – Term indicating the symmetrical arrangement of the various elements of a dish placed one upon the other.

CHEVALET – A slice of bread trimmed *en chevalet* and covered with wafer-thin slices of fat pork or butter, on which chicken *filets mignons* (breasts) are placed to give them a correct shape while cooking.

CHEVRET – See CHEESE.

CHEVRIER – A type of haricot *flageolet* (bean) which stays green. Cultivated especially in the neighbourhood of Arpajon, it bears the name of the originator of this variety. (See BEAN.)

CHEVROTIN – See CHEESE.

CHEVROTTON DE MÂCON – See CHEESE.

CHIANTI – Tuscany wine. (See INTERNATIONAL WINES.)

CHICHA – Mexican and Central American alcoholic beverage obtained from the fermentation of maize flour.

CHICKEN. POULETS, POULARDES, VOLAILLE – Chicken is the generic term used to describe the barnyard fowl and includes everything from the very young chicken (*poussin*) to the large hen suitable only for the stockpot. The young chickens (*poulet de grain* and *poulet de reine*) weigh from 600 to 1800 g. (1¼ to 4 lb.). *Poulet gras* weigh from 1800 g. to 2 kg. (4 to 4½ lb.), and fat hens or roasting chicken weigh from 1800 g. to 3 kg. (4 to 6½ lb.) or more and are called *poulardes* in French. Recipes for the different kinds of chicken are grouped together in alphabetical order in this section.

A good *poulet* has tender flesh, elastic, but not flabby; the feet can be black or white according to the breed, but never yellow. The comb should be small and unformed, the skin loose and white, and the parson's nose white or pinkish with a knob of fat above reaching the backbone.

Chicken flesh can replace meat and when grilled or roasted is suitable for all diets. Chicken in sauce, chicken with mushrooms, or creamed chicken are less so. Try to avoid buying 'battery' chickens.

The principal types of French hens are those of Bresse, Houdan, La Flèche, Crèvecoeur, Barbezieux, Faverolles and Le Mans.

General cooking instructions for chicken – When braising chicken there should be as little as possible of cooking liquid, so as not to dissipate the delicate flavour.

Sauces accompanying braised fowl are made with the liquor in which it was cooked, strained, all grease skimmed off, and finished according to the recipe.

Boiled or poached chicken is cooked in white stock (chicken or veal) or in a light beef stock.

A savoury stock can be made with the neck, head and crop, and the feet, cooked in water with aromatic vegetables and the usual seasonings.

Boiled chicken is accompanied by white or light sauce, made with the liquor in which it was cooked. A white *roux* should be made in advance, with butter and flour cooked gently together without colouring, and moistened with some of the chicken broth when the mixture is about three-quarters cooked.

Different ways of finishing these sauces are given in the list of white sauces (see SAUCE, *Compound white sauces*). Chicken baked in butter (cooked in the oven in a covered dish) is accompanied by the cooking juices skimmed of fat, diluted, and thickened. Cream is sometimes used.

Chicken baked *à la Matignon* is accompanied by the cooking juices diluted with wine, blended with veal or chicken stock, and bound with rich brown sauce. The garnish for a chicken dish is either cooked with the chicken or prepared separately, according to the recipe.

In none of the recipes that follow should all the sauce be used to coat the bird. A very little only should be poured over it, and the rest served separately.

Some instructions for cooking large fowls call for stuffings and prepared mixtures. Recipes for these will be found under FORCEMEAT.

In garnished chicken dishes, particularly those served at large dinners, the bird is often left whole. This calls for a decorative presentation. It is important, however, that the garnish should not cancel out the flavour of the dish. Garnishes should be arranged so that the bird can be quickly carved. Do not set all the accompaniments on the main dish but use only a small part as a garnish, and serve the rest separately when handing the sauce, all piping hot.

In making an ornamental arrangement set the fowl on a base of fried bread in order to keep it separate from the garnish.

To bake chickens and capons in butter. Clean, truss and bard the bird.

Put in a heavy-bottomed pot, pour melted butter over it, season, and cook quickly for a few moments over a good heat. Finish cooking in the oven, covered, basting frequently with its butter. Garnish according to the recipe. Serve with its cooking juices diluted according to the particular recipe.

To bake chickens and capons à la Matignon. Clean, draw, truss and bard the bird. Put it in a pan whose base is lined with *Matignon* (q.v.) half-cooked in butter.

Pour melted butter over, season, and cook covered in the oven, basting frequently with its butter.

When the chicken is cooked and golden brown, moisten with concentrated veal or chicken stock and baste with this juice.

Garnish and serve with its own cooking juice, diluted according to the recipe.

To bake chickens and capons à la Matignon (old style). Crisp in butter the flesh of a fowl prepared as for braising. Cover it in a thick layer of *Matignon* (q.v.); bard and wrap it in a sheet of buttered paper. Cook in the oven or on the spit. Unwrap the chicken, take off the bard and remove the *Matignon*. Put the bird in a saucepan, pour over Madeira. Boil down the liquid and add veal stock that has been boiled down and thickened. Remove all fat and strain.

Garnish according to the recipe and serve with its cooking liquor.

The recipes given below can be augmented by serving braised, boiled or baked chicken with different vegetables, with pasta and with other garnishes.

Braised chicken

To braise chickens and capons. Draw, singe, clean and truss the bird. Dip it for a moment into boiling stock to solidify the flesh, then lard the breast with bacon fat, truffles, or tongue.

Cover the breast with a bard of bacon fat big enough to protect this delicate part of the bird during cooking so that it does not become too dry. Brown the chicken in a hot oven, and then put it into a heavy braising pan with the ingredients used for braising white meat (see CULINARY METHODS, *Braising*).

Pour in the liquid indicated in the recipe, bring to the boil, cover the pot, return to the oven and cook, basting frequently.

Drain the chicken, remove the bard and trussing string and glaze in the oven, basting it with the cooking liquor.

Set it on a slice of fried bread (or directly onto the plate), garnish, and serve it with a sauce containing the liquid in which it was cooked.

How to truss a chicken

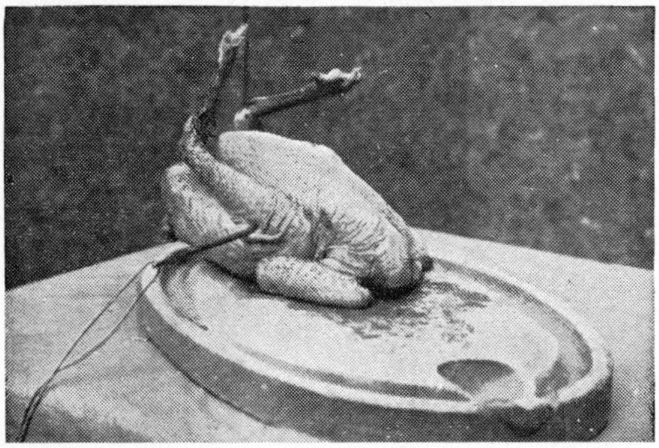

1. Pierce with threaded trussing needle the left thigh, the breast and the right thigh

2. Lay the chicken on its left side and sew through the right wing

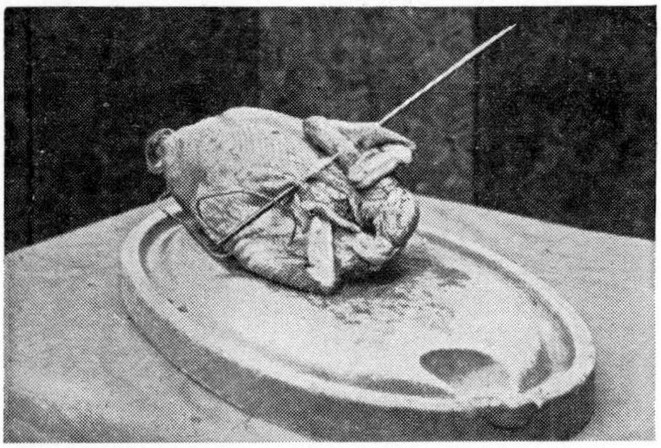

3. The chicken is on its right side; cross the back and pierce the left wing

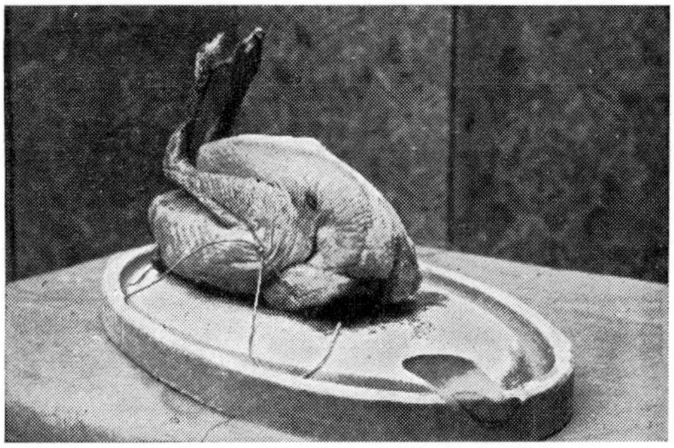

4. Bring the two ends of string together and tie them

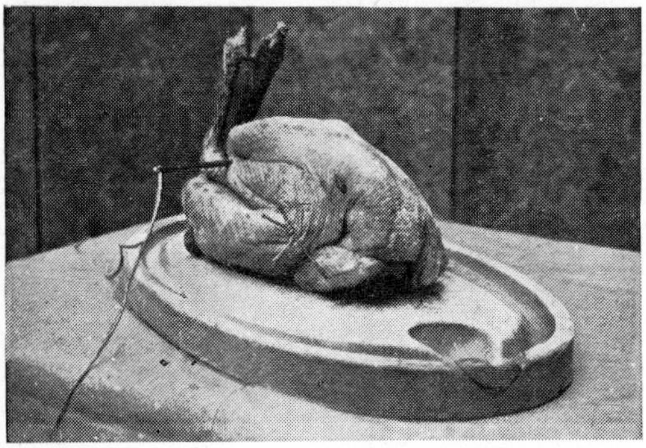

5. Pass the needle through the lower part of the drumsticks and under the breast from left to right

6. Next pierce the lower part of the body from right to left

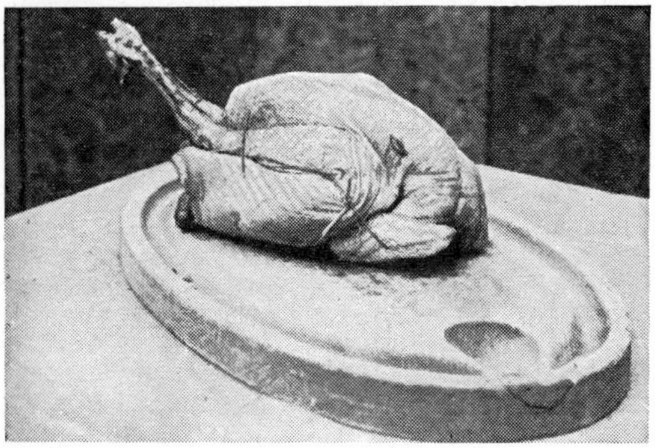

7. Pull the two ends of the string and tie them

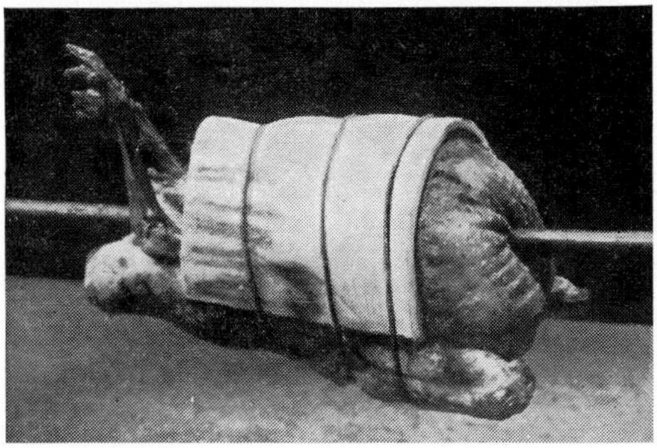

8. Chicken barded and trussed, ready to braise or roast

Carving a chicken into portions

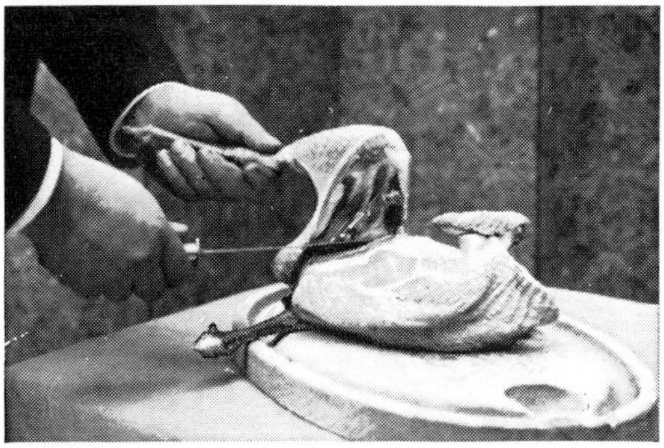

1. Raw chicken: first remove the right leg

2. Remove the right wing

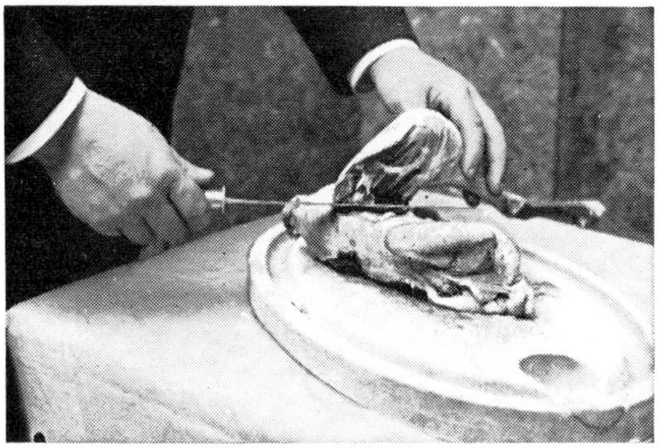

3. Place chicken on right side and remove the left leg

4. Remove the left wing

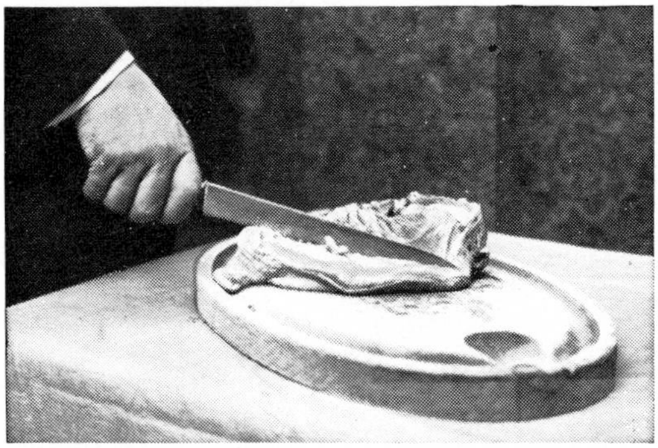

5. Cut away the fillets on either side

6. Cut the carcase in half

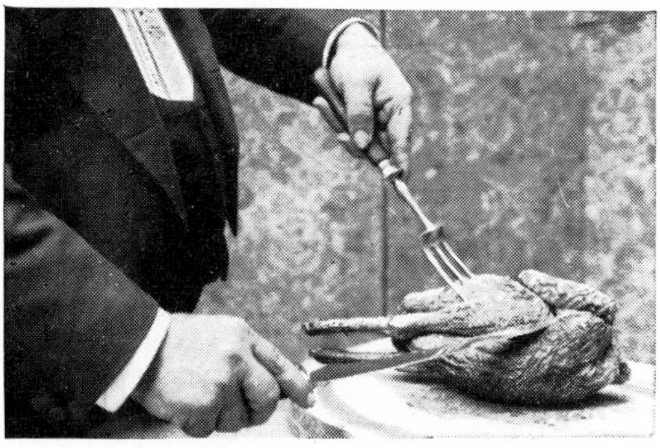

7. Roast chicken is cut up in the same way.

8. A small chicken can be cut in half lengthwise

To poach or boil chickens and capons. Clean and truss the bird. Rub the breast and legs with a slice of lemon to keep them white.

Lard or stud the breast with fat. Cover with a bard of bacon fat.

Bring to the boil in white stock and cook quickly for a few moments. Skim, cover the saucepan, and simmer very slowly.

To test whether the chicken is cooked, prick a fleshy part with the point of a knife. If a clear juice escapes it is done.

Drain the chicken, then remove the bard and the trussing string. Garnish and serve with a white sauce to which is added some of the liquor in which the chicken was cooked.

Chicken à l'allemande. POULARDE À L'ALLEMANDE – Poach the chicken in white stock. Coat with *Allemande sauce* (see SAUCE) to which part of the boiled-down cooking liquor has been added.

Chicken Ambassadrice. POULARDE AMBASSADRICE – Stuff the chicken with a mixture of lambs' sweetbreads, truffles and mushrooms bound with *Velouté sauce* (see SAUCE). Cook it covered, in the oven, *à la Matignon.*

Surround with pastry cases filled with sautéed chicken livers, cocks' combs and kidneys. Put a slice of truffle heated in butter on each.

Coat the chicken with the cooking juices diluted with Madeira and thickened brown veal stock.

Chicken à l'andalouse. POULARDE À L'ANDALOUSE – Stuff the chicken with rice mixed with small pieces of lean ham and seasoned with paprika.

Cook in butter in a heavy pan, adding (for flavouring) one large onion and a *bouquet garni* (q.v.). Serve garnished *à l'andalouse* (q.v.).

Surround the chicken with this garnish and sprinkle with its cooking juices diluted with white wine, to which thickened brown veal gravy and tomato purée have been added.

Chicken à l'anversoise. POULARDE À L'ANVERSOISE – Stuff the chicken with *Hop shoots* (see HOPS) in cream. Simmer in butter in a covered dish until the bird is three-quarters cooked. Transfer to a casserole with 400 g. (14 oz.) potatoes, lightly fried in butter. Complete cooking in the oven.

Pour a small quantity of the pan juices, diluted with white wine and thickened rich brown veal gravy, over the chicken. Serve in the casserole.

Chicken in aspic. POULARDE EN ASPIC – Cut the breast and wings of a cold, boiled chicken into thin slices, and coat with *White chaud-froid sauce* (see SAUCE). Decorate with truffles and glaze with chicken jelly.

Set these pieces in an aspic mould that has been lined with a layer of jelly. Fill the middle of the mould with *Chicken mousse* (see MOUSSES) made of the flesh of the chicken legs with the addition of *foie gras.* Fill the mould with the aspic jelly, leave to cool, and chill on ice.

Turn out onto a dish, or raised on a croûton of bread. Garnish with chopped jelly.

Chicken à l'Aurora. POULARDE À L'AURORE – Poach the chicken in white stock. Coat with *Aurora sauce* (see SAUCE) to which has been added a small quantity of the boiled-down cooking liquor.

Stuff with cream *Quenelle forcemeat* (see FORCEMEAT) flavoured with strong tomato purée.

Chicken ballottines. BALLOTTINES DE VOLAILLE – Use either a whole boned chicken, filled with stuffing, rolled in a ballottine and braised or poached (see BALLOTTINE), or legs of large chickens prepared in the same manner. The latter are usually called *Jambonneaux de volaille.*

Chicken à la banquière. POULARDE À LA BANQUIÈRE – Stuff the chicken with rice half-cooked in white stock mixed with 2 tablespoons (3 tablespoons) diced truffles. Poach in white stock.

Surround with *quenelles* (q.v.) of chicken forcemeat, mushrooms and thick slices of truffles. Coat with *Banquière sauce* (see SAUCE).

Boiled chicken à l'anglaise I. POULARDE POCHÉE À L'ANGLAISE – Poach in white stock. Surround with small slices of tongue, and with small mounds of celery, peas, carrots and turnips cooked in water.

Boiled chicken à l'anglaise II. POULARDE POCHÉE À L'ANGLAISE – Poach in water with a carrot cut in quarters, an onion stuck with a clove, a bunch of herbs and a piece of well-balanced lean bacon weighing 400 g. (14 oz.).

Surround with the bacon cut in squares.

Serve with *Parsley sauce* (see SAUCE) and chicken broth.

Boiled chicken à l'anglaise III. POULARDE POCHÉE À L'ANGLAISE – Poach the chicken in white stock with small carrots, pieces of turnip cut into balls, and celery hearts.

Surround with these vegetables, adding cooked French beans and cauliflower.

Serve with *Butter sauce* (see SAUCE), capers and chicken broth.

Chicken à la bonne femme. POULARDE À LA BONNE FEMME – Cook the chicken, covered in butter, in the oven. When it is half-cooked add 5 rashers blanched, diced lean bacon, and 20 small onions. Cook in the oven for 15 minutes.

Add 500 g. (generous 1 lb.) small potatoes. Finish cooking all together, basting frequently.

Put the chicken and its garnish in a *cocotte* or on a platter. Add 4 tablespoons ($\frac{1}{3}$ cup) thickened brown veal gravy to the cooking butter and pour over the chicken.

Chicken bouchées, canapés, croûtes and tartelettes – All these are filled with a *salpicon* (q.v.) of poultry finished off with truffles, mushrooms or other ingredients and bound with a white or brown sauce.

Chicken boudins à la Richelieu. BOUDINS DE VOLAILLE À LA RICHELIEU – Line small, well-buttered moulds with *Chicken forcemeat à la crème* (see FORCEMEAT). Fill the moulds with a *salpicon* (q.v.) of breast of chicken, truffles and mushrooms, blended with very thick *Allemande sauce* (see SAUCE). Cover with another layer of chicken forcemeat, which should be well smoothed over with the blade of a knife dipped in cold water.

Place the moulds in a baking tin of hot water in the oven, and poach. When cooked, turn out of the moulds, dry, dip in egg and breadcrumbs and fry in clarified butter until light golden.

Arrange in a turban shape on a dish, packing them in tightly. Garnish with fried parsley. Serve with *Périgueux sauce* or *Suprême sauce* with diced truffles added to it (see SAUCE).

Chicken à la bourgeoise. POULARDE À LA BOURGEOISE – Cook the chicken in butter in a covered casserole in the oven. When half-cooked add 5 rashers of diced lean bacon, 20 small onions and 20 small carrots. Finish cooking all together, basting frequently.

Dilute the cooking juices with white wine and thickened veal gravy, pour over the chicken and garnish.

Chicken à la bourguignonne. POULARDE À LA BOURGUIGNONNE – Brown 5 rashers blanched lean bacon in 25 g. (1 oz., 2 tablespoons) butter. Add 20 small onions and 20 sliced mushrooms.

Take these out and brown the chicken in the same butter. Remove the chicken. Dilute the juices with 4 dl. ($\frac{3}{4}$ pint, scant 2 cups) red wine and boil down by half. Add 4 dl. ($\frac{3}{4}$ pint, scant 2 cups) brown gravy, cook at boiling point for 5 minutes and add a *bouquet garni* (q.v.).

Put the chicken back in the pan. Cook gently for 20 minutes. Add the bacon, onions and mushrooms and continue cooking for 45 minutes to 1 hour.

Remove the *bouquet garni* and pour the sauce over the chicken.

Chicken brochettes. BROCHETTES DE VOLAILLE – Thread slices of chicken on metal skewers alternately with pieces of lean bacon and mushrooms. Coat in egg and breadcrumbs and grill.

Chicken broth (English and American cookery) – See SOUPS AND BROTHS.

Chicken capilotade. POULET EN CAPILOTADE – Use left-overs of boiled, braised, or roasted chicken for this dish.

Take the chicken off the bones, cut in thin slices, and simmer in a sauce such as *Chasseur, Italian, Portuguese, Provençal*, etc. (see SAUCE).

Chicken casserole. POULARDE EN CASSEROLE – Put the chicken, trussed for boiling and seasoned with salt and pepper, in a casserole in which some butter has been melted. Cook in the oven at a good heat.

Pour 4 to 5 tablespoons thickened rich brown veal stock over the dish.

Chicken casserole à la bonne femme. POULARDE EN CASSEROLE À LA BONNE FEMME – As above, adding to the chicken, when it has been well browned in butter, small pieces of blanched lean bacon, small onions that have been tossed in butter, and potatoes cut into pieces.

Chicken with celery (brown). POULARDE AUX CÉLERIS – Cook the chicken in butter in a covered casserole in the oven.

Surround with braised, quartered celery hearts. Dilute the cooking juices with white wine and thickened brown veal gravy, and pour over the bird.

Alternatively, the chicken may be braised with blanched celery.

Chicken with celery (white). POULARDE AUX CÉLERIS – As for *Chicken à l'allemande*. Surround the chicken with braised celery. Pour *Allemande sauce* (see SAUCE) over it.

Chicken à la Chantilly. POULARDE À LA CHANTILLY – Stuff the chicken with cooked rice mixed with truffles or diced *foie gras*. Cook in butter, in a covered dish in the oven, but do not allow to brown.

Surround with large whole truffles cooked in port wine, and slices of *foie gras* lightly fried in butter. Dilute the pan juices with white stock, add thick chicken *Velouté sauce* (see SAUCE) and simmer down by half. Add a few tablespoons whipped cream and pour over the chicken.

Chaud-froid of chicken (joints)

Chaud-froid of chicken. CHAUD-FROID DE VOLAILLE – A cold *entrée*. Poach joints of chicken in a flour-and-water stock, drain, and coat with white or brown *Chaud-froid sauce* (see SAUCE). Decorate with truffles, glazed in jelly.

Chicken à la chevalière. POULARDE À LA CHEVALIÈRE – Take off the wings of 2 chickens. Trim, and insert small pieces of bacon fat under the skin. Braise in Madeira-flavoured stock.

Detach the breasts. Trim and flatten them a little, stud with pieces of tongue and truffles, and put them in a buttered dish.

Cook the four leg joints, the ends of the wings and the divided carcases as for a *fricassée*. Drain and wipe the leg joints, coat with egg and breadcrumbs, and fry in clarified butter.

Arrange the pieces of carcase and wingtips in a pastry case. Pour over them the strained *fricassée* sauce.

Place the leg joints on top of the carcases and between each leg put a wing. Poach the breasts and place on top.

Serve with the rest of the *fricassée* sauce, to which mushrooms and truffles have been added.

Chicken chipolata. POULARDE CHIPOLATA – Braise the chicken in brown gravy. Surround with a garnish of chipolata sausages (see GARNISHES). Pour the pan juices diluted with Madeira and mixed with *Rich brown sauce* (see SAUCE) over the dish.

Chicken à la Chivry. POULARDE À LA CHIVRY – Poach the chicken in white stock. Surround with artichoke bottoms garnished with asparagus tips or fresh peas. Pour *Chivry sauce* (see SAUCE) over the chicken.

For a variation, serve the chicken with *Chivry sauce* and mixed vegetables served separately.

Chicken à la Clamart. POULARDE À LA CLAMART – Half-cook in butter a chicken trussed as for boiling. Add 1 litre ($1\frac{3}{4}$ pints, generous quart) fresh peas *à la française* which have been three-quarters cooked. Cover with a lid and finish cooking in the oven.

Small chickens prepared in the same way are called *poulets à la Clamart*.

Chicken in cocotte. POULARDE EN COCOTTE – Chicken cooked in a pot or casserole and served in the same receptacle.

Chicken compote. POULET EN COMPOTE – Truss the chicken as for boiling. Prepare as for *Compote of pigeon* (see PIGEON).

Chicken consommé – See SOUPS AND BROTHS.

Chicken côtelettes. CÔTELETTES DE VOLAILLE – Under this name are known the following:

1. Breasts of poultry removed when raw and cooked separately, to be served as a small *entrée*.
2. Croquettes made with a chicken croquette mixture, formed into the shape of cutlets, coated in egg and breadcrumbs, and fried in butter.
3. Variety of quenelles made with a poultry forcemeat and poached in a special mould.

To prepare chicken breasts. Remove the breasts of a small roasting chicken or a fat hen after having taken off the skin. Leave the wingtips on the joint. Flatten lightly.

To cook in butter à l'anglaise. Season the *côtelettes*, sprinkle with flour, coat with egg and breadcrumbs, and cook in clarified butter.

Garnish and add sauce according to the recipe.

Chicken *côtelettes* may be coated with breadcrumbs to which chopped truffles or other ingredients have been added.

To cook à blanc, or poach. Season the *côtelettes*, brush with melted butter, and lay them flat in a buttered sauté pan. Add a few drops of lemon juice; cover the pan and cook for 6 to 8 minutes in a very hot oven.

Garnish and add sauce according to the recipe.

The cooking of chicken *côtelettes à blanc* must be done extremely rapidly but without boiling. The liquid must be limited to the few drops of lemon juice indicated above.

To cook in butter à brun. Season the *côtelettes*, sprinkle with flour and quickly sauté in clarified butter. Cook very lightly as these pieces are extremely delicate and liable to become tough if over-cooked.

Garnish and add sauce according to the recipe. Put paper frills on the ends.

Côtelettes are served on croûtons, vegetables, etc.

Chicken côtelettes à l'anglaise. CÔTELETTES DE VOLAILLE À L'ANGLAISE – Season and coat the *côtelettes* in egg and breadcrumbs. Sauté in butter. Garnish with a green vegetable tossed in butter. Serve with thickened brown veal gravy.

Chicken côtelettes Helder. CÔTELETTES DE VOLAILLE HELDER – Cook the *côtelettes à blanc*. Dish and garnish with a *salpicon* (q.v.) of carrots, artichoke bottoms, truffles and mushrooms cooked slowly in butter.

Coat with rich chicken *Velouté sauce* (see SAUCE) diluted with 1 tablespoon tomato juice. Add strained butter.

Chicken côtelettes maréchale. CÔTELETTES DE VOLAILLE MARÉCHALE – Coat the *côtelettes* with egg and bread-crumbs, adding to the breadcrumbs a third of their volume of chopped truffles. Sauté in butter.

Top each *côtelette* with slices of truffles, and sprinkle with *Noisette butter* (see BUTTER, *Compound butters*).

Chicken crépinettes – See CRÉPINETTES.

Chicken à la crapaudine. POULET À LA CRAPAUDINE – Prepare, using a small roasting chicken, as *Pigeon à la crapaudine* (see PIGEON).

Chicken croquettes. CROQUETTES DE VOLAILLE – Combine finely chopped chicken with thick *Velouté sauce* (see SAUCE). Bind with an egg yolk and season well with salt, pepper and lemon juice. Cool thoroughly. Make into small oval croquettes. Coat with beaten egg and fine breadcrumbs and fry in deep fat.

Chicken with cucumber. POULARDE AUX CONCOMBRES – Follow recipe for *Chicken à l'allemande*. Surround with cucumber cut in chunks and simmered in butter. Pour over *Allemande sauce* (see SAUCE).

Chicken curry (Plumerey's recipe). CARI DE POULET – 'Toss in butter two chickens cut in pieces with 500 g. (generous 1 lb.) of uncooked ham cleaned of salt and cut in dice. Add a good tablespoon flour and moisten with light veal stock. Add also a *bouquet garni* (q.v.) and two teaspoons curry powder.

'After it is cooked, boil down the sauce without thickening it too much. It should look like a pale *espagnole sauce*, lightly coloured with saffron.' Serve with Indian style rice.

Chicken curry (Mont-Bry's recipe). CARI DE POULET – 'Draw, pluck and joint a medium-sized chicken. Divide each joint into 3 or 4 pieces (when cutting up chicken joints be careful not to splinter the bones into tiny fragments).

Cook in butter 2 chopped-up onions, 100 g. (4 oz.) ham cut in small pieces, and 2 peeled and chopped eating apples all seasoned with crushed garlic, thyme, bay leaf, cinnamon, cardamom and powdered mace. Add the chicken pieces.

'When quite firm, shake them about without letting them colour too much, and sprinkle them with 2 teaspoons curry powder. Add 2 peeled, seeded and crushed tomatoes and mix well.

'Put in $2\frac{1}{2}$ dl. (scant $\frac{1}{2}$ pint, generous cup) coconut milk (or almond milk). Cook very gently in a covered saucepan for about 35 minutes. 10 minutes before serving, add $1\frac{1}{2}$ dl. ($\frac{1}{4}$ pint, $\frac{2}{3}$ cup) thick fresh cream and the juice of 1 lemon. Thicken this sauce to the desired consistency by boiling down.

'Serve the chicken with rice cooked as follows:

'Cook 250 g. (9 oz., $1\frac{1}{4}$ cups) rice for 15 minutes in salt water, stirring often. Drain and wash several times in cold water. Dry, in the oven at a very low heat for 15 minutes.'

Chicken curry (Creole cookery). CARI DE POULET – Joint a medium-sized chicken. Brown the pieces very lightly in good fat, taking care not to let them become dry. Add 1 finely chopped onion and simmer very slowly. The onion must not be allowed to turn yellow. Add 2 small peeled, seeded and chopped tomatoes. Stir the mixture. Leave to simmer for 15 minutes. Add 2 teaspoons saffron, previously pounded in a mortar, with a sprig of thyme, a sprig of parsley, a clove of garlic, and a piece of stem ginger. Leave these spices to soak into the chicken before moistening the curry with a glass of lukewarm water, poured into the pan a little at a time. Simmer for 2 hours and serve with *Rice à la créole* (see RICE).

Chicken à la Cussy. POULARDE À LA CUSSY – Braise the chicken in brown butter. Surround with a *Cussy garnish* (see GARNISHES).

Pour the cooking juices diluted with port wine and *Rich Brown sauce* (see SAUCE. *Basic sauces*) over the chicken.

Chicken à la d'Albuféra. POULARDE À LA D'ALBUFÉRA – Stuff the chicken with rice half-cooked in white stock, mixed with small pieces of truffles and *foie gras*. Poach in white stock. Surround with pastry cases filled with small chicken quenelles, cocks' kidneys, slices of truffles and button mushrooms bound with *d'Albuféra sauce* (see SAUCE). Coat the chicken with *d'Albuféra sauce*.

Chicken demi-deuil. POULARDE DEMI-DEUIL – Poach the chicken in a white stock. Surround with pastry cases filled with a mixture of lambs' sweetbreads and mushrooms bound in thick chicken *Velouté sauce* (see SAUCE). Put a small truffle cooked in Madeira on each tartlet and pour on *Suprême sauce* (see SAUCE).

Chicken demi-deuil is also called *Poached chicken Lyonnaise*.

Chicken Demidoff I. POULARDE DEMIDOFF – Cook the chicken *à la Matignon* in a covered dish in the oven.

Surround with artichoke bottoms garnished with vegetable purée. Put an onion ring, dipped in batter and fried, on each artichoke, topped with a slice of truffle.

Mix the cooking juices with Madeira and *Rich brown sauce* (see SAUCE). Pour over the chicken.

Chicken Demidoff II. POULARDE DEMIDOFF – Cook the chicken in butter in a covered dish in the oven. When it is three-quarters cooked, add 3 dl. ($\frac{1}{2}$ pint, $1\frac{1}{4}$ cups) mixed vegetable purée, mushrooms and truffles. When cooked garnish with sliced truffles.

Mix the cooking juices with port wine and thickened brown veal stock, and pour over the chicken.

Chicken à la Derby. POULARDE À LA DERBY – Stuff the chicken with rice cooked in butter and mixed with truffles. Cook, covered, in the oven.

Surround with large truffles cooked in port wine, and slices of *foie gras* sautéed in butter. Mix the cooking juices with port wine and thickened brown veal gravy, and pour over the chicken.

Chicken à la Doria. POULARDE À LA DORIA – Poach the chicken in white stock. Take it out of the liquid, remove the barding and trussing string. Cut off the breast fillets and take out the small bones from the interior of the carcase.

Fill the chicken with the following mixture:

Bind 100 g. (4 oz.) each of cocks' combs and kidneys, 100 g. (4 oz.) button mushrooms and 100 g. (4 oz.) quartered truffles with 3 dl. ($\frac{1}{2}$ pint, $1\frac{1}{4}$ cups) very thick chicken *Velouté sauce* (see SAUCE). Chill.

Fill the chicken with this mixture, giving the bird its original shape. Arrange the breast fillets, cut into fine strips, on top. Pour very thick *Allemande sauce* (see SAUCE), over the chicken. Sprinkle with grated Parmesan and brown lightly in the oven.

Surround the bird with large chicken quenelles decorated with truffles, medium-sized truffles cooked in champagne, fried cocks' combs, and large mushrooms.

Pour into the bottom of the dish a few tablespoons *Suprême sauce* (see SAUCE).

Émincés of Chicken. ÉMINCÉS DE VOLAILLE – Left-over

chicken (poached, braised or roasted), boned, and cut into thin slices. Coat with sauce and heat without boiling.

Chicken fillets. FILETS DE VOLAILLE – Breasts of chicken removed when raw and cooked in various ways. See the recipes given under *Côtelettes* and *Suprêmes* below.

Chicken filets mignons. FILETS MIGNONS DE VOLAILLE – Long thin strips cut from the *Suprêmes* (see below) of poultry. These *filets*, encrusted with thin slices of truffles or pickled tongue, are formed into rings or arcs and placed on top of the *suprêmes*, which are cooked separately.

Chicken à la financière. POULARDE À LA FINANCIÈRE – Braise the chicken. Surround with a *Financière garnish* (see GARNISHES).

Pour *Financière sauce* (see SAUCE), to which has been added some of the juice in which the chicken was cooked, over the bird.

Chicken forcemeat – See FORCEMEAT.

Chicken fricassée – See FRICASSÉE.

Chicken fricassée à la minute (Plumerey's recipe). FRICASSÉE DE POULET À LA MINUTE – 'Cut up two chickens, put them in a saucepan with 175 g. (6 oz., ¾ cup) melted butter, and toss them so that they become firm without colouring. Add 2 tablespoons (3 tablespoons) flour, season with salt, pepper, and grated nutmeg, and add as much water as will make a slightly thickened sauce. Add 6 small blanched onions, and a *bouquet garni* (q.v.). Cook on a good heat, taking care that the chicken does not stick and that the sauce is boiled down little by little. At the end of 25 minutes test 1 of the legs to see if it is cooked. Add 250 g. (9 oz.) mushrooms, remove grease, bind the sauce with four beaten egg yolks, sprinkle with lemon juice.'

Chicken fritot. FRITOT DE VOLAILLE – *Entrée* prepared with slices of cooked chicken marinated in oil, lemon juice and herbs, dipped in batter and fried in deep fat or oil. (See also FRITTERS.)

Chicken galantine – See GALANTINE.

Chicken giblets. ABATIS DE VOLAILLE – Poultry giblets are composed of wingtips, neck, gizzard, liver, and heart. (See GIBLETS.)

Chicken à la Godard. POULARDE À LA GODARD – Braise the chicken. Surround with *Godard garnish* (see GARNISH). Pour over the chicken *Godard sauce* (see SAUCE) to which some of the cooking juices have been added.

Grilled chicken

Grilled chicken. POULARDE GRILLÉE – Cut the chicken open down the back, push the ends of the legs into the opening, flatten slightly, and season with salt and pepper. Brown on both sides in butter, cover both sides with fresh breadcrumbs and grill under gentle heat. The chicken can also be divided into joints as for *Sautéed chicken* (see below).

Grilled chicken is served with a highly seasoned sauce such as *Diable, Mustard, Béarnaise*, etc. (see SAUCE).

Grilled chicken à la diable. POULET GRILLÉ À LA DIABLE – Truss the chicken as for boiling and split it through the back. Flatten slightly, season with salt and pepper, spread with butter, and half-cook in the oven.

Smear the chicken with a little mustard to which some cayenne has been added. Coat with fresh breadcrumbs and sprinkle with melted butter. Finish cooking under a gentle grill, letting it colour well.

Garnish with gherkins and half-slices of lemon, and serve with *Diable sauce* (see SAUCE).

Chicken Grimod-de-la-Reynière – See below, *Chicken à la Nantua III.*

Chicken ham. JAMBON DE POULET – Name given in France to the thigh of a large chicken, which is boned, stuffed, trussed in the shape of a ham and braised in Madeira.

Chicken hash. HACHIS DE VOLAILLE – Made with left-over poultry (poached or braised), boned and chopped or cut in very small dice. (See HASH.)

Hungarian chicken. POULARDE À LA HONGROISE – Stuff the chicken with rice three-quarters cooked and seasoned with paprika.

Cook, covered with butter, in the oven. Dilute the pan juices with white wine and pour over the chicken. Serve with *Hungarian sauce* (see SAUCE).

Chicken à l'impériale. POULARDE A L'IMPÉRIALE – Stuff the chicken with a mixture of 150 g. (5 oz.) lambs' sweetbreads, 100 g. (4 oz.) button mushrooms, 3 medium-sized truffles shaped to look like olives, bound with 2 dl. (⅓ pint, scant cup) mushroom purée and 2 dl. (⅓ pint, scant cup) thick chicken *Velouté sauce* (see SAUCE). Cook, covered, in the oven without allowing it to colour.

Surround with pastry cases filled with small pieces of *foie gras*, large mushrooms cooked in butter and garnished with asparagus tips, and small artichoke bottoms simmered gently in butter and filled with chopped truffles.

Coat lightly with a sauce, using the cooking juices as for *Chicken à la Chantilly*.

Chicken à l'indienne. POULARDE À L'INDIENNE – Poach the chicken in white stock, or cook it, covered, in the oven with butter.

Pour *Curry sauce* (see SAUCE) over it, and serve with *Rice à l'indienne* (see RICE).

Cold chicken Isabelle (M. Apollon Caillat's recipe). CHAUD-FROID DE POULARDE ISABELLE – Cut the chicken in pieces, soak in cold water, drain and put in a shallow sauté pan. Pour over it 3 dl. (½ pint, 1¼ cups) concentrated veal stock, flavoured with mushroom essence, and cook.

Drain the bird. Strain the cooking juices and use them to moisten a *roux* (q.v.) made with 75 g. (3 oz., scant ½ cup) butter and the same quantity of flour, cooked together. Add 1 teaspoon paprika. Cook, and skim. Bind the sauce with 2 egg yolks beaten up in a little cream. Cook slowly, and strain over the pieces of chicken, which have been returned to the shallow pan. Add sweet pimentos cut in *julienne* strips. Simmer for a few minutes.

To serve, cover the chicken pieces completely with the sauce. When quite cold, decorate with small pieces of truffles and sweet pimentos.

Coat completely with a thin layer of jelly, which should be clear and almost colourless.

Chicken à l'ivoire. POULARDE À L'IVOIRE – Poach the chicken in white stock, surround with 20 mushroom heads and 20 chicken quenelles. Pour *Suprême sauce* (see SAUCE) over the bird.

Chicken jambalaya (Indian cookery). JAMBALAIA DE POULET – Pilaf made from rice cooked *à l'indienne* (see RICE).

Dice coarsely 150 g. (5 oz.) raw, lean ham. Sauté in butter in a heavy pan. When almost cooked, add 250 g. (9 oz.) cooked diced chicken.

Sauté and season with red pepper. Add 200 g. (7 oz., 1⅓ cups) *Rice à l'indienne* (see RICE) cooked separately.

Jellied chicken in casserole. POULARDE EN TERRINE À LA GELÉE – Bone a plump fowl. Stuff with a forcemeat made of equal parts of veal, fresh pork fat and *à gratin forcemeat,* the whole well seasoned, bound with two eggs, and flavoured with brandy and essence of truffles.

Put half a raw *foie gras* studded with 4 quarters of truffles on the forcemeat, and re-form the shape of the chicken. Truss as for boiling, bard with a slice of fat bacon, add Madeira, and cook, covered, in the oven. Remove from the dish and cool. Dilute the pan juices. Remove the trussing string and barding, wipe the chicken, and put it in an earthenware dish on a base of well-set jelly. Cover completely with jelly to which the diluted cooking juices have been added. Leave to chill for at least 12 hours.

Jellied chicken with champagne. POULARDE AU CHAMPAGNE EN GELÉE – This dish should be prepared well in advance.

Stuff a chicken with a whole *foie gras,* trimmed and studded with truffles, which has been soaked in brandy and spices, and cooked in butter for a few minutes.

Cook, covered, in the oven in butter. Dilute the cooking juices with 5 dl. (scant pint, 2¼ cups) dry champagne. Boil down. Add 5 dl. (scant pint, 2¼ cups) *Chicken jelly* (see JELLY). Boil for a few moments. Strain.

Put the chicken in a large earthenware dish and cover with the jelly. Cool completely. When the jelly is quite set scrape off any fat that sticks to the surface, and wipe the bird over 2 or 3 times with a cloth wrung out in very hot water.

Jellied chicken may be flavoured with different wines.

Jellied chicken with foie gras (canned). POULARDE AU FOIE GRAS À LA GELÉE – Prepare as for *Jellied chicken in casserole.* Drain, remove the trussing strings and wings. Put it breast downwards into a large tin just big enough to hold the chicken. Cover with the clarified cooking liquor. Solder the tin, make a mark on the top with solder. Put the tin into a pot and cover completely with water. Bring to the boil and continue to boil, without interruption, for 1 hour.

Drain the tin and leave to cool, keeping it upside down so that the breast of chicken is in jelly and the fat goes to the bottom of the tin.

Chicken with tarragon in jelly (*Scarnati*)

Chicken with tarragon in jelly. POULARDE À L'ESTRAGON DANS SA GELÉE – Truss the chicken as for boiling, put in a saucepan and cover with white stock. Add a generous quantity of tarragon.

Cook slowly for 1 hour. Leave to cool in its own liquid. Drain, take off the trussing string and wipe carefully.

Reheat the cooking liquor, from which all grease has been removed, and strain. Add to it the required quantity of gelatine, soaked in cold water, and heat slightly.

Pour this, when lukewarm, into a saucepan in which 100 g. (4 oz.) minced lean beef, 1 egg white and a handful of chopped tarragon leaves have been whisked together. Cook over a good heat for a moment, whisking lightly.

As soon as it comes to the boil, remove the saucepan to a very low heat and cook slowly for 25 minutes.

Strain the jelly through a cloth, adding, when it has cooled, 1 dl. (6 tablespoons, scant ½ cup) Madeira. When nearly cold, half-fill a dish with some of this jelly, and when it has set put the chicken on top.

Decorate with broad leaves of tarragon, blanched, trimmed, drained, and dipped one by one in half-set jelly. Arrange these leaves in a pattern on the breast of the chicken. Three-quarters cover the chicken with the rest of the jelly.

Place the dish on ice or in the refrigerator until ready to serve.

Chicken Katoff. POULET KATOFF – Grill a chicken (split down the back and lightly flattened) as for *Grilled chicken à la diable.*

Set it on a foundation of *Duchess potato* (see POTATOES), brushed with egg and browned in the oven. Surround with thickened brown veal stock to which butter has been added.

Chicken kromeskies. CROMESQUIS DE VOLAILLE – Prepared with a croquette mixture, wrapped in pig's caul (or pork fat), dipped in batter and fried. (See CROQUETTES.)

Chicken Lambertye. POULARDE LAMBERTYE – Poach a fat hen, trussed for boiling, in white chicken stock. Allow it to cool completely in its own liquid.

Make a circular incision round the breast and remove it. Fill the inside with a *Foie gras mousse* (see FOIE GRAS), rounding the top to re-form the shape of the chicken. Coat the chicken legs with *White chaud-froid sauce* (see SAUCE).

Place over the mousse the chicken breasts cut in slices, coated with the sauce and decorated with truffles and rounds of tongue glazed with jelly.

Serve on croûtons of bread, or on a bed of rice. Garnish with jelly shapes or chopped jelly.

Chicken à la languedocienne. POULARDE À LA LANGUEDOCIENNE – Cook the chicken, covered, in the oven with butter. Set on a dish and surround with tomatoes *à la languedocienne* and aubergines cut in slices and lightly fried in oil.

Dilute the cooking juices with white wine, season with a crushed clove of garlic, and add thickened brown veal gravy. Pour over the chicken and sprinkle with chopped parsley.

Chicken livers. FOIES DE POULETS – Chicken livers are used mostly as a garnish, and for forcemeat. They may, however, be served grilled on skewers, sautéed, with mushrooms, in pilafs and risottos, and used in *terrines* and *pâtés.*

Chicken loaf (cold). PAIN DE VOLAILLE FROID – Prepare cold *Chicken mousse* mixture (see below) and decorate as for all other cold loaves (game, *foie gras,* fish, shellfish). Coat a mould with jelly and decorate with pieces of truffles, hard-boiled eggs, white pickled tongue, etc.

Chicken loaf (hot). PAIN DE VOLAILLE CHAUD – Prepare a *Mousseline forcemeat* (see FORCEMEAT).

Butter a mould with a hole in the middle and fill with the above forcemeat to within 1 cm. (½ inch) of the top. Poach the loaf in the oven in a *bain-marie* (q.v.) for 45 minutes to 1 hour, depending on the size of the mould.

When the loaf is cooked, leave it to settle for a few moments before turning out. Surround with the garnish chosen and pour over it the sauce appropriate to the garnish.

The following garnishes and sauces are suitable for hot chicken loaves: *Clamart* (peas) and *Cream sauce*; mushrooms and *Allemande sauce*; *Hongroise* (*salpicon* (q.v.) of mushrooms and onions in separate groups) and *Sauce hongroise*; *Monselet* (coarsely diced artichoke hearts and truffles in separate groups) and *Suprême sauce*; *Montpensier* (asparagus tips in butter, slivers of truffles) and *Allemande sauce*; *Nantua* (crayfish tails, slivers of truffles) and *Nantua sauce*; asparagus tips and *Velouté sauce* cooked with cream. (See GARNISHES, SAUCE.)

Chicken à la lyonnaise or demi-deuil. POULARDE À LA LYONNAISE, DITE DEMI-DEUIL – Stuff the chicken with fine truffled forcemeat and poach in white chicken stock. Serve the chicken surrounded with vegetables cooked in the chicken broth, and accompanied by the strained poaching liquor.

This way of cooking chicken is the great speciality of the city of Lyons and is known as *Poularde de Madame Filloux*.

Chicken Maeterlinck (Mont-Bry's recipe). POULARDE MAETERLINCK – Stuff a chicken with a chopped-up mixture of cocks' combs and kidneys, lambs' sweetbreads, truffles and mushrooms, bound with very thick chicken *Velouté sauce* (see SAUCE) and fresh cream. Truss the chicken and wrap it in a bard of bacon fat. Put the bird in a deep pot with butter, strips of fresh bacon rind, sliced carrots and sliced onions. Season with salt. Cook in the oven, covered, for 45 minutes.

Drain the bird and remove the trussing string. Put it in an earthenware casserole and surround with 6 peeled truffles seasoned with salt, pepper and nutmeg, and 6 small slices of *foie gras* heated in butter. Dilute the cooking juices with $2\frac{1}{2}$ dl. (scant $\frac{1}{2}$ pint, generous cup) sherry and 4 dl. ($\frac{3}{4}$ pint, scant 2 cups) thickened and strained brown meat gravy. Add 4 tablespoons ($\frac{1}{3}$ cup) brandy and set alight. Seal the lid of the casserole with flour-and-water paste. Cook in the oven, in a good heat, for 35 minutes. Serve in the casserole.

Marinade of chicken. MARINADE DE VOLAILLE – Prepare in the same way as *Chicken fritot*, using uncooked chicken.

Chicken à la Matignon. POULARDE À LA MATIGNON – Stuff the chicken with *Forcemeat à gratin* mixed with one-third of its volume of *Quenelle stuffing* (see FORCEMEAT).

Brown in the oven. Take out, cool, and cover with a thick coating of *Matignon* (vegetable mixture). Wrap the chicken in salt pork, and tie firmly. Braise. When cooked surround with braised lettuces, and pour the cooking juices diluted with Madeira and *Rich brown sauce* (see SAUCE) over the bird.

Chicken mayonnaise. MAYONNAISE DE VOLAILLE – Slices of cooked chicken (or other poultry) seasoned with oil, vinegar, salt and pepper, set on shredded lettuce, coated with mayonnaise, and garnished with lettuce hearts and quartered hard-boiled eggs, capers and anchovy fillets. (See MAYONNAISE.)

Chicken médaillons. MÉDAILLONS DE VOLAILLE – There are several kinds. Some are prepared with a croquette mixture shaped into discs, coated in egg and breadcrumbs and sautéed in butter. Others, which belong to the category of *Chicken quenelles* (see QUENELLES) are made from quenelle forcemeat or chicken mousse, moulded into little cakes and poached. A third kind is made with the white flesh of a boned fowl, and, finally, some *médaillons* are cut from the breasts or *suprêmes* of raw chicken, lightly flattened and cut into oval pieces.

Methods of preparing these last two types are given below.

Chicken médaillons à l'algérienne. MÉDAILLONS DE VOLAILLE À L'ALGÉRIENNE – Coat in egg and breadcrumbs *médaillons* made with chopped chicken and sauté in butter. Set each *médaillon* on top of $\frac{1}{2}$ tomato which has been grilled and stuffed with rice pilaf mixed with diced sweet peppers. Surround with light *Tomato sauce* (see SAUCE).

Chicken médaillons Beauharnais. MÉDAILLONS DE VOLAILLE BEAUHARNAIS – Season the *médaillons*, cut from the breasts, and sauté in butter. Place each *médaillon* on a small artichoke bottom cooked in butter and garnished with 1 tablespoon *Beauharnais sauce* (see SAUCE), and topped with a slice of truffle. Surround with thickened brown veal gravy mixed with butter.

Chicken médaillons cut from the breast. MÉDAILLONS DÉTAILLÉS SUR FILETS DE VOLAILLE – Remove the breasts from a roasting chicken. Cut them into regular slices. Flatten these lightly and trim into rounds or ovals. Cook according to the recipe, following the instructions given under *Chicken côtelettes* and *Suprêmes of chicken* (see below).

The *filets mignons* may be left with the *médaillons*. They may also be cooked separately, as for *Suprêmes of chicken*, and served on top of the *médaillons*.

The legs, wings and carcases of the chickens used for the *médaillons* can be used up by following the recipes given under *Chicken ballottines* (see BALLOTTINES).

Chopped chicken médaillons. MÉDAILLONS EN CHAIR DE VOLAILLE HACHÉE – Bone the breasts of a roasting chicken. Chop them, adding 50 g. (2 oz., 1 cup) breadcrumbs soaked in milk and squeezed out, and 50 g. (2 oz., $\frac{1}{4}$ cup) butter. Add to the mixture 2 tablespoons (3 tablespoons) fresh cream, and season with salt, pepper and nutmeg.

Shape *médaillons* from the mixture, coat with egg and breadcrumbs, or dredge with flour, and sauté in clarified butter.

The carcase, neck, head and feet of the bird can be used to prepare chicken stock or soup, or in a sauce to accompany the *médaillons*.

Chicken médaillons Dunan. MÉDAILLONS DE VOLAILLE DUNAN – Make *médaillons* of chopped chicken mixed with a *salpicon* (q.v.) of lean ham and mushrooms. Coat in egg and breadcrumbs and sauté in butter.

Set in tartlets baked blind and filled with a *salpicon* of truffles *à la crème*. Serve with *Madeira sauce* (see SAUCE).

Chicken médaillons à l'écarlate. MÉDAILLONS DE VOLAILLE À L'ÉCARLATE – Season *médaillons* cut from the *suprêmes* and poach in white stock. Set in a dish in the form of a turban, alternating them with slices of pickled tongue heated in white stock.

Pour into the bottom of the dish a few tablespoons *Allemande sauce* (see SAUCE).

Chicken médaillons à l'égyptienne. MÉDAILLONS DE VOLAILLE À L'ÉGYPTIENNE – Season *médaillons* with paprika and sauté in butter.

Arrange in the form of a turban, alternating them with rounds of aubergines sautéed in butter. Garnish the middle of the dish with pilaf rice. Surround with *Tomato sauce* (see SAUCE) to which has been added the cooking juices diluted with white wine.

Chicken médaillons Fédora. MÉDAILLONS DE VOLAILLE FÉDORA – Season the *médaillons* and poach them in white stock. Set on croûtons of bread fried in butter. Garnish with cucumbers cut into uniform pieces and stewed in butter. Coat with the cooking juices diluted with cream and chicken *Velouté sauce* (see SAUCE).

Chicken médaillons Grignan. MÉDAILLONS DE VOLAILLE GRIGNAN – Make *médaillons* from chopped chicken meat. Sprinkle with flour, dip in beaten egg, and cover with finely chopped truffles. Cook in butter.

Arrange on artichoke bottoms cooked in butter. Garnish with a *ragoût* of *Chicken quenelles* (see QUENELLES), and cocks' combs and kidneys, bound with *Allemande sauce* (see SAUCE).

Chicken médaillons à la mantouane. MÉDAILLONS DE VOLAILLE À LA MANTOUANE – Season *médaillons* cut from the *suprêmes* and coat them *à la milanaise* (with egg and bread-crumbs mixed with grated Parmesan). Sauté in butter.

Set in tartlets which have been baked blind, each filled with macaroni bound with Parmesan, to which a *julienne* of lean ham and pickled tongue has been added. Put a slice of truffle on top of each *médaillon*.

Chicken médaillons à la turque. MÉDAILLONS DE VOLAILLE À LA TURQUE – Season *médaillons* with paprika, and sauté in butter. Set on top of *Rice pilaf* (see PILAF). Coat with the cooking juices diluted with white wine, and tomato-flavoured veal gravy.

Chicken à la milanaise I. POULARDE À LA MILANAISE – Stuff the chicken with *Macaroni à la milanaise* (see MACARONI). Cook, covered, in the oven in butter.

Dilute the cooking juices with white wine and thickened veal gravy to which tomato purée has been added, and pour over the chicken.

Chicken à la milanaise

Chicken à la milanaise II. POULARDE À LA MILANAISE – Stuff the chicken with a mixture of sliced lambs' sweet-breads, tongue, lean ham, mushrooms and truffles, bound with brown sauce flavoured with tomato. Braise the chicken.

Surround with *timbales* of *Macaroni à la milanaise* (made in dariole moulds). Dilute the cooking juices with Madeira and *Rich brown sauce* (see SAUCE) flavoured with tomato, and pour over the chicken.

Chicken mousse and mousselines. MOUSSE ET MOUSSELINES DE VOLAILLE – *Entrée*, cold or hot, prepared with *Chicken mousseline forcemeat* (see FORCEMEAT).

Chicken with mousseline forcemeat – Poach the chicken in white stock, drain and cut off the breast fillets as for *Chicken à la Doria*.

Fill the inside of the bird with *Mousseline forcemeat* (see FORCEMEAT), with the addition of one-third of purée of *foie gras*. Arrange this stuffing in layers, alternating with the pieces of breast fillets. Round off the top of the forcemeat to give it the shape of the chicken. Cook in a slow oven, setting the dish in a tray containing hot water.

Surround with one of the garnishes recommended for chicken poached in a white stock. (See GARNISHES.)

Chicken with mushrooms (brown). POULARDE AUX CHAMPIGNONS – Cook the chicken, covered, in the oven with butter. 10 minutes before the end of the cooking time add large mushrooms. When cooked dilute the pan juices with white wine and *Rich brown sauce* (see SAUCE) and pour over the chicken.

Chicken with mushrooms (white). POULARDE AUX CHAMPIGNONS – As for *Chicken à l'allemande*. Surround with large mushrooms cooked without allowing them to colour. Pour *Allemande sauce* (see SAUCE) over the chicken.

Chicken à la Nantua I. POULARDE À LA NANTUA – Poach the chicken in white stock. Surround with quenelles made of *Chicken forcemeat* (see FORCEMEAT) to which *Shrimp butter* (see BUTTER) has been added, and with boat-shaped pastry shells filled with shrimps in *Nantua sauce* (see SAUCE). Place on each boat a slice of truffle. Pour over the chicken *Suprême sauce* (see SAUCE) finished with shrimp butter.

Chicken à la Nantua II. POULARDE À LA NANTUA – Stuff the chicken with a purée of shrimps mixed with a very thick chicken *Velouté sauce* (see SAUCE). Poach in white stock.

Pour over it *Suprême sauce* (see SAUCE) finished with *Shrimp butter* (see BUTTER). Add a few pieces of truffle to the shrimp purée.

Chicken à la Nantua III. POULARDE À LA NANTUA – Poach the chicken, drain, cut off the breast fillets and stuff it in the same way as for *Chicken à la Doria*, replacing the mixture used in that recipe with purée of shrimps mixed with very thick chicken *Velouté sauce* (see SAUCE).

Re-shape the chicken, placing the breast fillets, cut in strips, on top. Pour *Allemande sauce* (see SAUCE) over the chicken. Sprinkle with Parmesan and brown the top.

Serve with *Suprême sauce* (see SAUCE), finished with *Shrimp butter* (see BUTTER).

Prepared in this way the chicken is also known as *Chicken Grimod-de-la-Reynière*.

Chicken à la Néva. POULARDE À LA NÉVA – Stuff the chicken with a fine *Chicken forcemeat* (see FORCEMEAT) to which has been added some raw *foie gras* and diced truffles. Truss as for boiling, and poach in chicken stock. Allow it to cool and when the chicken is quite cold, wipe it and coat with white *Chaud-froid sauce* (see SAUCE) prepared with some of the chicken broth. Glaze with jelly and allow to set firmly.

Set the chicken either on a bed of rice, on a slice of buttered bread, or directly onto the plate. Serve with vegetable salad in mayonnaise (the salad rounded into a dome and decorated with truffles). Garnish with jelly shapes.

Chicken à la Néva can also be served in the same way as *Chicken Lambertye*.

Chicken à la niçoise I. POULARDE À LA NIÇOISE – Cook the chicken, covered, in butter, in the oven. Serve surrounded by quartered artichokes which have been simmered in butter, braised courgettes (zucchinis), small new potatoes cooked in butter, and a few black olives.

Dilute the cooking juices with white wine, season with a crushed clove of garlic, thicken with brown veal gravy flavoured with tomato purée, and pour over the chicken. Sprinkle with chopped tarragon.

Chicken à la niçoise II. POULARDE À LA NIÇOISE – Cook the chicken in butter in the oven, covered. Arrange on a dish with tomatoes which have been slowly cooked in butter, diced courgettes tossed in oil, new potatoes cooked in butter, and black olives.

Pour the cooking juices, prepared as above, over the chicken, and sprinkle with chopped tarragon.

Chicken with noodles. POULARDE AUX NOUILLES – Stuff the chicken with noodles half-cooked in salt water, drained, and dressed with butter and grated cheese. Cook, covered in butter in the oven.

Dilute the pan juices with white wine, thicken with brown veal gravy flavoured with tomato purée, and pour over the chicken.

Chicken with oysters. POULARDE AUX HUÎTRES – Poach the chicken in white stock. Surround with oysters poached in their own liquor, and drained. Add boiled-down oyster liquor to *Suprême sauce* (see SAUCE) and pour over the chicken.

If preferred, the oysters may be served on pieces of fried bread or toast, or put in the sauce.

Chicken Panurge. ÉTUVÉE DE POULET PANURGE – Cut the chicken up as for a *fricassée*. Season with salt and pepper and put it in a shallow pan in 2 tablespoons (3 tablespoons) butter. Sauté the chicken over a hot flame until the flesh is quite firm, and remove from the pan.

Cut into thin pieces a 3-dl. (½-pint, 1¼-cup) mixture of carrots, onions and celery; toss lightly in butter, and put in the pan. Lay the chicken pieces on this vegetable foundation.

Pour in dry white wine. Boil down the liquid and pour in a little fresh cream. Cook gently, covered, for 25 minutes. Add stoned olives and simmer for a few minutes.

Put the chicken on a dish and pour the sauce, to which has been added a good tablespoon butter, over the bird. Place thin slices of the gizzard which have been peeled, trimmed, cooked in consommé and fried in butter; and thin slices of the liver, also fried in butter; on the chicken. Garnish with heart-shaped bread croûtons fried in butter.

Chicken à la parisienne. POULARDE À LA PARISIENNE – Remove the breast bone and stuff the chicken with a *Fine panada forcemeat* (see FORCEMEAT). Truss the bird and poach in white stock.

Drain the chicken when it is cold; cut off the pieces of breast. Take out the stuffing, cut in large dice and add to a cold chicken *Mousseline forcemeat* (see FORCEMEAT). Refill the interior of the bird with this mixture and coat with white *Chaud-froid sauce* (see SAUCE).

Slice the breasts thinly, coat with the sauce, and place on the chicken. Decorate with truffles and tongue. Serve the chicken on buttered bread, and surround with vegetable salad moulded in *darioles* lined with jelly and decorated with truffles.

Ornament the borders of the dish with jelly shapes and garnish with chopped jelly.

Chicken à la périgourdine. POULARDE À LA PÉRIGOURDINE – Stuff the chicken with *foie gras* and diced truffles, seasoned with salt and spice and moistened with brandy. Cook it, covered, in the oven with butter, or braise it.

Add truffles about 10 minutes before cooking is completed, and when serving surround the chicken with these. Pour over the chicken the cooking juices diluted with Madeira and *Rich brown sauce* (see SAUCE).

Chicken pie – See PIE.

Chicken pie à la créole. PÂTÉ DE POULET À LA CRÉOLE – Make some *Brioche pastry* (see PASTRY), very slightly sweetened and salted, tinted pale yellow with saffron. Prepare separately a chicken curry, boiling down the sauce as much as possible. Make a forcemeat with a blend of fat and lean pork, salted and very well peppered, and cook for a moment in fat. Spread out the pastry in the shape of a tart, hollow in the middle. Put a layer of forcemeat in the bottom, place the pieces of curried chicken on top, cover with another layer of forcemeat, and put on a lid of pastry.

Bake slowly in the oven. The middle should rise more than the sides. Serve hot or cold.

Chicken à la piémontaise I. POULARDE À LA PIÉMONTAISE – Stuff the chicken with risotto mixed with 100 g. (4 oz.) diced white truffles. Cook, covered, in the oven with butter.

Dilute the cooking juices with white wine, mix with thickened brown veal gravy, and pour over the chicken.

Chicken à la piémontaise II. POULARDE À LA PIÉMONTAISE – Cook the chicken, covered, in the oven with butter. When cooked garnish with cheese risotto. Cover the chicken with 100 g. (4 oz.) white truffles cut in thin slices. Pour the cooking butter mixed with 4 tablespoons (⅓ cup) thickened brown veal gravy over the dish.

Chicken pilaf. PILAF DE VOLAILLE – Cook the rice and arrange it in a border on a dish. Fill the middle with chicken prepared in the following manner:

Cut the chicken into small uniform pieces. Season with salt and pepper, sauté in butter and drain.

Dilute the pan juices with 1 dl. (6 tablespoons, scant ½ cup) white wine. Add 3 dl. (½ pint, 1¼ cups) brown veal stock and 1 tablespoon tomato purée. Boil for a few moments. Strain the sauce. Replace the chicken in the sauté pan and simmer for a few moments.

Chicken à la polonaise. POULET À LA POLONAISE – Stuff a chicken with *à gratin forcemeat* (see FORCEMEAT) mixed with a little bread that has been soaked and squeezed out, and chopped parsley. Truss as for boiling. Brown quickly in very hot butter. Put the bird in an earthenware casserole and finish cooking in the oven.

Take off the trussing strings and squeeze over the chicken a few drops of lemon juice. Sprinkle with browned butter in which some fine breadcrumbs have been fried, allowing 25 g. (1 oz., ⅓ cup) breadcrumbs to 150 g. (5 oz., generous ½ cup) butter.

Chicken à la portugaise I. POULARDE À LA PORTUGAISE – Cook the chicken, covered, in the oven with butter. To serve, surround with 8 tomatoes stuffed and topped with browned crumbs.

Dilute the cooking juices with white wine, thicken with brown veal gravy flavoured with tomato and a clove of garlic, and pour over the chicken.

Chicken à la portugaise II. POULARDE À LA PORTUGAISE – Cook the chicken, covered, in the oven with butter. When it is three-quarters cooked, put in the pot peeled, diced tomatoes which have been cooked in butter, and 1 tablespoon chopped onion.

To serve, pour the cooking juices over the chicken and sprinkle with chopped parsley.

Chicken princess. POULARDE PRINCESSE – Poach the chicken in a small quantity of white chicken stock.

Surround with a garnish of pastry cases filled with buttered asparagus tips, and truffles simmered in butter. Pour *Allemande sauce* (see SAUCE) over the chicken.

Chicken purée. PURÉE DE VOLAILLE – Purée of chicken poached in white stock, served alone or as a garnish or filling.

It is sometimes called *purée à la reine*, and used as a garnish for *entrées* made with pastry, such as *bouchées*, rissoles and *vol-au-vent*.

Chicken purée, finished off with cream, is also used for the soup called *coulis à la reine*.

Chicken quenelles. QUENELLES DE VOLAILLE – Prepared with various forcemeats (q.v.).

Chicken à la régence. POULARDE À LA RÉGENCE – Insert pieces of bacon fat into the chicken and braise it in brown butter. Surround with slices of calves' sweetbreads sautéed in butter, truffles cooked in Madeira, chicken quenelles, cocks' combs and large prawns cooked in bouillon.

Pour *Régence sauce* (see SAUCE), with some of the cooking liquor added, over the chicken.

Whole braised sweetbreads can be used instead of slices.

Chicken à la reine. POULARDE À LA REINE – Stuff the chicken with the same mixture as for *Chicken croquettes*. Poach in white stock, with the minimum of liquid. Surround with small pastry cases filled with *Chicken purée*.

Put on each pastry case, in the form of a lid, a thin slice of truffle. Pour *Allemande sauce* (see SAUCE) over the dish.

Chicken à la Renaissance. POULARDE À LA RENAISSANCE – Poach a chicken in white stock with the minimum of liquid. Surround with *Renaissance garnish* (see GARNISHES).

Pour *Suprême sauce* (see SAUCE), made with mushroom essence, over the chicken.

Chicken with rice à la Bourbon (Créole cookery). POULARDE AU RIZ À LA BOURBON – Lightly brown a chicken in fat. Add a finely chopped cooked onion, 2 carrots, a bunch of herbs, salt, pepper and 1 tablespoon tomato purée. Add stock and cook on very slow heat for about $1\frac{1}{2}$ hours. Boil down the liquid.

Scald, drain, and cook rice in chicken stock. When soft, arrange on a dish and place the chicken pieces round it. Strain the stock and pour over the dish. Decorate with slices of carrot.

Chicken and rice with suprême sauce. POULARDE AU RIZ SAUCE SUPRÊME – Half cook a chicken, trussed as for boiling and covered with bacon fat, in white stock. When half-cooked, drain the bird. Put the stock through a fine strainer and replace the chicken in the pot. Add 250 g. (9 oz., $1\frac{2}{3}$ cups) blanched and drained rice, stock, and 2 tablespoons (3 tablespoons) butter. Finish cooking all together, over slow heat.

Using part of the cooking liquor prepare a *Suprême sauce* (see SAUCE).

Flank the chicken with rice, and serve with *suprême sauce* and the chicken broth.

Roasting chickens, Angers (*French Government Tourist Office*)

Roast chicken. POULARDE RÔTIE – Truss the chicken and season inside and outside. Cover the breast with a thin slice of bacon fat, and roast in the oven or on the spit. For cooking times, see CULINARY METHODS, *Average cooking times for roasts.*

Serve with the cooking juices, and watercress.

Roast chicken à l'anglaise. POULARDE RÔTIE À L'ANGLAISE – Roast the chicken in the usual way. Surround with slices of bacon or grilled sausages, and serve with *Bread sauce* (see SAUCE).

Roast chicken à l'anglaise may also be prepared in the same way as *Roast turkey à l'anglaise* (see TURKEY).

Chicken with rock (coarse) salt. POULARDE AU GROS SEL – Poach the chicken in white stock. Serve with its strained cooking liquor and rock (coarse) salt.

An old-fashioned spit for chickens
(*Grün*)

Surround with carrots and onions cooked in the chicken broth.

Chicken Rosière. POULARDE ROSIÈRE – Stuff a chicken with *Chicken forcemeat with cream* (see FORCEMEAT). Truss it, laying the feet flat against the sides. Rub it all over with lemon juice and wrap it entirely in bards of bacon fat. Line the bottom of a casserole with strips of fresh bacon rinds, rounds of carrot and onion and a bunch of herbs. Place the chicken on top and add sufficient veal stock to cover the chicken. Simmer with the lid on for about 50 minutes.

Blanch, trim and press under a weight for 30 minutes 3 calves' sweetbreads, having removed all membranes. About 35 minutes before serving, cut the sweetbreads in slices 1 cm. ($\frac{1}{2}$ inch) thick, put in a pan, just cover with white veal stock, add a piece of butter and simmer.

Roast chicken (*A.B.C.*)

Prepare ¾ litre (1⅓ pints, 1¾ pints) fresh *Mushroom purée* (see MUSHROOMS). Add 2 dl. (⅓ pint, scant cup) fresh cream to bring it to the consistency of an ordinary sauce, and mix into it 150 g. (5 oz.) mushrooms chopped and cooked.

Drain the chicken, remove the barding and trussing strings and surround with the slices of sweetbread. Coat the chicken and the garnish with some of the sauce and serve the rest separately.

Chicken à la Rossini. POULARDE À LA ROSSINI – Cook the chicken, covered, in butter in the oven. Set it on a dish and surround it with slices of *foie gras* tossed in butter. Place 2 slices of truffle heated in butter on each slice of *foie gras*.

Pour over the chicken its cooking juices diluted with Madeira and truffle-flavoured *Rich brown sauce* (see SAUCE). The slices of *foie gras* may be placed in pastry cases, or on slices of bread fried in butter.

Chicken salad. SALADE DE VOLAILLE – Set sliced cooked chicken on a foundation of shredded lettuce, sprinkle with *Vinaigrette sauce* (see SAUCE) and garnish with lettuce hearts and quartered hard-boiled eggs.

Sautéed chicken. POULETS SAUTÉS – Small tender fowls, weighing from 900 to 1800 g. (2 to 4 lb.) are more suited to being cooked this way than fat fowls and capons. The chicken should be sautéed rapidly in butter, in oil or in fat, but should not be allowed to boil in its juices.

To cut up the chicken for cooking, divide it into joints. Cut away the leg at its thickest part, having cut through the joint. Heating the feet makes them easier to skin.

Spring chickens are simply divided into halves, which are lightly flattened.

To sauté à blanc. Season pieces of chicken and put them in a pan of heated butter. Sauté the pieces without allowing them to brown. Cover the pan and cook at moderate heat. Take out the wings and breasts first. Pour off the butter, dilute the pan juices with white stock, mushroom juice or cream, and add a sauce. Garnish.

To sauté à brun. Heat 3 tablespoons (scant ¼ cup) butter or oil in a pan and add seasoned pieces of chicken. Brown well on both sides, cover, and cook over a low heat. After 6 or 8 minutes, take out the wings and the pieces of breast, and keep them warm. (These parts, being the most delicate, are cooked the soonest.) Leave the legs and carcases to cook for 8 to 12 minutes, according to size.

Take out the pieces of chicken, remove the cooking fat, dilute the juices with the liquid specified in the recipe – wine, stock or meat juices, etc. Boil down this liquor by half and add a sauce.

Put back the pieces of chicken in the pan, cover and keep warm, but avoid boiling. Garnish.

To sauté à brun à la ménagère. Brown and cook the pieces of chicken as above. Take them out of the pan. Add 1 tablespoon flour to the liquor in the pan and allow to colour slightly. Dilute with wine or other liquid. Boil down and then add 2 dl. (⅓ pint, scant cup) white stock, consommé or water. Cook for 12 to 15 minutes, stirring with a wooden spoon, and strain.

Replace the pieces of chicken in the covered pan, pour the sauce over and keep warm, but avoid boiling.

The many garnishes for sautéed chicken include sautéed aubergines, glazed carrots, small pieces of celeriac, brussels sprouts in butter, cucumbers, baby marrows (zucchinis), sweetcorn in butter or cream, small glazed onions, noodles, macaroni, rice, etc.

In the recipes which follow, the diluted pan juices of the chicken sautées should have sauces added to them, such as thickened brown veal stock or *Rich brown sauce* (*demi-glace*) (see SAUCE). Tomato sauce can be added to them.

When the sauté preparations are diluted with wine and white stock or broth, the sauce may be thickened with a little butter and flour worked together. The same applies to *à blanc* chicken sautés.

Sautéed chicken Alexandra. POULET SAUTÉ ALEXANDRA – Sauté the chicken in butter *à blanc*. Dilute the cooking juices with 1 dl. (6 tablespoons, scant ½ cup) white stock and boil down. Stir in 1 dl. (6 tablespoons, scant ½ cup) chicken *Velouté sauce* (see SAUCE), add 2 tablespoons (3 tablespoons) *Soubise purée* (see PURÉE), 2 tablespoons (3 tablespoons) cream and 50 g. (2 oz., ¼ cup) butter. Strain the sauce.

Sautéed chicken a l'algérienne. POULET SAUTÉ À L'ALGÉRIENNE – Sauté the chicken in oil *à brun*. When half-cooked, add 1 tablespoon chopped onion.

Take out the chicken; put in the pan a crushed garlic clove and 2 peeled, drained and chopped tomatoes; cook for 8 minutes, stirring. Put back the chicken in the pan and simmer 8 to 10 minutes without boiling.

When serving the chicken, garnish with 2 diced aubergines sautéed in oil. Pour the sauce over the chicken and sprinkle with chopped parsley.

Sautéed chicken ambassadrice. POULET SAUTÉ AMBASSADRICE – Sauté the chicken and 8 mushrooms in butter *à brun*. Dilute the pan juices with ½ dl. (3 tablespoons, scant ¼ cup) Madeira. Boil down the liquid and pour in 1½ dl. (¼ pint, ⅔ cup) thickened veal gravy. Cook at boiling point for a few moments.

Garnish the cooked chicken with 8 cocks' combs and 8 cocks' kidneys cooked in light stock, 4 chicken livers sautéed in butter, the mushrooms, and 8 slices of truffle. Coat with the sauce.

Sautéed chicken à l'ancienne mode. POULET SAUTÉ À L'ANCIENNE MODE – Sauté the chicken in butter *à blanc*. Dilute the juices in the pan with 1½ dl. (¼ pint, ⅔ cup) white stock or mushroom stock, boil down to two-thirds of its volume, stir in 1½ dl. (¼ pint, ⅔ cup) chicken *Velouté sauce* (see SAUCE) and boil for 5 minutes. Add 50 g. (2 oz., ¼ cup) butter, and strain. Add 2 tablespoons (3 tablespoons) chopped truffles and 1 dl. (6 tablespoons, scant ½ cup) port.

Coat the chicken with the sauce and garnish with rosettes of puff pastry.

Sautéed chicken Annette. POULET SAUTÉ ANNETTE – Sauté the chicken in butter *à brun*. Dilute the pan juices with white wine and add 1 chopped shallot. Boil down the liquid, and add 1½ dl. (¼ pint, ⅔ cup) thickened brown gravy. Boil for a few moments. Add ½ tablespoon chopped parsley, chervil and tarragon, a squeeze of lemon juice and 1 tablespoon fresh butter.

Set the chicken in a crust of *Annette potatoes* (see POTATOES). Coat with the sauce.

The crust of Annette potatoes is made with straw potatoes cooked in butter like Anna potatoes, but with a small dish put in the middle of the potatoes to form a hollow cake.

Sautéed chicken Archduke. POULET SAUTÉ ARCHIDUC – Sauté the chicken in butter *à blanc*. When it is half cooked add 2 tablespoons (3 tablespoons) chopped onion lightly cooked in butter, and a pinch of paprika.

Dilute the cooking juices with 1 dl. (6 tablespoons, scant ½ cup) white wine, boil down, pour in 1½ dl. (¼ pint, ⅔ cup) cream and boil for a few moments. Add 50 g. (2 oz., ¼ cup) butter and a squeeze of lemon juice to the sauce and strain.

Garnish the chicken with cucumbers cut in chunks and simmered in butter. Coat with the sauce.

Sautéed chicken Archduke Salvator. POULET SAUTÉ ARCHIDUC SALVATOR – Prepare as for *Sautéed chicken Archduke*.

Set it on a *Potato galette* (see GALETTE) and garnish with cucumbers simmered in butter, sautéed mushrooms and slices of truffle.

There are numerous ways of cooking *Chicken Archduke*. The basic recipe is sautéed chicken to which has been added onion and cream. The method of diluting the juices may be varied by using brandy or Madeira, the sauce finished off with whisky or port, the garnish composed of cucumbers, mushrooms, quartered artichokes or truffles.

Sautéed chicken with artichokes. POULET SAUTÉ AUX ARTICHAUTS – Sauté the chicken in butter *à brun*. When it is half-cooked, add 12 quarters of well blanched artichokes. Finish cooking all these together.

Take out the chicken and artichokes. Dilute the pan juices with 1 dl. (6 tablespoons, scant ½ cup) white wine, boil down, pour in 1½ dl. (¼ pint, ⅔ cup) thickened rich brown veal gravy.

Set the chicken on a dish, garnish with the quarters of artichokes, and coat with the sauce. Sprinkle with chopped parsley.

The chicken may also be garnished with artichoke bases, cooked in a flour-and-water *court-bouillon*, sliced and sautéed with the chicken.

Sautéed chicken with basil. POULET SAUTÉ AU BASILIC – Sauté the chicken in butter, browning it. Dilute the pan juices with 2 dl. (⅓ pint, scant cup) white wine and add 1 tablespoon chopped basil. Boil down the liquid by half. Add 50 g. (2 oz., ¼ cup) butter; mix well. Coat the chicken with this juice.

Sautéed chicken à la biarrotte. POULET SAUTÉ À LA BIARROTTE – Sauté the chicken in oil *à brun*.

Dilute the pan juices with white wine, boil down, and pour in 1 dl. (6 tablespoons, scant ½ cup) *Tomato sauce* (see SAUCE). Add a crushed clove of garlic.

Garnish the chicken with 125 g. (4 oz.) *cèpes* (q.v.) sautéed in oil, 125 g. (4 oz.) diced potatoes sautéed in oil, a peeled, diced and sautéed aubergine and a medium-sized onion cut in rings and fried. Arrange in separate groups round the chicken.

Sautéed chicken à la bohémienne. POULET SAUTÉ À LA BOHÉMIENNE – Sauté the chicken, seasoned with paprika, in oil *à brun*. When it is half-cooked, add 4 sweet pimentos peeled and cut in large strips, 2 tomatoes peeled and cut in thick slices, a medium-sized onion cut in small dice and blanched, a crushed clove of garlic and a teaspoon chopped fennel.

Dilute the pan juices with white wine, add ½ dl. (3 tablespoons, scant ¼ cup) thickened rich brown veal gravy, and finish with a squeeze of lemon juice.

Set the chicken on a dish, coat with the sauce and serve with *Rice à l'indienne* (see RICE).

Sautéed chicken Boivin (Mont-Bry's recipe). POULET SAUTÉ BOIVIN – 'Cook a jointed chicken lightly in butter, browning a little on both sides. When the pieces are lightly browned, put in the pan 24 small onions that have been tossed in butter, 12 quarters of small blanched artichokes, and 24 small new potatoes of uniform size and shape. Season. Cook, covered, on a gentle heat.

'Drain the pieces of chicken. Set them on a dish and arrange the garnish of onions, artichokes and potatoes round them. Pour over the chicken the cooking juices diluted with *pot-au-feu* broth, with the addition of 2 tablespoons (3 tablespoons) dissolved meat glaze, sharpened with a squeeze of lemon juice, and with butter added.'

Sautéed chicken à la bordelaise. POULET SAUTÉ À LA BORDELAISE – Sauté the chicken in a mixture of oil and butter. Finish as in the recipe for *Sautéed chicken with white wine* (see below). Add to the sauce 1 tablespoon *Tomato sauce* (see SAUCE) and a crushed clove of garlic.

Garnish the chicken with 125 g. (4 oz.) sliced potatoes sautéed in butter, 2 blanched artichokes cut in quarters and cooked in butter, several sprigs fried parsley, and 2 medium-sized onions cut in rings and fried. Coat with the sauce.

Sautéed chicken à la bordelaise

Sautéed chicken à la bourguignonne. POULET SAUTÉ À LA BOURGUIGNONNE – Sauté the chicken in butter *à brun*. When three-quarters cooked add 12 small glazed onions, 12 mushrooms lightly cooked in butter and 2 slices blanched, diced lean bacon lightly fried in butter.

Take out the chicken and its accompaniments. Dilute the pan juices with 2 dl. (⅓ pint, scant cup) red wine and add a crushed clove of garlic. Boil down to two-thirds, add 1½ dl. (¼ pint, ⅔ cup) *Rich brown sauce* (see SAUCE), cook at boiling point for a few moments, and strain.

Surround the chicken with the garnish, and coat with the sauce. Heart-shaped croûtons fried in butter may be added.

Sautéed chicken à la bourguignonne or en matelote. POULET SAUTÉ À LA BOURGUIGNONNE, EN MATELOTE – Fry in butter 2 slices blanched lean bacon cut in big dice. Add 12 blanched small onions, cook till golden, and add 12 small mushrooms.

Remove these ingredients, which form the garnish, and brown quickly pieces of chicken in the same fat. When they are half-cooked, put the garnish back in the pan, cover, and cook for 15 minutes.

Take out the chicken and the garnish. Dilute the pan juices with 2 dl. (⅓ pint, scant cup) red wine, boil down to half, and thicken with 1 tablespoon butter mixed with a little flour. Strain.

Surround the chicken pieces with the garnish and pour the sauce over.

Sautéed chicken in butter or à la minute. POULET SAUTÉ AU BEURRE, À LA MINUTE – Sauté the chicken in butter *à brun*.

To serve, squeeze lemon juice over, pour on the very hot cooking butter, and sprinkle with chopped parsley.

Sautéed chicken with cèpes I. POULET SAUTÉ AUX CÈPES – Sauté the chicken in oil or in a mixture of oil and butter. When it is three-quarters cooked, add 300 g. (11 oz.) white *cèpes* (q.v.) which have been cut into thick slices and sautéed in oil. Sprinkle with chopped onion.

Drain the chicken and *cèpes*. Dilute the pan juices with 1 dl. (6 tablespoons, scant ½ cup) white wine, boil down and add 50 g. (2 oz., ¼ cup) butter.

Garnish the chicken with the *cèpes*, coat with the juice, and sprinkle with chopped parsley. A crushed clove of garlic may be added.

Sautéed chicken with cèpes II. POULET SAUTÉ AUX CÈPES – Prepare the chicken as for *Sautéed chicken with white wine* (see below). Garnish with *Cèpes à la bordelaise* (see MUSHROOMS). Coat with the sauce and sprinkle with chopped parsley.

Sautéed chicken chasseur

Sautéed chicken chasseur. POULET SAUTÉ CHASSEUR – Sauté the chicken in a mixture of oil and butter. When it is three-quarters cooked, add 125 g. (4 oz.) sliced mushrooms.

Dilute the pan juices with 1 dl. (6 tablespoons, scant ½ cup) white wine. Add a chopped shallot, boil down, add 1½ dl. (¼ pint, ⅔ cup) thickened veal gravy and ½ dl. (3 tablespoons, scant ¼ cup) *Tomato sauce* (see SAUCE). Boil for a few moments, add 1 tablespoon brandy and 1 tablespoon finely chopped parsley, chervil and tarragon.

Coat the chicken with the sauce and sprinkle with chopped parsley.

Sautéed chicken with chayotes. POULET SAUTÉ AUX CHAYOTTES – Proceed as for *Sautéed chicken with artichokes*.

Garnish the chicken with quarters of chayotes or custard marrows (q.v.) stewed in butter, and coat with the sauce.

Sautéed chicken with cream. POULET SAUTÉ À LA CRÈME – Sauté the chicken in butter *à blanc*. Dilute the pan juices with 2½ dl. (scant ½ pint, generous cup) cream. Boil down to half. Add 50 g. (2 oz., ¼ cup) butter. Coat the chicken with the sauce. The diluted cooking juices may be thickened with 1 or 2 tablespoons chicken *Velouté sauce* (see SAUCE).

Sautéed chicken curry. POULET SAUTÉ AU CURRIE – See below *Sautéed chicken à l'indienne*.

Sautéed chicken Demidoff. POULET SAUTÉ DEMIDOFF – Sauté the chicken in butter *à brun*. When it is half-cooked add 1½ dl. (¼ pint, ⅔ cup), purée of cooked chopped vegetables *à la Demidoff*.

At the end of cooking add 2 sliced truffles and 1 tablespoon blanched curly parsley leaves. Take out the chicken and its garnish, dilute the pan juices with ½ dl. (3 tablespoons, scant ¼ cup) Madeira. Boil down and add 1½ dl. (¼ pint, ⅔ cup) *Rich brown sauce* (see SAUCE).

To serve, cover the chicken with the vegetables, coat with the sauce and garnish with slices of onion dipped in batter and fried.

Sautéed chicken Duroc. POULET SAUTÉ DUROC – Proceed as for *Sautéed chicken chasseur*.

Garnish the chicken with 8 small tomatoes peeled and simmered in butter, and with 150 g. (5 oz.) small new potatoes cooked in butter. Coat with the sauce, sprinkle with chopped parsley.

Sautéed chicken à l'écossaise. POULET SAUTÉ À L'ÉCOSSAISE – Sauté the chicken in butter, browning it.

Dilute the pan juices with ½ dl. (3 tablespoons, scant ¼ cup) sherry. Boil down and add 1½ dl. (¼ pint, ⅔ cup) thickened brown veal gravy. Boil for a few moments, and add 50 g. (2 oz., ¼ cup) butter.

Garnish the chicken with buttered French beans, and truffles which have been cut in thick strips and heated in sherry. Coat with the sauce.

Sautéed chicken fermière or à la paysanne. POULET SAUTÉ FERMIÈRE, À LA PAYSANNE – Sauté the chicken as above. Add 1½ dl. (¼ pint, ⅔ cup) *Vegetable fondue* (see FONDUE). Finish cooking together.

Set the chicken and vegetables in an earthenware dish or casserole, add 2 tablespoons diced lean ham and simmer, covered, in the oven.

Dilute the cooking juices with 1½ dl. (¼ pint, ⅔ cup) thickened veal gravy and sprinkle over the dish.

Sautéed chicken aux fines herbes I. POULET SAUTÉ AUX FINES HERBES. Sauté the chicken in butter *à brun*.

Dilute the pan juices with 1½ dl. (¼ pint, ⅔ cup) white wine, add a chopped shallot. Boil down and add 1½ dl. (¼ pint, ⅔ cup) thickened brown veal gravy. Boil for a few moments. Add ½ tablespoon finely chopped parsley, chervil and tarragon, a squeeze of lemon juice, and 1 tablespoon fresh butter.

When ready to serve, pour this sauce over the chicken.

Sautéed chicken aux fines herbes II. POULET SAUTÉ AUX FINES HERBES – Sauté the chicken as above, and put on a dish. Dilute the cooking juices with ½ dl. (3 tablespoons, scant ¼ cup) white wine. Add a chopped shallot and ½ tablespoon finely chopped parsley, chervil and tarragon. Draw away from the heat and add 50 g. (2 oz., ¼ cup) butter and a squeeze of lemon.

Sautéed chicken à la florentine. POULET SAUTÉ À LA FLORENTINE – Proceed as for *Sautéed chicken with various wines*. Set the chicken in a border of *Risotto* (see RICE) mixed with 2 tablespoons (3 tablespoons) chopped truffles. Coat with the sauce, which has been well boiled down.

Sautéed chicken à la forestière. POULET SAUTÉ À LA FORESTIÈRE – Proceed as for *Sautéed chicken with mushrooms* (see below). Replace the mushrooms by 150 g. (5 oz.) morels sautéed in butter, 150 g. (5 oz.) diced potatoes sautéed in butter and 100 g. (4 oz.) small blanched cardoons.

Sautéed chicken with hop shoots. POULET SAUTÉ AUX JETS DE HOUBLON – Sauté the chicken in butter *à brun*. Dilute the pan juices with white wine, boil down and add thickened brown veal gravy. Garnish the chicken with 300 g. (11 oz.) hop shoots cooked in butter.

Sautéed chicken with hop shoots in cream I. POULET SAUTÉ AUX JETS DE HOUBLON À LA CRÈME – Prepare the chicken as for *Sautéed chicken with cream*, and garnish with hop shoots in cream.

Sautéed chicken with hop shoots in cream II. POULET SAUTÉ AUX JETS DE HOUBLON À LA CRÈME – Cook the chicken in butter and take it out of the pan. Put 1 tablespoon flour into the cooking butter and cook without allowing it to colour. Stir in 1 dl. (6 tablespoons, scant ½ cup) white stock or consommé. Boil down by one-third and add 3 tablespoons (scant ¼ cup) cream. Garnish as above.

Sautéed chicken à l'indienne I. POULET SAUTÉ À L'INDIENNE – Sauté the chicken in butter or oil *à blanc*. Add 1 large chopped onion and 1 tablespoon curry powder. As soon as the pieces of chicken are firm, sprinkle over them 1 tablespoon flour. Cook for a few moments, stirring, and pour in 2 dl. (⅓ pint, scant cup) white stock. Add a *bouquet garni* and cook with the pan covered.

Set the chicken in a *timbale* and coat with the boiled-down sauce, to which lemon juice has been added. Serve with *Rice à l'indienne* (see RICE).

Sautéed chicken à l'indienne II. POULET SAUTÉ À L'INDIENNE – Cut up the chicken into small pieces and put it into a casserole in which 1 large chopped onion, 100 g. (4 oz.) diced ham and 1 large grated eating apple have already been heated in butter (with oil or lard). Add a sprig of thyme, a bay leaf, a pinch of cardamom, a pinch of cinnamon, a pinch of mace and 2 crushed cloves of garlic. Sprinkle in 4 teaspoons curry powder and mix. Add 2 peeled and seeded tomatoes. Pour in 4 dl. (¾ pint, scant 2 cups) coconut milk and cook for 40 minutes. Add 1 dl. (6 tablespoons, scant ½ cup) double cream and the juice of 1 lemon. Serve with *Rice à l'indienne* (see RICE).

Each Indian cook has his own method of preparing curries of mutton, lamb, chicken, fish, etc. The basic principle, the curry seasoning, does not vary, but the recipes differ from each other in requiring different ingredients. As well as the traditional Indian-style rice – yellow (saffron) rice – boiled cabbage mixed with mashed potatoes and sprinkled with curry, thin pancakes made of fine wheaten flour, etc., are served.

In France, *Sautéed chicken à l'indienne* is often prepared by adding curry powder to a chicken sauté *à blanc*, its sauce bound with a chicken *Velouté sauce* (see SAUCE).

Sautéed chicken à l'italienne I. POULET SAUTÉ À L'ITALIENNE – Sauté the chicken in a mixture of oil and butter *à brun*. Dilute the juices with 1½ dl. (¼ pint, ⅔ cup) white wine; reduce and add 1½ dl. (¼ pint, ⅔ cup) *Italian sauce* (see SAUCE).

Sautéed chicken à l'italienne II. POULET SAUTÉ À L'ITALIENNE – Sauté the chicken in oil and butter. When half-cooked, add 1 tablespoon onion which has been partly cooked in butter, 1 chopped shallot, and 4 chopped mushrooms.

Dilute the pan juices with 1 dl. (6 tablespoons, scant ½ cup) white wine; boil down and add 1 dl. (6 tablespoons, scant ½ cup) thickened brown veal stock and ½ dl. (3 tablespoons, scant ¼ cup) *Tomato sauce* (see SAUCE). Boil for a few moments and add 1 tablespoon lean chopped ham and 1 tablespoon parsley, tarragon and chervil. Coat the chicken with this sauce.

Sautéed chicken à la japonaise. POULET SAUTÉ À LA JAPONAISE – Sauté the chicken in butter *à brun*. When it is half-cooked add 300 g. (11 oz.) blanched and drained Japanese artichokes. Continue cooking until the chicken is ready, then finish off as for *Sautéed chicken with artichokes*.

Sautéed chicken à la livonienne. POULET SAUTÉ À LA LIVONIENNE – Sauté the chicken in butter *à blanc*. When it is three-quarters cooked add 250 g. (9 oz.) morels sautéed in butter. Dilute the pan juices and finish as for *Sautéed chicken with cream*. Garnish with the morels and coat with the sauce, to which 1 tablespoon blanched and chopped chives have been added. Scatter 2 tablespoons (3 tablespoons) breadcrumbs fried in butter over the morels.

Sautéed chicken à la lyonnaise. POULET SAUTÉ À LA LYONNAISE – Sauté the chicken in butter *à brun*. When it is half cooked add 2 large chopped onions which have been sautéed in butter. Finish cooking. Dilute the pan juices with 2 tablespoons (3 tablespoons) vinegar. Boil down, and add 2 dl. (⅓ pint, scant cup) thickened brown veal gravy or *Rich brown sauce* (see SAUCE). Coat the chicken with the sauce and sprinkle with chopped parsley.

Sautéed chicken à la Marengo. POULET SAUTÉ À LA MARENGO – Sauté the chicken in oil *à brun*. Dilute the pan juices with 1 dl. (6 tablespoons, scant ½ cup) white wine, boil down and add ½ dl. (3 tablespoons, scant ¼ cup) thickened brown veal gravy, 1½ dl. (¼ pint, ⅔ cup) *Tomato sauce* (see SAUCE) and a crushed clove of garlic. Boil for a few minutes and strain.

Garnish the chicken with 8 fried mushrooms; 4 small fried eggs (or just the yolks); 4 crayfish trussed and cooked in *court-bouillon*; 4 heart-shaped croûtons fried in butter; and 8 slices of truffles sautéed in butter. Coat with the sauce and sprinkle with chopped parsley.

Sautéed chicken au matelote – See *Sautéed chicken à la bourguignonne*.

Sautéed chicken à la meunière. POULET SAUTÉ À LA MEUNIÈRE – Proceed as for *Sautéed chicken in butter*, adding chopped parsley, lemon juice and 3 or 4 tablespoons veal gravy or *Rich brown sauce*. (see SAUCE).

Sautéed chicken Mireille. POULET SAUTÉ MIREILLE – Sauté the chicken in butter *à brun*. Dilute the pan juices with 1 dl. (6 tablespoons, scant ½ cup) white wine; boil down and stir in 1½ dl. (¼ pint, ⅔ cup) thickened brown veal gravy and ½ dl. (3 tablespoons, scant ¼ cup) *Tomato sauce* (see SAUCE). Boil for a few moments.

Garnish the chicken with 8 endive hearts (gourilos) in cream and 8 small tomatoes, peeled, drained and cooked in butter. Coat the chicken with the sauce.

Sautéed chicken Monselet. POULET SAUTÉ MONSELET – Sauté the chicken in butter *à brun*. When it is three-quarters cooked, add 2 artichoke bottoms, blanched and cut in slices, and, when completely cooked, 2 medium-sized sliced truffles. Take out the chicken and its accompaniments, dilute the pan juices with 1 dl. (6 tablespoons, scant ½ cup) white wine and boil down. Add 1½ dl. (¼ pint, ⅔ cup) thickened brown veal gravy, and boil for a few moments. Garnish the chicken with the artichokes and truffles and coat with the sauce.

Sautéed chicken with morels and other mushrooms. POULET SAUTÉ AUX MORILLES – Proceed as for *Sautéed chicken with mushrooms* (see below), replacing the latter with 300 g. (11 oz.) morels (or an equivalent quantity of other mushrooms).

Sautéed chicken with mushrooms

Sautéed chicken with mushrooms. POULET SAUTÉ AUX CHAMPIGNONS – Sauté the chicken in butter *à brun*. When three-quarters cooked add 250 g. (9 oz.) sliced mushrooms. Dilute the pan juices with ½ dl. (3 tablespoons, scant ¼ cup) Madeira, boil down and add 1½ dl. (¼ pint, ⅔ cup) thickened brown veal gravy. Boil for a few moments. Garnish the chicken with the mushrooms and coat with the sauce.

Sautéed chicken niçoise. POULET SAUTÉ NIÇOISE – Sauté the chicken in oil *à brun*. Dilute the pan juices with 1 dl. (6 tablespoons, scant ½ cup) white wine, add a crushed garlic clove, boil down and add 1½ dl. (¼ pint, ⅔ cup) *Tomato sauce* (see SAUCE.)

Garnish the chicken with 8 artichoke quarters cooked in butter, 4 braised baby marrows (zucchini), 125 g. (4 oz.) small new potatoes cooked in butter, and 12 stoned black olives. Coat with the sauce and sprinkle with chopped tarragon.

Sautéed chicken with oysters I. POULET SAUTÉ AUX HUÎTRES – Sauté the chicken in butter *à blanc*. Dilute the pan juices with 1 dl. (6 tablespoons, scant ½ cup) white wine and the liquor from 12 poached oysters. Boil down and add 1 dl. (6 tablespoons, scant $\frac{1}{2}$ cup) chicken *Velouté sauce* (see SAUCE). Boil for a few moments. Add 50 g. (2 oz., $\frac{1}{4}$ cup) butter and a squeeze of lemon juice. Strain.

Garnish with the drained oysters and coat with the sauce.

Sautéed chicken with oysters II. POULET SAUTÉ AUX HUÎTRES – Sauté the chicken in butter *à blanc* and when half-cooked add 1 tablespoon blanched chopped onion.

Take out the chicken; add to the pan juices 1 tablespoon flour, the liquor from 12 poached oysters and 1 dl. (6 tablespoons, scant $\frac{1}{2}$ cup) mushroom or white stock. Cook for 10 minutes. Add 2 tablespoons (3 tablespoons) cream and 25 g. (1 oz., 2 tablespoons) butter. Strain and finish as above.

Sautéed chicken panetière. POULET SAUTÉ PANETIÈRE – Prepare as for *sautéed chicken with cream.* Place on a round of bread, trimmed, dried in the oven and spread with purée of *foie gras.*

Garnish with morels (or other mushrooms) in cream. Coat with the sauce.

Sautéed chicken with paprika. POULET SAUTÉ AU PAPRIKA – Season the chicken with paprika. Sauté in butter *à blanc* and finish as for *Sautéed chicken with cream.*

Sautéed chicken à la parisienne. POULET SAUTÉ À LA PARISIENNE – Proceed as for *Sautéed chicken with white wine* (see below). Put the chicken on a layer of *Duchess potato mixture* (see POTATOES) brushed with egg and browned in the oven. Garnish with buttered asparagus tips. Coat with the sauce.

Sautéed chicken Parmentier. POULET SAUTÉ PARMENTIER – Sauté the chicken in butter. When two-thirds cooked, add 4 blanched potatoes, cut in large dice and half-cooked in butter.

Finish as for *Sautéed chicken with white wine* (see below). Garnish with the potatoes, coat with the sauce and sprinkle with chopped parsley.

Sautéed chicken à la Périgord. POULET SAUTÉ À LA PÉRIGORD – See *Sautéed chicken with truffles.* The truffles may be cut to look like small olives.

Sautéed chicken petit-duc. POULET SAUTÉ PETIT-DUC – Sauté the chicken in butter *à brun.* Dilute the pan juices with $\frac{1}{2}$ dl. (3 tablespoons, scant $\frac{1}{4}$ cup) Madeira, boil down and add $1\frac{1}{2}$ dl. ($\frac{1}{4}$ pint, $\frac{2}{3}$ cup) *Rich brown sauce* (see SAUCE). Boil for a few moments.

Garnish the chicken with morels and truffle slices sautéed in butter. Coat with the sauce.

Sautéed chicken à la piémontaise. POULET SAUTÉ À LA PIÉMONTAISE – Proceed as for *Sautéed chicken with white wine* (see below). Put the chicken in a border of risotto mixed with diced white truffles, and garnish with slices of white truffle lightly heated in butter. Pour the sauce over it.

Sautéed chicken à la portugaise. POULET SAUTÉ À LA PORTUGAISE – Sauté the chicken in oil. When two-thirds cooked, add 1 tablespoon chopped onion. Take out the chicken, and put 4 peeled and pipped tomatoes and a clove of crushed garlic in the pan. Season, add 1 dl. (6 tablespoons, scant $\frac{1}{2}$ cup) white wine and boil down by half. Add 3 tablespoons (scant $\frac{1}{4}$ cup) thickened brown veal gravy. Coat the chicken with the sauce and sprinkle with chopped parsley.

Sautéed chicken à la provençale. POULET SAUTÉ À LA PROVENÇALE – Proceed as for *Sautéed chicken à la portugaise.*

Garnish the chicken with 20 stoned, blanched olives and 8 small mushrooms sautéed in oil. Coat with the sauce. Decorate with 8 anchovy fillets and sprinkle with chopped parsley.

Sautéed chicken Rivoli. POULET SAUTÉ RIVOLI – Sauté the chicken in butter *à brun.* When three-quarters cooked add 4 sliced potatoes sautéed in butter, and when completely cooked, 2 chopped medium-sized truffles.

Remove the chicken and garnishes and dilute the pan juices with $\frac{1}{2}$ dl. (3 tablespoons, scant $\frac{1}{4}$ cup) sherry. Boil down and add $1\frac{1}{2}$ dl. ($\frac{1}{4}$ pint, $\frac{2}{3}$ cup) thickened brown veal gravy. Pour the sauce over the chicken.

Sautéed chicken à la romaine. POULET SAUTÉ À LA ROMAINE – Sauté the chicken in oil, browning it. Dilute the pan juices with 1 dl. (6 tablespoons, scant $\frac{1}{2}$ cup) Asti wine. Boil down and pour in 1 dl. (6 tablespoons, scant $\frac{1}{2}$ cup) tomato sauce and $\frac{1}{2}$ dl. (3 tablespoons, scant $\frac{1}{4}$ cup) thickened brown veal gravy.

Put the chicken on a layer of leaf spinach, simmered in butter and mixed with 2 diced anchovy fillets. Coat with the sauce.

Sautéed chicken Stanley. POULET SAUTÉ STANLEY – Sauté the chicken in butter *à blanc.* When it is half-cooked add 2 finely chopped onions. Remove the chicken and garnish with mushrooms cooked in butter.

Add to the onions and cooking juices 2 dl. ($\frac{1}{3}$ pint, scant cup) cream. Cook for 10 minutes and sieve. Reduce the onion purée by a quarter, season with a pinch of curry powder and cayenne, and add 50 g. (2 oz., $\frac{1}{4}$ cup) butter. Coat the chicken with sauce; put 8 slices of truffle on top.

Sautéed chicken with tarragon. POULET SAUTÉ À L'ESTRAGON – Prepared as for *Sautéed chicken aux fines herbes I* but the shallot, parsley and chervil are replaced by an equivalent quantity of chopped tarragon. Decorate the chicken with blanched tarragon leaves.

Sautéed chicken with truffles. POULET SAUTÉ AUX TRUFFES – Sauté the chicken in butter *à brun.* When cooked, place 12 slices of raw truffle on it. Cover and cook for 5 minutes. Take out the chicken and truffles. Dilute the pan juices and finish as for *Sautéed chicken with mushrooms.*

Fresh or preserved truffles may be used. If the latter, add their boiled down juices to the sauce.

Sautéed chicken à la viennoise. POULET SAUTÉ À LA VIENNOISE – Proceed as for *Sautéed chicken Archduke,* but without the onion. Garnish with cooked, buttered cucumbers.

Sautéed chicken with various wines. POULET SAUTÉ AUX VINS DIVERS – Sauté the chicken in butter *à brun.* Dilute the pan juices with wine, add thickened brown veal gravy, and finish in the ordinary way.

Note. These preparations are designated by the name of the wine used: Chablis, Graves, Pouilly, Frontignan, Sauternes, Madeira, Port, Sherry, Champagne, etc.

Sautéed chicken with red wine is always called *à la bourguignonne.*

Sautéed chicken with white wine. POULET SAUTÉ AU VIN BLANC – Sauté the chicken in butter *à brun.* Dilute the juices with 1 dl. (6 tablespoons, scant $\frac{1}{2}$ cup) white wine, boil down, and pour in $1\frac{1}{2}$ dl. ($\frac{1}{4}$ pint, $\frac{2}{3}$ cup) thickened brown veal gravy. Boil for a few moments and finish with 50 g. (2 oz., $\frac{1}{4}$ cup) butter. Coat the chicken with the sauce.

Sautéed chicken à la zingara. POULET SAUTÉ À LA ZINGARA – Season the chicken with paprika, and sauté it in oil *à brun.* When it is cooked, add 4 tablespoons ($\frac{1}{3}$ cup) *zingara garnish* (q.v.).

Take out the chicken and its garnish. Dilute the cooking juices with $\frac{1}{2}$ dl. (3 tablespoons, scant $\frac{1}{4}$ cup) Madeira, boil down and add $1\frac{1}{2}$ dl. ($\frac{1}{4}$ pint, $\frac{2}{3}$ cup) *Rich brown sauce* (see SAUCE), flavoured with tomato.

Garnish the chicken with *zingara garnish* arranged on 4 small slices of toast with a thin slice of ham tossed in butter added to each one. Coat with the sauce and sprinkle with chopped parsley. The slices of ham may also be served in thin pastry tartlet shells.

Chicken in scallop shells – See HORS-D'ŒUVRE, *Scallop shells of poultry.*

Chicken soufflé. SOUFFLÉ DE VOLAILLE – *Using raw chicken.* Add 5 stiffly whisked egg whites to 1 kg. (2¼ lb.) *Chicken mousseline forcemeat* (see FORCEMEAT). Put in a buttered soufflé dish and cook gently in the oven for 35 to 40 minutes.

Using cooked chicken. Pound 500 g. (generous 1 lb.) cooked chicken meat adding 6 tablespoons (scant ½ cup) thick cold *Béchamel sauce* (see SAUCE). Season and rub through a sieve. Heat this purée, without allowing it to boil. Add 50 g. (2 oz., ¼ cup) butter, 5 egg yolks and 6 stiffly whisked egg whites. Put in a buttered soufflé dish and cook gently in the oven.

Cream of chicken soup. CRÈME DE VOLAILLE – Soup made with chicken cooked in a veal or chicken stock, pounded to a purée and finished with *velouté sauce* and cream. (See SOUPS AND BROTHS.)

Chicken Souvarov. POULARDE SOUVAROV – Stuff the chicken with chopped *foie gras* and truffles, seasoned with salt and spices and a few drops of liqueur brandy.

Put the chicken in a covered pan with some butter and cook until three-quarters done. Transfer the chicken to a casserole and add 8 medium-sized truffles which have been seasoned and simmered in butter for 5 minutes.

Moisten the chicken with the cooking juices diluted with Madeira, boiled down and mixed with *Rich brown sauce* (see SAUCE) made with the truffle juices. Cover, and seal the lid with flour-and-water paste. Finish cooking in the oven for 20 to 25 minutes.

Spring chicken. POUSSIN – This term can be used to describe a newly hatched chicken, but the flesh of such a young bird is so soft and insipid that it is scarcely edible. In culinary terminology the word *poussin* usually means a young chicken which is sufficiently well formed for its flesh to have all the necessary firmness and flavour.

The name is also given to a very small chicken, of which the best type is Hamburg chicken. These have delicate flesh and can be prepared in any of the ways given for small roasting chickens.

Spring chicken (cold). POUSSIN FROID – Prepared in any of the ways given for cold chicken or pigeon dishes. The chicken is stuffed with forcemeat or with *foie gras* and diced truffles. For some dishes the chickens are boned.

Spring chicken en compote. POUSSIN EN COMPOTE – Stuffed with a fine forcemeat (made with the chicken liver).

Prepared as for *Compote of pigeon* (see PIGEON).

Spring chicken (fried). POUSSIN FRIT – Cut the chicken into pieces of equal size and marinate in oil, lemon juice and salt and pepper. Roll the pieces in flour, coat with egg and breadcrumbs and fry in deep fat. Garnish with fried parsley and lemon quarters.

Spring chicken grilled à la diable. POUSSIN GRILLÉ À LA DIABLE – Prepared as for *Grilled chicken à la diable.*

Spring chicken in marinade (fried). POUSSIN EN MARINADE (FRIT) – Cut the chicken in quarters and take out the small bones. Marinate in oil, lemon juice, salt, pepper, and chopped herbs. Dip the pieces in a light batter and fry in deep fat.

Drain, and garnish with fried parsley. Serve with *Tomato sauce* (see SAUCE).

This dish is often incorrectly served under the name of *fritot* of chicken; but *fritot* denotes previously cooked substances.

Spring chicken with peas. POUSSIN AUX PETITS POIS – Prepared as for *Pigeon with peas* (see PIGEON).

Spring chicken à la piémontaise. POUSSIN À LA PIÉMONTAISE – Fill the chicken with fine forcemeat, the chopped liver and a little onion lightly cooked in butter. Truss as for boiling. Cook in butter, browning it all over. Drain, and remove the trussing strings. Surround the chicken with a risotto. Dilute the juices with white wine, thickened brown veal gravy and a little tomato purée. Boil down together and pour over the chicken.

Spring chicken à la polonaise. POUSSIN À LA POLONAISE – Stuff a chicken with *à gratin forcemeat* (see FORCEMEAT) mixed with soaked bread, butter and chopped parsley.

Cook in a casserole. Finish as for *Chicken à la polonaise.*

Roasted spring chicken. POUSSIN RÔTI – Put a *bouquet garni,* 1 tablespoon butter and the chopped liver, well seasoned with salt and pepper and grated nutmeg, inside the chicken. Truss, bard with bacon fat and put on the spit. Cook on a good heat, basting frequently.

Arrange on a long dish and garnish with cress. Hand the juices separately.

Spring chicken à la sicilienne (Prosper Salles' recipe). POUSSIN À LA SICILIENNE – Cook some lasagne (q.v.) in salt water. Drain and reheat for a few moments in hot butter. Bind with a purée of pistachio nuts. Season well and allow to cool. Stuff the chicken with this mixture and truss as for spit roasting. Cook at a good heat, basting frequently. When three-quarters cooked sprinkle with freshly grated breadcrumbs and let it colour. Hand the juices separately.

Spring chicken à la tartare. POUSSIN À LA TARTARE – Split the chicken down the back, season, brush over with melted butter and sprinkle with breadcrumbs. Grill on a gentle heat. Serve with *Tartare sauce* (see SAUCE).

Spring chicken à la viennoise. POUSSIN À LA VIENNOISE – Divide the chicken into quarters. Season, sprinkle with flour, and coat with egg and breadcrumbs. Brown them well on both sides in clarified butter (or lard), or fry in deep fat. Garnish with fried parsley and lemon quarters.

Chicken Stanley. POULARDE STANLEY – Poach the chicken in a white stock to which 4 large chopped onions have been added. Put the chicken on a dish and surround with 20 large mushrooms and 8 tartlets filled with chopped truffles.

Finish as for *Sautéed chicken Stanley.*

Stuffed chicken à l'ariégeoise. POULET FARCI À L'ARIÉGEOISE – Stuff the chicken with forcemeat made as follows: soak 250 g. (9 oz.) crustless bread in milk, squeeze and put in a basin. Add 100 g. (4 oz.) chopped raw ham, the chopped chicken liver and gizzard, 2 finely chopped cloves of garlic and 2 tablespoons (3 tablespoons) chopped onion cooked lightly in fat. Bind with an egg and the blood of the chicken. Season with salt, pepper and grated nutmeg. Add 1 tablespoon chopped parsley.

Truss the chicken as for boiling. Cook in a *pot-au-feu* with a piece of beef and a piece of chined salt pork (pork back). Take the trussing strings off the cooked chicken and garnish with balls of stuffed cabbage, potatoes sliced and cooked in the *pot-au-feu* broth, and the boned and sliced pork.

Serve with *Tomato sauce* (see SAUCE) seasoned with garlic.

The *pot-au-feu* broth is served as a soup, with rice or vermicelli.

Stuffed chicken à la mode de Sorges (Périgord cookery). POULET FARCI À LA MODE DE SORGES – Stuff the chicken with forcemeat made of chopped chicken liver, stale breadcrumbs, chopped bacon, chopped parsley, chopped spring onions, chopped shallot and chopped garlic, all well seasoned with salt, pepper and grated nutmeg, and bound with the blood of the chicken and eggyolks.

Brown the chicken all over in goose fat. Put it in a *marmite* and cover with boiling water. Season with salt and pepper. Bring to the boil and skim. Add 3 carrots, 2 turnips, the white parts of 3 leeks, 1 celery heart, 1 large onion stuck with 1 clove, and beet stalks tied in a bunch. Cook very slowly for 1 hour. Drain the chicken, remove the trussing strings, and garnish with the sliced carrots and turnips.

Serve with *Sorges sauce*, which is a highly seasoned *vinaigrette sauce* with chopped parsley, spring onions and shallots added, bound with 2 egg yolks cooked for 3 minutes in boiling water. Finish with the whites of these eggs, recooked in the chicken broth and cut in dice.

Suprêmes of chicken. SUPRÊMES DE VOLAILLE – The breast and wings of poultry, removed when raw. Also known as *côtelettes* or *filets*, and served as small *entrées*.

When *suprêmes* of *poulardes* or fat hens are used, they are divided into 2 or 3 slices, flattened, trimmed into oval shapes, and cooked like chicken *côtelettes*.

Suprêmes of chicken ambassadrice. SUPRÊMES DE VOLAILLE AMBASSADRICE – Sauté in butter. Garnish with chicken livers sautéed in butter, cocks' combs and kidneys, and truffles cut into the shape of olives. Dilute the pan juices with Madeira and thickened brown veal gravy. Pour over the dish.

Place on top of these *suprêmes* the *filets mignons* (pieces which lie against the breast bone), studded with truffles.

Suprêmes of chicken Camérani. SUPRÊMES DE VOLAILLE CAMÉRANI – Coat the *suprêmes* with a mixture of egg and breadcrumbs and chopped truffles. Sauté in butter.

Place on a bed of noodles. Make a sauce with the pan juices, mixed with Madeira and thickened brown veal gravy, to which has been added 1 tablespoon *julienne* (q.v.) of celery and truffles, cooked in butter until tender.

Suprêmes of chicken Carême. SUPRÊMES DE VOLAILLE CARÊME – Slit open the *suprêmes* and fill with a thick mushroom purée, to which a fine *julienne* (q.v.) of cocks' combs and truffles has been added. Sauté in butter.

Place on croûtons of bread fried in butter. Garnish with *Chicken quenelles* (see QUENELLES), truffles cut into olive shapes, and mushrooms. For sauce use thickened brown veal gravy with tomato and butter. Put the *filets mignons*, studded with pickled tongue, on top of the *suprêmes*.

Suprêmes of chicken à la florentine. SUPRÊMES DE VOLAILLE À LA FLORENTINE – Poach in veal or chicken stock until three-quarters cooked. Coat with *Mornay sauce* (see SAUCE) to which chicken essence has been added. Sprinkle with grated Parmesan and brown quickly.

Suprêmes of chicken Gabrielle. SUPRÊMES DE VOLAILLE GABRIELLE – Remove the *suprêmes*, without detaching the *filets mignons*. Cover with a thin layer of *mirepoix* (q.v.) cooked in butter until tender. Coat with egg and breadcrumbs. Sauté in butter.

Suprêmes of chicken à l'impériale. SUPRÊMES DE VOLAILLE À L'IMPÉRIALE – Stud the *suprêmes* with semi-circles of truffles and pickled tongue. Cook in white stock.

Fill cooked *barquettes* with a purée of truffles *à la crème* and put in the *suprêmes*. Coat lightly with *Suprême sauce* (see SAUCE). Put the *filets mignons*, studded with truffles, on top of the *suprêmes*.

Suprêmes of chicken marquise. SUPRÊMES DE VOLAILLE MARQUISE – Sauté in butter. Garnish with *bouchées* of puff pastry filled with a *salpicon* of cocks' combs, kidneys and truffles bound with cream. Dilute the pan juices with cream, to which has been added butter and 2 tablespoons (3 tablespoons) truffles. Coat the *suprêmes* with this sauce and put *filets mignons*, poached in white stock, on top.

Suprêmes of chicken Montpensier. SUPRÊMES DE VOLAILLE MONTPENSIER – Coat the *suprêmes* with egg and breadcrumbs and sauté them in butter. Garnish with asparagus tips in butter and put two slices of truffle on each *suprême*. Dot with *Noisette butter* (see BUTTER, *Compound butters*). For sauce use thickened brown veal gravy.

Suprêmes of chicken à la Périgueux. SUPRÊMES DE VOLAILLE À LA PÉRIGUEUX – Sauté in butter and put on croûtons fried in butter. Garnish with sliced truffles and coat with *Demi-glace sauce* (see SAUCE), flavoured with Madeira.

Suprêmes of chicken Pojarski. SUPRÊMES DE VOLAILLE POJARSKI – Chop the flesh of the *suprêmes*. Add 50 g. (2 oz., 1 cup) breadcrumbs, soaked in milk and squeezed, 50 g. (2 oz., ¼ cup) butter, and 1 or 2 tablespoons fresh cream. Season with salt, pepper and nutmeg. Reshape the *suprêmes*, flour lightly and sauté in butter.

Garnish with a green vegetable cooked in butter, and dot with *Noisette butter* (see BUTTER, *Compound butters*).

Suprêmes of chicken princesse. SUPRÊMES DE VOLAILLE PRINCESSE – Cook in veal or chicken stock. Put the *suprêmes* on croûtons fried in butter, garnish with asparagus tips in butter and coat with *Allemande sauce* (see SAUCE). Place two slices of truffles on each *suprême*. Put the *filets mignons*, studded with truffles, on top.

Suprêmes of chicken Richelieu. SUPRÊMES DE VOLAILLE RICHELIEU – Coat with egg and breadcrumbs and sauté in butter. Dot with *Maître d'hôtel butter* (see BUTTER, *Compound butters*) and put 4 slices of truffle on each *suprême*.

Suprême of chicken Rossini. SUPRÊMES DE VOLAILLE ROSSINI – Sauté in butter, and put on croûtons fried in butter. Garnish with slices of *foie gras* sautéed in butter, and sliced truffles. Coat with *Madeira sauce* (see SAUCE).

Suprêmes of chicken, with various vegetables. SUPRÊMES DE VOLAILLE AUX LÉGUMES DIVERS – Season the *suprêmes* and sauté in butter.

Garnish with any of the following vegetables: diced aubergines fried in butter, peeled mushrooms, braised endives, cucumber cut in chunks and simmered in butter, French beans in butter, braised lettuce, *macédoine* of vegetables in butter, peas in butter or *à la française*, asparagus tips in butter or cream, vegetable purées.

For sauce use the cooking juices, mixed with white wine and thickened brown veal gravy.

Suprêmes of chicken Verdi. SUPRÊMES DE VOLAILLE VERDI – Sauté the *suprêmes* in butter. Put them in a pastry shell filled with diced macaroni bound with purée of *foie gras*. Put two slices of truffle on top of each *suprême* and coat lightly with *Demi-glace sauce* (see SAUCE), finished with Marsala.

Add the *filets mignons*, cut in slices, coated in egg and breadcrumbs and sautéed in butter.

Chicken with tarragon I. POULARDE À L'ESTRAGON – Poach a chicken in white stock with a bunch of tarragon. Decorate with blanched tarragon leaves. Pour over the chicken several tablespoons of the cooking liquor, strained and thickened with arrowroot, to which chopped tarragon has been added.

Chicken with tarragon

Chicken with tarragon II. POULARDE À L'ESTRAGON – Cook the chicken in butter in a covered dish in the oven. To serve pour over it the cooking juices, diluted with white wine and thickened veal gravy, to which a handful of chopped tarragon has been added.

Chicken timbale. See TIMBALE, CROÛTES.

Chicken à la Toscane. POULARDE À LA TOSCANE – Stuff the chicken with 100 g. (4 oz., 1 cup) cooked spaghetti, 100 g. (4 oz., $\frac{1}{2}$ cup) of purée of *foie gras*, 2 diced truffles and 50 g. (2 oz., $\frac{1}{2}$ cup) grated Parmesan, seasoned and bound with 4 tablespoons ($\frac{1}{3}$ cup) thickened brown veal gravy. Cook the chicken, and prepare the sauce as for *Chicken à la Derby*.

Surround the chicken with 8 pastry cases filled with ham, tongue and truffles, bound with *Rich brown sauce* (see SAUCE), flavoured with tomato, and with 8 slices of *foie gras*, tossed in butter.

Pour the pan juices over the chicken.

Chicken Toulouse. POULARDE TOULOUSE – Poach the chicken in white stock. Garnish with *Toulouse garnish* (see GARNISH) and pour *Allemande sauce* (see SAUCE) over it.

Chicken with truffles. POULARDE AUX TRUFFES – Cook the chicken, covered, with butter in the oven. When cooked add 250 g. (9 oz.) sliced raw truffles. Cover, and keep on low heat for a few moments.

Dilute the cooking juices with Madeira and *Rich brown sauce* (see SAUCE).

Chicken with truffles à la périgourdine (Plumerey's recipe). POULARDE TRUFFÉE À LA PÉRIGOURDINE – 'Draw and singe a chicken without damaging the skin. Wash and peel 1 kg. (2 lb.) truffles and cut into pieces the size of pigeons' eggs. Keep the scraps. Simmer the truffles with salt, pepper, spices, half a bay leaf, a small sprig of thyme and some grated nutmeg, in 225 g. (8 oz., 1 cup) chicken fat and 225 g. (8 oz., 1 cup) melted, strained fat bacon, for 15 minutes. Stuff the chicken with the mixture, cover with the outside skin of the truffles and leave for 3 or 4 days. On the day it is served, remove the truffle skins and toss in butter with an onion, a carrot and a sprig of parsley. Put the chicken on a skewer, bard with fresh pork fat, cover with the vegetables and truffles, and wrap in oiled paper. Cook on a spit for $1\frac{1}{2}$ hours, sprinkling with water. 5 minutes before serving, unwrap the chicken and let it brown. Remove from the spit, discard the bards and serve with *Périgueux sauce*' (see SAUCE).

Chicken turban (ring). TURBAN DE VOLAILLE – Line a buttered *savarin* (ring) mould with thin slices of raw chicken, overlapping the edges. Cover with a thin layer of *Chicken mousseline forcemeat* (see FORCEMEAT). Fill the mould with a *salpicon* (q.v.) of cooked chicken, truffles and mushrooms, bound with *Allemande sauce* (see SAUCE). Cover with another thin layer of the forcemeat, folding the edges of the sliced chicken over it. Poach the 'turban' in the oven in a *bain-marie* for 40 minutes.

Leave for a few moments after cooking before unmoulding. Fill the middle with a garnish and serve with *Suprême* or *Allemande sauce* (see SAUCE).

Chicken à la viennoise. POULET À LA VIENNOISE – This method is for small spring chickens, but can be applied to small tender roasting chickens (*poulets de grain*). Joint the chicken. Season the pieces with salt and pepper, flour them, dip in egg beaten with oil, and cover with fresh breadcrumbs. Cook in clarified butter or lard. Serve on a napkin, garnished with fried parsley and quarters of lemon.

This chicken may also be fried in deep fat.

Chicken vol-au-vent – See VOL-AU-VENT.

Chicken wings – See PINIONS.

CHICK-PEA. POIS CHICHE – Plant (of the family *Leguminosae*) originating in the Mediterranean area, one species of which is cultivated in France.

In south-western France chick-peas are cooked *en estouffade* (q.v.). They are used in Spain a great deal, being an essential ingredient of many soups. Chick-peas are also very popular in North Africa, where they are part of the garnish for the classic *couscous*.

Chick-peas Catalan style. POIS CHICHES À LA CATALANE – Soak the chick-peas until they become quite soft. Boil in water with a vegetable garnish (for example, white dried beans), a *bouquet garni* (q.v.) and a piece of bacon. Season with salt and pepper. Add a few tablespoons oil to form a layer of fat on the surface. Add Spanish sausages called *chorizos*. Simmer very gently for about 4 hours.

Drain the chick-peas, remove the vegetable garnish and the *bouquet garni* and put the chick-peas into a saucepan. Add a few tablespoons tomato purée, the *chorizos* and the bacon cut in uniform pieces. Add a pinch of garlic and a few tablespoons of the liquid left over from boiling the chick-peas. Simmer for 1 hour.

CHICORY (U.S. Endive). ENDIVE – Magdebourg chicory is known in France and U.S.A. as *endive* and in Belgium, where it is grown in large quantities, as *chicorée de Bruxelles*, *witloof* or *barbe-de-bouc* (goat's beard).

Chicory roots, grown in the dark, are white and delicate. Chicory comes into season in October and is available throughout the winter. It is eaten raw in salads, or cooked in various ways.

Method of cooking. Trim and wash the chicory, leaving it in water for as short a time as possible. Place in a saucepan with 25 g. (1 oz., 2 tablespoons) butter, a pinch of salt, juice of $\frac{1}{4}$ lemon and 1 dl. (6 tablespoons, scant $\frac{1}{2}$ cup) water, for 500 g. (generous 1 lb.) chicory. Cover and bring to the boil. Simmer steadily for 45 minutes.

Another method. Trim and wash the chicory and place in a saucepan with 50 g. (2 oz., $\frac{1}{4}$ cup) butter, a pinch of salt and a few drops of lemon juice. Cover and stew for 45 minutes. Chicory cooked in this way can be used for the recipes given below. Chicory should never be parboiled before stewing.

Chicory à la béchamel. ENDIVES À LA BÉCHAMEL – Cook the chicory as above. Cover with *Béchamel sauce* (see SAUCE), and the cooking stock, boiled down with butter.

Chicory with brown or noisette butter. ENDIVES AU BEURRE NOIR – Cook the chicory as in the first recipe. Drain. Arrange on a dish. Pour on lemon juice and, just before serving, hot *Brown* or *Noisette butter* (see BUTTER, *Compound butters*).

Chicory with butter. ENDIVES AU BEURRE – Cook as in first recipe. Pour on the stock with a piece of butter added.

Chicory chiffonnade. CHIFFONNADE D'ENDIVES – Remove the outer leaves. Wash, dry and shred them finely. Cook in butter, in a covered pan, with a pinch of salt and sugar.

Chicory chiffonnade with cream. CHIFFONNADE D'ENDIVES À LA CRÈME – Cook as in the first recipe. Five minutes before serving, moisten with 2 dl. ($\frac{1}{3}$ pint, scant cup) boiling cream. Boil fast for a few seconds. Serve with the cooking stock and fresh butter.

Chicory à la flamande. ENDIVES À LA FLAMANDE – another name for *Chicory with butter*.

Chicory fritots. ENDIVES EN FRITOT – Cook the chicory as in the first recipe. Drain and dry. Quarter the shoots and steep in a marinade of oil, lemon juice, salt and pepper. Before serving, dip them in light batter and deep-fry. Serve garnished.

Chicory au gratin. ENDIVES AU GRATIN – Cook the chicory in butter. Sprinkle with grated cheese. Pour on melted butter. Brown in the oven.

Chicory in gravy. ENDIVES AU JUS – Cook as in the first

Chicory (*Nicolas*)

recipe. Arrange on a dish and pour on a few tablespoons concentrated brown veal stock and the cooking stock of the chicory.

Chicory à la grecque (hors-d'œuvre). ENDIVES À LA GRECQUE – Trim small chicory shoots. Wash and dry in a cloth. Plunge them into a stock prepared as for *Artichokes à la grecque* (see HORS-D'ŒUVRE). Finish as in that recipe.

Chicory à la meunière. ENDIVES À LA MEUNIÈRE – Name used for *Chicory with brown butter*.

Chicory à la milanaise. ENDIVES À LA MILANAISE – Cook the chicory as in the first recipe. Arrange on an ovenproof dish. Proceed as for *Asparagus à la milanaise* (see ASPARAGUS).

Chicory à la Mornay. ENDIVES À LA MORNAY – Cook the chicory as in the first recipe. Arrange in an ovenproof dish and cover with *Mornay sauce* (see SAUCE) and the concentrated stock of the chicory. Sprinkle with grated cheese. Pour on melted butter and brown in a very hot oven.

Chicory à la polonaise. ENDIVES À LA POLONAISE – Cook the chicory as in the first recipe. Arrange in a dish and proceed as for *Asparagus à la polonaise* (see ASPARAGUS).

Purée of chicory. PURÉE D'ENDIVES – Cook the chicory as in the first recipe. Rub through a sieve. Heat the purée and add a little butter or cream.

This purée can be thickened with a few tablespoons of *Béchamel sauce* or thick *Velouté sauce* (see SAUCE), or a third of its weight of mashed potatoes. Concentrated brown veal stock may be added.

Chicory salad. SALADE D'ENDIVES – Wash and dry the chicory. Remove faded leaves. Separate the remaining leaves and halve or shred them. Season with oil, lemon juice or vinegar, salt, and pepper.

Chicory, with the leaves whole or shredded, can also be dressed with *Mayonnaise* (see SAUCE, *Cold sauces*). Cooked chicory can also be made into a salad.

Chicory soufflé. SOUFFLÉ D'ENDIVE – Using cooked chicory rubbed through a fine sieve, proceed as for *Endive soufflé* (see ENDIVE).

CHICORY, COFFEE. CHICORÉE À CAFÉ – The wild chicory root has been used as a substitute for coffee since 1769. It was first used in Sicily, then in Germany and has given rise to an important industry. The roots, cut up into *cossettes*, are dried and powdered, more or less finely. The different types are known commercially as *gros-grains,* from selected *cossettes* (roots); *demi-grains*, from small *cossettes*; chicory *courantes*; and chicory in powder form.

Chicory has more food value than coffee, although this is not important as the amount consumed is small. It produces a dark infusion with laxative properties, and prevents caffeine poisoning which occurs when too much real coffee is drunk. Coffee addicts, justifiably, do not allow the addition of any chicory in coffee.

CHIFFONNADE – Term used in cooking for all plants, herbal or otherwise, cut into fine strips or ribbons. It is specially used for a mixture of sorrel and lettuce cut into *julienne* strips and cooked in butter.

Most of the *chiffonnades* are used as a garnish for soups.

Lettuce chiffonnade cooked in butter. CHIFFONNADE DE LAITUE AU BEURRE – Slice the leaves of a lettuce finely, leaving aside the coarser leaves. Put the sliced lettuce in a pan with 2 tablespoons (3 tablespoons) butter for every 250 g. (8 oz.) lettuce. Season and cook gently until the liquor has evaporated.

Lettuce chiffonnade with cream. CHIFFONNADE DE LAITUE À LA CRÈME – Prepared in the same way as *Lettuce chiffonnade cooked in butter*. When the lettuce has softened, moisten with a few tablespoons fresh cream and boil down until the liquor has evaporated.

This *chiffonnade* can also be moistened with cream sauce.

Mixed chiffonnade (garnish for soups). CHIFFONNADE MELANGÉE – Prepared in the same way as *Lettuce chiffonnade*, with a mixture of equal parts of sorrel and lettuce leaves.

Sorrel chiffonnade. CHIFFONNADE D'OSEILLE – Prepared with sorrel leaves in the same way as *Lettuce chiffonnade*. It is used specially for *Potage santé* (see SOUPS AND BROTHS).

CHIMNEY HOOK. CRÉMAILLÈRE – A toothed pot-hook used for suspending cauldrons and cooking pots in chimneys.

The symbolic expression *pendre la crémaillère* (to hang up the chimney hook) means the first meal in a new home.

CHINA – See INTERNATIONAL COOKERY.

CHINCHARD – See SAUREL.

CHINE. CHAINE – The bony part adhering to the fillet of a loin of veal, mutton, lamb or pork, or the bony part of a rib or sirloin of beef.

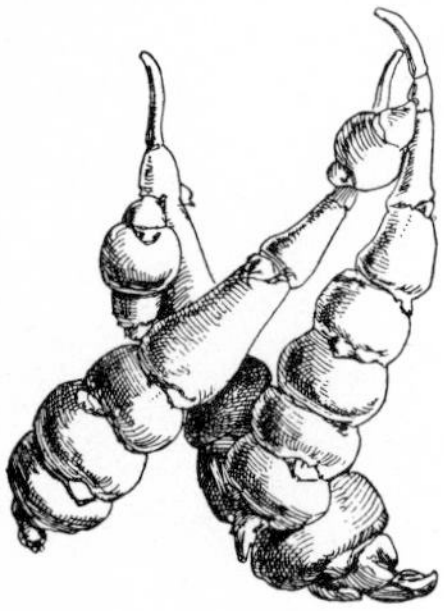

Chinese artichoke

CHINESE ARTICHOKE. CROSNE DE JAPON – Plant originating in China and Japan, first cultivated in France for its edible tubers, at Crosnes (Seine-et-Oise). It is also called *knotroot, chorogi* and *Japanese artichoke*.

This vegetable, delicious when fresh, is white. Tubers which have dried out and been revived by soaking, are sometimes sold as fresh, and can be recognised by a brown discolouration.

The Chinese artichoke is rich in carbohydrates, mostly sugars. It has a pleasant, though rather insipid, taste and is easily digested.

Put the tubers in a strong linen cloth with a handful of sea-salt, and shake them well. Wash them and remove any skin that is left. Blanch in salted water. Simmer in butter without allowing them to brown.

Tubers prepared in this way can be served as they are as a vegetable, or used to garnish a roast.

They can also be prepared *à la crème, aux fines herbes, au jus* and in all the ways given for Jerusalem artichokes (q.v.).

Chinese cabbage or Pe-tsai

CHINESE CABBAGE or PE-TSAI. CHOU DE CHINE – This fairly common cabbage has an oval heart with very tightly closed leaves.

All recipes given for green cabbage can be used. It can also be used in raw salad, or in a marinade, like red cabbage.

CHINOIS (Fruit) – French name for small green or yellow Chinese oranges, which are preserved in brandy.

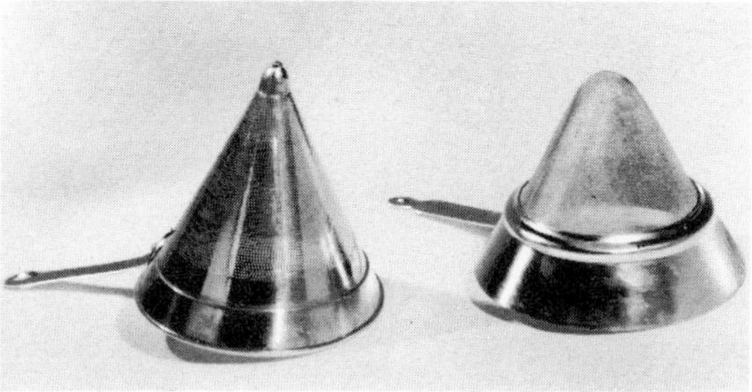

Two types of chinois
(*Larousse*)

CHINOIS (Utensil) – Conical strainer with a fine mesh.

CHIPOLATA – Garnish of braised chestnuts, small glazed onions, diced breast of pork, chipolata sausages, and sometimes glazed carrots (see GARNISHES). Applies also to cuts of butcher's meat and to chicken.

Chipolata was originally an Italian *ragoût* with an onion foundation. The word is also applied to small sausages enclosed in sheep's intestines.

CHIQUETER – To indent the margins of a *vol-au-vent* case, the rim of a tart, or gâteau, with a small knife.

Chives

CHIVES. CIBOULETTE, CIVETTE – Chives are used as a seasoning, mainly in salads.

CHLORIDE. CHLORE – Metalloid that enters the system in the form of sodium chloride. It is found in most of the body tissues and body liquids, particularly the blood.

In certain illnesses a salt-reduced (salt-free) diet is prescribed. This requires not only the drastic cutting down of condiments but also the elimination of foods rich in chloride.

CHOCOLATE. CHOCOLAT – The dried, roasted and polished 'nibs' or almonds of the cacao bean are crushed, and the resulting liquor, if of good quality, is about 50 per cent cocoa fat. When the liquor is partly defatted, it is cooled and solidifies into a hard block, known as *bitter chocolate*. This is used for baking in U.S.A. The cooking chocolate used

The manufacture of chocolate (l'*Encyclopédie*). From left to right: Sifting the almonds of the cacao beans; Roasting; Grating the almonds; Crushing the chocolate

most in England and France is a mixture of the chocolate liquor with some of the fat removed and sugar added. In England this is known as *pure chocolate* and in the U.S.A. as *bitter-sweet chocolate*. *Milk chocolate* has powdered or condensed milk added to the sweetened chocolate and is flavoured with vanilla, almond, cinnamon, etc. Chocolate used in confectionery to coat sweets has added cocoa fat. Cocoa is made from powdered chocolate which contains only 18 per cent fat.

Chocolate is a concentrated food, but should not be abused. The cocoa from which it is made contains theobromine – a nitrogenous substance similar to caffeine, which has a stimulating effect on the nervous system, and makes chocolate an excellent tonic for intellectual fatigue – but also calcium oxalate, which is harmful to the obese and those with rheumatic or liver complaints.

Chocolate is rich in calcium, phosphates and Vitamin D – which helps the bones to absorb calcium – and is therefore a valuable food for children, athletes, heavy workers and intellectuals, but in moderation. It is not recommended for sufferers from constipation, rheumatism, nor for diabetics, who have their own special chocolate. It is better eaten between meals.

Chocolate was brought to Europe by the Spaniards, who had discovered it in Mexico in 1519. Its use spread through Europe soon after.

Brillat-Savarin divulges the secret of increasing the flavour of chocolate which Mme. d'Arestrel, Mother Superior of the Convent of the Visitation at Belley, revealed to him: 'When you want to taste good chocolate, make it the night before in a faience coffee pot, and leave it. The chocolate becomes concentrated during the night and this gives it a much better consistency.'

Preparation of chocolate (beverage). CHOCOLAT – Use 40 g. (1½ oz.) good sweet chocolate for a breakfast cup of liquid. Break the chocolate into pieces, add a little water and hot milk and heat gently. Cover the pan, let the chocolate soften, remove from the heat and whip into a smooth paste. Add 2 or 3 tablespoons boiling water or milk to dilute the paste, then the rest of the liquid, stirring all the time. The chocolate or cocoa must never be allowed to boil.

CHOESELS (Belgian cookery) – A *ragoût* made of tripe and pancreas.

Cleaned, with the fat removed, pancreas resembles meat, but is flat and elongated. Beef pancreas, which is usually used for *choesels*, weighs about 500 g. (18 oz.).

The pancreas is often supplemented by other parts of the animal, which add their qualities to the flavour of the dish. Ox-tail, kidneys, quenelles of calves' sweetbreads, and breast and feet of lamb feature in *choesels*.

The seasoning usually consists of onions, thyme, bay, cloves, nutmeg, pepper and salt. The sauce is combined with a glass of Madeira, or strong Belgian beer (lambic).

Choesels à la bruxelloise (Paul Bouillard's recipe) – Brown an ox tail, cut into pieces, together with two calf (U.S. veal) sweetbreads in 100 g. (4 oz., ½ cup) smoking-hot, clarified beef fat. Reduce the temperature and cook gently for 45 minutes. Add 1 kg. (2¼ lb.) breast of veal, cut into pieces, and 1 large sliced onion. Cook for a further 30 minutes, stirring. Add 1 beef kidney, cut into large pieces. When the kidney has stiffened, moisten the stew with 3 dl. (½ pint, 1¼ cups) lambic (Belgian beer). Add a *bouquet garni* (q.v.). Season with salt and cayenne.

Cook gently for 30 minutes. Add to the *choesels* a bottle of lambic and 5 dl. (scant pint, 2¼ cups) of the cooking liquor from some mushrooms (see COURT-BOUILLON, *White court-bouillon for mushrooms*).

CHOLESTEROL. CHOLESTÉROL – Fatty substance rendered assimilable by the liver. The diets of sufferers from atheroma, arteriosclerosis, gout and liver complaints should contain only moderate amounts of cholesterol.

Below is the proportion of cholesterol contained in some common foods:

Brains	20·00 per 1000
Butter	4·00 ,, ,,
Calf's heart	1·50 ,, ,,
Calf's kidney	3·50 ,, ,,
Calf's lights	4·50 ,, ,,
Calf's liver	2·50 ,, ,,
Calf's sweetbread	2·80 ,, ,,
Egg yolk	20·00 ,, ,,

Other foods contain less than 1 per 1000.

Two substances found in plants (phytosterol and ergosterol) bear a strong resemblance to cholesterol. Therefore those on cholesterol-reduced diets must avoid vegetables that are particularly rich in these two substances, such as the pulses (peas, chick peas, haricot beans, broad beans, lentils) and mushrooms.

Cholesterol has a dual origin. It comes either from cholesterol-rich foods (egg yolk, offal, milk, cream, butter) or as the result of a synthesis effected mainly by the liver. Cholesterol can therefore continue to form itself in the body even when the intake of cholesterol-rich foods is reduced.

Cholesterol has a wide variety of functions. It forms part of the cellular membranes; it enters into the composition of tissue fats; it is present in the plasma to ensure the transference of acids by reserve fats to the liver where they are burned up.

Its oxidation in the liver produces bile acids which act as an emulsifying agent in the intestine.

The synthesis of the corticosurrenaloma hormones seems to follow a parallel course to that of cholesterol.

While it is a delicate matter to wrestle with the excessive formation of cholesterol internally, it is very easy to put a stop to excessive intake of cholesterol simply by eliminating certain foods from the diet.

One should avoid becoming overweight, especially in the early fifties, and it is wiser to limit the percentage of calories derived from fats to 30 per cent.

All foods containing animal fats should be avoided: offal (calves' and sheeps' livers, kidneys, sweetbreads), egg yolks, butter, margarine, oysters, chocolate, milk, cream cheese (apart from small quantities of Gruyère, Port-Salut, Dutch, and skimmed milk cheeses), *charcuterie*, pork, sauces, stews, fried foods. Small quantities of the following fats may be eaten: corn oil, soya oil, walnut oil, saffron oil, sunflower oil, grapeseed oil, and also virgin olive oil from first pressing.

Allowed. Grilled or roasted red meats (in moderation), fish.

Recommended. Vegetables (French beans, endive, spinach, celery, leeks, beetroot, carrots, tomatoes, aubergines, all types of green salad vegetables, asparagus, sorrel, onions, artichokes, melon, cucumber, radishes, potatoes), all kinds of fruit (but not walnuts, hazelnuts, chestnuts, and almonds).

CHOPE – Goblet of glass or earthenware, containing about ⅓ litre (12 fl. oz.), used for beer.

CHOPINE – Old measure for wine, equal to ½ litre (18 fl. oz.).

CHOPPING. HACHAGE – French term for chopping food is *hachage* or *hachement.*

Hachage can also mean food which has been chopped, as in onion *hachage*, though the more common word is *hachis.*

Meat is chopped on a chopping block, usually made of cross-grained planks set upright in a wooden frame. The chopping blocks or tables must not be washed with water but scraped with a special scraper, thoroughly dried with sawdust, and then rubbed clean.

'CHOPS'. BABINES – Slang name for lips of some animals, such as dogs or monkeys. The expression 'to lick one's chops' indicates satisfaction at a good dish.

CHOPSTICKS. BAGUETTES – The 'fork' of the Far East, indispensable to an Asian meal, made in ivory, ebony, or plastic. The Chinese call them 'lively fellows'. They are not difficult to manipulate and can be adapted to the requirements of various dishes. They are used, for example, to pick up pieces of food, also to push rice into the mouth whenever it is permitted to raise the bowl to chin level.

CHORON – *Chef de cuisine* of the Voisin restaurant.

CHOU (Pastry) – Bun made with *chou pastry*, which is pushed through a forcing (pastry) bag onto a metal baking tray. The *chou*, which is round, is either served as it is, or stuffed with cream or some other preparation.

Chou pastry or cream puff pastry. PÂTE À CHOU – Ordinary *chou pastry* is made as follows:

Ingredients. 1 litre (1¾ pints, generous quart) water, 375 g. (13 oz., generous 1½ cups) butter, 500 g. (18 oz., 4½ cups) sifted flour, 1 tablespoon salt, 25 g. (1 oz., 2 tablespoons) sugar, 16 eggs; 1 tablespoon orange blossom water or 1 teaspoon orange extract.

Method. Boil the water, butter, salt and sugar together in a deep flat-bottomed pan. When the mixture boils, remove the pan from the heat and pour in the sifted flour. Mix well. Dry out the mixture over a low heat, working it with a wooden spoon until it comes away from the sides of the pan and oils a little. Add the eggs, off the heat, two at a time, stirring vigorously, and then the flavouring.

Various cakes such as éclairs, Jacob's ladders, *Saint-Honoré, profiteroles*, are made with this pastry, as are soufflé fritters.

Cooking the choux or cream puffs. DRESSAGE ET CUISSON DES CHOUX – Put the mixture through a forcing-bag onto a buttered baking tray, allowing a space between each. Make them the size of a walnut or smaller if they are to be used as *profiteroles*. Brush with beaten egg. Cook in the oven at 200°C. (400°F., Gas Mark 6) for 15 minutes. When cold, these buns are filled with *French pastry cream* (see CREAMS) or with any other filling, according to the recipe.

Choux or cream puffs à la cévenole. CHOUX À LA CÉVENOLE – These are made like *Choux or cream puffs à la crème* (see below). When cold, fill with a purée of chestnuts mixed with whipped cream and flavoured with kirsch.

Squeezing chou paste onto baking tray (*Larousse*)

Choux or cream puffs à la Chantilly. CHOUX À LA CHANTILLY – Prepare and cook as for *Choux or cream puffs à la crème* (see below). Leave them to cool, split and fill with *Chantilly cream* (see CREAMS) flavoured with vanilla.

Chocolate choux or cream puffs. CHOUX AU CHOCOLAT – Prepared in the same way as *Coffee choux or cream puffs* (see below).

Coffee choux or cream puffs. CHOUX AU CAFÉ – Fill the cooked puffs with *French pastry cream* (see CREAMS) flavoured with coffee essence. Glaze with sugar flavoured with coffee.

Choux or cream puffs à la crème. CHOUX À LA CRÈME – When the puffs are cold, slit them on one side and fill with *French pastry cream* (see CREAMS). Close the puffs and sprinkle with icing sugar.

Choux or cream puffs à la frangipane. CHOUX À LA FRANGIPANE – The same as *Choux or cream puffs à la crème*, with *Frangipane cream* (see CREAMS).

Glazed choux or cream puffs. CHOUX GLACÉS – Ordinary puffs filled with cream or any other filling, and glazed with sugar cooked to the crack degree (see SUGAR, *Sugar boiling*).

Choux or cream puffs Montmorency. CHOUX MONTMORENCY – Made like *Choux or cream puffs à la crème.* Fill the puffs, when cold, with a mixture of cherries and *French pastry cream* (see CREAMS) flavoured with cherry brandy.

Choux or cream puffs à la normande – CHOUX À LA NORMANDE – *Choux* filled with a stiff apple purée mixed with a third of its weight of *French pastry cream* (see CREAMS) flavoured with calvados.

Plate of cream puffs

CHRISTMAS. NOËL – In the fourth century Pope Julius I fixed 25 December as the date on which the birth of Christ was to be celebrated.

In France, the main Christmas meal is served on the night

of 24 to 25 December, after the celebration of Midnight Mass. This meal is called the *reveillon*.

The menu for the *reveillon* and for Christmas Day itself – essentially a family celebration – must include dishes which have a ritual significance. Even if the *reveillon* menu includes expensive delicacies such as *foie gras*, truffles, game of various kinds, rare fish and shellfish, it must also include, in deference to tradition, a black or white pudding, sometimes both, and a goose or turkey with chestnuts, often enriched with truffles.

In Britain, Christmas Day is celebrated with even more gastronomic splendour than in France.

'For many of the islanders,' wrote Alfred Suzanne in his book *la Cuisine anglaise et americaine*, 'this anniversary is memorable (apart from all religious significance) because it evokes a great slaughter of turkeys, geese and all kinds of game, a wholesale massacre of fat oxen, pigs and sheep. They envisage garlands of black puddings, sausages and saveloys . . . mountains of plum-puddings and ovens-full of mince-pies. . . .

'On that day no-one in England may go hungry. . . . This is a family gathering and on every table the same menu is prepared. A joint of beef, a turkey or goose, which is usually the *pièce de résistance*, accompanied by a ham, sausages, and game; then follow the inevitable plum-pudding and the famous mince pies.'

Chub (*J. Boyer*)

CHUB. CHEVAINE, CHEVESNE – Freshwater fish with a long spindly body, the dorsal fin set below the ventral opening.

The common chub, called in English, *coheven, nab, botling,* and in French, *meunier, cabot, chabot, chavanne, testard, rotisson, caboda,* etc. sometimes reaches a size of 50 cm. (20 inches).

In U.S.A. chubs, known as the *longjaw, blackfin* and *bloater*, are found in the Great Lakes. Lake Superior is the source of most of the blackfin, which is the only chub used extensively as fresh fish.

All the recipes given for the féra (q.v.) (a fish belonging to the salmon family) are applicable to chub. This fish is also used in the *matelote* (q.v.).

CHUTNEY – Condiment of Indian origin which is made commercially. It is a purée made with seeded raisins, garlic, shallots, pimentos, apple, mustard, brown sugar and vinegar.

Bring 1 litre ($1\frac{3}{4}$ pints, generous quart) white vinegar to the boil. Add $1\frac{1}{2}$ kg. ($3\frac{1}{4}$ lb.) cooking apples, peeled and sliced. Cook them and add 500 g. (18 oz., $2\frac{1}{2}$ cups) brown sugar, 25 g. (1 oz., $\frac{1}{3}$ cup) finely chopped chillis, 200 g. (7 oz., $1\frac{1}{4}$ cups) seeded raisins, 500 g. (18 oz., 3 cups) finely chopped, preserved lemon peel, 500 g. (18 oz., 2 cups) diced preserved ginger, 2 crushed garlic cloves. Season with 4 teaspoons salt, 125 g. (4 oz., 1 cup) mustard grains, and 15 g. ($\frac{1}{2}$ oz., 2 tablespoons) powdered ginger. If possible, add 500 g. (18 oz.) preserved mangoes. Cook for 8 minutes. Put into warm glass jars while hot, and seal.

Ordinary bottling jars with rubber rings and screw caps are best.

CICADA. CIGALE – Insect common to southern countries. According to Aristotle, the Greeks were very fond of cicadas and their larvae.

CIDER. CIDRE – Fermented drink with an apple base. It was already being made in Normandy in the thirteenth century and is mentioned in the Chronicles of Charlemagne. Special apples are used, sweet, acid, and tart, which have given a reputation to the cider of the districts where they grow. There are early and late species. A good cider is made with $\frac{1}{3}$ sweet apples and $\frac{2}{3}$ sour and acid apples. Early ripening apples are put in the press as soon as they are ready; the rest should be stored in attics, and not in heaps at the foot of trees.

The apples are crushed and put in a press. The *marc* (what is left of the fruit after the juice has been pressed out) is sprinkled with water and pressed a second time.

Fermentation is started in the same way as with wine. Cider is subject to the same diseases as wine, and the same remedies can be applied to it.

There are different commercial brands of cider: sweet cider and bottled cider, sparkling or not, according to whether it has been bottled before or after complete fermentation in cask. It is a refreshing drink and less alcoholic than wine.

Apple press for cider

CIERP DE LUCHON – See CHEESE.

CIGAR, CIGARETTE – Tobacco rounds off a meal in a pleasant way for those who like it. Smoking before or even during the meal is a heresy and destroys the sense of taste. Professional tasters have to give up smoking altogether.

CINNAMON. CANNELLE – Bark of the cinnamon tree. The name is also given to other kinds of bark which resemble cinnamon in smell or flavour. The only medicinal species is the *Ceylon cinnamon* which is found in the shops in the form of thin sticks, about 1 cm. ($\frac{1}{2}$ inch) in diameter and up to 1 m. (1 yard) in length, consisting of rolled pieces of bark, each about $\frac{1}{4}$ mm. ($\frac{1}{80}$ inch) thick. It is yellow in colour, easily breakable, with a spicy aroma and a very fine, sweet, hot taste.

The *Chinese cinnamon* (*Cassia lignea*) is found in shorter, thicker sticks, formed of one layer of rolled bark, yellowish brown in colour, with a few brown or black spots, easily breakable but with a less pleasant aroma and taste.

Cinnamon contains a volatile oil. Powdered cinnamon is often made from inferior quality bark and adulterated. Cinnamon sticks are sometimes dried (with the essential oils extracted) before being sold, but such fraudulent practice is rare.

Cinnamon trees

CINNAMONE – Old name for a spice which is probably cinnamon (*cannelle*).

CISELER – French term for superficial incisions on the back of a fish to hasten its cooking. Also applied to the slicing of any kind of leafy herb which is to be cut up into *julienne* (q.v.) strips or into a *chiffonnade* (q.v.).

CITRIC ACID. CITRIQUE – Organic acid found in a great many fruits (lemons, oranges, gooseberries, raspberries, etc.) and some other plants. It is extracted from lemon juice, or it is prepared commercially by fermentation of glucose. It appears in large fragile crystals, with an agreeable acid flavour, and is soluble in water. It keeps well when dry, but solutions of citric acid are rapidly invaded by moulds.

Citric acid is used for making lemonade and also orange and lemon syrups, etc.

Citric acid syrup – See SYRUP.

Citron

CITRON. CÉDRAT – Species of lemon with a very thick coruscated skin, cultivated on the Mediterranean coast.

It is highly perfumed and, unlike the ordinary lemon or orange, is seldom eaten in a natural state. Because of its thick skin it is chiefly preserved, and is much used in cake-making and confectionery.

In Corsica, where it is widely cultivated, a liqueur called *cédratine* is made with the fruit.

CITRONELLA. CITRONELLE – Common name for *Collinsonia canadensis*, a coarse plant of the mint family. It exudes a penetrating scent, rather like lemon. The leaves are used for seasoning. Digestive liqueurs are made from its flowers.

CITRUS AURANTIUM (Seville orange). BIGARADIER, BIGARADE – Species of bitter orange used in confectionery and in distilling certain liqueurs and drinks. It is used in cookery for spicing various sauces for game, in particular for waterfowl, and also for making bitter orange marmalade.

The green leaves are principally used as an infusion (see TISANE).

The flowers, or orange blossoms, are used in confectionery, pharmaceutics and perfumery (distilled orange blossom water, essence of neroli).

CITRUS FRUIT. AGRUMES – Collective noun for oranges, lemons, tangerines, grapefruit and other cultivated *Rutaceae*.

CITRUS MEDICA – See AIGRE DE CÈDRE.

CIVET – Word mainly used for *ragoûts* of furred game, which are moistened with red wine, garnished with small onions, lardoons and mushrooms, and combined, when cooked, with the blood of the animal in question. This liaison with blood is essential to the dish.

The name of this preparation comes from the word *cive* (green onion) because the dish was flavoured with these onions.

It can be made with any furred game, and also with feathered game or fowl. There are even *civets de viandes* in some districts, and spiny lobster *civets* in Languedoc.

Civet of hare – See HARE.

Civet of spiny lobster – See SPINY LOBSTER, *Spiny lobster stew*.

CLAFOUTI – Fruit pastry or thick fruit pancake from the Limousin, usually made with black cherries.

Ingredients. 125 g. (4½ oz., generous cup) flour, 2 eggs, 100 g. (4 oz., scant cup) powdered sugar, half of which is kept to sprinkle over the fruit, 2 dl. (⅓ pint, scant cup) boiled milk, a pinch of salt, and 400 g. (14 oz.) cherries. Fill the pastry with the stoned cherries, and bake in a buttered flan case in the oven.

CLAIRE – Name of the marine enclosures in the Marennes region where the oysters are left to go green. (See OYSTER, *Green Marennes oysters*).

CLAIRET – Formerly, *clairet* was a spiced and flavoured wine.

It was well known at the time of Charlemagne, and was called *vin piment*, or simply *piment*. In this form it was drunk as an apéritif, made in the same way that vermouth and other mixed wines are made now.

This wine was not the same as *vin clairet*, which was a natural, raw wine, neither red nor white, a 'grey wine' as it would be called today. It was of *vin clairet* that poets sang in the eighteenth century.

Le Grand d'Aussy says of the other *clairet*: 'Something had been lacking at a feast if *piment* had not been served'; this being the name given to the wine in the thirteenth century. *Clairet* or *piment* was made in the religious houses. He also says the *pouillis* (statements of ecclesiastical profits in a province), prove that in the twelfth and fourteenth centuries the priors of the deanery of Châteaufort, on the Feast of the Assumption, were each in turn required to provide *piment* for the *chauvines* (nuns or postulants). This apéritif was made only with *vin clairet*. It had several different shades: grey, straw coloured, 'partridge-eye', etc.

Current legislation of *appellations d'origine* authorises the use of the word *clairet* in Bordeaux and Burgundy; Bordeaux clairet, Bordeaux supérieur clairet, Bourgogne clairet.

The expression *clairet* designates a pale red, light-bodied wine, not quite a rosé. It should be drunk young and slightly chilled.

CLAIRETTE – Name given to a sparkling white wine made in Drôme, where it is called Clairette de Die. Also the name of a white grape grown in the Mediterranean regions.

CLARET – Name given in England to red Bordeaux wines.

CLAM. PALOURDE – Name for many edible bivalve molluscs which live in slimy sand and are found at low tide.

Some of these molluscs are cultivated in special beds along the beaches of Auray, Croisic and in the Bay of Bourgneuf. Auray and Roscoff are the principal French centres of the clam trade.

In many of the places along the Atlantic coast the name *palourde* is also applied to other molluscs *Tapé à stries croisées, tapé virginal,* and *tapé à stries fines*, are called *palourdou* in La Rochelle. In Provence these molluscs are called *clovisses*.

They are mainly eaten raw in France but the North Americans, who are very fond of this shellfish, prepare it in many ways.

All recipes given for *clovisses*, oysters, mussels and other shellfish can be applied to them.

Clam chowder – See SOUP.

CLARIFICATION – Clarifying of food, usually liquids. The process varies for different substances.

Clarification of bouillon. See BOUILLON.

Clarification of butter. CLARIFICATION DU BEURRE – Heat the butter on a *very gentle heat*; the butter melts and appears as clear as olive oil while a white deposit forms on the bottom of the pan. Strain the clear butter into another receptacle.

Clarification of liquids and fruit juices. CLARIFICATION DES LIQUIDES ET DES SUCS DE FRUITS – Most liquids can be clarified by filtering; fruit juices are clarified by light fermentation.

Clarification of sugar – See SUGAR.

CLARY. ORVALE – Common name of the *Salvia sclarea* (herb of the sage family) formerly used in England for flavouring certain pastries. When infused in wine it has a muscat taste. It is one of the herbs used in making Italian vermouth.

CLAVARIA or CLUB-TOP MUSHROOM. BARBE-DE-CHÈVRE, CLAVAIRE – Capless, spindle-shaped mushroom which grows into branches of various colours, white, pink or purple. It is edible but tough, indigestible and rather insipid.

It can be prepared like other mushrooms: sautéed in oil or butter; *à la provençale; à la crème*, etc.

CLAYÈRE – Bed where oysters are fattened.

CLAYON – Small mat of rush or straw on which certain foods are placed. The same name is given to small wire trays.

CLEMENTINE. CLÉMENTINE – Fruit of the clementine tree, a hybrid of unknown origin discovered at the beginning of the twentieth century. It seems to be closely related to the mandarin tree.

The clementine is a small, round, orange-coloured fruit, flattened at both ends. The flesh is sweet, juicy and moderately acid. The true clementine is seedless. Recently the *Montreal clementine*, an earlier and more prolific variety containing about twenty seeds, has been developed.

The clementine is cultivated in North Africa and Spain, and is marketed between the middle of October and the end of January. Its development has been detrimental to that of the mandarin, as clementines have a more delicate flavour and are often seedless.

It is usually eaten as a fresh fruit.

CLIMAT – Certain vineyards, especially in the Côte de Nuits district, are so called because each has a specific climate.

CLISSE – Small tray or mat, made of wicker or rush, used to drain cheeses. Also a wicker covering round a bottle.

CLOCHE – Silver or plated cover for keeping dishes warm; also a glass cover under which cheese is kept, or a glass utensil used as a cover during cooking (see MUSHROOMS, *Mushrooms sous cloche*).

CLOSE (Jean-Joseph) – Famous pastry-cook born in Normandy, said to have invented the *pâté de foie gras aux truffes* in 1782, when he was in service with the maréchal de Contades, governor of the province of Alsace at the time. However, the *pâté* and the *terrine de foie gras* were known in the south-west of France before the time of Close. It is possible that Close popularised the dish in Alsace, and perhaps perfected it.

CLOS VOUGEOT – Famous vineyard of the Côte de Nuits (situated in the commune of Vougeot) which has the right to a special *appellation contrôlée* (see BURGUNDY). Apart from its wines, Clos Vougeot is famous for the fact that the château in the middle of the vineyards is the headquarters of the *Confrérie du tastevin* (see CONFRÉRIES VINEUSES).

The grape of the Clos Vougeot wines is the Pinot; the Gamay serves the remainder of the commune. The geological composition of the soil and subsoil are determinant factors in the particular flavour of the wine produced. Oenologists and gourmets attach great importance to which vineyard a wine comes from, and rightly so. In fact it is the vine, the microclimate, the year and the soil that determine the personality of a wine.

CLOTH FILTER. BLANCHET – White woollen cloth filter for straining syrup and thick liquids.

CLOUD. LOUCHIR – To become cloudy. This term is used of a liquid which is no longer clear.

CLOUTER (To stud) – An operation consisting of the insertion of small pieces of truffles, cooked ham, and scarlet tongue into meat, fowl, game.

Fish are studded with truffles, fillets of anchovy and gherkins.

CLOVE. GIROFLE (CLOU DE) – Flowers of the clove tree picked in bud and dried in the sun. The tree probably comes originally from China, but was first cultivated in the Moluccas by the Dutch, who had the monopoly. It was introduced into Réunion and Mauritius by Governor Poivre, and later into the West Indies, Cayenne and Zanzibar.

Cloves have a four-sided stem and a calyx with four sepals.

They have an aromatic scent and a hot spicy flavour, and are used for seasoning in cookery. They are sometimes sold mixed with cloves which have already been used in the manufacture of dyes or liqueurs. The clove matrix or fruits of the clove tree are also sold as cloves.

The clove is an excellent condiment and a powerful antiseptic.

CLOVISSE – Bivalve mollusc which is like the *palourde*; it is eaten fresh like oysters or cooked like mussels, and is served with or without lemon.

CLUPEIDAE. CLUPES – Family of seawater and freshwater fish which include shad, herring, sardine and anchovy.

CNICAUT – Edible wild cardoon, with a taste of cabbage.

COAGULATE. FIGER – To thicken or congeal, when applied to fats.

COAL FISH. CHARBONNIER – A kind of cod fished in the North Sea. Prepared like cod (see COD).

COASTER. GALERIE (BORDURE) DE PLAT – Ring of silver or silver-plate made to fit the inner diameter of round dishes. This ornamental circle is set in the well of the dish to hold in position the garnishes arranged round the main course.

COAT. ENROBER – To dip food either in batter or in a sauce which masks it entirely, such as *chaud-froid sauce*.

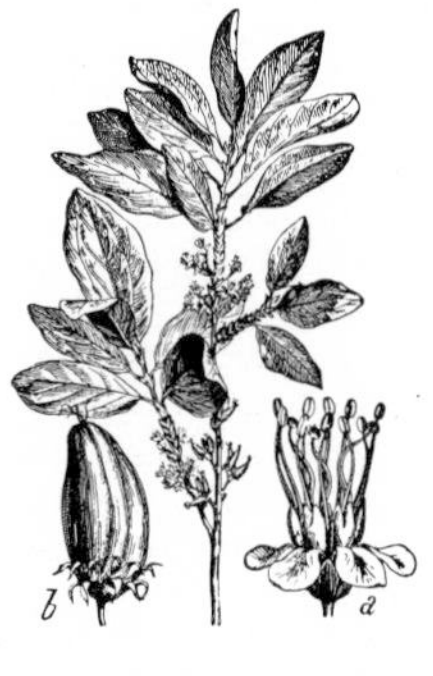

Coca:
a. Flower; b. Fruit

COCA – Peruvian shrub, the leaves of which are chewed by the Indians. Considered an economical food, its properties are due to the effect produced by its alkaloid, cocaine, which is as stimulating as tea or coffee.

It is used as an infusion, as a wine, as an elixir, and also used as an ingredient of certain cakes.

COCHINEAL. COCHENILLE – Insect used to prepare a red dye called carmine. The best-known cochineal is that of nopal (cochineal cactus).

The female insect is used, collected after she is fertilised and before the complete development of the eggs. Gray cochineals are the most sought after, but there are also red and black varieties.

They are put in the oven on metal sheets for a few moments, or plunged into boiling water, and dried.

Carmine is used for colouring in cooking and cake-mixing.

COCHLEARIA. COCHLÉARIA – Type of cruciferous plant, of which one species, the wild horseradish (*Cochléaria de Bretagne*) grows on the sea coast, particularly in Brittany, in England and in Ireland. It is known as scurvy-grass in the United States.

COCIDO (Spanish cookery) – Popular Spanish soup, also known under the name of *Olla podrida* (q.v.).

COCK-A-LEEKIE or COCKY-LEEKY (Scottish cookery) – Soup made of cock and leeks. (See SOUP.)

COCKLE. BUCARDE – European marine bivalve mollusc of the genus *Cardium*, found mainly at the mouth of rivers. The type found on the Atlantic coast of France, called *bucarde sourdon*, is edible. It is also known in France under the names of *coque, sourdon* and *poor man's oyster*.

Cockles are eaten raw and can also be prepared like mussels (q.v.).

COCK'S COMB. CRÊTE DE COQ – Fleshy excrescence, often voluminous, found on the heads of cocks and other gallinaceans. It is used chiefly as a garnish for *entrées*.

Method of cleaning and cooking cocks' combs. Prick the combs lightly with a needle and put them under the cold tap, pressing them with the fingers to dispel the blood.

Cover with cold water and cook until the water reaches a temperature of 40° or 45°C. (110°F.), when the skin of the combs begins to detach itself. Drain the combs and rub them one by one in a cloth sprinkled with fine salt.

Remove the outer skin; put the combs in cold water, and when they are white plunge them into a boiling *White court-bouillon* (see COURT-BOUILLON). Cook for 35 minutes.

Attelets of cocks' combs. ATTELETS DE CRÊTES DE COQ – Cook the cocks' combs, keeping them as white as possible and rather firm. Drain and wipe them, and thread on skewers, the frilled edge uppermost.

Cocks' combs en attereaux. CRÊTES DE COQ EN ATTEREAUX – Cook the cocks' combs in the manner described above and leave to cool. Drain, wipe, and marinate them in oil and lemon juice. Add chopped parsley.

Drain, and impale them three at a time on silver skewers. Dip in egg and breadcrumbs and fry in clarified butter.

Cocks' combs en attereaux à la Villeroi. CRÊTES DE COQ EN ATTEREAUX À LA VILLEROI – Cook the cocks' combs in a *White court-bouillon* (see COURT-BOUILLON), drain and dry them, and cover with *Villeroi sauce* (see SAUCE). Leave to cool on a grid. Cover the combs with egg, sprinkle with breadcrumbs, and fry in clarified butter.

Cocks' combs barquettes and tartlets. BARQUETTES ET TARTELETTES DE CRÊTES DE COQ – These are made in the same way as *barquettes* and tartlets filled with various *salpicon* preparations. (See HORS-D'ŒUVRE, *Hot hors-d'œuvre*.)

Salpicon of cocks' combs à blanc. SALPICON DE CRÊTES DE COQ À BLANC – Cook the cocks' combs in the manner described above, and dice them. Heat for a few moments in wine or liqueur. Add a few tablespoons *Velouté sauce* or *Allemande sauce* (see SAUCE).

This *salpicon* is used as a filling for *bouchées, barquettes*, tartlets, or other similar preparations.

Salpicon of cocks' combs à brun. SALPICON DE CRÊTES DE COQ À BRUN – Prepared in the same way as *Salpicon of cocks' combs à blanc*, but replace the white sauce with a concentrated, thickened brown stock, to which Madeira has been added before boiling down.

Stuffed cocks' combs. CRÊTES DE COQ FARCIES – Choose very large combs and cook them in *White court-bouillon* (see COURT-BOUILLON), keeping them rather firm. Leave to cool, drain and wipe them, and slit them down the centre of the fattest part. Stuff each with a small ball of forcemeat. Cover the combs in *Villeroi sauce* (see SAUCE). Dip in egg, sprinkle with breadcrumbs, and fry in clarified butter.

COCKTAIL – Drink of alcoholic liquor mixed with other liquid and aromatic ingredients, stirred or shaken with ice

Cocktail set (*Christofle. 'Manhattan'. Phot. Kollar*)

Cocktail accessories (*Christofle*)

and served ice-cold in special glasses. The origin of the word 'cocktail' is uncertain. Probably Anglo-American, it might refer to the shimmering which results from mixing coloured liqueurs, or, according to some etymologists, because the primitive cocktail of the Manhattan pioneers consisted of cocks' tails, dipped in a concoction of pimentos, with which they tickled their throats to incite them to drink. The French origin of the word *coquetel* is, however, told by a number of authors, who maintain that it was in Bordeaux, towards the end of the eighteenth century, that this kind of drink was invented.

The cocktail party is a phenomenon of the mid-twentieth century, and is used for entertaining small or large gatherings. On such an occasion one or more kinds of cocktails are served as well as 'straight' liquor, usually Scotch, Irish, Bourbon or rye whisky, poured over ice cubes ('on the rocks') or with crushed ice ('in a mist'), and served in short glasses; or mixed with water or carbonated water and served in long 'highball' glasses. Accompanying these drinks are *hors-d'œuvre* that can be eaten while holding the glass. These range from the simple to the elaborate.

There are a great many cocktails which have been in vogue from time to time, either because of their exotic nature or because of their fantastic names, but certain mixtures have stood the test of time and continue to win the approval of connoisseurs. These include the following:

Dry Manhattan (Bronx) – 3 parts whisky (Scotch, rye, or Bourbon), 1 part dry French vermouth. Garnish: twist of lemon peel.

Gin and Dubonnet (Dubonnet cocktail) – 2 parts Dubonnet and 1 part gin, combined with cracked ice, shaken hard in a cocktail shaker and strained into cocktail glasses.

Manhattan – 3 parts whisky (Scotch, rye or Bourbon), 1 part sweet Italian vermouth and a dash of Angostura bitters. Garnish (optional): a maraschino cherry.

Martini (gin and vermouth) – 3 parts gin, 1 part dry French vermouth, garnished with an olive, a twist of lemon peel or a pearl onion (in which case the drink is called a Gibson). Proportions may vary; some people prefer a straight Martini which means less gin and more vermouth. A sweet Martini would contain 5 parts gin and 1 part sweet Italian vermouth, and is garnished with a twist of orange peel.

Old-fashioned – Whisky (Scotch, rye, or Bourbon), Angostura bitters or cherry juice, sugar. Garnish: cherries, orange slices, lemon slices or pineapple wedges. A small lump of sugar moistened with the Angostura bitters or cherry juice is placed in an 'old fashioned' glass. Ice cubes are added and $\frac{1}{2}$ dl. (3 tablespoons, scant $\frac{1}{4}$ cup) whisky poured over them. One or more of the garnishes are added or, if preferred, a piece of lemon peel is twisted over the drink. A 'muddler' (stirring stick) is placed in each glass.

Pink gin – Made by putting Angostura bitters in a glass and agitating the glass so that the bitters coat the inside. The bitters are then poured away and gin added until the drink is pale pink.

Rum Daiquiri – 1 part lime juice, 1 part sugar syrup, 4 parts Bacardi rum. Blend syrup and lime juice. Add rum and finely crushed ice. Shake hard and strain into chilled glasses.

Whisky sour – 4 parts whisky (Scotch, rye, or Bourbon), 1 part orange juice, 1 part lemon juice, sweetening to taste. Garnish: maraschino cherry, orange peel or lemon peel.

The following is a selection of various types of cocktail, classified for easy reference:

Classic cocktails – *Adam I.C.D.* $\frac{1}{4}$ tin grapefruit, $\frac{1}{2}$ bitter Cinzano, $\frac{1}{4}$ dry Cinzano, $\frac{1}{4}$ gin.

Alexandra. $\frac{1}{3}$ fresh cream, $\frac{1}{3}$ Crème de Cacao, $\frac{1}{3}$ Cognac.

Americano. $\frac{1}{3}$ bitter Campari, $\frac{1}{3}$ sweet vermouth, $\frac{1}{3}$ dry vermouth, twist of lemon peel.

Arc-en-ciel. Pour in without mixing: $\frac{1}{4}$ grenadine, $\frac{1}{4}$ Marie Brizard, $\frac{1}{4}$ Véramint Ricqlès, $\frac{1}{4}$ green Chartreuse.

Bacardi. $\frac{3}{5}$ rum, $\frac{1}{5}$ grenadine, $\frac{1}{5}$ lemon juice.

Black velvet. $\frac{1}{2}$ stout, $\frac{1}{2}$ Champagne.

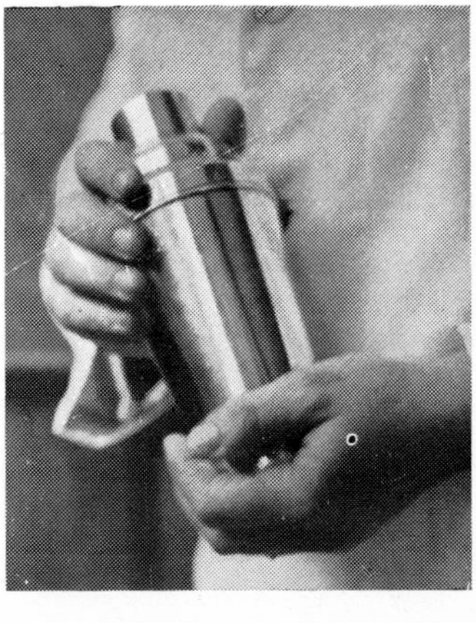

Cocktail shaker (*Larousse*)

Bloody Mary. 1 tin tomato juice, 1 dash lemon juice, 2 dashes Worcester sauce, 3 dashes vodka, salt and cayenne pepper.

Bronx. $\frac{3}{6}$ gin, $\frac{1}{6}$ Orange juice, $\frac{1}{6}$ Cinzano rosso, $\frac{1}{6}$ Cinzano bianco.

Canasta. $\frac{1}{3}$ Cinzano bianco, $\frac{1}{3}$ gin, $\frac{1}{3}$ maraschino.

Champagne cocktail. 1 glass Champagne, 1 dash Angostura bitters, twist of lemon peel, 1 sugar lump.

Champagne flip. 1 glass Champagne, 1 beaten egg yolk, twist of lemon peel. Sprinkle with grated nutmeg.

Cherry blossom. $\frac{1}{2}$ Cognac, $\frac{1}{2}$ cherry brandy, 1 dash Curaçao, 1 dash grenadine, 1 dash lemon juice.

Cinzano cobbler. $\frac{1}{2}$ Cinzano rosso, $\frac{1}{4}$ Curaçao, $\frac{1}{4}$ kirsch, 1 tablespoon sugar, 1 slice orange, diced fresh fruit.

Cuba libre. 1 glass rum, 1 glass Coca-Cola.

Curnonsky. $\frac{2}{5}$ Cognac, $\frac{3}{5}$ Cointreau, 1 tablespoon orange juice.

Daiquiri. $\frac{2}{3}$ rum, $\frac{1}{3}$ lemon juice, 1 tablespoon grenadine.

Dubonnet fizz. 1 glass Dubonnet, juice of $\frac{1}{2}$ orange. Top up with Champagne.

Evening delight. 1 glass rye whiskey, 1 dash Curaçao, 1 dash apricot brandy.

Gin fizz. 1 glass gin, juice of 1 lemon, 1 tablespoon sugar, soda water.

Half and half. $\frac{1}{2}$ pale ale, $\frac{1}{2}$ stout.

Maca. $\frac{1}{3}$ gin, $\frac{1}{3}$ sweet Martini, $\frac{1}{3}$ Noilly Prat, 2 dashes cassis, 1 slice orange.

Manhattan. $\frac{2}{3}$ Scotch whisky, $\frac{1}{3}$ Noilly Prat, 2 dashes Angostura bitters, 2 dashes Cointreau, 1 twist of lemon, 1 cherry. *Dry.* $\frac{1}{3}$ white vermouth, $\frac{2}{3}$ gin, 1 olive.

Mr. Callaghan. $\frac{2}{5}$ dry Cinzano, $\frac{1}{5}$ apricot brandy, $\frac{2}{5}$ Angostura bitters.

Negroni. $\frac{1}{3}$ gin, $\frac{1}{3}$ Campari, $\frac{1}{3}$ Cinzano rosso, twist of lemon peel.

Planter's. $\frac{2}{3}$ rum, $\frac{1}{6}$ lemon juice, $\frac{1}{6}$ orange juice.

Porto flip. 1 glass port, 1 egg yolk, 1 tablespoon sugar. Sprinkle with grated nutmeg.

Rose. $\frac{5}{10}$ gin, $\frac{3}{10}$ Noilly Prat, $\frac{2}{10}$ cherry Rocher, 1 cherry.

Sherry cobbler. 1 glass sherry, 2 dashes Curaçao, 3 dashes orange juice, 1 slice orange, 1 slice lemon.

Side car. $\frac{1}{4}$ lemon juice, $\frac{1}{2}$ Cognac, $\frac{1}{4}$ white Curaçao.

Sputnik. $\frac{2}{3}$ vodka, $\frac{1}{3}$ dry Cinzano, 1 cocktail onion.

Tom Collins. 1 glass gin, 1 tablespoon sugar, 1 tablespoon lemon juice, soda-water.

Coffee-based cocktails – *Roman holiday* (for 4 people). 100 g. (4 oz., $1\frac{1}{3}$ cups) very finely ground coffee, 3 dl. ($\frac{1}{2}$ pint, $1\frac{1}{4}$ cups) water, 2 to 5 teaspoons icing sugar, according to taste, 3 to 4 ice cubes per glass.

Make the coffee in a *bain-marie.* Crush the ice cubes and fill the glasses three-quarters full with them. Sprinkle with the sugar. Pour the boiling coffee over. Romans top this drink with a generous swirl of sweetened Chantilly cream flavoured with cinnamon.

Bourbon coffee. Black coffee, ice, Bourbon whiskey. Fill the glasses with ice and pour a liqueur glass of Bourbon whiskey in each. Top up with black coffee. If you like sugar or cream, or both, add these and stir. If the coffee is prechilled less ice is required.

Milk-based cocktails – *Tango.* 1 cup milk, 2 ice cubes, 2 tablespoons fruit syrup, (grenadine, cassis, raspberry, strawberry, pineapple or orange). Shake vigorously. The cocktail must be frothy.

Brésilien. Evaporated milk diluted with $\frac{1}{3}$ water, 2 teaspoons soluble coffee, $\frac{1}{4}$ teaspoon cinnamon, sugar to taste, ice cubes.

Prepare as for *Négrillonne* (see below), the chocolate being replaced by coffee.

Négrillonne. Evaporated milk diluted with $\frac{1}{3}$ water, 1 tablespoon chocolate powder, $\frac{1}{4}$ teaspoon vanilla or cinnamon, sugar to taste, ice cubes.

Blend the chocolate, vanilla and sugar. Add the milk diluted with the water and pour into the mixer or shaker. Shake until frothy. Serve with ice.

Tea-based cocktails – *Casbah.* This Algerian drink is an excellent thirst quencher. Drunk hot, even very hot, during the hottest season, it is delightfully refreshing.

1 tablespoon green tea, 1 tablespoon mint tea, 100 to 150 g. (4 to 5 oz., 1 cup) loaf sugar, $\frac{3}{4}$ litre ($1\frac{1}{3}$ pints) water.

Mix the green and mint tea together and leave them to infuse for some time. Crush the sugar and add gradually to the tea, until it all dissolves. The infusion must be very strong and sweet, almost syrup-like in consistency. Serve very hot with a fresh leaf of mint in each glass.

This beverage can be entirely prepared from powdered mint, in which case honey is substituted for sugar.

Tea punch (for 4 people). 2 teaspoons tea, rind of $\frac{1}{2}$ lemon, water, 3 tablespoons sugar, 1 dl. (6 tablespoons, scant $\frac{1}{2}$ cup) rum, ice cubes.

Make the tea, but add the lemon rind before pouring in the boiling water. Infuse for quarter of an hour. Add the sugar. Leave the tea to get quite cold; it can be placed in the refrigerator. To serve, place a large cube of sugar in each glass, pour in the rum and, lastly, the cold tea.

This cocktail is often drunk through a straw stuck through a slice of lemon.

Vitamin-based cocktails – The following cocktails have been specially devised by the dietician Gayelord Hauser.

Cocabacrem. 1 glass milk, 1 tablespoon yeast, 1 tablespoon honey, 1 tablespoon powdered milk, 1 sliced banana.

Cocabana. 1 glass pineapple juice, 1 tablespoon milk, 1 tablespoon honey, 1 mashed banana.

Cocabricot. 1 large glass apricot juice, $\frac{1}{4}$ cup skimmed milk, 1 tablespoon honey.

Cocktomate. 1 glass tomato juice, 1 tablespoon lemon juice, 1 tablespoon chopped parsley.

Complete cocktail. 1 glass pineapple juice, 1 tablespoon crushed walnuts, 1 tablespoon yeast, 1 tablespoon honey, 10 wild strawberries.

Maraîcher. $\frac{1}{3}$ celery juice, $\frac{1}{3}$ carrot juice, $\frac{1}{3}$ apple juice.

Milk shake. 1 glass orange juice, 2 tablespoons milk, 1 tablespoon honey.

COCOA (Beans). CACAO – Seeds contained in a pod which is the fruit of the cacao tree. The pod is gathered when ripe, and split. The beans, covered with fleshy pulp, are fermented; a process which destroys the germ, and enables them to be shelled. They are then dried in silos or in the open air. The highest quality cocoa comes from Venezuela, and Guatemala; it has a thick, ochre-coloured shell and a purple-blue bean. Ecuador cocoa beans are bigger, with a brown shell and a brown, almost black, bean. Brazil varieties of cocoa, including the Maragnan, are flatter in shape, with a purple-blue bean. Guiana cocoa beans are small, with a grey shell and brown bean.

Different characteristics make it possible to distinguish the cocoa of Jamaica, Martinique, Guadeloupe, etc. The beans should have a clean smell and should not have any wormholes, grit, or other foreign matter.

Columbus was, according to legend, the first European to see cocoa in use, but the specimens he took back to Spain were not considered of any value. Cortés found it widely grown and used in Mexico in 1519. The Aztecs grew it for many generations, and their Emperor Montezuma, and his court, are reputed to have consumed fifty large jars a day. There was no sugar at that time, and the drink was flavoured with vanilla and drunk cold.

In Europe, the Spaniards imitated the Aztecs' method of preparing 'chocolate', flavouring it with chillies and other hot spices and making it into a soup-like concoction.

Chocolate became a fashionable drink in France. The first record of its use in England was at Oxford in 1650. Seven years later a Frenchman opened a cocoa house in Bishopsgate Street, London. Under Charles II the duty payable on chocolate in its finished state was 8 shillings per gallon. Later, someone thought of adding sugar to chocolate. Pepys, in his diary, after his first taste of '*jucalette*' described it as 'very good'.

Cocoa pods

Chocolate houses were fashionable in the eighteenth century, each having a literary, political or gambling clientele. White's, the notorious gaming-house in St James's Street, began as a chocolate house.

Chocolate was first prepared by hand. Dr Joseph Fry of Bristol, having bought the patent rights from Walter Churchman, who had been making chocolate since 1728, was the first to manufacture it on a big scale in England, introducing a steam engine for grinding the cocoa beans in 1795. Dr James Baker founded the first chocolate factory in America in 1780. Both businesses still exist.

All this was still cocoa, or drinking chocolate. It is not definitely known when chocolate was first sold for eating; probably not until Victoria's reign. Cadbury's price list, as late as 1842, shows only one kind of eating chocolate.

Cocoa powder. POUDRE DE CACAO SOLUBLE – Cocoa with reduced fat content treated with potassium (of which it must not contain more than 3·5 g. per 100 g.). It is soluble.

Cocoa contains various alkaloids, the most important of which are theobromine and caffeine. It also contains about 17 per cent nitrogenous matter, 25·5 per cent fats and 38 per cent carbohydrates, all of which have important food value and a stimulating action. It is mainly taken in the form of chocolate.

Preparation of cocoa – To prepare an excellent breakfast beverage, cocoa can be used instead of slab chocolate. Boiling water and milk is poured on cocoa powder and mixed with sugar according to taste. A smooth paste can be made by mixing cocoa powder with sweetened condensed milk and then adding boiling water.

Roasted cocoa. CACAO TORRÉFIÉ – Cocoa beans have a very light smell and a bitter taste. Roasting, as in the case of coffee, is necessary to release the aroma. After roasting, the beans are pulverised and presented in various forms.

Cocoa shells. COQUES DE CACAO – The membranous shells of husked cocoa beans can be used to prepare a pleasant beverage, resembling chocolate, which possesses fortifying properties owing to the vitamin content. Allow 1 tablespoon cocoa shells per cup.

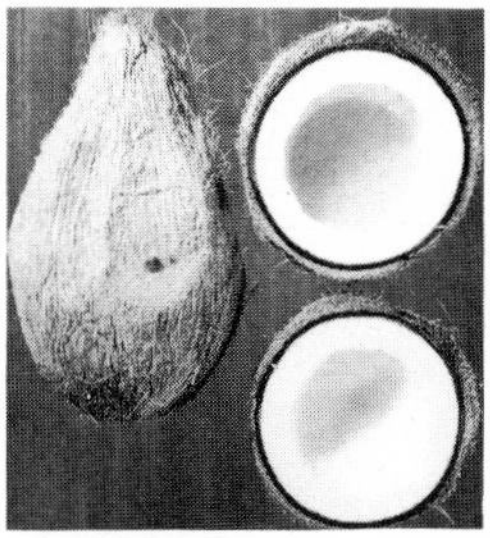

Coconut

COCONUT. NOIX DE COCO – Fruit of the coconut tree, belonging to the palm tree family. The sap is used to make fermented drinks called palm tree wines.

Gathered before the fruit is ripe, the coconut contains a kind of milk or cream. When ripe, the nut has a hollow centre and adheres to the shell. It is used mainly for cake-making and confectionery. Dried, and with the fibrous outer skin removed, coconut is called *copra*, and is used for making an industrial oil for soap manufacture.

Purified and deodorised, coconut oil, which has a firm consistency at ordinary temperatures, is called coconut butter. There are a number of commercial products under this name. It is fatty, almost without water content, odourless, tasteless, and very digestible. It is used in certain diets when butter cannot be assimilated, and especially in vegetarian cookery.

Coconut milk. LAIT DE COCO – Used to moisten curry sauces. Mix 400 g. (14 oz., 4 cups) finely grated coconut with 3 dl. ($\frac{1}{2}$ pint, $1\frac{1}{4}$ cups) warm milk. Strain through muslin.

COCO-PLUM. ICAQUE – Fruit of the tropical coco-plum tree. It is eaten fresh or preserved.

COCOSE – Butter made from coconut.

COCOTTE – Utensil in which certain foods are cooked, especially meat, fowl and game.

Cocottes are made in earthenware, fireproof porcelain or glass, tinned copper, nickel, aluminium, stainless steel, cast iron or silver. Dishes cooked in these utensils, in which they are usually served, are described as *en cocotte* or *en casserole*.

Cocottes

COD. CABILLAUD, CABLIAUD – Large fish of the genus *Gadus*, found in North Atlantic waters. It has an elongated body with soft grey scales, and yellow and brown spots on its back and flanks, which are white like its belly. A cod can weigh as much as 36 kg. (80 lb.). In France fresh cod is called *cabillaud* and salt cod is called *morue*. The flesh is white and flaky.

Its roe, smoked, is excellent.

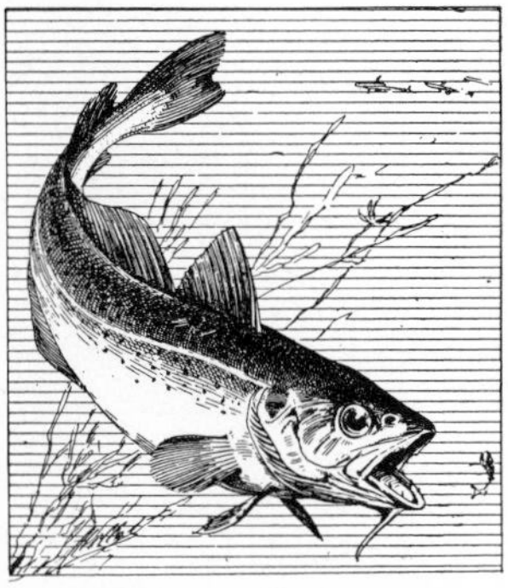

Cod

Fresh cod is prepared in many different ways. In addition to the recipes given below, this fish, whole or in steaks or fillets, can be prepared in any way suitable for brill (q.v.), turbot (q.v.), haddock (q.v.) and any other large fish.

The following recipes are particularly suitable for cod: *Bercy, bonne femme, normande, portugaise, provençale*.

Cod à l'anglaise. CABILLAUD À L'ANGLAISE – Cut the cod into slices 3 cm. ($1\frac{1}{4}$ inches) thick, taken from the middle of the fish for preference. Season with salt and pepper and dredge in flour. Dip in beaten egg mixed with oil, cover with white breadcrumbs, and cook in clarified butter until both sides are golden. Serve topped with half-melted *Maître d'hôtel butter* (see BUTTER, *Compound butters*).

Boiled cod (hot) with various sauces. CABILLAUD BOUILLI (CHAUD) – Poach the cod whole, or in steaks, in *Court-bouillon III* (see COURT-BOUILLON). Put the fish into the liquid when it is cold, bring to the boil then reduce the heat and leave to poach without allowing it to boil further.

Drain the fish and garnish with fresh parsley and boiled potatoes. Serve with one of the sauces recommended for boiled fish: *Anchovy, Butter, Caper, Shrimp, Fines herbes, Hollandaise, Lobster, Ravigote*, etc. (see SAUCE, *White sauces*).

Boiled cod (cold) with various sauces. CABILLAUD BOUILLI (FROID) – Cook the fish as described in the preceding recipe, but only until it is two-thirds done, so that the cooking process can be completed as it cools in the *court-bouillon*. Drain when it is cold, dry in a cloth, and garnish with fresh parsley or with lettuce hearts and quartered hard-boiled eggs. Serve with one of the sauces recommended for cold fish: *Gribiche, Mayonnaise, Ravigote, Rémoulade, Tartare, Green, Vincent* (see SAUCE, *Cold sauces*).

Cod à la boulangère. CABILLAUD À LA BOULANGÈRE – Season a piece of cod with salt and pepper, sprinkle with melted butter and brown lightly in the oven in a fireproof dish. Surround with sliced potatoes and sliced onions. Season the potatoes with salt and pepper, powdered thyme and bay and sprinkle with a little melted butter. Bake in the oven, basting frequently. Sprinkle with chopped parsley and serve in the dish in which it was cooked.

Cod braised in white wine. CABILLAUD BRAISÉ AU VIN BLANC – Proceed as described in the recipe for *Brill in white wine* (see BRILL).

Cod braised in white wine with various garnishes. CABILLAUD BRAISÉ AU VIN BLANC AVEC GARNITURES DIVERSES – All methods of preparation given for brill, sole, whiting and other braised and garnished fish can be applied to cod.

Cod with melted butter. CABILLAUD AI BEURRE FONDU – Cook the fish whole or in pieces in *Court-bouillon III* (see COURT-BOUILLON). Drain. Serve with melted butter and boiled potatoes.

Cold cod with various sauces. CABILLAUD FROID – Poach cod in salted water and leave to cool in the cooking liquid. Drain, and garnish with parsley. Serve with *Tartare, Mayonnaise, Vinaigrette* or any other sauce recommended as an accompaniment for cold fish (see SAUCE, *Cold sauces*). All the garnishes indicated for cold bass (q.v.) are suitable for cod.

Cod cooked in cream. CABILLAUD ÉTUVÉ À LA CRÈME – Bone a medium-sized cod. Skin the fillets and cut into 5-cm. (2-inch) pieces. Season with salt and pepper.

Fry 150 g. (5 oz., $1\frac{1}{4}$ cups) chopped onion lightly in butter without allowing it to colour, and add the fish. Fry the pieces on all sides. Moisten with 2 dl. ($\frac{1}{3}$ pint, scant cup) dry white wine. Simmer for several minutes. Add 4 dl. ($\frac{3}{4}$ pint, scant 2 cups) of *Cream sauce* (see SAUCE). Simmer slowly, with the lid on the pan, until cooked.

Cream cod gratin. CABILLAUD CRÈME GRATIN – Butter a dish and pipe a high border of *Duchess potatoes* (see POTATOES) round the edges. Put a few tablespoons *Mornay sauce* (see SAUCE) in the dish. Fill up to two-thirds of the height of the border with slices of cod, heated in butter. Cover with *Mornay sauce*, sprinkle with grated cheese, brush the border with beaten egg, sprinkle with melted butter and brown in a moderate oven.

Cod à la crème. CABILLAUD À LA CRÈME – Season slices of cod with salt and pepper. Fry in butter. When half-cooked, moisten with thick fresh cream. Finish cooking with the lid on the pan. Remove the fish, boil down the cream, add 2 or 3 tablespoons fresh butter to it and pour over the fish.

Cod à la dieppoise. TRONÇONS DE CABILLAUD À LA DIEPPOISE – Prepare 5 dl. (scant pint, $2\frac{1}{4}$ cups) concentrated fish stock (see FUMET). Clean, shell and open $\frac{1}{2}$ litre (scant pint, $2\frac{1}{4}$ cups) mussels and add 50 g. (2 oz.) shelled shrimps' tails. (To obtain this amount of shelled shrimps' tails allow 150 g. (5 oz.) shrimps.)

Make a *roux* with 25 g. (1 oz., 2 tablespoons) butter and 25 g. (1 oz., $\frac{1}{4}$ cup) flour. Dilute with the fish *fumet* and 1 dl. (6 tablespoons, scant $\frac{1}{2}$ cup) of the liquor in which the mussels were cooked, well strained. Season with a pinch of pepper and a little grated nutmeg. Bring to the boil, stirring all the time, add a small *bouquet garni* and 1 tablespoon mushroom peel. Simmer gently for 20 minutes.

Make a few small incisions on both sides of the cod fillets. Season with salt and cook in white wine and 25 g. (1 oz., 2 tablespoons) butter cut in pieces. Bring to the boil, transfer to the oven, and continue cooking in moderate heat for 15 to 18 minutes, basting frequently.

Strain the sauce into another saucepan. Add the liquor in which the fish was cooked and 2 egg yolks diluted with a few tablespoons mushroom stock. Stir for a few minutes over heat, add 50 g. (2 oz., $\frac{1}{4}$ cup) butter, remove from the heat, and add the mussels and the shrimps' tails. Do not allow to boil.

To serve, arrange the fish on a long dish and surround with the sauce and garnish. (Philéas Gilbert.)

Cod Dugléré. CABILLAUD DUGLÉRÉ – Cut the fish into steaks. Proceed as described for *Bass Dugléré* (see BASS).

Cod fillets. FILETS DE CABILLAUD – Skin the cod fillets and cut into pieces. Follow one of the recipes given for cod, or for whiting (q.v.), sole (q.v.) or bass (q.v.).

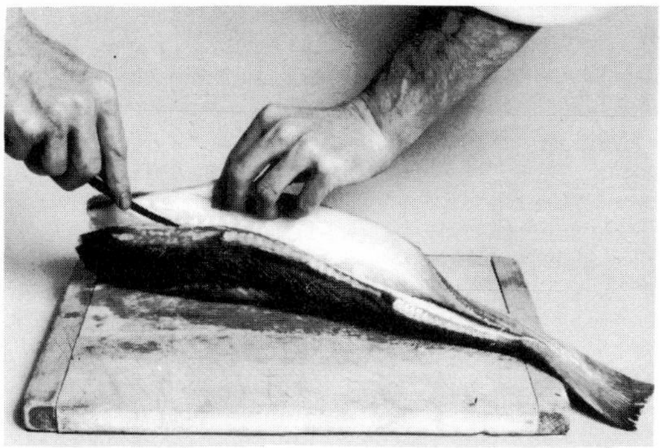

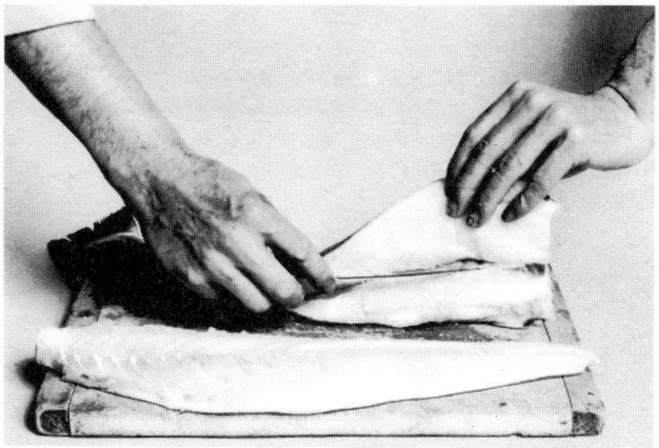

Filleting cod (*Ledoyen. Phot. Nicolas*)

Cod à la flamande. CABILLAUD À LA FLAMANDE – Season cod slices with salt and freshly ground pepper, and place in a buttered baking tin sprinkled with chopped shallots and chopped parsley. Cover with dry white wine and put a slice of peeled lemon on each piece of cod. Bring to the boil. Finish cooking in the oven, allowing about 12 minutes.

Drain the fish and arrange on a long dish. Bring the pan juices to the boil, add 1 tablespoon butter, pour the sauce over the fish, and sprinkle with chopped parsley.

Fried cod

Fried cod. CABILLAUD FRIT – Cut the fish into 2½-cm. (1-inch) thick slices. Dip in cold boiled milk. Dredge in flour and deep-fry in sizzling fat. Drain, dry in a cloth, and sprinkle with salt. Garnish with fried parsley and quarters of lemon.

Fried cod in breadcrumbs. CABILLAUD FRIT PANÉ – Dip slices of cod in egg and breadcrumbs and fry as above. Drain, season, garnish with fried parsley and lemon, and serve with *Maître d'hôtel butter* (see BUTTER, *Compound butters*).

Fried cod Orly. CABILLAUD FRIT ORLY – Cook cod fillets as in *Whiting Orly* (see WHITING).

Cod au gratin. CABILLAUD AU GRATIN – Prepare and cook cod steaks or fillets like *Brill au gratin* (see BRILL).

Grilled cod. CABILLAUD GRILLÉ – Season cod steaks with salt and pepper, sprinkle with melted butter or oil, and cook under a moderate grill. Put a slice of peeled lemon on each steak and garnish with fresh parsley. Serve with *Maître d'hôtel* butter or one of the sauces recommended for grilled fish (see SAUCE; BUTTER, *Compound butters*).

Cod à la hollandaise. CABILLAUD À LA HOLLANDAISE – Cook a piece of cod in *Court-bouillon III* (see COURT-BOUILLON), together with good, mealy potatoes. Drain the fish and surround with the potatoes, which have been dried off in the saucepan. Serve with melted butter.

This dish should not be confused with *cod with hollandaise sauce*, where the fish is cooked in a *court-bouillon* and served with *hollandaise sauce*.

Cod à l'indienne. DARNES DE CABILLAUD À L'INDIENNE – Season cod steaks with salt and pepper and put them into a pan on a foundation of 50 g. (2 oz., ½ cup) chopped onions lightly fried in butter, 2 peeled, seeded and chopped tomatoes, a pinch of grated garlic, and 1 tablespoon chopped parsley. Sprinkle with 2 teaspoons curry powder and 25 g. (1 oz., 2 tablespoons) butter cut in very small pieces. Moisten with 1½ dl. (¼ pint, ⅔ cup) dry white wine. Bring to the boil, then bake in the oven for 10 minutes. Baste with thick fresh cream and finish cooking, basting frequently. Serve with *Rice à l'indienne* (see RICE).

Cod steaks can also be cooked in a concentrated fish stock. Drain, season with salt and pepper, and cover with *Curry sauce* (see SAUCE) to which the concentrated pan juices have been added. Serve with *Rice à l'indienne* (see RICE).

Cod à la meunière. CABILLAUD À LA MEUNIÈRE – Slice the cod and proceed as described for *Bass à la meunière* (see BASS).

Cod Mornay. CABILLAUD MORNAY – Cook thin slices or fillets of cod in a very little white wine. Place them in an ovenproof dish, cover with *Mornay sauce* (see SAUCE), sprinkle with grated cheese and melted butter, and brown in the oven or under the grill.

Cod Mornay in shells. COQUILLES DE CABILLAUD MORNAY – This is useful for using up left-overs. Pour *Mornay sauce* (see SAUCE) into ovenproof shells. Fill with slices of hot cod and cover with *Mornay sauce*. Sprinkle with grated cheese and melted butter, and brown in the oven or under the grill.

Roast cod. CABILLAUD RÔTI – Use cod whole or cut in large pieces. Season with salt and pepper, sprinkle with oil and a dash of lemon juice, and leave to steep in this seasoning for 1 hour. Drain the fish, put on a spit and secure with string. Brush with melted butter and roast before a brisk fire, frequently basting with butter.

Remove the fish from the spit. Dilute the pan juices with white wine and serve with the fish.

The cod may also be roasted in the oven, placed on a grid to prevent its lying in the pan juices.

Cod in shells à la florentine. CABILLAUD EN COQUILLES À LA FLORENTINE – Proceed as described in the recipe for *Cod Mornay in shells* lining the bottom of the shells with 1 tablespoon leaf spinach, blanched and simmered in butter.

Cod in shells au gratin. CABILLAUD EN COQUILLES AU GRATIN – Put a border of sliced mushrooms round the edges of the shells. Pour in *Mornay sauce* (see SAUCE). Fill with small pieces of cod, put a cooked mushroom in the middle and cover with *Mornay sauce*. Sprinkle with grated breadcrumbs and melted butter, and brown under the grill.

Sprinkle with chopped parsley just before serving. To keep the fish from spilling out of the shells, a border of *Duchess potatoes* (see POTATOES) can be piped round the edges.

Cod in shells à la Nantua. CABILLAUD EN COQUILLES À LA NANTUA – Proceed as described in the recipes for *Cod Mornay in shells* replacing *Mornay sauce* by *Nantua sauce* (see SAUCE). Before serving put a large slice of truffle, heated in butter, into each shell.

Cod in white wine. CABILLAUD AU VIN BLANC – Using cod slices or fillets, proceed as for *Brill in white wine* (see BRILL).

SALT COD. MORUE – Wash thoroughly under a running tap, cut into pieces and soak for 24 to 36 hours in cold water. Drain the cod, put it in a pan and cover the fish with cold water. Heat, and at the first signs of bubbling, skim the water and lower the heat. Cover the pan, and poach for 15 to 18 minutes, according to the size of the pieces. The water must not boil. Drain well and prepare according to the recipe chosen.

Salt cod à l'anglaise I. MORUE À L'ANGLAISE – Poach the cod in water. Drain. Garnish with fresh parsley and serve with parsnips boiled in salt water and drained, and hard-boiled egg sauce.

Salt cod à l'anglaise II. MORUE À L'ANGLAISE – Wash and soak fillets of salt cod and cut into thin slices, gently flattening them. Dip in egg and breadcrumbs, fry in butter, and cover with partly melted *Maître d'hôtel butter* (see BUTTER, *Compound butters*). Serve with boiled potatoes.

Salt cod à la bamboche. MORUE À LA BAMBOCHE – Cut washed and soaked fillets of cod into thin slices. Dip in milk, then flour. Twist into spirals and deep-fry in boiling oil.

Drain, dry in a cloth. Fill a bowl with a *macédoine* (q.v.) of vegetables blended with butter or cream, and arrange the fillets on top.

Salt cod à la béchamel. MORUE À LA BÉCHAMEL – Poach the fish in water. Trim and flake, keeping the cod hot. Spread it in layers in a dish and pour over each layer a few tablespoons *Béchamel sauce* (see SAUCE), with butter and fresh cream added.

Salt cod à la bénédictine. MORUE À LA BÉNÉDICTINE – Wash and soak 1 kg. (2¼ lb.) cod. Poach, drain, remove skin and bone, and flake the fish. Dry in the oven for a few minutes. Mix in a mortar with 500 g. (generous 1 lb.) boiled potatoes which have been drained and dried in the oven. Work this mixture so that it absorbs 2 dl. (⅓ pint, scant cup) oil and 3 dl. (½ pint, 1¼ cups) boiled milk, taking care to add these ingredients alternately, a little at a time. When the mixture is smooth and moist, put it in a buttered baking dish, smooth the surface, pour on melted butter, and brown in the oven.

Brandade of salt cod with truffles is often served under the name of *salt cod à la bénédictine*. This dish is a kind of *brandade* of potatoes, browned in the oven.

Salt cod à la Benoiton. MORUE À LA BENOITON – Brown very lightly in oil and butter 150 g. (5 oz., 1¼ cups) finely sliced onions. Sprinkle with 25 g. (1 oz., ¼ cup) flour and cook for a few seconds. Moisten with 6 dl. (1 pint, 2½ cups) red wine and 1½ dl. (¼ pint, ⅔ cup) fish *fumet* (q.v.). Season with salt and pepper. Add a crushed clove of garlic and mix. Cook for 15 minutes. Add 5 sliced boiled potatoes, and 1 kg. (2¼ lb.) flaked boiled cod.

Tip the contents of the pan into a buttered baking dish in one movement (without mixing) and smooth the surface. Sprinkle with breadcrumbs, pour on melted butter and brown in the oven.

Boiled salt cod with various sauces. MORUE BOUILLIE – Wash and soak cod fillets and cut into pieces. Roll these into scrolls and tie them. Poach in water, as indicated in the introduction to this section.

Drain the cod scrolls, untie them and garnish with fresh parsley. Serve with boiled potatoes and a sauce: *Bâtarde, Caper, Cream, Curry, Parsley, Hollandaise, Mustard, Ravigote, Saint-Malo*, etc. (see SAUCE).

Bouillabaisse of salt cod. BOUILLABAISSE DE MORUE – Cook 100 g. (4 oz., 1 cup) chopped onion and 50 g. (2 oz., ½ cup) chopped leek in oil without browning. When these vegetables are tender, add 2 skinned, seeded, chopped tomatoes and a crushed clove of garlic. Cook rapidly for 5 minutes. Moisten with 1 dl. (6 tablespoons, scant ½ cup) white wine, and 5 dl. (scant pint, 2¼ cups) water or fish *fumet* (q.v.), and add a generous pinch of saffron. Bring to the boil. Put into this stock 750 g. (1¾ lb.) fillet of salt cod cut into pieces. Pour in 3 tablespoons (scant ¼ pint) oil. Season with a pinch of freshly ground pepper. Cover the saucepan and boil fast for 25 minutes. At the last moment add 1 tablespoon chopped parsley.

Serve the *bouillabaisse* with slices of toasted bread, or, if preferred, the soup can be served in a tureen with slices of French bread in it, and the fish served separately.

Bouillabaisse of salt cod à la ménagère. BOUILLABAISE DE MORUE À LA MÉNAGÈRE – Cook 100 g. (4 oz., 1 cup) finely chopped onion and 50 g. (2 oz., ½ cup) chopped leek in 1 dl. (6 tablespoons, scant ½ cup) oil. They should not brown. Add 2 crushed garlic cloves and moisten with 1 litre (1¾ pints, generous quart) water. Season with salt and pepper, add a pinch of saffron and a *bouquet garni*, and bring to the boil. Add 300 g. (11 oz.) thickly sliced potatoes and boil for 12 minutes. Now add 750 g. (1¾ lb.) salt cod cut into pieces. Pour 3 tablespoons (scant ¼ cup) oil into the pan. Cover, and boil fast. Before serving, remove the *bouquet garni* and add 1 tablespoon chopped parsley.

Serve the *bouillabaisse* with slices of toasted bread, rubbed with garlic and soaked in a little of the cooking stock.

Brandade of salt cod. BRANDADE DE MORUE – Wash and soak 1 kg. (2¼ lb.) salt cod and cut into pieces. Poach in water for 8 minutes. Drain, remove skin and bones, and flake the flesh. Heat 2 dl. (⅓ pint, scant cup) olive oil in a heavy, flat-bottomed saucepan until it begins to smoke. Put in the cod and add a a small crushed clove of garlic. Work the mixture on the stove with a hard wooden spoon until it is reduced to a smooth paste. Turn the heat very low and keep on working the *brandade*, adding, a little at a time, 5 dl. (scant pint, 2¼ cups) oil. Still stirring, add 2½ dl. (scant ½ pint, generous cup) boiled milk or fresh cream, pouring in a little at a time. Season with salt and white pepper.

When the *brandade* is ready, it should have the appearance of a white paste, very smooth, with the consistency of mashed potatoes.

Garnish with triangles of bread fried in butter or oil, or with croûtes of French bread, fried in oil.

Brandade of salt cod à la Nantua. BRANDADE DE MORUE À LA NANTUA – Prepare the *brandade* as indicated above, moistening it with fresh cream. Serve in a bowl, alternating the *brandade* with layers of a *ragoût* of crayfish tails. Surround with strips of truffle tossed in butter, and garnish with slices of bread fried in butter.

Brandade of salt cod with truffles. BRANDADE DE MORUE AUX TRUFFES – Make the *brandade* as indicated above. Add diced truffles tossed in butter. Cover with strips of truffle also tossed in butter. Surround with slices of bread fried in butter.

Salt cod with brown butter. MORUE AU BEURRE NOIR – Put the trimmed, poached and drained cod on a serving dish and

Brandade of salt cod (*Robert Carrier*)

dry for a minute or two in the oven. Pour over it a few drops of vinegar or lemon juice. Sprinkle with chopped parsley, and capers, if desired. Pour sizzling brown butter over the cod, allowing 225 g. (8 oz., 1 cup) butter for 1 kg. ($2\frac{1}{4}$ lb.) fish.

The cod can also be prepared as follows: Put the cooked fish on a serving dish, pour vinegar over it and sprinkle capers on the top. Fry sprigs of parsley in brown butter and add to the dish.

Salt cod with noisette butter. MORUE AU BEURRE NOISETTE – Poach and trim the cod, squeeze lemon juice over it and sprinkle with chopped parsley. Add a few tablespoons *Noisette butter* (butter heated in a frying pan until it is as brown as a hazelnut).

Salt cod à la crème. MORUE À LA CRÈME – Proceed as for *Salt cod à la béchamel*, using *béchamel sauce* enriched with cream.

Salt cod à la crème au gratin. MORUE À LA CRÈME AU GRATIN – Trim, poach and flake the cod, and proceed as for *Cream cod gratin*.

Salt cod à la créole. MORUE À LA CRÉOLE – Trim, poach, drain and flake the cod. Make a dome of it in a buttered *gratin* dish on a bed of a tomato fondue prepared as follows:

Cook 150 g. (5 oz., $1\frac{1}{4}$ cups) finely chopped onions in a mixture of oil and butter until they are very tender. Skin 4 tomatoes, remove seeds and crush. Add these to the onions, together with 4 skinned, diced sweet peppers. Season with salt and pepper, and flavour with a little chopped garlic. Put a few slices of tomato sautéed in oil, halved sweet peppers, skinned and sautéed in oil, on top of the cod, and pour a little of the hot oil over it. Bake in the oven for a few minutes. Before serving, squeeze a little lemon juice over the fish, and sprinkle with chopped parsley.

Croquettes of salt cod. CROQUETTES DE MORUE – Poach salt cod, leave to cool, dice into very small pieces, and make in the same way as other croquettes. Add cooked mushrooms and diced truffles, if desired. (See CROQUETTE.)

Curried salt cod, called à l'indienne. MORUE AU CURRIE, DITE À L'INDIENNE – Trim, poach, drain and flake the cod. Put it in 5 dl. (scant pint, $2\frac{1}{4}$ cups) *Curry sauce* (see SAUCE). Mix gently. Serve with *Rice à l'indienne* (see RICE).

Salt cod en escabèche. MORUE EN ESCABÈCHE – Wash and soak fillets of cod and cut into thin slices. Proceed as for *Anchovies à la grecque* (see HORS-D'ŒUVRE, *Cold hors-d'œuvre*).

Fillets of salt cod Orly. FILETS DE MORUE ORLY – Cut the raw cod into thin slices. Steep for 1 hour in a marinade of oil, lemon juice and chopped parsley. Dip in light batter and deep-fry. Garnish with fried parsley and serve with *Tomato sauce* (see SAUCE).

Fish balls of salt cod à l'américaine. CROQUETTES DE MORUE À L'AMÉRICAINE – Bind equal parts of *Duchess potato mixture* (see POTATOES) and cooked, flaked cod with a few tablespoons *Béchamel sauce* (see SAUCE). Season well and mix. Leave to cool. Divide into small parts and roll into balls on a floured board. Dip in egg and breadcrumbs and deep-fry. Garnish with fried parsley and serve with *Tomato sauce* (see SAUCE).

Fried salt cod. MORUE FRITE – Cut a fillet of cod into thin slices. Dip in boiled milk, drain, and flour lightly. Deep-fry in oil. Drain, dry in a cloth and season with fine salt. Garnish with fried parsley and lemon.

Fritot of salt cod. MORUE EN FRITOT – Poach and flake the cod. Steep in a marinade of oil, lemon juice, pepper and chopped parsley. Dip in a light batter and deep-fry in boiling oil. Garnish with fried parsley and serve with *Tomato sauce* (see SAUCE).

Salt cod à la hongroise. MORUE À LA HONGROISE – Cook chopped onions seasoned with paprika in butter until very tender. Cut 1 kg. ($2\frac{1}{4}$ lb.) cod into pieces and lay them on top of half the onions. Cover with the remaining onions. Moisten with $1\frac{1}{2}$ dl. ($\frac{1}{4}$ pint, $\frac{2}{3}$ cup) dry white wine. Add 150 g. (5 oz.) diced mushrooms. Cover the pan and cook for 6 minutes. Moisten with a few tablespoons thick fresh cream. Cover and simmer for 10 minutes.

Salt cod à la languedocienne. MORUE À LA LANGUEDOCIENNE – Cut 1 kg. ($2\frac{1}{4}$ lb.) desalted cod in pieces and cook in water. Drain, and put it into a *ragoût* of potatoes prepared as follows: Cut 1 kg. ($2\frac{1}{4}$ lb.) potatoes into quarters and brown lightly in oil. Sprinkle with 1 tablespoon flour and fry for a few seconds, shaking the pan all the time. Add a crushed clove of garlic. Moisten with a little of the fish cooking stock and add a *bouquet garni*.

Cover the dish and bake in the oven for 25 minutes, then remove the *bouquet garni*. Sprinkle with chopped parsley. Place the pieces of cod on top of the *ragoût*, pour oil over it and finish cooking in the oven for 5 to 6 minutes.

Salt cod à la lyonnaise (Carême's recipe). MORUE À LA LYONNAISE – Boil, drain and flake the cod. Dry in a saucepan over low heat, or in the oven.

Dice three large onions and cook in butter over a gentle heat until golden. Brown the cod in the same pan. Season with butter, grated nutmeg and lemon juice, and serve.'

Salt cod à la maître d'hôtel. MORUE À LA MAÎTRE D'HÔTEL – Poach and flake the cod. Put in a dish with alternate layers of sliced boiled potatoes, and cover with partly melted *Maître d'hôtel butter* (see BUTTER, *Compound butters*).

Salt cod mayonnaise. MAYONNAISE DE MORUE – Trim, poach and flake the cod. Prepare in the same way as *Cold salmon mayonnaise* (see SALMON).

Salt cod à la meunière. MORUE À LA MEUNIÈRE – Slice raw fillets of cod. Flour and fry in butter. Arrange on a long dish, sprinkle with lemon juice and chopped parsley. Pour sizzling butter over the fish.

Salt cod Mireille. MORUE MIREILLE – Cut cod fillets into pieces of equal size. Flour, and brown quickly in smoking-hot oil. Prepare a *fondue* of tomatoes as follows: Cook 50 g. (2 oz., $\frac{1}{2}$ cup) chopped onion with 4 skinned, seeded and chopped tomatoes and $\frac{1}{2}$ clove of chopped garlic in oil. Season with salt and pepper and 1 teaspoon saffron. Cook until almost all the liquid has evaporated. Moisten with 3 dl. ($\frac{1}{2}$ pint, $1\frac{1}{4}$ cups) white wine. Cook for 10 minutes.

Serve with a border of *Rice pilaf* (see PILAF). Cover with the tomato sauce. Arrange black olives on top and sprinkle with chopped parsley.

Salt cod Mornay. MORUE MORNAY – Trim, poach and drain pieces of cod. Put in an ovenware dish on a layer of *Mornay sauce*, and cover with more of the sauce. Sprinkle with grated cheese, add small pieces of butter, and brown in the oven.

Salt cod à l'occitane. MORUE À L'OCCITANE – Heat 5 tablespoons (6 tablespoons) oil with 1 clove of garlic in an ovenware dish. Add the following in layers: 750 g. ($1\frac{3}{4}$ lb.) cooked, flaked salt cod, 3 sliced hard-boiled eggs, 4 sliced boiled potatoes, 1 large peeled and diced tomato which has been cooked in oil, 24 black olives, 1 tablespoon capers.

Decorate the dish with sliced hard-boiled eggs, black olives and slices of peeled lemon. Pour on a few tablespoons oil, season with freshly ground pepper and heat gently. Garnish with chopped parsley.

Salt cod à la parisienne. MORUE À LA PARISIENNE – Trim, poach and drain slices of cod. Cover with diced hard-boiled eggs, capers and chopped parsley. Squeeze lemon juice over the fish, and pour on a few tablespoons brown butter in which 4 tablespoons ($\frac{1}{3}$ cup) fresh breadcrumbs have been fried.

Salt cod Parmentier. MORUE PARMENTIER – Cook and flake

the cod and put it in a buttered ovenproof dish. Cover with a light purée of potatoes. Sprinkle with grated cheese, pour on melted butter and brown in the oven.

Salt cod à la Provençale. MORUE À LA PROVENÇALE – Make 5 dl. (scant pint, $2\frac{1}{4}$ cups) tomato *fondue* with oil, flavoured with garlic. Add to it 1 kg. ($2\frac{1}{4}$ lb.) flaked cod poached in water. Add salt and pepper and sprinkle with chopped parsley. Cover the dish and simmer for a few minutes.

Salt cod en rayte. MORUE EN RAYTE – Brown 100 g. (4 oz., 1 cup) chopped onion in oil. Add 1 tablespoon flour. Cook for a few seconds, stirring. Moisten with $\frac{1}{2}$ litre (scant pint, $2\frac{1}{4}$ cups) red wine and the same quantity boiling water. Mix, season with pepper and a very little salt. Add 2 cloves garlic, 1 *bouquet garni* and 1 tablespoon tomato purée. Bring to the boil.

Deep-fry 750 g. ($1\frac{3}{4}$ lb.) floured, desalted cod fillets in oil. Add 2 teaspoons capers, cover the pan, and simmer for a few minutes.

Rougail of salt cod and tomatoes – See ROUGAIL.

Salt cod salad. SALADE DE MORUE – Mix slices of boiled potatoes and cooked, flaked cod. Add chopped onion, season with oil and vinegar, and sprinkle with chopped parsley, chervil and tarragon.

Salt cod with spinach au gratin. MORUE AUX ÉPINARDS GRATINÉE – Poach and flake the cod. Wash 500 g. (generous 1 lb.) spinach, parboil for 5 minutes in boiling salted water, drain and chop. Heat 2 dl. ($\frac{1}{3}$ pint, scant cup) oil until it begins to smoke. Put the spinach into the smoking oil. Season with salt, pepper, a touch of nutmeg and a little crushed garlic. Add the flaked cod and a few tablespoons *Béchamel sauce* (see SAUCE). Mix together and put it in a fireproof dish. Shape into a dome and smooth. Sprinkle with breadcrumbs, pour on a little oil and brown in the oven.

Salt cod with tomatoes à la marseillaise – MORUE AUX TOMATES À LA MARSEILLAISE – Cut the cod into pieces, flour, and deep-fry in oil. Simmer for 10 minutes in *Tomato fondue* (see TOMATO) strongly flavoured with garlic.

Vol-au-vent of salt cod. VOL-AU-VENT DE MORUE – Fill flaky pastry cases with *Brandade of salt cod. Vol-au-vent* can also be filled with flaked salt cod mixed with sliced truffles and mushrooms, and blended with either a meatless *velouté sauce* or a cream sauce.

COD-BURBOT – Freshwater fish of the codfish type. The cod-burbot is also known as *burbot, eel-pout* and *coney fish*. The method of cooking is the same as for burbot (q.v.). In U.S.A. the burbot, also called *freshwater cusk*, is found in the Great Lakes and smaller lakes and rivers across the northern latitude of the country.

COFFEE, COFFEE SHRUB. CAFÉ, CAFÉIER – The coffee shrub originated in Abyssinia and the Sudan. It is a large, evergreen bush with dark shiny leaves.

The cherry-like fruit is soaked, depulped and dried. The seed is then polished to remove the parchment-like husk and outer filament.

According to Balland, the coffee grains contain 6·15 to 15·30 per cent nitrogenous substances, 3·98 to 11·40 per cent fatty matter and 0·70 to 2 per cent caffeine (q.v.).

Coffee contains alkaloids, volatile aromatic products and various substances belonging to the phenolic series. It stimulates the central nervous system and the cardiac muscle.

History, or perhaps legend, tells us that the first man to drink coffee was the Mufti of Aden, who lived in the beginning of the ninth century. According to another tradition, we owe the discovery of coffee to a certain Mullah, or Moslem priest, called Chadely or Scyadly, whose name, it is said,

Coffee pot and grinder (*Nicolas*)

Special grinder and cup for Turkish coffee (*Delius*)

is still venerated in the Middle East. This holy man, upon finding himself often overcome by sleep in the middle of his prayers, attributed his drowsiness to the half-heartedness of his devotions, and his conscience tormented him. The Prophet, touched by his sorrow, led him to encounter a herdsman, who told him that each time his goats ate the berries of a certain shrub, they would remain awake, jumping and gambolling all night.

The Mullah wished to see this extraordinary plant, and the herdsman showed him a pretty shrub with a greyish bark and brilliant foliage, the slender branches of which, at the bases of their leaves, had bunches of small white flowers and clusters of small berries. Some were green, some were a clear yellow colour and others, which had reached full maturity, were the size, shape and colour of a cherry. It was the coffee shrub. The Mullah, testing these unusual berries, made himself a potent brew, and spent the night in a state of delicious intoxication which, however, in no way affected his intellectual capacities.

He told his Dervishes about his discovery and soon coffee became much in demand among devout Moslems, who looked upon it as a divine gift brought by an angel from heaven to the faithful. The use of coffee spread from Aden to Medina, Mecca, and throughout the whole of the Middle East. Coffee was taken during prayers, in the mosques, even in the Holy Temple at Mecca and before the Tomb of the Prophet.

Coffee, in the Middle East, is one of the first necessities of life. It was hardly known in Europe before the seventeenth century. Travellers who had acquired the habit of drinking this beverage in the East imported it at first for their personal use. Suleiman Aga, the ambassador of the Sublime Porte to the Court of Louis XIV in 1669 popularised coffee in France. As laid down by Turkish custom, he offered it to all who came to visit him. The vogue for coffee spread through high society; it was soon in demand and the price was high.

The Dutch founded the East India coffee trade when they introduced coffee into Java about 1690, but it was a Frenchman, Desclieux, who introduced it into the western hemisphere in the reign of Louis XIV. He brought one small seedling to Martinique. The plant flourished, and seedlings were taken to French Guiana. From there it spread to Central America. Brazil is the greatest producer of coffee.

The best varieties, known as *mocha* or *Yemen*, came from Arabia, Réunion Island and Martinique. The names have been preserved in the trade to distinguish three types of coffee, although the designation in no way implies its origin.

Bourbon. Medium-sized grains, yellowish, oblong.

Martinique. The biggest grains, rounded at the ends, greenish in colour.

Mocha. Small irregular grains, yellowish in colour and convex on both sides.

Like wine, coffee gives the greatest production in the plains, but the best qualities come from the highest parts of the torrid zone, particularly from Central America (Guatemala, Salvador, Honduras, Nicaragua and Costa Rica), as well as from the northern part of South America (Venezuela and Colombia) whose products are always highly rated.

After the fruit has been depulped and dried and the seed polished, the seeds are classified as to size and ripeness.

Coffees of various origins are usually blended in different proportions. When green, coffee keeps for a long time, provided it is protected from damp. It is entirely devoid of smell. To release the aroma, coffee has to be roasted, an operation which many coffee lovers insist on performing themselves. Well-roasted coffee should be brown, of varying degrees of darkness, but never black. If not sufficiently roasted it produces a colourless infusion which is rough and astringent. If over-roasted it produces a black, bitter infusion.

During the industrial roasting process a small quantity of sugar molasses or other product is sometimes added to 'coat' the berries. This is permissible by law. It gives the berries a better colour and more shiny appearance; it prevents the loss of aroma and has the further advantage, for the merchant, of increasing the weight. It also enables him to use inferior quality or damaged grains.

After roasting, coffee does not keep its aroma for long, and should not be roasted or purchased already roasted in quantities exceeding one's immediate needs. It is advisable to keep the berries in tins with well-fitting lids. Ideally, coffee should be ground immediately before being made, as ground coffee loses its aroma very quickly.

Soluble coffee, more commonly known as instant coffee, was the invention of a Mr G. Washington, an Englishman living in Guatemala. One day while waiting for his wife to join him in the garden for coffee, he noticed on the spout of the silver coffee-pot fine powder which seemed to be the condensation of the coffee vapours. This intrigued him, and led to his discovery of soluble coffee. In 1906 he started

When planning a kitchen, for convenience the cooking hob is often set into the working surface (*Marc Held. Phot. Larousse*)

Assorted coffee pots (*Larousse*)

'Melior'

Cona

Percolator

Two-colour stoneware pot

Coffee grinder 'Rallye' Peugeot

Neapolitan

experiments and put his product on the market in 1909. Since that time many varieties of instant coffee have appeared and with great commercial success.

Brewing coffee – There are four basic methods of brewing ground coffee – boiling, steeping, percolating and filtering. Coffee experts consider filtering the best method of extracting the soluble essences from the coffee which is contained in a paper or cloth filter. Boiling water is poured over, flowing into a container where it will not come into contact again with the grounds. For perfect coffee, earthenware or glass receptacles should be used, since contact with metal lowers the quality of the beverage.

The *Turkish* method consists of pouring coffee, ground to a powder, into a special receptacle containing boiling water, and heating until the coffee is on the point of boiling. This operation is repeated three times. A few drops of cold water are added to settle the grounds, and the coffee is ready.

The *French* method consists of pouring boiling water on finely ground coffee (but less finely ground than for Turkish coffee) contained between two perforated disks in a receptacle called a *cafetière*. Among the numerous types of *cafetières* the traditional *cafetière à la Dubelloy* is still the favourite with coffee connoisseurs.

Bourbon créole coffee. CAFÉ CRÉOLE BOURBON – Créole coffee must be strong and fragrant. Allow 1 heaped teaspoon ground coffee per cup. Press the coffee down well and proceed as follows:

Put the filter into a *bain-marie*, which must not be boiling. Keep some boiling water in a separate receptacle. Steep the coffee thoroughly, then, little by little, add tablespoons of the boiling water. Let it drip through until you have obtained the required amount of coffee. Serve very hot in a coffee-pot which has been scalded.

Coffee with cream, with milk. CAFÉ À LA CRÈME, AU LAIT – The addition of cream or milk to coffee reduces its stimulating properties and turns it into a real food. Dieticians, however, are very much against it because of its indigestibility.

Iced coffee. CAFÉ GLACÉ – Use 300 g. (11 oz., $3\frac{2}{3}$ cups) freshly ground coffee and $\frac{3}{4}$ litre ($1\frac{1}{3}$ pints, $1\frac{3}{4}$ pints) boiling water. Pour into a bowl with 575 g. ($1\frac{1}{4}$ lb., $2\frac{1}{2}$ cups) granulated sugar. Dissolve the sugar and chill the infusion.

Add to the coffee 1 litre ($1\frac{3}{4}$ pints, generous quart) vanilla-flavoured cold boiled milk, and $\frac{1}{2}$ litre (scant pint, $2\frac{1}{4}$ cups) fresh cream. Chill in an ice pail. If served with whipped cream it is called *café liégeois*.

Uses of coffee – Coffee is used for flavouring many hot and cold sweets. It is used in the form of an essence which is prepared with very strong coffee. To flavour creams, roast the coffee beans on a metal sheet in the oven, grind, and put them into boiling milk. Cover with a cloth and leave to infuse for a few minutes. (See CREAMS, ICE CREAMS AND ICES, PARFAIT.) Industrially produced coffee essence and instant coffee can also be used for flavouring creams.

Coffee with caffeine extracted. CAFE DÉCAFÉINÉ – To render coffee less harmful and extract the caffeine, attempts have been made to extract from coffee its alkaloid constituent (see CAFFEINE). This operation, which is nowadays done on a large scale, consists of breaking up the beans by steam, subjecting them to the action of chloroform or some other solvent, and then eliminating this liquid by heating and roasting.

After roasting, the coffee retains the same taste as ordinary coffee which has not been treated, without having any of its stimulating properties.

Coffee substitutes – Various grains and roots have been used to replace coffee, or for adulteration. Apart from chicory, the most important adulterants include figs, dates, acorns (mildly astringent), malt, barley and other roasted cereals, chick-peas and lupins (used a great deal in Brittany). The majority of these adulterants are harmless.

COGNAC – Town in the district of Charente which has given its name to famous brandies (see CHARENTE, SPIRITS).

The distillation of wines which provide the various Cognacs is done by the method of *brouillis* and *repasses*. The special qualities of the Champagnes, the Borderies and the Fins-bois are not apparent until the brandy has been allowed to age for 15 to 20 years in barrels of the white oak of the district, or in Limousin oak. Several brandies are blended together to obtain a perfect bouquet. The blend is left to age.

For the boundaries of the Cognac region and its various subdivisions, see map below.

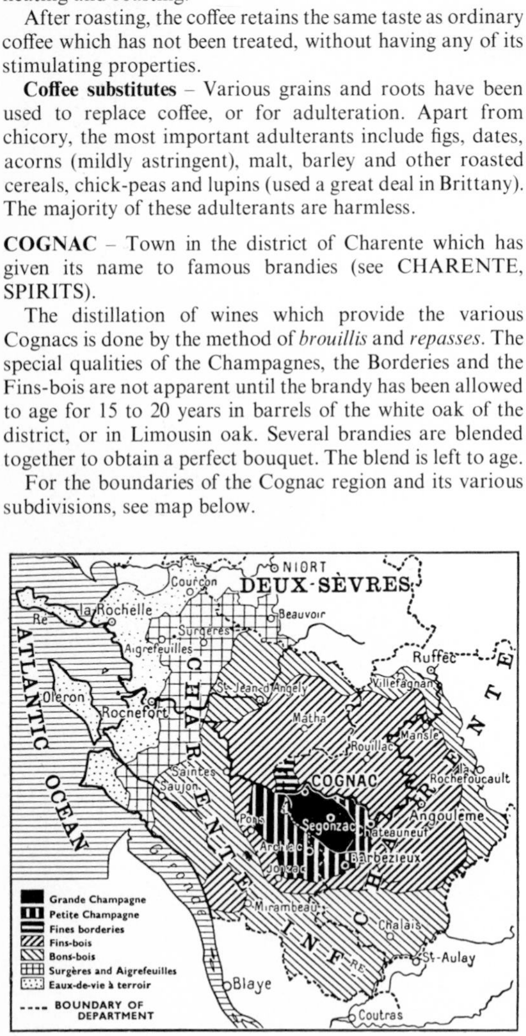

Map of the Cognac-producing areas

COLA. KOLA – African tree. Its seeds which are flattened oblong in shape, have a bitter, astringent flavour, and are chewed by the natives. They contain a high proportion of caffeine, theobromine, and a glucoside, cola red. Cola is a tonic and a stimulant but does not have any real nutritive value. It is used as a colouring matter, a liquid flavouring extract, in wines, etc.

Branch and nut of cola

Dieticians are firmly against all cola-based beverages.

Cola cream. CRÈME À LA KOLA – Made by adding a variable amount of essence of cola nut to some kind of sweetened substance. Often it is made by adding the extract to a thick French pastry cream (*crème pâtissière*), frangipane cream, or butter cream. Cola cream, flavoured with orange essence, is used to fill or decorate cakes and pastries such as Genoese cake, *choux*, éclairs, tartlets, etc.

COLBERT (À LA) – Name given to a preparation of fish which are dipped in egg and breadcrumbs before being fried (see SOLE, *Sole Colbert*).

The name is also applied to a special butter which is served with fish prepared *à la Colbert* (see BUTTER, *Compound butters*).

COLD FOODSTUFFS, PRESENTATION OF COLD DISHES. PLATS FROIDS – 'The basis of a cold buffet,' wrote Carême, 'is attractive presentation. Judicious cooking and careful seasoning are also supremely important. Good jellies are essential. These must be clarified, perfectly transparent, and of two colours only. One of these must be white, the other a beautiful bold colour.'

Carême gives the following recipe for a good jelly.

'Melt fine, dry sugar for 15 minutes on red embers to colour slowly. When it is reddish amber in colour moisten with ½ glass water and bring to the boil over a higher flame. After it has boiled for a few minutes it becomes a transparent caramel of a beautiful reddish amber colour.' Carême also recommends the use of 'beautiful *sauces magnonnaises*' (this was his name for mayonnaise) 'one white and the other a fine pistachio green.'

'*Entrées* must be dressed with care, glazed with an attractive light jelly, artistically presented, decorated as simply as possible with truffles, meat from the breasts of chicken and pickled ox tongue, and garnished with fine rounds of jelly arranged as elegant borders . . . these are the essentials in the presentation of handsome, cold dishes.'

The presentation of cold dishes should never be over elaborate or finicky. A dish of food should not be a work of architecture. In conclusion, Carême says that 'they should be put on smooth white plinths.' He was voicing the taste of his own day, which no longer prevails.

The simpler the presentation of a cold dish, the more handsome it is. But there are those who remain faithful to the old customs. It is for them that we quote Carême's rules for the presentation of cold dishes:

'*Fillets of beef.* Dressed in a long rectangle, glazed and decorated with jelly. The dish to be surrounded by a border of jelly.

'*Ribs of beef.* Dressed in their natural shape, garnished with their own bones, carefully scraped to make them white; border as above.

'*Chauds-froids of chicken.* Arrange in a pyramid and cover with a transparent sauce. Crown with a fine black truffle and a white double cock's comb. Scatter clumps of lightly chopped jelly on the peaks of the pile. Finish with a border of clear jelly. This is an *entrée* of great distinction.

'*Chicken salads.* Presented like *fricassées en chaud-froid.* Instead of a truffle, place ½ hard-boiled egg with the heart of a lettuce on top. Serve with a good white or green mayonnaise. Make a border of hard-boiled eggs or coloured butter, decorated with fillets of anchovy.

'*Galantines of poultry.* Garnish with a good forcemeat using plenty of truffles, whole and diced, pickled calf or ox tongue and calf's udder. Glaze lightly.

'*Salmis.* Presented as above.

'*Noix de veau* (see VEAL). Trimmed into an attractive shape and decorated with *tétine.* Glaze the remainder of the *noix* and decorate with jelly.' (By *tétine*, Carême means the layer of fat which covers part of the *noix de veau.*)

'*Eel galantines.* Should be tower shaped, set on a bed of *Montpellier butter* and decorated with jelly. Make a border of jelly or coloured butter garnished with sprigs of tarragon.

'*Salmon steaks.* May be masked with *Montpellier butter.* Decorate with jelly, truffle, breast of chicken or pickled tongue, so that the decoration is all the same colour. Make a border of coloured butter or jelly.

'*Salads of fillets of sole or other fish.* Arrange inside a border of moulded jelly. Fillets of turbot, trout, salmon, brill, pike and perch are arranged in the same way. For whole perch, cover the fish with white mayonnaise and decorate with truffles. Make a border of jelly in two colours'.

Carême writes, 'Cold dishes are everything in themselves, or they are nothing. The man of talent brings out all their inherent beauty; the man without taste detracts from it and makes them insipid.'

In modern practice the cold dish is presented more simply. The old methods, inspired by architecture rather than by the arts of the kitchen, have been abandoned and all the garnishes of a cold dish are grouped in the simplest manner possible round the main dish, without seeking after architectural effects.

Dishes are made in shapes adapted to their purpose. On these, food, simply presented and decorated, is much more elegant than formerly when wooden supports covered with butter, or plinths ornamented with so-called artistic figures were used.

The object is to make the most of the intrinsic shape and colour of the main dish, and to surround it only with garnishes which would normally be eaten with it.

Some time ago disciples of the Italian 'futurist' Marinetti attempted, unsuccessfully, to revive the decorative presentation of cold dishes.

COLD ROOM. CHAMBRE FROIDE – Room kept at an extremely low temperature and used for preserving and storing perishable foods.

COLIFICHET – A dry cake, without butter or salt, made for birds.

In *pâtisserie, pièces montées* (set pieces), which decorated the table and buffets were called *colifichets*, to distinguish them from the proper dishes. Although the *colifichets* were almost entirely edible, they were laden with ornament.

Nowadays, they are rarely made. They can occasionally be seen as specimens in culinary exhibitions.

COLIN – Name given in Paris markets to hake. This fish has delicate flaky flesh and is also called *saumon blanc* (white salmon). The head and back are grey, the stomach white and lightly silvered. Before the opening up of north Atlantic fishing, the *colin* was salted and used instead of salt cod in European markets.

The methods of preparation given for cod (q.v.) are suitable for *colin.*

COLLAGE – Clarification of alcoholic drinks by precipitation of the solids, which may spoil their keeping qualities (see WINE).

COLLE – Another word for gelatine. Butter sauce is sometimes called *sauce colle.*

COLLER – Adding dissolved gelatine to give body to a preparation.

COLLOP. ESCALOPER – To slice meat or vegetables.

COLOCASIA. CARAIBE (CHOU) – *Colocasia esculenta* (family *Araceae*), tuberous herb native of the Moluccas (Spice Islands). In the West Indies, leaves as well as tubers are eaten as cabbage, hence the French name *caraibe* (*chou*).

COLOCYNTH – Member of the gourd family. The multi-coloured fruit is rich and used as a table ornament. The pulp is bitter and a violent purgative.

COLOMBINES – Croquettes with an outer layer of semolina with Parmesan. (See HORS-D'ŒUVRE, *Hot hors-d'œuvre.*)

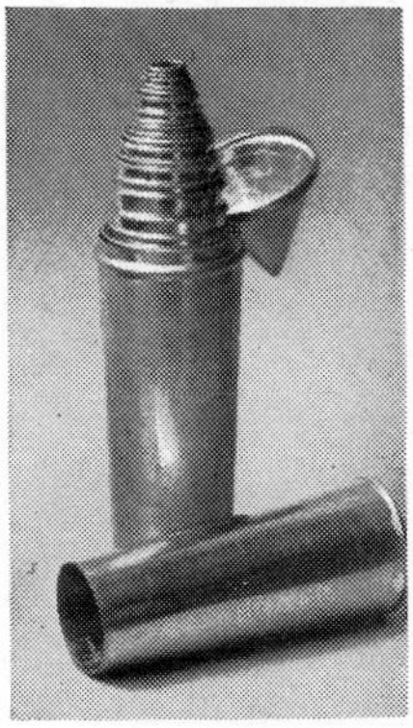

Moule à colonne
(*Dehillerin. Phot. Larousse*)

COLONNE – Implement used to core apples and cut vegetables into a column. Also called *moule à colonne.*

COLOURINGS. COLORANTS – The colourings used in cookery, cake-making, and confectionary, are mainly of vegetable origin, and are harmless; some are of insect origin, like the carmine of cochineal; or of mineral origin, such as those derived from coal.

The colouring most often used in cooking is caramel, especially to improve the look of the stock of *pot-au-feu*, meat glazes and sauces. Liquid caramel is obtained by cooking sugar with a little water until it turns dark (see SUGAR).

COLZA – Colza, or rape seed, is an oily plant sometimes used to adulterate mustard seed.

COMFITS. CONFITS – Fruits or vegetables preserved in sugar, brandy, or vinegar (see GHERKINS, CAPERS, FRUITS).

COMFREY. CONSOUDE – Name of various plants, some of which are edible and used in salad, or cooked, like corn-salad.

COMINÉE DE GELINES (Ancient recipe) – The ancestor of the *Chicken fricassée*, for which one of the oldest culinary treatises (1290), *le Traité où l'on enseigne à faire et appareiller et assaisonner toutes viandes*, gives the following recipe:

'If you wish to make *cominée de gelines*, take the chickens and cook them in wine and water, boil them, skim off the fat, and take out the chickens. Take egg yolks, beat them well, and dilute them with chicken stock. Put in some cumin, and put all together. There is your *cominée*.'

COMPOTE – Preparation of fresh or dried fruit in a thick or thin syrup, flavoured or not with various aromatics such as vanilla; lemon or orange zest; cinnamon; clove; etc.

Dried fruits, prunes, apricots, apples, pears, etc., must be soaked for some time in cold water before being cooked in the syrup.

Compotes are usually served cold. They can be sprinkled with kirsch or some other liqueur.

Simple compotes consist of one type of fruit cooked in syrup.

Compotes composées consist of a *macédoine* of various fruits, arranged in a dish. The syrup in which they have been cooked is poured over them, or they can be covered with a fruit jelly (quince, gooseberry, apple, etc.).

The word is also used for certain dishes (of pigeon, partridge) which have been cooked for a considerable time.

Fruit compote

COMPOTES OF FRESH AND DRIED FRUITS. COMPOTES DE FRUITS FRAIS ET SECS:

Apple compote. COMPOTE DE POMMES – Made with whole fruit, cored and peeled, or with fruit cut into halves or quarters, peeled and with the pips removed. Put the fruit in a syrup of 350 g. (12 oz., 1½ cups) sugar to 6 dl. (1 pint, 2½ cups) water, with or without vanilla flavouring.

Remove the pieces as soon as they are cooked, arrange them in a dish and pour the cooking syrup over the fruit.

Apricot compote. COMPOTE D'ABRICOTS – Halve the apricots; break open the stones and blanch the kernels; cook the fruit in a syrup – 350 g. (12 oz., 1½ cups) sugar to 6 dl. (1 pint, 2½ cups) water. Arrange the apricot halves in a dish and put half a kernel on each fruit. Pour over the cooking syrup.

Banana compote. COMPOTE DE BANANES – Peel the bananas and remove the strips of fibre. Cook for 5 minutes in a heavy sugar syrup – 450 g. (1 lb., 2 cups) sugar to 6 dl. (1 pint, 2½ cups) water. Flavour with kirsch.

Cherry compote I. COMPOTE DE CERISES – Put the stoned cherries in a sugar syrup which has been cooked to the large ball stage (119°–122°C., 246°–252°F.) (see SUGAR). Use 300 g. (11 oz., 1⅓ cups) sugar for each 1 kg. (2¼ lb.) cherries (net weight). Cook with the lid on for 8 minutes over low heat. Stir from time to time. Arrange the cherries in a dish and pour the cooking syrup over. Flavour with kirsch or cherry brandy.

Cherry compote II. COMPOTE DE CERISES – Put the stoned cherries in a deep dish with a bag containing 12 crushed kernels. Sprinkle generously with powdered sugar. When the cherries are swimming in their own juice, cook in the oven in a covered dish.

Fig compote (dried figs). COMPOTE DE FIGUES SÈCHES – Prepared in the same way as *Prune compote* (see below).

Fig compote (fresh figs). COMPOTE DE FIGUES FRAÎCHES – Peel the figs, which should be ripe and of equal size; put them in boiling syrup – 350 g. (12 oz., 1½ cups) sugar to 6 dl. (1 pint, 2½ cups) water – flavoured with vanilla. Poach for a few minutes. Pour the cooking syrup over the fruit arranged in a dish.

Pear compote. COMPOTE DE POIRES – If the pears are small, leave them whole, and peel them. If they are large, cut into quarters or halves and trim them.

Poach the fruit in boiling vanilla syrup – 350 g. (12 oz., 1½ cups) sugar to 6 dl. (1 pint, 2½ cups) water – cooking only lightly if soft.

If this compote is made with firm pears (cooking pears) rub the fruit with lemon and blanch them for a few minutes before putting them in the vanilla-flavoured cooking syrup.

Pineapple compote. COMPOTE D'ANANAS – Remove the skin and core of a pineapple. Slice the fruit and cook in vanilla-flavoured syrup. Arrange the fruit in a dish and pour the cooking syrup over it. Flavour with kirsch or any other liqueur.

This compote can be made with tinned pineapple.

Plum compote. COMPOTE DE PRUNES – Made particularly with mirabelle plums or greengages, but also with any kind of plum.

Stone the fruit and poach in a syrup of 350 g. (12 oz., 1½ cups) sugar to 6 dl. (1 pint, 2½ cups) water for 10 to 12 minutes.

Prune compote. COMPOTE DE PRUNEAUX – Soak the prunes in cold water until they swell. Cook in a syrup of 350 g. (12 oz., 1½ cups) sugar to 6 dl. (1 pint, 2½ cups) liquid, consisting of half red wine and half water, flavoured with cinnamon or with lemon zest. Cook very gently. This compote can also be prepared in a syrup made without the wine.

All dried fruit compotes are made in the same way, cooking the fruit in a thin syrup.

Raspberry compote. COMPOTE DE FRAMBOISES – Arrange the fruit in a deep dish. Pour over a few tablespoons of boiling syrup.

Strawberry compote. COMPOTE DE FRAISES – Prepared in the same way as *Raspberry compote*.

COMPOTES OF PRESERVED FRUITS. COMPOTES DE FRUITS EN CONSERVE:

Apricot compote. COMPOTE D'ABRICOTS – Choose slightly under-ripe fruit. Prick them and put in a basin. Cover with a very heavy cold syrup. Soak in the syrup for 3 hours.

While the fruit is soaking prepare a 26° syrup (see SUGAR) with lump sugar.

Clarify the syrup with white of egg – one white for 2 litres

($3\frac{1}{2}$ pints, $4\frac{1}{2}$ pints) syrup. Strain the syrup through a straining bag or cloth. Leave to cool.

Drain the apricots. Put them into wide-mouthed jars and cover with the boiling, clarified syrup so that it reaches at least 3 cm. (1 inch) above the level of the fruit. Fix on the tops and screw bands tightly, then give the bands one half-turn to loosen them.

Place a wire rack in the bottom of a large preserving pan and arrange the bottles on it so they do not touch. Fill the pan with cold water, making sure it covers the jars. Boil rapidly for a full 10 minutes. Remove the bottles, wipe and seal them. Keep in a cool place, away from the light.

Halved apricots can also be used for the compote. They are put in a basin and soaked in a heavy syrup. Half the number of stones are cracked, the kernels peeled and put into the preserving jars with the apricots.

The process for capping and boiling is the same as above.

Compote of cherries, peaches, plums and other fruits for preserving – All these fruits are prepared for preserving in the same way as apricots. They are boiled for a longer or shorter time, depending on their variety.

COMPOTIER – Deep dish on a raised base, used for fruits, compotes, jams and other cold sweets. China or crystal fruit dishes are also used for fresh fruits.

COMTÉ – See CHEESE.

CONCASSER – French term for rough chopping, or pounding in a mortar.

CONDÉ (Pâtisserie) – Roll out a piece of left-over *Flaky pastry* (see DOUGH) into a strip about 25 cm. (10 inches) long, 10 cm. (4 inches) wide and $\frac{1}{2}$ cm. ($\frac{1}{4}$ inch) thick. Cover with a layer of royal almond icing called *Condé* (see below). Divide the strip into rectangles 4 cm. ($1\frac{1}{2}$ inches) wide. Lift them with the blade of a large knife and put them on a baking tray. Powder with icing sugar. Cook in a gentle oven.

Preparation of the Condé – Beat together 100 g. (4 oz., scant cup) icing sugar and 2 egg whites. When the mixture is stiff, add enough finely chopped, peeled almonds to make a thick paste.

Two much used condiments: pickled gherkins and mustard

CONDIMENTS – Aromatic substances, added to food to improve its flavour.

The term 'seasoning' is used for substances which are added during cooking, while 'condiments' apply to those added at the table to food already prepared. The two words are interchangeable in current speech.

All condiments, except salt, and saltpetre, are of vegetable origin, and vegetarian peoples, particularly those who live in hot countries, use strong condiments the most.

Condiments are classed, according to their dominant flavour, into acid, aromatic, bitter, salt, sweet, etc.

Acid condiments – Vinegar, verjuice, the juice of lemon or tamarind, etc. affect the taste buds and encourage salivary secretion. So do all vegetables preserved in vinegar; salted cucumbers, which become acid through fermentation; capers; nasturtium flowers; Indian pickles; purslane; sweet-sour cherries; sea-fennel or samphire; little onions in vinegar; melon in vinegar.

Bitter aromatic condiments – Pepper is the chief example of this group; its aromatic qualities are largely lost in the process of cooking, and to preserve its flavour it should be added after cooking.

Paprika, the various types of pimento, and ginger can be used to reinforce the flavour of pepper.

Among the main aromatic condiments are dill, anise, basil, cocoa, coffee, cinnamon, chervil, coriander, cumin, turmeric, tarragon, fennel, juniper, clove, bay, mace, mint, nutmeg, parsley, saffron, sage, savory, thyme, vanilla, orange and lemon zest, and various aromatic vegetables.

Bitter condiments – Garlic, shallot, Welsh onion, spring onion, onion, rocamble (Spanish garlic), leeks, are vegetable seasonings rather than condiments, but are sometimes used raw as condiments; mustard and horseradish are true condiments, stimulating the appetite.

Fat condiments – The fatty elements (oils, butter, fats) are sometimes classed as condiments, because they are used for seasoning. They are really food, not condiments.

Ready-made condiments – There are many condiments, prepared industrially, which have a distinctive taste according to the proportions in which the specific ingredients are used. They include the English sauces (Worcestershire, Harvey, etc.), ketchups, curry powders, prepared mustards, soy sauce, etc.

Salt condiments – Sodium chloride or sea-salt is the only table condiment of mineral origin. Its importance is underlined by its frequent use in metaphors.

Condiment set by Nicolas Lefèvre (1763)
(*Arts décoratifs. Phot. Larousse*)

Salt is both an element which is an integral part of our tissues and body fluids, and an actual condiment. All our foods contain varying amounts of salt; in spite of this, there are few dishes which are not improved by the addition of it.

Saltpetre (azotate or potassium nitrate) is hardly used in cooking, but it is employed in the salting industry to accentuate the red colouring of meats.

Sweet condiments – Sugar and its derivatives (syrups, etc.) as well as honeys, are foods and condiments. In some countries, compotes (whortleberries, gooseberries) are used as condiments. Having a flavour which is sweet and sour at the same time, they are often served with roast or boiled meats, particularly game.

Sweet condiments also include the *aceto-dolce* of the Italians, a preserve of fruit and vegetables in vinegar, sweetened with concentrated grape must or with honey, and preserved fruits with mustard.

CONDIMENT SET. HUILLIER – Piece of tableware, often consisting of two glass bottles in a metal, wooden or pottery frame. Formerly, it was a magnificent piece of silver, placed on the table for decoration rather than use.

CONFECTIONER'S CUSTARD. CRÈME PATISSIÈRE – See CREAMS, *French pastry cream.*

CONFECTIONERY. CONFISERIE – The transformation of sugar into sweets. It tends more and more to be an industry of which the products are sold in special shops. One branch of confectionery is the making of chocolates. Long ago the Egyptians, the Arabs and the Chinese prepared sweetmeats based on various fruit juices and honey. In Europe the use of sugar was not widespread until after the Crusades, and even then remained for a long time in the hands of apothecaries. In the fifteenth century the crystallised fruits of Auvergne, the sugared almonds flavoured with amber or musk, and the '*gigembrats de Montpellier*' enjoyed a well-deserved reputation. In 1660, the regulations promulgated by Colbert underlined the importance of the manufacture of the sugared almonds of Verdun. In Diderot's *Encyclopédie* several plates show the work of the confectioner. With the discovery of sugar beet juice and the advance of machinery in the nineteenth century, sweet-making developed rapidly.

CONFIT – Meat of pork, goose, duck, turkey, etc., cooked in its own fat, and kept covered in the same fat to prevent it coming in contact with the air.

Confit d'oie (Preserved goose) (Gascon cookery) – Pieces of goose, cooked in goose fat and preserved in stoneware pots. (See GOOSE).

Confit de porc (Preserved pork) (Gascon cookery) – Pieces of pork, marinated in salt with spices, and cooked in melted pork fat.

Confit de porc, which is used a great deal in Gascon cookery, is preserved in stoneware pots in the same way as *Confit d'oie*.

CONFRÉRIES VINEUSES (Wine lodges) – The first wine lodges date back to the Middle Ages. Their principal aim was mutual brotherly aid, but some of them also took a protective interest in the quality of wine. The first of the present day *confréries* was founded in 1905 (the Sacavins d'Anjou). The Chevaliers du tastevin (1934), which followed it, was such a commercial success that after the Second World War more and more *confréries* were established. They all adhered to the spirit and tradition of mediaeval corporative *confréries* or ancient Bacchic societies. In fact, most of them are closer in character to the latter despite the fact that some of their ceremonial tends towards the mediaeval style.

Their celebrations are conducted according to a long established ruling: chapters, inauguration of members, banquets generously laced with local wines, traditional entertainment, all carried out in an atmosphere of high spirits and (usually rather earthy) good humour.

The importance of these *confréries* is undeniable. They have taught people, French and foreigners alike, to know and better appreciate French wines. There are almost enough of them now, however; if there are many more their effectiveness will be diminished.

The list of *confréries* that follows is divided into their regional categories, with comments on the most important of them.

ALSACE –

La Confrérie Saint-Etienne d'Alsace – Without question the oldest known *confrérie vineuse*; established in Ammerschwihr in the fourteenth century and reinstated after the Second World War in 1947.

It has preserved the mediaeval hierarchies inherited from the corporations. There are three progressive stages laid down for novices: apprentice, companion, master. There is also a special category, *hors cadre*, that of 'honorary member'. This is reserved for official personalities whom the *confrérie* considers worthy of the dignity.

BORDEAUX –

La Commanderie du bontemps de Médoc et des Graves – In Médoc, *bontemps* is the name for the wooden bowl in which the vine-grower beats the egg whites which will be used to

Confectioners at work
(from Diderot's *Encyclopédie*)

ALSACE
Confrérie
Saint-Étienne d'Alsace

BORDELAIS

Commanderie du bontemps de Médoc et des Graves

Connétablie de Guyenne

Jurat de Saint-Émilion

coller (clarify) his wine. This *confrérie*, founded in 1949, has chosen this object for its name and symbol, and for their traditional headgear, too, since the ruffle of white muslin that decorates the hat resembles stiffly whisked egg whites.

Every year, and particularly in June for the flower festival, and in September for the proclamation of the *vendanges* (vine harvest), the chapters of the *Commanderie* are celebrated in the splendid setting of some Graves or Médoc château. They are followed by marvellous spectacles and a banquet graced by the best wines.

La Commanderie du bontemps de Sainte-Croix-du-Mont – This, the most recent of the Bordeaux *confréries*, also comes under the banner of *bontemps*. It represents the white dessert wines of the right bank of the Garonne.

BOURGOGNE

Compagnon du Beaujolais

Chevalier du Tastevin

La Commanderie du bontemps de Sauternes et Barsac – The great white dessert wines of Sauternes and Barsac have rallied under the emblem of their neighbouring red wines. But while the robes of the latter are bordeaux-coloured, the vine-growers of Sauternes drape themselves in golden-hued velvet, the colour of their wines.

La Connétablie de Guyenne – The name of this *confrérie* refers to the administrative divisions of ancient France. It has taken upon itself the task of promoting the wines of the Premières Côtes de Bordeaux. The meetings are held in the magnificent château of the duc d'Epernon at Cadillac.

Le Grand Conseil du vin de Bordeaux – This is the amalgamation of several Bordeaux *confréries*.

La Jurade de Saint-Emilion – It was John 'Lackland', King of England, who signed a charter in Falaise in 1199 giving the freedom of the communes to Saint-Emilion. For six centuries this charter was to govern the *jurade*, the equivalent of the town council of Saint-Emilion.

The powers of the *jurade* extended to the domain of wine, and consisted of the proclamation of the *vendanges*, as well as control of the quality of the wines. It was in pursuance of these ancient functions that the *confrérie* of Saint-Emilion adopted the name of *Jurade* when it was 'resurrected' in 1948.

Nowadays the official chapters are held by torchlight in the monolithic church carved out of the rock. One of the most important occasions is the proclamation of the *vendanges* by the *jurats* from the top of the 'Tour du roi'.

BURGUNDY –

Les Compagnons du Beaujolais – This *confrérie*, as its name indicates, takes its inspiration from the ancient trade guilds; its Paris section is called *le Devoir parisien* (Parisian duty). Its aim is to make the wines of Beaujolais and the whole of this picturesque province better known and appreciated. Its headquarters are at Villefranche-sur-Saône.

La Confrérie des chevaliers du tastevin – Founded in 1934 at Nuits-Saint-Georges, this *confrérie* continues to be extremely successful. Its activities to publicise Burgundy wine have been considerable. It has branches in many foreign countries; the *commanderie* in the United States, for example,

RÉGION MÉDITERRANÉENNE

Chevalier
de la Méduse

SUD-OUEST

Confrérie Rabelais
de la «dive bouteille»

Viguerie royale
de Jurançon

is well known. Its headquarters are in the beautiful château of Clos-Vougeot, where the main celebrations of the *confrérie* take place: *tastevinages* and official chapters. The latter take the form of a spectacle enlivened by Burgundy *chants* and followed by copious *disnées* washed down with the best wines. It is attended by many foreigners as well as French people.

Celebrations of this kind are held several times a year, a special one being the wine sale of the Hospices de Beaune. This is the most important of the *Trois Glorieuses* of Burgundy. Each year, near 22 January, the *confrérie* organises a Saint-Vincent's day celebration in one of the villages of the Côte in honour of the patron saint of the vine-growers.

La Confrérie Saint-Vincent de Mâcon – This *confrérie*, also under the protection of the patron saint of the vine, has its headquarters in Mâcon and represents the wines of the whole region as well as those of Pouilly-Fuissé.

Les Piliers chablisiens – Why this name of *Piliers*? It is not because the members are 'pillars of wines', but because Chablis is nicknamed the 'Golden Gate' of Burgundy. This very lively *confrérie* has borrowed its name and its hierarchy from architecture. The grand master is called the *grand-architrave*. The chapters are conducted with earthy good humour in a Chablisien cellar. Each year, at the end of November, there is the joyous feast of 'Saint-Cochon' ('Saint Sucking-pig').

CHAMPAGNE –

L'Ordre des coteaux – This Champenois *confrérie* is the revival of a Bacchic society founded by Saint-Evremond, le marquis de Bois-Dauphin et le comte d'Olonne. Boileau alludes to this order in his third satire. The present-day *confrérie* holds its chapters in the cellars or estates of Champagne firms, as well as in other parts of France, and abroad. Its headquarters are in Reims. The great wines, however, do not associate themselves with it.

MEDITERRANEAN REGION –

Le Conseil des mestres tastaïres du Languedoc – This *confrérie* concerns itself with the wines produced in the *départements* of Tarn, Aude and Hérault.

L'Ordre des chevaliers du cep – This order was created in 1951 by M. Eugène Causse, editor-in-chief of the newspaper *la Journée vinicole*, a publication dedicated to the study and defence of wine development. Its headquarters are in Montpellier.

L'Ordre illustre des chevaliers de Méduse – This *confrérie* represents the wines of Provence, Cassis, Bandol, Côtes de Provence. It is the revival of an ancient Bacchic society of the same name initiated in Toulon towards the end of the seventeenth century. The founder was Girardin de Vauvray, general administrator of the Far Eastern seas.

Les Templiers de la Serre – To escape from the persecutions of the Pope and the French King, Philippe le Bel, a number of Templars took refuge in Banyuls, which was then a protectorate of Majorca. They gave a considerable impetus to viniculture and the wine-making industry. It is for this reason that when the vine-growers of Banyuls created an ancient order to publicise their wines, they chose the patronage of the Templars. The farm of la Serre, situated in the vineyards, is their headquarters.

LOIRE VALLEY –

La Confrérie des baillis de Pouilly – Based in Pouilly-sur-Loire, this *confrérie*, which was founded in 1949, has as its aim the promotion of the excellent dry wines of Pouilly-Fumé. Each year there is a tasting of these wines in Paris

La Confrérie des chevaliers de la chantepleure de Vouvray – *Chantepleure* is the picturesque name for the cask tap, the wooden spigot that the vine-grower places in the vat in order to extract the wine. When the tap is turned it 'sings'; then the wine 'weeps'.

The wine is Vouvray, dry or mellow, still or sparkling. Twice a year, in mid-June and mid-September, an official chapter is held in the Bonne Dame cellars hollowed out of the chalky soil on the banks of the Loire. This ancient *confrérie* was revived in 1937.

La Confrérie des chevaliers de Sancerre – This, the most recent of the *confréries vineuses*, aims at publicising the excellent dry white wines, rivals of the Pouilly wines, and is situated exactly opposite the Pouilly vineyards, on the Berry bank of the Loire.

La Confrérie des tire-douzils – Based in Marigny-Brizay in Vienne.

VAL DE LOIRE

Bailly de Pouilly-sur-Loire | Confrérie des tire-douzils | Chevalier bretvin | Chevalier de Sacavin

Les Entonneurs rabelaisiens – What more illustrious patron could one choose for the wine of Chinon than Maître François Rabelais, born in the town and a great lover of his 'Breton' wine. This *confrérie* was founded in 1962. It holds one chapter a year, at the end of September, in the Cave Peincte at Chinon. As is the custom, this chapter is accompanied by a bountiful repast, excellent wines and traditional entertainments.

L'Ordre des chevaliers bretvins – This *confrérie*, founded in 1948 and based in Nantes, aims at publicising Muscadet, the wine of this region, as well as regional dishes.

Les Sacavins d'Anjou – This is the oldest of the modern *confréries*, founded in 1905. Its headquarters are in Angers, and its purpose is to publicise the numerous Anjou wines. It organises a large number of celebrations, chapters, and tastings in Anjou and elsewhere.

SOUTH-WEST –

La Compagnie des mousquetaires d'Armagnac – Inspired by the glorious memory of D'Artagnon and his musketeers but instead of fighting against the protectorship of the Cardinal, it rallies to the cause of Armagnac. Its headquarters are in Condom.

La Confrérie des alambics charentais – This is the *confrérie* of Cognac. The purpose of its celebrations is, of course, to make the famous brandy even better known and appreciated.

La Confrérie Rabelais de la 'dive-bouteille' – For the wines of Gaillac.

Le Consulat de la vinée de Bergerac – For the wines of Bergerac.

La principauté de France-Pineau – This group, with its capital in Cognac, favours the Pineau of Charentes. It endeavours to make this wine better known and appreciated with the help of numerous celebrations held both in France and abroad.

La Viguerie royale de Jurançon – This *confrérie*, with its headquarters at Pau, has taken up the mission of defending and promoting the wine that was so dear to Henry IV.

CONGER EEL. CONGRE – Large fish, also called *anguille de mer* (sea eel), found in the seas of the temperate zone, particularly those of northern Europe.

Conger eels in an aquarium

The best-known type is the *common conger*, the flesh of which resembles that of eels, but is less delicate. The conger eel is chiefly used for making fish soups, notably the *bouillabaisse*, but can be cooked in all the ways given for eel (see EEL).

CONSOLANTE – Glass of wine, beer or cider served to the team of cooks in course of their work.

CONSOMMÉ – Meat stock which has been enriched, concentrated and clarified (see BOUILLON, *Clarification of bouillon*).

For the preparation of various consommés (simple consommés, chicken, game, fish consommés) see SOUP, *Clear soups*.

CONTISER – Term for encrusting chicken fillets, or those of game or fish (chiefly sole), with truffles or other ingredients cut in the shape of little cocks' combs. These are soaked in egg white in order to make them adhere properly and set at regular intervals into cuts made in the fillets.

CONVERSATION (Pâtisserie) – Roll out a piece of puff pastry (*pâte feuilletée*) which has already been rolled out five times (see DOUGH). Set out tartlet moulds close together on a table, moisten each one slightly and lay the pastry on top of the moulds. Flour a lump of pastry and press it gently into each mould so that the pastry adheres to the bottom and sides of the moulds. Half fill each tartlet with a preparation of almonds made according to the directions for *Dartois cakes* (q.v.), or with *French pastry cream* (see CREAMS) to which some powdered almonds have been added.

Moisten the edges of the tartlets lightly and place on them pastry rolled out thinner than the first.

Pass the pastry-roller over the tarts, cutting the pastry on the rim of the moulds and sealing the edges.

Make *Royal icing* (see ICING) with 250 g. (9 oz., 2 cups) icing sugar and one egg white worked well together, adding a pinch of flour to prevent it running.

Put thin bands of pastry crosswise on top of the tarts. Bake them at a moderate temperature.

COOK. CUISINIÈRE – Woman responsible for the preparation and cooking of food. The term is also used in France to describe a small household cooking-stove.

COOKIES – See BISCUIT.

COOKING. CUISINE – The French word *cuisine* is used for the art of preparing dishes (cooking) and the place (kitchen) in which they are prepared.

Cooking is an ancient art, born when primitive man first discovered that if a hunk of meat was placed near the fire it tasted better, and was easier to eat. Some ingenious man found a way of heating water in a stone hollowed out into a basin. The clay vase succeeded this primitive pot. The spit and the pot, however rudimentary in the beginning, made many culinary operations possible. Prehistoric finds such as fragments of pottery, flint and bronze implements and traces of hearths throw light on the origins of cooking.

Cooking among the Egyptians and Assyrians is described under BANQUET.

Greek cook

Greek cooking – In early Greece the only cook was the *mageiros*, who was not a real cook, but a baker. The name comes from *magis, madza*, barley bread or kneaded cake, or from *masso, matto*, to knead.

In Homer's time the *mageiros* did not exist. Female slaves ground the corn and prepared the food. According to the *Iliad* and the *Odyssey*, the host himself, however exalted, prepared and cooked the meals with the help of friends when he received distinguished guests.

Later, the *mageiros* cooked as well as baked for his masters. In time he became *archimageiros* or *chef de cuisine* and was given assistants.

Great houses had a hierarchy of slaves, under a steward, the *eleatros*. Each slave had definite duties. The *opsonomos* or *agorastes* (from *agora* or market place) bought the food, while the *opsartytes* looked after the fires, did rough jobs and prepared food for the household slaves. A woman, the *demiourga*, only made sweetmeats and other delicacies. Women had free access to the kitchen. Other slaves prepared meals or served at table. The *trapezopoios* laid the table and washed the dishes, the *oinophoros* had charge of the wine, the *oinochoikos*, a young slave, filled the wine cups of the guests.

In the fourth century B.C., Athenian cooks, as shown in the Greek theatre, were often slaves. They played an important rôle in the life of the city, judging by the taunts poets levelled at their pretensions.

'They were artists in their way; their apprenticeship lasted two years, under the direction of a cook of reputation, and during this time they wore the apron of the apprentice. In order to acquire this difficult *métier* the apprentice not only learnt from his masters, he was given books which set down the rules of his art, and, if zealous, spent his nights studying them.

'It was only after long study that he could aspire to become one of those artists whose names were quoted, and who became famous through the creation of a single dish.' (C. Daremberg and E. Saglio, *Dictionnaire des antiquités grecques et romaines*.)

In Greece, cooks had become persons of importance, ruling as masters over all the other slaves in the household. A special law permitted the cook who invented a new dish the privilege of making it and selling it to the public.

Many Greek cooks left famous names behind. Cadmos was cook to the King of Sidon in Phoenicia, and, according to legend, introduced writing into Greece. As a result of the burning of the library in Alexandria, only a few fragments and the authors' names remain from the Greek literature of gastronomy.

Although early Greek cooking equipment was rudimentary, kitchen utensils were gradually perfected. Casseroles, cauldrons and gridirons were sometimes made in precious metal and magnificently decorated. Objects from the Bosco-Reale Treasure, in the Louvre in Paris, show their splendour.

Cauldrons of bronze or iron were shaped like an egg, or truncated cone, with a rounded base, chains and a cover. Among them were the *chytra* and the *chutros*, common earthenware pots without ornament, the *kakkabe* (or *kakkabos*), a metal pot, the *lebes*, a large metal basin, the *olla*, an earthenware pot, ancestor of the *marmite*.

Casseroles and pans, generally made of bronze, and frying pans (the Greeks enjoyed fried food) were like those we use today. There were special dishes for cooking eggs, with cavities of different sizes. Athenaeus says: 'The first row belongs to the peacocks' eggs, the second to gooses' eggs, the third to chickens' eggs.' (*Deipnosophistai.*) These utensils were usually placed on a metal support, the *eugytheke*.

Graceful bronze kettles or double-bottomed amphorae, like a modern double-boiler, were used to heat drinks. Food was served on earthenware or metal utensils, such as the *kane*, a concave dish with two horizontal handles, and the *pazopsis*, a deep dish made from pottery, bronze, silver or even gold. Some dishes were served on *ichthuai*, plates decorated with fishes. Greek drinking vessels, richly decorated, were called *patarion* or *poterion*.

Roman cooking – In early Rome, as in Greece, there were no cooks as such. Bakers took their place. Cooking was rudimentary and there was no need for skilled cooks.

Not until after the war against Antiochus the Great (568 B.C.), did the Romans have banquets and employ skilled cooks. The rôle of the cook in society became more important with the return of the deputation sent to Athens to bring back the laws of Solon, and to study Greek Art and Letters.

Cooks and gastronomes were brought to Rome, and formed a society, one of their number calling himself *vicarius supra coenas*. Under Hadrian an academy, *Collegium coquorum* was formed. Cooks were highly paid. The triumvir Antony gave a house to Cleopatra's cook as a reward for an admirable meal.

In large Roman households, the kitchen slaves each had specific tasks. There was the *coquus*, who resembled the *gros bonnet* ('big noise'), the *focarius*, who kept the fires going, the *coctor*, who superintended certain dishes, the *pistor* or *pinsitor*, who was kitchen help, preparing the stuffings, pounding various foods (the Romans had a taste for purées), and grinding corn for bread and cakes.

Underground Roman kitchen
(from de Vogüé, *Antiquités civiles et religieuses de Syrie*)

Many slaves were attached to the kitchen and dining-room. The *condus* managed the household, and ordered and stored the food. The *doliarius* managed the cellar, the *structor* arranged the food on the serving platters, the *captor* carved the meat, the *proegustator*, a reliable man, tasted the dishes, and the *aquarius* was responsible for the supply of water.

In the *triclinium* (dining-room) was the *tricliniarcha*, who was like the butler in a large household today, the *pocillator*, who poured wine, and the *nomenclator*, a high-ranking servant, responsible for protocol.

For a long time in ancient Rome, and under the Republic, the chief food was a gruel, *puls* or *pulmentus*, made with barley or spelt (German wheat). This was roasted, pounded and cooked with water, to make a porridge like the *polenta* still eaten in Italy. This was made in a bronze cauldron.

Our terms for liquids like *potées, potages* and *pot-au-feu* derive from the Roman word *potus* from *potare* (to drink).

Under the Empire, decadence, gluttony and extravagant luxury became the characteristic of Roman cooking. Carême, who studied the Roman *cuisine*, declared that it was heavy and without refinement. The Romans carried their taste for meat to such extremes that restrictive measures had to be taken. They even ate elephant, of which Pliny tells us only the trunk found favour. He writes also of three roebuck, set on the table as a first course. Herds of these animals were set up in parks in the neighbourhood of Tarquinia.

The Romans did not confine themselves to wild animals, eating puppies: dormice especially fattened with chestnuts, acorns and nuts; and guinea pigs kept in a cage called the *gliriarium*.

Mazois, in the *Palais de Scaurus*, described the kitchen in the house of a great Roman:

'Scaurus' kitchen is arched, its dimensions are enormous, it is 45 m. (148 feet) long; and this will not astonish you when thinking of the banquets he gives and the great number of guests, freed men and slaves, he has to feed. Here the fireplace is elbow-high, but vast and made so as to draw off the smoke because, in winter, a house filled with smoke is uninhabitable, particularly if green wood or new brushwood are burnt. The decoration of the kitchen has a painting representing one of those ridiculous sacrifices made to the goddess Fortunax. This is surrounded with paintings of all the food necessary for a great feast: fish ready for cooking; hams; venison ready for the spit; birds, hares and many others objects. The floor is made of a composition used in Greece, producing a fine black paving, well drained so even those walking barefoot are warm.

'Near the kitchen are subsidiary rooms, such as the *olearium* where oil is kept in great *dolia* (earthenware pots 123 cm. (four feet) in diameter); the *horreum* where a great many things are kept, such as winter provisions, honey, fruits, dried raisins, salt meats, and all the provisions necessary for a great household. These storerooms are under the surveillance of a storekeeper called *promuscondus*, who checks on all the foodstuffs and supplies and delivers them to the servants when required. The steward sees to the maintaining of supplies; the amount of provisions the storerooms contain make them resemble actual shops.'

The kitchen utensils used by the Romans were similar in material and shape to those used by the Greeks. For cooking meat, they used a grill, called *craticula*. They also had a great many pastry moulds, sieves, skimmers, ladles, all more or less like those we use today.

Cooking and eating habits of the Gauls – Strabo wrote: 'The Celts eat bread in very small quantity with a great deal of meat either boiled, roast or grilled. Their rivers and the two seas which surround them provide fish, which they season with cumin and vinegar as oil is scarce. They add cumin to all their beverages.

'The rich drink wine, which they bring from Italy and Marseilles, and which is served as follows: a servant brings in each hand a bowl of earthenware or silver, similar to a *marmite*, and filled with wine. Each one draws from the bowl. Little is drunk at a time, but they drink often, and wine is almost always unadulterated.'

The Gauls loved spiced dishes. The recipes given below show their taste for strong condiments:

Method of preparing cranes and ducks. 'Wash and trim the crane (or the duck) and put it in an earthenware *marmite*. Add water, salt and dill. Let it reduce by half and then put the whole into a cauldron with oil and broth, a bouquet of marjoram and coriander. When the crane is on the point of being cooked, add a little heated wine. Pour over a mixture of honey, lovage, cumin, coriander, roots of benzoin, rue and pounded caraway, with vinegar. Put some starch in the pan and make the liquid boil. Put your crane on a dish and pour the sauce over it.'

Stuffing for dormice. 'Make this with the meat of the dormouse with powdered pepper, nuts, benzoin and broth. Put the dormice on a tile after sewing them up and put them in the oven. They can also be cooked in a copper boiler.'

Cooking and eating habits of the Franks and Merovingians – 'Once established in Gaul, the Franks imitated the luxurious example set by the Romanised Gauls. They ate reclining on couches in dining-rooms, around tables decorated with flowers. The Franks borrowed various dishes from the Gauls, and their cooking remained very much the same as that of the Romanised Gauls, entirely Roman. Pepper, honey, wine, vinegar, meat broth and aromatic plants formed the basis of all seasonings.' (From *l'Art Culinaire*, marquis de Cussy.)

At the end of the Merovingian period the convents, which had preserved all the traditions of the gourmands, increased in number in France, and great progress was made in cooking.

French cooking in the Middle Ages – Viollet-le-Duc gives a picture of what kitchens were like at the time:

'In the houses of the Middle Ages, chimneys were large and high; a man could get inside the chimney without bending, and ten or twelve people could sit easily round the hearth. Inside these chimneys strong andirons, called *landiers*, were needed to hold the enormous logs that were put on the fire, and to prevent them from rolling into the room. There were andirons for the kitchen and for other rooms; the former were complicated in form because they were put to various uses. Their uprights were furnished with supports or hooks to take the spits; they were surmounted by an extension in the form of a small brazier on which dishes could be prepared or kept warm.

'The division of stoves into several compartments as in our day, was seldom seen. The dishes were cooked on the fire itself, and these fierce fires did not allow for dishes which needed constant stirring, or to be made in frying pans.

'The andiron-braziers, filled with charcoal, were at a convenient height and at a distance from the fire. Sometimes they were divided into two compartments, in which case it was possible to prepare and cook four dishes outside the hearth. Over the hearth hung pots, suspended from hooks or tripods; in front of the fire one or two spits turned several pieces of meat. Only in this way could a large meal be prepared.

'Before the twelfth century, only roast meats and boiled vegetables were eaten, and the art of making stews was almost unknown. What was needed were good clear fires, large hearths on which many long spits could be set, and space for hanging vast cauldrons.

'The architects of the twelfth century began to put ovens in kitchens, and tables on which to arrange food before serving it. From the fourteenth century onwards, sauces were much appreciated. Ovens were needed to make the many dishes which were served at the big feasts of the time. The equipment of the kitchens began to improve.

'In the castles and convents of the Middle Ages, the chimney was not always built against the wall in the room kept for cooking, but was sometimes built in the middle of the vaulted roof, and the hearth set in the centre of the room. A kitchen like this resembled a tower, open at the top, without joists to separate the intervening space into floors, and with the diameter decreasing towards the top. Such a kitchen can still be seen in the Palace of the Popes at Avignon.'

View of the kitchen of Fontevrault Abbey

French cooking in the fourteenth and fifteenth centuries – Information on cooking at this time is found in *le Viandier* by Taillevent.

Soups were a gruel, made with milk, often flavoured with honey, saffron and sweet wine and thickened with *moyeux* (egg yolks) and butter. Rice soups were made and various purées like *garbures* (q.v.). They were called *soupes* (sops). *Brouet* was made of calves' meat, with fowl or conies (rabbits) cut into pieces, browned in *sein de lard* (lard) with onions and crushed almonds, and moistened with wine and stock. The *hochepot* (hotchpotch) was similar to *brouet*, but grilled bread or grated breadcrumbs were added as thickening. *Galimafrée* (which did not have its modern connotations with bad stew, *mauvais ragoût*), was made with mutton or fowl, cooked, chopped, simmered with onion and moistened with *cameline sauce*.

Taillevent gives recipes for seventeen sauces, including *sauce Robert,* so wholesome and necessary, according to Rabelais, for duck, rabbits, roasts, fresh pork, eggs, salt cod and other meats. Sauces were thickened with bread.

Italian kitchen of the sixteenth century.
After Christiano di Messiburgo, Ferrara, 1549

French cooking in the sixteenth century – Under François I, the days of feasting and drinking, as recounted by Rabelais, were revived. The first real cookery books date from this time. In 1543, *la Fleur de toute cuisine*, by Pierre Pidoux, and in 1570, the *Viandier de Taboureau*, appeared.

Cooking flourished in this reign. The refinements of the Italian Renaissance had penetrated into France, and French banquets became more splendid than ever. Menus included fish, fowl, feathered game and venison, but meat and vegetables featured little. Kitchen utensils were now augmented by vast copper *daubiers* (q.v.).

In the following reigns expense had to be cut down owing to imperial and religious wars. Prosperity returned under Henry II, and cooking made rapid progress. Feasts were magnificent. A meal served to Henry II himself included a profusion of lampreys in *Hippocras sauce*, hot-pots, ducklings *à la Malvoisie*, slices of *muraena* (an eel-like fish) served with a sauce of egg yolks and herbs, ducks *à la didone*, sturgeon fillets *à la lombarde*, quarters of roebuck, partridges *à la tonelette*, and a whole series of puddings such as *darioles* and *échaudes*.

At the end of the sixteenth century, Italian cooks and pastrycooks came to France under the influence of Catherine and Marie de Medici. At this time the Italian *maîtres queux* (head chefs) were considered the best in the world. They taught the French many recipes which have remained in the French culinary repertoire. Cooks were already aware of their rôle and social importance.

French cooking in the seventeenth century – The reign of Henry IV is symbolised by the famous 'hen' which the King wished all his subjects to be able to put in the pot on Sundays.

Although cooking had little significance during the reign of Louis XIII, it received an impetus founded on the *Cuisinier Français* by La Varenne, which appeared in 1651, the first book to fix the rules and principles of working, and to establish some order in cooking. In 1691 the *Cuisinier Royal et Bourgeois* by Massialot, giving precise instructions, appeared. It showed that cooking was growing more varied, and dishes were named after famous people or royal favourites. Menus mention the *olla* – the Spanish *olla podrida* – multiple *hors-d'œuvre*, monumental removes and *entremets* (q.v.). Courses were arranged in a logical way.

During the *Grand Siècle* cooking was spectacular rather than fine or delicate.

In the reign of Louis XIV the culinary utensils of the Middle Ages were replaced by a *Batterie de cuisine* (see KITCHEN EQUIPMENT) which included many new pots and pans in tinplate and wrought iron. Later, silver utensils were used.

The festivities of Superintendent Fouquet in his château de Vaux, and of the Prince of Condé at Chantilly, were particularly sumptuous. The famous Vatel was *maître d'hôtel* of the Grande Condé, a very important position.

Seventeenth century cook (*Mariette*)

All the *grands seigneurs* took a great interest in food, and master cooks, grateful for this interest, gave their masters' names to new dishes. This gave rise to the mistaken impression that dishes were created by those whose names they bore, as with *Béchamel*, called after the marquis de Béchamel.

Table manners were simpler than those in the preceding century. Although Louis XIV ate too heavily for a true gourmet, he established the habit of having dishes served separately. Before his time everything was thrown together, making a monstrous pyramid described by Boileau in his *Festin ridicule*:

Sur un lièvre flanqué de six poulets étiques,
S'élevaient trois lapins, animaux domestiques,
Qui, dès leur tendre enfance élevés dans Paris,
Sentaient encor le chou dont ils furent nourris.
Autour de cet amas de viandes entassées,
Régnait un long cordon d'alouettes pressées,
Et sur les bords du plat, six pigeons étalés
Présentaient pour renforts leurs squelettes brûlés.

On top of a hare surrounded by six emaciated pullets
Lay three rabbits, domestic animals,
Who, raised since their tender infancy in Paris,
Smelt still of the cabbage on which they had been fed.
Round this mass of piled up meats
Reigned a long border of pressed larks,
And on the edges of the dish, six pigeons spread out
Exposed their burnt skeletons as a reinforcement.

In the seventeenth century a great quantity of dishes were served at each meal, and there are many descriptions of the meals served at the royal table of Louis XIV.

The Palatine Princess wrote; 'I have seen the King eat, and that very often, four plates of different soups, an entire pheasant, a partridge, a large plateful of salad, mutton cut up in its juice with garlic, two good pieces of ham, a plateful of cakes, and fruit and jams.'

And according to Saint-Simon, 'All his life he had eaten very little bread, and for some time past only the soft part as he had no teeth. Soup in very large quantities, fine hashes and eggs were used as a supplement. Everything he ate was very highly spiced, at least twice as spiced as is ordinarily the case, and very strong indeed.' It was due to Louis XIV that the custom of serving sweets, formerly reserved for fête days, was introduced into daily use.

Menus were equally copious in the great houses and among the rich bourgeois of the time, and the master chefs, or *cordons bleus*, who prepared these meals had a great deal to do.

French cooking under the Regency – History has judged the eight years of Regency severely. But, if the years under Phillipe d'Orléans were disastrous politically and economically, they had at least some distinction as regards gastronomy. The true French cuisine dates from this time.

While the Regency lasted, the ovens of the great houses in the kingdom were hardly ever cold, and the gifted cooks who directed the kitchens of the Palais Royal, the Trianon and the other princely houses had to satisfy the refined table companions who were the guests of the Regent.

The Regent himself took a hand with the pastry. In *la vie privée d'autrefois*, Franklin wrote: 'For the little suppers given by the Regent, the dishes were prepared in special rooms on the same floor, where all the utensils were made of silver; the *roués* often worked with the cooks.'

The menu of one of these suppers gives a picture of the brilliant cuisine of the time. This meal is a key to the principal dishes in fashion:

First course. Joint of salt beef, garnished with carrots and potatoes.

Two soups. One made of a pike cullis, one of turnips with a duck thereon.

Two fish dishes. Carp *à l'anglaise*; freshwater fish consisting of twenty-four little perch and four little pikes.

Ten entrées. Mutton fillets larded and glazed with gherkins on top; two chickens stuck with parsley, *espagnole sauce*; pike *à la polonaise*; perch *à la genevoise* (six perch and one bottle of white wine); sauerkraut with one pike; twenty-five oysters cooked with a pint of cream; *noix de veau à la napolitaine*; three partridges *en levrault* (leveret); two fine eels *à la bavaroise*; and half a hundred fine crayfish; roebuck kidneys in marinade.

Two dishes of pâtisseries. A cake filled with apricot *marmelade*; an iced tart (six peaches iced and a pint of cream).

Four roasts. Fried smelts (crumbed), two *poulardes*, two fried soles, two wild ducks.

Four different salads, with sauces.

Four little hot entremets. Six veal sweetbreads larded and glazed; pig's trotters *Sainte-Menehould*; dried peas *à la crème*; dessert apples *à la chinoise*.

Until the beginning of the eighteenth century, cooking was done on the fire and on charcoal braziers. Kitchens were provided with a stove called a *potager* which had twelve or twenty grates (*foyers*), according to the size of the household. This arrangement lasted until the cast-iron stove heated with coal came into use.

French cooking under Louis XV – Cooking in the reign of Louis XV was much the same as under the Regency. The nobility were very interested in the culinary art. They were 'gastronomic snobs', and wished to have dishes named after them, whether invented in their own house or not. It is to this period that we owe *Bouchées à la Reine*, named in honour of Marie Leczinska, wife of Louis XV; *Cailles à la Mirepoix* (quails) and *Timbale Pompadour*.

The menus served at the court of Louis XV by Héliot, *écuyer de bouche* of Madame Dauphine de France, were grandiose. Carême published part of these menus, taken from the original source, in his *Maître d'hôtel français*. Philéas Gilbert notes that the menus were presented in the form of placards 'whose dimensions are those of electoral notices and in which figure: 4 ollas and 8 lesser soups; 12 fish *entrées*; 32 *entrées* and 44 lesser *entrées*; 12 removes; 4 *hors-d'œuvre* before the King; 2 grand *entremets*; 32 roasts; 2 lesser roasts at the ends of the table; 2 little dishes before the King; 40 cold *entremets* and 48 hot *entremets*.' Many master cooks were needed to execute such a menu.

In the time of Louis XV a number of culinary books appeared. The most interesting were *le Cuisinier moderne* by Vincent de la Chapelle, published in English in 1733, and translated into French in 1735, and the *Dons de Comus*, which appeared without the author's name but was written by Marin, *maître d'hôtel* of the maréchal de Soubise. This was preceded by a *Discours préliminaire*, remarkable both for its style and documentation, and attributed to the Jesuit fathers, Pierre Brunoy and Hyacinthe Bourgeant. Carême thought the work of de la Chapelle the best of the books which appeared in the seventeenth and eighteenth centuries, although he criticised the author for having given certain dishes inadmissible names, such as *Filet de boeuf en talon de botte,* and *Potage à la jambe de bois*, which he found grotesque.

Among the bourgeois at this time, meals were also simpler. Brillat-Savarin describes a typical meal served in the middle classes. In 1740 a dinner for ten people would consist of:

First course. Le bouilli (boiled meat); an *entrée* of veal cooked in its juice; an *hors-d'œuvre*.

Second course. A turkey; a dish of vegetables; a salad; a cream.

Third course. Cheese; fruit; a pot of jam. The plates were only changed three times – after the soup, for the second course, and for dessert. Coffee was seldom served, but quite often a ratafia of cherries or carnations, a recent introduction, was served.

French cooking at the time of Louis XVI – During the first years of the reign of Louis XVI, the tendency continued to refine culinary methods and to establish more order and logic, as well as greater elegance in menus for grand galas. Brillat-Savarin writes in his *Histoire de la cuisine* of great improvements in all branches of catering.

'Cooks, caterers, *pâtissiers*, confectioners, grocers, have multiplied on an ever increasing scale. . . . Physics and chemistry have been called to the aid of cooking. The most distinguished intellects have not thought it an unworthy task to occupy themselves with our basic needs, and have introduced improvements ranging from the workman's simple *pot-au-feu* to the transparent extracts (Brillat-Savarin means here the aspic jellies) which are served in gold and crystal. . . .

'The French *cuisine* has appropriated foreign dishes, such as caviare and beefsteak; seasoning such as curry and soya; drinks like punch and others. . . . Coffee has become popular, in the morning as nourishment, and after dinner as an exhilarating and tonic drink.

'Finally, the word gastronomy has been revived from the Greek.'

During the reign of Louis XVI the first restaurant came into being (see RESTAURANT). Menus of restaurateurs of the time provide information on cooking in general. These included 12 soups, 24 *hors-d'œuvre*, 15 or 20 *entrées* of beef, 20 *entrées* of mutton, 30 *entrées* of fowl or game, 12 or 20 *entrées* of veal, 12 dishes of *pâtisserie*, 24 dishes of fish, 15 roasts, 50 *entremets*, 50 desserts.

French cooking during the period of the Revolution and the Empire – The author of *Avant de quitter la table* described the French *cuisine* at the time of the Revolution:

'. . . the poor chefs were forgotten; a new austerity prevailed and the supreme *bon ton* was to assume a spartan simplicity.

'But the pleasures of the table never lose their rights, and the new masters of France soon tired of so much virtue, and once again in Paris and in the provinces, there was a return to good living. The chefs of the great houses of the nobility, finding themselves unemployed on the emigration of their masters, put themselves at the service of those who governed them, and soon the ovens were heated once again throughout the country, and particularly in Paris, in the Palais ex-Royal, rue Montorgueil, and the boulevard du Temple.

'Men of talent, such as Brillat-Savarin and Grimod de la Reynière, began to assemble their observations, and to experiment in order to write. In 1798, at the age of 16, Carême, the man who was going to write the new 'culinary charter', after 6 years in a modest cabaret on the outskirts of Paris, started as a pastry-cook with Bailly. The *maison Bailly* was one of the leading Paris *pâtisseries* and supplied the prince de Talleyrand, who kept a sumptuous table. Two years later Carême was first pastry-maker in this famous house'.

In the relatively calmer period of the Directory, the great bourgeois households reorganised themselves, new restaurants opened, and cooking again became as grandiose as in the time of Louis XV.

Under the Directory, an attempt was made to revive official dinners and suppers. Ostentation was re-established, and magnificent buffets with enormous, over-decorated cold *pièces* were prepared for balls. Even if the emphasis was on luxury rather than on a well-chosen ensemble in these great festivities, both in Paris and in the provinces, more rational menus were introduced.

A kitchen in the early nineteenth century

'The first Empire passed in the clash of arms and in triumphal trumpetings marked by splendid fêtes and immense banquets.' (Varras.)

The position of chef in the Imperial Court was no sinecure. The chefs came and went. Was it due to bad ventilation in the kitchens, or to the severe economy established in the household, which reduced wages to 2,400 francs?.

Among those who exercised their art at the Imperial Court, and contributed to the extravagance of the great galas which took place, was Chandelier, the man who was the most devoted of Napoleon's servants, followed him to St Helena, and in spite of countless difficulties applied himself to the task of encouraging the appetite of the fallen Emperor.

It was at this period that Carême himself, the great master of culinary art, collected his material for his works on French *cuisine* in the nineteenth century. While continuing his innovations in *pâtisserie*, he perfected his culinary knowledge. He was seen at the Tuileries, at the great dinners given by Talleyrand, at the fêtes of the Hotel de Ville where the new marshals of France, the new nobility, ministers and ambassadors came, and at the Elysée-Napoléon with the great Laguipière.

As a *pâtissier* he took the place of those who had come to the end of their careers: Tiroloy, one-time chef of the Soubise household, Feuillet of the house of Condé, Lecoq, who had worked in the royal household for Louis XVI. Carême was rapidly promoted under the famous chefs with whom he studied, and expresses his gratitude in his works.

French cooking at the beginning of the nineteenth century – Even the best equipped kitchens of this period had very mediocre implements, and cooking stoves were rudimentary. Carême has left us a picture of these kitchens at the hour of work.

'Imagine yourself in a large kitchen such as that of the Foreign Ministry at the moment of a great dinner. Twenty chefs are at their occupations, coming, going, moving with speed in this cauldron of heat. Look at the great mass of live charcoal, a cubic metre (yard), for the cooking of the *entrées*, and another mass on the ovens for the cooking of the soups, the sauces, the *ragoûts*, the frying and the *bain-marie*.

'Add to that a heap of burning wood in front of which four spits are turning, one of which bears a sirloin weighing 20 to 27 kg. (45 to 60 lb.), another a piece of veal weighing 16 to 20 kg. (35 to 45 lb.), the other two for fowl and game.

'In this furnace everyone moves with tremendous speed; not a sound is heard; only the chef has the right to make himself heard, and at the sound of his voice everyone obeys. Finally, to put the lid on our sufferings, for about half an hour the doors and windows are closed so that the air does not cool the dishes as they are being dished up. And in this way we pass the best days of our lives.

'But honour commands. We must obey even though physical strength fails. But it is the burning charcoal which kills us!'

During the Restoration, Brillat-Savarin's *la Physiologie du goût* appeared, and shows the importance that gastronomy and cooking had at that time. In the restaurants of the Palais Royal trade flourished. Thanks to the efforts of restaurateurs and master cooks to satisfy the tastes of their clientele, great progress was made in cookery.

Under the reign of Louis-Philippe the art of cooking was in lower favour. Everyone about the economical King lived with a simplicity close to stinginess. Dinners at the Tuileries were bourgeois in their presentation.

Louis-Philippe lived as a bourgeois, always with an eye on economy. He even assigned to the caterers the supplying of dinners at fixed prices to the château. The cost of these dinners was to be 5 to 10 francs per head, according to the importance of the guests.

Under such a régime the art of cooking could hardly make progress. However, it was in the reign of the 'bourgeois' King that the most famous clubs and gastronomic coteries were founded. These societies met in the best restaurants and were the forerunners of the *Académie des gastronomes*

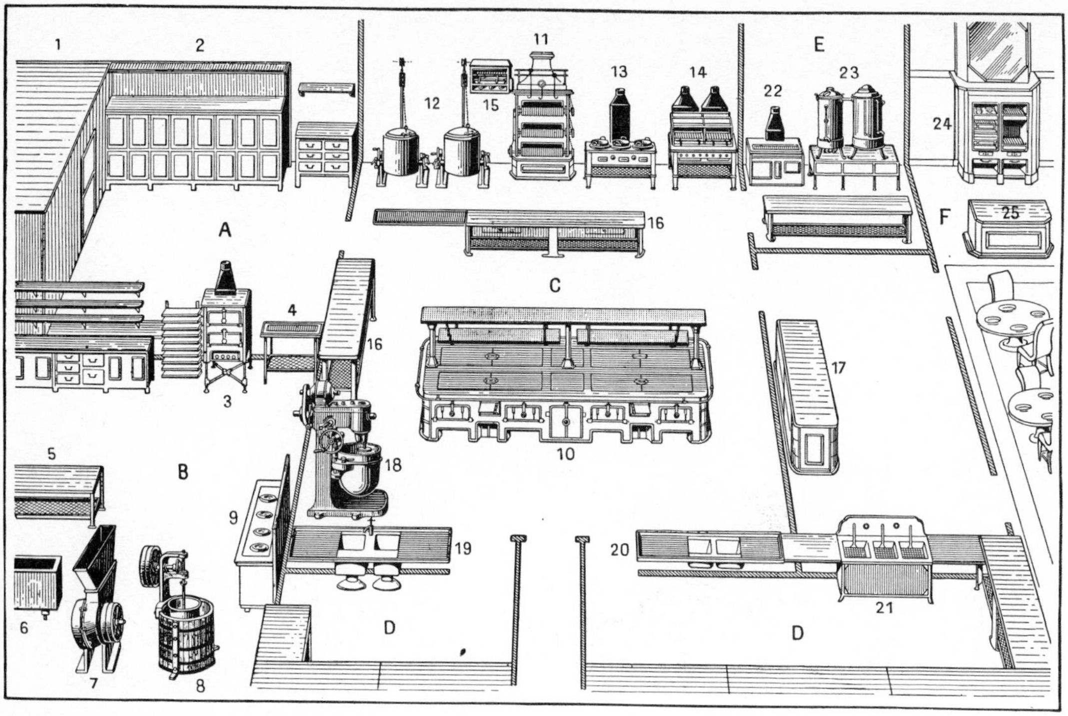

Diagrammatic installation of a kitchen (after the *Constructeurs associés de Paris*)

A. Storage room: 1. Cold room; 2. Refrigerating cabinet; 3. Oven; 4. Marble-topped table; 5. Table. B. Ice creamery: 6. Ice trough; 7. Machine for breaking up ice; 8. Motor turbine; 9. Ice cream containers. C. Kitchen: 10. Large central cooking range; 11. Spit; 12. Steam kettles; 13. Deep friers; 14. Grills; 15. Salamander stove; 16. Tables; 17. Hotplate; 18. Mixer. D. Washing-up space; 19. Sinks; 20. Washing-up range; 21. Washing-up sinks for glasses. E. Cafeteria; 22. Oven; 23. Percolators. F. Grill-room; 24. Grills; 25. Hotplate

founded by Curnonsky. Although Brillat-Savarin had predicted such an academy, its programme was nebulous.

The brief Republic of 1848 had its patriotic banquets, where the menu comprised only veal and salad.

French cooking during the period of the Second Empire – The Second Empire may have been 'the reign of electroplated ware and tinsel, the time of crinolines and prefects', but it was also a time that favoured the *cuisine*. Magnificent festivities and banquets took place at the Tuileries, and in the various châteaux in which the court of Napoleon III lived. The great dinners of the time achieved perfection. The first edition of the *Cuisine classique* by Urbain Dubois and Auguste Bernard appeared. This work is still an authority, and has done more for professional cooking than even the books of Carême, which are sometimes hard to read. Among the great chefs were Armand Gouffé and Joseph Gastilleur.

'On ordinary occasions,' says Madame de Carette, 'the table at the Tuileries was rich and elegant, and the food exquisite and delicate.' (*Souvenirs intimes de la cour des* Tuileries.)

'One ate at almost all seasons strawberries, peaches, little new peas, from the greenhouses of the châteaux of Versailles. . . . There were four double courses, (which means, today, two soups, two removes, four *entrées*, two roasts, etc.)

'The kitchens in the Tuileries were in the basement and the dishes arrived by lifts installed behind the Gallery of Diana'.

Despite the brilliance and delicacy of food in high social circles, many writers criticised the cooking of the time, complaining that it was mediocre. In the *Courrier de Paris* of 27 March 1858, cooking and chefs were severely rated:

'A good dinner is a rare thing today. Gastronomy is like poetry: it has fallen into a complete decadence. . . .

'The present generation eats and knows not how to eat . . . it is the enemy of that *grande cuisine* which was France's glory. The chefs are the cause of this indifference, which is blamed on us. They have muddled everything, spoilt everything, exhausted everything.'

On 7 June 1867, during the Universal Exhibition, the dinner of the three Emperors took place in the Café anglais. The guests were all illustrious, including the Czar, the

Old kitchen, Hospice de Beaune (*French Government Tourist Office*)

Commercial kitchen. Gaz de France (*Photothèque*)

Czarevitch, King William I of Prussia, and several Grand Dukes. A description of this meal will be found under the heading MENU. It cost 400 francs per head, a considerable sum at that time.

French cooking of the late nineteenth and early twentieth century – French cooking has reached its peak since the end of the nineteenth century. Many excellent cookery books were written at this time, starting with those by Urbain Dubois, Auguste Bernard, Gouffré, and Joseph Favre. After 1900 important books like Escoffier's *Guide culinaire* (in collaboration with Philéas Gilbert), *Plaisirs de la table* by Nignon, *le Grand livre de la cuisine* by Prosper Salles, were published. Interesting works came from the pen of master cooks such as Alfred Suzanne, Dietrich, Garlin, Werner, Bouzy, Alfred Guérot and Pellaprat.

These books deal only with theoretical instruction; often there is a gap between theory and practice. The fact that they were written at all proves that culinary practice was highly developed. The present-day chef must have the same qualities as those at the beginning of the last century, of whom Désaugiers wrote:

Un cuisinier, quand je dine,
Me semble un être divin
Qui, du fond de sa cuisine,
Gouverne le genre humain.
Qu'ici bas, on le contemple
Comme un ministre du ciel,
Car sa cuisine est un temple
Dont les fourneaux sont l'autel.

'A cook, when I dine, seems to me a divine being, who rules the human race from the depths of his kitchen. One considers him a minister of heaven, because his kitchen is a temple, in which his ovens are the altar.' (See also INTERNATIONAL COOKERY).

COOT. FOULQUE – Bird similar to the moorhen. It has dark flesh, dry and not strongly flavoured.

There are several varieties of coot in France: *foulque morelle, foulque macroule*, also known as *foulque judelle, foulque à crête du Cap* (African or crested coot) and *foulque bleue du Portugal.* It is found in England but is not so popular as it was. There are several species in the U.S.A., but they are not marketed.

The coot is classified by the church as Lenten fare. All ways of cooking a wild duck apply to a coot. It is good eaten fresh, if skinned immediately after it is shot (the skin is oily and smelly) and cooked in a casserole with a piece of larding bacon.

Coot

COPEAUX (Twists) – Small sweets or *petits fours* made from a mixture like that given for *langue de chat* (q.v.). They are squeezed from a forcing-bag on to a baking tray, and cooked in a hot oven. While still malleable, they are rolled round a stick into twists.

COPPER. CUIVRE – Metal used in the manufacture of many cooking utensils. It is a good conductor of heat, and copper cooking pans have the advantage of spreading heat evenly and cooking the food right through.

In minute but measurable doses, copper is one of the mineral elements in the human body and in some foods. Copper salts were long regarded as virulent poisons. Experiments have long proved this false, although salts, like sulphates and acetates (verdigris), tend to cause nausea and vomiting.

Coq au vin (*Robert Carrier*)

COQ – Chef aboard ship. Also the French word for cock and a synonym for chicken in certain dishes. *Coq* is usual on menus.

Coq en pâte – This dish is prepared with a fine chicken, and not a cock. It is much better if made as follows, in the old way:

Remove the breast bone from the dressed chicken. Stuff the bird generously with *foie gras* and truffles cut into large pieces, seasoned with salt and spices, moistened with Cognac and with some delicate forcemeat. Truss the chicken *en entrée* (i.e. the legs inserted into the sides).

Brown in butter on all sides. Cover with a *matignon*, made with 1 medium carrot, 1 onion, 1 small stick celery, all chopped, softened in butter and seasoned with salt, pepper, thyme and powdered bay. Add 75 g. (3 oz.) finely sliced lean raw ham at the end of cooking. Wrap the chicken in a pig's caul soaked in cold water, or in salt pork. Place on an oval base of *Lining pastry* (see DOUGH), made from 500 g. (18 oz., 4½ cups) flour, 300 g. (11 oz., 1⅓ cups) butter, 1 egg, 1½ dl. (¼ pint, ⅔ cup) water, 1½ teaspoons salt. Cover the chicken with more pastry, join the edges and pinch together. Brush with egg. Make an opening in the pastry to allow the steam to escape. Cook in a hot oven for 1 hour.

Chicken cooked in pastry is more often prepared like this: Stuff the chicken and brown it in butter, as described above. Place in a *terrine* which exactly contains it. Cover with *pâte à foncer* (as above). Brush with egg and cook in the oven.

Coq en pâte should be served with *Périgueux sauce* (see SAUCE).

Coq au vin (from an old recipe) – Cut a young chicken into six pieces. Heat 100 g. (4 oz.) diced lean breast of pork, and several button onions in 50 g. (2 oz., ¼ cup) butter in an earthenware pot. When browned, put in the pieces of chicken, a finely chopped garlic clove, a *bouquet garni*, morels (q.v.) or other mushrooms. Sauté, with the lid on, until golden. Remove the lid and skim off the fat. Add a little good brandy, flame, and then pour on ½ litre (scant pint, 2¼ cups) old Auvergne wine. Cook on a good heat for 15 to 20 minutes. Remove the chicken and pour over the sauce, thickened with the blood of the chicken, mixed with the pounded chicken liver and some brandy. Do not cook the sauce after this liaison, or it will curdle. The sauce may be thickened with *Kneaded butter* (see BUTTER), instead of the blood.

COQUE DU LOT – Cake made in the region of Lot for the Easter celebrations.

Ingredients. 1 kg. (2¼ lb., 9 cups) flour, 6 whole eggs, 125 g. (4 oz., ½ cup) butter, 125 g. (4 oz., ½ cup) sugar, 100 g. (4 oz., ¾ cup) citron, cut in long, thin slices, 25 g. (1 oz., 1 cake) yeast, flavouring made of a third each of lemon essence, orange-flower water and rum.

Method. Make a dough like *Brioche dough* (see DOUGH). When risen, shape into an oval loaf. Leave it to rise again. Bake in a hot oven.

COQUERET – Popular name for the strawberry-tomato, of which the fruit is edible. Common in the south of Europe.

COQUES À PETITS FOURS – Two of these are joined

with a stiff fruit *marmelade* or other composition, and glazed with *Fondant icing* (see ICING).

Pound 500 g. (18 oz., 3½ cups) dry blanched almonds with 500 g. (18 oz., 2¼ cups) fine sugar. Add 12 stiffly beaten egg whites. Mix well.

Pipe through a forcing-bag into balls on a sheet of greaseproof paper. Sprinkle with icing sugar. Cook in a slow oven.

The mixture can also be made as follows:

Grind 500 g. (18 oz., 3½ cups) blanched almonds and mix with 500 g. (18 oz., 2¼ cups) fine sugar, and 5 egg whites. Add 50 g. (2 oz., ⅓ cup) potato flour, 1 teaspoon powdered vanilla and 5 stiffly beaten egg whites.

COQUETIER – Egg-cup used to keep boiled eggs upright when served in their shells. Also applied to tradespeople dealing in eggs and poultry.

Coquille for roasting

COQUILLE – Kitchen utensil which is filled with charcoal. Used for roasting joints on a spit.

The name is also given to dishes of fireproof porcelain, tempered glass or metal made in the form of a shell. The deep shell of the scallop is used in the same way.

Various preparations are put in these shells: *salpicons*, purées, *ragoûts*, chicken fillets, fish or shellfish. These are covered in various sauces, sprinkled with grated breadcrumbs and grated cheese, and browned in the oven or under the grill (see HORS-D'ŒUVRE, *Scallop shells, garnished*).

CORDÉE – A pastry is said to be *cordée* when too much water has been used in the mixing. Such pastry is as hard as leather.

CORIANDER. CORIANDRE – The rounded fruits of this plant are about 5 mm. (¼ inch) in diameter, pale in colour, with an aromatic smell, and a taste both sweet and bitter. It is used to flavour spirits and to season many foods, including meats, cheeses, pickles, salads, soups, puddings and pastries.

CORKSCREW. TIRE-BOUCHON – Implement with a spiral thread, which can be flat or rounded, used to pull the cork from a bottle. There is less risk of cutting or breaking the cork with a rounded stem.

CORN (Maize). MAÏS – Also known as Indian corn and corn-on-the-cob. This plant is of South American origin. It was cultivated by the Peruvians before the arrival of the Spanish settlers.

Corn was introduced into France in the sixteenth century and many varieties are now grown there. It flourishes in the wine-growing districts.

The grain is enclosed in a fibrous casing with tasselled tops. Its flour makes a bread which is very popular in America. It contains a high proportion of oil but does not keep. Corn is relatively poor in nitrogenous substances, but quite rich in lipids and carbohydrates. In some regions it is eaten as porridge or polenta, cakes or bread. The grains can be grilled, boiled or made into popcorn or cornflakes.

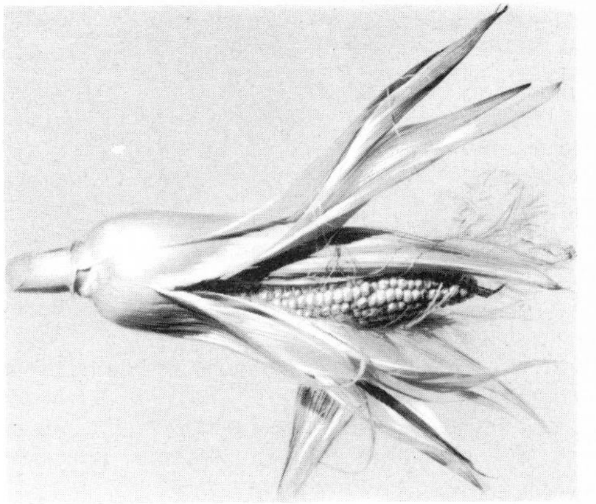

Ear of corn (maize) *(Nicolas)*

Fresh corn-on-the-cob is not much used in French cooking. In America, on the other hand, it is eaten in quantity.

Fresh corn à la béchamel. MAÏS FRAIS À LA BÉCHAMEL – Boil the cobs as for *Boiled fresh corn-on-the-cob I*. Strip the cobs and mix the corn with *Béchamel sauce* (see SAUCE).

Boiled fresh corn-on-the-cob I. MAÏS FRAIS AU NATUREL – Choose fresh corn cobs. They should be tender and milky. Boil them in salt water for 15 minutes, with or without their leaves.

Drain the cobs. Fold back the leaves, if not already stripped, to expose the cob. Serve fresh butter separately.

Corn-on-the-cob can also be steamed.

Boiled fresh corn-on-the-cob II. MAÏS FRAIS AU NATUREL – Sever the stem at the base. Remove the green leaves and the silky threads. Plunge into unsalted boiling water with milk – ½ litre (scant pint, 2¼ cups) milk to every 5 litres (4½ quarts, 5½ quarts) water. Boil quickly for 10 minutes.

Corn bread (American cookery). PAIN DE MAÏS – Mix 500 g. (18 oz., 3½ cups) cornmeal, 250 g. (9 oz., generous 2 cups) sieved wheat flour, 4 teaspoons sugar, 1½ tablespoons baking powder, 1½ teaspoons salt and 100 g. (4 oz., ½ cup) butter in a bowl.

Blend in 4 egg yolks beaten with ½ litre (scant pint, 2¼ cups) milk and 1 dl. (6 tablespoons, scant ½ cup) double cream, stirring as little as possible. Fold in 4 egg whites, whisked into a stiff froth, and pour into well-buttered muffin pans, filling them three-quarters full.

Bake in a hot oven for 25 or 30 minutes. This bread is served hot, straight from the oven, at breakfast.

Fresh corn in butter. MAÏS FRAIS AU BEURRE – Strip the cobs and proceed as for *Peas in butter* (see PEAS).

Fresh corn in cream. MAÏS FRAIS À LA CRÈME – Strip the cobs and proceed as for *Peas à la crème* (see PEAS).

Grilled fresh corn. MAÏS FRAIS GRILLÉ – Put the cobs on a gridiron and cook in a hot oven. When the grains have swollen and are a good colour, take the cobs out of the oven. Grilled corn may be stripped, or served on the cob.

Corn en suso with chicken giblets (Créole cookery). MAÏS EN SUSO AUX ABATIS DE POULET – Suso is a porridge made from cornmeal. It must not be too thick and should be simmered slowly for a long time.

Cut the giblets into equal pieces. Brown in fat and add a little water. Add 2 tablespoons (3 tablespoons) tomato purée and season. When completely cooked, drain off the stock and keep it to moisten the flour.

Wash some cornmeal. Put it in the pan in which the giblets have been browned, together with chopped onion. Add the giblets, the stock gradually, and cook slowly.

CORNELIAN CHERRY. CORNOUILLE – Tart, red fruit, the size of an olive, which is preserved in honey or sugar. It is preserved in pickle, like olives, and used for jelly. It is also called a *cornel.*

CORNET – This word has the following meanings:

1. A twist of paper used for wrapping.
2. A horn-shaped pastry.
3. A thin slice of ham, tongue, or other meat, rolled into the shape of a horn.
4. Term used in butchery, in France, for the larynx of a carcase.

Cornet for decorating. CORNET À DÉCORER – Paper cornet, which was used for decorating cold dishes. Replaced in *pâtisserie* by the forcing-bag (pastry bag).

Carême, in the *Discours préliminaire du Pâtissier royal*, says, 'I must give an honourable mention to the man who invented the paper cornet, used to decorate and embellish our modern sweets with meringue.

'I have been told that this ingenious idea belonged to a fashionable pastry-cook in Bordeaux; others have said that it was another pastry-cook in Bordeaux. Whoever he was, I am grateful to him for this delightful innovation; I regret not being able to associate his name with that of men of reputation.'

This remark implies that the paper cornet was not used in *pâtisserie* until the beginning of the nineteenth century. This seems improbable, if one thinks that in preceding centuries, especially in the eighteenth century, the decoration of cold dishes and sweets had been perfected.

Carême adds that one can use the cornet 'to form sponge fingers, *croquettes à la reine* and *biscottes à la parisienne*'.

CORNFLOUR or CORNSTARCH. FÉCULE DE MAÏS – White flour used for thickening, and in puddings. It is milled from corn (Indian corn or maize).

CORN OIL. HUILE DE MAÏS – Corn oil is used extensively in the U.S.A. for salad dressings, frying and as a shortening in baking.

CORN SALAD. MÂCHE – A variety of *valeriana* also known as *lamb's lettuce*. This plant grows wild in Europe, North America, North Africa and Asia Minor. It has been improved by cultivation, and is eaten in salad. In Europe it is on the market during the autumn. It was brought to America in the early part of the nineteenth century and is cultivated commercially and in gardens.

Corn salad can also be cooked like spinach (see SPINACH).

COROZO – White substance, used in industry, taken from the seed of the fruit of a palm tree. Corozo flour has been used as bran flour for bread, but this is forbidden today.

CORRECT. CORRIGER – In cooking, to correct a dish means to modify a too-predominant flavour by adding another savoury substance.

CORSICA. CORSE – Mediterranean island, which is a French *département*. Corsican cookery is simple. The Corsican is frugal. He no longer lunches *dans le tiroir* 'out of the drawer', (the main part of his meal consisting of chestnuts kept in the drawer of a cupboard); but he eats dishes based on fish, shellfish, and other *fruits de mer*, which are plentiful.

The sea around Corsica produces abundant fish, spiny lobsters and other shellfish. Lampreys and trout are found in the lakes and streams of the island. Corsica produces good

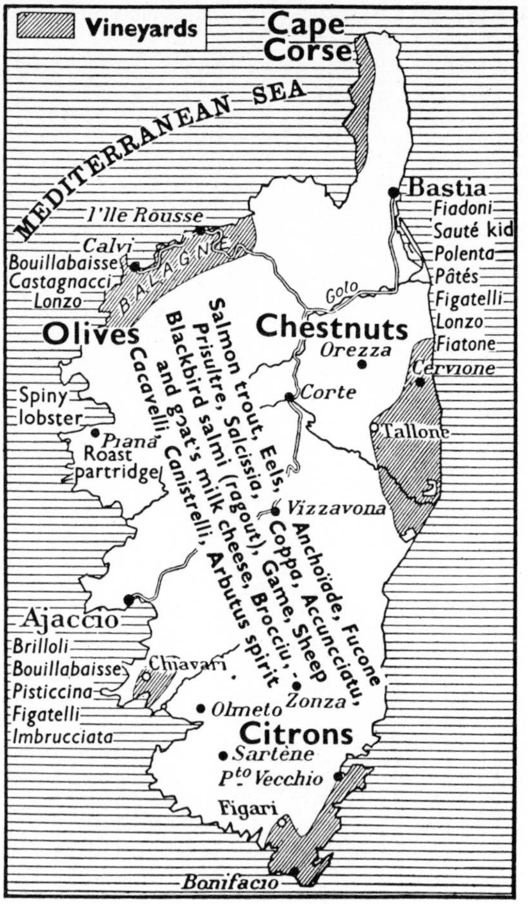

Gastronomic map of Corsica

vegetables, and plums, peaches, cherries, almonds, oranges and lemons grow in the orchards. Corsican figs are famous. Olives and chestnuts grow everywhere. Vines give wines of good quality. Arbutus trees, which produce red acid fruits reminiscent of strawberries, grow in the Maquis.

Sheep give good meat, goats are eaten young, and there are fine-quality pigs, from which several excellent types of *charcuterie* are made.

Game abounds in Corsica. Though rare, the *mouflon*, or wild sheep, is still found. In the forests are woodcock; and the blackbirds, fed on myrtle and arbutus, are succulent. The old French proverb which says *faute de grives, on mange les merles* (failing thrushes, one eats blackbirds) could hardly apply to Corsica, where the hunter who has killed a few of these delicate blackbirds, is upset if one or two thrushes are found among them.

The best Corsican cheese is Broccio, used for sweets such as *fritelles* and *figadones*. The ewes' milk cheese is sent to Roquefort, where it is made into blue cheese.

Corsican wines are varied, and some, without rivalling those of Guyenne, Burgundy, or the Côtes du Rhône, are excellent. Among them are those of Cap Corse, Porto-Vecchio, Cervione, Olmeto, Corte, and the heady Malvoisies, made in the neighbourhood of Cap Corse.

Culinary specialities – Among them are various fish soups, some of them like the Marseilles *bouillabaisse*, and flavoured with garlic, pimento, capsicum, and saffron; the *anchoïade*, similar to the one made in Nice; various *hors d'œuvre*; all kinds of shellfish and other *fruits de mer*, which are eaten raw or cooked in a *court-bouillon*. Also deserving special mention are stockfish, prepared in the same way as in Nice; *langoustes* cooked in a *court-bouillon* or braised; various local fish fried in olive oil, braised, baked in the oven, or cooked in various ways similar to those used on the mainland.

Other specialities are the *lonzo*, a fillet of pork, typical of the country (see LONZO); *coppa*, a highly flavoured sausage; *prisuttu*, raw ham; *omelette au broccio*; *figatelli*, a sausage made of pig's liver; *ragoût of pork with beans; stuffatu of mutton; assaignes; pebronata of beef*, braised beef flavoured with juniper; *missiasoga* made with goat's flesh cured in the sun; *cabris* and *cabiros* (kid), roasted or stewed; *mississa*, fillet of pork slashed, marinated, smoked and cooked on a grill; *tripa*, sheep's belly or intestines stuffed with a mixture of spinach, beet and *fines herbes*, combined with sheep's blood, tied up like a *boudin* (black pudding), and cooked in salted water.

Not to be forgotten are Corsican *polenta*, made as in Italy; *accuncciatu*, a stew of goat meat or lamb or mutton, with potatoes; and *tripettes*, made with sheep's small intestines cut into squares, fried, sautéed in lard with tomatoes and various condiments. The *ragoût de mouflon* is now rarely made, since the wild sheep have almost disappeared.

More exotic dishes include *blackbirds* which are roasted and wrapped in sage leaves, or made into *salmis* or *pâtés; woodcock à la cacciatore; salmis of partridges; wild boar with pibronata sauce*.

Among sweet dishes are *brioli*, made with chestnut flour; *fritelle*, a fritter with Broccio cheese; *fladène*, a tart made with Broccio and flavoured with vanilla; *fijadone*, a flan, *panette douce*, a bread made with eggs and sugar, decorated with raisins (eaten at Easter); *torta*, a cake decorated with pine kernels or almonds and flavoured with aniseed; *migliassis*, cakes baked in the oven on chestnut leaves; preserves made with citron and other fruits; chestnuts cooked in various ways.

There is also an excellent liqueur called *cédratine*.

COTEAUX, ORDRE DES – The name *coteaux* was given in the seventeenth century to people of refined taste, who not only were able to distinguish the best wines, but had the same taste for everything which concerned good living.

The poet, de Villiers, wrote:

Ces hommes admirables,
Ces petits délicats, ces vrais amis de tables,
Eux qu'on en peut nommer les dignes souverains,
Savent tous les coteaux où croissent les bons vins.
Et leur goût leur ayant acquis cette science,
Du grand nom de Coteaux on les appelle en France.

These admirable men,
These fastidious people, these true friends of good living,
One can name them worthy sovereigns,
They who know all the slopes on which the good wine grows.
Their science having been acquired through taste,
They are called in France by the great name of *Coteaux*.

Connoisseurs of good living were jokingly called '*profès dans l'ordre des coteaux*'.

The origin of this title is as follows: One day M. Lavardin, Bishop of Mans, was chaffing Saint-Evremond, who was dining with him, on his refinement. 'These gentlemen', he said, speaking of comte d'Olonne and of the marquis de Bois-Dauphin, 'exaggerate everything from the need to refine everything. They are not able to drink unless the wine comes from one of the hillsides of Aï, of Haut-Villiers, or Avenau.'

Saint-Evremond retold this criticism to his friends, and they repeated the words so often that in the end they were called '*les trois coteaux*' (the three hillsides), after which the *Ordre des coteaux* very soon came into being.

COTIGNAC – Quince paste. The most famous is the one made industrially at Orléans.

CÔTOYER – French culinary term which means to turn a joint in the oven.

COTRIADE or BRETON BOUILLABAISSE – As in the *bouillabaisse*, the more fish there are in the *cotriade*, the better.

These fish should be chosen from among the following: sardine, mackerel, John Dory, *daurade* (chrysophrys), *baudroie* (sea devil), hake, conger eel, gurnet, red mullet, etc. One or two large fish heads can be included.

Heat some butter or lard in a cauldron (on a wood fire) and cook quartered onions in it. When the onions turn pale gold, moisten with water, allowing $\frac{1}{2}$ litre (scant pint, $2\frac{1}{4}$ cups) per person. Add potatoes cut in quarters, thyme, bay and other herbs. Bring to the boil. Put the sliced fish on top of the potatoes. Cook rapidly.

Put slices of bread in a tureen and pour in the liquor. Serve the fish separately, on a large dish, with the potatoes.

COUCHER – French term, meaning to force stuffing, *pâté* or purée on to a baking sheet with a forcing-(pastry-) bag using a round or fluted nozzle.

COUCH GRASS. CHIENDENT – Common plant, the rhizomes of which are infused as a diuretic.

COUCOUZELLE – French name for the fruits of a variety of gourd which is picked before it is fully grown. They are called *courgettes* in France, and *zuchetti* or *zucchini* in Italy.

COULAGE – Disease of grapes. Also waste resulting from inadequate supervision in kitchen work.

COULIBIAC (Russian cookery) – A hot fish pie. Plumerey gives the following recipe in *L'Art de la cuisine française au XIXe; siècle*:

'In St Petersburg, this pie is made with salmon and *soudac*, but on state occasions with *sterlet* (the most prized fish in Russia).

'In Paris, where we have neither of these fish, they are replaced by turbot. The description given here is for twelve to fourteen persons. It is easy to increase or diminish it according to the number of guests.

'Take a 10-cm. (4-inch) slice of salmon and the same amount of turbot; remove the flesh and cut it into 12 square pieces. Chop plenty of parsley, spring onion, some chives and two punnets (small baskets) of mushrooms and put them in a large sauté pan with 225 g. (8 oz., 1 cup) butter; salt; pepper; allspice; clove; nutmeg and cinnamon. When they are softened, add $\frac{1}{2}$ glass Madeira, put in the pieces of fish and simmer gently until cooked.

Take out the pieces of fish and let them cool. Put a good tablespoon *Espagnole sauce* (see SAUCE) into the *fines herbes*, boil down, and put in a basin for use later on.

'Hard-boil 6 eggs and chop the whites and the yolks. Put 225 g. (8 oz.) *kache* (buckwheat) into a pan with the same volume of water, some butter, and salt. When it begins to boil, remove from the heat. Mix in 50 g. (2 oz., $\frac{1}{4}$ cup) fine butter, and cook for 15 or 20 minutes. The buckwheat will swell like Indian rice; the grains must be separate from one another. Pour out onto a plate.

'Take some *Brioche dough* (see DOUGH), less fine than usual. Roll it out twice. Make it into 2 sheets, one $2\frac{1}{2}$ cm. (1 inch) thicker than the other. Lay the thicker one on a baking sheet, spread some buckwheat on it, then a layer of fish, another layer of buckwheat, *fines herbes*, sauce, the eggs, and so on, until everything is used. Cover with the second sheet of dough, trim, moisten the edges, and draw up the edges of the lower sheet so that it covers the edge of the upper. The pie must be the shape of what is called a *pantin* in Paris. Moisten it outside and cover lightly with breadcrumbs. Put it in a gentle oven for 1½ hours, and serve straight from the oven, with melted butter.'

Petits coulibiacs de poulet à la russe (Russian chicken pie) (Plumerey's recipe) – 'Chop parsley, mushrooms and spring onions, and cook them in butter. Add a little blanched, chopped horseradish, salt, pepper and grated nutmeg. When this seasoning is browned, add a small spoonful *Espagnole sauce* (see SAUCE). Boil down, and take off the heat. Add cooked breast of chicken cut into large dice, 100 g. (4 oz., ¾ cup) rice which has been cooked in good consommé, and chopped hard-boiled eggs. Put on a plate to cool.

'Roll out some puff pastry four times. Let it rest for 10 minutes, roll it out to a thickness suitable for little patties and cut them out. Lay 24 rounds of pastry on a damp metal sheet and moisten them. Put a lump of the mixture on each, cover and press together to close. Moisten them, and sprinkle with freshly grated breadcrumbs.

'Cook in a medium oven for 25 to 30 minutes; give them a good colour and serve.'

These patties are served as a hot *entrée*.

COULIS – In the past, sauces in general were called *coulis* (cullis). More precisely, *coulis* are the juices which run out of the meat during cooking.

Some authors say that liquid purées should be called *coulis*, and that this word should not be used except for chicken purées, game purées, fish purées and those of shellfish and vegetables.

Some of these *coulis* can be served as soup. The principal type is *potage à la reine*.

As well as juice, *coulis* is what we call veal stock (*fonds de veau*), and what Carême called *blond de veau*.

In modern practice the word *coulis* is often used for thick soups which are made with a purée of shellfish: *coulis d'écrevisses* (crayfish cullis), *coulis de crabes* (crab), *de homard* (lobster), *de crevettes* (prawns), is often used instead of *bisque d'écrevisses*, etc.

COULOMMIERS CHEESE – See CHEESE.

COUPAGE – Mixing of various wines to obtain a commercial blend of colour, strength, and uniform taste.

COUP D'AVANT – The glass of wine, of liqueur or any alcohol which is taken immediately before a meal. This term is hardly used now. It is used more often for the generous glass of wine which is drunk after the soup. This custom has been passed from generation to generation, and is still found in different countries, in particular in rural communities.

The picturesque language of the Middle Ages gave names to the different drinks which were imbibed in particular circumstances. At court, and among the great, there was the *vin du coucher* (night-cap); in the middle of the meal, the *coup du milieu* (this custom still exists in Champagne). At a time when hardly anyone travelled except on horseback the glass of wine which was taken when setting out was given the name of *coup de l'étrier* (stirrup cup).

COUP DE FEU – The effect which is created by a joint being charred.

Also used in professional cookery for the hours devoted to serving up a meal.

COUP DE VIN – The amount of wine that can be drunk in a single gulp.

COUPE JACQUES – Fruit soaked in liqueurs and covered with various ices (see ICE CREAMS AND ICES).

COURGETTES – See ITALIAN MARROWS.

COURT-BOUILLON – An aromatic liquor (liquid) in which meat, fish and various vegetables are cooked.

Court-bouillon I, à la grecque, for marinating vegetables. COURT-BOUILLON À LA GRECQUE, POUR LÉGUMES MARINÉS – Put 1 dl. (6 tablespoons, scant ½ cup) olive oil, 7 dl. (1¼ pints, 1½ pints) water and the strained juice of 2 lemons in a pan. Add a *bouquet garni* of parsley roots, celery, fennel, thyme, bay; 12 to 15 coriander seeds and the same number of peppercorns. Boil for 20 minutes. Use according to instructions. This amount is enough for 25 to 30 small artichokes or an equal quantity of other vegetables prepared *à la grecque*.

Court-bouillon II, à la grecque, for marinating fish. COURT-BOUILLON À LA GRECQUE, POUR POISSONS MARINÉS – Gently simmer 100 g. (4 oz., 1 cup) finely chopped onion in 1½ dl. (¼ pint, ⅔ cup) olive oil. Do not allow the onion to brown. Moisten with 1½ dl. (¼ pint, ⅔ cup) white wine, 1½ dl. (¼ pint, ⅔ cup) water and the strained juice of 1 lemon.

Add an unpeeled, crushed garlic clove, a *bouquet garni* of 2 parsley roots, a sprig of thyme, a bay leaf, and a sprig of fresh fennel; 10 or 12 coriander seeds, and 2 sweet pimentos, skinned and cut into strips. Season with ¾ teaspoon salt and a pinch of freshly ground pepper.

Boil for 15 minutes. Use according to the recipe. This amount of *court-bouillon* is enough for 500 g. (generous 1 lb.) fish (net weight).

Court-bouillon III, salt water. COURT-BOUILLON À L'EAU SALÉE – This consists of salt water in the proportion of 1½ teaspoons salt to 1 litre (scant quart, generous quart) water. It is used to poach various fish such as sea perch, sea dace, coalfish, cod, white fish, haddock, etc.

Court-bouillon IV, for salmon and salmon trout. COURT-BOUILLON POUR SAUMONS ET TRUITES SAUMONÉES – Made with water; lemon juice or vinegar; sliced onions and carrots; parsley; thyme; bay leaf; salt and peppercorns. These fish can also be cooked in a white wine *court-bouillon*.

Court-bouillon V, for lobster and other shellfish. COURT-BOUILLON POUR LANGOUSTES ET AUTRES CRUSTACÉS – Made with water; thinly sliced carrots and onions; parsley; thyme; bay leaf; salt and peppercorns.

Court-bouillon VI, for lobster and other shellfish. COURT-BOUILLON POUR LANGOUSTES ET AUTRES CRUSTACÉS – Often used for cooking shellfish. It is made with salt water flavoured with thyme and bay.

Court-bouillon VII, au bleu, for river trout, carp, pike. COURT-BOUILLON AU BLEU, POUR TRUITES DE RIVIÈRE, CARPES ET BROCHETS – Made of salt water and vinegar, flavoured with carrots and sliced onions, parsley, thyme, bay leaf, salt and pepper. (see TROUT, *Blue trout*).

Court-bouillon VIII, white wine, à la hongroise. COURT-BOUILLON AU VIN BLANC, À LA HONGROISE – Melt 1 large tablespoon minced onion in 1 tablespoon butter until soft. Season with salt, paprika pepper, and a *bouquet garni*.

Moisten with 6 dl. (1 pint, 2½ cups) dry white wine. Boil for 8 minutes.

This *court-bouillon* is used for fish prepared as *hors-d'œuvre*. It can be made with olive oil instead of butter.

Court-bouillon IX, vegetable. COURT-BOUILLON AUX LÉGUMES – Cook 25 g. (1 oz., ¼ cup) finely chopped onion and 25 g. (1 oz., ¼ cup) finely chopped carrot in a tablespoon butter or oil. Season with salt and pepper. Add 2 crushed garlic cloves and a *bouquet garni*.

Moisten with 6 dl. (1 pint, $2\frac{1}{2}$ cups) dry white wine. Boil for 10 minutes. This is used for fish and other food served as *hors-d'œuvre*.

Court-bouillon X, au vert – Cook 100 g. (4 oz.) sorrel leaves; 25 g. (1 oz.) very young nettle leaves; a few sprigs of parsley; 1 tablespoon each of savory, burnet and green sage; 1 teaspoon tarragon and a sprig of thyme in 2 tablespoons (3 tablespoons) butter. Season with salt and pepper. Moisten with 6 dl. (1 pint, $2\frac{1}{2}$ cups) white wine. Cook for 8 minutes.

Used for small fish cooked *au vert* (set to stiffen in herbs before the white wine is added).

After the fish is cooked, the *court-bouillon* is thickened with egg yolks, and made acid with a few drops of lemon juice. (See EEL, *Eels au vert*).

Court-bouillon XI, white wine, for fish in marinade. COURT-BOUILLON AU VIN BLANC, POUR POISSONS MARINÉS – Put into a pan 2 small tender carrots cut in thin scalloped rounds; 1 small onion cut in thin slices; 2 finely chopped sticks of celery; 2 sliced shallots; a small handful of parsley stalks; 2 sprigs of thyme and a bay leaf.

Moisten with 2 dl. ($\frac{1}{3}$ pint, scant cup) white wine and 1 dl. (6 tablespoons, scant $\frac{1}{2}$ cup) vinegar. Season with salt and freshly ground pepper. Boil for 15 minutes. Pour, with the vegetables, over fish prepared *à la marinade* (see MARINADE). Cook according to the instructions given in the recipe.

The vegetables in this *court-bouillon* should be correctly sliced and scalloped, as they are usually served with the marinated fish.

Court-bouillon XII, white wine, à la mirepoix (for braised or poached fish). COURT-BOUILLON AU VIN BLANC, À LA MIREPOIX – Simmer 2 dl. ($\frac{1}{3}$ pint, scant cup) vegetable *mirepoix* (q.v.) (carrot, leek, onion, celery, thyme, powdered bay leaf) in butter, and moisten with 2 dl. ($\frac{1}{3}$ pint, scant cup) dry white wine.

Boil down by two thirds. Add 3 dl. ($\frac{1}{2}$ pint, $1\frac{1}{4}$ cups) fish *fumet* (q.v.). Boil for 10 minutes. Use according to instructions.

Court-bouillon XIII, Champagne, à la mirepoix. COURT BOUILLON AU VIN DE CHAMPAGNE, À LA MIREPOIX – Made in the same way as *Court-bouillon XII*, using Champagne instead of white wine.

Court-bouillon XIV, red wine, à la mirepoix. COURT-BOUILLON AU VIN ROUGE, À LA MIREPOIX – Made in the same way as *Court-bouillon XII*, using red wine from Burgundy or Bordeaux instead of white wine. Mushroom peelings can be used for all *court-bouillons à la mirepoix*.

Simple court-bouillon XV, for meats and offal – Cover 2 tablespoons (3 tablespoons) each of shredded carrot and onion; 1 *bouquet garni*; 10 peppercorns and 1 clove of garlic with salted water. Boil for 10 to 15 minutes before adding the meat.

Court-bouillon XVI, white, for meat. BLANC POUR VIANDES – Used for cooking certain offal (variety meats), such as sheeps' tongues and feet, calves' heads, and cocks' combs and kidneys.

Proceed as for *Court-bouillon XIX* (see below) adding one medium-sized carrot cut in quarters; one onion studded with a clove; and a *bouquet garni* (q.v.).

Put the meat into the boiling *court-bouillon*.

Court-bouillon XVII, white, for cooking calf's head. BLANC POUR CUIRE LA TÊTE DE VEAU – Mix flour with cold water, using 1 heaped tablespoon per litre (scant quart, generous quart) water, until smooth. Strain. Pour into a saucepan large enough to take the head, either whole, cut in half, or in pieces. Season with 1 teaspoon salt and add 1 tablespoon vinegar per litre (scant quart, generous quart) water. Bring to the boil, add 1 large onion studded with 2 cloves, and a *bouquet garni* made of a sprig of parsley, thyme and a bay leaf. When the stock is boiling, put in the calf's head wrapped in a fine muslin cloth. Add 250 g. (9 oz., generous cup) beef or veal fat, chopped and soaked in cold water. The fat will melt and form a protective layer over the calf's head and will prevent it from going black.

Court-bouillon XVIII, white, for mushrooms. BLANC POUR CHAMPIGNONS – Also used for other vegetables. Bring 50 g. (2 oz., $\frac{1}{4}$ cup) butter, the juice of $\frac{1}{2}$ lemon and 1 teaspoon salt to the boil in 1 dl. (6 tablespoons, scant $\frac{1}{2}$ cup) water.

Mushrooms or other vegetables are cooked in this liquor when it is boiling.

Court-bouillon XIX, white, for vegetables. BLANC POUR LÉGUMES – Used for cooking vegetables which are liable to turn dark, such as chards, cardoons, artichoke hearts, salsify, etc.

Mix 25 g. (1 oz., $\frac{1}{4}$ cup) flour into a smooth paste with 4 tablespoons ($\frac{1}{3}$ cup) water. Add 1 litre ($1\frac{3}{4}$ pints, generous quart) water, mix, and strain through a fine sieve. Season with 1 teaspoon salt. Add the juice of $\frac{1}{2}$ lemon and 2 or 3 tablespoons raw, chopped suet.

Boil for a few moments. Add the vegetable to be cooked.

This *court-bouillon* can be spiced with an onion studded with a clove, and a *bouquet garni* (q.v.), but this is not necessary if the ingredients cooked in it have to be seasoned at the final stage of cooking.

The *court-bouillon* cooks the vegetables and keeps them white. It is with this in view that suet (or butter) is added, as it forms a layer which protects the vegetables from contact with air.

A couscous bowl

COUSCOUS or COUSCOUSSOU – North African dish, dating from the earliest times. It is made with millet flour, or with crushed rice, and meat (mutton, chicken, etc.).

Some authors say the word *couscous* means *becquetée* (pecked at), from the food which a bird takes in its beak and rolls in small bits to feed its young. Leon Isnard wrote in a book on African cooking:

'It seems that the word *couscous* is a Gallic version of *rac keskes*, meaning *crushed small*. The word derives phonetically from the names *koskos, keuscass, koskosou, kouskous*, used in different parts of North Africa for a pot of earthenware or alfa glass in which semolina is steamed. The pot, which is pierced with holes is set on top of another similar one containing boiling water or stock.

'The inhabitants of North Africa used this name for all kinds of dishes made with flour, white or brown (buckwheat flour), and steamed in the *keskass*, a receptacle similar to a basin.

'But we think that the word *couscous* or *couscoussou* is onomatopoeic, simulating the noise made by the steam as it passes through the holes of the utensil in the process of cooking.

'In Kabylia, the word *sekjou* is used; in the Mozabite dialect *oucheou*. However, for some unknown reason the people of Oued-Rigt have adopted the word *gouni*, borrowed from the Berbers.'

There are many ways of preparing *couscous*.

Cooking the crushed grain by steaming. CUISSON DE LA SEMOULE À L'ÉTUVÉE – Soak the crushed grain in water until swollen. Place in the cooking vessel (a colander or strainer, fitted over a pan, can be used), without pressing it down.

Put some water or stock to boil in the pot, in the proportion of 1 litre (scant quart, generous quart) to 500 g. (generous 1 lb.) *couscous* (i.e. crushed grain). When the liquid begins to boil, put the uncovered vessel containing the crushed grain on top of the pot. (The vessel in which the grain is steamed must never come into contact with the boiling water.)

Place a damp cloth between the two vessels at the point of contact to prevent the steam escaping round the edge. When the steam begins to rise, cook for 40 minutes. Remove from the heat. Turn the grain on to a large plate. Fork it over to work out any lumps. Moisten with two glasses of water and a tablespoon oil. Add salt and pepper.

Leave for 15 minutes. Return the pot to the heat, and when the water boils put the *couscous* back in the steaming vessel. Steam for a further 20 minutes.

Cooking the crushed grain in boiling water. CUISSON DE LA SEMOULE PAR ÉBULLITION SPONTANÉE – The steaming vessel is dispensed with. Soak the *couscous* in the same way as above. Throw it into the boiling water or stock, stirring meanwhile. Use 1 litre (1¾ pints, generous quart) strained stock, or milk or water. Add butter and draw off the heat after 15 minutes. Leave it for a moment, but serve very hot, with meat or vegetables.

Armenian couscous. COUSCOUS ARMÉNIEN – Prepared like the Arab *couscous*, with crushed grain, chick-peas, slices of carrots and new turnips, pieces of white cabbage, and hashed mutton, all browned in oil. Hot pimento sauce is served separately.

Moroccan couscous. COUSCOUS MAROCAIN – Sieve 500 g. (18 oz.) finely ground hard wheat into a deep dish. Add water, drop by drop, working it with the hands until it is reduced to a fine consistency; without this working a lumpy mass will result. Put the grain in a strainer and steam it over a *bain-marie* or pan of hot water for 15 minutes. Put the *couscous* in a pan and separate the grains with the hands, adding lukewarm water. Cook for another 10 minutes, then separate it out again. Mix in butter and salt. Raisins can be added, if liked.

R. Pinet's recipe for *tagine*, which always accompanies the *couscous*, is as follows:

'For 12 people: 2 large quartered chickens, a neck of mutton cut for sautéing. Brown the meat in chicken fat with 4 large carrots and 4 diced onions. Sprinkle with a tablespoon ground red pepper, and moisten generously with mutton and chicken stock. Add crushed tomatoes, a *bouquet garni*, celery, and a sachet containing peppercorns, cloves, saffron, cinnamon and cumin.

Add equal quantities of quartered artichokes, *garbanzos*, (chick-peas), turnips, beans, marrow and diced courgettes.

Cook for 1 hour. The *ragoût* should be immersed in the stock and served in earthenware pots, without removing the fat.'

Mutton couscous 'chtitra'. COUSCOUS AU MOUTON 'CHTITRA' – For 6 or 8 persons, prepare and steam 500 g. (generous 1 lb.) *couscous*.

Put into a pot a leg of mutton cut into pieces; 3 chopped cloves of garlic; 3 small chopped red peppers; 2 soupspoons sweet red pepper powder; 1 teaspoon each of oil, salt, pepper, parsley and chopped chervil.

Moisten with 1 litre (1¾ pints, generous quart) water. Simmer for 3 hours or more. When cooked and ready to serve, add 100 g. (4 oz., ½ cup) butter to some of the liquor from the meat, and pour over the *couscous*.

Arrange the *couscous* on a large dish, place the meats on top, and serve with the rest of the sauce.

COUSINETTE (Béarnaise cookery) – Soup made with spinach, sorrel, lettuce, and other finely chopped green herbs.

COVER. COUVERT – Word used in various ways.

It is applied to the implements set out on a table which has been laid. The expression *lever* or *enlever le couvert* (to clear the table) means clearing the table once the meal is over. The word also applies to the number of guests present at a meal: *un dîner de 20, de 100 couverts* (a dinner of 20, or 100 people). More often the word *couvert de table* (table-setting) means the three implements used by the diner: the knife, the fork and the spoon.

Although together they form a logical collection, the knife for cutting, the fork for piercing solid food and the spoon for liquids, several centuries separate their discovery.

The oldest is the knife. Man's first need, even in primitive times, was to make a tool to cut up the meat obtained by hunting. As the use of bronze and iron was still unknown, he used flint and obsidian, a volcanic substance. Fragments of obsidian have the advantage of being both hard and sharp. Fitted between two bands of wood or bone, bound with plaited fibres, a piece of obsidian made one of the first knives. Placed at the end of an arrow or spear, it became a weapon. Later, bronze, iron and steel replaced obsidian for knives. According to Ammien Marcellin, bronze knives, made in one piece, were used by the Gauls, who used them to divide the largest pieces of meat. From the tenth century, the town of Beauvais had the monopoly for their manufacture.

The fork, which originally had only two prongs, was invented later than the knife.

The spoon was probably contemporary with the knife, as it would have been essential for liquids. At first it was a simple shell with a wooden handle. Metal spoons were made at least as early as metal knives. Many bronze spoons survive from excavations and can be seen in museums. They are of different shapes and sizes, some rounded, others elongated, similar to the spoons used today. Among these objects in museums there are only one or two early forks, which do not seem to have been used for eating. In the fourteenth century, even amongst the splendid silverware in palaces, there were far more spoons than forks. Piers Gaveston, the favourite of Edward II, owned sixty-nine silver spoons and three forks. These, according to the inventory, were designed for eating pears. Queen Clemence of Hungary (1328) left thirty spoons and a single fork at her death. M. le comte de Laborde writes, 'From the thirteenth century forks existed for exceptional dishes, but were not in common use.' Under the influence of a famous *beau*, M. de Montausier, the fork became generally used during the seventeenth century.

Not only has the *couvert* (place setting) made up of these three pieces become widely used today, but many implements, designed to fill particular needs have been developed. There are settings for luncheon, sweets, cakes, dessert, fruit, fish, or crayfish. There are spoons for absinth, porridge, jam, coffee, ices, infusions, liqueurs, mocha, eggs, syrup, soda, tea, or for glasses of water. There are special forks for winkles, snails, oysters, vegetables, fish and melons.

These three basic implements which make up the *couvert* are augmented by special implements for eating lobster, artichokes, asparagus, snails etc.

COW. VACHE – The cow is the female of the bovine species and is generally bred for milk or for reproduction. The meat of barren cows, or heifers, is more sought after than that of bullocks.

The flesh of old cows, worn out by bearing calves and by lactation, is tough and of inferior quality. Developments in milk production have meant that the herd is renewed more often, and milking cows discarded earlier. When they reach the butcher their meat is often of good quality, since breeders fatten them beforehand so that they are in the best possible condition.

COW-PARSNIP. BERCE – Weed of the family *Umbelliferae*, common in marshy places, in meadows and hedges. In Siberia its young shoots are eaten like asparagus. In Lithuania and Poland its leaves and seeds are made into a potent beer.

CRAB. CRABE – Shellfish of the order *Decapoda*. Many species are edible.

Crabs and shellfish in broth (Créole cookery). CRABES ET CRUSTACÉS EN BOUILLON – Soften chopped onion, tomato, pounded ginger, thyme, 2 cloves garlic, and the parts of the crab not usually eaten in some fat. Set aside the edible parts. Moisten the ingredients in the pan with broth and simmer gently for 2 hours. Sieve, pressing to obtain a thick sauce. Put some fat and a teaspoon each of saffron and chopped pimento in a casserole. Lightly brown the pieces of crab or other shellfish and pour the sauce over them. Cook for some minutes and serve hot with *Rice à la créole* (see RICE).

Cold crab. CRABE FROID – Cook a crab in *court-bouillon*, suitable for all shellfish, made from water, thyme, salt and a bay leaf. Leave to cool. Garnish with fresh parsley. Serve with *Mayonnaise sauce, Tartare sauce, Gribiche sauce* or *Green sauce* (see SAUCE).

In England, cold crab is sold already prepared (dressed crab). The meat, mashed with two forks, is seasoned with a sauce made from the crab's liver, English mustard, oil and vinegar, and is put back in the shell. The preparation is smoothed with a knife and decorated with egg yolks and chopped parsley. The crab is served with a *Mayonnaise sauce* (see SAUCE).

Dressed crab

Crab au gratin. CRABE AU GRATIN – Cook a large crab in *court-bouillon* (q.v.). Let it cool. When cold, remove the claws and legs. Using the point of a knife, make an incision underneath the crab's shell so as to detach the upper part.

Remove the meat from claws, legs and shell. Cut the meat into large dice, or mash with two forks. Clean the hollow shell with hot water and cover the bottom with a few tablespoons *Mornay sauce* (see SAUCE) to which the crab's liver and the creamy parts, finely pounded, are added. Replace the meat and cover with more sauce. Sprinkle with grated cheese. Pour on some melted butter and brown in a moderate oven.

CRACK (Small and large). CASSÉ (PETIT, GROS) – Degrees in cooking sugar (see SUGAR).

CRACKNEL (Biscuit). CRAQUELIN – Knead 250 g. (9 oz., $2\frac{1}{4}$ cups) sifted flour with 150 g. (5 oz., 10 tablespoons) butter, 2 egg yolks, 8 tablespoons ($\frac{2}{3}$ cup) cold milk, 25 g. (1 oz., 2 tablespoons) sugar and a pinch of salt.

Leave the pastry to rest for 2 hours. Roll it out $\frac{1}{2}$ cm. ($\frac{1}{4}$ inch) thick, and cut into 5-cm. (2-inch) squares. Arrange on a baking sheet. Brush with egg and cook in a very hot oven. Sprinkle with vanilla-flavoured sugar.

How to prepare crab

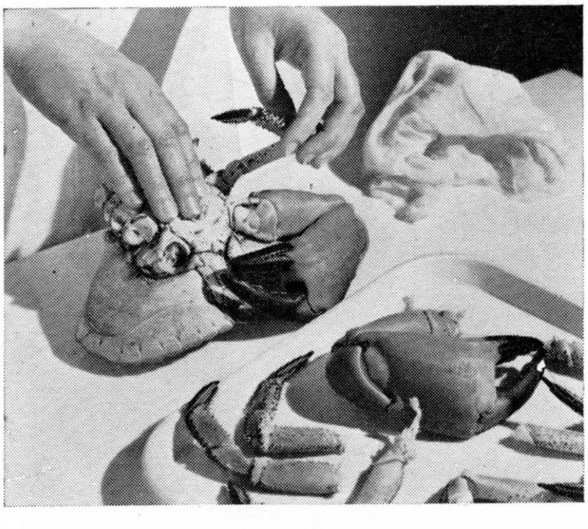

1. To twist off the legs and claws, wipe crab with damp cloth. Place on back with tail flap facing. Remove claws and legs by twisting inwards and towards you

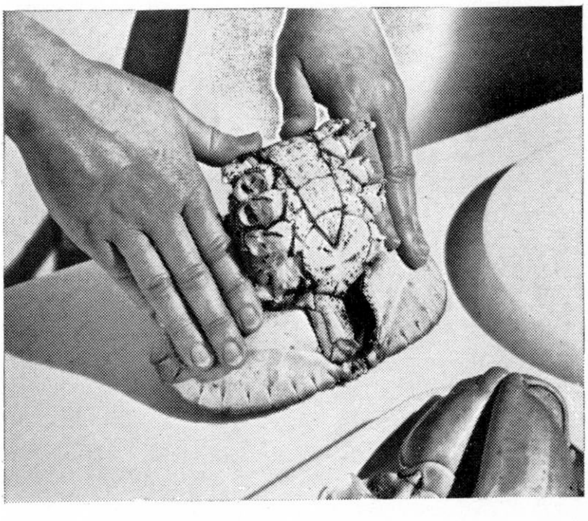

2. To separate body from shell, place thumbs under tail flap and push upwards until the body breaks away from the shell

3. To remove mouth and stomach bag, place shell with mouth facing you. Press thumbs down and forward on mouth until this, and stomach bag attached, breaks away with a click

4. To remove the stomach, take hold of the mouth and stomach bag and carefully remove them; they should come away in one piece. Discard them

5. To remove meat, ease around inside shell with handle of a spoon, loosening soft brown meat. Turn all the meat into a basin, leaving the shell clean

6. To trim shell, tap 'false line' around shell cavity with knife handle, press with thumbs until edges of shell wall break away neatly. Scrub and dry the shell and oil lightly

7. Taking body of crab, discard 'dead men's fingers'. Remove brown meat, adding to basin. Scoop white meat from leg sockets, keeping free from bone; put in second basin

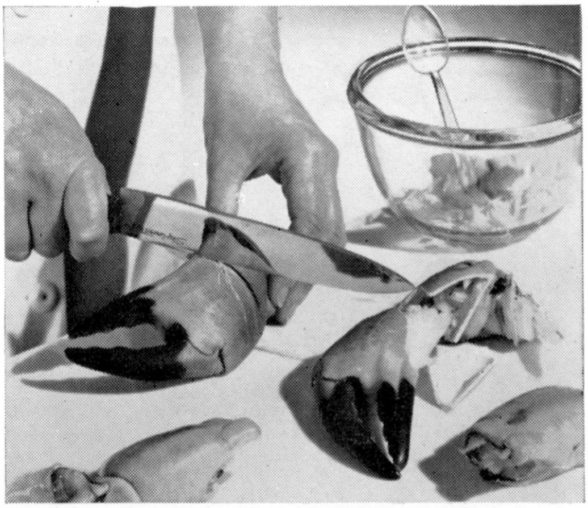

8. Twist first joint off claws to remove meat. With back of heavy knife tap sharply round centre of claw's broadest part until the shell cracks apart; empty both into white meat basin

CRAMIQUE (Belgian pâtisserie) – Brioche bread which has currants in it.

CRANBERRY or MOSSBERRY – Fruit of a small edible shrubby plant which grows in the boggy regions of North America and Europe. Cranberries look like small cherries and their colour varies from a clear pink to a deep red. They have an acid, slightly bitter flavour and are unpleasant eaten raw. They may be made into a compote or jelly, which has a delicate taste. Cranberry jelly is traditionally used with game and fowl, such as duck and goose.

Here is Dr Leclerc's recipe for cranberry jelly. Cover the berries with water and cook for 15 minutes, until they are soft. Add 350 g. (12 oz., 1½ cups) sugar for each 500 g. (generous 1 lb.) fruit and cook again until a thick syrup is made. This forms a jelly when cool.

CRANE. GRUE – Wader, seldom used for food nowadays. The Romans prized this bird, which they fattened specially to give it a richer flavour. In the Middle Ages, the crane was among the game birds eaten in the best society. It can only be eaten very young and is cooked in the same way as bustard (see BUSTARD).

CRAPAUDINE (À LA). – Preparation of fowl, particularly of pigeon (q.v.).

Some authors say that this name comes from the word *crapaud* (toad) and was given to the dish because the birds, trussed in this way, resemble toads.

CRAQUELIN – A cake which is so called because, being very dry, it crunches between the teeth. It is made in different ways; sometimes in the same way as Reims biscuits, sometimes with a dough (*pâte à echaudés*).

CRASSANE – Juicy variety of pear with aromatic flesh. (See PEAR.)

CRAYFISH (Freshwater). ÉCREVISSE – There are three principal varieties of crayfish: the *red-clawed crayfish* (underpart of the claws red) which is the largest of the French varieties and has delicate flesh; the *white-clawed crayfish* which is smaller – not more than 65 to 75 g. (2½ to 3 oz.); and the *slender-clawed crayfish* which is imported from central Europe and is of mediocre quality.

Whichever method of cooking is chosen for crayfish, it is necessary first of all to remove the *media lamina* of the tail flukes to which is attached a small black sac. If this is not discarded it spoils the delicate flavour. Approximately one fifth of the gross weight of a crayfish is edible.

Female and male crayfish

Crayfish bisque or coulis. BISQUE (COULIS) D'ÉCREVISSES – Thick soup made with crayfish cooked *à la mirepoix*. While pounding the crayfish in a mortar, add some cooked rice. (See SOUPS AND BROTHS, *Purée of crayfish soup*.)

Crayfish à la bordelaise. ÉCREVISSES À LA BORDELAISE – Make a fine *mirepoix* of vegetables. Toss the crayfish in butter separately. Season with salt, pepper and spices.

Pour brandy over the crayfish and set alight. Moisten with white wine. Add the *mirepoix* and cook together for 20 minutes. Drain the crayfish and put them in a deep dish. Bind the cooking stock with 3 or 4 egg yolks. Add a generous piece of butter. Season well. Mask the crayfish with this sauce and serve at once, piping hot.

Bush of crayfish. BUISSON D'ÉCREVISSES – A *buisson* is a small bush or clump. Cook the crayfish in *court-bouillon* as for *Crayfish à la nage* (see below). Leave them to cool.

Ingredients for crayfish à la bordelaise

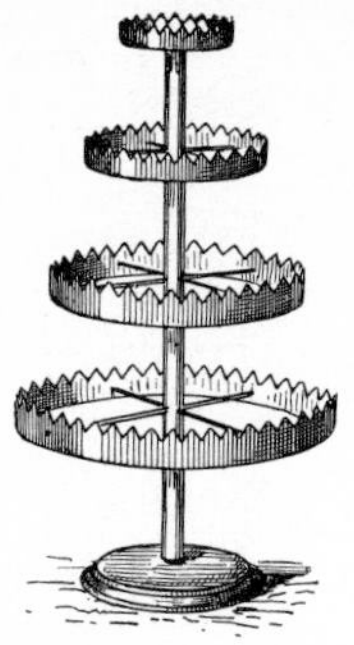

Special dish for arranging crayfish

Arrange them on a special dish, fixing them by their tails to the points on the dish. Garnish with bunches of fresh parsley.

Crayfish croûtes. CROÛTES AUX ÉCREVISSES – Using *Crayfish tail ragoût à la Nantua* (see below), proceed as for *Mushroom croûte* (see MUSHROOM).

Crayfish flan with cheese. FLAN AUX ÉCREVISSES GRATINÉ – Fill a flan crust baked blind (baked pie shell) with *Crayfish tail ragoût à la Nantua* (see below). Sprinkle with grated cheese. Pour on melted butter and brown in the oven.

Crayfish as a garnish. ÉCREVISSES POUR GARNITURE – Wash and gut the crayfish. Truss them (fasten the claws to the tail) or leave as they are, according to the recipe. Put them in a boiling *court-bouillon* of water, salt, thyme and bay leaf. Boil until cooked. Use them hot or cold.

Crayfish à la liégeoise. ÉCREVISSES À LA LIÉGEOISE – Cook the crayfish in a *court-bouillon* as for *Crayfish à la nage* (see below). Drain and arrange them in a deep dish. Strain the cooking stock and boil down to a quarter of its volume. Mix in 100 g. (4 oz., ½ cup) butter for 1 dl. (6 tablespoons, scant ½ cup) stock. Whisk thoroughly. Pour this sauce over the crayfish. Sprinkle with chopped parsley.

Crayfish à la marinière. ÉCREVISSES À LA MARINIÈRE – Sauté the crayfish in butter over a very hot flame. When they are browned, season with salt, pepper, powdered thyme and bay leaf, and moisten with enough dry white wine to cover them.

Cover the saucepan and boil for 12 minutes. Remove the crayfish. Boil down the stock and add some meatless *velouté*. Remove from the heat and mix in 2 or 3 tablespoons butter. Pour this sauce over the crayfish and sprinkle with chopped parsley.

Crayfish mousse à l'ancienne (cold). MOUSSE FROIDE D'ÉCREVISSES À L'ANCIENNE – Cook 36 medium-sized crayfish *à la mirepoix*. Drain them and shell the tails. Pound the shells in a mortar with the *mirepoix*, adding 50 g. (2 oz., ¼ cup) butter, 1½ dl. (¼ pint, ⅔ cup) cold meatless *velouté* and 1 dl. (6 tablespoons, scant ½ cup) melted aspic jelly.

Rub this mixture through a sieve and put it in a saucepan. Add 4 dl. (¾ pint, scant 2 cups) fresh partly whipped cream, and the crayfish tails, shelled and diced.

Line a charlotte mould with white paper and fill the mould with the mixture. Leave to chill on ice, or in a refrigerator, until just before serving.

Turn the mousse onto a serving dish. Decorate with slices of truffle dipped in half-set jelly. Surround with chopped aspic jelly.

Crayfish mousse (cold). MOUSSE FROIDE D'ÉCREVISSES – Make the mousse as in the previous recipe and arrange in a charlotte mould lined with aspic jelly and decorated inside with shelled crayfish tails and strips of truffles.

Crayfish mousse can also be served completely covered with aspic jelly.

Crayfish mousselines à la Nantua (hot). MOUSSELINES D'ÉCREVISSES À LA NANTUA – Use *Fine cream forcemeat* (see FORCEMEAT) made with fillet of pike or whiting mixed with a purée of crayfish tails. When the forcemeat is ready, add chopped crayfish tails. Fill small buttered moulds with this mixture. Stand in a dish of water and poach in the oven.

Turn out the *mousselines* on a dish, each one set on a round of bread fried in butter, or, if preferred, placed straight on the dish. Cover with *Nantua sauce* (see SAUCE). Decorate the top of each *mousseline* with a thick piece of truffle.

Crayfish *mousseline* can be served with various garnishes and covered with a sauce chosen to blend with these garnishes: *cancalaise, normande, cardinal, Victoria*, etc.

Mousselines are also used to garnish large braised fish. They can be served in tartlets baked blind (empty), or with artichoke hearts cooked in butter. The same mixture can be used to make large hot mousses which are poached in charlotte moulds standing in water.

Crayfish mousselines (cold). MOUSSELINES FROIDES D'ÉCREVISSES – These are made with a mousse mixture prepared as in the recipe for *Crayfish mousselines à la Nantua* (*hot*). Line small moulds with jelly, and decorate with crayfish tails and truffles. Fill the moulds with the mousse mixture and chill on ice.

Crayfish à la nage. ÉCREVISSES À LA NAGE – Remove the intestinal matter from the centre of the tails of 48 crayfish. Wash them and plunge immediately into a *court-bouillon* prepared as follows:

Slice 3 small carrots into thin rounds, and put them in a saucepan with 100 g. (4 oz., 1 cup) small finely chopped onions, 4 sliced shallots, a small crushed clove of garlic, a sprig of thyme, half a bay leaf, and a handful of parsley heads. Moisten with 4 dl. (¾ pint, scant 2 cups) white wine and 2 dl. (⅓ pint, scant cup) water. Season with salt and freshly ground pepper. Cook for 15 minutes.

Cook the crayfish in this *court-bouillon* for 10 minutes, tossing from time to time. Season with cayenne pepper and leave to cool in the cooking stock.

Crayfish puffs. FRIANDS AUX ÉCREVISSES – Proceed as for *Crayfish rolls* (see below) using flaky pastry cut into triangles.

Crayfish rolls. CHAUSSONS AUX ÉCREVISSES – Cut small rounds from a rolled-out layer of *Flaky pastry* (see DOUGH). Put a heaped tablespoon of *Crayfish tail ragoût à la Nantua* in the centre of each round when cold. Roll up and seal the edges. Brush the tops with egg and lightly score. Bake in a slow oven. Serve hot.

Crayfish rolls des Dames de Bous. CHAUSSON DE QUEUES D'ÉCREVISSES DES DAMES DE BOUS – 'Cook 100 crayfish *à la mirepoix* with white wine, seasoning rather highly.' According to Mme. de Loiseau, residuary legatee of the recipes of Mme. de Marron, this seasoning should be a mixture of 'all the main types of pepper'.

'With the shelled tails of the crayfish, make a *Ragoût à la Nantua* (see below), finishing it as indicated in the recipe for this *ragoût*. Leave to cool. At the same time, poach soft carp roes in white wine and also leave to cool.

'Roll out a round layer of *Flaky pastry* (see DOUGH) and place on a baking sheet. Spread it on one side only with the *ragoût* and with the soft roes enriched with thick slices of truffles seasoned with salt, pepper and spices, and sprinkled with liqueur brandy.

'Roll into a scroll, carefully sealing the edges. Score light diagonal lines on the scroll, brush with egg, and bake in a hot oven.

'When it is ready, pour a little hot *Crayfish butter* (see BUTTER, *Compound butters*) into the scroll through the opening.'

Fried crayfish rolls. RISSOLES AUX ÉCREVISSES – Proceed as for *Crayfish rolls.* Make the rolls as shown in the recipe. Deep-fry them instead of baking them in the oven. When they are a good colour, drain them and season with table salt. Garnish with fried parsley.

Crayfish tails au gratin. GRATIN DE QUEUES D'ÉCREVISSES – Prepare the crayfish tails as for *Crayfish tail ragoût à la Nantua* (see below). Put the *ragoût* in a buttered ovenware dish. Sprinkle with grated cheese, preferably Parmesan. Pour on melted butter. Brown slowly in the oven.

Crayfish tails au gratin à la façon de maître La Planche. GRATIN DE QUEUES D'ÉCREVISSES À LA FAÇON DE MAÎTRE LA PLANCHE – 'Using crayfish cooked *à la mirepoix*, prepare a *ragoût* of crayfish tails thickened with highly seasoned crayfish purée.

'Put this *ragoût* in a buttered ovenware dish with layers of fresh truffles cut into thick slices, seasoned and tossed in hot butter. Sprinkle with finely grated cheese. Brown in a moderate oven, standing the dish in warm water to prevent the sauce from curdling.'

Crayfish tail ragoût à la Nantua. QUEUES D'ÉCREVISSES À LA NANTUA – Make $1\frac{1}{2}$ dl. ($\frac{1}{4}$ pint, $\frac{2}{3}$ cup) *mirepoix* by cooking a mixture of finely diced carrots, onions, and celery, with powdered thyme and bay leaf, in butter until tender. Toss 48 crayfish tails in this mixture. Season with salt and pepper. Moisten with 2 dl. ($\frac{1}{3}$ pint, scant cup) white wine. Cover the saucepan and cook for 10 minutes.

Drain the crayfish. Shell the tails. Pound the shells and the *mirepoix* in a mortar and add *béchamel sauce* to this purée as shown in the recipe for *Nantua sauce* (see SAUCE).

Put the crayfish tails in a small pan with a tablespoon butter. Heat without browning. Sprinkle with 1 tablespoon flour and mix thoroughly. Moisten with 2 tablespoons (3 tablespoons) brandy and 1 dl. (6 tablespoons, scant $\frac{1}{2}$ cup) thick cream. Mix.

Leave to simmer on low heat for 8 minutes. Add the Nantua sauce, prepared separately. Remove from the heat and add 50 g. (2 oz., $\frac{1}{4}$ cup) butter.

According to how this *ragoût* is to be used, the whole or only part of the Nantua sauce made with the pounded shells is added to it. If it is to be used as the only filling of a *vol-au-vent* or pie, and if the tails of the crayfish are small, more tails will be needed. If intended as a garnish, it can be served with other garnishes such as mushrooms, truffles, oysters, etc.

Crayfish tails in shells. COQUILLES DE QUEUES D'ÉCREVISSES – Line silver, fireproof china or glass shells with *Mornay sauce* (see SAUCE) flavoured with *Crayfish butter* (see BUTTER, *Compound butters*). Pipe a narrow border of *Duchess potato mixture* (see POTATOES) round the shell.

Arrange 6 to 8 shelled crayfish tails on the sauce. Cover with more *Mornay sauce*, and sprinkle with grated cheese. Pour on melted butter and brown quickly in the oven.

Crayfish tails can be prepared in shells in the same way, using different sauces and garnishes, *à la normande, à la cardinal*, with mushrooms, etc.

Crayfish timbale à l'ancienne. TIMBALE DE QUEUES D'ÉCREVISSES À L'ANCIENNE – Prepare *Crayfish tail ragoût à la Nantua.* Line a shallow pie dish with *Fine lining paste* (see DOUGH). Line with a thin layer of *Fine pike forcemeat* (see FORCEMEAT). Mix coarsely diced truffles tossed in butter, and left to cool, with the *ragoût*; fill the pie with this.

Cover the *ragoût* with a layer of pike forcemeat, cover the pie with pastry and seal. Decorate with flaky pastry motifs.

Make a small hole in the pastry lid to allow the steam to escape. Brush with egg. Bake in a slow oven for 45 minutes to 1 hour.

When the pie is ready, pour into it a few tablespoons of thin *Nantua sauce* (see SAUCE).

Crayfish timbale à la mode de Chavillieu. TIMBALE DE QUEUES D'ÉCREVISSES À LA MODE DE CHAVILLIEU – Cook crayfish *à la mirepoix* with white wine. Drain them, shell the tails and put the tails in a pan with melted butter. Pound the shells in a mortar and divide the purée in half. With one half make *Crayfish butter* (see BUTTER, *Compound butters*). Mix the rest of the crayfish purée with an equal quantity of *Béchamel sauce* (see SAUCE), diluted with fresh cream. Rub this purée through a sieve with a spatula.

Heat the crayfish tails in the butter, without browning. Pour on some fresh cream and blend in the crayfish purée. Mix over heat. Moisten with thick fresh cream. When the *ragoût* has thickened, mix in some of the crayfish butter. Season with cayenne pepper and flavour with liqueur brandy. Keep hot in a double saucepan.

Prepare separately 24 forcemeat balls with lavaret stuffing. (This is a cream stuffing made with filleted fish, egg whites and thick fresh cream.) Poach the forcemeat balls slowly and keep them hot. Fill a pie crust of fine pastry, baked blind (empty), with alternate layers of crayfish tail *ragoût* and forcemeat balls. The pie must be hot when filled. Cover with *Nantua sauce* (made with the rest of the purée and the crayfish butter), and decorate with large slices of truffle, seasoned with salt and pepper, tossed in butter and flavoured with liqueur brandy. Serve very hot.

Crayfish vol-au-vent. VOL-AU-VENT AUX ÉCREVISSES – Make a *vol-au-vent* case (see VOL-AU-VENT). Fill with *Crayfish tail ragoût à la Nantua.*

Little crayfish vol-au-vent, barquettes or tartlets – See HORS-D'ŒUVRE, *Hot hors-d'œuvre.*

CREAM (from milk). CRÈME DU LAIT – Cream not only contains globules of fat, used for butter, but also a proportion of water, casein, lactose and mineral salts (see MILK).

There is a difference between single cream which is obtained by skimming milk that has been left to settle in shallow bowls, and which contains 10 to 20 per cent butter, and double cream, which is obtained by a separating machine and which must contain at least 30 per cent butter. Possible adulterants are starch, fecula (potato flour) and gelatine. These are easy to detect as they give the cream a mealy or gluey flavour.

Since cream is largely composed of fatty substances, sufferers from liver complaints should not eat it. Healthy people should use it sparingly.

CREAM CHEESES. FROMAGES À LA CRÈME – See CHEESE.

CREAM HORNS À LA CHIBOUST. CORNETS FEUILLETÉS À LA CRÈME, DITS À LA CHIBOUST – *Ingredients* (for 12 cornets). 500 g. (18 oz.) *Puff pastry* (see DOUGH), 150 g. (5 oz., generous $\frac{1}{2}$ cup) fine sugar, 5 egg yolks, 4 egg whites, 50 g. (2 oz., $\frac{1}{2}$ cup) flour, $\frac{1}{2}$ litre (scant pint, $2\frac{1}{4}$ cups) milk, $\frac{1}{2}$ vanilla pod or a few drops vanilla essence and a pinch salt.

Method. Make the pastry as for *Puff pastry* (see DOUGH) and roll it out 2 mm. ($\frac{1}{8}$ inch) thick. Cut into 12 strips, 3 cm. (1 inch) wide and 25 cm. (10 inches) long. Roll these strips round cornet moulds.

Arrange the cornets on a wet baking sheet; leave for 10 minutes. Brush them with egg and bake in a hot oven for 12 to 15 minutes. When nearly cooked, sprinkle with icing sugar, glaze, and take them out of the oven as soon as they glisten.

The cream. The base of this preparation is the *Crème pâtissière* (French pastry cream). Put the sieved flour, sugar and salt in a pan. Add the egg yolks and whip until the mixture is smooth.

Moisten with the milk, which has been boiled with $\frac{1}{2}$ vanilla pod. Mix carefully and cook on a good heat, beating until the cream is the right consistency. The cooking must be rapid, not more than 5 minutes. This makes the *crème pâtissière*. To obtain the *crème Chiboust*, add 4 stiffly beaten egg whites, while the mixture is still hot.

Fill the cornets with the cream when cold. Use a forcing-bag with a round nozzle, or a cornet of greaseproof paper.

CREAMS. CRÈMES – The French word *crème* applies to whipped cream; butter and custard creams used to garnish pastries and cakes; custard cream sauces; and soups.

Almond cream. CRÈME D'AMANDES – *Ingredients.* 500 g. (18 oz., $3\frac{1}{2}$ cups) almonds, 500 g. (18 oz., $2\frac{1}{4}$ cups) fine sugar, 500 g. (18 oz., $2\frac{1}{4}$ cups) butter, 8 eggs.

Method. Pound the peeled almonds with the sugar, moistening with two of the eggs. When the almonds have formed a paste, add the softened butter. Continue to work the mixture, adding the rest of the eggs one by one.

Butter creams. CRÈMES AU BEURRE – There are two ways of making butter creams, which are used for garnishing cakes and pastries. One combines butter with *Custard cream* (see below) and the other is made with sugar syrup, beaten egg yolks and butter. Both types of butter cream may be flavoured with mocha, praline, chocolate, vanilla or any liqueur.

Butter cream (with custard) I. CRÈME AU BEURRE – Make a *Custard cream* (see below). Beat it until it is lukewarm. Add 450 g. (1 lb., 2 cups) butter in small pieces for every 6 dl. (1 pint, $2\frac{1}{2}$ cups) custard, beating all the time. Flavour with vanilla sugar, or other flavouring, according to the recipe.

Butter cream (with custard) II. CRÈME AU BEURRE – *Ingredients.* 12 egg yolks, 500 g. (18 oz., $2\frac{1}{4}$ cups) fine sugar, 2 dl. ($\frac{1}{3}$ pint, scant cup) fresh cream, 450 g. (1 lb., 2 cups) butter, 1 vanilla pod, or 1 teaspoon vanilla essence.

Method. Work together the sugar, egg yolks, vanilla and cream in a basin.

Put the basin over a low heat or over a pan or casserole half-full of hot water, and whip the mixture until it becomes frothy, light and white. Remove from the heat and continue to whip until it cools. Mix this custard with the creamed butter.

Custard creams can be flavoured in various ways; with vanilla; lemon, orange or mandarin zest; with coffee, tea or liqueurs.

Butter cream with syrup. CRÈME AU BEURRE AU SYROP – Boil 450 g. (1 lb., 2 cups) sugar and $3\frac{1}{2}$ dl. (generous $\frac{1}{2}$ pint, $1\frac{1}{2}$ cups) water to 104°C. (220°F.), making generous 5 dl. syrup. Infuse the chosen flavouring (vanilla, zest, etc.) in the syrup. Gradually pour the boiling syrup over 12 egg yolks, beating constantly. Pass through a fine sieve and add 450 g. (1 lb., 2 cups) butter. Mix well.

Chantilly cream. CRÈME CHANTILLY – To make 1 litre ($1\frac{3}{4}$ pints, generous quart), put $\frac{1}{2}$ litre (scant pint, $2\frac{1}{4}$ cups) thick fresh cream in a basin. The cream should have been kept in a cool place, or on ice, for 24 hours, if possible. Beat the cream until it doubles its volume. Drain the cream on a fine sieve. Add 50 g. (2 oz., $\frac{1}{4}$ cup) fine sugar and 1 teaspoon vanilla sugar or a few drops vanilla essence.

Chantilly cream with fruit. CRÈME CHANTILLY AUX FRUITS – This can be made with all kinds of fruit pulp, but strawberry or raspberry are the most suitable. Add to the whipped cream a third of its volume of fruit pulp, passed through a fine sieve.

Chocolate cream I. CRÈME AU CHOCOLAT – Pour 2 dl. ($\frac{1}{3}$ pint, scant cup) warm water over 125 g. (4 oz., $1\frac{1}{3}$ cups) grated chocolate. Stir over a gentle heat until the mixture boils, then simmer for 15 minutes. Add 3 tablespoons (scant $\frac{1}{4}$ cup) fresh thick cream and 1 tablespoon butter.

Usually served hot but can be served cold.

Chocolate cream II. CRÈME AU CHOCOLAT – Add melted chocolate to $\frac{1}{2}$ litre (scant pint, $2\frac{1}{4}$ cups) *Custard cream* (see below).

Custard cream. CRÈME À L'ANGLAISE – Work 8 egg yolks, 250 g. (9 oz., generous cup) fine sugar, and a small pinch of salt in a pan with a spatula, over a gentle heat, until the mixture forms ribbons when the spatula is lifted. Moisten gradually with 5 dl. (scant pint, $2\frac{1}{4}$ cups) boiled milk, flavoured, according to taste, with vanilla or lemon or orange zest.

Mix well. Keep the pan on the heat, stirring all the time, until the contents almost boil. At this point the custard should cling to the spatula.

Pass the custard through a fine sieve and keep it warm in a *bain-marie* (double boiler) if required to accompany a hot pudding, or turn it out into a basin and keep in a cool place if to be served cold. In the latter case, it should be stirred while cooling to prevent a skin forming.

This custard can be made more cheaply by using fewer egg yolks (6 instead of 8) and by adding to the egg yolk and sugar mixture a teaspoon of arrowroot or fecula (corn or potato starch). This gives a thicker consistency to the custard and prevents it from clotting if allowed to overheat.

It is used cold, with the addition of gelatine, for cold sweets, such as *bavarois* (q.v.), charlottes (q.v.), *Rice à l'impératrice* (see RICE), etc.

Custard cream with gelatine. CRÈME À L'ANGLAISE COLLÉE – Used for cold sweets (desserts). Prepare the custard as described above. When it is cooked, add 25 g. (1 oz.) gelatine which has been soaked in cold water. Stir while it dissolves. Strain the custard, and stir while it cools.

Custard cream with liqueurs. CRÈME À L'ANGLAISE AUX LIQUEURS – Prepare the custard cream in the same way as *Custard cream with gelatine*. When it is cool, add a tablespoon of liqueur: Curaçao, kirsch, maraschino, rum, etc.

Custard cream au miroir. CRÈME AU MIROIR – Custard cream glazed with a salamander or hot poker.

Custard cream filling for waffles I. CRÈME POUR FOURRER LES GAUFRES – Whip 250 g. (9 oz., generous cup) butter, 250 g. (9 oz., 2 cups) icing sugar, 200 g. (7 oz., 1 cup) praline in a slightly warmed basin. When well blended, use as a filling for waffles.

Custard cream filling for waffles II. CRÈME POUR FOURRER LES GAUFRES – Cook 250 g. (9 oz., 2 cups) lump sugar and 1 dl. (6 tablespoons, scant $\frac{1}{2}$ cup) water till it reaches the ball stage (see SUGAR). Skim and strain the syrup. Put 15 egg yolks in a basin. Pour the sugar syrup over them, letting it fall in a thin thread. Mix. Add 250 g. (9 oz., generous cup) butter worked into a cream. Add 200 g. (7 oz., 1 cup) praline, beating all the time.

Although praline flavouring is given for these creams, one can also use coffee, chocolate, vanilla or orange flavouring.

Custard cream flavoured with tea. CRÈME À L'ANGLAISE AU THÉ – Prepare like *Mocha custard cream*, replacing the coffee with a strong infusion of tea.

The custard can also be made by adding to the egg yolk and sugar mixture milk in which tea leaves have been infused (without boiling).

Frangipane pastry cream. CRÈME PÂTISSIÈRE, DITE FRANGIPANE – *Ingredients.* 200 g. (7 oz., $1\frac{3}{4}$ cups) sifted flour, 4 whole eggs, 6 egg yolks, 1 litre ($1\frac{3}{4}$ pints, generous quart) milk, 50 g. (2 oz., $\frac{1}{4}$ cup) butter, 100 g. (4 oz. $\frac{1}{2}$ cup) fine sugar,

Method. Mix the whole eggs, egg yolks, flour and sugar in a pan over low heat. When they are smooth and form a ribbon when the spatula is lifted out of the pan add the milk and butter. Cook over the heat, stirring continuously with the spatula. Add the crushed macaroons. Cook, stirring from time to time, to prevent a skin forming.

French pastry cream or Confectioner's custard. CRÈME PÂTISSIÈRE – This filling is much used in *pâtisserie* for large and small gâteaux, and in the preparation of puddings, both hot and cold. We give two ways of making it, the first being the more economical.

First method. Put 50 g. (2 oz., ½ cup) sifted flour, 175 g. (6 oz., ¾ cup) fine sugar, a small pinch of salt, 1 tablespoon good quality butter and 4 whole eggs in a thick-bottomed pan. Work the mixture with a spatula or wooden spoon.

Add ½ litre (scant pint, 2¼ cups) boiling milk in which a vanilla pod has been infused, or to which a few drops of vanilla essence have been added. Stir and put the pan on the heat. Let it boil for a few minutes, stirring constantly to prevent the cream from catching on the bottom of the pan.

Turn into a basin. Stir the cream from time to time as it cools.

Second method. Follow the same procedure, but modify the ingredients: 65 g. (2½ oz., 10 tablespoons) flour, 250 g. (9 oz., generous cup) fine sugar, 6 egg yolks, ½ litre (scant pint, 2¼ cups) milk flavoured with vanilla, a pinch of salt.

Mocha custard cream. CRÈME ANGLAISE AU MOKA – Prepared in the same way as a simple *Custard cream*, but the mixture of egg yolks and sugar is moistened with milk in which some freshly roasted coffee beans have been infused. (The infusion is made by heating the milk and coffee beans without allowing it to boil.)

Plombières cream. CRÈME PLOMBIÈRES – 'Put 8 egg yolks and 1 tablespoon rice flour in a casserole. Add 3 glasses (cups) good milk which is almost boiling; put the pan on a moderate heat and stir continuously with a wooden spoon. When the mixture begins to thicken, remove from the heat and continue to stir until smooth. Cook for a few minutes longer. This cream must be of the same consistency as an ordinary *French pastry cream.* Mix in 175 g. (6 oz., ¾ cup) fine sugar and a minute pinch of salt. Pour the mixture into another pan and set it on ice, stirring from time to time. It thickens as it cools. Just before serving, mix in a good half glass of liqueur and a saucerful of whipped cream. The whole, well amalgamated, should produce a light, velvety cream of a perfect consistency. Arrange the cream in a silver dish, or in small pots, a pastry-case, a specially made biscuit-case, or in a dish-shaped container of almond paste'. (From *le Cuisinier royal* by Viard and Fouret, 1828).

Praline custard cream. CRÈME PRALINÉ – Add praline to *Custard cream.*

St Honoré cream. CRÈME SAINT-HONORÉ – This is *French pastry cream* to which stiffly beaten egg whites are added when the cream is still boiling. Use 16 egg whites for a cream made with 1 litre (1¾ pints, generous quart) milk, 500 g. (18 oz., 2¼ cups) fine sugar and 16 egg yolks.

CREAM SAUCE – See SAUCE.

CREAM SOUPS. CRÈMES, POTAGES – Thickened soups, based on cereal, vegetables, fowl, fish or shellfish. (See SOUPS AND BROTHS.)

CRÉCY (À LA) – Name for various preparations, especially a soup called *purée Crécy.* All dishes named in this way include a garnish of carrots and some are exclusively made from carrots (see SOUPS AND BROTHS).

This name has been given to various dishes because of the high quality of the carrots harvested at Crécy, a small town in the Seine-et-Marne.

Some authors insist that the name of this soup comes from that of a small town in the Somme, near which the Battle of Crécy took place in 1346. Monselet leans towards this view, as can be seen from his sonnet called la Purée Crécy:

Aux jours de dîme et de taille
Crécy fut une bataille,
Dont le pays maltraité
Garde la plaie au côté.
Combat d'estoc et de taille!
De cette cruelle entaille,
O contraste! Il n'est resté
Qu'un potage réputé.
Le temps a, pour nos détresses,
D'irrésistibles caresses
Dont chaque âge est adouci.
Légumes taillés en pièces
Disent seuls, en ce temps-ci
Les grands combats de Crécy!

This sonnet is a play on the word *taille*, and is really untranslatable. The sense is this: In the days of tithes and taxes there was a battle at Crécy from which the district suffered greatly. Of this cut-and-thrust fighting, this cruel slashing, nothing remains but a famous soup. Time has a way of healing distress, and vegetables cut into pieces are the only record of the great fights at Crécy.

CRÉMANT – Word used for Champagne wines which have only a small amount of creamy froth.

CRÈME (À LA) – Name given to meat and vegetable preparations, of which the pan juices are mixed with fresh cream e.g. *Mushrooms à la crème* (see MUSHROOMS).

CRÈME RENVERSÉE – Made like *Caramel custard* (see CUSTARD). Custard cream poured into a mould, cooked in the oven in a *bain-marie* and turned out when cold.

CRÉMETS D'ANGERS, DE SAUMUR – Cream cheeses to which egg whites are added. They are prepared by gradually adding fresh stiffly whipped cream and whipped egg whites, beating all the time, so that the various elements are properly amalgamated. The mixture is put in perforated moulds, covered with fine muslin, and left to drain in a cool place. To serve, the *crémets* are turned out of their moulds and covered with fresh cream.

CRÉOLE (À LA) – Term for various culinary preparations, usually containing a rice garnish, prepared as a pilaf or *à la créole* and finished with sweet peppers simmered in oil, and with tomatoes.

A la Créole can also apply to sweet dishes. Most of these are prepared with rice, and flavoured with orange.

CRÊPE. PANCAKE – A dish made of a batter of eggs and flour, poured sparingly into a frying-pan, and fried on both sides.

Crêpe batter I. PÂTE À CRÊPES – Mix 500 g. (18 oz., 4½ cups) sifted flour, 200 g. (7 oz., scant cup) fine sugar, a small pinch salt, and a vanilla pod (or a few drops vanilla essence, added after the eggs). Add 8 whole eggs and 4 yolks, one by one, working the batter with a wooden spoon until well mixed.

Add ¾ litre (1⅓ pints, 1¾ pints) milk, and 2 to 3 tablespoons Cognac or other liqueur, and 25 g. (1 oz., 2 tablespoons) butter, which has been heated until light brown.

The batter should be made in advance and left to stand.

Crêpe batter II. PÂTE À CRÊPES – Mix 500g. (18oz., 4½ cups) flour, 150 g. (5 oz., generous ½ cup) fine sugar, and a pinch of salt. Add 10 eggs. Work the mixture until it is smooth, and add 3 dl. (½ pint, 1¼ cups) fresh cream, ½ dl. (3 tablespoons, scant ¼ cup) Cognac, 75 g. (3 oz., 6 tablespoons) melted butter and 1 litre (1¾ pints, generous quart) milk. Strain through a fine sieve. Add ½ dl. (3 tablespoons, scant ¼ cup) orgeat syrup, and 100 g. (4 oz., 1 cup) finely crushed macaroons. Flavour to taste.

Crêpes filled with strawberries

Crêpe batter III. PÂTE À CRÊPES – Mix 500 g. (18 oz., 4½ cups) flour, 150 g. (5 oz., generous ½ cup) fine sugar, a pinch of salt, 10 eggs. Work the mixture and add 4 dl. (¾ pint, scant 2 cups) cream and ½ litre (scant pint, 2¼ cups) milk. Flavour to taste.

Crêpe batter IV. PÂTE À CRÊPES – Mix 500 g. (18 oz., 4½ cups) sifted flour, 150 g. (5 oz., generous ½ cup) fine sugar, a pinch of salt, 4 whole eggs and 5 yolks. Work the mixture; add 1 litre (1¾ pints, generous quart) milk and finish with 6 stiffly beaten egg whites. Flavour to taste.

Savoury crêpe batter. PÂTE À CRÊPES SALÉES – This is used for soup, garnishes and hot *hors-d'œuvre*. Work 250 g. (9 oz., 2¼ cups) sifted flour and 4 eggs together in a basin; season with 1½ teaspoons salt. Moisten with ¾ litre (1⅓ pints, 1¾ pints) milk, which has been boiled down by one third. The milk can be replaced by stock or broth.

Alsatian crêpes. CRÊPES ALSACIENNES – Pancakes made from a *crêpe* batter, filled with redcurrant or raspberry jelly, sprinkled with sugar and glazed in a hot oven.

Apple crêpes. CRÊPES DE POMMES – See APPLE, *Crêpes stuffed with apples.*

Buckwheat crêpes, called galetous. CRÊPES AU BLÉ NOIR, DITES GALÉTOUS – Put 2 tablespoons (3 tablespoons) olive oil in a basin with 2 small glasses brandy, 2 pinches salt, 2 cups sour milk, 500 g. (18 oz., 4½ cups) buckwheat flour. Mix well. Add 8 whole eggs, one by one, and work the mixture thoroughly to avoid lumps.

Cook the pancakes on a griddle which has been rubbed with butter or fat. This is a Breton speciality.

Crêpes à la cévenole. CRÊPES À LA CÉVENOLE – Make the *crêpes* in the usual way, with a sweetened batter. When they are cooked cover each one with a thin layer of a purée of *marrons glacés*, flavoured with rum.

Roll up the pancakes and arrange on a fireproof dish. Glaze them in the oven.

Potato crêpes – See POTATO, *Potato pancakes.*

Crêpes as a soup garnish, and for other purposes. CRÊPES POUR GARNITURE DE POTAGES – Prepared in the ordinary way, with unsweetened pancake batter, or with *Savoury crêpe batter.* (See GARNISHES.)

Crêpes Chartreux. CRÊPES DES CHARTREUX – Prepare a pancake mixture and add crushed macaroons, grated zest of an orange and some fine Champagne. Cook the pancakes in the usual way.

Serve with creamed butter blended with crushed meringues and flavoured with green Chartreuse. Finish as for *Crêpes Suzette* (see below).

Raspberry crêpes. CRÊPES AUX FRAMBOISES – Cover thin pancakes with raspberry purée, made by removing stems of raspberries and soaking them in sugar and liqueur. Thicken with *French pastry cream* (see CREAMS). Roll up the pancakes and trim them on a slant at both ends. Sprinkle with icing sugar and glaze in a hot oven.

Crêpes with Roquefort. CRÊPES AU ROQUEFORT – Make small pancakes with unsweetened batter. Spread them with the following mixture:

Work 2 tablespoons (3 tablespoons) Roquefort cheese into a paste. Add 4 tablespoons (5 tablespoons) *Béchamel sauce* (see SAUCE). Season with pepper and nutmeg.

Roll up the pancakes. Arrange them on a fireproof dish, sprinkle with grated cheese, and glaze in a hot oven.

Crêpes with Gruyère, Parmesan, Cantal, Brie, and Edam cheese can be made in the same way.

Crêpes Suzette – Make thin pancakes with a batter flavoured with Curaçao and mandarin orange juice.

Spread them with the following mixture:

Cream 50 g. (2 oz., ¼ cup) fine sugar with 50 g. (2 oz., ¼ cup) butter. Add the juice of a mandarin orange, its grated zest, and 1 good tablespoon Curaçao. Work the mixture with a spatula.

Spread the pancakes with this filling, fold them into four, and serve hot.

CRÉPINETTES – Small sausages, encased in caul. Most similar preparations are enclosed in a layer of forcemeat. Paper-thin slices of salt pork can be substituted for the caul.

Crépinettes, however made, are usually covered in melted butter or other fat, coated with fresh breadcrumbs and grilled. They can be sautéed or cooked in the oven.

Very small *crépinettes* are called *Pieds cendrillon.* In the past they were wrapped in sheets of special paper and cooked on hot cinders. Nowadays they are cooked in the same way as *crépinettes*, or enclosed in a thin sheet of fine pastry and cooked in the oven.

When they are grilled, or cooked in the oven, *crépinettes* are usually accompanied by a purée of potatoes. They can also be served with a strongly seasoned sauce, or, if they are truffled, with a *Périgueux sauce* (see SAUCE).

When *crépinettes* are truffled, the stuffing includes diced truffles, whatever the basic ingredient is, and a large slice of truffle is placed on top of the stuffing before enclosing it in the caul.

Crépinettes cendrillon – See PORK, *Cinderella pork crépinettes.*

Chicken crépinettes. CRÉPINETTES DE VOLAILLE – Made with minced fowl, combined with truffles and mushrooms in a concentrated *Velouté sauce* (see SAUCE) in the same way as *Lamb crépinettes* (see below).

Lamb crépinettes. CRÉPINETTES D'AGNEAU – Prepared with minced lamb, mushrooms, truffles and a white or brown sauce, enclosed in a delicate forcemeat and wrapped in caul.

Pork crépinettes. CRÉPINETTES DE PORC – Flat sausages.

Crépinettes Sainte-Menehould – Made with minced pig's trotters, bound with concentrated brown veal gravy (with or without diced truffles) enclosed in a fine pork forcemeat (with or without truffles), and wrapped in caul.

Truffled crépinettes. CRÉPINETTES TRUFFÉES – Made with sausage meat, or with a fine pork forcemeat and diced truffles. Divide into portions weighing 100 g. (4 oz.). Wrap each portion in a piece of caul.

Cover the *crépinettes* with melted butter and grill under a gentle heat. Serve with a purée of potatoes and *Périgueux sauce* (see SAUCE).

Veal crépinettes. CRÉPINETTES DE VEAU – Made with minced veal, combined with a white or brown sauce, in the same way as *Lamb crépinettes.*

CRESS. CRESSON – Name given to two separate plants which have similar properties. One is *watercress*, the other *garden cress.*

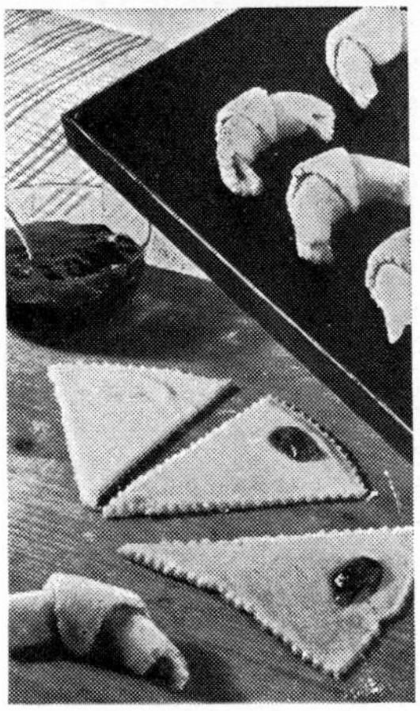

Jam croissants (Austrian pâtisserie)

To these two species should be added *lady's smock*, the leaves of which are sweeter than those of watercress. They are eaten in spring salads. *Rock cress* is eaten in the Vosges, and is more bitter than watercress. There is also *wild cress.*

Cress has a slightly bitter taste, like that of mustard.

The cress most used in cooking is watercress. It is used raw, to garnish grilled and roast meats, or in salad. Although it is excellent cooked, it is not often treated in this way.

Cress contains iron, sulphur, calcium and, most important, iodine (which is easily assimilable). It also contains a large quantity of antiscorbutic Vitamin C. Wild cress should not be eaten as it can transmit parasites. When cress is to be eaten raw, it should be picked over carefully, the thicker stems and yellowing or faded leaves removed, and the rest quickly washed and drained. It should not be left to soak in water. For recipes see WATERCRESS.

CRETAN DITTANY. DICTAME DE CRÈTE – Aromatic labinate formerly used in treacle. It is sometimes used in the manufacture of liqueurs.

CREUX – French term applied to wine which lacks body.

CREVER (To burst) – The use of the word *crever* gives many people the mistaken belief that rice should be cooked to the point of bursting, when it becomes a glutinous, insipid mass (see RICE).

CRICKET. CRIQUET – Insect of the same family as the grasshopper. It is eaten in some countries.

CROCK POT – A crock pot, commercially produced under a variety of trade names, is a well-insulated, electric, countertop cooking appliance that cooks food at a low temperature for many hours. Manufacturers' research kitchens have invented a large repertoire of recipes, but the crock pot, or slow cooker, as it is often known in Britain, is particularly useful for such dishes as stews, soups, casseroles, etc.

CROISSANT – Crescent-shaped roll generally made with *pâte feuilletée* (puff pastry), or with a leavened dough for which the recipe is given below.

This delicious pastry originated in Budapest in 1686, when the Turks were besieging the city. To reach the centre of the town, they dug underground passages. Bakers, working during the night, heard the noise made by the Turks and gave the alarm. The assailants were repulsed and the bakers who had saved the city were granted the privilege of making a special pastry which had to take the form of a crescent in memory of the emblem on the Ottoman flag.

Put 500 g. (18 oz., $2\frac{1}{2}$ cups) sifted flour on the table, and place 20 g. ($\frac{2}{3}$ oz.) dry yeast in the middle of the flour. Moisten the yeast with a little lukewarm milk and incorporate one quarter of the flour. Let the dough rise.

Add a pinch of salt, 200 g. (7 oz., scant cup) butter and 2 dl. ($\frac{1}{3}$ pint, scant cup) milk. Mix these well with the remaining flour and the other dough, working it all together and moistening it, if necessary, with a little extra milk. The dough should be firm, rather than soft. Roll it into a ball, cover with a cloth and leave to rise.

Divide it into pieces the size of an egg. Using a rolling-pin roll the pieces out into ovals and then roll them up into crescents. Place them on a baking sheet and leave to rise. Brush with milk and bake in a hot oven. As soon as they are ready, baste with a mixture of 3 tablespoons (scant $\frac{1}{4}$ cup) potato flour and $\frac{1}{2}$ litre (scant pint, $2\frac{1}{4}$ cups) boiled water.

Bakers usually sell two sorts of croissants, those made with butter, and 'the others', which no law obliges him to declare are 'made with margarine'.

Almond croissants. CROISSANTS AUX AMANDES – Pound 300 g. (11 oz., 2 cups) peeled almonds and 300 g. (11 oz., $2\frac{1}{3}$ cups) vanilla-flavoured sugar in a mortar, moistening little by little with egg white in sufficient quantity to obtain a paste which can be rolled out by hand. Add 2 tablespoons (3 tablespoons) flour to this paste.

Divide into pieces the size of a nut, and roll these with floured hands into cigar shapes. Dip in beaten egg and roll them in chopped almonds. Shape them into crescents on sheets of paper laid on baking sheets. Brush with egg yolk. Bake for 8 to 10 minutes in the oven at medium heat, and then brush with sweetened milk.

Jam croissants (Austrian pâtisserie). CROISSANTS AUX CONFITURES – Cut some *Puff pastry* (see DOUGH) into triangular pieces. Put a teaspoon of jam on one side of each triangle, and roll up as for ordinary croissants. Put them on a baking sheet, brush with egg yolk, and bake at a good heat. When ready, sprinkle with fine sugar.

CROMESQUI – Small *entrée* or hot *hors-d'œuvre* made with a *salpicon* (q.v.) enclosed in a pig's caul (or slices of salt pork) dipped in batter and deep-fried. (See HORS-D'ŒUVRE, *Hot hors-d'œuvre*.)

CROP. JABOT – A dilation of the gullet forming a pouch in birds, especially grain-eating birds. In the drawing of poultry and winged game, the crop is removed.

CROQUANT (Pâtisserie) – *Petit four* which, as its name indicates, crunches when bitten.

Pound in a mortar 250 g. (9 oz., $1\frac{3}{4}$ cups) almonds blended with 4 egg whites, added little by little. Add 500 g. (18 oz., $2\frac{1}{4}$ cups) fine sugar and 1 tablespoon vanilla sugar or a few drops vanilla extract. Strain through a fine sieve.

Make the paste into little boat-shapes, roll in brown sugar and put them on a buttered baking sheet. Bake in a very moderate oven.

CROQUE AU SEL (À LA) – Term for food which is eaten raw seasoned only with salt. *Artichokes à la croque au sel* are an example.

CROQUEMBOUCHE (Pâtisserie) – Made with ingredients which crunch between the teeth because they are glazed with sugar which is cooked *au cassé* (to the crack stage).

The typical *croquembouche* is that made of *choux profiteroles* filled with some kind of cream, glazed with sugar, and arranged one on top of the other.

Croquembouches can also be made of Genoese pastries, meringues, almond paste, and various fruits, the one most frequently made today being *croquembouche* of oranges.

Croquembouche of chestnuts (Carême's recipe)' CROQUEMBOUCHE DE MARRONS GLACÉS – 'Grill 60 fine Spanish chestnuts, and after having peeled them and removed any traces of burning, glaze by dipping them in sugar cooked to the crack stage (see SUGAR). Place them, as soon as glazed, into a mould.

'The *croquembouche* has to be piled up at the last minute before serving, because the moisture contained in the chestnuts tends to soften the sugar and make it lose both its consistency and its brilliance.'

Croquembouche of oranges

Croquembouche of oranges. CROQUEMBOUCHE D'ORANGES – Dip segments of orange in sugar cooked to crack stage. Arrange them one on top of the other in a *croquembouche* mould. When the sugar is cold, lightly heat the periphery of the mould and remove the *croquembouche*. Set it on a pastry base, and complete by adding more orange segments dipped in glazing sugar, topping it with an aigrette of spun sugar. Decorate with preserved cherries glazed in sugar cooked to crack stage.

CROQUE-MONSIEUR – Hot sandwich served as an *hors-d'œuvre* or small *entrée*.

Cut slices from a fresh or stale loaf. Spread with butter on one side, and lay a thin slice of Gruyère cheese on top, with a slice of lean ham on top of that. Close the sandwich and fry until golden in clarified butter.

CROQUETS – Dry *petits fours* of which the most famous are those of the Bordeaux area.

Bar almond croquets. CROQUETS DE BAR AUX AMANDES – *Ingredients.* 500 g. (18 oz., $2\frac{1}{4}$ cups) fine sugar, 250 g. (9 oz., $2\frac{1}{4}$ cups) ground almonds, 275 g. (10 oz., $2\frac{1}{2}$ cups) sifted flour, 8 egg whites, 1 tablespoon vanilla sugar.

Method. Moisten the sugar and ground almonds in a basin with the egg whites worked in one at a time. Mix in the sifted flour and vanilla sugar. Arrange on a baking sheet in the shape of leaves, using a thin piece of card bent into leaf shape, or a special metal cutter.

Bake in a gentle oven. When ready, leave to cool on a marble slab. Store in a jar or tin, and keep in a dry place.

Bordelais croquets. CROQUETS BORDELAIS – Pound 300 g. (11 oz., 2 cups) peeled almonds in a mortar with 150 g. (5 oz., scant cup) unpeeled almonds, 275 g. (10 oz., $1\frac{1}{4}$ cups) sugar, 100 g. (4 oz., $\frac{1}{2}$ cup) butter, 2 whole eggs, the grated zest of a lemon or orange, a packet of powdered yeast and a pinch of salt.

Chop up and roll into the form of a large *boudin* (black pudding), slightly flattened at the edges. Place on a baking sheet. Brush with egg, score it, and bake for 15 minutes in a moderate oven. Cut into slices.

CROQUETTES – Small preparations made with a *salpicon* (q.v.) bound with a white or brown sauce and containing, as well as the basic ingredient, chopped mushrooms, truffles and sometimes lean ham.

They can also be made with potatoes or other vegetables, fresh or dried; with rice cooked in stock or water; with various forms of pasta combined with cheese and *Béchamel sauce* (see SAUCE); or with a hash or a forcemeat of various meats or fish.

Sweet croquettes are made with rice cooked in milk, with semolina, or with a *salpicon* of fruit combined with stiff *French pastry cream* (see CREAM). *Croquets* is the name given to a number of croquettes made with a basic element of pasta.

Preparation of croquettes – Mix a *salpicon* (q.v.) of 500 g. (18 oz.) of the principal element (poultry, game, veal, lamb or offal) cut up into very small dice with 250 g. (9 oz.) cooked, diced mushrooms and 100 g. (4 oz.) diced truffles. Moisten with 1 dl. (6 tablespoons, scant $\frac{1}{2}$ cup) Madeira and heat in the oven in a covered pan.

Add 4 dl. ($\frac{3}{4}$ pint, scant 2 cups) *Velouté sauce* (see SAUCE) which has been boiled down and to which 3 egg yolks have been added after the desired thickness has been reached. Stir well over heat. Pour into a buttered baking dish, and dab the surface with butter to prevent a crust forming. Allow to cool completely before making the croquettes.

Croquettes made with fish or shellfish have only mushrooms and truffles added to them.

Divide the mixture into portions of about 50 to 75 g. (2 to 3 oz.). Roll these on a floured table, dip in a mixture of egg and olive oil beaten together, cover entirely with fine breadcrumbs, and shape them into corks, balls, eggs or rectangles.

Arrange them on a grill or in a frying basket, and plunge them into boiling oil. Cook until they are crisp and golden. Drain, wipe with a cloth, and sprinkle with fine salt.

Arrange the croquettes in the form of a pyramid or turban, and garnish with curled parsley.

When croquettes are served as an *entrée*, they are accompanied by a garnish of fresh vegetables to which butter has been added, or with a purée of vegetables.

Croquettes themselves if made very small can be used as a garnish for large roasts, for fowl, game or fish.

Recipes for the following croquettes will be found under HORS-D'ŒUVRE, *Hot hors-d'œuvre*: beef, brains, cress, *foie gras*, game, lobster, oyster, vegetables, macaroni, *Montrouge*, cod, fish, potatoes, *printanière*, various meats, *Viennoise*, poultry, etc.

Apricot croquettes I. CROQUETTES AUX ABRICOTS – Cook 500 g. (18 oz.) apricots in syrup, drain dry, and cut them into large dice. Bind with 4 dl. (¾ pint, scant 2 cups) *Fried custard* (see CUSTARD), and flavour with kirsch. Leave to cool.

Divide it into 50 g. (2 oz.) portions, roll them in flour and in egg and breadcrumbs. Deep-fry and serve with *Apricot sauce* (see SAUCE) flavoured with kirsch.

Apricot croquettes II. CROQUETTES AUX ABRICOTS – Cook halved apricots in a vanilla syrup. Drain well, and fill each half with 1 tablespoon *Frangipane pastry cream* (see CREAMS), flavoured with kirsch. Put two apricot halves together and envelop in a coating of cooked semolina (see SEMOLINA). Dip in egg and breadcrumbs and fry. Serve with *Apricot sauce* (see SAUCE) flavoured with kirsch.

Brie cheese croquettes. CROQUETTES DE FROMAGE DE BRIE – Put 25 g. (1 oz., ¼ cup) sifted flour in a casserole with 25 g. (1 oz., 3 tablespoons) rice flour. Moisten with 1 dl. (6 tablespoons, scant ½ cup) milk. Add 250 g. (9 oz.) Brie and 75 g. (3 oz., 6 tablespoons) butter, both cut into small pieces. Season with salt, a pinch of cayenne, and a little grated nutmeg. Cook on a good heat, stirring until the mixture is thick enough. Spread it out on a buttered baking sheet and leave to cool. Cut into rectangular pieces, dip in egg and breadcrumbs, and deep-fry.

This creamy mixture is also used to fill tartlets or *barquettes* served as a hot *hors-d'œuvre*.

Chestnut croquettes I. CROQUETTES DE MARRONS – Peel the chestnuts and cook them in a light syrup flavoured with vanilla. Sieve. Evaporate their moisture over heat, add 5 egg yolks and 50 g. (2 oz., ¼ cup) butter for 500 g. (18 oz., 2¼ cups) purée.

50 g. (2 oz., ¼ cup) of the purée makes 1 croquette. Dip in egg and breadcrumbs, and deep-fry in boiling oil. Serve with apricot sauce flavoured with kirsch.

Chestnut croquettes II. CROQUETTES DE MARRONS – Crumble 500 g. (18 oz.) *marrons glacés* (see CHESNUTS). Add 4 dl. (¾ pint, scant 2 cups) *French pastry cream* (see CREAMS) flavoured with kirsch. Leave to cool and make into croquettes. Finish in the same way as for *Apricot croquettes*.

Gruyère cheese croquettes. CROQUETTES DE FROMAGE DE GRUYÈRE – Mix 100 g. (4 oz., 1 cup) sifted flour in a pan with 50 g. (2 oz., ⅓ cup) rice flour, 3 eggs and 2 egg yolks. Moisten with 5 dl. (scant pint, 2¼ cups) boiled milk; season with a pinch of salt, a small pinch of cayenne, and a little grated nutmeg. Bring to the boil. Cook on a good heat for 5 minutes, stirring constantly to prevent it from sticking to the bottom of the pan. Remove from the heat.

Add 100 g. (4 oz., 1 cup) grated Gruyère. Spread out the mixture on a baking sheet and leave to cool. Cut into rectangles. Dip in egg and breadcrumbs and fry in boiling oil.

This cream can also be used to garnish *canapés*, *barquettes*, fried bread, or tartlets, which are then browned in the oven and served as hot *hors-d'œuvre*.

Mussel croquettes. CROQUETTES DE MOULES – Cook 2 litres (3½ pints 4½ pints) mussels in white wine with sliced onions, parsley, thyme and bay leaf. Drain the mussels, take them out of their shells and dry them on a cloth. Put them in a sauté pan with an equal quantity of diced mushrooms which have been simmered in butter.

Add *Béchamel sauce* (see SAUCE) which includes the liquor in which the mussels have been cooked and which has been boiled down. Leave to cool.

Make croquettes, dip in egg and breadcrumbs, and deep-fry.

Potato croquettes
(*Larousse*)

Potato croquettes. CROQUETTES DE POMMES DE TERRE – Prepare with a *Duchess potato mixture* (see POTATOES).

To vary the dish, when served as a hot *hors-d'œuvre* or used as a garnish, add various ingredients to the basic duchess preparation, such as finely hashed ham, mushrooms, truffles, thick tomato sauce, chopped onion lightly cooked in butter, *mirepoix* (q.v.), *duxelles* (q.v.) etc.

Rice croquettes (savoury). CROQUETTES DE RIZ – Prepare either with rice cooked in butter and bound with egg, or with cheese risotto. Make the croquettes and fry in smoking-hot fat. Garnish with fried parsley and serve with tomato sauce.

Rice croquettes (sweet). CROQUETTES DE RIZ – These can be served as a sweet course. Prepare 100 g. (4 oz., ¾ cup) sweetened rice (see RICE). As soon as it is cold, divide into portions of 50 g. (2 oz.). Make the croquettes in the shape of apples or pears, dip in egg and breadcrumbs, and deep-fry in very hot fat. Serve with a fruit sauce.

Rice croquettes (stuffed). CROQUETTES DE RIZ FOURRÉES – Divide cooked, sweetened rice into small balls. Put them on a floured board, slit them slightly, and fill with 1 teaspoon fruit marmalade (q.v.) or with thick *French pastry cream* (see CREAMS). Close the slit, dip the balls in egg and breadcrumbs, and deep-fry.

Rice croquettes old style (Carême's recipe). CROQUETTES DE RIZ À LA MANIÈRE ANCIENNE – 'Cook 175 g. (6 oz., ¾ cup) Carolina rice in good stock. Mix with 1 tablespoon thick *Velouté sauce* (see SAUCE), 2 tablespoons (3 tablespoons) grated Parmesan cheese, and a little nutmeg. Divide into 10 portions, make hollows in each, and fill them with a *salpicon* of game or fowl combined with *velouté sauce* which has been boiled down. Close up the balls, roll in fine grated Parmesan and then in the palm of the hand to make the croquettes completely round.' Dip in egg and breadcrumbs mixed with finely grated Parmesan cheese and deep-fry. Garnish with fried parsley.

La Varenne croquettes – Make large, thin *crêpes* (q.v.) with an unsweetened *crêpe* batter. Cover the *crêpes* with a layer of finely chopped mushrooms which have been cooked in butter and combined with thick tomato sauce. Roll up, cut into slices, dip in egg and breadcrumbs and deep-fry. Garnish with fried parsley.

CROQUIGNOLLES PARISIENNES (Pâtisserie) – *Ingredients.* 500 g. (18 oz., $4\frac{1}{2}$ cups) flour, 600 g. (21 oz., $2\frac{1}{2}$ cups) fine sugar, 10 egg whites, flavouring (vanilla, orange or lemon zest, liqueurs).

Method. Mix half the egg whites with icing sugar. Add the sifted flour, the rest of the egg and flavouring, and mix well. Press through a forcing-bag into various shapes on a buttered baking sheet. Leave to dry out for a few hours. Bake in a moderate oven.

In various regions of France *croquignolles* are slightly different. The best known are those of Navarre in the Basses-Pyrénées, which are made in the same way as above but with the following ingredients: 500 g. (18 oz., $4\frac{1}{2}$ cups) sifted flour, 500 g. (18 oz., $2\frac{1}{4}$ cups) fine sugar, 7 egg whites, 4 drops lemon essence or powdered vanilla, 2 tablespoons (3 tablespoons) brandy.

CROUSTADE (Pie, pasty) – Dishes made with flaky or puff pastry, filled with *ragoûts, salpicons* or other preparations.

Croustades are also made with bread which is hollowed out, brushed with egg and deep-fried, then filled with various purées (meat, fowl, fish, shellfish, or vegetable).

Bread croustade. CROUSTADE DE PAIN DE MIE – Made with stale bread. Cut a slice 5 cm. (2 inches) thick and trim to the desired shape. Decorate with knife-cuts in a pattern. Cut round the top with the point of the knife to mark the lid. Fry in deep fat until golden. Drain, and carefully prise off the marked lid. Remove the crumb from the inside, and line with a thin layer of forcemeat. Leave for a few moments at the open door of a warm oven. Fill the croustade with a *ragoût.* All the fillings given for *timbales* (q.v.) and *vol-au-vent* (q.v.) can be used.

Croustade made from a bread roll

Hollowed-out loaf of bread for making a croustade

Little croustades (hot). PETITES CROUSTADES (CHAUDES) – Line tartlet moulds with a sweet pastry dough (shortcrust with 1 egg and a little sugar added). Bake the tartlets blind, and fill with the chosen mixture (see HOR-D'ŒUVRE, *Hot hors-d'œuvre.*) They can also be filled with rice, semolina, duchess potato mixture, macaroni, noodles, etc.

Little duchess potato croustades: how to empty them using the handle of a small spoon

Little duchess potato croustades. PETITES CROUSTADES EN POMMES DE TERRE DUCHESSE – Spread out the *Duchess potato mixture* (see POTATOES) in a thick, even layer on a baking sheet, and leave to cool. Cut into *croustades* with a pastry-cutter, dip in egg and breadcrumbs and finish in the same way as for *Little noodle croustades* (see below).

Little noodle croustades (Carême's recipe). PETITES CROUSTADES DE NOUILLES – 'Prepare a noodle paste with 12 egg yolks (see NOODLE). Roll out the paste and cut into narrow strips. Boil for a few minutes in salted water. Drain the noodles and sauté them in 100 g. (4 oz., $\frac{1}{2}$ cup) butter and a little salt. Pour them into a large sauté pan and spread them out to a depth of 6 cm. ($2\frac{1}{2}$ inches).

'When they are cold, turn them onto a slab and cut *croustades* with a pastry-cutter. Mark lids with a smaller-size pastry-cutter, and fry in deep fat. Drain, remove the lids and remove the centres, leaving only a thin casing. Fill with a *salpicon.*'

Little rice croustades. PETITES CROUSTADES DE RIZ – Made with rice cooked in stock, left to cool, and cut into shapes with a pastry-cutter, in the same way as *Little noodle croustades.*

Little semolina croustades. PETITES CROUSTADES DE SEMOULE – The same as *Little noodle croustades*, using semolina cooked in stock. When quite cold, the semolina can be combined with egg yolks.

Little vermicelli croustades. PETITES CROUSTADES DE VERMICELLE – The same as *Little noodle croustades*, using vermicelli cooked in stock or plain water.

CROÛTES – Different preparations are designated under this name, some made of bread, some of brioche dough or other types of bread dough. They are used either with soups or as *hors-d'œuvre.*

Croûtes made of bread and served as a garnish are usually called croûtons.

CROÛTES FOR SOUP. CROÛTES À POTAGE –

Croûtes for croûte au pot – Divide a French loaf (*flûte*) into 5-cm. (2 inch) slices, cut each in half lengthwise, remove the soft part, and dry the crusts in a slow oven.

Alternatively, sprinkle them with the fat from the *pot-au-feu* and bake them in the oven until golden.

Diablotins. CROÛTES DITES DIABLOTINS – Cut a French loaf into slices 6 to 8 mm. ($\frac{1}{3}$ inch) thick. Cover with thick *Béchamel sauce* (see SAUCE) to which grated cheese seasoned with a

Preparation of croûtes
(*Larousse*)

little cayenne, has been added. Sprinkle with cheese and brown in the oven.

Stuffed croûtes. CROÛTES FARCIES – Cut a French loaf into slices 4 cm. ($1\frac{1}{2}$ inches) thick. Take out three-quarters of the soft part, and dry the crusts in the oven. Stuff them with chopped or sieved vegetables. Sprinkle with grated cheese, pour over them a little melted butter and brown in the oven. Serve as an accompaniment to soup.

CROÛTES FOR HORS-D'ŒUVRE or SMALL ENTRÉES. CROÛTES POUR HORS-D'ŒUVRE OU PETITES ENTRÉES – Small *croustades* made with stale bread, cut into $2\frac{1}{2}$-cm. (1-inch) thick slices. Press a small pastry-cutter half-way into the slices to mark the lids.

Fry the croûtes, drain, remove the incised portions, fill.

Croûtes with grated cheese. CROÛTES AU FROMAGE GRATINÉE – Cut 2-cm. ($\frac{3}{4}$-inch) slices from a stale loaf and trim into oval shapes. Fry in butter until they are golden.

Add grated cheese and thick cream to *béchamel sauce*, boil down, sieve, and pour over the croûtes. Put a thin slice of Gruyère on each croûte, pour some melted butter over, and brown in a hot oven.

Croûtes with mushrooms. CROÛTES AUX CHAMPIGNONS – Mushrooms prepared *à la crème* are used as a stuffing for brioche croûtes in the form of a *galette* (q.v.) – a round open tart made with puff pastry. The croûte is hollowed out, buttered, browned in the oven, and filled with *Mushrooms à la crème* (see MUSHROOMS). The croûtes are served hot.

Croûtes à la Nantua – Fry small rectangles of bread in butter, and cover with *Béchamel sauce* (see SAUCE) combined with a little *Crayfish butter* (see BUTTER). Add peeled crayfish tails, and cover with a cream sauce to which more crayfish butter has been added. Sprinkle with fine breadcrumbs, pour over a little melted butter, and brown quickly in a very hot oven. Shrimps can be substituted for the crayfish.

Croûtes à la reine – Cover slices of fried bread with a purée of fowl cooked *à la crème*. Sprinkle with fine breadcrumbs, pour over a little melted butter, and brown in a hot oven.

Croûtes Saint-Hubert – The same as *Croûtes à la reine*, but replace the purée of fowl with a game purée which has been combined with concentrated game stock.

Croûtes gratinées with truffles. CROÛTES GRATINÉES AUX TRUFFES – Cut cleaned, peeled truffles in thick slices, season with salt and pepper and dip in melted butter. Set these slices, overlapping, on slices of bread that have been lightly cooked in butter. Sprinkle with Parmesan cheese and pour over a few drops of melted butter. Brown in a very hot oven.

Croûtes with truffles. CROÛTES AUX TRUFFES – Made like *Croûtes with mushrooms* using truffles prepared *à la crème*.

CROÛTES FOR MIXED ENTRÉES. CROÛTES POUR ENTRÉES MIXTES – These are made of pastry or puff pastry left-overs, in the same way as for a pastry case. Cook the cases blind, and fill with the preparation indicated in the recipe.

CROÛTES FOR DESSERTS. CROÛTES POUR ENTREMETS –

Croûtes dorées – Cut stale brioche into slices 1 cm. ($\frac{1}{2}$ inch) thick. Soak the slices in cold sweetened milk flavoured with vanilla, then in slightly sweetened egg, and cook in clarified butter. Sprinkle with vanilla sugar. (See below, *Golden croûtes.*)

Fruit croûtes. CROÛTES AUX FRUITS – Cut a stale *savarin* (q.v.) into $\frac{1}{2}$-cm. ($\frac{1}{4}$-inch) slices, place on a baking sheet, sprinkle with fine sugar, and glaze in the oven.

Cut a piece of white bread into a conical shape, fry it, and place it in the centre of a dish. Arrange the *savarin* slices round it, alternating them with pineapple slices which have been cooked in syrup.

Cook quartered pear and apple slices in syrup and arrange them round the cone. Fill the inside of this border with a mixture of fruits which have been cooked in syrup and drained. Decorate with preserved cherries and lozenges of angelica, quartered preserved apricots, oranges preserved in brandy, and halved almonds. Stick a skewer (*attelet*) decorated with preserved fruits into the central cone.

Heat in a very moderate oven, and when ready to serve, cover with *Apricot sauce* (see SAUCE) flavoured with kirsch. Serve with more of the sauce. Other fruits cooked in syrup may be used.

Golden croûtes. PAINS À LA ROMAINE DITS AUSSI CROÛTES DORÉES – *Ingredients.* 250 g. (9 oz.) stale brioche, $\frac{1}{2}$ litre (scant pint, $2\frac{1}{4}$ cups) milk, 100 g. (4 oz., $\frac{1}{2}$ cup) butter, 125 g. ($4\frac{1}{2}$ oz., $\frac{1}{2}$ cup) fine sugar, $\frac{1}{2}$ vanilla bean, 2 eggs.

Method. Cut the brioche into thick slices and soak them in milk which has been boiled with the sugar and vanilla and left to cool. Dip the slices, one at a time, in the eggs, which have been beaten with a little fine sugar, and fry in butter. When both sides are golden, drain the slices and sprinkle with the rest of the sugar.

Croûtes with Madeira. CROÛTES AU MADÈRE – Made of slices of *savarin* and pineapple, like *Fruit croûtes.* Fill the centre with a *salpicon* (q.v.) of fruits cooked *en compote* to which have been added currants, sultanas and raisins that have been washed and left to swell in lukewarm water.

Cover the croûte with *Apricot sauce* (see SAUCE) flavoured with Madeira. Serve with a little more of this sauce.

Croûtes Montmorency – Cut a stale brioche into 1-cm. ($\frac{1}{2}$-inch) thick slices, and shape them into half moons. Sprinkle with sugar and glaze in the oven on a baking sheet. Cover each slice with a thin layer of *Frangipane pastry cream* (see CREAMS) flavoured with cherry brandy, and arrange them on a dish in the form of a crown, setting them very close together.

Fill the centre of the crown with a dome of stoned cherries which have been cooked in a vanilla syrup and drained. Decorate the border of the crown with preserved cherries, angelica lozenges and halved almonds. Cover with red-currant jelly laced with cherry brandy, and serve with a little of this sauce.

Croûtes à la normande – Glaze slices of stale brioche with sugar, cover with a thick purée of apple prepared as for *Apple charlotte*, (see CHARLOTTE) and finish with thick cream. Arrange on a dish in the shape of a crown. Fill the centre with quartered apples cooked in syrup flavoured with vanilla, and cover with *Apple sauce* (see SAUCE) flavoured with Calvados. Serve with this sauce.

CROÛTON – End of a long loaf. Also diced bread fried in butter, served as an accompaniment to soup.

Bread croûtons. CROÛTONS EN PAIN DE MIE – Slices cut from a stale white loaf which are fried in butter, grilled, or dried in the oven. Except for large croûtons used under game, croûton-supports are not considered edible. Their only rôle is to support large hot or cold joints in order to be able to display the various garnishes round them. All excessive trimmings should be avoided in these arrangements, which should be simple in order to be effective.

Bread croûtons

Croûtons for garnishes. CROÛTONS POUR GARNITURES – Croûtons made of white bread cut in different ways, often in the form of hearts. They are cooked in oil or butter and are used to garnish various dishes which are presented in sauce, such as *blanquette de veau, civet, chicken fricassée, chicken Marengo, salmis.* Croûtons used to garnish *salmis* are usually covered with *à gratin forcemeat* (see FORCEMEAT). Croûtons cut in the form of *dents de loup* (wolves' teeth) are used to garnish spinach and other vegetable dishes. Those cut in lozenge shapes are used for fish prepared *à la normande*.

Croûtons for scrambled eggs or omelettes. CROÛTONS POUR OEUFS BROUILLÉS OU OMELETTE – These are made of diced white bread fried in butter and added to scrambled egg or omelettes.

CROW. CORBEAU – The meat of this bird, except when young, is tough and fibrous. Nevertheless, in many forest regions where crows abound, they are used to make a poor soup. Cuniset-Carnot, in his *Vie aux champs*, gives a humorous recipe for cooking a crow. 'Make a good pot-au-feu. On the reversed lid of the pot put a plucked crow. After 5 or 6 hours of gentle cooking, throw the crow on the fire and enjoy the pot-au-feu.'

CROWN. COURONNE – Method of dressing a dish in the form of a crown or ring. *Brioche en couronne* is a type of dough-cake made in this shape.

CROWN-PIGEON (Squab). GOURA – This is cooked in the same way as the common pigeon, or squab.

CRU – The soil in which a plant or a fruit has grown. This applies particularly to vines.

CRUCHADE – A kind of porridge made with maize flour and milk or water. It has a great similarity to *miliasse* or *millat*, made in the south-west of France; and also to *polenta*, made in the south-east and in Italy. (See MILIASSE.)

CRUDITÉS – Food eaten raw. Man is the only living creature to use cooked foods. Children, however, have an innate taste for raw vegetables and even for unripe fruit, which indicates that raw food should be an essential part of man's diet.

The indigestibility of *crudités* is caused by the way they are sometimes presented; served finely chopped or grated, and chewed well, they are perfectly digestible.

Some foods are not pleasant to eat raw, or are only really edible when they are cooked. Meat, for instance, nearly always needs to be masked in various ways in order to be eaten raw, and is distasteful to many people even then. On the other hand, a cooked oyster can never have the flavour of an uncooked one, and this holds good for salads and fruit.

Gastronomes can see another advantage in *crudités*. Since their food value is generally minimal, they are useful for allaying the first pangs of hunger without spoiling the appreciation of the remainder of the meal; on the contrary, they rather enhance the main meal. Thus the perils of over-eating that so often menace those who love good food are avoided.

CRUET STAND (U.S. Castor set). MÉNAGÈRE – Table-set consisting of bottles and jars of glass, porcelain or metal, set in a base.

CRUSH. ÉCRASER – To flatten and break aromatic seeds, or bread which has been baked hard in the oven and is intended for breadcrumbs.

CRUSTACEANS. CRUSTACÉS – Animals, usually aquatic, with a hard, shelly crust and jointed extremities. Some species are used in cooking, e.g. crabs, crayfish, lobsters, etc. For the various dishes made with these different shellfish see recipes under their names.

Shellfish have a firm, close-grained flesh and an agreeable taste, but are not easy to digest. They have a reputation as aphrodisiacs, no doubt due to the very strong condiments with which they are often flavoured.

A crustacean: crab

CUCUMBER. CONCOMBRE – Genus of plants belonging to the gourd family, with large elongated fruits. Cucumbers originated in the north-west of India, where they have been cultivated in Hindustan for three thousand years. They also grow in a wild state. There are a large number of species, white or green, with smooth or rough skin, early or late fruiting. They are very watery and contain little nutritive value. Cucumbers are eaten raw in salads and are sometimes cooked. When they are to be cooked the rather bitter juice should be removed by salting and pressing before seasoning.

Cucumber contains Vitamins A and C, but it is indigestible, and should only be eaten by those with good digestions.

Cucumbers in butter. CONCOMBRES AU BEURRE – Peel the cucumbers, cut into pieces, blanch and drain. Season, and cook them slowly in a buttered sauté pan with the lid on.

Cucumbers à la crème. CONCOMBRES À LA CRÈME – Prepare the cucumbers as for *Cucumbers in butter*. When they are three-quarters cooked cover with boiling cream, and finish cooking. This dish can also be prepared by moistening the cucumbers with a *Cream sauce* (see SAUCE).

Cucumbers à la dijonnaise (hors-d'œuvre). CONCOMBRES À LA DIJONNAISE – Cut two green cucumbers into slices, then cut the slices into quarters. Boil for 2 minutes in salted water to which a few drops of wine vinegar have been added. Drain, put them in a colander under a cold tap, drain again, then simmer for 12 minutes in a casserole with 2 tablespoons (3 tablespoons) olive oil, 1 tablespoon vinegar, a pinch of salt and a pinch of paprika. Before serving add 2 teaspoons *Dijon mustard* and mix well.

Cucumbers au gratin. CONCOMBRES GRATINÉS AU PARMESAN – Cut the cucumbers into slices, blanch lightly, and cook them in butter. Put the slices in a buttered *gratin* dish sprinkled with grated Parmesan, sprinkle with more Parmesan, pour over some melted butter, and brown in the oven.

Cucumbers à la grecque (hors-d'œuvre). CONCOMBRES À LA GRECQUE – Quarter a large cucumber and cook in a *court-bouillon* made with 3 dl. (½ pint, 1¼ cups) water, 1 dl. (6 tablespoons, scant ½ cup) oil, the juice of lemon, a *bouquet* of celery, fennel, thyme, and a good pinch of coriander, salt and pepper.

Boil for 8 minutes. Drain the cucumbers, boil down the liquor in which they have been cooked to half, cool, and pour it over the cucumbers. Keep in a cool place and serve cold.

Cucumbers au jus. CONCOMBRES AU JUS – Prepare in the same way as *Cucumbers in butter*, adding a few tablespoons concentrated veal stock when cooked.

Cucumbers Mornay. CONCOMBRES MORNAY – Prepare in the same way as *Cucumbers in butter*. Put the cucumber pieces in a *gratin* dish lined with *Mornay sauce* (see SAUCE). Pour more sauce over them, sprinkle with grated cheese, pour over a little butter, and brown in the oven.

Cucumber purée. PURÉE DE CONCOMBRES – Peel two large cucumbers, split them lengthways and remove the seeds. Cut into slices and simmer in butter. Add half their quantity of potatoes, cut into quarters. Moisten with consommé or water, boil until soft, drain. Sieve the cucumbers and potatoes, and put this purée into a pan over low heat. Add a few teaspoons butter and thick cream, and work the mixture with a wooden spoon until it is smooth.

Cucumber salad. SALADE DE CONCOMBRES – Peel the cucumbers, split them in half lengthwise, remove the seeds, and slice the flesh finely. Spread the slices on a cloth, sprinkle with salt and leave for 30 minutes. Drain, season with salt, pepper, vinegar, oil and chopped chervil.

The cucumbers can be seasoned with *vinaigrette sauce* without first being salted.

Stuffed cucumbers. CONCOMBRES FARCIS – Peel cucumbers and cut into slices 5 cm. (2 inches) thick. Boil in salted water for 5 minutes. Drain, and scoop a hollow out of each slice.

Mix 2 tablespoons (3 tablespoons) *duxelles* (q.v.) with 250 g. (9 oz.) veal or pork forcemeat. Add 1 tablespoon chopped parsley, 50 g. (2 oz., ½ cup) chopped onion which has been cooked in butter and cooled. Fill the scooped-out cucumbers with the stuffing.

Line the bottom of a sauté pan with bacon rinds, slices of carrots and onion and a *bouquet garni* (q.v.). Set the cucumbers on this foundation and add enough slightly salted stock to reach two-thirds up the sides of the cucumbers. Bring to the boil. Put a buttered sheet over the cucumbers, cover the pan, and cook slowly in the oven for 35 minutes.

Strain the cooking liquor and boil down rapidly to 2 dl. (⅓ pint, scant cup). Thicken slightly with a brown sauce or with *Kneaded butter* (see BUTTER), and pour over the cucumbers when serving.

CUIRE VERT – Colourful expression once used to indicate to what degree certain meats should be cooked to keep them rare (*très saignantes*). Nowadays the expression is *cuire bleu*.

CUISINE – See COOKING.

CUISINE MINCEUR – A new method of French cooking. Based on the classic French principles, it maintains the characteristic flavours but reduces the proportion of foods which have a high calorie and saturated fat content such as butter and cream. Many authorities believe that by eating dishes prepared in this manner, the risk of a coronary may be reduced.

CUISSON – This term has several meanings in French.

1. The cooking of any kind of food.
2. Cooking time.
3. Liquid used in the cooking of certain foodstuffs for example, *cuisson* of mushrooms, *cuisson* of calves' heads. In this context the word means stock or clear soup.

CUISSOT – See HAUNCH.

CULINARY ART. ART CULINAIRE – For a short history of cookery see the entry on COOKING.

CULINARY METHODS. MÉTHODES CULINAIRES – All culinary operations, from the simplest to the most complicated, must be carried out according to precise rules. It is advisable to adhere scrupulously to these principles in order to achieve success in the preparation of all dishes.

The culinary rules governing the different methods of cooking foodstuffs are listed below in alphabetical order.

Braising meat. BRAISAGE DES VIANDES – Method of cooking meat chiefly used for red meats such as beef and mutton, but it can also be used for white meats such as lamb and veal. By slightly modifying the procedure it can also be used for pork and venison.

Large poultry is also braised, and the method may be used for large fish although, in fact, fish is stewed with a very little liquid rather than braised in the strict sense of the word.

Red meat should be interlarded before being braised; that is, thick lardoons, seasoned with spices, moistened with brandy and sprinkled with chopped parsley are threaded into it with a larding needle.

Large cuts of meat and venison are steeped in a marinade (q.v.) for a time before braising and then moistened with a braising stock prepared in advance, or from the stockpot or even with water. White or red wine, the marinade and aromatic vegetables should be added to the stock.

Instructions for braising large cuts are given under BEEF.

Garnishes for braised meat. Meat is usually braised *à la bourgeoise*, with carrots and onions added towards the end of cooking. Braised cuts can also be served with vegetables braised in stock, stuffed vegetables, macaroni prepared in different ways, risotto, etc.

Braising white meat. Strictly speaking, cuts of white meat, veal in particular, should be pot roasted rather than braised. However, cuts of white meat can be braised in the same way as red meat, but using very little stock. (See below *Pot roasting*.)

Braising large poultry. BRAISAGE DES GROSSES VOLAILLES – Large poultry is usually pot roasted rather than braised. Use very little stock in cooking.

Clarifying and enriching soups, stocks and jellies. CLARIFICATION DES BOUILLONS, FONDS ET GELÉES – The purpose of this operation is to make soups, stocks and jellies clearer and tastier. This applies to sweet jellies as well as to fish and meat stocks. After clarification, and enriching with chopped lean beef and egg white, the soup is known as consommé. Allow 250 to 350 g. (9 to 12 oz.) chopped lean beef to every litre (scant quart, generous quart) stock to ensure adequate clarification. For jelly stocks, which are very concentrated in themselves, 100 to 150 g. (4 to 5 oz.) per litre (scant quart, generous quart) is required.

Where appropriate chopped poultry may be used instead of chopped beef. A small quantity of egg white and finely diced vegetables should be used.

When clarifying sweet jellies (made with fruit and wine or liqueur) egg white only is used.

Clarified consommé and jellies of various kinds must be strained after boiling. Wet and wring out a cloth of closely woven material. Fix it to the four legs of an upturned stool. Under this cloth place a bowl large enough to take all of the stock. Skim off the fat, then pour the stock into this improvised strainer. For smaller amounts, lay the cloth on top of a bowl and lift up the corners.

Deep-frying. FRITURE – Method of cooking used a great deal in household kitchens. Fried foods, well prepared, are much prized by gastronomes. (See DEEP-FRYING.)

Gratin – Name given to dishes which, after being subjected to intense heat in the oven or under the grill, acquire a crisp, golden-brown crust. To assist in the formation of this crust, sprinkle the food either with fresh or lightly toasted breadcrumbs or with grated cheese, preferably Parmesan, and pour on melted butter.

Gratins can be made with either raw or cooked food. The most common raw *gratins* are made of fish covered with *Duxelles sauce* (see SAUCE.) A recipe for cooking raw vegetables *au gratin* is given under *Potatoes à la dauphinoise* (see POTATOES).

Fish prepared with a white *gratin sauce* are poached in concentrated fish stock, drained, covered with white sauce, sprinkled with cheese or breadcrumbs and browned quickly in the oven. When browning a *gratin* the dish should be set on a wire tray separating it from the oven shelf, or in a dish half-full of hot water. This prevents the fats from separating and the sauce from spoiling.

Grilling (U.S. broiling). GRILLADE – Grilling, like roasting, is a method of cooking by intense heat, the nourishing juices being sealed into the meat by the crust formed on the surface. The fuel traditionally used for grilling in France is small charcoal (known as *braise*). The charcoal, when thoroughly alight, is spread out to form a bed in a grille pan with a well-regulated draught. This bed of charcoal varies in depth according to the size and kind of meat to be grilled. Nowadays there are also gas and electric grills, both of which are very good and extremely practical.

The grill must be scrupulously clean, and heated before the meat is laid upon it or under it. The food to be grilled must be basted with clarified butter, oil or fat, and seasoned. Meat should be gently flattened and trimmed before cooking.

Fish should be scored with a knife, well coated with butter and oil, and seasoned. Fish which is rather dry has a tendency to stick to the bars of the grill, and should therefore be floured before being coated with butter or oil. This will form a covering which will enable the fish to cook without becoming too dry. Turn grilling meat or fish over once or twice during cooking, and baste frequently with the butter or oil, using a brush.

Grilled food is ready when it resists pressure if lightly touched with the fingertip. Tiny pinkish droplets appearing on the browned surface are another indication that it is fully cooked. Grilled white meat should be less browned than red meat and a less intense heat should be used. Grill fish at moderate heat, and baste frequently.

Grill poultry first if it is to be cooked in breadcrumbs. When three-parts cooked, cover with butter or oil and roll in the breadcrumbs as indicated for *Chicken à la diable* (see CHICKEN).

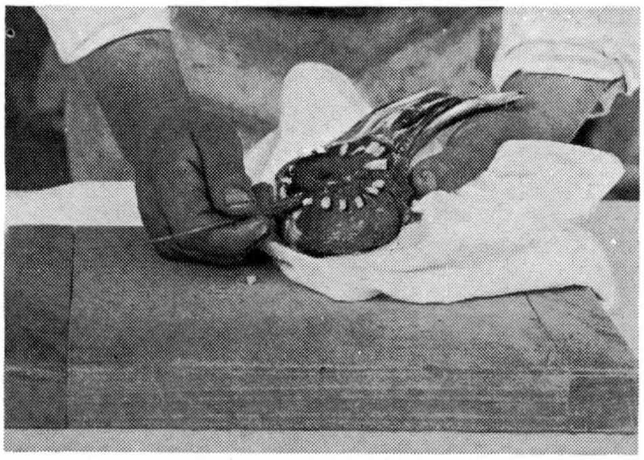

Interlarding a round piece of meat

Interlarding meat. PIQUAGE DES VIANDES – Certain cuts of meat, such as fillet of beef, leg of veal, etc., are interlarded with best pork fat cut into small lardoons. In the same way, poultry, veal sweetbreads, veal chops and large fish such as carp, sturgeon, etc. are interlarded with very small lardoons.

Interlarding a fillet of beef. Skin the meat and remove all tendons. Using a larding needle threaded with a lardoon, thread it into the fillet, following the grain of the meat. The depth of the stitch is determined by the length of the lardoon. Each lardoon should project 2 cm. (¾ inch) on either side.

Thread the second row of lardoons through the meat, alternating them with the first, at a distance of 2 cm. (¾ inch) making sure that the lardoons always project over the meat. Keeping the spacing even, thread as many double rows of lardoons into the meat as its length requires. After the fillet is completely interlarded, trim the lardoons so that the ends are of equal length. Tie the fillet crosswise to keep it round in shape. Put it on a spit or, if it to be roasted in the oven, in a roasting tin fitted with a grid.

Interlarding a fricandeau or leg of veal. Trim the joint as indicated under VEAL. Interlard as for fillet of beef.

Interlarding saddle of mutton or roebuck, baron of hare, haunch of venison, etc. Proceed as indicated above, adapting the thickness of the lardoons to the size of the meat.

Interlarding small cuts of meat. Lardoons must be cut very fine for small cuts and a finer needle should be used. Small round portions of meat may be interlarded by threading the lardoons into them in the form of a rosette. This method can also be used with beef and mutton *filets mignons*, and for veal sweetbreads. These last, before being interlarded, must be soaked in water, blanched, cooled under running water, and left to get quite cold under a weight.

Interlarding poultry and game. PIQUAGE DE VOLAILLES ET DU GIBIER – Only large poultry for braising is interlarded. Singe with a hot flame the part of the breast to be interlarded or dip it in boiling water to make the flesh firm.

Only old game for braising, such as partridge, pheasant or hazel-grouse, is interlarded. Proceed as for poultry, using very small lardoons.

Poaching. POCHAGE – Poaching is a gentle simmering in liquid. The amount of water or stock used depends on the food to be poached.

Meat, poultry and fish can all be poached, as well as eggs and meat balls, Mousses and *mousselines* are poached in a *bain-marie*. Sweetbreads are poached in a very little stock.

Red meat is poached in a white stock with vegetables, or in boiling salt water, as is customary with *Leg of lamb à l'anglaise* (see LAMB). White meat is seldom poached. But the term 'poaching' may be applied to the method of cooking used in preparing lamb and veal *en blanquette*.

Large poultry to be poached is put into cold white stock, the liquid brought to the boil, skimmed, and seasoned as with *pot-au-feu* (q.v.). The poultry is then simmered very slowly in the stock. Poultry for poaching can be stuffed or not, and trussed. It can be larded with best lardoons or studded with pieces of ham, tongue or truffles cut into the shape of little pegs. To protect the breast while cooking, poultry should be barded. To test whether the poultry is ready, prick the thigh. When the juice which runs out is white, the bird is cooked. After cooking, drain and untruss the poultry and remove the barding. Serve on fried bread, surrounded with an appropriate garnish. The stock, strained and skimmed, is boiled down and added to the sauce to be served with the dish.

Large fish can be poached whole or in slices, and moistened with concentrated fish stock (*fumet*). Thick slices of fish are prepared in the same way. Fillets of fish (brill, whiting, sole, turbot, etc.) to be poached are put in a buttered baking dish, seasoned, moistened with a few tablespoons concentrated fish stock and cooked in the oven.

Poached eggs are cooked in boiling salt water to which a few drops of vinegar have been added.

Fish or meat balls are put into a buttered pan, covered with boiling salt water and very slowly simmered.

Food poached on the *bain-marie* principle, such as mousses, *mousselines*, moulds, puddings, etc., are stood in baking tins or pans half full of hot water, and cooked in a very slow oven.

Pot roasting. POÊLAGE – Slow cooking by steam, using a casserole with a tightly fitting lid. The food is cooked with butter or fat, together with vegetables which have been slowly cooked in butter. Pot-roasted meat, poultry or fish must be frequently basted during cooking. When ready, take it out of the casserole and serve on a dish or in a *cocotte* (q.v.). Remove most of the cooking fat, add wine or stock, boil for a few moments, strain, and pour the liquor over the dish.

Pot roasting à la Matignon. Brown meat or fish to be pot roasted lightly in butter. Cover with a thick layer of *Matignon* (q.v.) or *fondue* of root vegetables. Wrap in buttered paper and cook in the oven. After cooking, unwrap, surround with garnishes and pour on the strained stock to which the *matignon* has been added.

Braising *à la matignon* can also be carried out by lining a braising pan with the *fondue* of root vegetables and placing the meat, fish or poultry, liberally basted with butter, on top.

Ragoûts – Details and recipes for the preparation of *ragoût* dishes are to be found under RAGOÛT.

Roasting. RÔTISSAGE – This is used in the cooking of meat, poultry, game, large fish and shellfish.

The distinctive feature of roasting is that the internal juices are preserved. In his *Principes et lois culinaires* Reculet defines the roasting process:

'Cooking by concentration works by means of transmission and not, as in the case of boiling, by means of insinuation. The concentrating agent, whether ponderable or imponderable, attacks and envelops the substance. The first coating is heated, the juices are driven inwards towards the centre, and the crust forms on the surface. The heat of the first coating is transmitted to the second. The juices sealed in by the outer coating, being unable to escape from the tissues, generate heat themselves, and contribute powerfully to the cooking of the whole.'

There are two ways of roasting: by the action of a naked flame on the spit; or by radiant heat in the oven. Spit roasts are superior to oven roasts because substances placed before an open fire can evaporate freely whereas those cooked in an enclosed oven are enveloped and radically altered by the vapour produced. However, roasts are usually cooked in coal, gas or electric ovens. These, being extremely well designed, produce good results, and they do sometimes incorporate an automatic spit.

Piece of beef ready to be oven roasted

Roasting in the oven. RÔTIS AU FOUR – The intensity of the cooking heat must be regulated to suit the roast. When the crust is formed, the heat must be lowered. With a solid fuel cooker, the roast should be moved to a cooler part of the oven and the roasting pan stood in another pan if necessary. It is essential for oven roasts to be raised above the bottom of the roasting pan on a grid. Basting of oven roasts should be carried out as for spit roasts (see below).

It does not take long to acquire the knack of knowing when the roast is ready. If in doubt, follow the instructions in the section on *Average cooking time for roasts* (see below), and look for the following indications.

When red meat (beef and mutton) is perfectly cooked, a small prick will make it exude pale pink blood. In the case of white meat (veal, lamb, pork) the juice is colourless. Poultry is perfectly cooked when, if tilted on a plate, pure white juice pours out of the body. As long as there are any reddish traces, the poultry is not fully cooked. Winged and ground game should, as a rule, exude a pinkish juice. It should be tested in the same way as red meat.

Poultry and game should be trussed and barded, or interlarded with best lardoons. The purpose of barding with pork fat or fat bacon is to protect the delicate parts of the breast from the intensity of the heat, and also to impregnate the flesh with fat to make it more tender. Barding is done by tying the fat to the bird with string. After cooking, the fat is removed.

Large cuts of meat are sometimes barded. More often, the delicate parts of these cuts are protected with well-flattened pieces of beef or veal fat.

Most roasts should be served directly they are removed from the spit or the oven. For red meat, however, it is advisable to take it out of the oven or off the spit a few minutes before it is quite ready, and to keep it hot in front of the open oven until it is ready to be served. While it is standing thus, the meat settles and is ready to carve.

Spit roasting. RÔTIS À LA BROCHE – Red meat, rich in juices, must always be browned and then subjected to an even heat, to ensure that the meat is cooked right through. Anthracite gives an intense heat without producing flames, and is very suitable for cooking red meat.

For white meat, the heat must be adjusted so that the external browning and internal cooking take place simultaneously. The same principles apply to poultry.

Spit-roasted food must be frequently basted. This is done with the fat floating on the top of the liquid in the dripping-pan, and not with the juice itself. Basting with pure fat produces a tender, well-browned roast, whereas basting with the cooking liquid prevents the roast from browning.

Gravy of the roast. JUS DE RÔTIS – It is essential to extract all the goodness in the roasting or dripping pan by immediate dilution with water or clear stock, and boiling. The gravy of a roast should not be completely skimmed.

The serving of roasts. DRESSAGE DES RÔTIS – The roast, if it is a joint or a bird, is laid on a very hot dish and garnished with fresh watercress which has been picked over, washed and thoroughly drained. The gravy is served separately, but just before serving, the cooking fat may be poured over the roast. In some parts of northern and eastern France, a thick purée of apples and stewed fruit is often served with roasts. These compotes and purées should be only slightly sweetened.

Winged game, other than wild duck, pintail and teal, are served on *canapés* or slices of bread fried in butter and spread with *à gratin forcemeat* (see FORCEMEAT).

Game birds are usually garnished with watercress and halved or quartered lemons. Orange is sometimes served instead of lemon with wild duck, teal, pintail and other wildfowl.

In England, roast winged game is often garnished with *Potato crisps* (see POTATOES). *Bread sauce* (see SAUCE) and fried breadcrumbs are served in addition to the gravy.

Redcurrant jelly and chestnut purée are often served with roast venison and small ground game.

Average cooking times for roasts. TEMPS MOYEN DE CUISSON DES RÔTIS –

Beef. Oven temperature 200°C. (400°F., Gas Mark 6) – except fillet.

Contre-filet or faux filet – Boned, 20 minutes per 500 g. (1 lb.) plus 20 minutes. On the bone, 15 minutes per 500 g. (1 lb.) plus 15 minutes.

Fillet – Oven temperature 230°C. (450°F., Gas Mark 8) 12 to 15 minutes per 500 g. (1 lb.); or 15 to 18 minutes per 500 g. (1 lb.) if using a spit.

Rib – 15 to 18 minutes per 500 g. (1 lb.) plus 15 minutes; or 20 minutes per 500 g. (1 lb.) plus 20 minutes if using a spit. As soon as the meat is taken off the spit it must be put in a warm oven for 30 minutes or longer, according to size. Under this very moderate heat cooking is completed and the rib retains all its internal juices.

Sirloin – 10 to 15 minutes per 500 g. (1 lb.) plus 10 minutes.

Sirloin roast à l'anglaise – 15 to 18 minutes per 500 g. (1 lb.) plus 15 minutes.

Lamb and mutton. Oven temperature 200°C. (400°F., Gas Mark 6).

Baron – 18 to 20 minutes per 500 g. (1 lb.) plus 18 minutes.

Breast – 20 to 25 minutes per 500 g. (1 lb.) plus 20 minutes.

Leg – 20 minutes per 500 g. (1 lb.) plus 20 minutes.

Saddle – 18 to 20 minutes per 500 g. (1 lb.) plus 18 minutes.

Shoulder – 18 to 20 minutes per 500 g. (1 lb.) plus 18 minutes.

Pork. Oven temperature 200°C. (400°F., Gas Mark 6).

Breast – 25 to 30 minutes per 500 g. (1 lb.) plus 25 minutes.

Fillet – 25 to 30 minutes per 500 g. (1 lb.) plus 25 minutes.

Veal. Oven temperature 200°C. (400°F., Gas Mark 6).

Breast – 24 to 28 minutes per 500 g. (1 lb.) plus 24 minutes.

Lengthwise cut of chump end (*U.S. tenderloin*) – 25 to 30 minutes per 500 g. (1 lb.) plus 25 minutes.

Top loin or fillet – 25 to 30 minutes per 500 g. (1 lb.) plus 25 minutes.

Poultry.

Chicken – Oven temperature 200°C. (400°F., Gas Mark 6), 15 minutes per 500 g. (1 lb.) plus 15 minutes; or 20 minutes per 500 g. (1 lb.) plus 20 minutes if using a spit.

Duck – Oven temperature 190°C. (375°F., Gas Mark 5), 15 minutes per 500 g. (1 lb.) plus 15 minutes; or 20 minutes per 500 g. (1 lb.) plus 20 minutes if using a spit.

Goose – Oven temperature 190°C. (375°F., Gas Mark 5), 15 minutes per 500 g. (1 lb.) plus 15 minutes.

Guinea-fowl – Oven temperature 200°C. (400°F., Gas Mark 6), 45 to 60 minutes per bird; or 1 to 1¼ hours if using a spit.

Pigeon – Oven temperature 200°C. (400°F., Gas Mark 6), 20 to 30 minutes per bird; or 30 to 40 minutes per bird if using a spit.

Turkey – Oven temperature 190°C. (375°F., Gas Mark 5), 15 minutes per 500 g. (1 lb.) plus 15 minutes for a bird weighing up to 5½ kg. (12 lb.), or 10 minutes per 500 g. (1 lb.) plus 10 minutes for a bird weighing over 5½ kg. (12 lb.).

Ground game. Oven temperature 200°C. (400°F., Gas Mark 6).

Hare (*baron*) – 15 to 20 minutes per 500 g. (1 lb.) plus 15 minutes; or 20 to 25 minutes per 500 g. (1 lb.) plus 20 minutes if using a spit.

Roebuck (*haunch or saddle*) – 20 minutes per 500 g. (1 lb.) plus 20 minutes; or 25 to 30 minutes per 500 g. (1 lb.) plus 25 minutes if using a spit.

Young rabbit – 15 minutes per 500 g. (1 lb.) plus 15 minutes; or 20 minutes per 500 g. (1 lb.) plus 20 minutes if using a spit.

Winged game. Oven temperature 200°C. (400°F., Gas Mark 6).

Grouse – 25 to 30 minutes per bird; or 30 to 40 minutes per bird if using a spit.

Partridge – 30 to 45 minutes per bird; or 45 to 60 minutes per bird if using a spit.

Pheasant – 50 to 60 minutes per bird; or 1 to 1¼ hours if using a spit.

Quail – 15 minutes per bird; or 20 minutes per bird if using a spit.

Snipe – 15 minutes per bird; or 20 minutes per bird if using a spit.

Teal – 30 minutes per bird; or 40 minutes per bird if using a spit.

Woodcock – 25 to 30 minutes per bird; or 30 to 35 minutes per bird if using a spit.

Sautés – Method of cooking in a wide, shallow frying pan, generally used for small portions of food. In France these pans are called *sautoirs, plats à sauter* or *sauteuses*.

The cooking is done in heated fat, butter or oil. The food is seasoned and when the butter or fat is thoroughly heated, it is laid flat in the pan so that it is thoroughly sealed.

Small cuts of meat treated in this way are rump and fillet steaks, *médaillons* and *tournedos* (beef); cutlets and *noisettes* (mutton or lamb); veal chops and escalopes or veal sweetbreads.

Red meat must be sautéed as quickly as possible in clarified butter. White meat can be sautéed in fresh butter and, after sealing, may cook more slowly. These cuts are sautéed with the pan uncovered.

Sautéed poultry (chicken of medium size, pigeon, etc.) is always jointed. The same principles apply as in the case of white meat.

Pieces of larger poultry are well browned on both sides and left to cook further with the pan covered.

Serving. Sauté dishes must be taken out of the pan and served as indicated in the selected recipe. The dishes are arranged with pieces of fried bread cut into shapes. After garnishing, the cooking stock which has been diluted with red or white wine, white or brown stock, or cream, is poured over the dish.

Mixed sautés – Name given to various *ragoûts* where the gravy is not thickened with flour. These *ragoûts*, made up of small pieces of boned lamb, beef, mutton or veal, are fried in butter, fat or oil.

They are cooked in their own stock diluted with various liquids, as with ordinary *ragoûts*, and served with various garnishes.

CUMIN – Plant whose long and spindle-shaped seeds are dull yellow or light brown in colour. They are five-sided and smooth or covered with tiny hairs. They are acrid and spicy in taste.

Cumin is used for seasoning and in the preparation of liqueurs. Bread is also made with cumin seeds. Wild cumin is sometimes used in certain cheeses, such as Munster cheese.

CUP. TASSE – Receptacle made of china or metal in various shapes and sizes, provided with a handle.

CUP-BEARER. ÉCHANSON – Official charged with the duty of pouring wine for a king or other great personage.

The title of senior cup-bearer or *bouteiller de France* was a purely honorary one under Louis XIV. This officer had no duties though there were twenty-four gentlemen under his command.

The armorial bearing of this office showed two silver-gilt bottles engraved with the arms of the king, supporting the arms of the holder of the office. His functions fell gradually into disuse, until finally they were exercised only at coronations, ceremonial feasts, at Communion Supper on Maundy Thursday, etc. The office itself was sometimes left vacant. The last *bouteiller de France* under the old monarchy was the marquis de Lamermary, appointed in 1702.

The Échansons de Paris was founded after the Second World War. Its aim is to publicise good wine.

CURAÇAO – Liqueur made from the rind of Seville oranges and brandy or gin.

CURCUMA – Indian plant whose yellowish rhizome has an acrid and bitter flavour and smells of saffron and ginger. Powdered, the rhizome is used in curry powder and English mustard.

CURD. CAILLÉ – Precipitate or coagulum formed in milk subjected to the action of rennet or acidified by lactic ferments. It is a result of the precipitation of casein and contains varying proportions of butter, depending on whether or not the milk has previously been skimmed. When curd is obtained by the action of rennet, the serum still contains a considerable proportion of casein, which can be precipitated by a second coagulation. The serum of milk curdled by acidification contains very little casein.

Curd can be eaten as it is or with cream. Curdling is the first operation in the manufacture of cheese (q.v.).

CURÉ – See CHEESE.

CURLEW. COURLIS – Wader, a marsh bird which is not highly esteemed from the culinary point of view. Cooked in the same way as plover (q.v.).

CURNONSKY – Maurice Edmond Sailland, the future Curnonsky, was born in Angers on 12 October 1872. After a secondary school education, he went on to study literature at the Sorbonne. The attractions of journalism speedily enticed him away from a university career, and in 1892 he began to frequent newspaper offices and literary circles. He made friends wherever he went.

Curnonsky at 80 years of age (*Keystone*)

On the advice of one of these friends, Alphonse Allais, the young Sailland decided to choose a pseudonym. It was the period of Franco-Russian *entente*. "Why not Sky?" someone suggested. He replied, '*Cur non Sky?*' The pseudonym had been found.

Simon Arbellot, his biographer, gives the following description of the life and career of this unrivalled prince-elect of gastronomes.

'Tracing Curnonsky's life through the early part of the century means reliving all the gay ostentation of the *boulevard*, and breathing again the perfumed air of what is called *la belle époque*. He was to be found wherever imagination triumphed over conformity. P. J. Toulet and Jean de Tinan were friends of his; Willy invited him into his circle and Curnonsky was later to become one of his favourite collaborators. Everyone knew that the old master humorist, author of so many licentious novels, had the knack of surrounding himself with young intellectuals who had fun ghosting for him. *Un petit vieux bien propre* is attributed to Curnonsky; Toulet is supposed to have written a part of *Maugis en ménage*; and the two together wrote a great many now-forgotten works signed 'Willy', the titles of which have a strong *fin de siècle* savour: *le Bréviaire des courtisanes, le Métier d'amant, Jeu de prince*, etc.

'Curnonsky was to be found wherever there was a meeting of minds. Léon Daudet, in his *Souvenirs*, gives us a picture of him as a regular visitor to Weber's, joining in the debates of Forain, Maxime Dethomas, Adrien Hébrard, Maurice de Fleury, while the slight, vaguely disturbing shadow of Marcel Proust hovered in the background. He was also to be found at Maxim's conversing with Feydeau and Maurice Bertrand. He used to join Paul Fort occasionally in the evenings at the *Closerie des lilas*, but secretly he preferred the poetry of George Fourest and Raoul Ponchon to symbolism.

'One day he yielded to the temptations of travel and distant horizons. On his return he wrote the account of the African expeditions of the duc de Montpensier. He was to become a skilful "biographer" of this hunting prince. He moved on to China where the *cuisine* of the country left an indelible imprint on his mind; he proclaimed it to be the best of the world.

'This somewhat bohemian way of life was, nonetheless, marked by a considerable literary output. Novels, short stories, an anthology, collections of anecdotes made the name of Curnonsky a familiar one in the press and in the publishing world. For Dranem he wrote *Une riche nature*, for Charles Barret, *Un homme qui a bien tourné*.

'Writing was his passion. And his masters? First and foremost was La Bruyère, whose advice he loved to repeat to his young friends: "If you wish to say it is raining, then *say* it is raining." Then Anatole France (the Anatole France of *Jacques Tournebroche* rather than of *M. Bergeret*), for the clarity of his old-fashioned, methodical style. I have heard Curnonsky cry out in indignation at the sight of a solecism. Language was no mere form of words to him.

'Then came the gastronomic period, together with princedom and public acclaim. Fifty or so academies and clubs fought for his presidency and solicited his presence at their feasts. "Cur" had always loved his food. The Anjou wine and the *rillauds* of his childhood had trained his appetite, and while the rue Jacob period – so discreetly touched on by Madame Colette – seems to have been somewhat disappointing in this respect, the Maxim and Weber era followed closely on its heels. Later, with the collaboration of an epicure and great amphitryon, Marcel Rouff, Curnonsky undertook what amounted to a tourist crusade. It was to this cause that he began to devote all his time. *La France gastronomique* (32 volumes, interrupted at the twenty-eighth by the death of his collaborator) is a monument of erudition, and a tribute to the richness of our soil. There are also dozens of cookery books, each one no less a literary than a gastronomic delight.

'A public referendum in May 1927 crowned him Prince of Gastronomes, and there was no respite for him after that. He went from *disnées* to light snacks, inaugurations and enthronements, *tastevins* and barbecues without a break. Wherever he went there was a table laid ready for him, the finest wines placed at his disposal.

'On 23 March 1928 he founded the Academy of Gastronomes, modelled on the *Académie française*, with forty seats and with symbolic titles ranging from Epicure to Talleyrand. His friends joined him – Maeterlinck in Vergilius Maro's seat, Marcel Rouff in that of Honoré de Balzac. For himself he chose the seat of Brillat-Savarin, in whose honour he gave an address.

'Curnonsky enjoyed a sprightly old age. Honoured and fêted wherever he went, he had the satisfaction of seeing his young disciples carrying on his good work and realising the idea that was so close to his heart, that of linking the route to the good restaurant to the interests of tourism. He died as the result of an accident in 1956.'

CURRANT. GROSEILLE – There are various types of currant, the best-known being *redcurrants, whitecurrants* and *blackcurrants*. Red and whitecurrants are cultivated in several regions of France, notably on the outskirts of Paris, and in the Meuse and Puy-de-Dôme districts. Blackcurrants are grown mainly on the Côte d'Or. In Dijon blackcurrants are used to make Cassis de Dijon, an internationally famous liqueur.

Red and whitecurrants can be eaten raw, as a dessert, but they are more commonly used in jellies, syrups and in various sweets. Red and whitecurrants are used at Bar-le-Duc to make a jelly which enjoys a great reputation.

Currant compote. COMPOTE DE GROSEILLES – Wash and clean the currants and put them in a bowl. Pour over them a boiling syrup (2 cups sugar plus $1\frac{1}{2}$ cups water) boiled to 121°C. (250°F.).

Currant jam – See JAM, *Jellies*.

Currant juice for ices. JUS DE GROSEILLE POUR GLACES – Proceed as for strawberry ice mixture. (See STRAWBERRY.)

CURRY. CARI – Combination of spices, thoroughly dried, ground to a powder, and cooked slowly in clarified butter, vegetable oil or soured milk before adding the fish, meat, eggs or vegetables that are to be curried. The curry powders sold in grocery shops are usually a combination of fifteen or twenty herbs, seeds and spices. Those who really appreciate curry choose special combinations of spices to go with various dishes, some of which call for mild, subtle seasonings and others for hotter ones. The strength of a curry depends on how much chilli is used.

The principal ingredients of curry powder are allspice, anise, bay leaves, cinnamon, caraway, celery seed, cloves, coriander, cumin, curry leaves, dill, fennel, fenugreek (seeds and leaves) , garlic, ginger, mace, mustard, nutmeg, pepper (white and black), paprika, poppy seeds, saffron, turmeric, mint, cubeb berries, sumach seeds, juniper berries, zedoary root, salt.

For the preparation of different curries see MUTTON, CHICKEN.

Bichique curry (Créole cookery). CARI DE BICHIQUES – The *bichique* is a minute fish found near the island of Réunion. It is exported in tins and prepared as follows:

Cook a finely chopped onion in good quality fat or oil until golden. For a small tin of *bichique* add a large peeled and seeded tomato cut into tiny pieces, and 1 coffeespoon Réunion saffron. Cover, and cook for a few seconds. Pound together in a mortar some ginger, 1 clove of garlic, a sprig of parsley, and salt. Mix with the ingredients in the pan. Carefully add the fish. Do not stir or they may break as they are very fragile. Leave to soak for 20 minutes. Cover the pan and put it in a moderate oven for 20 to 25 minutes. Serve with *Rice à la créole* (see RICE).

Bringelle curry (Créole cookery). CARI DE BRINGELLES – Cut some lean and fat pork into large cubes as for a stew. Brown them lightly in fat with finely chopped onion. Add 2 teaspoons saffron, parsley, thyme, garlic, a piece of well-crushed stem ginger and chopped tomatoes. Slice aubergines into rounds and dip them in water slightly seasoned with salt and vinegar. Drain thoroughly and put them in a saucepan with the pork. Moisten with a little olive oil and cover. Stir from time to time, crushing the aubergines with the spoon. Allow 2½ hours for cooking on a low flame. Serve when the sauce is thick.

CUSTARD. CRÈME – Custard is a mixture of beaten eggs and milk variously sweetened and flavoured, and cooked either over hot water or baked in the oven.

Caramel custard. CRÈME MOULÉE AU CARAMEL – Line a mould with caramel and fill it with a preparation of *Vanilla custard* (see below). Set the mould in a pan half-filled with hot water and cook slowly in the oven.

Caramel custard

Fried custard. CRÈME FRITE – Put 250 g. (9 oz., 2¼ cups) sifted flour in a pan with 125 g. (4 oz., ½ cup) fine sugar, 12 egg yolks, 4 whole eggs and a small pinch of salt. Moisten with 1 litre (1¾ pints, generous quart) milk which has been boiled with a vanilla pod. Add 50 g. (2 oz., ¼ cup) butter. Mix well and cook on the stove in the same way as *French pastry cream* (see CREAMS), stirring all the time. Spread out this cream on a buttered baking sheet in an even layer, about 5 mm. (¼ inch) thick, and leave to cool. Cut into pieces and dip in beaten egg and breadcrumbs.

Fry in deep boiling fat. Drain the pieces, dry them on a cloth, and sprinkle with powdered sugar. Serve with *Apricot sauce* (see SAUCE) flavoured with liqueur.

Vanilla custard. CRÈME MOULÉE À LA VANILLE – Dissolve 100 g. (4 oz., ½ cup) sugar in ½ litre (scant pint, 2¼ cups) boiled milk. Add ½ vanilla pod, and leave to infuse for 20 minutes. Pour this, little by little, over 2 whole eggs and 4 egg yolks which have been beaten together in a basin. Mix well and strain. Remove the froth which forms on the surface of the cream.

Fill a charlotte mould with the mixture and cook in a *bain-marie* in the oven. Let it cool thoroughly before turning it out.

CUSTARD APPLE COROSSOL – Common name for a species of *annona* and its fruit. It sometimes attains a weight of 4 kg. (8½ to 9 lb.), though the tree that produces it is stunted and bare.

The fruit, which resembles a large pimento in shape, has a smooth green skin with a few hairy protuberances. The pulp is white, compact and full of black seeds the size of apricot kernels which, when the fruit is ripe, give off an agreeable odour. The taste is slightly acid. When crushed and mixed with four or five times its volume of water, the pulp produces a liquid similar to milk. After being sweetened and chilled it makes a pleasant drink.

Custard apple:
a. Section of fruit

CUSTARD MARROW. CHAYOTE – Vegetable, also known in France as *brionne*, that is the fruit of a climbing plant belonging to the same family as marrows. The custard marrow is a native of Mexico and the Antilles. Its cultivation has spread to other hot countries, notably Algeria.

The fruit of the custard marrow is a large green pear with deep ribbing. Its surface is somewhat spiny. The flesh is white, firm, homogenous, without smell or too pronounced a taste. It is prepared in many ways. Before cooking it must be blanched or cooked *au blanc*, like cardoons (q.v.), being first cut into quarters and trimmed into lozenge-shaped pieces.

Custard marrows

Custard marrows in béchamel sauce. CHAYOTES AU BLANC – Prepared in the same way as *Custard marrows à la crème* (see below) but moistened with *Béchamel sauce* (see SAUCE) in place of fresh cream.

Braised custard marrows au jus. CHAYOTES BRAISÉES AU JUS – Trim into lozenge shapes and blanch in boiling salted water. Drain. Put them in a buttered pan lined with strips of bacon rind and sliced carrots and onions. Season. Cover with a consommé from which not all the fat has been skimmed, and cook with the lid on. When the liquor is reduced to a glaze add a few tablespoons rich brown veal stock. Simmer. Drain the custard marrows and pour over them a sauce made by boiling down the liquor remaining in the pan, adding butter and straining through a sieve.

Custard marrows with butter. CHAYOTES AU BEURRE – Cut the custard marrows into large lozenge-shaped pieces. Cook in *White court-bouillon for vegetables* (see COURT-BOUILLON) keeping them firm.

Drain and dry the pieces, put them into a sauté pan or heavy frying pan in which 3 tablespoons (scant ¼ cup) butter has been heated. Moisten with 3 tablespoons (scant ¼ cup) veal or chicken consommé, or water. Cover and cook gently until cooked. Pour over them the liquor in which they have cooked, with a little butter added.

Custard marrows à la crème. CHAYOTES À LA CRÈME – Cook the custard marrows in the same way as for *Custard marrows with butter*. When nearly cooked cover them with fresh boiled cream and finish cooking with the lid on.

To serve, pour over them the cream in which they were cooked.

Custard marrows à la créole. CHAYOTES À LA CRÉOLE – Quarter the custard marrows, blanch them well in salted water. Cook 100 g. (4 oz., 1 cup) chopped onions in butter and oil (half and half). Add 3 tomatoes, peeled, seeded and coarsely chopped, a *bouquet garni* (q.v.) a minced clove of garlic, and the custard marrows. Cook with the lid on.

Serve in a border of rice, cooked in *bouillon*. Sprinkle the custard marrows with chopped parsley.

Custard marrow fritters. CHAYOTES EN FRITOT – Quarter the custard marrows and cook in *White court-bouillon for vegetables* (see COURT-BOUILLON). Drain and dry them. Put them in a marinade of olive oil, lemon juice, salt and pepper. Dip each piece in a light batter and deep-fry in boiling oil. Garnish with fried parsley.

Custard marrows used as a garnish. CHAYOTES POUR GARNITURES – Quartered custard marrows, cooked in butter or braised, can be used as part of a garnish for eggs, fish, small pieces of meat, fowl, etc.

When used to garnish eggs or fish, the custard marrows are cut up into large dice, blanched and cooked in butter.

To garnish pieces of meat or fowl, trim the custard marrows into large lozenge shapes, cook in butter or braise, and when they are nearly cooked, add the juices of the meat or fowl which they are to accompany.

Custard marrows au gratin. CHAYOTES AU GRATIN – Quarter the custard marrows, cook in *White court-bouillon for vegetables* (see COURT-BOUILLON) then simmer in butter. Arrange in a buttered *gratin* dish and sprinkle with grated cheese. Pour melted butter over them and brown in a moderate oven.

Custard marrows à la grecque. CHAYOTES À LA GRECQUE – Dice the custard marrows. Blanch in salted water and cook in a *court-bouillon* in the same way as *Aubergines à la grecque* (see AUBERGINE). Leave to cool in their liquor before serving. Use as an *hors-d'œuvre*.

Custard marrows à la martiniquaise. CHAYOTES À LA MARTINIQUAISE – Press boiled custard marrow in a cloth to extract the maximum of water, then pound the pulp together with bread dipped in milk. Cook finely chopped onion in butter, add the custard marrow mixture with a little salt and pepper, and milk. Smooth the surface with breadcrumbs and cook in a moderately hot oven. (Recipe taken from the *Bulletin de la société d'horticulture d'Algérie*.)

Custard marrows mornay. CHAYOTES MORNAY – Prepare in the same way as *Custard marrows au gratin*. The custard marrows are arranged in a dish on a layer of *Mornay sauce* (see SAUCE), covered with the same sauce, sprinkled with grated cheese and browned in the oven.

Custard marrow salad. SALADE DE CHAYOTES – Quarter the custard marrows and cook in *White court-bouillon for vegetables* (see COURT-BOUILLON). Drain and slice them. Season with oil, vinegar, pepper and chopped herbs.

Stuffed custard marrows. CHAYOTES FARCIES – Halve the custard marrows crossways, trim and slightly hollow them out. Blanch in salted water, drain and dry them.

Simmer gently in butter. When nearly cooked, fill them with a mixture of pork forcemeat and dry *duxelles* (q.v.).

Arrange the forcemeat in the form of a dome. Put the custard marrows on a buttered *gratin* dish, sprinkle with breadcrumbs and melted butter, and brown gently in the oven.

Custard marrows prepared in this way can be served as a vegetable or used as part of the garnish of a particular dish.

Instead of pork forcemeat, they can be filled with one or other of the preparations indicated for various stuffed vegetables (see TOMATO, AUBERGINE, etc.).

CUTTING BOARD. PLANCHE À DÉCOUPER – Beechwood board used for cutting up meat, provided with a groove and a hole to catch the juices.

CUTTLEFISH. SEICHE, SÈCHE – Cephalopod mollusc with an internal shell (cuttlebone), secreting an inky liquid (sepia). The tough flesh becomes eatable if it is vigorously beaten. It was popular with the Romans and is still liked in certain countries, notably in Spain. Powdered cuttlebone was formerly used as an absorbent.

Cuttlefish is prepared like octopus.

CUVE – Large tun made of wood, cement or metal in which the grapes are pressed for wine and in which red wine is fermented.

CUVEAU – Small *cuve*.

CUVÉE – Product of a particular *cuve*. A *cuvée* can also be a mixture of grapes, either taken from different parts of a large vineyard, as in the Bordeaux district, bought from different growers under similar climatic conditions, as in Burgundy, or the product of different harvests in the same region, as in Champagne and on the slopes of the Rhône. The final result depends upon the quality of the vintage and the skilful balance of the mixture.

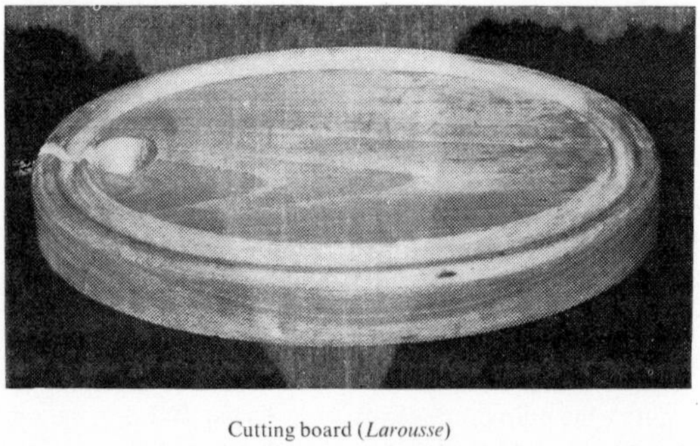

Cutting board (*Larousse*)

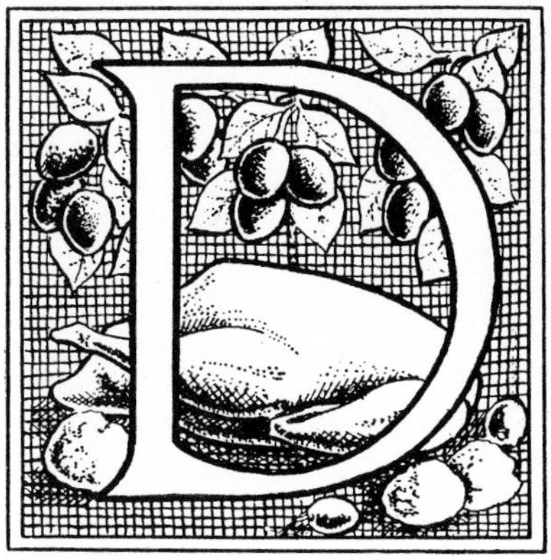

Dab

DAB. LIMANDE – Flat fish of the *Pleuronectidae* family, between 20 and 30 cm. (8 and 12 inches) long, with scales almost as rough as a file. It is oval and less elongated than the sole. Its right side, where the eyes are placed, is coloured, with a semi-circular lateral line running from head to tail; its blind side is white. The flesh is soft and easily digested. The American dab is not very different.

All recipes for plaice (q.v.) are suitable for dab.

DACE. DARD – Freshwater fish of the *Cyprinidae* family, also known in France as *aubourg*, *gravelet* or *vandoise*. It is caught in most of the rivers of central France but it is rather leathery to eat and is usually prepared *en matelote*.

DAGH KEBAB (Turkish cookery) – Pieces of shin veal skewered with slices of onions and tomatoes, grilled and sprinkled with thyme. It is served with pilaf of rice, okra (q.v.), or some other garnish.

DAHLIA – Ornamental plant, originally found in Mexico, which owes its name to the botanist Dahl of Antwerp. Dahlia tubers are edible and are similar to the Jerusalem artichoke in flavour. They are cooked in the same way as Jerusalem artichokes (q.v.).

DAIKON. DAÏKON – Large Japanese radish which can be eaten raw like the common radish, or parboiled and cooked like turnips.

DAISY. PÂQUERETTE – One of the commonest field flowers. Its young leaves and buds are eaten in salads.

DAME-BLANCHE (Cold sweet or dessert) – A kind of Plombières ice cream. (See ICE CREAMS AND ICES.)

DAMPFNUDELN (German pâtisserie) – *Ingredients*. 500 g. (18 oz., $4\frac{1}{2}$ cups) sieved flour, 100 g. (4 oz., $\frac{1}{2}$ cup) fine sugar, 5 egg yolks, 100 g. (4 oz., $\frac{1}{2}$ cup) melted butter, 2 dl. ($\frac{1}{3}$ pint, scant cup) milk, 10 g. ($\frac{1}{3}$ oz.) yeast, a small pinch of salt, lemon rind.

Method. Make a leaven with a quarter of the flour, the yeast and the milk, slightly warmed. Keep in a moderate temperature.

When the leaven has doubled in volume, mix in the melted butter, a little at a time, the salt, lemon rind, egg yolks, sugar and the rest of the flour.

Dredge with flour and roll out. Leave for 5 minutes. Cut into rounds with a pastry-cutter, put them on a floured cloth, and leave to rise in a moderate temperature for 1 hour. Baste with butter, sprinkle with fine sugar and bake in a slow oven.

Dampfnudeln are usually served with stewed fruit or jam. The rounds can also be filled with 1 teaspoon thick apricot purée flavoured with rum. Fold and seal, put them on a buttered baking sheet with the join downward, and bake.

DANDELION. PISSENLIT – Weed with toothed or pinnated leaves and yellow flowers, gathered in the fields from November to March. There are improved varieties, such as *plein coeur amélioré* and *très hâtif*, which are cultivated.

Tender young dandelion leaves are eaten raw, in salads. They can also be cooked like spinach (q.v.).

Daïkon

Dariole moulds (*Dehillerin. Phot. Larousse*)

DARIOLE – Small cylindrical mould. The name also applies to the cakes baked in these moulds.

Line *dariole* moulds with *Puff pastry* (see DOUGH) folded and rolled out 6 times. Fill with *Frangipane cream* (see CREAMS) mixed with almonds and flavoured with kirsch or some other liqueur. Bake in a hot oven, and sprinkle with sugar.

DARNE – Thick slice of a large raw fish. This cut used to be called, a *dalle* (slab).

Darnes of fish can be poached, braised, grilled, or sautéed in butter. This is a typical recipe.

Darne of salmon à l'ancienne. DARNE DE SAUMON À L'ANCIENNE – Season with salt and pepper a *darne* of salmon weighing between 500 and 600 g. (about $1\frac{1}{4}$ lb.) and place it in a buttered fireproof dish. Moisten with 1 dl. (6 tablespoons, scant $\frac{1}{2}$ cup) white wine and the same quantity of concentrated fish stock. Add a small sliced onion, a *bouquet garni* and the trimmings and peelings of mushrooms, the mushrooms themselves to be used later for the garnish.

Bring to the boil on the stove, and then place in the oven. Cook for 20 minutes, basting from time to time. About 10 minutes before taking it out of the oven, add the peeled and trimmed mushrooms. Drain the salmon, and garnish with the mushrooms arranged at each end of the dish. Top each mushroom with a poached oyster, decorated with a strip of truffle tossed in butter. Surround the salmon with freshwater crayfish which have been tossed and cooked in a *court-bouillon* (q.v.).

Boil down the cooking stock of the salmon and thicken with egg yolks and butter. Add 1 tablespoon liqueur brandy and a touch of cayenne pepper. Pour some of this sauce round the salmon and serve the rest separately.

Dartois (*Larousse*)

DARTOIS – Small snacks served as an *hors-d'oeuvre* or light main course. For recipes see HORS-D'ŒUVRE, *Hot hors-d'œuvre*.

DARTOIS (Pâtisserie) – Make two layers of *Puff pastry* (see DOUGH). Fill the middle of one layer with almond cream and cover with the second layer. Brush the top with egg, leaving the edges untouched or the pastry will not rise during baking.

Lightly mark dividing lines at evenly spaced intervals to indicate where the pastry is to be cut later. Bake in a moderate oven, then sprinkle the top lightly with icing sugar and put back in the oven until the sugar forms a glaze on top. Cut into sections at once, following the lines marked out before baking.

The base of this cake may be made with flaky pastry trimmings. It need only be 2 to 3 mm. ($\frac{1}{8}$ inch) thick – the upper layer about 5 mm. ($\frac{1}{4}$ inch) thick; or both layers may be of equal thickness of 4 mm. ($\frac{1}{6}$ inch).

Cream for filling dartois. Pound finely in a mortar 100 g. (4 oz., $\frac{1}{2}$ cup) sugar with 100 g. (4 oz., $\frac{3}{4}$ cup) blanched almonds, adding 2 eggs to prevent the mixture from becoming oily. Soften 100 g. (4 oz., $\frac{1}{2}$ cup) butter to a paste, and add to the mixture. Add also a small glass of rum and, if desired, 2 tablespoons (3 tablespoons) *French pastry cream* (see CREAM).

A good cream can be made by mixing ground almonds with *French pastry cream*, and flavouring the mixture with vanilla or rum. The greatest care must be taken to seal the layers of pastry as the cream boils during cooking and tends to ooze out.

Dates and date-palm

DATE. DATTE – The fruit of the date-palm was known to the Chaldeans in antiquity. It grows wild in the area bounded by the Euphrates and the Nile, and is cultivated in the desert oases of southern Algeria and Tunisia. The male and female principles grow on separate trees and artificial pollination is therefore necessary.

There are hard and soft dates, the latter being more highly prized. The best dates come from Tunisia, Algeria and western Asia. They are about the size of a thumb, with yellowish-red skin, and have a sweet flavour. Excellent dates are grown in South Carolina and Arizona (U.S.A.).

Since dates are a concentrate of sugar (73 per cent of their weight is rapidly assimilable sugar) they are full of nourishment. They contain appreciable quantities of phosphorus and calcium and are rich in Vitamins A and B. Some alcoholic drinks, including brandy, are made from dates.

Date fritters – See FRITTER, *Sweet* (*dessert*) *fritters*.

Stuffed dates (petits fours). DATTES FOURRÉES – Stone the dates, and stuff with almond paste flavoured with kirsch or rum, or with pistachio nut paste. Sprinkle with crystallised sugar.

DAUBE – Method of cooking meat. Although this method can be used for other meat, as well as poultry and game, the term *daube*, without qualification means a cut of beef cooked *en daube*, that is, braised in red wine stock well seasoned with herbs.

Stuffed dates
(*Scarnati*)

The name *daube à l'avignonnaise* means a dish made with mutton cooked in red wine.

For different kinds of *daube* see BEEF, MUTTON, TURKEY, PHEASANT.

Old daubière (*Larousse*)

DAUBIÈRE – Casserole of stoneware, earthenware or tinned copper for the cooking of *daubes*.

DAUCUS – Plant whose aromatic seeds, used medicinally in former times, are now used in the preparation of some liqueurs.

DAUMONT (À LA) – Method of preparing large fish. The *Daumont garnish* (see GARNISHES) comprises quenelles, soft roe, mushrooms and freshwater crayfish tails, served with *Nantua sauce*.

DAUPHINÉ – The Dauphiné region stretches from the Alps to the Rhône Valley. In the north it borders on the Lyonnais district and the Bresse area, from which it is separated by the Rhône. In the south it adjoins Provence without any clear-cut geographical demarcation line. Its north-eastern border is Savoy on the edge of the high, mountainous Isère valley. The diversity of geographical and climatic conditions of this region, explains the variety of its produce. The Rhône Valley has a climate favourable to the cultivation of

Dauphiné (*French Government Tourist Office*)

spring vegetables and fruit trees (especially peaches and apricots), and its sunlit slopes bear the famous Rhône vineyards. In the extreme south, olive trees are to be found. The valleys of the Alps provide rich pasture for rearing great numbers of cows which yield excellent milk. Here, too, are the groves from which the Lyons chestnuts are gathered. There are also hazelnut trees which yield an abundant crop. The honey from these upland pastures is highly prized. The lakes and rivers provide trout and crayfish. In some places truffles are found, and mushrooms are common in the woods.

Culinary specialities – Regional cookery shows a marked predilection for *gratin* dishes. These are made not only with macaroni and potatoes but also with chopped porridge, white beet, swedes, *cèpes* and crayfish tails.

Daubes are favourite dishes and those of Vienne enjoy a considerable reputation. Among the specialities of this region are *grillades marinière*; *défarde*; *baby quails*; *thrush with juniper berries*; *thrush pâtés des Alpes*; *salmis of thrush*; *pickled thrush*; the excellent *pickled truffles de Nyons*; and Chabeuil quails.

The dairy farms in these alpine pastures provide milk which is used to manufacture cheeses: Sassenage, Saint-Marcellin, Champoléon, Pelvoux, Briançon and the white cheese, *tomme* (a cheese made from fermented buttermilk). The characteristic regional pastry is the *pogne*, an immense tart filled in summer with fruit and in autumn with pumpkin. In the Drôme area, a *pogne* is a kind of *brioche*. The *pogne* of Romans enjoys an especially high reputation. Among the sweet specialities are Valence *pognes* and *meringues*, the *honey tourons* of Gap, the *sweetmeats* of Voiron and the famous *nougat* of Montélimar.

Wines – The Rhône slopes produce some very highly reputed wines, such as those of Hermitage and Crozes; white and red Hermitage and the famous Clairette de Die.

DAUPHINE (À LA) – Name given to several different dishes. Most commonly it is used for a potato preparation made from duchess potato mixture and *chou paste*. This mixture is shaped into balls and deep-fried. (See POTATOES.)

DAUPHINOISE (À LA) – Method of preparing potatoes (q.v.).

DECANT. DÉCANTER – To pour any liquid from one con-

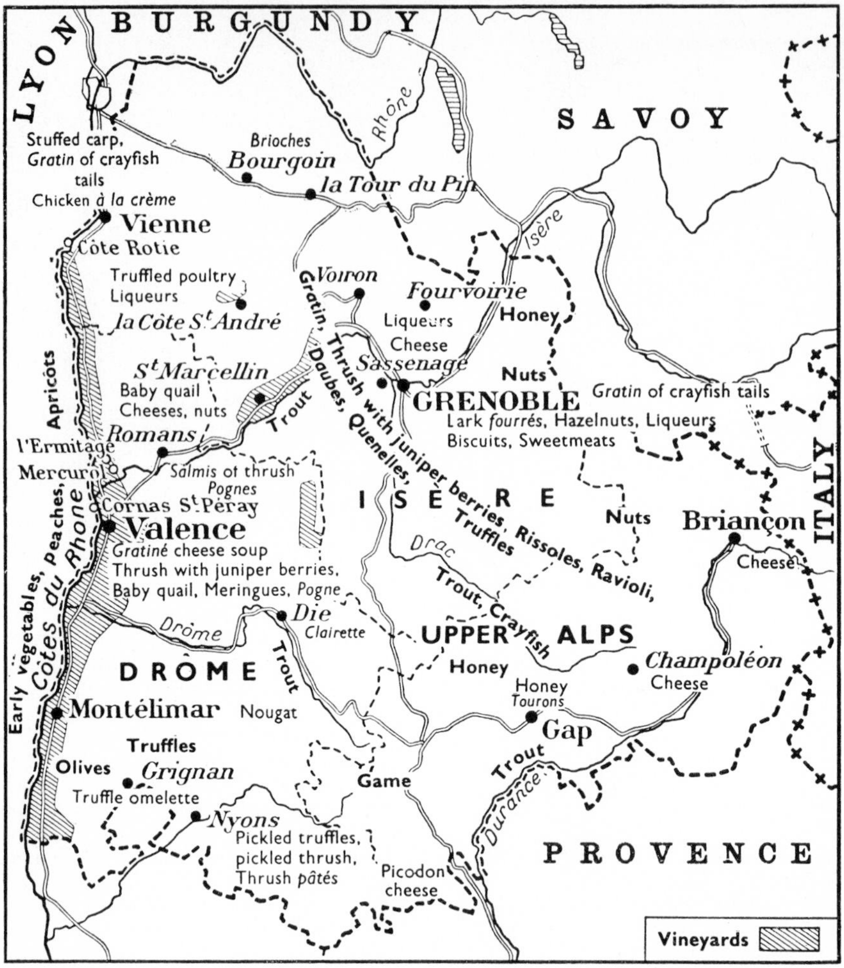

Gastronomic map of Dauphiné

tainer into another. Wine is decanted into a carafe to get rid of the deposit formed at the bottom of the wine bottle. Decanting has the added advantage of oxidising the wine.

This operation must be carried out with great care, training a light on the carafe to make sure that the wine is clear, and allowing as little as possible of the residue to get in.

Butter is also said to be decanted when it is melted and purified by being transferred from one container to another.

DECIZE – See CHEESE.

DECOCTION. DÉCOCTION – Process of boiling a solid for a period in water. Clear soup is a decoction of meat. The decoction of vegetable matter has the disadvantage of sapping many of its nutritive properties and evaporating its volatile elements.

DECOMPOSITION. DÉCOMPOSITION – Destruction of a body by the disintegration of its elements.

DEEP-FRYING. FRITURE – Immersing foods in a large, deep pan of boiling fat. The French term for deep-frying is *friture*, a word also applied to the fat used in deep-frying.

In the great kitchens of a hotel or restaurant, deep-frying is almost always carried out successfully, but this cannot be said of home cooking, where more often than not the methods and ingredients used are quite unsuitable.

In hotel kitchens a large number of different fats are available. These are chosen with care and used lavishly. In private households, the fats are not always pure, and, for reasons of economy, the housewife uses her fats too sparingly. This is false economy. Deep-frying can only be successful if a great deal of fat is used. The more fat the less waste, since, where too little fat is used, it is absorbed into the food and the pieces stick to one another and become soggy. Food fried in abundant fat is crisp, firm and cooked all through. It is properly sealed at the outset and therefore does not absorb the fat.

There must be ample space in the cooking utensil which should be made in a single piece, of sheet-iron or hammered copper.

As it is often necessary to fry a number of things at the same time, it is desirable to have at least two such pans in the kitchen. One of these should be kept exclusively for fish. Other necessary equipment for deep-frying are grids, baskets and skimmers. The pan must be carefully cleaned each time it is used, inside and out. The fat should be strained and poured back into the pan for storage.

Fats for deep-frying. LA GRAISSE DE FRITURE – The best fat to use in all deep-frying is beef kidney fat (suet), clarified and purified with scrupulous care. This fat is odourless and can be heated up to 180°C. (350°F.) without burning. If it is carefully looked after, it can be used over and over again.

A little veal fat can be added if desired, but veal fat must not be used alone, since it deteriorates very quickly. An alternative household fat can be prepared by mixing ox kidney-fat with an equal quantity of lard or oil, but these mixtures, apart from being more expensive, cannot be heated to the same high degree without burning, nor can they be used again as much. Mutton fat should never be used in deep-frying, since it impregnates the food with a taste of tallow.

Among the fats which are suitable for frying certain special foods are olive oil, which is suitable for fish, fritters, rice and cream croquettes, etc; clarified butter which may be used in the preparation of delicately flavoured sweets; and groundnut (peanut) oil and cereal oils.

The cheaper vegetable oils include various types of coconut butter. They are quite suitable in certain cases, but are still a poor substitute for ox kidney fat.

The fat of duck, goose and other fat poultry, as well as lard, may be used with butter for browning or in the preparation of *roux*, but ox kidney is more efficient.

In his book, *le Cuisinier praticien*, Reculet says:

'The amount of fat used in frying must always depend upon the size of the object to be fried; the greater the quantity of liquid, the more it can hold the heat, and it is able to counteract the cooling caused by the immersion of the object and the moisture given off during cooking.

'In a busy kitchen it is desirable to have two lots of cooking fat, one white and one brown. The white fat is fresh or at least little used: it should be used for all deep-frying except for fish. The brown fat, darkened by long service should be used for fish, though good white fat is preferable in all cases.

'There are several signs to be seen when frying-oil becomes hot:

1. A slight tremor on the surface.
2. A strong characteristic smell.
3. A dry whitish vapour given off by the fat.

Test the heat of the fat by adding a drop of water to it or by dipping any substance other than purified fat into it. If the sound is sharp and high, the fat is hot enough for frying.'

Vegetables and fruit, which have a high proportion of water in them, are fried in moderately hot fat. This applies particularly to potatoes. Fish and other large foodstuffs are also deep-fried in moderately hot fat; they would not be cooked right through if they were sealed at once by contact with too intense a heat.

Very hot fat is used for foodstuffs which must be sealed instantly, for example, anything dipped in egg and bread-crumbs or batter. This also applies to precooked foods such as croquettes and very small foodstuffs which must be sealed immediately. Soufflé potatoes must be dropped into very hot fat after having first been cooked in moderately hot fat.

This was Brillat-Savarin's theory of deep-frying:

'Not all liquids exposed to the action of fire can absorb the same amount of heat. Thus, one may with impunity dip one's finger into boiling spirits of wine, where one would withdraw it hastily from brandy, and still more hastily from water, while any contact with boiling oil would cause an intensely painful blister, since oil can hold at least three times as much heat as water.

'It is as a result of these differences that hot liquids act in different ways upon the foodstuffs which are immersed in them. Those cooked in water are softened and reduced by boiling; soups and extracts are their by-products. Foods cooked in fat, on the other hand, are compressed; they take on a dark colouring, and in the end become charred.

'In the first case, water dissolves and absorbs into itself the inherent juices of the foods cooked in it; in the second, the juices are preserved intact because they are insoluble in oil. If fried foods eventually become desiccated it is because over-exposure to heat has evaporated all the moisture in them.

'These two methods of cooking are known by different names, and the process of boiling foodstuffs in oil or fat is known as *frying*.

'The virtue of good frying lies in a kind of shell formed round the food, which prevents the fat from penetrating it and seals the juices inside. These juices are thus cooked within the shell so that the full flavour of the food is preserved. The boiling liquid must have attained a sufficient degree of heat for its action to be instantaneous; to reach this point, it must be heated for quite a long time over a very hot flame.

Olive oil should be used only for very quick frying or for processes which do not require great heat. This is because olive oil, if heated for a long time, develops an unpleasant taste which it is difficult to eradicate.' (*Physiologie du Goût*.)

Deep-frying basket
(*Dehillerin. Phot. Larousse*)

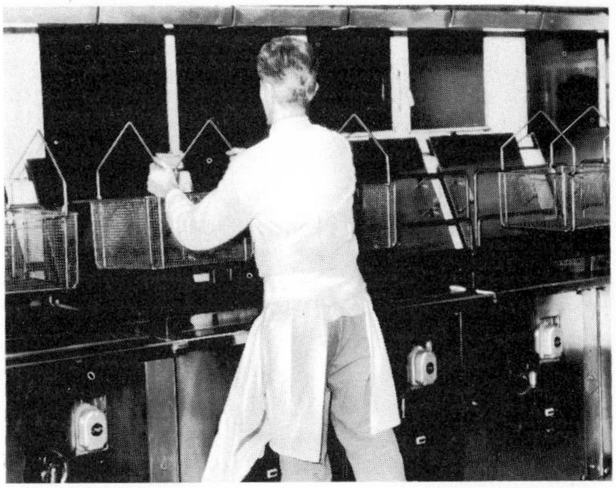

Electric deep-frying equipment, commercial
(*Brigaud. Phot. Photothèque E.D.F.*)

DEEP-FRYING BASKET. GRILLE – Wire utensil in which food is contained for deep-frying. Fried foods can be lifted out of the fat in this utensil.

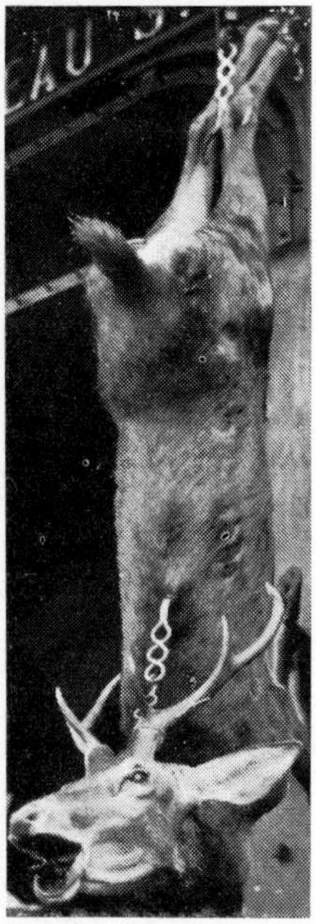

Deer on display in shop window

DEER. CERF – Wild mammal whose flesh is tender up to one year, and from then on becomes more and more tough. It is particularly indigestible and even poisonous when the deer has been brought down after a long chase.

All methods of preparation given for the buck are applicable to the doe.

DEFRUTUM – Latin term used by Apicius and found in ancient recipes to designate grape juice reduced by evaporation to a third of its volume. This juice was widely used in Roman cookery.

DÉGLAÇAGE – Technical term in French cookery for the operation of pouring any liquid into the pan in which food has been cooked in butter or other fat.

Wine is used for this purpose, heated and stirred in the pan so that all the concentrated juices are incorporated into it. White or brown stocks, cream, vinegar, or alcohol can also be used.

DÉGLACER – Technical term in French cookery for the dilution of the concentrated juices in a pan in which meat, poultry, game or fish has been roasted, braised or fried. White or red wine, Madeira or some other heavy wine, clear soup, stock and sometimes cream are used.

DÉGORGER – Term used in French cookery meaning to soak food for a variable length of time in cold water to free it from impurities. Thus, calves' heads and sweetbreads are soaked in water to make them very white.

The term is also used of the operation of clearing Champagne bottles of the impurities contained in the wine.

DÉGRAISSER – Term in French cookery meaning to skim off excess fat which forms on the surface of a liquid (clear soup, sauce, etc.). The term is also used to describe cutting away some of the fat which forms a coating on a joint of meat. All fat thus removed, whether from liquids or meat (except that of mutton or lamb) must be clarified. It can then be used for deep-frying.

DÉGRAISSIS – Term used in French cookery for the fat skimmed off clear soup, stock, or sauce. This fat, which must be clarified, is known in France as 'economy fat', and is used to fry certain vegetables, or as deep-frying fat.

DEHYDRATING. DÉSHYDRATER – Synonym for drying (q.v.).

DÉJEUNER – In France, the first meal of the day (breakfast) is called the *petit déjeuner* or *premier déjeuner* (i.e. little or first *déjeuner*) to distinguish it from *déjeuner*, which is taken in the middle of the day.

The institution of this midday meal dates back to the French Revolution. In the eighteenth century, the main meal of the day, *dîner* (dinner) was taken first at midday and later at 1 p.m. The *déjeuner*, taken upon waking, consisted of a soup or coffee with milk.

The Constituent Assembly began its deliberations at about midday, to rise at about 6 p.m. It was, therefore, necessary to change the dinner hour to 6 p.m., and since the members could not sit fasting, they were obliged to take a second breakfast at 11 a.m. This second *déjeuner* was more substantial than the first and included eggs and cold meat.

According to the Goncourt brothers, Edmond (1822–1896) and Jules (1830–1870), it was Mme. Handy who invented fork luncheons, by setting out cutlets, kidneys and sausages on a buffet in her café on the boulevards opposite the Comédie-Italienne, and pressing her clients to take these savouries with their meal.

Nowadays, in France, *déjeuner* has largely usurped the place of the original *dîner*. It includes the same dishes and is eaten later and later in the day.

The experts maintain that a substantial dinner does not necessarily cause a restless night, provided that there is a long enough interval between dinner and going to bed, and because too large a lunch makes work difficult in the afternoon, more and more people are following the British habit of having a substantial breakfast followed by a light lunch.

DÉLICE – This word, which in French strictly means a certain type of pastry, is nowadays misused by some pretentious *maîtres d'hôtel* in the drawing up of their menus.

Having no precise culinary meaning, the word (which implies delectability), is exploited for its very vagueness, implying in advance that the dish offered is delectable, though, in fact, all it does is to put the wary patron on his guard.

DEMI – In English the term 'half' is used of a glass of beer holding approximately 3 dl. ($\frac{1}{2}$ pint, $1\frac{1}{4}$ cups).

In France, a *demi* is a glass of beer also holding about 3 dl. ($\frac{1}{2}$ pint, $1\frac{1}{4}$ cups) which means that patrons get approximately three *demis* to a litre. (See TANKARD OR BEER-GLASS.)

DEMI-DEUIL (À LA) – This term (which, literally translated, means 'in half-mourning') is applied mainly to poached poultry and veal sweetbreads braised in a white sauce.

Food cooked in this way is dressed with *suprême sauce* and garnished with truffles.

DEMIDOFF – Name of a princely Russian family. Prince Anatole Demidoff, who married Princess Mathilde, daughter of King Jérôme Bonaparte (but was soon divorced), was one of the most celebrated gastronomes of the Second Empire.

Le petit déjeuner (*Boucher*)

For this reason, an elaborate method of preparing large poultry was called after him. (See CHICKEN, *Chicken Demidoff*.)

DEMI-ESPAGNOLE – By *demi-espagnole*, Carême means what today is called *demi-glace* (see SAUCE).

'Pour half the *grande espagnole* into a saucepan with the same volume of good clear chicken soup to which have been added the trimmings of mushrooms and truffles.' Carême adds instructions for the preparation of this soup:

'This consommé is made with the carcases and giblets of 2 chickens, moistened with good stock (too much salt must be particularly avoided). Next, add a carrot, a couple of onions, and, after having skimmed it carefully, let it simmer. About 2 hours later, strain it through muslin or sieve without pressure. Leave to stand, and strain thoroughly.

'Put the saucepan on a strong heat and stir with a special *espagnole* wooden spoon until the liquid is bubbling all over. Move it to the corner of the stove; skim carefully and remove every trace of fat. In this state, leave it for a full 45 minutes. Skim off the fat, and replace the stock on the strong heat. Stir the *espagnole* with a wooden spoon to prevent it from boiling over, which will otherwise happen because of the very rapid boiling necessary to preserve as far as possible the essence which is the sauce.

When it is suitably reduced, strain through a cloth.'

DEMI-GLACE – Brown sauce made by boiling and skimming *espagnole sauce* and mixing in white stock, *estouffade*, or clear soup.

This sauce is usually flavoured with Madeira or sherry. (See SAUCE.)

DEMI-JOHN. DAME-JEANNE – Large earthenware or glass bottle.

DEMI-SEL – See CHEESE.

DEMI-TASSE – In France a *demi-tasse* can mean either a very small cup or a cup of black coffee.

DÉNERVER – Term in French cookery denoting the removal of tendons, membranes, gristle, etc. from meat, poultry, game, etc.

DENIER (EN) – Potato crisps are sometimes called *en denier* in France because they are cut in the shape of a coin. (See POTATOES.)

DENSIMETER. DENSIMÈTRE – Instrument designed to measure the density of liquids. Anometers and alcoholometers are densimeters constant in weight but variable in volume, made in the form of a hollow glass rod weighted with lead or mercury. The rod sinks into the liquid and the density is recorded by means of a scale marked on the side.

There are a great many types of densimeter for different types of liquid. These are usually sold with conversion tables indicating the allowances to be made for temperature, and enabling the readings to be converted to other scales.

DENSITY. DENSITÉ – Degree of consistence of a body or substance, measured by the ratio of the mass to the volume, or by the quantity of matter in a unit of bulk. In practice, this is the ratio of the weight of a volume of a body to the weight of the same volume of distilled water at a temperature of 4°C. (39.2°F.). The measuring of density with special instruments makes it possible readily to assess the alcohol content of a liquid, the sugar content of a syrup, etc.

DENT-DE-LOUP (Wolves' fang) – Name given in France to several kinds of decorative motif used in the presentation of dishes:

1. Slices of sandwich bread cut into triangles and fried in butter or oil. These are used to garnish a number of different dishes.

2. Triangles cut out of strips of jelly, used to garnish cold dishes.

DENTEX. DENTÉ – Mediterranean fish. The *common dentex* can attain a length of up to 1 m. (40 inches); the *large-eyed dentex* grows to about 50 cm. (20 inches). Prepare as for sea bream (q.v.).

DENUTRITION. DÉNUTRITION – Nutritional disorder that occurs when deassimilation exceeds assimilation.

DE-OIL. DÉSHUILER – To remove excess oil from grain or flour, either by pressure or by some chemical process.

DERBY – Method of preparing large poultry (see CHICKEN, Chicken à la Derby). It was devised by M. Jean Giroix when he was in charge of the kitchens of the Hotel de Paris at Monte-Carlo.

DERMATITIS. DERMATOSE – Skin infection. Such complaints have led to food restrictions because certain foods (strawberries, shellfish, etc.) cause skin eruptions in some people. These people ought to avoid whatever upsets them or endeavour to desensitise themselves but it is unnecessary to forbid such foods to all sufferers from skin disorders.

In most cases of dermatitis a moderate diet is generally prescribed; not too much meat or fatty foods and especially not too much bread. Sometimes a restorative diet is indicated. Each case must be treated according to the type of dermatitis the person has, how efficient his digestive processes are, and his general state of health.

DÉROBER – French term used in cookery for the removal of the skins of shelled broad beans.

It can also mean the peeling of potatoes and other vegetables.

M.-A. Désaugiers
(1772–1827)

DÉSAUGIERS – Marc-Antoine Désaugiers, a talented writer of satirical songs, was born at Fréjus (Var) in 1772 and died in Paris in 1827.

Désaugiers, immortal author of *M. et Mme. Denis*, can be numbered among the gastronomic poets, for he wrote a great many songs extolling the joys of the table. Some of these songs are still sung today, when, as in our forefathers' time, each guest at table takes his turn at singing a song over the dessert. He was secretary of the *Caveau moderne*, a French literary, gastronomic and also somewhat bacchanalian society. He wrote his will, in a manner of speaking, in the last couplet of his *Chanson à manger* (Eating Song).

Je veux que la mort me frappe
Au milieu d'un grand repas;
Qu'on m'enterre sous la nappe
Entre quatre larges plats,
Et que sur ma tombe on mette
Cette courte inscription:
Ci-gît le premier poète
Mort d'une indigestion.

I pray that death may strike me
In the middle of a large meal.
I wish to be buried under the tablecloth
Between four large dishes.
And I desire that this short inscription
Should be engraved on my tombstone
Here lies the first poet
Ever to die of indigestion.

DESESSARTS – One of the greatest actors of the Comédie-Française in his day. He was born at Langres in 1740 and died at Barèges in 1793. He was also a celebrated gastronome.

'Desessarts,' says Emile Deschanel in *l'Histoire des comédiens*, 'had an appetite worthy of his size, but he was also a connoisseur. He was very witty. A good dinner sent his spirits soaring. He would analyse elegantly the qualities of each dish, and, in order to describe them more vividly, would coin amusingly bizarre words.

'If his fellow-diners were amiable and good trenchermen, the sybarite gaiety of Desessarts would express itself lyrically in poetic phrases such as "the boar, prince of the forests, whose ferocious pride is humbled when he is baked in a *pâté*".'

Desessarts was, like all gourmets, a splendid fellow. His talent was as straightforward as his character. Infectious gaiety mixed with *bonhomie* were distinctive traits both of his art and his disposition.

DESICCATION. DESSICCATION – Process of drying or dehydrating foodstuffs. (See PRESERVATION OF FOOD.)

DESSERT – Last course of a meal. Nowadays, in France, dessert comprises cheese, sweet dishes (which were formerly served before the dessert) and fruit.

In former times at great banquets, dessert, which was the fifth course of the meal, was often presented in magnificent style. Large set pieces fashioned in pastry, described often and in great detail by Carême, whose accounts are accompanied by splendid illustrations, were placed on the table at the beginning of the meal. These owed more to architecture than to the art of cooking, and had a purely decorative function. Just before the sweet course, a multitude of sweets were elegantly arranged on the table with the set pieces, for every ceremonial table was laid in accordance with a detailed plan. The dishes had to harmonise with gold plate, crystal, magnificent baskets of fruit, and the tall candelabra: a magnificent spectacle.

Flowers are used today for table decoration. Fruit too, is often placed on the table before the beginning of the meal and this, too, contributes to its embellishment.

Sweets, hot or cold, are served as dessert after the cheese in France. Although less ostentatious than in former times, modern desserts are no less sumptuous or succulent.

Dessert (after Carême, *le Confiturier royal*)

Modern dessert in France
(*Orfèvrerie Christofle*)

DESSERTE – French term for food that has been prepared but not used. In certain French restaurants, such food (apart from a few items) belongs to the waiters.

DÉTREMPE – Technical term in confectionery meaning a mixture of flour and water to be used in the preparation of pastries.

For example, *faire la détrempe du feuilletage* is the term used for making the flour-and-water mixture of flaky pastry.

DEVILFISH. DIABLE DE MER – Anglerfish, found on the North American and European sides of the Atlantic. It is also sometimes known as *sea-frog*, *miller's thumb*, and *bull-head*.

In the U.S.A. it is known as *goose fish*, *all-mouth monkfish*, and *fishing frog*.

DEVILLED. À LA DIABLE – Name given to a method of preparation, especially suitable for poultry. The bird is slit open along the back, spread out flat, seasoned, and grilled. After cooking it is sprinkled with fresh breadcrumbs and browned under the grill.

Poultry cooked in this way should be served with *Diable sauce* (see SAUCE).

DEXTRIN (British gum). DEXTRINE – Powdery substance, white or slightly yellowish, obtained by splitting starch. When mixed with water it forms a thick, viscous paste.

DEXTROSE – Scientific name for glucose, so called because in polarisation, it causes deviation to the right.

DIABETES. DIABÈTE – Serious nutritional disorder. There are two main types of diabetes; a mild form which does not prevent the sufferer from leading a normal life provided that he keeps to a special diet, and a severe form which requires medical treatment.

All diabetics require a special diet.

Cooking for diabetics. CUISINE DES DIABÈTIQUES – Once an intelligent cook knows the quantity of carbohydrates the diabetic is allowed (that is, floury and leguminous food) he can use the ration in many ways in order to vary the diet and make it pleasant and appetising. He will avoid thickened sauces and any food where flour or pulses are used in large amounts. Also to be avoided is the excessive use of salt, which would only increase the already pronounced thirst of the diabetic.

DIABLE – Cookery utensil made in the form of two porous earthenware pans, one of which fits onto the other as a lid. Some vegetables and fruit (potatoes, chestnuts) can be cooked in this type of pan without liquid.

In France a sheet-metal draught device for solid fuel cookers is also known as a *diable*.

DIABLE (À LA) – See DEVILLED.

DIABLOTINS – Slices of French bread about 5 mm. ($\frac{1}{4}$ inch) thick, covered with a mixture of thick *béchamel sauce* flavoured with grated cheese and cayenne pepper, sprinkled with grated Parmesan cheese and browned. They are served with soup.

Chocolates sold in paper cases and accompanied by a motto are also called *diablotins*.

DIAPHRAGM. COFFRE – Part of the body of man or beast which contains the ribs. The French word *coffre* is applied to the carapace of certain shellfish.

DIASTASIS. DIASTASE – Ferment which develops in grain and tubers at the moment of germination. This liquefies the starch and turns it into sugar.

DICING. COUPER EN DÉS – Cutting various foodstuffs, for example, ham, artichoke hearts, truffles, mushrooms, etc. into cubes or squares.

DIEPPOISE (À LA) – Method of preparing seawater fish. Fish *à la dieppoise* is cooked in white wine, garnished with mussels and shelled freshwater crayfish tails, and masked with a white wine sauce made with the cooking stock of the fish and mussels. (See BRILL, *Brill à la Dieppoise*.)

DIET. RÉGIME ALIMENTAIRE – Methodical and reasoned use of food in health as in sickness.

DIETETICS. DIÉTÉTIQUE – The study of everything concerned with diet and all that relates to the therapeutic use of food. Dietetics can be defined as the art of nourishing oneself naturally. The importance of a sensible, regulated, balanced diet has been amply proved where health is concerned.

Demi-johns and diables (*Nicolas*)

The science of dietetics is relatively new and unfamiliar. It is still mainly applied to invalid diets, diets for chronic diseases such as diabetes, rheumatism, etc. and slimming diets. But it is just as important for dietetics to be used in the service of the healthy. To feed oneself badly means depriving the body of nutrients that it requires, or providing these in over-generous or insufficient amounts, practices which often lead to disease and disorders.

It is important, therefore, to know the body's quantitative and qualitative requirements, and to discover what percentage of vital elements are present in the various foods. With this knowledge it is possible to compile diets suited to various needs.

Food is made up of certain percentages of three energising elements: proteids, glucides and lipids. *Proteids* (proteins) are the basic constituents of all living cells. There is no life without proteins. They should account for 11 to 14 per cent of the total calorie intake. *Carbohydrates* produce the sugars. Carbohydrates should account for about half the food eaten daily. *Lipids* (fats) have an important rôle in the diet. A minimum of 40 g. ($1\frac{1}{2}$ oz.) should be consumed each day, 25 g. (1 oz.) of which should be animal fat.

Mineral salts such as sodium chloride, calcium, phosphorus, etc. are present in food and these, too, are indispensable elements, as are trace elements such as zinc, iron, copper, etc., and vitamins. Approximately 25 g. (1 oz.) mineral salts should be consumed daily, half of which should be sodium salts.

Vitamins play a very important rôle. The table below indicates the properties and sources of the principal vitamins.

	Vitamins	*Sources*
A	Vitamin of growth. Strengthens resistance to illness. Vital for the production of retinal pigment.	Butter, milk, cheese, eggs, carrots, spinach, cabbage, fish liver oil.
B_1	Metabolism of glucides. Factor of appetite and the balance of the nervous system. Lack of this vitamin causes beriberi.	Yeasts, wheatgerm, sugar, bread, meat, dried vegetables, green vegetables.
B_2	Vitamin of general equilibrium. Nutritional and metabolic regulator.	Cereals, liver, eggs, milk, fish, meat.
B	Anti-pellagrous vitamin called nicotine acid. Essential for the release of energy from food.	Yeasts, cereal germ, dried vegetables, meat, fish.
B_{12}	Encourages the synthesis of proteins and helps in the growth and equilibrium of the red corpuscles.	Liver, fish.
C	Anti-scorbutic vitamin. Aids vascular resistance and strengthens resistance to infection. Hastens the healing of scars. Lack of this vitamin causes scurvy.	Fruit, vegetables.
D	Concerned with absorption and laying down of calcium and potassium in the bones. Important for children for bone formation and prevention of rickets.	Milk, butter, eggs, fish.
E	Plays an important role in fertility, pregnancy, sterility and muscular balance in rats. Uncertain function in human beings.	Green vegetables, cereal germ, pork fat, meat, fat.
K	Anti-haemorrhagic vitamin necessary for the coagulation of the blood. Its function is the formation of prothrombin.	Green vegetables, salads, fruit.

The problem that faces the dietitian is to calculate (according to the situation, temperament and tastes of the person concerned) the energy value (in calories) of a given food, as well as its richness in appropriate vitamins. It is then a case of combining the various foods so as to obtain a coherent, balanced, pleasant diet. In order to calculate calorie requirements we must bear in mind that:

1 g. protein produces 4 calories,
1 g. carbohydrate produces 4 calories,
1 g. lipids produces about 9 calories.

Each individual's needs, where calories are concerned, varies considerably according to the work he does, his age, the climate in which he lives, etc. As a general rule it is recognised that a man of average physical activity requires 2,800 calories daily, a woman, 2,200. Vitamin requirements are quantitative and qualitative.

WEIGHT AND CALORIE EQUIVALENTS

Food	*Weight*	*Calories*
Steak (average size)	120 g. (approx. $4\frac{1}{2}$ oz.)	300
Cutlet	50 g. („ 2 oz.)	150
Ham (1 slice)	50 g. („ 2 oz.)	175
Chicken (1 leg)	100 g. („ 4 oz.)	200
Egg	50 g. („ 2 oz.)	80
Sole (average size)	100 g. („ 4 oz.)	80
Fresh herring (large)	150 g. („ 5 oz.)	200
Potato (egg-sized)	50 g. („ 2 oz.)	40
Carrots	200 g. („ 7 oz.)	90
Noodles	200 g. („ 7 oz.)	150
Rice	150 g. („ 5 oz.)	150
Gruyère cheese	30 g. („ 1 oz.)	120
Apple	150 g. („ 5 oz.)	90
Pear (large)	200 g. („ 7 oz.)	120
Banana	80 g. („ 3 oz.)	80
Orange	150 g. („ 5 oz.)	75
Lemon	100 g. („ 4 oz.)	50
Oil (1 tablespoon)	15 g. („ $\frac{1}{2}$ oz.)	120
Sugar (1 lump)	5 g. („ $\frac{1}{6}$ oz.)	20

CALORIE REQUIREMENTS

		Activity	
	Intense	*Average*	*Slight*
Man	4500	2800	2200
Woman	3800	2200	1800
Child: up to 10 years		2000	
up to 15 years boy		3000	
up to 15 years girl		2600	
up to 20 years boy		3600	
up to 20 years girl		2400	

DIGESTER. DIGESTEUR – Piece of apparatus which works on the pressure cooker principle. It can be hermetically sealed and is fitted with a safety valve, enabling food to be subjected to higher temperatures than that of boiling water. (See PRESSURE COOKER.)

DIGESTIBILITY. DIGESTIBILITÉ – The assimilability of foodstuffs into the digestive system. The layman recognises food as digestible if it produces no unpleasant sensation in the course of digestion. To the expert, digestibility is determined by the proportion of elements in food which can be thoroughly assimilated into the human organism.

This portion is variable in different foods and depends also upon the state in which they are eaten, upon the manner in which they are cooked, upon the amount eaten and upon the other foods eaten at the same time, and is assessed only on the basis of a perfectly healthy digestion.

Some foods, such as sugar, which leaves no residue, are completely digestible; with most other foods there is a proportion of waste.

In a normal mixed diet the proportion of digestible matter is 97 per cent in meat and eggs, 94 per cent in milk, 79 per cent in bread, 80 to 85 per cent in pulses and potatoes. 95 per cent of the fats in meat, eggs, and milk are digestible. 100 per cent of the carbohydrates in milk are digestible, 99 per cent in cereals in the form of flour or bread, 96 per cent in pulses and potatoes. About 10 per cent of wastage is a fair average, especially as most people eat more than is strictly necessary.

DIGESTIVE. DIGESTIF – That which promotes digestion.

The digestive juices are elements in the secretions of the digestive glands which cause foodstuffs to undergo changes which render them assimilable. The principle digestive juices are: *ptyalin* in saliva, *pepsin* and *rennet* in the stomach, *amylase*, *trypsin* and *lipase* in the pancreas; *erepsin* and *invertin* in the intestine.

Several of these juices are taken in the form of medicine to supplement deficiencies in the natural secretions. Apart from these there are, strictly speaking, no medicines helpful to the digestion. Bitter medicines increase the appetite; alkalines and acids neutralise excess acids or alkalis in the stomach, but are not, in the exact sense of the word, digestives. As for liqueurs taken after meals with coffee, from the medical point of view, they do not deserve the name digestive which is sometimes bestowed upon them.

DIJON – Capital of the ancient province of Burgundy; a town of high gastronomic repute that has many specialities. Among these the most famous are Dijon *mustard*; *gingerbread*; *cassis*; *jambon persillé* (ham sprinkled with parsley); *gras-doubles à la dijonnaise* (tripe *à la dijonnaise*); *beef à la bourguignonne*; *ferchuse*; *snails à la bourguignonne*; *meurette*. There are many other special dishes which are described in detail under Burgundy (q.v.).

All sections of the gastronomic world meet at the international food fair held in Dijon every year. *La Commanderie des cordons-bleus* also has its headquarters in *la ville des Ducs*. (According to Curnonsky, the members of this *commanderie* would know how to make a dining-room out of a fireplace). A certain hotel in Dijon has wine taps in its bedrooms.

DILUTING. DÉLAYER – Adding liquid to another liquid or semi-solid substance.

DINATOIRE – French word for a midday dinner; a sort of late lunch substantial enough to render dinner unnecessary.

DINNER. DÎNER – Word derived from the low Latin *dicoenare, disnare*.

The ancient Greeks usually dined towards evening. In ancient Rome dinner or supper was taken at the ninth or tenth hour, (between 3 and 4 p.m.). The Roman dinner menu was made up as follows:

First course (*gustatus*). Eggs, various vegetables (probably seasoned with vinegar).

Second course (*mensa prima*). Various stews and roast veal.

Third course (*mensa secunda*). Pastries and various jams, fruit and sweetmeats.

Under Charles V (1337–1380), the main meal of the day was taken at 9 a.m. Under Louis XIII (1610–1643), dinner was served at midday. In the seventeenth century, it became customary to serve this meal after mass, between 11 a.m. and midday.

Under Louis XV (1715–1774), dinner became the main meal of the day, served at about two p.m. Nowadays the normal dinner hour is between 7 and 8 p.m., though in France it is commonly served much later than this and is often in the nature of supper.

DINOCHAU – See RESTAURANTS OF BYGONE TIMES.

DIPLOMAT. DIPLOMATE – Name given to several quite different dishes. (See PUDDING, *Diplomat pudding*, SAUCE, *Diplomat sauce*.)

DISH STAND. PORTE-PLAT – Basket used for carrying dishes. Also a metal or porcelain mat on which dishes are placed.

DISINFECTING. DÉSINFECTION – To purify or render aseptic by destroying harmful germs. Disinfecting is obligatory in contaminated areas, especially those where provisions are kept. In the case of foodstuffs which are in the least degree contaminated, chemical disinfectants are usually ineffectual and their use in such cases is condemned.

DISPENSAIRE – Name given in former times to a book of recipes.

DISSECTING. DISSECTION – Term sometimes used instead of jointing.

DISTILLATION – Process of separating the more volatile from the less volatile components in a liquid by vaporisation (through heating) followed by condensation (through chilling).

In industry, very large apparatus is used to distil fermented fruit juices or cereal decoctions in the production of commercial alcohol or spirits (q.v.).

DIURETIC. DIURÉTIQUE – Having the property of increasing the volume of urine. In the old *Codex Pharmacopoeiae*, the diuretic plants mentioned are the dried roots of smallage, asparagus, fennel, parsley and knee-holly.

DIVE – Old French word, short for *divin* (divine), now only used in the expression *la dive bouteille* (the divine bottle), a quotation from Rabelais' *Gargantua*.

DIVER or LOON. PLONGEON – Web-footed birds of the *Gaviiformes* order, similar to duck. The flesh is tough, oily, and fishy.

DOBULE – Common French name for the European chub, which is found in lakes, ponds, and rivers. This fish tastes a little like the *féra* (q.v.) and is cooked in the same way.

DOE. BICHE – The doe is the female of deer. The meat of this animal, when killed outside the mating season, is similar to that of the roebuck.

All methods indicated for venison are applicable to it. Doe meat should be marinated before preparing it for cooking.

DOE or ROEDEER. CHEVRETTE – See preceding entry.

DOG. CHIEN – Carnivorous domestic mammal whose meat is edible and is eaten in certain countries. In China there is a breed of dogs (Chow dogs) specially fattened for the table.

Dogfish

DOGFISH. AIGUILLAT – Common name for the fish of the *Squalus acanthias* species, also called the *piked dogfish* or *spur dogfish*. This fish is bluish grey on the back, dirty white on the belly, and has a horny spike in front which sometimes reaches 1 m. (39 inches) in length. It feeds on fish, shellfish, and molluscs, and has white, rather coarse flesh. Its liver oil is used in the treatment of animal skins; its own skin is used by turners for polishing wood and ivory.

Dogfish can be prepared by following the recipes given for cod (q.v.) and other large fish; its flesh can be made into a soup, which is thin but quite nutritive, especially if pasta products, cereals, or bread are added.

The name dogfish is given to other species of fish on both sides of the north Atlantic.

DOLIC. DOLIQUE – Group of pulses, several of which are edible. Among these the most important is the soya bean (q.v.).

DOLMAS or DOLMADES (Turkish cookery) – *Dolmas* are prepared by blanching vine leaves, draining them, and stuffing them with minced lamb and cooked rice. The leaves are rolled into balls and braised in very little stock with oil and lemon juice added.

Dolmas can also be made with cabbage leaves, fig leaves or the leaves of the hazelnut tree.

In Turkey, *dolmas* are often cooked in sheep-tail fat.

Dolma is also the term used in the Middle East for a dish of mixed stuffed vegetables (aubergines, tomatoes, artichoke hearts and courgettes).

DOM PÉRIGNON – A monk of the Abbey of Hautvilliers near Epernay, who achieved fame by discovering the process of making sparkling Champagne.

He gave his name to a celebrated Moët et Chandon Champagne.

DONKEY. ÂNE, ÂNON – Donkey's meat is tasty and superior in flavour to that of horse; it is used mainly in the manufacture of certain types of sausage. Wild donkey used to be considered choice venison in the Orient.

According to M. Alquier, donkey meat is less fatty and richer in albuminoids than equivalent cuts of beef.

The domesticated donkey is a descendant of the Nubian donkey.

Donkey meat, and that of donkey foals, was highly valued by the Romans. Maecenas, it is said, treated his guests to a stew of marinated donkey meat.

The Persians were great lovers of donkey meat. Thirty-two wild asses were served at a banquet given by Chah Abbas.

In France, in the sixteenth century, Chancellor Duprat had donkeys bred and fattened for his table. During the blockade of Malta by the English and the Neapolitans, the inhabitants, reduced to eating domestic animals like dogs, cats, rats, and donkeys, became so fond of donkey flesh that they preferred it to beef and veal. During the siege of Paris, donkey meat, as well as the flesh of other less edible animals, helped to appease the hunger of the besieged.

Culinary preparation of donkey meat is the same as for horsemeat or beef. The meat of young donkeys under two years old is very delicate and is used in making *pâtés*, which in quality rival those made of veal.

DORADE – See SEA BREAM.

DORMANT – Large silver or gold centrepiece which, in former times, stood on the dining-table. It was similar to an *épergne*.

DORURE (Gilding) – Term used in French cookery for beaten whole eggs or egg yolks, thinned with a little water, brushed onto pastry and other mixtures such as *Duchess potato* (see POTATOES) with a pastry-brush made of silk or feathers.

DOTTEREL. GUIGNARD – European bird of passage of the wader group. Its flesh is rather tasteless. All recipes for plover (q.v.) are suitable for dotterel.

DOUBLE-CREAM (Cheese) – See CHEESE.

DOUBLER – Term in French cookery, meaning to fold in two a layer of pastry, a cut of meat, or a fillet of fish. It also means to cover pastries on a baking sheet with another sheet to prevent overbaking by excessive heat.

DOUBLE SAUCEPAN (U.S. Double boiler). DOUBLE-FOND – Two saucepans which fit together. Food which must not come in contact directly with the heat of the cooker is placed in the upper saucepan. The lower pan contains water which is brought to the boil, thus heating the contents of the upper pan.

DOUGH, PASTRY, AND BATTER. PÂTE –

Brioche dough I. PÂTE À BRIOCHE – *Ingredients.* 500 g. (18 oz., $4\frac{1}{2}$ cups) sieved flour, 400 g. (14 oz., $1\frac{3}{4}$ cups) butter, 10 g. ($\frac{1}{3}$ oz.) dried yeast, 6 eggs, 25 g. (1 oz., 2 tablespoons) fine sugar, $1\frac{1}{2}$ teaspoons salt, 1 dl. (6 tablespoons, scant $\frac{1}{2}$ cup) warm water.

The leaven. Put a quarter of the flour in a circle on the table, with the yeast in the middle. Dilute with a little water, moisten and mix, keeping the dough rather soft. Roll into a ball, make a crossways incision on the top, put into a small bowl, cover, and leave in a warm place for the paste to ferment and double its volume.

The dough. Put the rest of the flour in a circle on the table, add 4 eggs and 2 tablespoons (3 tablespoons) warm water, mix, and knead the dough.

Add the sugar and salt dissolved in a few drops of water, soften the butter and add it to the dough.

Add the remaining 2 eggs, one by one, and mix the dough well.

Spread the dough on the table, indent, pour the leaven into the centre, and blend it in. Put the dough into a bowl, cover with a cloth, and leave in a warm place to rise.

5 or 6 hours later beat the dough, and keep in a cool place until needed.

Brioche dough II. PÂTE À BRIOCHE COMMUNE – *Ingredients.* 500 g. (18 oz., $4\frac{1}{2}$ cups) sieved flour, 200 g. (7 oz., scant cup) butter, 10 g. ($\frac{1}{3}$ oz.) yeast, 4 eggs, 1 teaspoon fine sugar, $1\frac{1}{2}$ teaspoons salt, 1 dl. (6 tablespoons, scant $\frac{1}{2}$ cup) warm water (or milk).

Method. Proceed as described in the recipe for *Brioche dough I* but keeping it rather firm.

When intended for pies to be served as an *entrée*, or for *coulibiacs* (q.v.), the sugar can be omitted, although the small amount of sugar indicated above is only meant to give a little colour to the dough.

Mousseline brioche dough. PÂTE À BRIOCHE MOUSSELINE – Prepare the dough as described in the recipe for ordinary *Brioche dough I.* Add 50 g. (2 oz., $\frac{1}{4}$ cup) softened butter per 450 g. (1 lb.) dough.

Shape the dough into a ball, put it into a well-buttered mould which has a band of greaseproof paper tied round it, taking care not to fill it above two thirds. Leave in a warm place until the dough rises to the top of the mould.

Bake in a slow oven.

Chou paste d'office (cream puff pastry). PÂTE À CHOU D'OFFICE – Put 1 litre ($1\frac{3}{4}$ pints, generous quart) water, 200 g. (7 oz., scant cup) butter, and $1\frac{1}{2}$ teaspoons salt into a pan. Bring to the boil, remove from heat and add 625 g. (1 lb. 6 oz., $5\frac{1}{2}$ cups) sieved flour, pouring it all in at once. Mix well.

Return to the heat and cook, stirring with a wooden spoon, until the mixture dries and comes away from the sides of the pan. Remove from the heat and, stirring vigorously, add 12 or 14 eggs (depending on size), putting them in 2 at a time.

Ordinary chou paste (cream puff pastry). PÂTE À CHOU ORDINAIRE – *Chou paste* can be moistened with milk instead of water, and the eggs can be added one by one. Stir the mixture with a wooden spoon all the time.

Dumpling dough. PÂTE À DUMPLING – *Ingredients.* 500 g. (18 oz., $4\frac{1}{2}$ cups) sieved flour, 300 g. (11 oz., $2\frac{1}{2}$ cups) suet (shredded), 50 g. (2 oz., $\frac{1}{4}$ cup) sugar, $1\frac{1}{2}$ teaspoons salt, 2 dl. ($\frac{1}{3}$ pint, scant cup) water.

Method. Put the flour in a circle on the table, put the suet in the middle, and add sugar, salt and water. Mix to a fairly stiff dough, shape into a ball, and keep in a cool place until needed.

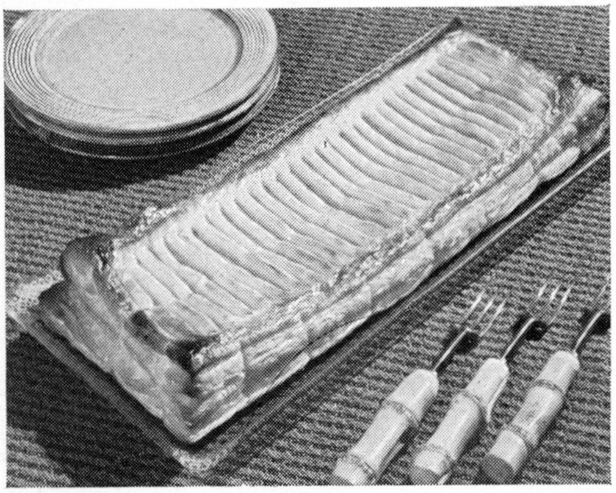

Flaky pastry

Flaky pastry. FEUILLETAGE – Flaky pastry, the most delicate of all pastries, is said by some historians to have been invented by Claude Gelée, called le Lorrain, the famous seventeenth century painter. Others say it was invented by a chef called Feuillet who was chief pastry-cook to the house of Condé.

Carême praises Feuillet, who was undoubtedly a great pastry-cook, and in his *Pâtissier Royal*, Carême says, 'Richard spurred me on to work twice as hard by speaking to me often of the great Feuillet'. But Carême stops there, and nowhere in his learned treatises on pastry does he say that Feuillet was the inventor of flaky pastry. But Joseph Favre is definite on this subject. In his *Dictionnaire universel de cuisine* he says that Feuillet was 'the inventor of flaky pastry.'

It appears, however, from the study of documents of a much earlier date, that flaky pastry was known not only in the Middle Ages but also in ancient Greece. In a charter drawn up by Robert, Bishop of Amiens (1311), flaky-pastry cakes are mentioned.

Claude Gelée who, it is said, served a pastry-cook's apprenticeship, was therefore not the inventor of this delicious pastry. He merely brought it back into fashion in his own time.

Flaky pastry or puff pastry (modern recipe). PÂTE FEUILLETÉE, FEUILLETAGE – Prepare a flour-and-water paste in the following manner:

Put 500 g. (18 oz., $4\frac{1}{2}$ cups) sieved flour on a board in a circle, making a well in the middle. Since flours differ, the exact proportion of water to flour is variable. Into the centre of this circle put in $1\frac{1}{2}$ teaspoons salt and about 3 dl. ($\frac{1}{2}$ pint, $1\frac{1}{4}$ cups) water. Mix and knead until the dough is smooth and elastic. Form into a ball and let it stand for 25 minutes.

Roll out the dough into a sheet about 20 cm. (8 inches) square and of even thickness throughout. Put 500 g. (18 oz., $2\frac{1}{4}$ cups) kneaded butter in the middle of this dough. The butter should be kneaded on a lightly floured board. Fold the ends of the dough over the butter in such a way as to enclose it completely. Leave to stand for 10 minutes in a cold place.

Give 2 turns to this dough. This operation is called *tourage* in French and it is done in two parts:

1. Roll the dough with a rolling-pin on a lightly floured board in such a way as to obtain a rectangle 60 cm. (24 inches) long, 20 cm. (8 inches) wide, and $1\frac{1}{2}$ cm. ($\frac{1}{2}$ inch) thick.
2. Refold the strip in three.

The second turn is done by rolling out the folded dough in the opposite direction, and so forth.

Give 4 more turns to the dough, leaving it to stand for 10 minutes between each operation. After having been given the 6 prescribed turns, the puff pastry is ready for use.

The purpose of turning and rolling is to spread the butter evenly in the dough.

During preparation, the dough should be kept in a cold place, but it should not be put directly on ice; this could cause the butter to harden and it would then not be easy to incorporate in the dough.

Flaky pastry or puff pastry (Carême's recipe). PÂTE FEUILLETÉE, FEUILLETAGE – 'Having put a litron (about 800 g., $1\frac{3}{4}$ lb., 7 cups) sieved flour on the board, place the tips of your fingers in the middle and spread it into a circle with an inside diameter of 10 cm. (4 inches); this operation is known as "making a well" because the flour, disposed in this manner, will have the water which is required for moistening it put in the middle.

'In the centre of this well, put 2 *gros* (see WEIGHTS AND MEASURES) fine salt, 2 egg yolks, a piece of butter the size of a walnut and nearly a glass of water. Stir this mixture with the tips of your fingers (using the right hand only and keeping the fingers spread out) and, little by little, mix in the flour, adding a little more water if necessary so that the dough is moistened, has the right consistency and is slightly firm. Then work it a little, pressing with the hand on the board in such a way as to achieve, after a few minutes, a dough which is soft to the touch and as smooth as satin.

1. Water is poured on the salt in the middle of the well

2. Mixing flour and water

3. Method of putting butter on the paste

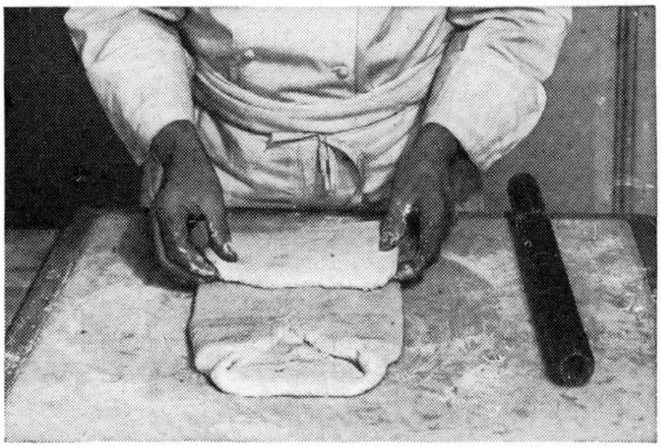

4. How butter is enclosed in the paste

5. Rolling out for the first time: the paste is rolled out in a rectangular sheet

6. Rolling out for the second time: the rectangle of paste is folded in three

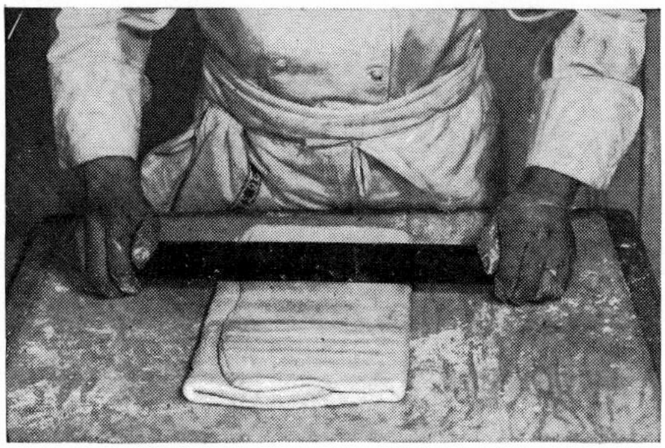

7. Second turn: turn the paste before rolling it out

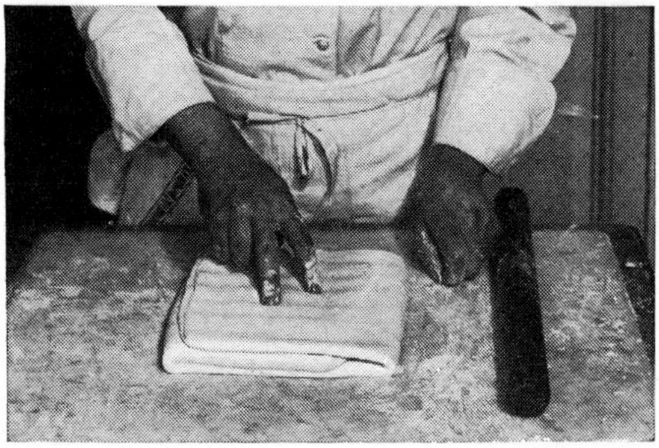

8. Making a mark on the paste to indicate that it has been given two turns

MAKING FLAKY PASTRY Cookery classes, Gaz de Paris (*Larousse*)

This dough should neither be too firm nor too soft. It is, however, better for it to be a little on the soft side rather than too hard.

'Roll the dough out in a rectangular sheet; put 400 g. (14 oz., 1¾ cups) butter in the middle and fold the edges of the dough over it. The butter should have been kneaded in a napkin to extract water and to make it supple and smooth. Make sure that it is entirely enclosed with an even thickness of dough all round. This should be done as quickly as possible. The dough should be folded in 3 layers of equal length. Roll out again to the same dimensions, turning it before rolling so that its former width becomes its length. Fold it again in the same way, and roll out so that it is 5 cm. (2 inches) longer than it is wide. Put it quickly onto a plate lightly sprinkled with flour and stand on crushed ice spread out to cover the same length and width as the pan. Cover the dough with a piece of paper, on which you stand a plate of crushed ice.

'After 3 or 4 minutes remove the top plate, turn the dough over and cover again. Begin the same operation all over again, after which you give the dough 2 turns as described above. Put the dough on ice again, turning it as carefully as before. Give another turn or two, depending on the use for which it is intended.

'Care should be taken to sprinkle the top and bottom of the paste with flour very sparingly when turning it, otherwise it goes grey in the baking.

'When the dough has been given the last turn, it should be used at once, being placed in the oven 4, 6 or, at the most, 8 minutes after the last rolling out. If it is ready 20 or 25 minutes before it can be put in the oven, it will be dull and tough.' (*Le pâtissier royale.*)

Flaky pastry or puff pastry made with oil (Carême's recipe). PÂTE FEUILLETÉE À L'HUILE – 'Proceed as described in the recipe for *Pudding pastry or suet flaky pastry* (see below), using oil, not lard. Add 3½ dl. (generous ½ pint, 1½ cups) oil during the rolling and turning of flaky pastry. Then cut as usual.'

Semi-flaky pastry or rough puff pastry. PÂTE DEMI-FEUILLETÉE, DEMI-FEUILLETAGE – Cut out puff pastry into patties, *vol-au-vent*, etc., and collect the left-over pieces together into a ball.

This dough, also called *rognures*, can be used for making boat-shaped tartlets, croustades, tartlets, etc.

Three-minute flaky pastry or puff pastry. PÂTE FEUILLETÉE EN TROIS MINUTES – *Ingredients.* 400 g. (14 oz., 3½ cups) sifted flour, 500 g. (18 oz., 2¼ cups) butter, 1½ teaspoons salt, 2½ dl. (scant ½ pint, generous cup) water.

Method. Mix the ingredients and give the dough 4 turns.

Viennese flaky pastry or puff pastry. PÂTE FEUILLETÉE À LA VIENNOISE – *Ingredients.* 500 g. (18 oz., 4½ cups) sifted flour, 500 g. (18 oz., 2¼ cups) butter, 2 egg yolks, 2½ dl. (scant ½ pint, generous cup) water, 1½ teaspoons salt.

Method. Mix half the flour with the yolks, water and salt. Mix the rest of the flour with a third of the butter, blending them with a knife.

Roll out the flour-and-water paste to a thin square sheet. Shape the butter-and-flour mixture into a square of a smaller size and put it on the other paste, enclosing it and folding the edges. Roll out as described in puff pastry recipes.

Flour-and-water paste. PÂTE À L'EAU – This is used for luting, or hermetically sealing, earthenware casserole and *cocotte* lids. It is made by mixing flour with enough warm water to obtain a soft paste. Use as indicated.

Leavened dough for tarts. PÂTE LEVÉE POUR TARTES – The best recipe for leavened paste for tarts is the same as for *Brioche dough I.*

A more ordinary dough can be made using 500 g. (18 oz., 4½ cups) sifted flour, 4 eggs, 1½ teaspoons salt, 1½ tablespoons sugar, 10 g. (⅓ oz.) yeast, 2½ dl. (scant ½ pint, generous cup) milk and 200 g. (7 oz., scant cup) butter.

Proceed as described in the recipe for *Brioche dough I.*

Fine lining paste or pastry dough I. PÂTE À FONCER FINE – *Ingredients.* 500 g. (18 oz., 4½ cups) sifted flour, 300 g. (11 oz., 1⅓ cups) butter, 1 egg, 1½ dl. (¼ pint, ⅔ cup) water, 50 g. (2 oz., ¼ cup) fine sugar, 1½ teaspoons salt.

Method. Spread the flour in a circle on the board, make a well in the middle and put in the egg, butter, water, sugar, and salt. Mix these ingredients together and incorporate the flour, little by little.

Knead twice, roll the paste into a ball, wrap in a cloth, and keep in a cold place until ready for use.

Lining paste should always be made several hours before it is needed. The less it is handled the better, as it quickly becomes tough.

Ordinary lining paste or pastry dough II (tart pastry). PÂTE À FONCER ORDINAIRE – *Ingredients.* 500 g. (18 oz., 4½ cups) sifted flour, 250 g. (9 oz., generous cup) butter, 2 dl. (⅓ pint, scant cup) water, 1½ teaspoons salt.

Method. Proceed as described in the recipe for *Fine lining paste.*

Pastry dough for hot or cold pies – see PASTRY.

Pudding pastry or suet flaky pastry (Carême's recipe). PÂTE FEUILLETÉE À LA GRAISSE DE BOEUF – 'Remove skin and fibre from 450 g. (1 lb.) of suet, chop it up very finely and pound in a mortar with 1 tablespoon good olive oil. Add several more tablespoons oil, little by little, as you pound it. This gives it body and softens it, so that the suet becomes as soft and easy to work as butter.

'Proceed to use it in place of butter, in the same proportions.

'Lard can be used instead of oil and by using suet and lard in equal proportions, very good puff paste is obtained, very agreeable to the palate, but it must be eaten hot.'

This type of puff paste is suitable for *entrée* pies. (See TOURTES (PIES).)

Puff pastry – See FLAKY PASTRY.

Savarin dough I. PÂTE À SAVARIN – *Ingredients.* 500 g. (18 oz., 4½ cups) sifted flour, 250 g. (9 oz., generous cup) butter, 50 g. (2 oz., ¼ cup) sugar, 1½ teaspoons salt, 10 g. (⅓ oz.) yeast, 6 to 8 eggs, 2 dl. (⅓ pint, scant cup) milk.

Method. Dissolve the yeast in about 2½ dl. (scant ½ pint, generous cup) warm water, adding it to a third of the flour. Blend and leave to rise until the leaven more than doubles its volume.

Spread the rest of the flour in a circle on the board, make a well in the middle and add salt and two thirds of the eggs. Work the mixture by hand to give it more body, then add the rest of the eggs and the milk. Knead until the paste no longer sticks to the hands.

Add the butter quickly and pour in the leaven. Blend the mixture to make it smooth and, last of all, add the sugar. Put the dough in a bowl, cover with a cloth, and stand in a cool place. Leave until the following day.

A mould with a special border, called a *savarin* mould, is used for baking this cake. Butter the mould and half-fill it with the dough. Stand in a warm place and leave the dough to rise until it completely fills the mould. Bake in a hot oven from 20 to 35 minutes, according to the size of the mould.

Savarin dough II. PÂTE À SAVARIN – This is a shorter formula. The ingredients are identical.

Put the sifted flour in a bowl. Mix the leaven and the dough in the order described above. Add the melted butter, still warm, to the dough. Add the leaven and sugar, and use at once.

Savarin dough III. PÂTE À SAVARIN – *Ingredients.* 500 g. (18 oz., 4½ cups) sifted flour, 375 g. (13 oz., generous 1½ cups) butter, 3 tablespoons fine sugar, 20 g. ($\frac{2}{3}$ oz., 1 cake) yeast, 8 eggs, 1 dl. (6 tablespoons, scant $\frac{1}{2}$ cup) milk, $1\frac{1}{2}$ teaspoons fine salt.

Method. Put the sifted flour in a bowl, make a well in the middle and put in the yeast. Moisten the yeast with the warm milk and stir. Add the eggs one by one, mixing the paste with the hands to blend well. Soften the butter, divide it into small pieces, and put them on the paste. Cover the bowl and stand in a warm place to ferment until the dough doubles its volume.

Add the salt. Knead the dough to blend in the butter and continue to do so until the dough acquires sufficient body to be lifted in one piece. Add the sugar and knead a few minutes longer to blend well.

Savarin dough IV. PÂTE À SAVARIN – *Ingredients.* 500 g. (18 oz., $4\frac{1}{2}$ cups) sifted flour, 350 g. (12 oz., $1\frac{1}{2}$ cups) butter, 2 teaspoons sugar, 10 g. ($\frac{1}{3}$ oz.) yeast, 7 eggs, 1 dl. (6 tablespoons, scant $\frac{1}{2}$ cup) milk, $1\frac{1}{2}$ teaspoons fine salt.

Method. Prepare a leaven, using a quarter of the flour, the yeast and the warm milk. Put this leaven in a small bowl, cover, and stand in a warm place to ferment.

Mix the rest of the flour with half the butter, the eggs, and the salt. Blend well, kneading the paste. Add the leaven, the rest of the butter, which has been softened, and the sugar. Continue to knead the dough for a few moments.

Short pastry I. PÂTE SÈCHE SUCRÉE – *Ingredients.* 500 g. (18 oz., $4\frac{1}{2}$ cups) sifted flour, 200 g. (7 oz., scant cup) butter, 3 eggs, 150 g. (5 oz., $\frac{2}{3}$ cup) fine sugar, $\frac{1}{2}$ tablespoon orange blossom water or $\frac{1}{2}$ teaspoon orange extract.

Method. Proceed as described in the recipe for *Fine lining paste or pastry dough I.*

Short pastry II. PÂTE SUCRÉE – *Ingredients.* 250 g. (9 oz., $2\frac{1}{4}$ cups) sifted flour, 75 g. (3 oz., 6 tablespoons) sugar, 200 g. (7 oz., scant cup) butter, 1 egg, a small pinch of salt, lemon peel or vanilla-flavoured sugar.

Method. Spread the flour in a circle, make a well in the centre and put in the sugar, well softened butter, salt, and egg. Mix these ingredients, with the exception of flour, into a soft paste. Incorporate the flour, kneading the paste as little as possible, only enough to make it hold together.

Leave for 2 hours, roll out, and cut as desired.

Baba batter. PÂTE À BABA – *Ingredients.* 500 g. (18 oz., $4\frac{1}{2}$ cups) sieved flour, 300 g. (11 oz., generous $1\frac{1}{4}$ cups) butter, 7 eggs, 20 g. ($\frac{2}{3}$ oz., 1 cake) yeast, $1\frac{1}{2}$ tablespoons sugar, 100 g. (4 oz., $\frac{2}{3}$ cup) raisins and sultanas (half and half), 1 dl. (6 tablespoons, scant $\frac{1}{2}$ cup) warm milk, $2\frac{1}{2}$ teaspoons salt.

Method. Proceed as for *Savarin dough.* When the dough is made, add the raisins, sultanas and sugar. Pour into buttered baba moulds, filling only one third of the moulds. Bake in a hot oven, like *savarins.*

When cooked, pour over them sugar syrup flavoured with liqueur.

Batter for small tea biscuits. PÂTE À PETITS GÂTEAUX – *Ingredients.* 500 g. (18 oz., $4\frac{1}{2}$ cups) sifted flour, 300 g. (11 oz., $1\frac{1}{3}$ cups) sugar, 1 whole egg, 4 egg yolks, 1 tablespoon orange blossom water.

Method. Mix the dough in the usual manner, knead it twice, roll it into a ball, and leave it to stand in a cold place for 1 or 2 hours.

Roll out the dough to a thickness of 1 cm ($\frac{1}{2}$ inch). Cut into biscuits with pastry cutters. Put them on a baking tray and brush with beaten egg. Decorate with halved almonds, cherries and candied peel, and bake in a hot oven. When ready, remove from the oven, brush with a solution of gum arabic, or boiling milk mixed with sugar and boiled down to a syrupy consistency. Treated in this manner, the biscuits keep better.

Crêpe batter – See CRÊPES.

Crêpe batter (sweet). PÂTE À PANNEQUETS – Put 250 g. (9 oz., $2\frac{1}{4}$ cups) sifted flour, 100 g. (4 oz., $\frac{1}{2}$ cup) fine sugar and a pinch of salt into a bowl. Add 6 whole eggs. Stir the mixture with a wooden spoon until smooth. Dilute with $7\frac{1}{2}$ dl. ($1\frac{1}{3}$ pints, $1\frac{2}{3}$ pints) boiled milk flavoured with vanilla, orange, or lemon, depending on the nature of the pancakes. Add 1 tablespoon butter heated to *noisette* colour (see BUTTER) and 1 tablespoon brandy or rum. Blend well.

Cussy batter. PÂTE À CUSSY – *Ingredients.* 250 g. (9 oz., generous cup) fine sugar, 150 g. (5 oz., scant cup) rice flour, 7 whole eggs, 65 g. ($2\frac{1}{2}$ oz., 5 tablespoons) butter, 1 tablespoon vanilla-flavoured sugar, a pinch of salt.

Method. Put the eggs, sugar, vanilla sugar, and salt into a basin. Whisk the eggs over a low heat. When the mixture is well whisked, add the rice flour and melted butter.

Batter for soufflé fritters. PÂTE À BEIGNETS SOUFFLÉS – Prepare in the same way as *Chou paste d'office*, adding 4 teaspoons sugar for the proportions indicated in that recipe.

Batter for Vienna fritters. PÂTE À BEIGNETS VIENNOIS – Proceed as described in the recipe for *Brioche dough* using 500 g. (18 oz., $4\frac{1}{2}$ cups) sieved flour, 200 g (7 oz., scant cup) butter, 6 eggs, 20 g. ($\frac{2}{3}$ oz., 1 cake) yeast, $2\frac{1}{2}$ teaspoons salt, 1 tablespoon sugar and 1 dl. (6 tablespoons, scant $\frac{1}{2}$ cup) milk.

Galette batter. PÂTE À GALETTE – *Ingredients.* 500 g. (18 oz., $4\frac{1}{2}$ cups) sifted flour, 375 g. (13 oz., generous $1\frac{1}{2}$ cups) butter, $1\frac{1}{2}$ dl. ($\frac{1}{4}$ pint, $\frac{2}{3}$ cup) water, 15 g. ($\frac{1}{2}$ oz., 1 tablespoon) fine sugar and $1\frac{1}{2}$ teaspoons salt.

Method. Mix as described in the recipe for *Fine lining paste.* Roll the dough into a ball without kneading. Leave to stand in a cool place for 2 hours.

Give the dough 3 turns, leaving it to stand for 10 minutes between each turn. Leave to stand for a few minutes before use.

Batter for little salted galettes (biscuits). PÂTE À PETITES GALETTES SALÉES – *Ingredients.* 250 g. (9 oz., $2\frac{1}{4}$ cups) sifted flour, 100 g. (4 oz., $\frac{1}{2}$ cup) butter, 1 dl. (6 tablespoons, scant $\frac{1}{2}$ cup) milk, 25 g. (1 oz., 2 tablespoons) fine sugar and $1\frac{1}{2}$ teaspoons salt.

Method. Pour the flour on a board, make a well in the middle and put the sugar and salt into it. Add the butter, and the milk which has been slightly warmed. Knead all the ingredients together, roll into a ball, and leave to stand for 30 minutes.

Roll the dough out to $\frac{1}{2}$ cm. ($\frac{1}{4}$ inch) in thickness. Prick over the surface with a fork. Cut out with a 6-cm. (2-inch) round pastry-cutter. Put the galettes on a metal tray and bake in a hot oven for about 10 minutes.

Genoese batter. PÂTE À GÉNOISE – *Ingredients.* 375 g. (13 oz., $3\frac{1}{4}$ cups) sifted flour, 500 g. (18 oz., $2\frac{1}{4}$ cups) fine sugar, 200 g. (7 oz., scant cup) melted butter, 16 eggs, flavouring.

Method. Blend the sugar and eggs, and cook very slowly over low heat or over a pan of hot water. Whisk until the mixture makes a ribbon. Remove from heat. Stirring gently with a wooden spoon, add the flavouring, flour and melted butter, pouring the latter in a small thread. Put into buttered, floured tins and bake in a hot oven.

Genoese batter may be flavoured with vanilla sugar, vanilla extract, lemon or orange peel, or liqueur.

Gougère batter. PÂTE À GOUGÈRE – Proceed as described in the recipe for *Ordinary chou paste.* After adding eggs to the paste, finish off with 250 g. (9 oz., generous 2 cups) Gruyère cheese cut in very small dice.

Manqué batter. PÂTE À MANQUÉ – *Ingredients.* 500 g. (18 oz., $2\frac{1}{4}$ cups) fine sugar, 400 g. (14 oz., $3\frac{1}{2}$ cups) sifted flour, 300 g. (11 oz., $1\frac{1}{3}$ cups) butter, 18 egg yolks, 16 stiffly beaten egg whites, 3 tablespoons (scant $\frac{1}{4}$ cup) rum.

Method. Cream the yolks and the sugar in a bowl until the mixture becomes white and light. Add the rum and flour, and mix. Fold in the stiffly beaten whites, and pour in the butter, melted.

Butter *à manqué* moulds, dust with flour, pour in the mixture and bake in a moderate oven.

Mazarin batter. PÂTE À MAZARIN – Mixture of baba and brioche dough in equal proportions.

This paste is usually baked in plain genoese cake tins.

Fine sponge cake or biscuit batter. PÂTE À BISCUITS FINS – *Ingredients.* 500 g. (18 oz., 2¼ cups) fine sugar, 10 eggs (yolks and whites separated), 125 g. (4 oz., 1 cup) sieved flour, 125 g. (4 oz., ⅔ cup) potato flour, 25 g. (1 oz., 2 tablespoons) vanilla-flavoured sugar, small pinch of salt.

Method. Blend the yolks with the sugar, vanilla sugar, and salt with a wooden spoon. When the mixture is quite smooth add the whites, whisked to a stiff froth, and then add the flour and potato flour.

Italian sponge cake or biscuit batter. PÂTE À BISCUITS ITALIENS – *Ingredients.* 250 g. (9 oz., 2 cups) lump sugar, 4 eggs (yolks and whites separated), 125 g. (4 oz., 1 cup) sieved flour, salt.

Method. Put the sugar in a pan, moisten with ½ dl. (6 tablespoons, scant ½ cup) water, cook to hard ball degree (see SUGAR) and allow to cool to half its temperature.

Add the yolks, then the flour and salt, and fold in the stiffly beaten whites.

Ordinary sponge cake or biscuit batter. PÂTE À BISCUITS ORDINAIRES – *Ingredients.* 250 g. (9 oz., generous cup) fine sugar, 8 eggs (yolks and whites separated), 150 g. (5 oz., 1¼ cups) sifted flour, salt.

Method. Proceed as described in the recipe for *Fine sponge cake or biscuit batter.*

Reims sponge cake or biscuit batter. PÂTE À BISCUITS DE REIMS – *Ingredients.* 12 eggs, 300 g. (11 oz., 1⅓ cups) fine sugar, 175 g. (6 oz., 1½ cups) sieved flour, 1 tablespoon vanilla-flavoured sugar, small pinch salt.

Method. Put the sugar, 12 egg whites and 10 yolks into a bowl and whisk over a low heat until the mixture becomes firm and smooth. Add the flour and vanilla sugar. Mix with a wooden spoon.

Swiss sponge cake or biscuit batter. PÂTE À BISCUIT DE SAVOIE – *Ingredients.* 500 g. (18 oz., 2¼ cups) fine sugar, 175 g. (6 oz., 1½ cups) sieved flour, 175 g. (6 oz., 1½ cups) cornstarch (cornflour), 14 eggs (separated), 1 tablespoon vanilla-flavoured sugar.

Method. Blend the sugar and the egg yolks together in a bowl until the mixture forms a ribbon. Add the flour, cornstarch, vanilla sugar and stiffly whisked egg whites. Mix quickly.

Butter a baking tin, sprinkle with cornstarch and pour in the mixture, filling two thirds of the tin. Bake in a slow oven.

Sponge cake or biscuit batter, whisked over heat. PÂTE À BISCUITS SUR LE FEU – Break 12 eggs into a pan. Add 500 g. (18 oz., 2¼ cups) fine sugar and a small pinch of salt. Keeping the pan on the edge of the burner, whisk the mixture until it becomes very firm and smooth.

Still whisking, add 225 g. (8 oz., 1⅓ cups) potato flour.

Sponge fingers batter. PÂTE À BISCUIT À LA CUILLER – *Ingredients.* 500 g. (18 oz., 2¼ cups) fine sugar, 375 g. (13 oz., 3¼ cups) sieved flour, 16 eggs (separated), 1 tablespoon orange blossom water.

Method. Mix the egg yolks and the sugar in a bowl, creaming the mixture until it forms a ribbon. Add the flavouring, mix in the flour, and fold in the stiffly whisked egg whites.

Pour the mixture into a pastry-bag with a 1½-cm. (¾-inch) nozzle. Pipe the biscuits onto strong paper and sprinkle with plenty of fine sugar. Shake off the surplus sugar by lifting the ends of the paper.

Moisten the biscuits with a few drops of cold water (which will ensure beading) and bake in a very slow oven.

DOUILLET or COCHON AU PÈRE (Pig au père) – Popular dish of an earlier age. Pierre de Lune, esquire of the household of the Prince de Rohan (1734–1803) gives the following recipe:

'Cut the pig into pieces. Blanch the pieces and interlard with pork fat cut partly from the outer layer and partly from the belly. Put them in a cloth and season with salt, pepper, whole cloves, nutmeg, bay leaves, green lemons and spring onions. Cook in a pot with stock and a little white wine. Make sure that the finished dish is highly seasoned. Leave to stand until lukewarm. Serve with slices of lemon.'

DOUZIL or DOUSIL – French word for the wooden spigot used to plug the hole in the vat from which the wine is extracted. (See CONFRÉRIES VINEUSES, *la Confrérie des tire-douzils.*)

DOVE. COLOMBE – See PIGEON.

DOYENNÉ – Variety of pear which melts in the mouth and is very sweet. (See PEAR.)

DRAFF. DRÈCHE – By-product of barley used in brewing. It is also used for fodder.

DRAGONET. DOUCETTE – Another name for corn salad (q.v.).

DRAINING. ÉGOUTTER – Draining off excess liquid from foodstuffs which have been washed, or blanched in boiling water and cooled under running water.

DRESSING (poultry, game, and fish). HABILLAGE – Poultry or winged game are dressed by being plucked, drawn, singed, trimmed, and trussed. The dressing of fish consists of scaling, gutting, and trimming.

DRINKING STRAW. CHALUMEAU – Hollow stem of straw, glass, metal, paper, or plastic used for drinking cold drinks.

DRIPPING PAN. LÈCHEFRITE – Rectangular pan, usually of metal, placed under food roasted on a spit. The juices of the roast drip into the pan.

DROMEDARY. DROMADAIRE – Camel (q.v.) with only one hump.

DRUM. ESTAGNON – Container in which liquids, especially oil, are transported.

DRUPE – French term for a fruit with a single stone.

DRYING. DESSÉCHER – Dehydrating a solid of any kind by putting it on the stove for a few seconds. Thus green vegetables boiled in salt water are dried or, more accurately, dehydrated when they are stood for a very short time over a hot flame to evaporate excess moisture absorbed by the vegetables during cooking. When they have been dried, the vegetables are tossed in butter.

In France, the term *dessécher* is also used of cooking panadas and dough on the stove.

The term 'drying' is not synonymous with 'reducing', which refers only to the process of boiling down certain liquids so that they are reduced in volume.

DUBARRY (À LA) – Garnish for meat which comprises small flowerets of cauliflower covered with *Mornay sauce* (see SAUCE), sprinkled with grated cheese and breadcrumbs, and browned.

DUBLIN BAY PRAWNS (Italian, scampi). LANGOUSTINE – Common names for the *Nephrops norvegicus.* This shellfish, about the size of a prawn, is orange in colour with white-tipped claws and legs. It does not change colour in cooking.

They are prepared in the same way as shrimps and served as *hors-d'oeuvre.*

All recipes for freshwater crayfish, and shellfish generally, are suitable for Dublin Bay prawns, which can also be prepared *à l'américaine* or *à la bordelaise.*

Duchesse d'Angoulême pears

DUCHESSE – Winter pear which makes an excellent table fruit.

DUCHESSE (À LA) – Name given to various preparations, especially a method of preparing potatoes. (See POTATOES, *Duchess potatoes.*)

DUCHESSE MIXTURE – Purée of potatoes blended with egg yolk. It is made into *Duchess potatoes* (see POTATOES) and into borders. savoury cases, etc.

DUCHESSES – *Petits fours* which are made as follows:

Pound in a mortar 60 g. ($2\frac{1}{2}$ oz., $\frac{1}{2}$ cup) sweet almonds with the same quantity of hazelnuts, and blend with 1 egg white. Add 300 g. (11 oz., $1\frac{1}{3}$ cups) fine sugar, 50 g. (2 oz., $\frac{1}{4}$ cup) vanilla-flavoured sugar, and 50 g. (2 oz.) chocolate. Add to this mixture 3 egg whites and mix thoroughly. Pipe into little balls on a baking sheet. Bake in a moderate oven.

DUCK. CANARD – Web-footed water bird of which many species are known. Varieties of domestic ducks are bred, some for food, others because of the beauty of their plumage. Their ancestor is the *wild duck* (*le canard sauvage*), which is found in Europe, Asia, North America and North Africa.

In French classical cookery, *Rouen* and *Nantes ducks* enjoy the highest esteem. The different types of ducks raised in France for food include *Duclair*, a variety of *Rouen duck*; *Barbary duck* which, when mated with a Rouen duck, produces the *mulard duck* which is bred specially for the production of *foie gras.*

The *Barbary duck* (which in French is also called *Canard d'Inde*) is raised mainly in the southern and south-eastern regions of France. Its flesh is rather mediocre and is sometimes too musky to be eaten. The young birds are fairly good to eat, the old are tough and have a strong odour which, it is said, they develop after they have acquired their red wattles.

The *Nantes duck* is a magnificent bird with fine, delicately flavoured flesh. It is smaller in size than the *Rouen duck.* When fully developed, that is at 4 months, it hardly ever exceeds 2 kg. ($4\frac{1}{2}$ lb.) in weight, whilst the *Rouen duck* weighs about $2\frac{1}{2}$ kg. ($5\frac{1}{2}$ lb.).

The *Rouen duckling* owes its reputation to the fine quality of its flesh and also to the method by which it is killed. It is smothered, not bled as are all other fowl (except guinea-fowl, which in the south-western part of France is often shot, like game). The fact that it loses none of its blood before being cooked makes the flesh of the *Rouen duck* stay red and gives it a special flavour much prized by connoisseurs.

Ducks which are killed without bleeding are rarely marketed in the U.S.A. Killed in this manner, they should be cooked the same day to avoid the development of dangerous toxins.

Other breeds of ducks raised for food are *Aylesbury duck*, a bird which has a certain similarity to the *Rouen duck* and which the English greatly appreciate; the black *Cayuga*, which is also called the *Great American duck*, and is a very large bird with delicate flesh; *Peking duck*, a small bird with yellow plumage and bright yellow feet and bill, which is excellent in quality.

In the U.S.A. domestic ducks are sold at about $2\frac{1}{2}$ kg. ($5\frac{1}{2}$ lb.), ducklings at about $1\frac{3}{4}$ kg. (4 lb.). Wild ducks are shot in large numbers during the hunting season. The most prized is the *Canvasback.*

The age and tenderness of ducks can be determined by the flexibility of their pinions and under-bill – these should be soft enough to be bent back easily.

Duck breeding. It is generally thought that the duck, being an aquatic animal, can only be raised in places situated near water or on river banks. This opinion is erroneous, as many poultry-breeders have proved.

The famous Rouen duckling is raised mainly around Yvetot, where you will not find a river or even a spring. The celebrated duck *pâtés* are made from the flesh of ducks raised a long way from running water.

In Languedoc and other parts of south-western France where big ducks are bred for the manufacture of *foie gras*, their flesh is preserved in fat, like that of geese. This preserved duck is esteemed by gastonomes even more than the *confit d'oie* (preserved goose). *Mulard ducks* are preserved in brine. The famous truffled *terrines* and *pâtés* are made from the livers of these ducks.

In French cookery, duck is always described as *caneton* (duckling).

Duckling d'Albuféra. CANETON D'ALBUFÉRA – 'Clean and truss 2 very young ducklings. Cut 12 pieces of uncooked Bayonne ham into heart-shaped slices. Melt 175 g. (6 oz., $\frac{3}{4}$ cup) best butter in a casserole, put in first the ham, then the 2 ducklings, and add a *bouquet garni* (q.v.), an onion studded with 2 cloves, and $\frac{1}{2}$ wine glass of Madeira.

'Cover with a piece of buttered paper, bring to the boil, and put on a *paillasse* (q.v.) (a brick oven with glowing charcoal), with hot coals above and below the casserole, without the heat being too lively, so that the ducklings are cooked without being fried. After 20 minutes turn the ducklings and remove the onion and the *bouquet garni.* Leave for another 20 minutes, then drain the ducklings, remove trussing string and arrange on a serving dish. The birds should be a lovely colour. Garnish with the slices of ham. Skim off surplus fat from the pan juices, add 2 tablespoons (3 tablespoons) *Financière sauce* (see SAUCE) and 100 g. (4 oz.) very small peeled mushrooms. Pour this sauce over the ducklings.' (From *L'art de la cuisine francaise au XIX siècle.*)

Duckling à l'alsacienne. CANETON À L'ALSACIENNE – Braise a Nantes duckling, arrange it on a serving dish, and surround with *sauerkraut* which has been braised separately with streaky bacon. Garnish the border of the dish with this bacon cut into rectangular pieces, and 6 smoked Strasbourg sausages poached in water.

Strain the braising liquor, spoon some over the duckling and serve the rest separately.

Ballottine of duckling (hot). BALLOTTINE DE CANETON – Bone a Nantes duckling and carefully remove all the flesh, leaving only the skin. Remove all sinews from flesh. Dice the fillets and chop the rest of the meat finely with an equal weight of fresh fat bacon, half of its weight of lean veal, and 75 g. (3 oz.) of panada (q.v.).

Pound the whole mixture in a mortar, adding 4 egg yolks. Season with salt, pepper, and spices. Rub this forcemeat through a sieve. Add 150 g. (5 oz.) uncooked *foie gras* (duck's liver) cut in large dice and briskly tossed in butter, 150 g. (5 oz.) diced truffles and the diced duck breast fillets. Add 2 tablespoons (3 tablespoons) brandy and blend well.

Spread the duck's skin on the table, on a piece of muslin which has been soaked in cold water and wrung out. Stuff the skin with the forcemeat and roll into a ballottine. Secure with string at both ends and in the middle.

Poach the ballottine in stock prepared by using a veal knuckle and the bones and trimmings of the duckling. Cook for about $1\frac{1}{4}$ hours, unwrap, and glaze in the oven.

Garnish and spoon over a little of the braising liquor which has been boiled down and strained. Serve the rest separately.

Hot ballottine of duckling may be served with most of the garnishes (q.v.) indicated for braised or broiled poultry. The following are the most suitable: *châtelaine*, chipolata, *forestière*, *godard*, braised chestnuts, braised lettuce, or other vegetables braised or cooked in butter.

Ballottine of duckling (cold). BALLOTTINE DE CANETON – Make in the same way as hot ballottine, but a greater quantity of duck's liver and truffles are added to the forcemeat.

After cooking, unwrap the ballottine, then wrap once again in the same cloth very tightly, and put to cool under a press. To serve, unwrap, glaze with liquid aspic jelly, arrange on a dish, and surround with chopped jelly.

Duckling à la bordelaise. CANETON À LA BORDELAISE – Stuff a duckling with fine pork forcemeat mixed with the chopped duck's liver, a little shallot, garlic, 1 tablespoon chopped parsley, blanched and chopped olives; seasoned with salt, pepper and spices; and bound with 1 egg.

Truss the duckling and fry in butter in a fireproof dish until it is golden on all sides. Add 500 g. (18 oz.) white, firm *cèpes* which have been trimmed, washed, lightly tossed in oil and seasoned with salt and pepper. Cook in a hot oven. When the duckling is done, remove trussing string and put back into the dish. Pour over 4 or 5 tablespoons thickened brown veal gravy, sprinkle with chopped parsley and serve in the dish in which it was cooked.

Braised duckling with various garnishes. CANETON BRAISÉ – Truss a large Nantes duckling and put it into a braising pan on a foundation of fresh bacon rinds, 1 carrot and 1 medium-sized onion sliced and tossed in butter. Add a *bouquet garni* (q.v.) of parsley, thyme and bay leaf. Season. Cook with the lid on for about 15 minutes. When the duckling is browned on all sides, moisten with $1\frac{1}{2}$ dl. ($\frac{1}{4}$ pint, $\frac{2}{3}$ cup) white wine.

Boil down, and add $3\frac{1}{2}$ dl. (generous $\frac{1}{2}$ pint, $1\frac{1}{2}$ cups) slightly thickened brown veal or chicken stock. Bring to the boil on the stove, then cook in a hot oven for about 1 hour with the pan covered.

Drain the duckling, remove trussing string, arrange on a serving dish, and garnish. Boil down and strain the braising liquor, spoon a little of it over the duck and serve the rest separately.

Nantes braised duckling may be served with all the garnishes (q.v.) recommended for braised and broiled poultry. The garnishes most suitable for this dish are: *fermière*, *languedocienne*, *macédoine*, *toulousaine*.

Braised Nantes duckling

Braised duckling can also be accompanied by carrots, turnips, celeriac, cucumbers, small glazed onions, peas, tomatoes, etc., sautéed in butter or braised.

Casserole of duckling with various garnishes. CANETON EN CASSEROLE – Prepare like *Chicken casserole*. (See CHICKEN.)

Serve with *bonnefemme*, *paysanne* or some other garnish which should be cooked with the bird in a casserole.

Duckling à la chipolata. CANETON À LA CHIPOLATA – Braise the duckling. When it is nearly done, drain and remove trussing string. Put it back in the casserole with a garnish of 10 braised chestnuts, 10 small glazed onions, 10 lean rashers of blanched and lightly fried bacon, and 18 carrots cut down to the size of olives and glazed. Boil down the braising liquor, strain, pour over the duckling, and finish cooking. Add 10 small chipolata sausages cooked in butter. Serve the duckling surrounded with the garnish arranged in separate groups. Pour over the sauce.

Cold duckling. CANETON FROID – Duckling can be prepared in any manner suitable for cold chicken (see CHICKEN).

Duckling with olives. CANETON AUX OLIVES – Braise the duckling, cooking it until three quarters done. Strain the braising liquor, put the duckling back in it and add 250 g. (9 oz., $1\frac{1}{2}$ cups) stoned, blanched olives. Finish cooking on a slow heat.

Duckling can also be cooked with stuffed olives.

Duckling à l'orange or à la bigarade I. CANETON À L'ORANGE, À LA BIGARADE – Braise a Nantes duckling. Drain, remove trussing string and arrange on a serving dish. Pour over *bigarade sauce* prepared in the following manner. Strain the braising liquor into a small saucepan in which 2 lumps of sugar, moistened with 2 tablespoons (3 tablespoons) vinegar, have previously been cooked to caramel degree. Boil down. Add the juice of 1 orange and $\frac{1}{2}$ lemon. Boil down again and strain. Add the blanched and drained rind of 1 orange and $\frac{1}{2}$ lemon shredded into a fine *julienne* (q.v.).

Duckling à l'orange or à la bigarade II. CANETON À L'ORANGE, À LA BIGARADE – Fry the duckling in butter, keeping it a little underdone. Drain, remove trussing string, and arrange on a serving dish.

Dilute the pan juices with 1 dl. (6 tablespoons, scant $\frac{1}{2}$ cup) white wine. Add 3 dl. ($\frac{1}{2}$ pint, $1\frac{1}{4}$ cups) clear veal stock or *Demi-glace sauce* (see SAUCE). Add sugar and vinegar cooked to caramel degree, as described above, and allow to boil for a few moments. Add the juice of 1 orange, $\frac{1}{2}$ lemon and finish off as described above.

Garnish with peeled slices of orange.

Sauce for *Duckling à l'orange* should be made of the rind of bitter oranges.

Duck pâtés. PÂTÉS DE CANETON – See PÂTÉ.

Duckling with peas I. CANETON AUX PETITS POIS – Brown together in butter 12 small onions and 200 g. (7 oz.) blanched, diced bacon. Remove these from the pan and in the same butter sear a trussed Nantes duckling. Brown it well on all sides, and drain.

Dilute the pan juices with 1 dl. (6 tablespoons, scant $\frac{1}{2}$ cup) white stock. Add $2\frac{1}{2}$ dl. (scant $\frac{1}{2}$ pint, generous cup) veal and chicken stock and put the duckling into this liquor. Add 1 litre ($1\frac{3}{4}$ pints, generous quart) fresh garden peas, the onions, pieces of bacon, and a *bouquet garni* (q.v.). Season and add 1 teaspoon sugar. Simmer gently with the lid on. When cooked, drain the duckling, arrange on a serving dish, and surround with the peas. Boil down the pan juices and pour over the bird.

A lettuce shredded into a *chiffonnade* (q.v.), or left whole and tied with string, can be added to the peas. If left whole, it should be cut into quarters when serving, and arranged on the peas.

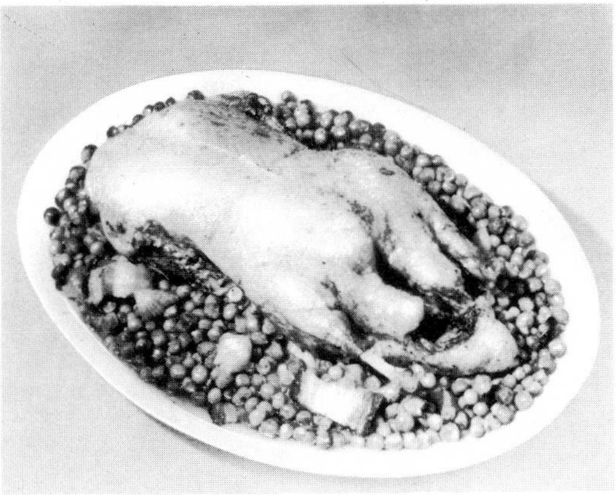

Duckling with peas (*Scarnati*)

Duckling with peas II. CANETON AUX PETITS POIS – Cook the duckling in a fireproof casserole, keeping it a little underdone.

Add 1 litre ($1\frac{3}{4}$ pints, generous quart) fresh garden peas, cooked *à la française* (see PEAS). Leave to infuse for a few moments without allowing to boil.

Roast duckling. CANETON RÔTI – Truss the duckling and roast it in the oven or on a spit. For cooking times see CULINARY METHODS, *Average cooking times for roasts*.

Duckling with sauerkraut. CANETON À LA CHOUCROUTE – This is prepared in the same way as *Duckling à l'alsacienne*. Surround with *sauerkraut* braised in the usual manner. Garnish with pieces of streaky bacon (cooked with the *sauerkraut*) and saveloys, Strasbourg or Frankfurt sausages. Pour the liquor in which the duckling was braised over the bird.

Duckling with turnips (braised). CANETON AUX NAVETS – Brown a trussed Nantes duckling in butter. When it is brown on all sides, take it out of the pan and drain. Remove the butter from the pan and make a sauce of $1\frac{1}{2}$ dl. ($\frac{1}{4}$ pint, $\frac{2}{3}$ cup) dry white wine and 4 dl. ($\frac{3}{4}$ pint, scant 2 cups) *espagnole sauce* (see SAUCE) or veal stock. Add a *bouquet garni* (q.v.). Place the duckling in the sauce and simmer gently.

Put the butter in another pan and add to it 3 or 4 small turnips, cut down to a uniform size. Season and sprinkle with 1 tablespoon sugar, which will enable them to be glazed more quickly. Cook on a brisk fire. Have ready 24 small onions, half cooked in butter.

When the duckling is half cooked drain it and strain the liquor. Put the duckling back into the pan and add the turnips, onions and sauce. Finish cooking in a slow oven.

To serve, garnish the bird and pour the sauce over it. Serve piping hot.

ROUEN DUCK. CANARD ROUENNAIS – See note under DUCK.

Ballottine of Rouen duckling. BALLOTTINE DE CANETON DE ROUEN – Prepare like *Ballottine of duckling*.

Rouen duckling à la bigarade. CANETON ROUENNAIS À LA BIGARADE – Prepare in either of the ways given for *Duckling à l'orange*.

Rouen duckling is rarely braised, but it can in fact be cooked in this manner and is excellent.

Rouen duckling au chambertin. CANETON ROUENNAIS AU CHAMBERTIN – Braise the duckling in liquor based on red wine. When it is nearly cooked, put it into another pan. Add 125 g. (4 oz.) pork or bacon cut in large dice, blanched and lightly fried, and 24 mushroom caps, peeled and tossed in butter.

Boil down the braising liquor in the other pan, strain, pour over the duckling and finish cooking in the oven with the lid on.

Rouen duckling in Champagne. CANETON ROUENNAIS AU CHAMPAGNE – Fry the duckling in butter. When nearly cooked, put it into an earthenware dish. Dilute the pan juices with 3 dl. ($\frac{1}{2}$ pint, $1\frac{1}{4}$ cups) dry Champagne, add a few tablespoons thickened brown veal stock, and pour over the duckling. Finish cooking in the oven with the lid on.

Chaud-froid of Rouen duckling. CHAUD-FROID DE CANETON DE ROUEN – Cook the duckling in the oven, keeping it a little underdone. Remove the legs and cut the breast fillets into strips. Using the carcase and the trimmings, roughly chopped, prepare a brown *Chaud-froid sauce* (see SAUCE, *Compound sauces*) and mix it with aspic jelly, flavoured with Madeira or other liqueur wine.

Coat the pieces of duckling fillets with this half-set sauce. Put on a grid to cool. Decorate with pieces of truffles, white of hard-boiled egg, and pickled tongue. Glaze with jelly.

Arrange in a dish in pyramid shapes. Garnish with chopped jelly and surround the border of the dish with jelly croûtons.

Rouen duckling en chemise I. CANTON ROUENNAIS EN CHEMISE – Remove the breast-bone of a Rouen duckling, stuff it as for *Duckling à la rouennaise*, and truss it. Roast as quickly as possible, for 8 to 12 minutes. Leave to get cold. Enclose the bird in a large pork bladder, previously soaked in cold water, placing the bird with the rump towards the opening of the bladder. Tie the opening with string. Poach in a clear braising stock for 45 minutes.

To serve, take the duckling out of the bladder and proceed as described in the recipe for *Duckling à la rouennaise*.

Rouen duckling en chemise II. CANETON ROUENNAIS EN CHEMISE – Remove the breast-bone, stuff the duck, and truss. Wrap in a cloth which has been soaked in water and wrung out. Tie like a galantine (q.v.). Poach in strong veal broth for 40 to 50 minutes.

Drain, unwrap, and serve surrounded with peeled orange quarters. Serve *rouennaise sauce* (see SAUCE) separately.

Rouen duckling with cherries. CANETON ROUENNAIS AUX CERISES – Truss the duckling and fry it in a pan with butter. When it is nearly cooked, put it into an earthenware dish with 250 g. (9 oz.) morello cherries, stoned. Dilute the pan juices with Madeira, add 1 or 2 tablespoons brown veal stock and pour over the duckling.

1

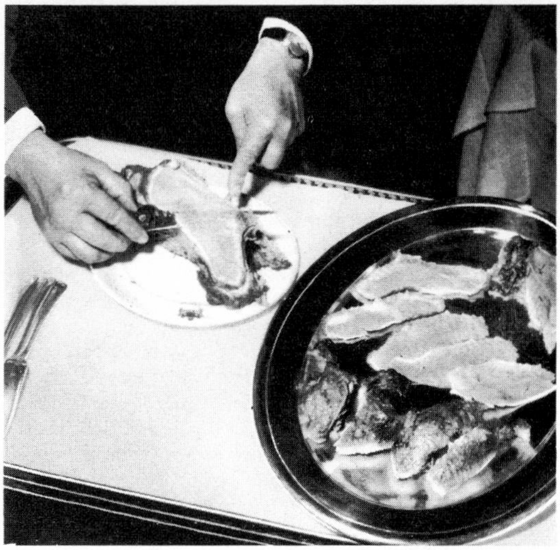

4

2

How to carve roast duck:

1. First cut off the legs
2. Place the bird on its back and cut vertically along the length of the breastbone
3. Cut off the breast meat in long thin slices
4. Repeat the operation on the other side
5. Finally cut off the two wings

(*Larousse*)

3

5

Simmer in the oven for a few minutes. Serve in the same dish.

Rouen duckling (cold). CANETON ROUENNAIS FROID – Rouen duckling, roast or fried, may be served cold garnished with watercress. It should be cooked longer than required for serving it hot.

Galantine of Rouen duckling. GALANTINE DE CANETON DE ROUEN – Prepare like *Galantine of chicken* (see GALANTINE) adding to the forcemeat a quantity of *à gratin forcemeat* (see FORCEMEAT).

Jellied Rouen duckling en daube. CANETON ROUENNAIS EN DAUBE À LA GELÉE – Prepare like *Daube of pheasant in jelly* (see PHEASANT).

Jellied strips of Rouen duckling à l'orange

Jellied strips of Rouen duckling à l'orange. AIGUILLETTES DE CANETON DE ROUEN GLACÉES À L'ORANGE – Prepare the duckling as described in the recipe for *Chaud-froid of Rouen duckling*. Cut the breast fillets into thin strips, and coat with *Chaud-froid sauce à l'andalouse* (see SAUCE). Decorate with truffles and orange peel cut into little strips, and glaze with jelly. Keep in a refrigerator. Using the flesh of the legs, make a mousse as described in the recipe for *Poultry mousse* (see MOUSSE), adding diced truffles. Fill a dome-shaped mould with the mousse and put it on ice to set.

When well chilled, turn it out onto a croûton of crustless bread, spread with butter, on a dish. Cover with duckling strips which have been coated in *chaud-froid sauce*. Spoon a little half-set jelly on the bottom of the dish. Cut oranges into basket-shapes, scoop out the pulp, half-fill with port jelly, decorate with peeled orange sections and arrange round the mousse shape.

Decorate the top by spiking on a skewer topped by half an orange with a big truffle in it.

Chill in the refrigerator.

Rouen duckling Lambertye. CANETON DE ROUEN LAMBERTYE – Proceed as described in the recipe for *Chicken Lambertye* (see CHICKEN), replacing the chicken mousse in that recipe by duck mousse.

Set in brown *Chaud-froid sauce* (see SAUCE).

Rouen duckling mousse I. MOUSSE DE CANETON DE ROUEN – Prepare like *Chicken mousse* (see CHICKEN), replacing the chicken by duck.

Rouen duckling mousse II and mousselines. MOUSSE ET MOUSSELINES DE CANETON ROUENNAIS – Prepare as described in the recipe for *Rouen duckling soufflé* (see below), the mousse, in a charlotte mould, poached in the oven in a *bain-marie* (q.v.); and the *mousselines*, in small moulds, poached in the oven in a *bain-marie*.

Rouen duckling pâté. PÂTÉ DE CANETON DE ROUEN – See PÂTÉ.

Rouen duckling in port. CANETON ROUENNAIS AU PORTO – Truss a Rouen duckling and cook in butter, keeping it slightly underdone. Drain and arrange on a dish. Dilute the pan juices with $2\frac{1}{2}$ dl. (scant $\frac{1}{2}$ pint, generous cup) port, and add $2\frac{1}{2}$ dl. (scant $\frac{1}{2}$ pint, generous cup) thickened brown veal gravy. Bring to the boil, simmer for a few moments, add some butter and strain. Pour a few tablespoons of this sauce over the duck and serve the rest separately.

Rouen duckling can be prepared in the same way with Madeira, Frontignan, or sherry instead of port.

Pressed Rouen duckling. CANETON ROUENNAIS À LA PRESSE – Cook the duckling for 18 to 20 minutes. Remove the legs, which will still be raw. Make a few shallow incisions on the underside of the legs, season with salt, pepper, and a little pounded clove. Brush with butter and grill briskly.

Carve the breast into thin slivers. Arrange these on a dish standing on a hotplate in which 1 dl. (6 tablespoons, scant $\frac{1}{2}$ cup) good red wine has been well boiled down. Season with freshly ground pepper.

Cut up the carcase, sprinkle with good red wine, and put it under a duck press. Add 2 tablespoons (3 tablespoons) brandy to the juice obtained, and pour over the sliced duckling. Scatter a few small pieces of butter on the slices. Heat on the hotplate without allowing the sauce to boil. Put the grilled legs at each end of the dish, and serve.

Duckling à la rouennaise. CANETON À LA ROUENNAISE – Fry 1 tablespoon chopped onion in 125 g. (4 oz., 1 cup) chopped bacon fat, without allowing it to colour. Add the duckling's liver, together with 1 or 2 chicken livers (or ducks' livers, if available), cut into thin slices. Season with salt and pepper, sprinkle with spices and chopped parsley, and fry as quickly as possible. Leave until cold, pound in a mortar, and rub through a sieve. Stuff the duckling with this forcemeat, and truss it. Cook in a very hot oven for 20 to 30 minutes, depending on the size of the bird. Serve with *Rouennaise sauce* (see SAUCE).

To serve *Duckling à la rouennaise*, remove the legs, make a few shallow incisions in them, season and grill. Cut the breast into thin slivers and arrange them on the borders of a buttered dish. Fill the middle of the dish with the stuffing contained in the carcase and put the grilled legs at each end.

Chop the carcase into big pieces, put it under a duck press, sprinkling it with 2 or 3 tablespoons brandy and a dash of lemon juice. Add the juice thus obtained to some *rouennaise sauce*, blend, and pour some over the sliced duckling. Serve the rest of the sauce separately.

Salmis of duckling à la rouennaise. CANETON EN SALMIS À LA ROUENNAISE – Remove the breast-bone and truss the duckling. Put it into a very hot oven to stiffen and sear it. Leave until just warm, then wipe on a cloth.

Remove the legs, make a few shallow incisions on the undersides, season and grill them. Carve the breast into thin slivers and put them in rows on a buttered dish. Sprinkle with 1 tablespoon finely chopped shallot, and season with crushed sea-salt, freshly ground pepper and spices.

Chop up the carcase, sprinkle with $\frac{1}{2}$ glass red wine, and put it under a duck press. Pour the juice obtained over the sliced duckling.

Heat the dish for a moment on the stove and put under the grill to glaze the meat. Place the grilled legs one at each end of the dish, and serve at once.

Different restaurants have different ways of preparing *Salmis of duckling à la rouennaise*. Quite often it is no more than *Duckling à la rouennaise*.

In some restaurants in Rouen, whence this dish originated,

the sliced duckling (cooked from 10 to 12 minutes) is covered with *Red wine sauce* (see SAUCE), spiced with shallots, flavoured with a tablespoon of brandy, and thickened with raw chopped duck liver.

In Duclair, the home of the famous ducklings, a different method is used. Bone the ducklings to the wing joints, put the liver inside the bird, trim and truss it, and roast on the spit for 20 to 22 minutes, depending on size.

Carve the breast into thin slices and arrange them on a dish around the carcase, which has been filled with the following purée: Fry a large chopped onion lightly in butter, sprinkle with port and Burgundy wine, boil down, add the duckling's liver pounded in a mortar and the blood from the carcase. Heat well.

Rouen duckling soufflé. CANETON ROUENNAISE SOUFFLÉ – This is very much a grand-style dish; it is excellent but rather expensive, as 2 ducklings should be used, the larger for serving and the smaller for making a forcemeat to stuff the other.

Truss the larger duck and roast in the oven, keeping it rather underdone. Remove the breast fillets and keep hot. Remove the breast-bone in such a way as to make the carcase hollow. Season the duck inside with salt, pepper, and spices, and sprinkle with 1 tablespoon brandy. Stuff the carcase with a forcemeat of 150 g. (5 oz.) uncooked *foie gras*, the ducks' livers, and the flesh of the second duck, prepared as described in *Mousseline forcemeat* (see FORCEMEAT). Spread this forcemeat in the carcase, piling it up to give the duck its original shape. Cover with buttered paper and tie with string. Lay the stuffed duck in a roasting pan, sprinkle with melted butter and cook in a slow oven for 20 to 25 minutes.

Remove the paper. Arrange the duck on a dish and surround with tartlets baked blind and filled with a *salpicon* (q.v.) of truffles and mushrooms blended with concentrated *Madeira sauce* (see SAUCE). Place a slice of duck on each tartlet and top with a sliver of truffle, heated in butter. Serve with *Rouennaise sauce* or *Périgueux sauce* (see SAUCE).

The same forcemeat can be used for making Rouen duck mousses and *mousselines*. The former are prepared in charlotte moulds with a hole in the middle, the latter in small individual moulds. They are cooked in the oven in a *bain-marie* (q.v.).

The same composition can also be used for preparing *Duck soufflé en timbale*. Put the mixture into buttered soufflé moulds and bake in the oven like an ordinary soufflé (see SOUFFLÉS, *Savoury soufflés*).

Suprêmes of Rouen duckling. SUPRÊMES DE CANETON ROUENNAIS – Remove the breast fillets of a Rouen duckling. Cut each fillet into 2 or 3 pieces lengthways. Beat to flatten them slightly, season with salt and pepper, put in a buttered dish, and cook with the lid on, keeping them rather underdone.

Duck fillets prepared in this manner are served with various garnishes and sauces. They can be prepared *à la bigarade*, with shredded orange and lemon rind and *bigarade sauce*; with morello cherries, stoned and cooked in Madeira with concentrated Madeira-flavoured veal gravy blended with a little butter; garnished with mushrooms sautéed in butter; *au chambertin*, arranged on croûtons fried in butter, garnished with sliced mushrooms fried in butter and slices of truffles in *chambertin sauce; au porto*, arranged on croûtons fried in butter with port sauce poured over them; *à la périgourdine*, arranged on fried croûtons, spread with *foie gras*, garnished with slivers of truffles and served with Madeira, port or sherry sauce; with truffles arranged on croûtons fried in butter, garnished with thick slices of truffles sautéed in butter and served with Madeira sauce *à l'orange*. Also on croûtons fried in butter, garnished with orange rind shredded into *julienne* (q.v.) strips, surrounded with peeled sections of orange, and served with orange sauce.

Terrine of Rouen duckling. TERRINE DE CANETON DE ROUEN – Using duck flesh, fine forcemeat and truffles, prepare like *Terrine of duckling* (see TERRINE).

Timbale of Rouen duckling Voisin. TIMBALE DE CANETON ROUENNAIS VOISIN – This dish was one of the specialities of the famous Voisin restaurant which no longer exists. The recipe was as follows:

Roast a Rouen duckling, keeping it a little underdone. When it is quite cold, remove the breast fillets.

Chop up the carcase and the trimmings and use them for making a *Salmis sauce* (see SAUCE, *Compound brown sauces*). Strain the sauce, remove surplus fat, add to it an equal quantity of meat jelly, boil down, and strain through a muslin cloth.

Coat a *timbale* with this sauce. When it sets, put in a layer of sliced fillets of duckling (previously coated with the same sauce and left to set), alternating with slivers of truffles. Spoon some half-set jelly over each layer and continue in this manner until the *timbale* is filled with alternating rows of sliced duck and truffles.

Finish off with a slightly thicker layer of jelly. Put the *timbale* on ice or in a refrigerator and chill well.

Rouen duckling with truffles. CANETON ROUENNAIS AUX TRUFFES – This method of preparation is suitable only for fillets or *suprêmes* (breasts) of Rouen ducklings.

Cook the duckling in the oven, keeping it a little underdone. Cut the breast fillets into thick slices. Arrange these in a dish with thick slices of truffles which have been tossed in butter. Keep hot.

Chop the carcase and the parings into pieces, moisten with Madeira, port or sherry, and boil down. Add a few tablespoons concentrated *Demi-glace* (see SAUCE). Allow to boil for a few moments, then strain. Bring this sauce to the boil, add 1 tablespoon brandy which has been set alight, and 2 tablespoons (3 tablespoons) butter. Pour the sauce over the duckling fillets.

WILD DUCKS. CANARDS SAUVAGES – Among the wild ducks used in cookery, the most popular, and the biggest, is the *green-head* or *mallard*, known in France as *Canard sauvage* or *Un sauvage*.

This duck, which has succulent flesh, is found in the vicinity of freshwater ponds and lakes from October to March. Its plumage varies, depending on sex, age, and season. The plumage of the male is green and red with touches of brown and grey. The female is brown.

The flesh of the other species of wild ducks, most of which are edible, is less delicate than that of the mallard. They include the *pintail*, the *sheld-duck* and the *gadwell*.

Other water game of the same family, which is defined by the generic term *waterfowl*, include the *spoonbill* or *shoveller-duck*, and the *teal*, a small but excellent bird.

Some waterfowl, for example, the pintail and teal are allowed as Lenten fare, whereas the mallard is considered as meat.

Wild duck à la bigarade. CANARD SAUVAGE À LA BIGARADE – Roast or fry the wild duck and prepare as *Duckling à l'orange*.

Fillets of duck à la bigarade (Plumerey's recipe). FILETS DE CANARD À LA BIGARADE – 'Remove the breast fillets and the legs of 2 wild ducks. Put them into an earthenware dish with salt, coarse-ground pepper, parsley, thyme, bay leaf, chopped shallots, lemon juice and $\frac{1}{4}$ glass good oil. Keep them in this seasoning for 45 minutes before they are required, turning frequently.

'Thread them on a skewer, without packing too tightly,

sprinkle with the seasoning in which they were steeped, and put on a spit.

'As soon as you feel them becoming firm to the touch, take them off the skewer. Wash the fillets and put them one by one into a sauté pan in which a piece of game jelly the size of a walnut has been melted, with an equal amount of butter and the juice of $\frac{1}{2}$ lemon. Arrange and serve with *Bigarade sauce* (see SAUCE).'

Wild duck au chambertin. CANARD SAUVAGE AU CHAMBERTIN – Roast or fry the duck, keeping it a little underdone. Prepare *Chambertin sauce* (see SAUCE), add to it some of the diluted pan juices left over from cooking the duck, and pour over the dish. Garnish with truffles and mushrooms.

Salmis of wild duck (Plumerey's recipe). SALMIS DE CANARD SAUVAGE – 'Cover a wild duck with a *mirepoix* (q.v.), wrap in a piece of paper and put to cook on a spit. After cooking for 30 minutes, unwrap, test to see if the duck is done, and cut up in the usual manner for a *salmis*.

'Put the joints into a casserole, together with the blood which comes out of them, making sure that it neither boils nor dries up, but keeps hot.

'Have some concentrated, thick *Financière sauce* (see SAUCE) ready in a *bain-marie* (q.v.). Put the bones and parings of the duck into a saucepan with $\frac{1}{2}$ glass good red Bordeaux wine, $\frac{1}{4}$ shallot, 1 clove, and a pinch of coarsely ground pepper. Boil down to half, add the *financière sauce*, and cook until it reaches the consistency of a *salmis sauce*. Strain, add 1 tablespoon olive oil and the juice of $\frac{1}{4}$ lemon. Arrange the pieces of duck on heart-shaped croûtons, garnish with sliced truffles and mushrooms, and pour the sauce over.'

Salmis of wild duck à la minute (Plumerey's recipe). SALMIS DE CANARD SAUVAGE À LA MINUTE – Prepare the duck and cook on the spit, as described in the preceding recipe. While it is cooking, chop parsley, mushrooms and shallots very finely, toss them in a pan in butter with salt, pepper, and a little grated nutmeg. Moisten with $\frac{3}{4}$ glass of white Chablis, boil down by half, and add a good tablespoon *Espagnole sauce* (see SAUCE). Remove from heat and add $\frac{1}{2}$ tablespoon of the best mustard.

'Take the duck off the spit, joint it, and put the pieces into a sauté pan, turning them gently. Put a little game jelly and a piece of butter the size of a small walnut into the pan. Serve the duck pieces with the sauce poured over.'

Wild duck à l'orange. CANARD SAUVAGE À L'ORANGE – Fry or roast the duck. Proceed as described in the recipe for *Duckling à l'orange*.

Wild duck in port. CANARD SAUVAGE AU PORTO – Fry or roast the duck and proceed as described in the recipe for *Rouen duckling in port*.

Wild duck à la presse. CANARD SAUVAGE À LA PRESSE – Roast the duck from 18 to 20 minutes. Proceed as described in the recipe for *Pressed Rouen duckling*.

Roast wild duck. CANARD SAUVAGE RÔTI – Roast the duck on brisk heat, either on a spit or in the oven.

Garnish with lemon and orange slices. Dilute the pan juices and serve separately.

Wild duck à la tyrolienne (Plumerey's recipe). CANARD SAUVAGE À LA TYROLIENNE – 'Stew cooking apples and add a little cinnamon and mace to infuse the hot apples. Truss the duck, stuff it with the stewed apples, and sew up the neck and the rump.

Duck press (*La Tour d'Argent. Phot. Nicolas*)

Bring to the boil $\frac{1}{3}$ glass vinegar with a piece of butter the size of a small walnut, $\frac{1}{2}$ coffee-spoon fine sugar, and a little coarsely ground pepper. Baste the duck with this during cooking on the spit, placing a pan beneath it to catch the juices. Cooking should be completed in 30 to 35 minutes. Take the duck off the spit, remove trussing strings and arrange on a dish. Strain the pan juices into a saucepan, heat, add $\frac{1}{2}$ tablespoon redcurrant jelly, and pour this sauce over the duck.'

DUCK PRESS. PRESSE À CANARD – Kitchen utensil, different from a meat press, in that it serves the sole purpose of extracting the juices from the carcase of duck.

DUNAND – There were two master chefs of this name, father and son, of Swiss origin, who were equally famous. The elder Dunand joined the French army and became chef to the prince de Condé. His son succeeded him and became controller of this great household. When the prince emigrated in 1793 the younger Dunand followed him, and for twelve years was in charge of his kitchens.

Then, being a sick man and with a nostalgic longing to see Paris once more, he returned to France. Having re-established himself, he entered the service of Napoleon I, as chef. He remained in the service of the Emperor until he left for Saint Helena but, to his great sorrow, was unable to go into exile with his master on account of his health, and he retired to Switzerland. He left to the Lausanne Museum the Emperor's personal table-service, which had been presented to him by Napoleon.

It is claimed that we owe the invention of the dish known as *Chicken sauté Marengo* to Dunand the younger.

DUXELLES – The name derives from *Uxel*, a small town of the Côtes-du-Nord. Some believe that this dish was so-called because it was created by La Varenne, an official of the household of the Marquis d'Uxelles.

Duxelles of mushrooms. DUXELLES DE CHAMPIGNONS – Clean and trim 125 g. (4 oz.) mushrooms, or peelings and stalks, and chop them finely. Put them in a cloth and twist tightly to extract all liquid. Lightly brown in butter half a chopped onion. Add 2 chopped shallots, salt, pepper, nutmeg and the squeezed mushrooms. Stir over brisk heat until the mushrooms are cooked. Leave to get cold and keep in a cold place, covered with buttered paper.

EARTH NUTS. TERRE-NOIX – Tuberous root of a plant whose scientific name is *Carum bulbocastanum*. It is black outside and white inside, tastes like chestnut and is prepared in the same ways. The seeds of the plant are sometimes used in place of caraway.

EASTER EGGS – See EGGS.

ÉCHAUDÉ – Pastry made with dough which is first poached in water, then dried in the oven.

The invention of this pastry is attributed to Charles-Paul Favart (father of the French dramatist) who, in 1710, was established as a pastry-cook in the rue de la Verrerie in Paris. It is probable that Favart's 'invention' consisted merely of improving and altering the shape of this pastry and thereby bringing it into fashion, for it was known in France long before Favart's time. It is mentioned in a charter of 1210, where it is described as 'buns called eschaudati', a name given to it because hot water was poured onto the dough to make it rise.

Carême's recipe is as follows: 500 g. (18 oz., $4\frac{1}{2}$ cups) flour, $1\frac{1}{2}$ dl. ($\frac{1}{4}$ pint, $\frac{2}{3}$ cup) oil, $1\frac{1}{2}$ teaspoons salt, 2 dl. ($\frac{1}{3}$ pint, scant cup) water.

Mix and knead the dough, and leave to stand, wrapped in a cloth, for 2 hours. Divide into small pieces, shape into balls, and press three fingers into them to make them hollow. Poach in water. Drain and dry in a cloth, and leave to dry thoroughly for 2 hours.

Bake in a hot oven for 25 to 30 minutes.

ÉCHIRÉ – One of the best French butters, made in the commune of this name (Deux Sèvres).

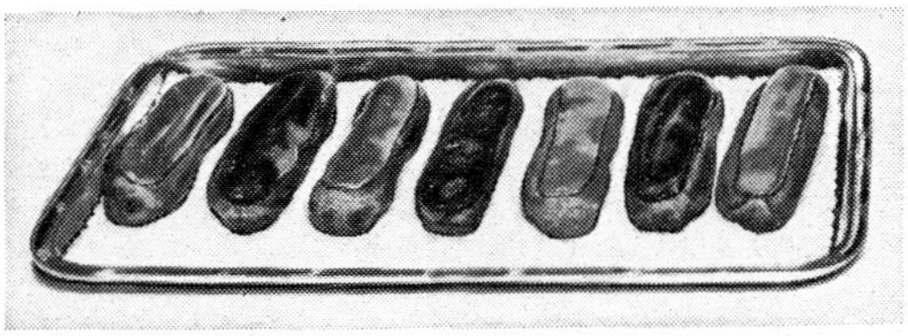

Coffee and chocolate éclairs (*Larousse*)

ÉCLAIR – Small pastry made with *Chou paste* (see DOUGH) filled with *French pastry cream* (see CREAM) flavoured with vanilla, coffee, or chocolate, and iced with *Fondant icing* (see ICING).

Pipe the éclairs on to a baking sheet in the shape of fingers. Brush with egg and bake in a hot oven. When the éclairs are cold, slit them along one side, and fill them, using a forcing-bag, with French pastry cream flavoured with vanilla, coffee or chocolate. Ice the top of the éclairs with hot fondant icing, flavoured to blend with the filling.

Éclairs can also be filled with different mixtures, such as *Crème Chiboust* (see CREAM), *Chantilly*, purée of *marrons glacés*, or *salpicons* of various kinds of fruit blended in French pastry cream.

Small éclairs à la hollandaise. PETITS ÉCLAIRS À LA HOLLANDAISE – These éclairs are served as *hors-d'œuvre*.

Make the éclairs of unsweetened *chou paste* and pipe them onto a baking sheet; they should be smaller than ordinary éclairs – about 4 cm. ($1\frac{1}{2}$ inches) long. Brush with egg and bake in a slow oven. Leave until they are quite cold.

Fillet a large herring, soak to remove all salt and dry in a cloth. Pound in a mortar, adding 2 yolks of hard-boiled eggs, and 75 g. (3 oz., 6 tablespoons) butter. Rub through a fine sieve. Add $\frac{1}{2}$ tablespoon chopped chives and $\frac{1}{2}$ tablespoon chopped parsley, and work to a smooth paste with a spatula. Slit the sides of the éclairs and fill them with this mixture, using a pastry forcing-bag. Brush the tops with melted butter and sprinkle with chopped yolk of hard-boiled eggs and chopped parsley.

ÉCUELLE – Deep dish used for serving vegetables.

EDAM – See CHEESE.

EEL. ANGUILLE – Snake-like fish with viscous and slippery skin. When caught in fast-flowing water its flesh is very delicate. It can be recognised by its light-brown skin, with shades of brown on the back and silver on the belly. The flesh of eels from a pool or stagnant water is slimy; the skin is dark brown on the back and dirty yellow on the belly.

Eels must be kept alive until the time of preparation. They should be kept in a fish pond or a large bucket of water which should be frequently changed. Eel's flesh is very nourishing, though a little heavy. It becomes more easily digestible if the layer of fat between the skin and the flesh is removed before cooking.

There are several varieties of sea eels, the best of which is *moray*. The *conger eel* is another sea eel which is chiefly used for *bouillabaisse* (q.v.). but it also makes excellent *matelotes* (q.v.).

Lamprey is similar to eel, and runs up rivers in spring. Its flesh is delicate in flavour and can be prepared in the same way as eel.

Eel in an aquarium

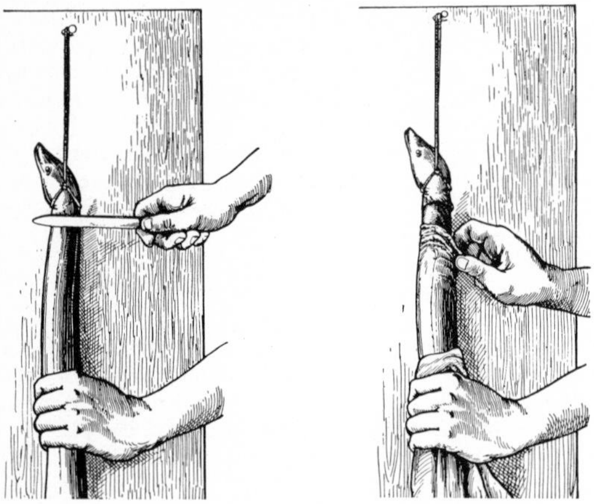

How to skin an eel

Before skinning the fish, kill it by banging the head hard against a stone. As soon as it is dead, hang it up on a hook by a string tied at the neck. Make a circular incision below the string. Turn the skin back all round the neck in such a way as to be able to hold it with a cloth and then tear the skin off.

Trim the eel and clean it by making a light incision along the belly. Cut off the head, which is thrown away, and cut the fish into slices or leave whole, as directed in the recipe.

Instead of skinning the eel whole, you can cut it into pieces. Grill them for a few moments under a brisk flame, turning them to catch the skin on all sides. Under the action of the heat the skin blisters and can be easily taken off. This method of skinning also has the advantage of removing the excess fat.

An eel weighing about 750 g. ($1\frac{3}{4}$ lb.) can be cooked in the following way in a wine *court-bouillon* (white or red wine) with vegetables. Cut the eel into 6-cm. ($2\frac{1}{2}$-inch) pieces, or leave whole, and cook in a well-buttered pan on a foundation of 50 g. (2 oz., $\frac{1}{2}$ cup) each of chopped onions and carrots per litre (scant quart, generous quart) liquid. Press well to make the fish lie flat. Add a crushed clove of garlic and a *bouquet garni* (q.v.). Season with salt and freshly ground pepper. Cover the fish with the wine and cook slowly on the side of the stove.

Eel cooked in *court-bouillon* can afterwards be prepared *à la bourguignonne*, fried, grilled, *à la tartare*, *en matelote*, in a white or brown sauce, etc. Small eels, and fillets or cutlets intended for frying are not cooked first in *court-bouillon*.

Eel à l'anglaise. ANGUILLE À L'ANGLAISE – Cut a boned eel into 5-cm. (2-inch) pieces. Flatten, and marinate for 30 minutes in oil, lemon juice or vinegar, salt and pepper. Coat the pieces with egg and breadcrumbs, and deep-fry. Serve with *Butter sauce* (see SAUCE) to which a little anchovy butter has been added.

Ballottine of eel, or stuffed eel. BALLOTTINE D'ANGUILLE (ANGUILLE FARCIE) – This dish is served hot or cold. When hot, it can be served with the garnishes and sauces recommended for large braised fish. When cold, all the recipes given for cold fish can be applied to it.

Cold ballottine of eel is also called galantine of eel.

Cold ballottine or galantine of eel, or eel sausage, or stuffed jellied eel. BALLOTTINE D'ANGUILLE FROIDE, GALANTINE, SAUCISSON D'ANGUILLE, ANGUILLE FARCIE À LA GELÉE – Bone the eel and fill with stuffing and wrap as described in *Hot ballottine of eel* (see below). Poach gently in red or white wine *court-bouillon* (q.v.).

Drain and unwrap, then rewrap the fish in the muslin cloth, rinsed out. Tie with string, tightening it a little, and put under a press. Leave for 12 hours to get quite cold.

Unwrap the ballottine, dry, trim, and coat with jelly or *Chaud-froid* (see SAUCE). Serve and garnish as described in the recipe.

The fish stock for cold ballottine of eel is made with red or white wine. After the ballottine is cooked, the stock is clarified as described in the recipe for *Fish jelly stock* (see JELLY), and used for coating and garnishing the eel. When the ballottine is prepared only in jelly, serve completely covered in its jelly, the dish being placed on a larger one and surrounded by crushed ice.

Hot ballottine of eel. BALLOTTINE D'ANGUILLE CHAUDE – Prepare a large eel, flatten slightly, season with salt, pepper and spices. Fill with forcemeat, stuffing the fish so as to retain its shape. Wrap the ballottine in a muslin cloth and tie it at both ends and in 3 or 4 places in the middle.

Put onto the grill of a buttered fish kettle. Cover with white or red wine *court-bouillon*. Bring to the boil, cover the pan, and poach gently. Drain and unwrap the eel. Place in a fireproof dish and glaze in the oven, basting frequently with the thickened pan juices.

The wine liquor for boiling ballottine of eel, which usually has diced vegetables sautéed in butter added to it, should be further strengthened by adding the bones and trimmings from other fish, if possible. After cooking the ballottine, the liquor should be used as a basis for the sauce which is to accompany it.

Stuffing for ballottine of eel will be found under *Forcemeats with fish* (see FORCEMEATS).

In addition to the recipes listed below for ballottine of eel all those given for large braised fish can be applied to it. The fish can be accompanied by a simple garnish such as mushrooms, various croquettes, *macédoine* of vegetables, potatoes prepared in various ways, rice pilaf, or risotto.

Ballottine of eel à l'ancienne. BALLOTTINE D'ANGUILLE À L'ANCIENNE – Stuff the eel with whiting forcemeat to which diced truffles have been added. Prepare as described above and poach in *court-bouillon* with white wine.

Drain, glaze, and arrange on a foundation of fish forcemeat or on a croûton of bread fried in butter. Surround with *à l'ancienne garnish* (see GARNISHES). Cover with *Normande sauce* (see SAUCE) diluted with the boiled down liquor in which the eel was cooked and finished with finely shredded *mirepoix* (q.v.) of vegetables and Madeira.

Ballottine of eel à la bourguignonne. BALLOTTINE D'ANGUILLE À LA BOURGUIGNONNE – Stuff the eel with a pike or whiting forcemeat mixed with chopped parsley. Prepare as described under *Hot ballottine of eel* and poach in a red wine *court-bouillon*. Drain, glaze, and arrange on a croûton of crustless bread fried in butter. Garnish *à la bourguignonne* (see GARNISHES) and cover with *Bourguignonne sauce* (see SAUCE) made with the liquor left over from cooking the fish.

Ballottine of eel à la gauloise. BALLOTTINE D'ANGUILLE À LA GAULOISE – Stuff the eel with pike or whiting forcemeat mixed with a *salpicon* (q.v.) of truffles and mushrooms. Prepare as described in *Hot ballottine of eel* and poach in white wine *court-bouillon*. Drain, and arrange on a crustless croûton of bread fried in butter. Surround with artichoke hearts filled with carps' soft roes cooked in butter, and pastry boats filled with *Crayfish tail ragoût à la Nantua* (see CRAYFISH).

Boil down the liquor in which the eel was cooked, thicken with *Espagnole sauce* (see SAUCE), add butter, strain, and pour over the dish.

Bastion of eel, after Carême

Bastion of eel. BASTION D'ANGUILLE – Bone 2 large eels, fill them with a pike or whiting stuffing and diced truffles. Wrap in a piece of muslin and tie with string. Cook in white wine and well-flavoured fish stock. Drain, unwrap, and cool under a press.

Cut the eels into pieces about 10 cm. (4 inches) long, and coat with *Chaud-froid sauce* (see SAUCE) prepared with the liquor in which the fish was cooked. Decorate with truffles and small pieces of hard-boiled egg whites. Glaze with liquid jelly. Arrange on a bed of cooked rice or on buttered croûtons of bread, placing the pieces upright, next to each other. Garnish the border of the dish with halved hard-boiled eggs and jelly croûtons.

Poached fillets of sole, cooled under a press and cut to look like loopholes, can be used as decoration for bastions of eel. The holes should be filled in with truffles, jelly croûtons, and *Montpellier butter* (see BUTTER, *Compound butters*). These dishes are prepared for grand occasions.

Eel à la bonne femme. ANGUILLE À LA BONNE FEMME – Place an eel of average weight, either cut in pieces or left whole and rolled into a ring, in a pan on a foundation of 4 tablespoons (5 tablespoons) chopped onion lightly fried in butter. Season with salt and pepper, add a *bouquet garni* and moisten with 3 dl. ($\frac{1}{2}$ pint, $1\frac{1}{4}$ cups) white wine. Poach gently, with the lid on the pan, for 25 minutes.

Drain the eel and arrange on croûtons of bread fried in butter. Garnish with diced potatoes fried in butter.

Boil down the pan juices by half, blend with 1 tablespoon kneaded butter, strain, and pour over the fish. Sprinkle with chopped parsley.

Collared eel, cold. ROULADE D'ANGUILLE, FROIDE – Bone and stuff an eel, make into a ring, and proceed as described in the recipe for *Ballottine of eel, cold.*

Collared eel à l'angevine. ROULADE D'ANGUILLE À L'ANGEVINE – Skin and bone an eel and season with salt and pepper. Stuff with pike forcemeat bound with an egg and a *salpicon* (q.v.) of mushrooms and truffles. Reshape the eel, wrap it in rashers of bacon, make into a ring and tie with string.

Fry sliced onion and carrot lightly in butter. Put the eel in a pan on this bed of vegetables, together with a leek, a branch of savory and a large *bouquet garni.* Cover the fish with white Anjou wine (not too sweet). Bring to the boil and remove scum. Simmer gently for 35 minutes with the pan covered.

Drain the fish. Unwrap and put it into another pan with peeled mushrooms which have been tossed in butter. Make a white *roux* (q.v.) of 50 g. (2 oz., $\frac{1}{4}$ cup) butter and 50 g. (2 oz., $\frac{1}{2}$ cup) flour. Dilute with the strained pan juices, blend well, and add the parings of the mushrooms. Boil down on full heat, and add $3\frac{1}{2}$ dl. (generous $\frac{1}{2}$ pint, $1\frac{1}{2}$ cups) fresh cream. Simmer until the sauce reaches the desired consistency, and add 100 g. (4 oz., $\frac{1}{2}$ cup) *Crayfish butter* (see BUTTER, *Compound butters*).

Collared eel à la bordelaise. ROULADE D'ANGUILLE À LA BORDELAISE – Stuff the eel with *Fish forcemeat* (see FORCEMEAT) flavoured with anchovy butter to which has been added chopped parsley. Make the eel into a ring and poach in a red Bordeaux wine *court-bouillon.* Drain, arrange on a dish, and put a pyramid of cooked *cèpes* in the middle.

Thicken the pan juices with kneaded butter, strain, as indicated for thin *Bordelaise sauce* (see SAUCE) and pour over the fish. Garnish with heart-shaped croûtons fried in butter.

Pieces of stuffed eel *à la bordelaise* are prepared in the same manner.

Collared eel à la royale. ROULADE D'ANGUILLE À LA ROYALE – Make a medium-sized eel into a ring, and poach in white wine *court-bouillon* with a *mirepoix* (q.v.) of vegetables. Leave to get cold in its liquor. Drain, dry, and coat with *Villeroi sauce* (see SAUCE). Fry in deep fat and drain.

Fill the centre with soft roes *à la Villeroi.* Surround with dressed crayfish cooked in *court bouillon,* alternating with bunches of fried parsley. Serve with *Normande sauce* (see SAUCE) to which chopped truffles have been added.

Eel coulibiac (Russian cookery). COULIBIAC D'ANGUILLE – Follow the recipe given for *Coulibiac of salmon* (see SALMON), replacing the salmon by boned, sliced eel.

Little eel coulibiacs. PETITS COULIBIACS D'ANGUILLE – See SALMON, *Small coulibiacs of salmon.*

Eel in cream with paprika, or à la hongroise. ANGUILLE À LA CRÈME, AU PAPRIKA, DITE À LA HONGROISE – Cut an eel into pieces and put them in a saucepan on a foundation of shredded onion lightly fried in butter. Sprinkle with paprika, add a *bouquet garni* and season.

Cover the fish with white wine and bring to the boil. Cover the pan and cook for 20 minutes. About 8 minutes before the end of cooking, add peeled mushrooms heads. Drain, arrange each piece of eel on a croûton of fried bread, and garnish with the mushrooms. Keep hot.

Boil down the pan juices by half and strain. Add 2 tablespoons (3 tablespoons) thin *Velouté sauce* (see SAUCE) and 2 dl. ($\frac{1}{3}$ pint, scant cup) cream. Cook until the sauce coats the surface of a spoon. Add 75 g. (3 oz., 6 tablespoons) butter, strain, and pour over the fish.

Eel à la diable. ANGUILLE À LA DIABLE – Make a medium-sized eel into a ring. Poach in white wine *court-bouillon,* and leave to cool in the liquor. Drain, dry, coat with mustard, sprinkle with melted butter, and dip in breadcrumbs mixed with a pinch of cayenne pepper. Sprinkle again with melted butter and grill gently.

Surround with a border of gherkins and half slices of

decoratively cut lemon. Serve with *Diable sauce* (see SAUCE).

Eel à la fermière. ANGUILLE À LA FERMIÈRE – Cut an eel into pieces and put them in a pan on a foundation of 2 dl. ($\frac{1}{3}$ pint, scant cup) of a *fondue* (q.v.) of vegetables. Season with salt and pepper. Moisten with $2\frac{1}{2}$ dl. (scant $\frac{1}{2}$ pint, generous cup) white wine and add a *bouquet garni.* Bring to the boil, cover the pan, and cook for 25 to 30 minutes. Drain, and arrange the pieces of eel on fried croûtons of bread. Boil down the pan juices, thicken with cream, and pour over the fish.

Fricassée of eel. ANGUILLE EN FRICASSÉE – Cut an eel into pieces of about 6 to 7 cm. ($2\frac{1}{2}$ inches), season with salt and pepper, and put into a well-buttered pan. Add 12 well-blanched onions and a *bouquet garni.* Moisten with water and white wine in equal proportions. Bring to the boil, cover the pan, and simmer for 25 to 30 minutes. About 5 minutes before the end of cooking add 10 sliced mushrooms.

Drain the fish, arrange on a shallow dish, and garnish with the well-drained onions and mushrooms. Strain the pan juices, add 3 tablespoons (scant $\frac{1}{4}$ cup) thin *Velouté sauce* (see SAUCE) and boil down by half.

Add 2 egg yolks mixed with 1 dl. (6 tablespoons, scant $\frac{1}{2}$ cup) cream and 50 g. (2 oz., $\frac{1}{4}$ cup) butter. Strain, and pour over the fish. Garnish with heart-shaped croûtons fried in butter.

Fried eel. ANGUILLE FRITE – Skin small eels, make light incisions on the backs, and twist into rings or figures of eight. Secure with skewers. Soak in milk, dredge with flour and fry in deep fat. Garnish with fried parsley and quarters of lemon.

Fried eel Orly. ANGUILLE FRITE ORLY – Slice an eel into fillets, flatten, season, dip in a light batter, and dry. Garnish with fried parsley and serve with *Tomato sauce* (see SAUCE). The eel slices can be dipped in beaten egg and breadcrumbs instead of butter.

Gallantine of eel arranged in a coil, after Carême

Galantine of eel arranged in a coil. GALANTINE D'ANGUILLE EN VOLUTE – Bone a large eel. Stuff with *Pike forcemeat à la crème* (see FORCEMEAT) and with a *salpicon* (q.v.) of fillets of sole to which truffles have been added. Twist the eel, coiling it upwards into a dome shape, and secure with string to help it keep this shape. Cook in a well-flavoured white wine fish stock.

Drain, and leave to cool. Cover with *Chaud-froid sauce* (see SAUCE) prepared with the liquor in which the fish was cooked. Decorate with truffles and hard-boiled egg white. Glaze with fish jelly. Serve on a bed of cooked rice, or on buttered bread croûtons.

Galantine of jellied eel. GALANTINE D'ANGUILLE À LA GÉLEE – Another name for *Cold ballottine of eel.*

Grilled eel maître d'hôtel. ANGUILLE GRILLÉE MAÎTRE D'HÔTEL – Prepare the eel as described for *Eel à la diable,* omitting the mustard. Cover with softened *Maître d'hôtel butter* (see BUTTER, *Compound butters*).

Grilled eel can be served with all the sauces recommended for grilled fish.

Eel à l'italienne. ANGUILLE À L'ITALIENNE – Cut a medium-sized eel in uniform pieces, season, and fry briskly in oil to stiffen the fish. Remove from the pan, and in the same oil brown 2 tablespoons (3 tablespoons) chopped onion. When nearly done, add 1 teaspoon chopped shallots and 125 g. (4 oz.) diced mushrooms or mushroom stalks. Put the eel back into the pan, add 1 dl. (6 tablespoons, scant $\frac{1}{2}$ cup) white wine and $2\frac{1}{2}$ dl. (scant $\frac{1}{2}$ pint, generous cup) tomato sauce. Simmer gently, with the lid on the pan, for 25 to 30 minutes. To serve, sprinkle with chopped parsley, chervil and tarragon.

Eel en matelote. ANGUILLE EN MATELOTE – Cut a skinned eel into pieces and prepare as described for *Matelote à la marinière* or *à la meunière* (see MATELOTE).

Eel en matelote à la normande. ANGUILLE EN MATELOTE À LA NORMANDE – Cut an eel into pieces and proceed as described for *Matelote à la normande* (see MATELOTE).

Eel à la meunière. ANGUILLE À LA MEUNIÈRE – Cut small eels into 10-cm. (4-inch) pieces. Season, dredge with flour and fry in butter. Scatter chopped parsley on top, sprinkle with lemon juice, and cover with *Noisette butter* (see BUTTER, *Compound butters*).

Hot eel pie (English cookery). PÂTÉ CHAUD D'ANGUILLE À L'ANGLAISE – Cut trimmed fillets of eel into slices of about 5 cm. (2 inches). Blanch in salted water, drain, and leave to cool. Season with salt, pepper, and grated nutmeg, and sprinkle with chopped parsley.

Arrange the eel slices in a pie dish, alternating with layers of sliced hard-boiled eggs. Cover the fish with white wine, and add a few dabs of butter. Cover with *Puff pastry* (see DOUGH). Brush with beaten egg, crimp the edges, and make a hole in the middle of the pastry to allow steam to escape. Bake in a moderate oven for $1\frac{1}{2}$ hours.

To serve, pour into the pie a few tablespoons thin *Demi-glace* (see SAUCE).

Hot eel pie aux fines herbes, called à la ménagère. PÂTÉ CHAUD AUX FINES HERBES DITE À LA MÉNAGÈRE – Cut eel slices into 5-cm. (2-inch) pieces. Flatten lightly and season with salt, pepper and spices. Put in a dish and sprinkle with white wine, a little brandy and a dash of olive oil. Leave in a cool place to marinate for 2 hours.

Drain and dry the pieces, fry them briskly in butter, and sprinkle liberally with chopped shallots and parsley. Remove the pan from the heat and pour into it the marinade. Leave to stand until quite cold.

Line a pie dish with pastry. Cover with a layer of pike forcemeat with chopped parsley added. Place the eel pieces on top, alternating with layers of the forcemeat. Sprinkle each layer with the marinade and finish with a 2-cm. ($\frac{3}{4}$-inch) layer of forcemeat. Sprinkle with melted butter and cover with pastry. Decorate the top with pastry cut in fancy shapes. Make an opening to allow steam to escape. Brush with egg, and bake in a moderate oven for 2 hours.

Before serving, pour a few tablespoons thin *Demi glace* (see SAUCE) through the opening into the dish.

Hot eel pie à la Nantua. PÂTÉ CHAUD D'ANGUILLE À LA NANTUA – Proceed as described in the recipe for *Hot eel pie aux fines herbes,* using eel slices studded with truffles, pike forcemeat flavoured with *Crayfish butter* (see BUTTER, *Compound butters*), and crayfish tails.

Pour into the pie a few tablespoons thin *Velouté sauce* (see SAUCE) flavoured with crayfish butter.

Hot eel pie with truffles. PÂTÉ CHAUD D'ANGUILLE AUX TRUFFES – Proceed as described in the recipe for *Hot eel pie aux fines herbes,* using slices of eel studded with truffles, and a mixture of pike forcemeat and diced truffles, alternating with thick slices of truffles.

Cold eel pie (English cookery). PÂTÉ FROID D'ANGUILLE À

Eel en matelote (*Robert Carrier*)

L'ANGLAISE – Proceed as described in the recipe for *Hot eel pie*. Leave to cool for several hours before serving.

Cold eel pie à la ménagère. PÂTÉ FROID D'ANGUILLE À LA MÉNAGÈRE – Proceed as described in the recipe for *Hot eel pie aux fines herbes*. When the pie is quite cold, pour in through the opening in the pastry, liquid aspic jelly made from fish bones. Leave for 12 hours to get cold again.

Cold eel pie with truffles. PÂTÉ FROID D'ANGUILLE AUX TRUFFES – As *Hot eel pie with truffles*. Finish with fish aspic jelly based on truffle essence. Leave for 12 hours to get cold.

Eel à la piémontaise. ANGUILLE À LA PIÉMONTAISE – Prepare a medium-sized eel, or eel slices, as described in the recipe for *Grilled eel maître d'hôtel*. Arrange on a foundation of *Risotto à la piémontaise* (see RICE). Surround with a border of *Tomato sauce* (see SAUCE).

Eel à la poulette. ANGUILLE À LA POULETTE – Fry 2 tablespoons (3 tablespoons) chopped onion gently in butter. Add eel slices, cooking them for a minute or two in the butter. Sprinkle with salt and pepper, and 1 tablespoon flour. Cover the fish with white wine and add a *bouquet garni*. Simmer gently, with the lid on the pan, for 25 to 30 minutes. About 10 minutes before serving add 12 peeled, sliced mushrooms. Serve the fish garnished with the mushrooms. Thicken the pan juices with egg yolks, as described for *Poulette sauce* (see SAUCE). Strain, pour over the fish, and sprinkle with chopped parsley.

Eel à la provençale. ANGUILLE À LA PROVENÇALE – Fry 2 tablespoons (3 tablespoons) chopped onion gently in oil, add eel slices and toss in the fried onion. Season with salt and pepper, add 4 peeled, deseeded, chopped tomatoes, a *bouquet garni*, and a little crushed garlic. Moisten with 1 dl. (6 tablespoons, scant $\frac{1}{2}$ cup) white wine. Simmer gently with the lid on the pan for 25 to 30 minutes. About 10 minutes before serving add 20 black olives. Simmer slowly. Sprinkle with chopped parsley just before serving.

Eel with risotto. ANGUILLE AU RISOTTO. See *Eel à la piémontaise*.

Eel à la romaine. ANGUILLE À LA ROMAINE – Cut a medium-size eel into 5-cm. (2-inch) pieces. Season with salt and pepper and fry briskly in butter. Add 350 g. (12 oz., $2\frac{1}{4}$ cups) freshly shelled garden peas, a small lettuce shredded into a *chiffonade* (q.v.), 50 g. (2 oz., $\frac{1}{4}$ cup) butter and 2 tablespoons (3 tablespoons) white wine. Cook slowly in an uncovered pan.

Just before serving, blend in $\frac{1}{2}$ tablespoon kneaded butter.

Eel on skewers à l'anglaise. ANGUILLE EN BROCHETTE À L'ANGLAISE – Marinate eel pieces in oil, lemon juice, pepper, salt, and chopped parsley for 1 hour. Drain, dredge in flour, dip in egg, and roll in breadcrumbs. Thread on metal skewers, putting a slice of fat bacon between each piece of fish. Grill on a low flame.

Garnish with parsley, and half slices of decoratively cut lemon. Serve with *Tartare sauce* (see SAUCE).

Eel à la tartare I. ANGUILLE À LA TARTARE – Cook eel slices in white wine *court-bouillon*. Leave to cool in this liquor. Drain, dry, dip in egg and breadcrumbs, and deep-fry. Garnish with fried parsley and serve with *Tartare sauce* (see SAUCE).

Eel à la tartare II. ANGUILLE À LA TARTARE – Cook the eel as described above. Drain, dry, coat with melted butter, and roll in finely grated breadcrumbs. Sprinkle with melted butter and grill on a gentle heat.

Surround with a border of gherkins and half slices of decoratively cut lemon. Serve with *Tartare sauce* (see SAUCE).

Hot eel tourte. TOURTE CHAUDE D'ANGUILLE – Proceed as described in the recipe for *Hot eel pie aux fines herbes*, using a pie dish with slightly raised edges.

Cold eel tourte. TOURTE FROIDE D'ANGUILLE – Proceed as described in the recipe for *Cold eel pie à la ménagère*, using a pie dish with slightly raised edges.

Cold eel tourte Rabelais. TOURTE FROIDE D'ANGUILLE RABELAIS – Bone an eel, flatten it, and put it into a shallow dish with salt, pepper and spices. Sprinkle with a few tablespoons white wine, a little brandy, and olive oil. Leave for 1 hour to marinate in a cool place.

Stuff the eel with whiting forcemeat (see FORCEMEAT, *Fish forcemeat II*) in alternate layers with shelled crayfish tails, olives stuffed with anchovy fillets, and pieces of truffle. Line with pie pastry a pie dish which has slightly raised edges. Cover the pastry with a layer of whiting forcemeat mixed with chopped parsley. Reshape the eel and put it into the pie dish.

Fill the middle of the pie with small rolled fillets of sole, half of them stuffed with whiting forcemeat mixed with *Crayfish butter* (see BUTTER, *Compound butters*), the other half with whiting forcemeat mixed with a purée of truffles. Cover the whole with a layer of whiting forcemeat *aux fines herbes* (see FORCEMEAT, *Fish forcemeat II*). Top the pie with pastry, seal the edges, and decorate with pastry cut in fancy shapes. Make an opening in the pie to allow steam to escape. Brush with beaten egg and bake in a moderate oven for about 1 hour. Leave to get quite cold. Pour in a few tablespoons fish aspic jelly.

Eel à la tyrolienne. ANGUILLE À LA TYROLIENNE – Cook the eel as described in the recipe for *Grilled eel maître d'hôtel*. Arrange on a *fondue* (q.v.) of tomatoes. Garnish with onion rings fried in butter. Sprinkle with chopped parsley.

Eels au vert. ANGUILLES AU VERT – Skin 2 eels and divide into 5-cm (2-inch) pieces. Fry 2 handfuls of spinach leaves, a few tarragon leaves, 2 tablespoons (3 tablespoons) pounded parsley leaves, a pinch of burnet, and a few sage leaves in 50 g. (2 oz., $\frac{1}{4}$ cup) butter. Toss the eel pieces in this mixture for a few minutes. Season with salt, freshly ground pepper, and a small pinch of powdered thyme and bay leaf.

Cover with 5 dl. (scant pint, $2\frac{1}{4}$ cups) white wine. Bring to the boil. Simmer, with the lid on the pan, away from the direct heat, for 10 minutes. Bind with 3 egg yolks and a dash of lemon juice. Transfer to an earthenware dish and keep in a very cold place.

EFFERVESCENCE – The release of gas in a liquid.

EGG-HOLDER. OEUFRIER – Utensil used for soft-boiling eggs.

EGGNOG. LAIT DE POULE – Nourishing drink made from egg yolk mixed with $\frac{1}{2}$ litre (scant pint, $2\frac{1}{4}$ cups) sweetened water or milk, flavoured with orange-flower water, vanilla, or grated nutmeg, and laced with rum or brandy.

The Germans make a beer eggnog which they call *biersuppe*. This is prepared as follows:

Boil 2 litres ($3\frac{1}{2}$ pints, $4\frac{1}{2}$ pints) beer with 500 g. (18 oz., $2\frac{1}{4}$ cups) sugar, a pinch of salt, a little grated lemon rind and a pinch of cinnamon. Add 8 egg yolks mixed with 1 tablespoon cold milk. Strain and chill. Just before serving add fried black bread croûtons and 100 g. (4 oz., $\frac{2}{3}$ cup) each of raisins and currants which have been cooked in 5 dl. (scant pint, $2\frac{1}{4}$ cups) water and well drained.

EGGPLANT – See AUBERGINE.

EGGS. OEUFS – The eggs of fish, birds and even reptiles can all be used as food. Hens' eggs, however, are mostly used in cookery, and it is with them that the following article mainly deals. Eggs are very nutritious. They are often eaten raw, particularly in country districts.

Composition of eggs – The average weight of a hen's egg

is 50 g. (2 oz.). The shell weighs about 12 per cent of the total weight of the egg and is made of a calcareous, porous substance which is pervious to air, water, and smells. It is lined with a delicate, pellucid membrane which separates itself from the shell at the larger end of the egg to form the air chamber. The size of this chamber is in inverse proportion to the freshness of the egg – the fresher the egg the smaller the chamber.

The albumen, or white of the egg, is a thick, viscous, transparent liquid, with a high percentage of water, and some mineral substances. Albumen is soluble in cold water, congeals at 70°C. (158°F.) and remains from then on insoluble. It forms about 58 per cent of the total weight of the egg.

The vitellus, or yolk of the egg (30 per cent of the total weight), is an opaque, soft substance which congeals in heat. The yolk is composed of albumins, fats containing vitamins, lecithins, nucleins, chlorestins, and mineral substances including a ferruginous pigment called *haematogen*, which gives it its colour.

The composition of the egg varies with the breed of the hen and its diet – the latter also influences the flavour of the egg.

The best eggs come from free-range hens, which eat the right proportion of grain and vegetable matter.

Dietetically, the fresh egg is almost a complete food. It contains easily assimilable proteins, fats, Vitamins A, B, D and E (only Vitamin C is absent), an appreciable amount of iron, and a number of valuable mineral salts: magnesium, a minute quantity of calcium, sodium, potassium, manganese, copper, zinc, chlorine, iodine, fluorine, etc. The egg, being a bearer of life, also contains precious oligo-elements.

The table below shows that the average egg yolk weighing 18 g. (¾ oz.) supplies 6 times more calories than the white, which weighs 35 g. (1½ oz.).

COMPOSITION OF AN AVERAGE EGG

	Weight	*Water*	*Albumen*	*Fats*	*Salts*	*Calories*
Shell	7 g.					
White	35 g.	30 g.	4·5 g.	0 g.	0·25 g.	10 g.
Yolk	18 g.	9 g.	2·9 g.	5·7 g.	0·25 g.	63 g.
Whole egg	60 g.	39 g.	7·4 g.	5·7 g.	0·50g.	73g.

From the tables of M. Alquier

Ostrich, turkey, peacock and duck eggs are bigger than chicken eggs; pigeon, guinea-fowl, pheasant, partridge, lapwing, plover and gull eggs are smaller. All these are of a similar composition except for duck and goose eggs, which are more oily.

Digestibility of eggs – Soft-boiled eggs, poached eggs, and *eggs en cocotte* are easily digested, unless served with a heavy garnish such as *foie gras*, truffles, mushrooms, etc.

The same applies to omelettes and scrambled eggs, although these, even without a garnish, are not as easily digested as those mentioned above.

Fried eggs are fairly digestible if they are not over browned in the butter or fat in which they are cooked.

Hard-boiled eggs take longer to digest than any of the others. A hard-boiled egg cut into very small fragments is more easily digested.

The average diet should not contain more than 2 or 3 eggs weekly (in whatever form they are served) and these should preferably be eaten at the midday meal.

Freshness of eggs – A fresh egg is heavy. When shaken, it should feel well-filled. As the shell is porous, the water which encloses the inner part of the egg evaporates. An egg loses a tiny fraction in weight every day. It is easy to gauge the freshness of an egg by plunging it into a 12 per cent solution of salted water (kitchen salt). If the egg is very fresh, it falls at once to the bottom of the water. If it is a few days old it floats, If it is bad it floats on top. This method does not apply to eggs that have been preserved in water and limestone, or other liquid.

Preservation of eggs – Eggs are preserved by the exclusion of air. They can either be dipped in a proprietary solution and then stored, or kept submerged in a solution of water-glass. Preserved eggs should not be used for boiling. Eggs can also be preserved by desiccation into powder.

BASIC EGG DISHES. MÉTHODES DE CUISSON DES OEUFS – In cooking and baking, only fresh eggs should be used.

Boiled eggs (hard). OEUFS DURS – Plunge the eggs into a pan of boiling water and boil for 8 to 10 minutes, according to size.

Drain the eggs and stand in cold water or under a cold tap. Peel them and use hot or cold, according to the recipe.

Boiled eggs (soft). OEUFS MOLLETS – Plunge the eggs into a pan of boiling water. Boil for 3 to 4 minutes. Shell them under cold water and keep warm in a pan of hot salted water until serving.

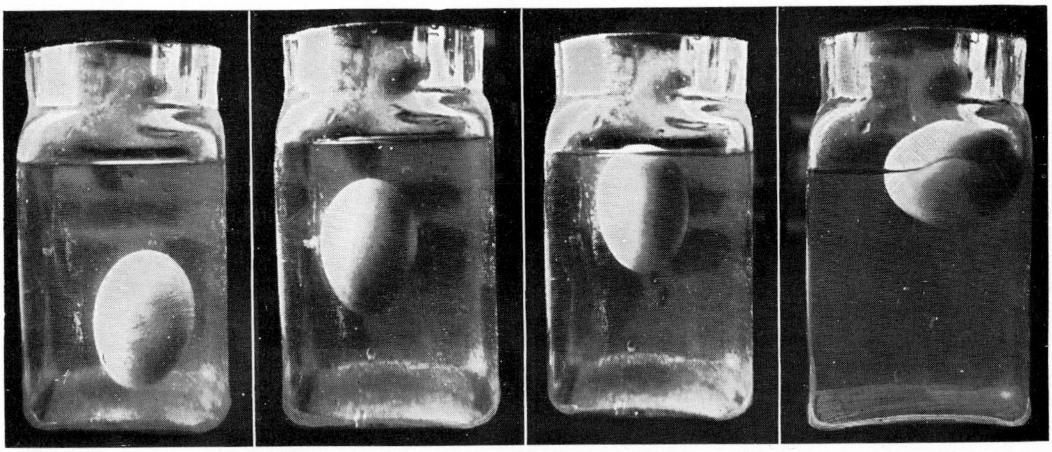

To test the freshness of an egg, plunge it into a 12 per cent solution of salted water: A fresh egg falls at once to the bottom; An egg 2 days old floats midway; An egg 4 days old rises to the surface; A 2-week old egg floats on top

Boiled eggs and garnished eggs en cocotte (*Robert Carrier*)

Drain the eggs and garnish them, or serve with sauce, according to the recipe. Soft-boiled eggs are served and garnished in the same way as poached eggs.

Eggs en cocotte, cassolettes or caissettes. OEUFS EN COCOTTE – This way of preparing eggs is a combination of *eggs à la coque* (see below) and *poached eggs* (see below).

Warm small round or oval dishes, made of china, earthenware, metal, or fireproof glass. Butter the dishes, or coat with a purée, according to the recipe. Use 1 or 2 eggs for each dish.

Place the dishes in the oven, in a pan half-filled with water. Leave for 6 to 8 minutes, according to the number of eggs in each dish. Salt the eggs when taking them from the oven.

Clean the outside of the dishes. Place them on a flat dish. Serve *au naturel* or garnished.

Eggs à la coque (boiled in their shells). OEUFS À LA COQUE – *First method.* Plunge the egg into boiling water. Leave a medium-sized egg for 3 minutes, a larger one, 30 seconds longer.

Second method. Plunge the eggs into boiling water. Boil for 1 minute. Remove from the heat, and leave in the hot water for 3 minutes.

Third method. Cover the eggs with cold water in a saucepan. Bring them to the boil and remove from the saucepan as soon as the water is boiling.

Fourth method. Steam the eggs, in special pans, for 3 minutes.

The times given above can be varied according to taste.

Fried egg and bacon

Fried eggs. OEUFS FRITS – There are 2 methods.

Fried. Cook 1 egg at a time in plenty of fat, oil, or butter. The white should cover the yolk.

Sautéed. Cook in a frying pan with fat, oil, or butter, on 1 side or both, and turn onto a dish or plate.

Heat oil in a small frying pan. Use enough to let the egg float. Break the egg into a cup and season with salt. Slide it into the hot oil and draw the white round the yolk with a wooden spoon to seal it.

Drain the eggs and garnish as shown for each recipe.

Eggs in a mould. OEUFS MOULÉS – This dish belongs to the *grande cuisine*, but can easily be prepared at home.

Coat the insides of *dariole* moulds with butter. Add chopped parsley, ham, truffles, etc. according to the recipe. Break the eggs into the lined moulds.

Cook in a *bain-marie* for 8 to 12 minutes. Leave in the moulds for a few minutes before taking out.

Place on slices of fried or toasted bread. Moulded eggs can also be served on tartlets or round *croustades* (q.v.), on artichoke hearts, or as shown in the recipe chosen. Garnish and serve with a suitable sauce.

Either simple or fluted moulds can be used.

Omelette

Omelette – It is less difficult to prepare an omelette than it seems. For success, observe the following points:

The flame must be very high.

Use an obsolutely clean frying pan, in which nothing else is ever cooked.

Beat the eggs lightly and only at the last moment.

Do not use too much butter or fat.

Have confidence in yourself.

For 4 people use the following quantities.

Lightly beat 8 eggs. Season with salt and freshly ground pepper.

Heat 35 g. ($1\frac{1}{2}$ oz., 3 tablespoons) butter in the frying pan and add the eggs. Cook over a high flame. Mix with a fork. Shake the pan so that the omelette is evenly cooked. Fold it over once and turn it upside down with 1 quick movement, onto a warmed dish.

Garnish the omelette and serve with a sauce from the omelette recipes in this section.

Poached eggs. OEUFS POCHÉS – Fill a pan with salted water – $1\frac{1}{2}$ teaspoons salt to 1 litre (scant quart, generous quart) water. Add 1 tablespoon vinegar. Bring to the boil. Break the eggs into the liquid exactly on the spot where it is bubbling. Simmer gently for 3 minutes.

Drain the eggs, one at a time, with a skimmer. Put each one separately into fresh water. Trim the eggs by removing the blisters (with fresh eggs this should hardly be necessary). Leave them in a dish of hot, salted water until they are served.

Drain and dry the eggs. Place them on fried or toasted slices of bread, according to the recipe. They can also be served on *croustades*, in tartlets, or on a bed of rice, semolina, potatoes, artichoke hearts, etc.

Garnish and cover with a sauce according to the recipe chosen.

Scrambled eggs. OEUFS BROUILLÉS – Well-made scrambled eggs are delicious, but they should be cooked with care – they must be smooth and creamy. They can be garnished in various ways.

First method. Use the following quantities for 4 people. Melt 50 g. (2 oz., $\frac{1}{4}$ cup) butter in a small frying pan with a heavy bottom, or a small saucepan. Break 8 eggs and beat together lightly, as for an omelette. Season them and add to the butter in the pan. Cook over a low heat, stirring constantly with a wooden spoon.

When the eggs are cooked, remove them from the stove and add 50 g. (2 oz., $\frac{1}{4}$ cup) butter, cut into small pieces. Mix well and keep hot in a *bain-marie* until serving.

Garnish according to the recipe chosen.

Second method. Use a double saucepan. Half-fill the bottom pan with warm water. Cook eggs and butter in the smaller pan, stirring with a wooden spoon.

When the eggs are cooked, add a little more butter, cut into small pieces.

2 or 3 tablespoons fresh cream can be added to scrambled eggs after they are cooked.

They can be served in small or large *croustades* (q.v.) made from puff pastry; in *timbales* (q.v.) made from plain pastry; in *cassolettes* (q.v.); in hollowed-out vegetables; or in metal or china pie dishes.

Eggs sur le plat, or shirred eggs. OEUFS SUR LE PLAT – For this simple way of cooking eggs special dishes are used, which are either for individual portions (1 or 2 eggs) or for cooking several at once.

For two eggs coat the dish with $\frac{1}{2}$ tablespoon butter. Heat on the stove. Break the eggs into the dish and pour melted butter on the yolks. Cook in the oven for as long as is liked and when ready, sprinkle with fine salt.

Garnish or cover with a sauce according to the instructions given alphabetically below.

EGG DISHES. LES DIVERS APPRÊTS D'OEUFS.

Eggs à l'africaine (soft-boiled or poached). OEUFS À L'AFRICAINE – Arrange the cooked eggs in a circle on a layer of *couscous* (q.v.).

Peel and dice aubergines, sauté them in oil and add to the ring.

Peel and dice sweet peppers and cook in a consommé. Make a *Tomato sauce* (see SAUCE), add the peppers and pour it over the eggs.

Eggs à l'agenaise (sur le plat). OEUFS À L'AGENAISE – Sauté chopped onions in goose fat. When cooked, add garlic and chopped parsley. Cook the eggs *sur le plat* on a bed of this onion mixture.

Garnish with peeled, diced aubergines, sautéed in goose fat.

Aladdin eggs I (sur le plat). OEUFS ALADIN – Bake the eggs in ovenproof dishes on a foundation of onions sautéed in butter until soft.

Garnish with *Sweet peppers à l'orientale* (see PEPPERS) and saffron-flavoured *Risotto* (see RICE). Surround with a border of *Tomato sauce* (see SAUCE).

Aladdin eggs II (soft-boiled or poached). OEUFS ALADIN – Arrange the cooked eggs in a circle on a layer of saffron-flavoured *Risotto* (see RICE).

Garnish with *Sweet peppers à l'orientale* (see PEPPERS) and mask the eggs with *Tomato sauce* (see SAUCE) spiced with a pinch of cayenne.

Eggs à l'alsacienne I (fried). OEUFS À L'ALSACIENNE – Arrange the fried eggs on a layer of braised *sauerkraut*, alternating them with slices of ham. Surround with a border of *Demi-glace sauce* (see SAUCE).

Eggs à l'alsacienne II (soft-boiled or poached). OEUFS À L'ALSACIENNE – Arrange the cooked eggs in a dish on a layer of braised *sauerkraut*. Garnish with thin slices of cooked ham. Cover with *Demi-glace sauce* (see SAUCE).

Eggs à l'alsacienne III (sur le plat). OEUFS À L'ALSACIENNE – Cook the eggs *sur le plat* in goose fat. Garnish with 1 tablespoon braised *sauerkraut* and a slice of ham. Surround with a border of *Demi-glace sauce* (see SAUCE).

Ambassadrice eggs I (soft-boiled or poached). OEUFS AMBASSADRICE – Make *croustades* (q.v.) with puff pastry and garnish with a *salpicon* (q.v.) of truffles and *foie gras*, blended with concentrated *Demi-glace sauce* (see SAUCE) flavoured with Madeira. Put the cooked eggs on the *croustades* and mask them with *Suprême sauce* (see SAUCE). Garnish with asparagus tips blended with butter.

Ambassadrice eggs II (en cocotte). OEUFS AMBASSADRICE – Line the *cocottes* with *Foie gras purée* (see PURÉE) and sprinkle with chopped truffles. Break the eggs into the lined dishes and cook in a *bain-marie*. When the eggs are cooked, take them out, garnish with asparagus tips, and surround the yolk with *Suprême sauce* (see SAUCE) to which sherry has been added.

Ambassadrice eggs III (sur le plat). OEUFS AMBASSADRICE – Cook the eggs *sur le plat* in the usual way. When ready, garnish with a *salpicon* of *foie gras*, truffles, and asparagus tips. Surround with *Suprême sauce* (see SAUCE) with sherry added.

Amélie eggs I (soft-boiled or poached). OEUFS AMÉLIE – Arrange the eggs on puff pastry *croustades* garnished with a fine *mirepoix* (q.v.) of vegetables (cooked in butter until they are soft) and with Madeira wine poured into the pan after the vegetables have been taken out.

Mask the eggs with a *Cream sauce* (see SAUCE). Garnish with morels cooked in cream.

Amélie eggs II (sur le plat). OEUFS AMÉLIE – Cook the eggs in ovenproof dishes on a *mirepoix* of vegetables with Madeira. Garnish with morels cooked in cream.

Eggs à l'américaine I (fried). OEUFS À L'AMÉRICAINE – Fry the eggs in butter. Garnish with 2 slices grilled or fried bacon and $\frac{1}{2}$ grilled tomato.

Eggs à l'américaine II (soft-boiled or poached). OEUFS À L'AMÉRICAINE – Arrange the cooked eggs on fried bread or *croustades*. Garnish with pieces of *Lobster* (*or spiny lobster*) *à l'américaine* (see LOBSTER). Pour *Américaine sauce* (see SAUCE) over the eggs.

Eggs à l'américaine III (sur le plat). OEUFS À L'AMÉRICAINE – Break 2 eggs onto 2 pieces of *Lobster* (*or spiny lobster*) *à l'américaine* (see LOBSTER) in a buttered ovenproof dish. Bake in the oven. Surround with *Américaine sauce* (see SAUCE).

Anchovy eggs I (soft-boiled or poached). OEUFS AUX ANCHOIS – Arrange the cooked eggs on bread fried in butter on both sides, or on puff pastry *croustades*.

Mask with *Anchovy Sauce* (see SAUCE). Garnish each egg with a desalted anchovy fillet.

Anchovy eggs II (sur le plat). OEUFS AUX ANCHOIS – Desalt and dice 1 anchovy per egg. Put them into a buttered ovenproof dish and break the eggs onto them. Cook in the oven and decorate with more anchovy fillets.

Anchovy eggs III (fried). OEUFS AUX ANCHOIS – Fry the eggs in oil. Arrange each one on an oval piece of bread, fried in butter on both sides. Garnish with anchovy fillets, arranged criss-cross. Sprinkle with *Noisette butter* (see BUTTER, *Compound butters*).

Eggs à l'ancienne I (soft-boiled or poached). OEUFS À L'ANCIENNE – Arrange the cooked eggs on a mound of rice, cooked in meat stock. Cover with *Veloute saucé* (see SAUCE). Put 1 teaspoon of *julienne* (q.v.) of truffles blended with thick *Madeira sauce* (see SAUCE) between the eggs.

Eggs à l'ancienne II (cold). OEUFS À L'ANCIENNE – Mask soft-boiled eggs or poached eggs with *White chaud-froid sauce* (see SAUCE) to which Madeira has been added. Decorate with truffles and glaze with jelly. Serve in a dish lined with a layer of chicken jelly.

Separate the eggs with slices of pickled tongue cut into fluted half-circles. Cover with thin jelly. Add chopped jelly to the middle of the dish. Keep cold until serving.

Eggs à l'andalouse I (sur le plat). OEUFS À L'ANDALOUSE – Cook the eggs *sur le plat* in oil in a dish which has been rubbed with garlic. Peel and dice sweet peppers and cook them in oil. Add them to *Tomato fondue* (see FONDUE) and garnish the eggs with the mixture.

Eggs à l'andalouse II (fried). OEUFS À L'ANDALOUSE – Fry the eggs in oil. Arrange alternately with grilled tomato-halves in the shape of a crown.

Garnish with sweet peppers and onion rings fried in oil.

Eggs à l'anglaise I (sur le plat). OEUFS À L'ANGLAISE – Break 2 eggs over a slice of grilled bacon in a buttered ovenproof dish. Cook in the oven.

Eggs à l'anglaise II (fried). OEUFS À L'ANGLAISE – Fry the eggs in butter. Cut them with a round biscuit-cutter, leaving only a thin rim of white round the yolk. Arrange on rounds of bread, toasted, or fried in butter.

Surround with veal stock, or serve the stock separately.

Eggs à l'antiboise. OEUFS À L'ANTIBOISE – Roll 4 tablespoons ($\frac{1}{3}$ cup) *nonats* (q.v.) in flour, and sauté in butter. When they are brown, add 1 tablespoon diced Gruyère cheese and a little garlic.

Break 4 eggs into the same pan and cook them in the oven. Turn upside down onto a hot dish. Sprinkle with chopped parsley.

Eggs à l'anversoise I (soft-boiled or poached). OEUFS À L'ANVERSOISE – Serve the cooked eggs on bread fried in butter on both sides. Garnish with hop shoots cooked in butter. Mask with *Cream sauce* or *Suprême sauce* (see SAUCE).

Eggs à l'anversoise II (sur le plat). OEUFS À L'ANVERSOISE – Garnish the cooked eggs with 1 tablespoon hop shoots cooked in butter or cream. Surround with a border of boiling cream.

Apicius eggs (soft-boiled or poached). OEUFS APICIUS – Serve the cooked eggs on grilled mushrooms. Garnish with *Crayfish tail ragoût à la Nantua* (see CRAYFISH). Mask the eggs with *Normande sauce* (see SAUCE). Put 1 tablespoon of a *salpicon*, made from truffles cooked in butter, between each egg.

Archduke eggs I (soft-boiled or poached). OEUFS ARCHIDUC – Arrange the cooked eggs on bread fried in butter on both sides, or on *croustades* of puff pastry. Coat with *Suprême sauce* (see SAUCE) to which paprika and chopped onion cooked in butter have been added. Garnish with diced truffles sautéed in butter.

Archduke eggs II (sur le plat). OEUFS ARCHIDUC – Break the eggs into an ovenproof dish lined with chopped onions which have been softened in butter and seasoned with paprika. Cook in the oven and garnish with diced truffles cooked in butter. Surround with *Suprême sauce* (see SAUCE) seasoned with paprika.

Argenteuil eggs I (soft-boiled or poached). OEUFS ARGENTEUIL – Arrange the cooked eggs on pieces of bread fried in butter on both sides, or on puff pastry *croustades*.

Mask with *White asparagus purée* (see PURÉE), to which *Velouté sauce* (see SAUCE) has been added in the proportion of 3 to 1. Garnish with white asparagus tips cooked in butter.

Argenteuil eggs II (sur le plat). OEUFS ARGENTEUIL – Break the eggs into a buttered ovenproof dish with 1 tablespoon fresh cream. Cook in the oven. Garnish with white asparagus tips cooked in butter.

Argenteuil eggs III (sur le plat). OEUFS ARGENTEUIL – Line an ovenproof dish with *White asparagus purée* (see PURÉE). Break the eggs into it. Cook in the oven.

Garnish with green asparagus tips cooked in butter. Surround with *Velouté sauce* or *Cream sauce* (see SAUCE).

Argenteuil eggs IV (cold). OEUFS ARGENTEUIL – Mask the soft-boiled or poached eggs with a *Chaud-froid sauce* (see SAUCE). Decorate with green asparagus tips and glaze with aspic jelly.

Make a salad of white asparagus tips seasoned with jellied *Mayonnaise* (see SAUCE). Arrange on a dish with eggs and chopped aspic in the middle.

Armenonville eggs (soft-boiled or poached). OEUFS ARMENONVILLE – Arrange the cooked eggs on oval pieces of toast made from unsweetened brioche dough. Mask with *Velouté sauce* (see SAUCE) to which sherry has been added. Garnish with small carrots cooked in cream, and asparagus tips sautéed with butter.

Auber eggs I (soft-boiled or poached). OEUFS AUBER – Stuff halved tomatoes with *Chicken forcemeat* (see FORCEMEAT) mixed with chopped truffles. Put 1 cooked egg on each half.

Mask the eggs with *Velouté sauce* (see SAUCE) flavoured with tomato paste and finished with a *julienne* of truffles cooked in sherry.

Auber eggs II (cold). OEUFS AUBER – Mask the eggs with a *White chaud-froid sauce* (see SAUCE) to which *Tomato essence* (see ESSENCE) has been added. Decorate with truffles and glaze with jelly.

Hollow out some tomatoes and fill with diced breast of chicken and truffles bound with mayonnaise made with gelatine. Put 1 soft-boiled or poached egg on each tomato. Arrange in a crown, and garnish with jelly.

Eggs with aubergines I (sur le plat). OEUFS AUX AUBERGINES – Line the ovenproof dish with diced aubergines sautéed in butter. Break the eggs onto the aubergines, and cook in the usual way for eggs *sur le plat*.

Eggs with aubergines II (fried). OEUFS AUX AUBERGINES – Fry the eggs in oil. Arrange them in a ring alternating with slices of aubergine, cut lengthwise and fried in oil, or grilled. Garnish with fried parsley.

Eggs with aubergines à la sicilienne (soft-boiled or poached). OEUFS AUX AUBERGINES À LA SICILIENNE – Cut the aubergines in half lengthwise. Score the pulp. Salt them and leave to sweat for 1 hour. Fry in oil.

Remove the pulp without tearing the skins and dry the pulp on the stove. Mix it with twice its volume of *Mornay sauce* (see SAUCE). Coat the bottoms of the aubergines with 1 tablespoon of this purée. Add 1 poached egg to each half. Arrange them in a buttered *gratin* dish and cover the eggs with the remaining purée, to which fresh cream has been added. Sprinkle with grated cheese. Brown in a hot oven.

Augier eggs (sur le plat). OEUFS AUGIER – Line a buttered dish with a purée made of sweetbreads and chopped chervil. Break the eggs onto the purée. Surround the yolks with a ring of fresh cream. Bake in the oven.

Aurora eggs I (soft-boiled or poached). OEUFS À L'AURORE – Arrange the cooked eggs on pieces of bread fried in butter on both sides, or on puff pastry *croustades*. Mask them with *Aurora sauce* (see SAUCE). Sprinkle with chopped hard-boiled egg yolks. Surround with *Tomato sauce* (see SAUCE).

Aurora eggs II (stuffed, hard-boiled). OEUFS DUR À L'AURORE FARCIS – Cut the hard-boiled eggs lengthwise. Remove the yolks. Mix two thirds of the yolks with an equal weight of thick *Béchamel sauce* (see SAUCE) and butter. Season and add chopped herbs. Stuff the eggs with this mixture, heaping it into a dome.

Arrange the eggs on a *gratin* dish masked with *Mornay sauce* (see SAUCE). Sprinkle them with grated cheese and pour on melted butter. Brown in a hot oven. Remove from the oven, sprinkle with the remaining chopped hard-boiled yolks, and surround with *Tomato sauce* (see SAUCE).

Eggs à l'auvergnate (soft-boiled or poached). OEUFS À

L'AUVERGNATE – Cook some cabbage in meat stock. Strain, and sauté in butter or lard. Arrange the cooked eggs on the cabbage, alternating with rounds of sausage, fried in butter.

Cover with concentrated veal stock to which butter has been added.

Babinski eggs (sur le plat). OEUFS BABINSKI – Garnish the cooked eggs with cork-shaped chicken croquettes and 1 tablespoon morels in cream. Surround with concentrated veal stock, to which butter has been added.

Bachaumont eggs (en cocotte). OEUFS BACHAUMONT – Butter the *cocottes* and line them with celeriac purée. Break the eggs onto the purée and cook in the oven in a *bain-marie* (q.v.).

Remove from the oven, season, and surround with *Cream sauce* (see SAUCE), mixed with chopped chervil.

Eggs and bacon I (sur le plat). OEUFS AU BACON – Break the eggs into an ovenproof dish lined with thin strips of bacon which have been lightly browned in butter. Pour the fat from the bacon over them and bake in the oven.

Eggs and bacon II (fried). OEUFS AU BACON – Fry the eggs in oil. Arrange in a ring, alternating with rashers of bacon, grilled or fried in oil. Garnish with fried parsley.

Bagration eggs I (soft-boiled or poached). OEUFS BAGRATION – Serve the cooked eggs in a flan case baked blind. Garnish with diced macaroni cooked in water, bound with cream, and mixed with diced truffles. Mask with *Cream sauce* (see SAUCE).

Bagration eggs

Bagration eggs II (in moulds). OEUFS BAGRATION – Line a buttered *dariole* mould with macaroni which has been cooked in water. Arrange the macaroni in a spiral. Spread *Quenelle forcemeat* (see FORCEMEAT) on the macaroni and break in the eggs. Cook in a *bain-marie*.

Unmould onto small round *croustades* and mask with *Cream sauce* (see SAUCE). Add to each egg a round slice of truffle cooked in butter.

Balmoral eggs (en cocotte). OEUFS BALMORAL – Line *cocotte* dishes with a layer of vegetable *mirepoix* (q.v.). Break the eggs onto the *mirepoix* and bake in the oven in a *bain-marie*.

Remove from the oven, season, and garnish with 1 tablespoon diced mushrooms fried in butter and blended with concentrated veal stock.

Bamboche eggs (fried). OEUFS BAMBOCHE – Fry the eggs in oil, and arrange in a circle on a *macédoine* (q.v.) of vegetables blended with cream. Garnish with thin strips of fried salt cod, as described for *Salt cod à la bamboche* (see COD, *Salt cod*).

Banville eggs (soft-boiled or poached). OEUFS BANVILLE – Cook artichoke hearts in *court-bouillon* (q.v.) and sauté them lightly in butter. Arrange the cooked eggs on the artichoke hearts and mask them with *Chivry sauce* (see SAUCE). Garnish with thickened *Chicken forcemeat à la crème* (see FORCEMEAT).

Eggs à la béarnaise (soft-boiled or poached). OEUFS À LA BÉARNAISE – Make small oval cakes using *Duchess potato mixture* (see POTATOES). Bake in the oven until golden brown and arrange 1 cooked egg on each one. Coat them with concentrated veal gravy to which butter has been added. Serve with *Béarnaise sauce* (see SAUCE).

Eggs à la Beauharnais (soft-boiled or poached). OEUFS À LA BEAUHARNAIS – Cook artichoke hearts in butter and garnish with *Beauharnais sauce* (see SAUCE). Arrange 1 egg on each. Coat with reduced *Demi-glace* (see SAUCE), to which butter has been added.

Eggs à la Beaumont (poached). OEUFS À LA BEAUMONT – For 10 eggs use 10 oval *croustades* made from left-over puff pastry, and $\frac{1}{2}$ litre (scant pint, $2\frac{1}{4}$ cups) thin *Béchamel sauce* (see SAUCE).

'Cook and trim 3 large artichoke hearts. Cut them into small squares and stew them gently in butter. Sieve one third of the stewed artichoke hearts. Mix the purée with the *Béchamel sauce*. Add 50 g. (2 oz., $\frac{1}{4}$ cup) butter.

Cook 175 g. (6 oz.) green asparagus tips in salt water. (In order to have the correct weight of asparagus tips, 400 g. (14 oz.) asparagus will be required.) Drain, but do not rinse in cold water. Season with salt, pepper and grated nutmeg. Dress with butter. Mix in the rest of the artichoke hearts.

'Poach the eggs which should be absolutely fresh. Drain them and plunge into lukewarm water. Then drain again and dry on a cloth. Trim the eggs and arrange them in a circle on individual *croustades*. Cover them with the sauce and put some chervil on each egg. Garnish with the artichokes and asparagus tips arranged in the centre of the circle.' (Philéas Gilbert.)

Eggs à la béchamel. OEUFS À LA BÉCHAMEL – See *Eggs with cream sauce* (below).

Belle-Hélène eggs (soft-boiled or poached). OEUFS BELLE-HÉLÈNE – Make oval croquettes from left-over poultry meat. Dip them in egg and breadcrumbs and fry in butter. Put 1 soft-boiled or poached egg on each. Mask the eggs with *Colbert butter* (see BUTTER, *compound butters*). Garnish with asparagus tips. Surround with a ring of *Velouté sauce* (see SAUCE).

Eggs à la bellevilloise (sur le plat). OEUFS À LA BELLE-VILLOISE – Line an ovenproof dish with chopped onion softened in butter. Put the eggs on the onions and garnish with 2 slices of grilled *andouillette* (q.v.). Bake them and when cooked surround the eggs with a ribbon of *Lyonnaise sauce* (see SAUCE).

Eggs à la bénédictine (soft-boiled or poached). OEUFS À LA BÉNÉDICTINE – Arrange the cooked eggs on a mixture of salt cod pounded with garlic, oil, and cream, and mixed with chopped truffles. Mask with *Cream sauce* (see SAUCE).

Béranger eggs (soft-boiled or poached). OEUFS BÉRANGER – Line a flan case, baked blind, with a layer of thick *Onion soubise* (see PURÉE). Put the cooked eggs on this layer and mask them with *Mornay sauce* (see SAUCE). Sprinkle grated cheese over the pie and pour melted butter over. Brown in the oven.

Bérangère eggs (en cocotte). OEUFS BÉRANGÈRE – Line buttered *cocottes* with a thin layer of forcemeat made from poultry and truffles. Break the eggs into the *cocottes* and cook in the usual way. When the eggs are cooked, garnish with 1 tablespoon of *ragoût* made from cocks' combs and kidneys, blended with *Suprême sauce* (see SAUCE).

Bercy eggs (sur le plat). OEUFS BERCY – Bake the eggs in the usual way. Garnish with a small grilled or fried sausage. Surround with *Tomato sauce* (see SAUCE).

Berlioz eggs (soft-boiled or poached). OEUFS BERLIOZ – Brown in the oven oval *croustades*, made from *Duchess potato mixture* (see POTATOES). Fill the *croustades* with a *salpicon* of truffles and mushrooms blended with a thick *Madeira sauce* (see SAUCE). Put the cooked eggs on the garnished *croustades*.

Mask the eggs lightly with *Suprême sauce* (see SAUCE). Fill the middle of the dish with cocks' combs fried *à la Villeroi*.

Bernis eggs I (soft-boiled or poached). OEUFS BERNIS – Make round *croustades*, with a small rim, from puff pastry. Garnish them with a layer of chicken purée. Arrange the cooked eggs in the *croustades*.

Mask the eggs with *Suprême sauce* (see SAUCE). Garnish with green asparagus tips blended with butter.

Bernis eggs II (cold). OEUFS BERNIS – Mask poached eggs in *White chaud-froid sauce* (see SAUCE). Decorate with truffles and glaze with jelly.

Line a dish with a layer of *Chicken mousse* (see CHICKEN). Arrange the eggs on the mousse, leaving space between each egg for a bunch of green asparagus tips. Spoon half-set jelly over the whole dish. Serve very cold.

If it is more convenient to serve the eggs in individual dishes, small *cassolettes* or shell dishes made from metal, crystal or china, can be used.

Bizet eggs (in moulds). OEUFS BIZET – Butter individual *dariole* moulds and line with finely chopped pickled tongue and truffles. Break the eggs into the moulds and poach them in a *bain-marie*.

Cook artichoke hearts in butter. Unmould the eggs and put 1 on each artichoke heart. Mask with *Périgueux sauce* (see SAUCE). Put a slice of truffle on each egg.

Eggs à la bohémienne (soft-boiled or poached). OEUFS À LA BOHÉMIENNE – Make *croustades* from puff pastry and garnish them with purée of *foie gras*. Put the cooked eggs on the purée. Cover them with *Velouté sauce* (see SAUCE). Cut lean ham into matchsticks and heat them in Madeira. Put the ham on the eggs and surround with a ring of light veal jelly.

Bonvalet eggs (soft-boiled or poached). OEUFS BONVALET – Hollow out rounds of bread, brown them in butter, and place the cooked eggs in the hollows.

Mask with *Velouté sauce* (see SAUCE) and surround with a ribbon of thick tomato-flavoured *Béarnaise sauce* (see SAUCE) piped through a paper forcing-bag. Put 1 slice of truffle, heated in butter, on each egg.

Eggs à la bordelaise I (sur le plat). OEUFS À LA BORDELAISE – Break the eggs onto a bed of chopped *Cèpes à la bordelaise* (see MUSHROOMS) and cook as usual.

Eggs à la bordelaise II (fried). OEUFS À LA BORDELAISE – Fry the eggs and oval croûtons in oil. Arrange the eggs on the croûtons, and garnish with *Cèpes à la bordelaise* (see MUSHROOMS).

Eggs as a border I (with various garnishes). OEUFS EN BORDURE – Hard-boil the eggs and cut them into quarters, thick rounds, or halves.

Butter a plain ring mould. Arrange the eggs with the yolks facing outward. Fill the mould, using a forcing-bag, with forcemeat made of meat, fish or vegetables. Press the forcemeat down to avoid empty spaces. Cover with a lid and cook in a *bain-marie* in a low oven.

Turn the mould out onto a dish so that the ingredients all come out together. Do not remove it too soon.

Fill the middle with a garnish such as creamed or sautéed mushrooms; a *macédoine* of vegetables; asparagus tips or other green vegetables in butter or cream; spinach leaves or spinach purée; sautéed aubergines; etc.

Spoon *Cream sauce* (see SAUCE) over the border.

Eggs as a border II. OEUFS EN BORDURE – Cut hard-boiled eggs into thick round slices. Bake a flan case and arrange the eggs round the edges of the flan, alternating them with

Eggs as a border to spinach

round slices of ham; pickled tongue; calves' brains sautéed in butter; aubergines or courgettes (zucchini) sautéed in butter; or with any garnish that goes well with hard-boiled eggs.

Fill the middle of the flan with one of the garnishes described in the previous recipe. Cover the eggs with *Cream sauce* (see SAUCE) or any other suitable sauce.

Eggs as a border III (cold). OEUFS EN BORDURE – Cut hard-boiled eggs into halves, quarters or thick rounds. Put them into ring moulds lined with white jelly, and decorate with pieces of truffle, pickled tongue, lean ham, or any suitable garnish. Fill with half-set jelly. Leave to set on ice.

Eggs as a border IV (cold). OEUFS EN BORDURE – Line a plain ring mould with jelly. Decorate with the whites of hard-boiled eggs, truffles, etc.

Use a forcing-bag to fill the ring with stuffing made from the yolks of the hard-boiled eggs sieved with purée of *foie gras*, in the proportion of 3 to 1. Fill the mould with half-set jelly. Leave to set in the refrigerator.

Turn the mould out onto a dish. Put a buttered croûton in the centre of the mould. Sieve together the yolks from halved hard-boiled eggs and some *foie gras*. Stuff the whites with this mixture and heap the eggs in a pyramid on the croûton. Decorate with truffles and spoon jelly over them. Garnish with jelly triangles.

In France these eggs are also called *jellied eggs à la française*.

Eggs à la bourguignonne (poached). OEUFS À LA BOURGUIGNONNE – Boil 6 dl. (1 pint, $2\frac{1}{2}$ cups) red wine, a pinch of salt, a pinch of pepper, a small handful of parsley, a twig of thyme, a fragment of bay leaf and a crushed clove of garlic, for a few minutes.

Strain, and poach 6 fresh eggs in the wine.

Drain the eggs and arrange them on croûtons fried in butter. Cover the eggs with *Bourguignonne sauce* (see SAUCE) made by blending kneaded butter into the red wine in which the eggs were cooked.

Alternatively, arrange the eggs on croûtons made from round slices of bread, fried in butter. Garnish with sautéed mushrooms and small glazed onions. Cover with *Bourguignonne sauce* (see SAUCE).

Eggs à la bretonne I (soft-boiled or poached). OEUFS À LA BRETONNE – Arrange the cooked eggs on croûtons, fried in butter. Cover them with *Bretonne sauce* (see SAUCE).

Alternatively, arrange the eggs in hollowed out croûtons, fried in butter (or in *croustades* or tartlets), and filled with white bean purée. Cover with concentrated veal gravy to which butter has been added.

Eggs à la bretonne II (sur le plat). OEUFS À LA BRETONNE – Bake the eggs *sur le plat* in the usual way. When they are cooked, surround them with a ribbon of *Bretonne sauce* (see SAUCE).

Alternatively, force through a forcing-bag, a thick purée of white beans along the edge of a buttered dish. Break the eggs into the dish and fry them in the usual way.

Brillat-Savarin eggs I (soft-boiled or poached). OEUFS BRILLAT-SAVARIN – Bake a flan case blind. Garnish with morels sautéed in butter. Put the cooked eggs on the mushrooms and mask with concentrated *Velouté sauce* (see SAUCE) to which sherry and butter have been added. Dress the centre of the dish with buttered green asparagus tips.

Brillat-Savarin eggs II (sur le plat). OEUFS BRILLAT-SAVARIN – Bake the eggs *sur le plat* in the usual way. Garnish them with morels sautéed in butter, and asparagus tips. Surround them with sherry-flavoured *Velouté sauce* (see SAUCE).

Brillat-Savarin eggs III (en caissettes). OEUFS BRILLAT-SAVARIN – Butter small ovenproof china dishes. Garnish them with 1 tablespoon sautéed morels. Break the eggs onto them and bake in the oven in a *bain-marie*.

Garnish with asparagus tips, and surround with a ribbon of *Velouté sauce* (see SAUCE), flavoured with sherry.

Brimont eggs (soft-boiled or poached). OEUFS BRIMONT – Fill a large puff pastry *croustade* with mushrooms cooked in cream. Put the cooked eggs on the mushrooms and mask with thick *velouté sauce* made from chicken stock with Madeira and cream added. Garnish the centre of the dish with small round chicken croquettes. Put a slice of truffle on each egg.

Eggs à la bruxelloise I (soft-boiled or poached). OEUFS À LA BRUXELLOISE – Arrange the cooked eggs on hollowed-out croûtons (which have been browned in the oven) or in tartlets (baked blind). Garnish with chopped chicory cooked in butter and bound with *Béchamel sauce* (see SAUCE). Coat with *Cream sauce* (see SAUCE).

Eggs à la bruxelloise II (sur le plat). OEUFS À LA BRUXELLOISE – Break the eggs onto halved, braised chicory in ovenproof dishes and cook them in the usual way. Surround them with a ribbon of *Cream sauce* (see SAUCE).

Cardinal eggs I (soft-boiled or poached). OEUFS CARDINAL – Garnish tartlets (baked blind) with spiny lobster blended with *Béchamel sauce* (see SAUCE). Put the cooked eggs on the lobster and mask with *Cardinal sauce* (see SAUCE). Garnish each egg with a slice of truffle.

Cardinal eggs II (in moulds). OEUFS CARDINAL – Butter *dariole* moulds and sprinkle them with lobster coral. Break the eggs in the moulds and cook them in a *bain-marie*. Empty the moulds into tartlets garnished with a mixture of lobster and *Béchamel sauce* (see SAUCE). Mask with *Cardinal sauce* (see SAUCE). Heat sliced truffles in butter and put one on each egg.

Carême eggs I (soft-boiled or poached). OEUFS CARÊME – Arrange the cooked eggs on artichoke hearts cooked in butter. Garnish with a *ragoût* of sweetbreads, truffles and mushrooms.

Mask with thick *Velouté sauce* (see SAUCE), one third of which should be veal stock, with cream and Madeira added.

Cut slices of pickled tongue with a fluted biscuit-cutter and put 1 slice on each egg.

Carême eggs II (in moulds). OEUFS CARÊME – Line small hexagonal moulds with pickled tongue and diced truffles. Break the eggs into the moulds and steam them. Garnish, and mask with sauce as in the recipe above.

Carême eggs III (cold). OEUFS CARÊME – Poach the eggs and trim them so that little of the white remains. Line small hexagonal moulds with jelly and decorate them with truffles and pickled tongue cut into small pieces. Put the eggs into the moulds. Fill the moulds with Madeira-flavoured jelly. Chill on ice.

Unmould the eggs and put each one on an artichoke heart which has been cooked in *court-bouillon* and masked with jelly. Arrange the eggs around an aspic of sweetbreads and truffles made in a conical mould.

Cook small mushrooms in *court-bouillon*. Mask them with *White chaud-froid sauce* (see SAUCE). Decorate with lozenge-shaped pieces of truffle. Put a decorated mushroom on each egg.

Eggs à la carmélite (soft-boiled or poached). OEUFS À LA CARMÉLITE – Bake a flan case blind. Garnish with *Mussels in cream* (see MUSSEL). Arrange the cooked eggs on the mussels; garnish with *White wine sauce* (see SAUCE).

Carmen eggs (sur le plat). OEUFS CARMEN – Bake the eggs *sur le plat* in the usual way. Cut them with a round biscuit-cutter, leaving only a narrow ribbon of white round the yolk. Deep-fry croûtons in oil. Cover each croûton with a slice of ham sautéed in a frying pan. Put 1 egg on each slice of ham. Mask the eggs with *Tomato sauce* (see SAUCE), seasoned with paprika and with butter added.

Carnavalet eggs (soft-boiled or poached). OEUFS CARNAVALET – Arrange the cooked eggs in a circle on *Subrics of spinach* (see SPINACH). Garnish the middle of the dish with a *macédoine* of vegetables blended with *Béchamel sauce* (see SAUCE). Mask the eggs with *Cream sauce* (see SAUCE).

Eggs à la catalane (fried). OEUFS À LA CATALANE – Fry halved tomatoes and thinly sliced aubergines in oil. Use a separate frying pan for each vegetable. When they are cooked, mix the vegetables together and season with salt and pepper. Add garlic and chopped parsley and arrange on a dish.

Cook the eggs in a frying pan and slide them on to the vegetables.

Eggs à la charcutière I (fried). OEUFS À LA CHARCUTIÈRE – Fry the eggs in lard. Arrange them on a dish in the shape of a crown, alternating them with grilled *Pork crépinettes* (see CRÉPINETTES). Garnish with fried parsley and serve with *Charcutière sauce* (see SAUCE).

Eggs à la charcutière II (soft-boiled or poached). OEUFS À LA CHARCUTIÈRE – Arrange the cooked eggs on small *Pork crépinettes* (see CRÉPINETTES) which have been fried or grilled. Cover with concentrated *Charcutière sauce* (see SAUCE).

Chartreuse eggs (in moulds). OEUFS EN CHARTREUSE – Cut carrots and turnips into tiny balls. Dice French beans. Cook these vegetables, and green peas, separately in salt water. Drain the vegetables, toss them in melted butter, and line buttered moulds with them. Break the eggs into the moulds and cook in a *bain-marie*.

Make round croûtes, hollow them out, and bake until golden. Fill them with well-drained braised cabbage.

Unmould the eggs and put them on the cabbage in the croûtes, separating each egg from the next with a slice of cooked sausage. Mask with concentrated veal stock to which butter has been added.

Eggs au chasseur I (sur le plat). OEUFS AU CHASSEUR – Garnish cooked eggs with sautéed chicken livers. Surround with a ribbon of *Chasseur sauce* (see SAUCE). Sprinkle with chopped parsley.

Finely sliced mushrooms can be added to the chicken livers.

Eggs au chasseur II (soft-boiled or poached). OEUFS AU CHASSEUR – Bake tartlets blind and fill them with sautéed chicken livers. Arrange the cooked eggs on the livers and cover with *Chasseur sauce* (see SAUCE). Sprinkle with chopped parsley.

Chateaubriand eggs (soft-boiled or poached). OEUFS CHATEAUBRIAND – Cook artichoke hearts in butter. Fill with thick *Béarnaise sauce* (see SAUCE). Arrange the eggs on the hearts, and mask with concentrated veal stock to which butter has been added.

Eggs à la châtelaine I (soft-boiled or poached). OEUFS À LA CHÂTELAINE – Bake tartlets blind. Garnish with *Chestnut purée* (see PURÉE) mixed with a quarter of its weight of *Onion soubise* (see PURÉE). Arrange the eggs on the purée and cover with a poultry *Velouté sauce* (see SAUCE).

Eggs à la châtelaine II (cold). OEUFS À LA CHÂTELAINE – Mask the soft-boiled or poached eggs with *Chaud-froid sauce* (see SAUCE). Decorate with pickled tongue and truffles, and glaze with jelly.

Arrange the eggs in a dish lined with a jellied chestnut mousse. Cover with a thin layer of half-set jelly.

Eggs à la Chaville (sur le plat). OEUFS À LA CHAVILLE – Line the ovenproof dish with 1 tablespoon *salpicon* of mushrooms cooked in butter. Break the eggs into the dish and cook in the usual way. Garnish the cooked eggs with 1 tablespoon *Tomato fondue* (see FONDUE) to which chopped tarragon has been added.

Chénier eggs (soft-boiled or poached). OEUFS CHÉNIER – Make a *Rice pilaf* (see PILAF) and add saffron. Make it into small cakes and put 1 egg on each. Garnish with sliced aubergines fried in oil. Mask with *Tomato sauce* (see SAUCE).

Eggs à la chevalière (soft-boiled or poached). OEUFS À LA CHEVALIÈRE – Bake a flan case blind. Arrange the eggs around the edge, and garnish the centre of the flan with a *ragoût* made of cocks' combs, kidneys, and mushrooms, blended with *Velouté sauce* (see SAUCE). Spoon *Suprême sauce* (see SAUCE) over the eggs. Dip cocks' combs in egg and breadcrumbs and fry them. Put 1 comb between each egg and 1 slice of truffle on each egg.

Eggs à la Chevreuse (sur le plat). OEUFS À LA CHEVREUSE – Pipe a layer of puréed French beans round the edge of a buttered ovenproof dish. Break the eggs into the middle of the dish. Sprinkle with grated cheese and bake.

Eggs à la Chimay (stuffed). OEUFS À LA CHIMAY – Cut hard-boiled eggs lengthwise. Remove the yolks and pound them, adding an equal quantity of dry *duxelles* (q.v.). Stuff the halved egg whites with this mixture.

Arrange the stuffed eggs in a buttered dish and cover with *Mornay sauce* (see SAUCE). Sprinkle with grated cheese. Pour melted butter over and brown in the oven or under a grill.

Eggs with chipolatas (sur le plat). OEUFS AUX CHIPOLATAS – Line an ovenproof dish with chopped onions softened in butter. Break the eggs onto the onions. Put a grilled chipolata sausage on either side of each yolk and pour melted butter over the dish. Cook in the oven. Surround with concentrated veal stock.

Eggs à la Chivry (soft-boiled or poached). OEUFS À LA CHIVRY – Arrange the cooked eggs on fried croûtons. Garnish with green asparagus tips cooked in butter. Cover with *Chivry sauce* (see SAUCE).

Choron eggs (soft-boiled or poached). OEUFS CHORON – Make oval croûtons with a deep groove round the edge and deep-fry them in butter. Put the cooked eggs on the croûtons and mask with *Cream sauce* to which *Tomato sauce* has been added (see SAUCE).

Pipe a ribbon of thick *Béarnaise sauce* (see SAUCE) into the groove round the croûtons. Garnish with small green peas cooked in butter.

Eggs à la Clamart (soft-boiled or poached). OEUFS À LA CLAMART – Bake tartlets and fill them with *Peas à la française* (see PEA). Arrange the cooked eggs on the peas and cover with *Cream sauce* (see SAUCE) to which *Green pea butter* (see BUTTER, *Compound butters*) has been added.

Eggs à la Clarence (soft-boiled or poached). OEUFS À LA CLARENCE – Bake tartlets and fill them with a *julienne* (q.v.) of pickled tongue, truffles, and mushrooms. Arrange the cooked eggs in the tartlets and cover with *Réforme sauce* (see SAUCE) to which butter has been added.

Garnished eggs en cocotte

Eggs en cocotte with cream. OEUFS EN COCOTTE À LA CRÈME – Put 1 tablespoon boiling cream in the *cocottes* and break in the eggs. Add a nut of butter to the yolk. Bake in the oven in a *bain-marie*.

Eggs en cocotte à la duxelles. OEUFS EN COCOTTE À LA DUXELLES – Line buttered *cocotte* dishes with dry *duxelles* (q.v.). Break the eggs into the *cocottes* and bake in the oven in a *bain-marie*. Remove from the oven and surround the yolks with concentrated veal gravy to which butter has been added.

Eggs en cocotte in gravy. OEUFS EN COCOTTE AU JUS – Cook as for *Eggs en cocotte with tarragon* (see below) leaving out the tarragon and reducing the veal gravy until it is very concentrated.

Eggs en cocotte au naturel – Cook as described under *Eggs en cocotte* (see EGGS, *Basic egg dishes*).

Eggs en cocotte with Parmesan cheese. OEUFS EN COCOTTE AU PARMESAN – Cook as for *Eggs en cocotte with cream.* Sprinkle grated Parmesan cheese over the eggs and pour melted butter over. Bake in the oven in a *bain-marie.*

Eggs en cocotte à la périgourdine. OEUFS EN COCOTTE À LA PÉRIGOURDINE – Break the eggs into *cocottes* lined with a purée of *foie gras*. Put a nut of butter on the yolks. Bake in the oven in a *bain-marie*. When cooked, surround the yolks with a ring of *Périgueux sauce* (see SAUCE).

Eggs en cocotte à la rouennaise. OEUFS EN COCOTTE À LA ROUENNAISE – Cook as for *Eggs en cocotte à la périgourdine*, using *à gratin forcemeat* (see FORCEMEAT) instead of purée of *foie gras*. Surround with a ring of *Wine sauce* (see SAUCE) to which butter has been added.

Eggs en cocotte à la strasbourgeoise. OEUFS EN COCOTTE À LA STRASBOURGEOISE – Line the *cocottes* with chopped truffles, add the eggs, and cook in the oven in a *bain-marie*. Garnish each *cocotte* with a knob of *foie gras* sautéed in butter. Surround with concentrated *Demi-glace sauce* (see SAUCE) to which Madeira and butter have been added.

Eggs en cocotte with tarragon. OEUFS EN COCOTTE À L'ESTRAGON – Cook the eggs as described under *Eggs en cocotte* (see EGGS, *Basic egg dishes*). When the eggs are cooked, pour a ring of concentrated veal gravy flavoured with tarragon round the yolks. Garnish with blanched tarragon leaves, arranged in a star. The *cocottes* can be lined with chopped tarragon, if desired.

Eggs en cocotte à la tartare. OEUFS EN COCOTTE À LA TARTARE – Mince raw beef finely. Add chopped chives and season with salt and pepper. Line the *cocottes* with this mixture and break in the eggs. Pour a ring of fresh cream round the yolks. Bake in the oven in a *bain-marie*.

Colbert eggs (soft-boiled or poached). OEUFS COLBERT – Arrange the cooked eggs in *croustades* garnished with a *macédoine* of vegetables blended with *Béchamel sauce* (see SAUCE). Mask the eggs with *Colbert butter* (see BUTTER, *Compound butters*).

Comtesse eggs (soft-boiled or poached). OEUFS COMTESSE – Bake tartlets and garnish them with a *salpicon* of truffles and mushrooms. Arrange the cooked eggs on top and mask with *Suprême sauce* (see SAUCE) flavoured with sherry. Put 1 slice of truffle on each egg.

Condé eggs I (sur le plat). OEUFS CONDÉ – Pipe a border of puréed red beans onto a buttered ovenproof dish. Grill or fry two slices of lean bacon and arrange them in the bottom of the dish. Break the eggs on top and cook in the usual way.

Condé eggs II (sur le plat). OEUFS CONDÉ – Bake the eggs as in the recipe above and when cooked garnish with 2 small chicken croquettes. Surround with *Suprême sauce* (see SAUCE).

Eggs Conti I (sur le plat). OEUFS CONTI – Line a buttered ovenproof dish with 1 tablespoon lentil purée. Break the eggs into the dish and bake in the usual way. 2 thin slices lean bacon, sautéed in butter or grilled, can be added.

Eggs Conti II (soft-boiled or poached). OEUFS CONTI – Line a pie dish with a thin purée of lentils and arrange the cooked eggs on the purée.

Eggs à la coque – See EGGS, *Basic egg dishes*.

Egg côtelettes (hard-boiled). OEUFS EN CÔTELETTES – Dice the whites and yolks of hard-boiled eggs and blend with a thick *Béchamel sauce* (see SAUCE) to which raw yolks of egg have been added. Chill.

Divide this mixture into 50-g. (2-oz.) pieces and shape into cutlets. Dip in egg and breadcrumbs and deep-fry. Arrange in a circle on a dish. Put a frill on each cutlet and garnish with fried parsley. Serve with *Tomato sauce* (see SAUCE) or other suitable sauce.

Egg côtelettes (cutlets) can also be served with other garnishes, such as green vegetables with butter or cream, *macédoine*, tomato *fondue*, risotto, and different kinds of pasta or purées.

The mixture for egg cutlets may be varied. Diced mushrooms and truffles may be added, or if a meat mixture is preferred, diced ham or diced pickled tongue.

Egg cutlets can be cooked in clarified butter instead of being deep-fried.

Eggs with cream (sur le plat). OEUFS À LA CRÈME – Break the eggs into individual buttered ovenproof dishes. Surround with fresh cream and cook in the usual way.

Alternatively, the cooked eggs can be surrounded with a ribbon of *Cream sauce* (see SAUCE).

Eggs with cream sauce (soft-boiled or poached). OEUFS À LA CRÈME – Put cooked eggs on croûtons fried in butter, and cover with *Cream sauce* (see SAUCE). This recipe is also called *Eggs à la béchamel.*

Eggs à la Crécy I (soft-boiled or poached). OEUFS À LA CRÉCY – Arrange the cooked eggs in a pyramid on a foundation of *Carrot purée* (see PURÉE). Cover with *Cream sauce* (see SAUCE).

Eggs à la Crécy II (sur le plat). OEUFS À LA CRÉCY – Spread 1 tablespoon *Carrot purée* (see PURÉE) on the bottom of small buttered ovenproof dishes and break in the eggs. Cook and then surround with *Cream sauce* (see SAUCE).

Eggs à la créole (fried). OEUFS À LA CRÉOLE – Fry the eggs in oil and arrange on grilled courgette halves. Fill the centre of the dish with *Rice à la créole* (see RICE). Pour *Noisette butter* (see BUTTER, *Compound butters*) over the eggs.

Eggs à la cressonière I (soft-boiled or poached). OEUFS À LA CRESSONIÈRE – Arrange the cooked eggs in a pie dish lined with *Watercress purée.* Cover with *Cream sauce* (see SAUCE). Bake in the oven, or with concentrated veal stock to which butter has been added.

Eggs à la cressonière II (sur le plat). OEUFS À LA CRESSONIÈRE – Pipe a border of thick *Watercress purée* (see WATERCRESS) onto a buttered ovenproof dish. Break in the eggs. Surround the yolks with *Cream sauce* (see SAUCE). Bake in the oven.

Egg croquettes (hard-boiled). OEUFS EN CROQUETTES – Prepare the croquette mixture as for *Egg côtelettes* binding with *White* or *Béchamel sauce* (see SAUCE).

When cold, form the mixture into eggs, or other shapes. Dip in egg and breadcrumbs and fry. Garnish with fried parsley. Serve with *Tomato* or *Cream sauce* (see SAUCE).

Daudet eggs (soft-boiled or poached). OEUFS DAUDET – Arrange the cooked eggs on puff pastry *croustades* covered with chopped breast of chicken. Cover with puréed truffles bound with rich *White sauce* (see SAUCE).

Daumont eggs (soft-boiled or poached). OEUFS DAUMONT – Arrange the cooked eggs on large mushrooms cooked in butter and garnished with a *salpicon* of crayfish tails *à la Nantua.* Cover with *Nantua sauce* (see SAUCE). Put a sliver of truffle on each egg.

Delmonico eggs (soft-boiled or poached). OEUFS DELMONICO – Coat the cooked eggs with *Mornay sauce* (see SAUCE) mixed with chopped truffles, and put them on a *croustade* of noodles filled with lambs' sweetbreads, mushrooms, and truffles, blended with concentrated *Madeira sauce* (see SAUCE). Glaze in the oven.

Demi-deuil eggs (soft-boiled or poached). OEUFS DEMI-DEUIL – Arrange the cooked eggs in a puff pastry shell filled with mushrooms in cream. Cover with *Suprême sauce* (see SAUCE). Garnish with diced truffles blended with concentrated *Madeira sauce* (see SAUCE).

Eggs à la diable (fried). OEUFS À LA DIABLE – Fry the eggs in sizzling (nearly brown) butter. Turn them without breaking the yolks. Arrange on a very hot dish. Sprinkle with brown butter and a dash of heated vinegar.

Eggs à la Diane (soft-boiled or poached). OEUFS À LA DIANE – Arrange the cooked eggs on hollowed-out slices of bread, fried in butter and garnished with puréed game. Cover with *Salmis sauce* (see SAUCE) to which diced truffles and butter have been added.

Dino eggs (soft-boiled or poached). OEUFS DINO – Arrange the cooked eggs in tartlets lined with finely shredded breast of chicken and *cèpes* (or small cultivated mushrooms) mixed with cream. Top with *Curry sauce* (see SAUCE).

Duchess eggs (soft-boiled or poached). OEUFS À LA DUCHESSE – Arrange the cooked eggs on oval potato cakes which have been baked golden. Boil down veal stock, add butter to it and pour over the eggs.

Duxelles eggs (soft-boiled or poached). OEUFS À LA DUXELLES – Arrange the cooked eggs on oval croûtons cooked in butter and garnished with thin slices of ham tossed in butter. Cover with *Duxelles sauce* (see SAUCE) with butter added. Sprinkle with chopped parsley.

Easter eggs. OEUFS DE PÂQUES – Hard-boiled eggs with dyed or painted shells; or sweets made of sugar, chocolate etc., shaped like eggs, which are offered at Easter.

We may owe Easter eggs to the Phoenicians. They

believed that night, the beginning of everything, begot an egg from which came love and the human race. Towards Easter the sun reaches the Equator, the long nights pass, the primeval egg breaks, and mankind is re-born.

In the past at Easter people were content simply to exchange dyed or decorated hens' eggs.

The most popular colour for Easter eggs is bright red. In Germany and some parts of France eggs used to be hidden in the garden and children would search for them, rejoicing when they found them in a green nest.

Hard boiled eggs can be dyed in the following ways.

Coral red. Boil salted water for 45 minutes with a dash of lemon juice, a sachet containing 150 g. (5 oz.) cochineal for 2 litres ($3\frac{1}{2}$ pints, $4\frac{1}{2}$ pints) water, and 50 g. (2 oz.) alum. Cook the eggs in this, keeping them on the boil for 12 minutes. Drain, dip in cold water and dry.

Dark maroon. Cook the eggs, as described above, in water mixed with 250 g. (9 oz.) camwood, and 1 teaspoon each of alum and salt.

Green. Cook the eggs, as described above, in water mixed with spinach which has been scalded, drained and pounded in a mortar.

Yellow. Cook the eggs, as described above, in salted water mixed with yellow onion peel, a pinch of saffron, and a dash of lemon juice.

Modern vegetable dyes make colouring eggs a simple process.

Eggs à l'écarlate I (cold). OEUFS À L'ÉCARLATE – Cover soft-boiled or poached eggs with half-set jelly, to which chopped pickled tongue has been added. Arrange the eggs on slices of pickled or smoked tongue. Cover with jelly.

Eggs à l'écarlate II (soft-boiled or poached). OEUFS À L'ÉCARLATE – Arrange the cooked eggs on croûtons fried in butter. Cover with *Tomato sauce* (see SAUCE) to which butter has been added. Sprinkle with diced, smoked, or pickled tongue.

Eggs à l'écarlate III (sur le plat). OEUFS À L'ÉCARLATE – Put 1 tablespoon concentrated *Tomato sauce* (see SAUCE) into a buttered heatproof dish. Break in the eggs, and sprinkle with finely diced pickled or smoked tongue. Bake until the white is set.

Edward VII eggs (soft-boiled or poached). OEUFS EDOUARD VII – Place the cooked eggs on *Risotto* (see RICE) mixed with diced truffles, alternating the eggs with slivers of pickled or smoked tongue cut in the shape of cocks' combs and heated in sherry. Cover the eggs with concentrated veal stock with butter added, and garnish each with a slice of truffle.

Elisabeth eggs (stuffed). OEUFS ELISABETH – Cut off the ends of hard-boiled eggs so they look like barrels. Take out the yolks without breaking the whites.

Rub the yolks through a fine sieve. Mix with an equal quantity of thick *Artichoke purée* (see PURÉE). Add chopped truffles, and season. Fill the eggs with this mixture, piling it up on top.

Place each egg on an artichoke heart which has been stewed in butter. Cover with *Mornay sauce* (see SAUCE). Sprinkle with grated cheese and melted butter. Brown the top. Arrange the eggs in a crown on a dish. Fill the centre with a *Ragoût of truffles* (see RAGOÛT) cooked in Madeira.

Esaü eggs (soft-boiled or poached). OEUFS ESAÜ – Arrange the cooked eggs in a pyramid on *Lentil purée* (see PURÉE). Garnish with heart-shaped croûtons fried in butter. Pour concentrated veal stock, with butter added, over the eggs.

Alternatively, arrange the eggs on a *croustade* of crustless bread, fried, hollowed out, and filled with lentil purée. Cover with concentrated veal stock with butter added.

Eggs à l'espagnole I (cold). OEUFS À L'ESPAGNOLE – Cover the cooked eggs with meat jelly to which tomato jelly has been added. Decorate each with a ring of blanched onion. Garnish with a pinch of chopped parsley, and cover with half-set jelly. Arrange the eggs on buttered rounds of toast. Surround with small de-seeded tomatoes dressed with oil, vinegar, salt, and pepper, and filled with diced sweet green pimentos seasoned *à la vinaigrette*.

Eggs à l'espagnole II (fried). OEUFS À L'ESPAGNOLE – Fry the eggs in oil. Arrange them in a crown, alternating with halved tomatoes fried in oil. Fill the centre of the dish with onion rings fried in oil. Pour a ring of *Tomato sauce* (see SAUCE) mixed with a *salpicon* of sweet pimentos round the eggs.

Eggs à l'espagnole III (soft-boiled or poached). OEUFS À L'ESPAGNOLE – Arrange the cooked eggs on tomatoes cooked in oil and filled with a *salpicon* of sweet pimentos. Fill the centre of the dish with onion rings fried in oil. Cover the eggs with *Tomato sauce* (see SAUCE) flavoured with red Spanish peppers.

Eggs à l'espagnole IV (sur le plat). OEUFS À L'ESPAGNOLE – Line a fireproof dish with 1 tablespoon chopped onion lightly fried in butter and seasoned with red Spanish pepper. Break in the eggs and cook in the usual way. Garnish with *Tomato fondue* (see FONDUE) mixed with diced sweet pimentos cooked in butter.

Favart eggs (soft-boiled or poached). OEUFS FAVART – Arrange the cooked eggs in small tartlet cases filled with a *salpicon* of calves' sweetbreads, truffles and mushrooms, blended with *Velouté sauce* (see SAUCE). Fill the middle with large truffled quenelles. Cover with *Suprême sauce* (see SAUCE).

Eggs à la flamande I (soft-boiled or poached). OEUFS À LA FLAMANDE – Arrange the cooked eggs on a layer of chicory (U.S. Belgian endive) cooked in butter. Cover with *Allemande* or *Cream sauce* (see SAUCE).

Alternatively, arrange the poached eggs on croûtons fried in butter. Put a head of chicory cooked *à la flamande* between each egg. Boil down the cooking liquor from the endives, add cream, and bring to the boil. Add fresh butter and pour over the eggs.

Eggs à la flamande II (sur le plat). OEUFS À LA FLAMANDE – This name usually means the same as *Eggs à la bruxelloise*, but poached, soft-boiled, or fried eggs, garnished with hop shoots cooked in butter or cream are also called *Eggs à la flamande*.

Florentine eggs (soft-boiled, poached, or sur le plat). OEUFS À LA FLORENTINE – Arrange the cooked eggs in *gratin* dishes on a layer of spinach cooked in butter. Cover with *Mornay sauce* (see SAUCE). Sprinkle with grated cheese and melted butter, and brown in a hot oven.

Eggs à la forestière I (poached). OEUFS À LA FORESTIÈRE – Arrange the cooked eggs on *croustades* filled with morels fried in butter and mixed with fried, diced bacon. Cover the eggs with *Chateaubriand sauce* (see SAUCE). Sprinkle with chopped parsley.

Eggs à la forestière II (sur le plat). OEUFS À LA FORESTIÈRE – Garnish the ovenproof dishes with diced, blanched bacon, lightly fried in butter. Break in the eggs and put 1 tablespoon morels, fried in butter, on each side. Cook in the oven and then season. Pipe *Chateaubriand sauce* (see SAUCE) round the edges.

Georgette eggs (poached). OEUFS GEORGETTE – Partly hollow out a baked potato and put in 1 tablespoon *Crayfish tail ragoût à la Nantua* (see CRAYFISH). Add a poached egg and cover with *Nantua sauce* (see SAUCE). Sprinkle with grated Parmesan and melted butter. Brown the top in a hot oven.

Grand Duke eggs I (soft-boiled or poached). OEUFS GRAND-

Florentine eggs (*Robert Carrier*)

DUC – Arrange the cooked eggs on oval croûtons fried in butter (or on puff pastry shells) with a sliver of truffle on each. Cover with *Mornay sauce* (see SAUCE). Sprinkle with grated cheese and melted butter. Brown the tops in a hot oven. Garnish with diced truffles and asparagus tips.

Grand Duke eggs II (sur le plat). OEUFS GRAND-DUC – Cover the eggs in their dishes with a light *Mornay sauce* (see SAUCE). Sprinkle with grated cheese and melted butter. Cook in a hot oven. Garnish with diced truffles and asparagus tips.

Eggs au gratin (soft-boiled or poached). OEUFS AU GRATIN – Prepare like *Mornay eggs* (see below).

Halévy eggs (soft-boiled or poached). OEUFS HALÉVY – Arrange the cooked eggs in tartlets baked blind. Garnish with a *salpicon* of chicken blended with *velouté sauce*. Cover half with *allemande sauce*, half with tomato sauce, to which butter has been added.

Hard-boiled eggs with endive. OEUFS DURS SUR CHICORÉE – Arrange the hard-boiled eggs on braised endive cooked in stock or cream. Cover with concentrated veal stock or a light *Cream sauce* (see SAUCE).

Hard-boiled eggs with various garnishes. OEUFS DURS AVEC GARNITURES DIVERSES – Shell the hard-boiled eggs and heat them in salted boiling water. Drain and dry them.

Arrange and garnish them as shown in the various recipes.

Hard-boiled eggs on a macédoine of vegetables. OEUFS DURS SUR MACÉDOINE DE LÉGUMES – Arrange the hard-boiled eggs on a *macédoine* of vegetables blended with butter or cream.

Hard-boiled eggs on various purées. OEUFS DURS SUR PURÉES DIVERSES – Hard-boiled eggs can be served with a purée of asparagus, carrots, celery, mushrooms, chicory, lettuce, chestnuts, sorrel, sweet potato, or Jerusalem artichokes.

Hard-boiled eggs with watercress. OEUFS DURS À LA CRESSONNIÈRE – Arrange the hard-boiled eggs on a bed of *Watercress purée* (see WATERCRESS). Cover with *Cream sauce* (see SAUCE).

Eggs in cups à la hollandaise. OEUFS EN TASSE À LA HOLLANDAISE – Butter 3 teacups and coat the insides with grated cheese. Add a layer of diced ham to each cup and pour in 1 egg whisked as for an omelette. Cover with a layer of ham and top with a thick layer of cheese. Cook for 12 minutes in a *bain-marie*. Serve with *Tomato sauce* (see SAUCE).

Eggs à l'italienne I (fried). OEUFS À L'ITALIENNE – Fry eggs in oil and arrange in a crown on a round dish. Alternate with thin slices of ham sautéed in butter. Pour *Italian sauce* (see SAUCE) over the eggs.

Eggs à l'italienne II (soft-boiled or poached). OEUFS À L'ITALIENNE – Fry slices of crustless bread in butter and spread with a *salpicon* of chopped ham blended with a Madeira-flavoured *Demi-glace sauce* (see SAUCE). Arrange the cooked eggs on top and pour *Italian sauce* (see SAUCE) with butter added, over the eggs. Sprinkle with chopped parsley.

Eggs à l'italienne III (sur le plat or en cocotte). OEUFS À L'ITALIENNE – Line buttered fireproof dishes or *cocottes* with

Preparing eggs à la hollandiase (*Claire*)

Placing the cups in a *bain-marie* (*Claire*)

lean, chopped ham. Break in the eggs and cook in the usual way. Pour a ring of *Italian sauce* (see SAUCE) round the eggs.

Jeannette eggs (en cocotte). OEUFS JEANNETTE EN COCOTTE – Line a *cocotte* with a layer of chicken *Quenelle forcemeat* (see FORCEMEATS). Break in the eggs and cook in the usual way. Garnish with asparagus tips. Surround with *Velouté sauce* (see SAUCE).

Jellied eggs à la française. OEUFS GLACÉS À LA FRANÇAISE – See *Eggs as a border IV*.

Jellied tarragon eggs, also called à la Chartres. OEUFS À L'ESTRAGON À LA GELÉE, À LA CHARTRES – Line moulds shaped like half an egg, or *dariole* moulds, with white tarragon-flavoured meat jelly. Decorate with blanched tarragon leaves. Arrange the eggs (poached or soft-boiled) in the moulds and fill them with jelly. Leave on ice to set.

Turn the eggs out and arrange them in a crown formation. Fill the centre with chopped jelly. Decorate with jelly croûtons.

Alternatively, decorate the cooked eggs with tarragon leaves and glaze with jelly. Arrange them in a deep dish on thin slices of cooked ham. Cover with half-set jelly. Chill on ice before serving. This is the method most often used in restaurants.

Poached or soft-boiled eggs can also be arranged in individual *cassolettes* lined with thin slices of ham and filled with jelly.

Jockey-club eggs (sur le plat). OEUFS JOCKEY-CLUB – Cook the eggs *sur le plat*. Trim with a cutter, leaving only a thin band of white. Place the eggs on grilled croûtons spread with purée of *foie gras* and arrange in a crown formation. Fill the middle of the dish with sliced calf's kidney sautéed in Madeira. Top each egg with a sliver of truffle.

Egg kromeskies (hard-boiled). OEUFS EN CROMESQUIS – Prepare an egg croquette mixture, as for *Egg côtelettes*, adding truffles and mushrooms. Bind with *Allemande sauce* (see SAUCE), allowing $3\frac{1}{2}$ dl. (generous $\frac{1}{2}$ pint, $1\frac{1}{2}$ cups) for 500 g. (18 oz.) *salpicon*. Leave the mixture to cool.

Divide into small portions and make them into oval or cork-shaped cakes. Dip in a light batter and fry in deep fat. Drain, and season with fine salt. Garnish with fried parsley. Serve with *Tomato sauce* (see SAUCE).

Egg kromeskies à la polonaise. OEUFS EN CROMESQUIS À LA POLONAISE – Prepare the mixture as above and divide into small portions when cold. Shape into rectangles. Wrap each one in a thin *crêpe* (pancake). Dip in a light batter and fry in deep fat. Serve with *Tomato* or *Piquante sauce* (see SAUCE).

Eggs à la languedocienne (fried). OEUFS À LA LANGUEDOCIENNE – Fry the eggs in oil. Arrange each on a slice of aubergine fried in oil. Fill the middle of the dish with garlic-flavoured *Tomato fondue*. Dot with Noisette butter (see BUTTER. *Compound butters*).

Eggs à la lorraine (sur le plat). OEUFS À LA LORRAINE – Line a buttered ovenproof dish with thin rashers of grilled bacon and slivers of Gruyère cheese. Break in the eggs. Pour a ring of fresh cream round the yolks and bake in the oven.

Lucullus eggs (soft-boiled or poached). OEUFS LUCULLUS – Arrange each cooked egg on an artichoke heart cooked in butter and garnished with a *salpicon* of lambs' sweetbreads, truffles, and mushrooms, bound with concentrated *Velouté sauce* (see SAUCE).

Cover the eggs with *Suprême sauce* (see SAUCE) to which coarsely diced truffles have been added. Put diced *foie gras* which has been seasoned with salt and pepper and tossed in butter in the centre of the dish. Alternate the eggs with cocks' combs *à la Villeroi*.

Eggs à la maraîchère (sur le plat). OEUFS À LA MARAÎCHÈRE – Line an ovenproof dish with 1 tablespoon *chiffonnade* (q.v.) of lettuce, sorrel, and chervil, tossed in butter. Break in the eggs. Add a thin rasher of bacon sautéed in butter. Bake in the usual way.

Marianne eggs (soft-boiled or poached). OEUFS MARIANNE – Arrange the cooked eggs on de-seeded tomato halves cooked in butter and filled with thick *Tomato fondue* (see FONDUE). Top each egg with a slice of black Madagascar potato cooked in butter, and coat with *Maître d'hôtel butter* (see BUTTER, *Compound butters*) mixed with dissolved meat jelly.

Marivaux eggs (soft-boiled or poached). OEUFS MARIVAUX – Garnish a flan case, baked blind, with a *salpicon* of mushrooms and truffles. Arrange the cooked eggs in the flan. Pour concentrated Madeira-flavoured *Demi-glace sauce* (see SAUCE) with butter added, over the eggs.

Masséna eggs (soft-boiled or poached). OEUFS MASSÉNA – Place each cooked egg on an artichoke heart cooked in butter and garnished with thick *Béarnaise sauce* (see SAUCE). Top each with a slice of poached marrowbone fat. Surround with *Marrow sauce I* (see SAUCE) and sprinkle with chopped parsley.

Massenet eggs (soft-boiled or poached). OEUFS MASSENET – Put the cooked eggs into *croustades* made of *Duchess potato mixture* (see POTATOES) and filled with a *salpicon* of French beans dressed with butter. Cover with *Marrow sauce I* (see SAUCE). Sprinkle with chopped parsley.

Eggs à la ménagère (fried). OEUFS À LA MÉNAGÈRE – Fry the eggs in butter. Arrange them on a bed of stock pot vegetables, sliced and sautéed in butter. Surround with a ring of *Tomato sauce* (see SAUCE).

Meyerbeer eggs (sur le plat). OEUFS MEYERBEER – Garnish cooked eggs with grilled lamb's kidney. Surround with *Périgueux sauce* (see SAUCE).

Eggs à la milanaise (fried). OEUFS À LA MILANAISE – Fry the eggs in oil. Arrange in a dish on a bed of *Macaroni à la milanaise* (see MACARONI), and surround with *Tomato sauce* (see SAUCE).

Mirette eggs (poached). OEUFS MIRETTE – Poach the yolks only. Place each in a tartlet case baked blind and garnished with a *salpicon* of chicken breast and truffles blended with Madeira-flavoured thick *Velouté sauce* (see SAUCE). Pour *Suprême sauce* (see SAUCE) over the eggs.

Miroir eggs. OEUFS MIROIR – Another name for eggs *sur le plat*.

Monselet eggs (soft-boiled or poached). OEUFS MONSELET – Arrange the cooked eggs on artichoke hearts cooked in butter. Cover with chicken *Velouté sauce* (see SAUCE), mixed with one third of its volume of veal stock and the same quantity of cream, flavoured with sherry and boiled down. Garnish with diced truffles cooked in butter, and small potato croquettes.

Montrouge eggs I (soft-boiled or poached). OEUFS MONTROUGE – Arrange the cooked eggs in tartlet cases baked blind, and garnished with *Mushroom purée* (see PURÉE). Cover with *Suprême sauce* (see SAUCE).

Montrouge eggs II (sur le plat or en cocotte). OEUFS MONTROUGE – Butter the ovenproof dishes and pipe a border of *Mushroom purée* (see PURÉE) through a forcing bag. Break in the eggs. Surround the yolks with fresh cream. Bake in the oven.

Alternatively, break the eggs into a *cocotte* lined with *Mushroom purée* (see PURÉE). Surround the yolks with fresh cream. Cook in the oven, in a *bain-marie*.

Mornay eggs I (soft-boiled or poached). OEUFS MORNAY – Arrange the cooked eggs in a fireproof dish on a layer of *Mornay sauce* (see SAUCE) or on croûtons fried in butter. Cover with *Mornay sauce*. Sprinkle with grated cheese and melted butter. Brown the top in the oven.

Mornay eggs sur le plat

Mornay eggs II (sur le plat). OEUFS MORNAY – Break the eggs into an ovenproof dish lined with *Mornay sauce* (see SAUCE). Cover with the sauce. Sprinkle with grated cheese and melted butter, and brown in the oven.

Eggs à la Nantua I (soft-boiled or poached). OEUFS À LA NANTUA – Arrange the cooked eggs in tartlets filled with *Crayfish tail ragoût à la Nantua* (see CRAYFISH). Cover with *Nantua sauce* (see SAUCE). Top each egg with a sliver of truffle.

Eggs à la Nantua II (sur le plat). OEUFS À LA NANTUA – Fill a buttered ovenproof dish with crayfish tails. Break in the eggs and cook in the oven. Put a sliver of truffle on each yolk. Cover with *Nantua sauce* (see SAUCE).

Eggs with noisette butter (sur le plat). OEUFS AU BEURRE NOISETTE – Heat the butter in a flameproof dish until light brown or *noisette*. Break the eggs into the heated butter and bake in the usual way.

Eggs à la normande (soft-boiled or poached). OEUFS À LA NORMANDE – Arrange the cooked eggs on puff pastry *croustades*, filled with a *salpicon* of mussels, mushrooms and shrimps' tails, bound with *Normande sauce* (see SAUCE). Put a poached and debearded oyster on each egg. Cover with *Normande sauce*. Top each egg with a sliver of truffle.

Omelette – See under separate heading at the end of this section.

Eggs opéra (sur le plat). OEUFS OPÉRA – Garnish the cooked eggs on one side with sliced chicken livers sautéed in Madeira, and on the other with asparagus tips. Surround with a ring of boiled-down veal stock, with butter added.

Eggs à la parisienne (sur le plat). OEUFS À LA PARISIENNE – Break the eggs into ovenproof dishes lined with chicken forcemeat mixed with pickled smoked tongue, truffles, and chopped mushrooms. Cook in the usual way. Surround with a ring of *Demi-glace sauce* (see SAUCE).

Parmentier eggs I. OEUFS PARMENTIER – Bake 4 large potatoes in the oven. Halve them and scoop out the pulp, taking care not to break the skin. Blend the pulp with butter and cream, and season. Line the potato skins with this pulp, and break 1 egg into each half. Sprinkle with cream and bake in the oven.

Alternatively, prepare the potatoes as described above, and put a poached egg into each potato half. Cover with *Mornay sauce* (see SAUCE). Sprinkle with grated cheese and melted butter and brown the top in the oven.

Parmentier eggs II (sur le plat). OEUFS PARMENTIER – Butter an ovenproof dish and line with diced potatoes, fried in butter. Break in the eggs. Surround with a ring of cream and cook in the oven.

Eggs à la Polignac (in moulds). OEUFS À LA POLIGNAC – Break the eggs into buttered individual *dariole* moulds, with a sliver of truffle in each. Cook in a *bain-marie*. Unmould the eggs onto croûtons fried in butter. Top with *Maître d'hôtel butter* (see BUTTER, *Compound butters*) mixed with dissolved meat jelly.

Eggs à la portugaise I (soft-boiled or poached). OEUFS À LA PORTUGAISE – Arrange each cooked egg on a tomato half which has been cooked in oil. Cover with *Portugaise sauce* (see SAUCE).

Eggs à la portugaise II (sur le plat). OEUFS À LA PORTUGAISE – Break each egg into a buttered ovenproof dish on 1 tablespoon *Tomato fondue* (see FONDUE). Cook in the oven.

Princess eggs (soft-boiled or poached). OEUFS PRINCESSE – Arrange the cooked eggs on croûtons or in puff pastry *croustades*. Cover with *Suprême sauce* (see SAUCE). Garnish with asparagus tips and chicken breasts shredded into *julienne* strips. Top each egg with a sliver of truffle.

Eggs à la printanière I (soft-boiled or poached). OEUFS À LA PRINTANIÈRE – Arrange the cooked eggs on a puff pastry base covered with a *printanière* (q.v.) of vegetables dressed with cream. Prepare *Suprême sauce* (see SAUCE) with *Printanier butter* added. Pour over the eggs. Garnish with asparagus tips in butter.

Eggs à la printanière II (cold). OEUFS À LA PRINTANIÈRE – Arrange the eggs (soft-boiled or poached) on a bed of *macédoine* (q.v.) of vegetables dressed with mayonnaise strengthened with gelatine. Garnish with green asparagus tips. Decorate the eggs with tarragon leaves. Cover with half-set jelly.

Eggs à la provençale I (soft-boiled or poached). OEUFS À LA PROVENÇALE – Arrange each cooked egg on a halved tomato cooked in oil. Cover with clear, garlic-flavoured *Tomato fondue* (see FONDUE). Garnish with coarsely diced aubergines fried in oil. Sprinkle with chopped parsley.

Eggs à la provençale II (sur le plat). OEUFS À LA PROVENÇALE – Rub individual ovenproof dishes with garlic and line them with slices of aubergines fried in oil. Break in the eggs and bake in the oven. Pour a ring of *Provençale sauce* (see SAUCE), round the yolks.

Eggs à la provençale III (fried). OEUFS À LA PROVENÇALE – Fry the eggs in oil and arrange each one on a halved tomato fried in oil. Garnish with slices of aubergine, fried in oil, and fried parsley.

Eggs à la provençale IV (fried). OEUFS À LA PROVENÇALE – Spread thinly sliced aubergines, fried in oil, on a dish. Alternate with halved tomatoes, pressed, seeded, and fried in oil. Arrange fried eggs on this layer, and sprinkle with sizzling butter to which 1 tablespoon chopped parsley mixed with chopped garlic has been added.

Eggs à la provençale V (glazed in jelly). OEUFS À LA PROVENÇALE – Coat the eggs (soft-boiled or poached) with tomato-flavoured, gelatine-strengthened mayonnaise. Decorate with tarragon leaves and glaze with jelly. Arrange each egg on a halved tomato, which has been seeded, steeped in oil, vinegar, salt and pepper, stuffed with diced potatoes and aubergines, and dressed with garlic-flavoured mayonnaise. Arrange the eggs in a crown and garnish with chopped parsley.

Rachel eggs (fried). OEUFS RACHEL – Fry the eggs in butter. Trim with a round pastry-cutter, leaving only a thin band of white.

Arrange each egg on a slice of bread fried in butter. Cover with *Marrow sauce* (see SAUCE). Top with a thin slice of marrow.

Eggs à la reine I (soft-boiled or poached). OEUFS À LA REINE – Arrange the cooked eggs in tartlets filled with *Chicken purée* (see PURÉE), and cover with *Suprême sauce* (see SAUCE).

Eggs à la reine II (sur le plat or en cocotte). OEUFS À LA REINE – Butter the ovenproof egg dishes or *cocottes* and pipe a border of *Chicken purée* (see PURÉE) through a forcing-bag. Break in the eggs. Surround the yolks with thick chicken *Velouté sauce* (see SAUCE) with cream. Cook in the oven.

Eggs à la romaine (fried). OEUFS À LA ROMAINE – Fry the eggs in oil. Toss chopped spinach in *Noisette butter* (see BUTTER, *Compound butters*) and mix with diced anchovies. Arrange the eggs on top, and sprinkle with more *noisette butter*.

Rossini eggs I (soft-boiled or poached). OEUFS ROSSINI – Arrange each cooked egg on a slice of *foie gras* sautéed in butter. Top with 2 slices of truffle tossed in butter. Cover with Madeira-flavoured *Demi-glace sauce* (see SAUCE).

Alternatively, arrange the eggs in puff pastry tartlets lined with coarsely diced *foie gras*. Garnish with slivers of truffles. Boil down a Madeira-flavoured *Demi-glace sauce* (see SAUCE), add butter, and pour over the eggs.

Rossini eggs II (sur le plat or en cocotte). OEUFS ROSSINI – Break the eggs into buttered ovenproof dishes or *cocottes* lined with a *salpicon* of *foie gras* and truffles. Bake in the oven. Surround with concentrated Madeira-flavoured *Demi-glace sauce* (see SAUCE) with butter added.

Rothomago eggs (sur le plat). OEUFS ROTHOMAGO – Line the ovenproof dishes with slices of ham tossed in butter. Break in the eggs and cook in the usual way. Garnish with grilled chipolata sausages. Surround with *Tomato sauce* (see SAUCE).

Eggs à la royale (soft-boiled or poached). OEUFS À LA ROYALE – Arrange the cooked eggs on puff pastry cases filled with a *salpicon* of truffles blended with concentrated Madeira-flavoured *Demi-glace sauce* (see SAUCE). Cover with chicken *Velouté sauce* (see SAUCE) mixed with puréed truffles diluted with cream and flavoured with Madeira.

Eggs à la Saint-Hubert (soft-boiled or poached). OEUFS À LA SAINT-HUBERT – Arrange the cooked eggs in a pie dish on a layer of minced venison or any other game. Cover with game *Poivrade sauce* (see SAUCE). Garnish with puff pastry crescents or heart-shaped croûtons fried in butter.

Scotch eggs I (soft-boiled or poached). OEUFS À L'ÉCOSSAISE – Arrange the cooked eggs on puff pastry croûtes covered with *Salmon purée* (see PURÉE). Cover with *Shrimp sauce* (see SAUCE). Decorate each egg with a sliver of truffle.

Scotch eggs II (cold). OEUFS À L'ÉCOSSAISE – Make a forcemeat using finely minced cooked ham, 2 to 3 pounded anchovy fillets and enough fresh breadcrumbs to give 'body'. Season with salt, pepper, and mixed spices. Bind with raw egg and blend well. Shell hard-boiled eggs and coat each with the forcemeat. Dip in egg and breadcrumbs and deep-fry in hot fat.

Scrambled eggs – See EGGS, *Basic egg dishes*.

Scrambled eggs à l'américaine. OEUFS BROUILLÉS À L'AMÉRICAINE – Add to the scrambled eggs, diced bacon fried in butter. Garnish with rashers of grilled bacon and halved grilled tomatoes.

The same name is used for scrambled eggs with sliced lobster or spiny lobster *à l'americaine*. Recipes for these dishes will be found under *Scrambled eggs à l'armoricaine* (see below).

Scrambled eggs à l'ancienne. OEUFS BROUILLÉS À L'ANCIENNE – Add mushrooms and diced truffles tossed in butter, to the scrambled eggs. Arrange in a flan case baked blind. Garnish with cocks' kidneys in sherry-flavoured *Velouté sauce* (see SAUCE) with cream. Surround with cocks' combs *à la Villeroi* and sherry-flavoured *Suprême sauce* (see SAUCE).

Scrambled eggs à l'antiboise. OEUFS BROUILLÉS À L'ANTIBOISE – Arrange scrambled eggs in a deep ovenproof dish, alternating with sliced courgettes sautéed in oil, and with *Tomato fondue* (see FONDUE). Finish with a layer of eggs. Sprinkle with grated Parmesan and melted butter. Brown in a hot oven.

Scrambled eggs Argenteuil. OEUFS BROUILLÉS ARGENTEUIL – Garnish the scrambled eggs with white asparagus tips, half cooked in salted water and then simmered in butter. Surround with *Cream sauce* (see SAUCE). Decorate with croûtons fried in butter.

Scrambled eggs à l'arlésienne. OEUFS BROUILLÉS À L'ARLÉSIENNE – Scramble the eggs with garlic-flavoured *Tomato fondue* (see FONDUE). Cook courgettes in butter. Halve them, remove the pulp and mix the chopped pulp with the scrambled eggs. Fill the halved courgette skins with the scrambled egg mixture and put them in a buttered fireproof dish. Sprinkle with grated Parmesan and melted butter. Brown the top. Surround with *Tomato sauce* (see SAUCE).

Scrambled eggs à l'armoricaine. OEUFS BROUILLÉS À L'ARMORICAINE – Arrange the scrambled eggs in a deep dish, alternating with a *salpicon* of *Lobster* or *Spiny lobster à l'américaine* (see LOBSTER). Put slices of lobster or spiny lobster on the eggs and surround with *American sauce* (see SAUCE).

Scrambled eggs with artichokes. OEUFS BROUILLÉS AUX ARTICHAUTS – Mix the scrambled eggs with cooked artichoke hearts, sliced or diced, and sautéed in butter.

Garnish with sliced artichoke hearts sautéed in butter,

and bread croûtons fried in butter. Surround with concentrated veal stock.

Scrambled eggs à la Bercy. OEUFS BROUILLÉS À LA BERCY – Arrange the scrambled eggs in a deep dish. Garnish with chipolata sausages, grilled or cooked in butter. Surround with *Tomato sauce* (see SAUCE).

Scrambled eggs with cèpes. OEUFS BROUILLÉS AUX CÈPES – Sauté sliced *cèpes* in butter or oil. Add them to the scrambled eggs. Arrange in a deep dish, with the *cèpes* in the middle. Garnish with croûtons fried in butter. Surround with concentrated veal stock.

Scrambled eggs with chicken livers. OEUFS BROUILLÉS AUX FOIES DE VOLAILLE – Heap the scrambled eggs on a heated dish. Garnish with sliced chicken livers, sautéed in butter and bound with *Demi-glace sauce* (see SAUCE). Sprinkle with chopped parsley.

Scrambled eggs Clamart. OEUFS BROUILLÉS CLAMART – Mix the eggs with *Peas à la française* (see PEA). Garnish with more peas.

Scrambled eggs with crayfish. OEUFS BROUILLÉS AUX ÉCREVISSES – Prepare as *Scrambled eggs with shrimps* (see below) using crayfish tails and *Nantua sauce* (see SAUCE).

Scrambled eggs 'l'échelle'. OEUFS BROUILLÉS 'L'ÉCHELLE' – Prepare scrambled eggs with cheese. Butter an earthenware dish and line it with croûtons of crustless bread fried in butter. Cover with thick slices of truffles heated in butter and seasoned with salt and pepper. Put the eggs in the dish.

Smooth the surface and sprinkle with grated cheese and melted butter. Brown the top.

Scrambled eggs à l'espagnole I. OEUFS BROUILLÉS À L'ESPAGNOLE – Fill halved, seeded tomatoes, cooked in oil, with scrambled eggs and a *salpicon* of sweet peppers. Garnish with onion rings fried in oil.

Scrambled eggs à l'espagnole II. OEUFS BROUILLÉS À L'ESPAGNOLE – Garnish the scrambled eggs with diced tomatoes cooked in oil and mixed with a *salpicon* of sweet pimentos. Top with onion rings fried in oil.

Scrambled eggs à la forestière. OEUFS BROUILLÉS À LA FORESTIÈRE – Garnish the scrambled eggs with morels fried in butter with chopped shallot and diced lean bacon. Top with a mound of morels. Surround with *Demi-glace sauce* (see SAUCE). Sprinkle with chopped parsley.

Scrambled eggs Georgette. OEUFS BROUILLÉS GEORGETTE – Bake large potatoes. Scoop out three-quarters of the pulp and fill with scrambled egg. Garnish with *Crayfish tail ragoût à la Nantua* (see CRAYFISH).

Scrambled eggs with ham or bacon. OEUFS BROUILLÉS AU JAMBON, AU LARD MAIGRE (OU BACON) – Add to the scrambled eggs, diced ham or bacon, blanched and lightly fried. Top with slices of lightly fried ham or rashers of bacon.

Scrambled eggs Massenet. OEUFS BROUILLÉS MASSENET – Garnish the scrambled eggs with diced artichoke hearts sautéed in butter. Arrange in a *timbale* and garnish further with small slices of *foie gras*, slivers of truffle, and asparagus tips. Surround with concentrated veal stock.

Scrambled eggs with mushrooms (various). OEUFS BROUILLÉS AUX CHAMPIGNONS – Add sliced or diced mushrooms, sautéed in butter and seasoned with salt and pepper, to the eggs.

Garnish with sliced mushrooms and croûtons. Surround with concentrated veal stock.

Scrambled eggs à la Nantua. OEUFS BROUILLÉS À LA NANTUA – Garnish the scrambled eggs with diced crayfish tails and truffles. Decorate with *Crayfish tail ragoût à la Nantua* and sliced truffles heated in butter.

Scrambled eggs à la normande. OEUFS BROUILLÉS À LA NORMANDE – Arrange the scrambled eggs in a flan case baked blind and garnished with shelled mussels bound with *Velouté sauce* (see SAUCE) based on fish stock and mixed with cream. Garnish with oysters poached in their own liquid and debearded, slivers of truffles tossed in oil, and shrimps' tails in *Shrimp sauce* (see SAUCE). Surround with croûtons fried in butter, and *Normande sauce* (see SAUCE).

Scrambled eggs panetière. OEUFS BROUILLÉS PANETIÈRE – Scramble the eggs and add mushrooms and diced ham fried in butter. Hollow out a round loaf, like a *croustade*. Butter the inside and brown lightly in the oven. Fill with the scrambled eggs and sprinkle with grated cheese and melted butter. Brown the top.

Scrambled eggs Parmentier. OEUFS BROUILLÉS PARMENTIER – Heap the scrambled eggs on a heated plate and garnish with diced potatoes sautéed in butter and rolled in meat jelly. Sprinkle with chopped parsley.

Scrambled eggs à la périgourdine. OEUFS BROUILLÉS À LA PÉRIGOURDINE – Prepare as for *Scrambled eggs Rossini* (see below). A *salpicon* of *foie gras* and truffles can be added to the scrambled eggs.

Scrambled eggs with potatoes. OEUFS BROUILLÉS AUX POMMES DE TERRE – Like *Scrambled eggs Parmentier*. It can also be made with potatoes boiled in their skins, peeled, sliced, and sautéed in butter.

Scrambled eggs princess. OEUFS BROUILLÉS PRINCESSE – Garnish the scrambled eggs with asparagus tips simmered in butter. Arrange in a *timbale* or in a flan case baked blind. Top with chicken breast cut into *julienne* strips and bound with *Suprême sauce* (see SAUCE), and with slivers of truffles tossed in butter. Surround with *suprême sauce*.

Scrambled eggs à la reine. OEUFS BROUILLÉS À LA REINE – Arrange the eggs in rows in a *vol-au-vent* case, alternating with thick *Chicken purée* (see PURÉE). Surround with *Suprême sauce* (see SAUCE).

Scrambled eggs à la romaine. OEUFS BROUILLÉS À LA ROMAINE – Scramble the eggs with grated Parmesan cheese. Arrange on a bed of leaf spinach cooked in butter and mixed with anchovy fillets. Sprinkle with grated Parmesan and melted butter. Brown the top.

Scrambled eggs Rossini. OEUFS BROUILLÉS ROSSINI – Arrange the eggs in a *timbale* or in a flan case baked blind. Garnish with slices of *foie gras* and slivers of truffles heated in butter. Surround with concentrated Madeira-flavoured *Demi-glace sauce* (see SAUCE).

Scrambled eggs Sagan. OEUFS BROUILLÉS SAGAN – Scramble the eggs with cheese. Arrange in a *timbale* or in a flan case baked blind. Garnish with escalopes of brains dredged in flour and sautéed in butter, and with slivers of truffles heated in butter. Surround with concentrated veal stock.

Scrambled eggs Saint-Hubert. OEUFS BROUILLÉS SAINT-HUBERT – Garnish the scrambled eggs with game purée bound with *Demi-glace sauce* (see SAUCE), based on concentrated game stock.

Scrambled eggs with a salpicon of lobster, spiny lobster or other shellfish. OEUFS BROUILLÉS AU SALPICON DE HOMARD (DE LANGOUSTE ETC.) – As *Scrambled eggs with shrimps* (see below) using a *salpicon* of the shellfish indicated. Serve with *Cream sauce* (see SAUCE) with white wine. Finish with the butter appropriate to the particular shellfish.

Scrambled eggs with shrimps. OEUFS BROUILLÉS AUX CREVETTES – Add peeled shrimps' tails, heated in butter, to the scrambled eggs. Garnish the top with a mound of shrimps' tails heated in butter or in *Shrimp sauce* (see SAUCE). Surround with croûtons fried in butter. Pour a ring of shrimp sauce round the eggs.

Sévigné eggs (soft-boiled or poached). OEUFS SÉVIGNÉ – Place each cooked egg on half a braised lettuce. Cover with *Suprême sauce* (see SAUCE). Top each egg with a sliver of truffle.

Eggs with shrimps I (sur le plat). OEUFS AUX CREVETTES – Bake the eggs in a buttered ovenproof dish with 1 tablespoon shrimp tails. Surround with *Shrimp sauce* (see SAUCE).

Eggs with shrimps II (soft-boiled or poached). OEUFS AUX CREVETTES – Line tartlets, baked blind, with shrimps blended with *Shrimp sauce* (see SAUCE). Arrange the eggs on this mixture and cover with the sauce.

Eggs with shrimps III (cold). OEUFS AUX CREVETTES – Coat *dariole* moulds with fish *aspic jelly* (see ASPIC). Line the sides with shrimps' tails. Pour over liquid jelly to set them. Place a soft-boiled egg in each mould. Fill with jelly and chill on ice.

Unmould the eggs onto grilled croûtons spread with *Shrimp butter* (see BUTTER, *Compound butters*). Arrange in a crown. Garnish with diced potatoes and shrimps' tails, dressed with mayonnaise strengthened with gelatine.

Decorate the top of each egg with three shrimps' tails arranged to look like a plume. Surround the croûtons with fish aspic jelly.

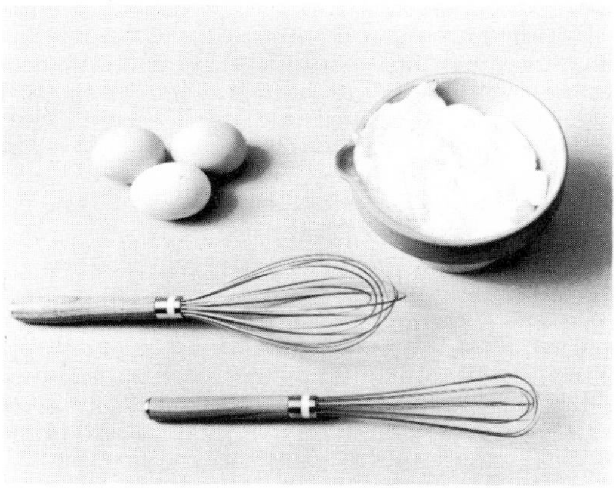

Snow eggs (*Nicolas*)

Snow eggs. OEUFS À LA NEIGE – Whisk egg whites and add sugar, as for a meringue. Take as much of the meringue mixture as 1 tablespoon will hold, which will give them an egg shape, and drop spoonful by spoonful into a saucepan of boiling milk sweetened with sugar and flavoured with vanilla. Poach the eggs, turning them so they cook evenly. When they are firm, drain in a fine sieve.

Use the milk left to make *Custard cream* (see CREAMS). Leave to cool.

Arrange the eggs in a dish and pour the custard over them.

Eggs à la soubise (hard-boiled). OEUFS DURS À LA SOUBISE – Arrange hard-boiled eggs on *Onion soubise* (see PURÉE). Cover with *Cream sauce* (see SAUCE).

Spanish eggs – See *Eggs à l'espagnole.*

Stanley eggs (soft-boiled or poached). OEUFS STANLEY – Arrange the cooked eggs in tartlet cases baked blind and filled with *Onion soubise* (see PURÉE). Cover with *Curry sauce* (see SAUCE).

Tarragon eggs (sur le plat). OEUFS À L'ESTRAGON – Break the eggs into a buttered ovenproof dish containing 1 tablespoon tarragon-flavoured veal stock. Cook until the whites are set. Surround with more stock. Decorate with blanched tarragon.

Tarragon eggs, also called eggs à la Chartres (soft-boiled or poached). OEUFS À L'ESTRAGON, À LA CHARTRES – Arrange the cooked eggs on croûtons fried in butter. Cover them with tarragon-flavoured veal stock. Decorate with tarragon leaves, blanched and well drained.

Eggs à la tripe, also called eggs à la béchamel soubisée (hard-boiled). OEUFS À LA TRIPE, À LA BÉCHAMEL SOUBISÉE – Cut hard-boiled eggs into quarters or thick round slices. Arrange in a pie dish. Cover with *Soubise sauce* (see SAUCE).

Verdier eggs (stuffed). OEUFS VERDIER – Sieve hard-boiled egg yolks and mix with cooked *foie gras*. Stuff the halves of egg white with this mixture.

Arrange in a *gratin* dish on a layer of sliced onions cooked in butter, blended with 1 tablespoon *Béchamel sauce* (see SAUCE), and seasoned with curry.

Cover with *béchamel sauce* mixed with a *julienne* of truffles. Sprinkle with Parmesan. Brown in a hot oven.

Victoria eggs (soft-boiled or poached). OEUFS VICTORIA – Arrange the cooked eggs in puff pastry cases lined with a *salpicon* of spiny lobster, or lobster, and truffles, bound with *Victoria sauce* (see SAUCE). Top each egg with a slice of lobster and a slice of truffle.

Eggs à la Villeroi (soft-boiled or poached). OEUFS À LA VILLEROI – Small cooked eggs are used for this dish. Coat with *Villeroi sauce* (see SAUCE) and leave to get cold. Dip in egg and breadcrumbs and fry. Arrange in a crown. Garnish with fried parsley and serve with *Tomato sauce* (see SAUCE).

Eggs à la Zingara (soft-boiled or poached). OEUFS À LA ZINGARA – Arrange the cooked eggs on oval croûtons fried in butter and covered with a thin slice of lean ham. Coat with *Zingara sauce* (see SAUCE).

OMELETTE – The etymology of this word is uncertain. It may have been derived from *amelette*, a corruption of *alemette*, derived from *alemelle* or *alumette*.

The name *ova mellita* was used by the Ancient Romans for eggs beaten with honey and cooked in an earthenware dish. This derivation seems more logical.

Recipes for sweet (dessert) omelettes will be found at the end of this section. The recipe for basic omelettes appears under EGGS, *Basic egg dishes*.

Filled omelettes. OMELETTES FOURRÉES – Omelettes, before being folded, can be filled with various mixtures (forcemeat, purée, salpicon), as indicated in individual recipes. The garnish should be hot, and folded carefully into the omelette.

Flat omelettes. OMELETTES PLATES – These are cooked in butter or other fat, and made flat like a thick pancake.

Garnished omelettes. OMELETTES GARNIES – The garnish, as indicated in individual recipes, can either be added while the eggs are being beaten, or put in the omelette when folding it. In addition to the inside filling, a little of the garnish is usually put on top of the omelette.

Agnes Sorel omelette. OMELETTE AGNÈS SOREL – Fill the omelette with sliced mushrooms which have been sautéed in butter and bound with *Chicken purée* (see PURÉE). Decorate the top with slices of pickled or smoked tongue. Boil down some veal stock, add butter, and pour round the omelette.

Omelette Albina – Add diced truffles to the eggs during beating. Cook the omelette in the usual way and fill with thick *Chicken purée* (see PURÉE). Pour *Velouté sauce* (see SAUCE) mixed with cream round the omelette.

Omelette à l'alsacienne – Cook the omelette in goose fat, and fill with braised, well drained *sauerkraut.* Cover the omelette with thin slices of ham and surround with *Demi-glace* sauce (see SAUCE).

Anchovy omelette. OMELETTE AUX ANCHOIS – Rub the fillets of desalted anchovy through a sieve, and add to the beaten eggs. Cook the omelette as usual. Cut desalted anchovy fillets into thin strips and place on top.

Omelette André-Theuriet – Fill the omelette with morels *à la crème*. Serve garnished with asparagus tips lightly cooked in butter, and with slivers of truffle tossed in the same butter. Surround with *Suprême sauce* (see SAUCE).

Archduke omelette. OMELETTE ARCHIDUC – Add chopped onion, lightly fried in butter and seasoned with paprika, to the seasoned beaten eggs before cooking. Garnish with slivers of truffle heated in butter, and surround with a paprika sauce.

Omelette Argenteuil – Fill the cooked omelette with white or green asparagus tips lightly cooked in butter, and put 1 tablespoon asparagus tips on top. Surround with *Allemande sauce* or *Cream sauce* (see SAUCE).

Artichoke omelette. OMELETTE AUX ARTICHAUTS – Add to the eggs, when beating, artichoke hearts which have been half-cooked then sliced and sautéed in butter. Cook. Garnish with a few of the artichoke hearts. Serve with concentrated veal stock with a little butter added.

Omelette with asparagus tips. OMELETTES AUX POINTES D'ASPERGES – Mix diced asparagus tips, which have been tossed in butter, into the beaten eggs. Garnish the cooked omelette with asparagus tips and sprinkle with melted butter.

Aubergine omelette. OMELETTE AUX AUBERGINES – Place slices of fried aubergine on the cooked omelette and surround with *Demi-glace sauce* or *Tomato sauce* (see SAUCE).

Bacon omelette. OMELETTE AU BACON – Add 4 tablespoons ($\frac{1}{3}$ cup) diced bacon, lightly fried in butter, to the beaten egg. Garnish the cooked omelette with thin rashers of cooked bacon.

Omelette à la Bércy – Add chopped *fines herbes* to the beaten egg. Garnish the cooked omelette with grilled or sautéed chipolata sausages, and surround with *Tomato sauce* (see SAUCE).

Omelette à la bigourdane – Fill the omelette with diced truffles and diced *foie gras*. Serve with *Madeira sauce* (see SAUCE).

Bone-marrow omelette. OMELETTE À LA MOELLE – *Flat*. Garnish the cooked omelette with slices of bone-marrow fat, poached in salt water and drained. Spoon a little liquid meat jelly over each slice of marrow and serve with *Marrow sauce* (see SAUCE).

Fluffy. Fill the omelette with a *salpicon* of bone-marrow fat bound with marrow sauce. Garnish with slices of marrow which have been poached in salted water and drained. Serve with marrow sauce.

Omelette à la bouchère – Fill the omelette with diced bone-marrow fat, poached and bound with liquid meat jelly. Put a row of poached marrow slices on top, and spoon liquid meat jelly over the omelette.

Omelette à la bruxelloise – Cook very small Brussels sprouts in salted water until three-quarters done. Drain, dry, and fry in butter. Stir the sprouts into beaten eggs before making the omelette. Surround with concentrated veal stock.

Carrot omelette – See *Omelette à la Crécy*.

Omelette with cèpes. OMELETTE AUX CÈPES – Add sliced *cèpes* (which have been fried in butter or oil) and chopped parsley to the beaten eggs. Top the cooked omelette with *cèpes*.

Omelette chasseur – Fill the omelette with sautéed chicken livers mixed with sliced mushrooms. Garnish the cooked omelette with the same ingredients. Serve with *Chasseur sauce* (see SAUCE) and sprinkle with chopped parsley.

Omelette à la châtelaine – Fill the omelette with braised and mashed chestnuts bound with concentrated veal stock. Serve with *Cream sauce* (see SAUCE).

Omelette with chervil. OMELETTE AU CERFEUIL BULBEUX – Add chopped turnip-rooted chervil, cooked in butter, and some chopped chervil, to the beaten eggs.

Chicken liver omelette. OMELETTE AUX FOIES DE VOLAILLE – Fill the omelette with sliced chicken livers which have been sautéed briskly in butter and bound with concentrated *Demi-glace sauce* (see SAUCE). Top the cooked omelette with chicken livers, as above, and serve with Madeira-flavoured *Demi-glace sauce* (see SAUCE).

Omelette Choisy – Fill the omelette with *Chiffonade of lettuce with cream* (see LETTUCE). Serve with *Cream sauce* (see SAUCE).

Omelette Clamart – Fill the omelette with *Peas à la française* (see PEA) keeping the mixture rather thick. When serving, put 1 tablespoon of the mixture on top of the cooked omelette.

Courgette omelette. OMELETTE AUX COURGETTES – *Flat*. Cut the courgettes in thin slices and sauté in butter. Beat the eggs with chopped parsley, season with salt and pepper, and pour over the marrows in the pan.

Fluffy. Fill the omelette with the diced courgettes sautéed in butter or oil and mixed with chopped parsley.

Omelette à la Crécy – Fill the omelette with 2 tablespoons (3 tablespoons) thick *Carrot purée* (see PURÉE). Decorate the top with a row of sliced carrots cooked in butter. Serve with *Cream sauce* (see SAUCE).

Omelette with croûtons. OMELETTE AUX CROÛTONS – *Flat*. Fry diced bread in butter. Beat the eggs with chopped parsley and pour over the croûtons. Make the omelette as a pancake.

Fluffy. Fry diced bread in butter and add to the eggs while beating them, together with chopped parsley. Make the omelette in the usual way.

Omelette Diane – Add seasoned sliced mushrooms, fried in butter, to the beaten egg. Fill the omelette with a *salpicon* of partridge or any other winged game, and truffles, bound with concentrated *Velouté sauce* (see SAUCE) based on game *fumet* (q.v.). Garnish the cooked omelette with a row of truffle slices tossed in butter. Serve with *Demi-glace sauce* (see SAUCE) based on game stock.

Diplomat omelette. OMELETTE DIPLOMATE – Make a flat omelette with 3 eggs. Cover with a layer of lobster and truffle *salpicon* bound with *Béchamel sauce* (see SAUCE) flavoured with lobster butter and brandy.

Top this omelette with another 3-egg omelette, keeping it creamy. Cover with *Mornay sauce* (see SAUCE) flavoured with lobster butter. Sprinkle with grated Parmesan and melted butter, and brown in a hot oven.

Omelette Du Barry – Boil cauliflower flowerets in salted water. Drain, and fry in clarified butter. Pour in the eggs, beaten with chopped chervil and seasoned with salt and pepper. Make a pancake omelette and serve with *Cream sauce* (see SAUCE).

Omelette à la duxelles – Fill the omelette with *duxelles* (q.v.) mixture to which diced ham has been added. Serve with tomato-flavoured *Demi-glace sauce* (see SAUCE).

Omelette à la fermière – Add to the beaten eggs 3 tablespoons (scant $\frac{1}{4}$ cup) of a *paysanne* (q.v.) of vegetables composed of sliced carrots, onions and celery, lightly fried in butter and seasoned with salt, pepper, and chopped parsley.

Fry 2 tablespoons (3 tablespoons) diced lean ham lightly in butter, pour the egg mixture over, and make a flat omelette.

Omelette à la flamande – Fill the omelette with shredded chicory (U.S. Belgian endive) cooked in butter and bound with cream. Serve with *Cream sauce* (see SAUCE).

Omelette Feydeau – Make a creamy omelette, keeping it rather liquid. Fill with *Mushroom purée* (see PURÉE).

Omelette Feydeau

Place a row of soft-boiled eggs on the cooked omelette. Cover with *Mornay sauce* (see SAUCE) mixed with a *julienne* of truffles. Sprinkle with grated Parmesan and brown the top.

Omelettes aux fines herbes – Add to the beaten eggs, chopped parsley, chervil, tarragon, and spring onion or chives. There should be enough of these herbs to make the omelette green.

Omelette à la florentine – Fill the omelette with leaf spinach cooked in butter. Serve with a light *Mornay sauce* (see SAUCE). Sprinkle with grated Parmesan and brown quickly.

Omelette à la forestière – Add 2 tablespoons (3 tablespoons) diced lean bacon, fried in butter, to the beaten eggs. Fill the omelette with morels which have been sautéed in butter, bound with concentrated veal stock, and sprinkled with chopped parsley. Serve with veal stock to which has been added a little butter.

Omelette à la gasconne – Add to the beaten eggs diced unsmoked ham, thinly sliced onions lightly fried in butter, chopped garlic and parsley. Make a flat omelette.

Omelette à la grecque – Add to the beaten eggs chopped onion lightly fried in butter, and diced sweet pimentos. Make 2 flat omelettes, spreading a layer of mutton hash between them. Serve with garlic-flavoured *Tomato sauce* (see SAUCE) and sprinkle with chopped parsley and *Noisette butter* (see BUTTER, *Compound butters*).

Ham omelette. OMELETTE AU JAMBON – As *Bacon omelette*, using diced lean ham.

Omelette with hop shoots. OMELETTE AUX JETS DE HOUBLON – Fill the omelette with hop shoots *à la crème*. Serve with *Cream sauce* (see SAUCE).

Hungarian omelette. OMELETTE À LA HONGROISE – Fry diced unsmoked lean ham lightly in butter. Add an equal quantity of diced onions, also fried in butter. Season with paprika. Add this mixture to the beaten eggs and make a flat pancake. Serve with *Hungarian sauce* (see SAUCE).

Japanese omelette. OMELETTE À LA JAPONAISE – Fill the omelette with Chinese artichokes cooked in butter and sprinkled with chopped parsley. Serve with *Cream sauce* (see SAUCE).

Omelette à la jardinière – Cook carrots, turnips, French beans, peas, potatoes, etc. in water or stock. Drain, and fry lightly in butter. Add to the beaten eggs and make a flat omelette. Garnish with cooked asparagus tips and cauliflower flowerets, and serve with *Cream sauce* (see SAUCE).

Omelette à la jurassienne – Add scalded, diced lean bacon, lightly fried in butter, and chopped spring onions to the beaten eggs. Fill the omelette with sorrel which has been cooked in butter.

Kidney omelette. OMELETTE AUX ROGNONS – Sauté diced calf's or lamb's kidneys in butter and bind with Madeira-flavoured, concentrated *Demi-glace sauce* (see SAUCE).

Lobster omelette. OMELETTE AU HOMARD – Prepare as *Shrimp omelette* (see below), using a *salpicon* of lobster bound with *Lobster sauce* (see SAUCE).

Omelette à la lorraine – Add to the beaten eggs diced lean bacon sautéed in butter, shredded Gruyère cheese, and chopped spring onion. Make a flat omelette.

Omelette Louis Forest – Beat the eggs with diced truffles cooked in butter, and make 2 flat omelettes. Spread one of them with slices of fresh *foie gras* sautéed in butter, and cover with the second omelette. Spoon over 1 tablespoon concentrated, Madeira-flavoured veal stock, and sprinkle with *Noisette butter* (see BUTTER, *Compound butters*).

Omelette à la lyonnaise – Add to the beaten eggs finely chopped onions, lightly fried in butter, and chopped parsley. Make a flat omelette. Sprinkle on the omelette a few drops of vinegar heated in the same pan, and pour over it *Noisette butter* (see BUTTER, *Compound butters*).

Omelette Maintenon – Fill the omelette with a *salpicon* of chicken, truffles, and mushrooms, bound with *Velouté sauce* (see SAUCE) diluted with cream. Keep the omelette creamy when cooking it. Cover with *Béchamel sauce* (see SAUCE) with onion, sprinkle with grated Parmesan and melted butter, and brown in the oven.

Omelette à la ménagère – Cut left-over pieces of beef into dice and fry lightly in butter. Add an equal quantity of diced onion, also cooked in butter. Beat the eggs with chopped parsley, season with salt and pepper, mix with the other ingredients, and make a flat omelette.

Omelette Mistral. Fry diced aubergines in oil. Fry diced tomatoes lightly in butter, add chopped parsley and a pinch of garlic, and mix with the aubergines. Add this mixture to the beaten eggs and make a flat omelette.

Omelette Monselet – Fill the omelette with a *salpicon* of artichoke hearts and truffles *à la crème*. Garnish with slivers of truffles heated in butter. Serve with Madeira-flavoured *Demi-glace sauce* (see SAUCE).

Omelette Montbry – Beat the eggs with grated horseradish, chopped spring onions, parsley, and seasoning. Make 2 flat omelettes. Spread one with a *salpicon* of celeriac bound with *Cream sauce* (see SAUCE) and seasoned with paprika. Cover with the second omelette. Spoon light *Mornay sauce* (see SAUCE) over them, sprinkle with grated Parmesan and melted butter, and brown under the grill or in a hot oven.

Omelette with morels. OMELETTE AUX MORILLES – Add to the eggs (while beating them) morels sautéed in butter, and chopped parsley. Make a flat omelette.

Omelette with morels à la crème. OMELETTE AUX MORILLES À LA CRÈME – Fill the omelette with morels *à la crème* and serve with *Cream sauce* (see SAUCE).

Omelette mousseline – Mix 6 egg yolks with 2 tablespoons (3 tablespoons) cream and season with salt and pepper. Add the stiffly whisked whites and fold into the mixture. Make a flat omelette.

Mushroom omelette. OMELETTE AUX CHAMPIGNONS – Add 2 tablespoons (3 tablespoons) sliced mushrooms, sautéed in butter, to the beaten eggs. Make a flat omelette and decorate with a row of mushroom slices.

Omelette à la nancéienne – *Flat.* Beat the eggs with chopped onion lightly fried in butter, and chopped parsley. Make 2 flat omelettes. Put slices of black pudding, lightly fried in butter, on 1 omelette and cover with the second. Pour over them concentrated veal stock, and sprinkle with *Noisette butter* (see BUTTER, *Compound butters*).

Fluffy. Beat the eggs with lightly fried chopped onion and chopped parsley. Fill with pieces of fried black pudding. Serve with boiled-down veal stock to which a little butter has been added.

Cheese mousseline omelette

Omelette à la Nantua – Fill the omelette with crayfish tails bound with *Nantua sauce* (see SAUCE). Garnish with crayfish tails and slivers of truffles. Serve with the sauce.

Omelette à la niçoise – Mix the eggs with *Tomato fondue* (see FONDUE), chopped parsley, and a pinch of garlic. Make a flat omelette and garnish with anchovies arranged in a criss-cross pattern. Sprinkle with *Noisette butter* (see BUTTER, *Compound butters*).

Omelette à la normande – Fill the omelette with a *ragoût* of shrimps' tails and mushrooms bound with *Normande sauce* (see SAUCE). Garnish with debearded oysters poached in their own liquid, and slivers of truffles. Serve with *normande sauce*.

Okra omelette à la créole. OMELETTE AUX GOMBOS À LA CRÉOLE – Add to the eggs, while beating them, diced onions, peeled and diced sweet pimentos – both of which have been cooked in butter – and chopped parsley. Fill the omelette with okra cooked in butter and mixed with *Tomato fondue* (see FONDUE) flavoured with a pinch of garlic. Serve with *Tomato sauce* (see SAUCE).

Omelette à la parisienne – Add chopped onion and chopped mushrooms, both sautéed in butter, to the beaten eggs. Cover the cooked omelette with chipolata sausages cooked in butter or grilled. Serve with concentrated veal stock to which a little butter has been added.

Omelette Parmentier – Fry diced potatoes, cooked or raw, in butter and add chopped parsley. Mix them with the beaten eggs for a flat omelette or use them to fill a fluffy omelette.

Omelette à la paysanne – Add to the beaten eggs chopped sorrel and sliced potatoes, both lightly fried in butter, together with pounded parsley and chervil. Make a flat omelette.

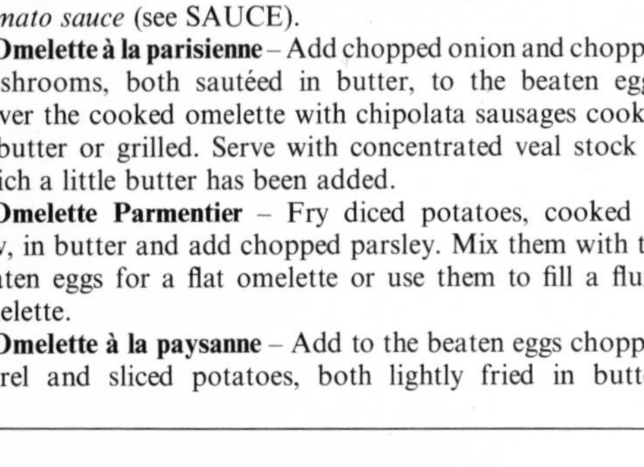

Omelette à la nancéienne

Polish omelette. OMELETTE À LA POLONAISE – Fill the omelette with mutton hash bound with *Demi-glace sauce* (see SAUCE). Garnish with *Tomato fondue* (see FONDUE). Sprinkle with chopped parsley and serve with *Tomato sauce* (see SAUCE).

Portuguese omelette. OMELETTE À LA PORTUGAISE – Fill the omelette with *Tomato fondue* (see FONDUE) and serve with *Tomato sauce* (see SAUCE).

Potato omelette – See *Omelette Parmentier*.

Princess omelette. OMELETTE PRINCESSE – Add green asparagus tips cooked in butter to the beaten eggs. Garnish with truffle slices heated in butter and serve with *Suprême sauce* (see SAUCE).

Omelette à la provençale – Cook peeled, seeded, and diced tomatoes in butter or oil. Season with salt and pepper and a pinch of garlic. Beat the eggs with pounded parsley and make a fluffy omelette, filling it with the tomato mixture.

Omelette à la romaine. Fry chopped onion lightly in butter and add chopped parsley. Make 2 flat omelettes. Spread one with leaf spinach cooked in *Noisette butter* (see BUTTER) and mixed with diced anchovy fillets. Cover with the second omelette.

Spoon *Mornay sauce* (see SAUCE) over the omelettes, sprinkle with grated Parmesan and melted butter, and brown under the grill or in a hot oven.

Omelette Rossini – Add a *salpicon* of *foie gras* and truffles to the beaten eggs. Garnish the flat omelette with slices of *foie gras* and slivers of truffles. Serve with Madeira-flavoured *Demi-glace sauce* (see SAUCE).

Omelette à la rouennaise – Fill the omelette with duck liver purée. Serve with red wine, boiled down and blended with meat jelly and butter.

Omelette à la royale – Make a small omelette using eggs mixed with truffle purée and fill it with a *ragoût* of cock's-combs and kidneys, mushrooms, and truffles, bound with *Velouté sauce* mixed with cream. Make a second, larger omelette with eggs mixed with fresh cream and seasoned with salt and pepper. Fold it over the smaller omelette and garnish with small slices of *foie gras* and slivers of truffles. Serve with port-flavoured *Suprême sauce* (see SAUCE).

Omelette à la Saint-Flour – Add to the eggs, while beating them, chopped onions and scalded, diced bacon, both lightly fried in lard. Make 2 flat omelettes. Spread one with a layer of braised, mashed cabbage and cover with the second omelette. Serve with *Tomato sauce* (see SAUCE).

Omelette à la Saint-Hubert – Fill the omelette with a purée of game-meat bound with thick *Demi-glace sauce* (see SAUCE) based on concentrated game stock. Garnish with sliced mushrooms lightly fried in butter and serve with *demi-glace sauce*.

Omelette with salsify and Brussels sprouts, called à la maraîchère. OMELETTE AUX SALSIFIS ET AUX CHOUX DE BRUXELLES, DITE À LA MARAÎCHÈRE – Slice salsify, cook in *court-bouillon*, cut into dice, toss in butter, and bind with thick *Velouté sauce*. Fill a fluffy omelette with this and garnish with small potatoes and Brussels sprouts sautéed in butter. Serve with concentrated *Demi-glace sauce* (see SAUCE) to which butter has been added.

Omelette de Savarin (according to Frédéric) – Philéas Gilbert relates that Frédéric, *chef de cuisine* to an archbishop, had many discussions with the *directeur de la table*, about Frédéric's Lenten mortification dish which was an omelette filled with soft roes and tunny fish.

The roes were cut into thin slices and cooked *à la meunière*. The tunny was dried in a cloth, cut into a coarse *salpicon*, seasoned, and simmered in butter. The eggs were beaten and mixed with thick cream. The tunny and roes were mixed in a shrimp sauce and seasoned. The omelette was filled with this sauce and garnished with slices of truffle or circled with fried frogs' legs.

Omelette à la savoyarde – Fry sliced potatoes and add the beaten eggs, mixed with shredded Gruyère to the pan. Make a flat omelette.

Sea-food omelette. OMELETTE AUX FRUITS DE MER – Beat the eggs with chopped parsley and chervil, season with salt and pepper, and make 2 flat omelettes.

Cover one with a *ragoût* of mussels, shrimps, cockles, and other shellfish, bound with *Shrimp sauce* (see SAUCE). Top with the second omelette, and pour *Cream sauce* (see SAUCE) flavoured with *Shrimp butter* (see BUTTER, *Compound butters*) over them. Glaze under the grill or in a hot oven.

Shrimp omelette. OMELETTE AUX CREVETTES – Fill the omelette with peeled shrimps' tails bound with *Shrimp sauce* (see SAUCE). Serve with the same sauce.

Sorrel omelette. OMELETTE À L'OSEILLE – Add to the beaten eggs, 4 tablespoons ($\frac{1}{3}$ cup) sorrel shredded into a *chiffonade* and lightly fried in butter. Make a flat omelette.

Spanish omelette. OMELETTE À L'ESPAGNOLE – Add to the beaten eggs, sweet pimentos, diced or shredded into *julienne* strips and cooked in butter, chopped parsley, and a pinch of garlic. Make a flat omelette.

Spinach omelette. OMELETTE AUX ÉPINARDS – Sweat leaf spinach in butter and mix with the beaten eggs. Make a flat omelette.

Spiny lobster omelette (crawfish omelette). OMELETTE À LA LANGOUSTE – Make as *Shrimp omelette*, using a *salpicon* of spiny lobster bound with a sauce flavoured with *Spiny lobster butter* (see BUTTER, *Compound butters*).

Spring onion omelette. OMELETTE À LA CIBOULETTE – Add chopped spring onions to the beaten eggs and make a flat omelette.

Sweetcorn omelette. OMELETTE AU MAÏS À LA CRÈME – Fill the omelette with *Fresh corn in cream* (see CORN) and serve with *Cream sauce* (see SAUCE).

Sweet pimento omelette. OMELETTE AUX PIMENTS DOUX – Add to the beaten egg coarsely shredded sweet pimentos (green, yellow or red) cooked in oil. Fry the flat omelette in oil.

Sweet potato omelette. OMELETTE AUX PATATES – Prepare as *Omelette Parmentier* using sweet potatoes fried in butter.

Tomato omelette and bacon

Swiss omelette. OMELETTE À LA SUISSE – Add Emmenthal cheese and cream to the beaten eggs. Make a flat omelette.

Omelette à la Talleyrand – Add to the beaten eggs, diced onions lightly fried in butter and seasoned with a pinch of curry powder. Make a flat omelette and garnish with slices of calves' sweetbreads dipped in egg and breadcrumbs and sautéed in butter. Serve with *Cream sauce*.

Tomato omelette. OMELETTE AUX TOMATES – Prepare like *Omelette à la provençale* but omit the garlic seasoning.

Truffle omelette. OMELETTE AUX TRUFFES – Add to the beaten eggs, diced truffles lightly tossed in butter. Garnish the flat omelette with slivers of truffle tossed in butter. Serve with *Demi-glace sauce* (see SAUCE) flavoured with Madeira and truffle essence.

Tunny omelette (Brillat-Savarin's recipe). OMELETTE AU THON – Wash and blanch soft carps' roes in slightly salted boiling water for 5 minutes. Drain and chop finely. Chop up a piece of tunny and add to the roes, together with a small, finely chopped shallot. Sauté the mixture in best butter, blending well.

Heat a second piece of butter with parsley and chopped spring onions. Pour this mixture onto a warmed dish intended for the omelette, sprinkle with lemon juice, and keep warm. Beat 12 fresh eggs and add the roe and tunny mixture to them. Make a long, thick omelette and transfer it to the prepared dish. Serve very hot. This recipe is also called *Omelette du curé*.

Two-coloured omelette. OMELETTE PANACHÉE – Beat 3 eggs with thick spinach purée or tomato pulp, and make an omelette, keeping the interior semi-liquid.

Make another omelette, using 6 eggs. When folding, put the smaller omelette inside it. Surround with *White, Brown*, or *Tomato sauce* (see SAUCE).

Omelette à la verdurière – Add to the beaten egg a *chiffonade* of sorrel and lettuce tossed in butter, chopped parsley, chervil, and tarragon. Make a flat omelette and sprinkle with *Noisette butter* (see BUTTER).

Omelette viveur – Cook 2 diced artichoke hearts in *court-bouillon*, drain, and fry briskly in clarified butter. Remove from the pan and fry 2 tablespoons blanched, diced, celeriac in the same butter. Drain.

Fry 75 g. (3 oz.) diced fillet of beef seasoned with salt and paprika, in the same butter. Put the artichokes and celeriac back into the pan and mix. Beat the eggs with chopped parsley and chervil and pour into the pan with the other ingredients. Make a flat omelette.

SWEET (DESSERT) OMELETTES. OMELETTES D'ENTREMETS –

Omelette à la Célestine – Three small omelettes, filled with apricot jam, arranged in a row on a dish, sprinkled with fine sugar and glazed in a hot oven.

Omelette à la dijonnaise – Beat the eggs with sugar, finely crushed macaroons, and double cream. Make 2 flat omelettes. Spread one with a thick layer of *French pastry cream* (see CREAM) mixed with ground almonds and flavoured with blackcurrant jam, and cover with the second omelette. Spoon meringue on the top and sides. Sprinkle with icing sugar, glaze in a very hot oven, and serve with blackcurrant jam.

Frangipane omelettes. OMELETTES À LA FRANGIPANE – Beat 10 eggs with 3 tablespoons (scant $\frac{1}{4}$ cup) fine sugar, 2 tablespoons (3 tablespoons) melted butter, and 1 dl. (6 tablespoons, scant $\frac{1}{2}$ cup) cream. Add a small pinch of salt.

Make 10 small flat omelettes. When cooked, put them on a baking sheet, spread each with a layer of *Frangipane cream* (see CREAM), fold, cut off the ends, sprinkle with fine sugar, and glaze in a very hot oven.

Norwegian omelette or Baked Alaska (*Robert Carrier*)

Jam omelette. OMELETTE AUX CONFITURES – Prepare like *Jam and fruit omelette* (see below) replacing the fruit by thick jam.

Jam and fruit omelette. OMELETTE À LA CONFITURE ET AUX FRUITS – Beat the eggs with fine sugar, adding a pinch of salt. Cook in butter in the usual way. When folding the omelette, fill with the desired fruit which is usually cooked *en compote* in vanilla-flavoured syrup, drained, bound with a jam suitable for the fruit, and flavoured with liqueur. Sprinkle with fine sugar and glaze under the grill or in a hot oven.

Liqueur omelette flambée. OMELETTE AUX LIQUEURS FLAMBÉE – Rum omelette is the most common of these omelettes. Beat the eggs with fine sugar, add a pinch of salt, and cook the omelette in butter, keeping it semi-liquid inside. Sprinkle with fine sugar and pour warmed rum over it. Set it alight when serving.

Armagnac, Calvados, Cognac, whisky, kirsch and other spirits and liqueurs made from various fruits can be used instead of rum.

Normandy apple omelette. OMELETTE À LA NORMANDE – Beat 10 eggs with sugar and fresh cream. Peel and cut 3 cooking apples into slices. Cook the apples in butter and vanilla-flavoured sugar. Add 4 tablespoons ($\frac{1}{3}$ cup) fresh double cream, and flavour with 2 tablespoons (3 tablespoons) Calvados. Make the omelette and fill with the apple mixture. Glaze under the grill and serve with double cream.

Norwegian omelette (U.S. Baked Alaska). OMELETTE À LA NORVÉGIENNE – The invention of the *omelette à la norvégienne* is attributed to an American-born physicist, Benjamin Thompson. But Baron Brisse, writing in 1866, states that a French chef learnt the secret of ice being baked in the oven from a Chinese colleague who came to Paris with a Chinese Mission. He describes the delicate operation:

'Chill the ice cream until hard, wrap it in a very light pastry crust and put in a hot oven. The pastry is baked before the ice can melt. This phenomenon is explained by the poor conductibility of certain substances. Gourmets can thus give themselves the double pleasure of biting through piping-hot crust, and cooling the palate on contact with the ice cream.'

Alternatively, put a piece of Genoa cake 2 cm. ($\frac{3}{4}$ inch) thick on an ovenproof dish, sprinkle with liqueur and put the ice cream on top. Enclose the entire cake with a layer of meringue and sprinkle with icing sugar. Bake in a very hot oven so that the meringue quickly becomes golden brown, but not long enough for the heat to penetrate through to the ice cream.

Norwegian omelette with pineapple. OMELETTE À LA NORVÉGIENNE À L'ANANAS – Proceed as described in the preceding recipe, using as a filling pineapple ice cream and pineapple cooked in syrup.

Omelette Reine Pédauque – Beat the eggs with fine sugar, fresh cream, and ground almonds. Make 2 flat omelettes. Spread one with a thick layer of apple purée mixed with fresh cream and flavoured with kirsch. Put the second omelette on top and cover the whole with a layer of meringue. Sprinkle with icing sugar and put in a very hot oven until the meringue is golden brown, and has set.

Soufflé omelette. OMELETTE SOUFFLÉE – Blend 250 g. (9 oz., generous cup) fine sugar and 6 egg yolks with vanilla flavouring or grated lemon or orange rind. Mix until the mixture turns white and forms a ribbon.

Whisk 8 egg whites into a very stiff froth and fold gently into the above mixture. Butter an ovenproof dish and sprinkle it with fine sugar. Pour in the omelette mixture (having reserved a little) and smooth it with the blade of a knife. Decorate the omelette by piping the reserved mixture on it through a forcing-bag. Sprinkle with very fine sugar and bake in a hot oven.

Strawberry omelette. OMELETTE AUX FRAISES – Make an omelette with eggs beaten with sugar, a pinch of salt, and a little cream. Steep strawberries in rum, or kirsch, and sugar, and fold them into the omelette. Sprinkle with fine sugar and glaze under the grill. Surround with crushed strawberries sprinkled with sugar and flavoured with liqueur.

Omelette with sugar. OMELETTE AU SUCRE – Beat the eggs with sugar and a small pinch of salt. Flavour the omelette with grated orange, lemon or tangerine rind, sprinkle with fine sugar, and glaze the omelette under the grill.

FISHES' EGGS. OEUFS DE POISSONS – Eggs of certain kinds of fish are used for food. The most highly esteemed are those of the sturgeon and sterlet, which are used for preparing caviare. Other edible fishes' eggs include those of the shad, of which the Americans are very fond, and those of fresh or pickled herring which are delicate in taste.

The eggs of various shellfish are also edible.

REPTILES' EGGS, TURTLE EGGS. OEUFS DE REPTILE, OEUFS DE TORTUE – Reptiles' eggs are very little used in European cookery. They are, however, much prized by the Arabs and the Indians who are particularly fond of the cayman's eggs. Turtle eggs are mainly used for soup.

EGG-TIMER. SABLIER – Small glass utensil made of two bulbous glass containers narrowing in the middle, where they communicate by means of a very small opening. One of the containers has a fixed quantity of sand which passes into the other when the egg-timer is turned upside down. It takes 3 minutes to do this – the usual time allowed for soft-boiling an egg.

EGLANTINE, DOG-ROSE. EGLANTIER – Wild rose-bush. The hips are red, ovoid, and elongated, and contain about a dozen small hairy ossicles.

Hip pulp has astringent properties, and is used to make jam. Dog-rose hip preserve is still sometimes used for chronic diarrhoea. It is prepared by steeping the hips, with the seeds and hair scraped out, in white wine, and cooking the pulp in $1\frac{1}{2}$ times its weight in sugar.

EGYPT. ÉGYPTE – Egyptian *cuisine* is influenced to a certain extent by that of Europe (especially in the luxury hotels) but its principal source of inspiration is Oriental. Present day Egyptian gastronomy is as good, if not better, than that of many European countries.

The staple diet of Egyptians is bread made from maize flour. Vegetables are highly esteemed and there are plenty of varieties to choose from. Rice is served both as a dish in its own right (such as the popular *rozzette*) and as a garnish.

A vegetable called *foul médames*, seasoned with mint, is considered by the Egyptians to be their national dish. *Molokheya* soup, with its special herb seasoning, is the national soup.

Green soup consists of a highly seasoned rabbit or chicken stock garnished with finely chopped green leaf vegetables. It is eaten with rice and tomato sauce.

Charcoal-grilled mutton is the favourite meat in Egypt. Since bullocks are used for farm work, their flesh is very tough and only suitable for stews.

The *bamia* is another much appreciated vegetable. Then there are sweet potatoes (sold in the streets in winter just as roast chestnuts are in Paris, London and Vienna). Potatoes and Jerusalem artichokes are also available as, in fact, are most of the vegetables cultivated in Europe.

Egg-timers (*Maison et jardin. Phot. Nicolas*)

There is a delicious variety of giant crayfish fished in the Red Sea (known by the Italian name, *gambari*) and *batarekh*, a kind of local caviare.

The most typical cakes are the marzipan *baklawa* and *konafa*; they are Syrian in origin.

The most widely cultivated Egyptian fruit is the date, of which there are fifteen varieties. There are excellent large, sweet, limes, and sugar cane. The latter is sold in special shops, the juice being extracted on the spot for the customer. Egypt, unlike other countries, does not use this juice to make rum. There are also oranges, mandarins, grenadines, mangoes, bananas, etc.

EGYPTIAN LOTUS. NELUMBO – Aquatic plant, also known as *Nile lily*. This magnificent plant, which was the sacred lotus of ancient Egypt, is now no longer found on the Nile, but it still grows in India and China. Its leaves and roots are edible and its fruit contains up to thirty kernels which are very delicate in flavour.

EIDER – Species of wild duck.

ELDERBERRY GOURILOS. MOELLE DE SUREAU – After paring away the woody outer casing, green elderberry stalks can be cooked in the same way as artichoke stalks or endive stumps.

ELECTRICITY. ÉLECTRICITÉ – A form of energy which is only apparent to our senses when it has been converted into chemical, calorific, illuminative, mechanical, or other energy.

Electricity was first used as a culinary aid during a dinner given under the French Restoration, when chickens were served that had been killed neither by wringing their necks nor slitting their throats, a fact that excited the curiosity of the guests when they were told. Upon hearing that the fowls had been electrocuted, they suddenly found a fine, distinctive flavour in the flesh.

Domestic fowls are no longer electrocuted, but electricity has come into use in the kitchen as a motive power for driving labour-saving devices, and as a heating medium. Electric cookers are clean and highly efficient, with sophisticated temperature control, and offer maximum precision in the preparation of food.

The development of electrical household equipment has made necessary the installation of high voltage electrical points in the kitchen. The installation of these points should be entrusted only to qualified electrical experts. There should be no plugs near water inlets; flex should be channelled through tubes or insulated in other ways (all connections should be carefully insulated, certain types of equipment should be earthed, etc.). Loose lengths of flex should be avoided; it is better to increase the number of electrical points, so that the various pieces of equipment can be plugged in as close as possible to their area of use. The strength of the power-feed must be sufficient to allow for any increase in the number of electrical appliances used at one time.

Modern electrical equipment, with its high level of efficiency, is usually safe, but it is advisable to buy from reliable manufacturers whose goods are quality-tested and guaranteed.

Household and kitchen aids can be divided into two categories: a basic machine that operates a number of appliances, or a number of appliances each with its own motor. In large-scale catering (restaurants, institutions, etc.) autonomous pressure cookers, griddles, deep-friers, etc., are used. Appliances like beaters, mixers, mincers, whisks, slicers, etc. help to cut time and labour costs. These, however, cannot entirely take the place of manual labour:

they are useful aids, no more. And not all machines are equipped with a sufficient number of speed variants.

ELEPHANT. ÉLÉPHANT – Elephant meat is edible but leathery. The trunk and feet are regarded as great delicacies in some Asian countries.

ELIXIR. ÉLIXIR – Liquid manufactured by dissolving various elements in alcohol or wine containing a high proportion of alcohol. The old *Codex Pharmacopoeia* included a large number of formulae for elixirs. The present Codex includes only 6, among which are the following:

Elixir of cola. ÉLIXIR DE COLA – 50 g. (2 oz.) fluid extract of cola, 100 g. (4 oz.) 60° proof alcohol, 100 g. (4 oz.) plain syrup and 750 g. ($1\frac{3}{4}$ lb.) Lunel wine.

Elixir of Garus. ÉLIXIR DE GARUS – Steep 1 g. vanilla and $\frac{1}{2}$ g. saffron in 1 kg. ($2\frac{1}{4}$ lb.) spirit of Garus for 2 days.

Infuse 20 g. ($\frac{3}{4}$ oz.) maidenhair fern in 500 g. (18 oz.) boiling water for 30 minutes. Add 200 g. (7 oz.) distilled orange-flower water and 1 kg ($2\frac{1}{4}$ lb., $4\frac{1}{2}$ cups) white sugar. Mix well. Add the spirit to this syrup. Leave to cool and filter.

Elixir of Grande-Chartreuse. ÉLIXIR DE LA GRANDE-CHARTREUSE – Steep the following for 8 days in 10 litres (9 quarts, 11 quarts) alcohol: 650 g. (scant $1\frac{1}{2}$ lb.) each of fresh melissa leaves and hyssop leaves, 300 g. (11 oz.) angelica leaves, 150 g. (5 oz.) cinnamon pod, 50 g. (2 oz.) each of mace and saffron. Distil. Add 1260 g. ($2\frac{3}{4}$ lb., $5\frac{1}{2}$ cups) white sugar.

ELK. ÉLAN – Wild ruminant found in northern Europe. The elk is now the largest stag in existence, and its flesh is edible. All recipes for stag and fallow deer are suitable for elk.

EMBONPOINT – This word once indicated a degree of corpulence in which fat was proportionate to size, but it is now commonly used as a euphemism for slight obesity. Connoisseurs of good food are usually proud of their *embonpoint* although whatever their weight might be they never admit to being fat.

ÉMINCÉ – Dish made with left-over meat. Thinly sliced, it is placed in an ovenware dish and covered with a sauce, such as *bordelaise*, mushroom, *chasseur*, Italian, *piquante*, Robert, Tomato, etc.

These slices of meat must be heated only in the sauce poured over them; they must not boil, especially if roast meat is used. Beef, roebuck, mutton, or lamb are most commonly used for this dish but it is sometimes made with poultry.

Émincés of beef with bordelaise sauce. ÉMINCÉS DE BOEUF SAUCE BORDELAISE – Arrange the slices of meat in a dish and garnish with strips of poached beef bone-marrow. Cover with *Bordelaise sauce* (see SAUCE).

Émincés of beef chasseur. ÉMINCÉS DE BOEUF CHASSEUR – Arrange slices of beef on a dish and cover with boiling *Chasseur sauce* (see SAUCE).

Émincés of beef à l'italienne. ÉMINCÉS DE BOEUF À L'ITALIENNE – Proceed as for *Émincés of beef chasseur*, covering the meat with *Italian sauce* (see SAUCE).

Émincés of beef à la lyonnaise. ÉMINCÉS DE BOEUF À LA LYONNAISE – Proceed as for *Émincés of beef chasseur*, covering the meat with *Lyonnaise sauce* (see SAUCE).

Émincés of beef with mushrooms. ÉMINCÉS DE BOEUF AUX CHAMPIGNONS – Arrange the slices of beef on a dish. Put whole or sliced mushrooms, tossed in butter, on top of the slices. Cover with boiling *Madeira sauce* (see SAUCE).

Émincés of beef with piquante sauce. ÉMINCÉS DE BOEUF SAUCE PIQUANTE – Proceed as for *Émincés of beef chasseur*, covering the meat with *Piquante sauce* (see SAUCE).

Émincés of beef with poivrade sauce. ÉMINCÉS DE BOEUF SAUCE POIVRADE – Proceed as for *Émincés of beef chasseur*, covering the meat with *Poivrade sauce* (see SAUCE).

Émincés of beef with Robert sauce. ÉMINCÉS DE BOEUF SAUCE ROBERT – Proceed as for *Émincés of beef chasseur*, covering the meat with *Robert sauce* (see SAUCE).

Émincés of beef with tomato sauce. ÉMINCÉS DE BOEUF SAUCE TOMATE – Proceed as for *Émincés of beef chasseur*, covering the meat with *Tomato sauce* (see SAUCE).

After being covered with the sauce indicated, *émincés* of beef can be garnished in various ways. The garnishes most suited to these dishes are: sauté potatoes; green vegetables tossed in butter or cream; braised vegetables; purées of pulses and chestnuts; pasta of various kinds; rice pilaf and risotto.

Émincés of mutton or lamb. ÉMINCÉS DE MOUTON, D'AGNEAU – Proceed as for *émincés* of beef, using left-over roast or braised mutton or lamb.

Émincés of pork. ÉMINCÉS DE PORC – Proceed, using slices of left-over pork, as for *émincés* of beef.

Émincés of poultry. ÉMINCÉS DE VOLAILLE – Make with thin slices of roast or poached left-over poultry. All methods of serving *émincés* of beef are suitable for *émincés* of poultry. They can also be covered with white sauces, such as cream sauce, curry, *supréme*, *ravigote*, *hongroise*.

Émincés of roebuck. ÉMINCÉS DE CHEVREUIL – Proceed, using slices of left-over roast roebuck, as for *émincés* of beef.

This dish, and other ground game, can be covered with all sauces especially suitable for ground game, e.g. *grand veneur*, *romaine*.

Émincés of veal. ÉMINCÉS DE VEAU – Prepared, *à brun*, like *émincés* of beef, *à blanc*, like *émincés* of poultry.

ÉMINCER – Term used in French cookery meaning to slice meat, vegetables or fruit very finely. Carrots and turnips are finely sliced for a *paysanne* preparation, mushrooms when they are to be sautéed in butter. Finely sliced potatoes, apples, etc. are also said to be *émincé*.

EMMENTHAL – See CHEESE.

EMPOTAGE – Term in French cookery referring to all the ingredients put in a braising pan.

EMPOTER – Term meaning to put various ingredients in a stockpot or braising pan.

EMULSION. ÉMULSION – Liquid of milky appearance containing minute drops of oil or fat in more or less stable suspension.

Emulsions have greater stability when the liquid is slightly alkaloid and proteid, with a somewhat viscous consistency. Milk, for instance, is an emulsion of cream globules.

The name emulsion is also given in cookery to a mixture of oil or butter with egg yolks, such as mayonnaise or *hollandaise sauce*.

Plain almond emulsion or milk of almonds. ÉMULSION SIMPLE D'AMANDES, LAIT D'AMANDES – 50 g. (2 oz., $\frac{1}{2}$ cup) blanched sweet almonds, 50 g. (2 oz., $\frac{1}{4}$ cup) white sugar, 1 litre ($1\frac{3}{4}$ pints, generous quart) distilled water (Codex formula).

Pound the almonds with the sugar and a little water to the consistency of a smooth paste. Dilute with the rest of the water and rub through a sieve.

EN-CAS – Term meaning 'in case' which is used in France to describe a meal (usually a cold meal) kept ready in case of need.

In the old châteaux, a table was always laid in readiness for unexpected guests. In the seventeenth and eighteenth centuries the *en cas de nuit* was the name given to a light meal kept in readiness near the king's bedchamber. It consisted of three loaves of bread, two bottles of wine and a flask of water. According to an anecdote dating from the time of Louis XIV, the great king once shared his *en-cas* with Molière in order to teach his courtiers a lesson after they had refused to allow the famous dramatist to sit at their table.

ENDIVE AND CHICORY
1. Louviers endive (U.S. chicory) 2. Barbe-de-Capucin (wild chicory)
3. Chicory (U.S. Belgian endive) 4. Endive (U.S. chicory, escarole)

ENDIVE (U.S. CHICORY). CHICORÉE – Genus of plant cultivated for its leaves. These are eaten in salads, but can be braised or stewed in butter as indicated in the following recipes.

There is confusion about the names *endive* and *chicory*. In England *endive* usually means the curly-leaved salad plant, generally called *chicory* in the U.S.A. What the French and Americans call *endive* or *Belgian endive* is called *chicory* in England. For the sake of clarity we are giving preference to the English usage.

Endive has very little nutritive value.

Endive with béchamel sauce. CHICORÉE À LA BÉCHAMEL – Braise in beef stock or cook in salted boiling water. Add several tablespoons *Béchamel sauce* (see SAUCE) and some fresh butter to the cooked endive.

Braised endive au gras. CHICORÉE BRAISÉE AU GRAS – Remove any hard leaves. Cut the rest from the stump. Wash the leaves in several clean lots of water, drain and blanch them for 10 minutes in rapidly boiling salted water. Drain, put under the cold tap, press the water from the endive and chop it up finely.

Make a white *roux* (q.v.) For 500 g. (generous 1 lb.) endive use 50 g. (2 oz., $\frac{1}{4}$ cup) butter and 50 g. (2 oz., $\frac{1}{2}$ cup) flour seasoned with salt, pepper, sugar and grated nutmeg, and moistened with 6 dl. (1 pint, $2\frac{1}{2}$ cups) consommé, or white stock. Add the endive. Bring to the boil on the top of the stove and then cook, covered, in the oven for $1\frac{1}{2}$ hours.

Buttered endive. CHICORÉE AU BEURRE – Braise in beef stock or cook in boiling salted water. Add to the cooked endive 50 to 75 g. (2 to 3 oz., $\frac{1}{4}$ to $\frac{1}{3}$ cup) butter for every 500 g. (generous 1 lb.) of vegetable.

Endive with cream. CHICORÉE À LA CRÈME – Cook in the same way as *Buttered endive*. Finish with $1\frac{1}{2}$ dl. ($\frac{1}{4}$ pint, $\frac{2}{3}$ cup) fresh cream.

Endive à la flamande. CHICORÉE À LA FLAMANDE – Trim and wash the endive. Blanch, drain, and cook it whole in butter. Finish in the same way as for *Endive with cream*.

Endive au gratin. CHICORÉE AU GRATIN – Put the braised endive in a fireproof dish and cover with *Béchamel sauce* (see SAUCE). Sprinkle with grated cheese, pour melted butter over it, and brown gently in the oven.

Endive au jus. CHICORÉE AU JUS – Braise the endive in beef stock on a foundation of sliced root vegetables (carrots, onions, etc.). Strain the boiled-down liquor and add to it several tablespoons rich veal stock.

Endive loaf. PAIN DE CHICORÉE – Combine 500 g. (generous 1 lb.) braised endive with 3 beaten eggs. Season with salt, pepper and nutmeg. Mix well. Pour into a buttered mould. Cook in the oven in a *bain-marie* for 25 minutes. Leave to cool for a few moments before turning it out onto a dish. Cover with *Allemande sauce* or *Cream sauce* (see SAUCE).

Endive au maigre. CHICORÉE ÉTUVÉE AU MAIGRE – Blanch the endive, put it in a colander under the cold tap, drain, and dry it. Put it in a casserole with 50 g. (2 oz., $\frac{1}{4}$ cup) butter for every 500 g. (generous 1 lb.) endive. Season. Moisten with 6 dl. (1 pint, $2\frac{1}{2}$ cups) water, and cook in the oven, covered, for $1\frac{1}{2}$ hours.

A white *roux* (q.v.) of flour and butter can be added.

Endive purée. PURÉE DE CHICORÉE – Rub braised or stewed endive through a sieve. Add *Béchamel sauce*, thick *Velouté sauce* (see SAUCE), rich veal stock, or fresh butter.

To improve the consistency of this purée, add a third or a quarter of its weight of potato purée.

Endive salad. SALADE DE CHICORÉE – See SALAD.

Endive soufflé. SOUFFLÉ DE CHICORÉE – Cook 250 g. (9 oz.) endive in beef stock or *au maigre* (in butter and water), and sieve. Combine with 3 egg yolks; season with salt, pepper, and nutmeg; and add 3 well-whisked egg whites.

Pour into a buttered soufflé dish. Smooth the surface and cook in the oven at 200°C. (400°F., Gas Mark 6) for 15 to 18 minutes. Serve at once.

Endive soufflé with Parmesan. SOUFFLÉ DE CHICORÉE AU PARMESAN – Made in the same way as *Endive soufflé*. Add 50 g. (2 oz., $\frac{1}{2}$ cup) grated Parmesan to the soufflé.

Little endive soufflés (hot hors d'œuvre). PETITS SOUFFLÉS DE CHICORÉE – The same as above. Put the mixture into individual soufflé dishes and cook in the oven at 200°C. (400°F., Gas Mark 6) 8 to 10 minutes.

Endive subrics. SUBRICS DE CHICORÉE – Prepared with braised endive in the same way as *Subrics of spinach* (see SPINACH).

ENDIVE GOURILOS. MOELLE DE CHICORÉE – The stumps of curly endive are often called *moelles* in France, but they are also known as *gourilos*.

Blanch in salt water containing lemon or vinegar, and drain well. Prepare in various ways: in butter or cream in a covered pan; fried; in *fritots* (q.v.); grilled; *à la grecque* (q.v.); curried; sautéed, etc. (See GOURILOS.)

ENGLISH COOKERY – See INTERNATIONAL COOKERY.

ENTOLOMA. ENTOLOME – Mushroom of the agaric family characterized by its pink spores and lamellae. The blackish-blue entoloma is poisonous and causes gastroenteritis accompanied by epigastric pains and vomiting.

ENTOMOPHAGOUS. ENTOMOPHAGE – Word of Greek origin meaning insect-eating. The ancient Athenians ate grilled cicadas. Even today many peoples, including the Arabs and the Egyptians, enjoy grasshoppers. The Chinese, too, eat certain insects, caterpillars, etc.

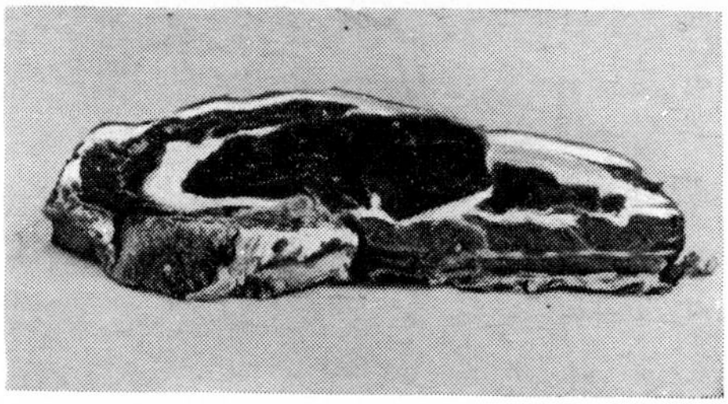

Piece of entrecôte from rib of beef
(*Boucherie Bernard. Phot. Larousse*)

ENTRECÔTE – Term which literally means 'between the ribs'. It is used of a steak taken between two ribs of beef.

The term also applies to a slice taken from the *contrefilet* or *faux filet* of beef, but a true *entrecôte* is that cut between the ribs. It is usually grilled or fried. For various recipes, see BEEF.

ENTRECUISSE – Term in French cookery for the fleshy thigh of poultry or winged game. This is to distinguish it from the lower half of the leg or 'drumstick'.

ENTRE-DEUX-MERS – Name given to the area of Bordeaux situated between the Garonne and the Dordogne, stretching to the south-eastern boundary of the Gironde *département* and overlapping the Lot-et-Garonne *département*.

The *appellation* Entre-Deux-Mers is reserved for the white wines, which are gradually becoming drier. The red wines have a right to the *appellation* Bordeaux or Bordeaux Supérieur.

ENTRÉE – The course which, in a full French menu, follows the *relevé* or intermediate course which, in its turn, follows the fish (or whatever dish may be served in place of it). In other words, the *entrée* is the third course, not the first, as it would seem to be.

It is usually a dish served with a white or brown sauce, but can also be a cold dish. At a large formal dinner, several *entrées*, all different from one another in character, are usually served.

Mixed *entrées*, that is to say composite dishes, can also be served.

Mixed entrées. ENTRÉES MIXTES – Under this heading there is an infinite variety of dishes, the chief of these being casseroles of rice with various garnishes; hot *pâtés* made with poultry, game, meat, offal (variety meats), fish and shellfish; pies; savoury tartlets and *vol-au-vent*. These are served after the principal *entrées*.

ENTRELARDER – French culinary term for slices of meat cooked with alternate layers of pork fat.

ENTREMETS – Literally 'between dishes'. In old French the term covered all the dishes which followed the roast, and included not only sweets but vegetables.

In the fourteenth, fifteenth, sixteenth and seventeenth centuries, *entremets* meant not only food but also entertainment in the middle of the meal, provided by buffoons, minstrels, troubadours, acrobats, dancers, and other performers.

Nowadays, the word means sweets (desserts), which, in France, are served after the cheese. Recipes are given under their names in alphabetical order.

Most sweets served nowadays fall into one of the following categories:

1. Batter sweets (crêpes, fritters, etc.).
2. Cooked creams and custards.
3. Egg sweets (sweet omelettes, etc.).
4. Fruit sweets (cooked or raw).
5. Ices and ice creams.
6. Meringue sweets.
7. Pastry sweets (tarts, pies, flans, etc.).
8. Puddings.
9. Rice and semolina sweets.
10. Whipped cream sweets.

EPERGNE. MÉNAGÈRE – Table-centre of glass, porcelain or metal bowls attached to an ornamental metal stem. In France, epergnes are still used as *hors-d'œuvre* sets for serving gherkins, salted cucumbers, small pickled melons, capers, and other delicacies. They are also used for serving stewed fruit or iced *petitsfours*.

ÉPIGRAMME – An *épigramme* of lamb consists of two cuts, both cooked 'dry'. These two pieces are a slice of breast and a cutlet or chop, dipped in egg and breadcrumbs and grilled or fried. Instructions for the preparation of *épigrammes* are given under LAMB.

Philéas Gilbert explains the origins of the term *épigramme* as follows:

'It was towards the middle of the eighteenth century. One day a young marquise overheard one of her guests at table remark that when he was dining the previous evening with the comte de Vaudreuil, he was charmingly received and, furthermore, had had a feast of excellent epigrams. The marquise, though pretty and elegant, was somewhat ignorant of the meaning of words.

'She later summoned Michelet, her chef.

'"Michelet," she said to him, "tomorrow, I shall require a dish of *épigrammes*!"

'The chef withdrew, pondering the problem. He looked up old recipes, but found no reference to anything of the kind. None of his colleagues had ever heard of the dish. But no French master chef is ever at a loss. Since he could discover nothing about the dish he set about to invent one. Next day, inspiration came and he created a most delicate dish.

'At dinner, the guests fell into ecstasies over the dish put before them and, after complimenting the lady of the house, desired to know its name. The chef was called. With perfect composure he replied, "*Épigrammes* of lamb à la Michelet".

'Everyone laughed. The marquise was triumphant, though she could not understand the amusement of her guests. From that moment, the culinary repertoire of France was enriched by a name still used to this day.

'But whereas this name was originally used for slices of breast of lamb dipped in breadcrumbs, fried in butter and arranged in a circle round a *blanquette* of lamb, by the end of the eighteenth century it had been completely transformed into what it is today, cutlets and slices of breast, dipped in egg and breadcrumbs and fried in butter or grilled.'

EPILEPSY. ÉPILEPSIE – Ancient doctors, in particular Hippocrates, recognised the importance of diet in the treatment of this disease, and since then all kinds of conflicting diets have been concocted. Some definite conclusions can be drawn from certain facts, however.

Epileptics are generally hearty eaters and bulimics: cutting down on food therefore diminishes the number of epileptic fits.

A vegetarian diet, or parrticularly a milk diet lessens the frequency of fits in the majority of cases.

These claims, however, are not true for all epileptics.

ÉPINE D'HIVER – Name of a winter pear, tender and fragrant to eat.

ÉPINÉE – French regional name for chine of pork.

EPIPHANY. ÉPIPHANIE – Epiphany or Twelfth Night (known in France as the Feast of the Kings) is celebrated on 6 January. In France it is an occasion for great feasting.

Twelfth-Night cake, the symbolic cake containing the traditional bean (or favour) is eaten on Twelfth Night. It is made either of risen dough in the shape of a ring, or flaky pastry in the shape of a *galette*, according to the region.

ÉPOISSES – See CHEESE.

ÉPONGER – Term in French cookery for the process of drying parboiled or boiled vegetables by putting them on a cloth after draining, to get rid of all surplus moisture.

Some deep-fried foods are drained in a cloth. This process is also known as *éponger*.

ERDBEERKUCHEN (German pastry) – A German strawberry tart. See TART, *Fruit tart à l'allemande*.

ERMITAGE (Wine) – This name is sometimes written with an 'H' (Hermitage). The wine, which is made in the Drôme *département*, enjoys a great reputation. There are both red and white Ermitage wines, made from grapes grown on the slopes of l'Ermitage in the commune of Tain on the left bank of the Rhône.

There are different types of soil in this area, and the vineyard is divided into three sections or *mas*, each very different in geological structure from the others. The *mas de Bossard* is a granite slope, the *mas de Méal* is alluvial soil, and the *mas de Greffieux* is clay.

Ermitage wine is perfect only when made from grapes from all three sections of the vineyard.

White Ermitage wine is a fine golden yellow. It has a fairly strong bouquet. The red wine, when it is young, is of a faded purple colour. It should be left to mature for a while, otherwise it tastes slightly bitter.

ERMITE – The name given in France to a very old wild boar which is also known as *solitaire*. The meat of old wild boar is leathery. Only young boar is eaten. In France, a young boar is known as a *marcassin* or *bête rousse*. (See WILD BOAR.)

ERVY – See CHEESE.

ERYTHRIN. ÉRYTHRIN – The generic name for several varieties of fish, rather thick and rounded in body with large heads.

Three or four varieties are to be found in the lakes and rivers of hot countries. This fish is excellent to eat. It is cooked in the same way as sea perch.

ESCABÈCHE – See HORS-DŒUVRE, *Cold hors-d'œuvre*. Word of Spanish origin. In Belgium it is *escavèche*, in North Africa, *scabèche*.

ESCALOPE or COLLOP – Slices of meat or fish of any kind, flattened slightly and fried in butter or some other fat.

In former times the term was used of a dish of sliced meat, for instance, sliced mutton would be called *une escalope de mouton*.

Veal escalopes are generally cut from the fillet (U.S. round) or the best end of neck (U.S. rib) or the topside or silverside (U.S. rump).

ESCAROLE. SCAROLE – Variety of salad plant with wide, curled, dark green leaves which are sometimes blanched by being surrounded with earth or being cultivated in cellars in the dark.

Escarole is chiefly eaten raw in salad, but can also be cooked in a great many ways. All the methods of preparation given for endive (q.v.) and chicory (q.v.) are applicable to this plant.

Auguste Escoffier in front of a sugar model of Grosvenor House, London

ESCOFFIER, AUGUSTE – Auguste Escoffier was born at Villeneuve-Loubet, a charming little town in the Alpes-Maritimes, in 1847. He began his career at the age of twelve, and became a very great cook.

In 1890, in association with Ritz and Echenard, two masters of the hotel business, he opened the Savoy Hotel in London, and remained in this illustrious establishment until 1898 when, for personal reasons, he gave up the direction of the Savoy kitchens to take charge of those of the Carlton Hotel, then one of the most famous in Europe.

As a reward for all he had done to enhance the prestige of French cooking throughout the world, Escoffier was made a Chevalier of the Legion of Honour in 1920, and Officer of the Legion in 1928.

Escoffier's culinary career was brilliant. He was regarded as the emperor of the world's kitchens, a title conferred upon him by the Emperor William II, who spent some time on the steamer *Imperator* of the Hamburg-America Line, which Escoffier had joined to take charge of the imperial kitchens. In the course of a conversation with Escoffier, the Emperor, congratulating him, said: 'I am the Emperor of Germany, but you are the Emperor of chefs.'

Escoffier retired in 1921. He was then seventy-four years of age and had practised his art for sixty-two years. In all the history of cookery, there is no other example of such a long professional career. He died in February 1935, nearly eighty-nine years old.

The culinary writings of Escoffier are works of authority. The best-known are *le Guide culinaire*, written in collaboration with Philéas Gilbert and Émile Fetu; *le Livre des menus; les Fleurs en cire; Ma cuisine; le Riz; le Carnet d'Épicure*.

It was Escoffier who, in 1893, honoured the Australian singer, Nellie Melba, by creating the peach dish that bears her name. He also invented the *dodine au Chambertin* and the *chaud-froid Jeannette*, the latter named after a ship that was trapped in the Polar ice. Many delicate culinary creations are associated with his name.

ESPAGNOLE SAUCE – One of the basic brown sauces. It is also called *sauce-mère* (mother-sauce) which indicates that it can be used as a basis for a large number of derivative brown sauces.

This is Carême's recipe for what he called *petite-espagnole*.

'Take a deep saucepan. Put in 2 slices of Bayonne ham. Place on top a *noix* of veal and 2 partridges. Add enough stock to cover the veal only. Boil down the liquid rapidly. Move the pan to a cooler part of the stove to extract all the juice from the contents.

When the stock is reduced to a coating on the bottom of the pan, remove it from the stove. Prick the *noix* of veal with the point of a knife so that its juice mingles with the essence. Put the saucepan back on the stove on a low heat and leave for about 1 hour. Watch the essence as it gradually turns to a clear red colour.

'To simplify this operation, scrape off a little of the essence with the point of a knife. Roll it between the fingers. If it rolls into a ball, the essence is perfectly reduced. If it is not, it will stick the fingers together.

'Remove the saucepan from the stove and put it aside for 15 minutes for the essence to cool. It will then dissolve more readily. Fill the saucepan with clear soup or stock and heat very slowly. As soon as it comes to the boil, skim it, and pour 2 ladles into a *roux*.'

For the preparation of this *roux*:

'Melt 100 g. (4 oz., ½ cup) butter and add to it sieved flour to make a rather liquid *roux*. Put it on a low heat, stirring from time to time so that little by little the whole of the mixture turns a golden colour. When adding the liquid, do not forget that the *roux* must not be on the stove while you are mixing in the first spoonfuls of stock; but it should be put on later, so that it may be added boiling hot to the rest of the stock.

'When the 2 ladles of stock are poured into the *roux*, stir so as to make the mixture perfectly smooth. Now pour it into the saucepan with the veal *noix*. Add parsley and spring onions, seasoned with ½ bay leaf, a little thyme, 2 chives, and mushroom trimmings. Leave to simmer, stirring frequently. After a full hour skim off the fat. 30 minutes later skim off the fat again.

'Strain through a cloth into a bowl, stirring from time to time with a wooden spoon so that no scum forms on the surface, as easily happens when the sauce is exposed to the air.' (Extract from *le Pâtissier royal; Traité des entrées chaudes*.)

Nowadays, a shoulder of veal is used instead of a *noix*, and partridge is not used in the stock. (See SAUCE, *Espagnole sauce*. See also DEMI-ESPAGNOLE.)

ESPRIT-DE-VIN – 84° proof alcohol.

ESQUIRE TRENCHANT – A servant or high dignitary officiating at ceremonial banquets. In former times, in great households, the *esquire trenchant* (or *écuyer trenchant*) was second to the *major-domo* in rank. In lesser households, the two offices were combined.

ESSAI or ESSAY – The *essai* at the French royal courts was the ceremony of tasting the king's food and drink. The cups which were used for tasting wines etc. were also called *essais*.

The fear of poison in the Middle Ages gave rise to a complicated ceremonial attending the sovereign's meals. In France, this was minutely regulated by court etiquette, which continued with slight modifications up to the Revolution, to be revived under the Empire.

The knife, fork, spoon, salt cellar, spices, and napkin were locked in the *cadenas* (q.v.) or *nef* (q.v.).

The *maître d'hôtel* rubbed all the cutlery and the dishes with balls of breadcrumbs which he made sure were eaten by the squires of the pantry, who, previously, had subjected the servants who had handed them the dishes to the same ordeal.

For drinks, the ceremonial was equally complicated. When the king called for a drink, the cup bearer made a sign to the wine butler and his assistant. The first of these brought the wine in a flagon, and the king's glass, covered; the second brought a silver jug full of water. The cup bearer took the glass and uncovered it; the wine butler poured in the wine, then the water. The cup bearer poured some of this watered wine into two little silver-gilt cups. He drank from one; the wine butler drank from the other. Only then did the cup bearer proffer the cup, now covered once more, across the table to the king. He did not uncover it until the very moment that the king was about to drink.

The same ceremonial took place for the queen. By special favour, Louis XIV bestowed the same prerogative upon the *dauphine* (the wife of the heir to the throne).

ESSENCE – A liquid, usually oily and volatile, extracted by the distillation of vegetable substances in water: essence of anise, cinnamon, lemon, oranges, roses, etc.

Essences are used in aromatherapy to combat various complaints. Fifteen of these appear in the Codex.

Anchovy essence. ESSENCE D'ANCHOIS – A commercial product which is used in the preparation of *Anchovy butter* (see BUTTER, *Compound butters*) and to flavour certain sauces, stuffings, salads, etc.

Bitter almond essence. ESSENCE D'AMANDES AMÈRES – A product which is made and sold commercially.

Chervil essence. ESSENCE DE CERFEUIL – Proceed as for *Tarragon essence*, using chervil in place of tarragon.

Coffee essence. ESSENCE DE CAFÉ – Pour 5 dl. (scant pint, 2¼ cups) boiling water on 200 g. (7 oz., 2⅓ cups) ground coffee placed in a filter. Pour the resulting liquid through the filter again. Cool and bottle it. Use to flavour creams, mochas, etc.

Fish essence. ESSENCE DE POISSON – For 5 dl. (scant pint, 2¼ cups), put in a saucepan: 1 kg. (2¼ lb.) bones and trimmings of sole, whiting, brill or other white fish, 1 small sliced onion, 100 g. (4 oz.) mushroom trimmings, a sprig of parsley, and a few drops lemon juice. Moisten with 1 litre (1¾ pints, generous quart) strained fish stock and 2 dl. (⅓ pint, scant cup) white wine.

Bring to the boil. Skim. Boil steadily for 30 to 35 minutes. Strain through muslin. Boil down to half its volume.

This essence, which is fairly rich, is used for poaching fish. It can also be used in the preparation of sauces to be served with fish.

Game essence. ESSENCE DE GIBIER – Game stock boiled down to the consistency of thick meat jelly.

Garlic essence. ESSENCE D'AIL – Pour boiling white wine or vinegar onto crushed cloves of garlic, strain and boil down.

Mushroom essence. ESSENCE DE CHAMPIGNONS – The liquid, greatly concentrated, in which mushrooms have been cooked. It is used to flavour sauces.

Onion and shallot essence. ESSENCE D'OIGNON, D'ÉCHALOTE – Infuse finely sliced onions or shallots in white wine or vinegar.

Parsley essence. ESSENCE DE PERSIL – Proceed as for *Tarragon essence*.

Tarragon essence. ESSENCE D'ESTRAGON – An infusion of fresh tarragon in white wine or vinegar, strained and reduced.

Tomato essence. ESSENCE DE TOMATES – Rub 500 g. (generous 1 lb.) very ripe raw tomatoes through a fine sieve. Boil the pulp until it is reduced to half its volume. Pass through a sieve, pressing hard with a spoon. Boil this pulp until it thickens to a syrupy consistency. Rub through muslin.

Cooked in this way, tomato pulp makes a kind of jelly which can be kept for several days. It is used as an additional ingredient for sauces, stuffings, and other mixtures.

Truffle essence. ESSENCE DE TRUFFES – Truffle peelings infused in Madeira or any other heavy wine.

ESTAMINET – Name given in former times in France to cafés where patrons were permitted to smoke.

Nowadays, the word is used of a basement tavern.

ESTOUFFADE – Name applied both to a dish whose ingredients are slowly stewed, and to a clear brown stock used to dilute sauces or to moisten braised meat and *ragoûts*.

ESTOUFFAT – Languedoc dialect form of the word *étuvée* (dish stewed very slowly). In that region it is mainly used to designate a stew of haricot beans and pork.

ÉTOUFFÉE – Method of cooking food in a tightly closed vessel with very little liquid or even without liquid, often called *à l'étuvée*.

ÉTOURDEAU – Name given in some parts of France to a young capon.

ÉTUVÉE – Method of cooking food. (See ÉTOUFFÉE.)

ÉTUVER – To cook food in a covered pan, without liquid. This method is suitable for all kinds of meat, poultry, vegetables, and fruit. A little butter, fat or oil should be added.

EUPHORISM. EUPHORISME – Euphorism is a new art of living that aims to encourage the expansion of the human personality through physical and moral equilibrium. In its attempt to cultivate an optimistic outlook of *joie de vivre* and good humour, euphorism depends to a large extent on gastronomy.

Doctor Pierre Vachet, a disciple of this philosophy, believes that gastronomy has an important rôle to play in the pursuit of happiness. Like art, it has its rules; whether it proposes a simple country meal or a sumptuous banquet, the taste buds and the mind must be equally satisfied.

The gourmet generally knows very well how to blend the delights of the palate with visual and mental stimulation. The pleasure it gives him to taste wines and savour the *chefs-d'œuvre* of French *cuisine* can be likened to the joy other people derive from listening to a beautiful symphony or gazing at a fine painting.

The author of *Maladies de la vie moderne* declares: 'Taste and flavours are precious elements of euphorism for, when properly applied, our sense of taste adds greatly to our physical and psychic pleasure.

'The sense of taste should therefore be educated and cultivated to a great extent in order to develop the taste buds, so that we learn to appreciate each separate flavour of whatever we consume. By analysing the qualities and defects of food, by knowing how truly to savour a wine, we shall acquire through practice a much wider range of sensory resources.

'Only by this kind of education and discipline can gastronomy take its rightful place in the epicurism of modern times, euphorism.'

There is a Euphorists' Club.

ÉVENT – French name for the deterioration which is caused, especially in wine, by too long exposure to the air. The taste of *évent* is the washy flavour in wine which has lost its aroma through oxidation.

EVERLASTING PEA. JAROSSE, JAROUSSE – Popular name for the cultivated vetch. In France, it is also sometimes called *Auvergne lentil.*

EWE. BREBIS – The flesh of a ewe, when young, is used as ordinary mutton (q.v.).

In some regions of south-western France, ewe's meat is pickled in the same way as pork.

EWER. AIGUIÈRE – Vessel for containing water for service at table. The word *aiguière* comes from Old French *aigue* (water).

The ewer goes back to antiquity. Its main features have not changed much. In general, it is a vessel of elongated form, with base, handle and spout. Gold, precious stones, and the finest enamels were used for the ewers on the tables of the French nobility in past centuries. One of the most beautiful examples is in chased silver and was part of the treasure discovered in 1830 at Berthonville, near Bernay, in the Eure. It is kept in the museum of medals in the French *Bibliothèque Nationale*.

EXCELSIOR – See CHEESE.

EXOCOETUS. EXOCET – This fish, commonly known as *flying fish*, is edible. It is prepared in the same way as mackerel (q.v.).

EXTRACT. EXTRAIT – Product obtained by evaporating animal or vegetable juice. The cooking stock of meat, boiled down to a coating in the pan, is an extract.

The extracts most commonly used are those of beef, veal, poultry and game.

Extracts of fish are called *essences* or *fumets*. The term can be extended to cover concentrated vegetable essences which are made from root vegetables and from mushrooms, tomatoes, and truffles.

Among the vegetable extracts used in the kitchen is soya sauce which, if added to *coulis* (q.v.), *ragoûts* (q.v.), and other meat or vegetarian dishes, enhances their flavour without destroying their own particular taste.

Chicken extract. GLACE DE VOLAILLE – Boil down clear chicken stock in the same way as indicated in the recipe for *Meat extract* (see below).

Fish extract. GLACE DE POISSON – See ESSENCE, *Fish essence*.

Game extract. GLACE DE GIBIER – Boil down clear game stock in the same way as for *Meat extract* (see below).

Meat extract. GLACE DE VIANDE – Boil down to half its volume 10 litres (9 quarts, 11 quarts) brown stock. Remove all fat, leaving the stock as clear as possible. Strain through muslin, and boil down further. Strain, and repeat the procedure until the stock coats the back of a spoon. Each time it is strained, transfer the stock to a smaller saucepan, and reduce the heat as the stock thickens.

Pour the extract into little jars and keep in a cool place.

Meat extracts (commercially prepared). EXTRAITS DE VIANDE DU COMMERCE – These extracts, which are manufactured commercially, are mainly used in household kitchens.

FAGOUE – Name given in the French tripe-trade to the pancreas, and sometimes to calves' sweetbreads.

FAÏENCE – Opaque type of pottery which is whitish in colour or tinted. The earthenware is covered with tin glaze (lead glaze made opaque by the addition of tin ashes) so that the colour of the earthenware is completely masked. This pottery takes its name from the Italian town of Faenza.

Very little is known about the origins of faïence pottery, but from the very earliest times a brilliant, vitreous lead glaze, coloured by means of metallic oxides, was known to potters. It is to be seen in the hypogeum of Ancient Egypt, on its vases, funeral images, and also on the glazed bricks which decorated the walls of Nineveh and Babylon.

The ancient mosques of Asia Minor have preserved for us the magnificent craftsmanship of the Persians, who passed on their skill to the Arabs.

From the thirteenth century there were important centres for the manufacture of faïence in Spain, at Malaga and Majorca, which gave its name to the Italian *majolica*. Up to the seventeenth century the most famous factories were in Valencia. But it was mainly through the discovery of tin glaze by Luca della Robbia towards the middle of the fifteenth century, that the ceramic industry was able to develop, first at Faenza and then in various other Italian towns, notably Urbino, Gubbio, Druta, Durante, Venice, Milan and Turin.

In France, in the sixteenth century, faïence pottery called Henry II faïence was made, the most important being the very individual pieces made by Bernard Palissy. During the same period Italian potters tried to introduce the faïence industry into France. The Conradi, coming from Savona, settled at Nevers. Early abortive attempts to make faïence in Rouen were made in the sixteenth century, but it was only in the seventeenth century that this town produced the beautiful specimens which remain one of the glories of the French faïence industry. These were very fashionable in the eighteenth century and were copied everywhere, both in France and other countries. Moustiers, from the end of the seventeenth century, made famous faïence pieces in the style of Tempesta, or copied from Bérain and from Bernard Toro. At Strasbourg, in the eighteenth century, the Hannong family created a style which was quickly adopted by the factories of Lunéville and Niederwiller. In Paris, Saint-Cloud, Meudon, Lille, and Marseille, there were also a large number of less important factories.

Outside France, some of the finest work was produced at Delft in Holland, which was, for a long time, the most active centre of the faïence industry in Europe.

Fine pottery, called clay pottery, made its appearance towards the middle of the eighteenth century, and this industry was most fully developed in England, in the towns of Leeds and Burslem. In France, this type of pottery was made especially at Pont-aux-Choux, Paris, Lunéville and Orléans.

With the advent of porcelain, faïence became less sought-after and less highly-prized. But modern faïence manufacturers have given a new lease of life to this type of pottery.

FAISANDAGE – French term for red meat in the condition which, in England, is known as 'high'. It is derived from *faisan* (pheasant).

When it is fresh, pheasant is tough and without much flavour. It grows tender and its aroma develops after it has been hung, the length of time depending upon the temperature. Nowadays, pheasant is no longer hung, as advocated by Montaigne, 'until it develops a marked smell'.

In Brillat-Savarin's time, pheasant was not considered fit for the gastronome's table except in a state of complete putrefaction. This authority recommends, in effect, that it should be kept, unplucked, until its breast turns green, so that for roasting on the spit it has to be held together by a slice of bread tied on with ribbon.

Apart from a few sportsmen in love with tradition, most people have today abandoned these excesses.

Winged game and ground game, when hung for a certain length of time, acquire a flavour similar to that of pheasant.

This habit of hanging meat until it is high is properly reprehended by those concerned with hygiene, and also by the true gastronome.

FAISANDEAU – Young pheasant.

FAISELLE. FAISSELLE – Osier or pottery basket used for draining cheese. Also the table on which the apple residue is drained after the brewing of cider.

FALCON. FAUCON – Bird of prey, trained to hunt on the wing. According to Tournefort, the French botanist and traveller, (1656–1708), it is delicate to eat and need not be hung.

FALERNIAN WINE. FALERNE – Campagna wine celebrated in verse by the poet Horace.

FALLOW-DEER. DAIM – Wild ruminant, somewhat rare in France. It is known as a *fawn* up to eight months. It loses its horns twice before it is fully grown. A fully grown fallow-

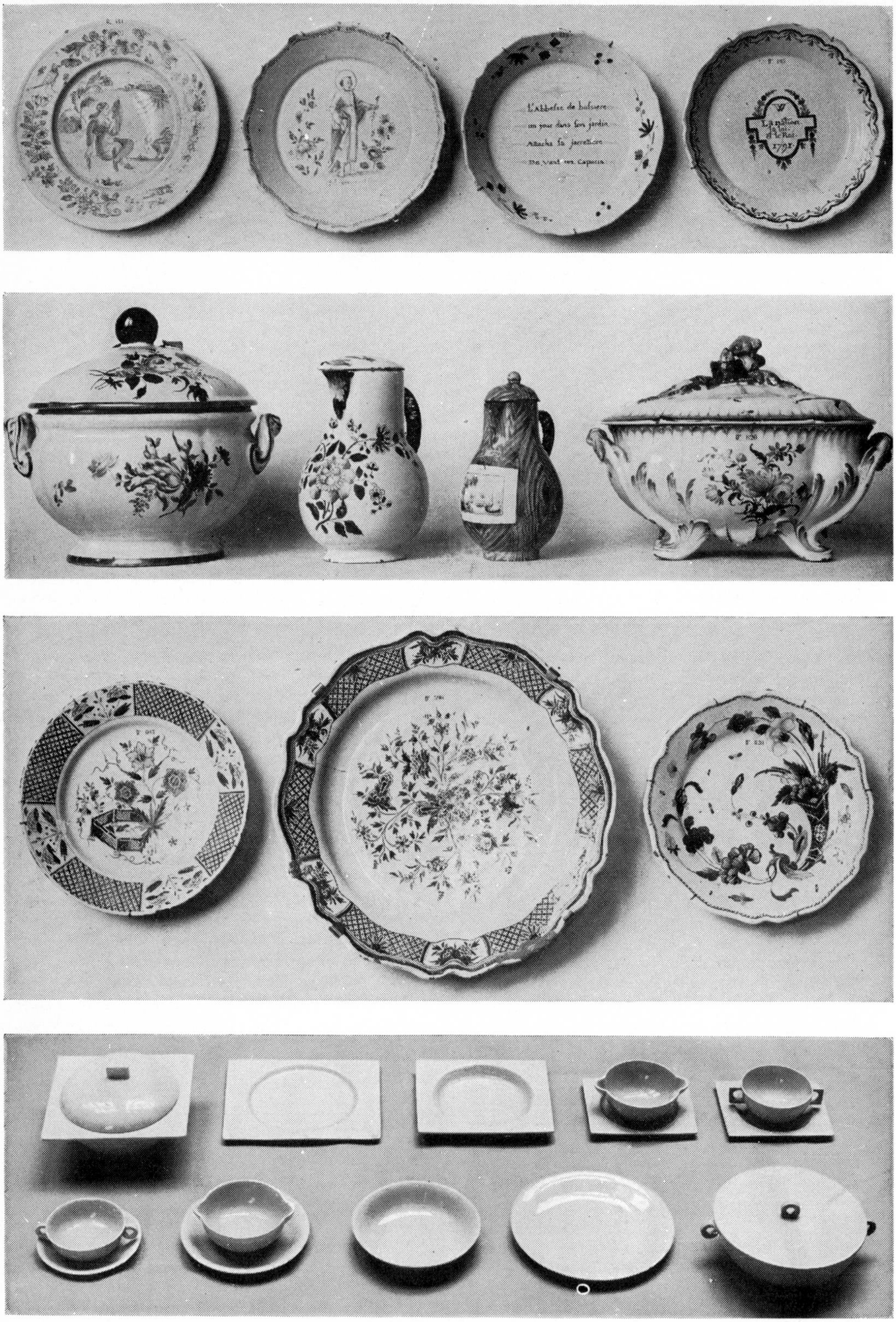

FAÏENCE TABLEWARE
From top to bottom: Antique faïence of Nevers, Strasbourg, Rouen; Modern faïence from Jean Luce

deer can be recognised by the palms between the branches of its antlers. The female of the fallow-deer is called a *doe*.

The meat of young fallow-deer is very delicate. That of the full-grown animal is leathery and must be steeped in a marinade.

All recipes for roebuck (q.v.) are suitable for fallow-deer.

Roast haunch of fallow-deer à l'anglaise. HANCHE DE DAIM RÔTIE À L'ANGLAISE – The haunch of fallow-deer (venison) is highly prized in England and is hung for quite a long time until it is high.

It keeps very well for several days if care is taken to hang it in a room well aired by a draught. Before hanging, the venison should be rubbed all over with a mixture of flour and pepper. The purpose of the flour is to keep out the damp and that of the pepper is to keep away the flies.

Before impaling the venison on the spit, trim it and coat with ordinary flour-and-water paste. Wrap it, coated with this mixture, in thick paper secured with several lengths of string.

Roast for 4 hours, basting frequently.

(Care must be taken not to cut the fat off the venison. The fatter it is the better.)

Ten minutes before removing the roast from the spit, unwrap it and scrape off the flour-and-water paste. Pour melted butter over the venison and sprinkle with salt and flour. Put it closer to the fire so that it is well browned.

With roast haunch of venison, it is usual to serve boiled French beans or chestnut purée, and redcurrant jelly. Haunch of stag is cooked in the same way, but is less highly prized than that of fallow-deer.

FANCHETTE or FANCHONNETTE (Confectionery) – This gâteau, which was very popular in the past, is scarcely ever made today. This is a pity because it is excellent. It is made in a deep, round baking tin similar to that used for hot *pâtés*.

Line a baking tin with flaky pastry dough which has been rolled out and folded into 3 upon itself, 6 times. Fill this crust with a cream which is made like French pastry cream, with the following ingredients: 12 egg yolks, 100 g. (4 oz., scant cup) powdered sugar, 100 g. (4 oz., 1 cup) flour, 5 dl. (scant pint, $2\frac{1}{4}$ cups) fresh thick cream, 1 tablespoon vanilla-flavoured sugar, a pinch of salt.

Bake the gâteau in a slow oven. When it is cold, cover with meringue. Decorate the top with meringue piped through a forcing bag. Sprinkle with sugar. Brown in the oven. Serve warm.

Coffee, chocolate, or almond cream, etc. may be substituted for vanilla cream.

FANES – Name given in France to the stalks, green or dry, of plants not cultivated for fodder.

The *fanes* of some pot vegetables are edible. Turnip stalks (turnip tops) can be cooked like spinach, but only if they are tender. An excellent soup is made from radish tops.

FANTAISIE – In France, the word *fantaisie* must appear on the label of synthetic products (*fantaisie* liqueurs, jams etc.). *Fantaisie* bread in France is bread sold by the piece and not by weight.

FAR – Porridge made from hard-wheat flour. The term is also used for a flan (tart) made in Brittany.

FARCI – Dish made in the south of France. It is cooked in stock and prepared in different ways. In its most usual form, the *farci* is cabbage stuffed with sausage meat or some other forcemeat, wrapped in muslin (U.S. cheesecloth) and cooked in stock.

Farci can also be prepared *à la niçoise* (see SOUFASSUM).

It can also be made by stuffing a breast of veal with forcemeat, cooking it in the liquid of a *pot-au-feu* (q.v.).

FARINACEOUS. FARINEUX – Containing flour or with a high starch content. Cereals, pulses, and potatoes are usually referred to as farinaceous foods.

FARINADA (Genoese cookery) – Gruel made from the flour of large white peas. When cooked it is poured onto an oiled board, cut into equal-sized pieces, and served as it is.

FARO – Belgian beer, only slightly fermented. It is relatively sour and often has sugar added to it.

FAR POITEVIN – A kind of *farci* (q.v.) made in Poitou from green vegetables and herbs (sorrel, green cabbage, white beet tops, lettuce). These are shredded raw, mixed with chopped pork fat, blended with cream and eggs, flavoured with chopped chives and parsley, highly seasoned, and wrapped in green cabbage leaves and lettuce leaves (put in a net). It is then cooked in a hotpot containing fresh and salt pork and flavoured with vegetables.

FASÉOLE – Species of haricot (U.S. shell) bean, cultivated in southern regions. Prepared in the same way as *Fresh white haricot beans* (see BEAN).

FAT. GRAISSE – Greasy substance which softens at a low temperature. It is found in animal tissue and in some vegetable substances.

There are fats in almost all muscular animal tissue. Fat also surrounds many animal organs. It forms deposits equal to at least a thirtieth of the weight of the whole body.

There are three principal constituents in fat: *stearin*, *olein* and *margarine*. Stearin is solid at normal temperatures, olein is liquid, margarine has intermediate consistency.

Fats have the highest calorific value of all foods and they are usually cheap, but two factors prevent their being the most valuable of all. They produce a feeling of satiety more rapidly than other foods, and the system can only tolerate a limited amount of fat (toleration point varies from individual to individual).

The normal diet must contain a proportion of natural fats: an average of 75 g. (3 oz.) daily for an adult.

In very cold countries a far greater amount is needed.

Economy fat. GRAISSE D'ÉCONOMIE – All fats produced in the preparation of *pot-au-feu*, and dripping of various kinds, should be carefully collected and preserved.

Once they are clarified, they can be used in the cooking of a variety of dishes.

Clarification of economy fat. Carefully skim off all the fat on the surface of the stockpot. Strain it through a fine sieve into an earthenware bowl. Leave it to get cold overnight. Next day, prick the layer of fat in 2 places and pour off, through the holes, all the liquid which is underneath the congealed fat.

Separated from its liquid, the fat can be used in the cooking of vegetables (it is especially recommended for braised cabbage) but, unless clarified, cannot be used for frying.

When fat is to be used for frying, process as follows:

Melt the fat in a saucepan first over low heat, then over a higher flame. Keep on the boil until it stops giving off steam. As soon as the steam stops rising, remove the pan from the stove; otherwise the fat will burn and acquire a bitter flavour. Strain through a fine sieve or muslin. Pour into an earthenware bowl and store in a cool, dry place.

This fat can be further improved by the addition of a third of its weight of lard.

Frying fat. GRAISSE À FRITURE – Generally made from clarified beef kidney fat (suet).

FATTENING. ENGRAISSEMENT – Fattening is the process of preparing animals for slaughter by increasing their weight and improving the quality of their flesh. This is made more nourishing and flavoursome by the penetration of fat between the muscles, and inside the muscles themselves.

FAUBONNE – A thick soup made with purée of white haricot (U.S. shell) beans with a plain *julienne* of vegetables added. (See SOUPS AND BROTHS.)

FAUVES (Wild animals) – French hunting term used especially of animals of the deer family, such as stag, fallow-deer, chamois, and roebuck, as opposed to black game such as boar, and red game such as fox.

FAUX FILET or CONTRE-FILET – See BEEF, Contre filet.

FAVEROLLES – Name used in the south of France for all kinds of haricot (U.S. shell) beans. These are also called *faverottes* and *favioles* in this region.

FAVRE – Joseph Favre was not only one of the greatest nineteenth-century chefs, but also one of the finest writers on culinary matters. He was the author of the *Dictionnaire universel de cuisine et d'hygiène alimentaire*, a work in four volumes, which contains not only a large number of recipes, but a very interesting history of cookery.

Joseph Favre was also the founder of the first Academy of Cookery. His bust was moved to *l'Académie culinaire de France* in 1953.

FAWN. FAON – The young of a roe-doe, hind or fallow-doe. For the preparation of fawn, see ROEBUCK.

FEDELINI – Italian pasta in the form of narrow ribbons. All recipes for macaroni (q.v.) are suitable for fedelini.

FENDANT (Wine) – Name of a Valais vine, cultivated in the Vaud Canton in Switzerland, said to be a variety of Chasselas. Wine made from Fendant grapes has a strong aroma and is very heady.

FENNEL. FENOUIL – Aromatic flowering umbelliferous plant of Italian origin which is now widely cultivated. It has a slight flavour of aniseed.

The edible part of this plant is the very fleshy bulbous stem at the base of the leaf stalk. This stem, which in French cookery is called *fenouil tubéreux*, and which the Italians, who are very fond of it, call *finocchio*, is cooked like celery. It can be eaten raw or cooked. In England it is called *Florence fennel*.

Both the bulbous stem and the leaves of the fennel plant are used in cookery to flavour a large number of dishes. Fennel is an excellent condiment.

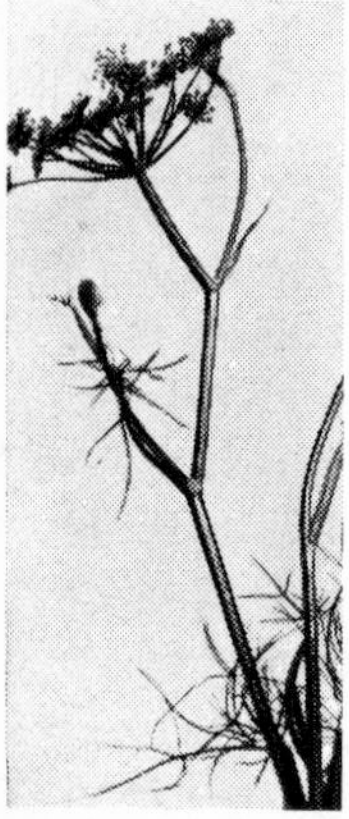

Sprig of fennel

Bulbous stem of fennel

Fennel with bone-marrow. FENOUIL À LA MOELLE – Braise in meat stock (see below). Complete cooking as for *Cardoons with marrow* (see CARDOON).

Fennel braised in meat stock. FENOUIL AU GRAS – Trim the fennel stems. Parboil for 5 minutes in boiling salt water. Cool under running water. Drain, and dry in a cloth. Quarter them or, if they are small, leave whole. Put them in an ovenproof dish lined with pork skin, and sliced onions and carrots. Moisten with a few tablespoons rather fat stock. Bring to the boil. Cover the pan and cook slowly in the oven.

Fennel in cream. FENOUIL À LA CRÈME – Fennel stems, simmered in butter or braised in meat stock as indicated above, can be put into a cream sauce and simmered for a few minutes before serving.

Fennel au gratin. FENOUIL AU GRATIN – Cook the fennel stems in butter or braise in meat stock. Put them in a buttered ovenware dish, sprinkle with grated cheese, and pour on melted butter. Brown in the oven.

Fennel in gravy. FENOUIL AU JUS – Braise in meat stock. Simmer for a few minutes in concentrated brown veal stock.

Fennel à la grecque. FENOUIL À LA GRECQUE – Proceed as indicated for *Artichokes à la grecque*. (See ARTICHOKE.) Fennel prepared in this way is served as an *hors-d'oeuvre*.

FENNEL-PEAR or FENOWLET. FENOUILLET – Variety of pear which tastes slightly of aniseed. Three varieties are grown in France: *fenouillet gris*, *fenouillet gros*, and the *fenouillet rouge*.

FENNEL-WATER. FENOUILLETTE – Liqueur made commercially, obtained from fennel seeds.

FENUGREEK. FENUGREC – Unusual Asiatic herb with slightly bitter aromatic seeds sometimes used in making curry.

FÉRA – Breed of salmon found in Lake Geneva and several other lakes in Switzerland, Bavaria, and Austria.

This fish is similar to the laveret, but the two differ in shape. The *féra*'s body is more compact, its scales are larger, and its jaws, sloping obliquely back, are somewhat truncated.

The colouring of the *féra* varies with the season, the age of the fish, and its habitat. It is easy to distinguish the different varieties because the *white fera* is found in very deep waters; the *black féra* in waters of average depth; the *blue féra*, which is really a young *féra*, has a bluish rather than greenish shimmer on the upper part of its body.

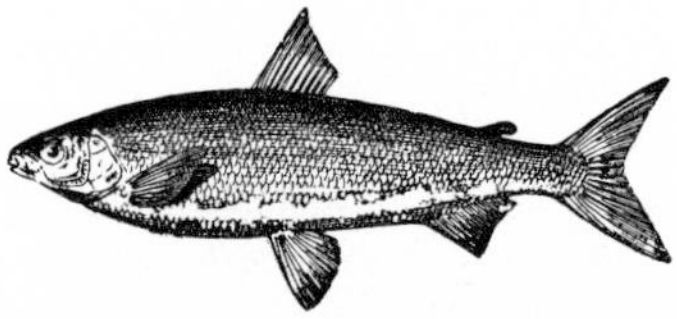

Féra

The Lake Geneva *féra* is the most highly prized. It is generally thought that the best Lake Geneva *féra* are those caught on the sandbank called the *Travers* where the water is very shallow and which forms a barrier across the lake near the port of Geneva. This fish, which fills out very rapidly by feeding on a winged insect called the caddis-fly, is very fat, white, and extremely delicate. The fishermen of Geneva sell it under the name of *Féra du Travers*.

Féra à la meunière – Scale, gut, and wash the *féra*. Dry thoroughly and season with salt and pepper. Dip in flour and cook in fresh butter over a moderate heat.

Baste frequently with the cooking butter. When cooked, drain the fish and sprinkle with chopped parsley. Pour on a few drops of lemon juice and the cooking butter, piping hot.

Serve at once.

FERCHUSE – Culinary speciality of Burgundy. In former times it was traditionally made on the day when the pig was killed. Its name *ferchuse* is a corruption of *fressure* (pluck) (q.v.).

Use a large saucepan with a heavy base. Melt in it 500 g. (generous 1 lb.) fresh chopped pork fat. Bring to the boil, put in all the pork pluck (heart, liver, and lungs) cut into pieces and seasoned with salt, pepper, and spices.

Brown the pluck very quickly. When browned, sprinkle with 3 tablespoons (scant $\frac{1}{4}$ cup) flour. Mix well, stirring with a wooden spoon, and cook until the flour is golden. Moisten with 2 parts red wine and 1 part of water or stock. There should be enough liquid to cover the pluck completely.

Bring to the boil. As soon as the liquid is boiling steadily, add 8 chopped shallots, 6 crushed cloves of garlic, and a large *bouquet garni*. Simmer slowly for 1 hour, then add 6 large, chopped onions which have been browned in lard, and 10 or 12 large, quartered potatoes. Continue to simmer for a further 45 minutes.

FERMENT – The agent, living or not, that induces fermentation.

FERMENTATION – The chemical change induced by the action of bacteria.

Alcoholic fermentation. FERMENTATION ALCOOLIQUE – See ALCOHOL, WINE, BEER.

Fermentation of milk. FERMENTATION LACTIQUE – See MILK, CHEESE.

Putrid fermentation. FERMENTATION PUTRIDE – See PUTREFACTION.

FERMIÈRE (À LA) – Special method of preparing braised or pot-roasted meat, with a garnish of carrots, turnips, celery, and onions cooked slowly in butter until very tender. (See FONDUE, *Vegetable fondue*.)

FERN. FOUGÈRE – The young shoots of certain ferns (such as the male fern and bracken) are edible and can be served like male hop-flower stalks.

FESTIVE COOKERY. CUISINE CALENDAIRE – Customs closely linked to certain days of the year, to religion or to legend, give plenty of opportunity for celebrations; and these, naturally enough, call for special food. Many so-called 'festive' dishes are similar to those eaten throughout the year; some belong *de rigueur* to certain occasions and may not be so popular at other times. This chapter includes specialities served in particular circumstances (such as the grain or grape harvest) as well as those offered on fixed and moveable feast days.

It would be impossible to include all traditional *cuisine* in the space at our disposal – that would require several volumes. Readers may expand the list for themselves, by noting the recipes of festive dishes they discover in their travels.

We have drawn largely from the *Manuel de folklore contemporain* (A. et J. Picard et Cie, Paris) by A. Van Gennep (no longer available), and *Vieux Dictons de nos campagnes* (New Editions of *la Toison d'Or*, 1952) by G. Bidault de L'Isle. We cannot speak too highly of these works.

Epiphany (6 January). ÉPIPHANIE – The Romans used to vote with beans, and it was with beans that they chose the traditional 'king of the feast' at the Saturnalian banquets: the king being the one who drew the bean. This pagan ceremony persisted but in a slightly different form – the bean being placed in the Twelfth-Night cake.

About a century ago there was controversy over the origin of this ceremony. Some maintained that the idea itself was blasphemous. Since no-one came forward with a better explanation, the bean was hastily replaced by a small china doll which was meant to represent the Child Jesus whom the Magi had come to adore on this day of Epiphany.

The custom had its detractors long before this. On 30 December 1972 a motion of censure proposed by the citizen Scipion Duroure encouraged the councillors of the municipality of Paris to pass a decree declaring that from 6 January 1793, the feast called *fête des Rois* (feast of the Magi) would be called *fête des Sans-Culottes* (feast of the Extreme Republicans) – and the bean continued to be drawn.

And so all over France and in many other countries besides, the tradition of the Twelfth-Night cake continues. It takes different forms according to the region. The gâteau of Savoy, for instance, is a brioche or fruit cake; that of Verviers has cinnamon and candied sugar among its ingredients. The flaky pastry gâteau belongs to Paris. It used to be made by the bakers, but the *pâtissiers* resented this, and parliament was on the side of the *pâtissiers* since butter and eggs were used to make it. All the same the bakers eventually won the day and, up to about 1914, they continued to sell the famous gâteau on 6 January.

Saint Vincent (22 January) – Since the body of Saint Vincent was transferred first to Burgundy and then to Champagne, this saint has, naturally enough, become the patron saint of the vine growers. At one time the people of Burgundy never let his day pass without holding a gargantuan 'pig feast'. The Chevaliers du Tastevin revived this custom in 1934.

At Ligny-le-Châtel, in Yonne, it used to be the custom to offer a figure made of pastry (the *mirlouzé*) along with the consecrated bread on this day.

In the region of Mâcon, the feast of Saint Vincent consisted of a dish called *couques* which was made of haricot beans cooked in goose fat, and a variety of fritters made with bread, brioche, or apples. Sometimes there were thick pancakes called *matefaims*.

Saint Charlemagne (28 January) – This was once a festival day for schoolchildren – especially for those at boarding school. A great banquet used to be held. (The young prince, son of Napoleon III presided over the one held at the lycée Louis-le-grand in 1868) and 'champagne' that consisted solely of bubbles was drunk! An address was given in Latin to which nobody listened, and next day, classes were presided over by sick or slumbering teachers, satiated once again for the year.

Candlemas (2 February). LE CHANDELEUR – Candlemas is the Feast of the Purification of the Virgin Mary; the one on which the virginal candle (*la chandelle*) is lit in remembrance of the presentation of Jesus at the temple of Jerusalem, in accordance with the law of Moses. In Roman times a pagan festival called *Lupercalia* was held near this date. Gelasius, who was Pope in 472, replaced this festival by Candlemas. Since Candlemas fell just as winter ended and spring began, the food was flour-based (old wheat to encourage the new). Fritters were served (butter and oil *rouligneaux*) and pancakes galore.

The pancake custom goes back a long way. The *Ménagier de Paris* cites that, in the fourteenth century, the rule for a good pancake batter was that it be '*ni clère ni espoisse*' (neither too thin nor too thick). And for superstition's sake, one had to toss the pancake higher than the kitchen cupboard while holding a coin in the hand.

Napoleon tossed one (badly) before he left for Russia.

At Montbard, biscuits are made from a mixture of flour and fat formed into human shapes whose features are marked with five haricot beans. These are called *mariottes* or *marionnettes*.

The feast of omelettes (10 February). LA FÊTE DES OMELETTES – This is how the villagers celebrate the return of the sun at Andrieux in the Hautes-Alpes. The valley in which this village lies is bereft of the sun's rays for about a hundred days a year. On 10 February the reappearance of the sun is the signal for general rejoicing. All the inhabitants busily prepare omelettes. At 10 a.m. these are carried to the square. The most venerable and aged of the inhabitants preside over the succeeding ceremony at which everyone dances the *farandole* holding their omelette pans in their hands. The whole gathering then goes to a stone bridge and the omelettes are placed on the parapets. When the sun peeps over the horizon about midday, the omelettes are offered to it. Home then, where every household makes and eats its own 'sacred' omelette in thanksgiving.

1st April – The sun happened to be in the constellation of Pisces on this date and the idea of *poisson d'avril* (April fish or fool) was born. Since 1 April was once the first day of the year, gifts were exchanged, particularly sweetmeats in the form of fish. These were the forerunners of the chocolate fish that we know today, which are just as characteristic of Easter as chocolate Easter eggs.

Saint Mark (25 April) – In the Baux de Provence, ring-shaped biscuits called *toques* are blessed and eaten.

Shrove Tuesday and Carnival. MARDI GRAS ET CARNAVAL – Depending upon when Easter Day falls, Shrove Tuesday is celebrated somewhere between 2 February and 9 March. Carnival begins on 6 January and can therefore last for anything between twenty-eight and sixty-six days. In the olden days it was particularly on Shrove Tuesday, the last day before Lent, that Carnival reached its height. The fattened ox with its accompanying traditions was one of the biggest attractions of the festival. Nowadays, in Burgundy and Dauphiné, Carnival delicacies are pancakes, fritters or *bugnes*, milk gruel, snake-shaped gâteaux called *fantaisies*. Another Burgundy speciality is cheese which is cooked in the cinders.

It's Mardi Gras
You mustn't go
I'll make you pancakes
And you will eat them-o!

In Champagne, pig's trotter always used to be eaten; its ear in Ardèche. In Touraine, it used to be leg of goat; in Limousin, a stuffed rabbit; in Quercy, an enormous *vol-au-vent* filled with jointed chickens and accompanied by salsify sauce) in the Confolens region, they used to feast upon stuffed breast of veal.

In Provence, the last big meal before Lent had to be an *aïoli*.

Pies and flans used to be eaten in Hérault.

In Nivernais, the Shrove Tuesday meal was:

Clear soup with pasta
Boiled beef and vegetables
Coq au vin or chicken in white sauce
Roast turkey or goose
Salad seasoned with garlic and nut oil
White goats' milk cheese with cream
Prune tart
Burnt marc brandy (indispensable)

And all over France, people feasted themselves on pancakes, fritters, waffles, and various biscuits and cakes.

In Les Landes, the cook knew that her *cruspets* were perfectly baked when, if she sharply rapped the *terrine* containing them with her knuckles, it broke.

There were also *cornious, merveilles* and *bottereaux* (fried biscuits). In Touraine, there were *russeroles* (small fried yeast biscuits).

The *faverolles* of Sainte-Menehould were made with butter, flour and eggs.

In Marne, they ate the defeated fighting cockerels; and in the Ardennes, a gigantic omelette marked the end of the egg-eating period.

In Sologne, they made *beugnons* (pasta browned in a frying pan) or slices of white bread dipped in frying batter.

The gâteaux of Reims were four-horned.

In Alsace, at Ossenbach and elsewhere, slices of dried apples and pears were served with bacon or ham. The same dish was called *séchu* in Territoire-de-Belfort.

In the Côte-d'Or and in Isère, a cheese soup began the meal.

Lent. CARÊME – No eggs, no fat, no meat. Lent is symbolised by the cod and the herring, two fish that could be conserved in various ways. In Bordeaux, this period of penitence began on a merry note by one journeying to Caudéran to eat the *lous limacs cendréis* (snails cooked in the ashes).

At Usclades, in Ardèche, a special dish was created for Lent: pieces of a cheese called Sarrasoune, and pieces of other varieties of cheese, were placed in an earthenware jar with salt, vinegar and mustard and set aside to ferment for three weeks. The result was a rather sticky mess with a very strong flavour.

One had to become slowly accustomed to the rigours of the long period of fasting, during which even eggs were forbidden under the *Ancien Régime*. The first Sunday of Lent offered some alleviation, and resulted in the *küchlis* of Alsace (crown-shaped gâteaux), the *bugnes* of Beaujolais, and *carpe brandonnière* (enjoyed by the inhabitants of Mareuil in Touraine as well as those of Saône-et-Loire).

In Franche-Comté and French Switzerland, there were the *piquerés, picrés* or *piconés* (peas fried in pork fat) which the young married couples offered to their guests. These appear again in Yonne, under the name of *guernaulée* or *grôlée*.

A dish of peas cooked first in water, then sautéed in lard, is variously called *dimanche au Piquerey, au Picoué, dé Pwé, des Boîdges, des Piquérés*, etc.

In Vermenton, *échaudés* and a pint of wine were distributed.

Mid-Lent. LA MI-CARÊME – Halfway through Lent was the signal for celebrations everywhere, accompanied by drinking sessions and feasts.

In Alsace, girls made special gâteaux which they distributed to the young men; in Hazebrouck, nuts were tossed into the streets. (These nuts, it was said, had the miraculous power of curing toothache.)

Palm Sunday. LES RAMEAUX – Or the first Sunday in

Spring, because the blossom appears on the boxwood and the first spring flowers are ready to be picked. In provincial France the children attend Mass bearing a large branch of boxwood hung with ribbons, chocolates or candies, apples or prunes, *croquets* (little crisp almond biscuits), candied fruit or waffles. In Brittany and Anjou, the branches are laurel or rosemary.

In the Nice region, the branches used to be decorated with candied fruit (apple, pear, orange) and little biscuit men. These biscuit figures are also found in Auvergne where they are called *bougeois*. In Savoy they are animal-shaped. In Dauphiné, besides these figures, there are *tortilles* which are crown-shaped gâteaux. In Sarlat, the biscuit figures are called *colombes* and their features are marked with aniseed. In Ardèche they are called *pantins, suisses*, or *estèves*. Elsewhere, gâteaux, sweetmeats, and 'red' eggs abound. In Aveyron, we find star-shaped biscuits called *chaudels*, along with aniseed dwarfs and biscuit figures. S-shaped or crown-shaped *pâtisseries* are the specialities in Perpignan. In Creuse, it is a cock; in Aubusson, a rosary of meringues with a ribbon threaded through them.

The *cornus, cornudos*, and *cornuelles* found in Limousin, Angoumois, and Périgord are triangular biscuits. In Berry, there are *marmottes* (little round biscuits). In Bergerac, around the year 1890, the branches were decorated with *sardinoux* (tiny salted fish); and in Quercy, real fish were served with the *fouaces* (girdle cakes).

Maundy Thursday. JEUDI SAINT – In Alsace, nothing but green vegetables are eaten in the home. But almost everywhere else this is the day where children (particularly choir boys) go from door to door collecting eggs and pennies.

Good Friday. VENDREDI SAINT – The most traditional dish is still cod; but in Selongey, on the Côte-d'Or, lentils have to be eaten to wash away one's sins; while in Alsace, *bretzels* crunched in unison by young engaged couples are a pledge of eternal love. Eggs 'gathered' on Good Friday were considered almost everywhere to have special qualities.

In Lorraine and in the Meuse valley, lasagne and other pasta are cut into lozenges and dipped in vinegar; or they become the *tâtelats* or *tâtelots* of Moselle by being cooked in water and seasoned with *vinaigrette*.

Easter. PÂQUES – The searching for eggs on Maundy Thursday and Good Friday was the preparation for the onslaught on hard-boiled eggs, pastries, and omelettes that marked the return to normal eating after Lent.

A long time before the advent of sugar-coated or chocolate eggs, it was the custom to dye and roll eggs. Children were told that Easter eggs were laid by hens, hares, or rabbits, depending upon the region.

However, there was other traditional Easter fare besides the indispensable omelettes. (In the Bray region, beechnut oil was set aside for making these.) Often it was roast kid or leg of mutton as in biblical days, but there were also parslied ham or pork brawn in Burgundy; specially fattened roast sucking pig in the Metz region; dried *saucisson* in Gascogne; and *saucisson* omelette in Lauraguais and Toulon.

In Ruffec and other Charentes provinces there are pies filled with minced meat. On Easter Saturday a pastry is made of flour, eggs, butter, and sugar. A large plate is lined with this, then a minced mixture of chicken or pigeon meat and hard-boiled eggs is placed upon it. This is covered with another layer of pastry. Before the pie is cooked, it is decorated by the daughter of the house with leaves, birds, and other simple shapes made of the leftover pastry. The pie is then glazed with yolk of egg and water and baked in the oven.

Pies, too, are served in Poitou; onion is added to those of Touraine.

In Louhans, a minced mixture of salt veal, chicken, and pork is the traditional filling for the pie.

In Souterraine (Creuse), the Easter pie is made of meat covered with halved hard-boiled eggs which give it a humped appearance.

The *galette pacaude* of Vendée (also called Easter bread) is made with bread dough rekneaded with butter and eggs to make a brioche dough. Sugar and orange-flower water are added, and the paste is formed into a large loaf and cooked in a slow oven like a brioche.

There are many other varieties of Easter *pâtisserie*: *cavagnats* at Menton; *cacavelli* or *campanili* in Corsica; flaky pastry pies filled with juicy chunks of lamb in Aveyron, etc.

The well-known *soupe dorée* (slices of white bread dipped in a mixture of beaten eggs and milk, then browned in butter) belongs traditionally to Easter. It is called *croûtes* in certain parts of Savoy.

Pâté en croûte is still the Easter Monday dish in Loches and Ligueil. In Marseille, it is pickled pork omelette.

Ascension – The traditional cheese dance is performed on this day at Vic-sous-Thil on the Côte-d'Or. A cream cheese is placed in a large bowl and crowned with a bunch of lilac. When the dancer makes her final curtsey, the inn-keeper steps forward and smears her face with the cream cheese.

In the Montbéliard region, fritters and spiced milk curds (*saizai*) are the order of the day.

Curdled milk blended with the seeds of cultivated cardoons (*caillebottes*) used to be the Ascension Day dish in Vendée. The whey was cut crosswise and eaten with fresh milk and sugar.

Pentecost. PENTECÔTE – A haricot bean soup called 'the soup of the Holy Ghost' is the traditional dish in the village of La Croix in the Alpes-Maritimes. It is made in two enormous cauldrons, each containing 150 litres (33 gallons, $41\frac{1}{2}$ gallons) soup, in a kitchen situated on the first floor of the church.

1 May – Roast pork and special gâteaux are offered on this day, in Burgundy. In Tours, everyone drinks the 'milk of May' to make them 'sweet and strong'.

Saint Isadore (10 May). SAINT ISIDORE – In Saint-Forgeux-l'Espinasse, the baker bakes 'Saint Isadores' which are large brioche figures 30 to 60 cm. (12 to 24 inches) high. These are exhibited in the church and later distributed.

Saint Phal (16 May) – At Viviers, in the Yonne, succulent duck pies are offered on this day. It is for this reason that the inhabitants are nicknamed 'ducklings'.

Corpus Christi. FÊTE-DIEU – Another type of cheese dance takes place on this day. A white cheese set in a bowl of cream is offered to the young girl who dances best.

15 August – At Ponts-de-Cé in Anjou, there is a net-fishing expedition. A banquet used to be held on this occasion at which everyone enjoyed a kind of fish stew laced with Anjou wine.

Harvest. MOISSONS – The harvest meal has always been a very important event. In Argonne, for example, at Pentecost, the master even used to offer a pre-harvest banquet to his future harvesters. The men who wielded the scythes, in particular, had a hard task before them out in the fields all day under the hot sun.

The following are a few examples of the kind of meals given. These, in a manner of speaking, formed part of their work contract in the Midi of France. There were five meals a day:

1. At 7 a.m. a crushed red anchovy spread on bread that had been dipped in oil and vinegar, along with a pickled onion or a piece of dry garlic-rubbed bread.
2. At 10 a.m. a hard-boiled egg and a piece of cheese.

3. At 1 p.m. lunch of soup followed by boiled vegetables or an onion omelette.

4. At 4 p.m. an enormous salad with a croûton of garlic-rubbed bread.

5. For supper, pork or mutton followed by an onion omelette called the *moissonneuse* (harvester) and *soupo courto* (a meat *ragoût* mixed with rice).

In the Aude, lunch consisted of white lamb stew, or an omelette, or sheep's tripe.

In Seine-et-Marne a stew accompanied by cheese and salad was carried out to the fields at 11 a.m. In the evening there was *charigot* (a mutton *ragoût* served with potatoes).

In Doubs, at 4 p.m., there was the *trempette* which was a bowl of sweetened wine in which one dipped *liches* (strips) of bread.

Harvest festival. À LA FIN DES MOISSONS – There was always a meal to mark the end of the harvest but it was served under a variety of names – reboule, paulée, passée, berlot, pochée, barbatto. Fritters and offal were served in Creuse and in Somme; sausages in Alsace and in Franche-Comté; cured knuckle of pork in the Massif Central; boiled beef in Normandy; jugged rabbit in Marne, Beauce, Perche and around Nice; rabbit *au sang* in Cher; roast goose in Alsace, Touraine and Seine-et-Marne; preserved goose (*confit d'oie*) in the regions that specialise in it; roast cockerel more or less throughout Marne, Isère, Angoumois and Sologne. There was a lot of pasta served too: ravioli or meat pasties, lasagne, *galettes* (girdle cakes) and *matafans*, waffles and *darioles*.

In the Massif Central the dish of the day is *patranque* (a potato and cheese dish) and *pountari* (a meatless stuffing cooked in a casserole).

In the Meuse, there are cream or jam puffs and *gouillates* (thin pastry squares eaten with milk or *vinaigrette*).

October – In Burgundy, neighbours and friends meet to crack nuts and to drink the new wine as the evenings draw in. There is much singing and story-telling on such occasions.

In some parts of Yonne, a light meal used to follow the wine and nuts. Small, very spicy, dumplings called *miottes* were served along with girdle cakes and haricot beans.

Grape harvest. LES VENDANGES – It used to be the general custom to offer the grape-pickers a meal during the harvest. In the upper Rhine valley this consisted of a soup thickened with flour or potatoes, and white cheese mixed with munster or herbstkas. In the region of Ay and Epernay, the freshly butchered pig's head was kept for this meal. In Touraine, jugged rabbit with prunes was the speciality. In Beaujolais, there were *chamoures* (marrow flans).

The *paulée*, the meal that marked the termination of the grape harvest, is still the signal for gargantuan feasts, where the speciality of each region has pride of place.

1 November – In the centre of France, this evening was spent doing the *pluche* which consisted of peeling chestnuts, then boiling and eating them. In other places, they used to make and eat the *milletée*, a kind of mash made from millet grain cooked in milk. These traditions were usually linked with some superstition or other.

Martinmas (11 November) – In some country districts, the custom is to eat a roast turkey stuffed with chestnuts, or a fattened goose (it is the end of the fattening period for these fowl). And the rue aux Oyers, aux Oues, and aux Ours (by deformation), used to be close to the abbey of Saint-Martin-des Champs. The Dijon gastronomic fair used to begin on 11 November.

North of the French border, in Flanders and in the Rhineland, the *cornes de Saint-Martin* (crescent-shaped gâteaux) were offered on this day.

Christmas Eve. LA VEILLÉE DE NOËL – The hearty Provençal supper becomes a meatless meal on Christmas Eve. It varies from district to district in Provence.

It can be cauliflower; cod in *raito* (cod, fried with wine sauce and capers); cardoons and chards in white sauce; snails; grey mullet with olives; celery *à la poivrade*; or omelettes with artichokes and fresh pasta.

But the highlight is the thirteen desserts: *nougat des capucins* made with figs, with nuts, and with honey; white nougat; the *fougasse* (girdle cake made with oil and orange-flower water); apples; pears; prunes; almonds; hazelnuts; the *calissons* of Aix; the *biscotins*; the *casse-dents* of Allanch, etc., washed down with hot wine and ratafi liqueur. Thirteen desserts, therefore, but not necessarily the same ones everywhere. And why thirteen? Simply in memory of the Last Supper which Christ shared with his twelve disciples.

Le réveillon (midnight feast) – Begins on return from Midnight Mass. (*Réveillon* means literally 'a new awakening').

The fasting of Christmas Eve, the length of the services (everyone used to attend laudes and matins before the three masses) and the (more often than not) long distance to cover coming and going, used to be justification enough for the *réveillon*. Also this was, materially speaking, the most important festival of all, the one that lent its name to all great rejoicings. On royal occasions, when large distributions of food were made to the people, the latter showed their delight by crying 'Noël! Noël!'.

In Armagnac, a stew is served.

In Alsace, there is *sauerkraut* and goose liver.

In Nivernais, a pig is slaughtered, and everyone tucks into the puddings while they wait for the girdle cakes.

In Poitou, there is poultry and game; partridges, capons, small game birds, herons, leverets, hutch rabbits, pheasants, etc.

In Provence, those who are still hungry after the 'big supper' find a turkey, stuffed with chestnuts, waiting for them on their return from church.

In Touraine, a pig is slaughtered and there are quantities of black and white puddings followed by *rillons* (potted pork), cutlets, and finally the *fouace* (girdle cake).

In Roussillon, like everywhere else, oysters and *foie gras* take the place of honour at the beginning of the meal, followed by the local ham and a roast turkey nestling beside a roast hare. The glowing Muscat, Banyuls and Rancio wines add gaiety to the feast. For dessert, there is pineapple bread, then the *tourrous* (the nougat of the region), the *rosquilles* of Amélie-les-Bains, and the *grebilles* (crisp biscuits). All these are highly esteemed varieties of local *pâtisserie*.

Roast goose is eaten in the south-west; turkey almost everywhere else.

In Britain, on Christmas Day there is an enormous joint of roast beef, or a goose, or a turkey, with plum pudding as dessert. At one time the royal Christmas dish was roast swan followed by plum pudding. Boar's head is served at Oxford.

In Austria, carp, potato chips, and pear flans are served at the *réveillon*. Then there is roast turkey or goose with apples, accompanied by a grilled noodle dish containing honey and poppyseeds for the midday meal on Christmas day.

In Denmark, there is hot rice sprinkled with cold milk, wheaten beer bread, ham and cod with horseradish sauce.

In Spain, there is almond soup and *besugo* (sea bream baked in the oven).

In Hungary, a substantial supper consisting of roast sucking pig and poppyseed cake is eaten before midnight mass.

In Switzerland, the Christmas patties are like apple turnovers except that they are made with pears.

Christmas cakes and biscuits. Cakes and biscuits have always been an integral feature of every feast day, to such an extent that they have taken on a ritual character, their shape and composition conforming to the solemnity of the occasion.

There are the Flemish *quegnolles*; the *cochelins* of the Beauce; the *nourolles* and *aguignettes* of Normandy; the *noulets* and *cornabeaux* of Berrichon; the *calendau* of Provence – and many others.

In Champagne, there is the *bourde*. This ritual gâteau used to be in the shape of a human figure and was eaten at Christmas time; now it is rectangular with two horns at either end. Bakers still make biscuits that are vaguely human-shaped. At Christmas, godparents used to give *bourdes* to their godchildren up to the period of their first Communion. These were placed in the children's shoes or under their pillows for them to eat when they awoke. The *bourdes* become *queugnots* in Châlons, *cogneux* in Lorraine, and *burdins* in Argonne. One Christmas in Moirement is described in the following few lines:

Early in the morning I baked for him
I made him a little *burdin*
Which is as big as our pitcher
I added a little lard
Because I hadn't enough butter

The gingerbread in Champagne takes the form of a Father Christmas, or of his ass. And all stuff themselves with waffles.

In Brittany, the black and white puddings and the cockerel make up the main part of the meal. But the *fouaces* (girdle cakes in the shape of a star, freshly made that morning) or the *nolets* topped with a cross, are still the most traditional of the delicacies. Best-known of all is the *far*, the cake that someone once said had the robustness of a nation.

At one time it was the custom to distribute among one's friends small gâteaux called *nieulles*. A huge loaf called *pain de calandre* was kneaded the night before and divided amongst the family, after a small piece had been cut off and marked with three or four crosses. This was kept as a remedy for all ills.

In Creuse, this loaf is made on Christmas Eve and a carefully prepared gâteau is put into the oven with it. This gâteau is said to have special properties and is put aside to be used in case of illness of man or beast. The belief is that all one has to do is to take a small piece to the ailing person in order to cure him immediately.

In Roussillon, the godfathers give their god-daughters a pineapple loaf called a *tortell*. Legend has it that Joseph gave this loaf to the Catalan shepherds who hastened to the stable at Christmas time.

FEUILLANTINE – Puff-pastries made with flaky pastry dough rolled out and folded into 3 upon itself 6 times. These pastries are cut out of the dough in strips 5 cm. (2 inches) long and 2 cm. ($\frac{3}{4}$ inch) wide. They are brushed with white of egg, sprinkled with granulated sugar and baked in a moderate oven.

Feuillantines are served with afternoon tea and also, instead of wafers, with ice cream.

FEUILLE DE DREUX – See CHEESE.

FEUILLETON – Preparation made from thin slices of veal or pork, beaten flat, spread with layers of stuffing, and laid one on top of the other. When it has been built up, the *feuilleton* is wrapped in thin slices of pork fat or pork caul, and braised in the usual way.

Feuilleton of veal à l'ancienne. FEUILLETON DE VEAU À L'ANCIENNE – For a *feuilleton* weighing 2 kg. ($4\frac{1}{2}$ lb.), cut 10 thin slices from the *noix* or *sous-noix* (U.S. loin) of veal. Flatten these with a beater to make them rectangular in shape. Season with salt, pepper, and a pinch of spices.

Cut a very thin slice of pork fat rather larger than the slices of veal. Spread a slice of veal with fine pork stuffing to which has been added a third of its weight of *à gratin forcemeat* (see FORCEMEAT) and a third of its weight of dry *duxelles* (q.v.), which has been bound with egg. Lay the slices of veal one on top of the other, spreading each with stuffing and ending with a layer of stuffing. Cover with a thin slice of pork fat. Fold the edges of the lower slice of pork fat so that they cover the sides of the *feuilleton*. Fold the edges of the upper slice over those of the lower slice. Tie the *feuilleton* neatly into shape. Put it in a buttered stewpan lined with bacon rinds and sliced onions and carrots. Add a *bouquet garni*. Cover, and simmer for 20 minutes. Moisten with $2\frac{1}{2}$ dl. (scant $\frac{1}{2}$ pint, generous cup) white wine. Boil down. Add $2\frac{1}{2}$ dl. (scant $\frac{1}{2}$ pint, generous cup) brown veal stock. Boil down to a concentrated jelly. Moisten with 5 dl. (scant pint, $2\frac{1}{4}$ cups) good stock. Cover, and cook in the oven for $1\frac{3}{4}$ hours, basting frequently.

Drain the *feuilleton*. Untie and put it on a serving dish. Pour on a few tablespoons of the fat of the braising stock. Glaze in the oven, basting frequently. Surround with a *Bourgeoise garnish* (see GARNISHES) or garnish with braised celery, chicory, lettuce, cucumbers, etc.

Remove the fat from the braising stock. Strain and, if necessary, boil down. Pour a few tablespoons of this stock over the meat and serve the rest separately.

To ensure that the *feuilleton* is perfectly rectangular in shape it can be boxed in with thin rectangular pieces of white wood laid on the top, bottom, and sides, and kept in position with string.

This dish can also be made with different mixtures, stuffings, and *salpicons*. It can be braised in Madeira instead of white wine.

Feuilleton of cold veal in jelly. FEUILLETON DE VEAU FROID À LA GELÉE – Prepare and cook the *feuilleton* as for *Feuilleton of veal à l'ancienne*. Cool under a weight. Trim and put it on a bed of well-set jelly in a bowl. Pour over it enough half-set jelly to cover it (the jelly having been enriched with the braising stock diluted with unthickened meat juice). Chill on ice.

Feuilleton of veal à la périgourdine. FEUILLETON DE VEAU À LA PÉRIGOURDINE – Prepare the *feuilleton* as indicated for *Feuilleton of veal à l'ancienne*, spreading the slices of meat with a stuffing made of two-thirds *foie gras* and one-third fine stuffing with diced truffles added. Braise in Madeira. Garnish with strips of truffle and slices of *foie gras* sautéed in butter.

Using the same method, *feuilletons* of pork or large poultry can be served hot or cold. Poultry *feuilletons* can be braised in white stock and served with a sauce and garnish especially suitable for poultry *entrées*.

FEUILLETTE – Cask roughly equivalent to the English quarter-cask, with a capacity of between 114 litres (25 gallons, 31 gallons) and 140 litres (31 gallons, 39 gallons). The *ordinary feuillette* holds between 133 litres (29 gallons, $36\frac{1}{2}$ gallons) and 135 litres ($29\frac{1}{2}$ gallons, 37 gallons), and the *large feuillette* holds up to 140 litres (31 gallons, 39 gallons). The *Burgundy feuillette* only holds between 112 litres ($24\frac{1}{2}$ gallons, $30\frac{1}{2}$ gallons) and 114 litres (25 gallons, 31 gallons).

FIASQUE – Wine flask (*fiasco* in Italian) with a wide base and long neck. It is usually wrapped in straw.

FIATOLE – Flat broad Mediterranean fish. It is striking in appearance with golden-yellow bars and spots on its leaden grey skin. It is fairly delicate to eat. All recipes for turbot (q.v.) are suitable for this dish.

FIÉLAS – Name given in Provence to the conger eel (q.v.), which is one of the ingredients of *bouillabaisse*. It can be stewed, cooked *en matelote*, etc. in the same way as eel.

FIELDFARE. LITORNE – Large type of thrush with greyish head-feathers. It is less delicate than the true thrush. All recipes for thrush (q.v.) are suitable for fieldfare.

FIELD-POPPY OIL. HUILE D'OEILLETTE – Edible oil obtained by pressing the seeds of the white poppy.

This oil is also known in France as white oil and *olivette*. It has the same culinary uses as olive oil.

FIG. FIGUE – Fruit of the fig tree.

There are three types of fig, the *white fig*, the *purple fig*, and the *red fig*. These three types are subdivided into a large number of varieties.

French figs are grown in the Midi, mostly in Var. The best-known varieties are *buissone, bellone, bourjasotte, célestine col de dame, dauphine violette*. These figs are exported fresh between June and November.

The fig is also grown throughout the whole of the Mediterranean basin. Algeria is the principal supplier of dried figs.

Branch of fig tree with fruits

Besides being the sweetest of all fruits, the fig contains appreciable quantities of Vitamins A, B, and C. It has laxative and digestive properties (although if eaten when under-ripe there is a risk of its causing an irritation of the mouth and lips). Figs are more nourishing when dried and, like prunes, are improved by soaking for twenty-four hours before use.

Fresh figs are usually eaten raw in their natural state. They can be served as *hors-d'œuvre* with raw ham in the same way as melon.

Figs can also be cooked in various ways. All recipes for apricots (q.v.) are suitable for figs.

A fermented drink is made from figs, and also a spirit which is highly prized by the Arabs.

In central Europe roast figs are used to flavour coffee, as chicory is in France.

Corsican anchoyade. ANCHOIADE CORSE – Pound some peeled fresh figs with a pinch of garlic, and desalted anchovy fillets. Spread the resulting paste on slices of bread moistened with olive oil. Cover with chopped onions.

Dried figs. FIGUES SÈCHES – In the south of France, figs are preserved by drying in the sun. Very ripe autumn fruit is used. The figs, spread out on hurdles, are exposed to the sun. They have to be turned over several times during the drying and, before they are completely dried, are slightly flattened. Treated in this way, figs will keep a very long time.

Dried figs are eaten as they are. They can also be stewed, like all other dried fruits, and are used in various sweets and pastries.

Fig fritters. BEIGNETS DE FIGUES – Peel and quarter the figs. Steep them for 30 minutes in brandy or some other liqueur, and sugar. Dip them in light batter and deep-fry. (See FRITTERS.)

Leg of wild pig with figs. CUISSOT DE MARCASSIN AUX FIGUES – Draw the sinews from the meat, wipe it, thread it with lardoons, and place it in a cooked marinade for 10 days. Wipe the meat and roast with herbs until cooked but slightly rare.

Make a caramel. Add half marinade, half vinegar to the residue in the roasting pan. Boil this down and poach some fresh figs in it. Drain these and arrange around the roast leg of pork. Continue to reduce the liquid, add kneaded butter, and serve this sauce separately.

Fig marmalade – See MARMALADES.

Pork stew with green figs. DAUBE DE PORC AUX FIGUES VERTES – Brown a fillet of lean pork in lard with chopped onions. Add 1 glass water, and a *bouquet* of parsley, thyme, and bay leaf. Season with salt and pepper. Simmer for 1 hour.

Poach small green figs in water. Crush a pimento in the juice of 1 lemon. Add this to the pork. Simmer for 1 or 2 minutes and then serve the pork surrounded by the figs.

Stewed figs. COMPOTE DE FIGUES – See COMPOTE.

Fig tart. TARTE AUX FIGUES – See TART.

Fig wine or figuette. VIN DE FIGUE, FIGUETTE – Medicinal drink made from dried figs.

FILBERT. AVELINE – Another name for the hazelnut. The filbert tree, which produces these nuts, is a variety of the common hazel tree. They are called this because they are ripe about Saint Philbert's day – 22 August.

Recipes for filbert nuts will be found under HAZELNUT.

FILLET. FILET – Undercut of the sirloin of beef. A cut taken from the fleshy part of the buttocks of other animals. For methods of preparation see BEEF, MUTTON, VEAL, PORK.

Filet mignon – Small cut of meat taken from the end of the beef fillet. *Filets mignons* are grilled or sautéed. (See BEEF.)

This term is also applied to fillet of lamb (q.v.), mutton (q.v.), veal (q.v.), and pork (q.v.).

Fillets of fish. FILETS DE POISSON – Fish cut lengthwise off the central bone before cooking, e.g. fillets of sole, whiting, etc.

Fillets of poultry and winged game. FILETS DE VOLAILLES ET DE GIBIERS DE PLUME – In France a *filet* as applied to game or poultry is, in the strict sense:

1. The under part of the breast of poultry and winged game.

2. The breasts themselves of poultry or game, cut off before cooking and prepared in various ways. They can be used whole or when they are too fat, as in the case of turkeys, cut into thin slices.

The breasts of poultry and game are more often known in cookery as *suprêmes*.

FILLETTE – Name for a small wine bottle used mainly for Anjou wines. Its capacity is about $\frac{1}{3}$ litre (generous $\frac{1}{2}$ pint, $1\frac{1}{2}$ cups).

FINANCIÈRE (À LA) – Method of preparing meat and poultry. *Financière garnish* (which is also used to fill pies and *vol-au-vent*) consists of cocks' combs and cocks' kidneys, quenelles, lambs' sweetbreads, mushrooms, olives and strips of truffles.

FIN DE SIÈCLE – See CHEESE.

FINE – Liqueur brandy (spirit of wine). The *appellation* must be followed by the name of the region whence it comes. (See COGNAC, *Fine Champagne*.)

FINES HERBES – This term is sometimes used to mean chopped parsley rather than a mixture of herbs and thus an omelette *aux fines herbes* contains only chopped parsley in addition to the usual seasoning.

Actually, *fines herbes* should be a mixture of herbs, such as parsley, chervil, tarragon, and chives.

FINTE – Fish somewhat similar to the shad. Like the shad, it returns to the rivers to spawn, but about a month later. It differs from the shad in shape, being rather more elongated, and unlike the shad it has very sharp teeth in both jaws. The *finte* is prepared in the same way as the shad (q.v.).

FIRECREST or FIRE-CRESTED WREN. ROITELET – Small singing bird which is prepared like lark (q.v.).

FIREDOG. LANDIER – Large kitchen andiron.

In his *Dictionnaire raisonné du mobilier français, de l'époque carolingienne à la Renaissance*, Viollet Le Duc defines antique firedogs and describes their uses in the kitchens of our ancestors:

'Stoves divided into several compartments were much less frequently used in kitchens than they are today. The food was cooked over the open fire. It will be readily understood that, in view of the great heat of the fire, it was impossible to use it for certain dishes which had to be stirred during cooking or which were prepared in small cooking pots.

'Stoves filled with live charcoal were propped on firedogs away from the hearth and at a convenient height for working. They made cooking very much easier. The kitchen staff even ate their food off these little stoves and kept themselves warm at the same time.

'Kitchen firedogs were simple in design, though they were forged with great care. Those designed for living apartments were often very richly ornamented with scroll work. Few firedogs made before the fifteenth century have much artistic merit.'

FISH. POISSONS – Most fish are edible and the fish world presents an enormous source of food. The most nourishing fish are river eels and lampreys, then come salmon, salmon trout, mackerel, turbot, fresh herring, and the conger eel. Among the least nourishing, although they are by no means to be despised, are bream, sole, and lemon sole.

Fish contains the same proportion of protein as meat. It has approximately the same food value and contains significant amounts of Vitamins B and D. It is rich in phosphorous and iodine, deficient in calcium, and contains less iron than meat.

The water content of all fish is much the same – 75 per cent. The albuminoids also vary little from species to species – they constitute about 18 per cent. The fats are found in more variable quantities. There are fish very rich in fat content, such as eel (26 per cent); fish fairly rich in fats such as lamprey (12·5 per cent), shad (8·42 per cent), mackerel (8·31 per cent), sturgeon (7·91 per cent), and herring (6 per cent); and lean fish such as pike, ray and bream.

Fish (*Nicolas*)

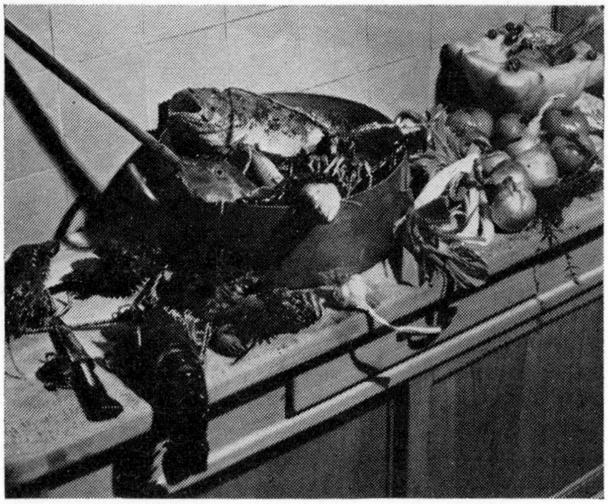

Fish for bouillabaisse (*French Government Tourist Office*)

The flesh of fish, therefore, does not differ greatly in content from the flesh of land animals: it may perhaps contain slightly less nitrogenous substances, but the fat content and the proportion of mineral is substantially the same, in particular that of phosphorated compounds. Owing to the fact that fish (particularly lean fish) is easily digestible, it is an excellent food for children and expectant mothers but it must be fresh, not oily, and served grilled, in soup, or baked.

From the practical point of view, it is interesting to note the quantity of waste of a whole fish. Thus carp, fresh cod, and sole carry 50 per cent waste, bass 47 per cent, perch and trout 44 per cent, small frying fish (such as gudgeon and smelts) from 40 per cent to 30 per cent, and the fresh sardine only 20 per cent.

Fish is subject to speedy decay by bacterial action and often causes food poisoning if it is not absolutely fresh.

At the market, the freshness of fish can be recognised by the firmness of the flesh; a clean fresh smell, without any suggestion of anything musty, unpleasant, sweetish or pungent; bright eyes, which should stand out and not be embedded in the orbits; bright scales and bright red gills.

Flat fish. POISSONS PLATS – There are two kinds of flat fish: *fish flattened vertically* (such as ray or skate) the upper, exposed side being dark and the underside white; and *fish flattened laterally*, which are the real flat fish, the white and dark sides representing the flanks, the back and the belly being represented by the flattened sides; the two eyes are both on the same side (the coloured side). Depending on the position of the eyes, flat fish are classified into *dextral species*, if the eyes lie on the right side of the head, and *sinistral species*, if they are on the left. The anus is always visible on the underside. Plaice, flounder, sole, and lemon sole are right-sided; while sardine, turbot, and brill are left-sided.

Poisonous fish – The flesh of certain varieties of fish, generally those inhabiting tropical seas, is permanently poisonous; other species, such as grey gurnard, carp-bream, garfish, etc., become poisonous at certain times.

Venomous fish – These fish, the flesh of which is often excellent, must not be confused with fish mentioned in the preceding paragraph. Venomous fish have dorsal fins armed with spines which are grooved and provided with poison glands. These can cause very painful and even dangerous wounds if they are handled without due precaution as, for instance, in the case of the weever or sting-fish.

Recipes for different fish are listed in their alphabetical order.

Fish mousse. MOUSSE DE POISSON – *Ingredients.* 1 kg ($2\frac{1}{4}$ lb.) fish (net weight), 4 to 5 egg whites, $1\frac{1}{4}$ litres ($2\frac{1}{4}$ pints, $5\frac{1}{4}$ cups) fresh thick cream, $1\frac{1}{2}$ teaspoons salt, $\frac{1}{4}$ teaspoon white pepper, pinch of spices.

Method. Season the fish with salt, pepper, and spices, and pound in a mortar as finely as possible. While pounding, add the egg whites a little at a time. Rub the mixture through a fine sieve.

Put it in a pan and leave to stand on ice (or in a cool place) for 2 hours. Add the cream, a little at a time, stirring with a wooden spoon.

Fill a mould three-quarters full with the mixture. Stand in water and poach in a moderate oven. When cooked, leave to stand for a few seconds before turning out.

Appropriate garnishes are: *cancalaise*; various species of mushrooms sautéed in butter; shrimps; *dieppoise*; fresh-water crayfish; *Joinville*; *Nantua*; *marinière*: *mussels*; *normande*; green peas in butter; asparagus tips in butter; *princesse*; *trouvillaise*; Victoria.

Recipes for all the garnishes are given under GARNISHES. Fish mousses are covered with one or other of the following sauces (q.v.) to blend with the garnish selected:

aurore, cardinal, cream, shrimp, curry, *diplomate*, parsley, lobster, *Joinville*, *marinière*, *Nantua*, *normande*, *ravigote*, *riche*, *vénitienne*, Victoria, *white wine*.

Fish roes on toast. CROÛTES AUX LAITANCES – Poach roes in a little butter and lemon juice, and place on rectangles of bread fried in butter. Sprinkle with breadcrumbs which have been fried in butter. Squeeze lemon juice over and put in a hot oven. Sprinkle with chopped parsley.

FISH KETTLE (Fish boiler). POISSONIÈRE – Kitchen utensil intended for cooking fish. It usually contains a removable grid which makes it possible to take out the fish without breaking it.

FISSURELLE – Species of gasteropod mollusc in a conical shell similar to that of the limpet or barnacle. It has radiating ribs and is perforated at the tip. *Fissurelles* live in temperate and tropical waters and there are about a hundred different types. The Greek *fissurelle*, called *Saint Peter's ear*, is very common in the Mediterranean.

All recipes for octopus (q.v.) are suitable for this mollusc.

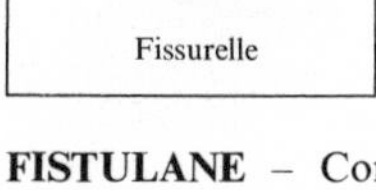

Fissurelle

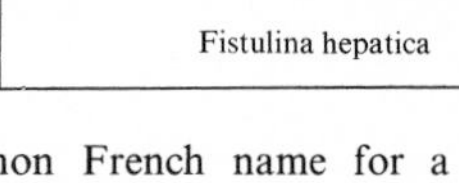

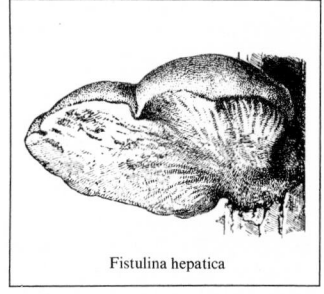

Fistulina hepatica

FISTULANE – Common French name for a headless mollusc also known as *gastrochère*. Its shell is tubular. *Fistulanes* are cooked in the same way as cockles (q.v.).

FISTULINA HEPATICA. FISTULINE HÉPATIQUE – A somewhat tasteless edible fungus which grows on the trunks of oak trees. It is commonly known in France as *langue-de-boeuf* (ox tongue) or *foie-de-boeuf* (ox liver). In U.S.A. it is known as *liver fungus*.

FLAGEOLET – See BEAN.

FLAKES. FLOCON – Name given to certain cereals, flattened in a rolling-mill and used (in France) as a garnish in soups or as an ingredient of porridges.

FLAKY PASTRY. FEUILLETAGE – See DOUGH.

FLAMANDE (À LA) – Name of a hotpot and of a garnish, which is used especially for large cuts of meat served as an intermediate course. It consists of braised cabbage, carrots, diced belly of pork, and potatoes. (See GARNISHES.)

The name *à la flamande* is also applied to a method of preparing asparagus (q.v.).

FLAMBER – To sprinkle a dish with spirits which are set alight just before serving.

FLAMICHE – Legrand d'Aussy (a French scholar, 1737–1800), thus described the *flamiche* as it was made in his day: 'It is a kind of *galette* made with baker's dough. It is rolled out with a rolling-pin and put in the oven while the wood is burning. As soon as it has been thoroughly heated, it is taken out of the oven and spread with butter. It is eaten as soon as it comes out of the oven.'

Nowadays the name *flamiche* is given to a kind of leek tart made in Burgundy and Picardy.

To make this tart, line a buttered tart tin with pastry, fill with sliced white leeks which have been cooked slowly in butter until very tender, blended with yolks of egg and well seasoned. Cover with a thin layer of lining pastry. Press the edges together and crimp them. Brush with egg and bake in a very hot oven.

In some parts of France, this tart is made with a mixture of flour, egg yolks, yeast, sugar, and rum or brandy.

FLAMINGO. FLAMANT – Wader with webbed feet. The Romans considered it a delicacy though it is now less highly prized. It is cooked in the same way as bustard (q.v.).

FLAMIQUE – A form of *flamiche* made in some parts of northern France.

FLAMRI – A semolina pudding, usually served cold, covered with a purée of raw red fruit. Boil $\frac{1}{2}$ litre (scant pint, $2\frac{1}{4}$ cups) white wine with the same quantity of water. Gradually pour into it 250 g. (9 oz., $1\frac{1}{2}$ cups) fine semolina. Mix. Simmer gently for 25 minutes. To this 'porridge' add 300 g. (11 oz., $1\frac{1}{3}$ cups) fine sugar, 2 whole eggs, a pinch of salt and 6 stiffly whisked egg whites. Pour the mixture into a buttered mould, put it in a pan of hot water, and bake. Leave to cool.

Turn out the pudding and pour over it a purée of sweetened raw red fruit (strawberries, redcurrants, raspberries).

FLAMUSSE (Burgundian pastry) – Flan made of lining pastry filled with a cheese-flavoured cream blended with eggs.

FLAN – Pastry preparation whose name comes from the metallurgical term *flan* (a metal disc). The flan has been in existence for many centuries. The Latin poet Fortunatus (530–609 A.D.) mentions it. He says that Saint Radegonde, as an exercise in mortification, made flans but ate only the coarse outer crust of rye or oatmeal dough.

A flan is an open tart filled with fruit, cream, etc.

Flans can be served as *hors-d'œuvre* or as a light main course, and as such have a savoury filling. They are also served as a sweet. Recipes for savoury flans and some sweet flans are given below. Recipes for sweet flans are also given under TART. (In U.S.A. a flan is known as a tart or pie.)

Flan cases – Made in the same way as tart cases, and are either baked blind (unfilled) or with the indicated filling.

How to prepare flan cases

Flan cases are made of short pastry, fine lining or ordinary pastry, sweet pastry, semi-flaky pastry, or with left-overs of puff pastry.

Apple flan Grimaldi. FLAN AUX POMMES GRIMALDI – Cut 4 big cooking apples into quarters and cook them in vanilla-flavoured syrup. Drain and arrange in a flan case (U.S. pie shell) filled with rice, prepared in the following manner:

Bake the flan case blind in a flan ring. When ready, fill with cooked sweetened rice, mixed with a *salpicon* (q.v.) of candied orange peel shredded very finely, flavoured with Curaçao, and with 1 tablespoon butter added to it.

Put the well-drained apple quarters on this rice, sprinkle with crushed macaroons and castor sugar and glaze in the oven.

This flan is served hot, accompanied by Curaçao-flavoured *Custard cream* (see CREAM).

Flan à la bordelaise – Bake a flan case blind. Fill with a coarse *salpicon* of beef bone-marrow mixed with diced, lean, cooked ham and blended with very thick *Bordelaise sauce* (see SAUCE). Decorate the top, alternating strips of poached and drained, bone-marrow with fresh mushrooms which have been sliced and sautéed in oil. Sprinkle with toasted breadcrumbs. Pour on melted butter. Brown quickly in a very hot oven. Sprinkle with chopped parsley.

Flan à la bourguignonne – Bake a flan case blind. Fill with a mixture prepared as follows: Simmer 10 sliced white leeks in butter, without browning. When very tender, add 3 dl. ($\frac{1}{2}$ pint, $1\frac{1}{4}$ cups) *Béchamel sauce* (see SAUCE) enriched with 1 dl. (6 tablespoons, scant $\frac{1}{2}$ cup) fresh cream, boiled and strained. Sprinkle with grated cheese. Pour on melted butter and brown in the oven.

Brillat-Savarin flan. FLAN BRILLAT-SAVARIN – Bake blind a flan case made of *Fine lining paste* (see DOUGH). Fill this crust with very creamy scrambled eggs and truffles. Decorate the top with strips of seasoned truffle dipped in melted butter. Sprinkle with grated Parmesan. Pour on melted butter. Brown in a very hot oven.

Carrot flan à la flamande. FLAN DE CAROTTES À LA FLAMANDE – Fill an unbaked flan with finely chopped carrots, boiled in a little water with butter, sugar, and flavouring to taste. Moisten with a few tablespoons custard, slightly thickened with potato flour or arrowroot.

Bake in a moderate oven. Just before it is cooked sprinkle with icing sugar and return to the oven until it is evenly glazed. This flan can be served hot or cold.

Cheese flan. FLAN AU FROMAGE – Line a flan ring, standing on a buttered baking sheet, with *Fine lining paste* (see DOUGH). Fill with a mixture prepared as follows: Boil $\frac{1}{2}$ litre (scant pint, $2\frac{1}{4}$ cups) thick fresh cream with 50 g. (2 oz., $\frac{1}{4}$ cup) butter. Season with salt, pepper and nutmeg. Add 100 g. (4 oz., 1 cup) sieved flour and mix on the stove to obtain a rather thick cream.

Take the pan off the heat and add to the cream 4 egg yolks and 150 g. (5 oz., $1\frac{1}{4}$ cups) grated Gruyère cheese. Blend into the mixture the whites of the eggs, beaten to a very stiff foam. Bake the flan in a hot oven.

Other types of cheese, such as Cantal, Dutch cheese, Parmesan, etc., can be used for this flan.

Selection of flans (*Debillot. Phot. Larousse*)

Cheese flan Juliette Récamier. FLAN AU FROMAGE JULIETTE RÉCAMIER – Stand a flan ring on a buttered metal baking sheet. Line with *Fine lining paste* (see DOUGH). Fill the bottom of the flan with beef bone-marrow dipped in concentrated veal stock and flavoured with chopped parsley and shallot cooked in white wine until all the moisture has evaporated. Season with salt, pepper, and grated nutmeg.

Fill the flan half-full of cream made like *French pastry cream* (see CREAM) but unsweetened, with grated cheese and a little fresh cream added. Bake in a moderate oven.

As soon as the flan is ready, turn it out and place on an ovenware dish. Decorate the top with a few tablespoons very soft scrambled eggs flavoured with cheese. Sprinkle with grated cheese and brown as rapidly as possible.

Chicken liver flan Chavette. FLAN DE FOIES DE VOLAILLE CHAVETTE – Make a flan case with *Fine lining paste* (see DOUGH) and bake blind.

Prepare a *ragoût* of chicken livers cut into thick pieces. Season with salt and pepper, and sauté quickly in sizzling butter. Drain the livers and keep hot. In the same butter, sauté 150 g. (5 oz.) sliced mushrooms. Season. Drain and keep warm with the chicken livers.

Pour 2 dl. ($\frac{1}{3}$ pint, scant cup) Madeira into the pan in which the livers and mushrooms have been cooked. Boil down. Add $3\frac{1}{2}$ dl. (generous $\frac{1}{2}$ pint, $1\frac{1}{2}$ cups) thin *Béchamel sauce* (see SAUCE) and 2 dl. ($\frac{1}{3}$ pint, scant cup) fresh cream. Add to this sauce the pieces of liver and mushrooms and cook until fairly thick. Strain the sauce through a sieve and put the livers and mushrooms back in it. Keep hot without bringing to the boil.

Scramble some eggs (they should be rather soft). Add 2 tablespoons (3 tablespoons) grated Parmesan and 2 tablespoons (3 tablespoons) butter. Put the chicken livers and mushrooms at the bottom of the flan. Cover with the scrambled eggs. Sprinkle with grated cheese. Pour on melted butter and brown in a very hot oven.

Freshwater crayfish flan à la Nantua. FLAN D'ÉCREVISSES À LA NANTUA – Bake a flan case blind. Fill with *Crayfish tail ragoût à la Nantua* (see CRAYFISH) mixed with truffles. Brown quickly in a very hot oven.

All shellfish flans, with shrimps, crabs, lobsters, and spiny lobster are prepared in this way. The truffles can be omitted.

Flan à la financière – Bake a flan case blind. Garnish with a *ragoût à la financière* thickened with concentrated *Demi-glace* (see SAUCE) flavoured with Madeira. Sprinkle with breadcrumbs. Brown in the oven.

Flan à la florentine – Bake a flan case blind. Fill with a layer of spinach (cooked whole, drained, squeezed, coarsely chopped, and simmered in butter). Cover with *Mornay sauce* (see SAUCE). Sprinkle with grated cheese. Pour on melted butter and brown in a hot oven.

Leek flan with cheese. FLAN DE POIREAUX AU FROMAGE – Stand a large flan ring on a buttered baking sheet. Line with *Fine lining paste* (see DOUGH) and bake blind. Remove the flan ring. Place the flan on an ovenware dish. Line the flan with a few tablespoons *Mornay sauce* (see SAUCE). Arrange on top a few white leeks, parboiled for a very short time and simmered in butter. Cover with *mornay sauce* enriched with butter. Sprinkle with grated Parmesan, pour on melted butter, and brown in the oven.

This flan can also be made with small onions instead of leeks. The onions must be well glazed first.

Raspberry cream flan. FLAN AUX FRAMBOISES À LA CRÈME – Remove the stems from the raspberries. Cover with sugar. Put a layer of *French pastry cream* (see CREAM) flavoured with vanilla on a baked flan case. Cover with raspberries and a small amount of raspberry jelly.

Flan à la reine – Bake a flan case blind. Fill with chicken *Salpicon à la reine* (see SALPICON). Sprinkle with toasted breadcrumbs and brown in a very hot oven. Decorate the top of the flan with strips of truffle.

Rice flan – See RICE.

Flan à la Sagan – Bake a flan case blind. Line the bottom with a *salpicon* (q.v.) of mushrooms and truffles blended in cream and seasoned with curry powder. Arrange slices of calves' brains sautéed in butter on top, with a strip of truffle on each slice. Cover with *Mornay sauce* (see SAUCE) flavoured with curry. Sprinkle with grated cheese, pour on melted butter, and brown in a hot oven.

Seafood flan. FLAN AUX FRUITS DE MER – Bake a flan case of *Fine lining paste* or *Flaky pastry* (see DOUGH). Fill with a seafood *ragoût* (oysters, mussels, freshwater crayfish tails, cockles, and other shellfish). Blend in rather thick *Normande sauce* (see SAUCE). Sprinkle with toasted breadcrumbs, pour on melted butter, and brown in a hot oven.

Shellfish flan. FLAN DE CRUSTACÉS – Using cooked lobster, crayfish, or some other shellfish, and a sauce appropriate to the fish chosen, proceed as indicated in the recipe for *Freshwater crayfish flan à la Nantua.*

Sole flan à la normande. FLAN DE SOLES À LA NORMANDE – Fillets of sole prepared *à la normande* arranged as a border in a flan crust. Cover with *Normande sauce* (see SAUCE) and garnish as indicated for *Fillets of sole à la normande* (see SOLE).

Fish flans of all kinds can be made in the same way. Fillets of fish are first poached in white wine or cooked in butter and arranged as a border in the flan. Any meatless garnish can be put in the flan and covered with a sauce appropriate to the garnish used.

FLANDERS. FLANDRE – The cookery of this northern province has much in common with that of Artois and Picardy.

Culinary specialities – *Baby chitterlings* of Cambrai and Armentières; *smoked tongues* of Valenciennes; *craquelots* of Dunkirk (herrings smoked with the leaves of the hazelnut tree); *soupe verte* (green soup); Flemish *hotpot*; *poule au blanc* (chicken in white sauce); *rabbit with prunes*; *tartine de beurre*.

Among the best-known sweets and pastries are: *apple pâté* of Avesnes; *craquelins* of Roubaix; *carrés* of Lannoy; *kokeboterom* of Dunkirk (small buns made with eggs and butter, sweetened and decorated with raisins); *red plum tarts*; *couques*; *bêtises* from Cambrai.

Good cheeses are made in French Flanders. Those of Bergues, Mont-des-Cats and Marolles (a very pungent cheese) are the best known.

Beer is the local drink, and good quality spirits are distilled from juniper and beetroot.

FLANGNARDE – This flan, which is sometimes called *flognarde*, is made in Auvergne and Limousin.

Put 3 tablespoons (scant $\frac{1}{4}$ cup) flour in a bowl. Break 3 eggs into it. Add a very little salt. Sweeten. Mix to a smooth paste, adding $\frac{3}{4}$ litre ($1\frac{1}{3}$ pints, $1\frac{3}{4}$ pints) milk, boiled and cooled. Flavour with vanilla or grated lemon rind.

Pour through a strainer into a deep buttered ovenware dish. Dot with small pieces of butter and bake in a hot oven. Serve hot or cold.

FLANK. FLANCHET – Cut of beef between the fat section and the breast. (See BEEF.)

FLATTEN. APLATIR – Action which renders a piece of meat (*entrecôte*, rump steak, escalope, cutlet, *noisette*, etc.) thinner by beating it with a beater or mallet. Flattening meat makes it easier to cook and makes it more tender.

FLAVOURING. PARFUM – Before the eighteenth century, flavourings very different from those in use today were employed often excessively. As well as the simple aromatic plants, such as thyme, bay leaf, savoury, coriander, aniseed, marjoram, and sage, more exotic aromatics like essence of roses or other flowers, benzoin, amber, etc., were quite common.

These aromatics are now only used in very small doses in the preparation of sweet courses, in pastry-making and confectionery.

Liqueur wines such as Madeira, Frontignan, port, sherry, etc. are widely used nowadays for flavouring.

Various brandies (Cognac, Armagnac, Calvados, etc.) are used for flavouring sauces and gravies and for bringing out the taste of preparations such as game stews, *salmis*, shellfish *à l'américaine* or *à la bordelaise*, woodcock *flambé*, pressed wild duck, etc.

The purpose of seasoning is to give relish to food. Information relative to aromatic plants and their uses in the kitchen will be found in the entry entitled CONDIMENTS.

FLETCHERISM. FLETCHÉRISME – Doctrine established by Horace Fletcher, American industrialist, who restored his gravely failing health by following an extremely austere diet (after having read Gornaro's book on the subject). He claimed to have discovered the 'golden key to health' in mastication pushed to its extreme limits: not swallowing a mouthful of food until it was reduced to the state of a liquid pap and had lost all its flavour.

FLEUR DE DECAUVILLE – See CHEESE.

FLEUR DE FARINE – Pure wheaten flour.

FLEURON – Small flaky pastry motif used to decorate certain dishes and the top of *pâtés* in pastry crust.

FLEURS DE VIN – Little whitish or bluish flakes, caused by the development of *mycoderma vini*, which appear in wines on the turn. The appearance of these flakes generally precedes acid fermentation.

FLOATING ISLAND. ÎLE FLOTTANTE – Cut into thin layers a stale *Savoie* (sponge) cake. Steep the slices in kirsch and maraschino. Spread each one with apricot jam and sprinkle with chopped blanched almonds and dried currants.

Build up the cake into its original shape by laying the slices one on top of the other. Ice with *Chantilly cream* (see CREAMS) flavoured with vanilla. Decorate with almonds, chopped pistachio nuts, and currants. Pour chilled vanilla-flavoured custard over the cake.

The pulp of strawberries, raspberries, or redcurrants, sieved and sweetened, may be used instead of custard.

FLORENTINE (À LA) – Method of preparation used mainly for fish and eggs, set on a bed of spinach cooked in butter, covered with *Mornay sauce* (see SAUCE), sprinkled with grated cheese, and browned.

FLOUNDER. FLET, FLÉTAN – Common name for a fish of the same family as the brill, dab, lemon sole, sole, and turbot. While these others never leave the sea, flounders, though also saltwater fish, are often found in fresh water. They are even caught in the River Seine between Pont-de-l'Arche and Les Andelys.

The flounder is oval in shape, covered with tiny scales. They vary in colour from greenish brown to blackish yellow, with yellow, orange, or reddish markings.

In France, the flounder is sometimes known as *flandre* (or *flondre*) *de rivière* or *de picard*. In former times it was incorrectly called *flétan* (halibut) which is in fact, a quite different fish, found in northern waters.

In northern countries of Europe, especially Norway, flounders are preserved by drying and smoking. All recipes for brill (q.v.) and turbot (q.v.) are suitable for flounders.

The flounder plays an important part in American cookery, often taking the place of sole and turbot which are not found in American waters and, having to be imported, are rather expensive.

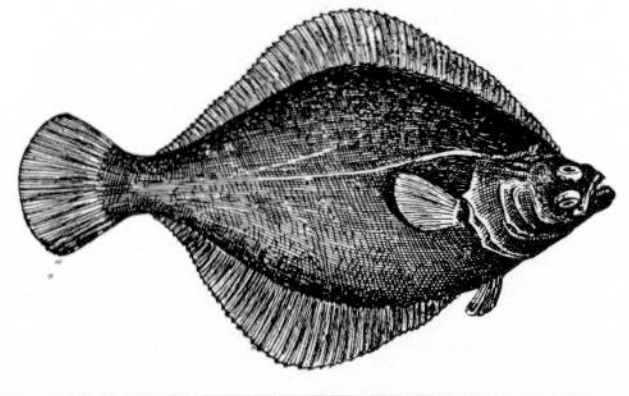

Flounder

FLOUR. FARINE – Flour is the finely ground and bolted meal of wheat and other cereals, including rye, buckwheat, rice oatmeal and maize (corn), but since wheat, with its content of gluten, is best for breadmaking, the word flour generally connotes wheat flour. The milling of grain for flour dates back to prehistoric times. What for centuries was the hard domestic job of producing flour that could be made into bread, has developed through the ages into a large industry. There is evidence that wheat or corn was crushed and used as food at least 6000 years ago; the pounding stones used for this purpose have been discovered in archaeological diggings in the British Isles, Switzerland, and elsewhere.

The Romans invented slightly conical millstones (querns) which were turned by hand or by slave and beast. Once the grain was crushed, the flour was bolted through horsehair sieves to produce different grades of flour. The invention of the water-propelled mill dates from about the time of the birth of Christ, and it was also at this time that flat millstones were used in preference to conical shapes.

Windmills first appeared in Europe about 1300 and were widely used until the invention of the steam engine in 1760. From then on rapid advances were made, culminating in roller mills, invented and perfected in Switzerland between 1834 and 1836. The roller system, with many modern mechanical improvements, is still in use in all large commercial mills.

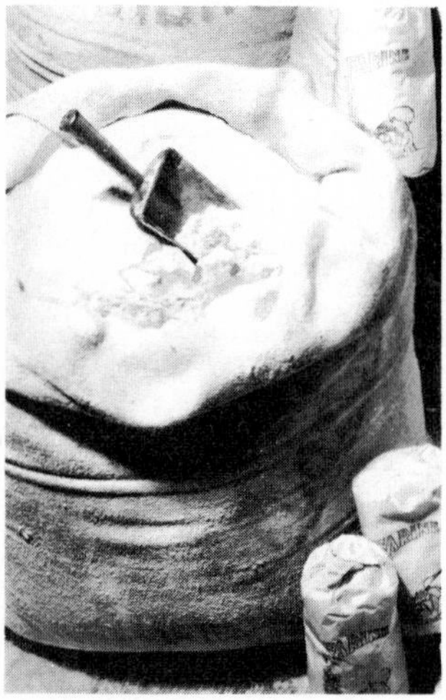

Flour (*Nicolas*)

The wheat kernel is composed of three parts; *endosperm*, *germ* or *embryo*, and *bran*. The object of milling is to separate the endosperm from the bran and germ, because white flour is derived from the endosperm which generally comprises 84 per cent of the kernel, as opposed to the 2 per cent content of germ and 14 per cent content of bran. Modern commercial milling of wheat first cleans the grain by means of air blasts and disk separators. After this the wheat is moistened and allowed to 'temper', a process which hardens the bran and makes the separation more complete.

Separation is accomplished by alternated reductions (rollings at varying tensions), and purifications (classifications by mechanised winnowing and sifting of the endosperm particles, the bran chips and the germ). The results of these successive reductions and purifications are blended into various standard and commercial blends (patents and clear grades) depending on the amount of germ and bran left in the endosperm flour. Freshly milled white flour is pale yellow but becomes white with ageing. To hurry this process most mills use a chemical agent which is rigorously controlled by the government. Vitamin content lost in this process is usually replaced.

Dietitians blame modern milling processes for causing the loss of certain essential elements of wheat. The proteic layer is one. It contains three times more protein substances, nine times more fatty substances, and ten times more mineral salts than the farinaceous kernel of grain. Then there are the vitamins, diastases, enzymes, which accumulate in the husks. The same applies to the wheatgerm, which contains in its very small volume, substances of immense nutritional value. The great elasticity of the wheatgerm prevents it being crushed in the course of modern milling processes, and it is consequently discarded with the other waste matter.

Graham flour is unbolted wheat meal ground from the whole kernel. Whole wheat, wholemeal or entire wheat contains all of the kernel except a portion of the bran.

FLOURING. FARINER – To sprinkle fish or other food lightly with flour.

To dip in flour small pieces of meat, usually escalopes and cutlets of veal, and lamb cutlets, before dipping in egg and breadcrumbs and frying in butter.

FLOUTES (Alsation cookery) – Quenelles made with mashed potatoes.

FLUKE. CARRELET – See PLAICE.

FLUORINE. FLUOR, FLUORURES – Under normal conditions, man absorbs small quantities of fluorine with his food, the most valuable source being drinking water. Children who drink water that is deficient in fluorine are much more susceptible to dental caries than children who live where the drinking water contains not less than 1 mg. fluorine per litre. Foods richest in fluorine are fish and tea. Small amounts of it are present in meat, egg, cow's milk, and fresh vegetables.

FLÛTE – The long French roll popular in the Paris region. The *flûte à potage* is a long French roll used for making *croûtes* served with broths and hotpots.

FLUTE. CANNELER – The operation of cutting vegetables, fruit, and the edges of some sweet courses in a decorative manner. Vegetables, mushrooms, and lemons can be decoratively cut with kitchen knives or with special tools. Circles of pastry cut with a fluted-edged pastry-cutter are said to be *cannelés*. The same term is used for the operation of marking the sides of a cake with a small knife, although this is more often called *chiquetage* (pinking).

FOGOSCH – This Hungarian fish is a pike-perch (q.v.).

FOIE GRAS – Preparations made from the livers of fattened geese and ducks were known in the ancient world.

The goose was regarded by the Romans not only as a sacred animal (from the time when a goose saved the Capitol), but also as a succulent one, for its meat and liver were highly prized by gourmets of the period.

The Romans used various methods of fattening ducks and of causing a considerable swelling of the liver.

Scipio Metellus, a Roman gastronome, had the idea of plunging the still warm livers in a bath of milk and honey, where they were left for several hours. When taken out of the milk, the livers were considerably swollen.

In cookery the name *foie gras* is used only of goose or duck liver fattened in a special way. The livers of Toulouse and Strasbourg geese sometimes weigh 2 kg. ($4\frac{1}{2}$ lb.).

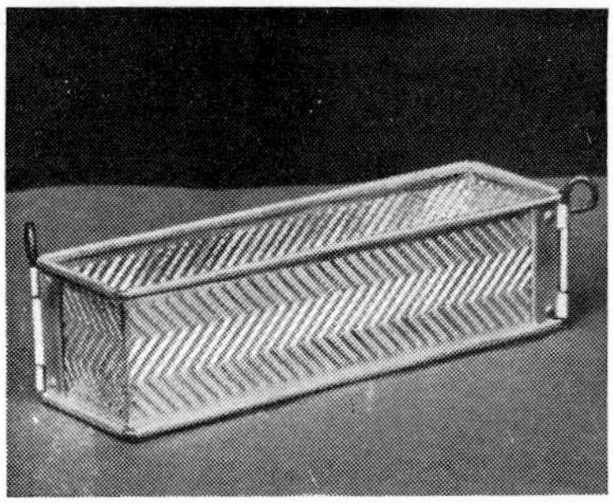

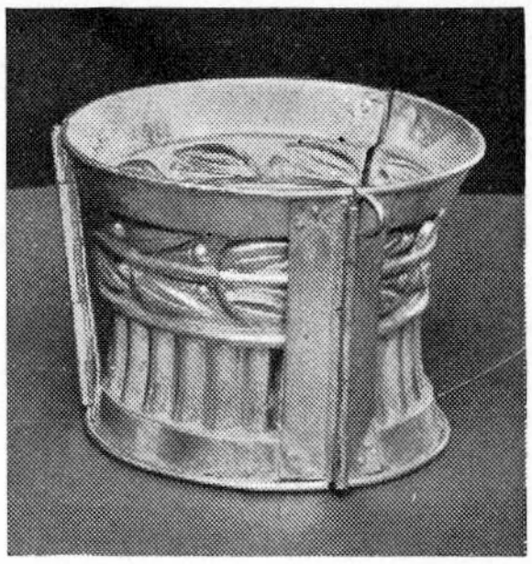

A hinged rectangular mould and a hinged round mould for pâté
(*Dehillerin. Phot. Larousse*)

Pâté de foie gras decorated by hand, from an 18th century document

Foie gras is regarded as one of the greatest delicacies available. 'The goose,' says C. Gérard, author of *L'Ancienne Alsace à table*, 'is nothing, but man has made of it an instrument for the output of a marvellous product, a kind of living hothouse in which grows the supreme fruit of gastronomy.'

This 'fruit' is *foie gras*, from which are made the succulent potted products and *pâtés* of Strasbourg, Toulouse, Périgueux, Nancy, etc.

The finest *foies gras* comes from geese reared in Alsace and south-western France. Toulouse *foies gras* are greatly sought after. Duck *foie gras* is also very delicate, but has a tendency to disintegrate in cooking. Other European countries besides France produce very good goose *foie gras*, notably Austria, Czechoslovakia and the Duchy of Luxemburg.

The quality of *foie gras* can be judged primarily by its colour and also by texture. It should be creamy-white, tinged with pink, and very firm.

Foie gras aspic – See ASPIC.

Foie gras en Bellevue – Line a plain mould with jelly. Decorate with strips of truffle and the whites of hard boiled egg. Cover these with a second layer of jelly. Leave on ice until thoroughly set. Add slices of poached *foie gras* or slices of potted *foie gras* with truffles. Fill the mould with half-set jelly. Chill on ice.

Foie gras en brioche (hot) – Season truffles and pour brandy over them. Take a large, very firm *foie gras* which will not disintegrate in cooking. Stud it with the truffles, and season with spiced salt. Pour brandy over it and leave to steep for several hours in this seasoning.

Wrap the *foie gras* in a piece of pork caul (or in very thin slices of pork fat) and cook in a slow oven for 18 to 20 minutes. Leave to cool. Put it in a buttered baking tin lined thickly with unsweetened *Brioche dough* (see DOUGH). Cover with a layer of dough. Tie a strip of buttered paper round the tin to prevent the dough from overflowing during baking. Leave to rise in a warm place.

Bake in a hot oven for 50 minutes to 1 hour. To test whether the *foie gras* is cooked, drive in a long skewer. If the skewer comes out quite clean, the *foie gras* is ready. Turn out the brioche and serve.

Foie gras en brioche (cold) – Proceed as for *Foie gras en brioche* (*hot*). Leave to cool before serving.

Foie gras en chausson – Proceed as for *Foie gras en brioche*. Stud the *foie gras* with truffles and cook for 18 to 20 minutes. Put it on a rather stiff layer of *Brioche dough* (see DOUGH). Roll in a scroll shape. Bake in the oven. Serve hot or cold.

Foie gras en cocotte or en casserole – Trim a large, firm *foie gras* and stud with truffles seasoned with *Spiced salt* (see SALT) and sprinkled with brandy. Season the *foie gras* with spiced salt, pour on brandy and leave to steep for 12 hours.

Brown the *foie gras* in very hot butter. Put in an ovenware dish. Moisten with the cooking butter mixed with Madeira or any other heavy wine and concentrated thickened brown veal stock. Cover the dish and seal with a strip of paste. Cook in a slow oven for 45 minutes to 1 hour, according to the size of the *foie gras*. Serve in the cooking dish.

Foie gras cutlets, croquettes and kromeskies. CÔTELETTES, CROQUETTES, CROMESQUIS DE FOIE GRAS – These different preparations, which are served as hot *hors-d'œuvre* or as a light main course, are made from *salpicon* (q.v.) of liver, with diced truffles added, in the same way as chicken cutlets, croquettes and kromeskies (see CHICKEN).

Foie gras 'eggs' (cold). OEUFS DE FOIE GRAS FROIDS – *Foie gras mousse* (see MOUSSE) shaped in little egg-shaped moulds. A truffle is placed in the middle of each mousse which is coated with jelly when it is quite cold and covered with brown or white *Chaud-froid sauce* (see SAUCE).

The 'eggs' are built up into a pyramid or put in a nest of butter piped through a forcing-bag.

Escalopes of foie gras Cambacérès – Sauté slices of *foie gras* in butter. Put each one on an artichoke heart cooked in butter and filled with a *salpicon* of mushrooms in cream.

On top of each escalope arrange 2 thick strips of truffle. Dilute the cooking butter with Madeira, thicken with *Demi-glace* (see SAUCE), flavour with *Truffle essence*, and pour over the dish.

Escalopes of foie gras en chaud-froid – Slices of *foie gras* (plain or truffled) covered with white or brown *Chaud-froid sauce* (see SAUCE). Decorate with truffles, whites of hard-boiled eggs, pickled tongue, and jelly.

The escalopes can be served in individual paper cases, or in silver, porcelain, or glass shells; each on a bed of chopped jelly. They can also be arranged in a circle on a bed of set jelly in a bowl, and covered with jelly.

Escalopes of foie gras with grapes. ESCALOPES DE FOIE GRAS AUX RAISINS – Sauté slices of *foie gras* in butter. Drain and put each on a slice of bread fried in butter. Decorate with peeled grapes. Dilute the cooking juices with Frontignan or other heavy wine. Boil down, add a few tablespoons thickened brown veal stock, and boil again. Cover the escalopes with this sauce.

Escalopes of foie gras with grapes and truffles (cold). ESCALOPES DE FOIE GRAS AUX RAISINS ET AUX TRUFFES – Cook the *foie gras* in its own fat. Cut in slices. On top of each slice place a wide strip of truffle, dipped in jelly so that it will stick to the escalope. Glaze with jelly.

Arrange the escalopes in a circle in a bowl. In the middle, heap a dome of fresh peeled grapes which have been steeped in a little liqueur brandy. Cover the dish with clear jelly flavoured with port or other heavy wine. Chill thoroughly on ice or in the refrigerator.

Escalopes of foie gras Montrouge – Sauté slices of *foie gras* in butter. Arrange in a circle, each on a slice of bread fried in butter. Pile thick *Mushroom purée* (see PURÉE) in the middle of the dish. Cover the escalopes with their cooking juices diluted with Madeira and veal stock.

Escalopes of foie gras Richelieu – Dip slices of *foie gras* in egg and breadcrumbs. Sauté in clarified butter. Arrange in a circle on a dish, and pour over them diced truffles in melted butter flavoured with a little Madeira or other heavy wine.

Escalopes of foie gras à la romaine – Sauté slices of *foie gras* in butter. Arrange on rounds of bread fried in butter. Cover with *Romaine sauce* (see SAUCE). Serve with rice cooked in butter.

Escalopes of foie gras with truffles. ESCALOPES DE FOIE GRAS AUX TRUFFES – Sauté slices of *foie gras* in butter. Arrange on rounds of bread fried in butter. Cover with slices of truffle heated in the butter in which the escalopes have been cooked. Dilute the cooking juices with Madeira or other heavy wine and *Demi-glace* (see SAUCE), and pour over the dish.

Foie gras à la financière – Stud a *foie gras* with truffles. Season with *Spiced salt* (see SALT). Pour on brandy and leave to steep for a few hours in this seasoning. Wrap the *foie gras* in pork caul or thin slices of pork fat. Cook in a braising stock, adding Madeira, for 40 to 45 minutes.

Drain, and serve on slices of bread fried in butter. Surround with *Financière garnish* (see GARNISHES) to which the braising stock, concentrated and strained, has been added.

Foie gras loaf (hot). PAIN DE FOIE GRAS – This dish is more a soufflé than a loaf and is usually described as such on restaurant menus. (See MOUSSE, *Foie gras mousse* (*hot*).)

Foie gras loaf in jelly. PAIN DE FOIE GRAS À LA GELÉE – Poach a large fat liver in Madeira-flavoured jellied stock. Cool, drain, and cut one lobe into slices.

Remove fat from the liquor in which the liver was poached, and add to it an equal quantity of jellied stock based on concentrated truffle stock. Add a small glass of fine Champagne brandy, boil down the liquor by half, and bind with a liaison of 4 egg yolks. Heat, incorporate 200 g. (7 oz., scant cup) butter and proceed as described in the recipe for *Hollandaise sauce* (see SAUCE).

When just warm, add to it 2 leaves (1 teaspoon) gelatine soaked in warm water, and the rest of the liver rubbed through a fine sieve. Blend without stirring too much.

Coat a mould with clear jelly. Decorate the walls of the mould with slivers of truffles. Fill with the liver composition in layers, alternating them with layers of the sliced liver and slivers of truffles. Cover with a layer of jelly. Leave to set on ice or in the refrigerator.

Serve on a buttered crustless croûton, or plain. Garnish with jelly croûtons.

Foie gras medallions. MÉDAILLONS DE FOIE GRAS – Slices of *foie gras* are sometimes called medallions. They can be served hot or cold (see *Escalopes of foie gras*).

Foie gras mousse (cold). MOUSSE DE FOIE GRAS – Rub cooked *foie gras* through a fine sieve. Put in a bowl with $2\frac{1}{2}$ dl. (scant $\frac{1}{2}$ pint, generous cup) melted jelly and 4 dl. ($\frac{3}{4}$ pint, scant 2 cups) *Chicken velouté* (see SAUCE) to every litre ($1\frac{3}{4}$ pints, generous quart) purée. Work this mixture gently on ice. Season. Add 4 dl. ($\frac{3}{4}$ pint, scant 2 cups) partly whisked fresh cream.

Put the mixture in a mould lined with jelly and decorated with truffles and the whites of hard-boiled eggs. Fill only to within 1 cm. ($\frac{1}{2}$ inch) of the top. Cover the mousse with a layer of jelly. Chill in the refrigerator.

Turn out onto a buttered slice of bread or onto a serving dish. Surround with chopped jelly and make a border of jelly cut out with a pastry-cutter.

Foie gras mousse (hot) – See MOUSSE.

Foie gras mousselines (cold). MOUSSELINES DE FOIE GRAS – Use the same mixture as for *Foie gras mousse* (cold). Put into little cups and decorate with truffles. Glaze with jelly.

Diced truffles may be added to the mixture.

Foie gras pancakes à la Périgourdine. PANNEQUETS DE FOIE GRAS À LA PÉRIGOURDINE – Make thin unsweetened pancakes. Fill them with *foie gras* mixed with chopped truffles and flavoured with a little Armagnac. Roll the pancakes into scrolls, trim at each end, and halve them. Put them on a buttered dish, sprinkle lightly with fried breadcrumbs, and warm for a few minutes in the oven.

Foie gras with paprika (cold). FOIE GRAS AU PAPRIKA – Stud the *foie gras* with truffles. Season with salt and paprika, and pour brandy over. Wrap it in a piece of pork caul and poach in Madeira. When cooked, drain and leave to cool. Unwrap, press into shape in a cloth. Cover with *Chaud-froid sauce* (see SAUCE) flavoured with paprika. Decorate with strips of truffle, and green and red sweet peppers, cut into rings and poached for a few seconds in jelly.

Glaze the *foie gras* with jelly. Put it in a dish and cover with clear jelly flavoured with port or other heavy wine.

Parfait of foie gras (cold) – Name given to several preparations which differ quite considerably from one another.

In former times a *parfait of foie gras* was a mousse of *foie gras* in jelly. Nowadays it is a whole *foie gras*, studded with truffles, poached in a Madeira-flavoured jellied stock, cooled and served in jelly.

Some writers on cookery describe as a *parfait* a *pâté of foie gras* in pastry crust which differs from an ordinary *pâté de foie gras*, only because instead of the empty pockets on the surface (which appear when the pâté is cold) being filled with butter or goose fat, they are filled with jelly.

Pâté of foie gras de Périgueux (old recipe) – 'To 1 kg. ($2\frac{1}{4}$ lb.) truffles add 12 *foies gras*; $1\frac{1}{2}$ kg. ($3\frac{1}{4}$ lb.) pork fat; parsley; spring onions; and mushrooms, all chopped. Make the *pâté* of chopped pork fat covered with a layer of sliced truffles, seasoned with fine salt and fine spices and *fines herbes*; next, another layer of pork fat, and on top of that a layer of *foie gras* seasoned as indicated above, and mushrooms, parsley, and spring onions. Continue building up the pâté in the same order until all the ingredients are used. Cover the whole with slices of pork fat. Cook and leave to cool.' (*Dictionnaire portatif de cuisine*, Paris, 1767.)

Truffled pâté of foie gras. PÂTÉ DE FOIE GRAS TRUFFÉ – *Ingredients.* 2 firm *foies gras*, 1 kg. ($2\frac{1}{4}$ lb.) pork and *foie gras* forcemeat, 400 g. (14 oz.) truffles, 1 kg. ($2\frac{1}{4}$ lb.) pastry dough, pork fat, bay leaf, thyme, salt, pepper, spices, brandy, Madeira.

Method. Stud the *foie gras* with truffles, peeled and quartered or, if small, left whole. Season with *Spiced salt* (see SALT) and sprinkle with brandy. Leave to steep in brandy and Madeira for 2 hours.

Line a *pâté* mould (a hinged round or oval mould) with the pastry dough (made with butter or lard). This must be made in advance and left to stand for a long time.

Line the bottom and sides of the pastry with part of the stuffing. Put in the *foie gras*, pressed close together. Cover with a domed layer of stuffing. On top of this lay a slice of pork fat, half a bay leaf, and a small sprig of thyme. Cover the *pâté* with a layer of dough and seal the edges. Decorate the top with decorative pastry motifs shaped with pastry-

Truffled pâté de foie gras (*Presse Moderne*)

cutters (lozenges, leaves, crescents, etc.) or strips of plaited dough. In the middle put 3 or 4 round pieces of dough shaped with a fluted pastry-cutter. Make a hole in the middle of these for the escape of steam during baking. Brush with egg. Bake in a fairly hot oven.

Cool. When it is luke-warm pour into it either half-melted lard, if it is to be kept for some time, or if it is to be used at once, Madeira-flavoured jelly.

Pâté de foie gras must be made at least 12 hours before using. The mould can be lined with a stuffing made entirely of *foie gras* instead of with pork and *foie gras* stuffing.

Small truffled pâtés of foie gras (old recipe). PETITS PÂTÉS DE FOIE GRAS AUX TRUFFES – 'Take *foies gras* and stud with truffles. Make a *foie gras* stuffing especially for the purpose. Prepare little individual *pâté* moulds. Put the stuffing at the bottom, a piece of *foie gras* on top and a truffle at each side. Cover with stuffing. Finish, brush with egg, and put them in the oven. When they are ready, uncover them, pour a little essence into them and serve.' (*Le Cuisinier gascon*, Amsterdam, 1747.)

Potted foie gras with truffles. TERRINE DE FOIE GRAS AUX TRUFFES – Cut a large *foie gras* in half. Trim the halves (the trimmings are used to make the forcemeat), and stud them with large pieces of truffle. Season the *foie gras* with *Spiced salt* (see SALT). Pour brandy over it and steep for 1 or 2 hours in this seasoning.

Line an ovenware dish with thin slices of pork fat. Put in it a fairly thin layer of a forcemeat made with 375 g. (13 oz.) lean pork, 450 g. (1 lb.) fresh pork fat, the trimmings of the *foie gras* – about 200 g. (7 oz.), 150 g. (5 oz.) diced or chopped truffles flavoured with $\frac{1}{2}$ dl. (3 tablespoons, scant $\frac{1}{4}$ cup) Madeira or brandy and seasoned with 4 teaspoons spiced salt. Put half of the *foie gras* on top of this forcemeat. Cover with another layer of the truffled forcemeat. Put the other half of the *foie gras* on top and cover with the remainder of the forcemeat. Press down well to flatten all the ingredients. Cover with a thin slice of pork fat. On top of this put half a bay leaf and a small sprig of thyme. Cover the dish and seal with flour-and-water paste. Cook in the oven, standing in a pan half-full of hot water, for 45 minutes to 1 hour, according to the size of the dish.

Leave to cool under a light weight until the following day. Next day, turn it out (this can be more easily done if the dish is first stood for a few seconds in hot water). Remove the slices of fat covering the potted *foie gras*. Dry the *foie gras* with a cloth, pressing a little so as to make the forcemeat quite firm. Before replacing it, line the bottom of the dish with a layer of lard mixed with goose fat (which was exuded in cooking). Pour a similar mixture of fat, almost cold, over the *foie gras*. Leave to chill in the refrigerator for at least 10 hours. Serve as it is in the cooking dish.

It is advisable to prepare potted *foie gras* (and other potted preparations containing *foie gras*) at least 24 hours before using.

To make it easier to serve in individual portions, potted *foie gras* is made in restaurant kitchens in rectangular earthenware, porcelain, or metal dishes.

Potted foie gras with truffles à la façon périgourdine. TERRINE DE FOIE GRAS TRUFFÉ À LA FAÇON PÉRIGOURDINE – Soak a large, firm *foie gras* overnight in cold water. Drain and dry in a cloth.

Make several incisions in the lobes of the *foie gras*, and put into each a piece of truffle. Season with salt and spices.

Line a *terrine* completely with thin slices of fresh pork fat. Put the *foie gras* into it and press well down. Cover with a thin layer of lean and fat pork, chopped together and seasoned. Pour on a few tablespoons brandy, and on top of the whole mixture pour a little luke-warm melted goose fat.

Cover the *terrine*, and seal the edges with flour-and-water paste. Place in a pan half-full of hot water and cook in a hot oven for about 1 hour. Leave the *foie gras* under a light weight until quite cold. Pour on a few tablespoons of goose fat, and when this is quite set, add a little melted lard. Cover the *terrine*. Seal with a strip of gummed paper. Keep in a cool, dry place.

Preserved potted foie gras in goose fat. CONSERVE DE FOIE GRAS AU NATUREL EN TERRINE – Season the *foie gras* with spiced salt. Steep in brandy for a few hours. Dry and poach in clarified goose fat. Drain, and put in a *terrine* just large enough to hold it. Cover with goose fat. Leave until quite cold. Pour over it a thin layer of melted lard and leave to cool. Cover the *terrine*, and seal the edges with a strip of gummed paper.

Prepared in this way and kept in a dry, cool place, *foie gras* will keep for a very long time.

Quenelles of foie gras – See QUENELLE.

Foie gras rissoles. RISSOLES DE FOIE GRAS – Cut a layer of *Flaky pastry dough* (see DOUGH) into small shapes with a fluted pastry-cutter. In the middle of each one put 1 tablespoon *salpicon* of *foie gras* with diced truffles added, seasoned and flavoured with a little brandy.

Roll the pastry into scrolls, carefully sealing the edges. Garnish with fried parsley. Serve with *Périgueux sauce* (see SAUCE).

Foie gras shells in jelly. COQUILLES DE FOIE GRAS À LA GELÉE – A method of serving in shells potted *foie gras*, cooked in its own fat. The shells are cut out with a shell-shaped scoop or a tablespoon can be used instead. To prevent the *foie gras* from sticking, dip the scoop or spoon in hot water before cutting. Decorate with chopped jelly.

Foie gras soufflé. SOUFFLÉ DE FOIE GRAS – Rub through a fine sieve 300 g. (11 oz.) carefully trimmed raw *foie gras* which has been pounded in a mortar with 3 egg whites. Put the mixture in a bowl and work on ice, incorporating about 3 dl. ($\frac{1}{2}$ pint, $1\frac{1}{4}$ cups) thick fresh cream little by little. Add 3 or 4 stiffly whisked egg whites. Fill a buttered soufflé dish with the mixture, stand in a pan of water, and cook for 30 to 35 minutes.

Serve with *Périgueux sauce, Madeira sauce* (see SAUCE) or with *Truffle essence* (see ESSENCE).

Foie gras soufflé can also be made with purée of cooked *foie gras*.

Foie gras Souvarov – Season a firm *foie gras*, steep in brandy, and brown in very hot butter. Put it in an oven-proof dish with large quartered truffles. Pour on a little *Demi-glace sauce* (see SAUCE) mixed with *Truffle essence* (see ESSENCE). Cover the dish and seal with a strip of paste. Cook in a moderate oven for 40 to 50 minutes according to the size of the *foie gras*. Serve in the cooking dish.

Foie gras tart à l'ancienne. TOURTE DE FOIE GRAS À L'ANCIENNE – Roll out a layer of *Fine lining paste* (see DOUGH) and cut it in a round shape. Cover the middle with a layer of *Mousseline forcemeat* (see FORCEMEAT) mixed with a little *Foie gras purée* (see PURÉE) and chopped truffles, leaving a border of 3 to 4 cm. ($1\frac{1}{2}$ inches).

Top with thick slices of raw truffle. Cover with a thin layer of the stuffing, and finally, with a lid of rolled-out pastry. Seal the edges. Make a hole in the pastry and decorate with pastry motifs, or score with shallow criss-cross lines. Brush with egg, and bake in the oven for 45 to 50 minutes. When the tart is ready, pour in through the hole in the middle, a few tablespoons concentrated *Demi-glace sauce* (see SAUCE) flavoured with *Truffle essence* (see ESSENCE). This tart can also be made with *Flaky pastry* (see DOUGH).

Foie gras tart with truffles (cold). TOURTE DE FOIE GRAS AUX TRUFFES – Using *Fine lining paste* (see DOUGH) make the tart as indicated for *Foie gras tart à l'ancienne*. When it is cold, pour into it (through the hole in the centre) a few tablespoons Madeira-flavoured jelly.

Tinned foie gras in goose fat. CONSERVE DE FOIE GRAS AU NATUREL – Put very firm *foies gras*, seasoned and steeped for 2 hours in brandy, into oval tins, adding a little goose fat. Seal. Stand them in water and boil steadily for $1\frac{1}{2}$ hours for tins weighing 1 kg. (2 lb.), and 1 hour for tins weighing 500 g. (1 lb.).

Drain, leave to cool, dry thoroughly, and keep in a cool, dry place.

Truffled foie gras in Madeira (hot). FOIE GRAS TRUFFÉ AU MADÈRE – Stud a *foie gras* with truffles and leave to steep in brandy. Wrap the *foie gras* in a piece of pork caul or thin slices of pork fat, and put it in a small braising dish lined with fresh pork skin and sliced onions and carrots, which have been tossed in butter. Cover, and simmer for 7 to 8 minutes. Moisten with $2\frac{1}{2}$ dl. (scant $\frac{1}{2}$ pint, generous cup) Madeira. Simmer for several minutes. Add 3 dl. ($\frac{1}{2}$ pint, $1\frac{1}{4}$ cups) concentrated brown veal stock. Cook in the oven for 45 minutes.

Drain and unwrap the *foie gras*. Strain, skim all fat off the stock, and pour over the *foie gras*.

Truffled foie gras in Madeira (cold). FOIE GRAS TRUFFÉ AU MADÈRE – Proceed as for *Truffled foie gras in Madeira (hot)*. When cooked, drain, unwrap the liver, and put it in a *terrine* just large enough to hold it. Strain the cooking stock and pour it over the *foie gras*. Leave to cool for 12 hours. Skim off the layer of fat which will have formed, and serve in the *terrine*.

When *Truffled foie gras in Madeira* is to be served cold, the veal stock must be of a kind that will readily set into a jelly.

Truffled foie gras in port (cold). FOIE GRAS TRUFFÉ AU PORTO – Proceed as for *Truffled foie gras in Madeira (cold)*, using jelly flavoured with port. Even when ruby port is used, the jelly should be amber-coloured.

Truffled foie gras in port
(*Battendier. Phot. Larousse*)

FOLLE-BLANCHE – Name of a vine bearing white grapes, which grows in the Charentes region. The wine made from these grapes is of rather poor quality, but it is used in the distillation of brandy.

FONDANT – See ICING.

FONDANTS (Croquettes) – See HORS-D'ŒUVRE, *Hot hors-d'œuvre*.

FOND-DE-PLAT – French term for an oval or round piece of wood which is placed on the bottom of a plate to form a raised base for cold dishes.

It is generally covered with foil and masked with a jelly or savoury butter, depending upon the dish.

FONDS – French term for stock. (See STOCKS, FUMET.)

FONDS DE PÂTISSERIE – Term for various sweet pastry bases used in French *pâtisserie*.

FONDUE – This name applies to a variety of different dishes. It can be a cheese sauce, originally from Switzerland, the recipe for which follows under *Cheese fondue I*.

It is also used for a dish of scrambled eggs with cheese, an original recipe of which can be found in Brillat-Savarin's *Physiologie du goût*. (See *Cheese fondue II*.)

Certain vegetable preparations are also called *fondue*. The vegetables are cooked for a very long time in butter, lard, or oil until they are reduced to pulp, i.e. become *fondues*. Different vegetable *fondues* can be used as constituent elements in a great many dishes.

Burgundy fondue. FONDUE BOURGUIGNONNE – This contemporary dish has nothing to do with Burgundy; it is a Swiss creation. A mixture of butter and oil is placed in a fondue dish which is set over its own individual heater on the table. Cubes of steak are served separately. With the aid of a fondue fork, each person plunges a steak cube into the smoking butter and oil mixture, cooking it to his taste, then dips it into one of a variety of sauces before eating it.

Carrot fondue. FONDUE DE CAROTTES – Gently cook very finely sliced or shredded carrots in butter, in a covered pan. Season with salt and a pinch of sugar.

Cook the carrots until they are reduced to a pulp. To avoid them being fried in the butter add a few drops of water or *bouillon* from time to time.

Celery fondue. FONDUE DE CÉLERI – Cook sliced or diced celery or celeriac gently in butter, adding a few drops water or *bouillon*. Season. Cook until the moisture has completely evaporated.

Cheese fondue I. FONDUE DE FROMAGE – This dish originated in the French-speaking part of Switzerland. It consists of grated cheese melted in white wine, seasoned with pepper, and flavoured with a little kirsch.

The *Valais fondue* contains no butter, no eggs, no flour or starch of any kind, and no chemical products in its original form. It is prepared in a small casserole and served on a hot plate or trivet. Each person round the table dips a piece of bread spiked on the end of his fork into the dish.

The *Fribourg (Freiburg) fondue* is prepared with Vacherin cheese, which is a soft cheese made in the Savoy from cows' milk.

A century ago, M. Victor Tissot gave Edmond Richardin the genuine recipe for this *fondue* with Vacherin.

'Take 1 kg ($2\frac{1}{4}$ lb.) fresh white Vacherin cheese; cut it into small cubes and place these in an earthenware or enamelled iron pot. Heat over a low flame, stirring frequently with a fork made of new wood. Try not to be distracted by the delicious aroma of the melting cheese. When the cheese begins to simmer and is ropy and cream-like in consistency,

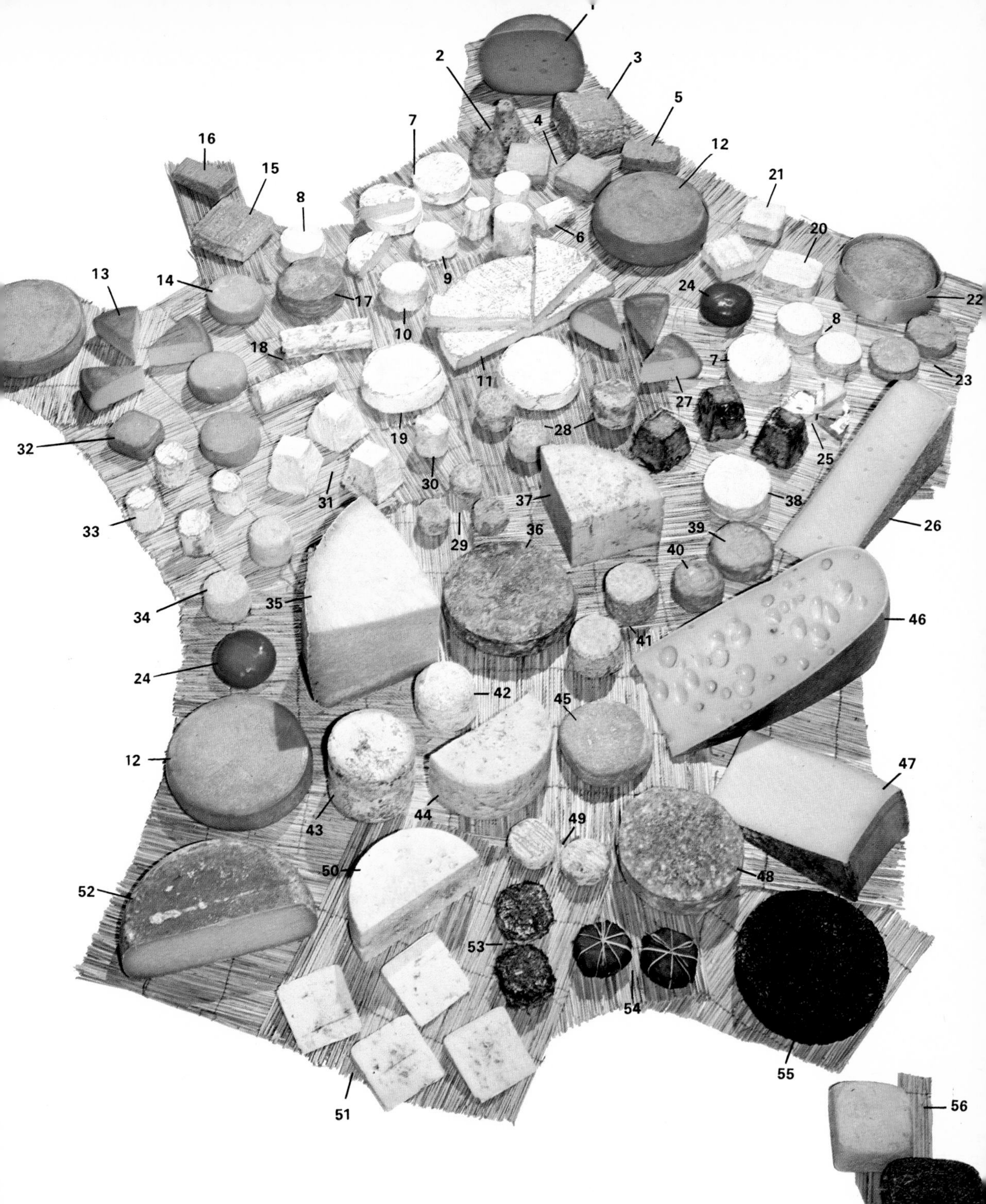

imolette
oulette d'Avesnes
aroilles
aroilles mignon
aguette d'Avesnes
ondard-neufchâtel
amembert
etit camembert
iple crème aromatisé
riple crème
rie
aint-paulin
aint-paulin en portions
etit saint-paulin

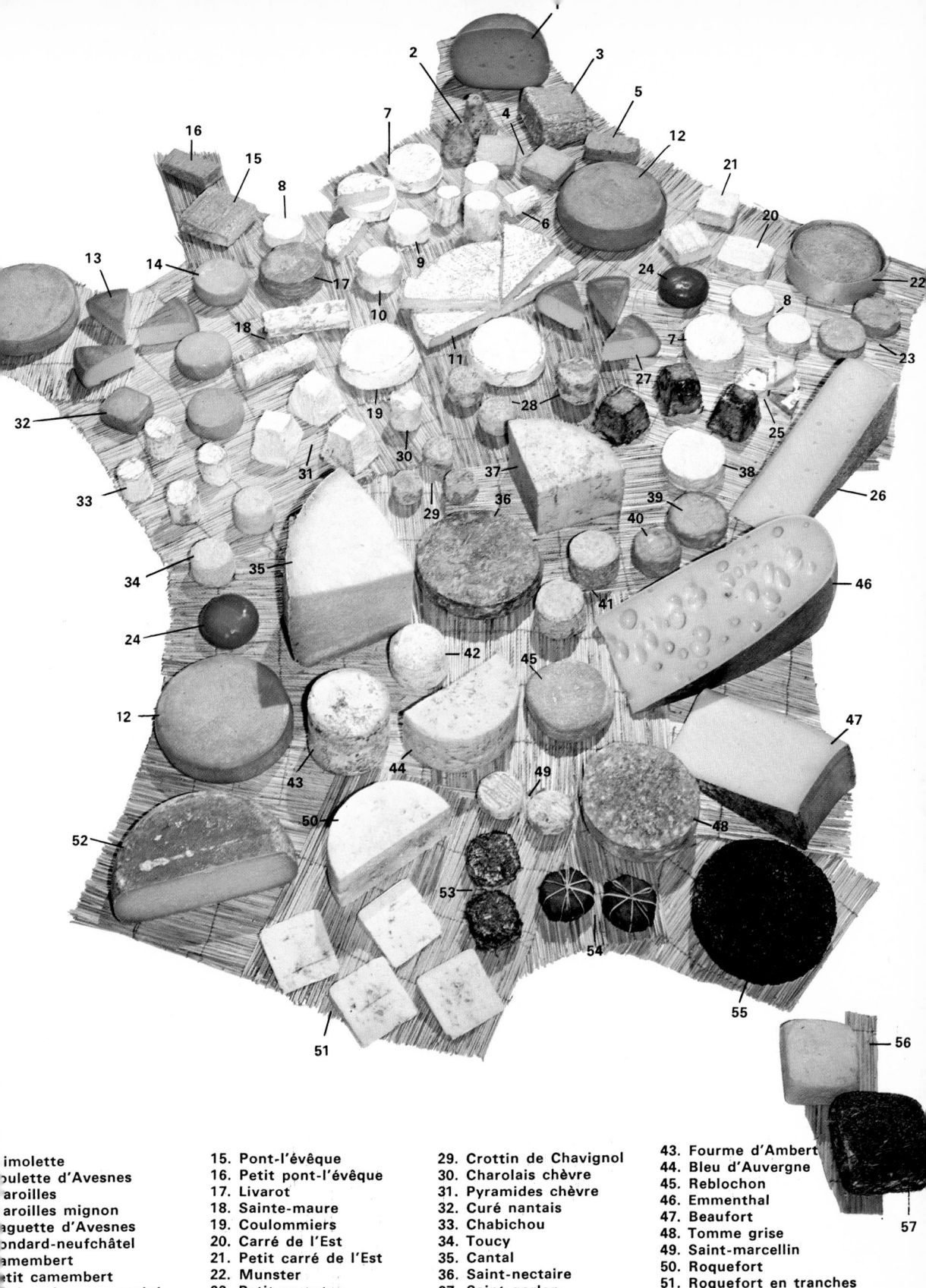

15. Pont-l'évêque
16. Petit pont-l'évêque
17. Livarot
18. Sainte-maure
19. Coulommiers
20. Carré de l'Est
21. Petit carré de l'Est
22. Munster
23. Petit munster
24. Baby
25. Fromage pour tartine
26. Comté
27. Valençay
28. Chèvre bondes
29. Crottin de Chavignol
30. Charolais chèvre
31. Pyramides chèvre
32. Curé nantais
33. Chabichou
34. Toucy
35. Cantal
36. Saint-nectaire
37. Saint-gorlon
38. Saint-florentin
39. Epoisses
40. Langres
41. Bleu de Bresse
42. Gaperon
43. Fourme d'Ambert
44. Bleu d'Auvergne
45. Reblochon
46. Emmenthal
47. Beaufort
48. Tomme grise
49. Saint-marcellin
50. Roquefort
51. Roquefort en tranches
52. Fromage des Pyrénées
53. Poivre d'âne
54. Banon de Provence
55. Fondu au raisin (grafcheese)
56. Niolo
57. Asco

Fresh fruits: pineapple, orange, black, red and white currants, melon, cherries, apricot, strawberries, mango, raspberries, peach, banana, avocado pear, grapefruit, apples (*Phot. Larousse*)

Cheese fondue

it is ready to eat. Place it in the centre of the table.

'Connoisseurs have small cubes of fresh bread ready on their plate in advance. These are speared with a fork, then plunged and turned in the fondue. Once a forkful is well coated with the smoking cream, it is removed and eaten, washed down with white wine.

'In this way the fondue is kept nicely warm and there is none of the bother of transferring it from one receptacle to another.

'1 kg. ($2\frac{1}{4}$ lb.) Vacherin cheese is sufficient to make ample *fondue* for four persons. It is a very nourishing dish.'

The *Neuchâtel fondue* has Gruyère cheese as a basis. For this dish stale and fresh cheese are mixed.

Cheese fondue II (Brillat-Savarin). FONDUE AU FROMAGE BRILLAT-SAVARIN – This is the name the author gives to a dish of scrambled eggs with cheese in his book *Physiologie du goût*. The following is a translation of the original recipe.

'Recipe of *fondue* as found in M. Trollet's papers. He was bailiff of Mondon in the Canton of Berne.

'Weigh the number of eggs which you want to use. This number depends on how many people are going to eat with you.

'Take a piece of good Gruyère weighing a third and butter weighing a sixth of the weight of the eggs.

'Break the eggs and beat them well in a casserole. Add the butter and the grated cheese.

'Put the casserole on a hot stove and stir with a wooden spoon until the mixture has suitably thickened and is smooth. Add a very little or hardly any salt, depending on the age of the cheese. Add a good portion of pepper, which is one of the distinguishing characteristics of this ancient dish. Serve on a lightly heated dish.'

Chervil tuber fondue. FONDUE DE CERFEUIL TUBÉREUX – Prepared in the same way as *Celery fondue*.

Chicory fondue. FONDUE D'ENDIVES – Cook finely minced chicory gently in butter in a covered pan. Season.

This *fondue* is served as a garnish for egg and fish dishes as well as cuts of meat and poultry, and vegetable dishes.

Fennel tuber fondue. FONDUE DE FENOUIL TUBÉREUX – Prepared and used in the same way as *Celery fondue*.

Leek fondue. FONDUE DE POIREAUX – Shred or cut into fine slices the white part of leeks and cook gently in butter until very soft. Season.

Used in sauces, stuffings, and stews, or as a garnish for eggs, fish, meat, poultry, and vegetables.

Mushroom fondue. FONDUE AUX CHAMPIGNONS – Mince the mushrooms, bind with cream, and brown in the oven.

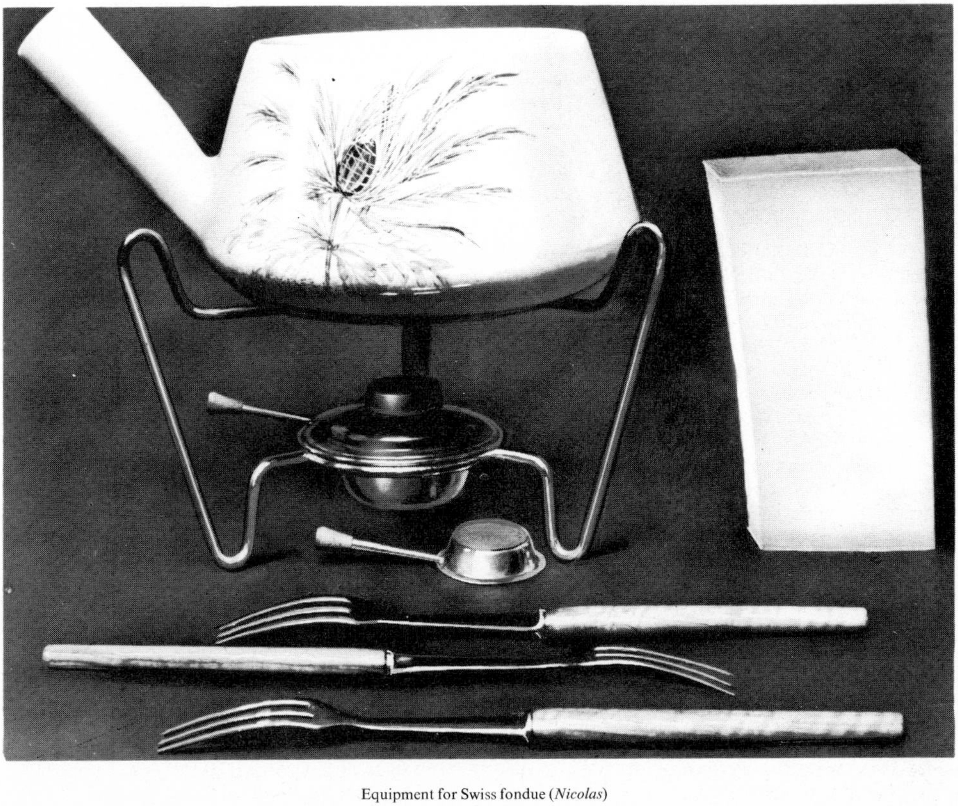

Equipment for Swiss fondue (*Nicolas*)

Onion fondue. FONDUE D'OIGNONS – Cook finely chopped onions gently in butter in a covered pan without allowing them to colour. To prevent the onions becoming fried, moisten them from time to time with water or stock. Season.

Sorrel fondue. FONDUE D'OSEILLE – Prepared in the same way as *Sorrel chiffonnade* (see CHIFFONNADE).

It is used in thick and thin soups, and as a garnish for eggs, small cuts of meat, and poultry.

Sweet pepper fondue. FONDUE DE PIMENTS DOUX – Cook finely chopped sweet peppers gently in butter or oil until soft. Season. Use in hot and cold sauces, in different kinds of stuffings, with soft eggs, in omelettes, with hot or cold fish, with shellfish, meat, poultry, and vegetables.

Tomato fondue. FONDUE DE TOMATES – Cook 1 chopped onion in butter or in a butter and oil mixture. When the onions begin to colour, add 6 peeled, seeded, and chopped tomatoes. Season with salt and pepper. Add 1 grated clove of garlic. Cook gently until the liquid of the tomatoes has almost disappeared. Add ½ tablespoon chopped parsley.

Tomato fondue is used for many dishes, mainly for those *à la provençale, à la portugaise*, or *à la madrilène*. It is used as a garnish for eggs, and for vegetables. When made with oil, and chilled, tomato fondue is often used in the preparation of cold *hors-d'œuvre*.

FONTAINEBLEAU – Town well known in the gastronomic world because of its famous grapes, which are found in and near Thomery (see GRAPES), and also because of its succulent cream cheese, which is eaten as a dessert.

FONTINA – See CHEESE.

FOOD PROCESSOR – A powerful time-saving appliance operated by electricity and equipped with a variety of cutting blades for puréeing, emulsifying, chopping, slicing and shredding.

FOOL – Fruit purée. Fruit of almost any variety is cooked with very little water and passed through a fine sieve. The pulp is sugared and kept cool – on ice if possible. Whipped cream is added to the pulp in the proportion of 2 to 1, mixed gently and served in sherbet glasses.

FORCE (Wine) – French term for incompletely fermented wine kept in small reinforced casks to develop a 'sparkle' just as Champagne wine develops it in bottles.

FORCEMEATS or STUFFINGS. FARCES – Forcemeats or stuffings, which are a mixture of ingredients minced or chopped and spiced, are among the preparations most widely used in cooking. They are often made from *charcuterie*, and are used in *pâtés*, potted preparations, galantines, and ballottines, to stuff or garnish eggs, fish, poultry, game, meat, vegetables, etc.

Forcemeats are also used in the making of forcemeat balls, borders, mousses, moulds, etc.

Forcemeats or stuffings can be made with or without meat, though all of them derive from 5 basic forcemeats. These are: Pork forcemeat; veal and fat forcemeat, known as *godiveau*; fine forcemeat, with cream; forcemeat made of special ingredients, with or without meat; *à gratin* forcemeat.

Forcemeats are given substance by the addition of various panadas (see below).

Most forcemeats made of meat, poultry, or game, are bound with eggs.

Panada for forcemeats or stuffings. PANADE – Preparation made with various flours or bread, usually boiled in water, milk, or stock, and used to bind stuffings or forcemeats.

Panadas are added to stuffings in the proportion of 2 parts basic ingredients to 1 part panada.

The panada should not be added to the forcemeat or stuffing until it is completely cold. To speed up the cooling process, spread out the forcemeat on a buttered dish. Cover with buttered paper to prevent a crust forming through exposure to the air. For the preparation of various panadas see PANADA.

FORCEMEATS or STUFFINGS MADE WITH BEEF, VEAL, PORK, GAME, AND POULTRY. FARCES DE CHAIR DE VEAU, DE PORC, DE GIBIER, DE VOLAILLE –

Beef forcemeat for agnolotti. FARCE DE BOEUF POUR LES AGNOLOTTI – This forcemeat is made of 500 g. (18 oz.) beef braised in red wine.

When completely cooked, remove the beef, chop, and add to it 250 g. (9 oz.) cabbage, chopped and braised, and 50 g. (2 oz., ½ cup) grated Parmesan cheese. Season with salt, pepper, and spices.

Strain the sauce in which the beef was braised, and use it for serving with agnolotti.

Chicken (or other poultry) forcemeat. FARCE DE VOLAILLE – Prepare like *Veal and pork forcemeat* (see below) using the following ingredients: 250 g. (9 oz.) chicken (or other poultry meat, such as turkey, pigeon, duck, guinea-fowl), 100 g. (4 oz.) lean veal, 100 g. (4 oz.) pork, 450 g. (1 lb.) fresh bacon, 2 eggs, 1½ dl. (¼ pint, ⅔ cup) brandy and 5 teaspoons *Spiced salt* (see SALT).

This forcemeat can also be prepared using only the meat of fowl and fresh bacon.

Forcemeat for galantines, pâtés and potted preparations. FARCE POUR GALANTINES, PÂTÉS, TERRINES –

Ingredients. 250 g. (9 oz.) lean veal, 500 g. (18 oz.) fresh pork fat, 2 eggs, 2 tablespoons *Spiced salt* (see SALT), 1½ dl. (¼ pint, ⅔ cup) brandy.

Method. Dice the veal, pork, and pork fat and pound in a mortar with the seasoning and brandy. Add the eggs and mix well. Rub through a fine sieve. Stir until very smooth.

Game forcemeat. FARCE DE GIBIERS – Prepare like *Chicken (or other poultry) forcemeat*, replacing chicken by game meat.

Game forcemeat for pâtés and potted preparations. FARCE DE GIBIER POUR PÂTÉS ET TERRINES – Using whatever game is indicated in the recipe, proceed as for *Chicken (or other poultry) forcemeat*.

To render this stuffing more delicate, the trimmings of fresh *foie gras* are added to it. It can also be enriched by the addition of *à gratin game stuffing* (see below) and *Game fumet* (see FUMET).

À gratin calves' liver forcemeat for borders and hot pâtés. FARCE À GRATIN DE FOIE DE VEAU POUR BORDURES ET PÂTÉS CHAUDS –

Ingredients. 300 g. (11 oz.) trimmed calves' livers, 250 g. (9 oz.) fat belly of pork, 75 g. (3 oz., 3 cups) mushroom peelings, 50 g. (2 oz., ½ cup) chopped shallots, 150 g. (5 oz., generous ½ cup) butter, 4 teaspoons salt, 1 teaspoon pepper, ½ teaspoon ground cloves, a small sprig of thyme, ½ bay leaf, 1½ dl. (¼ pint, ⅔ cup) white wine, 3 egg yolks.

Method. Brown the diced belly of pork in 50 g. (2 oz., ¼ cup) butter. Remove the pork from the pan, and, in the same butter, brown very quickly the diced calves' liver. Put the diced pork back in the pan. Add the mushroom peelings and shallots, seasoning and spices. Sauté the mixture on a very hot flame for 2 minutes. Take the calves' liver out of the pan. Dilute the juices with the white wine, boil down and add to the liver. Pound in a mortar, adding the rest of the butter and the egg yolks. Mix well. Rub through a sieve. Mix with a wooden spoon until it is very smooth.

The mixture is added to forcemeats for *pâtés* and potted products. It is also used in the preparation of borders and poultry or game moulds. Truffle peelings may be added to this forcemeat and pounded with the calves' liver. A little concentrated *Espagnole sauce* (see SAUCE) can also be added.

À gratin forcemeat for canapés and croûtons. FARCE À GRATIN POUR CANAPÉS ET CROÛTONS – Heat in a pan 150 g. (5 oz.) grated fresh pork fat. When it is very hot, put in 300 g. (11 oz.) trimmed chicken livers, 15 g. ($\frac{1}{2}$ oz., 2 tablespoons) chopped shallots, 25 g. (1 oz., 1 cup) mushroom peelings, a sprig of thyme, $\frac{1}{2}$ bay leaf. Season with salt, pepper, and a little spice. Brown the livers quickly over a very hot flame to seal them.

Leave to cool. Pound in a mortar and rub through a sieve, or reduce to a purée in an electric blender. Keep in an earthenware container in a cool place, and cover with buttered paper. Prepared in this way, the forcemeat will keep for several days.

It is spread on the croûtons of fried bread which are used as a base for small roast game birds, or served with *salmis* and civets.

À gratin game forcemeat. FARCE À GRATIN DE GIBIER – Proceed as for *À gratin calves' liver forcemeat*, using the following ingredients:

250 g. (9 oz.) livers of various types of game, 100 g. (4 oz.) belly of pork, 250 g. (9 oz.) young rabbit meat, 50 g. (2 oz.) *foie gras*, 25 g. (1 oz., 2 tablespoons) butter, 3 egg yolks, *Espagnole sauce* (see SAUCE) made with *Game fumet* (see FUMET), seasoning and spices as for *À gratin calves' liver forcemeat*, 1 dl. (6 tablespoons, scant $\frac{1}{2}$ cup) Madeira.

This stuffing is used for the same purposes as *À gratin calves' liver forcemeat*. It is especially used for hot *pâtés* and game pies.

À gratin poultry liver forcemeat. FARCE À GRATIN DE FOIES DE VOLAILLE – Proceed as for *À gratin calves' liver forcemeat*, substituting an equal quantity of trimmed poultry livers for the calves' livers. This is used for *pâtés* and potted preparations.

Mousseline forcemeat. FARCE À LA CRÈME, DITE MOUSSELINE – *Ingredients.* 1 kg. ($2\frac{1}{4}$ lb.) boned veal, poultry, or game, trimmed and with all gristle, tendons, etc. removed, 4 egg whites, $1\frac{1}{2}$ litres ($2\frac{3}{4}$ pints, $3\frac{1}{4}$ pints) thick fresh cream, 3 teaspoons salt, $\frac{3}{4}$ teaspoon white pepper.

Method. Pound the meat finely in a mortar. Season. Add the egg whites a little at a time, pounding well. Rub through a fine sieve. Stir vigorously with a wooden spoon. Keep it cool, on ice if possible, for 2 hours. Then add the cream a little at a time, stirring well, on ice if possible.

Use for fine forcemeat balls, mousses and *mousselines*.

Panada forcemeat with butter. FARCE À LA PANADE ET AU BEURRE – *Ingredients.* 1 kg. ($2\frac{1}{4}$ lb.) veal or poultry, boned and trimmed, with all gristle and tendons removed, 500 g. (18 oz.) panada, 500 g. (18 oz., $2\frac{1}{4}$ cups) butter, 4 whole eggs, 8 yolks, 2 teaspoons salt, $\frac{1}{2}$ teaspoon white pepper, pinch grated nutmeg.

Method. Dice the veal or poultry. Pound in a mortar with seasoning. Take out of the mortar and put in the panada. Add butter. Put back the meat and pound vigorously.

Add the eggs and the yolks, one at a time. Rub the forcemeat through a fine sieve. Work well with a wooden spoon until very smooth. This forcemeat may be made in an electric blender.

It is used for forcemeat balls, borders, moulds, and to stuff poultry, etc.

Panada forcemeat with butter (game). FARCE À LA PANADE ET AU BEURRE (GIBIER) – Proceed as for the above recipe using boned and trimmed game.

This stuffing is used for forcemeat balls, borders, moulds, and to stuff game birds.

Panada forcemeat with cream (fine). FARCE (FINE) À LA PANADE ET À LA CRÈME – *Ingredients.* 1 kg. ($2\frac{1}{4}$ lb.) veal or poultry, boned and trimmed, with all gristle and tendons removed, 400 g. (14 oz.) *Bread panada* (see PANADA), 4 egg whites, $1\frac{1}{2}$ litres ($2\frac{3}{4}$ pints, $3\frac{1}{4}$ pints) double cream, 1 teaspoon salt, $\frac{1}{2}$ teaspoon white pepper, pinch grated nutmeg.

Method. Pound the meat or poultry with the seasoning and the egg whites, adding a little at a time. Add the panada. Pound vigorously until the ingredients are thoroughly mixed. Rub through a fine sieve. Keep on ice for 1 hour. Add, a little at a time, a third of the cream, stirring with a wooden spoon. Add the rest of the cream, partly whipped.

This forcemeat may be prepared in an electric blender and is used for fine forcemeat balls.

Forcemeat for pâté of foie gras or potted foie gras. FARCE POUR PÂTÉ OUTERRINE DE FOIE GRAS – *Ingredients.* 375 g. (13 oz.) lean pork, 450 g. (1 lb.) fresh pork fat, 250 g. (9 oz.) fresh *foie gras*, 4 teaspoons *Spiced salt* (see SALT), 1 dl. (6 tablespoons, scant $\frac{1}{2}$ cup) brandy.

Method. Pound the meats finely in a mortar. Add the seasoning and the brandy. Rub through a sieve.

Périgourdine forcemeat. FARCE PÉRIGOURDINE – Make with breadcrumbs steeped in clear soup or milk, and chopped fresh pork or chopped ham or pork fat. Add chopped parsley and garlic and bind with egg yolks. Season with salt, pepper, and spices. Wrap in white cabbage leaves.

The stuffed cabbage, rolled into a large ball, is wrapped in muslin (U.S. cheesecloth) and braised.

This forcemeat is also used to stuff pot-roasted chicken. The liver and blood of the chicken are added to it.

Pork forcemeat, fine. FARCE FINE DE PORC – Make with lean pork and pork fat in the same way as *Pork forcemeat, ordinary* (see below) and rub the mixture through a sieve. It is used for the same purposes as ordinary pork forcemeat.

Pork forcemeat, ordinary. FARCE DITE CHAIR À SAUCISSES – Mix equal quantities of finely minced lean pork and pork fat. Season with *Spiced salt* (see SALT).

Used for *crépinettes*, sausages, stuffed vegetables, etc.

Poultry forcemeat for pâtés and potted preparations. FARCE DE VOLAILLE POUR PÂTÉS ET TERRINES – *Ingredients.* 575 g. ($1\frac{1}{4}$ lb.) poultry, 200 g. (7 oz.) veal, 900 g. (2 lb.) fresh pork fat, 3 eggs, 50 g. (2 oz., 3 tablespoons) *Spiced salt* (see SALT), $2\frac{1}{2}$ dl. (scant $\frac{1}{2}$ pint, generous cup) brandy.

Dice the poultry, veal, and fat. Pound finely in a mortar with the seasoning. Add the eggs and the brandy. Mix well. Rub through a sieve.

Forcemeat for poached, braised, or roast poultry. FARCE POUR VOLAILLES POCHÉES, BRAISÉES, RÔTIES – This stuffing is usually made with sausage meat, with chopped parsley added. Sometimes chopped onion, cooked slowly in butter until very soft, and breadcrumbs are added.

Forcemeat for truffled poultry. FARCE TRUFFÉE – Dice 1 kg. ($2\frac{1}{4}$ lb.) fresh pork fat and 250 g. (9 oz.) raw *foie gras*. Pound in a mortar. Add the cleaned peelings from 800 g. to 1 kg. ($1\frac{3}{4}$ lb to $2\frac{1}{4}$ lb.) truffles. Season with salt, pepper, and a pinch of spices. When the mixture is very smooth, take it out of the mortar and cook gently over a very low flame. Rub through a fine sieve.

Slowly melt 500 g. (18 oz.) of this truffled fat. Add to it the peeled truffles (the peelings having been used, as indicated above, to flavour the pork fat), quartered if large or whole if small. Season with salt, pepper, powdered thyme, and bay leaf. Poach on a low heat for 8 to 10 minutes. Leave the truffles to cool, covered. When they are quite cold, add them to the rest of the pork fat. Add a little brandy and mix thoroughly.

Quenelle forcemeat I. FARCE À GODIVEAU À LA GRAISSE, À

LA GLACE – *Ingredients.* 1 kg. ($2\frac{1}{4}$ lb.) lean veal with gristle and tendons removed, 500 g. (18 oz.) well-dried beef suet, 8 whole eggs, 4 teaspoons salt, 1 teaspoon white pepper, pinch grated nutmeg, 800 g. ($1\frac{3}{4}$ lb.) chopped ice, or failing this, 7 dl. ($1\frac{1}{4}$ pints, $1\frac{1}{2}$ pints) iced water.

Method. Mince the veal and the suet separately. Add the seasoning. Still keeping them separate, pound the veal and the suet. Then put them together and pound to a fine paste. Add the eggs, one by one, still pounding. Rub through a fine sieve. Spread the mixture out on a plate, and leave it on ice till the next day.

Pound the stuffing once more in the mortar, adding the ice, broken into small pieces and put in gradually. Mix well. Test the forcemeat by poaching a small piece. Add a little iced water if it is too firm; a little white of egg if too soft.

This stuffing is made into forcemeat balls which are served in *vol-au-vent* or pies, or used to garnish large cuts of meat or poultry.

Quenelle forcemeat II. FARCE À GODIVEAU À LA CRÈME – *Ingredients.* 1 kg. ($2\frac{1}{4}$ lb.) trimmed *noix* or loin of veal, 1 kg. ($2\frac{1}{4}$ lb.) beef suet, 4 whole eggs, 3 yolks, 7 dl. ($1\frac{1}{4}$ pints, $1\frac{1}{2}$ pints) fresh cream, 4 teaspoons salt, 1 teaspoon pepper, pinch nutmeg.

Method. Pound the chopped veal and suet in a mortar separately, then mix them. Add the seasoning, the eggs and yolks, one by one, mixing vigorously. Rub through a fine sieve and spread it out well on a board. Leave on ice until the next day.

Pound the stuffing once more in the mortar, adding the cream a little at a time.

Test the forcemeat as indicated in the preceding recipe, adjusting the consistency if necessary. This forcemeat is used in the same way as *Quenelle forcemeat I.*

Quenelle forcemeat balls. FARCE À GODIVEAU – These balls can be piped through a forcing-bag, but they are usually rolled by hand and poached in salt water.

They can also be poached dry, as follows:

Pipe the forcemeat through a forcing-bag onto buttered paper laid on a buttered baking sheet. Put the balls fairly close together. Cook in a moderate oven for 7 to 8 minutes. When little pinkish beads of fat begin to appear on the surface, the balls are ready.

Take them out of the oven. Overturn on a board or marble slab, peel off the paper, holding it at one corner. Use as required.

Veal forcemeat for borders, large stuffed forcemeat balls, linings (for the presentation of hot entrées). FARCE DE VEAU POUR BORDURES, GROSSES QUENELLES FOURRÉES, FONDS DE PLAT – *Ingredients.* 1 kg. ($2\frac{1}{4}$ lb.) lean veal, 300 g. (11 oz.) *Flour panada* (see PANADA), 5 whole eggs, 8 yolks, $1\frac{1}{2}$ dl. ($\frac{1}{4}$ pint, $\frac{2}{3}$ cup) very thick, cold *Béchamel sauce* (see SAUCE), 3 teaspoons salt, $\frac{3}{4}$ teaspoon white pepper, pinch grated nutmeg.

Method. Pound the veal finely in a mortar with seasoning. Take it out of the mortar and put the panada in its place. Pound until it is very creamy. Add the veal and pound thoroughly. Add the eggs and yolks, one at a time, then the *béchamel sauce*. Rub through a sieve. Work with a spatula until it is very smooth.

Veal and pork forcemeat. FARCE DE VEAU ET DE PORC – Chop 300 g. (11 oz.) round of veal, 250 g. (9 oz.) lean pork and 250 g. (9 oz.) fresh fat bacon.

Pound together in a mortar, add 2 whole eggs and 1 dl. (6 tablespoons, scant $\frac{1}{2}$ cup) brandy, season with *Spiced salt* (see SALT) and rub through a sieve.

FORCEMEATS or STUFFINGS MADE WITH FISH. FARCES DE POISSONS, CRUSTACÉS:

Anchovy forcemeat I. FARCE AUX ANCHOIS – Make a white *roux* of 1 tablespoon butter and 2 tablespoons flour. Moisten with 1 dl. (6 tablespoons, scant $\frac{1}{2}$ cup) boiling milk. Cook for a few minutes over a very hot flame, stirring with a wooden spoon. When very thick, remove from the stove.

Add 1 whole egg, 2 yolks, and the fillets of 4 desalted anchovies. Rub through a fine sieve. Cook for a few seconds, stirring. Rub through a fine sieve.

This stuffing is used as a filling for savoury tarts, *dartois*, small *pâtés*, pies, etc.

Anchovy forcemeat II. (Carême's recipe). FARCE D'ANCHOIS – 'Soak 275 g. (10 oz.) anchovies to remove the salt; clean and bone them. Toss for 2 minutes in 100 g. (4 oz., $\frac{1}{2}$ cup) butter, seasoned with 2 tablespoons (3 tablespoons) *fines herbes*, a pinch of nutmeg, and a very little *Spiced salt* (see SALT).

'When the mixture is cold, pound the fillets of anchovy with 175 g. (6 oz.) *Bread panada* (see PANADA). Add the cooking butter with the *fines herbes*. Pound this mixture for 5 minutes, add 100 g. (4 oz., $\frac{1}{2}$ cup) butter (crayfish butter or some other kind) and 3 egg yolks. Mix well.'

This mixture is used mostly for stuffing large fish. It can also be used to stuff vegetables, artichoke hearts, mushrooms, tomatoes, etc. to provide a Lenten dish.

Freshwater crayfish forcemeat. FARCE D'ÉCREVISSES Proceed as for *Prawn or shrimp forcemeat* (see below).

Cream fish forcemeat (Lenten). FARCE À LA CRÈME (MAIGRE) – Proceed as indicated for veal or poultry *Mousseline forcemeat*, using fish instead of meat. Pike, whiting, or some other suitable fish may be used.

Fish forcemeat I. FARCE DE POISSON – *Ingredients.* 1 kg. ($2\frac{1}{4}$ lb.) pike (or other white-fleshed fish), 400 g. (14 oz.) *Frangipane panada* or *Rice panada* (see PANADA), 4 egg whites, 4 teaspoons salt, 1 teaspoon pepper and a small pinch of grated nutmeg.

Method. Prepare as *Quenelle forcemeat II.*

Fish forcemeat II. FARCE DE POISSON – Chop finely 300 g. (11 oz.) whiting or other white fish. Add 200 g. (7 oz., $3\frac{1}{2}$ cups) breadcrumbs, soaked in milk and squeezed, 50 g. (2 oz., $\frac{1}{4}$ cup) butter, 1 tablespoon chopped blanched chives, 1 tablespoon chopped chervil and parsley. Season with salt, pepper, and nutmeg. Bind with 2 eggs. Mix thoroughly.

Mousseline forcemeat for fish mousses and mousselines. FARCE MOUSSELINE POUR MOUSSES ET MOUSSELINES DE POISSONS – *Ingredients.* 1 kg. ($2\frac{1}{4}$ lb.) skinned and boned pike, whiting, sole, salmon, or trout, 4 egg whites, $1\frac{1}{4}$ litres ($2\frac{1}{4}$ pints, $2\frac{3}{4}$ pints) fresh cream, $1\frac{1}{2}$ teaspoons salt, $\frac{1}{2}$ teaspoon white pepper, pinch grated nutmeg.

Method. Pound the fish in a mortar with the seasoning. Add the egg whites, a little at a time. Rub the mixture through a fine sieve. Stir on ice until very smooth and leave on the ice for 2 hours. Add the cream, a little at a time, stirring gently with a spatula.

This mixture is used for light fish quenelles, mousses, and *mousselines*, and also for stuffing large braised fish.

Panada forcemeat with butter (Lenten). FARCE À LA PANADE ET AU BEURRE (MAIGRE) – Proceed as for veal or chicken *Panada forcemeat with butter* using pike, whiting, or some other suitable fish.

This is used for plain fish quenelles, borders, moulds, and for stuffing large fish.

Panada forcemeat for fish and shellfish mousses. FARCE POUR MOUSSES DE POISSONS ET DE CRUSTACÉS (À LA PANADE) – Proceed as for *Mousseline forcemeat for fish mousses*, using the following ingredients: 1 kg. ($2\frac{1}{4}$ lb.) boned and skinned fish, 450 g. (1 lb.) *Frangipane panada* (see PANADA), 4 egg whites, $1\frac{1}{2}$ litres ($2\frac{3}{4}$ pints, $3\frac{1}{4}$ pints) cream, salt, pepper, grated nutmeg.

The addition of the panada to this forcemeat gives it body, but makes it less delicate in flavour. It is used for the same purposes as *Mousseline forcemeat for fish mousses.*

Pickled herring or sardine forcemeat. FARCE DE HARENGS SAURS, DE SARDINES – Use fillets of pickled herring or sardines, as for *Anchovy forcemeat I.*

Pike forcemeat à la lyonnaise, or Godiveau lyonnaise. FARCE DE BROCHET À LA LYONNAISE, DITE GODIVEAU LYONNAISE – *Ingredients.* 500 g. (18 oz.) skinned and boned pike, 500 g. (18 oz.) trimmed and minced beef suet, 500 g. (18 oz.) *Frangipane panada* (see PANADA) 4 egg whites, 2¼ teaspoons salt, ¾ teaspoon pepper, pinch nutmeg.

Method. Pound the fat, the panada, and the egg whites in a mortar. Add the pike and the seasoning. Work the stuffing vigorously with the pestle. Rub through a fine sieve and work with a spatula until the mixture is very smooth. An electric blender can be used.

This forcemeat is used for large fish balls known as *quenelles lyonnaises.* To make these, shape the forcemeat in a spoon and poach in salt water. Simmer for 10 minutes in the sauce to be served with them, usually a meatless *Espagnole sauce* (see SAUCE) containing mushrooms, stoned olives, truffles, and other small delicacies.

When pike quenelles are served with a thick sauce such as Nantua, lobster, shrimp, white wine or any other white sauce suitable for fish and shellfish, they should simply be poached in salt water. After draining and drying them in a cloth, serve them on bread fried in butter, on artichoke hearts, or on flaky pastry. Garnish, and cover with the sauce indicated in the selected recipe.

Prawn or shrimp forcemeat. FARCE DE CREVETTES – Pound in a mortar 100 g. (4 oz., ⅔ cup) prawns or shrimps with 100 g. (4 oz., ½ cup) butter. Rub through a fine sieve. Add to this mixture half its volume of yolks of hard-boiled eggs, rubbed through a fine sieve. Mix well.

This mixture is used for cold *hors-d'œuvre.*

Shellfish cream forcemeat, fine. FARCE FINE DE CRUSTACÉS À LA CRÈME – Proceed, using shellfish, as indicated for *Mousseline forcemeat for fish mousses.*

This is used for quenelles.

MISCELLANEOUS FORCEMEATS or STUFFINGS. FARCES DIVERSES –

Brain forcemeat – See OFFAL or VARIETY MEATS.

Forcemeat for fish. FARCE POUR POISSONS – Soak 250 g. (9 oz., 4½ cups) breadcrumbs in milk and squeeze them. Beat in a bowl. Add 75 g. (3 oz., ¾ cup) finely chopped onion, cooked slowly in butter until very soft, 25 g. (1 oz., ¼ cup) chopped shallot, cooked in white wine until all the moisture has evaporated, 100 g. (4 oz., 2 cups) chopped raw mushrooms, which have been squeezed (or 3 tablespoons (scant ¼ cup) dry *duxelles*), and 1 tablespoon chopped parsley. Bind with 2 whole eggs. Season with salt, pepper, and grated nutmeg.

According to the nature of the dish for which the forcemeat is to be used, a touch of garlic may be added.

Forcemeat à la provençale for fish. FARCE POUR POISSONS À LA PROVENÇALE – Cook slowly 100 g. (4 oz., 1 cup) finely chopped onions in 4 tablespoons (⅓ cup) oil until very tender. Add a finely chopped clove of garlic and 150 g. (5 oz., 2½ cups) chopped raw mushrooms. Brown for a few seconds.

Remove the pan from the stove and add 250 g. (9 oz., 4½ cups) freshly grated breadcrumbs, 1 tablespoon chopped chives, 1 tablespoon chopped parsley and chervil, and 3 chopped hard-boiled eggs.

Season with salt, pepper, and grated nutmeg.

Forcemeat of various fungi and mushrooms, cèpes, cultivated mushrooms, morels, St. George's mushrooms, etc. FARCE DE CHAMPIGNONS DIVERS – Proceed, using one or other of these fungi, first tossed in butter, as for *Truffle forcemeat* (see below). These forcemeats are used in the same way as truffle forcemeat.

Garlic forcemeat – See GARLIC.

Ravioli forcemeat – See RAVIOLI.

Sage and onion forcemeat (English cookery). FARCE À LA SAUGE – Used to stuff poultry, especially duck and goose. Bake 2 large onions in their skins in the oven. Leave to cool. Skin and chop them.

Mix with 150 g. (5 oz., 2½ cups) breadcrumbs, which have been dipped in milk and squeezed, and 150 g. (5 oz.) cooked and chopped beef suet. Add 2 tablespoons (3 tablespoons) chopped sage, season with salt and pepper, and mix thoroughly.

Truffle forcemeat (Carême's recipe). FARCE AUX TRUFFES – 'Chop 150 g. (5 oz.) black truffles, and toss them for a few minutes in 100 g. (4 oz., ½ cup) butter seasoned with *Spiced salt* (see SALT) and a touch of nutmeg. Drain the truffles on a plate, and pound 75 g. (3 oz.) *Bread panada* (see PANADA).

'When the truffles are cold, put them in the mortar and pound them with the panada for a few minutes. Add the butter in which the truffles were cooked, and pound together until the mixture is perfectly smooth. Mix in 3 egg yolks.'

This forcemeat is used for stuffing poultry and winged game, and for meat or fish *paupiettes* (q.v.). It is also used in various hot *pâtés.*

Stuffings for vegetables (various). FARCE POUR LÉGUMES – Used to stuff vegetables such as aubergines, small vegetable marrows (courgettes or zucchini), tomatoes, artichoke hearts, etc. It is really a thickened *Duxelles sauce* (see SAUCE) to which is added the pulp of the vegetables, scooped out after they have been cooked in oil.

Yolk of egg stuffing. FARCE DE JAUNES D'OEUFS – *Cold.* Rub the yolks of 10 hard-boiled eggs through a fine sieve. Add 100 g. (4 oz., ½ cup) butter softened to a paste. Season with salt and white pepper, and mix.

This is used as a spread in cold *hors-d'œuvre,* especially for *Canapés à la russe* (see HORS-D'ŒUVRE, *Cold hors-d'œuvre*). It is also used as filling for halved hard-boiled eggs, artichoke hearts, and small *barquettes* or tartlets served as garnishes with cold dishes.

Hot. Rub the yolks of hard-boiled eggs through a sieve. Season. Mix with half their weight of thick *Béchamel sauce* (see SAUCE) passed through a fine sieve.

This stuffing is used mainly to fill hard-boiled eggs prepared *au gratin* (see EGGS, *Eggs à la Chimay*). A teaspoon of dry *duxelles* (q.v.) and chopped parsley is added. It is also used to stuff vegetables which are then sprinkled with breadcrumbs, basted with melted butter and browned, and to fill small *vol-au-vent, barquettes,* tartlets, etc.

FORCING. FORÇAGE – Process of growing vegetables and fruit under glass in order to ripen them before their time. These products are then called 'forced' products.

The distinguishing quality of these fruits and vegetables is their rarity and their high price. Good cooks seldom buy them, preferring to use these products in their proper season.

FORCING-BAG (U.S. Pastry-bag). POCHE – Funnel-shaped bag which can be fitted with nozzles (French *douilles*) of different shapes and sizes. These nozzles are made with large or small apertures which can be plain or fluted, so that creamy mixtures can be piped in a wide range of decorative designs.

FORELEG HAM. JAMBONNEAU – The French word

jambonneau which is sometimes translated as foreleg ham, or picnic ham in the U.S.A., refers to the portion below the ham or shoulder of both fore and hind legs of the pig. (See HAM.)

FORESTIÈRE (À LA) – Method of preparation of small cuts of meat and poultry, garnished with morels, lean larding bacon cut in large pieces, and diced potatoes fried in butter. (See GARNISHES.)

FORK, FOURCHETTE – Table utensil designed to pick up meat and other food. It is of very ancient origin as it is mentioned in the Old Testament. It was first used as a ritual instrument to grip pieces of meat destined for sacrifices; later it was used in the kitchen. According to the eleventh century Italian scholar, Damiani, forks were introduced into Venice by a Byzantine princess and thence spread through Italy. They are mentioned in 1379 in an inventory of the French king, Charles V; and Edward II of England's favourite, Piers Gaveston, is recorded as having eaten a pear with a fork in the early fourteenth century. However, eating with forks did not become fashionable until the seventeenth century.

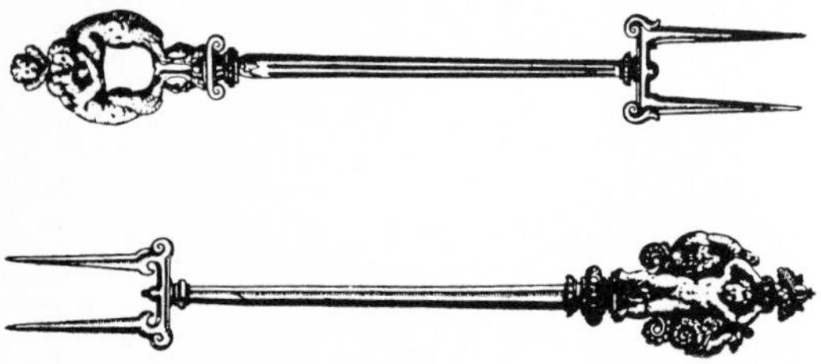

Renaissance forks

In the seventeenth century, use of the fork, which was originally two-pronged, then three-pronged, and later four-pronged, spread from Italy and Spain into France and England. An English traveller named Thomas Coryate is credited with bringing the use of the fork to England after a trip to Italy in 1608.

While in Paris in 1612, Coryate remarked that the fork was used in good society, though not yet amongst the common people. Hérouard in the *Journal of Louis XIV* speaks of the Dauphin beating the table with his fork and spoon.

Modern forks are made in many sizes and many metals, as well as in plastics and woods. Etiquette varies as to the proper way of holding and using a fork, and in which hand.

FORK LUNCHEON. DÉJEUNER À LA FOURCHETTE – A meal taken towards the middle of the day.

FOUNTAIN. FONTAINE – Term employed in pastry-making to describe placing flour on the board in a circle.

The various ingredients used to make the pastry are then placed inside the 'fountain'.

FOURDERAINE – Home-made liqueur which used to be common in the north of France and is still sometimes found there. The hedge sloes used in making it are picked after the first frost, when they are ripe. This liqueur is prepared in the same way as cassis.

FOURME – See CHEESE.

FOUR MENDICANTS. QUATRE MENDIANTS – Dessert made up of figs, raisins, hazelnuts, and almonds, whose colours recall those of the four mendicant Orders.

FOUR RED FRUITS. QUATRE FRUITS ROUGES – Strawberries, cherries, redcurrants and raspberries.

FOUR SPICES. QUATRE ÉPICES – A much used mixture, for which, formerly, each purveyor had a special formula. The most usual is the following:

125 g. (4 oz.) white pepper, 10 g. ($\frac{1}{3}$ oz.) powdered cloves, 30 g. (1 oz.) ginger, 35 g. (generous 1 oz.) grated nutmeg.

FOUR YELLOW FRUITS. QUATRE FRUITS JAUNES – Oranges, lemons, bitter oranges, and citrons.

FOX. RENARD – Animal ranking as vermin. Its flesh is very tough and with an extremely unpleasant 'wild' taste, but it is sometimes eaten after the animal has been skinned and the flesh soaked in running water or boiling water.

FRANCE – See INTERNATIONAL COOKERY, WINE.

FRANCHE-COMTÉ – Mountainous region in the western part of the Belfort Gap, surrounded by regions abundant in edible products and famous wines. In the north are Lorraine and Alsace; in the south Savoy, including the Bugey, which is a great centre of fine *cuisine*. To the west it borders on Burgundy, Bresse, and Champagne. To the east its immediate neighbour is Switzerland. The geographical position of Franche-Comté has influenced its inhabitants to be great gastronomes.

A variety of excellent foods is produced in this province. In Franche-Comté and the Jura, the beef cattle are famous for their well-flavoured meat and high-quality milk, from which cheese and other dairy products are made. In the orchards of Franche-Comté, excellent fruit, particularly stone fruit, is grown. This part of France has an abundant variety of game. In the rivers, streams, and ponds, numerous kinds of fish are found in great quantities. The inhabitants cook them in delicious ways, notably in succulent stews. Known for their delicacy are Saulon carp, red mullet, pike from Ognon, Doubs and Dessoubs trout, and Breuchin salmon trout the flesh of which is very well flavoured. In the Breuchin there are also good crayfish.

Cheeses from Franche-Comté include Septmoncel, which some knowledgeable people consider a rival to Roquefort, Comté cheese, which is a kind of Gruyère, Fromagère, and Fromage fort.

Franche-Comté (*French Government Tourist Office*)

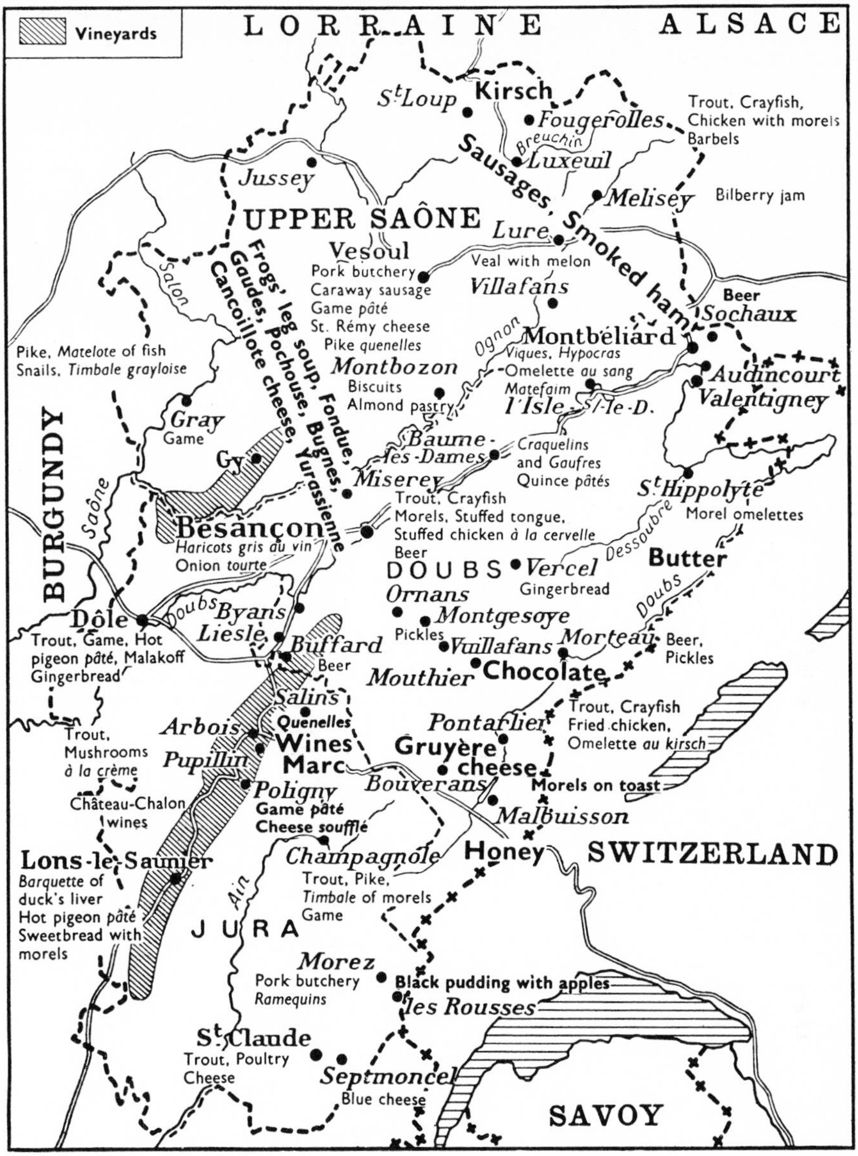

Gastronomic map of Franche-Comté

Culinary specialities – Foremost among the specialities are *maize porridge*, *potée franc-comtoise*, which is prepared like *potée* (q.v.) from other regions but has Morteau sausage added to it; *frog's leg soup*; *panada*, a dish like a soup with bread and butter boiled to a pulp; *cherry soup*; and a whole range of soups made with fresh vegetables.

All *charcuterie* is excellent in Franche-Comté and can be bought in Paris and many other large towns. It includes *smoked ham*, mainly from Luxeuil; different kinds of sausages including *caraway sausage* from Montbozon; and *stuffed tongue* from Besançon.

The most famous dishes to be found in Franche-Comté are *fish stews* made from freshwater fish with white or red wine, onions and herbs; *meat braised in wine*, cooked very slowly in a covered casserole to preserve all the meat juices; *pike quenelles* of Vesoul; *jugged hare à la franc-comtoise*; *cheese fondue*; *pain d'écrivisses*; *marrow au gratin*; *cheese potatoes; morels on toast*; *onion tourte*; pancakes called *matefaim*; *ramekins*; *fritters*; *flamusse*, cheese tart specially made in Burgundy; *sèche*, flat bread made with eggs and sugar; *craquelins* of Baume-les-Dames; *almond pastry and biscuits* of Montbozon; *viques* of Montbéliard; *malakoff* of Dôle; *quiche comtoise*; *galette de goumeau* of Saint-Amour; *gaufres de chanoinesses* of Baume-les-Dames; *chestnut cakes*; *pain d'épice* of Vercel and Dole; *paste* made from quinces growing in Baume-les-Dames; *bilberry and whortleberry jam* from Melisey.

Wines and liqueurs – Franche-Comté (and particularly the *département* of Jura) produces excellent white, red, and rosé wines, not to mention the celebrated yellow wine, which is a speciality of the region, and straw wines (*vins de paille*) which are difficult to find outside Jura and Hermitage.

The yellow wine is made from the Savagnin grape. The distinctive nutty flavour (*goût de jaune*) demands strictly controlled and highly specialised methods of vinification. fermentation, and conservation. The best yellow wine is that of Château-Chalon.

Straw wine is so-called because the grapes are sun-dried on straw mats before being pressed.

The Jura *appellations* are:

Yellow wines. Arbois, Côtes du Jura, Château-Chalon, Étoile.

Straw wines. Arbois, Côtes du Jura, Étoile.

Red and rosé wines. Arbois, Côtes du Jura.

White wines. Arbois, Côtes du Jura, Étoile.

Some well-known liqueurs are also made in Franche-Comté. The kirsch of Fougerolles is particularly well known.

FRANCILLON SALAD – Title of a Japanese salad, the recipe for which was given by the younger Alexandre Dumas in a play *Francillon* performed at the Comédie-Francaise. The recipe for this salad, of mussels, potatoes, and truffles, will be found under SALAD.

FRANCOLIN – Wild bird resembling a partridge, found in warm countries, especially in Sicily and Greece. Its flavour is something like that of partridge (q.v.), and it is prepared in the same way.

FRANGIPANE – Mixture of flour, egg yolks, butter, and milk, which is cooked like a *chou* (cream puff) *pastry*. Used in poultry and fish forcemeat.

FRANGIPANE CREAM – Cream used in the preparation of different desserts or sweets and cakes, made like *French pastry cream* (see CREAM).

Ingredients. 250 g. (9 oz., generous cup) sugar, 250 g. (9 oz., $2\frac{1}{4}$ cups) sifted flour, 4 whole eggs and 8 egg yolks, $1\frac{1}{2}$ litres ($2\frac{3}{4}$ pints, $3\frac{1}{4}$ pints) milk boiled and flavoured with vanilla, 50 crushed macaroons, 100 g. (4 oz., $\frac{1}{2}$ cup) butter, a pinch of salt.

Method. Put the sugar, sieved flour, and salt into a heavy saucepan with a flat bottom. Add the eggs and yolks. Mix all the ingredients thoroughly and add the milk very gradually. Cook slowly, stirring all the time, for 2 to 3 minutes. Add the butter and the crushed macaroons. Mix.

FRANKENTAL – Black grape also known as Black Hamburg, originating in Germany. The fruit is very large and juicy, and is often included in gift baskets of fruit.

FRASCATI – See RESTAURANTS OF BYGONE DAYS.

FRASCATI (À LA) – Garnish for meat dishes with consists of thin slices of *foie gras*, asparagus tips, mushrooms, and truffles. (See GARNISHES.)

FRAUDULENT MISREPRESENTATION OF FOOD. FRAUDE ALIMENTAIRE – Deception in the manufacture and sale of food products. Fraud occurs when the type and origin of the food product does not correspond to the name under which it is sold (for example, *pâte de foie gras* containing other than goose or duck liver) or when the quantity of goods is not as specified. (See also ADULTERATION.)

Fraudulence in such matters is nothing new, and it has always been the duty of the authorities to try to uncover it and stamp it out. When the corporations were in command and free trade did not exist, the legislator at that time had no scientific means of investigation and had to limit himself to preventive measures. All secret work was forbidden and consequently all night work was forbidden. It was forbidden to keep a variety of products in the same shop. Distinctive trademarks and certain symbols were compulsory on manufactured products. Offenders were severely punished.

Since 1888, various laws have defined the repression of fraudulent practices in the marketing of goods. Acts and decrees have been, and continue to be passed to protect drink and food produce.

In France, from the Middle Ages onwards, quality and quantity were under strict surveillance. River ports, markets, and shops were all controlled. Thus in 1577 Henri III ordered all bakers to keep a pair of scales and legitimate weights in their windows, workrooms, and carts, so that each customer might check the weight of his bread himself. In the eighteenth century, the Police Code added that the scales had to be hung sufficiently high to preclude the possibility of the seller tipping it with his thumb.

Fraudulent practices were severely reprimanded: penalties included the confiscation of goods, demolition of ovens, a fine or an *amende honorable*, and, in the Middle Ages, public flogging.

In 1431, if a cookshop proprietor sold a cat for a rabbit, he was condemned to go to the banks of the Seine in the busiest part of the day and shout an apology to the crowd while throwing the offending cat into the river. The butchers were forbidden to buy pigs nourished on human blood. It was forbidden to sell reheated meat, to keep meat more than two days in winter and one and a half days in summer, to sell meat by lamplight or candlelight (such lights made it easier for discoloured, putrid meat to be passed off as rosy and fresh). A regulation in 1399 controlled the time of day during which candles might be used.

On 22 June 1351 some suspect meat was confiscated in the master butcher Bardel's shop in rue Baudet-Saint-Antoine. The Corporation, outraged that one of their members should have disgraced himself, demanded that he be condemned. He was accused as a poisoner and was taken to the pillory in Les Halles where he was subsequently put to death. One hundred and twenty-seven bareheaded Paris butchers witnessed the execution of their *confrère*.

FREEZING – See PRESERVATION OF FOOD.

FRENCH CULINARY AND TABLE SLANG. ARGOT DE CUISINE ET DE TABLE – Slang, wrote Gaston Esnault in his *Dictionnaire historique des argots français* (Larousse) is 'a collection of non-technical spoken words that appeal to a social group. The group – corporative, schoolboy, fashionable society – is, he specifies, a more or less coherent one, adding, 'Slang varies from profession to profession'.

It is therefore only right and fitting that the culinary profession should have its own brand of slang.

The table is *la carante*. Then the food, in other words *la fripe, la croûte, la briffe, la cuistance, la béquetance, la jaffe, la graine, la tortore, la daronge, le frichti* arrives. Everyone has *un estome* (stomach), and one has to eat in other words, *claper, croquer, tortorer, cacher, grainer, claboter, clapoter, claquer, gousser, morfiler, morfier, to live. And if la jaffe* is good then *on se morfale, on fircote, on se bégale* (one enjoys oneself).

Bread and wine are placed on the table first. Bread, or *le gringue, l'artifaille, la brèque, le brigeton, le brignollet.* Wine, or *le sirop, le pivois, le jaja, le pive, le tutu, le busard, le picrate, le pichtegom.* If it is a robust red wine it is *le coaltair*; if it is a fine light wine, it is *le coulange.* It can be *rouquin* (red) or *beaujolpif* and will be in a bottle, that is to say *la betterave, la boutanche, la rouille.* If it is in litres, it is *le kil* or *kilo* and *on le pictera* (it will be quaffed with a right good will). If it is a bottle of *champ* (Champagne) it becomes a *roteuse.* It is drunk in *un guindal, un bennard* or *un glasse.*

The appetite begins with *l'apéro* (the alfa of the good old days has gone – *l'alfa* being the absinth (*la verte*) of *la Belle Epoque*). From *la bouillante* (soup) we move on to *la barbaque* or *bidoche, le saciflard* (saucisson), also called *du bits*, then came *les navarins* (turnips), *les loubiats* (haricot beans), then *le calendo* (Camembert) which is *un rême* (cheese), then *le caoua* (coffee) which, being black, can also be called *biffi*. At last it is time for *la consolante*, a bottle of wine drunk before leaving (or after the *coup de feu*). (Slang used by restaurant chefs around 1910. Taken from the *Dictionnaire* of Gaston Esnault).

FRENCH CULINARY NAMES. APPELLATIONS CULINAIRES – Information of the origin of certain culinary names is scattered throughout this volume. Here are a few more. The list is far from complete, and even the facts given here may be far from exact since most of it is based on hearsay. Curnonsky, for instance, had enormous difficulty in finally proving that *homard à l'américaine* (and not *à l'armoricaine*) was created by the chef Pierre Fraysse (native of Sète) for his restaurant called *Peter's*, in Paris, on his return from America. On the other hand, it is still a mystery who the Suzette was to whom a *maître d'hôtel* (from Paris or Monte-Carlo?) dedicated the *crêpes*. And was she really dining with the Prince of Wales when they were created for her?

Here then are a few more culinary terms:

Abrantès – The governor of Paris, Junot, duc d'Abrantès, had one of the best chefs of his time. This was Richard (who has a variety of chafing dish called after him). He created a number of dishes *à la d'Abrantès* as a tribute to his master.

Anna – Adolphe Dugléré, then head chef of the Café Anglais, invented Anna potatoes for the famous courtesan Anna Deslions.

Artois (À la d') – The calves' sweetbreads so called were invented by the Count of Artois, future Charles X.

Aurore – This was the Christian name of Brillat-Savarin's mother, to whom the author of *Physiologie du goût* dedicated some recipes.

Bagration – During the period of the *Restauration* (Restoration) (and what more suitable name for this epoch when French *cuisine* was at its peak!), the Princess Bagration had none other than Marie-Antoine Carême as her chef. He dedicated certain dishes to her, as he had done to Talleyrand.

Bellevue – Madame de Pompadour loved to please the palate of Louis XV; it was a finer one than that of his forebear, Louis XIV. She owned the château of Bellevue. Some of the recipes she devised were called after the château; some after herself.

Bénédictine, chartreuse, carmélite – Name for dishes prepared as they would have been in a monastic cell. Partridge or pheasant, for example, are cooked inside a mass of vegetable or herbs, or even wrapped in paper. Recipes are given under the appropriate headings.

Berry (À la) – The dish of fillets of young rabbits *à la Berry* owes its creation to the greedy and scandalous Duchess of Berry, favourite daughter of the Regent.

Bourdaloue (À la) – Invention of a *pâtissier* at the shop, *la Belle Époque* which was (and still is) situated in rue Bourdaloue, Paris. The specialities devised by its original owner are still sold there today.

Bresolles – *Ragoût* invented on the battlefield by the valet of the Marquis of Brezolles during the Seven Years' War.

Cardinal (À la) – It was Mazarin, a discerning man if ever there was one, who inspired the dishes thus named.

Chantilly – Name given to a number of preparations (and in particular to the cream of this name) by Vatel, when he was master chef to the Condé household.

Clamart (À la) – For a great many years, the *petits pois* eaten in Paris, and particularly at Court, came from the market gardens of Clamart in the suburbs.

Condé (À la) – Name given to certain preparations by Feuillet, master chef of the Condé household during the Restoration.

Conti (À la) – Name given to several recipes created by the chefs of the Prince of Conti.

But it was the Princess of Conti who 'invented' the loin of mutton that bears her name, the famous loin *gourmandé de persil* (gourmandised with parsley) that is mentioned in *le Bourgeois gentilhomme*.

Cussy (À la) – Louis de Cussy, one of the wittiest gourmets of the early nineteenth century was prefect of the palace under Napoleon I. and the chef dedicated some recipes to him.

Duroc (À la) – Véry, who owed much in his early days to the protection of Marshal Duroc and . . . to the love of Madame Véry, could hardly do less than dedicate a few recipes to his benefactor.

Frangipane (À la) – We owe this pastry cream to César Frangipani, an Italian nobleman. Catherine de Médicis introduced it into France.

Gérard (À la) – Gérard was assistant to Madame de Pompadour's chef. He called one of his creations after himself because he considered it too common to bear the name of such a personage as Madame de Pompadour. It was *manchon de veau à la Gérard*.

Maintenon (À la) – The marquise, who was a very good cook (she invented an oven when she was still the widow Scarron), created *côtelettes en papillotes* for her royal lover. They still bear her name.

Marengo – It is said that chicken *Marengo* was invented on the battlefield itself by Bonaparte's cook, a Swiss called Dunant.

Around the same period, a Parisian restaurateur used to serve a veal and tomato *ragoût* (the veal being first tossed in olive oil) in his restaurant *La Grâce de Dieu*. When news of the victory was circulated by the Paris stock exchange the humble restaurateur christened his veal dish *veau Marengo*.

Raymond Oliver, who runs the *Grand Véfour* (where Bonaparte used to dine occasionally with Josephine) maintains that it was not Dunant who created the dish. He assures us that chicken *Marengo* is of a more recent date and was served in Talleyrand's home nearing the end of Talleyrand's life. When his guests, entranced with the dish, begged him for the recipe, Talleyrand declared. 'To win victory at Marengo, Bonaparte had to sacrifice, *in extremis*, his friend Desaix; to make a success of this recipe, the tomato must be sacrificed at the very last moment. These two gestures have something in common, hence the name *poulet Marengo*'.

There are a few who think that this dish was concocted at an even later date, at Marengo in Algeria.

Melba – It was while he was working at the Savoy in London, that Escoffier invented his celebrated *pêche Melba* for the famous Australian singer Dame Nelly Melba (who loved her food). It was first served at a dinner given by the Duke of Orléans to celebrate the singer's triumph in *Lohengrin*. Escoffier conjured up a dish of a swan of ice, bearing peaches on its wings and resting on a bed of vanilla cream ice. Later he omitted the swan and sprinkled the peaches with raspberry syrup.

Montmorency (À la) – Cherry preserves. Once the only variety used was the 'Montmorency' type, a fresh, practically unsweetened cherry which it was said had been brought from Asia by Lucullus.

Orléans (À la) – Quince marmalade and other preserves have been named thus to commemorate Monseigneur de Jarente's, Bishop of Orléans', great love of food.

Père Faby (by distortion Fabri) – A Jesuit born in the

diocese of Belley (mentioned by Brillat-Savarin) who was particularly fond of *becfigues* (warblers). He was a great gourmet.

Reine (À la) – The *gourmandise* of Marie Leczinska gave birth to a whole host of recipes (*vol-au-vent*, chicken, consommés) all with the name *à la reine*.

But the creator of *potage à la reine* was Margot, the first wife of Henry IV.

Robert (À la) – The sauce *Robert* which Rabelais made such a fuss about was, it seems, invented by Robert, chef to the Abbot of Saint-Germain-des-Prés in the Middle Ages.

Salmis – Ought we really to attribute the *salmis de bécasse* (*salmis* of woodcock) to the Prince of Salm, who used to lodge in what is now the *Palais de la Légion d'honneur*? No. *Salmis* is a Gascon ellipsis of two Latin words: *salsa* (feminine of *salsus*, which means salted and is the root of the word 'sauce') and *mista* (feminine of *mistus*, past participle of *misceo* which means 'mixed up') so the exact definition of *salmis* is a 'mixed up sauce'.

Soubise (À la) – Sauce invented by Constant, head chef of the Soubise household.

Villeroy (À la) – Chickens *à la Villeroy* are attributed to the Marshal of Luxemburg, Duchess of Villeroy.

Xavier (À la) – Soup invented by Louis Stanislas Xavier of France, Count of Provence, the future Louis XVIII.

FRIANDISE – French word for a delicacy when referring to *pâtisserie* or sweetmeats.

This word is often used to describe iced *petits fours*.

FRICANDEAU – Rump (topside) of veal. Also describes a dish made of loin of veal (*noix de veau*) larded, braised, or roasted (see VEAL, *Noix de veau*).

The name is also applied to slices or fillets of fish, mainly those of sturgeon and fresh tunny (tuna fish), braised in a fish stock.

FRICASSÉE – In modern French usage, the word *fricassée* applies almost exclusively to a method of preparing poultry in a white sauce.

In earlier times the term denoted various kinds of stew made with white or brown stock, not only from poultry but from meat, fish and vegetables.

A *fricassée* of poultry is prepared in very much the same way as a *blanquette* (q.v.), a dish usually made with veal or lamb.

Fricassée of chicken à la berrichonne. FRICASSÉE DE POULET À LA BERRICHONNE – Brown in butter 250 g. (9 oz.) new carrots, whole if they are small, quartered if they are large. Remove them from the pan and brown the pieces of a jointed chicken in the same butter. Add $2\frac{1}{2}$ dl. (scant $\frac{1}{2}$ pint, generous cup) boiling water or white stock, the carrots and a bunch of mixed herbs. Season. Cover and cook for 30 minutes.

Pour off the chicken stock, add to it 5 tablespoons (6 tablespoons) cream and 2 egg yolks with a small pinch of fine sugar and 1 tablespoon vinegar. Mix well and pour the sauce over the chicken.

Warm the chicken in the sauce without bringing it to the boil.

Fricassée périgourdine – Name given in Périgord to the vegetables of a *pot-au-feu*. Before this is quite cooked, the vegetables are removed, drained, sliced, browned in butter or oil, sprinkled with flour, moistened with a little stock, and put back in the *pot-au-feu* to finish cooking.

The same name is given to a mixture of aromatic vegetables cooked in butter or oil with garlic and ham. This *fricassée* is used in various soups.

FRINGALE (Hunger pang) – This word comes from the ancient Norman *faim-valle* which meant *faim de cheval*, or a sudden hunger.

FRINOT – See CHEESE.

FRITOT – Type of fritter made with small pieces of poultry, lamb or veal sweetbreads, brains, or calves' heads.

Soak the pieces of meat for 30 minutes in oil, lemon juice (or vinegar), and mixed chopped herbs. Dip in a light batter and fry in deep fat.

Drain the fritters. Season with salt and garnish with fried parsley and quartered lemons. Serve with a sauce, usually Tomato.

A number of recipes are given under the heading *Fritot* in the section devoted to *Hot hors-d'œuvre* (see HORS-D'ŒUVRE).

Small pieces of meat and poultry prepared *à la Villeroi* are also called *fritots*.

FRITTER. BEIGNET – Food dipped in batter and fried in smoking-hot, deep fat (lard, oil, clarified butter, or vegetable fat). The batter for coating varies according to the nature of the food. (See BATTER.)

Another variety of fritter is made of a paste like *chou paste* and called soufflé fritters or *pets de nonne*.

A third variety is made of yeast dough, similar to brioche dough (see *Vienna fritters* below).

Cream fritters and fritters made of waffle batter (see WAFFLE), can be used like *croustades* (q.v.) for garnishes.

FRITTERS FOR HORS-D'ŒUVRE AND SMALL ENTRÉES. BIEGNETS POUR HORS D'OŒUVRE ET PETITES ENTRÉES – These fritters, the recipes for which are given below, should be served with tomato or other sauce.

Fritters

Anchovy fritters I. BEIGNETS D'ANCHOIS – Trim and desalt anchovy fillets. Spread them on one side with hard-boiled egg yolks rubbed through a sieve and mixed with a little butter and chopped parsley. Roll them up, dip in a light batter, and deep-fry. Garnish with fried parsley.

Anchovy fritters II. BEIGNETS D'ANCHOIS – Desalt, trim, and dry anchovy fillets. Sandwich them, two by two, with finely pounded fish forcemeat flavoured with anchovy purée and mixed with a little chopped parsley. Dip into batter and deep-fry.

Artichoke fritters. BEIGNETS D'ARTICHAUTS – See HORS-D'ŒUVRE, *Hot hors-d'œuvre*.

Aubergine fritters. BEIGNETS D'AUBERGINES – Peel the aubergines, cut into slices, and marinate for 1 hour in oil, lemon juice, chopped parsley, salt and pepper. Dip in batter and deep-fry.

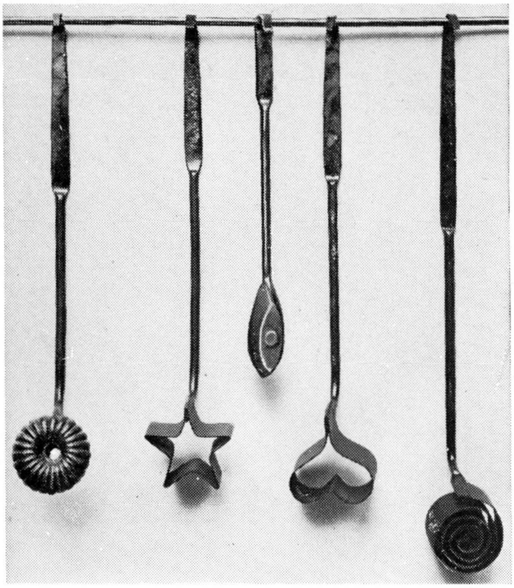

Moulds for fritters:
Left to right: mushroom, star, boat, heart, rose
(*Dehillerin. Phot. Larousse*)

Beef fritters. BEIGNETS DE BOEUF – See HORS-D'ŒUVRE, *Hot hors-d'œuvre.*

Brain fritters (lamb's or calf's). BEIGNETS DE CERVELLES D'AGNEAU, DE VEAU – Cook the brains in *court-bouillon* (q.v.). Cut into small slices and marinate in oil, lemon juice, and chopped parsley. Dip in batter and deep-fry.

Brussels sprout fritters. BEIGNETS DE CHOUX DE BRUXELLES – Half-cook, Brussels sprouts in salted water, drain, dip in cold water, dry, and marinate in oil, lemon juice, and chopped parsley. Dip in batter and deep-fry.

Cardoon or chard fritters. BEIGNETS DE CARDONS, DE CARDES – Cardoons or chards cooked, marinated and prepared as described for *Aubergine fritters.*

Cauliflower or broccoli fritters. BEIGNETS DE CHOUX-FLEURS, DE BROCOLIS – Divided into flowerets, marinated, and cooked as for *Mushroom fritters* (see below).

Celery fritters. BEIGNETS DE CELERI – Cook, marinate, and prepare as described for *Aubergine fritters.* Celeriac or ordinary celery may be used.

Chicken fritters. BEIGNETS DE VOLAILLE – Chicken left-overs, poached or braised and cut into small slices. Marinate in oil, lemon juice, and chopped parsley. Dip in batter and deep-fry.

Chicken liver fritters. BEIGNETS DE FOIES DE POULETS – Cut the livers into a *salpicon* (q.v.), brown briskly in butter, add diced mushrooms, also tossed in butter, and blend with thick *Béchamel sauce* (see SAUCE). When the mixture is cold, divide into small pieces and roll into balls.

Dip in batter and deep-fry.

Chicory fritters. BEIGNETS D'ENDIVES – Braise the chicory, dry well, and cut in two lengthways. Marinate for 30 minutes in oil, lemon juice, and chopped parsley. Dip in batter and deep-fry.

Courgette (zucchini) fritters. BEIGNETS DE COURGETTES – As *Aubergine fritters.*

Egg fritters. BEIGNETS D'OEUFS – Prepare a *salpicon* (q.v.) of hard-boiled eggs, mushrooms, and truffles (and lean ham, if liked) and blend with thick *Béchamel sauce*, or thick *Velouté sauce* (see SAUCE) if meat is being used. Spread the mixture on a metal sheet and allow it to cool, then divide into small pieces. Roll into balls. Dip in batter and deep-fry.

Egg fritters à la duxelles. BEIGNETS D'OEUFS À LA DUXELLES – Cut hard-boiled eggs into slices. Spread them with 1 teaspoon *duxelles* (q.v.). Sandwich them, two by two. Dip them in batter and deep-fry.

Egg fritters à la reine. BEIGNETS D'OEUFS À LA REINE – Make a flat, thin omelette. Allow it to cool, and then cut it into square or lozenge-shaped pieces. Put 1 tablespoon chicken purée bound with thick *Velouté sauce* (see SAUCE) mixed with chopped truffles on each piece. Sandwich the pieces, dip in batter and deep-fry.

Fish fritters (pickled or smoked fish). BEIGNETS DE POISSONS MARINÉS, FUMÉS – Prepare as described for *Anchovy fritters II.* Fritters can be made of different kinds of fish, such as herring fillets, smoked eel, sardines in oil, smoked salmon, tunny in oil, etc.

Fish, shellfish, and seafood fritters. BEIGNETS DE POISSONS, CRUSTACÉS, COQUILLAGES, FRUITS DE MER – Recipes for various kinds of fish fritters will be found under the heading HORS-D'ŒUVRE, *Hot hors-d'œuvre.*

Foie gras fritters à l'ancienne. BEIGNETS DE FOIE GRAS À L'ANCIENNE – Make thin unsweetened pancakes. Spread with *Foie gras purée* (see PURÉE) mixed with diced truffles and flavoured with brandy. Roll the pancake into scrolls. Cut these into 2 or 3 pieces. Dip in light batter and deep-fry.

Foie gras and truffle fritters. BEIGNETS DE FOIE GRAS AUX TRUFFES – Prepare a *salpicon* (q.v.) of cooked *foie gras* and truffles, blended with concentrated, Madeira-flavoured *Demi-glace sauce* (see SAUCE). Allow to cool. Divide into small pieces and wrap each in a piece of pig's caul or a very thin slice of salt pork, previously soaked in cold water. Dip in batter and deep-fry. Serve with *Périgueux sauce* (see SAUCE).

Jerusalem artichoke fritters. BEIGNETS DE TOPINAMBOURS – Cook, marinate, dip in batter, and deep-fry.

Meat fritters. BEIGNETS DE SALPICONS DE VIANDES – Prepare a meat *salpicon* and blend with a sauce, white or brown, depending on the type of meat chosen (cooked meat left-overs – lamb, beef, mutton, pork, veal, poultry). Add diced truffles and mushrooms. Spread on a metal sheet and allow to cool. Divide into small pieces, roll each into a ball, dip in batter and deep-fry.

Calf's mesentery fritters. BEIGNETS DE FRAISE DE VEAU – Cook the calf's mesentery in a *court-bouillon* (q.v.), drain, dry, marinate, and prepare like *Brain fritters.*

Mushroom fritters. BEIGNETS DE CHAMPIGNONS – Prepare a *salpicon* of mushrooms, adding diced ham if desired. Blend with *Béchamel sauce* (see SAUCE), divide into small pieces, roll into balls, dip in batter, and deep-fry.

Oyster fritters à la normande – See OYSTERS.

Potato fritters I. BEIGNETS DE POMMES DE TERRE – Bind a *salpicon* of boiled potatoes with *Béchamel sauce* (see SAUCE). Spread on a dish and leave until cold. Divide into small pieces and shape into balls. Dip in a light batter and fry in deep-fat.

Potato fritters II. BEIGNETS DE POMMES DE TERRE – Grate or mince raw potatoes, dry well, and season with salt, pepper, and grated nutmeg. Bind with egg yolks. Divide into small pieces, dip in a light batter, and deep-fry.

Salsify fritters. BEIGNETS DE SALSIFIS – Cook the salsify, cut into little pieces, marinate, dip in batter, and deep-fry.

Sorrel fritters. BEIGNETS D'OSEILLE – As for *Spinach fritters* (see below).

Spinach fritters I. BEIGNETS D'ÉPINARDS – Steep spinach leaves for a few minutes in oil, lemon juice, salt, and pepper. Press four leaves together at a time, dip them in light batter, and deep-fry.

Spinach fritters II. BEIGNETS D'ÉPINARDS – Prepare a *Quenelle forcemeat* (see FORCEMEAT) and put a thin layer on large spinach leaves, previously steeped in oil, lemon juice, salt, and pepper. Roll up, dip in batter, and deep-fry.

Sweetbread fritters (lamb's or calf's). BEIGNETS DE RIS D'AGNEAU. DE VEAU – Braise the sweetbreads in a *court-bouillon.* Marinate them for 30 minutes in oil, lemon juice, and chopped parsley. Dip in batter and deep-fry.

Tomato fritters. BEIGNETS DE TOMATES – Cut tomatoes into quarters, remove seeds, marinate, dip in batter, deep-fry.

Tongue fritters (ox or calf's). BEIGNETS DE LANGUE DE BOEUF, DE VEAU – Cook and cool the tongue and cut into small slices. Marinate, dip in batter, and deep-fry.

Truffle fritters. BEIGNETS DE TRUFFES – Cut raw truffles into thick slices and steep in brandy with salt, pepper, and spices. Dip in batter and deep-fry.

Vegetable-marrow (squash) fritters – See HORS-D'ŒUVRE, *Hot hors-d'œuvre.*

Vine tendril fritters. BEIGNETS DE VRILLES DE VIGNE – Steep the tendrils in oil, lemon, salt, and pepper. Taking a few at a time, dip in batter and deep fry.

SWEET (DESSERT) FRITTERS. BEIGNETS D'ENTREMETS –

Acacia blossom fritters. BEIGNETS D'ACACIA – Cut off the stalks, sprinkle the bunches of blossoms with sugar, pour over a little rum or brandy, and leave to steep for 30 minutes. Dip in batter and fry in deep, sizzling-hot fat. Drain, sprinkle with sugar and serve on a paper doyley.

Apple fritters. BEIGNETS DE POMMES – Core the apples and peel them. Cut them across in slices about 5 mm. ($\frac{1}{4}$ inch) thick. Steep for 30 minutes in brandy, kirsch or rum. Drain, dip in batter, and deep-fry. Drain, put on a baking tray, sprinkle with fine sugar, and glaze in a very hot oven.

Apricot fritters. BEIGNETS D'ABRICOTS – Halve the apricots and steep in sugar and liqueur.

Finish cooking as described in the recipe for *Crystallised fruit fritters* (see below).

Banana fritters. BEIGNETS DE BANANES – Peel the bananas and divide in half lengthways. Steep in sugar and liqueur.

Finish as described in the recipe for *Crystallised fruit fritters* (see below).

Blossom and flower fritters. BEIGNETS DE FLEURS – Divide acacia, elder, and marrow blossoms, lilies and violets, into bunches, or, depending on their nature, snip off stalks and separate into petals. Steep in sugar and liqueur for 30 minutes, and finish cooking as described in the recipe for *Acacia blossom fritters.*

Cherry fritters. BEIGNETS DE CERISES – Stone the cherries. Steep them in sugar and kirsch or cherry brandy.

Finish as described in the recipe for *Fresh fruit fritters* (see below).

Cherry soufflé fritters. BEIGNETS SOUFFLÉS AUX CERISES – Make the fritters as described in the recipe for *Soufflé fritters I* (see below). After cooking, garnish with stoned cherries cooked in syrup combined with a little cherry jam and flavoured with kirsch.

Chestnut fritters. BEIGNETS DE MARRONS – Prepare vanilla-flavoured *Chestnut purée* (see CHESTNUT). Taking pieces the size of a walnut, wrap them in leaves of unleavened bread (Matzos) dipped in water. Dip in batter and finish as described in the recipe for *Fresh fruit fritters* (see below).

Cold fritters, called Krapfuns. BEIGNETS FROIDS, DITS KRAPFUNS – Prepare and deep-fry the fritters as described in the recipe for *Vienna fritters* (see below).

As soon as they are cooked, drain them and drop into a hot, light syrup, flavoured as desired. When they are well steeped, strain and serve cold.

La marchande de beignets. Painting by Gerard Dou

Cream fritters. BEIGNETS DE CRÈME – Prepare a *Custard cream* (see CREAMS). Spread on a buttered metal baking sheet in a layer 2 cm. ($\frac{3}{4}$ inch) thick. Leave to cool.

Dip in batter and finish off as described in the recipes for *Crystallised fruit fritters* or *Fresh fruit fritters* (see below). Cream fritters are sometimes coated with egg and bread-crumbs before frying. In that case they go into the category of croquettes. They are also called fried creams.

Fritters à la créole. BEIGNETS À LA CRÉOLE – Slit and stone dates, and stuff them with sweetened rice mixed with finely chopped orange peel and flavoured with Curaçao.

Wrap each date in a very thin piece of *Vienna fritter dough.* Proceed as described in the recipe for *Vienna fritters* (see below).

Fritters à la Creppazi. BEIGNETS À LA CREPPAZI – Prepare large, thin, sweet pancakes (see CRÊPE). Coat with a light layer of *French pastry cream* (see CREAMS) flavoured with kirsch and mixed with crushed macaroons.

Put the pancakes on top of each other until the layer is about 5 mm ($\frac{1}{4}$ inch) thick. Cut into 5-cm. (2-inch) square pieces, dip in batter and finish as described in the recipe for *Fresh fruit fritters* (see below).

Crystallised fruit fritters. BEIGNETS DE FRUITS GLACÉS – Cut up peeled apricots, pineapple, peaches, pears, and apples, into slices.

Dust with sugar, sprinkle with brandy, kirsch, rum, or any other liqueur, and leave to steep for 30 minutes. Drain, dry, dip in batter, and deep-fry in smoking-hot fat.

Drain, dry in a cloth, arrange on a baking tray, sprinkle with fine sugar, and glaze either in a very hot oven or under a grill.

Currant fritters. BEIGNETS DE GROSEILLES – As *Strawberry fritters* (see below).

Date fritters. BEIGNETS DE DATTES – Stuff stoned dates with very thick *French pastry cream* (see CREAMS), flavoured with kirsch or some other liqueur.

Dip in light batter and deep-dry. Drain the fritters and dust with fine sugar.

Fig fritters. BEIGNETS DE FIGUES – Peel and quarter the figs. Steep them for 30 minutes in brandy and sugar. Dip in light batter and deep-fry.

Fresh fruit fritters. BEIGNETS DE FRUITS NON GLACÉS – Use cherries, strawberries, raspberries, redcurrants, tangerines, and oranges. Stone and hull the berries, and divide the oranges and tangerines into segments.

Sprinkle with sugar and leave to steep in liqueur for 30 minutes. Drain, dip in batter, and deep-fry. Drain, dry, and sprinkle with fine sugar.

Fruit jelly fritters I. BEIGNETS DE MARMELADES – Spread the jelly in a thin layer on a moist baking sheet. Cool. Cut into shapes and finish as described in the recipe for *Fresh fruit fritters.*

Fruit jelly fritters II. BEIGNETS DE MARMELADES – Wrap the fruit jelly in pieces of unleavened bread (Matzos) soaked in water.

Finish as described in the recipe for *Fresh fruit fritters.*

Mont-Bry fritters. BEIGNETS MONT-BRY – Prepare sweetened semolina as for a dessert and spread it on a buttered metal sheet in a layer 1 cm. ($\frac{1}{2}$ inch) thick.

Cool and cut into small rectangles. Coat with thick apricot jam mixed with a fine *salpicon* of walnuts and figs, and flavoured with rum. Dip in batter and deep-fry.

Nanette fritters. BEIGNETS NANETTE – Cut a stale brioche into slices. Spread with *French pastry cream* (see CREAMS) mixed with a *salpicon* of crystallised fruit steeped in kirsch. Sandwich the slices and steep in kirsch.

Dip in a light batter and finish as described in the recipe for *Crystallised fruit fritters* or *Fresh fruit fritters.*

Peach fritters. BEIGNETS DE PÊCHES – Divide ripe peaches in half, peel, and sprinkle with sugar and kirsch, rum, or brandy. Leave to steep in a cool place for 1 hour.

Dry, dip in batter, and fry in very hot deep fat. Drain the fritters, put them on a baking tray, sprinkle with fine sugar, and glaze in a hot oven.

Pear fritters. BEIGNETS DE POIRES – Proceed as described in the recipe for *Apple fritters.*

Pineapple fritters. BEIGNETS D'ANANAS – Cut the pineapple in slices, divide each slice in half, sprinkle with sugar, and steep in liqueur.

Finish as described in the recipe for *Crystallised fruit fritters.*

Plum fritters. BEIGNETS DE PRUNES – Steep halved greengages or plums for 1 hour in kirsch, brandy, or rum, and sugar.

Drain, dip in batter, and fry in deep fat.

Drain the fritters. Sprinkle with fine sugar and glaze in a hot oven. They may also be prepared without glazing.

Plum fritters à l'agenaise. BEIGNETS DE PRUNES À L'AGENAISE – Soak stoned, halved greengages in liqueur and sugar, stick them together to make whole fruit again, and coat with kirsch-flavoured plum purée. Dip in batter, fry in deep fat, and sprinkle with fine sugar.

Polenta fritters. BEIGNETS DE POLENTA – Using sweetened polenta cooked in milk, prepare as *Rice fritters* (see below).

Raspberry fritters. BEIGNETS DE FRAMBOISES – Remove stems, sugar lightly, and sprinkle with a little kirsch. Drain, dip in batter, and fry in very hot fat. Drain, sprinkle with sugar, and serve.

Rice fritters. BEIGNETS DE RIZ – Prepare sweetened rice, as for a dessert course. Spread in a thick layer on a flat tin, and cool. Cut into small pieces. Dip in light batter and finish off as described in the recipe for *Cream fritters.*

Rice fritters with various fillings. BEIGNETS DE RIZ FOURRÉS – Prepare the fritters as described in the preceding recipe, filling them with jam, jelly or a *salpicon* of various fruit.

Rice cream fritters. BEIGNETS DE RIZ À LA CRÈME – Prepare sweetened rice, spread it in a layer on a flat tin, and leave to cool. Cut into round pieces 4 cm. ($1\frac{1}{2}$ inches) in diameter. Sandwich these circlets together with a layer of a rather thick *French pastry cream* (see CREAMS).

Dip in batter and fry in very hot fat. Drain, and sprinkle with sugar.

Semolina fritters. BEIGNETS DE SEMOULE – Prepare sweetened semolina and proceed as described in the recipe for *Rice fritters.*

Shrove-Tuesday fritters (Alsatian cookery). BEIGNETS DE MARDI-GRAS – Prepare a noodle paste with the addition of butter. Roll out to a thickness of 5 mm. ($\frac{1}{4}$ inch). Cut into shapes with a pastry cutter, and deep fry in sizzling oil, drain. Sprinkle with sugar mixed with cinnamon.

Soufflé fritters (*Larousse*)

Soufflé fritters I (or Pets de nonne). BEIGNETS SOUFFLÉS (PETS DE NONNE) – Mix 1 litre ($1\frac{3}{4}$ pints, generous quart) water, 200 g. (7 oz., scant cup) butter, $1\frac{1}{2}$ teaspoons salt, and 100 g. (4 oz., $\frac{1}{2}$ cup) sugar and bring to the boil, in a saucepan. Remove from the heat. Pour in 625 g. (1 lb. 6 oz., $5\frac{1}{2}$ cups) sieved flour. Mix well. Put the saucepan back on the heat, stirring with a wooden spoon until the mixture comes away from the sides of the saucepan and becomes slightly oily. Remove from heat and add 12 eggs, one at a time, stirring vigorously.

Drop spoonfuls of the paste, one at a time, into hot, but not boiling, deep fat, then gradually increase the temperature of the fat.

When the fritters are golden, remove them from the fat and sprinkle with fine sugar. Fill as indicated in individual recipes, with various custards, creams, jams, etc.

Soufflé fritters II. BEIGNETS SOUFFLÉS – Prepare 250 g. (9 oz.) *Chou paste* (see DOUGH) without sugar. Divide the paste into portions the size of a small walnut. Drop one after the other into hot but not boiling fat.

Cook until the paste has risen and the fritters are crisp on the outside and golden coloured. Drain well on a cloth, and season.

Strawberry fritters. BEIGNETS DE FRAISES – Hull the strawberries and steep them in liqueur. Finish as described in the recipe for *Fresh fruit fritters.*

Stuffed fritters, called surprise fritters. BEIGNETS FOURRÉS, EN SURPRISE – Prepare the fritters as described in the recipe for *Soufflé fritters II.*

Drain, make a small slit on the side and fill them, using a forcing-bag, with *French pastry cream* (see CREAMS), jam, fruit purée or *salpicon,* as indicated.

Tangerine or orange fritters. BEIGNETS DE MANDARINES, D'ORANGES – Divide the tangerines or oranges into sections, trim them, steep in sugar and liqueur and finish as described in the recipe for *Fresh fruit fritters.*

Vienna fritters or Dauphine fritters. BEIGNETS VIENNOIS, BEIGNETS DAUPHINE – *Ingredients.* 500 g. (18 oz., $4\frac{1}{2}$ cups) sieved flour, 200 g. (7 oz., scant cup) butter, 6 eggs, 20 g. ($\frac{2}{3}$ oz., 1 cake) yeast, $2\frac{1}{2}$ teaspoons salt, 25 g. (1 oz., 2 tablespoons) sugar, 1 dl. (6 tablespoons, scant $\frac{1}{2}$ cup) milk.

Method. Mix the ingredients to make a paste as described in the recipe for *Brioche dough, ordinary* (see DOUGH). Roll out the pastry to a thickness of $\frac{1}{2}$-cm. ($\frac{1}{4}$-inch). Place spoonfuls of the filling indicated: cream, custard, *salpicon* of fruit, etc., regularly spaced on the pastry. Moisten the edges of the pastry and cover with a second piece of rolled-out pastry of the same size and thickness as the first. Stamp out the fritters with a round cutter, about 5 cm. (2 inches) in diameter. Lay them on a baking tray covered with a cloth sprinkled with flour. Leave to rise in a warm place for 30 minutes.

Drop the fritters into very hot deep fat and cook until they are well done and acquire a golden colour.

Drain, and sprinkle with fine sugar.

FRITTO-MISTO (Italian cookery) – In France this dish is called '*friture à l'italienne*'.

It is prepared from pieces of calves' head; brain; spinal bone-marrow (of sheep and calves); testicles; lambs' feet; rice and egg croquettes; fried bread; slices of sautéed calves' liver.

Some are dipped in flour-and-egg batter, others in egg and breadcrumbs. They are fried in deep fat or sautéed in butter. *Fritto-misto*, prepared in this way, makes an unusual and tasty luncheon dish.

FROG. GRENOUILLE – Web-footed amphibian of which there are about 20 species. Among those to be found in France are the *green* or *common frog*, the *rusty* or *mute frog*, so-called because the male has no voice-box. In the United States there is a very large species called the *bull frog* or *bellowing frog*. This creature is twice the size of the types indigenous to Europe.

Frog meat, which is no more than a titbit, is easily digestible.

The frogs eaten in France usually come from central Europe. They are very muscular, and plumper than the local varieties, but French frogs, especially those of Sologne and the Dombes, have more delicate flesh and a subtler flavour. The quality of the frogs of the Dombes fully justifies their being more expensive.

Preparation. Skin the frogs and remove the breast, retaining only the legs, which alone are edible. Cut off the feet. Skewer the legs and immerse them in very cold water. Change the water every 2 hours to whiten and swell the flesh. Dry the legs thus prepared and cook them according to one or other of the recipes set out below. Usually 3 pairs per serving are allowed.

Frogs' legs à l'anglaise. GRENOUILLES À L'ANGLAISE – Season the frogs' legs with salt and pepper. Flour them and dip in egg and breadcrumbs. Sauté in butter. Arrange them on a bed of *Maître d'hôtel butter* (see BUTTER, *Compound butters*). Serve with boiled potatoes.

This dish is called *à l'anglaise*, because this is the name given to food which is dipped in egg and breadcrumbs and then fried.

Frogs' legs à la béchamel. GRENOUILLES À LA BÉCHAMEL – Season the frogs' legs with salt and pepper. Put them in a frying pan with a little butter and 1 tablespoon white wine. Cover, and cook over a high flame.

Add a few tablespoons thick *Béchamel sauce* (see SAUCE) mixed with some fresh cream. Simmer for a few moments. Add 1 tablespoon butter.

Frogs' legs as a border, au gratin. GRENOUILLES EN BORDURES, GRATINÉES – Prepared like *Frogs' legs à la Mornay* (see below), but served as a garnish.

Frogs' legs in cream. GRENOUILLES À LA CRÈME – Cook the frogs' legs as for *Frogs' legs à la béchamel.* Boil some fresh cream and pour over the frogs' legs. Boil down and serve.

Curried frogs' legs. GRENOUILLES À L'INDIENNE – Sauté the frogs' legs in butter. Serve them in a border of curried rice, with *Curry sauce* (see SAUCE) poured over.

Fried frogs' legs. GRENOUILLES FRITES – Soak the frogs' legs in a marinade for 30 minutes, as for *Frogs' legs fritters* (see HORS-D'ŒUVRE, *Hot hors-d'œuvre*), and proceed in the same way as for that recipe.

The frogs' legs may also be dipped in flour and fried in the usual way.

Frogs' legs fritters. BEIGNETS DE GRENOUILLES – See HORS-D'ŒUVRE, *Hot hors-d'œuvre*.

Frogs' legs à la lyonnaise. GRENOUILLES À LA LYONNAISE – Season the frogs' legs and dip them in flour. Sauté in butter over a very high flame. When they are well browned, add 2 tablespoons (3 tablespoons) finely chopped onion lightly browned in butter. Sauté the frogs' legs and onions together. Sprinkle with chopped parsley. Serve with a sauce made by heating a little vinegar in the cooking butter.

Frogs' legs à la meunière. GRENOUILLES À LA MEUNIÈRE – Season and flour the frogs' legs, and sauté them in butter. Arrange them in a serving dish and sprinkle with chopped parsley. Squeeze a few drops of lemon juice over and pour on the cooking butter, which has been heated until it turns brown. If necessary, add a little fresh butter. Serve at once.

Frogs' legs à la Mirepoix. GRENOUILLES À LA MIREPOIX – Season and flour the frogs' legs, and sauté in butter. When they are cooked, add 2 tablespoons (3 tablespoons) vegetable *mirepoix* (q.v.) which has been slowly cooked in butter until tender.

Cook over a very high flame and mix well. To serve pour 2 tablespoons (3 tablespoons) concentrated meat stock over the mixture and sprinkle with chopped parsley.

Frogs' legs à la Mornay. GRENOUILLES À LA MORNAY – Cook the frogs' legs gently in a little white wine, butter, and lemon juice. Drain and dry them with a cloth.

Serve them on an ovenproof dish lined with *Mornay sauce* (see SAUCE) and surrounded with a border of *Duchess potatoes* (see POTATOES). Cover with *Morney sauce* to which the pan juices have been added. Sprinkle with cheese and pour on melted butter. Brush the border with beaten egg yolk. Brown in the oven or under the grill.

Frogs' legs à la niçoise. GRENOUILLES À LA NIÇOISE – Proceed as for *Frogs' legs à la mirepoix*, substituting *Tomato fondue à la niçoise* (see TOMATO) for the *mirepoix*.

Frogs' legs with chopped parsley. GRENOUILLES AUX FINES HERBES – Season the frogs' legs with salt and pepper. Dip in flour and sauté in butter over a high flame.

When they are cooked and well browned, sprinkle with chopped parsley. Squeeze the juice of a lemon over them and pour on the butter in which they have been cooked.

Frogs' legs à la poulette. GRENOUILLES À LA POULETTE – Cook the frogs' legs gently in a little white wine, with butter and a squeeze of lemon juice. Season with salt and pepper. Add a small onion and a *bouquet garni* (q.v.). As soon as the liquid comes to the boil, add peeled, sliced mushrooms. Cover and simmer.

Drain the frogs' legs and mushrooms. Strain the stock and boil it down. Thicken with egg yolks and cream, as for *Poulette sauce* (see SAUCE). Put the frogs' legs and mushrooms back in the sauce and heat. Add 1 tablespoon fresh butter, chopped parsley, and a squeeze of lemon juice.

Frogs' legs prepared in this way can be served in a pie crust or a *vol-au-vent*. They are then called *timbales* or *vol-au-vent of frogs' legs à la poulette*.

Frogs' legs sautéed à la provençale. GRENOUILLES SAUTÉES À LA PROVENÇALE – Sauté the frogs' legs in butter or oil, as for *Frogs' legs à la lyonnaise*. Add a little crushed garlic and chopped parsley.

Citrus fruits

Dried fruits (*Larousse*)

FROMAGE D'ITALIE – Dish made from pig's liver. (See OFFAL or VARIETY MEATS.)

FROMAGE GLACÉ – In former times, plain ices moulded into conical shapes were called *fromage glacé* in France.

The name *fromage bavarois* was used for the cold sweet made from a mixture of custard and whipped cream, now called *bavarois* (see BAVARIAN CREAM).

FROMAGER–To add grated cheese to a sauce, stuffing, or any kind of dough; or to sprinkle it over food to be browned in the oven. The cheeses most commonly used for this purpose are Parmesan and Gruyère.

FROMENTEAU – Variety of table grapes.

FRONTIGNAN – Small town of the Hérault district which has given its name to a heavy type of Muscatel wine.

FRUIT – Botanically speaking, fruit is the ovary of any growing plant. In current usage, however, 'fruit' refers only to those which may be eaten as dessert.

Some fruits, in fact, are eaten as vegetables, for example, aubergines, pumpkins, marrows, gourds, cucumbers, olives, tomatoes, etc.

In terms of calories some of the commoner fruits have little food value, except for those with a high starch, oil, or sugar content. However, it is from fruit that we get, in a form which is readily assimilated, essential minerals as well as all the precious health-giving vitamins. Also, because of its water content, fruit is an excellent thirst quencher.

Dried fruit. FRUITS SECS – Included under this heading are naturally dry fruits such as almonds, hazelnuts, walnuts, etc., rich in fats and albumen. Artificially dried fruits (apricots, cherries, figs, apples, pears, prunes, raisins, etc.) are eaten without further preparation. All these provide very concentrated nourishment. When they are soaked and cooked, although they have not quite all the qualities of fresh fruit, they provide a useful substitute.

Fruit ices. GLACES AUX FRUITS – The basic syrup consists of 4 cups sugar to 2 cups of water boiled for 5 minutes and cooled. This gives an approximate density of 18° to 22° when measured on a saccharometer. To this cold syrup various fruit pulps or juices are added.

Fruit juices. SUCS (JUS) DE FRUITS – Fruit juices, obtained by cooking fruit with a little water, or by squeezing it, are very popular especially as drinks for persons suffering from feverish illnesses.

Fruit juices are also extracted commercially. Most of these are excellent, especially those sterilised by some means other than boiling. They have considerable food value, comparable with that of milk.

Fruit mould. PAIN DE FRUITS – Coat a charlotte mould with a thick layer of jelly (made of the same fruit as the mixture to be used in the centre).

When this has set, fill the middle of the mould with a fruit *bavarois* mixture (see BAVARIAN CREAM) prepared in advance but without adding any cream. Cover with a layer of jelly. Chill on ice.

Pickled fruits. FRUITS CONFITS AU VINAIGRE – Pour vinegar into glass or stone pickling jars; add enough fine sugar to turn the mixture into a syrup which is sharp without being too sour. Add the fruit to be pickled. After a few weeks the fruit will be thoroughly impregnated with the syrup and will be ready for eating.

Pickled fruit may be used for the same purpose as fruit preserved in brandy, but is more commonly served as a condiment.

Fruit salad. FRUITS RAFRAÎCHIS – *Ingredients for* 10 *people.* 6 peaches, 6 apricots, 6 greengages, 3 ripe pears, 2 apples, 4 bananas, 100 g. (4 oz., scant cup) raspberries, 100 g. (4 oz., scant cup) white and black grapes (mixed), 100 g. (4 oz., scant cup) small strawberries, 24 fresh almonds, 3 dl. ($\frac{1}{2}$ pint, $1\frac{1}{4}$ cups) kirsch and/or maraschino, 5 or 6 tablespoons fine sugar.

Method. Peel the peaches, pears, and apples and cut them into little pieces. Peel the bananas and cut them into strips. Stone the apricots and greengages and cut them up.

Mix all this fruit in a bowl. Add two-thirds of the strawberries and raspberries. Decorate with two-thirds of the grapes. Sprinkle the sugar on top and pour on the liqueur. Gentle shake the dish so that the various fruits are properly mixed. Put the bowl into a larger bowl containing crushed ice. Leave for 1 hour.

Transfer the fruit salad to a glass bowl (or a special double container). Surround with crushed ice. Decorate the top of the fruit salad with the remaining strawberries, raspberries, grapes, and blanched and halved almonds.

The ingredients of a fruit salad vary according to the season. All kinds of fruit may be used, such as pineapples, oranges, nectarines, mirabelle plums, cherries, etc. It may also be made from fruit preserved in syrup.

Instead of sweetening it with sugar, syrup may be poured

onto the fruit salad, and any liqueur may be used for flavouring. Fruit salad can be served as a dessert course or as a salad course.

Fruit salad à la créole. FRUITS RAFRAÎCHIS À LA CRÉOLE – *Macédoine* of fruit made from bananas, pineapples and oranges finely sliced, sprinkled with rum and sugar and left to stand in ice. It is served in a glass bowl (or a special double container) on a bed of pineapple ice cream. Pour on lightly whipped sweetened fresh cream flavoured with rum. Decorate the top with orange segments and blanched pistachio nuts.

Fruit salad with kirsch. FRUITS RAFRAÎCHIS AU KIRSCH – Use all the fruits in season: strawberries, cherries, peaches, apricots, grapes, almonds, etc., with stalks, stones, skins removed. Some are sliced, others left whole.

Sprinkle with sugar, mix without bruising, pour kirsch over, and place in a larger bowl full of crushed ice.

Instead of sugar, the fruit salad may be sweetened with a very heavy syrup.

Fruit salad à la maltaise. FRUITS RAFRAÎCHIS À LA MALTAISE – *Macédoine* (q.v.) of fruit made from oranges, bananas, cherries, and pineapples, left to soak with sugar and Curaçao.

Serve in a glass bowl or special double container on a bed of orange ice cream. Cover with whipped cream. Decorate with segments of orange.

Fruit salad à la normande. FRUITS RAFRAÎCHIS À LA NORMANDE – Make a *macédoine* (q.v.) of fruit from russet or tart apples, fresh pineapple, and bananas. Soak this mixture in sugar and Calvados.

Serve in a glass bowl or special double container. Cover with lightly beaten fresh cream which has been sweetened with sugar and flavoured with calvados.

Fruit salad à l'occitanienne. FRUITS RAFRAÎCHIS À L'OCCITANIENNE – Place sliced pears, black and white grapes, and peeled figs cut into slices, in a bowl. Sprinkle with sugar and pour on Blanquette de Limoux (q.v.) and a little brandy. Surround the bowl with ice mixed with a little kitchen salt, so that the fruit may be slightly congealed.

Cover with *Chantilly cream* (see CREAMS) and decorate with grapes.

Fruit salad Tsarina (Czarina). FRUITS RAFRAÎCHIS TZARINE – Put mixed fruit, whole or sliced, soaked with sugar and kummel, on top of a layer of pineapple ice cream. Cover with *Chantilly cream* (see CREAMS) flavoured with kummel. Decorate with crystallised violets and lozenge-shaped pieces of angelica.

Fruit sauces – See SAUCE, *Dessert sauces.*

Sugar-coated and marzipan fruit. FRUITS DÉGUISÉS – Small fruit (strawberries, blackcurrants, cherries, gooseberries, plums, etc.), either fresh or preserved in brandy, coated with *Fondant icing* (see ICING).

Marzipan fruits are a kind of *petit four* (q.v.) made from very thick fruit purée mixed with almond paste, or sometimes with concentrated jam. These are moulded into the shape of various fruits and covered with caramel sugar.

FRUIT IN DIETETICS – The discovery of vitamins has highlighted the importance of fruit in the diet. It must be borne in mind, however, that digestive upsets frequently occur when raw fruit is eaten in conjunction with a meat diet.

Fruit salad

Fruit contains the following elements in variable proportions:

- Water (85 per cent average for juicy fruit).
- Organic acids (principally malic and citric acids).
- Carbohydrates.
- Proteic substances.
- Practically no lipids except in olives, almonds, and walnuts.
- Mineral salts.
- Vitamins.
- Aromatic essences (which give each fruit its particular flavour).

FRUITARIAN. FRUGIVORE – A person who lives exclusively on fruit and vegetables, believing that man should feed only on that which can be eaten in the natural state in which it grows.

FRUITERY. FRUITERIE, FRUITIÈRE – Special storage place for fruit. *Fruitière* is the name given to a cheese factory usually situated in the mountains near pastures.

FRUIT KERNEL. NOYAU – Soft part within hard shell of nut or stone fruit.

Fruit kernel liqueur. CRÈME DE NOYAUX – Liqueur which has fruit kernels as a basis. (See LIQUEUR.)

FRUIT STONE CRACKER. ÉNOYAUTEUR – Implement for cracking the stones of certain fruits, such as cherries, without crushing them completely.

FRUMENTY. FROMENTÉE – Porridge made from wheat flour.

FRYING – See DEEP FRYING; CULINARY METHODS, *Sautés.*

FRYING PAN. POÊLE – Shallow pan with a long handle, used for frying food.

A fish frying pan is oval in shape, and a pan for roasting chestnuts is perforated on the bottom.

FUCHSINE – Dye sold in the form of purple scales, rather sweet in taste and somewhat unpleasant in smell. It is sometimes used as artificial colouring for wines and foodstuffs.

FULBERT-DUMONTEIL – Jean-Camille Fulbert-Dumonteil was a French writer and a great gastronome. Born at Vergt in the Dordogne in 1830, he wrote charming articles on the art of cookery which were published in the form of a chronicle in various journals, notably the old *Figaro*. These were collected in one volume under the title *la France gourmande*.

FUMET – Name given to a number of different liquids which are used to flavour or give body to stocks and sauces. *Fumets* are prepared by boiling foodstuffs of one kind or another either in stock or in wine.

Fumets should not be confused with essences, extracts, or concentrates.

Chicken fumet. FUMET DE VOLAILLE – Chicken broth, made by boiling down chicken stock (see STOCKS).

This fumet is used to add flavour to various poultry dishes which are served with a sauce.

Fish fumet. FUMET DE POISSON – Stock made from the bones and trimmings of fish, the flesh being prepared separately. This fish stock is very much boiled down. It is used with white wine in the cooking of certain fish, and also in the preparation of special white or brown fish sauces.

For the preparation of fish *fumet*, see STOCKS.

Game fumet. FUMET DE GIBIER – Game stock made with the carcases and trimmings of different game boiled down to a concentrated consistency.

Mushroom fumet. FUMET DE CHAMPIGNONS – This *fumet* is prepared by almost completely reducing the cooking liquid of cultivated mushrooms. It is used to improve the flavour of certain sauces.

Pâté fumet – See PÂTÉ.

Truffle fumet. FUMET DE TRUFFES – *Fumet* used to enhance the flavour of certain sauces. Truffle peelings are simmered in Madeira or any heavy wine. The *fumet* is usually made when the truffles themselves are being used for some other purpose.

Vegetable fumet. FUMET DE LÉGUMES – This *fumet* is prepared by almost completely reducing a stock made from a variety of vegetables such as carrots, onions, leeks, celery, etc.

GADELLE – Name used in western France for the red-currant, which is called *gade* in Normandy.

GAILLAC – The white wines of this small town in the Tarn district enjoy a wide reputation. Some are sold in Paris as young wines; others are processed like Champagne and become *perlant*, *pétillant*, or *mousseux*, according to how 'bubbly' they are.

The vineyards of Gaillac (*French Government Tourist Office*)

GALANTINE – Dish made from boned poultry or meat, stuffed, and pressed into a symmetrical shape. Galantines are cooked in a gelatine stock.

The term probably derives from the words *géline* or *galine* which in old French meant chicken, for this dish was first made with poultry, and later, towards the end of the seventeenth century, with other types of bird, cuts of meat, and even fish. A *sous-presse* of fish was a form of galantine.

Nowadays, galantines are made from other meats besides poultry, but strictly the word 'galantine' without qualification denotes galantine of poultry.

There are many ways of preparing this cold dish.

Galantine of chicken I (Carême's recipe). GALANTINE DE POULARDE À LA GELÉE – *The forcemeat*. 'Chop 250 g. (9 oz.) veal with 500 g. (18 oz.) fat bacon and 225 g. (8 oz.) cooked ham. Mix in 4 teaspoons *Spiced salt* (see SALT), 2 egg yolks, and 2 tablespoons (3 tablespoons) chopped herbs with the same quantity of truffles. Mix well and place in an earthenware dish.

'Peel 750 g. ($1\frac{3}{4}$ lb.) very ripe truffles. Cut each truffle into quarters. Take a good red pickled tongue. Skin it and cut it lengthwise into 6 slices. Cut 500 g. (18 oz.) raw fat ham into thick fingers or use fresh pork fat or calf's udder.

The chicken. 'Singe, pluck, and bone a medium-sized plump chicken, and open it out on a cloth. Cut away half the meat of the breast and thighs. Use the pieces thus removed to line the bird wherever there is so little flesh that the skin is almost showing through, so that the flesh may be evenly distributed. Season with an appropriate amount of spiced salt, that is 2 teaspoons spiced salt per 500 g. (1 lb.) boned flesh.

'Spread half the forcemeat on the chicken, and lay half the truffles, tongue, and ham fat on top, making sure that the colours present a mottled effect. Season lightly with spiced salt. Cover the whole with half the remaining forcemeat and lay on top the truffles, the fat, and the pickled tongue, with a little added seasoning. Cover with the remaining forcemeat.

'Now fold the chicken back to its original shape, sewing it up with a trussing needle so that all the garnish is contained in the bird, which should be moulded into a round or slightly oval shape.

'Wrap slices of fat bacon round the chicken. Fold a piece of muslin round the whole, tying both ends tightly with string. Tie a piece of string round the middle to keep it in shape.

'Brown strips of fat bacon in a casserole. Place the galantine in it and surround with 4 onions, 4 carrots, a large bunch of parsley and spring onions. Season with thyme, laurel, basil and 4 cloves. Add the bones of the chicken, and 4 knuckles of veal or 2 calf's feet, enough stock or chicken broth to cover the galantine, then 1 glass dry Madeira or good white wine and 2 tablespoons (3 tablespoons) old brandy. Cover the whole with a piece of buttered paper and start to cook over a high flame. Then simmer slowly for 3 hours and remove from the stove.

'An hour later, carefully lift the galantine out of the casserole. Lay it breast downwards on a slightly curved earthenware platter and squeeze it gently, still wrapped in the muslin, to remove any moisture left in it.

'Cover with a lid and place on top a $3\frac{1}{2}$ kg. (8 lb.) weight, in order to flatten and spread the chicken.

'Next, strain the jelly through a fine sieve. Remove all fat and leave it to settle for 15 minutes. Clarify by one of the methods described under JELLY.

'When the galantine is cold, uncover it, dry it gently with a cloth, and remove all string. Cover it very carefully all over with a white glaze.

'Place on an *entrée* dish. Arrange a rosette of jelly on the top, surround with chopped jelly and then with rounds of jelly cut with a pastry cutter 1 cm. ($\frac{1}{2}$ inch) in diameter, and serve.'

Galantine of chicken II. GALANTINE DE POULARDE – *For the galantine.* 1 chicken, weighing 2 kg. ($4\frac{1}{2}$ lb.), 250 g. (9 oz.) finely minced pork, 250 g. (9 oz.) finely minced veal, 150 g. (5 oz.) each of fat bacon, lean cooked ham, and pickled tongue, 150 g. (5 oz.) truffles, 25 g. (1 oz., $\frac{1}{4}$ cup) pistachio nuts, 1 dl. (6 tablespoons, scant $\frac{1}{2}$ cup) brandy, 2 eggs, salt, pepper, spices.

For the stock or jelly. 2 calf's feet, 500 g. (18 oz.) fresh bacon rind, $2\frac{1}{2}$ kg. ($5\frac{1}{2}$ lb.) fleshy knuckle of veal, 2 carrots, 1 onion, 2 leeks, 1 *bouquet garni* (q.v.), 5 litres ($4\frac{1}{2}$ quarts, $5\frac{1}{2}$ quarts) white stock, 4 dl. ($\frac{3}{4}$ pint, scant 2 cups) Madeira, salt.

Singe and pluck the bird. Remove the feet and pinions. Slit the chicken along the back and with a small very sharp knife bone it without tearing the flesh. (This operation, which at first sight seems awkward, is actually fairly simple. It is necessary only to follow the joints of the chicken and to work inwards towards the carcase, shaving off the flesh as close to the bone as possible. This first boning operation separates the carcase from the body of the chicken, leaving them both whole.) Now remove the bones from the legs and wings, still being careful not to tear the skin.

Spread out the bird on the table and cut away the breast and the greater part of the fleshy portions of thighs and wings. Cut these pieces into squares, which will be used for the *salpicon* (q.v.) or meat *ragoût* in which the galantine is served.

The forcemeat. This is made of finely chopped lean pork and veal in equal quantities.

Pound in a mortar, seasoning it with salt, pepper, and spices. (To obtain a very fine forcemeat, rub the mixture, after pounding, through a sieve.)

The salpicon. Place in an earthenware dish the lean pieces cut away from the chicken, the fat bacon, the cooked lean ham, and the pickled tongue (all cut into squares), the diced truffles, and the blanched pistachio nuts. Add the forcemeat, the 2 eggs and the brandy. Mix thoroughly, adding seasoning if necessary.

Preparation of the galantine. Knead all the forcemeat into a ball and lay it on the chicken, which should be well spread out on the table. (From time to time, the hands should be dipped in water to make it easier to work the forcemeat.) Spread the forcemeat evenly over the chicken, forming it into a rectangular shape. Fold over the parts of the chicken skin which project at the sides and ends.

Dip a coarse linen cloth in water and wring it out, then spread it flat on the table. Place it so that a flap about 25 cm. (10 inches) wide hangs over the edge of the table. Place the galantine lengthwise on this cloth, about 10 cm. (4 inches) from the edge of the table, breast upwards. Wrap the galantine in the cloth as tightly as possible. Tie both ends of the cloth securely. Tie the galantine with string in 3 places to keep it in shape.

Method of cooking. The stock is made from the ingredients listed above. For the method of preparation see JELLY. To the ingredients listed, add the carcase and giblets of the chicken, with the exception of the liver.

Cook the stock for $1\frac{1}{2}$ hours, then lay the galantine in the stock and simmer gently for $1\frac{3}{4}$ hours. Remove the galantine. Let it stand for 15 minutes before unwrapping it. Remove the cloth, rinse in lukewarm water and wring thoroughly. Spread it on the table and carefully wrap the galantine in it as before, taking care to keep the slit part of the chicken underneath. Tie up the galantine. Press it on a slab, covering it with a wooden board with a weight on top. Allow to cool for at least 12 hours.

It can be kept for several days if it is stored in a cool place.

The galantine is served garnished with its own jelly, which must be clarified by the usual method (see JELLY).

OTHER GALANTINES – Galantines of other poultry may be prepared by the same method as that indicated for galantine of chicken. Galantines may also be made of various game birds such as pheasant, partridge, grouse, hazel-grouse, etc., altering the ingredients of the stuffing.

The recipes for the various galantines are given in alphabetical order under the name of each game bird.

Galantines may be prepared according to the method used by pork butchers. Instead of being wrapped in a cloth, they are put in special rectangular metal or earthenware moulds. To improve the flavour of these galantines, a certain amount of *foie gras* may be added to the stuffing. Diced *foie gras* may also be added to the *salpicon*.

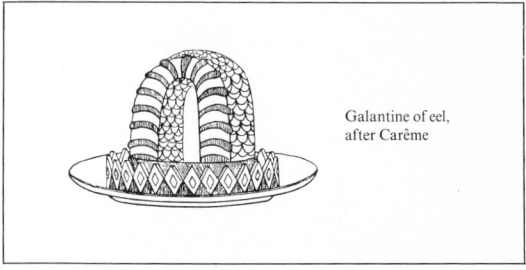

Galantine of eel, after Carême

Galantine of jellied eels. GALANTINE D'ANGUILLE À LA GELÉE – Prepare the eel according to the instructions for *Cold ballottine of eel* (see EEL). Cook it in a fish stock, drain, and allow to cool under a weight. Unwrap the galantine and cover with the half-set jelly. Place it on a long dish, and garnish with chopped jelly made from the eel stock.

GALATHÉE – Species of shellfish similar to freshwater crayfish. The parent species of this shellfish, the *galathée grêle*, is common on the European shores of the Atlantic and in the Mediterranean. *Galathée* is prepared as indicated for lobster (q.v.) and crayfish (q.v.).

GALAZYME, GALACTOZYME – Frothy milk, slightly fermented and with a very small alcoholic content. (See KÉFIR.)

GALETTE (French Twelfth-Night cake) – Cake made from flaky pastry. The galette is the symbolic cake eaten on Twelfth Night in most of the provinces north of the Loire, notably in the region of Paris.

South of the Loire, especially in the south of France, the Twelfth-Night cake is made from yeast dough in the form of a crown. In both cakes, the symbolic bean is baked in the dough. This is not always, as it used to be, a real bean, but is sometimes a small porcelain model either of a baby emerging from a bean or of some other figure. (See FESTIVE COOKERY.)

Flaky pastry galette. GALETTE FEUILLETÉE – Roll out flat some flaky pastry dough and cut from it a round piece 15 to 18 cm. (6 to 7 inches) in diameter. Place this on a slab. Crimp the edges and brush over with egg; mark out the top in lozenge-shaped segments. Bake in a hot oven.

Small orange galettes. PETITES GALETTES ORANGINES – Sieve 250 g. (9 oz., $2\frac{1}{4}$ cups) flour onto a table. In the centre place 125 g. ($4\frac{1}{2}$ oz., generous $\frac{1}{2}$ cup) sugar, 150 g. (5 oz., 10 tablespoons) butter, a pinch of salt, the zest of 2 oranges rubbed on

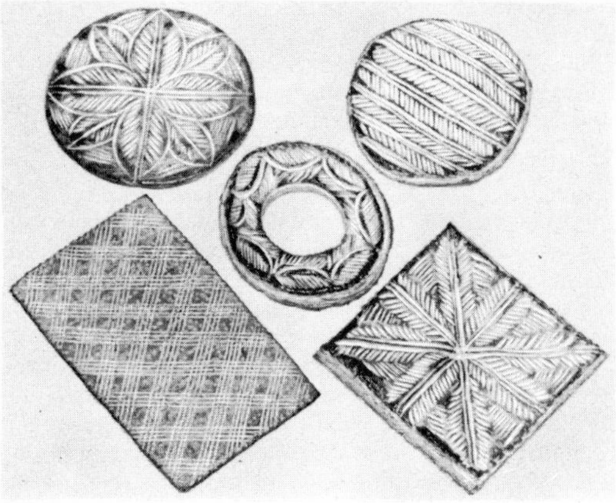

Flaky pastry galettes (*Scarnati*)

lumps of sugar and 6 egg yolks. Mix and work the flour into the mixture. Knead into a ball and allow it to stand for a few hours in a cool place.

Roll out the dough to a thickness of $\frac{1}{2}$ cm. ($\frac{1}{4}$ inch). Cut into rounds with a fluted cutter 5 cm. (2 inches) in diameter. Place them on a buttered baking sheet, brush with egg beaten with a pinch of sugar, and bake in a hot oven for 6 to 8 minutes.

Galette de plomb – *Ingredients.* 300 g. (11 oz., $2\frac{3}{4}$ cups) sieved flour, 200 g. (7 oz., scant cup) butter, 1 whole egg, 1 yolk, 1 teaspoon fine sugar, 2 teaspoons table salt, 1 to 2 tablespoons milk or cream.

Method. Sieve the flour onto a marble slab or table, and make a well in the centre. Dissolve the salt and sugar in 1 tablespoon milk or cream and pour into the well. Knead the butter until it is malleable, cut it up into very small pieces and dot these about in the circle of flour.

Work the butter and the flour until the mixture is very short. This is done by rubbing the hands together with the mixture of flour and butter between them. Continue to shorten the dough in this way until the butter is entirely broken up into very small particles. Spread out the dough. Beat the egg and yolk as for an omelette and pour over the dough. Work it in the same way as before, pressing the hands more and more tightly together as the kneading proceeds.

The ingredients in the dough should moisten it sufficiently to hold it together. The pastry should be fairly limp. If it is a little too firm, add a second tablespoon milk or cream. (The amount of moistening required may vary with the type of flour used.)

When the dough is thoroughly kneaded, cover with a damp cloth, and put it in a cool place for 30 minutes. Then flatten it on the table with the palm of the hand, flour it lightly, and fold into three. Roll into a ball. Flatten it into a round shape about $2\frac{1}{2}$ cm. (1 inch) thick. Crimp the edges with the back of a knife.

Place on a lightly buttered baking sheet and surround with a buttered tart ring. Brush the top with the beaten egg and trace on it either lozenges or rosettes. This last is the characteristic design for the *Galette de plomb*.

Bake for 20 to 25 minutes in a moderate oven. The *Galette de plomb* is eaten lukewarm or cold.

Potato galettes. GALETTES DE POMMES DE TERRE – These can be made either with potatoes prepared as for *Duchess potatoes* (see POTATOES) or with potatoes cut into thin discs. They are used as a garnish for various dishes, and are sometimes served topped with small pieces of meat, poultry, or fish.

Rich galette. GALETTE FONDANTE – *Ingredients.* 300 g. (11 oz., $2\frac{3}{4}$ cups) flour, 250 g. (9 oz., generous cup) butter, 1 egg and 1 yolk, 1 teaspoon salt, 25 g. (1 oz., 2 tablespoons) sugar, 1 dl. (6 tablespoons, scant $\frac{1}{2}$ cup) fresh cream, vanilla.

Work the flour with 50 g. (2 oz., $\frac{1}{4}$ cup) of the butter, then add the eggs, cream, salt, vanilla, and sugar. Leave to stand for 10 minutes.

Knead the dough and add the remaining butter. Roll out and fold the dough 4 times as is done for *Flaky pastry* (see DOUGH). Brush with egg and lattice it with a knife. Cook in a hot oven and sprinkle, while hot, with powdered sugar.

Savoury galettes. GALETTES SALÉES – Knead 250 g. (9 oz., $2\frac{1}{4}$ cups) sieved flour with 150 g. (5 oz., 10 tablespoons) butter, 8 tablespoons ($\frac{2}{3}$ cup) cold milk and $1\frac{1}{2}$ teaspoons salt. Leave to stand for 2 hours.

Roll out very thinly on a floured table, prick with a fork and cut into rounds 5 cm. (2 inches) in diameter. Place them on a buttered baking sheet and brush with milk to which salt has been added. Bake in a hot oven for 6 to 8 minutes.

As soon as the *galettes* are out of the oven, brush them again with salted milk.

GALICIEN – This sweet, which is a type of cake, was created in Paris at the old *Pâtisserie Frascati*, once situated on the corner of the boulevard de Richelieu and the rue de Richelieu. This pastry shop was built on the site of what was, during the years between 1796 and 1799 (the Directory) one of the most famous gaming-houses in Paris.

Ingredients. 500 g. (18 oz., $2\frac{1}{4}$ cups) fine sugar, 375 g. (13 oz., $3\frac{1}{4}$ cups) sifted flour, 16 eggs.

Method. Whisk the sugar and eggs in a pan, on the edge of a low flame. After the mixture has tripled in volume carefully stir in the sieved flour. Pour the mixture into a large, shallow, sloping-sided cake tin. Bake in a hot oven. Leave to cool.

Slice the cake across. Spread on each half a layer of *Butter cream* (see CREAMS) flavoured with pistachio nuts. Put the two halves together, exerting a little pressure to join them firmly. Spread the cake with apricot jam. Ice with *Pistachio icing* (see ICING) and decorate with more of the pistachio-flavoured butter cream, using a forcing-bag. Sprinkle with finely chopped pistachio nuts.

GALICHONS – Also called *calissons.* Little iced cakes made with pounded almonds, a speciality of Aix.

GALINGALE. SOUCHET – Common name of the plant *Cyperus* whose tubers are edible and known in French as *amandes de terre.*

GALL. FIEL – Secretion of the liver commonly called bile in humans. It is a very bitter greenish substance. The gall bladder is attached to the liver. In drawing poultry or winged game, the gall bladder must always be removed with the greatest care to avoid it breaking and giving a bitter flavour to the bird. Only pigeon liver contains no gall.

GALLIMAUFRY. GALIMAFRÉE – A chicken stew from mediaeval cookery. Taillevent, in his book *le Viandier*, gives the following recipe:

'For gallimaufry, take roast chickens or capons, cut them into sections, and afterwards fry them in bacon or goose fat. Add wine and verjuice, ground ginger, salt, and, to thicken it, treacle-mustard.'

Gallimaufry (old recipe) – 'Take a leg of mutton freshly cooked, and chop it as finely as possible in a dish of onions. Stew these ingredients with a little verjuice, butter, and ground white ginger, all mixed together and seasoned with salt.'

The word gallimaufry is now used in a disparaging sense, and means a badly cooked stew made from scraps.

GALL NUT. NOIX DE GALLE – Orientals eat a fleshy gall nut as big as a lady-apple that grows on a species of sage.

In other regions an edible type of gall nut grows on ground ivy.

GALLON – Liquid measure used in most English-speaking countries. It is equivalent to about $4\frac{1}{2}$ litres (U.S. gallon equals $3\frac{2}{3}$ litres).

GAMACHE – There is an episode in *Don Quixote* in which the hero and his faithful Sancho attend the wedding feast of a wealthy farmer called Gamache. The extraordinary number of dishes served at this repast has led to the word *gamache* being used to describe any similarly bountiful meal.

GAMAY – Village in Burgundy which has given its name to a vine. The *Petit gamay* is one of the most prolific vines in Burgundy. Although this vine is not of as fine a quality as the *Pinot*, Gamay grapes are much sought after for their yield, which is always fairly high. The grapes of the Gamay vine are sometimes used with those of the *Pinot*, but the *Pinot* are used by themselves in the best wines.

In districts to the west of the Côte d'Or and in the Beaujolais, Mâconnais, and Lyonnais districts, the grapes of the Gamay vine make wines of excellent quality. (See BURGUNDY.)

GAMBRA – Type of partridge of central European origin. All the recipes for partridge (q.v.) may be used in the preparation of this bird.

GAME. GIBIER – The term game applies to all wild animals and birds which are hunted and eaten.

Gibier, the French word for game, comes from *gibecer* which, in old French, meant hunting. *Gibecer* in turn derives from the Latin adjective *gibbosus*, meaning hunchback. This word was used to describe the various animals killed in the chase because, to carry home the game they killed, huntsmen were equipped with a bag, pouch, or box which they usually carried on their backs. Thus equipped, they had the appearance of hunchbacks. From this arose the word *gibecer*, followed by its derivative *gibecière* for the huntsman's bag or pouch. From the word *gibecière* it was an obvious step to the word *gibier*, 'that which was carried', and it was not long before the word was firmly established in the language.

Game can be divided into three categories.

1. Small birds, not larger than the quail or the thrush.
2. Game proper which can be subdivided into winged game (woodcock, partridge, pheasant, etc.) and ground game (wild rabbit and hare).
3. Large game or venison (roebuck, deer, and wild boar).

'Game,' writes Brillat-Savarin, 'is a healthy, warming, and savoury food, fit for the most delicate palate and easy to digest. In the hands of an experienced cook, game can provide dishes of the highest quality which raise the culinary art to the level of a science.

'There is game of all sorts. Certain types of game from Périgord will not have the same flavour as similar game killed at Sologne. Whereas a hare killed near Paris will make dull eating, a leveret from the Haut Dauphiné or the Burgundy district will be more deliciously flavoured than any other of its kind.'

In Britain there is a closed season for most game, i.e. a period when game may not be shot and killed. Several birds are protected all the year round, including blackbird, bustard, cygnet, heron, lapwing, lark, rail, swan, and swift.

Digestibility of game – Generally speaking, dieticians advise against the consumption of game, especially if it has been hung for too long. It can be extremely toxic and may cause food poisoning if putrefaction is advanced.

Fresh game should be eaten in moderation. It is important to remember that the quarry is shot down when moving fast and that there is a possibility of its muscular activity causing lactic acid to form in the flesh. The gun pellet wounds increase the toxicity of this acid, which encourages the spread of putrefaction. The latter begins almost immediately in the flesh of animals killed after a long struggle.

Game fowl left uncleaned is particularly toxic and indigestible.

The habit of marinating larger game in an effort to preserve it, reduces only very slightly the spread of microbes.

Game fumet – See FUMET.

Game. Painting by Frans Snyders

GAME BAG. CARNIER – Bag or net used to hold game.

GAME CHIPS. CROUSTILLES – Potatoes sliced very thinly and fried. They are served hot or cold.

GAMMELÖST – See CHEESE.

GANDER. JARS – See GOOSE.

GANGA – Hazel-grouse found in the Pyrénées.

GANTOIS (Flemish pastry) – Sieve 200 g. (7 oz., $1\frac{3}{4}$ cups) flour onto a table. Place in the centre 150 g. (5 oz., $\frac{2}{3}$ cup) refined brown sugar, 150 g. (5 oz., generous $\frac{1}{2}$ cup) butter, 2 medium-sized eggs, 1 teaspoon ground cinnamon, $\frac{1}{2}$ teaspoon ground cloves, a pinch of salt, and $\frac{1}{4}$ teaspoon bicarbonate of soda.

Knead, and when the flour and other ingredients are thoroughly mixed, work the dough with the palm of the hand. Leave to stand in a cool place for 1 hour.

Divide the dough into 5 parts and roll them out into rounds $\frac{1}{2}$ cm. ($\frac{1}{4}$ inch) thick. Place on a buttered baking sheet and bake in a moderate oven until golden brown. Leave to cool on a wire cake tray.

Spread each with a thin layer of greengage jam and place them one on top of the other. Trim, and cover the whole completely with concentrated apricot jam. Mix 25 g. (1 oz., 2 tablespoons) fine sugar, 25 g. (1 oz., $\frac{1}{4}$ cup) blanched and ground almonds, the finely diced candied peel of 1 orange (approximately 2 tablespoons), and 1 egg white.

Cover the cake with this mixture, sprinkle sugar over it and brown in the oven. Leave to cool before serving.

GAPERON – Cheese from Limagne which can be eaten from September to July.

GARBANZOS or GARVANCE – Spanish name for chick-peas.

These peas have rather a tough pulp and should be prepared like other dried vegetables by soaking overnight in cold water. Serve them with or without meat in the same way as haricot beans.

Garbanzos are an essential ingredient of *olla podrida*, a stew that is one of the most characteristic dishes of Spain.

GARBURE – Broth of the Béarnais district. The name also applies to many other broths and soups. Their common characteristics are the slices of bread covered with various savoury spreads, browned in the oven or simmered in fat in the stockpot, and served with the soup.

Simin Palay in his book *la Cuisine en Béarn* writes:

'Where does this term come from? The root is surely *garbe* (a sheaf or bunch). It is a bunch of vegetables which provides the basic stock of the *garbure*: cabbage, thyme, garlic, parsley, marjoram, French beans, peas . . . Moreover (in Béarn), the term *garburatye* is used for any collection or mixture of fresh green vegetables.

'Boil water in an earthenware pot glazed on the inside – cast iron or iron pots spoil the delicacy of the flavour. When it is boiling, throw in potatoes, peeled and cut into thick slices. Add other fresh vegetables in season: haricot or broad beans, peas, or French beans. Season with salt and pepper. Red pepper may be used in place of white. Flavour with garlic, a sprig of thyme, parsley or fresh marjoram. Leave to cook, making sure that the water is constantly on the boil. Shred tender green cabbage as finely as possible into strips, cutting across the width of the leaves, after having removed such portions as are too tough.

'Once the rest of the ingredients are thoroughly cooked, throw the cabbage into the boiling stock. Cover the pot to keep the cabbage leaves green and, 30 minutes before serving, put in a piece of pickled meat: *lou trébuc*; the fat adhering to this will be sufficient. If pork is used, a little goose fat will enhance the flavour. Cut stale wholemeal bread into thin slices and add to the stock and vegetables.

'The mixture must be thick enough for the ladle to stand up in it when set in the centre of the tureen.

'It is possible to make a good *garbure* without *trébuc*, but in that case it is necessary to put in the cold water a piece of ham bone, or a sausage, or, at the very least, lean bacon (thin flank). White cabbage may be used instead of green cabbage.

'For an everyday *garbure*, it is usual to make do with a piece of bacon or ham, or bacon chopped with crushed garlic.

'According to season, a few slices of pink swede or roast chestnuts are added. In winter, dried beans only being available, these have to be cooked in advance. They must be drained after cooking, as their water would destroy the characteristic flavour of the *garbure*. To thicken the broth, the beans are sometimes crushed and rubbed through a sieve.

'The meat is served separately from the broth, either by itself or with the vegetables, like the boiled beef of a hotpot. Some cooks brown the *trébuc* in a pan before putting it in the stock. In this case the necessary fat must be added, but the fat in which the *trébuc* was browned should not be used.

'A good *goudale* (q.v.) is an indispensable finish to every garbure.'

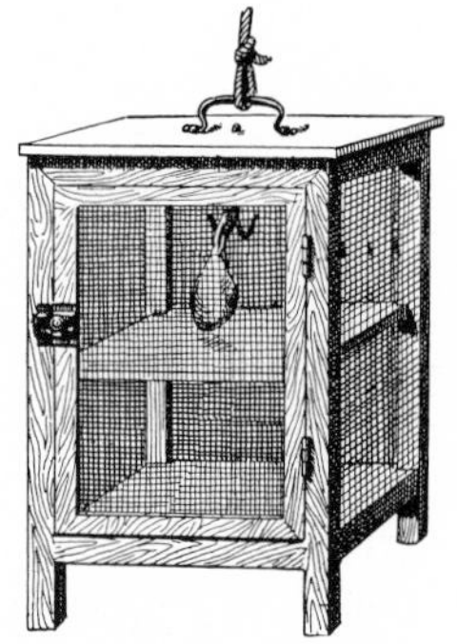

Garde-manger made with wire-mesh

GARDE-MANGER – Storage place, cool and well-aired, in large eating-houses, where the food required for the preparation of meals is kept. There are ice chests or refrigerators in which are stored meat, poultry, game, fish, and other provisions.

The cold buffet is prepared here, and all the preparatory work done on raw foodstuffs, such as boning and jointing meat, drawing and trussing poultry, and gutting fish.

The name is also used in France to designate the man whose special duty it is to supervise this part of the work of a large kitchen.

The word can also mean an ordinary larder.

GARDEN WARBLER. BECFIGUE – Bird found in great numbers in the south of France, particularly in Provence. It is called *béguinette* locally. Its French name *becfigue* dates back to the fig harvest in Roman times.

The garden warbler was greatly praised by Brillat-Savarin. He said that this bird, 'gets at least as plump as robins and ortolans, and nature has given its flesh a slight bitterness and a unique flavour which are so exquisite that they engage, gratify, and stimulate all the degustatory powers. If the garden warbler were the size of a pheasant it would certainly be worth the price of an acre of land.'

There are a number of recipes for preparing these little birds in addition to the recipes given for ortolans (q.v.).

Garden warblers à l'arlésienne. BECFIGUES À L'ARLÉSIENNE – Fill the middle of a round loaf of bread which has been hollowed out like a *croustade* (q.v.), buttered and baked in the oven, with St George's agarics (see AGARIC), briskly sautéed in butter.

On the mushrooms put 6 drawn and trussed warblers. Season with salt and pepper. Sprinkle with melted butter. Cook quickly in a very hot oven and serve in the bread croustade.

Garden warbler

Garden warblers in the manner of Father Fabri. BECFIGUES À LA FAÇON DU PÈRE FABRI – Put a piece of *foie gras* the size of a walnut, studded with a piece of truffle, inside each warbler. Brown briskly in sizzling butter.

Line an ovenproof dish with a layer of *à gratin forcemeat* (see FORCEMEAT) and put the birds on this, pressing them down into the forcemeat. Cover them with a few tablespoons of a fine *salpicon* (q.v.) of mushrooms tossed in butter. Sprinkle with a few drops of fine Champagne brandy and 2 tablespoons (3 tablespoons) melted butter. Cook in a hot oven.

Garden warblers à la landaise. BECFIGUES À LA LANDAISE – Wrap each warbler in a vine leaf and a thin rasher of bacon, and put them on metal skewers, 3 birds to a skewer, separated from each other by croûtons of bread lightly fried in butter.

Place them in a long fireproof dish, season with salt and pepper, sprinkle with butter or *foie gras* fat. Cook quickly in a hot oven. When cooked, pour over the birds a little Armagnac, previously heated, with fresh peeled grapes and 1 teaspoon dissolved meat jelly added to it.

Garden warbler à la piémontaise. BECFIGUES À LA PIÉMONTAISE – Heat butter in a sauté pan and lightly brown blanched, drained, and shredded rashers of bacon. In the same fat, sizzling hot, cook the warblers.

Arrange the birds in a pie dish or *timbale* on a foundation of smooth risotto (q.v.) with truffles. Dilute the pan juices with a little Madeira, add a few tablespoons thickened brown veal stock and pour over the birds.

Garden warblers à la polenta (called à la romaine). BECFIGUES À LA POLENTA, À LA ROMAINE – Put a fairly stiff layer of polenta (q.v.) with cheese into an ovenproof dish. With the back of a wet spoon press as many hollows in this layer of polenta as there are birds. Into each hollow put a garden warbler which has been briskly tossed in butter.

Pour over the birds the butter in which they were browned, adding a little flamed brandy to it. Cook in a very hot oven and serve in the same dish.

Roast garden warblers. BECFIGUES RÔTIS – Prepare like *Roast ortolans* (see ORTOLAN).

GARFISH. ORPHIE – The garfish, or sea eel, has dry, lean flesh, poisonous at certain times. Prepare like eel (q.v.).

GARGOTE – French term for a third-rate restaurant, with its proprietor being called the *gargotier*. *Gargote* is also used colloquially to describe bad cooking.

GARLIC. AIL – Perennial plant, distinguished by its strong smell, cultivated for its bulb. It is also called *poor man's theriac* and *herbe aux aulx* ('garlic herb'). In country districts some people consider garlic as a very powerful anthelmintic and also as an antifebrile.

Aristophanes wrote that the athletes used to eat garlic before their exercises at the stadium. Virgil said that garlic is the right food to maintain the strength of harvest reapers. Pliny, the naturalist, maintained that garlic is a cure for consumption. Celsius cited it as a cure for fever. Hippocrates classed garlic among the sudorific drugs and adds: 'garlic is hot, laxative, and diuretic, but it is bad for the eyes.' Dioscorides made a strong case in its favour as an anthelmintic (a cure for intestinal worms).

The prophet Mohammed said: 'In cases of stings and bites by poisonous animals, garlic acts as a theriac. Applied to the spot bitten by viper, or sting of scorpion, it produces successful results.' In Cayenne garlic is used against bites of certain snakes.

In his *Eléments d'histoire naturelle* published in 1792, Millin claimed that 'garlic is a preventive against the plague'. Bernardin de Saint-Pierre said: 'Garlic, the smell of which is so dreaded by our little mistresses, is perhaps the most powerful remedy in existence against the vapours and nervous maladies to which they are subject.'

In the sixteenth century, certain doctors, says Dr Félix Brémond in his *Dictionnaire de la table*, 'condemned themselves to constant carrying of several cloves of garlic in their pockets to protect themselves, and their patients, from the bad air and epidemic diseases.'

Garlic

Garlic butter. BEURRE D'AIL – This butter, which is used in sauces, forcemeats, or in the preparation of cold *hors-d'œuvre*, is made by pounding together 4 cloves of peeled, blanched and drained garlic and 100 g. (4 oz., $\frac{1}{2}$ cup) fresh butter. Pass the mixture through a fine sieve.

Garlic capons. CHAPONS À L'AIL – Crusts of bread rubbed with raw garlic, seasoned with oil, vinegar, salt, and pepper, and added to green salads.

Garlic forcemeat. FARCE D'AIL – Used for the preparation of cold *hors-d'œuvre* and various other dishes. Pound equal quantities of yolks of hard-boiled eggs and blanched cloves of garlic in a mortar. Add to this mixture half its volume of fresh butter, blend, and rub through a fine sieve.

Grated garlic. AIL RÂPÉ – Garlic is usually grated or pounded in a mortar. It is added to a great number of dishes. When added as a condiment to ingredients fried in butter, cooking fat or oil, do not allow it to fry, as this would render the dishes too pungent. Add it just before serving.

The expression *pointe d'ail* means the very small quantity of grated garlic which can be held on a point of a knife.

Garlic oil. HUILE D'AIL – Blanch and drain 15 cloves of garlic, and pound in a mortar to a fine paste. Add 3 dl. ($\frac{1}{2}$ pint, $1\frac{1}{4}$ cups) olive oil. Sieve through a muslin cloth.

This oil is used for seasoning salads. It can also be made by adding grated garlic to olive oil, which is then sieved through a cloth.

Powdered garlic. POUDRE D'AIL – Dry peeled garlic cloves slowly in an oven. When they are quite dry, pound them in a mortar and put to dry once again in the oven. Pound them again until they are reduced to a fine powder. Pass through a sieve. Pound the pieces left in the sieve and sift once more.

Put this powder into jars, seal, and keep in a dry place.

Garlic purée. PURÉE D'AIL – Blanch cloves of garlic and cook them in butter in a covered pan. Add a few tablespoons very thick *Béchamel sauce* (see SAUCE). Blend and pass through a sieve.

This purée is used in certain sauces and forcemeats.

Garlic sauce. SAUCE À L'AIL – Name sometimes used to describe *aïoli* (q.v.).

Garlic soup. SOUPE À L'AIL – This soup, the recipe for which will be found under SOUPS AND BROTHS, is very popular in the south of France.

Garlic toast. RÔTIE À L'AIL – Speciality of the south-west of France.

Lightly toast slices of wholemeal bread. Spread them with *Garlic purée*, sprinkle with grated breadcrumbs and olive oil, and brown briskly in the oven.

GARNISHES. GARNITURES – Garnishes are numerous and important to French *cuisine*. They are sometimes named after the man who originated them, or after an occasion, or after a place, etc.

Garnishes consist of various trimmings added to a dish or placed around meat, chicken, fish, etc., or served at the same time on a separate dish. Some garnishes are complicated and are made only by professionals; others are easily produced in the domestic kitchen.

Garnishes must always blend with the flavour of the basic dish. They may consist of one or several elements, and are termed simple or composite.

Simple garnishes. These consist of a single element, most commonly a vegetable, braised, sautéed, or bound with butter; a cereal (rice, etc.); or a farinaceous food (tart, croûton, etc.).

Composite garnishes. These are made from a number of ingredients, varying according to the basic dish. The ingredients must blend in flavour with the main dish and with one another.

Certain composite garnishes are often called *ragoûts* (*financière, Godard, Toulouse, etc.*). The various parts of these are generally arranged separately around the dish but they may also be mixed.

ARRANGEMENT OF GARNISHES. DRESSAGE DES GARNITURES –

For large cuts of meat, poultry, game – If there is no risk of their being spoilt by the stock or gravy of the main dish, the garnishes should be disposed round the main dish in separate groups.

The main meat should never be completely hidden by the garnish. If the meat is small, it is advisable to raise it on a croûton of fried bread or some other foundation.

This type of arrangement, being somewhat complicated, should be used only for formal banquets where dishes are presented to each guest and served by a waiter, and is only appropriate to certain garnishes made up of a large number of ingredients, such as *financière, Godard, Toulouse*, or *Tortue*.

To facilitate serving, large hot joints are often served to the guests already carved. Gravy and garnishes are served separately at the same time. Certain vegetable garnishes are always served separately. This applies especially to purées of vegetables or dried vegetables, to green vegetables in butter, which would become limp in the stock or gravy of the main dish, and to pastas and cereals (rice, semolina, etc.).

The stocks, gravies, and sauces appropriate to each garnish are listed under the various garnishes. The dressing should be very lightly sprinkled over the main dish. The remainder is served in a sauceboat.

Garnishes set out round the main dish should not be sprinkled with dressing, especially those made of fresh vegetables with butter, those served *au gratin*, or any deep-fried garnish.

Braised vegetables only should have the dressing poured over them.

For meat served in individual portions: cutlets, escalopes, noisettes, medallions, small fillets, fillet steaks, suprême of chicken, sautéed chicken – Apart from certain special dishes, to which attention is drawn under the appropriate heading, these small cuts of meat may be served with any of the garnishes indicated for large cuts.

It is advisable to prepare the garnishes in smaller shapes and quantities so that they may be in better proportion to the individual portions.

All the garnishes should be placed around or along the sides of the main dish. If sautéed, these portions should be served with their own cooking liquid. For grills it is preferable to serve a separate sauce.

The garnishes of individual portions may be served with sauce or not, according to the principles applicable to large cuts.

For cold dishes – Details of the ingredients and arrangement of garnishes for these dishes are given under the heading COLD FOODSTUFFS.

The quantities of garnish to be used depend upon the main dish, but they vary also according to the menu as a whole. The various ingredients of a composite garnish must be sufficient in number to serve all the guests. The quantities used in the preparation of garnishes, whether simple or composite, should be calculated at approximately 100 g. (4 oz.) for each guest.

For soups and broths – These garnishes may consist of a single item or may be composite. Some, such as tapioca and other similar ingredients, are cooked in the soup itself. Others are prepared separately and added to the soup at the last moment, or, where appropriate, served separately.

SIMPLE GARNISHES. GARNITURES SIMPLES –

For meat dishes –

Artichokes. Hearts or quarters: stewed; braised; sautéed. Hearts: stuffed, sprinkled with breadcrumbs and browned; puréed.

Artichokes, Jerusalem. Sautéed; in cream.

Aubergines. Stuffed, sprinkled with breadcrumbs and browned in cream.

Broad beans (fresh). In butter; in cream; puréed.

Brussels sprouts. Sautéed.

Cabbage (green or red). Braised; stuffed with forcemeat and rolled into balls; stuffed with small slices of meat and rolled into sausages.

Carrots (glazed). In gravy; with *Vichy sauce.*

Cauliflower. Sautéed; coated with *Mornay sauce*; in florets sprinkled with breadcrumbs and browned.

Celery or celeriac. Stewed; braised.

Cèpes. À la bordelaise; with chopped herbs; *à la provençale;* with cream.

Chestnuts. Stewed; braised.

Corn on the cob. In butter; in cream.

Cucumbers. Cut pear-shaped, stewed in butter; in thick slices, stuffed.

Endive. Braised; in butter; in cream.

Fennel (bulbous). Braised; stewed.

French beans. In butter; in cream; puréed.

Fungi. Cultivated mushrooms, chanterelles, morels, flap-mushrooms, St George's agaric, orange-milk agaric, etc. Sautéed, and cooked in various other ways.

Gourd (pumpkin). Quartered: stewed in butter; braised; stuffed; cooked in cream.

Hop panicles. In butter or cream.

Kidney beans (fresh or dried small). In butter or cream; puréed.

Ladies' fingers. In cream; in gravy.

Lentils. In butter; puréed.

Lettuce. Braised; stuffed.

Macaroni. Prepared in various ways.

Mixed beans. Mixture of French beans and small kidney beans, fresh or dried.

Noodles and other pasta of the same type. Prepared in various ways.

Onions. Glazed; stuffed.

Peas. À la française; cooked with lettuce leaves; *à la paysanne*; purée *St Germain.*

Potatoes. Boiled; Anna; croquettes; *fondantes*; fried in various ways; covered with breadcrumbs and browned; fried with minced onions previously browned; shaped as nuts and browned in butter; *parisienne*; sprinkled with parsley.

Red beans. À la bourguignonne; in gravy; puréed.

Rice. Cooked in fat; curried; pilaf; risotto croquettes; in cream.

Spinach. Whole leaves or as a purée; in butter; in cream; in stock.

Tomatoes. Stuffed in various ways, sprinkled with cheese and/or breadcrumbs and browned; grilled; sautéed.

Turnips. Glazed; stuffed.

White beans. In butter; *à la bretonne*; in cream; in stock; *à la maître d'hôtel;* puréed.

For poultry –

Artichokes. Hearts or quartered whole artichokes: stewed, braised, or sautéed for pot-roasted poultry; sautéed or cooked in a casserole for drumsticks or breasts of poultry.

Hearts: in cream for pot-roasted, poached, or sautéed poultry, for drumsticks or breasts of poultry; stuffed for braised or pot-roasted poultry; braised in white stock for poached poultry.

Cèpes. For braised or pot-roasted poultry, sautéed chicken or chicken casserole, for drumsticks or breasts of poultry.

Chestnuts. Braised or stewed for braised or pot-roasted chicken, for braised or pot-roasted young turkey, for pot-roasted pigeon.

Lettuce. Braised for braised, pot-roasted, or poached chicken, braised or pot-roasted young turkey, braised or pot-roasted pigeon.

Mushrooms. Cooked in a white stock for poached poultry, for drumsticks or breasts of poultry; cooked in a brown stock for braised, pot-roasted, sautéed, or casseroled poultry, drumsticks or breasts of poultry, pot-roasted pigeon, pot-roasted guinea-fowl.

Noodles and other pasta. For braised or pot-roasted poultry, sautéed or casseroled chicken, pot-roasted turkey.

Pilaf. With pot-roasted poultry, sautéed or casseroled chicken, drumsticks or breasts of poultry, pot-roasted turkey.

Rice. Cooked in fat, for poached poultry.

Risotto. For braised or pot-roasted poultry, chicken sautéed or cooked in a casserole, drumsticks or breasts of poultry.

Turnips. Glazed for braised poultry or braised or pot-roasted Nantes duckling.

Vegetables (various). Glazed carrots in gravy or *à la Vichy;* cauliflower sprinkled with cheese and/or breadcrumbs and browned; *Sauerkraut;* braised fennel; broad beans in butter or cream; glazed turnips; glazed onions; French beans in butter or cream; peas cooked in various ways; salsify sautéed or in cream; sautéed tomatoes; Jerusalem artichokes in butter, etc. All these vegetables may be served with braised, pot-roasted, or poached poultry, sautéed chicken or chicken casserole, cutlets, breasts, or fillets of chicken.

Young corn on the cob. In butter or cream for braised, pot-roasted, or poached poultry, sautéed chicken, cutlets, breasts, or fillets of poultry, pot-roasted guinea-fowl.

GARNISHES FOR EGGS. GARNITURES POUR OEUFS – Like all other basic foods, eggs, especially soft-boiled or poached in the ordinary way or in moulds, may be served with a great variety of garnishes. Detailed recipes for those garnishes and instructions for setting them out on the dish are to be found among the recipes for egg dishes (see EGGS).

GARNISHES FOR FISH. GARNITURES POUR POISSONS – Braised fish, whole or in thick slices, is garnished according to the instructions set out for main meat dishes.

Poached fish (fish cooked in a *court-bouillon*), whole or sliced, is invariably garnished with boiled or steamed potatoes and fresh parsley. The dressing is a sauce of some kind, served separately. To this standard garnish are sometimes added further ingredients such as very small fried fish, minute croquettes, or shells filled with various garnishes, etc.

Small fish, or fillets poached in a little *court-bouillon*, are served with various garnishes, simple or composite. Details of these garnishes are given with the recipe for the fish in question.

Small fish and their garnishes are normally covered with sauce prescribed for them, unless they are fried *à la meunière* or sprinkled with cheese or breadcrumbs and browned.

Grilled fish, whole or sliced, is garnished as a rule with boiled potatoes, slices of lemon cut with a fluted knife, and fresh parsley. Some types of grilled fish have special garnishes. Details of these are given with the recipe for the fish in question.

Fried fish is invariably garnished with fried parsley and halved or quartered lemons.

COMPOSITE GARNISHES. GARNITURES COMPOSÉES –

À l'africaine – Black potatoes (potatoes whose pulp is dark bluish in colour – see POTATOES), cut to look like marbles, blanched in salt water, and cooked in butter; braised courgettes (zucchini).

Serve with rice cooked in fat stock lightly flavoured with saffron.

Agnès Sorel – *Salpicon* (q.v.) of pickled tongue, mushrooms, and truffles, with little mounds of white rice.

Sauce. Stock of the main dish blended with Madeira and a *Demi-glace sauce* (see SAUCE).

Uses. For large cuts of meat; poultry; eggs.

Albigeoise – Potato croquettes prepared as for *Duchess potatoes* (see POTATOES) mixed with lean chopped ham; small tomatoes stuffed with chopped mushrooms (*duxelles*) which have been fried in butter with chopped onion and mixed with breadcrumbs, garlic, and chopped parsley.

Sauce. Demi-glace sauce (see SAUCE) flavoured with tomato.

Uses. For large and small cuts of meat.

Albufera – Small tartlets garnished with truffles shaped with a ball-scoop (the size of a pea) and chicken forcemeat balls of the same shape. Cocks' kidneys; mushrooms, and slices of pickled tongue shaped like cocks' combs are placed on top of each tartlet.

Sauce. Albufera sauce (see SAUCE).

Uses. For poached chicken. Chickens thus garnished are stuffed with rice mixed with a *salpicon* of *foie gras* and truffles.

Algérienne I – Sweet potato croquettes; small tomatoes stewed in oil.

Sauce. Clear veal stock flavoured with tomato.

Uses. For large or small cuts of meat; poultry.

Algérienne II – Croquettes of rice and sweet peppers; thick slices of aubergines.

Sauce. Clear veal stock flavoured with tomato.

Alsacienne – Braised *sauerkraut*; poached Strasbourg sausages cut into rounds; boiled potatoes.

Sauce. Veal stock or a thin *Demi-glace sauce* (see SAUCE).

Uses. For large cuts of meat; poultry, especially goose and duck.

Ambassadrice – Cocks' combs; cocks' kidneys; sautéed mushrooms; sautéed chicken livers; shredded truffles.

Sauce. Stock of the main dish blended with Madeira and thickened veal stock.

Uses. For small cuts of meat and poultry.

Américaine – Small slices of crayfish or lobster tails cooked *à l'américaine*.

Sauce. Sauce à l'américaine (see SAUCE) to which is added the concentrated stock of the fish used for the main dish. (See BRILL, *Brill à l'américaine*.)

Uses. For fish.

À l'ancienne I – Forcemeat balls of chicken and truffles; lamb sweetbreads; truffles shaped like olives; mushrooms; fresh crayfish cooked in a fish *court-bouillon* (q.v.).

Sauce. Suprême sauce (see SAUCE) to which has been added a fine vegetable pulp (*mirepoix*), flavoured with Madeira.

Uses. For calves' sweetbreads; poached or braised poultry; *vol-au-vent*; hot *pâtés*; savoury tarts.

À l'ancienne II – Little savoury nests made of fried *Duchess potatoes* (see POTATOES) filled with a mixture of diced calves' kidneys sautéed in butter, and diced mushrooms, bound with thickened veal gravy; stuffed braised lettuce; small potato balls browned in butter; French beans in butter.

Sauce. Braising liquor or pot-roast juices.

Uses. For large braised or pot-roasted cuts of meat, especially loin and saddle of veal.

Garnish à l'ancienne round a saddle of veal

À l'ancienne III – Small pastry boats garnished with a *salpicon* of soft roes blended with *Normande sauce* (see SAUCE); truffles trimmed to look like olives; mushrooms; freshwater crayfish cooked in a *court-bouillon.*

Sauce. Reduced pan juices of the main dish blended with a Madeira-flavoured *Velouté sauce* (see SAUCE) based on fish stock and cream, to which a fine vegetable *mirepoix* is added.

Uses. For baked or poached fish.

À l'anglaise I – Carrots cut in 5-cm. (2-inch) lengths and medium-sized onions cooked with leg of lamb; mashed turnips also cooked with leg of lamb, drained and mashed.

Sauce. Butter sauce (see SAUCE) with capers in vinegar added, served separately.

Uses. For poached leg of lamb.

À l'anglaise II – Carrots and turnips cut in 5-cm. (2-inch) lengths, cooked with chicken; celery hearts also cooked with chicken; French beans and cauliflower, boiled.

Sauce. Butter sauce (see SAUCE) with capers in vinegar added, served separately. (See CHICKEN, *Chicken à l'anglaise.*)

À l'Anversoise – Hop shoots in cream; potatoes cut to look like olives deep-fried in butter. Or small artichoke hearts stewed in butter and filled with hop shoots in cream; chicory (endive) *à la flamande.*

Sauce. Juices from the roast or clear veal stock.

Uses. For large or small cuts of meat; poultry.

Armenonville – Small *Anna potatoes* (see POTATOES); morels in cream; and tartlets filled with a *salpicon* of cocks' combs and kidneys.

Uses. For small pieces of meat; calves' sweetbreads.

À la banquière – Chicken quenelles; mushrooms; shredded truffles.

(According to the nature of the main dish, the ingredients of this garnish are either prepared separately or mixed in a *ragoût.*)

Sauce. Banquière sauce (see SAUCE).

Uses. For calves' sweetbreads and poultry poached or braised *à blanc*; *vol-au-vent.*

Béatrix – Morels sautéed in butter; glazed carrots; braised quartered artichokes; browned new potatoes.

Sauce. Diluted meat juices from the cooking pan.

Uses. For small cuts of meat.

À la Beauharnais – Very small artichoke hearts filled with *Béarnaise sauce* (see SAUCE) to which tarragon purée has been added; small potato balls browned in butter.

Sauce. Pan juices of the main dish diluted with Madeira and veal stock, together with chopped truffles.

Uses. For small cuts of meat.

Garnish Béatrix (*Debillot. Phot. Larousse*)

Beauvilliers – Small spinach kromeskies (prepared by filling pancakes with spinach, rolling them up, cutting them in rounds, dipping them in batter and frying them in deep fat); small tomatoes stuffed with cooked brain purée, browned with breadcrumbs; salsify cut into rounds, sautéed in butter.
Sauce. Braising stock.
Uses. For large cuts of braised meat.
À la bénédictine – Very small tartlets or pastry boats garnished with *Brandade of salt cod* (see COD, *Salt cod*) with chopped truffles added.
Sauce. White wine sauce (see SAUCE) if accompanying fish; *Cream sauce* for eggs.
Uses. For fish or coddled or poached eggs.
À la Berrichonne – Braised cabbage; small onions; chestnuts; rashers of lean bacon.
Uses. For meat, principally mutton, served in big cuts.
À la Biarrotte – Grilled *cèpes* and cakes of *Duchess potato* (see POTATOES) used as a foundation for meat.
Uses. For meat served in small portions.
Bonne-femme I – Potatoes trimmed into small ovals, small onions, lean larding bacon and mushrooms, cooked with chicken.
Uses. For poultry.
Bonne-femme II – Thinly sliced mushrooms cooked with fish.
Uses. For fish.
À la bordelaise I – *Cèpes à la bordelaise* (see MUSHROOMS); potatoes cut to look like olives and cooked slowly in clarified butter.
Sauce. Juices of the roast.
Uses. For large joints.
À la bordelaise II – Small quartered artichokes stewed in butter; raw, thinly sliced potatoes sautéed in butter; fried onion rings; fried parsley.
Sauce. Pan juices of main dish diluted with white wine and veal or chicken stock.
Uses. For jointed poultry.
À la boulangère – Thinly sliced or quartered potatoes and thinly sliced onions, cooked with the main dish.
Sauce. Juices of the roast.
Uses. For shoulder, leg, and other cuts of mutton and lamb; occasionally for poultry.
À la bouquetière I – Glazed carrots and turnips trimmed into very small ovals or shaped with a ball-scoop; peas and diced French beans, boiled separately and blended with butter; cauliflower divided into florets and boiled, covered with *Hollandaise sauce* (see SAUCE) or melted butter; new potatoes browned in butter.

Dispose these vegetables round the main dish in separate groups.
Sauce. Juices of the roast.
Uses. For large and small cuts of meat.
À la bouquetière II – Very small artichoke hearts simmered in butter, filled alternately with carrots and turnips; buttered French beans; small bunches of asparagus tips, held upright by a ring of carrots; cauliflower divided into florets and covered with *Hollandaise sauce* (see SAUCE); potatoes cut to look like olives and sautéed in butter.
Sauce. Juices of the roast.
Uses. For large and small cuts of meat.
À la bourgeoise (sometimes called à la mode) – Glazed carrots cut in ovals, and onions, both cooked with the meat. Sometimes braised fresh vegetables such as celery, lettuce, etc., are added.
Sauce. Braising liquor of the main dish.
Uses. For large braised cuts of meat, notably beef rump braised *à la bourgeoise* (see BEEF), but this garnish may be used with braised ox tongue, veal (*noix de veau*), or leg of lamb or mutton.
À la bourguignonne I – Small glazed onions; whole or quartered mushrooms sautéed in butter; diced, blanched, and browned salt (pickled) pork.
Sauce. Bourguignonne sauce (see SAUCE). This garnish, generally served with braised meat, should be added to the main dish a short time before it is completely cooked.
Uses. For large cuts of meat, especially beef.
À la bourguignonne II – The same as the previous garnish, but without the pork.
Sauce. Red wine sauce made with vegetable or fish stock with a little fresh butter added.
Uses. For braised fish.
À la brabançonne I – Braised chicory; *Potato fondantes* (see POTATOES).
Sauce. Reduced veal stock.
Uses. Large cuts of meat.
À la brabançonne II – Little tartlets garnished with Brussels sprouts simmered in butter, covered with *Mornay sauce* (see SAUCE), sprinkled with breadcrumbs and browned; potato croquettes.
Sauce. Reduced veal stock.
Uses. For large pieces of meat.
Brancas – *Anna potatoes* (see POTATOES) cooked in individual moulds and turned out; *Chiffonade of lettuce with cream* (see LETTUCE) quite dry.
Sauce. Thickened veal stock or a *Demi-glace sauce* (see SAUCE).
Uses. For small cuts of meat; white meat especially poultry.
À la bretonne I – Dry white beans or small kidney beans, cooked in meat stock and blended with *Bretonne sauce* (see SAUCE).
Sauce. Roast pan juices or veal stock flavoured with tomato.
Uses. For large cuts of meat (especially leg of lamb) pot-roasted or roasted.
À la bretonne II – Breton white bean purée (see PURÉE).
Sauce. Juices of the roast.
Uses. For large cuts of meat.
À la bretonne III – Leeks, onions, celery and mushrooms, cut in thin strips and cooked slowly in butter until they are very tender, and added to the main fish dish before it is fully cooked.
Sauce. Made with a *Velouté sauce* (see SAUCE) and cream.
Uses. For baked or poached fish.
Brillat-Savarin – Little nests made of *Duchess potatoes* (see

POTATOES) fried and hollowed to hold a *salpicon* of *foie gras* and truffles blended into a concentrated *Demi-glace sauce* (see SAUCE). Asparagus tips can be arranged on top.

Sauce. Thin *demi-glace sauce* for large cuts. Stock of the main dish flavoured with white Malaga wine, a third veal stock and two-thirds chicken *Velouté sauce* (see SAUCE), for small cuts.

Uses. For large and small cuts of meat.

À la bruxelloise – Brussels sprouts in butter; *Potato fondantes* (see POTATOES) or potatoes cut to look like olives and cooked slowly in clarified butter.

Sauce. Clear veal stock or thin *Demi-glace sauce* (see SAUCE).

Uses. For large and small cuts of meat.

Camérani – Small tartlets filled with *Foie gras purée* (see PURÉE); shredded truffles; slices of pickled tongue shaped as cocks' combs; *Macaroni à l'italienne* (see MACARONI).

Sauce. Suprême sauce (see SAUCE) to which the reduced pan juices have been added.

Uses. Poultry and poached calves' sweetbreads.

À la cancalaise – Lenten garnish of oysters and shrimps' tails in *Normande sauce* (see SAUCE).

À la cardinal – Fish garnish of little *coquilles cardinal*; mushrooms; slices of truffle.

Little carrot timbales. PETITS PAINS DE CAROTTES – Buttered custard cups or *dariole* moulds filled with carrots prepared as for *Carrot timbale* (see CARROT). Cook in a moderate oven in a pan of hot water or *bain-marie*.

Castiglione – Large mushrooms filled with risotto mixed with chopped lean ham, sprinkled with breadcrumbs and browned; rounds of aubergine sautéed in butter (to be used as *canapés*); strips of poached bone-marrow.

Sauce. Stock of the main dish flavoured with white wine to which chopped shallots and veal stock have been added. Butter should be added to this sauce after it has been reduced.

Uses. For small cuts of meat.

À la catalane – Aubergine, coarsely diced, sautéed in oil; *Rice pilaf* (see PILAF).

Sauce. A *Demi-glace sauce* (see SAUCE) flavoured with tomato.

Uses. For large cuts of meat.

Cavour – Small baked rounds of polenta (q.v.) made with cheese (to be used as *canapés*); large grilled mushrooms filled with purée of chicken liver; shredded truffles.

Sauce. Veal stock flavoured with Marsala or tomato.

Uses. For small cuts of meat, especially sautéed escalopes (U.S. cutlets) of veal and breaded calves' sweetbreads.

À la chalonnaise – Small tartlets garnished with cocks' kidneys blended with concentrated *Velouté sauce* (see SAUCE); cocks' combs *à la Villeroi*; slices of truffles; mushrooms.

Sauce. Suprême sauce (see SAUCE).

Uses. For poultry; calves' sweetbreads poached or braised in a white stock.

Chambord – Large and small fish quenelles; mushrooms; fillets of sole; soft roes sautéed in butter; truffles cut to look like olives; freshwater crayfish cooked in a *court-bouillon*; small fried croûtons.

Sauce. Red wine sauce (see SAUCE).

Uses. For large braised fish.

À la chanoinesse – Very small carrots in cream mixed with coarsely chopped truffles. Arranged as a filling for tartlets.

Sauce. Pan juices diluted with sherry and veal stock.

Uses. For calves' sweetbreads; *Suprême of chicken* (see CHICKEN); coddled or poached eggs.

À la châtelaine – Artichoke hearts filled with chestnut purée mixed with rice, sprinkled with breadcrumbs and browned; braised lettuce; potato balls browned in butter.

Sauce. Thickened veal stock or diluted pan juices of the main dish.

Uses. For large cuts of meat.

Chervil leaves. PLUCHES DE CERFEUIL – All traces of stalk and fibre should be removed from the leaves of chervil. Most soups with a base of whole or puréed vegetables should have chervil added – 1 teaspoon to every litre (scant quart, generous quart) soup. Because of the very delicate aromatic flavour of this herb, the leaves must be added to the soup at the last moment, when the soup is off the boil.

Uses. For soup.

Chiffonnade – Finely shredded lettuce leaves and sorrel stewed slowly in butter. This *chiffonnade* is used in many different soups.

À la chinonaise – Small rolls of green cabbage stuffed with sausage meat and braised; potatoes sprinkled with chopped parsley.

Sauce. Demi-glace sauce (see SAUCE).

Uses. For large cuts of meat.

Chipolata – Braised chestnuts; small glazed onions; chipolata sausages; mushrooms.

Sauce. Demi-glace sauce (see SAUCE) or the braising stock of the main dish.

Sometimes lean bacon, coarsely diced, blanched, and browned in butter with braised carrots, is also served.

Uses. For large cuts of meat or poultry.

Choron – Potato balls browned in butter; artichoke hearts filled with peas (or asparagus tips) and simmered in butter.

Sauce. Béarnaise sauce (see SAUCE) flavoured with tomato, arranged in a ring round the main dish.

Uses. For small cuts of meat, fried or grilled.

Chou paste balls. PROFITEROLES – Using *Chou paste* (see DOUGH) in a forcing-bag with a round nozzle, squeeze out onto a baking sheet little balls each the size of a nut. Bake in a moderately hot oven for 20 to 25 minutes.

Stuff the balls with a purée or whatever other ingredient is appropriate, according to the recipe for the soup in which they are to be served, and heat them up.

Uses. For soup.

À la Clamart I – Artichoke hearts filled with peas in butter; potato balls browned in butter.

Sauce. Veal stock blended with *Demi-glace sauce* (see SAUCE).

Uses. For large or small cuts of meat.

À la Clamart II – See *St Germain garnish II* (below).

À la Clermont – Rolls of green cabbage stuffed and braised; rectangular slices of salt (pickled) pork cooked with the cabbage; potatoes.

Sauce. Demi-glace sauce (see SAUCE) or the braising liquor.

Uses. For large cuts of meat.

Cocks' kidneys as garnish. ROGNONS DE COQ – Wash in several waters 100 g. (4 oz.) firm, white cocks' kidneys. Put them into a small saucepan with 1 dl. (6 tablespoons, scant $\frac{1}{2}$ cup) water, a pinch of salt, 25 g. (1 oz., 2 tablespoons) butter and a few drops of lemon juice.

Start cooking over a good heat. As soon as the liquid begins to boil turn the heat very low and continue cooking, covered, for 10 to 12 minutes, taking care to avoid boiling.

Use according to the recipe.

À la Conti – Small croquettes of purée of lentils (rolled into balls); potatoes cut to look like olives, fried in butter.

Sauce. Pan juices diluted with Madeira and *Demi-glace sauce* (see SAUCE).

Uses. For small cuts of meat.

Crêpes – Place in an earthenware dish 100 g. (4 oz., 1 cup) sieved flour and 1 teaspoon table salt. Add 2 whole eggs, mix well, and dilute the mixture with 2½ dl. (scant ½ pint, generous cup) boiled milk.

Make pancakes and use them as appropriate. Clear soup may be used instead of milk in the preparation of this garnish.

Uses. For soup.

Croûtes garnished and browned à l'ancienne. CROÛTES GARNIES ET GRATINÉES À L'ANCIENNE – Cut a long French loaf into slices 3 to 4 cm. (1½ inches) thick. Scoop out three quarters of the bread to make nests. Brush with butter or fat from a *pot-au-feu.* Toast lightly in the oven. Chop or sieve the vegetables from the *pot-au-feu,* add grated cheese, and garnish the bread with little mounds of this mixture. Place these croûtes on a baking sheet and sprinkle with grated cheese. Moisten with a few drops of the fat, and brown.

Uses. For clear soup.

Croûtons – Dice slices of sandwich loaf into cubes approximately ½ cm. (¼ inch) across. Fry them in clarified butter just before serving.

Uses. For soups. Allow 50 g. (2 oz.) fried bread for every litre (scant quart, generous quart) soup.

À la Cussy – Artichoke hearts filled with mushroom purée, sprinkled with breadcrumbs and browned; cocks' kidneys; shredded truffles.

Sauce. Sauce flavoured with Madeira or port.

Uses. For small cuts of meat; poultry, whole or jointed.

À la Daumont – *Crayfish tail ragoût à la Nantua* (see CRAYFISH) (in scallop shells or pastry boats); large fish quenelles (see QUENELLES), decorated with truffles; fillets of sole decorated with truffles cut in fancy shapes; slices of truffle; mushrooms cooked in *court-bouillon.*

Sauce. Normande sauce (see SAUCE) with *Crayfish butter* (see BUTTER, *Compound butters*).

Uses. For large baked fish.

À la Dauphine – *Dauphine potatoes* (see POTATOES).

Sauce. Roast pan juices or clear veal stock.

Uses. For large or small cuts of meat.

À la demi-deuil – Food prepared *à la demi-deuil* is covered with a *Suprême sauce* (see SAUCE) and garnished with truffles.

Uses. For poached poultry and veal braised *à blanc.*

À la dieppoise – Mussels (shelled) in white wine; tails of freshwater crayfish, grey or pink (shelled); mushrooms.

Sauce. White wine sauce (see SAUCE).

Uses. For fish poached in white wine.

Dubarry – Cauliflower shaped into balls, masked with *Mornay sauce* (see SAUCE) sprinkled with grated cheese and browned.

Uses. Large or small cuts of meat.

Garnish Dubarry (*Debillot. Phot. Larousse*)

À la duchesse – *Duchess potatoes* (see POTATOES) in different shapes according to the nature of the main dish.

Sauce. Thickened veal stock or roast pan juices.

Uses. For large or small cuts of meat.

Duroc – New potatoes (very small), browned in butter.

Sauce. Chasseur sauce (see SAUCE) cooked in the pan used for the main dish.

Uses. For small cuts of meat and poultry, sautéed.

Duxelles – Chopped mushrooms browned in butter and oil mixed with chopped onions and shallots, moistened with white wine, with chopped parsley added.

Uses. For small cuts of meat.

Favart – Chicken quenelles seasoned with chopped tarragon, tartlets of rich pastry filled with a *salpicon* of mushrooms (cèpes) in cream.

Sauce. Thick *Velouté sauce* (see SAUCE) of chicken with *Crayfish butter* (see BUTTER, *Compound butters*).

Uses. For poultry; veal; sweetbreads.

À la favorite – Small artichokes (or quarters of artichokes) braised; lettuces stuffed and braised; mushrooms cooked in butter and filled with mixed diced vegetables; small *Anna potatoes* (see POTATOES) baked in individual moulds and turned out.

Sauce. Thickened veal stock, *Demi-glace sauce* (see SAUCE) or the diluted pan juices of the main dish.

Uses. For large and small cuts of meat.

À la fermière – Artichoke hearts filled with a *fondue* (q.v.) of mixed vegetables; braised lettuces.

Sauce. Demi-glace sauce (see SAUCE).

Uses. For large cuts of meat.

À la financière – Chicken or veal quenelles; cocks' combs and kidneys; mushrooms; shredded truffles. Stoned and blanched olives, and freshwater crayfish are sometimes added.

Sauce. Financière sauce (see SAUCE).

Uses. For large and small cuts of meat; calves' sweetbreads; poultry; *vol-au-vent,* etc.

Garnish à la flamande round a fillet of beef

À la flamande – Green cabbage stuffed, rolled up, and braised; carrots and turnips trimmed into large oval shapes and glazed; potatoes. Diced pork fat and slices of sausage cooked with the cabbage are sometimes added.

Sauce. Demi-glace sauce (see SAUCE), veal stock, or the diluted pan juices of the main dish.

Uses. For large and small cuts of meat.

À la forestière – Morels sautéed in butter; potato balls browned in butter. Sometimes salt (pickled) pork, diced, blanched, and fried in butter is added.

Sauce. Demi-glace sauce (see SAUCE), reduced veal stock, or the diluted pan juices of the main dish.

Uses. Large and small pieces of meat; poultry.

À la française – Small nests made from *Duchess potatoes* (see POTATOES) hollowed out, dipped in egg and breadcrumbs, fried, and filled with diced mixed vegetables; bunches of asparagus tips; braised lettuces; florets of cauliflower coated with *Hollandaise sauce* (see SAUCE).

Sauce. Thin *Demi-glace sauce* (see SAUCE) or clear veal gravy.

Uses. For large cuts of meat.

A Frascati garnish round a fillet of beef

Frascati – Large baked mushrooms, some filled with a *salpicon* of truffles, others with buttered green asparagus tips; small slices of *foie gras* sautéed in butter.

Sauce. Demi-glace sauce (see SAUCE) flavoured with port.

Uses. For large cuts of meat.

À la gauloise I – Tartlets filled with cocks' kidneys; cocks' combs fried *à la Villeroi*; mushrooms; truffles.

Sauce. Pan juices of the main dish diluted with white wine.

Uses. For small cuts of meat; jointed poultry.

À la gauloise II – Pastry boats filled with a *salpicon* of truffles and mushrooms *à la crème*; *potato croquettes*; freshwater crayfish cooked in a *court-bouillon*.

Sauce. Matelote sauce (see SAUCE).

Uses. For large baked or poached fish.

Glazed carrots for garnish – See CARROTS.

Glazed Italian marrow (zucchini) garnish – See ITALIAN MARROW.

Glazed onions for garnish. OIGNONS GLACÉS – Skin small, uniform-sized onions. Fry them very lightly in butter in a shallow pan. Sprinkle with a little sugar and season.

Moisten with stock (or water, if the garnish is required for a Lenten dish) so that the liquid does not quite cover them. Simmer gently with the lid on the pan until the liquid has completely disappeared.

If, after this reduction of liquid, the onions are not yet cooked, add a few tablespoons of hot stock, finish cooking and glaze, without stirring them.

Godard – Large decorated quenelles; small poultry or veal quenelles with truffles; sheeps' sweetbreads, braised and glazed; cocks' combs and kidneys; small truffles, whole or cut to look like olives; mushroom caps.

When this garnish is for a substantial second course, calves' sweetbreads stuffed with bacon and braised may be substituted for the sheep's sweetbreads. (For fuller information, see CHICKEN, *Chicken à la Godard*.)

Sauce. Godard sauce (see SAUCE).

Uses. For large cuts of meat; poultry.

Gorenflot – Braised coarsely shredded red cabbage; rounds of Saveloy sausage cooked with the cabbage; *Potatoes à la ménagère* (see POTATOES).

Sauce. Braising stock.

Uses. For large braised cuts of meat.

Gouffé – Little nests of *Duchess potatoes* (see POTATOES) fried and hollowed out to hold morels cooked in cream; asparagus tips in butter.

Sauce. Stock of the main dish blended with Madeira and thickened veal stock.

Uses. For large and small cuts of meat.

Gratin dauphinois. Gratin of potatoes à la dauphinoise. GRATIN DE POMMES DE TERRE À LA DAUPHINOISE – Slice thinly 1 kg. ($2\frac{1}{4}$ lb.) potatoes. Season with salt and pepper and put them in an ovenproof dish previously rubbed with garlic and butter. Sprinkle grated cheese on the potatoes, spread out in the dish in even layers.

Pour over this a mixture of 2 eggs and 6 dl. (1 pint, $2\frac{1}{2}$ cups) boiled milk, a little salt, and a dash of grated nutmeg. Sprinkle with grated cheese and dot the top with butter.

Bring to the boil on the stove and complete the cooking in the oven for about 40 minutes. Serve in the baking dish.

The garlic and grated nutmeg may be omitted if desired, though, strictly speaking, they form an essential seasoning of this dish.

Gratin of potatoes à la savoyarde. GRATIN DE POMMES DE TERRE À LA SAVOYARDE – Prepared as for *Gratin dauphinois*, substituting clear stock for the milk.

Helder – Potato balls browned in butter; *Béarnaise sauce* (see SAUCE), traced in a circle on the meat; thick *Tomato fondue* (see FONDUE) placed in the middle of the *béarnaise sauce*.

Sauce. Meat juices of the main dish blended with reduced veal stock.

Uses. For small sautéed cuts of meat.

Henry IV – Artichoke hearts filled with *Béarnaise sauce* (see SAUCE) with concentrated veal stock added; potato balls browned in butter; shredded truffles.

Sauce. Stock of the main dish blended with Madeira and thickened veal stock.

Uses. For small cuts of meat.

À la hongroise I – Large florets of cauliflower coated with *Mornay sauce* (see SAUCE), seasoned with paprika, sprinkled with breadcrumbs and browned under the grill; *potato fondantes* (see POTATOES).

Sauce. Thin *Demi-glace sauce* (see SAUCE).

Uses. For large and small cuts of meat.

À la hongroise II – Nests of *Duchess potato* (see POTATOES) garnished with florets of cauliflower coated with *Mornay sauce* (see SAUCE), to which is added chopped onion simmered in butter and seasoned with paprika.

Sauce. Pan juices of the main dish blended with cream, seasoned with paprika and thickened with a little *Velouté sauce* or *Béchamel sauce* (see SAUCE).

Uses. For small cuts of meat.

À la hongroise III – Rice pilaf; diced tomatoes simmered in butter.

Sauce. Hongroise sauce (see SAUCE).

Uses. For poultry, poached or sautéed.

Japanese garnish – See JAPONAISE (À LA).

À la jardinière – Glazed carrots and turnips in small oval shapes (or rounded with a ball-scoop); peas; French beans; small kidney beans in butter – all disposed round the dish in separate groups.

Florets of cauliflower, coated with *Hollandaise sauce* (see SAUCE) or melted butter are sometimes added.

Sauce. Pan juices or clear veal stock.

Uses. For large and small cuts of meat.

Jessica – Tiny artichokes cooked in butter, stuffed with a *salpicon* of bone-marrow with shallots; morels sautéed in butter; *Anna potatoes* (see POTATOES) baked in individual moulds.

Sauce. Allemande sauce (see SAUCE) increased by a third with concentrated veal stock and *Truffle essence* (see ESSENCE).

Uses. For *Suprême of chicken* (see CHICKEN); veal escalopes (U.S. cutlets); coddled or poached eggs.

Joinville – *Salpicon* of shrimps, truffles and mushrooms, blended into *Velouté sauce* or *Normande sauce* (see SAUCE); sliced truffles.

Sauce. Normande sauce with *Shrimp butter* (see BUTTER, *Compound butters*).

Uses. For baked fish.

Julienne – Shred into matchstick strips, carrots, turnips, leeks, onions, and celery. Cook them in butter until tender. Add clear meat stock. If a vegetarian soup is required, water is added instead of stock. To this mixture add shredded cabbage and lettuce hearts, fresh peas, and 1 or 2 tablespoons shredded sorrel.

Uses. For soup.

À la languedocienne – Cèpes sautéed in butter or oil; diced or sliced aubergines fried in oil; potatoes cut to look like olives and cooked slowly in clarified butter.

Sauce. Demi-glace sauce (see SAUCE) flavoured with tomato.

Uses. For large and small cuts of meat; poultry.

À la lorraine – Red cabbage braised in red wine; *Potato fondantes* (see POTATOES).

Sauce. Diluted *Demi-glace sauce* (see SAUCE) or braising stock; in addition, *Horseradish sauce* (see SAUCE) served separately, or grated horseradish.

Uses. For large cuts of meat, particularly braised cuts.

À la lyonnaise – Medium-sized stuffed onions, braised; *Potato fondantes* (see POTATOES).

Sauce. Lyonnaise sauce (see SAUCE).

Uses. For large cuts of meat.

Macédoine – Mixture of vegetables which have been cooked in water separately, drained, and tossed in butter; carrots and turnips diced or shaped with a ball-scoop; diced French beans; small kidney beans; peas, etc. Cauliflower florets may be added.

Sauce. Juices of the roast or clear veal stock.

Uses. For large or small cuts of meat.

Maillot I (also called Porte-Maillot) – Glazed carrots and turnips in small oval lengths (or shaped with a ball-scoop); French beans in butter; braised lettuces. These vegetables, arranged round the dish in separate groups, are sometimes interspersed with little glazed onions and knobs of cauliflower sprinkled with melted butter.

Sauce. Demi-glace sauce (see SAUCE) flavoured with Madeira.

Uses. For large cuts of meat, especially ham.

Maillot II – Coarsely shredded carrots and turnips, simmered in butter in a covered pan; French beans in butter.

Sauce and uses. As *Maillot I.*

Maillot garnish round a ham

À la maraîchère – Carrots trimmed into large oval lengths and glazed; small glazed onions; thick slices of stuffed and braised cucumber; quartered artichokes which have been simmered in butter in a covered pan.

Sauce. Strained braising liquor, with all fat removed.

Uses. For large braised cuts of meat.

À la maréchale – Asparagus tips in butter; sliced truffles. Ingredients prepared *à la maréchale* are dipped in a mixture of two thirds breadcrumbs and one third finely chopped truffles.

Sauce. Maître d'hôtel butter (see BUTTER, *Compound butters*) or *Chateaubriand sauce* (see SAUCE).

Uses. For *Suprême of chicken* (see CHICKEN); escalopes (U.S. cutlets) of veal; sweetbreads; sometimes fillets of fish.

À la Marigny – Small artichoke hearts filled with corn kernels in cream; potato balls, browned in butter.

Sauce. Pan juices of the main dish diluted with white wine and thickened veal stock.

Uses. For small cuts of meat.

À la marinière – Shelled mussels cooked in white wine; shelled tails of freshwater crayfish.

Sauce. Marinière sauce (see SAUCE).

Uses. For fish.

Marivaux – Oval nests made of *Duchess potato* (see POTATOES), browned in the oven, filled with a mixture of finely chopped carrots, celery, artichoke hearts, and mushrooms – which have all been simmered in butter in a covered pan and blended with *Béchamel sauce* (see SAUCE) – sprinkled with Parmesan cheese and breadcrumbs and browned; French beans in butter.

Sauce. Thin *Demi-glace sauce* (see SAUCE) or thickened veal stock.

Uses. For large cuts of meat.

À la marocaine – Little mounds of rice pilaf, lightly seasoned with saffron (to be used as *canapés*); diced baby marrows (U.S. zucchinis) sautéed in oil; braised sweet peppers stuffed with chicken forcemeat.

Sauce. Pan juices diluted with tomato juice.

Uses. For *noisettes* of mutton or lamb.

À la mascotte – Sliced artichoke hearts sautéed in butter; potatoes trimmed into small oval lengths, browned in butter; sliced truffles.

Ingredients prepared *à la mascotte* are usually served in a deep pie dish or in earthenware dishes.

Sauce. Pan juices diluted with white wine and thickened veal stock.

Uses. For small cuts of meat; poultry.

Massena – Artichoke hearts garnished with strips of poached bone-marrow.

Sauce. Marrow sauce (see SAUCE) prepared by diluting the juices in which the marrow has been cooked.

Uses. For small cuts of meat.

Massenet – Anna potatoes baked in individual moulds and turned out (see POTATOES, *Anna potatoes for garnish*); small artichokes filled with a *salpicon* of bone-marrow; French beans in butter.

Sauce. Meat juices of the main dish or a *Demi-glace sauce* (see SAUCE) flavoured with Madeira.

Uses. For large or small cuts of meat.

Matelote – Small glazed onions; mushrooms; small croûtons fried in butter.

Sauce. Matelote sauce (see SAUCE) with red wine.

Uses. For fish.

Matignon – Artichoke hearts stuffed with a *matignon* (q.v.), sprinkled with breadcrumbs and browned; stuffed braised lettuces.

Sauce. Madeira sauce or *Port wine sauce* (see SAUCE).

Uses. For large and small cuts of meat.

Melba – Very small tomatoes filled with a *salpicon* of chicken, truffles, and mushrooms, blended in *Velouté sauce* (see SAUCE), sprinkled with breadcrumbs and browned; braised lettuce.

Sauce. Thickened veal stock flavoured with port.

Uses. For small cuts of meat.

Mentonnaise – Thick slices of small vegetable marrows stuffed with tomato-flavoured rice; small cooked artichokes simmered in butter in a covered pan; potatoes cut to look like olives and cooked slowly in clarified butter.

Sauce. Thickened veal stock or *Demi-glace sauce* (see SAUCE).

Uses. For large and small cuts of meat.

Mikado – Small mounds of curried rice to be used as *canapés*; tartlets filled with soya bean shoots in cream.

Sauce. *Curry sauce* (see SAUCE) with soya added.

Uses. For *suprêmes* of chicken, escalopes (U.S. cutlets) of veal.

Milanaise I – *Macaroni à l'italienne* (see MACARONI); cooked ham in *dariole* moulds.

Sauce. Veal stock flavoured with tomato.

Uses. For large pieces of meat.

Milanaise II – Semolina gnocchi (cut in lozenges and rectangles) sprinkled with cheese and browned.

Sauce. Thickened veal stock flavoured with tomato.

Milanaise III – *Macaroni à l'italienne* (see MACARONI); cooked ham, pickled tongue, mushrooms, and truffles, cut into strips and blended in concentrated veal stock flavoured with tomato, making a coarse *julienne*.

This *julienne* is either mixed with the macaroni or arranged in a circle round it.

Uses. For small cuts of meat especially veal cutlets (U.S. chops) in breadcrumbs.

Mirabeau – Stoned olives; anchovy fillets; blanched tarragon leaves. Watercress and occasionally matchstick potatoes are also included in this garnish.

Sauce. *Anchovy butter* (see BUTTER, *Compound butters*).

Uses. For small cuts of meat especially grilled steaks.

À la moderne – *Chartreuse* (q.v.) of vegetables in *dariole* moulds; stuffed, braised lettuces; small potatoes.

Sauce. Thickened veal stock with butter added.

Uses. Large cuts of meat.

Mont-Bry – Little cakes of spinach with Parmesan cheese; *cèpes* in cream.

Sauce. Pan juices of the main dish blended with white wine and thickened veal stock.

Uses. For small cuts of meat.

Montpensier – Green asparagus tips in butter; sliced truffles.

Sauce. Stock of the main dish blended with Madeira and thickened veal stock.

Uses. For small cuts of meat; jointed chicken.

Nanette – Small artichoke hearts cooked in butter in a covered pan, filled with *Lettuce chiffonnade with cream* (see CHIFFONNADE); mushrooms simmered in butter and filled with a *salpicon* of truffles blended with a concentrated *Demi-glace sauce* (see SAUCE).

Sauce. Pan juices of the main dish flavoured with Marsala and blended with chicken *Velouté sauce* (see SAUCE); cream and white chicken jelly.

Uses. For lamb cutlets (U.S. chops); escalopes (U.S. cutlets) of veal; calves' sweetbreads.

Nantua – Freshwater *Crayfish tails ragoût à la Nantua* (see CRAYFISH), arranged in shells, pastry boats, or tartlets, or set on a dish surrounding fish cooked in white wine. Shredded truffles are sometimes added.

Sauce. *Nantua sauce* (see SAUCE).

Uses. For fish.

Nichette – Grilled mushrooms filled with grated horse-radish; *ragoût* of cocks' combs and cocks' kidneys, blended in *Marrow sauce* (see SAUCE).

Sauce. *Marrow sauce*.

Uses. For small cuts of meat; *suprêmes*.

À la niçoise I – Small skinned tomatoes, simmered in butter; very small braised vegetable marrows (courgettes or zucchini); small artichokes stewed in butter; potato balls browned in butter.

Sauce. Thickened veal stock flavoured with tomato, or pan juices of the main dish flavoured with tomato.

Uses. Large and small cuts of meat; poultry.

À la niçoise II – Small tomatoes simmered in butter with a little chopped garlic; French beans in butter; new potatoes browned in butter, or potatoes cut to look like olives and cooked slowly in clarified butter.

Sauce and uses. As above.

À la niçoise III – *Tomato fondue à la niçoise* (see TOMATO); blanched green or black olives; anchovy fillets; capers.

When served with baked fish, the *fondue* is cooked in the same dish as the fish; for grilled fish, it is prepared separately.

Uses. For fish.

Ninon – Nests of *Duchess potato* (see POTATOES) filled with a *salpicon* of cocks' combs and kidneys blended in *Velouté sauce* (see SAUCE); asparagus tips in butter.

Sauce. *Marrow sauce* (see SAUCE).

Uses. For small cuts of meat.

Nivernaise – Carrots trimmed in small oval lengths; small glazed onions.

Sauce. *Demi-glace sauce* (see SAUCE) or, if the main dish is braised, the braising stock.

Uses. For large cuts of meat.

Normande – Oysters, trimmed and poached; mussels; shrimps; mushrooms; shredded truffles; freshwater crayfish cooked in a *court-bouillon*; fried breaded gudgeon; bread croûtons fried in butter.

Sauce. *Normande sauce* (see SAUCE).

Uses. For fish. See SOLE (*Sole à la normande*).

Olives for garnish – See OLIVES.

À l'orientale I – Small tomatoes stuffed with rice lightly flavoured with saffron; okras (ladies' fingers) cooked in butter; sweet peppers, skinned and simmered in butter in a covered pan.

The large cuts of meat served with this garnish must not be either interlarded or wrapped in bacon.

Sauce. *Tomato sauce* (see SAUCE) with butter.

Uses. For large and small cuts of meat.

À l'orientale II – Rice pilaf turned out of little conical moulds; cooked okra; small tomatoes stuffed with a tomato *salpicon*.

Sauce and uses. As above.

À la paloise – Potato balls browned in butter; French beans in cream.

Sauce. *Paloise sauce* (see SAUCE).

Uses. For small cuts of grilled meat.

À la parisienne I – *Potatoes à la parisienne* (see POTATOES); braised lettuce.

Sauce. Pan juices of the main dish diluted with white wine and veal stock.

Uses. For large and small cuts of meat; poultry.

À la parisienne II – As above, using quartered artichokes instead of lettuce.

Parmesan Génoise. GÉNOISE AU PARMESAN – Mix in a bowl 2 egg yolks seasoned with a little grated nutmeg, 2 stiffly beaten egg whites, 35 g. ($1\frac{1}{2}$ oz., 6 tablespoons) sieved flour, 50 g. (2 oz., $\frac{1}{2}$ cup) grated Parmesan cheese.

Spread the mixture $7\frac{1}{2}$ cm. (3 inches) thick on sheets of

A gourmet spread: duck *à l'orange*, turbot, lobster, *timbale* Elysée, assorted cheeses and wines (*Lasserre. Phot. Nicolas*)

paper on a buttered baking tin. Bake in a very slow oven and allow to cool. Cut into shapes.

Uses. For soup.

Pasta and cereals (soup garnish). PÂTÉS DIVERSES – 60 g. ($2\frac{1}{2}$ oz.) Italian pasta or vermicelli should be used for each litre ($1\frac{3}{4}$ pints, generous quart) soup. Cooking time varies from 8 to 14 minutes, according to the size and quality of the pasta used.

80 g. ($3\frac{1}{4}$ oz.) pastina or pasta beads should be used for each litre ($1\frac{3}{4}$ pints, generous quart) clear soup. Cooking time is 22 to 25 minutes.

Use approximately 70 g. ($2\frac{3}{4}$ oz.) tapioca, sago, or salep to 1 litre ($1\frac{3}{4}$ pints, generous quart) clear soup. Cooking time is 20 minutes.

50 g. (2 oz., $\frac{1}{4}$ cup) rice should be used for every litre ($1\frac{3}{4}$ pints, generous quart) clear soup. After pouring boiling water over it, the rice should be cooked in the clear soup for 25 minutes.

À la persane – Rounds or long slices of aubergines sautéed in oil; onion rings fried in oil; *Tomato fondue* (see FONDUE) with peppers (to decorate the other garnishes).

Sauce. Pan juices of the main dish or mutton or lamb stock flavoured with tomato.

Uses. Cutlets (U.S. chops) and *noisettes* of mutton or lamb.

À la piémontaise – Croquettes of risotto (mixed with a *salpicon* of truffles, mushrooms, pickled tongue, and ham) shaped to look like corks.

Sauce. Thin tomato sauce.

Uses. For large cuts of meat.

À la portugaise – Tomatoes stuffed with *duxelles* (q.v.); potatoes cut to look like olives and cooked slowly in clarified butter.

Sauce. Veal stock or *Demi-glace sauce* (see SAUCE) flavoured with tomato.

Uses. For large cuts of meat.

Prince Albert – Whole truffles simmered in butter in a covered pan.

The fillet of beef prepared according to this recipe is stuffed with *foie gras* (see BEEF, *Fillet of beef Prince Albert*).

Sauce. Juices of the main dish flavoured with Madeira or port; thickened veal stock.

Uses. For fillet of beef.

À la princesse – Asparagus tips in butter or cream; diced or sliced truffles.

Sauce. Allemande sauce (see SAUCE).

Uses. For poultry; calves' sweetbreads; small *vol-au-vent*; tartlets.

Printanier – Cut carrots or turnips in dice or fine strips about $2\frac{1}{2}$ cm. (1 inch) long. Blanch the vegetables and cook them in clear stock. When they are almost cooked, add peas and French beans which have been boiled and well drained. Asparagus tips and young kidney beans may also be added.

Uses. Add to boiling clear soup.

À la printanière – New carrots and turnips cut in small oval lengths, cooked in white stock, and tossed in butter; peas; asparagus tips in butter.

Sauce. Clear veal stock.

Uses. For large and small cuts of meat; poultry.

À la provençale – Aubergines cut in chunks, stuffed with *Tomato fondue* (see FONDUE), sprinkled with breadcrumbs and browned; French beans in butter; potatoes cut to look like olives and cooked slowly in clarified butter.

Sauce. Thickened veal stock flavoured with tomato and chopped tarragon.

Uses. For large and small cuts of meat.

Quenelles – Little balls about the size of a white bean, rounded or fluted. According to the recipe followed, they may be made of fine poultry, game or fish forcemeat. (See QUENELLES.)

Pipe through a forcing-bag and arrange in a buttered pan. Ten minutes before serving, cover with boiling salt water and simmer slowly. If no other garnish is used, 35 to 40 of these balls should be added to every litre ($1\frac{3}{4}$ pints, generous quart) clear soup. If other garnishes are used, 20 quenelles per litre ($1\frac{3}{4}$ pints, generous quart) will be sufficient.

Sometimes the balls are shaped in a teaspoon and sometimes stuffed with a *brunoise* (q.v.) of vegetables.

Uses. For soup.

Rachel – Slices of bone-marrow, poached, drained, grilled, and set on top of a piece of meat, which itself is set on artichoke hearts simmered in butter.

Sauce. Bordelaise sauce (see SAUCE).

Uses. For small pieces of grilled meat.

Ravioli – Prepare the ravioli as described in the recipe for ravioli (q.v.), but make very small. Fill them with chicken, *foie gras*, or any other delicately flavoured forcemeat. Simmer and drain.

Uses. Add to clear soup.

Régence – Large quenelles decorated with truffles, small chicken quenelles, slices of *foie gras* sautéed in butter, cocks' combs, mushrooms, thick slices of truffles (or truffles cut in ovals). For detailed instructions for the preparation of this dish see CHICKEN, *Chicken à la régence*.

Sauce. Allemande sauce (see SAUCE).

Uses. For cuts of white meat, calves' sweetbreads, poultry, savoury flans and tarts, *vol-au-vent*.

Régence garnish round veal sweetbreads

Réjane – Nests made of *Duchess potatoes* (see POTATOES), fried, hollowed-out and filled with leaf spinach in butter; quartered artichokes simmered in butter; slices of poached and drained bone-marrow.

Sauce. Braising stock.

Uses. For braised veal sweetbreads.

Renaissance – A variety of spring vegetables, disposed round the dish in individual groups. They are separately glazed, braised, tossed in butter or fried, as appropriate.

Sauce. Gravy of the roast or clear veal gravy.

Uses. For large cuts of meat.

Richelieu – Medium-sized stuffed tomatoes, sprinkled with breadcrumbs and browned; braised lettuce; potatoes cut as for small chips and cooked slowly in clarified butter, or new potatoes fried in butter.

Sauce. Thickened veal stock or a rather liquid *Demi-glace sauce* (see SAUCE).

Uses. For large cuts of meat.

À la romaine – Individual spinach *timbales* with anchovies; individual *Anna potatoes for garnish* (see POTATOES) turned out of small moulds.

Sauce. Thin tomato sauce or thickened veal stock flavoured with tomato.

Uses. For large cuts of meat.

Romanov – Cucumber stuffed with *duxelles* (q.v.), sprinkled with breadcrumbs and browned; *Duchess potatoes* (see POTATOES) filled with a *salpicon* of celeriac and mushrooms in a *Velouté sauce* (see SAUCE), sprinkled with grated horseradish.

Sauce. Demi-glace sauce (see SAUCE) flavoured with Madeira.

Uses. Garnish for large and small cuts of meat.

Rossini – Thick slices of truffle; slices of *foie gras* sautéed in butter.

Sauce. Stock of the main dish blended with Madeira and thickened veal stock.

Uses. For small cuts of meat.

Royale – This garnish for soup is prepared either from a flavoured consommé (q.v.) thickened with eggs, or from a purée of some kind, also thickened with egg.

Fill small *dariole* moulds with the chosen ingredients and cook in a *bain-marie* (q.v.) until firm. When completely cold, turn out of the moulds and dice neatly or cut into lozenges, squares, rounds, stars, leaves, etc.

Uses. Royales are used as garnishes for clear soups.

The measures given below are for 1½ litres (2¾ pints, 3¼ pints) clear soup.

Royale of asparagus tips. ROYALE DE POINTES D'ASPERGES – Boil 75 g. (3 oz.) asparagus tips in salt water and add 5 or 6 leaves young spinach. Drain, add 1½ tablespoons (2 tablespoons) *Béchamel sauce* (see SAUCE) and 2 tablespoons (3 tablespoons) consommé, and rub through a sieve. Blend in 4 egg yolks and cook as for other *royales*.

Royale of carrots, called à la Crécy. ROYALE DE CAROTTES, DITE À LA CRÉCY – Cook 1 sliced carrot, seasoned with salt and a little sugar, in butter. Add 2 teaspoons *Béchamel sauce* (see SAUCE), 2 tablespoons (3 tablespoons) cream, and sieve. Blend in 4 egg yolks. Pour into a buttered mould and cook in a *bain-marie* in a moderate oven until firm.

Royale of celery. ROYALE DE CÉLERI – Cook in butter in a double saucepan 75 g. (3 oz., ⅔ cup) finely shredded stick celery. Add 1 tablespoon *Béchamel sauce* (see SAUCE) and 2 tablespoons (3 tablespoons) consommé, and blend in 4 egg yolks.

Royale of chicken purée. ROYALE DE PURÉE DE VOLAILLE – Pound to a fine pulp 50 g. (2 oz.) cooked white meat of poultry. Add 2 tablespoons (3 tablespoons) *Béchamel sauce* (see SAUCE) and 2 tablespoons (3 tablespoons) cream, and strain. Blend in 4 egg yolks. Poach as for other *royales*.

Royale of game purée. ROYALE DE PURÉE DE GIBIER – Pound to a fine pulp 50 g. (2 oz.) flesh of ground game (hare or roebuck) or of winged game (partridge or pheasant). Add 1½ tablespoons (2 tablespoons) *Demi-glace sauce* (see SAUCE), 3 tablespoons (scant ¼ cup) consommé, and strain. Blend in 1 whole egg and 2 yolks. Pour into a mould and poach like other *royales*.

Plain royale. ROYALE ORDINAIRE – Put a large pinch of chervil into 1½ dl. (¼ pint, ⅔ cup) boiling consommé and leave it to infuse for 10 minutes. Beat together 1 whole egg and 2 yolks. Blend the eggs slowly into the stock. Strain, skim, and pour into a buttered mould. Cook as for other *royales*.

Royale of fresh pea purée. ROYALE DE PURÉE DE POIS FRAIS – Blend 2 tablespoons (3 tablespoons) fresh pea purée with 4 tablespoons (⅓ cup) consommé. Season with salt and a little sugar. Blend in 1 whole egg and 2 yolks. Pour into a mould and poach like other *royales*.

Royale of tomato purée. ROYALE DE PURÉE DE TOMATES – Dilute 1 dl. (6 tablespoons, scant ½ cup) concentrated tomato purée with 4 tablespoons (⅓ cup) consommé. Season with salt and sugar, thicken with 4 egg yolks and poach as for other *royales*.

Sagan – Risotto as a foundation, adding mushrooms stuffed with purée of brain mixed with a *salpicon* of truffles.

Sauce. Stock of the main dish blended with Madeira and thickened veal stock.

Uses. For escalopes of veal (U.S. veal cutlets); veal sweetbreads; *suprêmes* of chicken.

Saint-Germain I – Thick purée of green peas, served separately.

Sauce. Clear veal stock.

Uses. Large and small cuts of meat.

Saint-Germain II – Artichoke hearts simmered in butter and garnished with purée of green peas. This garnish is sometimes referred to as *Clamart*.

Sauce and uses. As above.

Saint-Saëns – Fritters of truffles and *foie gras*; cocks' kidneys; asparagus tips.

Sauce. Suprême sauce (see SAUCE) flavoured with *Truffle essence* (see ESSENCE).

Uses. For *suprêmes* of poultry.

À la sarde – Cork-shaped croquettes of rice cooked with cheese; mushrooms sautéed in butter; French beans in butter.

Sauce. Thin tomato sauce or veal stock flavoured with tomato.

Uses. For large cuts of meat.

À la sarrasine – Small buckwheat cakes, browned in butter; little rice tartlets, filled with *fondue* (q.v.) of tomatoes with sweet peppers added. Place 1 or 2 fried onion rings on each tartlet.

Sauce. Thin *Demi-glace sauce* (see SAUCE).

Uses. For large cuts of meat.

Sauerkraut. CHOUCROUTE – Wash and drain the *sauerkraut*; squeeze it dry and simmer in clear soup or white stock.

Semolina gnocchi (Hungarian cookery). GNOCCHI DE SEMOULE – Work 75 g. (3 oz., 6 tablespoons) butter in a bowl with a spatula. During this process add 1 egg, 65 g. (2½ oz., scant ½ cup) semolina and 2 teaspoons flour. Season with salt and a pinch of grated nutmeg. Work vigorously with the spatula until the mixture is slightly frothy. Leave to stand for 1 hour.

Make large oval balls shaped with a tablespoon and put them into a buttered pan. Add boiling water and leave to simmer for 20 minutes.

Uses. For soup.

Serge – Very small quartered cooked artichokes simmered in butter; coarsely shredded ham simmered in Madeira.

Ingredients prepared *à la Serge* are dipped in a mixture of breadcrumbs mixed with chopped truffles and mushrooms.

Sauce. Demi-glace sauce (see SAUCE) flavoured with *Truffle essence* (see ESSENCE).

Uses. Escalopes of veal (U.S. veal cutlets); calves' sweetbreads.

Spun eggs. OEUFS FILÉS – For 1 litre (1¾ pints, generous quart) soup, beat 1 egg and strain it through muslin. Put it in a fine strainer held over a frying pan containing boiling consommé. Move the strainer backwards and forwards over the stock. Drain the threads of egg thus prepared and add them to the soup.

Uses. For soup.

À la strasbourgeoise – Braised *sauerkraut*; thin rectangles of salt (pickled) pork cooked with the sauerkraut; slices of *foie gras* sautéed in butter.

Sauce. Boiled-down pan juices of the main dish.

Uses. For braised or pot-roasted poultry.

À la sultane – *Canapés* of chicken forcemeat (shaped like cutlets) on which chicken *suprêmes* are placed; very small tartlets filled with purée of truffles with pieces of blanched pistachio nut on top; cocks' combs.

Suprêmes prepared *à la sultane* are dipped in a mixture of breadcrumbs and chopped truffles.

Sauce. Suprême sauce (see SAUCE) very slightly seasoned with curry powder.

Uses. For *suprêmes* of chicken.

Tomatoes. TOMATES – Peel small, very firm tomatoes, remove liquid and pips, dice the flesh into squares 1 cm. ($\frac{1}{2}$ inch) across and add these to boiling consommé. Leave to simmer for 7 minutes and drain.

Uses. Add to soup.

Tortue – Little veal quenelles; stoned olives; mushrooms; sliced truffles and gherkins; freshwater crayfish cooked in a *court-bouillon*; fried egg yolks; heart-shaped pieces of fried bread; small pieces of tongue and calves' brains.

Sauce. Tortue sauce (see SAUCE).

Uses. For veal.

À la toscane – Thick diced macaroni mixed with a purée of *foie gras*; coarsely diced truffles sautéed in butter.

Ingredients prepared *à la toscane* must be dipped in a mixture of breadcrumbs and grated Parmesan cheese.

Sauce. Thickened veal stock.

Uses. For escalopes (U.S. cutlets) of veal; calves' sweetbreads; breasts of chicken.

À la toulousaine, also called à la Toulouse – Chicken quenelles; cocks' combs and kidneys; braised lamb or calves' sweetbreads; mushrooms; shredded truffles.

The elements of this garnish are arranged in separate groups and sometimes include chicken livers sautéed in butter.

Sauce. Allemande sauce (see SAUCE).

Uses. For calves' sweetbreads; poultry; savoury pies; tarts; *vol-au-vent*.

À la trouvillaise – Shelled shrimps; mussels; mushrooms.

Sauce. Shrimp sauce (see SAUCE).

Uses. For fish.

Truffles. TRUFFES – This garnish is very occasionally added to soups.

Shred fresh truffles into fine strips, or dice them into small squares. Put these in the boiling soup at the last minute. The heat of the soup is sufficient to cook the truffles.

À la tyrolienne – Tomatoes cut into quarters and cooked slowly in butter until very tender; onion rings fried in oil.

Sauce. Reduced veal stock with butter added.

Uses. For grilled cuts of meat or poultry.

Garnish à la tyrolienne (*Debillot. Phot. Larousse*)

À la Valenciennes – Rice cooked in meat stock (or plain boiled rice) mixed with a *salpicon* of sweet peppers.

Sauce. Pan juices of the main dish diluted with white wine or tomato-flavoured thickened veal stock.

Uses. For small cuts of meat or poultry.

À la Valois – Thinly sliced potatoes and slices of artichoke hearts sautéed together in butter, served in the *terrine* in which the meat is cooked.

Sauce. Pan juices with white wine added and veal stock with butter added.

Uses. For small cuts of meat.

Au vert-pré – Matchstick potatoes; watercress.

Sauce. Maître d'hôtel butter (see BUTTER, *Compound butters*).

Uses. For small cuts of meat and poultry, grilled.

Victoria – Small tomatoes stuffed with purée of mushrooms; quartered artichokes simmered in butter.

Sauce. Meat juices of the main dish blended with Madeira or port and thickened veal stock.

Uses. For small cuts of meat.

À la viennoise – Whites and yolks of hard-boiled egg, chopped separately; anchovy fillets; stoned olives; rounds of lemon with rind and skin removed; capers; chopped parsley. All these ingredients are arranged round the dish in separate groups.

Sauce. Brown butter (see BUTTER, *Compound butters*).

Uses. For small cuts of meat or poultry.

This garnish is especially suitable for cutlets (U.S. chops) and escalopes (U.S. cutlets) of veal; breasts of poultry, dipped in breadcrumbs and sautéed in butter. It can also be served with fillets of fish, chiefly brill (U.S. flounder) and sole.

Vladimir – Cucumbers cut in small oval lengths and simmered in butter; very small vegetable marrows (courgettes, zucchinis) coarsely diced, sautéed in butter.

Sauce. Stock of the main dish blended with sour cream, seasoned with paprika, and with grated horseradish sprinkled on top.

Uses. For small cuts of meat.

GARUM – Type of condiment, much used as a spice in ancient Roman cookery. It was probably pickling brine derived from salting seawater fish – scomber or mackerel in particular – and squeezing them to extract the liquid.

The best known, extracted from scomber, was called *garum nigrum.* It was put in little pots, as mustard is nowadays, and each guest flavoured it to his own liking, one with vinegar (*oenogarum*), another with water (*hydrogarum*), another with oil (*oleogarum*).

The *garum piperatum* was, as its name indicates, strongly flavoured with pepper.

GASCONY. GASCOGNE – Ancient province which once included the Landes, Basque, Chalosse, Condomois, Armagnac, Comminges, Couserans, Lomagne, Astarac and Bigorre districts and part of the Bordelais and Bazadais districts. It has always been a land of high gastronomic repute.

The inhabitants have maintained the cult of good eating in the *départements* which have been formed within the boundaries of Gascony – Hautes-Pyrénées, Gers, Landes, part of the Basses-Pyrénées, Haute Garonne, Lot-et-Garonne and Tarn-et-Garonne.

Gallimaufry was created in this region. This is the dish for which Taillevent, master chef of King Charles VII, gave the recipe, and the name of which, no-one quite knows why, has become a synonym for a bad stew.

Culinary specialities – The good things of this province are many. They include the *hams* of the Landes and of Ossau, eaten raw like those of Parma, or used in *fricassés* of various

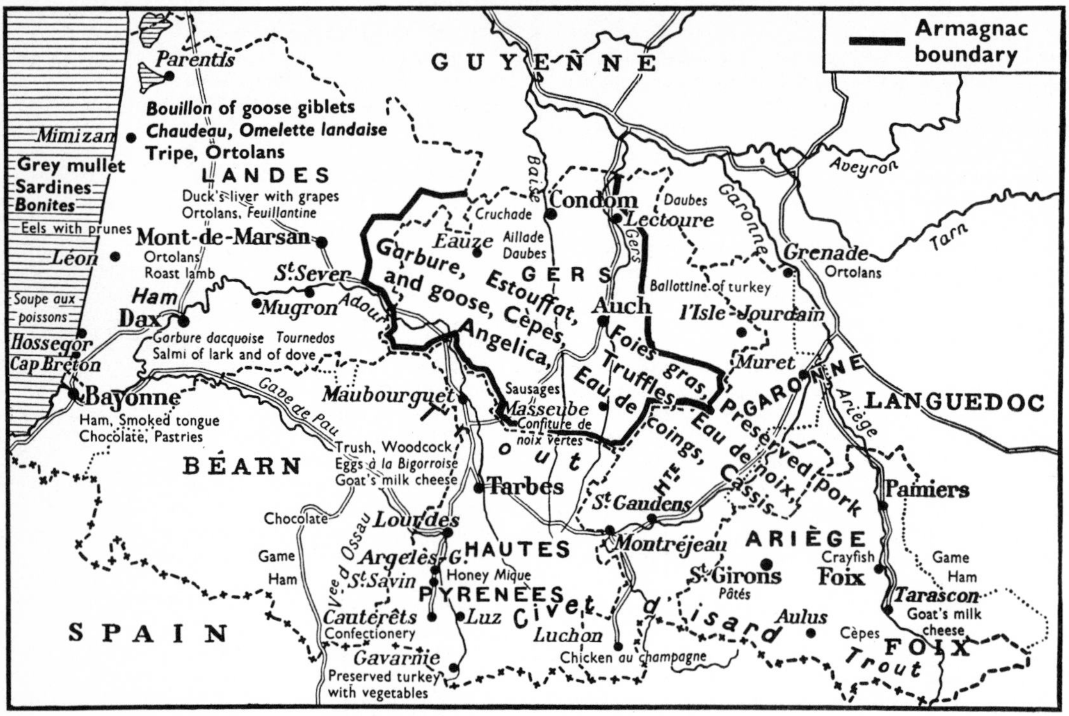

Gastronomic map of Gascony

kinds; *goose livers* and *duck livers; buntings; preserves of goose* and of *pork*; the savoury *oysters* of Cap Breton; and the *potted meats* and *pâtés* and *truffled foie gras* of the Gers, the Landes and the Lot-et-Garonne.

Nor must we forget Madarin wine and the rich and heady *Armagnac.*

GASTRONOME – Slightly pedantic term, dating back to the beginning of the nineteenth century, signifying experts in gastronomy. Genuine connoisseurs in matters of good food are satisfied with the name *gourmand* which, though normally translated as 'greedy', has no derogatory overtones in French.

The true gastronome, while esteeming the most refined products of the culinary arts, enjoys them in moderation, and, for his normal fare, seeks out the simplest dishes. While he is not himself a practitioner of the culinary art, he knows enough of its methods to be able to pass judgment on a dish and to recognise the ingredients of which it is composed.

GASTRONOMIC ASSOCIATIONS. GASTRONOMIQUES (ACADÉMIES, ASSOCIATIONS, GROUPEMENTS) – The *Académie des Gastronomes* was founded by Curnonsky in 1927. It admits forty members, consisting of gourmets, lovers of good food, culinary writers, and amphitryons. Each occupies the seat of a former great gourmet and upon election is called upon to deliver an address in honour of his predecessor.

But the *Académie des Gastronomes* was not the first of its kind. Without going so far back as the ancient *confréries*, the earliest of the modern associations is the *Club des cent* founded in 1912 by the gourmand-journalist Louis Forest. The *Club des cent* is a very active body with its own confidential (and very severe) personal guide. It awards diplomas, but rarely. It awards a substantial gastronomic literary prize annually.

The *Académie des psychologues du goût* is called the 'Jockey club of eating' and was founded in 1922. It counts many ambassadors among its members.

The *Académie Rabelais* groups together writers, painters, and designers interested in food.

The *Association amicale des amateurs d'authentiques andouillettes* (A.A.A.A.A.) is the most rigid and most exclusive (five members) of the gastronomic associations. Its members believe in simple, substantial and wholesome fare. A rare diploma, designed by Henry Monier, is awarded to the most outstanding amphytryons of the A.A.A.A.A.

The *Association des gastronomes amateurs de poisson* (1937) is the fish lovers' association.

The *Association des gastronomes régionalistes* (1924) is the association of gastronomes interested in regional cookery.

The *Belle Table* was founded by the engraver and painter Georges Villa. It concerns itself as much with the décor of the table as with the food served thereon.

The *Club de la casserole*, founded by René Lasserre, is the gourmet club of fashionable Paris. Its insignia is a tiny saucepan key ring. Its formal galas, which include fashion shows of *haute couture*, *coiffures*, furs and jewels, attract many of the leading personalities of stage and screen. The grand finale of a typical gala is the release of doves.

At the *Club des gourmettes*, the conversation is of cooking, and the members really know what they are talking about.

The *Club Prosper-Montagné* is where restaurateurs, *pâtissières, charcutiers*, and similar foregather.

The *Club des purs cent* is a splinter group of the *Club des cent* and numbers about fifty gourmets.

The *Commanderie des cordons-bleus*, in Dijon, awards diplomas to the best restaurateurs.

The *Compagnie des gentilshommes de gueule* (1928) organises monthly informal dinners presided over by a cultured and refined speaker.

The *Confrérie de la pochouse* extol this eminent regional dish of Verdun-sur-le-Doubs.

The *Échansonnes de France* is an association of female gourmands reluctant to leave all there is to say about wine to men alone.

The *Fin Palais* (1927) is an association of gourmand lawyers.

The *Galants de la verte marennes* wed their oysters to the whole range of white wines of the territory.

The *Société de gastronomie médicale* groups together the medical gourmets.

The *Taste-Moungettes* of Comminges extol the haricot beans of the region, indispensable ingredient of the *cassoulet*, the Luchon *pistache* and several other dishes.

GASTRONOMIC CALENDAR. CALENDRIER GASTRONOMIQUE – Below, month by month, is the best period of the year to eat the following:

Meat. VIANDES DE BOUCHERIE – *All the year round.* Beef, mutton, veal.

All the year round except July, August. Pork.

All the year round except July, August and September. Lamb.

Poultry. VOLAILLES – *January.* Duck, turkey, goose, pigeon, guinea fowl, poulard, chicken.

February. Duck, turkey, pigeon, guinea fowl, poulard.

March. Duck, pigeon, poulard.

April. Duck, pigeon, poulard, chicken.

May, June. Duck, turkey, goose, pigeon, poulard, chicken.

July to December. Duck, turkey, goose, pigeon, guinea fowl, poulard, chicken.

Game. GIBIER – *January.* Hutch rabbit, venison, quail, woodcock, snipe, capercaillie, wild duck, curlew, grouse, plover, teal.

February, March. Hutch rabbit, woodcock, snipe, capercaillie, wild duck, curlew, grouse, plover, teal.

April. Woodcock, snipe, capercaillie, wild duck, curlew, grouse, plover, teal.

May to August. Capercaillie, grouse, plover, teal.

September to December. Hare, hutch rabbit, venison, partridge, quail, pheasant, woodcock, capercaillie, wild duck, curlew, grouse, plover, teal.

Fish. POISSONS – *January.* Freshwater fish: eel, barbel, bream, carp, perch, salmon, tench.

Sea fish: bar (rare), brill, plaice, sea bream (rare), smelt, sturgeon, gurnet, herring, dab, mackerel (rare), whiting, cod, mullet, ray, sardines, sole, salmon trout (rare), turbot.

February. Freshwater fish: eel, gudgeon, perch, salmon.

Sea fish: bar (rare), brill, plaice, sea bream (rare), smelt, sturgeon, gurnet, herring, dab, mackerel (rare), whiting, cod, mullet, ray, sardines, sole, salmon trout (rare), turbot.

March. Freshwater fish: eel, gudgeon, salmon.

Sea fish: shad (rare), brill, plaice, sea bream, smelt, sturgeon, gurnet, herring, dab, mackerel (rare), whiting, cod, mullet, ray, sardines, sole (rare), salmon trout (rare), turbot.

April. Freshwater fish: eel, gudgeon, salmon, river trout.

Sea fish: shad, bass, brill, plaice, sea bream, smelt (rare), sturgeon, gurnet, dab, mackerel, whiting, cod, mullet, ray, sardines, sole (rare), salmon trout, turbot.

May. Freshwater fish: eel, gudgeon, salmon, river trout.

Sea fish: shad, bass, cod, sea bream, smelt (rare), gurnet, dab, mackerel, whiting, mullet, ray, sardines, sole (rare), tuna, salmon trout, turbot.

June. Freshwater fish: eel, gudgeon, salmon (rare), tench, river trout.

Sea fish: shad, bass, cod, sea bream, smelt (rare), gurnet, mackerel, mullet, plaice, ray, sardines, sole (rare), tuna, salmon, trout, turbot.

Frogs.

July. Freshwater fish: eel, pike, gudgeon, tench, trout, salmon (rare).

Sea fish: shad, bass, cod, sea bream, smelt (rare), gurnet, mackerel, plaice, ray, sardines, sole (rare), tuna, salmon trout, turbot.

Frogs.

August. Freshwater fish: eel, bream, pike, carp, grayling, perch, tench, river trout.

Sea fish: bass, brill (rare), cod, sea bream, smelt, gurnet (rare), mackerel, plaice, ray, sardines, sole (rare), salmon trout, turbot.

September. Freshwater fish: eel, bream, pike, carp, grayling, perch, tench, river trout.

Sea fish: bass (rare), brill (rare), cod, sea bream, smelt, gurnet (rare), plaice, ray, sole, salmon trout (rare), turbot (rare).

October. Freshwater fish: eel, barbel, bream, pike, carp, gudgeon, grayling, perch, tench, river trout (rare).

Sea fish: bass (rare), brill (rare), sea bream (rare), smelt, gurnet (rare), herring, dab, cod, plaice, ray, sole, salmon trout (rare), turbot (rare).

November. Freshwater fish: eel, barbel, bream, pike, carp, gudgeon, grayling, perch, tench.

Sea fish: bass (rare), brill, gilthead (rare), smelt, gurnet, herring, dab, whiting, cod, plaice, ray, sole, salmon trout (rare), turbot (rare).

December. Freshwater fish: eel, barbel, bream, pike, carp, gudgeon, grayling, perch, tench.

Sea fish: bass (rare), brill, sea bream (rare), smelt, sturgeon, gurnet, herring, dab, whiting, cod, mullet, plaice, ray, sole, salmon trout (rare), turbot.

Crustaceans. CRUSTACÉS – *January, February, March.* Lobster, crayfish.

April and May. Lobster, crayfish, crab, prawns, shrimps, freshwater crayfish.

June, July, August. Crab, prawns, shrimps, freshwater crayfish.

September. Lobster, crayfish, crab, prawns, shrimps, freshwater crayfish.

October, November, December. Lobster, freshwater crayfish.

Molluscs. MOLLUSQUES – *January, February, March, April, September, October, November, December* (that is to say the months with an 'r' in their name). Oysters, mussels.

GASTRONOMIC CUSTOMS. USAGES GASTRONOMIQUES – Gastronomic customs vary according to the period and the country.

The narrow-minded person admits as orthodox only the methods and seasonings to which he is accustomed, and considers those who have a different conception of the art of eating quite barbarous.

In America it is quite usual to add sugar to a salad. Heresy! Abomination! exclaim certain French authorities, who nevertheless think it nothing out of the ordinary to add slices of sweet beetroot to a salad of *mâche* (lamb's lettuce or corn salad). In Germany and in England, sweet cooked fruit is often served with the meat, and the same critics denounce this depraved taste; yet they would permit a garnish of chestnut purée (which is nothing but a purée of fruit much sweeter than some cooked apples or cranberries), or seasoning a haunch of venison with redcurrant jelly, or regaling themselves with *caneton à l'orange* or *cailles aux racines* or other savoury dishes garnished with sweet fruits.

In any case gastronomic usages are not the same everywhere in France, and the description of each province found in this dictionary in alphabetical order shows this clearly.

Not only are the culinary preparations different but the way the food is served and the arrangement of the meals vary. Thus in Flanders it is the established custom to serve soup at the beginning of the principal meal of the day. In other regions the habit of drinking a *trou de milieu* or, in Normandy, a *trou Normande*, has persisted.

The *trou de milieu* consists of serving, in the middle of the meal, generally before the service of the roast, small glasses of spirituous liqueurs of various kinds; Cognac, Armagnac, *marc*, *quetsche*, Calvados, *kirsch*, etc. In the south-west of France, where this custom used to be traditional, the young daughter of the house offered the guests these liqueurs placed on a great silver tray.

In modern practice, although the custom of the *trou de milieu* still persists in some parts, the *sorbet*, still made with a base of liqueur or liqueur wine, has for the most part taken its place.

GÂTEAU – See CAKE.

GAUDES – The name given in Franche-Comté, Burgundy, and other districts to a kind of maize flour porridge or pudding somewhat similar to the Italian polenta, or to hasty-pudding.

Franche-Comté gaudes. GAUDES DE FRANCHE-COMTÉ – Pour into a saucepan containing $3\frac{1}{2}$ litres (3 quarts, $7\frac{1}{2}$ pints) salted boiling water, 500 g. (18 oz., 3 cups) maize flour which has been mixed in cold water to a smooth consistency. Mix well. Cook this pudding, stirring constantly with a large wooden spoon, until it is thick. Add 100 g. (4 oz., $\frac{1}{2}$ cup) butter. Serve hot.

Sometimes this pudding, after it is cooked, is poured into small bowls where it is left to cool. It is then cut into slices which are heated in butter and sprinkled with fine sugar.

The *gaudes* may also be served cold, in which case the maize flour mixture is poured into moulds. When the gaudes have cooled, they are turned out of the moulds and eaten with sugar.

GAULOISE (À LA) – Name used for a garnish consisting of cocks' combs and kidneys which is served with clear soup (see SOUPS AND BROTHS).

It is used, too, for a garnish served with large and small *vol-au-vent* or pies, having cocks' kidneys as its chief ingredient, with pickled tongue and truffles added. This filling is blended in *Suprême sauce* (see SAUCE) flavoured with Madeira.

The name is used for little cakes made of Genoa cake mixture (see CAKE, *Genoa cake*) cooked in special moulds (*moules à diplomates*), spread with apricot jam and grilled chopped almonds.

GAYETTES (Provençal cookery) – Type of flat sausage made of pork liver and fresh bacon encased in pork caul and cooked in the oven.

They are generally served cold, as an *hors-d'œuvre*. (See PORK, *Pork liver gayettes*.)

GAZELLE – Antelope found in northern and western Asia and in central Africa.

The meat of the gazelle is very good to eat. It should first be left in a mild marinade. All the recipes appropriate to roebuck (q.v.) and venison (q.v.) are suitable for gazelle.

GAZPACHO (Spanish cookery). GASPACHO – Soup-salad made of fresh cucumber, tomatoes, sweet peppers, and slices of bread moistened with water.

Soak the skinned, sliced, and deseeded tomatoes, and the sliced, deseeded peppers in a dressing prepared as follows: Pound in a mortar 2 cloves of garlic. Season with salt, pepper, and a little cumin. Blend with oil and vinegar; add a little finely sliced shallot, chopped chervil and a cup of iced water.

Leave to soak for 30 minutes. Ten minutes before serving, add thinly sliced cucumber, slices of bread, more water, if necessary, and cubes of ice. Serve very cold.

GEANS CHERRIES. GUIGNES – Species of red, black, or white cherry. They are firm and fairly sweet.

Geans are mainly used in France to make a liqueur called Guignolet, which is a speciality of the town of Angers.

GEBIE – Small shellfish, whitish in colour, found in French coastal waters. It can be cooked like shrimps, and is used mainly as bait for large fish.

GELATINE. GÉLATINE – Amorphous, colourless solid, without smell, which swells in water. When mixed in hot water, it forms a viscous substance which turns to jelly when the mixture is cold, provided that it has not been allowed to boil for too long.

Gelatine is produced by the action of heat upon a substance contained in bones, cartilage and tendons. It is used in the preparation of jellies.

Leaf gelatine. GRÉNÉTINE – A pure and transparent form of gelatine used in pharmacy and cookery.

GELOSE. GÉLOSE – Synonym of agar-agar. A viscous substance extracted from certain marine algae. Much used in Japan in the preparation of fruit and other jellies.

GENDARME – French popular name for pickled herring. This name is also given to a type of sausage, dry and very hard, which is made in Switzerland and bears some slight resemblance to a herring in appearance.

GENEVOISE SAUCE – Sauce, originally called *Génoise*, served only with fish. It is flavoured with red wine. (See SAUCE.)

GENISTA (Broom). GENÊT – Botanical name for a number of plants of the broom family. They have butterfly-like flowers. Broom buds are sometimes pickled in vinegar and used as a substitute for capers.

GENOESE. GÉNOISE – *Génoise* was the name of a sauce served only with fish cooked in a *court-bouillon* (salmon and salmon trout in particular). Nowadays, this sauce is called *Genevoise*.

In confectionery, cakes made from a Genoese mixture are called Genoese cakes.

Genoese cake I. PÂTÉ À GÉNOISE – *Ingredients.* 500 g. (18 oz., $2\frac{1}{4}$ cups) fine sugar, 500 g. (18 oz., $4\frac{1}{2}$ cups) sieved flour, 500 g. (18 oz., $2\frac{1}{4}$ cups) butter, 16 eggs, a pinch of salt, 1 vanilla bean.

Gazelle (*Grün*)

Method. Put the sugar, eggs, salt, and vanilla bean in a pan and whisk over very gentle heat. When the mixture begins to foam and rise well up in the pan, remove from the stove and continue whisking until it is cold. Still beating the mixture, add the flour, using a dredger, and the butter, which should be melted and tepid.

Pour into baking tins and bake in the oven at 190°C. (375°F., Gas Mark 5) for 40 to 45 minutes.

Genoese cake II. PÂTÉ À GÉNOISE À L'ANCIENNE – *Ingredients.* 500 g. (18 oz., $2\frac{1}{4}$ cups) fine sugar, 500 g. (18 oz., $4\frac{1}{2}$ cups) sieved flour, 175 g. (6 oz., 1 cup) sweet almonds, 25 g. (1 oz., $2\frac{1}{2}$ tablespoons) bitter almonds, 300 g. (11 oz., $1\frac{1}{3}$ cups) butter, 12 eggs, small pinch of salt.

Method. Blanch and pound the almonds to a fine powder in a mortar. Put in a bowl and mix in 2 eggs. Add the sugar, flour, and 5 whole eggs. Beat with a wooden spoon for 5 minutes. Add 5 egg yolks, the melted butter, and the remaining whites, beaten.

Put the mixture into buttered baking tins and bake in a hot oven.

Apricot Genoese cake. GÉNOISE À L'ABRICOT – Bake a Genoese cake. Slice it horizontally into 3 layers of equal thickness. Rub apricot jam through a sieve and flavour it with kirsch. Spread on 1 layer of cake. Cover with the middle slice. Spread with apricot jam. Set the last slice carefully on top of the other. See that the edges of the cake fit together as neatly as possible.

Spread the top and sides of the cake with apricot jam, and ice it with a *Fondant icing* (see ICING) flavoured with kirsch.

The cake may be sprinkled with blanched and chopped pistachio nuts or with chopped browned almonds, and decorated with crystallised fruits or *Royal icing* (see ICING).

Genoese cake with chocolate filling (*Kollar*)

Genoese cake with chocolate filling. GÉNOISE FOURRÉE AU CHOCOLAT – Slice a Genoese cake horizontally into 3 layers of equal thickness. Spread a layer of *Chocolate butter cream* (see CREAMS) on 1 slice of cake. Cover with another slice. Spread with the butter cream. Lay the last slice on top of the others. Press gently to stick the three parts firmly together. Spread the top and sides with apricot jam and sprinkle with chocolate hundreds and thousands.

Genoese cake with mocha cream. GÉNOISE FOURRÉE AU MOKA – Made like Genoese cake with chocolate filling. Instead of chocolate butter cream, coffee butter cream is put between the layers. Apricot jam is then spread on the top and sides of the cake and it is iced with mocha *Fondant icing* (see ICING).

Genoese cake with filling à la normande. GÉNOISE FOURRÉE À LA NORMANDE – Slice a round Genoese cake horizontally into 2 layers of equal thickness. Moisten the halves with Calvados. Spread one half with thick apple jam mixed with half its weight of *French pastry cream* (see CREAMS) flavoured with Calvados. Place the other half of the cake on top. Spread apricot jam over the cake and ice with *Fondant icing* (see ICING) flavoured with Calvados. Decorate with quartered apples cooked in syrup, halves of almonds, and lozenges of angelica.

GENTIAN. GENTIANE – General name given to several species of plants. The large gentian or yellow gentian, as well as other flowers of this family, are used in the preparation of certain apéritifs. Gentiane, a digestive liqueur, is distilled from the gentian in France and Switzerland, and has a distinctive taste much prized in these countries.

The large, bitter-tasting root of the gentian is treated either by soaking or infusion.

GEOPHAGIST (Earth-eater). GÉOPHAGE – Certain American Indians in times of scarcity used to eat a type of clay soil. This soil has no food value, and serves only to create an illusion of satiety.

In different parts of Asia, Africa, and America, there are whole tribes of geophagists. The yellow races are especially addicted to this peculiar custom, although it has been observed in several peoples belonging to other ethnic groups. Geophagists are to be found in almost all latitudes.

In Java and Sumatra, the clay which provides food for the inhabitants undergoes some preparation in advance. According to Hekmeyer, it is mixed into a paste with water after all foreign bodies (such as sand and stones and other hard matter) have been removed. It is then rolled out into thin cakes and baked in an iron pan over a charcoal fire.

GEORGETTE – Name for certain foods, especially potatoes, which are stuffed with a *ragoût* of freshwater crayfish tails.

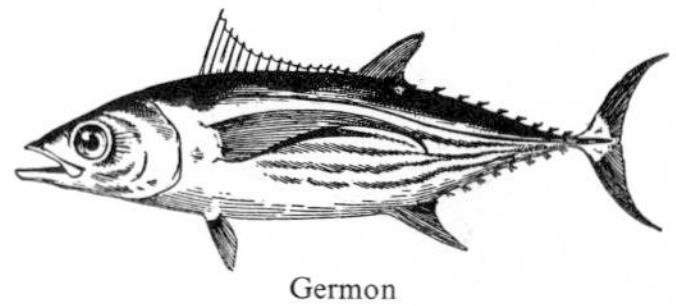

Germon

GERMON – Another name for tunny (tuna) sometimes also called white tunny, because of its resemblance to that fish.

The *common germon*, which is to be found in the Mediterranean, has white flesh which makes quite good eating. All recipes suitable for tunny (tuna) may be used for germon. In U.S.A. the Pacific coast *albacore* is a white-meat tunny (tuna fish).

GÉROMÉ – See CHEESE.

GEX – See CHEESE.

GHERKIN. CORNICHON – Gherkins are very young fruits of certain varieties of cucumber. They are gathered green, preserved in vinegar, and used as a condiment.

Gherkins in vinegar (cooked). CORNICHONS AU VINAIGRE (À CHAUD) – Trim and rub the gherkins and soak them in salt for 24 hours. Drain in a sieve, and wipe them well with a cloth, one by one.

Put them in a large basin and cover with vinegar which has been boiled in a copper pan. Leave for 10 hours. Put the vinegar back to boil, adding some fresh vinegar. Allow $\frac{1}{2}$ litre (scant pint, $2\frac{1}{4}$ cups) for 3 litres ($5\frac{1}{4}$ pints, $6\frac{1}{2}$ pints) boiled vinegar. Pour the boiling vinegar on the gherkins.

The next day, drain the gherkins, put them in jars or pots, with small white onions, chillis, sprigs of thyme, fragments of bay, tarragon sprigs, and cloves, and cover with the vinegar. Seal the pots or jars hermetically and keep in a cool place.

Gherkins in vinegar (uncooked). CORNICHONS AU VINAIGRE (À CRU) – Rub the gherkins with a cloth, or brush them, to remove the down which covers them. Steep in a basin of sea-salt. Leave for 24 hours. Drain, wash them in vinegar water, drain again, and wipe them one by one.

Arrange them in a glass jar or in a stoneware pot, adding small white onions, chillis, sprigs of thyme, fragments of bay leaf, tarragon sprigs and cloves. Cover with wine vinegar. Seal the pots hermetically, and keep in a cool place.

Gherkins prepared in this way can be kept for 4 to 5 weeks.

Fresh salt gherkins à la russe. CORNICHONS FRAIS SALÉS À LA RUSSE – Wash 24 fresh gherkins in lukewarm water without trimming them. Leave to cool in a large basin of cold water. Drain and wipe them. Put in a jar in layers with blackcurrant leaves and sprays of fennel between.

Put shavings of horseradish and a layer of blackcurrant leaves on the last layer of gherkins, which should reach 2 cm. ($\frac{3}{4}$ inch) below the top of the receptacle. Press the leaves down. Boil salt water, cool, and pour over the gherkins. Leave to soak for 24 hours.

Gherkins are used as an *hors-d'œuvre* in Russia.

GIBLETS. ABATIS – The head, neck, heart, pinions, feet, gizzard, and liver of poultry, as well as cocks' combs and kidneys.

The giblets of turkeys and large chickens are used for making *ragoûts*, and improving the taste of stocks and clear soups.

Cocks' combs, and kidneys and livers of fowl are used for certain classic garnishes such as *financière*, *Toulouse*, and *ambassadrice*, and other dishes of a similar type.

The livers of geese and ducks are not considered as giblets. These are expensive delicacies and require special preparation.

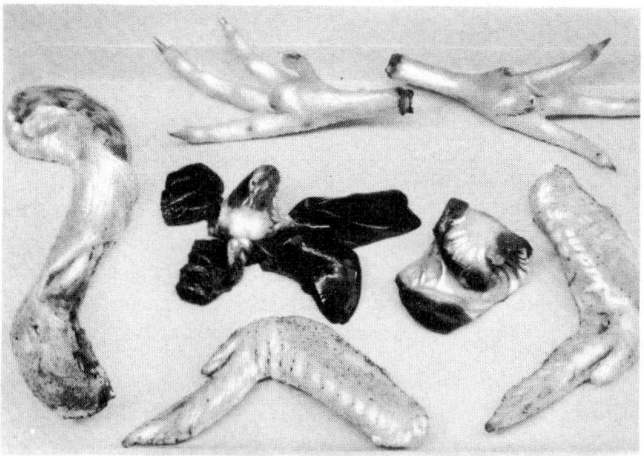

Chicken giblets (*Scarnati*)

Methods of preparing poultry giblets – The giblets of turkeys and geese are those most frequently used for *ragoûts*. Before being used, giblets should be thoroughly washed and trimmed. Singe the neck, head, and pinions, and remove all feathers. Scald the feet, peel off the outer skin which covers them, and pare off the end of the spurs. Slit the gizzard on the curved side, open it and remove the inner bag, taking care not to break it, as it is full of grit. Remove the gall bladder from the liver and trim off the upper part of the heart. The pinions, neck, and head of turkeys, geese, and ducks should be scalded to make plucking easier. Plunge them into boiling water and pluck immediately.

The giblets of various kinds of poultry are all prepared in a similar manner. Recipes are therefore given only for turkey giblets, which are the biggest. Depending on how tender the giblets are, it will be sufficient to increase or decrease the period of cooking.

Only stocks made of the same kind of meat as that which forms the basis of the *ragoût* should be used; otherwise use water. A chicken *ragoût* should be moistened with chicken or veal stock, but never with lamb or mutton stock.

In addition to the recipes given below, all those given for lamb, mutton, veal or chicken *ragoûts* can also be applied to giblets. (See RAGOÛTS.)

The livers of duck, turkey, goose and chicken should not be added to the various giblet *ragoûts* earlier than 10 minutes before removing from the heat.

These livers are used separately, sautéed, cooked on skewers, in pilaf or risotto, or prepared in other ways. (See OFFAL or VARIETY MEATS.)

Duck and chicken giblets. ABATIS DE CANARDS ET DE POULETS – Prepared in the same ways as turkey giblets (see below).

Giblet soup – See SOUPS AND BROTHS.

Turkey giblets à l'anglaise. ABATIS DE DINDE À L'ANGLAISE – *Ingredients.* One large set (or 2 small sets) giblets: head, neck, pinions, gizzard, liver, feet – 700 to 800 g. ($1\frac{3}{4}$ lb.) – 2 medium large onions, 2 large potatoes, a *bouquet garni* (a sprig of parsley, thyme and half a bay leaf), 1 tablespoon chopped parsley, 1 tablespoon chopped chervil, salt, pepper.

Method. Scald the head, neck, pinions and feet, and remove all feathers. Slit and clean the gizzard, remove the gall bladder from the liver, cut up the giblets into uniform pieces. Slice the onions and potatoes.

Put half the onions and the potatoes into a shallow pan, and sprinkle with half the chopped parsley. Put the pieces of giblets, except the liver, on this layer of vegetables. Cover with the rest of the onions, potatoes and chopped parsley. Put the *bouquet garni* in the middle, season with salt and pepper, and pour in enough water to cover.

Boil fast on a high flame. Then draw the pan to the edge of the burner, cover, and keep it simmering moderately but continuously for 45 minutes. Ten minutes before serving add the liver.

Serve the giblets in a shallow dish, and sprinkle with chopped chervil.

Turkey giblets bonne femme. ABATIS DE DINDE BONNE FEMME – *Ingredients.* One large set (or 2 small sets) giblets – 700 to 800 g. ($1\frac{3}{4}$ lb.), 25 g. (1 oz., 2 tablespoons) butter, 100 g. (4 oz.) lean unsalted bacon, 100 g. (4 oz.) small onions, 24 small new carrots or 3 large carrots cut to size of new carrots, 25 g. (1 oz., $\frac{1}{4}$ cup) flour, 1 dl. (6 tablespoons, scant $\frac{1}{2}$ cup) white wine, a *bouquet garni*, 1 clove of garlic, $1\frac{1}{4}$ litres ($2\frac{1}{4}$ pints, $2\frac{3}{4}$ pints) water, salt, pepper.

Method. Follow the instructions given in the recipe for *Turkey giblets à la bourgeoise* (see below).

Turkey giblets à la bourgeoise. ABATIS DE DINDE À LA BOURGEOISE – *Ingredients.* One large set (or 2 small sets) giblets – 700 to 800 g. ($1\frac{3}{4}$ lb.), 25 g. (1 oz., 2 tablespoons) butter, 100 g. (4 oz.) lean unsalted bacon, 100 g. (4 oz.) small onions, 24 small new carrots or 3 large carrots cut to size of new carrots, 25 g. (1 oz., $\frac{1}{4}$ cup) flour, 1 dl. (6 tablespoons, scant $\frac{1}{2}$ cup) white wine, a *bouquet garni*, a clove of garlic, $1\frac{1}{4}$ litres ($2\frac{1}{4}$ pints, $2\frac{3}{4}$ pints) water, salt, pepper.

Method. Prepare the giblets as indicated in the recipe for *Turkey giblets à l'anglaise*. Blanch and dice the bacon. Peel the onions and new carrots, peel and chop the clove of garlic.

Heat the butter in a shallow pan. Add the bacon, brown it lightly, and remove it. Fry the onions until golden. Drain and put with the bacon.

Brown the giblets, except the liver, on a high flame, turning with a spoon to ensure even cooking. Add the chopped garlic and sprinkle with the flour. Stir to blend, and as soon as the flour begins to brown, moisten with the white wine and boil down for a few minutes. Complete the moistening with enough water or stock to cover.

Add the *bouqet garni*, bacon, onions and carrots. Add salt and pepper. Cover the pan and as soon as it begins to boil fast reduce the heat and leave to finish cooking on moderate heat for 45 minutes. Ten minutes before serving, add the liver. Arrange the giblets in a shallow dish and add the garnish. Pour the sauce over.

Turkey giblets à la bourguignonne. ABATIS DE DINDE À LA BOURGUIGNONNE – *Ingredients.* One large set (or 2 small) turkey giblets – 700 to 800 g. (1¾ lb.), 25 g. (1 oz., 2 tablespoons) butter, 100 g. (4 oz.) desalted lean bacon, 100 g. (4 oz.) small onions, 100 g. (4 oz.) cultivated mushrooms, 1 tablespoon flour, ½ litre (scant pint, 2¼ cups) red wine, a *bouquet garni*, a clove of garlic, ½ litre (scant pint, 2¼ cups) water or stock, salt, pepper.

Method. Follow the instructions given in the recipe for *Turkey giblets à la bourgeoise*.

Turkey giblets chasseur. ABATIS DE DINDE CHASSEUR – Season the giblets with salt and pepper and fry them in a shallow pan, using oil and butter in equal proportions. Drain, and keep hot.

In the same pan put 100 g. (4 oz.) thinly sliced mushrooms and cook on a high flame. Add 2 chopped shallots, moisten with half a glass white wine, and boil down.

Add 1 dl. (6 tablespoons, scant ½ cup) *Tomato sauce* (see SAUCE) and 2 dl. (⅓ pint, scant cup) thickened brown veal stock. Put the giblets into this sauce. Reheat without boiling and add 1 tablespoon chopped parsley, chervil and tarragon.

The dish should not be too thick. The tomato sauce is sufficient to give it the desired consistency.

Turkey giblets with chipolata sausages. ABATIS DE DINDE À LA CHIPOLATA – *Ingredients.* One large set (or 2 small sets) turkey giblets – 700 to 800 g. (1¾ lb.), 25 g. (1 oz., 2 tablespoons) butter, 5 or 6 blanched and glazed small onions, 24 chestnuts, peeled and three-quarters cooked in stock with a pinch of sugar and 1 tablespoon butter, 8 cooked chipolata sausages, 50 g. (2 oz.) desalted, diced and browned bacon, 1 tablespoon flour, 1 dl. (6 tablespoons, scant ½ cup) white wine, a *bouquet garni*, 1¼ litres (2¼ pints, 2¾ pints) water, salt, pepper.

Method. Follow the instructions given in the recipe for *Turkey giblets à la bourgeoise*. The cooked chestnuts should not be added to the *ragoût* until 15 minutes before serving.

Turkey giblets à l'écossaise. ABATIS DE DINDE À L'ÉCOSSAISE – Follow the recipe for *Turkey giblets bonne femme* with 2 dl. (⅓ pint, scant cup) Brunoise garnish made up of finely shredded carrots, celery and onions half cooked in butter, and hulled barley, previously soaked in warm water and cooked in salted water for 35 minutes.

Turkey giblets à la fermière. ABATIS DE DINDE À LA FERMIÈRE – Follow the recipe for *Turkey giblets à la bourgeoise* but replace the garnish given for that recipe by 4 dl. (¾ pint, scant 2 cups) *Vegetable fondue* (see FONDUE).

Fricassée of turkey giblets (early French recipe). ABATIS DE DINDE EN FRICASSÉE AU BLANC – Prepare turkey giblets, put into a saucepan with 2 tablespoons (3 tablespoons) butter, a *bouquet garni* of parsley, a scallion, 1 clove of garlic, 2 cloves, thyme, bay leaf, basil, and some mushrooms. Add a pinch of flour, moisten with water or stock, season with salt and coarsely ground pepper, and cook. Boil down and thicken the sauce. Remove the herbs, add gradually 3 egg yolks blended with 3 tablespoons (scant ¼ cup) cream, without bringing to the boil. A dash of vinegar or lemon juice may be added to the *roux* before binding the sauce.

Turkey giblets fried in batter. ABATIS DE DINDE EN FRITOT – Cook the giblets in stock. Drain, and leave to cool. Soak for 30 minutes in a marinade of 1 tablespoon oil, a few drops vinegar or lemon juice, chopped parsley, salt and pepper. Coat the giblets in batter made from 75 g. (3 oz., ¾ cup) flour, 1 tablespoon oil, 1 dl. (6 tablespoons, scant ½ cup) warm water, salt, pepper, and 1 stiffly whisked egg white added after the mixture has been left to stand.

Fry the giblets in smoking-hot deep fat. Drain, sprinkle with fine dry salt, and garnish with fried parsley and quarters of lemon. Serve with tomato sauce.

Turkey giblet ragoût (basic method). ABATIS DE DINDE EN RAGOÛT À BRUN – Cut the neck, pinions and gizzard into pieces; also the feet, if they are being used.

Put the giblets into a shallow pan in which butter has been heated. Cook, stirring from time to time. Sprinkle with flour and brown lightly. Add a little crushed garlic. Moisten with stock or water and a little white wine. Add a *bouquet garni*. Bring to the boil, season, cover the pan with a lid and cook for 30 to 35 minutes. Strain the giblets, trim them, and carefully remove all bone splinters. Put the boned giblets back in a clean pan.

Garnish with blanched and lightly fried vegetables, according to the recipe chosen. Sieve the juices left in the pan, remove surplus fat, add tomato purée, and pour over the giblets. Bring to the boil, cover, and finish cooking in the oven; 10 minutes before serving, add the liver. Take care not to break the giblets or vegetables when serving.

The moistening of brown giblet *ragoûts* is usually done with veal or chicken broth and light stock. They could also be moistened with water, supplemented by a small quantity of tomato purée.

Turkey giblets with turnips. ABATIS DE DINDE AUX NAVETS – 'Take 2 sets of turkey giblets. Open the gizzards to empty them; scald the pinions and the necks, pluck them and singe them, cut into pieces and wash under a running tap, then drain. Put a piece of butter with 225 g. (8 oz.) bacon cut into large dice into a saucepan; when it is fried, put in the giblets to colour them a little. Sprinkle with a little flour and moisten with stock or water. Add an onion stuck with 4 cloves, salt, pepper, and a *bouquet garni*. Cut the turnips to look like large olives, put them with some butter and sugar into a saucepan to brown lightly. Moisten with the sauce in which the giblets were cooked, add the turnips to the giblets, boil down the sauce to the desired consistency. Simmer gently to allow fat to rise, which should then be removed. Taste to see if there is enough salt, remove the *bouquet* and the onions stuck with cloves. Serve hot.' (From *La Grande Cuisine simplifiée*, by Robert, Paris, published by Audot, 1845.)

Giblets can be prepared in the same manner with mushrooms, celeriac, artichoke hearts, cucumbers etc.

Turkey livers. FOIES DE DINDES – All recipes for chicken livers are suitable for the livers of turkeys.

Turkey livers are sometimes very large and delicately flavoured. They are similar to duck and goose livers and the same methods of preparation can be applied to them.

Young pigeon livers. FOIES DE PIGEONNEAUX – Usually the pigeon liver, which contains no gall, is left inside the bird if it is to be braised, stewed, pot-roasted or roasted.

All recipes for chicken livers are suitable for pigeon livers.

GIGOT, MANCHE DE – Small metal appliance attached to the bone or 'handle' of the leg of mutton after cooking, to keep it steady while carving.

GIGUE – See HAUNCH.

GILD. DORER – Some types of pastry and other preparations are brushed with egg (gilded or glazed) before browning in the oven.

GIMBLETTE – See RING-BISCUIT.

GIMLET. FORET – Steel point used to penetrate wood and casks. Also used by wine waiters to uncork bottles.

GIN – Spirit, distilled from grain (barley, wheat, oats) and flavoured with juniper berries.

Ginger in root form, preserved and powdered
(*Fauchon. Phot. Nicolas*)

GINGER. GINGEMBRE – Root-stock of a tropical plant which grew originally in Bengal and Malabar. It is sold in two forms. *Grey ginger* has the stronger smell and comes in tubercles 4 to 10 cm. ($1\frac{1}{2}$ to 4 inches) long and 1 to 2 cm. ($\frac{1}{2}$ to $\frac{3}{4}$ inch) thick, covered with a greyish-yellow skin and well-defined rings. *White ginger* is sold skinned and cut up into smaller pieces.

It is used as a condiment. Jam is also made with ginger.

GINGER BEER – See BEER.

GIRAFFE. GIRAFE – Ruminant African mammal. Its flesh is edible.

GIRAUMON – West Indian pumpkin. Its flesh is sweet and delicate, sometimes with a musky flavour. It is eaten raw in salads like cucumber, or cooked with other types of gourd and pumpkin. (See GOURD, PUMPKIN.)

GIRDLE (U.S. GRIDDLE). GALETTOIRE – Flat iron pan without an edge or with a very shallow edge, used for baking pancakes of wholemeal flour called *galetons*, drop scones or girdle cakes (U.S. griddle cakes).

GIRELLA. GIRELLE – Small, graceful sea-fish. It is beautifully coloured and has no scales.

The *common girella* is violet with an orange stripe; the *red girella*, a rich scarlet; the *Turkish girella*, green with turquoise blue stripes. These are all Mediterranean fish.

Girella is used mainly in *bouillabaisse* (q.v.), but it can be served fried. Its flesh is fairly delicate.

Girella

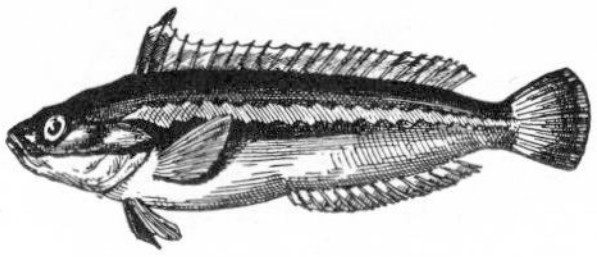

GIZZARD. GÉSIER – Third digestive pouch in birds. In birds of prey, it has a membraneous lining. In grain-eating birds, it is very muscular and thick.

GJETÖST – See CHEESE.

GLAÇAGE – There is no single English equivalent for this word. It is used for several quite distinct operations for which there are various terms in English.

In its proper sense, *glacer* means to freeze a liquid until it turns to ice. Thus a creamy or other mixture may be put in a freezer with salt, saltpetre and natural ice to make *une glace*, that is to say an ice cream or water ice. (See ICE CREAMS AND ICES.)

But *glaçage* is also used for browning or glazing in a very hot oven. A braised cut of meat, poultry or game is *glacé* (browned or glazed) by being subjected to intense heat in the oven after basting in its own stock. Meat is said to be browned if served hot, and glazed (with jelly) if served cold.

Glaçage is used for glazing when it is applied to fish, eggs or anything else covered with a white sauce. It can also mean glazing in the sense of sprinkling sweets and confectionery with icing sugar and subjecting them to intense heat. This last form of *glaçage* is also applied to carrots, turnips and onions. The term is applied also to the icing of cakes.

GLACIÈRE – The term *glacière* has two meanings; ice box or refrigerator, or a sugar-dredger.

GLASS AND GLASSES. VERRE, VERRERIE – Ever since glass was invented it has been used to make receptacles to contain and store drinks and foodstuffs. Glass utensils were used side by side with the pottery which had served the same purpose since ancient times. Glass, which by its transparency allowed the liquid inside to be seen, was preferred for flagons containing drinks and for drinking vessels because it afforded

Old bottles and old champagne glasses

Left: Three series of glasses

Above: Glasses for Burgundy, Bordeaux, Moselle and Rhine wine ('*Au vase étrusque*'. *Phot. Nicolas*)

pleasure to the eye at the same time as the pleasure to the palate. There exist, in museums and private collections, bottles, carafes and drinking vessels of every period and every country.

When glass-makers were sufficiently masters of their technique to be able to seek artistic effects, objects made of glass sometimes became purely ornamental.

The shape of the glass is so very important for the full appreciation of wine, that each region has produced the shape that best enhances its particular wine. As a general rule, the glass should be as fine as possible, roomy (it must never be filled to the brim), with *bombé* shoulders so that the wine has ample room to develop its aroma. Champagne, on the other hand, should be served in narrow glasses to prevent the bouquet from being dissipated. A flute glass or, better still, a tulip glass is the most suitable.

GLAZES. GLACES – Glazes are stocks reduced to a syrupy consistency used as a finish for certain sauces in order to enhance their flavour and improve their consistency.

A *demi-glace sauce* is one obtained from the combination of *Espagnole sauce* (see SAUCE), light brown stock, and Madeira.

GLUCOMETER. GLUCOMÈTRE, GLYCOMÈTRE – Graduated hydrometer used for the instantaneous assessment of the sugar content of liquids. Special glucometers are used for measuring the sugar density of wines and syrups.

GLUCOSE – A sugar found in its natural state in many fruits, and in particular in grapes.

It is made industrially by heating starch with various acids. This produces first dextrins and then an impure form of glucose itself. Two forms of glucose are used commercially, viscous and semi-solid. Glucose has many industrial uses, notably to increase the sugar content of wine and beer. It is also used in the manufacture of syrup and jam. French law lays down that when glucose is used in this way the fact must be indicated on the label.

GLUTEN – Albuminous substance in flour.

When flour is kneaded under running water, a paste is first formed, then – the starch having been gradually washed away – a greyish elastic dough is produced. This is the gluten. It is because of its gluten content that flour can be made into bread. Ordinary bread contains about 7 per cent gluten.

Gluten dough, bread and biscuits. PAINS, PÂTÉS, BISCUITS DE GLUTEN – These products, manufactured especially for diabetics, have a quantity of gluten added. Gluten bread still retains an average of 40 per cent of starch while potatoes contain only 23 per cent. These products are not recommended, except in very mild cases of diabetes, since they contain such a high proportion of starch. In cases where the starch content has been appreciably reduced, the product no longer bears any real resemblance to bread.

GLUX – See CHEESE.

GLYCERINE. GLYCÉRINE – Colourless, sweetish, syrupy liquid, a by-product of soap manufacture. It can be extracted from most fats.

Glycerine can be used in industrial confectionery without injury to health. It is also regarded as a valuable substitute for sugar in the sweetening of diabetic foods.

GNOCCHI – This dish, made from flour or semolina, can be prepared in two ways, either from *Chou paste* (see DOUGH) made with milk, or from a semolina porridge.

Gnocchi can also be made from potatoes. These various dishes, of Italian or Austro-Hungarian origin, can be served as a hot *hors-d'œuvre* or as a separate course.

Gnocchi au gratin (Austro-Hungarian cookery) – Make a *Chou paste* (see DOUGH) in the usual way, using milk instead of water. When it is ready add 50 g. (2 oz., $\frac{1}{2}$ cup) grated Parmesan for every 450 g. (1 lb.) paste.

Poaching gnocchi with the aid of a forcing-bag (*Maison Desmeuzes*)

Put the paste in a large forcing-bag with a round nozzle. Force it through by pressing with the hand. The *gnocchi* are dropped into a pan of boiling salted water, each one the size of a small walnut. Simmer for a few minutes. As soon as the *gnocchi* rise to the surface of the water, drain them and put on a cloth to dry.

Place them in a *gratin* dish lined with a layer of *Mornay sauce* (see SAUCE). Cover with the same sauce. Sprinkle grated cheese on the top and pour on melted butter. Brown in a slow oven.

Potato gnocchi (German cookery). GNOCCHI DE POMMES DE TERRE – Boil 1 kg. ($2\frac{1}{4}$ lb.) potatoes. Drain, and dry in the oven. Rub them through a fine sieve. While still hot, add to this purée 2 whole eggs, 2 yolks, 50 g. (2 oz., $\frac{1}{4}$ cup) butter, 150 g. (5 oz., $1\frac{1}{4}$ cups) flour. Season with salt, pepper and grated nutmeg. Mix.

Divide the mixture into pieces the size of a walnut and roll into balls. Flatten them gently, pressing on them with the back of a fork so that they have ridges along the top. Simmer in salted boiling water. Drain, and place them in a dish in layers, sprinkling grated cheese on each layer. Pour melted butter over and brown in the oven.

Gnocchi à la romaine – Shake, through a dredger, 250 g. (9 oz., $1\frac{1}{2}$ cups) semolina into 1 litre ($1\frac{3}{4}$ pints, generous quart) boiling milk. Season with salt, pepper and grated nutmeg. Mix well and cook for 20 minutes.

Remove from the stove and add 2 egg yolks. Spread out evenly on a moistened slab so that it is about 1 cm. ($\frac{1}{2}$ inch) thick. Leave to cool. Cut into shapes.

Put the *gnocchi* in a buttered dish lined with grated Gruyère or Parmesan cheese. Sprinkle with the same cheese. Pour melted butter over and bake in a slow oven.

Goat with kid

GOAT. CHÈVRE – Goats are raised especially for dairy production. Goats' meat, when the animal is still too young for breeding, has an agreeable flavour although it is tougher than mutton. As a rule, only animals which are old and worn-out by milking are slaughtered. The meat is as nutritive as mutton, but its smell is disagreeable. Goat is eaten in Spain, in Italy and in the South of France. In the high mountains goats' meat is dried in the open air; this is the *bindenfleisch* of the Canton des Grisons. Male goats' flesh can be eaten only when the animals are very young, from six weeks to four months.

GOAT'S BEARD. BARBE-DE-BOUC – Wild salsify, of which several varieties are known. The tender shoots of some are eaten like asparagus, the roots of others are prepared like *scorzonera* (see SALSIFY).

There is a variety of goat's beard cultivated in Belgium called *witloof*, which in France is called *endive*.

GOBLET. GOBELET – Wide-mouthed drinking vessel which used to be made of silver or silver-plate.

Antique goblets are often exquisitely engraved. Small silver wine-tasters are also called *gobelets* in French, though the more usual name for them is *tâte-vin* (wine-taster).

The goblet service. SERVICE DU GOBELET – At the French court, 'serving the goblet' was one of the most important ceremonies of the royal household. The master of the goblet, who was the head functionary of the royal kitchens, was in sole charge of the household bread, fruit and linen for the royal table.

GOBY. GOBIE – Fish known in France as the *goujon de mer*. It is to be found in all the oceans, and some kinds are also found in large rivers. This tiny fish, which has very delicate flesh, is usually eaten fried, like river gudgeon.

GODARD – Garnish for certain meat dishes served as a second course, and for poultry *entrées*. (See GARNISHES.)

GODIVEAU – Delicate forcemeat from which quenelles are made.

The etymology of this word is uncertain. Scheler suggests that it comes from the old French verb *goder* which means to make *godinettes*. Lacam believes that *godiveau* is derived from the old word *godebillaux*. He says that formerly *godebillaux* meant a pie filled with meat balls made of chopped veal and *béatilles* (titbits) such as cocks' combs and kidneys, lambs' sweetbreads, etc., made into a stew.

Godiveau forcemeat can be prepared in different ways (see FORCEMEATS OR STUFFINGS, *Quenelle forcemeat*). In addition to the recipes given elsewhere, here is the one given by Carême for this forcemeat.

Godiveau with chives (Carême's recipe). GODIVEAU À LA CIBOULETTE – 'Trim 450 g. (1 lb.) fillet of veal and 675 g. ($1\frac{1}{2}$ lb.) suet. Chop the veal finely and mix in the fat. After all of it has been chopped, add 4 teaspoons spiced salt, a pinch of nutmeg, and 4 eggs. Chop for several minutes.

'Pound the *godiveau* in a mortar, remove from the mortar and place it on ice or in a cool place for 2 hours. Divide the mixture into 2 parts and pound each part separately, moistening little by little with pieces of washed ice, each the size of an egg. This will make the *godiveau* very firm and smooth.

'Put it in a large bowl and pound the rest in the same way, putting it in the bowl when it is ready, with 2 tablespoons (3 tablespoons) *Velouté sauce* (see SAUCE) and 1 tablespoon chives chopped very fine. This mixture is used like forcemeat.'

Carême goes on to explain the rôle played by the ice in this preparation:

'Ice helps in binding and giving body to the *godiveau*, which is what gives it its desirable smooth softness.'

GODWIT. BARGE – Marsh bird, also found along river banks and near the sea shore, commonly called *oyster-catcher* or *cricket-teal*.

The two varieties, the *black tailed godwit* and the *bar tailed godwit* are found in Europe. In America there are the large *marbled godwit* and the small *Hudsonian godwit*.

All recipes given for woodcock (q.v.) can be applied to godwit.

GOÉLAND – Colloquial French name for large seagulls. The flesh of this bird, which is oily, leathery and unpleasant in flavour, used to be eaten as Lenten fare. Its eggs are edible. It is prepared in the same way as bustard, cooked like domestic goose or duckling.

GOÉMON – Type of seaweed.

GOGUES (Angevin cookery) – Chop finely equal quantities of onions, spinach, beet and lettuce. Season with salt and leave for 12 hours. Next day cook the vegetables in lard until they are very soft.

Dice fat bacon equal in weight to the mixed vegetables. Cook the bacon a little, and add it to the vegetables. Season with pepper, salt and allspice. Add enough pig's blood to make a thin mixture.

Mix thoroughly and wrap in thin pieces of beef, 20 cm. (8 inches) long. Secure the ends. Simmer the *gogues* in salt water for $2\frac{1}{2}$ hours. Drain and leave to cool.

When the *gogues* are quite cold, slice them and toss in butter, browning them slightly on both sides.

GOGUETTE – Old name for a flat sausage made from highly spiced pork stuffing.

GOLD. OR – Precious non-rusting metal sometimes used in the Middle Ages in thin leaves for wrapping certain *patés* and roast birds. Gold is still used for this purpose in the Far East.

GOOD KING HENRY (Allgood, English mercury). BON-HENRI – Plant commonly found in wild places, frequently growing against walls. It is also called *wild spinach*. The leaves are cooked like spinach. They should be cooked in two waters and the first, green and bitter, should be thrown away. The young shoots are sometimes eaten like asparagus.

GOOSE. OIE – All the species of geese which are used as food in Europe are the issue of the *wild goose*.

In France two varieties of geese are raised, the *petite* and the *grosse*. The smaller goose (*petite*) weighs about 3 kg. ($6\frac{1}{2}$ lb.) on average. After methodical fattening they attain the weight of 5 kg. (11 lb.) and are excellent roasting birds. This common goose can be treated in any way suitable for poultry, especially turkey.

The big goose (*grosse*) is a heavy bird, weighing 5 kg. (11 lb.) on the average and reaching 10 to 12 kg. (22 to $26\frac{1}{2}$ lb.) after fattening.

Geese of this type are found mainly around Toulouse, where they are bred, and in the Garonne basin. The bird is usually called the *Toulouse goose*; the *Strasbourg goose* is a species of the same breed. This bird carries its body almost perpendicularly; its behind, called 'artichoke', drags on the ground even before the fattening process. The skin covering its breast is loose and slack, forming a lappet, or wattle, which constitutes a fat store. It is this variety of goose that is used in the south-west of France for the *confit d'oie*.

The Toulouse geese also provide the livers which are made into the famous *pâtés de foie gras with truffles*, produced in Toulouse, in the Gers, the Landes, in Strasbourg and other parts of France. This variety, however flavoursome its flesh, is used only for making *confit d'oie* and cannot be treated by any of the culinary methods applied to the common goose.

The *confit* and various other specialities made of preserved goose of the Toulouse species are excellent, but the most delicate part of this bird is, of course, the liver, especially when an intensive cramming, coupled with total immobilisation, have enlarged this organ to the state of complete fatty degeneration.

For many centuries the goose was considered the best of poultry. In Paris, *rôtisseurs* principally sold roast geese, hence the name of *oyers* by which they were, for many years, described in their statutes.

In England the goose has always been greatly appreciated. On Michaelmas Day it was the custom to serve roast goose, prepared in the traditional English way, stuffed with sage and onions. This tradition goes back to the sixteenth century and Alfred Suzanne in his book *la Cuisine Anglaise*, described its origins as follows:

'The 29th September, Michaelmas Day, is the anniversary of a great naval victory won by the English against the Spaniards. Queen Elizabeth was at table when the news of the sinking of the Spanish Armada was brought to her.

'The principal dish that day was roast goose, to which the Queen, it was said, was particularly partial, and in an excited outburst of patriotism and . . . gourmandism, she decreed that this glorious occasion be commemorated by serving roast goose on that day every year.'

The flesh of adult geese is rather tough and requires prolonged cooking, usually braising, but the flesh of young goose is tender and delicate. In northern France, where the common goose is more appreciated than in the south, it is customary to expose the birds to cold for a time during winter, to make the flesh tender.

In his book *l'ancienne Alsace à table*, Charles Gérard wrote:

'The bird itself is nothing, but the art of man has turned it into an instrument which produces marvellous results, a kind of living greenhouse in which the supreme fruit of gastronomy is grown.'

The *foie gras* is indeed the 'supreme fruit of gastronomy', especially when prepared as it is in Strasbourg or Toulouse, but the flesh of a young goose, or *gosling*, as the bird is called up to 7 months old, is not to be despised, and a great many gastronomes rank it highly. A young goose, like duck, can be recognised by the pliability of its underbill.

Goose à l'alsacienne. OIE À L'ALSACIENNE – Stuff the goose with sausage meat. Truss it for roasting and pan-roast it in butter. Garnish with *sauerkraut* (q.v.) braised separately, with cooking juices added. Alternate the *sauerkraut* with pieces of lean bacon and poached Strasbourg sausages. Dilute the pan juices with white wine and veal stock and pour over the goose.

Male (right) and female goose

Toulouse geese

Goose à l'anglaise (English style). OIE À L'ANGLAISE – Stuff the goose with the following:

Bake 1 kg. ($2\frac{1}{4}$ lb.) unpeeled onions in the oven and allow to cool. Peel and chop, adding to them an equal weight of soaked and pressed crustless bread. Season with $1\frac{1}{2}$ teaspoons salt, a pinch of pepper, a little grated nutmeg and 3 tablespoons (scant $\frac{1}{4}$ cup) chopped sage.

Truss the goose and roast in the oven or on a spit. Arrange on a dish, spoon over some of the diluted pan juices, and serve with apple sauce, cooked without sugar or only very slightly sweetened.

Ballottine and galantine of goose. BALLOTTINE, GALANTINE D'OIE – Prepare like *Galantine of chicken* (see CHICKEN) using boned goose, fine pork or chicken forcemeat, truffles, pickled tongue and ham cut in dice or thin strips.

Ballottine of goose is usually served cold, the liquor in which it was cooked being made into jelly. It can also be served hot accompanied by a garnish.

Goose à la bourguignonne. OIE À LA BOURGUIGNONNE – Prepare as for *Chicken à la bourguignonne* (see CHICKEN).

Braised goose with various garnishes. OIE BRAISÉE – Prepare like *Braised turkey* (see TURKEY).

Goose à la chipolata. OIE À LA CHIPOLATA – Prepare, pan-roasted or braised, as *Turkey à la chipolata* (see TURKEY).

Civet of goose. CIVET D'OIE – Prepare like *Civet of hare* (see HARE) using goose cut into uniform pieces.

Confit d'oie I – Bleed the goose, pluck and singe it and leave until quite cold before cutting. Slit open the back completely, clean out the bird and remove the liver, taking care not to damage it. (The liver can be used separately for making *terrines* and *pâtés*.) Divide the goose into 4 pieces. Leave intact the bones connected to these pieces in order to prevent the flesh losing its shape too much during cooking.

Salt the pieces of goose, put them into a large earthenware pot and leave in a cold place for 24 hours.

When they are thoroughly impregnated with salt, take them out, brush off the salt and wipe with a cloth.

Cook in clarified goose fat. When the fat has solidified, cut it into small pieces, put into a deep pot, moisten with a few tablespoons of water, and add a muslin bag containing several cloves of garlic, a few cloves, and some peppercorns, and heat. Do not put the pieces of goose in until this is three quarters melted. Cook on a moderate heat for about 1 hour.

Test with a big needle to make sure the goose is done. The juice which comes out should be perfectly clear, which indicates that the cooking is complete.

Drain the pieces of goose and remove the carcase bones. Put a thick layer of the fat in which the goose was cooked, clarified and strained, into a big earthenware jar, glazed on the inside. When the fat is completely solid, put in the pieces of goose, so that they do not touch the wall of the jar. Cover with warm goose fat.

Leave for 2 days. Strain into the pot some hot fat to seal any holes. When this is well congealed, pour a layer of lard over it, and when this is set, put a circle of greaseproof on top, pressing it down to make it adhere. Cover the top of the jar with a double thickness of paper and tie with string.

Confit d'oie prepared in this way will keep for a very long time. It can also be canned, the cans being placed in boiling water.

Confit d'oie II – Cut the goose into quarters and rub whole surface with spiced salt, prepared by mixing 1 kg. ($2\frac{1}{4}$ lb.) salt, 6 g. ($\frac{1}{4}$ oz.) saltpetre, 4 crushed cloves, 2 pounded bay leaves, a good pinch of pounded thyme.

Put the pieces of goose into an earthenware pot, glazed on the inside. Cover with spiced salt. Leave to steep in this seasoning for 24 hours.

Take the pieces of goose out, shake off surplus salt, and wipe the pieces carefully. Put them into a big pot in which goose fat has been left to melt slowly. Cook on low heat for $1\frac{1}{2}$ hours.

Test the pieces of goose with a thick straw, which should penetrate the flesh easily. Drain the quarters, put them into the earthenware jar. Strain the hot fat over them, making sure the meat is covered completely. When quite cold and the goose fat has become congealed, pour a layer of lard, about 1 cm. ($\frac{1}{2}$ inch) thick, over the surface. The lard is denser in consistency and this operation will ensure that the *confit* will keep for a long time. Store in a cool, dry place.

When taking pieces of goose out of the jar for use, care must be taken to see that the remaining pieces are completely covered by the fat.

Confit d'oie is one of the specialities of Languedoc and Gascogne, and an essential ingredient for the *garbure* (q.v.), the most characteristic of Béarn dishes.

'Leg of preserved goose,' says Simin Palay, 'is a dish which is always ready should a relative or a guest arrive unexpectedly. An old country saying assures us:

'Lou qui a coéche d'auque a hourrup de bi,
Que pot embita parent ou besi'

which means:

'He who has a goose leg and a little wine can safely invite relatives or neighbours.'

In Languedoc *confit d'oie* is used for the preparation of *cassoulet* (q.v.). It can also be served on its own, hot or cold, with or without garnish. Here are some recipes for serving it hot:

Confit d'oie, Basque. CONFIT D'OIE À LA BASQUAISE – Heat the quarters of goose in their own fat, drain, and garnish with *cèpes* cooked in a mixture of oil and goose fat in equal proportions, and mixed with chopped parsley and garlic.

Confit d'oie à la béarnaise – Heat the pieces of goose in their own fat, and drain. Garnish with thin slices of raw potato fried in goose fat and sprinkled with 1 tablespoon chopped parsley mixed with a pinch of pounded garlic.

Confit d'oie with green cabbage. CONFIT D'OIE AUX CHOUX VERTS – Prepare green cabbage as described in the recipe for *Braised cabbage* (see CABBAGE). When nearly done, add a piece of goose coated with the fat. Arrange the piece of goose on a dish, surround with the cabbage, and garnish with boiled potatoes.

Confit d'oie with kidney beans. CONFIT D'OIE AUX HARICOTS BLANCS – Add the pieces of goose to beans cooked *à la bretonne* (see BEANS), simmer for a few minutes and serve in a *timbale*.

Confit d'oie with lentils. CONFIT D'OIE AUX LENTILLES – Cook 1 litre ($1\frac{3}{4}$ pints, generous quart) lentils with the usual aromatics. Drain, and simmer with a few tablespoons thickened brown veal stock. Add the pieces of goose about 25 minutes before serving. Heat gently with the pan covered.

Confit d'oie with peas, or à la landaise. CONFIT D'OIE AUX PETITS POIS, DIT À LA LANDAISE – Remove the surplus fat covering a piece of *confit d'oie*.

Melt some goose fat in an earthenware casserole and fry in it 8 small onions and 2 tablespoons (3 tablespoons) diced Bayonne ham. Add 1 litre ($1\frac{3}{4}$ pints, generous quart) freshly shelled peas. Cook for 5 minutes. Sprinkle in 1 tablespoon flour, cook for a few moments, stirring with a wooden spoon, moisten with 1 dl. (6 tablespoons, scant $\frac{1}{2}$ cup) water and season with a little salt and 1 teaspoon sugar. Add a *bouquet garni* consisting of parsley, chervil, tarragon and bay leaf. Cook with a lid on for 40 minutes. Put in the piece of *confit d'oie* and finish cooking, with the casserole covered, for 25 minutes.

Confit d'oie à la périgourdine, à la sarladaise – Prepare as *Confit d'oie à la béarnaise* with a garnish of sautéed potatoes (sliced raw and fried in goose fat) mixed with slivers of truffles.

Goose en daube Capitole. OIE EN DAUBE CAPITOLE – Stuff the goose with a fine forcemeat mixed with *foie gras* and diced truffles. Truss and braise in the usual way. When the goose is nearly done, strain the braising liquor through a fine strainer.

Remove trussing string and put the goose back into the pan with 250 g. (9 oz.) small mushrooms, 250 g. (9 oz.) stoned blanched olives, and 250 g. (9 oz.) small chipolata sausages tossed in butter. Pour in the braising liquor and finish cooking in a low oven.

Goose à la flamande. OIE À LA FLAMANDE – Braise the goose in the usual manner. Garnish *à la flamande* (see GARNISHES). Boil down the braising liquor, strain and pour over the goose.

Goose frittons or grattons. FRITTONS, GRATTONS D'OIE – Name for the residue which remains in the pot after goose fat melts.

Minute fragments of flesh, which are trimmed off the quarters of goose while preparing *confit d'oie*, are sometimes added to this residue.

The *frittons* are drained, pressed to extract all the fat contained in them, seasoned with salt and then left to get cold. *Frittons* are eaten as *hors-d'œuvre*. They can be pressed into a block by moulding them in a bowl or other receptacle.

Goose giblets and pinions. ABATIS, AILERONS D'OIE – Prepare in any of the ways given for turkey giblets (see GIBLETS).

Goose livers. FOIES D'OIE – Livers of roasting geese are prepared as for livers of all other poultry. They can be cooked on skewers, sautéed with mushrooms, in Madeira, with truffles, pilaf, risotto, etc. They can be used as a garnish for eggs prepared in different ways, or with various *entrée* dishes.

They are also used for preparing *à gratin forcemeat* (see FORCEMEATS).

Foie gras, that is, liver of fattened geese, can be prepared in innumerable ways, both hot and cold. (See FOIE GRAS.)

Goose pâté, cold. PÂTÉ FROID D'OIE – Using goose meat prepare like *Chicken pâté, cold* (see PÂTÉ, *Cold pâtés*).

Goose pâté, hot. PÂTÉ CHAUD D'OIE – Prepare, using goose meat, like *Chicken pâté, hot* (see PÂTÉ, *Hot pâtés*).

Goose ragoûts. RAGOÛTS D'OIE – Use goose meat cut in uniform pieces.

These *ragoûts* can be garnished in various ways. They can be made *à la bourgeoise*, *à la chipolata*, with celeriac, with turnips, chestnuts, olives, etc. (See RAGOÛT.)

Goose ragoût à la bonne femme. RAGOÛT D'OIE À LA BONNE FEMME – Cut a medium-sized goose into uniform pieces. Season with salt and pepper and put the pieces into a sauté pan in which 2 tablespoons (3 tablespoons) clarified butter (or goose fat) have been heated. Add a big onion and a carrot, cut into quarters. Brown the pieces of goose and the vegetables well.

When the pieces of goose are well browned, sprinkle in 2 tablespoons (3 tablespoons) flour and fry, stirring the *ragoût* on the fire. Add a small crushed clove of garlic, moisten with half a glass of white wine and add 4 dl. ($\frac{3}{4}$ pint, scant 2 cups) stock. Add a *bouquet garni*, and cook for 40 minutes, keeping the pan covered.

Drain the pieces in a sieve placed over a bowl. Trim them and put into the cleaned pan. Add 250 g. (9 oz.) small onions, lightly tossed in butter, 250 g. (9 oz.) lean bacon cut into small pieces, scalded and lightly fried, and 1 kg. ($2\frac{1}{4}$ lb.) quartered potatoes. Skim off surplus fat from the sauce, add 2 tablespoons (3 tablespoons) *Tomato purée* (see PURÉE) and pour it over the goose. Put on the stove for a moment, cover the pan and cook in a hot oven, without stirring, for 45 minutes.

Roast goose. OIE RÔTI – This method of cooking is suitable only for a very young and tender goose. It can be roasted in the oven or on a spit, and should be left a little underdone.

Roast goose à l'anglaise is stuffed with sage and onions.

Smoked breast of goose. POITRINE D'OIE FUMÉE – This preparation, which is made in Alsace and in Germany, can be found in shops, cooked ready for use. It is eaten cold, like smoked ham, and is also a garnish for *sauerkraut*.

Stuffed goose necks. COUS D'OIE FARCIS – This makes an excellent *hors-d'œuvre* and is eaten as a sausage. It is prepared in various regions of south-western France when **confit d'oie** is being made.

Bone the necks, leaving a good deal of the skin covering the breast attached to them. Using the flesh taken off the bones, make a forcemeat, adding some minced pork, mixed with a small quantity of goose liver and diced truffles. Season and stuff the necks. Cook them in goose fat, and keep in earthenware jars as pieces of *confit d'oie*.

Goose tongues. LANGUES D'OIE – In Béarn, the tongues of big geese, which are used for making *confit*, are cooked on a grill.

Goose à la mode de Visé, also called à l'instar de Visé (Flemish cookery). OIE À LA MODE DE VISÉ, À L'INSTAR DE VISÉ – Cook a young goose that has not yet started laying, in white stock spiced with 2 bulbs of garlic. Drain, cut into pieces, sprinkle with goose fat, and simmer in a sauté pan with the lid on.

Prepare a *Velouté sauce* (see SAUCE), mixing flour with goose fat for the *roux* (q.v.) and using the liquor in which the goose was poached. Keep on simmering the *velouté* for an hour; it should be rather thick. Make a liaison with 4 egg yolks as for *Chicken fricassée* (see CHICKEN). Strain the sauce, add to it a few tablespoons cream and 1 good tablespoon *Garlic purée* (see PURÉE), using the garlic cooked with the goose.

Drain the pieces of goose dry and put into the sauce. Heat well and serve heaped on a dish.

GOOSEBERRY. GROSEILLE – Large berry, green in colour or streaked with red. In French one variety of gooseberry is called *groseille à maquereau* because it is used in the preparation of a sauce which, traditionally, is served with mackerel.

In France, gooseberries are mainly grown in Normandy and other northern districts.

GORENFLOT (Pâtisserie) – Name of a sweet made of baba (q.v.) dough baked in a hexagonal mould. This cake was first made at the Maison Bourbonneaux in the middle of the nineteenth century. It was called Gorenflot by its creator, in memory of the hero of Alexandre Dumas' play *la Dame de Monsoreau*.

GORGONZOLA – Italian cheese (see CHEESE).

GOUDALE – A *garbure* (q.v.) to which red or white wine is added. Simin Palay, in his *la Cuisine en Béarn*, says that a *goudale* is the traditional conclusion to every *garbure*. When the bread and vegetables of this broth have been eaten, the diner pours into his plate a generous cup of red or white wine, mixes it with the soup left at the bottom of the plate, and drinks it.

The *goudale* is considered in Béarn to be a sovereign remedy for illness, if a local proverb is to be believed:

'Goudale pla adoubado,

'Tiro un escut de la pocho deu medecin.'

('A well-made *goudale* keeps a coin from the doctor's pocket.')

GOUFFÉ – Jules Gouffé was one of the greatest chefs of the nineteenth century.

Born in Paris in 1807, he had a talent for cookery from his early youth. His father, an established pastry-cook in the Saint-Merri quarter, taught him the basic principles of cookery. It was then that Carême, hearing of the talent of the young Gouffé – who at 17 was already showing promise in the decoration and presentation of set pieces – took him into his kitchens in the Austrian Embassy in Paris. Carême turned him into a model craftsman, a celebrity of his day.

In 1840, Jules Gouffé set up on his own in the Faubourg Saint-Honoré; his restaurant became one of the best in Paris. In 1855 he retired, but went back to work in 1867, encouraged by those famous gourmets, Dumas the elder and Baron Brisse. This pair of epicures offered him the post of head chef at the Jockey Club. It was at this time that Gouffé began work on his *Livre de cuisine*, a magnificent book which deserves a place in every library of cookery, side by side with the works of Carême, Plumerey, Urbain Dubois, Emile Bernard, Escoffier, etc.

A few lines from the master's preface will suffice to show the importance of his work:

'Having, from my earliest youth, embarked upon a career of cookery, I saw much, observed much, practised much in every sense of the word. I am not one of those who declare that French cookery – that part of our national heritage of which we have reason to be proud – is lost today and that it will never recover. The good and true things never die. No doubt there may be periods of decline, but sooner or later, with hard work, intelligence and good will, there must be a recovery.

'If, thanks to the reforms and the methods which I propose, I find that in a few years' time everyone, whatever his rank in society, is eating as well as he possibly can; that, on the one hand, household cookery is at last being carried out with care, economy and comfort; and on the other hand the *grande cuisine* goes forward under progressive conditions, with that good taste and brilliance which is so appropriate to a century of enlightenment and luxury like our own; then I shall have truly attained the goal which I have set myself... I shall feel myself well paid for all my pains.'

In 1872, Jules Gouffé published *le Livre de pâtisserie*, then *le Livre des conserves*.

In 1875 *le Livre des soupes et des potages* was published. This was the crowning point of a whole lifetime devoted to remarkable work in the field of cookery.

Gouffé died at Neuilly in 1877.

GOUGELHOF or GOUGELHOPF – See KUGELHOPF.

GOUGÈRE (Burgundian pastry) – This pastry, which is said to have originated at Sens, is made not only in Burgundy but also at Troyes, in Champagne, and in other districts of France.

The dough. Place in a thick, flat-bottomed saucepan $2\frac{1}{2}$ dl. (scant $\frac{1}{2}$ pint, generous cup) water, 100 g. (4 oz., $\frac{1}{2}$ cup) butter, and 1 teaspoon salt. As soon as the water is boiling, move the saucepan away from the flame and add 200 g. (7 oz., $1\frac{3}{4}$ cups) sieved flour. Mix, then dry the dough over a high flame, stirring it with a wooden spoon, like *Chou paste* (see DOUGH) until it comes away easily from the sides of the saucepan.

Remove the pan from the stove and beat into the mixture 5 whole eggs, one by one, 100 g. (4 oz., 1 cup) finely diced Gruyère cheese, and a pinch of white pepper.

Making the cake. With a tablespoon, scoop out pieces of dough, each the size of an egg. Put them straight into a buttered pie dish, one against the other in a circle. Smooth the circle on top and round the inside with the back of a spoon. Brush with beaten egg. Sprinkle with very finely diced cheese. Bake in a slow oven.

The more usual way to serve a *gougère* is cold, but it may also be served hot as *hors-d'œuvre*.

GOUGNETTES (Lot cookery) – Type of doughnut. Prepare a dough from 500 g. (18 oz., $4\frac{1}{2}$ cups) flour, 5 eggs, 75 g. (3 oz., 6 tablespoons) sugar and 10 g. ($\frac{1}{3}$ oz.) dried or compressed yeast. Leave to rise for about 1 hour.

Roll out the dough on a floured table. Shape flattened dough into small thin loaves, and cut them into 5-cm. (2-inch.) pieces.

Fry the pieces in very hot fat. Drain the *gougnettes* when they are crisp and evenly browned. Sprinkle with sugar.

GOULASCH (Hungarian cookery) – Goulasch (sometimes called gulyas) is a kind of beef stew made with diced onions and seasoned with Hungarian paprika. Several kinds of goulasch are made in Hungary, and recipes for them are given under BEEF.

Goulasch soup (Hungarian broth). GOULASCH (POTAGE) – Dice coarsely 350 g. (12 oz.) beef sirloin, trimmed and with all fat removed. Brown in butter in a casserole with 2 tablespoons (3 tablespoons) finely chopped onion. Season with salt and a large pinch paprika. Add a little cummin and a small crushed clove of garlic.

When the meat is well browned all over, sprinkle 1 tablespoon flour over it. Mix and let it cook for 1 to 2 minutes, but without allowing it to brown. Add $1\frac{1}{2}$ litres ($2\frac{1}{4}$ pints, $2\frac{3}{4}$ pints) consommé. Bring to the boil and cook slowly for about 3 hours.

An hour before serving, add to the broth 2 diced potatoes. Serve with bread croûtons fried in butter.

GOURD. COURGE – Name given to many species of the *Cucurbitaceae* family including summer and autumn pumpkins (yellow gourds), vegetable marrows, various summer squashes, Canada or cushaw, Quaker or Japanese squashes (or pumpkin).

Different varieties of gourd:
Pumpkin, squashes, vegetable marrow

Gourds are one of the oldest vegetables known to man although it is doubtful if any of those grown today could be identified with the original species. The word *gourd* is reserved in North America for the decorative inedible variety. Winter and summer squash as well as pumpkin are grown on a very large scale. Winter squash can often be used in place of pumpkin.

GOURILOS – Gourilos are the stumps of endive. When fully grown and tender, they make a delicately flavoured vegetable.

They can be prepared *à la grecque* as an *hors-d'œuvre*; or as a vegetable in butter or cream, in gravy, fried, gilled etc.

Method. Trim and wash the stumps. Boil them in salt water until tender.

Drain and leave to cool. Dry them and cook according to the following recipes.

Gourilos in butter. GOURILOS AU BEURRE – Blanch 12 gourilos. Place in a frying pan with 50 g. (2 oz., $\frac{1}{4}$ cup) butter and 2 tablespoons (3 tablespoons) water. Cover and cook for 40 minutes. Arrange in a dish and pour on the butter in which they have been cooked, to which has been added a tablespoon water or white stock.

Gourilos in cream. GOURILOS À LA CRÈME – Cook as for *Gourilos in butter*. When they are ready, add $1\frac{1}{2}$ dl. ($\frac{1}{4}$ pint, $\frac{2}{3}$ cup) hot fresh cream. Simmer for 8 minutes. Arrange the gourilos in a dish and pour on the cream.

Endive gourilos. GOURILOS FRITS – Blanch the gourilos, drain, leave to cool, chill and dry them. Steep them in oil, lemon juice, salt and pepper for 25 minutes. Coat them with a thin frying batter and fry in deep fat. Drain. Sprinkle with salt.

Gourilos in gravy, bone-marrow sauce, velouté sauce or other sauces. GOURILOS AU JUS, À LA MOELLE, AU VELOUTÉ – Proceed as in recipes for cardoons (q.v.) or celery (q.v.), using any of these sauces.

Grilled gourilos. GOURILOS GRILLÉS – Blanch the gourilos and soak in oil and lemon juice as for *Fried gourilos*. Grill them under a low flame, moistening them with oil from time to time.

Gourilos à la grecque. GOURILOS À LA GRECQUE – Blanch the gourilos and prepare as for *Artichokes à la grecque* (see HORS-D'ŒUVRE).

GOURMAND, GOURMANDISM. GOURMAND, GOURMANDISE – Many people take the word 'gourmandism' to be synonymous with 'gluttony'.

Brillat-Savarin is sternly critical of this interpretation.

'Authorities who thus interpret *gourmandise* have completely forgotten social *gourmandise* which combines the elegance of Athens, the luxury of Rome and the delicacy of France. Such *gourmandise* orders with discernment, supervises with wisdom, savours with enthusiasm, judges with profundity. It is a precious attribute which may well be esteemed a virtue, for it is the source of our purest delights.

'*Gourmandise* . . . is a passionate, rational and habitual preference for all that flatters the palate.

'*Gourmandise* is the enemy of excess; every man who gives himself indigestion or gets drunk, runs the risk of no longer being a true gourmand.

'Delicacy (*friandise*) is an essential part of *gourmandise*, for delicacy is the same kind of discrimination applied to delicate titbits such as preserves, pastries and sweets. . . .'

From the social point of view, the advantages of gourmandism are innumerable. 'It is *gourmandise*,' continues Brillat-Savarin, 'which stimulates the transport from pole to pole of wines, spirits, sugar, spices, pickles, savouries, indeed provisions of every kind, down to eggs and melons.

'It is this which affords a livelihood to the industrious multitude of cooks, confectioners, pastry-cooks and other diversely named purveyors of food, who, in their turn, rely for the satisfaction of their needs on workers of all kinds. This gives rise, always and everywhere, to a wealth of economic activity, of which even the most lively mind cannot calculate the extent nor assess the value.' (*Physiologie du goût.*)

The gourmand
(*Collection of J.-J. T. de Lusse*)

GOURMET – Formerly, the word *gourmet* was never used in the inexact sense which is current nowadays.

The *gourmet*, whose full title was *courtier-gourmet-piqueur*, was not a *gourmand*, in other words a connoisseur of good things, but rather a sworn official, charged with the duty of tasting wines and spirits. *Gourmets-piqueurs* were once part of a confraternity. Nowadays they are organised into syndicates.

GOURNAY – See CHEESE.

GRAHAM BREAD. PAIN DE GRAHAM – Wholemeal bread made from a mixture of different cereal flours. This bread was invented in 1840 by an American, Silvester Graham.

GRAIN – Small weight used in former times. It weighed approximately $\frac{1}{20}$ g.

GRAMOLATES or GRAMOLATAS – Sherbet made from a *granité* (q.v.) mixture. (See ICE CREAMS AND ICES.)

GRAND MAÎTRE – Under the old French monarchy, the *grand maître*, who was also called *souverain maître de l'hôtel du roi* was chief of all the officers of the royal kitchens.

GRAND VENEUR SAUCE – Brown sauce, served with ground game and venison. (See SAUCES, *Brown sauces*.)

GRANITÉS – Type of sherbet. No Italian meringue is added to this mixture, as is done with ordinary sherbet mixture. (See ICE CREAMS AND ICES.)

GRAPE. RAISIN – Fruit of the vine.

The stem of the grape bunch, which is more or less woody according to the species, contains a little free acid and tannin. The seeds contain a tannin, a resinous substance, an essential oil and volatile acids which come into play later in the development of the bouquet.

The pulp is held in place by very thin membranous cell walls (hardly $\frac{1}{2}$ per cent of the weight of the fruit) so thin that the weight of the juice is just about equal to that of the pulp; it consists mainly of sugar in proportions which vary according to the type of plant and the year, sometimes rising as high as $23\frac{1}{2}$ per cent of sugar in weight, corresponding to 15 per cent of alcohol in volume. In a good year most choice types give comparable figures.

Chasselas grapes (*Fauchon. Phot. Nicolas*)

Dessert grapes. RAISINS DE TABLE – A few varieties of grapes listed according to their season: earliest first.

Angevine is the earliest variety of all, fruit pale yellow, flesh juicy and sweet; *Saint-Jacques*, with transparent yellow fruit, ripens very soon after; *Cardinal* is a red grape with a slightly musky flavour; *Chasselas* is the most popular cultivated variety and it alone accounts for more than half French production (there are numerous types of *Chasselas* grape); *Admirable*; *Dattier*; *Alphonse Lavallée* is deep blue in colour and cultivated extensively; *Oeillade* is a deep blackish violet; *Muscat de Hambourg* is purplish-black with plump oval fruit; *Gros Vert, Servant, Olivette blanche, Muscat d'Alexandrie* are all white grapes.

The great dessert grape producing regions of France are Vaucluse, Bouches-du-Rhône, Hérault, Gard, the valley of the Garonne, and the Moissac region which is particularly famous for its golden *Chasselas*.

For the varieties of grapes used for making wine (*cèpages*) see VINE.

Keeping grapes. The system used at Thomery, for the Chasselas grape, consists of cutting off the bunch, with a piece of the main stem attached, before it is quite ripe, and soaking the thick stem in a bottle half filled with water.

Dried grapes. RAISINS SECS – Gathered when perfectly ripe, and dried in the sun. The principal commercial types in France are:

Raisins. Mainly from the Midi. Gathered very ripe, plunged into a wash of boiling water and ash, then dried in the sun on their stalks.

Sultanas. Large fruit, practically seedless and with a muscat flavour.

Currants. Mainly from the Greek islands. Small, seedless, washed with ash and stripped from their stalks.

Dried grapes are used in cookery, pastry-making and confectionery. They can still be used to make wine after being soaked.

Grape jelly. CONFITURE DE RAISINS – Like *Currant jelly II* (see JAMS AND JELLIES) using 250 g. (9 oz., generous cup) sugar to 500 g. (18 oz.) grape juice.

GRAPEFRUIT. PAMPLEMOUSSE – Citrus fruit the size of a very big orange, pale yellow in colour. The Chinese eat this fruit at the beginning of a meal as an apéritif, and this custom was copied by the Americans when they acclimatised the fruit in their country.

Cut the fruit in half horizontally with a very sharp knife (a special knife is used for this purpose), make a circular incision around the central cone and remove it. Slide the knife into each section of the fruit to loosen the pulp from the skin surrounding it. Sprinkle with fine sugar. It can be flavoured with liqueur and served on ice.

Preparing grapefruit (*Claire*)

GRAPPA – Piedmontese marc brandy in which a sprig of rue is infused.

GRASSHOPPER. SAUTERELLE – Orthopterous, herbivorous insect, often constituting a plague to agriculture. Grasshoppers are greatly relished by African natives who eat them in the most diverse forms, boiled, roasted, grilled, salted, dried and reduced to a paste. Moses permitted the Hebrews to eat four different species, described in Leviticus.

GRASS SNAKE. COULEUVRE – Non-poisonous snake. The common grass snake is sometimes eaten in France under the name of *anguille des haies* (hedge eel). It is prepared in the same way as Eel (q.v.).

GRATER. RÂPE – Utensil with a rough surface, pierced with holes, used to reduce to a coarse powder certain vegetables, fruits or other commodities (cheese, nutmeg, almonds, etc.).

GRATERON – Common French term for rennet.

GRATIN – The term means the thin crust formed on the surface of certain dishes when they are browned in the oven or under the grill.

It is extended to denote certain methods of preparation. Thus we speak of macaroni *au gratin*, sole *au gratin*. (See CULINARY METHODS.)

Gratin languedocien – Half cook in oil 4 peeled, sliced aubergines, seasoned with salt and pepper, and 12 halved seasoned tomatoes. Arrange them in alternate layers in a baking dish. Cover with a mixture of breadcrumbs and chopped garlic and parsley. Sprinkle with olive oil. Begin cooking on the top of the stove, then bake slowly in the oven until the top is well browned.

GRATTONS or GRATTERONS – Names given in certain regions of France, especially in the south-west, to the residue of the melted fat of pork, goose or turkey. It is sometimes called *frittons*, and is salted while still hot, and eaten cold as an *hors-d'œuvre*.

Grattons must not be confused with *rillettes*, which are prepared by pounding in a mortar a mixture of fat and lean pork which has been slowly cooked beforehand.

Grattons (speciality of the Ile Bourbon). GRATTONS À L'ÎLE DE LA RÉUNION (ÎLE BOURBON) – Take the skin from the back of a young pig, leaving on it 2 cm. ($\frac{3}{4}$ inch) of fat. Cut it into 10-cm. (4-inch) squares. Score the fat without touching the skin with criss-cross lines, making little squares about 8 mm. ($\frac{1}{3}$ inch) across. Put the pieces of skin in a pan with some melted fat. Leave them to cook very slowly for 3 to 4 hours. When the skin is tender and transparent, raise the heat and cook for a further 40 minutes, until the pieces of skin bubble up and become crisp. They should swell up like fritters. Remove them from the pan with a perforated spoon or skimmer and put them in a dish. Sprinkle with table salt. This dish should always be cooked uncovered.

GRAVENCHE – Fish of the salmon family found mainly in Lake Geneva. It closely resembles the *féra* with which it is often confused. The *féra* has a more curved back and lighter coloured scales.

The *gravenche* is usually much smaller than the *féra*. Its flesh is fairly firm and delicate but has much less flavour.

All recipes suitable for *féra* and river trout may be used for *gravenche*. (See FÉRA, TROUT.)

GRAVES – Les Graves is the name of the sandy and gravelly territory that lies in the *département* of the Gironde. The hills and plateaux of this region yield excellent wines.

The Graves or Graves of Bordeaux also occupy a strip of land, about 15 km. (9 miles) wide, running parallel to the Gironde between Bordeaux and Langon.

The red wines of Graves are full-bodied and lively. Their very delicate bouquet evokes the aroma of truffles and the perfume of the resin of the nearby pine forests. Like Médoc, the region has some outstanding wines.

Apart from Château Haut-Brion, classified *premier cru* in 1855, most of the Graves wines were classified in 1953 (decree of 18 October 1958). The classification is as follows:

Châteaux	*Communes*	*White (W) or Red (R)*
Bouscaut	Cadaujac	W and R
Carbonnieux	Léognan	W and R
Chevalier (Domaine de)	Léognan	W and R
Couhins	Villenave-d'Ornon	W
Fieuzal	Léognan	R
Haut-Bailly	Léognan	R
La Mission-Haut-Brion	Talence	R
La Tour-Haut-Brion	Talence	R
La Tour-Martillac	Martillac	W and R
Laville-Haut-Brion	Talence	W
Malartic-Lagravière	Léognan	W and R
Olivier	Léognan	W and R
Pape-Clément	Pessac	R
Smith-Haut-Lafite	Martillac	R

The white wines of Graves are dry and elegant with a delicate bouquet. They are an excellent accompaniment to seafood, shellfish, grilled fish, and subtle sauces. In the south of the region, the white wines are sweeter and lighter, more akin to Sauternes wines.

Grayling

GRAYLING. OMBRE COMMUN – Rare freshwater fish resembling trout, from which it differs by its bigger and more brilliant scales, smaller snout, an enormous dorsal fin of bluish-grey colour. Its sides are silvery, sometimes tinged with pink or purple and flecked with dark spots.

The flesh is very delicate and has a slight flavour of thyme. It is prepared like trout (q.v.).

GRECQUE (À LA) – Dishes *à la grecque* should be of Greek origin in their method of preparation, but in practice this is seldom the case. Though it sometimes happens that a dish called *à la grecque* on a restaurant menu really is of Greek origin, more often than not the name is given to dishes of French origin.

Among the dishes called *à la grecque* are *Artichokes à la grecque* (see ARTICHOKE) and other vegetables prepared in the same way.

GREENGAGE. REINE-CLAUDE – Plum with a yellowish-green skin, lightly tinted with red on the side of the fruit exposed to the sun. (See PLUM.)

GREENHOUSE, HOTHOUSE. SERRE – Building made of glass where plants are raised in artificial heat. The vegetables or fruit cultivated under glass have less flavour than plants grown in the open air.

GRENACHE – The word *grenache* is derived from the Italian word *granaccio* which means 'large seeds'. The Grenache grape accounts for much of the vine stock of the Côtes du Rhône wines of the south of France and the Mediterranean basin. It is used to make straight, unfortified sweet wines. The best-known *appellations* of Roussillon are all Grenache wines. The most important of these are Banyuls, Maury, Côtes-d'Agly, Rivesaltes.

GRENADIER – Fish thus named in France because of the shape of its head, which is reminiscent of a French Grenadier's cap. It is never more than 40 cm. (16 inches) long, and its white flesh is delicate. It is served poached, with half-melted *Maître d'hôtel butter* (see BUTTER, *Compound butters*); boiled (hot or cold) with various sauces; *à la boulangère*, with sliced potatoes and onion rings.

GRENADINS – Small slices of fillet of veal (*noix de veau*) cut in the shape of triangles or rectangles which are interlarded with best larding bacon and braised.

Braised veal grenadins. GRENADINS DE VEAU BRAISÉS – Using fillet or under-fillet of veal, cut narrow thick escalopes.

Flatten them gently, trim them, and stud them with thin strips of larding bacon or salt pork.

Grills (*La Carpe. Phot. Nicolas*)

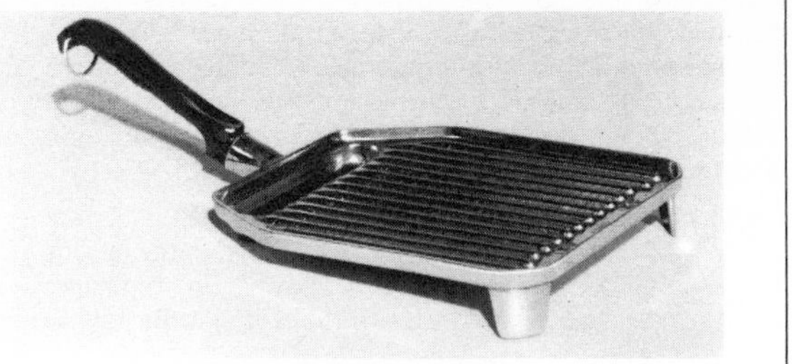

Above: Grilling pan for meat (*Larousse*)
Below: Electric toaster (*Nicolas*)

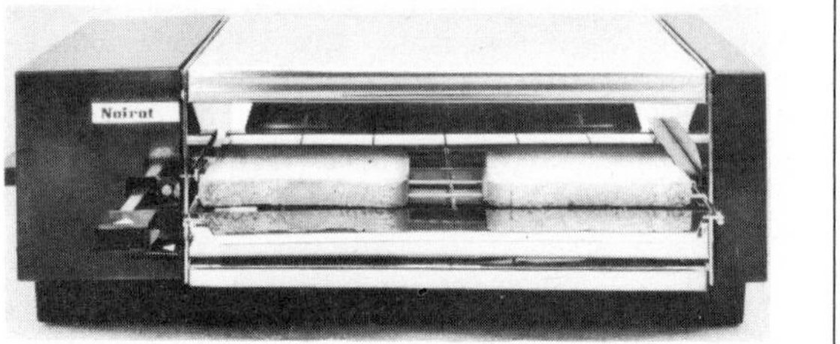

Brown in butter, fresh crackling (or bacon rind), a medium-sized onion, a carrot cut into thin slices, and the trimmings of the veal. Lay the *grenadins* flat in the pan and brown them lightly. Cover, and cook gently on a low flame for 15 minutes.

Moisten with 2 dl. ($\frac{1}{3}$ pint, scant cup) white wine. Boil down the juices almost completely, and add a little water. Bring to the boil again, cover, and bake in a slow oven for about 45 minutes, basting from time to time.

Drain the *grenadins* and lay them on a dish. Strain the juices and pour a few tablespoons over the *grenadins*. Brown in the oven, basting frequently. Dilute the cooking juices in the pan with clear veal stock or consommé. Scrape the sides of the pan and stir the fragments into the gravy. Strain through a fine sieve. Remove fat and boil down if necessary. Pour over the *grenadins*.

Serve braised veal grenadins with all the garnishes suitable for veal chops, escalopes, fillet of veal or *fricandeaux* (q.v.). *Grenadins* are, in fact, small *fricandeaux*.

Among the garnishes best suited to this dish are *bouquetière*, *bourgeoise*, glazed carrots, braised celery, braised endive, chicory, spinach, *fermière*, *jardinière*, braised lettuce, *macédoine*, *nivernaise*, green peas, *printanière*, purée of fresh or dried vegetables, quartered artichokes, or artichoke hearts. (See GARNISHES.)

Poultry grenadins. GRENADINS DE VOLAILLE – The term *grenadin* includes slices of white meat of large poultry, especially turkey. This dish is prepared in the same way as *Braised veal grenadins*.

GRÉSILLER – To shrink or shrivel by heating. The real meaning of the word *grésiller* is to patter. It is applied also to foodstuffs which in cooking make a pattering sound like falling hail.

GRIBICHE – Cold sauce served with cold fish. It is an oily sauce made of the yolks of hard-boiled eggs, oil and vinegar, seasoned with mustard. To this mixture add capers, chopped gherkins, parsley, chervil and tarragon, and whites of hard-boiled eggs cut into short matchsticks. (See SAUCE, *Cold sauces*.)

GRIDIRON, GRILL. GRIL – Kitchen implement with a long history. It is a contemporary of the spit. The cooking of meat on a spit is far older than the preparation of foodstuffs in earthenware or bronze containers.

The metal gridiron was one of the first implements used by our remote ancestors for cooking meat.

GRIGNON – Piece of dry bread, baked very hard, which can be nibbled (*grignoter*). The name *grignon* is also given to the end crust of a long or round loaf. It is also called *quignon*.

GRILLARDIN – Name given by the French to the chef who, in large restaurants, is concerned entirely with the grilling (U.S. broiling) of various types of food.

GRILLETES – Old name for thin slices of fresh pork fried in butter or fat.

GRILLING (U.S. BROILING). GRILLADE – Method of cooking food by putting it on a gridiron over embers, or, in modern cookers, under a grill.

In former times grilling was done on an open wood or charcoal fire. Nowadays, food is grilled by gas or electricity.

GRILSE. SAUMONEAU – Name for a young salmon that has been only once to sea. Before that the salmon is called a parn.

All methods of preparation given for salmon (q.v.) are applicable to the young fish.

GRIMOD DE LA REYNIÈRE – Famous gastronome, born in Paris in 1758, died in 1838. His father, who was Farmer General, was himself the son of a pork butcher.

Grimod de la Reynière, barrister-at-law, did not devote much time to his profession. He preferred sessions at the table to sessions in the Palace of Justice. The first edition of his *Manuel des Amphitryons* came out in 1808, and the series *Almanacs des Gourmands* were published between 1803 and 1812. These books have since been republished several times and form an integral part of every gastronome's library.

'Grimod de la Reynière,' says Carême, 'was familiar with the *ancien régime*, and lived through the horrors of the Revolution. After the reign of terror, he considered it both necessary and wise to write his *Manuel des Amphitryons*, so as to instruct the new rich in the conventions and proprieties which they must observe.

'His *Almanac des Gourmands* is full of flashes of gastronomy and wit. Doubtless, he had some good influence on the science of cookery, but he played no part in the rapid progress which modern cookery has made since the renaissance of the art.'

Grimod de la Reynière set up a 'jury of tasters', who awarded a kind of academic certificate called *légitimation* to various dishes.

Grimod de la Reynière (1758–1838)

This jury of tasters met at intervals at the home of the gastronome, who lived in the Champs-Elysées. There, in solemn fashion, they tasted the dishes sent to Grimod de la Reynière by tradesmen who sought publicity by making known to their customers the judgement, always favourable, pronounced by this gastronomic Areopagus.

The jury of tasters, however, had to give up its sittings because some of its judgements aroused protest. Grimod de la Reynière was even accused of interested partiality.

GRIND. ÉGRUGER – To reduce to powder. This term is used especially of sea-salt ground in a mortar or mill.

GRISSINI – Long sticks of hard-baked bread varying in length from 25 to 75 cm. (10 to 30 inches).

Grissini, of Italian origin, can be bought at large bakeries.

GROG – Drink containing rum or some other spirit, lemon, sugar and hot water.

Old Grog was the nickname given to the English admiral Vernon because of the grogram coat he used to wear.

In 1740 he ordered his men to put water in their ration of rum, and thus a new beverage called 'grog' was invented.

GROS-BLANQUET – Variety of pear with a greenish-yellow skin. It is quite sweet, but rather gritty in texture.

GROSSETÊTE – See RESTAURANTS OF BYGONE DAYS.

GROUSE. TÉTRAS – Game bird of which there are several varieties.

The largest is the *capercaillie*, a superb creature, with very delicate flesh. Quite common in countries of northern Europe, it is rarely found in France. It is prepared like pheasant or ordinary grouse.

The *black grouse*, a bird about the size of the pheasant and cooked in the same way, the British *red grouse* or *Scotch grouse*, the French *gelinotte* (hazel grouse or hazel hen), and the *ganga* or pin-tailed grouse which is found in the south of France and Algeria, all belong to the same family. The last bird, whose flesh is extremely delicate, is the size of a good partridge. It is usually spit-roasted but may be prepared in any way suitable for the *gelinotte*.

This bird should not be confused with that from the same region called *ganga-cata*, or *gelinotte des Pyrenées*, which is equally good to eat, but smaller in size.

All these birds have very good flesh. But they have a pronounced pine flavour, the leg meat in particular, so normally the legs are not served.

In North America there are many species, including *ruffed grouse* (partridge), *blue grouse*, *sage grouse*, *sharp-tailed grouse* and *prairie chicken*.

This game is much prized in England and in U.S.A. It is scarcer in France, where it is known as *gelinotte* (hazel grouse or hazel hen), a bird of much poorer quality than the British or American grouse.

Young grouse is best roasted but may be cooked in the same way as hazel grouse (q.v.).

Marinated grouse (Roman cookery). TÉTRAS MARINÉ – 'Make a good marinade using white wine. After having skinned and cleaned out the bird, marinate it for 3 or 4 days.

'Bard it in bacon fat. Braise it, adding a good *mirepoix* (q.v.) of vegetables lightly cooked in butter, a *bouquet garni* (q.v.), veal stock and the marinade.

'Allow to cool in its cooking liquid, remove all fat from this to clarify it, then boil it down to the point where it can be put in a border mould. When it is turned out, put the sliced meat of the grouse in the middle.

'Serve with slices of buttered toast.' (Recipe of B. Farrep.)

GRUYÈRE – Valley in the Swiss canton of Fribourg after which Gruyère cheese is named. (See CHEESE.)

GRYPHAEA. GRYPHÉE – Species of mollusc sold commercially under the name of Portuguese oysters.

GUAVA. GOYAVE – Fruit of the guava tree, a bush which grows in the tropical regions of America and Asia.

There are several species of guava, some are pear shaped, others orange shaped. One type is shaped like a fig.

The pulp of the guava is somewhat insipid. It is usually eaten raw, but can be stewed or made into jam, jelly or paste.

GUDGEON. GOUJON – Small fish found on the sandy bottom of the lakes and rivers of Europe. Gudgeon live in shoals. There are various kinds.

The parent species, the *common gudgeon*, is the one found in large numbers in the rivers of France. Another kind is found in the Somme, and another in the Danube. One species, *gremille* (pope), is found in almost all French rivers, especially the Seine and the Moselle, and is sometimes called in French, *goujonnière* or *perche goujonnière*.

The flesh of the gudgeon is very delicate. It is usually eaten fried, like the smelt.

Gudgeon en manchon. GOUJON EN MANCHON – Coat with egg and breadcrumbs the bodies of the gudgeon, leaving the heads and tails uncoated. Deep fry. These are used as a garnish for braised fish. Other small fish can be sprinkled with breadcrumbs before frying.

GUERBIGNY – See CHEESE.

GUÉRET – See CHEESE.

GUIGNETTE – Name given in some parts of France to the sand piper, a bird of the snipe family.

All recipes for snipe (q.v.) are suitable for this bird. In some parts of France the name *guignette* is applied to a mollusc, the *littorine*, found in French coastal waters.

GUINEA FOWL. PINTADE, PINTADEAU – Genus of bird of the *Gallinaceae* family which includes several species. It is a native of Africa and was known to the Romans, who called it Numidian hen or Carthaginian (Carthage) hen. The flesh of young guinea fowl is delicate and similar to that of pheasant.

Guinea fowl à la languedocienne (*Robert Carrier*)

The guinea fowl often figures on the menu of banquets and wedding receptions as 'Bohemian pheasant', a name which is somewhat exaggerated.

Guinea poults, which are found in the markets of France towards the end of July, are excellent. They can be prepared in any way suitable for pheasant or partridges.

Fully grown guinea fowls are prepared (hot or cold) in any way suitable for chicken.

Guinea fowl liver. FOIE DE PINTADES – All recipes for chicken livers are suitable for guinea fowl livers. These are also used as an ingredient in stuffings.

Guinea fowl

GUINEA PIG. COCHON D'INDE – Domestic rodent of South American origin. Its flesh is edible, but it is chiefly used for laboratory experiments.

GUINGUET – French expression used to describe mediocre, rather acid wine of low alcoholic content.

GUINGUETTE – Name given to a French suburban place of refreshment with music and dancing. Some etymologists believe that this name is derived from *guinguet*, a type of grape cultivated in the Paris suburbs. A rather sour wine was made from these grapes and this was mainly drunk in taverns on the outskirts of Paris.

GULL. MOUETTE – Sea-bird whose flesh is leathery with an unpleasant taste, but whose eggs are edible.

GULYAS – See GOULASCH.

GUM. GOMME – Term applied to a number of diverse substances which flow either naturally or by inducement from the stems of certain plants. When mixed with water these substances have adhesive properties. The stems of the plants exude gum when they are punctured by insects or when incisions are made in them.

One of these gums, *gum tragacanth*, is used in cookery, and also in the preparation of medicinal pastes and in the manufacture of syrup gum.

It is said that some resinous gums were used as condiments by the Romans.

Gum arabic. GOMME ARABIQUE – Product of secretion of various species of acacia trees. It is found in the form of yellowish or reddish fragments, soluble in water, contact with which gives them a viscous consistency. This property renders it useful in pharmaceutics and cookery for the preparation of mucilages. Gum arabic is the basis of jujube, marshmallow and liquorice paste.

Syrup gum. SIROP DE GOMME – Crush 500 g. (18 oz.) gum arabic and soak for 24 hours in $\frac{1}{2}$ litre (scant pint, $2\frac{1}{4}$ cups) cold water. Add to a syrup made with 2 kg. ($4\frac{1}{2}$ lb., 9 cups) sugar and 1 litre ($1\frac{3}{4}$ pints, generous quart) water boiled to 105°C. (220°F.). Boil the mixture, skim, and filter it when quite cool. Store in bottles.

GURNEAU – French name for a species of gurnet. It is found in the Mediterranean, in British coastal waters and in the Baltic.

All recipes for gurnet (q.v.) are suitable for this fish.

GURNET. GRONDIN – This European fish is often sold in France as red mullet, but erroneously, since though quite delicate in flavour, it cannot be compared with the true red mullet.

The gurnet is called *grondin* (grunter) in French because of the grunting sound it is said to make when it comes out of the water. It is quite different in shape from the true red mullet.

There are various types of gurnet. Among those to be found in France are the *red gurnet*, whose scales are a beautiful clear red or rose colour; the *cuckoo gurnet*, red in colour; the *trigle lyre*, whose back is a beautiful clear red with silvery and rose-coloured belly and sides; the *grey gurnet*, grey with whitish spots on back and flanks; the *shining gurnet*, also called the *long-finned gurnet*, which is the largest of the species – it can be as much as 60 cm. (24 inches) in length – coloured yellowish pink along the back, pinkish white on the belly. The shining gurnet, when its fins are outspread, has the appearance of a butterfly, with delicately tinted 'wings' ranging from blue to deep purple.

Gurnet is quite good to eat. Its flesh is white and flaky.

All recipes for red mullet (see MULLET) are suitable for gurnet, which can be fried, grilled or cooked in butter *à la meunière* (q.v.). They can be stewed or cooked in white wine, and they are used in *bouillabaisse* (q.v.).

GUYENNE – This vast province has been divided into the *départements* of the Gironde, Dordogne, Lot, Aveyron, Lot-et-Garonne and Tarn-et-Garonne.

The *cuisine* of this region is dominated by the truffles of Périgord and Lot, and garlic which is used liberally in most of the local dishes.

The products of the region include the celebrated Roquefort cheese; the truffles of Périgord and Lot; the geese and duck livers which are potted or made into *pâtés*; the *confit d'oie* of Montauban; the lamb of Pauillac; and all the succulent partridge, woodcock and thrush *pâtés* made almost everywhere here, but especially in the little town of Lomogne, a centre of delicious cooking.

Culinary specialities – Among the special local dishes of Guyenne those deserving of special mention are *estouffat of haricot beans*; *lampreys à la bordelaise*; *tripe with saffron*; *tripe à la ruthénoise*; *leg of lamb à la ficelle*; *white pudding quercinois*; *stuffed chicken*; *potted truffles*; *cèpes à la bordelaise*; *millas girondin*; Agen *prunes*; *hearth-cake*.

The broths and *pots-au-feu* include the *garbure Gasconne* and, no less delectable, the *chaudeau* and the *tomato tourin*.

Most famous of the fish dishes of Guyenne are *matelotes of lampreys and eels* and *trout à la meunière*. Exclusive to this region are *oyster sausages*; *bunting en caisses*; *old fashioned galimaufry*; *foie-gras with grapes*; *jugged mountain hare*; *tripe à la landaise*; *leg of lamb à la gasconnade*; *stuffed chicken*; *alicuit of goose or chicken*; *stuffed goose hearts*; *roast wood pigeon*; *woodcock salmi*, and, the dish extolled by Marcel Prévost, the *Christmas estouffat*.

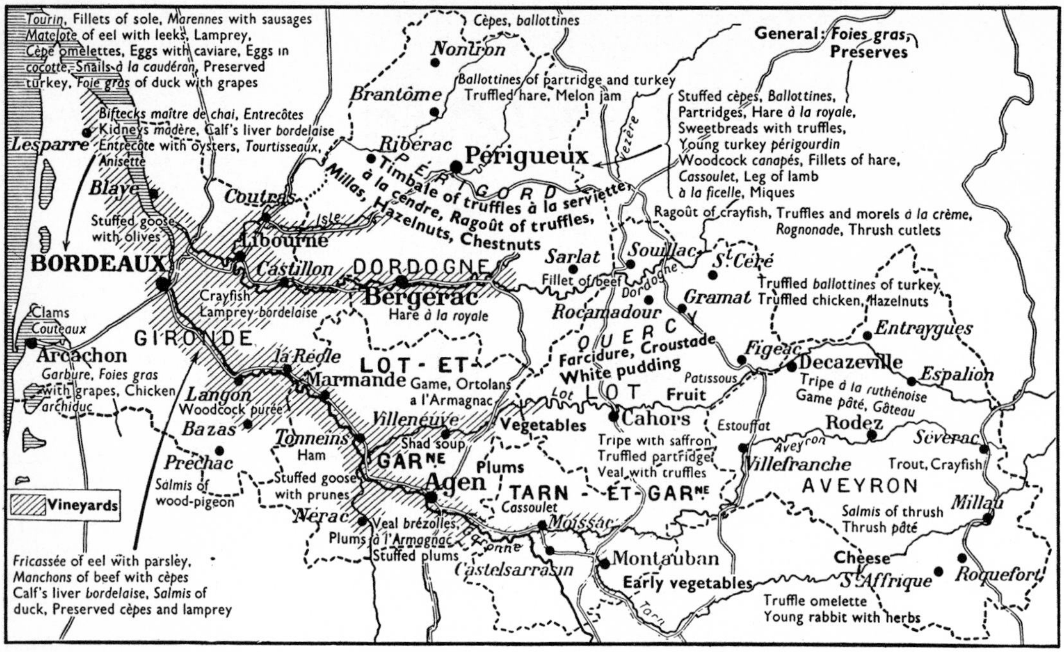

Gastronomic map of Guyenne

Among the sweets of the district are *tourtisseaux, cruchade gasconne* and *lou pasti.* The *feuillantines* of Gers and the *gâteau à la broche* must not be forgotten.

We end this list with a brief reference to the excellent red and white wines of the district (see BORDEAUX) and above all to the *eau-de-vie* of Armagnac (see GASCONY).

GYMNÈTRE – Species of fish which tastes rather like fresh cod.

The *gymnètre faux,* which is found in the Mediterranean, is about 45 cm. (18 inches) long, flat, silver in colour with red fins.

All recipes for cod (q.v.) are suitable for this fish.

HADDOCK. ÉGLEFIN, AIGLEFIN, AIGREFIN – Sea-fish of the cod family, but smaller than the true cod. This fish is also known in France as *égrefin, morue noire* (black cod), *morue Saint-Pierre* and in Newfoundland as *âne* or *ânon.*

Fresh haddock is white and delicate. All recipes for cod (q.v.) are suitable for fresh haddock.

Smoked haddock

Smoked haddock is very popular in England and the U.S.A. As soon as it is caught, the fish is split lengthwise, lightly rubbed over with salt, hung by the tail, and left to smoke for 24 hours. Smoked haddock keeps fresh for several days.

Cod and haddock, when they are fresh, lend themselves to a great number of culinary treatments and suitable recipes will be found under BASS, BRILL, EEL, WHITING, TUNNY, TURBOT.

Baked haddock

Baked haddock à l'irlandaise. AIGREFIN AU FOUR À L'IRLANDAISE – Stuff a haddock with suet. Truss in an S-shape and make light incisions on the sides. Put in a buttered baking pan, season with salt and pepper, and moisten with $1\frac{1}{2}$ dl. ($\frac{1}{4}$ pint, $\frac{2}{3}$ cup) Madeira. Cover with a buttered paper and bake in the oven, basting frequently. Untie the fish, arrange on a hot dish and sprinkle with the pan juices.

Serve with *Oyster sauce* or *Shrimp sauce* (see SAUCE).

Curried smoked haddock. HADDOCK À L'INDIENNE – Bone, skin and dice the fish. Cook chopped onion in butter and add the haddock. Cook for 5 minutes. Add a fairly thin *Curry sauce* (see SAUCE). Cover, and simmer for 10 minutes. Serve with *Rice à l'indienne* (see RICE).

Grilled smoked haddock. HADDOCK GRILLÉ – Brush the fish with oil or melted butter and cook slowly under the grill.

Serve with melted butter and boiled potatoes, or with *Maître d'hôtel butter* (see BUTTER, *Compound butters*).

Smoked haddock with paprika. HADDOCK AU PAPRIKA – Proceed as for *Curried haddock*, substituting *Hungarian sauce* (see SAUCE) for curry sauce.

Poached smoked haddock. HADDOCK POCHÉ – Simmer the fish in slightly salted boiling water, without allowing it to boil, for 6 to 10 minutes, according to its size. Haddock can also be poached in milk. Serve with melted butter and boiled potatoes.

HAGGIS (Scottish cookery) – Haggis may be regarded as the national dish of Scotland. When this dish is served at certain large banquets in Scotland, it is accompanied by an escort of pipers.

Here is the recipe given by Alfred Suzanne in his book *la Cuisine anglaise*.

'To make a haggis, take a sheep's stomach, clean thoroughly and turn inside out.

'Take the heart, liver and lungs of the sheep. Boil all these for 30 minutes in salt water. Take out the offal and mince it very finely, except for part of the liver which must be allowed to get quite cold so that it can be grated.

'Spread the mince on a table and season with salt, pepper, nutmeg, cayenne pepper and chopped onion. Add the grated liver, a handful of oatmeal and 500 g. (18 oz., 4 cups) chopped beef suet. Now fill the stomach with the mixture, a little more than half full, leaving plenty of space at the top to prevent it from bursting during cooking. Add a glassful of good gravy. Prick the haggis here and there with a large needle and sew up the opening. Place in a large pan with plenty of water and boil for 3 hours.

'It sometimes happens that the bladder bursts during

cooking and spills out its contents. To avoid this, wrap the haggis in a napkin, as though it were a galantine, before putting it into boiling water.'

Haggis is normally served wrapped in a well-starched napkin and whisky is the traditional drink that goes with it.

HAKE – Sea-fish called *merlan* (whiting) in Provence, *colin* (cod) in Paris and *saumon blanc* (white salmon) on some French menus. Its flesh is tender, white, flaky and easy to digest. When dried, it is called *merluche* (stockfish).

All recipes for cod (q.v.) are suitable for hake.

HALBRAN. ALBRAN – Name given to very young wild duck. When a little older it is called duckling, then duck. It is cooked like duck (q.v.).

HALCYON (kingfisher). ALCYON – The name of this bird comes from the Greek *alkuon* (formed of *als*, the sea, and *kuon*, one who nurses its young). According to a Greek legend the halcyon built its nest on the waves of the sea.

This bird, remarkable for its brilliant blue plumage, with varying shades of red on the breast, is the Australian version of our kingfisher, or laughing jackass. From Australia the species has spread to China and Japan.

The halcyons built their nests with the aid of a gelatinous substance secreted during the laying period by their crops. These nests are much esteemed by the Chinese. In their dried state they are imported into Europe and are greatly prized at the best tables, where they are known as birds' nests.

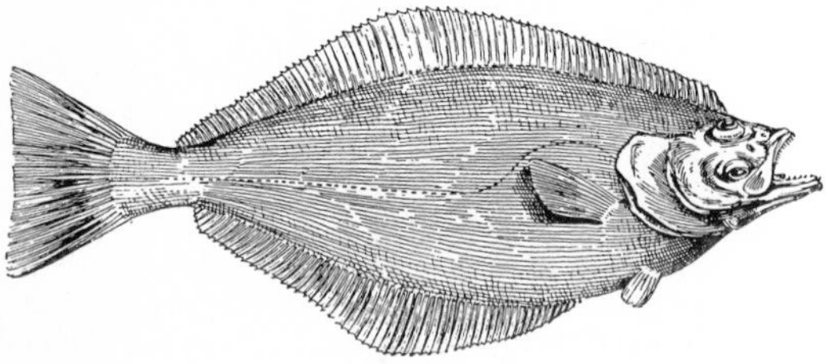

Halibut

HALIBUT. FLÉTAN – Large flat fish found in northern waters. The body is more elongated in shape than other flat fish, the eyes are on the right side, and the mouth is large. A halibut can be as much as 2 m. ($6\frac{1}{2}$ feet) long and weighs between 150 and 200 kg. (330 and 440 lb.).

The firm white flesh of halibut is greatly valued as food, and all recipes for brill (q.v.) may be used for this fish.

HALICOT OF MUTTON. HALICOT DE MOUTON – A mutton stew garnished with turnips, potatoes, onions, and, sometimes, with haricot beans. See MUTTON, *Haricot or halicot of mutton.*

HAM. JAMBON – Strictly, a ham is a leg of pork, salted and smoked. In current usage, however, the term is also applied to the shoulder of pig that is cured in the same fashion. This cut, though excellent, is nevertheless a good deal less delicate than the leg.

In French cookery the term *jambon* not only means ham but also applies to a leg of fresh pork. This cut can be cooked in a great many ways, either whole or divided into smaller cuts. It is also used as an ingredient for stuffing, and in various manufactured pork products (see PORK). A Ham Fair is held regularly in Paris and several other large French cities. This fair which, in former times, was held during the three days preceding Good Friday, and which was then called *Foire du lard* (the Bacon Fair), took place in the square in front of Notre-Dame. The canons leased the ground to the butchers and pork butchers. The site was changed several

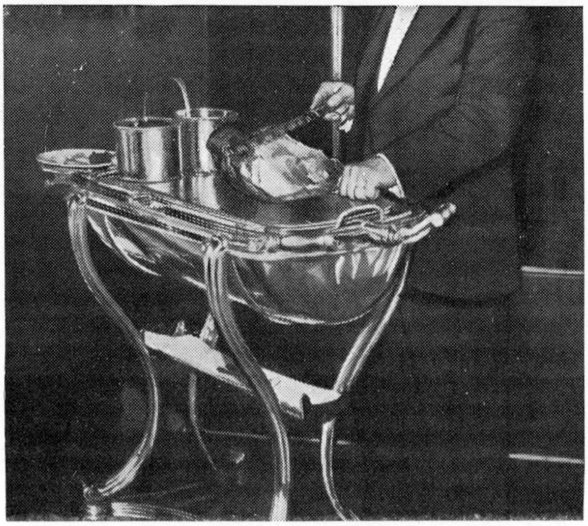

Slicing and serving ham in a large restaurant

times. In 1813, the fair was transferred to the quai des Grands-Augustins, where it remained until 1832. It was moved to faubourg Saint-Martin, and in 1848 was transferred to the boulevard Bourdon. At the end of the Second Empire it was moved, for the last time, to the boulevard Richard-Lenoir, where it is still held today.

The salting and smoking of pork to produce ham is of French origin. It was the Gauls, great devotees of pig meat and efficient pig breeders, who first became renowned for the salting, smoking and curing of the various cuts of pork.

After salting, the Gauls subjected them for two days to the smoke of certain selected woods. They then rubbed them with oil and vinegar and hung them up, to dry and preserve them. The Gauls ate ham either at the beginning of a meal to sharpen their appetites, or at the end to induce thirst.

Many different kinds of salt and smoked ham are obtainable in France. Almost every region has its own local ham. Among the best known are the *jambon de Bayonne*, cured at Orthez, but known the world over as *jambon de Bayonne*. This ham is eaten raw, as an *hors-d'œuvre*. It is also used in cooking in various ways, but unlike York ham or other lightly smoked hams, it must not be boiled. *Jambon de Bayonne* is served with eggs cooked in various ways, and it also forms an ingredient of various sauces and *ragoûts*. The *jambon de Toulouse* is merely salted and dried. It is eaten raw like the *jambon de Bayonne*, and is also used in cooking.

There are a large number of salted and smoked hams called in France *jambons de campagne*. Among these are the hams of Brittany, Morvan, Burgundy, Montagne-Noir (Cévennes), Lorraine, Alsace, Touraine, Limousin, Auvergne, the Vosges, Savoy, etc. Almost all these hams are eaten raw, or may be used in cooking, like the *jambon de Toulouse*. Some may be boiled like York ham.

French cooking hams, similar to English cooking hams, are *jambon blanc* or *jambon demi-sel*, also known as *jambon de Paris*. This ham, which is either not smoked at all or only very lightly smoked, is sold by all French pork butchers under the name of *jambon glacé*.

The food value of ham is more or less equivalent to that of meat. However, salted or smoked raw ham is not to be recommended for fragile digestions, and more robust constitutions should not consume too much of it. Cooked ham, on the other hand, may be given to children and invalids. Home-cooked ham is best boiled in plenty of water to remove fats and toxic substances. Boiled ham bought commercially, tinted pink by the addition of potassium nitrate, is better avoided.

American hams (preserved). JAMBONS D'AMÉRIQUE – Excellent hams are cured in the U.S.A. However, almost all American hams exported to Europe, and particularly to France, are cooked and preserved.

English hams. JAMBONS D'ANGLETERRE – English hams are usually described on French menus as York ham, but a distinction must be made between the various methods of processing. This is indicated by their trade mark.

York ham, which is smoked (lightly or heavily), is usually boiled. It is served either hot or cold. When hot, a special sauce is served with it, flavoured with Madeira, sheery, port, etc. York ham can also be boiled and then baked in the oven, covered with brown sugar, spice and cloves.

Raw York ham, thinly sliced and sautéed in butter, is often served with eggs.

Baked York ham

German, Czechoslovakian and Hungarian hams. JAMBONS D'ALLEMAGNE, DE BOHÊME, DE HONGRIE – The best-known is Mainz ham which, like Westphalian ham, is mostly eaten raw, but may also be boiled whole and served before the main course. Other well-known German hams come from Hamburg, Gotha and Stuttgart.

The best Czechoslovakian ham is Prague ham; it is cooked whole, and makes a delicious prelude to the main course. It is served cold. Excellent smoked hams are made in Hungary.

Italian hams. JAMBONS D'ITALIE – The best-known Italian ham is Parma ham. This is usually eaten raw as an *hors-d'œuvre* and is one of the most delicate of hams. It can be used in cooking, though it must not be boiled, but cut into thin slices or diced and sautéed in butter or fat. Cooked in this way it can be served with eggs, various meat dishes, poultry or risottos.

There are other kinds of Italian ham which are either boiled whole and eaten hot or cold, or used in the same way as Parma ham.

Spanish hams. JAMBONS D'ESPAGNE – Asturias ham is the best-known Spanish ham. It is mild, very delicate in flavour, and is eaten hot or cold after having been boiled. It is also used in cooking like the hams of Bayonne and Toulouse.

Salted and smoked ham. JAMBON DE PORC SALÉ ET FUMÉ – Salted and smoked hams, whether of French or foreign origin, after having been boiled as described below, provide an intermediate course (*remove*) much prized by connoisseurs. These boiled hams are also served cold.

Boiled and cold hams of various kinds are to be found in all the pork butchers of Paris and the big provincial towns. In these shops are sold, apart from the *jambon de Paris* (*jambon glacé*), boiled hams boned and moulded with jelly, smoked hams boiled and cold, boiled rolled hams, Dijon hams, Dijon hams prepared with parsley, and the foreleg hams of Paris, Reims, Strasbourg, Nancy etc.

The curing of ham, which is now a great industry, involves two main operations, salting and smoking. The hams are either salted in brine, or dry salt, or rubbed over with dry salt, saltpetre and sugar and left for three days well covered with this mixture. They are then put into brine, washed, brushed and dried, and finally smoked in special chambers, starting with a light smoke which grows denser as the operation proceeds.

Poaching. Ham should be soaked in cold water for at least 6 hours before cooking. It is then scrubbed, boned at the chump end and put into cold water to cook, without any seasoning or aromatics.

Although ham cooked in this way is sometimes described as 'boiled', it should, in fact, be poached and so as soon as the water boils, reduce the heat and leave to poach, simmering very gently so that the water just shivers. Allow 20 minutes cooking time per 500 g. (1 lb.) of York, Hamburg or Paris ham. Czechoslovakian and Spanish hams require a little less cooking time.

If the ham is to be served cold, leave it to cool in the water in which it was cooked. If it is to be served hot, drain, remove the skin, and glaze.

Cold ham is served with jelly.

Hot ham is served with vegetables, most frequently spinach, and with Madeira or other wine sauce.

Glazing. Having poached the ham as described, remove the skin. Put the ham into a pan, sprinkle with sugar and brown in the oven or under the grill.

The sugar, upon caramelising, forms a light glaze on the surface of the ham, which not only makes its appearance more appetising, but also gives it a good flavour.

The ham can also be glazed by following the method given for braised meats (see CULINARY METHODS).

Jambonnière or braising pan for ham (*Larousse*)

Braising. Soak the ham as described above and poach very gently, so that boiling is hardly perceptible.

Remove the ham 40 minutes before it is completely cooked. Skin it and put into a braising pan. Add 5 dl. (scant pint, $2\frac{1}{4}$ cups) Madeira or any other liqueur wine (port, sherry, Frontignan, Lunel, Marsala etc.).

Cover with a lid and cook in the oven for between 45 minutes and 1 hour. Glaze the ham as described above. Arrange on a serving dish and put a paper frill around the knuckle. Garnish as described in the recipe, or serve the garnish and the appropriate sauce separately.

Garnishes and sauces suitable for York and other hams served hot. Alsacienne (Madeira sauce), *berrichonne* (Madeira sauce), *brabançonne* (Madeira sauce), chipolata (Madeira sauce), braised celery or celeriac (Madeira sauce), glazed cucumbers in big chunks (Madeira sauce), chicory (Madeira sauce), leaf or chopped spinach (Madeira sauce), *flamande* (*demi-glace sauce*), *hongroise* (*demi-glace sauce*), *macédoine*

Ham glacé (*Robert Carrier*)

(*demi-glace sauce*), *nivernaise* (*demi-glace sauce*), noodles with *noisette butter* (Madeira, sherry or port sauce), garden peas or other green vegetable dressed with butter or cream (Madeira sauce, or wine-flavoured cream sauce), various fresh or dried vegetable purées (*demi-glace sauce* flavoured with Madeira or other liqueur wine), *romaine* (Marsala sauce). (See GARNISHES, SAUCE.)

Ham à l'alsacienne I. JAMBON À L'ALSACIENNE – Braise the ham and glaze it as described above. Garnish with braised *sauerkraut*, Strasbourg sausages and boiled potatoes.

Ham à l'alsacienne II. JAMBON À L'ALSACIENNE – Heat cooked, thinly sliced York ham in a few tablespoons of stock without allowing it to boil. Serve on a foundation of braised *sauerkraut*.

Garnish with Strasbourg sausages and boiled potatoes.

Ham à la bayonnaise. JAMBON À LA BAYONNAISE – Poach a well de-salted Bayonne ham in water until three quarters cooked. Take out of the pan, remove skin and trim off surplus fat on the surface only.

Put it into a pan and finish braising in Madeira. Glaze and arrange on a long dish. Serve with *Rice pilaf* (see PILAF), chopped tomatoes, small button mushrooms and little chipolata sausages fried in butter. Serve with *Madeira sauce* (see SAUCE) based on the braising liquor.

Burgundian ham with parsley (cold). JAMBON PERSILLÉ DE BOURGOGNE – This is an Easter luncheon dish in Burgundy.

Wash and desalt the ham. Blanch it thoroughly, drain, skin, and cut into big pieces. Put these into a large pan with 500 g. (18 oz.) sliced veal knuckle, 2 calf's feet, boned, blanched and tied with string, and a big *bouquet garni* (q.v.) with, in addition to the usual herbs, chervil and tarragon, and 10 peppercorns (tied in a piece of muslin). Season with a little salt. Add enough dry white wine to cover all the meat. Bring to the boil on a high flame, reduce heat, cover, and simmer gently on a low heat, to obtain a very clear stock. This will be used for making the jelly to accompany the ham.

When the ham is well cooked, drain, flake with a fork and put into a salad dish, pressing it down well.

Strain the liquor. Add 1 tablespoonful tarragon vinegar. When it begins to coagulate, add 2 tablespoons (3 tablespoons) chopped parsley. Pour this jelly over the ham. Leave in a cool place until cold. It is advisable to prepare this dish the day before it is required.

Ham in Chambertin. JAMBON AU CHAMBERTIN – Cook a York or Prague ham in water until three quarters done. Drain, trim and skin.

Braise in a liquor based on Chambertin. When cooked, drain the ham and glaze.

Surround with small glazed onions and button mushrooms fried in butter. Strain the braising liquor and pour over the ham.

Cold ham. JAMBON FROID – Poach the ham in water and, if it is to be served whole, leave it to cool in its poaching liquor, then trim, remove skin, and cover with *Aspic jelly* (see JELLY).

If it is to be moulded, bone it, trim, remove skin, put into a special mould, and leave to cool under a press.

Cold ham mousse. MOUSSE FROIDE DE JAMBON – Pound finely in a mortar 500 g. (18 oz.) cooked lean ham adding 2 dl. ($\frac{1}{3}$ pint, scant cup) cold, thick *Velouté sauce* (see SAUCE). Rub through a sieve.

Put this purée into a bowl, season, stand it on ice and stir with a wooden spoon for a few minutes, adding, little by little, $1\frac{1}{2}$ dl. ($\frac{1}{4}$ pint, $\frac{2}{3}$ cup) liquid jelly. Fold in 4 dl. ($\frac{3}{4}$ pint, scant 2 cups) half-whipped cream. Pour into a jelly-lined mould and leave on ice to set.

Turn out onto a dish, or a buttered bread croûton, and garnish with jelly.

Ham mousse

Ham à la crème. JAMBON À LA CRÈME – Cook a York or Prague ham in salted water until two thirds done, skin, and braise in a Madeira *mirepoix* (q.v.). Drain and glaze.

Boil down the braising liquor by two thirds, and add 5 dl. (scant pint, $2\frac{1}{4}$ cups) fresh double cream. Boil down sauce by one third, strain, and serve with the ham.

Ham en croûte. JAMBON EN CROÛTE – See *Prague ham in pastry à l'ancienne*.

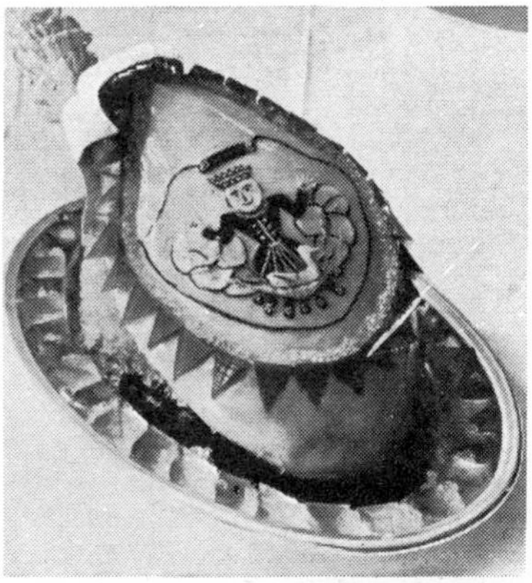

Ham glacé Reine Pédauque (*Larousse*)

Ham glacé Reine Pédauque (cold buffet dish). JAMBON GLACÉ REINE PÉDAUQUE – Cut into thin slices the pope's eye (U.S. eye of the round) of a York ham, poached in Meursault wine and left until cold. Put the slices together again, sandwiching them with layers of *Foie gras purée* (see PURÉE) mixed with diced truffles, reshaping the ham into its original form. Coat with port-flavoured *Chaud-froid sauce* (see SAUCE). Decorate with truffles, glaze with port-flavoured aspic jelly, and surround with jelly croûtons.

Ham with lettuce, chicory and endives. JAMBON AU LAITUES, AUX ENDIVES À LA CHICORÉE – Braise the ham in Madeira, garnish with halved braised lettuces (or chicory or endive) and serve with Madeira-flavoured *Demi-glace sauce* (see SAUCE).

Ham à la maillot. JAMBON À LA MAILLOT – Desalt the ham, wrap it in a cloth, put in a large braising pan and cover with cold water. Simmer gently.

When the ham is cooked, drain and skin. Put it into a small braising pan with a grid, add $\frac{1}{2}$ litre (scant pint, $2\frac{1}{4}$ cups)

Madeira. Cover and simmer for 30 minutes. Glaze. Garnish with glazed carrots cut into balls, French beans, small onions glazed in stock, and braised lettuce. Arrange these vegetables in separate groups and serve with Madeira sauce (see SAUCE).

Ham in pastry, or ham turnover with foie gras and truffles. JAMBON EN CHAUSSON, CHAUSSON DE JAMBON AU FOIE GRAS ET TRUFFES – Braise a ham in Madeira, port or sherry. When cooked, take out the pope's eye and the round, trim them, and cut each into 8 or 10 slices of uniform thickness.

Put these on an oval-shaped piece of rolled out *Lining paste* (see DOUGH) on a foundation of *duxelles* (q.v.) mixture and chopped truffles, alternating with layers of *foie gras* tossed in butter, and slivers of truffles. Cover the ham with a layer of *duxelles* mixture and chopped truffles, put another piece of rolled-out lining paste on top, seal, and pinch up the edges. Brush the top with beaten egg, make a few light incisions and a hole in the middle to allow steam to escape. Bake in a hot oven for about 45 minutes.

Pour a few tablespoons of *Port sauce* (see SAUCE) through the hole and serve the rest of the sauce separately.

Ham in pastry can be prepared with various garnishes, such as *ragoût à la financière, ragoût à la Godard,* morels fried in butter, spinach or any other braised vegetable.

Another variation is to place the ham and its garnish on a round piece of pastry, which is then folded over, forming the classic turnover.

Ham pie. PÂTÉ DE JAMBON – Using thin slices of ham, fine forcemeat (see FORCEMEAT) and truffles, prepare as *Veal and ham pâté* (see PÂTÉ).

Prague ham in pastry à l'ancienne. JAMBON DE PRAGUE EN PÂTE À L'ANCIENNE – Poach the ham in water until it is two-thirds done. Drain, skin and glaze.

When cold, put it, glazed side down, on a big piece of rolled-out *Lining paste* (see DOUGH), spread with a layer of fine *mirepoix* (q.v.) of vegetables which have been softened in butter and mixed with dried *duxelles* (q.v.) and chopped truffles.

Prague ham in pastry à l'ancienne
(*Larousse*)

Enclose the ham in the pastry and seal the edges. Turn it over and put into a buttered baking tin, sealed side down. Brush the top with beaten egg, and decorate with fancy pieces of pastry. Make a hole in the middle to allow steam to escape and bake in a hot oven for about 45 minutes.

Pour into it a few tablespoons of *Périgueux sauce* (see SAUCE) through the hole in the middle.

Ham with sauerkraut. JAMBON À LA CHOUCROUTE – The same as *Ham à l'alsacienne.* Serve with *Demi-glace sauce* (see SAUCE) or a sauce based on Alsation wine.

Ham with spinach. JAMBON AUX ÉPINARDS – Braise the ham in Madeira. Serve with leaf spinach cooked in butter, or chopped spinach cooked in stock. Serve with *Demi-glace* or *Madeira sauce* (see SAUCE).

Ham in pastry (*Robert Carrier*)

York ham à la financière. JAMBON D'YORK À LA FINANCIÈRE – Braise the ham in Madeira. Glaze and surround with *Financière garnish* (see GARNISHES). Skim off surplus fat from the braising liquor, boil down, strain, and pour over the ham.

HAMBURGER STEAK, (Austro-Hungarian cookery). KEFTEDES – This dish is made from minced beef browned in butter or fat. Similar 'steaks' are made from minced veal, poultry and game. Here is a Hungarian recipe for hamburger steak:

1 kg. ($2\frac{1}{4}$ lb.) finely minced lean beef or veal, 10 rashers chopped bacon.

Mix the beef or veal with the bacon and add to it 200 g. (7 oz.) of crustless bread soaked in milk and squeezed out. Season with salt, pepper and grated nutmeg.

When all the ingredients are well mixed, divide into pieces of equal weight. Shape each piece into a steak $7\frac{1}{2}$ cm. (3 inches) in diameter and 2 cm. ($\frac{3}{4}$ inch) thick. Flour, and fry in fat. When they are cooked, dip in concentrated meat stock. Serve with mashed potatoes or other vegetables.

Hamburger steak (German cookery). KEFTEDES DE BOEUF – Proceed as for *Hamburger steak (also called à l'allemande)* (see BEEF), but leave out the chopped fried onions.

Hamburger steaks à la berlinoise. KEFTEDES DE BOEUF À LA BERLINOISE – Mince finely 300 g. (11 oz.) lean beef and 75 g. (3 oz.) fat bacon or salt pork. Add 75 g. (3 oz.) soft bread soaked in milk and squeezed dry. Season with salt, pepper and nutmeg and mix thoroughly.

Divide the mixture into 4 parts. Shape each piece so that it is round and flat. Dip in flour and fry in boiling lard. Brown the steaks well on both sides. Pour *Demi-glace sauce* (see SAUCE) over them to serve.

Game hamburger steaks. KEFTEDES DE GIBIER – Remove fat and sinews from the game. Mince finely, adding 1 tablespoon chopped onion browned in butter. Divide into pieces of equal size and pat into little round or oval shapes. Dip in flour and fry in butter. Serve with an appropriate sauce and garnish.

Poultry hamburger steaks. KEFTEDES DE VOLAILLE – Proceed as for *Game hamburger steaks*, substituting poultry for game.

HAMMERHEAD SHARK. MARTEAU – Type of porbeagle. Its flesh, which is oily and leathery, is salted and eaten in some parts of the world.

HANGING. MORTIFIER – Process for tenderising meat or game by leaving it to hang for a period.

Hang meat on a hook in a cool, well-ventilated, very dry place.

HARE. LIÈVRE – Wild rodent with dark flesh, highly flavoured and excellent to eat. The mountain hare is more delicate than that of the plains.

The male hare is called a *buck* and the female a *doe*. In France a young leveret up to 3 months is called a *financier*; up to 6 months a *trois-quarts* and at a year a *capucin* or *lièvre fait*. Young hares can be recognised by the fact that their ears tear easily and by a little rounded prominence on a bone under the leg joint which disappears as it grows older.

Hare can be eaten fresh, as soon as it is shot, or, if it is left to get cold, two or three days after killing, depending on the time of the year. It must never be eaten 'high'.

How to choose a hare. A hare is always tender in its first year. As it grows older its flesh becomes tough and stringy, but the female is still tender in its second year.

First-year hares can be recognised by their slender paws and by the smoothness of their coat which, in older hares, becomes slightly wavy and shows traces of greying.

In a young hare, the claws, hidden under the fur of the paws, are invisible. With age, the claws grow and project slightly beyond the fur.

French hares. The best are those of Beauce, Brie, Normandy, Champagne and Touraine.

The hares of northern France and Brittany are of inferior quality. This is due to the nature of the soil, which is poor feeding ground for hares.

The hares of Beauce, Brie and Champagne have golden coats, the colour of ripe corn.

The hares of Normandy and Touraine are usually small, with tan coats, darker than those of Beauce, Brie and Champagne.

The hares of Brittany are small, and have very dark tan coats mottled with black.

Many of the hares of southern France are of fine quality, especially those of Périgord and Gascony, though these are seldom to be found on sale in Paris.

English hares. Similar to those from Normandy.

German hares. Larger than the French varieties but inferior in flavour.

Hare à l'allemande. LIÈVRE À L'ALLEMANDE – For this dish the saddle and haunch of the hare are used. Roast the hare in the usual way and pour sour cream into the roasting pan. Strain the sauce through a fine sieve and serve separately. Sometimes this sauce is poured over the hare. (See also *Saddle of hare à l'allemande* below).

Ballotine of hare (cold). BALLOTTINE DE LIÈVRE – Made of slices of hare, lean ham, pickled tongue, pork fat, *foie gras*, truffles and hare stuffing, in the same way as *Galantine of chicken* (see GALANTINE).

Ballottine of hare à la périgourdine (hot). BALLOTTINE DE LIÈVRE À LA PÉRIGOURDINE – Bone a young hare. Spread it on a cloth covered with thin slices of pork fat. Season with spiced salt and pour brandy over it. Cover with a layer of game stuffing made from the flesh of a leveret, with chopped truffles added. On top of this stuffing put alternate thin strips of hare, cut from the thighs and browned in butter, strips of *foie gras* and slices of truffles. Season and pour brandy over these ingredients. Cover with a layer of *à gratin game stuffing* (see FORCEMEAT). Fold the hare into a roll and tie with string. Braise it in a Madeira braising stock made from shin of veal, the bones and trimmings of the hare and the leveret, and the usual pot vegetables. Cook for $1\frac{1}{2}$ hours. Drain the hare and remove the string. Brown in the oven. Boil down the braising liquor, strain, add shredded truffles and pour over the ballottine.

Civet of hare. CIVET DE LIÈVRE – Skin and draw a young hare. Collect the blood and put it aside with the liver, removing the gall bladder.

Joint the hare, cutting the body into 3 or 4 pieces. Put these in a dish, season with salt, pepper, thyme and powdered bay leaf. Add a sliced onion. Moisten with 2 or 3 tablespoons oil and 1 tablespoon brandy. Leave the hare in this marinade for 3 hours.

For a medium-sized hare parboil and then brown in butter 200 g. (7 oz.) lean bacon, cut into squares. Remove from the pan and, in the same butter, brown 2 quartered onions. Add 2 tablespoons (3 tablespoons) flour. Cook, stirring with a wooden spoon until the flour is a golden colour.

Add the pieces of hare, well dried. Brown them in the roux, stirring. Moisten with enough red wine just to cover the hare. Add a *bouquet garni* (q.v.), to which has been added a clove of garlic. Cover the pan and simmer slowly for 45 minutes to 1 hour.

Drain the pieces of hare. Scrape off any fragments of skin or bone clinging to them. Clean out the saucepan and put in the hare. Add the fried bacon, 24 small braised onions and 24 small mushrooms tossed in butter. Add the marinade to the cooking stock. Strain and pour over the hare. Cover the pan and cook in a moderate oven for about 45 minutes.

A few minutes before serving, add the chopped liver to the *civet*. Thicken the sauce with the hare's blood mixed with 3 or 4 tablespoons fresh cream.

Garnish with slices of bread cut into the shape of hearts, fried in butter.

Civet of hare au chaudron. CIVET DE LIÈVRE AU CHAUDRON – Prepared in the same way as *Civet of hare*, except that the hare is cooked in a pot hanging from a hook in the chimney of an open wood fire. Also, the sauce is thickened with kneaded butter and flour – 100 g. (4 oz., $\frac{1}{2}$ cup) butter and 2 tablespoons (3 tablespoons) flour for a young hare.

Garnish with blanched, coarsely diced belly of pork browned in butter, and small onions.

Civet of hare à la flamande. CIVET DE LIÈVRE À LA FLAMANDE – Brown pieces of hare in butter. Sprinkle with 2 tablespoons (3 tablespoons) flour, and cook for a few seconds, stirring with a wooden spoon.

Moisten with 1 litre ($1\frac{3}{4}$ pints, generous quart) red wine to which has been added the liver rubbed through a sieve, the blood, and 2 dl. ($\frac{1}{3}$ pint, scant cup) vinegar. Season with salt and pepper. Add 25 g. (1 oz., 2 tablespoons) brown sugar and a large *bouquet garni* (q.v.). Cover, and cook for 12 minutes. Add 4 onions finely sliced and tossed in butter. Complete the cooking in the oven, keeping the pan covered.

When the pieces of hare are cooked, drain, dry, and put them in a frying pan. Sieve the sauce with the onions, pour over the hare and simmer for a few minutes.

Surround the *civet* with slices of bread cut into the shape of hearts, fried in butter and spread with redcurrant jelly.

Civet of hare à la lyonnaise. CIVET DE LIÈVRE À LA LYONNAISE – Proceed as for ordinary *Civet of hare*, replacing the mushrooms by chestnuts cooked in stock and browned.

Hare cutlets. CÔTELETTES DE LIÈVRE – There are three different ways of preparing hare cutlets.

1. Make a croquette forcemeat using scraps of hare, mushrooms and truffles, blended with a thick brown or white sauce. Leave to cool. Shape into cutlets, and cook in clarified butter. Serve with a game sauce.

2. Chop finely the raw flesh of a hare. Add a quarter of its weight of bread, soaked and squeezed dry, and the same quantity of butter. Season well. Shape the mixture into cutlets. Flour them and fry in clarified butter.

Serve with *Demi-glace sauce* (see SAUCE) based on concentrated game stock.

3. Using raw hare, make a forcemeat with bread boiled to a pulp, and butter. Fill buttered cutlet moulds and poach. Serve on pieces of bread fried in butter. Garnish to taste. Pour over them a brown or white sauce based on concentrated game stock.

Fillets of hare. FILETS DE LIÈVRE – Fillet a raw saddle of hare so that the meat comes away in long slices. Remove the tendons. Interlard with best lardoons. Season and put the fillets in a baking dish. Pour melted butter and a little brandy over them and bake in a moderate oven.

Serve each fillet on a slice of bread fried in butter. Garnish according to the recipe used. Mask with a sauce suitable for ground game.

The *filets mignons*, the slender strips of meat inside the saddle, can be prepared in the same way as the larger fillets. Usually, however, they are left with the larger fillets. Garnishes and sauces for *Saddle of hare* are suitable for fillets.

In some restaurants, special *entrées* are made with fillets of hare. They are folded into crescent shapes and cooked as indicated above. They are then presented on a foundation of *Mousseline forcemeat* (see FORCEMEAT) made from the remaining meat of the hare, and served with garnishes such as *Financière Périgourdine, Rossini*, etc. (see GARNISHES). All these *entrées*, which are in the realm of *grande cuisine*, are served with *Demi-glace sauce* (see SAUCE), based on concentrated stock made from the bones and trimmings of the hare.

Fillets of hare en chaud-froid. FILETS DE LIÈVRE EN CHAUD-FROID – Stud the fillets with truffles. Fold into the shape of crescents. Simmer in Madeira and leave to cool. Mask with a brown or white *Chaud-froid sauce* (see SAUCE) based on concentrated stock.

Decorate with truffles, the whites of hard-boiled eggs or other garnish. Glaze with jelly and pour over clear jelly flavoured with Madeira or some other heavy wine.

Fillets of hare in cream. FILETS DE LIÈVRE À LA CRÈME – Interlard the fillets. Steep them for 1 hour in a marinade of brandy, oil, salt, pepper and spices. Proceed as for *Saddle of hare à l'allemande* (q.v.).

Fillets of hare à la Lucullus. FILETS DE LIÈVRE À LA LUCULLUS – Decorate the fillets of hare with pickled tongue and truffles cut in the shape of cocks' combs and dipped in white of egg. Fold them into crescent shapes and simmer gently in brandy and butter.

Drain the fillets. Arrange them in a flaky pastry crust filled with a *salpicon* (q.v.) of truffles and *foie gras* blended with *Demi-glace sauce* (see SAUCE) based on concentrated game stock.

Fillets of hare sautéed with truffles. FILETS DE LIÈVRE SAUTÉS AUX TRUFFES – Cut the fillets into slices. Season, and brown them in butter, taking care that they keep their pinkish colour.

Drain. Toss 12 thick strips of truffle in the cooking butter, so that they are barely cooked. Put these on the slices of hare. Pour a little Madeira into the cooking pan and add a few tablespoons *Demi-glace sauce* (see SAUCE) based on concentrated game stock. Pour over the pieces of hare.

Pâté of hare. PÂTÉ DE LIÈVRE – Bone a hare. Set aside the breast meat, the *filets mignons* and the loins. Remove the gristle from these parts and interlard them with best lardoons. Season with *Spiced salt* (see SALT). Steep in a brandy marinade, adding equal quantities of fine strips of fresh ham (not smoked), fresh pork fat and quartered truffles.

Make a forcemeat with the rest of the meat as described in the recipe for *Game forcemeat* (see FORCEMEAT). Rub through a sieve. Bind with the hare's blood.

Grease a hinged mould with butter. Line with *Pastry dough* (see PASTRY). Cover the dough with thin slices of larding bacon. Line the bottom and sides with a layer of hare forcemeat. Alternate the meats, truffles, etc. on this foundation of forcemeat.

Cover with a layer of forcemeat. Continue to fill the mould with alternate layers of meat and forcemeat, finishing with a layer of forcemeat. Cover with a thin slice of pork fat. Put a layer of rolled-out pastry on top, pressing the edges of the dough together to seal. Flute the edges. Decorate the top with dough motifs and make a hole in the middle to allow the steam to escape during baking. Brush with beaten egg.

Bake in the oven, allowing 15 to 20 minutes per 500 g. (1 lb.) Leave the *pâté* to cool in the mould. When it is cold pour a few tablespoons of Madeira-flavoured meat jelly into it. If the *pâté* is to be kept for any length of time, substitute a mixture of butter and lard for the jelly.

Hare *pâté* must be made at least 24 hours before serving.

Potted hare. TERRINE DE LIÈVRE – Made from strips of hare, pork fat, *foie gras*, truffles and hare stuffing, in the same way as *Potted duck* (see TERRINE).

Roast legs of hare. CUISSES DE LIÈVRE RÔTIES – Remove the tendons from a hare's legs. Stud with best larding bacon to form rosettes, and roast them. Serve with *Poivrade sauce*

(see SAUCE) and *Chestnut purée* (see CHESTNUT).

All recipes for saddle of hare are suitable for the legs.

Saddle of hare. RÂBLE DE LIÈVRE – For a baron of hare the whole body of the hare from the base of the neck to the tail is used; but for the saddle alone, the portion of the trunk which ends at the top of the thigh is served.

This is one of the most delicate parts of the hare. Before cooking it remove all the thin membrane which covers the flesh.

The saddle is barded with a thin slice of pork fat or studded with truffles.

Saddle of hare is generally roasted and served with *Poivrade sauce* (see SAUCE) and *Chestnut purée* (see CHESTNUT), which are served separately.

Saddle of hare à l'allemande. RÂBLE DE LIÈVRE À L'ALLEMANDE – Interlard the saddle with best lardoons. Steep for 2 hours in a raw marinade (q.v.).

Put the marinated vegetables in a roasting pan. Dry the saddle of hare and lay it on top. Roast in a hot oven. When the saddle is almost cooked, take out the vegetables. Pour the marinade over the hare and add 2 dl. ($\frac{1}{3}$ pint, scant cup) cream.

Place the saddle on serving dish, squeeze some lemon into the cream sauce, strain, and pour it over the hare. Serve with redcurrant jelly or unsweetened apple sauce.

Saddle of hare au chambertin. RÂBLE DE LIÈVRE AU CHAMBERTIN – Interlard the saddle. Roast in the oven, taking care that it retains its pinkish colour.

Fry a slice of bread and spread it with *à gratin game forcemeat* (see FORCEMEAT). Lay the saddle on top. Garnish with mushrooms cooked in butter, small strips of belly of pork, parboiled and fried in butter, and truffles cut into thick strips. Mask with *Chambertin sauce* (see SAUCE), to which the pan juices, diluted with red wine, have been added.

Saddle of hare, roast. RÂBLE DE LIÈVRE RÔTI – Interlard the saddle. Roast in a hot oven for 18 to 20 minutes, or on a spit, allowing an extra 2 to 5 minutes.

Garnish with a bunch of watercress and half a lemon. Make a border of alternate slices of lemon and beetroot cut with a fluted knife. Serve with the diluted cooking juices or a thin *Poivrade sauce* (see SAUCE).

Hare soufflé. SOUFFLÉ DE LIÈVRE – Made with hare in the same way as *Chicken soufflé* (see SOUFFLÉ).

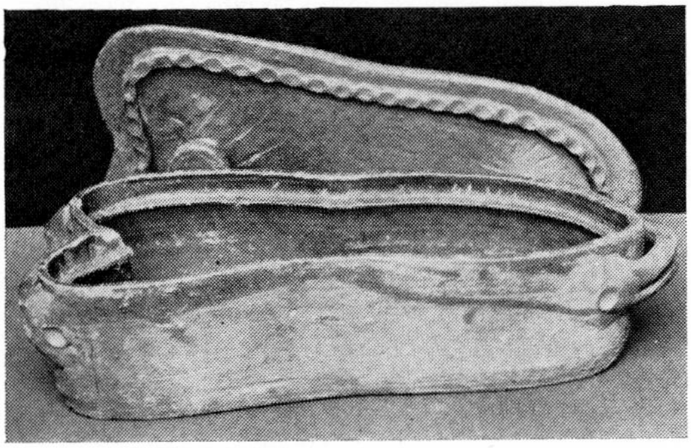

17th century terrine for preparing hare à la royale

Stuffed hare à la périgourdine or à la royale (Périgord cookery). LIÈVRE FARCI À LA PÉRIGOURDINE, À LA ROYALE – In the Périgord region this dish bears the high-sounding title of *lièvre à la royale*.

When drawing the hare, collect all the blood and set it aside to bind the stuffing, which will be used later.

Crush the paws of the hare and remove the tendons. Interlard the fillets and legs with best lardoons.

Chop the liver, heart and lungs. Add to this 200 g. (7 oz.) raw goose *foie gras* and 100 g. (4 oz.) fresh pork fat, 100 g. (4 oz.) bread soaked in stock and squeezed dry, 1 tablespoon chopped onion cooked very slowly in butter until tender and left to cool, a very little pounded garlic, 150 g. (5 oz.) chopped truffles and a pinch of chopped parsley. Bind this stuffing with the blood of the hare. Season well.

Stuff the hare with this mixture. Sew up the skin so as to hold the stuffing in and truss the hare. Braise in a little white wine for about 2 hours, basting frequently. Brown the hare in the oven. Drain and untie it. Add to the braising stock a few tablespoons *Demi-glace sauce* (see SAUCE) based on concentrated game stock and 2 tablespoons (3 tablespoons) Armagnac. Strain, and add 150 g. (5 oz.) shredded or diced truffles. Pour this sauce over the hare.

This dish is often braised in red wine.

Stuffed hare à la périgourdine (cold). LIÈVRE ÉTOFFÉ À LA PÉRIGOURDINE – Bone a hare, slitting it along the back before drawing it, so that the skin of the belly remains intact. Draw it and cut off the legs and shoulders.

Set aside the liver, heart, kidneys and blood. Keep the blood in a bowl, with 1 tablespoon vinegar to prevent it from clotting.

Using the boned meat of the thighs and shoulders, some lean veal, fresh pork and pork fat, make a *Game forcemeat* (see FORCEMEAT). Add to this a quarter of its weight of *à gratin forcemeat* (see FORCEMEAT), made from the liver, heart and kidneys of the hare with an equal quantity of raw *foie gras*. Bind with 2 eggs. Season well. Add spices and 2 tablespoons (3 tablespoons) brandy.

Season the hare with *Spiced salt* (see SALT) and sprinkle with a little brandy. Put a layer of stuffing on top. In the middle of the stuffing lay alternate thin strips of lean veal browned in butter, thin strips of *foie gras* seasoned with spiced salt and moistened with brandy, lardoons of pork fat (or blanched salt pork) and pieces of truffle. Cover with a layer of stuffing. Add further layers of meat and stuffing.

Fold the hare into shape and sew it up. Wrap it in a cloth and tie it in the shape of a ballottine (q.v.). Cook in a strong game stock flavoured with Madeira. This stock should be prepared in advance, using the bones and trimmings of the hare, a knuckle of veal, fresh pork skin (or bacon rinds) and a boned and blanched calf's foot.

Simmer the hare very gently for about $1\frac{1}{2}$ hours. When it is cooked, drain and unwrap it, then put it back in the cloth, wrapping it tightly. Cool under a weight. Next day, unwrap the hare. Glaze with jelly. Surround with jelly croûtons.

Stuffed hare à la périgourdine en cabessal or chabessal. LIÈVRE FARCI À LA PÉRIGOURDINE EN CABESSAL, CHABESSAL – Stuff a hare with fillet of veal, fresh pork and ham, seasoned with salt, pepper, spices, shallots and garlic. Sew up the skin. Bard the hare and braise in red wine. Tied into a ring, the hare is said to be *en cabessal* or *chabessal*. (The *cabessal* was the folded ring of cloth which women wore on their heads to support pails or jars of water.)

Bone the braised hare. Pound the liver with garlic and blend it into the sauce. Add the hare's blood and a little vinegar.

This method of preparing hare or leveret is popular in Périgord, and in the Aveyron region.

HARICOT OF MUTTON. HARICOT DE MOUTON – Mutton stew made with turnips and potatoes. (See MUTTON.)

HASH. HACHIS – A hash is usually made from left-overs of scraps of beef, mutton, pork, veal, poultry, fish or shell-fish, and is prepared in various ways.

Dice the meat very small, rather than mince it. In this way, it will taste better and look more appetising. French hashes are usually blended with white or brown sauces. Hashes made from left-overs of roast or pot-roasted meat must not boil after the sauce has been added, but should only be warmed up over a low flame. Hashes made from boiled or braised meat should simmer on the stove for a time.

Hashes are piled inside a border of *Duchess potatoes* (see POTATOES), or sprinkled with breadcrumbs and browned, or served in a border of pilaf or risotto.

Sometimes hash is served in a pie dish as a garnish with hard-boiled, poached or coddled eggs.

Boiled beef hash I. HACHIS DE BOEUF – Dice very finely 500 g. (18 oz., 4 cups) boiled beef scraps. Bind with $1\frac{1}{2}$ dl. ($\frac{1}{4}$ pint, $\frac{2}{3}$ cup) *Demi-glace sauce* (see SAUCE), cover and bring to the boil. Cook in the oven for 25 minutes. Stir from time to time and add a few tablespoons *demi-glace* if the sauce appears too thick.

Boiled beef hash II. HACHIS DE BOEUF – Slowly cook 2 tablespoons (3 tablespoons) chopped onion in 1 tablespoon butter until very tender. Sprinkle with 1 tablespoon flour. Brown. Add 2 dl. ($\frac{1}{3}$ pint, scant cup) veal stock, season and bring to the boil, stirring all the time. Simmer for 15 minutes.

Dice the boiled beef very finely and add to the mixture. Proceed as indicated in the previous recipe.

Curried beef hash I. HACHIS DE BOEUF À L'INDIENNE – Proceed as for *Roast beef hash* (see below). Bind the diced meat with *Curry sauce* (see SAUCE). Serve in a border of rice. Serve with curry sauce.

Curried beef hash II. HACHIS DE BOEUF À L'INDIENNE – Cook 2 tablespoons (3 tablespoons) chopped onion in 1 tablespoon butter until very tender. Sprinkle with 1 teaspoon curry powder and 1 tablespoon flour. Add 2 dl. ($\frac{1}{3}$ pint, scant cup) white stock or broth. Mix well. Cook for 15 minutes.

Add the finely diced beef. Serve in a border of rice with *Curry sauce* (see SAUCE).

Beef hash with herbs. HACHIS DE BOEUF AUX FINES HERBES – Proceed as for *Roast beef hash* (see below). Just before serving sprinkle with 1 tablespoon of chopped parsley and 1 tablespoon chopped chervil.

Beef hash à la hongroise. HACHIS DE BOEUF À LA HONGROISE – Proceed as for *Roast beef hash* (see below). Bind the diced meat with *Hungarian sauce* (see SAUCE).

Beef hash à l'italienne. HACHIS DE BOEUF À L'ITALIENNE – Proceed as for *Roast beef hash* (see below). Bind with *Italian sauce* (see SAUCE).

Beef hash à la languedocienne. HACHIS DE BOEUF À LA LANGUEDOCIENNE – Proceed as for *Roast beef hash* (see below). Add 1 tablespoon chopped parsley and a little grated garlic.

Serve on a layer of sliced aubergines sautéed in oil or butter. Smooth the surface of the hash. Surround with a very thick *Tomato fondue* (see FONDUE). Sprinkle with breadcrumbs and cheese. Pour melted butter over it and brown.

Beef hash à la lyonnaise. HACHIS DE BOEUF À LA LYONNAISE – Proceed as for *Beef hash à la languedocienne*, binding the diced meat with *Lyonnaise sauce* (see SAUCE).

Serve with a border of *Duchess potatoes* (see POTATOES). Decorate the top with fried onion rings.

Beef hash à la Parmentier. HACHIS DE BOEUF À LA PARMENTIER – Proceed as for *Roast beef hash* (see below). Serve in large, partly scooped-out baked potatoes. Sprinkle with breadcrumbs. Pour melted butter over; brown in oven.

Beef hash with poached eggs. HACHIS DE BOEUF AUX OEUFS POCHÉS – Proceed as for *Boiled beef hash II*.

Garnish with well-drained poached eggs. If desired, cover with *Tomato sauce* (see SAUCE).

Beef hash à la polonaise. HACHIS DE BOEUF À LA POLONAISE – Proceed as for *Roast beef hash* (see below). Garnish with poached eggs and *Tomato sauce* (see SAUCE).

Beef hash à la portugaise. HACHIS DE BOEUF À LA PORTUGAISE – Proceed as for *Roast beef hash* (see below). Bind with *Tomato sauce* (see SAUCE).

Cover the bottom of an ovenproof earthenware dish with slices of tomato tossed in butter or oil. Spread the hash over the tomatoes. Cover with a further layer of tomatoes cooked in the same way. Sprinkle with breadcrumbs and season with a touch of garlic. Pour melted butter or oil over the top and brown in the oven.

Beef hash with potatoes. HACHIS DE BOEUF EN BORDURE – Proceed as for *Roast beef hash* (see below).

Pile the hash in a border of *Duchess potatoes* (see POTATOES). Sprinkle with breadcrumbs and grated cheese. Brush the border with beaten egg, pour on melted butter and brown.

Beef hash with mashed potatoes. HACHIS DE BOEUF À LA PURÉE DE POMMES DE TERRE – Mix 300 g. (11 oz.) $2\frac{1}{4}$ cups) finely diced boiled beef with 200 g. (7 oz., scant cup) *Potato puree* (see POTATOES). Season. Arrange in a buttered ovenproof earthenware dish. Cover with a thin layer of the potatoes. Smooth the surface, sprinkle with breadcrumbs and grated cheese, pour melted butter over and brown.

This hash can be prepared in the same way with purée of white or red haricot beans, lentils or split peas.

Roast beef hash. HACHIS DE BOEUF – Dice the beef very finely. Bind with boiling *Demi-glace sauce* (see SAUCE). Heat in a double saucepan and serve in a pie dish.

Fish hash. HACHIS DE POISSONS – Use finely diced pieces of cooked fish (cod, turbot, brill, sole or salmon). Bind with vegetable-based *Velouté, Béchamel*, or any other sauce suitable for fish (see SAUCE).

Fish hash is often used as a filling for pastry boats, large or small *vol-au-vent* (q.v.), tartlets, etc.

Hash of ground game. HACHIS DE GIBIERS DE POIL – Made from left-overs of braised venison, or roast roebuck, deer or wild goat. Bind with a brown stock to which *Espagnole sauce* with game essence, *Demi-glace sauce* or Madeira, has been added (see SAUCE).

Hash of winged game. HACHIS DE GIBIERS DE PLUME – Made from left-overs of game, braised, pot-roasted or roast (pheasant, hazel grouse, partridge). These are cooked in white stock which is thickened with *Allemande, Béchamel* or *Velouté sauce* (see SAUCE), which has been boiled down with concentrated game stock. They can also be cooked in brown stock, to which *Demi-glace, Madeira* or *Salmi sauce* (see SAUCE) are added.

This hash is most commonly used as a filling for *vol-au-vent*, pies or tartlets, and can also be served on fried bread.

Lobster and shellfish hash. HACHIS DE HOMARD – Made from lobster or any other similar shellfish, finely diced, warmed up and mixed with *Velouté, Béchamel* or any other sauce suitable for fish and shellfish served hot (see SAUCE). Shellfish hash is used as a filling for pastry boats, large or small *vol-au-vent*, tartlets, etc.

Mutton or lamb hash. HACHIS DE MOUTON, D'AGNEAU – Use roast, braised or boiled left-overs of lamb or mutton. All recipes for beef are suitable for mutton or lamb hash.

Pork hash. HACHIS DE PORC – Made from left-overs of roast, braised or boiled pork. Use a suitable recipe for beef hash if a brown sauce is used, or use a white sauce and follow the recipe for *Veal hash à l'allemande*.

Poultry hash. HACHIS DE VOLAILLE – Use left-over pieces of braised, stewed, pot-roasted or roast poultry. This dish is usually made with a white sauce, as described in the recipe for *Veal hash à l'allemande*, but it may also be made with brown stock as described in the recipes for beef hash.

Poultry hash *à blanc* has *Allemande, Béchamel, Cream* or *Velouté sauce* (see SAUCE) added. It must be heated in a double saucepan.

Poultry hash, whether a white or brown sauce is used, is often served with poached or coddled eggs. It can be used as a filling for large or small *vol-au-vent*, tartlets and other pastry cases, and also as a stuffing for artichoke hearts or mushrooms. These are sprinkled with breadcrumbs and browned, and are served as a garnish for main dishes.

Sweetbread (veal or lamb) hash. HACHIS DE RIS DE VEAU, D'AGNEAU – This can be made with a white or brown sauce. Dice the sweetbreads very small and proceed as for veal or poultry hash.

Veal hash. HACHIS DE VEAU – Left-over pieces of braised, stewed, pot-roasted or roast veal can be prepared in a brown sauce like a beef hash or in a white sauce as below.

Veal hash à l'allemande. HACHIS DE VEAU À L'ALLEMANDE – Dice the veal very finely. Bind with *Allemande sauce* (see SAUCE). Heat in a double saucepan.

Serve in a pie dish or, if desired,in a pie crust or *vol-au-vent*.

Veal hash à la béchamel. HACHIS DE VEAU À LA BÉCHAMEL – Proceed as for *Veal hash à l'allemande*, using *Béchamel sauce* (see SAUCE).

Veal hash with cream sauce. HACHIS DE VEAU À LA CRÈME – Proceed as for *Veal hash à l'allemande* (q.v.), using *Cream sauce* (see SAUCE).

Veal hash à la Mornay. HACHIS DE VEAU MORNAY – Bind the hash with *Béchamel sauce* (see SAUCE). Serve in a border of *Duchess potatoes* (see POTATOES). Cover with *Mornay sauce* (see SAUCE). Sprinkle with grated cheese, pour on melted butter, and brown.

HÂTEREAU – Old French word for little balls of pork liver, similar to *gayettes* (q.v.).

Nowadays, this is the name given to a hot *hors-d'œuvre* or a light main course of small pieces of food, dipped in egg and breadcrumbs and fried, skewered and coated with a sauce.

HATTELLE or HÂTTELETTE – Old French words for small birds, giblets, etc., roasted on skewers. It is derived from *hâtelet* or *attelet* (skewer).

HAUNCH. CIMIER – Hindquarters of the ox and of certain wild animals. This word is applied particularly to deer.

For detailed recipes see ROEBUCK or VENISON.

The French also use the words *gigue* and *cuissot* to describe haunch of game.

HAUT-BRION – Bordeaux wine of great repute. The Château Haut-Brion, in the Pessac commune, is in the Graves and not the Médoc district. According to the list drawn up in 1855 by the Bordeaux Chamber of Commerce, this is the only Graves wine given a 'first growth' classification. The other first growth Bordeaux wines are Château-Lafite, Château-Margaux, and Château-Latour.

HAWFINCH. GROS-BEC – European seed-eating bird. It is known in France as *gros-bec, casse-noix* or *pinson royal*. It is usually roasted.

HAWKSBILL TURTLE. CARET – Aquatic tortoise, native of the warm American and Indian seas. It furnishes the valuable tortoiseshell of commerce; its flesh is not worth eating but its eggs are highly esteemed.

HAY BOX or FUELLESS COOKER. MARMITE NORVÉGIENNE – An ordinary pot, when its contents have been brought to the boil, is enclosed in an insulating box, embedded in materials which are poor heat conductors. In this way, the temperature drops very slowly, remaining at 70°C. (158°F.) even after five or six hours or, with the most up-to-date equipment, even longer. In this way, food can be cooked without supervision and without the use of fuel once it has been brought to the boil.

HAZEL GROUSE. GELINOTTE – Bird also known as wood grouse and ruffled grouse. Hazel grouse lives in woods. There are two species, one a native of Europe, the other of Asia. The common hazel grouse, which is on sale in France during the winter months, is a bird about the size of a partridge, whose plumage, reddish in colour, is speckled with brown, black, white and grey.

Hazel grouse

The hazel grouse, which was once very common in France, especially in Alsace, the Ardennes and the Pyrénées, is rarer nowadays, and the greater number of hazel grouse sold in France come from Russia and are frozen. The best come from Vologda, Archangel and Kazan.

The meat is white and tender, but tastes rather strongly of fir cones, which some people find unpleasant. This flavour can be made less strong by soaking the bird in milk for some time before cooking.

All the recipes given for partridge (q.v.) are suitable for hazel grouse.

Hazel grouse à l'allemande. GELINOTTE À L'ALLEMANDE – Truss a hazel grouse. Season. Brown the bird in 1 tablespoon butter in a covered saucepan. When it is three-parts cooked, drain, remove the breasts and cut them into thin strips. Put them back on the bird, taking care to restore it to its original shape.

Cover the hazel grouse with *Béchamel sauce* (see SAUCE) mixed with sour cream. Sprinkle with breadcrumbs, and pour on a little melted butter. Let it brown a little in the oven. Serve with *Demi-glace sauce* (see SAUCE).

Casserole of hazel grouse à la polonaise. GELINOTTE EN CASSEROLE À LA POLONAISE – Stuff the hazel grouse with *à gratin game forcemeat* (see FORCEMEAT) flavoured with 1 or 2 crushed juniper berries. Truss. Cook in butter in an earthenware casserole. After removing the string, pour over it 3 tablespoons (scant $\frac{1}{4}$ cup) game stock or concentrated thickened veal stock and a little lemon juice. Add browned melted butter with a handful of freshly grated breadcrumbs fried in it.

Chaud-froid of hazel grouse. GELINOTTE EN CHAUD-FROID – Prepared in white or brown stock, as for *Chaud-froid of partridge* (see PARTRIDGE).

Hazel grouse à la crème. GELINOTTE À LA CRÈME – Wrap larding bacon round the hazel grouse and truss it. To lessen the taste of fir cones, soak it for 1 hour in milk before cooking.

Brown the bird in 1 tablespoon butter heated in a flame-proof earthenware casserole. Put the casserole in the oven, uncovered. Cook in a hot oven (220°C., 425°F., Gas Mark 7), basting frequently, for about 18 minutes.

Remove the bird from the casserole, take off the string and larding bacon, and put it back in the casserole. Pour over it 1 dl. (6 tablespoons, scant ½ cup) fresh thick cream. Complete the cooking in a moderate oven (160°C., 325°F., Gas Mark 3), basting frequently.

Grilled hazel grouse. GELINOTTE GRILLÉE – Slit the hazel grouse along the back. Open it and remove most of the small bones. Gently flatten the bird, season it with salt and paprika, brush with melted butter, cover it all over with freshly grated breadcrumbs and cook under the grill on a gentle heat. Brown well on all sides.

Garnish with watercress and surround with a border of half-slices of lemon and slices of gherkin.

Serve either with *Maître d'hôtel butter* (see BUTTER, *Compound butters*), with *Diable sauce* (see SAUCE) or with any sauce suitable for grilled poultry and wildfowl.

Hazel grouse à la hongroise. GELINOTTE À LA HONGROISE – Cook 2 tablespoons (3 tablespoons) chopped onion seasoned with paprika in butter. Put the trussed hazel grouse in a casserole with the onion. Cook in the oven in gentle heat. When the bird is almost cooked, remove the string and put it back in the casserole, pouring over it 4 tablespoons (5 tablespoons) cream. Season with paprika. Complete the cooking, basting the bird frequently with the cream.

Hazel grouse loaf. PAIN DE GELINOTTE – This is prepared like *Partridge loaf* (see LOAVES, *Winged game loaf*).

Hazel grouse mousse, hot or cold. MOUSSE DE GELINOTTE – Made from fillets of hazel grouse in the same way as *Quail mousse* (see QUAIL).

Pâté of hazel grouse and potted hazel grouse. PÂTÉ, TERRINE DE GELINOTTE – *Pâtés* of hazel grouse or potted hazel grouse are prepared in the same way as *pâtés* of partridge and potted partridges (see PARTRIDGE).

Roast hazel grouse. GELINOTTE RÔTIE – Wrap the bird in larding bacon and truss. Cook in a hot oven for 15 to 18 minutes, and on the spit for 18 to 20 minutes. Add a little water to the roasting pan to make a gravy. Serve with the bird.

In England, bread sauce, fried breadcrumbs and potato crisps are usually served with this game.

Salmi of hazel grouse. GELINOTTE EN SALMIS – Prepared in the same way as *Salmi of woodcock* (see WOODCOCK).

Suprêmes of hazel grouse. SUPRÊMES DE GELINOTTE – Remove the breasts from an uncooked hazel grouse. Trim and bone them. Flatten them carefully, season with salt and pepper, and cook in butter. Lay them on a dish, garnish as indicated in the appropriate recipe, and serve with the sauce recommended.

All recipes given for cooking and serving *suprêmes* of chicken and game birds are suitable for *suprêmes* of hazel grouse.

HAZELNUT. NOISETTE – Fruit of the hazelnut or cobnut bush, which grows all over Europe. This nut is rich in oil and pleasant to taste. Hazelnuts are used in confectionery. Cultivated hazelnuts are called filberts.

Hazelnut butter – See BUTTER, *Compound butters.*

HEADY. CAPITEUX – Applied to wines which go to one's head, that is, wines which are rich in alcohol.

HEART. COEUR – See OFFAL or VARIETY MEATS.

HEARTH-CAKE. FOUACE – Old form of pastry like a *galette* of fine wheaten flour. It is made of unleavened dough and was originally baked under the ashes in the hearth. Hearth-cake is made in all the provinces of France.

Hearth-cake makers from Lerné have acquired a universal reputation, thanks to the novel *Gargantua*. In the sixteenth century the guild of hearth-cake makers consisted largely of inhabitants of the market town of Lerné. In almost all the houses there was an oven to cook the hearth-cakes. Some of these ovens, hewn in the rocks, still exist, going back to the eleventh century.

The fashion for Lerné hearth-cakes, of which the peasants from Chinonais were so fond, continued until the end of the eighteenth century.

E. Johanneau, who published an edition of the works of Rabelais with interesting commentaries, tells of his trip to Lerné in September 1821.

In this village he was given '*Galettes*, called hearth-cakes, which have a high reputation in this part of the country.'

Since 1821, the trade in these cakes has become negligible at Lerné, and soon only their memory will remain. Since they have fallen into such undeserved disfavour, it is well to recall what Rabelais said about them:

'*Notez que c'est viande céleste, manger à déjeusner, raisins avec fouache fraische.*'

'It is heavenly fare to lunch on grapes and fresh-baked hearth-cakes.'

Hearth-cakes are still made in the Auvergne, but in quite a different way from these famous hearth-cakes.

Auvergne hearth-cakes. FOUACES D'AUVERGNE – *Ingredients.* 500 g. (18 oz., 4½ cups) flour, 100 g. (4 oz., ½ cup) butter, 15 g. (½ oz.) yeast, 3 eggs, a small glass Cognac, a few drops orange-flower water, 1 dl. (6 tablespoons, scant ½ cup) milk.

Method. Work all ingredients together in a bowl. Leave for 12 hours. Set out like a crown on buttered paper and brush with yolk of egg. Bake in moderate oven.

HEDGEHOG. HÉRISSON – Insect-eating mammal, regarded by some people as very good to eat.

HELDER – See RESTAURANTS OF BYGONE DAYS.

HELVELLE – Type of fungus which grows in Europe in damp grass, or in upland woods at the base of trees, especially fir trees.

Most types of *helvelle* are edible. They are sometimes called monks' morels, baby morels. The best of them is the *crinkled helvelle*, which tastes a little like the true morel.

HEMIONE. HÉMIONE – Wild animal found in Asia, akin to the donkey and horse. For suitable recipes, see DONKEY, HORSE.

HEMLOCK. CIGUË – Name of a number of poisonous plants of the *Umbelliferae* family. The poisonous qualities of some of these plants have been greatly exaggerated. The *great hemlock* (which might be confused with parsley) is in fact hardly poisonous. It seems improbable that Socrates should have been poisoned with the juice of this plant alone.

The *little hemlock* is distinguished from parsley and chervil, with which it could be confused, by its thicker and larger leaves which are marbled with black or violet on the lower side and on the edges, and particularly by the unpleasant smell which is released when the leaves are rubbed. Some poisonous effects are attributed to it, but as with the preceding species, its poisonous qualities are exaggerated.

HERB-BENNET. BENOÎTE – The roots of this plant, which gives out a smell of cloves, possess stimulating and tonic properties.

Its yellow leaves, picked before the appearance of the flowers, are sometimes eaten in salad.

HERB-IVY. IVE – Species of chive, used in the flavouring of salads and sauces.

HERBS. HERBES – A large number of aromatic plants used in the kitchen come under the general heading of herbs.

Among the most common are chervil, tarragon, chives and

parsley. Herbs are also used as trimmings in salads. (See AROMATIC PLANTS, FINES HERBES.)

Herb broth. POTAGE AUX HERBES – Refreshing soup made with leeks and pot herbs. (See SOUPS.)

Pot vegetables or 'herbs'. HERBES POTAGÈRES – Generally, six vegetables only are included among the pot herbs. They are orach (rarely found), spinach, lettuce, sorrel, seakale-beet and purslane. All these vegetables are used in the preparation of soups and broths, but this list is a somewhat arbitrary selection, as there are many other vegetables equally suitable for the pot.

Turtle herbs. HERBES À TORTUE – Mixture of aromatic herbs of which the main ones are basil, marjoram, savory and thyme.

These herbs are used in the flavouring of turtle soup, and also in turtle sauce (see SAUCE, *Tortue sauce*) which is served with calf's head.

HÈRE – French term for a stag between eighteen months and two years old, from the time bumps appear on its forehead to the time when the antlers are fully formed.

HERMETICAL SEALING. HERMÉTIQUE – When a lid or stopper of a container fits so exactly that the container is rendered airtight, it is said to be hermetically sealed. Casseroles and saucepans can be made almost airtight by using flour-and-water paste to seal them.

HERMITAGE WINE – See ERMITAGE.

HERMIT CRAB. BERNARD-L'ERMITE – This shellfish has one particularly interesting characteristic. Nature having neglected to give it a hard shell except just round the middle, to protect itself from its enemies it creeps into shells of molluscs, abandoned by the rightful owner.

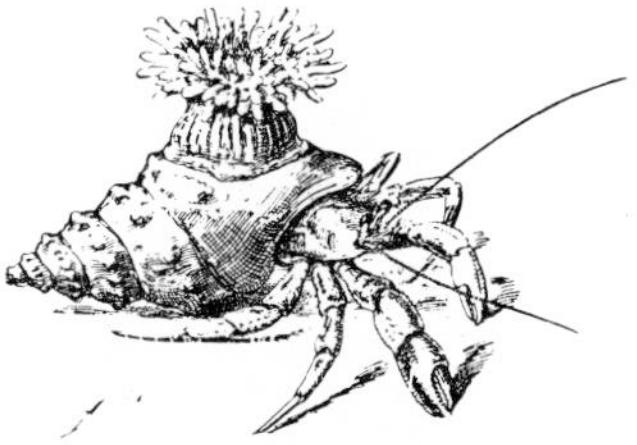

Hermit crab

Alexander Dumas the elder, writing about this crustacean in his *Dictionnaire de la cuisine*, says 'the Creator, who had started to dress him as a lobster, was disturbed, or became absent-minded in the middle of the job, and finished him dressed as a slug.

'And so, to protect those parts of its body which are vulnerable and so tempting, as soon as it sees a shell which fits its size, it eats the owner of the shell and proceeds to take its place while it is still warm.'

Hermit crabs can be cooked in the same ways as shrimps (q.v.). Having been taken out of the shell, it is cooked in salted *court-bouillon* (q.v.) flavoured with thyme and bay leaf. It can also be cooked in sea water.

One can also, after having cleaned the hermit crab, sprinkle it with butter and cook it in its borrowed shell under the grill, or bake it on hot coals.

HERRING. HARENG – the *common herring*. Fish with bluish scales along its back and silvery sides and belly.

These fish, which are found in the North Sea, are prodigiously fertile. Every year, in March, they migrate from the polar seas to the French Atlantic coastal waters, or the Channel, where they congregate in immense shoals.

The herring fisheries in the Channel extend from Calais to the mouth of the Orne. The fishing season lasts from the middle of October to the end of December. Boulogne can claim to be the real centre of the French herring industry.

The fresh herring is among the most delicately flavoured of fish. It can be cooked in a great many different ways.

Herrings

How to prepare herrings – *Dressing of fresh fish.* Cut them through the gills, leaving the hard and soft roes. Scale, wash and dry thoroughly. According to the way in which they are to be cooked, slit them along the back or sides, fillet them or, if they are to be poached, braised or grilled, leave them whole.

Kippers and bloaters. Grill or fry them as they are.

Salt herrings. Fillet them. To remove the salt, soak them in milk or a mixture of equal parts of milk and water. Drain, dry and trim them, and cook according to the recipe.

Smoked herrings. Fillet, skin and trim them. Soak, if necessary, to remove salt. Cook according to the recipe.

FRESH HERRINGS. HARENGS FRAIS –

Devilled grilled herrings. HARENGS GRILLÉS À LA DIABLE – Slit the herrings along back and sides. Season and coat them with mustard. Sprinkle with white breadcrumbs and oil, and cook slowly under the grill.

Serve with *Mustard sauce* or *Ravigote sauce* (see SAUCE).

Fillets of herrings à l'anglaise. FILETS DE HARENGS À L'ANGLAISE – Fillet and trim the herrings. Dip them in egg and breadcrumbs and deep-fry in boiling fat. Serve with *Maître d'hôtel butter* (see BUTTER, *Compound butters*) mixed with boiled, mashed, soft roes.

Fried herrings. HARENGS FRITS – Slash the herrings along the sides. Dip them in milk and flour and deep-fry in boiling fat. Drain them, and dry in a cloth. Season with salt and garnish with fried parsley and quartered lemons.

Grilled herrings. HARENGS GRILLÉS – Cut, scale and dry the herrings. Slash the sides. Coat them with oil or melted butter. Season and cook slowly under the grill. Serve with *Maître d'hôtel butter* (see BUTTER, *Compound butters*). *Mustard sauce* (see SAUCE) or any other sauce suitable for grilled fish.

Herrings à la boulangère. HARENGS À LA BOULANGÈRE – Grease an oval flameproof earthenware dish liberally with butter. Lay 6 herrings in the dish and sprinkle with salt. Surround with 2 thinly sliced potatoes and 1 chopped onion, which have been lightly cooked in butter.

Season with salt, pepper, a little thyme and powdered bay leaf. Pour 2 to 3 tablespoons melted butter over the dish. Add enough water to cover. Bring to the boil and cook in the oven, basting from time to time. Sprinkle with chopped parsley and serve in the cooking dish.

Herrings à la meunière. HARENGS À LA MEUNIÈRE – Proceed as for *Féra à la meunière* (see FÉRA).

Herrings in white wine. HARENGS ÉTUVÉS AU VIN BLANC – Cut the herrings into thick slices and put them in a buttered pan. Season with salt. Moisten with 2 dl. ($\frac{1}{3}$ pint, scant cup) white wine, season with salt and pepper. Dot with butter cut into small pieces. Bring to the boil over a high flame. Cover, and simmer for 8 to 10 minutes.

Drain the herrings, and place on a dish. Simmer the cooking liquor to evaporate some of the liquid, add a little butter, and pour over the fish.

Marinade of fresh herrings (hors-d'œuvre). HARENGS FRAIS MARINÉS – Steep 12 soft-roed herrings in salt for 6 hours and dry with a cloth. Put a layer of finely sliced onions and carrots in a flameproof earthenware dish with sprigs of parsley and thyme, $\frac{1}{2}$ bay leaf, a few peppercorns and 1 or 2 cloves. Lay the herrings in the dish.

Pour over a mixture of equal parts of white wine and vinegar, which should not quite cover the fish. Put another layer of sliced onions and carrots on top. Cover the dish with oiled paper. Bring to the boil. When the liquid is bubbling, cover the dish and simmer slowly for 15 minutes.

Leave the herrings to cool in the stock.

Sautéed herrings à la lyonnaise. HARENGS SAUTÉS LYONNAISE – Slash the herrings along the sides. Season and dip in flour. Sauté them on one side in butter. Turn the herrings over and add 3 to 4 tablespoons finely chopped onions, previously lightly fried in butter.

Finish cooking the onions and herrings together and then put the herrings in a dish. Pour the butter and onions over. Sprinkle with chopped parsley. Pour 1 tablespoon of vinegar into the pan and heat in a little butter. Pour this over the fish.

Soft herring roes. LAITANCES DE HARENGS – Remove the soft roes from fresh herrings. Use any recipe indicated for carp soft roes (see SOFT ROES).

SALT HERRINGS. HARENGS SALÉS – In the Boulogne fishing industry herrings are either salted at sea or in port. Salt herrings are processed industrially by the following methods:

When the Boulogne herring fleet trawls in the North Sea from June to October, the trawlers are at sea for long periods at a time and the herrings are salted on board as soon as they are caught. They are put down with alternate layers of salt, in barrels which are then hermetically sealed.

Fishing vessels which operate in the Pas-de-Calais and the Channel ports put into port each day as soon as the nets are hauled in. The fish is transported from the boat to the salting sheds. After it has been mixed with salt in a long wooden trough it is thrown into cement vats. The salt mixes with the moisture from the herrings to form a brine with a salt-density of 25°. The fish must remain steeped in this brine for at least ten days, to ensure its preservation.

SMOKED HERRINGS. HARENGS FUMÉS – There are two ways of smoking fish, 'hot' and 'cold'.

In cold smoking, the fish is hung some way away from the fire and is smoked at a temperature of about 25°C. (77°F.).

In hot smoking, the fish is hung close to the fire and is partially cooked. Cold smoking is carried out almost exclusively in France, notably in Boulogne. The fuel used is always wood, preferably beech, and sawdust. Resinous wood is avoided, as it imparts an unpleasant flavour to the fish.

Hot smoking is scarcely ever used except in the preparation of bucklings, which are much in demand in Alsace.

Smoked herrings are processed in the following way:

The herrings are salted to a greater or lesser degree according to the type of smoked herring required. Pickled smoked herrings must be salted for at least eight days. Slightly salted or mild smoked herrings are made from fresh herrings salted for twenty-four to forty-eight hours. Bloaters are salted for a few hours only.

Once they are salted, the herrings are strung on rods threaded through their gills, and are put to drain on trolleys or racks, then set up in the smoking chimneys. In modern smokeries, the racks are fitted into the chimney, thus avoiding a great deal of handling.

When the herrings are in the chimney, a beechwood fire is lit. This produces a powerful draught, which dries the herrings, and at the same time draws off any excess oil. Next, the fire is damped with beech sawdust and chips. This causes the fire to send off a dense smoke which smokes the herrings and gives them their special flavour.

When the herrings have been sufficiently smoked, they are removed from the chimney and taken to the smokery worksheds, where girls sort and grade them, and crate the sound ones according to size and quality.

Generally, very large herrings are crated in twenties, weighing from 4 to 5 kg. ($8\frac{3}{4}$ to 11 lb.) according to season. Medium herrings are packed in batches of twenty-five, weighing from $3\frac{1}{2}$ to 4 kg. ($7\frac{3}{4}$ to $8\frac{3}{4}$ lb.) Small herrings are also packed in batches of twenty-five and weigh from 3 to $3\frac{1}{2}$ kg. ($6\frac{1}{2}$ to $7\frac{3}{4}$ lb.). Smoked herrings are also packed in wooden barrels which hold from sixty to a hundred fish, according to size.

Bloaters are made from herrings which are very slightly salted and smoked. They do not keep for any length of time, and should be eaten without delay, like fresh fish.

Kippers are lightly smoked herrings slit from top to bottom and opened out. In recent years, kippers have become very popular in France.

Fillets of fresh and salt herring are very much sought after. Skilled girls cut off the head and tail of the herring, slit it open, bone and skin it. In this way fillets are obtained of which every part can be eaten, and there is no waste. 200 g. (7 oz.) of fillets are packed in little wooden boxes, or parcels of 1 kg. ($2\frac{1}{4}$ lb.) of fillets are made up.

Irish smoked herrings. HARENGS SAURS À L'IRLANDAISE – Wash and dry the herrings. Cut off the heads. Split the fish in half lengthwise and spread them out flat in a deep dish. Cover them with whisky and set light to them. When the whisky has all burnt away and the flame extinguished, the herrings are ready for eating.

Smoked fillets of herring in oil. FILETS DE HARENGS SAURS MARINÉS À L'HUILE – Fillet and trim 24 smoked herrings. Soak them in milk for 2 hours to remove salt. Drain, and dry them in a cloth. Put them in a pie dish in layers, with alternate layers of finely chopped onions, sprigs of thyme and broken-up bay leaves. Place the soft and hard roes of the herrings on top. Cover with olive oil, and leave them to soak for 24 hours.

Smoked fillets of herring with soft roes. FILETS DE HARENGS SAURS AUX LAITANCES – Fillet several smoked, soft-roed herrings. Remove the skin, and bone them as completely as possible. Cut each fillet into strips. Put them in a pan with enough milk almost to cover them. Leave to soak for 30 minutes, or longer if the herrings are very salty.

Rub the soft roes through a sieve, collecting the purée in a bowl underneath. Add 1 teaspoon mustard, 1 dl. (6 tablespoons, scant $\frac{1}{2}$ cup) oil (stirring it in a little at a time), and a little vinegar. Add further seasoning if necessary.

Drain the fillets and dry them in a cloth. Arrange them in *hors-d'œuvre* dishes. Pour the soft roe sauce over them and sprinkle with chopped parsley.

HIPPOCRAS – Spiced aromatic wine much enjoyed by our ancestors. It was so called because it was filtered through a bag of a type said to be invented by Hippocrates, the great physician who lived in the fifth century B.C.

Properly speaking Hippocras was a type of apéritif similar to the vermouths made nowadays, rather than a table wine. Our forebears, in fact, drank it before meals or, if it was served at table, at the end of the meal.

Arnaud de Villeneuve, famous thirteenth century physician, gives a number of different recipes for the spiced wine. In one recipe he recommends bringing the wine to the boil and putting in it a sachet containing, for 3 litres ($5\frac{1}{4}$ pints, $6\frac{1}{2}$ pints) wine, 75 g. (3 oz.) each of the following spices: cubeb, cloves, nutmeg and raisins. Boil the wine until it is reduced by a third of its volume. Add sugar.

In another recipe, the wine is spiced with a mixture of cinnamon, ginger, paradise nuts, cloves, sugar and a pinch of musk.

Hippocras was drunk cooled or even iced whenever possible.

This wine remained popular for a very long time; it was still in fashion in the eighteenth century. Presents of it were made to the king and to foreign nobility.

Here is a more recent recipe for Hippocras:

Put 700 g. ($1\frac{1}{2}$ lb., 3 cups) sugar in a saucepan with 4 dl. ($\frac{3}{4}$ pint, scant 2 cups) water and the following spices: 4 teaspoons ginger, 2 cloves, $\frac{1}{4}$ of a nutmeg (ground), $1\frac{1}{2}$ to 2 tablespoons cinnamon and the zest of 2 Seville oranges.

Boil this syrup for a few minutes. Add 2 litres ($3\frac{1}{2}$ pints, $4\frac{1}{2}$ pints) of old wine (white or red). Leave the mixture on the stove until the surface turns white, then pour it into a large jug and leave to infuse for 30 minutes. Strain through muslin, and bottle.

HIPPOPOTAMUS. HIPPOPOTAME – Large amphibious pachyderm whose flesh is much sought after for food by the African natives.

HOAXES (Gastronomic). SUPERCHERIES GASTRONOMIQUES – By gastronomic hoaxes we mean the substituting of one product for another, or practical jokes and tricks of a similar nature. The various forms of falsification involving fraud are not dealt with here. Hoaxes intended to mystify and surprise are usually harmless; while commercial falsification is downright dishonest. The latter involves adding to or detracting from a wholesome, high-grade product and offering an inferior (or even harmful) one in its place for the purpose of illicit gain.

The gastronomic hoax may take several forms. It may be the jest of a host who takes unfair advantage of his guests before serving them with a proper meal; it may be to test the gastronomic skills of a particular guest in order to amuse the others; it may even be dictated by events with the tacit agreement of all; finally, it may be a practical joke, where the host mystifies everybody by suddenly producing from out of the blue some startling novelty (which may not be all that it appears to be)!

Jest of a host – Grimod de la Reynière sent out invitations for a luncheon party, a so-called 'Economists' luncheon', reserved for specialists in the business and agricultural world. When they arrived, the master of the house announced that he had gathered his guests together so that they could taste all sorts of breads (baked for varying lengths of time) and grain-based beverages.

Knowing the reputation of Grimod de la Reynière's table, the guests had fasted the day before. So one can imagine their surprise at this announcement. However, they set to with a will and greedily swallowed hot, warm and cold bread made variously of barley, wheat, chestnuts, maize, Jerusalem artichokes and potatoes. This they washed down with beer and spirits made from grain. They could hardly swallow another morsel when their host announced that it was time to proceed to the examination of other substances. At this point, a delicate feast was served, which only Grimod de la Reynière could enjoy (not having eaten anything beforehand). He did so in front of the bloated 'economists' who were satiated but not satisfied.

To test the palate and discernment of a guest – The most typical example is the meal served to Monselet. Monselet, famous journalist and staunch defender of gastronomy was considered to be anything but a connoisseur. Chavette, who ran the *Brébant* restaurant, one day took it into his head to invite Monselet to dinner. The menu was:

Swallow's nest soup
Brill
Izard cutlets
Capercaillie
Wines from Tokay, the Rhine, Cape of Good Hope, etc.

Monselet gave the highest praise to each of these dishes. Joseph Hémard describes how Chavette, looking stern and tragic, pointed an accusing finger at Monselet when the meal had ended:

'You have just, he jeered with a fiendish laugh, publicly admitted your ignorance. The swallow's nest soup was a purée of noodles and kidney beans; the brill was cod cooked on a fine comb (and to illustrate his point he showed him the carefully preserved backbone made of two yellow combs sewn together back to back); the izard cutlets were lamb cutlets marinated in bitters; the capercaillie was a small turkey sprinkled with a glass of absinth! The Clos-Vougeot was made by adding a spoonful of cognac and a flower of violet to an ordinary wine; the Tokay was nothing but a Mâçon with a little punch added; and as for the South African wine, it was simply a Chablis.'

'But . . .', Monselet protested timidly, 'I recognised the perfume of the little Rhine flower . . .'

'Which we obtained with a few drops of essence of thyme.'

Overcome, Monselet lowered his head. Then confronted by the unrestrained laughter of the other guests and their exhortations for penance, for an *amende honorable*, and other encouragements of that sort, he flung himself to his knees in front of Chavette, hands clasped, and entreated in a trembling voice:

'Mercy! Pray don't betray me! Don't spread this abroad! Save me from dishonour, I beg of you! I have children!'

The soirée probably concluded with much drinking and merriment. At all events, the secret does not seem to have been well kept. No more, in fact, than on yet another occasion when the same Monselet was the guest of the author of the *Grand Dictionnaire de cuisine*, Joseph Favre. The latter had written:

'Dear Maître, tomorrow at midday, there will be a fork luncheon party at the home of our friend Fulbert Dumonteil. I shall be doing the cooking.'

There was to be a fourth guest, the journalist, novelist and politician, Tony Révillon. The menu was as follows:

Burbot liver *en caisse*
Saucisson de Lyon – Isigny butter
Salmon escalopes, tartare sauce
New potatoes
Omelette à l'ambre gris
Dessert

It appeared to be quite an ordinary menu, apart from the ambergris.

Monselet started off by being late and lunch was already over when he eventually arrived at 4 o'clock. But, undismayed, the guests began again, for they were as eager as Favre that the plot should succeed. As he savoured the various dishes, Monselet discoursed knowledgeably upon each one. The omelette particularly delighted him; he could not find words enough to do it justice. Finally, Favre was unable to contain himself any longer and showed him the real menu. The result was catastrophic.

We must add that a few days previously the celebrated physiologist, Paul Bert, had received a number of crocodiles from Egypt which he planned to dissect in order to study their nervous system. Favre, who was present at the anatomy, declared that these reptiles were good to eat, so Paul Bert set aside two brains and a piece of tail for himself, while Favre carried away a whole tail, four brains and six eggs just about ready for laying.

And so it was that the crocodiles' brains became burbot livers; the escalopes of crocodile tail became escalopes of salmon; and the omelette of crocodile eggs became *omelette à l'ambre gris*.

To crown it all, Favre substituted ordinary horsemeat sausage for the *saucisson de Lyon*, and as for the Isigny butter, it was simply margarine.

Hoaxes dictated by events – At the time of the Continental System, beet sugar took the place of cane sugar (and still does). During the Second World War, grape sugar (which did not require coupons) was preferred to saccharin as a substitute for ordinary sugar. Certainly the most famous period under this heading was the Siege of Paris 1870–1871. Because of the lack of food people had to have recourse to substitutes, a number of which, as presented by the best chefs, gave some pleasant evenings to the fortunate few. The mutton-flavoured rat is famous, but the equally famous elephant pie was, in fact, made with mice. It seemed to be the general opinion that the zoological gardens possessed a whole troop of elephants (instead of only two) to provide the wherewithal to fill all the pies. And it was a bone, a mouse's bone, found in a pie dish that led to the discovery of what lay at the bottom of the affair. But it was very good. And that, after all, was the main thing.

And what about the *concierge* in Paris who, in 1917, raised a few chickens so that he could sell dozens of fresh eggs daily?

The practical joke – The prototype is certainly the *'bouribout'*, a dish invented comparatively recently by the humorist Henry Monier. He had discussed the dish with some of his journalist colleagues, gastronomes like himself, mentioning that there was no restraurant in Paris where it could be found. A restaurateur upon hearing this declared that he knew how to prepare it. The late Marius Richard described the event in his column, praising the marvellous dish eaten in the same restaurant. And they say that Monier himself was quite astonished to know that the '*bouribout*' was nothing but a duck with cherries, otherwise known as *canard à la Montmorency*.

HOCCO – Type of gallinaceous bird of which there are a dozen species to be found in the equatorial regions of Central America. They are similar to the European turkey and have a delicious white flesh. A certain number are bred in the poultry-runs of France.

In his *Souvenirs d'émigration*, Brillat-Savarin mentions this kind of wild turkey and remarks upon its succulent flesh. It is cooked in the same way as turkey (q.v.).

HOG-FISH. RASCASSE – Fish oblong in shape and rather high backed, with a large and spiny head. It has spikes, whose prick is poisonous, on its dorsal fins. Its colouring is varied, but mostly greyish with black markings. The Provençal fishermen know the hog-fish under such names as *scorpion*, *crapaud* (toad) or *diable de mer* (sea-devil).

The flesh of the hog-fish is tough, and is not used other than for *bouillabaisse* or similar fish soups.

HOG'S FAT. PANNE – The fat which covers the pig's kidneys and fillets. It is used for making fine forcemeats and black (blood) puddings. Rendered down it produces superior quality lard which in French is called *axonge*.

HOG'S HEAD CHEESE or PORK BRAWN. FROMAGE DE TÊTE DE PORC – A kind of galantine (q.v.) made from hog's head.

HOLLAND – See INTERNATIONAL COOKERY.

HOLLANDAISE SAUCE – Name of a hot sauce made with egg yolks and butter. It is served with eggs, fish and vegetables. (See SAUCE.)

HOLLY. HOUX – Evergreen shrubs. In some countries, notably Corsica, holly berries are roasted and powdered and are used to make a drink similar to coffee.

There is an excellent clear holly spirit produced in Alsace.

Butcher's-broom or knee-holly. HOUX-FRÉLON, PETIT-HOUX – European plant used in pharmacy. Its root has diuretic properties. The young shoots of the plant are edible and can be cooked in the same way as asparagus.

HOLLYHOCK. ALCÉE – Plant originating in Lebanon. It has an appreciable nutritive content. A nourishing starch flour is obtained from its roots.

HONEY. MIEL – Sweet liquid manufactured in the sac of the worker bee from the nectar secreted in certain flowers and introduced by the insect into the cells of the hive. Honey was the chief sweet food of ancient times when cane sugar was a rarity.

It is a particularly energising food, providing 300 calories per 100 g. The sugars it contains are completely assimilable by the body. Honey contains hardly any vitamins; only in the proportion of 2 mg. to 100 g.

Several grades of honey are sold commercially:

1. Virgin or superfine honey, extracted from the combs by exposure to the sun or gentle heat.
2. Common or yellow honey, extracted under greater heat.
3. Brown honey, extracted by pressure under heat.

Honey is a very rich and concentrated food. Its effect is similar to that of sugar but it is more readily assimilated. Apart from this, it is medically prescribed or prohibited in the same cases as sugar, and in particular is forbidden to diabetics. It is slightly laxative.

In diet, especially that of children, honey can take the place of sugar in almost all its uses, though there are people who find it indigestible.

Hocco

The quality, consistency, aroma and flavour of honey vary according to the type of flowers most widespread in the region where it is gathered. The best is made from the nectar of labiates (thyme, mother of thyme). Narbonne honey owes its distinctive flavour to the nectar of rosemary. The most highly reputed honey is that of Hymetus in Greece, and in France that of Narbonne, Gâtinais, Champagne and Savoy. Spring honey is superior to autumn honey.

Certain plants impart a distinctive flavour to honey which is sometimes unpleasant (for instance, honey gathered from pines, which has a resinous taste). Honey made from the nectar of poisonous plants such as belladonna can itself be poisonous.

HONGROISE (À LA) – Dishes prepared *à la hongroise* are cooked in a cream sauce seasoned with paprika. Eggs, fish, meat (other than pork products), poultry, etc., can be prepared *à la hongroise*. Recipes for these dishes are given in alphabetical order under appropriate headings.

HOP. HOUBLON – Hardy plant grown in many countries.

The cones of the female plant are used in the brewing of beer.

Hop shoots. JETS DE HOUBLON – In French cookery, the name *jets de houblon* is given to the edible flowers of the male plant, or panicles. The edible tip of the panicle is broken away from its woody stem in the same way as green asparagus tips.

Hop shoots are boiled in salt water, with a few drops of lemon juice. Once they are cooked they can be treated in a number of different ways:

In butter. Toss for a few seconds in butter.

In cream. Toss in butter and simmer in fresh cream.

In stock. Toss in butter. Simmer for a few seconds in concentrated brown veal stock.

Hop shoots may be served as a vegetable or a garnish with various dishes. In particular they are used as a garnish with eggs.

Branch of hop with cones

In Belgium, where this vegetable is much prized, hop shoots, when they are served as a vegetable, are always garnished with poached eggs arranged in a circle on top and interspersed with croûtons of bread cut in the shape of cocks' combs and fried in butter.

In U.S.A. hop panicles or shoots are not sold in the market, but there are some large hop producing regions where they may be found.

HORN. CORNE – Little horn utensil, used to scrape up the remains of mixtures in mortars, in basins, or on marble slabs.

HORS-D'ŒUVRE – By definition, these snacks are additional to the menu. They should therefore be light and delicate, especially when served before a rather heavy menu consisting of a number of courses.

With a light luncheon, the *hors-d'œuvre* may be more substantial and nourishing.

There are two main types: cold *hors-d'œuvre* and hot *hors-d'œuvre*.

Cold *hors-d'œuvre*, usually served with luncheon, are of two kinds: those which can be bought ready for the table and those which require some preparation at home.

Formerly, hot *hors-d'œuvre* were called *entrées volantes* or *petites entrées*. They generally formed part of the dinner menu, and were served after the soup. Hot *hors-d'œuvre* can, however, be served at luncheon at the same time as cold *hors-d'œuvre*.

Nowadays, it is customary to serve a wide variety of *hors-d'œuvre* at the beginning of a luncheon.

France has also adopted a custom imported from Russia, of serving *hors-d'œuvre* in a special way; as *zakouski*, a kind of meal-before-the meal, entirely made up of *hors-d'œuvre*, washed down with liberal draughts of wine and liqueur. Formerly, in Russia, this was served in an ante-chamber adjoining the dining room.

In France, the custom has been somewhat modified. Under the name of *zakouski* or *hors-d'œuvre à la russe*, these snacks are arranged on trays and served to the guests at the table itself.

Presentation of cold hors-d'œuvre – These snacks must be presented elegantly.

Here are a few hints to help the hostess.

1. *The dishes.* Apart from special *hors-d'œuvre* sets, china or glass plates and dishes or antique gold or silver plate may be used. Old rustic-style plates, pottery or silver porringers, crystal bowls, etc, can be used very effectively.

2. *The garnishes.* Garnishes, though purely decorative, must all be edible. There is a great variety of such garnishes. Tastefully chosen and arranged, they give a very attractive appearance to the *hors-d'œuvre*. The most common garnish is parsley, which must be very green and curly. It can be used in sprigs or chopped.

Hors-d'œuvre can also be garnished with chervil, tarragon, watercress and lettuce hearts. As a contrast to these greenstuffs, half slices of lemon and beetroot can be used. Beetroot is served diced, cut into matchsticks and in other ways.

The decoration of *hors-d'œuvre* can be varied by using any of the following: capers, gherkins, red pomegranate seeds, hard-boiled eggs (halved, quartered or chopped), small pickled onions, large onions sliced into rings or chopped, small kidney beans, French beans, green peas, asparagus tips, boiled carrots and turnips, radishes, black radish, the leaves and stalks of leeks, yellow, red and green peppers, mushrooms, truffles, etc.

To achieve greater variety in form and colour, flowers can also be used. Nasturtiums (whose leaves are also edible), borage, violets, chrysanthemums and daisies all enhance the decorative effect.

Presentation of hot hors-d'œuvre – Unless otherwise stated under the entry relating to a particular item, hot *hors-d'œuvre* are served on a dish, a folded napkin or a paper doily, and garnished with fresh or fried parsley according to their nature. Fried *hors-d'œuvre* such as fritters, *cromesquis* croquettes, etc., may be served in nests of matchstick potatoes.

COLD HORS-D'ŒUVRE. HORS-D'ŒUVRE FROIDS – These usually consist of one or several ingredients, cut into dice, seasoned, with an oil and vinegar dressing or with a mayonnaise sauce. Compound butters, forcemeats, special purées and *salpicons* may also be added.

Hors-d'œuvre vegetables (*Robert Carrier*)

Some cold hors-d'œuvre: salad of ox muzzle, artichokes à la grecque, mushrooms, cucumber

The following are the most usual *hors-d'œuvre*.

Aceto-dolce – See *Sour-sweet pickles* below.

Allumettes – See *Pastry straws* below.

Anchovies. ANCHOIS – These must first be freed from salt.

For different mixtures (compound butters, stuffings, purées, *salpicons*, sauces, etc.). Wash the anchovies, soak them in cold water, cut into fillets, clean and dry them. The method of preparation after this varies according to the particular dish for which they are intended.

For hors-d'œuvre and different garnishes. Soak the anchovies and cut them into fillets as above. Scrape and clean them well to ensure that all the scales have been removed. Dry lightly in a cloth.

Cut the fillets into small strips or leave them whole, according to the dish for which they are intended.

Arrange anchovy fillets in a deep dish or *terrine*. Cover with olive oil. Put the lid on the dish and keep in a cool place. Use as indicated.

Anchovies and hard-boiled eggs I. ANCHOIS ET OEUFS DURS – Two thirds hard-boiled eggs and one third anchovy fillets cut into small dice. Season with oil, vinegar, salt, pepper and finely chopped herbs, or with mayonnaise.

Anchovies and hard-boiled eggs II. ANCHOIS AUX OEUFS DURS – Proceed as for *Anchovies in oil* (see below). Garnish with the yolks and white of hard-boiled eggs chopped separately, capers and chopped parsley.

The dressing, garnish and decoration of marinated anchovy fillets can be varied. Apart from the additional ingredients mentioned above, a variety of other items can be used, e.g. *Lettuce chiffonnade* (see CHIFFONNADE), olives, beetroot, lemon, chervil, tarragon, etc.

Anchovies à la grecque. ANCHOIS À LA GRECQUE – Put fresh anchovies, cleaned and dried in a cloth, into salt for 2 hours. Soak in cold water, and shake them individually to ensure that all the salt falls off. Sear for 1 minute only in smoking oil.

Drain the anchovies and arrange in layers in a *terrine*. Each layer should be sprinkled with thyme, sweet bay, coriander and pepper grains. Make *Court-bouillon II* (see COURT-BOUILLON) and pour, while still boiling, over the anchovies. Marinate them in this *court-bouillon* for 24 hours.

Serve in an *hors-d'œuvre* dish. Sprinkle with the marinade, garnish with slices of peeled lemon and sprinkle with freshly chopped fennel.

In France this dish is also known as *Escabèche d'anchois à la grecque*.

Anchovies à la normande. ANCHOIS À LA NORMANDE – Arrange the marinated anchovy fillets on a *salpicon* (q.v.) of rennet apples seasoned with mayonnaise. Surround with a border of beetroot cut into very small dice. Dress with a thin trickle of oil.

Norwegian anchovies (kilkis). ANCHOIS DE NORVÈGE – These can be bought ready prepared. Arrange the anchovies on an *hors-d'œuvre* dish and surround with half slices of lemons cut with a fluted cutter, and with fresh parsley. Sprinkle with several tablespoons of their marinade.

Norwegian anchovies or *kilkis* can be used in all ways indicated for anchovies in brine.

Anchovies in oil. ANCHOIS À L'HUILE – Free anchovies from salt. Cut into thin strips. Arrange on an *hors-d'œuvre* dish, in a pattern. Garnish with capers and chopped parsley. Dress with a thin trickle of oil.

Anchovy salads, various. SALADES D'ANCHOIS – Anchovy fillets in oil or with hard-boiled eggs accompanied by a salad.

Anchovy salad can be served with a great variety of dishes: *Lettuce chiffonnade* (see CHIFFONNADE), boiled potatoes cut into fine slices or dice, celeriac cut into a fine *julienne* (q.v.), etc.

These various additions are accompaniments; the anchovies dominate the dish.

Anchovy scrolls. PAUPIETTES D'ANCHOIS – Free anchovy fillets from salt, scrape, and dry in a cloth. Flatten the fillets and coat them with a thin layer of fish purée or any other mixture suitable for cold *hors-d'œuvre*. Roll the fillets into scrolls.

Arrange them in an *hors-d'œuvre* dish and garnish with the yolks and whites of hard-boiled eggs chopped separately, capers, and chopped parsley. Dress with a thin trickle of oil.

Bargeman's anchovy scrolls. PAUPIETTES D'ANCHOIS BATELIÈRE – Make anchovy scrolls and stuff them with tunny (tuna fish) purée blended with mayonnaise. Arrange them two by two in small baked *barquette* shells. Garnish with a *salpicon* made with hard-boiled eggs and gherkins, seasoned with mayonnaise. Arrange on a paper doyley and garnish with fresh parsley.

Monselet anchovy scrolls. PAUPIETTES D'ANCHOIS MONSELET – Fill anchovy scrolls with a stuffing made with the yolks of hard-boiled eggs. Arrange each scroll on a toasted *canapé* of bread covered with *Anchovy butter* (see BUTTER, *Compound butters*).

Surround the scrolls with a ring of capers and put a small sprig of tarragon in each.

Arrange on a paper doyley and garnish with fresh parsley.

Anchovy scrolls à la niçoise. PAUPIETTES D'ANCHOIS À LA NIÇOISE – Fill anchovy scrolls with *Tarragon butter* (see BUTTER, *Compound butter*).

Hollow small raw tomatoes, marinate them and two-thirds fill each with a fish purée. Place the scrolls in the tomatoes on the foundation of fish purée.

Decorate to taste. Arrange on an *hors-d'œuvre* dish and dress with a trickle of oil.

Vatel anchovy scrolls. PAUPIETTES D'ANCHOIS VATEL – Stuff anchovy scrolls with *Anchovy butter* (see BUTTER, *Compound butters*) to which chopped tarragon has been added.

Make small patty cases of puff pastry. Fill these two-thirds with a *salpicon* of marinated tunny (tuna fish) and truffles seasoned with mayonnaise. Put 1 scroll on each patty, and a sliver of truffle on each scroll, topped with a dot of butter mixed with the yolk of hard-boiled eggs.

Arrange on a paper doyley and garnish with fresh parsley.

Artichokes. ARTICHAUTS – Small artichokes, quartered artichokes and hearts of artichokes, prepared according to the methods described under the heading ARTICHOKE, can be used as ingredients for a variety of *hors-d'œuvre*.

Artichokes

Artichokes Baron-Brisse. ARTICHAUTS BARON-BRISSE – Cut the hearts of artichokes into thin slices and cook them lightly for a few moments in boiling oil, moving them around. Moisten with a few tablespoons of *Tomato essence* (see ESSENCE). Add lemon juice, salt, pepper, parsley and chopped chervil. Boil together for a few minutes.

Leave to cool. Arrange on an *hors-d'œuvre* dish with rounds of peeled lemon.

Artichokes à la grecque. ARTICHAUTS À LE GRECQUE – Trim 20 small tender artichokes (see ARTICHOKE). Flavour with lemon and plunge one after the other into a liquid prepared as follows:

Boil together for 5 minutes in a casserole 5 dl. (scant pint, $2\frac{1}{4}$ cups) water, 1 dl. (6 tablespoons, scant $\frac{1}{2}$ cup) olive oil, the juice of 1 lemon, a pinch of salt, 10 coriander seeds, 10 peppercorns, and a large *bouquet garni* composed of parsley, thyme, bay leaf, celery and fennel.

Cook the artichokes in this *court-bouillon* for 18 to 20 minutes. Take them out of the liquor and keep in a cool place. Arrange on an *hors-d'œuvre* dish and serve as cold as possible – iced if desired.

This *hors-d'œuvre* keeps fairly well, particularly if the artichokes are put in a narrow pickling jar and kept in a very cool place. For a larger quantity (100 artichokes) see ARTICHOKE, *Pickled artichokes à la grecque*.

Artichokes à la poivrade. ARTICHAUTS À LA POIVRADE – Name given to a dish of small young artichokes eaten raw with *Vinaigrette sauce* (see SAUCE) strongly flavoured with pepper.

Artichoke à la vinaigrette. ARTICHAUTS À LA VINAIGRETTE – Another name for *Artichokes à la poivrade*.

Boiled artichokes, either hot or cold, accompanied by a *Vinaigrette sauce* (see SAUCE), are also served under this name.

Garnished artichoke hearts. FONDS D'ARTICHAUTS GARNIS – Prepare and cook very small artichoke hearts (see ARTICHOKE).

Drain and dry them. Garnish with vegetable salad, asparagus tips, different *salpicons* (q.v.), etc.; dress with mayonnaise or *vinaigrette sauce*.

Artichoke hearts may be garnished with different purées and with caviare. Arrange the hearts in an *hors-d'œuvre* dish. Decorate with fresh parsley, hard-boiled eggs, chopped jelly, etc.

Artichoke hearts à la grecque. FONDS D'ARTICHAUTS À LA GRECQUE – Proceed as indicated for *Artichokes à la grecque*, using very small artichoke hearts or large hearts cut into slices.

Artichoke hearts à la tartare. FONDS D'ARTICHAUTS À LA TARTARE – Cook artichoke hearts in a white *court-bouillon* (q.v.); drain, dry and cut into slices. Arrange in an *hors-d'œuvre* dish with *Tartare sauce* (see SAUCE).

Garnish with a border of the yolks of hard-boiled eggs and chopped parsley, arranged in separate rows. Surround with half slices of cooked beetroot, cut with a fluted-edged knife.

Quartered artichokes. QUARTIERS D'ARTICHAUTS – Tender quartered artichokes are prepared as an *hors-d'œuvre*, following the instructions given for artichoke hearts and whole artichokes.

Assiette anglaise – Assortment of different kinds of cold meat, usually York ham; pickled tongue; *entrecôte*, fillet or roast beef; veal; pork, arranged on a plate.

Garnish with chopped jelly, watercress and gherkins.

Assiette anglaise is mainly served for luncheon.

Assorted hors-d'œuvre. ASSIETTE ASSORTIE, ASSIETTE VOLANTE – An assortment of different kinds of *hors-d'œuvre*, mainly salted items, cut into very small slices.

Barquettes – Small oval-shaped patties made of pastry, baked blind, garnished with different fillings (see BARQUETTES). Items which can be used as garnishes for pastry boats include anchovy in *salpicon* or anchovy scrolls, smoked eel, beetroot, special compound butters for *hors-d'œuvre*, caviare, pickled cucumber, prawns, shrimps, crayfish, *foie gras*, pickled herrings, lobster and crawfish, different vegetables in *salpicon* or cut into slices, poached mussels, olives, hard-boiled eggs, plovers' eggs, red and green peppers, different sausages, marinated tunny, tomatoes, truffles.

The following serve as decorations for these various pastry boats: capers, gherkins, beetroot, chopped jelly, hard-boiled eggs, fresh parsley, chervil, tarragon, lettuce.

The following are a few examples. All recipes given for filling patties, *canapés* and tartlets apply to *barquettes*, which are generally served on a paper doyley. On the menu they are often called *frivolités*, a name originally given them by Escoffier.

Bagration barquettes. BARQUETTES BAGRATION – Garnish the *barquettes* with a thin layer of cold *Chicken purée* (see CHICKEN). Cover this purée alternately with thin slices of breast of chicken and truffles. Spoon half-set jelly into the *barquettes*.

Beauharnais barquettes. BARQUETTES BEAUHARNAIS – Garnish the *barquettes* with a *salpicon* of breast of chicken and truffles. Cover this garnish with a layer of mayonnaise, to which a purée of tarragon and a little gelatine has been added. Decorate with tiny pieces of truffles and cover with jelly.

Barquettes à la cancalaise – Garnish the *barquettes* with a mousse made from whiting or other white fish. Poach, drain and trim some oysters. Lay these on the mousse in each *barquette* and spoon over some jelly.

Marivaux barquettes. BARQUETTES MARIVAUX – Fill the *barquettes* with a *salpicon* of shrimps and mushrooms, blended with gelatine-strengthened mayonnaise. Decorate with rounds of hard-boiled eggs and chervil. Coat with jelly.

Barquettes à la normande – Garnish the *barquettes* with a *salpicon* of fillets of sole, mussels and truffles.

Coat the *barquettes* with a white meatless *Chaud-froid*

sauce (see SAUCE). Put 1 poached oyster and 2 shelled crayfish tails on each boat. Spoon over some jelly.

Beef, smoked. BOEUF FUMÉ – Cut the meat into very thin slices. Serve in an *hors-d'œuvre* dish or on a plate, arranged flat or rolled into cornets. Garnish with parsley. Smoked beef is also used as a garnish for *canapés*.

Beetroot. BETTERAVE – Beetroot can be bought cooked in greengrocers' shops or it can be prepared at home. It is mainly used for salads.

Peel the cooked beetroot and cut it into thin slices. Arrange in an *hors-d'œuvre* dish. Season with oil, vinegar, salt and pepper. Sprinkle with chopped parsley.

Beetroot cassolettes – See BEETROOT.

Beetroot à la crème. BETTERAVE À LA CRÈME – Cut the beetroot into fine matchsticks. Season with a *Mustard cream sauce* (see SAUCE). Serve in *hors-d'œuvre* dish.

Beetroot and hard-boiled eggs. BETTERAVE ET OEUFS DURS – Take equal quantities of cooked beetroot and hard-boiled eggs, both cut into dice. Season as for *Anchovies and hard boiled eggs* (see above).

Beetroot à la normande. BETTERAVE À LA NORMANDE – Cut beetroot and tart apples into slices and arrange alternately on an *hors-d'œuvre* dish. Surround with a ring of chopped chives. Season with *Vinaigrette sauce* (see SAUCE) made with cider vinegar.

Beetroot salad. SALADE DE BETTERAVE – This salad is served with a *Vinaigrette* or a *Cream sauce* (see SAUCE) as indicated above. Serve in an *hors-d'œuvre* dish or in a salad bowl.

Bouchées – See *Patties* below.

Brioches, small garnished. BRIOCHES MIGNONNES GARNIES – Take very small *Brioches à tête* (see BRIOCHE) scoop out three-quarters of the dough and fill with any of the garnishes usually served with tartlets and other similar preparations.

Cabbage, green. CHOUX VERTS – Prepare in the same way as *Red cabbage*, below.

Cabbage, red. CHOUX ROUGE – Trim and wash a medium-sized cabbage. Cut it into very fine small strips, put them into a dish and pour over 3 dl. ($\frac{1}{2}$ pint, $1\frac{1}{4}$ cups) boiling vinegar. Mix well and leave for 5 hours. Drain and season with oil, salt and pepper.

Red cabbage can be blanched before it is steeped in the vinegar.

Canapés – Small garnished pieces of toast make a very attractive *hors-d'œuvre*. They can be served in two ways.

First method. Cut the crusts off a sandwich loaf and cut the bread into thin slices. Cut the slices into small pieces of various shapes and forms. Toast these on both sides without over browning.

When cool, spread on one side with a compound or plain butter, or any other suitable preparation, according to the kind of *canapé* desired. Garnish accordingly. Instructions for decorating can be found below. Arrange on a paper doyley, napkin, plate or dish.

Second method. Toast large slices of a sandwich loaf lightly on both sides. When cool spread with butter or any other suitable preparation. Garnish, and cut into *canapés* of various shapes. Decorate.

If a great many *canapés* of the same kind are to be served, the second method is recommended. The toast can also be made of black bread or with ordinary unsweetened brioche (baked in a rectangular tin if possible).

In addition to the recipes listed below, *canapés* may be prepared in many ways. Different kinds of meat, fish, vegetables, truffles, etc., cut into thin slices or made into *salpicons*, can be used as garnishes.

Decorate *canapés* with hard-boiled eggs, capers, gherkins, olives, beetroot, cucumber, truffles, mushrooms, parsley, chervil, tarragon, etc.

Preparation of various canapés: radishes, tomatoes, cucumber

Anchovy canapés – See ANCHOVY.

Aurora canapés. CANAPÉS À L'AURORE – Slice a round unsweetened brioche loaf, toast, and spread with yellow butter. Garnish with a thin slice of smoked salmon, put a round of beetroot in the middle, sprinkle with minced yolk of hard-boiled egg, and surround with a border of yellow butter.

Canapés à la bayonnaise – Slice a sandwich loaf, toast, and spread with parsley butter. Garnish with very thin slices of Bayonne ham.

Canapés à la bordelaise – Slice a sandwich loaf, toast, and spread with *Shallot butter*. Garnish with a *salpicon* of cooked *cèpes* and lean ham, and surround with a border of *Paprika butter* (see BUTTER, *Compound butters*).

Canapés with caviare. CANAPÉS AU CAVIAR – Slice a sandwich loaf, brown loaf or unsweetened brioche; the slices should be round. Toast, and spread with *Caviare butter* (see BUTTER, *Compound butters*) or with fresh butter. Surround with a fairly high border of caviare butter. Garnish the centre with fresh caviare. Sprinkle with a pinch of chives.

These *canapés* can also be made with pressed caviare, but they will not be so delicate.

Crayfish canapés. CANAPÉS AUX ÉCREVISSES – Follow the recipe for *Shrimp canapés* (see below), using *Crayfish butter* (see BUTTER, *Compound butters*) and crayfish tails instead of shrimps.

Canapés à la danoise – Slice a dark rye loaf of rectangular shape, toast, and spread with *Horseradish butter* (see BUTTER, *Compound butters*), and garnish with thin strips of smoked salmon alternating with fillets of herring. Separate the strips of fish by a little fresh caviare, and surround with a border of chopped chives.

Harlequin canapés. CANAPÉS ARLEQUIN – Slice a sandwich loaf, toast, and spread with a compound butter. Garnish with chopped yolks and whites of hard-boiled eggs, smoked tongue, ham, truffles, parsley, etc. Surround with a thin border of compound butter.

These canapés can be garnished with a mixture of different preparations. The garnish is prepared last, so the left-overs of special canapés can be used up for this dish.

Herring canapés. CANAPÉS AUX HARENGS – Use the recipe for *Anchovy canapés* (see ANCHOVY), substituting *Herring butter* (see BUTTER, *Compound butters*) and fillets of herring for the anchovy.

These *canapés* can be garnished with different kinds of herrings.

Canapés à la hollandaise – Slice a sandwich loaf, toast, and spread with a purée of soft herring roes. Garnish with fillets of herring arranged in a criss-cross pattern. Fill each opening with chopped parsley.

Canapés Laguipière – Lozenge-shaped *canapés* of ordinary unsweetened brioche bread, toasted, and spread with *Truffle butter* (see BUTTER, *Compound butters*). Garnish with slices of breast of chicken, and decorate the points of the lozenges with chopped pickled or smoked tongue and chopped truffles. Surround with a border of yellow butter.

Canapés à la livonienne – Slice a rectangular rye loaf, toast, and spread with *Horseradish butter* (see BUTTER, *Compound butters*). Garnish with slivers of herring fillets alternating with thin ribbons of tart apples. Brush lightly with oil and surround with a border of chopped chives.

Canapés decorated with hard-boiled eggs and green beans

Lobster canapés. CANAPÉS AU HOMARD – Follow the recipe for *Shrimp canapés* (see below), substituting *Lobster butter* (see BUTTER, *Compound butters*) and pieces of lobster.

Monselet canapés. CANAPÉS MONSELET – Trim slices of sandwich loaf into oval shapes, toast, and spread with yellow butter. Garnish with a border of small round slices of breast of chicken, alternating with equally small rounds of pickled or smoked tongue. Fill the centre with a *salpicon* of truffles and surround with a border of yellow butter.

Mont-Bry canapés. CANAPÉS MONT-BRY – Slice unsweetened brioche, toast, and spread with *Herring butter* (see BUTTER, *Compound butters*). Garnish with fillets of herring, alternating with evenly cut strips of beetroot and gherkins. Surround with a border of chopped yolks of hard-boiled eggs.

Canapés à la moscovite – Slice a square black rye loaf, toast, and spread with *Horseradish butter* (see BUTTER, *Compound butters*). Surround with a border of butter mixed with the coral of spiny lobsters. Fill the centre with fresh caviare and decorate with shrimp tails.

Canapés à la nantaise – Slice sandwich bread thin and trim the slices into long oval shapes. Toast, and spread with *Sardine butter* (see BUTTER, *Compound butters*). Garnish with fillets of sardines in oil from which all the bones and skin have been carefully removed, and garnish with sardine butter in such a way as to make the *canapés* look like fish.

Canapés Ninon – Trim slices of sandwich bread into oval shapes, toast, and spread with *Printanier butter* (see BUTTER, *Compound butters*). Garnish with a border of small thin rounds of breast of chicken, alternating with rounds of truffles. Fill the centre with lean ham cut into very small dice.

Canapés à la parisienne – Slice a rectangular sandwich loaf, toast, and spread with butter mixed with pounded chervil. Garnish with small, thin slices of breast of chicken coated with gelatine-strengthened mayonnaise and decorated with truffles and tarragon leaves. Surround with a border of chopped jelly.

Canapés à la printanière – Trim slices of sandwich loaf into rounds, toast, and spread with *Montpellier butter* (see BUTTER, *Compound butters*). Garnish with leaves of watercress, alternating with thin round slices of carrots cooked in clear stock. Spoon over a thin layer of meat jelly and surround with a border of chopped yolks of hard-boiled eggs.

Canapés à la reine – Trim slices of unsweetened brioche into rounds, toast, and spread with *Truffle butter* (see BUTTER, *Compound butters*). Garnish with a *salpicon* of breast of chicken, decorate with lozenge-shaped slices of truffle, and surround with a border of yellow butter.

Russian salad canapés. CANAPÉS À LA RUSSE – Slice a sandwich loaf, toast, and spread with butter *aux fines herbes*. Surround with a border of yellow butter, fill the centre with *Russian salad* (see SALAD) decorate with truffles, and cover with a thin coat of jelly.

Shrimp canapés. CANAPÉS AUX CREVETTES – Slice a rounded sandwich loaf or cut out rounds from square slices. Toast, and spread with *Shrimp butter* (see BUTTER, *Compound butters*). Garnish with shrimps arranged in a rosette. Surround with a border of shrimp butter or with chopped parsley.

Smoked eel canapés. CANAPÉS À L'ANGUILLE FUMÉE – Slice a round sandwich loaf, toast, and spread with *Mustard butter* or with *Horseradish butter* (see BUTTER, *Compound butters*). Garnish with thin slices of smoked eel, and surround with hard-boiled egg yolks and chives, chopped separately.

Canapés with spiny lobster. CANAPÉS DE LANGOUSTE – Follow the recipe for *Shrimp canapés*, using *Spiny lobster butter* (see BUTTER, *Compound butters*) and slices of spiny lobster or spiny lobster cut into dice.

Canapés with pickled tongue. CANAPÉS À L'ÉCARLATE – Slice a sandwich loaf, toast, and spread with *Paprika butter* (see BUTTER, *Compound butters*). Garnish with thin slices of pickled or smoked tongue or with tongue cut into very small dice. Surround with a border of paprika butter.

Canapés à la Veron – Slice a square black rye loaf, toast, and spread with *Horseradish butter* (see BUTTER, *Compound butters*). Garnish with thin slices of Bayonne ham and surround with a border of hard-boiled egg yolks and parsley chopped up in equal proportions.

Watercress canapés. CANAPÉS AU CRESSON – Slice a sandwich loaf, toast, and spread with a butter made like *Tarragon butter* (see BUTTER, *Compound butters*), substituting watercress leaves for the tarragon. Garnish with leaves of blanched watercress and surround with a border of chopped hard boiled eggs.

Canapés with York ham. CANAPÉS À LA YORKAISE – Slice a sandwich loaf, toast, and spread with *Chivry butter* (see BUTTER, *Compound butters*). Garnish with thin slices of York ham, and surround with a border of chopped parsley.

Carolines – Small éclairs made of unsweetened *Chou paste* (see DOUGH), garnished to taste with different preparations such as mousses or purées made of shrimps, prawns, crayfish, lobster, spiny lobster, *foie gras*, salmon, sole, poultry, game, etc. The éclairs are coated with a *Chaud-froid sauce* (see SAUCE) in keeping with the filling, and glazed with jelly. Arrange them on a paper doyley.

Caroline éclairs can also be filled with *salpicons* blended with *chaud-froid sauce*, or with mayonnaise or jelly. They can also be garnished with fresh caviare.

Caviare – The word 'caviare' generally indicates fresh caviare, i.e. the roe of one of the members of the sturgeon family.

In Russia, the roe of other fish such as *soudac*, trout, salmon, perch, pike and *sigui* are prepared in the same way. These inferior products cannot be sold in France as caviare.

Salted and pressed caviares are also on the market, but their flavour is not as good as that of the real caviare.

Fresh caviare is served in its original container surrounded by crushed ice, or in special containers also surrounded by ice. Caviare should be delicately handled. It is usually served with thin slices of rye bread lightly buttered, or with a Russian pancake called *blini* (q.v.).

Lemon and chopped chives are provided when serving caviare for each diner to help himself.

Caviare barquettes or tartlets. BARQUETTES, TARTELETTES AU CAVIAR – Use very small *barquettes* or tartlets. Garnish with fresh caviare. Serve on a paper doyley.

Small brioches with caviare. PETITES BRIOCHES AU CAVIAR – Use very small *Brioches à tête* (see BRIOCHE) made from unsweetened dough. Hollow out the brioches and fill with fresh caviare. Serve on a paper doyley.

Celeriac. CÉLERI-RAVE – Cut into dice, cook quickly, drain, season with oil and vinegar, mayonnaise or mustard.

Celery à la grecque. CÉLERI À LA GRECQUE – Trim and wash the celery, cut the hearts into quarters and prepare in the same way as *Artichokes à la grecque* (see above).

Cherries in vinegar, also called preserved cherries. BIGARREAUX AU VINAIGRE – Choose very firm white heart cherries. Cut their stalks by two-thirds.

Put them in an earthenware jar. Sprinkle with very small pieces of thyme and bay leaf. Pour over boiling vinegar seasoned with salt, and 2 cloves. Cover the jug with a lid and keep cool. Leave to infuse for 15 days.

Serve the cherries in an *hors-d'œuvre* dish. Sprinkle with the marinade.

Cherries preserved in vinegar are served separately as *hors-d'œuvre* or with cold or hot meat dishes.

Crayfish. ÉCREVISSES – Diced crayfish tails seasoned with oil, vinegar, salt and pepper, or with a mayonnaise.

Cucumbers. CONCOMBRES – Dice fresh cucumbers, put them in a dish and sprinkle with salt. Serve seasoned with salt, pepper, vinegar and oil.

Cucumber à la grecque. CONCOMBRES À LA GRECQUE – Cut the cucumber into pieces and proceed as for *Artichokes à la grecque* (see above) but cook only for 10 or 12 minutes.

Cucumber salad. CONCOMBRES EN SALADE – Peel the cucumbers and cut them lengthwise into very thin slices.

Put them on a cloth, sprinkle with fine salt and leave them to render their liquor for 30 minutes. Drain, dry, and season with oil, vinegar, pepper, parsley and chopped chervil. Fresh cream may be added.

Cucumber stuffed with vegetable salad. CONCOMBRES FARCIS À LA PRINTANIÈRE – Cut a large cucumber into pieces and blanch in salted water. Drain, dry, and hollow out to give them the shape of *cassolettes*. Fill with a vegetable salad: carrots, turnips, diced French beans, and peas blended with thick mayonnaise. Sprinkle with oil and vinegar.

Éclairs à la Karoly – Stuff éclairs with a game purée, coat with a brown *Chaud-froid sauce* (see SAUCE) and glaze over with jelly.

Eel. ANGUILLE – For the general method of cleaning and cooking, see EEL. Various dishes which can be served as hot or cold *hors-d'œuvre*, particularly *Eels au vert*, are also described in the section EEL.

Commachio eel. ANGUILLE DE COMMACHIO – This kind of salted and smoked eel is only used as *hors-d'œuvre*. Serve in an *hors-d'œuvre* dish.

Eel à l'indienne. ANGUILLE À L'INDIENNE – Proceed as for *Eel à l'italienne* (see below). Moisten with a *court-bouillon* seasoned with curry powder. Put into a *terrine* with the liquid. This dish must be completely cooled before it is served.

Garnish eels with quartered pimentos and thin slices of raw tomatoes which have been sprinkled with salt. Sprinkle the whole dish with the liquor in which the eel has been cooked.

Eel à l'italienne. ANGUILLE À L'ITALIENNE – Cut an eel weighing 750 g. (1¾ lb.) into 5-cm. (2-inch) pieces.

Thread the pieces, separated by bay leaves, on small wooden skewers. Put all the skewers in an oiled dish, season and sprinkle with oil. Cook for 12 minutes in the oven. Drain and remove the pieces of eel from the skewers. Arrange them in a *terrine*.

Put 2 dl. (⅓ pint, scant cup) vinegar and 1 dl. (6 tablespoons, scant ½ cup) water into the dish in which the eel has been cooked. Add a lump of sugar, 4 cloves and a pinch of salt. Boil this *court-bouillon* for 5 minutes, and pour over the eel. Cover the *terrine*, put into a very cool place, and leave for 2 or 3 days before serving.

Arrange on an *hors-d'œuvre* dish and cover with the jelly which has formed in the *terrine*.

Jellied eel in Chablis. ANGUILLE AU VIN DE CHABLIS, EN GELÉE – Cut small eels into pieces and cook in concentrated fish stock prepared with Chablis. Drain the pieces and put into a small *terrine*. Clarify the liquid in which the eel has been cooked and pour over the dish. Cool on ice.

Eel marinated in red wine. ANGUILLE MARINÉE AU VIN ROUGE – Proceed as described for *Eel marinated in white wine* (see below), but use red wine for the *court-bouillon*.

Eel marinated in vinegar. ANGUILLE MARINÉE AU VINAIGRE – Proceed as described for *Eel marinated in white wine* (see below) but use vinegar instead of white wine for the *court-bouillon*.

Eel marinated in white wine. ANGUILLE MARINÉE AU VIN BLANC – Cut the eel into pieces. Cook minced onions in butter until soft. Line a shallow pan with the onion and place the eel on them. Cover with *Court-bouillon XII* (see COURT-BOUILLON). Add a large *bouquet garni*. Cook for 20 minutes and cool the eel in its liquor.

Eel à l'orientale. ANGUILLE À L'ORIENTALE – Proceed with eel, cut into pieces, as for *Red mullet à l'orientale* (see below).

Preparing sections of cucumber to be stuffed with vegetable salad

Smoked eel (Kiel). ANGUILLE FUMÉE DE KIEL – Cut the eel into fillets or very thin slices. Garnish with fresh parsley and half slices of lemon cut with a fluted cutter.

Smoked eel canapés – See *Canapés* above.

Eel in verjuice. ANGUILLE AU VERJUS – Cut the eel in pieces. Cook chopped onions gently in butter. Line the bottom of a flat pan with the onions and place the pieces of eel on top. Season. Add a *bouquet garni*. Moisten with verjuice and white wine in equal quantities. Finish the dish as for *Eel marinated in white wine* (see above).

Eggs, hard-boiled. OEUFS DURS – Cut into dice, or slice. Season with oil, vinegar, salt and pepper or with mayonnaise.

Eggs, stuffed. OEUFS FARCIS – Hard-boil the eggs. Cut into halves. Take out the yolks and mix these with whatever preparation is used as stuffing. Another way of stuffing eggs is to cut a little off at both ends so that they can stand. Carefully take the yolks out without breaking the white. Stuff the eggs to taste. Arrange them standing up looking like little barrels.

Salads and *salpicons* can be used as stuffings for eggs.

Decorate the halved eggs or the little barrel-shaped eggs, glaze over with jelly and arrange on an *hors-d'œuvre* dish or on a plate garnished with curly parsley.

Egg stuffing à la moscovite. FARCE D'OEUFS À LA MOSCOVITE – Pound 2 hard-boiled egg yolks. Add 2 tablespoons (3 tablespoons) thick mayonnaise, 1 tablespoon finely chopped onions cooked in oil until tender, and 1 tablespoon chopped parsley. Season with salt and paprika and mix well.

Plovers' or lapwings' eggs. OEUFS DE PLUVIER, DE VANNEAU – Hard-boil the eggs and peel two-thirds of each one. Put the part of the egg which is left in the shell on a bed of watercress, made to look like a nest. The merits of this *hors-d'œuvre* lie mainly in the rarity of the eggs and their high price. Lapwings' eggs appear on the market in France round about Easter.

Escabèche of various fishes (Spanish and Provençal cookery). ESCABÈCHE DE POISSONS DIVERS – Wash smelts, mackerels, whitings, red mullets, etc., and dry in a cloth. Dip in flour and fry in olive oil until both sides are lightly coloured. Pour boiling *court-bouillon* over them. This is prepared as follows:

Heat the oil in which the fish were fried until it begins to smoke. Add, for $2\frac{1}{2}$ dl. (scant $\frac{1}{2}$ pint, general cup) oil, 5 cloves unpeeled garlic, and a sliced onion and carrot. Fry for a few minutes and add $1\frac{1}{2}$ dl. ($\frac{1}{4}$ pint, $\frac{2}{3}$ cup) vinegar, $\frac{1}{2}$ dl. (3 tablespoons, scant $\frac{1}{4}$ cup) water, a sprig of thyme, half a bay leaf, some parsley, 3 pimentos, salt and pepper. Cook for 10 to 12 minutes, pour over the fish, and leave to soak for 24 hours. Serve cold with the marinade.

Fanchonnettes – See *Patties, Fanchonnette patties*, below.

Fennel roots. FENOUIL BULBEUX – Peel and wash the bulbous part of the fennel, cut into halves or quarters, and serve with *Vinaigrette sauce* (see SAUCE).

Fennel roots à la grecque. FENOUIL BULBEUX À LA GRECQUE – Cut the bulbous roots into halves or quarters and proceed as indicated for *Artichokes à la grecque* (see above).

Figs, fresh. FIGUES FRAÎCHES – Serve as they are. Arrange the figs on vine leaves or, preferably, on small fig leaves. Or roll them in thin slices of Parma ham.

French beans. HARICOTS VERTS – Cook in salt water, drain, cut into dice, season with oil and vinegar, salt and pepper, or with mayonnaise.

Frogs' legs. GRENOUILLES – For the general preparation of dishes with frogs legs see FROG.

Frogs' legs à la grecque. GRENOUILLES À LA GRECQUE – Cook frogs' legs in *Court-bouillon I* (see COURT-BOUILLON). Leave to cool in the cooking stock.

Garnish with rounds of peeled lemon.

Frogs' legs à la parisienne. GRENOUILLES À LA PARISIENNE – Cook frogs' legs in white wine to which a squeeze of lemon has been added and which has been seasoned with salt and pepper. Drain the frogs' legs and dry them in a cloth. Cover with *Mayonnaise III* (see SAUCE).

Serve on diced potato salad. Garnish with chopped hard-boiled eggs (yolk and white chopped separately) and parsley.

Frogs' legs with pimentos. GRENOUILLES AUX PIMENTS DOUX – Cook the frogs' legs as described in the recipe for *Frogs' legs à la parisienne* above. Add finely cut red and green peppers and vinegar or lemon juice to the cooking stock and dress with a trickle of oil. Leave to cool.

Frogs' legs à la vinaigrette. GRENOUILLES À LA VINAIGRETTE – Poach the frogs' legs as described in the recipe for *Frogs' legs à la parisienne* above.

Drain, season with oil, vinegar, pepper, salt and chopped parsley. Sprinkle some of the boiled-down cooking stock over the dish.

Gherkins. CORNICHONS – Gherkins in vinegar are served cut into dice.

Goose, smoked. OIE FUMÉE – Cut the breast into very thin slices. Serve with fresh parsley.

Ham (Bayonne, Parma, Westphalia, Ardennes, Toulouse). JAMBONS – Cut the raw ham into very thin slices and arrange in slices or rolled into cornets. Garnish with fresh parsley.

Herrings. HARENGS – Cut desalted smoked herrings into small dice. Season with an oil and vinegar dressing or with mayonnaise. Add hard-boiled eggs cut into dice and sprinkled with chives or chopped onions.

Fillets of salted herrings. FILETS DE HARENGS SALÉS – Fillet 6 salted herrings, skin them and free them from salt by soaking in milk and water. Drain, dry in a cloth and arrange in a *terrine*. Put rounds of blanched onions on them and add thyme, bay leaf and cloves. Pour 2 dl. ($\frac{1}{3}$ pint, scant cup) vinegar over and marinate them in this mixture for 5 hours. Cover with oil and keep in a cool place. Garnish with capers, gherkins and lemon.

These fillets can also be prepared in a *court-bouillon* (q.v.), or dressed with a mayonnaise, or used as a garnish for *canapés* if thoroughly dried on a cloth.

Fillets of smoked herring. FILETS DE HARENGS SAURS – Fillet smoked herrings, skin them, and soak in milk and water. Drain, dry in a cloth, arrange in a *terrine*, put blanched rounds of onions on them, sprinkle with thyme, add a bayleaf and some cloves, and cover with oil. Keep cool.

Garnish with hard-boiled eggs, chopped parsley, and rounds of fluted lemon slices.

Fillets of smoked herring prepared in this way can be dressed with mayonnaise, or used as garnish for *canapés*. The soft and hard roes are steeped in oil and served with the fillets.

Fresh herrings, marinated. HARENGS FRAIS MARINÉS – Divide 6 herrings with soft roes into pieces. Arrange in a buttered or oiled pan.

Make *Court-bouillon XII* (see COURT-BOUILLON), pour over the herrings and bring to the boil. Cover, and cook for 10 to 12 minutes. Put into a *terrine* with the cooking stock. Leave to cool before serving. Sprinkle with some of the stock, decorate with the vegetables cooked in the *court-bouillon* and thin rounds of lemon.

Herrings à la livonienne. HARENGS À LA LIVONIENNE – Choose large smoked herrings. Fillet, skin and trim them. Keep the heads and tails. Cut the fillets into dice and add an equal quantity of cooked potatoes and diced tart apples.

Season with oil, vinegar and pepper, and add chopped parsley, chervil, tarragon and fennel. Mix well.

Arrange on a dish in the shape of herrings and complete by adding the heads and tails.

Hors-d'œuvre (*Robert Carrier*)

Herrings à la portugaise. HARENGS À LA PORTUGAISE – Cut herrings into large pieces and cook in 2 dl. ($\frac{1}{3}$ pint, scant cup) *Tomato fondue* (see FONDUE).

Serve as above.

Smoked herring à la russe. HARENGS FUMÉS À LA RUSSE – Soak smoked herring fillets in milk or cold strained tea, skin, and cut crosswise into thin slices. Arrange in a dish, giving them their original shape. Season with several tablespoons *Vinaigrette sauce* (see SAUCE) to which chervil, tarragon, fennel and chopped shallots have been added. Add 2 to 3 tablespoons sour cream to the dressing.

Kilkis or Norwegian anchovies – See under *Anchovies* above.

Leeks à la grecque. POIREAUX À LA GRECQUE – Use the white part of large tender leeks. Cut into pieces $7\frac{1}{2}$ cm. (3 inches) long. Blanch and cook as indicated for *Artichokes à la grecque* (see above).

Lobster, spiny lobster and other shellfish. HOMARD, LANGOUSTE, CRUSTACÉS – Cut into dice, season with oil and vinegar, salt and pepper, or with mayonnaise.

Mackerel, marinated. MAQUEREAUX MARINÉS – can be bought ready prepared and should be served in an *hors-d'œuvre* dish or in the original container.

Marinated mackerel can also be prepared at home. Choose very small fish and proceed as for *Smelts in marinade* (see below).

Melon – Cut melons in half, drain, and take the seeds out. Cut in slices. Serve on a dish covered with green leaves. Surround with crushed ice.

The Italians serve thin slices of Parma ham with melon.

Small preserved melons. PETITS MELONS CONFITS – Proceed with very small melons as indicated in the recipe for *Gherkins in vinegar* (see GHERKINS).

Leave to soak for 10 days before serving. Serve in an *hors-d'œuvre* dish or in an earthenware jar.

Mortadella. MORTADELLE – Cut the Mortadella into thin slices. According to their diameter, divide the slices into halves or quarters. Arrange on an *hors-d'œuvre* dish, flat or rolled into cornets. Garnish with fresh parsley.

Mousse Fanchon – In France this *hors-d'œuvre* is also called *mousse mignonne*. It consists of various kinds of mousses.

Coat small moulds with jelly, fill them with the various mousses and decorate with small pieces of truffle. Put in the refrigerator.

Turn out the moulds just before serving. Put them on *canapés* of sandwich bread toasted and spread with a compound butter in keeping with the mousse. Arrange on a paper doyley.

Mousses Fanchon can also be served on tartlets or on artichoke hearts.

Mulberries. MÛRES FRAÎCHES – Serve plain in a fruit dish or on a plate covered with green leaves.

Mushrooms. CHAMPIGNONS – Cook in a white *Court-bouillon III* (see COURT-BOUILLON) mushrooms cut into small dice. Season with an oil and vinegar dressing, or with mayonnaise.

Marinated cèpes and mushrooms. CÈPES, CHAMPIGNONS MARINÉS – Use small firm white mushrooms. Parboil for 4 minutes in salted boiling water. Drain and dry. Put them in an earthenware dish and cover them with a boiling marinade, prepared as follows:

For 1 kg. ($2\frac{1}{4}$ lb.) mushrooms, boil together for 10 minutes, 5 dl. (scant pint, $2\frac{1}{4}$ cups) vinegar, $1\frac{1}{2}$ dl. ($\frac{1}{4}$ pint, $\frac{2}{3}$ cup) oil, 3 crushed cloves of garlic, a *bouquet garni* made of 2 parsley roots, $\frac{1}{2}$ bay leaf, a sprig of thyme and a little fennel, 1 teaspoon coriander, 6 to 8 peppercorns.

Leave the mushrooms in the marinade for 4 to 5 days. Serve in an *hors-d'œuvre* dish.

These mushrooms can be bottled in the prescribed marinade. Bottling jars of 1 litre (scant quart, generous quart) capacity must be boiled for 35 minutes; those of $\frac{1}{2}$ litre (scant pint, $2\frac{1}{4}$ cups) capacity need only 25 minutes.

Mussels. MOULES – Cook in white wine. Shell, dry, season with oil and vinegar, salt and pepper, or with mayonnaise.

Mussels à la ravigote. MOULES À LA RAVIGOTE – Cook and drain large mussels. Put them in a *terrine*. Season with *Vinaigrette sauce* (see SAUCE) to which hard-boiled eggs, parsley, chervil, tarragon and chopped gherkins have been added. Arrange on an *hors-d'œuvre* dish.

Mussel salad. SALADE DE MOULES – Prepare the mussels as for *Mussels à la marinière* (see MUSSEL). Shell them and dress with oil, vinegar, pepper and *fines herbes*. Serve in an *hors-d'œuvre* dish.

Mussels à la tartare. MOULES À LA TARTARE – Prepare some large mussels as for *Mussels à la marinière* (see MUSSEL). Shell them and arrange in an *hors-d'œuvre* dish. Mask with *Tartare sauce* (see SAUCE). Surround with half slices of lemon cut with a fluted knife.

Olives – Arrange on an *hors-d'œuvre* dish without dressing them.

Black olives. OLIVES NOIRES – These can be bought ready for the table and are served without dressing. Arrange on an *hors-d'œuvre* dish.

Stuffed olives. OLIVES FARCIES – Choose large stoned olives, which have been soaked to free them from salt. Stuff with a compound butter. The most usual stuffing for olives is *Anchovy butter* (see BUTTER, *Compound butters*). Arrange the stuffed olives on an *hors-d'œuvre* dish and dress with a few tablespoons oil.

Stuffed olives can also be bought.

Onions. OIGNONS – Cut raw onions into dice, blanch, drain, and season with oil, vinegar, salt and pepper, or with mayonnaise.

Onions à la grecque. OIGNONS À LA GRECQUE – Prepared like *Artichokes à la grecque* (see above).

Onions à l'orientale – See ONION.

Ox muzzle salad. MUSEAU DE BOEUF EN SALADE – Blanch, cool and drain the muzzle. Scrape and wash. Boil the muzzle in a white *court-bouillon* (q.v.), and leave it to cool in the pot. Drain, wipe dry and cut into very thin slices. Season with a strong *Vinaigrette sauce* (see SAUCE) to which onion and chopped parsley have been added.

Arrange on an *hors-d'œuvre* dish. Decorate with tiny rings or raw onions and chopped hard-boiled eggs.

This *hors-d'œuvre* can be bought ready-made.

Ox tongue salad. PALAIS DE BOEUF EN SALADE – Proceed as above.

Oysters

Oysters. HUÎTRES – Oysters are usually eaten raw. There are a number of recipes for serving oysters as a cold *hors-d'œuvre*. The most famous are *Oysters à l'andalouse, Oysters in barquettes, Oysters with caviare, The gastronome's oyster* and *Marinated oysters*. (See OYSTER.)

Pastry straws with anchovies. ALLUMETTES AUX ANCHOIS – Proceed as for *Allumettes with anchovies* (see *Hot hors-d'œuvre*) but serve cold.

Pastry straws with caviare. ALLUMETTES AU CAVIAR – Prepare pastry as for *Allumettes* (q.v.). Cover with a thin layer of *Fish forcemeat* (see FORCEMEATS) and cook in the oven. Cool and cover with fresh caviare.

Norwegian pastry straws. ALLUMETTES À LA NORVÉGIENNE – Prepare the pastry as for *Allumettes* (q.v.). Cover with a thin layer of a *salpicon* (q.v.) of hard-boiled eggs, blended with *Béchamel sauce* (see SAUCE). Bake in the oven. Leave to cool and garnish with Norwegian anchovy fillets.

Parisian pastry straws. ALLUMETTES À LA PARISIENNE – Prepare the pastry as for *Allumettes* (q.v.). Coat with a thin layer of chicken *Mousseline forcemeat* (see FORCEMEATS) and bake in the oven.

Cool, garnish with thin strips of breast of chicken alternating with slices of truffles and pickled tongue. Glaze with jelly.

Vladimir pastry straws. ALLUMETTES VLADIMIR – Prepare the pastry as for *Allumettes* (q.v.), coat with a thin layer of *Pike forcemeat* (see FORCEMEATS) and *Crayfish butter* (see BUTTER). Bake in the oven. Leave to cool, and garnish with small slices of smoked salmon, alternating with slices of truffles. Glaze with jelly.

Patties. BOUCHÉES – Very small patties made of puff pastry garnished with different mousses; prawns, shrimps, crayfish, *foie gras*, game, poultry, etc.

Fanchonnette patties. BOUCHÉES FANCHONNETTE – Make very small patties of puff pastry. Garnish with a salad of breast of chicken and a *salpicon* (q.v.) of red and green peppers with mayonnaise. Put a thick slice of truffle on each patty.

Small patties can be garnished in the same way as *canapés*, tartlets, and other similar preparations.

Peppers, sweet. PIMENTS DOUX – Skin the peppers, open them and take out the seeds. Cut into sticks and season with oil, vinegar, salt and pepper. Arrange in an *hors-d'œuvre* dish, sprinkle with chopped parsley, and garnish with thin rings of raw onion.

Peppers, small green. PETITS PIMENTS VERTS, POIVRONS – Proceed as indicated for *Sweet peppers* above.

Pickles – Arrange in an *hors-d'œuvre* dish or serve in the original container.

Pissalat (condiment) – This can be bought ready-made.

To make it yourself pickle a mixture of small shad, herrings, sardines and anchovies, for 8 days. Rub through a sieve and dilute with a few tablespoons of the brine in which the fish were pickled. Add some cloves and put into jars. Seal well and keep in a cool place.

Pissalat condiment can be used as it is, or with oil added to it.

Potatoes. POMMES DE TERRE – Cooked in water, cut into dice or sliced, seasoned with oil, vinegar, salt and pepper, or with mayonnaise.

Printanière – See *Spring vegetables* below.

Radishes, black. RADIS NOIRS – Scrape the radishes and cut into thin slices. Sprinkle them with salt and leave them to render their liquor for 30 minutes. Dry, and arrange in an *hors-d'œuvre* dish.

A little *Vinaigrette sauce* (see SAUCE) can be added. In Russia, black radish is generally served with a sour cream dressing.

Radishes, red and white. RADIS ROSES, RADIS GRIS – Scrape the radishes, cut the green part short, wash and arrange in an *hors-d'œuvre* dish. Serve with salt and fresh butter.

Red radishes are often used to decorate cold dishes and salad arrangements.

Red mullet à l'orientale or red mullet with saffron. ROUGETS À L'ORIENTALE, AU SAFRAN – Choose very small fish. Season with salt and pepper, roll in flour, deep-fry in hot oil.

Arrange the fish on an oiled baking dish. Cover with *Tomato fondue* (see FONDUE) spiced with a little saffron, fennel, thyme, powdered bayleaf, some grains of coriander, garlic and chopped parsley. Bring to the boil. Cover the dish and finish the cooking in the oven for 6 to 8 minutes.

Serve in an *hors-d'œuvre* dish with slices of peeled lemon. Sprinkle with chopped parsley.

Rollmops – Fillets of herring, marinated and strongly spiced. They are stuffed with a gherkin, rolled up and secured with a little wooden stick. Rollmops are served on an *hors-d'œuvre* dish decorated with rounds of onions.

Rollmops

Rolls, garnished. PETITS PAINS GARNIS – Choose very small oblong-shaped rolls made with butter. Similarly shaped rolls made from ordinary *Brioche dough* (see DOUGH) can also be used. Fill them *à la française*, or *à la russe*:

À la française. Cut open on one side only. Spread with butter (either ordinary butter or mustard butter). Garnish with thin slices of breast of chicken (or other poultry), ham, pickled tongue, fillet of beef, smoked salmon or similar items according to taste. Various purées or *foie gras* can also be used as stuffing.

À la russe. Take a round slice off the top of the rolls. Empty the rolls through this opening without breaking the crust. Fill the roll with a purée, a salad, or a *salpicon* (q.v.).

Arrange on a paper doyley, or on a napkin.

Rolls *à la française* are served at luncheon or as sandwiches.

Rolls *à la russe* should always be very small. They belong to the Russian *hors-d'œuvre* called *zakouski.*

Salami – Cut into thin slices, arrange on an *hors-d'œuvre* dish, garnish with fresh parsley.

Salmon à la canadienne. SAUMON À LA CANADIENNE – Cut the salmon in squares and sauté in oil. Season with salt and paprika.

Add okra pods (ladies' fingers) which have been poached separately. Moisten with white wine and lemon juice. Cover with a lid and simmer for a few seconds. Leave to cool.

Arrange in an *hors-d'œuvre* dish. Garnish with red and green peppers, peeled and cut into dice. Pour a little olive oil over the dish.

Fresh salmon can be served as an *hors-d'œuvre* following the instructions given for different kinds of fish as *hors-d'œuvre.*

Salmon paupiettes à l'impériale. PAUPIETTES DE SAUMON À L'IMPÉRIALE – Flatten thin narrow slices of salmon, season, coat lightly with a layer of *Pike forcemeat* (see FORCEMEATS) with a little shallot and some chopped parsley added. Roll up into the shape of *paupiettes* and secure with string.

Put the *paupiettes* into an oiled pan, packing them in fairly tightly. Moisten with a few tablespoons white wine and a squeeze of lemon juice. Season and add a little bouquet of fennel. Simmer very slowly with the lid on.

Drain the *paupiettes*, untie, and place each on a small artichoke heart cooked in a white wine stock. Arrange in an *hors-d'œuvre* dish, sprinkle with the stock in which the *paupiettes* have been cooked, and add a little olive oil and a few spices. Decorate with capers, half slices of lemon cut with a fluted cutter, and fresh parsley.

Salmon paupiettes au vert. PAUPIETTES DE SAUMON AU VERT – Prepare the *paupiettes* as in the preceding recipe. Cook them according to the instruction for *Eels au vert* (see EEL).

Smoked salmon. SAUMON FUMÉ – Cut the smoked salmon into very thin slices. Arrange on an *hors-d'œuvre* dish, flat or rolled into cornets. Garnish with fresh parsley.

Smoked salmon Boston style. SAUMON FUMÉ À LA BOSTONNAISE – Cut 100 g. (4 oz.) smoked salmon into very thin short strips. Add 100 g. (4 oz.) cooked mushrooms and 75 g. (3 oz.) each of green and red peeled pepper, cut in the same way. Season with mayonnaise mixed with a very little Tabasco sauce (commercial product). Arrange on an *hors-d'œuvre* dish, surround with the chopped yolks and whites of hard-boiled eggs, and sprigs of parsley. Sprinkle with chopped parsley and serve.

Smoked salmon à la moscovite. SAUMON FUMÉ À LA MOSCOVITE – Roll very small slices of smoked salmon into cornets. Fill with fresh caviare. Arrange the cornets in a circle on a plate. Decorate with the chopped yolks and whites of hard-boiled eggs, parsley and capers.

Salt cod, curried. ESCALOPES DE MORUE À L'INDIENNE – Soak the salt cod and cut into thin slices. Wash and dry the slices in a cloth. Flour lightly and cook in boiling oil.

Take the fish out of the pan. Cook 2 tablespoons (3 tablespoons) finely minced onion in the pan, sprinkle in 1 tablespoon curry powder, moisten with $1\frac{1}{2}$ dl. ($\frac{1}{4}$ pint, $\frac{2}{3}$ cup) white wine and a little lemon juice, and add a little crushed garlic. Boil for a few minutes and put the slices of cod into this *court-bouillon*. Bring to the boil again, cover and remove from the heat.

Cool, arrange in a dish and surround with lemon slices.

Salt cod tongues à la madrilène. LANGUES DE MORUES À LA MADRILÈNE – Cook an unpeeled clove of garlic in very hot oil. Toss the cod tongues in this oil.

Pour over the tongues a sufficient quantity of vinegar to cover them. Season with thyme, powdered bay leaf and red Spanish pepper. Cook in an open pan for 12 minutes, and sprinkle in a generous amount of freshly chopped fennel. Leave to cool in the stock.

Salt cod tongues, marinated. LANGUES DE MORUES MARINÉES – Soak the cod tongues to remove the salt. Dry, and fry in olive oil.

Moisten with white wine *court-bouillon* (q.v.) adding just enough to cover them. Cook slowly for 12 minutes. Put the tongues and the cooking liquor into a *terrine*. Leave to cool. Sprinkle with chopped parsley.

Sardines in oil. SARDINES À L'HUILE – Arrange on an *hors-d'œuvre* dish, dress with oil, and garnish with capers and fresh parsley.

Sardine purée. PURÉE DE SARDINES – Put in a mortar 12 well-boned sardines which have been kept in olive oil. Pound them in the mortar together with 4 yolks of hard-boiled eggs. Pass through a fine sieve and use for cold or hot *hors-d'œuvre*.

Sausages, various. SAUCISSONS – There are many different sausages which can be bought ready-made and served as *hors-d'œuvre*.

Cut into thin slices and arrange on an *hors-d'œuvre* dish with fresh parsley.

Saveloys (sausage). CERVELAS – Cook various kinds of saveloys and leave to cool. Cut into thin slices and serve like other sausages.

Sheep's trotters à la vinaigrette. PIEDS DE MOUTON À LA VINAIGRETTE – Cook the sheep's trotters in the usual way (see OFFAL or VARIETY MEATS). Drain, bone and cut into very small pieces. Season the meat while it is still hot, with oil, vinegar, salt, pepper, onions and chopped parsley. Arrange in small salad bowls or in an *hors-d'œuvre* dish.

Shellfish, mixed. FRUITS DE MER – Different kinds of shellfish served raw.

Shrimps. CREVETTES – Shrimps seasoned with oil, vinegar, salt and pepper, or with mayonnaise.

Shrimp salad. SALADE DE CREVETTES – Shell the shrimps and put them in a deep dish. Cover with mayonnaise. Garnish the dish with lettuce, leaving the centre free; fill this with rounds of hard-boiled eggs.

Sigui, smoked. SIGUI FUMÉ – Cut smoked *sigui* into very thin slices, arrange on an *hors-d'œuvre* dish and garnish with fresh parsley. You can also use smoked sigui for filling *barquettes, canapés*, tartlets, etc.

Smelts in marinade. ÉPERLANS MARINÉS – Clean and dry carefully chosen smelts. Roll in flour and fry them in boiling oil so that they quickly colour on both sides. Season.

Drain the smelts. Arrange them in a deep dish, cover with rounds of blanched onions and sprinkle with thyme and bay leaf. Add peppercorns and cloves. Cover with cold concentrated vinegar. Leave the smelts for 12 hours in this marinade. Serve in an *hors-d'œuvre* dish.

Sour-sweet pickles (aceto-dolce) – Different kinds of vegetables and fruits are commercially preserved in vinegar. They are then put in a syrup of must and honey spiced with mustard.

Arrange in an *hors-d'œuvre* dish or serve in the original jar.

Sprats – Take the heads and the tails off the fish and skin them. Arrange on a plate and sprinkle with chopped shallots and parsley. Moisten with oil and vinegar and leave to steep for several hours in this marinade before serving. Arrange on an *hors-d'œuvre* dish and garnish with fresh parsley.

Spring vegetables

Spring vegetables (printanière) – Cook diced French beans, carrots and turnips cut into very small squares, peas and asparagus tips in water. Drain and season with oil, vinegar, salt and pepper.

Tapenade (Provençale recipe) – This consists of olives pounded with desalted anchovy fillets and capers, the whole being blended with olive oil and lemon juice, then seasoned with pepper. Serve on toast.

Tartlets, garnished. TARTELETTES GARNIES – Garnished tartlets are prepared and filled in the same way as *barquettes*; the only difference lies in their shape. Tartlets are baked in small round tins with plain or fluted borders.

Toast, garnished. TOASTS GARNIS – All recipes for garnished *canapés* can be used for garnished toast.

Tomatoes. TOMATES – Peel and seed the tomatoes. Cut them into dice or slices. Sprinkle with salt, leave them to stand for a time and season with oil, vinegar, salt and pepper.

Tomatoes à l'antiboise. TOMATES À L'ANTIBOISE – Choose red, uniform, small tomatoes. Take out the seeds without damaging the flesh. Leave them for 1 hour in oil, vinegar, salt and pepper. Garnish with a mixture of chopped tunny (tuna fish) in oil, hard-boiled eggs, capers, parsley, chervil and tarragon blended with a strongly flavoured mayonnaise to which anchovy essence has been added. Arrange on

Stuffed tomatoes

an *hors-d'œuvre* dish or plate, sprinkle with the marinade, and garnish with fresh parsley and half slices of lemon cut with a fluted cutter.

Tomatoes, stuffed. TOMATES FARCIES – Prepare tomatoes as described in the recipe for *Tomatoes à l'antiboise* (see above). Garnish with a compound butter, purée, Russian salad, or a *salpicon* (q.v.).

Stuffed tomatoes presented in a hollowed-out cucumber

Tomatoes à la vinaigrette. TOMATES À LA VINAIGRETTE – Skin the tomatoes, take out the seeds and water and cut into slices or quarters. Put on a towel, cover with salt and leave them to render their liquor for 1 hour.

Arrange in an *hors-d'œuvre* dish, sprinkle with oil and vinegar, chopped parsley, chervil and tarragon. Sprinkle with freshly ground pepper and garnish with thin rounds of raw onion.

Tongue, pickled and smoked. LANGUE ÉCARLATE, FUMÉ – Cut into thin slices and serve in an *hors-d'œuvre* dish.

Trout, marinated. TRUITES MARINÉES – Cook very small trout in *Court-bouillon XII* (see COURT-BOUILLON). Leave them to cool in their cooking stock. Arrange in an *hors-d'œuvre* dish. Pour the stock over the fish and garnish with seeded and peeled slices of lemon, and fresh parsley.

Trout à l'orientale. TRUITES À L'ORIENTALE – Prepare and cook very small trout as indicated for *Red mullet à l'orientale* above. Arrange on an *hors-d'œuvre* dish.

Trout, smoked. TRUITES FUMÉES – Garnish and serve with toast and lemon.

Truffles. TRUFFES – Cut cooked or raw truffles into dice or strips, season with oil, vinegar, salt and pepper, or with mayonnaise. Truffles can also be blended with jelly or with a brown *Chaud-froid sauce* (see SAUCE).

Tunny (tuna fish). THON – Marinate in oil, cut into dice, season with oil, vinegar, salt and pepper, or mayonnaise.

Tunny (tuna fish) à la nantaise. THON À LA NANTAISE – Cut the fish into slices. Cover with a thin coating of *Horseradish butter* (see BUTTER, *Compound butters*). Arrange the slices two by two in a circle on a plate, alternating with rounds of cooked beetroot. Garnish the centre with a salad of mussels and potatoes. Sprinkle with chives and chopped tarragon.

Tunny (tuna fish) in oil. THON À L'HUILE – Arrange canned tunny on an *hors-d'œuvre* dish, dress with oil and garnish with capers or fresh parsley.

Vegetable boats, garnished. BARQUETTES DE LÉGUMES GARNIES – Pieces of vegetables, mainly beetroot and cucumber, shaped like boats, hollowed out and garnished in different ways.

All the fillings given for *barquettes* apply as garnishes for vegetable boats. The most usual garnishes for this kind of *hors-d'œuvre* are caviare, vegetable *macédoine*, purées, butter compounds, *salpicons* of shellfish.

Vegetable julienne. JULIENNE DE LÉGUMES – Cook the following fine *julienne* (q.v.) slowly in oil in a covered pan: 100 g. (4 oz., 1 cup) of the white part of leeks, 100 g. (4 oz., 1 cup) celery and 50 g. (2 oz., $\frac{1}{2}$ cup) onions. Season.

When three-quarters cooked add 50 g. (2 oz., 1 cup) raw mushrooms cut into *julienne* strips. Blend with fresh cream or mayonnaise, or leave as it is, according to what other dishes you are serving.

Whitebait, marinated. NONATS MARINÉS – Put the fish in a deep dish, and pour in a boiling marinade made with white wine. Cover and leave to cool before serving. Arrange in an *hors-d'œuvre* dish, sprinkle with chopped parsley, and surround with half slices of lemon cut with a fluted cutter.

Whitebait salad. SALADE DE NONATS – Put a twig of thyme, a bay leaf and some salt into a pot of water. Bring to the boil, put the fish in and boil for 1 minute. Drain, arrange in a salad bowl or an *hors-d'œuvre* dish, and sprinkle with *Vinaigrette sauce* (see SAUCE).

Zampino – Boned and stuffed pigs' trotters. Cook and leave to cool. Cut into thin slices and arrange on an *hors-d'œuvre* dish, garnished with parsley. *Zampino* can be bought ready cooked in shops selling Italian produce.

HOT HORS-D'ŒUVRE. HORS-D'ŒUVRE CHAUDS –

Allumettes – Puff pastry rectangles, spread with a suitable mixture and baked in the oven.

Make *Puff pastry* (see DOUGH). Roll out to a thickness of $\frac{1}{2}$ cm. ($\frac{1}{4}$ inch) and cut into ribbons $7\frac{1}{2}$ cm. (3 inches) long. Spread with a cold forcemeat of poultry or fish, and add the garnish appropriate to the recipe.

Cut the ribbons into rectangles about $2\frac{1}{2}$ cm. (1 inch) wide. Put on a baking sheet and bake in the oven for 12 to 15 minutes. Arrange on a napkin and serve very hot.

Allumettes with anchovies I. ALLUMETTES AUX ANCHOIS – Spread with *Fish forcemeat* (see FORCEMEAT) with *Anchovy butter* (see BUTTER, *Compound butters*.) Garnish with fillets of anchovy.

Allumettes with anchovies II. ALLUMETTES AUX ANCHOIS – Spread with *Salpicon* (q.v.) of fillets of anchovies and hard-boiled eggs blended with thick *Béchamel sauce* (see SAUCE).

Allumettes à l'andalouse – Spread with *Poultry forcemeat* (see FORCEMEAT) seasoned with paprika, mixed with a *salpicon* of lean ham and onions cooked in butter, also seasoned with paprika.

Allumettes à la chalonnaise – Spread with *Poultry forcemeat* (see FORCEMEAT) to which diced cocks' combs and kidneys, mushrooms and truffles have been added.

Allumettes Chavette – Spread with *Fish forcemeat* (see FORCEMEAT) with *Crayfish butter* (see BUTTER, *Compound butters*). Garnish with crayfish tails and truffles.

Allumettes à l'écarlate – Spread with *Veal forcemeat* (see FORCEMEAT) to which a *salpicon* of pickled or smoked tongue has been added.

Allumettes à l'écossaise – Spread with purée of haddock blended with thick *Béchamel sauce* (see SAUCE).

Allumettes à la florentine – Spread with spinach cooked in butter, blended with thick *Béchamel sauce* (see SAUCE), to which grated cheese has been added. Sprinkle with Parmesan cheese and brown in the oven just before serving.

Anchovy tart with pissalat. TOURTE D'ANCHOIS AU PISSALAT – Roll out *Lining paste* (see DOUGH) 1 cm. ($\frac{1}{2}$ inch) thick.

Line a large tart tin with the pastry, crimp the edges. Desalt fillets of anchovy, dry them well in a cloth and cover the pastry with them in a criss-cross pattern. Sprinkle with 1 tablespoon finely chopped onions and distribute 20 black olives on top. Dress with 3 tablespoons (scant $\frac{1}{4}$ cup) olive oil mixed with 2 tablespoons (3 tablespoons) *pissalat* (q.v.). Cook in a slow oven. Serve very hot.

Anchoyade I – Desalt and scrape fillets of anchovy and steep them for several minutes in olive oil to which chopped garlic and ground pepper have been added.

Arrange the fillets on large pieces of crust cut from the lower part of home-made bread. Crush the fillets onto the bread by pressing them with other pieces of bread cut into squares, which are then removed. The diners eat these squares one after the other, as they become impregnated with anchovy.

Moisten the crusts with the oil in which the fillets have soaked, and grill.

This Provençal dish is known in the Bouches-du-Rhône district under the name of *quichet*.

Anchoyade II – Desalt fillets of anchovy. Pound, moistening with a few tablespoons olive oil and vinegar.

Spread this purée on large slices of bread. Cover with slices of hard-boiled eggs and minced onions. Add a few drops of olive oil, season with freshly ground pepper and heat lightly in the oven.

Attereaux – Name given to the method of cooking on skewers, in which the ingredients, instead of being grilled, are coated with a sauce, dipped into egg and breadcrumbs, and fried.

All the ingredients are first cooked, then cut into pieces. Any ingredient used for *attereaux* must be quite cold before it is put on a wooden or metal skewer. The different ingredients used are garnished according to their nature with mushrooms, truffles, etc.

The sauce must be thick and almost cold. When the skewer is full and coated with sauce it is left to get quite cold before it is dipped into egg and breadcrumbs. *Attereaux* are fried just before serving, drained and dried, arranged on a napkin and garnished with fresh parsley.

If wooden skewers are used they are taken out when the cooking is finished and replaced by silver skewers for serving.

Use short metal skewers instead of wooden ones if possible. This does away with the necessity of replacing the skewers after cooking.

In ancient times *attereaux* were served as an *entrée volante* or small *entrée*. They were served in a circle on a crust of fried sandwich bread, or on a foundation of rice.

All kinds of meat, fish, shellfish and a variety of other food, cut into small square pieces, can be used for *attereaux*.

The sauce can be white or brown, made from meat, fish or vegetable stock, according to the principal ingredient of the *attereaux*. This ingredient determines the name given to the *attereaux* on the menu.

Attereaux à l'écarlate – Pickled or smoked tongue, mushrooms and truffles coated with thick *Velouté sauce* (see SAUCE) with tomato purée added.

Attereaux à la Villeroi – Brains, cocks' combs or combs of other birds, *foie gras*, sweetbreads, cocks' kidneys, etc. The dish may be completed with the additions of mushrooms, truffles, artichoke hearts, pickled tongue, ham, etc. Poultry or other cold meat can be used in the same way. Coat with *Villeroi sauce* (see SAUCE).

Attereaux of brain à l'ancienne. ATTEREAUX DE CERVELLE À L'ANCIENNE – Poached brain, mushrooms and truffles coated with *Villeroi sauce* (see SAUCE).

Attereaux of brain à l'italienne. ATTEREAUX DE CERVELLE À L'ITALIENNE – Poached brain, ham and mushrooms coated with *Duxelles sauce* (see SAUCE).

Attereaux of brain à la mirepoix. ATTEREAUX DE CERVELLE À LA MIREPOIX – Poached brain and ham coated with *mirepoix* (q.v.) of vegetables blended with *Villeroi sauce* (see SAUCE).

Attereaux of chicken livers à la duxelles. ATTEREAUX DE FOIES DE VOLAILLE À LA DUXELLES – Chicken livers browned lightly in butter and mushrooms coated with *Duxelles sauce* (see SAUCE).

Attereaux of cocks' combs à l'ancienne. ATTEREAUX DE CRÊTES DE COQ À L'ANCIENNE – Cocks' combs stuffed *à la duxelles* (q.v.), ham and mushrooms coated with *Villeroi sauce* (see SAUCE) with tomatoes.

Attereaux of lobster. ATTEREAUX DE HOMARD – Lobster, mushrooms and truffles coated with *Villeroi sauce* (see SAUCE) or *Shellfish butter* (see BUTTER, *Compound butters*).

Attereaux of oysters. ATTEREAUX D'HUÎTRES – Poached oysters and mushrooms coated with *Villeroi sauce* (see SAUCE) based on fish stock.

Attereaux of Parmesan, also known as à la royale and à la princesse. ATTEREAUX AU PARMESAN – Cook a stiff semolina with Parmesan. Spread out to cool on a baking sheet in a $\frac{1}{2}$-cm. ($\frac{1}{4}$-inch) layer. When quite cold, cut into circlets $2\frac{1}{2}$ cm. (1 inch) in diameter. Put these on the skewers, alternating with rounds of Gruyère cheese. Coat with egg and breadcrumbs, but not with any sauce.

Attereaux of sweetbreads. ATTEREAUX DE RIS D'AGNEAU, RIS DE VEAU – Sweetbreads, mushrooms and truffles coated with *Villeroi sauce* (see SAUCE).

Attereaux of various vegetables. ATTEREAUX DE LÉGUMES – Cooked or parboiled vegetables, such as artichoke hearts, carrots, celeriac, pumpkin, etc. One of these or various combinations can be used.

Coat with thick *Béchamel sauce* (see SAUCE).

Barquettes, garnished. BARQUETTES GARNIES – Oval-shaped tartlets lined with different kinds of pastry (puff pastry, ordinary lining (pie) pastry, etc.) baked blind and filled with different ingredients.

Roll out the pastry $2\frac{1}{2}$ mm. ($\frac{1}{8}$ inch) thick. Stamp the dough out with a fluted oval pastry-cutter. Butter *barquette* baking tins, plain or fluted. Put the cut-out pieces of pastry into the moulds, pressing well down so that they cling to all sides of the tins.

Prick the pastry lining the base of the tins to prevent blistering. Put greaseproof paper in each and fill the tins with dried peas or rice. Bake in a moderate oven for 12 to 15 minutes. Remove the paper and the peas or rice. Take the pastry out of the tins, brush with egg and put back into the oven for a few minutes to dry, leaving the oven door open.

This way of preparing pastry is called baking blind (unfilled). The reason for filling the tartlets with dried vegetables or cereals (which are taken out after cooking and can be used again) is to keep the pastry uniformly hollow.

Fillings for barquettes. The ingredients of the fillings vary according to the recipe chosen. The most usual are purées, *ragoûts* and *salpicons*. You can also fill *barquettes* with the garnishes given for patties, tartlets, etc.

Once filled, serve the *barquettes* as they are, or sprinkle with fried breadcrumbs or grated cheese and brown under the grill. Decorate as indicated in the recipe.

Serving barquettes. Cover a dish with a napkin or a paper doyley and arrange the *barquettes* on it. Garnish with parsley.

Barquettes can be served as a small *entrée* or *entrée volante*. In this case they should be baked in slightly bigger moulds than for *hors-d'œuvre*.

Barquettes à l'américaine – Fill with a *salpicon* (q.v.) of spiny lobster and *Lobster à l'américaine* (see LOBSTER), sprinkle with fried breadcrumbs and put in the oven for a short time.

Barquettes with anchovies. BARQUETTES AUX ANCHOIS – Desalt anchovy fillets. Dice mushrooms and onions and cook slowly in butter. Blend all together with *Béchamel sauce* (see SAUCE). Bake the *barquettes* blind and fill them with the above *salpicon*. Sprinkle with breadcrumbs fried in butter and drained. Put into a very hot oven for a few minutes.

Barquettes à la bouquetière – Blend mixed vegetables with *Béchamel* or *Velouté sauce* (see SAUCE). Fill the *barquettes* and put on each a small bouquet of asparagus tips.

Barquettes with chestnuts. BARQUETTES AUX MARRONS – Use *Fine lining paste* (see DOUGH) and bake cases for *barquettes*, as indicated above. Fill with *Chestnut purée* (see CHESTNUT). Pile the purée into a dome and smooth the surface. Sprinkle with grated Parmesan cheese. Pour melted butter over it and brown in a hot oven.

Barquettes with mussels. BARQUETTES DE MOULES – Prepare *Mussels à la poulette* (see MUSSELS), fill the *barquettes*, sprinkle fried breadcrumbs over them, and put in the oven for a few minutes.

Barquettes with oysters. BARQUETTES D'HUÎTRES – Poach the oysters and drain. Fill the *barquettes* and cover with *Oyster sauce* (see SAUCE). Brown in a very hot oven.

Barquettes with shrimps. BARQUETTES DE CREVETTES – Make a *ragoût* of shrimp tails. Fill the *barquettes*. Spoon over some *Mornay sauce* (see SAUCE). Sprinkle with cheese and brown under the grill.

Beurrecks à la turque I – Dice 225 g. (8 oz., 2 cups) Gruyère cheese, mix with 1 dl. (6 tablespoons, scant ½ cup) thick, almost cold, *Béchamel sauce* (see SAUCE) and leave to get quite cold.

Divide the mixture into small portions of about 50 g. (2 oz.) and mould into cigar shapes. Make some ordinary noodle paste (see NOODLES, *Fresh noodles*), roll out wafer thin, enclose each portion of cheese mixture in an oval piece of noodle paste, dip in egg and breadcrumbs and fry just before serving.

Beurrecks à la turque II – Make the mixture of cheese and *Béchamel sauce* as in the above recipe.

Make ordinary noodle paste, roll out wafer thin, cut into round pieces, put the cheese and *Béchamel* mixture on the paste and fold it like a turnover. Dip in egg and breadcrumbs and fry just before serving.

Blinis (Russian cookery) – *Blinis* are pancakes made with yeast, very popular in Russia. They are often served with fresh caviare sprinkled with melted butter, or with sour cream.

First method. Dilute 7 g. (¼ oz.) yeast in 2 dl. (⅓ pint, scant cup) warm milk. Mix, do not let curdle, pass through a strainer. Sieve 125 g. (4½ oz., generous cup) white flour and 150 g. (5 oz., 1¼ cups) buckwheat flour, and mix together with a pinch of salt. Put in a bowl and add the liquid. Mix in the yolks of 3 eggs. The paste should have the consistency of pancake batter and care should be taken to keep it light.

Leave to rise in a warm place for 2 hours.

Add 2 beaten egg whites and 2½ dl. (scant ½ pint, generous cup) whipped cream. Cover and leave to rise for 20 minutes.

Second method. Make a yeast batter using 250 g. (9 oz., 2¼ cups) sifted flour, 15 g. (½ oz.) yeast, and 2½ dl. (scant ½ pint, generous cup) warm milk. Leave in a warm place for 2 hours.

Add 125 g. (4½ oz., generous cup) flour, a pinch of salt, 2 egg yolks and 1½ dl. (¼ pint, ⅔ cup) warm milk. Mix. Add 2 beaten egg whites.

Cover and leave to rise for 30 minutes.

Third method. Put into a bowl 250 g. (9 oz., 2¼ cups) buckwheat flour and 25 g. (1 oz.) yeast. Moisten with 2½ dl. (scant ½ pint, generous cup) warm water. Leave to ferment in a cool place for 4 hours.

Add 125 g. (4½ oz., generous cup) fine white flour, a pinch of salt, 2 egg yolks and 1½ dl. (¼ pint, ⅔ cup) warm cream.

Mix, add 2 firmly beaten egg whites and half their volume of whipped cream, and leave to rise for 20 minutes.

Blinis can also be made of rice flour or maize (corn) flour.

Cooking of blinis. In France, *blinis* are cooked in the same way as ordinary pancakes (*crêpes*).

In Russia, *blinis* are fried in special cast-iron frying pans, divided into flat 'nests', in which up to 6 small, individual pancakes can be cooked at once. They are served very hot, with melted butter, sour cream, chopped hard-boiled eggs in melted butter, caviare, smoked salmon, *kilki*, salted herring, and other similar 'fishy' foods.

Blinis with carrots. BLINIS AUX CAROTTES – Dice 1 tablespoon carrots, cook in butter and pour the *blini* mixture over. Continue as usual.

Blinis with caviare. BLINIS AU CAVIAR – Prepare the *blinis* according to one of the methods described above.

Serve piping hot with fresh caviare, melted butter and sour cream.

Blinis with eggs. BLINIS AUX OEUFS – Before putting the *blini* mixture into a buttered frying pan, sprinkle into the pan 1 tablespoon chopped hard-boiled eggs.

Cook the *blinis* in the usual way.

Lithuanian blinis. BLINIS LIVONIENS – Mix in a bowl 4 tablespoons (⅓ cup) flour and 4 whole eggs. Add, little by little, 4 glasses of milk, a pinch of salt and a pinch of sugar.

Add 4 beaten egg whites and 4 tablespoons (⅓ cup) whipped cream.

Cook the *blinis* in the usual way.

Brioches, garnished. BRIOCHES GARNIES – These brioches must be very small. They are often served as patties.

Use ordinary unsweetened brioche dough. Bake the brioches in very small fluted moulds in the shape of *Brioches à tête* (see BRIOCHE).

Leave them to cool. Remove the heads, keeping them to serve as lids. Scoop out the brioches, taking care not to break them. Dry them for a few minutes in the oven with the door open.

Small *Brioches à tête* may be filled with the same ingredients as given for *Patties* (see below). When garnished, put the heads back on the brioches and put in the oven for a few seconds.

Small garnished brioches can be used as an accompaniment for large dishes of various kinds.

Brochettes – Prepare *brochettes* according to the recipes given in their alphabetical order. (See SKEWER, BEEF,

Fillet of beef on skewers, MUTTON, *Fillets of mutton on skewers*.)

Brochettes served as an *hors-d'œuvre* should be very much smaller than those prepared for an *entrée*.

Brochettes de Parme – Another name for *Attereaux of Parmesan*. (See *Attereaux* above.)

Brochettes of sweetbreads. BROCHETTES DE RIS D'AGNEAU, RIS DE VEAU – Parboil or braise lamb or calf sweetbreads, cut into square pieces. Put them on metal skewers, alternating with rectangles of lean blanched bacon or lean ham and, if desired, with cooked, sliced mushrooms.

Brush the *brochettes* with melted butter, roll in fine breadcrumbs and grill under a moderate heat.

Caissettes (small garnished cases) – Round or oval receptacles made of ovenproof china, glass or metal, filled with *ragoûts* (q.v.), *salpicons* (q.v.) or similar ingredients. Recipes for these are given elsewhere; they are the same as for *barquettes*, patties, pies, tartlets, etc.

According to the nature of the garnish used the cases are sprinkled with breadcrumbs or grated cheese and put under the grill. Alternatively, they may be sprinkled with well-drained fried breadcrumbs, and put in the oven. A third possibility is to decorate the cases with truffles, mushrooms, etc.

Canapés or garnished toast. CANAPÉS, TOASTS GARNIS – Cut the *canapés* from a sandwich loaf, having first removed the crust. Shape them, as required, into squares, rectangles, ovals or rounds. Toast the slices on both sides, butter them or spread with whatever ingredient is indicated in the chosen recipe (forcemeat, scrambled eggs, purées, *salpicon* (q.v.), etc.).

Garnish the *canapés* as indicated, sprinkle with freshly grated breadcrumbs, fried breadcrumbs or grated cheese, according to the garnish used, and grill, or brown them in the oven. Arrange on a paper doyley or napkin and decorate with green curly parsley.

Garnishes for *canapés* are numerous. Apart from those given in the recipes which follow, you can use all those indicated in the section on *Croûtes* (see below).

Canapés with bloater. CANAPÉS AU BLOATER – Cut sandwich loaf into rounds and toast. Heap the bloater purée, to which *Béchamel sauce* (see SAUCE) and butter have been added, on the rounds, and heat in the oven.

Alternatively, garnish the *canapés* as indicated above, but sprinkle them with grated Parmesan cheese and brown them in the oven.

Canapés with hard-boiled eggs. CANAPÉS AUX ŒUFS DURS – Spread a *salpicon* of hard-boiled eggs blended with *Béchamel sauce* (see SAUCE), on rectangular pieces of toast. Cover each piece with two rounds of hard-boiled egg. Fry breadcrumbs in butter, drain well, sprinkle on the *canapés*, and brown lightly in the oven.

Canapés with scrambled eggs. CANAPÉS AUX ŒUFS BROUILLÉS – Cover rounds of toast with scrambled eggs arranged in a dome. Sprinkle with grated Parmesan cheese and brown in the oven.

Canapés à la florentine – Toast rounds of sandwich bread. Parboil some spinach, drain and rub through a sieve. Blend with thick *Béchamel sauce* (see SAUCE) and spread on the toast. Sprinkle with grated Parmesan cheese and brown in the oven.

Canapés with Gruyère cheese. CANAPÉS AU FROMAGE DE GRUYÈRE – Spread the *canapés* with a layer of thick *Béchamel sauce* (see SAUCE) to which grated Gruyère cheese and a pinch of cayenne have been added. Scatter diced Gruyère cheese over the *canapés* and brown in the oven.

Canapés can be made in the same way with Cheshire, Edam or Parmesan cheese.

Canapés with ham. CANAPÉS AU JAMBON – Cut a sandwich loaf into oval-shaped slices and toast. Make a *salpicon* of York or Prague ham and blend it with a concentrated *Demi-glace sauce* (see SAUCE) to which chopped parsley has been added. Spread the *salpicon* on the toast.

Fry slices of ham in butter and put one on each *canapé*. Sprinkle with breadcrumbs fried in butter.

Canapés with sardines. CANAPÉS AUX SARDINES – Toast rectangular pieces of bread. Cover with fillets of sardines. Heat for a few moments in the oven. Arrange on a napkin.

Altnernatively, make a purée of sardines in oil, mixed with hard-boiled eggs. Rub through a sieve and add a little English mustard. Spread on the *canapés* and arrange fillets of sardines in oil on top.

Sprinkle with breadcrumbs which have been fried in butter and drained well. Put in the oven for a few minutes. Season with a pinch of cayenne and serve.

Canapés Victoria – Make a *salpicon* of lobster or spiny lobster, truffles and mushrooms, all cut into very small dice, blended with thick *Béchamel sauce* (see SAUCE) and finished off with *Crayfish butter* (see BUTTER, *Compound butters*).

Spread toast with this *salpicon*. Fry breadcrumbs in butter, drain well, and sprinkle on the *canapés*. Put them in the oven for a few moments.

Cannelons, garnished. CANNELONS GARNIS – These can be of rectangular shape or made as cornets.

Rectangular. Roll out puff pastry in rectangles measuring 4 cm. ($1\frac{1}{2}$ inches) by 10 cm. (4 inches).

Using a forcing-bag with a plain nozzle make a line of cold forcemeat or other mixture in the middle of the rectangles. Moisten the border all around the forcemeat, and cover with another rectangle of puff pastry. Brush over with egg and bake in the oven.

Cornets. Cut the dough into straight ribbons and roll around special 'funnels' (see CORNETS).

When the cornets are baked, take the funnels out and fill the cornets. Use *salpicons* (q.v.), meat purée, fish or shellfish purée, etc., as fillings. The purées should be rather thick.

All the garnishes given for *barquettes*, patties, *cassolettes*, and similar dishes can be used for *cannelons*.

Cassolettes – Individual glass, metal or porcelain containers. The most usual ingredients for *cassolettes* are purées, *ragoûts* (q.v.), *salpicons* (q.v.) and similar preparations.

Cassolettes without a border. Fill the *cassolettes* with the preparation indicated.

Sprinkle with breadcrumbs fried in butter and drained, or, according to the recipe used, with grated cheese. Brown for a few moments in the oven.

Cassolettes with a border of Duchess potato. Use a forcing-bag and pipe a thin border of *Duchess potato* (see POTATOES) round the edge of the *cassolette*.

Fill with the preparation indicated, sprinkle with breadcrumbs fried in butter and drained, or with grated cheese, and brown in the oven.

Cassolettes topped with Duchess potato. Prepare the *cassolettes* as indicated in the above recipe. Fill as described and cover with a layer of *Duchess potato* (see POTATOES) pressing down on the edges to seal in the contents. Brush the top with egg and brown in the oven.

Cassolettes with border and covered with puff pastry. Put a narrow band of puff pastry round the rim of the *cassolettes*. Fill them with the desired preparation, which should be cold or lukewarm.

Cover the *cassolettes* with a round of puff pastry. Press well onto the border. Decorate with flower-shaped ornaments or other motifs made from puff pastry. Brush with egg and bake in the oven for 10 to 12 minutes.

Cassolettes ambassadrice – Make a lid and a border for the *cassolettes*, using *Duchess potatoes* (see POTATOES). Fill with a *ragoût* of chicken livers. Put in the oven for a few minutes.

Cassolettes bouquetière – Make the border of the *cassolettes* with *Duchess potatoes* (see POTATOES). Fill with a *macédoine* of vegetables with cream.

Put in the oven. When removed from the oven put 1 tablespoon asparagus tips cooked in butter, and a little knob of cauliflower, on each *cassolette*.

Cassolettes à la florentine (with meat) – Use *Duchess potatoes* (see POTATOES) to make the top of the *cassolettes*. Put 1 tablespoon spinach leaves cooked in butter at the bottom. Put 1 tablespoon *salpicon* of chicken blended with *Velouté sauce* (see SAUCE) on the spinach. Brown in the oven.

Cassolettes à la gauloise – Use *Duchess potatoes* (see POTATOES) to make the border of the cassolettes. Fill with a *salpicon* of cocks' combs and kidneys, truffles and mushrooms blended with *Velouté sauce* (see SAUCE).

Brown in the oven. When removed from the pan put a cock's comb fried *à la Villeroi* on each *cassolette*.

Cassolettes with lobster or spiny lobster. CASSOLETTES AU HOMARD, À LA LANGOUSTE – Make the border or top of whatever preparation you desire. Fill with a *salpicon* of lobster or spiny lobster blended with cream and finished off with *Crayfish butter* (see BUTTER, *Compound butters*). Brown in the oven.

Cassolettes marquise – Make the border of puff pastry. Fill with *Crayfish tail ragoût à la Nantua* (see CRAYFISH) to which diced truffles and mushrooms have been added. Bake in the oven.

Cassolettes Régence – Make a border of *Duchess potatoes* (see POTATOES). Fill with a *salpicon* of breast of chicken and truffles cooked in *Velouté sauce* (see SAUCE).

Bake in the oven. Put a large slice of truffle on each *cassolette* when removed from the oven, and cover with a small bouquet of asparagus tips cooked in butter.

Cassolettes Sagan (without a border) – Fill with a *salpicon* of truffles and mushrooms cooked in *Velouté sauce* (see SAUCE). Sprinkle with grated Parmesan cheese. Brown in the oven. When taken out, put on each *cassolette* a very small slice of calf's brain sautéed in butter.

Cassolettes of sweetbread. CASSOLETTES DE RIS D'AGNEAU, RIS DE VEAU – These can have a border or be served plain. Fill with a *salpicon* of sweetbread blended with *Velouté sauce* (see SAUCE) to which truffles and mushrooms can be added, if desired. Sprinkle with fried breadcrumbs and brown in the oven.

Cassolettes à la vénitienne (without a border) – Line the bottom of the *cassolettes* with diced macaroni *à l'italienne*. Add 1 tablespoon *ragoût* of sweetbreads, truffles and mushrooms, if desired. Sprinkle with fried breadcrumbs and brown in the oven.

Choux (U.S. cream puffs) – Using *Ordinary chou paste* (see DOUGH), make small *choux* (cream puffs), the size of pigeons' eggs.

After the *choux* are cooked, split the sides open and fill with whatever preparation is indicated in the recipe used. Heat for a few moments in the oven.

If the choux are small enough they can be used as a garnish for large dishes, or served as savouries. *Choux* can be filled with all the preparations recommended for *barquettes, cassolettes*, tartlets and other similar dishes.

Choux with cheese. CHOUX AU FROMAGE – Filled with a cream made with Cheshire, Gruyère or Parmesan cheese.

Choux à la maraîchère – Filled with a *salpicon* (q.v.) of carrots, leeks, celery – all cooked in butter and blended with thick *Béchamel sauce* (see SAUCE).

Choux à la Nantua – Filled with a purée of crayfish to which chopped truffles have been added.

Choux à la royale – Filled with a purée of truffles with cream.

Choux à la Saint-Hubert – Filled with a purée of game blended with *Demi-glace sauce* (see SAUCE) based on concentrated game stock.

Choux à la strasbourgeoise – Filled with a *salpicon* of *foie gras* and truffles blended with concentrated *Demi-glace sauce* (see SAUCE).

Choux à la toulousaine – Filled with a *salpicon* of sweetbreads, cocks' combs and cocks' kidneys, mushrooms and truffles blended with *Allemande sauce* (see SAUCE).

Choux au vert-pré – Filled with a purée of green beans, green peas and asparagus tips blended with cream.

Cierniki (Polish cookery) – Mix in a *terrine* 225 g. (8 oz.) pressed white cheese, 100 g. (4 oz., 1 cup) sifted flour, 50 g. (2 oz., $\frac{1}{4}$ cup) melted butter and 3 eggs. Season with salt, pepper and grated nutmeg. Blend these ingredients with a spatula and gradually work in a further 75 g. (3 oz., $\frac{3}{4}$ cup) flour.

Experiment with poaching 1 teaspoon of this mixture in boiling water. If it is not thick enough add a little more flour, if it is too thick, lighten it with 1 or 2 tablespoons cream.

Sprinkle flour on a table and roll the mixture out on it. Shape into small *galettes* 5 cm. (2 inches) in diameter and 1 cm. ($\frac{1}{2}$ inch) thick. Poach for 15 to 18 minutes in boiling water, drain, arrange in a pie dish and pour melted butter over them.

Cocks' combs. CRÊTES DE COQ – For two recipes using cocks' combs see *Attereaux* and *Fritot* in this section.

Cocks' combs Villeroi. CRÊTES DE COQ VILLEROI – Drain cocks' combs cooked in a white *court-bouillon* (q.v.) and put them in a lukewarm *Villeroi sauce* (see SAUCE).

Take them out and dip them one by one in finely grated breadcrumbs. Each cock's comb must be completely covered. Dip in beaten egg and again in breadcrumbs.

Fry just before serving and heap on a napkin or arrange in a nest of straw potatoes. Garnish with fried parsley.

Serve with *Tomato sauce* or *Périgueux sauce* (see SAUCE).

Stuffed cocks' combs Villeroi. CRÊTES DE COQ FARCIES VILLEROI – Choose very large cocks' combs. Cook, and then open them on the fleshy side without cutting right through. Stuff them with a little forcemeat. Complete the cooking and serving as in the preceding recipe.

Cocks' combs can be stuffed with forcemeats, or purées of mushrooms, *foie gras*, different vegetables, *duxelles* (q.v.), *brunoise* (q.v.), *portugaise* (q.v.), etc.

Cocks' kidneys. ROGNONS DE COQ – Cook kidneys in *Court-bouillon I* (see COURT-BOUILLON). Then follow any of the recipes for cocks' combs in this section.

Colombines – Line buttered tartlet tins with a semolina mixture flavoured with Parmesan cheese. Fill the tins with a *salpicon* (q.v.), a purée or any other mixture generally used for *barquettes*, patties and similar dishes. Cover with a thin layer of semolina.

Dip the tins into warm water and turn out the tartlets. Dip them in egg and breadcrumbs and deep-fry. Serve with fried parsley.

Craquelins – *Croquettes* prepared with stuffed pancakes (*crêpes*). This *hors-d'œuvre* is better known under the name of *pannequet*.

Crayfish. ÉCREVISSES – Small crayfish, cooked *à la nage*, *à la marinière*, or *à la liégeoise*, can be served as hot *hors-d'œuvre*. Crayfish tails are often used as the principal ingredient in hot *hors-d'œuvre* such as fitters, croquettes, stuffed potatoes, rissoles, soufflés or tartlets.

Cromesquis – See *Kromeskies* in this section.

Croquets – A variety of croquettes made of pasta, macaroni, spaghetti, etc.

Begin by poaching the pasta in salted water. Drain, and cut into dice. Blend with thick *Béchamel sauce* (see SAUCE) and add grated cheese.

This preparation can be finished off with lean ham or scarlet tongue cut into *julienne* (q.v.) strips. Serve with *Tomato sauce* (see SAUCE).

Croquettes – Croquettes served as hot *hors-d'œuvre* are composed of one or several preparations cut into small dice (or, in certain cases, chopped). They are blended with a white or brown sauce based on meat, fish or vegetable stock. (See CROQUETTES.)

Beef croquettes I. CROQUETTES DE BOEUF – Minced boiled beef, blended with a beaten egg; and chopped parsley. Shape according to taste.

Serve with *Tomato sauce* (see SAUCE).

Beef croquettes II. CROQUETTES DE BOEUF – *Salpicon* of boiled beef, mushrooms and lean ham, blended with concentrated *Demi-glace sauce* (see SAUCE), and shaped according to taste.

Serve with *Piquant sauce* (see SAUCE).

Beef croquettes III. CROQUETTES DE BOEUF – *Salpicon* of boiled beef and lean ham, blended with thick *Béchamel sauce* (see SAUCE). Shape according to taste. Serve with *Tomato sauce* (see SAUCE).

Beef croquettes IV. CROQUETTES DE BOEUF – Two-thirds *salpicon* of boiled beef, one-third rice cooked in meat stock. Shape according to taste.

Serve with *Tomato sauce* (see SAUCE).

Beef croquettes V. CROQUETTES DE BOEUF – *Salpicon* of corned beef (pressed beef) blended with *Demi-glace sauce* or *Béchamel sauce* (see SAUCE).

Serve with *Tomato sauce* (see SAUCE).

Beef croquettes made of left-overs. Many preparations can be made by adding to the boiled beef different ingredients like spinach, lettuce, celery or other chopped vegetables, grated cheese, chopped onion cooked in butter, tomato *fondue*, purées of fresh and dried vegetables, *mirepoix* of vegetables, bread soaked in *bouillon* or in milk, etc.

Bone-marrow croquettes. CROQUETTES D'AMOURETTES – *Salpicon* of bone-marrow and mushrooms blended with *Allemande sauce* (see SAUCE). Shape to look like corks and serve *Tomato sauce* (see SAUCE) separately.

Brain croquettes. CROQUETTES DE CERVELLE – Prepare like *Bone-marrow croquettes* using a *salpicon* of sheep's or calf's brain. Shape according to taste.

Cod croquettes. CROQUETTES DE MORUE – These are also called fish balls or fish cakes. They are made of two-thirds cod, which should be cooked. drained, and cut into pieces, mixed with one-third *Duchess potatoes* (see POTATOES) blended with thick *Béchamel sauce* (see SAUCE). Shape into balls.

Serve with *Tomato sauce* (see SAUCE).

Cress croquettes. CROQUETTES CRESSONNIÈRE – Purée of watercress to which *Duchess potatoes* (see POTATOES) have been added. Blend with *Velouté sauce* (see SAUCE) flavoured with mixed herbs. Shape according to taste.

Fish croquettes. CROQUETTES DE POISSONS – A *salpicon* composed solely of the fish prescribed, blended with *Béchamel* or *Allemande sauce* (see SAUCE). Shape according to taste and serve with a sauce in character with the fish used for the croquettes.

These croquettes are usually served in the shape of balls. *Duchess potatoes* (see POTATOES) should be added to the ingredients and the croquettes served with *Tomato sauce* (see SAUCE).

Diced mushrooms and truffles can also be added to the ingredients of fish croquettes.

Foie gras croquettes à la Périgueux. CROQUETTES DE FOIE GRAS À LA PÉRIGUEUX – *Salpicon* of *foie gras* and truffles, blended with a very strong *Demi-glace sauce* flavoured with Madeira, or with *Allemande sauce* (see SAUCE). Shape into little flat cakes, and serve with *Périgueux sauce* (see SAUCE).

Foie gras croquettes à la reine. CROQUETTES DE FOIE GRAS À LA REINE – *Salpicon* of *foie gras*, bound with *Allemande sauce* (see SAUCE). Shape into little flat cakes and serve with *Suprême sauce* (see SAUCE), adding truffles.

Game croquettes. CROQUETTES DE GIBIER – *Salpicon* of game left-overs, mushrooms and truffles, blended with very concentrated *Demi-glace sauce* (see SAUCE). Serve with *demi-glace sauce* based on concentrated game stock.

On the menu, name the croquettes after the game which is predominant in their preparation, e.g., *pheasant croquettes, venison croquettes*, etc.

Croquettes can be prepared from a mixture of different kinds of game.

Lobster croquettes I. CROQUETTES DE HOMARD – *Salpicon* of lobster to which diced mushrooms and truffles have been added, blended with thick *Béchamel sauce* (see SAUCE).

Serve with *White wine sauce* (see SAUCE).

Lobster croquettes II. CROQUETTES DE HOMARD – *Salpicon* of lobster, mushrooms and truffles, blended with *Allemande sauce* (see SAUCE), finished with *Crayfish butter* (see BUTTER, *Compound butters*) or any shellfish butter.

Serve with *Lobster sauce* (see SAUCE).

Lobster croquettes III. CROQUETTES DE HOMARD – Two-thirds *salpicon* of lobster, one-third rice cooked in meat or fish stock.

Serve with *Lobster sauce* (see SAUCE) made with white wine.

This method of preparation applies to all shellfish. It is a practical way of using up left-overs.

If there is not a sufficient quantity of left-overs, potato purée or rice can be added to the *salpicon*.

Macaroni croquettes valentinoise. CROQUETTES DE MACARONI VALENTINOISE – *Salpicon* of big macaroni, blended with thick *Béchamel sauce* (see SAUCE) to which grated cheese has been added.

Spread the macaroni on a shallow dish in a layer 1 cm. ($\frac{1}{2}$ inch) thick. Add a layer of *salpicon* (q.v.) *à la Nantua* to which diced truffles have been added. Cover with a second layer of the macaroni mixture. Leave to cool.

Divide into portions, shape into little rectangles. Dip into egg and breadcrumbs and fry. Serve with *Nantua sauce* (see SAUCE).

Meat croquettes (made with various meat left-overs). CROQUETTES DE VIANDES – *Salpicon* of the meat blended with *Allemande sauce, Demi-glace sauce* or *Tomato sauce* (see SAUCE), depending on the meat used.

The *salpicon* can be finished off with diced mushrooms and truffles, smoked or pickled tongue or ham.

Montrouge croquettes. CROQUETTES MONTROUGE – Mushroom purée blended with yolks of eggs, mixed with chopped lean ham.

These croquettes are mainly used as garnish and should be very small. If they are used as garnish for a fish dish, the chopped ham must be left out. Shape to look like very small eggs.

Mussel croquettes. CROQUETTES DE MOULES – *Salpicon* of mussels and mushrooms, blended with thick *Béchamel* or *Allemande sauce* (see SAUCE) based on fish stock.

Serve with *White wine sauce* (see SAUCE).

Noodle croquettes. CROQUETTES DE NOUILLES – Prepare, cook and serve as *Macaroni croquettes valentinoise* (see above) using ordinary or small noodles instead of macaroni.

Oyster croquettes à la normande. CROQUETTES D'HUÎTRES À LA NORMANDE – *Salpicon* of poached oysters, mushrooms and truffles blended with *Allemande sauce* (see SAUCE). Shape into flat cakes and serve with *Normande sauce* (see SAUCE).

Veal croquettes (*Scarnati*)

Oyster croquettes Victoria. CROQUETTES D'HUÎTRES VICTORIA – *Salpicon* of lobster, mushrooms and truffles blended with *Béchamel sauce* (see SAUCE). Put in the middle of each croquette a poached oyster coated with *Allemande sauce* (see SAUCE) and finished with *Crayfish butter* (see BUTTER, *Compound butters*) or any other shellfish butter. Shape into flat cakes.

Serve with *Lobster sauce* (see SAUCE).

Potato croquettes. CROQUETTES DE POMMES DE TERRE – Potato croquettes are usually served without sauce.

Potato croquettes Dauphiné – See POTATOES, *Dauphiné potatoes.*

Potato croquettes à la florentine – CROQUETTES DE POMMES DE TERRE À LA FLORENTINE – Two-thirds *Duchess potatoes* (see POTATOES) mixed with one-third spinach cooked in butter. Add 50 g. (2 oz., $\frac{1}{2}$ cup) grated Parmesan cheese for each 500 g. (18 oz., $2\frac{1}{4}$ cups) potato and spinach mixture.

Potato croquettes à la niçoise. CROQUETTES DE POMMES DE TERRE À LA NIÇOISE – *Duchess potatoes* (see POTATOES) mixed with 2 dl. ($\frac{1}{3}$ pint, scant cup) thick *Tomato fondue à la niçoise* (see TOMATO) for each 500 g. (18 oz., $2\frac{1}{4}$ cups) potato.

Potato croquettes with Parmesan cheese. CROQUETTES DE POMMES DE TERRE À LA PARMESANE – *Duchess potatoes* (see POTATOES) with grated Parmesan cheese. For each 500 g. (18 oz., $2\frac{1}{4}$ cups) potato add 50 g. (2 oz., $\frac{1}{2}$ cup) cheese.

Cheshire or Gruyère cheese can also be added to potato croquettes.

Poultry croquettes. CROQUETTES DE VOLAILLE – *Salpicon* of poultry meat, mushrooms and truffles, blended with *Allemande sauce* (see SAUCE).

Serve with *Demi-glace sauce, Périgueux sauce* or *Tomato sauce* (see SAUCE).

Printanière croquettes – Spring vegetables blended with *Béchamel sauce* or *Allemande sauce* (see SAUCE).

Serve with a *Cream sauce* (see SAUCE) to which parsley and chervil have been added.

Rice croquettes. CROQUETTES DE RIZ – Rice cooked in meat, fish or vegetable stock, plain or with grated cheese added.

Serve with *Tomato sauce* (see SAUCE).

Rice croquettes à l'américaine. CROQUETTES DE RIZ À L'AMÉRICAINE – Rice cooked in fish stock to which a *salpicon* of *Lobster à l'américaine* (see LOBSTER) has been added.

Serve with *American sauce* (see SAUCE).

Curried rice croquettes. CROQUETTES DE RIZ À L'INDIENNE – Rice cooked in a meat, fish or vegetable stock to which is added a *salpicon* of onions, cooked in butter until soft, and blended with a few tablespoons of *Curry sauce* (see SAUCE).

Rice croquettes à la piémontaise. CROQUETTES DE RIZ À LA PIÉMONTAISE – *Risotto à la piémontaise* (see RICE) served with *Tomato sauce* (see SAUCE).

Spiny lobster croquettes. CROQUETTES DE LANGOUSTE – As for *Lobster croquettes* (see above) using a *salpicon* of spiny lobster instead of lobster.

Vegetable croquettes (various). CROQUETTES DE LÉGUMES – *Salpicon* of cooked vegetable, blended with *Béchamel sauce* (see SAUCE).

Serve with *Tomato sauce* or *Cream sauce* (see SAUCE).

Vegetable croquettes are usually made from artichoke hearts, carrots, celeriac or French beans. They can also be prepared using a *macédoine* of vegetables.

Croquettes à la viennoise – *Salpicon* of lamb sweetreads, lean ham, mushrooms and chopped onions, cooked in butter until soft, and blended with thick *Velouté sauce* (see SAUCE) seasoned with paprika. Shape into small rectangles, and fry. Arrange in a circle and garnish the centre with a heap of fried onions.

Serve with *Tomato sauce* (see SAUCE) seasoned with paprika.

Croustades – Small, filled *croustades*, made of *Duchess potatoes* (see POTATOES), rice, semolina or *Lining paste* (see DOUGH) are used as *hors-d'œuvre.*

Croustades of duchess potatoes. Make a very thick duchess potato mixture. Roll out on a floured table to a thickness of about $3\frac{1}{2}$ cm. ($1\frac{1}{2}$ inches).

Cut out pieces about 5 cm. (2 inches) across, using a pastry-cutter. Dip in egg and breadcrumbs twice.

With a smaller pastry-cutter mark out the lid of the *croustade* by pressing on it. Fry the *croustades.* Remove the lids. Hollow out the *croustades* and fill as directed in the recipe chosen. Cover with the lids.

Serve the *croustades* on a napkin or paper doyley.

Croustades of rice or semolina. Prepare as described above, but using rice or semolina cooked in a meat, fish or vegetable stock, bound with egg yolks, and spread on a slab to cool.

Croustades made of lining paste (*tart pastry*). Line *croustade* moulds with lining paste, following the directions given for *barquettes.* Bake the pastry blind. Garnish as described in the recipe chosen.

Croustades à l'alsacienne – Make the *croustades* using *Duchess potatoes* (see POTATOES). Fill with braised *sauerkraut.* Put on each *croustade* a slice of ham and a round of poached Strasbourg sausage.

Croustades à l'anversoise – Make the *croustades* using duchess potatoes. Fill with hop shoots with cream.

Croustades à la bretonne – Make the *croustades* using duchess potatoes. Fill with a purée of *Fresh white beans à la bretonne* (see BEAN).

Croustades à la forestière – Make the *croustades* using duchess potatoes. Cut out with an oval pastry-cutter. Fill with morels sautéed with parsley. Put on each *croustade* a small rectangle of blanched lean bacon browned in butter.

Croustades à la grecque – Make rice *croustades* and cut into oval shapes. Fill with *Tomato fondue à la grecque* (see TOMATO). Put on each *croustade* 3 onion rings which have been dipped in batter and fried.

Croustades à la marinière – Make the *croustades* using *Lining paste* (see DOUGH). Fill with a *ragoût* of *Mussels à la marinière* (see MUSSEL).

Croustades à la Montrouge – Make the *croustades* using lining paste. Fill with a purée of mushrooms with cream.

Croustades à la napolitaine – Make the *croustades* using lining paste. Fill with *Spaghetti à la napolitaine* (see SPAGHETTI).

Croustades à la nivernaise – Make the *croustades* using *Duchess potatoes* (see POTATOES). Fill with very small glazed carrots. Put on each *croustade* a bouquet of very small glazed onions.

Croustades à la toulousaine – Make the *croustades* using lining paste. Fill with a *ragoût* of cocks' kidneys and forcemeat blended with *Suprême sauce* (see SAUCE). Put on each *croustade* a small slice of calf's sweetbread, a slice of truffle and a cock's comb.

Croustades vert-pré – Make the *croustades* using duchess potatoes. Fill with a mixture of equal parts diced French beans, peas and asparagus tips blended with butter.

Croustades Vichy – Make rice *croustades*. Fill with *Carrots à la Vichy* (see CARROTS).

Apart from all the special recipes given for *croustades* they can also be made according to the recipes given for *barquettes* and similar dishes.

Croûtes, garnished. CROÛTES GARNIES – Cut slices of stale sandwich loaf into rounds 5 cm. (2 inches) in diameter and $2\frac{1}{2}$ cm. (1 inch) thick, using a biscuit-cutter.

With a biscuit-cutter of smaller diameter, mark the top of the croûtes firmly but without cutting right through.

Fry in butter until golden brown. Drain and hollow out.

Garnish according to the selected recipe.

Alternatively, instead of frying the croûtes in butter, spread them with butter and brown in the oven.

Croûtes à l'ambassadrice – Garnish with a purée of breast of chicken (or other poultry) in *Velouté sauce* (see SAUCE). Put a large slice of truffle and a small bouquet of *mirepoix* of vegetables on each croûte.

Anchovy croûtes. CROÛTES AUX ANCHOIS – Cut slices of a sandwich loaf in round or rectangular pieces. Fry them in sizzling butter. Desalt anchovy fillets and cut into thin strips. Put these strips on the croûtes.

Sprinkle with breadcrumbs fried in butter and seasoned with cayenne. Put in a very hot oven for a few moments.

Arrange on a napkin or on a paper doyley and garnish with fresh parsley.

Croûtes with bone-marrow. CROÛTES À LA MOELLE – Garnish with bone-marrow cut into dice and poached. Sprinkle with a little chopped shallot. Pour concentrated and thickened veal stock on the croûtes and brown in the oven. Before serving put 2 or 3 slices of bone-marrow on each croûte. Sprinkle with chopped parsley.

Croûtes Brillat-Savarin – Garnish with a *salpicon* of hard-boiled eggs, mushrooms and truffles blended with *Béchamel sauce* (see SAUCE). Make a criss-cross pattern of anchovy fillets on each croûte. Sprinkle with fried breadcrumbs and brown.

Croûtes cardinal – Garnish with a *salpicon* of lobster and truffles blended with *Béchamel sauce* (see SAUCE) finished with *Lobster butter* (see BUTTER, *Compound butters*). Sprinkle with breadcrumbs and brown. When ready, put a slice of lobster and 2 slivers of truffles on each croûte.

Cheese croûtes. CROÛTES AU FROMAGE – Garnish with a *salpicon* of Gruyère cheese. Season with paprika and grated nutmeg. Sprinkle grated cheese and melted butter on the croûtes and brown.

Croûtes à la Clamart (Vegetarian recipe) – Garnish with a purée of fresh peas mixed with fresh cream.

Devilled croûtes. CROÛTES À LA DIABLE – Garnish with a *salpicon* of York ham and mushrooms blended with a strong *Demi-glace sauce* (see SAUCE), seasoned with a pinch of cayenne. Sprinkle with fried breadcrumbs and brown.

Croûtes Dubarry – Garnish with florets of cauliflower cooked in butter. Coat with *Mornay sauce* (see SAUCE), sprinkle with grated cheese, and brown.

Croûtes à la livonienne – Garnish with a purée of soft roes of smoked herring with the addition of *Béchamel sauce* (see SAUCE). Put a little *salpicon* of fillets of smoked herrings and tart apples on each croûte. Sprinkle with fried breadcrumbs and brown.

Croûtes à la lyonnaise – Garnish with diced boiled beef sautéed in butter and mixed with an equal quantity of diced onions tossed in butter. Sprinkle with breadcrumbs, pour butter over the croûtes, and brown. Pour a little lemon juice or vinegar on them and sprinkle with chopped parsley.

Mushroom croûtes. CROÛTES AUX CHAMPIGNONS – Garnish with a *ragoût* of small mushrooms *à l'allemande*.

Mushroom croûtes are made from small, round, crusty rolls. Scoop out the rolls, butter them and brown in the oven. The croûtes can also be made from French bread cut thick slices and prepared in the same way as the rolls.

Tourte de champignons à la crème is also sometimes called *mushroom croûte*.

Croûtes à la paysanne I – Garnish with coarsely chopped vegetables cooked in butter until soft. Sprinkle with grated cheese and brown.

Croûtes à la paysanne II – Garnish with stock-pot vegetables chopped and mixed with grated cheese. Finish as in the previous recipe.

Croûtes à la provençale – Garnish with *Tomato fondue* (see FONDUE). Put 4 black, stoned olives, each surrounded by a fillet of anchovy, on each croûte. Sprinkle with fried breadcrumbs. Heat in the oven. Sprinkle with chopped parsley.

Croûtes à la reine – Garnish with a *salpicon* of poultry, truffles and mushrooms, blended with thick *Velouté sauce* (see SAUCE), sprinkled with fried breadcrumbs. Brown in the oven.

Croûtes à la rouennaise – Garnish with *à gratin forcemeat* (see FORCEMEAT) made, whenever possible, of Rouen duckling livers (see DUCK). Heat for a minute in the oven. Put a grilled mushroom on each croûte. Fill the hollow of the mushroom with a little very thick *Bordelaise sauce* (see SAUCE).

Croûtes with skate liver. CROÛTES DE FOIE DE RAIE – Garnish with a *salpicon* of skate liver cooked in a *court-bouillon* (q.v.). Pour melted butter, seasoned with salt and pepper and a squeeze of lemon juice, over the *salpicon*. Put in the oven. Arrange the croûtes with the liver on a dish, sprinkle with chopped parsley, squeeze a few drops of lemon juice over, and before serving pour a little brown butter on them.

Croûtes with soft roes. CROÛTES AUX LAITANCES – Garnish with soft roes of fresh herrings. Sprinkle with fried breadcrumbs and put in the oven.

Croûtes à la zingara – Garnish with ham, smoked or pickled tongue and truffles cut into strips and blended with tomato-flavoured *Demi-glace sauce* (see SAUCE). Put a round slice of heated ham and a grilled mushroom on each garnished croûte. Sprinkle with chopped parsley.

Apart from the above recipes, recipes given for *barquettes*, *cassolettes*, etc., can be applied to garnished croûtes.

Cutlets (compound) (U.S. chopettes). CÔTELETTES COM-

POSÉES – Make up the mixture given in the chosen croquette recipe.

Spread a layer of this mixture on a dish, leave to cool completely, and divide into portions of 50 to 75 g. (2 to 3 oz.).

Dip in egg and breadcrumbs and shape into the form of cutlets (chops). Deep-fry in clarified butter or sauté in butter, depending on recipe. Arrange in the shape of a crown. Add appropriate garnish. Put a piece of raw macaroni, decorated with a tiny paper frill, on each cutlet. Serve with an appropriate sauce.

These cutlets, when made very small, can be used as a garnish for large dishes.

All the directions given for making croquettes also apply to these cutlets, which differ from croquettes only in their shape.

They can also be made from purée of poultry, game, fish, etc., dipped in egg and breadcrumbs, and sautéed in butter. Cutlets which have purées as a basic ingredient can have a filling of plain or compound *salpicon* blended with very thick sauce.

Dartois – Similar to *Allumettes* (see above). Their difference lies in the fact that the garnish in a *dartois* is enclosed in two pieces of puff pastry, which are not cut into rectangles until after the cooking is finished.

Roll the puff pastry out as for *allumettes*, cut into bands and put on a moistened baking tray. Spread the middle of the band with the chosen filling, which must be cold, leaving 1 cm. (½ inch) clear on each side.

Put on each garnished band another band of pastry the same length and width as the bottom one, but a little thicker. Moisten the border of the lower band with water and press the upper band on it. Make a few light cuts along the edges. Brush with egg and score the surface lightly. Mark into divisions to make subsequent cutting easier. Bake in a hot oven for 20 to 25 minutes. Cut into rectangles about 2½ cm. (1 inch) long, and arrange on a napkin.

All fillings given for *allumettes* can be used for *dartois*. They can also be garnished with *salpicons* (q.v.) of meat, poultry, fish, etc., blended with white or brown stock.

Anchovy dartois (Sausselis). DARTOIS AUX ANCHOIS – Fill with *Anchovy forcemeat* (see FORCEMEAT). Decorate with anchovy fillets, cover with a layer of puff pastry and bake in the oven.

Dartois à la florentine – Fill with spinach cooked in butter, blended with *Béchamel sauce* (see SAUCE) to which grated cheese has been added.

Dartois Grimod de la Reynière – Fill with fine *Pike forcemeat* (see FORCEMEAT) with *Crayfish butter* (see BUTTER, *Compound butters*). Decorate with crayfish tails and sliced truffles.

Dartois Laguipière – Fill with a *salpicon* (q.v.) of calves' sweetbreads and truffles to which is added a *brunoise* (q.v.) of vegetables, blended with thick *Velouté sauce* (see SAUCE).

Dartois Lucullus – Fill with a *salpicon* of *foie gras* and truffles blended with concentrated *Demi-glace sauce* (see SAUCE).

Dartois à la reine – Fill with a *salpicon* of poultry, truffles and mushrooms blended with *Velouté sauce* (see SAUCE).

Sardine dartois. DARTOIS AUX SARDINES – Made like *Anchovy dartois*, using well-trimmed fillets of sardines in oil instead.

Tunny (tuna fish) dartois. DARTOIS AU THON – Made like *Anchovy dartois*, using finely cut-up slices of tunny in oil.

Eggs mignons. OEUFS MIGNONS – Name given to very small egg-shaped cases made of *Duchess potato* (see POTATOES). They are dipped in egg and breadcrumbs, deep-fried, hollowed out and filled in various ways.

Make a duchess potato mixture and leave until quite cold. Divide into portions of 1 tablespoon. Roll these in flour and shape to look like eggs. Roll them in egg and breadcrumbs twice. Fry in hot, deep fat, drain and dry them.

Make a small round opening in the top and through the opening hollow out the 'egg' completely, without breaking the crust. Fill with the selected mixture. Arrange them on a napkin-covered dish or in a nest of straw potatoes and garnish with fried parsley.

Eggs mignons d'Aigrefeuille. OEUFS MIGNONS D'AIGREFEUILLE – Fill with a purée of poultry finished with *Crayfish butter* (see BUTTER, *Compound butters*).

Eggs mignons à l'andalouse. OEUFS MIGNONS À L'ANDALOUSE – Fill with a purée of *foie gras* to which grated orange peel has been added.

Eggs mignons Beauharnais. OEUFS MIGNONS BEAUHARNAIS – Fill with a purée of poultry finished with *Tarragon butter* (see BUTTER, *Compound butters*).

Eggs mignons à la cévenole. OEUFS MIGNONS À LA CÉVENOLE – Fill with *Chestnut purée* (see CHESTNUTS), mixed with a purée of onions.

Eggs mignons à la Clamart. OEUFS MIGNONS À LA CLAMART – Fill with a purée of fresh peas with cream.

Curried eggs mignons. OEUFS MIGNONS À L'INDIENNE – Fill with a *salpicon* of poultry blended with *Curry sauce* (see SAUCE).

Eggs mignons à la nivernaise. OEUFS MIGNONS À LA NIVERNAISE – Fill with a *fondue* (q.v.) of diced carrots and onions blended with veal stock.

Eggs mignons à la normande. OEUFS MIGNONS À LA NORMANDE – Fill with a *ragoût* of oysters with *Normande sauce* (see SAUCE).

Eggs mignons à la royale. OEUFS MIGNONS À LA ROYALE – Fill with a *salpicon* of French beans and asparagus tips, blended with butter.

In addition to these fillings, all those given for *barquettes*, patties, *croustades*, etc., can be used for eggs mignons.

Fondants (croquettes) – The French call very small croquettes *fondants*. They are made of vegetable purée or of a cream preparation with cheese.

Vegetable purée fondants. Prepare the purée of the selected vegetables and add an appropriate sauce to it. The sauce should be very thick. The proportion of sauce to vegetable purée should be one to three.

Divide the purée into small portions of about 50 g. (2 oz.). Roll in flour and coat with egg and breadcrumbs as for croquettes. Shape to look like eggs or pears.

Fry just before serving. Drain, and arrange on a napkin. Garnish with fried parsley.

These croquettes can be made from any one vegetable purée or a combination of purées. The basic purée must, however, always weigh two-thirds of the whole preparation.

Cream fondants with cheese. Prepare a very thick unsweetened *French pastry cream* (see CREAMS). Add grated cheese.

Spread on a slab to a thickness of about 1 cm. (½ inch). Leave to cool. Cut into shapes. Dip in egg and breadcrumbs and finish as for vegetable croquettes.

Argenteuil fondants. FONDANTS ARGENTEUIL – Asparagus purée with *Béchamel sauce* (see SAUCE).

Cheese fondants. FONDANTS DE FROMAGES – A creamy cheese mixture made of Brie, Camembert, Cantal, Cheshire, Gruyère or Dutch cheese.

Fondants Crécy – Purée of carrots with *Béchamel sauce* (see SAUCE).

Fondants with foie gras Taillevent. FONDANTS DE FOIE GRAS TAILLEVENT – Purée of *foie gras* and purée of the white meat of poultry mixed with *Allemande sauce* (see SAUCE).

Fondants with foie gras and truffles. FONDANTS DE FOIE

GRAS AUX TRUFFES – Purée of *foie gras* and purée of truffles with a very concentrated *Madeira sauce* (see SAUCE).

Meat fondants. FONDANTS DE VIANDES – Prepare in the same way as *Fondants à la reine* (see below) using different kinds of meat purées. Blend these purées with a sauce appropriate to the meat.

Fondants à la Nantua – Purée of sole with *Béchamel sauce* (see SAUCE) and *Crayfish butter* (see BUTTER, *Compound butters*).

Fondants with poultry liver or à la rouennaise. FONDANTS DE FOIES DE VOLAILLE À LA ROUENNAISE – Purée of poultry liver with *Rouennaise sauce* (see SAUCE).

Fondants à la reine – Purée of poultry, to which diced mushrooms and truffles have been added, blended with *Allemande sauce* (see SAUCE).

Fondants Vladimir – Purée of calves' sweetbreads mixed with purée of truffles, blended with *Allemande sauce* (see SAUCE).

Fondants à la Yorkaise – Purée of ham with *Béchamel sauce* (see SAUCE).

Fritots – A kind of fritter, the commonest ingredients of which are offal (variety meats), poultry, left-overs of fish and shellfish.

Beef fritots. FRITOTS DE BOEUF – Cut boiled beef into square pieces of 4 cm. (1½ inches). Finish as for *Bone-marrow fritots* (see below).

Bone-marrow fritots. FRITOTS D'AMOURETTES – Cook the bone-marrow in a white *court-bouillon* (q.v.). Divide into pieces 5 cm. (2 inches) long. Marinate the pieces, dip them in batter and deep-fry. Arrange on a napkin and garnish with fried parsley. Serve with *Tomato sauce* (see SAUCE).

Fritots of calves' and sheeps' brains – FRITOTS DE CERVELLE D'AGNEAU, DE VEAU – Cut the brains into thick slices and cook in a *court-bouillon*. Marinate and finish as for *Bone-marrow fritots*.

Fritots of cocks' combs. FRITOTS DE CRÊTES DE COQ – Cook the cocks' combs in a white *court-bouillon*. Marinate and finish as for *Bone-marrow fritots*.

Fritots of cooked fish. FRITOTS DE POISSONS DE DESSERTE – Divide the pieces of fish into pieces. Marinate them, dip in batter and finish as for *Bone-marrow fritots*.

Fritots of calf's or sheep's foot. FRITOTS DE PIEDS DE MOUTON, DE VEAU – Bone the calf's (or sheep's) foot. Cook in *Court-bouillon I* (see COURT-BOUILLON) and marinate. Finish as for *Bone-marrow fritots*.

Fritots of calf's head. FRITOTS DE TÊTE DE VEAU – Cook the calf's head in *Court-bouillon I* (see COURT-BOUILLON). Marinate and finish as for *Bone-marrow fritots*.

Frogs' legs fritots. FRITOTS DE GRENOUILLES – Trim the frogs' legs, put them in an uncooked marinade (q.v.) and leave for 30 minutes. Dip in frying batter and finish as for *Bone-marrow fritots*.

Fritots of cold meat. FRITOTS DE VIANDES DE DESSERTE – Boiled or braised left-overs of lamb, mutton or veal can be used. Marinate and finish as for *Beef fritots*.

Fritots of calf's mesentery. FRITOTS DE FRAISE DE VEAU – Cook and marinate the mesentery and finish like *Bone-marrow fritots*.

Mussel fritots. FRITOTS DE MOULES – Prepare in the same way as *Oyster fritots* (see below).

Oyster fritots. FRITOTS D'HUÎTRES – Poach the oysters, drain, dry, marinate, and dip in frying batter. Finish as for *Bone-marrow fritots*.

Fritots of cold poultry. FRITOTS DE VOLAILLE DE DESSERTE – Left-overs of poached or braised poultry are best. Remove all the bones. Cut into very small regular pieces. Marinate, and dip into frying batter. Finish as for *Bone-marrow fritots*.

Sweetbread fritots. FRITOTS DE RIS D'AGNEAU – Braise lambs' sweetbreads and marinate. Finish as for *Bone-marrow fritots*.

Vegetable fritots. FRITOTS DE LÉGUMES – Cut into quarters or into long pieces, vegetables such as cardoons or salsify (which should be cooked in a white *court-bouillon*), or artichokes and asparagus (which should only be blanched). Marinate, and dip in frying batter. They are finished in the same way as *Bone-marrow fritots*.

Fritters. BEIGNETS – Fritters served as *hors-d'œuvre* or small *entrées* can be made from a variety of ingredients – meat, poultry, fish and cooked vegetables – dipped in batter and fried.

Different kinds of batter can be used.

Fritters with frying batter. Whatever ingredients you use, they should be cooked first and then cut into slices, square pieces or any other shape desired.

Some recipes require the basic ingredient to be left to soak for 30 minutes in oil, lemon juice or vinegar, chopped parsley, salt and pepper.

When ready to fry, dip the pieces, one by one, into a light batter, and deep-fry them in very hot fat until they are a good colour. Dry them on a cloth, season with fine dry salt and arrange them in a pile on a dish.

For fritters incorporating forcemeat, mince, purées or various *salpicons* (q.v.), prepare the ingredients as directed in the recipe and leave until quite cold. Divide into small portions, shape into balls, corks, rissoles, flat round cakes, etc. Roll in flour. Dip in batter and finish as described above.

Fritters (*Scarnati*)

Fritters with chou paste (*soufflé fritters*). Prepare *Chou paste I* (see DOUGH). Add whatever ingredients are indicated in the recipe chosen.

Divide the paste with a spoon into pieces as small as a hazelnut or as large as a walnut, depending on the ingredients. Drop one by one into hot, but not boiling, oil. Cook on a high flame until the fritters are well shaped, dry and golden brown. Drain on paper or linen towelling, sprinkle with fine dry salt and serve.

Anchovy fritters I. BEIGNETS D'ANCHOIS – Roll anchovy fillets into rings and put them on thin round slices of bread, about 4 cm. (1½ inches) in diameter.

Sandwich these rounds together, two by two, dip in batter, and fry just before serving.

The rounds of bread can be coated with a layer of *fish*

forcemeat (see FORCEMEATS) or spread with *Anchovy butter* (see BUTTER, *Compound butters*).

Alternatively, spread the rounds of bread with a *salpicon* (q.v.) of hard-boiled eggs and fillets of anchovies blended with *Béchamel sauce* (see SAUCE).

Finish in the usual way.

In all the recipes bread can be replaced by small savoury pancakes.

Anchovy fritters II. BEIGNETS D'ANCHOIS – Soak unleavened bread (matzos) in cold water and cut into small circles. Put a little *salpicon* made of anchovies and hard-boiled eggs blended with *Béchamel sauce* (see SAUCE) on each circle. Seal the fritters like turnovers, dip in frying batter and finish as indicated above.

Artichoke fritters. BEIGNETS D'ARTICHAUTS – Trim very tender artichokes and divide into quarters. Lay them on a dish and dress with a trickle of oil and a squeeze of lemon juice. Season with salt and pepper. Leave to marinate for 30 minutes.

Dip the artichokes in batter and fry them. If they are a little hard, blanch them lightly before putting them into the marinade.

Beef fritters à la lyonnaise. BEIGNETS DE BOEUF À LA LYONNAISE – Make *Beef hash à la lyonnaise* (see HASH), using beef left-overs.

Divide the mince into pieces the size of a walnut. Dip in batter and fry.

Bernois fritters. BEIGNETS BERNOIS – Cut Gruyère cheese into rounds $2\frac{1}{2}$ cm. (1 inch) in diameter. Make a thick *Béchamel sauce* (see SAUCE) and add minced ham. Coat the rounds of cheese with this sauce and sandwich together in pairs. Finish the fritter in the usual manner.

Fish fritters. BEIGNETS DE POISSONS – Use left-over braised or poached fish. Cut into slices or pieces and marinate for 30 minutes in oil, lemon juice, chopped parsley, salt and pepper.

Dip the pieces one by one in batter and finish in the usual manner.

Fritters à la florentine. BEIGNETS À LA FLORENTINE – Prepare 225 g. (8 oz., 1 cup) spinach purée, making it as dry as possible. Add 2 dl. ($\frac{1}{3}$ pint, scant cup) thick *Béchamel sauce* (see SAUCE) and 2 to 3 tablespoons grated cheese.

Leave to cool, divide into balls the size of a pigeons' eggs, roll in flour, dip in batter and finish in the usual manner.

Herring fritters I. BEIGNETS DE HARENGS – Use marinated herrings. Drain, and dry on a cloth. Coat with a thin layer of *Fish forcemeat* (see FORCEMEATS) and roll them up. Dip in batter and finish in the usual way.

Herrings fritters II. BEIGNETS DE HARENGS – Make a *salpicon* of marinated herrings and *Fish forcemeat* (see FORCEMEATS) and spread it on pancakes (*crêpes*) made without salt. Roll up the pancakes, cut them in uniform pieces, dip in batter and finish in the usual way.

Lucullus fritters. BEIGNETS LUCULLUS – Cut truffles into thick slices, coat with a purée of *foie gras* and sandwich together in pairs. Dip in batter and finish in the usual manner.

In France these fritters are also known as *Fritters à la périgourdine*.

Meat fritters. BEIGNETS DE VIANDES – Use braised or poached left-overs of meat. Cut into squares, slices or any other shape.

Marinate for 30 minutes in oil, lemon juice, chopped parsley, salt and pepper. Dip the pieces one by one in batter. Finish in the usual manner.

Mussel fritters à la duxelles. BEIGNETS DE MOULES À LA DUXELLES – Cook large mussels in white wine, take them out of their shells, dry well, cover with 1 teaspoon thick *Duxelles sauce* (see SAUCE). Dip the mussels in batter and finish in the usual manner.

Pasta fritters. BEIGNETS DE PÂTES – Prepare *Macaroni à l'italienne* (see MACARONI) cut into dice, shell-shaped pasta, noodles or vermicelli. Leave to cool. Divide into portions the size of pigeons' eggs.

Dip in batter and finish in the usual manner.

Rice fritters. BEIGNETS DE RIZ – Cook the rice and mix with Parmesan cheese. Divide into portions the size of pigeons' eggs. Dip in batter and finish in the usual manner.

Polenta and semolina fritters are prepared in the same way as rice fritters.

Soft roe fritters. BEIGNETS DE LAITANCES – Poach the soft roes in *Court-bouillon XV* (see COURT-BOUILLON). Drain and put them in a marinade of oil, lemon juice or vinegar, and chopped parsley. Dry, dip in batter and fry in the usual way.

Soufflé fritters. BEIGNETS SOUFFLÉS – Prepare *Chou paste* (see DOUGH) without sugar. Divide with a spoon into pieces the size of a hazelnut. Drop one by one into hot, but not boiling, oil. Cook over a high flame until the fritters are well shaped, dry, and golden in colour.

Drain on paper or linen towelling and serve.

Soufflé fritters with anchovy I. BEIGNETS SOUFFLÉS AUX ANCHOIS – Prepare 250 g. (9 oz., 1 cup) *Chou paste* (see DOUGH) and add 2 tablespoons (3 tablespoons) *salpicon* of desalted anchovies.

Proceed as for *Soufflé fritters*.

Soufflé fritters with anchovy II. BEIGNETS SOUFFLÉS AUX ANCHOIS – Make the fritters as directed for *Soufflé fritters*.

As soon as they are cooked and drained, stuff them with *Anchovy butter* (see BUTTER, *Compound butters*).

Soufflé fritters à la hongroise. BEIGNETS SOUFFLÉS À LA HONGROISE – Make 250 g. (9 oz., 1 cup) batter as for *Soufflé fritters*. Add 3 tablespoons (scant $\frac{1}{4}$ cup) chopped onions cooked in butter and season with $\frac{1}{2}$ teaspoon of paprika.

Soufflé fritters à la parmesane I, or cheese soufflé fritters. BEIGNETS SOUFFLÉS À LA PARMESANE, BEIGNETS AU FROMAGE – Prepare 250 g. (9 oz., 1 cup) *Chou paste* (see DOUGH), add 50 g. (2 oz., $\frac{1}{4}$ cup) grated Parmesan cheese and season with a little grated nutmeg.

Soufflé fritters à la parmesane II. BEIGNETS SOUFFLÉS À LA PARMESANE – Make the fritters as indicated for *Soufflé fritters*. As soon as they are cooked and drained, stuff them with *Cream sauce* (see SAUCE) to which Parmesan cheese has been added.

Soufflé fritters à la toscane. BEIGNETS SOUFFLÉS À LA TOSCANE – Proceed as indicated for *Soufflé fritters à la parmesane*, adding chopped lean ham and truffles to the *chou paste*.

Sweetbread fritters. BEIGNETS DE RIS D'AGNEAU, DE VEAU – Braise or poach the sweetbreads. Cut into square pieces. Marinate for 30 minutes in oil, lemon juice, chopped parsley, salt and pepper.

Dip the pieces in batter, fry, and finish in the usual manner.

Truffle fritters. BEIGNETS DE TRUFFES – Cover large slices of truffle with poultry purée and sandwich together in pairs. Dip in batter and finish in the usual way.

Vegetable fritters. BEIGNETS DE LÉGUMES – Vegetables for fritters must be cooked or parboiled, according to their nature. Cut them into pieces, slices or strips.

Marinate for 30 minutes in oil, lemon juice or vinegar, chopped parsley, salt and pepper.

Dip one by one in batter and fry in the usual manner.

The best vegetables for fritters are artichokes, white asparagus tips, Brussels sprouts, cauliflower, salsify, tomatoes.

Hors d'œuvre: potato crisps, fennel, pâté served in a napkin shaped like a gondola, avocado, prawn cocktail (*Moustache. Phot. Nicolas*)

Vegetable marrow (U.S. squash) flower fritters. BEIGNETS DE FLEURS DE COURGES – Dip the flowers one by one into a light batter and then fry.

Vegetarian fritters à la printanière. BEIGNETS VÉGÉTARIENS À LA PRINTANIÈRE. Make 250 g. (9 oz.) vegetable *macédoine* (q.v.) and blend with 2 dl. ($\frac{1}{3}$ pint, scant cup) thick *Béchamel sauce* (see SAUCE). Leave to cool. Finish in the usual manner.

Vegetarian fritters à la romaine. BEIGNETS VÉGÉTARIENS À LA ROMAINE – Blanch some spinach, chop and simmer it in butter. Mix 250 g. (9 oz., $1\frac{1}{4}$ cups) spinach with 2 dl. ($\frac{1}{3}$ pint, scant cup) thick *Béchamel sauce* (see SAUCE) and 3 tablespoons (scant $\frac{1}{4}$ cup) grated cheese. Leave to cool. Finish in the usual manner.

Kromeskies. CROMESQUIS – Kromeskies are generally made of the same ingredients as *Croquettes* (see above), and can also be made of mince, purée, forcemeat and all kinds of left-overs of meat, fish or vegetables.

À la française. Prepare the ingredients as croquettes according to the recipe chosen. Let this get quite cold. Divide into portions of about 60 to 75 g. ($1\frac{1}{2}$ to 2 oz.). Roll in flour and shape into corks or rectangles.

Dip in batter and drop them one by one into a pan of boiling fat. Fry until golden brown, drain, dry in a cloth, and sprinkle with salt. Garnish with fried parsley and serve with an appropriate sauce.

À la russe. Prepare according to the recipe chosen and divide into pieces as directed above.

Wrap each portion in a very thin piece of salt pork and shape like a cork. Dip in batter and finish as indicated above.

À la polonaise. Proceed as directed in the preceding recipe, using large, thin, unsweetened pancakes (*crêpes*) instead of caul.

À l'ancienne. Wrap each portion in a thin layer of *Duchess potatoes* (see POTATOES), and then in an unsweetened pancake (*crêpe*). Finish as directed in the preceding recipes.

Kromeskies are generally served with *Tomato sauce* (see SAUCE) or any other suitable sauce.

As kromeskies are very much like croquettes we give only a few special recipes. They are made, as far as the basic ingredients are concerned, in every way like croquettes, for which the recipes are given above.

Kromeskies à la bonne femme. CROMESQUIS À LA BONNE FEMME – *Beef hash à la lyonnaise* (see HASH) coated in batter.

Kromeskies à la carmélite. CROMESQUIS À LA CARMÉLITE – Salt cod pounded with garlic, oil, and cream to which chopped truffles have been added. Wrap in pancakes and coat with batter.

Serve with a *White wine sauce* (see SAUCE).

Kromeskies à la florentine. CROMESQUIS À LA FLORENTINE – Thick *Béchamel sauce* (see SAUCE) to which grated Parmesan cheese and spinach cooked in butter have been added. Wrap in pancakes and coat with butter.

When the kromeskies are made of preparations which are difficult to divide into portions and to shape into corks or rectangles, (as, for instance, in the case of *Kromeskies à la florentine*), coat the pancakes with *béchamel sauce*, then add the spinach. Roll the pancakes, cut them into pieces and dip in frying batter. Finish as directed above.

Kromeskies à la mirepoix. CROMESQUIS À LA MIREPOIX – *Mirepoix* (q.v.) of vegetables, blended with *Velouté sauce* or *Béchamel sauce* (see SAUCE). If a meatless *mirepoix* is used it should be blended with *béchamel sauce*; if minced raw ham is added to the *mirepoix, velouté sauce* should be used for blending. In either case wrap in pancakes and coat with batter. Serve *Tomato sauce* (see SAUCE) separately.

Kromeskies Saint-Hubert. CROMESQUIS SAINT-HUBERT – *Salpicon* (q.v.) of game blended with *Demi-glace sauce* (see SAUCE) based on concentrated game stock. Wrap in caul and coat with batter.

Kromeskies with various vegetables. CROMESQUIS DE LÉGUMES – *Salpicon* of cooked vegetables blended with *Béchamel sauce* (see SAUCE). Wrap in pancakes and coat with batter.

The most usual vegetables for this dish are artichoke hearts, asparagus, carrots, salsify and celeriac.

Kromeskies à la Vladimir. CROMESQUIS À LA VLADIMIR – *Salpicon* of fillet of sole, truffles and crayfish tails blended with thick *Velouté sauce* (see SAUCE), based on fish stock. Wrap in duchess potatoes and pancakes and coat with batter. Serve with *Normande sauce* (see SAUCE).

Mazagrans – *Moulded mazagrans.* Butter tartlet tins, and line them with a thin layer of rolled out *Duchess potato* (see POTATOES).

Fill the tartlets with a *salpicon* (q.v.) or any other preparation indicated in the recipe. The filling should be quite cold. Cover each tartlet with a circle of potato mixture cut out with a fluted biscuit-cutter, and brushed with egg. Brush again with egg and brown in a very hot oven.

Take the *mazagrans* out of the tins when they are ready and arrange on a plate.

Large mazagrans. Line deep fireproof plates with rolled-out duchess potato mixture.

Fill with a *salpicon* or other cold preparation. Cover with another layer of the potato mixture. Decorate with rolled-out pieces of duchess potato mixture cut in fancy shapes. Bake in a moderate oven. Serve on the plate on which the *mazagran* has been baked.

Unmoulded mazagrans. Roll out a layer of duchess potatoes. Cut it into circles, using a fluted biscuit-cutter about 5 cm. (2 inches) in diameter.

Put these circles on a buttered baking tray. Fill with a *salpicon* or any other suitable cold preparation, putting a piece the size of a walnut on each.

Cover with a second circlet of duchess potatoes. Seal the edges and brush with egg. Brown lightly in a very hot oven.

All garnishes, *salpicons*, or other preparations given for patties, *croustades*, rissoles, tartlets, etc., can also be used for *mazagrans*.

Médaillons – The only difference between *médaillons* and *Croquettes* (see above) is their shape. *Médaillons* are shaped like small flat cakes. They are made of the same preparations as croquettes and left until quite cold. Dip them in egg and breadcrumbs and sauté in clarified butter.

Arrange in a circle. Garnish with fried parsley.

Médaillons are served with a sauce appropriate to the basic ingredients. They can also be garnished with vegetables blended with butter or with a fairly thick vegetable purée.

Oysters. HUÎTRES – There are several ways of serving cooked oysters as a hot *hors-d'œuvre*, including *Oysters à l'américaine* (see OYSTERS), *Attereaux of oysters* (see *Attereaux* above) *fritots*, patties, oysters on skewers, fried oysters, etc.

Pannequets – Pancakes served as *pannequets* in an *hors-d'œuvre* are made from unsweetened *Crêpe batter* (see CRÊPE).

Anchovy pannequets. PANNEQUETS AUX ANCHOIS – Cut the pancakes into rectangles and garnish with *Pike forcemeat* (see FORCEMEATS) with *Anchovy butter* (see BUTTER, *Compound butters*).

Pannequets à la brunoise – Roll the pancakes and fry them. Stuff with a *brunoise* (q.v.) of vegetables cooked in butter and blended with *Béchamel sauce* (see SAUCE).

Cheese pannequets (Cheshire, Gruyère or Parmesan). PANNEQUETS AU FROMAGE – Cut the pancakes into rectangles.

Vegetables: radishes, carrots, celery, artichokes
and pumpkin with cooking pan and saucepans (*Phot. Nicolas*)

Fill them with cream cheese. Sprinkle with grated cheese, and brown.

Pannequets à la florentine – Cut the pancakes into lozenge shapes. Garnish with spinach cooked in butter and blended with *Béchamel sauce* (see SAUCE) to which grated cheese has been added. Sprinkle with more grated cheese, and brown.

Fried pannequets in breadcrumbs. PANNEQUETS PANÉS ET FRITS – Prepare the pancakes and stuff them as described below under *Stuffed pannequets.*

Roll into scrolls, cut them into pieces, dip in egg and breadcrumbs, and fry.

Pancakes prepared in this way are also known in France under the name of croquettes or *craquelins*.

Apart from the recipes given here, pancakes can be stuffed with all kinds of preparations: purées, *salpicons*, creams, etc. as given in recipes for *barquettes*, patties, *canapés*, tartlets and other small dishes of the same kind.

Pannequets à la grecque – Rolled pancakes garnished with a *salpicon* of braised mutton, aubergines sautéed in oil, and pimentos, blended with *Tomato sauce* (see SAUCE) seasoned with paprika. Dip in egg and breadcrumbs and fry.

Pannequets are often made from very small pancakes spread with forcemeat, folded in two and browned under the grill.

Pannequets à la hongroise – Rolled pancakes garnished with a *salpicon* of onions and mushrooms cooked in butter until very soft, seasoned with paprika and blended with *Béchamel* or *Velouté sauce* (see SAUCE).

Pannequets à l'italienne – Rolled pancakes garnished with *duxelles* (q.v.) to which lean chopped ham, blended with very thick *Tomato sauce* (see SAUCE), has been added. Dip in egg and breadcrumbs and fry.

Pannequets à la ligurienne – Make very small pancakes and fold in two. Garnish with a *salpicon* of anchovies and hard-boiled eggs blended with *Tomato fondue* (see FONDUE), seasoned with tarragon.

Sprinkle with breadcrumbs and brown.

Pannequets à la Saint-Hubert – Cut the pancakes into rectangles or into lozenge shapes. Garnish with a purée of ground game with *Demi-glace sauce* (see SAUCE) based on concentrated game stock.

Pannequets à la strasbourgeoise – Cut the pancakes into rectangles. Garnish with a purée of *foie gras* to which chopped truffles have been added.

Stuffed pannequets. PANNEQUETS FOURRÉS – Make the pancakes large and very thin.

Spread them on a table, coat with a thin layer of the selected forcemeat, roll them up and cut each roll into two or three pieces. Put these on a baking tray and heat in the oven.

If preferred, instead of rolling them up, put two together and cut with a biscuit-cutter into rectangles, squares, lozenges or circles. For further recipes see CRÊPES.

Small pâtés au gastronome. PETITS PÂTÉS AU GASTRO- pastry approximately 5 mm. ($\frac{1}{4}$ inch) thick. Cut into rounds or ovals with a pastry-cutter.

Collect the remains of the dough and roll them out into another layer, which should be a little thinner than the first layer. Cut the same number of shapes out of it. Put the second lot of circles on a moistened baking tray.

Slightly moisten the edges of the circles with water. Put in the centre of each a portion of filling the size of a hazelnut. This can be forcemeat, minced meat or any other preparation according to the recipe chosen.

Cover with the circles cut out of the first layer of dough. Press with the back of a spoon so that the two circlets stick together. Brush with egg and put in a hot oven for 12 to 15 minutes.

In addition to the recipes given below, small *pâtés* can be filled with all the ingredients given for *barquettes*, patties, tartlets, etc.

Small pâtés straight from the oven (*Larousse*)

Small pâtés with anchovy. PETITS PÂTÉS AUX ANCHOIS – Make small *pâtés*. Garnish with *Fish forcemeat* (see FORCEMEATS) with *Anchovy butter* (see BUTTER, *Compound butters*) to which a *salpicon* (q.v.) of anchovy fillets has been added.

Small pâtés à l'andalouse. PETITS PÂTÉS À L'ANDALOUSE – Make small *pâtés*. Garnish with sausage meat to which a *salpicon* of pimentos cooked in butter, and chopped onions lightly fried in butter, has been added.

Small pâtés à la charcutière. PETITS PÂTÉS À LA CHARCUTIÈRE – Small *pâtés* garnished with sausage meat to which chopped parsley has been added.

Small pâtés à la duxelles. PETITS PÂTÉS À LA DUXELLES – Garnish with *Pork forcemeat* (see FORCEMEATS) to which an equal part of dry *duxelles* (q.v.) has been added.

Small fish pâtés. PETITS PÂTÉS DE POISSONS – These can be made in any shape. Garnish with a forcemeat of pike, whiting or any other fish, or a *salpicon* of cooked fish, blended with thick *Velouté sauce* (see SAUCE) based on fish stock. If desired, diced mushrooms and truffles can be added to the *salpicon*.

Small game pâtés with stock. PETITS PÂTÉS DE GIBIER AU JUS – Proceed as indicated in the recipe for *Small pâtés with stock* (see below) but use a *salpicon* of game instead of forcemeat.

Small pâtés au gastronome. PETITS PÂTÉS AU GASTRONOME – Small oval *pâtés* garnished with a *salpicon* of cocks' combs, pickled or smoked tongue, truffles and mushrooms, blended with strong Madeira-flavoured *Demi-glace sauce* (see SAUCE).

Small pâtés à la lyonnaise. PETITS PÂTÉS À LA LYONNAISE – Small square *pâtés* garnished with finely chopped braised or boiled beef to which have been added chopped onions cooked in butter until soft, and blended with concentrated veal stock.

Small meat pâtés. PETITS PÂTÉS DE VIANDES – Any shape. Garnish as for *Small pâtés à la Saint-Hubert* (see below) replacing the purée of game by any kind of meat.

Small pâtés à la moscovite. PETITS PÂTÉS À LA MOSCOVITE – Make a *Brioche dough* (see DOUGH), less fine than usual and cut it into circles of approximately $7\frac{1}{2}$ cm. (3 inches) in diameter.

Put a piece of *Pike forcemeat* (see FORCEMEAT) the size of a walnut in the middle of each circle.

Top with a little cooked semolina and a slice of raw white fish. Season with salt and spices. Fold the dough over towards the centre from the sides, making small oval-shaped pies. Press the rims together and crimp the edges. Make a small hole in the middle. Put on a tray in a warm place and leave to rise for 30 minutes. Brush with egg and bake in a hot oven for 25 minutes.

Just before serving pour into the opening of each pie a little concentrated *Demi-glace sauce* (see SAUCE) to which chopped parsley and lemon juice have been added.

Small mutton pâtés. PETITS PÂTÉS DE MOUTON À L'ANGLAISE – Line deep tartlet moulds with *Lining paste* (see DOUGH). Fill with small dice of mutton, half lean half fat. Season with salt and pepper and sprinkle with chopped herbs.

Make some puff pastry and give it 8 turns. Cover the *pâtés* with little circles of pastry. Brush with egg and make a small hole in the middle of each pie.

Bake in a cool oven for 35 minutes. As you take the *pâtés* out of the oven pour into each 2 teaspoons *Demi-glace sauce* (see SAUCE).

Small poultry pâtés with stock. PETITS PÂTÉS DE VOLAILLE AU JUS – As described in the recipe for *Small pâtés with stock* (see below) using a *salpicon* of poultry.

Small pâtés à la reine. PETITS PÂTÉS À LA REINE – Small round *pâtés* garnished with poultry purée to which chopped truffles, blended with thick *Velouté sauce* (see SAUCE), have been added.

Small pâtés à la Saint-Hubert. PETITS PÂTÉS À LA SAINT-HUBERT – Small round *pâtés* garnished with game purée blended with *Demi-glace sauce* (see SAUCE) based on concentrated game stock.

Small pâtés with stock. PETITS PÂTÉS AU JUS – Line small pastry moulds with *Lining paste* (see DOUGH).

Fill them with a *salpicon* of forcemeat, mushrooms and truffles blended with strong *Demi-glace sauce* (see SAUCE).

Cover each mould with a round of puff pastry. Press the rims together. Put on each a small ring of puff pastry cut out with a fluted pastry-cutter of a smaller diameter than the lid.

Make a small hole in the middle of the lid. Brush with egg and bake in a hot oven for 15 to 18 minutes. Take the *pâtés* out of the moulds. Pour into each a few drops of thickened veal stock, piping hot.

Small *pâtés* with stock can be prepared in the same way using all kinds of other meat.

Small pâtés à la strasbourgeoise. PETITS PÂTÉS À LA STRASBOURGEOISE – Garnished with a purée of *foie gras* to which chopped truffles have been added.

Garnished patties. BOUCHÉES GARNIES – Puff pastry baked blind, garnished with meat, fish or vegetable *salpicon* (q.v.).

Roll out puff pastry 6 times, and then to a thickness of 5 mm. ($\frac{1}{4}$ inch). Cut out circles $6\frac{1}{2}$ cm. ($2\frac{1}{2}$ inches) in diameter with a fluted pastry-cutter. Place on a slightly moistened metal tray. Brush with egg, mark the lid by pressing each circle lightly with a smaller pastry-cutter.

Bake the patties in a hot oven. Remove the lids and scoop out the soft part from the interior of the patty.

Very small, hollowed out and variously filled brioches are also called patties.

To prepare bouchées, roll out puff pastry and cut out circles with a fluted pastry-cutter

Place the circles of pastry on a slightly moistened metal tray (*Larousse*)

Mark the lid with a smaller pastry-cutter

Baked bouchées ready for filling (*Larousse*)

Filling the patties. Fill with a simple or compound meat, fish or vegetable *salpicon*, blended with white or brown stock, purées of meat, fish or vegetables.

All the fillings recommended for *barquettes*, croûtes, tartlets and similar dishes can also be used for patties. Very small patties can be used as a garnish for large dishes of various kinds. Slightly bigger patties can be served as small *entrées*.

Just before filling, put them in the oven for a few seconds. If at all possible, arrange the cooking so that garnishing can take place the minute they come out of the oven. This makes a great difference to the flavour. The same applies to all kinds of pastry dishes filled with a *salpicon* or other hot garnish.

Patties à l'américaine. BOUCHÉES À L'AMÉRICAINE – Fill with a *salpicon* of spiny lobster or *Lobster à l'américaine* (see LOBSTER).

Patties à la bénédictine. BOUCHÉES À LA BÉNÉDICTINE – Fill with salt cod pounded with garlic, oil and cream, to which diced truffles have been added. Cover the patties with slices of truffles.

Patties à la bouquetière. BOUCHÉES À LA BOUQUETIÈRE – Fill with vegetable *macédoine* (q.v.), blended with *Béchamel* or *Velouté sauce* (see SAUCE).

Patties à la Clamart. BOUCHÉES À LA CLAMART – Fill with a purée of fresh peas with cream.

Crayfish patties. BOUCHÉES AUX ÉCREVISSES – Fill with a *ragoût* of crayfish tails bound with *Nantua sauce* (see SAUCE).

Patties à la Crécy. BOUCHÉES À LA CRÉCY – Fill with a purée of carrots cooked in vegetable stock.

Patties à la dieppoise. BOUCHÉES À LA DIEPPOISE – Fill with a *salpicon* of mussels and prawns blended with *White wine sauce* (see SAUCE).

Patties à la financière. BOUCHÉES À LA FINANCIÈRE – Fill with *Salpicon à la financière* (see SALPICON). Cover with sliced truffles.

Patties à la julienne. BOUCHÉES À LA JULIENNE – Fill with vegetables cut into matchsticks, stewed in butter and blended with cream.

Patties with lobster, spiny lobster, or other shellfish. BOUCHÉES AU HOMARD, À LA LANGOUSTE – Fill with a *salpicon* of the chosen shellfish, blended with *Béchamel* or *Velouté sauce* (see SAUCE) based on fish stock and finished with *Crayfish butter* (see BUTTER, *Compound butters*) or any other shellfish butter.

Patties Montglas (square shape). BOUCHÉES MONTGLAS – Fill with a *salpicon* of lamb sweetbreads, cocks' combs and kidneys, truffles and mushrooms, blended with a Madeira-flavoured *Demi-glace sauce* (see SAUCE). Top with small slices of *foie gras* and slices of truffles.

Patties with mussels. BOUCHÉES AUX MOULES – Fill with mussels with *Allemande* or *Poulette sauce* (see SAUCE).

Patties with oysters. BOUCHÉES AUX HUÎTRES – Fill with poached oysters, drained and debearded, mixed with *Normande sauce* (see SAUCE) made with white wine.

Patties à la périgourdine. BOUCHÉES À LA PÉRIGOURDINE – Fill with a *salpicon* of truffles and *foie gras*, blended with Madeira-flavoured *Demi-glace sauce* (see SAUCE).

Patties with poultry. BOUCHÉES DE VOLAILLE – Fill with a *salpicon* of poultry or purée of poultry with cream.

Patties à la reine. BOUCHÉES À LA REINE – Fill with a purée of poultry with cream or *Salpicon à la reine* (see SALPICON).

Patties à la Saint-Hubert. BOUCHÉES À LA SAINT-HUBERT – Fill with a purée of game or *salpicon* made from the meat of ground game. These patties should be oval.

Sévigné patties. BOUCHÉES SÉVIGNÉ – Fill with a *salpicon* of chicken quenelles with truffles cooked in *Velouté sauce* (see SAUCE). Put half a heart of braised lettuce on each patty.

Patties with shrimps. BOUCHÉES AUX CREVETTES – Fill with a *ragoût* of shrimp tails with *Shrimp sauce* (see SAUCE).

Patties with soft roes. BOUCHÉES AUX LAITANCES – Fill with a *salpicon* of soft roe with cream or with *Velouté sauce* (see SAUCE).

Patties with truffles. BOUCHÉES AUX TRUFFES – Fill with a *salpicon* of truffles stewed in butter, with cream or with Madeira or similar wine.

Piroghi (Russian cookery). PIROGUI – This is the Russian name for pies of various kinds. Piroghi can be made from different doughs: *chou paste*, pancake batter, puff pastry, etc., and filled with mixtures such as meat, poultry, game, fish, vegetables, rice, cheese. (See PIROGHI.)

Pirozhki. PIROJKI – Plural of *pirozhok* – a diminutive of *piroghi* – i.e. small pie or patty, filled with all kinds of different ingredients. (See PIROGHI.)

Pomponnettes – Rissoles made in the shape of a very small pouch.

Roll out best quality *Lining paste* (see DOUGH), to a thickness of 5 mm. ($\frac{1}{4}$ inch). Cut circles with a fluted pastry-cutter $7\frac{1}{2}$ cm. (3 inches) in diameter.

Fill with a portion of purée the size of a walnut. Lightly moisten the rim of the dough and fold in towards the middle to make the shape of a small pouch. Fry in deep fat over a hot flame. *Pomponnettes* can be made from left-over puff pastry. All fillings given in the recipes for rissoles can be used.

Stuffed potatoes. POMMES DE TERRE FOURRÉES – After potatoes have been baked in the oven and two-thirds of their pulp scooped out, fill with *Ragoût à la cancalaise, Ragoût à la Nantua* (see RAGOÛT) or with a *salpicon* (q.v.) of poultry.

Quiche lorraine – Flan filled with a cream garnished with thin slices of lean bacon and served piping hot. The method of preparing *quiches* is described under QUICHE.

Patties à la reine
(*Larousse*)

Ramekins. RAMEQUINS – Tartlets with cream cheese. This name is also given to a small pastry made of *chou paste* to which cheese is added. For their preparation see RAMEKINS.

Rastegai – Russian patty, made of a yeast dough and sealed only at the ends. Divide the yeast dough into 150 g. (5 oz.) pieces, roll into balls, allow to stand for 8 to 10 minutes then roll out into circles. Put on each, 1 tablespoon minced beef with chopped eggs and onion, fish forcemeat, or chopped mushrooms. Crimp up the ends, making a boat-shaped patty, leaving the middle unsealed and the filling exposed. Hence the name, which in Russian means 'unbuttoned'. Leave to stand for 10 minutes, then bake in a hot oven. When ready, brush the *rastegai* with melted butter and add garnish appropriate to the filling. Thus, a fish *rastegai* should have a slice of cooked salmon or sturgeon, for a mushroom *rastegai* a teaspoon of small pickled *cèpes* or slices of hard-boiled egg, etc. Fish *rastegais* are served as an accompaniment to *ukha*, (clear fish soup), meat *rastegais* to strong beef consommé, and mushroom *rastegais* to mushroom consommé.

Ravioli – Small pasta envelopes filled with different purée stuffings, and poached. Serve in a clear soup with grated cheese. (See RAVIOLI.)

Ravioli à la lituanienne – See *vareniki* in this section.

Rissoles – Small pastries of various shapes (round, oval, rectangular or turnovers). Rissoles are made from a variety of doughs, including lining paste, left-over puff pastry or ordinary brioche pastry. They are filled mainly with croquette ingredients. The filling should only be put on the pastry when it is quite cold. For the method of preparation see RISSOLES.

Generally speaking rissoles should be fried, but sometimes they are baked in the oven.

Rissoles à la bohémienne – Using *Brioche dough* (see DOUGH) make the rissoles in the shape of turnovers. Fill with a *salpicon* of *foie gras* and truffles blended with rich *Demi-glace sauce* (see SAUCE).

Rissoles à la chalonnaise – Round rissoles of puff pastry. Fill with a *salpicon* of cocks' combs and kidneys, truffles and mushrooms, blended with thick *Velouté sauce* (see SAUCE) based on chicken stock.

Cinderella rissoles. RISSOLES CENDRILLON – Make the rissoles using *Brioche dough* (see DOUGH) in the shape of turnovers. Fill with a *salpicon* (q.v.) of poultry and truffles blended with a purée of *foie gras*.

Rissoles à la dauphine – Make Brioche dough rissoles in the shape of turnovers.

Rissoles filled with all kinds of garnishes, *salpicons* (q.v.), etc. are served under this name.

The name of the main ingredients should appear on the menu, e.g. *Foie gras rissoles à la dauphine, Lobster rissoles à la dauphine,* etc.

Farm rissoles. RISSOLES À LA FERMIÈRE – Made from *Lining paste* (see DOUGH) cut into circles. Fill with a *salpicon* of equal quantities of ham and *mirepoix* (q.v.) of vegetables cooked in butter, blended with rich *Demi-glace sauce* (see SAUCE).

Foie gras rissoles. RISSOLES AU FOIE GRAS – Choose your dough according to taste. Fill with a purée of *foie gras* to which chopped truffles can be added, if desired.

Pompadour rissoles. RISSOLES POMPADOUR – Roll out left-over puff pastry and cut into circles. Fill with a *salpicon* of pickled or smoked tongue, truffles and mushrooms blended with *Demi-glace sauce* (see SAUCE).

Sausages. SAUCISSES – Small chipolata sausages, Strasbourg, Frankfurt and Vienna sausages are served as *hors-d'œuvre*.

Devilled chipolata sausages. SAUCISSES CHIPOLATAS À LA DIABLE – Cook chipolata sausages under a grill. Put each sausage on a slice of bread which has been fried in butter and spread with mustard. Sprinkle with fried breadcrumbs, season with a little cayenne and put in the oven for a minute.

Garnish with fresh parsley.

Sausages à la duchesse. SAUCISSES À LA DUCHESSE – Fry the sausages quickly in butter. Make oval cakes of *Duchess potato* (see POTATOES) brown them in the oven and put a sausage on each potato cake.

Add white wine and *Demi-glace sauce* (see SAUCE) to the butter in which the sausages were cooked. Boil down, add more butter and pour this sauce over the sausages. Sprinkle with chopped parsley.

Frankfurt, Strasbourg and Vienna sausages. SAUCISSES DE FRANCFORT, DE STRASBOURG, DE VIENNE – Poach the sausages in boiling water for 10 minutes. Drain, and serve with grated horseradish.

Sausages à l'italienne. SAUCISSES À L'ITALIENNE – Proceed as for *Sausages à la duchesse*. Pour very thick *Italian sauce* (see SAUCE) over the sausages.

Sausages à la languedocienne. SAUCISSES À LA LANGUEDOCIENNE – Fry the sausages in butter. Cut an aubergine into slices. Dip in flour and fry in oil. Put 1 sausage on each slice of fried aubergine, and top with 1 tablespoon *Tomato fondue* (see FONDUE) seasoned with a little chopped garlic. Sprinkle with fried breadcrumbs, put in the oven for a minute, sprinkle with chopped parsley and serve.

Sausage à la lyonnaise. SAUCISSON CHAUD À LA LYONNAISE – Poached saveloy sausage served with hot potato salad.

Saveloys are often made with truffles, and also with pistachio nuts added.

Sausages à la maltaise. SAUCISSES À LA MALTAISE – Fry the sausages in butter.

Cut a sandwich loaf into thick rectangular pieces. Hollow out and fry in butter. Put 1 sausage on each piece.

Add white wine to the butter in which the sausages were fried, stirring well. Season with a little chopped shallot. Make a rich *Demi-glace sauce* (see SAUCE). Blanch some orange peel, drain, cut into very thin strips and add to the sauce. Pour over the sausages.

Sausages à la tyrolienne. SAUCISSES À LA TYROLIENNE – Cook the sausages under the grill.

Cut a sandwich loaf into thick rectangular pieces. Hollow them out and fry in butter. Garnish with *Tomato fondue* (see FONDUE). Put 1 sausage on each piece of fried bread. Fry onion rings in oil and put 2 rings on each sausage.

Sausages à la zingara. SAUCISSES À LA ZINGARA – Fry the sausages in butter.

Grill some mushrooms and fill with a *julienne* (q.v.) of lean ham, scarlet tongue, truffles and mushrooms, blended with tomato-flavoured *Demi-glace sauce* (see SAUCE).

Put 1 sausage on each garnished mushroom. Sprinkle with chopped tarragon.

Scallop shells, garnished. COQUILLES GARNIES – Using a forcing-bag, make a thin border of *Duchess potatoes* (see POTATOES) round the edge of the scallop shell. You can also use thin rounds of boiled potatoes.

Put 1 tablespoon of the desired sauce on the bottom of the shell. Garnish according to the recipe chosen, and spoon over some more of the same sauce. Sprinkle with breadcrumbs or grated cheese, depending on the ingredients used, and with melted butter. Put the shells into a baking-dish containing warm water, and brown in a very hot oven.

When scallop shells are *gratiné* (sprinkled with breadcrumbs and grated cheese and browned in the oven) or glazed (heated quickly in a hot oven), the shells can be prepared without a potato border.

The function of the border is to contain the ingredients of the garnish. It can be made of different preparations, which go well with the main ingredient of the garnish. You can, for instance, make a rim of chicken, veal or fish forcemeat for the shells, or pipe a border of spinach, rice, etc.

The shells can be made without breadcrumbs or glazing. If they are made with a border of duchess potato they should be baked quickly in the oven, to give the potato a good colour before the garnish is added.

After the shells have been coated with a sauce, browned or glazed, they can be decorated with truffles, mushrooms, asparagus tips, etc. Care should be taken to use only decorations which are in harmony with the basic ingredients.

Scallop shells of bone-marrow à la duxelles. COQUILLES D'AMOURETTES À LA DUXELLES – Make a border of *Duchess potatoes* (see POTATOES). Garnish with slices of bone-marrow, mushrooms and *Duxelles sauce* (see SAUCE).

Sprinkle with breadcrumbs and melted butter and brown the top. After cooking, sprinkle a few drops of lemon juice on the shells and garnish with chopped parsley.

Scallop shells of brains à l'allemande. COQUILLES DE CERVELLE À L'ALLEMANDE – Make a border of duchess potatoes. Garnish with slices of lamb's or calf's brain and *Allemande sauce* (see SAUCE). Glaze in the oven.

Scallop shells of brains à l'aurore. COQUILLES DE CERVELLE À L'AURORE – Make a border of duchess potatoes. Garnish with brains, mushrooms and *Aurore sauce* (see SAUCE).

Sprinkle with grated cheese, pour melted butter over the shells, and brown. When cooked, sprinkle with chopped hard-boiled eggs and chopped parsley. Pour round them a ring of *Tomato sauce* (see SAUCE).

Scallop shells of brains à la duxelles. COQUILLES DE CERVELLE À LA DUXELLES – Prepare in the same way as *Scallop shells of bone-marrow à la duxelles*, using slices of brains instead of bone-marrow.

Scallop shells of brill Mornay. COQUILLES DE BARBUE MORNAY – Make a border of duchess potatoes. Garnish with slices of cooked brill with *Mornay sauce* (see SAUCE). Sprinkle with cheese, pour melted butter over the shells and brown.

(In U.S.A. grey sole or flounder can be substituted for brill.)

Scallop shells of brill à la trouvillaise. COQUILLES DE BARBUE À LA TROUVILLAISE – Make a border of duchess potatoes. Brown the border before garnishing with slices of brill, mussels, shrimps and *Shrimp sauce* (see SAUCE). These shells are not glazed, but they should be decorated with small mushroom heads.

Scallop shells of crayfish. COQUILLES D'ÉCREVISSES – Make a rim of duchess potatoes and garnish with *Crayfish tail ragoût à la Nantua* (see CRAYFISH).

Finish as for *Scallop shells of shrimps* (see below).

The shells used should be very small.

Scallop shells of eggs au gratin. COQUILLES D'OEUFS AU GRATIN – Make a border of duchess potatoes and garnish with hard-boiled eggs cut into large dice, and *Mornay sauce* (see SAUCE). Sprinkle with cheese and brown in the oven.

Scallop shells of fish. COQUILLES DE POISSONS – Prepare as described in the recipes for scallop shells of brill, shrimps, crayfish, skate liver, lobster, oysters, soft roes and mussels.

Fill the shells with garnishes and sauces, as directed in the recipe chosen. The sauces used most often for fish in scallop shells are the following: *Aurore, Béchamel,* shrimp, *duxelles,* lobster, Hungarian, curry, Italian, Mornay, Nantua, *niçoise, normande* and white wine sauce.

According to the recipe chosen, scallop shells of fish are sprinkled with breadcrumbs or grated cheese, or they are simply glazed.

For all these dishes of fish in scallop shells you can use up left-overs of boiled or braised fish such as perch, cod, coalfish, whiting, hake, skate, salmon, sole, trout, turbot, etc.

Scallop shells of left-overs. COQUILLES À LA MÉNAGÈRE – Make a border of *Potato purée* (see POTATOES) and garnish with minced left-over pieces of boiled beef blended with *Tomato sauce* (see SAUCE). Sprinkle the shells with breadcrumbs and brown in the oven.

Left-overs in shells can also be prepared with minced mutton or veal. If minced veal is used, blend with a thick *Velouté* or *Béchamel sauce* (see SAUCE).

Scallop shells of lobster. COQUILLES DE HOMARD – Make a border with duchess potatoes and garnish with pieces of lobster, or *salpicon* (q.v.) of lobster with *Béchamel, Lobster* or *Mornay sauce* (see SAUCE). Sprinkle the shells with grated cheese and brown the top.

Scallop shells of meat. COQUILLES DE VIANDES – Follow the directions given for *Scallop shells of bone-marrow.* Left-overs of boiled, braised or roast lamb, mutton, beef or veal can be used.

Scallop shells of mussels. COQUILLES DE MOULES – Prepare as described in the recipes for *Scallop shells of oysters* or *Scallop shells of soft roes.* You can also follow any of the recipes for fish in scallop shells.

Scallop shells of oysters à la diable. COQUILLES D'HUÎTRES À LA DIABLE – Make a border of duchess potatoes and garnish with poached oysters, drained and bearded, and thick *Béchamel sauce* (see SAUCE) made with the water in which the oysters have been poached, seasoned with a pinch of cayenne. Sprinkle the shells with fried breadcrumbs. Brown.

Shells with oysters cooked in this way are often known as *Oysters à la diable.*

Scallop shells of oysters Mornay. COQUILLES D'HUÎTRES MORNAY – Make a border of duchess potatoes and garnish with poached oysters, drained and debearded, and *Mornay sauce* (see SAUCE). Sprinkle with grated cheese, pour butter over the shells, and brown.

Scallop shells of poultry. COQUILLES DE VOLAILLES – In principle, only the white meat should be used, but in ordinary home kitchens, where these shells are served mainly to use up left-overs, all parts of the poultry can be used.

Scallop shells of poultry à l'allemande. COQUILLES DE VOLAILLE À L'ALLEMANDE – Make a border of duchess potatoes and garnish with slices of white poultry meat and *Allemande sauce* (see SAUCE). Glaze in a hot oven.

Scallop shells of poultry Monselet. COQUILLES DE VOLAILLE MONSELET – Make a border of duchess potatoes. Garnish with slices of white poultry meat, artichoke hearts and *Mornay sauce* (see SAUCE).

Sprinkle with grated cheese and brown in the oven. After taking out of the oven, garnish each shell with 2 slices of truffle alternating with sliced artichoke hearts cooked in butter.

Scallop shells of poultry princesse. COQUILLES DE VOLAILLE PRINCESSE – Make a border of duchess potatoes.

Garnish with slices of white poultry meat and *Allemande sauce* (see SAUCE).

Do not glaze. Just before serving, put on each shell 2 slices of truffle and a bouquet of asparagus tips cooked in butter.

Scallop shells of poultry Rossini. COQUILLES DE VOLAILLE ROSSINI – Make a border of Duchess potatoes and brown before adding the garnish.

Garnish with slices of white poultry meat, truffles and thick *Madeira sauce* (see SAUCE).

Just before serving, put on each shell 1 slice of *foie gras* sautéed in butter, and a slice of truffle.

Scallop shells of poultry with smoked or pickled tongue. COQUILLES DE VOLAILLE À L'ÉCARLATE – Make a border of duchess potatoes and brown in the oven.

Garnish with slices of white poultry meat, smoked or pickled tongue and *Allemande sauce* (see SAUCE).

Do not glaze, but sprinkle the shells just before serving with chopped tongue.

Scallop shells of shrimps. COQUILLES DE CREVETTES – Make a border of duchess potatoes. Garnish with a *ragoût* of shrimps' tails with *Béchamel* or *Velouté sauce* (see SAUCE) finished with *Shrimp butter* (see BUTTER, *Compound butters*).

Sprinkle with grated cheese, pour melted butter over the shells and brown in the oven.

Scallop shells of skate liver and brown butter. COQUILLES DE FOIE DE RAIE AU BEURRE NOIR – Make a border of duchess potatoes and brown in the oven. Garnish with slices of cooked skate liver.

Sprinkle with pounded parsley, and a few drops of lemon juice. At the last moment pour *Brown butter* (see BUTTER, *Compound butters*) over the shells.

Scallop shells of skate liver à la polonaise. COQUILLES DE FOIE DE RAIE À LA POLONAISE – Dress and garnish as directed for *Scallop shells of skate liver and brown butter.*

Sprinkle with the chopped yolks of hard-boiled eggs and chopped parsley.

Brown fine breadcrumbs in *Noisette butter* (see BUTTER, *Compound butters*) and sprinkle over the shells.

Scallop shells of soft roes à la florentine. COQUILLES DE LAITANCES À LA FLORENTINE – Make a border of duchess potatoes. Garnish with slices of soft carp roes or herring roes arranged on a layer of spinach cooked in butter, and *Mornay sauce* (see SAUCE). Sprinkle with grated cheese and brown in the oven.

Scallop shells of sweetbreads. COQUILLES DE RIS D'AGNEAU – Prepare with lambs' sweetbreads as described in the recipes for *Scallop shells of bone-marrow* or *Scallop shells of brains.*

Small soufflés. PETITS SOUFFLÉS – These are made in *cassolettes* from all the different mixtures described in the section on SOUFFLÉS.

Small soufflés à l'américaine. PETITS SOUFFLÉS À L'AMÉRICAINE – Fill the *cassolettes* with alternate layers of the mixture used for *Lobster soufflé* or *Spiny lobster soufflé* (see SOUFFLÉS) and *Salpicon à l'américaine* (see SALPICON).

Finish in the ordinary way as described in the section on SOUFFLÉS.

Small soufflés à l'aurore. PETITS SOUFFLÉS À L'AURORE – Garnish the *cassolettes* with the mixture for *Chicken soufflé* (see SOUFFLÉ) and add concentrated tomato juice.

When the soufflés come out of the oven sprinkle them with the chopped yolk of hard-boiled eggs and chopped parsley.

Small crayfish soufflés à la Nantua I. PETITS SOUFFLÉS D'ÉCREVISSES (À LA NANTUA) – Rub through a sieve 125 g. (4 oz.) white fish (whiting, cod or sole) cooked in butter. Add to this purée $1\frac{1}{2}$ dl. ($\frac{1}{4}$ pint, $\frac{2}{3}$ cup) crayfish purée blended with thick *Béchamel sauce* (see SAUCE). Season with a little cayenne. Blend with 3 egg yolks and, at the last minute, work 3 stiffly beaten egg whites into the mixture.

Small crayfish soufflés à la Nantua II. PETITS SOUFFLÉS D'ÉCREVISSES (À LA NANTUA) – Prepare the mixture as described in the preceding recipe.

When putting it into the *cassolettes* arrange alternate layers of *salpicon* (q.v.) of crayfish tails with truffles.

Finish as described in the preceding recipe.

Small crayfish soufflés with Parmesan. PETITS SOUFFLÉS D'ÉCREVISSES AU PARMESAN – Fill the *cassolettes* with a layer of the mixture used for *Parmesan soufflé* (see SOUFFLÉ). On this put 1 tablespoon *Crayfish tail ragoût à la Nantua* (see CRAYFISH). Cover with another layer of Parmesan soufflé mixture. Finish as described in the preceding recipes.

Small oyster soufflés à la cancalaise. PETITS SOUFFLÉS AUX HUÎTRES, DITS À LA CANCALAISE – Poach 12 oysters in their own juice. Drain, and dry in a cloth.

Boil down the cooking stock and add $1\frac{1}{2}$ dl. ($\frac{1}{4}$ pint, $\frac{2}{3}$ cup) thick *Béchamel sauce* (see SAUCE). Strain, and blend with 3 egg yolks. Add the oysters cut in two and the beaten egg whites.

Finish as described in the preceding recipes.

Small soufflés à la princesse. PETITS SOUFFLÉS À LA PRINCESSE – Fill the *cassolettes* with alternate layers of the mixture used for *Chicken soufflé* (see SOUFFLÉ) and a *salpicon* of truffles and asparagus tips.

Finish as described in the preceding recipes.

Small soft roe soufflés. PETITS SOUFFLÉS DE LAITANCES – Poach, cool and drain the soft roe of carp or other fish. Rub through a fine sieve. To each 125 g. (4 oz.) of this purée add $1\frac{1}{2}$ dl. ($\frac{1}{4}$ pint, $\frac{2}{3}$ cup) thick *Béchamel sauce* (see SAUCE).

Blend with 3 egg yolks and add the 3 beaten egg whites.

Finish as described in the preceding recipes.

Subrics – Similar to small croquettes except that they are not dipped in egg and breadcrumbs and fried in deep fat, but are cooked in butter in a shallow pan. For their general preparation see SUBRICS.

Brain and bone-marrow subrics. SUBRICS DE CERVELLE, D'AMOURETTES – Poach a calf's brain, drain, and cut into large dice. Put into a *terrine*.

Add $\frac{1}{2}$ dl. (3 tablespoons, scant $\frac{1}{4}$ cup) *Allemande* or *Béchamel sauce* (see SAUCE), and 1 egg beaten as for an omelette. Season with salt, pepper and nutmeg. Mix carefully so as not to crush the brain. Finish as described under SUBRICS. Serve with *Tomato sauce* (see SAUCE).

Instead of calf's brain an equivalent amount of sheep or ox brains can be used.

Subrics made of sweetbreads and bone-marrow are prepared in the same manner.

Brain subrics à l'italienne. SUBRICS DE CERVELLE À L'ITALIENNE – Dice the brains and blend with 2 eggs beaten as for an omelette, mixed with 1 tablespoon flour seasoned with pepper and nutmeg.

Add 2 tablespoons (3 tablespoons) grated Parmesan cheese. Finish as described under SUBRICS. Serve with *Tomato sauce* (see SAUCE).

Subrics à la florentine – Make a preparation for *subrics* with spinach and finish off with 50 g. (2 oz., $\frac{1}{2}$ cup) grated Parmesan cheese.

Finish as described under SUBRICS.

Subrics of goose liver. SUBRICS DE FOIE GRAS – Put 50 g. (2 oz., $\frac{1}{2}$ cup) sifted flour into a bowl. Add 1 egg beaten as for an omelette, and 2 or 3 tablespoons thick cream. Season with salt and pepper, and mix.

Cook 250 g. (9 oz.) goose liver. Cool and dice. Mix carefully into the above preparation.

Finish as described under SUBRICS. Serve with *Périgueux sauce* (see SAUCE).

Subrics à la menagère – Dice 250 g. (9 oz., 2 cups) cold braised or boiled beef. Add 1 tablespoon chopped onion cooked in butter until very soft, and 1 tablespoon chopped parsley.

Blend this mixture with 2 beaten eggs and 1 tablespoon flour. Season with salt, pepper and nutmeg. Mix well.

Finish as described under SUBRICS.

Subrics can be prepared in the same way, using all kinds of cold cooked meat and fish.

Poultry liver subrics. SUBRICS DE FOIES DE VOLAILLE – Cook chicken (or other poultry) liver in butter. Cool and dice. Blend with 2 beaten eggs, 1 tablespoon flour, salt, pepper and nutmeg.

Finish as described under SUBRICS.

Rice subrics à la piémontaise. SUBRICS DE RIZ À LA PIÉMONTAISE – Blend 250 g. (9 oz. 1½ cups) cheese risotto with 2 beaten eggs. Add 1 to 2 tablespoons lean, chopped ham, and mix.

Finish the *subrics* in the usual manner. Serve with *Tomato sauce* (see SAUCE).

Semolina subrics. SUBRICS DE SEMOULE – Proceed as for *Rice subrics à la piémontaise*, using semolina cooked in a clear stock or in milk. Omit the chopped ham, if desired.

Sweetbread subrics. SUBRICS DE RIS DE VEAU, D'AGNEAU – Proceed as described for *Brain subrics*, using a *salpicon* (q.v.) of sweetbreads.

Talmouse – This can be made in many different ways but it should always have cheese as a basis.

Line fluted tartlet tins with *Fine lining paste* (see DOUGH) and fill with whatever cheese preparation is given in the recipe chosen. Brush with egg, sprinkle with Gruyère cheese, dice, and bake in a slow oven. Take the *talmouses* out of the tins.

Talmouses which have *Gougère batter* (see DOUGH) as a basis are often filled with a cream cheese mixture after they are cooked.

Talmouses à l'ancienne – Roll out some left-over puff pastry to a thickness of 5 mm. (¼ inch). Cut into squares of 6 cm. (2½ inches). Coat with a thin layer of the mixture used for *Cheese soufflé* (see SOUFFLÉ).

Put very small dice of Gruyère cheese on each *talmouse*. Lift its four corners so as to enclose the filling. Put these turnovers on a baking sheet. Bake in a slow oven.

Talmouses à la pâtissière – Line fluted tartlet tins with *Fine lining paste* (see DOUGH). Fill with a cheese *Chou paste* (see DOUGH) piped through a forcing-bag. Brush over with egg, sprinkle with very small dice of Gruyère cheese and bake in a slow oven.

Take the *talmouses* out of their tins, and fill the *choux* with a cream cheese mixture piped through a forcing-bag.

Saint-Denis talmouses. TALMOUSES DE SAINT-DENIS – Recipe from *Cuisinier gascon*, Amsterdam 1747.

'Make ordinary puff pastry; take a preparation of cream cheese and drain well; work it thoroughly with your hands; add as many eggs as the cheese will absorb, a grain of salt, and a pinch of flour; when this is all well mixed, put a layer of the cheese mixture on the rolled-out puff pastry and fold over both layers. Brush over with egg, bake in the oven and serve.'

This kind of *talmouse* is very similar to a cheese *quiche*.

Spinach talmouses. TALMOUSES AUX ÉPINARDS – Prepare the *talmouses* as described in any of the previous recipes and fill them with a *Spinach soufflé* (see SOUFFLÉ) to which grated cheese has been added.

Finish the *talmouses* as described in the preceding recipes.

Tartlets, garnished. TARTELETTES GARNIES – The preparation of garnished tartlets is the same as for *barquettes*, from which they differ only in their shape. These tartlets can be prepared from all kinds of doughs but are usually made from *Fine lining paste* (see DOUGH).

Line some round or fluted tartlet moulds as described for *Barquettes* (see above). Bake the tartlets blind. Take them out of their tins and finish as described in the chosen recipe.

In addition to the fillings given in the recipes which follow, all those given for *barquettes* and similar dishes can be used for tartlets.

Agnes Sorel tartlets. TARTELETTES AGNÈS SOREL – Coat the bottom of the tartlets with a layer of *Chicken purée* (see PURÉE). Surround with a border of very small slices of breast of chicken and pickled or smoked tongue. Put a mushroom head in the middle.

Heat through in the oven. Pour a little *Allemande sauce* (see SAUCE) on the mushrooms.

Argenteuil tartlets. TARTELETTES ARGENTEUIL – Fill with *Chicken purée* (see PURÉE). Cover with asparagus tips cooked in butter.

Beatrix tartlets. TARTELETTES BÉATRIX – Garnish with *Mushroom purée* (see PURÉE). Make a border of shrimps. Put a poached oyster on each tartlet. Cover with *Normande sauce* (see SAUCE).

Curried tartlets. TARTELETTES À L'INDIENNE – Fill with a prawn *ragoût* made with curry. Put 1 teaspoon *Rice à l'indienne* (see RICE) on each tartlet.

Tartlets à l'écossaise. TARTELETTES À L'ÉCOSSAISE – Garnish with *Salmon purée* (see PURÉE). Cover with *Mornay sauce* (see SAUCE). Sprinkle with grated cheese, and brown. Put a piece of sliced truffle on each tartlet.

Tartlets à la japonaise. TARTELETTES À LA JAPONAISE – Fill with Chinese artichokes with cream. Sprinkle with fried breadcrumbs. Warm through in the oven.

Metternich tartlets. TARTELETTES METTERNICH – Garnish with a *salpicon* (q.v.) of sweetbreads and truffles seasoned with paprika. Put a small slice of calf's brain on each tartlet. Cover with *Hungarian sauce* (see SAUCE).

Tartlets à la mirepoix. TARTELETTES À LA MIREPOIX – Fill with a *mirepoix* (q.v.) of vegetables cooked in butter with a *salpicon* of ham blended with rich veal gravy. Cover with a thin layer of *Chicken forcemeat* (see FORCEMEATS). Cook in the oven.

Printania tartlets. TARTELETTES PRINTANIA – Fill with morels in cream. Sprinkle with fried breadcrumbs. Warm through in the oven and then put 1 teaspoon asparagus tips cooked in butter on each tartlet.

Regina tartlets. TARTELETTES RÉGINA – Fill with a *salpicon* of mushrooms and truffles with cream. Sprinkle with fried breadcrumbs. Warm through in the oven and then put a very small slice of sweetbread sautéed in butter on each tartlet.

Timbales, garnished. TIMBALES GARNIES – This name covers a variety of small dishes which are all similar in shape but their ingredients differ.

Use buttered *dariole* moulds. Decorate with tiny motifs of truffle, scarlet tongue or lean ham. Alternatively, sprinkle with chopped truffle or chopped tongue. Line with a layer of fine forcemeat of poultry, fish or anything else suitable.

Fill the middle with a cold *salpicon* (q.v.) prepared according to the recipe selected. Cover the garnish with a layer of the same forcemeat as the one chosen for lining the inside of the mould. Cook in the oven, standing in a pan of water, for 15 to 18 minutes. Leave in the moulds for a few minutes before taking out. Cylindrical or six-sided *dariole* moulds can be used.

Garnished *timbales* are often masked with a sauce in character with the main ingredient; or the sauce can be served separately. These *timbales* can be served on croûtes of bread fried in butter, or on artichoke hearts.

Apart from the recipes which follow, small *timbales* can be garnished in the same way as *Barquettes, Croquettes* and *Croustades* (see above).

Timbales à l'amiral – Decorate the buttered moulds with truffles and line with fine *Fish forcemeat* (see FORCEMEATS).

Fill with a *salpicon* (q.v.) of crayfish tails, oysters and truffles blended with *Velouté sauce* (see SAUCE) based on fish stock and finished with *Crayfish butter* (see BUTTER, *Compound butters*). Cover with the fish forcemeat, poach, and serve with *Normande sauce* (see SAUCE).

Bagration timbales. TIMBALES BAGRATION – Sprinkle the buttered moulds with chopped truffles and chopped, pickled or smoked tongue. Line them with a fine *Chicken* *forcemeat* (see FORCEMEATS). Fill with diced macaroni, blended with cream, to which a *salpicon* of truffles and chopped tongue has been added. Finish in the usual way and serve with *Suprême sauce* (see SAUCE).

Beauvilliers timbales. TIMBALES BEAUVILLIERS – Line buttered moulds with an unsweetened *Brioche dough* (see DOUGH). Bake and leave to cool.

Empty the brioches, leaving a crust 5 mm. (¼ inch) thick. Warm slightly in the oven. Fill them with a *salpicon* of breast of chicken and truffles blended with *Allemande sauce* (see SAUCE). Put a bouquet of asparagus tips cooked in butter on each *timbale*.

Timbales à l'épicurienne – Sprinkle the buttered moulds with breadcrumbs and line them with a layer of rice, cooked in meat stock, to which chopped truffles have been added. This layer should cover the sides of the moulds evenly and be about 5 mm. (¼ inch) thick.

Fill with a *salpicon* of lambs' sweetbreads, truffles and scarlet tongue blended with *Mushroom purée* (see PURÉE). Cover the *salpicon* with a layer of the rice cooked in meat stock. Cook these small *timbales* in the oven for 8 minutes. Leave them to settle a little before turning out. Serve with *Tomato sauce* (see SAUCE).

Timbales à la fermière – Butter the moulds and coat with a *brunoise* (q.v.) of vegetables cooked in butter. Line with a thin layer of forcemeat, and fill with a *macédoine* (q.v.) of vegetables mixed with thick *Béchamel sauce* (see SAUCE).

Serve with a light *Demi-glace sauce* (see SAUCE).

Timbales à la milanaise – Butter the moulds and line with macaroni cooked in water, drained and dried. Lay the macaroni in a spiral shape against the sides of the moulds. Cover them with a thin layer of fine *Chicken* or *Veal forcemeat* (see FORCEMEATS).

Fill with a *salpicon* of pickled or smoked tongue, lean ham, truffles and mushrooms, blended with rich tomato-flavoured *Demi-glace sauce* (see SAUCE). Serve with tomato-flavoured *demi-glace sauce*.

Timbales à la Montrouge – Decorate the buttered moulds with lean ham and line with fine *Chicken forcemeat* (see FORCEMEATS). Garnish with a *salpicon* of chicken mixed with *Mushroom purée* (see PURÉE). Serve with *Allemande sauce* (see SAUCE).

Timbales à la nantuatienne – Decorate buttered moulds with crayfish tails and truffles. Line them with a fine *Fish forcemeat* (see FORCEMEATS) with *Crayfish butter* (see BUTTER, *Compound butters*). Fill with crayfish purée (see PURÉE, *Shrimp purée*) to which a *salpicon* of crayfish tails has been added. Serve with *Nantua sauce* (see SAUCE).

Timbales à la piémontaise – Decorate the buttered moulds with pickled or smoked tongue and truffles cut into very small dice. Fill with *risotto* made with saffron, to which a fine *julienne* (q.v.) of white truffles has been added. Serve with *Tomato sauce* (see SAUCE).

Timbales à la polonaise – Butter the moulds and line with strips cut from thin unsweetened pancakes (*crêpes*). Add a light layer of *Chicken forcemeat* (see FORCEMEATS) with cream. Fill with a purée of brains to which chopped truffles have been added. Serve with *Allemande sauce* (see SAUCE).

Timbales à la printanière – Cook carrots, turnips and French beans. Cool, and cut into short narrow strips. Decorate the buttered moulds with these. Line with a thin coating of *Quenelle forcemeat* (see FORCEMEATS).

Fill with a *macédoine* of vegetables blended with *Béchamel sauce* (see SAUCE). Serve with a light *Demi-glace sauce* (see SAUCE).

Timbales à la Rossini – Decorate the buttered moulds with truffles and line them with fine *Chicken* or *Veal forcemeat* (see FORCEMEATS).

Fill with a *salpicon* of *foie gras* and truffles blended with a rich *Demi-glace sauce* (see SAUCE). Serve with *demi-glace sauce* flavoured with truffle essence.

Timbales à la Saint-Hubert – Decorate the buttered moulds with chopped truffles and chopped, pickled or smoked tongue, and line them with *Game forcemeat* (see FORCEMEAT). Fill with a *salpicon* of game to which truffles and mushrooms have been added. Blend with *Demi-glace sauce* (see SAUCE) based on concentrated game stock.

Serve with *demi-glace sauce* based on concentrated game stock.

Polish valesniki. VALESNIKIS POLONAIS – To 125 g. (4 oz., ½ cup) white pressed cream cheese, add 125 g. (4 oz., ½ cup) well-softened butter. Season with salt, pepper and grated nutmeg. Add 1 egg and mix well.

Divide into portions of 50 to 75 g. (2 to 3 oz.). Put each portion on a small, thin, unsweetened pancake (*crêpe*). Fold over and dip in butter. Deep-fry in very hot fat, drain, and sprinkle with fine salt. Garnish with fried parsley.

Lithuanian vareniki. VARÉNIKIS LITUANIENS – Chop a large onion finely and cook in butter. When it has turned a golden colour add 125 g. (4 oz.) raw fillet of beef and 125 g. (4 oz.) raw, finely chopped beef kidney fat. Season with salt, pepper and nutmeg. Brown the meat, blend with 2 tablespoons (3 tablespoons) thick *Béchamel sauce* (see SAUCE). Add 1 tablespoon chopped parsley.

Make a noodle paste (see NOODLES, *Fresh noodles*). Cut into squares of 6 cm. (2½ inches) and put in the middle of each square a portion of the above mixture as for ravioli. Poach these *vareniki* in salted boiling water for 15 to 18 minutes. Drain, put in a dish and sprinkle with melted butter.

HORSE BUTCHERY. HIPPOPHAGIE – The slaughter of horses for human consumption.

Horseflesh, forbidden in Mosaic law, was eaten from time immemorial in Tartary and northern lands. For centuries it has been the principal food of the Gaucho Indians of South America. For a very long time the Teutons, too, lived on horsemeat, and continued to do so until their conversion to Christianity.

The people of Paris have always eaten horsemeat, in spite of numerous eighteenth-century police ordinances forbidding its sale in the hope of 'preventing those diseases which the consumption of such meat cannot fail to induce'. In spite of the fact that horsemeat was in use during the critical revolutionary period, the order prohibiting its sale was re-enacted in 1803, and again in 1811.

There followed special orders permitting the use of horsemeat as animal food, especially for the animals in the zoo. The interdict was finally revoked about 1830. This followed reports by Parmentier and Parent-Duchatelet, arising out of the publicly expressed views of Baron Larrey, who had used horsemeat extensively to feed his wounded men during the Napoleonic wars.

After the battle of Eylau, being entirely cut off from supplies on the Isle of Lobau, he made soup of it in the breastplates of the dismounted cavalry, and seasoned it with gunpowder in place of salt. More provident than the rest, he had kept a little salt for himself, and was thus able to invite Marshall Masséna to share his hotpot.

At the instigation of Geoffrey-Saint-Hilaire, there followed a propaganda campaign in favour of horsemeat. This was crowned with success when on 6 February 1865, a horsemeat banquet was held at the Grand Hotel. In the following year, on 9 July, another horsemeat banquet took place at the establishment of Lemardelay, a Paris horse butcher.

Since then, horsemeat has become more and more popular, and the number of horse butchers has greatly increased.

A variety of recipes for beef (q.v.) can be used for horsemeat.

HORSE CHESTNUT. MARRON D'INDE – Seed fruit, very rich in starch. Once the acid has been extracted from it, the horse chestnut can be made into flour suitable for human consumption.

HORSE PARSLEY. MACERON – Herbaceous plant of the umbelliferous group. This herb has a strong aromatic fragrance similar to that of parsley. It grows wild by the roadside and in ditches, especially in cool and shady places.

The common horse parsley is fairly prolific in the south of France. In former times, the root of this plant was eaten. The tender leaves of the horse parsley are used in cooking as a substitute for parsley.

HORSERADISH. RAIFORT – Plant originating in the East, growing both wild and cultivated. Its cylindrical root, brown outside, white inside, has a sharp and piquant flavour and a very penetrating smell. This root is used grated as a condiment. It is a great favourite in Germany (where it is called 'German mustard') and accompanies a wide range of dishes.

Horseradish butter – See BUTTER, *Compound butters.*

Canapés of horseradish à l'anglaise. CANAPÉS DE RAIFORT À L'ANGLAISE – Spread thin slices of black bread with butter to which English mustard and chopped chives have been added. Cover with grated horseradish and surround with a border of chopped, hard-boiled egg yolks.

Grated horseradish. RAIFORT RÂPÉ – Wash and peel a root of horseradish. Grate on a cheese-grater. Serve in an *hors-d'œuvre* dish as accompaniment to boiled meat or cold meat.

Horseradish sauce or Albert sauce (hot). SAUCE AU RAIFORT DITE ALBERT-SAUCE – Cook 4 teaspoons grated horseradish in 2 dl. ($\frac{1}{3}$ pint, scant cup) white consommé. Add $2\frac{1}{2}$ dl. (scant $\frac{1}{2}$ pint, generous cup) *Butter sauce II* (see SAUCE).

Boil down and sieve. Bind with 2 egg yolks. Add 1 teaspoon mustard blended with 2 teaspoons wine vinegar.

Serve with boiled or braised beef.

Horseradish sauce (cold). SAUCE AU RAIFORT – Mix grated horseradish with breadcrumbs soaked in milk and squeezed dry. Season with salt and sugar. Add thick cream and vinegar.

HOSPICE DE BEAUNE – The Beaune hospital – a jewel of Gothic architecture – was founded in 1443 by Nicolas Rolin, chancellor to the Duke of Burgundy, Philippe le Bon.

The vinicultural district called the Hospices is the result of charitable donations made to the hospital, and is situated in one of the best regions of the Côte de Beaune.

The famous public auction of the Hospices wines takes place every November. Buyers come from all over the world, while restaurateurs consider themselves honour-bound to purchase a vat of Hospices wine because although 'Hospice de Beaune' does not boast a special *appellation contrôlée*, the name alone gives the wine an added lustre.

HOTCH-POTCH. HOCHEPOT – This is a corruption of the name given in France to a fatty broth made from pigs' ears and tails, breast of beef, breast and shoulder of mutton, salt bacon, and mixed sliced vegetables, mainly cabbage, carrots, onions, leeks and potatoes. (See SOUPS, *Hochepot à la flamande.*)

There is also a spiced oxtail stew which is called a hotch-potch. (See OFFAL or VARIETY MEATS, *Oxtail en hochepot*).

The French *hochepot* may be derived from the verb *hocher*, to shake. Meats of various kinds cooked in a sauce are 'shaken' in the pot to prevent them from sticking.

Hotch-potch (Scottish cookery) – Scottish national soup prepared as follows.

Put in a stewing pot 1 kg. ($2\frac{1}{4}$ lb.) boned shoulder of mutton and 1 kg. ($2\frac{1}{4}$ lb.) rump of beef. Cover with cold water and bring it to the boil. Remove scum, add salt, and simmer for 2 hours. Put a celeriac cut into quarters into the pot, add 1 small cabbage, 1 large onion with 2 cloves, the white part of 4 leeks tied in a bundle, 2 turnips, 4 carrots and a clove of garlic. Simmer together for 35 minutes. Add 200 g. (7 oz., $1\frac{1}{4}$ cups) potatoes cut into pieces, 150 g. (5 oz., $\frac{2}{3}$ cup) diced French beans, 5 tablespoons (6 tablespoons) fresh white beans, a lettuce cut into quarters, and a handful of fresh peas. Cook all these ingredients together on a low heat.

HUSK. GRUAU – The part of the wheat encasing the grain. It is the most nourishing part of the wheat and the richest in gluten. The husk is also the toughest part of the wheat. In the first stage of milling it is very coarsely ground. At the second grinding, the husks are ground finer to produce wholemeal flour from which wholemeal bread is made.

The outer casings of oats, separated from the grain by a special milling process, are also called husks. (Oat husks cannot be used in the making of bread.) When the husks are removed from barley and the grain is smoothed it becomes pearl barley.

The French word for husk, *gruau*, is also given to a very small pasta, made from potatoes, which looks like sago.

HYDROMEL – A drink made from honey, much used by the Greeks and Romans. Plain hydromel is a solution of honey in water. Vinous hydromel (mead) is the result of the alcoholic fermentation of honey diluted with five times its volume of water. It has an alcoholic content of 11° to 13°.

Hydromel may be made according to the following recipe:

Heat 100 litres (22 gallons, $27\frac{1}{2}$ gallons) water to 50°C. (122°F.) in a copper kettle. Add 50 kg. (110 lb.) honey.

Gradually raise the temperature of the water to boiling point, taking care to skim the liquid constantly. Pour into a vat and leave to cool. When it is quite cold, transfer to a barrel where it must be left to ferment for 5 to 6 weeks. Draw off the hydromel.

Spirits can be distilled from hydromel. It can also be used in the manufacture of vinegar.

HYDROMETER. ARÉOMÈTRE – Instrument for measuring density. Hydrometers are principally used for the comparison of liquid densities at a constant weight and variable volume. These instruments, on being placed in the liquid under examination, by a simple reading of their graduated stems, show the density for a given temperature. Special tables enable necessary adjustments to be made when operating at a different temperature. There are many of these instruments in existence (syrup gauge, salinometer, acidimeter, alcoholometer, etc.). Only the Gay-Lussac centesimal alcoholometer is legal in France.

HYSSOP. HYSOPE – Small plant with a pungent aromatic smell and a slightly bitter flavour. It is used in the distillation of a number of liqueurs. In particular, in the composition of the elixir of Grande-Chartreuse.

IBEX. BOUQUETIN – A type of wild goat which lives in the high mountains. It is becoming increasingly rare in Europe.

ICE. GLACE – Water in its solid state. Ice used in conjunction with food ought to yield drinking water when melted. To analyse the ice, wash a cube with distilled water and melt it. Test as for drinking water.

ICE CREAMS AND ICES. GLACES – Flavoured ices have been made since the very earliest times, and it is generally recognised that the Arabs and the Chinese knew the art of making iced sweets, especially water ices (sherbets). The Chinese, it is said, taught the art of ice cream making to the Indians, the Persians and the Arabs.

Ice creams and water ices were introduced into France about the year 1660 by a Sicilian, Francisco Procopio. Some ten years later he opened a café in Paris, in the rue des Fossés-Saint-Germain (now the rue de l'Ancienne-Comédie). It was here that Procopio (who had changed his name to the more Gallic-sounding Procope) sold variously flavoured ice creams and water ices to the Parisians, who acquired a taste for these sweets, still a novelty to them.

Other Parisian *limonadiers* quickly followed Procope's example, and soon there were so many of them that, in 1676, it was necessary to give statutory recognition to their corporation and to authorise its members officially to sell ice creams and water ices. It is said that there were in Paris, at that time, 250 *limonadiers* who were selling ices.

Until about the middle of the eighteenth century, ices were only sold in Paris in the summer. In 1750, Procope's successor, Buisson, started making ices all the year round. His competitors at once followed suit. But the ices were of poor quality. It was not until 1776 that ices more delicate in flavour began to be made. These had more body than those of earlier times and could be moulded into different shapes. It was about this time that *fromages*, as well as a number of frozen desserts, were invented. Some of these are still made today.

Although the Romans used to cool drinks with ice or snow, this practice was not introduced into France until the seventeenth century, and even then it was only adopted by persons of great refinement.

In the *Dictionnaire de Monnet*, 1636, the word *glacière* (ice chest) does not even appear. Yet some forty years later the custom of drinking iced wines was so general in France that any departure from it was much frowned upon, if one may judge from what Boileau says in his *Repas ridicule*:

Mais qui l'aurait pense? Pour comble de disgrâce,
Par le chaud qu'il fasait, nous n'avions point de glace,
Point de glace, bon Dieu! Dans le fort de l'été,
Au mois de juin . . .
'The worst of disasters. But who would have thought it?
'In spite of the heat, we had no ice.
'No ice, good God! At the height of the summer,
'In the month of June . . .'

At the end of the eighteenth century, the manufacture of ices developed considerably, especially in Paris. This was the age which saw the invention of the ice bombe. It was soon the custom to serve a *bombe glacée* at the end of any formal meal, and the savouring of ices at the cafés of the Palais-Royal had by this time become fashionable.

During the period of the First Empire, thanks to the Italian ice cream manufacturers, of whom there were many in Paris, ice cream and water ices of various kinds improved still further in quality. Ices began to be made from a basic mixture of egg yolks and syrup, which led to the creation of more elaborate sweets. These took the place of cylindrical ice cream blocks at formal dinners.

Pratti and Tortoni became famous for the delicacy of their ices.

Under the Second Empire the 'surprise omelette', sometimes called *omelette à la norvégienne*, was invented. This remarkable sweet, with a centre of cold fruit and ice cream and a hot crust of meringue browned in the oven, was cleverly devised to produce a gastronomic paradox, a ball of ice in a piping hot casing. (See EGGS, *Omelette à la norvégienne*.) Under the Second Empire, too, *coupes*, mousses, and *parfaits* were first made.

The manufacture of ices, sherbets and ice creams has developed into an industry of some magnitude being, as it is, an important outlet for agricultural dairy produce, eggs and fruit.

The enormous advances made by the refrigeration industries have resulted in much improved methods of manufacture, conservation and distribution. Domestic appliances, too, have been considerably improved.

The manufacture of ice cream products, now mainly automatic, is carried out under strictly hygienic conditions. Electrically-operated ice cream freezers are available for domestic use.

General method for the preparation of ices – *Using a churn freezer.* Having prepared the appropriate mixture (for syrup ice or cream ice), pour it into a metal freezer lodged in a bucket containing layers of chipped ice, salt and saltpetre. This mixture should be well pressed down in the bucket. Replace the lid and start to churn, continuing until freezing is accomplished.

If a hand-operated churn freezer is used close it tightly. Turn it up first one way and then the other by the handle attached to the lid. This operation throws some of the mixture against the sides of the freezer so that it solidifies. It is therefore necessary from time to time to scrape the sides of the freezer with a special spatula and mix the frozen ice cream with the rest. During the freezing process, stir the mixture thoroughly with the spatula so that it remains smooth and creamy.

Using a food freezer. Ice cream mixtures can be frozen quickly and easily in a household food freezer. This does not produce the same perfect texture as an ice cream churn freezer, but if the mixture is frozen quickly and stirred frequently, satisfactory results can be obtained.

Presentation of ices – Ice cream and water ices can be presented in many different ways. They can be shaped with a ball-scoop and served in shells or in special glasses, or – still shaped with a ball-scoop – formed into a pyramid on a dish covered with a folded napkin or paper doyley.

Ice cream and water ices can also be transferred, after freezing, to special moulds which are conical in shape. These are hermetically sealed and placed, with their contents, in a bucket where they are packed round with chopped ice and salt. To ensure that the ices are quite firm when they are turned out of the moulds, they should be left in the ice bucket for at least 1 hour.

To turn out these ices, run cold water rapidly over the mould. Dip it for a second into warm water. This will warm the mould slightly and detach the ice from the sides. Tip the mould upside down on a dish and lift it up carefully, leaving the ice cream in the centre of the dish.

Ices can be prepared in small moulds in the same way as those shaped in large moulds.

Small moulds are available in a variety of shapes.

When they are filled, their edges are sealed with butter. They are then pressed down into a bucket of crushed ice and salt, like other types of ice cream moulds.

ICE CREAM AND WATER ICE MIXTURES. COMPOSITIONS POUR GLACES DIVERSES – These are of three kinds: those with a syrup base, used in the preparation of water ices flavoured with fruit juices, essences or liqueurs; those with a custard base, made from a mixture of egg yolks, sugar and milk; and those with a mousse base.

Mixture for fruit ices. GLACE AUX FRUITS – Rub the fruit (peeled if necessary) through a fine sieve. Add to the purée thus obtained an equal quantity of cold sugar syrup (4 cups sugar and 2 cups water boiled for 5 minutes and cooled) and add lemon juice according to the nature of the fruit purée. Mix all these ingredients on ice, where possible testing the sugar content of the mixture with a saccharometer. Fruit ices are made from a mixture registering a standard density of 18° to 22°.

Fruit ices may also be prepared thus:

Pound the fruit in a mortar with 300 g. (11 oz., $1\frac{1}{3}$ cups) fine sugar to every 500 g. (generous 1 lb.) fruit.

Electric churn freezer 'Sirem' (*Nicolas*)

Rub through a fine sieve. Add to this mixture as much water as is required to bring it to the right density. (This must be tested with a saccharometer.)

Mixture for ices flavoured with liqueurs and essences. GLACES AUX LIQUEURS, AUX ESSENCES – Add the liqueur or essence desired to cold sugar syrup (see SYRUP). Usually, 1 dl. (6 tablespoons, scant $\frac{1}{2}$ cup) liqueur is required for every litre (scant quart, generous quart) syrup. A little lemon juice is added to this mixture.

These are the basic ingredients of ices flavoured with anisette, Armagnac, Crème de cacão, Curaçao, cherry brandy, kirsch, rum, maraschino, or any other liqueur.

As in the case of fruit ices, this mixture whenever possible must be tested with a saccharometer, which should register between 18° and 22°.

Ice cream mixture (custard). GLACE À LA CRÈME – Place in a saucepan 300 g. (11 oz., $1\frac{1}{3}$ cups) fine sugar and 10 egg yolks. Work this mixture with a spatula until it reaches ribbon consistency (when it drops off the spatula like a ribbon).

Blend in little by little, 1 litre ($1\frac{3}{4}$ pints, generous quart) flavoured boiling milk. Cook on the stove, stirring until it coats the spoon. It must not be allowed to come to the boil or the mixture will curdle.

Rub through a fine conical sieve into a bowl. Stir from time to time until it is quite cold.

The mixture most commonly used is 400 g. (14 oz., $1\frac{3}{4}$ cups) fine sugar and 8 egg yolks to 1 litre ($1\frac{3}{4}$ pints, generous quart) milk. This is a very good recipe, producing a firm, creamy ice, not too sweet, to which may be added a liquid flavouring (brandy, rum, kirsch, Chartreuse or any other) without risk of spoiling its consistency. By using less milk and making up the liquid content with fresh cream, an ice cream of smoother texture can be obtained.

A drier and firmer ice is made by using less sugar and fewer

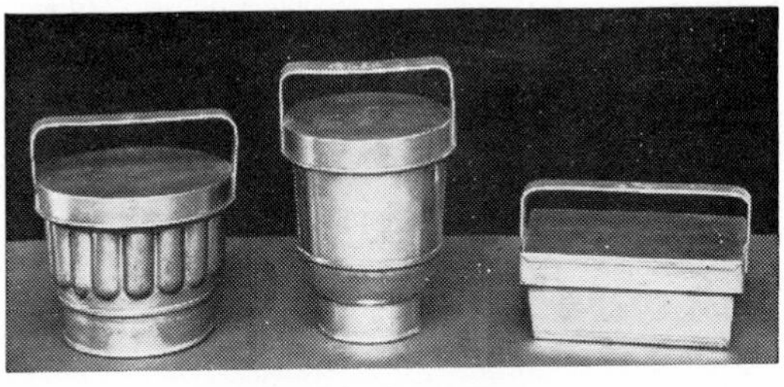

Various moulds for ice puddings (*Dehillerin. Phot. Larousse*)

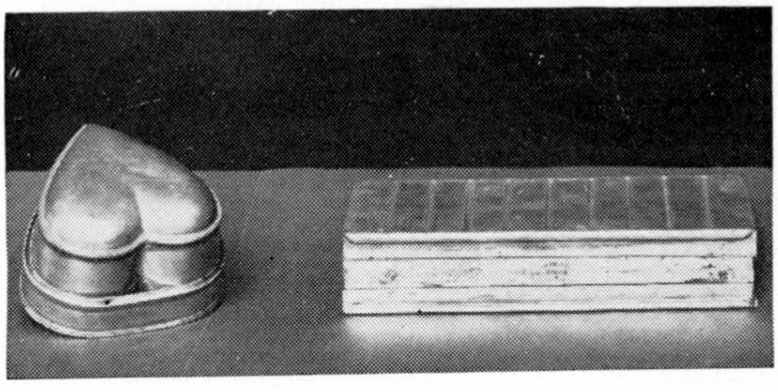

Old-fashioned ice cream moulds

egg yolks. If, however, too little sugar or too few eggs are used, the result will be a disappointingly tasteless mixture.

In no circumstances should less than 300 g. (11 oz., $1\frac{1}{3}$ cups) fine sugar and 6 egg yolks be used. Even these quantities will not yield an ice of good quality.

Mousse (bombe) mixture. PÂTE À BOMBE – Make 1 litre ($1\frac{3}{4}$ pints, generous quart) syrup boiled to 104°C. (220°F.). Put the syrup and 32 egg yolks in a double saucepan on the stove over a high flame. From time to time stir with a whisk. When the mixture reaches the consistency of thick cream, rub it through a fine seive into a bowl. Whisk until it is quite cold, when it should be light, frothy and whitish in colour. Add an equal quantity of whipped cream, and liqueur or fruit purée.

Keep in a stone or porcelain container, and place in a bucket of ice without salt, or in the refrigerator.

Recipes for a number of different ices are given below.

PLAIN FRUIT ICES WITH A SYRUP BASE. GLACES SIMPLES, AUX FRUITS, AU SIROP –

Apricot ice. GLACE À L'ABRICOT – Equal quantities of fresh apricot pulp or purée and syrup. The juice of 2 lemons is added to every litre (scant quart, generous quart) of this mixture. (Density: 18° to 19° – see SUGAR.)

Banana ice. GLACE À LA BANANE – Proceed as for *Pineapple ice* (see below), using syrup and banana purée. Add lemon juice. Flavour with kirsch or rum. (Density: 20° to 21° – see SUGAR.)

Cherry ice. GLACE AUX CERISES – Soak $\frac{1}{2}$ litre (scant pint, $2\frac{1}{4}$ cups) crushed stoned cherries for 1 hour in $\frac{1}{2}$ litre (scant pint, $2\frac{1}{4}$ cups) syrup. Soak pounded kernels with the cherries. Add a few drops of lemon juice and a little kirsch. Rub through a fine sieve. (Density: 20° to 21° – see SUGAR.)

Lemon ice. GLACE AU CITRON – Soak the rind of 3 lemons for 2 hours in $\frac{1}{2}$ litre (scant pint, $2\frac{1}{4}$ cups) cold syrup. Add the juice of 4 lemons (and, if desired, the juice of 2 oranges). Strain. (Density: 21° to 22° – see SUGAR.)

Melon ice. GLACE AU MELON – Proceed as for *Apricot ice*, using melon pulp rubbed through a fine sieve. Add a little brandy to the mixture.

Orange ice. GLACE À L'ORANGE – Proceed as for *Tangerine ice* (see below) with the peel and juice of 4 to 5 oranges and the juice of 1 lemon. (Density: 20° to 21° – see SUGAR.)

Peach ice. GLACE À LA PÊCHE – Proceed as for *Apricot ice*, using peach pulp. (Density: 18° to 19° – see SUGAR.)

Pear ice. GLACE À LA POIRE – Pound in a mortar 500 g. (18 oz., $2\frac{1}{4}$ cups) fine sugar with 500 g. (18 oz.) peeled and cored pears stewed until very soft. Add the juice of a lemon. Rub through a sieve. Add enough filtered water to bring the sugar density to 21° to 22° (see SUGAR.)

Pineapple ice. GLACE À L'ANANAS – Soak $\frac{1}{2}$ litre (scant pint, $2\frac{1}{4}$ cups) finely pounded pineapple (fresh or tinned) for 2 hours in an equal quantity of syrup. Add a little lemon juice and kirsch. (Density: 18° to 20° – see SUGAR.)

Plum ice. GLACE AUX PRUNES – Proceed as for *Apricot ice*, using purée of plums.

Raspberry ice. GLACE À LA FRAMBOISE – Proceed as for *Strawberry ice* (see below) using crushed raspberries.

Redcurrant ice. GLACE À LA GROSEILLE – Add $\frac{1}{2}$ litre (scant pint, $2\frac{1}{4}$ cups) redcurrant juice to an equal quantity of syrup. Add only a few drops of lemon juice, as the fruit is acid enough. (Density: 19° to 20° – see SUGAR.)

Strawberry ice. GLACE AUX FRAISES – Add $\frac{1}{2}$ litre (scant pint, $2\frac{1}{4}$ cups) crushed strawberries (fresh or preserved) and the juice of 2 lemons and 2 oranges to $\frac{1}{2}$ litre (scant pint, $2\frac{1}{4}$ cups) cold syrup. Sieve. (Density: 16° to 18° – see SUGAR.)

This ice may also be prepared as follows: pound together 1 kg. ($2\frac{1}{4}$ lb.) strawberries and 500 g. (18 oz., $2\frac{1}{4}$ cups) fine sugar. Add the juice of 2 lemons and of 2 oranges. Rub through a sieve.

Add to this mixture enough filtered water to bring the mixture to a density of 16° to 18° (see SUGAR).

Tangerine ice. GLACE À LA MANDARINE – Infuse the peel of 4 tangerines in $7\frac{1}{2}$ dl. ($1\frac{1}{3}$ pints, $1\frac{2}{3}$ pints) boiling syrup. When the mixture is cold, add the juice of 6 tangerines, 2 oranges and 1 lemon. Strain. (Density: 20° to 21° – see SUGAR.)

PLAIN ICE CREAMS. GLACES SIMPLES À LA CRÈME –

Almond ice cream. GLACES AUX AMANDES – Add to 1 litre ($1\frac{3}{4}$ pints, generous quart) boiled milk, 100 g. (4 oz., scant cup) fresh almonds and 5 bitter almonds which have been blanched and pounded with a few tablespoons water. Infuse for 25 minutes.

Use to prepare custard cream as described in the basic recipe for *Ice cream mixture*. Freeze the ice cream in the usual way.

Chocolate ice cream. GLACE AU CHOCOLAT – Add 250 g. (9 oz., 3 cups) grated chocolate, dissolved in 2 dl. ($\frac{1}{3}$ pint, scant cup) water to 1 litre ($1\frac{3}{4}$ pints, generous quart) boiled milk flavoured with vanilla.

The chocolate being sweet in itself, only 250 g. (9 oz., generous cup) fine sugar should be used instead of the larger quantities indicated in the basic instructions for *Ice cream mixture*.

Coffee ice cream (*Debillot. Phot. Larousse*)

Coffee ice cream. GLACE AU CAFÉ – Infuse 50 g. (2 oz., $\frac{2}{3}$ cup) freshly roasted and ground coffee in a 1 litre ($1\frac{3}{4}$ pints, generous quart) hot, boiled milk for 25 minutes. Use this to prepare the cream according to the basic instructions for *Ice cream mixture*. It can also be made by adding to the milk 2 dl. ($\frac{1}{3}$ pint, scant cup) very strong liquid coffee.

Hazelnut ice cream. GLACE AUX AVELINES – Proceed as for *Almond ice cream*, substituting for the almonds 100 g. (4 oz., 1 cup) slightly roasted, pounded hazelnuts.

Pistachio ice cream. GLACE À LA PISTACHE – Pound together 75 g. (3 oz., $\frac{2}{3}$ cup) blanched pistachio nuts and 25 g. (1 oz., 3 tablespoons) blanched fresh almonds. While pounding, add a few tablespoons milk.

Infuse in 1 litre ($1\frac{3}{4}$ pints, generous quart) boiling milk.

Hazelnut ice cream (*Larousse*)

Use to prepare the cream according to the basic instructions for *Ice cream mixture*.

Plombières ice cream. GLACE PLOMBIÈRES – Pound thoroughly in a mortar 300 g. (11 oz., 2 cups) blanched fresh almonds and 25 g. (1 oz., 3 tablespoons) blanched bitter almonds. Moisten with a little milk. Add $1\frac{1}{2}$ litres ($2\frac{1}{4}$ pints, $2\frac{3}{4}$ pints) cream.

Strain, pressing the mixture down in the strainer to extract all the milk.

Stir 10 egg yolks thoroughly with 300 g. (11 oz., $1\frac{1}{3}$ cups) fine sugar in a saucepan. Add the milk to this mixture. Heat on the stove without bringing to the boil, as for *Custard cream* (see CREAMS). Remove from the stove and stir vigorously for 3 minutes. Rub through a sieve. Freeze in a churn freezer, stirring from time to time with a spatula. When the mixture is partly frozen, add 6 dl. (1 pint, $2\frac{1}{2}$ cups) whipped cream. Continue the freezing process.

Drain off any water in the bucket and immerse the freezer once more. Cover it completely with ice and salt and leave for 2 hours.

Scoop out the ice cream with a ball-scoop and arrange in a pyramid on a dish covered with a folded napkin. Pour apricot jam over the ice cream.

Chestnut Plombières ice cream. GLACE PLOMBIÈRES AUX MARRONS – Mix 250 g. (9 oz., 1 cup) chestnut purée (made from skinned chestnuts cooked in milk) with 1 litre ($1\frac{3}{4}$ pints, generous quart) hot *Custard cream* (see CREAMS). Rub through a fine sieve. Freeze. When it is firm and smooth, mix in $\frac{1}{2}$ litre (scant pint, $2\frac{1}{4}$ cups) whipped cream, and 5 tablespoons (6 tablespoons) maraschino.

Put this mixture in a cylindrical ice cream mould and leave in the ice bucket for $1\frac{1}{2}$ hours.

Praline ice cream. GLACE AU PRALINÉ – Add to 1 litre ($1\frac{3}{4}$ pints, generous quart) vanilla custard cream, prepared as described in the recipe for *Vanilla ice cream* (see below), 125 g. (4 oz., $\frac{2}{3}$ cup) praline (q.v.) of burnt almonds, pounded and rubbed through a sieve or put through a grinder.

The same method is used for burnt hazelnuts, walnuts, pistachio nuts or peanuts.

Tea ice cream. GLACE AU THÉ – Prepare the cream in the usual way with a mixture of $7\frac{1}{2}$ dl. ($1\frac{1}{3}$ pints, $1\frac{2}{3}$ pints) milk and 3 dl. ($\frac{1}{2}$ pint, $1\frac{1}{4}$ cups) very strong, strained tea.

The same method is used for the preparation of ice creams flavoured with peppermint, lime-flower or verbena infusions.

Vanilla ice cream. GLACE À LA VANILLE – Proceed as for the basic *Ice cream mixture*, using milk in which a vanilla pod has been infused for 20 minutes, or to which 1 tablespoon of vanilla extract has been added.

Vanilla and strawberry ice cream (*Debillot. Phot. Larousse*)

Walnut ice cream. GLACE AUX NOIX – Proceed as for *Almond ice cream*, using 100 g. (4 oz., 1 cup) pounded walnuts.

Ice cream without eggs (American cookery). GLACE SANS OEUFS – Boil 1 litre ($1\frac{3}{4}$ pints, generous quart) milk with the same quantity of cream and 250 g. (9 oz., generous cup) fine sugar. Bind with 50 g. (2 oz., $\frac{1}{2}$ cup) cornflour. Rub through a hair sieve. Let it cool, stirring often.

Flavour with vanilla, lemon or orange zest, coffee, chocolate, liqueurs, etc. Freeze in the usual way.

BOMBE ICES. BOMBES GLACÉES – In former times, *bombes* were made of water ice or ice cream mixtures and were shaped in spherical moulds. This is how they got their name. Nowadays, *bombe* ices are more delicate in flavour, being made from the *Mousse* (*bombe*) *mixture* described in the basic recipes above.

A *bombe* should be made of two different ice cream mixtures, one to line the mould (this is usually a plain ice cream or a fruit or water ice), the other, which fills the casing, made from *Mousse* (*bombe*) *mixture*. *Bombes* are made in conical moulds, slightly rounded at the top, with tight-fitting lids, and are hermetically sealed with butter. They should be left to stand in ice and salt for 2 hours.

Bombe Aïda – Line the mould with *Tangerine ice*. Fill with *Mousse* (*bombe*) *mixture* flavoured with vanilla and kirsch.

Algerian bombe. BOMBE ALGÉRIENNE – Line the *bombe* mould with *Tangerine ice*. Fill with *Pineapple ice*, to which pieces of crystallised pineapple steeped in kirsch have been added.

Bombe Alhambra – Line the mould with *Vanilla ice cream*. Fill with strawberry-flavoured *Mousse* (*bombe*) *mixture*. After turning out, surround the *bombe* with large strawberries steeped in kirsch.

American bombe. BOMBE AMÉRICAINE – Line the mould with *Strawberry ice*. Fill with *Mousse* (*bombe*) *mixture* flavoured with tangerine. Decorate the *bombe* with *Pistachio ice cream* put through a forcing-bag.

Apricot bombe – See APRICOT.

Bombe Bourdaloue – Line the mould with *Vanilla ice cream*. Fill with *Mousse* (*bombe*) *mixture* flavoured with anise. Decorate the *bombe* with crystallised violets.

Bombe cardinal – Line the mould with ice cream flavoured with strawberry and raspberry. Fill with vanilla *Mousse* (*bombe*) *mixture* flavoured with praline.

Bombe Chateaubriand – Line the mould with *Apricot ice*. Fill with *Mousse* (*bombe*) *mixture* flavoured with vanilla, mixed with crystallised (candied) apricots, diced and steeped in kirsch.

Bombe dame-blanche – Line the mould with *Vanilla ice cream.* Fill with *Mousse (bombe) mixture* flavoured with almond milk.

Bombe dauphinoise – Line the mould with *Pineapple ice.* Fill with whipped cream flavoured with green Chartreuse.

Bombe diplomate – Line the mould with *Vanilla ice cream.* Fill with *Mousse (bombe) mixture* flavoured maraschino, mixed with crystallised fruit steeped in liqueur.

Bombe Doria – Line the mould with *Pistachio ice cream.* Fill with *Mousse (bombe) mixture* flavoured with vanilla, mixed with pieces of *Marrons glacés* (see CHESTNUT) steeped in Curaçao.

Bombe duchesse – Line the mould with *Pineapple ice.* Fill with *Mousse (bombe) mixture* flavoured with pears and kirsch.

Bombe Francillon – Line the mould with *Coffee ice cream.* Fill with *Mousse (bombe) mixture* flavoured with fine Champagne brandy.

Bombe Gismonda – Line the mould with *Praline ice cream.* Fill with *Mousse (bombe) mixture* flavoured with aniseed, and a praline (q.v.) made from filberts.

Bombe Grimaldi – Line the mould with *Vanilla ice cream.* Fill with *Mousse (bombe) mixture* flavoured with kummel. Decorate the *bombe* with crystallised (candied) violets and halved pistachio nuts.

Bombe Héricart – Line a large, shallow mould with *Strawberry ice.* Fill with *Mousse (bombe) mixture* flavoured with Champagne brandy, with whole strawberries from strawberry jam dotted about here and there.

Bombe impératrice – Line the mould with *Redcurrant ice.* Fill with *Rice à l'impératrice* (see RICE) mixed with diced crystallised (candied) fruit steeped in liqueur.

Bombe Médicis – Line the mould with *Pear ice.* Fill with *Mousse (bombe) mixture* flavoured with peach, and pieces of peach steeped in kirsch.

Bombe Monselet – Line the mould with *Tangerine ice.* Fill with *Mousse (bombe) mixture* flavoured with port and mixed with candied orange peel cut into little pieces and steeped in Champagne brandy.

Bombe Montmorency – Line the mould with kirsch ice (see the basic recipe above for ices flavoured with liqueurs). Fill with *Mousse (bombe) mixture* flavoured with cherry brandy, mixed with cherries steeped in kirsch.

Nelusko ice cream – *Mousse (bombe) mixture* enclosed in a layer of ice cream flavoured with praline.

Bombe Nesselrode – Line the mould with *Vanilla ice cream.* Fill with *Mousse (bombe) mixture* to which a purée of *Marrons glacés* (see CHESTNUT) flavoured with kirsch has been added.

Bombe succès – Line the mould with *Apricot ice.* Fill with *Chantilly cream* (see CREAMS) flavoured with kirsch, mixed with diced apricots.

Bombe tutti-frutti – Line the mould with *Strawberry ice.* Fill with *Mousse (bombe) mixture* flavoured with vanilla, and with a *salpicon* (q.v.) of crystallised fruit steeped in liqueur.

Bombe Véronique – Line the mould with *Pistachio ice cream.* Fill with chocolate-flavoured *Mousse (bombe) mixture* mixed with diced candied orange peel steeped in Champagne brandy.

ICED COUPES or SUNDAES. COUPES GLACÉES – These are a delicious composite sweet with ice cream as their main ingredient. They are served in glass or silver ice cups, and for this reason they are known as *coupes* in France.

The glasses are usually filled with one or more kinds of ice cream and decorated on top with fresh or crystallised fruit, or with *Chantilly cream* (see CREAMS).

Sundaes may be presented in a great many different ways.

Preparation of coupes

The *coupe Jacques* may be regarded as the classic sundae, the model for all others. (See also SUNDAES.)

Apricot coupe. COUPE GLACÉE AUX APRICOTS – Put 2 tablespoons (3 tablespoons) fresh (or canned) sliced apricots, steeped in kirsch, into a Champagne glass or ice cup.

Top with a layer of *Apricot ice.* Smooth down the surface. Decorate with half an apricot, steeped in kirsch, and halved, blanched almonds. Sprinkle with a few drops of kirsch.

Cherry coupe. COUPE GLACÉE AUX CERISES – Put 2 tablespoons (3 tablespoons) stoned cherries which have been steeped in cherry brandy and sugar in the bottom of the ice cups. Cover with *Cherry ice.*

Decorate the ices with cherries and halved almonds.

Coupe Crapotte. COUPE GLACÉE CRAPOTTE – Fill Champagne glasses or ice cups three-quarters full with a smooth layer of *Peach ice.* Arrange on top a mixture of equal quantities of alpine strawberries and raspberries, previously steeped in kummel and chilled.

Cover the fruit with a layer of whipped cream piped through a forcing-bag with a fluted nozzle.

Decorate the top with blanched almonds and crystallised violets.

Coupe Jacques – Fill Champagne glasses or ice cups with equal quantities of *Lemon ice* and *Strawberry ice.* Put 1 tablespoon fresh fruit steeped in kirsch in the middle. Decorate with crystallised cherries and halved almonds. Sprinkle a few drops of kirsch on top.

Peach coupe. COUPE GLACÉE AUX PÊCHES – Put 1 tablespoon of a *salpicon* (q.v.) of raw peaches, steeped in liqueur, in Champagne glasses or ice cups. Cover with a smooth layer of *Peach ice.* Place in the centre a ripe peach which has been peeled and chilled on ice. Sprinkle with kirsch or any other liqueur.

SHERBETS AND WATER ICES. SORBETS – See SHERBETS.

Gramolates – A *granité* (see below) served between main courses, like sherbets. They are also served as refreshments in the course of an evening's entertainment.

Granités – These ices, which are presented in special glasses, are made from fruit syrups, with a density of not more than 14° by the syrup saccharometer.

They are frozen in a churn freezer or deep freeze. Unlike other types of ice, they are not stirred during freezing. As their name suggests, *granités* should have a somewhat granular texture.

Iced Marquises. MARQUISES GLACÉES – Make from a

mixture similar to that used in the preparation of *granités* but frozen to a somewhat stiffer consistency.

It is flavoured with kirsch and should register 17° on the syrup saccharometer.

Mix in, for 1 litre ($1\frac{3}{4}$ pints, generous quart) of the syrup, 4 dl. ($\frac{3}{4}$ pint, scant 2 cups) very stiffly beaten *Chantilly cream* (see CREAMS) mixed with a purée of strawberries or some other fruit. Serve in glass goblets.

Iced punch à la romaine. PUNCH GLACÉ À LA ROMAINE – Iced punch is served between main courses, like sherbets and *granités*.

To $\frac{1}{2}$ litre (scant pint, $2\frac{1}{4}$ cups) syrup (density 22°) add enough dry white wine or dry Champagne to reduce the density to 17°. Add to this mixture a little lemon and orange rind and the juice of 2 oranges and 3 lemons. Leave, covered, for 1 hour. Strain and bring to a density of 18°.

Ice this mixture in a churn freezer until it is rather stiff. Add a quarter of its volume of *Italian meringue* (see MIXTURES), made from 2 egg whites and 100 g. (4 oz., $\frac{1}{2}$ cup) sugar.

Just before serving, mix in 1 dl. (6 tablespoons, scant $\frac{1}{2}$ cup) rum. Serve like sherbet.

Spooms – A sherbet with a sugar density of 20°. When it is frozen, *Italian meringue* (see MIXTURES) is added – twice as much as would be used in an ordinary sherbet.

Spooms are made from fruit juices or wines such as Champagne, muscatel, Frontignan, sherry, port, etc. They are served in glasses, like sherbets.

MISCELLANEOUS ICES AND ICE CREAMS. GLACES DIVERSES –

Iced mousses or mousselines. MOUSSES, MOUSSELINES GLACÉES – Iced mousse or *mousseline* may be made in two different ways, using either syrup or custard cream.

Ingredients for the syrup. Make a thick syrup (4 cups sugar, 2 cups water boiled to 104·5°C. (220°F.) and cooled). Add equal quantities of fresh fruit pulp and very stiff *Chantilly cream* (see CREAMS).

Ingredients for the cream. Make a custard using 500 g. (18 oz., $2\frac{1}{4}$ cups) sugar, 16 egg yolks and $\frac{1}{2}$ litre (scant pint, $2\frac{1}{4}$ cups) milk. Leave to cool. Add $\frac{1}{2}$ litre (scant pint, $2\frac{1}{4}$ cups) fresh cream, 20 g. ($\frac{3}{4}$ oz., $2\frac{1}{2}$ tablespoons) powdered gum tragacanth and flavouring (vanilla, orange or lemon rind, various liqueurs, etc.). If the mousse is made with fruit, add to the cream mixture $\frac{1}{2}$ litre (scant pint, $2\frac{1}{4}$ cups) fresh fruit pulp.

Beat the mixture on ice until it is very frothy. Put into moulds lined with white paper. Seal them hermetically and leave to stand in ice and salt for 2 to 3 hours, according to the size of the moulds.

Iced parfaits. PARFAITS GLACÉS – In former times the term *parfait* was used exclusively for an iced sweet flavoured with coffee. Nowadays, *parfaits* are made from all kinds of ices. They differ from *bombes* in that they are not encased in a simple water ice or ice cream.

Mix 32 egg yolks in 1 litre ($1\frac{3}{4}$ pints, generous quart) syrup of 28° density, strained and cooled.

Cook over a low flame like a custard. Strain through a fine sieve, and whisk on ice until it is quite cold. Flavour with 1 dl. (6 tablespoons, scant $\frac{1}{2}$ cup) rum or brandy, and blend in 1 litre ($1\frac{3}{4}$ pints, generous quart) cream, stiffly beaten.

Put the mixture in a *parfait* mould. Leave in ice and salt for 2 to 3 hours, or place in a food freezer.

This mixture can be flavoured with coffee, chocolate, praline, vanilla and many other flavourings.

Ice puddings. POUDINGS GLACÉS – Ice puddings can be made in many ways. They are shaped in pudding-basin moulds or in *bombe* moulds.

Line the moulds with wafers, sponge fingers steeped in liqueur as for a *Charlotte russe* (see CHARLOTTE), or with finely sliced Genoese cake cut into thin strips.

Fill with a *Mousse (bombe) mixture*. The pudding can be made more attractive by using different coloured layers of variously flavoured ice cream for the filling. It may also be made from a mixture similar to that used in a Bavarian cream (q.v.).

Ice puddings are frozen with a great deal of ice or placed in a food freezer.

Iced pudding capucine. POUDING GLACÉ CAPUCINE – Make a *Genoese cake* (see GENOESE) in a charlotte mould. Leave it until it is completely cold. Remove the top and scoop out the cake almost completely, being careful not to break the crust. Fill with alternate layers of tangerine-flavoured *Iced mousse* and kummel-flavoured *Iced mousse*, prepared in advance.

Cover the Genoese cake with its top. Surround it with ice and salt in a bucket and leave for 1 hour, or place in a food freezer.

Place it on a base of clear sugar, decorated with flowers and ribbons of spun sugar. Pipe *Chantilly cream* (see CREAMS) through a forcing-bag onto the cake.

Iced soufflés. SOUFFLÉS GLACÉS – These are prepared with a mixture similar to that used for cream iced mousses, or with a fruit mixture.

Ingredients and method for fruit iced soufflés. Whisk 10 egg whites to a stiff foam. Add 500 g. (18 oz., $2\frac{1}{4}$ cups) sugar cooked with 1 cup water to 116°C. (240°F.) (see SUGAR). Put this mixture in a bowl and chill. Add $\frac{1}{2}$ litre (scant pint, $2\frac{1}{4}$ cups) of whatever fruit purée is desired and $\frac{1}{2}$ litre (scant pint, $2\frac{1}{4}$ cups) stiffly beaten cream.

Large soufflés are served in an ordinary soufflé dish, surrounded by a white paper frill tied with string or stuck together with butter. The frill should be about $2\frac{1}{2}$ cm. (1 inch) deeper than the dish. Fill the dish until the soufflé is flush with the top of the frill. Put it in a bucket of ice and salt, or in a food freezer.

Small soufflés are served in the same way, either in little metal cases or in frilled paper cases. They, too, should be put to freeze in a bucket of ice and salt, or placed in a food freezer.

Before serving remove the paper frills from the dish or cases.

Neapolitan ice cream or ice gâteau. BISCUITS GLACÉS – These ices are made of *Ice cream mixture* shaped in rectangular boxes. Layers of ice cream are alternated with layers of water ices of different colours and flavours.

They are left to freeze in ice and salt in the usual way, or placed in a food freezer.

When the block of ice cream is taken out of the mould, it is cut into neat slabs and served either unadorned, or decorated with plain ice cream piped through a forcing-bag.

Neapolitan ice cream Comtesse-Marie. BISCUIT COMTESSE-MARIE – This is made in a special square mould (called a *Comtesse-Marie* mould). It is lined entirely with *Strawberry ice* and filled with sweet vanilla-flavoured whipped cream.

Turn the ice out of the mould into a special waxed paper case. Decorate with large strawberries steeped in kirsch, and sweet whipped cream.

ICED DESSERTS or SWEETS. ENTREMETS GLACÉS – Sweets or desserts of this kind may either be served in addition to ice cream or may include ice cream in their composition. Among these sweets are Bavarian cream (q.v.), *Charlotte russe* (see CHARLOTTE), fruit salads flavoured with liqueurs, various jellies including fruit moulds, puddings, *Rice à l'impératrice* (see RICE), stewed suédoise (q.v.).

Iced apples à la normande. POMMES GLACÉES À LA NOR-

MANDE – Scoop out large, sound cooking apples without damaging the skins. Immerse the hollowed-out apples for a few minutes in boiling syrup, so that they are slightly cooked.

From the pulp, make either an *Ice cream mixture* or a *Mousse* (*bombe*) *mixture* (see above). Flavour with Calvados.

If the apples are filled with mousse mixture, chill them in plenty of ice and salt for about 2 hours. If they are filled with ice cream, freeze the mixture first and fill the skins just before serving.

Iced grapefruit (filled). PAMPLEMOUSSE GLACÉ – This sweet can be prepared in the same way as *Iced tangerines and oranges* (see below), by filling the skins with a plain ice or *Mousse* (*bombe*) *mixture* made from the pulp.

Iced melon (filled). MELON GLACÉ – Slice off the top of a large cantaloupe melon near the stem. Remove all liquid and seeds.

Using a large spoon, scoop out the pulp, being careful not to damage the rind. Make a kirsch-flavoured water ice or ice cream with the pulp.

Just before serving, fill the melon with this ice. Serve in a large glass dish, surrounded with crushed ice.

Iced melon filled à la Chantilly. MELON GLACÉ À LA CHANTILLY – Prepare the melon as indicated above. Cook the pulp sugar and rub it through a fine sieve. When quite cold, mix it with stiffly beaten *Chantilly cream* (see CREAMS) flavoured with kirsch. Sprinkle the inside of the melon rind with sugar and kirsch, leave for a time, and then fill the rind with the mixture.

Stand the melon in an ice bucket for 2 hours before serving.

Iced pears belle angevine. POIRES BELLE ANGEVINE – Cut each pear at the stalk end, core it, scoop out some of the flesh without damaging the skin and pour boiling syrup over the fruit.

Fill the pears with pear *Iced mousse* flavoured with kirsch or with ordinary *Pear ice* made from the scooped-out flesh.

Arrange the pears on a napkin-covered dish, or on a foundation of nougat.

Iced pears, filled. POIRES DUCHESSE GLACÉES – Scoop out, without damaging the skins, some large, sound, well-shaped pears. Using the pulp, prepare a *Mousse* (*bombe*) *mixture*. Immerse the hollowed-out pears for 5 minutes in boiling syrup. Drain and leave to cool. Fill with the mousse mixture and chill for 2 hours in an ice bucket with plenty of ice and salt.

Iced pineapple. ANANAS GLACÉ – Choose a large pineapple, regular in shape, with the plume of its tufted top left on.

Remove the tufted top by a clean cut about 2 cm. ($\frac{3}{4}$ inch) below the crown. Keep it to use as a lid.

Carefully remove all the flesh, leaving on the sides and bottom of the unbroken rind, pulp about 1 cm. ($\frac{1}{2}$ inch) thick. Dust inside with 2 tablespoons (3 tablespoons) sugar, sprinkle with 2 tablespoons (3 tablespoons) kirsch and leave in a cold place for about 2 hours.

Just before serving, fill the rind with *Pineapple ice* prepared from the pulp removed earlier, with shredded pineapple steeped in kirsch added to it.

Put the pineapple on a napkin or a block of ice slightly hollowed out in the middle, and replace the tufted crown on top.

Iced pineapple à la bourbonnaise. ANANAS GLACÉ À LA BOURBONNAISE – Slice off the top of a large fresh pineapple. Keep this part with its leaves intact to cover the pineapple later.

Carefully scoop out all the flesh of the pineapple. Core it, and cut the remainder into little cubes. Sprinkle with rum and sugar and stand it on ice.

Iced pineapple mounted on a pedestal of ice
(*Modern Press*)

Make a rum ice cream.

Before serving, sprinkle the inside of the scooped-out shell with rum and sugar and embed it in an ice-bucket to chill. Fill the shell with alternate layers of pineapple cubes and rum ice cream.

Cover with the top of the pineapple. Serve surrounded with crushed ice.

Iced pineapple à la Chantilly. ANANAS GLACÉ À LA CHANTILLY–Proceed as described in the recipe for *Iced pineapple* above, replacing pineapple ice by *Vanilla ice cream* with whipped cream added to it.

Arrange the pineapple on a napkin or on a block of ice and replace the tufted top.

Iced pineapple à la créole. ANANAS GLACÉ À LA CRÉOLE – Scoop out the pineapple as indicated above. Fill with an *Iced mousse* made from the pulp of the pineapple alternating with layers of chopped crystallised fruit steeped in rum.

Replace the top of the pineapple. Serve on a dish covered with a napkin, or on a block of ice.

Iced pineapple à la parisienne I. ANANAS GLACÉ À LA PARISIENNE – Prepare a *Banana ice* and flavour with Champagne brandy.

Cut off the top of the pineapple and scoop out three-quarters of the pulp without damaging the rind. Cut the pulp into small dice and steep in a bowl with 125 g. (4 oz., $\frac{3}{4}$ cup) wild strawberries and 125 g. (4 oz., 1 cup) black grapes, sugar, and Champagne brandy. Keep in a cool place until ready to serve.

Fill the pineapple rind with banana ice, alternating with layers of the fresh fruit. Sprinkle each layer of fruit with blanched, finely shredded almonds. Finish with a layer of ice cream and cover with the tufted top.

Put on a block of ice, slightly hollowed out in the middle, or on a napkin-covered dish.

Serve with *Apricot sauce* (see SAUCE) laced with kirsch.

Iced pineapple à la parisienne II. ANANAS GLACÉ À LA PARISIENNE – Scoop out the pineapple as indicated above. Fill with alternate layers of *Strawberry ice* and a *salpicon* (q.v.) of pineapple pulp, diced and steeped in kirsch.

Iced tangerines and oranges. MANDARINES ET ORANGES GLACÉES – Slice off the top of the fruit near the stem. Scoop out the pulp carefully so as not to damage the skins. Fill the skins with a plain *Tangerine ice* or *Orange ice* made from the fruit pulp.

Cover with the top of the fruit and serve on a napkin.

Melon frappé – Two melons are used in the preparation of

Iced pineapple à la Chantilly (*Robert Carrier*)

this sweet. Using the pulp of one of them, make a *granité* flavoured with kirsch.

Slice off the top of the second melon near the stem. Remove all liquid and seeds. Using a spoon, scoop out the pulp, being careful not to damage the rind. Steep the pulp on ice in Frontignan, port, sherry, kirsch, maraschino or Curaçao.

Put the shell of the melon in an ice bucket until it is very cold. Fill with alternate layers of the *granité* and the iced flesh of the second melon.

Replace the top of the melon. Serve in a glass dish.

Peaches cardinal. PÊCHES CARDINAL – Stew the peaches in a syrup flavoured with vanilla. Leave until completely cold. Drain them. Put them in a dish on a fairly thick layer of *Strawberry ice*. Cover with iced redcurrant jelly flavoured with kirsch, and scatter wild strawberries on top.

Peach Melba. PÊCHES MELBA – This sweet was first made in London by Escoffier. Line a silver dish with a fairly thick layer of *Vanilla ice cream*. Place on top peeled peaches which have been steeped in a syrup flavoured with vanilla, and left until they are completely cold. The peaches are then covered with raspberry purée.

Many other kinds of fruit may be served in the same way. For instance, large fresh strawberries steeped in sugar or kirsch; pears (halved or quartered) stewed in vanilla-flavoured syrup, and chilled; nectarines (peeled, stewed in syrup and chilled), etc.

Pear Melba. POIRES MELBA – Poach the pears in vanilla-flavoured syrup. Drain and dry them. Arrange in a glass dish or a *timbale* on a foundation of *Vanilla ice cream* and cover with raspberry purée.

ICHTHYOPHAGY. ICHTYOPHAGIE – The practice of eating nothing, or almost nothing, but fish. Ichthyophagy is mainly practised among seaboard peoples. A fish diet is said to be less nourishing than a meat diet, but there are no substantial grounds for this view. Fish has been credited with aphrodisiac properties. It is also said to stimulate the brain. These properties were attributed to fish because of a misguided belief that it contains a high proportion of phosphorus. In fact there is less phosphorus in fish than in meat, less even than in some vegetables. Fish on the whole is very easily digested. As a result it gives the impression of being less filling than some other foods, and so it is not favoured by manual workers.

ICING. GLACES DE SUCRE – Sugar icing, which may be prepared with or without cooking, is used in confectionery of all kinds. Pastries, cakes and *petits fours* (q.v.) of various kinds may all be decorated with icing.

Blackcurrant icing. GLACE AU CASSIS – Mix ½ dl. (3 tablespoons, scant ¼ cup) blackcurrant juice with 1 dl. (6 tablespoons, scant ½ cup) syrup cooked to hard ball stage (121°C., 250°F.). Add enough icing sugar to produce a fairly stiff paste. Mix. This icing must be warmed slightly before use. It is often coloured with a little liquid carmine.

Using the same method, icing may be made with strawberries, raspberries, redcurrants and other red fruit.

Chocolate icing. GLACE AU CHOCOLAT – Place 125 g. (4 oz., 4 squares) unsweetened, softened chocolate in a bowl. Add a few tablespoons lukewarm syrup, boiled to short thread stage (see SUGAR), and icing sugar. This icing must be used at once.

Coffee icing. GLACE AU CAFÉ – Add to ½ litre (scant pint, 2¼ cups) very strong coffee (coffee essence) enough icing sugar to make a fairly stiff paste. This icing must be used at once.

Fondant icing. GLACE AU FONDANT – Put in a basin 2½ kg. (5½ lb.) lump sugar. Add 1½ litres (2¼ pints, 2¾ pints) water and 100 g. (4 oz., 1 cup) glucose.

Cook over a high flame, skimming from time to time, until the sugar has reached 116°C. (240°F.) or soft ball stage (see SUGAR).

Pour the sugar onto a marble slab and let it cool a little. Work it with a spatula by folding the edges towards the centre until it is a white and very smooth fondant. Put in a bowl, cover with a damp cloth and leave in a cool place.

To use the fondant. Soften a few tablespoons of the mixture in a small saucepan over a low flame, stirring constantly. Add a little syrup cooked to short thread stage. Flavour with any appropriate liqueur, or add a little coffee essence or melted chocolate.

Colour the fondant with carmine or any other vegetable colouring if desired.

Lemon icing – GLACE AU CITRON – Made with the rind and juice of lemons, as for *Orange icing* (see below).

Orange icing. GLACE À L'ORANGE – Put the peel of 2 oranges in 1 dl. (6 tablespoons, scant ½ cup) syrup cooked to the hard ball stage (see SUGAR) and let it stand for 15 minutes. Add the strained juice of the fruit. Put the mixture in a bowl, add icing sugar, and proceed as for other kinds of icing.

This icing may be coloured with a little liquid carmine and a yellow vegetable dye. It must be used at once.

Royal icing. GLACE ROYALE – Put 2 egg whites in a small bowl. Add enough icing sugar to make a fairly stiff paste, though it must be soft enough to spread easily on cakes and pastry.

Mix, without working the eggs and sugar too hard.

Royal icing for desserts or sweets. GLACE ROYALE – Prepared in the same way as ordinary royal icing with egg whites and very fine icing sugar. Add to the mixture 6 to 8 drops of lemon juice and work with a spatula for 8 to 10 minutes. When the icing is ready, cover with damp paper. Keep in a cool place.

Strawberry fondant icing. GLACE AU FONDANT À LA FRAISE – Cook sugar to 116°C. (240°F.) or soft ball stage (see SUGAR). Add a little strawberry juice and a few drops of lemon juice. Pour it on a marble slab and work it with a spatula until very smooth.

Using the same method, fondant icing may be made with raspberry juice, lemon (rind and juice), or orange (rind and juice), or from the pulp or juice of other kinds of fruit.

Icing flavoured with rum and other liqueurs. GLACE AU RHUM – Put in a bowl 1 dl. (6 tablespoons, scant ½ cup) syrup cooked to soft ball stage (see SUGAR), 1½ tablespoons rum and 1 teaspoon lemon juice. Add icing sugar. Mix. Use at once.

Icing made in this way may be flavoured with other liqueurs.

IERCHI – Russian name for a small fish similar to gudgeon. It is much used in Russian cooking, served fried or in soup.

Iguana

IGUANA. IGUANE – A kind of lizard, very scarce except in the tropics. Iguanas are to be found in both hemispheres, but there is one species which exists only in America.

In spite of its size, which precludes its assimilation with European lizards – though it is akin to these in its habits, and is almost as graceful and no less agile – the iguana should be included among those harmless animals which are worthy of preservation.

Its flesh is among the foods most highly prized by the gourmets of Central and South America.

ÎLE-DE-FRANCE – Some people say that Paris, the symbol and home of the whole gastronomic tradition of the Île-de-France, does not possess culinary specialities which are particularly her own. Such people take no account of the magnificent work carried out by the master chefs of Parisian restaurants, from Carême to Escoffier. There were also Gouffé, Urbain Dubois, Philéas Gilbert, Marguery, Paillard, Mourier, Nignon and a host of others.

In this vast city there are the best cooks and most skilful *cordons bleus* of all France. Paris abounds with foodstuffs imported from abroad and brought in from every corner of France, not to mention the produce of the fertile soil of the Île-de-France, and the livestock reared in all the *départements* around Paris, which provide it with savoury fish, delicate poultry, every kind of game and a host of other delicious things.

Les Halles (*French Government Tourist Office*)

The finest vegetables are grown in the Île-de-France, and the most delicately flavoured fruit is picked in the orchards of Paris. Here is a list of a few of the gastronomic delights to be found in the Île-de-France, and in the Paris region in particular:

Argenteuil asparagus, which with that of Lauris has the reputation of being the best in France; Clamart green peas; the French beans of Bagnolet; the cauliflower of Arpajon; the carrots of Crécy-sur-Morin; Laon artichokes and asparagus; the white beans of Soissons, or more accurately of Noyon; the lettuces of Versailles; the fragrant morels of the woods of Verrières, Viarmes and Rambouillet; the cultivated

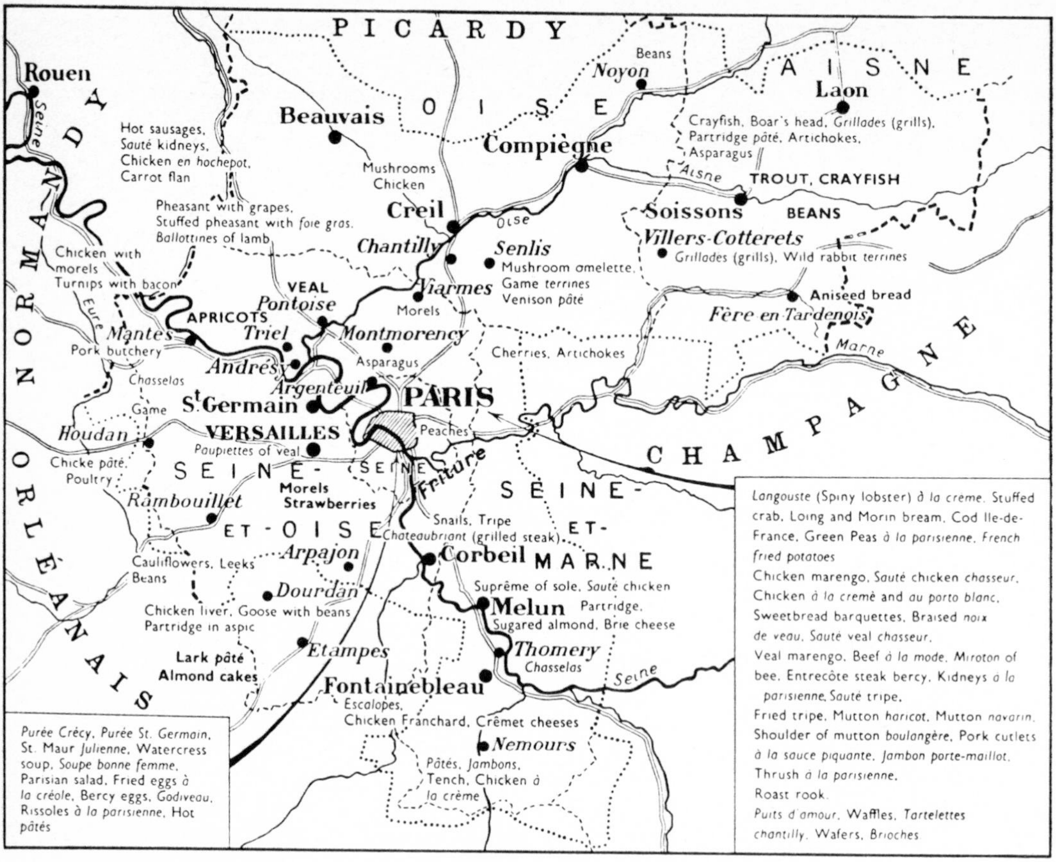

Gastronomic map of Île-de-France

mushrooms of the Paris region, called *champignons de Paris*; the pot-vegetables grown at Bagneux, Châtillon, Saint Denis and other places in the area; onions, small and large, leeks, cabbages, carrots, turnips, cucumbers, shallots, various salads, spinach, sorrel, chervil, parsley, parsnips, horse-radish, beetroot.

The fruits of the Paris orchards have a great reputation; the Chasselas of Fontainebleau (those from the king's vine-arbour), of Thomery and Andrézy; the peaches of Montreuil; the strawberries of the Bièvre valley, the Héricart strawberry which the barrow-men call 'Ricart', and many other sweet-smelling fruits which melt in the mouth, such as pears, apples, plums, figs, apricots and nectarines.

Excellent meat is sold in Paris. What is more, the Paris butchers are true artists, and their cuts are flawless. Pontoise veal, called river veal, is as tender and as delicate as any to be found.

In the woods and forests around Paris, in the regions of Versailles, Marly and Saint-Germain-au-Laye, there is an abundance of excellent game.

The poultry of Houdan is held in high repute for its delicate flavour. The freshwater fish caught in the Seine, the Marne, the Oise and the Aisne are especially delicious.

Very good cheeses are made round about Paris, among which are Coulommiers, Brie, Brie de Melun, and the fresh cream cheese known as the Crèmet of Fontainebleau, which rivals the famous fresh cream cheese of Saumur and Angers.

On the hillsides of the Marne, which are an extension of the neighbouring Champagne vineyards, the grapes gathered produce table wines that are fresh and pleasant to taste.

Excellent cider is brewed in the Aisne and Oise districts, and among the liqueurs distilled in the Paris region there is one, the *Noyau de Poissy*, which enjoys a great and long-established reputation.

Culinary specialities – The following soups were invented in Paris, in Parisian restaurants by Parisian chefs, and may be classed among the culinary specialities of Paris and the Paris region: *Crêcy, Saint-Germain, Parisien, Bonne-femme, Cressonnière, Santé, Bonvalet, Compiègne, Cormeilles, Briard, Soissonnais, Argenteuil, Ambassadeurs, Balvet, Faubonne, Germiny* (invented by Dugléré at the *Café Anglais*), *Darblay, Longchamp, Saint-Cloud.*

Among the pork specialities of the Paris region are: *Andouillettes* (chitterling sausages); *boudins noirs et blancs* (black and white puddings); *petit-salé*; *veau piqué* (misnamed since it is not made from veal but from pork); *friands parisiens; Pâté de foie de cochon* (pig's liver *pâté*); *fromage de tête de porc* (pork brawn); *hure de porc à la parisienne* (boar's head *à la parisienne*) *Roulade de tête de porc; pâté de porc de Paris; rillons* and *rillettes; cervelas* or *saucisson à cuire* (saveloy or cooking sausage); *jambon glacé de Paris* (glazed Paris ham); *côtes de porc à la charcutière* (ribs of pork *à la charcutière*)*; pieds de porc à la parisienne* (pig's trotters *à la parisienne*).

Among the dishes made from other meat are: *Beef miroton; shoulder of mutton à la boulangère; entrecôte Bercy* and *entrecôte marchand de vin*; the celebrated *navarin of mutton*, and the old *halicot* of mutton with turnips, now called *haricot of mutton; fillet of beef à la bèarnaise* (*béarnaise sauce* having been created at Saint-Germain-en-Laye); *rib of veal à la bonne femme; calves' tendons à la paysanne*; the old-fashioned *fricandeau; calves' head du Puits Certin; sauté of veal chasseur; mutton chops Champvallon; sheep's trotters à la poulette; épigrammes of mutton, lamb*, etc.

Among the special poultry and game dishes of Paris are: *Sautéed chicken Bercy, Boivin-Champeaux, Chasseur, Durand, fines herbes, Lathuile, Parmentier; spring chicken en cocotte, à la Clamart, à la bonne-femme, à la diable; squab à la crapaudine, en compote, en papillotes; duckling nantais with turnips, green peas; duckling rouennais à la presse; timbale of duckling Voisin; gibelotte of young rabbit; young garenne rabbit chasseur; pheasant à la Sainte-Alliance*, a majestic creation from the hands of Brillat-Savarin; *snipe à la fine Champagne, à la Riche; wild duck à la presse.*

Vol-au-vent, flans and tarts filled in many different ways have for a very long time been regarded as culinary specialities of Paris.

Special Parisian fish (sea and freshwater) and shellfish dishes are: *Lobster à l'américaine*; the various *matelotes* of eels and freshwater fish, for example *matelotes du Moulin de la Râpée* and *à la canotière; eel à la tartare; carp à la canotière; bouillabaisse à la parisienne* (doubtless disapproved of by natives of Marseilles, but excellent all the same, and invented by a Parisian master chef); *whiting Bercy, Colbert, au gratin*; all manner of dishes made of sole, brill, turbot, sea perch, etc., *brill Dugléré, young turbot au plat, sole à la normande, sole Marguery, turbot à la parisienne, spring lobster à la parisienne, coquilles Saint-Jacques à la parisienne, frogs' legs à la poulette.*

The sauces in the Paris repertoire are numerous. Among the brown sauces may be mentioned: *Charcutière, chasseur, Colbert, diable, hachée, moelle* and *Robert.*

Among the white sauces the following are the best known: *Béarnaise, Bercy, Bonnefoy, Chantilly, Choron, Fayot, Laguipière, marinière, mousseline, moutarde, poulette, ravigote, Riche* and *Véron.*

Here is a random selection of some other Parisian specialities: *Green peas à la française, à la parisienne; Matelote de Beauvais*; the partridge *pâtés* of Laon; the poultry *pâtés* of Houdan; the lark *pâtés* of Étampes; *échaudés; puits d'amour; oublies*; the Paris brioche; the aniseed bread of Fère-en-Tardenois; the stuffed pears of Provins; the cakes of Compiègne and Étampes; the green walnuts of Faucaucoure; the barley-sugar of Moret and the sugared almonds of Melun.

IMPÉRATRICE (À L') – Name applied to various dishes and cakes. Among these is *Rice à l'impératrice*, a cold dessert, a recipe for which is given under RICE.

IMPERIAL. IMPÉRIALE – The name given to a variety of plum and also to a large bottle holding about 4 litres ($3\frac{1}{2}$ quarts, $4\frac{1}{2}$ quarts), which is used for Bordeaux wines and for spirits.

IMPÉRIALE (À L') – Name applied to various dishes garnished with truffles, *foie gras*, cocks' combs and kidneys, and other similar garnishes.

IMPROMPTU – An improvised meal which would be described as a pot-luck meal in English.

INCISE. INCISER – To make shallow incisions with a sharp knife in the skin of fish that is to be grilled or fried.

INFUSE. INFUSER – To steep herbs or other flavouring in boiling liquid, until the liquid absorbs the flavour.

Milk used in the preparation of creams and custards is flavoured by infusing vanilla, cinnamon, or lemon or orange rind in it.

Wine used in the preparation of sauces is flavoured by the infusion of mushroom peelings, truffles or any kind of herb.

INSECTS, EDIBLE. INSECTES COMESTIBLES – Considering the prodigious number of insects, which, for the most part, feed on the greenstuffs which are also eaten by man and his flocks and cattle, one cannot help being surprised that in the west, even in times of famine, no one dreams of eating them.

They are usually objects of disgust among western peoples who do not, however, hesitate to eat prawns and other shellfish. On the other hand, the Arabs and other peoples of Africa and Asia look upon certain insects as great delicacies, and are surprised at our taste for shellfish.

The Hebrew tribes ate insects, long before Saint John the Baptist was forced to feed exclusively on locusts and other creatures of the same kind. In Leviticus (II, 21–22), Moses enumerates the animals which the Hebrews were permitted to eat. Among these he mentions four insects which Saint Jerome in his Latin translation calls *locusta, bruchus, ophimachus* and *attacus.*

The *locusta* must have been the locust, but naturalists have been unable to identify the other three.

Several other insects, such as white ants, are used as food by savage tribes. In ancient times, the Greeks prized grasshoppers very highly, especially the larvae. The Chinese, too, greatly enjoy eating certain insects, and feast upon the chrysalis of the silk-worm, while in Mexico, fried palm and agave grubs are sold in the streets like chestnuts.

INTERLARDING. PIQUAGE DES VIANDES – See CULINARY METHODS.

INTERNATONAL COOKERY. CUISINE ÉTRANGÈRE – AMERICAN COOKERY. CUISINE AMÉRICAINE – **Canada** – Traditions of home cooking persist in Canada despite the growing dependence on convenience foods elsewhere. The type of home cooking varies according to which part of Europe the family originally came from.

The native inhabitants had little to offer. The Huron and Iroquoi Indians cooked their beans in the embers, and lived mainly on a porridge made of water and crushed maize, to which they added fish or meat. However, pork trotter stew is said to be of Indian origin.

Otherwise it is European cookery, or rather European provincial cookery that forms the basis of Canadian *cuisine*. In Labrador, and on the shores of Newfoundland, we rediscover specialities of Mecklenburg, Swabia and Switzerland. Elsewhere, it is English cookery that reigns supreme. And naturally the whole of French Canada guards the secrets of the traditional regional dishes of France, especially those of Normandy. Certain religious communities in Canada still possess old recipes long since forgotten, even in France: a type of gingerbread made by the Ursuline nuns of Quebec, for example.

Canada is a rich country, with immense reserves of game; the Canadians eat bear, caribou, moose, and the goats of the Rocky Mountains. Fish abound in the innumerable lakes. Wheat, maize, oats and barley grow in abundance. These energy-giving cereals form the principal part of most Canadians' midday meal. The Ministry of Agriculture publishes booklets of cereal recipes, in order to encourage housewives to be adventurous in their presentation of cereals.

Canada is, above all, the country of the maple, the tree that is the country's national emblem. Whenever the thaws come, its bark is pierced by the sap collectors, and the sap flows like water: clear and slightly sweet. It is boiled to a syrup, which, together with the light brown maple sugar, form the basis of cakes, biscuits, sauces and jams, perfuming the Canadian air with the aroma of honey.

Central and South America – The cookery of South America is a spicier version of Spanish or Portuguese *cuisine* (depending upon the region), while that of Central America, and of Cuba in particular, is individual in character. (Cuba boasts a wide range of food produce, all of excellent quality.)

Delicately fleshed fish are caught in the Caribbean Sea and in the Gulf of Mexico. The best of these are *cabrilla, cabra mora, cherna criolla*, and *cherna americana*. They are all spindle-shaped and vividly coloured.

In the same seas are found fish that belong to the same family as the perch: the *rabirrubia*, the *pargo colorado*, the *pargo amarillo*, to name only a few.

A species closely related to the above includes the *ronco carbonero*, the *boca colorada*, the *ronco amarillo*, the *jeniguana*, etc. Fish of the mackerel family also abound in these waters.

All these fish are served boiled, grilled or fried. Some are considered more suitable for marinating.

The oysters caught off the shores of Cuba are delicious. They include a variety with a completely white shell.

Among the shellfish is a type of giant prawn (some weighing as much as 400 g. (14 oz.). These prawns are a blackish-blue colour when they emerge from the water but cooking changes them to red.

High-quality meat is imported from the United States; the poorer home-produced beef is consumed by the country people. The latter comes from oxen which, working in a hot country as they do, yield lean, not very tasty meat.

Veal is better, mutton is mediocre, but pork is of good quality. Poultry is scarce and of inferior quality in Central America. Eggs, of course, are also scarce.

Cuba grows a wide range of vegetables, many of them similar to those found in our markets. In Central America there are edible plants such as manioc, Chinese potatoes, yams, Indian corn, plantain (the large banana used in cooking), and the small Indian pumpkin (*calabaza*). There are grapefruit, citrons, several varieties of oranges, lemons, sour limes, mangoes, guavas, red and yellow bananas, anonas, coconuts, avocado pears, custard apples, etc.

The special dishes of Central America are all highly spiced and most of them contain green peppers. Fish dishes include *cod à la créole* (*bacalao à la criolla*)*; cod Biscay-style; marinated fish; West Indian red prawns (camarones)* fried in oil; *cherna with onions; octopus with pimentos*.

Meat dishes include *olla podrida*, a hearty stew made from a variety of meats, found in the parts of the country of Iberian origin; *sancocho*, which is a type of *olla podrida; puchero*, a Spanish-style *pot-au-feu; monteria*, a chicken and tomato hash garnished with yams, potatoes and white Indian corn cobs and served with Cuban-style rice surrounded with bananas fried in oil; various types of meat balls called *albondiguillas de carne; tasajo à la cubaine* (minced cured beef simmered in tomato sauce and served with Cuban-style rice and fried bananas); *pork chops Cuban-style*, or *with rice*, or *à l'espagnole; marinated rabbit; tamales*.

Nearly all South American dishes are served with rice. This is prepared, Cuban-style, *à la créole* or *à la valencienne*. The vegetable specialities of the country include a variety of ways of preparing potatoes which along with rice, bananas and Indian corn take the place of our bread and most of our vegetables in the diet of the natives of the West Indies and Central America; bananas and plantain, eaten raw and used in cooking; Japanese and Porto Rican yams, served braised, or in hazelnut butter, or *à la créole*; roots of cassava or manioc prepared like yams; gombos prepared *à l'espagnole* or *à la créole;* avocado *à la créole* or in salad, palm cabbage in salad.

The orchards of Central America contain many delicious fruits, most of which are exported to Europe.

The large custard apple is the biggest member of the anona family. This fruit, which can weigh as much as 3 kg. ($6\frac{1}{2}$ lb.) is sometimes called sour sop in English. When it reaches maturity it exudes a pleasant aroma. Its dense white flesh, with large black seeds, is slightly acid and a tasty beverage is obtained by crushing the pulp and mixing it with four or five times its volume of water.

Anonas (small custard apples) are shaped rather like artichokes. The cream-coloured flesh is sweet but rather insipid. They are eaten raw.

The mamey of Santo Domingo can grow to the size of a small melon. Its skin is thick and its flesh yellow. It contains a very large stone. Called the apricot of the Tropics, it has, apart from the colour of its pulp, no similarity to this fruit. The fruit is usually stewed. A certain bitterness remains whatever method of preparation is chosen.

The red mamey, despite its name, belongs to a different family. Its other name in Central America is sapota. The skin of this fruit is woody and its strawberry-coloured flesh has the consistency of a ripe banana. It is usually eaten raw.

Guavas come in several varieties. Some are orange-shaped, others pear-shaped, others again look like large figs. The flesh is insipid and is generally eaten raw. It may also be stewed or made into jellies.

Mangoes vary in shape according to their species. Usually they resemble pears both in colour and shape. Their pulp is very juicy but slightly bitter in flavour.

The citron is the biggest fruit of the lemon family. This fruit is hardly ever eaten raw. It is usually preserved.

The grapefruit is the biggest fruit of the orange family. In Central America it is called either *pomelos*, or by its English name.

Kumquats are small fruits of the orange family. They are about the size and shape of olives and may be eaten raw like almonds since their skin is tender and not bitter. They may also be stewed, or pickled in vinegar.

From the Argentine (Spanish influence) to Brazil (Portuguese influence), from Peru to Bolivia the same dishes (with only slight variations) and the same spices appear again and again. Beer and rum are drunk in Columbia, excellent beer and *chica* in Bolivia. There are vineyards in the Argentine, Uruguay and Peru. Chile is the largest wine-producing area (see WINES).

United States – The history of cooking of the United States is closely related to the history of the country. When the early settlers arrived, they found the Indians, who had been living off the land for centuries, eating the animals and birds of the plains and forests; fish and shellfish from the seas, lakes, rivers and streams; and wild fruits and nuts; a great variety of greens, and corn (maize). Most of the settlers, beginning with the Spanish explorers in the 1500s, followed by the British in the 1600s, and not long after, the Dutch, French, Germans, and Scandinavians, arrived in the New World with domestic animals and native plants to start a new life comparable to the one they had left behind. Many of them incorporated into their traditional eating habits certain Indian foods, especially corn.

By the nineteenth century, people from every corner of the globe had come to this country, settling in different areas. Thus regional cooking in the United States can be attributed in part to the resources of an area, but also to the people who settled there and adapted their native cooking habits to what nature had to offer.

Many factors enter into the American gastronomical picture. Most important are the natural resources of the whole country, modern food handling and rapid transportation, food technology, nutritional emphasis, and communication.

The climatic and geographical conditions of the United States are so varied that from the fertile valleys, vast forests and plains, lakes, rivers and streams, and extensive coastal regions, almost every food known to man can be produced within its borders. With modern technology, the produce of any one section of the country can be enjoyed in any other. For example, oranges and grapefruit grown in Florida or California are sold in every State in the Union. Maine lobsters are served in Texas, and oysters and crabs from Maryland are served fresh in Chicago. This means that very few foods are unique to any one area, but there are still special dishes that certain localities claim as their own. To mention a few, baked beans and brown bread belongs to Boston, and lobster stew to Maine. Fried chicken, hominy grits and pecan pie are at home south of the Mason-Dixon line; roast pork tastes best in Iowa; and New Orleans is where one finds the best Creole cooking.

Food technology, which concerns itself in part with the processing and packaging of food, takes much of the hard work of food preparation out of the home or restaurant kitchen. This, together with country-wide distribution, tends to standardise American food. The whole country is highly nutrition-conscious. Great emphasis is placed on the importance of eating foods with high vitamin and mineral content; food is advertised and sold quite as much for its food value as for its enjoyment. Food fads extolling the health-giving properties of one food or another come and go, but the basic requirements for nutritional health remain constantly in the minds of most Americans, professional and domestic, who plan meals.

The food business, with its main contributing subdivisions, represents a major part of American industry. One subdivision is communication, with cookbooks, magazine articles, newspaper columns, radio and television programmes all dealing with the production and preparation of food. The United States can boast its share of gourmets who strive constantly, through the various media of communications, to raise the gastronomic standards of the country.

Hotels and restaurants in the United States, as in most countries, range from the simplest to the most luxurious. In large cities such as New York, Chicago and San Francisco, there are many restaurants which specialise in food from other countries. In large cities generally, the better restaurants combine American cooking with international cooking, the French variety having the predominant influence. Outside the cities and across the length and breadth of the country there are thousands of small inns, restaurants and hotels. Some of the establishments specialising in regional cookery have attained national reputations. Peculiarly American are the eating-places dedicated to eating as quickly as possible for as little money as possible. These include lunch counters where quick-order meals are served, cafeterias where customers serve themselves from a wide variety of foods, the ubiquitous hot-dog and hamburger stands, and drive-ins where meals are served to patrons in their cars.

Certain American gastronomical habits that surprise visitors to the country are the speed with which most people eat, the number of foods that are served together on a plate, the sweet jellies and conserves served with meat and vegetables, and the great quantities of dairy produce used. These are admittedly American characteristics, but the nature of the country, and the international nature of its population, make it impossible to define United States cookery as such, other than to say that America is capable of producing and cooking the finest food in the world. Favourite American foods are: steaks, lamb chops, ham, chicken, lobster, corn on the cob, apple pie and ice cream.

When Spanish monks planted a few vines around Los Angeles in the eighteenth century, they had little idea that 200 years later America would be the second biggest wine-producing continent in the world.

It was not until a century ago, however (thanks to a Hungarian called Harszthy) that California became the centre of the American wine industry.

American wines are classified as 'dry' wines (white or red wines not exceeding 14°), and 'sweet' or 'dessert' wines. Some bear the name of the grower; others have European names.

A great deal of alcohol is consumed in the United States. This is mainly derived from cereals. There is also home-produced gin and imported Scotch whisky. On the whole, however, Americans prefer their own Bourbon whisky which is distilled from maize, or Canadian rye whisky.

Small pastries filled with jam: gefüllte Tascherl
(pâtisserie viennoise)

AUSTRIAN COOKERY. CUISINE AUTRICHIENNE – Austrian *cuisine* is refined and contains Italian, German and Oriental influences. The traditional *goulasch*, which is of Hungarian origin, consists of sautéed beef cooked in a very thin sauce, garnished with sweet peppers. Sweet peppers are also served stuffed. Viennese boiled beef is well known. It is made with well-hung, tender meat and is accompanied by salads and various compotes. *Wiener-schnitzel* is a veal escalope, breadcrumbed, then fried in clarified butter.

Austria is above all the country of puddings and pastries: *Mehlspeisen, Linzer torte* and *Sacher-torte* are well known. *Nockerl* are quenelles made of flour and eggs bound with milk, similar to the *Spätzle* of Baden but sweeter and more delicate. They are sprinkled with poppyseeds and served with cream. *Strudel* consists of a very stiff dough rolled out thinly then folded over and over with layers of a kind of apple jam. *Kaiser-schmarren* is a thick sweet pancake which is divided in the pan as the mixture firms. The triumph of these Viennese sweets is the *Zchwetschgen-knödel* – prunes with their stones replaced by lumps of sugar, then wrapped in a very light potato pastry and fried.

Austria makes an excellent lager. Large quantities of red and white wines are also produced. See *Central European Cookery* in this section.

BELGIAN COOKERY. CUISINE BELGE – Belgium is the country of 'pudding fairs'. The citizens of the city and suburbs of Brussels, for example, spend three days celebrating theirs. It is a country with a great love of food, for although surrendering wholeheartedly to the delicacies of French *cuisine*, the Belgian gourmet has remained faithful to his own national specialities. These include *eel au vert* (a spring and summer dish); Flemish *carbonade* for which the celebrated national beer, *gueze lambic*, seems specially designed; *choezels au madère; fricadelles bruxelloises* (fried mince balls); *l'oie à l'instar de Visé* (goose Visé-style); *hochepot gantois* (Ghent hotchpot); *kouyn met pruneu* (rabbit with prunes), essentially a Flemish dish; *hop shoots; Brussels endive; pâté namurois brioché* (Namur brioche pastry pie); and the succulent dishes *à la liégeoise* (calves' kidneys, larks, crayfish, etc.) which for many food lovers are the jewels of Belgian *cuisine*. The sauces are all seasoned predominantly with juniper berries, giving the dishes a distinctive flavour.

One of Belgium's national dishes is *waterzoii* (spouting water). Once made of fish from the Flemish coast, it now consists of chickens from the farmlands, especially those round Ghent. It is also one of the most ancient of Belgian dishes. Legend has it that Charles V considered it one of the best (and there is a painting in humorous vein by Herbo to illustrate this).

Brillat-Savarin, once initiated into the delights of Belgian *cuisine*, greatly enjoyed *waterzoii*, Namur pie, and the dishes with a distinctly Latin flavour such as those *à la liégeoise*. *L'oie à l'instar de Visé* surprised but did not tempt him. The origin of the recipe, although comparatively recent, is much disputed. It is said to owe its creation to an angry police inspector who, sixty years ago, was in charge of police headquarters in the charming Meuse village of Visé. One day he was called upon to settle a dispute concerning a goose that had wandered onto the public highway and been run over by a carter. The owner of the goose demanded nine francs compensation from the carter and said that he could keep the dead bird. The carter refused to pay more than six francs since, he said, the goose was no use to him.

'As you do not wish to have the bird,' the police inspector said to the carter, 'pay him the six francs you have offered.'

Then he said to the owner of the goose, 'As for you, since you are determined to rid yourself of the creature, here are this fellow's six francs and here are three from me. That makes nine, which is the amount you asked. I'll take the goose myself.'

The police inspector took the goose home and prepared it in the following way. He trussed and placed it in a large cooking pot, together with the giblets, and covered it with salted water. This was brought to the boil and skimmed. He added 2 heads of garlic, some onion, a few carrots, a *bouquet garni*, 2 cloves and several white peppercorns.

When the bird was cooked, he carefully jointed it and simmered the pieces gently in equal parts of goose fat and butter. He then made a white *roux* from goose fat, flour, and a little goose stock. This, when boiled, produced a rather thick sauce. He then added 4 egg yolks, a few pats of butter, and cream. He sieved the sauce, and tossed in a few cloves of garlic previously cooked in milk. Finally he arranged the goose portions on a large plate and poured the sauce over them.

Another recipe appears under GOOSE.

CENTRAL EUROPEAN AND BALKAN COOKERY. CUISINE DE L'EUROPE CENTRALE ET DES BALKANS – First in importance and distinction comes **Hungary**, symbolised for us by *goulasch* and paprika. The latter, however, is a recent innovation, dating from the Turkish occupation. Paprika-flavoured dishes include *goulasch* (meat soup or stew), *pörkölt* (a thicker stew in which onion predominates), *tokany* (with the meat thinly sliced); *paprikache* (stew made with white meat or fish and flavoured with sour cream) and *szekelygylyas* (pork, sour cream and *sauerkraut*).

Characteristic ingredients of Hungarian *cuisine* are pork and goose fat, and large quantities of onion.

The *fogas* of Lake Balaton is a famous variety of fish.

The national *pâtisserie* speciality is *rétèche*: flaky pastry stuffed with vegetables, cheese or fruit. Hungarian wines are excellent, the most famous being Tokay. There is also an apricot liqueur called barack.

Beer (Pilsen) is the national beverage in **Czechoslovakia**. Pork, a beef *pot-au-feu* (*hovesy maso*), potatoes, goose, and cabbage are the staple foods.

The Orient has been the main influence in **Rumanian** cookery, which is based on fish, pork and game. The wines are excellent.

Bulgarian cookery is a blend of Turkish and Russian influences. *Tchorba* soup and yogurt reign supreme. There is a plum spirit called slivovitz.

Yugoslavian cookery is as varied as the races and the climate. Serbs, Croats, Slovenes and Bosnians all eat Hungarian stews, Italian pastas and Turkish pastries, and drink beer and wine.

In **Greece**, there is beef in the north, lean mutton in the south, fish, olive oil, *mézés* (see *Turkish cookery* below) and ouzo (the raki of the other Mediterranean coast) everywhere.

Greek wines are generally very sweet. Samos is one of them, counterpart of the hydromel of the Ancient Greeks. Retsina is flavoured with resin.

CHINESE COOKERY. CUISINE CHINOISE – 'China and France,' Curnonsky said, 'are the only two peoples to have created a *cuisine* that is inseparably linked with good manners and courtesy.' Since the time of the Celestial Empire, the Chinese have considered their *cuisine* an art and an important expression of their country's civilisation.

Chinese cookery in restaurants abroad may not be a true reflection of the original. Preparation is a painstaking business, with the cook carefully scooping out bones and shredding fowl, meat and fish into strips that can be easily manipulated by chopsticks. These existed a long time before Europe had the fork, and are made of bamboo, blackwood, ivory, silver or plastic.

Most of the dishes are common to the whole of China, with rice as the principal ingredient. Besides taking the place of bread, it can be a main course, an accompaniment, steamed, boiled or fried. Northern China (including Pekin) is where highly seasoned dishes are to be found; Nankin, Shanghai, central China and Szechuan prefer sweet dishes. Canton, in the south, is the gastronomic capital of China.

The soya bean is the other basic ingredient. Soy sauce (*cho-you*) like the Vietnamese *nuoc nam*, is one of the reasons why Chinese *cuisine* is described as 'a form of dietetics, 5,000 years old'.

Salangane's nest soup and *shark's fin soup* are based on chicken stock. The classical method of cooking is by steaming. Eel, goose and duck are cooked in this way. A philosopher, Lao Tesu, once said: 'Govern the Empire as carefully as you would cook a small fish.' The fruits of the sea are much respected in China.

Lacquered duck (prepared twenty-four hours in advance) is a great classical dish. Chicken is prepared with pineapple, almonds, bamboo shoots, Chinese mushrooms or in sweet-and-sour sauce (like pork).

Only a glass of warm yellow wine (rice wine) is drunk with the meal. Jasmine tea is served afterwards. It has been known there since the year 2000 B.C. There are two main types of tea: green tea (*tsing tcha*) which is dried in the sun, and red tea which is artificially dried and destined for export.

It is practically impossible to imitate Chinese cookery outside the Far East, but dishes can be given a 'Chinese flavour' by using such products as rice, soya beans, spices, ginger, black or scented mushrooms (sold dried in food shops that specialise in exotic foods). Swallows' nests and

Dutch cookery

Fruit pudding (*Claire*)

Soup with meat balls and vermicelli

sharks' fins are sold tinned, rice pancakes in packets. *Sauerkraut* is of Chinese origin.

DUTCH COOKERY. CUISINE HOLLANDAISE – Dutch cookery is closely related to that of Belgium and north Germany. Being a country of rich pasture lands, there is an abundance of high quality dairy produce, and a feature of the large towns are the milk parlours (*melksalons*), which also sell excellent sandwiches. Holland's rich dairy produce goes into its excellent cheeses, which represent one of the country's largest exports. Edam cheese (*edammerkaas*), Purmerend and Alkmaar cheeses are spherical in shape and painted red. Another famous cheese is Gouda (*goudschekaas*), a cream cheese manufactured mostly in the south of Holland. It is shaped like a flattened cylinder with rounded ends.

Holland is a country equally devoted to stock farming and fishing, so the Dutch table features a wide variety of *charcuteries* and salted and smoked fish. The oysters of Zealand are of excellent quality.

There is a Dutch proverb which says: '*Haring in't land, dokter aan de kant*': 'As long as the herring is there, the doctor stays away.' Herring is the staple food of the Dutch people. (Herring fishing was transferred to deeper waters after the enclosure of the Zuyder Zee. In 1965 the total catch amounted to 450 million fish.) So it is not surprising that the herring is the centre-piece of countless feasts. One of these is the 'New Hollanders' (first fishing of the year) celebrated in gaily decorated coastal villages. The first barrel of herring is offered to the queen.

In restaurants specialising in French food, the favourite dishes are *jugged hare* (*hazepeper*), and *veal escalope with sauce brunoise*, accompanied by potatoes and peas. Cheese is usually served with butter and small salted biscuits. Rice is imported in large quantities from the former Dutch colonies and often appears in both savoury and sweet dishes.

From Indonesia comes excellent coffee, tea, and high quality cocoa and chocolate. The Dutch love good coffee and drink it often, from small porcelain coffee cups.

Apart from their own national beer, the Dutch drink French and Rhine wines. They have a famous liqueur: Curaçao (Wynand Fockink), which is sold in big-bellied, narrow-necked ceramic flagons.

ENGLISH COOKERY. CUISINE ANGLAISE – The essence of English cookery lies in choosing ingredients of the finest quality and cooking them so that their flavour and texture are fully developed. This is done with the minimum addition of ingredients to mask the fine natural taste of the original food.

England has long been a producer of beef, mutton, lamb, pork, pheasant, grouse, partridge, duck, salmon, sole, plaice, turbot, halibut, butter and cheese, etc., of a quality unsurpassed anywhere else in the world. Dishes from these prime materials cooked by roasting, grilling, frying or baking can be relied on to give food which is not only good to eat but is also easily digested.

Puddings, pies and tarts are another important part of English cooking. A great number of different recipes for baked, boiled and steamed puddings use mainly flour, fat, eggs and fruit are given in any English basic cookery book – the variety of puddings available is probably greater than in any other country in the world. The main meal of the day usually includes one of these puddings or one with milk as the main ingredient, or it may be a pie or tart having pastry as one of its main ingredients.

Cakes, scones and biscuits also feature in English cookery, and are usually eaten at the tea meal in the late afternoon. There are many varieties, a number of which are fairly plain, having a smaller proportion of fat, sugar and eggs than those of other countries. Another basic constituent of the tea meal is thinly sliced brown or white bread and butter.

Vegetable cookery is not a highly developed art in England. As long ago as the eighteenth century foreigners said that English cooks seemed incapable of turning out a good vegetable dish. A German named Moritz in 1872 wrote of his landlady's meal that 'An English dinner for such lodgers as I am, generally consists of a piece of half-boiled or half-roasted meat, and a few cabbage leaves boiled in plain water, on which they pour a sauce made of flour and butter.' It is usual for a main meal to include potatoes as one of the two vegetables served, both of which are cooked by boiling in plenty of water.

Popular dishes for which England is justly famous include pork pies, the best ones being made in the Midlands; bacon and egg – thin smoked back rashers lightly fried and served with slices of bread crisply fried and a lightly fried egg – a delicious dish whether served for breakfast, lunch or supper; Lancashire hotpot – a stew of meat, potatoes and onions cooked slowly for a long period in the oven; Cornish pasties – diced lamb, potato and shredded onion cooked in individual cases of short pastry and served either hot as part of the main meal or cold as a snack or picnic dish. Other delicious specialities are Christmas pudding, mince pies, stew with dumplings, Welsh rarebit, Yorkshire pudding, steak and kidney pudding, and kippers (particularly those cured in wood smoke).

FRENCH REGIONAL COOKERY. CUISINE RÉGIONALE – Every French province has its particular *cuisine*, although all so-called regional dishes are not necessarily authentic. Nevertheless, there are a great number of genuine French regional specialities. These are given under the names of the provinces listed alphabetically.

GERMAN COOKERY. CUISINE ALLEMANDE – There is more to this substantial *cuisine* than the dishes we are so

German cookery: slices of black pudding with rounds of sour apple (*Claire*)

familiar with abroad. The German gastronomic map is a reflection of the geographical one, which extends from the North Sea to the Alps, and offers much variation, each region offering special dishes depending upon its ancestry and climate.

The soups, like French soups, are mostly the hearty type. Beginning from the north and working towards the south, there is *Hamburger Aalsuppe* (eel soup) which, although it gets its name from the great German port, is, in fact, common to the whole of Schleswig-Holstein. A typical German soup is *Haferschleimsuppe*, a *consommé* made of oats. Then there is *Arfensuppe mit Snuten und Poren* which is a pea soup flavoured with pig's snout and trotters. Another Hamburg speciality is brisket of beef garnished with veal, semolina quenelles and diced seasonal vegetables.

Bremen eel soup is flavoured with a wide variety of herbs. In Wurttemberg and Baden there is *Spätzle* soup (*Spätzle* are squares of fresh noodle paste, plain, or filled with liver, ham, mushrooms). In Swabia there are many vegetable soups: cauliflower soup, bean soup, lentil soup, pea soup, potato soup.

The North Sea and the Baltic provide fresh fish and shellfish. In Berlin, fresh herring (or green *Grüner Hering*) are eaten fried, hot or cold, together with jacket potatoes. They are sometimes marinated after they are fried. The red herring is also much prized. Another outstanding dish is herring salad with gherkins and potatoes.

Hamburg offers oysters, lobster, and large prawns. One speciality is fried oysters and Cheshire cheese; and there is a delicious crayfish soup. All varieties of sea and river fish are found here. Holstein is best known for its tench. At Emden a veritable meal is made of the herring; while elsewhere along the coast there is smoked fish accompanied by spirits (*schnapps*, brandy, etc.).

The Rhine is the river for salmon, and the chefs of the region have many ways of preparing it. One of the trout recipes is paper-wrapped trout (*Forelle in Papier-Hûlle*). Moselle pike is garnished with cream and grated Parmesan. Further south, in Wurttemberg and Baden, eels and salmon are served Basle-style, steamed with onions. The trout of the Black Forest are cooked *au bleu* in a mixture of water, wine and vinegar; those of Wiesent in melted butter, garnished with small potatoes. The fish of the Danube are served in the same fashion.

In the mountain lakes of Upper Bavaria there are trout (*Saiblinge*) and a variety of salmon (*Renken*).

The Hamburg *Stubenkûcken* are spring chickens as popular as the caponised ducks eaten in the same city. The *cuisine* of the ancient town of Bremen has an international flavour, one of its specialities being chicken curry. Smoked breast of goose is a typical Pomeranian dish; goose is eaten almost everywhere.

In the Rhineland, an item on the menu called *Halbe Hahn* does not mean 'half a chicken', but a roll of wholemeal bread filled with Dutch cheese.

Charcuterie is important in the country of *Sauerkraut*. In Hamburg, *Gefüllte Schweinerippchen* are pork cutlets stuffed with currants, apples, biscuits and rum. The pork butchers of Holstein have ham comparable in quality to that of Westphalia; there are also some very good varieties of sausage. In Berlin, *Sauerkraut* is served with *Eisbein*, which is boiled salted knuckle of pork accompanied by pea purée. In Bremen, any feasts dedicated to the honourable pig are bound to include *Pinkel-Wurst* (a sausage made of wheaten flour and diced bacon), and Oldenburg hams smoked in the hearth.

The smoked juniper-flavoured hams of Westphalia are rivalled by the excellent *charcuterie* of Münsterland. Smoked bacon is served with beans and seasoned with savory; and there is a sausage wrapped in flaky pastry. *Mettwurst* and dried sausage are found in Lower Saxony; sausage garnished with horseradish and mustard in Hanover is eaten with *Lüttje Laage*, a glass of beer topped with a small glass of brandy.

Smoked pork loin is a favourite dish of the Hessians, while the Rhinelanders feast upon grilled puddings served with onions mixed with potato purée and christened 'Heaven and Earth'. Mainz offers succulent pickled pork and various types of sausages, while the whole of the Palatinate offers *Schweinepfeffer mit Knödel*, which is a *poivrade* of pork garnished with quenelles.

Swabian *Schlachtplatte* is a generous heap of cooked meats. The grilled sausages of Nuremberg are as good as those of Ratisbon and Coburg, the former short and fat, the latter thin and served stuffed into bread rolls. Both are rich in herbs and spices. In Upper Bavaria, there are grilled smoked pork; pig's ear and pea purée; pig's tongue with onion; and *Rostbratwürste* (grilled Franconian sausages).

The *Hamburger Steak* is well known internationally. A similar dish is *Holsteiner Schnitzel*, a breadcrumbed veal escalope, slightly browned, topped with a poached egg, a grilled sardine, and surrounded by various vegetables, including cucumbers. This is a favourite festive dish in the region.

Meat balls served with a piquant caper sauce is a Pomeranian delicacy. Westphalia is the country of *Pfefferpotthast*,

Black Forest Christmas gâteaux with cinnamon (*Claire*)

meat cut into small pieces and boiled with bay leaf, cloves, and the weight of the beef in onions. The whole is then bound with breadcrumbs and seasoned generously with pepper. A fine beef stew is produced in Munster, and a tripe dish, *Soester Wamme*, a speciality of Soest, is well known throughout the region.

In the Kassel district, the speciality is a mixture of veal and pork (*Weckewerk*) simmered with bread rolls and eaten cold. Spit roasts are a Rhineland delicacy. In upper Nahe, near Idar-Aberstein, there is the custom of marinating beef for twenty-four hours in wine, salt, pepper, onions and herbs, before cooking. They use a spit rod or beechwood, and roast over wood charcoal. In Stuttgart, there is a unique dish called *Gaisburger Marsch*, which consists of sliced potatoes, *Spätzle* and beef. These are cooked to such a degree of tenderness that they may be eaten with a spoon as a soup. Muzzle of beef salad is a Nuremberg dish. Veal knuckle, boiled, then grilled, and accompanied by *Knödel*, comes from around Munich.

Fresh vegetables accompany almost all specialities, from Schleswig-Holstein to Hamburg. In Bremen a sign of autumn is the appearance of *Brunten oder gepflückten Finten*, a dish of white haricot beans, french beans, carrots and potatoes. Winter is the season of red cabbage cooked with bacon, and of stuffed cabbage. In Berlin, favourite dishes are peas with bacon with squares of toasted bread added; and potato pancakes (grated raw potatoes, or potatoes bound with flour, called *Kartoffelpuffer*). In summer, Berliners enjoy the small turnips of Teltow, and the asparagus grown on the Brandenburg marshes.

Westphalia offers a dish made of raw potatoes blended with buckwheat flour, served fried. The vegetables grown in the countryside around Brunswick are tinned and sold throughout the country; the asparagus in particular is excellent. The green cabbages of Lower Saxony are served with a popular sausage stuffed with brains. The Hessen region offers *Beulsches*, potato quenelles made with a forcemeat of leeks and savoury pudding; and *zwiebelkuchen*, an onion cake.

The staple diet of the people of Wurttemberg is boiled flour quenelles. There are many varieties of these, ranging from the *Spätzle* with added liver, ham, etc., to the *Maultasche*, a kind of highly seasoned canelloni stuffed with brains, veal and pork.

Upper Bavaria is the country of *Knödel* (potato balls). These are varied by the addition of white breadcrumbs, liver stuffing, or bacon.

There are also the small round cumin-flavoured cheeses of Harz; the Hessian *Schmierkäse* (a white cheese blended with green sauce containing nine varieties of herbs); cream cheese made of ewes' milk, from the Palatinate, including that of Mayence called *Mainze Handkäse*; the cheeses of Allgäu; *Kraeuter* (a kind of Roquefort); and the assorted cheesecakes that German beer complements so perfectly. The salads of Baden contain Emmenthal cheese, together with bitter-sweet melon, red bilberries, and hard-boiled eggs.

Pâtisseries are excellent throughout Germany and very varied. There are the *Napfkuchen* of Berlin; *Streuselkuchen*, a yeast cake made with butter, flour and sugar; Berliner *Pfannkuchen* (jam fritters dusted with sugar); and many varieties of rolls, some made with milk. In Dresden there are custard tarts speckled with raisins, Christmas *Mohnspielen* (slices of white bread steeped in milk and sprinkled with ground poppyseeds and sugar). Lübeck has its almond paste, Bremen its *Bremer Klaben* (white bread dough mixed with raisins and crytallised lemon). Brunswick has gingerbread made with honey from the moors of Lüneburg, and *Zuckerkuchen*, a sugary cake baked on a metal tray. Hanover has its *petits-beurre* (*Liebnitz Keks*), the Rhineland has its *Muzen* (variety of fritters), and Cleves has its almond *Spekulatius*. The gâteaux (*Printen*) of Aix-la-Chapelle are coated with chocolate or caramel; the Black Forest offers cherry tart and bilberry cake; a fruit loaf called *Hutzelbrot* and the *Zuckerbrot* of Ulm are favourites of the people of Wurttemberg. The *Kuchle* of Baden are fritters fried in deep fat. Then there are the aniseed-flavoured *Springerle* from Heidelberg and the macaroons and chocolate-covered nougat of Nuremberg.

'Let there by beer . . . And there was beer.' A Bavarian monastery attributes these words to Saint Gambrinus, and they are sufficient to show the influence of this legendary figure over the great country of hops. There is a wide variety of German beers. They include Holstein beer, Berlin beer (which in summer is a low fermentation wheat beer kept in stone jugs and drunk with raspberry syrup: *Weisse mit Himbeer*), Franconian beer (Rauchbier of Bamberg, Bäck'bier of Bayreuth, fortified beer of Kulmbach), Munich beer, etc.

German wines are often excellent. There are two principal denominations: *Auslese*, first-class quality wines, and *Spätlese* wines made from grapes that have been allowed to ripen on the vine for as long as possible (see WINE).

Assortment of Italian produce: Gorgonzola, Bel paese, Parma ham, Asti spumante and Chianti (*Maison Biletta. Phot. Larousse*)

ITALIAN COOKERY. CUISINE ITALIENNE – The Italian *cuisine* does not begin and end with pasta dishes, risotto, *fritto misto* and *zuppa inglese* (which despite its name was certainly not invented in England).

Italian *cuisine* is much more than that. Besides the above (which are all excellent) there are succulent *charcuteries* made in Milan and Bologna, such as *mortadella* and *salami*, the famous Parma ham, and the *zampone* (stuffed pig's trotter) of Modena. Then there is Gorgonzola cheese (which is quite unlike Roquefort or any of the other French blue cheeses) and Parmesan cheese which goes so well with all Italian pasta dishes and which is the secret of the creaminess of Italian risotto.

Italian *cuisine* is one of the oldest in Europe. It is derived from Greek gourmet traditions, these being derived in their turn from Oriental *cuisine*. Throughout the centuries these culinary traditions became firmly established in Italy. They gradually attained perfection in the country that had adopted them. Choose any ordinary Italian dish and it is the replica of one that was once enjoyed by gourmands reclining on their triclinia in Ancient Rome.

Italian polenta is the same as the pulse that the Romans

prepared *en route* when they set out to conquer the world. They toasted grains of wheat, crushed them, and made a gruel from the result. The only difference is that polenta is now made from coarse maize flour, not wheaten flour.

Contemporary Italian dessert wines are almost identical to those the Romans made. They left them to thicken in the attics of their villas then drank them diluted with snow.

Italian *cuisine* can be considered the 'mother' of all European Latin *cuisines*.

Catherine de Medicis took Italian pastry-makers, cooks and ice cream makers with her to France. These craftsmen imparted the secrets of their delicate pastries (especially their *pasta frolla*), luscious creams and flavoured ices to their French counterparts. Italian culinary methods were thus introduced into France, and there is hardly a restaurant menu in that country today that does not include dishes of Italian origin. In Paris, and in most of the large towns, are restaurants (and some of these the best in town) that offer solely Italian dishes, accompanied by the appropriate Italian wines. Wines such as Valpolicella from Verona, Bardolino from Garda, Chianti from Tuscany and Frascati and Orvieto the white wines from Castelli Romani and Umbria. Piedmont has red and white *moscati spumanti* from Asti (Barbera and Freisa) and the famous Emilian wine, Lambrusco. Italy is the second largest wine-producing country of Europe. There is also a traditional spirit, grappa, and a herb-flavoured liqueur called strega (witch). Another liqueur, from the Adriatic coast, is maraschino.

Italian food produce is of excellent quality. Italian *charcuteries* are known everywhere. The pork butchers are culinary artists, making *mortadelle* where the skin of a boned piglet is stuffed without there being the slightest apparent trace of an incision.

The poultry of Piedmont has delicate, tender flesh although it is rather too yellow for some tastes. The young guinea fowl of the province, no bigger than pigeons, are delicious, the butter of Piedmont is excellent, Italian pasta is extremely good, and the coarse maize flour with which polenta is made is better here than anywhere. Italian olive oil is comparable to the olive oil of Provence, and Italian tomatoes are sweeter than the tomatoes of most other European countries. The meat (apart from pork) may not quite match the delicacy and flavour of the meat of some other European countries, but it is still quite good.

Pasta asciutta, the general name for various types of pasta, should be served *before* the main course.

For Italian wines see WINE.

JAPANESE COOKERY. CUISINE JAPONAISE – Japan is an agglomeration of densely populated islands lacking in cattle, sheep or pigs. The people live mainly on fish and various sea products, supplementing their diet with rice and other plants and vegetables.

The abundance of sea-food explains why fish form the basis of Japanese *cuisine*. The people are skilful cooks, and have devised many ways of serving food of marine origin. They use not only all the types of fish and shellfish found in their seas, but also edible seaweed, and many other marine products unknown in the West, which they eat both in their fresh and preserved states. Tinned sea urchins, crabs, mussels, fish quenelles, etc., are widely available in Japan.

Dried fish, which the Japanese call *sashimi*, is very popular. They also eat solid-fleshed fish such as sea bream (*taï*), tuna (*maguro*), carp (*koi-no-araï*), turbot (*hirame*) and, less frequently, mackerel (*saba*), usually seasoned with soy sauce.

Raw fish seasoned with soy sauce is easily digestible and (in the opinion of Nipponese gourmets) a most delicate dish. Another national dish is *sukiyaki*, which means 'roasted on the spit'. This has a history. In former times roast beef was prohibited by the Buddhist monks who forbade the domestic eating of animal meat. Such edicts were regarded lightly in rural areas, and the peasants used to get over them by building a fire between two stones in the fields and roasting the mutton and pork over it there. *Sukiyaki* dates from this time. Each guest prepares the dish according to his taste using the foods that are available: thin slices of meat, raw diced vegetables, mushrooms, bamboo shoots, raw egg, etc.

The following are among the most popular fish dishes in Japan:

Kabayaki. Grilled eel fillets (*unagi*). This is prepared in a very special way in Japan. The eel is gorged with beer or spirits, bled, then immediately split in half lengthwise with one blow from a chopper and completely deboned. This requires much skill. It is first steamed, then grilled over a wood fire and served sprinkled with sauce.

Katsus-buski. Dried bonito (a species of tuna). When the drying process is completed the fish becomes like a piece of wood. It is then grated as it is required. Bonito powder is added to certain soups with the dual purpose of seasoning them and making them more nutritious. It is widely used in Japan.

Maguro-no-suhki. A bowl of cooked rice containing powdered egg wrapped in a thin slice of raw tuna (or other substance).

Musi-yaki. Fish cooked in the oven in a sauce made of potato flour; or cooked dry and sprinkled afterwards with the same sauce.

Nosi-maki. A bowl of rice garnished with seaweed.

Nuta. A mixture of raw fish and vegetables. This dish is strongly seasoned with horseradish, mustard and other condiments.

The Japanese drink tea, water, beer and hot rice wine before a meal.

RUSSIAN AND POLISH COOKERY. CUISINE RUSSE ET POLONAISE – Russian *cuisine* is composed of two contrasting gastronomic influences: Asian and west European. Contemporary Russian *cuisine*, then, is a blend of these, and not at all as the great French chefs have imagined it since the eighteenth century.

A rare book of the sixteenth century, *le Ménagier russe*, describes the Russian *cuisine* of that time. Festive occasions were frequent, and drink flowed with every meal. There was Greek and Italian wine (hot and cold), hydromel, beer, sparkling *kvas*, brandy, cherry and raspberry liqueurs. But, according to the advice of *Le Ménagier*, these wines and

Russian specialities: vodka, caviare, eel and smoked salmon (*Nicolas*)

spirits were not to be offered too liberally – 'There should be no disputes and certainly no knock-out blows.'

Other picturesque details of Russian *cuisine* are supplied by the descriptions of the traditional, quasi-ritual meal (similar to that offered on Christmas Eve in Europe) eaten on the return from midnight mass between Holy Saturday and Easter Sunday.

The Easter meal is a mixed cold table, with savoury and sweet dishes, pastries, and desserts laid out together. All these dishes remain on the table during the whole of Easter Sunday and Easter Monday; empty ones being replaced by full ones as the food is consumed.

The composition of the Easter meal is traditional. Certain dishes, such as roast lamb and sucking pig, must always be included, and one or more lambs made of butter must be prepared. This is done in the following way:

A reclining lamb is modelled from a block of fresh butter. Its wool is fashioned by placing a piece of canvas on some butter and attaching it to the modelled lamb's body. The head is carefully sculpted. The horns may be covered with gold or silver foil, and peppercorns or grape seeds serve as eyes. The lamb is then placed on a mount consisting of a piece of wood placed on a bottle. The wood is covered with damp hemp on which grass, oats or lentils have been sown and germinated to give an attractive surround.

An orthodox Russian Easter meal consists of a roast lamb and sucking pig, a cold ham, a turkey or piece of feathered game, also roasted, roast leg of veal, variously coloured eggs, a *paskha* of white cheese (pyramid of pressed white cheese), one or more Easter gâteaux (*koulitch*), one or several *babas* (cylindrical cake made of leavened dough which can be as much as 1 m. (39 inches) high and 40 cm. (16 inches) in diameter), plates of Polish pastries (*plietzki*), and several salt cellars of salt which has been blessed. A large number of non-ritual dishes also appear on the Easter table. These, like the dishes above, are constantly replenished throughout the night.

Apart from this Easter fare there are Russian *zakouskis*, closely related to the *smörrebrod* and *smorgasbord* of Scandinavia. The *zakouskis* are arranged on immense buffet tables, pride of place being given to caviare. Today, as in former times, the sumptuousness of the display of *zakouskis* is an indication both of the social status of the host and the prestige of the guest. Vodka accompanies the meal.

Russian *hors-d'œuvre* (hot and cold) are many and varied.

The following are some of the hot *hors-d'œuvre* (most of which are found under HORS-D'ŒUVRE, *Hot hors-d'œuvre*): Variously garnished *barquettes, beurrecks à la turque, blinis, ciernikis, kromeskies à la polonaise* or *à la russe, cheese croûtes, anchovy dartois, herrings à l'estonienne, nalesnikis, Siberian pel'meni* (see PEL'MENI), *Caucasian pirozhki* and other varieties (see PIROGHI), *rastegaïs, cabbage sausselis, Lithuanian varenikis, game tartlets, visnisekis*, etc.

Cold *hors-d'œuvre* include a great variety of *canapés* and *barquettes, agourois*, various types of *caviare, herrings à la livonienne, rolls à la varsovienne*, etc.

A distinguishing feature of Russian *cuisine* is the use of *smetana* (whey) and beetroot, which forms the base of *bortsch*, without which no Russian meal would be complete.

Russian soups, like those of Poland, are very nourishing, for besides vegetables they contain a variety of meats.

The following are the soups most commonly served in Russia and Poland: Polish *bortsch, stschi à la russe, cucumber rossolnick, oukha de sterlet, meschanski soup, nettle soup, Livonian soup, botwinia* (served iced). *Polish kolodnik, kliotskis soup, cream of ham soup, game okrochka, morel soup, Finnish soup, kalstchale* (a *macédoine* of glacé fruits), *calves' kidney soup*, iced *ockrochka fish soup*, etc.

Scandinavian specialities: marinated mackerel, cod liver à la scandinave (*Nicolas*)

The Russians make excellent pies. The best-known is the *coulibiac*, which goes back as far as the sixteenth or seventeenth century. It used to be filled with cabbage, but nowadays it is usually contains salmon or other fish. Other pies include: *Polish pie, Vesiga patties, burbot liver patties, Smolensk pies, Troitski patties, sour cabbage patties, Caucasian pies, Saracen pies, Russian fish tourte, small croustades of fish*, and the numerous pastry items included in the *hors-d'œuvres* list.

Vodka (46° alcohol) made from fermented wheat, or occasionally from maize or potatoes, is odourless and colourless and should traditionally be drunk in one gulp. It helps digest the predominantly fatty food. Russian tea (black tea from China) is drunk all day from the ever-simmering samovar. Some wine is produced, mainly in the Caucasus.

SCANDINAVIAN COOKERY. CUISINE SCANDINAVE – In the Scandinavian countries of Sweden, Norway and Denmark almost everything on the restaurant menus is *à la carte*. These countries have a buffet table in the dining-room, called *smörgåsbord* which is covered with all kinds of cold meats, fish, cheeses and spirits. One can help oneself before the meal unless it constitutes the meal proper. These *hors-d'œuvre* consist principally of preserved fish (smoked or tinned), anchovies, mackerel, brisling, etc., and are accompanied by a wide range of seasonings. There is, for example, *gaffel-biter*, oyster sauce or anchovy sauce made with white wine. Other parts of the *smörgåsbord* include salt beef, rolled breast of pork or mutton (*rullepölse*), various items of *charcuterie* such as Danish *saucisson*, which resembles Italian *salami* but is fattier and more savoury. There are also various salads of which the most original is *sill-salade*, made of cooked beetroot, anchovies, herrings and salted gherkins.

National dishes include *leg of pork with caramelised apples, fresh apples, prunes and red cabbage; knuckle of ham with turnip cabbage; brisket of beef with horse-radish; veal stew with dill sauce*. The famous *pytt-i-panna* is composed of diced beef, ham and apples topped with a poached egg. Even more original is roast reindeer (*rensdyrsteg* in Norwegian, *radjurstek* in Swedish) served with a cream sauce seasoned with goat's cheese (*gjetöst*) and accompanied by bilberry jam. Then there is the snow hen, a speciality of Scandinavia. Wheat, rye and barley bread are served with the meal.

Every housewife knows the secret of how to make a good sandwich – there are as many as fifty-nine varieties.

Scandinavian beers are world-famous, especially Danish beer. Then there is the well-known akvavit, a light fragrant spirit that aids the digestion and is drunk at the end of the meal, like the Calvados.

SPANISH COOKERY. CUISINE ESPAGNOLE – There is an old Spanish saying, 'All you find to eat in a Spanish inn is what you bring with you.' Fortunately, the advent of tourism has changed all this.

Dishes vary from the south (rice and pork), to the north (beef and potatoes) while the poor central provinces generally eat lean mutton and chick peas. Fish and shellfish are caught all along the coast, and are usually fried in oil.

There is one dish better known than any of the others: *olla podrida* (q.v.) which is possibly the forerunner of the *grande ouille* that used to be made in south-west France and is a soup that combines the flavours of meats and vegetables. Another good Spanish soup is *puchero* (q.v.) which is often a substitute for *olla podrida*.

Paella is a hearty dish that includes pork, chicken, duck, *chorizos*, fish, shellfish, frogs, snails and a large number of vegetables, pulses and cereals. Simpler *paellas* are made in the home.

Other special Spanish dishes are *marinated fish, marinated game, chicken Valencia, bacalao à la biscaïenne* (cod served with tomatoes, onions, green peppers and hard-boiled eggs), *monteria, roast veal Spanish-style* (topside of veal which, before being roasted, is marinated with red peppers, origano, garlic, white wine and the juice of bitter oranges), ham and eggs, *chorizos with garbanzos* (see GARBANZOS), etc.

In the course of this volume you will find a great many recipes of Spanish origin.

In the streets of Spain, vendors sell *churros* (hot fritters), water melon, and *touron* (a kind of almond paste). Water melon is offered with a glass of Manzanilla.

Spain is the third wine-producing country in Europe. The principal wines are: Jerez, Manzanilla, Malaga, Moscatel, Valdepanas, etc. (See WINE.)

SWISS COOKERY. CUISINE SUISSE – Swiss hotels, catering for a large tourist industry, have an international *cuisine*.

Home cooking in private households, small local restaurants and country inns is surprisingly good and has a distinctive local character. There is no lack of produce for good cooking – abundant milk, cream and butter, excellent quality meat, poultry and game, succulent fruit and vegetables. Excellent transport facilities ensure that a wide variety of products from all over Europe and from other continents are available on the market.

Swiss *charcuterie* is a highly developed art and deserves its excellent reputation.

Although it is easy nowadays to enjoy perfectly fresh seafish and other sea products, Swiss gourmets prefer the rich and varied local river and lake fauna. Pride of place goes to the *fario*, a red-spotted trout with delicate flesh that lives in the mountain streams and is far superior to the rainbow trout artificially bred for table use.

The char comes a close second to the trout for flavour, while the burbot with its delectable liver is fairly abundant in Switzerland. All western and central European varieties of fish are found in the Swiss lakes and rivers. Some species, however, are found only in the Swiss lakes. One example is the *féra* of Lake Geneva, a delicious salmonid that can reach a very large size. The same fish is found in Lakes Zurich and Constance, where it is called *fellschen*. Lake Neuchatel has its *bondelles*; and in the tiny lake of Zoug, a species of small, rosy-fleshed trout called *zuger röthli* is fished in springtime. These are served with a cream sauce flavoured with aromatic herbs.

Another great delicacy is fried baby perch caught in Lake Leman, and eaten, washed down with a bottle of Dézaley, on the shores of the lake itself.

Cheese is a basic ingredient of Swiss *cuisine*. To the uninitiated there are only two types: Gruyère, a pleasantly piquant, fatty cheese (minimum 45 per cent fat), and Emmenthal, fatty and sticky with large vacuoles, a rarer cheese with a less pronounced flavour. To the initiated, however, there are infinite variations of quality in these two cheeses depending on their provenance and age.

In the Vaud part of the Jura mountains there is a special cheese called Vacherin, creamy with a delicate flavour. Another special cheese, Schabzieger, is produced in the canton of Glarus. This cheese is very close-textured because the whey undergoes a double coagulation process. The Berne section of the Jura mountains possesses a cheese speciality called Tête de moine (monk's head). This is a close-grained, tender cheese. Although Reblochons and Tommes are manufactured on the borders of Savoy, they are eaten mainly in Geneva, where gourmets give first prize to the distinctive Tomme au marc, coated with vintage marc.

Pâtisserie has always been a speciality of the Swiss, and Swiss chocolates enjoy a world-wide reputation for quality. The raw materials are all imported, since Switzerland does not produce cocoa or a sufficient quantity of sugar. The industry came into its own after a law passed limiting the duty payable on sugar and other foreign produce.

Swiss vineyards produce some highly regarded white and red wines, both of which consistently improve in quality (see WINE).

Gastronomic customs vary from region to region. In French-speaking Switzerland, customs are more or less the same as in France, though with a tendency to make the main meal of the day the midday meal, as they do in German-speaking Switzerland. For most families the evening meal consists of a cup of white coffee and potatoes browned in butter (*rösti*), which the Béarnaise housewives do well.

There are many specialities, especially those devised for festive occasions like carnival. Swiss cooks have also adopted classic dishes from France, specialities from Savoy and Franche-Comté, dishes from southern Germany, and pastas, risottos and fried dishes from northern Italy.

In Geneva there is *soupe aux fidés* which is a *pot-au-feu* soup garnished with very fine vermicelli; and *longeole*, which the Genevese go to the mountain inns to eat. This is a kind of fresh moist *andouille* based on fat pork rinds, seasoned with coriander and fennel and served poached, accompanied by boiled potatoes. Then there are *atriaux*, which are highly seasoned, flat pigs' liver sausages, served fried. A wide variety of cheese dishes are served including soufflé fritters, ramekins, cheese steaks (a thick slice of Gruyère dipped in white of egg and breadcrumbs and fried in clarified butter), cheese croûtes (slices of stale bread soaked in white wine or milk, sometimes sprinkled with onion rings, covered with a slice of cheese and baked or fried).

One of the best-known dishes in cheese *fondue* for which there are many recipes. Here is Brillat-Savarin's. 'The *fondue* begins in the kitchen in a glazed earthenware casserole or cast-iron enamelled pan (*caquelon* they call it in French-speaking Switzerland) which is rubbed with a clove of garlic. The cheese is finely grated, allowing 150 to 200 g. (5 to 7 oz.) of good, full-flavoured Gruyère per person. Enough local wine is added to cover. Correct the seasoning with salt if necessary, and add a grinding of pepper (a little grated nutmeg does not harm, either). While the *fondue* is being prepared, the guests cut their bread into small pieces. The *fondue* is brought in on a spirit heater. At the last moment a small glass of pure fruit kirsch is added. Everyone eats from the same dish, dipping their forkful of bread right to the bottom to ensure that the fondue does not stick to the pan while cooking. No wine is drunk, but halfway through the meal, a small glass of kirsch is offered.' The experts disapprove of short cuts, such as thickening the mixture with cornflour, or making it more frothy by adding bicarbonate. However, when one is not very sure of success, it is advisable to add a little cornflour with the wine before heating, rather than spoil the fondue. This guarantees perfect binding when the mixture is brought to the boil. Thin it with hot white wine if evaporation causes it to thicken too much.

In the canton of Vaud, we find excellent *charcuterie*. Payerne sausages are not unlike those of Morteau but fattier, more moist and more highly seasoned. Cabbage and liver stuffed sausages have a pronounced smoky flavour, and are eaten Vaudois-style, garnished with leeks and potatoes. Tongue marinated *à la vaudois* is delicious and a well-known dish in Paris today. Vevay *bricelets* (variety of wafer) are exported all over the world.

Fribourg is renowned for its salted and smoked beef. Smoked cows' udders are considered a delicacy. The *fondue* of this canton is made with Vacherin cheese.

Neuchâtel *fondue* is made of equal proportions of Gruyère and Emmenthal. Fried *bondelles* are accompanied by Auvernier wine.

In Valais, the shepherds prefer *raclette* to *fondue*. A piece of Valaisian cheese is stuck on a fork and held over the fire. As the surface of the cheese softens and begins to bubble, it is scraped with a knife onto a heated plate. This is eaten with boiled potatoes and with an appetite sharpened by the altitude and a glass or two of *fendant*, what could be better!

Berne also produces *cochonnailles* (cooked meats); the saveloy, ham, smoked bacon, smoked pork shoulder are renowned, and with the addition of cabbages and *sauerkraut* form a rich stew called *bernerplatte*. A good classical *sauerkraut* is also made in Berne.

Basle is principally a town of pastry-makers, and the *leckerlis* of Basle, with their hard, brittle, full-flavoured base are well known. There is a wide variety of home-made pastries, and these increase in number at carnival time.

The culinary art of Zurich has borrowed much from countries on the other side of the Rhine. There is *leberknödel* (calf's liver quenelles), *knöpli* (a pastry made of flour, milk and eggs cut into small pieces and poached in boiling water, like the *spoetzle* of Baden). *Dampfnüdeln* (steamed pastry balls) come from Wurttemberg. Roast sausages are typical Zurich fare, made of a mixture of finely minced pork and veal. Another local dish is *leberspiessli*, which are *brochettes* (skewers) of cubes of calf's liver and bacon interspersed with leaves of sage. This is cooked in clarified butter and served with creamed kohlrabi, small white turnip cabbages (not to be confused with *rutabaga*, which is a swede turnip). Zurich *leckerlis* have a marzipan base and bear no resemblance to those of Basle. *Trichterküchli* are home-made pastries made with a thin *choux pastry* mixture. This is placed in a funnel and left to flow into hot fat, where it forms unexpected amusing shapes. They are a carnival speciality. Millet porridge (*hirsenbrei*) was once a traditional dish. At the time of their alliance with Strasbourg, the delegates of Zurich paid an official visit to their allies, bearing an immense cauldron of this porridge which was still hot on their arrival, and symbolised how promptly they would bring aid if called upon. It is rarely served now.

The canton of Glarus manufactures *schabzieger*, which forms the basis of various food products. *Birnbrot* is a rather heavy *pâtisserie* made of bread dough mixed with figs, pears softened in red wine, almonds and walnuts. It forms a dense loaf and is served very thinly sliced.

Saint-Gall no longer enjoys the gastronomic *fastes* of its famous abbey, but still retains some delicious *charcuterie*, such as *schiblig* (a kind of dried saveloy) and *därre landjaeger* (steam-dried and known as *gendarmes suisses*).

In the canton of Girsons is *bindenfleisch* (beef, mutton or goat's flesh dried out-of-doors). This can only be done in the upper valleys where the air is dry and pure. The meat becomes as hard as leather and is eaten raw, in shavings.

Tessin *cuisine* has a distinctly Italian flavour, and is, in fact, only distinguishable from that of Lombardy by a greater refinement in its preparation. The ravioli of this canton are very large.

In the Swiss Alps, apart from the bread, flour and coffee that reach them from the valley, the shepherds have to depend upon the resources of the Alps. Milk, whey, buttermilk, cream, butter and cheese, supplemented by salted meats, constitute their basic diet during the season. They do, however, have a few traditional dishes. In the Appenzell pastures there is *fenz*, a thick, lightly salted porridge made of flour and buttermilk, cooked over the fire in a cauldron or in the traditional three-legged pot. This porridge may also be prepared with milk and with cream (*nidel-fenz*). *Room-zonne* is another cream-based porridge that is cooked over the fire. As much flour as it will absorb is added to it, followed by a generous slab of butter. *Chääs schoppe* or *alte mâ* is prepared by placing alternating layers of stale bread and slices of cheese in a cauldron, and sprinkling with milk. Once the preparation is thoroughly soaked, it is fried gently in butter until golden brown, rather like a thick waffle.

These dishes, perhaps named differently and varying slightly in their preparation, are found in all the chalets of the Central Swiss Alps. Polenta has been recently introduced into Valais and Grisons. Milk or water is drunk, the latter sometimes with a dash of kirsch.

TURKISH COOKERY. CUISINE TURQUE – Because of the country's long subjugation to the Greeks, there is no such thing as Turkish *cuisine*. What exists is a local *cuisine* influenced by the various races that make up the nation, dominated by the more refined Greek *cuisine*.

The Turkish *cuisine*, then, enjoyed by Persians, Kurds, Armenians, Rumanians, Albanians, the island population, European colonials and the Jewish people (for it conforms to the principles of the Talmud) comprises quite a wide range of dishes.

In Constantinople and its immediate vicinity, the water is of such purity and digestibility that it is looked upon as a kind of elixir. People make pilgrimages to drink the Taxim and Buyuk Dere waters, and carry bottles of it away with them. A proverb says that 'whoever has once drunk the waters of Taxim will always return to drink it again'.

Apart from lamb and mutton, meat is far from good. Buffalo meat takes the place of ox meat; veal is scarce and lean; pork is forbidden for religious reasons; poultry is poor. This means that most meat dishes are made of mutton or lamb.

There is an abundance of vegetables: artichokes, tomatoes, courgettes, aubergines, giant french beans, gombos. Rice is the national dish; Turks soak their rice for a few minutes in strongly salted water before cooking it using a large quantity of Alep butter, the surplus of which is poured off at the end of cooking.

Oriental cooking is savoury and spicy. It is also very rich, as oil plays an important part in its preparation.

Pâtisserie is heavy and generally too sweet. It is always served with large glasses of water.

The milk used is buffalo milk.

Fruits come mostly from Asia, Smyrna and Jaffa: figs, peaches, oranges, melons, water melons, muscat grapes, Jerusalem grapes, strawberries, apricots, plums, almonds, cherries, apples, etc.

Cooking is done in hemispheres of beaten copper called *djindjères*.

In the cheaper restaurants, *djindjères*, each containing a different *ragoût*, are ranged side by side on a 'silo', which is covered with cinders to conserve the heat. They stay there from one meal to another, just as lamb and mutton remain constantly on the spit.

In Constantinople, some restaurants stay open all night, and there are many itinerant food sellers, offering cooked rice, chick peas, spit-roasted lamb and chicken offal, white cheese, grilled fish, tea, coffee, salep, ices, *simits*, waffles, melons, water melons, chicory, *mézés*, etc.

One habit that has been passed from the Greek to the Turks is that of eating *mézés* in the cafés in the evening between 5 o'clock and 8 o'clock, together with numerous glasses of raki and ouzo. *Mézés* are *hors-d'œuvre* consisting of radishes, cucumbers, pieces of cheese, fried fish, horse-radish, haricot bean salad, tomato and onion salad, olives, sweetcorn, diced swordfish, salted almonds, etc.

Kacher cheese and yogurt are essential items of the Turkish diet, together with olives and raw onions.

Jams, flower and fruit syrups and Turkish delight are delicacies, as are melons, water melons, cucumbers, tomatoes and chicory, all of which are eaten raw.

The most typical Turkish specialities are *aïoli à la grecque* (see AÏOLI), *Armenian couscous, dagh kebabs, dolmas à la turque, keftes-kebabs, macaroni à la persane, aubergine purée, red caviare purée, rice pilaf, lamb's tripe soup, tourlouyouvetsch, Jaffa oranges in syrup.* (Most of these may be found in alphabetical order in this volume.)

INTOXICATION – The general effect of the phenomena produced by the action of a poison.

Alcoholic intoxication. INTOXICATION ALCOOLIQUE – See ALCOHOLISM.

Food intoxication. INTOXICATION ALIMENTAIRE – It is essential to differentiate between the two categories of food intoxication: that caused by food which is already poisonous (or has become so through putrefaction) before ingestion; and that caused by wholesome food rendered toxic by fermentations or putrefactions produced by it in the intestine.

Dietetic remedial treatment for the latter consists of reducing the quantity of the troublesome food and offering it in a more digestible form. The residues that encourage the growth of microbes are thus eliminated since the digestive juices transform the food completely.

This is why, in the case of proteic putrefaction, the proportion of albumins in the diet is reduced and that of farinaceous foods increased. Inversely, when a child suffers from intestinal catarrh caused by hydrocarbonic fermentations, a starch-reduced, albumin-rich diet is prescribed (albuminous milk, buttermilk, etc.).

IRIDESCENT SEAWEED. IRIDÉE – Edible seaweed remarkable for its variegated colouring. It is eaten raw in salad or cooked like French beans.

IRISH STEW (British cookery) – This dish really belongs to the Irish culinary repertoire. It is mutton stewed in white stock with potatoes and sliced onions. (See MUTTON.)

IRON. FER – Although iron is present in very small quantities in the human body (5 or 6 g.), it has a very important part to play in the body's functioning.

IRON CONTENT OF CERTAIN FOODS
(*in mg. per 100 g.*)

Beef	3·5	Whole eggs	3·1
Mutton	0·46	Cow's milk	0·15
Very fat pork	1·5	Butter	0·2
Offal	7·9	Wheatgerm	4·07
Eel	1	Wholemeal bread	3
Salmon	1	White bread	1·2
Smoked herring	1·2	Root vegetables	0·7
Oysters	5·7		

IRRORATEUR (Spray gun) – Piece of apparatus, invented by Brillat-Savarin, which was used to perfume rooms, especially the dining-room.

Brillat-Savarin writes in the preface to *la Physiologie du goût*: 'I submitted to the council of the Society for the Encouragement of National Industries my *irrorateur*, a piece of apparatus invented by me, which is none other than a compressor spray which can fill a room with perfume.

'I had brought the spray with me, in my pocket. It was well-filled. I turned on the tap and, with a hissing sound, out came a sweet-smelling vapour which rose right up to the ceiling and then fell in tiny drops on the people present and on their papers.

'It was then that I witnessed, with indescribable pleasure, the heads of the wisest men in the capital bending under my '*irroration*'. I was enraptured to note that the wettest among them were also the happiest.'

ISIGNY – A small town in Calvados where some of the best butter in France is made from its famous cream.

ISINGLASS (Gelatine). COLLE DE POISSON CLARIFIÉE – 'Take a 25-g. (1-oz.) sheet of gelatine; after cutting it into small pieces, wash it, put it in a pan with 8 glasses of filtered water and 50 g. (2 oz., $\frac{1}{4}$ cup) sugar. Put it on the fire.

'As soon as rapid boiling is established, put the pan on the side of the fire in such a way as to keep it boiling.

'Take care to remove the scum as it rises and when the reduction produces a good glass of gelatine, strain it through a napkin into a clean vessel.

'The proper clarification of the sugar and the gelatine can be considered the secret of success of attractive fruit and liqueur jellies.' (Carême.)

ITALIAN MARROWS, COURGETTES (U.S. zucchini). COURGETTES – Variety of gourd with short fruits. Courgettes are also known under the name of *courgeron, coucourzelle,* and *zuchetti*. In U.S.A. they are called *Italian squash* or *zucchini*.

Courgettes have a very delicate taste.

Method of preparation. Courgettes may be peeled or not. When the vegetable is to be fried it is peeled, cut into thick rounds or little sticks, soaked in milk, drained, rolled in flour, and deep-fried in boiling oil.

Italian marrows, à la créole. COURGETTES À LA CRÉOLE – Peel the courgettes, remove the seeds, dice the flesh, and brown in good fat. Add salt, put the lid on the pan and cook slowly on low heat, stirring from time to time. Crush them with a spoon and cook until all the moisture has evaporated. Let the pulp acquire a golden colour before serving.

Glazed Italian marrow garnish. COURGETTES GLACÉES – Divide the courgettes in quarters and trim them into lozenge shape of even size. Blanch for a few minutes and drain.

Put them in a sauté pan with 2 tablespoons (3 tablespoons) butter, a pinch of salt, and a little sugar. Cover with cold water. Bring to the boil, cover, and cook gently until the liquid has almost entirely disappeared. Sauté the courgettes in the remaining liquor so that they are coated with it.

Courgettes à la niçoise II

Italian marrow à la grecque (hors-d'œuvre). COURGETTES À LA GRECQUE – Divide the courgettes into small slices without peeling them, or trim them into lozenge shapes. Put them into a *court-bouillon* prepared in the manner described for *Artichokes à la grecque* (see HORS-D'ŒUVRE). Finish in the same way.

Italian marrows à l'indienne. COURGETTES À L'INDIENNE – Prepare the marrows the same as for *Glazed Italian marrow*. Simmer them in butter. Season with salt and a good pinch of curry powder.

When they are cooked, pour over a few tablespoons *Béchamel sauce* (see SAUCE). Mix without breaking the courgettes.

Italian marrows à la mentonnaise. COURGETTES À LA MENTONNAISE – Prepare the courgettes in the way described for *Italian marrow à la niçoise II* (see below).

Stuff the halved courgettes with their chopped pulp, to which an equal quantity of blanched, drained and chopped spinach simmered in butter, has been added. Add a little Parmesan cheese to the stuffing, a little garlic and some chopped parsley.

Sprinkle with browned breadcrumbs. Pour olive oil over the courgettes and brown in the oven.

Italian marrows à la mingrélienne (Russian cookery). COURGETTES FARCIES À LA MINGRÉLIENNE – Peel the courgettes and cut them into slices 5 cm (2 inches) thick. Remove the seeds, blanch and drain the slices.

Blanch and drain some rice, put it under the cold tap, and drain again. Add some fat chopped mutton, chopped onion softened in butter, chopped fennel, a little garlic, salt and pepper. Mix well.

Fill the courgettes with this stuffing, rounding the tops. Arrange in a buttered sauté pan, packing them in fairly tightly. Moisten with tomato-flavoured veal stock. Start cooking on the stove, and continue gently in the oven with the lid on. Baste the dish with its own juice during cooking.

Italian marrows à la niçoise I. COURGETTES À LA NIÇOISE – Pare the courgettes, cut them into thin slices, salt them, wipe with a cloth, sprinkle flour and sauté them in oil in a pan on a strong flame.

Put them in a dish, alternating them with skimmed and seeded tomatoes which have been sliced and lightly fried in oil.

Pour 2 tablespoons (3 tablespoons) boiling oil, in which some garlic and chopped parsley have been rapidly browned, over the slices. A little sliced onion, browned in oil, can also be added to this dish.

Italian marrows à la niçoise II. COURGETTES À LA NIÇOISE – Divide the courgettes in half lengthways. Make an incision (around the pulp, $\frac{1}{2}$ cm. ($\frac{1}{4}$ inch) from the edge, and several little cuts in the middle of the pulp.

Season the courgettes with salt, put them on a cloth and leave them to get rid of excess moisture. Dry and cook them gently in oil, without letting them brown too much. Drain.

Take out three-quarters of the pulp, without damaging

Italian pasta: Spaghetti alla bolognese

the skin. Chop the pulp. Add two-thirds of its weight of risotto flavoured with Parmesan and 2 tablespoons (3 tablespoons) thick tomato purée, flavoured with a touch of grated garlic. Stuff the halved courgettes with this mixture. Smooth the stuffing with a fork, giving it a lightly domed shape. Put the courgettes in an oiled *gratin* dish. Sprinkle with breadcrumbs, pour over some oil, brown gently in the oven.

To serve, surround them with a few tablespoons good veal stock and sprinkle with chopped parsley.

Italian marrows à la provençale. COURGETTES À LA PROVENÇALE – Cut the courgettes into thick slices, without peeling them. Salt, dry, sprinkle with flour and sauté them in oil.

Arrange the slices in layers in a *gratin* dish, alternating them with rice cooked in stock, and tomatoes lightly fried in oil, with sliced onions, parsley, and chopped garlic.

Smooth the surface of the dish, cover with grated cheese, and brown in the oven.

Italian marrow salad. COURGETTES EN SALADE – Divide the courgettes lengthways into quarters. Blanch them in boiling salt water for 6 to 8 minutes. Drain and wipe them on a cloth.

Put them in a salad bowl. Pour over them a few tablespoons *Vinaigrette sauce* (see SAUCE). Sprinkle generously with chervil and chopped tarragon.

This salad can be served with mayonnaise.

Italian marrows sautéed. COURGETTES SAUTÉES – Peel the courgettes, cut them in slices, flour them and sauté in oil or butter.

ITALIAN PASTA (Pasta products). PÂTES ALIMENTAIRES – Dried wheaten flour preparation, mostly made from durum wheat. The flour is well kneaded into a stiff dough and forced through specially perforated cylinders from which it comes out in various shapes, known by different names (macaroni, spaghetti, vermicelli, crescioni, ditalini, fedelini, ravioli, reginette, strichetti, tagliarini, tagliatelli, tortellini, etc.)

They are made by kneading vigorously hard (red) wheat with boiling water. After kneading, the paste is put in a bronze cylinder equipped with a die, and pressure is applied to it by a hydraulic press. A fan is placed near the outlet of the die to begin the drying process, which ends in the drying oven. The small pasta products are cut as they emerge from the cylinder bt means of a circular knife; the others are produced in different lengths. Egg pasta is made by adding dry or fresh eggs to the mixture. The slightly yellow colour of ordinary pasta is due to the addition of turmeric or to various chemical colourings.

The food value of pasta products is the same as that of the cereals from which it is made. It contains glucides or carbohydrates and mineral salts, but only very small amounts of protein, fats and vitamins (mostly Vitamin B1).

Pasta is essentially an energy food providing the body with 350 calories per 100 g. (4 oz.) pasta. It is an excellent staple food.

For the preparation of home-made noodles, see NOODLES.

ITALIENNE (À L') – Name given to various dishes made of meat, poultry, fish and vegetables. In all these dishes finely diced or chopped mushrooms are used.

The name *à l'italienne* is also given to a method of preparing macaroni or other pastas.

ITALY – See INTERNATIONAL COOKERY, WINE.

IVA – Name given in some districts of France to the yarrow, and to a type of gentian.

IVOIRE (À L') – Method of preparation used especially for poultry. (See CHICKEN, *Chicken à l'ivoire*.)

IVROGNE DE MER – Small fish with red scales found in the Atlantic, and in the Mediterranean and Adriatic. Its flesh is tough, but it is edible.

IZARD. ISARD – Name given to the wild goat of the Pyrénées. For methods of cooking it see ROEBUCK.

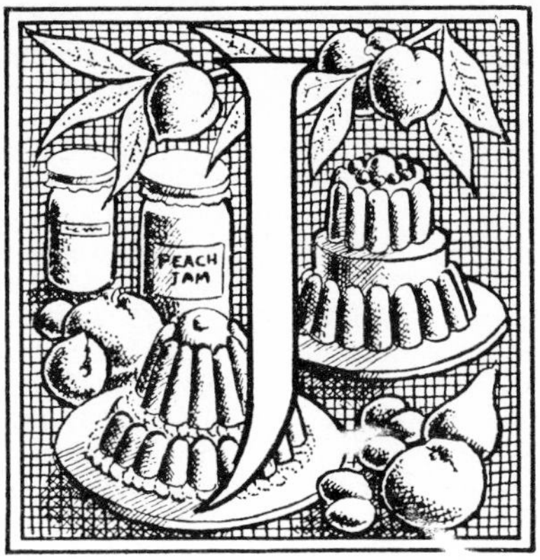

JALOUSIES – Little cakes made of flaky pastry.

Method I. Roll out a piece of *Flaky pastry dough* (see DOUGH) and cut it into strips about $7\frac{1}{2}$ cm. (3 inches) wide.

Leaving a margin of 1 cm. ($\frac{1}{2}$ inch) around the edges, spread a layer of *Almond paste* (see ALMOND) flavoured with vanilla on the slices.

Decorate with twisted strips of dough to make a criss-cross pattern. Secure this by pressing down at each edge of the slice a narrow strip of dough moistened with water so that it sticks firmly. Crimp the edges. Brush with beaten egg. Bake in a medium oven. When cooked, spread apricot jam on top. Cut into pieces of equal size.

Method II. Roll out a piece of flaky pastry, cut it into 2 pieces, each 10 cm. (4 inches) wide).

Place one of these on a slightly moistened baking sheet. Brush the edges of the dough with water. Spread with jam, leaving a border. Fold the second length of dough in half lengthwise. Using the back of a large knife, carefully cut the folded dough into strips of equal width, leaving a border at each end. Open out the dough and lay it carefully on the slice spread with jam. Press the edges to join them. Trim the edges neatly and crimp them.

Brush the top with beaten egg. Bake in a medium oven for 25 to 30 minutes. Take the tart out of the oven, spread jam on it and sprinkle sugar crystals round the edge.

Cut into strips about 4 cm. ($1\frac{1}{2}$ inches) wide. Leave to cool on a wire tray.

JAMS AND JELLIES. CONFITURES, GELÉES – A preparation of fruit for which the legal definition in France is as follows: 'Products constituted solely of refined or crystallised sugar and fresh fruits or juice of fresh fruits, or preserved in some way other than by drying.' (Decree of 25 September 1925). They must contain a maximum of 40 per cent moisture, and in consequence hold 60 per cent dry extract, of which 55 per cent must be sugar. (Fruit already contains 5 to 7 per cent.)

Only those products which correspond to this definition have a right to be labelled *pure fruit, pure sugar*.

The law authorises the mixing of fruits (in practice, apple juice is used a great deal, particularly for jellies), on condition that the fruit used in the highest proportion is put first on the label.

Marmelades (q.v.) must correspond to the same definition as jams, but the dry extract can fall as low as 55 per cent, and the use of brown sugar, or sugar which has already been used for crystallising fruit, is allowed.

If tartaric acid or citric acid is added, the label must contain the word *fantaisie*. When artificial essences are added, the words *fantaisie* or *arome artificiel* (artificial flavouring) must appear on the label. When colouring matter is added, this must be indicated.

A product made with essences, acids and colouring matter cannot bear the name of a fruit, and can only be sold under the name of *produit artificiel* (artificial product) with, if necessary, the mention of pure sugar.

Jams made of fruit or of mixtures of fruit, or *marmelades* made with syrup which has been used to preserve fruits (syrup containing about 5 per cent glucose) must bear the words *au sirop de fruits confits* (made with preserved fruit syrup).

Jams, all of which are obtained from a basis of fruit and sugar, can be divided into various categories:

1. Jams made by cooking stoned fruit with sugar. Apricots, cherries, strawberries, oranges, plums, etc., are used and, according to its kind, the fruit is prepared whole or halved.
2. Jellies made only with the juice of fruits and sugar.
3. *Marmelades* prepared with strained fruit pulp and sugar.
4. Jams made with a multiple base, such as the *raisinés* (q.v.), or other similar preparations.

Preserving pan with skimming ladle
(*Dehillerin. Phot. Larousse*)

Jam-making. FABRICATION – The quantity of sugar used varies according to the fruit in question. Sugar is used not only to sweeten the preparation, but to preserve it. When rather watery fruits with slight acidity are used, sugar must be introduced in a quantity to equal that of the fruit.

For fruits of more substance, containing mucilaginous

matter, the quantity of sugar should be reduced. The best quality sugar should be used.

Too much sugar oversweetens the jam, noticeably diminishes the flavour of the fruit, and risks rapid crystallisation. On the other hand, jams or jellies prepared with an insufficient quantity of sugar are in danger of fermenting, or, if they have been overcooked, of lacking all flavour.

Cooking. This cannot be properly done without an untinned copper or aluminium utensil.

The time taken to cook the jam depends upon the intensity of the heat to which it is submitted. It cannot be precisely measured. The cooking period is divided into two phases: during the first the evaporation of the moisture contained in the fruit takes place. The process of dehydration is complete when the steam rising from the pan is less dense and the surface begins to seethe rather than to bubble. Then the real cooking begins, effected at greater or less speed according to whether the fruit is watery or easily jelled.

During the first phase, the jam should be skimmed with an untinned skimming ladle, to remove all the impurities which rise to the surface.

Once evaporation has taken place, you must follow very closely the progress of the cooking, which from then on will be very rapid. Put the skimming ladle frequently into the pan to see whether, on lifting it out, the drops of jam fall off easily or slowly. As soon as these drops collect in the centre of the skimmer and slide slowly off, the jam is ready. It is cooked to a degree called jelling – 32°–33° (104·5°C., 220°F. on the sugar thermometer).

Potting, sealing and conservation. As soon as the jam has achieved the stage known as jelling, remove the pan from the fire. Allow the jam to cool for a few minutes. Fill the pots, having heated them gradually beforehand so as to prevent them from cracking. Put the pots on a table and leave them till the following day. Then cover the surface of the jam with a glycerine paper or paraffin wax, and seal the top of the pot with a double paper tightly tied with string.

Gum on labels indicating the type of jam and store in a very dry place.

Failures in jam-making and remedies.

The jam remains runny. – There is lack of pectin. Add some apple jelly.

The jam crystallises. – The fruits are insufficiently acid. Cook again, adding lemon juice, or tartaric or citric acid.

The jam develops mould. – The jars are inadequately sealed. Remove the mould and cover with melted paraffin wax.

The jam ferments. – The cooking has been insufficient. Cook again.

Recipes for jams and jellies are given below; recipes for marmalade will be found under the separate heading MARMALADE.

JAMS. CONFITURES –

Apricot jam I. CONFITURE D'ABRICOTS – For 1 kg. (2 lb.) apricots which are ripe, net weight stoned, 750 g. (1½ lb., 3 cups) sugar.

Put the sugar in a pan with 1 dl. (6 tablespoons, scant ½ cup) water. Let the sugar dissolve, then boil for 5 minutes and skim.

Add the apricots. Cook till the jelling stage is reached, as described above. Finish according to the instructions above adding, at the last moment, some of the apricot kernels which have been previously shelled and divided in two.

Apricot jam II. CONFITURE D'ABRICOTS – For 1 kg. (2 lb.) net weight of apricots, 800 g. (1¾ lb., 3½ cups) sugar, 1 dl. (6 tablespoons, scant ½ cup) water.

Put the fruit, sugar and water in a pan. Let the sugar melt, stirring all the time on a gentle heat. Raise the heat and continue to cook until the jelling stage is reached. Add shelled apricot kernels. Finish as directed above.

Cherry jam I. CONFITURE DE CERISES – For 1 kg. (2 lb.) stoned cherries, use 1 kg. (2 lb., 4 cups) sugar and 1 dl. (6 tablespoons, scant ½ cup) water. Proceed in the same way as for *Apricot jam I.*

If the cherries are very sweet, only 750 g. (1½ lb., 3 cups) sugar should be used for 1 kg. (2 lb.) fruit.

Cherry jam II. CONFITURE DE CERISES – 1 kg. (2 lb.) cherries, 1 kg. (2 lb., 4 cups) sugar, 5 dl. (scant pint, 2¼ cups) gooseberry juice, 1 dl. (6 tablespoons, scant ½ cup) water. Dissolve the sugar in the water and boil for 5 minutes. Add the cherries and the gooseberry juice. Cook and finish in the usual way.

The addition of gooseberry juice makes for more rapid cooking and a more fragrant jam as well.

Chestnut jam. CONFITURE DE MARRONS – See CHESTNUTS.

Melon jam. CONFITURE DE MELON – For 1 kg. (2 lb.) melon, net weight, after removing rind and seeds, 750 g. (1½ lb., 3 cups) fine sugar.

Cut the flesh of the melon into little pieces. Put these in layers in a large basin, sprinkling each layer with sugar. Leave to stand in a cool place for 3 or 4 hours, then put the contents of the basin into a pan and cook to the jelling stage as described above.

Orange jam. CONFITURE D'ORANGES – For 1 litre (1¾ pints, generous quart) orange purée, 1 kg. (2 lb., 4 cups) sugar, 1 dl. (6 tablespoons, scant ½ cup) water and 3 dl. (½ pint, 1¼ cups) apple juice.

Choose oranges of the same size, sound and with a thick skin. Prick them here and there rather deeply with a little pointed stick. Put them in a pan of boiling water and leave to cook rapidly for 30 minutes.

Drain, and soak them in a basin of cold water, renewing the water frequently, for 24 hours. This rather prolonged operation removes the bitterness from the orange rind and softens it more completely.

Drain the oranges, divide them into quarters, remove the pips and pith and pass through a sieve.

Dissolve the sugar with the water in a pan. Boil for a few moments, and skim. Add the orange purée and the apple juice. Finish in the same way as the recipes above.

Peach jam. CONFITURE DE PÊCHES – Proceed with stoned and skinned peaches in the same way as for *Apricot jam.*

Pineapple jam. CONFITURE D'ANANAS – For 1 kg. (2 lb.) fresh pineapple (net weight, after removing the outside and hard core), 750 g. (1½ lb., 3 cups) sugar, 1 dl. (6 tablespoons, scant ½ cup) water.

Cut the pineapple into small, square pieces. Dissolve the sugar in the water and cook it to the ball stage (116°C., 240°F.), then put in the pineapple chunks.

Cook the jam as usual until it reaches the jelling stage.

Finish in the usual way.

Plum jam. CONFITURE DE PRUNES – For every 1 kg. (2 lb.) stoned plums, add 750 g. (1½ lb., 3 cups) sugar and 1 dl. (6 tablespoons, scant ½ cup) water. Prepare as for *Apricot jam.*

Raspberry jam. CONFITURE DE FRAMBOISES – Remove stems from raspberries. Choose ripe but firm fruit. Put in a copper pan. Cover with sugar cooked to 116°C. (240°F.). For 1 kg. (2 lb.) of fruit use 1 kg. (2 lb., 4 cups) sugar.

Heat gently on a small flame or in a double cooker so that the sugar thoroughly penetrates the fruit. Remove from the heat, and leave overnight.

Next morning drain the raspberries very carefully without crushing them, and put the syrup back on the stove. Add an equal quantity of currant juice. Cook this syrup until it coats a silver spoon. Put the raspberries in it and bring to the boil.

Pot the jam. Cover with a layer of currant jelly. When the jam is absolutely cold, cover the pots.

Rhubarb jam. CONFITURE DE RHUBARBE – For 1 kg. (2 lb.) rhubarb (net weight, with outer fibres removed), 800 g. ($1\frac{3}{4}$ lb., $3\frac{1}{2}$ cups) sugar, 1 dl. (6 tablespoons, scant $\frac{1}{2}$ cup) water.

Skin the stems of young red or green rhubarb, according to whether one wishes to obtain a jam of one or the other colour, and divide into pieces 5 cm. (2 inches) long.

Wash the pieces, drain, and put them in with the sugar, which has been dissolved with the water and boiled for a few minutes.

Draw the pan to one side of the stove and cover it. Leave for 10 minutes so that the rhubarb softens. Return the pan to full heat and cook, stirring until the jam reaches the jelling stage. Finish in the usual way.

Strawberry jam. CONFITURE DE FRAISES – The strawberries must be selected for perfect unblemished ripeness. It is advisable not to wash them unless absolutely necessary. In this case they should be well drained and dried before cooking.

1 kg. (2 lb.) strawberries (net weight), 750 g. ($1\frac{1}{2}$ lb., 3 cups) sugar, 1 dl. (6 tablespoons, scant $\frac{1}{2}$ cup) water.

Dissolve the sugar in a pan with the water and cook to ball stage (116°C., 240°F.), skimming well.

Put the strawberries, stalks removed, in the dissolved sugar. Keep the pan on the side of the stove for a few minutes. When the juice from the strawberries has thinned the sugar to a syrupy consistency, drain the fruit through a silk strainer. Cook the syrup again in the pan until it reaches 116°C. (240°F.) once more. Put the strawberries back in the pan and cook for 5 or 6 minutes, to the point at which the jam reaches the jelling stage. Finish in the usual way.

Tomato jam. CONFITURE DE TOMATES – 1 litre ($1\frac{3}{4}$ pints, generous quart) drained tomato pulp, 1 kg. (2 lb., 4 cups) sugar, 1 dl. (6 tablespoons, scant $\frac{1}{2}$ cup) water, 3 dl. ($\frac{1}{2}$ pint, $1\frac{1}{4}$ cups) apple juice, 1 vanilla pod.

Dissolve the sugar in the water with the vanilla pod. Cook to the ball stage (116°C., 240°F.).

Add the tomato pulp to the pan, sieving it first. Cook on a lively heat, stirring all the time with the skimmer until the jam reaches the jelling stage.

Finish in the usual way.

Instead of apple juice, gooseberry juice may be used. The addition of juice is necessary to supply the jelling element to the tomatoes, so that the jam sets properly.

Watermelon jam. CONFITURE DE PASTÈQUES – For 1 kg. (2 lb.) watermelon, net weight after removing rind and seeds, 750 g. ($1\frac{1}{2}$ lb., 3 cups) fine sugar.

Proceed in the same way as for *Melon jam*.

JELLIES. GELÉES –

Apple jelly. GELÉE DE POMMES – This jelly is made by cutting good cooking apples into slices without peeling them or removing the pips. The fruit should be ripe and perfectly sound.

Cook them in a preserving pan with $1\frac{1}{2}$ litres ($2\frac{3}{4}$ pints, $3\frac{1}{4}$ pints) water for every 1 kg. (2 lb.) fruit. As soon as the apples are cooked, turn them into a jelly-bag placed over a large basin.

Add 800 g. ($1\frac{3}{4}$ lb., $3\frac{1}{2}$ cups) sugar for every litre (scant quart, generous quart) juice, which must be obtained without pressure. Cook until it begins to jell. This stage is reached when a drop of jelly is let fall from the skimmer onto a plate without spreading.

Fill the pots when the jelly is lukewarm, and cover them the following day.

Cherry jelly. GELÉE DE CERISES – For 1 litre ($1\frac{3}{4}$ pints, generous quart) cherry juice use 850 g. (1 lb. 14 oz., $3\frac{3}{4}$ cups) sugar, ($\frac{1}{2}$ pint, $1\frac{1}{4}$ cups) apple juice, 1 dl. (6 tablespoons, scant $\frac{1}{2}$ cup) water.

Proceed in the same way as for *Currant jelly* (see below).

Currant jelly I. GELÉE DE GROSEILLES – Use two-thirds redcurrants and one-third white. 125 g. (4 oz.) raspberries are added to each 1 kg. (2 lb.) currants.

Crush the currants and raspberries together and strain them through a cloth which is wrung at both ends.

Dissolve the sugar, slightly moistened with hot water, allowing 1 kg. (2 lb., 4 cups) for each litre (scant quart, generous quart) fruit juice. Cook to the jelling stage on a good heat.

Currant jelly II. GELÉE DE GROSEILLES – Add the currants and the raspberries to the sugar, which has been dissolved in a pan, allowing 600 g. ($1\frac{1}{4}$ lb., $2\frac{1}{2}$ cups) sugar for every 1 kg. (2 lb.) fruit.

Allow the fruit to swell, keeping the pan on a corner of the stove. Then boil quickly until the jelling stage is reached. Strain the jelly and decant into pots.

Redcurrant juice can also be obtained in the following way. Put the currants in a pan with the raspberries. Add a glass of water for every 1 kg. (2 lb.) fruit. Keep at a low temperature until the skins burst and the juice comes out. Strain juice as described above.

Orange jelly. GELÉE D'ORANGES – Rub the zest of 12 oranges with 100 g. (4 oz., scant cup) lump sugar. Add this sugar, which has absorbed the fragrant oil of the oranges, to 1 litre ($1\frac{3}{4}$ pints, generous quart) apple juice, obtained as described for *Apple jelly*.

Add the strained juice of the 12 oranges and 900 g. (2 lb., 7 cups) lump sugar. Add, if desired, 100 g. (4 oz., $\frac{2}{3}$ cup) crystallised orange peel which has been soaked in lukewarm water and shredded into fine strips.

Cook the jelly to the jelling stage and finish as described.

Quince jelly. GELÉE DE COINGS – Cut ripe, peeled quinces into slices. Put them into a basin of cold water as soon as they have been sliced. Cook them in a copper pan with water in the proportion of 1 litre (scant quart, generous quart) water for 500 g. (1 lb.) fruit, without stirring. As soon as the fruit is cooked turn it into a sieve and drain.

Put the juice into a pan and add 800 g. ($1\frac{3}{4}$ lb., $3\frac{1}{2}$ cups) sugar for each litre (scant quart, generous quart) liquid. Dissolve the sugar. Cook on a lively heat until the jelly has reached the jelling stage.

JAMBE DE BOIS SOUP – This was the name given, in former times, to a clear soup whose principal ingredient was a piece of leg of beef on the bone. When it was ready, the meat fell away from the bone. (It was as though a wooden leg was floating in the soup, hence its name.)

JAMBON – See also HAM.

Jambon de Prague sous la cendre – Name which is often used in menus to describe ham (Prague, York or other) cooked in pastry.

JAPAN – See INTERNATIONAL COOKERY.

JAPONAISE (À LA) – A number of different dishes are called *à la japonaise*. Most of them have this in common, that Chinese (in French, called Japanese) artichokes are included in the ingredients. *Francillon salad* is sometimes called *salade à la japonaise*. It is made from mussels, potatoes and truffles, and was invented by Alexandre Dumas the younger (see SALADS, *Mixed salads*).

The term *japonaise* is also applied to an iced *bombe* made of peach ice cream filled with tea-flavoured mousse.

JARDINIÈRE (À LA) – Name given to a garnish made of

fresh vegetables – carrots and turnips (shaped with a plain or fluted ball-scoop, cut with a hollow tubular cutter, or diced), green peas, small kidney beans, French beans (diced or cut into lozenges), cauliflower, etc. These vegetables are cooked separately, some boiled, others glazed. They are arranged round the main dish in separate groups. This garnish is served with roast, stewed or braised meat and pot-roasted poultry. (See GARNISHES.)

JASMIN – Plant containing a powerfully scented substance which is used in oriental cookery and confectionery.

JAY. GEAI – Bird regarded as a delicacy when it is young. The fully grown birds may also be eaten, but they must be boiled before roasting. These jays differ from the jays of North America. European jays have a pinkish-brown body, white rump, black tail, white patch on wings, black and white crown feathers, blue and black wing coverts.

JELLY. GELÉE – A jelly is, first of all, a clear meat or fish stock which solidifies when cold, by virtue of the gelatinous substances contained in it.

In former times, meat and fish jellies were prepared with hart's horn. Nowadays, these jellies are prepared in a more natural way, by including gelatinous bones in the stock or by adding a quantity of gelatine to it. It is this preparation which was once called aspic.

Gelatine should not be used to excess in the preparation of meat jellies. Whenever possible it should be left out altogether, and this is possible where the stock is made from naturally gelatinous parts of the meat, such as veal knuckles and calves' feet, fresh bacon rind, and poultry.

In jam-making, the name jelly is given to a preserve, made from fruit juice and sugar, which, by a careful control of temperature in cooking, is reduced to the required consistency. Jelly may be made from quinces, currants, apples and other fruits containing pectin (see JAMS AND JELLIES).

Certain sweets are also called jellies. These are made from various fruit juices with sugar and a variable quantity of gelatine added, or made by the old method, with calf's foot jelly.

Jellies are also made from fresh and dried vegetables, and cereals. These are mainly used as invalid foods. Recipes for them are given further on in this section and elsewhere in this volume.

Clarification of jellies. Jelly stocks must always be clarified to ensure perfect transparency, whether they have a meat, fish or vegetable base, and after they have been prepared according to the instructions and have been reduced (with or without gelatine) to the desired consistency.

Instructions for clarification of jelly stocks are given under ASPIC. Methods for clarifying meat, fish and vegetable stocks are also given in the article on CULINARY METHODS.

Chopped jelly. GELÉE HACHÉE – Chopped meat or fish jelly is used as a garnish for cold dishes. To obtain the best results, place the jelly on a cloth which has been dipped in cold water, wrung out thoroughly and spread out on the table. Chop the jelly with a large knife. It must be arranged round the dish with a spoon and not, as is often done, squeezed through a forcing-bag. Treated in the latter way, the jelly tends to lose its colour and becomes cloudy.

Set pieces in jelly. ATTELETS DE GELÉE – These set pieces, which were much used in former times to enhance the appearance of a cold dish, have now almost disappeared, although, on occasions, they still appear as a feature of a cold buffet.

Jelly triangles. CROÛTONS DE GÉLEE – These croûtons or triangles are used to provide a decorative border for a cold dish.

They are made from very stiff meat or fish jelly which is first cut into strips about 5 cm. (2 inches) wide, and then shaped into elongated triangles to produce a dog's tooth effect.

The jelly may also be cut into other shapes, using pastry-cutters.

MEAT JELLIES. GELÉES DE VIANDE –

Meat jelly stock. FONDS POUR GELÉE DE VIANDE – *Ingredients.* For 5 litres ($4\frac{1}{2}$ quarts, $5\frac{1}{2}$ quarts) of jelly:

Nourishing ingredients. 2 kg. ($4\frac{1}{2}$ lb.) beef (leg), $1\frac{1}{2}$ kg. ($3\frac{1}{4}$ lb.) knuckle of veal, $1\frac{1}{2}$ kg. ($3\frac{1}{4}$ lb.) veal and beef bones sawn in small pieces, 3 calves' feet (boned and blanched, with the bones ground), 250 g. ($\frac{1}{2}$ lb.) bacon rinds.

Aromatic ingredients. 2 or 3 large carrots, 2 medium onions, 2 leeks, 3 stalks of celery, bouquet of herbs, salt and pepper.

Liquid. $8\frac{1}{2}$ litres ($7\frac{1}{2}$ quarts, 9 quarts) water.

Put the beef, the veal (tied with string) and the bones in a pan and brown slightly in butter. Transfer the meat and bones to a large stockpot, brown them further with the carrots, onions, leeks and celery. Pour in the water.

Rinse the pan in which the meat and bones were first browned with a little water, and add this to the ingredients in the stockpot. Bring to the boil, skim, and add the calves' feet and bacon rinds, tied with string, and the bouquet of herbs. Season. Simmer gently for about 5 to 6 hours.

Strain this stock through muslin or a fine strainer. To turn it into aspic jelly, clarify it in the usual way.

Chicken jelly stock. FONDS POUR GELÉE DE VOLAILLE – Use the same method of preparation as for ordinary jelly adding, over and above the basic ingredients, a pullet which has been browned in the oven or, alternatively, $1\frac{1}{2}$ kg. ($3\frac{1}{4}$ lb.) chicken carcase and giblets, also browned in advance in the oven.

When this jelly stock is intended as a garnish for galantine, the galantine takes the place of the pullet and should be cooked in the stock.

Fish jelly stock. FONDS POUR GELÉE DE POISSON – This stock is made in the same way as concentrated fish stock (see STOCKS) from the following basic ingredients.

For 5 litres ($4\frac{1}{2}$ quarts, $5\frac{1}{2}$ quarts): 500 g. (1 lb.) fish bones and trimmings of turbot, brill or sole (U.S. flounder or haddock) or an equivalent quantity of fish such as whiting, gurnet, weever, etc., 2 medium onions (finely sliced), mushroom peelings, celery, parsley roots, thyme, laurel.

This stock may be made with water but it is better made with *fish fumet* (see FUMET) prepared in advance.

Fish jelly stock with red wine. FONDS POUR GELÉE DE POISSON AU VIN ROUGE – This stock is used in cooking the various fish served in red wine jelly (salmon trout, brown trout, carp, etc.).

It may be prepared like ordinary fish jelly, with the same basic ingredients and flavourings, to which are added equal parts of red wine (Burgundy or Claret) and *Fish fumet* (see FUMET).

Game jelly stock. FONDS POUR GELÉE DE GIBIER – The same method is used as that given for ordinary jelly. Use the same basic ingredients, adding about $1\frac{1}{4}$ kg. (3 lb.) game carcases and trimmings which have been previously browned in the oven. Add celery, thyme, bay leaf and 8 to 10 juniper berries to the usual flavourings.

White jelly stock. FONDS POUR GELÉE BLANCHE – Made from the same basic ingredients and flavourings as ordinary jelly, but without browning the meat or bones.

VEGETABLE JELLIES. GELÉES DE LÉGUMES – These jellies, which are prepared from various dried vegetables, cereals and fresh herbs, are used particularly as invalid foods. Pectose is a constituent of all these vegetables. In unripe fruit and vegetables, it is present in an insoluble state but, as the fruit or vegetable ripens, it changes into soluble pectin.

Fresh bean jelly. GELÉE DE FÈVES FRAÎCHES – Put ripe, shelled beans in a saucepan. Add a little water, cover tightly, and cook. From time to time, while they are cooking, add a little water so that the liquid level in the pan remains constant.

When the beans are cooked, sieve them. Press the vegetables gently to extract all the juice, which makes a jelly with a very high albumen content.

In the same way, jellies can be extracted from small kidney beans, French (string) beans, green peas and various other fresh vegetables.

DESSERT (SWEET) JELLIES. GELÉES D'ENTREMETS – Sweet jellies are made with a base of powdered gelatine or French leaf gelatine dissolved in water or (rarely) from calf's foot jelly plus sugar and water. This base is flavoured either with liqueur, a dessert wine, or a fruit juice.

For liqueur jellies, the liqueur is added after clarifying the jelly. 1 dl. (6 tablespoons, scant 1½ cup) liqueur is used to 9 dl. jelly (1½ pints, 2 pints) base.

Jellies made from juicy fruits. GELÉES DE FRUITS AQUEUX – Use lemons, oranges, tangerines, pineapple, grapes, etc. The filtered juice of the fruit is added to the dissolved gelatine.

Muscovite jelly. GELÉE À LA MOSCOVITE – This jelly is made in the usual way, flavoured with liqueur or fruit juice and poured into a hinged mould, called a 'Muscovite' mould, which must be completely airtight, as in the preparation of ice cream.

The special feature of this jelly is that it is covered with a thin coating of frost.

Red fruit jellies. GELÉES DE FRUITS ROUGES – Cherries, strawberries, raspberries, redcurrants, etc. Only very ripe fruit should be used. Put the fruit through a fine sieve. Add between 1 dl. (6 tablespoons, scant ½ cup) and 3 dl. (½ pint, 1¼ cups) water to ½ litre (scant pint, 2¼ cups) juice, according to the pectin content of the fruit.

Filter this fruit juice, and add it in two stages to the calf's foot jelly or the gelatine, dissolved in advance, to ensure the right consistency.

Russian jelly. GELÉE À LA RUSSE – This sweet is made like other jellies, with various flavourings. It is whisked on ice until it begins to set, poured into a mould as quickly as possible, and put on ice to set completely. Turn out on a napkin.

Stone fruit. GELÉES DE FRUITS À NOYAUX – Apricots, nectarines, peaches, plums, etc., are often used as a garnish with different fruit jellies.

The jelly itself may also be made from these fruits.

Dip the fruit in boiling water and peel. Cook slowly in syrup. Leave in the syrup until cold. Make the jelly from the syrup and clarify in the usual way.

Generally, fruit jellies should be flavoured with kirsch, maraschino or some other liqueur.

Swedish fruit jelly. GELÉE DE FRUITS À LA SUÉDOISE – Fruit jelly, garnished after it is put in the mould, with various kinds of fruit which have been cooked in syrup and thoroughly drained.

Various wine jellies. GELÉES AUX VINS DIVERS – Champagne, Frontignan, Madeira, Marsala, port, sherry, etc. 3 dl. (½ pint, 1¼ cups) wine should be used to every 7 dl. (1¼ pints, 1½ pints) jelly base.

PASTE JELLIES (Confectionery). PÂTES – These confections are made by mixing fruit or flower pulp with sugar.

Apple paste jelly. PÂTE DE POMMES – 'Choose good, sound, cooking apples, peel them and remove cores. Put into a pan with water, and cook, turning with a wooden spoon from time to time, until they have been softened. Remove, strain the juice into a bowl leaving the apples in the sieve until cold, then rub the pulp through a sieve. Put over the fire and cook down by half. Remove from heat, transfer from the pan into an earthenware or glazed china bowl – a precaution which cannot be stressed too much.

'Clarify the same amount of sugar, cook it to small crack degree (see SUGAR), take the pan off the fire, pour in the apple pulp, stir the mixture thoroughly with a wooden spoon and place on a low heat. Allow to heat until the mixture shivers very slightly. Stir all the time until you begin to see the bottom of the pan. Then proceed to pour into moulds as described (below.' (*Le Confiseur moderne.*)

Apricot paste jelly. PÂTE D'ABRICOTS – 'Choose sound, ripe apricots, stone them, put into a pan with water, stand over the fire and, as soon as boiling is established, remove and drain. Rub through a sieve at once to extract all pulp, collecting it in a bowl. Throw away the skin. Weigh the pulp and boil down by half. Take out of the pan and transfer into an earthenware or china bowl. Clarify the same quantity of sugar as you have pulp and cook to small crack degree (see SUGAR). Pour the pulp into it, stirring with a wooden spoon. When the mixture is smooth, stand the pan on low heat again, stirring all the time until the bottom of the pan can be seen, then remove from the heat.

'Put moulds of different shapes (round, heart-shaped, etc.) on a tinned metal sheet, fill them with the apricot and sugar confection, smoothing the surface with a knife. When the moulds are filled, dust them with sugar and put them into a hot drying-oven. Two days later take the confections out of the mould, turn them out onto a sieve, dust with sugar, leave in a drying-oven for a day, then store in tins with well-fitting lids, placing the confections in rows and putting a sheet of white paper between each layer.' (*Le Confiseur moderne.*)

Cherry paste jelly. PÂTE DE CERISES – 'Choose very ripe red cherries. Remove stalks and stones, putting the cherries into a bowl as you do so. Then transfer them into a pan and put over the fire. Bring them to the boil, stirring with a wooden spoon. Rub through a sieve to extract all the pulp, collecting it in a bowl. Boil down by half, weigh the pulp and pour into a china bowl. Clarify the same weight of sugar, cook to ball degree (see SUGAR), add the cherry pulp and proceed as described in the recipe for *Apricot paste jelly*.' (*Le Confiseur moderne.*)

Grape paste jelly. PÂTE DE VERJUS – 'Pick good green grapes off the bunches and put into a basin with a little water. Bring to the boil on a high flame. When the grapes swell and burst, strain the juice into a bowl, leaving the grapes to drip. Then rub them through a sieve, collecting the pulp in a bowl. Put it into a pan, set on a low flame, boil down by half and weigh. Clarify the same amount of sugar, cook to small ball degree (see SUGAR), take off the heat, pour in the grape pulp and add 100 g. (4 oz., ½ cup) apple pulp per 450 g. (1 lb., 2 cups) grape pulp. Mix well and proceed as described above.' (*Le Confiseur moderne.*)

Greengage paste jelly. PÂTE DE REINES-CLAUDES – 'Pick the greengages when they are very ripe. Stone, put into a pan with a little water, and bring to the boil. Strain the juice, leaving the greengages on the sieve to cool. When they are cold, rub them through the sieve, weigh the pulp and, allowing the same amount of sugar, proceed as described above.' (*Le Confiseur moderne.*)

Mirabelle paste jelly. PÂTE DE MIRABELLES – 'Choose sound mirabelles, peel, stone them and put into cold water. Place them in a pan over the fire, stirring with a wooden spoon until they are cooked. Drain, leave the mirabelles in a sieve until cold, then rub them through. Boil down the quantity by half and pour from the pan into a china bowl. Weigh the pulp, clarify the same amount of sugar and cook to small crack degree (see SUGAR). Pour the pulp into it, stirring with a wooden spoon to mix, and proceed to make the jellies as described in the recipe for *Apricot paste jelly*.' (*Le Confiseur moderne*.)

Peach paste jelly. PÂTE DE PÊCHES – 'Proceed as above using the following ingredients: 2 kg. (4 lb.) peaches and $1\frac{1}{2}$ kg. (3 lb., 6 cups) sugar.' (*Le Confiseur moderne*.)

Pear paste jelly. PÂTE DE POIRES – 'Prepare as *Apple paste jelly*, using the pulp of juicy pears.' (*Le Confiseur moderne*.)

Quince paste jelly. PÂTE DE COINGS – 'Choose very ripe quinces, cut into quarters, remove the skins and pips, put into a pan with water and place over the fire to soften. Drain, and proceed as described in the recipe for *Apricot paste jelly*.' (*Le Confiseur Moderne*.)

Raspberry paste jelly. PÂTE DE FRAMBOISES – 'Choose ripe raspberries, rub through a sieve to extract the pulp. Put over the fire and boil down the pulp by half. Weigh, add the same amount (by weight) of sugar cooked to ball degree (see SUGAR), and proceed as described above.

'Strawberry jellies are made in the same way as raspberry jellies.' (*Le Confiseur moderne*.)

Violet paste jelly. PÂTE DE VIOLETTES – 'Take 1 kg. (2 lb.) clean violets, reduce to pulp by bruising in a mortar and add the juice of 2 lemons.

'Cook 1 kg. (2 lb., 4 cups) sugar to ball degree (see SUGAR), take the pan off the fire, add the bruised violets and 500 g. (1 lb., 2 cups) apple jelly, mix, and make the jellies as described above.

Various other flowers, such as orange blossom, roses, etc., can be made into jellies in a similar manner.' (*Le Confiseur moderne*.)

JERBOA. GERBOISE – Small rodent about the size of a squirrel. It is to be found in all parts of Europe, and is prepared for the table like squirrel (q.v.). Found in south-western U.S.A. and Mexico, under the name of *kangaroo-rat* or *pouched mouse*.

JERUSALEM ARTICHOKE. TOPINAMBOUR – Plant originating in North America and imported into France at the beginning of the seventeenth century. Jerusalem artichokes, also known as *artichauts du Canada* and *poires de terre*, were not much liked at the start, but were established, like the potato, by Parmentier. They are at their best on the borderline of winter and spring.

Jerusalem artichokes are firm in consistency. They resemble real artichokes to some extent in flavour and may be substituted for them in certain preparations. They have a pleasant taste, but one that soon palls.

Jerusalem artichokes à l'anglaise. TOPINAMBOURS À L'ANGLAISE – Peel the artichokes, divide in quarters and cut them to look like pigeons' eggs. Blanch lightly in salted water and cook gently in butter. Season, and stir in a few tablespoons of rather thin *Béchamel sauce* (see SAUCE). Simmer for a few minutes. Serve in a deep dish.

Jerusalem artichokes in butter. TOPINAMBOURS AU BEURRE – Cut to look like pigeons' eggs. Cook in butter like *Château potatoes* (see POTATOES).

Jerusalem artichokes à la crème. TOPINAMBOURS À LA CRÈME – Cut to look like pigeons' eggs and simmer gently in butter. When they are almost cooked, cover with boiling fresh cream and finish cooking as slowly as possible. Season.

At the last moment add a few tablespoons of fresh cream. *Jerusalem artichokes à la crème* may also be prepared with rather thin *Béchamel sauce* (see SAUCE).

Fried Jerusalem artichokes. TOPINAMBOURS EN FRITOT – Cut the artichokes in thick slices and cook them in butter. Dip in light batter and fry in smoking-hot fat or oil.

Purée of Jerusalem artichokes. PURÉE DE TOPINAMBOURS – Peel the artichokes, cut them in thin slices and simmer them in butter and a little water in a covered pan. Rub through a sieve. Heat this purée and add to it a sufficient quantity of potatoes to give it the desired consistency. Add a few tablespoons boiling hot milk or cream and 2 or 3 tablespoons fresh butter.

Salad of Jerusalem artichokes. SALADE DE TOPINAMBOURS – Made like *Potato salad* (see SALAD).

Soufflé of Jerusalem artichokes. SOUFFLÉ DE TOPINAMBOURS – Using purée of Jerusalem artichoke, made like *Potato soufflé* (see SOUFFLÉ).

JERUSALEM MELON. ABDELAVIS – This melon, which originally came from Egypt, has sweet, juicy and succulent flesh which is much valued as it quenches thirst. Its seeds are used for making sedative and tranquilising drinks, and its flesh is used in the manufacture of excellent ices, bombes, etc. It is eaten like melon.

JESSE – Fish found in almost all the rivers of Europe, rather similar in shape to the carp. It turns yellowish when cooked. It is fairly delicate but has many bones and is cooked in the same way as carp (q.v.).

JÉSUITE – A small pastry made of left-overs of *Flaky pastry dough* (see DOUGH).

Roll out the dough. Cut it into lengths 15 cm. (6 inches) wide. Spread half the lengths with almond paste, and cover with the remaining lengths. Sprinkle with praline (q.v.). Cut into triangles. Bake in a moderate oven.

JÉSUS – Type of pork-liver sausage made in Switzerland and Franche-Comté. It is also called *Jésu*. The *Jésu de Morteau* is particularly well known.

JOHANNISBEERKUCHEN (German cookery) – A German redcurrant tart. (See TARTS, *Fruit tart à l'allemande*.)

JOHANNISBERG – A village of Hesse-Nassau, in Prussia, where two special vines are grown, the large and the small Riesling. A famous dry white wine is made from the grapes of these vines.

JOHN DORY. SAINT-PIERRE – Fish, also known to the French as *dorée*, *Jean-Doré* and *poule de mer*. It is very oddly shaped, oval in form, and flat, with a large spiny head. Its skin is thick and it is covered with very small scales.

The first dorsal fin consists of nine spines held together by a membrane which ends in a long filament. On the flanks is a round blackish mark, surrounded by a light grey circle.

The flesh of the John Dory is delicate and rivals turbot and sole. In U.S.A. the Atlantic fish, the porgy (called scup in New England), could be used for John Dory recipes.

It may be cooked whole, grilled, braised or poached in a *court-bouillon* (q.v.), but most often it is filleted and cooked in the same way as fillets of brill (q.v.), turbot (q.v.) or sole (q.v.).

The John Dory is also used as an ingredient of *bouillabaisse* (q.v.).

Fillets of John Dory Pierre Chapelle. FILETS DE SAINT-PIERRE PIERRE CHAPELLE – Fillet a raw medium-sized John Dory. Season with salt and pepper and coat with egg and breadcrumbs. Use the skin and bones to prepare a white wine fish stock. Use this stock for a rice pilaf made of 100 g. (4 oz., $\frac{1}{2}$ cup) rice tossed in butter with chopped onions and cooked in the stock for 20 minutes. In another pot cook 50 g.

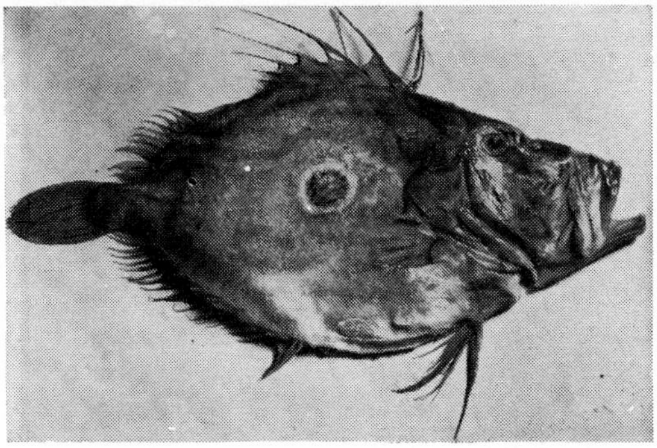

John Dory

(2 oz., $\frac{1}{2}$ cup) chopped onions gently in butter. Add 4 to 6 large tomatoes, peeled, squeezed to remove seeds and chopped. Season with salt, pepper, garlic and 1 teaspoon curry powder. Cook together for 20 minutes. Cook the fillets of fish in butter. Serve on top of the pilaf. Surround with the tomatoes.

JOINTING. DÉPEÇAGE – The action of cutting up meat, poultry, etc. (See CARVING.)

JONCHÉE – See CHEESE.

JUDAS-TREE. GAINIER – Judean tree which also grows in southern Europe, North America and Asia. Its strongly scented flowers are pickled in vinegar like capers.

JUDRU – A very short, thick *saucisson* made at Chagny in Burgundy.

JUICE. JUS – The French use the term *jus* in a somewhat wider sense than the English 'juice'.

Jus is used:

1. As in English, of the juice squeezed out of foodstuffs, whether animal or vegetable, e.g. herbal juice, orange juice, lemon juice, meat juice, etc.

2. Of the gravy of a roast made by diluting the juices of the roasting pan or dripping pan (in the case of spit roasts), with clear stock, water or any other suitable liquid, and then boiling it until all the goodness in the pan has been absorbed into the stock.

3. Of meat juice, extracted by pressing slices of lightly grilled beef in a special press. This juice is taken as a tonic.

4. Of *coulis* (q.v.) or brown stock, thickened or clear, of various kinds of meat, especially veal. (See STOCKS, *Veal stock.*)

Fruit and vegetable juices are very valuable in dietitics. Fruit juice is an excellent beverage containing vitamins, minerals and retaining the diuretic qualities of whole fruit. In fact, it has all the assets of the latter without its disadvantages (e.g. indigestibility).

Fruit juice is given to babies who cannot digest milk, or as a means of compensating for the vitamin deficiency in certain tinned milks. Invalids, post-operative patients and convalescents all must have fruit or vegetable juices in their diets.

Vegetable juice is particularly suitable for those who cannot tolerate raw vegetables or cooked green vegetables and, generally speaking, for people who find cellulose indigestible.

Apple juice. JUS DE POMMES – This is made from apple pulp. (See APPLE, *Apple pectin.*)

Herb juices. JUS D'HERBES VERTES – Made from various raw herbs (watercress, chervil, parsley, tarragon, etc.) pounded in a mortar and strained through muslin.

Meat juice. JUS DE VIANDE – This is extracted by putting slices of lightly grilled beef into a special press. The juice dripping from the press is collected in a cup standing in a bowl of hot water.

Orange, Seville orange or lemon juices. JUS D'ORANGE, BIGARADE, CITRON – These juices have many uses in the kitchen, in confectionary and in *pâtisserie*. They are extracted by squeezing the fruit. The flavour is enhanced if a little grated rind is added before straining.

Pineapple juice. JUS D'ANANAS – Pound fresh pineapple pulp in a mortar. While pounding, mix in a few tablespoons plain sugar syrup. Strain the pulp through muslin. This juice, like all other fruit juices, is used in the preparation of desserts.

Red fruit juices. JUS DE FRUITS ROUGES – Made from strawberries, raspberries, redcurrants or cherries. Rub the raw fruit through a fine sieve.

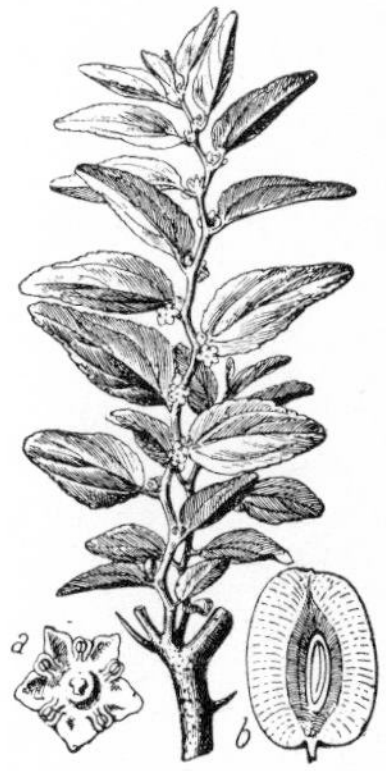

Jujube
a. Flower; b. Fruit

JUJUBE – The fruit of the jujube tree which is of Syrian origin. It grows in warm climates, including the south of France. The ovoid fruit is about the size of an olive, covered with a smooth, leathery, red skin. The pulp is yellowish, mild and sweet. It has a long stone.

Dried jujubes are used to sweeten medicines. They are soothing to the throat and chest, and are used in infusions, decoctions and in the form of paste, etc.

JULIENNE – Term used in French cookery to designate:

1. A clear vegetable soup made from clear consommé. To this stock is added a mixture of finely shredded vegetables cooked very slowly in butter until they are tender. (See SOUPS AND BROTHS, *Consommé julienne.*)

2. Any coarsely or finely shredded foodstuffs. Thus one may say *julienne* of breast of chicken, *julienne* of mushrooms, *julienne* of truffles, *julienne* of gherkins, etc.

JUNIPER BERRIES. GENIÈVRE – The berries of a bush which grows wild in woods and mountain gullies.

Juniper berries are used to add flavour to marinades, and as seasoning with certain foods (*sauerkraut*, thrushes, blackbirds, etc.). They are also used in the distillation of gin.

JUNIPER WINE. GENEVRETTE (VIN DE GENIÈVRE) – Medicinal drink made from juniper berries. (See BEVERAGES, *Juniper hippocras.*)

This name is also given to a wine which used to be made in the Gâtinais district from absinthe and juniper seeds.

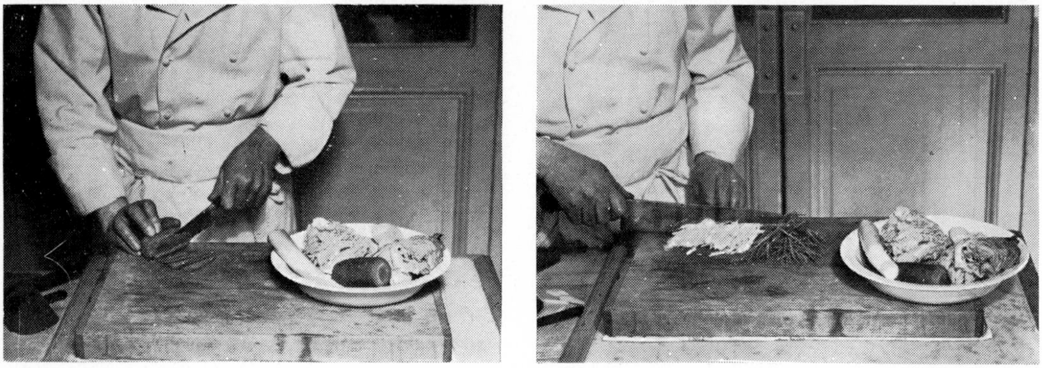

Slicing vegetables *julienne*: first and second steps (*Larousse*)

Juniper berries (*Rap*)

JUPITER'S BEARD. JOUBARBE – Name given to several plants with fleshy leaves. Among these are the houseleek or wild artichoke, and the white stonecrop, which is edible, its leaves being eaten in salad.

JURANÇON – Small town in the Basses-Pyrénées, 1 km. ($\frac{3}{4}$ mile) from Pau. A fine wine is made there which, it is said, was greatly prized by King Henry IV of France.

Legend has it that when the king was born, his grandfather, the King of Navarre, after having rubbed the baby's lips with a clove of garlic, made him swallow a few drops of Jurançon. The royal infant having come through this bacchic ordeal very creditably, his grandfather, in a frenzy of enthusiasm, cried: 'You are a real Béarnais.'

White Jurançon is a full-blooded and intoxicating wine. With age, it acquires a strong flavour of Madeira.

A red Jurançon is also made, but is less popular than the white. These wines are made by mixing the grapes of several different vines in the vat, but, curiously enough, the grapes of the Jurançon vine are not among them.

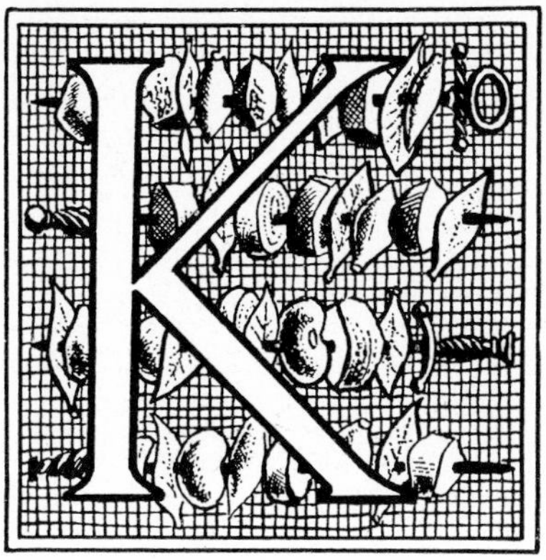

KALTSCHALE (Russian cookery) – A fruit salad liberally moistened with liqueur, wine or syrup.

Take a selection of mixed fresh fruit such as apricots, pineapple, peaches, strawberries, raspberries, melon and watermelon. Where necessary, skin the fruit. Cut it all up into small, thick slices and place in a bowl pressed down into a bucket of crushed ice.

Bring to the boil 1 bottle Champagne, $\frac{1}{2}$ litre (scant pint, $2\frac{1}{4}$ cups) red Bordeaux wine, 1 dl. (6 tablespoons, scant $\frac{1}{2}$ cup) Madeira, 2 or 3 tablespoons sugar and a pinch of ground cinnamon. Chill this mixture on ice and pour it over the fruit. Chill again and serve.

Kaltschale with strawberry purée. KALTSCHALE À LA PURÉE DE FRAISES – Embed a bowl in crushed ice. Fill it with fruit as indicated above. Make a purée of strawberries as follows: Rub through a fine sieve 1 kg. ($2\frac{1}{4}$ lb., 7 cups) very ripe strawberries and 225 g. (8 oz., 2 cups) redcurrants. Dilute this purée with 1 litre ($1\frac{3}{4}$ pints, generous quart) light sugar syrup and $\frac{1}{2}$ bottle Champagne previously brought to the boil and chilled. Pour over the fruit and serve chilled.

KANGAROO. KANGOUROU – The flesh of this Australian mammal is edible. Kangaroo tail soup is a delicacy in Germany. It is also sold commercially.

KASHA (Russian cookery). KACHE – Russian dish of cooked buckwheat. There are several ways of preparing it.

Ingredients. 500 g. (1 lb.) buckwheat, 1 teaspoon salt, 25 g. (1 oz., 2 tablespoons) butter.

1. Sort the buckwheat to pick out any black grains. – these are still covered with the hard husk which people find unsightly. Cook in a frying pan without grease or liquid, until the grains acquire a light golden colour. Put into an ovenproof dish, season with salt, add the butter, and pour in just enough boiling water to cover. Bake in a slow oven for $2\frac{1}{2}$ to 3 hours. It will have a thin crust but the grains should fall apart easily.

2. Using the same proportions, put the buckwheat in a double saucepan, add salt and melted butter, cover with cold water, stir, and cook on a low heat for 3 hours.

3. Wash the buckwheat, scald with boiling water and pour off the liquid. Put in a saucepan with salt and butter, cover with boiling water, bring again to the boil, stir, and transfer into a double saucepan. Cook for 3 hours.

Kasha croûtons. CROÛTONS DE KACHE – Soak 500 g. (1 lb.) crushed buckwheat in warm water until it forms a thick porridge. Season with salt and put it in a large earthenware pot.

Bake in a hot oven for 2 hours. Remove the thick crust formed on the surface. Scoop out all the porridge not sticking to the sides of the pan and put in a bowl. Add a piece of butter about the size of an egg. Mix well with a spatula. Press the porridge between 2 saucepan lids to make a 'dough' 1 cm. ($\frac{1}{2}$ inch) thick. Cut into shapes with a pastry-cutter and brown them in clarified butter.

These buckwheat croûtons are served with *shchi, borshch* and other soups.

Kasha with mushrooms. KACHE AUX CHAMPIGNONS – Prepare the buckwheat porridge as indicated above, adding to it sliced mushrooms tossed in butter before putting it in the oven.

Serve in the cooking pot, with fresh butter handed separately.

Kasha with Parmesan. KACHE DE SARRASIN AU PARMESAN – Make the buckwheat porridge as indicated above. When it is baked, remove the crust from the top and use part of the soft porridge to line a buttered boat-shaped dish, or a deep *gratin* dish. Sprinkle the porridge with grated Parmesan cheese and melted butter. Spread another layer of porridge on top and sprinkle with grated Parmesan and melted butter. When it is full, smooth the surface, sprinkle with Parmesan and melted butter and brown in the oven. Serve with melted butter and *estouffade* (q.v.) stock.

Polish kasha. KACHE POLONAIS – Pick over, blanch and hull 250 g. (9 oz.) barley. Simmer it gently in 3 litres ($5\frac{1}{4}$ pints, $6\frac{1}{2}$ pints) milk with a piece of butter about the size of an egg. Stir until the barley is fully cooked. Remove from the stove. Add 250 g. (9 oz., generous cup) butter, 6 eggs beaten as for an omelette, and 1 dl. (6 tablespoons, scant $\frac{1}{2}$ cup) sour cream.

Put this mixture in a buttered charlotte mould. Bake in a hot oven. Wrap the mould in a napkin and serve the kasha in it. Serve with double cream.

Semolina kasha. KACHE DE SEMOULE – Pour 500 g. (18 oz., 3 cups) Smolensk semolina on a slab. Beat 2 eggs as for an omelette and pour over the semolina. Mix well so that the semolina is thoroughly moistened. Leave the mixture to dry in a very moderate oven. Put through a food mill or strainer.

Boil 2 litres ($3\frac{1}{2}$ pints, $4\frac{1}{2}$ pints) milk with 250 g. (9 oz., generous cup) butter. Pour in the semolina. Season. Simmer gently, stirring frequently. Put into a serving dish and brown in a hot oven. Serve with melted butter.

KAUNAS – See CHEESE.

KEBAB (Turkish cookery) – Name used in Turkey for various dishes whose principal feature is skewered meat.

The skewers are of metal or wood. The meat – mutton, lamb or buffalo – is cut into squares, seasoned with pepper, salt, thyme and powdered bay leaves. Square pieces of mutton fat are placed on the skewer between the pieces of meat. In Turkey, mutton fat takes the place of bacon. The skewered meat is grilled over hot embers, and is served plain, with lemon or with various garnishes.

Kebab galette. KEBAB EN GALETTE – Cut into thick squares a boned shoulder of lamb. Steep the pieces in milk, and place them on skewers with squares of green pepper, tomato, onion and bay leaves between. Sprinkle with powdered thyme. Grill over hot embers.

Take the pieces off the skewers. Arrange them on a *galette* (q.v.) (thin cake) made of wheaten flour. Cover with finely chopped onions previously browned in butter. Moisten with brown stock and cover with another wheaten *galette*, which should be piping hot.

Shish-kebab, which is the Turkish name for skewered mutton cooked in this way, is also served with pilaf of rice or with chick peas and raw finely sliced onions.

Tchevir me kebab – Place on an upright spit some thin slices of mutton, alternating with pieces of mutton fat. This spit turns itself in front of an upright grill.

As the meat is cooked the pieces are slit lengthwise, taken off the spit one after another, and served with yogurt, pilaf of rice, etc.

KÉFIR – Fermented milk of Caucasian origin. Strictly it should be made of camels' milk but, in practice, it is made from cows' milk, skimmed or not, according to taste. Fermentation is induced by means of *kéfir* bacteria. When the bacteria have been added to the milk it is put in bottles with patent stoppers and kept for a period in a hot cupboard. After a day, mild *kéfir* is obtained. This is slightly laxative. After two days, medium *kéfir* is obtained, which is not laxative. Strong *kéfir* is obtained after three days of fermentation. It is slightly constipating and contains 2·5 per cent alcohol.

Kéfir has a rather sour taste. It is frothy and contains a greater or lesser proportion of alcohol according to the period of fermentation. The casein shows signs of peptinisation in the form of thin flakes. *Kéfir* is easily digestible and is often recommended for invalids.

KEFTES-KEBABS (Turkish cookery) – Made from small slices of raw meat (mutton, veal or buffalo), skewered, grilled and served with pilaf of rice and the juices of roast meat.

KETCHUP or CATSUP – Ketchup is a condiment rather than a sauce in the proper sense of the word. It is manufactured commercially and much used in England and North America. It is also made in home kitchens.

Mushroom ketchup or catsup. KETCHUP AUX CHAMPIGNONS – Put in a salting jar layers of fresh sliced mushrooms – about 1 cm. ($\frac{1}{2}$ inch) deep – and sprinkle each layer with table salt, pepper and allspice.

Leave the mushrooms in the salt for 5 or 6 days in a cool place. Press to extract all the juice. Boil this juice. Season with pepper, thyme, bay, ginger, marjoram and a little tomato paste. Leave to cool. Filter and bottle.

Tomato ketchup. KETCHUP AUX TOMATES – Cut up $3\frac{1}{2}$ kg. (8 lb.) unpeeled tomatoes, 6 medium onions, 2 sweet red peppers and 2 garlic cloves. Cover with water and boil gently until the vegetables are soft. Strain through a sieve. Tie in a bag 1 red pepper, 2 bay leaves, 1 tablespoon chopped celery, 1 tablespoon mustard seeds, 1 teaspoon peppercorns and 1 stick cinnamon, and add this, with 1 tablespoon salt, to the juice. Boil down by half, stirring frequently. Add 100 g. (4 oz., $\frac{1}{2}$ cup) brown sugar, 100 g. (4 oz., $\frac{1}{2}$ cup) white sugar and 4 dl. ($\frac{3}{4}$ pint, scant 2 cups) vinegar. Continue simmering for 15 to 20 minutes or until the sauce is thickened to the desired point. Seal in hot sterilised jars or bottles.

KETMIE – Plant, the fruit of which is edible and known as okra, gumbo or ladies' fingers. (See OKRA.)

KHLODNIK (Polish and Russian cookery). KOLODNIK – Iced soup, very popular in Poland, its country or origin, and in Russia.

It is made as follows:

Wash and blanch 4 large handfuls of tender beetroot leaves. Chop finely. Add to these a handful of finely chopped, blanched and drained chervil, tarragon, chive, fennel and shallot.

Put these herbs in a dish embedded in chopped ice, and moisten them with $\frac{1}{2}$ litre (scant pint, $2\frac{1}{4}$ cups) cucumber brine. Add the same amount of *kvass* (q.v.), a drink very popular in Russia. Just before serving, season the soup with salt and a pinch of fine sugar. Add the following garnishes: 48 crayfish tails, 500 g. (1 lb.) diced, braised sturgeon, 4 or 5 tablespoons diced, fresh cucumber. Add 3 dl. ($\frac{1}{2}$ pint, $1\frac{1}{4}$ cups) sieved sour cream and 1 or 2 pieces of ice. Serve with quartered hard-boiled eggs sprinkled with finely chopped chervil and fennel.

KID. CHEVREAU, CABRI – Young goat, slaughtered before being weaned. The meat of the kid is not very substantial but it is not unwholesome, as some people believe.

In French butchery sucking kids thirty to forty days old are called *têtards*, the other, three or four months old, are called *broutards*.

All the methods of preparation given for very young lamb are applicable to kid (see LAMB). As the meat is rather tasteless it has to be well seasoned.

The roast kid of Israel perfumes the pages of the Bible with its appetising aroma. It is the roast of patriarchs and kings. To this day, the bedouin in his tent solemnly 'stews' his kid on festive occasions; and in Cambodia and Burma, the kid is the traditional dish for engagement celebrations.

In the Middle Ages, it held its own among quarters of venison and heads of boar, dressed herons and white swans. Even at the time of the kings of Navarre, the kid of the Pyrénées was considered the chief attraction of the Easter feasts. And the gallant Béarnais who was to become Henry IV had occasion more than once to wash down the Easter kid with a fine Jurançon wine.

KIDNEYS. ROGNONS – Pigs' and sheep's kidneys are the shape of a haricot (shell) bean; calves' and ox kidneys are multi-lobed.

Calves' and lambs' kidneys are delicate and sought-after foodstuffs. Pigs' kidneys, a little richer and with a sweetish taste, are less well thought of. Ox and sheep's kidneys are tough and often taste of urine.

Cocks' kidneys. ROGNONS DE COQ – These are used mainly as an ingredient in garnishes, but they may also be used, cooked in various ways, as hot *hors-d'œuvre* or small *entrées*, in the same way as cocks' combs (q.v.).

To prepare a garnish, wash firm, white cocks' kidneys in several waters. Put them into a small saucepan with water, a pinch of salt, a little butter and a few drops of lemon juice.

Start cooking over a good heat. As soon as the liquid begins to boil turn the heat very low and cook, covered, for 10 to 12 minutes, taking care to avoid boiling.

Use according to the recipe chosen.

Kidneys sautéed with Madeira. ROGNONS SAUTÉS AU MADÈRE – Calves' or lambs' kidneys sliced and sautéed in butter. Madeira is poured into the cooking pan and this sauce is diluted with *Demi-glace sauce* (see SAUCE.)

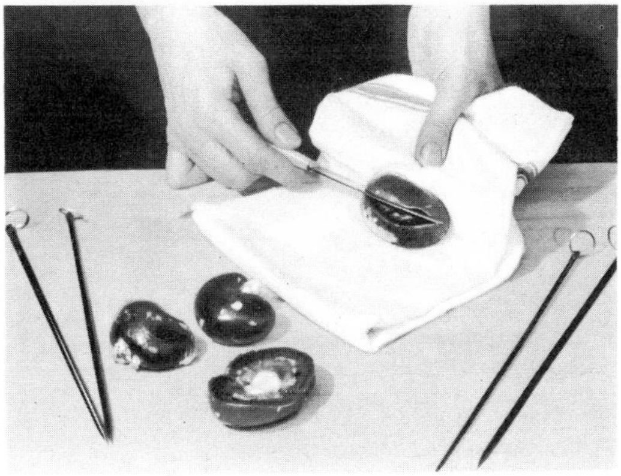

Preparing kidneys on a skewer *(Scarnati)*

KILKIS or NORWEGIAN ANCHOVIES – Tiny fish found mainly in northern European waters. It is preserved like the anchovy and is very well liked in Russia. It is served as an *hors-d'œuvre* (see HORS-D'ŒUVRE, *Hot hors-d'œuvre*).

KIMALI BUREK (Turkish and Russian cookery). KIMALI BEURRECK – Stuffed pancake rolled into the shape of a cigar, filled with forcemeat or some other filling, and fried. (See HORS-D'ŒUVRE, *Hot hors-d'œuvre, Beurrecks à la turque.*)

KINGFISH. TASSARD – Large fish found in all oceans. There are many different species. The flesh is firm and white and it is prepared in the same way as tunny fish.

KIPPER – These, strictly called kippered herrings, are herrings which are slit open and smoked.

Kippers are very good to eat. They are usually grilled and served with melted butter or *Maître d'hôtel butter* (see BUTTER, *Compound butters*). They can also be boiled. (See HERRINGS.)

KIRSCH – Spirit with a very strong bouquet, chiefly manufactured in easten France and in Germany. The finest kirsch comes from Alsace. Black Forest kirsch also enjoys a great reputation. It is distilled from fermented ripe wild cherries.

Kirsch is highly prized by connoisseurs. It is used a great deal for flavouring in confectionery and *pâtisserie.*

KISEL. KISSEL – Russian dessert made from all kinds of berries. It is served in a charlotte mould with thick cream and can be eaten either hot or cold.

KISSING CRUST. BAISURE – Bakery term describing the pale soft crust where one loaf has touched another in baking.

KITCHEN EQUIPMENT. BATTERIE DE CUISINE – This term covers all the utensils used in the kitchen for the preparation and cooking of food. The utensils, of various shapes, are made of copper or other metals such as nickel, aluminium or bimetals, silver-plated copper, iron, cast-iron, bronze, sheet-iron, wrought-iron, etc., of special fireproof earthenware or china, or of hardened glass which is also fireproof.

We know very little about the first kitchen utensils. The Egyptians, the Assyrians and the Persians principally used earthenware and bronze vessels, big-bellied in shape, with and without handles. They also used the spit and, for cooking cakes and biscuits, they had baking dishes rather like those we use nowadays.

The Jews did not generally use earthenware vessels for cooking purposes; most of their pots and pans were made of metal. To extract the meat from the big pots in which food destined to be offered to God was prepared, they used a big two-pronged fork, the forerunner of our table fork, which did not make its appearance until the seventeenth century.

The Greeks, for their culinary preparations, used greatly improved bronze, iron or silver vessels. They also had some in earthenware. Almost all these vessels were conical in shape and therefore not very deep. They were provided with lids, and either handles or detachable rings.

Among the principal kitchen utensils used by the Greeks was the *chytra*, a kind of earthenware pan used for cooking meats and stews. It was apparently in these utensils that the famous Spartan broths were prepared. Or perhaps this historical dish was made in the *kakkabi*, a fairly large three-legged pot. The Greeks also had another pot, which can be considered as the prototype of the earthenware casserole which we use nowadays for the *pot-au-feu*. This, filled with cooked fruit (probably cooked in wine and sweetened with honey) was carried to the altar of the god, Bacchus, on the third day of the feast of Anthesteria, the famous festival in honour of Dionysus.

The Greeks also had bronze casseroles which resembled those now in use. For cooking meat and fish cut in pieces they had a pan similar to the type which in France today is called *coupe lyonnaise*, and which the Greeks called *teganon*. In order to place all these metal or earthenware receptacles on the fire, the Greeks used a triangular support, the tripod, that is still in use in country kitchens.

Kitchen utensils used by the Romans were similar to those of the Greeks. It is also a known fact that Greek cooks brought the art of cooking to Rome. The Romans, who were sensual, voluptuous people, with a great love of luxury in all things, made kitchen utensils not only of bronze but also of silver. Among the treasures of Bosco-Reale, which are kept in the Louvre, various kitchen utensils of this type can be seen. Kitchen utensils used by the Romans included the *clibanus*, an earthenware utensil with holes pierced in it, used for cooking various dishes, mainly pastry, in hot ashes; *craticula*, a grill for cooking meat and fish on the glowing embers; and the *apala*, a dish with cavities of varying sizes hollowed out, which was used for cooking eggs.

The Gauls and the Gallo-Romans had earthenware and metal kitchen utensils somewhat similar to those of the Greeks and the Romans. The Celts knew nothing of the

Water heaters found in the excavations at Pompeii provided with pipes to make the best possible use of the heat from the fireplace; the principle is the same as for our most perfectioned tubular boilers

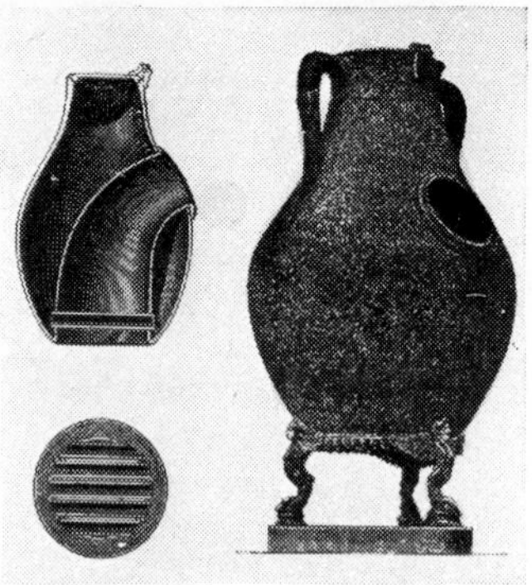

refinements of the sumptuous cookery of Imperial Rome and their pots and pans were rudimentary. With the coming of the Merovingian era, kitchen utensils began again to improve. Some specimens of these have survived, and we can see in museums the magnificent bronze vessels in which the food was prepared.

From reading Charlemagne's *Capitularies*, it seems evident that in succeeding centuries French kitchen utensils were improved still further. After the Crusades a great number of richly worked metal utensils – ewers, salvers, cauldrons – were brought to Europe and served as models for the artisans of the West in the manufacture of magnificent utensils.

In French museums and private collections can be seen, for example, cooking pots in engraved bronze or artistically beaten copper; wrought-iron pot-hangers, which are veritable works of art; kitchen forks, which in those days were called *roables*; turning gridirons; big-bellied pots and kettles; the *acoste-pot* (old version of the *accote-pot*, 'tilt-pot'), and other kitchen implements which are all excellent examples of ironmongery.

To show what a collection of kitchen utensils in the sixteenth-century manor house was like, we reproduce an extract from an inventory made in 1530 at the château of La Mothe-Chandenier:

'In the kitchen of the aforesaid château of la Mothe:

'18 silver dishes and 18 *escuelles* (mediaeval version of *écuelle* – bowl) bearing the coat of arms which the late Master and the late Lady brought with them from Javarzay when they came here to the château of la Mothe.

'The following utensils were found in the said kitchen:

'Six large dishes, three small, and ten bowls, all utensils engraved with the late Master's coat of arms;

'One pot-hanger;

'Two beaten-iron cookers;

'One big iron spit;

'Then two more smaller spits;

'One iron fish slice, one grid;

'*Item*, one big cooking pot;

'*Item*, one big cast-iron pot with perforations;

'*Item*, another iron pot of one *seilée* (a measure of capacity);

'*Item*, two big cauldrons of three *seillées*, without rims;

'*Item*, another cauldron, of two *seillées*;

'*Item*, another, of one *seillée*;

'*Item*, two small cauldrons of half *seillées*;

'*Item*, two big round bronze pans of about four *seillées* each;

'*Item*, plus another round pan of two *seillées* (with a piece broken off;

'One wooden press for pressing capons;

'Two iron spoons;

'One small skimmer;

'One round bronze pan with a long handle for cooking fish;

'Two old dripping pans;

'One small metal mortar and pestle;

'Three iron frying pans with long handles;

'A table on two trestles;

'One old bench with bar back;

'One cupboard with two glass doors, which can be locked with a key;

'Another old cupboard, for keeping plates and dishes, with two glass doors, which can be locked with a key;

'Six big copper candlesticks;

'Six other medium-sized candlesticks;

'One deep copper basin for washing hands;

'Two deep bronze candlesticks, in the shape of a cup;

'In the larder near the said kitchen:

'Three long shelves, but there was no meat there except for one piglet, which was kept for the Master in case he wanted it while he was here.

'The following bottle-ware:

'Barrel of Gascony wine;

'Pitcher with a spout;

'Half-litre mugs;

'One stone mustard pot, for making mustard, etc.;

'One small table for making pastry.'

Our ancestors used many other utensils in addition to those mentioned in the inventory quoted above.

They had, among others, the horsehair sieve or tammy, which, it is said, was invented by the Gauls. The following utensils were also in use: the *couloir*, a large strainer with a handle which was used for draining foods; the *rastels* or *rastelrier*, iron hooks on which food was hung; pots and kettles of all sizes; *tartières* (baking tins); skillets, saucepans, frying pans, etc.; the *féral* – a large metal vessel used as a water container; the *becdasne*, a pot with a handle and a long curved spout; funnels, mostly in copper; the *esmieure*, a grater used for grating nutmeg and cheese. Nutmeg was greatly valued in those days, as we know. 'Do you like nutmeg? They put it in everything,' Boileau was to write a few hundred years later.

In the kitchens of those times they also used gridirons, mortars; spice-grinders; various ladles which were called *potlouches* and *poches; minchoirs*, long-bladed knives used for slicing pork fat into rashers; mincers and various other utensils which are still in use in the present day.

Tin plating of pots and pans was already known at that time. In the Homeric era tin, along with silver, gold and

French kitchen and table utensils of the Middle Ages and the Renaissance: 1. Trencher (16th century); 2. Lidded cup (14th century); 3. Copper pot with two handles (9th century); 4. Metal jug (15th century); 5. Knife (16th century); 6. Marmite with two handles (14th century); 7. Copper kettle (15th century); 8. Copper ewer with its oriental-style stand (9th century); 9. Pitcher sculpted in the decoration of the Saint-Benoit church in Paris (15th century); 10. Two-branched candlestick (16th century); 11. Cauldron (15th century).

bronze, was considered to be one of the precious metals. History tells us that the Aedui, the people who inhabited ancient Gaul, invented metal plating and it is thanks to this discovery that vessels and kitchen utensils were made in such a way that tin, applied on copper, could not be distinguished from silver.

There are many people who protest against the disappearance of the archaic spits or such other utensils formerly used in the kitchen. They are even capable of lamenting the passing of those inconvenient charcoal ranges – the stoves about which Carême complained when he said: 'The coal is killing us!' These were the old-fashioned *paillasses*, laboriously kept up, where, in live charcoal embers, stews and braised dishes simmered and sometimes caught fire.

In 1849, Michel Chevalier wrote in the *Magasin Pittoresque*: 'The improvement of household utensils has more to do with real freedom than is generally realised, for it contributes a great deal to freedom from drudgery in the home, which matters no less to human happiness than liberty in a public place. One utensil may free the servants from one type of arduous or unhealthy task, another allows one person to do the work of three and, consequently, frees two from domestic drudgery.'

Modern kitchen equipment – Modern kitchen equipment, either in domestic or institutional kitchens, includes such utensils as well-sharpened knives, wire whisks, saucepans, frying pans, casseroles, braising pans, kettles and strainers, and many inventions which in recent years have contributed much to make culinary operations easier and have taken the drudgery out of cooking.

The kitchen in many modern homes is the centre of family living, especially in the ever increasing number of areas where domestic service does not exist. This means that the kitchen must be an attractive room to be in, as well as an efficient place in which to produce meals. Such a room in many cases includes a dining area, either a table or counter space. The basic requirements, the stove and the refrigerator, are designed for appearance as well as usefulness, but besides these appliances there are many others designed for home use which make the preparation of food not only easy but enjoyable. Included in an ever expanding list of such appliances are electric beaters, electric blenders for chopping, pulverising and puréeing, pressure cookers, machines for slicing and shredding vegetables, rôtisseries, thermostatically controlled frying pans, waste disposal units, automatic dish washers and home freezers. But all this equipment does not assure good food. On the contrary, gourmets agree that much in texture and flavour can be sacrificed to the speed and efficiency of many of the modern gadgets. One must retain a sense of proportion.

Kitchens in small restaurants and inns are usually an elaboration of a domestic kitchen, but the modern kitchen designed for large hotels, restaurants and institutions may be compared to a factory. Here the utensils are tools of the trade and are built on a large scale and of sturdy materials. The kitchen is divided into many departments, each of which has its head chef and assistants. There may be departments for baked goods, soups, roasts, fish, salads and *hors-d'œuvre*, vegetables, desserts, beverages. In some kitchens these departments are further subdivided; in others they are combined. All these departments are under the direction of a manager or head chef who is responsible for the whole operation. On his staff there are usually one or more dietitians to plan the menus. Trained kitchen engineers design kitchens of various types and specifications, but each must meet public health requirements, which are today more rigid and closely controlled than ever before. Specifications for a modern kitchen designed in the U.S.A. to feed 2000 people a day, but capable of feeding 5000, include the following equipment:

3 electric ranges
3 compartment steamers
2 large tilting kettles used for soups and vegetables
2 undercounter refrigerators
1 bakers' revolving tray oven
2 cooks' tables with sinks
1 60-quart (70-litre) electric mixer
2 salad preparation tables
Salad refrigerator
Fish refrigerator
80-quart (90-litre) electric mixer
Mobile flour bin
Room refrigerators for meat
Room refrigerator for vegetables and dairy products
Room refrigerator for frozen foods
Baker's refrigerator
'Pass-through' refrigerator which can be filled from the kitchen side and opened on the serving side
5 10-quart (12-litre) tilting pans used for soups and sauces
Hot food table
Refrigerated cold table
Milk dispenser
Cream dispenser
Tea urn
Coffee urn
Electric juice dispenser
Electric ice maker

Classic French pots and pans: 1. Casserole russe; 2. Sauté pan (plat à sauter); 3. Frying pan (sauteuse); 4. Small casserole russe; 5. Round cocotte; 6. Oval copper cocotte for cooking chicken *en cocotte*; 7. Small copper cocotte for game; 8. Stew pan (marmite à ragoût); 9. Large stock pot (grande marmite); 10. Double saucepan (marmite) for steaming potatoes; 11. Braising pan (braisière) (*Larousse*)

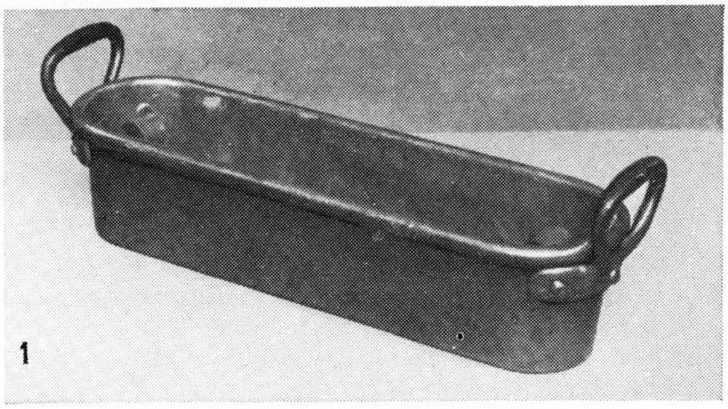

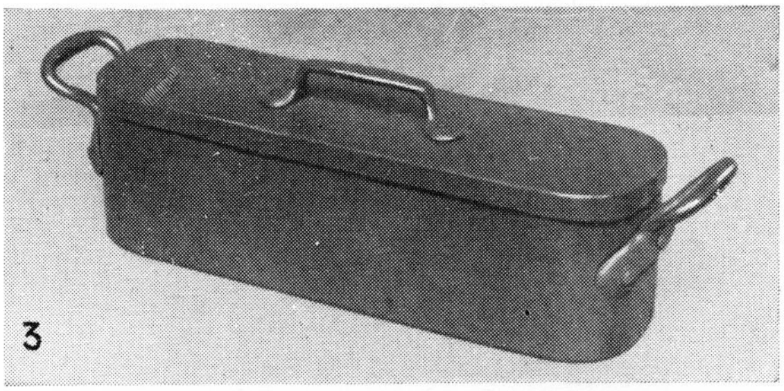

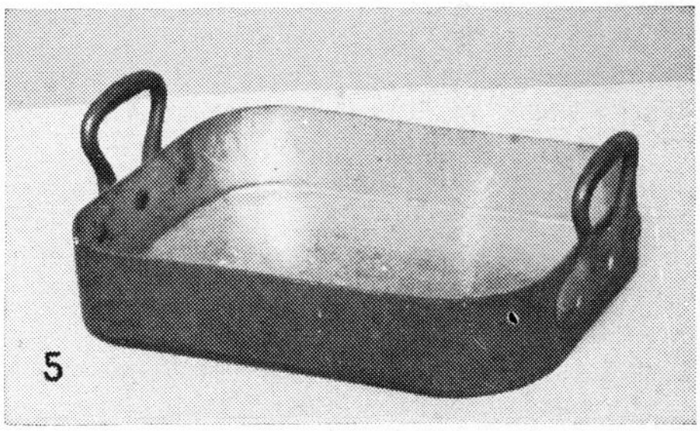

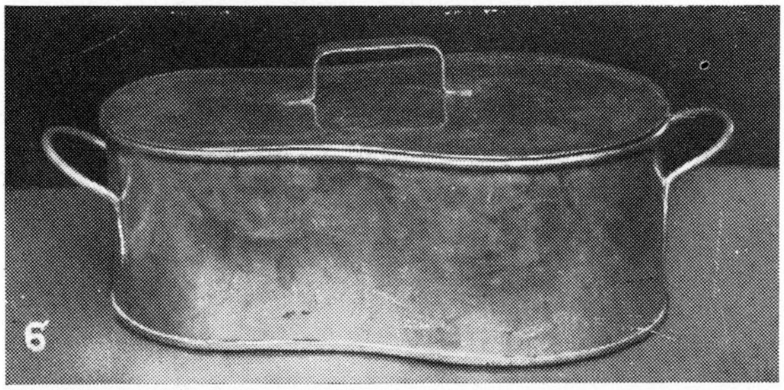

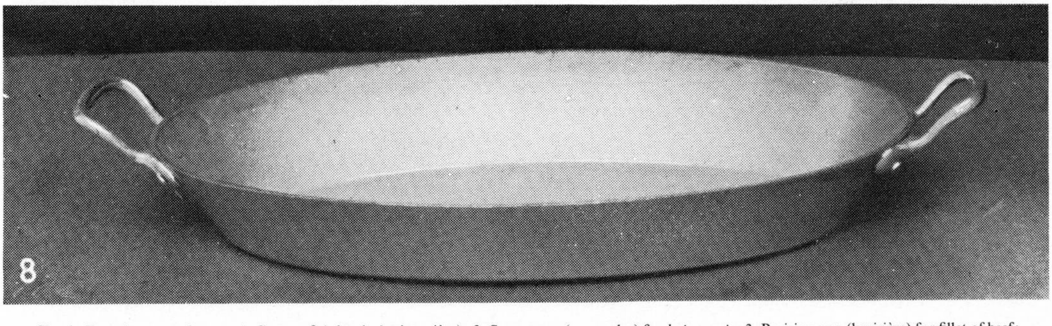

Classic French pots and pans: 1. Copper fish kettle (poissonière); 2. Saucepans (casseroles) for *bain-marie*; 3. Braising pan (braisière) for fillet of beef; 4. Round stew pan (bassine or rondin à ragoût); 5. Copper pan (plaque d'office); 6. Pan for cooking ham (jambonnière); 7. Turbot kettle (turbotière); 8. Fish pan (plaque à poisson) (*Larousse*).

Added to these utensils there are many machines for serving food, for disposing of rubbish and for washing dishes.

Many hotels catering to a luxury clientele have charcoal broilers and rôtisserie spits rotating before open fires.

KITCHEN TEAM. BRIGADE DE CUISINE – In a hotel or restaurant this term applies to the staff of a kitchen.

In principle, a kitchen team of a relatively important establishment, a team which takes its orders from a chef, referred to as the *gros bonnet* ('big-hat') in professional jargon, consists of a *chef saucier* (sauce chef), who is considered to be the deputy head of the team; an *entremettier*, who has charge of the preparation of soups, vegetables and sweet courses; a *rôtisseur* who, in addition to various roasts, also prepares fried dishes and grills; and, finally, a *garde-manger* (larder chef), who has charge of all the supplies, raw and cooked, and prepares cold dishes such as galantines, *terrines, pâtés*, mousses, etc. He also prepares the jellies, sees to the cutting up of meat, fish, poultry, game, etc., and does all the cold *hors-d'œuvre* relevant to the kitchen service. Kitchen assistants, called *commis*, are attached to the chef of each section.

If the establishment is an important and busy one, some of these sections (each team service is called a section, or *partie*, in France), are doubled. Thus the sauce section might have a second service under a special chef – the fish chef. *Entremets* becomes a separate section, also with a chef at its head, usually the soup chef, called *potagiste* or *potager*. The *rôtisserie* (the section in charge of roasts) may be supplemented by a cook who would have charge of all grills and would, therefore, be called the *grillardin*.

In an establishment of still greater importance, the roasting section, in addition to the roast chef proper and the *grillardin*, would also have a *friturier* (fryer), a noun which probably does not exist in any dictionary but is accepted in culinary terminology and means exactly what it says.

Equally, the *garde-manger*, in addition to the actual head of this important section, might be supplemented by the inclusion of other chefs, each with his own speciality. One might have the charge of *hors-d'œuvre*, another of meat, etc. chef and an assistant chef, there are also special teams dealing with pastry. These would include a *chef pâtissier* and several assistants, a *chef confiseur* and a *chef glacier*.

The art of managing the kitchen team of a big restaurant or hotel is a difficult one. A chef in charge of a kitchen must not only be a man who knows his job – his art, we should say – inside out, but he must also have the qualities of an ideal administrator. The time is long past (if it ever existed at all) when kitchens in big establishments were run without some system of accounting. Today, more than ever, the kitchen of a restaurant or of a hotel must be well organised, everything must be foreseen and carried out in such a way that the dishes, whilst being excellent in quality, cost only what they should cost and no more. In a modern establishment the kitchen is a department which must never show a loss – always a profit.

At the end of the nineteenth century and at the beginning of the twentieth there were a great number of *chefs de cuisine* (famous *gros bonnets*), who had charge of kitchen teams: M. Prat, who for a long time had charge of the kitchens at the Grand-Hotel in Paris; Jean Giroix, who directed the kitchen at the Hotel de Paris in Monte Carlo; Léopold Mourier, who, after having directed the kitchen of the Maire restaurant (now no more) became the *grand maître* of various famous restaurants, such as the Café de Paris, Armenonville, the Pré-Catelan, Fouquet, etc.

The great Escoffier, who died in 1935, was first the chef of the Petit Moulin-Rouge, then took charge of the no less famous kitchens of the old Maire restaurant, then the Grand-Hotel at Monte Carlo and the Savoy in London. He finished his active career at the Carlton Hotel in London. Philéas Gilbert was the author of the best culinary works of our time. Other illustrious names include Tony Girod, Ninlias, Argentier, Prosper Drenault, Prosper Salles and Deland.

It is impossible for us to give the names of all the *gros bonnets* of the past who have improved the status of the culinary art. We can only mention chefs of the great private houses, such as Urbain Dubois, Émile Bernard, Armand Gouffé, Joseph Favre and Gastilleur, some of whom had charge of the imperial and royal kitchens.

KNEADING OF DOUGH. FRAISAGE – This operation consists of breaking up the dough once it has become elastic, by working it with the palm of the hand. The object of handling the dough in this way is to obtain a perfect mixture of all the ingredients.

Selection of cooks' knives: 1. Palette knife; 2. Carving knife; 3. Slicing knife; 4. Chopping knife; 5. Filleting knife for fish; 6. All-purpose knife (*Coutellerie André. Phot. Larousse*)

KNIFE. COUTEAU – A cutting instrument, with a handle and a blade.

Kitchen knives. COUTEAUX DE CUISINE – For the various culinary operations it is essential to have good tools, and in particular very good knives. Each has its proper use. In order of size they are: vegetable knife for peeling vegetables; knife with a larger blade for cutting fish fillets; slicing knife with a fairly large blade for slicing raw or cooked meat perfectly; straight-bladed chopper, with which it is possible to break up bones of a certain size, and to hash meat in the same way as with a four-bladed chopper; carving knife, which is used for cutting bards of fat pork or bacon and which resembles the so-called 'English' knife used to carve large joints of beef and hams, but which, instead of having a rounded point, is sharply pointed.

There is also the knife for boning meat. It is used mostly in butchery but can be used in cooking.

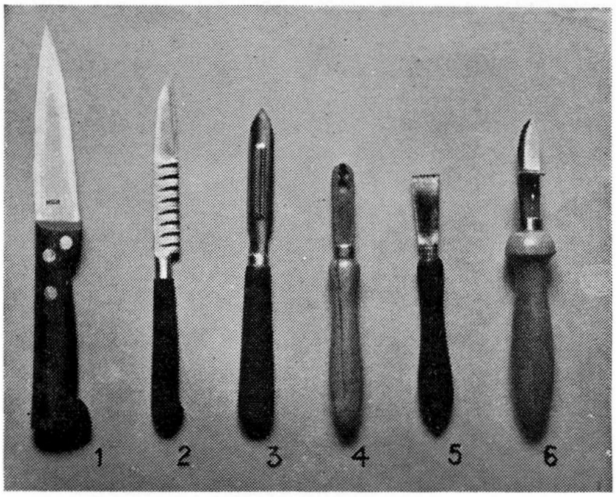

Some special knives: 1. Boning knife; 2. Fluted knife; 3. Potato peeler; 4. Cannelling knife; 5. Knife for scraping lemon zest; 6. can opener (*Coutellerie André. Phot. Larousse*)

Among the cutting tools which it is necessary to have in a well-ordered kitchen, are the following: a cleaver, which is a fairly large instrument with which a carcase can be cut in half; a chopper, to crack the hardest bones; a chopping knife, which is made with one, two or four blades; the whole series of small knives used for chopping, peeling and paring vegetables, especially potatoes, and for cutting potatoes into ribbons; knives for opening oysters; tin-openers.

Little tools, such as knives with a fluting device or one for scraping lemon zest, should be mentioned, as should little instruments for cutting ravioli; special knives for cutting grapefruit; scissors for jointing chicken; the cutlet beater; the butcher's saw; and the scraper for the butcher's table.

Table knives should be of excellent quality, with good cutting blades in pure steel. Many table knives are made today in stainless steel. Their principal advantage is that they do not stain. For serving fruit, knives are made in silver plate. For fish, special knives are made of silver plate.

KNIFE-REST. PORTE-COUTEAU – Utensils of various shapes, in glass or silver, on which the knife is placed to prevent soiling the tablecloth.

KNUCKLE. SOURIS – Small, fleshy muscle on the leg of mutton. It is much appreciated by connoisseurs.

KOHLRABI. CHOU-RAVE – This is not, properly speaking, a root, but a swelling of the stem above ground in the form of a plump, pithy ball. Some varieties have quite a delicate flavour. All the recipes given for turnips (q.v.) and for celeriac (q.v.) may be used for this vegetable.

Kohlrabi à la paysanne. CHOU-RAVE À LA PAYSANNE – Cut the kohlrabi into slices. Brown in lard in which some chopped onion has been softened. Add some fresh breast of pork and season with salt. Moisten with white wine and stock in equal proportions. Cook in the oven.

KOUMISS – Fermented mares' milk, originally made in Turkestan and Tartary, rather similar to *kéfir*. The ferment used is prepared by working 250 g. (8 oz.) barm (brewer's yeast) and 125 g. (4 oz., 1 cup) flour with a little honey and a glass of milk. Leave overnight. Next day add 3 litres ($5\frac{1}{4}$ pints, $6\frac{1}{2}$ pints) milk to this leaven. It contains a great deal of carbonic acid gas and from 1·65 to 3·23 per cent alcohol.

KROMESKY – See CROMESQUI.

Kugelhopf with mould (*Nicolas*)

KUGELHOPF or KOUGLOFF (Alsation pastry). KOUGELHOF, KOUGLOF – It is said that Queen Marie Antoinette was very fond of this pastry, which contributed a great deal to the fashion in her day for sweets made with risen dough. These were no longer made with leaven, as they had been until the middle of the eighteenth century, but with brewer's yeast, which had been in use for a very long time in Austria and Poland.

Some authorities, however, believe that it was Carême who popularised this pastry in Paris, when he established himself as a pastry-cook. It is said that he was given the recipe by M. Eugène, at that time master chef to Prince Schwartzenberg, the Austrian ambassador.

Ingredients. 500 g. (18oz., 4½ cups) sieved flour, 200 g. (7 oz., scant cup) butter, 90 g. (3½ oz., ½ cup) fine sugar, 4 eggs, 25 g. (1 oz.) yeast – or 15 g. (½ oz.) in summer, 50 g. (2 oz., ⅓ cup) currants, 1½ teaspoons salt.

Make the dough according to the instructions for *Brioche dough* (see DOUGH), but make it a little less firm.

Butter a large *kugelhopf* mould and line the sides with shredded almonds. Half-fill with dough. Leave the dough in a warm place, until it has risen above the sides of the mould.

Bake in a hot oven 40 to 45 minutes.

KULICH (Russian cookery). KOULICH – Cake of risen dough, made in Russia for the ceremonial Easter dinner. After it has been baked and cooled, it is decorated with a cluster of artificial roses.

Kulich, Russian Easter cake

KUMMEL – Russian liqueur extracted from caraway seeds.

One type of Russian kummel has a deposit of crystals at the bottom of the bottle. This is sugar with which the liqueur is supersaturated under heat and which resumes its crystalline state upon cooling four or five days later. The same phenomenon also occasionally occurs in jam-making.

Danzig liqueur is a well-known, potent type of kummel with a particularly large amount of crystallisation. It is an essential ingredient of Rothschild soufflé.

Kummel or *Leidsche kaas* is also the name of a Dutch cheese. (See CHEESE.)

KUMQUAT – Very small orange shaped like an elongated olive. This fruit, which is nowadays sold in certain food stores, is eaten raw, like oranges and tangerines.

It can be used in salads or marmalade.

KVASS. KWASS – Slightly gaseous, mildly alcoholic drink similar to beer. It is made in Russia by adding fermented yeast to a must of rye flour mixed with a little sprouted barley. It is sometimes flavoured with mint leaves or juniper berries.

LA BOUILLE – See CHEESE.

LABRUS. LABRE – European sea fish, also called *wrasse*. It is remarkable for its brilliant colouring, but is tasteless, and limp in texture. It is served fried, or may be used as an ingredient of *bouillabaisse* (q.v.).

LACHE – Small sea-fish, very delicate to eat, cooked in the same way as the smelt (q.v.). It is rather scarce.

LACRIMA-CHRISTI. LACRYMA-CHRISTI – Wine made from grapes grown on the slopes of Vesuvius. It is rather sweet and delicate.

LACTARY. LACTAIRE – Fungus of the agaric type. It contains a white or coloured milky juice. Some lactaries are poisonous, others are edible, though of rather poor flavour in spite of the fact that one type is called *delicious*.

LACTIC ACID. LACTIQUE – An acid present in sour milk and certain fermented substances. It is an antiseptic and is particularly effective in preventing putrefaction. A primitive method of preserving meat was to immerse it in sour milk.

LACTIC FERMENTS. LACTIQUES – These are microbes which are very widespread and of many kinds. When they are introduced into milk the lactose (milk sugar) molecules are split and lactic acid is produced. It is these microbes which breed on the teats of cows in cowsheds and in dairies. They cause the curdling of milk and are one of the agents in the production of cheese.

Sour milk is produced either by introducing indigenous ferments into the milk or by using ferments imported from the Balkans, Egypt and the Caucasus. These latter, being adapted to higher temperatures, produce a larger quantity of lactic acid. (See CHEESE, KÉFIR, KOUMISS, YOGURT.)

LACTOMETER. LACTOMÈTRE – A graduated densimeter which shows the density of milk, from which the cream content can be calculated.

LADIES' FINGERS. GOMBO, GOMBAUT – See OKRA.

LADLE. POCHE – Large spoon with cup bowl and a long handle, used mainly for serving liquid dishes.

LADY APPLE – Tiny variety of pale yellow apple, tinged with carmine. The white flesh is firm and crunchy; the flavour sweetish, but with a touch of bitterness.

LAGOPUS. LAGOPÈDE – The lagopus or *Pyrenean partridge* has tawny plumage with thin black streaks in summer. In winter it turns almost completely white, except for touches of black on the tail. It is sometimes called *snow partridge* because of its winter plumage.

This bird is much sought after for the table, in spite of its slightly bitter flavour which is due to the fact that it feeds on birch-shoots, myrtle berries and other mountain berries.

All recipes for grouse (q.v.), which belong to the same family as the lagopus, are suitable for this bird.

LAGUIPIÈRE – Laguipière, who was born in the middle of the eighteenth century and died in 1812, was one of the great masters of French cookery. Carême described him as 'the most remarkable chef of our times'. Carême's tutor in all branches of cookery was, in fact, Laguipière, who accompanied Murat to Naples and later followed him to Russia. He froze to death at Vilno (later Vilnius) during the 1812 retreat from Moscow.

At the beginning of his book, *le Cuisinier parisien*, Carême wrote the following words about his great master: 'Awake, shade of Laguipière! Listen to the voice of a pupil, a friend, a devotee! You should have died in Paris, surrounded by the reverence evoked in all of us by the memory of your great work . . . Laguipière, accept the pious homage of a faithful disciple. I couple my works with your name. I have cited you with pride in all my books, and, today, I invoke your memory and dedicate to you my finest work.'

It is regrettable that so learned a practitioner of the art of cooking as Laguipière should not have left any written record of his teachings for posterity.

LAITIAT – Name given in the Franche-Comté to a refreshing drink made by steeping wild fruit in whey.

LAMB. AGNEAU – Young ovine animal before it is a year old.

After the age of one year, when the animal has already grown its first two nippers (the incisor teeth of herbivorous animals), it is called a yearling. When the other permanent teeth appear, the animal becomes a ram or a ewe.

In the culinary sense lamb is known in two forms:

1. The milk-fed (or baby) lamb. This animal has not yet been weaned and has not yet been put out to graze. The best French lamb of this type is Pauillac lamb.

2. Ordinary lamb or salt meadow lamb. This is a young sheep which has not yet reached its full growth.

Good quality lamb can be recognised by the width of its loins, which should be well covered with flesh, and by the whiteness of its fat, which should be firm and abundant, especially round the kidneys. Its freshness can be judged from the firmness of its legs and the colour of the kidneys,

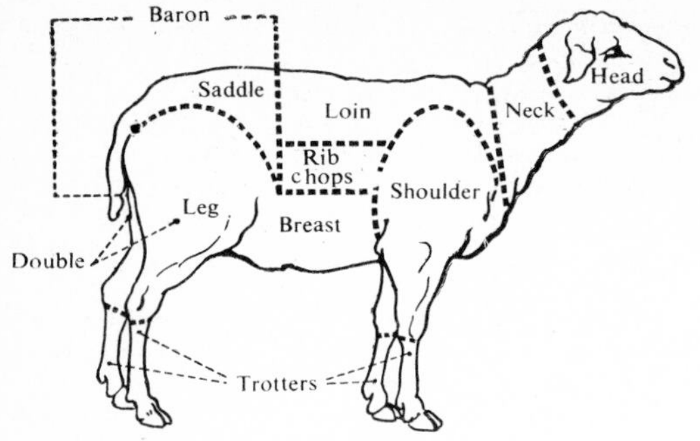

Lamb: division of the live animal

which should be pale pink. Baby or milk-fed lamb is generally sold whole, with its pluck. It is also sometimes sold in quarters.

Lamb should be eaten at its freshest. This meat does not keep for very long. Ordinary lamb and milk-fed lamb are sold in butchers' shops and, in France, in poultry shops. Ordinary lamb is divided into cuts like mutton.

The best parts are the legs, the saddle and the loins. The neck and breast are principally used for making *blanquettes*, *fricassées*, *ragoûts* and sauté dishes.

The legs are generally used for roasting. They are served as they are, plain or with a garnish of vegetables – baked, dressed with butter, or braised.

The shoulders, whether boned or not, are usually prepared in the same manner as legs.

Two legs are called a double. When the saddle, and sometimes a part of the loins, is left with the legs, then such a joint is called a baron. Half of this joint is known as a quarter.

The best way to prepare these various joints is to roast or pot-roast them. The loins can also be cooked whole (on the spit or in the oven) but they are usually divided into cutlets, which can be grilled or fried and served plain or with various garnishes. All lamb offal (variety meat) is delicate in flavour.

Lamb plays an important part both in classical French cookery and in home cookery.

Baby or milk-fed lamb is divided into the same cuts as ordinary lamb: baron, loin, double, shoulder, leg, quarter, saddle. All these cuts can be served with garnishes recommended for ordinary lamb and for mutton. Bearing in mind the particularly delicate flavour of this meat, however, it is advisable to serve it grilled, pot-roasted or as a roast, with its own juice – thickened or clear – as the only accompaniment. Other parts of milk-fed lamb are used for *blanquettes*, *ragoûts* and sauté dishes.

BABY or MILK-FED LAMB. AGNEAU DE LAIT –

Leg of baby or milk-fed lamb in pastry à la périgourdine. GIGOT D'AGNEAU EN PÂTE À LA PÉRIGOURDINE – A method of preparation for leg of baby or milk-fed lamb.

Trim the leg and remove most of the bone. Cook in a hot oven for 10 minutes to brown it. Allow to cool. Cover completely with sausage meat mixed with one-third of its weight of uncooked goose liver rubbed through a sieve, 2 diced truffles, 1 egg. Wrap the leg in a sheet of salt pork or a piece of pig's caul, previously soaked in cold water.

Put the leg on an oval-shaped sheet of rolled-out pastry. Cover with another sheet of pastry. Seal the edges by crimping them. Make a hole in the middle to allow steam to escape. Brush the top of the pastry with beaten egg, and put

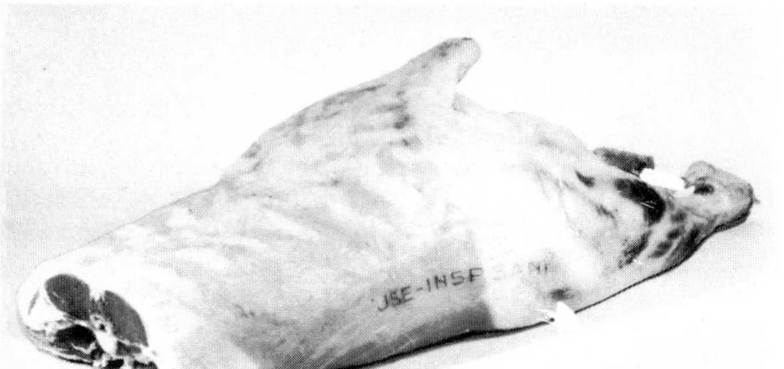

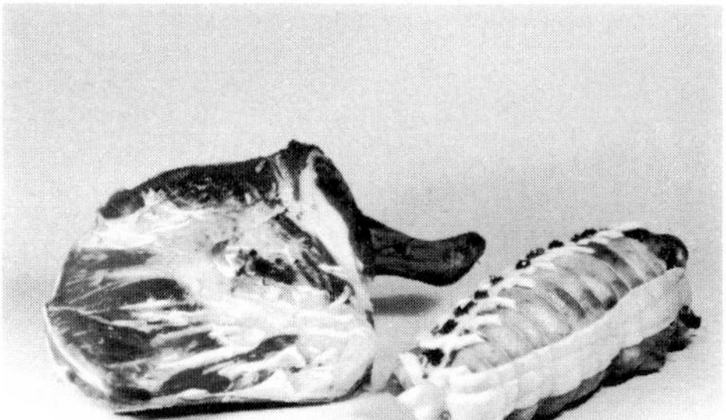

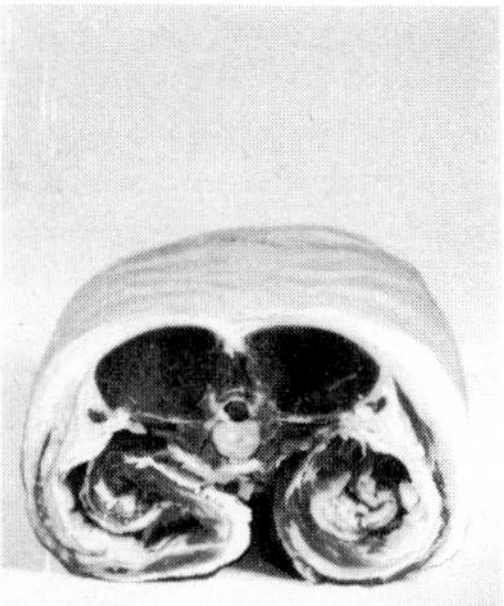

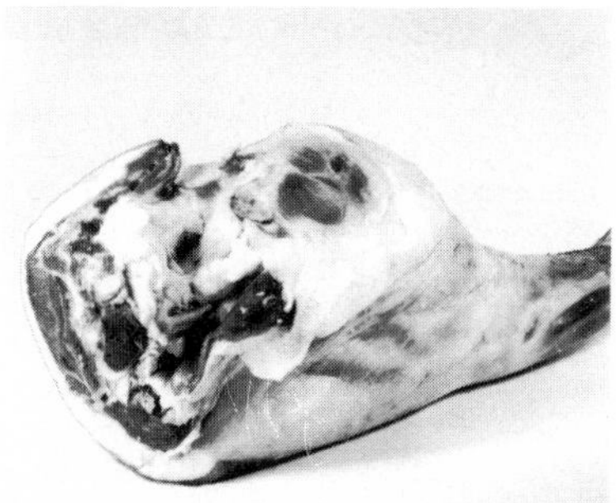

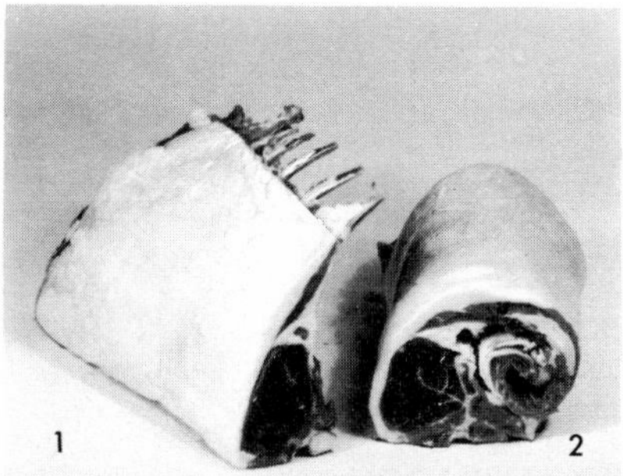

CUTS OF LAMB
Baron 1. Shoulder; 2. Rolled shoulder
Saddle Leg 1. Loin; 2. Boned chops

it on a baking sheet. Cook in a moderate oven for 1½ hours.

When removed from the oven, pour through the hole in the top 1½ dl. (¼ pint, ⅔ cup) *Périgueux sauce* (see SAUCE). Serve on a napkin-covered dish.

This kind of hot pie can also be made with a boned and rolled leg of ordinary lamb.

Loin of baby or milk-fed lamb à la Clamart. CARRÉ D'AGNEAU À LA CLAMART – Trim the loin of baby or milk-fed lamb and pot-roast it in butter. When cooked, add to the casserole 350 g. (12 oz., 2¼ cups) fresh garden peas prepared *à la française* (see PEAS). Leave to simmer for 5 minutes under a lid.

Loin of baby or milk-fed lamb La Varenne. CARRÉ D'AGNEAU LA VARENNE – Bone a trimmed loin of baby or milk-fed lamb. Beat it to flatten slightly, season with salt and pepper, dip in beaten egg and cover with breadcrumbs, pressing down well to make the crumbs adhere. Cook the loin in clarified butter until both sides are a golden colour.

Arrange on a dish on a foundation composed of a *salpicon* (q.v.) of cultivated *Mushrooms cooked in cream* (see MUSHROOMS). Sprinkle with *Noisette butter* (see BUTTER, *Compound butters*).

Loin of baby or milk-fed lamb maharajah. CARRÉ D'AGNEAU MAHARADJAH – Trim a loin of milk-fed lamb and pot-roast in butter.

When half-cooked, add 75 g. (3 oz., ¾ cup) chopped onion lightly cooked in butter. Season with salt, 1 teaspoon curry powder and a clove of garlic. Cook with a lid on.

Serve garnished with *Rice pilaf* (see PILAF) and small tomatoes cooked in oil. Dilute the pan juices with 1½ dl. (¼ pint, ⅔ cup) white wine, add 2 dl. (⅓ pint, scant cup) fresh cream, simmer, and pour over the curry.

Loin of baby or milk-fed lamb Monselet. CARRÉ D'AGNEAU MONSELET – Trim a loin of baby or milk-fed lamb and cook under a grill. When nearly cooked, sprinkle with freshly grated breadcrumbs and put back under grill to turn golden.

Put on a foundation of *Anna potatoes* (see POTATOES). Garnish with quarters of small artichokes cooked in butter. Surround with a border of buttered *Demi-glace sauce* (see SAUCE).

Loin of baby or milk-fed lamb à la périgourdine. CARRÉ D'AGNEAU EN CRÉPINE À LA PÉRIGOURDINE – Trim and bone a loin of milk-fed lamb and cook in butter until three-quarters done. Allow to cool.

Coat on both sides with finely minced pork forcemeat mixed with diced truffles. Wrap in a thin piece of pig's caul previously soaked in cold water. Make sure the fat covers the meat completely. Spread with melted butter, cover with white breadcrumbs, sprinkle with more butter and grill or broil on low heat. Put the loin on a dish, garnish with small potato balls cooked in butter. Serve with *Périgueux sauce* (see SAUCE).

Fried loin of baby or milk-fed lamb à la viennoise. CARRÉ D'AGNEAU FRIT À LA VIENNOISE – Method of preparation suitable only for loin of milk-fed (or baby) lamb.

Divide the loin in half. Marinate for 1 hour in oil, lemon juice, salt, pepper and chopped parsley. Drain the pieces of lamb and dry; dredge in flour and dip in egg and breadcrumbs. Fry in clarified butter or deep-fry in sizzling fat. Garnish with fried parsley and quarters of lemon.

Quarter of lamb. QUARTIER D'AGNEAU – Joint comprising the leg and half the saddle. It is mainly taken from baby or milk-fed (Pauillac) lamb, and is usually roasted. All the garnishes recommended for baron or saddle of ordinary lamb are applicable to quarter of lamb.

Roast baby or milk-fed lamb. AGNEAU DE LAIT RÔTI – This method of preparation is suitable for small lambs. Dress the skin over the knuckles and shoulders. Truss the lamb to give it a regular shape. Put on a spit, season with salt and pepper, brush with melted butter and roast before a brisk fire, allowing 20 to 25 minutes per 500 g. (1 lb.).

Take it off the spit, put on a long dish, and garnish with bunches of watercress and quarters of lemon. Dilute the pan juices with a little stock and serve with the lamb.

Roast lamb is generally served with mint sauce and garnished with various vegetables. Lamb can also be roasted in the oven.

Grilled shoulder of baby or milk-fed lamb. ÉPAULE D'AGNEAU DE LAIT GRILLÉE – Trim the shoulder, make a few slits on both sides, season, and brush with melted butter.

Grill under a moderate flame for 20 to 25 minutes. Sprinkle with white breadcrumbs, brush with melted butter, and put under the grill or broiler to colour.

Arrange on a long dish. Serve garnished with watercress.

Baby or milk-fed lamb stuffed with rice. AGNEAU DE LAIT FARCI AU RIZ – Stuff the lamb with half-cooked *Rice pilaf* (see PILAF), to which have been added the animal's liver, heart, sweetbreads and kidneys, cut into small slices, briskly fried in butter, and seasoned.

Sew up the opening, and truss the lamb. Cover the back with strips or rashers of bacon tied in place. Put on a spit and roast before a lively fire, allowing 20–25 minutes per 500 g. (1 lb.).

Remove from the spit, take off the bacon and cut away trussing string. Put on a long dish, garnish with watercress and quarters of lemon. Serve with the pan juices, diluted with a few tablespoons of stock.

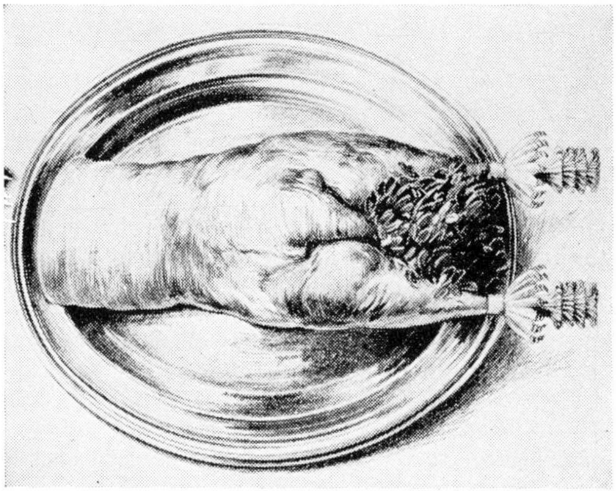

Roast baron of lamb

LAMB. AGNEAU –

Baron of lamb. BARON D'AGNEAU – The cut comprising the two legs and the saddle. This joint is roasted on a spit or pot-roasted, but may also be served as a roast in its own juice.

It is accompanied by a garnish of vegetables, either arranged around the joint or served separately, and with its own juice, left as it is or thickened, depending on the nature of the garnish.

For cooking time see CULINARY METHODS, *Average cooking times for roasts*.

Garnishes suitable for baron of lamb. Green vegetables dressed with butter or cream; braised vegetables; *Anversoise; bouquetière; bretonne; Clamart; Dauphine; duchesse; jardinière; macédoine; parisienne; provençale; renaissance; Richelieu.* (See GARNISHES.) *Anna potatoes* (see POTATOES) and potatoes prepared in various other ways would also be suitable.

Blanquette of lamb. BLANQUETTE D'AGNEAU – This method of preparation is often described as a *fricassée*.

Soak the pieces of lamb and dry well. Fry in butter without allowing to brown. Season. Sprinkle with 2 tablespoons (3 tablespoons) flour, blend over heat, add white stock and garnish as for *Blanquette of lamb à l'ancienne* (see below). Bring to the boil, simmer with the lid on from 45 minutes to 1 hour.

Transfer to another pan. Add small onions, mushrooms, and the sauce. Blend in egg yolks as described below.

Blanquette of lamb à l'ancienne. BLANQUETTE D'AGNEAU À L'ANCIENNE – This is made of shoulder and ribs of ordinary or salt meadow lamb. Cut $1\frac{3}{4}$ kg. (4 lb.) lamb into uniform pieces. Soak for 1 hour in water, blanch, dip in cold water to cool, and dry.

Put into a shallow pan. Add enough white stock (or a light *pot-au-feu* broth – see SOUPS AND BROTHS) to just cover the meat. Add 2 medium-sized carrots cut in quarters, 2 medium-sized onions – one studded with a clove – and a *bouquet garni* consisting of a sprig of parsley, a stalk of celery, 2 leeks, a sprig of thyme and a bay leaf. Season with salt.

Bring to the boil, remove scum and simmer with the lid on the pan 45 minutes to 1 hour.

Take out the pieces of lamb and remove small pieces of bone and skin which have become detached during cooking. Put the lamb into a shallow pan with 12 small onions previously cooked in a *court-bouillon* (q.v.), and the same number of cooked mushrooms.

Make a *roux* (q.v.) of 60 g. ($2\frac{1}{2}$ oz., 5 tablespoons) butter and 75 g. (3 oz., $\frac{3}{4}$ cup) flour. Add the strained stock in which the lamb was cooked, simmer for 15 minutes, skim, strain, and pour over the lamb.

Simmer gently for 20 to 25 minutes. Blend in 4 egg yolks mixed with 1 dl. (6 tablespoons, scant $\frac{1}{2}$ cup) cream, a dash of lemon juice and a pinch of grated nutmeg. Keep the *blanquette* hot but do not allow to boil.

Alternatively, cook the lamb in stock, and put it into a shallow pan with onions cooked in *court-bouillon*, and the mushrooms. Keep hot with the pan covered. Prepare *Velouté sauce* (see SAUCE) with the stock in which the lamb was cooked. Blend with egg yolks, cream and lemon juice, to the desired consistency, strain through a tammy cloth, and pour over the lamb.

Lamb's brains – See OFFAL or VARIETY MEATS.

Lamb's breast. POITRINE D'AGNEAU – This is generally used for making *ragoûts* or sauté dishes. It can also be made into *épigrammes* (q.v.) and is used instead of beef to prepare country soups (see SOUPS AND BROTHS, *Mutton broth*).

Lamb's breast à l'anglaise. POITRINE D'AGNEAU À L'ANGLAISE – Cook the breast as in the recipe for *Lamb's breast à la diable* (see below) and leave to get cold under a press. Cut into rectangular pieces, dip in beaten egg and breadcrumbs and fry in clarified butter. Arrange on a long dish, dot with dabs of half-melted *Maître d'hôtel butter* (see BUTTER, *Compound butters*).

Lamb's breast fried in batter. POITRINE D'AGNEAU EN FRITOT – Braise, bone, cool under a press and cut the breast of lamb into small, square pieces. Steep for 1 hour in oil, lemon juice, chopped parsley, salt and pepper.

Dip the pieces in light batter and deep-fry. Drain, dry, season with finely ground salt. Arrange on a napkin in a pyramid, garnish with fried parsley, and serve with tomato sauce.

Lamb's breast in breadcrumbs with various garnishes. POITRINE D'AGNEAU PANÉE – Cook pieces of breast, dipped in egg and breadcrumbs, in clarified butter as described in the recipe for *Lamb's breast à l'anglaise*.

Arrange in a crown on a dish. Fill the middle of the dish with the garnish indicated. Surround with a border of thickened veal stock.

Garnishes suitable for breast in breadcrumbs. Green vegetables blended with butter or cream; purées of various vegetables; spinach, leaf or purée; rice pilaf or risotto; various pasta products with butter or *à l'italienne*, new potatoes in butter; carrots, glazed, or *à la Vichy*.

Lamb's breast à la diable. POITRINE D'AGNEAU À LA DIABLE – Braise the breast or cook it in a little white stock. Drain, and remove all the rib bones. Leave to cool under a press. Cut into rectangular pieces, spread these with mustard and a pinch of cayenne pepper. Dip in melted butter and breadcrumbs. Sprinkle with butter and cook on a low grill.

Arrange in a circle on a dish, and garnish with watercress. Serve with *Diable sauce* (see SAUCE).

Épigrammes of lamb's breast. POITRINE D'AGNEAU EN ÉPIGRAMMES – Braise a lamb's breast or poach it in very little white stock. Drain, bone, and cool under a press.

Cut into heart-shaped pieces of uniform size. Dip in egg and breadcrumbs.

At the same time dip in egg and breadcrumbs a number of lamb chops, similar in shape and size to the pieces of breast. Cook the chops and the pieces of breast under a low grill or sauté them both in butter.

Arrange in a crown on a long dish. Decorate the end bones with paper frills. Put the recommended garnish in the middle of the dish. Pour a few tablespoons of *Demi-glace sauce* (see SAUCE) on the *épigrammes*, or the stock left over from braising the breast, boiled down and strained.

Garnishes suitable for épigrammes of lamb. All those recommended elsewhere for lamb chops or *noisettes*.

Stuffed breast of lamb. POITRINE D'AGNEAU FARCIE – Slit the pieces of breast to form pockets. Fill them with fine forcemeat bound with an egg. Sew up the opening. Wrap the pieces in thin rashers of bacon. Braise them in a small quantity of liquid.

Drain the pieces. Unwrap and glaze. Arrange on a dish and garnish as indicated. Sprinkle with the strained pan juices.

Stuffed breast of lamb can be served with all the garnishes recommended for pieces of braised lamb or mutton.

Lamb chops. CÔTELETTES D'AGNEAU – Rib lamb chops are cut from the rib roast. In France they are called *côtelettes* and in England they are called cutlets.

Loin lamb chops are cut from the loin and are known in French as *côtes*. In England they are known as lamb chops.

Chops are most often grilled, but all preparations recommended in the following recipes are suitable for rib chops (cutlets) or lamb chops cut from the loin. They can be served with any of the garnishes recommended for *Mutton cutlets* (see MUTTON). Most frequently these garnishes consist of a green vegetable, such as beans, peas, asparagus tips, etc. dressed with butter.

Lamb chops à l'ancienne. CÔTELETTES D'AGNEAU À L'ANCIENNE – Fry the chops in butter. Arrange in a crown on a dish. Garnish the middle with a *ragoût* of lambs' sweetbreads, cocks' combs and kidneys, truffles and mushrooms, bound with *Velouté sauce* (see SAUCE) and cream. Dilute the pan juices with Madeira, sherry or other similar wine, add a little light *Demi-glace sauce* (see SAUCE) and pour over the chops. Garnish the bones with paper frills.

Lamb chops à l'anglaise. CÔTELETTES D'AGNEAU À L'ANGLAISE – These are prepared in two ways:

Grilled. Season the chops, dip in melted butter and breadcrumbs and grill or broil.

Arrange on a dish. Garnish with grilled strips or rashers of bacon, boiled potatoes and watercress.

Sautéed. Dip in beaten egg and breadcrumbs and sauté in clarified butter. Arrange in a crown on a dish and sprinkle with *Noisette butter* (see BUTTER, *Compound butters*).

Lamb chops in aspic jelly. CÔTELETTES D'AGNEAU À LA GELÉE – Braise a large lamb loin, neatly trimmed, in very little *court-bouillon* (q.v.). Allow to cool in its own strained juices.

Drain and cut into chops. Dry them and glaze with jelly. (The pan juices left over from braising the cutlets should be added to the jelly before its clarification.) Arrange the chops in a turban on a dish. Garnish with chopped jelly, hard-boiled eggs cut into quarters, lettuce hearts, or with mixed salads. Serve with *Mayonnaise* or *Tartare sauce* or, as is customary in England, with *Mint sauce* (see SAUCE, *Cold sauces*.)

Instead of cooking the loin whole and then cutting it, the chops can be prepared as described in the recipe for *Chaud-froid of lamb chops* (see below).

Bar-man lamb chops. CÔTELETTES D'AGNEAU BAR-MAN – Grill the chops. Garnish with whole, grilled tomatoes and mushrooms. Put a rasher of grilled bacon on each cutlet, and garnish with watercress.

Lamb chops in breadcrumbs, garnished. CÔTELETTES D'AGNEAU PANÉES GARNIES – Dip the chops in egg and breadcrumbs if they are to be fried, and in butter and breadcrumbs if they are to be grilled.

Fry in clarified butter, or cook under the grill on low heat. Surround with the recommended garnish.

All the garnishes for fried lamb chops are applicable to lamb chops in breadcrumbs.

Lamb chops Brossard. CÔTELETTES D'AGNEAU BROSSARD – Dip the chops in beaten egg and breadcrumbs mixed with chopped truffles. Sauté in butter. Arrange in a crown on a dish. Garnish the middle of the dish with mushrooms cooked in cream. Put a border of *Demi-glace sauce* (see SAUCE) round the chops.

Lamb chops Champvallon. CÔTELETTES D'AGNEAU CHAMP-VALLON – Choose lower ribs from salt meadow lamb, cut fairly thick. Proceed as with *Mutton chops Champvallon* (see MUTTON).

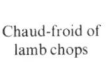

Chaud-froid of lamb chops

Chaud-froid of lamb chops. CÔTELETTES D'AGNEAU EN CHAUD-FROID – Braise thick chops in very little liquid. Leave to get cold under a press in the stock in which they were braised, strained and with surplus fat removed.

When they are quite cold, drain, trim, and cover with *Chaud-froid sauce* (see SAUCE) using the pan juices in which the cutlets were cooked.

Decorate with pieces of hard-boiled egg whites, truffles, pickled tongue, etc. Glaze with liquid jelly and leave in a cold place to set.

Lay the chops in a circle on a dish. Garnish with chopped jelly. Serve with mint sauce. *Chaud-froid* of lamb chops can be served with a vegetable salad or mixed salad.

Lamb chops Conti. CÔTELETTES D'AGNEAU CONTI – Coat the chops on both sides with a *mirepoix* (q.v.) of vegetables finely chopped and cooked in butter. Dip in breadcrumbs and fry in clarified butter. Arrange in a crown on a dish, alternating with slices of ham cut in triangles and fried in butter. Garnish the centre of the dish with a fairly thick *Lentil purée* (see PURÉE). Surround with a border of *Demi-glace sauce* (see SAUCE).

Lamb chops in crépinettes. CÔTELETTES D'AGNEAU EN CRÉPINETTES – Prepare as *Mutton chops in crépinettes* (see MUTTON), or, instead of braising them, fry them in butter before wrapping them in pieces of thin salt pork or pig's caul.

Lamb chops Dubarry. CÔTELETTES D'AGNEAU DUBARRY – Grill or fry the chops and garnish with cauliflower divided into florets and covered with *Mornay sauce* (see SAUCE), sprinkled with Parmesan cheese. Brown in the oven or under a grill.

Lamb chops à la financière. CÔTELETTES D'AGNEAU À LA FINANCIÈRE – Fry the chops. Add Madeira to the pan and finish off the sauce with *Demi-glace sauce* (see SAUCE).

Arrange the chops in a circle in a puff pastry shell (not too raised) and garnish the middle with a *Ragoût à la financière* (see RAGOÛT).

If there is no time to make a pastry shell, the chops can be arranged in a crown, putting each on a heart-shaped croûton fried in butter.

Lamb chops à la française. CÔTELETTES D'AGNEAU À LA FRANÇAISE – 'Fry 12 cutlets, put them under a press; when they are cold, coat with chicken quenelle forcemeat.

'Put them on a metal sheet greased with clarified butter and glaze with egg. Cook in the oven, painting them with melted butter from time to time, until nicely golden.

'Prepare a *croustade* (q.v.) from a piece of bread about 10 cm. (4 inches) in diameter, scooped out in the middle and fried in deep fat. Put this *croustade* in the middle of an *entrée* dish, place the cutlets around it and fill the middle with fried lambs' sweetbreads and truffles. Glaze and serve.' (*La Grande Cuisine simplifée*, by Robert, 1845.)

Lamb chops with garnish. CÔTELETTES D'AGNEAU SAUTÉES GARNIES – Season the chops and sauté them in butter. Arrange them in a crown on a dish. Garnish with vegetables or any other garnish recommended below. Dilute the pan juices with white wine, add *Demi-glace sauce* (see SAUCE) or veal stock, boil down, strain, and pour over the chops.

Grilled lamb chops served with rice

Garnishes suitable for lamb chops. Green vegetables dressed with butter or cream; various braised vegetables; potatoes prepared in various ways; purées of fresh or dried vegetables; pasta products; rice; risotto; and the garnishes, simple or mixed, recommended for small fillet steaks, *tournedos*, escalopes of veal, *noisettes* and *médaillons* of mutton or lamb.

Grilled lamb chops garnished with various vegetables. CÔTELETTES D'AGNEAU GRILLÉES GARNIES DE LÉGUMES – Season the cutlets, brush with melted butter or oil, and cook under a moderate flame. Garnish with vegetables. Put paper frills on end bones.

Grilled chops can be garnished with various green vegetables, dressed with butter or cream (asparagus tips, French beans, kidney beans, young broad beans, garden peas, etc.); potatoes prepared in different ways; braised vegetables (celery, lettuce, endive, etc.); purées of fresh vegetables; small marrows (zucchini) or aubergines cut in dice and sautéed in butter or oil; tomatoes lightly sautéed in butter or oil; Brussels sprouts or cauliflower sautéed in butter; cucumbers cut into uniform pieces and cooked in butter; artichoke hearts fried lightly in butter, etc.

Lamb chops à l'italienne. CÔTELETTES D'AGNEAU À L'ITALIENNE – See MUTTON, *Mutton chops à l'italienne.*

Lamb chops Maintenon. CÔTELETTES D'AGNEAU MAINTENON – See MUTTON, *Mutton chops Maintenon.*

Lamb chops à la maréchale. CÔTELETTES D'AGNEAU À LA MARÉCHALE – Dip in egg and breadcrumbs and fry in clarified butter.

Arrange the chops in a crown, and put on each a sliver of truffle heated in butter. Garnish with asparagus tips dressed with butter. Put a border of *Demi-glace sauce* (see SAUCE) mixed with Madeira and butter around the chops.

Lamb chops à la mexicaine. CÔTELETTES D'AGNEAU À LA MEXICAINE – Fry the chops in butter. Arrange in a crown on a dish and garnish the middle with bananas cut in slices, dipped in batter and fried.

Add to the pan juices (for 6 chops) 2 tablespoons (3 tablespoons) wine vinegar. Pour in 2 dl. ($\frac{1}{3}$ pint, scant cup) brown veal stock. Simmer to thicken. Add to it the peel of 1 orange, blanched, rinsed in cold water, well drained, and finely shredded. Pour over the chops.

Minute lamb chops. CÔTELETTES D'AGNEAU À LA MINUTE – Beat the chops flat and season. Sauté as briskly as possible in sizzling butter.

Arrange in a crown. Pour over the chops the butter left in the pan, with a dash of lemon juice and some chopped parsley added to it.

Lamb chops Montrouge. CÔTELETTES D'AGNEAU MONTROUGE – Dip in egg and breadcrumbs and fry in clarified butter. Arrange in a crown on a dish. Garnish the middle with fairly thick *Mushroom purée* (see PURÉE). Put a border of buttered *Demi-glace sauce* (see SAUCE) around the chops.

Lamb chops Paul Mounet. CÔTELETTES D'AGNEAU PAUL MOUNET – Fry 6 chops in goose fat. Arrange them in a crown, alternating with rows of fried heart-shaped croûtons.

Put into the pan 2 tablespoons (3 tablespoons) Bayonne ham which has been blanched, drained, dried, and finely shredded. When the ham is lightly browned add 2 tablespoons (3 tablespoons) shredded *cèpes* or mushroom caps, and sauté lightly. Add 2 cloves of garlic, also finely chopped. Dilute with 1 tablespoon wine vinegar, add 2 dl. ($\frac{1}{3}$ pint, scant cup) tomato-flavoured *Demi-glace sauce* (see SAUCE). Cook for 5 minutes. Pour over the chops.

Lamb chops en papillotes. CÔTELETTES D'AGNEAU EN PAPILLOTES – Prepare as described in the recipe for *Veal chops en papillote* (see VEAL).

Lamb chops, instead of being fried, can be braised, allowed to get cold in the juices and then put into buttered papers.

The juices left over from braising will be used for moistening the *duxelles* (q.v.).

Lamb chops à la parisienne. CÔTELETTES D'AGNEAU À LA PARISIENNE – Dip the chops in beaten egg, then in breadcrumbs mixed with chopped truffles. Cook in clarified butter. Arrange in a crown in a dish. Garnish the middle of the dish with mushrooms cooked in cream. Put a border of asparagus tips dressed with butter round the chops.

Lamb chops Périnette. CÔTELETTES D'AGNEAU PÉRINETTE – Dip the chops in egg and breadcrumbs mixed with finely chopped cooked ham. Fry them in clarified butter.

Arrange in a crown alternating with rows of baby marrows (zucchini) cut in long slices and fried in oil. Garnish the middle of the dish with a *Tomato fondue* (see FONDUE) mixed with sweet pimentos, cut in large dice and fried in oil.

Lamb chops à la portugaise. CÔTELETTES D'AGNEAU À LA PORTUGAISE – Fry the lamb chops in butter. Garnish with very small, stuffed tomatoes, cooked in the oven or under a grill. Dilute the pan juices with white wine, add a little tomato purée with a finely chopped or pounded clove of garlic blended in, and pour this sauce over the chops.

Lamb chops princesse. CÔTELETTES D'AGNEAU PRINCESSE – This name describes the following two methods of preparation:

1. Dip the chops in egg and breadcrumbs, fry them in clarified butter, arrange in a circle on a dish. Garnish with little bunches of asparagus tips dressed with butter and coarsely shredded truffles. Serve with *Allemande sauce* (see SAUCE) based on concentrated mushroom stock.

2. Cook the chops in butter. Arrange in a circle. Cover with *Allemande sauce* based on concentrated mushroom stock. Put a sliver of truffle on each chop and garnish the middle of the dish with asparagus tips dressed with butter. Dilute the pan juices with Madeira and thickened brown stock. Pour this over the chops.

Lamb chops à la romaine. CÔTELETTES D'*k*GNEAU À LA ROMAINE – Fry the chops in butter. Arrange in a crown on a dish, alternating with rows of heart-shaped croûtons of bread fried in butter. Garnish the middle of the dish with small potato balls, cooked in butter and tossed in concentrated meat stock. Pour over the chops *Romaine sauce* (see SAUCE) to which the pan juices, diluted with 2 tablespoons (3 tablespoons) wine vinegar, have been added.

Lamb chops Rossini. CÔTELETTES D'AGNEAU ROSSINI – Fry the chops in butter, and arrange on a dish. Put on each a slice of *foie gras* fried in butter and 2 or 3 slivers of truffle tossed in butter. Dilute the pan juices with Madeira (or any similar wine), add some *Demi-glace sauce* (see SAUCE), boil down, strain and pour over the chops.

Lamb chops à la rouennaise. CÔTELETTES D'AGNEAU À LA ROUENNAISE – Fry the chops in butter. When half cooked, add to the pan 2 tablespoons (3 tablespoons) chopped onion lightly cooked in butter, and 1 teaspoon chopped shallots. Drain the chops. Arrange in a crown on a dish, alternating with rows of heart-shaped croûtons fried in butter. Pour over the following sauce:

Dilute the pan juices with 3 dl. ($\frac{1}{2}$ pint, $1\frac{1}{4}$ cups) *Demi-glace sauce* (see SAUCE). Boil for 5 minutes, remove from the heat and stir in 3 uncooked chicken livers rubbed through a fine sieve, blended with 2 tablespoons (3 tablespoons) Calvados. Heat without allowing to boil. Put the sauce through a strainer. Heat gently and blend in 2 teaspoons butter.

Lamb chops à la sarladaise. CÔTELETTES D'AGNEAU À LA SARLADAISE – Grill the chops or fry them in butter. Arrange in a ring on a layer of *Potatoes à la sarladaise* (see POTATOES). Pour around the potatoes several tablespoons of *Périgueux sauce* (see SAUCE).

Lamb chops soubise. CÔTELETTES D'AGNEAU SOUBISE – Grill or fry the chops. Arrange in a crown. Garnish with a fairly thick *Onion soubise* (see PURÉE).

Lamb chops Talleyrand. CÔTELETTES D'AGNEAU TALLEYRAND – Sauté the chops in butter. Arrange in a crown. Garnish the middle of the dish with a fairly thick *Onion soubise* (see PURÉE). Pour over the chops the following sauce:

In the butter left over in the pan, lightly fry diced mushrooms and diced truffles. Dilute with sherry and add thick fresh cream. Simmer for a few moments and pour over the chops.

Lamb chops à la Toulouse. CÔTELETTES D'AGNEAU À LA TOULOUSE – Braise the chops and glaze in the oven. Boil down the stock until thick and add to it 2 tablespoons (3 tablespoons) Madeira.

Arrange the chops in a slightly raised puff pastry shell (or in a circle on croûtons fried in butter) and garnish them, in the centre, with *Ragoût à la toulousaine* (see RAGOÛT). Sprinkle the chops with the pan juices. Put paper frills on end bones.

Lamb chops à la turque. CÔTELETTES D'AGNEAU À LA TURQUE – Fry the chops in butter. Arrange in a circle on a dish. Garnish the middle of the dish with *Rice pilaf à la turque* (see PILAF). Dilute the pan juices with stock and *Tomato sauce* (see SAUCE), add a pounded clove of garlic and pour over the chops.

Lamb chops Villeroi. CÔTELETTES D'AGNEAU VILLEROI – See MUTTON, *Mutton chops à la Villeroi*.

Crépinettes of lamb. CRÉPINETTES D'AGNEAU – Prepare like *Crépinettes of pork* (see PORK) using lamb *salpicon* (q.v.).

Crépinettes of lamb à la périgourdine. CRÉPINETTES D'AGNEAU À LA PÉRIGOURDINE – Flatten and trim 6 lamb cutlets, season with salt and pepper, and braise. Allow to cool in the pan juices.

Prepare 200 g. (7 oz.) finely pounded *Pork forcemeat* (see FORCEMEATS), add to it 100 g. (4 oz.) *foie gras*, and 2 diced truffles. Mix well.

Drain the chops and dry them off. Coat on both sides with a layer of the above forcemeat. Wrap each cutlet in a thin piece of pig's caul or salt pork, making sure that it is entirely closed.

Brush the *crépinettes* with melted butter, coat with breadcrumbs, and cook under a low flame.

Lamb curry. CARI D'AGNEAU – Follow directions for *Curried mutton* (see MUTTON), reducing the cooking time slightly to allow for the tenderness of the meat.

Double of lamb. DOUBLE D'AGNEAU – This is a joint comprising the two legs of the animal. You can either roast or pot-roast it. Garnish with vegetables and serve with its own gravy, clear or thickened, depending on vegetable chosen.

Cook for 18 to 20 minutes per 500 g. (1 lb.) plus 18 minutes at 200°C. (400°F., Gas Mark 6).

All the garnishes recommended for the baron are suitable for a double of lamb.

Filets mignons of lamb. FILETS MIGNONS D'AGNEAU – Small pieces of lean meat found on the bone of the saddle. In general, these small fillets are left with the big fillets of the saddle when the saddle is boned, but they can also be prepared separately. (See MUTTON, *Filets mignons of mutton*.)

Fillets of lamb (U.S. loin of lamb). FILETS D'AGNEAU – Half of the saddle, boned, rolled and secured with string. It can be roasted, pot-roasted or braised.

All methods of preparation given for loin or shoulder of lamb are applicable.

Fricassée of lamb. FRICASSÉE D'AGNEAU – This is the same as the second recipe for *Blanquette of lamb* above.

Lamb's head à l'écossaise. TÊTE D'AGNEAU À L'ÉCOSSAISE – Singe and carefully clean the lamb's head. Cut in two lengthwise. Leave to soak thoroughly in cold water.

Remove the brains, which are cooked separately in *court-bouillon* (q.v.).

Cook the 2 halves of the head in water with carrots, onions and celery as a *pot-au-feu* (q.v.). (Cooking time about 2 hours.) Drain the head, put it in an ovenproof dish, brush with melted butter and put in a very hot oven.

Serve with a white sauce to which 1 tablespoon chopped and blanched sage and the diced brains have been added.

Stuffed lamb's head à l'anglaise. TÊTE D'AGNEAU FARCIE À L'ANGLAISE – Scald the lamb's head and remove all bones. Fill it with a stuffing *à l'anglaise*, made of chopped suet and breadcrumbs, well seasoned and mixed with forcemeat made from minced lamb's liver and bacon.

Wrap the lamb's head in a napkin and secure both ends with string.

Brown chopped bacon rinds, carrots and onions in butter in a braising pan. Put in the head. Add a *bouquet garni* (q.v.) and a clove. Braise for 30 minutes.

Serve with *Pascaline sauce* prepared as follows:

Toss 1 chopped onion in 2 tablespoons (3 tablespoons) butter, and moisten with 2 dl. ($\frac{1}{3}$ pint, scant cup) white wine. Boil down and add 3 dl. ($\frac{1}{2}$ pint, $1\frac{1}{4}$ cups) white sauce. Bring to the boil, bind with 2 egg yolks and add 1 tablespoon chopped, blanched parsley, a dash of lemon juice and a pinch of cayenne pepper.

Lamb's kidney – See OFFAL or VARIETY MEATS.

Leg of lamb. GIGOT D'AGNEAU – The best way to prepare leg of lamb is to roast, pot-roast or braise it. This joint, when it is big, can also be boiled, according to the English method.

Roast, pot-roast or boiled leg of lamb can be served with all the garnishes recommended for leg, baron, double or shoulder of mutton.

For cooking time see CULINARY METHODS, *Average cooking times for roasts*.

The leg of baby or milk-fed lamb is either roasted or pot-roasted.

Roast leg of lamb is served garnished with watercress and quarters of lemon and accompanied by its own gravy. It can also be served, as is customary in England, with *Mint sauce* (see SAUCE, *Cold sauces*).

Leg of lamb à l'anglaise. GIGOT D'AGNEAU À L'ANGLAISE – Season a leg of lamb, trim and bone it almost completely. Wrap it in a napkin, lightly buttered and sprinkled with flour. Secure with string.

Put it into lightly salted boiling water with 2 quartered carrots, 2 medium-sized onions, one stuck with a clove, and a *bouquet garni* consisting of a sprig of parsley, thyme, a bay leaf and a clove of garlic.

Cook the leg, simmering gently, allowing 15 to 20 minutes per 500 g. (1 lb.). Drain, unwrap it, and arrange on a long dish. Put vegetables around it. Serve with *Butter sauce II* (see SAUCE), to which has been added 2 teaspoons capers and the strained stock.

Leg of lamb boiled *à l'anglaise* can be served with purée of turnips or celery which has been cooked with the leg, mashed potatoes, or purée of white beans.

Leg of lamb à la bonne femme. GIGOT D'AGNEAU À LA BONNE FEMME – Using a leg of lamb, prepare as described in the recipe for *Leg of mutton à la bonne femme* (see MUTTON).

Leg of lamb à la bordelaise. GIGOT D'AGNEAU À LA BORDELAISE – Cook a leg of lamb in a mixture of butter and oil in a casserole. When one-third done, add 600 g. ($1\frac{1}{4}$ lb.) tiny potato balls and 250 g. (9 oz.) fresh *cèpes* or button mushrooms, lightly tossed in oil. Season. Cook in a slow oven. When the leg and garnish are cooked, sprinkle with *Noisette butter* (see BUTTER, *Compound butters*) in which 4 tablespoons ($\frac{1}{3}$ cup) breadcrumbs with 1 tablespoon chopped parsley and garlic have been fried.

Leg of lamb à la boulangère. GIGOT D'AGNEAU À LA BOULANGÈRE – Prepare like *Shoulder of mutton à la boulangère* (see MUTTON).

Braised leg of lamb with various garnishes. GIGOT D'AGNEAU BRAISÉ – Prepare like *Braised shoulder of lamb* (see below), and serve with the usual garnishes suitable for braised, pot-roasted or roast mutton or lamb.

Leg of lamb en chevreuil. GIGOT D'AGNEAU EN CHEVREUIL – Prepare, using a leg of lamb, as described in the recipe for *Leg of mutton en chevreuil* (see MUTTON).

Parslied leg of lamb. GIGOT D'AGNEAU PERSILLÉ – Leg of ordinary or milk-fed lamb, cooked in the oven or on a spit. When cooked, coat it with fresh breadcrumbs mixed with chopped parsley. Press well to make this mixture adhere evenly all over the joint and put the leg back in the oven until the surface turns golden. Arrange on a long dish, garnish with watercress and lemons cut in half. Serve with its own gravy.

In the south-east of France chopped garlic is added to the parsley and breadcrumbs mixture.

Pot-roasted leg of lamb with various garnishes. GIGOT D'AGNEAU POÊLÉ – Leg of lamb trimmed and pot-roasted in a casserole in butter or other fat, but without adding any liquid.

When the leg is cooked, put it on a long dish and surround it with the garnish desired (all garnishes recommended for baron, double, or loin of lamb). Pour over it the pan juices mixed with white wine and thickened brown stock.

Roast leg of lamb. GIGOT D'AGNEAU RÔTI – Trim the leg at the knuckle end, loosen the flesh around the knuckle and remove most of the bone. Tie this part of the leg with string. Cook on a spit or in the oven. For cooking times see CULINARY METHODS, *Average cooking times for roasts.*

Arrange the leg on a long dish and garnish with a bunch of watercress. Serve with the diluted pan juices (keeping a little fat in them), halves of lemons, and *Mint sauce* (see SAUCE).

Lamb's liver. FOIE D'AGNEAU – This is generally used with the rest of the lamb's pluck to prepare a special dish called *fressure.*

All recipes for calf's liver can also be used for lamb's liver (see OFFAL or VARIETY MEATS).

Loin of lamb. CARRÉ D'AGNEAU – Loin of lamb is often roasted. All garnishes recommended for baron or double of lamb are applicable to this cut. They are served with their own juices, clear or thickened, depending on the nature of the garnish. They are also served with *Mint sauce* (see SAUCE).

Cook for 15 to 20 minutes per 500 g. (1 lb.) plus 15 minutes at 200°C. (400°F., Gas Mark 6).

Baby or milk-fed lamb loins, which are not very big, are usually pot-roasted in butter or grilled.

Loin of lamb (U.S.) – See *Fillets of lamb.*

Loin of lamb à la Beauharnais. CARRÉ D'AGNEAU À LA BEAUHARNAIS – Trim the loin, season, brush with melted butter and grill or broil under a gentle heat. When it is nearly

Parslied leg of lamb (*Robert Carrier*)

cooked, sprinkle with white breadcrumbs and finish cooking under the grill or broiler to brown the surface.

Put the meat on a long dish, garnish at each end with *Noisette potatoes* (see POTATOES) and with little artichoke hearts boiled in *court-bouillon* (q.v.), sautéed in butter, and filled with *Beauharnais sauce* (*Béarnaise sauce* (see SAUCE) finished off with a purée of tarragon). Surround the loin with a border of buttered *Demi-glace sauce* (see SAUCE).

Loin of lamb à la bonne femme. CARRÉ D'AGNEAU À LA BONNE FEMME – Trim the loin and brown in butter in a *cocotte* (earthenware fireproof casserole). Add 12 lightly fried bacon rashers and 250 g. (9 oz., $1\frac{1}{2}$ cups) tiny potato balls. Season, sprinkle with 2 tablespoons (3 tablespoons) butter, cook in a slow oven, and serve in the *cocotte*.

Loin of lamb à la bordelaise. CARRÉ D'AGNEAU À LA BORDELAISE – Pare and trim the loin and brown it lightly in a mixture of butter and oil in equal proportions in a *cocotte* (q.v.). Add *cèpes* fried in oil, and potatoes cut down to look like small olives. Season, and cook in a slow oven. Add several tablespoons of brown stock mixed with tomato purée and flavoured with a crushed clove of garlic. Sprinkle with chopped parsley. Serve in the *cocotte*.

Loin of lamb à la boulangère. CARRÉ D'AGNEAU À LA BOULANGÈRE – Trim the loin. Prepare in an earthenware dish as *Shoulder of lamb à la boulangère* (see below).

Loin of lamb in a cocotte à la maraîchère. CARRÉ D'AGNEAU EN COCOTTE À LA MARAÎCHÈRE – Trim the loin and brown it in butter in an earthenware dish. Put into the *cocotte* 24 small potatoes tossed in butter, 150 g. (5 oz.) salsify cooked in *court-bouillon* (q.v.) and tossed in butter, and 24 Brussels sprouts lightly blanched and tossed in butter.

Finish cooking everything together. Add 4 tablespoons (5 tablespoons) thickened brown stock. Serve in the *cocotte*.

Grilled loin of lamb. CARRÉ D'AGNEAU GRILLÉ – Trim the loin. Make a few surface incisions in the skin, season, brush with melted butter and grill (or broil) under a low flame until both sides are golden.

Arrange on a long dish, garnish with watercress and serve with half-melted *Maître d'hôtel butter* (see BUTTER, *Compound butters*).

Loin of lamb à la languedocienne. CARRÉ D'AGNEAU À LA LANGUEDOCIENNE – Trim the lamb and brown it lightly in butter (or goose fat) in an earthenware dish. Add 2 small onions tossed in butter with 12 small pieces of smoked ham, 6 blanched garlic cloves and 200 g. (7 oz.) small white *cèpes* or button mushrooms fried in oil. Season. Cook in a slow oven, basting frequently. Sprinkle with chopped parsley and serve in the dish in which it was cooked.

Loin of lamb à la niçoise. CARRÉ D'AGNEAU À LA NIÇOISE – Trim a loin of lamb and brown in butter in an earthenware *cocotte* (q.v.). Add zucchini (or a baby marrow) peeled, diced, and tossed in butter; a large peeled, seeded tomato cut into pieces and fried in oil; and about 20 small new potatoes, cut to a uniform size. Season with salt and pepper. Cook in a slow oven. Sprinkle with chopped parsley. Serve in the *cocotte*.

Loin of lamb with noodles. CARRÉ D'AGNEAU AUX NOUILLES – Trim the loin of lamb and cook it in butter in a *cocotte* (q.v.). When nearly cooked, remove it from the *cocotte*. Add noodles, freshly boiled in salted water, drained, and tossed in *Noisette butter* (see BUTTER, *Compound butters*), to the *cocotte*. Put the loin back. Finish cooking together in the oven. Sprinkle with a few tablespoons of thickened brown stock.

Loin of lamb Parmentier. CARRÉ D'AGNEAU PARMENTIER – Brown a trimmed loin of lamb in butter. Put in a pan 250 g. (9 oz., $1\frac{1}{2}$ cups) diced potatoes. Season and sprinkle with melted butter. Finish cooking together in a slow oven. Place on a dish. Dilute the pan juices with white wine, add thickened veal stock, and pour over the loin. Sprinkle with chopped parsley.

Pot-roasted loin of lamb with various garnishes. CARRÉ D'AGNEAU POÊLÉ – Trim a loin of lamb and pot-roast in butter. When half cooked, add the vegetables chosen as garnish and finish cooking together.

Arrange the loin in a dish and surround with garnish. Dilute the pan juices with white wine, blend in thickened brown stock, and pour over the meat.

The pot-roasted loin may be cooked separately, and garnished with one or other of the garnishes recommended for baron or double of lamb.

The following garnishes can be added to the loin during cooking: artichokes (hearts or quarters), diced aubergines previously tossed in butter or oil, new carrots half-cooked in butter and water, *cèpes* fried in oil or butter, various types of mushrooms, Brussels sprouts, marrows cut in large dice, half-braised Chinese artichokes, half-cooked turnips, glazed small onions, diced or shredded potatoes, salsify cooked in *court-bouillon* (q.v.), drained and tossed in butter.

Pot-roasted loin of lamb can also be garnished with the following: pasta prepared in various ways, purées of fresh or dried vegetables, rice pilaf or risotto, *fondue* of tomatoes, *soubise*, etc.

Medallions of lamb. MÉDAILLONS D'AGNEAU – Another name for *Lamb noisettes* (see below).

Mignonnettes of lamb. MIGNONNETTES D'AGNEAU – Name often used for *Lamb noisettes* (see below).

Minced lamb. HACHIS D'AGNEAU – Prepare as *Beef hash* (see HASH).

Lamb moussaka. MOUSSAKA D'AGNEAU – Prepared with minced lamb and aubergines like *Mutton moussaka* (see MUTTON).

Lamb noisettes. NOISETTES D'AGNEAU – Delicate pieces of meat taken from the rib or loin of lamb. They are trimmed into round, rather thick fillets. Their weight varies between 75 and 100 g. (3 and 4 oz.).

Sautéed noisettes of lamb. NOISETTES D'AGNEAU SAUTÉES – Trim the *noisettes* and flatten them lightly. Season and sauté briskly in clarified butter, oil, or a mixture of butter and oil. Garnish.

Sautéed *noisettes* are sometimes served on croûtons fried in butter or on various garnishes as foundations.

Garnishes and sauces for them will be found in the recipes which follow. In addition to these recipes, all those given elsewhere for *tournedos* or *médaillons* of beef, as well as those indicated for lamb or mutton cutlets, can be applied to *noisettes*.

The stocks and gravies most commonly used in cooking are based on veal, chicken or beef. Stock can also be made of lamb and mutton trimmings and bones.

Lamb noisettes à l'algérienne. NOISETTES D'AGNEAU À L'ALGÉRIENNE – Proceed as described in the recipe given for *Tournedos à l'algérienne* (see BEEF).

Lamb noisettes Armenonville. NOISETTES D'AGNEAU ARMENONVILLE – Sauté the *noisettes* in butter, arrange on a foundation of *Anna potatoes* (see POTATOES), garnish with morels in cream and cocks' combs and kidneys. Serve with a sauce made of the pan juices, mixed with white wine and thickened veal stock.

Lamb noisettes Béatrix. NOISETTES D'AGNEAU BÉATRIX – Sauté the *noisettes* in butter and place on fried croûtons. Garnish with morels or other mushrooms fried in butter, very small quarters of artichokes cooked in butter, small glazed carrots and new potatoes in butter. Serve with a sauce made from the pan juices mixed with sherry and thickened veal stock.

Lamb noisettes Beauharnais. NOISETTES D'AGNEAU BEAUHARNAIS – Sauté the *noisettes* in butter. Place on fried croûtons. Garnish with very small artichoke hearts filled with thick *Béarnaise sauce* (see SAUCE) with a purée of tarragon added to it, and tiny potato balls. Serve with a sauce made from the pan juices mixed with Madeira and *Demi-glace sauce* (see SAUCE) with chopped truffles added to it.

Lamb noisettes Carignan. NOISETTES D'AGNEAU CARIGNAN – Sauté the *noisettes* in butter and place on a foundation of *Anna potatoes* (see POTATOES).

Garnish with very small quarters of artichokes cooked in butter, and asparagus tips dressed with butter. Put between the noisettes very small 'eggs' made of *Duchess potato mixture* (see POTATO), dipped in egg and breadcrumbs, fried, hollowed out and filled with a purée of *foie gras* with truffles. Serve with a sauce made from the pan juices mixed with port and *Demi-glace sauce* (see SAUCE).

Lamb noisettes chasseur. NOISETTES D'AGNEAU CHASSEUR – Sauté the *noisettes* in a mixture of butter and oil. Serve with a sauce made from the pan juices mixed with *Chasseur sauce* (see SAUCE).

Alternatively one can remove the *noisettes* as soon as they are cooked and put into the same pan (for 8 *noisettes*) 125 g. (4 oz., 2 cups) chopped mushrooms and 1 teaspoon chopped shallots. Dilute with white wine and moisten with veal stock and a little *Tomato sauce* (see SAUCE).

Lamb noisettes Cussy. NOISETTES D'AGNEAU CUSSY – Sauté the *noisettes* in butter and arrange on fried croûtons. Garnish with little artichoke hearts filled with mushroom purée and sprinkled with breadcrumbs. Serve with a sauce made from the juices mixed with Madeira and *Demi-glace sauce* (see SAUCE).

Lamb noisettes Duroc. NOISETTES D'AGNEAU DUROC – Proceed as for *Lamb noisettes chasseur*. Garnish with very small potato balls fried in butter. Sprinkle with chopped tarragon.

Lamb noisettes à l'italienne. NOISETTES D'AGNEAU À L'ITALIENNE – Sauté the *noisettes* in oil. Arrange on fried croûtons and put on each *noisette* a small slice of lean ham fried in oil. Serve with a sauce made from the pan juices mixed with *Italian sauce* (see SAUCE).

Lamb noisettes Melba. NOISETTES D'AGNEAU MELBA – Sauté the *noisettes* in butter, arrange on fried croûtons, garnish with braised lettuce hearts, or with small tomatoes stuffed with a mixture of chicken, truffles and mushrooms, bound with *Velouté sauce* (see SAUCE). Brown in the oven or under a grill. Serve with a sauce made from the pan juices mixed with Madeira and *Demi-glace sauce* (see SAUCE).

Lamb noisettes Montpensier. NOISETTES D'AGNEAU MONTPENSIER – Sauté the *noisettes* in butter, arrange on fried croûtons, and garnish with coarsely shredded truffles and asparagus tips both fried in butter. Serve with a sauce made from the pan juices mixed with Madeira and *Demi-glace sauce* (see SAUCE).

Lamb noisettes Nichette. NOISETTES D'AGNEAU NICHETTE – Grill the *noisettes* and put each on a cake made of *Duchess potato* (see POTATOES) cooked in the oven until golden. Garnish with cocks' combs and kidneys. Put a grilled mushroom filled with grated horseradish on top of each *noisette*. Serve with *Marrow sauce* (see SAUCE).

Lamb noisettes à la niçoise I. NOISETTES D'AGNEAU À LA NIÇOISE – Sauté the *noisettes* in oil and garnish *à la niçoise* (see GARNISHES). Serve with a sauce made from the pan juices diluted with white wine and tomato-flavoured veal stock.

Lamb noisettes à la niçoise II. NOISETTES D'AGNEAU À LA NIÇOISE – Sauté the *noisettes* in oil and garnish with small new potatoes tossed in butter, and French beans in butter. Put on each *noisette* 1 tablespoon *Tomato fondue* (see FONDUE). Serve with a sauce made from the pan juices diluted with white wine and tomato-flavoured veal stock.

Lamb noisettes Rivoli. NOISETTES D'AGNEAU RIVOLI – Sauté the *noisettes* in butter, arrange on *Anna potatoes* (see POTATOES), and serve with a sauce made from the pan juices mixed with Madeira and *Demi-glace sauce* (see SAUCE) with truffles added to it.

These can be served in a *cocotte* (q.v.).

Lamb noisettes Saint-Germain. NOISETTES D'AGNEAU SAINT-GERMAIN – Proceed as described in the recipe for *Tournedos Saint-Germain* (see BEEF).

Lamb noisettes à la turque. NOISETTES D'AGNEAU À LA TURQUE – Sauté the *noisettes* in butter, garnish with *Rice pilaf à la turque* (see PILAF) and aubergines cut in large dice and fried in oil. Serve with a sauce made from the pan juices diluted with tomato-flavoured veal stock.

Lamb noisettes à la Valenciennes. NOISETTES D'AGNEAU A LA VALENCIENNES – Sauté the *noisettes* in butter and put each on a little mound of rice *à la Valenciennes* (see GARNISHES). Serve with a sauce made from the pan juices diluted with white wine and tomato-flavoured veal stock, with a pounded clove of garlic added to it.

Lamb noisettes garnished with vegetables. NOISETTES D'AGNEAU GARNIES AUX LÉGUMES – Sauté the *noisettes* in butter or grill them, garnish with the vegetables recommended. Sprinkle the sautéed *noisettes* very lightly with a sauce made from the pan juices, diluted and boiled down, or with a thickened *Demi-glace sauce* (see SAUCE).

The following vegetables are used for garnishing *noisettes*: quartered hearts of artichokes, sautéed or fried aubergines, fried *cèpes* and other mushrooms, braised endive, kidney beans in butter, sautéed Brussels sprouts, cucumbers cut into uniform pieces and cooked in butter, stewed Chinese artichokes, stewed gumbos (okra), French beans in butter, braised lettuce, peas in butter or *à la française*, asparagus tips in butter, etc.

The *noisettes* can also be garnished with purée of fresh vegetables, such as chicory or spinach.

Pascaline of lamb. PASCALINE D'AGNEAU – Plumerey, who continued Carême's work, gives a recipe for this rather complicated dish. He says that he wrote it from the dictation of the old controller of the Prince de Conti's household, but he himself never tried it out.

'Scald perfectly 4 lambs' heads and put them to soak, as well as the 4 sets of brains and 4 tongues. Take 3 lambs' livers, and mince with fresh bacon, *fines herbes*, salt, pepper and spices, to make into forcemeat. Cook 12 lambs' feet with the tongues in a *court-bouillon*.

'Cook the brains separately in a white *court-bouillon*. When the tongues and brains are cooked, cut them into large dice with mushrooms, and shape them into 12 croquettes.

'Now take the 4 blanched heads of lamb and fill with the forcemeat. Sew them up securely. Put on top of them several slices of lemon. Cover with bacon and cook them in a covered casserole on a bed of vegetables.

'Have a dozen larded lambs' sweetbreads ready. Keep the throats. Prepare a smooth sauce (*Velouté* – see SAUCE), into which you have put 2 handfuls of mushrooms. Boil down and bind with 6 egg yolks. Take the heads out of the casserole, drain, remove thread, arrange on a long dish, nose part facing outwards. Cut each foot in two and put 3 halves between each head. Pour the sauce over and put around them 12 fried croquettes, 12 larded lambs' sweetbreads and 12 croûtons of bread cut to look like cocks' combs, fried in butter. Add the lambs' throats and mushrooms to the sauce and cover the heads with it.

Alexandre Dumas père, who wrote a gastronomical

dictionary, gives for the preparation of *Pascaline of lamb* the following recipe, different from that given by Plumerey:

Pascaline of lamb à la royale. PASCALINE D'AGNEAU À LA ROYALE – 'The custom of serving a lamb whole on Easter Sunday was kept in France until the time of Louis XVI. This is how the dish was prepared:

'The neck of a six-month-old lamb was boned, the breast bone sawn through and the shoulder bone broken and trussed to the breast. The 2 shank bones of the legs were also broken and fastened in the same manner.

'It was stuffed with a forcemeat of pounded lamb, yolks of hard-boiled eggs, stale breadcrumbs and chopped *fines herbes*, and seasoned with 4 spices.

'The flesh was carefully larded and put to roast before a big fire. It was served whole, as a separate course, after the soup, either with a green sauce or on a *ragoût* of truffles cooked in ham jelly.'

Pâté of lamb à la périgourdine – See PÂTÉ.

Lamb pie à la languedocienne. TOURTE D'AGNEAU À LA LANGUEDOCIENNE – Puff pastry pie with a filling of small lamb *noisettes* sautéed in butter; salsify cooked in *Court-bouillon IX* (see COURT-BOUILLON), cut into pieces and tossed in butter; sliced mushrooms; stoned and blanched olives. Put these ingredients into a pastry-lined dish on a layer of finely pounded *Pork forcemeat* (see FORCEMEAT). Dot with a few dabs of butter. Cover with a piece of rolled-out pastry, brush with egg and bake in the oven for 40 or 45 minutes. Pour into the pie a few tablespoons of boiled down *Demi-glace sauce* (see SAUCE), flavoured with Madeira.

Lamb pilaf. PILAF D'AGNEAU – Prepared like *Mutton pilaf* (see PILAF).

Lamb's pluck – See OFFAL or VARIETY MEATS.

Lamb ragoût. RAGOÛT D'AGNEAU – The parts which are most suitable for this dish are lower ribs, neck, shoulder and breast.

Ragoût of lamb à l'anglaise. RAGOÛT D'AGNEAU À BLANC (À L'ANGLAISE) – Put into a pan, in alternate layers, 750 g. ($1\frac{1}{2}$ lb.) lamb cut in pieces and 3 medium-sized sliced potatoes mixed with 2 medium-sized chopped onions. Season, and add a *bouquet garni* (q.v.). Pour in enough water or light stock to cover the meat. Cook fairly briskly with a lid on the pan.

Heap in a deep dish and sprinkle with chopped parsley.

Ragoût of lamb à la bonne femme. RAGOÛT D'AGNEAU À LA BONNE FEMME – Brown 750 g. ($1\frac{1}{2}$ lb.) lamb in clarified fat, and season with salt, pepper and a pinch of sugar. Sprinkle with 2 tablespoons (3 tablespoons) flour and brown lightly. Moisten with $\frac{3}{4}$ litre ($1\frac{1}{3}$ pints, $1\frac{3}{4}$ pints) water, add a *bouquet garni* (q.v.) and $\frac{1}{2}$ crushed clove of garlic.

Cook with a lid on the pan for 40 minutes. Drain the lamb, trim, and put the pieces back in the pan.

Add 500 g. (18 oz., 3 cups) small potato balls and 12 small onions lightly fried in butter. Cook with a lid on the pan for 40 to 45 minutes. 2 tablespoons (3 tablespoons) tomato sauce can be added.

All the *ragoûts* given for mutton (q.v.) can be used for lamb.

Rib roast of lamb (U.S.) – See *Loin of lamb*.

Saddle of lamb. SELLE D'AGNEAU – The saddle of lamb can be prepared by roasting, pot-roasting or braising, like *Saddle of mutton* (see MUTTON). All the garnishes recommended for mutton can be applied to it.

The saddle of baby or milk-fed lamb is either roasted or pot-roasted. This saddle usually remains attached to two legs of the animal, which constitutes the joint known as the baron of lamb.

Sautéed lamb. SAUTÉ D'AGNEAU – Prepared from the same parts of the animal as are used for *ragoûts*.

Cut $1\frac{1}{2}$ kg. ($3\frac{1}{4}$ lb.) boned lamb into pieces. Brown in butter with a carrot and an onion cut in quarters. Season.

Remove the lamb with a perforated spoon and put into a sauté pan with the garnish indicated in the recipe chosen.

Dilute the pan juices with 2 dl. ($\frac{1}{3}$ pint, scant cup) white wine or other wine, depending on recipe, and add 4 dl. ($\frac{3}{4}$ pint, scant 2 cups) thickened brown stock and 1 dl. (6 tablespoons, scant $\frac{1}{2}$ cup) tomato purée. Strain through a fine strainer and pour over the lamb.

Add a *bouquet garni* (q.v.) and finish cooking in the oven for 25 minutes with a lid on the pan.

Sautéed lamb à l'ancienne. SAUTÉ D'AGNEAU À L'ANCIENNE – Bone and cut the lamb into pieces and sauté in butter. Add 125 g. (4 oz.) lambs' sweetbreads (soaked, blanched and half cooked in butter), 225 g. (8 oz.) small mushrooms lightly tossed in butter, and 125 g. (4 oz.) cocks' combs and kidneys, cooked in a white *court-bouillon* (q.v.). Moisten with the pan juices diluted with 2 dl. ($\frac{1}{3}$ pint, scant cup) Madeira, to which 3 dl. ($\frac{1}{2}$ pint, $1\frac{1}{4}$ cups) *Velouté sauce* (see SAUCE) and 2 dl. ($\frac{1}{3}$ pint, scant cup) thick fresh cream have been added. Season and strain. Leave to simmer gently for 20 minutes.

Garnish with heart-shaped croûtons fried in butter.

Sautéed lamb with artichokes. SAUTÉ D'AGNEAU AUX ARTICHAUTS – Fry in butter or oil 750 g. ($1\frac{1}{2}$ lb.) neck or shoulder of lamb, boned and cut in pieces. Season with salt and pepper and cook until done.

Decorate with 4 artichoke hearts, blanched and cut in large dice, or sliced and fried in butter or oil.

Dilute the pan juices with 1 dl. (6 tablespoons, scant $\frac{1}{2}$ cup) white wine, boil down, add 2 dl. ($\frac{1}{3}$ pint, scant cup) thickened veal stock and pour over the lamb. Sprinkle with chopped parsley.

Sautéed lamb with aubergines. SAUTÉ D'AGNEAU AUX AUBERGINES – Cut $1\frac{1}{2}$ kg. ($3\frac{1}{4}$ lb.) boned and trimmed lamb's neck into pieces. Season with salt and pepper and cook until brown in a mixture of butter and oil in equal proportions. When the lamb is cooked, heap in a shallow dish. Put on top 3 small aubergines, peeled, cut in pieces and fried in oil. Mix the pan juices with white wine, thickened brown veal stock and tomato purée, flavoured with a pinch of chopped garlic. Boil down, strain, and pour over the lamb. Sprinkle with chopped parsley.

Sautéed lamb with cèpes, morels, St. George's agaric. SAUTÉ D'AGNEAUX AUX CÈPES, MORILLES, MOUSSERONS – Cook the lamb as described in the recipe for *sautéed lamb with aubergines*, replacing the aubergines by 250 g. (8 oz.) *cèpes*, morels or St. George's agarics, fried in butter or oil.

Sautéed lamb chasseur. SAUTÉ D'AGNEAU CHASSEUR – Proceed as described in the recipe given for *Sautéed veal chasseur* (see VEAL).

Sautéed lamb à la crème. SAUTÉ D'AGNEAU À LA CRÈME – Bone and cut the lamb into pieces. Season with salt and paprika and fry in butter.

Heap on a shallow dish. Dilute the pan juices with $2\frac{1}{2}$ dl. (scant $\frac{1}{2}$ pint, generous cup) cream. Boil down by one-third, add 50 g. (2 oz., $\frac{1}{4}$ cup) butter, strain, and pour over the lamb.

Sautéed lamb aux fines herbes. SAUTÉ D'AGNEAU AUX FINES HERBES – Proceed as described in the recipe for *Sautéed lambs à la minute* (see below), adding to the sauce 1 tablespoon chopped shallots and 2 tablespoons (3 tablespoons) of a mixture of chopped parsley, chervil and tarragon.

Sautéed lamb à l'indienne. SAUTÉ D'AGNEAU À L'INDIENNE – Proceed as described in the recipe for *Sautéed veal à l'indienne* (see VEAL).

Sautéed lamb à l'italienne. SAUTÉ D'AGNEAU À L'ITALIENNE – Proceed as described in the recipe for *Sautéed lamb à la minute* (see below). Dilute the pan juices with white wine and *Italian sauce* (see SAUCE).

Sautéed lamb à la minute. SAUTÉ D'AGNEAU À LA MINUTE – Cut a boned neck or shoulder of lamb into small pieces. Sauté on lively heat in butter or oil.

When the pieces are cooked and sufficiently browned, put them in a dish, sprinkle with chopped parsley and a dash of lemon juice, and pour over them the pan juices diluted with 1 dl. (6 tablespoons, scant $\frac{1}{2}$ cup) white wine and thickened veal stock.

Sautéed lamb with mushrooms. SAUTÉ D'AGNEAU AUX CHAMPIGNONS – As in the recipe for *Sautéed lamb with cèpes, morels, St. George's agarics*, but use cultivated mushrooms, peeled and fried in butter, whole, if they are small, sliced, if they are large.

Sautéed lamb with paprika (à la hongroise). SAUTÉ D'AGNEAU AU PAPRIKA (À LA HONGROISE) – Cut into pieces $1\frac{1}{2}$ kg. ($3\frac{1}{4}$ lb.) boned lower ribs or shoulder of lamb. Brown in butter. As soon as the lamb is well browned, add 2 chopped onions. Season with salt and 1 tablespoon paprika. Sprinkle in 2 tablespoons (3 tablespoons) flour. Moisten with 2 dl. ($\frac{1}{3}$ pint, scant cup) white wine. Boil down, and then add 3 dl. ($\frac{1}{2}$ pint, $1\frac{1}{4}$ cups) white stock, 2 tablespoons (3 tablespoons) tomato purée, and a *bouquet garni* (q.v.). Cook with a lid on the pan for 30 minutes. Take the pieces of lamb out with a perforated spoon, and put them in a pan with 250 g. (8 oz.) mushrooms which have been sliced and lightly tossed in butter. Add fresh cream seasoned with paprika to the sauce left in the first pan. Boil down, strain, and pour over the lamb. Simmer gently with a lid on the pan for 25 minutes.

Sautéed lamb Parmentier. SAUTÉ D'AGNEAU PARMENTIER – Cook the meat and sauce as described in the recipe for *Sautéed lamb with aubergines*, replacing the aubergines with 4 diced potatoes fried in butter or oil.

Sautéed lamb à la printanière. SAUTÉ D'AGNEAU À LA PRINTANIÈRE – Proceed as in the recipe for *Sautéed veal à la printanière* (see VEAL).

Sautéed lamb with tomatoes. SAUTÉ D'AGNEAU AUX TOMATES – Proceed as described in the recipe for *Sautéed lamb with artichokes*, replacing the artichokes by 8 small peeled, seeded tomatoes, cooked in butter or oil. A grated clove of garlic can be added.

Shoulder of lamb. ÉPAULE D'AGNEAU – All the recipes given for *Shoulder of mutton* (see MUTTON) are applicable to shoulders of ordinary lamb. They can be boned and stuffed before cooking.

Shoulders of baby or milk-fed lamb and Pauillac lamb should not be boned. These are grilled or roasted, and served with various garnishes.

Shoulder of lamb à l'albigeoise. ÉPAULE D'AGNEAU A L'ALBIGEOISE. Bone the shoulder and stuff with forcemeat made of sausage meat and minced pig's liver in equal proportions, flavoured with chopped garlic and parsley, and well seasoned. Roll the shoulder and secure with string.

Fry it lightly until golden in sizzling goose fat in an earthenware casserole. Surround with quartered potatoes or whole new potatoes, and 12 lightly blanched cloves of garlic. Season, sprinkle with a little goose fat and cook in the oven. Sprinkle with chopped parsley. Serve in the dish in which it was cooked.

Shoulder of lamb à la boulangère. ÉPAULE D'AGNEAU À LA BOULANGÈRE – Bone the shoulder, season it on the inside, roll, and secure with string. Cook for 30 minutes in an earthenware fireproof dish in which 3 to 4 tablespoons butter have been heated.

Surround with 3 sliced or quartered large potatoes and 3 onions, finely chopped and lightly fried in butter. Season the garnish, sprinkle with the butter left over in the pan and finish cooking in the oven, basting frequently. Just before serving add 4 tablespoons ($\frac{1}{3}$ cup) thickened brown stock.

Braised shoulder of lamb with various garnishes. ÉPAULE D'AGNEAU BRAISÉE – Bone a shoulder of lamb. Season inside, roll and secure with string.

Put into a braising pan finely chopped bacon rinds, 2 carrots and 1 onion, and fry lightly in butter. Place the shoulder of lamb on top. Leave to cook with the lid on the pan for 10 minutes. Moisten with $1\frac{1}{2}$ dl. ($\frac{1}{4}$ pint, $\frac{2}{3}$ cup) white wine and boil down. Add $2\frac{1}{2}$ dl. (scant $\frac{1}{2}$ pint, generous cup) thickened brown stock, 1 dl. (6 tablespoons, scant $\frac{1}{2}$ cup) tomato purée, a *bouquet garni* (q.v.) and the bones and trimmed scraps of the shoulder. Cover with a lid and cook in a moderate oven for 1 to $1\frac{1}{2}$ hours, depending on the size of the shoulder.

Glaze in the oven, and arrange on a dish. Surround with the recommended garnish. Heat the pan juices left over from braising, remove fat, boil down, strain if necessary and pour over the shoulder.

Garnishes suitable for braised shoulder of lamb. All the garnishes indicated for the baron, double, loin and saddle of roast or braised mutton, and beans or *Bean purée à la bretonne* (see PURÉE).

Shoulder of lamb à la catalane or with pistachio nuts. ÉPAULE D'AGNEAU À LA CATALANE (EN PISTACHE) – See MUTTON, *Shoulder of mutton à la catalane.*

Shoulder of lamb à la gasconne. ÉPAULE D'AGNEAU À LA GASCONNE – Stuff the boned shoulder with a forcemeat made of raw ham (fat and lean), stale bread (without crusts) soaked in stock and squeezed out, chopped onion, and chopped garlic and parsley, all bound with an egg, and well seasoned.

Brush the shoulder with goose fat and brown lightly in the oven.

Put into a braising pan with coarsely shredded, blanched green cabbage, 2 quartered carrots, 1 onion stuck with a clove, and a *bouquet garni* (q.v.). Moisten with slightly fat stock. Cook in the oven for 45 minutes. Add quartered potatoes and finish cooking together for another 45 minutes.

Roast shoulder of lamb. ÉPAULE D'AGNEAU RÔTIE – Shoulder of lamb is usually boned, rolled and secured with string before being roasted in the oven or on a spit. It is garnished with watercress and its gravy is served separately.

The shoulder of baby or milk-fed lamb is not boned. It should be roasted in the oven or on a spit on a brisk fire. Garnish with watercress and serve the gravy separately.

Rolled shoulder of lamb (Carême's recipe). ÉPAULE D'AGNEAU EN BALLOTTINE – 'Bone 2 shoulders of lamb to the shank bone; season with salt, pepper and nutmeg and stuff it with a finely pounded forcemeat.

'With a butcher's needle thread a string through to the end of the shoulder in such a way as to make it serve as a draw string. Lard each shoulder with lardoons of bacon, working them in in the shape of a rosette. Put into a casserole trimmings from the shoulders and veal scraps, 1 carrot, 2 onions and a *bouquet garni*. Cover with rashers of bacon. Moisten with *bouillon* and a good glass of white wine to cover the larded shoulders, and cook for $1\frac{1}{2}$ hours. Take care to glaze the larded shoulders gradually. Drain, remove string, arrange on a dish and garnish with small glazed carrots and onions, or braised lettuce or celery. Strain the pan juices and remove surplus fat, boil down, pour some over the rolled shoulder of lamb and serve the rest separately.

Lamb on skewers. BROCHETTES D'AGNEAU – Using pieces of lean lamb cut from the neck or lower ribs, and pieces of bacon, prepare as described in the recipe for *Brochette of veal* (see VEAL).

Sliced lamb. ÉMINCÉS D'AGNEAU – Best cuts of lamb, pot-roasted or braised.

Lamb sweetbreads – See OFFAL or VARIETY MEATS.

Lamb on skewers or brochettes (*Robert Carrier*)

Timbale of lamb à l'ancienne. TIMBALE D'AGNEAU À L'ANCIENNE – Line a Charlotte mould with pie pastry. Put in it small lamb *noisettes* braised in *court-bouillon* (q.v.), lamb sweetbreads cooked in butter, and truffles and mushrooms, all blended with *Velouté sauce* (see SAUCE) diluted with cream and flavoured with Madeira. Alternate with layers of macaroni cooked in water and blended with cream, butter and grated cheese. These fillings must be completely cold before being put into the pie dish. Cover the dish with a pastry lid and decorate the top with pastry leaves. Make an opening to allow steam to escape and brush over with beaten egg. Bake in a hot oven for 40 to 45 minutes. Before serving, pour into the pie through the opening, a few tablespoons of the *Velouté sauce*.

Lamb's trotters (feet). PIEDS D'AGNEAU – These are prepared as *Sheep's trotters (feet)* (see OFFAL or VARIETY MEATS).

Vol-au-vent of lamb with truffles and mushrooms I. VOL-AU-VENT D'AGNEAU AUX TRUFFES ET CHAMPIGNONS – Fill a *vol-au-vent* case, as soon as it is out of the oven, with a *ragoût* of braised thin *noisettes* of lamb, lamb sweetbreads cooked in butter, and sliced truffles and mushrooms, all moistened with white or brown thickened stock.

Vol-au-vent of lamb with truffles and mushrooms II. VOL-AU-VENT D'AGNEAU AUX TRUFFES ET CHAMPIGNONS – Prepare a *vol-au-vent* case in the usual way. As soon as it is removed from the oven, fill with a *ragoût* of lamb sweetbreads braised in *court-bouillon* (q.v.), with truffles and mushrooms added, the whole blended with a piping hot *Allemande sauce* (see SAUCE).

LAMBALLE – Name given to various dishes. It is usually applied to a meat broth made by adding consommé with tapioca cooked in it to a purée of fresh peas (see SOUPS AND BROTHS, *Potage Lamballe*).

LAMBICK – Highly intoxicating Belgian beer, rather sour in taste. (See BEER.)

LA MOTHE-SAINT-HÉRAYE – See CHEESE.

LAMPREY. LAMPROIE – There are three types of edible lamprey: the *lamprey-eel* or *sea-lamprey*, the *lampern* or *river lamprey* and the *lamprey* proper.

The lamprey-eel found in the Atlantic and the Mediterranean is the most highly prized. It is similar to the eel in general appearance, but different from it in a number of details: its skin is yellowish with brown markings, its dorsal fins are spaced along its back, and it has seven bronchial orifices which form two vertical lines on either side of its neck.

In spring, the lamprey-eels migrate to the mouths of rivers. They are to be found in large numbers in the Loire, the Rhône and the Gironde.

The flesh of the lamprey is delicate but, being very fatty, it is somewhat indigestible. Lampreys of medium size are the most sought after, especially those caught in the mouths of rivers.

Scald the fish so that the skin can be easily removed. According to the manner in which it is to be cooked, cut it into thick slices or leave it whole. Prepare according to the selected recipe.

The lamprey can be cooked in a great many different ways. Most commonly it is stewed in wine (*en matelote*) flavoured with the blood of the fish. All recipes for eel (q.v.) are suitable for lamprey.

Lamprey à la Bordelaise (Bordeaux cookery). LAMPROIE À LA BORDELAISE – Bleed a medium-sized lamprey. Keep the blood aside to flavour the sauce. Scald the fish and scrape off the skin. Remove the central nerve. (To do this, cut off the tip of the lamprey's tail, make an incision round the neck below the gills and, through this opening, catch hold of the nerve and pull it out.)

Cut the fish into slices 5 cm. (2 inches) thick. Butter a pan and line it with sliced onions and carrots. Put in the slices of lamprey. Place a *bouquet garni* (q.v.) and a clove of garlic in the middle of the dish. Season with salt and pepper. Moisten with enough red wine to cover the fish. Boil for 12 minutes.

Cook 12 slices of white leek with 4 tablespoons ($\frac{1}{3}$ cup) raw diced bacon in butter in a covered pan. Drain the slices of lamprey and put them in a pan, alternating with the slices of white leek. Make a *roux* (q.v.) of flour and butter. Moisten with the cooking stock of the lamprey. Cook this sauce for 15 minutes, strain, and pour over the lamprey. Simmer very slowly until the fish is cooked. Arrange the fish on a serving dish and pour over it the sauce mixed with some of the blood. Garnish with slices of bread fried in butter.

LAMPSANA, NIPPLEWORT. LAMPSANE – Plant of the endive family, similar to the sow-thistle. Its leaves are eaten raw in salad. Cooking turns them bitter.

LANGUE-DE-CHAT (Cat's tongue) – In the view of some experts, this biscuit derives its name from its shape – thin, flat and narrow, somewhat like a cat's tongue in appearance.

Langues-de-chat, which are crisp, dry biscuits, can be made and flavoured in various ways. Only biscuits made according to one of the recipes given below, however, can properly be called *langues-de-chat*.

These keep for a long time and are served with some liqueurs and sparkling wines. They are also served with iced sweets (desserts) and used as an ingredient of various puddings.

Langue-de-chat I – Work together, in a bowl, 250 g. (9 oz., 2 cups) fine sugar and $2\frac{1}{2}$ dl. (scant $\frac{1}{2}$ pint, generous cup) fresh cream. Add 250 g. (9 oz., $2\frac{1}{4}$ cups) sieved flour, 1 tablespoon vanilla-flavoured fine sugar, and, when the mixture is quite smooth, 5 stiffly beaten egg whites.

Rub a metal baking sheet with pure wax or line with heavy waxed paper and, using a forcing-bag with a round nozzle, pipe the mixture to make little strips about $2\frac{1}{2}$ cm. (1 inch) apart, so that they will not run into one another during baking.

Bake in a hot oven for about 8 minutes.

Langue-de-chat II – *Ingredients.* 125 g. ($4\frac{1}{2}$ oz., generous $\frac{1}{2}$ cup) butter, 125 g. ($4\frac{1}{2}$ oz., generous cup) sieved flour, 100 g. (4 oz., scant cup) fine sugar, 25 g. (1 oz., $\frac{1}{4}$ cup) vanilla-flavoured fine sugar, 2 eggs.

Method. Cream the butter in a warmed bowl. Add the sugar and vanilla-flavoured sugar. Work the mixture for 2 minutes, and mix in the eggs, one at a time. Add the sieved flour.

Pipe this mixture onto a baking sheet as indicated above.

LANGUEDOC, ROUSSILLON, COMTÉ DE FOIX – The land of Oc (Languedoc) is a district which for centuries has had a tradition of fine cooking. Its people have always been connoisseurs of good food. Not only have they provided substantial dishes in abundance, such as the famous *cassoulet* (q.v.) of Castelnaudary and the *daube languedocienne,* but also subtly flavoured and delicate appetisers such as the *pâté de foie gras* with truffles, gem of the Languedoc culinary repertoire, which has made famous throughout the world the names of Toulouse, Cazères, Albi and other cities where for so long these delicacies have been made.

In Languedoc, the Roman and Arab influences which gradually determined the character of its cooking are still

Ambialet, Tarn (*French Government Tourist office*)

recognisable. In this province, which was called *Gallia Narbonensis* under the Romans, was invented the *ragoût* of mutton with white beans which was the prototype of that robust dish known as *cassoulet*.

The Languedoc larder is well stocked. In the south-western provinces of France are to be found excellent meat, succulent poultry, and good winged and ground game. The finest *foie gras* is made in this region from goose and duck liver and their indispensable foil, the truffle, the 'subterranean empress' as it was called by the Marquis de Cussy.

To these delicacies must be added excellent saltwater and freshwater fish. Among the latter are the trout of the icy Pyrenean streams, the perch, bream, tench, pike, etc., which are found in abundance in the Garonne, Ariège, Tarn and Aude rivers.

The Languedoc kitchen gardens are well stocked with vegetables and the orchards with delicious fruit. Languedoc also has its vineyards and produces excellent wine.

Culinary specialities – With such natural resources, it is no wonder that the *cuisine* of Languedoc is excellent and that the region has a large number of succulent specialities.

Here, first, are some typical Languedoc broths and soups: *Pot-au-feu à la poule farcie* (stuffed chicken hotpot); *soup au farci; pot-au-feu albigeois* (with stuffed goose neck); *pot-au-feu carcassonnais* (with ribs of beef, neck of mutton, lean bacon, stuffed cabbage and white beans); *ouillade catalan; braou bouffat de Cerdagne; boullinade des pêcheurs* (Roussillon); *bouillabaisse Catalane* (which is nothing like the *bouillabaisse* of Marseille); *soupe aux poissons de Sète* (fish soup); *soupe aux clovisses* (cockle soup); *soupe à l'ail* (garlic soup); *soupe à la courge* (pumpkin soup); *soupe aux choux* (cabbage soup); *soupe aux tomates* (tomato soup); *tourin*; and succulent *garbure*.

Among the *hors-d'œuvre* of the area are: Black Mountain and Ariège ham; sausages from Luchon, Toulouse, the Black Mountain and Ariège; *fritons* or *grattons of pork, goose and turkey; dried fèche with radishes* from Tarn; *melsat* from Dourgne; *languettes* (little tongues) from Tarn; *anchovy pâté* from Collioure; *little pâtés* of Pézenas or Béziers (which are also eaten as a dessert); *anchoiade; fresh white beans à la croque-au-sel*; fresh figs.

Among the special egg dishes of Languedoc are: *Omelettes à la cansaldo; omelettes with ham, blood, wild asparagus tips, hop shoots* (called *omelette à la Saint-Jean*), *agaric, peppers, pine kernels, garlic, tomatoes and Quercy truffles; poached* or *fried eggs with ham, tomatoes, aubergines, garlic; poached* or *fried eggs à la cansalado.*

The following dishes are made from saltwater and freshwater fish, shellfish of all kinds, snails and frogs: *Cod à l'ailloli; ragoût of cod à la carcassonnaise; cod à la persillade* (with parsley); *brandade of cod; cod bouillabaisse; shad à la persillade; stuffed shad on the spit; lamprey en matelote; fricandeau of tunny* (*tuna*) *fish à la catalane, with olives or with anchovy; chopped tunny* (*tuna*) *à la palavasienne;* river *trout à la meunière; river trout in court-bouillon; small fry in court-bouillon; Eel à la catalane; elver fry; pike on the spit; matelotes of various freshwater fish; civet of spiny lobster* (Roussillon); *freshwater crayfish in court-bouillon; mussels à la ravigote; mussels à la catalane; mussels with rice; cockles à la persillade; snails à la languedocienne, à la lodévoise, à la narbonnaise, à la sommeroise; mourguettes à la meridionale; frogs legs à la persillade.*

Here are some of the meat, poultry and game dishes of Languedoc: *Daube of beef à l'albigeoise, à la carcassonnaise; estouffat of beef à la catalane; veal slices with agaric; roll of veal en papillote; veal en persillade; ragoût of veal with olives; chump end of veal with salsify; pistache of mutton; gasconnade of mutton; braised leg of mutton with salsify; ragoût of mutton with white beans; leg of mutton with garlic;* Luchon *salted ewe;* Toulouse *quarter of lamb à la persillade; blanquette of lamb; cutlets of milk-fed lamb en culotte; leg of lamb with agaric; galimaufry of pork; ribs of pork à la persillade; ribs of pork en papillotes; lumbet of pork with potatoes, cassoulets* from Carcassonne, Castelnaudary and Toulouse; *estouffat of white beans* from Carcassonne; *saupiquet ariégeois* (with white beans); *roast sucking pig with piglet skins; tripe à l'albigeoise; tripe à la mode narbonnaise; cabassols* (Hérault); *manouis* (Hérault); *tripe with saffron; petarram* of Luchon; *lamb's pluck à la languedocienne; lamb's sweetbread pie with salsify; calf's head with olives; calf's brain en papillote; veal kidneys à la catalane.*

Fricassée of chicken; poultry pie with agaric, salsify, mushrooms and truffles; stuffed chicken; truffled capon; capon à la carcassonnaise (stuffed with sausage, olives, chicken livers, the neck stuffed with garlic bread, roasted on the spit); *truffled young turkey; young turkey with olives; duck à la bigarade; duck with olives; salmi of duck; pigeon à la catalane; compte of pigeon; pigeon in blood; goose with chestnuts; ragoût of goose with celery; salmi of guinea fowl; alicuit of chicken, turkey and goose; sanguette of chicken; turkey livers with capers, olives, or sautéed with garlic and lemon; foie gras of duck or goose with capers, grapes truffles, Frontignan wine, in pies, charcoal-grilled, potted;* Toulouse, Cazères and Luchon *pâtés de foie gras with truffles; pickled goose and duck; partridge à la catalane; salmi of partridge;*

Gastronomic map of Languedoc

partridge with cabbage; salmi of larks; larks en caisse; small birds baked in a pie; bunting en caisse; salmi of thrush; teal à la bigarade; hare au saupiquet; civet of hare; civet of izard (Pyrenean mountain goat); *pâté of young rabbit with truffles; hare pâté.*

The vegetable dishes, sweets and preserves made in Languedoc include: *Gratin of tomatoes and aubergines; aubergine stuffed à la catalane; agarics sautéed with garlic; cèpes à la persillade; green peas with ham; salsify deep-fried with sugar; stuffed cabbage, green cabbage sautéed and stewed; French beans with tomato sauce.*

Biscuits from Bédarieux; *honey croquettes* from Narbonne; *grape tart; touron* from Limoux; *Montpellier pie; Limoux cake; dry pepper cakes* from Limoux; *Alleluias* from Castelnaudary; *ring-biscuits* and *janots* from Albi; *flaky pastry* and *rauzel* from Carcassonne; *flaunes* or *flauzonnes* from Lodève; *heartcakes* from Tarn; *bras de Venus* from Narbonne; *pancakes; oreillettes* ('rabbits ears'); *pickled plums; crystallised fruit* from Carcassonne.

Wines – The province of Languedoc is very large and covers several wine-producing areas.

Côtes du Rhône. The best-known vineyards of the northern part of this area are situated on the right bank of the Rhône (opposite Valence and Tain-L'Hermitage) in the *département* of Ardèche. This is where the white and red wines of Saint-Joseph and the red wines of Cornas are produced. The Saint-Péray white wines, also from this area, are made into excellent sparkling wines following the *méthode champenoise*.

The *appellations* of the southern part of the right bank of the Côtes du Rhône are situated in the *département* of Gard. This is the home of the dry, fruity rosés of Tavel and Chusclan, the red and rosé wines of Lirac, and the red and white wines of Laudun. Another exceptional wine produced here is the V D.Q.S. *Costières du Gard.*

Aude and Hérault. Besides a large production of *vin ordinaire*, Aude produces the excellent red wines Fitou, Corbières and Minervois; also a sparkling wine called Blanquette de Limoux.

A very fine famous Muscat wine is produced in the *département* of Hérault in Frontignan.

Eastern Pyrenees. This *département* is the home of such great dessert wines as Rivesaltes and Muscat de Rivesaltes, Banyuls and Banyuls Grand Cru, Maury, Côtes d'Agly and Grand Roussillon.

Gaillac wine, from the *département* of Tarn, can be drunk as a still or sparkling wine.

LANGUEDOCIENNE (À LA) – Name given to a number of different dishes mostly served with a garnish of tomatoes, aubergines and *cèpes.* The sauce served with dishes prepared *à la languedocienne* is flavoured with garlic.

LAPWING. VANNEAU – Bird of passage with crested head, considered very good to eat. Its eggs are much sought after. The lapwing is cooked like plover (q.v.).

LARD. SAINDOUX – Cooking fat obtained from the melting down of pork fat. This fat, well prepared and free from impurities, is excellent and in certain regions of France, notably the south-west, is used in place of butter or oil for the greater part of their culinary preparations.

Preparation. Cut the fat in very small pieces and put it in a deep pot with 1 dl. (6 tablespoons, scant $\frac{1}{2}$ cup) water per 500 g. (1 lb.) fat.

Start cooking over a good heat, stirring with a wooden spoon, then cook over a gentle but sustained heat, stirring often, until the fat is completely melted. At this point the pieces of pork fat will appear well fried and crisp, while the liquid part will be very clear and will give off no more steam.

As soon as it is ready, strain through a very fine strainer or close woven cloth. Put into pots, which should be filled to the top. When the fat is completely set, cover the pots with paper, tie with string, and put them in a cool, dry place. The lard will keep for several months.

After the melting process is complete the strained pork fat leaves a residue that is considered very good to eat in the districts of France where lard is used.

Lard gras (pork fat) – The fat of pork lying between the skin and the flesh which is found all along the chine.

This fat, usually eaten fresh, is in two layers. The first layer, which is next to the flesh, is used chiefly in the preparation of lard. It is called melting fat. The second layer, next to the skin, is firmer and melts less readily. It is used in various ways in pork butchery and also for barding. It is known as hard fat.

Lard maigre – This is the fat of the pig's belly, streaked with muscular tissue. It can be salted or smoked.

In France this fat is usually eaten fresh but in England and in U.S.A. it is smoked and known as bacon, or salted and known as salt pork.

LARDING. LARDER – Threading lardoons of varying thickness into large cuts of meat, by means of a larding needle.

Larding fat. LARD À PIQUER – Pork fat used for interlarding meat. This fat should be white, firm and dry. In summer it must, if possible, be kept on ice before being cut into lardoons. The purpose for which the lardoons are used determines their length and thickness.

To make them, first cut the fat into rectangular slabs. When measured across, these slabs should correspond to the desired length of the lardoons.

Lay these slabs flat on a table, skin downwards. Slice the fat evenly. With the flat of the knife smooth the surface of the fat, and slice horizontally to obtain the lardoons.

They must be kept in a cool place until they are needed. Larding needles of different thicknesses are available for threading the lardoons into the meat.

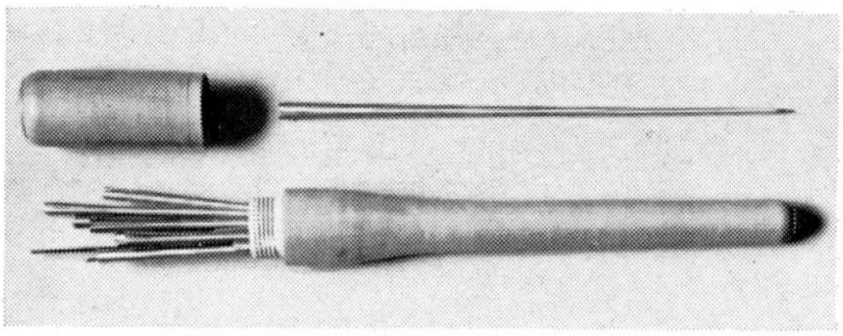

Larding needles (*Coutellerie André*)

LARDING NEEDLE. LARDOIRE – Implement used for larding cuts of meat, poultry and game.

LARDOONS. LARDONS – Strips of larding fat of varying lengths and thicknesses, threaded into meat, poultry and game by means of a larding needle.

In French, the name *lardon* is also used for blanched and fried diced bacon which is added to certain dishes such as *civet of hare, beef à la bourguignonne* etc., and to a number of garnishes.

LARK. ALOUETTE, MAUVIETTE – Bird, of which numerous species are known, including the *calandra* and *crested lark.* The lark has a very delicate flesh but, in some countries, it is in great demand more as an aviary bird than as food, because of its varied and harmonious song.

In France, larks are eagerly sought for the preparation of lark *pâté*, greatly esteemed by gastronomes.

Although the lark is found in Asia and in Africa, it belongs more to northern parts of Europe. Larks abound in Provence, in Languedoc, in the plains of Champagne and Burgundy, as well as in the steppes of southern Russia.

In France, the lark is always referred to as *mauviette* when it is used for the table. In former times this savoury bird was called *mauvis*, which derives from the Latin *mala avis*, meaning bad bird. It is strange that the qualification *mauvais* (bad) should have been applied to a bird which is so delicate to eat.

Larks à la bonne femme. MAUVIETTES À LA BONNE FEMME – Prepared in a casserole in the same way as *Thrushes à la bonne femme* (see THRUSH).

Larks in breadcrust. MAUVIETTES EN CROÛTE – Slit the birds along the back and bone them. Stuff them with a piece of *foie gras* about the size of a small nut. Press in a piece of truffle. Fold the birds back into shape. Place them in a buttered casserole, pressing them closely one against the other so that they keep their shape in cooking. Season. Pour on melted butter. Cook for 5 minutes in a very hot oven.

Drain the larks. Scoop out a round loaf and butter the inside. Line with *à gratin forcemeat* (see FORCEMEAT). Brown in the oven. Put the larks in the crust and finish cooking them in the oven for 8 minutes. Pour over them a few tablespoons Madeira-flavoured concentrated *Demi-glace sauce* (see SAUCE). Put the 'pie' on a dish covered with a napkin, and serve.

Larks en caisses. MAUVIETTES EN CAISSES – Proceed as for *Thrushes en caisses* (see THRUSH).

Larks à la minute. MAUVIETTES À LA MINUTE – Slit the larks along the back. Open and flatten them gently. Season with salt and pepper. Fry quickly in a frying pan, using best butter. Place each bird on a slice of bread fried in butter, and serve. Pour a little liqueur brandy and *Demi-glace sauce* (see SAUCE) into the pan and stir. Pour this sauce over the larks.

Lark pâté, cold. PÂTÉ FROID DE MAUVIETTES – Made with boned larks stuffed in the same way as cold *Partridge pâté* (see PÂTÉ).

Lark pâté, hot. PÂTÉ CHAUD DE MAUVIETTES – Made with boned larks stuffed with *foie gras* and truffles, in the same way as hot *Quail pâté* (see PÂTÉ).

Larks à la piémontaise. MAUVIETTES À LA PIÉMONTAISE – Stuff each lark with a piece of *à gratin forcemeat* (see FORCEMEAT) about the size of a small nut. Cook quickly in butter. Serve in a deep earthenware dish on a bed of polenta (q.v.) made with cheese. Press the birds down into the polenta, pour on melted butter and bake in the oven for 5 minutes. Sprinkle with a few tablespoons of game stock flavoured with Marsala.

Pilaf of larks. PILAF DE MAUVIETTES – Cook the larks quickly in butter. Arrange them in a circle on a bed of *Rice pilaf* (see PILAF). Pour a few tablespoons of game essence flavoured with Madeira over them.

Larks with risotto. MAUVIETTES AU RISOTTO – Proceed as for *Pilaf of larks*. Serve the larks on a bed of *Risotto* (see RICE).

LARUE – See RESTAURANTS OF BYGONE DAYS.

LASAGNE. LAZAGNE – Italian pasta cut in the shape of wide ribbons. It is cooked in the same way as macaroni (q.v.).

LATEX – The milky sap of a number of plants. The latex of the galactodendron of Columbia is drunk and used in cooking in the same way as milk.

LATOUR (Château) – One of the five great wines of Bordeaux (Paulliac-Médoc).

Latticed apple flan

LATTICED FLAN or TART. GRILLÉ – Flan or tart pastry shell filled with fruit, cream or other filling, covered with narrow criss-cross strips of pastry.

LATUILLE, LE PÈRE – See RESTAURANTS OF BYGONE DAYS.

LA VARENNE – A great chef who lived in the seventeenth century. La Varenne began his career as kitchen minion or *marmiton* in the home of the Duchesse de Bar, sister of Henry IV of France.

The King, author of the legendary 'poule au pot', observing that La Varenne was a bright lad, entrusted him with certain negotiations in an affair of the heart. As a result of this, he made such a great fortune that the Duchess remarked jestingly to him one day: 'You have done better by carrying my brother's "*poulets*" (amorous notes) than by larding mine'.

But La Varenne also had great talents as a chef. He was the author of the first systematically planned books on cookery and confectionery. These books are now rare, but they have been consulted for centuries and contain recipes which can still be used today. Here are their titles: *le Pâtissier français* (first edition 1653); *le Confiturier français* (1664); *le Cuisinier français* (first edition 1651, published by Pierre David at Lyons, now virtually unobtainable); and *l'École des ragoûts* (published at Lyons by Jacques Carnier in 1725).

LAVARET – Fish of the salmon family found in very deep lakes. There are also saltwater lavarets which periodically run to the rivers. The most sought after is that of Lake Le Bourget.

This fish is very delicate. All recipes for river trout and salmon trout are suitable for lavaret. (See TROUT.)

LAYON. COTEAUX DU LAYON – The vineyards of Anjou are to be found on these slopes. Some of the best white wines of the Maine-et-Loire *département* come from the vineyards on these slopes on the right bank of the Layon river.

LEAF. FEUILLE – Aerial part of plants, usually flat and green. A great many leaves are edible.

Vine leaves. FEUILLES DE VIGNE – Young vine leaves have various uses in cookery. They are used to wrap game (quail and partridges especially) along with strips of bacon or pork fat.

Turkish *dolmas* (balls of meat and rice) are wrapped in vine leaves.

Young tender vine leaves are sometimes used to make fritters, or finely chopped and added to green salads.

Vine leaves may also be used in decorative arrangements of fresh fruit.

LEAF CHERVIL. PLUCHES DE CERFEUIL – See GARNISHES, *Chervil leaves.*

LEAKAGE. COULAGE – Loss of liquor from a cask.

LEAVEN. LEVAIN – Sour wheat paste which has begun to ferment and which is in a fit state to induce fermentation, and thus cause kneaded dough to rise. The term leaven is often used instead of barm (brewer's yeast).

LEBERKNÖDELN (Hungarian cookery) – See SOUPS AND BROTHS.

LEBER-SUPPE (Hungarian cookery) – See SOUPS AND BROTHS.

LECITHIN. LÉCITHINE – Fat containing phosphorus which is found in egg yolks, brain, etc.

Leckerli (Swiss pâtisserie)

LECKERLI (Swiss pâtisserie) – Type of spiced biscuit, rectangular in shape and about 1 cm. ($\frac{1}{2}$ inch) thick.

Ingredients. 150 g. (5 oz., generous $\frac{1}{2}$ cup) fine sugar, 350 g. (12 oz., 1 cup) honey, 500 g. (18 oz., $4\frac{1}{2}$ cups) sieved flour, 25 g. (1 oz., $\frac{1}{4}$ cup) chopped fresh almonds, 50 g. (2 oz., $\frac{1}{3}$ cup) chopped candied lemon or orange peel, 1 teaspoon bicarbonate of soda, 25 g. (1 oz., $\frac{1}{4}$ cup) spices (ground cloves, nutmeg and ginger).

Method. Arrange the flour in a ring on the table. Put the honey in the centre of the ring and work with a spatula. Add all the other ingredients and knead well.

Put the mixture in rectangles on well-buttered baking trays. Bake in the oven. Cut into small rectangles and brush with milk just before taking out of the oven.

LEEK. POIREAU – Hardy biennial plant, the origins of which go back a very long way, which has never been found in its wild state and is believed to be a cultivated variety of oriental garlic.

The Egyptians held the leek in great esteem, as did the Romans. Nero had leek soup served to him every day. The Romans attributed to leeks the property of imparting and keeping up the sonority of the voice, and it is known that Nero was anxious to have a clear and sonorous voice for delivering his orations.

The leek has little nutritional value apart from being rich in Vitamin C and containing a variety of mineral salts and a little iron. Leek *bouillon* is a diuretic.

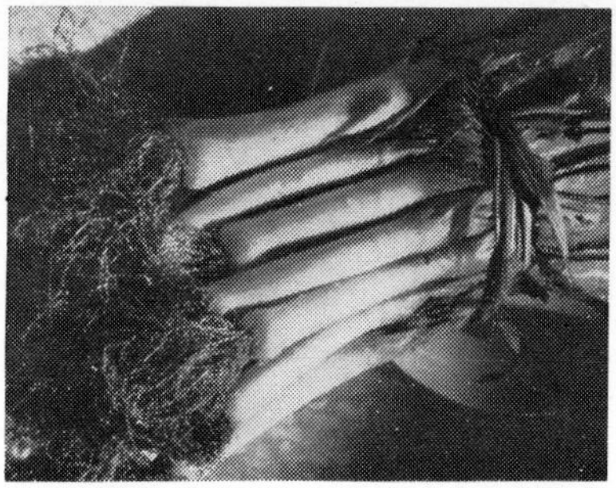

Bunch of leeks (*Kollar*)

This plant, which is mainly used as a flavouring for the stockpot or an ingredient of home-made soups, can also be prepared in various ways as a vegetable.

Leeks à la béchamel. POIREAUX À LA BÉCHAMEL – Trim the leeks, leaving only the white part. Parboil for 5 minutes in salted water, and drain. Cook in butter and arrange in a *timbale* or dish.

Cover with not too thick *Béchamel sauce* (see SAUCE.)

Boiled leeks. POIREAUX À L'ANGLAISE – Trim off the roots of the leeks and the greater part of the green ends, leaving only the white part. Take off the outside skin and wash the leeks. Tie them in bunches like asparagus and cook in boiling salted water.

Drain and dry them, serve on a folded napkin or in a perforated asparagus dish. Garnish with fresh parsley. Serve with melted butter.

Braised leeks. POIREAUX BRAISÉS –

Trim 12 large leeks, leaving only the white part. Cut into pieces and put into a sauté pan in which 3 tablespoons (scant $\frac{1}{4}$ cup) butter have been heated. Season with salt and pepper. Moisten with 5 tablespoons (6 tablespoons) water, cover the pan and simmer for about 40 minutes. Put the leeks into a vegetable dish. Sprinkle with the braising liquor to which an extra tablespoon of butter has been added.

Alternatively, the leeks can be moistened with clear meat stock instead of water.

Leeks with melted butter or other sauces. POIREAUX AU BEURRE FONDU – Boil in water and serve with melted butter or any other sauce, such as *Cream, Hollandaise, Mousseline, Vinaigrette* (see SAUCE).

Leeks à la creme. POIREAUX À LA CRÈME – Put the white part of the leeks into a buttered sauté pan. Season and cook gently for 15 minutes with a lid on. Moisten with fresh cream, covering the leeks. Simmer gently for 30 minutes with the lid on the pan. Put into a vegetable dish. Add a few tablespoons fresh cream to the pan juices and pour over the leeks.

Deep-fried leeks. POIREAUX EN FRITOT – Trim the leeks, leaving only the white part, and cut this into pieces. Marinate for 30 minutes in oil, lemon juice, salt and pepper, then parboil in salted water for 8 minutes.

Dip in a light batter and fry in smoking hot deep fat. When the leeks become golden and crisp, drain them, dry, season with fine salt, arrange in a heap on a folded napkin or on a paper doyley, and garnish with fried parsley.

Leeks au gratin. POIREAUX AU GRATIN – Trim the leeks, leaving only the white part. Parboil in salted water and cook gently in butter in a covered sauté pan. Put into a buttered ovenproof dish, sprinkle with grated cheese (Parmesan, for preference), pour over some melted butter, and brown in a slow oven or under a low grill.

Leeks à la grecque. POIREAUX À LA GRECQUE – White part of the leeks cooked in a *court-bouillon* (q.v.) consisting of water, oil and lemon juice, spiced with coriander. (See HORS-D'ŒUVRE, *Cold hors-d'œuvre*.)

Leeks Mornay. POIREAUX MORNAY – Cook the white part of the leeks in butter. Put them into a fireproof dish on a layer of *Mornay sauce* (see SAUCE). Sprinkle with grated cheese and melted butter and brown in the oven.

Velouté or cream of leek. VELOUTÉ, CRÈME DE POIREAUX – Recipes for these soups will be found in the section entitled SOUPS AND BROTHS.

Leeks à la vinaigrette. POIREAUX À LA VINAIGRETTE – Cook the white parts of the leeks in salted water. Drain and dry them, arrange in an *hors-d'œuvre* dish and season with oil, vinegar, salt and pepper.

LEFT-OVERS. RESTES – Sometimes foodstuffs are served in large quantity when, for example, they will be served at a subsequent meal as cold meat. It is done with roast meat or poultry or braised meat (*boeuf à la mode*, for example), when it is intended to reheat these meats to serve them again.

LEGUMIN. LÉGUMINE – Proteid substance resembling casein found in pulses (peas, beans, lentils). It is less well assimilated than animal protein, and combines with chalk to form an insoluble deposit. For this reason pulses cannot be satisfactorily cooked in hard water.

Lemons on a branch

LEMON. CITRON – Fruit of the lemon tree, very acid and highly scented. It originally came from India, but now grows out of doors in the Mediterranean region and extensively in California, U.S.A.

The juice and the zest of lemons are used in cooking to flavour and season a large number of dishes. Various creams, puddings and sauces are flavoured with the zest (the outside part of the skin). The juice is used to enhance the flavour of certain dishes and to season salads and mayonnaise instead of vinegar.

For the use of lemon as a flavouring for *bavarois*, creams, mousses, puddings, sauces, soufflés, see these words in their alphabetical order.

The food value of the lemon is a matter of some controversy; however, being exceptionally rich in Vitamin C it is undoubtedly the specific remedy for scurvy.

Lemon custard. CRÈME AU CITRON – Make a *Custard cream* (see CREAMS) using milk which has been boiled with lemon zest. Pass through a very fine strainer or silk tammy.

Lemon essence. ESSENCE DE CITRON – A commercial product used in cooking and *pâtisserie* in place of fresh lemon juice. It is very concentrated.

Lemon jam. CONFITURE DE CITRON – Blanch the skins of 24 lemons. When they are half cooked drain them. Chop up half the lemon skins and rub them through a sieve. Cut the rest into thin strips. Mix these ingredients and moisten with the juice of 8 lemons. Add an amount of sugar equal in weight to the lemon skins. Cook in a copper pan in the same way as other jams.

Lemon manqué. MANQUÉ AU CITRON – See MANQUÉ. Use lemon-flavoured sugar for the mixture and add diced crystallised citron or ½ teaspoon lemon essence to it.

When the *manqué* is baked and turned out, mask it completely with egg whites whisked with sugar until stiff. Frost with icing sugar. Sprinkle pistachio nuts on top. Dry in the oven but do not brown.

Preserved lemon peel. ÉCORCE DE CITRON CONFITE (CITRONNAT) – Blanch pieces of fresh lemon peel, from which the pith has been removed. In this way only the zest is used. Drain the pieces and put them in syrup (q.v.). Leave all night in the syrup.

Next day take out the peel and cook the syrup until it measures 25° on the saccharometer or until it drops in a short thread from the spoon. Put back the peel. Leave to soak in syrup overnight again and repeat the operation for several days, cooking the syrup for the last time to the point of crystallisation.

Lemon syrup. SIROP DE CITRON – Soak the zest of 12 fine lemons in their own juice. Prepare 1 litre (1¾ pints, generous quart) hot sugar syrup measuring 36° on the saccharometer. Add the juice and zest to this syrup. Leave for 5 to 6 days. Filter.

Lemon zest. ZESTE DE CITRON – This is used to flavour creams and other preparations for sweets by grating the skin with a lump of sugar. The sugar becomes impregnated with the essential oil of the lemon and is then put in the mixture to be flavoured.

Milk can also be flavoured with lemon zest and used in creams and custards. The zest which is used to flavour certain culinary preparations is prepared in this way:

Remove the zest from the fruit with a sharp knife. According to the use to which it is to be put, chop the zest finely, or slice it into fine strips. In the latter case, blanch the lemon *julienne*, drain and dry it.

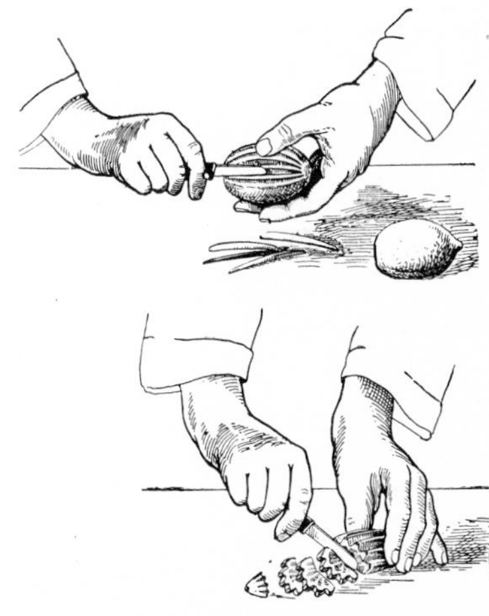

How to groove and slice a lemon for garnishing

LEMONADE. CITRONNADE, LIMONADE – Drink consisting of lemon juice, sugar and water.

Lemonade I. CITRONNADE – Dissolve 250 g. (9 oz., 2 cups) lump sugar in 1 litre ($1\frac{3}{4}$ pints, generous quart) filtered water. Add the juice and zest of 2 lemons to the syrup. Leave to infuse for 3 hours in a cool place.

Strain through a fine strainer. A siphon of soda water, or fresh water, can be added to the lemonade. Serve cold and put a slice of lemon in each glass.

Lemonade II. LIMONADE CUITE – Cut a lemon into thin slices. Remove the seeds. Infuse for 1 hour in $\frac{1}{2}$ litre (scant pint, $2\frac{1}{4}$ cups) boiling water. Add 25 g. (1 oz., 2 tablespoons) sugar.

Fizzy lemonade. LIMONADE GAZEUSE – This lemonade is usually artificially made and aerated with carbonic acid gas, like manufactured soda water. It is sold in bottles or siphons.

Lemon sole

LEMON SOLE. LIMANDE-SOLE – The name lemon sole is a corruption of the French *limande-sole*. This fish is really a kind of dab but, unlike the dab and other flat fish such as flounder and plaice, it is elongated and oval in shape, and is thus somewhat similar to a sole in appearance.

Some authorities assert that lemon sole is very little inferior in quality to the sole, but this opinion is not shared by gastronomes, who find this fish comparatively stringy and tasteless. It corresponds to the *yellowtail flounder* in U.S.A.

All recipes for brill (q.v.) and sole (q.v.) are suitable for lemon sole.

LENT. CARÊME – Forty-day fast imposed by the Catholic religion, from Ash Wednesday till Easter. This period of fasting in the early Church had excellent physical effects by imposing on the digestive system, worn out by gastronomic excess during the winter season, a much needed rest.

Brillat-Savarin tell us that towards the middle of the eighteenth century the normal régime in bourgeois families consisted of four meals:

Breakfast, which took place before 9 a.m. and consisted of bread, cheese, fruit, sometimes a *pâté* or cold meat. (The habit of drinking coffee had not yet penetrated into provincial life.)

Lunch, which took place between noon and 1 p.m., with soup, the boiled meat of the *pot-au-feu*, and vegetable accompaniments according to the season.

Around 4 p.m. there was a light meal enjoyed as a rule by the ladies of the household and the children.

Supper was at 8 p.m., with *entrée*, roast, side-dishes, salad and dessert.

During Lent breakfast was omitted, meat was excluded from the lunch menu, and in the evening supper was replaced by a meal which contained no eggs, butter, or anything of a live nature.

Battle between Carême (Lent) and Mardi-Gras (from an 18th century print)

The real test of culinary art was to create a rigorously apostolic meal which had all the appearances of an excellent supper.

Little by little the Church relaxed its original severity, and permitted the use of butter and eggs and, later, the flesh of 'cold-blooded' animals, such as fish. Still later, certain aquatic game considered to be cold-blooded, such as the spoonbill, pintail, scoter-duck, moorhen, coot, teal, water-rail, curlew, heron, godwit and sandpiper were allowed.

A Lenten meal could also include an impressive list of sumptuous removes, *entrées* and roasts. Understood in these terms the Lenten diet does not differ from normal diet from the health point of view.

For Lent menus see FESTIVE COOKERY.

Lent anecdotes. CARÊME ANECDOTIQUE – 'Madame Victoire (sister of Louis XV), good, sweet and kindly, lived in the most refreshing simplicity in a society that loved her dearly; her household adored her. In exemplary fashion (and without stirring from her luxurious *bergère* in Versailles) she fulfilled all her religious duties by giving all she possessed to the poor and by diligently observing fastings and Lent. In fact, the same lady's table was so noted for its meagreness that the parasite gourmets kept well away from it. It was not that Madame Victoire did not appreciate good food, but she had the strictest religious scruples concerning what should be eaten during penance. I have seen her tormented by doubt over a duck served to her during Lent. The question was whether the bird was lean or fat. She solicited the opinion of a bishop who happened to be attending the dinner. He immediately assumed the demeanour and tone of a judge at the last court of appeal. He told the princess that doubts such as these necessitated placing the cooked bird upon a very cold silver platter. If the creature's juices congealed within a quarter of an hour, it was to be considered fat; if, on the other hand, the juices remained liquid, it could be eaten without misgiving. Madame Victoire lost no time in putting the matter to the test: the juices did not congeal, a fact that delighted the princess since she was very partial to that particular type of wildfowl. The truth was that the period of fasting which Madame Victoire so diligently observed also upset her. She waited impatiently for the midnight bell on the Saturday before Easter and saw to it that she was immediately brought a plump fowl with rice and other succulent dishes.'

'Desbarreaux, upon hearing a peal of thunder while eating a bacon omelette, opened the window and flung his plate out into the night muttering: "All that fuss just for an omelette!"'

'One town celebrated Lent with a procession in which a beautiful, frail young maid played the part of a poor, wretched, barefooted girl. The moment the procession was over, the hypocrite went off to dine with her lover on a quarter of lamb and a ham. The odour of these drifted down the street, whereupon several people went up to the room where she was enjoying herself and dragged her downstairs, obliging her to parade through the town with the spit-roasted quarter of lamb slung round her shoulders and the ham strung round her neck.' (Brantôme.)

LENTIL. LENTILLE – A pulse (leguminous seed), originally from central Asia, where it was cultivated in prehistoric times. There are numerous varieties. This vegetable contains more protein than any other; 100 g. (4 oz.) provide 337 calories.

Lentils are rich in mineral salts, especially phosphorous and iron. They are particularly recommended for children, anaemics, nursing and expectant mothers, provided that none of these suffers from digestive troubles. It is advisable to purée them or to mix them with potatoes to counteract the effect of the unassimilable lentil husks.

Cooking of lentils. CUISSON DES LENTILLES. Proceed as for *Dried white beans* (see BEAN). Like these, lentils must be soaked in cold water before cooking, but not for long. If they are soaked too long, they begin to germinate, which renders them, if not actually poisonous, at least more difficult to digest.

After cooking in meat or vegetable stock, lentils can be prepared in any way suitable for dried white beans.

LENTISK. LENTISQUE – Bush of the same family as the turpentine tree. It is grown in the Greek Archipelago. Its fruit yields an edible oil. A resin known as mastic is collected from its trunk by making incisions in it. This resin is used to flavour the spirit known as Raki.

LÉOGNAN – Among the excellent Graves wines produced in this Gironde commune are the Château-Haut-Bailly, Château-Carbonnieux, Domaine de Chevalier, Château-Malartic-Lagravière and Château-Olivier.

LÉOVILLE – Red Bordeaux wine classed among the second growths of the great Médoc wines.

Léoville-Las-Cases, Léoville-Poyferré and Léoville-Barton, which are made in the commune of Saint-Julien, are highly prized by connoisseurs.

LEPIOTA. LÉPIOTE – Species of fungus of which a number of varieties are edible, the best-known in France being the *cultivated lepiota*, also known as the *coulemelle*.

LEPIDOSTEUS (Gar-pike). LEPIDOSTÉE – The peculiarity of this fish is that it has very hard, pebbly scales, so that it is encased in a veritable suit of armour.

It is to be found in the rivers and lakes of Central America. Its flesh is fairly delicate. All recipes for pike (q.v.) are suitable for this dish.

LES LAUMES – See CHEESE.

LESSER CELANDINE. FICAIRE – Plant whose leaves are sometimes eaten after being blanched. They are cooked in the same way as spinach (q.v.).

LETTUCE. LAITUE – Plant which grows wild all over Europe, in the Caucasus and in India. It has been cultivated in Egypt and China from time immemorial.

The word 'lettuce' comes from the Latin *lactuca*, because lettuce, when it is cut, exudes a milky juice. In ancient times, the lettuce was looked upon as a sacred plant (it figures in the Passover ritual of the Hebrews at the same time as the paschal lamb). It was brought into favour in ancient Rome by Antonius Musa, physician to the Emperor Augustus.

Galen asserts that this plant cured him of stomach disorders when he was young. He adds that lettuce brought him restful sleep in his old age.

Among the Romans, lettuce was usually served at the end of the evening meal. Under the Emperor Domitian, the fashion changed and it became customary to serve lettuce at the beginning of the meal.

The Romans now regarded lettuce, especially when dressed as a salad, as an appetiser, and so took to serving it as an *hors-d'oeuvre*.

Lettuce is in season all the year round, except in winter. All the common varieties can be eaten raw, in salads. Cabbage lettuces are mainly used in cookery, but cos lettuces can also be cooked. Lettuce can be braised, like endive.

Braised lettuce in meat stock. LAITUES BRAISÉES AU GRAS – Trim the lettuces by removing the tough green outer leaves. Parboil them for 5 minutes in salt water. Cool them under running water. Squeeze the leaves to extract all the water. Tie 2 or 3 lettuces together.

Butter a pan and line it with bacon rinds, sliced onions and carrots. Lay the lettuces in this pan. Cover with rather fat stock. Bring to the boil. Cover and cook in a moderate oven for 50 minutes.

Drain the lettuces, and untie them. Cut each in half, lengthwise. Trim the leaves at both ends and fold each half in two. Boil down the cooking stock, strain it through a fine sieve, and pour over the lettuces.

Lettuces prepared in this way can be served as they are, as a vegetable, as a garnish for various main dishes, or may be cooked further with various sauces as indicated below.

Vegetarian braised lettuce. LAITUES BRAISÉES AU MAIGRE – Proceed as above, omitting the bacon rind. Moisten with water instead of stock.

Lettuce with bone-marrow. LAITUES À LA MOELLE – Arrange braised lettuces in a circle in a shallow pie dish, alternating with slices of bread fried in butter. Put on top of each lettuce 2 slices of poached beef marrow. Add a little *Demi-glace sauce* (see SAUCE) to the braising stock. Boil down the stock, add butter, strain and pour over the dish. Sprinkle a little chopped parsley on top of each slice of marrow.

Lettuce in browned butter. LAITUES AU BEURRE NOISETTE – Braise the lettuces, and halve and roll them. Arrange in the form of a rosette on a dish. Before serving, pour a few tablespoons *Brown butter* (see BUTTER) over them.

Chiffonnade of lettuce in butter for garnishing. LAITUES EN CHIFFONNADE AU BEURRE – Shred very finely 4 trimmed and washed lettuces. Put them in a pan with 2 tablespoons (3 tablespoons) butter. Season with table salt. Moisten with 3 tablespoons (scant $\frac{1}{4}$ cup) *bouillon* (q.v.). Cover and simmer gently. Use as indicated in the recipe for whatever main dish is to be served with this garnish.

Chiffonnade of lettuce for cold dishes. LAITUES EN CHIFFONNADE – Shred very finely some trimmed and washed lettuces. Squeeze them to extract all moisture. Season with oil, vinegar, salt and pepper.

This *chiffonnade* is used mainly to decorate salads and mayonnaise of fish, shellfish or poultry.

Chiffonnade of lettuce with cream as garnish. LAITUES EN CHIFFONNADE À LÁ CRÈME – Prepare and cook finely shredded lettuce as for the preceding recipe.

When the lettuce is soft, moisten it with $1\frac{1}{2}$ dl. ($\frac{1}{4}$ pint,

$\frac{2}{3}$ cup) cream. Simmer for a few minutes. Serve as garnish with a suitable main dish.

Lettuce Colbert (Vegetarian cookery). LAITUES COLBERT – Cook the lettuces in butter in a covered pan. Drain and halve them. Fold the halves into pear shapes. Squeeze them gently, dip in egg and breadcrumbs, and deep-fry.

Arrange them in a circle on a dish, and cover with *Maître d'hôtel butter* (see BUTTER, *Compound butters*).

Creamed lettuce. LAITUES À LA CRÈME – Halve or quarter braised lettuces if they are too big and arrange them neatly in a buttered frying pan. Simmer for 5 minutes. Cover with boiling fresh cream and simmer until this is reduced by half. Arrange the lettuces in a shallow serving dish, alternating them with croûtons of fried bread. Coat with the cream.

Deep-fried lettuce. LAITUES EN FRITOT – Braise the lettuces as for *Braised lettuce*. Fold the quarters and put them in a dish. Season with oil, lemon juice, salt and pepper. Leave them in this marinade for 30 minutes. Just before serving, dip them in a light batter and deep-fry. Garnish with fried parsley.

Lettuce au gratin (in white sauce). LAITUES AU GRATIN – Arrange halved braised lettuces in a *gratin* dish. Pour *Mornay sauce* (see SAUCE) over them. Sprinkle with grated cheese, pour on melted butter, and brown.

Lettuce in gravy. LAITUES AU JUS – Braise lettuces, halve them, and place them in a buttered pan. Sprinkle with a few tablespoons of well-seasoned brown veal stock. Simmer. Arrange the lettuces in a ring, alternating with slices of bread fried in butter. Boil down the cooking stock, add butter and pour over the dish.

Lettuce à la hollandaise. LAITUES À LA HOLLANDAISE – Arrange on a dish, alternating with slices of bread fried in butter, halved lettuces braised in a vegetable stock. Cover with *Hollandaise sauce* (see SAUCE, *Cold sauces*).

Lettuce à l'italienne. LAITUES À L'ITALIENNE – Proceed as for *Lettuce in gravy*, using *Italian sauce* (see SAUCE) instead of the stock.

Lettuce Mornay. LAITUES MORNAY – See *Lettuce au gratin (in white sauce)*.

Lettuce purée. PURÉE DE LAITUE – Sieve lettuces braised in meat or vegetable stock through a fine sieve. Heat this purée. To give it body, add a few tablespoons of concentrated and strained *Béchamel sauce* (see SAUCE). Season. Mix and add butter.

Mashed potatoes can be added, as they can be added to the purées of all watery vegetables.

Lettuce salad. SALADE DE LAITUE – See SALAD.

Lettuce soufflé. SOUFFLÉ DE LAITURE – Made with purée of lettuce in the same way as for *Endive soufflé* (see ENDIVE).

Lettuce soup. POTAGE DE LAITUE – See SOUPS AND BROTHS, *Purée of lettuce soup*.

Stuffed lettuce. LAITUES FARCIES – Blanch the lettuces. Cool under running water and squeeze dry. Slit them in half without cutting the stump. Season them inside. Fill each lettuce with a fine forcemeat mixed with *duxelles* (q.v.). Each piece of mixed forcemeat should be the size of an egg. Close up the lettuces, tie, and braise them.

Stuffed lettuce can be served as a vegetable, arranged in a circle on a dish with fried bread between and covered with any suitable sauce, or it may be used as a garnish.

Lettuce stumps. MOELLE DE LAITUE – The stumps of cos lettuces which have gone to seed are mainly used. These stumps, after trimming, are cooked like asparagus, or in any of the ways suitable for artichoke stalks or endive stumps.

LEVERET. LEVRAUT – Young hare. (See HARE.)

LEVROUX – See CHEESE.

LIAISON – See THICKENING.

LIÉGEOISE (À LA) – Method of cooking, applied to various foodstuffs. Its characteristic feature is the use of juniper flavouring. (See OFFAL or VARIETY MEATS, *Calves' kidneys à la liégeoise*; THRUSH, *Thrushes à la liégeoise*.)

LIGHTEN. DÉTENDRE – To make a mixture lighter by the addition of eggs or some liquid.

LIGHTS. MOU – In the tripe trade this term is used to designate the lungs of certain animals. For the preparation of lambs' and calves' lights, see OFFAL or VARIETY MEATS.

LIMANDELLE – A flat fish, also called *cardine* or *mère de sole*, very good to eat. It has an elongated oval body, about 25 to 35 cm. (10 to 14 inches) long, with fragile, shaded scales. Its eyes are placed on the left side, which is pale yellow with brown shading. Its blind side is white. All recipes for plaice (q.v.) and brill (q.v.) are suitable for this fish.

LIME. LIMON – Thin-skinned citrus fruit.

Lime tree. TILLEUL – Tree of which there are several species in Europe. The scented flowers are used in infusions for their soothing and antispasmodic properties. The American species (*Tilia Americana*) is called a linden tree.

The flowers are also used in pastry-making and confectionery to flavour creams, ices and sweets (desserts) of various kinds.

LIMONADIERS – Name given in France in former times to sellers of non-alcoholic drinks. In the Middle Ages the only drinks available were beer, hippocras (mead), sweet or heavy wines. Anyone was free to stock and sell wines, without seeking permission of any authority. In the sixteenth century, spirits began to be widely drunk. They were sold by the small glassful at vinegar shops.

It was the Italians, many of whom followed Catherine de Medici into France, who introduced a number of entirely new drinks. Among these were lemonade, orangeade, bitter citron cordial, frangipane water, sherbets, *populo*, etc. The drink which found most favour with the public was lemonade, and the name *limonadiers* stuck to shop keepers who sold other drinks as well.

LIMOUSIN – See MARCHE AND LIMOUSIN.

LIMOUSINE (À LA) – Method of preparing red cabbage.

Cuts of meat and poultry garnished with red cabbage cooked in this way are also called *à la limousine*.

LIMOUX, BLANQUETTE DE – Sparkling wine, fairly heavy, made at Limoux in the Aude district.

LIMPET. BERNICLE – See BARNACLE.

LINE. FONCER – To cover the bottom of a stewpan or saucepan with strips of bacon and rounds of vegetables; or to cover the inside of a *terrine* with strips of pork fat; or to cover the sides and bottom of a mould or dish with pastry.

LING. LINGUE – Fish of the cod family, also called *sea burbot* or *long cod*. It is fished in the same latitudes as cod. It is quite good to eat, is often salted like cod, and is prepared in the same way as cod (q.v.) or codling.

In U.S.A. the name ling is sometimes given to the freshwater burbot.

LINNET. LINOT-LINOTTE – Small, edible but rather tasteless bird which feeds on linseed or hempseed. It is prepared in the same way as lark (q.v.).

LION – Lion meat, though edible, is seldom used in cookery. It is rather tasteless and must be steeped in an aromatic marinade before cooking.

All recipes for beef (q.v.) are suitable for lion.

LIQUEUR – Name given to various composite alcoholic drinks. Nowadays these are made from a mixture of spirits and syrups. There are innumerable liqueurs with many different names. Their alcoholic content varies.

Liqueurs can be made in the home. Their quality varies according to the spirits or alcohol used.

All home-made liqueurs are made by steeping fruit and other basic ingredients in alcohol or spirits. The best spirits to use are 70° (US 80°) proof. Liqueurs made in this way are often called ratafias.

Acacia liqueur or ratafia I. LIQUEUR, RATAFIA D'ACACIA – Remove stalks from acacia flowers and steep 100 g. (4 oz.) of the flowers in 1 litre ($1\frac{3}{4}$ pints, generous quart) spirits, preferably white, proof 88° (US 100°).

Leave to infuse for 1 month, keeping the hermetically sealed container in a warm place.

At the end of a month add 125 g. (4 oz., $\frac{1}{2}$ cup) sugar. Stir from time to time until all the sugar has dissolved. This takes about 2 weeks. Filter through filter paper, and bottle.

Acacia liqueur or ratafia II (old recipe). LIQUEUR, RATAFIA D'ACACIA – Put 200 g. (7 oz.) acacia flowers in a deep dish with alternate layers of fine sugar. Steep for 24 hours.

Moisten with $2\frac{1}{2}$ dl. (scant $\frac{1}{2}$ pint, generous cup) water and strain. Add to the strained liquid a syrup made with $1\frac{1}{2}$ dl. ($\frac{1}{4}$ pint, $\frac{2}{3}$ cup) water and the remaining sugar – 750 g. ($1\frac{1}{2}$ lb., 3 cups) are needed in all. Finally, add 6 dl. (1 pint, $2\frac{1}{2}$ cups) spirits.

Leave to steep for a few months. Filter and bottle.

Angelica liqueur or ratafia. LIQUEUR, RATAFIA D'ANGÉLIQUE – *Ingredients.* 900 g. (2 lb.) angelica, 900 g. (2 lb., 7 cups) lump sugar, 5 litres ($4\frac{1}{2}$ quarts, $5\frac{1}{2}$ quarts) spirits, $1\frac{1}{2}$ tablespoons (2 tablespoons) cinnamon, 1 teaspoon nutmeg, 1 clove, $\frac{1}{2}$ litre (scant pint, $2\frac{1}{4}$ cups) filtered water.

Method. Cut the angelica into small pieces and put them together with the sugar, spirits, and other ingredients in a large jar. Seal the jar hermetically and leave for 2 months.

Sieve through a fine strainer over a large bowl. Press the pieces of angelica to extract all the juice.

Filter through filter paper. Bottle, cork well, and keep at a moderate temperature, in a cupboard rather than a cellar.

Anise or anisette liqueur or ratafia I. LIQUEUR, RATAFIA D'ANIS (ANISETTE) – Put 25 g. (1 oz.) green, crushed anise, $\frac{1}{4}$ teaspoon cinnamon, $1\frac{1}{2}$ tablespoons (2 tablespoons) coriander into 1 litre ($1\frac{3}{4}$ pints, generous quart) spirits. Infuse for 1 month. Add 500 g. (18 oz., $2\frac{1}{4}$ cups) sugar dissolved in a little water. Filter and bottle.

Anise liqueur or ratafia II. LIQUEUR, RATAFIA D'ANIS – Make a syrup of $2\frac{1}{2}$ kg. ($5\frac{1}{2}$ lb., 11 cups) sugar and 1 litre ($1\frac{3}{4}$ pints, generous quart) water. Strain through muslin.

Dissolve 3 g. ($\frac{1}{10}$ oz.) essence of Chinese anise, $\frac{1}{2}$ g. ($\frac{1}{60}$ oz.) essence of Seville orange, $\frac{1}{2}$ g. ($\frac{1}{60}$ oz.) essence of cinnamon, 5 g. ($\frac{1}{6}$ oz.) essence of anise, 1 g. ($\frac{1}{30}$ oz.) essence of nutmeg, 1 g. ($\frac{1}{30}$ oz.) tincture of vanilla in 15 g. ($\frac{1}{2}$ oz.) spirits 70° (US 80°) proof.

Mix thoroughly and add $1\frac{1}{2}$ litres ($2\frac{3}{4}$ pints, $3\frac{1}{4}$ pints) alcohol 85° (US 97°) proof. Leave to stand for 24 hours. Filter and bottle.

Anise liqueur III or cream of aniseed (old recipe). LIQUEUR, CRÈME D'ANIS – 100 g. (4 oz.) whole aniseed, 4 litres ($3\frac{1}{2}$ quarts, $4\frac{1}{2}$ quarts) spirits 36° (US 42°) proof.

Infuse for 6 days and strain through muslin.

Add 3 kg. ($6\frac{1}{2}$ lb., 13 cups) sugar dissolved in 2 litres ($3\frac{1}{2}$ pints, $4\frac{1}{2}$ pints) water.

Leave to stand for several days, until the liqueur is clear. Strain through muslin.

Apricot liqueur. LIQUEUR D'ABRICOT – *Ingredients.* 30 apricots, 4 litres ($3\frac{1}{2}$ quarts, $4\frac{1}{2}$ quarts) white wine, 1 kg. ($2\frac{1}{4}$ lb., $4\frac{1}{2}$ cups) sugar, 1 litre ($1\frac{3}{4}$ pints, generous quart) 58° (US 66°) proof spirits, $1\frac{1}{2}$ tablespoons (2 tablespoons) cinnamon.

Method. Put the apricots in a large pan. Moisten with the white wine and bring to the boil. Add the sugar, cinnamon and spirits.

Take the pan off the heat. Cover and leave to infuse for 4 days. Strain, filter, and bottle. Cork the bottles tightly. Keep in a dry place.

Blackcurrant liqueur I. LIQUEUR DE CASSIS – *Ingredients.* 1 litre ($1\frac{3}{4}$ pints, generous quart) spirits, 1 kg. ($2\frac{1}{4}$ lb.) blackcurrants, 750 g. ($1\frac{3}{4}$ lb. $3\frac{1}{2}$ cups) sugar, 1 clove, 1 g. ($\frac{1}{30}$ oz.) cinnamon stick. To give a stronger flavour, add 10 blackcurrant leaves, the greenest available, from the top branches.

Method. Put the clove, cinnamon and blackcurrant leaves in a bowl. On top lay the blackcurrants, picked over and well crushed by hand. Pour the spirits over them, mix, add the sugar and mix again. Put the mixture in a stone jar and seal. Keep the jar in a warm place (in the sun, if possible) for at least 1 month to ensure a thorough infusion. At the end of this time strain the liqueur through a sieve over a bowl. Extract all liquid by squeezing the pulp in a coarse linen cloth.

Filter and bottle the liqueur.

Water should not be added to help dissolve the sugar, since this would lower the alcohol content of the liqueur. If too strong, add a plain syrup of 500 g. (18 oz., $2\frac{1}{4}$ cups) sugar to $\frac{1}{2}$ litre (scant pint, $2\frac{1}{4}$ cups) water. Dissolve cold.

Blackcurrant liqueur II (old recipe). LIQUEUR DE CASSIS – Infuse 1 kg. ($2\frac{1}{4}$ lb.) blackcurrants, 1 teaspoon each of ground cloves and ground cinnamon, 3 litres ($5\frac{1}{4}$ pints, $6\frac{1}{2}$ pints) spirits and 750 g. ($1\frac{3}{4}$ lb., $3\frac{1}{2}$ cups) sugar in a jar. Leave for 15 days, mixing every day.

Strain through muslin, filter, and, when perfectly clear, bottle.

Carnation liqueur or ratafia. LIQUEUR, RATAFIA D'OEILLET – Steep in 1 litre ($1\frac{3}{4}$ pints, generous quart) alcohol, at 39° (US 44°) proof, 250 g. (9 oz.) carnation petals. Spice with a clove and $\frac{1}{2}$ teaspoon cinnamon. Leave for 1 month, then filter.

Add a syrup made from 500 g. (18 oz., $2\frac{1}{4}$ cups) sugar and $\frac{1}{2}$ litre (scant pint, $2\frac{1}{4}$ cups) water. Filter once more. Bottle.

Cherry liqueur or ratafia. LIQUEUR, RATAFIA DE CERISE – Crush 4 kg. ($8\frac{3}{4}$ lb.) Montmorency cherries with the stones. Put them in a bowl and leave to ferment for 4 days.

Add 4 litres ($3\frac{1}{2}$ quarts, $4\frac{1}{2}$ quarts) alcohol, 39° (US 44°) proof spirit, and 1 kg. ($2\frac{1}{4}$ lb., $4\frac{1}{2}$ cups) sugar. Put the mixture in a jar and leave to infuse for a month. Squeeze through muslin. Filter and bottle.

Cherry liqueur or ratafia, Grenoble style. LIQUEUR, RATAFIA DE CERISE À LA FAÇON DE GRENOBLE – Infuse in 2 litres ($3\frac{1}{2}$ pints, $4\frac{1}{2}$ pints) brandy 125 g. (4 oz., $\frac{3}{4}$ cup) blanched cherry stone kernels, 10 g. ($\frac{1}{3}$ oz.) peach blossom or leaves, 1 teaspoon cinnamon, 12 cloves.

When the brandy is thoroughly impregnated with the aroma of these ingredients, pour it over 2 litres ($3\frac{1}{2}$ pints, $4\frac{1}{2}$ pints) cherry juice with 500 g. (18 oz., $2\frac{1}{4}$ cups) sugar dissolved in it. Mix. Filter and bottle.

Liqueur or ratafia of cherry stones. LIQUEUR, RATAFIA DE NOYAUX DE CERISES – This can be made from the stones of cherries used for jam-making.

Wash and dry the stones. When they are quite dry, crush them. Put them to infuse in alcohol, allowing 1 kg. ($2\frac{1}{4}$ lb., 6 cups) stones to 1 litre ($1\frac{3}{4}$ pints, generous quart) spirits.

Proceed as indicated in the previous recipe.

Citron liqueur or ratafia. LIQUEUR, RATAFIA DE CÉDRAT – Made with the peel and juice of citrons, in the same way as *Orange ratafia* (see below).

Coffee liqueur (old recipe). LIQUEUR DE CAFÉ – Roast $1\frac{1}{2}$ kg. ($3\frac{1}{4}$ lb., 13 cups) best mocha beans and grind very fine. Infuse in 5 litres ($4\frac{1}{2}$ quarts, $5\frac{1}{2}$ quarts) alcohol 58° (US 66°) proof, and 4 litres ($3\frac{1}{2}$ quarts, $4\frac{1}{2}$ quarts) water. After 10 days of infusion, distil in a *bain-marie* to obtain 5 litres ($4\frac{1}{2}$ quarts, $5\frac{1}{2}$ quarts). If a stronger flavour of coffee is desired, more fresh coffee can be infused in the liqueur. Next, dissolve $2\frac{1}{2}$ kg. ($5\frac{1}{2}$ lb., 11 cups) sugar in $2\frac{1}{2}$ litres ($4\frac{1}{2}$ pints, $5\frac{1}{2}$ pints) water and add this to the liqueur. Leave to stand overnight and filter next day.

Curaçao liqueur. LIQUEUR DE CURAÇAO – *Ingredients.* 50 g. (2 oz.) bitter orange peel, 1 teaspoon cinnamon, 30 g. (1 oz.) Pernambuco bark, 1 clove, 1 litre ($1\frac{3}{4}$ pints, generous quart) pure wine alcohol 79° (US 90°) proof, 500 g. (18 oz., $2\frac{1}{4}$ cups) sugar, $\frac{1}{2}$ litre (scant pint, $2\frac{1}{4}$ cups) water.

Method. Infuse the orange peel, Pernambuco bark, cinnamon and clove for 3 weeks. Make a syrup of the sugar and water and pour it over these ingredients.

Filter and bottle. If necessary, colour with carmine and caramel.

Dantzig liqueur. LIQUEUR DE DANTZIG – This liqueur is made from sweetened 85° (US 97°) proof grain spirits with water added, and flavoured with various herbs.

The characteristic feature of this liqueur is that it has tiny specks of gold leaf floating in it.

Fennel liqueur. LIQUEUR DE FENOUIL – This is made from fennel stalks in the same way as *Angelica liqueur*.

Grande-Chartreuse – The liqueur of the Grande-Chartreuse, generally called Chartreuse, is one of the most famous liqueurs now being made. It is produced by the distillation of herbs gathered in Alpine regions, and is named after the monastery of the Grande-Chartreuse, where it was first manufactured by the monks.

Juniper liqueur or ratafia. LIQUEUR, RATAFIA DE GENIÈVRE – Make a syrup of 4 kg. ($8\frac{3}{4}$ lb., $17\frac{1}{2}$ cups) sugar dissolved in a little water. With this syrup, moisten 4 litres ($3\frac{1}{2}$ quarts, $4\frac{1}{2}$ quarts) juniper berries placed in a stone crock with 4 litres ($3\frac{1}{2}$ quarts, $4\frac{1}{2}$ quarts) alcohol.

Seal and leave to infuse for 15 days, shaking the crock from time to time after the first 3 or 4 days. Strain the liqueur through a muslin bag. Bottle.

This liqueur is good only when it has been kept a very long time.

Lemon liqueur or ratafia. LIQUEUR, RATAFIA DE CITRON – Made with the peel and juice of lemons, in the same way as *Orange liqueur* (see below).

Orange liqueur or ratafia. LIQUEUR, RATAFIA D'ORANGE – *Ingredients.* 6 oranges, 1 litre ($1\frac{3}{4}$ pints, generous quart) brandy or pure white spirits of wine, 500 g. (18 oz., 4 cups) lump sugar, $\frac{1}{2}$ teaspoon cinnamon, $\frac{1}{2}$ teaspoon coriander.

Method. Peel the oranges carefully, so that none of the white pith is mixed with the outer rind. Chop the rind finely.

Squeeze the juice of the oranges into a jar. Add the sugar to the juice. Add the chopped rind, cinnamon and coriander. Pour on the spirits and mix all together. Leave to infuse for 2 months.

Filter and bottle.

Orange blossom liqueur or ratafia. LIQUEUR, RATAFIA DE FLEURS D'ORANGER – Made from the petals of orange blossom in the same way as *Carnation liqueur*.

Liqueur or ratafia of peach and apricot stones. LIQUEUR, RATAFIA DE NOYAUX – Made from peach and apricot stones, or a mixture of the two.

Half-fill a stone crock with whole stones. Fill up with white alcohol. Leave to infuse for $1\frac{1}{2}$ months, placing the crock either in the sun or in a hot place.

Take out a quarter of the stones. Crack them and put the shells and kernels back in the crock. Leave to infuse for another 15 days. Draw off the liqueur. Add an equal quantity of water with 350 g. (12 oz., $1\frac{1}{2}$ cups) sugar per litre (scant quart, generous quart) dissolved in it. After 10 days, filter and bottle.

Peppermint liqueur (old recipe). LIQUEUR DE MENTHE – Dissolve $2\frac{1}{2}$ kg. ($5\frac{1}{2}$ lb., 11 cups) white sugar on the stove in $1\frac{3}{4}$ litres (3 pints, 4 pints) water. Add 2 litres ($3\frac{1}{2}$ pints, $4\frac{1}{2}$ pints) alcohol, 58° (US 66°) proof, and 1 g. ($\frac{1}{30}$ oz.) essence of mint.

Leave for 30 days. Filter through filter paper.

Persico or persicot – Alcoholic liqueur, made of *eau-de-vie*, peach stone kernels, sugar and aromatic substances. It is used for flavouring pastry desserts.

Quince liqueur or ratafia (quince water) I. LIQUEUR, RATAFIA DE COING (EAU DE COING) – Cut the quinces into quarters. Remove pips and shred the fruit without peeling.

Place in a bowl, cover and leave to stand in a cool place for 3 days. Squeeze through muslin. Add to the quince juice an equal quantity of spirits. To every litre (scant quart, generous quart) of this mixture add 350 g. (12 oz., $1\frac{1}{2}$ cups) sugar, a clove and a small piece of cinnamon. Infuse in a jar for 2 months.

Strain through a muslin bag. Bottle.

Quince liqueur or ratafia II. LIQUEUR, RATAFIA DE COINGS – Prepare the quince juice as for the previous recipe. To every $1\frac{1}{2}$ litres ($2\frac{3}{4}$ pints, $3\frac{1}{4}$ pints) juice add $\frac{1}{2}$ litre (scant pint, $2\frac{1}{4}$ cups) alcohol, 85° (US 97°) proof. Add $\frac{1}{2}$ teaspoon cloves, 1 teaspoon cinnamon, a pinch of ground mace and 1 or 2 teaspoons bitter almonds.

Leave the mixture to infuse for 2 months. Then add a syrup (cold) made from 225 g. (8 oz., 1 cup) sugar dissolved on the stove in 2 dl. ($\frac{1}{3}$ pint, scant cup) water.

Filter and bottle.

Raspberry liqueur or ratafia. LIQUEUR, RATAFIA DE FRAMBOISE – Put 1 kg. ($2\frac{1}{4}$ lb.) very ripe raspberries in a jar. Cover with 4 litres ($3\frac{1}{2}$ quarts, $4\frac{1}{2}$ quarts) spirits. Cork the jar and leave to infuse for 2 months, putting the jar in the sun whenever possible.

Add to the liqueur 500 g. (18 oz., $2\frac{1}{4}$ cups) sugar, barely moistened to dissolve it.

Filter and bottle.

Tangerine liqueur or ratafia. LIQUEUR, RATAFIA DE MANDARINE – Proceed as for *Orange liqueur*, using the peel and juice of tangerines.

Vanilla liqueur or ratafia. LIQUEUR, RATAFIA À LA VANILLE – Infuse 3 vanilla pods in 1 litre ($1\frac{3}{4}$ pints, generous quart) spirits for 15 days. Mix with a very thick syrup. Filter and bottle.

Verbena liqueur or ratafia. LIQUEUR, RATAFIA DE VERVEINE – Made with verbena leaves in the same way as *Vanilla liqueur*.

Violet liqueur or ratafia. LIQUEUR, RATAFIA DE VIOLETTE – Made with violets in the same way as *Carnation liqueur*.

Walnut liqueur or ratafia (walnut water or cordial). LIQUEUR RATAFIA DE NOIX (BROU, EAU DE NOIX) – Split in half 20 green walnuts and put them in a jar with $1\frac{1}{2}$ litres ($2\frac{3}{4}$ pints, $3\frac{1}{4}$ pints) spirits. Cork tightly.

Leave this mixture to infuse for 6 weeks in a cool place, shaking the jar from time to time.

Strain through a cloth. Add a syrup made from 500 g. (18 oz., $2\frac{1}{4}$ cups) sugar and $2\frac{1}{2}$ dl. (scant $\frac{1}{2}$ pint, generous cup) boiled water, also a little cinnamon and a pinch of coriander.

Leave to infuse for another month. Strain and bottle.

Walnut liqueur or ratafia (walnut water or cordial) à la carmélite. LIQUEUR, RATAFIA DE NOIX (BROU, EAU DE NOIX À LA CARMÉLITE) – Proceed as indicated in the previous recipe, using 100 green walnuts and ½ tablespoon cloves. The walnuts must be unripe so that they can be pierced with a thick pin.

When the mixture has infused for 2 months, add 2 kg. (4½ lb., 9 cups) sugar.

Proceed as indicated in the previous recipe.

LIQUEUR or DESSERT WINES. VINS DE LIQUEUR – Name given to any wine which is both sweet and intoxicating. Among these wines, which are mainly drunk as apéritifs and used in cooking and confectionery, the following are well known: Frontignac, Muscatel, Lunel, Grenache, Banyuls, Madeira, Malaga, Malmsey, Marsala, Port, Sherry, Lacrima-Christi.

LIQUORICE. RÉGLISSE – Leguminous plant found mainly in Spain and Sicily. Its rhizome contains a sweet substance, and when soaked or infused in water, provides a sweet drink.

Solidified liquorice comes from a watery extract obtained by strong pressure, which is then evaporated to a solid consistency. It is black in colour, and is generally moulded into cylindrical sticks, glossy when broken, sweet tasting, a little bitter and sharp, soluble in water to some extent when pure.

Litchis on a branch

LITCHI or LICHEE. LETCHI – This fruit, probably of Chinese origin, is also cultivated in India, the Philippine Islands and other countries of the Far East. It has the appearance of a berry about the size of a cherry, and has a large stone. The pulp is white, sweet and musky in flavour. It has a thin, hard and scaly shell which comes away easily from the fruit. The shell is greenish at first, then it turns pink, and when fully ripe, red.

For export, the fruit is usually left to dry in its shell. It then turns black like a prune, is very sweet with a slightly acid flavour, and is called lichee or litchi nuts.

Fresh lichees are sold in some delicatessen stores and those specialising in exotic fruits.

LITRON – Old French liquid measure. An old bushel measured about 13 litres (2¾ gallons, 3½ gallons) and a litron was a sixteenth of a bushel.

LITTLE BUSTARD (Field duck). CANEPETIÈRE – Migratory European wild bird of the wader family.

LIVAROT – See CHEESE.

LIVER. FOIE – The liver is the largest and most important of the glands attached to the digestive organs.

The livers of slaughtered animals, poultry and game are all used in cookery, as are those of one or two fish, such as turbot and skate. (See OFFAL or VARIETY MEATS.)

LIVESTOCK. BÉTAIL – This word is used to describe all the animals, particularly animals intended for food, raised on cattle-breeding farms.

Erroneously this word is also applied to small farmyard animals, various types of poultry and hutch rabbits.

The only animals which should come under this heading are bullocks, oxen, cows, calves, sheep, lambs and pigs.

Livre d'or of Alex Humbert
(*Phot. X*)

LIVRE D'OR – French term for the visitors' book, especially (in this context) the one offered by the restaurateur to enthusiastic clients. All too often it becomes the repository of banal compliments and tasteless jokes; sometimes, however, it contains clever witticisms and humorous drawings and becomes a worthy logbook of the establishment.

Can you imagine, for example, what the *livre d'or* of the Rocher restaurant of Cancale could be today with the signatures of Balzac, Victor Hugo, Baudelaire, Eugène Sue, the Goncourts and Flaubert?

Some *livres d'or* are veritable treasures. That, for example, of Camille Renault of Puteaux, restaurateur-cum-patron of the arts, which runs to seven volumes and contains paintings, watercolours and drawings signed by Villon, Reynold Arnould, Picasso, Braque, Fernand Léger, etc.

In the *livre d'or* of the Grand Saint-Antoine restaurant of Albi, the Rieux family can trace its lineage from the first entry by Jaurès. Then there is the *livre d'or* of Sam, the troubadour-restaurateur of Pontchartrain, which boasts all the signatures of the famous of its time – and many more.

During the war, Picasso and his friends passed the time drawing on the paper tablecloths of the Catalan restaurant. The poet Georges Hugnet published these collected drawings (some coloured with mustard, coffee and red wine) in a luxury edition known as the *Nappe du Catalan*. If only all *livres d'or* were of this calibre!

LLAMA. LAMA – Ruminant mammal found in Peru. It is edible and is cooked in the same way as beef (q.v.).

LOACH. LOCHE – Name given to several European freshwater fish, all long in shape and barbed.

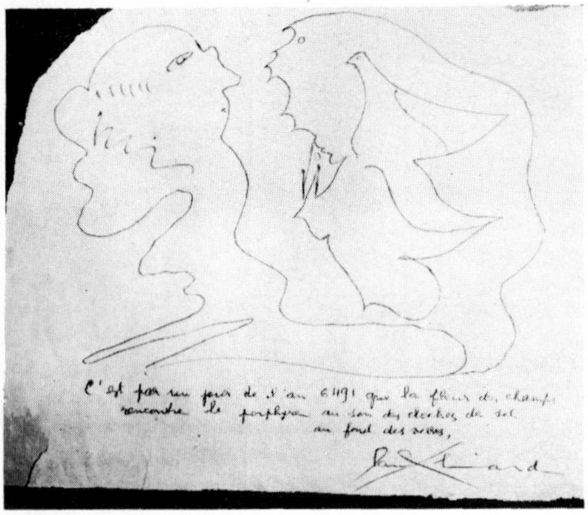

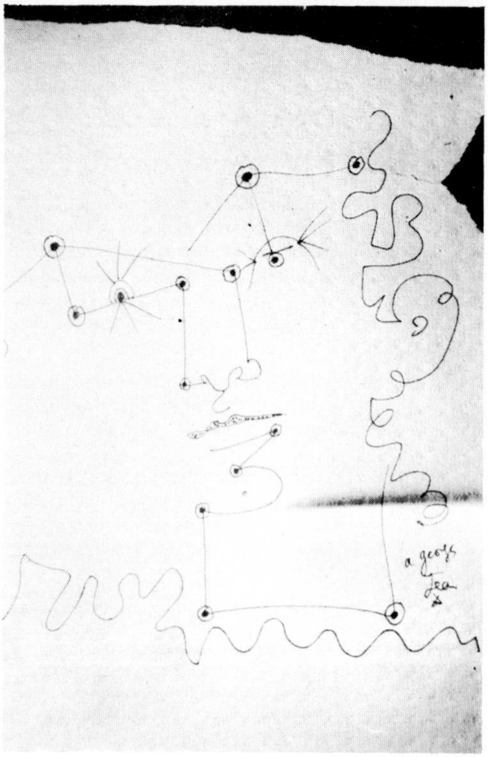

Drawings on paper tablecloths of the Catalan restaurant. *Top left:* Drawing by Pierre de Mandiargues. *Bottom left:* Drawing by P. Eluard. *Above:* Drawing by J. Cocteau (*Phot. X*)

There are three types: the *common loach*, a delicate fish found in mountain streams; the *spined loach* or *groundling*, a small fish found in rivers and streams, about the size of a gudgeon, and rather leathery; the *rockling*, about the same size as the other two, but less delicate in flavour. The loach is eaten fried, *en matelote* or *à la meunière*.

LOAVES. PAINS – Culinary term applied to dishes, served cold or hot, made of a forcemeat placed in a special mould and poached in a *bain-marie* (q.v.) if served hot, and set in a mould lined with aspic jelly and chilled if served cold.

This type of *entrée* was once very popular. It has been replaced by mousses (q.v.), which are also prepared hot or cold.

The various ingredients used for the forcemeats are, as indicated in individual recipes, liver (*foie gras*), game meat (winged and ground game), poultry and vegetables, fish and shellfish.

FISH AND SHELLFISH LOAVES. PAINS DE POISSONS, CRUSTACÉS.

Pike loaf (hot). PAIN DE BROCHET – Dice 500 g. (18 oz.) pike flesh (net weight, after cleaning the fish). Season with 1 teaspoon salt, a pinch of white pepper and a little grated nutmeg. Pound in a mortar into a fine paste.

Remove the fish from the mortar and in its place put 250 g. (9 oz., 1 cup) *Flour panada* (see PANADA). After pounding the panada thoroughly, add to it 250 g. (9 oz., generous cup) butter. Blend by pounding together.

Put the pike back in the mortar and pound vigorously to obtain a perfectly smooth mixture. Add, still pounding, 1 whole egg and, one by one, 4 egg yolks.

Remove the forcemeat from the mortar, rub through a fine sieve, transfer to a bowl and stir with a wooden spoon until very smooth.

Butter a mould and fill with the mixture. Cook in a *bain-marie* (q.v.) in the oven from 45 to 50 minutes, depending on the size of the mould. Turn out onto a serving dish, either straight onto the dish or on a fried croûton of bread. Serve with the garnish and sauce as indicated in the recipe.

Various fish loaves (hot). PAINS DE POISSON – Using carp, salmon or turbot flesh, prepare as described in the recipe for *Pike loaf*.

The forcemeat can also be prepared as described in the recipe for *Mousseline forcemeat* (see FORCEMEATS).

Garnishes and sauces. Cancalaise (poached oysters) and *Normande sauce*; *Américaine* (slices of spiny lobster) and *American sauce*; *Cardinal* (slices of spiny lobster or lobster, truffles and mushrooms) and *Cardinal sauce*; *Normande* (mussels, oysters, crayfish, mushrooms and truffles) and *Normande sauce*; *Trouvillaise* (shrimps' tails, mussels and mushrooms) and *Shrimp sauce*. (See GARNISHES, SAUCES.)

Shellfish loaves (hot). PAINS DE CRUSTACÉS – Prepare a lobster, spiny lobster, crab or any other shellfish forcemeat, as described in the recipe for *Panada forcemeat with butter* (see FORCEMEATS), pour into a well-buttered mould with a hole in the middle and poach in the oven in a *bain-marie*.

Turn out onto a dish and serve with the garnish indicated. Pour over a sauce appropriate to the garnish.

Garnishes and sauces. All the garnishes and sauces recommended for fish loaves are applicable to shellfish loaves.

FOIE GRAS LOAVES. PAINS DE FOIE GRAS – In the old days the *foie gras* loaves (today replaced by *foie gras* mousses and *mousselines*) were prepared using panada (q.v.) to bind them. This is no longer used nowadays; a more delicate composition is obtained and the binding of the mixture is assured by using meat jelly. Here is an old recipe for this type of *entrée*:

Jellied foie gras loaf (*Carême*)

Jellied foie gras loaf (Carême's recipe). PAIN DE FOIE GRAS À LA GELÉE – This *entrée* can be made from fattened goose liver although Carême uses capon liver.

'Trim 450 g. (1 lb.) fat capon liver, which you have previously soaked in water.

'Weigh out 175 g. (6 oz., $\frac{2}{3}$ cup) panada and the same amount of butter or grated bacon fat.

'Begin to pound the panada, then add butter to it. Take this mixture out of the mortar and proceed to pound the liver into a perfectly smooth paste. Add the panada and pound together for a good 15 minutes, adding 5 egg yolks, 4 teaspoons spiced salt, 2 tablespoons (3 tablespoons) *fines herbes* tossed in butter (by *fines herbes*, Carême meant a mixture of chopped mushrooms, truffles, shallots and aromatic herbs) and 1 tablespoon *Velouté sauce* (see SAUCE).

'When the whole has been well blended, rub it through a sieve and put this forcemeat into a bowl. Add 50 g. (2 oz.) blanched, diced udder, 50 g. (2 oz.) pickled tongue and 50 g. (2 oz.) truffles (50 g. (2 oz.) pistachio nuts can also be added).

'Transfer the mixture into a cylindrical-shaped mould, lined with thin rashers of bacon, in such a way as to have the whole inside surface covered completely. Press down the mould with a napkin to make the forcemeat take shape. Cover with more bacon rashers and stand the mould in a casserole 10 cm. (4 inches) larger than the mould. Pour enough boiling water into the casserole to reach to within 1 cm. ($\frac{1}{2}$ inch) of the rim. Place on red coals and put some glowing coals on the lid as well, to ensure that the water maintains the same temperature – almost boiling – all the time. (Or you can cook the loaf in a *bain-marie* in a slow oven.)

'A good 2 hours later take out the mould (1 hour later if the cooking is done in the oven) and put it on ice or in a cold place. When the loaf is quite cold, heat the mould on the stove to loosen it and turn out onto a casserole lid. Remove the bacon rashers covering the loaf, and spoon over some warm, clear jelly on top and all round.

'Put the loaf on an *entrée* dish, the bottom of which should be lined with some liquid jelly, and set. Garnish the edges of the dish first with chopped jelly, then with jelly croûtons, and decorate the top with jelly.'

GAME LOAVES. PAINS DE GIBIERS –

Ground game loaf (hot). PAIN DE GIBIER DE POIL – This is prepared, using the flesh of leveret, hare or deer, like *Chicken loaf (hot)* (see CHICKEN).

Ground game loaf in jelly. PAIN DE GIBIER DE POIL À LA GELÉE – Like *Winged game loaf in jelly* (see below).

Winged game loaf (hot). PAIN DE GIBIER DE PLUME – Use the meat of woodcock, pheasant, partridge, like *Chicken loaf (hot)* (see CHICKEN). The garnish and sauces suitable for hot game loaf are: mushrooms and *Demi-glace sauce* (see SAUCE) based on buttered, concentrated game stock boiled down to the consistency of a *fumet* (q.v.); chipolata sausages with buttered *Demi-glace; Rossini* (escalopes of liver and truffles) and *Demi-glace sauce* based on a truffle *fumet*; truffles and *Demi-glace* based on truffle *fumet*.

Winged game loaf in jelly. PAIN DE GIBIER DE PLUME À LA GELÉE – Prepare like *Foie gras loaf in jelly* (see FOIE GRAS) replacing the liver by 500 g. (18 oz.) (net weight) of game meat, as indicated.

loaves are made of braised vegetables mixed with eggs beaten as for an omelette, poured into a buttered plain mould and poached in a *bain-marie*.

By following the recipe given for *Endive loaf* (see ENDIVE) various other vegetable loaves can be made: artichoke, aubergine, carrot, cauliflower, turnip, etc.

This type of loaf, made in large moulds, is served as a small *entrée*, with a cream sauce poured over it.

Small vegetable loaves are used as a garnish for meat and poultry. They can also be used for garnishing fish dishes, or poached or soft-boiled eggs. Some recipes are given below.

Small cauliflower loaves. PETITS PAINS DE CHOU-FLEUR – Prepare a cauliflower purée bound with egg yolks, pour it into small buttered *dariole* moulds and cook in the oven in a *bain-marie*.

Small lettuce loaves. PETITS PAINS DE LAITUES – Using lettuces, braised, chopped and bound with egg, prepare as for *Small spinach loaves* (see below).

Various other vegetable loaves or vegetable purées such as carrot, mushrooms, endive, Brussels sprouts, chicory, tomato, etc. can be prepared in the same manner.

Small spinach loaves à la romaine. PETITS PAINS D'ÉPINARDS À LA ROMAINE – Prepare a leaf spinach purée, tossed in

Lobster (*Robert Carrier*)

Noisette butter (see BUTTER, *Compound butters*), mixed with diced anchovy fillets, and bound with eggs beaten as for an omelette. Pour the mixture into buttered *dariole* moulds and cook in a *bain marie*.

LOBSTER. HOMARD – Large seawater crustacean similar in shape to the crayfish. There are two main types; one is found in European waters, the other in American waters.

The shell of the lobster is smooth. Its claws are armed with pincers of unequal size; one is large and oval, the other more slender and elongated.

The lobster found in European waters is of a rich, dark blue colour tinged with purple. Its joints are orange and its feelers, which are as long as its body, red.

The lobster reaches full size very slowly. At 5 years old, it is about 12 cm. (5 inches) long, having shed its tail some

20 times in the course of this period. Later it grows very much larger, attaining 30 to 50 cm. (12 to 20 inches) in length and weighing up to 5 kg. (11 lb.).

The female lobster carries its eggs in the tail. The French have a special name, *paquette*, for the female lobster with fully formed eggs, and connoisseurs assert that it is when the eggs are formed and not laid that the flesh of the female lobster is at its most delicate and savoury.

The American lobster lives only on the Eastern coast of North America, running from Labrador to North Carolina, although the most important sources are off the coast of Nova Scotia and the state of Maine. According to United States fisheries authorities, the 5-year-old lobster measures about 27 cm. ($10\frac{1}{2}$ inches) and has moulted 25 times. It is a dark mottled green when caught. The flesh of the lobster is more highly flavoured than that of the spiny lobster or crayfish.

There are many ways of preparing lobster. It can be eaten hot or cold like the spiny lobster (q.v.).

Lobster à l'américaine. HOMARD À L'AMÉRICAINE – This

How to cut up a lobster à l'américaine (*Larousse*)
1. Cut off the right claws; 2. Cut off the left claws; 3. Cut off the tip of the tail; 4. Cut the carcase in two; 5. Cut the head in two lengthwise; 6. Lobster completely cut up

dish is of Provençal origin. Raw lobster sautéed in oil and the use of tomatoes are characteristic features of Mediterranean cookery.

Towards the middle of the nineteenth century, this dish was called *lobster à la provençale* (Gouffé). The name *lobster à l'américaine* was applied at that time to a dish made from poached lobster.

A certain confusion had arisen over these two names. *Lobster à la provençale*, simpler to prepare and less subtle in flavour, usurped both the name and the position of *lobster à l'américaine*. There is still some doubt as to who invented the name *lobster à l'américaine*, the dish itself having been known for a very long time.

Was it some anonymous cook, as the master chef Escoffier would have us believe, who, having known the dish in Nice, exported it to America, whence it was subsequently re-imported into France? Was it some restaurateur, perhaps Fraisse of Noel and Peter's Restaurant, who gave this name to the dish in honour of some transatlantic patron?

Curnonsky settled this controversy once and for all by investigating the matter. He discovered that a certain Pierre Fraisse, born in Sète, chef for a number of years in the United States (mainly in Chicago), set up a restaurant called Peter's in the boulevard des Italiens. It was the period of the Second Empire. One evening, in an attempt to serve a party of tourists who had little time to spare, he followed the Provençal recipe, starting with the living lobster. The delighted clients asked for the name of the wonderful dish. Still under the influence of his American sojourn, Fraisse replied: 'Homard à l' américaine'.

This lobster would be even more American, perhaps, if whisky were used instead of Cognac.

To those who object to the dissection of a live lobster we dedicate the following lines:

An American was uncertain
Of the best way to cook lobster
Why not just leave it for now
Said the *homard à l'Américaine* . . .

Provençal cooks prepare lobsters and spiny lobsters in the Provençal fashion, in a *coulis* (q.v.) of tomatoes flavoured with onion, garlic and parsley.

Take a hen lobster weighing 1 kg. (generous 2 lb.). Cut the tail into slices, following the marks of the joints. Split the carcase in two, lengthwise. Crack the shell of the claws. Remove all the gritty substance near the head. Keep the coral and the liver, which will be used to thicken the sauce. Season the portions of the lobster with salt and pepper.

Heat 4 to 6 tablespoons olive oil in a pan. Put in the pieces of lobster, brown quickly on both sides and remove from the pan. Put 2 tablespoons (3 tablespoons) finely chopped onion in the pan. Cook slowly until very tender, stirring frequently with a wooden spoon. When almost cooked, add 2 chopped shallots. Stir, mixing thoroughly. Put 2 coarsely chopped tomatoes (peeled, squeezed and with seeds removed) into the pan. Add a touch of garlic, and 1 tablespoon chopped parsley and tarragon.

Lay the pieces of lobster on this foundation of herbs and vegetables. Moisten with $1\frac{1}{2}$ dl. ($\frac{1}{4}$ pint, $\frac{2}{3}$ cup) dry white wine, 1 dl. (6 tablespoons, scant $\frac{1}{2}$ cup) fish *fumet* (q.v.) and 4 tablespoons ($\frac{1}{3}$ cup) brandy. Season with cayenne pepper.

Bring the mixture to the boil, cover the pan, and cook on the stove or in the oven for 20 minutes.

Drain the lobster pieces and pick out the flesh from the claws and the tail.

Serve in the halves of the shells. Keep warm while the sauce is being made.

The sauce. Boil down the pan juices by half. Add the coral and liver of the lobster pounded and mixed with butter. Whisk over a high flame. Remove the pan from the fire and, still whisking to ensure a smooth and creamy sauce, add 100 g. (4 oz., $\frac{1}{2}$ cup) butter cut into fragments.

Season with a little cayenne pepper and a squeeze of lemon juice. Pour this sauce, piping hot, over the lobster, and sprinkle with chopped parsley.

Lobster aspic. ASPIC DE HOMARD – Line a mould with jelly and lay in it thick slices of lobster interlaced with strips of truffle, decorated with jelly. Fill the mould to the top with clear white fish jelly. Leave on ice to set.

It can either be turned out straight onto the dish or served on a slice of buttered bread. Decorate with jelly.

Boiled lobster. HOMARD BOUILLI – Proceed as for *Lobster à la nage* (see below).

This dish is served hot with a sauce usually served with boiled fish or shellfish. When it is eaten cold, it should be served with a sauce suitable for cold fish or shellfish.

Lobster à la bordelaise. HOMARD À LA BORDELAISE – Use small lobsters called *demoiselles of Cherbourg*, or large lobsters split in half lengthwise.

Large lobsters can be prepared *à la bordelaise* by splitting them into sections as for lobster *à l'américaine*. Proceed as for *Crayfish à la bordelaise* (see CRAYFISH).

Lobster Brillat-Savarin. HOMARD BRILLAT-SAVARIN – Cook a large lobster in *Court-bouillon XII* (see COURT-BOUILLON). Drain. Cut off the tail and shell it. Simmer slices of the flesh in a thick *American sauce* (see SAUCE), which has been prepared separately, adding to it some of the *court-bouillon* in which the lobster was cooked, boiled down almost to a jelly.

Shell the claws and the carcase. Chop the flesh into a coarse *salpicon* (q.v.). Add equal quantities of *salpicon* of cooked truffles and mushrooms. Simmer all these ingredients in a *Curry sauce* (see SAUCE) made with the rest of the lobster *court-bouillon*.

Cook courgettes, cut into thick slices – the same number as there are lobster slices – slowly in oil.

Place the slices of lobster and courgette alternately in a ring inside a baked flan crust. Put the *salpicon* in the middle and cover with American sauce. On top of each slice of lobster place a thick strip of truffle.

Lobster cardinal. HOMARD CARDINAL – Boil the lobster in *Court-bouillon XII* (see COURT-BOUILLON) until it is cooked. Drain, cool a little, and split it lengthwise. Remove the flesh from the tail and cut it into slices of equal thickness. Cut off the claws, take out the flesh, and dice it to make a *salpicon* (q.v.). Add an equal quantity of diced truffles. Bind the *salpicon* with a *Lobster sauce* (see SAUCE).

Fill the halves of the lobster shell with the *salpicon*. Place on top the slices of lobster interspersed with strips of truffles. Pour on some lobster sauce. Sprinkle with grated cheese and melted butter.

Place the halves on a baking sheet and brown them quickly in the oven. Garnish with curly parsley.

Lobster en chemise. HOMARD EN CHEMISE – Plunge a lobster into boiling water to kill it. Season with salt and pepper. Baste with oil or melted butter. Wrap it in a double thickness of oiled greaseproof paper and tie with string.

Place on a baking sheet, and bake in a hot oven for 40 to 50 minutes for a medium-sized lobster. Untie, and serve it in the paper in which it has been cooked.

Suitable dressings are half-melted *Maître d'hôtel butter* (see BUTTER, *Compound butters*), or any sauce usually served with grilled fish: *Américaine, Béarnaise, Bercy, Bordelaise, Hongroise, Indienne, Ravigote* (see SAUCE).

Lobster in cream. HOMARD À LA CRÈME – Cut up the lobster as for *Lobster à l'américaine*. Sauté the portions in butter. Drain off the butter. Pour 3 tablespoons (scant $\frac{1}{4}$

cup) brandy into the pan and mix with the pan juices. Add 5 dl. (scant pint, $2\frac{1}{4}$ cups) cream. Season with salt and a touch of cayenne pepper. Cover the pan and simmer.

Serve the lobster in a pie dish (in or out of its shell). Boil down the cooking sauce to half its volume, add 50 g. (2 oz., $\frac{1}{4}$ cup) butter and a few drops of lemon juice, and strain through muslin. Pour this sauce over the lobster.

Lobster croquettes. CROQUETTES DE HOMARD – Made from lobster *salpicon* (q.v.) in the same way as plain croquettes. If desired a *salpicon* of mushrooms and truffles may be added. (See HORS-D'ŒUVRE, *Hot hors-d'œuvre, Croquettes.*)

Lobster à la franco-américaine. HOMARD À LA FRANCO-AMÉRICAINE – This method of cooking lobster is a variant of the recipe for *Lobster à l'américaine*.

Plunge 2 lobsters in boiling water. Cut off the claws and crack them. Split the lobsters in half lengthwise. Drain the carcases and scrape them out, keeping the liver and the liquid.

Simmer 2 tablespoons (3 tablespoons) chopped onion and 1 tablespoon chopped shallot in 4 tablespoons ($\frac{1}{3}$ cup) oil. Add the lobsters, and season with salt and freshly ground pepper.

Pour over 3 dl. ($\frac{1}{2}$ pint, $1\frac{1}{4}$ cups) rather thin *Tomato sauce* (see SAUCE). Boil for 5 minutes. Add 2 small glasses of brandy. Cover the pan and bake in the oven for 16 to 18 minutes.

Drain the lobsters. Put them on a serving dish and keep warm. Strain the sauce and put it back in the pan. Add the liquid and liver, 2 tablespoons (3 tablespoons) meat essence, $\frac{1}{2}$ glass Madeira, 2 tablespoons (3 tablespoons) flaming brandy and 1 or 2 small chopped sweet peppers. Boil down this sauce, add butter, and pour over the lobsters.

Grilled lobster. HOMARD GRILLÉ – Plunge a medium-sized lobster into boiling salt water for 3 minutes. Drain, split it in two lengthwise, season, and pour melted butter over it. Grill on a moderate heat.

Crack the claws so that the flesh can be easily removed, and serve on a napkin garnished with fresh parsley.

Serve with melted butter, *Maître d'hôtel butter* or *Ravigote butter* (see BUTTER, *Compound butters*).

Lobster Henri Duvernois. HOMARD HENRI DUVERNOIS – Split a lobster lengthwise or joint it as for *Lobster à l'américaine*. Season with salt and paprika. Sauté it in butter.

Take it out of the pan. Add to the butter 4 tablespoons ($\frac{1}{3}$ cup) *julienne* (q.v.) of leeks and 4 tablespoons ($\frac{1}{3}$ cup) mushrooms tossed in butter.

Put the lobster back in the pan. Moisten with $1\frac{1}{2}$ dl. ($\frac{1}{4}$ pint, $\frac{2}{3}$ cup) sherry and 2 tablespoons (3 tablespoons) brandy. Boil down, add fresh cream, cover with a lid and simmer.

Put the lobster on a long dish. Garnish with a pilaf of rice arranged along each side. Boil down the sauce, add 2 tablespoons (3 tablespoons) butter and pour over the lobster.

Lobster kromeskies. CROMESQUIS DE HOMARD – This dish is served as a hot *hors-d'œuvre* or as a light main course. It is made from lobster *salpicon* (q.v.) either plain or with a *Velouté* or *Béchamel sauce* (see SAUCE), to which diced truffles and mushrooms have been added. For further details see HORS-D'ŒUVRE, *Hot hors-d'œuvre*.

Lobster à la marinière. HOMARD AU COURT-BOUILLON À LA MARINIÈRE – Very small lobsters are used for this dish. Proceed as for *Crayfish à la marinière* (see CRAYFISH).

Lobsters cooked in this way are often called *Lobsters à la nage*.

Lobster Mornay. HOMARD MORNAY – Proceed as for *Lobster cardinal*, substituting *Mornay sauce* (see SAUCE) for lobster sauce.

Lobster Mornay in scallop shells (hot). COQUILLES DE HOMARD MORNAY – Proceed as for *Brill in scallop shells* (see BRILL) or any other fish in scallop shells, using a *salpicon* (q.v.) and thick slices of lobster coated with *Mornay sauce* (see SAUCE). Brown in a very hot oven.

As with all other scallop shells, whether filled with poultry, fish or other ingredients, the shells should be decorated with a border of *Duchess potato mixture* (see POTATOES) piped through a forcing-bag with a fluted nozzle, before they are filled.

Hot lobster scallop shells can also be made with other sauces such as *Cardinal, Nantua, Normande, White wine sauce* (see SAUCE).

Cold lobster mousse. MOUSSE DE HOMARD FROIDE – Add to a *mirepoix* (q.v.) some dry white wine and 3 tablespoons (scant $\frac{1}{4}$ cup) flaming brandy. Cook the lobster in this and leave to cool. Drain the lobster and take it out of the shell. Pound the flesh finely in a mortar, slowly adding for every 500 g. (18 oz.) flesh (net weight) 2 dl. ($\frac{1}{3}$ pint, scant cup) cold *Velouté sauce* (see SAUCE) based on fish stock. Rub this mixture through a sieve. Put the purée thus obtained in a pan on ice. Stir with a spatula for a few minutes. Add 4 to 5 tablespoons cold *Fish aspic jelly* (see ASPIC) and about 2 dl. ($\frac{1}{3}$ pint, scant cup) fresh, slightly whipped cream. Season.

Line a plain mould with fish jelly. Fill with the lobster mousse and decorate with truffles or some other garnish. Put it on ice to set.

Turn the mousse out onto a serving dish or on a slice of thickly buttered bread. Surround with chopped jelly and a border of jelly croûtons.

The mousse may also be served in a bowl and covered with fish aspic jelly. A *salpicon* of lobster and truffles may be added to the mixture.

Cold lobster mousselines (mousses served in individual portions). MOUSSELINES DE HOMARD FROIDES – These are made from the same mixture as *Cold lobster mousse*. Serve either in small cylindrical moulds lined with jelly and decorated with truffles, or in little silver or porcelain cups.

Lobster *mousselines* can be served as *hors-d'œuvre* or as a light main course, or may be used as a garnish with large cold fish.

Lobster à la nage

Lobster à la nage (cold). HOMARD À LA NAGE – Proceed as for *Lobster à la nage* (*hot*) (see below). Leave the lobsters to cool in the *court-bouillon* and serve them in it. Serve with a *Mayonnaise sauce* or *Tartare sauce* (see SAUCE, *Cold* *sauces*), or any other sauce usually served with cold fish or shellfish.

Lobster à la nage (hot). HOMARD À LA NAGE – Boil some small lobsters, of the type known as *demoiselles of Cherbourg or Dieppe*, in white wine *Court-bouillon XII* (see COURT-BOUILLON).

Serve hot in the *court-bouillon*, with sauce suitable for poached fish.

Lobster Newburg. HOMARD À LA NEWBURG – *Ingredients.* 2 lobsters weighing about 400 to 500 g. (1 lb.) each, 175 g. (6 oz., $\frac{3}{4}$ cup) butter, 3 dl. ($\frac{1}{2}$ pint, $1\frac{1}{4}$ cups) sherry, 3 dl. ($\frac{1}{2}$ pint, $1\frac{1}{4}$ cups) concentrated fish stock, 3 dl. ($\frac{1}{2}$ pint, $1\frac{1}{4}$ cups) *Velouté sauce* (see SAUCE), 4 dl. ($\frac{3}{4}$ pint, scant 2 cups) cream, salt, paprika.

Method. Wash the lobsters and joint them as for *Lobster à l'américaine.* Remove the liver and keep for use later. Season the lobsters with salt and paprika. Brown the lobsters in 75 g. (3 oz., 6 tablespoons) butter. Cover the pan and cook for 12 minutes.

Drain off the butter and add the sherry. Boil down over a high flame. Add the fish stock and the *velouté sauce.* Keeping the pan covered, simmer gently for 20 minutes.

Take out the pieces of lobster and arrange them in a deep dish. (The tail pieces may be shelled.)

Boil down the sauce, add the cream, and test the sauce. When it coats the back of a spoon, add the liver, previously rubbed through a fine sieve and blended with the rest of the butter. Mix the sauce quickly by whisking. Pour over the pieces of lobster.

This dish is sometimes called *lobster sauté a la crème.*

Lobster à la parisienne. HOMARD À LA PARISIENNE – Cut into slices of equal thickness the tail of a medium-sized lobster, cooked in a *court-bouillon* and cooled. Coat with gelatine-strengthened mayonnaise and decorate with strips of truffle dipped in the half-set mayonnaise jelly.

Line a mould with jelly, fill with vegetable salad mixed with the rest of the lobster, diced, and diced truffles in mayonnaise. Turn out onto a dish, arrange the prepared lobster slices round it in a border, and garnish with chopped jelly.

The slices coated with jelly may also be served as a border to *Parisian salad* (see SALAD) which should be piled up into a small dome in the middle.

Cold lobster à la parisienne or à la russe. HOMARD FROID À LA PARISIENNE, À LA RUSSE – Proceed according to the recipes for *Spiny lobster à la parisienne* or *à la russe* (see SPINY LOBSTER).

Lobster pilaf. PILAF DE HOMARD – Coarsely dice the flesh of boiled lobsters or cut it into pieces. Brown lightly in butter.

Line a domed mould with *Rice pilaf* (see PILAF), and fill with the lobster. Turn out the mould on a serving dish. Surround with *Lobster sauce* (see SAUCE) or any other sauce suitable for shellfish.

Lobster risotto. RISOTTO DE HOMARD – Proceed as for *Lobster pilaf.* Fill a ring mould with risotto. Turn it out, and heap pieces of lobster in the middle.

Lobster salad. SALADE DE HOMARD – See SALAD, *Lobster salad.*

Cold lobster with various sauces. HOMARD FROID AVEC SAUCES DIVERSES – Boil the lobster in a *court-bouillon* (q.v.). Leave to cool. Split it in two lengthwise. Crack the shell of the claws so that the flesh can be taken out easily. Garnish with fresh parsley or lettuce hearts. Serve with *Mayonnaise sauce* or any other cold sauce, such as *Gribiche, Rémoulade, Tartare* (see SAUCE, *Cold sauces*).

Lobster in scallop shells (cold). COQUILLES FROIDES DE HOMARD – This dish is usually made from scraps.

Line the scallop shells with shredded lettuce seasoned with salt, pepper, oil and vinegar. On this foundation put a lobster *salpicon*, seasoned with French dressing and sprinkled with chopped chervil and parsley.

Put 1 or 2 thick slices of lobster in each shell. Cover with mayonnaise. Decorate the top with fillets of anchovy, capers and olives. Garnish with lettuce hearts and quartered hard-boiled eggs.

Lobster in scallop shells à la parisienne. COQUILLES DE HOMARD À LA PARISIENNE – Proceed as for *Lobster in scallop shells* (*cold*), using vegetable salad dressed with mayonnaise or French dressing, instead of lettuce. Decorate with strips of truffle, capers, lettuce hearts and quartered hard-boiled eggs.

Lobster in scallop shells vert-pré. COQUILLES DE HOMARD VERT PRÉ – Line the shells with shredded watercress leaves in a French dressing. Place a *salpicon* and slices of lobster on top. Coat with green mayonnaise. Decorate with slices of gherkin and chopped yolks of hard-boiled eggs. Surround with a border of French beans which have been boiled in salt water, drained, diced and seasoned with French dressing.

Lobster soufflé. SOUFFLÉ DE HOMARD – Pound in a mortar 300 g. (11 oz.) cooked lobster (net weight). Rub through a fine sieve. Add 2 dl. ($\frac{1}{3}$ pint, scant cup) *Béchamel sauce* (see SAUCE) previously cooked with a little of the lobster stock. Season with salt, pepper and grated nutmeg. Blend in 4 egg yolks. Add 4 stiffly beaten egg whites.

Put the mixture in a buttered soufflé dish and cook in a slow oven for 25 to 30 minutes. Serve at once.

Little lobster soufflés can be served as an *hors-d'œuvre* or light main course. These are made from the same mixture as lobster soufflé, but are cooked in small buttered cups or cases.

Lobster on the spit. HOMARD À LA BROCHE – Plunge a large live lobster into boiling salt water for a few seconds to kill it instantly.

Put the lobster on a spit. Season with salt, pepper, thyme, and powdered bay leaf. Baste with melted butter or oil, with a dripping pan or other suitable dish underneath. Put into the pan a few tablespoons of dry white wine and 2 tablespoons (3 tablespoons) butter. Cook in front of a very hot fire, basting frequently. A lobster weighing $1\frac{1}{2}$ kg. (about 3 lb.) needs to be cooked for 40 to 45 minutes.

Remove the lobster from the spit and arrange on a long dish. Serve with the juice collected in the dripping pan.

Lobster on the spit can be served with spicy sauces such as *Béarnaise, Curry, Ravigote* (see SAUCE).

Lobster thermidor. HOMARD THERMIDOR – Split a lobster in two, lengthwise. Crack the shell of the claws and pick out the meat. Season both halves of the lobster with salt. Pour oil over them and roast in the oven for 15 to 20 minutes.

Dice the flesh. Make a stock of white wine, fish *fumet* and meat juices, flavoured with chervil, tarragon and chopped shallots. Boil it down to a concentrated consistency. Add to this a little very thick *Béchamel sauce* (see SAUCE) and some English mustard.

Boil the sauce for a few seconds, then whisk in fresh butter (one-third of the volume of the sauce). Line the two halves of the carcase with a little of this sauce. Fill them with the flesh of the lobster, cover with the remainder of the sauce, sprinkle with grated Parmesan and melted butter and brown quickly in the oven.

(This is the recipe for *lobster thermidor* given to us by M. Tony Girod, for many years master chef of the famous Parisian restaurant, the *Café de Paris.*)

This dish is often prepared in a different way. The tail of the lobster is split in half and grilled, then the flesh is cut into thick slices and put back in the shells, which have been coated with a little cream sauce seasoned with mustard. They are covered with the same sauce and browned in the oven. (See FRENCH CULINARY APPELLATIONS.)

LOCUST or CAROB TREE. CAROUBE – Leguminous plant which grows in the East and in the Mediterranean. The long pod contains numerous seeds and a rather insipid sweet pulp.

LOIN. CARRÉ – The front part of a hindquarter of beef, mutton, lamb, pork or veal with the flank removed.

LONGCHAMP – A broth fundamental to Parisian cooking. It is made by cooking shredded sorrel and vermicelli in consommé and adding a purée of fresh green peas. (See SOUPS AND BROTHS.)

LONGE – This French term should refer only to the top part of the loin of veal (see VEAL).

It is, however, inaccurately extended to refer to the same part of any slaughtered animal.

LONZO (Corsican cookery) – Pork product eaten raw as an *hors-d'œuvre*, like raw salt ham, made from boned fillet of pork. This is steeped in brine with herbs and then dried.

LOQUAT or JAPANESE MEDLAR. NÈFLE DU JAPON – Fruit of the Japanese *biwa.* It looks something like a small plum. Its seeds are enclosed in a large stone. Loquats ripen in Provence from April onward. They are quite sweet, slightly tart, and refreshing.

LORDS AND LADIES. PIED-DE-VEAU – Common name for *wild arum*, the tuberous roots of which contain edible fecula. It is also known as *cuckoo-pint* and *wake-robin.*

LORRAINE – District of high gastronomic repute. Here the connoisseur of good cooking will savour many succulent dishes, and will find white, red and rosé wines, all delightful, though some are more fragrant than others.

Culinary specialities – The dishes of Lorraine are, for the most part, substantial. Heading the list of the culinary specialities of what was once the ancient province of Lotharingie is the *potée*, the national soup of this region.

Then there is the *quiche*, a dish which goes back centuries in the gastronomic history of Lorraine. This is a tart made with eggs, cream and lean bacon. It is also called *féouse.*

Another characteristic local dish is the *tourte à la Lorraine*, made with two kinds of meat, veal and pork. These are first steeped with herbs in a marinade and then baked together on a bed of savoury egg custard in a pie crust of fine pastry.

Other specialities include *ramequins; kneppes; oeufs à l'escargot* (eggs with snails); *choucroute* (*sauerkraut*) *à la messine; tourte aux oignons* (onion tart similar to the Strasbourg onion tart); *pâtés; quenelles de foie de veau* (calves' liver forcemeat balls); *civet de pork frais* (civet of fresh pork); and a whole series of local pork products, the finest being the famous *black pudding* of Nancy. The *potted meats* and *pâtés de foie gras* of Lorraine rival in delicacy those of neighbouring Alsace.

A local writer, Auricoste de Lazarque, devoted a book of some 300 pages to the gastronomy of his homeland. He speaks with eloquence of the *matelote de Metz; crayfish à la mode de Boulay; frogs' legs à la mode de Riom; partridge with cabbage à la Lorraine;* and the *daube of goose.* He gives recipes for the *soupe au lard de Lorraine*; the *soupe au boudin* (black pudding soup); *sucking pig in aspic; ham au foin;*

Gastronomic map of Lorraine

the *goose pâté* of Rupt-de-Mad; *soupe dorée; meillat* or *miot; rouyats* (apple pies); *chaudée* (a kind of apple tart); *chemitrés* (a kind of waffle); and many other delicious dishes.

Among the delicate pastries made in Lorraine are the *macaroons* and *bergamotes* of Nancy; the *madeleines* of Commercy; the *kugelhupf* (similar to that of Alsace); *Nancy cake*; the *nonettes* of Remiremont; *aniseed bread*; and *mirabelle plum tart*. There are, too, the *myrtle jams*; the famous *sugar almonds* of Verdun; and many other sweet dishes.

The cheeses include Gérardmer cheese, admirable partner to the local wines, Lorraine cheese made from scalded curds, and Fromgey, a kind of white cheese, which is spread on a slice of bread and sprinkled with chopped onions and shallots.

Wines – Among the wines of this region are the white, red and rosé wines of Côtes de Toul in Meurthe-et-Moselle, and the white and red wines of Moselle. Both varieties are in the V.D.Q.S. category (vins délimités de qualité supérieure).

LOTUS – In ancient Egypt the tuberous stump of white lotus was eaten, grilled or boiled. The pink lotus, on the other hand, being regarded as a sacred plant, was forbidden food.

LOUBINE – French local name for the grey mullet.

LOUISE-BONNE – Variety of pear.

LOVAGE. LIVÈCHE – Herb of the angelica family, much used in Roman cookery. The young leaves, ribs and leaf stalks are eaten like celery. The seeds are used in confectionery.

LOVE-IN-A-MIST. POIVRETTE – Common name for the cultivated *nigella* (q.v.).

LUMPY. GRENU – Stuffings or doughs are said to be lumpy when they are not thoroughly mixed and smooth.

LUNEL WINE – Muscatel wine made in the Hérault commune, round about Lunel. This is a sweet dessert wine.

LUPIN – A pulse (leguminous plant) used as fodder. Its bitter seeds can only be eaten after soaking in water.

LUTE. LUT – A paste which hardens as it dries. It is used to seal containers hermetically. Almond lute is made by mixing powdered almonds, from which the oil has been extracted, with starch paste. In cooking, a flour-and-water paste is used, which is also called *repère* or *repaire*.

LYONNAIS – The Lyonnais district, more industrial than agricultural, has a few fertile plains, notably those of Forez and Roannais, and market gardening is carried out on a large scale in the area. There is an abundance of good quality potatoes as well as excellent onions, such as those of Roanne, which are used in the preparation of a large number of special dishes, for example *tripe à la lyonnaise*.

Many other vegetables are grown. Fruit production is also an important industry, and some fruit, such as the apricots of Ampuis have a well-deserved reputation. So, too, have the sweet chestnuts which come from the many trees that flourish on the mountain sides.

The neighbouring regions converge on Lyons, a town of high gastronomic repute, with many excellent foodstuffs, such as the succulent poultry of Bresse.

Excellent meat is to be found in the Lyonnais district. Pigs, bred in large numbers, provide Lyons with the many well-known pork products made there. The game of this region is also of fine quality.

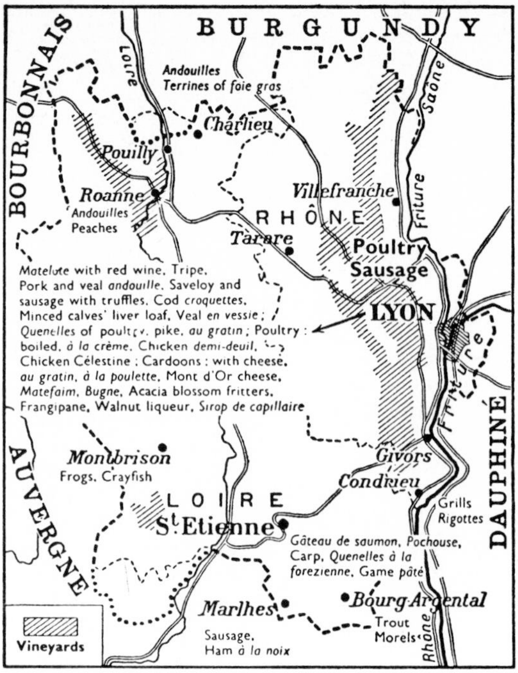

Gastronomic map of Lyonnais

Excellent fish is caught in the Loire, the Saône and the Rhône, as well as in the local ponds.

Culinary specialities – The well-known *Lyons sausage; pike au bleu; quenelles* (fish balls) *of pike à la lyonnaise; gratin of crayfish tails; matelots of Loire and Saône fish; omelette à la lyonnaise; black pudding with apples; tripe à la lyonnaise; poached saveloy with pistachio nuts and truffles; roulade of pig's head; Charlieu chitterlings; ham with walnuts; Marlhes sausage; chicken en demi-deuill*; the celebrated *poached chicken de la mère Filloux; chicken à la crème; chicken en vessie* (chicken sausage); *chicken célestine; veal en vessie* (veal sausage); *cardoons au gratin*.

Among the special sweets of this region are *bugnes lyonnaises* (a special type of fritter); *acacia blossom fritters; frangipane*; the substantial *matefaim* (a type of pancake); and *pumpkin cake*.

Wines – Worthy accompaniment of the dishes made in the Lyonnais district, are the wines drunk by the gourmets of this food-loving region.

Beaujolais wines. See BURGUNDY.

Côtes du Forez. Under this V.D.Q.S. *appellation* Lyonnais produces a light and fruity Gamay red wine not unlike Beaujolais.

LYOPHILISATION – Lyophilisation or freeze-drying is a method of drying prefrozen products. The process is carried out in several stages and results in a perfectly dry, stable, end product, unaltered in quality. Foods of animal and vegetable origin treated thus (delicate fruit, fruit juices, vegetables, coffee, tea, milk, fish fillets, certain meats) have the same texture, taste, aroma, vitamins, fatty acids and proteins.

Other advantages are easy rehydration of the treated foods; instant consumption; long-term conservation; ease of transport, storage and distribution (weight and volume are reduced, due to the elimination of water).

MACARONI – A farinaceous food, originally from Italy (some authorities give Naples as its place of origin), where it has been eaten for centuries. Macaroni, like all other pasta, is very nourishing.

Cooking macaroni. CUISSON DE MACARONI – Put 2 litres ($3\frac{1}{2}$ pints, $4\frac{1}{2}$ pints) water in a pan, adding salt in the ratio of $1\frac{1}{2}$ teaspoons per litre (scant quart, generous quart). Bring it to the boil and put in 150 g. (5 oz.) macaroni, broken into pieces.

Boil very fast for 16 to 20 minutes according to the thickness of the macaroni. Like all pasta products, macaroni must not be overcooked. Remove the saucepan from the stove. Cover it and leave the pasta to swell in the water for a few minutes.

Drain the macaroni and put it back in the saucepan. Evaporate all moisture by leaving it on the stove for a few seconds. This is necessary to get rid of any water absorbed by the macaroni during cooking.

Proceed according to the recipe used.

Macaroni à l'anglaise – Boil the macaroni as indicated above. Heap on a serving platter. Serve with butter.

Macaroni à la béchamel – Add several tablespoons *Béchamel sauce* (see SAUCE) to the cooked macaroni. Season. Mix. Just before serving, add 3 tablespoons (scant $\frac{1}{4}$ cup) butter.

Macaroni pieces (*Nicolas*)

Macaroni with butter. MACARONI AU BEURRE – Add 75 g. (3 oz., 6 tablespoons) fresh butter, cut into small pieces, to the cooked macaroni. Season. Toss so that the butter is well mixed in.

Macaroni with cheese. MACARONI AU FROMAGE – Another name for *Macaroni à l'italienne* (see below).

Macaroni with cream. MACARONI À LA CRÈME – Boil the macaroni until it is three-parts cooked. Drain and put back in the saucepan on the stove to evaporate all moisture. Moisten with 2 dl. ($\frac{1}{3}$ pint, scant cup) boiled fresh cream. Simmer slowly for 10 to 12 minutes. Season with a pinch of salt and a little grated nutmeg. Remove the pan from the stove and mix in 60 g. ($2\frac{1}{2}$ oz.,.5 tablespoons) butter cut into small pieces.

Macaroni à la créole – Proceed as for *Macaroni à l'italienne* (see below). Make a coarse *salpicon* (q.v.) of sweet peppers (green and red), very small vegetable marrows (zucchini, courgettes) tossed in oil, tomatoes tossed in oil, and a touch of garlic. Bind with cheese. Mix this *salpicon* with the macaroni.

Macaroni croquettes. MACARONI EN CROQUETTES – These are made in the usual way (see CROQUETTES) using macaroni, boiled in salt water, drained, diced and blended with *Allemande* or *Béchamel sauce* (see SAUCE).

Macaroni à la fermière – Proceed as for *Macaroni à l'italienne* (see below). Serve in a deep dish alternating with layers of a vegetable *fondue* of carrots, turnips, celery, onion and leek, finely sliced and cooked slowly in butter until very tender.

Macaroni au gratin

Macaroni au gratin – Proceed as for *Macaroni à l'italienne* (see below). Serve in an ovenware dish lined with butter and grated cheese. Sprinkle the top of the macaroni with mixed breadcrumbs and grated cheese. Pour melted butter over and brown in the oven.

Macaroni à l'italienne – Add 50 g. (2 oz., $\frac{1}{2}$ cup) grated cheese (a mixture of Gruyère and Parmesan) and 50 g. (2 oz., $\frac{1}{4}$ cup) butter cut into small pieces, to the cooked macaroni. Season with salt and a little grated nutmeg. Toss to mix thoroughly. Heap on a serving plate. One kind of cheese only need be used, though a mixture of Parmesan and Gruyère gives better results.

Macaroni à la Lucullus – Proceed as for *Macaroni à l'italienne.* Serve in a dish with alternate layers of a coarse *salpicon* of *foie gras* and truffles blended in a very concentrated *Madeira sauce* (see SAUCE). Decorate the top of the macaroni with strips of truffle.

Macaroni à la milanaise – Proceed as for *Macaroni à l'italienne.* Add 2 to 3 tablespoons *Demi-glace sauce* (see SAUCE) flavoured with tomato, and 2 to 3 tablespoons of Milanaïse garnish (coarsely shredded ham, pickled tongue, mushrooms and truffles).

Mix well and heap on a serving platter.

Macaroni à la mirepoix – Make a *mirepoix* (q.v.) of vegetables, rather coarsely diced, cooked slowly in butter until very tender and blended with cheese. It should be a quarter of the weight of the macaroni. Mix the *mirepoix* with the cooked macaroni. Put in an ovenproof dish lined with butter and grated cheese. Sprinkle the top of the macaroni with cheese. Pour butter over and brown in the oven.

Macaroni à la Nantua – *Macaroni à l'italienne* served in a pie crust of lining pastry baked blind, with alternate layers of *Crayfish tail ragoût à la Nantua* (see CRAYFISH).

Macaroni à la napolitaine I – Proceed as for *Macaroni à l'italienne.* Add 3 tablespoons (scant $\frac{1}{4}$ cup) *Tomato sauce* (see SAUCE) to the macaroni. Mix. Serve in a deep dish. Sprinkle with grated cheese.

Macaroni à la napolitaine II – Break some thick macaroni into short sticks, and boil in salt water until the macaroni is three-parts cooked. Drain and mix with butter.

Put the macaroni in an ovenproof dish lined with butter and grated cheese, with alternate layers of cooked *Braised beef* (see BEEF) rubbed through a sieve. Sprinkle the layers with grated cheese. Warm over a low heat and serve.

Macaroni à la piémontaise – Proceed as for *Macaroni à l'italienne.* After adding the butter and cheese, add very finely sliced white truffles. Mix and serve in a deep dish.

The white truffles are cooked by the heat of the macaroni.

Macaroni with seafood. MACARONI AUX FRUITS DE MER – Proceed as for *Macaroni à l'italienne.* Serve in a deep dish with alternate layers of *Seafood ragoût* (see RAGOÛT).

Macaroni à la sicilienne – Proceed as for *Macaroni à l'italienne.* Add, at the same time as the butter and cheese, a few tablespoons of purée of chicken livers mixed with *Velouté sauce* (see SAUCE). Serve in a deep dish.

Macaroni in stock. MACARONI AU JUS – Boil the macaroni until it is three-parts cooked. Drain and put in a saucepan with brown veal or beef stock. Cover and leave to simmer slowly for 12 to 15 minutes.

Heap on a serving dish and pour over it 2 tablespoons (3 tablespoons) concentrated brown stock.

Macaroni with tomato sauce. MACARONI À LA TOMATE – Proceed as for *Macaroni in stock*, substituting tomato sauce for the stock.

Macaroni with truffles. MACARONI AUX TRUFFES – Mix butter, cheese and coarsely shredded truffles tossed in butter with the macaroni. Decorate the top with strips of truffles.

MACAROON. MACARON – Small round dry pastry made of almond paste, sugar and egg white.

The origin of this pastry is unknown. Some authorities suggest that this little biscuit was invented in Italy, and from there came to France, where it was appreciated by connoisseurs, and was subsequently mass produced.

Delicately flavoured macaroons are made in various parts of France. Those of Nancy are considered the best. They have been made for nearly two centuries by successive generations of the same family, and are known as the macaroons of the 'Macaroon Sisters'.

In the eighteenth century, it became the custom in many convents for the nuns to make macaroons. The nuns of the Convent of the Visitation of Our Lady at Melun made these and other sweetmeats.

When, in 1748, the Court was at Fontainebleau, the Dauphin and his wife went to visit the Convent of the Visitation of Our Lady at Melun, at the Port de Bière the procession was addressed by the Mayor, who offered the visitors a ceremonial bottle of wine with a basket of biscuits, macaroons, sugar sticks and other sweetmeats.

Plain macaroons. MACARONS ORDINAIRES – Pound in a mortar 200 g. (7 oz., $1\frac{1}{2}$ cups) blanched almonds (4 of which should be bitter almonds) moistened with 1 egg white. As soon as the almonds are well pounded, add 150 g. (5 oz., $\frac{2}{3}$ cup) sugar. Mix and add $\frac{1}{2}$ egg white. Still mixing, add 150 g. (5 oz., $\frac{2}{3}$ cup) sugar and the rest of the egg white.

The mixture must be rather soft but not runny. If necessary at this stage add another $\frac{1}{2}$ egg white and mix thoroughly.

Pipe the mixture onto a sheet of rice paper. The macaroons should be 3 to 4 cm. ($1\frac{1}{2}$ inches) in diameter, and far enough apart to prevent them from running into one another during baking.

Sprinkle with icing sugar and bake at 180°C. (350°F., Gas Mark 4) for 20 minutes or until the macaroons are a rich golden colour.

Crisp macaroons. MACARONS CROQUANTS – Pound in a mortar 250 g. (9 oz., $1\frac{3}{4}$ cups) blanched almonds with a little egg white. Add 250 g. (9 oz., generous cup) sugar flavoured to taste. Mix well. Add to the mixture 250 g. (9 oz., generous cup) sugar and enough egg white to make a fairly soft but not runny paste. Spoon small heaps of this mixture onto rice paper. Bake at 180°C. (350°F., Gas Mark 4) for 18 to 20 minutes.

Hazelnut macaroons. MACARONS AUX NOISETTES – Hazelnuts, egg whites and sugar are used for these macaroons. The hazelnuts are not blanched. The method is the same as for plain macaroons.

Pine kernel macaroons can also be made in the same way.

In accordance with a regulation regarding the naming of foodstuffs, the above biscuits may no longer commercially be called macaroons in France.

Montmorillon macaroons. MACARONS DE MONTMORILLON – These macaroons are shaped through a fluted nozzle into rings. They are a speciality of Vienna.

Niort macaroons. MACARONS DE NIORT – Pound in a mortar 375 g. (13 oz., $2\frac{1}{2}$ cups) blanched almonds with 5 egg whites and 500 g. (18 oz., $2\frac{1}{4}$ cups) sugar. Transfer the mixture to a small saucepan and dry out on the stove. Add 4 teaspoons finely chopped crystallised angelica.

Proceed as usual.

Macaroons à la parisienne. MACARONS À LA PARISIENNE – Pound in a mortar 250 g. (9 oz., $1\frac{3}{4}$ cups) blanched almonds with 4 egg whites. Add 375 g. (13 oz., 3 cups) fine sugar and a little vanilla. Mix well. Put the mixture in a bowl and blend in 2 more egg whites. Whisk the mixture. Pipe onto rice paper. Sprinkle with sugar and bake as indicated above.

Soft macaroons. MACARONS MOELLEUX – Pound in a mortar 250 g. (9 oz., $1\frac{3}{4}$ cups) almonds with 250 g. (9 oz., 2 cups) lump sugar. Pound into this mixture enough double cream and egg white to make a paste which is soft but not runny.

Spoon the mixture onto sheets of rice paper and bake as indicated above.

MACE. MACIS – Dried shell of the nutmeg. Its flavour is midway between that of nutmeg and cinnamon. It is used to flavour marinades, brines and sauces.

MACÉDOINE – Mixture or raw or cooked fruit or vegetables. It can be served either hot or cold.

The name *macédoine* is derived from Macedonia, the country formed by small states which were conquered by Alexander the Great.

MACÉDOINE OF FRUIT. MACÉDOINE DE FRUITS –

Macédoine of fruit, chilled (fruit salad). MACÉDOINE DE FRUITS RAFRAÎCHIS – Mix in a bowl, fruit in season, such as quartered or sliced pears, peeled and sliced bananas, sliced apricots, strawberries, whole raspberries, blanched fresh almonds, etc.

Pour a heavy sugar syrup over the fruit, or sprinkle each layer of fruit with fine sugar. Flavour with a few teaspoons of kirsch, maraschino, or other liqueur.

Embed the bowl of fruit in a bucket of crushed ice. Leave to chill for 2 hours.

MACÉDOINE OF VEGETABLES. MACÉDOINE DE LÉGUMES –

Macédoine of vegetables with butter. MACÉDOINE DE LÉGUMES AU BEURRE – Shape carrots and turnips into balls with a ball-scoop, or dice them finely. Dice French beans or cut them into lozenges. Dice green asparagus tips. Boil each of these vegetables and some green peas separately in salt water.

Heat the vegetables together and blend in butter. Season.

Cold macédoine of vegetables. MACÉDOINE DE LÉGUMES FROIDS – Prepare, cook and mix in a bowl the same vegetables as in the recipe for *Macédoine of vegetables with butter*. Dress with oil, vinegar, salt and pepper or with mayonnaise.

This dish can be eaten either as a salad or an *hors-d'œuvre*.

Macédoine of vegetables with cream. MACÉDOINE DE LÉGUMES À LA CRÈME – Prepare and cook the same mixture of vegetables as above. Blend in fresh cream.

Macédoine of vegetables in jelly. MACÉDOINE DE LÉGUMES À LA GELÉE – This type of *macédoine*, which is usually served with mayonnaise mixed with concentrated jelly stock, is set in a mould lined with jelly. It is also known as *aspic of vegetables*.

MACKEREL. MAQUEREAU – A long, slender, saltwater fish. Its scales are small and smooth, its back steely blue or greenish, its belly an opalescent silvery white. It is fatty and savoury, and is eaten fresh, smoked, salted or soused.

Its real name is *soombrid.* The name mackerel is derived from the French word *maquereau* which also means a 'procurer' or 'pimp'. It was given to this fish because of its habit of escorting the young shad (known as 'virgins') to the males. The male mackerel is polygamous.

The French name for young mackerels is *sansonnets*.

Mackerel à l'anglaise. MAQUEREAU À L'ANGLAISE – Cut the fish into thick slices. Poach in a *court-bouillon* (q.v.) flavoured with fennel. Serve with a rather liquid gooseberry purée.

Mackerel à la boulonnaise. MAQUEREAU À LA BOULONNAISE – Cut the mackerel into thick slices. Poach in a *court-bouillon* with a good deal of vinegar. Drain and skin. Arrange on a dish and surround with shelled, poached mussels. Cover with *Butter sauce* (see SAUCE) moistened with a little of the mackerel and mussel cooking stocks.

Mackerel with browned butter I. MAQUEREAU AU BEURRE NOISETTE – Poach the mackerel, sliced or filleted, in a *court-bouillon*. Put it on a serving dish and pour lemon juice over it. Before serving, pour on 2 to 3 tablespoons butter heated in a pan until nut brown.

Mackerel with browned butter II. MAQUEREAU AU BEURRE NOIR – Cut the mackerel into thick slices or fillet it. Poach in a vinegar *court-bouillon*. Drain. Put on a serving dish and dry it a little in the oven. Sprinkle with chopped parsley and capers. Pour a little lemon juice or vinegar over it. Before serving, pour on 2 tablespoons (3 tablespoons) butter heated in a frying pan until very dark brown.

The mackerel can also be prepared as follows:

Put it on a serving dish. Dry in the oven and sprinkle with capers. Pour a little lemon juice or vinegar over it. Pour on browned butter as indicated above, with 2 tablespoons (3 tablespoons) parsley leaves fried in it.

Mackerel Colbert. MAQUEREAU COLBERT – Slit the fish along the back. Open it and remove the bone. Season with salt and pepper. Dip in egg and breadcrumbs and deep-fry. Serve with *Maître d'hôtel butter* (see BUTTER, *Compound butters*).

Mackerel in court-bouillon. MAQUEREAU AU COURT-BOUILLON – Poach the fish, whole or sliced, in a *court-bouillon* of water with vinegar or lemon juice, seasoned with salt and flavoured with thyme and bay leaves.

Drain. Garnish with fresh parsley. Serve with one of the following sauces: *Butter, Parsley, Hollandaise, Lobster, Ravigote, Venetian* (see SAUCE).

Fillets of mackerel à la dieppoise. FILETS DE MAQUEREAU À LA DIEPPOISE – Poach the fillets in white wine, and drain. Arrange on a dish surrounded by a *Dieppoise garnish* (see GARNISHES). Cover with *White wine sauce* (see SAUCE), with the cooking liquor of the mussels and fillets added to it. Sprinkle the garnish with chopped parsley.

Fillets of mackerel with aubergines. FILETS DE MAQUEREAU AUX AUBERGINES – Season the fillets and fry them in butter *à la meunière*. Put them on a serving dish. Surround with slices of aubergine fried in butter. Squeeze lemon juice over the fillets. Pour on the cooking butter, piping hot.

Fillets of mackerel à la florentine. FILETS DE MAQUEREAU À LA FLORENTINE – Cook the fillets in a very little white wine. Cook leaf spinach in butter. Arrange the fillets on this bed of spinach. Cover with *Mornay sauce* (see SAUCE) with the fish cooking stock added to it. Sprinkle with grated cheese and melted butter and brown in the oven or under a grill.

Fillets of mackerel au gratin. FILETS DE MAQUEREAU AU GRATIN – Proceed as for *Sole au gratin* (see SOLE).

Fillets of mackerel with various garnishes. FILETS DE MAQUEREAU AVEC GARNITURES DIVERSES – Cook in butter and surround with one of the following garnishes: *cèpes* sautéed in oil; thick slices of mushrooms cooked in butter; cucumber cut into small oval chunks and cooked in butter; very small vegetable marrows (courgettes or zucchinis) cut into rounds and sautéed in butter or oil; tomatoes sautéed in oil or butter and flavoured with garlic; coarsely diced potatoes sautéed in butter.

Pour lemon juice and the cooking butter, piping hot, over the fillets.

Fillets of mackerel à la lyonnaise. FILETS DE MAQUEREAU À LA LYONNAISE – Line a dish with 2 tablespoons (3 tablespoons) chopped onion which has been gently cooked in butter and moistened with 1 tablespoon vinegar. Season the fillets, lay them on top of the onion and cover them with more onion prepared in the same way. Moisten with $\frac{1}{2}$ dl. (3 tablespoons, scant $\frac{1}{4}$ cup) white wine. Sprinkle with breadcrumbs, and dot with tiny pieces of butter. Bake in the oven. Sprinkle with chopped parsley.

Fillets of mackerel à la piémontaise. FILETS DE MAQUEREAU

How to fillet mackerel: Trace the contours of the fillet with a knife (*Larousse*)

Slide the knife along the backbone and detach the fillet (*Larousse*)

À LA PIÉMONTAISE – Season the fillets and dip in egg and breadcrumbs. Fry in butter.

Serve on a foundation of risotto (q.v.) and surround with a border of *Tomato fondue* (see FONDUE).

Fillets of mackerel à la vénitienne. FILETS DE MAQUEREAU À LA VÉNITIENNE – Cook the fillets in white wine with chopped shallots and chervil. Drain. Put on a serving dish. Cover with *Venetian sauce* (see SAUCE) to which the boiled-down pan juices have been added.

Fillets of mackerel in white wine. FILETS DE MAQUEREAU AU VIN BLANC – Trim the fillets and season them with salt and pepper. Put in a buttered baking tin. Moisten with concentrated white wine fish *fumet* (q.v.) and bake in the oven for 8 to 10 minutes. Drain, boil down the pan juices and use as a basis for *White wine sauce* (see SAUCE). Pour the sauce over the mackerel and serve.

Fried mackerel. MAQUEREAU FRIT – This is especially suitable for small mackerel. Dip in cold, boiled milk. Flour lightly and deep-fry in very hot fat. Drain, dry on a cloth and season with dry table salt. Garnish with fried parsley and lemon.

Grilled mackerel. MAQUEREAU GRILLÉ – Snip off the tip of the mackerel's jaw and slit the fish along the back. Open it and cut the bone in two places without separating the halves. Season, baste with melted butter and grill slowly.

Shape the mackerel in its original form. Pour on half melted *Maître d'hôtel butter* (see BUTTER, *Compound butters*).

Any sauce suitable for grilled fish, e.g. *Bordelaise, Provençale, Saint-Malo* (see SAUCE) can be served with mackerel.

Mackerel à la meunière. MAQUEREAU À LA MEUNIÈRE – Prepare like *Bass à la meunière* (see BASS).

Mackerel soft roes. LAITANCES DE MAQUEREAU – See SOFT ROES.

Soused mackerel. MAQUEREAUX MARINÉS – Usually served as a cold *hors-d'œuvre*. Proceed as for *Marinade of fresh herrings* (see HERRING).

MÂCON WINE. VIN DE MÂCON – The name of Mâcon is well known, thanks to the excellent wines made from the grapes grown around this town in the Saône-et-Loire *département*.

The *Côte mâconnaise* extends along the slopes which run almost parallel to the right bank of the Saône between Tournus and the boundary of the Rhône *département*.

Mâconnais wines (known as Mâcon wines) are full bodied and very smooth, with a delicate and distinctive aroma.

The most famous of the white Mâcon wines are Pouilly-Fuissé, Pouilly-Loché and Pouilly-Vinzelles, all from the Solutré region, south of Mâcon. (See BURGUNDY.)

MÂCONNAISE – Wine cask in use in the Mâconnais district. It holds about 212 litres ($46\frac{1}{2}$ gallons, 58 gallons).

This name is also applied to a bottle, containing 8 dl. ($1\frac{1}{3}$ pints, $1\frac{2}{3}$ pints), which is used for Mâconnais wines.

MÂCONNAISE (À LA) – Name given to various meat dishes flavoured with red wine.

MADDER-WORT. GARANCE – Plant used in dyeing, from which a kind of beer can be brewed.

MADEIRA CAKE – Mix 500 g. (18 oz., $4\frac{1}{2}$ cups) sifted flour with $\frac{1}{2}$ teaspoon salt. Cream 450 g. (1 lb., 2 cups) butter and 450 g. (1 lb., 2 cups) sugar. Beat 10 egg yolks until light and add to the butter mixture. Sift in the flour gradually. Add $\frac{1}{2}$ teaspoon lemon essence and the grated rind of $\frac{1}{2}$ lemon. Beat the egg whites until stiff, and fold in. Line 2 900-g. (2-lb.) bread tins with buttered paper or waxed paper. Pour the batter into the pans and sprinkle the surface with sugar. Bake $1\frac{1}{4}$ hours at 150°C. (300°F., Gas Mark 2). Place small slices of candied citron on the surface of the cake after the first 15 minutes of baking.

MADEIRA WINE. VIN DE MADÈRE – This wine, which is made from grapes grown on the island of Madeira in the Atlantic Ocean, is one of the finest of fortified wines.

Various types of wine are made in Madeira, such as Malmsey, Muscatel, Dry Madeira, made from the grapes of vines which are said to have been imported into Madeira from Cyprus in about the fifteenth century. Funchal, the capital of the island, is the storehouse of these wines.

Madeira is a tonic and an exhilarating wine. It is drunk as an apéritif before meals and is used a great deal in cooking.

Madeira pie. CROÛTE AU MADÈRE – Fruit pie served with apricot sauce flavoured with Madeira.

Madeira sauce. SAUCE AU MADÈRE – A *demi-glace sauce* boiled down with Madeira. (See SAUCE.)

Madeira sherbets. SORBETS AU MADÈRE – Sherbets served in sherbet glasses with Madeira poured over them just before serving.

MADELEINE – A small cake made of flour, butter, eggs and sugar.

A chronicler of the history of pastry-making says that the great pastry-cook, Avice, invented the madeleine when he was working for Prince Talleyrand. 'He had the idea of using *tôt-fait* (q.v.) or *quatre-quarts* (q.v.) mixture for little cakes baked in an aspic mould. M. Boucher and Carême approved

Madeleines made in old-fashioned moulds

the idea. He gave the name of madeleines to these cakes.' (Lacam, *Mémorial de la pâtisserie*.)

Other authorities, however, hold that far from having been invented by Avice, these little cakes were known in France long before his time. They believe that they were first made at Commercy, and were brought into fashion about 1730, first at Versailles and then, in Paris, by Stanislas Leczinski, father-in-law of Louis XV, who was very partial to them.

The recipe for madeleines remained a secret for a very long time. It is said that it was sold for a very large sum to the pastry-makers of Commercy, who made of this great delicacy one of the finest gastronomic specialities of their town.

Commercy madeleines

Commercy madeleine. MADELEINE DE COMMERCY – Work together in a bowl 625 g. (1 lb. 6 oz., 5 cups) fine sugar, 625 g. (1 lb. 6 oz., $5\frac{1}{2}$ cups) sieved flour, 12 eggs, $1\frac{1}{2}$ teaspoons bicarbonate of soda, the grated rind of a lemon, a pinch of salt.

When this mixture is very smooth, add to it 300 g. (11 oz., $1\frac{1}{3}$ cups) melted butter. Mix well. Put in buttered madeleine moulds. Bake in a very slow oven.

Plain madeleines. MADELEINES ORDINAIRES – *Ingredients.* 250 g. (9 oz., 2 cups) fine sugar, 250 g. (9 oz., $2\frac{1}{4}$ cups) sieved flour, 250 g. (9 oz., generous cup) melted butter, 4 eggs, a pinch of salt, vanilla or other flavouring.

Method. Put the sugar, flour, eggs, salt and flavouring into a bowl. Work with a spatula until the mixture is smooth. Add the melted butter.

Butter and flour the required number of madeleine moulds. Spoon in the mixture. The moulds should be two-thirds full. Bake at 190°C. (375°F., Gas Mark 5) for 15 to 20 minutes.

MADERISED. MADÉRISÉ – Certain white wines acquire with age a flavour of Madeira. These are said to be maderised.

The term *madérisé* in modern French also applies to the unpleasant bottle smell of a wine kept for too long a period.

MADRILÈNE (À LA) – Name given to a clear soup (generally served cold or chilled) which is flavoured with tomato juice. The name is also applied to other dishes, flavoured with tomato juice.

MAGISTÈRES – Name given to a number of nourishing soups invented by Brillat-Savarin, author of *la Physiologie du goût.*

'The first of the *magistères*', says Brillat-Savarin, 'is made as follows:

'Take 6 large onions, 3 carrots, a handful of parsley. Chop all these ingredients and put them in a pot to warm and brown with a piece of good fresh butter.

'When the mixture is just right, throw in 175 g. (6 oz.) candied sugar, 20 grains pounded amber, with a slice of toast and 3 bottles of water. Boil for 45 minutes and add fresh water to make up the small amount lost through evaporation, so that 3 bottles full of liquid remain.

'Pound an old fowl, flesh, bones and all, in a mortar with an iron pestle. Chop 900 g. (2 lb.) carefully chosen beef.

'When this is done mix the two meats, adding salt and pepper. Put the mixture in a saucepan over a high flame, so that the heat penetrates right through, and from time to time add a little fresh butter so that the mixture is well browned without sticking to the pan.

'When the stock begins to brown, strain the soup which is in the first saucepan. With this, moisten little by little the mixture in the second saucepan, and, when it is all mixed in, boil it for 45 minutes so that the surface of the liquid ripples throughout. Care must be taken to add hot water from time to time so that the liquid level remains constant. The result is a potion whose beneficial effect is certain as long as the invalid, however exhausted he may be, is still able to digest food.'

Brillat-Savarin goes on to explain how the *magistère* should be given to the invalid.

'On the first day he should be given a cup every 3 hours until he settles down for the night; on the following days, a large cup in the morning only and the same amount in the evening, until the 3 bottles are used up. The invalid should be kept on a light though nourishing diet, such as legs of poultry, fish, sweet fruit and jam.

'Towards the fourth day the invalid should be able to return to normal life.

'This *magistère*,' Brillat-Savarin points out, 'is intended for robust and dynamic characters and for people who generally wear themselves out by burning up their energies.'

The master suggests another *magistère* made from shin of veal, pigeons and crayfish, intended for 'the weak and the infirm'.

MAGNY – See RESTAURANTS OF BYGONE DAYS.

MAGPIE. PIE – Common bird in France, sometimes eaten in the country. The flesh is very dry and is used mainly for stock. Young magpies are more tender and more edible.

MAIA – Name given in the Balkans to milk soured by previous fermentation and used as a leaven in the preparation of yoghourt.

MAIGRE – French word describing foods prescribed by the Church for consumption during Lent and days of abstinence. In the early days, only foods of vegetable origin were permitted, but gradually the Church authorised butter and eggs; then the flesh of cold-blooded creatures such as fish; then certain waterfowl (considered to be cold-blooded, too) such as the shoveller duck, the pintail, the scoter, the waterhen, the coot, the teal, the water-rail, the curlew, the heron, the godwit, the sandpiper and the wheatear.

MAILLOT – See GARNISHES.

MAINE – See ORLÉANAIS.

MAINTENON (À LA) – See MIXTURES, *Maintenon mixture*.

MAIRE – See RESTAURANTS OF BYGONE DAYS.

MAISON – The term *maison* is often abused in restaurants. All too often one reads: *sole* (or some other fish) *maison, chicken maison,* etc.

The epithet *maison*, in its origin and in the minds of restaurateurs who use it honestly, indicates that the dish in question has been made by the restaurateur himself or his staff, following a recipe which he can claim as his own.

Nevertheless, the term does lack precision. It would be more satisfactory to say *de notre maison* or *à la manière de notre maison*, since *maison* as it stands is vague enough for unscrupulous restaurateurs to offer as a *Tarte maison*, for instance, a pastry which comes from a *maison* other than their own, from a wholesale confectioner, in fact!

There would be no great harm in this, were it not that more serious abuses may arise from it, when, for instance *maison* is applied to a product whose name implies its place of origin. *Fine maison*, i.e. Fine Champagne (a liqueur brandy) would be suspect, because, by law, the designations 'Cognac' and 'Fine Champagne' are reserved exclusively, under pain of prosecution and severe penalties, for brandies made in Cognac or within the official boundaries of the Fine Champagne region. Thus, the expression *fine maison* is a purely fanciful one. It suggests to the consumer a Fine Champagne which the *maison* has imported for its own exclusive use from the Fine Champagne region. In fact it merely enables the restaurateur to sell, without risk of prosecution, adulterated brandy, made from spirits which might come from anywhere.

MAISON DORÉE – See RESTAURANTS OF BYGONE DAYS.

MAISON DU ROI (Royal Household) – Under the old French monarchy, this was the name given to all the departments and personnel of the court. Chief among these was the *bouche du roi* (royal kitchens), which was made up of a very large number of officials.

MAITRANK – Drink very popular in Germany. The name is made up of the words *mai* (May) and *trank* (drink), indicating that it is made in the spring.

It is prepared from young, fragrant, asperula shoots. This plant is also known as woodruff.

Put some young asperula shoots in a large soup tureen. Moisten with a bottle of white Rhine wine and 2 to 4 tablespoons of brandy. Cover the tureen and leave to infuse for 30 minutes. Add 100 g. (4 oz., $\frac{1}{2}$ cup) sugar dissolved in a little water. Mix.

This drink can also be made with white Alsace wine or white Graves.

MAÎTRE D'HÔTEL – Nowadays, the title of *maître d'hôtel* is reserved for the man in charge of the dining-room in a hotel or restaurant. He is assisted by a team of senior, junior and assistant waiters.

Formerly this title was used also of a hotel proprietor, but only in the provinces.

Previously in royal, princely, and other noble households, the office of *maître d'hôtel* was always held by persons of the highest rank, sometimes princes of the blood royal. Although at that time the office was a sinecure, the *maître d'hôtel* was, at least nominally, in charge of all departments of the royal household, including the kitchens and cellars, and all the functionaries and servants.

The *maître d'hôtel* of a modern restaurant or a great private establishment today, must have a very extensive range of technical knowledge. He must have qualities of leadership which will enable him to command his staff with authority and courtesy. He must be a first-class administrator and a tactful diplomat.

He must be thoroughly familiar with details of the special work of the dining-room, kitchens and cellars. He must be able to talk to the clients – in several languages – politely but not obsequiously. He must be able to advise his clients, to guide them in their choice of dishes, the wines to go with them and the fruit to follow.

These are the qualities which the modern *maître d'hôtel* must possess. If he is no longer a *grand seigneur*, as were the important personages who filled this office in the great royal households, he is usually a man of distinction, good education and, particularly, a master of his art, for service at the table is as much an art as cooking.

MAÎTRE D'HÔTEL BUTTER. BEURRE À LA MAÎTRE D'HÔTEL – A seasoned butter served with grilled meat or fish, fried fish and other dishes. It is prepared by creaming fresh butter with chopped parsley, lemon juice, salt and pepper. (See BUTTER, *Compound butters*.)

MAIZE – See CORN.

MALAGA – A sweet wine made in Andalucia, which enjoys a great reputation and is used in cooking and confectionery. There is white Malaga, which is a golden colour, and red Malaga.

MALAXER – French word meaning to knead a substance in order to soften it.

MALIC ACID. MALIQUE – An organic acid present in most fruit and some vegetables.

MALLOW. MAUVE – Plant whose leaves, which contain a viscous substance, are used as an emollient in poultices and infusions.

The flowers are soothing to chest troubles. The leaves can be eaten in salad or as a vegetable, like spinach.

MALMSEY (MALVOISIE) WINE. VIN DE MALVOISIE – This famous wine made in Madeira, Cyprus and the Canary Islands is named after a vine originating in the Greek island, Malavosia. The transplanted vine yields a slightly musky wine, sometimes a little bitter, and heavy and, occasionally, perfectly dry.

It is very similar to Frontignac, and is drunk as an apéritif. It is also used a great deal in cooking in the preparation of sweets, and to flavour certain sauces, instead of Madeira and other heavy wines.

MALT – Barley prepared for brewing by steeping, germination or kiln drying. (See BEER.)

Malt extract. EXTRAIT DE MALT – A concentrated infusion of germinated barley which is made into syrups or crystals. It is used as a food, especially to moisten porridges for very young babies, because of its enzyme content.

MANCHE – In French cookery, the projecting bone of a cutlet is called a *manche*.

MANCHETTE – A paper frill for the projecting bones of cutlets or joints. (See PAPILLOTE.)

MANCHON – This is a name for:

1. A small cake made of flaky pastry and baked in a mould in the shape of a muff.

2. A *petit four* made of almond paste rolled out rather thin, baked for a few seconds in the oven, then rolled on a wooden handle to make a kind of little muff.

When these *manchons* are cold they are filled with butter cream flavoured with praline (q.v.). Each end of the biscuit is then dipped into very finely shredded green almonds.

MANGE-TOUT – Sugar pea or bean of which the pod is eaten as well as the seeds. They are cooked in the same way as French beans (see BEANS, *French beans*).

MANGO. MANGUE – The mango tree, of which the mango is the fruit, is of East Indian origin. It is cultivated in the East Indies, Cayenne, Malaya, China, the island of Mauritius and in southern Florida and California in U.S.A.

The mango is an oblong fruit about the size of a big pear, green in colour, turning orange-yellow when ripe with a rosy blush on the side exposed to the sun. The flesh is orange-yellow in colour, similar to that of a carrot. It is pleasant in flavour but a little acrid and does not appeal to all tastes.

Besides being eaten raw, mangoes can also be made into jam and are used in the preparation of Indian chutney, a pickle with a great reputation, used as a condiment.

MANGOSTEEN. MANGOUSTAN – This tree grows in India and the Spice Islands. Its fruit (not to be confused with the mango) is about the size of an orange, with a delicious raspberry-flavoured pulp. It is eaten raw, used to make jams and other preserves and as an ingredient of desserts.

MANICAMP – See CHEESE.

MANICLE – Vine grown in Bugey. It yields a 'muddy' (*épais*) wine. Brillat-Savarin says that this vine was planted by the Romans.

MANIER – French culinary term for working a mixture by hand. It is particularly applied to thoroughly mixing a quantity of flour with butter or other fat. This mixture is used to rapidly thicken sauces, gravies and stews, and is called kneaded butter.

MANQUÉ – A cake very popular in Paris.

One recipe for *manqué* is given under SPONGE CAKE. *Ingredients.* 250 g. (9 oz., $2\frac{1}{4}$ cups) sifted flour, 375 g. (13 oz., 3 cups) fine sugar, 125 g. (4 oz., $\frac{1}{2}$ cup) butter, 9 eggs, a small pinch of salt, vanilla.

Method. Work the egg yolks with the sugar, vanilla and salt in a mixing bowl. When the mixture is light and fluffy, add the melted butter, flour, then, stirring gently, the stiffly beaten whites of egg. Fill a brioche mould with this mixture. Bake in a slow oven. Sprinkle with *praline* (q.v.) and decorate the top with a piece of crystallised fruit.

MANZANILLA WINE – Kind of sherry.

MAPLE. ÉRABLE À SUCRE – A true native of South America, and cultivated in the United States and Canada. The trunk of this tree, tapped in the spring, yields abundant sap which can be fermented or made into vinegar, but which is usually eaten in the form of syrup (maple syrup) or sugar (maple sugar).

A maple tree can yield, in 24 hours, as much as 30 kg. (66 lb.) sap containing 2 kg. ($4\frac{1}{2}$ lb.) sugar.

Several varieties of maple yield sugar.

MARAÎCHÈRE (À LA) – Method of preparation applied especially to large roast or braised cuts of meat. The main ingredients are carrots, small onions, braised stuffed cucumbers, salsify, artichokes, *Château potatoes* (see POTATOES).

MARASCHINO. MARASQUIN – Liqueur made chiefly in Zara, in Dalmatia. Its main ingredient is a type of black cherry called *marasca* in Italy.

The cherries are pounded and the stones crushed (which is not the case with kirsch). Honey is added and the mixture is left to ferment. It is then distilled and sugar is added.

MARBLED. PERSILLÉ – Meat is said to be marbled when it is flecked with tiny particles of fat. This marbling only occurs in meat of the finest quality.

In French the term *persillé* is also applied to various green-veined cheeses.

MARC – The residue of various fruits and vegetables after pressing. The word is often used as an abbreviation for *eau-de-vie de marc*, a spirit distilled from the marc of grapes. It can also mean the residue of substances like tea or coffee from which the goodness has been extracted by boiling or steeping.

MARCHE AND LIMOUSIN – Geographically and historically these two ancient French provinces are different from each other. Gastronomically, however, they can be regarded as one, for not only are they neighbours but they share the same produce and the same culinary specialities.

The province of Limousin is now divided into the *départements* of Corrèze and Haute-Vienne. The famous *hare à la royale* was created in this province.

Potted foie gras and *pâtés de foie gras* are made in Brive.

Limoges china, as well as its *cuisine*, is famous.

In these two ancient provinces are to be found foodstuffs of every kind and of the highest quality.

The cattle of Limousin are famous, as are its pigs, from which excellent pork products are made. Ground and winged game abound in the Marche and Limousin provinces. Freshwater fish (carp, perch, pike and others) fill the rivers, lakes and ponds of the region. The trout of Vienne, Maulde and Vézère are very delicate in flavour. Crayfish abound in the waterways. Notable, too, are the salmon of Vézère.

The market gardens produce excellent vegetables, and there is an abundance of fruit and chestnuts.

In the woods and fields of this region, all kinds of fungi are to be found, in particular *cèpes* and morels.

Excellent cheeses are made in the Marche and Limousin provinces.

The slopes of Argentat and Queyssac in Corrèze produce pleasant wines. The rosé wines of Chabanais, Étagnat, Saint-Brice, Verneuil and Aise, in the Vienne Valley, have a high reputation.

Culinary specialities – *Soupe bouillie d'avoine* (oat porridge); *soupe au pain de seigle* (rye-bread soup); *soupe aux choux* (cabbage soup); *soupe Bréjauda* (a soup made from cabbage and bacon. With this soup the people of Limousin make *chabrol*; they add half a glass of red wine to the last few spoonfuls of soup left in the plate).

Farcidures (balls made from buckwheat flour mixed with sorrel and beetroot and wrapped in cabbage leaves. These are sometimes made small and cooked in cabbage soup). *Trout à la meunière; matelotes of fish de la Corrèze; crayfish in court-bouillon; broccana* (meat *pâtés*, made from sausage meat and veal); *hare au Cabessal* or *Chabessal* (this dish, which is the great culinary speciality of the region, is known among connoisseurs as *hare à la royale*). *Cèpes* stuffed *à la corrézienne; farcidure of fried potatoes; chou farci* (stuffed cabbage).

Among the sweets and desserts are Limousin *clafoutis; flognarde; fruit tart; cheese pâté; tourtons* (buckwheat *galettes*); the *macaroons* of Dorat; the *croquants* (biscuits) of Bort-les-Orgues; the *meringues* of Uzerches.

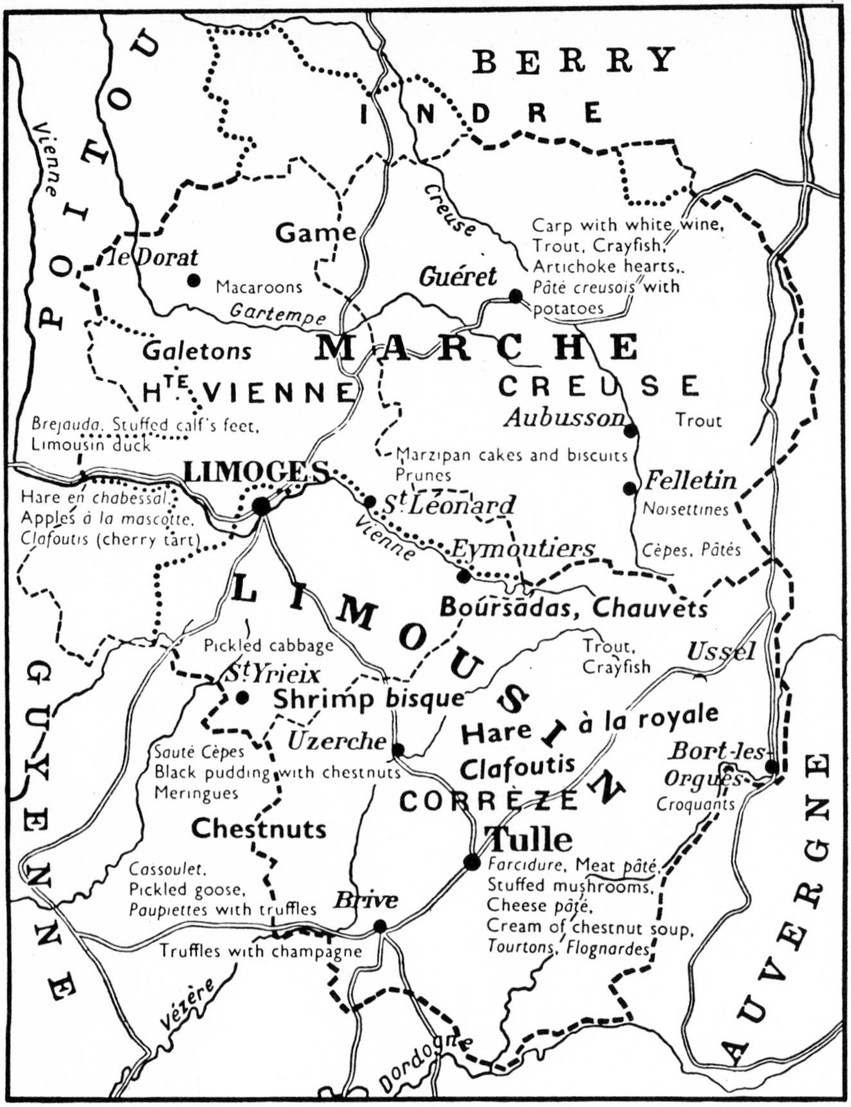

Gastronomic map of Marche and Limousin

MARÉCHALE (À LA) – Method of preparing escalopes, wings and breasts of poultry and other small cuts, dipping them in egg and breadcrumbs and frying them in butter. These small cuts are usually garnished with green asparagus tips and truffles.

MARÉE – French collective name for all the seawater fish, shellfish and seafood sold in a fish market.

Paris had a regular daily supply of fresh fish as early as the sixteenth century, thanks to the sturdy fish cart ponies which raced to and fro between the Channel ports and the capital.

MARENGO – Name of the battle in which Napoleon Bonaparte defeated the Austrians on 14 June 1800. This battle has given its name to a chicken dish which was cooked on the battlefield itself by Dunand, chef to Napoleon.

Bonaparte, who on battle days ate nothing until the fight was over, had gone forward with his general staff and was a long way from his supply wagons. Seeing his enemies put to flight, he asked Dunand to prepare dinner for him. The master chef at once sent men of the quartermaster's staff and ordnance corps in search of provisions. All they could find were 3 eggs, 4 tomatoes, 6 crayfish, a small hen, a little garlic, some oil and a saucepan. Using his bread ration, Dunand first made a *panade* with oil and water, and then, having drawn and jointed the chicken, browned it in oil, and fried the eggs in the same oil with a few cloves of garlic and the tomatoes. He poured over this mixture some water laced with brandy borrowed from the General's flask and put the crayfish on top to cook in the steam.

The dish was served on a tin plate, the chicken surrounded by the fried eggs and crayfish, with the sauce poured over it. Bonaparte, having feasted upon it, said to Dunand: 'You must feed me like this after every battle.'

The originality of this improvised dish lay in the garnish, for *chicken à la Provençale*, sautéed in oil with garlic and tomatoes, was known in Paris under the Directory (1796–1799). Dunand was well aware that the crayfish were out of place in this dish, and so he later substituted wine for the water and added mushrooms. But one day, when he had served the dish improved in this way, Bonaparte said angrily: 'You have left out the crayfish. It will bring me bad luck. I don't want any of it.'

Willy-nilly, the crayfish garnish had to be restored, and it has remained to this day the traditional garnish for the dish.

For detailed recipes see CHICKEN, and also VEAL, *Veal sauté marengo*.

MARENNES – Small port in the Charente-Maritime district where, in vast beds at La Tremblade, fine white and green oysters are bred.

There is a *confrérie* called the *Galants de la Verte Marennes*.

MARES-TAILS. PRÊLE – Common plant of the fields, especially in damp places, which is hard stemmed and rich in silica. In their first week of growth the young shoots, not yet silicious, are edible and can be used like asparagus. The Romans valued them and the habit of eating them is maintained in certain regions. They are also pickled in vinegar.

MARGARINE – Cooking fat made from the most soluble parts of beef and veal fat, purified by heating and decanting, and churned with a little cream. Vegetable oil, groundnuts, sesame or coconut is added.

This type of margarine is intended especially for pastry-making. The type called table margarine which is used in household cooking is made entirely from vegetable fat.

MARGUÉRY – See RESTAURANTS OF BYGONE DAYS.

MARIGNAN – Cake very popular in Paris. Bake a *savarin* (q.v.) in a *manque* (q.v.) mould. When ready, soak it in syrup flavoured with liqueur. Cut 2 horizontal channels on top of the cake. Decorate them with *Meringue à Marignan* (see MERINGUE). Cover the cake with apricot jam, leaving the meringue plain.

MARIGOLD. SOUCI – Name of several plants, among them the cultivated marigold whose yellow flowers are sometimes used to colour butter. The fully blown buds of the marsh marigold are sometimes pickled in vinegar, masquerading as capers.

MARINADE – A seasoned liquid, cooked or uncooked, in which foodstuffs, notably meat and fish, are steeped.

The purposes of a marinade is to season the food steeped in it by impregnating them with the flavour of its condiments. It also softens the fibres of some kinds of meat a little, and enables fish and meat to be kept rather longer than is generally possible.

The time during which foodstuffs should be left in a marinade depends upon their size and texture. In winter large cuts of meat and venison can be left in a marinade for 5 to 6 days. In summer, they should not be steeped for longer than 24 to 48 hours, except in the case of large cuts of venison, which require longer steeping.

COOKED MARINADES. MARINADES CUITES –

Preservation of cooked marinades. CONSERVATION DES MARINADES CUITES – These marinades can be kept for quite a long time provided they are brought to the boil every other day in summer and every four days in winter. Each time the marinade is boiled a little wine and vinegar should be added to it.

Cooked marinade for meat and venison. MARINADE CUITE POUR VIANDES DE BOUCHERIE ET VENAISON – Brown very slightly in oil the vegetables and herbs indicated for *Uncooked marinade* (see below). Add white wine and vinegar, and simmer gently for 30 minutes.

Season the meat with salt and pepper. Put it in a bowl and cover with the marinade, which must be quite cold. Keep in a cool place.

Cooked marinade for mutton, called 'en chevreuil'. MARINADE EN CHEVREUIL – Proceed as indicated above, adding juniper and rosemary.

Red wine marinade for meat. MARINADE AU VIN ROUGE – Proceed as indicated above, using red wine instead of white wine. Leave to steep for 2 hours.

UNCOOKED MARINADES. MARINADES CRUES –

Uncooked marinade I (for meat and game). MARINADES CRUES POUR VIANDES DE BOUCHERIE ET VENAISON – Chop 1 medium-sized carrot, 1 large onion, 2 shallots, 2 sticks celery and 2 clove of garlic. Put half these vegetables in a deep dish, which must be large enough to contain the meat. Add a sprig of chopped parsley, a few shreds of thyme and bay leaf, 6 to 8 peppercorns and a clove.

Season the meat with salt and pepper and put it in the dish. Cover with the rest of the vegetables. Moisten with 6 dl. (1 pint, $2\frac{1}{2}$ cups) dry white wine and $2\frac{1}{2}$ dl. (scant $\frac{1}{2}$ pint, generous cup) oil. Keep in a cool place. Turn the meat over frequently so that it is thoroughly impregnated with the flavour of the herbs.

When this marinade is to be used for venison, 6 coriander seeds and 6 crushed juniper berries should be added.

Uncooked marinade II (for large cuts of meat). MARINADE CRUE POUR GROSSES VIANDES DE BOUCHERIE – Season the cut (haunch, rib, shoulder, etc.) with salt, pepper and spices. Put it in a bowl. Cover with a chopped onion and carrot. Add 2 crushed garlic cloves, a sprig of parsley and thyme, a quarter of a bay leaf and a clove. Moisten with cooking wine (dry white wine or red wine). Add a few drops of brandy. Cover with a plate, face downwards, and leave to steep in a cool place for 6 hours (or longer, in cool weather). Turn the meat over from time to time so that it is thoroughly impregnated with the marinade.

The meat is moistened with this marinade when braised.

Uncooked marinade III (for small individual portions of meat, poultry, fish, etc.). MARINADE CRUE POUR MENUES PIÈCES DE BOUCHERIE, VOLAILLES POISSONS, ETC. – Season the meat, poultry or fish with salt and pepper before putting it in the marinade. Lay the pieces in a deep dish. Sprinkle with finely chopped onions or shallots, coarsely chopped parsley, shreds of thyme and bay leaf, and garlic if desired. Pour oil and a squeeze of lemon juice over this mixture.

Leave to steep for 2 hours, turning frequently.

Uncooked marinade IV (for garnishes to be served with pâtés, potted meats, galantines, etc.). MARINADE CRUE POUR ÉLÉMENTS DE GARNITURE DES PÂTÉS, TERRINES, GALANTINES, ETC. – Season the garnish indicated with salt, pepper and spices. Pour on white wine, brandy and oil. Leave to steep in this marinade for 2 hours.

MARINIÈRE (À LA) – Method of preparing mussels and other shellfish (see MUSSELS). This name is also applied to certain dishes made of fish cooked in white wine and garnished with mussels (see BRILL, *Brill à la marinière*).

MARIVAUX – See GARNISHES.

MARJORAM. MARJOLAINE – This aromatic herb, which is used in cookery, flowers in the middle of summer.

MARMALADES. MARMELADES – In French the word *marmelade* is applied to fruit stewed for a very long time until it is reduced to a thick purée. Recipes are given below for various fruit marmalades (*marmelades*). For general instructions on jam-making, see JAMS AND JELLIES.

Apple marmalade. MARMELADE DE POMMES – Put the peeled

A salad basket of fresh brown eggs (*Phot. Nicolas*)

and quartered apples into a copper pan. Moisten with a few tablespoons water. Cook on the stove over a gentle heat.

Rub the apples through a sieve set over a large basin. Return this purée to the pan, with the liquor in which it has been cooked. Add 300 g. (11 oz., $1\frac{1}{3}$ cups) sugar for every 500 g. (18 oz., $2\frac{1}{4}$ cups) pulp. Mix and boil the marmalade, stirring all the time with the skimmer.

To determine whether the marmalade is cooked drop a little onto a plate. If this remains in a blob without spreading out the marmalade is cooked.

Apricot marmalade. MARMELADE D'ABRICOTS – *Ingredients.* 1 kg. ($2\frac{1}{4}$ lb.) stoned apricots (net weight), 750 g. ($1\frac{1}{2}$ lb., 3 cups) sugar, 1 dl. (6 tablespoons, scant $\frac{1}{2}$ cup) water.

Method. Simmer the apricots in the water for 20 minutes, stirring them with a copper or wooden spatula.

Rub through a sieve and put the pulp into a pan with the sugar. Cook to the jelling stage. Finish as described above.

Fig marmalade. MARMELADE DE FIGUES – Peel and slice figs which should be ripe but firm.

Prepare a syrup made of 200 g. (7 oz., scant cup) sugar and a little water for every 1 kg. ($2\frac{1}{4}$ lb.) fruit. Add the sliced figs. Boil until the jelling stage is reached.

Melon marmalade. MARMELADE DE MELON – Remove the rind of the melons and the seeds, and rub the pulp through a sieve. Add 100 g. (4 oz., $\frac{1}{2}$ cup) sugar per 450 g. (1 lb.) pulp if this is very sweet, or more if it is less sweet. Boil until it sets.

Orange marmalade. MARMELADE D'ORANGES – Pierce 10 oranges in several places with a pointed stick, and blanch in boiling water for 25 to 30 minutes.

Put them under the cold tap for some time. Divide them into quarters, remove the seeds, the pith and the fibrous parts, and rub through a wide meshed wire sieve. Add an equal quantity of sugar and one-third of the weight of the pulp in apple juice, obtained in the manner described for *Apple jelly* (see JAMS AND JELLIES). Boil in the usual way.

Peach marmalade. MARMELADE DE PÊCHES – Prepare with peaches in the same way as *Apricot marmalade.*

Pear marmalade. MARMELADE DE POIRES – Prepare with quartered pears in the same way as *Apple marmalade.*

Plum marmalade. MARMELADE DE PRUNES – Prepare with plums in the same way as *Apricot marmalade.*

Quince marmalade. MARMELADE DE COINGS – Prepare in the same way as *Apple marmalade*, using quinces.

MARMITE – Metal or earthenware covered pot, with or without feet, depending on whether it is used for cooking in the hearth or on the stove.

Straight-sided *marmites* for stove cooking can have a capacity of as much as 200 litres (44 gallons, 55 gallons). These very large pots have a tap fitted near the base.

Cooking pots of this size or even larger are often required in large establishments such as hospitals, etc. They may be either fixed or swinging, and should be made with a false bottom so that their contents are heated by steam.

There are special types for medium- or high-pressure cooking. Large swinging *marmites* are balanced in such a way as to ensure their stability at all angles. Pots of this type intended for use on board ship have a concave lip to prevent spilling in heavy seas.

There is also a type of double cooking pot called a *marmite.*

Earthenware marmites (*Nicolas*)

Newly baked bread (*Poilane. Phot. Nicolas*)

In this pot the water in the bottom is heated by vapour passing through a coil of copper tubing. Baskets are used for cooking rice, fish, meat, etc.

MARMITE, PETITE – Name of a clear savoury broth, a type of hotpot, cooked and served in an earthenware pot.

This broth was invented in Paris and is much prized by gourmets. (See PETITE MARMITE, SOUPS AND BROTHS.)

MARMOT. MARMOTTE – Rodent about the size of a large cat, which lives at high altitudes in the Alps and the Pyrenees. Marmots grow very fat towards the end of the autumn. In the winter they hibernate and live on their fat. Their flesh, which has a pronounced musky flavour, is edible after long steeping in a marinade.

MAROILLES – Small town in northern France which has given its name to a cheese, also known as Marolles. (See CHEESE.)

MAROUETTE – Type of rail which is very good to eat.

It is said that King Charles X of France gave orders that he should be immediately informed whenever a flight of *marouettes* was sighted, even if he were in council with his ministers.

This bird is prepared in the same way as quail. (q.v.).

MARQUER – In French cookery, this term covers all operations connected with the preparation of foodstuffs prior to cooking.

'Food fully prepared, and put in a saucepan, when nothing remains but to cook it,' is how Plumerey defined this cooking term. *Marquer*, however, is generally used in a more limited sense, meaning to place food in a buttered or greased pan, lined with pork skin, and carrots and onions cut into rings.

MARQUISE – Name of a variety of very tender and sweet pear. This fruit, which is pyramid shaped, is in season in France in November and December.

MARRON – A kind of chestnut, improved by cultivation, which is bigger and better than the common variety.

It is eaten boiled or grilled, or prepared in various ways for use in cooking, *pâtisserie* and confectionery.

The chestnut is a concentrated source of nourishment (250 calories per 100 g., 4 oz.) although it is rather indigestible owing to the fact that its starch is not easily assimilable. The chestnut is not very rich in vitamins, but contains a high proportion of mineral salts. Its high calcium and phosphorus content make it an excellent food for children and convalescents, provided they have healthy digestions.

Peeling chestnuts. Slit the surface of the chestnuts on the domed face. Put them in a baking tin with a little water and roast them in the oven for 8 minutes. Peel while they are still hot.

Another method. Slit the chestnuts as indicated above. Put them, a few at a time, into boiling fat. Deep-fry for 2 minutes. Drain. Peel them while they are still hot.

MARRONS GLACÉS – See CHESTNUT.

MARSALA – Dessert wine made in Italy from grapes grown in Sicily. This wine, which has something in common with sherry or Madeira, contains about 24 per cent of alcohol.

It is drunk as an apéritif before meals, and is also used in cooking and *pâtisserie*.

MARSEILLAN – Wine generally known as *pelure d'oignon* (onion skin). It is made at Marseillan, a little town in the Hérault district.

Above: Aluminium marmite (*Larousse*)

Right: Marmite for steaming potatoes (*Larousse*)

Stainless steel marmite and stew pan (*Chorand*)

MARSHMALLOW. PÂTE DE GUIMAUVE – This confection contains no real marshmallow, in spite of its name. It is made of egg whites.

MARTAGON – Variety of Alpine lily, also found in Russia, where the bulbs are used for food.

MARTINIQUE – Island in the Lesser Antilles colonised by the French in the seventeenth century and renowned for its rum, considered the best in the world. Sugar cane is grown extensively in this part of the world, and rum is one of the products of sugar cane.

Martinique coffee has a great reputation. The island also produces cocoa and fine spices.

MARTIN-SEC – Variety of pear in season in France from November to January. It is ovoid in shape and of medium size with a russet skin. The pulp is gritty and rather dry, but quite sweet.

MARTIN-SIRE – Variety of pear, also known as *rouville*, in season in France in November. It is rather large and elongated. Its skin is yellowish with grey flecks, the pulp firm and quite sweet.

MARTYRS, (BRASSERIE DES) – See RESTAURANTS OF BYGONE DAYS.

MARZIPAN. MASSEPAIN – Marzipan is made from ground almonds, sugar and egg whites. It can be coloured and flavoured and made into *petits fours* (q.v.) of different shapes, known in France as *massepains*. Marzipan is also used to make little sweets in the form of fruit, vegetables, etc.

Marzipan is of very ancient origin, and was probably made originally by some order of nuns, who made many little cakes and sweets.

In 1844, a rumour began to circulate that the author of *la Comédie humaine* (Balzac) had set himself up as a confectioner.

'No one talked of anything else on the Stock Exchange, in the foyer of the Opéra, at the Théâtre-Français, and in all the cafés on the Paris boulevards.

'Several thousands of copies of a curious circular had just made their appearance in Paris. They read as follows:

ISSOUDON MARZIPAN!

"Gentlemen,

"I have just opened a shop at 38 bis rue Vivienne to exploit this product which, in the province of Berry, enjoys a reputation almost a hundred years old. The most remarkable novelist of our era speaks of it thus in one of his works:

'This worthy woman was given the recipe by those most famous nuns to whom we owe Issoudon marzipan, one of the greatest creations of French confectionery, and which no master chef, cook, pastry-cook or confectioner has been able to imitate. M. de Rivière, French Ambassador in Constantinople, ordered large quantities every year for the seraglio of the Sultan Mahmoud.' – H. de Balzac.

"This unique sweetmeat, which to this day has been made only for the rich man's table, will now come within the reach of many more people by virtue of our new selling policy. Issoudon marzipan costing from 60 francs to 5 francs will be on sale to the people of Paris. In order to popularise the extraordinary qualities of this sweetmeat, slices of it will be sold for 50 centimes in the shop."

'This circular bore no signature, and it was inferred that it came from the pen of Balzac or that of a friend, editor or colleague. No one else had ever thought of the idea of launching a confectioner's shop with a paragraph from a novel.

'After making enquiries it was discovered that Balzac, though he did not go to the length of taking a hand in the work, patronised the confectioner's shop in the rue Vivienne.

'For a fortnight, there were long queues of curious visitors and, though there were few takers at 60 francs, the 50-centime slices were sold in large numbers.

'Then Paris turned its attention to other matters and the sale of marzipan sweets slumped.' (Dr Cabanès)

According to this story it seems certain that marzipan sweets, if they were not actually invented in the province of Berry, were once very popular there, and that those of Issoudon enjoyed a great reputation.

Marzipan is very popular in Flanders; marzipan of the finest quality is manufactured industrially all over Belgium.

OLD MARZIPAN RECIPES. RECETTES ANCIENNES DE MASSEPAINS – The following recipes are taken from the *Confiturier royal*, published by Claud Prud'homme in 1732.

Plain marzipan sweets. MASSEPAINS COMMUNS – 'Take $1\frac{1}{2}$ kg. ($3\frac{1}{4}$ lb., $10\frac{1}{2}$ cups) sweet almonds. Peel them in hot water. Drain and dry them. After this, pound them in a marble mortar, pouring egg white over them from time to time to prevent them from becoming too oily.

'When the almonds are pounded to a smooth paste, cook 700 g. ($1\frac{1}{2}$ lb., 3 cups) sugar to the feather stage. Next, put in your almonds and blend all the ingredients with a spatula, carefully scraping the sides of the pan to prevent sticking, which may occur even though the pan is taken off the stove. You will know that your paste is ready if none sticks to the back of your hand when you touch it. Next, take the paste out of the pan and put it on a pastry board. Sprinkle it with fine sugar on both sides. Leave to cool.

'Roll it out to a moderate thickness. Cut your shapes out of the paste with biscuit-cutters. Press them down slightly with the tip of your finger onto sheets of rice paper, to bake them. Expose them to heat on one side only. Next, ice them on the other side and then cook in the same way.

'They can be made round, oval, fluted, heart-shaped, etc. You can also make your paste very moist and squirt it through a syringe. Your marzipan sweets will have as many special names as they have shapes, though they will differ from one another only in shape and the manner in which they are iced, as will be seen below.'

Iced marzipan sweets. MASSEPAINS GLACÉS – 'When your marzipan sweets, cut round, long, oval or fluted, are baked and ready on one side, gently lift them off the paper with a knife. Then ice them on the unbaked side in one of the two following ways:

'Take water scented with orange blossom or some other flavouring, or cooked fruit juice, according to the type of marzipan sweets you wish to make. Mix in little by little some fine powdered sugar, stirring the mixture well until it is as thick as porridge. Take out some of this icing with a knife and spread it neatly on your marzipan sweets. Then, put them back on the rice paper and warm them gently in the oven to set the icing. Put them in a tin for use when required.

'The other type of icing is made with the egg white and fine sugar only, or mixed with some cooked fruit pulp, working and using as indicated above. You can make both types of icing at the same time, so as to distinguish between differently shaped sweets by icing them differently.'

Royal marzipan sweets. MASSEPAINS ROYALS – 'The paste is the same as for the first kind. Take a piece and stretch it out on the table to about the thickness of a finger. Cut the strip into as many pieces as will make a ring around your finger. Press the ends firmly together so that they will not come apart. Dip these rings in egg white into which a little apricot jam has been mixed, then, dip them in fine sugar. Blow on them to shake off surplus sugar. Put them on rice paper to bake on both sides in the oven, as they have been iced top and bottom.'

MODERN MARZIPAN RECIPES. RECETTES MODERNES DE MASSEPAINS –

Plain marzipan sweets. MASSEPAINS ORDINAIRES – Pound in a mortar 250 g. (9 oz., $1\frac{3}{4}$ cups) blanched sweet almonds and

4 or 5 bitter almonds, moistening from time to time with a little cold water.

As soon as the almonds are reduced to a smooth, rather stiff paste, put them in a copper pan with 500 g. (18 oz., 4 cups) fine sugar, a pinch of powdered vanilla and a few drops of orange-blossom water. Mix well over a low flame, stirring with a wooden spoon until the mixture is thoroughly dried. Put it back in the mortar and work well with the pestle until it becomes very smooth. To make it even smoother, put it on the table and work by hand, mixing in a small handful of fine sugar sifted through a hair sieve.

Roll out the paste to a thickness of 2 cm. ($\frac{3}{4}$ inch). Put it on a sheet of rice paper and cut into shapes. Put these shapes on a baking sheet covered with paper. Dry in a very cool oven.

Soft marzipan sweets. MASSEPAINS DITS MOELLEUX – *Ingredients.* 500 g. (18 oz., $3\frac{1}{2}$ cups) almonds, 500 g. (18 oz., 4 cups) fine sugar, 250 g. (9 oz., 1 cup) *Royal icing* (see ICING), 10 egg whites, 10 drops essence of bitter almonds or $\frac{1}{2}$ teaspoon almond essence.

Method. Proceed as indicated above. Pipe onto buttered paper in various shapes or in rings. Sprinkle with sugar and bake in a moderate oven.

Marzipan sweets. MASSEPAINS – Pound finely in a mortar 500 g. (18 oz., $3\frac{1}{2}$ cups) blanched almonds with 450 g. (1 lb., 2 cups) sugar and 50 g. (2 oz., $\frac{1}{4}$ cup) vanilla-flavoured sugar, adding 4 egg whites little by little.

Leave this mixture to stand for a few minutes. Roll it out to a thickness of 3 mm. ($\frac{1}{8}$ inch). Cut the sweets into different shapes. Ice with rather liquid *Royal icing* (see ICING) flavoured with a few drops of orange-blossom water or orange essence. Put on a baking sheet and bake in a slow oven.

Marzipan sweets à la russe. MASSEPAINS À LA RUSSE – Work together in a bowl 100 g. (4 oz., 1 cup) sieved flour and 375 g. (13 oz., 3 cups) fine sugar, adding 8 egg whites, 2 at a time.

Working the mixture well, add 375 g. (13 oz., $3\frac{1}{4}$ cups) ground almonds and 250 g. (9 oz., $1\frac{1}{2}$ cups) finely chopped candied orange peel. Pipe the paste onto buttered and floured baking sheets and bake in a hot oven. Lift the sweets off the baking sheet while they are still hot.

MASCOTTE – A cake made by filling a Genoese cake with *Butter cream* (see CREAMS) flavoured with mocha and mixed with finely pounded roasted hazelnuts. The Genoese cake is iced with this cream.

MASCOTTE (À LA) – Name of a garnish served with small cuts of meat and poultry. It consists of quartered artichoke hearts sautéed in butter, small potatoes cut into the shape of olives and cooked in butter, and truffles.

MASKING. NAPPER – Masking is the covering of food with its appropriate sauce after it is dished up for serving.

MASSÉNA (À LA) – The name of a garnish served with small cuts of meat, *tournedos* and fillets. It consists of artichoke hearts filled with thick *Béarnaise sauce* (see SAUCE) and strips of poached beef bone-marrow.

MASILLONS – *Petit four* (q.v.) of almond paste in the shape of a tartlet.

Ingredients. 125 g. (4 oz., $\frac{3}{4}$ cup) blanched almonds, 250 g. (9 oz., 2 cups) fine sugar, 125 g. (4 oz., $\frac{1}{2}$ cup) butter, 6 egg whites, 125 g. (4 oz., 1 cup) cornflour (cornstarch), vanilla.

Method. Pound the almonds with 2 egg whites, the sugar and the vanilla. Rub this mixture through a sieve. Put it in a bowl and work it, adding the rest of the egg whites to make it very frothy. Add the butter, melted, then dredge in the cornflour (cornstarch). Mix thoroughly.

Fill little buttered tartlet cases with this mixture and bake in a hot oven. As soon as they are taken out of the oven, spread the tartlets with apricot jam and ice with kirsch-flavoured *Fondant icing* (see ICING).

MASTIC – Resin which exudes in the form of pale yellow drops from incisions made in the mastic tree. These drops are floury on the surface and have an aromatic and resinous flavour. Mastic comes mainly from the island of Chios. It is chewed in the East and is also used in the spirit known as Raki (q.v.).

Silver vessel for the preparation of an infusion of maté. The hollow stem serves as a drinking straw. Its base is a perforated hollow ball which serves as a strainer (*Larousse*)

(*Collection Dr Gottschalk. Phot. Larousse*)

MATÉ – Plant sometimes known as *Paraguay tea.* Its leaves, which are rich in caffein, are used in the preparation of an infusion which is both a stimulant and a tonic.

This drink, which is relatively cheap, is much used in Peru, Chile, the Argentine, Brazil, Bolivia, Paraguay, etc.

In South America, maté tea is made in a somewhat eccentric fashion. The powdered maté is placed in hollowed-out gourds which have been dried and decorated. These are called *matés* in some countries and *culha* in Brazil. Boiling water is poured over the powder. The tops are then replaced on the gourds. The drinkers take it in turns to suck the tea contained in the gourds through a special straw known as a *bombilla*.

This infusion is also made in containers of precious metal, with a *bombilla* of the same metal through which the tea is drunk.

Maté can be prepared in different ways. It is best in an infusion, prepared as follows:

Put in a teapot 25 g. (1 oz.) maté (leaves or powder). Pour on 1 litre ($1\frac{3}{4}$ pints, generous quart) boiling water. Leave to infuse in a hot place for at least 10 minutes. Strain.

Drink hot or cold, with or without sugar, according to taste.

The infusion of maté, which must always be carried out in a hot place, can be prolonged beyond 10 minutes. Some authorities assert that this plant only yields up all its properties after long simmering, and that it should be left to infuse, with the teapot standing on the stove or in a basin of boiling water, for 1 hour.

As in the case of tea, maté can be flavoured in various ways. Thus lemon juice, rum, kirsch, etc., may be added. After straining, the leaves or grounds can be stirred once or twice into hot water, producing a second and third drink which is still quite pleasant.

MATEFAIM – Name given in certain regions of France, notably the Loire, Ain and Jura, to a rather coarse but nourishing type of pancake which appeases or dulls the edge of appetite.

MATELOTE – Name given in French cooking to a fish stew made with white or red wine.

Strictly, *matelotes*, which are also called *meurettes* or *pochouses* according to district and method of preparation, should be made from freshwater fish. Only the dish known as *matelote à la normande* is made from sea fish, mainly sole, conger eel and gurnet. This *matelote* is moistened with cider and thickened with *Velouté sauce* (see SAUCE) based on fish stock and fresh cream.

The term *matelote* is also loosely and incorrectly applied to dishes made of veal and poultry.

Most *matelotes* of freshwater fish should be garnished. In addition to the small onions and mushrooms which must always be cooked with the fish, add freshwater crayfish cooked in a *court-bouillon* (q.v.), and heart-shaped pieces of fried bread.

With some types of *matelote*, such as *pochouse* and *matelote à la tourangelle*, lardoons of belly of pork are cooked with the fish at the same time as the small onions and mushrooms.

The method used in the preparation of most *matelotes* is indicated below under *Matelote à la canotière*.

Matelote à la bourguignonne or matelote de meunière – This *matelote*, known as *meurette*, is made from freshwater fish: small carp, pikerel, eel, barbel. These fish, cut into chunks, are put in a copper pan on a foundation of finely sliced carrots and onions, sprigs of parsley, thyme, bay leaves and crushed cloves of garlic. The mixture is moistened with red wine. Blazing Burgundy marc brandy is added, and the sauce is thickened with butter and flour kneaded together. Garnish with bread cut into squares, fried in butter, and rubbed with garlic.

Matelote à la canotière – Made with carp and eel.

Butter a deep frying pan. Line with 150 g. (5 oz., 1¼ cups) finely chopped onion and 4 cloves of crushed garlic. Put in 1½ kg. (3¼ lb.) fish cut into pieces of equal thickness, with a large *bouquet garni* (q.v.) in the middle of the pan. Moisten with 1 litre (1¾ pints, generous quart) dry white wine. Bring to the boil, add 1 dl. (6 tablespoons, scant ½ cup) brandy, flame it and cook with the pan covered.

Drain the pieces of fish and put them in another pan. Add 125 g. (4 oz.) small cooked mushrooms and 125 g. (4 oz.) small glazed onions. Moisten with the stock in which the fish has been cooked, boiled down to two-thirds of its volume. Thicken with butter and flour kneaded together, allowing 50 g. (2 oz., ½ cup) flour 100 g. (4 oz., ½ cup) butter to every litre (scant quart, generous quart) stock. Finally add 150 g. (5 oz., 10 tablespoons) butter. Simmer gently. Serve the *matelote* in a deep dish or bowl.

Garnish with fried gudgeon dipped in egg and breadcrumbs (apart from the head and tail), and freshwater crayfish cooked in a *court-bouillon*.

Matelote à la marinière – Made with a mixture of freshwater fish. Proceed as for *Matelote à la canotière*, moistening the stew with white wine. Thicken the sauce with a *Velouté sauce* (see SAUCE) made by moistening a white *roux* of butter and flour with concentrated fish stock. This stock is made from the heads and trimmings of the fish moistened with white wine and flavoured with onions, parsley, thyme and bay leaves.

Garnish the *matelote* with small glazed onions, mushrooms, freshwater crayfish and heart-shaped pieces of fried bread.

Matelote à la meunière – Made with one kind of fish only (usually eel) or with several different kinds of fish. Proceed as for *Matelote à la canotière*, moistening the fish with red wine. Thicken the sauce with butter and flour kneaded together.

Garnish the *matelote* with freshwater crayfish and pieces of bread fried in butter.

Matelote à la normande – Made with saltwater fish cut into thick slices. Moisten the fish with cider. Add Calvados and set alight. Thicken with *Velouté sauce* (see SAUCE) based on concentrated fish stock. Bring the sauce to the required consistency by adding thick fresh cream, allowing 1½ dl. (¼ pint, ⅔ cup) per litre (scant quart, generous quart) sauce.

Garnish with mushrooms, mussels, poached oysters, crayfish, and small heart-shaped pieces of bread fried in butter.

MATIAS – A rather solid, unleavened *galette* (q.v.) made of ordinary dough mixed with onions, chopped leeks and mashed potatoes. It should be eaten hot.

MATIGNON – A *fondue* (q.v.) of vegetables served as a garnish with a large number of dishes. (See also GARNISHES.)

Meatless matignon. MATIGNON AU MAIGRE – Stew gently in butter 125 g. (4 oz., 1 cup) chopped carrot, 50 g. (2 oz., ½ cup) chopped celery, 25 g. (1 oz., ¼ cup) finely chopped onions. Add half a bay leaf and a sprig of thyme. Season with salt and a pinch of sugar.

When the vegetables are very tender, moisten with 1 dl. (6 tablespoons, scant ½ cup) Madeira. Boil down until well reduced.

Matignon with meat. MATIGNON AU GRAS – Prepared as indicated above, with the addition of 100 g. (4 oz.) lean raw ham cut into small thin slices.

MAYONNAISE – A cold sauce of which the basic ingredients are egg yolks and oil blended into an emulsion. For recipes, see SAUCE, *Cold sauces*.

'Culinary purists,' writes Carême in his *Cuisinier parisien*: *Traité des entrées froides*, 'are not in agreement regarding the name. Some say *mayonnaise*, others *mahonnaise* and other *bayonnaise*. We always refer to this sauce by the name of *magnonaise*.'

Mayonnaise is probably a corruption of *moyeunaise*, derived from the old French word *moyeu*, which means egg yolk.

The term *mayonnaise* is also used of cold dishes made from fish, shellfish or poultry, covered with mayonnaise sauce and garnished with lettuce hearts, hard-boiled eggs, anchovy fillets, olives and capers.

Fish mayonnaise. MAYONNAISE DE POISSONS – Made from various kinds of fish, cooked and cut into small slices, in the same way as *Lobster mayonnaise* (see below).

Lobster mayonnaise. MAYONNAISE DE HOMARD – Boil a lobster in a *court-bouillon* (q.v.) and leave to cool. Take the meat of the tail and cut into pieces of equal thickness. Season with salt, pepper, oil, vinegar or lemon juice, chopped parsley and chervil. Dice the rest of the lobster separately and season in the same way.

Take the outer green leaves of a number of lettuces (setting aside the hearts for garnishing). Shred them coarsely and dress.

Line a salad bowl with shredded lettuce. Put the diced lobster on this and arrange the slices on top. Cover with mayonnaise. Decorate with fillets of anchovy, olives and capers, and surround with quartered hard-boiled eggs and lettuce hearts.

Poultry mayonnaise. MAYONNAISE DE VOLAILLE – Proceed as for *Lobster mayonnaise*, using cooked poultry (usually poached chicken) cut into small slices.

This mayonnaise can also be made with the chicken jointed and skinned, especially when a small bird is used.

Mayonnaise of Mediterranean or Dublin Bay prawns. MAYONNAISE DE LANGOUSTINES – Prepared in the same way as *Lobster mayonnaise*, using Mediterranean or Dublin Bay prawns.

Mayonnaise of all kinds of shellfish, crabs, shrimps, crayfish tails, etc., can be made in the same way.

Spiny lobster mayonnaise. MAYONNAISE DE LANGOUSTE – Spiny lobster slices may be arranged on a bed of shredded lettuce and served in their shell, cut lengthwise.

Mayonnaise of fillets of sole à l'ancienne with a border of jelly. MAYONNAISE DE FILETS DE SOLES À L'ANCIENNE, SUR BORDURE DE GELÉE – Poach fillets of sole in a very little white wine. Leave them to cool. Trim into rectangles. Cover with gelatine-strengthened mayonnaise.

Fill a ring mould with fish aspic jelly. Turn it out onto a dish when set. Fill the centre of this jelly border with a salad of potatoes, artichoke hearts and diced truffles dressed with gelatine-strengthened mayonnaise.

Arrange the fillets of sole on top of the jelly.

MAZAGRAN – Cold or hot coffee served in a glass.

The word also means a kind of tartlet lined with *Duchess potatoes* (see POTATOES), filled with a *salpicon* (q.v.) or any other preparation, and baked in the oven.

MAZARIN (Pâtisserie) – Fill a plain baking tin 6 to 8 cm. ($2\frac{1}{2}$ to 3 inches) deep with best *Genoese batter* (see DOUGH). Bake the cake and allow it to cool. Scoop out the middle, making a funnel-shaped cavity which does not quite reach the bottom. Ice the cone removed from the cake with pale pink fondant icing.

Fill the well of the cake with chopped crystallised fruit (angelica, candied orange and lemon peel, stem ginger, etc.), with a little syrup, thick apricot purée, and kirsch added. Spread the cake with apricot jam. Cover the well with the iced core and decorate with crystallised fruit.

MEADOW-SWEET. REINE-DES-PRÉS – Plant whose tender leaves and flower tips, put to infuse in wine or hydromel, give them an agreeable taste. They are used in making certain types of vermouth.

Tea made from the meadow-sweet blossoms is antispasmodic, diuretic and sudorific.

MEAL. REPAS – A grouping together of various kinds of nourishment taken at a fixed and traditional time.

Preparation for a meal. MISE EN PLACE – In large kitchens this covers all the preparatory operations involved in the cooking of a meal.

It is useful, in a small as well as a large establishment, to prepare the various ingredients required for the meal in advance, peeling the vegetables, etc. When the small tasks are done the actual cooking is much simplified.

MEAT. VIANDE – The word *viande* derives from the Latin *vivenda* which meant that 'which maintains life,' and was, like the word 'meat' in English, synonymous with foodstuff in general. Cynegetic (hunting) language, preserving an archaic tradition, keeps up this meaning in the words *viandis* and *viander* to describe pasture or the action of pasturing where wild beasts are concerned. Today, the meaning is restricted to the muscular flesh of edible animals.

When a piece of meat is examined closely it is seen to be formed of small reddish fibres enclosed in a thin skin. These fibres are grouped into bundles, and their covering skin, thickening, forms the tendons. Certain muscles are surrounded or separated from other groups by thicker coverings of tendon tissue, the mucous membranes. Round the muscular masses, and sometimes between their bundles of fibre, there can be seen deposits of fat varying in quantity.

The connective tissue which holds them together and forms the tendons and muscular fibres is broken down in cooking, and then attacked by the gastric juices. But these juices leave intact the corresponding tissue in raw meat, and it is broken down only in the intestines.

Muscular tissue is formed from albumens and fats; there are only traces of carbohydrates (except in horsemeat, which is richer in glycogen and glucose than the meat of other animals). It contains a large proportion of water (sometimes as much as 70 per cent in certain cuts), mineral salts, among which phosphorus and iron are the most important, and gelatine.

As with all albumens, muscular tissue coagulates in heat from 70° to 80°C. (158° to 176°F.).

Muscular flesh also contains some soluble substances called extractives, because they are found in the extract obtained from the evaporations of their solutions. Some substances can be identified by chemical means, while others remain unknown. They belong to the chemical group of purines, which relates them to the alkaloids in coffee, tea and chocolate. They are transformed by heat into aromatic substances which act as stimulants to the digestive system, the nervous system and the heart.

Freshness of meat. FRAÎCHEUR DE LA VIANDE – Immediately after slaughter meat is slightly acid, because of the presence of lactic acid in the muscular tissue, and hard as a result of stiffening in death. In this state it can be used for dishes that involve long cooking, like *pot-au-feu*. For all other purposes it must be 'hung', (kept in a cool place for a day or two according to the season) for a certain degree of decomposition to take place. This is due to the action of soluble ferments which exist in the muscles as in all organic tissue, and which soften the fibres by the phenomenon of autolysis (spontaneous decomposition). This autolysis, if it is allowed to proceed to its extreme limits, will continue to the point of complete liquefaction. This process must not be confused with the putrefaction due to bacteria.

The longer it is hung, the more tender the meat becomes. In some places, for example in Vienna, everything is sacrificed to tenderness, and meat is often hung for seven or eight days.

Quality of meat. QUALITÉS DES VIANDES. Variable proportions of fat are found in different kinds of cuts of meat. It may be found around or between the muscular fibres or even in the middle of them, and between the bundles of fibre, in well-nourished animals.

The choicest cuts always have some fat, which is very desirable in cooking, but this should not be excessive. Analyses show that nutritional value in terms of calories depends chiefly on the fat content, since the latter contains more calories than do albumens; but instructions based on such facts should not be followed to the letter, since few people eat very fatty pieces, and would normally leave them on the side of the plate.

Meat that is only moderately fat is generally easier to digest than meat with a very high fat content.

The dark meats (*viandes noires*) of game and venison contain more extractives, and even toxic substances (when the animal has been hunted hard or when the flesh is very 'high'); they are usually more difficult to digest than butcher's meat.

Red meats are those of adult animals (bullock, cow, bull, sheep, horse, donkey, mule); they can be digested and tolerated by most people, provided their use is not abused.

The way in which the animals are fed has a great effect on the quality of the meat.

Meat in dietetics. VIANDE EN DIÉTÉTIQUE – For the vast majority of Europeans, meat is the most important of all foods. Dieticians do not share this view and blame meat for many of our current health problems.

Meat contains 15 to 25 per cent of protein substances; variable amounts of fat ranging from 20 to 30 per cent (pork) to less than 5 per cent (rabbit). Meat contains no carbohydrate, so its calorific value is not very high (206 calories per 100 g.). (The calorific value of wheat flour is 350; that of dried nuts over 600.) It is rich in mineral salts such as phosphorus and iron, but lacking in calcium.

Meat leaves little intestinal residue and is liable to cause constipation and intestinal troubles. For these reasons, dieticians recommend either a strict vegetarian diet, which calls for a long and difficult period of adaptation, or a reduction in the daily consumption of meat: 100 g. (4 oz.) maximum for an average adult. The type of meat eaten should be chosen to suit each person's temperament, deficiencies and taste.

Beef. This has the highest protein count of all butcher's meats (23 to 24 per cent).

Horse meat. Equivalent to that of beef.

Veal. Not as rich in protein as beef.

Lamb, mutton. Mutton contains less protein than veal but is fatter.

Pork. Contains least protein of all (on average only 16 per cent). It is particularly indigestible because of its high fat content (more than 30 per cent). This is true not only of pork but of all pork butchery products.

Game. Not recommended by dieticians because of its toxicity (especially game that has been hung).

Tripery. Viscera and offal (variety meats) are not recommended dietetically. Brains, for example, have a high cholesterol count and contain much fat so they are not the light food suitable for children and invalids that they were once considered to be.

Meat extract. EXTRAIT DE VIANDE – Stock that has been concentrated by heat or in a vacuum. Extracts contain part of the extractive substances of the meat, some mineral salts and the same aromatic ingredients (celery, etc.) which give stocks their savoury taste.

There are a great many of these extracts on sale. They should be regarded as condiments which permit any liquid to be given approximately the same flavour as beef stock.

Meat juice. JUS DE VIANDE – The name juice or 'gravy' properly belongs to the liquid which escapes from a piece of meat during cooking, and which is served with roast meats.

There exist commercial substitutes for this juice, very similar to meat extracts.

Meat pulp. PULPE DE VIANDE – Describes meat which has been pulped, that is to say, scraped while raw. It has the appearance of a homogeneous paste, and is used for additional nourishment in special diets.

MEAT CLEAVER. FEUILLE – Implement used to split carcases in half. It is also used in the kitchen for cutting up meat for stews, etc.

MEATBALLS (German and Austrian cookery). KLÖSSE Very popular in Austria and Germany, *klösse* are a kind of round ball made of different forcemeats. They are boiled in salt water, thoroughly drained, and served with browned butter and fried breadcrumbs poured over them.

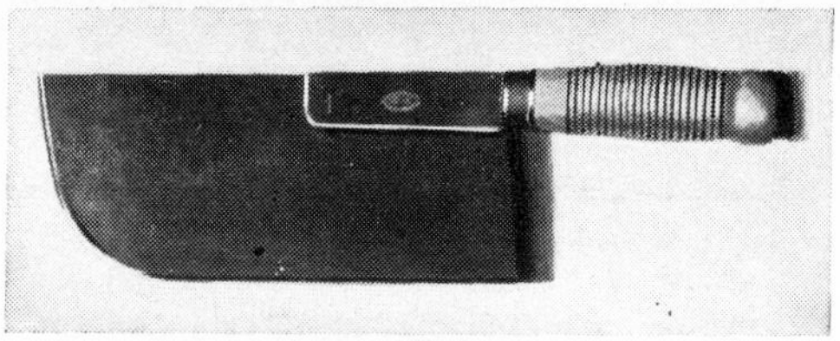

Meat cleaver (*Coutellerie André. Phot. Larousse*)

Meatballs à la viennoise. KLÖSSE À LA VIENNOISE – Dice finely 500 g. (18 oz.) sandwich bread. Toss in butter until golden. Place in a dish and pour on a few tablespoons boiling milk. Leave to soak. Add 250 g. (9 oz., generous cup) finely diced lean ham tossed in butter, 175 g. (6 oz., $1\frac{1}{2}$ cups) chopped onion, cooked slowly in butter until very tender, and 1 tablespoon chopped chervil and tarragon. Add 1 tablespoon flour and 3 or 4 eggs beaten as for an omelette. Season with salt, pepper and nutmeg. Mix thoroughly.

Divide this mixture into pieces each weighing about 50 g. (2 oz.). Shape into balls. Dip the balls in flour and poach in salt water for 10 to 12 minutes. Drain. Toss a handful of breadcrumbs in browned butter and pour over the meatballs.

MÉCHOUI (Arab cookery) – Arabic word meaning roasted. Arab roasts are made with various animals such as gazelle, sheep, mouflon (wild sheep), young camel or lamb. The animal must always be very fat.

'The cooking demands very special care, for a *méchoui* cannot be perfect unless it is constantly basted with melted butter and roasted slowly on red hot charcoal embers, which must be kept at the same temperature the whole time. Care must also be taken that the meat is not charred outside and raw inside.

'A *méchoui* is perfectly cooked when, on pricking it with a large needle, no drops of pink juice exude through the puncture. Care must be taken that the kidneys are properly cooked. These are the most precious part of the roast. A successful *méchoui* must be of a fine golden-brown colour and the meat must be well roasted and crackling. This is how it is done:

'Kill, skin an eviscerate a sucking lamb. Impale it from head to tail on a pointed wooden spit.

'Tie the shoulders to the neck with string. Stretch the legs out to the full length of the spit, binding them with a strip of linen. Season well with salt and pepper. Rest each end of the spit on a tall stone or Y-shaped support on which the spit can be turned. Near the spitted carcase, dig a hole 1 m. (39 inches) in length and 50 cm. (20 inches) in depth. Light a wood fire. Place the lamb about 50 cm. (20 inches) from the fire. Rotate the spit slowly so that the whole lamb is exposed to the embers. Using a brush, baste with melted butter.

'When it is cooked, take it off the spit. Lay it on a dish and place it in the middle of the table. According to tradition, the diners must abandon the use of knives and forks. Custom requires that the *méchoui* should be eaten with fingers, the guests tearing off the flesh as desired. The host must serve himself first and must pluck out the kidneys to offer to his guests.

'When the *méchoui* is all eaten, the servants pass round the ewer containing warm water scented with rose leaves, so that the guests may rinse their hands.

'The whole beauty of this dish lies in the incomparable flavour of the crackling skin and browned flesh. So that it may lose none of the delicacy which makes it so much sought-after by gourmets, it must be speedily dismembered as soon as it appears on the table. If it is left to get cold, the skin, firm and crackling at the outset, grows soft very quickly. One should therefore never forget to provide the guest with hot plates for a *méchoui*.

'In different regions of Morocco and Tunisia, the *méchoui* differs only in the method of cooking. It is braised in a glazed earthenware oven.' (L. Isnard, *L'Afrique gourmande*.)

MEDALLION. MÉDAILLON – This is a name applied to various foodstuffs which must, by definition, be cut in the shape of round or oval medallions.

The word is synonymous with *tournedos* (q.v.) when applied to small cuts of beef, with collops (q.v.) when applied to slices of mutton, veal or large poultry. The term is extended to designate slices of *foie gras* served hot or cold.

Medallions of anchovy à la niçoise – See ANCHOVY.

Medallions of lamb – See LAMB.

Medlars

MEDLAR. NÈFLE – The fruit of the medlar tree, a rosaceous plant, which grows wild in all the temperate regions of Europe.

The medlar is a very tart fruit which can only be eaten when it is thoroughly ripe and soft. It has then quite a pleasant flavour of wine.

MÉDOC – Wine-producing region of Bordeaux situated on the left banks of the Garonne and Gironde, stretching from Blanquefort to Graves. It is subdivided into two regions: Bas Médoc in the north and Haut Médoc in the south. The best wines come from the latter. The following communes of Haut Médoc have been given a special *appellation*: Moulis, Listrac, Margaux, Saint-Julien, Pauillac, and Saint-Estèphe.

Médoc wines have a character of their own, distinguished by a slight tartness (quite unlike that of any other wine), by their delicacy, aroma, smoothness, and a bouquet that improves with age.

They are full bodied without being highly intoxicating. When young, they are of a beautiful garnet colour which changes to burnt ruby with maturity. (See BORDEAUX.)

MEHLSUPPE (German cookery) – For this soup made from flour, known also as sweet-and-sour soup, see SOUPS AND BROTHS.

MELBA – See GARNISHES.

MÉLILOT – Fragrant herb which, in country districts, is used to stuff a freshly killed rabbit to flavour the meat.

The dried leaves and flowers are used to flavour marinades and stews. It is also used in the making of Gruyère cheese.

MELISSA. MÉLISSE – Plant of Mediterranean origin, known also as lemon balm. It has oblong, light green, slightly velvety leaves, and smells rather like lemon.

Melissa

Melissa cordial. EAU DE MÉLISSE – Spirit distilled from melissa. The best-known melissa cordial is that of Carmes, made by infusion of spirits of kidney vetch and spirits of melissa.

Fresh melissa blossoms	900 g. (2 lb.)
Zest of fresh lemons	150 g. (5 oz.)
Ceylon cinnamon	80 g. (3 oz.)
Cloves	80 g. (3 oz.)
Nutmeg	80 g. (3 oz.)
Coriander	40 g. ($1\frac{1}{2}$ oz.)
Angelica roots	40 g. ($1\frac{1}{2}$ oz.)
Alcohol (80°)	5000 g. (11 lb.)

Slit or crush the various ingredients. Put them with the alcohol in the steam chamber of a distilling apparatus. Leave to infuse for 4 days in a cool place, then distil.

Melissa leaves placed on meat keep away flies and other insects.

MELON – Fruit of a number of herbaceous plants, it is of Asian origin and was first transplanted to Italy, then to France, well before the sixteenth century. The melon was known in early times and was much prized by the Greeks and Romans.

Melon is eaten raw and in its natural state, either at the beginning of the meal as an *hors-d'œuvre* or at the end, as a fruit.

Melon

As an *hors-d'œuvre* it is often seasoned with salt and spiced with ginger. As a dessert it is sprinkled with sugar, though a great many connoisseurs consider that the only admissible seasoning is salt, often with pepper added.

To choose a melon, tap it lightly to discover whether it is well fleshed or hollow. Look to see whether it has round its stem that 'crown' which indicates that the melon is perfectly ripe and whether or not it is sweet.

Chilled melon with Frontignan wine. MELON RAFRAÎCHI AU FRONTIGNAN – Take a large cantaloup melon. Make a circular incision round the stem. Remove the top and scoop out the seeds. Put the melon in a bowl full of crushed ice. Sprinkle the inside with 2 tablespoons (3 tablepoons) sugar and pour into it $2\frac{1}{2}$ dl. (scant $\frac{1}{2}$ pint, generous cup) Frontignan wine or any other dessert wine. Replace the top of the melon and leave to chill thoroughly. Serve in a bowl full of crushed ice.

Melon prepared in this way is not cut into slices. The pulp is scooped out with a large silver spoon.

Chilled melon can be flavoured with grenache, Madeira, Marsala, muscatel, port, sherry, tokay, etc.

Chilled melon en surprise or melon à la parisienne. MELON RAFRAÎCHI EN SURPRISE (MELON À LA PARISIENNE) – Scoop out a large cantaloup melon as indicated for *Iced melon* (see below). Dice the scooped-out pulp. Add various fruits in season: pineapple, apricots, peaches, pears, cherries, plums, oranges, bananas, apples, grapes, etc., cut into pieces, coarsely diced or stoned. Add sugar, and moisten with kirsch, maraschino or any liqueur, as for *Fruit salad* (see FRUIT).

Chilled melon en surprise (*Larousse*)

Fill the melon with this mixture. Put it in a large bowl filled with crushed ice. Leave to chill thoroughly before serving.

Crystallised melon. MELON CONFIT – In high-grade industrial confectionery, whole melons are crystallised in their rind.

In household kitchens, melons can be crystallised in slices or cubes.

Cut into slices of equal size a cantaloup melon which is not over ripe. Skin the slices and remove the seeds. Put in a bowl and sprinkle with sugar. Leave to steep in the sugar for a few hours. Drain. Keep the juice. Put the melon in cold water and leave overnight.

Next day pour the melon juice into a pan. Add enough water and sugar to make a syrup with a density of 14° as measured on a saccharometer. Put the slices of melon in this syrup and boil them. Leave the melon, covered with its syrup in an earthenware bowl, to stand overnight. Next day, drain the pieces of melon, taking them out with care so as not to break them. Boil the syrup until it is reduced to 16° density and pour over the melon. Repeat this operation several times, reducing the syrup each time until it reaches a density of 32°. In French confectionery this process is called *façon*.

When the melon has undergone the required number of *façons*, drain and dry it. Keep in a very dry place.

Fresh melon. MELON AU NATUREL – Melon should be well chilled before serving. If possible, leave it on ice for 1 or 2 hours.

If melon is to be served as an *hors-d'œuvre*, each guest will season it himself with salt, sometimes pepper, or with fine sugar. It can also be spiced with ground ginger. When melon is served as a dessert, if it is fragrant and rich in flavour, serve it plain or with fine sugar.

Melon, in common with other fruit, must not be sliced with an ordinary steel knife. Whether for slicing or eating, a silver, silver-plated or stainless steel knife or a silver spoon should be used.

Iced melon. MELON GLACÉ – Cut a circle of rind round the stem of a large cantaloup melon. Scoop out the pulp, leaving only a thin layer on the rind.

Make a melon ice cream with the pulp (see ICE CREAMS AND ICES). Just before serving, fill the melon rind with the ice cream.

Melon jam. CONFITURE DE MELON – Proceed as for *Apricot jam* (see JAMS).

Melon pickled in vinegar. MELON CONFIT AU VINAIGRE – Choose small, not very ripe melons. Cut into pieces of equal thickness, and proceed as for *Gherkins in vinegar* (see GHERKIN).

Melon in vinegar is used in the same way as gherkins, as an accompaniment to boiled meat and cold meat.

Small green melons are generally used. The rind of large melons can be pickled in the same way. Remove the outer skin only, and dice.

MELON DE MALABAR – Name given in France to the Siamese pumpkin. It is cooked in the same way as ordinary pumpkin (q.v.).

MELONGÈNE – French name for the aubergine (q.v.).

MELTING HOUSE. FONDOIR – This is where the melting of fats and tallow from slaughter houses takes place.

MENDIANTS – Common name for a dessert made of almonds, figs, hazelnuts and raisins, whose colours recall the dress of the four Roman Catholic mendicant Orders.

MENTONNAISE (À LA) – Method of cooking certain foodstuffs, especially rock-pool fish. The characteristic ingredients are tomatoes, black olives and garlic seasoning. (See GARNISHES.)

MENU – A sheet of paper or card on which is written, in a specific order, the names of all the dishes which are to be served in succession at a given meal.

The idea of providing a 'bill of fare', which in old French was called an *escriteau*, is not new.

Here, for instance, is a list of dishes which were served on the occasion of the marriage of a counsellor and master of the Counting House in 1571. This curious document, preserved in the archives of the Northern *département* of France, is entitled:

'Bill of fare for the nuptial supper of Master Baulde Cuvillon.'

FIRST COURSE

Salads of various kinds
Flesh of *prinsel* with parsley and vinegar (savoury preserves)
Mutton broth
Fricassée of gosling
Spring chickens with spinach
Cold *saille*
Pigeons *à la Trimoulette*
Roast joint of mufton
Roast breast of veal
Small pastries with hot sauce
Roast roebuck
Dainty *pâté*
Spring chickens in aspic
Sweetened mustard

SECOND COURSE

Venison broth
Roast capon
Orange salad
Roast pheasants
Roast rabbits
Roast spring chickens, some stuffed, others larded
Chériots
Roast quails
Roast *crousets*
Smoked tongues
Boulogne sausages
Pheasant *pies*
Meaux ham pies
Crousets pies
Turkey or peacock pie
Venison pie
Leg of lamb *daube*
Capon in aspic
Roast swan
Sweetened mustard
Olives

DESSERT

Mousse tart
Apple tart
Chervil tart
Jam tart
Cream flan
Gohière
Waffles
Pear pies
Clove apples
Pears in mead
Sartelles pears
Angelots
Morbecque cream
Green walnuts
Fresh fruit
Ample jelly
Cheese

A great many menus of this kind are to be found in the archives of large French towns, but most of them are no more than the accounts of the money spent in buying the food to be served at great feasts.

The 'bills of fare' and *escriteaux* were working menus, instructions to indicate to the kitchen staff of a royal or princely household the order in which the various courses should succeed one another at a great dinner.

The individual menu as we know it today did not come into use until the early nineteenth century, at the time of the first Restoration in France, appearing in the celebrated restaurants of the Palais-Royal, which at that time was the gastronomic centre of Paris. It was customary to show at the door enormous posters on which were inscribed the names of the dishes provided by the establishment. One or two ot these poster-menus have come down to us, notably that of the ancient *Rocher de Cancale*, one of the most celebrated restaurants of the time, and that of the equally famous *Hotel des Américains*.

As soon as individual menus came into being, every effort was made to make them artistic and elaborate. The greatest artists did not consider it beneath their dignity to illustrate them with their own hands, and these little cards were afterwards much sought after by collectors and bought at very high prices.

Other individual menus, though less artistic, were also sought by collectors. Written out by hand on plain cards, they recorded meals which have become historic.

Sixteenth century menu – This menu is taken from a *mémoire* on the preparation of an *escriteau* for a banquet.

Ragoûts. Woodcock *à la Quesat* – Capons *pèlerins* – Stuffed roebuck – Civet of venison with turnips – Rabbit *à la grenade* – Lion of white capon – Stuffed birds – Goslings with Milanese cheese – Partridge *à la tonnelette* – Partridge *à l'orange* – Partridge with capers – Wood pigeon *en poivrade* – Pickled teal – *Soleil* of white capon – Venison with turnips – White jelly, decorated, shredded, moulded – Chitterlings in jelly – Jelly *angelots* – *Orissan* in jelly – Quails with bay leaves – Roebuck with Milanese cheese – Roebuck head – Salt venison frumenty – Sheep's tongues *à la vinaigrette* – Mock hedgehog – Goslings in Malmsey wine – Peacocks in their feathers – Devilled trotters with sturgeon – Spring chickens in vinegar – Boar with chestnuts – Veal sausages – Tench *à la lombarde* Amber jelly, plain and fancy – Jelly shield – Jelly escutcheon – Jelly fountain.

Roasts. Larks – Bitterns – Capons – Herons – Young rabbits – Side of beef – Partridge – Plovers – Boar-Doves – Woodcock – Quail – Roebuck – Pheasant – Rabbit – Young hare – Goslings – Young pigeons – Chickens – Teal.

Salads. White – Green – Hop shoots – Olives – Pickled purslane – Lemon – Pomegranate – Lettuces – Samphire – *Bon-Chrétien* pear.

Final courses. Saveloys – Mainz ham – Pies of artichokes, capon, ox tongue, ox feet, sheep's feet, teal – Small hot *choux pastries* – Rissoles – Pickled cucumbers – Rosemary snow – Rosemary cream – Apples *au gatelin* – *Etrier* of plums – Tarts, old style, with cream, beef bone-marrow, plums – Cream gâteau – *Gâteau joyeux* – Boar's head – *Pies à la tonnelette* with woodcock, quince, chestnuts, apples, chickens – Venison pies – Cheese tarts – Asparagus – Blancmange – Frumenty cream – *Baudrier* of apples – Fritters – *Tarte angoulousée* – *Tarte d'Angleterre* – *Tarte fanaïde* – Chopped apple tart – White wine tart – Flaky pastry – Italian gâteau.

Seventeenth century menu – Under Louis XIV, the menus were magnificent.

Here is the menu of the dinner offered by Madame la Chancelière to Louis XIV in 1656 in her Château of Pontchartrain.

First course. Eight potted meats and vegetables and sixteen hot *hors-d'œuvre.*

Second course. Eight important intermediate dishes called broths. Sixteen *entrées* of fine meats.

Third course. Eight roast dishes and sixteen vegetable dishes cooked in meat stock.

Fourth course. Eight pies or cold meat and fish dishes and sixteen raw salads, with oil, cream and butter.

Fifth and last course. Twenty-four different kinds of pastries – twenty-four jars of raw fruit – twenty-four dishes of sweetmeats – preserves, dried and in syrup and jams.

There were, in all, 168 garnished dishes, not counting the various foodstuffs served as dessert.

Eighteenth century menu – Here is the menu of a meal which Marshal the Duke de Richelieu offered to all the princes and princesses and the members of their courts taken prisoner by him during the Hanoverian war. President Hénault tells us how the menu for this memorable supper was drafted by the Duke de Richelieu himself. Its peculiarity lay in the fact that it was made up entirely of one kind of meat, beef, because, on that particular day, there was little in the Marshal's larder.

'My lord,' said Rullières to the Marshal, 'there is nothing in the kitchens except a carcase of beef and a few roots . . .'

'Very good,' said the Marshal, 'that is more than is needed to provide the prettiest supper in the world.'

'But, my lord, it would be impossible . . .'

'Come, Rullières, calm yourself, and write out the menu that I am about to dictate to you.'

And the Marshal, seeing Rullières more and more alarmed, took the pen out of his hand and, seated in his secretary's place, wrote the following menu which, later, was brought into the collection of Monsieur de la Popelinière.

SUPPER MENU

Centrepiece

The large silver-gilt salver with the equestrian figure of the King, the statues of Du Guesclin, Dunois, Bayard, Turenne. My silver-gilt plate with the arms embossed and enamelled.

First course. Tureen: A tureen of *garbure gratinée*, made of beef consommé.

Four *hors-d'œuvre*: Palate of beef *à la Sainte-Menehould* – Little pies of chopped fillet of beef with chives – Kidneys with fried onion – Tripe *à la poulette* with lemon juice.

To follow the broth: Rump of beef garnished with root vegetables in the meat juices. (Trim these vegetables into grotesque shapes on account of the Germans.)

Six *entrées*: Oxtail with chestnut purée – Civet of tongue *à la bourguignonne* – *Paupiettes* of beef *à l'estouffade* with pickled nasturium buds – Fillet of beef braised with celery – Beef rissoles with hazelnut purée – Beef marrow on toast.

Second course. Roast sirloin (baste it with melted bone-marrow) – Endive salad with ox tongue – Beef *à la mode* with white jelly mixed with pistachio nuts – Cold beef gâteau with blood and Jurançon wine. (Don't make a mistake!)

Six final dishes: Glazed turnips with the gravy of the roast – Beef bone-marrow pie with breadcrumbs and candy sugar – Beef stock aspic with lemon rind and pralines – Purée of artichoke hearts with stock (beef) and almond milk – Fritters of beef brain steeped in Seville orange juice – Beef jelly with Alicante wine and Verdun mirabelles.

To follow, all that is left in the way of jams or preserves.'

And, as a coda to this majestic menu (which we should like to regard as authentic and of its period, although in some respects it strikes us as somewhat odd), the Marshal added:

'If by any unhappy chance, this meal turns out not to be very good, I shall withhold from the wages of Maret and Roquelère (his *maître-d'hôtel* and master chef, no doubt) a fine of 100 pistols. Go, and entertain no more doubts!

Signed: RICHELIEU'

This menu, strange as its composition may seem, is perfectly orthodox. Structurally, it obeys all the rules which were in force at this period concerning the organisation of important meals.

Nineteenth century menu – Here is a menu of a historic dinner, known as the dinner of the 'Three Emperors', served on 7 June 1867, at the Café Anglais, which no longer exists.

Among the illustrious guests who attended were Alexander II, Czar of all the Russias, the Czarevich (the future Alexander III) and the King of Prussia who afterwards became the Emperor William I.

This dinner, it is said, cost 400 francs a head.

MENU

SOUPS

Impératrice – Fontanges

INTERMEDIATE COURSE

Soufflé *à la Reine*
Fillet of sole *à la vénitienne*
Collops of turbot *au gratin*
Saddle of mutton with Breton purée

ENTRÉES

Chickens *à la portugaise*
Hot quail *pâté*
Lobster *à la parisienne*
Champagne Sherbets

RÔTS

Duckling *à la rouennaise*
Canapés of bunting

FINAL COURSE

Aubergines *à l'espagnole*
Asparagus
Cassolettes princesse
Iced *bombe*
Fruit

WINES

Madère retour des Indes, 1846
Sherry 1821
Château-Yqem 1847
Chambertin 1846
Château-Margaux 1847
Château-Latour 1847
Château-Lafite 1848

Composition of a banquet menu – Generally speaking, the menu of a great banquet should be made up as follows:

A soup. Often for an important dinner two soups are served, one clear and one thick.

Hot hors-d'œuvre. This type of dish is more often than not omitted at great dinners.

Cold hors-d'œuvre. In former times, these were obligatory at great dinners. They are now no longer served in the evening, but only at luncheons at the beginning of the meal.

Intermediate fish courses. These consist as a rule of large fish braised and served with various garnishes and sauces, or poached, with special sauces served separately.

Intermediate meat, poultry or game courses. Usually the intermediate course consists of a large cut of meat (beef, mutton or lamb), roast or braised and garnished with vegetables.

Less commonly, a large bird is served as an intermediate course. A cut of venison can also be used for this purpose. It should be served with chestnut purée and a special venison sauce. Very rarely, winged game is served as an intermediate course. Usually it is presented as an *entrée* or *rôt*.

Entrées. A large number of dishes can be served as *entrées.*

To ensure efficient service at an important dinner, there should be not more than one *entrée*, and this should be chosen from among those which are easy to serve.

Very seldom, in a well-planned menu, is a cold dish such as aspic, *chaud-froid*, mousse, mould, *pâté de foie gras*, galantine of chicken, etc., served as an *entrée*. These dishes belong more properly in the category of cold *rôts*.

Rôt. This is usually poultry or winged game. Less commonly, a cut of venison is served as a *rôt*. Even more rarely, roast red meat is served, such as fillet, rib or sirloin. This rule holds not only for large dinners but also for those where there are only a small number of guests. Such cuts should only be served as *rôts* at intimate dinners where the laws governing the composition of a menu may be transgressed. At the family table full licence is permitted.

To follow, or even to be served with the *rôt*, there must be a salad. At a large dinner it is advisable to keep to plain salads, *salade en saison*, but a composite salad may also be served. Recipes for these salads are to be found under SALAD.

Cold rôt. Name given to a cold dish served after the hot *rôt*. The cold *rôt* is usually either a *pâté de foie gras* with truffles or a *foie gras* in aspic. Salad should not be served with this delicate dish.

The following may also be served as cold *rôts*: Spiny lobster prepared *en bellevue, à la parisienne* or *à la russe*; jelly with a border of slices of various shellfish; mousses or moulds of *foie gras* or ham; galantines of various types of poultry or winged game; freshwater crayfish served *en buisson*; and most of the cold fish, meat or poultry dishes given in this book.

Entremets. In former times this term covered not only the vegetable side dishes served after the roast, but also the various sweets which nowadays form the dessert.

In France the correct procedure is to serve the sweet after, not before, the cheese.

The above text is retained from the first edition of Larousse for its interest (and amusement) value. Modern banquets are naturally less copious and much less elaborate.

Here is the menu of a solemn chapter of the *confrèrie* Chantepleure de Vouvray (1951):

Gargamelle cocktail snacks
Pike of the Loire valley *à la vouvrillonne*
Grilled *andouille* cooked over wine roots
Perles du tuffeau (special pastry) pies
Roast turkey with chestnut purée
Salad of tender vine leaves with nut oil
Goats' milk cheese
Prune tart stuffed with marzipan
Fruit

MÉOT – See RESTAURANTS OF BYGONE DAYS.

MERCUREY – This wine, made from grapes grown in the commune of Mercurey in the Saône-et-Loire district, is classified as a first growth of the Chalon slopes.

It is similar to the wines of the Beaune slopes, but is a little less sweet. (See BURGUNDY.)

MÈRE DE SOLE – Fish, also called in France *cardine* or *limandelle*. It is cooked in the same way as plaice (q.v.).

MÈRE GOUTTE – Wine made from the juice extracted from the grapes when they are first crushed, and before they are put in the press.

MERGA (Arab cookery) – Name of the sauce served with couscous (q.v.). It is made from the cooking stock of the meat served with the couscous, and can be made either mild or strong. Strong merga is spiced with red pepper.

MERINGUE – Small *pâtisserie* made from egg white and sugar.

Historians of cookery say that this little *pâtisserie* was invented in 1720 by a Swiss pastry-cook called Gasparini, who practised his art in Mehrinyghen, a small town in the State of Saxe-Coburg-Gotha.

The first meringues made in France were served in Nancy to King Stanislas who, it is said, prized them highly. It was he, no doubt, who gave the recipe for this sweetmeat to Marie Leczinska. Queen Marie-Antoinette had a great liking for meringues. Court lore has it that she made them with her own hands at the Trianon, where she also made *vacherins*, for which a similar mixture is used.

Up to the beginning of the nineteenth century, meringues were shaped in a spoon, as the pastry forcing-bag had not yet been invented.

Ingredients. 12 egg whites, 500 g. (18 oz., $2\frac{1}{4}$ cups) sugar, $1\frac{1}{2}$ teaspoons table salt, flavouring to taste.

Method. Whisk the whites to a stiff foam. When they have risen well, add the salt and sugar. Fill a forcing-bag with this mixture, and pipe the meringues in the desired shape and size onto buttered and floured baking sheets. Sprinkle with sugar. Bake in a very slow oven.

After taking the meringues out, press the base of each one with the thumb to make a little hollow. Keep in a dry place.

Meringue Chantilly (*Larousse*)

Border of meringues with Chantilly cream. BORDURE DE MERINGUES À LA CHANTILLY – Take some oval meringues, half of them white, flavoured with vanilla, half pink, flavoured with strawberry or raspberry essence.

Arrange them in a circle, sticking them together with

boiled sugar. Put them in a ring on a dish to form a border. Before serving, fill the middle of the dish with *Chantilly cream* (see CREAMS) flavoured with vanilla or fruit juice.

Meringue croquembouche or pyramid. CROQUEMBOUCHE DE MERINGUES – Using small oval or round meringues made in different colours and differently flavoured, make a pyramid by joining them together with sugar boiled to crack degree (see SUGAR). Alternate the colours in forming the pyramid.

Meringue crust. MERINGUE – A raw or cooked sweet, once it is made, may be covered with meringue mixture and put in the oven to bake the meringue crust.

Italian meringues. MERINGUES À L'ITALIENNE – Proceed as for plain meringues, using the cooked meringue called *Italian meringue mixture* (see MIXTURES).

Meringue à Marignan – Cook to ball degree (see SUGAR) 500 g. (18 oz., $2\frac{1}{4}$ cups) sugar dissolved in a little water. Add kirsch, maraschino or any other liqueur. Cook a little longer to bring it back to the ball degree. Pour this sugar onto 5 stiffly beaten egg whites.

Marignan meringue is usually decorated with a long strip of crystallised angelica stuck at each end like the handle of a basket.

Swiss meringues. MERINGUES SUISSES – *Ingredients.* 6 egg whites, 500 g. (18 oz., 4 cups) fine sugar, 3 drops acetic acid or $\frac{1}{2}$ teaspoon lemon juice, vanilla, a pinch of salt.

Method. Work the sugar with 2 egg whites, the acetic acid, vanilla and salt. When the mixture is very white and smooth, add the 4 remaining egg whites, whisked to a stiff froth. Mix well. Pipe through a forcing-bag. Bake in the oven.

Decorate with crystallised fruit and sprinkle with sugar of different colours.

MÉROU – Fish found in Mediterranean coastal waters. A *mérou* can be as much as 1 m. (39 inches) in length. It is rather tasteless.

All recipes for tunny (q.v.) are suitable for *mérou*.

MERVEILLE – Name of a French pastry made from dough cut into different shapes and deep-fried.

Make a dough with 500 g. (18 oz., $4\frac{1}{2}$ cups) sifted flour, 150 g. (5 oz., $\frac{2}{3}$ cup) butter, 25 g. (1 oz., 2 tablespoons) sugar, 4 eggs and a small pinch of salt. Leave this dough to stand for 1 hour. Roll it out to a thickness of $\frac{1}{2}$ cm. ($\frac{1}{4}$ inch). Cut into various shapes with fluted pastry-cutters. Deep-fry in boiling fat. Drain, and sprinkle with vanilla-flavoured sugar.

MESCAL – Alcoholic drink tasting of bitter almonds. It is made in Mexico and South America from the Mexican agave.

MESENTERY OF CALF. FRAISE DE VEAU – Membrane which envelopes the intestines of the calf. This is cooked like *Calf's head* (see OFFAL or VARIETY MEATS).

MESSIRE-JEAN – French variety of pear of medium size which ripens in autumn. Its skin is russet in colour with a greyish tinge. It is rather gritty in texture, but very fragrant.

METS – The French apply this term to any food prepared for the table. It derives from the Latin *missus*.

METTON – See CHEESE.

Milk (*Nicolas*)

MEUNIÈRE (À LA) – Method of cooking fish, which is seasoned, lightly floured and fried in butter. To serve, squeeze a few drops of lemon juice over it, sprinkle with parsley, and pour on the cooking butter, piping hot.

MEURSAULT – A great white Burgundy wine classified among the wines of Côte de Beune. Meursault also yields excellent, though less well-known, red wines.

MICROWAVE OVEN – An electrically operated counter-top appliance that works on the principle of radiation reaction on the water molecules within foods of all kinds, so that foods are cooked evenly throughout in a comparatively short time. Much prized for its cleanliness and speed in cooking and defrosting, it has gained great popularity. Manufacturers have met all government safety and health requirements, but scientists have no definite data on possible radiation damage from prolonged use.

MIGNONETTE – French name for coarsely ground pepper.

In former times, this was the name given to a muslin sachet containing red pepper, nutmeg, coriander, cinnamon, ginger and cloves. This aromatic sachet was dipped for a few moments in the cooking pot to season the food.

MIGNOT – A celebrated restaurateur of the seventeenth century. He was immortalised by Boileau who, in his satire *le Repas ridicule*, called him a poisoner.

Mignot who, it is said, was a cook of some talent and a conscientious restaurateur, was much enraged by such criticism and took his complaint to court. His suit was rejected and he resolved to take vengeance himself. At that time he was making a kind of dry pastry much prized by Parisians. He conceived the idea of wrapping these little cakes in a sheet of paper upon which, at his own expense, he had printed a violent satire on Boileau written by the latter's enemy, the Abbé Cottin.

The success of these pastries, which were called *biscuits Mignot*, was enormous. All Paris wanted to taste them so as to be able to savour, at the same time, the verses in which Cottin reviled Boileau. The rage of Mignot subsided somewhat when he discovered that, far from doing him any harm, the couplet had contributed to his greater prosperity.

MIGRAINE – Wine made from grapes grown in the neighbourhood of Auxerre.

MIKADO – See GARNISHES.

MILANAISE (À LA) – Food prepared *à la milanaise* is generally dipped in egg and breadcrumbs mixed with grated Parmesan cheese, and fried in clarified butter.

The name also described a method of preparing macaroni, and a garnish for cuts of meat, made from macaroni with cheese, coarsely shredded ham, pickled tongue, mushrooms and truffles, all blended in tomato sauce.

This garnish is also used with *Macaroni timbales à la milanaise* (see TIMBALE).

MILANESE CAKE. MILANAIS – Heat on the stove, as for a Genoese cake, 250 g. (9 oz., 2 cups) fine sugar and 6 eggs until the mixture begins to heat. Add 200 g. (7 oz., scant cup) melted butter and 200 g. (7 oz., $1\frac{3}{4}$ cups) sieved flour. Flavour with 1 dl. (6 tablespoons, scant $\frac{1}{2}$ cup) anisette liqueur.

Pour the mixture into ornamental tins and bake in a medium oven. Turn out the cakes, spread with apricot jam and ice with aniseed-flavoured *Fondant icing* (see ICING).

MILK. LAIT – Opaque white alkaline liquid with a yellowish or bluish tinge, secreted by the mammary glands.

The composition of the milk varies according to the type and breed of animal, its state of health and the diet on which it has been reared.

Milk analysis laboratory
Laiterie Servas (Ain) (*Rayot*)

A litre ($1\frac{3}{4}$ pints, generous quart) milk supplies the body with 30 g. protein, 35 g. fats, 54 g. milk sugar, 7 g. mineral salts (calcium, phosphorus, sodium, etc.) and an appreciable quantity of Vitamins A, B, B_1, B_2, C. It is indispensable to babies, but not the complete food for adults that many suppose it to be: its nutritive value is inadequate. For example, to obtain sufficient carbohydrates for his needs, the average adult would have to drink 3 litres ($5\frac{1}{4}$ pints, $6\frac{1}{2}$ pints) milk; in which case the protein intake (120 g.) would be excessive, equivalent to 500 g. (18 oz.) of beef. Lime salts would also be in excess of his needs.

In spite of the fact that it is a liquid, milk should always be regarded as a food and not as a drink, and should be sipped and swallowed slowly. Taken in this way, it coagulates in

Concentrated milk
(*Nicolas*)

little fragments in the stomach, and these can be dealt with readily by the digestive juices. On the other hand, if it is gulped down it forms a large indigestible clot in the stomach, and the digestive juices have difficulty in breaking it down. For the same reason, milk is more digestible in the form of soups and porridges because, mixed with carbohydrates, the clot breaks up into fragments more readily. Even persons suffering from enteritis can take milk in this form.

Condensed milk. LAITS CONDENSÉS – Milk collected with the utmost care, with or without added sugar, is evaporated in a vacuum at 60 per cent so as to reduce its water content by 40 to 50 per cent.

Sweetened condensed milk keeps better, once the tin is opened, than unsweetened milk. It has the consistency of thick cream.

Dried milk. LAITS DESSÉCHÉS – Milk, usually partly skimmed, is evaporated very rapidly by passing through heated cylinders. Powdered milk keeps very well. The partial skimming of the milk makes it less likely that the powder will turn rancid. This milk, suitably diluted, can be given to young babies.

Fermented milk. LAITS FERMENTÉS – All agricultural communities make use of fermentation to preserve milk and alter its flavour. Apart from spontaneous coagulation, due to the action of the lactic microbes, which produces curds, and curdling by means of rennet, which is the basis of cheese-making, there are many other types of fermented milk. Examples of these are the *dahdi* of India, the *mazyn* of Armenia, the *huslanka* of the Carpathians and Bukovina, the *lab an zebadi* of Egypt, the *yoghurt* of Bulgaria and the *taetta* of Scandinavia. This last is a runny, viscous milk to which vegetable juices are added to prevent coagulation.

All these types of sour milk are produced by the action of lactic ferments of varying degrees of purity and obtained from a number of different sources.

Kefir (q.v.) and *koumiss* (q.v.) are produced by the combined action of the lactic ferments and barm (brewer's yeast), which forms lactic acid, alcohol, and carbonic acid, rendering the milk frothy.

Almond milk – See ALMOND.

Buttermilk – See BUTTERMILK.

Coconut milk – See COCONUT.

MILL. MOULIN – Small machine used to pulverise foodstuffs such as coffee, breadcrumbs, pepper, block salt, etc.

MILLAS or MILIASSE – Name given in the Languedoc region to a kind of porridge or hasty-pudding made either with maize flour (cornmeal) or with a mixture of wheaten flour and maize flour.

Though the true millas is made in Languedoc, similar porridges are made in various parts of south-eastern and south-western France. In different areas they are given other names: *cruchade* in Guyenne and Gascony; *broye, gaudines* or *yerbilhou* in Béarn; *pous* or *rimotes* in Périgord; *gaudes* in Franche-Comté.

Polenta (q.v.), which is made in Corsica and in Provence, is a porridge of the same type as millas.

The millas of Languedoc is a dish in rustic style. Formerly, in the countryside of the region, it was eaten like bread with certain dishes cooked in gravy, such as beef *daube*, *civet* of hare, etc. When used in this way, the millas, when it is quite cold, is cut into slices and browned in fat in a frying pan, or toasted under the grill. In Languedoc, various sweets are made from millas.

Cherry millas. MILLAS AUX CERISES – Put a layer of hot millas in a buttered pie dish. Add sugar and flavour with kirsch. Smooth the millas carefully. Part-cook some stoned cherries in syrup. Drain, and steep in kirsch. Spread them on top of the millas and cover with another layer of millas. Smooth the surface carefully. Make a border of cherries, prepared as indicated above. Sprinkle with crushed macaroons. Pour on melted butter and brown in a slow oven.

A millas sweet (dessert) can be made in the same way using various kinds of cooked fruit such as apricots, bananas, peaches, pears, apples, plums, etc.

Fried millas. MILLAS FRIT – Cut the millas into slices of equal thickness. Flour the slices and brown them lightly in butter or fat. Prepared in this way millas can be used in place of bread with various dishes in gravy.

Millas with frittons. MILLAS AUX FRITTONS – In Languedoc this type of millas is made on the day when, according to the local phrase, the housewife *fait le cochon* (cooks the pig). The porridge is cooked in the cauldron used to clarify the fat of the pig. At the end of the cooking, the *frittons* (the residue of the pork fat after melting) are added to the millas.

When it is ready, the porridge is poured onto a floured linen cloth and left to cool. It is then sliced into squares or rectangles before being fried or grilled.

Millas with grape jam. MILLAS AU RASINÉ – Spread slices of millas with *raisiné* (q.v.) and arrange them in a circle on a dish. Sprinkle the slices with crushed macaroons. Pour on melted butter and brown gently in the oven.

The millas may be spread with other types of jam, or thick purées.

Lot-et-Garonne millas. MILLAS DE LOT-ET-GARONNE – This kind of millas is called a *rimote* and also a *cruchade* in Lot-et-Garonne.

Pour water into a large pan and bring to the boil. Flavour with lemon essence and orange-flower water.

Sprinkle into the boiling liquid freshly milled maize flour (cornmeal) until a thick porridge is produced. Pour into shallow plates.

Rimotes are eaten hot, sprinkled with sugar. When they are cold, they can be cut into quarters, browned on both sides in a frying pan, and sprinkled with sugar.

Millas with sugar. MILLAS AU SUCRE – Cut a layer of millas into slices. Cook the slices in hot butter or fat. (In Languedoc pork or goose fat is used for this purpose.) Brown the slices on both sides. Drain. Sprinkle liberally with fine sugar flavoured with vanilla or lemon rind.

Toasted millas. MILLAS GRILLÉ – Spread slices of millas with fat or butter. Toast them gently under the grill.

Mille-feuilles

MILLE-FEUILLE – A pastry very much in vogue in Paris. It is made by arranging thin layers of flaky pastry one on top of the other with layers of cream or some other filling in between.

Mille-feuille can be baked in the form of a large sweet, decorated in various ways. Or, as in Paris *pâtisseries*, in small individual portions, by cutting the flaky pastry into pieces 5 cm. (2 inches) wide and laying them one on top of the other, sandwiched together in the same way with cream or some other filling.

Large mille-feuille. GROSS MILLE-FEUILLE – Roll out the *Flaky pastry* (see DOUGH) 2 cm. (¾ inch) thick. Cut circles 15 to 18 cm. (6 to 7 inches) in diameter. Put these on a baking sheet, dredge with sugar and bake in a hot oven. Leave to cool, trim, and spread each circle with *French pastry cream* (see CREAMS) or with any other sweet cream. Place the circles one on top of the other to produce a cake 18 to 20 cm. (7 to 8 inches) deep, regular in shape. Ice it with plain meringue, carefully smoothed with a knife. Sprinkle with sugar and put the cake in the oven for a few minutes to set the meringue.

Decorate the top of the cake according to taste.

Large *mille-feuilles*, after being covered with a thin layer of meringue, may be sprinkled on the top and sides with dried sultanas, currants and pistachio nuts, either whole or chopped.

When they are intended to be used for a cold buffet they can be further decorated with sugar ornaments arranged as a border on top of the cake, and with plumes of spun sugar. This type of decoration for large cakes is hardly ever used nowadays. Most commonly, *mille-feuilles* are made square and simply sprinkled with icing sugar.

Mille-feuille can also be filled with any kind of confectioner's cream or thick fruit purées or jams in alternate layers. The layers of a large *mille-feuille* can also be spread at the last moment with thick *Chantilly cream* (see CREAMS) flavoured with vanilla.

Small mille-feuille. PETIT MILLE-FEUILLE – Individual portions are made in the same way as large *mille-feuilles*, but the square layers, spread with cream, are laid one on top of the other, and cut into pieces 5 cm. (2 inches) wide. The top is left plain.

MILLER'S THUMB. MEUNIER – Common name for a freshwater fish, also known as a *bull-head*. It is eaten fried.

MILLÉSIME – French term for a wine (whatever its region or vineyard) that has the vintage year (*millésime*) marked both on the label and the cork. Since the year helps to distinguish the character and worth of a wine, these are the ones preferred by connoisseurs.

All dated wines are not by any means equal in quality. There are exceptional, excellent, good and mediocre wines. The qualities of a particular year also vary from region to region and occasionally from vineyard to vineyard.

In Champagne, only the bottles of the best vintage years are marked; the others are used for blending.

MILLET – Cereal grain which is one of several species of panic-grass. There are two main edible varieties, the *common millet* and what is now called *Italian* or *German millet*.

This plant has been cultivated from very ancient times, the common millet in the Egypto-Arab countries and the 'Italian' variety in Japan. Millet was cultivated in India in prehistoric times. The Romans used it to make a kind of milk porridge from the grains after removing the husks. It is still used in this way by some African tribes.

MILLIASSOUS (Pâtisserie) – Put in a bowl 200 g. (7 oz., 1½ cups) flour made from small millet, 400 g. (14 oz., 1¾ cups) sugar and 8 eggs. Work this mixture thoroughly. Add the finely chopped rind of 2 lemons. Moisten with 1½ litres (2¾ pints, 3¼ pints) boiling milk and mix well.

Fill small buttered baking tins with the mixture. Bake in a hot oven for 20 to 30 minutes.

MIMOSA SALAD – Sprinkle mimosa with coarsely chopped yolks of hard-boiled eggs and serve in a salad bowl.

MINCEMEAT (English cookery) – Mincemeat should steep for a month in Madeira, rum or brandy.

Mince pie is popular in the United States, but the mincemeat is different.

Meat is not an ingredient of English mincemeat. In the United States meat (beef or venison) is almost always included, although several recipes for meatless mincemeat exist, some using green tomatoes and others more closely resembling the English variety.

English mincemeat. MINCEMEAT ANGLAIS – 450 g. (1 lb., 3 cups) shredded suet, 450 g. (1 lb., 3 cups) currants, 450 g. (1 lb., 3 cups) chopped seeded raisins, 450 g. (1 lb., 4 cups) chopped apples, 450 g. (1 lb., 2 cups) sugar, 450 g. (1 lb., 3 cups) sultanas, 100 g. (4 oz., ⅔ cup) chopped, mixed candied fruit peel, 3 tablespoons (4 tablespoons) brandy or rum, juice and rind of 1 lemon, 1 teaspoon each of cinnamon, nutmeg, clove and mace.

Combine the ingredients. Pack closely in jars and cover tightly. This yields about 2 kg. (4 to 5 lb.) mincemeat.

American mincemeat. MINCEMEAT AMÉRICAIN – Put the following ingredients in a large bowl: 450 g. (1 lb., 3 cups) minced beef suet, 450 g. (1 lb., 3½ cups) cooked and finely diced beef, 450 g. (1 lb., 3 cups) seeded and chopped raisins, 450 g. (1 lb., 3 cups) cleaned and washed currants and sultanas, 450 g. (1 lb., 4 cups) peeled and chopped rennet apples, 150 g. (5 oz., 1 cup) finely diced candied citron, 100 g. (4 oz., ¾ cup) chopped candied orange peel, the chopped rind and juice of 1 orange, 450 g. (1 lb., 2 cups) light brown moist sugar, 25 g. (1 oz., ¼ cup) mixed spices, 2½ teaspoons salt, a half-bottle brandy, 1 dl. (6 tablespoons, scant ½ cup) rum, 1 dl. (6 tablespoons, scant ½ cup) Madeira.

Mix all the ingredients thoroughly. Leave the mixture to steep for 1 month in a cool place. Stir every 8 days.

Mincemeat fritters. BEIGNETS DE MINCEMEAT – Dip rounds of rice paper in water. Fill them with mincemeat and shape into balls. Dip them in batter and deep-fry. Serve with apricot sauce flavoured with rum.

Mincemeat omelette, or Christmas omelette. OMELETTE DE MINCEMEAT (OMELETTE DE NOËL) – Beat the eggs, adding a few tablespoons fresh cream, a little rum, grated lemon rind, and sugar.

Cook the omelette in butter and, just before folding it over, fill it with a few tablespoons mincemeat, heated with fresh cream. Sprinkle the omelette with sugar, pour plenty of rum over it, set alight and serve.

Mincemeat rissoles. RISSOLES DE MINCEMEAT – Proceed as for plain rissoles (q.v.).

Mincemeat vol-au-vent. BOUCHÉES DE MINCEMEAT – Bake small *vol-au-vent*. While they are still hot, fill them with mincemeat with fresh cream added.

Mince pie – 'This little pie', wrote Suzanne, French historian of English cookery, 'is especially esteemed and popular in England. With the legendary plum pudding, it presides as master at the gargantuan love feast of Christmas. Its absence from a Christmas dinner would be looked upon as a breach of the traditional rules and customs.'

To make the pies, line large, deep, buttered tartlet tins with plain lining dough or with flaky pastry trimmings. Fill with one of the mincemeats indicated above. Cover with a thin layer of *Flaky pastry* (see DOUGH). Press the edges together. Make a hole in the centre of each pie to allow the steam to escape. Brush with egg and bake in a hot oven. Serve the mince pies hot.

MINCERS AND CHOPPERS. HACHOIRS – In butcher's shops and restaurant kitchens, precision implements are used for mincing and chopping. Many of them are electrically operated.

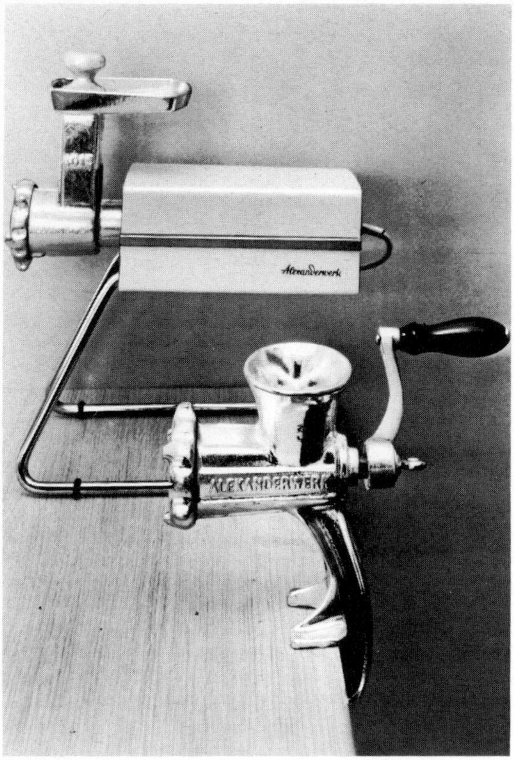

Mincers and choppers (*La Carpe. Phot. Nicolas*)

In French private kitchens, one of the implements used is the four-bladed, double-handled chopper. An ordinary meat chopper can be used, too, though this is really intended for chopping bones.

Chopping boards are sometimes made of cross-grained plywood, like the chopping blocks described under CHOPPING.

MINERAL WATERS. EAUX MINÉRALES – Some natural mineral water is produced by the disintegration of the rocks under intense heat in the bowels of the earth. This water is sometimes hot when it reaches the earth's surface (thermal water), sometimes cold. Each mineral spring has its own special properties which seem to be unrelated to its chemical composition, since two springs very close together can have different properties.

MINESTRA – Italian word for a thick soup. The best-known of Italian *minestras* is *minestrone*, for which a recipe is given under SOUPS AND BROTHS.

MINNOW. VAIRON – Small freshwater fish whose bronze-coloured back has olive lights. It is often substituted for gudgeon in *fritures* of small fish. Its flesh, however, is less fine and more bitter in taste than that of gudgeon. Prepare in the same way as gudgeon (q.v.).

Minnow

MINT. MENTHE – Fragrant plant of which there are a great many varieties. These most commonly used in France are *menthe pouliot, menthe crépue* (curly mint) or *menthe rouge* (red mint). Peppermint is a variety of mint used in dispensing. It has a four-sided stem which is green or reddish, and contains an oily essence (essence of peppermint) from which crystals of camphor mint or menthol can be extracted.

Mint, which is used a great deal in infusions, is also an ingredient in a large number of liqueurs. It is also used in cooking, especially in England, where it is cultivated.

Spirit of mint is made by steeping 1 kg. ($2\frac{1}{4}$ lb.) fresh mint leaves in 3 litres ($5\frac{1}{4}$ pints, $6\frac{1}{2}$ pints) alcohol, 70° (U.S. 80°) proof, for 3 days, and distilling it by condensation.

Mint sauce (English cookery). SAUCE-MENTHE – This sauce is an almost indispensable adjunct to hot or cold lamb in England.

Add $1\frac{1}{2}$ dl. ($\frac{1}{4}$ pint, $\frac{2}{3}$ cup) vinegar, 4 tablespoons ($\frac{1}{4}$ cup) water, 25 g. (1 oz., $\frac{1}{4}$ cup) fine sugar, a pinch of salt and a little pepper to 50 g. (2 oz., 2 cups) finely shredded mint leaves. Leave to marinate in a bowl. For an alternative recipe see SAUCE, *Cold Sauces*.

MIQUES DE MAÏS (Périgord cookery) – Make a fairly stiff dough with 250 g. (9 oz., $1\frac{3}{4}$ cups) maize flour (cornmeal) 250 g. (9 oz., $2\frac{1}{4}$ cups) sifted flour, 1 tablespoon pork fat, a pinch of salt and a glass of tepid water.

When this dough is well kneaded, break it into small pieces of 100 g. (4 oz.) each. Shape the pieces into balls by rolling them in floured hands.

Drop these dough balls into a saucepan of salted boiling water. Poach like forcemeat balls. Turn them over once or twice so that they are fully cooked.

When they are ready, after 25 to 30 minutes' boiling, strain the *miques*, put them on a cloth and keep them warm.

Miques are eaten as bread. In the countryside around Périgord, they are an accompaniment to dishes such as pickled pork with cabbage, *civet* of hare or rabbit, etc.

They can also be served as a sweet (dessert) by frying them in butter and sprinkling with sugar.

MIRABEAU (À LA) – Garnish served mainly with grilled meat. It consists of strips of anchovy fillets arranged in a criss-cross pattern on the meat, stoned olives, blanched tarragon leaves and anchovy butter.

MIRABELLE – Small plum, golden yellow in colour with a penetrating smell. It is eaten stewed, made into jam, preserved, and used in the manufacture of a spirit. It is also used in confectionery.

Mirabelle plum flan. FLAN AUX MIRABELLES – Proceed as indicated for *Apricot tart* (see TART).

MIRBANE. Name given to an artificial essence of bitter almonds. It is a yellow liquid with a powerful smell, and is used in perfumery and occasionally in inferior confectionery.

MIREPOIX – Mixture used in meat, fish and shellfish dishes to enhance their flavour.

Mirepoix with meat. MIREPOIX AU GRAS – Cook 150 g. (5 oz., $1\frac{1}{4}$ cups) diced carrot, 100 g. (4 oz., 1 cup) chopped onion, 50 g. (2 oz., $\frac{1}{2}$ cup) chopped celery, and 100 g. (4 oz., $\frac{1}{2}$ cup) chopped raw ham or blanched belly of pork in 25 g. (1 oz., 2 tablespoons) butter in a covered saucepan with a sprig of thyme and a quarter of a bay leaf. Simmer slowly until the vegetables are very tender.

Mirepoix is added to certain sauces, notably *Espagnole sauce* (see SAUCE), to enhance the flavour. It can also be added to braised or pot-roasted meat or poultry.

Bottling plant for Vichy mineral water (*Mougins*)

Vegetable mirepoix. MIREPOIX AU MAIGRE – This *mirepoix* is often called *brunoise*. It is used mainly in the preparation of shellfish *à la bordelaise*. It is also used as an additional ingredient in some white sauces.

Cook 150 g. (5 oz., $1\frac{1}{4}$ cups) diced carrot, 100 g. (4 oz., 1 cup) chopped onion and 50 g. (2 oz., $\frac{1}{2}$ cup) chopped celery slowly in butter. Season with salt, a pinch of powdered thyme, and bay leaf. Cook until the vegetables are very tender.

MIRLITONS DE ROUEN – Small pastry in the form of a tartlet which is speciality of Rouen.

Ingredients. 250 g. (9 oz.) flaky pastry dough, 4 egg yolks, 50 g. (2 oz., $\frac{1}{4}$ cup) sugar, 125 g. (4 oz., $\frac{1}{2}$ cup) butter, 1 vanilla pod, $\frac{1}{2}$ tablespoon orange-blossom water.

Method. Make *Flaky pastry* (see DOUGH). Mix the sugar, yolks and vanilla (the part taken from the inside of the pod). Add the butter, heated until it is nut-brown in colour, and the orange-blossom water. Line tartlet tins with the flaky pastry. Fill two-thirds full with the mixture. Sprinkle with fine sugar and bake in a hot oven for about 15 minutes.

MIROIR (AU) – Descriptive term for eggs baked in the oven so that the white forms a polished film over the yolk. It is also more loosely applied to other dishes which have a mirror-bright finish. (See EGG, *Baked eggs au miroir.*)

MIROTON – Type of stew made from cooked meat and flavoured with onions.

In a number of old French recipe books this dish is called *mironton*, and was used not only of a meat dish but also of dishes made with fruit.

For the preparation of *miroton* see BEEF, *Miroton of beef.*

MISSEL THRUSH. DRAINE – Species of thrush called missel thrush because it feeds on mistletoe berries. Its plumage is darker than that of the common thrush, and it is longer. It is cooked in the same way as thrush (q.v.).

MISSION HAUT-BRION WINE – Mission Haut-Brion vineyards are among the oldest of the Bordeaux region. They are situated in the Pessac commune of Graves.

MITAN (Middle-cut) – Old French word, a synonym of middle. It is used in cooking for the middle cut of salmon.

MITE. CIRON – Common name for all the animalcules which live in food matter, in cheese for instance, or in vegetable refuse.

MITONNER – French cooking term meaning to simmer bread for a long time in soup.

MIX. DÉLAYER – To blend various ingredients thoroughly into a homogenous mixture.

MIXTURES. APPAREILS –

Cream cheese mixture for hot hors-d'œuvre à la russe. APPAREIL TWAROGUE – Prepared from pressed creamed cheese mixed with an equal quantity of fresh butter, blended until it is very smooth.

Dauphine potato mixture. APPAREIL À POMMES DE TERRE DAUPHINE – *Duchess potatoes* (see POTATOES) mixed with *Chou paste* (see DOUGH) prepared without sugar, in the proportion of one part *chou paste* to three parts duchess potatoes.

Duchess potato mixture. APPAREIL À POMMES DE TERRE DUCHESSE – Potato purée bound with eggs. (See POTATOES.)

Mixtures for kromeskies and croquettes. APPAREILS À CROMESQUIS, À CROQUETTES – These mixtures, which are similar for both preparations, are composed of one or more ingredients, cut into small dice, blended for a white mixture with *Velouté sauce* (see SAUCE) with egg yolks added to it, or for a brown mixture with *Béchamel sauce* (see SAUCE) with rich *demi-glace* (meat jelly) or thickened brown stock.

Maintenon mixture. APPAREIL À MAINTENON – Mixture of *Onion soubise* (see PURÉE) and thick *Béchamel sauce* (see SAUCE), bound with egg yolks, incorporating sliced or shredded mushrooms cooked in butter, truffles, and *Pickled tongue* (see OFFAL or VARIETY MEATS).

Matignon mixture. APPAREIL À MATIGNON – Vegetables cut in thin slices, cooked in a covered pan in butter with ham, and then mixed with Madeira. (See MATIGNON.)

This is used as a supplementary ingredient for various mixtures, also for braised and fried dishes *à la Matignon.*

Mirepoix mixture. APPAREIL À MIREPOIX – Vegetables cut *en brunoise* (q.v.), the degree of fineness depending on the use for which it is intended. Very small pieces of lean ham or bacon lightly cooked in butter are added. (See MIREPOIX.)

This is used as a supplementary ingredient for sauces, forcemeats and various mixtures; it is also used for braised and fried dishes *à la Mirepoix*.

Semolina mixture for hot pies à la russe (Semolina kasha) – See KASHA.

MIXTURES FOR SWEET DISHES. APPARAEILS POUR ENTREMETS –

Bavarois mixture. APPAREIL À BAVAROIS – A mixture of English custard and dissolved gelatine, variously flavoured, with whipped cream added to it. (See BAVAROIS.)

Butter cream mixture. APPAREIL À CRÈME AU BEURRE – This mixture, which is used in the preparation of various cold pastry desserts (coffee gâteaux, praline, chocolate gâteaux, etc.), is made with 28° syrup, egg yolks, and fresh butter, or with custard to which fresh butter has been added while it was still warm. (See CREAMS.)

Caramel cream mixture. APPAREIL À CRÈME AU CARAMEL – A mixture of eggs, sugar, milk and the flavouring chosen, cooked in a *bain-marie* (q.v.) in a mould coated with light caramel. (See CUSTARD, *Caramel custard*.)

Chou paste or cream puff pastry mixture. APPAREIL À PÂTE À CHOU – This mixture is used for making cakes of various kinds, cream buns, éclairs, etc. and also for the preparation of various dishes, such as soufflé fritters, *gnocchi, profiteroles*, etc. (See DOUGH.)

Condé mixture. APPAREIL À CONDÉ – *Ingredients.* 250 g. (9 oz., 2¼ cups) chopped almonds, 375 g. (13 oz., 3 cups) fine sugar, egg whites, powdered vanilla.

Method. Put the sugar, almonds and vanilla into a bowl. Moisten with egg white, in sufficient quantity to make an easily spreadable, non-runny paste. (See CONDÉ.)

This mixture is used for icing various dessert pastries.

French pastry cream mixture. APPAREIL À CRÈME PÂTISSIÈRE – Cream cooked to a firm consistency, made by diluting egg yolks blended with flour and sugar, with boiled milk flavoured as desired. (See CREAMS.)

Crème Saint-Honoré mixture. APPAREIL À CRÈME SAINT-HONORÉ – Mixture of French pastry cream with egg whites beaten to a stiff foam, added while it is still cooking. (See CREAMS.) Used for various sweet dishes.

English custard mixture. APPAREIL À CRÈME ANGLAISE – Custard made of 500 g. (18 oz., 4 cups) fine sugar, 16 egg yolks, 1 litre (1¾ pints, generous quart) boiled flavoured milk. Cook on the stove, stirring constantly, until the first sign of boiling.

This custard is also known under the name of English sauce. It can be served alone, but is more often served as an accompaniment to puddings.

It can be blended with gelatine, dissolved in a little cold water; allow 25 g. (1 oz.) powdered gelatine to 1 litre (1¾ pints, generous quart).

This custard is served hot or cold, as indicated in the recipe. (See CREAMS.)

Custard mould mixture. APPAREIL À CRÈME RENVERSÉE – Mixture prepared like English custard, using 1 litre (1¾ pints, generous quart) boiled milk, 4 whole eggs, 7 egg yolks, and 200 g. (7 oz., 1½ cups) fine sugar. Blend the ingredients well.

Fruit soufflé mixture. APPAREIL À SOUFFLÉ AUX FRUITS – Cook 250 g. (9 oz., generous cup) sugar in a copper pan to crack stage (see SUGAR). Add 200 g. (7 oz., scant cup) fruit pulp, rubbed through a sieve.

Bring the syrup to ball stage. Pour it gradually on 5 egg whites whisked into a very stiff froth. Bake like a soufflé.

Meringue mixture. APPAREIL À MERINGUE ORDINAIRE – Whisk 8 egg whites into a very stiff froth. Add 500 g. (18 oz., 2¼ cups) slightly moistened sugar to the mixture, folding it gently with a wooden spoon.

The proportion of egg whites for the meringue can be increased. Up to 12 egg whites for 500 g. (18 oz., 2¼ cups) of sugar can be used.

Italian meringue mixture. APPAREIL À MERINGUE ITALIENNE – Whisk 8 egg whites until very stiff. Make a syrup of 500 g. (18 oz., 2¼ cups) sugar and 1 cup water cooked to 121°C. (250°F.).

Pour this syrup in a thin thread on the egg whites, whisking vigorously throughout this operation.

Italian meringue mixture en genoise. APPAREIL À MERINGUE ITALIENNE EN GENOISE – Blend 500 g. (18 oz., 2¼ cups) sugar and 8 egg whites in a copper pan on a hot plate whisking until the mixture reaches a consistency when it can be held on the whisk.

This meringue can be kept in a bowl for a time. Cover it with a circle of paper.

MOCHA. MOKA – Variety of coffee bean grown in Mocha in Arabia. These fragrant beans are roasted rather less than those of Réunion Island and Martinique, which are blended in the coffee commonly used in France.

Coffee made from pure mocha is generally served in special cups, smaller than those used for ordinary coffee.

Mocha cake. GÂTEAU MOKA – Cake made by covering layers of cake, made from best Genoese mixture, with butter cream flavoured with mocha. Put one layer of cake spread with mocha cream on top of the other.

Ice with mocha-flavoured fondant icing or mocha-flavoured butter cream. Decorate the iced cake by piping the same icing or cream through a fluted nozzle onto the sides and top.

Mocha cream. CRÈME AU MOKA – Custard flavoured with coffee essence. Butter cream can also be flavoured with mocha.

French pastry cream (see CREAMS) used for filling *choux* and *éclairs* may be flavoured with mocha coffee. Mocha is sometimes added to *Chantilly cream*.

Mocha essence. ESSENCE DE MOKA – Made with unadulterated roasted mocha coffee infused in the same way as any other coffee essence.

Put in the upper compartment of a large coffee filter 200 g. (7 oz., 2⅓ cups) freshly roasted and ground coffee. Pour onto this, a little at a time, 5 dl. (scant pint, 2¼ cups) very strong coffee prepared in advance, and poured on hot but not boiling.

During this process the filter should stand in hot water.

Coffee essence can also be made with skimmed milk, but only if it is to be used to flavour creams or ice cream mixtures. To make this essence, completely skim 5 dl. (scant pint, 2¼ cups) milk. Bring to the boil. Put in 200 g. (7 oz., 2⅓ cups) roasted coffee, still hot and crushed with a rolling-pin. Cover the container with a cloth. Leave to infuse for 15 minutes.

Mocha ice cream. GLACE AU MOKA – Ice cream flavoured with mocha coffee. (See ICE CREAMS AND ICES, *Coffee ice cream*.)

MOCHATINE CAKES. MOKATINE – Individual portions of mocha cake or *petits fours* made from best Genoese mixture, filled with mocha-flavoured butter cream and iced with mocha-flavoured fondant icing.

MOCK TURTLE SOUP (English cookery). POTAGE FAUSSE TORTUE – Soup made with calf's head. (See SOUPS AND BROTHS.)

MODE (À LA) – Name given mainly to large cuts of braised beef. (See BEEF, *Top of rump à la mode.*)

MOISTENING. MOUILLEMENT – Moistening is the process of adding a liquid of some kind to *ragoûts*, stews, braised meat, fish or poultry, etc.

The term is applied to the broth, consommé stock, wine, etc., used in this way.

MOLASSES. MÉLASSE – Thick brownish substance which is the residue of sugar refining. It will not crystallise.

Sugar cane molasses has quite a pleasant smell and taste, and is used in the distillation of tafia, generally known as rum, a name once used only of the spirit distilled from cane juice, the natural juice of the sugar cane.

MOLLUSCS. COQUILLAGES – Univalve or bivalve edible mollusc. Nearly all are of marine origin; the snail is the one land mollusc that is eaten.

Many types are eaten raw, sprinkled with a little lemon juice or vinegar. Molluscs are used as a garnish for numerous dishes, especially for fish.

Some molluscs can cause poisoning and infectious diseases but the majority of those caught in clear water can be consumed without danger.

Oysters (q.v.) hold first place by reason of their delicate taste and substance. They are easily digested and have the advantage of being able to be consumed alive. It is possible to eat a very large quantity of oysters without loss of appetite; an equivalent quantity of meat with a far lower nutritive value would bring about satiety. The quantity of diluted sea water which oysters contain is a mineralizing element of the first order.

Mussels (q.v.), perhaps richer in food value than oysters, are rather more difficult to digest. They are usually eaten cooked.

Among the other shellfish, scallops (q.v.) deserve a place apart. They have a flavour approaching that of lobster.

MONACO – Monaco consommé is a clear chicken broth thickened with arrowroot, with a special garnish of small rounds of cake mixture made with cheese.

Monaco cream soup is a cream of chicken soup served with the same garnish.

MONBAZILLAC – White wine, very rich and somewhat similar to Sauternes. It is made from grapes grown at Monbazillac, a small commune in the Dordogne 8 km. (5 miles) from Bergerac. A ministerial decree of May 1936 lays down the boundaries of the Monbazillac vineyards. Wine grown beyond these boundaries may not bear the name Monbazillac.

MONSELET – The author Charles Monselet was born at Nantes in 1828 and died in Paris in 1888. He was one of the well-known writers of his day.

He was also a great gastronome, or, more exactly, a poet of gastronomy, for he wrote a number of pleasant poems on the good things of the table. He published several gastronomic works, among them being the *Almanach des gourmands*, the *Lettres gourmandes* and *Cuisinière poétique*. He also wrote a large number of sonnets on cooking.

MONSELET (À LA) – Name given to a great many dishes which contain artichoke hearts and truffles, with potatoes fried in butter where appropriate.

MONSIEUR FROMAGE – See CHEESE.

MONT-BLANC – See CHESTNUTS.

MONT-BRY – See GARNISHES.

MONT-CENIS – See CHEESE.

MONTE-CRISTO *Montpensier gâteau* is often called by this name. The recipe for this cake is given under MONTPENSIER.

MONTGLAS – *Salpicon à la Montglas* is made from *foie gras*, pickled tongue, truffles and mushrooms blended in *Demi-glace sauce* (see SAUCE) flavoured with Madeira. This *salpicon* is used as a filling for very small *vol-au-vent*, tartlets and other pastry cases.

MONTHÉLIE – Red Burgundy wine produced in Monthélie (north of Volnay) in the Côte de Beaunne. (See BURGUNDY.)

MONTMAUR – Pierre de Montmaur was a great French scholar and a distinguished Hellenist. He was born in about 1576 at Bétaille, a village of Bas-Limousin between Tulle and Brive. He became a professor of Greek at Paris in 1623, and died in 1648.

Montmaur was mean, parasitic (a sponger as we would say today) and also a slanderer. Because of this he made many enemies. Among these was Ménage, a French literary

Main types of edible molluscs: 1. Common oyster (huître); 2. Portuguese oyster; 3. and 4. Mussels (moules); 5. Clam; 6. and 7. Clovisse; 8. Praire; 9. and 10. Cockles (coques); 11. Lavignon; 12. Vernis; 13. Fléon; 14. Razor shell; 15. and 16. Scallops (coquille Saint-Jacques); 17. Amande-de-mer; 18. Dosinie exolète; 19. Ormer; 20. Winkle; 21. Whelk; 22. Limpet

figure (1613–1692), tutor to Marc de Sévigné, who averred that Montmaur had above all been a teacher of adulation and cookery.

'He gave his lessons in flattery in the morning and his cookery lessons in the evening.'

Ménage said that Montmaur, in his theories of cookery, gave an inflated importance to the position of the chef. He taught that anyone who aspired to become an expert in this important branch of human knowledge should first study the science of government, medicine, painting, astrology, architecture and arithmetic, and gave specious and absurd reasons for this.

'It is necessary for the chef to consider with care the place, the time, the guests and the host; it is necessary for him to be able to direct a meal as though he were directing a battle. He has to be versed in chemical analysis, so as to distinguish between wholesome and dangerous foodstuffs, and those more or less resistant to the action of heat. He has to be able, like a painter, to make attractive designs and blend colours with skill, and so on.'

MONTMORENCY – Name given to a variety of cherry cultivated in the neighbourhood of Paris.

MONTMORENCY (À LA) – Name given to various dishes, cakes or sweets, all of which have cherries added to them in one form or another. For example: *Duck à la Montmorency; aiguillettes* (thin slices of breast) of Rouen duck with cherries, called Montmorency; cherry ice cream, called Montmorency; iced mousse with cherries, called Montmorency; cherry tarts and tartlets, called Montmorency.

Border of cream à la Montmorency. BORDURE DE CRÈME À LA MONTMORENCY – Fill a turban (ring) mould with rich custard flavoured with kirsch and cook in a saucepan of water. Leave to cool. Turn out on a dish. Fill the middle with stoned cherries, poached in syrup flavoured with kirsch. Mask with *Chantilly cream* (see CREAMS) shaped into a dome and decorated with large stoned cherries cooked in syrup.

Montmorency cake. GÂTEAU MONTMORENCY – Cook some stoned cherries in syrup. Drain and mix with cherry jam flavoured with kirsch.

Using best *Genoese batter* (see DOUGH) make a round cake. Spread with the cherry mixture. Cover the cherries with *Italian meringue* (see MIXTURES). Smooth the meringue and decorate with meringue piping.

Sprinkle with icing sugar and brown in the oven. Decorate the top of the cake with cherries, lightly sprinkled with sugar.

MONTPELLIER BUTTER. BEURRE DE MONTPELLIER – A fancy butter, coloured green, used in the presentation and decoration of cold dishes. This butter is edible, but it is intended primarily for decoration rather than for food. (See BUTTER, *Compound butters.*)

MONTPENSIER – See GARNISHES.

MONTPENSIER (Pâtisserie) – *For the dough.* 250 g. (9 oz., $2\frac{1}{4}$ cups) sifted flour, 125 g. (4 oz., $\frac{1}{2}$ cup) sugar, 125 g. (4 oz., $\frac{1}{2}$ cup) butter, 2 whole eggs.

For the filling. 125 g. (4 oz., scant cup) blanched almonds, 250 g. (9 oz., generous cup) sugar, 50 g. (2 oz., $\frac{1}{4}$ cup) butter, 1 teaspoon powdered vanilla, 2 dl. ($\frac{1}{3}$ pint, scant cup) water, 5 egg whites.

Sieve the flour in a ring on the table. Put the sugar, butter and eggs in the middle. Mix quickly and, when the dough is of a good consistency, knead into a ball. Leave to stand while the filling is prepared as follows:

Pound the almonds finely in a mortar, adding the water. Put them in a bowl. Add the sugar, vanilla and the butter, previously melted. Mix well and add the stiffly beaten egg whites a little at a time.

Roll out the sweetened dough and lay it on a flan ring 20 to 25 cm. (8 to 10 inches) in diameter. Press it well down into the ring, making sure that it is firmly attached to the sides. A pie dish may be used as a substitute for the ring and baking sheet. In this case the tart is served in the dish.

Trim the edge with a knife. Prick the bottom of the flan with the point of a knife.

Pour the filling into the flan. Sprinkle with fine sugar and bake in a slow oven for 45 minutes.

A few seconds before the flan is cooked, turn it out. Put it back in the oven to brown the sides. Sprinkle once more with fine sugar, and leave to cool before serving.

MONTRACHET – One of the great wine-growing localities of the Côte de Beaune, distinguished by an *appellation contrôlée spéciale* and situated partly in the commune of Puligny, partly in that of Chassagne. It produces one of the greatest dry white wines, with a bouquet reminiscent of fresh almonds. In the best vintage years this wine matures wonderfully well.

The name Montrachet enters into the names of neighbouring *appellations*; Puligny-Montrachet, Chevalier-Montrachet, Bâtard-Montrachet, Bienvenues-Bâtard-Montrachet, Criots-Bâtard-Montrachet, Chassagne-Montrachet (which also produces fine red wines). (See BURGUNDY.)

MOOSE or ELK. ORIGNAL – The largest member of the deer family. The flesh of Canadian moose is comparable to venison. It is prepared like deer.

MOQUE (Belgian Pâtisserie) – 500 g. (18 oz., $4\frac{1}{2}$ cups) sieved flour in a ring on the table. In the middle put 4 or 5 crushed cloves, a pinch of bicarbonate of soda, a pinch of salt, 100 g. (4 oz., $\frac{1}{2}$ cup) moist brown sugar, the same weight of melted molasses and 300 g. (11 oz., $1\frac{1}{4}$ cups) butter.

Mix thoroughly, working the flour in a little at a time. Roll the dough into the shape of a long sausage. Stand it in a cool place and leave overnight.

Next day, cut the dough 'sausage' into slices $\frac{1}{2}$ cm. ($\frac{1}{4}$ inch) thick. Put these rounds of dough, spaced out a little, on a buttered baking sheet.

Bake in a moderate oven.

MORAY. MURÈNE – The histories of ancient Rome speak with enthusiasm of this fish. Wealthy gourmets of imperial Rome, it is said, bred moray, whose flesh grew more succulent in the magnificent breeding grounds which were maintained at great expense.

The moray, which is somewhat similar to an eel in appearance, is a carnivorous fish of extreme voracity. It is prepared in the same way as eel (q.v.).

MOREL. MORILLE – Name of a fungus found in the spring on the fringe of woods. There are various species, the most highly prized being the little black pointed morels found in mountainous country. (See MUSHROOM.)

To prepare for cooking, trim, wash in several waters and very carefully remove any dirt in the interstices of the honeycombed caps. Simmer them in butter in a covered pan in the same way as *cèpes*. When the morels are large, divide them in halves or quarters before cooking. Morels can also be fried without first simmering them in butter. In this case they must be thoroughly dried after washing.

MORELLO CHERRY. GRIOTTE – This species of cherry is dark red or almost black and it has a tough skin. The pulp, which is red, is firm and sweetish, but sometimes bitter.

Morels
(*Kollar*)

All recipes for the preparation of cherries are suitable for morello cherries. (See CHERRY.)

MORNAY (À LA) – Method of preparing certain food, principally fish. All dishes *à la Mornay* are covered with *Mornay sauce* (see SAUCE).

MORTADELLA. MORTADELLE – A large type of sausage of Italian origin. The *mortadella* of Bologna has the highest reputation. *Mortadella sausages* are also made in France, notably in Lyons and Paris. These are excellent.

They are served, thinly sliced, as an *hors-d'œuvre*.

MORTAR. MORTIER – Bowl made of marble, stone, metal or wood in which forcemeats and other mixtures are pounded or mixed using a pestle made of hard wood.

MOSCOVITE – Sweets *à la moscovite* are prepared in various ways.

Cold moscovites are similar to *bavarois* (Bavarian creams). Moscovites, however, are different in that they are usually made in a hexagonal mould with a hinged lid and embedded in crushed ice and salt.

The name moscovite is also used of an iced *bombe* with kummel and almonds, and of an ice pudding flavoured with vanilla, also made in a hexagonal mould. In this case the ice cream is made with a hole in the centre which is filled with fresh fruit and *Chantilly cream* (see CREAMS).

Moscovite jellies are made with fruit or liqueurs in a hermetically sealed mould and embedded in ice and salt. The distinctive feature of these jellies is that they are covered with a frosting of rime.

Fruit moscovite. MOSCOVITE AUX FRUITS – Rub through a fine sieve enough fruit to produce 8 dl. ($1\frac{1}{3}$ pints, $1\frac{3}{4}$ pints) pulp. Add 300 g. (11 oz., $1\frac{1}{3}$ cups) sugar and 20 g. ($\frac{3}{4}$ oz.) gelatine dissolved in water. Mix well and put it to set on ice, stirring constantly. Flavour with kirsch.

When it begins to set, add 6 dl. (1 pint, $2\frac{1}{2}$ cups) very stiffly whipped fresh cream. Mix. Fill a moscovite mould. Close it, and rub a little butter round the rim of the lid to ensure that it is hermetically sealed.

Put the mould in a bucket on a bed of crushed ice sprinkled with coarse salt. Surround and cover with more crushed ice and salt. Wrap in a cloth. Leave to stand for 2 hours. Turn out like an ordinary ice cream.

Proceeding as indicated above, moscovites can be made using apricots, pineapple, cherries, strawberries, peaches, pears, etc. They can also be frozen in a deep-freeze.

This sweet can be flavoured with various liqueurs.

MOSTELLE – Mainly Mediterranean fish which is very delicately flavoured, and should be eaten in the places where it is caught, as it deteriorates when transported.

All recipes for whiting (q.v.) are suitable.

MOTHE-SAINT-HÉRAYE – See CHEESE.

MOTHER OF VINEGAR. MÈRE DE VINAIGRE – A thick, corrugated film which forms during the acidulation of wine, as a result of the action of *mycoderma aceti*.

MOUFFLON. MOUFLON – Name given to various breeds of wild sheep. The *European moufflon*, which is the parent stock of the domestic sheep, is mainly found in Sardinia and Corsica, where it is known as *mufione* or *mufoli*. The *African cuffed moufflon* is about the size of an ordinary sheep. The *American moufflon*, also called *mountain ram*, is a slender animal with very long legs. Its horns, which in the male are very large and thick, come right down to the eyes, and form an almost complete spiral. Its coat, short and wiry, is brown in colour.

All these animals are edible. Their meat is very similar to that of the chamois. Before cooking in any way, moufflon meat must be steeped for a long time in an aromatic marinade. It can be roasted or made into a *ragoût* or *civet*. All recipes for mutton and roebuck are suitable for moufflon.

MOULD. MOULE – Hollow receptacle made in different materials and different shapes, used in cooking and confectionery.

MOULDING. MOULAGE – The process of putting a liquid or semi-liquid in a mould, whose shape it takes when it sets or thickens either by congealing or cooking.

In former times, moulded plinths were much used for the presentation of cold dishes, but this practice has disappeared today.

MOULIN-À-VENT – A famous wine-growing district in the Saône-et-Loire *département* of Beaujolais. Its red wines, stronger and more full-bodied than most Beaujolais wines, are distinctive in being delicious when young and also capable of maturing graciously, especially those of good vintage years. (See BURGUNDY, BEAUJOLAIS.)

MOUSSACHE – Manioc flour used in the manufacture of tapioca.

MOUSSAKA – Dish of Rumanian origin, now made also in a number of Eastern countries. (See MUTTON, *Moussaka of mutton*.)

MOUSSES – In cooking and confectionery this term is used of a number of different dishes, mostly served cold and even iced, though a few can be eaten hot.

SAVOURY MOUSSES. MOUSSES D'ENTRÉES –

Fish mousse – See FISH.

Foie gras mousse (hot). MOUSSE DE FOIE GRAS – Pound in a mortar 125 g. (4 oz.) raw chicken or veal with 1 egg white. Rub through a fine sieve.

Put this mixture in a bowl and add 125 g. (4 oz.) raw *foie gras* and 50 g. (2 oz.) raw truffles, both rubbed through a sieve. Season.

Mix these ingredients on ice, working with a spatula and blending in, a little at a time, 1 dl. (6 tablespoons, scant $\frac{1}{2}$ cup) thick cream. Add 2 stiffly beaten egg whites. Put in a soufflé dish, cover, stand in a pan of water and cook for 25 to 30 minutes.

Serve with *Madeira* or *Périgueux sauce* (see SAUCE).

This dish is sometimes called *soufflé of foie gras*. It is served as an *hors-d'œuvre* or light *entrée*.

Foie gras mousse (cold) – See FOIE GRAS.

Chicken mousse – See CHICKEN.

Cold quail mousse – See QUAIL.

DESSERT MOUSSES. MOUSSES D'ENTREMETS –

Chocolate mousse. MOUSSE AU CHOCOLAT – Make *Chantilly cream* (see CREAMS) using 6 dl. (1 pint, $2\frac{1}{2}$ cups) fresh cream. Melt 200 g. (7 oz.) vanilla-flavoured (bitter-sweet) chocolate with 4 tablespoons hot water over a gentle heat until it forms a smooth paste. Add to this paste 200 g. (7 oz., scant cup) sugar and 6 tablespoons water. When it is thoroughly mixed, bring to the boil, and leave to stand until quite cold before adding the cream.

Chocolate mousse

Fruit mousses. MOUSSES DE FRUITS – *Apricot mousse.*

Rub through muslin 625 g. (1 lb. 6 oz.) very ripe apricots into a bowl. Mix with it 250 g. (9 oz., 2 cups) fine sugar and 4 tablespoons kirsch. Instead of the sugar, syrup may be used, made with 250 g. (9 oz., 2 cups) lump sugar dissolved in a few spoonfuls of hot water, boiled for 2 minutes and left to get quite cold before it is added to the apricot purée.

Line a mould with fine white paper.

Whisk 4 dl. ($\frac{3}{4}$ pint, scant 2 cups) thick fresh cream until it is stiff. Add to the apricot purée. Put in the prepared mould, cover with a disc of white paper, close the mould, and seal round the rim with butter. (In contact with the ice the butter will harden. The mould being thus hermetically sealed, there can be no seepage of salt water.) Place the mould in a container on a deep bed of ice, salt and saltpetre. Surround with layers of ice and saltpetre and cover with the same. Leave to chill for 2 hours.

Before serving, wash and dry the mould, turn out the mousse and remove the paper.

Following this same recipe, mousses can be made with various kinds of fruit, such as pineapple, cherries, peaches, pears, plums, etc.

The term mousse is also used to describe sweet jellies made with fruit or flavoured with liqueurs. These jellies are whisked on ice until they begin to set. They are then poured into jelly moulds and left to set on ice.

Iced mousses. MOUSSES GLACÉES – These are iced sweets, usually made from *Bombe mixture* (see ICE CREAMS AND ICES).

MOUSSEAU – A type of French bread made from wheaten flour.

MOUSSELINE – Name given to various preparations, most of which have a large or small quantity of whipped cream added to them. This term is in particular used of moulds made of various pastes enriched with cream (poultry, game, fish, shellfish, *foie gras*).

Mousselines are served hot or cold. If cold, they are also known as small aspics.

Mousseline is used as an adjective to denote a sauce enriched with whipped cream (*mayonnaise mousseline, hollandaise mousseline*). It is also used of the paste or forcemeat used to make fish balls and mousses.

The term *mousseline* is much used in confectionery to describe certain cakes and pastries made of delicate mixtures (e.g. *brioche mousseline*).

MOUTARDELLE – A kind of horseradish, which is eaten in the same way as horseradish.

MOUTON BLANC – See RESTAURANTS OF BYGONE DAYS.

MOYEU – Old French word for the yolk of an egg.

MUGWORT. BARBOTINE – Name sometimes given to *tansy*, a plant which is also called *herbe aux vers* (worm herb) in French because of its anthelmintic properties. In the north of France, this aromatic plant is used for flavouring certain cakes and dishes.

In the olden days, tansy or mugwort was used in England for flavouring ale.

MULBERRY. MÛRE – Fruit of the mulberry tree, which the Romans are said to have prized highly. It is sweet but rather tasteless, and is seldom eaten raw. A syrup is made from it and its juice is used to colour wines.

The fruit of the bramble or wild mulberry is stewed and used in jams and jellies. A syrup which has a slightly tart flavour is also made from it.

MULE – Mule meat is highly prized, except when it is musky in flavour. All recipes for horsemeat are suitable for mule.

MULLET, GREY. MUGE, MULET – Fish found in coastal waters. It has a protuberance in the middle of the lower jaw which corresponds to an indentation in the upper jaw. Its body is elongated, with rather narrow flanks. It is covered with large broad scales. There are a number of varieties, the most common being the *striped mullet* and the *grey mullet*.

In France this fish is sometimes called *poisson sauteur* (leaping fish), because of its great agility. Flattening itself on the surface of the water and spreading its tail in a brusque movement, the mullet leaps sideways to great heights.

The flesh of mullet is white, fatty, delicate and easy to digest. All recipes for bass (q.v.) are suitable for grey mullet.

MULLET, RED. ROUGET – The name *rouget* is given in French to quite different types and species of sea fish which have nothing in common except their red colouring.

Two kinds may be distinguished: *red mullet*, which have two barbels on their lower jaw; and *gurnets*, which are recognised by their large bony heads and three pectoral rays. The Mediterranean *rouget*, which is of the mullet type, has a red back, and flanks and belly that are pink and silver without longitudinal bands. Its head is heavy and has two barbels on the lower jaw. Its tail is cankerous. The white fish is very fine and delicate.

The American mullet is the most important food fish in southern U.S.A.

Those who enjoy red mullet eat it grilled and accompanied by *Maître d'hôtel butter* (see BUTTER) or one of the special sauces for grilled fish.

For many connoisseurs this fish must be cooked without having its scales removed. It is sometimes known as *bécasse de mer* (sea woodcock) a name which suggests that its inside may be eaten.

Red mullet à la Bercy. ROUGET À LA BERCY – Make a few shallow cuts across the mullet if it is scaled; season with salt and pepper, brush with oil and grill (broil) at a gentle heat.

Set on a serving dish. Cover with half-melted *Bercy butter* (see BUTTER, *Compound butters*).

Red mullet à la bordelaise. ROUGET À LA BORDELAISE – Make a few shallow cuts across the back of the mullet. Brush with oil, season, and grill (broil) under a gentle heat.

Garnish with fresh parsley and lemon and serve with *Bordelaise sauce* (see SAUCE) with white wine.

Red mullet en caisse. ROUGET EN CAISSE – Grill the mullet or sauté it in butter. Put it into a rectangular paper case, oiled and dried in the oven. Coat the bottom with *Duxelles sauce* (see SAUCE) and coat the fish with the same sauce. Cover with breadcrumbs, sprinkle with oil or melted butter. Put in the oven for a few moments.

Red mullet with fennel. ROUGET AU FENOUIL – Make a few light incisions across the back of the mullet and season with salt and pepper. Put into a fireproof dish lined with 25 g. (1 oz., $\frac{1}{4}$ cup) chopped onions gently cooked in oil, mixed with 1 tablespoon chopped fresh fennel.

Cover with breadcrumbs. Sprinkle with a little oil, and cook in the oven at a gentle heat. Sprinkle with a little lemon juice and chopped parsley.

Fillets of red mullet à l'anglaise. FILETS DE ROUGET À L'ANGLAISE – Fillet the mullet. Trim the fillets, season with salt and pepper, flour them, coat in egg and breadcrumbs and cook in butter, browning them on both sides. Set on a serving dish with *Maître d'hôtel butter* (see BUTTER) on top.

Fried red mullet. ROUGET FRIT – Make a few light incisions on the mullet and proceed as for *Fried bass* (see BASS).

Red mullet au gratin. ROUGET AU GRATIN – Cooked like *Sole aù gratin* (see SOLE).

Grilled red mullet. ROUGET GRILLÉ – Make a few light incisions on the mullet, season, oil and grill the mullet on a gentle heat, as for *Grilled bass* (see BASS). Serve with *Maître d'hôtel butter* (see BUTTER) or with any sauce suitable for grilled fish.

Red mullet à l'indienne. ROUGET À L'INDIENNE – Lightly score the mullet across the back, season and flour, and sauté in oil.

Set on a serving dish. Pour *Curry sauce* (see SAUCE) over it. Surround with tomatoes cooked in butter. Serve with *Rice à l'indienne* (see RICE).

Red mullet à l'italienne. ROUGET À L'ITALIENNE – Score the mullet, season, sauté it in butter or grill it.

Line a serving dish with *Italian sauce* (see SAUCE), and set the mullet on it.

Coat with the same sauce, cover with breadcrumbs, sprinkle with melted butter and brown in the oven for a few minutes. Sprinkle with chopped parsley.

Red mullet à la meunière. ROUGET À LA MEUNIÈRE – Proceed as for *Bass à la meunière* (see BASS).

Red mullet à la moelle. ROUGET À LA MOELLE – Grill the mullet and serve it with *Marrow sauce* (see SAUCE).

Red mullet à la Nantaise. ROUGET À LA NANTAISE – Season the mullet with salt and pepper, brush with oil, and grill. Take the liver from the fish, taking care not to tear it. Add the liver, crushed, to the following sauce.

Boil down $1\frac{1}{2}$ dl. ($\frac{1}{4}$ pint, $\frac{2}{3}$ cup) white wine to which has been added 1 tablespoon finely chopped shallot. Add a little dissolved meat glaze, a little butter and some lemon juice. Put this sauce in a dish, set the mullet upon it, and surround with half slices of lemon with fluted edges.

Red mullet à la niçoise I. ROUGET À LA NIÇOISE – Season the mullet with salt and pepper, flour lightly and brown quickly on both sides in oil in a frying pan. Put the fish in a fireproof dish, the bottom of which has been lined with a layer of tomatoes cooked to a pulp and flavoured with tarragon.

Put anchovy fillets cut into thin strips on top of the mullet. Cover with breadcrumbs, sprinkle with olive oil, and cook in the oven for 6 to 8 minutes. Set a round of peeled lemon on the fish.

Red mullet à la niçoise II. ROUGET À LA NIÇOISE – Season a mullet with salt and pepper, brush with olive oil and grill under a gentle heat.

Set on a dish on a layer of tomatoes cooked up to a pulp and flavoured with tarragon. Put fillets of anchovies cut into thin strips, and rounds of lemon, on the fish.

Red mullet à la niçoise is often garnished with unstoned black olives and also with capers.

Red mullet à l'orientale – See HORS-D'ŒUVRE, *Cold hors-d'œuvre*.

Red mullet en papillote. ROUGET EN PAPILLOTE – Grill the mullet and enclose it, between 2 layers of *Duxelles sauce* (see SAUCE), in a sheet of oiled paper cut into a heart shape. Close up the paper, set it on a dish, and put it in the oven for a few moments to make it puff up. Serve immediately.

Red mullet à la provençale. ROUGET À LA PROVENÇALE – Prepared as for *Bass à la provençale* (see BASS).

Red mullet with shallots. ROUGET À L'ÉCHALOTE – Make a few light incisions down the back of the mullet and season with salt and pepper. Spread with a layer of chopped shallots cooked almost dry in white wine, and sprinkle 2 tablespoons (3 tablespoons) dry white wine over it. Dot with small pieces of butter and cook first on the stove, then in the oven at a moderate temperature, basting frequently. Sprinkle with chopped parsley and a little lemon juice. Serve in the dish in which it was cooked.

MULLIGATAWNY HOTPOT (Créole cookery). MOULOUCOUTANI, BOUILLON DE FEU – A highly spiced dish which contains curry powder and a special curry paste, served in soup plates, with *Rice à la créole* (see RICE) served separately.

Brown a young chicken slightly in a pan. Remove it and keep hot. Cook a saucerful of finely chopped onions in the fat. Do not brown. Cook also a large chopped tomato. When these ingredients are tender, add 1 tablespoon of Indian curry powder, garlic, thyme, parsley and ginger thoroughly pounded together in a mortar. Stir the mixture several times. Cut up the chicken as for *Sautéed chicken* (see CHICKEN) and put it in the pan with the other ingredients. Allow the chicken to become coated with the mixture, then moisten slowly with clear chicken stock. Before serving, mix 1 tablespoon curry paste in a little of this stock and pour into the sauce. Simmer gently for at least 4 hours.

MUROL – See CHEESE.

MUSCADEL. VIN DE MUSCAT – Sweet dessert wine made from Muscat grapes.

MUSCADELLE – Winter pear with a musky flavour.

MUSCADET – Light dry white wine from the region of Nantes. (See BRITTANY.)

MUSCAT – White or black grapes with a musky flavour.

MUSETTE (EN) – In former times this was the name given to a shoulder of beef boned, rolled in the form of a bladder and braised. This joint, rolled in the same way, was also called *en ballon*.

SUSPECT

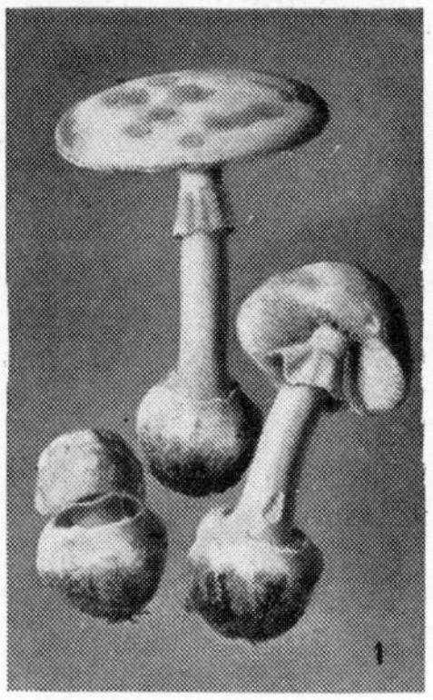

1. Amanita citrina

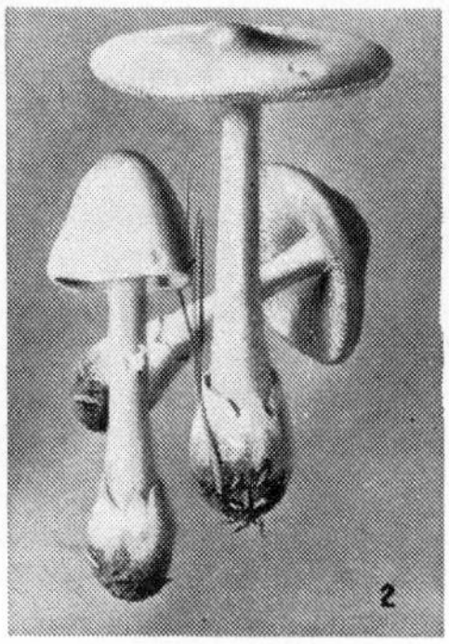

2. Volvaria gloiocephala

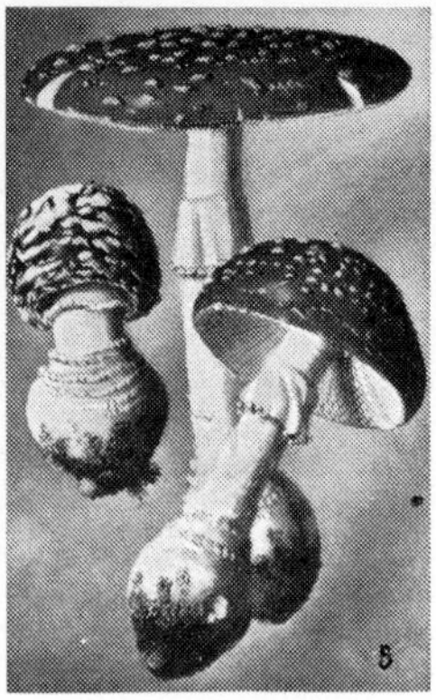

5. Amanita muscaria

6. Amanita pantherina

POISONOUS

7. Entoloma livida

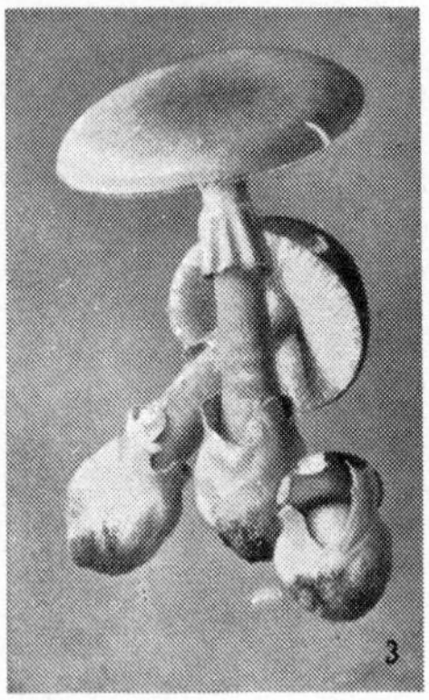

DEADLY
3. Amanita phalloides
4. Amanita verna

MUSHROOMS. CHAMPIGNONS – Cryptogamus plants, devoid of chlorophyll, of which there are a great number of species, some edible, some poisonous. Apart from their botanical characteristics, there is no empirical means of distinguishing the good from the bad. The blackening of a silver object or of an onion provides no guarantee, and even if it is possible to make certain fungi safe for consumption by a preliminary boiling in salted water or vinegar, this procedure is without avail for fungi which contain amanita toxin, the most deadly of all.

It is wise, therefore, if one has no knowledge and no experience of identifying mushrooms, to be satisfied with cultivated mushrooms, which are found at all greengrocers and markets and are perfectly safe.

If one wishes to gather wild mushrooms it is necessary to learn to identify the edible kinds, recognised as such in the locality, and at the same time to recognise the dangerous species.

One can make an arbitrary division of mushrooms into three groups: the species which are very poisonous and dangerous; those which are not only edible, but of excellent flavour and worth cooking; and between these two groups the immense quantity of mushrooms, some suspect, some edible, but without gastronomic interest, except for those passionate devotees whose attention we should direct to the treatises of experts so that they may distinguish the suspect from the edible.

The consumption of these species would only be of interest if their nutritive value had been clearly demonstrated, which is not the case. Certainly analyses indicate an impressive proportion of albuminous substances and of mineral salts, a special sugar, rehalose, and a little lecithin; unfortunately most of these substances are without value, either because they are not assimilable in this particular form, or because the cellulose which encloses them is not soluble by the digestive juices.

It follows that mushrooms can hardly be considered as food, but more as a condiment, a rôle which classic cookery has always allotted to them.

Among the dangerous mushrooms the following should be recognised:

Amanita phalloides (death cap). L'AMANITE PHALLOÏDE (ORONGE VERTE, ORONGE CIGUË) – The most dangerous of all, nearly always deadly. The mushroom has a rounded cap which later flattens out, dirty green in colour, fading to a yellowish brown, sometimes bluish, sometimes a paler yellow. It has white gills, sometimes with greenish shades; a white ring; a long stem, narrower at the top, swollen at the base, in the form of a cup enclosed in a sheath or volva, which is only seen on digging it out of the ground. The spores are colourless.

Amanita verna (gill). L'AMANITE VERNA (PRINTANIÈRE) – This is probably only a variety of *Amanita phalloides*. It has a cap of the same form which is white, shiny, dotted with the remains of the volva; white flesh; white gills; and a white ring around the stalk which has a tendency to drop away.

Both these species are particularly poisonous and are responsible for the majority of deaths from eating mushrooms.

Amanita pantherina (panther cap). L'AMANITE PANTHÉRINA (FAUSSE GOLMOTTE) – Has first of all a rounded cap, which becomes curved, then flattens out. The colour is variable, brown, greyish red, the colour of dead leaves, sometimes dark yellowish green, almost always covered with scales (the debris of the volva) which sometimes disappear after prolonged rain. It has white gills; a white ring; and a white stalk whose swollen base buried below ground bears two or three circular ridges. Similar to *Amanita pantherina* is *Amanita brunnescens* which is typical of North America.

Amanita muscaria (fly agaric). L'AMANITE MUSCARIA (TUE-MOUCHES, FAUSSE ORONGE) – Its cap, of the same form as the preceding species, is a brilliant vermillion red or orange red covered with whitish debris from the volva, except after heavy rain; white or yellowish gills; a white ring. The base of the stem, underground, is covered with white scales.

Amanita citrina (false death cap). L'AMANITE CITRINE – Less poisonous than the preceding species. It is eaten in certain areas, but it should be regarded at least as suspect. This fungus has a citron yellow cap, or greenish yellow, sometimes almost white, covered with the debris of the yellowish volva.

The gills are white, the stalk is fairly tall, swollen at the base. There is a white or yellowish ring which does not become detached.

Apart from *Amanita verna* which grows from spring to autumn, these species appear particularly in summer and autumn in the woods.

Besides these poisonous species the *Amanita* group includes some highly esteemed mushrooms:

Amanita caesarea (Caesar's mushroom). L'ORONGE – A magnificent mushroom, rather rare. It has in the first place the form of an egg as long as it is enclosed in the volva, then, when this tears, the red or orange cap appears, first domed, then convex, never covered with scales, but sometimes one can see the traces (two or three fragments) of the volva. The cap is gleaming, sometimes a little slimy in damp weather. It is easily detachable and reveals very white flesh. The gills are large, yellow, never attached to the stem; the stalk is cylindrical, yellow, swollen at the foot, surrounded with a white volva; the yellow ring, tends to drop off. Found in the woods at the end of summer and in autumn. Similar to *Amanita caesarea* is *Amanita calyptroderma* which grows in North America in the autumn.

Amanita rubescens (blusher). LA GOLMOTTE, ORONGE VINEUSE – Has a convex cap which later on becomes flatter. It is brownish red or wine-coloured, sometimes quite dark, sometimes faded, with whitish or whitish-yellow scales. The flesh is pinkish or white, turning to pink when in contact with the air; the stalk is hollow, thick, yellow or whitish pink, with a deepening wine-coloured tinge at the base. The gills are white or pinkish. Found in clearings from the end of spring until autumn, it is toxic when raw but excellent when properly cooked.

Amanitopsis fulva and Amanitopsis vaginata (grisette and tawny grisette). COUCOUMELLE – These have domed caps, later spreading out, which are grey, lead coloured, yellowing brown, or beige, usually free of debris from the volva, but sometimes bearing large white patches of volva. They never have a ring on the stalk. The stems are slender, white or slightly coloured, hardly swollen at the base, which remains enclosed by the persistent white or coloured volva. The gills are white, and are never joined at the stalk. Found particularly in autumn, they are toxic when raw but excellent when cooked.

Below are some other good spring mushrooms:

Morchella esculenta (common morel). MORILLES – These do not usually lend themselves to any confusion with dangerous species, and are among the most sought-after mushrooms. They have a rounded or oval shape, beige, greyish or almost black according to the species, the cap indented with honeycombing; the stalk is often shorter than the cap. Morels are found in spring in clearings and copses. In U.S.A. they are found in sandy soil during warm weather in May and June.

Tricholoma (Lepista) saevum (blewit). MOUSSERON VRAI – This has a convex cap, often wavy at the edges, matt, smooth, creamy in colour, sometimes greyish, pinkish or lilac coloured. The stem is short, thick, cylindrical, full. The gills are sinuous, white or cream, joined to the stem. The blewit grows in rings in the spring in meadows or on the borders of woods. It is found sometimes, but rarely, in autumn. In U.S.A. this species is found from September to freezing weather in thin woods and open grassy places.

Marasmius oreades (fairy-ring champignon). FAUX MOUSSERON – Sometimes found in spring but more often in autumn, it grows in circles in dry meadows and pastures or on the edges of paths. The cap is tan or yellow, thin, without much substance, with a central prominence, smooth at the edges; the gills are whitish, uneven, fairly wide apart, and not joined to the stalk. This mushroom, which is never attacked by insects, is sought for its aroma. In U.S.A. it is found from May to October.

Boletus. LES BOLETS – Found in spring and autumn. There are numerous species. Instead of gills they have fleshy tubes on the underside of the cap, white or yellowish, sometimes red, turning to a greenish hue in time, when they are detachable from the cap in the same manner as the choke of an artichoke when cooked. According to the species, the cap is light or dark brown, sometimes very dark brown; the thick stalk which is substantial, is white or brown, and never has a trace of red in the edible species; the white flesh does not turn green when it comes in contact with the air. Even though there are edible species with red tubes, one would do well to avoid them, in spite of the fact that the most suspect, *Boletus satanas*, only gives rise to serious indigestion. There is one *cèpe* of a pale yellow colour which without being poisonous is uneatable on account of its bitterness.

The mushrooms that follow are only found in summer and autumn:

Psalliota arvensis (horse mushroom). PRATELLE, *boule de neige* – Has a globular cap of a rosy tint, which later spreads out, thick and white; a strong stem, thickened at the base; rosy white gills; white flesh, yellowing a little when in contact with the air; and a large double ring.

Lepiota procera (parasol). COULMELLE – Has an ovoid cap, becoming rounder and finally spread out, domed in the centre, brown or brownish grey; and a hollow stem, rather tall. The gills are numerous and stand away from the stalk. The flesh is rather soft, insubstantial and white, turning pink or reddish in the air.

Cantharellus cibarius (chanterelle). CHANTERELLE, GIROLLE – Has a form in the shape of a cup, with a frilled edge, and thick swollen vein-like gills, the colour of egg yolk, dark or paler (according to humidity). The stalk is fleshy, short, sometimes non-existent. This mushroom cannot be confused with any other.

Craterellus (Cantharellus) cornucopioides (horn of plenty). CRATERELLE – In France called the *horn of plenty* or *trumpet of death*. It appears in the woods at the end of summer and in autumn. The mushroom is in the form of a horn, with vein-like gills and frilled edges, nearly black on top, and dark grey on the underside, smooth on top, slightly veined on the underside. The stem is tubular, ash grey or black. Unattractive and tough as it is, this mushroom is sought for as a condiment on account of its smell which recalls that of the truffle.

In U.S.A. *Cantharellus floccosus* is found from July to September in woods. Many edible and poisonous mushrooms not mentioned here are found in U.S.A. Cultivated mushrooms are very widely marketed and are government supervised.

Mushroom poisoning – Leaving aside the mushrooms which are suspect and can produce serious indigestion, there exist two types of poisoning according to the type of poison contained in the fungi.

Muscarine poisoning (*Amanita muscaria, Amanita pantherina*, etc.) resembles atropine intoxication.

The start is rapid (1 to 4 hours after eating). It is characterised by an indefinable malaise, rapidly followed by colic, vomiting, diarrhoea, stomach cramps, abundant salivation, followed by nervous disorders (delirium, excitement, fainting, reeling, dilation of the pupils) followed by prostration.

Avoid the use of alcohol which dissolves the poison, and attempt to empty the stomach by administering vomitives (lukewarm water, soapy water, never emetics); the patient must be kept warm, given frictions, made to inhale ether. The recovery often occurs in 1 or 2 days, the convalescence is short. There are, nevertheless, more serious cases, even fatal (20 per cent of cases for *Amanita pantherina*).

Phalline poisoning (more correctly, amanita toxin) is much more serious; it is above all caused by *Amanita phalloides* and *Amanita verna*. The beginning of the symptoms is much more delayed (12 to 24 hours after eating, sometimes more), and they manifest themselves by fainting fits, great pain, burning stomach, cramp in various parts of the body; intestinal disturbances take the appearance of cholera symptoms, with incessant vomiting, diarrhoea, often bleeding, pain, cold sweats, cold extremities. The stomach is hypersensitive, and rejects everything, the liver is enlarged and painful. The symptoms occur, reach a crisis, are followed by periods of calm.

The mind is not affected until the final period, when the pulse slows down, breathing becomes difficult, the patient turns yellow, and then prostration and collapse ensue, all these symptoms manifesting themselves over 2 or 4 days at least, lasting sometimes for 8 or 10; death follows in 60 per cent of cases; if a recovery is possible it still necessitates a long convalescence.

Preparation of mushrooms (*Larousse*)

The emptying of the stomach, which must always be attempted by means of vomitives and stomach douches, has only a small chance of success, the poison being already absorbed.

We must apologise for introducing a rather terrifying picture in a work dedicated to gastronomy, but when one thinks of the too frequent fatal accidents which occur every year from eating poisonous mushrooms, one cannot too often sound a note of warning.

Preparation of cultivated mushrooms. PREPARATION DES CHAMPIGNONS DE COUCHE – Choose 500 g. (1 lb.) very white mushrooms, and remove the earthy bottom of the stalk. Wash quickly and carefully in a lot of water. Drain the mushrooms and dry them. Slice off the stalks on a level with the caps. Pare the caps neatly or groove them by cutting minute and regular incisions.

When one is dealing with cultivated mushrooms which are fresh and firm, it is best not to attempt any kind of embellishment when peeling them, but simply to pare them neatly. It is, however, common practice in restaurant cookery to groove them.

Throw them into a boiling liquor prepared in the following way: Boil together 1 dl. (6 tablespoons, scant $\frac{1}{2}$ cup) 50 g. (2 oz., $\frac{1}{4}$ cup) butter, the juice of half a lemon and 1 teaspoon salt. Boil the mushrooms in this liquor for 5 minutes. Turn out into an earthenware vessel with the liquor.

The *court-bouillon* having once served to cook the mushrooms is used for various preparations: added to white sauces, such as *velouté, suprême, allemande,* white wine, etc. It can also be used to prepare *hors-d'œuvre* cooked in a marinade.

Another method. Pare or groove the mushrooms and rub them with half a lemon. Put them in a pan in which a little butter has been melted.

Season with a pinch of salt, moisten with 2 tablespoons (3 tablespoons) white stock or Madeira and simmer with the lid on for 8 minutes. Use according to instructions.

Prepared in this way mushrooms are less white but of better flavour.

RECIPES SUITABLE FOR CULTIVATED MUSHROOMS. RECETTES RELATIVES AUX CHAMPIGNONS DE COUCHE –

Mushroom barquettes (hot hors-d'œuvre). BARQUETTES AUX CHAMPIGNONS – Fill puff pastry *barquettes* with a *ragoût* of mushrooms cooked in cream, or *à la poulette* (see below). (See HORS-D'ŒUVRE, *Hot hors-d'œuvre*.)

Mushrooms cooked in butter. CHAMPIGNONS AU BEURRE – Slice the mushrooms into 2 or 3 pieces according to their size, and season with salt and pepper. Sauté them in butter in a frying pan over a lively heat. Transfer to a vegetable dish.

This recipe can be used for *cèpes*, field mushrooms, chanterelles, morels, blewits and Caesar's mushrooms.

Mushrooms cooked in cream I. CHAMPIGNONS À LA CRÈME – Slice the mushrooms, season them and simmer in butter for 8 to 10 minutes.

Cover with boiling cream and leave to cook until the cream is almost completely boiled down.

Stir in a little fresh cream.

This recipe can be used for *cèpes*, morels, Caesar's mushrooms, and to field mushrooms.

Mushrooms cooked in cream II. CHAMPIGNONS À LA CRÈME – Simmer in butter and add *Cream sauce* (see SAUCE).

Mushroom croûte I. CROÛTE AUX CHAMPIGNONS – Simmer

Mushrooms cooked in cream

the mushrooms in butter. Add a few tablespoons of *Allemande sauce* (see SAUCE), or *Béchamel sauce* (see SAUCE) if the dish is to cooked *au maigre* (q.v.). Mix together.

Arrange this preparation in a round bread roll which has been hollowed out, buttered and lightly browned in the oven. Heat for a moment.

This recipe can be used for *cèpes*, morels, etc.

Mushroom croûte II. CROÛTE AUX CHAMPIGNONS – Simmer the mushrooms in butter. Dust lightly with flour and moisten with fresh cream. Season. Cook very gently for 12 minutes. Add butter, and finish in the same way as the recipe above.

Little mushroom croûtes (hot hors-d'œuvre). PETITS CROÛTES AUX CHAMPIGNONS – Prepare a *Mushroom purée* (see below) and fill bread rolls which have been scooped out, or spread on biscuits.

Mushroom essence – See ESSENCE.

Mushrooms aux fines herbes. CHAMPIGNONS AUX FINES HERBES – The same as *Mushrooms cooked in butter* with the addition of chopped parsley.

This recipe is applicable to *cèpes*, field mushrooms, chanterelles, morels, blewits, Caesar's mushrooms.

Mushroom forcemeat or duxelles. FARCE DE CHAMPIGNONS, DUXELLES – This stuffing is usually prepared with cultivated mushroom stalks and peelings, the caps being used for other purposes, but it can be made with other types of mushroom.

Cook gently some chopped onion in a mixture of butter and oil, to which a little chopped shallot is added when the onion is almost cooked. Put in the stalks and peelings of the mushrooms, which have been chopped up and pressed to extract the moisture. For 500 g. (1 lb.) mushrooms use 50 g. (2 oz., $\frac{1}{2}$ cup) onion, 25 g. (1 oz., $\frac{1}{4}$ cup) shallot, 50 g. (2 oz., $\frac{1}{4}$ cup) butter, 3 tablespoons (4 tablespoons) oil.

Cook on a lively heat until all the moisture has evaporated. Season with salt and pepper. Add 1 teaspoon chopped parsley.

Duxelles prepared in this way is used in a large number of preparations.

Mushrooms fumet. FUMET DE CHAMPIGNONS – Term given to the liquor in which mushrooms have cooked. The liquor is boiled down to about a quarter of its original volume.

Mushroom garnish. GARNITURE DE CHAMPIGNONS – Mushrooms which have been sautéed, grilled or cooked in liquor are added to many preparations such as *blanquettes, fricassées*, escalopes, *noisettes* (small slices of fillet, loin, or leg of lamb, pork, etc.), *tournedos*, chicken, sweetbreads, fish, eggs, etc.

Mushrooms à la grecque (cold hors-d'œuvre). CHAMPIGNONS À LA GRECQUE – Choose very small mushrooms. Cook in the same way as for *Artichokes à la grecque* (see HORS-D'ŒUVRE).

Grilled mushrooms. CHAMPIGNONS GRILLÉS – Choose large, even-sized mushrooms, and remove the stalks. Wash and wipe them, soak in butter or oil, season, and grill under a gentle heat.

Set on a dish with *Maître d'hôtel butter* (see BUTTER, *Compound butters*), as they are, or use according to the directions of the recipe.

Mushrooms à la hongroise. CHAMPIGNONS À LA HONGROISE – Prepare in the same way as *Cèpes à la hongroise* (see below).

Mushroom julienne. JULIENNE DE CHAMPIGNONS – Trim, wash, wipe and pare the mushrooms. Cut them into *julienne* (q.v.) strips, thick or thin according to the use to which they will be put. Season and simmer in butter.

Mushroom ketchup – English condiment made and sold commercially. It is used in English cookery to season sauces and as a condiment with cold meat. Prepare as follows:

Peel, trim and wash some fresh mushrooms. Slice them finely. Put them in layers in an earthenware bowl, sprinkling each layer with fine salt. Cover the bowl and leave to macerate for 3 days in a cool place. Skim each day.

Strain the juice through a stout cloth. Measure the liquid and put it in a saucepan. Add the following spices for every litre (scant quart, generous quart) juice: 10 g. ($\frac{1}{3}$ oz.) fennel flower, 1 tablespoon ground mace, 1 tablespoon ground ginger, 1 teaspoon cayenne pepper, 1 teaspoon grated nutmeg, 1 teaspoon powdered cloves.

Cook until the liquid forms a syrup. Pour into small bottles. Cork and seal.

Mushrooms à la lyonnaise. CHAMPIGNONS À LA LYONNAISE – The same as *Mushrooms cooked in butter*, with chopped onion softened in butter.

Set in a vegetable dish, sprinkle with drops of lemon juice and chopped parsley, and pour over the mushrooms the hot butter in which they were cooked. All edible mushrooms can be prepared in this way.

Mushrooms in Madeira or in other liqueur wines (garnish). CHAMPIGNONS AU MADÈRE – Sauté the mushrooms in butter. Drain them, deglaze the sauté pan with the wine chosen, and boil down. Add a few tablespoons thick *Spanish sauce* (see SAUCE). Boil down by half and strain through a sieve. Put the mushrooms back into this sauce.

Cultivated mushrooms, field mushrooms, morels, etc., are prepared in this way.

Mushrooms in marinade (hors-d'œuvre). CHAMPIGNONS MARINÉS – *Cèpes* and cultivated mushrooms can be prepared in a marinade (see HORS-D'ŒUVRE, *Cold hors-d'œuvre, Marinated cèpes and mushrooms*).

Mushroom omelette. OMELETTE AUX CHAMPIGNONS – Slice the mushrooms thinly, or cut them into dice. Season and sauté in butter. Add to the beaten eggs and make the omelette in the usual way (see EGGS).

Mushrooms prepared in this way can be used to garnish fried eggs, poached eggs or soft-boiled eggs.

Mushroom patties (hot hors-d'œuvre or garnish). TARTELETTES AUX CHAMPIGNONS – Cook them in cream, or in a *Poulette sauce* (see SAUCE). Put the mixture in short pastry tarts which have been baked blind. Sprinkle with dried breadcrumbs or with breadcrumbs fried in butter and drained, or with grated cheese. Brown in the oven.

These patties can also be prepared with mushrooms cut in *julienne*, or in dice, sautéed in butter and combined with a brown or white sauce.

Mushrooms à la poulette I. CHAMPIGNONS À LA POULETTE – Simmer the mushrooms in butter. Add a few tablespoons of *Poulette sauce* (see SAUCE). Set in a vegetable dish, sprinkle with chopped parsley.

Cultivated mushrooms, field mushrooms, *cèpes* and morels are prepared in this way.

Mushrooms à la poulette II. CHAMPIGNONS À LA POULETTE – Soften the mushrooms in butter and drain. Put 1 tablespoon flour in the sauté pan. Mix, and moisten with *bouillon* or white stock. Boil down, and combine with 1 or 2 egg yolks. Finish the sauce with cream and butter, season, and pass through a sieve.

Mushroom powder. POUDRE DE CHAMPIGNONS – Trim and clean the mushrooms. Slice them. Put them on a baking sheet on layers of paper and dry very slowly in the oven or near an open fire. When they are perfectly dry pound them in a mortar, and pass through a fine sieve. The powder is used to flavour various preparations such as *ragoûts*, sauces and stuffings.

Preserved mushrooms (au naturel). CONSERVES DE CHAMPIGNONS – Sterilise the mushrooms as soon as they have been gathered. Peel, scrape and wash them in several waters until they are tender. Drain, leave to cool, and put into glass jars. Sterilise by cooking at boiling point for $1\frac{1}{4}$ hours.

See also HORS-D'ŒUVRE, *Cold hors-d'œuvre, Marinated cèpes and mushrooms.*

Mushroom purée. PURÉE DE CHAMPIGNONS – See PURÉE.

Mushroom rissoles – See RISSOLE.

Mushroom salad. SALADE DE CHAMPIGNONS – Only freshly gathered mushrooms are used (agarics, morels, or cultivated mushrooms).

Trim, wash, wipe, and cut them up finely, seasoning with oil, lemon juice or vinegar, salt, pepper and chopped herbs. Put in a salad bowl.

One can also add a salad dressing to cultivated mushrooms which have been pared and cooked as described above under *Preparation of cultivated mushrooms*. Serve as an *hors-d'œuvre*.

Mushroom salpicon. SALPICON DE CHAMPIGNONS – The mushrooms are cut into dice, big or small, according to the use to which they are put, and cooked in butter.

Little mushroom soufflés. PETITS SOUFFLÉS AUX CHAMPIGNONS – Make the soufflé preparation with mushroom purée according to the method given for all soufflés with a vegetable purée base.

Put the preparation into little soufflé dishes. Cook in the oven. (See SOUFFLÉ.)

Cream of mushroom soup. POTAGE CRÈME DE CHAMPIGNONS – See SOUPS AND BROTHS, *Mushroom velouté soup*.

Mushrooms sous cloche. CHAMPIGNONS SOUS CLOCHE – Choose mushrooms of medium size. Trim, wash, remove the stems, and season them. Put each, gills uppermost, on a slice of bread which has been fried in butter or toasted. Fill each cap with a little *Maître d'hôtel butter* (see BUTTER, *Compound butters*) and a few drops of cream. Set on a *gratin* dish. Cover with a glass cloche of the same diameter as the plate. Cook on top of the stove at a low temperature for 15 to 18 minutes.

This recipe is suitable only for cultivated mushrooms.

Stuffed mushrooms. CHAMPIGNONS FARCIS – Choose mushrooms of the same size and weight for this garnish. Break the stalks away from the cap. Wash and wipe the caps. Arrange them on an oiled or buttered baking tray, season them, moisten lightly with oil or melted butter and set in the oven for 5 minutes.

Stuff each cap with a spoonful of *duxelles* (see above). Dust with fine dried breadcrumbs, sprinkle with oil or butter and brown in the oven.

Mushrooms can be filled with various preparations such as *brunoise* (q.v.) or *mirepoix* (q.v.), different purées, risotto, various *salpicons*, etc., in the manner indicated for all those vegetables which are stuffed and browned in the oven (see GRATIN).

Mushroom tart. TOURTE AUX CHAMPIGNONS – Prepare the mushrooms by cooking them in cream or in *Poulette sauce* (see SAUCE). Arrange in flaky pastry open tart pastry case.

Mushrooms on toast (hot hors-d'œuvre). TOASTS AUX CHAMPIGNONS – Grill the mushrooms or sauté them in butter. Arrange them on bread cut in rectangles or rounds, grilled or fried. Sprinkle with fried breadcrumbs. Put in the oven for a moment. Season with freshly ground pepper, and sprinkle with chopped parsley.

Mushroom vol-au-vent. VOL-AU-VENT AUX CHAMPIGNONS – Fill a *vol-au-vent* case with a *ragoût* of mushrooms cooked in cream or in *Poulette sauce* (see SAUCE).

RECIPES SUITABLE FOR CÈPES AND OTHER VARIETIES. RECETTES S'APPLIQUANT AUX CÈPES ET À QUELQUES AUTRES ESPÈCES –

Cèpes à la béarnaise. CÈPES À LA MODE BÉARNAISE – Trim, wash and wipe the *cèpes*, and dry them by putting them under the grill or in the oven.

Insert small pieces of raw garlic into the caps, in the same way as garlic is inserted into a leg of mutton. Season with salt and pepper and grill them.

Arrange them on a hot plate and cover with a mixture of breadcrumbs fried in very hot oil. Sprinkle with chopped parsley.

Cèpes à la bordelaise. CÈPES À LA BORDELAISE – Trim and wash the *cèpes* and simmer them in butter and lemon juice. Drain and sponge them dry. Cut them into slices if they are very large, leave whole if they are small. Season with salt and pepper and sauté them in oil, browning slightly.

At the last moment for each 500 g. (18 oz.) *cèpes*, add the chopped-up stalks, 2 teaspoons chopped shallot, 2 tablespoons freshly grated breadcrumbs, and a teaspoon of chopped parsley.

Arrange the *cèpes* in a dish, sprinkle over them a little lemon juice and some chopped parsley.

This is how *cèpes à la bordelaise* are prepared in Paris restaurants. In Bordeaux and in south-west France, the *cèpes* are not seasoned with shallots but with chopped garlic, (as in the case of *cèpes a la provençale*) and breadcrumbs are not added to the preparation.

In that same region, *cèpes* prepared *à la bordelaise* are never browned. They are sometimes cooked in oil, not in a frying pan but in an earthenware casserole.

Cèpes cooked with cream I. CÈPES À LA CRÈME – *Cèpes* which are white-fleshed and firm are cooked in this way. According to their size they are cut into slices or left whole.

Put them into a pan in which some butter has been heated. Season with salt and pepper, and simmer them in the butter. When cooked, cover them with fresh boiling cream. Cook until the cream has almost disappeared. Add 3 to 4 tablespoons fresh cream. Mix. Arrange the *cèpes* in their sauce in a dish.

One tablespoon chopped onion which has been lightly fried in butter can be added to the *cèpes* when they are simmering in butter.

Cèpes cooked with cream II. CÈPES À LA CRÈME – Simmer the *cèpes* in butter. Moisten with a *Cream sauce* (see SAUCE) which is not too thick. Cook for a further few minutes. Finish with a little fresh cream.

Cèpes au gratin. CÈPES AU GRATIN – Trim, wash and remove the stalks from *cèpes* chosen for their firmness. Season with salt and pepper, and simmer in a little butter.

Arrange them in a buttered fireproof dish, tops downwards. Put into each cap 1 tablespoon stuffing prepared with the chopped stalks mixed with breadcrumbs, chopped onion lightly fried in oil or butter, parsley, chopped garlic and seasoning. Press the stuffing into the caps so that it adheres to them. Sprinkle with grated dried breadcrumbs, and pour over each cap a little melted butter or oil. Brown gently in the oven.

Cèpes à la grecque (hors-d'œuvre). CÈPES À LA GRECQUE – Choose small *cèpes* which are not yet fully grown. Cook them in a *court-bouillon* (q.v.) as for *Artichokes à la grecque* (see HORS-D'ŒUVRE).

Grilled cèpes. CÈPES GRILLÉS – Large white-fleshed *cèpes* are prepared in this way. Make superficial cuts in the domed caps. Season with salt and pepper. Brush over with oil or melted butter. Cook them under the grill at a moderate temperature.

Serve with *Maître d'hôtel butter* (see BUTTER, *Compound butters*) separately or placed on the *cèpes*.

Cèpes à la hongroise. CÈPES À LA HONGROISE – Cook 500 g. (1 lb.) cèpes in butter with 2 tablespoons (3 tablespoons) chopped onion which has been cooked in butter. Leave the *cèpes* whole if they are small, slice them if they are large. Season with salt and paprika pepper. Cover with boiling cream or with a *Cream sauce* (see SAUCE) which is not too thick. Cook until the cream is almost entirely boiled down. Add a little butter.

Cèpes with Indian sauce. CÈPES À L'INDIENNE – Sauté 500 g. (1 lb.) pared, washed and dried *cèpes* in butter. When they are cooked, add 2 tablespoons (3 tablespoons) chopped onion which has been cooked in butter. Mix, shaking the pan. Simmer gently, and add a few tablespoons *Indian sauce* (see SAUCE).

Cèpes à la provençale. CÈPES À LA PROVENÇALE – Cook in the same way as for *Cèpes à la bordelaise,* but replace the shallot with finely chopped onion, and add a little crushed garlic.

Smothered or stewed cèpes I. CÈPES ÉTUVÉS – Choose 500 g. (1 lb.) fresh *cèpes* of even size. Trim the earthy part of the stem. Wash, drain and wipe dry. Slice off the stalks on a level with the cap; leave the caps whole or divide them in two if they are too large. Wipe them.

Put them in a pan with 1 tablespoon butter, some drops of lemon juice and a pinch of salt. Simmer with the lid on for 5 minutes. Turn out into an earthenware *terrine* with their liquor. Use according to the instructions in the recipe.

Smothered or stewed cèpes II. CÈPES ÉTUVÉS – Wash and trim the *cèpes*, oil them lightly and put them for a few minutes under the grill to enable them give off their liquor.

Morels. MORILLES – Trim them, wash in several waters, and carefully remove any dirt in the interstices of the honeycombed caps. Cook them in butter in the same way as *cèpes*.

When the morels are large, divide them in halves or quarters before cooking.

Morels can also be fried without first simmering them in butter. In this case they must be thoroughly dried after washing.

Chanterelles, blewits, Caesar's mushrooms. SIROLLES, MOUSSERONS, ORONGES – All these mushrooms are usually prepared according to the methods prescribed for *cèpes* and morels. If they are cooked as soon as picked they can be fried in oil or butter without any other treatment except for thorough washing and drying in a cloth.

MUSHROOM BED. CHAMPIGNONNIÈRE – Place given over to the cultivation of mushrooms, nearly always established in old chalk pits.

MUSK DEER. CHEVROTIN – Small wild deer found in India, Tibet, and also in Africa. It is hunted for its musk, the product secreted in an abdominal pocket. The animal is edible when young.

All the preparations suitable for lamb (q.v.) can also be applied to it.

MUSLIN BAG. NOUET – A bag used in cooking. Anything to be cooked or infused in liquid and later taken out can be put in one of these bags, which is knotted or tied with string, thus flavouring the liquid without leaving any solid particles in it.

MUSSEL. MOULE – Edible mollusc found in all the oceans of the world, especially in cold regions.

There are two main species of mussel, the *common mussel*, which is the most widespread, and which has a long shell with a very slight roughness along the back, and the *Provence mussel*, with a larger shell, sharper along the edges, found at Biarritz, at Bidassoa and on the Mediterranean seaboard. The Provence mussel is bred in salt-water pools along this sheltered coast, at Toulon and Marseilles. It is a little tougher and less highly prized than the common mussel.

A distinction must also be made between wild mussels, gathered in their natural beds and on rocks, and cultivated mussels, bred on wooden hurdles. In places exposed to the pounding of the waves, wild mussels are small and leathery; those found in slimy places are uneatable. On the other hand, a number of natural beds in France produce very good mussels (Villerville, Dives, Port-en-Bessin, Quiberon). The

Mussels growing in natural surrounds

Mussels cultivated on wooden hurdles

mussel beds of Isigny, which are permanently under water, have to be dredged. These mussels, which can be up to 12 cm. (4½ inches) in length and are very curved in shape, enjoy a great reputation under the name of *caïeu d'Isigny*.

Breeding on hurdles produces tender and delicately flavoured mussels. They remain small but are very plump. Hurdle-bred mussels can generally be distinguished from wild mussels by the following characteristics: in the hurdle-bred mussel the edge of the shell opposite the hinge (the frontal edge) is always slightly convex, whereas with wild mussels found in French coastal waters it is always slightly concave.

Poisoning and allergy – Mussels can cause skin eruptions and digestive disturbances to some people. Anyone with this kind of sensitivity should avoid eating them.

Mussels gathered in polluted water can spread typhoid infection if they are eaten raw, as is sometimes the case in Provence, but as they are almost always cooked the dangerous microbes are destroyed.

On the other hand, a poison secreted by certain diseased mussels cannot be destroyed by cooking, and may cause serious illness and sometimes death. At the very first onset of the symptoms, while the doctor is on his way, purgatives and emetics must be given.

It was once thought that, to avoid the danger, it was enough to put a piece of silver in the cooking water and discard the mussels if the coin turned black. This, however, is not an adequate precaution, because the coin will in fact turn black when the mussels are not very fresh and give off hydrogen sulphide which is not in itself poisonous. The poison in question does not turn silver coins black. A useful precaution is to add a pinch of bicarbonate of soda to every litre (scant quart, general quart) of cooking water. This is sufficient to destroy the poison. A little vinegar, added as seasoning, also has a beneficial effect.

It must not be thought that mussels taken from the hulls of ships covered with copper plating are unhealthy because they contain copper salts. These mussels should, however, be rejected because harbour water is contaminated, and mussels collected in this way often smell of sewage.

Mussels à la bordelaise. MOULES À LA BORDELAISE – Cook in white wine 2 litres (3½ pints, 4½ pints) mussels, trimmed, scraped and washed, with a sliced onion, parsley, thyme and bay leaf as for *Mussels à la marinière* (see below). When the mussels split open, drain them. Put them in a bowl or deep dish after having removed 1 shell from each mussel. Keep hot.

Make 2 dl. (⅓ pint, scant cup) vegetable *mirepoix* (q.v.) by cooking the vegetables slowly in butter until very tender. Just before it is ready, add 1½ dl. (¼ pint, ⅔ cup) *Velouté sauce* (see SAUCE). Strain the stock in which the mussels were cooked and moisten the *mirepoix* with it. Add 2 dl. (⅓ pint, scant cup) fresh cream and 2 tablespoons (3 tablespoons) tomato purée. Boil down and whisk in 50 g. (2 oz., ¼ cup) fresh butter, a squeeze of lemon juice and seasoning. Pour this sauce, boiling hot, over the mussels. Sprinkle with chopped parsley.

Mussels in cream. MOULES À LA CRÈME – Cook 2 litres (3½ pints, 4½ pints) mussels as for *Mussels à la marinière* (see below). Put them in a bowl and keep hot.

Strain the stock in which the mussels were cooked and add it to 3 dl. (½ pint, 1¼ cups) *Béchamel sauce* (see SAUCE). Mix a few tablespoons fresh cream into this sauce and simmer until it is quite thick. Finish with 4 tablespoons (⅓ cup) cream and 1 tablespoon butter. Season and strain through muslin. Bring this sauce to the boil and pour over the mussels.

Curried mussels. MOULES AU CURRIE (À L'INDIENNE) – Proceed as for *Mussels à la hongroise* (see below), substituting 1 teaspoon curry powder for the paprika.

Rice à l'indienne (see RICE) is served with mussels prepared in this way.

Fried mussels. MOULES FRITES – Steep shelled mussels for 30 minutes in a marinade of oil, lemon juice and chopped parsley, after having cooked them as for *Mussels à la marinière* (see below). Dip in a light batter and deep-fry in boiling fat. Drain and dry in a cloth. Garnish with fried parsley.

Mussels as a garnish. MOULES POUR GARNITURES – Wash the mussels in several changes of water. Scrape. Cook them in white wine with sliced onions, parsley, thyme and bay leaves. Drain and shell them. Use as indicated in the selected recipe.

The cooking stock of the mussels is added to the sauce after having been boiled down and strained through muslin.

Mussels à la hongroise. MOULES À LA HONGROISE – Cook the mussels as for *Mussels à la marinière* (see below), seasoning them with paprika. Strain the cooking stock through a fine sieve. Cook 100 g. (4 oz., 1 cup) chopped onions slowly in butter until very tender. Season with 1 teaspoon paprika. Moisten with the stock. Add 3 tablespoons (scant ¼ cup) *Béchamel sauce* (see SAUCE) and a little fresh cream. Cook until quite thick. Add 2 tablespoons (3 tablespoons) butter to this sauce. Strain and pour, boiling hot, over the mussels.

Mussels à la marinière

Mussels à la marinière I. MOULES À LA MARINIÈRE – Line a buttered saucepan with 2 tablespoons (3 tablespoons) chopped shallot. Add 1 or 2 sprigs of parsley, 1 sprig of thyme and ¼ bay leaf. Put in 2 litres (3½ pints, 4½ pints) mussels, trimmed, scraped and washed.

Add 2 tablespoons (3 tablespoons) butter cut into very small pieces. Moisten with 2 dl. (⅓ pint, scant cup) dry white wine. Cook, covered, over a very high flame.

As soon as the mussels are fully opened, drain them. Remove 1 shell from each, and put them in a bowl. Keep hot. Take the parsley, thyme and bay leaf out of the saucepan. Add 3 tablespoons (scant ¼ cup) butter to the stock. Mix well and pour over the mussels. Sprinkle with chopped parsley.

Mussels à la marinière II. MOULES À LA MARINIÈRE – Put chopped onion instead of shallot in the buttered pan. Add chopped parsley, a sprig of thyme and a shred of bay leaf. Lay the mussels on top. Moisten with dry white wine. Season with freshly ground pepper. Cover and cook quickly. Drain the mussels, put them in a bowl and keep hot.

Add to the stock 2 tablespoons (3 tablespoons) *Velouté sauce* (see SAUCE), based on fish stock, and a squeeze of lemon. Add butter and mix. Pour this sauce over the mussels. Sprinkle with chopped parsley.

Mussel farmers' mouclade. MOUCLADE DES BOUCHOLEURS – 'Clean and wash the mussels, place them in a saucepan and toss over a high heat until they open. Remove the empty shells and place the remainder on a heated plate. Strain the juice of the mussels through a fine sieve.

'Chop 1 clove of garlic and a sprig of parsley finely. Blend with 100 g. (4 oz., ½ cup) butter. Pour the juice of the mussels into a saucepan and warm over a gentle heat. Add flavoured butter, a pinch of curry powder, a touch of pepper and finally the mussels. Stir well and simmer for 5 minutes. Sprinkle with 1 teaspoon arrowroot or cornflour, stir again and simmer for 2 minutes. Add 1½ dl. (¼ pint, ⅔ cup) fresh cream and serve immediately.' (Recipe from M. Guy Epaillard of La Rochelle).

Mussels à la poulette. MOULES À LA POULETTE – Cook 2 litres (3½ pints, 4½ pints) mussels as indicated for *Mussels à la marinière*. Drain and put in a bowl.

Decant the cooking stock. Strain and boil down. Add it to 3 dl. (½ pint, 1¼ cups) *Poulette sauce* (see SAUCE) based on concentrated fish stock. Add butter to this sauce and a squeeze of lemon juice, and pour over the mussels. Sprinkle with chopped parsley.

Mussel rissoto. RISOTTO DE MOULES – Prepare the mussels as indicated for *Mussels à la poulette*. Shell them. Strain the cooking sauce and add butter. Put the mussels back in the sauce. Pile this *ragoût* in the middle of a border of risotto. (See RICE).

Mussel sauce. SAUCE AUX MOULES – A white wine sauce made with the concentrated and strained cooking stock of the mussels, with shelled mussels added.

Mussels skewered. MOULES EN BROCHETTES – See SCALLOP SAINT-JACQUES, *Scallops, skewered.*

Mussel soup. SOUPE AUX MOULES – Cook the mussels as for *Mussels à la marinière*. Drain and shell them. With the cooking stock make a thin *Velouté sauce* (see SAUCE). Enrich this *velouté* with a few tablespoons fresh cream. Add butter. Rub through a sieve. Put the shelled mussels in the sauce.

MUSTARD. MOUTARDE – Name of various plants whose seeds are used in the preparation of the condiment known as mustard. The most commonly used are the *white mustard*, with reddish-yellow seeds, *black mustard*, with smaller blackish-red seeds (the leaves of this plant are sometimes used in salad) and *wild mustard*, whose oily seeds are mainly used to adulterate the other two varieties.

Mustard was known to the Romans. They imported it into Gaul, where it quickly gained favour as a condiment.

There are a great many formulae for mustard, differing with each manufacturer. *English mustard* is usually sold as a fine powder, a mixture of black and white mustard, with curcuma added. It is mixed with water before use. *French mustards*, which are sold in the form of paste, are made with a mixture of white and black powdered mustard seed, often with herbs added. They are mixed with verjuice (Dijon mustard) or unfermented wine (Bordeaux mustard). In Italy, *Cremona mustard* contains crystallised fruit.

Leaf or Chinese mustard. MOUTARDE DE CHINE – Herbaceous plant, used in cooking like spinach, of which two varieties are cultivated in France. They are the *moutarde de Chine à feuille de chou* (*Brassica juncea*, cabbage-leaf variety) and the *moutarde de Chine frisée* (curly variety). They are in season from October into the winter.

This vegetable has rather a strong smell.

Mustard sauce. SAUCE MOUTARDE – This sauce is usually served with fish. It is made by adding mustard to *Butter sauce* (see SAUCE). One tablespoon is used to 2½ dl. (scant ½ pint, generous cup) sauce.

MUSTÈLE – Fish found mainly in the Mediterranean, which the Italians call *galea* or *pesce moro*. It is somewhat similar to the turbot. Its liver is highly prized by connoisseurs.

MUTTON. MOUTON – Mutton, somewhat fatter and darker in colour than beef, has much the same properties as other red meat. It is believed to be a little more digestible, though this depends on the cut.

In France salt meadow mutton is highly prized. This comes from sheep pastured on the coast where aromatic plants are prolific. The English cross-breed (Southdown cross-breed) is also well liked for its fat and tasty meat, as well as the Dishley cross-breed, which provides small legs and large cutlets. In some districts mutton tends to taste of wool grease. In Africa and several Asian countries sheep are bred with especially large tails. This fat takes the place of butter in the cooking of meat in Moslem communities.

Best quality mutton is bright red, close-grained and firm. It has a great deal of fat which is white and firm and evenly spread over the muscular tissue and in the tissue itself. A fleshy leg of mutton has a thick layer of fat at the base. In second-grade mutton, there is less fat, and the meat is less red and firm. In third-grade mutton there is only a very thin layer of fat on the kidneys and none on the surface of the meat.

In France the cuts of mutton, as with beef, are divided into three categories for sale.

First category. Leg, rib, fillet, chump cutlets (U.S.A. English lamb chops), loin cutlets (U.S. loin chops).

Secondary category. Shoulder, chuck, neck cutlets (U.S. rib chops).

Third category. Flank, neck, breast and shin.

Baron of mutton. BARON DE MOUTON – A cut comprising the entire hind-quarters of the sheep; the saddle and the two hind legs.

Salt meadow lamb and Paullac lamb are usually cut in this way. Barons of mutton are less commonly found.

These large cuts, which are always roasted, are served as an intermediate course (see CULINARY METHODS, *Roasting*), with a garnish of vegetables and their own gravy, slightly thickened, according to the nature of the garnish.

Cooking time. See CULINARY METHODS, *Average cooking times for roasts*.

Garnishes for baron of mutton. Bouquetière; Bretonne; Clamart; Dauphine; Duchesse; Jardinière; Potatoes Château, Fondantes, with parsley, *Anna* or prepared in some other way; *Portugaise; Provençale; Renaissance; Richelieu*. (See GARNISHES and POTATOES).

Mutton or lamb brains – See OFFAL or VARIETY MEATS.

Breast of mutton. POITRINE DE MOUTON – This part of the sheep is used mainly in the preparation of *ragoûts*.

All recipes for breast of lamb are suitable for breast of mutton. This cut is especially suitable for *épigrammes* (see LAMB, *Breast of lamb en épigrammes*).

The breast may be used with the neck in the preparation of *Mutton broth* (see SOUPS AND BROTHS).

Grilled breast of mutton (Carême's recipe). POITRINE DE MOUTON GRILLÉE AU NATUREL – 'Take 2 fine well-fleshed breasts of mutton. With a single stroke of the knife remove the part of the bone above the gristle. Tie the breasts. Put them in an oval casserole with 2 carrots, 2 onions and a *bouquet garni* (q.v.). Moisten with good clear soup (enough to cover the meat). Bring to the boil. Skim and cook for 2½ hours. Drain the breasts and put them in a press. When they are cold, trim them and gently take off the skin without touching the fat. Round off the meat on the side where the

Pâtés: terrines of truffled duck *au fois gras*; veal and ham pie; country pâté (*Phot. Nicolas*)

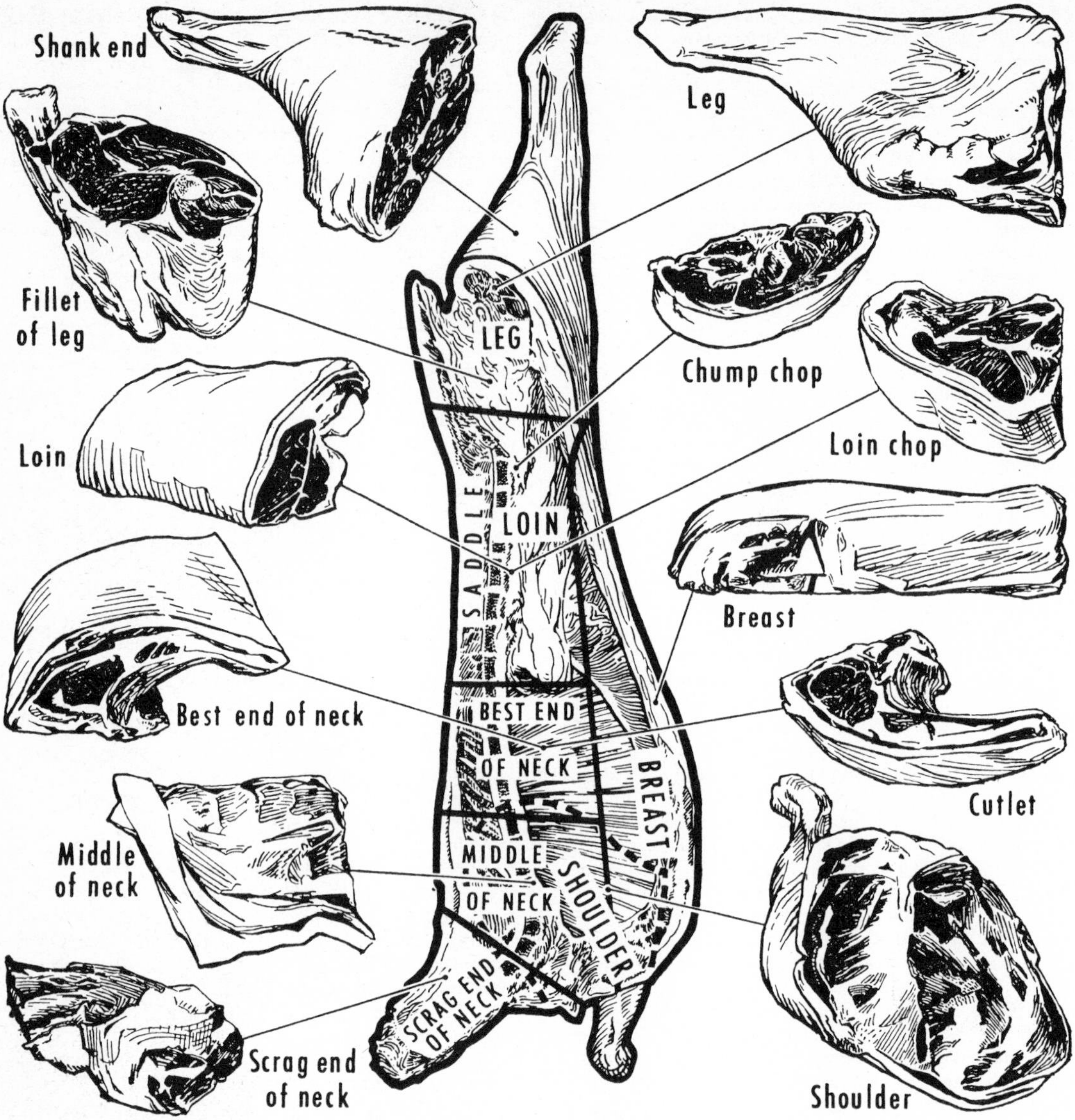

English cuts of mutton

gristle is. Saw off the bones, if they are too long, at the lower edge of the breast. Dip them in melted butter. Grill over a gentle heat, making sure that they are a good colour and that, while grilling, they are gradually warmed through.'

Prepared in this way, grilled breast of mutton is served with *Diable sauce* (see SAUCE) or any other sauce especially suitable for grilled meat.

Grilled breast of mutton in breadcrumbs (Carême's recipe). POITRINE DE MOUTON PANÉE GRILLÉE – Prepare 2 breasts of mutton as indicated in the previous recipe. Leave to cool, and cut each breast into 6 pieces. Trim these pieces, leaving the bone. Dip them in melted butter and breadcrumbs. Grill them and serve with *Poivrade sauce* (see SAUCE).

Stuffed breast of mutton à l'ariégeoise. POITRINE DE MOUTON FARCIE À L'ARIÉGEOISE – Cut open a breast of mutton to form a pouch. Season inside. Stuff with breadcrumbs dipped in clear soup and squeezed, chopped raw ham, and chopped parsley and garlic. Bind with eggs and season well. Sew up the opening in the breast.

Put in a buttered braising pan, lined with fresh pork skin or bacon rinds, sliced onions and carrots. Add a *bouquet garni* (q.v.). Cover and cook gently for 15 minutes. Moisten with $1\frac{1}{2}$ dl. ($\frac{1}{4}$ pint, $\frac{2}{3}$ cup) dry white wine. Boil down. Add 3 tablespoons (scant $\frac{1}{4}$ cup) tomato purée and 3 dl. ($\frac{1}{2}$ pint, $1\frac{1}{4}$ cups) thickened brown stock. Cover and cook in the oven for 45 minutes to 1 hour.

Drain and serve on a large dish. Surround with a garnish of stuffed cabbage rolled into balls and potatoes cooked in clear stock and butter. Skim all fat off the braising stock. Boil down and strain. Pour over the dish.

Mutton broth (English cookery) – Broth made with the breast and neck of mutton, a mixture of coarsely chopped pot vegetables and pearl barley. (See SOUPS AND BROTHS.)

Mutton chops. CÔTELETTES DE MOUTON ANGLAISES – Mutton chops (U.S. English lamb chops) are cut from the fillet of mutton. They are cut very thick, 4 to 5 cm. ($1\frac{1}{2}$ to 2 inches). Roll the end of the chop inwards and fix with a skewer.

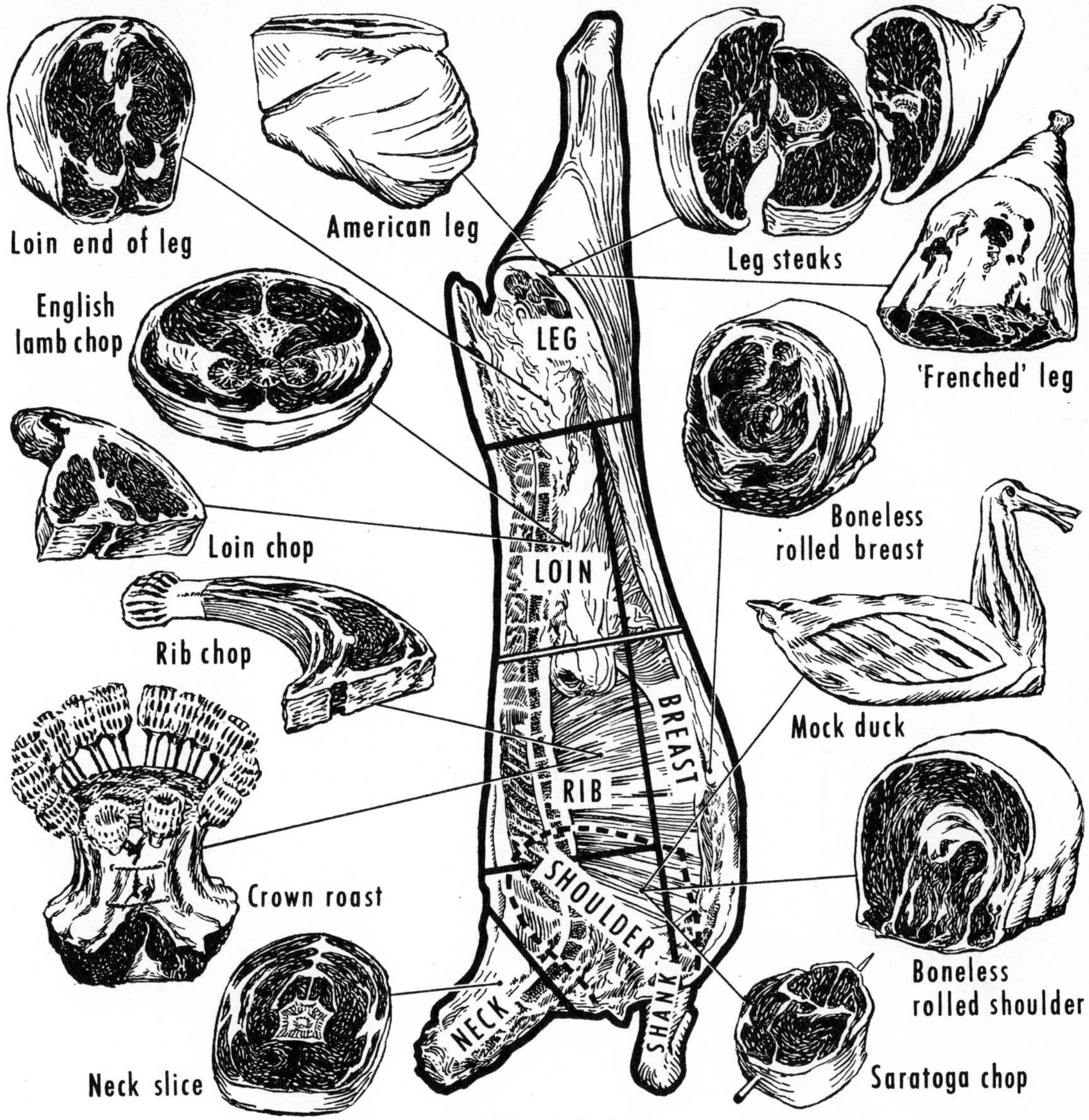

American cuts of mutton

Mutton chops are always grilled. They are served plain as a rule, garnished with parsley, though any of the garnishes suitable for mutton cutlets may be served with these chops.

Mutton cutlets (U.S. chops). CÔTELETTES DE MOUTON – The cutlets are cut from the rib. According to the part from which they are taken, they have different names.

Chump cutlets (U.S. loin chops) are taken from the covered part of the rib. These must be cut rather thick. They are trimmed by cutting off the end of the bone and paring away the narrow strips of meat on either side of this bone, as well as excessive fat along the top. After trimming, the cutlets are slightly flattened.

Chump cutlets are usually grilled, since this method of cooking suits them best. They may, however, be sautéed or braised.

The *neck cutlets* (U.S. rib chops) are those cut from the uncovered part of the rib. These are prepared in the same way as chump cutlets, but generally they are sautéed or braised.

Untrimmed cutlets are taken either from the covered or uncovered part of the rib. The French call them *bouchères*.

The term *undressed* is also applied to a cutlet whose bone meat, after having been detached from the bone and folded back on itself, is kept in this shape by the bone.

Fillet cutlets (U.S. sirloin chops) are cut from the saddle of mutton, split in two, lengthwise.

Mutton cutlets (chops) à l'albigeoise. CÔTELETTES DE MOUTON À L'ALBIGEOISE – Sauté the cutlets in oil. Arrange in a circle. Garnish the middle of the dish with sliced *cèpes* (q.v.) sautéed in oil and flavoured with garlic. Dilute the pan juices with white wine poured into the pan and heated. Season with a touch of garlic. Add fairly thin *Tomato sauce* (see SAUCE). Pour this sauce over the cutlets. Sprinkle with chopped parsley.

Mutton cutlets (chops) à l'anglaise. CÔTELETTES DE MOUTON À L'ANGLAISE – Season with salt and pepper. Dip in egg and breadcrumbs and fry in butter.

Garnish with potatoes or green vegetables tossed in butter.

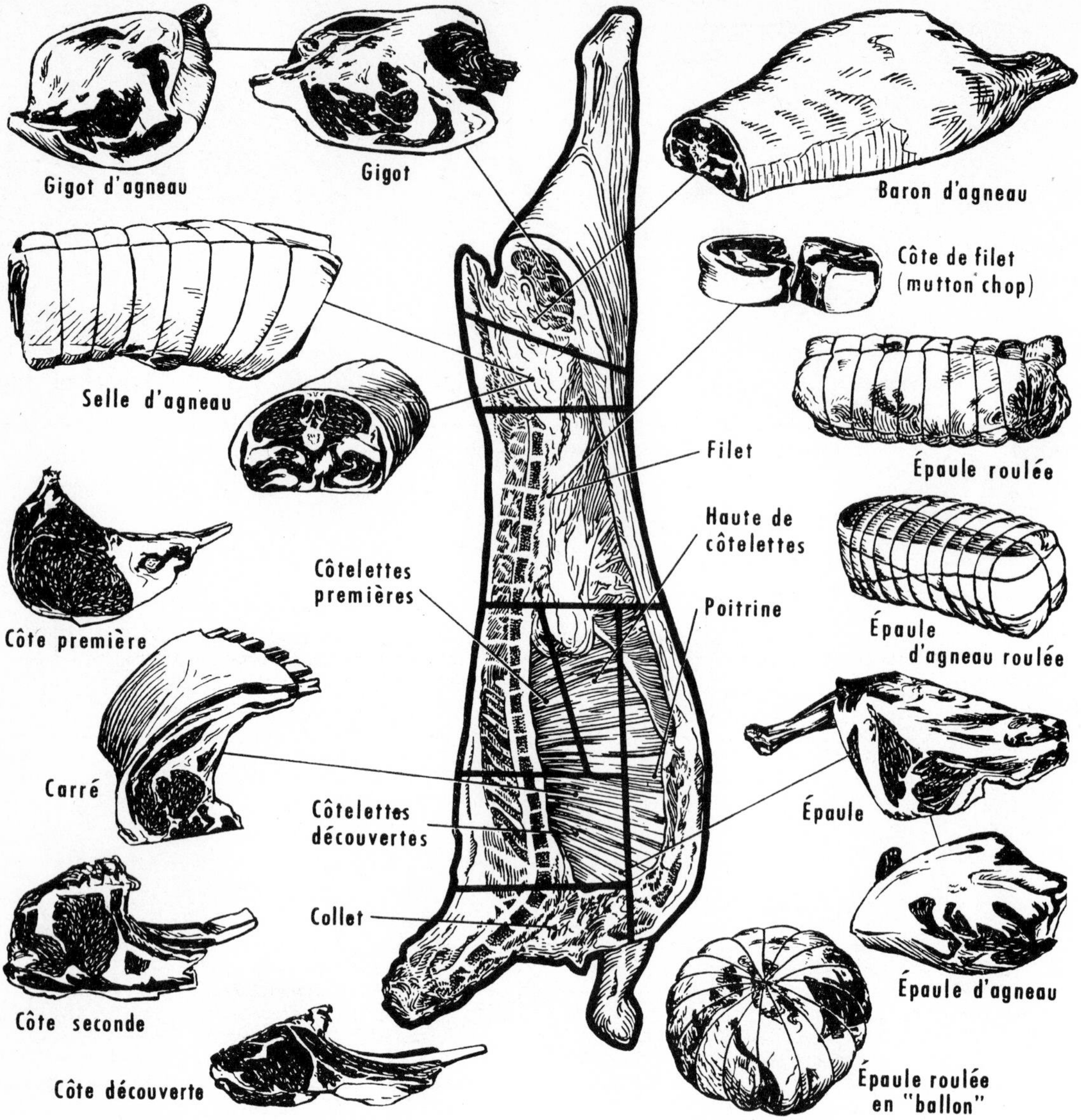

French cuts of mutton

Mutton cutlets (chops) à la bouchère. CÔTELETTES DE MOUTON À LA BOUCHÈRE – Name given to neck cutlets (U.S. rib chops) whose bone is not scraped, and to cutlets of which the meat on the bone is cut away and rolled back. These cutlets are grilled.

Braised cutlets (chops) with various garnishes. CÔTELETTES DE MOUTON BRAISÉES – These should be cut rather thick. Season. Put in a buttered frying pan lined with pork skin, finely sliced onions and carrots. Cover and cook gently for 10 minutes. Moisten with white wine and a few tablespoons thickened brown gravy. Boil down. Add a *bouquet garni*. Cover and cook in the oven for 45 minutes to 1 hour, according to the size of the cutlets. Drain the cutlets. Garnish with the vegetables indicated. Boil down the braising liquor, strain, and pour it over the cutlets.

Mutton cutlets (chops) à la bretonne. CÔTELETTES DE MOUTON À LA BRETONNE – Sauté in butter. Arrange in a circle. Garnish the middle of the dish with white beans or small kidney beans *à la bretonne* (see BEANS). Dilute pan juices with a little clear stock; pour round the cutlets.

Mutton cutlets (chops) à la bruxelloise. CÔTELETTES DE MOUTON À LA BRUXELLOISE – Sauté in butter. Garnish with Brussels sprouts sautéed in butter. Pour white wine and *Demi-glace sauce* (see SAUCE) into the pan. Heat and serve with the cutlets.

Mutton cutlets (chops) à la cévenole. CÔTELETTES DE MOUTON À LA CÉVENOLE – Braise the cutlets in very little stock. When they are three-parts cooked, put 18 chestnuts, three-parts cooked, 18 small glazed onions, and 12 small lardoons of belly of pork, blanched and fried, in the saucepan. Finish cooking all together. 5 minutes before removing from the stove, add 12 small chipolata sausages, cooked in butter. Arrange the cutlets in a circle on a dish. Put the other ingredients in the middle. Pour on the braising stock. Carrots cut into uniform pieces can be added to the garnish.

Mutton cutlets (chops) Champvallon. CÔTELETTES DE MOUTON CHAMPVALLON – Season 6 neck cutlets (U.S. rib chops) and brown them quickly in butter on both sides. Line

Chump cutlets (*Karquel*)

Chump cutlets (*Karquel*)

an earthenware dish with 3 tablespoons (scant $\frac{1}{4}$ cup) sliced onions cooked in butter without browning. Lay the cutlets on top. Pour white stock or water into the pan in which the cutlets were fried, and heat. Moisten the cutlets and onions with this stock. Add a *bouquet garni* and $\frac{1}{2}$ clove crushed garlic. Bring to the boil on the stove, cover and put in the oven. Cook for 35 minutes.

Put on the top of the cutlets 500 g. (1 lb. 2 oz., 3 cups) potatoes cut into thin slices. Season, moisten a little if necessary, and finish cooking in the oven, basting frequently.

Remove the *bouquet garni*. Sprinkle with chopped parsley and serve.

Mutton cutlets (chops) chasseur. CÔTELETTES DE MOUTON CHASSEUR – Sauté the cutlets in butter and drain. For 6 cutlets, put in the frying pan 1 tablespoon chopped shallots and 6 sliced mushrooms. Brown for a few seconds over a very hot flame. Moisten with $1\frac{1}{2}$ dl. ($\frac{1}{4}$ pint, $\frac{2}{3}$ cup) white wine. Boil down. Add $2\frac{1}{2}$ dl. (scant $\frac{1}{2}$ pint, generous cup) thickened brown stock and 1 tablespoon *Tomato sauce* (see SAUCE). Boil for a few seconds. Add 2 teaspoon chopped chervil and tarragon and 1 tablespoon butter. Arrange the chops in a circle on a dish and pour the sauce over them.

Mutton cutlets (chops) en chaud-froid and in jelly. CÔTELETTES DE MOUTON EN CHAUD-FROID ET À LA GELÉE – Proceed as indicated for *Chaud-froid of lamb chops* and *Lamb chops in aspic jelly* (see LAMB).

Mutton cutlets are rarely served cold. It is usually lamb cutlets which are served in this way.

Mutton cutlets (chops) à la Clamart. CÔTELETTES DE MOUTON À LA CLAMART – This dish can be prepared in two ways.

1. *Grilled* or *sautéed* and garnished with *petits pois à la française* (young peas cooked in butter with onions and shredded lettuce) or, green peas tossed in butter.

2. *Braised.* Brown the cutlets on both sides in butter. For 6 cutlets put in the pan 1 litre ($1\frac{3}{4}$ pints, generous quart) newly shelled peas, 1 shredded lettuce, 12 small onions; all these ingredients previously mixed with 75 g. (3 oz., 6 tablespoons) butter, salt and a pinch of sugar.

Add a *bouquet garni* parsley and chervil. Moisten with 4 tablespoons ($\frac{1}{4}$ cup) slightly thickened brown veal stock. Cover and cook for 45 minutes to 1 hour.

Arrange the cutlets in a circle on a deep dish. Pile the peas in the middle.

Neck cutlets (*Karquel*)

Mutton cutlets (chops) en crépinettes à l'ancienne. CÔTELETTES DE MOUTON EN CRÉPINETTES À L'ANCIENNE – Cut the cutlets (chops) rather thin and chop off the end of the bone. Braise them and leave to cool in their stock. Drain and dry in a cloth. Coat them on both sides with fine stuffing mixed with diced truffles, well seasoned and flavoured with a few drops of brandy. Wrap each cutlet in a piece of pig's caul or thin slice of salt pork, dipped in cold water. Dip the cutlets in melted butter and breadcrumbs, baste with melted butter and grill slowly.

Arrange the cutlets in a circle on a dish. Garnish the middle with thick mushroom purée (see MUSHROOMS). Serve with *Périgueux sauce* (see SAUCE) made with the braising stock of the cutlets.

Curried mutton cutlets (chops). CÔTELETTES DE MOUTON AU CURRIE – Sauté the cutlets in oil. Arrange in a circle on a dish. Cover with *Curry sauce* (see SAUCE) to which the diluted pan juices left from cooking the cutlets have been added. Serve with *Rice à l'indienne* (see RICE).

Mutton cutlets (chops) à la duxelles. CÔTELETTES DE MOUTON À LA DUXELLES – Sauté the cutlets in butter, or a mixture of equal parts of oil and butter. Drain them and place on a dish. Pour white wine into the cooking pan; add *Duxelles sauce* (see SAUCE) and boil for a few seconds. Pour this sauce over the cutlets and sprinkle with chopped parsley.

Mutton cutlets (chops) à la fermière. CÔTELETTES DE MOUTON À LA FERMIÈRE – Fry in butter thick loin chops, seasoned with salt and pepper, in a fireproof casserole. For 6 chops, add 3 dl. ($\frac{1}{2}$ pint, $1\frac{1}{4}$ cups) *Vegetable fondue* (see FONDUE) and 4 or 5 tablespoons ($\frac{1}{4}$ or $\frac{1}{3}$ cup) fresh green peas. Season. Moisten with $1\frac{1}{2}$ dl. ($\frac{1}{4}$ pint, $\frac{2}{3}$ cup) white wine. Boil down. Add 2 dl. ($\frac{1}{3}$ pint, scant cup) slightly thickened brown stock, and a small *bouquet garni*. Cook for 20 minutes. Add 20 small potatoes trimmed into pear shapes. Cover and finish cooking in the oven for about 45 minutes. Serve in the casserole.

Grilled mutton cutlets (chops). CÔTELETTES DE MOUTON GRILLÉES – Trim the cutlets and flatten them slightly. Baste with melted butter or oil; season. Cook under the grill. Serve the cutlets on a very hot dish. Decorate the bones with paper frills and garnish with watercress.

Grilled mutton cutlets (chops) à l'anglaise. CÔTELETTES DE MOUTON À L'ANGLAISE – Season. Dip in melted butter and breadcrumbs. Grill slowly. Garnish to taste.

Grilled mutton cutlets (chops) in breadcrumbs. CÔTELETTES DE MOUTON GRILLÉES PANÉES – Baste the cutlets with melted butter. Season. Coat both sides with freshly made breadcrumbs. Pour on melted butter and cook under the grill. Serve on a very hot dish, garnished with watercress. Decorate the bones with cutlet frills.

Mutton cutlets (chops) à la hongroise. CÔTELETTES DE MOUTON À LA HONGROISE – Season the cutlets with salt and paprika. Sauté in butter. When they are browned on both sides, put in the frying pan 2 tablespoons (3 tablespoons) chopped onion, cooked slowly in the butter until very tender. Season with paprika. Finish cooking all together. Serve the cutlets in a circle on a dish. Heap potatoes or any other vegetable sautéed in butter in the middle.

Pour 1 dl. (6 tablespoons, scant $\frac{1}{2}$ cup) white wine into the frying pan. Add 4 dl. ($\frac{3}{4}$ pint, scant 2 cups) thick fresh cream and simmer until quite thick. Blend in 2 tablespoons (3 tablespoons) butter. Pour this sauce over the cutlets.

Mutton cutlets (chops) à l'italienne. CÔTELETTES DE MOUTON À L'ITALIENNE – Sauté the cutlets in a mixture of oil and butter. Place them on a dish. Put in the pan 3 dl. ($\frac{1}{2}$ pint, $1\frac{1}{4}$ cups) *Italian sauce* (see SAUCE). Add 2 tablespoons (3 tablespoons) very finely diced lean cooked ham, 1 tablespoon butter and 2 teaspoons chopped parsley. Pour this sauce over the cutlets.

Mutton cutlets (chops) Maintenon. CÔTELETTES DE MOUTON MAINTENON – Fry the cutlets in butter on one side only. Drain and dry in a cloth. Put on the cooked side 1 heaped tablespoon of *Maintenon mixture* (see MIXTURE): a *Soubise* (see PURÉE) with shredded truffles, mushrooms and pickled tongue added. Smooth this mixture carefully into a dome. Heat some butter in a baking tin and lay the cutlets in it. Sprinkle with breadcrumbs and pour on melted butter. Brown in the oven.

Arrange the cutlets in a rosette on a dish. Decorate the bones with cutlet frills. Serve with *Périgueux sauce* (see SAUCE).

This dish can also be prepared as follows:

Braise the cutlets in a very little stock. Leave to cool under a weight in the strained braising stock. Drain, trim, and heap *Maintenon mixture* (see MIXTURE) on one side. Finish cooking as indicated above. (The *périgueux sauce* is made with the cooking stock.)

Minced mutton cutlets (chops) sautéed and garnished. CÔTELETTES DE MOUTON HACHÉES, SAUTÉES, GARNIES – Cut the medallion of lean meat out of the cutlet without touching the fat part on the bone. Mince the meat finely, adding to it $\frac{1}{3}$ its weight in butter. Season with salt and pepper. Using this minced meat, reshape the cutlet medallion. Sauté in butter. Garnish with vegetables tossed in butter.

Minced mutton cutlets (chops) in breadcrumbs, sautéed. CÔTELETTES DE MOUTON HACHÉES, PANÉES, SAUTÉES – Prepare the cutlets as indicated above. After reshaping them, dip in egg and breadcrumbs. Sauté in butter.

Garnish with vegetables tossed in butter.

Mutton cutlets (chops) à la niçoise. CÔTELETTES DE MOUTON À LA NIÇOISE – Sauté the cutlets in oil. Drain and arrange in a circle on a dish. Fill the middle with new potatoes fried in butter. Arrange French beans in butter and small tomatoes stewed in butter alternately round the edge. Pour a little white wine into the cooking pan. Add a sauce composed of $\frac{1}{3}$ thickened brown stock and $\frac{2}{3}$ *Tomato sauce* (see SAUCE). Season with a touch of garlic and butter. Pour this sauce over the cutlets and sprinkle with chopped parsley.

Mutton cutlets (chops) Parmentier. CÔTELETTES DE MOUTON PARMENTIER – Sauté the cutlets in butter. When they are well browned on both sides, add to the pan diced potatoes three-parts cooked in butter. Finish cooking all together. Arrange the cutlets in a circle and heap the potatoes in the middle. Pour white wine and a few spoonfuls of stock into the cooking pan. Heat, and pour this sauce over the dish. Sprinkle with chopped parsley.

Mutton cutlets (chops) Pompadour (Carême's recipe). CÔTELETTES DE MOUTON POMPADOUR – 'Prepare the cutlets in the same way as those called *à la Soubise* (braised). Do not heat them but coat with a concentrated *Soubise purée* (see PURÉE). Coat the purée once with breadcrumbs. Dip in egg, then in breadcrumbs a second time and brown in clarified butter. Arrange on a dish. Put a *macédoine* (q.v.) in the middle. Boil down the pan juices and pour over the dish.'

Mutton cutlets (chops) à la provençale. CÔTELETTES DE MOUTON À LA PROVENÇALE – Sauté the cutlets in oil. Garnish with small tomatoes stewed in butter or oil, sautéed mushrooms and blanched olives.

Pour white wine into the cooking pan. Add tomato-flavoured veal stock with a touch of garlic added. Pour this sauce over the dish.

Mutton cutlets (chops) à la Réforme. CÔTELETTES DE MOUTON À LA RÉFORME – Season the cutlets and baste with butter. Coat with white breadcrumbs mixed with $\frac{1}{3}$ finely chopped lean ham. Sauté in butter. Garnish with the white of 1 hard-boiled egg, 2 cooked mushrooms, 1 small truffle, 1 gherkin and a small slice of pickled tongue; all these ingredients cut into short, thick strips and mixed.

Pour *Poivrade sauce* (see SAUCE) into the cooking pan. Heat and pour over the shredded mixture only. Serve with redcurrant jelly.

Mutton cutlets (chops) à la russe. CÔTELETTES DE MOUTON À LA RUSSE – Leaving the fat on the bone, cut the medallion of meat out of each cutlet. Prepare a mince as for *Beefsteak à la russe* (see BEEF). Reshape the cutlets. Dip in egg and breadcrumbs. Sauté in clarified butter.

Arrange in a circle on a dish. On each cutlet place a little mound of onions fried in butter. In the middle of the dish heap sautéed potatoes.

Serve with a *sour cream sauce* prepared as follows: Pour the sour cream into the pan in which the cutlets have been cooked. Enrich this cream with a few tablespoons of *Demi-glace sauce* (see SAUCE). Boil down and strain.

Mutton cutlets (chops) sautéed in breadcrumbs. CÔTELETTES DE MOUTON SAUTÉES, PANÉES – Season the cutlets. Dip in egg and breadcrumbs and sauté in butter.

Arrange on a dish. Serve as they are, with the cooking butter poured over them, or garnished with vegetables.

Mutton cutlets (chops) sautéed with garnish. CÔTELETTES DE MOUTON SAUTÉES, GARNIES – Saute the cutlets in butter so that they remain pinkish inside.

Arrange on a very hot dish. Pour dry white wine into the cooking pan and add a few tablespoons thickened brown stock. Heat and pour over the dish.

Garnishes for sautéed mutton cutlets. All those indicated for medallion of mutton. The cutlets can also be garnished with purées of various vegetables, especially *Purée bretonne* (see PURÉE); green vegetables tossed in butter or cream; potatoes cooked in various ways; various cheese pastes; risotto.

Mutton cutlets (chops) Soubise. CÔTELETTES DE MOUTON SOUBISE – Grill or sauté the cutlets. Serve *Soubise purée* separately (see PURÉE).

Stuffed cutlets (chops) with various garnishes. CÔTELETTES DE MOUTON EN PORTEFEUILLE – Make an incision in the thickest part of rather thick cutlets. Pull the edges a little apart to form a pouch. Season the cutlets. Fill with a *Quenelle forcemeat* (see FORCEMEAT) mixed with diced mushrooms and truffles tossed in butter. Close up the pouch in the cutlets and cover with a thin strip of pork fat or bacon rasher, securing it with string. Brown the cutlets in butter on both sides. Moisten with slightly thickened brown stock. Braise the cutlets. Drain and remove the pork fat. Glaze them. Arrange in a circle on a dish, and garnish as indicated. Boil down and strain the cooking stock and pour over the dish.

Prepared in this way, cutlets can be garnished with vegetables, tossed in butter or braised, and served with garnishes such as *Chipolata, Forestière, Financière*, etc. (see GARNISHES). They can also be garnished with vegetable purées, pasta prepared in different ways, risotto, etc.

Mutton cutlets (chops) La Varenne. CÔTELETTES DE MOUTON LA VARENNE – Cut the medallions out of 6 cutlets. Finely chop this meat with $\frac{1}{3}$ its weight of dry *Duxelles* (q.v.), 2 tablespoons (3 tablespoons) butter, 2 teaspoons chopped parsley, salt and pepper. Reshape the cutlets with this mixture, and put them back on the bone. Dip the cutlets in egg and breadcrumbs and sauté in clarified butter. Arrange in a circle on a dish. Fill the middle of the dish with very thick *Mushroom purée* (see PURÉE), made with the addition of 100 g. (4 oz., 2 cups) diced truffles tossed in butter. Make a sauce of a few tablespoons of *Demi-glace sauce* (see SAUCE) cooked with Madeira. Add butter and strain. Pour over the dish.

Mutton cutlets (chops) à la villageoise. CÔTELETTES DE MOUTON À LA VILLAGEOISE – Braise and leave to cool in their stock. Make a *Soubise* (see PURÉE) with very concentrated veal stock and add sliced mushrooms sautéed in butter. Heap some of this mixture on one side of each cutlet. Proceed as for *Mutton cutlets Maintenon.*

Mutton cutlets (chops) à la Villeroi. CÔTELETTES DE MOUTON À LA VILLEROI – Braise the cutlets and leave to cool in their stock. Drain and trim. Dip in *Villeroi sauce* (see SAUCE) and in egg and breadcrumbs. Cook in clarified butter and drain. Arrange in a circle on a paper doyley and garnish with fried parsley. Serve with *Périgueux sauce* or *Tomato sauce* (see SAUCE).

Civet of mutton. CIVET DE MOUTON – Brown in butter 24 small onions and 200 g. (7 oz., $1\frac{3}{4}$ loosely packed cups) diced and blanched belly of pork.

Take them out of the pan and, in the same fat, brown thoroughly 750 g. (generous $1\frac{1}{2}$ lb.) lower mutton cutlets (U.S. rib chops), boned and trimmed into squares. Season with salt, pepper and spices. Add 1 crushed clove of garlic and sprinkle with 2 tablespoons (3 tablespoons) flour. Cook until the flour is golden-brown. Moisten with equal parts red wine and clear stock. Add a *bouquet garni* and 2 tablespoons) brandy. Cover and cook in the oven for an hour.

Drain on a sieve. Put the pieces back in the pan and add the pork lardoons, small onions and 24 small mushrooms previously tossed in butter. Strain the sauce and pour it over the mutton. Cover and cook in the oven for an hour.

The sauce of this civet is thickened with the blood of a chicken or rabbit.

Curried mutton. RAGOÛT DE MOUTON À L'INDIENNE (CURRIE DE MOUTON) – Dice $1\frac{1}{2}$ kg. ($3\frac{1}{4}$ lb.) lean mutton (neck chops or shoulder) into pieces 4 cm. ($1\frac{1}{2}$ inches) square. Brown in lard with 150 g. (5 oz., $1\frac{1}{4}$ cups) chopped onions. Season with salt and 1 teaspoon curry powder. Brown for a few seconds on the stove. Add a clove of crushed garlic. Sprinkle with 50 g. (2 oz., $\frac{1}{2}$ cup) flour. Mix and moisten with clear stock or water, just enough to cover the meat. Add 1 chopped peeled tomato, with the seeds removed, and a *bouquet garni.* Cover and cook for $1\frac{1}{2}$ hours.

Take out the *bouquet*. Put the meat in a bowl. Pour on the sauce, boiled down if necessary, flavoured with lemon juice. Serve with *Rice à l'indienne* (see RICE).

Curried mutton can also be prepared in the same way as *Chicken curry* (see CHICKEN).

It is also possible, still preparing it in the French way as indicated above, to moisten it with coconut milk instead of clear soup. This milk is made by diluting a grated coconut with its own milk mixed with water, or ordinary milk, and sieving this pulp through muslin.

Mutton daube à l'avignonnaise. DAUBE DE MOUTON À L'AVIGNONNAISE – Cut a boned leg or shoulder of mutton into pieces. Following the grain of the meat, interlard each piece with a thick lardoon, and season with salt, pepper and spices.

Steep for 2 hours in a marinade of red wine, oil, finely sliced carrots and onions, crushed garlic, parsley, thyme and bay leaves.

Line a deep earthenware dish with layers of thin slices of pork fat. Intersperse each layer with 2 tablespoons (3 tablespoons) chopped onion, belly of pork and fresh pork skin, diced and blanched, and a little crushed garlic. Put the pieces of mutton on top. Season with salt, pepper, thyme and powdered bay leaf. Put a large bouquet of parsley stalks with a piece of dried orange peel in the middle of the meat. Moisten with the strained marinade, adding enough clear stock to cover the meat. Put slices of pork fat on top. Cover the dish and seal hermetically with flour-and-water paste. Cook slowly in the oven for 5 hours.

Éclanche of mutton. ÉCLANCHE DE MOUTON – Old French word for shoulder of mutton.

Épigrammes of mutton. ÉPIGRAMMES DE MOUTON – Made with a piece of the breast, braised or boiled, trimmed to the shape of a heart, dipped in egg and breadcrumbs, sautéed in butter or grilled, and a grilled mutton chop.

Épigrammes can be garnished with different vegetables. For a recipe, see LAMB, *Breast of lamb en épigrammes.*

Filets mignons of mutton en chevreuil (venison style). FILETS MIGNONS DE MOUTON EN CHEVREUIL – Proceed as for *Beef filets mignons en chevreuil, venison style* (see BEEF).

Grilled filets mignons of mutton. FILETS MIGNONS DE MOUTON GRILLÉS – Flatten the fillets slightly. Season; baste with melted butter or oil and coat with breadcrumbs. Pour melted butter over them and grill slowly. Serve with *Maître d'hôtel butter* (see BUTTER, *Compound butters*) or any other sauce suitable for grilled meat.

Fillet of mutton (U.S. Sirloin roast). FILET DE MOUTON – Name given to the half-saddle, split lengthwise.

This cut is rolled and tied after boning. It can be roasted, pot-roasted or braised, as for rib or shoulder. All garnishes for rib or shoulder are suitable for fillet of mutton.

The term *filets mignons* (of mutton or lamb) is used of the two thin slivers of meat found under the saddle.

Fillets of mutton on skewers. BROCHETTES DE FILET DE MOUTON – Cut a well-trimmed loin of mutton or lamb into pieces about $\frac{1}{2}$ cm. ($\frac{1}{4}$ inch) thick. Thread these on skewers alternating with blanched pieces of lean bacon. Season, dip into melted butter, cover with white breadcrumbs, sprinkle with melted butter, and grill.

Pieces of bacon, and sliced mushrooms, lightly tossed in butter, can also be added.

Proceeding as described above, various dishes on skewers, such as chicken livers, lamb's sweetbreads or escalopes of calf's sweetbreads, fillets of beef, mutton, lamb or veal, fillets of various fish (for the latter omit the bacon), fillets of chicken, etc., can be prepared. Lean bacon can be replaced by square pieces of smoked bacon, which does not need to be blanched.

Fillets of mutton in red wine. FILETS DE MOUTON AU VIN ROUGE – Cut the fillets into little square pieces. Season with salt and pepper. Cook in sizzling butter, keeping slightly underdone on the inside. Drain. Toss 125 g. ($4\frac{1}{2}$ oz., generous 2 cups) thickly sliced mushrooms in the same butter. Take the mushrooms out of the pan and put them with the meat.

Pour 3 dl. ($\frac{1}{2}$ pint, $1\frac{1}{4}$ cups) red wine into the pan. Boil down, add a few tablespoons thickened brown veal stock, simmer to a concentrated consistency, blend in some butter, strain, and pour over the mutton and mushrooms.

Haricot or halicot of mutton. HARICOT (HALICOT) DE MOUTON – Mutton *ragoût* whose name is no doubt derived from the old French *halicoter*, to cut into tiny morsels.

There are recipes for this dish which date back to a time before the vegetable bean (*haricot*) was generally known. In one of the oldest formulae given by Taillevent, the following recipe is given.

'Put them all raw to fry in lard, cut into tiny pieces with sliced onions and some beef broth, verjuice, parsley, hyssop and sage, and boil together, with fine-powdered spices.'

Thus in former times haricot (or halicot) of mutton was made without haricot beans. The only garnish was turnips, potatoes and onions.

Haricot of mutton is made like a *ragoût* of mutton with potatoes, and has nothing in common with the *ragoût of mutton* with white haricot beans for which the recipe is given below.

Mutton hash. HACHIS DE MOUTON – Made from cooked meat, braised or roasted in the same way as *Beef hash* (see BEEF).

Mutton head – See OFFAL or VARIETY MEATS, *Sheep's head*.

Mutton hindquarter. DOUBLE DE MOUTON – This cut is made up of the two hind legs of the animal. They are not split. The hindquarter is usually roasted and served as an intermediate meat course.

All garnishes and sauces indicated for *Baron of mutton* can be served with this dish.

Mutton kidneys – See OFFAL or VARIETY MEATS.

Leg of mutton à l'anglaise I. GIGOT DE MOUTON À L'ANGLAISE – Take a leg of mutton, trim, cut off the end of the bone, wrap in a buttered and floured cloth and plunge into a pan of boiling salt water. Add 4 medium-sized carrots cut to look like big olives, 6 medium-sized onions (one studded with 2 cloves), a *bouquet garni* (q.v.) and 2 cloves garlic. In the same pan put 1 dozen large, tender turnips, quartered and tied in a cloth.

Boil steadily, allowing 30 minutes per pound of meat. Drain and unwrap the leg of mutton. Put it on a serving dish, and surround with the carrots and onions.

With it serve the turnips, rubbed through a sieve, and a *Butter sauce* (see SAUCE) made with the cooking stock of the mutton, with 2 tablespoons (3 tablespoons) capers added. Skim and drain the rest of the stock and serve separately.

Leg of mutton à l'anglaise II. GIGOT DE MOUTON À L'ANGLAISE – Proceed as indicated above, substituting a purée of celery for the purée of turnips. (Like the turnips, the celery must be cooked with the mutton.)

Mashed potatoes cooked with the mutton can be served in place of turnips or celery.

Leg of mutton cooked according to the English method should be served with a purée of turnips only, which are cooked with the meat.

Carême, in his *Traité des grosses pièces de mouton*, advises glazing the leg after boiling with the usual ingredients. He also advises garnishing with cauliflower covered with a very smooth *Espagnole sauce* (see SAUCE).

He adds that all kinds of vegetables and sauces can be served with leg of mutton cooked in this way.

'It is a strange error on the part of many chefs,' he concludes, 'to suppose that English gourmets will eat this leg only if served with boiled carrots and turnips. What the English like best is to see the juice coming from the leg when they slice it.'

Leg of mutton à la bonne femme. GIGOT DE MOUTON À LA BONNE FEMME – Proceed as indicated for *Shoulder of mutton à la bonne femme* (see below).

Leg of mutton à la bordelaise (Carême's recipe). GIGOT DE MOUTON À LA BORDELAISE – 'Take a leg of mutton which has been hung until very tender. Bone it, except for the projecting bone. Stuff with ham and fillets of anchovy from which all salt has been removed, and also with chopped parsley, 2 shallots and 1 clove of garlic, chopped and blanched. Tie the leg to keep in all the stuffing. Brown lightly in butter. Moisten with a bottle of good red Bordeaux wine. Add 2 carrots, 3 onions (1 studded with 2 cloves), a *bouquet garni* of thyme, bay leaves and basil. Cover and stew slowly, but in such a way as to reduce the stock to a *Demi-glace* (see SAUCE). Cook for $1\frac{1}{2}$ hours. Have ready $1\frac{1}{2}$ litres ($2\frac{3}{4}$ pints, $3\frac{1}{4}$ pints) perfectly skinned cloves of garlic. Boil in a lot of water. Drain. Cool under running water and sauté in the best butter. Keep them hot. Drain the leg of mutton. Put it on a serving dish. Boil down the stock with 2 tablespoons *Espagnole sauce* (see SAUCE).

'After taking out the vegetables and the *bouquet garni*, strain the stock through muslin. Pour over the joint. Dress the garlic with 1 tablespoon *Allemande sauce* (see SAUCE) and a small pinch of Cayenne pepper. Serve in a sauceboat or silver bowl.'

How to cut a leg of mutton:
Left: parallel to the bone
Right: perpendicular to the bone
(*Larousse*)

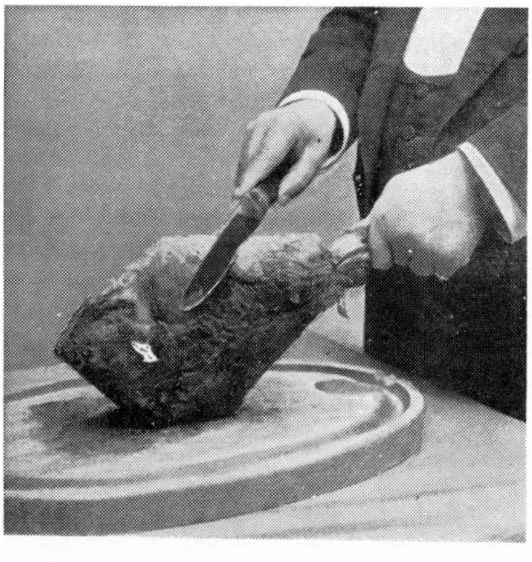

Leg of mutton à la boulangère. GIGOT DE MOUTON À LA BOULANGÈRE – Proceed as for *Shoulder of mutton à la boulangère* (see below).

Braised leg of mutton. GIGOT DE MOUTON BRAISÉ – Proceed as for *Braised shoulder of mutton* (see below).

Leg of mutton à la bretonne. GIGOT DE MOUTON À LA BRETONNE – Roast a leg of mutton. Serve with it the diluted pan juices with a little fat left in them. Garnish with white haricot beans, small kidney beans *à la bretonne,* or *Purée of haricot beans à la bretonne* (see BEANS). The garnish must be served separately.

Leg of mutton en chevreuil (venison style). GIGOT DE MOUTON EN CHEVREUIL – Bone the chump end of a leg of mutton and fix the bone into the smaller end so that it projects. Completely skin the meat and interlard with best lardoons, as for a haunch of roebuck.

Put the leg to steep in a special marinade (see MARINADE). Leave it in this marinade for some time, depending on the tenderness of the meat and on the weather (2 days in summer and 4 to 5 days in winter).

Dry the leg of mutton in a cloth. Roast it. Serve *Roebuck sauce* or *Poivrade sauce* (see SAUCE) separately.

Roast leg of mutton. GIGOT DE MOUTON RÔTI. Bone the chump (U.S. loin) end of the leg. For cooking time see CULINARY METHODS, *Average cooking time for roasts.* Serve the diluted pan juices with it.

It is customary to stud the leg near the projecting bones with 2 or 3 small cloves of garlic.

Cold leg of mutton is cooked in the same way as roast leg of mutton. It is served plain, garnished only with watercress.

Leg of mutton de sept heures or à la cuiller. GIGOT DE MOUTON DE SEPT HEURES (À LA CUILLER) – Trim the leg and cut off the end of the bone. Braise in the usual way, but cook for a long time at a moderate temperature.

After cooking, this mutton should be so tender that it can be cut with a spoon.

Serve with the braising liquor, strained and boiled down. All garnishes indicated for *Braised rib* or *Shoulder of mutton* (see below) are suitable for *Leg of mutton à la cuiller.*

Leg of mutton à la Soubise. GIGOT DE MOUTON À LA SOUBISE – Trim the leg of mutton and braise in the usual way. When it is half-cooked, drain it. Strain the briasing stock. Put the leg back in the braising pan. Surround with 2 kg. ($4\frac{1}{2}$ lb.) parboiled quartered onions. Pour on the braising stock. Finish cooking all together.

Drain the onions. Crush them in a saucepan, and add 250 g. (9 oz., $1\frac{1}{4}$ cup) rice cooked in clear chicken soup. Simmer for 10 minutes. Rub the onions through a fine sieve (or through a tammy cloth, pressing hard). Heat this purée, and add butter to it. Glaze the joint. Put it on a serving dish and pour over it a few tablespoons of stock, strained and boiled down, if necessary. Serve with the braising stock and the *soubise* (onion purée).

The leg can also be braised in the usual way, with the *soubise* prepared separately as indicated in the recipe for this purée (see PURÉE).

Mutton and lamb's liver, heart and spleen. FOIE, COEUR ET RATE DE MOUTON – These parts constitute what is called the *pluck*.

Sheep and lamb pluck is used mostly in *ragoûts*.

Moussaka of mutton (Rumanian cookery). MOUSSAKA DE MOUTON – *Ingredients prepared in advance.* Using cooked mutton make 1 kg. ($2\frac{1}{4}$ lb., $4\frac{1}{2}$ cups) mince.

Cook in oil 6 aubergines, halved lengthwise and lightly scored with a knife. Scoop out the pulp and chop it. Keep the skins to line the mould.

Cook in oil 2 peeled aubergines, cut into slices and chopped. Add to the mutton mince, and add also 125 g. ($4\frac{1}{2}$ oz., $2\frac{1}{4}$ cups) chopped mushrooms tossed in butter, 75 g. (3 oz., $\frac{3}{4}$ cup) chopped onions cooked very slowly in butter until tender, 1 tablespoon chopped parsley, a touch of garlic, and 1 dl. (6 tablespoons, scant $\frac{1}{2}$ cup) *Espagnole sauce* (see SAUCE) strongly flavoured with tomato. Season with salt, pepper and spices.

Bind with 2 or 3 eggs. Mix thoroughly.

Final preparations for the moussaka. Completely line a large buttered charlotte mould with the aubergine skins, purple side downward. Fill this mould with alternate layers of mince and round slices of fried aubergine. Press these ingredients well down into the mould. Cover with aubergine skins. On top of the skins lay a sheet of buttered greaseproof paper. Stand the mould in a pan of water and cook the *moussaka* in the oven for 1 hour.

Let it stand for a few minutes before turning out on to a serving dish.

If aubergines are not available the *moussaka* may be made with very small vegetable marrows (*zucchini*, courgettes).

For individual portions served in a restaurant, the *moussaka* is usually made in a large rectangular mould.

Navarin of mutton. NAVARIN DE MOUTON – A *ragoût* garnished with different vegetables.

Navarin of mutton with potatoes. NAVARIN DE MOUTON AUX POMMES DE TERRE – Name given to *Ragoût of mutton à la bonne femme* cooked without belly of pork (see below).

Navarin of mutton printanier. NAVARIN DE MOUTON PRINTANIER – The chuck and shoulder of mutton cut into pieces each weighing about 60 g. ($2\frac{1}{2}$ oz.) Season with salt, pepper and a pinch of fine sugar.

With 2 tablespoons (3 tablespoons) stock fat or butter, brown the pieces thoroughly. Sprinkle with 2 tablespoons (3 tablespoons) flour, mix, and brown lightly in the oven. Add enough tepid water to cover the meat. Bring to the boil, stirring constantly, to ensure that the *roux* is well blended into the stock. Add chopped tomatoes, 1 clove crushed garlic, and a *bouquet garni* (q.v.). Bring to the boil, cover and simmer in the oven for 1 hour. Remove the pieces of meat and strain the sauce. Rinse the saucepan in hot water to detach bone splinters. Put all the ingredients and the sauce back in the pan. Bring to the boil once more and add small onions, quartered carrots, turnips cut to look like olives and new potatoes. Continue cooking, still very slowly, for 1 hour. Add 175 g. (6 oz., 1 scant cup) shelled peas and 100 g. (4 oz., $\frac{1}{2}$ cup) French beans. Finish cooking the *navarin,* still simmering very gently, for a further $\frac{1}{2}$ hour.

Skim all fat off the *navarin* and serve.

Noisettes of mutton. NOISETTES DE MOUTON – These small pieces should be cut from the *noix* of the leg, since *noisette* is the diminutive of *noix*. In practice, however, these very

Noisettes of mutton Armenonville

delicate cuts are taken from the fillet (loin) or the rib of the animal.

Noisettes cut from the rib are more regular in shape than those cut from the loin.

These may be sautéed or grilled, and served with all garnishes suitable for *Mutton cutlets* and *Noisettes of lamb* (see LAMB).

Noisettes of mutton Armenonville. NOISETTES DE MOUTON ARMENONVILLE – Sauté the *noisettes* in butter. Set each one on a small *Anna potato* (see POTATOES) cooked in a tartlet.

Garnish with cocks' combs and cocks' kidneys, alternated with the *noisettes*, and morels in cream, piled in the middle of the dish. Dilute the pan juices with white wine, heat and pour over the meat.

Noisettes of mutton Nichette. NOISETTES DE MOUTON NICHETTE – Grill the *noisettes*. Put each one on a bed of browned *Duchess potatoes* (see POTATOES). On top of each put a large grilled mushroom. In the middle of the dish heap morels sautéed with chopped parsley.

Pour concentrated veal stock, enriched with butter, round the dish.

Noisettes of mutton à la tyrolienne

Noisettes of mutton à la tyrolienne. NOISETTES DE MOUTON À LA TYROLIENNE – Sauté the *noisettes* in butter. Set each on a small *Anna potato* (see POTATOES), and decorate the top with a spoonful of *Tomato fondue* (see TOMATO, FONDUE). Fill the middle of the plate with fried onion rings. Pour the cooking stock over the *noisettes*.

Mutton pie (English cookery) – See PIE.

Pistache of mutton or mutton à la catalane (Languedoc cookery). PISTACHE DE MOUTON (MOUTON À LA CATALANE) – Made from boned shoulder of mutton or part of the leg. The distinctive feature of this dish is that it is garnished with a considerable amount of garlic. (See *Shoulder of mutton à la catalane*, below).

Ragoût of mutton. RAGOÛTS DE MOUTON – *Ragoûts* are made with the shoulder, neck, neck chops and breast of the sheep. These are trimmed, boned and cut into pieces weighing up to 100 g. (3 to 3½ oz.).

Ragoûts may be prepared in white or brown stock. Different vegetables, fresh or dried, and rice or barley are served with them.

Ragoût of mutton à l'anglaise I (Irish stew). RAGOÛT DE MOUTON À L'ANGLAISE – Cut into pieces of equal size 750 g. (1½ to 1¾ lb.) mutton. Put these in a saucepan in alternating layers with 500 g. (18 oz., 3 cups) sliced potatoes and 200 g. (7 oz., 1¾ cups) sliced or chopped onions. Put a *bouquet garni* in the middle of the pan. Season with salt and pepper. Moisten with enough water just to cover the meat and potatoes.

Bring to the boil. Cover the pan. Cook in a hot oven for about 1 hour. Remove the bouquet and serve in a deep dish.

This stew has no thickening other than the potatoes, which in cooking should thicken the stock sufficiently.

Ragoût of mutton à l'anglaise II (Irish stew). RAGOÛT DE MOUTON À L'ANGLAISE – Prepare the stew as indicated in the previous recipe, but using only half the quantity of potatoes and onions. Boil the stew for 35 minutes.

Drain on a sieve. Put the pieces of meat back in the saucepan. Cover with 400 g. (14 oz., 2⅓ cups) potatoes cut into ovals and 24 small parboiled onions. Pour strained cooking stock over all these ingredients. Cover, and cook in the oven for 35 to 40 minutes. Serve in a deep dish.

Ragoût of mutton with barley. RAGOÛT DE MOUTON À L'ORGE – Use the same ingredients and procedure as for *Ragoût of mutton with white haricot beans* (see below), leaving out the belly and substituting for the beans 150 g. (5 oz., scant cup) pearl barley, previously cooked in salt water for 1 hour. The cooking water of the barley should be used to moisten the *ragoût*.

Ragoût of mutton with red beans. RAGOÛT DE MOUTON AUX HARICOTS ROUGES – Proceed as for *Ragoût with white haricot beans* (see below), substituting for the white beans the same quantity of red beans, three-parts cooked in red wine.

Ragoût of mutton with white haricot beans. RAGOÛT DE MOUTON AUX HARICOTS BLANCS – This *ragoût* should not be confused with *haricot of mutton*.

Brown in fat 125 g. (¼ lb., 1 cup) diced and blanched belly of pork. Take these lardoons out of the pan and in the same fat brown 750 g. (1½ to 1¾ lb.) mutton cut into square pieces and seasoned with salt and pepper.

Dust flour over the *ragoût* and proceed as indicated for the first stage of *Ragoût of mutton à la bonne femme* (see below).

Drain the mutton and put the pieces back in the pan. Add ½ litre (scant pint, 2¼ cups) white beans, three-parts cooked, and the browned lardoons. Skim all fat off the sauce. Strain and pour over the *ragoût*.

Cover and cook in the oven for 1½ hours.

Ragoût of mutton à la bonne femme. RAGOÛT DE MOUTON À LA BONNE FEMME – Cut into square pieces 750 g. (1½ to 1¾ lb.) mutton. Season with salt and pepper and brown with 1 quartered onion in cooking fat. Pour off some of the fat. Add a pinch of fine sugar (this sugar, turning into caramel, will give the necessary colouring to the sauce), and 2 tablespoons (3 tablespoons) flour. Mix. Add 1 small clove of crushed garlic. Moisten with 1 litre (1¾ pints, generous quart) water or clear stock. Add 3 tablespoons (scant ¼ cup)

Ragoût of mutton with white haricot beans

Tomato purée (see SAUCE) 100 g. (4 oz., ½ cup) fresh, pulped tomatoes, and a *bouquet garni* (q.v.). Cover and cook in the oven for an hour.

Drain the pieces of mutton on a sieve. Remove the skin and splinters of bone separated during cooking. Put the meat back in the pan. Add 400 g. (14 oz., 2⅓ cups) potatoes cut to look like big olives, 24 small glazed onions and 125 g. (¼ lb., 1 cup) blanched and browned belly of pork cut into little squares. Skim all fat off the sauce. Strain and pour over the *ragoût*. Bring to the boil. Cover and cook in the oven for 1 hour.

Ragoût of mutton with celeriac. RAGOÛT DE MOUTON AU CÉLERI-RAVE – Proceed as indicated for *Ragoût of mutton à la bonne femme*, substituting for the garnish indicated an equal quantity of celeriac cut into large oval pieces and parboiled.

Ragoût of mutton with chick-peas, à la catalane. RAGOÛT DE MOUTON AUX POIS CHICHES (À LA CATALANE) – Proceed as for the first stage of *Ragoût of mutton à la bonne femme*, using a little more *Tomato purée* (see SAUCE, *Tomato sauce*) and seasoning liberally with crushed garlic. Put the pieces of mutton back in the pan. Add chick-peas, cooked separately. Strain the sauce and pour it over the dish. Finish cooking in a slow oven.

Ragoût of mutton with kohl-rabi. RAGOÛT DE MOUTON AUX CHOUX-RAVES – Proceed as indicated for *Ragoût of mutton with celeriac*, substituting kohl-rabi, cut to look like big olives and parboiled, for celeriac.

Ragoût of mutton with macaroni, à la milanaise. RAGOÛT DE MOUTON AU MACARONI (À LA MILANAISE) – Proceed as for the first stage of *Ragoût of mutton à la bonnae femme*, using a larger quantity of *Tomato purée* (see SAUCE) and cooking the meat completely in one stage.

Put the pieces of mutton, drained and trimmed, in a flat earthenware dish. Cover with macaroni half-boiled in salt water, drained, cut into lengths of 6 cm. (2½ inches), and then cooked in butter. Thoroughly mix grated Parmesan into the macaroni. Pour over this the sauce strained through a fine sieve, sprinkle with melted butter, and brown slowly in the oven.

Ragoût of mutton à la niçoise. RAGOÛT DE MOUTON À LA NIÇOISE – Bone and cut into square pieces 750 g. (1½ to 1¾ lb.) shoulder of mutton. Brown in oil, sprinkle flour over it, and add 2 cloves of crushed garlic.

Moisten with 1½ dl. (¼ pint, ⅔ cup) white wine. Boil down. Add enough clear stock to cover the meat, 4 tablespoons (⅓ cup) *Tomato purée* (see SAUCE) and a *bouquet garni* (q.v.). Cook for one hour. Drain the meat, trim it, and put the pieces back in the pan. Add about 30 small new potatoes and 12 small browned onions. Strain the sauce and pour it over the mutton. Cover and cook in the oven for 45 minutes. Without stirring the *ragoût*, add to it 4 very small vegetable marrows, peeled, coarsely diced and browned in oil. Cook in a slow oven for 15 minutes.

Ragoût of mutton à la paysanne. RAGOÛT DE MOUTON À LA PAYSANNE – Proceed as for *Ragoût of mutton à la bonne femme*, cooking the meat with carrots, turnips, onions and quartered potatoes.

This *ragoût* is also made with carrots, turnips, onions and celery cut into triangles and tossed in butter, and potatoes cut to look like olives.

Ragoût of mutton printanier. RAGOÛT DE MOUTON PRINTANIER – Another name for *Navarin of mutton printanier*.

Ragoût of mutton with rice. RAGOÛT DE MOUTON AU RIZ – Proceed with the same ingredients as for *Ragoût of mutton with barley*, substituting for the barley 150 g. (5 oz., ⅔ cup) rice, added to the *ragoût* 30 minutes before serving.

Rib of mutton. CARRÉ DE MOUTON – Rib of mutton is usually divided into cutlets. It can also be roasted or braised whole, and garnished with vegetable. It should be served as intermediate course. A rib of mutton should not include more than 8 to 9 cutlets, starting from the chump.

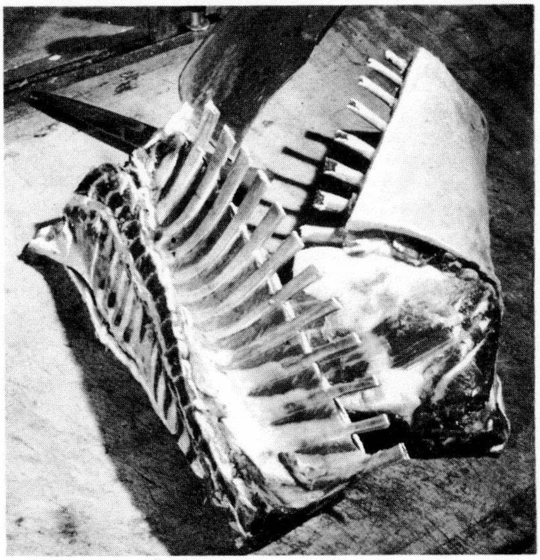

Ribs of mutton (*Karquel*)

Preparation of a whole rib: Sever at the chuck. Remove the thin parchment-like skin which covers the meat, and remove the backbone. Loosen the tips of the cutlet bones. Bard the skinned meat with pork fat tied on with several lengths of string.

Rib of mutton à l'ancienne (Carême's recipe). CARRÉ DE MOUTON À L'ANCIENNE – 'Cut two ribs of mutton from the fillet (loin) to the fourth cutlet (rib) from the neck.

'Completely remove all the skin covering the fillet, after having removed the backbone, and trim the fillet. Detach to the width of a thumb the meat covering the ribs at the top end. Saw through one bone of each pair of cutlets so that the remainder are only 2½ inches long. Interlard one of the ribs with best square lardoons. Thread sprigs of parsley into the other.

'Put the ribs in a marinade composed of an onion cut into rings, parsley, thyme, bay leaf, salt, pepper and half a glass of good oil.

'Three-quarters of an hour before serving, put it on the spit. Wrap in a sheet of buttered paper. Baste frequently. Five minutes before serving, unwrap, glaze, serve and pour clear stock over it.'

Rib of mutton à la boulangère. CARRÉ DE MOUTON À LA BOULANGÈRE – Proceed as for *Shoulder of lamb à la boulangère* (see LAMB).

Rib of mutton à la bretonne. CARRÉ DE MOUTON À LA BRETONNE – Roast the rib in the oven or on the spit. Serve with *white beans* or small *kidney beans à la bretonne* (see BEANS). Serve the gravy of the roast separately.

A *Purée bretonne* (see PURÉE) can also be served with rib of mutton.

Rib of mutton à la boulangère. CARRÉ DE MOUTON À LA MOUTON BRAISÉ – Put the trimmed, barded and tied rib in a buttered braising pan lined with pork skin, and a sliced onion and carrot which have been tossed in butter. Add a *bouquet garni*. Season. Cover and cook gently for 15 minutes. Moisten 1½ dl. (¼ pint, ⅔ cup) white wine. Boil down to an essence. Moisten with 3 dl. (½ pint, 1¼ cups) thickened veal stock or clear soup. Cover and cook in the oven for 45 minutes to 1 hour, according to the size of the joint.

Drain the rib. Glaze and garnish it as indicated. Pour over it the reduced and strained braising stock with the fat skimmed off.

Garnishes for rib of mutton. Most garnishes indicated for *Baron of mutton* are suitable for this cut. It can also be garnished (these garnishes are very suitable for the rib) with purées of fresh or dried vegetables, especially pulses (lentils, dried beans, etc.), risotto and pasta prepared in different ways.

As appropriate, these garnishes are arranged round the meat or served separately.

Cold rib of mutton. CARRÉ DE MOUTON FROID – Roast the rib in the oven or on the spit, and leave until cold.

Trim. Glaze with jelly. Serve on a long dish. Garnish, at each end of the dish, with bunches of watercress and, along the sides, with chopped jelly.

In England it is customary to serve mint sauce with cold lamb or mutton (see SAUCE, *Cold Sauces*).

Rib of mutton à la Maintenon. CARRÉ DE MOUTON À LA MAINTENON – Proceed as for *Saddle of mutton à la Maintenon* (see below).

Rib of mutton à l'orientale. CARRÉ DE MOUTON À L'ORIENTALE – Trim a rib of mutton and braise in the usual way. Drain it. Garnish along the sides with small tomatoes stuffed with a *salpicon* (q.v.) of sheep's (lamb's) liver, sautéed in butter, blended with thick brown stock with a *salpicon* of sweet peppers cooked in oil added to it, and with small artichokes, filled with a *salpicon* of onions cooked in butter until very tender. Garnish each end of the serving dish with saffron-flavoured *Pilaf of rice* (see PILAF). Serve with the braising liquor.

Roast rib of mutton. CARRÉ DE MOUTON RÔTI – Trim all skin from the rib. Bard with pork fat and tie the joint. Roast in the oven or on the spit. When it is ready, the inside of the meat should be pinkish in colour.

Garnish with watercress. Serve with its pan juices, with the surplus fat skimmed off. (See CULINARY METHODS, *Average cooking time for roasts*).

Roast rib of mutton with various garnishes. CARRÉ DE MOUTON RÔTI – Prepare and cook as indicated in the previous recipe. Surround with the garnish indicated. Serve with the pan juices, clear or slightly thickened, according to the nature of the garnish.

Garnishes suitable for roast rib of mutton. All those indicated for *Baron of mutton*.

Saddle of mutton. SELLE DE MOUTON – This cut is most commonly roasted and sometimes braised (see CULINARY METHODS). It provides an intermediate meat course. It is served surrounded by the desired garnish and with the pan juices, clear or thickened, depending on the nature of the garnish. All garnishes indicated for *Rib* or *Leg of mutton* are suitable for saddle of mutton.

Cold saddle of mutton. SELLE FROIDE DE MOUTON – Proceed as for *Roast of leg of mutton*, served cold.

Saddle of mutton à la Maintenon. SELLE DE MOUTON À LA MAINTENON – Trim a saddle of mutton cut near the upper leg. Braise until it is three-parts cooked. Strain the stock and leave the meat to cool in it.

Drain, and cut thin long slices inside the saddle, leaving the overhang on either side. Put these slices back inside the saddle with layers of *Maintenon mixture* between (see MIXTURES), all pressed close together, so as to reshape the saddle. Cover with *Soubise purée* (see PURÉE) bound with egg. Put the saddle on an oven-proof dish. Sprinkle with breadcrumbs and pour on melted butter. Pour round a few tablespoons of the strained braising stock. Cook in a slow oven until the top of the saddle is lightly browned. Serve with it the braising stock, strained and boiled down.

Shoulder of mutton en ballon

Saddle of mutton à la Maintenon is usually garnished with braised vegetables.

Shoulder of mutton en ballon or en musette. ÉPAULE DE MOUTON EN BALLON (EN MUSETTE) – Bone the shoulder. season, and shape it into a ball. This type of rolled mutton is called *en ballon* or *en musette.* Braise the shoulder in the usual way (see CULINARY METHODS). Drain and untie.

Glaze. Garnish according to the recipe selected. Pour the braising stock over it.

Shoulder of lamb en ballon may be stuffed.

Shoulder of mutton à la bonne femme I. ÉPAULE DE MOUTON À LA BONNE FEMME – Bone the shoulder and season. Stuff with sausage meat. Roll lengthwise and tie. Half-cook it in butter or lard. Put it in an earthenware dish lined with 600 g. (1 lb. 5 oz., $3\frac{1}{2}$ cups) potatoes cut to look like big olives or new potatoes, 150 g. (5 oz., generous cup) small half-cooked onions and 150 g. (5 oz., generous cup) blanched and fried pork lardoons. Season these ingredients well. Pour on melted butter. Add a *bouquet garni.* Cook in a moderate oven, basting frequently.

Shoulder of mutton à la bonne femme II. ÉPAULE DE MOUTON À LA BONNE FEMME – Trim a shoulder of mutton. Cut off the end of the bone, but do not bone the meat. Brown it in butter in an earthenware dish and remove it from the dish. In the same butter, lightly brown 150 g. (5 oz., generous cup) blanched and drained pork lardoons and about 20 small onions. Take these ingredients out of the dish and put back the shoulder of mutton. Surround with 600 g. (1 lb. 5 oz., $3\frac{1}{2}$ cups) quartered potatoes, the small onions and the lardoons. Pour butter over the dish. Season. Cook in the oven, basting frequently.

Shoulder of mutton à la boulangère. ÉPAULE DE MOUTON À LA BOULANGÈRE – Bone the shoulder, season inside. (Roll lengthwise, if desired.) Tie. Cook for 30 minutes. Surround with 300 g. (11 oz., $2\frac{3}{4}$ cups) sliced onions or about 20 small onions tossed in butter. Season and pour the cooking butter over them. Finish cooking in the oven, basting frequently. Just before serving, add a few tablespoons thickened brown stock.

Shoulder of mutton à la bourgeoise. ÉPAULE DE MOUTON À LA BOURGEOISE – Bone the shoulder and stuff it if desired. Braise. When the joint is half-cooked, drain and put it in another braising pan or in a deep earthenware dish with 6 small carrots (200 grams, 7 oz.), cut to look like big olives and half-cooked in butter, 20 small glazed onions (150 grams, 5 oz.), 175 g. (6 oz., $1\frac{1}{2}$ cups) coarsely diced belly of pork, blanched and browned. Moisten with the strained cooking stock. Cover and finish cooking all together in the oven.

Braised shoulder of mutton with various garnishes. ÉPAULE DE MOUTON BRAISÉE – Bone the shoulder. Season inside with salt and pepper. Roll lengthwise and tie.

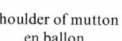

Put it in a buttered braising pan lined with pork skin or bacon rinds, carrots and onions sliced and tossed in butter. Surround the shoulder with its bones and trimmings cut into small pieces and tossed in butter. Add a large *bouquet garni* (q.v.). Season. Cover and cook gently for 15 minutes. Moisten with 2 dl. ($\frac{1}{3}$ pint, scant cup) dry white wine. Boil down. Add 4 dl. ($\frac{3}{4}$ pint, scant 2 cups) thickened brown stock and 3 tablespoons (scant $\frac{1}{4}$ cup) *Tomato sauce* (see SAUCE). Bring to the boil.

Cover and cook in the oven for about $1\frac{1}{2}$ hours. Drain and untie the shoulder. Glaze in the oven. Put it on a dish and surround with a suitable garnish. Boil down the braising stock, remove surplus fat, strain and pour over the meat.

Suitable garnishes for braised shoulder of mutton. All garnishes indicated for *Braised rib of mutton*, especially *Bretonne garnish* (see GARNISHES), various vegetable purées, dried vegetables in particular (see PURÉE), risotto, and pasta prepared in various ways.

Shoulder of mutton à la bretonne. ÉPAULE DE MOUTON À LA BRETONNE – Bone and braise. Garnish with *white haricot beans* or small *Kidney beans à la bretonne* (see BEANS), or with a purée of *White haricot beans à la bretonne* (see PURÉE). Pour the strained braising stock over the shoulder.

Shoulder of mutton with red cabbage à la flamande. ÉPAULE DE MOUTON AUX CHOUX ROUGES, À LA FLAMANDE – Bone the shoulder and stuff if desired. Roll lengthwise and tie. Braise until half-cooked. Line a deep earthenware dish with red cabbage prepared *à la flamande* (see CABBAGE) but which is only half-cooked. Lay the shoulder on this bed and cover with more red cabbage. Cover and cook slowly in the oven.

When the shoulder is ready, drain and untie it. Put it back in the dish on top of the cabbage. Pour over it a few tablespoons of stock.

Shoulder of mutton à la catalane or en pistache. ÉPAULE DE MOUTON À LA CATALANE (EN PISTACHE) – Bone the shoulder, roll lengthwise and tie. Put it in a saucepan lined with 1 large slice of raw ham (not smoked), 1 sliced onion and carrot.

Season. Pour over it 2 tablespoons (3 tablespoons) goose fat or lard. Cover and cook gently on the stove for 25 to 30 minutes. Take the shoulder and the slice of ham out of the pan. Brown 2 tablespoons (3 tablespoons) flour in it. Moisten with 2 dl. ($\frac{1}{3}$ pint, scant cup) white wine. Add 4 dl. ($\frac{3}{4}$ pint, scant 2 cups) brown stock or clear soup. Mix well; strain. Put the joint, and the slice of ham, diced, back in the saucepan. Add 50 blanched cloves of garlic and a *bouquet garni* (q.v.) containing 1 piece dried orange peel. Moisten with the cooking stock. Cover and cook in a moderate oven for about 1 hour.

Drain and untie the shoulder. Put on a dish. Pour over it the sauce and the cloves of garlic.

The sauce for *pistache* of mutton can also be thickend with breadcrumbs.

Shoulder of mutton à la chipolata. ÉPAULE DE MOUTON À LA CHIPOLATA – Bone and braise. Proceed as for *Shoulder of mutton à la bourgeoise,* garnishing with chipolata sausages. (See GARNISHES.)

Shoulder of mutton in jelly. ÉPAULE DE MOUTON EN GELÉE – Bone the shoulder. Stuff with a *Fine forcemeat* (see FORCEMEAT) mixed with lean diced ham with 1 or 2 eggs to bind it. Roll lengthwise and tie. Put the shoulder in a stock mixed with *mirepoix* (q.v.). Cook for 1 hour. Drain the meat and leave it to cool under a weight. Untie. Skim off surplus fat from the stock. Mix in a little concentrated and strained aspic jelly. Pour over the meat and leave to cool. Put the shoulder in an earthenware dish on a foundation of jelly set firmly; cover completely with half-set jelly. Leave until quite cold. Serve in the earthenware dish.

Shoulder of mutton with rice. ÉPAULE DE MOUTON AU RIZ – Bone. Roll lengthwise and tie. Braise until three-parts cooked, moistening with a fair amount of rather thin stock. Drain and put it in another saucepan. Add 500 g. (1 lb. 3 oz., $3\frac{1}{2}$ cups) parboiled rice. Moisten with the strained stock. Finish cooking all together.

Stuffed shoulder of mutton, braised. ÉPAULE DE MOUTON FARCIE BRAISÉE – Bone the shoulder and season inside. Stuff with *Fine pork stuffing* (see FORCEMEATS, *Pork forcemeat or stuffing, fine*) mixed with 150 g. (5 oz., $1\frac{1}{4}$ cups) chopped onions cooked in butter until very tender and 1 tablespoon chopped parsley. These quantities are for 500 g. (1 lb. 3 oz., generous 2 cups) stuffing. Season well with salt, pepper and spices. Roll the shoulder lengthwise and tie. Braise as indicated in the recipe for *Braised mutton with various garnishes.*

Garnish as indicated in the preceding recipe. Pour on the braising stock, boiled down and strained.

Stuffed shoulder of mutton en daube à la bourguignonne. ÉPAULE DE MOUTON FARCIE EN DAUBE À LA BOURGUIGNONNE – Bone the shoulder. Stuff it with fine pork stuffing (see FORCEMEATS FOR STUFFINGS), adding to this 1 chopped onion cooked slowly in butter until very tender, 3 tablespoons (scant $\frac{1}{4}$ cup) dry *duxelles* (q.v.), and some chopped parsley.

Roll the shoulder into a ball (*en ballon* or *en musette*, see above), and braise in red wine. When it is half-cooked, drain, untie and put it in a deep earthenware dish. Add 200 g. (7 oz., 2 cups) mushrooms tossed in butter, 20 small glazed onions (150 grams, 5 oz.), 125 g. ($4\frac{1}{2}$ oz., 1 cup) coarsely diced belly of pork, blanched and browned. Moisten with the strained cooking stock. Add 2 tablespoons (3 tablespoons) blazing brandy. Cover the dish. Seal with flour-and-

Untrimmed shoulder of mutton (*Larousse*)

Rolled shoulder of mutton (*Larousse*)

water paste and cook in the oven for 45 minutes to 1 hour, according to the size of the shoulder.

Shoulder of mutton with turnips. ÉPAULE DE MOUTON AUX NAVETS – Bone the shoulder and stuff if desired. Roll lengthwise and tie. Braise until three-parts cooked. Drain, put the shoulder in another saucepan with 1 kg. (2 lb. 3 oz., scant 6 cups) tender turnips, cut to look like big olives and browned in butter, and 30 small onions 250 g. (9 oz.) also browned in the frying pan.

Skim all fat off the braising stock, strain, and pour over the dish. Finish cooking all together.

Sliced mutton. ÉMINCÉS DE MOUTON – Prepare with cooked mutton, in the same way as *Sliced beef* (see BEEF).

Braised sheep's tails (Carême's recipe). QUEUES DE MOUTON BRAISÉES – 'Take 12 medium-sized tails. Soak in cold water for 1 hour. Pour boiling water over them. Line a saucepan with mutton trimmings, a *bouquet garni* (q.v.), 2 onions, 2 carrots. Cover with thin strips of belly of pork. Tie the tails in pairs. Moisten with good clear soup. Cook for $1\frac{1}{2}$ hours. Drain the tails and put them in a press. Skim all fat off the stock; boil down almost to a jelly. When the tails are cold, trim them and heat slowly in the stock, reducing this slowly to a liquid jelly. Turn the tails over and over so that they are thoroughly impregnated with this liquid jelly. Serve them like cutlets, with *Espagnole sauce* (see SAUCE), boiled down (reduced) to half its volume.'

Grilled sheep's tails (Carême's recipe). QUEUES DE MOUTON PANÉES GRILLÉES – Prepare 12 sheep's tails as indicated in the previous recipe, trim them, dip them in melted butter and breadcrumbs, and grill until they are a good colour. Serve with *Hachée sauce* or a thin *Tomato sauce* (see SAUCE).

Sheep's tongues – See OFFAL OR VARIETY MEATS.

Sheep's trotters – See OFFAL OR VARIETY MEATS.

MYRTLE. MYRTE – Fragrant evergreen shrub common all over Europe. Myrtle berries were used in place of pepper among the ancients, and even gave their name to a stew, *myrtalum*. There was also a spiced wine made from myrtle (*Myrtidanum*).

The pepper myrtle has leaves similar to those of the bay tree. Its powdered berries are known as *Jamaican pepper*.

MYSÖST – See CHEESE.

NAGE (À LA) – Method of preparing freshwater crayfish, spiny lobsters and small lobsters. These are cooked in a *court-bouillon* (q.v.) flavoured with herbs. Shellfish prepared in this way can be eaten cold or hot, and are served in this *court-bouillon.* (See CRAYFISH, LOBSTER, SPINY LOBSTER.)

NALESNIKI (Russian cookery) – *Cromesqui* (q.v.) made from a mixture of white cheese and butter, used to fill a pancake made without sugar. The pancake is then dipped in butter and deep-fried.

NANDU. NANDOU – A kind of ostrich. The flesh of its young is tender and its eggs are edible.

NANTAIS – Nantes duckling sometimes appears on French menus simply as *Nantais* (see DUCKLING).

NANTAIS – Small almond biscuit.

Put 500 g. (18 oz., $4\frac{1}{2}$ cups) sieved flour in a circle on the table. In the middle place 125 g. ($4\frac{1}{2}$ oz., generous cup) almonds pounded in a mortar, 250 g. (9 oz., scant $1\frac{1}{4}$ cup) fine sugar, 250 g. (9 oz., scant $1\frac{1}{4}$ cup) butter, 3 eggs and 1 dl. (6 tablespoons, scant $\frac{1}{2}$ cup) kirsch. Work this dough in the usual way. Leave to stand in a cool place.

Roll out the dough. Cut it into circles with a fluted pastry-cutter, put the biscuits on a baking sheet, brush with egg, dust with sugar mixed with chopped almonds, and bake in a moderate oven.

Nantes cookies. PETITS PAINS DE NANTES – Put 100 g. (4 oz., $\frac{1}{2}$ cup) softened butter into a bowl with 100 g. (4 oz., $\frac{1}{2}$ cup) castor sugar, a pinch of salt, $\frac{1}{2}$ teaspoon baking powder and the rind of 1 lemon or orange grated on to the sugar. Mix until a creamy consistency is reached. Then, whisking vigorously, incorporate 2 whole eggs, and 125 g. ($4\frac{1}{2}$ oz., scant $1\frac{1}{4}$ cup) sieved flour.

Put the mixture into tartlet tins, buttered and sprinkled with finely shredded, well-dried almonds. Bake in a moderate oven.

Turn out on to a wire tray. Brush the top with apricot jam, then ice with maraschino-flavoured *Fondant icing* (see ICING) and sprinkle with pink sugar.

NANTUA (À LA) – Name given to various dishes, which are garnished with freshwater crayfish tails or, where appropriate, covered with crayfish purée.

NAPKINS. SERVIETTES DE TABLE – Table napkins should be folded simply, and not in the fanciful shapes that they used to be given.

NAPOLITAIN – Large cakes which, like *breton* and *Savoie* cakes, *millefeuilles* and *croquembouche*, were once used to decorate elaborate buffets.

In former times it was customary to place at each end of a table set for a large dinner party either an imposing decorated pastry or a heap of crayfish or other shellfish. This practice has now been abandoned, and although *napolitains* are still made, they are now usually small.

The name of this cake suggests that it was created in Naples. It is more probably the invention of Carême, who made great set pieces of large and magnificent pastries to which he himself gave the names.

Ingredients. For a large napolitain: 365 g. ($\frac{3}{4}$ lb., $2\frac{1}{2}$ cups) blanched sweet almonds, $12\frac{1}{2}$ g. ($\frac{1}{2}$ oz., 1 tablespoon) blanched bitter almonds, 175 g. (6 oz., $\frac{3}{4}$ cup) fine sugar, 250 g. (9 oz., scant $1\frac{1}{4}$ cups) butter, 500 g. (18 oz., $4\frac{1}{2}$ cups) sieved cake flour, 30 g. (1 oz., 2 tablespoons) sugar flavoured with lemon (or any other flavouring) a pinch of salt.

Method. Pound the almonds in a mortar to a fine paste with a little white of egg to bind them. Add the fine sugar, the flavoured sugar, the butter and flour. Pounding constantly, add as many whole eggs as are required to make a smooth and rather stiff paste. Take it out of the mortar and leave to stand in a cool place for a time.

Roll out the paste. Cut it into square, round or hexagonal pieces. With a pastry cutter 2 inches in diameter, cut out the middle of each piece, except for 2, which will serve for the top and bottom layer of cake.

Bake these layers of pastry in a hot oven and when they are quite cold spread each one with a different fruit purée or jelly. Put the layers one on top of the other, using an uncut layer to form the base, with alternate layers of jam or jelly. Cover with the other uncut layer. When the cake is built up, coat with apricot jam, pipe with *Royal icing* (see ICING).

NARBONNE – Town in the Aude district, regarded as one of the capitals of French viticulture, for it is in the Narbonne region that many of the ordinary table wines are made.

NARCISSUS. NARCISSE – The bulbs of this plant are edible and are used for food in some regions. They are cooked in the same way as Jerusalem artichokes.

NARWHAL. NARVAL – A cetacean found in Arctic seas. It has a unique defensive weapon in the form of the left canine tooth which can be up to 3 m. (9 ft.) in length. This weapon, believed to belong to the fabulous unicorn, changed hands at very high prices in the Middle Ages, for it was believed to have the power of divining poisons.

Nowadays, the narwhal is chiefly used for the oil processed from its fat. The flesh is eaten by the people of Greenland, probably when no other food is available.

NASTURTIUM. CAPUCINE – Edible and decorative plant. Its flowers and leaves are similar to watercress in taste. It used, at one time, to be called Mexican cress and Jesuits' cress because it was brought into Europe by the Jesuits.

Nasturtium flowers are used in salads. The leaves when young can also be used in salads, like cress. The buds and the seeds, when they are still tender, are pickled in vinegar like capers.

NATURISM, NATURIST. NATURISME, NATURISTE – A doctrine which preaches the return to nature, with regard to clothing as well as food.

Naturism prescribes a much more rigorous diet than vegetarianism. According to the apostles who preach this regenerative doctrine, diet must be made up entirely of raw fruit and vegetables, with some relaxation which permits the seasoning of these natural foods and the preparation of cereal porridges.

NAVARIN – This name is used expressly for a *ragoût* of mutton made either with small onions and potatoes or with different vegetables such as carrots, turnips, small onions, new potatoes and green peas. In this case the dish must be described as *à la printanière* (see MUTTON).

The term *navarin* is sometimes wrongly applied to *ragoûts* of shellfish or poultry; it should only be used of mutton dishes or, in exceptional cases, lamb.

NEAPOLITAN SLICES. TRANCHES NAPOLITAINES – Mass-produced Neapolitan ice creams sold in cafés and some restaurants. They are made of alternate layers of plain ice cream and mousse mixture, cut into slices from a larger block.

NECTARINE – Smooth-skinned variety of peach. It is eaten raw, like the peach, and can be cooked like peaches (see PEACH). It is also called *brugnon* in French.

NEEDLE. AIGUILLE –

Larding needle. AIGUILLE À PIQUER – Small-size larding needle, pointed at one end and pronged at the other, used for piercing and larding various substances with thin strips of bacon. It is with a larding needle that we stud fillet of beef, calves' sweetbreads, small pieces of meat, poultry and winged game and different cuts of venison with pieces of bacon, pork or ham fat.

Trussing needle. AIGUILLE À BRIDER – Steel pin pointed at one end and pierced at the other. A trussing needle is used for trussing poultry and game.

NEF (Ship) – This name was given in France to a piece of goldsmith's work made in the form of a ship, which contained cutlery, napery, etc., used at the royal table, such as the salt cellar, the great carvers and the table napkins in scented sachets.

All persons, even princesses, passing by the royal *nef* had to salute it.

NÉGUS – Wine spiced with sugar, lemons and nutmeg.

NEIGE DE FLORENCE – Delicate pasta product used in clear soup. This pasta, which the guests themselves put into their plates of consommé, is presented in the form of flakes, white and very light. Hence its name, 'Florentine snow'.

NELUSKO – Iced *petits fours* which are made as follows:

Steep cherries in brandy. Drain them. Put them on a napkin to dry them slightly. Make a *Fondant icing* (see ICING) and warm it gently. While it is being warmed in a *bain-marie* (q.v.), slit and stone each cherry. Put them back on the napkin with the holes upward. Fill the cherries with a little *Bar-le-Duc* redcurrant jam, without pips (see JAMS AND JELLIES, *Bar-le-Duc currant jelly*). A forcing bag may be used for this operation. Flavour the fondant icing, which must remain thick, with a little of the brandy from the cherries. Heat the fondant.

Using a skewer and taking care to keep the holes in the cherries upward, dip them in the icing. The thicker it is, the more liqueur and the better the sweet.

The dipping must be carried out quickly, for the stoned cherries, filled with *Bar-le-Duc* jam, are very moist, and the moisture will immediately mix with the icing and melt it.

As soon as the *neluskos* are cold, put them in silver-paper cases, as the syrup always manages to ooze through ordinary paper.

NEMOURS (Tartlets) – Line tartlet tins with *Flaky pastry dough* (see DOUGH). Put a little mirabelle jam (see MARMALADE, *Plum marmalade*) at the bottom of each one. On top of the jam, pipe some *Chou paste* (see DOUGH). Bake in a hot oven. Sprinkle with icing sugar.

NÉNUPHAR (Water lily) – Aquatic plant with a starchy root which is used as food in certain parts of the world. The seeds, too, are used, mostly in Chinese cookery.

NÉROLI – A volatile oil extracted from orange blossom.

This oil is used in confectionery, and in the manufacture of some liqueurs.

NÉROLI (Pâtisserie) – Pound in a mortar 125 g. ($4\frac{1}{2}$ oz., 1 cup) blanched almonds with 3 eggs. Add 200 g. (7 oz., scant cup) fine sugar, the candied peel of 3 oranges chopped fine, and $\frac{1}{2}$ dl. (3 tablespoons, scant $\frac{1}{4}$ cup) orange-blossom water or 1 teaspoon orange extract. Work this mixture thoroughly with the pestle.

Put the mixture in a bowl. Add 60 g. ($2\frac{1}{2}$ oz., 5 tablespoons) melted butter and 30 g. (1 oz., $\frac{1}{4}$ cup) cornflour (cornstarch). Mix well.

Fill small buttered tins with the mixture, sprinkle with chopped almonds and bake in a moderate oven.

NESSELRODE – An iced sweet, usually known as *Nesselrode pudding* (see PUDDING).

NESTS. NIDS – Edible nests are made in various ways. They are used for the presentation of small tit-bits.

Potato nests. These are like little baskets made with matchstick potatoes, which are put in small wire baskets shaped like nests, and deep-fried in boiling fat. Fried food of various kinds is served in these nests. Or, after lining them with pancakes, various *ragoûts* (q.v.) may be served in them. (See QUAIL, *Quails in a nest*.)

Swallows' nests. NIDS D'HIRONDELLES – Nests built by salanganes. They are much sought after by Chinese gourmets.

The salangane builds its nest with its saliva. Just before the mating season, the bird's saliva glands become enlarged and secrete a thick, viscous, glutinous liquid containing 90 per cent of a protein which is insoluble in water.

The nests, constructed in layers, placed one on top of the other, are font-shaped and are attached to the sides of rocks in almost inaccessible grottos on the coast of Annam, in Java, and on one or two islands of the Malay Archipelago.

Collecting these nests is a difficult and dangerous occupation, and only the high price paid for them can explain the risks taken by men engaged in 'hunting the nests'.

Before being sold for food, the nests undergo complicated processing. They are washed several times in hot water, kneaded with groundnut oil which is then washed out in a

Swallow's nest

further bath of hot water. The nests are then very carefully cleared of all down and feathers with pincers.

Particularly enjoyed by gourmets of China, swallows' nests are generally eaten in the form of soup. After being dipped in hot water they are added to carefully clarified beef or chicken broth, and cooked for half an hour in a double saucepan. For every bowl of soup of 300 to 400 g. (11 to 14 oz.), a nest weighing 8 to 15 g. ($\frac{1}{4}$ to $\frac{1}{2}$ oz.) is required (see SOUPS AND BROTHS, *Consommé with birds' nests*).

NETTLE. ORTIE – Weed with stinging hairs on leaves, full of formic acid, which provokes skin eruption. Some species of this plant, such as *white dead nettle* and *blind nettle*, or *Lamium album*, are edible and used like sorrel, as a vegetable or in soups.

The young leaves, buds and roots are used as a purifier of the digestive and renal tracts, and to combat malaria.

NEUFCHÂTEL – See CHEESE.

NÉVA (À LA) – Method of preparing poulards (see CHICKEN).

NIÇOISE (À LA) – Method of preparing various dishes, all of which have tomatoes among their ingredients. They are usually flavoured with garlic.

NIGELLA. NIGELLE – Name given to a number of plants of the *Ranunculus* family, whose seeds are used as a spice. Some varieties have aromatic and pungent seeds which can be used instead of pepper. Nigella is also known as *fennel flower* or *devil-in-the-bush*.

Cultivated nigella is used as a spice in Egypt.

NIOLO – See CHEESE.

NITROGEN. AZOTE – Colourless, tasteless, scentless permanent gas forming 78·1 per cent of the atmosphere; it enters into the composition of many of the substances used as food. (See ALBUMINOIDS.)

NIVERNAIS AND MORVAN – The culinary repertoire of this ancient province, which roughly corresponds to the Nièvre *département* of today, has no dishes in the grand manner, but the foodstuffs produced in this area are excellent. The livestock produce meat of the highest quality, cattle reared and nurtured in the rich plains of the Loire (Charolais cattle, locally bred) are especially prized for the fine quality of their meat. For delicacy of flavour, the sheep rival those reared in the Bourbonnais and Berry districts. The pigs of the Nivernais province are equally excellent, and very good poultry is bred here. That of Morvan is especially delicate. Succulent winged and ground game is fairly abundant in this region.

In the rivers and small lakes of the Nivernais and Morvan provinces fish of all kinds abound. These provide the materials for delicious *matelotes* (q.v.). River trout and crayfish are plentiful.

The kitchen gardens and orchards also yield very good products. Pot vegetables such as carrots and onions are especially flavoursome, and it is because of the fine quality of its vegetables that the name *Nivernaise* is given to one of the best garnishes for meat dishes in the classic culinary repertoire (see GARNISHES).

The best known cheese of the region is that called *fromage sec* (dry cheese) made by drying white cheese in straw baskets, draining them well and dusting them with pepper.

Culinary specialities – *Cabbage soup with pork fat; Nivernais hot-pot; mixed vegetable soup, country style; chitterlings and baby chitterlings of Clamecy, Saveloy; cooking sausage* (*with garlic*)*; beursaudes* (pork greaves); *Morvan smoked ham; black puddings with wild thyme; griaudes; matelotes of Loire fish; fricassée of pike; river trout à la meunière; freshwater crayfish in court-bouillon; Nivernaise omelette* (a flat omelette, filled with sorrel, ham and chives); *beef daube* (made with a lot of carrots); *grilled beef à la marinière* (similar to charcoal grilled beef); *veal stewed in red wine; grenadins of veal of Corbigny; tripe à la morvandelle* (similar to *tripe à la mode de Caen*)*; pig's liver with onions; eel galette; griaude galette; chicken en barboille* (chicken in red wine, the sauce thickened with chicken's blood); *rabbit en barboille; civet of hare* (in the Nivernais district turnips are added to the civet); *saupiquet des Amognes; potato pâté; treuffes* (potatoes) *en tourtière* (baked in a pie-dish); *leek tart* (a kind of *flamiche*)*; dandelion salad with bacon; grapiaux* (large pancakes cooked in melted pork fat).

Among the Nivernais sweets, pastries and confectionery are: *Flamusse aux pommes* (a special kind of apple flan); *pâté aux poires* (pear paste); *sour milk fritters; galettes aux griaudes; croquets* (*petits fours*) from Nevers and Prémery; *nougatines* from Nevers; *barley-sugar* from Morvan; *négus* (a kind of soft caramel); *marzipan sweets* from Decize.

Wines – Nivernais is the region that produces those excellent white wines, Pouilly-sur-Loire and Pouilly-Fumé. The *appellation* is determined by the variety of grape used.

Pouilly-sur-Loire is made from the Chasselas grape. It is fresh and versatile and should be drunk young. Pouilly-Fumé is derived from the Sauvignon grape. It is a distinguished wine, dry and elegant with a delicate bouquet. Connoisseurs choose it to drink with fish, shellfish and seafood.

Both wines are produced in the region around the town of Pouilly, situated on the right bank of the Loire.

NOEKKELÖST – See CHEESE.

NOËL PETERS – See RESTAURANTS OF BYGONE DAYS.

NIVERNAISE (À LA) – Name of a garnish served with intermediate meat courses. It is made up of carrots cut to look like olives, and small glazed onions.

NOISETTE – Small individual portion of meat, particularly a slice cut from the fillet, rib or leg of mutton or lamb.

A *noisette*, as its name suggests, must be round in shape. Its average weight should be from 70 to 90 g. (2 to 3 oz.).

For the preparation of *noisettes*, see LAMB, MUTTON.

More loosely, the term is used to describe a small slice of veal fillet or fillet of beef.

NOISETTE BUTTER – See BUTTER.

NOISETTE POTATOES – Potatoes shaped with a ball scoop to look like hazelnuts (see POTATOES), cooked in butter and slightly browned.

NOISETTE SAUCE – See SAUCE.

NOISETTINES – Small cakes made by putting together two oval layers of short pastry with *Frangipane cream* (see CREAMS) flavoured with hazelnuts.

They can also be made of large round layers of short pastry filled with hazelnut cream.

NONAT – There is some doubt as to whether this tiny Mediterranean fish is a separate species or, according to a view quite widely held, merely the fry of the goby. The *nonat* is a great delicacy. It can be eaten only in places close to its fishing grounds.

The best way of preparing nonats is deep-frying. They can also be used as an *hors-d'œuvre*, and as a garnish for omelettes.

NONNETTE (Iced gingerbread) – Small round gingerbread which is made industrially. The chief centres for the manufacture of *nonnettes* are Dijon and Reims.

NONPAREILLE – Name given in France to small capers pickled in vinegar.

The same name is given to coloured granulated sugar used to decorate sweets and cakes.

There is also a French variety of pear called *nonpareille*. It is large, ripens in the autumn, and is somewhat tart in flavour.

NOODLES. NOUILLE – Pasta made with flour, eggs and water. Noodles can be eaten fresh or dried.

For the food value of noodles, see ITALIAN PASTA.

DRIED NOODLES OR VERY SMALL NOODLES. NOUILLES SÈCHES, NOUILLETTES – These can be bought ready-made. They are poached in salt water as described for freshly made noodles and macaroni. After poaching they are prepared like the latter.

Dried noodles are served by themselves or are used as garnish for meat, fish, eggs, etc. When noodles are used as garnish, they are prepared with butter or stock.

Pasta should not be poached in a *bouillon* or in stock, as that toughens them without improving their flavour. Three-quarters cook the pasta in salted water, drain, and simmer gently for a few minutes in a *bouillon*.

FRESH NOODLES. NOUILLES FRAÎCHES – Fresh noodles can be bought ready-made in food stores. In France, especially in Alsace, housewives make them at home.

Ingredients. 500 g. (18 oz., $4\frac{1}{2}$ cups) sifted flour, 3 whole eggs and 6 yolks, 2 teaspoons salt and about 3 tablespoons (scant $\frac{1}{4}$ cup) water. The pasta is more delicate if only yolks of eggs are used. This depends on what the noodles are to be used for; in some cases they are made with whole eggs.

Method. Sieve the flour. Arrange it in a circle on the table. Put the salt in the middle, dissolving it in water. Add the eggs and the yolks. Mix the flour a little at a time with the eggs. Knead thoroughly to make sure that the flour is well mixed and to ensure a smooth mixture.

The pasta must be very firm. Wrap in a thin cloth to prevent it from drying, and leave to stand for at least an hour, until it loses its elasticity. When a large quantity of noodles is required, make them several hours beforehand. It is then easier to cut them into strips.

Divide the dough into pieces about the size of an egg and roll into balls. Roll out each piece into the shape of a large thin pancake.

Spread the rolled-out dough on baking sheets covered with sheets of paper. Leave to dry for 50 minutes. Lightly dust the pancakes with flour. Roll them and cut into whorls 2 mm. ($\frac{1}{16}$ inch) wide. Spread them out on a baking sheet.

These are very fine noodles. If the noodles are required for garnishing they should be cut about $\frac{1}{2}$ cm. ($\frac{1}{4}$ inch) wide.

Fresh noodles à l'alsacienne. NOUILLES FRAÎCHES À L'ALSACIENNE – Prepare the noodles as indicated for *Fresh noodles in butter* (see below).

Put them in a pie dish and sprinkle on the top a handful of noodles which have been lightly browned in butter.

Boiled fresh noodles. NOUILLES AU NATUREL – Plunge 250 g. (9 oz.) fresh noodles into $2\frac{1}{2}$ litres ($4\frac{1}{2}$ pints, $5\frac{1}{2}$ pints) boiling water, with $1\frac{1}{2}$ teaspoons salt per litre ($1\frac{3}{4}$ pints, generous quart). Boil fast for 8 to 10 minutes. Drain the noodles. Put them in a shallow pan and evaporate excess moisture over low heat. Serve in a well-heated deep dish.

Fresh noodles in butter. NOUILLES FRAÎCHES AU BEURRE – Cook the noodles in salted water and drain. Put them in a pan and dry them slowly on the stove.

Cut 75 g. (3 oz., 6 tablespoons) butter into small pieces so that the butter will melt quickly. Add to the noodles and mix well. Season. Serve in a pie dish.

Fresh noodles with brown butter. NOUILLES FRAÎCHES AU BEURRE NOISETTE – Cook the noodles in salted water and drain. Dry and put them in a warm dish. Heat 75 g. (3 oz., 6 tablespoons) butter in a frying pan until it has become a nut-brown colour. Pour it over the noodles and mix gently with a fork.

Fresh noodles au gratin. NOUILLES FRAÎCHES AU GRATIN – Cook the noodles in salted water as described in the recipe for *Fresh noodles in butter*.

Drain the noodles. Add 50 g. (2 oz., $\frac{1}{2}$ cup) mixed grated Gruyère and Parmesan cheese and 50 g. (2 oz., $\frac{1}{4}$ cup) butter. Season with salt and pepper and a little grated nutmeg. Spread the noodles evenly on a buttered dish, sprinkled with grated cheese.

Sprinkle more grated cheese on the noodles, add a little melted butter and brown in a hot oven.

Fresh noodles with stock. NOUILLES FRAÎCHES AU JUS – Cook and drain the noodles and sprinkle them with several tablespoons of thick brown veal stock, beef stock or any other slightly strengthened meat stock.

Leave to simmer for a few minutes on the side of the stove and serve in a pie dish.

Fresh noodles à l'italienne. NOUILLES FRAÎCHES A L'ITALIENNE – Cook the noodles, drain, and finish off with butter and grated cheese as described in the recipe for *Fresh noodles au gratin*, but do not brown them. Serve in a pie dish.

This dish can be made with Parmesan cheese only or with Gruyère cheese only, but the mixture of both cheeses gives a better result.

Fresh noodles à la lyonnaise. NOUILLES FRAÎCHES À LA LYONNAISE – Prepare the noodles as described in the recipe for *Fresh noodles in butter*. Arrange them in a pie dish and garnish the top with 3 tablespoons (scant $\frac{1}{4}$ cup) finely minced onions fried in butter.

Fresh noodles à la milanaise. NOUILLES FRAÎCHES À LA MILANAISE – Cook the noodles, drain, and finish them as described in the recipe for *Macaroni à la milanaise* (see MACARONI).

Fresh noodles à la napolitaine. NOUILLES FRAÎCHES À LA NAPOLITAINE – Cook the noodles, drain, and finish the dish as described in the recipe for *Macaroni à la napolitaine* (see MACARONI).

NOQUES (Alsatian cookery) – Work to a paste, in a warmed bowl, 250 g. (9 oz., scant $1\frac{1}{4}$ cups) butter seasoned with salt, pepper and a touch of grated nutmeg, adding 2 whole eggs and 2 yolks, 150 g. (5 oz., $1\frac{1}{4}$ cups) sieved flour and a stiffly beaten egg white. Divide this mixture into parts, each about the size of a hazelnut. Poach in boiling salt water. Drain. To serve, sprinkle with grated Parmesan, and browned butter.

Noques are also served in soup.

Noques à la viennoise (Austrian sweet) – These *noques* are

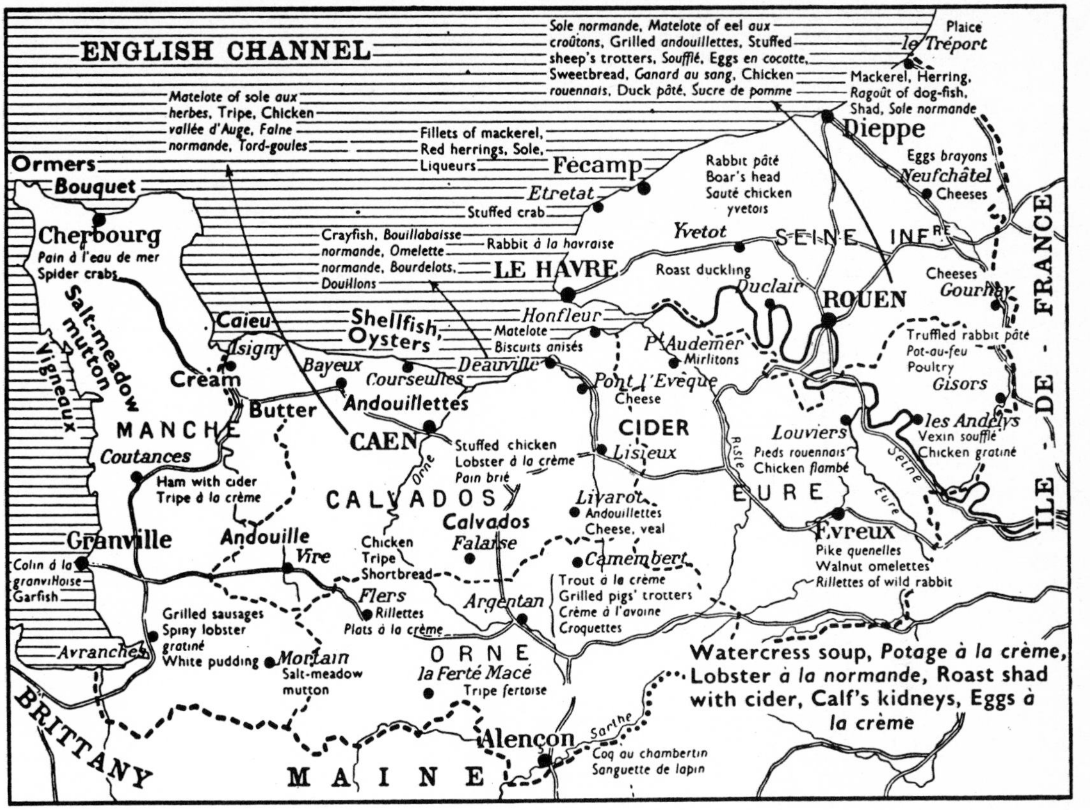

Gastronomic map of Normandy

a kind of small *quenelle* (q.v.), similar to *Snow eggs* (see EGGS), but less delicate. They can be made lighter by beating the egg whites. These *noques* are served with vanilla-flavoured custard.

Ingredients. 125 g. ($4\frac{1}{2}$ oz., generous $\frac{1}{2}$ cup) butter, 100 g. (4 oz., $\frac{1}{2}$ cup) sugar, 100 g. (4 oz., 1 cup) sieved flour, 9 eggs, 1 pod vanilla, 5 dl. (scant pint, $2\frac{1}{4}$ cups) milk, 1 dl. (6 tablespoons, scant $\frac{1}{2}$ cup) double cream, a pinch of table salt.

Put the butter in a bowl and work with a spatula until it is smooth and creamy. Work in a pinch of salt, 2 tablespoons (3 tablespoons) sugar, and 5 yolks of egg added one by one. Add half the double cream.

Beat all the ingredients vigorously together. When the mixture is very fluffy, whisk with an egg-whisk in place of the spatula. While whisking, sprinkle in the flour, and mix. Beat a white of egg to a stiff foam and blend it in. Mix in, one by one, 3 unbeaten egg whites.

The *noques* are poached in sweetened milk in the same way as *Snow eggs* (see EGGS).

Poach the *noques* without bringing the liquid to the boil. (If the milk is allowed to boil, this causes the *noques* to swell unduly.) While they are poaching, turn them over gently with a skimmer. When they are ready, drain them.

To make the custard which goes with the *noques*, use the milk in which they have been poached, adding the double cream and 4 egg yolks. Beat the yolks and the cream with an egg-whisk, and when they are well mixed blend in the boiling sweetened milk. Thicken this custard by heating it on the stove for a few seconds, but do not let it boil. Strain it through a fine sieve on to the *noques*.

This sweet can be served hot or cold.

NORMANDE (À LA) – Method of preparation used mainly for fish braised in white wine, especially sole.

The usual garnish for these fish, which are coated with *Normande sauce* (see SAUCE), comprises poached oysters, shelled shrimps, mushrooms, strips of truffle, fried gudgeon (or smelt), freshwater crayfish in *court-bouillon* (q.v.), and lozenge-shaped pieces of bread fried in butter. Poached and shelled mussels are often added to this garnish (see SOLE, *Sole à la normande*).

Small cuts of meat and chicken can be prepared *à la normande*. After they are cooked they have cider poured over them. The sauce is enriched with a little Calvados.

Some species of winged game, especially partridge, can be prepared *à la normande* (see PARTRIDGE).

There are also a large number of preparations called *à la normande* in pastry-making.

NORMANDY – Province of high gastronomic repute; the Normandy table is regarded as one of the best in all the provinces of France.

Normandy produces excellent butter and cream, which are used in all characteristic dishes of the region.

The cattle and sheep nurtured on its rich pastures provide high-grade meat. Its salt-meadow sheep are particularly good.

Fruit production is a very important industry. Normandy apples have a great reputation.

Its coastal waters provide an abundance of sole, brill, turbot, mackerel and many other delicate fish. The Seine shad and the salmon and trout of Bresles and the Arques are very delicate fish.

There is no lack of shellfish. There are the white oysters of Dives, Luc-sur-mer and Courseulles, the mussels from the natural mussel-beds, which are as fat as one could wish; clams; *fléons* (*donax*) cockles. Giant mussels, called *caieu*, are found at Isigny, and there are the *ormiers* (or haliotis) of the Cap de la Hague, the winkles or periwinkles and also the prawns (*bouquet*) of Cherbourg, and the *demoiselles* (small lobsters) of Caen, Cherbourg and Dieppe.

The milk and cream of Normandy have a well-deserved reputation. The most famous butter is that of Isigny. This butter is the basis of excellent cheeses: Camembert, Livarot, Pont-l'Évêque.

The winged and ground game shot in Normandy is highly prized.

This region has no vineyards. Wine, moreover, is not much drunk by its people. They have, however, excellent cider and perry to drink with the special dishes of their province. The cider of the Auge Valley has the highest reputation. The pears of Clécy, Alemon, Argentan, Écouche and Domfront are highly prized. And there is the cider spirit called Calvados, and the celebrated Benedictine liqueur made at Fécamp.

Culinary specialities – A distinctive feature of a large number of the dishes of Normandy is that they are cooked in cream. Many dishes are cooked with a special fat called *graisse normande*, which is made by melting together and clarifying equal quantities of pork fat and suet, flavoured with pot vegetables and herbs and seasoned with salt and pepper. This fat gives a special flavour to food cooked in it.

Among the culinary specialities of the region are: *soup normande*; the famous *Madame Poulard omelette; omelette aux coques; Matelote normande*, made with saltwater fish; the true *sole à la normande*, which is a way of stewing soles in cream, and has nothing in common with the *sole à la normande* served in Paris restaurants; *sole à la dieppoise* (and other sea fish prepared in the same way); *mussels à la marinière; seine shad stuffed and baked; tripe à la mode de Caen* and *tripe à la mode de la Ferté-Macé; sheep's trotters à la rouennaise; casserole of veal in cream; white pudding of l'Avranchin; duckling à la rouennaise*, which is prepared in different ways in Rouen and Duclair; *wood partridges flambés*; and the famous *Poulet à la crème* (chicken in cream) called *vallée d'Auge*.

Among the vegetables are *French beans in cream* and *salsify à la normande*.

The pork products of Rouen, Vire and other places, such as the chitterlings of Vire and the baby chitterlings of Caen, black and white puddings, sausages, etc., are excellent.

Large farm in Normandy

The cheeses of this region have a high reputation. The best known are: Pont-l'Évêque, Camembert, Livarot, Neufchâtel, Bondon, Gournay, and the famous small double-cream cheeses among which is the celebrated Gervais Petit-suisse.

Among the sweets and confectionery of Normandy are *terrinée* which is also called *tord-goule*; Normandy *bourdelots* (apple turnovers), made by cooking whole apples in a coating of pastry; *douillons*, made in the same way with pears; *galette normande; fouace* (hearth cake) from Caen, *roulettes* from Rouen, *mirlitons* from Rouen and Pont-Audemer, delicious *Normandy shortbread; duchesses de Normandie; norelles; boulots; rivets* and *chemineaux*, and the famous *sucres de pomme*.

NORVÉGIEN (Pâtisserie) – Pound in a mortar 250 g. (9 oz., scant 2 cups) sweet almonds and 1 tablespoon blanched apricot kernels, with 4 whole eggs. When the almonds are pounded to a smooth paste, add 275 g. (10 oz., $1\frac{1}{4}$ cups) fine sugar.

Blend this mixture thoroughly in a bowl and add 200 g. (7 oz., scant cup) softened butter. Work with a spatula until the mixture is frothy. Still stirring, add 25 g. (1 oz., $\frac{1}{4}$ cup) cornflour (cornstarch) and 1 small glass of kirsch.

Put the mixture into buttered moulds lined with buttered paper. Bake in a moderate oven.

NORVÉGIENNE (À LA) – Name given to various preparations in cookery and confectionery. It is more precisely used for ice cream inside a piping hot casing. This sweet is called *Omelette à la norvégienne* (see EGGS, *Norwegian omelette*).

The same name is also applied to certain methods of presenting cold fish or shellfish, such as salmon, lobster and spiny lobster.

NOUGAT – Sweet made with roasted almonds or walnuts, and honey or syrup.

The word derives from the Latin *nux*, nut (walnut) for it would appear that originally this sweet was made mainly with walnuts; nowadays it is generally made with almonds and sugar, honey being substituted occasionally for the latter. Industrially, it is made with hazelnuts or pistachios.

There are a great many kinds of nougat: hard or soft, white or coloured. White nougat is usually made industrially; Montélimar nougat enjoys a great reputation.

In the South of France, the oil-cake made from the residue of walnut oil is called *nougat*.

Almond nougat. NOUGAT AUX AMANDES – See ALMOND.

White nougat. NOUGAT BLANC – Cook together to the small crack degree (see SUGAR) 250 g. (9 oz., $\frac{3}{4}$ cup) honey and an equal quantity of sugar. Add 1 tablespoon orange-blossom water, and a stiffly beaten egg white.

Melt over a gentle flame, stirring, and bring the sugar to the ball degree. Add 500 g. (18 oz., $4\frac{1}{2}$ cups) sweet almonds which have been blanched, dried, chopped and heated.

Put this mixture in a flat baking tin lined with sheets of rice paper. Cover with sheets of the same paper. Place on top of the nougat a wooden board with a 1-kg. (2-lb.) weight on it. Leave until lukewarm. Cut into squares or other shapes.

Nougat with filberts, hazelnuts, pine kernels or pistachio nuts can be made in the same way.

NOUGATINE CAKES – Put into a deep, square, well-buttered baking tin, about $7\frac{1}{2}$ cm. (3 inches) in depth, *Genoese cake* mixture (see GENOESE) flavoured with vanilla. Bake, and leave to cool.

Cut the cake into squares and slice each across into 3 or

4 layers. Spread *Praline cream* (see CREAMS) on each layer. Build them up by putting the layers one on top of the other, and ice with *Chocolate fondant icing* (see ICING).

These cakes can be made separately in small square pieces instead out of one large cake.

NULLES – Amber and musk-flavoured dessert creams that used to be very popular in France.

'Whip together 4 or 5 egg yolks, a quantity of very fresh cream, lots of sugar and a pinch of salt.

'Cook in a shallow casserole. Brown quickly under a hot grill, sprinkle with perfumed water and musk-flavoured sugar, and serve.' (Lavarenne.)

NUT. NOIX – Name for a number of different types of fruit with a woody outer casing and a soft inner skin enclosing an edible kernel.

NUT-GALL. NOIX DE GALLE – Eastern peoples eat fleshy nut-gall. It is about the size of a lady apple, and grows on a species of sage bush.

In some places a nut-gall which grows on a species of ground-ivy is eaten.

NUTMEG. MUSCADE – Seed of the nutmeg tree, which grows in warm countries and is similar in appearance to the pear tree.

The nutmeg is oval in shape, rounded, greyish brown in colour, usually with a whitish coating of milk of lime. It contains 25 per cent fat (nutmeg butter), volatile oil, acid and starch. It is an aromatic spice, stimulating to the palate, and is used a good deal in cooking.

Nutmeg

OATMEAL. GRUAU D'AVOINE – Oats with the husk removed, the grain separated from the chaff and ground. Oatmeal is used in broths and porridge.

Oatmeal porridge – See PORRIDGE.

Oatmeal soup. POTAGE AU GRUAU D'AVOINE – Pour 4 tablespoons ($\frac{1}{3}$ cup) oatmeal into 1 litre ($1\frac{3}{4}$ pints, generous quart) stock. Mix well and simmer gently for 30 minutes. Add 50 g. (2 oz., $\frac{1}{4}$ cup) fresh butter and blend well. This soup can also be made with milk or water.

Cream of oatmeal soup. POTAGE CRÈME D'AVOINE – Boil the oatmeal as described in the recipe for *Oatmeal soup*. Strain through a coarse muslin cloth and bind with egg yolks, cream and fresh butter.

Oatmeal soup au naturel. POTAGE À L'AVOINE AU NATUREL – Soak crushed oat grains in warm water. Add salt, and cook in plenty of water, simmering very gently, for 4 hours.

Strain through a muslin bag, bind with a few tablespoons of cream or milk and a little fresh butter.

OATS. AVOINE – Cereal, the grain of which excels all others as fodder for horses, cattle and poultry.

It is also used as food for man in the form of fine flour (oatmeal), slightly coarser groats, and also flattened into what is known as rolled or flaked oats. It is used for porridge and for soups.

Oats are rich in phosphorus, iron and vitamins. They are a safe, recommendable food for children (especially as a breakfast dish), convalescents and anaemics. Oats contain a valuable growth-promoting hormone called *auxin*.

Roast oat grains have a smell which strongly resembles that of vanilla.

Because of its low gluten content, oatmeal flour does not produce malleable paste when mixed with water; it is, therefore, not a bread crop.

Sweetened cream of oats gruel. BOUILLIE À LA CRÈME D'AVOINE SUCRÉE – This dish is recommended mostly for children, elderly people and invalids. To ensure that the gruel is smooth, the oatmeal should be diluted, little by little, with cold liquid, then poured into sweetened boiling liquid (usually milk). Cook for 10 minutes, stirring with a wooden spoon.

OBA – Species of mango from Gabon (Africa) of which the fruit is called *ibas*; it contains a white oily almond which can be used in its natural state to prepare *pain de dika*. It tastes like cocoa.

The mango from Gabon was introduced into Europe in 1855.

OBLADE – Mediterranean fish, similar to bream (q.v.). It is cooked *à la meunière*, fried or boiled.

OCA, OKA-PLANT – This plant (*Oxalis tuberosa*) was introduced from South America into England in 1829. It is extensively cultivated in Peru and Bolivia and grows very well in England and Wales. It also grows wild in the forests of France. It has edible tubers which are washed, parboiled in salted boiling water and then prepared in different ways: *au beurre* (lightly fried); *à la crème*, in stock, etc.

OCTOPUS. POULPE – Marine cephalopod mollusc, known in Brittany under the names of *pieuvre* and *minard*; tough-fleshed, edible after prolonged beating.

Octopus à la provençale. POULPE À LA PROVENÇALE – Clean an octopus and leave it for as long as possible in running water. Drain, and beat it hard with big sticks so as to soften the flesh, which is always rather leathery.

Discard the eyes and mouth. Cut up the tentacles and middle into chunks of equal size. Blanch, drain and wipe them, and cook lightly in oil with some chopped onion. Simmer for a few moments. Pour in $\frac{1}{2}$ bottle dry white wine and an equal quantity of water. Add a *bouquet garni* (q.v.) and a crushed clove of garlic.

Cook until the pieces are quite tender, with the saucepan covered. Sprinkle with chopped parsley.

Octopus with rice. POULPE AU RIZ – Prepare the chunks of octopus as in the preceding recipe. When two-thirds cooked, put in the casserole 250 g. (9 oz., $1\frac{1}{4}$ cups) rice. Season with a pinch of saffron. Continue cooking for another 20 to 25 minutes.

Octopus may also be cut in pieces, deep-fried in oil, and served with spinach.

OFFAL (G.B.) or VARIETY MEATS (U.S.A.). ABATS DE BOUCHERIE – Terms which define various parts of the carcase. The offal or variety meats for beef, mutton and lamb, pork and veal are as follows:

Beef. BOEUF – *White*. Feet and stomachs (generally used in the preparation of tripe), tripe and brain.

Red. Lights, heart, liver, tongue and kidneys.

Mutton and Lamb. MOUTON, AGNEAU – Kidneys, tongue, brain, feet, animelles, stomachs and the 'pluck', that is, the heart, liver and lungs.

Pork. PORC – Kidneys, liver, brain, trotters and head. All the pig's entrails are used in pork butchery. The intestines are used as containers in the manufacture of sausages, saveloys, dried sausages and black (blood) puddings. Pig's blood is used in the manufacture of black puddings.

Veal. VEAU – Lights, heart, liver, mesentery, spinal marrow (amourette), head, sweetbread, trotters and kidneys.

BEEF or OX OFFAL or VARIETY MEATS. ABATS DE BOEUF – In the U.S.A., all parts of beef are called *beef*, whereas in England only the best cuts are called beef and the less choice are termed *ox*. Example: rump of beef, fillet of beef; ox liver, ox tongue.

Beef amourettes (ox marrow). AMOURETTE DE BOEUF – In French the name *amourette* defines the spinal marrow. The spinal marrow of beef or ox is used in cookery and even more so the spinal marrow of calves.

All methods of preparation given elsewhere for *Calves' (veal) amourettes* (which are more delicate in flavour than those of beef or oxen) are applicable to the *amourettes* of beef or ox.

Beef or ox brain. CERVELLE DE BOEUF – *Method of preparation.* Soak the brain at least 4 hours in cold water. Clean well; remove all the membranes which cover the brain. Soak once again in cold water to make quite white. Put into boiling strained *court-bouillon* (q.v.), prepared with water, sliced carrots and onions, a dash of vinegar or lemon juice, salt, sprig of thyme, bay leaf. Cook for 20 to 25 minutes.

Drain, and prepare as described in appropriate recipes.

If the brain is not to be used at once, keep in the *court-bouillon* in which it was cooked.

All the recipes given in this section for the preparation of *Calves' brains* (see below) can be applied to ox brains.

Beef or ox feet. PIEDS DE BOEUF – These are only used as a garnish for tripe cooked *à la mode de Caen*.

Beef or ox heart. COEUR DE BOEUF – Prepared like *Calf's heart* (see below).

Beef or ox kidneys. ROGNONS DE BOEUF – This variety meat or piece of offal, which is mediocre in taste and often tough, can be prepared as described in the recipes given in this section for *Calf's (veal) kidneys* (see below).

Beef or ox liver. FOIE DE BOEUF – Beef or ox liver, although inferior in flavour, can be prepared as described in the recipes given for *Calf's (veal) liver* (see below).

Beef or ox muzzle. MUSEAU DE BOEUF – This can be prepared as described in most of the recipes given for *Ox tongue* (see below). More often, muzzle is served cold, seasoned with oil and vinegar dressing, as *hors-d'œuvre*.

For this method of preparation cook the muzzle, previously soaked in salted water, from 6 to 8 hours. When it is cold, cut into thin slices, season with oil, vinegar, salt, pepper and chopped fine herbs. This salad is often sprinkled with chopped onion.

Beef or ox palate. PALAIS DE BOEUF – Piece of offal (variety meat) not much used nowadays. In the olden days it was very popular.

Method of preparation. Soak the palate for a long time in cold water. Blanch it, allow to cool, and drain. Remove the skin which covers it.

Cook in white *court-bouillon* as for *Calf's head* (see below).

Beef or ox palate attereaux. ATTEREAUX DE PALAIS DE BOEUF – See ATTEREAUX.

Beef or ox palate fried in batter. FRITOT DE PALAIS DE BOEUF – Cook and allow to cool as described above; cut into uniform pieces. Marinate for 1 hour in a mixture of oil, lemon juice and chopped parsley. Soak in a light batter and deep-fry in sizzling fat. Garnish with fried parsley, and serve with *Tomato sauce* (see SAUCE).

Beef or ox palate au gratin. PALAIS DE BOEUF AU GRATIN – Cook the palate as above and slice. Arrange in a crown on a buttered dish. Cover with *Duxelle sauce* (see SAUCE), sprinkle with grated breadcrumbs and brown the top.

Beef or ox palate à la lyonnaise. PALAIS DE BOEUF À LA LYONNAISE – Cook an ox palate as described above; cut into thick slices like *Tripe à la lyonnaise* (see below).

Beef or ox palate à la poulette. PALAIS DE BOEUF À LA POULETTE – Cook the palate as described above, and cut into thick slices. Simmer with cooked, sliced mushrooms.

Ox tail. QUEUE DE BOEUF – Used for making various soups, particularly *Oxtail soup* (see SOUPS AND BROTHS). It can also be prepared independently in a great many ways.

Ox tail is normally sold in butchers' shops completely skinned, but there are some dishes which require unskinned ox tail, for instance for the preparation of boned, stuffed ox tail.

Generally speaking, before being cooked in any way, the ox tail is cut into uniform chunks. The same applies to unskinned ox tail, except in cases when, before being boned and stuffed, it has to be left whole.

Cut into pieces, the ox tail is usually braised, as indicated for this type of dish (see BEEF; CULINARY METHODS, *Braising*). It can be served with the garnishes recommended for braised top rump (see BEEF, *Top rump*).

The following garnishes are the most suitable for ox tail: *berrichonne; bourgeoise; bourguignonne;* chipolata sausages; *compote; fermière; flamande*; various fresh, buttered, braised or glazed vegetables; *maraîchère*; braised chestnuts; *macaroni à l'italienne* (or other pasta products); *nivernaise*; fresh noodles; *piémontaise*; purées of various vegetables (fresh or dried); *tortue*.

Depending on its nature, the garnish is either disposed around the ox tail or served separately in a *timbale*. After the ox tail has been arranged on a serving dish, its braising liquor should be boiled down, strained and poured over it.

Braised stuffed ox tail. QUEUE DE BOEUF FARCIE BRAISÉE – Soak a whole, unskinned ox tail in cold water. Bone it carefully, without damaging the skin. Spread it on the table, season with salt, pepper and spices and fill along the entire length with some forcemeat – finely pounded *Pork forcemeat* (see FORCEMEATS or STUFFINGS) is the most suitable – mixed with chopped onion lightly fried in butter and chopped parsley, bound with an egg. Reshape the tail, sew up the slit side, wrap in a cloth and tie with string as a long ballottine.

Braise in brown stock as described in the recipe for *Top rump, braised* (see BEEF).

Stuffed ox tail can be accompanied by the garnishes recommended above for ox tail cooked in pieces.

Grilled ox tail Sainte-Menehould. QUEUE DE BOEUF GRILLÉE SAINTE-MENEHOULD – Cut the ox tail into rather big chunks and cook in a stockpot as a *pot-au-feu* (q.v.).

Drain the pieces, bone them, and cool under a press in the strained liquid in which they were cooked. Drain, spread with mustard slightly flavoured with cayenne pepper, sprinkle with melted butter, roll in fresh breadcrumbs, and cook under a low grill.

Serve with a spiced sauce, such as *Diable, Piquante, Poivrade*, etc. (see SAUCE).

Ox tail en hochepot. QUEUE DE BOEUF EN HOCHEPOT – Cut the ox tail, whether skinned or not, into uniform chunks. Put into a stockpot with 2 pig's trotters, cut into pieces, and a whole pig's ear. Add enough water to cover, bring to the boil, remove scum and simmer gently for 2 hours. Add 1 small blanched cabbage cut in quarters, 3 carrots and 2 turnips, cut into pieces, and 10 small onions. Simmer gently for 2 hours.

Drain the pieces of ox tail and pig's trotters. Arrange them on a large dish. Put the vegetables in the middle, and surround with grilled chipolata sausages and the pig's ear cut into strips. Serve with boiled potatoes.

Beef tongue

Beef or ox tongue. LANGUE DE BOEUF – Ox tongue can be used fresh or salted, when it should be steeped in salt 24 hours.

If used fresh, soak in cold water for several hours, trim and skin and braise or poach the tongue.

Braised. The tongue is prepared in the same way as a piece of braised beef, and can be accompanied by garnishes recommended for this dish (*Bourgeoise; Bourguignonne; Sauerkraut; Milanaise*; etc., see GARNISHES).

Poached. Poach like *Top rump* (see BEEF), and add the same garnishes.

Salted. Poach and serve cold as *Pickled (scarlet) beef or ox tongue* (see below), or hot with various vegetable purées (see PURÉE).

Beef or ox tongue à l'alsacienne. LANGUE DE BOEUF À L'ALSACIENNE – Poach the tongue, soaked, skinned and trimmed in stock with a *bouquet garni* (q.v.) until half-cooked. Finish cooking with separately prepared *sauerkraut* (q.v.) and lean bacon.

Drain the tongue. Arrange it on a bed of *sauerkraut*. Surround with thin slices of bacon and *Strasbourg sausages* (see SAUSAGE) which have been poached for 10 minutes in boiling water. Serve with boiled potatoes.

Beef or ox tongue à la bourgeoise. LANGUE DE BOEUF À LA BOURGEOISE – Braise the tongue in the usual way. (See BEEF, *Braised beef*.) When it is nearly cooked, remove from saucepan. Strain the stock in which the tongue was boiled through a fine strainer. Put the tongue back into the pan. Add *bourgeoise garnish*: half-cooked carrots cut to uniform size, little half-cooked glazed onions and pieces of larding bacon lightly fried in butter. Pour the strained stock over the tongue. Finish cooking everything together in a moderate oven (180°C., 350°F., gas Mark 4).

Braised beef or ox tongue with various garnishes. LANGUE DE BOEUF BRAISÉE – Braise the tongue slowly in the usual way. (See BEEF, *Braised beef*.) Drain and surround with the garnish specified. Strain the stock, remove surplus fat, boil down the sauce to thicken it, pass through a strainer, and pour over the tongue.

Cold beef tongue

Garnishes for braised tongue: *bourguignonne; bruxelloise; cévenole*; chipolata sausages; braised chicory; buttered spinach purée; *fermière; flamande; jardinière; macédoine; milanaise, nivernaise*, noodles (or other pasta with an Italian sauce); purées of fresh or dried vegetables; various green vegetables braised or dressed with butter; risotto.

The sauce is made with white wine, red wine or Madeira.

Beef or ox tongue à la diable. LANGUE DE BOEUF À LA DIABLE – Cut braised or poached cold tongue crossways into rather thick slices. Spread with mustard, dip in melted butter and breadcrumbs and sprinkle with melted butter. Grill under gentle heat, browning on both sides. Serve with *Diable sauce* (see SAUCE).

Braised beef or ox tongue with various sauces. LANGUE DE BOEUF BRAISÉE – Braise the tongue and serve with one of the following sauces: *Mushroom; Chasseur; Lyonnaise; Madeira* (or other wine sauces); *Piquante; Poivrade; Tomato sauce*, etc. (see SAUCE).

Beef or ox tongue au gratin. LANGUE DE BOEUF AU GRATIN – Cut braised cold tongue into slices, not too thin. Arrange them in a circle on a buttered dish, alternating with rows of thin slices of lean boiled ham. Put cooked mushrooms on the tongue. Pour over *Duxelles sauce* (see SAUCE) to which has been added the juices in which the tongue was cooked. Sprinkle with breadcrumbs and melted butter and brown under a grill or in the oven.

Pickled (scarlet) beef or ox tongue. LANGUE DE BOEUF À L'ÉCARLATE – Soak the trimmed tongue for several hours in cold water, drain and dry. Prick it all over and rub thoroughly with a mixture of salt and saltpetre (sodium nitrate).

Put the tongue into a wooden or earthenware container. Cover with the pickling brine described below, and allow to cool. Put on a wooden lid, pressing down well, and leave in the brine for six days in the summer and eight days in the winter.

Pickling brine for ox tongue. Pour into a large saucepan 5 litres ($4\frac{1}{2}$ quarts, $5\frac{1}{2}$ quarts) water, $2\frac{1}{4}$ kg. (5 lb., $6\frac{2}{3}$ cups) sea salt (coarse salt), 150 g. (5 oz.) saltpetre, 300 g. (11 oz., $1\frac{1}{2}$ cups) brown sugar, 1 sprig of thyme, 1 bay leaf, 12 juniper berries and 12 peppercorns.

Boil for a few minutes. Allow to cool completely before pouring the liquid over the tongue.

Method of cooking ox tongue. After pickling the tongue, drain it, and soak in cold water for several hours to free from salt. Boil it in water without any seasoning or condiments from 2 to 3 hours, depending on size.

Tripe. GRAS-DOUBLE – The best part of beef or ox stomachs. It is sold fresh, pickled, uncooked and cooked. If uncooked, it requires 3 to $3\frac{1}{2}$ hours of cooking in a salt water *court-bouillon* (q.v.). Pickled tripe requires 1 to $1\frac{1}{2}$ hours of cooking in salted water.

Tripe en blanquette. GRAS-DOUBLE DE BOEUF EN BLANQUETTE – Brown lightly 2 large tablespoons (scant $\frac{1}{4}$ cup) chopped onion with 50 g. (2 oz., $\frac{1}{4}$ cup) butter. Sprinkle with 1 tablespoon flour and add 6 dl. (1 pint, $2\frac{1}{2}$ cups) stock. Mix, and boil for a few minutes.

Add to this sauce 750 g. ($1\frac{3}{4}$ lb., $3\frac{1}{2}$ cups) cooked tripe cut into pieces. Season with salt and pepper, add a *bouquet garni* (q.v.) and cook, uncovered, for $1\frac{1}{2}$ hours.

Before serving, bind with 2 egg yolks mixed with 2 tablespoons (3 tablespoons) cold water. Blend well, add 2 tablespoons (3 tablespoons) fresh butter, 1 tablespoon chopped parsley and several drops of lemon juice. To serve, heap high on a serving plate.

Tripe à la bourgeoise. GRAS-DOUBLE DE BOEUF À LA BOURGEOISE – Brown lightly 12 small onions in 50 g. (2 oz.,

$\frac{1}{4}$ cup) butter. Sprinkle with 1 tablespoon flour, brown slightly, and moisten with 6 dl. (1 pint, $2\frac{1}{2}$ cups) stock. Mix and boil for a few minutes.

Put in a saucepan 750 g. ($1\frac{3}{4}$ lb., $3\frac{1}{2}$ cups) cooked tripe cut into pieces. Season, add a *bouquet garni* (q.v.), and boil fast. Add 24 small new carrots, lightly blanched, and the same number of small half-cooked onions. Cover the saucepan and cook for $1\frac{1}{2}$ hours. When served, sprinkle with chopped parsley.

Tripe à la fermière. GRAS-DOUBLE DE BOEUF À LA FERMIÈRE – Brown lightly 4 tablespoons ($\frac{1}{3}$ cup) chopped onion and 4 tablespoons ($\frac{1}{3}$ cup) young diced carrots in 50 g. (2 oz., $\frac{1}{4}$ cup) butter. Sprinkle with 2 tablespoons (3 tablespoons) flour, allow to colour slightly, add 6 dl. (1 pint, $2\frac{1}{2}$ cups) stock and boil for a few minutes.

Add cooked tripe seasoned with salt and pepper. Cover and cook $1\frac{1}{2}$ hours. Ten minutes before serving, add 2 tablespoons (3 tablespoons) sliced mushrooms fried in butter.

Fried tripe in breadcrumbs. GRAS-DOUBLE DE BOEUF, FRIT PANÉ – Cut cooked tripe into little pieces, season with salt and pepper, dip in egg and breadcrumbs and fry in fat or oil.

As soon as the tripe turns golden and becomes crisp, drain, and serve with *Diable, Piquante, Rémoulade, Tartare, Tomato* or any other spiced sauce (see SAUCE).

Grilled tripe à l'espagnole. GRAS-DOUBLE DE BOEUF GRILLÉ À L'ESPAGNOLE – Cut 750 g. ($1\frac{3}{4}$ lb., $3\frac{1}{2}$ cups) cooked and well-drained tripe into pieces. Marinate for 1 hour in 4 tablespoons ($\frac{1}{3}$ cup) oil, 1 teaspoon lemon juice, 1 teaspoon salt, 3 to 4 peppercorns and 1 tablespoon chopped parsley.

Drain the pieces, cover with breadcrumbs and grill under gentle heat.

Arrange the tripe in a crown, alternating with rows of halved tomatoes fried in oil. Put onions sliced in rounds and fried in oil in the centre.

Tripe à la lyonnaise. GRAS-DOUBLE DE BOEUF À LA LYONNAISE – Cook and drain the tripe and cut into thin strips. Fry in sizzling butter or lard. Season, and add 4 large tablespoons (generous $\frac{1}{3}$ cup) chopped onion fried in butter or lard. Mix and cook together until the tripe is browned. When serving add a dash of vinegar heated in the frying pan, and sprinkle with chopped parsley.

Tripe à la mode de Caen. TRIPES À LA MODE DE CAEN – In Paris and several other big cities in France one can find *Tripes à la mode de Caen*, cooked and ready to serve and frequently of excellent quality, as these dishes are prepared in large quantities by first-rate specialists.

But this dish is very easy to make. As tripe is usually sold cleaned, washed and blanched, all that remains is to stew it slowly in a *marmite* or casserole, with aromatics and moistening. The cooking takes a long time, about 10 to 12 hours in a slow oven.

Tripe will be better and will stay whiter after cooking if it is prepared in a special *marmite*, with a very small opening, used principally in Normandy. One can, however, cook the tripe in an ordinary casserole or in an earthenware fireproof dish. What is of the greatest importance in the cooking is to make sure that it is done in a hermetically sealed utensil, in a moderate but sustained heat. Seal, before putting on the lid, with a strip of flour-and-water paste. This paste is not edible; its purpose consists entirely of forming a protective coating under which the tripe, cooking without bubbling, remains very white. The paste is prepared by kneading some ordinary flour with hot water.

Ingredients. The basic ingredients of *Tripe à la mode de Caen* include ox mesentery, composed of the honeycomb or reticulum, the psalterium or manyplies, rennet or reed and the belly. To these should be added a gelatinous substance provided by the feet and fatty matter, which is to form a protective layer above the liquid. This is fat taken off beef cut in slices.

The net weight of the basic ingredients should be 2 kg. ($4\frac{1}{2}$ lb.), and the following ingredients are then added:

1 whole ox or calf's foot, 500 g. (18 oz.) beef fat, 5 medium onions, 5 medium carrots, 300 g. (11 oz.) leeks, a *bouquet garni* (with the accent on thyme and bay leaf), 4 cloves garlic, 15 g. ($\frac{1}{2}$ oz., 2 teaspoons) salt, 1 teaspoon pepper, a pinch of allspice.

In principle, the liquid used should be cider, strengthened with a few spoonfuls of Calvados or other spirits with a cider base. But, as it often happens that tripe prepared with cider turns dark, it is best to use plain water.

The amount of liquid should be sufficient for the tripe to be completely submerged. The quatity, therefore, will depend on the type of utensil used.

Method. Line the bottom of the *marmite* or casserole with onions and carrots cut into pieces. On top of these put the ox foot, boned and cut into pieces, and its bone, split into two lengthways. Add the tripe, cut into 6 cm. ($2\frac{1}{2}$-inch) square pieces. Insert the garlic, *bouquet garni* (q.v.) and the leeks, tied in a bunch, among the pieces of tripe. Season with salt, freshly ground pepper and spices. Cover the whole with beef fat cut into slices and flattened, and pour in enough water to cover.

Put the paste lid, rolled out rather thick, on the casserole, so as to seal the top hermetically. Cook in the oven until the paste is well set. Cover, and leave in a slow oven for about 10 hours.

Remove the paste lid. Take out the layer of fat. Drain the tripe, remove the vegetables, *bouquet garni*, bunch of leeks and all the bones. Put the tripe into a serving dish; strain the gravy, skim off surplus fat, and pour the gravy over the tripe.

Keep hot in a *bain-marie* until ready to serve.

Tripe à la polonaise I. TRIPES DE BOEUF À LA POLONAISE – Blanch (see BLANCHING) the tripe, drain, allow to cool and put into boiling water to cook for 4 or 5 hours, with a garnish of vegetables as for *Pot-au-feu* (see SOUPS AND BROTHS). Drain the tripe and cut into slices.

Prepare a *julienne* (q.v.) of celery, parsley root or parsnips and carrots, and boil in strained tripe stock until the vegetables are done. Add the tripe to the vegetables. Season with salt and pepper and add a little powdered sweet marjoram. Blend in some *Kneaded butter* (see BUTTER, *Compound butters*). Bring to the boil. Serve in a flat dish.

Tripe à la polonaise II. GRAS-DOUBLE DE BOEUF À LA POLONAISE – Fry the cooked tripe, cut in thin strips, in butter until it is brown. Arrange in a dish and sprinkle with chopped hard-boiled egg yolks and parsley. Dress with a dash of vinegar or lemon juice and pour on the butter from the pan, in which 50 g. (2 oz., 1 cup) breadcrumbs have been browned.

Tripe à la portugaise. GRAS-DOUBLE DE BOEUF À LA PORTUGAISE – Cut 750 g. ($1\frac{3}{4}$ lb., $3\frac{1}{2}$ cups) tripe, previously cooked and drained, into pieces. Simmer with 3 dl. ($\frac{1}{2}$ pint, $1\frac{1}{4}$ cups) *Tomato fondue* (see FONDUE), for 20 minutes with a lid on.

Arrange on a dish, sprinkle with chopped parsley.

Tripe à la poulette I. GRAS-DOUBLE DE BOEUF À LA POULETTE – 'Cut the tripe into pieces $2\frac{1}{2}$ cm. (1 inch) square; keep hot in a double boiler or *bain-marie* with a little butter and meat jelly. Make some light *Allemande sauce* (see SAUCE) adding some lightly fried blanched chopped parsley. Mix half of it with the tripe; add the juice of 1 lemon. Heat in a dish, and cover with the rest of the *allemande*, adding 250 g. (9 oz., $2\frac{1}{4}$ cups) peeled mushrooms.' (From Carême and Plumerey.)

Tripe à la poulette II. GRAS-DOUBLE DE BOEUF À LA POULETTE

Preparation of tripe à la mode de Caen (*Robert Carrier*)

– Cut cooked and drained tripe into small pieces and simmer for a few minutes in 3 dl. ($\frac{1}{2}$ pint, $1\frac{1}{4}$ cups) *Poulette sauce* (see SAUCE). Add 12 lightly cooked mushrooms and 1 tablespoon chopped parsley. Heat in a serving dish.

Tripe à la provençale. GRAS-DOUBLE DE BOEUF À LA PROVENÇALE – Proceed as described in the recipe for *Tripe en blanquette*, using shredded bacon fat or pork fat instead of butter. After binding the sauce with egg yolk, add a few leaves of basil pounded with bacon fat or pork fat.

Tripe sautéed in butter. GRAS-DOUBLE DE BOEUF SAUTÉ AU BEURRE – Cut cooked tripe into square or rectangular pieces. Season with salt and pepper, sprinkle with flour, and fry in butter until golden brown.

Place on a serving dish and sprinkle with chopped

parsley and a little vinegar or lemon juice. Heat the butter remaining in the pan until sizzling and pour over the tripe.

LAMB or MUTTON OFFAL or VARIETY MEATS. ABATS D'AGNEAU, DE MOUTON:

Animelles (U.S. fry) – Culinary term for the testicles of male animals, in particular those of lambs and sheep. In the past *animelles* were very much in vogue in France, Spain and Italy.

This is a delicate piece of offal (variety meats) and there are many recipes for preparing it, some of which are given below.

Before preparing them, scald, skin and soak the *animelles* in cold water for 2 to 3 hours.

Animelles (U.S. fry) in cream sauce. ANIMELLES À LA CRÈME – Cut in thin slices. Season with salt and pepper. Cook in butter. Add a few tablespoons *Cream sauce* (see SAUCE) and simmer gently. Before serving add a little cream and some fresh butter. Mix well.

Prepared in this manner, the *animelles* are mostly used as a garnish for patties, pies and *vol-au-vent* dishes. Mushrooms and truffles can be added to them.

Fricassée of animelles (U.S. fry). ANIMELLES EN FRICASSÉE – Slice the *animelles* into escalopes and cook in *Court-bouillon XII* (see COURT-BOUILLON). Drain, put into a shallow pan with cooked, sliced mushrooms (or left whole, if they are small). Add *Poulette sauce* (see SAUCE). Simmer gently without allowing to boil. Before serving, add some fresh butter.

Fried animelles (Plumerey's recipe). ANIMELLES DE MOUTONS FRITES – 'Choose 3 fresh sheep's (mutton) *animelles*, remove the skin and cut each into 8 pieces of uniform size. Put into an earthenware bowl with salt, pepper, 2 teaspoons tarragon vinegar, 2 teaspoons olive oil, a little thyme, $\frac{1}{2}$ bay leaf, 1 sliced onion and a few sprigs of parsley. Cover the bowl. After one hour they should give out their liquid. Drain, put back into the bowl with the rest of the ingredients, and sprinkle with the juice of half a lemon. Before serving, drain on a cloth, pressing lightly; dredge with flour and fry until golden. Arrange in a heap on a napkin and garnish with fried parsley.'

Animelles (U.S. fry) fried in batter. ANIMELLES FRITES – Cut the *animelles* into broad, thin slices. Marinate for 1 hour in oil, lemon juice, chopped parsley, salt and pepper.

When required, dip them into light batter (see BATTERS FOR FRYING). Fry, and garnish with fried parsley. Serve with *Tomato sauce* (see SAUCE).

Fried animelles (U.S. fry) with mushrooms. ANIMELLES SAUTÉES AUX CHAMPIGNONS – Scald, skin and thoroughly soak the *animelles*, then slice and dry.

Sauté on a brisk flame in sizzling butter and finish off as described in the recipe for *Calves' kidneys sautéed with mushrooms* (see below).

Animelles (U.S. fry) à la vinaigrette. ANIMELLES À LA VINAIGRETTE – Cook the *animelles* in a white *court-bouillon* as for *Calf's head* (see below). Serve with *Vinaigrette sauce* (see SAUCE).

Sheep's (lambs') brains. CERVELLE DE MOUTON, D'AGNEAU – All methods of preparation given for ox (beef) and calves' brains can be applied to sheep's and lambs' brains.

The brains must be first soaked, the membranes covering them removed, and the brains cooked in *Court-bouillon III* (see COURT-BOUILLON).

Sheep's (lambs') brains fried in batter. CERVELLE DE MOUTON, D'AGNEAU, EN FRITOT – Like *Calves' brains fried in batter* (see below).

Sheep's (lambs') brains à la bordelaise. CERVELLE DE MOUTON, D'AGNEAU, À LA BORDELAISE – Cut the brains, cooked in *Court-bouillon III* (see COURT-BOUILLON) into slices. Dredge with flour and brown lightly in clarified butter. Arrange in a crown, alternating with rows of oval-shaped croûtons of bread fried in butter. Add a few tablespoons of *Bordelaise sauce with red wine* (see SAUCE).

Sheep's (lambs') brains à l'indienne. CERVELLE DE MOUTON, D'AGNEAU, À L'INDIENNE – Like *Calves' brains à l'indienne* (see below).

Sheep's (lambs') brains with red wine. CERVELLE DE MOUTON, D'AGNEAU, AU VIN ROUGE – Like *Calves' brains with red wine*, or *à la bourguignonne* (see below).

Sheep's head. TÊTE DE MOUTON – Only the tongue and brain of the sheep are used in cookery, though sheep's head can be prepared in the same way as lamb's head (see LAMB).

Sheep's (lambs') kidneys à l'anglaise. ROGNONS DE MOUTON, D'AGNEAU, À L'ANGLAISE – Remove the skin of the kidneys and slit on the bulging side. Open without separating the two halves completely. Put on a skewer to keep the kidney open (2 pieces of kidney per skewer). Season with salt and pepper, brush with melted butter, dip in breadcrumbs and grill. Garnish with grilled rashers of bacon, boiled potatoes and watercress. Put a pat of *Maître d'hôtel butter* (see BUTTER, *Compound butters*), the size of a walnut, on each kidney.

Kidneys *à l'anglaise* can also be prepared without being dipped in butter and breadcrumbs.

Sheep's (lambs') kidneys Carvalho. ROGNONS DE MOUTON, D'AGNEAU, CARVALHO – Remove the skin and cut in two lengthways. Season and sauté them briskly in sizzling butter.

Arrange the halved kidneys in a crown on a dish, placing them on croûtons of the same shape, fried in butter. Put on each half of a kidney 2 thin slices of truffle and 1 mushroom cap fried in butter.

Lace the pan juices with Madeira, dilute with *Demi-glace* (see SAUCE), add butter, strain, and pour over the kidneys.

Sheep's (lambs') kidneys au gratin. ROGNONS DE MOUTON, D'AGNEAU, AU GRATIN – Sauté the halved kidneys, seasoned with salt and pepper, in butter over a brisk flame, just to stiffen them.

Arrange them, bulging side up, on sausage stuffing or forcemeat (see FORCEMEATS or STUFFINGS) mixed with a third of its weight in dry *duxelles* (q.v.) piped in a circle on a buttered dish. Press them slightly into the forcemeat. Put 1 cooked mushroom on each half kidney and surround with forcemeat studded with slices of uncooked mushrooms. Pour over *Duxelles sauce* (see SAUCE). Sprinkle with breadcrumbs and melted butter and brown in a very hot oven.

Remove from the oven, squeeze a few drops of lemon juice over and sprinkle with chopped parsley.

Sheep's (lambs') kidneys sautéed with mushrooms or with various wines. ROGNONS DE MOUTON, D'AGNEAU, SAUTÉ AUX CHAMPIGNONS – Like *Calves' kidneys sautéed with mushrooms* and *Calves' kidneys sautéed with various wines* (see below).

Sheep's (lambs') kidneys on skewers. BROCHETTES DE ROGNONS DE MOUTON, D'AGNEAU – Thread on skewers sheep's kidneys cut into small slices, square pieces of lightly fried bacon, and sliced mushrooms tossed in butter (see below, *Calves' kidneys on skewers*).

Sheep's (lambs') kidneys Turbigo. ROGNONS DE MOUTON, D'AGNEAU, TURBIGO – Divide the kidneys in halves and fry briskly in butter. Arrange in a circle on a dish. Put in the middle peeled mushrooms fried in the butter in which the kidneys were cooked. Between each half of kidney put 2 chipolata or small link sausages, grilled or fried in butter, and on each of the halves place 1 mushroom cap fried in butter.

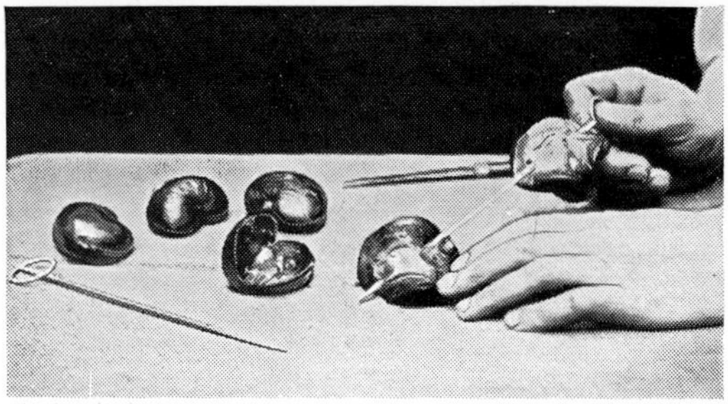

Kidneys on skewers. How to open kidneys and how to skewer them

Add white wine to the pan juices with tomato-flavoured *Demi-glace sauce* (see SAUCE), blend, and pour over the dish.

Sheep's (lambs') kidneys au vert-pré. ROGNONS DE MOUTON, D'AGNEAU, AU VERT-PRÉ – Prepare as for *Sheep's kidneys on skewers*. Arrange on a dish and garnish with potato straws and watercress. Place on the kidneys a pat of *Maître d'hôtel butter* (see BUTTER, *Compound butters*).

Lamb's liver. FOIE D'AGNEAU – Lamb's liver is rarely prepared by itself. It forms a part of the animal's pluck, which is used for *ragoûts*.

The liver can be cooked on skewers as *Calf's liver on skewers* (see below), or it can be fried in butter like *Calf's liver à l'anglaise* (see below).

Lamb's pluck à l'anglaise. FRESSURE D'AGNEAU À L'ANGLAISE – Slice the lamb's liver, heart, spleen and lungs (the last two having previously been blanched for 10 minutes in salted water).

Slice the lamb's sweetbread. Season with salt and pepper and dredge all the above ingredients in flour. Fry in a shallow pan in clarified butter. Drain and arrange on a dish. Put 1 tablespoon flour into the pan in which the pluck was fried and cook for a few moments to brown lightly; add 1 dl. (6 tablespoons, scant $\frac{1}{2}$ cup) Madeira, a few tablespoons of veal stock and a few drops of *Harvey sauce* (English spice sauce). Pour this sauce over the pluck.

Lambs' tongues. LANGUES D'AGNEAU – These are usually braised. They can also be cooked in white *court-bouillon* (q.v.) like *Calf's tongue* (see below) and treated in the same way.

Serve with a garnish of vegetables, dressed with butter or braised; as a *ragoût*, with mushrooms, with chipolata or link sausages, with young carrots, *à la bouguignonne*, etc. The tongue can also be prepared grilled *à la diable*, fried in butter, in buttered papers (as rib chops of veal) *à la Sainte-Menehould* (as pig's trotters, see below), in *crépinettes* (q.v.) etc.

Lambs' sweetbreads. RIS D'AGNEAU – Most of the recipes

Lambs' sweetbreads Villeroi on skewers (*Larousse*)

given for *Calves' sweetbreads* can be used for lambs' sweetbreads.

Soak the sweetbreads and put them into a pan. Moisten with a few tablespoons white stock. Add 1 teaspoon butter and a few drops of lemon juice. Cover and simmer for 25 minutes. Leave to cool in the stock (strained) in which they were cooked, and proceed as indicated in the selected recipe.

Lambs' sweetbreads are used as a garnish for *vol-au-vent*, patty shells, raised pies, *timbales*, various decorative borders, etc.

They can also be served fried with *Cream*, *Poulette*, *Curry* or *Hungarian sauce* (see SAUCE), on skewers, in scallop shells, in batter, as *cromesquis* or croquettes, with pilaf, etc.

They are also used as garnish for eggs, and for small *entrée* dishes of meat, chicken, etc.

(For these dishes, see *Calves' sweetbreads* below.)

Hot pâté of lambs' sweetbreads à l'ancienne. PÂTÉ CHAUD DE RIS D'AGNEAU – Line the sides and bottom of a buttered *pâté* mould with *Lining paste* (see DOUGH).

Cover the inside of the baking dish with a thick layer of *Forcemeat à la crème* (see FORCEMEATS or STUFFINGS).

On this put a layer of lambs' sweetbreads half-cooked in butter, slices of mushrooms lightly fried in butter, and thick slices of truffles. Cover with another layer of forcemeat, another layer of sweetbreads, mushrooms and truffles, and finish with a layer of forcemeat.

Cover the *pâté* with a piece of rolled-out pastry and seal the edges. Make an opening in the pastry lid to allow steam to escape. Decorate the top with small pastry decorations and brush with beaten egg. Bake in a moderate oven for 45 minutes to 1 hour, depending on the thickness of the pastry.

Put the *pâté* on a dish. Through the opening in the top pour in several tablespoons *Allemande sauce* (see SAUCE), flavoured with truffles.

Lambs' sweetbreads pilaf. PILAF DE RIS D'AGNEAU – Prepare like *Chicken liver pilaf* (see PILAF) replacing the latter by lambs' sweetbreads cooked in butter which have been previously soaked in cold water and blanched.

Vol-au-vent of lambs' sweetbreads with truffles and mushrooms. VOL-AU-VENT DE RIS D'AGNEAU AUX TRUFFES ET CHAMPIGNONS – Prepare the *vol-au-vent* case (see VOL-AU-VENT).

Fill with a *ragoût* of lambs' sweetbreads braised in *court-bouillon* (q.v.), together with sliced truffles and mushrooms in very hot *Allemande sauce* (see SAUCE).

Ragoûts of lambs' sweetbreads intended for filling *vol-au-vent* cases or similar dishes can be cooked either in a white or brown stock.

In addition to truffles and mushrooms, these *ragoûts* can

be supplemented with various ingredients such as quenelles, cocks' combs and kidneys, brains in large dice, sliced artichoke hearts, etc. The lambs' sweetbreads must, of course, be the predominating ingredient.

Sheep's (lambs') tongues. LANGUES DE MOUTON, D'AGNEAU – These can be prepared in various ways. First soak in cold water and scald for skinning.

Braised sheep's (lambs') tongues with various garnishes. LANGUES DE MOUTON, D'AGNEAU, BRAISÉES – Braise in a very little stock. Arrange on a dish and surround with a suitable garnish. Pour the braising stock, boiled down and strained, over the dish.

All garnishes indicated for *Braised shoulder or rib of mutton* (see MUTTON, GARNISHES), are suitable.

Sheep's (lambs') tongues en crépinettes. LANGUES DE MOUTON, D'AGNEAU, EN CRÉPINETTES – Braise the tongues and leave to cool in their stock. Cut them in half, enclose each half in *Fine pork stuffing* (see FORCEMEATS or STUFFINGS) with truffles; wrap in a piece of pork caul.

Baste the *crépinettes* with melted butter. Dip in bread-crumbs, and grill slowly. Serve with *Périgueux sauce* (see SAUCE).

Devilled sheep's (lambs') tongues. LANGUES DE MOUTON, D'AGNEAU, À LA DIABLE – Braise the tongues and leave to cool in their stock. Cut them in half and spread each half with mustard seasoned with a touch of cayenne pepper. Baste with butter. Dip in breadcrumbs, pour butter over them and grill slowly. Serve with *Diable sauce* (see SAUCE).

Fritot of sheep's (lambs') tongues. LANGUES DE MOUTON, D'AGNEAU, EN FRITOT – Braise the tongues (or poach them in very little liquid). Leave to cool in their stock. Drain. Cut into thin slices, and steep them for 1 hour in a marinade of oil, lemon juice, chopped parsley, salt and pepper.

Dip in light batter and deep-fry in boiling fat. Garnish with fried parsley. Serve with *Tomato sauce* (see SAUCE).

Sheep's (lambs') tongues au gratin. LANGUES DE MOUTON, D'AGNEAU, AU GRATIN – Braise the tongues and cut them in half lengthwise. Put them in an ovenware dish masked with *Mornay sauce* (see SAUCE). Decorate each half tongue with a cooked mushroom. Cover with Mornay sauce, dust with breadcrumbs, and pour on melted butter; brown slowly. Sprinkle with chopped parsley.

Sheep's (lambs') tongues à la hongroise. LANGUES DE MOUTON, D'AGNEAU, À LA HONGROISE – Half-cook the tongues in clear soup. Drain; skin them. Cook 100 g. (4 oz., 1 cup) chopped onions slowly. Put the tongues on top. Season with salt and paprika, cover and stew. Moisten with $1\frac{1}{2}$ dl. ($\frac{1}{4}$ pint, $\frac{2}{3}$ cup) white wine. Boil down.

Moisten with a rather thin *Velouté sauce* (see SAUCE). Cover and cook. Pour sauce over tongues in a deep dish.

Sheep's (lambs') tongues à l'italienne. LANGUES DE MOUTON, D'AGNEAU, À L'ITALIENNE – Braise and simmer in *Italian sauce* (see SAUCE).

Pickled sheep's (lambs') tongues. LANGUES DE MOUTON, D'AGNEAU, À L'ÉCARLATE – Wash the tongues, and put them in brine, as for *Pickled ox tongue*, for 3 or 4 days. Cook in the same way as ox tongue.

These tongues can be served hot with any garnish (especially with purée of lentils or chestnuts), or with green or red cabbage, in which the tongues should be simmered. They can be served cold, like ox tongue, after having been coloured with carmine or caramel.

Sheep's (lambs') tongues à la poulette. LANGUES DE MOUTON À LA POULETTE – Cook the tongues in white stock. Drain and slice. Proceed as indicated for *Sheep's (lambs') trotters à la poulette* (see below).

Skewered sheep's (lambs') tongues. LANGUES DE MOUTON, D'AGNEAU, EN BROCHETTES – Braise the tongues and leave to cool. Slice and thread the pieces on skewers. In between each piece put a slice of mushroom tossed in butter and a square piece of bacon, lightly browned.

Baste with butter and coat with breadcrumbs. Pour butter over them and grill slowly.

Serve with *Piquante sauce* made with the braising stock of the tongues, or with *Diable sauce* (see SAUCE).

Sheep's (lambs') tongues à la vinaigrette. LANGUES DE MOUTON, D'AGNEAU, À LA VINAIGRETTE – Cook in a white stock, as for *Calf's head.* Drain and skin. Garnish with fresh parsley. Serve with *Vinaigrette sauce* (see SAUCE), capers, onions and chopped parsley.

Sheep's (lambs') trotters. PIEDS DE MOUTON, D'AGNEAU – Sheep's or lambs' trotters, which can be bought in the shops already blanched, must be boned, singed and the little tufts of hair between the cleavage in the hoof removed.

Cook in a light white *court-bouillon* (q.v.) and proceed as described in the given recipe.

Sheep's (lambs') trotters en blanquette. PIEDS DE MOUTON, D'AGNEAU, EN BLANQUETTES – This is the same as *Sheep's (lambs') trotters à la poulette* (see below) to which, in addition to the mushrooms, small onions cooked in a veal or chicken consommé are added.

Sheep's (lambs') trotters in crépinettes à la périgourdine. PIEDS DE MOUTON, D'AGNEAU, EN CRÉPINETTES À LA PÉRIGOURDINE – Braise the trotters and allow to cool in their braising stock and drain. Put half each trotter between two layers of finely minced truffled forcemeat. Wrap in pieces of pig's caul or paper-thin slices of salt pork. Brush with melted butter, dip in breadcrumbs and grill under a gentle flame. Serve with the pan juices in which the trotters were braised, boiled down with 1 wine glass of Madeira, strained, and with a few diced truffles added.

Croquettes of sheep's (lambs') trotters. CROQUETTES DE PIEDS DE MOUTON, D'AGNEAU – These are prepared with a *salpicon* (q.v.) of sheep's trotters mixed with mushrooms and truffles, and bound with *Allemande sauce* (see SAUCE) like ordinary croquettes. (See HORS-D'ŒUVRE, *Hot hors-d'œuvre.*)

Fried sheep's (lambs') trotters. PIEDS DE MOUTON, D'AGNEAU, FRITS – Cook halved sheep's trotters in white *court-bouillon* (q.v.), drain and dry. Marinate for 30 minutes in oil, lemon juice, chopped parsley, salt and pepper.

When needed, dip into batter and deep-fry in sizzling fat. Garnish with fried parsley. Serve with *Tomato sauce* (see SAUCE).

Fried sheep's (lambs') trotters a l'ancienne. PIEDS DE MOUTON, D'AGNEAU, FRITS À L'ANCIENNE – Cook the trotters in white *court-bouillon* (q.v.), or braise them. Drain, dry, split, and cover each half with a layer of finely pounded forcemeat or stuffing (q.v.) mixed with chopped truffles. Put the halves together, sandwiching tightly. Wrap in a piece of pig's caul or a paper-thin sheet of salt pork. Leave to marinate. When required, dip in batter and fry. Serve with *Périgueux sauce* (see SAUCE).

Sheep's (lambs') trotters à la hongroise. PIEDS DE MOUTON, D'AGNEAU, À LA HONGROISE – Prepare like *Sheep's (lambs') trotters à la poulette* (see below), with finely chopped onion, slightly browned in butter, and seasoned with paprika.

Sheep's (lambs') trotters à la poulette. PIEDS DE MOUTON, D'AGNEAU, À LA POULETTE – Cook 250 g. (9 oz., 3 cups) sliced mushrooms. Bone 12 trotters, split in half, and cook in white *court-bouillon* (q.v.). Put into a shallow pan with the cooked mushrooms. Add 4 tablespoons ($\frac{1}{3}$ cup) white stock and the same amount of mushroom stock (see STOCK). Boil down almost entirely. Add 3 dl. ($\frac{1}{2}$ pint, $1\frac{1}{4}$ cups) *Velouté sauce* (see SAUCE) and 3 tablespoons (scant $\frac{1}{4}$ cup) cream. Simmer for 5 to 6 minutes.

Bind the sauce with a liaison of 3 or 4 egg yolks mixed with 3 or 4 tablespoons (scant $\frac{1}{4}$ or $\frac{1}{3}$ cup) cream. Simmer the trotters but do not boil. Add 3 tablespoons (scant $\frac{1}{4}$ cup) butter, a dash of lemon juice and 1 tablespoon chopped parsley. Mix well.

Sheep's (lambs') trotters à la rouennaise I. PIEDS DE MOUTON, D'AGNEAU, À LA ROUENNAISE – Blanch the trotters whole and braise them in a good strong stock. Drain, and remove all bones. Fill the inside with sausage meat mixed with 1 lightly browned chopped onion, chopped parsley and the stock left over from the braising, boiled down and strained.

Dip the trotters in egg and breadcrumbs. Just before serving, deep-fry in sizzling fat. Garnish with fried parsley.

Sheep's (lambs') trotters à la rouennaise II. PIEDS DE MOUTON, D'AGNEAU, À LA ROUENNAISE – Braise the trotters and divide in halves. Sandwich them between two layers of stuffing or forcemeat prepared as described in the preceding recipe. Wrap in pieces of pig's caul or paper-thin slices of salt pork. Brush with melted butter, roll in breadcrumbs and grill under a low flame.

Sheep's (lambs') trotters à la vinaigrette. PIEDS DE MOUTON, D'AGNEAU, À LA VINAIGRETTE – Cook the trotters in a white *court-bouillon* (q.v.). Drain, and bone them completely. Season while hot with oil, vinegar, salt, pepper and finely chopped herbs.

This salad (which is served as an *hors-d'œuvre*) is generally flavoured with chopped spring onions.

PORK OFFAL or VARIETY MEATS. ABATS DE PORC –

Pig's bladder. VESSIE DE PORC – This part of the animal, after careful washing, is blown up and dried, and then used as a casing for big sausages, and for wrapping lard. Pig's bladder is also used in the kitchen for wrapping ducks and other poultry prepared *en chemise* (see DUCK).

Pigs' brains. CERVELLE DE PORC – Pigs' brains can be prepared in any way suitable for *Calves' brains.*

Smoked pig's cheek (bath chap). JOUE DE PORC FUMÉE – This part of the animal is much prized in England. Smoked pigs' cheeks (bath chaps) are boiled in water and eaten cold, like ham.

Pigs' ears. OREILLES DE PORC – Pigs' ears are mainly used in the preparation of various pork butchery products, chiefly for brawn or head cheese.

They can also be served separately, as a small *entrée.* Boil in a *court-bouillon* (q.v.) as for *Pigs' feet* (see below), or braise.

Boiled pigs' ears. OREILLES DE PORC BOUILLIES – Singe the ears, clean the inside thoroughly and boil them in salted water, allowing $1\frac{1}{4}$ teaspoons salt per litre ($1\frac{3}{4}$ pints, generous quart) with carrots, 1 onion studded with a clove and a *bouquet garni* (q.v.). Simmer gently for about 50 minutes. Drain the ears and prepare as indicated in individual recipes.

Having been boiled in this manner, pigs' ears can be treated in various ways, coated with batter and fried in deep fat, *à la lyonnaise* (cut into coarse *julienne* strips and fried in butter with sliced onions), *à la vinaigrette* (see below, *Calf's head*), etc.

Braised pigs' ears with various garnishes. OREILLES DE PORC BRAISÉES – Singe 4 pigs' ears and clean the inside thoroughly. Blanch for 5 minutes in boiling water. Drain and cut each in half lengthways.

Lay them flat in a buttered sauté pan on a foundation of bacon rinds and sliced onions and carrots. Put a *bouquet garni* (q.v.) in the middle of the dish. Cover and cook on top of the stove. Moisten with 2 dl. ($\frac{1}{3}$ pint, scant cup) white wine, boil down completely, add 4 dl. ($\frac{3}{4}$ pint, scant 2 cups) thickened brown veal stock and finish cooking in the oven, with a lid on, for 50 minutes.

Drain the ears, arrange on a serving dish and garnish as indicated in the recipe. Boil down the braising liquor, strain it and pour over the ears.

Pigs' ears au gratin. OREILLES DE PORC AU GRATIN – Braise the ears and cut in two lengthways. Put them into a buttered oven-proof dish. Surround with sliced mushrooms. Cover with *gratin sauce* (made of *Duxelles mixture* (q.v.) and the liquor left from braising the ears). Sprinkle with grated breadcrumbs and melted butter. Brown the top slowly in the oven. Before serving squeeze a few drops of lemon juice over the ears and sprinkle them with chopped parsley.

Grilled pigs' ears. OREILLES DE PORC GRILLÉES – Boil or braise the ears and cut in two lengthways. Coat with melted butter and breadcrumbs. Sprinkle with melted butter and grill gently. Serve with a well-spiced sauce.

Grilled pigs' ears are generally accompanied by mashed potatoes, served separately.

Grilled pigs' ears Sainte-Menehould. OREILLES DE PORC GRILLÉES SAINTE-MENEHOULD – Boil the pigs' ears in a spiced *court-bouillon* (q.v.), like pigs' feet. Drain and cool under a press. Cut in two, coat with melted butter and breadcrumbs and cook either under the grill or in the oven.

Pigs' ears à la hongroise. OREILLES DE PORC À LA HONGROISE – Boil the pig's ears as described above and cut into uniform pieces. Melt some butter in a sauté pan, soften in it (for 2 ears) 100 g. (4 oz., 1 cup) diced onions, season with salt and paprika, and put in the pig's ears. Cook, covered, for 10 minutes. Add 4 tablespoons ($\frac{1}{3}$ cup) mushrooms cut in large dice and tossed in butter. Moisten with 4 dl. ($\frac{3}{4}$ pint, scant 2 cups) *Velouté sauce* (see SAUCE).

Cook with a lid on for 14 minutes. Before serving, add 3 tablespoons (scant $\frac{1}{4}$ cup) butter.

Stuffed pigs' ears. OREILLES DE PORC FARCIES – Prepare like *Calves' ears Villeroi* (see below).

Pigs' feet (trotters). PIEDS DE PORC – Tie the pig's feet two by two, boil in stock prepared like a meat stock, and add carrots, onions and a *bouquet garni* (q.v.). Drain, straighten by placing between two thin boards tied with string, and cool under a press.

When cold, cut each trotter in two lengthways, brush with butter or lard, and grill gently. Pigs' feet are usually accompanied by mashed potatoes served separately.

Pigs' feet can be braised. They are cooked in this way when they are intended for preparing a *salpicon* (q.v.) or when they are used as an element of various garnishes.

They can also be prepared in any way suitable for *Calves' feet.*

Pigs' feet Sainte-Menehould. PIEDS DE PORC SAINTE-MENEHOULD – This is a special way of cooking pigs' feet to obtain a particular softening of the bones so that they can be easily crunched.

Cook the feet very slowly for a long period. Brush them with melted butter and coat with white breadcrumbs. Sprinkle with melted butter or lard and cook in the oven until golden. Serve with mashed potatoes.

Truffled pigs' feet I. PIEDS DE PORC TRUFFÉS – Cook the pigs' feet (either boil or braise them) and bone completely. Cut the flesh into large dice. Mix with *Fine pork forcemeat* (see FORCEMEATS or STUFFINGS) to which some diced or chopped truffles have been added. Season with salt, pepper and spices, and add a dash of brandy.

Divide into 100-g. (4-oz., $\frac{1}{2}$ cupful) parts and shape them into *crépinettes* (q.v.), pointed at one end. Put 2 or 3 fine truffle slices on each *crépinette* and wrap in a piece of pig's caul. Brush with melted butter, coat with breadcrumbs and grill gently. Serve with mashed potatoes.

Truffled pigs' feet II. PIEDS DE PORC TRUFFÉS – Braise the pigs' feet in Madeira-flavoured stock. Leave in the braising liquor until cold, then drain and bone. Cut half the flesh into as many pieces as there are feet to be served. Chop the rest, mix with *Fine truffled forcemeat* (see FORCEMEATS or STUFFINGS) and add the braising liquor, boiled down and strained.

Pork intestine. INTESTIN DE PORC – The small intestine, known in French *charcuterie* trade as *menus* or *menuises*, is used for making various kinds of sausages and black puddings. The caecum, which is also called *sac* or *poche* in French, is used for making *andouilles* and other sausages.

The colon, which is also called *chaudin*, and the rectum, which is known under the names of *rosette, boyau gras* or *fuseau*, is used for the same purposes.

Pig's kidney. ROGNON DE PORC – Prepare in the same way as *Calf's kidney*.

Pig's lights (lungs). MOU DE PORC (POUMON DE PORC) – The pig's lights, or lungs, are not very substantial. They acquire a little nutritive value from the garnish and sauces which accompany them.

They are used by pork butchers in making pork *pâtés de foie*, and in cookery for making stews in the same way as *Lamb's* or *Calf's pluck*.

Blanquette of pig's lights. MOU DE PORC EN BLANQUETTE – Cut the lights into pieces, season and cook as described in the recipe for *Tripe en blanquette*.

Ragoût of pig's lights. MOU DE PORC EN RAGOÛT – Beat the lungs to expel all air from them and cut into 40 to 50-g. (2-oz.) pieces.

Season with salt and pepper and fry in butter or lard, stirring frequently so that all the pieces get well browned. Sprinkle with flour and let this colour slightly in the oven. Moisten with white stock, add a little crushed garlic and a *bouquet garni* (q.v.).

Cook in the oven 1 to 1½ hours. Drain and trim the pieces, put into another casserole with the garnish indicated. Strain the sauce over the lights, cover, and cook in the oven 20 to 30 minutes.

Pig's lights à la bonne femme. MOU DE PORC À LA BONNE FEMME – Cut 1 kg. (2¼ lb.) lights into pieces, season with salt and pepper, and fry in butter or lard.

Sprinkle in 2 tablespoons (3 tablespoons) flour, moisten with 1½ litres (2¾ pints, 3¼ pints) white stock or water, and add a *bouquet garni* (q.v.) and a crushed clove of garlic. Bring to the boil, and cook in the oven for 1½ hours.

Drain and trim the pieces, put into another casserole with 12 small, glazed onions, 125 g. (4½ oz., 7 slices) bacon, lightly fried, and 400 g. (14 oz., 2⅓ cups) potatoes, quartered or cut to look like large olives. Cook in the oven 25 to 30 minutes.

Pig's lights en civet, or in red wine. MOU DE PORC EN CIVET (AU VIN ROUGE) – Proceed as described in the recipe for *Pig's lights à la bonne femme*. Moisten with 1 litre (1¾ pints, generous quart) red wine and ½ litre (scant pint, 2¼ cups) white stock. Add small glazed onions, 125 g. (4½ oz., 7 slices) diced and fried bacon, and 125 g. (4½ oz., 2½ cups) raw mushrooms, sliced or cut into quarters. Cook in the oven for 25 minutes. Thicken with 2 dl. (⅓ pint, scant cup) pig's blood.

Pig's lights à la ménagère. MOU DE PORC À LA MÉNAGÈRE – Fry the lights in butter or lard. When half-cooked, add 2 big onions and 2 carrots cut into quarters.

Moisten with 2 dl. (⅓ pint, scant cup) white wine, boil down, add 1 crushed garlic clove, a *bouquet garni* (q.v.), and 1½ litres (2¾ pints, 3¼ pints) white stock or water. Cook in the oven for 1 hour.

Add 4 or 5 potatoes (500 g., 18 oz., 3 cups), cut into quarters, and leave to cook in the oven for 30 minutes.

Pig's lights à la provençale. MOU DE PORC À LA PROVENÇALE – Cut the lights as described above and fry in oil. Add 2 crushed garlic cloves and a big *bouquet garni* consisting of thyme, bay leaf, parsley and basil.

Dilute with 2 dl. (⅓ pint, scant cup) white wine and boil down. Moisten with 2 dl. (⅓ pint, scant cup) thickened veal stock and 8 dl. (generous 1⅓ pints, 1¾ pints) light *Tomato sauce* (see SAUCE). Cook in the oven for 1½ hours.

Drain the pieces, trim them and put into another casserole with 250 g. (9 oz., scant 1½ cups) black olives. Strain the sauce over them and cook in the oven for 25 minutes. When serving, sprinkle with chopped parsley.

Fresh tomatoes, peeled, seeded and coarsely chopped, can be used instead of tomato sauce.

Pig's liver. FOIE DE PORC – Pig's liver is mainly used as a forcemeat ingredient for various *charcuterie*, such as pork brawn and *gayettes* (q.v.). It can also be served hot cooked in various ways. All the recipes given for *Calf's liver* (see below) are applicable to it.

Pig's liver gayettes (Provençale cookery). GAYETTES DE FOIE DE PORC – Cut 500 g. (18 oz.) pig's liver and the same amount (4½ cups) fresh fat bacon (or pig intestine fat) into very small dice. Add 2 cloves finely pounded garlic. Season with 3 teaspoons (1 tablespoon) salt, ½ teaspoon freshly ground pepper and a little spice. Mix.

Divide this forcemeat into 100-g. (4-oz.) parts. Wrap each in a piece of pig's caul (or fat pork), well softened in water. Secure with string.

Put the *gayettes* into a greased pan. Sprinkle with a few tablespoons of lard. Cook in the oven 25 to 30 minutes. The *gayettes* are generally served cold as an *hors-d'œuvre*.

Pig's snout. GROIN DE PORC – This part of the animal is mainly used for preparing brawn. It can also be cooked like *Pigs' ears* or *Pigs' feet* (*trotters*), allowed to cool and grilled like trotters.

Pig's spleen. RATE DE PORC – This part of the viscera is rather mediocre in taste. It is mainly used in *charcuterie* for making sausages.

The spleen, together with the lungs and the heart, can be made into a stew.

Pig's stomach. ESTOMAC DE PORC – The hog's stomach or paunch is used only for making sausages, after it has been washed thoroughly and cooked for a long time.

Pigs' tails. QUEUES DE PORC – These are usually grilled, as *Pigs' feet* (*trotters*).

Singe and clean the tails. Cook them as described in the recipe for *Pigs' ears*. Cool under a press to straighten them. Coat with melted butter and breadcrumbs and grill gently. Serve with mashed potatoes.

Stuffed, braised pigs' tails with various garnishes. QUEUES DE PORC FARCIES, BRAISÉES – Bone the pigs' tails completely in such a way as to obtain long bags, taking care not to tear the skin. Stuff with fine pork or other forcemeat (see FORCEMEATS or STUFFINGS), truffled if desired. Secure with string and braise in very little liquid.

Drain, put on a serving dish and surround with the garnish indicated. Boil down the braising liquor, strain, and pour over the tails.

All the garnishes recommended for sautéed, pot-roasted or braised meat served in small portions are applicable (see GARNISHES).

Stuffed, grilled pigs' tails. QUEUES DE PORC FARCIES, GRILLÉES – Stuff the tails and braise as described above, or cook them in stock as indicated for *Pigs' ears*. Cool under a press.

Brush with melted butter, coat with grated breadcrumbs and grill gently. Serve with mashed potatoes.

Pig's tongue. LANGUE DE PORC – Pig's tongue can be pre-

Pig's tongue in jelly

pared in any way suitable for *Calf's tongue* (see below). After pickling in brine it can be prepared as *Ox tongue a l'écarlate*.

Pig's tongue is also used as an ingredient for potted heads (head cheese) and head brawn.

VEAL OFFAL OR VARIETY MEATS. ABATS DE VEAU –

Veal amourette. AMOURETTE DE VEAU – This is calf's spinal marrow. Calf's *amourette* is principally used; that of oxen (beef) more rarely.

This substance has a very great similarity to brains. It must be soaked in cold water and all membranes covering it removed before preparing it.

After careful washing, boil it in *court-bouillon* (q.v.), then follow any of the recipes given for *Calves' brains* (see below).

The *amourette*, cut into little pieces and cooked in *court-bouillon*, can be used as a garnish for pie dishes, raised pies, *vol-au-vent* and other similar dishes. It can also be served as *hors-d'œuvre*, with oil and vinegar dressing, or with mayonnaise.

Calves' brains. CERVELLE DE VEAU – 500 g. (18 oz.) calves' brains serves 4 people. Soak the brains in cold water for 1 hour. Remove the skin and any traces of blood. Unless otherwise specified in a particular recipe, simmer them (do not boil) in *Court-bouillon III* (see COURT-BOUILLON), to which 1 tablespoon of vinegar has been added, for 15 to 20 minutes. Drain, plunge in very cold water, and allow to cool. Drain and dry. Follow succeeding recipes for final preparation.

Calves' brains à l'allemande. CERVELLE DE VEAU À L'ALLEMANDE – Cook the brains in *court-bouillon* as above and drain. Cut into 3 or 4 uniform slices and dip in flour. Sauté the slices in butter until browned. Arrange on croûtons of bread fried in butter, and cover with *Allemande sauce* (see SAUCE).

Calves' brains à la bourguignonne. CERVELLE DE VEAU À LA BOURGUIGNONNE – Proceed as described in the recipe for *Calves' brains à l'allemande* but use *Bourguignonne sauce* instead of *Allemande* (see SAUCE).

A *Bourguignonne garnish* can also be added (see GARNISHES).

Calves' brains in browned butter I. CERVELLE DE VEAU AU BEURRE NOIR – Cook the brains in *court-bouillon* (q.v.), drain and cut into slices. Arrange them on a dish, season, and sprinkle with 3 to 4 tablespoons ($\frac{1}{4}$ cup) butter, browned in a shallow pan. Add 1 tablespoon chopped parsley, and a dash of vinegar heated in the same pan after the butter has been poured off.

Calves' brains in browned butter II. CERVELLE DE VEAU AU BEURRE NOIR – Season and flour slices of brains. Fry them lightly in butter, arrange on a dish, and finish off as described above.

Calves' brains in noisette butter. CERVELLE DE VEAU AU BEURRE NOISETTE – Season and flour slices of brains, brown lightly in butter, arrange on a dish, sprinkle with chopped parsley, add a dash of lemon juice, and pour over a few tablespoons browned *Noisette butter* (see BUTTER, *Compound butters*).

Fried calves' brains à l'anglaise. CERVELLE DE VEAU FRITE À L'ANGLAISE – Cut cooked brains in slices and marinate for 25 minutes in 2 tablespoons (3 tablespoons) oil mixed with lemon juice, salt, pepper and chopped parsley.

Dip the slices in beaten egg and breadcrumbs, fry in very hot fat, drain, and arrange on a plate with fried parsley. Serve with *Tomato sauce* (see SAUCE).

Calves' brains fried in batter. CERVELLE DE VEAU EN FRITOT – Boil 500 g. (18 oz.) calves' brains in *court-bouillon*, cool and cut in squares. Soak for 25 minutes in a mixture of oil, lemon juice, chopped parsley, salt and pepper. Dip the pieces in *Frying batter VI* (see BATTERS FOR FRYING) and deep-fry in sizzling fat. Drain, dry, season with fine salt. Arrange on a dish in the shape of a pyramid and garnish with fried parsley. Serve with *Tomato sauce* (see SAUCE).

Fried calves' brains à la provençale. CERVELLE DE VEAU SAUTÉE À LA PROVENÇALE – Proceed as described in the recipe for *Calves' brains à l'italienne* (see below), but instead of using *Italian sauce*, put some *Tomato fondue* (see FONDUE) in the middle of the dish.

Garnish with black olives and sprinkle with chopped tarragon.

Fried calves' brains à la romaine. CERVELLE DE VEAU FRITE À LA ROMAINE – Prepare the brains as described in the recipe for *Calves' brains à l'anglaise.*

Arrange in a circle, put some leaf spinach cooked in butter in the middle, place 1 rolled anchovy on each slice of brains, and sprinkle with a few tablespoons of *Noisette butter* (see BUTTER, *Compound butters*).

Calves' brains au gratin. CERVELLE DE VEAU AU GRATIN – Cook slices of calves' brains in *court-bouillon* (q.v.), drain, coat with a few tablespoons *Duxelles sauce* (see SAUCE) and place in a fireproof dish. Put a slice of cooked mushroom on each.

Cover with *duxelles sauce*, sprinkle with white breadcrumbs and melted butter, and brown in a slow oven. Sprinkle with chopped parsley and add a dash of lemon juice.

Calves' brains à la hongroise. CERVELLE DE VEAU À LA HONGROISE – Cut 1 pair of cooked brains into slices. Season with paprika, sprinkle with flour and fry lightly in butter. Arrange in a crown on croûtons of bread fried in butter.

Put a mixture of diced mushrooms, hard-boiled eggs and truffles, all tossed in butter, in the middle. Top each slice with a small sliver of ham heated in butter. Pour some *Paprika sauce* (see SAUCE, *Hungarian sauce*) over the middle of the dish and sprinkle with chopped parsley.

Calves' brains à l'indienne. CERVELLE DE VEAU À L'INDIENNE – Cut cooked brains in slices and fry lightly in butter. Arrange in a crown with some *Rice à l'indienne* (see RICE) and cover with *Curry sauce* (see SAUCE).

Calves' brains à l'italienne. CERVELLE DE VEAU À L'ITALIENNE – Cut cooked brains in slices, season, sprinkle with flour, and fry lightly in oil, or oil and butter in equal proportions.

Arrange in a circle and cover with *Italian sauce* (see SAUCE).

Calves' brains in jelly. CERVELLE DE VEAU À LA GELÉE – Soak 500 g. (18 oz.) calves' brains in salted water for 5 minutes. Skin them, and cook with 4 dl. ($\frac{3}{4}$ pint, scant 2 cups) jellied meat stock. Boil for 5 minutes, then leave to cool in the pan.

Drain the brains, divide in halves, dry, put into a dish and pour over the pan juices, clarified and strained through a napkin. Put on ice to set.

Cold jellied calves' brains. CERVELLE DE VEAU EN CHAUD-FROID – Cook 500 g. (18 oz.) calves' brains as described in the recipe for *Calves' brains in jelly*. Leave to cool in the liquid in which they were boiled. As soon as they are quite cold, drain, divide in halves, dry without damaging them, and coat them with *White chaud-froid sauce* (see SAUCE).

Cold jellied calves' brains à la parisienne. CERVELLE DE VEAU EN CHAUD-FROID À LA PARISIENNE – Prepare the brains as described in the preceeding recipe and garnish with *Parisian salad* (see SALAD).

Calves' brains loaf à l'ancienne. PAIN DE CERVELLE DE VEAU À L'ANCIENNE – Cook 500 g. (18 oz.) calves' brains in butter. Add 50 g. (2 oz., $\frac{1}{4}$ cup) butter and 100 g. (4 oz., $\frac{1}{2}$ cup) *Frangipane panada* (see PANADA) and pound in a mortar.

Season with salt, pepper and ground nutmeg and add two eggs, pounding well to achieve a smooth mixture.

Pass through a fine sieve, blend with a spoon, and put into a buttered mould. Cook in a pan of hot water, or in a *bain-marie* 25 to 30 minutes in the oven. Leave for 5 minutes before turning out.

Put the loaf on a dish and surround with mushrooms cooked in *Court-bouillon IX* (see COURT-BOUILLON). Pour over 2 dl. ($\frac{1}{3}$ pint, scant cup) *Allemande sauce* (see SAUCE), and decorate with 12 slivers of truffles.

Calves' brains en matelote. CERVELLE DE VEAU EN MATELOTE – Boil 500 g. (18 oz.) calves' brains in 8 dl. (generous $1\frac{1}{3}$ pints, $1\frac{3}{4}$ pints) *Court-bouillon with red wine* (*XIV*) (see COURT-BOUILLON). Drain, cut in thick slices and put into a shallow pan with 24 small glazed onions and 24 small mushrooms fried in butter.

Boil down the *court-bouillon* by half, blend in 50 g. (2 oz., $\frac{1}{4}$ cup) *Kneaded butter* (see BUTTER, *Compound butters*), strain, and pour over the brains.

Simmer for a few moments without boiling. Garnish with heart-shaped croûtons of bread fried in butter.

Calves' brains à la poulette. CERVELLE DE VEAU À LA POULETTE – Cut the cooked brains into thick slices and cook for a few moments, without allowing to boil, in *Poulette sauce* (see SAUCE). Heap in a shallow platter.

Brain stuffing or forcemeat. FARCE DE CERVELLE – Cook a brain in a *court-bouillon* (q.v.). Drain, and rub through a fine sieve. Heat the purée in a double saucepan. According to the recipe used, add a little butter, cream, *Béchamel* or *Velouté sauce* (see SAUCE).

This stuffing is used to fill small *vol-au-vent*, tarts or tartlets, *barquettes*, etc.

Calves' ears braised à la mirepoix. OREILLE DE VEAU BRAISÉES À LA MIREPOIX – Blanch four calves' ears for 8 minutes. Cool them in cold water, drain, trim, dry and thoroughly clean the inside.

Put into a saucepan, cover with 2 dl. ($\frac{1}{3}$ pint, scant cup) *mirepoix* (q.v.), add a *bouquet garni* (q.v.), season with salt and pepper, add 1 dl. (6 tablespoons, scant $\frac{1}{2}$ cup) white wine and cook to thicken.

Add 3 dl. ($\frac{1}{2}$ pint, $1\frac{1}{4}$ cups) slightly thickened brown veal stock and cook in the oven with a lid on for $1\frac{1}{2}$ hours.

Drain the ears, remove the skin which covers the thin part of the inside and the outside with the aid of a spoon. Beat this part flat and slit it.

Arrange the ears on croûtons of bread fried in butter. Strain pan juices, remove surplus fat, and pour over dish.

Braised calves' ears Mount-Bry. OREILLES DE VEAU BRAISÉES MONT-BRY – Cook the ears as described in the recipe for *Calves' ears braised à la mirepoix*.

Drain them, put each on a little *Anna potato cake* (see POTATOES), and garnish with 4 lettuce hearts braised in the juice. Strain the pan juices, remove surplus fat, pour over the ears and serve.

Fried calves' ears I. OREILLES DE VEAU FRITES – Cook the ears as described in the recipe for *Calves' ears braised à la mirepoix*, drain, cool, divide into uniform pieces, dip in beaten egg and breadcrumbs and deep-fry in sizzling fat.

Arrange in a pyramid, decorate with fried parsley and serve with the pan juices, strained and finished off as *Diable* or *Piquante sauce* (see SAUCE).

Fried calves' ears II. OREILLES DE VEAU FRITES – Cut the ears into strips, leave to soak in batter and finish off as described above.

Fried calves' ears III. OREILLES DE VEAU EN FRITOT – Cook the ears in a flour-and-water stock. Drain and wipe them. Cut each into 8 or 10 pieces of regular shape and size. Marinate for 30 minutes with oil, lemon juice, chopped parsley, salt and pepper. Dip in a light batter and fry in smoking hot deep fat. Garnish with fried parsley. Serve with *Tomato sauce* (see SAUCE).

Grilled calves' ears à la diable. OREILLES DE VEAU GRILLÉES À LA DIABLE – Cut the braised ears in two lengthways, put them under a press for a few moments, spread with mustard, sprinkle with melted butter, dust with white breadcrumbs and cook on both sides under a gentle grill. Serve with *Diable sauce* (see SAUCE).

Calves' ears à la hongroise. OREILLES DE VEAU À LA HONGROISE – Cook the ears in a flour-and-water *court-bouillon* (q.v.), cut them into uniform pieces and put them into a sauté pan in which 100 g. (4 oz., 1 cup) finely diced onions (for every 2 ears), seasoned with salt and paprika, have been cooked in butter. Stew the ears for 10 minutes. Add 4 tablespoons ($\frac{1}{3}$ cup) mushrooms cut into large dice and lightly cooked in butter. Stir in 4 dl. ($\frac{3}{4}$ pint, scant 2 cups) thin *Velouté* or *Béchamel sauce* (see SAUCE). Cook, covered, for about 15 minutes. Add 3 tablespoons (scant $\frac{1}{4}$ cup) butter.

Calves' ears à l'indienne. OREILLES DE VEAU À L'INDIENNE – Cook in flour-and-water *court-bouillon* (q.v.). Cut into squares and treat like *Calves' feet à l'indienne* (see below).

Calves' ears à l'italienne. OREILLES DE VEAU À L'ITALIENNE – 'Prepare and cook the calves' ears as described in the recipe for *Calves' ears braised à la mirepoix*, but instead of slitting them, cut the tendons to round off the end, and dress the inside with a mixture of truffles, mushrooms and calf's tongue cut up very small, and bound with 2 tablespoons (3 tablespoons) thick *Financière sauce* (see SAUCE). Bring the whole to the boil and serve with an *Italian sauce*.' (From Carême and Plumerey.)

Calves' ears en tortue. OREILLES DE VEAU EN TORTUE – Cook the ears as described in the recipe for *Calves' ears braised à la mirepoix* but replacing the white wine by Madeira.

Drain, arrange on fried croûtons, and surround with the garnish *en tortue* (see GARNISHES). Strain the pan juices, skim off fat, and finish as described for *Tortue sauce* (see SAUCE). Pour over the dish and serve.

Calves' ears stuffed en tortue. OREILLES DE VEAU FARCIES EN TORTUE – Soak the ears and part cook in a flour-and-water *court-bouillon* as for *Calf's head* (see below).

Stuff them with a forcemeat composed of one half *Fine pork forcemeat* and one half *Veal forcemeat* (see FORCEMEATS or STUFFINGS) with the addition of diced truffles, the whole bound with eggs.

Finish cooking the ears in a Madeira-flavoured braising stock. Finish off as for *Calf's head en tortue* (see below).

Calves' ears Villeroi. OREILLES DE VEAU VILLEROI – Cook

the ears as described in the recipe for *Calves' ears braised à la mirepoix* and drain.

Trim, fill the inside with a finely pounded *Chicken forcemeat* (see FORCEMEATS or STUFFINGS), dip in *Villeroi sauce* (see SAUCE), then in breadcrumbs, and fry.

Arrange on a plate with fried parsley and serve with *Tomato* or *Périgueux sauce* (see SAUCE).

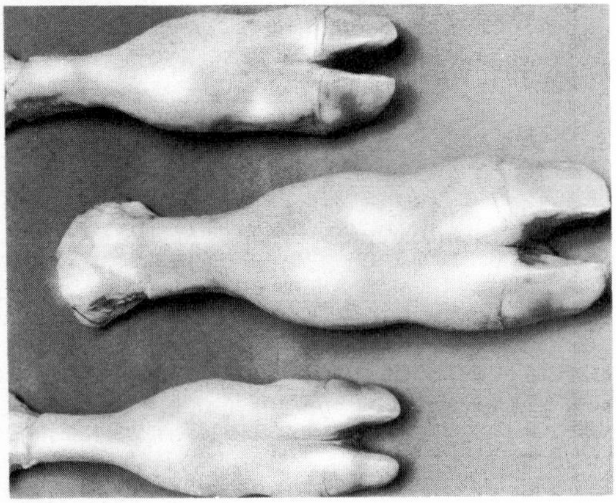

Calves' feet (*Nicolas*)

Calves' feet. PIEDS DE VEAU – Soak the feet in cold water, bone and blanch them, cook in a *court-bouillon* as for *Calf's head* (see below).

Cut into pieces, marinate for 1 hour in oil, lemon juice, chopped parsley, salt and pepper, dip in a light batter and deep-fry in sizzling fat.

All the recipes given for *Calf's head* can be used for *Calves' feet*.

Calves' feet à l'indienne. PIEDS DE VEAU À L'INDIENNE – Cook as for *Calves' feet* and serve with *Rice à l'indienne* (see RICE), the feet covered with *Curry sauce* (see SAUCE).

Calves' feet à l'italienne. PIEDS DE VEAU À L'ITALIENNE – Cut cooked calves' feet into uniform pieces and put into *Italian sauce* (see SAUCE).

Calves' feet with tartare sauce. PIEDS DE VEAU À LA TARTARE – Cut into uniform pieces, dip in egg and breadcrumbs, deep-fry and serve with *Tartare sauce* (see SAUCE, *Cold sauces*).

Calves' feet à la vinaigrette. PIEDS DE VEAU À LA VINAIGRETTE – Prepare like *Calf's head in oil* (see below).

Calf's head. TÊTE DE VEAU – Calf's head should be boned and soaked for a long time in cold water, then blanched, cooled, and cut into pieces, or – depending on the method of preparation – it can be left whole. Then it is cooked in a *White court-bouillon* (see below).

When calf's head is being cooked *à l'anglaise* it does not have to be boned. After a long soaking and blanching, it is cooked in the white *court-bouillon*. It should always be served with the tongue cut in slices, and the brain, cooked separately in white *court-bouillon* and sliced. The brain can also be pounded and blended with a cold sauce.

White court-bouillon for calf's head. Mix flour with cold water, using 1 heaped tablespoon per litre ($1\frac{3}{4}$ pints, generous quart) water, until smooth. Pass this mixture through a fine strainer. Pour into a saucepan, big enough to take the head, either whole or divided in halves, or cut into pieces. Season with 1 teaspoon salt and add 1 tablespoon vinegar per litre ($1\frac{3}{4}$ pints, generous quart) water. Bring to the boil. Add 1 large onion studded with two cloves, and a *bouquet garni* consisting of parsley, thyme and a bay leaf. When this stock is boiling, put in the calf's head wrapped in a fine muslin cloth.

Add 250 g. (9 oz., generous 2 cups) beef (or veal) fat, chopped and soaked in cold water. This fat, upon melting, will form a protective layer over the calf's head and will prevent it from going black.

Calf's head à l'anglaise. TÊTE DE VEAU À L'ANGLAISE – Cook the calf's head in a white *court-bouillon* (see *Calf's head*), whole or split in half, but without boning.

Arrange the head on a dish and serve with a piece of boiled bacon and *Parsley sauce* (see SAUCE).

Calf's head à la bonne femme. TÊTE DE VEAU À LA BONNE FEMME – Boil the calf's head in a white *court-bouillon* (see *Calf's head*) cut into uniform pieces and simmer gently in a *Demi-glace sauce* (see SAUCE) with pieces of bacon, lightly browned in butter, glazed mushrooms, olives and small onions. Heap on a dish.

Calf's head Caillou. TÊTE DE VEAU CAILLOU – For 6 persons, cook half a blanched calf's head, cut into 6 pieces, and half the calf's tongue in a large saucepan. The head should only be three-quarters cooked, the final cooking taking place in the sauce.

Fry 1 large chopped onion in 3 tablespoons (scant $\frac{1}{4}$ cup) butter without allowing it to brown, adding 50 g. (2 oz., $\frac{1}{4}$ cup) lean smoked ham cut into little pieces. Sprinkle in 4 tablespoons ($\frac{1}{3}$ cup) flour, brown lightly, blend with 5 dl. (scant pint, $2\frac{1}{4}$ cups) stock. Add 2 tablespoons (3 tablespoons) *Tomato sauce* (see SAUCE), a *bouquet garni* (q.v.) consisting of 2 sprigs parsley, 1 small clove of garlic, 1 sprig of thyme, $\frac{1}{4}$ bay leaf and 1 stalk of celery. Mix well and cook for 20 minutes.

Put the calf's head and the tongue, cut into 6 slices, into a sauté pan, add 48 peeled chestnuts, half-cooked in consommé, 48 large, stoned olives, and 12 mushrooms, skinned and washed with the stalks removed. Add 1 dl. (6 tablespoons, scant $\frac{1}{2}$ cup) Madeira. Simmer for 10 minutes. Cover with the strained sauce and cook under a lid for 35 minutes.

Arrange the calf's head and the chestnuts on a large shallow dish. Garnish with little escalopes of brains dipped in slightly beaten egg and breadcrumbs and fried in butter, and with heart-shaped croûtons fried in butter.

Calf's head in crépinettes. TÊTE DE VEAU EN CRÉPINETTES – Cut 500 g. (18 oz.) of calf's head cooked in a white *court-bouillon* (see *Calf's head*) into pieces. Add to this $\frac{1}{3}$ its weight in diced mushrooms lightly fried in butter, and 4 tablespoons diced truffles. Blend with *Madeira sauce* (see SAUCE) based on truffle essence and boiled down. Add some diced calf's tongue and brain. Allow to cool.

Divide this mixture into parts of 50 g. (2 oz.) each. Enclose each of these in 3 tablespoons (scant $\frac{1}{4}$ cup) finely-minced *Pork forcemeat* (see FORCEMEATS or STUFFINGS). Roll each into the shape of a flat sausage, and wrap in a piece of caul, cut paper-thin, moistened with cold water. Smear with melted butter, roll in white breadcrumbs, sprinkle with melted butter and grill under a gentle flame. Serve with *Périgueux sauce* (see SAUCE) or with any other sauce recommended for grilled meats.

Calf's head à la financière. TÊTE DE VEAU À LA FINANCIÈRE – Cut the head, boiled in a white *court-bouillon* (see *Calf's head*) and well drained, into 2-inch pieces. Stew in Madeira. Arrange in a dish. Cover with *Financière garnish* (see GARNISHES), to which pieces of sliced or diced calf's tongue, and brain sliced into escalopes, have been added.

Fried calf's head. TÊTE DE VEAU FRITE – Cut the head into square pieces. Marinate for 1 hour in oil, lemon juice, salt, pepper and chopped parsley. Dip the pieces into a light batter (see BATTER) and deep-fry in sizzling fat.

Garnish with fried parsley. Serve with *Tomato sauce* (see SAUCE) or any other sauce recommended for calf's head.

Calf's head fried in batter. TÊTE DE VEAU EN FRITOT – This is the same recipe as that for *Fried calf's head.*

Fried calf's head à la piémontaise. TÊTE DE VEAU FRITE À LA PIÉMONTAISE – Cook the calf's head in a white *court-bouillon* (see *Calf's head*) and cut in small square pieces. Slice the tongue and the brain. Marinate for 1 hour in oil, lemon juice, salt, pepper and chopped parsley.

Dip in a light batter (see BATTERS FOR FRYING) and deep-fry in sizzling fat.

Drain on a cloth, season with finely ground salt. Arrange in a heap on a dish, surrounded by a border of *Risotto à la piémontaise* (see RICE). Pour a few tablespoons of a not too thick *Tomato sauce* (see SAUCE) over the risotto.

Calf's head Godard. TÊTE DE VEAU GODARD – This is prepared like *Calf's head à la financière.*

In the olden days, calf's head Godard used to be served whole and almost always stuffed. (See below, *Stuffed calf's head à l'ancienne.*)

Calf's head with Gribiche sauce. TÊTE DE VEAU SAUCE GRIBICHE – Cook the calf's head and the tongue in a white *court-bouillon* (see *Calf's head*) and cut into uniform pieces. Drain. Garnish with escalopes of tongue, and slices of brain cooked separately in *court-bouillon* with fresh parsley. Serve with *Gribiche sauce* (see SAUCE, *Cold sauces*).

Calf's head à l'italienne. TÊTE DE VEAU À L'ITALIENNE – This is cooked calf's head cut into square pieces and put into *Italian sauce* (see SAUCE). Sprinkle with chopped parsley.

Calf's head à la lyonnaise. TÊTE DE VEAU À LA LYONNAISE – Cook the calf's head in a white *court-bouillon* (see *Calf's head*), cut into pieces and put them into an ovenproof dish lined with a layer of thinly sliced onions lightly fried in butter and mixed with chopped parsley. Cover with *Lyonnaise sauce* (see SAUCE). Sprinkle with breadcrumbs and melted butter. Brown in the oven.

Calf's head à l'occitane (Languedoc cookery). TÊTE DE VEAU À L'OCCITANE – Cut half a well-soaked calf's head into 8 uniform pieces and cook in a white *court-bouillon* (see *Calf's head*). In the same *court-bouillon* cook half a calf's tongue. Poach the brain separately in *Court-bouillon V* (see COURT-BOUILLON). Put 3 tablespoons (scant $\frac{1}{4}$ cup) chopped onion, lightly fried in butter, into a shallow fireproof dish and add 1 garlic clove towards the end of cooking. Place the dish in a pan of boiling water and put in the pieces of calf's head and the sliced tongue and brain. Garnish with black olives, 2 peeled, deseeded tomatoes cut into little pieces and tossed in oil, and 2 sliced hard-boiled eggs. Season with salt and pepper. Put 75 g. (3 oz., 6 tablespoons) butter divided into tiny dabs, 5 tablespoons (6 tablespoons) oil, juice of $\frac{1}{2}$ lemon and 1 teaspoon chopped parsley on the calf's head. Heat in a pan of water, keeping the dish covered. Before serving, baste the head well with the sauce.

Calf's head in oil. TÊTE DE VEAU À L'HUILE – Serve with slices of tongue and brain, garnished with fresh parsley and *Vinaigrette sauce* (see SAUCE).

Calf's head with olives. TÊTE DE VEAU AUX OLIVES – Cut the head into pieces. Put into a shallow pan with some *Demi-glace sauce* (see SAUCE) or rich meat stock laced with Madeira. Add stoned and blanched olives. Simmer slowly.

Calf's head à la portugaise. TÊTE DE VEAU À LA PORTUGAISE – Cut the boiled calf's head and tongue into square pieces. Cook gently in a not too thick *Tomato fondue* (see FONDUE).

Put the sliced calf's brain on top. Sprinkle with chopped parsley.

Calf's head à la poulette. TÊTE DE VEAU À LA POULETTE – Boil in a white *court-bouillon* (see *Calf's head*) and cut into little slices. Prepare as described in the recipe for *Sheep's trotters à la poulette.*

Calf's head à la ravigote. TÊTE DE VEAU À LA RAVIGOTE – Cook the calf's head in *court-bouillon* (see above). Drain and cut into square pieces. Cover with *Ravigote sauce* (see SAUCE) and garnish with slices of brain.

Hot calf's head with various cold sauces. TÊTE DE VEAU CHAUDE – Arrange the cooked head on a dish with slices of tongue and brain. Garnish with fried parsley. Serve with various cold sauces, such as: *Aïoli, Gribiche, Mayonnaise, Ravigote* (or *Vinaigrette*), *Rémoulade, Tartare, Vincent* (see SAUCE, *Cold sauces*).

Hot calf's head with various hot sauces. TÊTE DE VEAU CHAUDE – Cook the calf's head in a white *court-bouillon* (see above) and drain; arrange on a dish with slices of tongue and brain, garnish with fried parsley, and serve with sauces such as: *Caper, Fines herbes, Hungarian, Ravigote* (see SAUCE, *Compound white sauces*); *Charcutière, Diable, Fines herbes, Piquante, Robert* (see SAUCE, *Compound brown sauces*).

Stuffed calf's head. TÊTE DE VEAU FARCIE – Cook the calf's head in a white *court-bouillon* (see *Calf's head*), divide in half or cut into pieces. Cut the lean parts into 6-cm. (2- to 3-inch) slices.

Arrange these inside the head with a stuffing made of chopped minced veal, panada (q.v.) and cream, and a mixture of chopped dried mushrooms, chopped hard-boiled eggs and chopped parsley. Press this forcemeat into a dome shape. Put the pieces of head, stuffed side up, into a buttered ovenproof dish, with several tablespoons of white stock. Sprinkle with breadcrumbs and melted butter. Put the dish in a pan half-filled with hot water, and brown in a slow oven.

Serve with a well-spiced sauce, such as *Piquante, Poivrade, Tartare, Ravigote* or *Béarnaise* (see SAUCE).

Calf's head can also be served with one of the garnishes which usually go with braised calf's head, *Financière, Godard, Tortue, etc.* (see GARNISHES).

Stuffed calf's head à l'ancienne. TÊTE DE VEAU FARCIE À L'ANCIENNE – Boil a boned calf's head in a white *court-bouillon* (see *Calf's head*) until three-quarters done. Drain and dry the head. Remove the ears. Spread the head, skin side down, on a damp, wrung-out napkin, stretched taut on the table. Remove some of the lean flesh inside the head, cover the hole made in the skin by the removal of the ears with a thick slice of bacon. Season with salt, pepper and all-spice. Fill with a *Veal forcemeat* (see FORCEMEATS or STUFFINGS) made of minced veal, panada and cream, adding a mixture made of the lean flesh taken out of the head, trimmed and diced, the tongue, and some truffles.

Enclose this stuffing in the skin and sew up the opening. Wrap in the napkin and mould the head into its original shape. Secure with string.

Brown pieces of bacon rinds, carrots and sliced onions in butter and put the calf's head in the pan, surrounded by pieces of knuckle browned in butter. Add a large *bouquet garni* (q.v.). Simmer, covered, on the top of the stove, for 15 minutes. Add 3 dl. ($\frac{1}{2}$ pint, $1\frac{1}{4}$ cups) Madeira and boil down. Add 5 dl. (scant pint, $2\frac{1}{4}$ cups) thickened veal stock. Put the ears into the saucepan, wrapped in a piece of muslin to enable them to be taken out easily. Bring to the boil. Finish cooking in a slow oven with a lid on. Before the cooking is complete, remove the ears, which consist of more delicate flesh and are, therefore, cooked sooner.

Drain the head. Unwrap it and arrange on a large, long dish. Fix the ears in their place by means of small skewers.

Surround the head either with *Financière* or *Godard garnish* (see GARNISHES) arranged in bunches.

Add sliced calf's brain, cooked in *court-bouillon* (q.v.). Strain the pan juices, remove surplus fat, boil down and pour over the calf's head.

Calf's head à la Tertillière. TÊTE DE VEAU À LA TERTILLIÈRE – Cook the head in a white *court-bouillon* (see *Calf's head*), drain, cut into pieces and put into a shallow pan with 150 g. (5 oz., generous cup) pickled tongue, 150 g. (5 oz., scant 2 cups) mushrooms, 6 small truffles, all coarsely shredded, and $3\frac{1}{2}$ dl. (generous $\frac{1}{2}$ pint, $1\frac{1}{2}$ cups) *Madeira sauce* (see SAUCE) with truffle essence. Cook gently for 30 minutes. Add 1 teaspoon finely shredded, blanched and drained lemon peel.

Garnish with halves of hard-boiled eggs and small slices of calf's brain.

Calf's head en tortue. TÊTE DE VEAU EN TORTUE – In the old days, a large *entrée* demanded a certain number of garnishes. Nowadays, this dish is served in a *timbale* and the various garnishes are put in a mixed *ragoût* over it.

This garnish is made of the following ingredients: quenelles of minced veal (see FORCEMEAT or STUFFINGS, *Quenelle forcemeat*); cocks' combs and kidneys, cooked mushrooms, stuffed poached olives, slivers of truffles and escalopes of calf's tongue. To this *ragoût*, stewed with Madeira and blended with *Tortue sauce* (see SAUCE), add gherkins, cut in uniform pieces. Arrange the head on a dish, dress with the garnishes and *Tortue sauce*, decorate with fried eggs, slices of calf's brain cooked in *court-bouillon* (q.v.), dressed crayfish, also cooked in *court-bouillon*, and heart-shaped fried croûtons.

Pieces of calf's head, after having been slowly cooked in *Tortue sauce*, can also be arranged on croûtons of bread fried in butter, with the garnishes disposed around.

Calf's head can also be served whole, stuffed and cooked in braising stock spiced with *Turtle herbs* (see HERBS).

Calf's head à la toulousaine. TÊTE DE VEAU À LA TOULOUSAINE – Cut the cooked head into square pieces. Fill a dish with pieces of tongue and brain and add *Garnish à la toulousaine* (see GARNISHES). Heat, cover with *Allemande sauce* (see SAUCE) based on mushroom essence. Garnish with slivers of truffle.

The head can also be served, cut in round pieces, on circular croûtons fried in butter, with the garnish laid out in separate groups. Pour over *Allemande sauce*.

Calf's head à la vinaigrette. TÊTE DE VEAU À LA VINAIGRETTE – Prepared like *Calf's head in oil*.

Calf's heart à l'anglaise I. COEUR DE VEAU À L'ANGLAISE – Cut the calf's heart into slices about 2 cm ($\frac{3}{4}$ inch) thick. Remove the little clot of blood which forms in the centre between the compartments. Season with salt and pepper, brush with melted butter, roll in freshly grated breadcrumbs and grill under a gentle flame. Arrange in a dish alternating with grilled slices of bacon. Garnish with boiled potatoes. Dot the slices of heart with dabs of half-melted *Maître d'hôtel butter* (see BUTTER, *Compound butters*).

Calf's heart à l'anglaise II. COEUR DE VEAU À L'ANGLAISE – Cut into slices and fry in butter as described in the recipe for *Calf's liver à l'anglaise I* (see below).

Casserole of calf's heart. COEUR DE VEAU EN CASSEROLE – Season the heart with salt and pepper and put into an earthenware casserole in which 3 tablespoons (scant $\frac{1}{4}$ cup) butter have been heated. Cook in a moderate oven from 30 to 35 minutes, basting frequently with the juice.

Baste with a few tablespoons thickened veal stock. Serve in the casserole in which it was cooked.

Casserole of calf's heart à la bonne femme. COEUR DE VEAU EN CASSEROLE À LA BONNE FEMME – Brown the calf's heart in sizzling butter in an earthenware fireproof casserole as described above. Add very small potatoes, small glazed onions and lean rashers of bacon, fried in butter. Cook all the ingredients together. Finish off as described in the preceding recipe.

Casserole of calf's heart can be garnished with various vegetables, some of which may be cooked with the heart, or added to the casserole; others may be added after the heart is cooked.

Roast calf's heart. COEUR DE VEAU RÔTI – Season calf's heart with salt and pepper, sprinkle with olive oil and a dash of lemon juice. Leave to soak for 30 minutes in this seasoning. Wrap in a sheet of pork fat or in a piece of pig's caul. Roast on a spit before a brisk fire for 35 minutes or bake $1\frac{1}{2}$ to 2 hours in the oven. Serve with the diluted pan juices poured over.

Sautéed calf's heart. COEUR DE VEAU SAUTÉ – Cut the heart into thin small slices. Season with salt and pepper. Toss quickly in sizzling butter and finish cooking as described in the recipe for *Calf's kidney à la bordelaise* (see below).

Sautéed calf's heart can be prepared with a *Mushroom sauce, Chasseur sauce, Madeira* or other wine sauce (see SAUCE).

An alternative, after having tossed it in butter, is to add *Rice pilaf* (see PILAF) or risotto (see RICE).

Stuffed calf's heart with various vegetables. COEUR DE VEAU FARCI AVEC LÉGUMES – Open the heart without separating the halves completely. Remove the clot of blood which forms in the middle. Season with salt and pepper and fill with finely minced *Pork forcemeat* (see FORCEMEATS or STUFFINGS), or other stuffing. Wrap it in a sheet of salt pork cut paper thin, in a piece of caul, or in thin slices of bacon. Secure with string. Put into a casserole, sprinkle with melted butter, season, and cook in a slow oven for about 1 hour.

Arrange the heart on a dish and garnish with the vegetables indicated. Dilute the pan juices with dry white wine, blend in thickened veal stock, boil down, add butter, pour over the heart and serve.

Calves' kidneys. ROGNONS DE VEAU – When a calf's kidney is cut into slices or escalopes for frying or grilling cut off all fat and remove membranes. If it is to be cooked whole, in a casserole or otherwise, it is trimmed less drastically, so as to leave a light coating of fat around it.

Calves' kidneys à la Bercy. ROGNONS DE VEAU À LA BERCY – Cut the kidneys across into slices 2 cm. ($\frac{3}{4}$ inch) thick. Brush them with melted butter, season and dip in breadcrumbs. Grill under a brisk flame. Serve with *Bercy butter* (see BUTTER, *Compound butters*).

Calves' kidneys à la bordelaise. ROGNONS DE VEAU À LA BORDELAISE – Skin the kidneys and cut them open without dividing the halves completely. Put two skewers through each kidney to keep the shape. Season, spread with butter, sprinkle with breadcrumbs and grill under a brisk flame, cooking the open side of the kidney first.

Arrange on a dish, garnish with slivers of marrow poached in salted water and drained. Pour a border of *Bordelaise sauce* (see SAUCE) around the kidneys.

Casserole of calves' kidneys. ROGNONS DE VEAU EN CASSEROLE – Take some of the fat off the kidneys. Season, and cook them whole, in an earthenware casserole in which 2 tablespoons (3 tablespoons) butter have been heated. Baste with 2 tablespoons (3 tablespoons) thickened veal stock. Serve in the casserole.

Casserole of calves' kidneys à la bonne femme. ROGNONS DE VEAU EN CASSEROLE À LA BONNE FEMME – Cook 50 g. (2 oz., 3 slices) diced bacon and 4 small onions in butter in a casserole. Remove these from the casserole and in the same butter toss a whole kidney, with the fat partly taken off, just to stiffen it. Add the diced bacon and onions, and surround the kidney with a dozen new potatoes, or old potatoes cut down to the size of olives, three-quarters cooked in butter.

Season with salt and pepper. Cook in the oven, uncovered. Baste with 4 tablespoons (⅓ cup) veal stock. Serve in the casserole.

Sometimes mushrooms lightly tossed in butter are added to the garnish of the kidney.

Grilled calves' kidneys. ROGNONS DE VEAU GRILLÉS – Slit the kidney lengthways without completely dividing it into halves. Put 2 metal skewers through it to keep it open. Season, brush over with melted butter and cook under a grill. Serve with *Maître d'hôtel butter* (separately or on the kidney), *Bercy butter*, or any other sauce specially recommended for grills. (See BUTTER, *Compound butters*; SAUCE.)

Calves' kidneys à la liégeoise. ROGNONS DE VEAU À LA LIÉGEOISE – Cook the kidneys as described in the recipe for *Casserole of calves' kidneys*. Add to the casserole 4 crushed juniper berries, 2 tablespoons (3 tablespoons) gin which has been set ablaze, and 1½ tablespoons (2 tablespoons) thickened veal stock. Serve as it is.

Calves' kidneys with pilaf. ROGNONS DE VEAU EN PILAF – Prepared like *Calf's liver with pilaf* (see below).

Calves' kidneys sautéed à la bordelaise. ROGNONS DE VEAU SAUTÉS À LA BORDELAISE – Skin the kidney and cut into small slices. Season with salt and pepper. Sauté briskly in sizzling butter, remove the kidney and keep hot.

Add 1 dl. (6 tablespoons, scant ½ cup) white wine to the butter. Put in 1 tablespoon finely chopped shallots. Boil down; add 2½ dl. (scant ½ pint, generous cup) thickened brown veal stock, and the pan juices left over from frying the kidney. Boil down to the desired consistency. Put the kidney into the sauce with 2 tablespoons (3 tablespoons) diced beef marrow, poached and well drained. Mix, and serve in a dish sprinkled with chopped parsley.

Calves' kidneys sautéed with mushrooms. ROGNONS DE VEAU SAUTÉS AUX CHAMPIGNONS – Cut the kidney into small slices, season with salt and pepper and sauté briskly in sizzling butter. Remove the slices and keep hot.

Fry 4 sliced mushrooms in the same butter. Remove them and add to the kidney.

Pour 1 dl. (6 tablespoons, scant ½ cup) Madeira into a saucepan, add 1½ dl. (¼ pint, ⅔ cup) thickened brown veal stock or *Demi-glace sauce* (see SAUCE) and the juices left over from the kidney. Boil down by a good third.

Put the kidneys and the mushrooms into this sauce, which should be quite thick. Add 1 tablespoon butter. Shake the pan to mix well. Heap on a shallow dish.

Sautéed calves' kidneys with various wines. ROGNONS SAUTÉS AU VIN – Prepare as described above (with or without mushrooms) and replace Madeira by Chablis, Sauternes, Graves or another white wine or a red wine: Burgundy, Bordeaux, Côtes du Rhône, Alsatian wine, Rhine wine, etc.

Calves' kidneys on skewers. ROGNONS DE VEAU EN BROCHETTES – Skin the kidneys and cut into uniform pieces. Season with salt and pepper. Put on metal skewers, alternating with pieces of bacon, lightly fried in butter. Dip in breadcrumbs and grill under a brisk flame. Serve with *Maître d'hôtel butter, Bercy butter* or a special sauce recommended for grills (see BUTTER, *Compound butters*; SAUCE).

Calf's liver à l'anglaise. FOIE DE VEAU À L'ANGLAISE – Cut the calf's liver into thin slices, season with salt and pepper, dredge lightly with flour and fry very quickly in sizzling butter. Brown on both sides. Arrange on a dish with thin rashers of bacon, fried in butter in the same pan as the liver.

Serve with potatoes cut down to the same size, boiled in salted water and well drained, or with steamed potatoes.

Sprinkle with chopped parsley and a few drops of lemon juice, and pour over it the butter in which the liver was cooked.

Calf's liver *à l'anglaise* can also be prepared by grilling the liver and the bacon, garnishing the dish with boiled potatoes and dabbing with *Maître d'hôtel butter* (see BUTTER, *Compound butters*).

Calf's liver Bercy. FOIE DE VEAU BERCY – Slice, season, dredge with flour and grill. Serve with *Bercy butter* (see BUTTER, *Compound butters*).

Calf's liver à la bordelaise. FOIE DE VEAU À LA BORDELAISE – Slice, season, dredge with flour and fry in butter. Arrange on a dish in alternate rows with slices of ham fried in butter. Serve with *Bordelaise sauce* (see SAUCE).

Calf's liver à la bourgeoise. FOIE DE VEAU À LA BOURGEOISE – Lard the liver with thick strips of bacon fat ½ cm. square (¼ inch square) and 5 to 7½ cm. (2 to 3 inches) long, seasoned with pepper, spices and chopped parsley. Sprinkle with brandy. Secure with string. Braise like *Top rump à la bourgeoise* (see BEEF).

Calf's liver à la bouguignonne. FOIE DE VEAU À LA BOURGUIGNONNE – Proceed using sliced calf's liver as described in the recipe for *Entrecôte à la bourguignonne* (see BEEF).

Calf's liver à la créole (Créole cookery). FOIE DE VEAU À LA CRÉOLE – Cut the liver in slices and lard with small pieces of larding bacon. Leave to marinate in a few drops of oil. Dust lightly with flour. Brown on both sides in fat and leave in the corner of the pan. In the same pan, fry lightly 1 teaspoon finely chopped onion, and add the same quantity chopped parsley, breadcrumbs and salt. Blend a little *Tomato purée* (see SAUCE, *Brown basic sauces*) with 1 tablespoon white wine and add to the pan. Remove the slices of liver, and put on each a little of the mixture in the pan. Heat a dish, put a knob of butter at the bottom, and fill with the slices of liver. Pour over the sauce, which should be thick.

Calf's liver à l'espagnole. FOIE DE VEAU À L'ESPAGNOLE – Cut in slices, season, dredge with flour and fry in butter. Arrange on a bed of *Tomato fondue à la Niçoise* (see FONDUE). Garnish with fried onion rings and fried parsley.

Calf's liver à l'italienne. FOIE DE VEAU À L'ITALIENNE – Cut into thin slices, season with salt and pepper, and fry briskly in sizzling butter. Serve with *Tomato sauce* (see SAUCE).

Calf's liver à la lyonnaise. FOIE DE VEAU À LA LYONNAISE – Cut into thin strips. Season, dredge with flour, fry briskly in butter, or butter and oil mixed. Fry lightly sliced onion in butter and put on top of the liver. Add a few tablespoons rich veal stock or meat jelly. Sprinkle with a dash of vinegar heated in the same pan and with chopped parsley.

Calf's liver with pilaf. FOIE DE VEAU EN PILAF – Cut the liver into pieces, season and dredge with flour. Fry briskly in butter. Serve in a dish with *Rice pilaf* (see PILAF). Sprinkle with a little veal stock, flavoured with *Tomato purée* (see SAUCE, *Brown basic sauces*) and boiled down to thicken it.

Calf's liver à la provençale. FOIE DE VEAU À LA PROVENÇALE – Cut in slices and proceed as given in the recipe for *Calves' brains à la provençale*.

Roast calf's liver. FOIE DE VEAU RÔTI – Lard the liver with lardoons of bacon fat ½ cm. (¼ inch) wide and 5 cm. (2 inches) long. Season with pepper, spices and chopped parsley, and sprinkle with brandy. Wrap in a caul or thin sheet of salt pork, previously soaked in cold water, and tie with string.

Cook on a spit or roast in the oven (see CULINARY METHODS, *Average cooking time for roasts*). Dilute the pan juices with white wine or clear veal stock, pour over the liver and serve.

Calf's liver on skewers. FOIE DE VEAU EN BROCHETTES – Cut the liver into pieces 3½ cm. (1½ inches) square and ½ to

1 cm. ($\frac{1}{4}$ to $\frac{1}{2}$ inch) thick. Fry these quickly in butter to stiffen them. Put them on metal skewers, alternating with rows of lean bacon cut to the same size and lightly fried. Brush with melted butter and dip in breadcrumbs. Grill, and serve with *Maître d'hôtel butter* (see BUTTER, *Compound butters*), or serve with one of the sauces specially recommended for grills, such as *Diable, Piquante, Bordelaise* (see SAUCE).

Mushrooms, cut into thick slices and lightly tossed in butter, can also be added to the liver.

Calf's liver soufflé. SOUFFLÉ DE FOIE DE VEAU – Pound 500 g. (18 oz.) braised calf's liver in a mortar or purée in electric blender with 75 g. (3 oz., 6 tablespoons) butter and 2 dl. ($\frac{1}{3}$ pint, scant cup) very thick *Béchamel sauce* (see SAUCE). Bind with 3 egg yolks and $\frac{1}{2}$ dl. (3 tablespoons, scant $\frac{1}{4}$ cup) double cream. Season with salt, pepper and nutmeg. Rub through a sieve with a wooden spoon. Add 3 very stiffly beaten egg whites.

Pour into a buttered soufflé dish and bake in the oven (see SOUFFLÉ).

Calves' lungs à la bourgeoise. MOU DE VEAU À LA BOURGEOISE – Calves' lungs can be prepared *à la bourgeoise* (see GARNISHES). See below, *Stewed calves' lungs* for method.

Calves' lungs à la poulette. MOU DE VEAU À LA POULETTE – Cut in small pieces, simmer in butter in covered pan and finish cooking as described in the recipe for *Sheep's* (*lambs'*) *trotters à la poulette*.

Stewed calves' lungs. CIVET DE MOU DE VEAU – Cut the lungs into 50 g. (2 oz.) pieces. Season with salt and pepper. Brown in butter.

When the pieces are brown, sprinkle in 3 tablespoons (scant $\frac{1}{4}$ cup) flour. Allow the flour to cook for a few moments, stirring it. Add enough red wine (undiluted red wine or half wine and half stock) to cover the lungs. Add a good *bouquet garni* (q.v.) and 1 crushed clove of garlic and mix. Cook in a moderate oven with a lid on for $1\frac{1}{2}$ hours.

Remove the pieces of lung, put them into a shallow pan with 250 g. (9 oz., generous cup) lean diced bacon, blanched and fried in butter, 250 g. (9 oz., 3 cups) mushrooms, sliced if they are big, whole if small, 24 small fried onions. Strain the pan juices and pour over. Continue to cook in the oven for 30 minutes.

Garnish with heart-shaped croûtons of bread fried in butter.

Calf's mesentery. FRAISE DE VEAU – The fold of peritoneum which attaches part of the intestinal canal to the posterior wall of the abdomen. It is not sold in the U.S.A.

Fried calf's mesentery. FRAISE DE VEAU FRITE – Drain the mesentery cooked in the special *court-bouillon* given for *Calf's head* (see above). Dry, cut in square pieces, season the pieces, dip in lightly beaten egg and breadcrumbs and deep-fry in sizzling fat.

Garnish with fried parsley. Serve with a spiced sauce such as *Diable, Piquante*, etc. (see SAUCE).

Calf's mesentery à la hongroise. FRAISE DE VEAU À LA HONGROISE – Cut the mesentery into uniform pieces, fry briskly for a few minutes in butter, sprinkling them with a good pinch of paprika.

Serve with *Hungarian sauce* (see SAUCE).

Calf's mesentery à l'indienne. FRAISE DE VEAU À L'INDIENNE – Cut the mesentery into uniform slices, put them for a few moments into *Curry sauce* (see SAUCE). Serve with *Rice à l'indienne* (see RICE).

Calf's mesentery à la lyonnaise. FRAISE DE VEAU À LA LYONNAISE – Cook the mesentery as described above, cut it into thin strips and proceed as described in the recipe for *Tripe à la lyonnaise* (see above).

Calf's mesentery à la poulette. FRAISE DE VEAU À LA POULETTE – Cook the mesentery as above, cut into uniform pieces and proceed as described in the recipe for *Tripe à la poulette* (see above).

Calves' sweetbreads. RIS DE VEAU – Soak the sweetbreads in cold water until they become white. Cover with salted cold water in a saucepan, and bring slowly to the boil, stirring frequently with a wooden spoon. At the first sign of boiling, cool under running water.

Drain the sweetbreads, trim, put between two cloths under a board with a weight on top.

With a larding needle insert into the sweetbreads strips of bacon, stud with pieces of truffle, tongue, ham; or leave them as they are, according to the use for which they are intended. Cook according to the recipe chosen.

Calves' sweetbreads à l'anversoise. RIS DE VEAU À L'ANVERSOISE – Braise in white stock, serve with *Anversoise garnish* (see GARNISHES) and the pan juices, with veal stock added and boiled down to the desired consistency.

Attereaux of calves' sweetbreads – See ATTEREAUX.

Calves' sweetbreads à la banquière. RIS DE VEAU À LA BANQUIÈRE – Braise in white stock (see below). Serve with *Banquière garnish* (see GARNISHES).

Calves' sweetbreads braised in brown stock. RIS DE VEAU BRAISÉS À BRUN – Put the calves' sweetbreads, prepared as described above, into a shallow pan with butter, in which 1 tablespoon diced salt pork or bacon rinds have been browned. Add thinly sliced onions and carrots. Season, and add a *bouquet garni* (q.v.).

Cook gently in the covered pan, add a few tablespoons white wine, boil down to a glazed condition, and add a few tablespoons brown veal stock.

Finish cooking as described in the recipe for *Calves' sweetbreads braised in white stock* but glaze for a little longer.

Serve and garnish as indicated in the chosen recipe.

The liquid used for moistening sweetbreads should be very thick.

Calves' sweetbreads braised in white stock. RIS DE VEAU BRAISÉS À BLANC – Put the blanched, cooled and pressed sweetbreads (larded, studded or left plain, according to recipe) into a shallow pan in which some bacon rinds have been browned in butter, with finely sliced carrots and onions. Season and add a small *bouquet garni* (q.v.).

Stew under a lid on a gentle fire. Add a few tablespoons white stock. Bring to the boil, cover, cook in the oven from 35 to 45 minutes, basting frequently with the juices.

As soon as the sweetbreads are cooked, glaze them very lightly (if the recipe calls for such glazing) by exposing them for a few minutes, uncovered, to the heat of the oven, and basting them with the fat of the pan juices. Remove the sweetbreads, strain the pan juices. Serve and garnish as indicated in the recipe.

Calves' sweetbreads Clamart. RIS DE VEAU CLAMART – Braise in brown stock. Serve with *Clamart garnish* (or with green peas and butter) and the pan juices poured over (see GARNISHES).

Escalopes of calves' sweetbreads à l'ancienne. ESCALOPES DE RIS DE VEAU À L'ANCIENNE – Cut the sweetbreads into thick slices and braise in white stock as in recipe above. Arrange on the inner edge of a large puff pastry shell. Fill the centre with a *ragoût* of cock's combs and cock's kidneys, truffles and mushrooms, blended with *Velouté sauce* (see SAUCE) made with chicken stock boiled down with cream and flavoured with Madeira. Put a sliver of truffle on each escalope.

Escalopes of calves' sweetbreads in breadcrumbs. ESCALOPES DE RIS DE VEAU PANÉES – Cut the escalopes as described above. Dip in lightly beaten egg and breadcrumbs.

Fry them in clarified butter (see CLARIFICATION). Serve with garnish and sauce recommended in the recipe.

Escalopes of calves' sweetbreads à l'ancienne

The escalopes can be coated with mushrooms, ham, chopped parsley, truffles, grated Parmesan, *mirepoix* (q.v.), etc. (See GARNISHES; SAUCE.)

Escalopes of calves' sweetbreads in butter. ESCALOPES DE RIS DE VEAU AU BEURRE – Blanch and cool under a press. Cut the sweetbreads into 3 or 4 escalopes each, depending on thickness. Season, dredge with flour and sauté in butter. Serve with the garnish and sauce recommended in the recipe (see GARNISHES, SAUCE).

Fried escalopes of calves' sweetbreads in allemande sauce. ESCALOPES DE RIS DE VEAU SAUTÉES À L'ALLEMANDE – Fry in butter, arrange on fried croûtons, and serve with *Allemande sauce* (see SAUCE).

Escalopes of calves' sweetbreads au gratin. ESCALOPES DE RIS DE VEAU AU GRATIN – Braise and slice the sweetbreads, arrange in a circle on a buttered dish, surround with sliced mushrooms, cover with *Duxelles sauce* (see SAUCE), sprinkle with breadcrumbs and brown the top.

When ready to serve, sprinkle with a little lemon juice and chopped parsley.

Escalopes of calves' sweetbreads à l'italienne. ESCALOPES DE RIS DE VEAU À L'ITALIENNE – Fry escalopes of braised sweetbreads in oil. Pour over *Italian sauce* (see SAUCE).

Escalopes of calves' sweetbreads à la maréchale. ESCALOPES DE RIS DE VEAU À LA MARÉCHALE – Dip in beaten egg and breadcrumbs and fry in butter. Garnish with slivers of truffles and cooked asparagus tips dressed with butter. Sprinkle with the butter left in the pan in which the escalopes were cooked.

Escalopes of calves' sweetbreads à la milanaise. ESCALOPES DE RIS DE VEAU À LA MILANAISE – Coat with a mixture of grated cheese and breadcrumbs, and finish off as described in the recipe for *Veal chops à la milanaise* (see VEAL).

Escalopes of calves' sweetbreads Rossini. ESCALOPES DE RIS DE VEAU ROSSINI – Fry in butter, and complete as described in the recipe for *Tournedos Rossini* (see BEEF).

Escalopes of calves' sweetbreads Saint-Germain. ESCALOPES DE RIS DE VEAU SAINT-GERMAIN – Cut a sweetbread which has been soaked, blanched and cooled under a press into four escalopes. Season with salt and pepper, dredge with flour and fry in butter.

Escalopes of calves' sweetbreads served in a pastry case (*Robert Carrier*)

Arrange each on a little cake of *Anna potatoes* (see POTATOES). Top with a trickle of very thick *Béarnaise sauce* (see SAUCE) and in the centre of the sauce put a small teaspoon meat jelly. Add a little butter to the boiled-down pan juices, and spoon around the escalopes.

Escalopes of calves' sweetbreads can be grilled instead of being fried in butter.

Escalopes of calves' sweetbreads with truffles

Escalopes of calves' sweetbreads with truffles. ESCALOPES DE RIS DE VEAU AUX TRUFFES – Cook the escalopes in butter. Arrange on croûtons of bread fried in butter and put on each escalope 3 or 4 slivers of truffle heated in butter. Garnish the middle of the dish with *Noisette potatoes* (see POTATOES). Add Madeira and veal stock to the pan juices, boil down, and pour over the escalopes.

Escalopes of calves' sweetbreads Villeroi. ESCALOPES DE RIS DE VEAU VILLEROI – Braise and slice the sweetbreads, coat with *Villeroi sauce* (see SAUCE), dip in breadcrumbs and fry.

Arrange in a ring on a dish, and garnish with fried parsley. Serve with *Périgueux* or *Tomato sauce* (see SAUCE).

Calves' sweetbreads à la fermière. RIS DE VEAU FERMIÈRE – Braise in brown stock (see above). When half-cooked add *Fermière garnish* (see GARNISHES). Finish cooking together and serve with its own juices.

Calves' sweetbreads à la financière. RIS DE VEAU À LA FINANCIÈRE – Stud the sweetbreads with pieces of truffle and *Pickled (scarlet) beef or ox tongue* (see above). Braise in brown stock, serve with *Financière garnish* and *Financière sauce* with the pan juices added (see GARNISHES; SAUCE).

This is usually served either on fried croûtons or in a pie crust.

Grilled calves' sweetbreads. RIS DE VEAU GRILLÉS – Rinse, blanch, cool and press the sweetbreads. Brush with melted butter, season and grill under a moderate flame. Serve and garnish as indicated in the recipe.

If the sweetbreads are too big, divide them horizontally in halves before grilling them.

Grilled calves' sweetbreads with various garnishes. RIS DE VEAU GRILLÉ – Garnish with braised or buttered vegetables, purées of green or dried vegetables (the purées are usually served separately), fried mushrooms, grilled or sautéed tomatoes, spinach, braised chicory, noodles, risotto, etc. (see GARNISHES).

According to the garnish chosen, serve with *Maître d'hôtel butter* (see BUTTER, *Compound butters*), or one of the sauces specially recommended for grills: *Diable, Italian, Marrow, Piquant, Robert*, etc. (see SAUCE).

Calves' sweetbreads à la japonaise. RIS DE VEAU À LA JAPONAISE – Braise in brown stock as in above recipe. Serve with the boiled-down pan juices and garnish with Chinese artichokes (see GARNISHES).

Calves' sweetbreads à la jardinière. RIS DE VEAU À LA JARDINIÈRE – Braise in brown stock as in above recipe; serve with *Jardinière garnish* (see GARNISHES) and the pan juices boiled down.

Calves' sweetbreads à la macédoine. RIS DE VEAU À LA MACÉDOINE – Braise in brown stock, as described above. Serve with garnish *à la macédoine* (see GARNISHES).

Calves' sweetbreads à la Nantua I. RIS DE VEAU À LA NANTUA – Braise in white stock, without larding (see above). Scoop about two-thirds out of the top part. Fill with *Crayfish tail ragoût à la Nantua* (see CRAYFISH), substituting, if necessary, 2 small lobsters for the crayfish. Garnish the main part of the sweetbreads with this mixture.

Cover with *Allemande sauce* (see SAUCE), sprinkle with breadcrumbs, glaze lightly in the oven. Arrange on croûtons, garnish with very small patty shells filled with the crayfish garnish and slivers of truffles. Serve with *Suprême sauce*, to which *Crayfish butter* is added. (See SAUCE; BUTTER, *Compound butters*.)

Calves' sweetbreads à la Nantua II. RIS DE VEAU À LA NANTUA – Braise in white stock (see above). Garnish with crayfish tails, shrimps or pieces of lobster meat and slivers of truffle. Cover with *Suprême sauce* with the boiled-down pan juices, to which *Crayfish butter* has been added. (See SAUCE; BUTTER, *Compound butters*.)

Calves' sweetbreads à la périgourdine. RIS DE VEAU À LA PÉRIGOURDINE – Braise in brown stock (see above). Garnish with truffles cut in thin slices or diced. Serve with *Madeira sauce* (see SAUCE) made with boiled-down pan juices.

Poached calves' sweetbreads. RIS DE VEAU POCHÉS – Prepare the sweetbreads as described at the beginning of this section and put into a saucepan. Cover with white stock. Bring to the boil, remove scum and simmer gently 35 to 40 minutes, depending on size. Drain the sweetbreads and strain the stock.

Serve and garnish as described in the recipe used.

Calves' sweetbreads poêlé. RIS DE VEAU POÊLÉS – Prepare the sweetbreads as described above. Heat 1 generous tablespoon butter in a shallow frying pan, put in the sweetbreads, season, and cook covered on gentle heat 35 to 40 minutes.

Garnish, and serve as described in the particular recipe.

Calves' sweetbreads princesse. RIS DE VEAU PRINCESSE – Poach or braise in white stock (see above). Serve with *Princess garnish* (see GARNISHES) and white *Allemande sauce* (see SAUCE) made with the boiled-down pan juices.

Calves' sweetbreads with various purées. RIS DE VEAU AUX PURÉES – Braise in brown stock (see above). Serve with purée of any of the following vegetables: artichokes, asparagus, aubergines, carrots, mushrooms, cucumbers, kidney beans, French beans, lentils, onions, green peas, *soubise*.

Calves' sweetbreads Régence. RIS DE VEAU RÉGENCE – Stud with slivers of truffle. Braise in white stock (see above). Serve with *Régence garnish* and *Allemande sauce* made with the concentrated pan juices (see GARNISHES, SAUCE).

Roast calves' sweetbreads. RIS DE VEAU RÔTIS – Prepare sweetbreads as described above. Lard them with strips of fat bacon, or leave plain. Season, wrap in a sheet of salt pork or in a piece of caul, and put on a spit.

Cook over brisk heat for 35 minutes. Serve and garnish as described in the particular recipe.

Soufflé of calves' sweetbreads. RIS DE VEAU SOUFFLÉ – Braise sweetbreads in white stock (see above) and hollow out. Prepare the scooped-out pieces as a soufflé (q.v.) and fill the hollowed-out parts with it. Bake in a slow oven 12 to 15 minutes. Arrange on a croûton. Serve with the garnish and sauce recommended in the recipe.

Calves' sweetbreads Talleyrand. RIS DE VEAU TALLEYRAND – Stud with truffles, braise in brown stock as described above, serve with *Talleyrand sauce* (see SAUCE) made with the boiled-down pan juices.

Calves' sweetbreads Toulouse or Toulousaine. RIS DE VEAU TOULOUSE, TOULOUSAINE – Poach or braise in white stock (see above). Serve with *Toulouse garnish* and *Allemande sauce* made with the boiled-down pan juices (see GARNISHES; SAUCE).

Calves' sweetbreads with various vegetables. RIS DE VEAU AUX LÉGUMES – Braise in brown stock (see above), and garnish with various buttered or braised vegetables: young carrots, mushrooms, celery, *cèpes*, chicory, cucumbers, endives, young beans, shoots of young hops, kidney beans, French beans, lettuce, sweet corn, morels, glazed onions, green peas and the boiled-down pan juices.

Calf's tongue. LANGUE DE VEAU – All the methods of preparation given for beef or ox tongue: braised, with various garnishes, grilled, *à la diable*, fried, with Italian sauce, etc., can be used for cooking calf's tongue.

Calf's tongue, cooked in a special *court-bouillon* (see recipe for cooking *Calf's head*), is always served with calf's head.

POULTRY OFFAL or VARIETY MEATS – See also GIBLETS.

Chicken livers. FOIES DE VOLAILLE – These are prepared skewered, in a pilaf or risotto, sautéed with various garnishes, etc. They are also used as garnishes themselves, and as an ingredient of various forcemeats, particularly of *À gratin forcemeat* (see FORCEMEATS or STUFFINGS).

Chicken livers on skewers à l'indienne. BROCHETTES DE FOIES DE POULET À L'INDIENNE – Cut the trimmed livers into 3 or 4 pieces. Season with salt and pepper and fry in sizzling butter. Thread them on metal skewers in rows, alternating with blanched bacon cut in thick square pieces and slices of mushrooms, both lightly tossed in butter.

Dip the threaded skewers in the butter left in the pan, and roll in freshly grated breadcrumbs. Grill on a brisk fire. Serve with *Rice à l'indienne* (see RICE) and a *Curry sauce* (see SAUCE).

Duck livers. FOIES DE CANETON – These are prepared in the same way as those of other poultry: on skewers, in a pilaf, as a risotto, sautéed with various garnishes. They are also used as an ingredient in forcemeats, especially for *À gratin forcemeat* (see FORCEMEATS or STUFFINGS).

OFFICINAL PASTILLES. PÂTES OFFICINALES – Substances of a firm consistency (small aromatic confections, usually hard gums or jelly jujubes), which do not stick to the fingers and are composed of gum and sugar dissolved in water, with aromatic flavourings or medicaments. They are transparent if they have been moulded and brought to the right consistency by a slow process of evaporation and dried in a drying oven, and opaque if they have been evaporated in a very high temperature and stirred with a wooden spoon. 'Sugared pastilles' are covered with a light coating of crystallised sugar, which increases their keeping quality.

OGNONNADE or OIGNONADE – Stew containing a large proportion of onions. The term also applies to finely chopped onion, melted in butter or cooked in white wine.

OIL. HUILE – Fat which is liquid at normal temperatures. There are animal and vegetable oils but vegetable oils are more common. Oil does not mix with water but can be emulsified. It is soluble in alcohol, ether, benzine, etc.

In industry, oils are divided into two categories: siccative or quick-drying oils (which thicken but do not turn rancid when exposed to the air), and non-siccative oils, which tend to turn rancid when exposed to the air, but do not thicken.

Oil in dietetics. HUILE EN DIÉTÉTIQUE – Dieticians and gastronomes both agree that vegetable oils are the best of all food fats, provided that they have not been adulterated in the process of manufacture.

The ideal oil is unrefined oil. It is made from carefully selected grain, nuts or fruit, which are husked, shelled or stoned as the case may be.

The fruits and almonds are then pressed in a hydraulic press, ideally, that is, in a cold press. Other types of presses can raise the temperature of the product to between 60° and 90°C. (140° and 194°F.).

The oil thus obtained is guaranteed 'virgin' oil. It is considered the best from a culinary point of view and is the only one which is authorised to be labelled 'guaranteed virgin oil'. The addition of 'guaranteed first cold-press extraction' indicates that no solvents have been used in its manufacture.

This does not mean that the use of refined oils is discouraged, nor that they are harmful. In fact, some oils are not edible unless they are refined. Such is the case with maize, soya and peanut oils. Even though refined, their quality is indisputable. Certainly their vitamin content may be slightly reduced, but they retain many other valuable properties. Corn oil, for example, is anticholesterol; soya oil is excellent for diabetics, since it is rich in albuminoids and deficient in carbohydrates. Nevertheless, gourmets prefer to cook with unrefined olive oil; just as the diet-conscious prefer unrefined sunflower, sesame or even pumpkin oil.

Virgin olive oil is undoubtedly the best of all food fats. It should be used frequently and preferably in its raw state (for seasoning, salads, etc.), bearing in mind, however, that the daily intake of fat ought not to exceed 50 g. ($1\frac{3}{4}$ oz.) for a sedentary adult; 65 g. ($2\frac{1}{4}$ oz.) for a labourer or very active individual.

Oil of sweet and bitter almonds. HUILE D'AMANDES DOUCES ET AMÈRES – Extracted from almonds put in linen bags and subjected to pressure. This oil is used in confectionery.

Cotton-seed oil. HUILE DE COTON – Extracted from cotton seed. Now that this oil can be purified and rendered colourless, it is used in cookery, chiefly as an ingredient of vegetable cooking fats or oleomargarine.

Groundnut oil (peanut oil). HUILE D'ARACHIDES – A clear, non-siccative oil extracted from peanuts. It is tasteless and odourless, and used as a table oil by people who prefer an oil entirely without taste.

Olive oil. HUILE D'OLIVE – The oil *par excellence*, since etymologically the word 'oil' is derived from 'olive'. There are different grades of olive oil.

Pure oil is extracted cold from the finest fresh olives, which are simply crushed. This oil has a distinctive flavour, is greenish in colour and keeps fresh for a long time.

Second grade oil is extracted by pressure under heat. It is white in colour and becomes rancid more quickly when exposed to the air.

Third grade oil (lubricating oil) is extracted from windfalls or fermented or preserved olives. It is often treated with sulphate of carbon, and then neutralised and rendered odourless. This oil is intended only for industrial use, but is all too often used for adulteration.

Connoisseurs distinguish between the various 'vintages' of olive oil, and hold the oil of Provence in particularly high esteem.

Palm oil. HUILE DE PALME – This oil is solid at normal

Pounding olives to extract olive oil (after Stradanus)

temperatures. It is used in cooking by Africans. In the West, it is chiefly used in the manufacture of soap.

Poppy-seed oil. HUILE D'OILLETTE – Extracted from the seeds of the black, white or purple poppy. A quick-drying oil, which is used a great deal as a table oil in northern France and in Paris because of its lack of taste. It is called *huile blanche* in France.

Sesame oil. HUILE DE SÉSAME – Extracted from the seeds of the sesame plant, grown in warm climates. It has a rich nutty flavour and is non-siccative. It is a staple food in India and the Orient and is growing increasingly popular in the Western world in preparing confectionery and baked foods.

Shellfish oil. HUILE DE CRUSTACES – Pound finely in a mortar the trimmings and shells of shellfish of which the flesh has been used for some other purpose. While pounding, add olive oil, equivalent in weight to the shells. Pound thoroughly with the pestle so as to obtain a smooth mixture. Rub the first through a fine sieve and then strain through coarse muslin.

This mixture is used to season mayonnaise and other cold sauces, as a seasoning in shellfish and fish salads, and in the preparation of cold *hors-d'œuvre.*

Walnut oil. HUILE DE NOIX – A quick-drying oil. The pure oil extracted cold from dried walnuts is used in cookery. It has a very pronounced nutty flavour, well liked by some people but disliked by those who are unaccustomed to it. Walnut oil extracted under heat is not edible.

OILLE – In the olden days the name *oille* was applied to a kind of *potée* made of various meats and vegetables.

The word, according to some authorities, comes from the Spanish *olla*, but it probably derives from *oule*, which in the south-west of France is used to describe an earthenware pot in which this dish is prepared.

There are three kinds of *oilles*. The first is an old French soup which, in the days of Louis XIII, was called *grand-ouille* and which is the *ouille-en-pot* mentioned in the letters of Madame de Maintenon.

The second is *olla-podrida*, a complicated dish of foreign origin. Spanish ambassadors served this dish as a part of diplomatic representation and official ceremonial. Protocol decreed that this soup be served for a dinner given for a Spanish grandee.

The third is *oille-moderne à la française.*

Here is the method of preparing this *oille*, according to an old recipe:

'Take a plump chicken and 2 big pigeons. Trim and clean them and stuff with a forcemeat composed of crustless bread soaked in stock, blended with 8 egg yolks, 1 white onion baked on hot coals, and 3 chopped artichoke hearts, the whole seasoned with a few leaves of chervil and a pinch of grated nutmeg. Sew up the 3 birds to keep in the forcemeat, and truss them, to prevent deformation during cooking. Take an earthenware pot, put into it 6 or 8 pounds of beef cut into thin slices, 1 veal knuckle cut into 4 pieces, 3 onions, 1 parsnip, 2 carrots, 2 turnips, 2 white leeks tied with 2 stalks of purslane, orach and Swiss chard. On this foundation put the stuffed birds. First heat on a very hot fire, then place the pot on a moderate heat. Remove scum and leave to simmer gently. After 5 hours' cooking, cut crusts of bread, toast them lightly, put into dish, moisten with stock, and simmer. Arrange the chicken and the pigeons but none of the other meat on the toasted bread, untruss the 3 birds, strain the stock to remove fat, and pour over the *oille*.'

OISEAUX SANS TÊTE – Name given in some regions to stuffed fillets of various meats, particularly beef.

Oiseaux sans tête 'Loose vinken' (Belgian cookery) – Beat slices of beef until very thin. Season, put a little sausage meat, or, if preferred, a small piece of lean blanched bacon, in the middle, roll up the slices and tie with string.

Fry these in butter or lard, with sliced onions. When they are browned on all sides, sprinkle with flour, moisten either with beer or stock in sufficient quantity just to cover the rolls. Cook gently, covered, and serve in the same dish.

Okra

OKRA or LADIES' FINGERS. GOMBO, GOMBAUT – Plant of the mallow family, very prolific in South America and southern United States, West Africa and India where it is cultivated and eaten as a vegetable.

There are a number of different species, most of them edible. In most cases it is the pods which are eaten, but one species, from New Guinea, has sorrel-like leaves which are eaten like sorrel.

The best-known variety with edible pods is known as *okra* or *gumbo*, or in the Near East and in France as *bamia*. Another variety, commonly called the *royal marshmallow*, whose flowers are like those of the hollyhock, bears a juicy fruit called *nafé* in France; it is used in the preparation of a poultice for the chest.

Okra, or ladies' fingers, are eaten fresh when they are young with tender seeds. They can also be dried and kept for a long time. They look like haricot (white) beans and should be steeped in warm water before use.

However they are to be prepared, okra should always be slightly blanched first in salt water.

Okra braised with bacon. GOMBOS BRAISÉS AU GRAS – Chop onions and cook in butter until very tender. Put them in a shallow buttered saucepan lined with slices of blanched lean bacon. Blanch and drain the okra and lay them on the onions. Cook as described in the recipe for *Okra in butter*.

Arrange slices of bacon in a ring on the dish in which they are to be served. Place the okra in the middle.

Okra in butter. GOMBOS AU BEURRE – Blanch and drain the okra. Put them in a buttered frying pan. Season with salt and pepper and add a few tablespoons consommé or water. Cover, and cook slowly. This is used as a garnish for eggs cooked in various ways, for braised fish, individual servings of meat, or poultry. If okra is to be served with meat or poultry, the pan juices should be added just before the end of cooking. Okra in butter may also be served as a separate vegetable.

Okra in cream. GOMBOS À LA CRÈME – Cook the okra as for *Okra in butter*. When they are ready, cover with a *Cream sauce* (see SAUCE). Let them simmer for a few minutes. Serve in a deep dish.

Okra à la Créole. GOMBOS À LA CRÉOLE – Prepare the okra as for *Okra in tomato sauce*, seasoning them with saffron. Serve in a dish with a border of rice, cooked with meat stock.

Fried okra. GOMBOS EN FRITOTS – Blanch the okra. Drain and dry them with a cloth. Soak them for half an hour in oil, lemon juice, chopped parsley, salt and pepper. Dip in frying batter (see BATTERS FOR FRYING) and deep-fry. Garnish with fried parsley and lemon.

Okra in tomato sauce. GOMBOS À LA TOMATE – Brown the okra lightly in a frying pan in which 1 large onion, chopped fine, has been slowly cooked in oil until tender. Add 1 kg. ($2\frac{1}{4}$ lb.) okra, and 4 peeled, seeded and coarsely chopped tomatoes. Season. Add a clove of garlic. Cover and cook slowly for 45 minutes.

Okra à la turque. GOMBOS À LA TURQUE – Use dried okra, which is called *bamia*. These are usually to be found in oriental food stores.

Each pod is the size of a haricot (white) bean. Steep them for at least 12 hours in cold water. Drain them. Brown 100 g. (4 oz.) lean diced mutton and 1 medium-sized chopped onion. Add 1 kg. ($2\frac{1}{4}$ lb.) okra and brown lightly. Moisten with a few tablespoons clear soup or water. Season. Add a pinch of cayenne pepper. Cover and cook slowly.

Olive branch with fruits

OLIVE – Native of eastern Mediterranean countries, but now grown throughout the Mediterranean regions, as well as in tropical and sub-tropical areas. It has been cultivated for hundreds of years and is recorded as grown in Egypt in the seventeenth century B.C. Olives are also grown in South Australia. They were introduced into Mexico and California in the seventeenth century by Jesuit missionaries and are now very abundant there.

The fruit is grown primarily for its oil; the Latin term (*olea*) applies exclusively to olive oil (see OIL).

The olives, which are hard-stoned berries, are used as condiment, seasoning and *hors-d'œuvre* in two forms:

Gathering olives at St Jean de Fos, Hérault
(*French Government Tourist Office*)

Green olives. Picked unripe, treated with hot, weak alkali (potassium or ash solution), which removes their bitter taste, and then pickled in spiced brine.

Black olives. Picked ripe, washed in several waters, put into boiling brine without the alkali treatment, then dried and pickled in oil.

The species of olives known in French as *picholines* are cultivated specially for the table. They are large, of elongated form and reddish-black colour.

Olives with anchovy butter. OLIVES AUX BEURRE D'ANCHOIS – Wash and dry 5 salted anchovy fillets. Pound in a mortar and add 60 g. ($2\frac{1}{2}$ oz., 5 tablespoons) butter. Mix, season with pepper, and rub through a sieve. Stuff stoned olives with this mixture through a paper forcing bag.

Olives for garnish – Stone the olives with a special utensil or a knife, or buy stoned olives. Blanch them, drain and rinse in cold water. Put in to simmer with the dish for which the garnish is intended.

Stuffed olives for garnish – Stone big olives, blanch for 3 minutes, rinse in cold water and drain.

Stuff with *Quenelle forcemeat* (see FORCEMEATS or STUFFINGS) mixed with *fines herbes* or chopped truffles, depending on the nature of the dish.

OLIVET CHEESE – See CHEESE.

OLLA-PODRIDA – Spanish soup in a grand style, somewhat similar to the *hochepot flamand.*

The French translation of the word is *pot-pourri.* This term, in the olden days, was used to describe not a soup, but a stew made of various meats.

The word *olla-podrida* is rarely used nowadays to describe this national soup, which is also called *puchero* or *cocido.*

The following recipe for an *olla-podrida* is intended for twenty guests.

Ingredients. 2 kg. ($4\frac{1}{2}$ lb.) beef (brisket or forequarter flank), 500 g. (18 oz.) shoulder of mutton, 500 g. (18 oz.) breast of mutton, 500 g. (18 oz.) uncooked ham, 500 g. (18 oz.) salt pork, 2 each pig's ears, feet and tails, 1 plump chicken, 2 partridges (when in season), 6 *chorizos* (Spanish sausages).

Vegetables: 4 medium-large carrots, 8 big leeks (white only), 2 big onions, 1 cabbage, 2 heads of lettuce, 8 potatoes, 500 g. (18 oz.) chick-peas (*garbanzos*), well soaked; garlic, salt, pepper and a large *bouquet garni* (q.v.).

Method. Put all the meat, except the chicken, partridge and *chorizos*, into a pit pot. Cover with plenty of cold water. Season with salt, making allowances for the salt content of some of the meats. Bring to the boil, remove scum, and add crushed garlic and a *bouquet garni.* Put in the chick-peas, previously well soaked in cold water. Cook for 2 hours. Add the chicken and partridges (lightly browned) together with the *chorizos*; cook for 30 minutes. Add the various vegetables roughly sliced, except the potatoes, which, similarly sliced, should be put into the soup only 35 minutes before serving.

Simmer gently for 2 hours. As cooking progresses, take out the meats which are done; some being more tender than others will require less time.

Arrange all the meats and the vegetables on a big dish and serve the soup in a soup tureen.

OLORON – See CHEESE.

OMELETTES – See EGGS.

OMNIBUS – In restaurant terminology (Paris restaurants particularly) this name is applied to the *commis*, or chef's assistant or waiter, whose work consists of passing on the orders to the kitchen and fetching the food from there. *Omnibus* is a kind of apprentice.

ONAGER. ONAGRE – Wild ass which in Persia is considered highly prized game. This is the wild ass of the Bible.

ONION. OIGNON – Biennial plant, native of Asia and Palestine, which has been cultivated from earliest times. This vegetable of the *Liliaceae* family was so greatly prized in Egypt that it was worshipped.

The bulb has many concentric coats. It contains a strong and acrid sulphuretted essence, which causes watering of the eyes and rubefaction of the skin, but disappears in the cooking process. Its taste is pungent.

Raw onion is rather indigestible and should be eaten in moderation.

Chopped onion. OIGNONS HACHÉS – Peel the onion, cut in half; cut each half into very thin slices without separating them from the root, and make 5 to 6 horizontal cuts through the whole thickness of the onion.

Now cut the onion again vertically. You will thus have minute dice which will need very little chopping to obtain finely chopped onion.

If prepared in advance, it should be tied in a corner of a cloth and placed under a cold water tap to 'revive' it. Then squeeze the onion in the cloth to drain it well, and spread it in a saucer.

Proceed in the same way if very white chopped onion is required as an accompaniment for calf's head, or any dish *à la vinaigrette.*

Fried onions. OIGNONS FRITS – Cut medium-sized onions into round slices about $\frac{1}{4}$ cm. ($\frac{1}{8}$ inch) thick. Shake out the slices into rings. Season with salt, dredge with flour and fry in smoking hot oil. Drain the onions, dry on a cloth and sprinkle with salt.

Fried onions are used as a garnish, particularly for *Entrecôte à la tyrolienne* (see BEEF) and *Chicken sauté à la bordelaise* (see CHICKEN).

Onions fried in batter. OIGNONS EN FRITOT – Cut the onions into round slices, as described above. Shake out the slices into rings. Season with salt and pepper and sprinkle with oil and lemon juice. Leave to marinate in this seasoning for 30 minutes. Shake dry.

Dip the onion rings into light batter and fry. Onions fried in this way are used as a garnish.

Glazed onions. OIGNONS GLACÉS – *White*: Skin button onions. Put them into a shallow pan with enough white stock almost to cover them. Add butter, allowing 125 g. (4 oz., generous ½ cup) per litre (1¾ pints, generous quart) of liquid. Season and simmer with a lid on. Turn the onions in their liquor, boiled down to a glaze – so that they can be coated with this glaze all over.

Brown: Heat some butter in a shallow pan and put in the onions. Season with salt and a pinch of castor sugar. Cook, covered, on a moderate heat, in such a way as to allow the onions to cook and acquire their colour at the same time.

Glazed onions for garnish. OIGNONS GLACÉS (POUR GARNITURES) – See GARNISHES.

Onions à la grecque (Hors-d'œuvre). OIGNONS À LA GRECQUE – Skin small uniform-sized onions. Blanch them, dip in cold water and drain. Cook in a *court-bouillon* as indicated for *Artichokes à la grecque* (see HORS-D'ŒUVRE). Leave to cool in the *court-bouillon*.

Onions à l'orientale (Hors-d'œuvre). OIGNONS À L'ORIENTALE – Blanch medium-sized onions thoroughly in salted water and remove three-quarters of the insides.

Stuff with a composition of chopped onion (using the scooped-out parts), half its weight of rice cooked in stock, *Tomato fondue* (see FONDUE) cooked with oil and flavoured with garlic, and sweet pimentos, stewed in butter and chopped. Season with saffron. Put the stuffed onions into an oiled dish, sprinkle with oil, bake slowly in the oven, and leave to get cold before serving.

Onion purée or soubise – See PURÉE, *Onion soubise*.

Onion soup. SOUPE À L'OIGNON – See various recipes for the preparation of this soup in the section SOUPS AND BROTHS.

Preparing stuffed onions (*Claire*)

Stuffed onions. OIGNONS FARCIS – Peel medium-sized onions, taking care not to damage the first white layer. Cut transversely, at the stalk end, at about three-quarters of their height. Blanch thoroughly in salted water, plunge into cold water and drain.

Remove the inside, leaving a thickness all round of two layers of onion skins. Chop the scooped-out part finely and mix with some pork, veal, beef or mutton forcemeat (see FORCEMEATS or STUFFINGS).

Stuff the onions with this mixture, put them into a buttered sauté pan, moisten with a few tablespoons slightly thickened brown veal stock, bring to the boil with a lid on the pan and finish cooking in the oven, basting frequently, to glaze the onions. A few moments before removing from the oven, sprinkle the surface with toasted or fresh breadcrumbs, and brown the top.

This method is applied mainly to sweet Spanish onions.

They may be served separately, as a vegetable, but are principally used as a garnish.

Stuffed onions à la catalane. OIGNONS FARCIS À LA CATALANE – Prepare the onions as described above. Stuff them with a mixture of chopped onion, rice cooked in meat stock, sweet pimentos, stewed in oil and chopped, and hard boiled eggs – the whole well blended, seasoned and spiced. Put the stuffed onions into a well-oiled, oven-proof dish. Pour in enough stock to cover the onions halfway and cook gently in the oven. A few moments before removing from the oven, sprinkle with white breadcrumbs and brown the top.

Stuffed onions à la duxelles, called à la parisienne. OIGNONS FARCIS À LA DUXELLES (À LA PARISIENNE) – Prepare the onions as described above. Stuff with a mixture of chopped onions, *Duxelles sauce* (see SAUCE) and chopped, lean, cooked ham. Braise in the usual manner.

Stuffed onions à l'italienne. OIGNONS FARCIS À L'ITALIENNE – Prepare the onions as described above. Stuff them with a risotto, mixed with chopped onions and chopped cooked lean ham. Braise in the usual manner. A few moments before removing from the oven, sprinkle with grated Parmesan and brown the top.

ONOPORDON – Genus of coarse thistle-like herbs of the *Compositae* family; also called *Onopordum*. One species is a wild artichoke, which grows on hillsides and roadsides.

The leaf receptacles of this plant are eaten as cultivated artichokes. The stalks are also eaten as cardoons and the roots as salsify.

ONOS. APHIE – Fish caught in the Mediterranean which is also called *rockling*.

Some doctors maintain that the flesh of the rockling is very indigestible. This was not so in the opinion of the ancients who, justly, greatly appreciated this fish for its very nourishing flesh. It is prepared like whiting.

OPHIDIUM. DONZELLE – Small Mediterranean fish similar to the eel. It is sometimes known in France as *demoiselle* and *girelle* (potter's wheel). This fish is used as an ingredient of *bouillabaisse* (q.v.).

OPOSSUM – Marsupial, reaching the size of a hare, which abounds in certain regions of North America. The flesh is edible and resembles that of rabbit.

ORACH or ORACHE. ARROCHE – Common name of several species of plants frequently cultivated in gardens, among them a type called *mountain spinach*, the leaves of which are eaten, cooked like spinach. In U.S.A. this is called *French spinach* or *sea purslane*.

ORANGE. Fruit of the orange tree.

The orange tree (*Citrus sinensis*) is an elegant tree with pleasantly scented blossom and sweet, aromatic fruit. It originated in China and Cochin-China.

The Greeks and the Romans did not know the sweet orange, but they did perhaps know the bitter orange (*Citrus aurantium*). The Sanscrit name of this was *nagrunga*, from which the Italian words *naranzi* and *d'aranzi*, the Latin terms (of the Middle Ages) of *arantium, arangium*, and later, *aurantium* – which produced the French word *orange* – were all derived.

The crusaders brought bitter oranges from Palestine into Italy. The Arabs introduced them into Spain and the south

Oranges

of France, as well as into East Africa. Nice has been trading in bitter oranges since 1332.

A historic orange tree, planted in 1422, by Eléonore de Castille, the wife of Charles III, the King of Navarre, came into the possession of the Constable of Bourbon, was confiscated with all his possessions in 1552 and later graced first the gardens of Fontainebleau, under the name of Lord High Constable, then the gardens of Versailles. It died in 1858.

The sweet orange tree is classified as a native of China and the Chinese consider oranges wild fruit. Vasco de Gama brought a root of this tree to Portugal and it is from this tree, preserved in Lisbon at the home of Count de Saint-Laurent, that all the oranges of Portugal, Spain, Provence, etc., have come.

The orange tree is cultivated in all sub-tropical countries (Mediterranean Basin, North America, South America, South Africa). The production of oranges exceeds that of all other fruits.

Orange blossom and leaves. FLEURS, FEUILLES D'ORANGER – The flowers and the leaves of orange trees, particularly those of the bitter orange which are more strongly scented, are used as an infusion.

The essential oil of orange flowers is called *neroli*; that of the bitter orange *essence de petit-grain*. It is used for perfuming creams, custards, pancake batter, etc.

Orange flower water is used as an antidote for cardiospasms, palpitations and chronic diarrhoea (1 to 3 drops on a lump of sugar several times daily).

Orange flower water. EAU DE FLEUR D'ORANGER – Orange flower water has a subtle fragrance and is used in pastry-making and confectionery.

Orange flower water is manufactured industrially.

Orangeade – Very refreshing beverage made by adding the juice of one or several oranges to sweetened water.

To improve the taste of the orangeade, a little curaçao, brandy, rum or some other spirit can be added.

This beverage should be served as cold as possible, preferably iced.

Orangeat – French name for finely chopped, candied orange peel.

Orange cake. GÂTEAU À L'ORANGE – Cake made of Genoese pastry mixture, flavoured with orange. It is usually called *orangine* (q.v.).

Candied orange peel. ÉCORCE D'ORANGE CONFITE – Candied orange peel is used in pastry-making and confectionery. It is prepared in the following manner.

Scrape the orange rind with a spoon to remove all the white pith lining it on the inside, blanch, and put into syrup. Leave in the syrup for 24 hours. On the following day drain, cook the syrup to 102°C. (215°F.), or until it threads from the spoon, and put in the rind. This constitutes *façon* in confectionery terms. Repeat this operation several times, bringing the sugar to the desired degree of crystallisation at the last boiling.

Orange compote. COMPOTE D'ORANGES – Divide the oranges into segments, remove skin and pips and put into a bowl. Pour over them boiling syrup flavoured with orange peel. Cover the bowl. Leave to steep in the juice in a cold place. Serve in a fruit dish.

Orange cream. CRÈME À L'ORANGE – Custard cream flavoured with orange peel (see CREAMS).

Orange fritters. BEIGNETS D'ORANGES – Prepare like all fruit fritters, using orange segments. (See FRITTERS, *Sweet (dessert) fritters.*)

Glacé orange segments. QUARTIERS D'ORANGE GLACÉS – Remove all the white pith, taking care not to damage the thin skin in which the pulp is contained. Put the orange segments in the oven for a few moments to dry.

Spike them on a cocktail stick or a needle and dip them,

Orange salad (*Claire*)

Orangeade (*Claire*)

one by one, into sugar cooked to crack degree (see SUGAR). Leave them to cool on a wire mesh or a metal sieve. Put each segment into a little frilly paper case.

It is of orange segments prepared in this manner that orange *croquembouches* (q.v.) are made. They are also used for decorating sweet dishes.

Orange granité. GRANITÉS GLACÉS À L'ORANGE – This is served like sherbet. (See ICE CREAMS AND ICES *Granités*.)

Orange ice and iced mousse. GLACÉ ET MOUSSE GLACÉE À L'ORANGE – Orange ice is made of sugar syrup flavoured with orange, in the same way as all other water ices. (See ICE CREAMS AND ICES.) This ice is set in special forms, or served in glasses, or *en rocher*. It can also be served in scooped-out orange peel.

Orange iced mousse is prepared using orange-flavoured mousse (*bombe*) mixture and set in iced biscuit moulds. The mousse is often served under the name of *Biscuit glacé à l'orange*. It is also used as an ingredient of mixed ice *bombes* (see ICE CREAMS AND ICES).

Orange jelly. GELÉE À L'ORANGE – Jelly served as a sweet course (not to be confused with *Orange jelly* preserve, see JAMS AND JELLIES) which is set in special moulds or served in cups of orange peel.

Orange jelly is prepared as all other fruit jellies (see JELLY) and is usually flavoured with a few drops of Curaçao.

Orange jelly (preserve). GELÉE D'ORANGE – This is made of the juice of sweet oranges in the usual way (see JAMS AND JELLIES).

Orange liqueur – See LIQUEUR.

Orange marmalade. MARMELADE D'ORANGES – As described in recipes for other fruit marmalades (see MARMALADE).

Bitter (Seville) orange marmalade. CONFITURE (MARMELADE) DE BIGARADES – Prepare like *Orange marmalade* (see MARMALADE), using bitter oranges.

Orange pudding. POUDING À L'ORANGE – See PUDDINGS, *Lemon, Tangerine or Orange soufflé pudding*.

Orange salad. SALADE D'ORANGE – The word 'salad' is incorrectly used in this case, as no salt enters into the preparation of the dish. But it has become common usage to call the dish by this name.

Peel the oranges and remove all the pith covering them. Cut into round slices $\frac{1}{4}$ cm. ($\frac{1}{8}$ inch) thick and remove all pips. Arrange the slices in a fruit dish, sprinkle with castor sugar and a little Curaçao or any other liqueur such as rum, brandy or kirsch, and serve.

Bitter (Seville) orange salad. SALADE DE BIGARADES – This is served as a sweet course. Prepare, using bitter oranges, as *Orange salad*.

Orange soufflé. SOUFFLÉ À L'ORANGE – Using orange-flavoured soufflé mixture, prepare like any other cream soufflé (see SOUFFLÉS).

Striped oranges. ORANGES RUBANÉES – Choose big oranges

Oranges

Orange marmalade (*Fauchon. Phot. Nicolas*)

and scoop out the pulp, taking care not to damage the skins. Using this pulp make a clear orange jelly. Prepare a *Bavarois mixture* (see BAVARIAN CREAM), keeping it as white as possible, to contrast with the red of the orange jelly.

Fill the orange-peel cups with these two compositions, putting them in alternate, well-marked layers. Do not pour any jelly or *bavarois mixture* into the orange skins until the previous layer is completely set. This result is achieved if the orange-peel cups are placed in a pan filled with crushed ice. Chill.

Cut each orange-peel cup into quarters and serve in a fruit dish.

Oranges in syrup (Turkish cookery). ORANGES AU SIROP – Remove the yellow part of the peel of Jaffa oranges. Remove the pith and shred the peel into thin, long *julienne* strips. Poach the oranges in thick, slightly caramelised syrup. Leave them in this until the syrup thickens once more.

Towards the end of cooking, put in the shredded rind.

Orange wine. VIN D'ORANGE – The word 'wine' is incorrectly applied to this beverage, which, however, is excellent and very refreshing.

Choose very ripe oranges, peel them and cut into transverse slices. Press them to extract all the juice.

For every 4 litres ($3\frac{1}{2}$ quarts, $4\frac{1}{2}$ quarts) of this juice add 1 kg. ($2\frac{1}{4}$ lb.) sugar. Bottle, cork, tie with string and leave to ferment.

ORANGE MILK AGARIC. ORONGE – Common name for a mushroom of the *amanita* genus (see MUSHROOMS).

ORANGINE – Genoese pastry, flavoured with candied orange peel, cut transversely into three layers, sandwiched with *French pastry cream* (see CREAM) and iced with *Fondant icing* (see ICING).

Cut a *Genoese cake* (q.v.), flavoured with candied orange peel and baked in a flan ring with high sides, into three layers. Cover each with an orange-flavoured *French pastry cream* (see CREAMS). Reshape the cake. Ice with orange-flavoured *Fondant icing* (see ICING). Decorate with candied orange peel.

This gâteau can also be made by putting Genoese cakes, each baked in a flan ring in layer cake tins of different dimensions, one on top of another, sandwiching with orange-flavoured *French pastry cream*.

OREILLER DE LA BELLE AURORE (The Pillow of Belle Aurore) – In his book, *la Table au pays de Brillat-Savarin*, Lucien Tendret gives a recipe for this grandiose game pie, which, he says, was one of Brillat-Savarin's favourite dishes.

'At midday', wrote Tendret, 'we would sit at table, drink Côte-Grêle wine, from Brillat-Savarin's vineyard, and eat the traditional pie, square shaped and for that reason called *l'Oreiller de la Belle Aurore* after Brillat-Savarin's mother, Claudine-Aurore Récamier.'

Lucien Tendret's recipe for this pie was modified by Philéas Gilbert, and it is from this version that we quote below:

'In a pie in which game is the principal element the flavour of game meat must be the predominating flavour.

'Choose a plump, tender pheasant, bone it, having first cut off the drumsticks; season with a good pinch of *Spiced salt* (see SALT) and put into an earthenware casserole with 5 tablespoons (6 tablespoons) fine Champagne brandy and the same amount of Madeira.

'Remove all sinews from a big fat goose liver, and stud it generously with quarters of fresh, peeled truffles. Season with spiced salt and put it with the pheasant. Leave to marinate for one hour, turning both the pheasant and the liver from time to time.

'Cut into big dice 350 g. ($\frac{3}{4}$ lb.) wild rabbit meat, the flesh from the drumsticks, 150 g. (5 oz.) fillet of pork, 150 g. (5 oz.) round of veal and 400 g. (14 oz.) fresh fat bacon. Pound each of these ingredients separately, then put them all into the mortar, with 200 g. (7 oz.) raw goose liver and 45 g. ($1\frac{1}{2}$ oz., 3 tablespoons) spiced salt. Continue to pound until all the ingredients have blended into a homogeneous mixture, adding, little by little, 2 eggs beaten as for an omelette. Rub this forcemeat through a sieve into a bowl; add 100 g. (4 oz., 2 cups) finely chopped truffles and keep in a cool place. When ready to use, add the marinated pheasant and goose liver to the forcemeat.

'Bone two woodcocks. Sauté in butter 100 g. (4 oz.) chicken livers, as well as the livers of the pheasant and the woodcocks, which should be fried lightly, enough to stiffen them. Add 1 teaspoon chopped shallot, a pinch of spiced salt and 20 g. (1 scant oz., scant cup) fresh mushroom parings. Put on the fire for 2 minutes and dilute with 2 tablespoons (3 tablespoons) Madeira.

'Pound these livers in a mortar, then the woodcock meat. Combine the two ingredients, add 100 g. (4 oz.) raw goose liver, 50 g. (2 oz., 3 slices) finely shredded bacon, the trail of woodcocks, a pinch of spiced salt, 1 fresh, peeled truffle, and continue to pound in a mortar until the mixture is perfectly smooth. Rub through a sieve and keep by.

'Using 600 g. ($1\frac{1}{4}$ lb., 5 cups) sieved flour, 12 g. (2 scant teaspoons) salt, 3 dl. ($\frac{1}{2}$ pint, $1\frac{1}{4}$ cups) water and 30 g. (1 oz., 2 tablespoons) butter, prepare semi-puff pastry, allowing $5\frac{1}{2}$ turns. Roll out two-thirds of the pastry into 31-cm.-square (12-inch-square) sheets. Line the middle of this rolled-out piece of pastry with thin bacon rashers leaving a border of pastry of about 13 cm. (5 inches). Spread half of the first forcemeat on the bacon rashers in an even layer.

'Spread the pheasant on the table skin downwards, cover with half the woodcock forcemeat, put the goose liver on top and cover with the rest of the forcemeat. Bring the edges of the pheasant's skin and flesh together, so as to enclose the liver and to form a kind of slightly flattened galantine. Place this on the layer of forcemeat spread on the pastry. Cover completely with the other half of the forcemeat and on top of that lay a few thin rashers of bacon.

'Sprinkle with a pinch of spiced salt, add a small pinch of crushed bay leaf and a little powdered dry thyme.

'Roll out the rest of the pastry into a sheet a little thinner than the first piece. Pinch up the edges of the first piece of pastry all round the filling. Cover with the second piece of pastry and seal up the edges. Trim away surplus pastry, crimp the edges and decorate the sides with fancy pastry shapes, crescents, circles, lozenges, which are made to adhere by moistening the pastry slightly. Decorate the top with pastry leaves.

'Put 3 scallop-edged pieces of pastry, each of a different size, one on top of the other in the middle of the pie, and make a hole in the centre to allow steam to escape during cooking.

'Brush the pie with beaten egg. Surround it with a piece of buttered greaseproof paper fastened with string, all round; this can be removed after the pie has been in the oven for three-quarters of an hour.

'Put into a hot oven, keeping a regular heat. Allow from 30 to 32 minutes per kg. (15 to 16 minutes per pound).

'When cooked and the pastry is no more than warm, pour $1\frac{1}{2}$ dl. ($\frac{1}{4}$ pint, $\frac{2}{3}$ cup) game liquid aspic jelly through the hole in the top.

'This pie should be prepared at least 24 hours in advance.' (Philéas Gilbert.)

ORGEAT – Beverage made from an emulsion of almonds

with sugar. In the past this was made from a barley decoction.

Orgeat syrup. SIROP D'ORGEAT – Beverage prepared in the olden days from a barley emulsion to which an almond decoction was added. This syrup is nowadays made only from almonds.

Ingredients. 1 kg. ($2\frac{1}{4}$ lb.) almonds including 30 to 40 bitter almonds, $1\frac{1}{4}$ kg. ($2\frac{1}{2}$ lb., $5\frac{1}{4}$ cups) sugar, $\frac{3}{4}$ litre ($1\frac{1}{3}$ pints, $1\frac{3}{4}$ pints) water or milk and 3 teaspoons tartaric acid (cream of Tartar).

Method. Scald the almonds for a few moments in boiling water to loosen the skin, blanch, wash and pound them into a fine paste. Squeeze out the oil, reduce the rest to a powder, mix with enough water to make it into a liquid paste, and leave to stand for 24 hours. Add the rest of the water and dissolve the tartaric acid in the emulsion.

Filter through paper. Dissolve the sugar, either cold or on a low heat, and add to the emulsion.

ORIENTALE (À L') – Term applied to the preparation of various ingredients (fish, eggs, vegetables) cooked with tomatoes, flavoured with garlic and sometimes spiced with saffron.

ORIGAN (Wild Marjoram) – Aromatic herb, possessing a pungent smell and slightly bitter taste, somewhat similar to sweet marjoram.

It is used to flavour Italian *pizza.*

ORLÉANAIS – This ancient province of France can be classed among the gastronomical centres of the country, by virtue of the succulent game *pâtés* made there.

The gastronomical resources of Orléanais are great and all the produce – agricultural and livestock – is of the highest quality.

In Perche, cattle are raised, producing meat of excellent quality. The region specialises in raising very big sheep, which are perhaps less delicate than the smaller ones raised in Sologne.

In Beauce excellent poultry is found. The best comes from Romorantin, Selles-sur-Cher, Montargis and Dreux. Sologne produces fine game, and Sologne winged game is considered the best in France.

Loire fish (carp, pike, shad) is known for its delicate flavour, and is used in the preparation of delicious *matelotes.* Loire salmon is a highly prized fish, and crayfish abound in the waterways of this region.

Val-de-Loire is extremely fertile. The produce of its admirable market gardens and orchards are in great demand, especially Vendôme asparagus.

Beauce wheat produces one of the best quality flours to be found in France. At Boynes, near Pithiviers, saffron is grown. Among the food products of this region are wine vinegar, made of pure wine, which has for centuries been produced at Orléans.

Culinary specialities – Among the culinary specialities of this region is the celebrated *Pithiviers lark pâté,* made for 200 years to an old recipe in the shop of master-pastrycook Gringoire. There is the whole range of succulent pies made for centuries in this region.

There are many other excellent specialities, of which the following are the best known: *Blois and Vendôme rillettes* (potted mince); the succulent *Jargeau andouilles* and various other local pork products; *pike à la marinière; pike in saffron* (Gàtinais-grown saffron); *baked carp; matelote of eel; braised beef à la beauceronne; boiled leg of Sologne mutton; calf's mesentery à la blaisoise; young rabbit à la solognote; terrine of hare; stuffed potatoes; stuffed cabbage; croûte aux champignons de Montargis.*

Orléanais can be justly proud of its puff pastries with almonds, known as *Pithiviers almond cakes*; the '*demoiselles Tatin*' tart, made in Lamotte-Beuvron; *Beaugency fruit pâtés; crisp biscuit* from Sully, Montoire and Romorantin; *Orléans quince marmalade* and a natural product, *Gâtinais honey.*

Wines – Orléanais and Maine have no great wines, only pleasant regional varieties much valued by gourmets. Among the A.O.C. (*Appellation d'Origine Contrôlée*) wines are the excellent white Jasnières wine and the white, red and

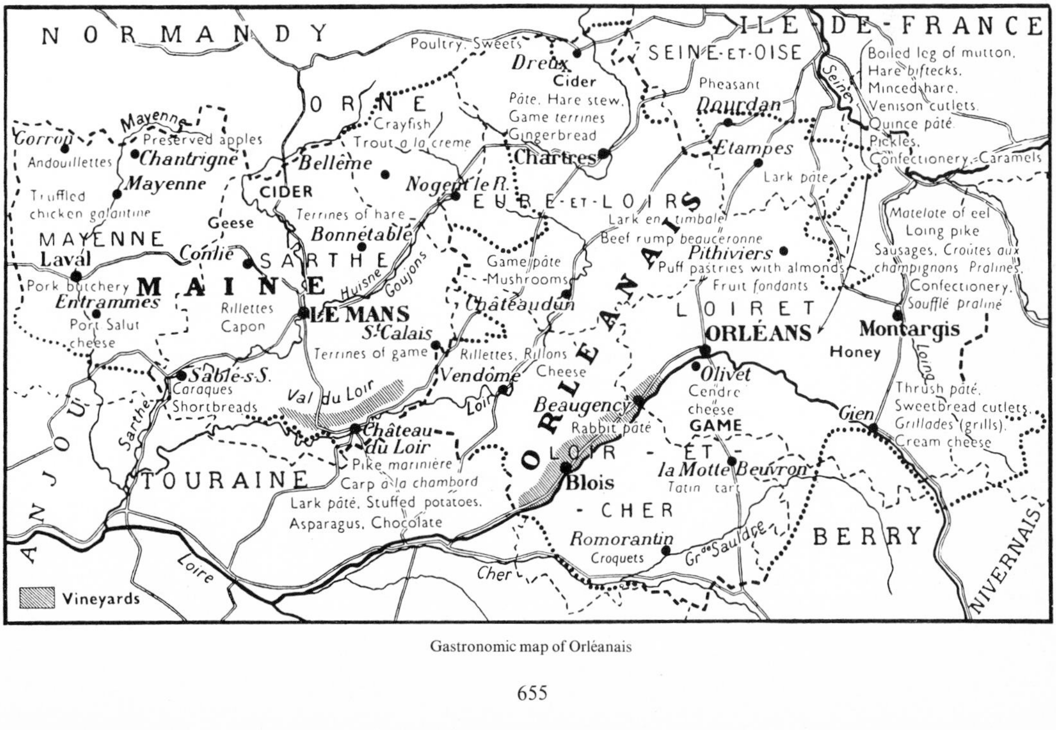

Gastronomic map of Orléanais

rosé wines of the Coteaux du Loir. V.D.Q.S. (*Vins Délimités de Qualité Supérieure*) wines are found in all three colours: Côtes de Gien or Coteaux du Giennois, and the Orléanais wines, including the delicious pale red Gris Meunier. All these wines are drunk young and chilled.

ORLY (À LA) – Method of preparation applied mostly to fish. The fish is filleted, the fillets skinned, dipped into a light batter, fried in deep fat and accompanied by tomato sauce. (See WHITING, *Whiting Orly*.)

ORMER. ORMEAU, ORMIER – Shellfish which are usually eaten raw or in soup as they are so small. Ormers should be beaten before being cooked.

ORTOLAN or GARDEN BUNTING – This small bird enjoys a high reputation as a table delicacy. Ortolans are found in central and southern Europe. They are plentiful in the south of France, particularly in Landes, a region which specialises in fattening them, and also in Spain, Italy and Greece.

They can be prepared in any way suitable for *Garden warblers* or *Larks*.

Gastronomes say that the only way to cook this bird is to roast it in the oven or on the spit, and insist that it should not be cooked in anything but its own fat.

Ortolans à la Brissac (Plumerey's recipe) – 'Cut a desalted ham pope's eye, from the part where the lean merges with the fat, into little squares. Thread the ortolans on thin skewers alternating with pieces of ham. Put them on a spit, back to back. Cook before a clear, lively fire, basting continuously with clarified butter.

'When nearly cooked, sprinkle with breadcrumbs and do not baste any more, to allow the birds to colour well. Take off the skewers, arrange on a dish and add small croûtons of bread to the ham. Peel 2 small baskets of mushrooms, slice them and sauté in a glass of Aix oil until they acquire a pale golden colour. Add sliced truffles and drain off all the oil. Add a piece of concentrated meat jelly about the size of a walnut, 1 tablespoon *Espagno le demi-glace* (see SAUCE) and a dash of lemon juice. Pour in the middle of the ortolans and serve.'

Ortolans à la Carême – 'Stuff the ortolans, boned through the back, with a little *foie gras* (q.v.) encrusted with a piece of truffle. Wrap each one in a piece of muslin and tie with string at both ends. Plung them into boiling port and poach for 5 minutes. Drain and unwrap.

'Arrange each in a tartlet case, baked blind and filled with a *salpicon* (q.v.) of lambs' sweetbreads, truffles and mushrooms, bound with chicken *Velouté sauce* (see SAUCE) boiled down with the port and a little cream.'

Ortolans in cases à la royale. ORTOLANS EN CAISSE À LA ROYALE – Bone the ortolans through the back. Stuff each one with a piece of *foie gras* (q.v.), encrusted with a slice of truffle, seasoned with spiced salt and sprinkled with brandy.

Reshape the ortolans. Brown them quickly in butter. Put each into a frilly paper case or individual oven-proof dishes on 1 tablespoon truffles shredded into *julienne* (q.v.) strips. Sprinkle with melted butter, cook in the oven for 5 or 6 minutes and serve.

Cold ortolans. ORTOLANS FROIDS – All the methods of preparation given for quails, thrushes and larks are applicable to ortolans. Ortolans, however, whether served hot or cold, should be prepared in the simplest manner and roasted.

Ortolans à la landaise – This recipe was supplied by Felix Campagné, Hôtel de France, at Pau.

'Arrange the ortolans in rows in a dripping pan and stand it in a big open fireplace before a great log fire. They cook in their own melting fat.

Salt and spice them with one turn of the pepper mill.'

Ortolans à la périgourdine – Heat 2 tablespoons (3 tablespoons) butter in an earthenware casserole and put in 6 trussed ortolans. Brown them quickly in the sizzling butter. Cover with 12 thick slices of truffles. Season with salt and pepper. Cover the casserole and cook in the oven for about 8 minutes, basting the birds with 1 generous tablespoon Armagnac which has been set alight. Serve in the same casserole.

Ortolans à la provençale (Carême's recipe) – 'Twenty ortolans would be enough for an entrée. Cut 24 thick, oval-shaped croûtons. Hollow out on one side, put 1 ortolan on each croûton, then place in a sauté pan in which you have put some best olive oil, spiced with a pounded ½ clove of garlic. Heat the oil with the croûtons and the ortolans, then place in the oven.

'As soon as the croûtons begin to colour lightly, remove the pan from heat, drain them on a cloth to wipe off the oil, and arrange on a dish. Prepare a truffle *ragoût* (q.v.) and *Parisian sauce* (see SAUCE, *Cold sauces*), add to it anchovy butter made from two de-salted anchovy fillets, put in 1 tablespoon cold olive oil and the juice of ½ lemon, pour this in the middle of the dish containing the ortolans, and serve.'

Roast ortolans. ORTOLANS RÔTIS – Truss the ortolans and wrap in vine leaves. Pack them in rows, fairly tightly, in a pan moistened with a little salted water. Roast in a very hot oven for about 5 minutes. Arrange each on a croûton fried in butter. Serve with lemon halves.

Cooked in this way, the birds don't lose their fat, which is greatly enjoyed by gastronomes.

Ortolans on skewers. BROCHETTE D'ORTOLANS – Wrap the trussed ortolans in thin rashers of fat bacon. Thread on skewers, 4 birds to a skewer, separated from each other by little croûtons, cut to look like cocks' combs and lightly fried in butter. Put the skewers into a roasting pan in which a little butter has been heated. Cook briskly in a hot oven for about 5 minutes.

Arrange the skewers on a long dish. Garnish with watercress and quarters of lemon. Pour the pan juices over the birds.

ORVAL or CLARY. SAUGE SCLARÉE, ORVALE – Variety of sage used in the manufacture of Turin Vermouth.

OSTRICH. AUTRUCHE – The flesh of this bird, forbidden to the Jews and the Moslems, was much valued by the Romans. The second Apicius dedicated a special sauce to it.

An ostrich, on the average, gives about 30 kg. (66 lb.) meat and 20 kg. (44 lb.) fat. But only the wings are sufficiently tender to be edible. Its eggs, on the other hand, are excellent.

OTTER. LOUTRE DE RIVIÈRE – Carnivorous water mammal. Its flesh, which is oily and leathery, has a very unpleasant taste.

OUBLIE (Wafer) – Furetières defines the *oublie* as a 'thin round wafer cooked between two irons'. According to him, him, the word *oublie* is a corruption of *oblaye*, derived from *oblata*, which used to define non-consecrated Eucharist host. It was called *oblée* or *oublie*.

The most famous of these wafers were made in Lyons, and it is in this town that they were first rolled into a cone. In Paris they were flat and insipid.

These wafers, made out of any pastry remnants, were once left to bakery boys – it was their profit. On winter evenings they would offer them to passers-by and sell them from door to door; they sold 7 or 8 at a time. This was called '*une main d'oublies*' (a handful of wafers).

The wafer vendors cast dice with their clients for their wares. Towards the middle of the eighteenth century these vendors were called '*marchands de plaisir*', because their cry was '*Voilà le plaisir*'.

Here is a recipe for making the wafers.

Oublies à la parisienne (Parisian wafers) – *Ingredients.* 250 g. (9 oz., 2 cups) sieved cake flour, 150 g. (5 oz., $\frac{2}{3}$ cup, firmly packed) castor sugar, 2 eggs, 65 g. (2 oz., $\frac{1}{4}$ cup) melted butter, 7 dl. ($1\frac{1}{4}$ pints, $1\frac{1}{2}$ pints) milk, flavouring, orange-blossom water, lemon rind.

Method. Blend the flour, sugar, eggs and flavouring in a bowl. When the mixture has been worked into a smooth paste, add the milk, little by little, then the melted butter and, last of all, the grated lemon rind.

Heat the wafer irons and grease them evenly. Pour in 1 tablespoon of the mixture and cook on a very lively heat, turning the irons. Take out the cooked wafer, roll it into a cone round a conical piece of wood, or leave it flat.

OUILLAT or TOURRI (Béarn cookery) – 'Put 1 chopped onion to cook in fat or olive oil in an earthenware casserole. When the onion colours, add some crushed garlic and cook. Pour in hot water. Add a bouquet of thyme and parsley, season with pepper and salt, simmer for 30 minutes, then strain on to slices of bread.

'Water in which French beans, dried peas, broad beans and asparagus were cooked is sometimes used for this purpose. An egg and a dash of vinegar can be added at the moment of straining into the soup tureen. Grated Gruyère cheese can be substituted for egg. When in season, tomatoes, peeled and sliced, are put to cook with the onion.' (Simin Palay.)

OUKA (Russian cookery). OUKA DE LOTTE À L'OSEILLE – This soup is made by cooking squares of burbot in a fish stock made from perch, *siguis* and *ierchis*, then adding a *julienne* of parsley roots and celery (previously softened in butter). Simmer for a few minutes. A *chiffonade* (q.v.) of blanched, drained sorrel and the burbot's liver (previously cooked separately) is added just before serving.

Modern electric oven
(*Brigaud. Phot. Photothèque E.D.F.*)

OVEN. FOUR – Enclosed space which can be brought to a high temperature and into which dishes are put to cook. Cooking in the oven has been known for a very long time. The baker's oven is still today constructed almost in the same way as in ancient times (see BAKERY). A pastry oven is a little smaller and has certain special characteristics (see PÂTISSERIE). The oven for cooking is usually part of the whole cooking range or stove, though separate ovens are also sometimes used. The great progress which has been made in our time in the construction of ovens consists mainly in the use of metals, insulating materials, and double walls, which are a great economy and assure perfect regularity of heat. Further advances are the use of other combustibles than wood, such as gas, oil, steam and electricity for baker's and pastry-cooks' ovens. The most modern and practical kitchen stoves are those heated by gas or electricity. Infra-red grills and electronic ovens are another innovation.

OVERLAP. IMBRIQUER – Overlapping is sometimes used for decorative effect in the garnishing of dishes. For instance, little strips of truffle can be laid one against the other and set in jelly to decorate certain cold dishes. The effect is reminiscent of tiling.

OX. BOEUF – See also BEEF, OFFAL or VARIETY MEATS.

Ox belly (tripe). GRAS-DOUBLE DE BOEUF – This part of the offal comes from the animal's paunch. It is generally sold cooked and can be prepared in various ways.

For all recipes for preparing ox belly, see OFFAL or VARIETY MEATS.

Ox brain. CERVELLE DE BOEUF – See OFFAL or VARIETY MEATS.

Ox cheeks. JOUES DE BOEUF – Boned and trimmed ox cheeks are used for preparing *pot-au-feu*.

Ox cheeks can be braised or made into stews. They can also be prepared like *Pickled tongue* (see OFFAL or VARIETY MEATS).

Ox heart, Ox muzzle, Ox palate, Ox tail. COEUR, MUSEAU, PALAIS, QUEUE DE BOEUF – See OFFAL or VARIETY MEATS.

Oxtail soup – See SOUPS AND BROTHS.

Ox (beef) tongue. LANGUE DE BOEUF – See OFFAL or VARIETY MEATS.

Ox tripe. TRIPES DE BOEUF – This term applies equally to the ox belly and the tripe itself. (See OFFAL or VARIETY MEATS.)

OXFORD SAUCE (English cookery) – Sauce served with cold venison. The ingredients are redcurrant jelly, port, chopped shallot, grated orange and lemon rind, orange and lemon juice, mustard and powdered ginger.

OXYMEL – Syrup made from a mixture of honey and vinegar. It is obtained by cooking 1 part vinegar with 4 parts honey.

OYSTER. HUÎTRE – Bivalve mollusc usually eaten raw.

The oyster has been known to man from the earliest times, though there is no positive evidence that the Egyptians and Assyrians ate this delicious mollusc. It seems to have been unknown to the Jews. The Celts gathered oysters and fed on them abundantly. The Greeks prized oysters highly and knew how to prepare them in a number of ways. They were especially fond of Hellespont (Dardanelles) oysters. The people of Greece used oyster shells for casting their votes. The voter inscribed his choice with a sharp point on the white mother-of-pearl of the shell. The Romans were great lovers of oysters, and prized those gathered in the Lucrine Lake, as well as the oysters of Brindisi, Taranto and Circeo. It is said that they seasoned their oysters with *garum* (q.v.).

In France, up to the beginning of the nineteenth century, it was thought that the coastal oyster beds were inexhaustible; the Ordinance of 1681, enacted to protect mussels, left the oyster fisheries free from control. However, by 1754 it became necessary to prohibit the gathering of oysters between 1st April and 31st October each year. Similar measures had to be taken in Brittany.

In spite of these precautions, the devastations of the natural oyster beds continued in all coastal areas, until in

'Bélon' oysters

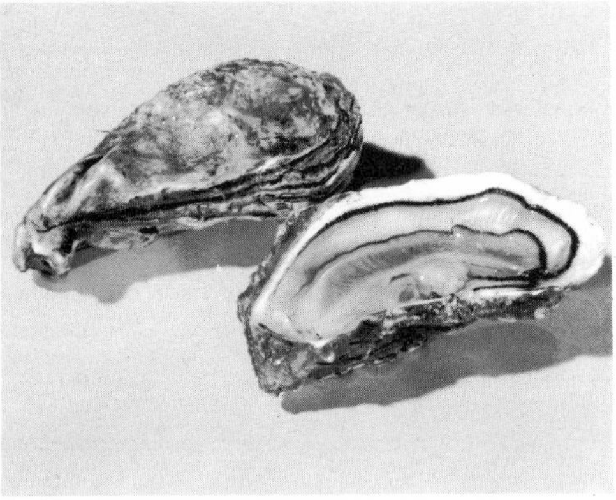

Portuguese oysters

Marenne oysters
(*Marveilles de mer – Charlot I. Phot. Larousse*)

1840 it became necessary to call in a naval vessel at Arcachon to guard the oyster beds in the bay. But the beds, once depleted, could not be replenished by 'spontaneous generation'. The Administration of Fisheries realised that new oysters would have to be brought to the depleted beds.

Coste, the true father of the oyster industry, went to Lake Fusaro and studied the methods by which the Italians maintained a supply of excellent oysters. The man-made oyster beds of Tarento consisted of stakes tied together with ropes from which were suspended traps in the form of small faggots. The stakes and faggots were encrusted with oysters of every size. The saleable oysters were put on the market. The smaller ones were put into osier baskets to attain full growth.

On his return to France, Coste succeeded in stocking the Bay of Saint-Brieuc with oysters collected at Cancale on the English Channel and Tréguier, Côte de Nord. He replenished the Thau pool and the Bays of Toulon and Brest with British oysters. The Concarneau reserve came into being, and finally model beds were built up at Arcachon in the Cès, at Crastorbe and then at Lahillon.

The American Indians ate large quantities of oysters. Oyster fisheries and farming represent a large industry in North America today.

Nutritive value of oysters – Raw oysters contain vitamins, phosphorus salts, chalk, iron, copper and manganese in a readily assimilable form. They also contain a very high proportion of iodine and are sometimes eaten to combat anaemia. Green American oysters (different from the Marenne oyster) have been used in the treatment of anaemia with results equal to those obtained from calves' liver. Oysters contain appreciable amounts of Vitamins A, B_1, B_2, and C.

The risk of infectious diseases being spread through the water contained in oysters is small, provided they are bought from a conscientious supplier who has made it his business to know where they come from.

Improved methods and conditions of transport have put an end to the prejudice of avoiding oysters in 'the months without an R'. Nowadays, oysters may be safely consumed all the year round. However, since the 'months without an R' correspond to the oysters' period of reproduction, oyster farmers prefer not to deplete the beds at this time. It is better, therefore, to eat the oysters on their own home ground rather than to rely on finding them elsewhere.

Various types of oyster – There are two main types: the *wild oyster*, which has a very pronounced sea-water flavour, and the *cultivated oyster*. In the cultivation of oysters, seed-oysters are affixed to tiles and reared in areas some way out to sea. When they have reached a certain size, they are transferred to the fattening beds which are always situated at the mouth of a river, the mixture of fresh and sea water being essential to induce over-growth of the liver in which the fattening consists.

The green *Marenne oysters* owe their colouring to the algae and microscopic diatoma which live in the fattening pools in which they are embedded.

This colouring was an accidental discovery. During the siege of La Rochelle, some oysters were thrown into the old salt marshes. When they were fished out again, everyone was astonished at their green colour. After a good deal of hesitation, it was decided that they should be tasted and it was noticed that, far from being spoiled, they had acquired a more delicate flavour.

The name *Portuguese oyster* is given to a sub-variety of oyster whose proper name is *gryphacea*. Since it has become customary to bed and treat them like the Marenne oysters, their flavour has improved noticeably, though they are still not comparable with genuine oysters.

Oysters can be prepared in a great many different ways. They can be served as hot or cold *hors-d'œuvre*. They can be used in the preparation of elegant and elaborate garnishes, and excellent soups and sauces can be made from them.

OYSTERS AS COLD HORS-D'ŒUVRE. HORS-D'ŒUVRE FROIDS – Oysters must not be opened until just before serving, and are best served very cold. It is therefore ad-

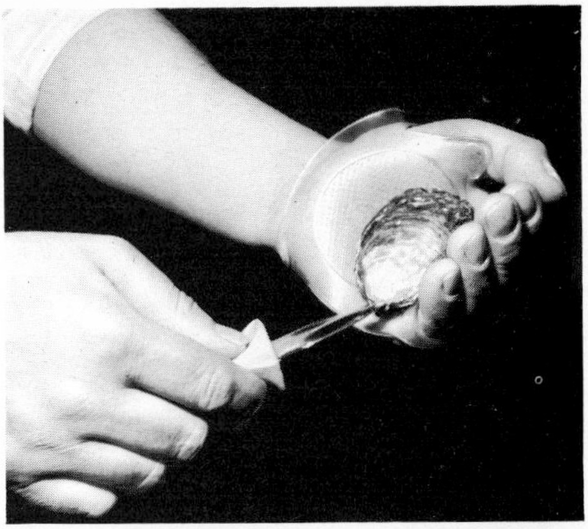

How to open an oyster at the hinge; Using an oyster knife (*Marveilles de mer – Charlot I*), with the hand protected by a special glove; Using the oyster opener (*La Samaritaine. Phot. Larousse*)

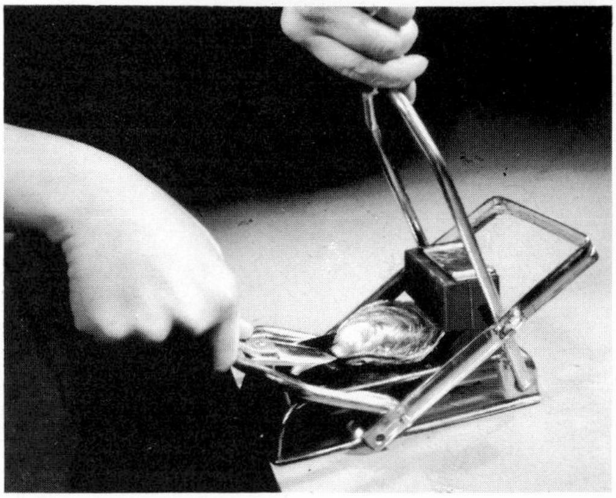

visable whenever possible to lay them as soon as they are opened on a bed of crushed ice. Eaten in this way, with the midday or evening meal, the oyster provides a nourishing and delicious *hors-d'œuvre*. Its dressing is usually simple, consisting of lemon juice or shallot vinegar with coarsely ground pepper.

Slices of buttered brown or white bread are usually served with fresh oysters.

Oysters à l'andalouse. HUÎTRES À L'ANDALOUSE – Poach 24 oysters in their own liquor. Drain them and dry in a cloth. Remove the beards and leave them to cool.

Decorate each with a little sliver of truffle, making them stick with jelly, then spoon over some half-set jelly and leave till they are quite cold.

Choose 12 deep halves of oyster shells as regular in shape as possible. Wash them thoroughly, and fill them with *Tomato mousse* (see TOMATO, *Cold tomato mousse*), doming it a little. Put 2 oysters on each shell. Mask with half-set jelly and leave to set.

Arrange the oysters in a bed of crushed ice on a dish.

Oysters in barquettes. HUÎTRES EN BARQUETTES – Poach the oysters, drain and remove the beards. Mask them with glazing mayonnaise (see SAUCE). Decorate with truffles and the roe of a spiny lobster (crayfish). Mask with jelly.

Set them in pairs in little *barquettes* baked blind. Garnish with *Russian salad* (see SALAD) a vegetable mousse or other *hors-d'œuvre* filling. Garnish with green curly parsley.

Oysters with caviare. HUÎTRES AU CAVIAR – Bake blind tartlet shells, using *Fine lining paste* (see DOUGH). Fill each with 1 tablespoon fresh caviare. Place on top a single shelled oyster. Garnish with fresh parsley and serve with lemon.

The tartlets must be filled at the last moment, and the oysters opened and shelled just as they are about to be served. Oysters and caviare can also be served in well-washed oyster shells.

The gastronome's oyster. HUÎTRES DU GASTRONOME – Poach the oysters and drain them. Remove the beards and leave to cool. Coat them with a *Chaud-froid sauce à la hongroise* based on vegetable stock (see SAUCE). Cover with jelly.

Cook tiny artichoke hearts in a white *court-bouillon* (q.v.). Steep them in oil and lemon juice. Just before serving, fill these with a salad of crayfish tails and diced truffles dressed with gelatine-strengthened mayonnaise. Put an oyster on top of each one.

Arrange the artichoke hearts on a dish and garnish with chopped jelly.

Marinated oysters. HUÎTRES MARINÉES – Shell the oysters. Put them in a marinade of white wine, oil and lemon juice, well seasoned with herbs and prepared in advance.

Bring to the boil and remove them at once from the stove. Pour the stock and oysters into a bowl. Leave until they are quite cold. Serve them in *hors-d'œuvre* dishes with the marinade.

OYSTERS AS HOT HORS-D'ŒUVRE. HORS-D'ŒUVRE CHAUDS – There are a great many recipes for cooked oysters, the best known of which are given in this section.

However oysters are to be prepared, they must always first be poached in their own liquor.

To poach oysters. Open the oysters. Prise them away from the shells without tearing the flesh. Put them in a pan, with their own liquor strained through muslin. Bring to the boil. As soon as the liquid begins to bubble, remove the pan from the stove.

Cooked oysters are often served in the deep halves of their shells. If they are to be glazed or sprinkled with cheese and browned, the shells must be embedded in a layer of salt spread on a baking sheet, to keep them upright.

Glazing and browning must be accomplished very quickly, to prevent the oysters from becoming tough.

Oysters à l'américaine I. HUÎTRES À L'AMÉRICAINE – Put the oysters in the deep halves of their shells. Lay them on a baking sheet lined with cooking salt. Squeeze a few drops of lemon juice on each oyster and season with a touch of cayenne pepper.

Sprinkle with fried breadcrumbs. Pour over them melted butter seasoned with lemon, salt and pepper. Brown in a very hot oven. Garnish with fresh parsley.

Oysters à l'américaine II. HUÎTRES À L'AMÉRICAINE – Put

Oysters à la florentine (*Robert Carrier*)

the oysters back in the deep halves of their shells. Cover with *American sauce* (see SAUCE, *Compound white sauces*) with the concentrated liquor of the oysters added. Garnish with fresh parsley.

Attereaux of oysters – See HORS-D'ŒUVRE, *Hot hors-d'œuvre*.

Oyster barquettes à l'américaine. BARQUETTES D'HUÎTRES À L'AMÉRICAINE – Bake *barquettes* blind. Fill each with 1 tablespoon *American sauce* (see SAUCE). Place on top 2 or 3 poached, drained and trimmed oysters. Sprinkle with freid breadcrumbs, and season with a touch of cayenne pepper.

Oyster barquettes à la Nantua. BARQUETTES D'HUÎTRES À LA NANTUA – Fill cooked *barquettes* with 1 tablespoon of *ragoût* of *Crayfish tails à la Nantua* (see RAGOÛT). Put 2 poached oysters on top of each. Coat with *Nantua sauce* (see SAUCE). Sprinkle with grated cheese, and brown quickly in the oven.

Oyster barquettes à la normande. BARQUETTES D'HUÎTRES À LA NORMANDE – Fill *barquettes* with a *salpicon* (q.v.) of crayfish tails, mussels and mushrooms blended in a *Normande sauce* (see SAUCE). Put 2 poached oysters on top of each. Mask with *Normande sauce*. Put a strip of truffle on top of each *barquette*.

Oyster bouchées. BOUCHÉES AUX HUÎTRES – See HORS-D'ŒUVRE, *Patties with oysters*.

Oyster coquilles – See HORS-D'ŒUVRE, *Scallop shells of oysters*.

Oysters à la crème. HUÎTRES GRATINÉES À LA CRÈME – Detach the oysters from the shell, remove beards, and put 1 tablespoon cream in each shell with the oyster. Sprinkle with a little melted butter and Parmesan cheese and grill under a fairly high flame.

Oyster croquettes – See HORS-D'ŒUVRE, *Croquettes*.

Devilled oysters – See below, *Grilled oysters*.

Oysters à la florentine. HUÎTRES À LA FLORENTINE – Fill the deep halves of the oyster shells with a layer of spinach cooked in butter. Put an oyster on top of each. Cover with *Mornay sauce* (see SAUCE). Sprinkle with cheese and brown in the oven.

Fried oysters. HUÎTRES FRITES – Poach, drain and remove the beards from the oysters. Dip in milk and flour them, shaking off any excess flour. Deep-fry in boiling fat. Drain and dry on a cloth. Season with fine salt. Garnish with lemon and fried parsley.

Fried oysters Colbert. HUÎTRES FRITES COLBERT – Poach, drain and remove the beards of the oysters. Dip them in egg and breadcrumbs and fry them. Garnish with lemon and fried parsley. Serve with *Maître d'hôtel butter* (see BUTTER, *Compound butters*).

Oyster fritot – See HORS-D'ŒUVRE, *Fritot*.

Oyster fritters à la normande. BEIGNETS D'HUÎTRES À LA NORMANDE – Poach the oysters and leave them to cool in their own liquor. Drain and wipe them with a cloth. Dip them one by one in *Villeroi sauce* (see SAUCE) adding chopped truffles and vegetables. Dip them in batter (see BATTERS FOR FRYING) and deep-fry in very hot fat until the fritters have swelled to their full extent and are a golden colour.

Drain them on a cloth. Season with dry fine salt.

Oysters for garnishing. HUÎTRES POUR GARNITURES – Shell the oysters and poach them in their own liquor.

Remove the pan from the heat as soon as the liquor begins to boil. Drain and trim the oysters and proceed according to the recipe used.

If the oysters are not to be used at once, keep them hot in their own strained liquor. Care must be taken to see that they do not boil. The oyster liquor is strained and added to the sauce.

Oysters au gratin I. HUÎTRES AU GRATIN – Fill the deep halves of oyster shells with a layer of *duxelles* (q.v.). Put an oyster on each shell and a mushroom on top of each oyster. Cover with *Duxelles sauce* (see SAUCE), with the oyster liquor added. Sprinkle with breadcrumbs. Pour on melted butter seasoned with salt and pepper and a few drops of lemon. Brown in a very hot oven. After they have been taken out of the oven, squeeze a few drops of lemon juice over them. Sprinkle with chopped parsley and garnish with fresh parsley.

Oysters au gratin II. HUÎTRES AU GRATIN – Proceed as for *Oysters à l'américaine I*.

Grilled oysters, also called devilled oysters. HUÎTRES GRILLÉES, À LA DIABLE – Poach, drain and remove the beards of the oysters. Thread them on little metal skewers.

Pour melted butter, seasoned with lemon, salt and pepper, over the oysters. Dip them in fine breadcrumbs seasoned with a little cayenne pepper. Grill under a low flame. Serve in the same way as *Oysters on skewers* (see below). Serve with *Diable sauce* (see SAUCE).

Oysters à la Mornay. HUÎTRES À LA MORNAY – Line the deep halves of the oyster shells with *Mornay sauce* (see SAUCE). Put an oyster on top of each. Cover with the same sauce. Sprinkle with grated Parmesan, pour on melted butter and brown in a very hot oven. Garnish with fresh parsley.

Oysters à la polonaise. HUÎTRES À LA POLONAISE – Put the oysters back in the deep halves of their shells. Sprinkle with chopped yolks of hard-boiled egg and chopped parsley and warm in the oven. Just before serving, pour 1 tablespoon browned butter with fried breadcrumbs over each oyster.

Oysters on skewers. BROCHETTES D'HUÎTRES – Thread poached oysters on little metal skewers with slices of cooked mushroom in between. Pour melted butter seasoned with lemon juice and pepper over them. Dip them in fine breadcrumbs and grill under a low heat.

When serving, surround with a border of fluted half-slices of lemon and garnish with parsley.

Sprinkle with melted *Maître d'hôtel butter*, or with one of the sauces especially suitable for grilled fish (see BUTTER, *Compound butters*; SAUCE).

Oyster soufflés. HUÎTRES SOUFFLÉES – Pound 12 raw oysters in a mortar. Mix in, little by little, the white of 1 raw egg.

Rub through a sieve. Put the mixture in a bowl and stir it on ice. Add 30 g. (1 oz., 2 tablespoons) *Fine pike forcemeat* (see FORCEMEATS or STUFFINGS) and about 2 dl. ($\frac{1}{3}$ pint, scant cup) thick fresh cream.

Put 2 teaspoons of the mixture in each oyster shell. Put a poached and drained oyster on top of this forcemeat and cover with a layer of soufflé mixture. Smooth, doming it slightly.

Bake in the oven for 6 to 8 minutes.

Oyster soup. SOUPE AUX HUÎTRES – Shell 24 oysters and put them in a pan. Pour over their strained liquor. Add 2 dl. ($\frac{1}{3}$ pint, scant cup) white wine.

Bring to the boil, then turn the flame very low. Skim. Add 2 dl. ($\frac{1}{3}$ pint, scant cup) cream, 3 tablespoons (scant $\frac{1}{4}$ cup) crushed biscuit crackers, and 100 g. (4 oz., $\frac{1}{2}$ cup) butter cut into tiny fragments. Season. Spice with a touch of cayenne pepper. Mix. Pour the soup into a tureen and serve with crushed crackers.

Oysters Villeroi. BROCHETTES D'HUÎTRES VILLEROI – Poach and drain the oysters. Cover them with *Villeroi sauce* (see SAUCE). Thread them on little metal skewers and fry them just before serving. Drain and garnish with parsley.

OYSTER CATCHER. HUÎTRIER – A wader, sometimes called sea-magpie. The flesh of the young bird is quite delicate. It is prepared in the same way as plover.

OYSTER PLANT – See SALSIFY.

PACARET – This word, which is a variation of Pascarete, is used to define wine of the Jerez district of Spain. The name of the wine is derived from the name of the small town of Paxarete or Pajarete in the Jerez sherry-producing district. The grapes gathered there yield very sweet juice, which is treated with brandy to prevent it fermenting, and results in the Paxarete or Pajarete liqueur wine. This used to be much in vogue in England in the eighteenth century.

PAËLLA – Spanish rice dish which has gained international fame. Different regions of Spain vary the paëlla according to the local produce. Vegetables, meat, chicken and sausage, characterise the paëllas of interior Spain; Valencia and Barcelona specialise in combining sea foods with chicken and vegetables in the rice base. The name of the dish comes from the iron frying pan with two handles, the paëlla, in which the rice is cooked and served.

The following is a Valencian paëlla: Heat 3 tablespoons (scant $\frac{1}{4}$ cup) oil in a deep iron frying pan with 2 cloves of garlic, finely chopped. Add 2 chopped onions, and 2 diced sweet red peppers. Add to this 1 small chicken cut in small pieces, and 225 g. (8 oz.) pork, ham or beefsteak cut in small dice. Brown the meat and add 4 peeled and quartered small tomatoes. Stir in 675 g. ($1\frac{1}{2}$ lb.) rice and cook gently for 5 minutes. Cover with well-seasoned stock to which a pinch of saffron has been added. Add 175 g. (6 oz.) shelled peas, 175 g. (6 oz.) fresh kidney beans and several artichoke hearts. Cook 10 minutes more and then add 450 g. (1 lb.) cod, whiting or hake cut in small pieces, 1 lobster or crayfish, also cut in small pieces, 225 g. (8 oz.) shrimps or prawns, 6 dl. (1 pint, $2\frac{1}{2}$ cups) thoroughly washed mussels or small clams. Boil hard for 5 minutes and simmer for 15 more, adding more stock as necessary. The rice should be moist but not soupy. When the rice is cooked, place the paëlla in the oven for a few minutes. Chopped parsley is added before serving. Small inkfish or squid and garlic sausages may also be added to the above ingredients. The inkfish are usually fried in the oil before adding the rice, and the garlic added after the meat has been browned.

PAILLARD – See RESTAURANTS OF BYGONE DAYS.

PAILLASSE – French name for a charcoal fire which was used in kitchens of long ago to prepare dishes which needed prolonged cooking, especially braised meat.

Meat was also grilled on glowing embers in a bucket-shaped brick brazier.

The term *paillasse* is also used to describe the layer of glowing charcoal embers spread out on the grill.

PAINS – French term for dishes, served cold or hot, made of a forcemeat placed in a special mould and poached in a *bain-marie*, in the case of a dish being served hot; and set in a mould, lined with aspic jelly and chilled when served cold.

This type of *entrée* has been replaced by mousses, which are also prepared hot or cold. The various ingredients used for the forcemeats are, as indicated in individual recipes, liver (*foie gras*), game meat (winged and ground game), poultry, vegetables, as well as fish and shellfish. For recipes see LOAVES.

PALADRU – See CHEESE.

PALAIS-ROYAL (Café du) – See RESTAURANTS OF BYGONE DAYS.

PALATE OF OX. PALAIS DE BOEUF – See OFFAL or VARIETY MEATS, *Ox palate.*

PALE ALE – Light English beer.

PALETS DE DAMES – Little dry *petit fours* (fancy biscuits).

Into a hot bowl put 250 g. (9 oz., 1 generous cup) fine sugar, and 6 eggs. Stir well with a wooden spoon. When the mixture is frothy add 250 g. (9 oz., $2\frac{1}{4}$ cups) sieved flour, still stirring.

Put on a buttered baking sheet, lightly sprinkled with flour. Bake in a hot oven. Glaze with water icing (confectioners' frosting).

Palets de dames (which are sometimes written *palais*) can be flavoured with vanilla, lemon or orange rind or any other flavouring.

PALETTE KNIFE. AMASETTE – Small utensil used in pastry-making for picking up dough.

PALMAE. PALMIER – Name of a large family of trees, of which the fruit (dates), the nuts (coconut), the terminal shoots (cabbage palm), the pith or interior of the stem (sago), and the sap (palm wine) are used in cookery.

Palm hearts. COEURS DE PALMIER – The hearts or tender shoots of palms are cooked like asparagus. Peel the stalks completely and boil in salted water. Serve hot with various white sauces or cold *à la vinaigrette.*

Palm hearts can also be prepared in various other ways: *à la crème*, stewed in butter, in gravy, *au gratin*, with Parmesan cheese, *à la polonaise*, and in general in any way suitable for asparagus (q.v.) or cardoon (q.v.).

PALM OIL. HUILE DE PALME – See OIL.

PALMIER (Pâtisserie) – Paris speciality, prepared in the following way.

How to fold the pastry to make palmiers (*Larousse*)

How to cut and shape palmiers (*À l'Alsacienne. Phot. Larousse*)

Roll out puff pastry 1 cm. ($\frac{1}{2}$ inch) thick on a table sprinkled with icing sugar instead of flour. Cut into strips 30 cm. (12 inches) wide. Bring the two ends of these strips together towards the centre and fold in two, lengthways.

Leave to settle for a few moments, then cut them across into pieces 6 mm. ($\frac{1}{4}$ inch) thick.

Put these on a baking sheet, placing them at a little distance from each other. Bake in a hot oven.

PALM NUT. NOIX DE PALME – Fruit of the elaeis of New Guinea, varying from the size of a hazel nut to that of a walnut. Palm oil is extracted from these nuts.

PALOURDE – Name given to a kind of squash (vegetable marrow) in some parts of France.

PALUS – Vineyards planted on the alluvial tracts of land in the Bordeaux region and on the estates bordering the banks of the Garonne, Dordogne and Gironde.

PANADA. PANADE – This name applies to two different preparations: one a kind of soup, made of bread, stock, milk or water and butter; the other a paste of flour, bread, toast (*biscottes*) or various starches, used for binding meat or fish forcemeats.

Bread panada. PANADE AU PAIN – Soak 250 g. (9 oz.) white crustless bread in 3 dl. ($\frac{1}{2}$ pint, $1\frac{1}{4}$ cups) boiled milk until the milk is absorbed. Blend the mixture, stirring all the time, as described in the recipe for *Flour panada* (see below).

Leave until quite cold, as for flour panada.

Uses. For fish forcemeats.

Flour panada for forcemeat. PANADE POUR FARCE À LA FARINE – Pour 3 dl. ($\frac{1}{2}$ pint, $1\frac{1}{4}$ cups) water into a saucepan, add 50 g. (2 oz., $\frac{1}{4}$ cup) butter and $\frac{1}{3}$ teaspoon salt. Pour in 150 g. (5 oz., $1\frac{1}{4}$ cups) sieved flour. Mix well on the heat, stirring with a wooden spoon. Cook until the mixture thickens, leaving the sides of the pan clean.

Put into a buttered dish, spread in an even layer, cover with a piece of buttered paper and leave until quite cold.

Uses. For all quenelle forcemeats.

Frangipane panada. PANADE À LA FRANGIPANE – Mix 125 g. ($4\frac{1}{2}$ oz., generous cup) sieved flour and 4 egg yolks in a pan, stirring with a wooden spoon. Add 100 g. (4 oz., $\frac{1}{2}$ cup) melted butter, $\frac{1}{3}$ teaspoon salt, pepper and a pinch of grated nutmeg.

Stirring all the time, dilute the mixture with $2\frac{1}{2}$ dl. (scant $\frac{1}{2}$ pint, generous cup) boiling milk, poured in little by little. Cook for 5 or 6 minutes, beating vigorously with a whisk.

Leave until cold, as above.

Uses. For chicken and fish forcemeats.

Potato panada. PANADE À LA POMME DE TERRE – Season 3 dl. ($\frac{1}{2}$ pint, 1 $\frac{1}{4}$ cups) milk with $\frac{1}{3}$ teaspoon salt, a pinch of pepper and a touch of grated nutmeg. Boil until it has been reduced by one-sixth, then add 25 g. (1 oz., 2 tablespoons) butter and 250 g. (9 oz., $1\frac{1}{2}$ cups) thinly slice boiled potatoes. Cook gently for 15 minutes. Blend well to obtain a smooth mixture.

Use this panada, while it is still warm, for white meat quenelles.

Rice panada. PANADE AU RIZ – Cook 200 g. (7 oz., 1 cup) Italian rice in 6 dl. (1 pint, $2\frac{1}{2}$ cups) white stock to which 25 g. (1 oz., 2 tablespoons) butter have been added, allowing about 50 minutes' cooking time in the oven. Blend well to obtain a smooth mixture.

Leave until cold, as described in the recipe for *Flour panada.*

Uses. For various forcemeats.

PANCAKES – See CRÊPES.

PANCHO-VILA (Chilean cookery) – Small white haricot beans sautéed with onion and garlic, then bound with tomato *sauce.* The mixture is spooned into individual ramekins, topped with a poached egg, sprinkled with Parmesan cheese, and glazed.

PANETIÈRE – Small sideboard dresser, usually carved with lattice work, in which, in some regions of France, bread is kept.

PANETIÈRE – Method of preparation applied to various articles (lambs' sweetbreads, chicken livers, cocks' combs and kidneys, etc.), or to small birds. After cooking they are placed in *croustades* (q.v.), and baked golden in the oven.

PANETONE (Italian cake) – *Ingredients.* 500 g. (18 oz., $4\frac{1}{2}$ cups) sieved flour, 125 g. (4 oz., $\frac{1}{2}$ cup) butter, 75 g. (3 oz., 6 tablespoons) brown sugar, 3 eggs and 4 egg yolks, 25 g. (1 oz.) dried or compressed yeast, 3 teaspoons salt, 25 g. (1 oz., 2 tablespoons) fine sugar, 25 g. (1 oz., 3 tablespoons) sultanas, 50 g. (2 oz., $\frac{1}{3}$ cup) candied citron peel cut in small dice.

Method. Spread the flour in a circle on the table, make a well in the middle and put in the salt, eggs, sugar, in a little warm water, 75 g. (3 oz., 6 tablespoons) butter (just softened), and yeast. Mix these ingredients, adding a few tablespoons warm water, little by little. Then incorporate the flour, a little at a time. When the moistening is complete, stir the dough vigorously until it becomes elastic and does not stick to the hands.

Spread it in a layer and sprinkle with castor (fine) sugar. Add 2 egg yolks and the rest of the butter softened to a paste. Scatter sultanas and candied citron peel on top and blend in all the ingredients, kneading the dough for a few minutes. Roll into a ball, put in a buttered and floured baking tin, and stand in a warm place to allow the dough to ferment until little air bubbles appear on the surface. Dilute the 2 remaining egg yolks with a few teaspoons of water, and mix with a pinch of flour and the same amount of icing (confectioner's) sugar.

Brush the top liberally with this mixture. Mark the top with a crossways incision and sprinkle with sugar. Bake in the oven in moderate heat.

PANICUM. PANIC – Old Latin name for one of the millets. *Panicum miliaceum* is milled into flour in Italy, and used to prepare a kind of meal, with milk or stock.

PANIER – Wickerwork basket with a handle. In cookery and pastry-making various substances are fashioned to look like wickerwork baskets.

Potato paniers. PANIERS EN POMMES DE TERRE – These baskets, used for arranging various fried objects, are made from potatoes cut in thin ribbons and fried in deep fat.

Pulled sugar paniers. PANIERS EN SUCRE TIRÉ – These baskets are used for arranging petits fours, especially iced *petits fours*. *Bombes*, mousses and iced cakes are also served in them.

They are often extremely decorative pieces, carried out by pastry-cooks and confectioners who are artists in this work.

PANNEQUETS – Pancakes spread with cream, jam, marmalade or any other mixture, then rolled or folded in four, sprinkled with icing sugar or crushed macaroons, and glazed in the oven or under a grill. (For the preparation of pancake batter, see CRÊPE.)

These pancakes can also be spread with savoury mixtures, especially cream cheese. They are served as a hot *hors-d'œuvre* or as a small *entrée*. (See also HORS-D'ŒUVRE, *Hot hors-d'œuvre*.)

SAVOURY PANNEQUETS FOR HORS-D'ŒUVRE AND SOUP. PANNEQUETS DE HORS-D'ŒUVRE:

Anchovy pannequets. PANNEQUETS AUX ANCHOIS – Spread the pancakes made of unsweetened batter with thick *Béchamel sauce* (see SAUCE) mixed with *Anchovy purée* (see PURÉE) and desalted anchovy fillets cut in large dice. Fold the pancakes in four. Put into a buttered, ovenproof dish, sprinkle with breadcrumbs fried in butter and drained, and put in a very hot oven or under a grill for a few moments.

Pannequets with crayfish, called à la Nantua. PANNEQUETS AUX ÉCREVISSES, À LA NANTUA – As *Pannequets with shrimps* (see below), using *Nantua sauce* (see SAUCE) and diced crayfish tails.

These pancakes can be sprinkled with grated Parmesan, instead of fried breadcrumbs, and browned in the oven or under a grill.

Pannequets Mornay – Spread the pancakes with a *salpicon* (q.v.) of ham and mushroom bound with *Béchamel sauce* (see SAUCE). Roll them. Arrange on a buttered fireproof dish, cover with a thin layer of *Mornay sauce* (see SAUCE), sprinkle with grated Parmesan and melted butter, and brown the top.

Pannequets à la reine – Spread the pancakes with *Chicken purée* (see PURÉE) mixed with diced truffles. Roll the pancakes and cut each roll into 2 lozenges. Cover each with 1 tablespoon chicken *Velouté sauce* (see SAUCE) cooked with cream. Sprinkle with grated Parmesan and brown the top.

Pannequets with shrimps, or other shellfish. PANNEQUETS AUX CREVETTES – Prepare as *Anchovy pannequets*, spreading the pancakes with shrimp or other shellfish purée mixed with a *salpicon* (q.v.) of the chopped tails of the shellfish.

Pannequets with soft roes. PANNEQUETS AUX LAITANCES – Spread the pancakes with a *salpicon* (q.v.) of soft roes and mushrooms bound with *Velouté sauce* (see SAUCE), based on a fish stock and cooked with cream. Roll the pancakes, sprinkle with grated Parmesan and melted butter, and brown the top.

Pannequets for soup garnish. PANNEQUETS (GARNITURES DE POTAGE) – Make some very thin pancakes (see CRÊPE). Fill each with a basic forcemeat or add dry diced mushrooms (*duxelles*), chopped truffles, or cooked diced vegetables (*mirepoix*). Cover with another pancake. Cut rounds with a fluted cutter. Add to boiling clear soup.

Pannequets la Varenne – Spread the pancakes with *duxelles* (q.v.) mixed with a fine *salpicon* (q.v.) of ham, bound with a thick *Velouté sauce* (see SAUCE). Sprinkle with grated Parmesan and brown the top.

SWEET PANNEQUETS. PANNEQUETS D'ENTREMETS:

Pannequets with apples – See APPLE, *Crêpes stuffed with apples*.

Apricot pannequets. PANNEQUETS AUX ABRICOTS – Spread the pancakes with a mixture composed of diced apricots bound with *French pastry cream* (see CREAMS) and mixed with the blanched, chopped apricot kernels, sprinkled with kirsch. Roll up the pancakes, cut each into 2 lozenges, put on a baking sheet, sprinkle with icing sugar, glaze in a very hot oven and serve.

Pannequets à la cévenole – Spread the pancakes with *Chestnut purée* (see CHESTNUTS) mixed with fresh double cream and flavoured with kirsch. Finish off as described above.

Pannequets à la créole – Spread the pancakes with a *salpicon* (q.v.) of pineapple bound with rum-flavoured *French pastry cream* (see CREAMS). Finish off as described above.

Pannequet with various fruit. PANNEQUETS AUX FRUITS DIVERS – Prepare using *salpicon* (q.v.) of fruit (bananas, cherries, strawberries, peaches, pears, apples, etc., cooked in syrup) bound with *French pastry cream* or *Frangipane* (see CREAMS). Finish off as described above.

Jam pannequets. PANNEQUETS AUX CONFITURES – Spread the pancakes with jam. Roll or fold in four and finish off as described above.

Pannequets with pineapple – See PINEAPPLE.

Pannequets au praliné – Spread the pancakes with an almond or hazelnut praline bound with *French pastry cream* (see CREAMS), flavoured with kirsch or other liqueur. Roll up the pancakes, cut each roll into 2 lozenges, put on a baking sheet, sprinkle with finely crushed macaroons (q.v.) and glaze.

PANOUFLE – Term for the under part of the top of sirloin.

PANTIN (petit) – Small oval or rectangular-shaped patty, usually filled with a fine pork forcemeat, which may be truffled.

PANTLER. PANETIER – Officer in charge of the pantry and master dispenser of the bread.

The Lord Pantler (*le grand panetier*) was the officer of the French royal household who had jurisdiction over all the bakers of the capital and all the officers of the pantry (Royal and common). Under Louis XIV his function consisted of 'placing the King's knife and fork on ceremonial occasions,

Arms of the Lord Pantler

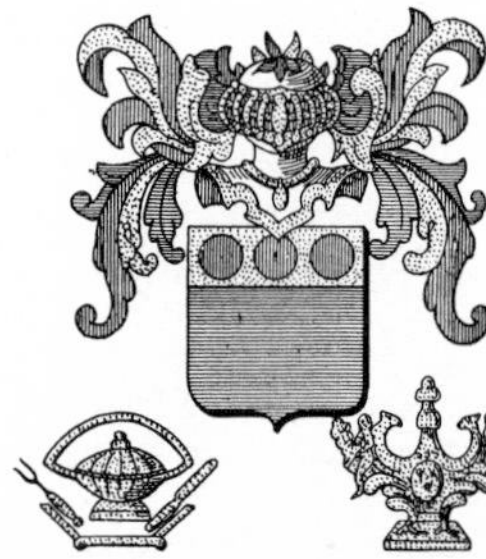

assisted by esquire-trenchants, and to taste the dishes set before the King.'

In England in the Middle Ages the pantler had to put the salt cellar and the knives on the table. The pantler's office was amalgamated with the office of master dispenser of the bread, and was allowed as hereditary to the Beauchamps of Elmley, afterwards Earls of Warwick.

In France the pantler had under his command 24 gentlemen servants each quarter (with a token surety of 700 pounds in 1661). His coat of arms bore the insignia of his office – the *nef* (a vessel-shaped gold or silver receptacle in which the King's salt cellar, cutlery, etc. were kept) and the *cadenas*.

PANURE – French culinary term for the coating of breadcrumbs adhering to some substance either by means of melted butter or beaten egg.

It should be a fine golden colour and slightly crusty after frying in deep fat or butter.

PAPAYA or PAWPAW. PAPAYER – Tree found extensively in the Malay Archipelago, India, Cochin-China, Réunion Island, Tahiti, Senegal, Gabon, Guinea and Martinique. Its fruit is sweet and easily digestible because of its enzyme content.

PAPILLOTE – Term which applies to paper frills used for putting on end bones of lamb, mutton, and veal cutlets, *suprêmes* of chicken, cutlet-shaped croquettes, etc.

It is also used to describe small joints, principally chop end of veal, which, after preliminary cooking, are enclosed in a sheet of oiled white paper cut in the shape of a heart and put in the oven, where the paper swells under the action of heat. (See VEAL, *Veal chops en papillotes*.)

It once described sweets wrapped in gold or silver paper. These used to be very popular but are no longer in vogue. They were pulled like crackers and there was a piece of paper inside with the inscription of a poem or motto.

PAPRIKA – Hungarian name for sweet pepper. Powder made from this pepper is red in colour, has a slightly pungent taste and is used as a condiment. It is also used as seasoning for goulasch, the Hungarian national dish.

PARADISE NUTS. MANIGUETTE, GRAINE DE PARADIS – Aromatic and acrid condiment much used in former times. Nowadays, it is sometimes used to adulterate pepper.

PARASOL MUSHROOM. COULEMELLE – Edible mushroom with a ring but without a volva. The best of all, but the most fragile, in the opinion of the connoisseurs.

PARFAIT – The term *parfait* once applied only to an iced sweet based on a coffee cream. It is now applied to an ice made of a single flavour mousse (*bombe*) mixture set in plain moulds. (See ICE CREAMS AND ICES.)

On the menu one can describe light ices made of variously flavoured mixtures as *parfaits*.

PARFAIT-AMOUR – Liqueur flavoured with grated citron peel, coriander and cinnamon. Also called citron liqueur.

PARIS (Café de) – See RESTAURANTS OF BYGONE DAYS.

PARIS-BREST (Pâtisserie) – Name of a Paris speciality, a pastry made of *chou paste*, forced through a forcing bag in the form of a crown, sprinkled with grated or chopped almonds.

After baking, the pastry is slit open and filled with *Praline butter cream* (see CREAMS, *Butter creams*).

PARISIEN GÂTEAU – This gâteau used to be called *polonais*.

Paris-Brest
(*Maison Desmeuzes. Phot. Larousse*)

Prepare a fine sponge mixture with 250 g. (9 oz., generous cup) sugar, 65 g. ($2\frac{1}{2}$ oz., 10 tablespoons) sieved flour, 65 g. ($2\frac{1}{2}$ oz., 10 tablespoons) cornflour (cornstarch), 7 egg yolks, 7 stiffly beaten egg whites, a pinch of salt, and vanilla or lemon peel, using the method described under DOUGH, *Fine sponge cake batter*.

Butter a round tin with a hole in the middle, sprinkle with sugar and cornflour and fill up to three-quarters with the cake mixture. Bake in a slow oven for 40 minutes.

Lift the cake out of the tin and leave to cool on a wire tray or a sieve. Cut into layers 1 cm. ($\frac{1}{2}$ inch) thick. Spread each layer with a coating of *Frangipane pastry cream* (see CREAMS) and sandwich together, reshaping the cake. Put a piece of sponge cake on the bottom of the hollow part and fill the centre with a *salpicon* (q.v.) of crystallised fruit bound with frangipane or very thick apricot jam. Cover with another piece of sponge cake. Coat the top and the sides with diluted apricot jam and cover with *Italian meringue* (see MIXTURES, *Italian meringue mixture*). Pipe meringue decorations on top. Sprinkle with icing sugar. Bake in a slow oven, to make the meringue golden. Serve with kirsch-flavoured apricot jam.

This gâteau can also be made by sandwiching several layers of sponge cake, spread with frangipane cream and sprinkled with diced crystallised fruit. The gâteau is then covered with Italian meringue and baked golden in the oven.

PARISIENNE (À LA) – Name of a garnish, the elements of which vary, but should always include *Potatoes à la parisienne* (see POTATOES).

This garnish is served with meat and poultry.

PARMENTIER (Antoine-Auguste) – Economist and agronomist, born in 1737, died in 1817, who wrote numerous works on food and to whom we owe the popularisation of potatoes, scorned as food in France before his time.

PARMENTIER – Method of preparing various dishes, which always include potatoes in one form or another. (See SOUPS AND BROTHS, *Purée of potato soup Parmentier*; BEEF, *Boiled beef sautéed Parmentier, Miroton Parmentier*; CHICKEN, *Chicken Parmentier*.)

PARMENTIÈRE – Name sometimes given to potato.

PARMESAN – Italian cheese made in the Parma region. See also CHEESE.

Parmesan straws. PAILLETTES AU PARMESAN – Give 10 turns to puff pastry. Work it on a table sprinkled with very finely grated Parmesan; add a little cayenne pepper.

As soon as all the cheese has been absorbed by the paste, roll it out into strips 13 to 15 cm. (5 to 6 inches) long. Cut these into small sticks $\frac{1}{4}$ cm. ($\frac{1}{8}$ inch) wide. Put these on a buttered baking tray and cook in a very hot oven. Serve piping hot.

Cheshire and Gruyère cheese straws are prepared in the same way as Parmesan straws. In France Parmesan straws are also called *Paillettes dorées*. Cheese straws are often served as a garnish for clear soups.

PARMESANE (À LA) – Term applied to a great many preparations which invariably include Parmesan cheese, usually grated.

PARR. TOCAN – Name for very young salmon, less than one year old.

PARROT FISH. PERROQUET DE MER – One of the numerous species of coral fish.

PARSLEY. PERSIL – Hardy biennial plant used as a flavouring in cookery.

There are four edible varieties of parsley: *common parsley, curly-leaved parsley, Neapolitan* or *celery-leaved parsley* and *Hamburg* or *turnip-rooted parsley*, the fleshy roots of which are eaten like celeriac.

In cookery parsley is used in several forms: in sprigs, mixed with other aromatic plants, especially thyme and bay leaf (see BOUQUET GARNI); chopped or rough-chopped, in which case it is added to the dish at the end of cooking; sometimes sprinkled on the dish ready for serving; *en pluches*, i.e. picked off leaf by leaf, blanched in salted boiling water, drained and added to the dishes at the end of cooking, or fried quickly in butter and poured over dishes served with browned butter; and fried in deep fat until crisp and used as a garnish for fried dishes.

Fresh parsley, picked over and washed, is also used for garnishing cold dishes. Parsley roots are used as a condiment.

Chopped parsley. Pick over, wash and dry the parsley. Put together in a tight bunch; cut it first, then chop as quickly as possible, either with a kitchen knife or with a multiple-blade chopping knife.

When parsley is not to be used immediately after chopping, to keep it fresh for several hours, tie it in a corner of a cloth and leave it under a running tap. Dry it well by twisting the cloth. Pour into a small receptacle.

Fried parsley. Wash the parsley well, dry it and pick off in little sprigs. Put it in a wire basket, and plunge into a pan of sizzling fat. Keep in the fat for a few moments; dry on a cloth.

Parsley en pluches. Wash the parsley and pick off leaf by leaf, then blanch or fry, as required.

Rough-chopped parsley. Pick over and wash the parsley and chop it coarsely.

PARSNIP, PANAIS – Root used as condiment, particularly for flavouring stocks. It can also be served as a vegetable.

Parsnips are prepared in any way suitable for carrots (q.v.) and kohlrabi (q.v.).

PARTRIDGE. PERDREAU, PERDRIX – Name covering several genera of the game bird family *Phasianidae*, all of which are edible.

The partridge is rather indigestible and can become toxic if hung. Sufferers from hepatitis, rheumatism, gout and dyspepsia are advised not to eat it.

The name 'partridge' applies to both sexes of adult birds after the hunting season opens. As the saying goes:

'On the feast day of Saint Rémi (1st. October)
All partridges have the same gender.'

Partridges were introduced into France in the fifteenth century by René, King of Naples, who brought several pairs from the island of Scio for breeding in Provence.

The principal species found in France is the *common* or *grey partridge*, brownish grey in colour, speckled with white on the back, ash coloured on the breast. The male has a brown spot.

Red-legged partridge is bigger than the common species; it is brownish, slightly darker on the back, with a grey breast, red below, and with a pure white neck and red bill and legs. It is found mainly in the South of France.

Rock partridge

The *rock partridge* and the *snow partridge* or *lagopus* are also found in France.

The *American partridge* can now be obtained frozen in France.

Ballottine of partridge with various garnishes. BALLOTTINE DE PERDREAU – Bone the partridge and stuff with *foie gras*, truffles and game forcemeat, as described in the recipe for *Ballottine of pheasant* (see PHEASANT).

Wrap in a piece of muslin and tie with string. Cook for 45 minutes in a little Madeira-flavoured braising liquor, made from the bones and scraps pared off the partridge, a veal knuckle and the usual aromatic vegetables.

Drain the ballottine, unwrap and glaze in the oven. Arrange on a serving dish and surround with the garnish recommended. Boil down the braising liquor, strain and pour over the ballottine.

Ballottines of partridges can be served with all the garnishes recommended for roasted or braised pheasant, woodcock and other winged game.

Jellied ballottine of partridge. BALLOTTINE DE PERDREAU À LA GELÉE – Prepare like *Ballottine of partridge*. Cook the ballottine in Madeira-flavoured liquid game jelly.

When cooked, drain and cool under a light press. Arrange in a *terrine* or glass dish. Clarify the jelly in the usual way (see ASPIC, *Clarification of aspic jelly*) and pour over the ballottine.

Partridges with cabbage. PERDRIX AUX CHOUX – Cook half a big cabbage, 1 piece of lean bacon, 1 uncooked sausage, 2 big carrots and the usual aromatics in a casserole.

Lard the breasts of 2 partridges and put them in the casserole. After about 30 minutes, remove the bacon and sausage and continue cooking the partridges and cabbage for a further $1\frac{1}{2}$ hours.

Arrange the partridges on the cabbage in a deep dish or *timbale*. Garnish with rectangles of the bacon, and the sausage and carrots cut in slices. Baste with a few tablespoons of good stock.

The partridges can also be served in a buttered *timbale* lined with the pieces of bacon and sliced carrot and sausage, garnished with a layer of cabbage. Put the partridges on top, cover with the rest of the cabbage, and heat in the oven for 5 minutes.

Turn out the *timbale* onto a dish and pour over a few tablespoons of *Demi-glace sauce* (see SAUCE) based on a game *fumet* (q.v.), or brown veal stock.

The same method of preparation can be applied to pheasant, hazel grouse or guinea fowl.

Casserole of partridge (or partridge en cocotte). PERDREAU EN CASSEROLE, EN COCOTTE – Prepare like *Casserole of pheasant* (see PHEASANT) making allowances for cooking time according to the size of the partridge.

Partridge à la catalane, en pistache (Languedoc cookery). PERDREAU À LA CATALANE, EN PISTACHE – Stuff the partridge with a forcemeat made of its chopped liver, freshly grated breadcrumbs, chopped lean ham, parsley and garlic, bound with an egg. Truss the bird, bard it, season, and put in an earthenware casserole in which 3 tablespoons (scant $\frac{1}{4}$ cup) butter or goose fat has been heated. When the partridge acquires a golden colour, remove it from the casserole. Put 1 large tablespoon diced raw ham into the casserole. Sprinkle with 2 tablespoons (3 tablespoons) flour and cook for a few moments. Moisten with $\frac{1}{2}$ dl. (3 tablespoons, scant $\frac{1}{4}$ cup) dry white wine and 1 dl. (6 tablespoons, scant $\frac{1}{2}$ cup) stock. Add 1 tablespoon tomato purée, a *bouquet garni* of parsley, thyme, bay leaf and a small piece of orange peel. Cook for 10 minutes. Remove the ham and the *bouquet garni* and strain the sauce. Return the partridge to the casserole, add the ham and *bouquet garni*, and pour in the sauce. Bring to the boil, cover, and simmer for 10 minutes. Add 12 cloves of garlic, previously boiled in salted water and drained. Finish cooking together, simmering gently, for 35 minutes. Remove the *bouquet garni* and serve the partridge in the casserole.

In western Languedoc this sauce is usually thickened with breadcrumbs.

Partridge in chambertin. PERDREAU AU CHAMBERTIN – Stuff the partridge, and prepare as described in the recipe for *Woodcock au chambertin* (see WOODCOCK).

Partridge à la champenoise. PERDREAU À LA CHAMPENOISE – Stuff the partridge with *foie gras* cut in large dice, seasoned and sprinkled with 1 tablespoon brandy. Truss as for an *entrée* and pot roast in butter. When three-quarters done, add 8 peeled mushroom caps and finish cooking together. Drain the partridge, untruss, and arrange on a croûton fried in butter and spread with a layer of *À gratin game forcemeat* (see FORCEMEATS or STUFFINGS). Dilute the pan juices with $2\frac{1}{2}$ dl. (scant $\frac{1}{2}$ pint, generous cup) champagne, add some fresh cream, simmer until the sauce thickens, blend in some butter, strain, add 3 tablespoons (scant $\frac{1}{4}$ cup) fresh truffles shredded into a fine *julienne* (q.v.) and lightly tossed in butter, and pour over the partridge.

Chartreuse of partridge. CHARTREUSE DE PERDRIX – Pluck, draw and singe 2 partridges. Truss them and lard the breast with thin lardoons of bacon fat. Brush them with butter, season, and brown on all sides in a hot oven for 7 or 8 minutes.

Put some bacon rinds and sliced carrots and onions on the bottom of a deep casserole. Add a layer of blanched, well-drained and seasoned cabbage.

Place the partridges on the cabbage. Add 200 g. (7 oz.) lean scalded bacon, 1 small uncooked sausage, 1 medium-sized carrot cut into quarters, 1 onion studded with a clove, and a *bouquet garni* (q.v.). Cover the ingredients with another layer of cabbage and moisten with the pan juices diluted with 8 dl. (scant $1\frac{1}{2}$ pints, scant 2 pints) stock.

Bring to the boil on the stove, then put in the oven and cook with a lid on from $1\frac{1}{2}$ hours to 2 hours, depending on how tender the birds are. Before the cooking is complete, remove the bacon and sausage, to avoid their being overcooked.

Preparation of the chartreuse. Chartreuse of partridge (or any other game) is a variation of partridge with cabbage, differing mainly in its more decorative and elaborate arrangement, which requires great attention to detail. In addition to the lean bacon and sausage cooked with the cabbage, add the following ingredients, which should be prepared separately while the partridges are cooking: 2 young turnips, cut with a small vegetable tube into sticks $3\frac{1}{2}$ cm. ($1\frac{1}{2}$ inches) long, cooked in stock, 3 carrots, cut and cooked in a similar way, 150 g. (5 oz., generous $\frac{1}{2}$ cup) French beans cooked in salted water, drained and dressed with butter, 5 tablespoons (6 tablespoons) fresh garden peas, cooked in salted water and well drained, and 75 g. (3 oz., 6 tablespoons) *Quenelle forcemeat II* (see FORCEMEATS or STUFFINGS).

Remove the partridge, untruss and cut into quarters. Drain the cabbage. Remove the vegetables, *bouquet garni* and bacon rinds and keep all these ingredients hot.

Butter a big charlotte mould and decorate it with little turnip and carrot sticks, placing them in rows, separated from each other by a row of peas.

Cover these vegetables with a thin layer of *Quenelle forcemeat II* (see FORCEMEATS or STUFFINGS), to solidify the vegetable garnish. Line the mould with well-drained and pressed-out cabbage.

Place the pieces of partridge, and the lean bacon trimmed and cut into small rectangles, on the cabbage. Cover with the rest of the pressed cabbage. Cover the whole with a layer of forcemeat and smooth the forcemeat evenly.

Put the filled mould into a pan half-filled with boiling water. Cook in a slow oven for about 40 minutes. Let the *chartreuse* stand for 5 minutes before turning it out. Garnish the top with a skinned sausage, cut in slices and arranged in a circle.

Chartreuse of partridge poult. PERDREAU EN CHARTREUSE – Young partridges, which are roasted, jointed and arranged in a mould or a *timbale*, on a foundation of braised cabbage, cooked with old partridges to give them more flavour. See *Chartreuse of partridge* above.

Chaud-froid of partridge. CHAUD-FROID DE PERDREAU – Roast the partridge in the oven, allow to cool and joint. Skin the pieces and trim them. Cover with *Brown chaud-froid sauce* based on concentrated game stock (see SAUCE). Decorate with pieces of truffle, hard-boiled egg whites and pickled tongue, and glaze with jelly.

Arrange in a dish on a foundation of well-set jelly. Cover completely with semi-liquid jelly flavoured with Madeira or other liqueur wine. Chill well on ice.

The *chaud-froid* of partridge can also be served on a buttered croûton, as described in the recipe for *Chaud-froid of chicken* (see CHICKEN), and garnished with chopped jelly.

Partridge à la chipolata. PERDREAU À LA CHIPOLATA – Truss the partridge as for an *entrée* and cook in a casserole. When it is nearly cooked, untruss and replace in the casserole. Add *Chiplata garnish* (see GARNISHES) and simmer gently.

After being cooked the partridge can also be placed on a croûton fried in butter, and surrounded with chipolata garnish. Dilute the pan juices with Madeira and concentrated game stock and pour over the partridge.

Partridge à la crapaudine. PERDREAU À LA CRAPAUDINE – Prepare as *Pigeon à la crapaudine* (see PIGEON).

Serve with *Diable sauce* to which some game *fumet* (q.v.) has been added, or with *Périgueux sauce* (see SAUCE).

Partridge à la crème. PERDREAU À LA CRÈME – Prepare as *Pheasant en cocotte with cream* (see PHEASANT), making allowances for cooking time, depending on size of bird.

Crépinette of partridge Brillat-Savarin. PERDREAU EN CRÉPINE BRILLAT-SAVARIN – Split the partridge along the back, as for grilled chicken. Remove all the small bones. Flatten slightly and season with salt and spices. Fry the partridge quickly in butter to stiffen the flesh.

Coat on both sides with *foie gras* forcemeat (see FORCEMEATS, *Forcemeat for pâté de foie gras*) mixed with truffles, and wrap in a piece of pig's caul or pounded fat pork. Arrange on a foundation of *Lentil purée* (see PURÉE). Simmer a few tablespoons of game *fumet* (q.v.) with Madeira, strain, add a little butter and pour around the dish.

Crépinette of partridge à la périgourdine. PERDREAU EN CRÉPINE À LA PÉRIGOURDINE – Truss the partridge as for an *entrée,* slit open the back and remove the small bones, leaving only the drumsticks and the bones of the pinions. Flatten the partridge slightly, season with salt and pepper, and fry it quickly in butter to stiffen the flesh.

Put the bird on a layer of *Fine pork forcemeat* (see FORCEMEATS), mixed with a *salpicon* (q.v.) of *foie gras* and truffles, and enlivened with 1 tablespoon flaming brandy. Spread on a piece of pig's caul or pounded pork fat big enough to enclose the partridge and forcemeat. Put a layer of forcemeat over the partridge and cover it well. Wrap the whole in the piece of pig's caul.

Brush with melted butter, dip in freshly ground breadcrumbs and cook on a low grill until both sides are golden. Arrange in a dish, and surround with a *ragoût* of truffles and mushrooms in Madeira-flavoured game *fumet* (q.v.).

Jellied partridge en daube. PERDREAU EN DAUBE À LA GELÉE – See PHEASANT, *Daube of pheasant in jelly.*

Estouffade of partridge. PERDREAU EN ESTOUFFADE – Truss the partridge as for an *entrée,* season it, brush with butter and roast until golden in the oven. Put into an oval-shaped earthenware *cocotte* (q.v.), on a foundation of a *mirepoix* (q.v.) of vegetables, well softened in butter. Cover the partridge with a layer of the same *mirepoix.* Sprinkle with melted butter and add 2 tablespoons (3 tablespoons) flaming brandy. Put the lid on and seal it with flour-and-water paste. Cook in a hot oven for 25 to 30 minutes. Serve in the *cocotte.*

Estouffade of partridge à la cévenole. PERDREAU EN ESTOUFFADE À LA CÉVENOLE – Stuff the partridge with *Fine pork forcemeat* (see FORCEMEATS) mixed with one-third of its weight of a forcemeat *à gratin* (see FORCEMEATS) 1 tablespoon chopped truffles. Truss as for an *entrée.* Season with salt and pepper and brown quickly in butter, to stiffen it. Untruss, put into an earthenware casserole, surround with a garnish of 12 chestnuts three-quarters cooked in concentrated veal stock, 6 mushrooms tossed in butter and 6 scalded lardoons (q.v.) of breast of pork, fried in butter. Moisten with 4 tablespoons (5 tablespoons) concentrated game stock or concentrated brown veal stock flavoured with Madeira. Sprinkle with 1 tablespoon flaming brandy. Put the lid on the casserole and seal it with flour-and-water paste. Cook in a hot oven from 40 to 45 minutes. Serve in the casserole.

Partridge à la financière. PERDREAU À LA FINANCIÈRE – Cook the partridge in butter in an earthenware *cocotte.* When it is nearly cooked, untruss it and put it back in the *cocotte* and garnish *à la financière* (see GARNISHES) bound with 4 tablespoons ($\frac{1}{3}$ cup) Madeira-flavoured game stock.

Finish cooking in a slow oven. Serve in the same *cocotte.*

Instead of cooking and serving the partridge in a *cocotte,* it can be pot-roasted in butter, placed on a croûton fried in butter and spread with an *à gratin* forcemeat (q.v.), and surrounded with the various elements of *financière garnish* disposed in separate groups.

Partridge à la forestière. PERDREAU À LA FORESTIÈRE – Stuff the partridge with forcemeat *à gratin* (see FORCEMEATS). Truss it as for an *entrée* and fry it in butter, to stiffen it. Take out of the casserole and put 1 teaspoon of chopped shallot into the casserole. Replace the partridge and surround it with 150 g. (5 oz.) sliced mushrooms, 12 lean lardoons scalded and tossed in butter, and 4 to 6 tablespoons ($\frac{1}{3}$ to $\frac{1}{2}$ cup) diced potato, tossed in butter. Finish cooking together in the oven with a lid on.

When the partridge is cooked, untruss it, baste with 3 tablespoons (scant $\frac{1}{4}$ cup) of game *fumet* (q.v.) and serve in the casserole.

Galantine of partridge. GALANTINE DE PERDREAU – Bone the partridge and prepare as described in the recipe for *Ballottine of pheasant* (see PHEASANT).

Grilled partridge à la diable. PERDREAU GRILLÉ À LA DIABLE – Split the partridge down th the back, open it out and flatten slightly. Brush with melted butter, season with salt and pepper, and cook under a moderate grill, 4 minutes each side. Brush with melted butter and dip in freshly grated breadcrumbs.

Put the partridge back under the grill and finish grilling gently, basting frequently with melted butter.

To serve, decorate with watercress and a lemon quarter at each end. Garnish the edges of the dish with fluted-edged half-slices of lemon, and thin slices of gherkins. Serve with *Diable sauce* (see SAUCE).

Grilled partridges can also be served with *Maître d'hôtel butter* (see BUTTER, *Compound butters*).

Partridge à la mirepoix. PERDREAU À LA MIREPOIX – Stuff the partridge with *À gratin game forcemeat* (see FORCEMEATS), mixed with diced truffles. Truss it as for an *entrée.* Fry quickly in butter to stiffen it. Remove trussing and cover with a fine *mirepoix* (q.v.) of vegetables, gently cooked in butter and mixed with a little Madeira. Wrap the partridge in a piece of pig's caul or pork fat. Cook it in very little Madeira-flavoured braising stock.

Drain the partridge, unwrap and arrange on a croûton fried in butter, spread with more forcemeat and browned under a grill. Add 3 tablespoons (scant $\frac{1}{4}$ cup) Madeira and 1 tablespoon flaming brandy to the braising liquor; boil down, strain, and pour over the partridge.

Partridge à la moldave (Moldavian style). PERDREAU À LA MOLDAVE – Split open the partridge, flatten it, season, dip in egg and black breadcrumbs mixed with a little powdered coriander. Sauté in clarified butter until both sides are golden.

Arrange on a cake made of baked potato pulp mixed with a *brunoise* (q.v.) of carrot, celery and mushrooms. Bind this mixture with yolks of egg, shape it into a pancake, dredge with flour and fry in butter.

Pour a ring of concentrated veal stock around the partridge. Squeeze a few drops of lemon juice on the bird and sprinkle with 1 tablespoon *Noisette butter* (see BUTTER, *Compound butters*).

Partridge Monselet. PERDREAU MONSELET – Stuff the partridge with *foie gras* and truffles cut in large dice. Truss it, season, and cook in butter in an earthenware cocotte. When half-cooked, add 2 artichoke hearts, sliced and tossed in butter, and 1 medium-sized truffle, cut in thick slices. Moisten with 3 tablespoons (scant $\frac{1}{4}$ cup) game *fumet* (q.v.) and 1 tablespoon flaming brandy. Cover the cocotte and leave in the oven for 3 minutes. Serve in the cocotte.

Partridge mousses and mousselines. MOUSSES, MOUSSELINES DE PERDREAU – Using boned partridge prepare like *Cold quail mousse* (see QUAIL).

Partridge à la normande. PERDREAU À LA NORMANDE – Truss the partridge as for an *entrée* and brown it in butter. Put into an earthenware casserole on a foundation of peeled, sliced cooking apples, tossed in butter. Surround the partridge with similar slices. Moisten with fresh cream. Cook in a hot oven under a lid.

Serve in the casserole.

Cold partridge pâté. PÂTÉ FROID DE PERDREAU – Prepare like *Pheasant pâté* (see PHEASANT).

Hot partridge pâté. PÂTÉ CHAUD DE PERDREAU – Using

boned partridges, forcemeat *à gratin*, *foie gras* and truffles, prepare like *Hot woodcock pâté* (see WOODCOCK).

Partridge à la Périgueux. PERDREAU À LA PÉRIGUEUX – Stuff the partridge with truffles as described below in the recipe for *Truffled partridge (roast)*. Cook it gently in butter in an earthenware casserole. When three-quarters cooked, add 20 thick slices of truffles, seasoned with salt, pepper and a pinch of spices. Sprinkle with $1\frac{1}{2}$ dl. ($\frac{1}{4}$ pint, $\frac{2}{3}$ cup) Madeira-flavoured game *fumet* (q.v.) and 1 tablespoons flaming brandy. Serve in the casserole.

Roast partridge. PERDREAU RÔTI – Cover the partridge with a vine leaf, then with a thin rasher of bacon enclosing the breast completely, and tie with string.

Roast the bird in the oven (see CULINARY METHODS, *Average cooking time for roasts*).

Untruss, arrange the partridge on a croûton of bread fried in butter or in the fat collected in the dripping pan, spread with a layer of *À gratin game forcemeat* (see FORCEMEATS) and brown lightly on top.

Garnish with watercress and half a lemon. Serve with the pan juices left from cooking the bird.

Salmis of partridge. SALMIS DE PERDREAU – Using roast partridge, underdone and cut into joints, prepare as *Salmis of woodcock* (see WOODCOCK).

Partridge sautéed with truffles. PERDREAU SAUTÉ AUX TRUFFES – Choose a plump partridge and cut up into joints, as in the case of *Sautéed chicken* (see CHICKEN). Season with salt and pepper and sauté briskly in butter. Remove the joints, and arrange them on a croûton, fried in butter, spread with a forcemeat *à gratin* (see FORCEMEATS) and browned on top.

Toss 12 thick slices of truffles quickly in butter and season with salt and pepper. Cook the truffles very lightly, taking care not to let them dry up. Put them on the partridge. Dilute the pan juices with Madeira, add a few tablespoons brown *Game stock* (see STOCK), boil down, blend in a little butter, strain, and pour over the partridge.

Partridge soufflé. SOUFFLÉ DE PERDREAU – Old partridges are prepared in this way. The soufflé mixture is made from partridge meat in the same manner as *Woodcock soufflé* (see WOODCOCK).

Partridge à la Souvarof. PERDREAU À LA SOUVAROF – Stuff the partridge with *foie gras* and truffles cut in large dice, seasoned with salt and pepper and sprinkled with a dash of brandy. Truss as for an *entrée*. Brown quickly in butter, to stiffen it. Put into an oval-shaped earthenware *cocotte*. Surround with 3 truffles cut in large pieces, or whole truffles, peeled and seasoned.

Moisten with 1 dl. (6 tablespoons, scant $\frac{1}{2}$ cup) Madeira-flavoured game *fumet* (q.v.), to which the pan juices, diluted with Madeira, have been added. Sprinkle with a dash of brandy.

Cover the *cocotte* with its lid and seal with fiour-and-water paste. Cook the partridge in a hot oven for 40 minutes. Serve in the *cocotte*.

Stuffed partridge in aspic. PERDREAUX FARCIS À LA GELÉE – Slit the partridges along the back, bone, open them out and season with diced spiced salt. Stuff each with truffled *Game forcemeat* (see FORCEMEATS), placing in the middle a piece of *foie gras*, encrusted with 1 peeled truffle, seasoned with spiced salt and sprinkled with brandy.

Reshape the partridges. Truss them, wrap each one in a thin slice of bacon fat or a piece of pig's caul. Cook in a little Madeira-flavoured aspic jelly (see JELLY, *Game jelly stock*) made from the scraps trimmed off the birds, a veal knuckle and fresh bacon rinds.

When the partridges are cooked, drain them, unwrap, untruss and dry on a cloth. Put into an oval-shaped *terrine* and leave until cold. Then cover completely with the jelly, clarified in the usual manner (see ASPIC, *Clarification of aspic jelly*).

Chill thoroughly before serving.

Stuffed partridges in aspic (tinned or canned). PERDREAUX FARCIS À LA GELÉE – Partly bone the partridges. Stuff them with a big piece of raw fat goose liver, encrusted with one or two medium-sized truffles which have been peeled, seasoned with spiced salt and sprinkled with brandy, and enclosed in a layer of truffled *Fine pork forcemeat* (see FORCEMEATS). Truss the partridges as for an *entrée*, wrap each in a thin rasher of bacon fat or a piece of pig's caul. Put them into a sauté pan on a foundation of chopped bacon rinds, carrots and onions and the giblets of the birds, all lightly tossed in butter. Moisten with Madeira or any other liqueur wine. Cook gently, with the lid on, for 10 minutes. Moisten with good strong jelly prepared from calves' feet and fresh bacon rinds (but no gelatine). Cook in the oven for 30 to 35 minutes.

Drain the partridges, remove barding and trussing string, and dry the birds on a cloth. Put each into a tin-plated can, breast downwards, and leave to cool. When quite cold, cover them with the jelly in which they were cooked, clarified in the usual manner (see ASPIC, *Clarification of aspic jelly*). Leave until quite cold. Solder the tins (cans). Boil them in water for 45 minutes, making sure that during this operation boiling does not cease for a single moment.

Take the tins out of the water, put them on the table in such a way that the partridges are breast downwards. Cool. Mark the tin on the top to make sure it is breast side up when you open it.

Terrine of partridge. TERRINE DE PERDREAU – Prepared like *Potted pheasant* (see PHEASANT).

Timbale of partridge. TIMBALE DE PERDREAU – Prepared like *Timbale of woodcock* (see WOODCOCK).

Truffled partridge (roast). PERDREAU TRUFFÉ (RÔTI) – Partly bone a plump partridge, opening it on the back, near the neck (the bird having been cleaned from the front). Through this opening stuff it with 100 g. (4 oz., 1 cup) pork fat studded with pieces of truffle, and 75 g. (3 oz.) truffles cut in quarters. Truss the partridge and wrap it in a thin slice of bacon fat. Roast in a slow oven (see CULINARY METHODS, *Average cooking times for roasts*).

Serve either with the diluted pan juices or with *Périgueux sauce* (see SAUCE) to which the diluted pan juices have been added.

The truffling of game or poultry should be done at least 24 hours in advance. This will render the flesh more flavoursome. When the bird is being cooked on a spit, cover it completely with a piece of buttered greaseproof paper; remove a few minutes before taking the bird off the spit, so as to brown it.

Truffled partridge, like all other truffled winged game, can also be cooked in a casserole or a *cocotte*.

Partridge à la vigneronne. PERDREAU À LA VIGNERONNE – Truss the partridge as for an *entrée* and cook it in butter in a casserole or a *cocotte*. Untruss it, and put into the casserole 24 peeled and seeded grapes. Add 3 tablespoons (scant $\frac{1}{4}$ cup) game *fumet* (q.v.) and 1 tablespoon flaming brandy. Simmer with a lid on for 5 minutes. Serve in the casserole in which it was cooked.

PASKHA (Russian cookery) – This dish used to be an essential part of the Easter table in Russia.

Press out any excess moisture from 2 kg. ($4\frac{1}{2}$ lb.) cream (U.S. cottage) cheese, blend with 1 kg. ($2\frac{1}{4}$ lb.) sour cream, 250 g. (9 oz., generous cup) butter, 1 teaspoon salt, 125 g. (4 oz., $\frac{1}{2}$ cup) vanilla flavoured sugar, 2 tablespoons (3 tablespoons) finely grated lemon rind, 50 g. (2 oz., $\frac{1}{2}$ cup) chopped almonds and 5 tablespoons (6 tablespoons) seedless raisins. When the mixture is very smooth, place in a muslin-lined receptacle (traditionally pyramid shaped) which will allow the mixture to drain. Put a weight on top and leave in a cool place.

Turn out on a dessert dish and decorate with sultanas, chopped pistachio nuts or crystallised fruit.

PASSARELLE – Dried Muscatel grapes, prepared in the Frontignan region as well as in Smyrna and Damascus.

The process of turning these grapes into raisins is called *passerillage* or *passarillage*.

Passe-Crassane pears (*Wide World*)

PASSE-CRASSANE – Variety of very fragrant winter pear.

PASSE-POMME – Name given to three varieties of apple which ripen in August: *white, red* and *Jerusalem*.

PASSE-TOUT-GRAIN or PASSE-TOUS-GRAINS – Name of a red Burgundy wine made partly from black Pinot grapes and partly from Gamay grapes (the proportion of Pinot being at least one third).

PASSION FRUIT. BARBADINE – Edible fruit of the passion-flower tree or giant granadilla, used as a dessert.

PASTA – See ITALIAN PASTA, MACARONI, NOODLES, RAVIOLI, SPAGHETTI.

PASTA FROLLA – Italian name for a very delicate sweet pastry similar to Savarin pastry (see DOUGH, *Savarin dough*).

PASTEURISATION – Process of heating a liquid up to a temperature between 70° and 80°C. (158° and 176°F.), then cooling quickly. Pasteurisation arrests development of certain bacteria and increases the duration for which the product can be kept, without assuring complete sterilisation. Unfortunately, pasteurisation often removes valuable nutrients.

PASTILLAGE – Paste which was much in demand in the past for decorating big pastry and confectionery creations, as well as pillars and ornaments used for dressing big cakes. This paste was made from icing sugar, powdered starch, gum tragacanth and water. Pastillage is not much used nowadays.

PASTILLE – Small round confection made from dissolved sugar and water, poured hot, drop by drop, onto a cold marble slab. The sugar is usually flavoured with various aromatic flavourings. Pastilles are manufactured almost entirely in factories.

General rules for making pastilles. 1. Choose very white, well grained and odourless sugar. Pound it into powder, sift through a horsehair sieve, and remove the finest part by means of a silk sieve. This powder, being too fine, has the drawback of making the pastilles too heavy and compact, and less shiny.

2. Dilute the sugar with aromatic essence and a quantity of water. Use a small silver pan, if possible, as it will not communicate any unpleasant taste to the mixture.

3. Watch the sugar carefully while it is on the heat, stirring from time to time when the mixture begins to simmer.

4. Make sure that the mixture is not too liquid for pouring. Should that be the case, take the mixture off the heat and stir with a wooden spoon until it acquires the desired consistency.

5. Make sure that the flavourings used, which are juices pressed out from various kinds of fruit, are fresh.

Coffee pastilles. PASTILLES AU CAFÉ – Prepare $1\frac{1}{4}$ kg. (3 lb.) finest quality sugar as described above. Bring 25 g. (1 oz., $\frac{1}{2}$ cup) ground coffee to the boil several times in $\frac{1}{2}$ litre (scant pint, $2\frac{1}{4}$ cups) water. Pour through a straining bag in which a piece of gelatine has been put, to make the grounds settle.

When the liquid is cold, strain and use for diluting the sugar, then proceed to pour the pastilles.

Jasmine pastilles. PASTILLES AU JASMIN – Pound and sift $1\frac{3}{4}$ kg. (4 lb.) sugar, put it into a china bowl and dilute with 50 g. (2 oz.) jasmine essence, adding water until it forms a paste. Roll, and make into pastilles.

Mignonette, jonquil and tuberose pastilles are made in a similar manner, using the same quantity of the essence of these flowers per pound of sugar.

Orange-blossom pastilles. PASTILLES À LA FLEUR D'ORANGER – Pound $1\frac{3}{4}$ kg. (4 lb.) white superfine sugar in a marble mortar. Sift it through a horsehair or silk sieve to extract the finest part, which can be kept for other uses.

Put the rest of the sugar into a china bowl and add double orange-blossom water, stirring with a wooden spoon. Pour a little water on at a time and stir continuously until the paste is quite firm. If too much water has been added, and the paste

Pastillage (*Maison Morat*)

has become too liquid, thicken it with a little powdered sugar (some of which should be kept in reserve for such an emergency).

To test whether the composition has reached the desired degree, take a little of it on a wooden spoon, hold it up, and if it becomes detached it is just right.

Put 100 g. (4 oz.) of this paste into a small pan with a long spout. Heat on the stove until it becomes liquid, stirring with the wooden spoon. Remove from the heat when the paste is just about to boil. Stirring it a few more times, begin to pour onto tin-plated metal sheets in the following manner:

Hold the pan with your left hand and, tipping the spout very gently, pour the paste with the aid of a knitting needle fixed in a small piece of wood, held in your right hand. Move the saucepan and the needle in such a way as to make the paste drop on the metal sheet in the shape of little buttons (which are called pastilles).

There are special droppers for shaping boiled sugar drops.

Take care to space the pastilles properly when pouring them, and to pour the same quantity of paste for all of them. Leave for 1 hour, take the pastilles off the metal sheets, put them on a paper-covered sieve, and leave in a warm place for a day. Longer than that would diminish the aroma.

Rose pastilles. PASTILLES À LA ROSE – 'Pound $1\frac{3}{4}$ kg. (4 lb.) best sugar in a marble mortar, sift through a horse-hair sieve into a bowl, dilute with attar of roses until it forms a fairly thick paste, and drop from the pan with the aid of a knitting needle as described above.' (*Le Confiseur moderne, 1821.*)

PASTIS (Béarn cake) – 'Mix 12 eggs with 1 tablespoon orange blossom water, 1 small glass of brandy, 400 g. (14 oz., $1\frac{3}{4}$ cups) fine sugar, a little milk and 100 g. (4 oz., $\frac{1}{2}$ cup) melted butter and whisk vigorously.

'Add a little baker's yeast and stir, adding flour until the paste is sufficiently thick.

'Blend the dough well, roll into a loaf in the bowl, sprinkle with flour, cover with a cloth and lave, near the fire, until next day.

'Put the dough into a buttered tin and bake in a hot oven.' (*Simin Palay: La Cuisine en Béarn.*)

There is an Armagnac pastry delicacy also called by this name.

PASTIS – Popular name for an aniseed apéritif enjoyed in the south of France. There are several varieties.

Pastis has taken the place of absinth (called '*la verte*'), the popular pre-1914 drink, now prohibited. There is an Order called Anysetiers du Roy.

PASTRY. PÂTE – See also DOUGH.

Pastry dough for hot or cold pies. PÂTE ORDINAIRE – *Ingredients.* 1 kg. ($2\frac{1}{4}$ lb.) sifted flour, 250 g. (9 oz., generous cup) butter, 2 whole eggs, 1 tablespoon salt, about 4 dl. ($\frac{3}{4}$ pint, scant 2 cups) water. The quantity of water may vary depending on the quality of flour used. The better the quality of flour, the more water it can absorb.

Method. Spread the flour in a circle on the board and put the salt, water, eggs and butter in the middle. Mix in the usual manner and knead the paste to make it smooth and homogeneous. Roll into a ball, wrap in a cloth and keep in a cool place until required for use.

Pie pastry, like all pastry, should be prepared at least 12 hours before it is to be used. A well-rested pastry (and the pastry made according to this recipe can rest up to 24 hours) is easier to work and takes on less colour during baking.

Common brioche dough. PÂTE À BRIOCHE COMMUNE – Some small pies, especially those made in the shape of oval or rectangular patties or turnovers, are shaped by hand, without a mould, and are made of unsweetened common brioche dough or short pastry. Recipes for both these will be found in the section entitled DOUGH.

Lard pastry dough. PÂTE AU SAINDOUX – *Ingredients.* 1 kg. ($2\frac{1}{4}$ lb.) sifted flour, 250 g. (9 oz., generous cup) warm, melted lard, 2 whole eggs, 4 dl. ($\frac{3}{4}$ pint, scant 2 cups) warm water and 1 tablespoon salt.

Method. Prepare in the same manner as ordinary pastry dough (see above). Use for big cold pies.

Puff pastry shells. CROÛTES DE BOUCHÉES FEUILLETÉES – Prepare with puff pastry rolled out six times, and leave to rest. Roll out 8 mm. ($\frac{1}{3}$ inch) thick. Cut out pastry rounds about 6 cm. ($2\frac{1}{2}$ inches) in diameter.

Put these onto a wet baking sheet, turning them over. Using a round cutter, 3 cm ($1\frac{1}{4}$ inches) across, dipped in hot water, mark out the lids of the pieces of pastry, and mark the edges with a knife.

Cook in a hot oven. When baked take out of the oven and remove the lids. Fill them with whatever preparation is indicated.

Raised pastry case cooked blind. CROÛTE DE GRANDE TIMBALE CUITE À BLANC – Butter the interior of a charlotte mould and decorate the sides with pieces of noodle paste (see NOODLES).

Roll some short pastry into a round about 20 cm. (8 inches) in diameter. Sprinkle lightly with flour and fold in half.

Draw the points of this half-circle together in such a way as to form a dome. Roll it out once 8 mm. ($\frac{1}{3}$ inch) thick. Press into the mould, without disturbing the noodle paste decorations.

Line with a fine buttered paper and fill it up with dried raw beans. Put a dome-shaped piece of paper on top of the dry filling, and a thin sheet of pastry on top of this, joining the edges together by gently pressing with the fingers. Make the rim of the pie by pinching this border with pastry pincers both inside and out. Moisten with water the part forming the lid, and put leaves and roses cut from a thin sheet of pastry on it.

Put on top of the lid 3 or 4 small circles of pastry. Stick these together and make an opening in the middle to allow for the escape of steam during cooking. Brush the outside of the pie with egg and cook in the oven at moderate heat for 30 to 35 minutes.

When the pastry is cooked, take off the lid. Remove the paper and provisional filling; brush the interior with egg and dry off in a warm place. Fill it with whatever preparation is indicated.

Raised pies, or *timbales*, cooked blind in this way, are used for a number of mixed *entrées*. They can be filled after cooking with various *ragoûts* or with macaroni arranged in layers alternating with a *ragoût* composed of various ingredients combined with a white or brown sauce.

Pastry sticks – See ALLUMETTES, STRAWS.

PASTRY CREAM, FRENCH. CRÈME PÂTISSIÈRE – Custard made of eggs, sugar, flour, milk and flavouring, which is used in pastry-making as filling for various cakes, such as *choux, éclairs, batons de Jacob.* (See CREAMS.) This preparation is also known as confectioner's custard.

PASTRY CRIMPER or PINCER. PINCE – Tool used for pinching the edges of pies, tarts, etc.

PASTRY CUTTER. COUPE PÂTE – Instrument used to cut sheets of pastry into round or oval shapes. They are either plain or fluted, and can be bought in various sizes.

PASTRY WHEEL. GAUFREUSE – Small pastry tool of hardwood, used in place of metal pastry pincers to crimp the edges of tarts and pastries.

PASTRIES, BASES FOR. FONDS DE PÂTISSERIE – Many

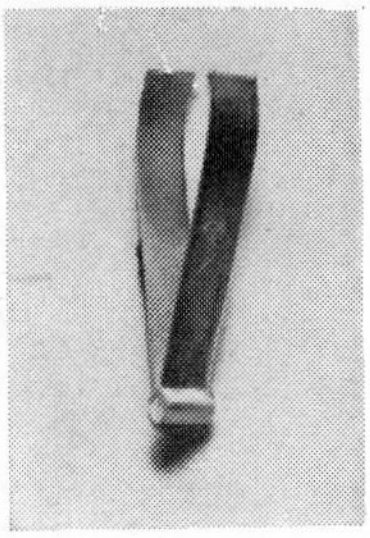

Pastry crimper

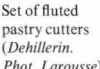

Set of fluted pastry cutters (*Dehillerin. Phot. Larousse*)

French sweets (desserts), *gâteaux* and *petits fours* are based on one of the following mixtures.

Fonds de Berrichons – 250 g. (9 oz., generous cup) sugar, 250 g. (9 oz., scant 2 cups) dried blanched almonds, 10 egg whites, stiffly beaten.

Pound the almonds and add with the sugar to the egg whites. Bake in a slow oven on greased, floured trays.

Fonds brésiliens – Pound 250 grams (9 oz., generous cup) sugar with 250 grams (9 oz., scant 2 cups) unblanched almonds and blend with 3 egg whites and 50 g. (2 oz., 3 tablespoons) honey. Add to this mixture 100 g. (4 oz., 1 cup) cocoa powder and 7 egg whites, stiffly beaten. Bake in a slow oven on greased, floured trays.

Fonds napolitains – 250 g. (9 oz., generous cup) butter, 250 g. (9 oz., $2\frac{1}{4}$ cups) flour, 250 g. (9 oz., generous cup) sugar, 250 g. (9 oz., generous 2 cups) ground almonds, 3 egg yolks.

Knead the butter and flour, then add the sugar and the egg yolks. Mix without kneading and roll out. Cut or shape as required and bake in a moderate oven.

Fonds noix or noisette – 250 g. (9 oz., generous cup) sugar 250 g. (9 oz.) walnuts or hazelnuts, 100 g. (4 oz., $\frac{1}{2}$ cup) butter, 125 g. ($4\frac{1}{2}$ oz., 1 cup) cornflour or arrowroot, 30 egg yolks, 24 egg whites, stiffly beaten.

Pound the nuts and the sugar, then work together with the egg yolks and butter. Add the cornflour or arrowroot and the egg whites. Bake in a slow oven on greased floured trays.

Fonds perlés – Fold 250 g. (9 oz., generous cup) sugar and 250 g. (9 oz., generous 2 cups) ground almonds into 12 egg whites, stiffly beaten. Butter and flour a baking tray. Rinse a cake ring with hot water. Place it on the baking tray and fill with the mixture. Dust with icing sugar. Unmould the mixture onto the tray and dust again with sugar. Bake in a slow oven.

If preferred, the cake may be dusted with sugar only after the cake ring has been removed.

Fonds progrès – 125 g. ($4\frac{1}{2}$ oz., scant cup) unblanched almonds, 125 g. ($4\frac{1}{2}$ oz., $\frac{3}{4}$ cup) hazelnuts, 250 g. (9 oz., generous cup) sugar, 10 egg whites, stiffly beaten.

Toast the almonds and hazelnuts in the oven. Pound them and blend with the sugar and egg whites. Bake in a slow oven on greased, floured trays.

Fonds réserve – Pound 100 g. (4 oz., 1 cup) fresh blanched almonds and add with 250 g. (9 oz., generous cup) sugar to 2 egg whites. Whip 200 g. (7 oz., scant cup) sugar and 12 egg yolks over hot water. Add the first mixture to this along with 100 g. (4 oz., 1 cup) flour, 100 g. (4 oz., scant cup) cornflour or arrowroot and 10 egg whites, stiffly beaten. Pour thinly onto greased, floured baking trays and bake in a slow oven.

Fonds sablés – 250 g. (9 oz., $2\frac{1}{4}$ cups) flour, 125 g. ($4\frac{1}{2}$ oz., generous $\frac{1}{2}$ cup) sugar, 125 g. ($4\frac{1}{2}$ oz., generous $\frac{1}{2}$ cup) butter, 175 g. (6 oz., $1\frac{1}{2}$ cups) ground almonds, 2 eggs, vanilla.

Knead the butter and flour, then blend all ingredients together without further kneading. Set aside in a cool place. Cut into shapes and bake in a moderate oven.

This is excellent for lining moulds for iced sweets.

Fonds succès – Pound 250 g. (9 oz., scant 2 cups) dried, blanched almonds with 250 g. (9 oz., generous cup) sugar. Blend with 12 egg whites, stiffly beaten. Bake in a slow oven on greased, floured trays.

Pâte – *Pâte* is a general term used for pastry doughs, bread doughs, sweet pastes and batters. For recipes, see DOUGH and PASTRY.

PÂTÉ – This word is used in three ways in French: *pâté, pâté en terrine* and *pâté en croûte*. In France the word *pâté* on its own should, strictly speaking, only be applied to a dish consisting of a pastry case filled with meat, fish, vegetables or fruit, which is baked in the oven and served hot or cold. The best English translation of this word is 'pie', although many of these dishes are much richer and more elaborate than the sort of pie usually eaten in England, and are often prepared in moulds rather than pie dishes. A selection of such recipes will be found under PIE.

Pâté en terrine is a meat, game or fish preparation put into a dish (*terrine*) lined with bacon, cooked in the oven and always served cold. The correct French abbreviation of this is *terrine* but in common usage the French also call it *pâté*. The English have adopted both names but as the strictly correct and less confusing term is *terrine*, instructions on the preparation of such dishes are given under TERRINE.

Pâté en croute (see below) is a rich meat, game or fish mixture cooked in a pastry crust and always served cold.

Amiens duck pâté. PÂTÉ DE CANARD D'AMIENS – There are two kinds of *pâté* made in Amiens: one with boned duck, the other with unboned duck.

The duck *pâté* is made without a mould; it is shaped by hand. Here is a recipe for a *pâté* of unboned duck as it was made in Amiens towards the middle of the last century.

The pastry. Use 500 g. (18 oz., $4\frac{1}{2}$ cups) sifted flour, 100 g. (4 oz., $\frac{1}{2}$ cup) lard, 1 tablespoon olive oil, 1 whole egg, $1\frac{1}{2}$ teaspoons fine salt and about $1\frac{1}{2}$ tablespoons (2 tablespoons) water.

'Spread the flour on a board in a circle, make a well in the middle and put in the salt. Break in the egg and dissolve the salt in it. Add olive oil. Knead the lard if it is hard, and mix it with the liquid part of the ingredients in the middle of the flour. Rub the lard mixture and flour together without moistening. When the paste is well mixed, spread it on a marble slab and sprinkle with cold water. Keep it on the firm side. Roll together into one lump and leave to rest in a cool place for at least 2 hours before using.

The duck. 'Only young ducklings which take very little cooking time should be used for these *pâtés*.

'The duck having been killed, plucked, cleaned out and singed, remove carefully any innards which may have been left in. Cut off the pinions a little below the first joint from the shoulder.

'Cut off the feet at the joint. Season the duck with spiced salt, inside and outside. Cut up a scalded breast of bacon

(streaky), and fry it in a little fat on a low fire. Remove it and fry the duck on low heat, browning it on all sides. Drain, and leave to cool before making the *pâté*.

The forcemeat. '*À gratin forcemeat* is always used for this *pâté*, composed either of calf or duck liver. The duck's liver will be added to this forcemeat.

'Use 500 g. (18 oz.) calf or chicken livers, 150 g. (5 oz., 1 cup) shredded fat bacon, 1 medium-sized onion, 2 teaspoons spiced salt, a few fragments of thyme and bay leaf and 2 chopped shallots.

'Render down the fat bacon on a low fire and fry in this fat the livers, trimmed and cut in large dice. Add the onion and shallots and season with spiced salt, thyme and bay leaf. Cover and leave for a minute or two at the side of the stove. Remove and leave to get cold, then pound in the mortar and rub the forcemeat through a fine sieve.

The pâté. 'When the pastry, the forcemeat and the duck are ready, proceed to make the *pâté*.

'Divide the pastry into two equal parts. Using half, roll it out into an oval-shaped piece 1 cm. ($\frac{1}{2}$ inch) thick. This piece of pastry should be a little longer and wider than the duck. Put it in a baking tin, slightly moistened with a little cold water to make the paste adhere. Spread the middle with a quarter of the forcemeat, place the duck in the forcemeat and season with spiced salt and a little cayenne pepper. Cover the duck with the rest of the forcemeat, enclosing it completely.

'Put another oval-shaped piece of pastry over the duck, seal the edges, crimp up the sides and decorate the top with dough cut out in fancy shapes. Make a hole in the centre to allow for steam.

'Brush the pastry crust with beaten egg. Bake in a hot oven for $1\frac{1}{4}$ to $1\frac{1}{2}$ hours, depending on size.' (M. Dumont-Lespine's recipe.)

Rouen duckling pâté. PÂTÉ DE CANETON ROUENNAIS – Shape by hand as *Lark pâté* (see below), or in a mould as *Woodcock pâté* (see below), using boned duckling stuffed with *À gratin forcemeat* (see FORCEMEATS), *foie gras* and truffles.

Pâté of foie gras with truffles. PÂTÉ DE FOIE GRAS AUX TRUFFES – *The forcemeat*. Pound finely in a mortar (for a *pâté* for 10 persons) 375 g. (13 oz.) lean pork, 475 g. (1 lb.) fresh bacon and 150 g. (5 oz.) raw goose liver parings. Season this forcemeat with 4 teaspoons *Spiced salt* (see SALT) and rub through a sieve.

The foie gras. Stud a big, pared goose liver (or 2 small livers) generously with pieces of truffle, seasoned with spiced salt. Marinate this liver in brandy and Madeira and season with spiced salt.

The pâté. Following the instructions given under PIE, line a round or a hinged mould with *Fine lining paste* (see DOUGH) made with butter or lard. Coat the sides and bottom of the mould with a layer of the forcemeat, to which 1 tablespoon brandy and liquor left from marinating the liver have been added. Put the liver in the middle of the mould. Cover with a layer of forcemeat, piling it up in a dome. Place on top 1 rasher of bacon and a small bay leaf.

Cover with a piece of rolled-out pastry, seal and crimp the edges. Decorate the top with pieces of pastry cut out in fancy shapes. Make a hole in the centre. Cut several pastry rings with a fluted-edged pastry-cutter, and place them on top of one another round the hole. Brush with beaten egg.

Bake in a moderate oven, allowing 30 minutes per kg. (15 minutes per lb.). Leave the *pâté* to cool in the mould. When it is just warm, pour into the *pâté* through the hole on top, warm lard if it is to be kept for some time; or some Madeira-flavoured aspic jelly (see ASPIC).

The *pâtés* are cut in different ways, according to their shapes. Those made in round moulds are served in slices, cut from top to bottom. Bigger *pâtés* are served in scallop shells, as follows: Remove the pastry lid, scrape off the surface fat layer and ladle out the *pâté* with a big spoon dipped into hot water. Scoop up enough *pâté* to fill a shell. Put the filled shells on a plate.

Arrange the empty *pâté* crust on a dish, placing the pastry lid on it upside down. Garnish the lid with a layer of chopped jelly. Dispose the scallop shells of *foie gras* on it, piling them up in a heap.

Rectangular-shaped *pâtés*, the type most commonly found in shops, are cut in slices, which are then halved and arranged, overlapping slightly, on a long dish.

Lark pâté en pantin. PÂTÉ D'ALOUETTES EN PANTIN – Bone the larks completely and stuff with *À gratin forcemeat* (see FORCEMEATS) studded with a piece of truffle. Wrap each lark in 1 thin rasher of bacon.

Roll out a rectangular piece of *Lining paste* (see DOUGH), put on top 1 thin bacon rasher, spread with a layer of forcemeat (truffled, if desired) and lay the larks on top of that. Cover the larks with a layer of forcemeat topped with 1 rasher of fat bacon.

Thin down the edges of the rolled-out piece of pastry with a rolling-pin, bring the edges together and seal them. Put the *pâté* upside down on a baking tray. Make one or two holes to allow steam to escape during baking, brush with beaten egg and bake in a moderate oven.

Leave the *pâté* to get cold. Pour into it through the holes in the top some game aspic jelly (see ASPIC, *Game jelly stock*) or, if the *pâté* is not to be eaten at once, some melted butter.

Pithiviers lark pâté. PÂTÉ D'ALOUETTES – For this *pâté* the larks can be boned or left whole, according to taste.

Stuff each with a little *À gratin forcemeat* (see FORCEMEATS), one large cube of *foie gras* and a medium-sized truffle. Season the larks with spiced salt, wrap in thin bacon rashers and lay them out side by side on a piece of pastry spread with a thin layer of forcemeat. Cover the larks with the same forcemeat and finish making the *pâté*. Leave to rest for a night and bake on the following day. When the *pâté* is cold, pour into it some aspic jelly (see ASPIC).

To serve, cut the *pâté* into rectangular pieces in such a way as to make sure that each piece contains a whole lark. Discard the crust surrounding the sides of the *pâté* and serve only the top and bottom crust.

Partridge pâté. PÂTÉ DE PERDREAU – Prepare in an oval or rectangular mould like *Woodcock pâté* (see below).

Pheasant pâté. PÂTÉ DE FAISAN – Using boned and stuffed pheasant, prepare like *Woodcock pâté* (see below).

This *pâté* can also be made using a boned pheasant, cut into thin slices. The *pâté* is lined with the slices alternating with rows of slivers of foie gras and truffles, the whole sealed down with *Game forcemeat* (see FORCEMEATS).

Pâtés made from various kinds of poultry. PÂTÉS DE VOLAILLES – These *pâtés* can be made from chicken, turkey, pigeon, or guinea fowl, boned, stuffed with an appropriate forcemeat, *foie gras* and truffles, or with the flesh of the appropriate bird cut in thin slices, with *foie gras*, truffles and forcemeat. Shape by hand or bake in oval or rectangular moulds lined with *Fine lining paste* (see DOUGH).

Woodcock pâté. PÂTÉ DE BÉCASSES – Bone the woodcocks and stuff with *À gratin forcemeat* (see FORCEMEATS) mixed with the chopped trail of the birds, pieces of *foie gras* and truffles. Reshape the woodcocks. Wedge them tightly against one another in an oval mould lined with pastry and bacon rashers and coated with *Game forcemeat* (see FORCEMEAT). Cover with a layer of forcemeat, place 1 rasher of bacon on top. Cover with pastry, seal and crimp the edges, and decorate the top with pieces of pastry cut in fancy shapes. Make a hole in the centre, brush with beaten egg and bake in a moderate oven.

When the *pâté* is quite cold, pour some aspic jelly (see ASPIC) based on a game *fumet* (q.v.) into it.

PATELLA. PATELLE – Name applied to various gastropod molluscs. They are univalve, edible and known also by the name of *limpets*. They are eaten raw, like clams.

PATIENCE DOCK. PATIENCE – Name of various plants of the *Rumex* genus, among them *herb patience*, which has a bitter root, used in making depurative and anti-scorbutic decoctions. The leaves and petioles of the *alpine dock*, known also as *monk's rhubarb*, are eaten in the Alps, the Pyrenees and in the Auvergne; they are put in soups and cooked as a vegetable. *Rhubarb sorrel*, which was already known as a pot herb in the times of antiquity, is mentioned by Horace.

PÂTISSERIE – Name for various preparations made of pastry, generally baked in the oven. The term also applies to the art of the pastry-cook, as well as to the place where pastries are made and sold.

The Greeks made pastry. Bourdeau, in his *Histoire de l'Alimentation*, even attributes the invention of plum pudding to the Greeks.

In the Middle Ages in France the pastry-cooks were called *oubleyeurs*, after *oublie*, wafer cooked in irons or *gaufre* moulds, which was their main product.

In 1268, Etienne Boileau in his *Livre des Métiers* laid down rules and statutes, and fixed the duration of the apprenticeship, wages, and fines incurred for an infraction of the statutes. The preamble stated: 'Whoever wishes to become an *oubleyeur* in the city of Paris may do so freely and openly, provided he knows the trade, has the wherewithal and keeps to the usages and customs of the trade.'

These statutes were modified from century to century, embodying ever more restrictive clauses. The terms and conditions for obtaining the Master's certificate became more and more in favour of the Treasury and the King.

Rabelais in his *Pantagruel* (Book 4, Chapter 59) enumerates some of the pastries which were in great vogue at the time, such as big puff pastry gâteaux, *carves*, *casse-museaux* (small cream buns), *brides à veaux*, *caillebottes* (curd cakes), *poupelins* ('baby dolls'), macaroons, quince pies, 20 kinds of tarts, 16 kinds of tourtes (q.v.), etc.

As the years went by, numerous disagreements arose between the pastry-cooks, the bakers and the pork butchers, all accusing the others of trespassing on each other's trades. In the seventeenth century the bakers added the sale of small cakes to their trade. The pastry-cooks protested, started a court case and the Lieutenant-General of Police issued an order forbidding the master bakers to encroach on the trade of the pastry-cooks. Later, another dispute arose in connection with Twelfth Night cakes, which the bakers were in the habit of offering to clients who brought their bread to be baked in their ovens. They were forbidden to do so, but nevertheless continued to bake and offer these cakes. In 1794, however, the Twelfth Night cakes aroused the wrath of the revolutionaries, who seemed to see monarchist tendencies in this custom, and they ordered the practice to cease.

But no decree could eradicate a time-honoured tradition. The pastry-cooks got round the order by substituting Liberty cakes for Twelfth Night cakes, complete with Phrygian cap traced on the cake.

The main dispute between the pastry-cooks and the pork butchers, ending in a long court case, arose in connection with a ham pie. This was a ham, cooked as usual and enclosed in pastry. The pork butchers maintained that as the crust did not adhere to the ham it could not be considered a pie. Only raw ingredients enclosed in pastry and cooked at the same time as the pastry could be considered as pies. The pork butchers won their case.

From the beginning of the nineteenth century French pastry-making made great strides forward with Carême, the creator of large display pieces and of numerous elements of what is called '*pâtisserie de main*'. He perfected the existing cakes and created new ones, such as the *croquembouche*, *mille-feuille*, *sultanes*, decorated with pulled sugar, etc. This was also the epoch of great *pâtissiers*, such as Rouget, Leblanc, Jacquet, Félix and Lesage, the specialist of display pieces. Later, towards 1844, came the Julien dynasty, founders of cake shops in the Bourse, Favart and boulevard des Italiens, prolific creators to whom we owe such cakes as *trois-frères*, *savarin*, *gorenflot*, *régent*, *richelieu* and *Paris-pâté*. Along with them, the cake shops of Seugnot, Bourbonneux,

A pastry-cook's shop in the eighteenth century, from Diderot's *Encyclopédie*. Victuals can be seen hanging from the ceiling; there is also the butcher's block (No. 8), which shows how much pastry-cooks competed with the pork butchers

Quillet, Chiboust, Frascati, Petit vied with each other. These houses specialised in the creation of numerous cakes, such as *bourdaloue*, *saint-honoré*, *napolitain*, *châteaubriand*, *cussy*, *ambroisie* (or Genoese cake) and many others.

Little Russian patties (*Claire*)

Twelfth Night cake – A decorated cake which used to be eaten on the Feast of the Epiphany (6 January). Usually a bean (or, in later years, a silver coin) was baked in the cake. The person getting this at the Twelfth Night feast was accepted as King for the occasion.

PÂTISSIÈRE (Noix) – Culinary term for the chump end of the loin of veal, which is situated in the fillet. It is sometimes called round of veal.

PATRONNET – French name for a pastry-cook's young apprentice.

PATTIES. PETITS PÂTÉS – **Small hot patties.** PETITS PÂTÉS CHAUDS – As their name indicates, small hot patties are the diminutive versions of big hot *entrée* pies and *pâtés*. They are served as *hors-d'œuvre* and as small *entrées*.

'Small patties,' said Carême, 'are perfect only when eaten straight out of the oven. If they are allowed to get cold and are then reheated, they lose some of their quality.'

In days gone by patties used to be sold in the streets of Paris to the accompaniment of the cry: 'Piping hot! Piping hot!'

Some bakers and caterers still sell a patty filled with sausage meat or a *salpicon* (q.v.) of pork, known as *friands*.

In the section devoted to hot *hors-d'œuvre* (q.v.), various recipes for the preparation of patties will be found.

Little Russian patties. PETITS PÂTÉS À LA RUSSE – These are served as an accompaniment to soup, and are made of *Puff pastry* or common *Brioche dough* (see DOUGH). They are filled with various mixtures, especially various fish forcemeats, principally salmon.

PAUCHOUSE – See POCHOUSE.

PAUILLAC – Commune of the *département* of Gironde where the famous Pauillac milk-fed lambs are raised. (See LAMB.)

PAUNCH (Belly). ESTOMAC – See OFFAL or VARIETY MEATS.

PAUPIETTES – Thin slices of beef or other meat stuffed with some forcemeat, rolled into *paupiettes* (the shape of big corks) wrapped in a thin rasher of bacon and braised in very little liquid. *Paupiettes* are served with a vegetable garnish. (See BEEF, *Paupiettes of beef*.)

Paupiettes can also be made from fillets of fish. (See SOLE, *Paupiettes of sole*.)

Paupiettes of lamb à la créole. PAUPIETTES D'AGNEAU À LA CRÉOLE – Cut some lamb taken from the leg or the shoulder into escalopes, flatten them well and spread with a *Fine pork forcemeat* (see FORCEMEATS) mixed with chopped onion, fried in butter, with half its weight of sweet pimentos cut in very small dice.

Roll the escalopes into *paupiettes* and tie them with string. Put into a sauté pan in which 100 g. (4 oz., 1 cup) chopped onion has been softened in butter. Brown the *paupiettes* with the onion. Add 2 peeled, seeded and chopped tomatoes. Season with salt and pepper and add a *bouquet garni* (q.v.), a pinch of garlic and a small piece of lemon rind. Cook in the oven, uncovered, for 45 minutes.

Drain the *paupiettes*. Arrange them on a dish. Garnish the middle of the dish with *Rice à la créole* (see RICE). Boil down the pan juices, strain, and pour over the *paupiettes*.

PAVÉ – Term describing a cold dish composed of some kind of a mixture, frequently a mousse, set in a special square or rectangular mould, coated with jelly and decorated with truffles, etc.

The name *pavé* also applies to certain square cakes, made of Genoese or sponge layers, sandwiched with a butter cream, and to spice cake.

Pavé of chicken à l'écarlate. PAVÉ DE VOLAILLE À L'ÉCARLATE – Coat a square mould with clear chicken aspic jelly flavoured with Madeira. Line the mould with circlets of pickled tongue, thin slices of chicken breast and round slivers of truffles, alternating the colours. Spoon a little aspic jelly over.

Fill the mould with alternate layers of chicken mousse and pickled tongue mousse, both mousses bound with aspic jelly. Put slivers of truffles between each layer. Cover with a layer of chicken aspic jelly and chill on ice. Turn out the *pavé* onto a dish and surround with slices of pickled tongue, decorated with slivers of truffle and glazed with jelly. Garnish with chopped jelly.

Pavé of foie gras à la king. PAVÉ DU ROI, AU FOIE GRAS – This *pavé* is composed of a fat goose liver, generously studded with truffles, enclosed in *Fine lining paste* (see DOUGH), rolled out in a circle and shaped into a crescent. Decorate with fleurs-de-lys cut out of pastry. It is a *foie gras* pie made by hand instead of being baked in a mould.

When the pie is cold pour in some port-flavoured jelly (q.v.).

Pavé of foie gras with truffles (cold). PAVÉ DE FOIE GRAS AUX TRUFFES – Line a mould with jelly (q.v.) flavoured with sherry (or other liqueur wine), decorate with slivers of truffles and fill with *Foie gras mousse* (see FOIE GRAS) and slices of *foie gras* and truffles, putting them into the mould in alternate layers. Cover with a layer of jelly. Chill on ice. Turn out onto a serving dish and garnish with chopped jelly.

Pavé of pheasant or other game à la Saint-Hubert. PAVÉ DE FAISAN À LA SAINT-HUBERT – Make in a square or rectangular mould, using pheasant or other game mousse, slices of the appropriate game and slivers of truffles, prepared as described in the recipe for *Pavé of foie gras with truffles*.

Pavé of salmon à la Nantua. PAVÉ DE SAUMON À LA NANTUA – Coat a square mould with fish aspic jelly (see JELLY, *Fish jelly stock*), decorate with crayfish tails dipped in *Chaud-froid sauce à la Nantua* (see SAUCE), and slivers of truffles, and fill with salmon mousse (see FISH, *Fish mousse*) bound with aspic jelly.

Cover the mousse with a layer of jelly and chill on ice. Turn out onto a dish. Garnish with little *barquettes* baked blind and filled with more crayfish tails, covered with the sauce and glazed with jelly. Put chopped jelly between each tartlet.

Pavés of soles or other fish. PAVÉS DE SOLES – Prepare as *Pavé of salmon* using sole mousse (see FISH, *Fish mousse*), fillets of sole, cooked in white wine and well drained, and slivers of truffles.

These *pavés* are decorated with truffles, slices of hard-boiled egg yolks, blanched tarragon or chervil leaves, lobster coral, etc.

They can be garnished, in addition to fillets of soles and truffles, with slices of lobster or spiny lobster, crayfish tails, well-dried, poached oysters, and glazed with aspic jelly (q.v.).

SWEET PAVÉS. PAVÉS D'ENTREMETS:

Chocolate pavé. PAVÉ AU CHOCOLAT – Sandwich Genoese or chocolate sponge layers together with chocolate *Butter cream* (see CREAMS). Trim the sandwich, giving it a square shape. Ice with *Chocolate icing* (see ICING).

As in the case of all cakes filled with butter cream, the *pavés* should be put in the ice box to allow the cream to set.

Coffee pavé. PAVÉ AU MOKA – Prepare as *Chocolate pavé*, using coffee *Butter cream* (see CREAMS) and *Coffee icing* (see ICING).

Fruit pavé. PAVÉ AUX FRUITS – Spread Genoese sponge layers with vanilla-flavoured *Butter cream* (see CREAMS), putting a layer of various fruit, cooked in syrup, well drained and chopped into a *salpicon* (q.v.), on the cream. Sandwich the layers of cake, pressing down to make them adhere. Trim the cake to give it an even, square shape. Ice with kirsch-flavoured *Fondant icing* (see ICING). Decorate with crystallised fruit, angelica lozenges and almonds.

Hazelnut pavé. PAVÉ AUX NOISETTES – Prepare as *Chocolate pavé*, using burnt hazelnut *Butter cream* (see CREAMS) and kirsch-flavoured icing.

Praline pavé. PAVÉ AU PRALINE – Prepare as *Chocolate pavé*, using burnt almond butter cream and kirsch-flavoured icing.

Small rice pavés à la cévenole. PETITS PAVÉS DE RIZ À LA CÉVENOLE – Prepare the *pavés* as described in the recipe for *Small rice pavés with fruit* (see below), using a purée of *marrons glacés* or vanilla-flavoured *Chestnut purée* (see CHESTNUTS). Deep-fry and arrange in a pyramid.

Small rice pavés à la créole. PETITS PAVÉS DE RIZ À LA CRÉOLE – Spread the *pavés*, prepared as described below, with a *salpicon* (q.v.) of pineapple cooked in syrup, cut in very small dice and bound with stewed apricots. Deep-fry and arrange in a pyramid.

Small rice pavés with fruit. PETITS PAVÉS DE RIZ AUX FRUITS – Cook 100 g. (4 oz., $\frac{1}{2}$ cup) sweetened rice. Spread it on a buttered pan in a layer 1 cm ($\frac{1}{2}$ inch) thick. Cover the surface with a little butter to prevent a crust forming, and leave to cool.

Turn out the rice and cut into an even number of rectangular pieces, 4 cm. ($1\frac{1}{2}$ inches) wide and about 6 cm. ($2\frac{1}{2}$ inches) long. Spread half of these rectangles on one side with a layer of stewed fruit: apricots, chestnuts, peaches, apples, or any other. Cover the remaining rectangles with rice, then dip in egg and breadcrumbs, and shape the pieces into straight-sided *pavés*.

Deep-fry in smoking hot fat, drain, arrange in a pyramid on a dish and serve with a fruit sauce, flavoured with kirsch or any other liqueur.

Small rice pavés à la normande. PETITS PAVÉS DE RIZ À LA NORMANDE – Spread the *pavés*, prepared as described above, with stewed apples. Fry and arrange in a pyramid.

Small rice pavés Pompadour. PETITS PAVÉS DE RIZ POMPADOUR – Spread the *pavés*, prepared as described above, with a *salpicon* (q.v.) of crystallised fruit, cut in very small dice and bound with a few tablespoons of rum-flavoured *French pastry cream* (see CREAMS). Fry and arrange in a pyramid.

Small semolina pavés. PETITS PAVÉS DE SEMOULE – Prepare like *Small rice pavés*, using sweetened, cooked semolina.

Pavés can be endlessly varied by spreading with various jams, stewed fruit and *salpicons* (q.v.), as well as variously flavoured *French pastry cream* (see CREAMS).

PAVÉ DE MOYAUX – See CHEESE.

PAVIE – Firm-fleshed peach, similar to a clingstone, with the pulp adhering to the stone.

PAYSANNE (À LA) – Method of preparing butcher's meat and poultry, usually braised and accompanied by a garnish of carrots, turnips, onions and celery sliced and lightly cooked in butter, pieces of scalded and fried lean bacon, and potatoes cut down to a uniform small size.

Fresh peas (*Claire*)

PEA. POIS – Plant thought by some to have originated in western Asia and been derived from the wild pea. According to whether the pod is tender or parchment-lined, peas are classified as edible-podded (also called sugar peas) or as shelling peas. They can be either tall or dwarf. The most esteemed French varieties, which are eaten 'green', before they reach complete maturity, when they are still *petits pois* (small peas), are *pois de Clamart* and *pois Michaux*. The late varieties are preserved by means of drying. Whole dried peas, of greyish yellow colour, are preferred in France to split peas, which are of a greyish green colour.

Cultivated by the Hebrews, Persians, Greeks and later the Romans, peas are now found throughout most of the world. This vegetable is very rich in nitrogen and mucilage, contains a strong proportion of oxalic acid and has a pleasant taste recalling that of chestnuts.

Shelled peas are very nutritious, rich in protein, but hard to digest. The peas should be well cooked, and if possible, served mixed with other vegetables in stews, purées or soups.

The best of the '*mange-tout*' variety (the edible-podded pea) are *Corne de bélier* and *Carouby*.

Shelling peas or '*petit pois*' are divided into two categories depending upon whether the pea is round or wrinkled. Some of the best known round varieties are: *large-podded Express, Express Alaska, Petit Provençal.* The wrinkled varieties include: *Téléphone, Merveille d'Amérique, Centurion, Progrès de Laxton*, etc.

FRESH GARDEN PEAS. POIS FRAIS –

Boiled peas. PETITS POIS À L'ANGLAISE – Cook the peas in boiling salted water as quickly as possible, keeping the saucepan uncovered.

Drain and dry off by tossing them in a saucepan on the stove. Serve with fresh butter.

Peas à la bonne femme. PETITS POIS À LA BONNE FEMME – Melt some butter in a saucepan and in it brown lightly 12 small onions (new, when in season) and 100 g. (4 oz., ½ cup) diced, scalded lean bacon. Remove the onions and bacon from the pan.

Add 2 tablespoons (3 tablespoons) flour to the butter and cook for a few minutes, stirring with a wooden spoon. Dilute with 2 dl. (⅓ pint, scant cup) white stock. Boil for 5 minutes. Put 1 litre (1¾ pints, generous quart) fresh garden peas into this sauce, add the onions, bacon and a *bouquet garni* (q.v.), and simmer with a lid on.

Peas in butter. PETITS POIS AU BEURRE – Cook the peas in salted boiling water. Drain them and dry off by tossing in a saucepan on brisk heat. Season with a pinch of castor (fine) sugar. Dress with fresh butter cut in tiny pieces, allowing 100 g. (4 oz., ½ cup) butter per litre (1¾ pints, generous quart) shelled garden peas.

Peas à la crème. PETITS POIS À LA CRÈME – Boil the peas in water, drain, and toss in a pan on heat for a few moments to dry off. Cover with boiling fresh cream. Simmer until the liquid is boiled down by half and season with salt and a pinch of sugar. Add 2 tablespoons (3 tablespoons) fresh cream, blend well, and serve in a *timbale*.

Peas with fennel. PETITS POIS AU FENOUIL – Boil the peas in salted water with a good bunch of fresh fennel tied with a string. Drain, dress with butter and add 1 tablespoon chopped fennel. Serve in a *timbale*.

Peas à la fermière. PETITS POIS À LA FERMIÈRE – Cook 500 g. (18 oz.) small new carrots with 12 small onions, as described in the recipe for *Glazed carrots* (see CARROTS). When the carrots are half-cooked add to the pan 8 dl. (scant 1½ pints, scant 2 pints) freshly shelled garden peas, 1 head of lettuce shredded into a coarse *julienne (q.v.)* and a *bouquet garni* composed of parsley and chervil. Season with salt and sugar. Moisten with 2 tablespoons (3 tablespoons) water. Simmer with the lid on. Add butter before serving.

Peas à la française. PETITS POIS À LA FRANÇAISE – Put into a large saucepan 1 litre (1¾ pints, generous quart) fresh garden peas, 1 lettuce heart shredded into a *chiffonnade* (q.v.), 12 small onions (new, if in season), a *bouquet garni* composed of parsley and chervil, 100 g. (4 oz., ½ cup) butter, 1½ teaspoons salt and 25 g. (1 oz., 2 tablespoons) sugar. Mix well.

Add 3 to 4 tablespoons (scant ¼ to ⅓ cup) cold water. Bring to the boil then simmer gently with the lid on. When the peas are cooked, remove the *bouquet garni*, take the pan off the stove and add 3 or 4 teaspoons fresh butter. Mix and serve in a *timbale*.

Peas with ham (Languedoc cookery). PETITS POIS AU JAMBON – Cut 1 medium-sized onion into quarters and brown with 100 g. (4 oz.) lean, raw (not smoked) ham in butter. Add 1 litre (1¾ pints, generous quart) garden peas to the pan. Toss them lightly in the butter, sprinkle in 1 tablespoon flour and cook for a few minutes. Moisten with 3 dl. (½ pint, 1¼ cups) water, season with salt and sugar, add a small *bouquet garni* (q.v.) and simmer, covered, from 45 to 50 minutes. Remove the *bouquet garni* and serve in a *timbale*.

Peas with lettuce. PETITS POIS AUX LAITUES – Prepare as *Peas à la française*, using tied lettuce heads and omitting the small onions.

When the peas are cooked, drain the lettuces and cut into quarters. Put these on the peas. Finish off with fresh butter and serve in a *timbale*.

Peas with mint. PETITS POIS À LA MENTHE – Proceed as described in the recipe for *Peas with fennel*, substituting fresh mint for the fennel. Serve the peas in a *timbale*, dress with butter and put scalded mint leaves on top.

Peas à la paysanne. PETITS POIS À LA PAYSANNE – Prepare, using big fresh garden peas, like *Peas à la française*, with coarsely shredded lettuce and onions cut in quarters. When the peas are cooked, mix with kneaded butter, allowing 25 g. (1 oz., 2 tablespoons) butter and 10 g. (½ oz., 2 tablespoons) flour per litre (1¾ pints, generous quart) of peas.

Peas à la paysanne are often called *à la bonne femme*.

Purée of fresh garden peas, called Saint-Germain. PURÉE DE POIS FRAIS, DITE SAINT-GERMAIN – Cook large peas as described in the recipe for *Peas à la française*, drain, and rub through a fine sieve.

Heat this purée and add the liquor left from cooking the peas, boiled down and strained. Blend in fresh butter, allowing 100 g. (4 oz., ½ cup) per litre (1¾ pints, generous quart) of purée.

This purée can also be made using peas boiled in salted water and well drained.

DRIED PEAS. POIS SECS – Three kinds of dried peas are used in the kitchen: split peas, yellow peas and chick-peas.

Yellow peas are used only in some parts of eastern France as a purée. This is often served in Germany as an accompaniment to *sauerkraut*. Yellow peas can also be cooked in the same manner as dried white beans.

Chick-peas, dried whole, come from a plant of the family *Leguminosae*, which in France is also called *pois chiche* or pois cornu.

Split peas are more commonly used in France, served mainly as a purée.

To cook split peas. Soak the split peas in water to soften them.

Put them into a saucepan and cover with water, allowing 1½ litres (2¾ pints, 3¼ pints) water per 500 g. (18 oz.) split peas. Add 1 ham knuckle and a coarse *mirepoix* (q.v.) composed of 1 carrot, 1 medium-sized onion and 75 g. (3 oz., scant ½ cup) scalded lean bacon – all these ingredients cut in large dice and softened in butter. Add a *bouquet garni* of parsley, thyme, bay leaf and the green part of 3 leeks. Season, bring to the boil and simmer gently with the lid on for about 1½ hours. A few leaves of lettuce can also be added as a garnish.

Split pea purée. PURÉE DE POIS CASSÉS – Cook the split peas as described above and rub through a sieve. Heat the purée, stirring with a wooden spoon. Dilute with a few tablespoons of the liquid left over from cooking the peas, strained through a fine strainer. Take off the heat and, just before serving, add butter.

If this purée is served as a vegetable or garnish, a few tablespoons of fresh cream can be added to it.

Split pea soup or purée aux croûtons. POTAGE DE POIS CASSÉS – Soup made of split peas, cooked as described above and rubbed through a sieve. (See SOUPS AND BROTHS, Purée of split pea soup.)

EDIBLE-PODDED or SUGAR PEAS. POIS MANGE-TOUT, PRINCESSES – These are peas the pods of which have no parchment lining; they can therefore be eaten seed, pod and all.

Top and tail the pods and break in 2 or 3 pieces. Cook them in any way recommended above for fresh garden peas.

PEACH. PÊCHE – The peach is the fruit of the peach tree, one of the *Rosaceae* family. It is said to have originated in Persia and is one of the best and most attractive of French fruits.

Peaches can be divided into two main categories: white-fleshed peaches, of which the best known are (in order of maturity): *Madeleine Pouyet*; *May Flower*; *Amsden*; *Charles Ingouf*; *Charles Roux*; and yellow-fleshed peaches often

Peaches (painting by W. Volker)

wrongly called 'apricot peaches'. Yellow-fleshed peaches generally mature later than the white-fleshed variety and are less aromatic. However, they are larger, stand up much better to transport, are more pleasant to the eye, being more attractively coloured, and make good preserving fruits. Moreover, they grow more rapidly than their white-fleshed counterparts. The principal varieties of yellow-fleshed counterparts. The principal varieties of white-fleshed peaches are: *Dixired, Red Haven, Fair Haven, Hale Haven, Southland, Elberta* and *J. H. Hale*. The last two are particularly late maturing fruits and less tasty than the others.

Almost half of French peach production takes place in the Rhône Valley. There is also extensive peach cultivation in the Garonne Valley, Bouches-du-Rhône, Gard, Roussillon and in the Fréjus region. The season lasts from 10 June to 10 September.

Peaches are eaten raw as a dessert fruit, or cooked, and in the latter form they enter into the making of a vast number of sweets and pastries, and are used in a great many confectionery preparations. Various excellent beverages are also made from peaches; highly flavoured brandies and liqueurs are distilled from them.

The following can be classed among the best varieties of French peaches: *Amsdem*, a round fruit, slightly flattened, of medium size, with red flush and mottling, and greenish-white, juicy flesh of good flavour; *Early Croncels*, a big ovoid fruit, amber coloured with purplish flush, with a delicate flesh and pleasant flavour; *Felignies* (end of August) medium-sized fruit, yellow with crimson flush, creamy white flesh of very good flavour; *Victoria*, round medium-sized fruit, yellow with crimson flush, white melting flesh tinted next stone, very good; *Hale's early*, medium-sized fruit, slightly flattened, flushed and mottled, very juicy flesh of good flavour; *France*, big round fruit with very downy skin, yellow and crimson in colour, with white flesh, slightly tinted next stone, very good; *Grosse mignonne*, very big almost round fruit, skin flushed with purple, white juicy flesh, very melting and sweet; *Reine des vergers*, big slightly elongated fruit, crimson-purplish flush, white flesh, slightly pink next stone, melting and sweet; *Admirable yellow* or *Apricot peach*, a round fruit, with orange tinted yellow skin, very good white juicy flesh; *Venus's breast*, big round fruit with a nipple on the top, crimson flush, rather fine, semi-melting flesh, quite good in flavour.

Peaches Bourdaloue. PÊCHES BOURDALOUE – Halve the peaches, peel and poach in vanilla-flavoured syrup. Drain and dry them. Arrange in a flan case, baked blind, on a foundation of *Frangipane cream* (see CREAMS), not too thick and mixed with crushed macaroons. Cover the peaches with a layer of the same cream. Sprinkle with crushed macaroons and a little melted butter and glaze quickly in the oven.

This dessert can be made without covering the peaches with frangipane cream. They should be decorated with crystallised cherries, lozenges of angelica and halved almonds. The flan case can be filled with sweetened semolina, bound with eggs and butter and flavoured with kirsch.

A *salpicon* (q.v.) of crystallised fruit, steeped in some liqueur, can be added to either of the above compositions.

Peaches in brandy. PÊCHES À L'EAU-DE-VIE – Prepare like *Apricot comfits in brandy* (see APRICOT).

Chilled peaches with raspberries. PÊCHES RAFRAÎCHIES AUX FRAMBOISES – Poach choice peaches in vanilla-flavoured syrup. Chill on ice. Just before serving arrange in a fruit dish, cover with a purée of fresh raspberries diluted with a little of the syrup in which the peaches were cooked, boiled down and laced with a few drops of kirsch. Scatter fresh raspberries on top.

Peaches Colbert. PÊCHES COLBERT – Using halved peaches, poached in vanilla-flavoured syrup, prepare like *Colbert apricots* (see APRICOT).

Compote of peaches. COMPOTE DE PÊCHES – Plunge the peaches into boiling water for a moment then peel immediately. Poach them, whole or halved, in vanilla-flavoured 18° syrup (see SUGAR).

Serve hot or cold.

Peaches Condé. PÊCHES CONDÉ – Poach halved peaches in vanilla-flavoured syrup. Prepare like *Apricots condé* (see APRICOT).

Peach coupe – See ICE CREAMS AND ICES.

Peach croûte. CROÛTE AUX PÊCHES – Cook halved or quartered peaches in vanilla-flavoured syrup, drain and prepare as described in the recipe for *Apricot croûte* (see APRICOT).

Crystallised peaches. PÊCHES CONFITES – Prepare like *Crystallised apricots* (see APRICOT).

Peach flambé Brillat-Savarin. PÊCHES FLAMBÉES BRILLAT-SAVARIN – Prepare as many little *savarins* (q.v.) (crown-shaped) as you have halves of big peaches.

Arrange the *savarins*, soaked in syrup, in a circle on an ovenproof dish. Put into each *savarin* 1 tablespoon very thick *French pastry cream* (see CREAMS), mixed with a *salpicon* (q.v.) of crystallised fruit, steeped in kirsch or maraschino.

Poach the halved and peeled peaches in vanilla-flavoured syrup. Drain and dry them. Arrange on the *savarins*. Sprinkle with crushed macaroons and a little melted butter. Brown lightly in the oven. Before serving, sprinkle with kirsch and set alight. Serve with apricot sauce, made by diluting apricot jam with the syrup in which the peaches were cooked, heating it and straining.

Peach flambé au kirsch. PÊCHES FLAMBÉES AU KIRSCH – Peel the peaches and poach them in vanilla-flavoured syrup. Drain, and arrange in a dessert dish. Pour over a few tablespoons of the syrup in which they were cooked, thickened with arrowroot. Sprinkle with heated kirsch,

Armagnac, brandy, Calvados, rum, and set alight.

Instead of serving all the peaches together in one dish, they can be arranged in individual *cassolettes*.

Peach flan

Peach flan or tart. FLAN, TARTE AUX PÊCHES – Prepare as described in the recipe for *Apricot tart (flan)* (see TART) using halved or quartered peaches.

Peach fritters – See FRITTERS.

Peaches in Frontignan. PÊCHES AU FRONTIGNAN – Peel the peaches and cook in vanilla-flavoured syrup. Drain, and arrange in a dessert dish. Boil down the syrup by two-thirds, add several tablespoons of Frontignan wine, and pour over the peaches. Serve hot or cold.

Peach ice – See ICE CREAMS AND ICES.

Peaches à l'impératrice. PÊCHES À L'IMPÉRATRICE – Peel the peaches, halve and poach in vanilla-flavoured syrup. Drain and dry. Arrange them in a dish filled up to two-thirds with *Rice à l'impératrice* (see RICE), chilled in a refrigerator. Cover the peaches with a layer of raspberry or strawberry jelly.

Peach jam – See JAMS AND JELLIES.

Penelope peaches. PÊCHES PÉNÉLOPE – Poach the peaches in syrup, strongly flavoured with vanilla. Leave to cool in the syrup.

Prepare an iced strawberry mousse (see ICE CREAMS AND ICES, *Iced mousses or mousselines*) using a 35° syrup, (see SUGAR) mixed with an equal quantity of strawberry pulp and twice its volume of *Chantilly cream* (see CREAMS) whisked very stiffly. Fill individual moulds with this mousse, seal hermetically, and chill for 2 hours. Before serving, turn out the strawberry mousse into fruit dishes. Arrange the peaches, drained, dried and chilled in a refrigerator, on the mousse.

Garnish the middle with fresh chilled strawberries. Cover with a film of sugar cooked to pearl degree. Serve with *zabaglione* (q.v.) flavoured with parfait-amour (q.v.) liqueur.

Peach pulp (raw). PULPE DE PÊCHES (CRUE) – Peel and rub the flesh of the peaches through a fine sieve. Add a third of its weight in castor sugar. Mix well. Flavour with liqueur.

This pulp is used for covering chilled fruit, as a compote, and for certain cold sweets, such as charlottes, fruit moulds, puddings, etc.

Peaches à la Madame Récamier. PÊCHES MADAME RÉCAMIER – René de Beauvoir gave the following recipe for this dish in *Monde Illustré* (May 1857), dictated by Chevrier, the illustrious *maître d'hôtel* of the early nineteenth century:

'Madame Récamier,' says Chevrier, 'had lost all interest in food and we could see her fading away. No one dared disobey the doctor's orders for her – a diet. Very well, I said to myself, she likes peaches – I'll serve her some in my own way.

'And I put one, the best I could find, to cook in a *bain-marie* (q.v.). I smothered it with exquisite sugar syrup, poured some cream over it – and there it was.'

Peaches with rice and meringue. PÊCHES MERINGUÉES AU RIZ – Proceed as described in the recipe for *Apricots with rice and meringue* (see APRICOT), using halved peaches, poached in vanilla-flavoured syrup.

Ring (border) of peaches à la Chantilly (Cold sweet or dessert). BORDURE DE PÊCHES À LA CHANTILLY – Bake a *Vanilla custard* (see CUSTARD) in a ring mould. Leave until cold and turn out onto a dish. Halve 6 peaches, poach in vanilla-flavoured syrup, drain, dry and arrange in the middle of the ring.

Cover the peaches with vanilla-flavoured whipped cream, piling it up in a dome. Decorate with crystallised cherries and halved pistachio nuts.

Peach soufflé. SOUFFLÉ AUX PÊCHES – Use peach purée, mixed with sugar syrup cooked to crack degree (see SUGAR) then with egg whites whisked into a stiff froth. Prepare as indicated in the recipe for fruit soufflés. (See SOUFFLES, *Fruit base mixtures*.)

Peach soufflés can also be made using a cream composition, mixed with peach pulp and pieces of peaches cooked in vanilla-flavoured syrup, well drained and dried.

Peaches Sultana. PÊCHES SULTANE – Poach whole or halved peaches in vanilla-flavoured syrup and leave until cold.

Drain them and arrange in a *timbale* or dessert dish on a foundation of *Pistachio-nut ice cream* (see ICE CREAMS AND ICES). Cover with syrup flavoured with attar of roses. Pour on a film of sugar cooked to pearl degree (see SUGAR).

Peaches in red wine à la bordelaise. PÊCHES AU VIN ROUGE, DITES À LA BORDELAISE – Halve and peel 4 peaches. Sprinkle with sugar and leave to stand for 1 hour. Boil 3 dl. ($\frac{1}{2}$ pint, $1\frac{1}{4}$ cups) Bordeaux wine with 8 lumps of sugar and a small piece of cinnamon bark, in a copper pan. Poach the halved peaches in the wine. When they are cooked, drain and arrange in a glass dish. Boil down the syrup, pour over the peaches and leave to get cold.

Serve with slices of brioche, sprinkled with sugar and glazed in a hot oven.

PEACOCK. PAON – This magnificent bird was once esteemed by gastronomes as a rarity. Today it is still greatly admired for its ornamental qualities but has lost its gastronomical value.

In the Middle Ages it held pride of place at great state banquets. Its cooking needed all the skill of an experienced master-cook. The bird was skinned carefully, the skin was treated and dressed, the tail spread in a fan, the head with its crest wrapped in a piece of linen, constantly moistened with water during roasting. The feet and the beak were gilded, and the bird, dressed in full feather, was carried to the table in a solemn procession. At great feasts it was served either buried under flowers or with flames shotting out of its beak (this effect being achieved by putting a piece of cotton dipped in spirit, or a piece of camphor, in its beak).

The bird was set before the master of the house or the most distinguished guest present. Only the noblest present had the right to carve it, and only if he could do it with such skill as to allow each guest, however many there might be at table, to have a piece.

This operation was accomplished amid the praise and approval of the company, acknowledging the knight-trenchant's skill. He, fired with enthusiasm, would rise and with his hand on the dish, take an oath vowing to be worthy of the eulogies, either by being the first to raise his standard on a town which was about to be besieged, or by leading a lance attack upon the enemy.

Then each knight, receiving his piece, would make his own vow to the peacock, and failure to carry it out would be a blot on his escutcheon.

For culinary preparation of peacock, see PHEASANT.

Peanut plant with pods buried in the earth

PEANUT. ARACHIDE – Plant originating from America which is cultivated in all hot countries. Its pods, which bury themselves in the earth to mature the seeds, produce nuts which are eaten either raw or roasted. They are also known under the names of *earthnuts*, *groundnut* and *monkey-nut*. The nutrition value of the peanut is considerable.

Peanut oil and peanut butter are made from this nut. The latter can be eaten in sandwiches or on pieces of toast, accompanied by lettuce leaves, cream, chervil and tarragon, or on gingerbread, with jam or jelly.

Peanut oil – See OIL, *Groundnut oil.*

Peanut paste. PÂTE D'ARACHIDE – Prepare using blanched peanuts in the same way as *Almond paste* (see ALMOND).

PEAR. POIRE – Fruit of the pear tree of the family *Rosaceae* which does not seem to have been known in the distant past. It was cultivated by the Romans, and Pliny mentions 38 varieties of it, whilst Virgil only mentions three. Today, a whole volume would be required to enumerate them.

They are classified as follows: early varieties, usually sold in summer as they ripen; mid-season varieties, picked at the end of August or beginning of September and consumed in autumn; and late varieties, which are refrigerated and eaten in winter and early spring.

Among the early varieties are the *Doyenné de juillet*, *Beurré Giffard*, both of these in season from the beginning of July. *Docteur Guyot*, the earliest of the wide range of cultivated varieties appears next. The tasty *Williams's* or *Bon Chrétien* (*Bartlett* in U.S.A.) is sold throughout France from mid August to early October. It is a knobbly pear, yellow in colour, often tinged with pink. It has delicate, slightly musk-flavoured flesh.

The best known of the mid-season varieties are: *Louise-Bonne*, a large pear, red in colour, fading to yellow, with very delicate flesh; *Alexandrine Douillard*; *Beurré Hardy*, a russet pear streaked with dark red; *Belle Epine du Mas*. Other lesser known varieties are also popular: *Beurré Clairgeau*, for example, *Beurré Diel*, *de Curé*, and *Beurré d'Arenberg*, etc.

The best known of the late varieties are, first, the most esteemed of all, the *Doyenné du comice*, pale green shaded with darker green and red. It has an excellent flavour and is marketed from the end of October to the end of December. Then there is *Passe-Crassane*, big, round, with flattened extremities, a musky flavour but rather gritty flesh. It refrigerates successfully and is marketed from Christmas to Easter.

French pears and some imported Italian pears keep the French market supplied from July to April. For the remainder of the year, there are pears from the southern hemisphere (Argentine, Australia, South Africa) mostly *Beurré d'Anjou*, and *Packam's Triumph*.

The pears of Provence and of the Rhône Valley account for half the bulk of French production. They are mostly early varieties (*Docteur Guyot* and *Williams'*). The Paris region, Loire Valley and Anjou grow mainly autumn and winter varieties (*Beurré Hardy*, *Doyenné du comice* and *Passe-Crassane*).

Cooking pears generally have rather crisp flesh, sometimes rather gritty and often tart. They are in season from December to May and should only be eaten cooked.

Perry pears are used in the making of perry or pear cider.

Dessert pears, among the best of dessert fruits, are usually eaten raw but may be cooked and used as a filling or garnish for tarts, flans, pies, iced mousses, charlottes, etc.

With only 2 per cent acid content, the pear is suitable for the most fragile digestions, provided it is well masticated. Its flesh contains a large number of mineral salts (notably manganese); its sugar is assimilable even by diabetics.

Excellent preserves are also made of dessert pears. They can be crystallised like any other fruit, whole or quartered. They are then partly dried in the oven and flattened on one side – these dried pears can be found in the shops and are called *poires tapées* in France.

Baked pears, also called poires en douillon and poires cartouches. POIRES EN RABOTTE – Peel and core the pears, half-cook in butter and wrap each in a piece of *Fine lining paste* (see DOUGH). Put on top of each a circlet cut out of the same pastry. Brush with beaten egg and bake in a hot oven for 25 minutes, or longer, if the pears are large.

The *douillons* or baked pears can also be prepared without peeling. Half-cook them in the oven before enclosing in pastry.

Pears Bourdaloue. POIRES BOURDALOUE – Cut the pears in half if they are of medium size, or in quarters if they are large. Trim and poach in vanilla-flavoured syrup.

Put them in a flan case, filled with *Frangipane cream* (see CREAMS) and proceed as described in the recipe for *Peaches Bourdaloue* (see PEACH).

Beurré Clairgeau pears (*Wide World*)

Pears à l'impératrice (*Robert Carrier*)

Pears Brillat-Savarin. POIRES BRILLAT-SAVARIN – Poach 8 pear halves in vanilla-flavoured syrup. Drain them, dry, and arrange in a circle on a *Genoese cake* (q.v.) cut into two layers and sandwiched together with thick, rum-flavoured stewed pear mixture. Decorate with crystallised cherries and lozenges of angelica. Heat in the oven. Pour over some rum-flavoured, thinned-down apricot pulp. Serve with rum-flavoured *Custard cream* (see CREAMS) thickened with arrowroot.

Cardinal pears. POIRES CARDINAL – Poach the pears in vanilla-flavoured syrup. Leave them to cool, drain, and arrange in a fruit dish or in a *timbale*. Cover with kirsch-flavoured, sweetened raspberry purée, and sprinkle with chopped almonds.

Pear charlotte. CHARLOTTE DE POIRES – Using stewed pears, prepare as described in the recipe for *Apple charlotte* (see CHARLOTTE).

Pear compote. COMPOTE DE POIRES – Using whole pears if they are small, halved or quartered if they are large, prepare as described in the recipe for *Peach compote* (see COMPOTE).

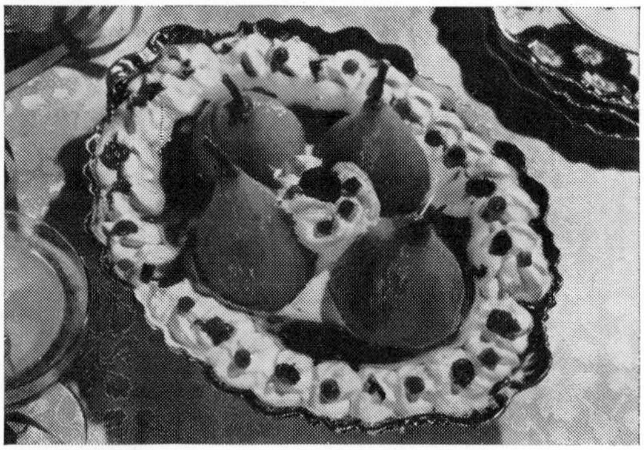

Pears Condé

Pears Condé. POIRES CONDÉ – Using pears cooked in syrup, prepare like *Condé apricots (see* APRICOT).

Pear croûtes. CROUTES AUX POIRES – Using halved or quartered pears poached in vanilla-flavoured syrup, prepare as described in the recipe for *Apricot croûte* (see APRICOT).

Pear flambé au kirsch. POIRES FLAMBÉES AU KIRSCH – Using whole or halved pears cooked in vanilla-flavoured syrup, prepare like *Peach flambée au kirsch* (see PEACH).

Pear fritters – See FRITTERS.

Pears Hélène. POIRES HÉLÈNE – Poach the pears in vanilla-flavoured syrup and arrange on vanilla-flavoured ice. Serve with hot *Chocolate sauce* (see SAUCE).

Pear ice and Iced mousse – See ICE CREAMS AND ICES.

Iced pears Mourier. POIRES GLACÉES MOURIER – Peel Crassane pears to as uniform a size as possible and poach in syrup strongly flavoured with vanilla. Drain and chill on ice.

Arrange in a meringue flan case filling the middle with kirsch-flavoured *Iced pear mousse* (see ICE CREAMS AND ICES). Pipe whipped cream over the mousse through a forcing bag and decorate with glacé cherries, angelica lozenges and almonds.

Pears à l'impératrice. POIRES À L'IMPÉRATRICE – Using whole or halved pears, poach in vanilla-flavoured syrup and proceed as described in the recipe for *Peaches à l'impératrice* (see PEACH).

Pear Melba – See ICE CREAMS AND ICES.

Pears with rice and meringue. POIRES MERINGUÉES AU RIZ – Proceed as described in the recipe for *Apricots with rice and meringue* (see APRICOT), using halved or quartered pears poached in vanilla-flavoured syrup.

Pear flan à la crème (*Café de Paris*) *Phot. Larousse*)

Ring (border) of pears Chantilly. BORDURE DE POIRES CHANTILLY – These cold sweets are made using quartered pears, cooked in syrup like *Border of peaches à la Chantilly* (see PEACH).

Pears with semolina. POIRES À LA SEMOULE GRATINÉES – Peel the pears, cut into quarters and cook in a light vanilla-flavoured syrup. Drain and arrange in a circle in a buttered oven-proof dish on a thick layer of semolina, cooked as described in the recipe for *Semolina pudding* (see SEMOLINA).

Sprinkle with crushed macaroons and melted butter. Brown the top in a slow oven and serve in the same dish.

Pear soufflé. SOUFFLÉ AUX POIRES – Prepare like a cream soufflé (see SOUFFLÉ) using a cream composition mixed with pear pulp and a *salpicon* (q.v.) of crystallised pears, steeped in kirsch.

Pear tarts. FLANS, TARTES AUX POIRES – Prepare like any fruit flan or tart using sliced or quartered pears (see TART).

Timbale of pears d'Aremberg. TIMBALE DE POIRES D'AREMBERG – Butter a charlotte mould and line it with slightly firm *Brioche dough* (see DOUGH). Fill the mould with quarters of pears, half-cooked in vanilla-flavoured syrup, putting them in rows alternating with stewed apricots.

Cover with a piece of rolled-out brioche dough, sealing the edges. Make a small hole in the middle to allow steam to escape. Bake in a hot oven for about 45 minutes. Turn out on to a serving dish and pour over kirsch-flavoured *Apricot sauce* (see SAUCE).

PEARL. PERLE – Pearl-like. Hulled and polished barley is called pearl barley (see BARLEY).

A degree of the boiling of sugar is also called pearl degree (see SUGAR).

PEC – French word used only in the expression *hareng pec*, i.e. freshly salted herring, barrelled without being smoked.

PECCARY. PÉCARI – Species of South American wild pig. Its flesh is much prized but sometimes has a musky flavour. Peccary is prepared like young wild boar (q.v.).

PECTEN. PEIGNE – Genus of bivalve molluscs of the family *Pectinidae* with rounded shells, divided into grooves radiating from the middle of the hinge, the most important species being the scallop.

In many respects scallops can be compared to oysters, but, while oysters are stationary, stuck to the rocks, scallops are mobile, rising and whirling on the surface of the water.

Pilgrims to the shrine of Saint James at Santiago de Compostela always wore the 'palmer's cockle' (*Pecten jacobaeus*) on their shoulder, having gathered them on the seashore. Thus this mollusc first acquired in French the name of *peigne Saint-Jacques* and later became merely Saint-Jacques. (See SCALLOP, *Scallop Saint-Jacques.*)

PECTIN. PECTINE – Mucilaginous substance occurring as a constituent in certain fruits (quince, apples, oranges, lemons,

Pediments for cold dishes, after Carême

etc.) and vegetables (split peas, lentils, etc.) which causes their pulp, when boiled with sugar in the presence of sufficient acid, to set as a jelly. The skin and pips of these fruits contain a great deal of pectin and should, therefore, be used in the preparation of jellies.

PEDIMENTS. SOCLES – Ornamental pediments once played a great part in the serving of cold dishes, important sweet dishes, etc.

In modern practice their use has been abandoned.

PEEL. ÉCALURE – Name given to the outer skin, whether hard or soft, of some fruit and vegetables.

PEELING. ÉPLUCHAGE – The action of removing the skin of fruit or vegetables. Not all vegetables are peeled. Strip green vegetables, such as sorrel, spinach and watercress, discarding all faded leaves. Other vegetables such as peas are shelled.

The process of preparing French beans and runner beans for the pot is known as stringing. When they are young they are simply topped and tailed.

PÉGOT – Sticky coating which covers Roquefort cheese.

PELAMIS (BONITO). PÉLAMIDE – *Katsuwonus pelamis*, a species of fish related to the tunny. If differs from the latter by its more elongated body, a longer and more pointed muzzle and a big jaw.

The prototype of the species of the common pelamis is the *Sardinian pelamis* or *red-backed bonito*. This fish, which reaches a length of 68 cm. (27 inches), is silvery with light blue tints on the back. It is found in the Mediterranean and in the Atlantic and can be prepared in any way suitable for tunny (q.v.).

PÉLARDON DE RUOMS – See CHEESE.

PELICAN – Large web-footed water fowl, with a large naked pouch or gular sac, which hangs from the long bill, serving as a temporary storage place for fish. They live mainly in freshwater lakes and lagoons, but there are a few marine species, like the Chilean and the Brown pelicans.

Their flesh is oily and tough but is, nevertheless, eaten in some countries.

PEL'MENI (Russian cookery). PELLMÈNES SIBÉRIENS – A kind of ravioli with a filling of beef, or a mixture of beef and pork. The *pel'meni* are generally served in soup or they can be served boiled with a dollop of sour cream. The Siberians like a mustard and vinegar dressing with the dish.

PELURES – French culinary term for usable parings, such as truffle or mushroom parings.

PEMMICAN – North American Indian cake of dried and pounded meat mixed with melted fat, a food product famous since the early expeditions to North America, It is no longer in demand.

Pemmican could be kept for a long time, did not deteriorate, and took up little space.

It was first made from the meat of bison (wild ox, now almost completely extinct), or from venison. The rump of the animal was cut into thin slices, dried in the sun and pounded finely. This meat powder was then mixed with melted fat in the proportion of two parts meat to one part fat, and enclosed in bags made from the animal's skin. It was eaten raw, or boiled in water.

Two pounds of pemmican were enough for the daily ration of a working man.

PÉNIDE – French term for sugar cooked with a decoction of barley, then poured on an oiled marble slab and twisted, like a cord, with oiled hands. This manipulation renders the sugar opaque, unlike barley sugar, which is left transparent.

PENNYROYAL. POULIOT – A kind of wild mint with a strong, pungent flavour, sometimes used as a condiment in cookery.

PEPPER. POIVRE – Fruit of the pepper plant, a genus of vine-like shrubs, a native of the Indian Archipelago. It is extensively cultivated throughout the whole of tropical Asia and equatorial America.

Pepper was one of the first spices to be introduced into Europe. It was used by Hippocrates in his prescriptions.

There are two kinds of pepper in commerce: black pepper, with a greenish-black wrinkled surface, and white pepper, which is the same seed freed from the skin and the fleshy part of the fruit. It is less pungent and less aromatic than black pepper. The berries are picked before they are ripe.

Ground pepper rapidly loses its flavour and aroma; it is therefore advisable always to grind it as and when required. A pepper mill is used for this purpose. With this one avoids possible substitutes and adulterations.

Pepper is a much-used condiment, entering into almost all culinary preparations. It is a strong stimulant, and its over-use should be avoided.

Red pepper or pimento. PIMENT – *Capsicum frutescens* has many varieties and is a native of America. It is now cultivated in most warm parts of the world. Dried and ground it becomes, according to the variety, cayenne pepper, chilli powder, paprika and red pepper.

All these peppers are used mainly as condiments.

Red pepper (pimento) paste (Créole cookery). PÂTE DE

Branch of pepper shrub

PIMENTS – This can be bought in delicatessen shops ready for use, but it can also be made at home.

Seed and pound long, strong red peppers with a little onion, ginger and salt in a mortar. Put this thick paste into a jar and cover it with best oil. Close with a well-fitting lid. Leave to macerate. This paste will keep indefinitely, as long as there is a protective layer of oil on top.

Sweet peppers. PIMENTS DOUX – The big sweet peppers or pimentos, which are cultivated in Spain, Italy, the South of France and in the United States, are used in cookery and are served, red or green, as *hors-d'œuvre*, as a vegetable and as a salad.

Sweet peppers fried in batter. PIMENTS DOUX EN FRITOT – Choose small-sized peppers, put them under a grill for a few moments to loosen the skin, peel and remove seeds. Stuff them with a *salpicon* (q.v.) of onions and mushrooms, softened in butter and bound with a little *Tomato sauce* (see SAUCE), mixed with some chopped garlic and parsley. Leave to macerate for 1 hour in oil, lemon juice, salt and pepper.

A few minutes before serving, dip the peppers one by one in a light batter (see BATTER) and fry in smoking hot deep fat, drain on a cloth, season with fine dry salt and arrange in a heap on a dish. Garnish with fried parsley. Serve with tomato sauce.

Sweet peppers au gratin. PIMENTS DOUX GRATINÉS – Seed and peel the peppers, and cook in butter. Line the bottom of an ovenproof dish with *Mornay sauce* (see SAUCE), mixed with a good tablespoon of chopped onion softened in butter. Put in the peppers, cover with *Mornay sauce*, sprinkle with grated cheese and melted butter and brown in a slow oven.

Sweet peppers or pimentos with black olives (Créole cookery). PIMENTS, PIMENTOS DOUX AUX OLIVES NOIRES – Put 4 big green peppers under a grill to make peeling easier. Remove seeds, shred the pimentos into fine *julienne* (q.v.) strips and season with a few tablespoons of *Vinaigrette sauce* (see SAUCE).

Arrange this *julienne* as a border in an *hors-d'œuvre* dish and fill the middle with small black olives, marinated in oil.

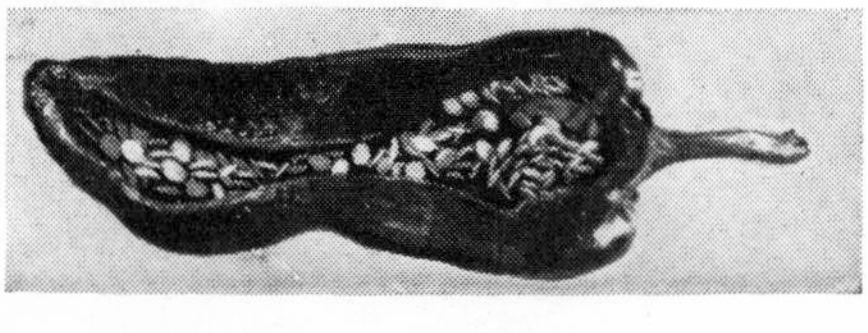

Section of pepper

Sweet peppers à l'orientale. PIMENTS DOUX À L'ORIENTALE – Peel and seed the peppers, and cut into large dice. Put into a casserole and for 500 g. (18 oz.) peppers add 100 g. (4 oz., 1 cup) chopped onion which has been softened in oil without allowing it to colour. Add a pinch of garlic. Moisten with $1\frac{1}{2}$ dl. ($\frac{1}{4}$ pint, $\frac{2}{3}$ cup) stock and simmer gently for 35 minutes.

Sweet peppers à la petite russienne (Russian cookery). PIMENTS DOUX À LA PETITE RUSSIENNE – Cut 24 green sweet peppers open at the stalk end and remove the seeds. Parboil slightly and stuff with a forcemeat prepared in the following manner:

Chop coarsely 2 handfuls of sorrel leaves, 4 peeled and seeded tomatoes, 3 sweet Spanish onions, 3 green peppers and 1 stalk of fennel. Put these into a saucepan in which a little olive oil has been heated. At the first sign of boiling drain in a sieve to remove excess liquid. Fill the peppers with this forcemeat mixed with a little rice, parboiled in salted water and drained.

Put the peppers into an oiled sauté pan, packing them in fairly tightly. Moisten with tomato purée, which should not be too thick. Add the juice of 2 lemons and 2 dl. ($\frac{1}{3}$ pint, scant cup) olive oil. Cook for 25 minutes. Transfer to a deep dish and leave until cold.

These peppers are served as *hors-d'œuvre*, which in Russia are called *zakuski*.

Sweet peppers à la piémontaise. PIMENTS DOUX À LA PIÉMONTAISE – Seed and peel the peppers, and cook in stock for 15 minutes. Butter an ovenproof dish and put in the peppers in rows, with alternating rows of cheese risotto (see RICE, *Risotto à la piémontaise*). Finish with a layer of peppers. Sprinkle with grated Parmesan cheese and melted butter and brown gently in the oven.

Sweet pepper purée – See PURÉE.

Ragoût of sweet peppers à l'espagnole. RAGOÛT DE PIMENTS DOUX À L'ESPAGNOLE – Seed and peel 6 peppers, cut into quarters and put into a sauté pan in which 100 g. (4 oz., 1 cup) finely sliced onion has been softened in oil. Season with salt and red pepper. Add 1 clove of pounded garlic, sprinkle in 1 tablespoon flour and moisten with 3 dl. ($\frac{1}{2}$ pint, $1\frac{1}{4}$ cups) stock and 2 tablespoons (3 tablespoons) tomato purée. Simmer gently for 35 minutes. Serve in a vegetable dish or *timbale*. Sprinkle with chopped parsley.

Sweet pepper salad à la créole. SALADE DE PIMENTS DOUX À LA CRÉOLE – Mixture of sweet peppers and boiled rice, seasoned with oil, vinegar, salt and paprika. (See SALAD, *Sweet pimento salad à la créole*.)

Stuffed sweet peppers à la turque (*Scarnati*)

Sweet peppers à la turque. PIMENTS DOUX FARCIS À LA TURQUE – Peel the peppers, open them at the stalk end and

Silver perch

River perch

remove seeds. Parboil for 5 minutes and stuff with a forcemeat composed of two-thirds cooked, chopped mutton and one-third rice, boiled in stock, seasoned with salt and pepper, flavoured with a little garlic and bound with 4 tablespoons ($\frac{1}{3}$ cup) tomato purée.

Put the peppers into a sauté pan on a foundation of chopped onions lightly fried in oil. Moisten with a few tablespoons light *Tomato sauce* (see SAUCE). Bring to the boil on the stove, then cook in the oven with a lid on from 30 to 35 minutes. Serve in a *timbale* with the pan juices poured over.

Sweet peppers à la vinaigrette. PIMENTS DOUX À LA VINAIGRETTE – Choose small-sized peppers and cut them into quarters or slices. Arrange in an *hors-d'œuvre* dish. Season with oil, vinegar, salt and pepper. Sprinkle with chopped parsley and chervil.

Sweet peppers prepared as an *hors-d'œuvre* may be garnished with finely sliced young onions, tomatoes cut in small pieces, chopped hard-boiled eggs and other ingredients normally used as *hors-d'œuvre* garnish.

PERCH. PERCHE – Genus of freshwater fish.

The common or river perch is considered in France one of the best freshwater fishes. It can be recognised by its closely spaced dorsal fins, with hard spines in the first, its scalloped scales sticking closely to the skin, and its bright colours, greenish above, golden yellow below, with 6 transverse brown bars. River perch reach a length of 35 cm. (14 inches) and attain a weight of almost 2 kg. (4 pounds). Its flesh is delicate and easily digestible.

The young of the species, called *perchettes*, are generally fried in deep fat; the medium-sized perch are prepared *à la meunière* and the large can be stuffed and prepared like shad (q.v.).

Perdrix (partridge)

grey (*Rödle*)

red (*Scaïoni*)

The name of perch is also given to other species of spiny-finned freshwater fish, such as *silver perch, black bass, perch-trout*, etc.

The silver perch, which originated in North America is now quite common in French rivers and is also found in lakes.

Black bass, also of North American origin, has been acclimatised in French waters for some years past. Its flesh is white, delicate and has few bones. In flavour it resembles river trout a little and can be prepared in any way suitable for this fish (see TROUT).

The American perch-trout, also now acclimatised in French waters, is prepared like river trout.

'Bass' is derived from '*barse*', an old English name for the perch.

PERCOLATOR. PERCOLATEUR – Big coffee pot with a filter used for making black coffee in big quantities (see COFFEE).

PERDRIX – Term for old partridges.

These can be used only for preparing game forcemeats and purées. When they are not too tough, they can also be used for galantines, *terrines*, *pâtés*, game stocks and *fumets*.

If they are not too old and their flesh is not too dry, they can also be stewed with cabbage or used for *Chartreuse of partridge* (see PARTRIDGE). Tender old partridges can be prepared in any way suitable for young partridge.

PÉRIGOURDINE (À LA) – All dishes prepared *à la périgourdine* include a garnish of truffles, to which *foie gras* (q.v.) is sometimes added.

PERIWINKLE. BIGORNEAU – See WINKLE.

PERLOT – Name used in Manche for a small oyster.

PERRY. POIRÉ – Fermented beverage, made in the same way as cider, using pear juice.

The most famous perry is made in Normandy, from *Coq* pears.

PERSICO, PERSICOT – Liqueur made from brandy, almonds, peach stones, sugar and spices.

PERSILLADE – Term for chopped parsley, often mixed with varying quantities of chopped garlic, added to certain dishes at the end of cooking. The term also applies to left-over meat, fried in butter, cooking fat or oil and sprinkled with *persillade*. Thus we have the household expression *persillade de boeuf*, which means sauteed beef with chopped parsley.

PERSILLÉ – French term used to describe beef that is flecked with fat. Such *persillage* is only present in top-quality beef.

Persillé is also used to describe certain greenish-veined cheeses.

PERSILLER – Term which means to sprinkle a dish with chopped parsley.

PERSIMMON. KAKI – Fruit of a tree of Japanese origin. It has been cultivated for centuries in Japan and China, and is cultivated commercially in France, Italy, Spain and other Mediterranean countries and, in the U.S.A., in the South and in California. It is rather like a tomato in appearance. As it ripens, it turns from yellow to red. It is a soft, sweet fruit, quite pleasant in taste.

Iced persimmon à la créole. KAKIS GLACÉS À LA CRÉOLE – Cut a hole in the fruit round the stalk. Scoop out the pulp without breaking the skin. Sprinkle kirsch or some other liqueur inside the scooped-out fruit. Leave to steep for 1 hour in a cool place.

Rub the pulp through a fine sieve, add to *Pineapple ice* (see ICE CREAMS AND ICES) and fill the scooped-out fruit with the mixture.

Persimmon à l'impératrice. KAKIS À L'IMPÉRATRICE – Steep the scooped-out fruit in liqueur, as in the previous recipe. Dice the pulp finely and mix it with *Rice à l'impératrice* (see RICE). Fill with this mixture.

Persimmon jam. CONFITURE DE KAKIS – Made from very ripe fruit in the same way as *Apricot jam* (see JAMS AND JELLIES).

Persimmon with kirsch. KAKIS AU KIRSCH – Taking ripe persimmons, cut a hole in each. Sprinkle with sugar and pour kirsch into them. Serve on a bed of ice shavings.

Stewed persimmon. COMPOTE DE KAKIS – Made from very ripe fruit, in the same way as stewed apricots (q.v.).

PESTLE. PILON – Wood, metal or porcelain instrument used for pounding in a mortar.

PETERAM – Sheep's tripe as prepared in Luchon.

PETITE MARMITE – The *petite marmite* is one of the best specialities of Paris restaurants. This method of serving consommé in the earthenware receptacle in which it was cooked was invented in Paris some 80 years ago, and the vogue for *petite marmite* soup spread to the restaurants of the old world and the new.

The *petite marmite* contains all the ingredients which go to make up this dish, i.e. lean pieces of meat, oxtail, poultry, marrow bones and stock-pot vegetables, with the addition of little cabbage balls. The soup is usually served with small pieces of toast spread with bone marrow, rusks sprinkled with stockpot fat and dried in the oven, or thin slices of French bread dried in th the oven and sprinkled with grated cheese.

For the method of preparation of the *petite marmite*, see SOUPS AND BROTHS, *Clear soups*.

PETIT MAURE – See RESTAURANTS OF BYGONE DAYS.

PETITS FOURS (Pâtisserie) – Name adopted for many kinds of small fancy cakes and biscuits.

The name, according to Carême, comes from the fact that they are usually baked in a slow oven, after the big cakes have come out and the temperature of the oven has gone down.

There are two kinds of *petits fours*. The first includes all the little fancy biscuits (cookies), *tuiles*, *palets de dames*, macaroons, shortbreads, etc. The second covers the iced *petits fours*, usually small Genoese cake fancies dipped into Fondant icing.

There are other *petits fours* which belong more in the realm of confectionery than pastry-making, such as candied fruit sold in the shops in France under the name of *fruits déguisés*, as well as marzipan fruits, moulded in different shapes and coloured.

PETITS-PIEDS – French menu term used to describe all the small birds, such as blackbirds, thrushes, ortolans, larks, etc.

PETITS POIS – Term for fresh garden peas.

PETS-DE-NONNE – See FRITTERS, *Soufflé fritters*.

PFANNKUCHEN (Austrian cookery). FAN-KOUKE – Roll out *Brioche dough* (see DOUGH) $\frac{1}{2}$ cm. ($\frac{1}{4}$ inch) thick. Cut rounds with a pastry cutter, about 6 to 8 cm. ($2\frac{1}{2}$ to 2 inches) in diameter. In the middle of these put 1 tablespoon rather thick apricot purée. Moisten the edges with water, cover with rounds of the same size, and press the edges firmly together.

Put the *pfannkuchen* on a floured cloth and leave in a warm place to rise. Fry them, drain, and immerse in hot rum syrup.

PFLAUMENKUCHEN (German cookery) – Plum tart made in the German way. (See TART, *Fruit tart à l'allemande*.)

PHEASANT. FAISAN – *Phasianus* is the Latin name of this succulent bird, which the ancients called the bird of Phasis, the river of Colchide which separated Europe from Aisa. This bird of Phasis, originally a native of the Caspian region, has multiplied in game preserves in Europe, without losing anything of its distinctive flavour, which is essentially that of a wild bird.

Brillat-Savarin, who prized it very highly, tells us in his *Variétés* that 'the pheasant is an enigma to which only experts have the key, and they alone can savour it in all its excellence.

Petits fours (*Claire*)

Iced petits fours (*Larousse*)

Cock (left) and hen (right) pheasant
(*J. Boyer*)

'Eaten at precisely the right moment, its flesh is tender, sublime and highly flavoured, for it has at once something of the flavour of poultry and of venison.

'This ideal moment is when the pheasant begins to decompose. Then its aroma develops in an oily essence which requires a little fermentation to reach perfection, like the aroma of coffee which manifests itself only through roasting.'

Experiment has proved that birds preserved in their feathers have much more aroma than those left stripped for a long time, either because exposure to the air robs them of some of their aroma, or because (in the case of unplucked birds) some of the oil in the feathers is absorbed into the flesh and gives it added flavour.

The common pheasant is now found all over Europe, as far away as Siberia. Various breeds have sprung from the original Phasis species. Among them the following provide the best eating: the *common pheasant*, the *golden pheasant* and the *silver pheasant*. The common pheasant, almost alone, is used for the table. The other breeds are rather for ornament.

True connoisseurs of this savoury bird prefer the hen pheasant to the cock. The distinctive features of the cock pheasant are the shape of its tail, which is longer than its whole body, and its neck feathers, which are iridescent and shot with blue and green. The hen has a short tail, and its plumage is much less brilliant in colouring than that of the cock.

A yearling pheasant can be distinguished from an old bird by the first wing-tip feather, which is pointed in a young bird and rounded in an old one. When the upper part of the pheasant's beak is pliable to the touch, one can be certain that it is a yearling bird.

HOT PHEASANT DISHES. FAISANS CHAUDS –

Pheasant à l'alsacienne. FAISAN À L'ALSACIENNE – Name given to pheasant with *sauerkraut*, prepared as indicated in the recipe below.

Pheasant à l'américaine. FAISAN À L'AMÉRICAINE – Slit a pheasant along the back. Open and flatten gently. Season with salt and pepper. Sauté quickly in butter on both sides. Coat both sides with freshly made breadcrumbs seasoned with a touch of cayenne pepper. Grill the pheasant slowly. Cover with slices of grilled bacon and garnish with grilled tomatoes and mushrooms, bunches of watercress and potato crisps. Serve with *Maître d'hôtel butter* (see BUTTER, *Compound butters*).

Pheasant à la bohémienne. FAISAN À LA BOHÉMIENNE – Slit along the front. Draw the pheasant and remove the breastbone. Stuff with a small cold *foie gras* (q.v.) studded with truffles, seasoned with salt and paprika and cooked for 15 minutes in Madeira.

Truss the bird, with the legs pressed tightly against the breast. Cook in a casserole in butter for about 45 minutes. Just before serving, pour 2 tablespoons (3 tablespoons) blazing brandy over the pheasant, and a few tablespoons of game essence. Serve in the cooking dish.

Pheasant with cabbage. FAISAN AUX CHOUX – Proceed as for *Partridge with cabbage* (see PARTRIDGE).

Casserole of pheasant. FAISAN EN CASSEROLE, EN COCOTTE – Truss the pheasant with the legs pressed tightly against the breast. Cook in butter in an earthenware casserole. When it is cooked, pour a little brandy and 2 to 3 tablespoons (3 tablespoons to scant $\frac{1}{4}$ cup) game stock over it.

Casserole of pheasant with mushrooms. FAISAN EN CASSEROLE AUX CHAMPIGNONS – Prepare th the pheasant as for *Casserole of pheasant*. When it is half-cooked, add 12 mushrooms without the stalks. Finish cooking all together. Finish as for *Casserole of pheasant*.

Pheasant en chartreuse. FAISAN EN CHARTREUSE – Brown a pheasant in the oven and proceed as indicated for *Chartreuse of partridge* (see PARTRIDGE).

Pheasant en cocotte. FAISAN EN COCOTTE – Another name for *Casserole of pheasant*, for which the recipe is given above. In former times this dish was garnished with large mushrooms and potatoes trimmed into small pear shapes, cooked with the pheasant.

With or without this garnish, proceed as for *Casserole of pheasant*.

The term *en cocotte* indicates the method of pot-roasting in a fireproof earthenware dish (*cocotte*). *Pheasant en cocotte* can be served with various garnishes but in this case it is desirable to indicate the garnish by the name of the dish (see GARNISHES).

Pheasant en cocotte with cream. FAISAN EN COCOTTE À LA CRÈME – Truss the pheasant with the legs pressed against the breast. Cook in butter until three-parts cooked. Pour on $2\frac{1}{2}$ dl. (scant $\frac{1}{2}$ pint, generous cup) fresh cream. Finish cooking, basting the pheasant frequently with the cream. Just before serving, add a squeeze of lemon juice.

Soured cream may be used for this dish.

Pheasant croquettes. CROQUETTES DE FAISAN – Proceed as for *Chicken croquettes* (see CHICKEN), using a *salpicon* (q.v.) of pheasant, truffles and mushrooms blended in white or brown sauce (see SAUCE).

Pheasant cutlets. CÔTELETTES DE FAISAN – These are made with the breast of the bird, cut off before cooking, as for *Chicken côtelettes* (see CHICKEN). All recipes and garnishes for these are suitable for pheasant cutlets.

Small cuts are often called *suprêmes*.

Pheasant à la géorgienne (Russian cookery). FAISAN À LA GÉORGIENNE – Truss the pheasant *en entrée*, with the legs pressed against the breast. Bard it.

Put it in a casserole with 30 shelled and skinned walnuts.

Moisten with the juice of 3 oranges and 750 g. ($1\frac{3}{4}$ lb.) grapes squeezed and strained, 1 glass of malmsey and the same amount of a very strong infusion of green tea. Add 3 tablespoons (scant $\frac{1}{4}$ cup) butter. Season with salt and pepper. Cover the pheasant and cook in this mixture for about 45 minutes. Drain. Untruss and remove barding. Brown it, and put it on a dish surrounded with fresh walnuts. Pour on the cooking stock, boiled down with a few tablespoons of brown stock added or game essence, and strained.

Grilled pheasant. FAISAN GRILLÉ – This method is generally used for very young pheasant. Slit the bird along the back. Open and flatten gently. Season with salt and pepper. Coat with butter, and dip in breadcrumbs; grill slowly, as for *Grilled chicken diable* (see CHICKEN).

Grilled pheasant is served with devilled sauce (see SAUCE, *Diable sauce* or *Périgueux sauce*).

Pheasant à la languedocienne. FAISAN À LA LANGUEDOCIENNE – Joint a pheasant. Season with salt and pepper. Make a *mirepoix* (q.v.) of carrots, onions, celery and lean raw ham seasoned with salt, pepper, powdered thyme and bay leaf. Cook slowly until very tender. Put the pheasant in the pan with this *mirepoix*. Brown and sprinkle with 2 tablespoons (3 tablespoons) flour. Cook the flour until it is golden in colour. Moisten with 3 dl. ($\frac{1}{2}$ pint, $1\frac{1}{4}$ cups) red wine and mix well. Add a few tablespoons clear stock and a small *bouquet garni* (q.v.). Cover, and cook for 35 minutes.

Drain the pheasant. Put it in an ovenware dish with 8 small mushrooms and 12 thick strips of truffle. Pour on 2 tablespoons (3 tablespoons) brandy. Moisten with the strained sauce and add butter. Put the lid on the dish, seal the edges with flour-and-water paste. Stand in water and cook in the oven for 35 minutes. Serve in the baking dish.

Pheasant à la normande. FAISAN À LA NORMANDE – Brown the pheasant in butter and put it in an ovenware dish or casserole lined with a layer of peeled, sliced sweet apples lightly browned in butter. Surround the pheasant with apples prepared in the same way. Cook in a slow oven. Just before serving, pour fresh cream and a little Calvados over it.

Pheasant à la périgueux. FAISAN À LA PÉRIGUEUX – Truffled pheasant, pot-roasted instead of roasted. It is served on a slice of bread fried in butter and surrounded by large forcemeat balls made from *Game forcemeat* with truffles (see FORCEMEATS or STUFFINGS). Serve with *Périgueux sauce* (see SAUCE) with the cooking stock added to it.

Hot pheasant pie – See PIE, *Game pies*.

Pheasant pie with truffles. TOURTE DE FAISAN AUX TRUFFES – Proceed, using pheasant, as indicated for *Woodcock pie with truffles* (see WOODCOCK).

Pheasant purée. PURÉE DE FAISAN – Purée made from pot-roasted pheasant or pheasant scraps. It is used for filling small *vol-au-vent*, *barquettes*, or tartlets. Proceed as indicated for *Purée of woodcock* (see WOODCOCK).

Roast pheasant. FAISAN RÔTI – Truss and bard the breast with a large slice of pork fat. Tie the fat with string. Baste the pheasant with melted butter. Season. Roast in a hot oven for about 30 minutes. If the pheasant is roasted on the spit, allow a few minutes longer for cooking.

Untruss the pheasant and put it on a slice of fried bread, spread with *à gratin game forcemeat* (see FORCEMEATS) if desired. (The stuffing should be made with the chopped liver of the pheasant.) Garnish with watercress and lemon. Serve the cooking stock, diluted, with it.

Pheasant à la Sainte-Alliance. FAISAN À LA SAINT-ALLIANCE – 'Take a pheasant, hung until it is perfect to eat. Pluck it and interlard it carefully with the freshest and firmest pork fat you can find.

'Take 2 woodcocks. Bone and draw them and make 2 piles, one of the meat, the other of the entrails and livers.

'With the meat, make a stuffing by chopping it with steamed beef bone-marrow, a little grated pork fat, pepper, salt, *fines herbes* (q.v.), and a quantity of good truffles enough to stuff the pheasant completely.

'Take care to put in the stuffing in such a way that none falls out. This is sometimes difficult when the bird is rather old. There are various ways of achieving this end. One is to cut a slice of bread and tie it to the bird with string, so as to seal its breast.

'Cut a slice of bread which overlaps the laid-out pheasant from neck to tail by 5 cm. (2 inches). Next take the liver and entrails of the woodcock. Pound in a mortar with 2 large truffles, 1 anchovy, a little grated pork fat and a piece of good fresh butter.

'Toast the bread and spread this paste evenly on it. Put it under the pheasant, prepared as indicated above, so that the bread will be thoroughly impregnated with the roasting juice. When the pheasant is cooked, serve it, elegantly couched, on the slice of bread. Surround with Seville oranges.' (Brillat-Savarin, *Physiologie du goût*.)

Salmis of pheasant. SALMIS DE FAISAN – Roast the pheasant in the oven or on the spit until it is three-quarters cooked. Joint it. Trim the pieces and skin them. Put them in a buttered pan. Cover with 150 g. (5 oz., $1\frac{1}{2}$ cups) mushrooms tossed in butter (whole if they are small, sliced if they are large) and 150 g. (5 oz., $1\frac{1}{2}$ cups) shredded truffles. Pour on 4 tablespoons ($\frac{1}{3}$ cup) *Espagnole sauce*, based on concentrated game stock (see SAUCE). Keep hot, but do not boil.

Chop the carcase and the trimmings. Brown them slightly in a pan in which 4 tablespoons ($\frac{1}{3}$ cup) *mirepoix* (q.v.) has been cooked. Moisten with the cooking stock of the pheasant, diluted with 2 dl. ($\frac{1}{3}$ pint, scant cup) white wine. Boil down. Moisten with $1\frac{1}{2}$ dl. ($\frac{1}{4}$ pint, $\frac{2}{3}$ cup) *Espagnole sauce* (see SAUCE) based on concentrated game stock. Cook for 15 minutes. Strain the sauce through a fine strainer, pressing with the back of a spoon so as to extract all the juice from the meat and vegetables. Strain this sauce once more through muslin. Boil down. Add 2 tablespoons (3 tablespoons) blazing brandy and 4 tablespoons ($\frac{1}{3}$ cup) butter. Mix and pour over the pheasant. Heat, but do not boil.

Drain the pheasant and arrange the joints in a pyramid on a slice of bread fried in butter, spread with *À gratin game forcemeat* (see FORCEMEATS) and brown in the oven. Put the mushrooms and truffles on top. Pour the sauce, piping hot, over the dish.

Instead of serving the *salmis* on a slice of bread it may be put in a deep dish or a shallow bowl. Pour the sauce over it and garnish with slices of fried bread cut into heart shapes and spread with *à gratin game forcemeat*.

Salmis of pheasant in red wine. SALMIS DE FAISAN AU VIN ROUGE. Proceed as indicated above, moistening with red instead of white wine.

Sautéed pheasant. FAISAN SAUTÉ, SAUTÉ DE FAISAN – Pheasant is seldom prepared in this way. A tender young pheasant can, however, be sautéed.

Joint the bird, season with salt and pepper, and sauté slowly in butter, taking care not to dry it.

Pour over it the cooking stock diluted with white wine or any other wine, according to the recipe, flavoured with a little concentrated game or veal stock, with butter added.

Pheasant à la Souvarov. FAISAN À LA SOUVAROV – Stuff the pheasant with a coarse *salpicon* (q.v.) of *foie gras* and truffles seasoned with salt, pepper and spice, and with brandy poured over it.

Truss the bird with the legs pressed against the breast. Bard it and cook in butter until three-quarters cooked. Untruss and untie the barding. Put it in an earthenware dish with 12 medium-sized truffles, tossed in butter. Moisten with the cooking stock diluted with Madeira. Add 2 dl. ($\frac{1}{3}$ pint, scant cup) *Demi-glace sauce* based on concentrated game stock with a little brandy (see SAUCE).

Cover the dish and seal with flour-and-water paste. Finish cooking in the oven for 15 to 18 minutes.

Suprêmes of pheasant. SUPRÊMES DE FAISAN – Cut off the the wings and breasts of the pheasant before cooking (these are the *suprêmes*). Poach them or sauté them in butter, and serve with various sauces and garnishes.

All recipes for *suprêmes* of chicken (see CHICKEN) are suitable for *suprêmes* of pheasant.

Truffled pheasant. FAISAN TRUFFÉ – Pheasant is truffled in the same way as young turkey (see TURKEY).

For a medium-sized truffled pheasant use 350 g. (12 oz.) fresh pork suet and 250 g. (9 oz.) truffles. Cook for 50 to 55 minutes in a medium oven, or for 55 minutes to an hour on the spit.

The bird must be truffled at least 24 hours before cooking.

COLD PHEASANT DISHES. FAISANS FROIDS.

Pheasant aspic à l'ancienne. ASPIC DE FAISAN À L'ANCIENNE – Truss a pheasant with the legs pressed against the breast. Pot-roast in butter, keeping the meat slightly pinkish in colour. Cut off the breasts. Separate the *mignon* fillets (underpart of breast meat) from the *suprêmes*. Cut each *suprême* in 3 thin *aiguillettes* (q.v.).

Spread one side of these *aiguillettes* thickly with pheasant purée made from the legs and some *foie gras* (q.v.), blended with a little concentrated game stock, flavoured with a little liqueur brandy, with $\frac{1}{3}$ its weight of whipped cream added. Dome the purée slightly on top of the *aiguillettes* of pheasant. Cover them with *White chaud-froid sauce* based on game stock (see SAUCE).

Put a strip of truffle dipped in jelly on top of each. Glaze with game jelly (see JELLY, *Game jelly stock*). Line an aspic

Chaud-froid of pheasant
(French Government Tourist Office)

mould with jelly and put in the *aiguillettes*. Decorate with slices cut from the *mignon* fillets and with strips of truffle.

Fill the mould with clear game jelly. Leave to set in a refrigerator or cooler. Turn out the aspic straight on to a dish or on to a slice of bread cut to the size of the mould and buttered.

Surround the aspic with chopped jelly and a border of rounds of jelly shaped with a pastry-cutter.

Ballottine of pheasant in jelly (Carême's recipe). BALLOTTINE DE FAISAN À LA GELÉE – 'Take a Strasbourg *foie gras*. Soak in cold water and blanch. Cut each half into 4 fillets and trim.

'Pound 2 of these fillets in a mortar with the trimmings and the meat of a red partridge with an equal weight of pork fat. Season the mixture very well. Add 2 egg yolks and *fines herbes* tossed in butter. Pound the lot thoroughly.' (By '*fines herbes*', Carême means cultivated mushrooms.)

'Rub the stuffing through a quenelle sieve. Carefully bone a well-hung, fat pheasant. Lay it on a cloth and season very well. Lay on top of it half the the stuffing, and then 3 fillets of *foie gras*, interspersing these with halved truffles. Add as much *Spiced salt* (see SALT) as required. Cover the whole with half the remaining stuffing.

'Lay on top the rest of the *foie gras* and the halves of truffle. Season and cover with the rest of the stuffing. Fold the pheasant into shape. Wrap in a cloth. Tie and cook in jelly stock flavoured with Madeira, to which have been added the bones and trimmings of the pheasant and partridge.

'Leave the ballottine to cool under a light weight. Glaze with jelly in the usual way.'

Chaud-froid of pheasant. FAISAN EN CHAUD-FROID – Truss a pheasant with the legs pressed against the breast. Cook in butter, taking care that the meat remains pinkish. Joint the bird, skin the pieces and trim them.

Coat with *Chaud-froid sauce, brown* (see SAUCE) prepared in the usual way, with game stock flavoured with essence of truffles. Decorate the pieces of pheasant with truffles cut into fancy shapes, the whites of hard-boiled eggs and other decorative motifs, dipped into half-set jelly (see JELLY, *Game jelly stock*) before they are put on the bird. Glaze the joints with jelly. Chill in a refrigerator.

Line a dish with buttered sandwich bread. Arrange the pheasant on it, with the legs on the platform of bread and the breast and wings on top. Surround with chopped jelly (use a spoon for this; if the jelly is piped it may be discoloured). Make a border of rounds of jelly, cut out with a pastry cutter. As with all *chauds-froids* of poultry or winged game the pheasant *en chaud-froid* can be served in a glass bowl or deep silver dish, and coated with clear jelly.

Daube of pheasant in jelly. FAISAN EN DAUBE À LA GELÉE – Slit a pheasant along the back and bone it. Season inside and stuff with a forcemeat made of lean veal, *À gratin game forcemeat* (see FORCEMEATS) and *foie gras* with 3 tablespoons (scant $\frac{1}{4}$ cup) game essence and 2 tablespoons (3 tablespoons) brandy added. Season well and bind with 1 or 2 egg yolks. Spread the stuffing evenly on the pheasant and put in the middle half a raw *foie gras* studded with 4 large raw quarters of truffle. Season with spiced salt and pour on a little brandy. Fold the pheasant into shape. Truss with the legs pressed against the breast. Bard with a thin slice of pork fat and pot-roast in Madeira for 45 minutes to 1 hour.

Drain the pheasant. Untruss and remove the pork fat. Put it in an earthenware dish. Moisten with the cooking stock with 5 dl. (scant pint, $2\frac{1}{4}$ cups) jelly added (game jelly for preference).

Leave to cool thoroughly for at least 12 hours. Before serving skim off the film of fat on the surface of the jelly.

Galantine of pheasant in jelly. GALANTINE DE FAISAN À LA GELÉE – Proceed as for *Ballottine of pheasant in jelly*.

Pheasant pâté (*Debillot. Phot. Larousse*)

Pheasant loaf à l'ancienne – See LOAVES, *Winged game loaf*.

Pheasant pâté. PÂTÉ DE FAISAN – Bone a large pheasant. Cut the wings and breasts into thin slices, and steep in brandy. With the rest of the meat prepare a stuffing, flavour with a little brandy and bind with an egg. Line an oval *pâté* mould with a hinged lid with *Fine lining paste* (see DOUGH), and cover with thin slices of pork fat.

Put a layer of stuffing at the bottom of the mould. On this arrange slices of breast alternating with thin slices of *foie gras* and quartered truffles. Cover these with a layer of stuffing and continue to fill the mould in this way to within $\frac{1}{2}$ cm. ($\frac{1}{4}$ inch) of the rim, ending with a layer of stuffing. On top of this last layer, put $\frac{1}{2}$ bay leaf. Fold the overlapping ends of the pork fat inward. Cover the *pâté* with an oval layer of rolled-out pastry and press down at the edges. Pink the edges with pastry pincers to form a coxcomb design. Make a hole in the middle of the *pâté* for the escape of steam. Decorate the top with pastry motifs. Brush the top of the *pâté* with egg and bake in a moderate oven for $1\frac{1}{4}$ hours, or longer if the *pâté* is large.

Leave to cool without turning out. When it is cold, pour in half-set jelly (see JELLY, *Game jelly stock*).

Pheasant *pâtés* (like all cold *pâtés*) must be prepared at least 24 hours before using.

In addition to those listed above, other ingredients may be used, such as thin slices of lean cooked ham or pickled tongue, thin slices of fresh pork fat, etc.

Another way of preparing the *pâté* is to dice coarsely the slices of pheasant and other whole ingredients and mix them with the stuffing.

Potted pheasant. TERRINE DE FAISAN – Made with the same ingredients as those indicated for *Pheasant pâté*: thin slices of breast of pheasant, *foie gras*, truffles, game stuffing.

Fill a bowl lined with thin slices of pork fat and the ingredients in alternate layers. On top of the last layer of stuffing put a thin slice of pork fat. Cover the bowl, sealing the edges with flour-and-water paste. Stand in water and cook in the oven for 1 to $1\frac{3}{4}$ hours, according to the size of the bowl. Leave the mixture to cool under a light weight.

Turn it out next day. Dry it with a cloth. Line the bowl with a layer of lard $\frac{1}{2}$ cm. ($\frac{1}{4}$ inch) thick, and leave to set. Put the mixture on top. Pour on cool lard to cover and seal the edges with lard.

Thus encased in fat, the potted pheasant will keep for several days. If it is to be eaten at once, concentrated game jelly may be used instead of lard.

Preserved pheasant with foie gras and jelly. CONSERVE DE FAISAN AU FOIE GRAS À LA GELÉE – Prepare the pheasant as indicated for *Daube of pheasant in jelly*.

Drain, untruss and remove barding. Dry well in a cloth. Put it in a tin just large enough to take it whole. Cover with clear jelly made from the cooking stock and clarified (see ASPIC, *Clarification of aspic jelly*), flavoured with Madeira or some other heavy wine. Solder the tin. Mark the lid with a touch of solder. Put it in a pan with enough water to cover. Boil steadily for $1\frac{1}{4}$ hours. Take the tin out of the pan and put it upside down on a table so that the breast of the pheasant is glazed with jelly. Leave to get cold.

Pheasant Prince Orloff in jelly. FAISAN PRINCE ORLOFF À LA GELÉE – Bone a pheasant, leaving the bones in the wing tips and lower part of the leg. Season the bird inside, and stuff with a forcemeat made of the boned meat of another pheasant, trimmed and minced, with an equal quantity of chopped pork fat and $\frac{1}{4}$ its volume of cooked *foie gras* coarsely diced, and diced truffles. Season the mixture well and flavour with 1 tablespoon brandy.

Fold the pheasant into shape and sew it up. Baste with melted butter. Wrap in a cloth and tie with string. Put the pheasant in a braising pan lined with fresh pork skin and sliced carrots and onions tossed in butter. Moisten with game stock, made separately from the bones and trimmings of the two pheasants. Cover, and cook slowly for 15 minutes.

Drain the pheasant. Unwrap it, then wrap it again after washing the cloth in hot water and wringing it out. Tie and leave until it is quite cold, unwrap it and dry it well in a cloth. Coat it completely with *White chaud-froid sauce* (see SAUCE) made with the cooking stock. Decorate the breast of the bird with truffles, and the whites of hard-boiled egg and jelly flavoured with Madeira. Serve on a slice of sandwich bread, cut to the size of the pheasant and spread with melted butter. Surround with 8 truffles, cooked in Madeira, scooped out and filled with *Foie gras purée* (see PURÉE). Separate the truffles with 1 tablespoon chopped jelly, and make a border of jelly cut into triangles.

Pheasant with sauerkraut or à l'alsacienne. FAISAN À LA CHOUCROUTE, À L'ALSACIENNE – Truss the pheasant with the legs pressed tightly against the breast. Cook in butter, keeping the meat pinkish inside. Put in a braising pan in which *sauerkraut* has been cooked, flavoured with *Essence of game* (see ESSENCE) and goose fat. Garnish with fat bacon and saveloy. Cook in the oven for 25 minutes.

Put the pheasant on a bed of *sauerkraut*, surround with the saveloy and the fat bacon cut in rectangles.

PHOSPHORUS. PHOSPHORE – Phosphorus is a chemical element which is a constituent of animal tissues, including the brain, and forms a major part of bone material. In combination with albumen (nuclein) or the fats (lecithin), it enters into the composition of the muscles, the glands and the nerve tissues.

The food we eat contains too great a proportion of phosphorus substances, much of which is eliminated. The substance which is easiest to assimilate is vegetable phosphorus matter.

PHYSALIS PERUVIANA – Botanical name for *Cape gooseberry*. See also STRAWBERRY TOMATO.

PICARDAN – Variety of Languedoc vine plant, producing Muscat wines.

PICARDY. PICARDIE – This region of France, according to some authorities, is the least favoured from the gastronomical point of view.

Leek flan, or *flamique*, enjoys great popularity in Picardy and in the Champagne region, though it is not a dish of transcendent quality.

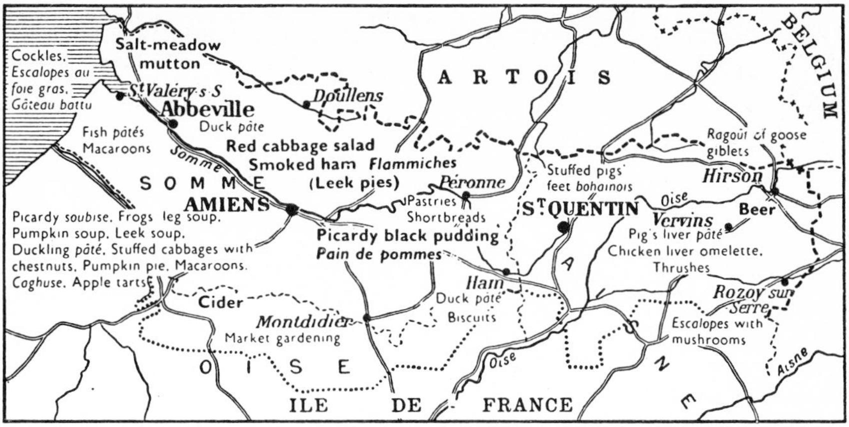

Gastronomic map of Picardy

There are many other culinary specialities in the Picardy region, for example, the duck *pâtés* of Amiens and Abbeville.

The market gardens of the region produce very good vegetables, most of which are exported to England.

Cattle raised for food in the Picardy pastures produce meat of the first quality. The Baie-de-Somme salt meadow sheep are famous. Picardy pork is excellent and is made into *charcuterie*.

Although the coast of Picardy does not stretch very far, sea fish and shellfish are found in great abundance. Cockles, which are called *hénons* locally, are found in prodigious quantities in the Baie de la Somme. Excellent fish is found in the River Somme.

This region abounds in birds of passage: wild duck, teal and garganey, and sometimes bustards, or wild geese. Thrushes, too, are found in Picardy in great numbers.

Excellent cheeses are made in Picardy: those of Maroilles, usually called Marolles, and those of Mouchelet are well known.

Cider is the local drink, but beer is also popular.

Culinary specialities – *Andouilles*, *andouillettes*, various small sausages, *black puddings*, *smoked ham*, etc.

Tripe soup, which is made as an ordinary *pot-au-feu* using pork offal and parings, muzzle, ears, liver, heart, spleen, etc.; *pumpkin soup*; *frogs' legs soup*; *leek soup*; *flamiques* or *flamiches*, a kind of country flan made of leeks, onions and marrows; various fish *pâtés*; *Amiens* and *Abbeville duck pâté*; *caqhuse*, a fresh piece of braised pork; *potato flan*, *potato pie*.

Among the sweet and confectionery specialities of Picardy are *apple tart*; Péronne shortbreads; *vitalons*, a kind of quenelle made of batter and poached in sweetened, aromatised milk; *gâteau battu*; *plum tart*, *taliburs aux pommes*, similar to Normandy *douillon*; bissale, made of buttered bread dough; and the Amiens, Abbeville and Ham macaroons and biscuits.

PICAREL – French name for small Mediterranean fish, which is prepared like anchovy.

PICAUT – The turkey is called by this name in Normandy.

PICCALILLI – A pickle, originally East Indian, of chopped vegetables in vinegar, mustard and spices. This product is found in the shops ready for use.

PICHOLINE – French name for big green table olives.

PICKEREL. BROCHETON – Young pike. It can be prepared in any manner given for large pike (see PIKE), and is used mainly for *matelotes* (q.v.) and freshwater fish stews.

PICKLED. À L'ÉCARLATE – Pork or beef are pickled by steeping in brine with saltpetre added, and then boiled.

The addition of saltpetre to the brine causes the meat to turn red and is known in France as pork or beef *à l'écarlate* (scarlet meat).

PICKLES – Gherkins, cucumbers and various vegetables pickled in vinegar and spices. This product is found in the shops ready for use, and is often bottled in the home.

PICNIC. PIQUE-NIQUE – Meal taken in the open, or a meal to which each participant contributes a dish.

PICODON DE DIEULEFIT – See CHEESE.

PICQUEPOUL or PICPOUILLE – Variety of vine plant grown in Gers, from which Armagnac is distilled.

PIED-DE-MOUTON – Common name in France for an excellent edible fungus.

PIE. PÂTÉ – Dish consisting of a pastry crust with various kinds of filling.

Some of the recipes given below are for rich pies (*pâtés*) made in moulds rather than pie dishes. General instructions for doing this are as follows:

Lining the mould. Choose a hinged mould, round, oval or rectangular, depending on the nature of the pie in question, and butter it carefully.

Take three-quarters of the pastry (prepared in advance and well rested). Roll into a ball, roll out, and fold in the shape of a *calotte* (flattened dome). Roll out this *calotte*, unfold and repeat the same process, rolling it in the opposite direction to a thickness of $\frac{1}{2}$ cm. ($\frac{1}{4}$ inch). Unfold the *calotte* of pastry and put it in a mould placed on a metal baking sheet. Press the pastry down round the sides of the tin, taking care to see that it is pressed evenly all the way to the bottom and rises about 2 cm. ($\frac{3}{4}$ inch) above the edge of the tin, to form a rim which will later be sealed with a pastry lid.

Filling the pie. Line the bottom and the walls of the pie with very thin rashers of bacon.

Put a thin layer of the prescribed forcemeat over the bacon. Smooth this carefully, to ensure that it is even all over. Fill the pie with thin slices of veal browned in butter, diced or sliced poultry or game meat, fresh pork prepared in the same manner as the veal, ham, etc. Alternate with bacon cut in thin slivers, or truffles peeled and steeped in brandy with spiced salt and cut into pieces.

This filling should be put into the pie in layers sealed down with a small quantity of the forcemeat. Cover the last layer of forcemeat with a thin rasher of bacon.

Sealing the pastry. Roll the remainder of the pastry into a piece of the same diameter as the opening of the mould. Moisten the edges of the rim with water, put the rolled-out pastry lid on top and seal the edges, pressing lightly. Crimp the edges with a pastry crimper.

Decorate the top with pieces of dough cut in fancy shapes, and brush with beaten egg. Make a hole in the middle. Butter a piece of thin cardboard, roll it into a tube and place in the hole. (This chimney provides an outlet for steam during cooking.) Brush the top with beaten egg once again.

Baking the pie. Bake the pie in a hot oven, allowing 35 to 40 minutes per kg. (18 to 20 minutes per lb.). When cooked, leave until completely cold. Pour a few tablespoons of melted butter or warm lard through the 'chimney' to fill up any gaps in the forcemeat. If the pie is intended for immediate consumption, pour into it some meat, chicken or semi-liquid game jelly, depending on the nature of the pie.

Do not turn out until the butter or the jelly are cold, and sufficiently solidified. Keep in a cool place until ready to serve.

The above method of preparation for meat, poultry or game pies is also applicable to fish or shellfish pies.

FISH AND SHELLFISH PIES. PÂTÉS DE POISSONS, DE CRUSTACÉS –

Eel pie. PÂTÉ D'ANGUILLE – Cut boned eel fillets into thin slices about 6 cm. (2½ inches) long. Stud them with truffles or desalted anchovy fillets. Marinate for 2 hours in white wine, brandy, oil, salt, pepper and dried *fines herbes* (chopped parsley, tarragon and chives).

Fry the fillets briskly in butter and sprinkle with chopped shallots. Line a mould with pastry dough and line the sides and the bottom with a layer of *Pike forcemeat* or other fish forcemeat (see FORCEMEATS) mixed with diced truffles.

Fill the pie with the eel, alternating with layers of pike forcemeat, and pour the marinating liquor over the top. Cover with another layer of forcemeat, sprinkle with melted butter, and put on a pastry lid. Decorate the top of the pie with pieces of pastry cut in fancy shapes. Make a hole in the middle to allow steam to escape.

Bake in a moderate oven for 1½ to 2 hours, depending on the size of the pie. Pour in a few tablespoons of *Demi-glace* or *Velouté sauce*, based on fish stock (see SAUCE) through the opening in the top.

Diced mushrooms tossed in butter and sprinkled with chopped *fines herbes* (q.v.) can be put into the forcemeat.

Eel pie can be garnished inside with shelled crayfish tails, in which case *Crayfish sauce* (see SAUCE) is poured in at the end. The pie can also be filled simply with the fish, each layer of the eel slices being covered with a layer of truffle slivers.

Eel pie to be served cold is prepared in the same manner. When it is cold, pour a few tablespoons of fish aspic jelly (see ASPIC, *Aspic of fish*) made from the bones and parings of eel into it, or, if the pie has to be kept for some time, a few tablespoons of melted, almost cold butter.

Lamprey pie à la bordelaise. PÂTÉ DE LAMPROIE À LA BORDELAISE – Prepare as *Eel pie* using fillets of lamprey and *Fish forcemeat* (see FORCEMEATS) mixed with chopped parsley and chives. Put a layer of the white part of leeks, sliced and lightly cooked in butter, and a layer of truffle slivers, between each layer of lamprey fillets.

Salmon pie. PÂTÉ DE SAUMON – Line a mould with *Fine lining paste* (see DOUGH). Prepare as *Eel pie*, using slices of salmon, *Pike forcemeat* (see FORCEMEATS), truffles, and other garnishes.

Salmon pie en pantin. PÂTÉ DE SAUMON EN PANTIN – Prepare with slices of salmon, *Pike forcemeat* (see FORCEMEATS), truffles, and other garnishes, arranged in layers on a sheet of *Fine lining paste* (see DOUGH) rolled out into an oval shape.

Cover with pastry, seal and crimp the edges. Decorate the top with pieces of pastry cut in fancy shapes. Brush with beaten egg, make a hole in the middle to allow steam to escape, and bake in a slow oven.

This pie can be made of *Brioche dough* (see DOUGH). It can also be made as a turnover.

Salmon pie à la russe I. PÂTÉ DE SAUMON À LA RUSSE – 'I shall give you the details of this hot pie as I have seen it made in the house of the Russian Ambassador (Prince Kurakin), by his Russian cook,' writes Carême.

'Having cut a small fillet of salmon into slices, season with *fines herbes* (q.v.), salt salt, pepper and grated nutmeg. Dredge a small Strasbourg *foie gras*, cut in slices, in the same seasoning and herbs. Chop 12 hard-boiled egg yolks. Line the pie mould as usual for a hot pie, garnish the sides and bottom with rice cooked in good chicken stock (the rice, as well as the rest of the garnish, should be cold). Put in a layer of salmon slices, sprinkle with chopped yolks, cover with slices of *foie gras*, and follow up with a sprinkling of yolks. Repeat the process again with the same filling of salmon and *foie gras*. Pour over butter flavoured with *fines herbes* in which the *foie gras* and the salmon have been tossed. Cover the rest with a layer of rice and finish making the pie as usual. Bake it for 1½ hours and serve at once.

'The Russian cook put no sauce in, but a good concentrated *Espagnole sauce* (see SAUCE) will give more taste and will render this strange *ragoût* more delicate.' (*Traité des entrées chaudes de pâtisseries*, by Carême.)

Salmon pie à la russe II – See COULIBIAC.

Sole pie. PÂTE DE SOLES – Prepare as *Eel pie* in an oval or rectangular mould, lined with *Fine lining paste* (see DOUGH), using fillets of sole, *Fish forcemeat* (see FORCEMEATS), truffle and other garnish.

This pie can be made by filling it with rolled fillets of sole, stuffed with truffled fish forcemeat.

Spiny lobster and other shellfish pie. PÂTÉ DE LANGOUSTE – Prepare as *Eel pie* replacing the eel by slices of the shellfish. The forcemeat used for this pie should have some compound butter, flavoured and coloured with the appropriate shellfish, added to it (see BUTTER).

Turbot pie. PÂTÉ DE TURBOT – Prepare as *Eel pie*, in an oval or rectangular mould, replacing the eel by fillets of turbot.

Proceeding as described in the recipe for *Eel pie* and other recipes, pies can be made of all kinds of fish, such as brill, pike, cod, carp, sturgeon, eel-pout, whiting, grayling, salmon, trout, etc.

All these pies can be served cold.

GAME PIES. PÂTÉS DE GIBIER.

Blackbird pie. PÂTÉ DE MERLES – Prepare as described in the recipe for *Thrush pie* below.

Hare pie. PÂTÉ DE LIÈVRE – Prepare as *Rabbit pie* below, using sliced hare meat, *Game forcemeat* (see FORCEMEATS) and truffles.

Lark pie I. PÂTÉ DE MAUVIETTES – Using boned larks, *foie gras* or *à gratin forcemeat* and truffles, prepare as *Quail pie*.

Lark pie II or Dijon roussotte. PÂTÉ D'ALOUETTES, DIJONNAIS ROUSSOTTE – For 6 persons take 18 larks, 350 g. (12 oz.) fresh pork fillet, 100 g. (4 oz.) fat pork, 100 g. (4 oz.) cooked ham.

Bone the larks, leaving only the leg bones (keeping all the trail) and marinate them for 2 days in brandy, Madeira, salt, pepper and spices.

Cut the pork fillet and fat pork into large dice and brown lightly over a high flame. Leave until quite cold, then pound in a mortar, incorporating the cooked ham, 5 or 6 good truffles and the larks' trail, lightly fried in butter. Taste, add seasoning if necessary, and rub through a fine sieve.

Reshape the larks, stuffing with a little of this forcemeat, a piece of truffle and a piece of *foie gras*.

Line a mould with *Fine lining paste* (see DOUGH). Cover with very thin rashers of bacon, spread a little forcemeat on the bottom and put in the larks, placing them in rows and interspersing each row with a thin layer of forcemeat. Put on a pastry lid (without making any hole in the centre, as for other pies). Scatter 2 or 3 pieces of fresh butter on the top and bake in a slow oven for about 1¼ hours. Turn out and serve as it is.

The pie can be served cold. In this case, alternate the larks with good pieces of truffled *foie gras*. When the pie is cold, pour in some game aspic jelly (see JELLY, *Game jelly stock*).

The larks can be replaced by thrushes, quails, etc. This pie is also known as *Pâté Racouchot*.

Pheasant pie. PÂTÉ DE FAISAN – Prepare, using jointed roast pheasant, kept very underdone, as described in the recipe for *Woodcock pie*.

Quail pie with truffles. PÂTÉ DE CAILLES AUX TRUFFES – Line a low round mould with *Fine lining paste* (see DOUGH) and coat the sides and the bottom with *A gratin forcemeat* (see FORCEMEATS). Stuff the quails with *foie gras* and truffles, roll into little ballottines and half-cook in Madeira-flavoured braising stock. Arrange the quails in a circle. Fill the middle of the mould with truffles lightly tossed in butter. Cover with a pastry lid and finish making the pie in the usual manner. Bake in a moderate oven for about 1 hour.

Before serving, pour in a few tablespoons of *Demi-glace sauce* (see SAUCE) having added to it the liquor left from braising the quails.

This type of pie is usually made in shallow moulds; it is really a *croustade* (q.v.) more than a pie and is usually described on the menus as *croustade of quails*.

Rabbit pie with truffles. PÂTÉ DE LAPEREAU AUX TRUFFES – Slice the fillets of 2 young rabbits and brown them briskly in butter without actually cooking them. Using the shoulder flesh and boned legs, prepare a fine forcemeat and add to it half its weight of *Pork forcemeat* (see FORCEMEATS).

Line an oval or round mould with *Fine lining paste* (see DOUGH) and spread the sides and the bottom with a layer of the forcemeat.

Fill the pie with slices of rabbit meat putting them in rows, covering each row with slivers of truffles, lightly tossed in butter, and a layer of the forcemeat.

Cover with a pastry lid and finish making the pie in the usual way. Bake in a moderate oven for 1 to 1¼ hours, depending on the size.

Thrush or blackbird pie. PÂTÉ DE GRIVES, DE MERLES – Prepare, using boned and stuffed thrushes and blackbirds, as described in the recipe for *Lark pie* or *Woodcock pie*.

Thrush pie à l'ardennaise. PÂTÉ DE GRIVES À L'ARDENNAISE – Bone the thrushes and stuff with juniper-flavoured *À gratin game forcemeat* (see FORCEMEATS). Arrange like *Quail pie*, but without the truffles. Put a piece of lean bacon, lightly fried in butter, between each thrush.

Just before serving pour into the pie a few tablespoons of concentrated game stock, made from the carcases and parings of thrushes, flavoured with juniper berries.

Thrush pie à la cévenole. PÂTÉ DE GRIVES À LA CÉVENOLE – Prepare as *Quail pie*, using boned thrushes stuffed with *À gratin game forcemeat* (see FORCEMEATS). Garnish the pie with half-cooked braised chestnuts and lean rashers of bacon, scalded and lightly fried.

Pour in a few tablespoons of Madeira-flavoured game *fumet* (q.v.).

Woodcock pie with truffles. PÂTÉ DE BÉCASSES AUX TRUFFES – Line a pie mould with *Fine lining paste* (see DOUGH). Coat the sides and bottom with a layer of *À gratin game forcemeat* (see FORCEMEATS), mixed with the livers and the trail of the birds, rubbed through a sieve.

Put into the pie the breasts of 2 woodcocks, roasted and kept very underdone. Bone the legs, pound the flesh in a mortar and add to the forcemeat. Cover the breasts with thick slices of truffles lightly tossed in butter, and over these spread a layer of forcemeat. Cover the pie with pastry and bake in the oven for about 1 hour.

This pie can also be made of boned woodcock stuffed with *foie gras* and truffles.

Pies of wood-pigeon, partridge and other game. PÂTÉ DE PALOMBE, PERDREAU – Using the meat of the game chosen, prepare as pheasant or woodcock pie.

MEAT PIES. PÂTÉS DE VIANDES DIVERSES.

Beef pie à la parisienne. PÂTÉ DE BOEUF À LA PARISIENNE – Line a pie mould with *Fine lining paste* (see DOUGH). Coat the bottom and the sides with *Quenelle forcemeat* (see FORCEMEATS) made of a mixture of beef and veal – half-and-half. Marinate for 1 hour thin slices of fillet of beef in white wine and brandy with *fines herbes* (q.v.) and chopped shallots, seasoned with salt, pepper and spices. Fry the slices quickly in butter until they are half-cooked, and leave to get cold.

Put the slices into the pie in layers, scattering sliced mushrooms, fried in butter, on each layer. Add a layer of forcemeat, sprinkle with melted butter, cover with pastry and finish the pie. Bake in a slow oven from 1 to 1¼ hours.

Before serving, pour in a few tablespoons of *Demi-glace sauce* (see SAUCE), boiled down with the marinating liquor.

Beefsteak pie – See BEEF.

Beefsteak and kidney pie – See BEEF.

Calves' sweetbreads pie a l'ancienne. PÂTÉ DE RIS DE VEAU À L'ANCIENNE – Line a low pie dish with *Fine lining paste* (see DOUGH). Coat the bottom and sides with a layer of *Quenelle forcemeat II* (see FORCEMEATS) mixed with chopped truffles. Put in a layer of truffles and mushrooms, sliced and lightly fried in butter. On top of this add 2 calf sweetbreads, half-braised in a *court-bouillon* (q.v.). Cover with truffles and mushrooms. Sprinkle with melted butter. Put on a pastry lid and finish the pie. Bake in a moderate oven for 45 minutes to 1 hour, depending on its size.

Before serving, pour in a few tablespoons of *Velouté sauce* (see SAUCE) cooked with cream.

This pie can also be filled with calves' sweetbreads sliced and lightly fried in butter.

Lamb pie à la périgourdine I. PÂTÉ D'AGNEAU À LA PÉRIGOURDINE – Line a pie mould with pastry. Cover the sides with finely pounded *Veal and pork forcemeat* (see FORCEMEATS).

Fill the dish with alternate rows of lambs' sweetbreads half-cooked in butter, slices of *foie gras* and slivers of truffles, lightly fried in butter, ending with a layer of forcemeat. Cover with a piece of pastry. Bake for 45 minutes to 1 hour. Pour in a few tablespoons of *Périgueux sauce* (see SAUCE).

Lamb pie à la périgourdine II. PÂTÉ D'AGNEAU À LA PÉRIGOURDINE – Prepare as in previous recipe, but replace lambs' sweetbreads by little escalopes of loin or fillets of lamb, briskly fried in butter for just long enough to stiffen them.

Lamb sweetbreads pie. PÂTÉ CHAUD DE RIS D'AGNEAU – Prepare as *Calves' sweetbreads pie*, using lambs' sweetbreads, blanched and lightly fried in butter.

Anglo-French mutton pie (Carême's recipe). PÂTÉ DE MOUTON ANGLO-FRANÇAIS – 'Having trimmed the fillets of 4 loins of mutton, cut and trim into slices and season on both sides with salt, coarsely ground pepper and nutmeg. Then warm slightly 225 g. (8 oz., 1 cup) Isigny butter, add 2 tablespoons (3 tablespoons) parsley, twice the amount of mushrooms and the same quantity of truffles, all finely chopped, and a blanched and chopped shallot.

'Line the pie dish with *Fine lining paste* (see DOUGH), dip the fillets into the butter *aux fines herbes* and, one by one, put them in the pie dish, arranging them in a circle. Fill the middle with cooked white mushrooms, sliced truffles or artichoke hearts, or some escalopes of lambs' or calves' sweetbreads. Sprinkle the rest of the butter *aux fines herbes* on top.

'Finish making the pie and put in a lively oven. Bake for $1\frac{1}{2}$ hours. When ready to serve, remove any fat, cover with mutton *demi-glace* (see SAUCE, *Demi-glace sauce*) blended with mushroom or truffle essence, and add the juice of 1 lemon.

'Or you can remove surplus fat from the hot pie and pour over a good *Espagnole sauce* with mushrooms, truffles, artichoke hearts and lambs' sweetbreads, or *Tomato sauce* (see SAUCE).'

Mutton pie (English cookery). PÂTÉ DE MOUTON À L'ANGLAISE – This pie is made with mutton in the same way as *Beefsteak pie* (see BEEF).

Small mutton pies or mutton patties. PETITS PÂTÉS DE MOUTON À L'ANGLAISE – Line deep tartlet tins with *Ordinary lining paste* (see DOUGH). Fill with diced mutton, half fat half lean. Season with salt and pepper and sprinkle with chopped *fines herbes* (q.v.).

Cover with lids of *Puff pastry* (see DOUGH), sealing the edges. Brush the tops with beaten egg and make a small hole in the middle of each pie. Bake in a moderate oven for 40 minutes. Pour into each patty 1 tablespoon *Demi-glace sauce* (see SAUCE).

These patties are eaten hot or cold.

Pork pie – See PORK.

Pork pie à la hongroise. PÂTÉ DE PORC À LA HONGROISE – Line a pie mould with *Fine lining paste* (see DOUGH). Coat the sides and the bottom with *Quenelle forcemeat II* (see FORCEMEATS) spiced with chopped chives and seasoned with paprika.

Line the bottom of the pie with a thick layer of diced onions and mushrooms, cooked gently in butter, seasoned with salt and paprika and bound with a few tablespoons of *Velouté sauce* (see SAUCE).

On this garnish put thin slices or pork, previously marinated and browned quickly in butter. Cover with a layer of forcemeat, put on a pastry lid and finish the pie. Bake in a slow oven for 1 or $1\frac{1}{4}$ hours.

Just before serving, pour in a few tablespoons of *Hungarian sauce* (see SAUCE).

This type of pie is usually served as a *croustade* (q.v.).

Fillet of veal pie. PÂTÉ DE FILET DE VEAU – Proceed as for *Beef pie à la parisienne*, using slices of veal and *Quenelle forcemeat* (see FORCEMEATS).

POULTRY PIES. PÂTÉS DE VOLAILLES.

Chicken pie I. PÂTÉ DE POULET À L'ANGLAISE – Joint a medium-sized chicken. Sprinkle the pieces with finely chopped shallots, onion, mushrooms and parsley, and season with salt and pepper.

Line a pie dish with thin, seasoned slices of veal.

Put in the joints, first the legs, then the wings and breast. Cover with 150 g. (5 oz.) bacon cut into thin rashers. Add 4 halved yolks of hard-boiled eggs. Pour in chichen stock to cover the ingredients up to three-quarters.

Wet the edges of the pie dish and press on a band of pastry. Brush this over with a little water and cover with a lid of *Puff pastry* (see DOUGH). Press the edges well together, and scallop the sides. Make a hole in the middle of the lid and brush with beaten egg. Bake in a moderate oven for $1\frac{1}{2}$ hours.

When the pie is cooked, pour in a few tablespoons of concentrated chicken stock.

Chicken pie II. PÂTÉ DE POULARDE EN PANTIN – This pie is shaped by hand using a boned fowl, stuffed with a fine *foie gras* forcemeat; or slices of chicken and truffle rolled into ballottines, half cooked in chicken stock, and left to get cold.

Put the chicken, covered with bacon rashers, on an oval-shaped piece of pastry. Cover with pastry and seal the edges. Decorate the top of the pie with pastry cut out in fancy shapes. Brush with beaten egg, make a hole to allow steam to escape. Bake in a moderate oven for $1\frac{1}{2}$ to 2 hours depending on the size of the pie.

Just before serving pour in a few tablespoons brown chicken stock flavoured with truffle *fumet* (q.v.) or chicken *Velouté sauce* cooked with cream (see SAUCE).

The sauce can be served separately.

Chicken pie III. PÂTÉ DE POULARDE – Prepare the pie in a mould, following the general instructions given for the preparation of such pies.

Fill with slices of fillets of fowl fried in butter; *Poultry* or *Quenelle forcemeat* (see FORCEMEATS), truffles and other garnish. Cover the pie, decorate the top, brush with beaten egg and bake in a moderate oven. Serve hot or cold.

Rouen duckling pie à la rouennaise. PÂTÉ DE CANETON DE ROUEN À LA ROUENNAISE – Roast a plump Rouen duckling keeping it very underdone. Cut the breast into slices. Skin the legs, remove the bones, pound the flesh in a mortar and rub it through a sieve. Add to it three times its weight of *À gratin forcemeat* (see FORCEMEATS) and some diced truffles. Add the blood, pressed out of the duckling's carcase, to the forcemeat. Season well and add 2 tablespoons (3 tablespoons) Calvados which has been set alight.

Choose an oval-shaped mould (either a hinged mould or one with low sides), and line it with *Fine lining paste* (see DOUGH) mixed with truffles shredded into a fine *julienne* (q.v.). Coat the sides and bottom with a layer of *Poultry* or *Quenelle forcemeat* (see FORCEMEATS). Fill the pie with slices of duckling, alternating with layers of the truffled forcemeat *à gratin* and sliced mushrooms and truffles, lightly tossed in butter. Finish with a layer of poultry forcemeat, cover with a piece of rolled-out pastry and finish making the pie in the usual manner.

Bake in a moderate oven for 1 to $1\frac{1}{4}$ hours, depending on the size, then pour in a few tablespoons of *Rouennaise sauce* (see SAUCE).

Foie gras and truffle pie. PÂTÉ DE FOIE GRAS AUX TRUFFES – This type of pie is usually made by filling a pie crust baked blind, lined with a layer of *Foie gras purée* (see PUREE) or *À gratin forcemeat* (see FORCEMEATS), with a whole *foie gras* cooked in liqueur wine. Garnish with sliced truffles fried lightly in butter, and a few tablespoons of sauce, flavoured with liqueur wine and mixed with the concentrated liquor left from cooking the liver.

Foie gras pie can also be prepared as *Chicken pie*. The liver is half-cooked with port, placed in a mould lined with *Fine lining paste* (see DOUGH), coated with a layer of forcemeat, covered with a lid of pastry, and finished as described in the general instructions on making pies.

After baking, a few tablespoons of *Demi-glace sauce* (see SAUCE) cooked with truffle *fumet* (q.v.) are poured into the pie.

Guinea fowl pie. PÂTÉ DE PINTADE – Prepare as *Chicken pie*, using a boned guinea fowl, stuffed with *foie gras* and truffles.

This pie can also be prepared using cooked and jointed guinea fowl.

Pigeon pie. PÂTÉ DE PIGEON À L'ANGLAISE – Line the bottom and sides of a pie dish with thin rashers of smoked bacon.

Sprinkle with finely chopped shallots and put in the pigeons, cut each in 4 pieces, seasoned with salt and pepper and sprinkled with chopped parsley. Add ½ hard-boiled egg yolk for each pigeon.

Pour in some light brown stock to about half-way. Wet the edges of the pie dish and put a border of pastry around them. Brush with a little water and cover with a lid of puff pastry. Press the edges well together, make a hole in the centre and brush over with beaten egg. Bake in a moderate oven for 1½ hours.

Pour a few tablespoons of stock into the pie.

Pigeon pie à la languedocienne. PÂTÉ DE PIGEON À LA LANGUEDOCIENNE – Proceed as described for *Pigeon pie with mushrooms and truffles* (see below), replacing the last two ingredients by a garnish of salsify, cooked in a *court-bouillon* (q.v.), cut into little sticks and fried in butter; stoned and blanched olives; button mushrooms; sliced chicken livers sautéed in butter; and cut up, scaled and fried lean bacon.

Before serving put a few tablespoons of concentrated brown veal stock into the pie.

Pigeon pie with mushrooms and truffles. PÂTÉ DE PIGEON AUX CHAMPIGNONS ET AUX TRUFFES – Line a shallow mould with *Fine lining paste* (see DOUGH).

Coat the sides and bottom with truffled *Quenelle forcemeat* (see FORCEMEATS). Put the truffles and mushrooms, sliced and lightly tossed in butter, in the pie dish. Add 2 pigeons, each cut in 4 pieces and browned in butter. Cover with truffles and mushrooms. Sprinkle with melted butter. Cover with pastry, finish making the pie in the usual manner and bake in the oven for about 1 hour.

Pour in a few tablespoons of chicken *Velouté sauce* (see SAUCE) cooked with cream and flavoured with Madeira or any other wine.

Hot pies made of various kinds of poultry. PÂTÉS CHAUDS DE VOLAILLES – These pies can be made of turkeys and geese etc., by following the recipes given for *Chicken pie*.

The birds are used whole, boned and stuffed, or sliced.

COLD PIES. PÂTÉS FROIDS –

Various fish pies (cold). PÂTÉS DE POISSONS – These pies are made in the same way as those which are to be served hot. They can be shaped by hand or made in moulds lined with fine lining paste.

Ham pie. PÂTÉ DE JAMBON – This is made in an oval-shaped mould, like *Veal and ham pie* (see below). Use forcemeat indicated in that recipe, mixed with chopped lean ham; or *Panada forcemeat with butter* (see FORCEMEATS), also mixed with chopped ham and slices of raw ham. When the pie is cold, pour into it some Madeira-flavoured aspic jelly (see ASPIC). The use of truffles in this pie is optional.

Veal and ham pie. PÂTÉ DE VEAU ET JAMBON – *Ingredients.* 300 g. (11 oz.) lean veal, 300 g. (11 oz.) lean pork, 200 g. (7 oz.) ham, 500 g. (18 oz., generous 2 cups) fine *Veal and pork forcemeat* (see FORCEMEATS), 200 g. (7 oz.) fat bacon, 1 dl. (6 tablespoons, scant ½ cup) Madeira and 3 to 4 teaspoons *Spiced salt* (see SALT).

Method. Remove all sinews from the veal taken from the chump end of loin, and cut into strips about 10 cm. (4 inches) long. Prepare the pork and the ham in a similar manner and put all these meats into a bowl. Season with spiced salt. Sprinkle with Madeira and leave to steep for several hours.

Sprinkle with a small quantity of *fines herbes* (q.v.) and chopped shallots.

Line the mould (round, oval or rectangular in shape) with *Lining paste* (see DOUGH), prepared in advance and left to rest for some time. Cover with thin rashers of fat bacon and coat with a layer of fine *Veal and pork forcemeat* (see FORCEMEATS). Fill the pie with veal, pork and ham in alternate rows, sealing them down with a thin layer of forcemeat. Add truffles cut in quarters. Finish off with a thick layer of forcemeat.

Roll out the rest of the pastry into a circle of the same diameter as the opening of the mould. Put it over the pie and seal and crimp the edges.

Brush the top with beaten egg and decorate with pieces of pastry cut in fancy shapes.

Make a hole in the middle. Roll a piece of buttered cardboard and put it into the hole, to hasten the cooking process and to prevent the pie walls from subsiding.

Brush with beaten egg once again. Bake the pie in the oven for about 1¼ hours at moderate heat.

Leave the pie until it is completely cold. Pour into it some melted butter or lard to seal any gaps. When this is solidified, turn out the pie. If it is to be eaten immediately, pour in a few tablespoons of aspic jelly (see ASPIC).

SWEET PIES. PÂTÉS D'ENTREMENTS –

Apple pie à l'anglaise. PÂTÉ DE POMMES À L'ANGLAISE – *Ingredients.* 500 g. (18 oz., 4½ cups) sifted flour, 350 g. (12 oz., 1½ cups) butter, 25 g. (1 oz., 2 tablespoons) fine sugar, 2 egg yolks, 2 dl. (⅓ pint, scant cup) water and 1½ teaspoons salt.

Put the flour in a circle on the board, make a well in the middle, put into it the salt and sugar and dissolve these in the water. Add the yolks. Mix the pastry without kneading too much. Roll into a ball and leave to stand in a cool place for 2 hours.

Cut the apples into quarters, remove core, peel and cut into thick slices. Put into a pie dish, piling them up into a dome. Sprinkle with sugar mixed with a little powdered cinnamon.

Wet the edges of the pie dish and put a border of pastry around them. Brush this over with a little water and cover with the pastry, rolled out to form a lid, pressing the edges well together. Scallop the sides, decorate with fancy pieces of pastry, brush with beaten egg and bake in a slow oven for 45 minutes to 1 hour.

Mince pies. GÂTEAUX DE NOËL – These pies are especially popular in England. They are, wrote A. Suzanne, 'the cakes which, with the traditional plum pudding, are pre-eminent among the dishes of the copious Christmas dinner.'

Fill small deep tartlets made of pie crust or flaky pastry with mincemeat. Cover with thin flaky pastry with a hole pricked in the middle. Brush with egg, bake in a hot oven, and serve hot. Here is a French recipe for mince pies:

Mincemeat. Prepare and leave to soak for 6 to 8 days the following ingredients:

100 g. (4 oz.) finely chopped fillet of beef, 50 g. (2 oz.) pickled tongue very finely diced, 50 g. (2 oz.) chopped fat bacon, 100 g. (4 oz., ⅔ cup) sultanas, 100 g. (4 oz., ⅔ cup) currants, 50 g. (2 oz., ½ cup) blanched and chopped almonds, 50 g. (2 oz., ¼ cup) brown sugar, a pinch of mixed spices, the grated rind and juice of a lemon. Mix these ingredients together, adding half a glass of brandy.

Special pie crust – 500 g. (18 oz., 4½ cups) sieved flour, 100 g. (4 oz.) beef suet, 100 g. (4 oz., ½ cup) butter, 1 egg, 1½ teaspoons salt, 1 dl. (6 tablespoons, scant ½ cup) water. Knead all these ingredients into a rather firm dough. Leave it to stand, then roll it out and fold it into three. Repeat this operation twice more. Divide the dough into small pieces and line deep buttered tartlet tins with the pieces, making sure the dough is evenly spread. Fill each tartlet with mincemeat and cover with a pastry lid. The pies should be sealed at the edges with pastry pincers. Brush the tops of the pies with milk and sprinkle lightly with brown sugar. Cook in a hot oven.

PIÈCES MONTÉES – In old-fashioned culinary practice much use was made of decorative pieces, which were often made of inedible ingredients. They were frequently monumental affairs and now only survive to a small extent in pastry-making.

PIED-DE-CHEVAL – Variety of large oysters, not greatly esteemed in Europe.

PIÉMONTAISE (À LA) – Garnish served with meat and poultry. It is composed of *timbales* of risotto, mixed with blanched, shredded truffles, served in a mound with the meat or poultry.

PIERRY – Name of a vineyard on the Épernay slope, producing grapes from which excellent champagne is made.

PIG. COCHON – See PORK.

Wood pigeons

PIGEON, SQUAB – PIGEONNEAU – Granivorous bird of which there are many domestic and wild species. The principal of these are *rock pigeons* or *carrier pigeons*, from which the domesticated varieties evolved, the *ringdove* or *wood pigeon* whose flesh is much esteemed by gastronomes, and *turtledove* or *passenger pigeon*.

The word pigeon rarely figures on the French menu. *Pigeonneau* (squab) is used instead. This applies to a young, tender bird, which can be prepared in many different ways.

Unlike other birds, pigeon's liver contains no gall, and it is customary to leave the liver inside the bird when dressing it. Pigeon is drawn and prepared for cooking like all other domesticated birds. It should be barded before being roasted on a spit or cooked in a casserole or a *cocotte*.

Casserole of pigeon or pigeon en cocotte. PIGEONNEAU EN CASSEROLE, EN COCOTTE – Prepare like *Casserole of chicken* or *Chicken en cocotte* (see CHICKEN).

Pigeon à la catalan (Catalan style) or en pistache. PIGEONNEAU À LA CATALANE, EN PISTACHE – Proceed as described in the recipe for *Partridge à la catalane* (see PARTRIDGE).

Cold pigeons. PIGEONS FROIDS – Pigeons and squabs can be prepared in any way suitable for poultry, particularly for spring chickens and grain-fed poulets. (See CHICKEN.)

Cold pigeons can be prepared as ballottines, *en chaud-froid, en daube à la gelée*, galantines, mousses or *mousselines*, loaves, pies and *terrines*.

Compote of pigeon I. PIGEONNEAU EN COMPOTE – Brown the pigeon in butter and drain. Dilute the pan juices with 1 dl. (6 tablespoons, scant $\frac{1}{2}$ cup) white wine, boil down by two-thirds, add $1\frac{1}{2}$ dl. ($\frac{1}{4}$ pint, $\frac{2}{3}$ cup) *Demi-glace sauce* (see SAUCE) and strain.

Put the pigeon back in the casserole with 12 small glazed onions, 12 mushrooms and 50 g. (2 oz., $\frac{1}{2}$ cup) fat bacon cut in dice, scalded and fried. Cover with the sauce, bring to the boil, cover the casserole and cook in the oven from 25 to 30 minutes.

Arrange the pigeon on a serving dish, surround with garnish and pour the sauce over it.

Compote of pigeon II. PIGEONNEAU EN COMPOTE – Fry scalded fat bacon, in 1 tablespoon butter. Add blanched onions and mushrooms. Fry together, then drain all the garnish.

Brown the pigeon in the same fat and remove it. Put 1 tablespoon flour into a casserole, moisten with 1 dl. (6 tablespoons, scant $\frac{1}{2}$ cup) white wine, boil down, add 2 dl. ($\frac{1}{3}$ pint, scant cup) white stock and boil down by one-third.

Put the pigeon and its garnish back in the casserole, add a *bouquet garni* (q.v.) and cook with a lid on for 25 to 30 minutes.

Pigeon à la crapaudine. PIGEONNEAU À LA CRAPAUDINE – Split the pigeon horizontally, from the tip of the breast to the wings. Open it, flatten slightly, spread with melted butter and season with salt and pepper. Grill slowly until both sides are golden.

Arrange the pigeon on a dish and decorate the border with a row of gherkins cut in slices. Serve with *Diable sauce* (see SAUCE).

Pigeon à la diable. PIGEONNEAU À LA DIABLE – Prepare as described in the recipe for *Grilled chicken à la diable* (see CHICKEN).

Fried pigeon. PIGEONNEAU EN FRITOT – Prepare like *Chicken fritot* (see CHICKEN).

Grilled pigeon à la Saint-Germain. PIGEONNEAU GRILLÉ À LA SAINT-GERMAIN – Split the pigeon open, remove most of the bones, flatten slightly, season with salt and pepper, spread with melted butter, cover on both sides with freshly grated breadcrumbs, sprinkle with butter, and grill slowly.

Arrange the pigeon on a dish. Put some rather thick *Béarnaise sauce* (see SAUCE) on both sides and garnish wth *Potatoes à la parisienne* (see POTATOES). Boil down a few tablespoons of veal stock, add butter and pour round the pigeon.

Pigeon à la Maître-Jacques (old recipe). PIGEONNEAU À LA MAÎTRE-JACQUES – 'Bone 2 pigeons completely. Season with salt, pepper and spices and stuff with the following forcemeat: 50 g. (2 oz., $\frac{1}{2}$ cup) chopped onion softened in butter, 100 g. (4 oz., 4 cups) dried *duxelles* (parings and stalks of chopped mushrooms), 2 tablespoons (3 tablespoons) chopped parsley, the chopped livers of the pigeons, 1 egg, 1 tablespoon of brandy, salt and pepper, 150 g. (5 oz.) *Fine pork forcemeat* (see FORCEMEATS). Roll the pigeons into ballotines (q.v.) and wrap each in a very thin, large escalope of veal seasoned with salt, pepper and spices. Tie the pigeons as ballottines.

Put into a casserole on a foundation of bacon rinds, carrots and onions chopped and fried in butter. Simmer on the stove with a lid on for 15 minutes. Moisten with 1 glass Madeira, boil down and add a few tablespoons of thickened brown veal stock in sufficient quantity to cover the pigeons. Cook in the oven for 30 minutes. Drain the ballottines and remove the string. Put them into an earthenware *cocotte*. Add 500 g. (18 oz., 6 cups) sliced mushrooms, tossed in butter, and 20 thick slices of truffles. Strain the braising liquor, boil down, add 3 tablespoons (scant $\frac{1}{4}$ cup) flaming brandy, and pour over the pigeons. Seal the lid of the *cocotte* with flour-and-water paste. Cook in the oven for 40 minutes and serve in the *cocotte*.

Pigeon à la minute. PIGEONNEAU À LA MINUTE – Split the pigeon in half and remove all small bones. Flatten slightly, and fry quickly in sizzling butter. When the pigeon is almost cooked, add 1 tablespoon chopped onion lightly fried in butter. Finish cooking together.

Arrange the pigeon on a dish. Dilute the pan juices with a

dash of brandy, add a little dissolved meat jelly and $\frac{1}{2}$ tablespoon chopped parsley, and pour over the pigeon.

Pigeon mousse and mousselines. MOUSSE, MOUSSELINES DE PIGEONNEAU – Prepare like *Chicken mousse and mousselines* (see CHICKEN).

Pigeon with olives. PIGEONNEAU AUX OLIVES – Prepare like *Duckling with olives* (see DUCK).

Pigeon en papillote. PIGEONNEAU EN PAPILLOTE – Split the pigeon in half lengthways, partially bone the halves, season with salt and pepper, and fry in butter to stiffen them. Wrap each half in buttered greaseproof paper cut in the shape of a heart, spread with *Duxelles sauce* (see SAUCE) and lined with a slice of ham, as described in the recipe for *Veal chops en papillote* (see VEAL). Close the *papillote* securely and cook in the oven.

Pigeon pie with mushrooms and truffles – See PIE, *Poultry pies.*

Pigeon with peas I. PIGEONNEAU AUX PETITS POIS – Fry 50 g. (2 oz., $\frac{1}{2}$ cup) diced and blanched fat bacon and 12 small onions in butter. When done remove these ingredients from the sauté pan.

In the same butter brown a pigeon trussed as for an *entrée*. Remove the pigeon. Dilute the pan juices with white wine and thickened veal stock. Replace the pigeon in the sauté pan and add $4\frac{1}{2}$ dl. (generous $\frac{3}{4}$ pint, 2 cups) peas, a *bouquet garni* (q.v.), the onions and lardoons. Season and finish cooking together.

Pigeon with peas II. PIGEONNEAU AUX PETITS POIS – Truss the pigeon as for an *entrée* and brown in butter. Prepare *Peas à la française* (see PEAS) and put the pigeon into the same casserole. Moisten with the diluted pan juices and an equal amount of water. Finish cooking together.

Pigeon à la Richelieu. PIGEONNEAU À LA RICHELIEU – Split the pigeon down the back and open it out. Remove most of the bones from the inside. Dip in egg and breadcrumbs and fry in clarified butter until both sides are golden. Arrange on a serving dish, garnish with slivers of truffle and put on top some softened *Maître d'hôtel butter* (see BUTTER, *Compound butters*).

Roast pigeon. PIGEONNEAU RÔTI – Truss and bard the pigeon, season on the inside and roast (see CULINARY METHODS, *Average cooking time for roasts*).

Garnish with watercress. Serve with the diluted pan juices.

Salmis of pigeon. PIGEONNEAU EN SALMIS – Proceed as described in the recipe for *Salmis of woodcock* (see WOODCOCK).

Pigeon stewed with blood, also called pigeon stew with blood (old recipe). PIGEONNEAU ÉTUVÉ AU SANG, DIT AUSSI ÉTUVÉE DE PIGEON AU SANG – 'Bleed two pigeons keeping all the blood and adding $\frac{1}{2}$ tablespoon vinegar to prevent it from coagulating.

'Pluck, draw, singe and split the pigeons in half. Season with salt and pepper and brown in a casserole with 1 tablespoon grated bacon fat. Remove and keep hot in the oven.

Put 24 small onions and 100 g. (4 oz., 6 slices) blanched lean bacon, cut in large lardoons into the casserole.

'Fry a pale golden colour and sprinkle in 1 tablespoon flour. Cook for a moment, then moisten with 4 dl. ($\frac{3}{4}$ pint, scant 2 cups) good red wine and 2 dl. ($\frac{1}{3}$ pint, scant cup) stock or water. Season, add a *bouquet garni* (q.v.) and a little chopped garlic. Put the pigeons into this stock and simmer for 45 minutes. Two minutes before serving, thicken with the blood kept for this purpose.

Garnish with 8 croûtons of home-made bread fried in butter and pour the stock over the pigeons.'

Pigeon Villeroi. PIGEONNEAU VILLEROI – Split the pigeon in half lengthways. Remove most of the bones and flatten the pigeon halves slightly. Season and cook in butter, or braise. Leave to get cold under a press.

Dip in *Villeroi sauce* (see SAUCE), dip in egg and breacrumbs and fry. Garnish with fried parsley. Serve with *Périgueux sauce* (see SAUCE).

Pike

PIKE. BROCHET – Freshwater fish with a long body, large flat jaw, mouth stretching to the eyes and armed with numerous strong teeth. The back is slightly flattened and dark green, the belly white; the sides have golden glints and the fins are reddish. Pike likes fresh water, whether fast flowing or calm, where it devours enormous quantities of fish. Its white, firm flesh is greatly esteemed. Pike milt and roe are slightly toxic, especially during the spawning season (February to April). In U.S.A. the best-known species of pike are *common pike, muskellunge* and *pickerels.*

Pike au beurre blanc. BROCHET AU BEURRE BLANC – In Anjou, as well as in the Nantes region, there are numerous recipes for preparing *beurre blanc* served with pike and Loire shad. Here are some local recipes for this dish:

First recipe. Prepare a *court-bouillon* (q.v.) and boil for 30 minutes. Put in the pike. As soon as boiling is again established, draw the fish kettle to the edge of the stove and leave to poach for 25 to 30 minutes.

Boil down some vinegar. Add to it 2 or 3 chopped shallots, a pinch of salt and a little freshly ground pepper (one turn of the mill). Boil down by half and remove from the heat.

Soften a piece of butter on a plate and incorporate it, little by little, in the vinegar, beating vigorously with a whisk. The sauce will become frothy without being liquid and acquire the whiteness which is its feature.

Drain the pike, arrange it on a hot dish and pour the *beurre blanc* over it, adding a little freshly chopped parsley.

Second recipe. Cook a 750 g. ($1\frac{3}{4}$ lb) pike in a little *court-bouillon* made of white wine, water, and the usual vegetables, seasoning and aromatics. When the fish is cooked, drain, arrange on a hot dish and cover with *beurre blanc* prepared in the following manner: put 1 chopped shallot and a pinch of salt into a saucepan, moisten with 2 tablespoons (3 tablespoons) water and 1 tablespoon vinegar, and boil down by two-thirds.

Remove the pan from the heat and add to it 150 to 200 g. (about 6 oz., $\frac{3}{4}$ cup) fresh butter, stirring all the time. Sprinkle with chopped parsley.

Third recipe. For 8 persons allow a 2 kg ($4\frac{1}{2}$ lb.) pike. Clean it thoroughly, cut off the fins and tail, wash carefully in several waters, dry, sprinkle with fine salt and leave for 15 minutes. Wash again, put into a fish kettle surrounded with fresh parsley, 2 sliced onions, 2 quartered shallots, 2 cloves garlic, 8 to 10 chives, or the green of 1 leek, a branch of fresh thyme, 1 small bay leaf, a few slices of carrot, some fine salt and ground pepper. Sprinkle with sprigs of parsley, pour in enough white wine to cover and leave to marinate for 1 hour

About 45 minutes before serving put the fish kettle on brisk heat. At the first sign of the surface beginning to 'shiver' or ripple gently, draw aside and keep near boiling point.

Separately, put 1 tablespoon chopped shallot into a

saucepan, add a pinch of freshly ground pepper and 1 glass best quality white wine vinegar (not just any commercial vinegar with a rough taste). Boil down gently by three-quarters. Take 1 kg. (2 lb.) best fresh butter, and chop it into small pieces.

Strain the vinegar. Put it into a strong copper pan with 1 tablespoon shallots, very finely chopped and lightly squeezed with the flat of the knife. Add a few pieces of butter and put over a high flame. Stir all the time with a wooden spoon, and little by little add $\frac{2}{3}$ of the butter. As soon as the light white mousse is formed, remove from the heat but do not stop stirring. Add the rest of the butter, stir until it has been absorbed and keep hot without allowing the sauce to boil. Season to taste. The sauce should be creamy.

To serve, drain the pike as soon as it is cooked, wipe it on a cloth, put on a long, deep, very hot dish. Cut the skin deftly along the backbone, slip the point of the knife under the incision, quickly remove the main bone in one movement, holding the head with the left hand. Reshape the fish, stir the *beurre blanc* a couple of times just to make sure the shallots are well mixed, spread over the pike and serve.

Fourth recipe. Prepare a *court-bouillon* made of water, 1 large onion, 1 sliced carrot, 2 dl. ($\frac{1}{3}$ pint, scant cup) vinegar, salt, peppercorns, a sprig of parsley, thyme and a bay leaf. Allow to cook for 20 minutes.

Put a 2-kg. ($4\frac{1}{2}$-lb.) pike, carefully scaled, cleaned and washed, into this composition. Keep on a low heat with the water just simmering for 20 or 25 minutes.

Meanwhile, put 2 medium-sized chopped shallots, 3 tablespoons (scant $\frac{1}{4}$ cup) vinegar, some salt and freshly ground pepper into a flat-bottomed saucepan. (When adding salt, bear in mind that the butter may be salted.) Add a piece of butter cut in large dice.

Put the sauce on brisk heat and keep stirring with a wooden spoon until the surface whitens slightly. Remove the saucepan from the fire and continue to stir.

When ready to serve, drain the fish, dry on a cloth, put on a long hot dish (white china for preference), cover the pike with *beurre blanc*, sprinkle with chopped parsley and serve very hot. (Recipe from *Phare de la Loire*.)

Fifth recipe. Le beurre blanc de ma tante. Scale a pike and clean it out: one slit under the gills, otherwise no cuts at all, as the pike must remain intact.

Cook the fish in a fish kettle in *court-bouillon* made of white wine, water and a sprinkling of vinegar, with a sprig of thyme, bay leaf, parsley, carrot cut in very thin slices, onion, a clove of garlic, black peppercorns and coarse salt.

When the *court-bouillon* is ready put it on lively heat. When you see it boiling and when it begins to diffuse a delicious aroma, put in the pike.

The cooking must not take longer than 15 minutes. If a fork penetrates the flesh easily the pike is cooked to a turn.

Remove the fish kettle from the heat without uncovering, so that the pike becomes completely saturated with the *court-bouillon*.

The sauce is the most delicate part of the operation. Put into a saucepan 1 tablespoon chopped shallot, 1 pinch ground pepper, 1 tablespoon flour and some butter – 250 g. (9 oz., generous cup) will be sufficient for a $1\frac{1}{2}$-kg. (3-lb.) pike. Add 1 tablespoon vinegar. Put the sauce to heat, stirring from time to time with a wooden spoon. When the butter melts, the liaison is achieved by adding a ladleful of previously prepared *court-bouillon*. Leave to simmer.

To serve, take the pike out of the fish kettle and put it on a long dish. Pour over some of the sauce, very hot. Mix the remainder with 3 or 4 tablespoons well-beaten fresh cream, and put it around the fish. Sprinkle with chopped parsley and finely grated lemon rind.

Pike au bleu. BROCHET AU BLEU – This method is mainly used for small pike.

Put the pike into a *court-bouillon* prepared as described in the recipe for *Blue trout* (see TROUT).

Drain the fish, arrange on a napkin and garnish with fresh parsley. Serve with boiled potatoes and melted butter or one of the other sauces specially recommended for poached fish.

Braised fillets of pike with various sauces and garnishes. FILETS DE BROCHET BRAISÉS – Cut the fillets from a large uncooked pike. Trim them and remove bones and skin. Cut the fillets into slices of uniform size. Cook them in a very little concentrated fish stock. Drain, dry, arrange on a serving dish, surround with the garnish recommended, and pour over a sauce that goes with the garnish, adding to it the liquor in which the fish was cooked, greatly concentrated.

Note. All the sauces and garnishes recommended for brill (q.v.), sole (q.v.) and young turbot (q.v.) are suitable for fillets of pike.

Pike cutlets I. CÔTELETTES DE BROCHET – Using *Pike forcemeat* (see FORCEMEATS) shape in small buttered moulds having the form of cutlets, and poach. Arrange them on a serving dish, placing them either straight on the dish, on heart-shaped croûtons, or on a puff pastry foundation. Serve with the garnish and sauce indicated in the recipe. All the sauces and garnishes recommended for *Poached fillets of sole* (see SOLE) are applicable to these cutlets.

Pike cutlets II. CÔTELETTES DE BROCHET – Prepare a croquette mixture, using a *salpicon* (q.v.) of cooked pike as the main ingredient, with truffles and mushrooms added. These cutlets, which are really a variety of croquettes (q.v.), are deep-fried like croquettes.

Pike mousse – See FISH, *Fish mousse*.

Pike mousselines. MOUSSELINES DE BROCHET – These are made of *Mousseline forcemeat* (see FORCEMEATS) poached in small *dariole* moulds.

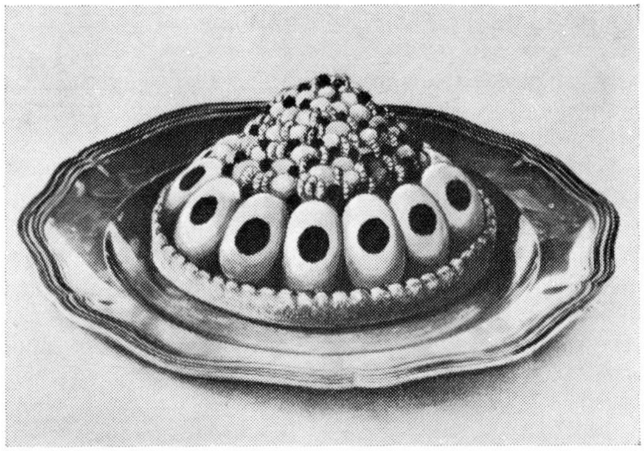

Pike quenelles en croustade

Pike quenelles. QUENELLES DE BROCHET – Prepare 300 g. (11 oz.) bread panada, using 3 dl. ($\frac{1}{2}$ pint, $1\frac{1}{4}$ cups) milk and 250 g. (9 oz., $4\frac{1}{2}$ cups) soft breadcrumbs or a flour panada using 3 dl. ($\frac{1}{2}$ pint, $1\frac{1}{4}$ cups) hot water, 50 g. (2 oz., $\frac{1}{4}$ cup) butter and 150 g. (5 oz., $1\frac{1}{4}$ cups) flour well in advance, so that it is cold when needed for use.

Pound finely 500 g. (18 oz.) pike flesh, carefully boned and skinned, with 2 teaspoons salt, a pinch of pepper and a little grated nutmeg.

Remove the fish and leave on a plate. Pound the panada until it is reduced to a completely smooth pulp, put the fish back into the mortar with 200 g. (7 oz., scant cup) butter and continue to pound well. Add, one at a time, 2 whole eggs and 4 yolks and rub through a sieve.

Transfer the resulting forcemeat into a bowl, stir with a wooden spoon to blend well. To test the seasoning and the texture of the forcemeat, take a piece the size of a hazelnut and drop it into salted water to poach.

There are special moulds for these quenelles and all that has to be done is to butter them and fill with forcemeat. When no such moulds are available, shape the quenelles in a large spoon and put them in rows into a buttered sauté pan. Or pipe through a forcing bag and cut off in 3½-cm. (1½-inch) lengths. Allow 50 g. (2 oz., ¼ cup) forcemeat for each quenelle. Cover the quenelles with salted boiling water, allowing 1½ teaspoons salt per litre (1¾ pints, generous quart). Cover, and poach on the edge of the burner for 10 minutes, keeping the water just simmering. Make sure that the poaching is complete just at the right time, so that the quenelles are ready when needed for serving, or only a few minutes before.

Drain them on a cloth, arrange in a crown on a dish and serve with the sauce and garnish indicated in the recipe.

The use of an electric blender can greatly facilitate this process.

Pike quenelles à la crème. QUENELLES DE BROCHET À LA CRÈME – Pipe the quenelles through a forcing bag with a plain nozzle, or mould them with a large spoon, and drop them into a buttered sauté pan. Poach in boiling salted water 10 minutes, simmering so gently that the boiling is imperceptible.

Drain the quenelles and dry on a cloth. Place each on a croûton fried in butter. Pour boiling *Cream sauce* over (see SAUCE).

Pike quenelles à la florentine. QUENELLES DE BROCHET À LA FLORENTINE – Poach in salte salted water, drain and dry. Arrange in an oven-proof dish on a bed of spinach leaves cooked in butter and seasoned with salt, pepper and grated nutmeg.

Cover with *Mornay sauce* (see SAUCE), sprinkle with grated cheese, pour over some melted butter and brown quickly in the oven.

Pike quenelles à la lyonnaise

Pike quenelles à la lyonnaise. QUENELLES DE BROCHET À LA LYONNAISE – These are made of *Pike forcemeat à la lyonnaise* (see FORCEMEATS), moulded with a spoon or shaped by hand and poached in salted water.

Drain and put them into a sauté pan containing thin *Espagnole sauce* (see SAUCE). For 12 quenelles of medium size add 36 cooked mushrooms, 36 stoned, blanched olives, and 24 thick slices of truffles.

Simmer for 10 minutes with a lid on without turning the quenelles, which should swell.

Arrange in a pyramid or in a flan crust baked blind.

Quenelles of pike mousseline – See QUENELLES.

Quenelles of pike princesse – See QUENELLES.

Roast pike à la mode de Bugey. BROCHET RÔTI À LA MODE DE BUGEY – Stuff a pike with a forcemeat made of whiting mixed with diced truffles bound with *Cream sauce* (see SAUCE) and finished off with *Crayfish butter* (see BUTTER, *Compound butters*).

Put the pike on a spit, brush with melted butter, season with salt and pepper, and roast before a lively fire. When nearly cooked, baste with fresh cream.

Arrange on a dish and surround with little *barquettes*, some filled with *Crayfish tail ragoût à la Nantua* (see CRAYFISH) and others with *Truffles à la crème* (see TRUFFLE). Add some fresh cream to the pan juices, boil down, strain, and pour over the fish.

The same recipe can be used for salmon, salmon trout and char.

PIKE-PERCH. SANDRE – Type of fish of the *Percidae* family found mostly in the watercourses of central and eastern Europe. In France it is found only in the Doubs and the Saône. Its flesh is white, flaky and very delicate in taste. All the cooking methods given for perch are applicable to the pike-perch.

PILAF, PILAU or PILAW – Method of preparing rice which originated in the East.

Rice prepared in this manner may be served without any garnish, but some ingredients are usually added to it, such as shrimps, chicken livers, lobster or various other shellfish, lambs' or sheep's sweetbreads, kidney, poultry, meat, etc.

Rice pilaf or pilaw. RIZ PILAF – Heat 100 g. (4 oz., ½ cup) butter, without allowing to colour. Add 500 g. (18 oz.) Patna rice.

Stir over the heat until all the grains are lightly cooked, then add 1 litre (1¾ pints, generous quart) *pot-au-feu* broth or white stock. Season, cook in the oven, covered, and without disturbing, for 18 to 20 minutes.

When the rice is cooked, mix with it 50 g. (2 oz., ¼ cup) butter cut into small pieces.

Rice pilaf (Turkish cookery). RIZ PILAF – Soak the rice for an hour or two in strongly salted water, drain, and cook for a few minutes in plenty of butter without colouring it.

Add a *bouquet garni* (q.v.) and pour in twice its volume of liquid. Cook, covered, until little holes form on the surface of the rice.

It is sometimes mixed with cooked chick-peas, currants and pine kernels.

Chicken liver pilaf. PILAF DE FOIES DE VOLAILLE – Put the rice into a buttered mould. Fill the middle with chicken livers, sliced and sautéed in butter. Finish as described in the recipe for *Shrimp pilaf* (see SHRIMP). Turn out the pilaf on to a dish and pour round it a few tablespoons *Demi-glace sauce* (see SAUCE), adding to it the butter in which the chicken livers were cooked.

Foie gras pilaf. PILAF DE FOIE GRAS – Arrange the rice on a dish in a circle. Fill the middle with slices of *foie gras* sautéed in butter. Pour over them the pan juices diluted with Madeira and moistened with *Demi-glace sauce* (see SAUCE).

Truffle slivers, sautéed in butter, can be added.

Pilaf with mussels. PILAF DE MOULES – Cook the mussels as indicated for *Mussels à la poulette* (see MUSSEL). Shell them. Moisten with a few tablespoons of their cooking sauce. Pile them inside a border of *Rice pilaf.* Pour a few tablespoons of *Poulette sauce* (see SAUCE) round the border.

Mutton pilaf I. PILAF DE MOUTON – There are various ways of preparing this dish.

Sauté in butter 500 g. (18 oz.) lean coarsely diced mutton. Season with salt and pepper. Drain and keep hot.

Pour 1½ dl. (¼ pint, ⅔ cup) white wine into the frying pan. Heat and stir. Add 2 dl. (⅓ pint, scant cup) *Demi-glace sauce* (see SAUCE), or thickened veal stock, or brown stock made from the bones and trimmings of the mutton, and 1 dl. (6 tablespoons, scant $\frac{1}{2}$ cup) tomato purée. Bring to the boil. Put the mutton into this sauce. Heat but do not boil.

Butter a deep dish or basin and line it with *Rice pilaf.* Put aside most of the mutton sauce and pour the meat, with a little of the sauce, into the dish. Cover with rice. Unmould onto a platter. Pour the remaining sauce around the edge.

Mutton prepared as indicated above can also be served in a border of pilaf rice. This is made by filling a buttered turban (ring) mould with rice, pressing down well before turning out. Pour the sauce over the dish.

Another method is to bone the mutton and cut it into pieces. Braise in a very little tomato-flavoured stock. Serve in a border of rice pilaf as indicated above.

Mutton pilaf II (Turkish cookery). PILAF DE MOUTON – Make a *ragoût* (q.v.) of mutton, flavouring it strongly with tomatoes and spicing with a little ginger (or, if preferred, with saffron) and a touch of garlic.

When the mutton is almost cooked, drain it. Put it in another saucepan with peeled sweet peppers, coarsely diced. Add parboiled rice. Moisten with the strained cooking stock. Finish cooking all together. Serve in a bowl or deep round dish.

Sheep's (lamb's) kidney pilaf. PILAF DE ROGNONS DE MOUTON – This is made with kidneys cut in slices. (See OFFAL or VARIETY MEATS, *Calf's liver with pilaf.*)

Veal pilaf. PILAF DE VEAU – Prepare with fillet (U.S. sirloin) of veal cut into small square pieces and sautéed in butter, in the same way as *Mutton pilaf.*

PILCHARD – Small fish of the *Clupeidae* family, sold mainly tinned (canned) in spiced oil like sardines.

PILOT-FISH. FANFRE – Fish somewhat similar to mackerel. It is cooked in the same way. The pilot-fish is quite tasty, but indigestible.

PIMENTO – See PEPPER.

PINCER – Culinary term which describes the operation of browning certain substances in fat. It is applicable mainly to meat and vegetables before adding stock or any other liquid to them.

Pincer also applies to the operation of pinching up the edges of pies, tarts, etc.

PINCH. PINCÉE – The term 'pinch' frequently occurs in this book and corresponds to about 5 g. (1 scant teaspoon) in the case of salt and about 2 g. ($\frac{1}{2}$ teaspoon) in the case of pepper or mixed spices.

The term, however, is used only in application to quick seasoning. Seasoning for dishes requiring prolonged cooking must be expressed in more precise quantities.

PINEAPPLE. ANANAS – Herbaceous hardy perennial plant, rather similar to aloes in the structure of its leaves, although they are less thick than those of aloes. The flowers, bluish in colour, produce an ovoid globular fruit, yellowish in colour when ripe.

The pineapple is a native of America. It has, however, naturalised admirably in Asia and Africa, where it is generally cultivated.

Pineapple contains a strong proportion of sugar (more than 15 per cent), citric and malic acids and a ferment called *bromeline* very close to pepsin and papain (vegetable pepsin). It is a ferment which can be dissolved in proteinic substances and which acts very energetically on albumin contained in egg white, in meat and in milk, which it first curdles.

This ferment appears to be destroyed by heating and it is not present in sterilised, tinned pineapple. Pineapple contains a large quantity of Vitamins A and B.

When it is quite ripe this fruit has a very pleasant smell. Its firm, melting flesh, of a clear yellow colour, contains an abundance of fragrant juice in which the flavours of apple, strawberry and peach seem to mingle all at once.

Pineapple is eaten as it is, as a dessert, or is used for preparing various sweet dishes, ices, sherbets, jams, cakes and refreshing drinks. A kind of wine is made from fermented pineapple juice. When distilled, this produces a very pleasant liqueur.

When they are of good quality, tinned pineapples, preserved in syrup, can replace fresh ones, but they do not equal them in fragrance and delicacy of flavour.

Duck with pineapple (Chinese cookery). CANARD À L'ANANAS – Remove the bones from a small duck. Cut the flesh into strips and sauté these in fat along with garlic and chopped onions. Blend a little flour with the juice of a tin of pineapple and pour into the pan. To this add 1 tablespoon tomato purée, salt and pepper, a pinch of sugar. Simmer for 30 minutes.

Cut the pineapple slices into small pieces. Add them to the duck along with a handful of French beans. Simmer for 15 minutes. Just before serving add 1 tablespoon soya sauce.

Pineapple à la bavaroise. ANANAS À LA BAVAROISE – Hollow out and prepare a large pineapple as described in the recipe for *Iced pineapple* (see ICE CREAMS AND ICES).

Fill it with a pineapple-flavoured *Bavarian cream* (q.v.) with grated pineapple, steeped in kirsch, added to it.

Pineapple Bourdaloue. ANANAS BOURDALOUE – Proceed as described in the recipe for *Apricots Bourdaloue* (see APRICOTS), replacing the halved apricots by half slices of pineapple.

Dust with crushed macaroons, sprinkle with melted butter and glaze in the oven.

Pineapple compote. COMPOTE D'ANANAS – Peel a ripe, sound pineapple. Remove the eyes, which penetrate a little into the flesh beneath the rind.

Divide the pineapple in halves lengthways, remove the hard core and cut each half into regular slices. Cook in a light syrup, plain or flavoured with vanilla. Arrange in a fruit dish, and sprinkle with its syrup laced with kirsch or rum. Serve cold.

The pineapple can also be cooked whole, according to various recipes. Remove the core with the aid of a special corer and cut into slices.

Pineapple Condé. ANANAS CONDÉ – Arrange half slices of fresh pineapple cooked in syrup, or tinned pineapple, in a shallow oven-proof dish, three-quarters filled with *Dessert rice* (see RICE).

Decorate with halved glacé cherries and lozenges of angelica.

Heat in a moderate oven and serve with *Apricot sauce* (see SAUCE) laced with kirsch, either poured over or served separately.

Alternatively, arrange the half slices on a border of dessert rice prepared as described in the recipe for Apricots condé (see APRICOT).

Pineapple fritters. BEIGNETS D'ANANAS – Cut a fresh or tinned pineapple into slices. Dust with sugar, sprinkle with kirsch or rum, and leave to steep for 30 minutes.

Proceed as described in recipes for *Fresh fruit fritters* (see FRITTERS).

Pineapple fritters à la Carême. BEIGNETS D'ANANAS À LA CARÊME – Slice the pineapple and leave to steep as described in the preceding recipe.

Dry the slices, coat them with a thin layer of very thick apricot jam and stick them together in pairs. Dip into a light batter (see BATTERS FOR FRYING) and fry in deep fat.

Pineapple ice cream. GLACE À L'ANANAS – Add to $\frac{1}{2}$ litre (scant pint, $2\frac{1}{4}$ cups) syrup, prepared as described for fruit ices, ½ fresh shredded or grated pineapple. Leave to steep for 2 hours. Pass this mixture through a sieve and flavour it with kirsch. Measure it with a syrup gauge and rectify until it registers from 18° to 20°.

Chill in a freezer (see ICE CREAMS AND ICES). Serve in wine glasses, goblets or sundae glasses.

Iced pineapple – See ICE CREAMS AND ICES.

Pineapple with vanilla ice cream. COUPES GLACÉES À L'ANANAS À LA VANILLE – Fill dessert glasses with vanilla ice cream and diced pineapple steeped in kirsch.

Decorate with pineapple cut in lozenges, and sprinkle with kirsch.

Pineapple à l'impératrice. ANANAS À L'IMPÉRATRICE – Proceed as described in the recipe for *Apricots à l'impératrice* (see APRICOT), replacing the latter by half slices of pineapple cooked in syrup. Or prepare the pineapple as described for *Iced pineapple* (see ICE CREAMS AND ICES).

Fill the rind with *Rice à l'impératrice* (see RICE), and diced pineapple steeped in kirsch.

Leave to set in a cold place, or on ice, and serve like iced pineapple.

Pineapple manqué. MANQUÉ À L'ANANAS – Add diced crystallised pineapple to a *manqué* (q.v.) mixture. Bake and turn out. Ice with *Fondant icing* (see ICING) flavoured with pineapple. Decorate the top with pieces of crystallised pineapple.

Pineapple pancakes (crêpes). CRÊPES FOURRÉES, PANNEQUETS À L'ANANAS – Prepare *pannequets* (q.v.). Coat them with thick apricot jam, with pineapple cooked in syrup and cut into minute dice added to it. Roll up the pancakes.

Glaze in the oven as described in the recipe for *Apricot pannequets* (see PANNEQUETS).

Or coat the pancakes with *French pastry cream* (see CREAMS) with a grated pineapple added to it and finish as indicated above.

Pineapple à la piémontaise. ANANAS À LA PIÉMONTAISE – Proceed as described in the recipe for *Pineapple Condé*, replacing dessert rice by a layer of polenta (q.v.) bound with egg and flavoured with vanilla.

Or arrange the half slices of pineapple, cooked in syrup, on crescent-shaped polenta croquettes.

Pineapple with rice. ANANAS AU RIZ – Proceed as described for *Apricots with rice* (see APRICOT), replacing the halved apricots by half slices of pineapple in syrup.

Pineapple with rice and meringue. ANANAS MERINGUE AU RIZ – Proceed as described in the recipe for *Apricots with rice and meringue* (see APRICOT) using slices of pineapple poached in vanilla-flavoured syrup.

Pineapple sauce – See SAUCE.

Pineapple savarin. SAVARIN À L'ANANAS – Prepare a *savarin* (q.v.). Saturate it with syrup and flavour with kirsch or rum. Arrange it in a dish and garnish with half slices of pineapple cooked in syrup, or fill the middle with diced pineapple cooked in syrup. Serve hot or cold.

Pineapple surprise. ANANAS EN SURPRISE – Scoop out and prepare a large pineapple as described in the recipe for *Iced pineapple* (see ICE CREAMS AND ICES).

Fill it with a *macédoine* (q.v.) composed of the scooped-out pineapple pulp cut in thin slices, fresh blanched almonds and all kinds of fruit, previously steeped in kirsch and castor sugar.

Put the pineapple upright in a dish filled with crushed ice and leave to chill for 2 hours before serving.

Serve like *Iced pineapple*.

Pineapple tart. CROÛTE À L'ANANAS – Proceed as described in the recipe for *Fruit croûtes* (see CROÛTES) using, instead of mixed fruit, only pineapple cut in half slices for the border and in large dice for the interior.

Decorate with cherries and angelica and finish off as described in that recipe.

Pineapple tart à la royale. CROÛTE À L'ANANAS À LA ROYALE – Arrange a border of half slices of pineapple and slices of *savarin* (q.v.). Fill the middle with thick *French pastry cream* (see CREAMS) mixed with a grated pineapple flavoured with kirsch. Sprinkle with crushed macaroons. Decorate with crystallised fruit.

Pineapple tourte – See TOURTE, *Apricot tourte*.

Pork with pineapple. PORC À L'ANANAS – Brown some diced smoked bacon in a frying pan, then add a piece of pork chine. Brown. Remove the meat and place in a casserole. Sprinkle with thyme, bay leaf, cloves and 1 cup pineapple juice. Bake for 2 hours in a moderate oven, basting frequently. Serve with *Rice à la créole* (see RICE).

PINÉE – French word for first quality dried cod.

PINE SEED (Nut). PIGNON – Kernels of pine cones, which in taste resemble almonds and have various uses in cookery and confectionery.

This nut is known as *pignoli* in cookery.

PINION or POULTRY WING. AILERON – The terminal segment of a bird's wing, also called wing tip.

The pinions of large birds, which are classed as giblets, can be made into a great number of dishes (see GIBLETS).

The word 'pinion' also means the bones which support the fin rays of fish.

The recipes which follow are intended for pinions of turkeys or turkey-poults, but they are also suitable for preparing pinions of other big poultry.

Pinions of turkey à l'anglaise. AILERONS DE DINDONNEAU À L.ANGLAISE – See GIBLETS, *Turkey giblets à l'anglaise*.

Pinions of turkey à la bourgeoise. AILERONS DE DINDONNEAU À LA BOURGEOISE – See GIBLETS, *Turkey giblets à la bourgeoise*.

Turkey pinion broth. POT-AU-FEU AUX AILERONS DE DINDONNEAU – This is prepared like ordinary broth with stuffed turkey pinions. (See SOUPS AND BROTHS, *Pot-au-feu*.)

Pinions of turkey chasseur. AILERONS DE DINDONNEAU CHASSEUR – Cut the pinions in 2 pieces. Season with salt and pepper, fry them in butter, and finish cooking as described in the recipe for *Sautéed chicken chasseur* (see CHICKEN).

Consommé with pinions I. CONSOMMÉ AUX AILERONS – Prepare a chicken consommé (see SOUPS, *Clear soups*). Bone and stuff the pinions with a *Quenelle forcemeat* (see FORCEMEATS). Put the pinions into the consommé to cook. Pass the consommé through a muslin cloth and serve with trimmed pinions.

Rice cooked in consommé is sometimes added to this soup.

Consommé with pinions II. CONSOMMÉ AUX AILERONS – Prepare meat stock. Trim 6 pinions, put in a muslin bag and cook in the stock. Strain the stock and serve with the pinions, removing all the little bones which have come loose during cooking.

Serve with bread cut into small pieces and dried in the oven. Carrots and leeks, cooked in stock and cut into pieces are sometimes added to this soup.

Fricassée of turkey pinions. AILERONS DE DINDONNEAU EN FRICASSÉE – Cook the pinions, stuffed as described in (I) above, until two-thirds done, in chicken or veal stock. Put them into a sauté pan with small onions and mushrooms half-cooked in chicken or veal stock. Moisten with *Velouté sauce* (see SAUCE) made from the stock in which the pinions were cooked. Finish cooking together, simmering gently. Bind the sauce with egg yolks and cream, as described in the recipe for *Fricassée of chicken à la berrichonne* (see FRICASSÉE).

Turkey pinions à la niçoise. AILERONS DE DINDONNEAU À LA NIÇOISE – Season the pinions with salt and pepper. Fry briskly in a mixture of butter and oil. Remove when golden. Into the same pan put (for 6 pinions) 50 g. (2 oz., $\frac{1}{2}$ cup) chopped onion. Fry lightly, add 3 peeled, seeded, chopped tomatoes, and a little grated garlic. Cook for 5 minutes, put the pinions back in the pan, add a *bouquet garni* (q.v.), moisten with $1\frac{1}{2}$ dl. ($\frac{1}{4}$ pint, $\frac{2}{3}$ cup) dry white wine, season, bring to the boil, cover, and simmer for 20 minutes. Add 24 black olives and the same number of small button mushrooms. Finish cooking, simmering gently for 15 minutes. Sprinkle with chopped tarragon.

Turkey pinions en tortue. AILERONS DE DINDONNEAU EN TORTUE – Bone 12 turkey pinions in such a way as to shape them into pockets. Stuff with a *Quenelle forcemeat* (see FORCEMEATS). Sew up the opening. Fry thinly sliced carrots and onions in bacon fat and add the pinions. Season with salt and a little allspice. Add a *bouquet garni* (q.v.), sprinkle with melted butter and put the pan on brisk heat. Brown both sides of the pinions lightly. Moisten with 1 glass Madeira. Leave to boil down completely. Add a few tablespoons thickened brown veal stock and braise in a slow oven, uncovered.

Remove the pinions with a perforated spoon, and put into another pan with *Tortue garnish* (see GARNISHES). Add *Tortue sauce* (see SAUCE) to the braising pan juices, boil down, strain, and pour over the pinions. Leave to simmer for a few minutes. Arrange the pinions on a serving dish with the garnish around them. Add supplementary garnish: gherkins cut in small uniform pieces, fried yolks of egg, dressed crayfish, heart-shaped croûtons fried in butter. Pour the sauce over the pinions.

Stuffed turkey pinions in aspic jelly. AILERONS DE DINDONNEAU FARCIS À LA GELÉE – Stuff the pinions with a finely pounded *Pork forcemeat* (see FORCEMEATS), adding diced truffles or a forcemeat made of minced pork, *foie gras* and truffles. Wrap each pinion in a piece of muslin and secure with string. Cook in a stock made from Madeira-flavoured meat jelly or a rich broth flavoured with Madeira. Drain, cook, and put in a dish. Clarify the liquid jelly in which they were cooked and pour over the pinions. (See JELLY, *Meat jelly stock*.)

Stuffed braised pinions of turkey. AILERONS DE DINDONNEAU FARCIS, BRAISÉS – Singe and pluck 6 turkey pinions. Bone them carefully, so as not to damage the skin. Stuff them with forcemeat: finely pounded pork forcemeat, chicken forcemeat, quenelle forcemeat, or any other (see FORCEMEATS or STUFFINGS). Wrap each one in a thin rasher (slice) of bacon and secure with thread.

Melt some butter in a sauté pan, and in it brown bacon rinds, 50 g. (2 oz., $\frac{1}{2}$ cup) onion and 50 g. (2 oz., $\frac{1}{2}$ cup) carrot, cut in thin slices. Arrange the pinions on these. Add a *bouquet garni* (q.v.), and season with salt and pepper. Simmer under a lid on top of the stove for 15 minutes.

Moisten with 2 dl. ($\frac{1}{3}$ pint, scant cup) dry white wine or Madeira, according to recipe, boil down, and add 4 dl. ($\frac{3}{4}$ pint, scant 2 cups) brown chicken or veal stock. Bring to the boil. Cook in the oven, covered, for 40 minutes. Remove the pinions, unwrap them and glaze in a hot oven. Arrange them on a dish and pour over them the pan juices in which they were braised, with the fat skimmed off, boiled down and strained.

The pinions can be completed with various garnishes.

Stuffed turkey pinions in chaud-froid sauce. AILERONS DE DINDONNEAU FARCIS EN CHAUD-FROID – Cook the stuffed pinions in liquid aspic jelly laced with Madeira. Leave to cool in the stock. Drain and dry well.

Cover with white or brown *Chaud-froid sauce* (see SAUCE), depending on the nature of the dish. Glaze the pinions with a jelly. Garnish with chopped jelly.

Pinions in *chaud-froid sauce* can be decorated with truffles, tongue *à l'écarlate*, hard-boiled egg white, etc., croûtons of bread spread with butter. Place them in a glass dish and cover with jelly.

Stuffed turkey pinions with chipolata sausages. AILERONS DE DINDONNEAU FARCIS CHIPOLATA – Prepare like Turkey giblets *with chipolata sausages* (see GIBLETS).

Stuffed turkey pinions à la fermière. AILERONS DE DINDONNEAU FARCIS À LA FERMIÈRE – Stuff the pinions with a finely pounded forcemeat of chopped onions cooked in butter until transparent, mixed with chopped parsley. Braise the pinions until half done and put in an earthenware casserole. Cover them with garnish *à la fermière* (carrots, turnips, celery and onions, sliced and lightly fried in butter). Remove fat from the pan juices, boil down, strain, and pour over the ingredients in the casserole. Finish cooking in the oven with a lid on.

Stuffed turkey pinions fried in batter. AILERONS DE DINDONNEAU FARCIS EN FRITOT – Stuff and cook the pinions as described above. Strain the stock in which they were cooked and leave them to cool in it.

Drain and marinate for 30 minutes in oil, lemon juice, salt, pepper and chopped parsley. Dip them in a light batter (see BATTERS FOR FRYING) and deep-dry in sizzling fat.

Drain, dry, season with dry fine salt. Garnish with fried parsley and quarters of lemon. Serve with tomato or other sauce.

Stuffed turkey pinions à la périgourdine. AILERONS DE DINDONNEAU FARCIS À LA PÉRIGOURDINE – Stuff the pinions with *foie gras* and diced truffles, to which a little *Pork forcemeat* (see FORCEMEATS) can be added. Season with salt, pepper and spices, and sprinkle with brandy.

Wrap in rashers of bacon. Braise in stock laced with Madeira. When three-quarters cooked, remove, unwrap, put in an earthenware dish with 200 g. (7 oz., 2 cups) quartered truffles for 6 pinions. Skim the fat off the stock, boil down, strain, and pour the stock over the pinions. Cook in the oven for 15 minutes.

Stuffed turkey pinions Sainte-Menehould. AILERONS DE DINDONNEAU SAINTE-MENEHOULD – Stuff the pinions as described above and braise in white wine or in clear veal stock. Drain and cool under a press.

Brush with butter, dip in toasted or grated breadcrumbs, sprinkle with melted butter and grill on a low heat until both sides are golden.

Serve either with *Diable sauce* or with *Sainte-Menehould sauce* (see SAUCE) made from the stock in which the pinions were braised.

Grilled pinions *Sainte-Menehould* can be served with various vegetables, cooked in water and dressed with butter, or with purées of vegetables. Serve with mustard.

Stuffed turkey pinions à la Soubise. AILERONS DE DINDONNEAU FARCIS À LA SOUBISE – Stuff and braise the pinions as described above. Drain and glaze. Arrange on a dish and sprinkle with the boiled-down pan juices. Serve with *Onion soubise* (see PURÉE).

PINOT – Variety of grapes of which the black is used exclusively for making red Burgundy wines. In Champagne the white Pinot is used.

PINTAIL (Duck). PILET – Variety of wild duck. Prepare like wild duck or spoonbill or shoveller duck (see DUCK).

PIPERADE – Basque dish. Cooked tomatoes and peppers to which eggs are added, one by one, to obtain a fluffy purée. To this is added Bayonne ham.

PIPIT – Small edible bird which can be prepared in the same way as lark (q.v.).

PIPKIN. HUGUENOTE – Old-fashioned cooking pot with or without little feet.

PIQUEPOULT – Wine made in the Gers *département*, from which Armagnacs are distilled.

PIQUETTE – Wine of second or third pressing obtained by flooding husks of grapes with unsweetened warm water. It is a light, refreshing drink which does not travel, and is used either for home consumption or for distilling purposes. Common usage has also extended the word to mean 'mediocre wine'.

PIROGHI or PIROZHKI. PIROGUI – In Russian the name *piroghi* means pies large enough to be cut into portions. *Pirozhki*, meaning little pies, are small enough to be eaten out of the hand.

Carrot pirozhki. PIROGUI AUX CAROTTES – Roll some puff pastry about 6 or 7 mm. ($\frac{1}{4}$ inch) thick and cut into circles 10 cm. (4 inches) in diameter.

Shred the carrots into a *brunoise* (q.v.), cook in butter, mix with chopped hard-boiled eggs, parsley and chives, bind with thick *Béchamel sauce* (see SAUCE) and put 1 tablespoon of this mixture on each circlet of pastry.

Moisten the edges of the pastry and seal, enclosing the filling and giving the *pirozhki* an oval shape. Put them on a baking sheet, brush with beaten egg and bake for 18 minutes in a hot oven.

Caucasian pirozhki. PIROGUI CAUCASIENS – Spread a thin layer of cheese-flavoured *Chou pastry* (see CHOU) on a baking sheet. Bake in the oven. Put the pastry on a table, divide into 2 parts and sandwich them together, having first coated them with a light layer of thick *Béchamel sauce* (see SAUCE), to which some grated cheese and cooked sliced mushrooms have been added.

Cut into rectangles 6 cm. ($2\frac{1}{2}$ inches) long and 3 cm. ($1\frac{1}{4}$ inches) wide.

Cover these with cheese-flavoured *Béchamel sauce*, and coat with breadcrumbs. Fry in smoking hot deep fat and drain.

Cream cheese pirozhki. PIROGUI AU FROMAGE – Butter *dariole* moulds and line them with unsweetened *Common brioche dough* (see BRIOCHE). Fill with cream cheese, cover with a circlet of the same dough and seal the edges. Leave to rise in a warm place for 30 minutes. Bake in a hot oven from 20 to 25 minutes.

Fish pirozhki. PIROGUI AU POISSON – Proceed as described in the recipe for *Game pirozhki* (see below), replacing the game meat by chopped cooked white fish.

Game pirozhki. PIROGUI AU GIBIER – Prepare *Puff pastry* (see DOUGH), roll it out $\frac{1}{2}$ cm. ($\frac{1}{4}$ inch) thick and cut into circles about 7 to 8 cm. (3 inches) in diameter.

Put 1 tablespoon game hash (q.v.), mixed with chopped hard-boiled eggs, cooked buckwheat or rice cooked in meat stock, on each circlet. Moisten the edges of the pastry, and cover with another circlet of the same size and thickness. Brush with beaten egg, and bake in a hot oven from 18 to 20 minutes.

Moscow pirozhki. PIROGUI À LA MOSCOVITE – Roll out unsweetened *Common brioche dough* (see BRIOCHE) into oval pieces about 6 cm. ($2\frac{1}{2}$ inches) wide and 10 cm. (4 inches) long. Put on each a piece of filling, the size of a walnut, prepared in the following manner.

Chop and mix 100 g. (4 oz.) white flaked fish, 75 g. (3 oz.) cooked visiga (dry spinal cord of the sturgeon) and 2 hard-boiled eggs. Season.

Moisten the edges of the dough slightly and enclose the filling by bringing the edges together and sealing them. Keep in a warm place to rise for 25 minutes. Bake in a hot oven for 20 minutes.

Polish pirozhki. PIROGUI POLONAIS – Roll out puff pastry 6 to 7 mm. ($\frac{1}{4}$ inch) thick and cut into oval-shaped pieces about 6 cm. ($2\frac{1}{2}$ inches) wide and 10 cm. (4 inches) long.

Put the following filling on each, in pieces the size of a walnut.

Sauté gently 50 g. (2 oz., $\frac{1}{2}$ cup) chopped onion in butter, add 250 g. (9 oz.) veal udder and 250 g. (9 oz.) lean veal, cut in small dice and also fried in butter. Season with salt, pepper and nutmeg and leave to cool before using.

Seal as described in the recipe for *Moscow pirozhki*, and bake in a hot oven for 20 minutes.

Pirozhki with truffles. PIROGUI AUX TRUFFES – Cut cooked truffles into thick round slices. Cover with thick *Béchamel sauce* (see SAUCE) and leave until cold.

Sandwich these between two *blini* (q.v.) circlets cut out with a pastry cutter, and press down well to seal the edges. Dip in beaten egg, roll in breadcrumbs and fry in clarified butter.

Pirozhki with various vegetable fillings. PIROGUI AUX LÉGUMES – Proceed as described in the recipe for *Carrot pirozhki*, replacing carrots by a *salpicon* (q.v.) of various vegetables cooked in butter and bound with *Béchamel sauce* (see SAUCE).

The filling of vegetable *pirozhki* may be supplemented by buckwheat or rice cooked in stock or water.

Visiga pirozhki. PIROGUI AU VÉSIGA – Roll out puff pastry $\frac{1}{2}$ cm. ($\frac{1}{4}$ inch) thick and cut into circlets 10 cm. (4 inches) in diameter. Put on each some of the following mixture:

Cook 100 g. (4 oz.) visiga (dry spinal cord of the sturgeon) in white stock, 4 parsley roots and 1 stalk of celery. Drain the visiga, chop it, as well as the parsley roots and celery, add 2 chopped hard-boiled eggs and 1 tablespoon chopped parsley. Bind with 3 tablespoons (scant $\frac{1}{4}$ cup) thick *Béchamel sauce* (see SAUCE). Season with salt, pepper and nutmeg and leave to get cold before using.

Moisten the edges of the pastry, fold in the shape of a turnover, seal well, brush with beaten egg, and bake in a hot oven from 18 to 20 minutes.

PISSALADIÈRE – Flan made mainly in the Nice region, filled with onions, anchovy fillets and black olives.

PISTACHE (EN) – Term used in the south-western part of France, mainly in the Catalan country, to describe a special method of preparing leg of mutton. Its only garnish consists of cloves of garlic. (See MUTTON, *Pistache of mutton.*)

Pigeons and partridges can also be prepared *en pistache*.

PISTACHIO. PISTACHE – Seed of the *Pistacia vera*, a deciduous tree, native of the Levant, which, it is said, was brought to Rome by Vitellius. It yields an edible nut, about the size of an olive, brown-reddish in colour, with a thin husk, inside which a ligneous membrane is found. This is easily separated into 2 pieces and contains a very pale almond enclosed in a reddish skin.

Pistachio nuts have a sweet and pleasant flavour and are used as flavouring in cookery, *charcuterie*, pastry-making and confectionery.

This is the name given to a Comminges mutton *ragoût* garnished with haricot beans. Here is the recipe given by M. Jean Peyrafitte of the hotel 'Poste et Golf' at Luchon:

'Soak 500 g. (18 oz.) white Tarbes haricot beans for 12 hours, changing the water twice. Cook the beans in an earthenware casserole with a *bouquet garni*, some whole carrots, garlic, 1 onion stuck with 2 or more cloves, a good hock of home-cured ham and 150 g. (5 oz.) fresh pork rinds.

'Sauté a piece of mutton (shoulder preferably). When this is three-quarters cooked, drain it and add the haricot beans. Simmer over a low heat until the mutton is cooked. Check the seasoning and serve in the casserole.'

PISTOU (Italian cookery) – This soup, the recipe for which is given in the section headed SOUPS AND BROTHS, is made of various vegetables and thick vermicelli. Its main characteristic is that pounded garlic with basil and grilled tomatoes mixed with oil are used.

Pistou actually means pounded basil. Its meaning has been extended to include soups incorporating the latter.

PITHIVIERS GÂTEAU – This gâteau is a speciality of Pithiviers. It is made of *Puff pastry* (see DOUGH) and almond paste, which can be prepared from the following ingredients: 50 g. (2 oz., $\frac{1}{2}$ cup) blanched almonds, 50 g. (2 oz., $\frac{1}{4}$ cup) fine sugar, 50 g. (2 oz., $\frac{1}{4}$ cup) butter, 3 eggs and $\frac{1}{2}$ dl. (3 tablespoons, scant $\frac{1}{4}$ cup) rum.

Pound the almonds in a mortar, adding 1 egg. When they are reduced to a fine paste, put into a bowl, add castor sugar and butter, and blend the mixture, stirring with a wooden spoon until very smooth. Add 2 eggs, one by one, and flavour with rum. Roll out half the puff pastry into a round piece 20 cm (8 inches) in diameter and 2 mm ($\frac{1}{10}$ inch) thick. Turn the pastry and put on a moistened metal sheet.

Spread this with the almond paste, leaving about 2 cm ($\frac{3}{4}$ inch) of the edge uncovered. Roll out the rest of the pastry into a circle of the same diameter as that forming the bottom of the gâteau. To seal, moisten the bottom piece of pastry around the edges and cover with the second piece, taking care to turn it. Press well all round to seal the edges properly, brush with beaten egg and leave for 5 minutes. With the point of a knife mark the top with faint lines in the shape of a rosette and bake in the oven from 25 to 30 minutes. Two minutes before taking it out of the oven, sprinkle the gâteau with very fine sugar and glaze in the hottest part of the oven.

PITHIVIERS AU FOIN – See CHEESE.

PLAFOND – French word for tinned copper metal baking sheets, which were used in the olden days for browning small pieces of meat.

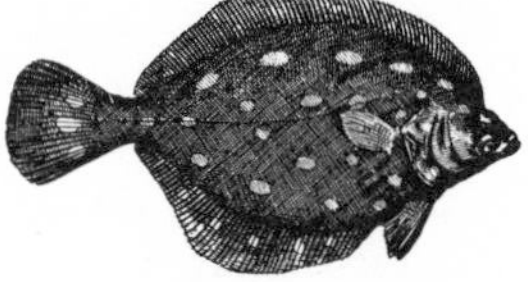

Plaice

PLAICE. CARRELET, PLIE FRANCHE – Seawater fish which is flat, diamond-shaped with rounded angles. The two eyes are

How to fillet plaice

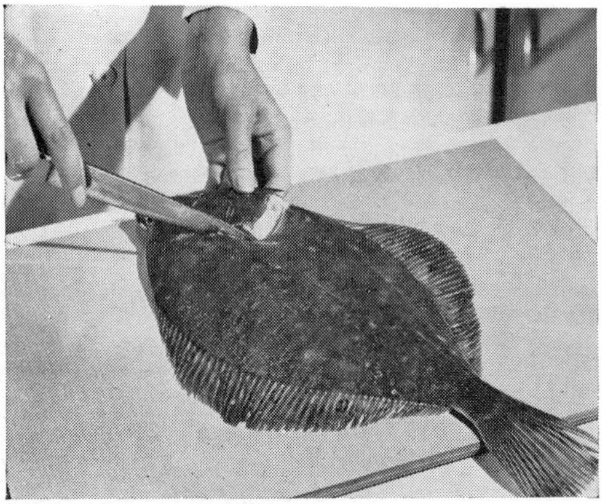

Remove head

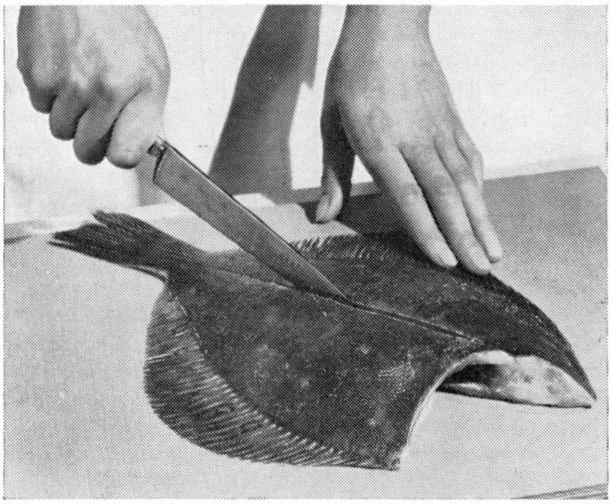

Make an incision down the back base

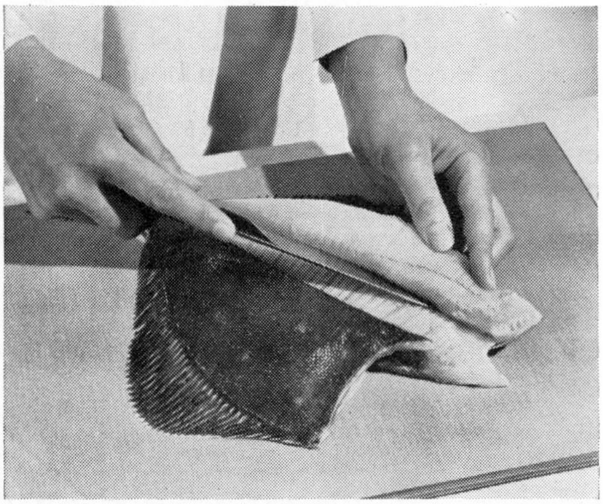

Cut into fillets

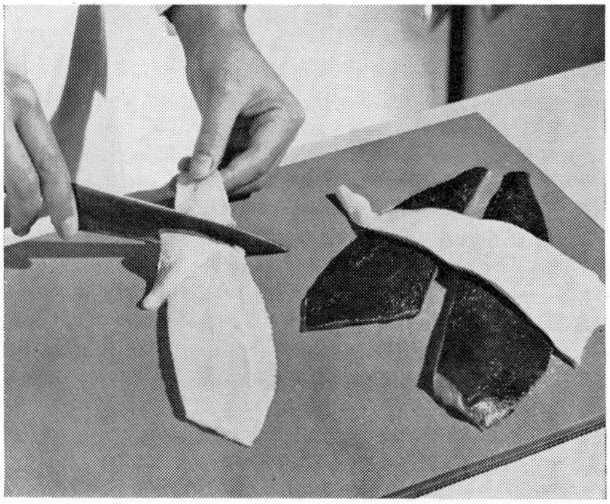

Skin

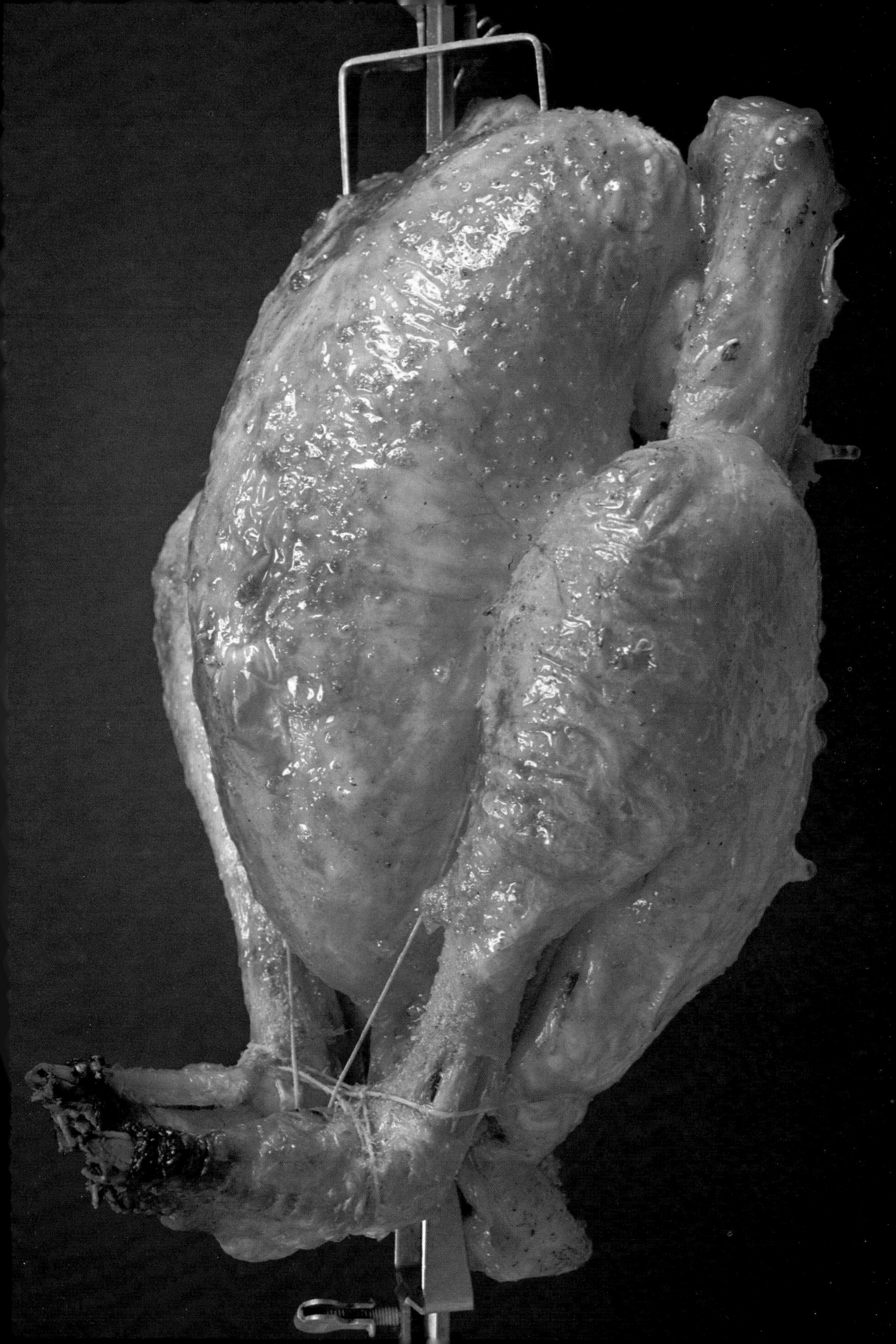

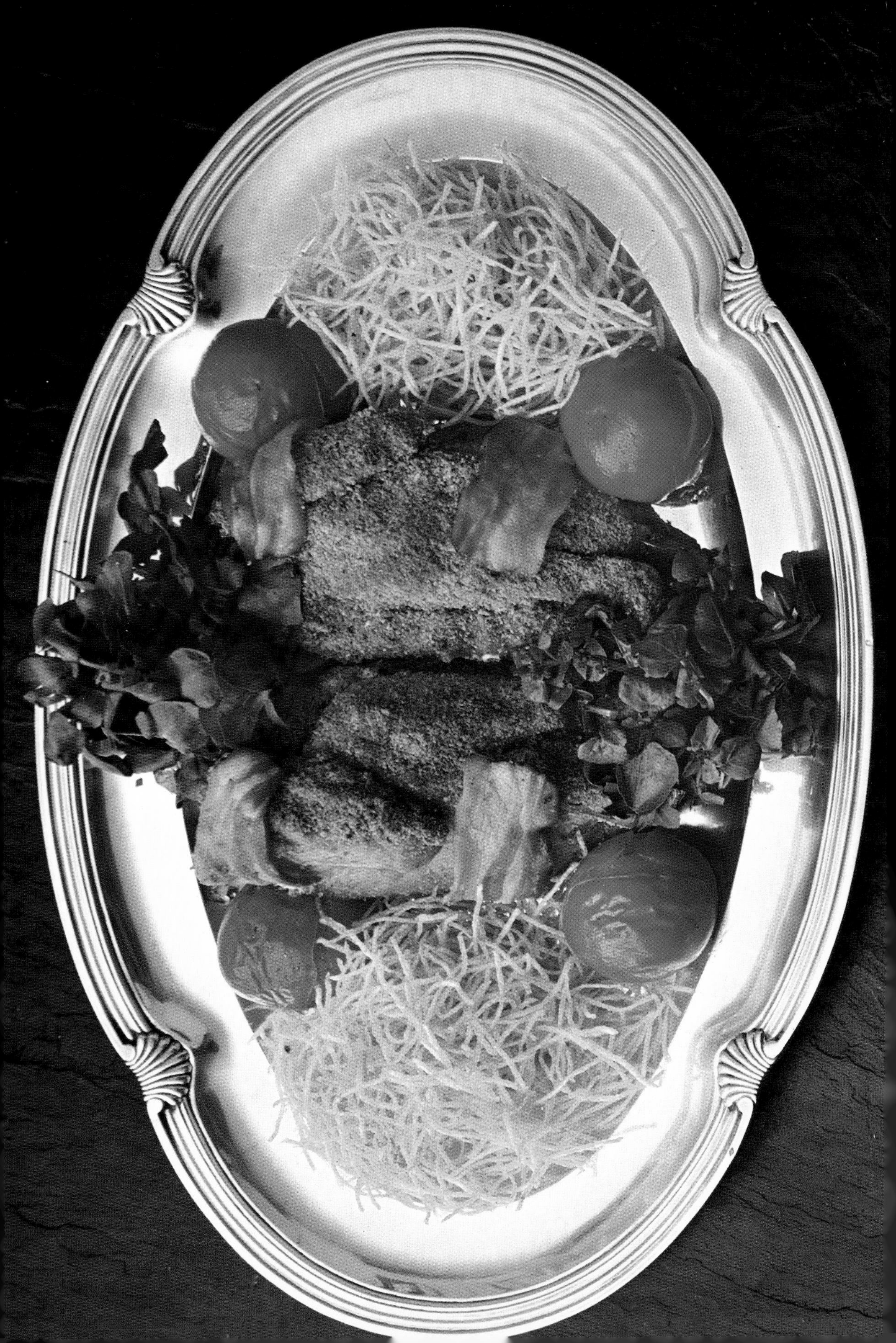

set on the left side of the head. The left side is brownish with rounded or oval spots, red or orange. Plaice have 5 or 6 bony tubercles well marked between the eyes. The reverse side is white.

This fish, though of medium quality, is quite good, provided it is perfectly fresh.

Boiled plaice with various sauces. CARRELET BOUILLI – Only large plaice are used in this way, cooked whole, or cut into slices. Cook them in a *court-bouillon* of water, milk, salt, and lemon slices, in the same way as for brill (q.v.).

Drain the plaice and garnish with fresh parsley. Serve with boiled potatoes in a dish and with one of the sauces which are normally served with boiled fish.

Plaice à la bonne femme. CARRELET À LA BONNE FEMME – Proceed as for *Brill à la bonne femme* (see BRILL).

Plaice Dugléré. CARRELET DUGLÉRÉ – Cut a large plaice into slices and cook in the same way as for *Bass Dugléré* (see BASS).

Chef's lore maintains that it was for plaice that Dugléré (then chef of the one-time *Café Anglais*) invented this method of preparation, which in actual practice is used for bass, brill and chicken-turbot.

Fried plaice. CARRELET FRIT – Use only small plaice and cook in the same manner as *Fried brill* (see BRILL).

Plaice à l'indienne. CARRELET À L'INDIENNE – Cut a large plaice into slices. Season with salt and pepper and put them in a pan on a base of chopped onions softened in butter and seasoned with curry powder.

Stew the plaice with the lid on. Sprinkle it with curry powder, pour over it 2 dl. ($\frac{1}{3}$ pint, scant cup) white wine for 750 g. ($1\frac{1}{2}$ lb.) fish. Boil down the liquor, and cover with *Béchamel sauce* (see SAUCE), not too thick. Cook for a further 15 minutes on a low heat.

Place the slices in a dish, cover them with the boiled-down sauce to which butter has been added, flavoured with a little lemon juice. Serve with *Rice à l'indienne* (see RICE).

Plaice à la niçoise. CARRELET À LA NIÇOISE – Make some light incisions in the plaice. Season with salt and pepper. Brush it with oil and grill under a gentle heat.

Put it on a serving dish on a layer of tomatoes softened in butter, seasoned with garlic and chopped tarragon. Lay a grid of anchovies on top of the fish, and sprinkle with capers. Surround it with green olives which have been stoned and blanched, or unstoned black olives. Sprinkle with chopped basil.

As well as the methods indicated above, see also those given for BRILL; TURBOT; SOLE.

PLAISIR – French word for a small wafer or *oublie*, rolled into a cone (see OUBLIE.)

PLANTAIN TREE. FIGUIER D'ADAM – A type of banana tree (see BANANA).

PLASTRON – Ventral part of the shell of turtles. This part, as well as the dorsal one, after being taken out of the horny plate or shell, is used for making turtle soup.

PLATE. ASSIETTE – Small table utensil, mostly of porcelain or china nowadays, of various materials in the past. The centre of the plate is called the 'well' and the border, which forms the band around the hollow part, is called the 'rim'. This band is also sometimes referred to as the 'shoulder'.

The Greeks had two types of plates: the first, *tryps*, were quite large and could serve as a dish; the other, *tryblion*, was smaller.

The Romans had plates in pottery, glass, silver and gold. The common people used wooden bowls.

In the Middle Ages, the individual plate disappeared. It was replaced by a round slice of bread which was called a trencher. After the meal this bread was distributed to the poor.

At the end of the fifteenth century everybody wanted to have silver plates and dishes. Juvenal des Ursin sorrowfully protested against this abuse.

In the sixteenth and seventeenth centuries plates became magnificent works of art, in which gold, enamel and even precious stones were combined. There exist today wonderful plates which were made by the enamellers of Limoges. Plants, shells and animals can be seen worked in relief on the plates of Bernard Palissy.

Although the greater part of the plates in precious metals and enamels are of the same size as present-day plates – about 20 cm. (8 inches) in diameter – they were rather show pieces than table utensils in daily use. Plates manufactured at Sèvres come very near to the art of bygone days.

The faïence of Moustiers, remarkable for its decorative qualities and the purity of its enamel, was for a long time attributed to the factories of Rouen.

At the end of the seventeenth century Pierre Clerissy, coming from a family of potters, created in Moustiers a pottery industry, which, according to Davillier, 'must have brought him a fortune, and to his town a century of prosperity'. His nephew, who succeeded him in 1728 and bore the same name, was elevated by Louis XV in 1743 and took the title of Seigneur de Trevans. He was appointed secretary of the king's chancellery in 1847 by the Parliament of Provence, when he joined forces with Joseph Fouque, a skilled artist, and handed over his factory to him. The factory by now employed 28 painters and remained the first and most important of all those soon to be established by his competitors at Moustiers and in several neighbouring localities. Its products enjoyed a well-merited reputation, which they maintained for a long time, for Abbé Delaporte, in his *Voyageur français*, published in Paris in 1788, speaks of it in these terms:

'There is in the little town of Moustiers a factory of faïence which is considered the best and finest in the kingdom.'

Other factories in the south of France included those at Marseille. Some of these, notably those of Savy, produced remarkable pieces, decorated with landscapes and still life, painted with great perfection.

The decoration of plates offers a great variety of subjects and curiosities. The décor of Italian plates, or *majolica*, is very varied. At the beginning, the ornaments were mixed with figures, then scenes reproduced from the works of great masters began to take precedence, often taking up the whole surface. Finally, the central motive was framed with so-called grotesque ornaments. At Nevers, Italian influence is felt; later we find white decorations on Persian blue background. Still later comes the Chinese style. Nevers also produced popular china plates, particularly so-called 'patronymic' plates, bearing the name of the person for whom they were destined as wedding presents, with a figure of his or her patron saint painted on it; plates bearing professional emblems and plates made during the revolutionary period, with mottos and symbols.

Historical events have often been represented on popular plates. The conquest of Algeria, depicting military scenes, such as the award of the *croix d'honneur*; the consuls of Damascus congratulating Abd el-Kader on his intervention on the side of the Lebanese Maronites massacred by the Turks; the Syrian Maronites welcoming French troops, and episodes from the 1914 War. Puzzle pictures and Béranger songs also decorated popular plates.

Rouen plates have had several styles of decoration: the *lambrequin* design, composed of symmetrical patterns, repeated or alternating, and converging towards the centre of

Rouen (18th century)

Moustier

Moustier

Old Sèvres　　Old Sèvres　　Sèvres (Empire period)　　Sèvres (Fontainebleau service)

Wedgwood: Dinner and dessert plates

Goupy: soup and dinner plates

Woodhouse: dinner, soup, dessert, salad and side plates

SOME EXAMPLES OF OLD PLATES

the plate; the design inspired by the rococo style, armorial bearings, and couplets with the music carefully noted down. Floral pieces, in fresh and brilliant colours, decorate Strasbourg plates.

Decoration of plates is in fact a very active branch of art, even in modern times.

PLATINE – French name for a small low baking pan.

PLEUROTUS – Genus of fungi, some species of which are edible and excellent.

PLOMBIÈRE (Ice) – Iced sweets (see ICE CREAMS AND ICES).

Golden plover
(*W. E. Higham*)

PLOVER. PLUVIER – Genus of wading birds of which there are several species: the *great plover* is about the size of a lapwing or peewit and, like them, haunts marshlands and water meadows near the sea. The *golden plover* is the size of a turtle dove and its plumage is speckled with yellow.

Plovers are considered excellent game and some gastronomes insist that they should be cooked undrawn. This tradition is an old one: in the sixteenth century, according to Lucien Tendret, only three kinds of birds (larks, turtle doves and plovers) were roasted without 'breaking into them'.

Plover can be prepared in any way suitable for woodcock (q.v.).

PLUCHES – French name for the leaves of certain plants, such as chervil and parsley. These leaves are generally used raw, chervil leaves being put into some soups. In some cases the leaves are blanched in boiling water.

PLUCK. ISSUES – The lights, heart and entrails of slaughtered animals. (See OFFAL or VARIETY MEATS, *Lamb's pluck à l'anglaise*).

The French word *issues* is wrongly used for the giblets of poultry. The expression *issues de table* was used formerly to describe the last tit-bits served at the end of a great banquet. These included sweets, sugared almonds, crystallised fruit, and other delicacies which went with the sweet. Sometimes these were not served at the table but in a room next to the dining-room.

PLUM. PRUNE – Fruit of the plum tree, of the family *Rosaceae*. It is cultivated everywhere in Europe. There is an infinite variety of plum trees in France which all produce sweet-tasting fruit. Among the best of these are the *greengage (reine-claude)* which ripens at the end of July and whose flesh is very sweet and well flavoured; the *golden greengage (reine-claude dorée)* which ripens towards the end of August; the *mirabelle*, a small round plum, yellow in colour streaked with red, the flesh very well flavoured, which is fully ripened at the end of August; violet, black, and white *damsons*; the *Saint Catherine*; the *early yellow*; the *quetsche* (the fruit from which

Greengages

the famous liqueur is made and which is also used for compotes, jams and in *pâtisserie*) which matures during the month of August; the *ente* or *Agen* plum, medium-sized fruit, pinkish violet in colour which ripens in September (usually sold as prunes).

All these varieties of plums are eaten as fresh fruit. They may also be used to make compotes, jams and a large number of pastry desserts. The plum is an excellent dessert fruit.

Plums Bourdaloue. PRUNES BOURDALOUE – Large greengages are used in this way. Proceed as for *Apricots Bourdaloue* (see APRICOT).

Plums in brandy. PRUNES À L'EAU-DE-VIE – Wipe some greengages and prick them 2 or 3 times with a big needle. Weigh the fruit. Make a syrup of sugar in the ratio of 250 g. (9 oz., 1 generous cup) sugar and 3 tablespoons ($\frac{1}{4}$ cup) water to each kg. (2 lb.) fruit, and cook to 105°C. (220°F.).

When this syrup is ready, immerse the plums in it. Let them boil twice before touching with the skimmer.

Drain and put them in a jar. Let the syrup cool completely. Add to it a quantity of good quality brandy equal to the quantity of syrup. Strain the liquid through muslin and fill the jar with it. Cork and secure firmly. Leave to soak well before using.

'Agen' plums

Candied plums. PRUNES CONFITES – Prepared as for *Candied apricots* (see APRICOT).

Compote of plums – See COMPOTE, *Plum compote*.

Plums Condé. PRUNES CONDÉ – Large greengages are used for this recipe. Proceed as for *Apricots Condé* (see APRICOT).

Plums flambé Lorraine. PRUNES FLAMBÉES À LA LORRAINE – Cook lightly in a vanilla syrup some stoned mirabelle plums. Drain, and put them in ovenware dishes. Pour over a little syrup bound with arrowroot. Sprinkle with hot Quetsche. Set alight when serving.

Plum fritters – See FRITTERS.

Plum fritters à l'agenaise – See FRITTERS.

Ice and iced mousse of plums. GLACE, MOUSSE GLACÉE AUX PRUNES – Follow the same procedure as for *Apricot ice* or *Iced mousse* (see ICE CREAMS AND ICES).

Plum jam. CONFITURE DE PRUNES – Allow 350 g. (12 oz., $1\frac{1}{2}$ cups) sugar for 500 g. (18 oz.) stoned fruit. Proceed as for *Apricot jam* (see JAMS AND JELLIES).

Plum soufflé Lorraine. SOUFFLÉ AUX PRUNES À LA LORRAINE – Prepare a purée of 200 g. (7 oz.) mirabelle plums and mix it with 250 g. (9 oz., generous cup) sugar cooked to a heavy syrup. Add 5 egg whites beaten to a very stiff foam and then diced preserved plums, soaked in plum brandy. To cook, proceed as for sweet soufflés (see SOUFFLÉ).

Alsatian plum tart – See TART, *Fruit tart à l'alsacienne*.

POACHING. POCHAGE – Method of cooking meat, poultry, fish, etc., in a clear spiced and flavoured stock, or in water. (See CULINARY METHODS.)

Poached eggs. OEUFS POCHÉS – The eggs selected must be small and very fresh (see EGGS, *Poached eggs*).

POCHARD. AYTHYA – Species of duck known as *pochard, pockard* or poker (the female of which is known as *dunbird*).

A fully-grown male pochard has a bright red head and neck; the back and breast partly a dull black, partly ash-grey with thin black stripes. The sides are similarly striped; the lower region of the abdomen is black, the bill is dark blue, the culmen and the tip are black, the tarsus and the scutes blueish and the eyes orange-red. The plumage of the female of the species, even in the spring, is less brilliant.

This species frequently nests in the marshy plains of Holland, Northern Germany and Belgium and crosses France twice a year during winter migrations. They are then keenly pursued by sportsmen for the succulence and the distinctive taste of their flesh, which is greatly prized by connoisseurs.

All the methods of preparation given for wild duck can be applied to pochard (see DUCK).

POCHOUSE – The *pochouse* (also written *pauchose*) is a *matelote* (q.v.) made of all kinds of freshwater fish, with eel predominating, which should be cooked with white wine and thickened with *Kneaded butter* (see BUTTER), as with *Matelote à la meunière* (see MATELOTE).

Cut the fish into uniform chunks and put into a buttered sauté pan on a foundation of onions and carrots cut in slices. Season and put on a big *bouquet garni* (q.v.) containing 1 clove of garlic in the middle. Pour in enough dry white wine to cover the fish. Bring to the boil, then cover and simmer from 20 to 25 minutes.

Drain the pieces of fish. Put them into another sauté pan with diced bacon, mushrooms and small onions. Thicken the liquor in which the fish was cooked with kneaded butter. Strain and pour over the fish. Simmer for a few moments. Just before serving add a few tablespoons fresh cream.

The word comes from the fisherman's *'poche'*, the game bag he fills with the various fish that go to make up this freshwater *bouillabaisse*. The dish is a speciality of Verdun-sur-le-Doubs (where there is a *confrerie* dedicated to it). The true *pochouse* never contains larding fat and must contain burbot.

Pochouse de Verdun-sur-le-Doubs – Made with fish of different kinds: eel, pike, carp, barbel, chub and bream.

Cut them up and place in a tinned copper cauldron. Pour in 1 glass white Burgundy wine, covering the fish.

For a pochouse requiring about 2 kg. (4 to 5 lb.) of fish, you will need a fair amount of garlic, 100 g. (4 oz.) bacon cut into lardoons, thyme, bay leaf, enough salt and a good pinch of pepper. Grill the bacon.

Knead 250 g. (9 oz., generous cup) fresh butter mixed with flour, for thickening the sauce. Cook for 30 to 45 minutes. At first boil fast, then simmer for 12 minutes, after the butter has been added.

To serve, take the chunks out one by one, put them on a dish on a foundation of croûtons of bread fried in butter and rubbed with garlic. Strain the sauce over the fish.

Take care not to stir the chunks of fish during cooking; just shake the pan.

Avoid cooking the hard roes of pike, barbel and chub.

POD. COSSE – Vessel enclosing certain leguminous seeds: pea pod, bean pod, etc.

POÊLAGE – Method of cooking applied to various substances, which are cooked *à l'étuvée*, that is, in a covered pan with butter or other fat. (See CULINARY METHODS, *Pot-roasting*.)

Poêle (pan) for crêpes, fish and ordinary frying
(*Larousse*)

POÊLON – An earthenware utensil or a pan made of copper or some other metal, with a long handle. Such aluminium or copper pans are used for cooking sugar.

POGNE DE ROMANS – Cake which is a kind of sweet brioche and is prepared in the following manner: sift 500 g. (18 oz., $4\frac{1}{2}$ cups) flour and spread it on the table in a circle. In the middle of this circle put $1\frac{1}{4}$ teaspoons salt, 1 tablespoon orange blossom water, or $\frac{1}{2}$ teaspoon orange extract, 25 g. (1 oz.) yeast, 250 g. (9 oz., generous cup) softened butter and 4 eggs. Mix all the ingredients well, working the dough vigorously to give it body. Add 2 more eggs, one by one and, finally, still kneading the dough, incorporate 200 g. (7 oz., scant cup) castor (fine) sugar little by little. Put this dough into a small bowl sprinkled with flour, cover, and keep in a warm place from 10 to 12 hours.

Turn out the dough on to a board and pummel it to arrest

fermentation. Divide into 2 parts, mould into balls, shape the top (as in the case of ordinary brioche). Put the cakes into buttered baking tins, leave the dough to rise for another 30 minutes in a warm place, brush with beaten egg and bake in a moderate oven (the *pogne* can be eaten hot or cold). It can be served with redcurrant jelly.

POISSONNIER – Chef of an important restaurant who is in charge of all fish dishes, with the exception of fried or grilled fish, which are the domain of the *rôtisseur* or the *grillardin. Poissonnier* also means fishmonger.

POITOU – The Poitou gastronomic folklore extends to several *départements* (Vendée, Vienne, Deux-Sèvres, Maine-et-Loire). The culinary specialities are in fact local dishes, as they are everywhere, varying in detail according to tastes in different places.

The cattle raised in Parthenay and Bressuire provide excellent meat, mutton is of good quality and the pork, owing to the good pig food, is of excellent flavour.

Poultry farming produces a whole range of birds: turkeys, capons, table fowl, guinea fowl, and in the cantons of Chef-Boutonne and Sauzé-Vaussay ducks are raised for the production of foie gras. Civray *pâte de foie gras* is famous; *confits de canard* are also made here.

Ground game is of high repute, as well as winged game (partridges, woodcock, snipe, quail, rail and field-ducks) and waterfowl abounds here.

Coastal parts of Vendée abound in excellent fish. Almost every kind of shellfish is found there. The Portuguese oysters of Tranche and Groin-du-Cou, the mussels from the Aiguillon mussel farms and the spiny lobsters of the island of Yeu are greatly prized. The rivers provide a great variety of freshwater fish, the brooks and streams furnish crayfish and the marshes abound in eels and frogs.

The land of Poitou is fertile and produces an abundance of onions, artichokes, garden peas, Marac haricot beans, Niort cauliflowers and Vendée green cabbages.

The wooded district north-west of Poitou produces choice chestnuts and Vienne equally good walnuts.

Among the cheeses made in this district are La Mothe Saint-Héraye, Saint-Loup, Goat cheese, Vienne chabichou, etc. Local butter, Charente, is good.

Culinary specialities – Among the typical local dishes is *potée à la tête de porc,* which furnishes both a soup and the main course; the pig's head is cut into pieces and eaten sprinkled with sea salt and a dash of vinegar. Among the fish dishes are: *grilled eels* from Saint-Trojan; *bouilleture,* a *matelote* of eel in red wine, with prunes added to the garnish; *chaudrée,* a fish stew, its main feature being the variety of the fish used; the *cotriade,* a kind of *bouillabaisse,* which is not specifically a Vendée dish but is made all along the coast, particularly in the canton of Noirmoutier. *Frogs' legs à la luconnaise* are first soaked for 1 hour in vinegar-flavoured water, then drained, dried, dredged with flour, fried in *noisette butter* and served with fried cloves of garlic.

Among meat dishes, is the *Vendée fressure*; it is the pluck, including the pig's lungs, liver, heart and spleen, chopped and mixed with congealed pig's blood. The whole is then cooked with chopped fat bacon, slowly, for a long time. It is usually eaten cold.

Pâté de Paques, or Easter pie, is long, crescent shaped and filled with balls of hashed meat, hard-boiled eggs, and slices of pork, chicken or rabbit, sautéed in butter and left to get cold. The *Vendée pie* is made of fillets of wild rabbit and forcemeat of the flesh mixed with an equal quantity of pork, half cooked and chopped. *Easter loaf* or *galette piquante* is made of bread dough mixed with butter, sugar, eggs and orange-blossom water, and shaped into a cob.

Vegetable dishes include the *chouée,* which is green cabbage boiled in salted water, drained and pressed, with plenty of butter added to it; *mogettes,* French beans cooked in the ordinary way and dressed with butter and cream; the *far* (or *farci*), which is composed of different vegetables, such as Swiss chard leaves, spinach, leeks, and cabbage, first cooked in salted water, then drained, pressed, chopped and stewed for a long time with pork fat, onion and diced bacon. Beaten eggs and cream are added to the mixture.

Notable sweets and pastries include the *tourteau fromagé,* cream cheese or goat cheese reduced to a fine paste, to which is added a quarter its weight of flour, fine sugar, butter, egg yolks, whites beaten into a stiff froth, and flavourings. It is then put into a mould, allowed to ferment, and baked in the oven. The *fouée* ('faggot'), a circlet of bread dough covered with cream, melted butter or oil, which used to be baked in a blazing oven; *bottereaux de Langon,* a kind of *oreillettes* deep-fried in oil; and *plum pies.* The following are among

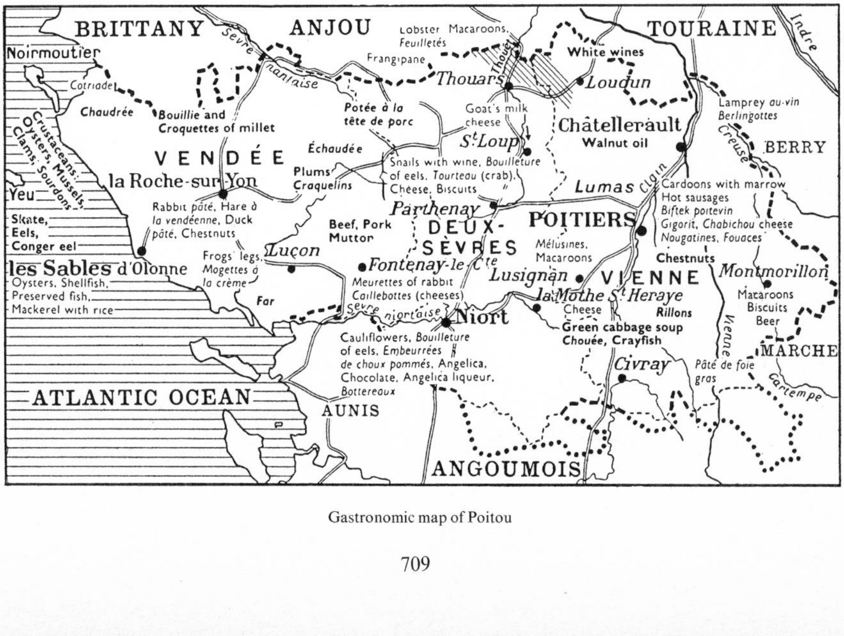

Gastronomic map of Poitou

noted local products: Montmorillon *macaroons and biscuits*; Lusignan *melusines and macaroons*; Parthenay *biscuits*; Chatellerault *caramels*; Niort *angelica*.

Wines – Poitou offers a selection of excellent non-vintage local wines. The angelica liqueur of Niort is very well known.

POIVRADE. Method of preparing certain meats, mainly ground game. (See SAUCE, *Pepper or poivrade sauce*).

The name also applies to small young artichokes which are eaten *à la croque-au-sel* (with salt as the only accompaniment).

POIVRON – French common name for red pepper or pimento.

POLAND – See INTERNATIONAL COOKERY.

POLENTA – Piedmont form of maize (corn) meal porridge. It is made of maize flour dried in the open and not in the oven, as for *gaudes* (hasty puddings). It can also be made of chestnut flour, as is done in Corsica.

Polenta is used as a garnish for garden warblers and other similar small birds; this is a traditional north Italian dish and was a great favourite of Napoleon I.

To cook polenta. Bring 1 litre ($1\frac{3}{4}$ pints, generous quart) water to the boil, add salt, allowing $2\frac{1}{2}$ teaspoons per litre. Sprinkle in 250 g. (9 oz.) maize flour gradually, stirring with a wooden spoon. Cook from 25 to 30 minutes. Add, for the above quantity of polenta, about 65 g. ($2\frac{1}{2}$ oz., 5 tablespoons) butter and 75 g. (3 oz., $\frac{3}{4}$ cup) grated Parmesan cheese.

Spread the polenta on a moistened baking tray in an even layer. When cold, cut into square or lozenge-shaped pieces. Fry these pieces golden brown in butter. Arrange on a dish and sprinkle with grated cheese and *Noisette butter* (see BUTTER).

Polenta can be used as a garnish for various meat and fish dishes.

Polenta fritters – See FRITTERS.

Thrushes or other small birds with polenta. GRIVES À LA POLENTA – Prepare polenta with cheese as described above. Pour it into a buttered oven-proof dish, spreading it in a layer 3 cm. ($1\frac{1}{2}$ inches) thick.

With the aid of a spoon dipped in water indent as many 'nests' as there are thrushes (or other birds). Sprinkle with grated cheese. Half roast the birds in the oven and put one in each little cavity. Sprinkle with a little melted butter and finish cooking in the oven. Dilute the pan juices with white wine and pour round the dish.

POLONAISE (À LA) – Method of preparing certain dishes. (See ASPARAGUS, CAULIFLOWER.)

POMEGRANATE. GRENADE – Fruit of the common pomegranate tree which is believed to be of North African origin. It is used widely in France.

Pomegranates can be eaten raw like other fruit, but generally it is the juice only which is used. From this juice the popular grenadine syrup is made. Pomegranates are also used in the preparation of ices and jellies. A type of alcoholic drink is also made from this fruit.

POMEROL – *Appellation contrôlée* vineyard of the Gironde situated in the commune of the same name on the right bank of the Dordogne. Production is limited to vigorous, aromatic red wines of outstanding quality and excellent bouquet.

POMFRET. BRÈME DE MER – Fish (*Brama brama*) which is also known as *Ray's bream* and *sea bream*, and is found in the North Atlantic and Pacific Oceans. Pomfret is also the name of flat fish found in the Indian Ocean.

POMMARD – This wine, which is produced in the little commune of Côte-d'Or (Côte de Beaune), is classed among the finest growths of Burgundy wines.

POMME DE PIN – See RESTAURANTS OF BYGONE DAYS.

POMPE or GIBASSIER (Provence cake) – Traditional cake eaten in Provence at the *gros soupa* on Christmas Eve. It is also called *gibassier* ('gibbous'), because of the lumps on its surface.

The *grøs soupa* is the meal which precedes the midnight mass. As the fast entails abstinence from meat, the meal invariably consists of Lenten dishes, such as cod *en rayte* or *en brandade* and cardoons in cream.

'The dessert is by no means the least attraction of this traditional meal and consists mainly of locally manufactured nougat, dates, and – above all – the *pompe* or *gibassier*, another local product, the whole washed down liberally with the customary mulled wine.

'Here is the recipe for this cake:

'*Ingredients.* 500 g. (18 oz.) bread dough leaven, 500 g. (18 oz., $2\frac{1}{4}$ cups) brown sugar, 2 kg. ($4\frac{1}{2}$ lb.) flour, 6 eggs, 1 dl. (6 tablespoons, scant $\frac{1}{2}$ cup) best oil and finely grated rind of 1 lemon and 1 orange.

'*Method.* Spread the flour on a board in a circle, make a well in the middle and put into it the leaven with the brown sugar, oil and half the eggs. Mix well, incorporating the flour little by little. Knead the dough well and add the rest of the eggs one by one. This dough should be quite soft.

'Leave to rise for about 6 hours in a warm temperature, then beat it out, divide into pieces of about 200 g. (7 oz.), shape into crowns and put on boards sprinkled with fine bran.

'Keep in a warm place, as the dough takes a long time to rise.

'Bake in a lively oven. When ready, take out of the oven and moisten the surface of each cake with a cloth dipped in a mixture of water and orange-blossom water.' (A. Caillat.)

POMPONNETTES – Small preparations served as *hors-d'œuvre.* (See HORS-D'ŒUVRE, *Hot hors-d'œuvre.)*

PONT-L'ÉVÊQUE – See CHEESE.

PONT-NEUF (Pâtisserie) – Line buttered tartlet tins with *Puff pastry* (see DOUGH). Fill with *Frangipane cream* (see CREAM) mixed with crushed macaroons. Put 2 thin strips of puff pastry criss-cross fashion on each tartlet. Bake in a moderate oven. When ready, remove from oven and sprinkle with fine sugar.

POPE. GREMILLE – Fish of the perch family, sometimes called ruff. It is a freshwater fish found in most of the rivers of

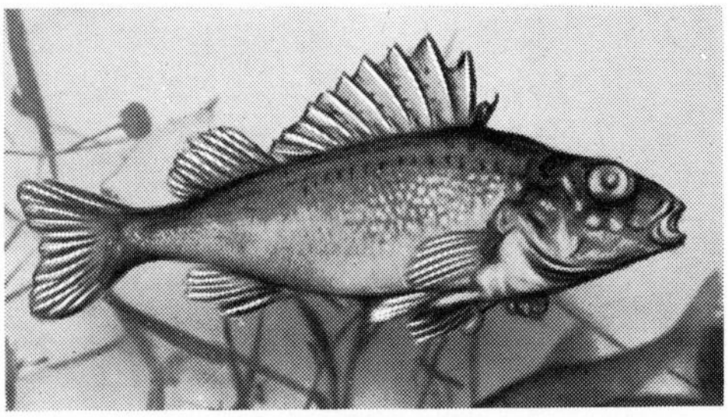

Pope

France, especially in the Seine and the Moselle. The pike-perches of middle western U.S.A. are very similar.

The flesh is quite delicate. All the recipes for perch may be used in the preparation of this fish (see PERCH). It is used especially in fish stews (*matelotes*).

POPPY. COQUELICOT – Common plant in cornfields, the petals of which are used to dye certain liquids. The leaves, in spite of being slightly narcotic, are sometimes used as a vegetable like spinach.

The white poppy is cultivated principally for the extraction of poppy seed oil. The aromatic seeds were used in pastry-making in times of antiquity (they were known to the Egyptians earlier than 1500 B.C.), and are still used in many regions for sprinkling cakes and bread.

PORCELAIN. PORCELAINE – Fine earthenware. It owes its name to the cowrie, or porcelain shell, which in old French was called *pourcelline* or *pourcellaine* and in Italian and Latin *porcellana* or *porcellina*.

There are two kinds of porcelain: *hard-paste* or *Chinese porcelain* and *soft-paste* or *French porcelain*.

Hard-paste porcelain dates back to the Han period, 206 B.C. The best period was during the reign of Ch'eng Hua, 1465–1488 (Ming dynasty). From China the industry spread to Japan in the sixteenth century.

For a long time Chinese and Japanese porcelain aroused the admiration of connoisseurs and the envy of European potters.

Soft-paste porcelain does not owe its name to the degree of hardness of the actual paste but to its weak resistance to high temperature and to the softness of its glaze, easily scratched by steel. Its discovery is probably due to a Rouen earthenware maker by the name of Poterat.

A century earlier, however, in 1585, a first attempt, soon to be abandoned, was made in Florence. At the end of the seventeenth century the first pottery works producing soft-paste porcelain was established at Saint-Cloud. In the eighteenth century rival establishments sprang up in Paris, Lille, Chantilly and, finally, under the patronage of Madame de Pompadour and Louis XV, at Vincennes, which in 1753 became the Royal pottery works. In 1756 it was transferred to Sèvres where it is active to this day.

This small workshop, in which Orry and Fuloy were able to establish themselves, thanks to the patronage of Madame de Pompadour, produced far better results than were achieved before that in France or abroad, in spite of the competition set up by Meissen in Saxony, where hard-paste porcelain has been made since 1709, following the discovery of kaolin clay deposits in the region. The problem of manufacturing porcelain similar to that made in China and Japan, which had for so long occupied the minds of potters, was solved, and that period saw the rise of numerous potteries in Germany. Potteries were also established in Austria, Holland, Denmark, Russia, Switzerland and Italy. In 1776, kaolin deposits were found in France, first at Alençon, then at Saint-Yrieux, near Limoges. It was then that Sèvres began to modify its production and potteries were opened all over France, in Limoges, Paris, and other places.

The pottery industry was neglected for a time but now beautiful porcelain is once again in favour. The Sèvres porcelain factory, with its workshops and laboratories, has made important improvements in the manufacturing process and the decoration of the porcelain.

PORCHERONS (AUX) – See RESTAURANTS OF BYGONE DAYS.

PORCUPINE. PORC-ÉPIC – Animal whose rather fat flesh is good to eat, especially when young.

PORK. PORC – Domestic pachyderm which is not usually referred to by this name until after slaughter. The male is called a boar, the female a sow, the castrated animal is called fig or stag and the young animal is called piglet, porker or sucking pig.

Pork is fat and firm and has more red meat than white. It only acquires this colour when the animal is killed by complete bleeding. It is lacking in albuminoids (16 per cent only) and is particularly indigestible because it contains such a high proportion of fats. For this reason pork is taboo for sufferers of hepatitis and is not recommended for persons with intestinal troubles or poor digestions.

There are three principal breeds of pig which have produced the many species which exist in Europe: the Asiatic, Neapolitan and Celtic.

The Asiatic breed, with small straight, pointed ears, has been used for cross-breeding, as it produced bacon of soft and inferior quality.

The Neapolitan breed, with pointed, horizontally placed ears, without cross-breeding and living in the open, has retained its purity of strain.

The Celtic breed, with long, wide, lop ears, which formerly inhabited Gaul and the British Isles, has, as a result of cross-breeding, undergone various changes in various regions of France. Today there is a great variety of species, including the following: Alsace, Anjou, Bayonne, Bresse, Brittany, Bugey, Champagne, Charolais, Craon, Corsican, Landes, Lauraguaise, Limousin, Lorraine, Manche, Marche, Nevers, Normandy, Périgord, Picardy, Rouergue, Vendée, etc.

Among the different breeds, five can be singled out:

The Normandy breed, with a lean body and saddle-back, which gives superior quality flesh; Craon or Anjou breed, raised in the Loire basin; Lorraine breed, raised mainly in the *départements* of Muerthe and Moselle, greatly prized for the quality of its flesh and bacon; the Périgord breed, which produces pigs with a very highly developed sense of smell, used for finding truffles; the Bresse breed, black pigs with a white band encircling the middle of the body.

Among the English cross-breeds, all of which have been introduced into France, is the Yorkshire, white or yellowish skinned pigs, which produce the famous hams. Other principal breeds of British pig include: Large White Ulster, Large Black, Tamworth, Wessex Saddle-back, Berkshire, Gloucester Old Spots, Lincoln Curly-coated, Cumberland, Essex.

Pork is eaten either fresh or cured. Its flesh lends itself particularly to salting, smoking and many other processes of pork butchery.

Pork andouilles and andouillettes (sausages). ANDOUILLES, ANDOUILLETTES DE PORC – Big pork sausages made of the large intestine and the stomach of the pig, cut into strips and mixed with lardoons of pork fat. These sausages are salted and can be kept for a long time.

The most famous *andouilles* are those made in Vire and in Brittany. They are eaten as *hors-d'œuvre*, cut into thin slices like saveloys and other sausage.

They can also be served hot. For this they should first be boiled in slightly salted water, left to cool, then grilled and served with mashed potatoes or other vegetable.

The best *andouillettes* come from Troyes, Nancy, Tours, Strasbourg, Lyons, Cambrai, Caen and Paris.

All these varieties of *andouillettes* are grilled and served with mashed potatoes or other vegetables. Before being put under the grill, the *andouillettes* should be cut slightly and brushed with melted butter.

They can also be fried in butter or lard.

Home-made andouilles. ANDOUILLES DE MÉNAGE – Soak pig's intestines in cold water and wash well. Drain, dry on a cloth, cut into thin strips and put into a bowl with half their weight of lean bacon, cut into very small pieces. Add 1 glass white wine and chopped onion, shallot and parsley. Season with salt, pepper and spices, mix well and leave to marinate in this seasoning for several hours. Fill the pig's intestines with this mixture.

Cook and finish off as described in the recipe for *Nancy andouilles*.

Nancy andouilles. ANDOUILLES DE NANCY – Soak 750 g. ($1\frac{1}{2}$ lb.) pork belly and 750 g. ($1\frac{1}{2}$ lb.) calf's mesentery in cold water. Wash them carefully and cook in salted water for 2 hours. Drain, rinse in cold water, dry on a cloth and cut into very small pieces.

Put into a bowl, season with salt, pepper and spices, moisten with 2 dl. ($\frac{1}{3}$ pint, scant cup) white wine and add 100 g. (4 oz., 2 cups) chopped mushrooms lightly fried in butter with chopped onion, shallot and parsley. Chopped truffles can also be added.

Fill pig's intestines, thoroughly soaked and washed, with this mixture. Form the andouilles by twisting the intestine at intervals of 15 to 20 cm. (6 to 8 inches). Prick the *andouilles* with a big needle and plunge them into a pan of boiling water. Season with salt, and add sliced onions and carrots, 2 cloves garlic and a good *bouquet garni* (q.v.).

As soon as boiling is established, draw the pan to the side of the stove, cover, and simmer very gently for 2 hours.

Take the pan off the stove and leave the *andouilles* in the liquid in which they were cooked until almost quite cold.

Drain, put in a shallow baking pan, cover with a board, put a weight on top and leave in a cool place until quite cold.

To serve, slash the *andouilles* with a few very light incisions, grill and serve with mashed potatoes.

Fine pork andouillettes. ANDOUILLETTES FINES DE PORC – Cook a calf's mesentery, cut into big square pieces, and half its weight of lean bacon, similarly cut, in 1 litre ($1\frac{3}{4}$ pints, generous quart) meat stock, to which 1 onion studded with a clove and a good *bouquet garni* (q.v.) have been added. Season and bring to the boil. Cover with a lid and simmer very gently for about 2 hours.

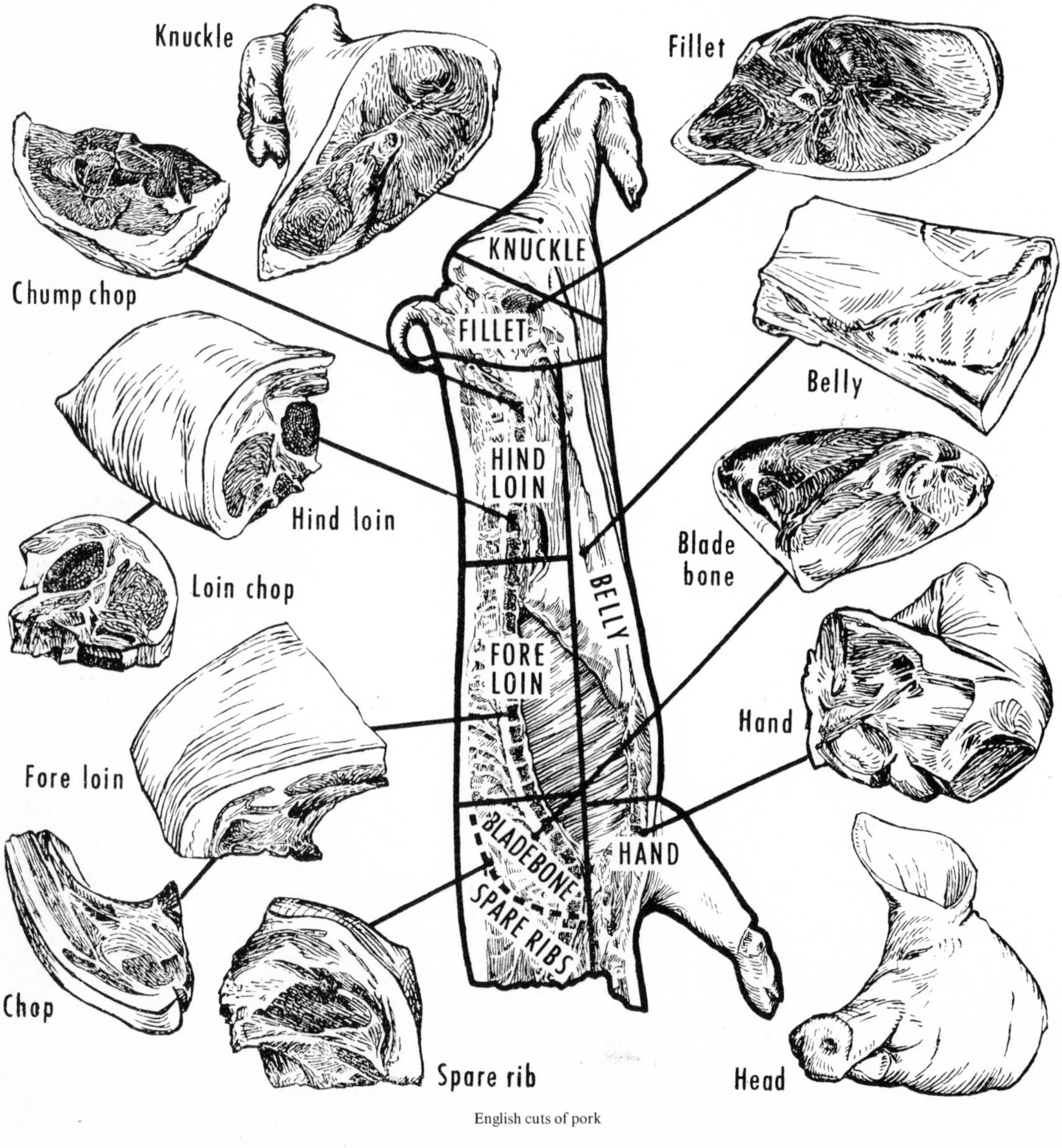

English cuts of pork

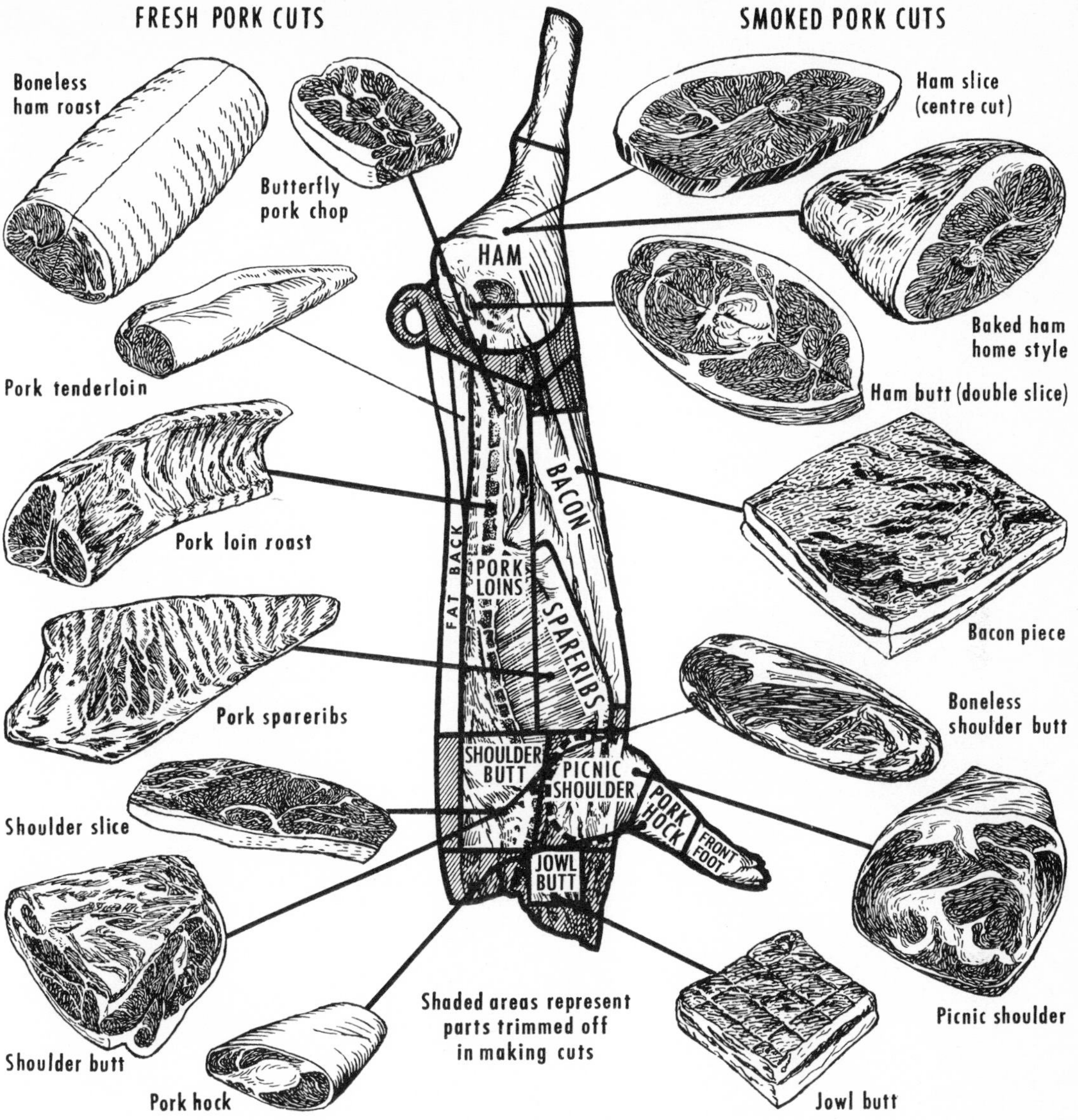

American cuts of pork

Drain the meats and chop coarsely, put into a bowl, and add 100 g. (4 oz., 2 cups) chopped mushrooms, lightly fried with chopped onions, shallots and parsley, and bound with a few tablespoons concentrated stock.

Add 6 raw egg yolks and mix all the ingredients well. Stuff this mixture into pig's intestines which have been well soaked and washed, and tie the *andouillettes* into 10-cm. (4-in.) pieces. Cook and finish off as described in the preceding recipes.

Pig's blood. SANG DE PORC – This is almost solely used for making black puddings. It can also be used for clarifying jellies, and as an element of liaison for red wine sauces of the *civet* type.

Breast of pork. POITRINE DE PORC – This part of the animal is used fresh for making *ragoûts*. It can also be boned and grilled, after some of the fat has been removed.

In its salted or smoked state it provides bacon.

Carbonades of pork. CARBONADES DE PORC – The word *carbonades*, which in the past applied to all meat cooked on a grill ('*sur des charbons ardents*', i.e. *on glowing coals*) today only applies to thin slices of pork cut from the neck end, as well as lean parts of top of rump, which are grilled on hot coals.

The term *carbonades* also applies to thin slices of pork braised like *Carbonades of beef à la flamande* (see BEEF).

Grilled *carbonades* of pork, which are generally dipped in butter and breadcrumbs before cooking, and sautéed carbonades, can be served with all the garnishes recommended for veal or pork chops.

Chine of pork. ÉCHINE DE PORC – Cut taken from the back of the animal, which includes part of the backbone and surrounding flesh. In some regions of France it is also called *échinée* and *épinée*. The term is principally used to describe that part of the chine next to the neck.

All the methods of preparation given for loin and fillet of pork are suitable for chine. This cut is also used for making stews.

After cutting it into slices, it can be grilled or sautéed in the

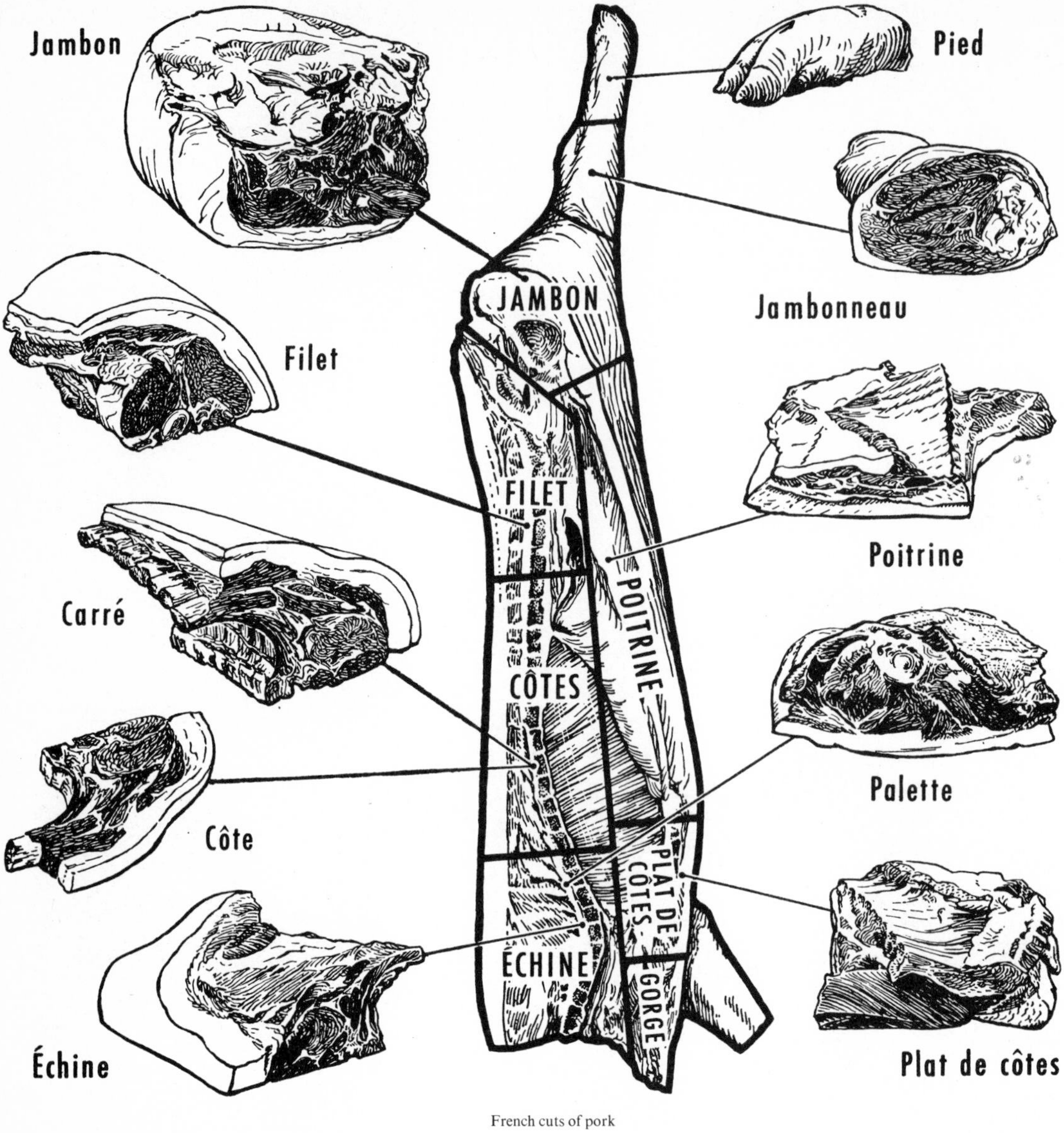

French cuts of pork

same way as pork chops. All methods of preparing chops can be applied to chine. Prepared in this way and grilled they are usually called *carbonades*.

Chine of pork can be half or fully salted and in this form used as an ingredient of *potées* and *estouffades*. This cut is not marketed in the U.S.A.

Pork chops à l'alsacienne. CÔTES DE PORC À L'ALSACIENNE – Season the chops and sauté them in butter or lard, or braise them. Arrange them in a turban on a dish. Fill the middle with *sauerkraut* (q.v.) piled up into a dome, and top with poached Strasbourg sausages. Garnish the dish with boiled potatoes. Pour over the chops some of the diluted pan juices, or, if the chops are braised, some of the strained braising liquor.

Pork chops à l'ardennaise. CÔTES DE PORC À L'ARDENNAISE – Sauté the chops in butter or lard. Arrange in a turban on a dish. Put in potatoes sautéed in butter and mixed with diced, fried bacon, and chopped onion lightly fried in butter.

Dilute the pan juices with white wine, add a few crushed juniper berries, moisten with *Demi-glace sauce* (see SAUCE), strain, and pour over the chops.

Pork chops à la bayonnaise. CÔTES DE PORC À LA BAYONNAISE – Insert slivers of garlic into the meaty part of the chops. Season with salt, pepper, powdered thyme and bay leaf, sprinkle with oil and a dash of vinegar. Leave them to marinate in this seasoning for 1 hour. Sauté briskly in lard in an earthenware dish. When the chops are browned on both sides, surround with new potatoes tossed in lard, and sliced *cèpes* or mushrooms sautéed in oil. Finish cooking everything together in the oven. Sprinkle with chopped parsley.

Braised pork chops with various garnishes. CÔTES DE PORC BRAISÉES – Cut the chops a little on the thick side. Braise and garnish them in the same way as *Veal chops (see VEAL)*.

Pork chops charcutière. CÔTES DE PORC CHARCUTIÈRE – This dish, which is found ready for use in pork butchers' shops, is prepared in restaurants as follows:

Flatten the chops slightly, season, coat with melted butter, dip in breadcrumbs and grill gently. Arrange in a crown, fill the middle of the dish with mashed potatoes and serve with *Charcutière sauce* (see SAUCE) to which shredded gherkins are added.

Pork chops charcutière are fried in lard and simmered in *charcutière sauce* to which some sliced gherkins have been added.

Fried pork chops with garnish. CÔTES DE PORC SAUTÉES GARNIES – Trim and lightly flatten 4 loin pork chops. Season with salt and pepper and cook in a sauté pan in which 1 tablespoon butter or lard has been heated.

Cook the chops on a lively heat. Brown well on both sides. When they are cooked, remove from the pan, surround with the garnish indicated in the recipe and pour the pan juices over, diluted as indicated in the recipe and strained through a fine sieve or strainer.

Pork chops à la gasconne. CÔTES DE PORC À LA GASCONNE – Marinate the pork chops as described in the recipe for *Pork chops à la bayonnaise*. Fry them quickly in butter or goose fat, to stiffen them.

Put 6 peeled and slightly blanched cloves of garlic for each chop into the pan. Cover and finish cooking on low heat. When the chops are nearly cooked, add 8 stoned and blanched olives per chop. Arrange the chops in a crown and put the garnish in the middle of the dish. Dilute the pan juices with $\frac{1}{2}$ glass white wine, add a few tablespoons thickened veal stock, boil for a few moments, and pour over the chops. Sprinkle with chopped parsley.

Grilled pork chops. CÔTES DE PORC GRILLÉES – Season loin chops with salt and pepper, brush them with melted butter, oil or lard and cook under a moderate grill.

Grilled pork chops garnished with apple rings

Arrange on a dish and garnish with watercress.

Grilled pork chops are served plain, or with a garnish of vegetables, most often with mashed potatoes.

Pork chops à la milanaise. CÔTES DE PORC À LA MILANAISE – Beat loin pork chops flat, season with salt and pepper, coat with egg and breadcrumbs and proceed as described in the recipe for *Veal chops à la milanaise* (see VEAL).

Pork chops Pilleverjus. CÔTES DE PORC PILLEVERJUS – Flatten slightly and trim loin chops. Season them with salt and pepper.

Pork chops charcutière (*Robert Carrier*)

Fry in lard. When both sides are well browned, put into the pan (for 4 chops) 4 tablespoons ($\frac{1}{3}$ cup) finely chopped onion, three-quarters cooked. Add a *bouquet garni* (q.v.), cover the pan and cook on low heat for 35 minutes.

Shred a young cabbage heart into a *julienne* (q.v.) and cook covered, in butter or lard, as slowly as possible. As soon as the cabbage is done, moisten it with cream and simmer for a few moments, stirring all the time.

Arrange the chops on a foundation of the cabbage *julienne*. Garnish with boiled potatoes.

Dilute the pan juices with 1 good tablespoon vinegar, add 4 tablespoons ($\frac{1}{3}$ cup) stock and pour over the chops.

Pork chops with Robert sauce. CÔTES DE PORC SAUCE ROBERT – Season and grill the chops. Serve with *Robert sauce* (see SAUCE) and mashed potatoes.

Or: Sauté the chops in butter or lard. When they are half-cooked, put into the sauté pan (for 4 chops) 100 g. (4 oz., 1 cup) finely chopped white onions.

Drain the chops and arrange them on a dish. Dilute the pan juices with 2 dl. ($\frac{1}{3}$ pint, scant cup) white wine. Boil down almost completely. Add 3 dl. ($\frac{1}{2}$ pint, $1\frac{1}{4}$ cups) *Demi-glace sauce* (see SAUCE). Boil for 5 minutes. Remove from the heat, add a pinch of sugar and 1 good teaspoon mustard to the sauce, mix, and pour over the chops.

In a home kitchen, dilute the pan juices with white wine, add some meat stock, boil for a few minutes, bind with 1 tablespoon butter kneaded with flour, and add 1 or 2 tablespoons tomato purée.

Alternatively, proceed as follows:

Cook the chops and remove them from the pan. Into the same butter put 1 or 2 tablespoons flour, mix, and lightly cook. Moisten with white wine and stock, blend well, and cook for a few minutes.

Pork chops à la vosgienne. CÔTES DE PORC À LA VOSGIENNE – Sauté the chops in lard or butter. When half done add 1 tablespoon chopped onion lightly fried in butter (1 tablespoon per chop). Finish cooking together on gentle heat.

Arrange the chops in a crown. Fill the middle of the dish with stoned mirabelles (plums), cooked without sugar.

Dilute the pan juices with vinegar and white wine, add some concentrated veal stock and pour over the chops.

Pork crépinettes. CRÉPINETTES DE PORC – *Crépinettes* or small flat sausages are made of *Fine pork forcemeat* (see FORCEMEATS) mixed with chopped *fines herbes* and flavoured with brandy.

The forcemeat is divided into 90 or 100 g. ($3\frac{1}{2}$- to 4-oz.) pieces, each of which is wrapped in a piece of pig's caul, previously soaked in cold water, and moulded into a rectangular shape.

The *crépinettes* are coated with butter and freshly sifted breadcrumbs, sprinkled with melted butter and grilled gently.

Grilled *crépinettes* are usually served with mashed potatoes but they can also be served with various vegetables dressed with butter.

Cinderella pork crépinettes. CRÉPINETTES DE PORC CENDRILLON – These *crépinettes* are made of fine truffled pork forcemeat. Put 1 good tablespoon *salpicon* (q.v.) of pig's feet, mixed with truffles and mushrooms cut into dice and bound with greatly concentrated veal stock, in the middle of each *crépinette*.

Cinderella *crépinettes* are grilled and served with *Périgueux sauce* (see SAUCE) and mashed potatoes.

Pork fat. LARD – The adipose tissue of the pig. In French, the term *lard*, which is sometimes used of fat of animals other than pig, usually means fresh raw pork fat. The French equivalent of the English term 'lard' is *saindoux*.

Fillet (U.S. Tenderloin) of pork. FILET DE PORC – The fillet (tenderloin) of pork is the part of the animal from the first ribs to the leg. It is the part which in the case of veal or mutton is called saddle.

Cinderella pork crépinettes

The pig's back, or saddle, is generally cut in half, lengthways. The fillet of pork can be prepared in any way suitable for the loin. Escalopes and *noisettes*, as well as *filets mignons*, are cut from boned fillets of pork, and prepared in any way suitable for chops. Roast or pot-roasted fillet of pork is often referred to in French as *longe*.

Pork fricadelles. FRICADELLES DE PORC – Prepare, using pork meat, in the same way as *Fricadelles of beef* (see BEEF).

Pork gelatine. COLLE DE COUENNES – Soak 3 kg. ($6\frac{1}{2}$ lb.) fresh pork skins in cold water. Put them in a casserole, cover with water, bring to the boil and drain. Put under the cold tap, scrape and wash them; put them back in the casserole, cover with water. Boil, skim and simmer for 6 or 8 hours, skimming often.

Pass the contents of the pan through a strainer into a basin. Leave to cool. When it is cold and has set, remove all fat from the surface and rub the gelatine with a cloth dipped in boiling water, so as to remove every trace of fat.

Add this gelatine to the prepared stock (see JELLY).

Ham. JAMBON – See HAM.

Hand of pork. JAMBONNEAU – Cook in the same way as ham (see HAM, *Salted and smoked ham*) until the flesh comes away from the bones. Reshape it by wrapping tightly in a cloth, leave to cool in the liquid it was cooked in, grease slightly and roll in breadcrumbs.

Pork hash. HACHIS DE PORC – Prepare like *Beef hash* (see BEEF), using left-over pieces of pork.

Potted head (brawn or head cheese). HURE DE PORC – This is generally sold in pork butchers' shops ready for the table. It used to be made in the country.

Potted head (brawn or head cheese) à la pistache (old recipe). HURE À LA PISTACHE – Clean and scrape a pig's head, remove the tongue, brains and all the fat part of the throat and cut off the ears. Steep the head, ears and tongue and 2 calves' tongues in brine for 3 or 4 days. Drain. Wrap the head in a cloth and put into a braising pan, together with the ears, also wrapped, and cook gently in the usual manner (see CULINARY METHODS, *Braising of meat*) for 4 or 5 hours. Add the tongues 2 hours later. Take off the best piece of skin and spread it on a napkin. Cut the fleshy part of the head into long strips, rejecting all pieces tinged with blood.

Sprinkle this meat with four spices (q.v.) and chopped shallots. Lay out these strips, mixing the various meats as well as possible. Scatter a few pistachio nuts here and there. Fold the skin over these pieces, wrap tightly in a napkin, tying it securely with string. Put back to cook. Bring the braising liquid to the boil, then simmer. One hour later, drain, remove string, and put the contents of the napkin into a brawn mould, with a weight on top. Press down well, leave until quite cold.

Potted head (brawn or head cheese) with truffles. HURE DE

Potted head, large Lyon potted head in centre; on either side small Paris potted heads, whole and cut (*Charcuterie Chèdeville. Phot. Larousse*)

PORC AUX TRUFFES – As above, adding raw truffles cut into strips.

Leg of pork (ham). JAMBON – French and imported hams are listed under the entry entitled HAM. Leg of pork can be eaten fresh, salted or smoked.

Braised fresh leg of pork. JAMBON DE PORC FRAIS BRAISÉ – This joint is cooked as described under CULINARY METHODS, *Pot-roasting*, allowing 20 to 25 minutes cooking time per 500 g. (per pound) plus 20 minutes.

Fresh braised leg of pork can be accompanied by any of the garnishes recommended for braised meat. The braising liquor is boiled down, and the surplus fat removed. Strain and pour over the leg.

A few hours before putting fresh leg of pork to braise, season it with salt flavour flavoured with powdered thyme and bay leaf.

Roast leg of pork. JAMBON DE PORC FRAIS RÔTI – Trim the leg of pork, removing the bone up to the knuckle, and skin it. A few hours before roasting the leg cover it with salt. Wipe and roast in the oven, or on a spit (see CULINARY METHODS, *Average cooking times for roasts*). Serve the leg with the pan juices diluted with white wine or Madeira. Any of the garnishes recommended for roast meat can be used.

Stuffed pig's leg or Zampino (Italian cookery). JAMBE DE PORC FARCIE, ZAMPINO – Soak the leg in cold water for 3 hours and scrape the skin thoroughly. Prick in a few places with a trussing needle. Wrap in a fine cloth and tie at both ends and in the middle. Put it into a braising pan and cover with cold water. Bring to the boil, then simmer for 3 hours.

Roast leg of pork

The *zampino* is served hot, with potato or lentil purée. It can also be served cold, cut in slices like sausage.

Pig's liver. FOIE DE PORC – All recipes for calf's liver are suitable for pig's liver, though it is mainly used as an ingredient in stuffings. (See OFFAL or VARIETY MEATS.)

Pig's liver with mustard. FOIE DE PORC À LA MOUTARDE – Lard a pig's liver and daub it generously with mustard. Sprinkle with parsley and chopped garlic and bake in a covered casserole with butter. Three-quarters of an hour in a gentle oven should be enough.

Remove the liver and place on a warm serving plate. Slice it. Dilute the juices in the casserole with 1 tablespoon mustard and 2 tablespoons (3 tablespoons) vinegar. Pour this concentrated sauce over the sliced liver.

Serve *Potato galettes* (see GALETTE) as an accompaniment.

(Recipe of Madame Simone Nouyrigat, of the *Pierre Traiteur* restaurant.)

Loin of pork. CARRÉ DE PORC – This cut can be roasted or pot-roasted. It is usually accompanied by its own juices, suitably diluted, and most often with a garnish of potatoes, especially mashed potatoes, or a purée of dried vegetables, or fresh braised vegetables (celery, chicory, endive, lettuce, etc.).

It is advisable before roasting or pot-roasting a loin of pork, as well as all other pork joints cooked in the same way, to season it several hours before cooking with salt mixed with powdered thyme and bay leaf. Seasoned thus in advance, the flavour of fresh pork is rendered more delicious.

Loin of pork à l'alsacienne. CARRÉ DE PORC À L'ALSACIENNE – Season the loin of pork in advance and cook in the oven until three-quarters done.

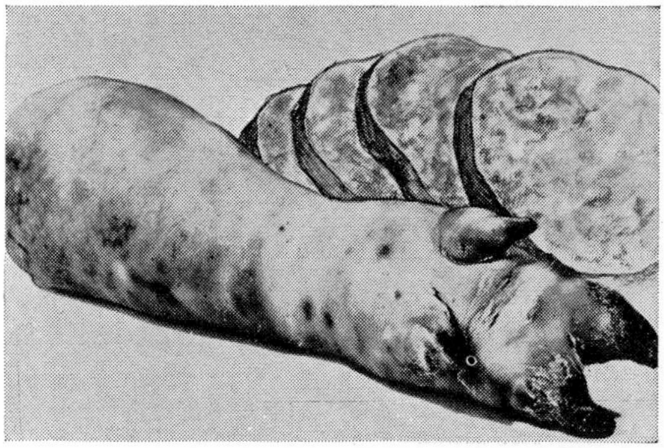

Zampino (stuffed pig's leg) (*Larousse*)

Finish cooking with *sauerkraut* (q.v.) prepared separately in the usual manner and with a garnish of lean smoked bacon, *Strasbourg sausages*.

Drain the loin. Arrange on a large oval-shaped dish. Garnish at the two ends with *sauerkraut*, surround with sausages and bacon cut in rectangles, and serve with boiled potatoes.

Loin of pork à l'alsacienne can also be made by roasting or pot-roasting the loin and serving it surrounded with *sauerkraut*. Pour over the pan juices left over from roasting.

Loin of pork à la bonne femme. CARRÉ DE PORC À LA BONNE FEMME – Season the loin of pork in advance and put it into an earthenware dish in which several tablespoons of butter or lard have been heated.

Roast the loin in the oven until half done, browning well. Put into the roasting pan, for a loin weighing about 1 kg. ($2\frac{1}{4}$ lb.), 500 g. (18 oz., 3 cups) potatoes cut to look like large olives or into quarters, and 24 small onions, fried in butter or lard. Season the garnish, add a *bouquet garni* (q.v.) and finish cooking together in the oven, basting frequently. Take out of the oven, sprinkle with chopped parsley and serve in the same dish in which it was cooked.

Loin of pork à la boulangère. CARRÉ DE PORC À LA BOULANGÈRE – Trim the loin of pork and proceed as described in the recipe for *Shoulder of lamb à la boulangère* (see LAMB).

Loin of pork with green cabbage, or with Brussels sprouts. CARRÉ DE PORC AUX CHOUX VERTS, AUX CHOUX DE BRUXELLES – Roast or pot-roast the loin. Arrange it on a serving dish. Surround with a garnish of *Braised green cabbage* (see CABBAGE), or Brussels sprouts boiled in water, drained, and tossed in the fat in which the loin was cooked. Pour over the pan juices left from roasting the loin.

Loin of pork with red cabbage. CARRÉ DE PORC AUX CHOUX ROUGES – Roast or pot-roast the loin of pork as described above. Arrange it on a serving dish. Surround with red cabbage braised separately.

Loin of pork à la chipolata. CARRÉ DE PORC À LA CHIPOLATA – Season the loin of pork in advance and pot-roast it. Arrange it on a serving dish. Surround with chipolaya garnish, composed of braised chestnuts, small glazed onions, chipolata sausages and glazed carrots. Pour over the pan juices left from cooking the loin.

Cold loin of pork. CARRÉ DE PORC FROID – This is generally served with a green salad, potato salad, or red cabbage salad, accompanied by *Mayonnaise sauce* (see SAUCE) and pickled gherkins.

Loin of pork à la limousine. CARRÉ DE PORC À LA LIMOUSINE – Roast or pot-roast the loin. Garnish with *Red cabbage à la limousine*, braised with mashed chestnuts (see CABBAGE).

Pour over the pan juices left from roasting the loin.

Roast loin of pork. CARRÉ DE PORC RÔTI – Trim and season the loin in advance. Roast it in the oven, or on a spit (see CULINARY METHODS, *Average cooking time for roasts*).

Arrange on a serving dish. Garnish with watercress. Serve with the pan juices, suitably diluted.

It is customary in certain parts of France to serve roast loin of pork with unsweetened apple purée.

Roast loin of pork à la languedocienne. CARRÉ DE PORC RÔTI À LA LANGUEDOCIENNE – Twelve hours before roasting the loin, insert into it some pieces of garlic cut into little strips. Season it with salt and spices and sprinkle with oil. Leave to marinate in this seasoning. Roast in the oven or on a spit. Serve with its own juices.

Roast loin of pork à la provençale. CARRÉ DE PORC À LA PROVENÇALE – Twelve hours before roasting the loin insert into it some sage leaves. Season with salt and powdered thyme and bay leaf. Cover with crushed cloves of garlic and pour over a few tablespoons olive oil.

Roast loin of pork

Roast the loin in the oven, putting the garlic cloves into the roasting pan. Arrange on a serving dish and pour over the pan juices.

Roast loin of pork with various sauces and garnishes. CARRÉ DE PORC RÔTI – Roast the loin in the oven. Arrange on a serving dish. Surround with the garnish indicated (or dish up the garnish separately in a *timbale*) and serve with the sauce recommended.

All the garnishes which are suitable for meat courses (lamb, beef, mutton, veal) can be served with loin of pork (see GARNISHES). It can also be served with various sauces, such as *Charcutière, Mustard, Piquante, Robert, Tomato,* etc. (see SAUCE).

Roast loin of pork à la soissonnaise. CARRÉ DE PORC RÔTI À LA SOISSONNAISE – Trim the loin of pork, season, and roast it in an earthenware dish, cooking it until it is three-quarters done. Add some kidney beans, cooked separately (see BEANS, *Fresh red beans*).

Finish cooking in the oven, basting frequently. Serve in the same dish.

Loin of pork with sauerkraut – See *Loin of pork à l'alsacienne*.

Pork offal or variety meats. ABATS DE PORC – The major parts of pork offal are used as ingredients for various

Roast loin of pork garnished with orange

products known in U.S.A. as variety meats or cold cuts and in England as preparations or pork butchery: brawn (U.S. head cheese), sausages, etc.

The feet (trotters), brains, liver, kidneys and the head – especially the ears – can be prepared as independent dishes by following the instructions given in the recipes for veal and mutton offal or variety meats. All recipes for preparing pig's ears and trotters will be found under OFFAL or VARIETY MEATS.

Pork pie

Hot pork pie. PÂTÉ CHAUD DE PORC À L'ANGLAISE – Line the sides and bottom of a pie dish with thin slices of raw ham. Put into this dish, in alternate layers, 500 g. (18 oz.) slices of fresh pork, seasoned with salt, pepper and powdered thyme and bay leaf, and sprinkled with dried *duxelles* (q.v.) mixture; also chopped parsley and sage, 500 g. (18 oz., 3 cups) raw potatoes cut in thin slices and 100 g. (4 oz., 1 cup) chopped onion.

Moisten with $1\frac{1}{2}$ dl. ($\frac{1}{4}$ pint, $\frac{2}{3}$ cup) water, cover with a lid of *Lining paste* or *Puff pastry* (see DOUGH), as described in the recipe for *Beefsteak pie* (see BEEF). Brush the top with beaten egg, crimp up the edges and bake in a moderate oven for about 2 hours.

Piglet. PORCELET – Name applied to a young pig up to the age of two months. In culinary parlance it is called sucking or suckling pig.

Suckling pig, whether stuffed or not, is usually roasted on a spit. It is best to roast it in such a way as to make the skin golden and crisp. Cooking time for a medium-sized suckling pig varies between $1\frac{1}{2}$ and 2 hours. If the animal is stuffed, the cooking time should be increased by 15 minutes for each 500 g. (1 lb.) of stuffing.

Suckling pig can also be braised, or boiled – as is done in Russia – in which case it can be served either hot or cold, in aspic.

Black pudding (U.S. blood pudding). BOUDIN – Large sausage made of pig's blood and suet enclosed in an intestine.

According to some historians, black pudding, as we know it today, is one of the few Assyrian dishes which have come down to us still greatly resembling those made by the pork butchers of Tyre, who, it is said, excelled in this type of preparation.

The preparation of black puddings has greatly improved in the course of the centuries and those made today are superior to those of our grandparents' time.

Black pudding is the traditional French dish served at supper after Christmas midnight mass. Large quantities of both black and white puddings are eaten at this meal. The Christmas dinner generally includes many other traditional dishes, such as truffled turkey, goose stuffed with chestnuts, and *foie gras* with truffles, served in a *terrine*, in jelly or in a pie crust.

Achille Ozanne, cook and poet, wrote of black puddings:

'Préparez des oignons, hachés menus, menus,
Qu'avec autant de lard sur un feu doux l'on passe,
Les tournant tant, qu'ils soient d'un blond devenus,
Et que leur doux arome envahisse l'espace . . .
Mêlez le tout au sang, puis, bien assaisonnez,
De sel, poivre et muscade, ainsi que des épices;
Un verre de Cognac; après: vous entonnez
Dans les boyaux de porc, dont l'un des orifices
Est d'avance fermé, et dès qu'ils sont remplis,
Ficelez l'autre bout, et dans l'eau frémissante
Plongez tous les boudins! Ces travaux accomplis,
Egouttez-les après vingt minutes d'attente.'

'Chop the onions, finely, finely,
Toss them in an equal amount of fat on a low fire,
Stirring them, until they are a beautiful golden colour,
And their fragrance pervades all round . . .
Blend them with blood then season well with
Salt, pepper, nutmeg and the spices;
A glass of brandy and then you stuff the mixture
Into the pig's intestine, one end of which
Has previously been sealed. As soon as this is filled,
Tie up the other end and into simmering water
Plunge the black pudding! Once this is done,
You give them twenty minutes, and drain.'

Black puddings can be made using blood of animals other than pig, but any addition to pig's blood, or even its complete substitution by the blood of ox, calf or sheep, produces black puddings of mediocre quality.

Black puddings can be made from the blood of various fowls, rabbits, and wild animals such as deer, wild boar, etc., but these puddings can only be made if the blood of these animals can be obtained, and they must therefore be blooded, as is done with the domestic pig.

In France the name *boudin* also applies to various preparations made from poultry and game, which are really no more than quenelles.

A great variety of black and white puddings are made in France. Each region has its special *boudin*. Among the best known are the black and white puddings of Nancy, Metz, Strasbourg, Lyons, Dijon, Rouen, Pau, Albi, Toulouse, Auvergne, Limousin, Roussillon, Berry, Brittany, Flanders and, last but not least, those made in Paris.

Black pudding and white pudding (U.S. blood sausage and white sausage). BOUDIN DE PORC – These pork sausages are generally found in the shops ready for use. They can be grilled or cooked in the oven, as well as fried in butter or lard.

The black pudding is made of pig's blood and fat.

The white pudding is a sausage made of white pork meat and fat.

Black puddings (U.S. blood sausage). BOUDINS NOIRS DE PORC – Into a large bowl put 1 kg. ($2\frac{1}{4}$ lb.) fresh hog's fat cut in large dice and half-melted, 400 g. (14 oz., $3\frac{1}{2}$ cups) chopped onion, fried lightly in lard without allowing it to colour, 6 teaspoons salt, a good pinch of freshly ground pepper and a good pinch of spices. Add 8 dl. (scant $1\frac{1}{2}$ pints, scant 2 pints) pig's blood and 2 dl. ($\frac{1}{3}$ pint, scant cup) fresh cream.

Mix all these ingredients. Fill pig's intestines with the mixture, without stuffing them too much, as the mixture swells during cooking. Tie the black puddings into the desired lengths, or leave whole, as the case may be.

Lay them out on a wicker tray and plunge this tray into a big pan of boiling water. Draw the pan to the side of the burner and poach the black puddings at a temperature of 95°C. (203°F.) for about 20 minutes. As they rise to the surface, prick them with a pin to let our air, otherwise, when heated, the casings may burst.

Drain the puddings. Leave them to get cold on the wicker tray, covered with a cloth to prevent their drying up too much.

Make a few shallow incisions on both sides and grill very gently on moderate heat. Serve with mashed potatoes.

Black puddings (U.S. blood sausage) à l'anglaise. BOUDINS NOIRS À L'ANGLAISE – Prepare as ordinary black puddings, adding to the mixture 500 g. (18 oz.) rice well cooked in stock, or an equal quantity of pearl barley, also cooked in stock. Season with plenty of spices.

Grill like ordinary black puddings.

Black puddings (U.S. blood sausage) à la flamande. BOUDINS À LA FLAMANDE – Use mixture similar to that for ordinary black puddings, adding to it 200 g. (7 oz., scant cup) brown sugar, 100 g. (4 oz., $\frac{2}{3}$ cup) currants and the same amount of sultanas, washed, allowed to swell in warm water, and drained well.

These black puddings are grilled in the usual way and served with sweetened apple purée.

Black puddings (U.S. blood sausages) with apples, called à la normande. BOUDINS NOIRS AUX POMMES, DITS À LA NORMANDE – Cut the black puddings into uniform little chunks and sauté in butter in a frying pan. When they are lightly browned, add peeled, sliced cooking apples, cooked in butter, allowing 500 g. (18 oz.) apples per 1 kg. ($2\frac{1}{4}$ lb.) black puddings.

Sauté the apples and the black puddings for a few moments. Serve in a deep dish.

White puddings (U.S. sausage). BOUDINS BLANCS DE PORC – Chop finely together 500 g. (18 oz.) lean pork and 800 g. ($1\frac{3}{4}$ lb.) fresh pork fat.

Pound this mixture in a mortar, adding to it 100 g. (4 oz., $\frac{1}{2}$ cup) butter, and an equal quantity of raw fat goose liver.

Rub this mixture through a sieve, put into a bowl and stir with a wooden spoon. Add, one by one, 4 whole eggs, 100 g. (4 oz., 1 cup) chopped onion fried lightly in butter without allowing it to colour, and 2 dl. ($\frac{1}{3}$ pint, scant cup) fresh cream. Season with 5 teaspoons salt, a good pinch of white pepper and a pinch of spices. Mix well.

Fill pigs' intestines (casings) with this mixture and poach as described in the recipe for black puddings.

Grilled white puddings (sausage). BOUDINS BLANCS GRILLÉS – When the white puddings are quite cold, prick them (do not make incisions with a knife) on both sides, wrap each in a piece of buttered greaseproof paper and cook gently under a grill. Serve with mashed potatoes.

Bacon rinds and pork skin. COUENNE DE PORC – Bacon rinds and pork skin are used in a great number of culinary preparations, mainly as an element of garnish for braised meats and, along with calves' feet, as the gelatinous element in preparing jellies.

Pork skin, boiled in well-spiced stock, can also be prepared as ballottines or *roulades*, which are served cold.

Salt pork. PETIT SALÉ DE PORC – This term covers various joints of pork pickled in brine. Forequarter flank, cutlets, ears, knuckles, pig's snout, etc., can be treated in this way.

Wash the pork in plenty of water, then put into brine and leave from 3 to 6 days, depending on the season. These cuts are boiled in water and served hot, with potato salad.

The term *petit salé* applies to salt chine of pork, which is boiled and served with various vegetables, most frequently with boiled or braised cabbage or mashed potatoes.

This cut is also used as an ingredient for *potée*.

Boiled salt pork à l'anglaise. PORC SALÉ BOUILLI À L'ANGLAISE – Boil a piece of salt pork (shoulder or breast) in water with the usual vegetables and 6 parsnips. Arrange on a dish and surround with the vegetable garnish. Serve with pease pudding, which is prepared in the following manner:

Blend together in a bowl 500 g. (18 oz., 2 cups) rather thick purée of split peas, 100 g. (4 oz., $\frac{1}{2}$ cup) butter, 3 whole eggs, salt, pepper and grated nutmeg.

Put this purée into a buttered pudding basin and cook in the oven in a *bain-marie*.

The mixture can be put in a scalded, buttered and floured cloth, tied and cooked with the pork.

Purée of yellow split peas can be served with *boiled salt pork à l'anglaise* instead of pease pudding.

Pork sausages. SAUCISSES DE PORC – Pork sausages, whether they be long or flat, are made of sausage meat, which can include various ingredients.

Sausages which are not made of pork, as well as sausages of foreign origin (Cambridge sausages, Frankfurt sausages, etc.) are dealt with under SAUSAGE.

Sausage meat. Chop separately equal quantities of lean pork, having removed all sinews, and fresh pork fat. Pound this forcemeat in a mortar to varying degrees of fineness, depending on the type of sausage for which they are intended. Season with *Spiced salt* (see SALT), allowing about 4 to 5 teaspoons salt per kg. (2 teaspoons per lb.).

Or: Use half fat, half lean pork, remove all sinews, and chop finely. Season with salt as above.

Or: Chop lean beef and neck end of pork in equal proportions.

Making sausages. When the forcemeat is ready, stuff pigs' intestines with it, using a special utensil. To facilitate this operation, incorporate a little cold water or 2 whole eggs per kg. (1 whole egg per lb.) of meat in the forcemeat while mixing it.

Truffled sausage meat. Prepare as above, adding 150 g. (5 oz., $2\frac{1}{2}$ cups) fresh truffles, cut in small dice, to the forcemeat.

Truffled sausages are mostly made of forcemeat to which truffle parings have been added.

Sausages with red or green cabbage. SAUCISSES AUX CHOUX ROUGES, CHOUX VERTS – Grill the sausages, or poach them in white wine. Arrange them on a bed of braised green cabbage, or red cabbage prepared as described in the recipe for *Red cabbage à la flamande* (see CABBAGE).

If the sausages are poached, add the liquor in which they are cooked to the cabbage braising liquid.

Sausages à la catalane. SAUCISSES À LA CATALANE – Fry in lard 1 kg. ($2\frac{1}{4}$ lb.) of big sausage twisted into a coil. When it is well browned, remove from the pan.

Put 2 tablespoons (3 tablespoons) flour into the same fat and colour lightly. Moisten with white wine and meat stock, add 1 tablespoon tomato purée, and mix well. Cook for 10 minutes and strain.

Put the sausage back into the pan. Add 2 to 4 blanched cloves of garlic and a *bouquet garni* (q.v.), to which a small piece of bitter orange rind has been added. Pour the sauce over the sausage. Cover and simmer gently for 30 minutes.

The sauce can be thickened with white breadcrumbs instead of flour.

Chipolata sausages. SAUCISSES CHIPOLATAS – Sausages made in very small-sized casings. These are divided into pieces from 4 to 5 cm. ($1\frac{1}{2}$ to 2 inches) long.

They are used as a garnish for various dishes and can be grilled, fried in butter or poached in white wine.

Country sausages I. SAUCISSES DE CAMPAGNE – Stuff pigs' intestines with a forcemeat composed of 2 parts lean beef and 1 part lean fresh bacon, seasoned with 6 teaspoons salt, 1 teaspoon pepper, $\frac{1}{2}$ teaspoon pounded pimento, a pinch of saltpetre and 1 clove of garlic, per kg. ($2\frac{1}{4}$ lb.) forcemeat. Make the sausages from 10 to 12 cm. (4 to 5 inches) long.

When they are ready, dry them on the top part of the oven. Poach in boiling water or stock from 10 to 12 minutes.

This type of sausage is used mainly as an element of garnish for *potées*.

Country sausages II. SAUCISSES DE CAMPAGNE – Use forcemeat composed of 2 parts lean pork and 1 part firm bacon fat, seasoned as above, flavoured with savory, coriander, marjoram, thyme and bay leaf, and moistened with 1 dl. (6 tablespoons, scant $\frac{1}{2}$ cup) red wine per kg. ($2\frac{1}{4}$ lb.).

Stuff small ox intestines with this forcemeat. Join the sausages two by two and dry on the top part of the oven.

These sausages are poached in water or cooked in *potées*.

Pig's liver sausage. SAUCISSES DE FOIE DE PORC – Use forcemeat composed of 3 parts pork (fat and lean) and 1 part pig's liver, previously parboiled and seasoned with *Spiced salt* (see SALT), allowing from 4 teaspoons per kg. (2 teaspoons per lb.), and mixed with 2 tablespoons (3 tablespoons) pig's blood. Stuff in beef intestine casings.

Divide into lengths of 10 to 12 cm. (4 to 5 inches). Poach in water like black puddings.

Pig's liver sausage is also grilled like black pudding.

Shoulder of pork. ÉPAULE DE PORC – Fresh shoulder of pork is used in the same way as chine. Bone and roll the shoulder, then roast, pot-roast or braise it. Serve with all the garnishes suitable for *Loin of pork*. The shoulder can also be cut into pieces and made into stews. Salted shoulder of pork is used as an ingredient for *potées*.

Boned, salted and smoked shoulder of pork is prepared like leg.

Cold pork slices. ÉMINCÉS DE PORC – Use left-over pork cut into thin slices, as described in the recipe for *Sliced beef* (see BEEF).

This dish is usually served with *Charcutière* or *Robert sauce* (see SAUCE) and accompanied by mashed potatoes or a purée of any other starchy vegetable.

Pork stew. RAGOÛT DE PORC – Pork is seldom cooked as a stew. The cuts most suitable for this method of preparation are the shoulder, chine and breast. Care should be taken to remove all surplus fat.

Sucking pig, suckling pig. PORCELET – See *Piglet*.

Stuffed suckling pig à l'occitane. PORCELET ÉTOFFÉ À L'OCCITANE – Clean out the suckling pig through a short incision on the belly. Bone it, leaving only the leg bones. Season inside with salt and spices, sprinkle with brandy, and leave to marinate for a few hours.

Stuff it with the following mixture:

Cut the pig's liver and an equal quantity of calf's liver into small slices. Season and brown briskly in sizzling butter, to stiffen them. Drain, and put in a dish.

In the same butter, quickly brown the heart and the kidneys of the suckling pig, cut into small slices, and 150 g. (5 oz.) lambs' sweetbreads, soaked, parboiled, rinsed in cold water and sliced.

Drain all these ingredients and put together with the liver.

Add 3 tablespoons (scant $\frac{1}{4}$ cup) butter to the same pan and lightly fry 200 g. (7 oz., scant 2 cups) finely chopped onion without allowing it to colour. When the onion is well softened, add 2 tablespoons (3 tablespoons) chopped shallots and 2 dl. ($\frac{1}{3}$ pint, scant cup) dried *duxelles* (q.v.). Fry for a few moments, and add a pinch of pounded garlic. Moisten with dry white wine, boil down, and add 4 dl. ($\frac{3}{4}$ pint, scant 2 cups) rich veal broth.

Bring to the boil, add 150 g. (5 oz.) fresh bacon rinds, cooked and cut in small pieces, and stoned and blanched green olives. Cook for a few minutes. Put the above ingredients into this sauce. Heat, without allowing the sauce to boil, stir, and leave this *ragoût* to cool.

Mix it with sausage meat, bind with eggs, season well, add chopped parsley and a dash of brandy and blend.

Stuff the suckling pig the day before it is to be cooked and leave in a marinade of oil, brandy, sliced carrots and onions, parsley, thyme, bay leaf, crushed cloves of garlic and spices.

Truss and skewer the suckling pig and sew up the opening. Put it into a long braising pan on a foundation of bacon rinds, and the carrots and onions used for the marinade. Add fresh sliced carrots and onions. Sprinkle with lard, cover, and cook gently on the top of the stove until the vegetables begin to brown.

Moisten with 3 dl. ($\frac{1}{2}$ pint, $1\frac{1}{4}$ cups) dry white wine. Boil down this liquid. Add a few tablespoons thickened brown veal stock and a good *bouquet garni* (q.v.). Cook in the oven. When done, the skin of the suckling pig should be golden and crisp.

Drain the piglet, untruss, and put on a serving dish. Garnish all round with small pork *crépinettes* (see above) *aux fines herbes* and small black puddings fried in butter. Add the onions and carrots from the braising pan. Pour over the strained braising liquor. Serve with a purée made of mashed celeriac and potatoes in equal proportions.

Instead of braising the piglet with slices of onions and carrots, it can be garnished with medium-sized whole onions and carrots cut down to a uniform size, disposing them around the dish along with black pudding and *crépinettes*.

The stuffing should be of an adequate consistency (which is achieved by binding it with egg) to ensure that when the suckling pig is cut, it does not spill out but remains intact, together with the cut slice.

PORKER. GORET – Name given to a piglet which, having reached the age of six months, is no longer a suckling pig.

PORPOISE. MARSOUIN – The smallest of the puffing cetaceans, valuable mainly for the oil extracted from it. The porpose is edible, though oily. In former times it was sold in Paris during Lent. It is prepared in various ways and eaten in Scotland, Iceland and Newfoundland.

Porridge (*Claire*)

PORRIDGE (English cookery). BOUILLIE D'AVOINE – A popular food, made of specially treated oatmeal and water. Porridge is greatly appreciated in Scotland, Ireland and throughout England. Here is the recipe:

Boil 1 litre ($1\frac{3}{4}$ pints, generous quart) water with $2\frac{1}{2}$ teaspoons salt. As soon as boiling is established, pour 300 g. (11 oz., scant 2 cups) oatmeal into it in a steady rain. Stir all the time, until the porridge acquires the desired consistency.

Leave to simmer for 20 minutes, stirring from time to time. Serve with cold milk or cream. Each person at table is left to season porridge to his or her taste.

Porridge or hasty-pudding. BOUILLIE – Bring salt water to the boil in a pan. Pour in maize flour (corn meal, or a mixture of maize and wheaten flour) to obtain a fairly thick mixture. Cook on moderate heat, stirring frequently with a wooden spoon, until the mixture is very thick. Add a few tablespoons pork fat. Mix well.

While it is still hot, pour this porridge on to a coarse linen cloth and spread it out in a layer about 2½ cm. (1 inch) thick. Leave to cool. When it is quite cold, cut it into squares or rectangles, and proceed as indicated in the selected recipe.

Arrowroot porridge. BOUILLIE À L'ARROWROOT – See ARROWROOT.

Buckwheat porridge. BOUILLIE DE SARRASIN – See KASHA.

Maize porridge or las pous (Périgord cookery). BOUILLIE DE MAÏS DITE LAS POUS – This *bouillie* or porridge, which in Périgord is also called *rimotes*, is somewhat similar to the *gaudes* of Franche-Comté and also to polenta, as it is made in Italy, Corsica and Provence.

The *bouillie* is eaten instead of bread with certain dishes, such as salt pork with cabbage and jugged hare, and is also served as a soup. It is prepared like polenta (q.v.).

It can also be eaten as a sweet course. For this, when the maize is cooked, pour it into a baking pan or some other shallow receptacle, spread it in an even layer, and allow to cool. Cut into uniform pieces, dip in flour and fry in lard or butter. Arrange on a dish and sprinkle with sugar.

Béarn millas. MILLAS DU BÉARN – The porridge, which in this region is also called *paste, pastel, gaudines* and *yerbilhou*, is prepared in the same way as *broye* (q.v.).

Périgord millas or las pous. MILLAS PÉRIGOURDIN, LAS POUS – Proceed in the usual way with a mixture of equal quantities of maize (corn meal) and wheaten flour.

If the porridge is too thick it can be made lighter with a little hot milk. It can be made more delicate by the addition of a little fresh butter just before the porridge is ready.

Dr. Bircher-Benner's muesli. BOUILLIE CRUE DU DOCTEUR BIRCHER-BENNER – This is not strictly speaking a porridge, because it is not boiled, but its consistency is so mushy that it has the appearance of porridge.

Attaching great importance to the nutritive value of raw food, Dr. Bircher-Benner prescribed this mixture as a breakfast and supper dish. At lunch time he allowed various cooked foods and even meat, in addition to raw vegetables and fruit served as an *hors-d'œuvre*.

The *muesli* is prepared overnight. Soak 2 or 3 tablespoons rolled oats in cold water for 12 hours. On the following morning, drain and mix with condensed milk, raw grated unpeeled apples, or with any other fruit in season, sometimes with grated carrots. Add honey and lemon juice.

PORRINGER. ÉCUELLE – Bowl made of wood, earthenware or metal to hold an individual portion of food. In the Middle Ages it was usual for two people to share a porringer, hence the French expression: *'Manger à la même écuelle'* (which means, roughly, to live in one another's pocket).

PORT. PORTO – A great wine, of international renown, grown in the valley of Douro in Portugal, east of the town of Oporto. This wine matures splendidly and reaches its plenitude when it is between 25 and 30 years old. The types of port wines usually consumed are the result of blendings of several different vintage years. However, connoisseurs naturally prefer 'vintage' port with a *millésime*, that is a single specified vintage year. Port is drunk as an apéritif in France, but the English custom of drinking it after the meal is often adopted where old vintage port is concerned. Port has its part to play in the composition of various dishes, such as eel *matelote* (See MATELOTE, *Matelote à la canotière*), calves' sweetbreads (see OFFAL), *zabaglione* and, of course, cocktails (port flip, etc.).

PORTER – English beer, very strong and dark, almost black.

PORT-SALUT – See CHEESE.

PORTUGAISE – Tomato fondue made with butter or oil and flavoured with onion, garlic and parsley. (See FONDUE, *Tomato fondue*).

PORTUGUESE OYSTER. GRYPHÉE – Type of mollusc (see OYSTERS).

POSSET – Hot drink made of milk and white wine or beer.

POT-AU-FEU – An essentially French method of cooking a broth which provides at one time soup, meat and vegetables (see SOUPS AND BROTHS).

POTASH. POTASSE – Oxide of potassium. Alkaline substance which plays an important rôle in nutrition.

POTASSIUM NITRATE – See SALTPETRE.

POTATOES. POMMES DE TERRE – Tuber-bearing plants, native of South America, introduced into France, as an ornamental plant, towards 1540.

The potato was brought from Quito in South America, first into Spain, where it was cultivated in Galicia, and later from North America into England.

In 1563 Sir John Hawkins is said to have introduced the potato into England, but its cultivation was neglected there and it was reintroduced in 1586 by Sir Francis Drake. Sir Walter Raleigh grew potatoes in Ireland.

In 1593, Gaspard Bauhon praised it and engaged several farmers around Lyons and the Vosges region to grow it, but in 1630 the Parliament of Besançon, from fear of leprosy, forbade the cultivation of potato.

The potato must have been introduced into Lorraine in 1665, for on the 28th June, 1715, the Court of Nancy issued a decree exacting a tithe, which was only payable after 50 years of cultivation.

In 1597, the botanist Gérard, who received some potatoes direct from Virginia, gave the following description of this crop: 'These tubers are a nourishing as well as a pleasant dish, equal in wholesomeness and salubrity to the batata (sweet potato), whether they be baked in hot ashes, or boiled and eaten with oil, vinegar or pepper, or prepared in any other way by the hands of an able cook.'

In 1619 potato figures among the foods to be served at the Royal table in England. It did not, however, become an article of import until 1662.

In Scotland it has been cultivated since 1683 – and in open fields, for the first time, by Thomas Prentice in 1728.

It was introduced into the Low Countries in 1588 by Clusius, who got it from Gérard.

The English introduced it into Flanders during the wars against Louis XIV.

In France the potato was still considered suspect in 1771; it was said to be unfit for human consumption and dangerous, because of its weakening properties. It was Parmentier who rehabilitated it. In 1771, in a thesis, he listed it among the vegetables which could be used in times of food shortage along with horse chestnuts, acorns, and the roots of bryony, iris, gladioli and couch grass. In 1773 he published his work entitled *Chemical examination of potato, wheat and rice* and began his research into the panification of potato flour.

In 1787, during a period of scarcity, he obtained the concession of 50 arpents (old French measure roughly equivalent to an acre) of poor land in the Sablon plain. The cultivation proved successful, contrary to all expectations, and a short while later Parmentier was able to offer King Louis XVI a bouquet of potato flowers, which set a fashion for this plant.

We know the way in which he aroused the cupidity of the Parisians: the field was closely guarded during the day by soldiers of the Garde Française, but was left unsupervised during the night.

Parmentier had his precursors – and he never denied this: Turgot acclimatised potatoes in the Limousin; Lavoisier, on the advice of Parmentier, cultivated them in his lands in Fréchines, in Vendôme; La Rochefoucauld-Liancourt in Beauvais, Chalaire in the Boulogne region in 1763; Dottu, the great agriculturist of Villers-Bretonneux, in Picardy from 1766.

Denigration gave place to a period of enthusiasm and a craze for the potato flower, which was used as a decorative design for plates. After its popularisation, thanks to Parmentier, the potato became one of the staple foods at the beginning of the nineteenth century.

The potato is an energy food, 100 calories per 100 g. (4 oz.), rich in carbohydrates (20 to 25 per cent), lacking in albuminoids. It contains a few mineral salts (potassium mostly) Vitamins B and C, and a very small amount of iodine. Its starch is one of the most assimilable of all and for this reason it can be included in the diet of diabetics. There are only traces of fats and calcium.

Some label the potato solanaceous, in other words of the same family as tobacco, henbane and belladonna. In fact the infinitesimal amount of solanum detectable in potatoes is found just under the skin and is therefore discarded with it. Yellowy-fleshed potatoes are considered the best, since white-fleshed potatoes are usually demineralized. Some people find potatoes hard to digest, especially mashed potatoes, often due to insufficient mastication and salivary impregnation. Potatoes ought to be thoroughly masticated.

Weight for weight, the potato contains two and a half times less carbohydrates than bread, which makes it a highly desirable food in diets for diabetics, as 40 g. ($1\frac{1}{2}$ oz.) bread can be replaced by 100 g. (4 oz.) potato. It is rich in potassium and constitutes a highly alkaline food.

To avoid the loss of mineral salts, and in particular of potassium salts, it should not be boiled in too much water (or at least the water in which it is boiled should be kept for soup). This loss is decreased by cooking in fat, such as butter, lard or oil. The best method of cooking potato to preserve the maximum of its mineral elements and taste is to bake it in the ashes or in the oven. The taste is incomparably better and makes it possible to eat potatoes without salt, should this be necessary.

The potato plays a very important part throughout Europe as an article of food.

In certain Central European countries the potato plays a greater part than in Western Europe, often taking the place of bread.

Among the numerous French-cultivated varieties of potatoes are: *Bintje, B.F.15, Belle de Fontenay, Eerstelingen* or *Sterling, Royal Kidney, Viola, Ratte* or *Quenelle de Lyon* (the best variety of all, perhaps, from a culinary point of view), *Roseval, Saucisse, Rosa*, etc.

Black potato, or rather purple potato, called *Négresse* in French, is a gastronomical curiosity.

Potatoes à l'anglaise. POMMES DE TERRE À L'ANGLAISE – Peel the potatoes down to as uniform a size as possible and either boil them in salted water or steam them. *Potatoes à l'anglaise* are used as a garnish for boiled fish and some meat dishes.

Anna potatoes, also called potato cake with butter. POMMES DE TERRE ANNA, GALETTE DE POMMES DE TERRE AU BEURRE – Peel long yellow potatoes, trim them to shape into big uniform-sized cylinders. Slice them thinly, wash and dry. Put them into a straight-sided dish with a lid, with plenty of clarified butter. Arrange the potato slices in uniform overlapping layers. Fill the dish with rows of potato slices, season each layer and sprinkle with clarified butter. Cover the dish, start cooking on the stove, then put into a very hot oven and cook from 30 to 35 minutes.

When three-quarters cooked, turn the potato cake upside down to colour the other side. Drain off the butter and arrange on a dish.

Anna potatoes for garnish. POMMES DE TERRE ANNA – Proceed as described in the previous recipe, piling the potatoes into well-buttered, tinned-copper *dariole* moulds and using slices of potato of the same diameter as the mould used.

Cook in the oven. Turn out and use as indicated in the recipe.

Anna potatoes (home method). POMMES DE TERRE ANNA – Peel the potatoes as uniformly as possible, slice them thinly, wash, dry and season.

Sauté them in the butter until they are completely impregnated. Shape into a big cake, pressing them with the back of a fork. Brown on one side on moderate heat, and turn it and brown the other side.

Annette potatoes. POMMES DE TERRE ANNETTE – Cut the potatoes into thin *julienne* (q.v.) strips, wash, dry, season and fill a well-buttered casserole with them. Bake in the oven as described in the recipe for *Anna potatoes*.

This dish, which is a variation of Anna potatoes, can also be cooked in a frying pan like a pancake.

Potatoes cooked in the ashes. POMMES DE TERRE SOUS LA CENDRE – Wash big long potatoes. Dry them and bake in hot ashes with glowing embers on top.

Wipe the potatoes and serve with fresh butter.

Potatoes baked in the oven. POMMES DE TERRE AU FOUR – Wash the potatoes, dry them and bake in a hot oven. Serve with fresh butter.

Potatoes with bacon. POMMES DE TERRE AU LARD – Fry 100 g.

Potatoes as garnish:
duchess, parisienne, croquettes, straw potatoes

(4 oz.) diced and blanched bacon in a sauté pan in 1 tablespoon butter, lard, or goose fat. Add 10 small onions.

Remove the bacon and the onions. Put 1 tablespoon flour into the pan, allow it to colour slightly. Moisten with $3\frac{1}{2}$ dl. (generous $\frac{1}{2}$ pint, $1\frac{1}{2}$ cups) stock or water, season, add a *bouquet garni* (q.v.) and bring to the boil.

Put 500 to 600 g. (18 to 21 oz., 3 to $3\frac{1}{2}$ cups) potatoes, cut to look like olives (or into quarters), the bacon and the onions, into this sauce. Bring to the boil, cover the pan, and cook in a slow oven. Sprinkle with chopped parsley.

Potatoes with basil. POMMES DE TERRE AU BASILIC – Cook the potatoes, cut down to a uniform size, in butter, keeping the pan covered. When ready, sprinkle with coarsely chopped fresh basil, allowing 1 good tablespoon for 500 g. (generous lb.) potatoes.

Potatoes à la basquaise. POMMES DE TERRE À LA BASQUAISE – Choose long potatoes and hollow them out lengthways. Parboil for 5 minutes, drain and dry. Stuff them, with garlic-flavoured *Tomato fondue* (see FONDUE), mixed with a *salpicon* (q.v.) of sweet pimentos cooked in butter (or oil), chopped Bayonne ham and chopped parsley.

Butter a deep *à gratin* dish, put the potatoes into it, season, sprinkle with melted butter (or oil), heat on the stove, and finish cooking in a slow oven.

When the potatoes are done, scatter some breadcrumbs on top, sprinkle with butter and brown. Pour on a few tablespoons thickened brown veal stock.

Potatoes à la berrichonne. POMMES DE TERRE À LA BERRICHONNE – Peel 500 g. (18 oz.) potatoes, cutting them down to a uniform size to look like large olives, as for *Potatoes in butter* (see below). Put them into a sauté pan in which 2 tablespoons (3 tablespoons) chopped onion and 100 g. (4 oz., $\frac{1}{2}$ cup) diced and scalded bacon have been fried together in 1 tablespoon butter. Brown lightly, pour in enough stock to cover the potatoes, season, add a *bouquet garni* (q.v.) and cook with a lid on.

Serve in a vegetable dish, sprinkled with chopped parsley.

Black potatoes, also called négresses or pommes de Madagascar. POMMES DE TERRE NOIRES, DITES NÉGRESSES, POMMES DE MADAGASCAR – This variety of potato is remarkable only for its colour, which after cooking is not really black, but a dark purple. They are used mainly as an element of mixed salads and cold *hors-d'œuvre*. They can be prepared in most of the ways suitable for ordinary potatoes.

Boiled potatoes. POMMES DE TERRE BOUILLIES – Wash the potatoes, put them into a saucepan, cover with water, season with coarse salt and cook.

Drain the potatoes, peel them and use as indicated in the recipe: creamed; *lyonnaise*, *maître d'hôtel*, in salad, sautéed, etc.

Potato borders. BORDURES DE POMMES DE TERRE – These borders are made of *Duchess potato* (see below), piped through a forcing-bag around the edges of dishes, brushed with beaten egg, and browned lightly in the oven.

Potato borders can also be made by moulding duchess potato mixture by hand.

Potatoes à la boulangère (garnish). POMMES DE TERRE À LA BOULANGÈRE – These potatoes are usually cooked round a joint of meat baked in the oven, as described in the recipe for *Shoulder of lamb à la boulangère* (see LAMB).

They can also be cooked separately, in a baking pan, in the oven.

Potatoes in butter (garnish). POMMES DE TERRE AU BEURRE – Cut the potatoes to look like large olives, or if new potatoes are used, peel them.

Wash, drain, put into a sauté pan in which some butter has been heated, season with salt, and sauté to impregnate them with scalding butter.

Cook in the oven or on the stove until the potatoes acquire a golden colour. Shake the pan from time to time during cooking. Sprinkle with chopped parsley.

Potato cakes. GALETTES DE POMMES DE TERRE – These can be prepared in several ways.

1. Using *Duchess potato* (see below), shaped into round or oval cakes, brush with beaten egg and cook in the oven until golden.

2. Prepare the potato cakes as above. Dredge them in flour and fry until pale golden in clarified butter.

3. Make small or large potato cakes, as described in the recipe for *Anna potatoes* but making them thinner.

Finish off as indicated in individual recipes, putting different ingredients between each layer of potatoes, such as: *brunoise* (q.v.) or *mirepoix* (q.v.) of vegetables, sliced mushrooms, spinach cooked in butter, chopped ham, various vegetables thinly sliced and cooked in butter, truffles, etc.

These potato cakes can be made big or small, depending on the final use for which they are intended. When small, they are used as a garnish, or as foundations for escalopes, medallions, *noisettes*, *tournedos*, etc.

Little potato cakes (Carême's recipe). PETITS PAINS DE POMMES DE TERRE – 'Bake 12 peeled kidney potatoes in the ashes. Remove all the reddish parts and use only the white flesh. Weigh out 350 g. (12 oz.) of this and pound with 100 g. (4 oz.) Isigny butter. When the mixture becomes smooth, add to it 100 g. (4 oz.) castor (fine) sugar, 50 g. (2 oz.) sieved flour, 2 egg yolks and a grain of salt. Pound everything together into a perfectly smooth paste. Take it out of the mortar, put on a lightly floured board, roll, and cut into 4 parts. Roll each part, making it twice its original length, then cut into little balls the size of walnuts, giving them the shape of boats. Place them on a buttered baking sheet. Brush with beaten egg and bake in a moderate oven.'

Château potatoes. POMMES DE TERRE CHÂTEAU – (See above, *Potatoes in butter*.)

Château potatoes are a traditional garnish for grilled *chateaubriand* steak.

Chatouillard potatoes. POMMES FRITES CHATOUILLARD – Cut the potatoes into ribbons, peeling them off spiral-fashion, 3 mm. ($\frac{1}{8}$ inch) thick (see CHATOUILLARD).

Cook like *Soufflé potatoes* (see below). Drain, season, and arrange around grilled meat.

Potatoes copeaux. POMMES FRITES COPEAUX – Like *Chatouillard potatoes* but cut into irregular ribbons.

Crainquebille potatoes. POMMES DE TERRE CRAINQUEBILLE – Put some big, long, peeled potatoes into a sauté pan on a foundation of chopped onion fried in butter. Pour in enough stock to cover the potatoes half-way.

Season with salt and pepper, add a *bouquet garni* (q.v.) with 1 clove of garlic added to it, place on each potato 1 slice seeded tomato and sprinkle with melted butter. Bring to the boil on the stove, then cook in the oven. A few moments before taking out of the oven, sprinkle with white breadcrumbs and brown the top.

Potatoes à la Crécy, also called à la Vichy. POMMES DE TERRE À LA CRÉCY, À LA VICHY – Prepare like *Anna potatoes*, putting a layer of *Carrots à la Vichy* (see CARROTS) between each layer of potato.

Potatoes à la crème. POMMES DE TERRE À LA CRÈME – Boil the potatoes in water, peel them when cooked, cut into thick slices and put into a sauté pan. Cover with boiling milk or boiling fresh cream. Cook briskly until the liquid is reduced. Season with salt, pepper and grated nutmeg. Add a few tablespoons fresh cream.

Potato curly crisps (U.S. chips). POMMES FRITES COLLERETTES – Like *Fried potatoes (potato crisps)* (see below), but cut with a fluted cutter.

Potato croquettes
(*Larousse*)

Potato croquettes. CROQUETTES DE POMMES DE TERRE – Divide *Duchess potato* (see below) into small (40- to 50-g., 1½- to 2-oz.) pieces. Mould into the shape of corks or other shapes, rolling them in flour. Dip in egg and breadcrumbs and fry in very hot deep fat. Use as indicated in the recipe.

Potato croquettes Chevreuse. CROQUETTES DE POMMES DE TERRE CHEVREUSE – As above, adding chopped chervil to the duchess potato mixture.

Potato croquettes à la lyonnaise. CROQUETTES DE POMMES DE TERRE À LA LYONNAISE – As above, adding chopped onion lightly fried in butter and chopped parsley to the duchess potato mixture.

Potato croquettes à la parmesane. CROQUETTES DE POMMES DE TERRE À LA PARMESANE – As above, adding grated Parmesan cheese to the duchess potato mixture.

Potato croquettes à la périgourdine. CROQUETTES DE POMMES DE TERRE À LA PÉRIGOURDINE – As above, adding chopped truffles to the duchess potato mixture.

Potato croustades (hors-d'œuvre or entrée). CROUSTADES DE POMMES DE TERRE –

1. Roll out *Duchess potato* (see below) to a thickness of 2½ cm. (1 inch) and with a pastry-cutter cut out circles 5 or 6 cm. (about 2¼ inches) in diameter.

Dip in egg and breadcrumbs. Mark the middle in each circlet with a smaller pastry-cutter, pressing in to penetrate only one-third of the circlet's thickness.

Fry in very hot deep fat. Drain on a cloth, remove the small circle forming the lid and hollow out the *croustades* without breaking them. Fill as indicated in the recipe.

These *croustades* are used as hot *hors-d'œuvre* or as a garnish for meat, poultry and fish.

2. Line some well-buttered, fluted, brioche tins with duchess potato mixture. Put in a layer of purée.

Brush the inside of the *croustades* with beaten egg and cook golden in the oven. Turn carefully out of the tins, brush the outside with beaten egg and put in the oven for a few moments. Fill as indicated in the recipe. The same uses as above.

3. Mould duchess potato mixture on a round, buttered dish in such a way as to obtain a *croustade* deep enough to contain the filling indicated.

Decorate the edges by piping some mixture through a forcing bag. Fill as indicated in the recipe.

These *croustades* can be made large or small depending on the final use for which they are intended. They are used as a foundation for meat, poultry, fish, etc., served in small pieces and accompanied by a sauce.

4. Shred the potatoes into *julienne* strips (as described in the recipe for *Annette potatoes*) and line a well-buttered dish with them.

In the middle of the potatoes put a cast iron form (rather like a layer-cake tin), buttered on the outside.

Press hard on this to make the potatoes go up the sides of the dish and form a lining layer ½ inch thick. Fill the inner mould with deep-frying fat. Cook in the oven like *Annette potatoes*.

When it is cooked, remove the inner mould, press down the potatoes with a fork and brown the inside part lightly.

Turn out carefully on to a dish and fill as indicated in the recipe.

They can be made without the inside mould, by pressing the potatoes, when half cooked, against the sides of the dish.

Dauphine potatoes. POMMES DE TERRE DAUPHINE – Mix *Duchess potatoes* (see below) with one-third their weight of unsweetened common *Chou paste* (see DOUGH). Leave until cold. Divide into 40- or 50-g. (about 1½-oz.) pieces. Shape into balls, roll in flour and fry in very hot deep fat.

Drain, dry, sprinkle with salt and arrange in a heap on a plate or in a potato nest. Or use as a garnish, as indicated in the recipe.

These potatoes can be moulded into different shapes. They can also be dipped in egg and breadcrumbs before deep-frying.

Potatoes à la dauphinoise
(*Claire*)

Potatoes à la dauphinoise, also called Gratin de pommes à la dauphinoise. POMMES DE TERRE DAUPHINOISE – Slice 500 g. (18 oz.) potatoes very finely, put them in a bowl and moisten with 3 dl. (½ pint, 1¼ cups) boiled milk with a beaten egg added to it.

Season with salt, pepper and grated nutmeg. Add 50 g. (2 oz., ½ cup) grated Gruyère cheese and mix. Put into an earthenware dish, buttered and rubbed with garlic.

Sprinkle with grated Gruyère cheese, scatter 25 g. (1 oz., 2 tablespoons) butter in tiny pieces over the top, wipe the edges of the dish carefully and bake in a slow oven for 45 minutes.

Duchess potatoes. POMMES DE TERRE DUCHESSE – Cut 500 g. (18 oz.) peeled potatoes into thick slices or quarters. Boil them briskly in salted water. Drain, put in the oven for a few moments to evaporate excessive moisture, and rub through a sieve.

Put the purée into a saucepan, dry off for a few moments, turning with a wooden spoon. Add 50 g. (2 oz.) butter, season with salt, pepper and a little grated nutmeg, bind with a whole egg and 2 yolks and mix. Spread the purée on a buttered metal sheet, leave until cold, and shape as indicated in the recipe.

When this mixture is intended for borders to be piped through a forcing-bag, it is used while still hot. It is then not so thick as when it is intended for croquettes, or to be served as duchess potatoes proper.

Duchess potatoes for garnish. POMMES DE TERRE DUCHESSE –

These potatoes are prepared from *Potato purée* described below, moulded by hand into various shapes, or forced through a bag on to a buttered baking sheet.

As soon as the purée has been piped through, brush with beaten egg and put in the oven to brown. Use as indicated in the recipe.

Potatoes with fennel. POMMES DE TERRE AU FENOUIL – Like *Potatoes with basil* replacing the basil by fresh chopped fennel.

Potato fondantes. POMMES DE TERRE FONDANTES – Cut the potatoes to uniform size to look like small eggs. Put them into a buttered sauté pan, cover and cook gently on the top of the stove. Turn them carefully, one at a time, once during cooking. They should be golden on the outside and very soft inside when cooked.

They can also be prepared as follows:

Cook the potatoes, cut as described, in lard. When they are done, drain off the lard and replace it by butter.

Sliced potatoes should be dried in a cloth before frying (*Claire*)

Fried potatoes. POMMES DE TERRE FRITES – This is the most popular form of potatoes eaten, also the least digestible. If the frying is carried out correctly, at the right temperature, the potatoes should be crisp, very pleasant to the taste and easier to digest; if badly done, the potatoes are impregnated with fat and become indigestible.

They are immersed in deep cooking fat or oil, at a temperature of 180°C. (356°F.), when the fat is beginning to smoke. This temperature falls at once to 160°C. (320°F.) then to 150°C. (302°F.) when fresh cold potatoes are put in so the fat must be reheated each time. The potatoes should acquire a golden colour.

If cut very finely (straw potatoes), and immersed in special fat heated to 190°C. (374°F.), in five minutes' cooking time the temperature of the fat will fall to only 177°C. (350°F.).

Under the entry DEEP-FRYING all instructions relative to the clarification of the fat in which the potatoes are cooked are given, as well as all information dealing with utensils, pans, etc., which are used for deep-frying.

Fried potatoes, or potato crisps (U.S. chips). POMMES FRITES CHIP, EN LIARDS – Cut the potatoes into the shape of corks then into very thin slices. Soak in cold water for 10 minutes. Drain, dry on a cloth and fry in very hot deep fat. Drain and season.

These potatoes are often used as an accompaniment to roast game *à l'anglaise*.

Fried potatoes pont-neuf. POMMES FRITES PONT-NEUF – Cut the potatoes into pieces 1 cm. ($\frac{1}{2}$ inch) thick and 6 to 7 cm. (about $2\frac{1}{2}$ inches) long. Fry in boiling fat.

Potato fritters: scallops garnished with duchess potatoes

Potato fritters – See FRITTERS.

Gastronome potatoes, also called potatoes à la Cussy (Plumerey's recipe). POMMES DE TERRE GASTRONOME, POMMES DE TERRE CUSSY – 'Take big yellow potatoes, cut off the two ends, and cut them with a special cutter (called in French, a *colonne*) into cork-shaped chunks, about $2\frac{1}{2}$ cm. (1 inch) in diameter. Cut them into slices 5 mm. ($\frac{1}{4}$ inch) thick, putting them into water as you cut them. Dry on a cloth to absorb all water.

'Put them into a big pan with 225 g. (8 oz., 1 cup) hot clarified butter, so that they cook gently, colouring without sticking to the pan or drying up. In the meantime, slice 6 or 8 truffles, toss them in butter with 1 tablespoon of Madeira and a piece of chicken jelly the size of a walnut. When the potatoes are cooked and acquire a fine golden colour, remove them from the fire, add the truffles and the juice of $\frac{1}{2}$ lemon and serve piping hot.

'We owe this side dish to the late Monsieur de Cussy, a fine gourmet and former administrator of Napoleon's palace.'

This method of preparing potatoes is somewhat similar to the one called '*à la scarlandaise*'.

Potatoes Georgette. POMMES DE TERRE GEORGETTE – These are principally served as a hot *hors-d'œuvre*. Choose medium-sized potatoes, bake in the oven and cut a circle on one side'

Through this opening scoop out three-quarters of the pulp. While still hot fill them with *Crayfish tail ragoût à la Nantua* (see CRAYFISH).

Heat the potatoes in the oven and serve.

Grilled potatoes. POMMES DE TERRE GRILLEES – Choose big, long potatoes and cut them lengthways into slices $1\frac{1}{2}$ cm. ($\frac{1}{2}$ inch) thick. Parboil them in salted boiling water for 4 minutes. Drain and dry on a cloth. Brush with oil or melted butter. Cook under a low grill. Arrange on a dish and top with half-melted *Maître d'hôtel butter* (see BUTTER, *Compound butters*).

Hashed browned potatoes (American cookery). POMMES DE TERRE HACHÉES BRUNES À L'AMERICAINE – Boil the potatoes in salted water, drain well and chop up.

Fry them in butter in a frying pan, browning well. Season with salt and pepper. Give them the shape of a turnover and allow to colour.

Chopped onions fried in butter are sometimes added to this dish.

Potatoes à la hongroise. POMMES DE TERRE À LA HONGROISE – Soften 75 g. (3 oz., $\frac{3}{4}$ cup) chopped onions in butter in a sauté pan. Season with $\frac{1}{2}$ teaspoon paprika. Add 1 peeled, seeded and chopped tomato, and 500 g. (18 oz.) long potatoes cut into thick round slices. Season with salt. Moisten with meat stock in sufficient quantity to cover the potatoes. Bake in the oven. Sprinkle with chopped parsley.

Potatoes à la landaise. POMMES DE TERRE À LA LANDAISE – Fry 100 g. (4 oz., 1 cup) diced onions and 150 g. (5 oz., generous $\frac{1}{2}$ cup) diced Bayonne ham, in goose fat or lard. When the onions and the ham are browned, add 500 g. (18 oz.) potatoes cut in large dice. Season with salt and pepper. Cook with a lid on, stirring from time to time. Add 1 tablespoon chopped garlic and parsley.

Potato loaves. PAINS DE POMMES DE TERRE – Bake big floury potatoes in the oven and scoop out the pulp with a spoon. Rub this through a sieve as quickly as possible. Put the purée thus obtained into a saucepan with butter, allowing 100 g. (4 oz., $\frac{1}{2}$ cup) butter per 1 kg. ($2\frac{1}{4}$ lb.) purée. Add salt, pepper and grated nutmeg. Stir on the fire for a few moments to dry off excessive moisture, then remove from heat and add 1 whole egg and 4 yolks. Mix well. Divide into 50-g. (2-oz.) pieces, and mould them into small boat-shaped cakes slit in the middle. Put on a baking sheet, brush with beaten egg and cook in a very hot oven until golden.

Potatoes Lorette. POMMES DE TERRE LORETTE – Divide *Dauphine potato* (see above) into small (about 50-g., 2-oz.) parts, shape into crescents and fry in deep fat.

Potatoes à la lyonnaise. POMMES DE TERRE À LA LYONNAISE – Prepare as described in the recipe for *Sautéed potatoes* (see below). When three-quarters cooked, add 4 tablespoons ($\frac{1}{3}$ cup) sliced onions fried in butter.

Finish cooking together, shaking the pan frequently to mix well. Sprinkle with chopped parsley.

Macaire potatoes. POMMES DE TERRE MACAIRE – Bake big potatoes in the oven. Halve them and scoop out the pulp with a fork. Mash this pulp with several tablespoons butter, allowing 100 g. (4 oz., $\frac{1}{2}$ cup) butter per 1 kg. ($2\frac{1}{4}$ lb.) pulp. Season with salt and pepper.

Put the pulp into a frying pan in which some butter has been heated. Spread in a flat cake. Fry until golden on both sides.

Maire potatoes. POMMES DE TERRE MAIRE – The same as *Potatoes à la creme*.

Potatoes à la maître d'hôtel. POMMES DE TERRE À LA MAITRE D'HÔTEL – Boil the potatoes in salted water. Peel and slice them. Put them into a sauté pan and cover with boiling milk. Add 2 or 3 tablespoons butter, season, and cook until the liquid is boiled down.

Sprinkle with chopped parsley.

Potato matches (U.S. potato sticks). POMMES FRITES ALLUMETTES – Cut the potatoes into little sticks $\frac{1}{2}$ cm. ($\frac{1}{4}$ inch) wide and 6 or 7 cm. ($2\frac{1}{2}$ inches) long. Fry in very hot deep fat in order to obtain crisp golden potatoes.

Drain, dry and season with fine, dry salt.

Potatoes with mint. POMMES DE TERRE À LA MENTHE – Boil new potatoes with a sprig of mint. Serve in a vegetable dish and put a green mint leaf on each potato.

Potatoes Mont-Dore. POMMES DE TERRE MONT-DORE – Prepare creamy mashed potatoes mixed with grated cheese, heap in a dome in a buttered fireproof dish, sprinkle with grated cheese, pour on some melted butter and brown.

Potatoes mousseline. POMMES DE TERRE MOUSSELINE – Bake the potatoes, remove pulp and rub it through a sieve. Stir the pulp in a pan on heat, adding to it, for 1 kg. ($2\frac{1}{4}$ lb.) pulp, 250 g. (9 oz., generous cup) butter and 4 egg yolks. Season with salt, pepper and grated nutmeg. Remove from heat and add 2 dl. ($\frac{1}{3}$ pint, scant cup) whipped cream. Pile in a dome in a buttered fireproof dish, sprinkle with melted butter and brown quickly in the oven.

This purée can also be put into a flan case made of *Lining paste* (see DOUGH).

Potatoes au naturel

Potatoes nature or au naturel. POMMES DE TERRE NATURE, AU NATUREL – One or other of these names is often given to boiled potatoes (see above, *Potatoes à l'anglaise*).

Potato nests. NIDS DE POMMES DE TERRE – Shred the potato into fine *julienne* (q.v.) strips, as described in the recipe for *Straw potatoes* (see below). Wash, dry and use them for lining special moulds or wire baskets.

Press the potatoes well against the sides of the wire baskets. Trim away any overlapping parts, close the baskets and plunge them into very hot deep fat.

Take out of the pan, drain and season.

Noisette potatoes (garnish). POMMES DE TERRE NOISETTE – Scoop out with a vegetable scoop pieces of potato the size and

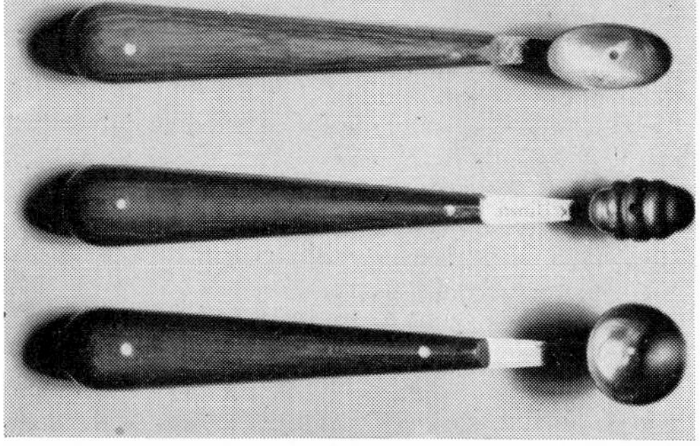

Spoons for scooping out potatoes and for shaping potato noisettes (*Larousse*)

shape of hazelnuts. Fry them in butter, season, and cook until golden all over.

Potatoes à la normande. POMMES DE TERRE À LA NORMANDE – Cut 500 g. (18 oz.) potatoes into thin slices. Wash and dry them, season with salt and freshly ground pepper, and put into a buttered sauté pan in layers, alternating with the shredded white part of 2 big leeks and 1 heaped tablespoon chopped parsley.

Add a *bouquet garni* (q.v.) and enough white veal stock, meat stock or water – if the dish is intended to be served as Lenten fare – to cover the potatoes. Scatter 50 g. (2 oz., $\frac{1}{4}$ cup) butter in tiny dabs.

Bring to the boil, cover, and cook in the oven.

Potato pancakes. CRÊPES DE POMMES DE TERRE – Peel, wash and dry the potatoes, put them through a mincer. Dab the pulp obtained with a cloth, put it into a bowl, season with salt, pepper and grated nutmeg, and add, for 500 g. (18 oz.) potatoes, 2 eggs beaten with 1 dl. (6 tablespoons, scant $\frac{1}{2}$ cup) milk and 50 g. (2 oz., $\frac{1}{4}$ cup) *Noisette butter* (see BUTTER, *Compound butters*). Add cheese if desired.

Make the pancakes in the usual manner, keeping them a little thicker than for sweet pancakes.

Potatoes à la parisienne

Potatoes à la parisienne (garnish). POMMES DE TERRE À LA PARISIENNE – Like *Noisette potatoes*, but smaller in size. As soon as the potatoes are cooked, toss them in greatly concentrated veal stock or dissolved meat jelly. Sprinkle with chopped parsley.

Parmentier potatoes. POMMES DE TERRE PARMENTIER – Cut potatoes into pieces about 1 cm. ($\frac{1}{2}$ inch) square. Cook them in butter. Sprinkle with chopped parsley.

These potatoes are more often cooked with the meat with which they are served.

Parsley potatoes. POMMES DE TERRE PERSILLÉES – Boil the potatoes, drain well and add melted butter and chopped parsley. Potatoes with bacon the recipe for which is given above, are often served under this name.

Potatoes à la paysanne. POMMES DE TERRE À LA PAYSANNE – Cut the potatoes into very thin round slices. Put them into a buttered sauté pan in alternate layers with chopped sorrel cooked in butter mixed with pounded chervil and a pinch of grated garlic. Season with salt and pepper, add meat stock (or water, if th the dish is to be served as Lenten fare). Scatter tiny dabs of butter over and cook in the oven.

Potato purée. PURÉE DE POMMES DE TERRE – Cut potatoes into thick slices or quarters and cook them in fast-boiling salted water.

Drain, put in the oven for a few moments to evaporate surplus moisture and rub through a sieve, pressing down with a wooden masher. Put the purée into a pan set on the stove and blend in about 175 g. (6 oz., $\frac{3}{4}$ cup) butter per kg. ($2\frac{1}{4}$ lb.) purée. Add a few tablespoons of boiling milk, stir vigorously with a wooden spoon and serve.

The purée should not be allowed to boil after the butter has been added to it.

Potato purée à la crème. PURÉE DE POMMES DE TERRE À LA CRÈME – As above, replacing milk by fresh cream.

Potato purée au gratin. PURÉE DE POMMES DE TERRE AU GRATIN – Prepare the purée as described above. Add grated cheese and put into a buttered fireproof dish; smooth the surface, working it into a slight dome shape. Sprinkle with grated cheese and melted butter and brown the top.

Potato purée soup. POTAGE PURÉE DE POMMES DE TERRE – See SOUPS AND BROTHS, *Purée of potato soup Parmentier*.

Potato quenelles à l'alsacienne, called floutes (Alsatian cookery). QUENELLES DE POMMES DE TERRE À L'ALSACIENNE, DITES FLOUTES – Prepare 500 g. (18 oz., $2\frac{1}{4}$ cups) very fine potato purée. Add 2 whole eggs and 75 g. (3 oz., $\frac{3}{4}$ cup) unsifted flour in order to obtain a fairly firm paste. Season with salt, pepper and grated nutmeg.

Shape into balls, roll to look like corks, or mould with a soup spoon. Drop the quenelles one by one into a pan of salted boiling water. Poach for 8 to 10 minutes. Drain and put into a buttered dish. Pour over some piping hot *Noisette butter* (see BUTTER, *Compound butters*) in which a handful of fine, freshly grated breadcrumbs have been lightly fried.

Potato quenelles with Parmesan cheese. QUENELLES DE POMMES DE TERRE AU PARMESAN – Prepare the quenelles as described above. After poaching, put them into a dish, buttered and sprinkled with grated Parmesan cheese. Sprinkle with more grated Parmesan, spoon over some melted butter, and brown the top in a very hot oven.

Rissole potatoes. POMMES DE TERRE RISSOLÉES – Another name for *Sautéed potatoes* (see below).

Roast potatoes. POMMES DE TERRE RÔTIES – Peel big, long potatoes, and put them into a sauté pan in which some butter or lard has been heated. Season with salt. Cook in the oven, basting frequently, until golden all over.

Potatoes Saint-Flour. POMMES DE TERRE SAINT-FLOUR – Line the bottom of a deep fireproof dish with a layer of green cabbage braised in fat and cooked slightly crisp. Over the cabbage put a layer of potatoes cut in thick slices, mixed with lean diced bacon, scalded and fried. Season with salt and pepper. Moisten with stock, flavoured with a little crushed garlic. Sprinkle with grated cheese. Cook in a slow oven.

Potato salad – See SALAD.

Potatoes à la sarladaise. POMMES DE TERRE À LA SARLADAISE – Prepare like *Anna potatoes* putting the potatoes into a deep dish in layers, alternating with rows of thinly sliced truffles.

Sautéed potatoes I. POMMES DE TERRE SAUTÉES – Slice boiled, peeled, potatoes. Season, and fry in butter until golden, shaking the pan frequently to ensure even browning. Sprinkle with chopped parsley.

Sautéed potatoes II. POMMES DE TERRE SAUTÉES À CRU – Cut 500 g. (18 oz.) uncooked Dutch potatoes into very thin slices, wash, dry on a cloth and season.

Cook in butter in a frying pan. Shake the pan frequently to ensure even cooking and to give all the potatoes a golden colour.

Sprinkle with chopped parsley.

Sautéed potatoes à la provençale. POMMES DE TERRE SAUTÉES À LA PROVENÇALE – Use either raw or boiled potatoes and

Potatoes, roast, noisette, saute, mashed, boiled, fried

prepare like *Sautéed potatoes I or II.* Add 1 good tablespoon chopped parsley and garlic.

These potatoes can also be cooked in oil instead of butter.

Potatoes à la savoyarde. POMMES DE TERRE À LA SAVOYARDE – Prepare like *Potatoes à la dauphinoise*, replacing the milk by white stock.

Potato soufflé – See SOUFFLÉ.

Soufflé potatoes (or puffed potatoes). POMMES DE TERRE SOUFFLÉES – Choose uniform-sized potatoes. Peel, trim and cut them lengthways into slices, 3 mm. ($\frac{1}{8}$ inch) thick. Wash and dry on a cloth.

Plunge into not too hot deep fat, which should be heated gradually. Cook the potatoes until they begin to rise to the surface. Drain in a frying basket.

Just before serving, plunge them into a second pan of very hot deep fat. Drain the potatoes, which should be well puffed up, spread them on a cloth and sprinkle with salt.

This method of cooking potatoes was discovered by accident. It is claimed that the discovery took place at Pecq in 1837, when the train had great difficulty in clambering up the final slope. The proprietor of the restaurant in which the Company was giving lunch to its guests had prepared some fried potatoes for the appointed time and let them get cold, and then, taken by surprise by the unexpected arrival of the party, only had time to plunge them into boiling fat quickly and, to his amazement, saw them puff up.

The famous analytical chemist Chevreul, who was informed of this phenomenon, studied it experimentally and established the conditions under which it occurred and could be reproduced at will.

It is perhaps the only time that a train being late had happy consequences!

Soufflé potatoes require double cooking and fat which can be brought to a very high temperature without burning, which is best achieved with beef suet. The potatoes should first be plunged into fat at a temperature of 180°C. (356°F.) contained in a big pan (which reduces the degree of cooling); this temperature is reduced to 135°C. (275°F.) in 2 minutes. After 7 minutes – the time needed for cooking through slices 3 mm. ($\frac{1}{8}$ inch) thick – the temperature is lowered to 120°C. (248°F.). The potatoes are then cooked and soft. They are taken out, the heat is increased and the potatoes are reimmersed, a few at a time, in hot fat which should register at least 190°C. (374°F.) to ensure puffing up. At this temperature the surface of the slices is transformed into a waterproof skin, which will swell as a result of the volatilisation of the water contained inside.

Steamed potatoes. POMMES DE TERRE À LA VAPEUR – Steam the potatoes in a special steamer as described in the recipe for *Potatoes à l'anglaise*.

Potatoes in stock. POMMES DE TERRE AU JUS – Cut the potatoes into quarters and put into a sauté pan with butter. Pour in enough clear brown veal stock to cover. Season, cover, and cook in the oven.

Straw potatoes. POMMES FRITES PAILLE – Cut the potatoes into very thin *julienne* (q.v.) sticks. Wash and dry on a cloth. Fry in hot, deep fat. Drain in a frying basket. Just before serving, plunge into smoking hot fat.

Stuffed potatoes I. POMMES DE TERRE FARCIES – Bake long potatoes in the oven and scoop out two-thirds of the pulp. Rub through a sieve and mix with ingredients such as *duxelles* (q.v.), *fines herbes* (q.v.), grated cheese, chopped ham, *mirepoix* (q.v.), chopped onion softened in butter, or various chopped meats, etc. Season well, add butter and fill the potato skins with the mixture.

Sprinkle with grated cheese or breadcrumbs, pour on a little melted butter and brown the top.

Or: Peel some very big potatoes. Cut them to look like cylinders, slice off the ends to make them all the same height, say about 6 to 7 cm. ($2\frac{1}{2}$ inches).

How to empty a potato ready for stuffing

Hollow them out with a vegetable scoop, to form a cavity capable of containing about 50 g. (2 oz., $\frac{1}{4}$ cup) forcemeat. Blanch in fast-boiling salted water, drain, dry, arrange in a well-buttered sauté pan and season. Stuff with the filling indicated, either through a forcing-bag or with a spoon. Smooth the top layer of the filling into a dome shape.

Moisten the potatoes with meat stock without covering them. Bring to the boil on the stove, cover the pan, and cook in a slow oven from 35 to 40 minutes. Remove the potatoes carefully, arrange them in a fireproof dish, sprinkle with breadcrumbs and melted butter and brown the top in the oven. Boil down the pan juices, skim off any surplus fat, strain, and pour over the potatoes.

Stuffed potatoes II. POMMES DE TERRE FOURRÉES – Bake medium-sized, uniform-shaped potatoes. Cut a circular opening on one side and keep the cut-out pieces to use as lids. Scoop out three-quarters of the pulp, taking care not to damage the skin. Stuff the potatoes with the filling indicated. Sprinkle the top with breadcrumbs or grated cheese and brown the top, or simply replace the cut-out circles as lids.

Serve on a folded napkin.

If the stuffed potatoes are to be browned later, it is better to cut them in half, lengthways, instead of hollowing them out through a circular opening.

Stuffed potatoes à la cancalaise. POMMES DE TERRE À LA CANCALAISE – Prepare like *Stuffed potatoes I*, using a filling of poached oysters, mushrooms, and *White wine sauce* (see SAUCE).

Stuffed potatoes à la cantalienne. POMMES DE TERRE À LA CANTALIENNE – Scoop pulp out of the potato, mash and mix with two-thirds of its weight of braised, chopped cabbage.

Sprinkle with grated cheese and brown the top.

Stuffed potatoes à la chasseur (Hunter style). POMMES DE TERRE CHASSEUR – Cook potatoes as above and stuff with sliced chicken livers and mushrooms, sautéed in butter, and *Chasseur sauce* (see SAUCE).

Stuffed potato with cheese

Stuffed potatoes with cheese. POMMES DE TERRE AU FROMAGE, GRATINÉES. Cook potatoes as above, and stuff with the mashed pulp, seasoned, and with butter added to it.

Sprinkle with grated cheese and brown the top.

Stuffed potatoes à la duxelles. POMMES DE TERRE FARCIES À LA DUXELLES – Prepare like *Potatoes stuffed with sausage meat* (see below) and stuff with a *duxelles* (q.v.) mixture.

Stuffed potatoes fermière. POMMES DE TERRE FERMIÈRE – Fill with the pulp scooped out of the potatoes, mashed and mixed with two-thirds of its weight of chopped stock-pot vegetables. Sprinkle with grated cheese and brown the top.

Stuffed potatoes à la florentine. POMMES DE TERRE À LA FLORENTINE – Fill with spinach cooked in butter. Cover with *Mornay sauce* (see SAUCE), sprinkle with grated cheese and brown the top.

Stuffed potatoes à la hongroise. POMMES DE TERRE À LA HONGROISE – Fill with the pulp scooped out of the potatoes, mashed with a fork, mixed with one-third of its weight of chopped onion gently fried in butter and seasoned with paprika.

Stuffed potatoes Maintenon. POMMES DE TERRE MAINTENON – Fill with a *salpicon* (q.v.) of breast of chicken, pickled tongue, truffles and mushrooms bound with *soubise* (q.v.).

Sprinkle with grated cheese mixed with breadcrumbs and brown the top.

Stuffed potatoes à la ménagère. POMMES DE TERRE FARCIES À LA MÉNAGÈRE – Prepare like *Potatoes stuffed with sausage meat* (see below) and stuff with chopped meat left-overs.

The chopped meat, beef or mutton, can be mixed with one-third of its weight of fine forcemeat or sausage meat.

Stuffed potatoes princesse. POMMES DE TERRE PRINCESSE – Fill with asparagus tips with *Cream sauce* (see SAUCE). Cover the potatoes with slivers of truffles.

Stuffed potatoes à la provençale. POMMES DE TERRE À LA PROVENÇALE – Fill with a *salpicon* (q.v.) of marinated tunny (tuna fish) and hard-boiled eggs, bound with *Tomato fondue* (see TOMATO). Sprinkle with breadcrumbs and brown the top.

Potatoes stuffed with sausage meat. POMMES DE TERRE FARCIES CHARCUTIÈRE – Prepare as described in the second method of the recipe for *Stuffed potatoes I*. Fill with sausage meat stuffing, mixed with chopped parsley and, if desired, chopped onions lightly fried in butter.

These potatoes can also be stuffed with sausage meat mixed with the pulp of cooked potatoes, as described in the first method of the same recipe.

Stuffed potatoes soubise. POMMES DE TERRE SOUBISE – Fill with thick *Onion soubise* (see PURÉE) with cream.

Sprinkle with breadcrumbs and brown the top.

Stuffed potatoes à la Vichy. POMMES DE TERRE À LA VICHY – Fill with *Carrots à la Vichy* (see CARROTS).

Sprinkle with breadcrumbs and brown the top.

Stuffed potatoes Yorkshire style. POMMES DE TERRE À LA YORKAISE – Bake the potatoes in the oven and fill with chopped York ham and mushrooms bound with *Béchamel sauce* (see SAUCE), mixed with chopped onion lightly fried in butter and seasoned with a little paprika.

Potato subrics. SUBRICS DE POMMES DE TERRE – Cut the potatoes into small dice, parboil in salted water for 2 minutes, drain dry, and cook lightly in butter in a covered pan.

Remove from the heat and bind with thick *Béchamel sauce* (see SAUCE), allowing $2\frac{1}{2}$ dl. (scant $\frac{1}{2}$ pint, generous cup) sauce per 500 g. (18 oz., $2\frac{1}{4}$ cups) potatoes. Add 3 yolks and 1 whole egg to the mixture. Season with salt, pepper and grated nutmeg and mix.

Heat some clarified butter in a frying pan and drop the mixture 1 tablespoon at a time into the hot butter, taking care to allow space for the *subrics* to spread during cooking, and to prevent their sticking to each other.

Turn the *subrics* with a palette knife to make both sides golden. Serve with *Cream sauce* (see SAUCE).

Potatoes à la toulousaine. POMMES DE TERRE À LA TOULOUSAINE – Cut the potatoes into quarters and brown them lightly in a mixture of $\frac{2}{3}$ goose fat and $\frac{1}{3}$ oil in a sauté pan.

Season, sprinkle with flour, add 1 tablespoon chopped garlic and parsley. Pour in enough stock or water to cover the potatoes. Stir, bring to the boil, cover, and cook in the oven. Sprinkle with chopped parsley.

Potatoes à la Vichy. POMMES DE TERRE À LA VICHY – Name sometimes given to *Potatoes à la Crécy*.

Potatoes Voisin. POMMES DE TERRE VOISIN – Prepare like *Anna potatoes* sprinkling each layer of potatoes with grated cheese.

Potatoes Yvette. POMMES DE TERRE YVETTE – Name under which *Annette potatoes* are sometimes served.

POTÉE – All preparations cooked in an earthenware pot. In particular the word describes soup made with pork and vegetables, mostly cabbage and potatoes, of which cabbage soup is the most characteristic.

Potée Lorraine – Line the bottom of an earthenware vessel with pieces of pork skin or bacon rind. Place on top some fresh pork fat, a knuckle of ham or bladebone of pork, carrots, turnips, bunches of leeks and a whole blanched cabbage. Barely cover with cold water. Cook for 3 hours. Thirty minutes before taking it from the fire, put in a large, well-pricked sausage. Serve with boiled potatoes.

POT-ROASTING. POÊLAGE – Method of slow cooking by steam. A casserole with a tightly fitting lid is used. The food is cooked in butter or fat and flavoured with vegetables which have been cooked slowly in butter until very tender.

Pot-roasted meat, poultry or fish must be basted frequently during cooking. When it is ready, take it out of the casserole. Serve on a dish, or, where appropriate, in a *cocotte* (q.v.). Remove most of the cooking fat.

Dilute the juices in the casserole with wine or stock as

indicated in the recipe. Boil for a few seconds. Strain and pour over the dish.

Pot-roasting à la Matignon. POÊLAGE À LA MATIGNON – Brown lightly in butter the meat or fish to be pot-roasted. Cover with a thick layer of *Matignon* (q.v.) or *fondue* (q.v.) of root vegetables. Wrap in buttered greaseproof paper and cook in the oven in a braising pan, or on the spit. After cooking, unwrap, place on a dish, surround with the appropriate garnishes and pour on the stock.

Braising *à la Matignon* can also be carried out by lining the braising pan with the fondue of root vegetables and placing the meat, fish or poultry, liberally basted with butter, on top.

POTTED CHAR (English cookery) – Fish conserve formerly held in great esteem in England, where it was eaten at breakfast.

Cook the char in a prepared vegetable stock and let them cool in the liquid. Remove all skin and bones and arrange the fillets of fish, well drained, in shallow earthenware pots. Cover with clarified butter and set in the oven for 15 minutes. Allow to get quite cold. Add a few more tablespoons clarified butter, if necessary, so that the fish is completely covered.

Potted char, kept in a cool place, will keep for 2 weeks.

In U.S.A., char is the name given to certain types of red-fleshed trout. Trout may be used in this recipe.

POUILLARD – Name given to a young partridge. It is prepared in the same way as a fully grown partridge.

POULE-AU-POT – *Pot-au-feu* prepared with beef and a stuffed chicken. (See SOUPS AND BROTHS, *Pot-au-feu à la béarnaise*.)

POULETTE (À LA) – Method of preparing a diversity of ingredients, notably offal or variety meats. Previously cooked, these are moistened with a *Velouté sauce* (see SAUCE) bound with egg yolks and cream, and are usually garnished with little onions and mushrooms. (See OFFAL or VARIETY MEATS, *Sheep's (lambs') trotters à la poulette*; MUSHROOMS, *Mushrooms à la poulette*.)

POULIGNY-SAINTE-PIERRE – See CHEESE.

POULTRY. VOLAILLE – See CHICKEN.

POUPELIN – Gâteau made by cooking *Chou paste* (see DOUGH) in a plain mould. Three-quarters of the pastry spills outside the mould during cooking. Cool and fill the crust with *Chantilly cream* (see CREAMS), fruit mousse or ice cream.

POUPETON – Method of preparing certain butcher's meats, which are rolled one inside the other into a meat roll. These pieces are generally braised.

POUSSIN – See CHICKEN, *Spring chicken*.

POUSSOIR – Small machine used in *charcuterie* (pork butchery), with which the minced meats are pressed into the gut to make sausages. Air is prevented from entering the gut, an essential condition of perfect sausage making.

Mushrooms à la poulette (*Robert Carrier*)

POUTARGUE, BOUTARGUE – See HORS-D'ŒUVRE, *Cold hors-d'œuvre*.

POUTINE – Tiny undeveloped fish (larvae or post-larvae or 'fry') of various kinds, mainly the early stages of sardines and anchovies. They are treated in the same way as nonats (q.v.).

PRAIRE – Popular name in France for the clam, a bivalve mollusc, most often eaten raw like oysters but which may also be cooked like mussels.

This shellfish is found on the sandy Atlantic coasts of France and also in the Mediterranean. It is known, as *coque rayée* in the bays of Cancale and St. Malo, and as *rigadelle* down the length of the Atlantic Coast from St. Brieuc to Lannion.

PRALINE. PRALIN – A preparation used by pastry-cooks, made in the following way:

Ingredients. 100 g. (4 oz., scant cup) almonds, 100 g. (4 oz., $\frac{1}{2}$ cup) sugar, $\frac{1}{2}$ vanilla pod.

Method. Put the sugar and vanilla in a copper pan and melt over a good heat until it is brown. Remove the vanilla pod. Add the almonds, previously browned in the oven. Mix. Pour into a greased baking tin, cool, then pound in a mortar as finely as possible.

Gâteau 'praliné'

PRALINÉ. PRALINÉ. – Cake made with layers of Genoese cake separated by a layer of praline butter cream, covered with a layer of the same cream and sprinkled with chopped almonds.

Praline butter cream is made by adding 200 g. (7 oz., 1 cup) powdered praline to 1 kg. ($2\frac{1}{4}$ lb., $4\frac{1}{2}$ cups) *Butter cream* (see CREAMS).

PRALINE (Confectionery) – Very delicate sweet, an almond covered with a coating of cooked sugar, variously flavoured and coloured.

The history of this confection goes back to the reign of Louis XIII. At this period, the maréchal duc de Choiseul-Praslin divided his time between the battlefield and the boudoirs of famous women. He had already established quite a reputation for himself through his ingenuity and wit when one day he surpassed himself: he offered some sweets along with his proposals. These were such a novelty at the time that people had never tasted anything like them. His friends besieged the marshal for the recipe, pleading with him at the same time to part with some more. When they asked what the delicacies were called, the duc de Praslin was unable to put a name to them. 'I leave it to you,' he said 'to christen them.' A voice rang out in the company, 'Prasline', pronouncing for the first time a name that was to become famous throughout the world.

The head of maréchal de Praslin's household later settled in Montargis where he founded the *Maison de la Prasline*, which later became the *Confisérie du Roy*.

PRATELLE – Variety of mushroom, large and pinkish, cultivated in beds.

PREIGNAC – White wine which comes from a district of the same name in the Gironde.

PRÉ-SALÉ – See SALT MEADOW.

PRESENT – Dutch cheese, also known under the name of Edammer Kaas.

PRESENTATION OF DISHES. DRESSAGE DES PLATS – To present a dish is to arrange food on a serving dish in accordance with certain accepted rules, e.g., a joint of meat surrounded by its appropriate garnish.

In former times the presentation of dishes was somewhat elaborate. There are many fine drawings of these masterpieces of culinary architecture in the works of Carême.

The presentation of dishes is now as simple as possible. Cold dishes are generally served on a layer of jelly straight on the dish surrounded by a suitable garnish or jelly motifs. Or in glass or crystal bowls, completely covered with very clear jelly.

Aspics, mousses, moulds and other moulded dishes are sometimes set on a slice of sandwich bread cut to the shape of their base and surrounded with a border of jelly, but they are more commonly served straight on the dish, decorated with jelly, or in a glass bowl.

Fish is generally served surrounded by the appropriate garnish interspersed with sprigs of curly parsley, or, where appropriate, skinned, trimmed and masked with jelly and decorated with whatever jelly is indicated in the recipe.

This simplification in the serving of cold dishes, especially sweets (desserts), was recommended by Carême himself, who urged the use of crystal bowls.

In the 'introductory discourse' to the *Cuisinier parisien*, Carême says that, for the presentation of these dishes he had furnished manufacturers with 'several models of bowls for sweets, some of which should be presented in crystal containers.' He advised the cooks of his own day to 'stand jelly sweets on ice to set', which is now current practice.

'In general', wrote Carême, 'I would wish to see these new bowls carried out in future in handsome silverware. They would do honour to the goldsmiths and silversmiths of France.'

PRESENTOIR – Dish on which a tureen, vegetable dish, etc. rests.

PRESERVATION OF FOOD. CONSERVE – The art of preserving food is extremely ancient, but it is only since the mid nineteenth century that it has moved out of the empirical realm into the scientific.

Since the earliest times man has tried to guard against famine by preserving foods during their season of abundance; in particular, meat obtained by hunting.

The only means of preserving food in prehistoric times was by drying. This method is still employed today, particularly in Switzerland, where beef is preserved (*Bindenfleisch*) in the Grisons, being dried solely in the strong pure air.

But once man knew how to use fire to cook meat, he very soon used it for curing it. This was the first scientific method of preserving. Having noticed the effect that fire had on meat, an effect which altered its substance, made it more tasty and easier to masticate, the possibility dawned on primitive man of delaying its decomposition by smoking it. This method of preserving, assisted by a preliminary salting, is still used today, and it is in this manner that all hams and smoked meats are prepared and preserved.

Freezing played a part in preserving meat in those remote days. There was also salting, but only in regions near the sea where rock salt was found.

Fruit and vegetables were first preserved by drying in the sun or by the fire. Later, recourse was made to the system of enveloping food substances in fat. Although rather imperfect, this procedure is still used today to preserve, for a limited period, meat which has first been cooked in fat, put in stoneware pots and covered entirely with fat. Once congealed it makes an almost completely airtight cover.

The basic ways of preserving food, i.e., canning and bottling, freezing, salting and dehydrating are still in use, but modern methods have revolutionised the processes. The preservation of food in the home as well as in the factory is very important.

CANNING AND BOTTLING. CONSERVATION EN BOITE – The process of hermetically sealing food for future use was invented in 1795 by a Frenchman, Nicholas Appert. In 1810 a patent was taken out in England for Appert's method and from there it quickly spread to America, where lobsters and salmon were the first foods preserved in this way. In 1823 Thomas Kensett, an American, invented the tin can for packing food, including meat, poultry, fish, vegetables and fruit. Glass containers, earthenware jars and tin cans are now used in commercial and home canning and bottling.

This method of preservation is basically a process whereby the action of moulds, yeasts and bacteria that spoil fresh food is stopped by subjecting them to high heat long enough to stop the action. Most vegetables as well as poultry, meat and fish must be processed in pressure canners under a $4\frac{1}{2}$-kg. (10-lb.) pressure at 115°C. (240°F.). Most fruits and tomatoes are processed in a boiling water bath. Several varieties of containers are used; all are equipped with covers or seals and directions to make the containers airtight. With the advent of freezers, home canning of poultry, meat and fish is now rare, but canning and bottling of vegetables and fruit is still quite common.

CURING. SALAISON – The curing of meat is an ancient practice. Cato the Censor gives a recipe for the salting of ham which goes back to 200 B.C. In England, by the fourteenth century, it was indeed a sign of poverty to be without bacon. Until the middle of the nineteenth century bacon and ham could only be cured in the winter. When a method of cooling curing cellars with ice was introduced, curing began to be carried out all the year round. Mechanical refrigeration, introduced in Britain in 1877, was the beginning of the modern curing industry, which revolutionised the whole approach.

The success of home curing largely depends on the extent to which unspecialised premises can be adapted for the purpose. The ideal curing room should have a temperature of between 3° and 10°C. (38° and 50°F.), a free circulation of fresh cool air and a means of darkening, as light has a bad effect on the fat of the meat. Most cellars are even in temperature and are suitable provided they are not too damp.

For drying the best room is one which keeps a temperature of about 15°C. (60°F.), preferably with a current of air. The ceiling of a large kitchen not too near the fire, or of a passage leading from the kitchen, is good for this purpose. Rooms in which there is a hot water tank may be used, if the meat is not placed too near the source of heat.

For storage the essentials are absence of light and steady though not necessarily low temperature. (Most attics are too hot in summer and subject to variations in temperature, which lead to condensation on the surface of the bacon or ham and in time produce slime and other evils. Cellars are often too damp and lack adequate air circulation.) A good larder or unheated ground floor room facing north is best.

The equipment for home curing need not be elaborate but should include a boning knife, a carving knife, scales for weighing meat, a large basin or tub for brining head and trotters, a curing trough, shelf or floor, depending on the type of cure, and a thermometer.

For dry salting a stone or brick floor or slate shelf will be needed. If a 'box' cure is contemplated, a strong box with pieces of wood and weights; for pickle curing, tubs or barrels are suitable. It must be remembered that the meat will float in the pickle and boards with weights (large clean stones will do) must be provided as a cover.

For a combination of dry and pickle cures, a stone or lead trough is ideal, preferably with a plug hole for drawing off the liquor, but wooden troughs and basins may be used.

When the meat is being dried, meat hooks and strong twine will be needed and, for storage, greaseproof paper and clean muslin or calico.

Curing ingredients – The preservation of meat consists partly of drying the meat and partly of impregnating it with a sufficiently high concentration of salt and saltpetre (sometimes sugar as well).

Salt is the really essential ingredient in curing. Saltpetre is not a substance required for human nutrition and, except in small concentrations, could be regarded as an irritant or a weak poison, like many other preservatives. Common salt, differs in being a necessary ingredient of the human diet, yet in high concentrations it can become an irritant or even a poison. Sugar has none of the objectionable qualities of the other preservatives and is supposed to help keep the meat soft by counteracting the hardening effects of saltpetre.

Curing ingredients also include vinegar (mostly acetic acid), pepper (the essential oil probably has a preservative effect), beer, wines and spirits (alcohol being a preserving agent) and wood smoke in which are found formaldehyde, alcohols, tars, creosote, etc.

Fruits, berries, spices, etc., have practically no preservative effect, apart from some of the acids or essential oils contained in them, and their main function is to add flavour to the cured product.

Cleansing – The first operation in treating a fresh cut is to cleanse it by dipping it for a short time in a strong brine. This has several advantages; it is rapid and allows the full cure to be carried out at once. It provides the wet salt surface which starts the penetration of salt into the meat without the laborious process of rubbing. This brine can be watered down after cleansing and used for the light pickling of small cuts or offal (variety meats).

The brine is prepared by dissolving 6 kg. (13 lb.) salt and 100 g. (4 oz.) saltpetre in 23 litres (5 gallons, $6\frac{1}{4}$ gallons) boiling water. Mix thoroughly, strain through a cloth and cool to 10°C. (50°F.) or even lower before using.

The loin should be immersed for 10 minutes, until clean. The ham will require longer, about 1 hour, and while in the brine the large veins should be squeezed from the hock end to the fillet end. After cleansing, place the cut skin-side upwards to drain, but do not allow to dry.

Pickling – Dilute above quantity of brine by adding it to 7 litres (6 quarts, $7\frac{1}{2}$ quarts) water. Stir well and use as a pickling brine for head, trotters, tongue, etc.

Salting – Weigh the meat and allow one-tenth of its weight of salt. The amount of saltpetre required is one-fortieth of the weight of salt.

Owing to the small amount of saltpetre the mixing should

be very thorough. To ensure this, use dry, sieved salt. Divide it into three equal parts and add to each the appropriate amount of crushed and sieved saltpetre. Mix each pile of salt and saltpetre thoroughly and sift the mixture, but do not mix the three piles of curing mixture, as one will be used for rubbing in, one for sprinkling and the last for sprinkling at the time of rebedding.

Drain the cleansing brine from the cut and, using one-third of the curing mixture, rub thoroughly first on the skin side, forcing some of it down the shank of the ham, then rub the flesh side lightly.

Prepare a bed of salt about 5 cm. (2 inches) thick and press down the cut into it, skin side down. Sprinkle lightly with the second third of the curing mixture. Cover the cut entirely with $2\frac{1}{2}$ to 5 cm. (1 to 2 inches) salt, taking care to pack the salt tightly at the sides. (The meat tends to shrink and draw away from the salt, causing the surface to become dry and the salting uneven.)

After five days, break the pack, remove any discoloured salt and repack the cut, sprinkling as before with the remainder of the curing mixture.

Different cuts should be kept in salt for varying periods, depending on their thickness. Ham is usually kept in salt 6 to 7 days per $2\frac{1}{2}$ cm. (1 inch) of thickness. In the case of several cuts being cured, care should be taken to repack the salt after each removal of meat.

Washing and maturation – Remove meat from the salt bed, wash the surface in cold water, or leave the ham or bacon in the room where it has been salted for a further period of 2 to 4 weeks, to enable the salt and saltpetre to go on penetrating, until enough curing mixture has been absorbed to prevent the growth of undesirable bacteria. During this period the maturation begins and continues through the subsequent operations of drying, smoking and storage. After this preliminary maturation, wash off excess salt from the surface of the meat, soaking it in a little cold water overnight, if necessary.

Drying – Hang the meat in a warm place with a temperature of about 15°C. (60°F.), not exceeding 21°C. (70°F.). As the drying proceeds, a white surface layer of crystalline salt appears, but if the washing has been thorough, this is not excessive. Where it is difficult to obtain dry storage conditions it is particularly important to remove this surface salt, as it attracts moisture.

Smoking – This should be considered as an alternative method of drying. In addition, however, smoking introduces preservatives and flavouring substances into the meat. Smoking should be carried out at a temperature below 32°C. (90°F.), otherwise the fat will melt, and it is essential to ensure that sufficient moisture has been removed from the bacon or ham.

Storage – This should be, as far as possible, in the dark, at a temperature of about 15°C. (60°F.), but it does no harm to store at lower temperatures provided variations are avoided. Should the temperature of the meat surface at any time be below the dewpoint, a film of moisture will be deposited and the value of the drying process will be partly lost.

If bacon and hams can be kept under dry conditions, they may be hung up without any covering. Added protection is supplied by wrapping the meat in paper or cloth and surrounding with some substance which will take up moisture from the air, such as kiln-dried salt (so long as it does not come into actual contact with the meat), slaked lime, charcoal, wood ashes, malt culms, dried oat hulls or oat meal (provided it is free from mites). Cured meat may be stored by hanging up in clean linen or calico bags, lime-washing the bags two or three times. (With acknowledgement to the Controller of Her Majesty's Stationery Office. Part of this article is taken from *Bulletin No. 127* of the Ministry of Agriculture and Fisheries.)

DEHYDRATION. DESSICCATION – Evaporation of water from foods is another time-honoured technique which has a modern development, but except in time of war, when dehydrated foods are used extensively because of the small shipping space they take, foods processed by canning or freezing are more acceptable, both for reasons of flavour and of keeping qualities. Comparatively few dehydrated foods are sold extensively. Exceptions to this are dried fruits (raisins, prunes, apricots, peaches, pears, etc.), milk (dried to a soluble powder which is used for reconstituted milk in liquid form and for cake and bread 'mixes') and potatoes. Dried whole eggs can be successfully used and egg whites can be dried and used for meringues and icings.

FREEZING. SURGÉLATION – Frozen foods when properly processed resemble the fresh variety more closely than foods preserved by any other method, although no preserved food can claim equality with absolutely fresh food. Freezing in ice is an ancient practice, but the modern method of quick freezing plays a major role in gastronomy in both commercial and domestic areas. To have complete success, food must be used when at its peak, packaged so as to exclude all air and frozen as quickly and thoroughly as possible. Such food is stored at −18°C. (0°F.).

Home freezers are used for storage of commercially frozen products, produce of the garden, orchard or farm, meat, fish, breads, pies, cakes and ice creams, dairy products and pre-cooked meat and vegetable dishes. Well planned use of a home freezer is a great boon to the modern housewife. Most frozen foods should be consumed within one year of being processed. Some foods do not retain their good quality so long. The following should not be stored in a freezer longer than four months: ham; bacon; duck; goose; rich fish like salmon; offal (variety meats) or sausage.

Meat – Properly aged and trimmed cuts of meat are packed in heavy 'freezer' paper. Pork should be used within about 4 months but other meats (beef, veal and lamb) may be kept a year. If the package is neither heavy nor tight enough, 'freezer burn' will develop.

Poultry and game – Chicken, ducks, wild game and rabbits to be cooked whole should be cleaned and trussed before freezing. Giblets are wrapped in freezer paper and stored in the body cavity. Small birds may be cut up (jointed) and wrapped in small packages.

Fish – Fish should be chilled, cleaned and washed before freezing. Small fish are frozen whole; large fish are cut into steaks or filleted. It is important to freeze fish as soon as possible after it is caught.

Vegetables – Some vegetables freeze more successfully than others. All vegetables must be blanched in boiling water or steam before freezing. Following is a representative list of vegetables with instructions for home processing and freezing. The vegetables are packed in airtight plastic containers.

PRESS. PRESSE – Culinary implement serving to extract by pressure fruit juice, or the juice from the carcase of a fowl or of a piece of cooked meat.

According to their use (juice press, lemon squeezer, etc.) these presses take various forms.

PRESS. FOULER – Pressing a purée or some other substance through a strainer with a wooden spoon.

PRESSURE COOKER. MARMITE À PRESSION – Hermetically sealed cooking pan with a lid. In this type of saucepan the pressure forces the temperature up to as much as 130°C. (266°F.) whereas, in an ordinary saucepan, it cannot rise

HOME FREEZING OF VEGETABLES

Vegetable	*Preparation*	*Blanching time in boiling water*	*Processing*
Asparagus	Select young, tender stalks. Sort according to thickness of stalk. Wash and discard tough sections. Leave in lengths to fit package or cut into pieces.	Small stalks, 2 minutes; medium, 3 minutes; large, 4 minutes.	Blanch, cool, drain and pack. When packing spears alternate tips and stem ends.
Beans, Broad Lima, Kidney	Select well-filled pods. Beans should be ripe but not starchy or mealy. Shell, wash and sort according to size.	Small, 2 minutes; medium, 3 minutes; large, 4 minutes.	Blanch, cool and drain. Pack into containers, seal and freeze.
Beans, French, Runner	Select young, tender beans. Wash, cut off stem and tips. Leave whole, slice or cut into pieces.	3 minutes.	Blanch, cool and drain. Pack, seal and freeze.
Beetroot	Select beetroots not more than $7\frac{1}{2}$ cm. (3 inches) across. Wash and sort according to size. Trim tops, leaving 1 cm. ($\frac{1}{2}$ inch) of stems. Cook in boiling water until tender – small beets 30 to 35 minutes, medium size 45 to 50 minutes. Cool, peel, cut into slices or cubes.	—	Pack, seal and freeze.
Broccoli	Select tight, compact, dark-green heads with tender stalks. Wash and trim. To remove insects, soak for 30 minutes in a solution made of 4 teaspoons salt to $4\frac{1}{2}$ litres (4 quarts, 5 quarts) cold water. Split into sprigs.	3 minutes.	Blanch, cool and drain. Pack leaving no headspace. Seal and freeze.
Cabbage	Wash well and shred.	2 minutes.	Blanch, cool thoroughly and drain well. Pack, seal and freeze.
Carrots	Select tender carrots. Remove tops, wash and peel. Leave small carrots whole. Cut others into small cubes, thin slices or strips.	Whole carrots (small), 5 minutes; cubes, slices or strips, 2 minutes.	Blanch, cool and drain. Pack, seal and freeze.
Cauliflower	Select firm, tender, snow-white heads. Break into sprigs. Wash well. If necessary to remove insects, soak for 30 minutes in a solution made of 4 teaspoons salt to $4\frac{1}{2}$ litres (4 quarts, 5 quarts) cold water. Drain.	3 minutes.	Blanch, cool and drain. Pack leaving no headspace. Seal and freeze.

Vegetable	*Preparation*	*Blanching time in boiling water*	*Processing*
Corn-on-the-cob	Trim off leaves and remove silks. Wash, and sort according to size.	Small ears, 4 minutes; medium, 7 minutes; large, 9 minutes.	Blanch, cool thoroughly and drain. Pack ears in containers or wrap in moisture-vapour-resistant material. Seal and freeze.
Mushrooms	Wash and trim. Soak 5 minutes in 4dl. ($\frac{3}{4}$ pint, 2 cups) water with 1 teaspoon lemon juice.	Steam 3 minutes for small or sliced mushrooms, 5 minutes for large whole ones.	Cool, pack, seal and freeze.
Okra	Select young tender green pods. Wash thoroughly. Cut off stems.	Small pods 3 minutes; large pods 4 minutes.	Blanch, cool and drain. Leave whole or slice crosswise. Pack, seal and freeze.
Peas	Select plump, firm pods with sweet, tender peas. Shell and sort out tough or immature peas.	$1\frac{1}{2}$ minutes.	Blanch, cool and drain. Pack, seal and freeze.
Peppers	Peppers frozen without heating are best for use in uncooked foods. Blanched peppers are easier to pack and good for use in cooking. Select firm, crisp, thick-walled peppers. Wash, cut in half, cut out stems and remove seeds. If desired, cut in strips or rings.	Halves, 3 minutes; slices, 2 minutes.	Blanch, cool and drain. Pack, leaving 1 cm. ($\frac{1}{2}$ inch) headspace. Seal and freeze. Unblanched peppers – pack leaving no headspace. Store for 3 months only.
Tomatoes	Wash, sort and trim, and cut up the tomatoes. Simmer for 5 to 10 minutes. Press through a sieve. If desired, add 1 teaspoon salt to each generous litre (2 pints, $2\frac{1}{2}$ pints) of juice for seasoning.	—	Fill containers, leaving 1 cm. ($\frac{1}{2}$ inch) headspace. Seal and freeze. Whole unblanched tomatoes can be stored for 3 months.

Fruits – Some fruits such as apples, apricots and peaches darken when frozen. To prevent this the fruit is packed in a sugar syrup and a little ascorbic acid (Vitamin C) is added. Following is a representative list of fruits that can be frozen. A 40 per cent syrup contains 300 g. (11 oz., $1\frac{1}{3}$ cups) sugar to 6 dl. (1 pint, $2\frac{1}{2}$ cups) water. A 50 per cent syrup contains 450 g. (1 lb., 2 cups) sugar to 6 dl. (1 pint, $2\frac{1}{2}$ cups) water. A 60 per cent syrup contains 700 g. (1 lb. 9 oz., 3 cups) to 6 dl. (1 pint, $2\frac{1}{2}$ cups) water.

HOME FREEZING OF FRUIT

Fruit	*Preparation*	*Processing*
Apples	Select crisp, firm apples. Wash, peel and core. Slice medium apples into twelfths, larger sizes into sixteenths. Blanch 1 minute. Use 40 per cent syrup. For a better quality product add $\frac{1}{2}$ teaspoon ascorbic acid to each generous litre (2 pints, $2\frac{1}{2}$ pints) syrup.	Pack well and cover with syrup. Leave headspace, seal and freeze.
Apple sauce	Select full-flavoured apples. Wash, peel if desired, core and slice. Add a little water. Cook until tender. Cool and strain or liquidise. Sweeten to taste.	Pack into containers, leave headspace, seal and freeze.

Fruit	*Preparation*	*Processing*
Apricots	Select firm, ripe, uniformly-coloured fruit. Sort, wash, halve and stone. Peel and slice if desired. If not peeled, heat in boiling water ½ minute to keep skins from toughening during freezing. Cool and drain. Use 40 per cent syrup. To keep from darkening, add ¾ teaspoon ascorbic acid to each generous litre (2 pints, 2½ pints) syrup. Can also be frozen crushed or puréed. Use fully ripe fruit. For crushed apricots, heat in boiling water ½ minute, cool and peel. Stone and crush. For purée, stone, quarter and press through a sieve or liquidise; or heat apricots in small amounts of water and press through sieve or liquidise. With each generous litre (2 pints, 2½ pints) prepared apricots mix 225 g. (8 oz., 1 cup) sugar. Add ¼ teaspoon ascorbic acid dissolved in 1 dl. (6 tablespoons, scant ½ cup) water to fruit before adding sugar.	Pack, cover with syrup, leave headspace. Seal and freeze.
Berries	Select firm, fully ripe juicy berries. Sort, wash and drain well. Do not wash raspberries or strawberries unless necessary.	Pack berries into containers and cover with 40 or 50 per cent syrup, depending on sweetness of fruit. Leave headspace. Seal and freeze. Can also be open frozen and then packed with or without sugar.
Cherries	Select bright red, tree-ripened cherries. Stem, sort and wash. Drain.	Pack cherries into containers and cover with cold 60 per cent syrup. Or open freeze and then pack mixed with sugar in the proportion of a quarter the weight of fruit.
Peaches and nectarines	Select firm, ripe, well-coloured fruit. Wash, stone (pit) and peel. Cut into halves, quarters or slices. Cover with 40 per cent syrup. To prevent darkening, add ½ teaspoon ascorbic acid for each generous litre (2 pints, 2½ pints) syrup.	Seal and freeze.
Plums and prunes	Select firm, ripe fruit. Wash, cut in halves or in quarters and stone. Pack cut fruit into containers. Cover fruit with cold 40 or 50 per cent syrup depending on tartness of fruit. For improved quality, add ½ teaspoon ascorbic acid to each generous litre (2 pints, 2½ pints) syrup.	Leave headspace. Seal and freeze. Can be frozen as cooked purée.
Rhubarb	Select firm, tender, well-coloured stalks with good flavour and few fibres. Wash, trim and cut into 2½ to 5 cm. (1 to 2 inch) pieces or in lengths to fit the package. Blanching in boiling water for 1 minute and cooling promptly helps retain colour and flavour.	Pack either raw or blanched rhubarb into containers, and cover with cold 40 per cent syrup. Leave headspace. Seal and freeze. Can be frozen without syrup.

above 100°C. (212°F.). The cooking of meat and vegetables can be speeded up considerably in a pressure cooker.

PRÊTRE – Small sea fish about the size of a smelt, 10 to 18 cm. (4 to 7 inches) long, with a silvery star-shaped mark on its sides. Its flesh is delicate.

PRETZEL. BRETZEL – German and Alsatian savoury biscuit, baked in the shape of a loose knot, hard, sprinkled with salt and cumin seeds. Pretzels are served with beer.

Prepare separately the paste and the liquid for cooking the pretzels.

Paste. Allow 2½ dl. (scant ½ pint, generous cup) water for 500 g. (18 oz., 4½ cups) flour, 25 g. (1 oz.) yeast, 2½ teaspoons salt and 4 teaspoons caraway seed. Make a stiff paste and knead it well. Leave to rise for 30 minutes in a warm place, covered with a cloth.

Liquid. 5 dl. (scant pint, 2¼ cups) water, 2 teaspoons bicarbonate soda, 1¼ teaspoons carbonate of ammonia.

Making pretzels, and the finished article

Shape the paste into pretzels and plunge them into the boiling liquid. They will fall to the bottom of the pan. When they rise to the surface, dry, put them on a baking sheet, sprinkle with coarse sea salt, brush with beaten egg, sprinkle with cumin seeds, and bake in the oven.

Prickly pear

PRICKLY PEAR. FIGUIER DE BARBARIE – Cactus with edible fruit, which is generally eaten raw but can be stewed.

PRIMEUR – Fruit, vegetable or any other foodstuff obtained before the normal season of its maturity.

PRINCESSE (À LA) – Name for various preparations in cookery and pastry-making.

The garnish known as *princesse*, composed of green asparagus tips and truffles, is chiefly used to accompany *Suprêmes of chicken* (see CHICKEN).

PRINTANIER. PRINTANIER, PRINTANIÈRE – A mixture of vegetables, scooped out in the shape of little balls with a special vegetable baller, or cut into dice or lozenges, cooked separately in water and dressed with butter.

The term *à la printanière* is applied to various dishes, but mainly to meat *entrées* garnished with early or mixed vegetables.

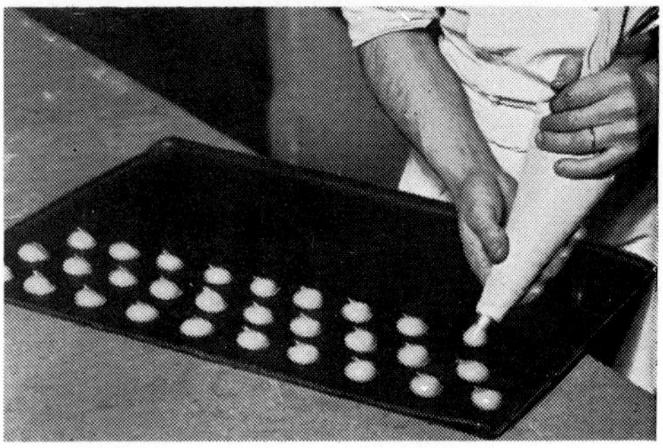

Preparing profiteroles
(*Maison Desmeuzes. Phot. Larousse*)

PROFITEROLE (Pâtisserie) – Little balls of Chou paste (see DOUGH) piped through a forcing-bag.

After cooking, they are filled with various substances; game or other purée, cheese mixtures, etc.; or with sweet custards, jams, etc.

Profiteroles, filled with vanilla custard and iced with caramelised syrup, are used for making *croquembouches* (q.v.) and gateaux Saint-Honoré (q.v.).

Profiteroles with a savoury filling are used to garnish soup.

Profiteroles are forced through a forcing bag with a round nozzle on to a baking tin. They are brushed with egg and baked in a moderate oven.

Garnish the *profiteroles* with *French pastry cream* (see CREAMS) or sweetened whipped cream. Arrange in a

Profiteroles

pyramid on a dessert platter and pour *Chocolate sauce* over (see SAUCE).

PROVENÇALE (À LA) – Describes certain preparations characterised by the use of tomato and garlic mixed, and sometimes of garlic alone.

PROVENCE, COMTÉ DE NICE – Garlic is the base of

almost all Provençal dishes, but it must be remembered that the Midi garlic has not such a strong taste or such a bitter flavour as that of the northern districts.

Culinary specialities. Among a long list of Provençal dishes are

Soups: *garlic*; *aïgo-saou* (a kind of *bouillabaisse* with white fish, the fish used being eaten with *aïoli* or other sauce); *conger*; *aïgo-bouido* with poached eggs; *mariage*, a very thick soup made of beef, mutton or chicken stock and rice; *poutine*, made with tiny fish fry; *nonats* (a minute Mediterranean fish), in the region of Nice; *pistou*, which contains French beans, potatoes, tomatoes and vermicelli, and is finished with an *aillade* of basil and grated cheese.

Fish: bouillabaisse; *bourride*, a kind of *bouillabaisse* made with white fish, but without saffron seasoning. Part of the liquid serves to soak slices of bread put in a dish; the rest, with 2 tablespoons (3 tablespoons) *aïoli* and 1 egg yolk per person, is used to prepare a sauce which is poured over the slices of bread.

Fish is eaten with *aïoli*, a kind of mayonnaise made with garlic purée, allowing, per person, 1 large whole clove garlic, 1 egg yolk, salt, 1 dl. (6 tablespoons, scant $\frac{1}{2}$ cup) oil and a little lemon juice.

Dried salt cod en rayte; *grilled red mullet with fennel*; *sartadagnano* (a *macédoine* of little fish cooked in oil in the frying pan, pressed together in cooking so that they can be turned like a pancake, sprinkled with hot vinegar on the plate).

Stockfish, belonging more particularly to the region of Nice, is dried salt cod, hard as wood, and needing long soaking before use; a kind of stew made with stockfish includes intestines, onions and leeks, garlic, sweet pimentos, aromatic plants, potatoes and black olives (*stocaficada*).

Esquinado of Toulon consists of crabs cooked in vinegar and water, dressed and mixed with an equal quantity of mussels, then the crab shells are refilled with the mixture, sprinkled with breadcrumbs and browned.

Poutine and *melet* are used to prepare savoury purées, such as *pissalat*, *tapenade*, etc. The *fissaladière*, a speciality of Nice, is an open tart of ordinary pastry or bread dough filled with chopped onions cooked in oil, covered with fillets of anchovy and black olives.

Pan bagna is a slice of bread moistened with olive oil and covered with anchovy fillets, thin slices of tomato and capers.

Panisso is a porridge of chick-peas or corn meal cooled in very small saucers and fried in oil. It is eaten sprinkled with sugar.

Meat: *Beef en daube*; *leg of mutton Avignonnaise*; *pieds paquets* of the Pomme district; *gayettes* sausages (made of pig's liver); *sou-fassum*, a kind of stuffed cabbage cooked in a *pot-au-feu* or with mutton, a speciality of the Grasse-Antibes region; *liver à la moissonneuse*.

Vegetables and cereals: *Stuffed marrow (squash) flowers*; *Swiss chard au gratin*; *tart of soft fruits* in the Nice style; *stuffed baby marrows (zucchini)*; *ravioli, cannelloni, capelletti.*

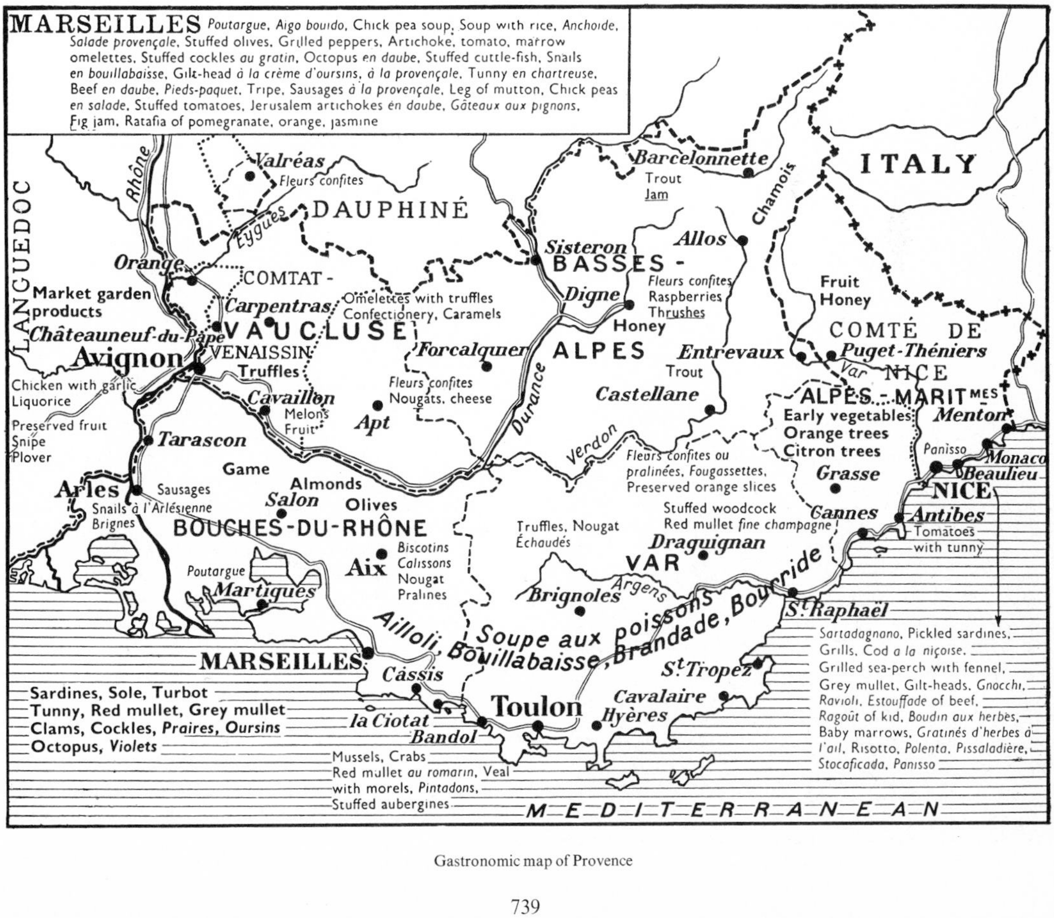

Gastronomic map of Provence

Cheeses: Strong cheese of Mont-Ventoux; goats' milk cheese of the Alpilles, the Maures and the Esterel; sheeps' milk cheese of Banon, Brousse, Valdebleou.

Pastry and specialities: *Gibassier*, *fougasse*, and *pompe gâteaux* (this last particularly for Réveillon, the Christmas morning feast); *bugnes* of Arles, *biscuits* and *calissons* of Aix, and *praline flowers* from Grasse.

Wines – Provence, birthplace of the French wine, offers a wide variety of wines: generous, full-bodied reds; dry, aromatic white wines (fitting accompaniment to *bouillabaisse*, fish soups, sea food, grilled crustaceans and fish). The best known are those of Cassis (Bouches-du-Rhône), Bandol (Var), Palette (Bouches-du-Rhône) and Bellet (Alpes-Maritimes). The wines of the Côtes de Provence and Côteaux d'Aix are in the V.D.Q.S. category.

Since the *département* of Vaucluse is now part of Provence, we must include the wines of the left bank of the Côtes du Rhone méridionales. Most important of all are the splendid Châteauneuf-du-Pape wines, strong, glowing reds and an excellent dry white wine. Then there are the four communes of Vinsobres, Cairanne, Gigondas and Vacqueyras, the natural sweet wine of Rasteau and the muscat wine of Beaumes-de-Venise.

PRUNE. PRUNEAU – Red or purple plum, dried in the sun or in the oven, after which treatment it will keep for a long time in a perfect state. Most plums can be dried, but particularly the *Ente*, or *Agen, the Large Damson* of Tours, the *Catherine* and the *Imperial*.

The *Perdrigon*, when it has been peeled, stoned, dried in the sun and flattened, is commercially known under the name of *Pistole*. The same plum, unpeeled, unstoned, scalded, then dried in the shade, is called a *Brignole* or *Pruneau fleuri*.

In France the most renowned prunes are those of Agen and of Touraine.

Californian prunes are good. Their flesh, however, is less delicate than that of French prunes.

Prunes are most often cooked in a compote. Cooked and stoned prunes are used for the preparation of various sweets, such as cakes, puddings, soufflés, tarts, etc.

The prune is very nutritious and excellent for athletes, children and expectant mothers. It is also a laxative.

Puyrémas, Vaucluse (*French Government Tourist Office*)

Prunes should preferably be eaten raw having been previously soaked for 24 hours in cold water. Cut lengthwise to remove the stone. They are usually served for breakfast.

Compote of prunes (stewed prunes). COMPOTE DE PRUNEAUX – Soak the prunes in cold water. When they have swollen sufficiently, drain and put them in a saucepan and cover with cold water. Add 100 g. (4 oz., $\frac{1}{2}$ cup) sugar for 500 g. (18 oz.) fruit. Flavour with lemon or orange rind, vanilla or cinnamon.

Cook gently for about 1 hour.

Compote of prunes with red or white wine. COMPOTE DE PRUNES AU VIN ROUGE, BLANC – The same as above, substituting red or white wine for water.

PUANT MACÉRÉ – See CHEESE.

PUCHERO (Spanish cookery) – Stew made of different kinds of meat and vegetables.

PUDDING. POUDING – Name given to numerous dishes, both sweet and savoury, served hot or cold, which are made up in many different ways.

SAVOURY PUDDINGS. POUDINGS D'ENTRÉES –

Beefsteak pudding (English cookery) Mix 1 kg. ($2\frac{1}{4}$ lb., $8\frac{3}{4}$ cups) sieved flour with 600 g. ($1\frac{1}{4}$ lb., 4 cups) suet (having first removed the skin and strings from the suet and shredded it finely), a good pinch of salt and about 2 dl. ($\frac{1}{3}$ pint, scant cup) water. The mixture should be a smooth and soft dough.

Using two-thirds of the pastry, line a buttered pudding basin or a round-bottomed mould. Arrange in layers $1\frac{1}{2}$ kg. ($3\frac{1}{4}$ lb.) beef, cut in slices about 1 cm. ($\frac{1}{2}$ inch) thick, season with salt, pepper and grated nutmeg and sprinkle with chopped onion and parsley. Moisten with water in sufficient quantity to cover the meat. Roll out the rest of the pastry, cover the pudding and seal the edges.

Tie a scalded, floured cloth over the top, not forgetting to make a pleat in the cloth. Cook in a pan of boiling water, for 3 hours if fillet of beef is used, for 4 hours if the meat is taken from some other part of the animal. Keep the water boiling constantly, adding more if necessary.

Beefsteak and kidney pudding (English cookery) – This is made like *Beefsteak pudding*, using slices of beef and beef kidney.

Beefsteak and oyster pudding (English cookery) – Prepare in the same way as *Beefsteak pudding*, adding uncooked oysters to the filling.

Chicken puddings à la Richelieu. BOUDINS DE VOLAILLE À LA RICHELIEU – Line small, well-buttered moulds with fine *Chicken forcemeat* (see FORCEMEATS). Fill with a *salpicon* (q.v.) of breast of chicken, truffles and mushrooms, blended with very thick *Allemande sauce* (see SAUCE). Cover with another layer of chicken forcemeat, which should be smoothed over with the blade of a knife dipped in cold water. Place the moulds in a pan of hot water and poach in the oven. Turn out of the moulds, dry, dip in egg and breadcrumbs and fry in clarified butter until light golden.

Arrange the puddings in a circle on a dish, packing them fairly tightly. Garnish the middle of the dish with fried parsley. Serve with *Périgueux* or *Suprême sauce* (see SAUCE) with diced truffles added to it.

Chicken puddings can also be prepared in the following manner: roll the chicken forcemeat, which should be of a fairly firm consistency, into little cylinders. Poach them. Slit open on one side, stuff with the *salpicon* indicated, and close the opening. Dip in egg and breadcrumbs and fry in clarified butter.

Game pudding (stuffed). BOUDINS DE GIBIERS – Prepare,

using various game forcemeats and suitable *salpicons* (q.v.), as described in the recipe for *Chicken puddings à la Richelieu.*

Mutton pudding (English cookery). POUDING DE MOUTON – Proceed as for *Beefsteak pudding* using mutton instead of beef.

SWEET (DESSERT) PUDDINGS. POUDINGS D'ENTREMETS –

English almond pudding. POUDING AUX AMANDES À L'ANGLAISE – Cream together 125 g. ($4\frac{1}{2}$ oz., generous $\frac{1}{2}$ cup) butter and 150 g. (5 oz., $\frac{2}{3}$ cup) sugar in a basin. Add 250 g. (9 oz., generous 2 cups) almonds, blanched and chopped finely. Season with a pinch of salt. Add 1 teaspoon orange-flower water or $\frac{1}{2}$ teaspoon orange extract, 2 whole eggs and 2 yolks and 4 tablespoons ($\frac{1}{3}$ cup) thick, fresh cream. Blend well.

Pour into a pudding basin. Cook in a *bain-marie* in a slow oven, and serve in the same dish.

American pudding. POUDING À L'AMÉRICAINE – Put in a basin 75 g. (3 oz., $1\frac{1}{2}$ cups) breadcrumbs, 100 g. (4 oz., 1 cup) unsifted flour, 100 g. (4 oz., $\frac{1}{2}$ cup) brown sugar and 75 g. (3 oz.) chopped beef marrow. Add 100 g. (4 oz., scant cup) crystallised fruits cut in dice and a little finely shredded orange and lemon peel.

Bind with 1 whole egg and 3 yolks. Add a little cinnamon and grated nutmeg and 1 small glass of rum or brandy. Mix well.

Pour the mixture into a buttered, floured mould. Cook in a bain-marie. Serve with rum-flavoured *zabaglione* (q.v.).

English apple pudding. POUDING DE POMMES À L'ANGLAISE – Line a pudding basin with suet pastry (see DOUGH, *Dumpling dough*), rolled out to 8 mm. ($\frac{1}{4}$ inch) thick.

Fill with cut-up apples, adding sugar and a flavouring of grated lemon rind and powdered cinnamon. Put a flat piece of pastry on top of the pudding, joining it carefully at the edges. Wrap the basin in a cloth, tied very firmly, and put it into a saucepan of boiling water. Keep the water constantly boiling; cook for about 2 hours. Turn out onto a dish.

The pudding may be made in the same way with pears instead of apples.

Pudding mould

Biscuit pudding POUDING DE BISCUITS – Put into a saucepan 250 g. (9 oz) crumbled sponge finger biscuits and moisten with 6 dl. (1 pint, $2\frac{1}{2}$ cups) boiling milk sweetened with 150 g. (5 oz., $\frac{2}{3}$ cup) sugar.

Stir this mixture over the heat, with a wooden spoon. Add 150 g. (5 oz., 1 cup) currants and diced crystallised fruits, soaked in kirsch. Add 3 egg yolks, 125 g. (4 oz., $\frac{1}{2}$ cup) melted butter and 3 stiffly beaten egg whites.

Fill a mould which has been buttered and sprinkled with breadcrumbs with this mixture. Cook in the oven in a *bain-marie*. Serve with *Apricot sauce* (see SAUCE).

Brazilian pudding. POUDING BRÉSILIEN – Prepare the same mixture as for *Tapioca pudding* (see below). Put it into a plain mould coated with caramel. Poach in a *bain-marie*. Serve without sauce or any accompaniment.

French bread pudding. POUDING AU PAIN À LA FRANÇAISE – Soak 300 g. (11 oz., $5\frac{1}{2}$ cups) breadcrumbs in 1 litre ($1\frac{3}{4}$ pints, generous quart) boiled milk with vanilla and 250 g. (9 oz., generous cup) sugar. Sieve the mixture. Add 4 whole eggs and 6 yolks. Fold in 4 stiffly beaten egg whites.

Fill a mould sprinkled with fine breadcrumbs with this mixture. Cook in the oven in a *bain-marie*. Leave a few moments before turning it out of its mould. Serve with *Custard sauce* (see SAUCE), *zabaglione* (q.v.), or a fruit sauce, separately or poured over the pudding.

German bread pudding. POUDING AU PAIN À L'ALLEMANDE – Soak 300 g. (11 oz., $5\frac{1}{2}$ cups) breadcrumbs in 1 litre ($1\frac{3}{4}$ pints, generous quart) Rhine wine or Moselle, to which has been added 200 g. (7 oz., scant cup) brown sugar and a little cinnamon.

Sieve this mixture, add 4 whole eggs, 6 yolks and 150 g. (5 oz., generous $\frac{1}{2}$ cup) melted butter, and 4 stiffly beaten egg whites.

Put the mixture in buttered moulds sprinkled with breadcrumbs. Cook in the oven in a *bain-marie*. Serve with fruit sauce flavoured with kirsch or any other liqueur.

German bread and fruit pudding. POUDING AU PAIN ET AUX FRUITS À L'ALLEMANDE – Put in a basin 150 g. (5 oz.) bread cut in small dice and fried in butter. Pour on this bread $2\frac{1}{2}$ dl. (scant $\frac{1}{2}$ pint, generous cup) boiled milk. Let it soak in well. Add 2 cooked apples cut in small dice, 50 g. (2 oz., $\frac{1}{4}$ cup) diced candied orange peel, 50 g. (2 oz., $\frac{1}{2}$ cup) ground almonds and the same quantity of stoned raisins, put to swell in water and drained.

Add 75 g. (3 oz., generous $\frac{1}{4}$ cup) sugar, a little grated lemon peel and 3 egg yolks. Mix all these ingredients well together and finally add to them 3 stiffly beaten egg whites. Fill a buttered pudding basin with this mixture. Cook in the oven in a *bain-marie* for 45 minutes. Let the pudding rest before turning it out of the mould on to a dish. Coat it with a white wine sauce made with 2 dl. ($\frac{1}{3}$ pint, scant cup) wine and 2 tablespoons (3 tablespoons) apricot jam.

Bread pudding with red wine. POUDING AU PAIN AU VIN ROUGE – Prepare in the same way as *German bread pudding* but replace the white wine by red wine.

Cabinet pudding. POUDING DE CABINET – *Ingredients.* 150 g. (5 oz.) sponge finger biscuits (lady fingers), 2 tablespoons (3 tablespoons) crystallised fruits cut into dice, 2 tablespoons (3 tablespoons) stoned and cleaned raisins, 6 dl. (1 pint, $2\frac{1}{2}$ cups) mixture for baked *Vanilla custard* (see CUSTARD), 25 g. (1 oz., 2 tablespoons) butter, 1 small glass kirsch, 1 small glass maraschino, 4 dl. ($\frac{3}{4}$ pint, scant 2 cups) vanilla-flavoured *Custard cream* (see CREAMS).

Method. Butter a cylindrical mould and arrange in it alternate layers of the sponge fingers broken up and soaked in liqueur and the raisins, also soaked in liqueur. Fill up the mould with the baked custard mixture prepared in the usual way (see CUSTARD).

Put the mould in a pan two-thirds full of hot water and cook in the oven for 30 minutes. Let the pudding rest a little before turning it out of the mould. Serve with *Custard cream* (see CREAMS).

Cabinet puddings can be prepared with all sorts of flavours, and they can be served with *zabaglione* (q.v.) or different fruit sauces.

Chestnut soufflé pudding. POUDING SOUFFLÉ AUX MARRONS – Rub through a fine sieve 1 kg. ($2\frac{1}{4}$ lb.) peeled chestnuts, cooked in a light vanilla-flavoured syrup and well drained.

Add to the purée, stirring with a wooden spoon, 150 g. (5

Ingredients for fruit pudding (*Claire*)

German bread and fruit pudding (*Claire*)

oz., $\frac{2}{3}$ cup) sugar and 100 g. (4 oz., $\frac{1}{2}$ cup) butter. Dry out over heat. Remove from heat, add 8 egg yolks and fold in carefully 6 stiffly beaten egg whites. Cook in a *bain-marie*.

Serve with *Custard cream* (see CREAMS) flavoured with vanilla, or *Apricot sauce* (see SAUCE) flavoured with kirsch.

Chocolate pudding. POUDING AU CHOCOLAT – Soften in the oven 100 g. (4 oz.) semi-sweet chocolate. Work by hand in a cloth 150 g. (5 oz., generous $\frac{1}{2}$ cup) butter until very soft. Put it in a basin previously scalded with boiling water, and beat with a wooden spoon. When it is creamy in consistency add 75 g. (3 oz., generous $\frac{1}{4}$ cup) castor sugar and 25 g. (1 oz., 2 tablespoons) vanilla sugar; or 100 g. (4 oz., $\frac{1}{2}$ cup) sugar plus a few drops vanilla essence. Beat to a froth, then add 8 egg yolks, one by one, the chocolate beaten to a fine paste with a little of the butter and sugar mixture, 40 g. ($1\frac{1}{2}$ oz., 6 tablespoons) sifted flour and 40 g. ($1\frac{1}{2}$ oz., $\frac{1}{4}$ cup) potato flour. Complete with 5 stiffly beaten egg whites.

Put this mixture in a buttered and floured mould of about $1\frac{1}{4}$ litres ($2\frac{1}{4}$ pints, $2\frac{3}{4}$ pints) in capacity. Poach in a *bain-marie* for about 45 minutes. Let the pudding rest before turning it out of the mould onto a dish. Pour chocolate-flavoured *Custard cream* (see CREAMS) over it.

Clermont pudding (cold). POUDING CLERMONT – Add to a *Bavarian cream* (q.v.) flavoured with rum a quarter its volume of *Chestnut purée* (see CHESTNUTS), and for every litre ($1\frac{3}{4}$ pint, generous quart) of the mixture 100 g. (4 oz.) broken-up *marrons glacés*. Put the mixture into a mould greased with sweet almond oil, and put on ice or in a deep-freeze to set. Serve in the mould, with a liqueur-flavoured fruit sauce.

Diplomat pudding (cold). POUDING DIPLOMATE – Decorate an oiled mould with crystallised fruit, and fill it with alternate layers of sponge finger (lady finger) crumbs soaked in kirsch or other liqueur, and a *Bavarian cream* (q.v.) flavoured with vanilla.

Put on each layer of sponge biscuits currants and sultanas (seedless raisins) which have been swelled in warm syrup and well drained; and, here and there, spoonfuls of apricot jam. Put on ice or in a deep-freeze to set. Serve with a fruit and liqueur sauce.

Diplomat pudding with fruit (cold). POUDING DIPLOMATE AUX FRUITS – Prepare as described in the preceding recipe with the addition of layers of various fruits, peeled, sliced and soaked in sugar and liquer.

Set the pudding on a serving dish; surround the base with fruit cooked in syrup and well drained.

Fruit pudding. POUDING DE FRUITS – Put a buttered mould in a *bain-marie*. Pour into it a few tablespoons custard mixture prepared as for *Cabinet pudding* but made with 6 whole eggs and 6 yolks to each litre ($1\frac{3}{4}$ pints, generous quart) milk, and with the addition of $\frac{1}{3}$ fruit purée.

Cook the custard until set, then put on top a layer of the same fruit used for the purée, previously cut up and soaked in sugar and liqueur. Pour over another layer of custard, and continue to fill the mould with alternate layers of fruit and custard, cooking the layer of custard each time. Finish cooking in the *bain-marie* over gentle heat. Let the pudding rest a few minutes before turning it out. Serve with a fruit sauce flavoured with kirsch or any other liqueur.

Fruit puddings can be prepared with apricots, nectarines, peaches, pears, apples, etc.

Lemon, tangerine or orange soufflé pudding. POUDING SOUFFLÉ AU CITRON, À LA MANDARINE, À L'ORANGE – Prepare the same mixture as for *Saxon pudding* (see below). Flavour with lemon, tangerine or orange. Cook in a *bain-marie*. Serve with *Custard cream* (see CREAMS) flavoured with lemon, tangerine or orange.

Macaroni pudding. POUDING AUX NOUILLES – Prepared in the same way as *Semolina pudding* (see below).

Marrow pudding. POUDING À LA MOELLE – Melt in a *bain-marie* 250 g. (9 oz.) marrow and 50 g. (2 oz., 6 tablespoons) beef suet. Let the mixture cool a little, and beat in a basin with 200 g. (7 oz., scant cup) sugar. Add 75 g. (3 oz., $1\frac{1}{2}$ cups) bread, soaked in milk and squeezed out, 3 whole eggs and 8 yolks, 200 g. (7 oz., scant $1\frac{1}{2}$ cups) chopped crystallised fruit, 50 g. (2 oz., 6 tablespoons) stoned raisins and 75 g. (3 oz., $\frac{1}{2}$ cup) sultanas or seedless raisins. Mix well together.

Fill a buttered and floured mould with this mixture. Cook gently in a *bain-marie*.

Serve with a *zabaglione* (q.v.), flavoured with rum.

Nesselrode pudding I (cold). POUDING NESSELRODE – Add to 1 litre ($1\frac{3}{4}$ pints, generous quart) *Custard cream* (see CREAMS) 250 g. (9 oz., 1 cup) fine *Chestnut purée* (see CHESTNUTS), 100 g. (4 oz., $\frac{3}{4}$ cup) candied orange peel and 100 g. (4 oz., $\frac{1}{2}$ cup) crystallised cherries cut in dice and soaked in Malaga, 100 g. (4 oz., scant $\frac{3}{4}$ cup) each of currants and sultanas, or seedless raisins, picked over, set to swell in warm water and then soaked in Malaga.

Add an equal amount of whipped cream flavoured with maraschino.

Put the mixture in a large charlotte mould with a lid,

having lined the base and sides with white paper. Close the mould and fill in the lid opening with butter to seal it hermetically. Put the mould in ice and salt to set, or place in a deep-freeze.

Turn out the pudding on to a serving dish. Take off the paper covering it and surround the base with *marrons glacés*.

Nesselrode pudding II. POUDING NESSELRODE – Put 40 peeled chestnuts cooked in a 16° light syrup with a vanilla pod or a few drops of vanilla essence through a fine sieve.

Mix custard sauce made from 8 egg yolks, 200 g. (7 oz., scant cup) sugar and 8 dl. ($1\frac{1}{3}$ pints, $1\frac{3}{4}$ pints) boiled fresh cream. Flavour with 1 dl. (6 tablespoons, scant $\frac{1}{2}$ cup) maraschino and strain through a cloth.

Freeze in an ice cream freezer. As soon as it sets add to it 3 dl. ($1\frac{1}{2}$ pint, $1\frac{1}{4}$ cups) whipped cream and 100 g. (4 oz., scant $\frac{3}{4}$ cup) each of currants, carefully picked over and cleaned, and stoned raisins, both previously cooked in a 30° heavy syrup.

It is said these puddings were invented by Monsieur Mouy, chef to the Comte de Nesselrode.

Plum pudding – Sweet which is served in England and in the United States at Christmas time and called Christmas pudding.

Ingredients (for a pudding to serve 15 to 20 persons).

500 g. (18 oz., $3\frac{2}{3}$ cups) suet (net weight, after skinning, etc.), 300 g. (11 oz., $5\frac{1}{2}$ cups) fresh breadcrumbs, 300 g. (11 oz., $2\frac{3}{4}$ cups) sifted flour, 150 g. (5 oz., 1 cup) stoned Malaga raisins, 150 g. (5 oz., 1 cup) best currants, 150 g. (5 oz., 1 cup) sultanas or seedless raisins, 100 g. (4 oz., $\frac{3}{4}$ cup) candied citron, 100 g. (4 oz., $\frac{3}{4}$ cup) candied orange peel, 150 g. (5 oz., scant cup) stoned prunes, 250 g. (9 oz., 3 cups) peeled and grated cooking apples, 150 g. (5 oz., $1\frac{1}{4}$ cups) blanched and chopped almonds, 250 g. (9 oz., scant $2\frac{1}{4}$ cups) brown sugar, the grated rind and juice of 1 orange and 1 lemon, 4 whole eggs, 8 dl. ($1\frac{1}{3}$ pints, $1\frac{3}{4}$ pints) rum, 2 tablespoons (3 tablespoons) mixed spices (cinnamon, nutmeg, ginger), $1\frac{1}{2}$ teaspoons salt.

Method. Remove all skin and fibre from the suet and chop it finely. The chopping is rendered easier if the suet is sprinkled with a third of the flour indicated.

Stone the raisins carefully and pick over the currants and sultanas. Rub them in a cloth with 1 or 2 tablespoons flour – in addition to the flour allowed above – and wash them.

Stone the prunes, and chop them with a knife or put them through a mincer. (This addition of prunes to the plum pudding is optional, but they give the pudding mixture a richer dark colour.) Peel and grate or chop the apples.

Cut the candied citron and orange peel in minute dice. Blanch and chop the almonds. Grate the orange and lemon peel and press the juice out. Strain through a muslin bag.

Put all the ingredients, except the eggs, into a big basin. Stir until the mixture is smooth, then add a quarter of the rum. Cover the basin with a cloth and leave in a cool place for 2 or 3 weeks.

Stir the mixture every day, adding a few tablespoons of rum each time. In England this preparation is done at least 1 month before Christmas.

On the day the pudding is to be cooked, add the eggs. Stir the pudding to ensure perfect blending. If the mixture is too thick and difficult to stir, soften by adding a few tablespoons of milk, or – more strictly in conformity with the English tradition – stout. Put the mixture into small basins greased with butter and sprinkled with flour.

Cook the pudding in boiling water for at least 6 hours.

Remove from the pan and leave for a few minutes before turning out. Remove the cloth and turn out the pudding on to a dish. Sprinkle it with sugar. When ready to serve, heat the rum, pour over the pudding and set it alight. The pudding can also be set alight with kirsch, brandy or whisky and it can be served with rum-flavoured *zabaglione* (q.v.) or with hot custard. In England it is often served with brandy butter, which is prepared as follows:

Heat a bowl and put into it 200 g. (7 oz., scant cup) butter. Beat the butter to turn it into a paste, adding to it 1 tablespoon castor sugar and $\frac{1}{2}$ dl. (3 tablespoons, scant $\frac{1}{4}$ cup) brandy. Whisk vigorously to make the mixture frothy. Serve cold.

The making of plum pudding is simple and easy. This sweet (dessert), which is one of the most nourishing dishes, has the advantage that it can be made well in advance and keeps for a long time. Thus one can have an excellent sweet course ready in reserve.

Pumpkin pudding. GÂTEAU DE POTIRON – Prepare as for *Purée of pumpkin soup* (see SOUP), pressing the purée vigorously to remove the water. For each 500 g. (18 oz., 2 generous cups) purée add $\frac{1}{2}$ litre (scant pint, $2\frac{1}{4}$ cups) milk, 100 g. (4 oz., $\frac{1}{2}$ cup) sugar and 50 g. (2 oz., $\frac{1}{4}$ cup) butter, and bring to the boil. Now add 2 tablespoons (3 tablespoons) potato flour blended with a little water. Stir, and simmer for 30 minutes, stirring from time to time. Remove from the heat and cool a little, then add 3 egg yolks and flavouring (orange-flower water or $\frac{1}{2}$ teaspoon orange or vanilla essence). Beat the 3 egg whites stiffly and fold them into the mixture. Turn it into a buttered mould. Cook for 45 minutes in a slow oven.

Rice pudding. POUDING AU RIZ – Wash 250 g. (9 oz., $1\frac{1}{4}$ cup) rice, blanch and drain it and put it in a saucepan. Pour in 1 litre ($1\frac{3}{4}$ pints, generous quart) milk previously boiled with 150 g. (5 oz., $\frac{2}{3}$ cup) sugar, $\frac{1}{2}$ pod of vanilla or a few drops vanilla essence (or other flavouring according to taste) and a pinch of salt. Add 50 g. (2 oz., $\frac{1}{4}$ cup) butter.

Cook on the stove. As soon as boiling begins, cover the pot and continue cooking in the oven at low heat for 25 to 30 minutes. Do not stir.

Remove from the oven, add 8 egg yolks, mix with care so as not to break the grains of rice, and add 7 or 8 stiffly beaten egg whites. Fill buttered moulds with this mixture and sprinkle with fine breadcrumbs. Cook in the oven in a *bain-marie*.

Serve with *Custard cream* (see CREAMS), *zabaglione* (q.v.) or a liqueur-flavoured fruit sauce.

Chocolate rice pudding. POUDING AU RIZ AU CHOCOLAT – Prepare and cook in a mould or pudding dish as for *Rice pudding*, but with the addition of 50 g. (2 oz.) semi-sweet melted chocolate for every 500 g. (18 oz.) rice pudding.

English rice pudding I. POUDING AU RIZ À L'ANGLAISE – Prepare the mixture as described in the recipe for *Rice pudding* with 175 g. (6 oz., scant cup) rice, 1 litre ($1\frac{3}{4}$ pints, generous quart) milk flavoured to taste, 50 g. (2 oz., $\frac{1}{4}$ cup) sugar, 75 g. (3 oz., 6 tablespoons) butter and a small pinch of salt. Keep the rice rather firm. Bind the mixture with 3 whole eggs.

Cook in the oven in a pudding dish in a *bain-marie*. Sprinkle the pudding with sugar and glaze.

English rice pudding II. POUDING DE RIZ AU PLAT, DIT À L'ANGLAISE – Prepare the mixture in the usual way. Add to it 50 g. (2 oz., $\frac{1}{4}$ cup) butter and 3 whole eggs. Mix and pour into a buttered pudding dish.

Cook in the oven in a *bain-marie* for 25 minutes. Sprinkle with sugar and glaze.

Sago pudding. POUDING AU SAGOU – Prepare as described in the recipe for *Semolina pudding* (see below), using sago.

Saxon pudding. POUDING SAXON – Beat 100 g. (4 oz., $\frac{1}{2}$ cup) butter to a cream with a wooden spoon in a saucepan. Add 100 g. (4 oz., $\frac{1}{2}$ cup) sugar and 3 dl. ($\frac{1}{2}$ pint, $1\frac{1}{4}$ cups) boiled milk and mix.

Bring to the boil, stirring all the time with the wooden

spoon, until it is firm and dry like *chou pastry*. Remove from the heat, add 5 egg yolks, and fold in 5 stiffly beaten egg whites.

Fill a buttered mould with the mixture, and cook in a slow oven in a *bain-marie*. Serve with a *zabaglione* (q.v.) or *Custard cream* (see CREAMS).

Scotch pudding. POUDING ÉCOSSAIS – Put in a basin 500 g. (18 oz., $4\frac{1}{2}$ cups) freshly made breadcrumbs and moisten with a little boiled milk. Add 375 g. (13 oz.) finely chopped beef marrow, 100 g. (4 oz., $\frac{1}{2}$ cup) sugar, 1 cup 100 g. (4 oz., $\frac{3}{4}$ cup) currants, 100 g. (4 oz., $\frac{3}{4}$ cup) sultanas, 100 g. (4 oz., $\frac{3}{4}$ cup) raisins, 175 g. (6 oz., 1 cup) chopped crystallised fruits. Add 4 eggs and 4 tablespoons (5 tablespoons) rum and beat well together.

Put this mixture in a large well-buttered mould, filling to not more than 1 cm. ($\frac{1}{2}$ inch) from the top. Cook in a *bain-marie* in the oven for 1 hour. Serve with *zabaglione* (q.v.) or *Custard cream* (see CREAMS) flavoured with Madeira.

Semolina pudding. POUDING À LA SEMOULE – Sprinkle 250 g. (9 oz., $1\frac{1}{3}$ cups) semolina gradually into 1 litre ($1\frac{3}{4}$ pints, generous quart) boiling milk with 100 g. (4 oz., $\frac{1}{2}$ cup) sugar, a pinch of salt, 100 g. (4 oz., $\frac{1}{2}$ cup) butter and flavouring. Mix well. Cook in a low oven for 25 minutes. Turn the mixture out of the basin, incorporate 6 egg yolks, 75 g. (3 oz., 6 tablespoons) butter and 4 stiffly beaten egg whites. Butter a mould, sprinkle it with semolina and fill it with the pudding mixture. Poach in a *bain-marie* in a moderate oven. It is cooked when the composition becomes a little elastic to the touch.

Let the pudding rest for a few minutes before turning out. Serve with *Custard cream* (see CREAMS), *zabaglione* (q.v.) or liqueur-flavoured fruit sauce.

English suet roll pudding. POUDING ROULÉ À L'ANGLAISE – Prepare 1 hour before it is needed, a suet pudding pastry made with 500 g. (18 oz., $4\frac{1}{2}$ cups) sifted flour, 300 g. (11 oz.) very dry beef suet, 50 g. (2 oz., $\frac{1}{4}$ cup) sugar, $2\frac{1}{2}$ teaspoons salt and 2 dl. ($\frac{1}{3}$ pint, scant cup) water.

Roll out into a rectangle about $\frac{1}{2}$ cm. ($\frac{1}{4}$ inch) thick. Spread on this strip of pastry some jam or marmalade and roll up into a sausage. Wrap in a buttered, floured cloth and tie it. Cook in boiling water, or steam, for $1\frac{1}{2}$ hours. Drain the pudding, unwrap it, cut it into slices about 1 cm. ($\frac{1}{2}$ inch) thick, and arrange them in a circle. Serve with fruit sauce.

Sweet potato pudding. POUDING DE PATATES AU PLAT – Peel 750 g. ($1\frac{1}{2}$ to $1\frac{3}{4}$ lb.) Sweet potatoes, cut into thick slices, and boil in water with a pinch of salt. As soon as they are cooked, drain, put in the oven to dry off excess moisture, and rub through a small mesh sieve.

Put this purée into a bowl. Add 100 g. (4 oz., $\frac{1}{2}$ cup) sugar and 3 whole eggs and blend, stirring with a wooden spoon. When the mixture is quite smooth, moisten with $\frac{1}{2}$ litre (scant pint, $2\frac{1}{4}$ cups) milk with a few drops of vanilla essence added. Mix, and pour into a buttered pudding dish, or other ovenproof receptacle. Put the dish into a pan half filled with hot water. Bring to the boil on the stove, then cook in a slow oven for 35 minutes (if the oven is too hot cover the pudding to prevent it browning too quickly).

Five minutes before taking out of the oven, sprinkle with sugar and glaze the top, placing the dish in the hottest part of the oven. Serve in the same dish.

This pudding can be served hot or cold. It can be flavoured with kirsch, rum, orange, lemon, etc.

Tapioca pudding. POUDING AU TAPIOCA – The same method of preparation as for *Semolina pudding*, see above, but using tapioca.

Vermicelli pudding. POUDING AU VERMICELLE – The same method of preparation as for *Semolina pudding*, using vermicelli.

PUFFER (German cookery) – Fritter made with a batter made of flaked oats, worked with warm water, adding sugar, a little salt, and eggs, flavoured with cinnamon. Puffers are cooked in butter.

PUITS D'AMOUR (Pâtisserie) – Using *Flaky pastry* (see DOUGH) that has been rolled and turned six times, cut out rounds of about $7\frac{1}{2}$ cm. (3 inches) in diameter with a fluted cutter.

Put half of these on a lightly moistened baking sheet, keeping them a little apart from each other. Cut out the centres of the other pastry rounds with a smaller cutter, so as to leave rings or 'crowns'.

Moisten the pastry circles on the baking tin and carefully set one of the crowns on each. Press them gently so that the two stick together. Brush the top of the crowns with egg and cook for about 15 minutes in a medium oven. Draw the baking tin to the front of the oven without taking it right out, and powder the pastry cases lightly with icing sugar. Put them for a moment in the hottest part of the oven to melt this sugar, which will form a glaze. Take them out and put on a rack to cool. They will look rather like *bouchées*.

When they are quite cool, fill with *French pastry cream* (see CREAMS) with the aid of a spoon, or forcing-bag; or alternatively fill with very thick gooseberry jelly.

PULP. PULPE – The soft and fleshy parts of fruit or vegetables reduced to a moist paste by rubbing through a sieve.

PULQUE – A drink which has some relation to cider. The agave from which it is made was cultivated on a large scale by the ancient Aztecs.

PULTÖST – See CHEESE.

Pumpkin (*Sougez*)

PUMPKIN. POTIRON, COURGE – Gourd with orange-coloured flesh which has a distinctive and sweet flavour. In France it is used to make soup, jam and a dessert (sweet). In U.S.A. almost its only use in cooking is as a filling for pies. In England the name is sometimes used to describe a variety of gourds known as squash in U.S.A.

Pumpkin au gratin. COURGE AU GRATIN – Pare the pumpkin and divide into quarters. Blanch for a short time in boiling salted water; drain and dry.

Arrange the pieces on a *gratin* dish, buttered and sprinkled with grated cheese. Sprinkle the pieces with more cheese, pour on some melted butter, and brown in a warm oven.

This dish can be prepared by alternating the slices of

Pumpkins at the Paris market
(*French Government Tourist Office*)

pumpkin in the dish with slices of onion which have been softened in butter. It could also be prepared with North American winter squash.

Gratin of pumpkin with rice. GRATIN DE COURGE AU RIZ – Simmer slices of pumpkin in butter and put in a *gratin* dish which is well buttered and sprinkled with grated cheese. Fill with alternate layers of pumpkin and rice, which has been cooked in unskimmed stock. Sprinkle with grated cheese and pour melted butter over the dish. Brown in a warm oven. This could be made with North American winter squash.

Pumpkin jam. CONFITURE DE COURGE – Prepare with very ripe pumpkin in the same way as *Apricot jam* (see JAMS).

Pumpkin au jus. COURGE AU JUS – Divide the pumpkin into quarters or into lozenge-shaped pieces. Blanch for a few minutes in boiling salted water. Drain, dry and put in a sauté pan with a few spoonfuls boiled down veal stock. Simmer for 25 minutes with the lid on.

Pumpkin pudding – See PUDDING.

Pumpkin purée. PURÉE DE COURGE – Divide the pumpkin into quarters, season with salt and a pinch of sugar and cook slowly in butter with the lid on the pan.

When the pumpkin is very soft, put it through a sieve. Heat the purée and add, off the heat, a little butter. Add one-third of its weight in potato purée, and fresh cream or concentrated meat stock. This dish can be made with any of the North American winter squashes.

Pumpkin salad. SALADE DE COURGE – Pare the pumpkin; divide it into quarters. Blanch in salt water, put under the cold tap, drain and dry. Season with oil, vinegar or lemon juice, and salt and pepper.

Pumpkin soufflé. SOUFFLÉ DE COURGE – Bind 250 g. (9 oz., generous cup) pumpkin purée flavoured with sugar and vanilla, with 3 egg yolks. Add 3 stiffly beaten egg whites.

Turn out into a buttered soufflé dish and cook in the usual way (see SOUFFLÉ).

Pumpkin soup – See SOUPS AND BROTHS, *Purée of pumpkin soup.*

Sweet-sour pumpkin à l'allemande (cold hors-d'œuvre). COURGE À L'AIGRE-DOUX, À L'ALLEMANDE – Pare the pumpkin, cut it into square pieces or trim into lozenge shapes, and put the pieces in a jar, strewing each layer with grated cinnamon, cloves, thyme, bay and grated nutmeg. Cover with vinegar which has been boiled with 150 g. (5 oz., $1\frac{1}{4}$ cups) cinnamon per litre ($1\frac{3}{4}$ pints, generous quart) and allowed to cool.

Cover the jar and leave to soak for 10 to 12 days.

PUNCH – A drink said to have originated among English sailors, and which, about 1552, consisted of a simple mixture of cane spirit and sugar, heated.

Iced punch. PUNCH GLACÉ – Prepare a mixture similar to that for *Punch marquise* (see below). While the wine is hot, add to it 5 tablespoons (6 tablespoons) tea and infuse.

Strain through a silk strainer. Add 1 orange and 1 lemon, peeled and cut in slices, and 2 dl. ($\frac{1}{3}$ pint, scant cup) hot rum. Set alight, allow to cool, strain, add water if too syrupy and freeze like a water ice.

Kirsch punch. PUNCH AU KIRSCH – Infuse 6 tablespoons ($\frac{1}{2}$ cup) tea for 8 minutes in 1 litre ($1\frac{3}{4}$ pints, generous quart) boiling water. Strain this infusion into a punch-bowl with 500 g. (18 oz., $2\frac{1}{4}$ cups) sugar. Stir with a silver spoon to dissolve the sugar.

Add $\frac{3}{4}$ litre ($1\frac{1}{3}$ pints, $1\frac{3}{4}$ pints) kirsch. Set alight and serve in punch glasses.

Punch cake – See CAKE.

Punch marquise – Put in a copper pan 1 litre ($1\frac{3}{4}$ pints, generous quart) Sauternes (or any other rather sweet white wine), 250 g. (9 oz., generous cup) sugar and the rind of a lemon tied in muslin with a clove. Dissolve the sugar. Heat the wine to the point where a fine white froth rises to the surface. Pour the mixture into a punch-bowl. Add $2\frac{1}{2}$ dl. (scant $\frac{1}{2}$ pint, generous cup) Cognac. Set alight. Serve in punch glasses with a thin slice of lemon in each glass.

Rum punch. PUNCH AU RHUM – Prepare an infusion of tea in the same way as for *Kirsch punch.* Pour into a punch bowl with sugar and some thin slices of lemon. Add $\frac{3}{4}$ litre ($1\frac{1}{3}$ pints, $1\frac{3}{4}$ pints rum. Set alight.

PURÉE – Preparation obtained by mashing and sieving certain foodstuffs. Any kind of food, whether from the animal or the vegetable kingdom, can be reduced to a purée after having been cooked.

According to the uses for which they are intended purées are made of varying consistency. Those to be served as a vegetable or a garnish are kept to a thickish consistency; those meant to make soup are made rather thinner.

Some vegetables, being too watery to make a sufficently thick purée, have a complementary thickening ingredient added to them, most frequently another more floury vegetable, a cereal or a thick sauce.

Meat purées of all kinds and fish purées have the addition of sauce, brown or white according to the nature of the purée, and well boiled down.

The use of a kitchen blender greatly facilitates the making of purées.

PURÉES OF FISH, CRUSTACEANS AND MOLLUSCS. PURÉES DE POISSONS, CRUSTACÉS ET MOLLUSQUES –

Anchovy purée (cold). PURÉE D'ANCHOIS – Pound in a mortar 50 g. (2 oz.) anchovy fillets desalted and well cleaned, with the yolks of 4 hard-boiled eggs and 50 g. (2 oz., $\frac{1}{4}$ cup) butter. Rub through a fine sieve.

According to the individual recipe the purée can be completed with chopped herbs or other savoury additions.

Use as garnish for various *hors-d'oeuvre*, to stuff hard-boiled eggs, artichoke bottoms, olives, etc.

Anchovy purée (hot). PURÉE D'ANCHOIS – Add 2 tablespoons (3 tablespoons) anchovy purée to $1\frac{1}{2}$ dl. ($\frac{1}{4}$ pint, $\frac{2}{3}$ cup) thick *Béchamel sauce* (see SAUCE). Strain through a cloth. Heat and add butter.

According to the individual recipe this purée can also include hard-boiled eggs and chopped parsley. Use as filling for pastry cases, fritters, rissoles, etc.

Herring purée. PURÉE DE HARENGS – Prepared like *Anchovy purée*, replacing anchovies with desalted herring fillets. The same uses.

Mussel purée. PURÉE DE MOULES – Prepared in the same way as *Oyster purée* and used in the same way as *Shrimp purée* (see below).

Oyster purée. PURÉE D'HUÎTRES – *Hot.* Pound in a mortar 24 oysters which have been poached in their liquor and well drained. Rub through a sieve. Add to it 3 dl. ($\frac{1}{2}$ pint, $1\frac{1}{4}$ cups) *Béchamel sauce* (see SAUCE), which has had the oyster liquid added to it and has then been boiled down, mixed with cream and strained through a cloth.

Use like *Shrimp purée* (see below).

Cold. Crush in the mortar 24 oysters, poached and well drained, with 4 yolks of hard-boiled eggs and 40 g. ($1\frac{1}{2}$ oz., 3 tablespoons) butter. Put through a fine strainer.

Salmon purée. PURÉE DE SAUMON – *With fresh salmon.* Put through a sieve 250 g. (9 oz.) salmon flesh cooked in butter. Heat this purée and bind it with 2 dl. ($\frac{1}{3}$ pint, scant cup) thick *Béchamel sauce* (see SAUCE). Season. Add butter.

Used for garnishing eggs, pastry cases and shells, bread etc.

With smoked salmon. Put through a sieve 250 g. (9 oz.) smoked salmon. Add to this purée 4 yolks of hard-boiled eggs rubbed through a fine sieve, 50 g. (2 oz., $\frac{1}{4}$ cup) butter and mix well.

Use for *canapés*, pastry shapes and various *hors-d'œuvre*.

Sea-urchin purée. PURÉE D'OURSINS – Clean the sea-urchins, and remove the yellow substance which adheres to the inside of the shell. Add this substance to thick *Béchamel sauce* (see SAUCE) which has been mixed with cream, allowing 1 litre ($1\frac{3}{4}$ pints, generous quart) sauce to 36 sea-urchins. Mix well. Put through a fine strainer.

The same uses as for *Shrimp purée* (see below).

Shrimp purée. PURÉE DE CREVETTES – Pound finely in a mortar the shells of the shrimps (or prawns or other shellfish), whose flesh is being otherwise used.

Add this to an equal quantity of thick *Béchamel sauce* (see SAUCE) which has been mixed with cream. Put through a fine sieve, pressing with a wooden spoon.

Use as a complementary ingredient of sauces, forcemeats, etc. for fish and shellfish and for hot *hors-d'œuvre*.

Tunny (tuna fish) purée. PURÉE DE THON – Like *Anchovy purée*. The same uses.

GAME PURÉES. PURÉES DE GIBIER –

Game purée I. PURÉE DE GIBIER – Pound in a mortar the cooked flesh of any game bird or animal, together with half its weight of rice cooked in stock.

Put through a fine sieve. Add this purée to *Derni-glace sauce* (see SAUCE) made with the cooking juices of game. Mix well over heat, season, and add butter.

Game purée II. PURÉE DE GIBIER – Pound cooked game in a mortar and add to it some thick *lentil purée* (see below). Finish as above.

Use as a garnish for poached or soft-boiled eggs, or as a filling for omelettes, stuffing for vegetables and garnish for pastry shells.

MEAT AND POULTRY PUREES. PURÉES DE VIANDES –

Beef purée. PURÉE DE BOEUF – Pound in a mortar 500 g. (generous lb.) braised beef, carefully trimmed and with all gristle removed. Add this purée to 4 dl. ($\frac{3}{4}$ pint, scant 2 cups) *Derni-glace sauce* (see SAUCE). Mix over heat, stirring with a wooden spoon. Strain through a fine sieve. Bind with egg if desired.

Use as a filling for various pastries and pasta dishes, or as a stuffing for vegetables (onions, tomatoes, artichoke bottoms, etc.), veal or beef olives, etc.

Brain purée. PURÉE DE CERVELLE D'AGNEAU, DE VEAU – Rub cooked lambs' or calves' brains through a fine sieve. Add this purée to *Béchamel* or *Velouté sauce* (see SAUCE), which has been mixed with cream, allowing 2 dl. ($\frac{1}{3}$ pint, scant cup) sauce to each set of brains. Mix over heat, season, and put through a fine sieve.

Use as garnish for poached eggs or soft-boiled eggs, as a forcemeat for fowl, as filling for pastry cases, tartlets, artichoke bottoms, mushrooms, etc.

Brain purée, and in general all white meat purées, may have diced truffles, mushrooms or ham added to them, or may be enriched by *duxelles* (q.v.) or mixed vegetables cooked in butter.

Calf's liver purée. PURÉE DE FOIE DE VEAU – Pound in a mortar calf's liver cut in pieces, sautéed in butter, seasoned and cooled. Rub through a fine sieve.

Use for borders and moulds.

Chicken purée (cold). PURÉE DE VOLAILLE – Pound in a mortar the flesh of a chicken poached in chicken stock. Turn this purée into a bowl, add to it a few tablespoons very thick fresh cream, season, and put through a fine strainer. Mix till very smooth.

Use for cold *hors-d'œuvre*, *canapés* and pastry cases.

Chicken purée (hot). PURÉE DE VOLAILLE – Pound in a mortar the bones and trimmed flesh of a chicken poached in chicken stock. Rub through a fine sieve. Heat in a sauté pan. Bind it with one-third of its weight of thick chicken *Velouté sauce* (see SAUCE). Season, and add butter and fresh cream.

Use as garnish with poached and soft-boiled eggs, in pastry shells, in small cases made of other crusts, and to stuff vegetables such as artichoke bottoms, cucumbers, tomatoes, mushrooms, etc.

Chicken liver purée. PURÉE DE FOIES DE VOLAILLE – See FORCEMEATS, *À gratin poultry liver forcemeat*.

Foie gras purée. PURÉE DE FOIE GRAS – *Hot.* Mix thick chicken *Velouté sauce* (see SAUCE) with twice its volume of cooked *foie gras* (truffled or not, as desired) which has been rubbed through a fine sieve. Mix well over heat and bind with egg yolks.

Use to garnish pastry shells and tartlets, as stuffing for various vegetables such as artichoke bottoms, mushrooms, etc., in which case white breadcrumbs are added.

Cold. Rub cooked *foie gras* through a fine sieve. Work till very smooth.

Use for cold *hors-d'œuvre* and for cold eggs, poached or soft-boiled.

Sweetbread purée. PURÉE DE RIS DE VEAU – Prepare with braised sweetbreads as described in the recipe for *Brain purée*. The same uses.

Veal purée. PURÉE DE VEAU – Prepare with braised veal in the same way as *Beef purée*. Bind with chicken *Velouté sauce* or *Béchamel sauce* (see SAUCE). The same uses.

VEGETABLE PURÉES. PURÉES DE LÉGUMES –

Artichoke purée I. PURÉE D'ARTICHAUTS – Half cook 6 large artichoke bottoms in a flour-and-water *court-bouillon* (q.v.), slice, and simmer in butter. Add $2\frac{1}{2}$ dl. (scant $\frac{1}{2}$ pint, generous cup) *Béchamel sauce* (see SAUCE). Pass through a fine strainer, heat, and add 15 g. ($\frac{1}{2}$ oz., 1 tablespoon) butter. Use as a vegetable or ganish for meat or poultry.

Artichoke purée II. PURÉE D'ARTICHAUTS – Add to the artichoke bottoms cooked in butter 1 large potato cut in thick slices. Moisten with $1\frac{1}{2}$ dl. ($\frac{1}{4}$ pint, $\frac{2}{3}$ cup) stock. Cook together. Finish the purée as above.

The same uses as the preceding purée.

Green asparagus purée. PURÉE D'ASPERGES VERTES – Prepare, with green asparagus, as the next recipe.

White asparagus purée. PUREE D'ASPERGES BLANCHES – Cook the asparagus tips in salt water, drain and rub through fine sieve. Heat the purée, remove from the heat and add a little fresh butter.

This purée is rather thin so a quarter of its weight of *Potato purée* (see POTATOES) may be added to it. Or, depending on its final use, one-third of its volume in thick *Béchamel sauce* (see SAUCE) may be added.

The uses are the same as for *Artichoke purée*.

Aubergine purée. PURÉE D'AUBERGINES – Simmer 4 peeled, sliced, aubergines in butter. Add 2 sliced potatoes. Moisten with $1\frac{1}{2}$ dl. ($\frac{1}{4}$ pint, $\frac{2}{3}$ cup) stock. Season and cook gently. Rub through a fine sieve and finish the purée as described in the recipe for *Artichoke purée*. The same uses.

Broad bean purée. PURÉE DE FÈVES FRAÎCHES – Cook broad beans in salted water, season with a sprig of savory and rub through a fine sieve. Heat this purée and bind with butter or cream.

Alternatively, cook the beans like *Peas à la française* (see PEA) rub through a fine sieve and bind the purée with butter or cream. To make a thicker consistency the beans may be augmented by a quarter of their volume of potatoes, added during cooking.

Use as garnish to eggs, small cuts of meat and poultry.

Fresh flageolet bean purée. PURÉE DE FLAGEOLETS FRAIS – Prepare with fresh flageolet beans cooked in water in the same way as for *Broad bean purée*, and used in the same way.

French (string) bean purée. PURÉE DE HARICOTS VERTS – *Hot.* Rub through a sieve French beans, cooked in salted water and drained. Heat this purée and bind with butter or cream.

Use as garnish for eggs, small cuts of meat, poultry, or as a vegetable.

Cold. Rub through a fine sieve French beans, cooked in salted water and drained. Bind this purée with thick mayonnaise.

Use as filling for artichoke bottoms, tomatoes and pastry cases, and, by itself, as garnish for cold dishes.

Haricot bean purée. PURÉE DE HARICOTS – Rub through a fine sieve dried haricot beans which have been soaked and then cooked in stock or water. Heat this purée and bind with fresh butter.

Use as garnish for large or small cuts of meat, particularly mutton.

Breton white bean purée. PURÉE DE HARICOTS BLANCS À LA BRETONNE, DITE PURÉE BRETONNE – Haricot beans cooked in a meat stock, drained, bound with *Bretonne sauce* (see SAUCE) and rubbed through a sieve.

Use as garnish for roast, baked or braised meat, especially mutton. It is also served as a vegetable.

White bean purée or purée soissonnaise. PURÉE DE HARICOTS, DITE À LA SOISSONNAISE, PURÉE SOISSONNAISE – Haricot beans cooked in water or in a meat stock and rubbed through a sieve when still hot. Stir the purée over the heat, adding 100 g. (4 oz., $\frac{1}{2}$ cup) butter for each 500 g. (18 oz., $2\frac{1}{4}$ cups) purée. Dilute if necessary with a few tablespoons of boiling milk or the water in which the beans were cooked.

Use in the same way as *Breton white bean purée*.

Beetroot purée. PURÉE DE BETTERAVES – *Hot.* Rub through a fine sieve 2 large beetroots cooked in the oven (as for salad beetroots) and peeled. Heat this purée in a sauté pan. Add to it $2\frac{1}{2}$ dl. (scant $\frac{1}{2}$ pint, generous cup) concentrated *Demi-glace sauce* (see SAUCE). Season, and bring to the boil, stirring with a wooden spoon. Add 25 g. (1 oz., 2 tablespoons) butter.

The purée may also be thickened with concentrated *Béchamel sauce* (see SAUCE). Use as garnish to small pieces of game meat.

Cold. Add to the cold beetroot pulp, 2 dl. ($\frac{1}{3}$ pint, scant cup) very thick mayonnaise.

Use as filling for *canapés*, boat-shaped pastry cases and *hors-d'œuvre* tartlets.

Carrot purée. PURÉE DE CAROTTES – Simmer carrots in butter in a covered pan until they are very tender (new carrots should be used if possible). Bind with *Béchamel sauce* (see SAUCE). Finish like *Artichoke purée*.

Use as garnish for small or large cuts of meat. It is also served by itself as a vegetable.

Cauliflower purée. PURÉE DE CHOU-FLEUR – Cook the cauliflower in water and rub through a fine sieve. Heat the purée. Bind it with a third of its volume of *Béchamel sauce* (see SAUCE). Add butter.

To make a thicker consistency a small quantity of potatoes may be added.

Use as a garnish for eggs, small pieces of meat, and sweetbreads. This purée can also be served as a vegetable.

Celery purée. PURÉE DE CÉLERI – Simmer in butter in a covered pan celery stalks or celeriac, previously blanched in salted water. Finish as described in the recipe for *Artichoke purée*.

This purée can be thickened with concentrated *Béchamel sauce* (see SAUCE), or with potato cooked with the celery.

Use as a garnish with eggs and with large or small cuts of meat. It is also served as a vegetable.

Chestnut purée. PURÉE DE MARRONS – This purée is mainly used as accompaniment to game meats and venison. (See CHESTNUTS.)

Cucumber purée. PURÉE DE CONCOMBRES – As *Artichoke purée*, using peeled sliced cucumbers, cooked in butter in a covered pan.

Used as garnish with salmon steaks cooked in butter or *court-bouillon* (q.v.), and with small cuts of meat.

Garlic purée. PURÉE D'AIL – Blanch lightly in salted water 50 g. (2 oz.) garlic. Drain, and cook them for 15 minutes in butter without letting them colour. Add $2\frac{1}{2}$ dl. (scant $\frac{1}{2}$ pint, generous cup) thick *Béchamel sauce* (see SAUCE). Rub through a fine sieve. Heat and add 15 g. ($\frac{1}{2}$ oz., 1 tablespoon) butter.

Used as garnish for small cuts of sautéed meat (most of all *noisettes* or mutton or lamb cutlets), poached eggs and hot *hors-d'œuvre*.

Jerusalem artichoke purée. PURÉE DE TOPINAMBOURS – Cook the Jerusalem artichokes in butter in a covered pan. Put them through a fine sieve. Heat the purée and bind with butter or cream.

For a thicker consistency, potato purée to the amount of one-half or one-third the volume of the artichoke purée may be added. Japanese artichoke, root chervil and salsify purées are made in the same way.

Use as garnish for eggs, small cuts of meat and game meat.

Lentil purée. PURÉE DE LENTILLES – As *Haricot bean purée*, using lentils cooked in stock or water.

Use as garnish with large and small cuts of meat and game.

Lettuce purée. PURÉE DE LAITUES – Rub lettuces braised in stock or water through a fine sieve. Heat the purée, and bind with butter or cream.

Use as garnish with eggs or small cuts of meat, sweetbreads, poultry, etc.

Chicory, endives, the leaves of red or white beet or other similar vegetables may be made into purée in the same way.

Marrow or gourd (U.S. squash) purée. PURÉE DE COURGE – Prepared in the same way as *Pumpkin purée* (see PUMPKIN).

Baby marrow (zucchini) purée. PURÉE DE COURGETTES – Prepare in the same way as *Aubergine purée*. The same uses.

Mushroom purée. PURÉE DE CHAMPIGNONS – Trim, wash and dry 500 g. (18 oz.) firm, white cultivated mushrooms and rub them through a sieve as rapidly as possible (peel them if they are not white enough).

Add this purée to 2 dl. ($\frac{1}{3}$ pint, scant cup) *Béchamel sauce* (see SAUCE) which has been thickened in a pan with a few tablespoons of cream. Boil down for a few moments over a good heat, season and strain through a fine sieve. Heat the purée once more, remove from the heat and blend in 50 g. (2 oz., $\frac{1}{4}$ cup) butter.

Use as garnish for meat, chicken and fish, and to stuff artichoke bottoms, eggs, fillets of fish, etc. It is also used as filling for pastry shells and *canapés* served as a hot *hors-d'œuvre* or small *entrée*.

Onion soubise I. PURÉE D'OIGNONS, DITE SOUBISE – This purée, which is used as a garnish for meat, can be prepared in two ways:

Blanch 1 kg. ($2\frac{1}{4}$ lb.) chopped onions thoroughly in salted water. Five minutes before draining them add 250 g. (9 oz., generous cup) rice. Drain these ingredients, then hold under a cold water tap to cool. Dry, and season with salt, white pepper, grated nutmeg and a pinch of sugar.

Line a deep casserole with thin rashers of fat bacon.

Add the onions and rice. Moisten with white stock in sufficient quantity to cover the mixture. Bring to the boil on the stove, then cook covered in the oven.

Take the onions and rice out of the casserole without touching the bacon rashers. Rub through a sieve, pressing with a wooden spoon.

Reheat the purée. Add 150 g. (5 oz., 10 tablespoons) butter and 1 dl. (6 tablespoons, scant $\frac{2}{3}$ cup) fresh double cream. Blend.

Or: Blanch 1 kg. ($2\frac{1}{4}$ lb.) chopped onions thoroughly and cook gently in butter. Add 1 litre ($1\frac{3}{4}$ pints, generous quart) thick *Béchamel sauce* (see SAUCE). Season with salt, white pepper and grated nutmeg. Simmer gently, stirring frequently. Rub through a sieve, pressing with a wooden spoon. Finish cooking the purée as above.

Onion soubise II. PURÉE SOUBISE – Blanch 500 g. (18 oz.) chopped onions, drain, and cook in the oven with 50 g. (2 oz., $\frac{1}{4}$ cup) butter, a pinch of salt, a pinch of white pepper and a pinch of fine sugar.

When the onions are cooked, without getting brown, add 4 dl. ($\frac{3}{4}$ pint, scant 2 cups) thick *Béchamel sauce* (see SAUCE). Blend and finish cooking in the oven, with a lid on the pan, for 30 minutes.

Rub through a sieve, and add 75 g. (3 oz., 6 tablespoons) butter, whitening it, if necessary, with several tablespoons of cream.

Prepared in this way, the soubise is thinner in consistency and is mainly served as a sauce for grilled meat.

Chick-pea purée. PURÉE DE POIS CHICHES – Prepared like *Split pea purée* (see below).

Fresh pea purée. PURÉE DE POIS FRAÏS – Rub through a fine sieve some fresh garden peas cooked in water or *à la française* (see PEA). Heat this purée and add butter.

Use as garnish for eggs, small cuts of meat, sweetbreads and poultry. It is also served as a vegetable and as a soup.

Split pea purée. PURÉE DE POIS CASSÉS – Like *Haricot bean purée*, using split peas cooked in stock or water.

Use as garnish for large and small cuts of meat, braised or roast goose, ham and venison.

Sweet pepper purée. PURÉE DE PIMENTS DOUX – Peel the peppers, remove seeds, cook in butter, and pound them finely in a mortar with half their weight of thick *Béchamel sauce* (see SAUCE). Rub through a sieve, reheat and add butter.

Use as a garnish for grills, and for poached or soft-boiled eggs.

Potato purée. PURÉE DE POMMES DE TERRE – See POTATOES.

Pumpkin purée. PURÉE DE COURGE – See PUMPKIN.

Spinach purée. PURÉE D'ÉPINARDS – Cook the spinach in salted water. Drain, cool it in cold water, drain it again, and squeeze as dry as possible. Rub through a fine sieve. Heat, and bind it with butter and cream.

Use as garnish with meat, and poached or soft-boiled eggs. May also be used as a vegetable.

Tarragon purée. PURÉE D'ESTRAGON – *Hot.* Blanch rapidly in salted water 250 g. (9 oz.) fresh tarragon leaves. Drain, cool in cold water, drain again, squeeze as dry as possible and rub through a fine sieve.

Add to 2 dl. ($\frac{1}{3}$ pint, scant cup) thick *Béchamel sauce* (see SAUCE). Heat well, add butter, season, and mix well.

Use as filling for mushrooms, artichoke bottoms and pastry shells, or as garnish for large or small cuts of meat, chicken, eggs or fish.

Cold. Bind the tarragon purée, prepared as above, with very thick mayonnaise instead of sauce. (See also TARRAGON.)

Use as an ingredient of cold *hors-d'œuvre*.

Watercress, chervil, parsley or other herb purées, hot or cold, are prepared in the same way.

Truffle purée. PURÉE DE TRUFFES – Rub through a fine sieve 250 g. (9 oz.) fresh truffles, raw or cooked. Mix with 2 dl. ($\frac{1}{3}$ pint, scant cup) *Béchamel sauce* (see SAUCE) which has been cooked with fresh cream. Boil for a few moments. Strain through a fine sieve.

Use as filling for pastry cases, little shells of bread, potato crust, etc., which accompany elaborate dishes; and as stuffing for artichoke bottoms, mushrooms, etc., as well as a liaison for various sauces.

PURÉE-PRESSER. PASSE-PURÉE – Kitchen utensil, of which there are many types, used for pressing through purées of meat, fish, vegetables or fruit.

QUAIL. CAILLE – This word comes from the old Flemish word *quakele*. Quail is a bird of passage, a native of hot countries. It comes to Europe in the spring and returns to hot climates at the beginning of winter.

The common quail (*Coturnix vulgaris*) is the only species which comes to Europe but there are many exotic varieties of quail in Asia and the Indian Archipelago.

The American quail belongs to the American partridge family. It is a little bigger than the common quail and its flesh has a delicate flavour. It can be found in the markets in France in winter, and can be prepared in any manner suitable for ordinary quail.

In September and October the quails begin to migrate to Africa and India. In the spring they cross the Mediterranean, covering the whole distance without stopping, and go to France. There they are trapped alive and put into cages for systematic fattening.

Charles Jobey says that the quail 'belongs to the highest aristocracy of the bird world', and this is true in so far as wild quail is concerned, but applies much less in the case of quail bred for food.

Common quail

American quail:
a. Male
b. Female

There are many recipes for the preparation of this bird. It should never be allowed to get high. In addition to the recipes given below, quail can also be prepared by following any of the recipes given for partridge (q.v.).

Quails in cases (stuffed). CAILLES EN CAISSES (FARCIES) – Bone the quails. Stuff each with a little *À gratin game forcemeat* (see FORCEMEATS) adding to it the quails' livers and mixing in some chopped truffles. Reshape the birds to give them their proper form and wrap each in a piece of buttered greaseproof paper. Put them into a buttered pan, placing them tightly against each other. Sprinkle with a little melted butter, cover with a lid and cook in the oven for 15 to 18 minutes. Remove the birds from the pan and, after taking off the papers, put each into a paper case which has been brushed with oil and dried in the oven. Dilute the pan juices with Madeira, moisten with a little concentrated game stock and pour over the quail. Put the cases back in the oven for 5 minutes before serving.

Quails in cases à l'italienne. CAILLES EN CAISSES À L'ITALIENNE – Prepare the quails as described in the recipe for *Quails in cases (stuffed)*. Put 1 tablespoon *Italian sauce* (see SAUCE) into each case before putting in the birds. Finish cooking as described in the recipe for *Quails in cases.*

Quails in cases à la Lamballe. CAILLES EN CAISSES À LA LAMBALLE – Prepare the quails as described above. Before putting in the birds, line the cases with a *julienne* (q.v.) of mushrooms and truffles blended with cream. Dilute the pan juices with port, add fresh cream and pour this sauce over the quails.

Quails in cases à la mirepoix. CAILLES EN CAISSES À LA MIREPOIX – Prepare the quails as described above. Add some *Vegetable mirepoix* (see MIREPOIX) to the pan juices and pour over the birds.

Quails in cases Mont-Bry. CAILLES EN CAISSES MONT-BRY – Prepare the quails as described above, replacing *à gratin* forcemeat by *Chicken forcemeat* (see FORCEMEATS) mixed with chopped truffles. Dilute the pan juices with champagne and brown veal stock. Place the quails into cases and garnish with a *ragoût* (q.v.) of cocks' combs and kidneys.

Quails in cases à la Périgueux. CAILLES EN CAISSES À LA PÉRIGUEUX – Prepare the quails as described above. Arrange them in cases, put a thick slice of truffle on each and pour over *Périgueux sauce* (see SAUCE), adding the pan juices diluted with Madeira.

Quails in cases à la strasbourgeoise. CAILLES EN CAISSES À LA STRASBOURGEOISE – Bone the quails and stuff them with a *salpicon* (q.v.) of *foie gras* and truffles, seasoned with salt and a pinch of spices and sprinkled with a few drops of brandy.

Wrap the birds in buttered papers and cook as described in the recipe for *Quails in cases*. Arrange in paper cases, put a thick slice of truffle on each and cover with *Périgueux sauce* (see SAUCE).

Quails in cases à la vigneronne. CAILLES EN CAISSES À LA VIGNERONNE – Bone the quails, leaving the legs and wings intact. Stuff with *foie gras* and diced truffles sprinkled with brandy and well seasoned. Reshape the quails, wrap each in a piece of muslin and tie with string.

Cook in jelly stock made out of a veal knuckle and the quails' bones and trimmings and add some white Bordeaux wine. Drain the quails and cool thoroughly under a light press. Unwrap, coat with *Brown chaud-froid sauce* (see SAUCE) prepared with a part of the liquor in which the quails were cooked. Glaze with jelly made from the rest of the liquor and flavoured with Madeira.

Arrange the quails, each in a frilly paper case, or in little individual dishes. Put 1 large round slice of truffle on each quail and 3 large grapes on top.

Quails in cases à la vigneronne

Casserole of quails (or quails en cocotte). CAILLES EN CASSEROLE, EN COCOTTE – Put into each quail a piece of butter, the size of a cobnut, kneaded with a little salt and pepper. Truss the birds. Put them into an earthenware casserole or *cocotte* in which butter has been heated. Season and cook in the oven for 15 minutes. Add a dash of brandy and baste with a few tablespoons of game stock.

The quails may be wrapped in vine leaves or in thin rashers of bacon, served with croûtons fried in butter, spread with *à gratin game forcemeat* (see FORCEMEATS), if desired.

Casserole of quails à la bonne femme. CAILLES EN CASSEROLE À LA BONNE FEMME – Cook the quails in a casserole with a garnish of diced potatoes tossed in butter and blanched diced bacon. Finish cooking as described in the recipe for *Casserole of quails*.

Casserole of quails with grapes. CAILLES EN CASSEROLE AUX RAISINS – Clean out and singe 6 quails. Pluck them, truss, and wrap each in a vine leaf and thin rasher of fat bacon. Put them into a sauté pan in which 1 good tablespoon of butter has been heated, and cook in a hot oven for 8 minutes. Take the quails out of the pan, remove trussing strings and arrange them in an ovenproof dish. Add 60 large fresh peeled and seeded grapes. Sprinkle with the fat given out by the birds. Put the dish in the oven, uncovered, for 5 minutes.

At the moment of serving, sprinkle the birds with their pan juices diluted with 2 tablespoons (3 tablespoons) brandy and 4 tablespoons (5 tablespoons) brown veal stock. Serve at once.

Chaud-froid of quails. CAILLES EN CHAUD-FROID, CHAUD-FROID DE CAILLES – Bone 10 quails and stuff with *à gratin game forcemeat* (see FORCEMEATS). In the middle of the forcemeat put a piece of uncooked *foie gras* studded with a piece of truffle, seasoned with salt and spices and sprinkled with brandy. Reshape the quails, wrap each in a piece of muslin and tie both ends with string, in such a manner as to make little ballottines.

Put these into a sauté pan on a foundation of fresh bacon rinds (pork rind), carrots and onions – all chopped and fried in butter. Cover the birds with their bones and trimmings, previously tossed in butter. Moisten with $2\frac{1}{2}$ dl. (scant $\frac{1}{2}$ pint, generous cup) Madeira. Boil down almost completely. Add veal stock simmered with a few tablespoons *Game jelly stock* (see JELLY). Bring to the boil, cover the sauté pan, and cook in a hot oven for 20 minutes.

Drain the quails and put them into a flat *terrine*. Strain the liquor in which they were cooked and pour over them. Leave to cool in this liquor. Drain the quails again, unwrap, and dry thoroughly. Coat each quail with a *Brown chaud-froid sauce* (see SAUCE) made from the liquor left over from cooking the quails and flavoured with Madeira or some other wine. Decorate the quails with pieces of truffles and hard-boiled egg white. Glaze the decorations with half-set jelly and chill. Arrange them in a crown in a deep dish and cover completely with half-set jelly. Keep on ice until ready to serve.

Quails *en chaud-froid* prepared as above can be arranged in different ways. Serve on the dish, surrounding them with chopped jelly; or put them into a glass dish and cover them with a clear jelly.

The quails can also be served individually, each in a frilly paper case on a foundation of chopped jelly, or in porcelain, glass or silver dishes.

Confit of quails. CAILLES CONFITES – Decapitate 4 plump quails, putting the heads aside for use later. Season the birds with salt and freshly ground pepper. Flame in a frying pan with Armagnac or Cognac.

Melt 200 g. (7 oz.) goose fat in a pan, adding a few drops of water. When the fat is almost melted, add the quails. Bring slowly to the boil, then simmer for 35 to 40 minutes.

Remove the pan from the heat and cool the quails. Place them in the refrigerator in order to set the film of fat that covers them.

Prepare 4 rectangular *canapés* (q.v.). Spread them with a thin layer of fresh *foie gras*, about 25 g. (1 oz.). Place 1 quail in the centre of each *canapé* and fix the heads in position. The eyes are made of hard-boiled egg white and a speck of truffle.

Decorate each quail with small pieces of truffle and surround with 6 large skinned, de-seeded grapes. Glaze the birds with savoury jelly.

The quails should be served on a large dish and decorated to taste (usually with a piping of chopped savoury jelly). (Recipe used in the restaurant *Lasserre*.)

Quails en chemise. CAILLES EN CHEMISE – Stuff the quails with *à gratin game forcemeat* (see FORCEMEATS). Truss them as for an *entrée* and enclose each one in a piece of small intestine. Tie up at both ends and wrap in muslin, which should also be tied at both ends. Poach from 15 to 18 minutes in boiling clear stock. Drain, remove the muslin and serve the quails in a *timbale* (q.v.), wrapped in their *chemises*, sprinkled with a few tablespoons of the liquor in which they were cooked. Serve with *Rouennaise sauce* (see SAUCE) to which concentrated game stock, boiled down to the consistency of a *fumet* (q.v.), has been added.

Quails with cherries. CAILLES AUX CERISES – Cook the quails, trussed as for an *entrée*, in butter in a casserole or earthenware *cocotte*. When three-quarters done add 12 stoned cherries for each quail.

Stoned cooked or fresh cherries can be used. Put them in an ovenproof dish and cook in a low oven, without any liquid except the juice rendered by the fruit.

Cold quails. CAILLES FROIDES – In addition to various recipes in this section, all the methods of preparation given for cold partridge are suitable for cold quail. (See PARTRIDGE.)

Devilled quails. CAILLES GRILLÉES À LA DIABLE – Split the quails down the back and flatten them slightly. Brush with melted butter, season with salt and freshly ground pepper and dip in white breadcrumbs. Grill the quails on both sides under a low heat. Arrange on a dish and garnish with a border of sliced lemons and gherkins. Serve with *Diable sauce* (see SAUCE) flavoured with concentrated game stock boiled down to the consistency of a *fumet* (q.v.).

Quails à la financière (stuffed) I. CAILLES À LA FINANCIÈRE – Prepare and cook the quails as described in the recipe for *Quails in cases (stuffed)*. When they are cooked, sprinkle with a few tablespoons *Demi-glace sauce* (see SAUCE) and glaze in the oven, placing each bird on an oval croûton fried in butter. Surround with *à la financière* garnish (see GARNISHES). Put a thick slice of truffle on each quail. Dilute the pan juices with Madeira, add *Demi-glace sauce* (see SAUCE) based on game *fumet* (q.v.) and pour over the birds.

Quails à la financière II. CAILLES À LA FINANCIÈRE – Proceed as described in the above recipe and arrange the quails with their garnish in a puff pastry shell or in a *timbale* made of *Fine lining paste* (see DOUGH), baked blind.

Quails à la financière with a rice border. CAILLES À LA FINANCIÈRE EN BORDURE DE RIZ – Prepare the quails and the garnish as described in the recipe for *Quails à la financière* and serve them in a rice border (see BORDER, *Rice ring with garnishes)*.

Quails à la gourmande. CAILLES À LA GOURMANDE – Stuff the quails with a mixture of butter, lean ham and chopped truffles and cook them in butter. Dilute the pan juices with champagne and chicken stock. Add fresh truffles shredded into a *julienne* (q.v.). Arrange the quails on a dish, on a foundation of large mushrooms stewed in butter and filled with a *salpicon* (q.v.) of *foie gras*. Heat the sauce until piping hot and pour over the birds.

Quails à la grecque. CAILLES À LA GRECQUE – Truss the quails as for an *entrée* and cook in butter. Arrange in a pyramid on a foundation of *Rice à la grecque* (see RICE) and pour over the pan juices diluted with game stock concentrated to the consistency of a *fumet* (q.v.).

Grilled quails à la duchesse. CAILLES GRILLÉES À LA DUCHESSE – Grill the quails as described for *Devilled quails*. Arrange them on small cakes of *Duchess potato* (see POTATOES), garnish with asparagus tips dressed with butter, and surround with a ring of *Demi-glace sauce* (see SAUCE), based on a game *fumet* (q.v.), with butter added to it.

Grilled quails à l'indienne. CAILLES GRILLÉES À L'INDIENNE – For 12 quails prepare the following mixture in a bowl: 300 g. (11 oz., generous $1\frac{1}{4}$ cup) butter, blended into a paste, 1 tablespoon curry powder, 1 tablespoon Mulligatawny paste, 2 teaspoons Worcester sauce, 2 teaspoons Harvey sauce, 2 tablespoons (3 tablespoons) unsweetened chutney, 1 teaspoon paprika and salt. Blend into a paste.

Remove the breastbone and put a little of the paste into each bird. Sear them quickly in the oven, and cool them under a light press. Coat the outside of each quail with the same paste and grill. When they are brown, finish cooking in the oven. Prepare a border of *Game forcemeat* (see FORCEMEATS), put the rice in the middle, arrange the quails on top, pour over a little of the sauce and serve the rest separately. Serve straw potatoes at the same time.

Rice for the garnish. Brown chopped shallots lightly and moisten with the stock in which the rice is to be cooked. Season with curry powder, Mulligatawny paste and paprika. Cook for a moment, then strain through a fine strainer. Pour this stock over the rice, bring to the boil, add a good piece of butter, cover, and cook in the oven for 20 minutes.

Indian sauce. Fry 2 onions and 2 cloves of garlic lightly in butter. Add a little curry powder and 2 diced cooking apples. Moisten with brown veal stock, cook, and pass through a sieve. Pour into a saucepan and taste the sauce to make sure the flavour is good. Pour over the quails. (Recipe by M. A. Menager, chef to King Edward VII of England.)

Jellied quails à la périgourdine. CAILLES À LA PÉRIGOURDINE, À LA GELÉE – Bone and stuff the quails with *À gratin game forcemeat* (see FORCEMEATS), *foie gras* and truffles, allowing quite a lot of truffles. Reshape the quails, wrap each in a piece of muslin and tie at both ends. Poach from 20 to 25 minutes in liquid *Game jelly stock* (see JELLY), flavoured with Madeira or any other wine. Leave the quails to cool in their liquor. Drain, unwrap, and dry on a cloth. Put them into a *terrine* or glass bowl. Clarify the jelly and pour over the quails. Chill thoroughly before serving.

Quails à la limousine. CAILLES À LA LIMOUSINE – Arrange the quails, grilled as described for *Devilled quails*, on a foundation of artichoke hearts cooked in a *court-bouillon* (q.v.), simmered in butter and filled with *Chestnut purée* (see CHESTNUTS). Pour round the border a ring of *Demi-glace sauce* (see SAUCE) based on concentrated game *fumet*, with butter added to it.

Quails Lucullus. CAILLES LUCULLUS – Bone the quails, put into each bird about 25 g. (1 oz.) uncooked *foie gras*, seasoned with salt and spices and studded with a small peeled truffle. Put the quails into a sauté pan and cook as described in the recipe for *Quails in cases*. Arrange in a low pastry shell filled with a *ragoût* of *Truffles à la crème* (see TRUFFLE). Dilute the pan juices with Madeira, add brown veal stock, boil down by half and pour over the birds.

Minute quails. CAILLES À LA MINUTE – Open the quails down the back and remove the small bones from the inside. Beat lightly to flatten. Season with salt and pepper and sauté the birds briskly in butter, browning them slightly on both sides. When done, sprinkle with a little chopped onion fried in butter and chopped parsley. Put thinly sliced mushrooms (1 per quail) into the sauté pan to brown, add a dash of brandy, moisten with game *fumet* (q.v.) and brown veal stock, boil for a few moments, add a dash of lemon juice and pour this sauce over the birds.

Quails à la Monselet. CAILLES À LA MONSELET – Half bone the quails. Stuff them with a *salpicon* (q.v.) of truffles and *foie gras*. Wrap each bird in a piece of muslin and poach in Madeira-flavoured game stock made from the quails' bones and trimmings. Drain the birds, unwrap, put into an earthenware *cocotte* or casserole with a garnish of sliced artichoke hearts tossed in butter, cultivated mushrooms and thick slices of truffles. Strain the liquor in which the quails were cooked, add an equal quantity of thick fresh cream, boil down and pour over the birds. Cover the *cocotte* and put in a slow oven for 5 minutes.

Cold quail mousse. MOUSSE FROIDE DE CAILLES – Truss 12 quails as for an *entrée* and braise them in Madeira-flavoured stock, with the usual vegetables and truffle and mushroom trimmings added to it. Leave the quails to cool in the braising liquor.

Drain and bone them completely, taking care to preserve the wings intact, as they will be used for garnishing the mousse.

Using the trimmings, bones and skins of the quails, make a *Brown chaud-froid sauce* (see SAUCE).

Prepare *Game jelly stock* (see JELLY), flavoured with Madeira or some other wine.

The mousse mixture is made as follows:

Pound the rest of the quails' flesh finely in a mortar, adding to it 175 g. (6 oz., $\frac{3}{4}$ cup) cooked *foie gras* and 3 or 4 tablespoons of the *chaud-froid sauce*. When the mixture is quite smooth take it out of the mortar and rub it through a fine sieve, or use an electric blender. Transfer the mixture to a bowl on ice. Stir vigorously, add a dash of brandy, 2 or 3 tablespoons concentrated liquid game jelly and $2\frac{1}{2}$ dl. (scant $\frac{1}{2}$ pint, generous cup) fresh cream, very stiffly whipped. Blend carefully.

Line the bottom and sides of a mousse mould with a layer of game jelly. Arrange a border on the bottom of alternating rows of thick slices of truffles, cooled in Madeira, and half of the quails' wings, cooled under a press and coated with the *chaud-froid sauce*. Fill the mould with the mousse mixture to within 2 cm. (1 inch) of the edge. Lay the remaining wings on top, alternating with rows of truffle slices. Finish off with a layer of game jelly, filling the mould right up to the top.

Leave the mousse on ice or in a refrigerator until it sets completely. Turn out on a dish or on a buttered croûton. Surround with chopped game jelly and put a border of small pieces of jelly, cut in the shape of wolf's teeth, around the edge of the dish.

Instead of putting the quail mousse into a mould, it can be put into a dish on a layer of well-set jelly. Pile the mixture into a dome, garnish with quails' wings coated with the *chaud-froid sauce* and slivers of truffles, and pour half-set jelly over the top.

Quails in a nest

Quails in a nest. CAILLES AU NID – Bone the quails, stuff with *À gratin game forcemeat* (see FORCEMEATS) mixed with chopped truffles, wrap each bird in a small piece of muslin and make into a roll. Poach for 18 minutes in stock prepared from the bones and trimmings, with clear veal stock and Madeira. Drain the quails, unwrap, press in a cloth to give them their proper shape and glaze lightly in the oven. Arrange them in a nest of straw potatoes, prepared as described in the recipe for *Potato nests* (see POTATOES). Line with a salted batter pancake (see CRÊPES) and fill with a *ragoût* of cocks' kidneys, small button mushrooms and truffles, blended with a few tablespoons of *Financière sauce* (see SAUCE) to which the liquor left over from poaching the quails has been added. Put the rest of the *ragoût* on top.

Quail pâté. PÂTÉ DE CAILLES – Bone the quails. Stuff each with a piece of *À gratin forcemeat* (see FORCEMEATS) about the size of a hazelnut, and the same amount of *foie gras*, studded with a piece of truffle, the whole well seasoned with salt and spices and sprinkled with a dash of brandy. Wrap each quail in a very thin rasher of bacon.

Line a hinged oval or rectangular mould with fine pastry, then with thin rashers of bacon. Cover with a layer of finely pounded forcemeat made of veal and lean and fat pork in equal proportions, bound with an egg, well seasoned, sprinkled with a little brandy and mixed with diced truffles. Over this forcemeat put a layer of *À gratin game forcemeat* (see FORCEMEATS), then half the stuffed quails, pressing down well. Cover with another layer of forcemeat, put in the rest of the quails and follow with a layer of forcemeat. Cover this with a layer of truffled forcemeat, flatten it, and cover again with a layer of thin rashers of lean bacon. Seal with a pastry lid. Decorate with pieces of pastry cut in fancy shapes. Make a hole in the middle of the lid to allow steam to escape, and brush the top with beaten egg. Bake in a hot oven for about $1\frac{1}{2}$ hours.

When cooked, leave the *pâté* to get cold, and pour liquid *Game jelly stock* (see JELLY) through the hole in the top.

Hinged mould for quail pâté

Quails with peas. CAILLES AUX PETITS POIS – Cook the quails in a casserole as described in the appropriate recipe. Have ready $\frac{1}{2}$ litre (scant pint, $2\frac{1}{4}$ cups) fresh garden peas, cooked in butter, and some small young onions. Put the peas into the *cocotte* and leave the whole to simmer together without boiling.

Quails petit-duc. CAILLES PETIT-DUC – Split the quails on the back and season with salt and paprika. Sprinkle with melted butter and dip in white breadcrumbs. Grill them and arrange each one on a little cake of *Anna potatoes* (see POTATOES), baked in tartlet tins. Put 1 large grilled mushroom, filled with grated horseradish, on each quail. Heat a few tablespoons of *Game fumet* (see FUMET), add Madeira and butter, and pour over the birds.

Quails with rice. CAILLES AU RIZ – Truss the quails as for an *entrée*, season and cook in butter. Arrange them in a pyramid on a foundation of a *Rice pilaf* (see PILAF) to which the butter left in the pan has been added. Add a dash of brandy to the pan juices, moisten with concentrated brown veal stock or concentrated *Game fumet* (see FUMET). Pour over the quails.

Quails with rice (stuffed). CAILLES AU RIZ – Prepare and cook the quails as described in the recipe for *Quails in cases*. Arrange them on a foundation of *Rice pilaf* (see PILAF). Dilute the pan juices with brown veal stock, simmer for a few moments and pour over the quails.

Quails with risotto. CAILLES AU RISOTTO – Proceed as described in the recipe for *Quails with rice*, replacing the rice pilaf with *Risotto with cheese*.

Quails with risotto à la piémontaise. CAILLES AU RISOTTO À LA PIÉMONTAISE – Arrange quails cooked in butter on *Risotto à la piémontaise* (see RICE), mixed with finely sliced white truffles. Dilute the pan juices with concentrated brown veal stock and pour over the quails.

Roast quails. CAILLES RÔTIES – Wrap the quails first in vine leaves, then in thin rashers of bacon and secure with string. Roast on a spit before a lively fire for 15 to 20 mins (or in the oven, for 12–15 mins). Arrange each quail on a garnished *canapé*. Garnish with watercress and quarters of lemon. Dilute the pan juices and serve with the resulting sauce.

Quails à la romaine. CAILLES À LA ROMAINE – Heat some butter in a flameproof earthenware casserole and brown the quails all over. Add fresh peas which have been prepared in the following manner: fry finely chopped young onions with lean diced ham in butter. Add freshly shelled peas. Season with salt and a pinch of sugar. Cover and cook from 35 to 40 minutes.

Cover the casserole and finish cooking together in the oven. Serve in the same casserole.

Quails Saint-Mars. CAILLES EN COCOTTE SAINT-MARS – Put the quails, trussed as for an *entrée*, into a sauté pan. Cover them with a *julienne* of coarsely shredded carrot, onion and celery, lightly fried in butter and moistened with veal stock flavoured with sherry. Season and cook without a lid. Drain the quails, untruss them and arrange in an earthenware *cocotte* or casserole. Cover with a *julienne* of coarsely shredded truffles and mushrooms. Pour the pan juices over the *julienne*. Sprinkle with 2 tablespoons (3 tablespoons) brandy and dot with small pieces of butter. Cover the *cocotte* and seal the lid with flour-and-water paste. Cook in the oven, in a *bain-marie*, from 15 to 18 minutes.

Quails à la Souvarof. CAILLES À LA SOUVAROF – Stuff the quails with a *salpicon* (q.v.) of *foie gras* and truffles, season and sprinkle with a dash of brandy. Truss as for an *entrée*. Fry briskly in butter for 6 minutes. Put into an earthenware *cocotte* with cooked truffles, allowing 2 truffles per quail. Season with salt and pepper. Dilute the pan juices with Madeira, moisten with *Demi-glace sauce* (see SAUCE) based on *Game fumet* (see FUMET). Simmer for a few moments and pour over the quails. Add a dash of brandy. Cover the *cocotte*, seal the lid on and cook in the oven for 12 minutes.

Quails à la Talleyrand. CAILLES À LA TALLEYRAND – Split the quails open, flatten them lightly and season. Coat on both sides with a thin layer of *Vegetable mirepoix* (see MIREPOIX), mixed with 1 tablespoon lean, chopped cooked ham and chopped truffles. Wrap each quail in a piece of pig's caul or salt pork. Sprinkle with melted butter and roll in fresh breadcrumbs. Grill the quails on a low flame and arrange on puff pastry tartlets, baked blind and filled with *Mushroom purée* (see PURÉE). Serve with *Périgueux sauce* (see SAUCE) based on a game *fumet*.

Tinned (canned) quails in jelly. CONSERVE DE CAILLES À LA GELÉE – *Forcemeat ingredients.* 200 g. (7 oz.) fine pork, minced, 100 g (4 oz., $\frac{1}{2}$ cup) *À gratin game forcemeat* (see FORCEMEAT), 200 g. (7 oz., generous $\frac{3}{4}$ cup) cooked *foie gras*, 75 g. (3 oz.) truffles (net weight), brandy, salt, pepper and spices.

Liquor for stewing. Strong meat jelly stock made from beef, 1 veal knuckle, calves' feet, chicken, bacon rinds and the usual vegetables and aromatics, 4 dl. ($\frac{3}{4}$pint, scant 2 cups) Madeira.

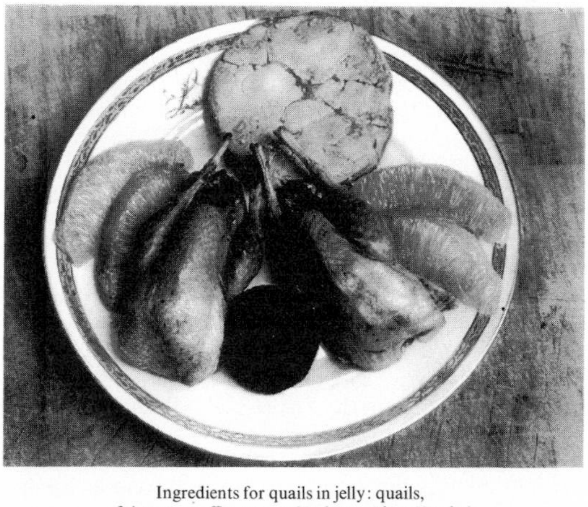

Ingredients for quails in jelly: quails, foie gras, truffle, orange (*Ledoyen. Phot. Nicolas*)

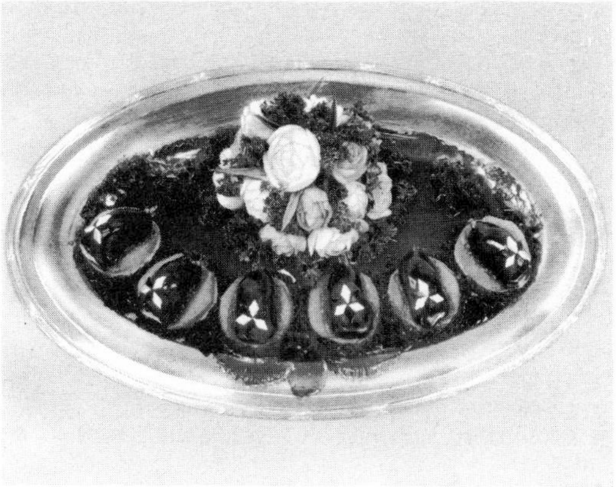

Canapé of jellied quails garnished with foie gras (*Ledoyen. Phot. Nicolas*)

Method. Truss the quails as for an *entrée*. Remove the backbone and the breastbone and spread the quails flat on the table. Season and sprinkle with brandy. Inside each quail put a piece of the forcemeat the size of an egg, with a piece of *foie gras*, studded with a quarter of a truffle, in the middle. Reshape the quails and wrap each in a piece of buttered paper. Pack them tightly into a buttered sauté pan. Cover with the bones and trimmings, which should previously be tossed in butter.

Moisten with 2 dl. ($\frac{1}{3}$ pint, scant cup) Madeira and bring to the boil. Cover with a sheet of buttered paper. Cook in the oven, covered, for 25 minutes. Test the quails gently with the point of a trussing needle: if no blood comes out, they are cooked. Cool in the braising liquor.

Drain the birds, unwrap and dry them. Put them into tins, breast downwards. Cover with clarified liquid *Game jelly stock* (see JELLY), to which the diluted braising liquor has been added.

When the jelly is quite cold, solder the lids of the tins. Mark them and put the tins into a big pan. Cover with cold water. Put a weight on the tins so as to make sure they are well submerged. Give them 1 hour 10 minutes of uninterrupted boiling for tins containing 1 quail, and $1\frac{1}{4}$ hours for tins containing 2 quails. Drain the tins, put them on the table separated from each other, placing them marked side up. Leave until quite cold.

QUARTANIER – French name for a four-year-old wild boar.

QUARTER. QUARTIER – The quarter of the forepart of beef includes the shoulder and the sides. The hindquarter is made up of the thigh and sirloin.

In French butchery a 'fifth' quarter is spoken of to describe all the inedible parts of the slaughtered animal: skin, horns, hoofs and tallow.

QUASI – Piece from the rump of veal.

QUATRE-QUARTS (Four quarters) – Household cake mixture, made up of equal quantities of eggs, flour, butter and sugar. (English pound cake.)

Beat together in a bowl 100 g. (4 oz., $\frac{1}{2}$ cup) sugar with either 2 large eggs or 3 small ones until the mixture becomes white and frothy. Add 100 g. (4 oz., 1 cup) sifted flour, and 100 g. (4 oz., $\frac{1}{2}$ cup) melted butter. Flavour with orange-blossom water, orange or lemon peel, or any liqueur, and pour into a buttered mould. Cook in the oven at a gentle heat for 25 or 30 minutes.

QUENELLE – Dumpling made with fish or meat forcemeat bound with eggs. The word is said to come from the Anglo-Saxon *knyll*, meaning to pound, to grind, because the flesh of the meat or fish, before being turned into quenelles, must be pounded in a mortar.

Quenelles are made with all kinds of meat, poultry, game, fish and shellfish. They are made in different shapes, large and small. The most important is the quenelle prepared with the forcemeat called *godiveau* or *Quenelle forcemeat* (see FORCEMEATS).

Quenelles, particularly the small kind, are used as an element in such garnishes as *financière*, *Godard*, *Toulouse*, etc. Large quenelles, which are generally embellished with truffles, pickled tongue, etc., are used as a more elaborate garnish for large braised fish or *entrées*. They are also used to prepare tarts, *timbales* and other preparations of the same kind.

Quenelles of foie gras. QUENELLES DE FOIE GRAS – Pound a raw *foie gras* and rub it through a fine sieve. Pound half as much raw chicken flesh as there is *foie gras*, mixing in with it, little by little, half its weight of *Bread panada* (see PANADA). Rub this forcemeat through a sieve. Put it back in the mortar and pound again, adding to it, little by little, the purée of *foie gras* and 3 or 4 egg yolks. Season with salt, pepper and spices. Beat this forcemeat on ice.

Make the quenelles in the usual way (with a spoon or with a forcing bag) and poach them in salted water.

Quenelles of meat, veal, chicken, game. QUENELLES DE VIANDES, VEAU, VOLAILLE, GIBIER – Prepare in the same way as those for pike. (See FORCEMEATS, *Quenelle forcemeat*; PIKE, *Pike quenelles*.)

Quenelles of pike mousseline. QUENELLES DE BROCHET MOUSSELINE – Made with *Mousseline forcemeat* (see FORCEMEAT). Mould in a tablespoon, lay in a buttered sauté pan, and poach in boiling salted water from 8 to 10 minutes according to size.

Drain, dry, and place on a croûton of bread fried in butter or on puff pastry crusts. Garnish and sauce are according to the particular recipe. *Mousseline* quenelles may be prepared in the same way, using other fish: whiting, brill, sole, salmon, trout.

Quenelles of pike princesse

Quenelles of pike princesse. QUENELLES DE BROCHET PRINCESSE – Set the above quenelles on a border of *Pike forcemeat* (see FORCEMEATS) with truffles. Decorate the middle of the dish with asparagus tips. Coat with *Normande sauce* (see SAUCE).

QUICHE – The *quiche* or *kiche*, as the word is sometimes spelt, originates in Lorraine.

There are several kinds of *quiche*. Each region of Lorraine or Alsace has its own. The name is also used for some custard tarts served as a sweet, though the real *quiche*, that of Lorraine, is always served as *hors-d'œuvre* and never for the sweet course.

Line with ordinary short crust pastry (see DOUGH, *Lining paste*) a pie dish or plate with fluted edges, 20 cm (8 inches) in diameter and well buttered. The pastry should extend a little beyond the edges.

Put thin slices of streaky bacon, blanched and lightly fried in butter, in the bottom of this flan case. Fill the crust with a mixture composed of 4 eggs and 4 dl. ($\frac{3}{4}$ pint, scant 2 cups) thick fresh cream, seasoned with salt and well beaten. When the flan is filled, add 2 teaspoons butter cut into tiny pieces. Cook in the oven at moderate heat for 30 to 35 minutes. Serve very hot.

Sometimes the flan pastry is enriched with thin slices of Gruyère cheese, set alternately with the bacon.

Quiche Lorraine

Quiche Lorraine (old recipe) – 'Roll out as thinly as possible some bread dough. Put this sheet of dough on a metal dish with raised and fluted edges, sprinkled with flour. Put small pieces of very fresh butter all over the dough.

'Fill the pie dish with a mixture of thick cream and eggs well beaten together and seasoned with salt. Cook in a very hot oven for a maximum of 10 minutes. Serve very hot.'

Little quiches with cheese. PETITES QUICHES AU FROMAGE – Line tartlet cases with short crust pastry (see DOUGH, *Lining paste*). Put Gruyère cheese, cut into very small pieces, in the bottom of these cases. Fill them with a mixture of cream and eggs. Cook in the oven for 14 or 15 minutes. Turn out and serve very hot.

Little quiches with ham. PETITES QUICHES AU JAMBON – Proceed as in the last recipe, replacing the cheese by lean cooked ham cut up into small pieces.

QUIGNON – Big wedge of bread cut from one of the larger French loaves.

QUILLET (Pâtisserie) – This sweetmeat was created in a Parisian *pâtisserie* which was managed for a long time by M. Charabot, one of the masters of French pastry-making. This is the recipe:

Put in a copper basin 500 g. (18 oz., $2\frac{1}{4}$ cups) sugar, and 15 whole eggs, powdered vanilla and a very small pinch of salt. Beat with a whisk over a gentle heat, without letting it get too hot.

When the mixture is half thickened remove it and continue to beat it away from the heat until it is almost cold. Then add 500 g. (18 oz., $4\frac{1}{2}$ cups) sieved flour, sprinkled in a shower, and 500 g. (18 oz., $2\frac{1}{4}$ cups) melted butter.

Fill round cake tins with the mixture. Bake in the oven at a moderate heat. Cool the cakes and fill them with the following butter cream:

Heat together in a saucepan 1 dl. (6 tablespoons, scant $\frac{1}{2}$ cup) milk, 5 dl. (scant pint, $2\frac{1}{4}$ cups) 28° syrup (see SUGAR), 2 dl. ($\frac{1}{3}$ pint, scant cup) *Orgeat syrup* (see ORGEAT) and a vanilla pod. Cook this mixture for a few moments, then pour it over 8 egg yolks in a basin. Blend well with a whisk. Reheat the mixture gently without allowing it to boil. Cool. Pour onto 250 g. (9 oz., generous cup) butter which has been put through a sieve. Mix well. Keep this butter cream in a cool place until it is needed.

Fill the cake with the cream, and pipe some through a forcing-bag over the top. Decorate with sugar.

QUINCE. COING – Fruit of the quince, a common tree which used to be as well known as the apple and the vine. It has a tart and astringent flavour, a very sweet smell, and cannot be eaten raw. It is full of pectin and is used for jellies, jams, marmalade, syrups, and home-made liqueurs. (See JAMS AND JELLIES.)

Quince compote. COMPOTE DE COINGS – Cut ripe quinces into quarters. Trim, and blanch them for a few minutes in boiling water. Drain, and cook them in a vanilla syrup. Arrange them in a dish or *timbale*, and pour over them the syrup in which they were cooked.

Quince jelly. GELÉE DE COINGS – Made with an equal weight of sugar and quince juice, like *Apple jelly* (see JAMS AND JELLIES).

Quince liqueur or ratafia (quince water) – See LIQUEUR.

Quince marmalade. MARMELADE DE COINGS – Made in the same way as *Apple marmalade* (see MARMALADES).

Quince paste. PÂTE DE COINGS – Make some quince marmalade in the same way as *Apple marmalade* (see MARMALADES). Boil down to a good thick consistency. Put it on a shallow baking dish and dry in a warm oven. Cut the paste into square or rectangular slices. Dust them with crystallised sugar. Keep in a dry place.

QUINTAL – Name of a variety of cabbage.

Quinces (*Evereinoff, Copyright George Truffaut*)

RABBIT. LAPIN – Small rodent of the hare family, of African origin. There are several breeds of rabbit. The fur is sometimes white, sometimes grey, or black and tan, or mottled.

The domestic rabbit should be eaten young, when it is from 3 to $3\frac{1}{2}$ months old. A young rabbit can be recognised by the following: a short neck, plump knees, and very flexible front legs, which can be bent about at will.

The warren rabbit, the typical species of wild rabbit, is prodigiously fertile.

Fulbert-Dumonteil, the poet of good eating, praised it in these terms:

'It provides a feast for countryman and labourer. It is the youngster's game. It is present on all festive occasions, be it a suburban wedding or a village christening. Its appetising aroma pervades farmhouse and cottage alike.'

The flesh of rabbit is fairly white and somewhat less fatty than that of poultry. Its flavour depends a great deal on its feeding. It is more stringy and less delicate than white poultry, but quite as readily digestible.

However, sufferers from dyspepsia, hepatitis, colitis are advised to avoid fricassée of rabbit, and all similar sauce-based rabbit dishes.

Rabbit Coquibus. LAPIN COQUIBUS – Joint a rabbit and put it for a time in a marinade. Sauté it very quickly. Add 24 small onions and the same number of strips of lean blanched bacon. Fry all these ingredients. Sprinkle with 1 heaped tablespoon flour, and brown for a few seconds. Moisten with 2 dl. ($\frac{1}{3}$ pint, scant cup) white wine, a few tablespoons clear soup and the marinade, strained. Add a large *bouquet garni* of parsley, thyme, bay leaves and savory. Boil for 15 minutes. Put 400 g. (14 oz.) small new potatoes in the saucepan. Cover and cook for 45 minutes.

Fricassée of rabbit. GIBELOTTE – This *fricassée*, which is called *gibelotte* in French, is made with white or red wine. (See below, *Young wild rabbit en gibelotte.)*

Sautéed rabbit with curry. LAPIN SAUTÉ AU CURRIE – Proceed as for *Sautéed rabbit with paprika*, substituting Indian curry powder for paprika. Serve with *Rice à l'indienne* (see RICE).

Sautéed rabbit with paprika. LAPIN SAUTÉ AU PAPRIKA –

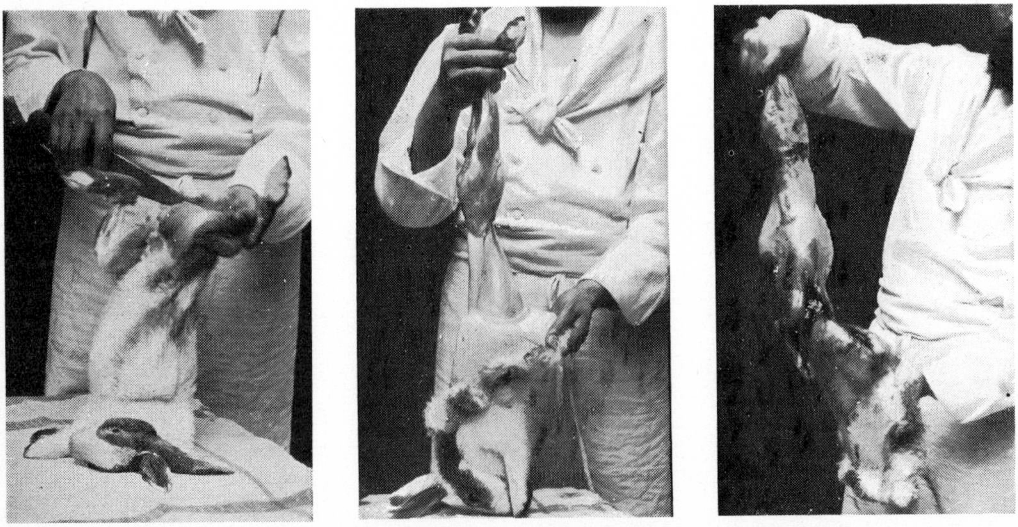

To skin a rabbit, first make two cuts from the abdomen along each thigh to free the hindlegs; then holding the animal by the hindlegs in the right hand, peel off the skin with the left hand

How to clean and cut a rabbit (*Larousse*)

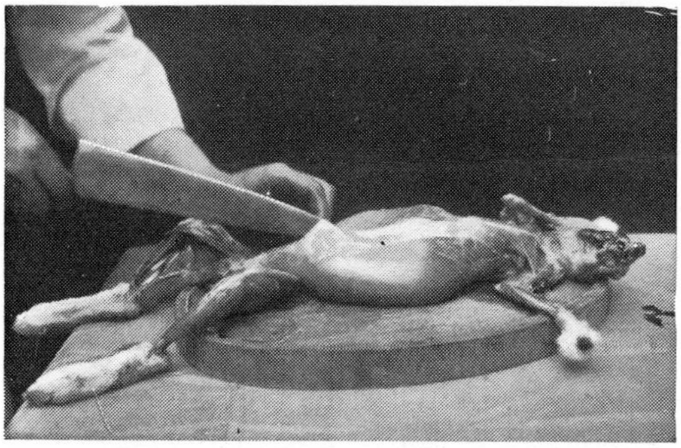

Place the rabbit on its back and slit open the stomach

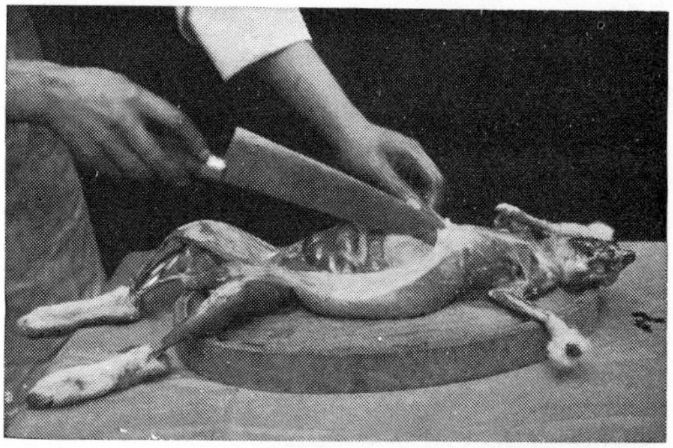

Make an incision as far as the breast

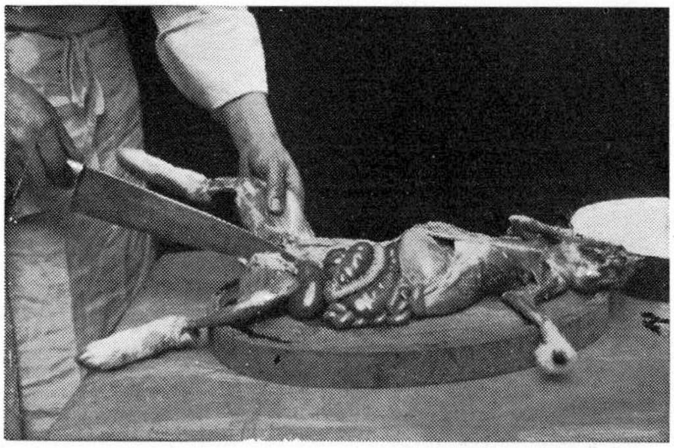

Cut away the contents of the abdomen

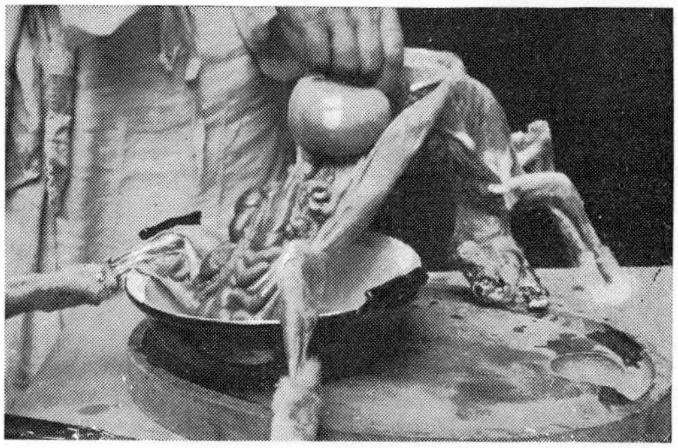

Empty the intestines into a bowl

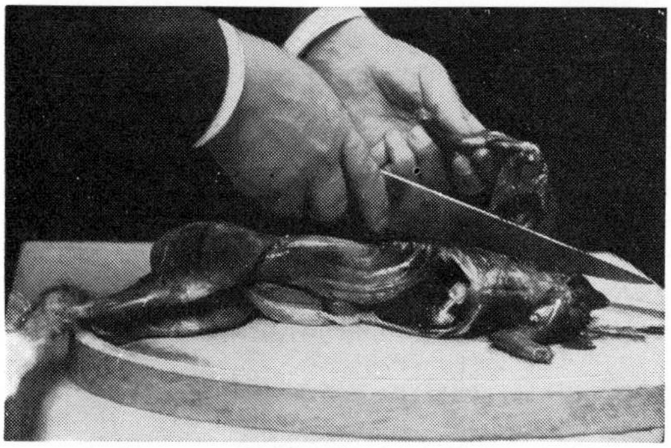

Lay the rabbit on its side and remove the front legs

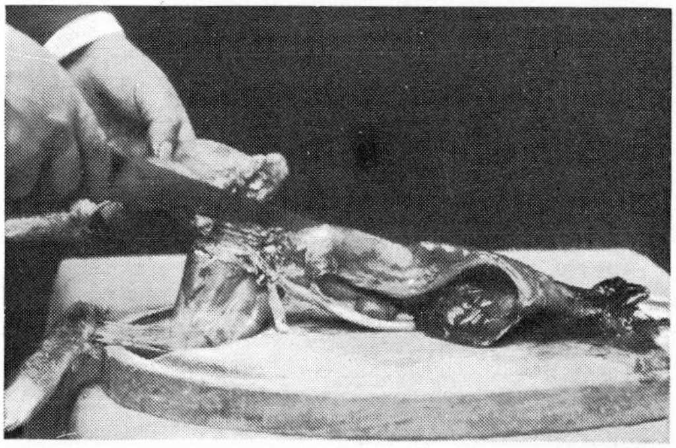

Cut off the hindlegs

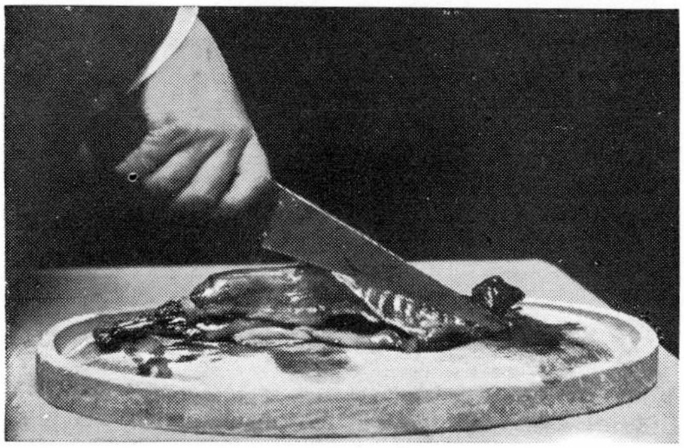

Cut away the front portion of the thorax to be thrown out

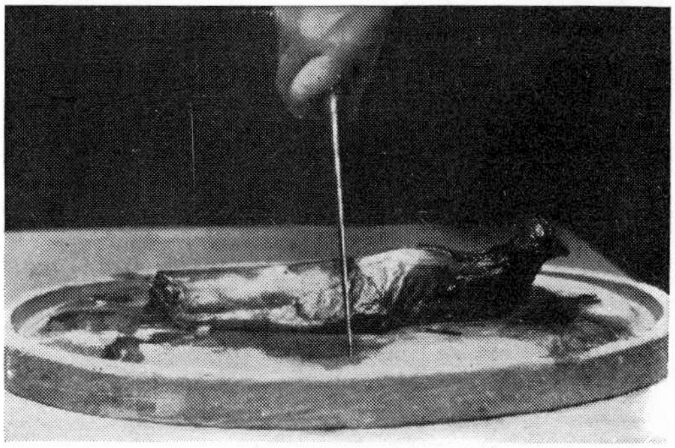

Divide the rabbit in two

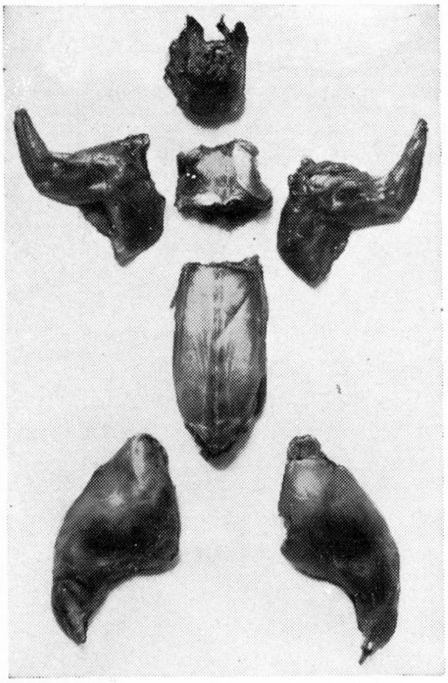

Pieces of cut rabbit

Joint the rabbit and steep it in a marinade. Cook very slowly in butter, until tender, 100 g. (4 oz., 1 cup) sliced onion. Brown the rabbit in the same pan. Season with 2 teaspoon paprika.

When the pieces of rabbit are well fried, sprinkle with 1 heaped tablespoon flour, which should take on a golden colour but should not brown. Moisten with $\frac{1}{2}$ glass white wine. Boil down and add enough clear stock just to cover the rabbit. Strain the marinade and add it to the stock. Dice coarsely 150 g. (5 oz., $2\frac{1}{2}$ cups) mushrooms and put them in the pan. Cover and cook for 35 minutes. Add 5 tablespoons (6 tablespoons) thick fresh cream. Keeping the pan covered, simmer for about 35 minutes until the rabbit is cooked. Before serving, add a little more fresh cream.

YOUNG WILD RABBIT. LAPEREAU – The flesh of this rabbit is somewhat firmer than that of the domestic rabbit. It has also more flavour, though frequently it is spoiled by mustiness.

Blanquette of young wild rabbit. LAPEREAU EN BLANQUETTE – Cut the rabbit into sections and proceed as for *Blanquette of lamb* (see LAMB).

Boiled young wild rabbit à l'anglaise. LAPEREAU BOUILLI À L'ANGLAISE – Draw the rabbit by making a very small incision in the belly. Stuff it with a stuffing *à l'anglaise* made from one-third veal or ox kidneys, one-third best veal fat or udder, one-third sandwich bread soaked in milk and squeezed dry. Add 1 egg to every $\frac{1}{2}$ kg. (18 oz.) stuffing. Season with salt, pepper and spices. Having stuffed the rabbit, sew up the opening and truss. Simmer it in salted water for about 1 hour. Serve with *Caper sauce* (see SAUCE).

Young wild rabbit chasseur, or sautéed with mushrooms. LAPEREAU SAUTÉ AUX CHAMPIGNONS, CHASSEUR – Joint the rabbit. Season with salt, pepper, thyme and powdered bay leaf and cook with mushrooms or *chasseur*, following the recipes given under VEAL, *Sautéed veal chasseur*, or *with mushrooms*.

Young wild rabbit en gibelotte. LAPEREAU EN GIBELOTTE – This is prepared in exactly the same way as *Civet of hare* (see HARE) except that white wine is often used instead of red wine. It is also quite usual to add quartered potatoes or small potato balls to this *gibelotte*.

Potted wild rabbit or pâté. PÂTÉ OU TERRINE DE LAPEREAU – These preparations are made with boned rabbit stuffed with pork in the same way as *Potted hare* or *Pâté of hare* (see HARE).

Roast young wild rabbit. LAPEREAU RÔTI – Proceed as for *Roast hare* (see HARE).

Young wild rabbit sautéed à la minute. LAPEREAU SAUTÉ À LA MINUTE – Skin, draw and joint the rabbit, taking care the bones do not splinter. Season with salt and pepper.

Brown it quickly in very hot butter in a heavy iron pan until all the pieces are a good colour. Shake the pan frequently and turn over the pieces so that they are cooked all through. As soon as it is ready, put the rabbit in a pie dish and keep it warm.

Dilute the pan juices with $1\frac{1}{2}$ dl. ($\frac{1}{4}$ pint, $\frac{2}{3}$ cup) white wine. Add 1 chopped shallot. Boil down the sauce until it is very concentrated. Add thickened brown veal stock.

Boil for a few seconds. Add 1 tablespoon butter and a squeeze of lemon juice. Pour over the rabbit. Sprinkle with chopped parsley.

RABIOLE – Variety of kohl-rabi or turnip.

RABOTTE or DOUILLON – Fruit dumpling of Norman origin. The fruit, mostly apple or pear, is enclosed in a shortcrust pastry to make a *douillette* (a priest's overcoat), from which word comes its name. It is then cooked in the oven.

RACAHOUT – Mixture of starches which, according to Dorvault, must be made in the following proportions: 50 g. (2 oz.) each of cocoa, acorn flour and rice flour; 45 g. ($1\frac{1}{2}$ oz.) potato flour, 15 g. ($\frac{1}{2}$ oz.) salep, 250 g. (9 oz.) white sugar, 5 g. ($\frac{1}{5}$ oz.) vanilla sugar. Prepared like drinking chocolate.

RACHEL – See GARNISHES.

RACLETTE – Variety of Swiss cheese *fondue*, speciality of the canton of Valais, made by holding a big piece of the local cheese to the fire and scraping off the softened part as it melts. The cheese scrapings are eaten with jacket potatoes and accompanied by Fendant, the heady white wine of Valais.

RACOON. RATON-LAVEUR – Small wild animal, with longish grey fur, living in the forests of America. It is edible and cooked like wild rabbit.

RADISH. RADIS – Plant of the *Cruciferae* family, of which the root is edible. Cultivated in China, Japan and the Indies in the most remote areas, the radish is found now in all the temperate regions of Europe.

There are a great many varieties of radish: round, long, pink, black, white and purple.

All the radishes are eaten raw as *hors-d'œuvre* with butter and salt.

The tender leaves of pink radishes can also be eaten. Raw, they are put in salad; cooked, they are used like spinach.

Pink radishes may also be served hot, cooked like new turnips.

Black radishes. RADIS NOIRS – After having been peeled, black radishes are cut into rounds and put to soak in salt for 30 minutes.

The rounds are then washed and served in a radish dish.

Pink radishes in cream. RADIS ROSES À LA CRÈME – Peel the radishes and blanch in salted water. Drain and stew in butter. When they are cooked add the cream, allowing $3\frac{1}{2}$ dl. (generous $\frac{1}{2}$ pint, $1\frac{1}{2}$ cups) cream for every 500 g. (18 oz.) radishes. Boil down the cream by one-third. Serve in a deep dish.

Glazed pink radishes. RADIS ROSES GLACÉS – Peel the radishes, blanch them for 5 minutes in salted water, drain and cool in cold water. Toss in butter over a good heat, sprinkling them with a little sugar. When they are lightly coloured moisten them with sufficient stock or water barely to cover them. Simmer covered, until they have absorbed all the liquid. At this point the radishes should be cooked and well glazed.

If they are still hard, add more liquid and boil down once more.

Pink radishes in stock. RADIS ROSES AU JUS – Cook the radishes in salt water. When they are cooked drain them and moisten with a few tablespoons of meat stock boiled down until it is thick and brown. Simmer gently.

Pink radishes poulette. RADIS ROSES À LA POULETTE – Cook the radishes as above, moistening them with *Poulette sauce* (see SAUCE). Simmer gently in the sauce.

RAGOÛT – *Ragoûts* are made from meat, fowl or fish cut in pieces of regular shape and size, browned or cooked without colouring and with or without an accompaniment of vegetables.

The 'brown' *ragoûts*, of which the best-known type is the *Ragoût of mutton* or *Navarin of mutton* (see MUTTON), are prepared by frying the meat lightly, sprinkling with flour and adding stock, meat juices or water.

The uncoloured *ragoûts* – *à blanc*, sometimes described as *à l'anglaise*, which must not be confused with *blanquettes* and *fricassées* – belong to the category of poached food. They have no thickening other than that created by the addition of potatoes to their preparation. Typical of these *ragoûts* is Irish stew.

Also included under the name of *ragoûts* are various garnishes, composed of one or more ingredients, bound with a white or brown liaison, with a meat or meatless stock, used in preparing *entrées*, or to embellish fish, fowl, eggs and other preparations. (See GARNISHES.)

It is as well to note that meat *ragoûts*, especially those incorporating a *roux* (q.v.), are particularly indigestible. According to the dieticians, only those with excellent constitutions should eat *ragoûts*.

Round pan for ragoûts (*Larousse*)

Method of cooking 'brown' ragoûts. Cut up the meat, whether boned or not, into pieces about 5 cm. (2 inches) long. Brown them over a good heat in a sauté pan, in smoking hot clarified fat. Season with salt, pepper and a pinch of sugar (the addition of sugar gives the preparation a good natural colour).

As soon as the pieces of meat are browned, pour off three-quarters of the fat. Sprinkle with flour and let it colour a little, shaking the pan over the heat. Stir in water, stock or meat juice; add a *bouquet garni* (q.v.) and, if the type of *ragoût* calls for it, crushed garlic and tomato sauce. Cook, covered, in the oven or on a very low heat for 45 minutes to 1 hour.

Drain the pieces of meat; trim them, put them in another pot or in the same pot – cleaned – in which they were cooked, cover them with the specified vegetables and pour over the sauce, strained and with the fat removed.

Cook covered, simmering very gently, for 45 minutes to 1 hour according to the kind of meat being used. Cooking in the oven is best.

Serve in a dish or deep plate, putting the pieces of meat below and the vegetables on top. Pour the boiling hot sauce over all.

The method recommended above (trimming the drained pieces and putting them in another pot with the strained and de-greased sauce) gives a better-looking dish. In home cooking, this complication can be avoided and the accompanying vegetables can be put directly into the *ragoût* without changing pots.

Method of cooking for ragoûts à blanc or à l'anglaise. Put the pieces of meat, cut in pieces as above, in a sauté pan, alternately with layers of potatoes cut in slices, and chopped onions. Season with salt and pepper and put a *bouquet garni* in the centre.

Pour over water or stock in sufficient quantity to cover meat and vegetables. Start cooking on a good heat, then cover and cook in the oven or over a very low heat for about $1\frac{1}{2}$ hours.

Serve in the same way as for the brown *ragoût*.

Ragoût à la banquière – Ingredients given in the recipe for *Banquière garnish* (see GARNISHES) mixed and bound with a good thick sauce.

Used as filling for pastry cases, *timbales*, pies, *vol-au-vent*.

Ragoût à la cancalaise – Poached oysters, bearded; shrimps; *Normande sauce* to bind (see SAUCE).

Used as filling for pastry cases, *timbales*, pies, *vol-au-vent*, etc.

Ragoût of celeriac. RAGOÛT DE CÉLERI-RAVE – Celeriac cut to look like 'pigeon's eggs', stewed in butter and bound in a *Cream sauce* (see SAUCE).

Same uses as *Ragoût à la banquière*.

Ragoût à la cévenole – Composed of braised chestnuts, small glazed onions, and coarsely diced streaky (lean) bacon, blanched and lightly fried, the whole bound with the cooking liquor of the braised meat which this garnish should accompany – or with thick, rich *Demi-glace sauce* (see SAUCE) flavoured with Madeira.

Ragoût à la Chambord – See CARP, *Carp Chambord*.

Ragoût chipolata – Composed of braised chestnuts, small glazed onions, mushrooms and chipolata sausages. This *ragoût*, which is bound with *Demi-glace sauce* (see SAUCE) flavoured with Madeira, is used as garnish for large cuts of braised or oven-roasted red meat.

Ragoût of cocks' combs and kidneys. RAGOÛT DE CRÊTES ET DE ROGNONS DE COQ – This *ragoût*, used to garnish poultry, as filling for *vol-au-vent* or other pastry cases, for rice borders, etc., is made up of cocks' combs and kidneys cooked in a flour-and-water *court-bouillon* (q.v.) and bound with a white or brown sauce according to the type of preparation.

Ragoût à la financière – This *ragoût* is used to accompany meat and poultry, as well as for filling *timbales*, pies, *vol-au-vent*, rice borders and other mixed *entrées*. It is made up of quenelles, cocks' combs and kidneys, truffles and mushrooms, completed sometimes with peeled olives and bound with *Financière sauce* (see SAUCE).

Ragoût à la Godard – See GARNISHES.

Ragoût of lobster à la cardinal. RAGOÛT DE HOMARD À LA CARDINAL – *Ragoût* composed of a mixture of sliced, cooked lobster, and slices of cooked truffles and mushrooms bound with very thick *Cardinal sauce* (see SAUCE).

Used as filling for pastry cases, *timbales*, *vol-au-vent*, etc.

Ragoût à la marinière – Composed in principle of mussels cooked in white wine and taken out of their shells, and shelled shrimps, bound in a *Marinière sauce* (see SAUCE).

This *ragoût* is used to garnish braised fish or as filling for tarts, tartlets, *timbales, vol-au-vent,* etc. It can be finished off with all kinds of shellfish cooked in white wine, with their shells removed.

Ragoût of molluscs. RAGOÛTS DE COQUILLAGES – Prepared by binding shellfish (mussels, oysters, cockles, clams, etc.) cooked in white wine and shelled, in a white sauce suitable to the nature of the dish.

Ragoût of mushrooms. RAGOÛT DE CHAMPIGNONS – Sliced, sautéed mushrooms bound with *Velouté sauce* (see SAUCE) mixed with cream, or with brown sauce boiled down with Madeira. The same uses as above.

Ragoût Nantua I – Shell 40 medium-sized crayfish tails, previously cooked in *mirepoix* (q.v.). Put them in a sauté pan with 1 tablespoon butter. Sauté for a moment over a good heat. Sprinkle with 1 tablespoon flour, moisten with 1 tablespoon of brandy and cover with fresh cream. Mix, cook over a gentle heat for 10 minutes, stirring often. At the last moment add 75 g. (3 oz., 6 tablespoons) *Crayfish butter* (see BUTTER, *Compound butters*) made with the scraps and shells of crayfish.

Ragoût Nantua II – Cook the crayfish tails for a moment in butter, moisten with brandy and cream and cook until it is reduced to half its quantity.

Add 2 dl. ($\frac{1}{3}$ pint, scant cup) crayfish purée prepared with the scraps and shells and *Béchamel sauce* (see SAUCE).

Crayfish tail ragoût à la Nantua (see CRAYFISH) is used to fill pastry cases, tarts, tartlets and *vol-au-vent.* It is also used to garnish egg and fish dishes of various kinds. Sometimes truffles cut in slices or little olive-shaped pieces are added to the *ragoût.*

Offal (variety meats) ragoût. RAGOÛT D'ABATS – *Ragoût* of this kind, used as a garnish for braised, poached or oven-roast poultry, and also to garnish *entrées* made with pastry, is made with white offal (variety meats), brains, and lambs' or calves' sweetbreads, sliced or cut in dice, with or without the addition of mushrooms and truffles, and bound with brown or white sauce.

Ragoût à la périgourdine – Mix *foie gras* cut in large dice and sautéed briskly in butter, with truffles cut in dice in the same way and cooked very lightly in butter. Bind them with concentrated cooking juices of the fowl or game to be garnished, flavoured with Madeira or some other wine.

Used as garnish for oven-roasted or braised poultry or game, and also as accompaniment to egg dishes of various kinds, pilaf, risotto, various borders of garnish and *entrées* made with pastry.

Seafood ragoût. RAGOÛT DE LANGOUSTE, CRUSTACÉS – Small slices of crawfish, lobster, prawns or shrimps, shelled, bound with a *Cream sauce* or *White wine sauce* (see SAUCE) and finished with *Shrimp* (or other crustacean) *butter* (see BUTTER, *Shrimp butter*).

Ragoût Talleyrand – Heat in a small sauté pan with a few tablespoons Madeira, 100 g. (4 oz.) cocks' kidneys cooked in flour-and-water *court-bouillon,* and 100 g. (4 oz.) mushrooms also cooked in flour-and-water *court-bouillon.* Bind with $1\frac{1}{2}$ dl. ($\frac{1}{4}$ pint, $\frac{2}{3}$ cup) chicken *Velouté sauce* (see SAUCE) mixed with cream, strained and with the addition of 2 tablespoons *mirepoix* (q.v.) of root vegetables and 1 tablespoon truffles cut in very small dice.

Ragoût à la tortue – This *ragoût* is the special accompaniment of calf's head cooked *à la tortue.* It is composed of quenelles, mushrooms, stuffed olives, sliced truffles, gherkins cut in small olive-shaped pieces, slices of tongue and calf's brain, all bound with *Tortue sauce* (rich brown sauce with Madeira added, flavoured with *Turtle herbs,* see HERBS) and completed with small fried eggs, heart-shaped pieces of bread fried in butter and crayfish cooked in *court-bouillon* (q.v.) these last ingredients added to the garnish when it is being set round the dish. (See OFFAL or VARIETY MEATS, *Calf's head en Tortue.*)

Ragoût à la toulousaine – *Ragoût* used to garnish poultry, *vol-au-vent* and other preparations served as *entrées.* Composed of chicken forcemeat quenelles, slices of lambs' or calves' sweetbreads, cocks' combs and kidneys, mushrooms and truffles, the whole bound with *Allemande sauce* (see SAUCE).

Ragoût of truffles. RAGOÛT DE TRUFFES – Under this name is described a garnish of truffles cut in thick slices or big dice and bound with either *Rich brown sauce* flavoured with Madeira or with a *White sauce* (see SAUCE).

Ragoût of vegetables or Ragoût à la printanière. RAGOÛT DE LÉGUMES DIT À LA PRINTANIÈRE – Put in a well-buttered sauté pan the following vegetables: 500 g. (18 oz.) new carrots, 12 little new onions, 3 medium-sized artichokes divided into quarters (blanched for 5 minutes in water with salt and lemon juice), and 2 lettuces, trimmed, blanched, divided in quarters and folded over as for braising. Pour over the vegetables either water or white stock just to cover them. Season, and start cooking over a good heat. Cook at boiling point for 8 minutes with the pot covered, then add $\frac{1}{2}$ litre (scant pint, $2\frac{1}{4}$ cups) freshly shelled peas and 12 peeled new potatoes. Cook in the oven, covered, for 40 to 45 minutes. Set in a deep dish. Pour the cooking liquor, boiled down and enriched with butter, over the vegetables.

This *ragoût* can be made with all kinds of new vegetables: fresh kidney beans, new broad beans, courgettes (zucchini) cut in quarters, asparagus tips, either white or green, cucumbers cut into small chunks, French beans, new turnips.

The *ragoûts* should be cooked in earthenware casseroles or in fireproof porcelain or bi-metal pots, and served in the pot.

RAGUENEAU – Parisian pastry-cook described by Cyrano de Bergerac in his *Voyage aux états de la lune,* and again by Edmond Rostand.

A pastry-cook of renown, keeping shop near the Palais, as fat as was suitable for a shopkeeper whose sign carried the words: *Aux amateurs de haulte graisse,* his days were spent happily between the supervision of his oven and the service of his clientele, which was composed of attorneys and lawyers, among whom had slipped in some hungry-looking writers.

Why did he have to begin to write? History suspects one Béis – an author today completely forgotten – of having maliciously drawn him into it.

The *pâtisserie* of Ragueneau became a kind of academy, where the pastries and tarts served as attendance tallies. Ragueneau set himself to write a Pindaric ode, then a tragedy: *Don Olibrius, l'Occiseur d'Innocents.*

He neglected his oven, neglected his clients; the effect on his business was such that he felt constrained to shut up shop.

Packing up his belongings into a miserable little cart, he set off for the Midi with his wife. At Béziers he sought out Molière, to whom he offered *Don Olibrius.* One may guess the response of the great humorist; but out of pity he offered the ex-pastry-cook a modest part as a valet in his troupe. Ragueneau was as bad an actor as he was a writer and he had to resign himself to the function of a candle-snuffer.

These functions he carried out subsequently at Lyons until his death, leaving as his whole fortune a hat with holes in it and a washed-out cloak. Among his papers were found four hundred and fifty-six sonnets, eight tragedies, seven epithalamiums, four elegies, sixty-three odes and nineteen heroic plays.

RAIDIR – Culinary term meaning to sear a foodstuff quickly in butter or other smoking hot fat.

RAIL. RÂLE – Name of two species of migrant waders, the *rail,* or in French 'king of quails', and the *water-rail,* very inferior to the former. Prepared like quail (q.v.).

RAISINÉ – Jam made by reducing grape juice or must to a jellied consistency. Often another fruit is added, principally pears.

Simple raisiné. RAISINÉ SIMPLE – Choose very sweet grapes, either green or black, strip them from their bunches and keep only the perfectly sound fruit. Put them in a pot over a gentle heat, and crush with a wooden spoon. Rub through a sieve, gathering the juice in a basin. Pour half this juice into a rinsed-out pan and cook over a strong heat, skimming from time to time. When the liquid rises, add a little of the juice reserved in the basin, repeat this each time it rises. Do not stop stirring until the cooking is done, which will be when the *raisiné* is boiled down by two-thirds.

Raisiné de Bourgogne – Prepare the must as described above, add sugar if necessary, boil down to half, then put in fruit (pears, quinces, apples, peaches, melon, etc.) peeled, seeded and cut into thin slices. Cook like the simple *raisiné* until the preserve is so thick that if taken between thumb and forefinger, it forms a gluey thread.

RAISINS. RAISINS DE MALAGA – Made from dried muscat grapes and eaten as dessert. They are also used in confectionery as an ingredient of cakes and puddings, and in cookery to garnish various dishes.

RAITON – Small-sized skate, usually cooked by frying. (See SKATE.)

RAKI – Alcoholic drink with a basis of plum or grape *eau-de-vie,* flavoured with aniseed and mastic.

RAMBOUR or RAMBOURG – Variety of apples whose name comes from the Rambour (Somme) district, where they were first cultivated. This fruit ripens in August. There is a *White* and a *Red Rambour.*

RAMEKIN. RAMEQUIN – Formerly toasted cheese was served under this name. Nowadays ramekins are tarts or tartlets filled with creamed cheese, this designation having, however, different interpretations in different regions.

Small pastries made with cheese-flavoured *chou pastry* are called ramekins. Individual earthenware baking dishes are also called ramekins.

Cheese ramekin I. RAMEQUIN DE FROMAGE – Add to 500 g. (18 oz.) *chou pastry* made without sugar, called ramekin pastry (see DOUGH, *Gougère batter*), 50 g. (2 oz., $\frac{1}{2}$ cup) Gruyère cut in small dice.

Pipe the paste on to a baking tin in the form of medium-sized *choux*, through a forcing-bag with a plain nozzle. Brush with egg. Put on top of each a pinch of Gruyère cut into very small dice. Cook in the oven at moderate heat for 12 to 15 minutes.

The ramekins may also be made in the form of elongated *choux*.

If a forcing-bag is not available they may be shaped with a spoon.

Cheese ramekin II (old recipe). RAMEQUIN DE FROMAGE – 'Take some cheese, melt it with butter, onion, whole or pounded, salt and pepper, spread over some bread, pass the shovel from the hot fire above it and serve hot.'

This recipe, an extract from an old instruction book, resembles *Welsh rarebit*, which is given in its alphabetical order.

Ramekin (Mont-Bry's recipe). RAMEQUIN – 'Put in a saucepan 1 glass of milk. Season with a good pinch of salt, a very small pinch of sugar and a very little white pepper. Add 25 g. (1 oz., 2 tablespoons) butter. Bring to the boil.

'As soon as the milk is boiling, put into the pot, which you will have taken off the heat, 100 g. (4 oz., 1 cup) sifted flour. Mix. Stir over the heat with a wooden spoon to dry out the dough, exactly as is done for *chou pastry*. When the dough is well dried, remove from heat and add 3 eggs, one by one, and 50 g. (2 oz., $\frac{1}{2}$ cup) Gruyère cheese cut in small dice.

'Put the dough into a forcing-bag fitted with a plain nozzle and squeeze it into *choux* on a baking tin. Brush with egg and put on top of each a pinch of Gruyère cut in very little dice. Cook in a low oven.'

RAMEREAU – Young woodpigeon. For its culinary preparation see PIGEON.

RAMPION. RAIPONCE – Plant cultivated in gardens, but also growing wild in the fields.

The root of rampion may be eaten raw or cooked. It is prepared like salsify. The leaves can be eaten raw in salad or cooked like spinach.

RAMPONNEAU – See RESTAURANTS OF BYGONE DAYS.

RANCIO – Red rosé wine of the Midi with Madeira-like taste. This wine is very sweet, and its taste is reminiscent of Spanish wines.

RÂPÉ – Abbreviation for *fromage râpé (grated cheese)*.

RASPBERRY. FRAMBOISE – Fruit of the raspberry bush which grows wild in woods or which can be cultivated in the garden. It is one of the most delicately flavoured fruits.

It can also be prepared in various ways – in jelly, jam, compote, sweet pastry and liqueurs. Distillation of raspberries results in delicious brandy.

The following are the best cultivated varieties in France: *Belle de Fontenay; Perpétuelle de Billard; Merveille des quatre-saisons* (red or white); *Hornet* or *Pilate* (non-climbing). The best are found on the Côte-d'Or, and in the neighbourhood of Paris. Raspberries are available from July to October.

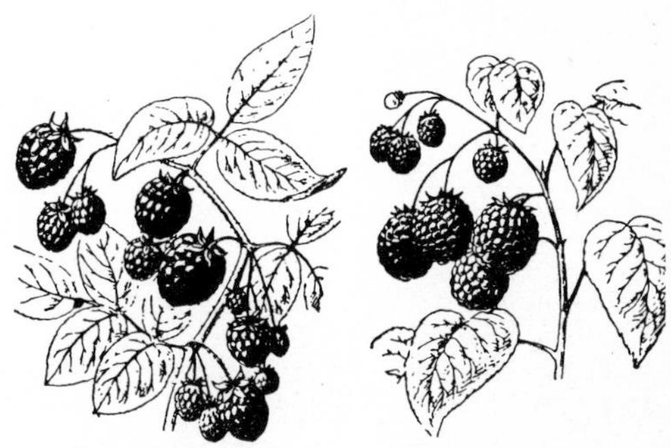

Raspberry: Merveille des quatre-saisons — Raspberry: Belle de Fontenay

Raspberry Bavarian cream. BAVAROIS AUX FRAMBOISES – This is prepared in the same way as other Bavarian creams with the addition of pulped raspberries. (See BAVARIAN CREAM.)

Raspberry charlotte. CHARLOTTE AUX FRAMBOISES – Line a mould with sponge fingers as for *Charlotte russe* (see CHARLOTTE). Fill the mould with a charlotte composition adding raspberry pulp. Put in the refrigerator. Turn out of the mould on to a dish covered with a folded napkin.

Raspberry compote. COMPOTE DE FRAMBOISES – Remove stems of very ripe large raspberries. Put in a fruit dish. Pour several tablespoons boiling syrup on the fruit.

Raspberry cream. CRÈME AUX FRAMBOISES – Add cooked raspberry pulp to custard made with a little arrowroot or cornstarch. (See CREAMS, *Custard cream.*)

Iced raspberry mousse or purée. MOUSSE, MOUSSELINE GLACÉE À LA FRAMBOISE – Made from raspberry juice or pulp (fresh or tinned) like other iced fruit mousses and purées. (See ICE CREAMS AND ICES.)

Raspberry juice or pulp. JUS, PULPE DE FRAMBOISES – Proceed with fresh raspberries as described for *Strawberry pulp* (see STRAWBERRY).

Raspberry desserts etc. – See also CRÊPES, FLAN, FRITTER, ICE CREAMS AND ICES, JAMS, LIQUEUR, SAUCE, SOUFFLÉS, SYRUP, TART.

RASTEGAÏS (Russian cookery) – See HORS-D'ŒUVRE, *Hot hors-d'œuvre*.

RAT – Rodent which was elevated to the rank of comestible during the siege of Paris in 1870, and which is eaten in certain regions. The flesh of well-nourished rats can be, it seems, of good quality, but sometimes with a musky taste. Rats nourished in the wine stores of the Gironde were at one time highly esteemed by the coopers, who grilled them, (after having cleaned out and skinned them) on a fire of broken barrels, and seasoned them with a little oil and plenty of shallot. This dish, which was then called *cooper's entrecôte,* would be the origin of the *entrecôte à la bordelaise*.

RAT-MORT, CAFÉ DU – See RESTAURANTS OF BYGONE DAYS.

RATAFIA – Liqueur obtained without distilling, by simple infusion (see LIQUEUR).

RATATOUILLE – Peel and slice 2 or 3 aubergines and 500 g. (1 lb.) Italian marrows (courgettes), sprinkle with salt and leave covered with a weighted plate for 1 hour. Slice 2 large onions, and 500 g. (1 lb.) skinned, deseeded tomatoes. Slice 2 peppers very thinly, removing core and seeds. Crush 3 garlic cloves.

Heat $1\frac{1}{2}$ dl. ($\frac{1}{4}$ pint, $\frac{2}{3}$ cup) olive oil in a heavy pan, fry the onion until slightly coloured, add the garlic. Cook for 5 minutes, then add aubergines, courgettes, peppers and tomatoes. Season with salt and pepper, add a *bouquet garni* and cook, covered, for 1 hour. This dish may be served hot or cold.

RATON – Pastry with a cream cheese basis..

Raton with macaroni (old recipe). RATON AUX MACARONI – Mix together 4 tablespoons (5 tablespoons) flour, 2 tablespoons (3 tablespoons) sugar, 10 lengths macaroni (broken into pieces) and 4 crushed almonds. Add 2 whole eggs. Mix well. Add 4 dl. ($\frac{3}{4}$ pint, scant 2 cups) milk and mix again.

Heat 1 tablespoon butter in a casserole. Pour the mixture over it. Begin cooking on top of the stove, stirring all the time, then bake in the oven for 20 to 25 minutes. Serve hot.

RAVIER – Small dish varying in shape and material, in which *hors-d'œuvre* are served.

RAVIGOTE – White sauce, hot or cold, which must, as its name indicates, be highly seasoned. (See SAUCE.)

RAVIOLI – Light preparation of pasta enclosing forcemeat of one kind or another.

The name of this preparation probably comes from the fact that in times past food left over from preparing meals on board ship was put into it. Until the beginning of the nineteenth century it was called *rabiole*, a word meaning something of little value.

Ravioli is made with pasta (see ITALIAN PASTA). After being stuffed with various mixtures the pieces are poached in salted water, moistened with veal or beef stock, and sprinkled with cheese.

To make ravioli. Roll out the pasta very thinly and cut out with a fluted cutter into rounds or squares about 5 cm. (2 inches) across. Put in the middle of each a piece of forcemeat about the size of a walnut, moisten the edges, and fold the pasta over like an apple turnover.

Or: Roll out the pasta into a piece about 8 cm. (3 inches) wide and as long as space permits. Set on this length of pasta a row of little balls of forcemeat about 2 cm. ($\frac{3}{4}$ inch) apart. Moisten the edges of the pasta and double them over, then cut into half-moons with a fluted pastry cutter.

Or: A square sheet of thin pasta may have little balls of forcemeat set out on it 2 cm. ($\frac{3}{4}$ inch) apart, lengthways and crossways. Moisten the spaces between them. Cover with a second sheet of pasta the same size. Cut out the ravioli with a special wheel cutter.

To poach ravioli. Plunge the ravioli into boiling salted water. Boil steadily for 8 to 10 minutes, according to size.

Drain the ravioli and set in layers on a *gratin* dish which has been buttered and sprinkled with grated cheese. Pour a few tablespoons veal or beef stock over each layer and sprinkle with grated cheese. Reheat or brown according to recipe.

To make ravioli: Using a forcing-bag place little balls of forcemeat onto a square of thinly rolled pasta (*Larousse*)

Cover each ball of forcemeat with a second layer of pasta and cut out the ravioli with a special wheel cutter (*Larousse*)

Ravioli forcemeats. FARCES À RAVIOLI – The fillings for ravioli are numerous, and meat and poultry left-overs may be used for them.

For a classic ravioli the forcemeat should be made with *Daube of beef* (see BEEF) that has been very well cooked, allowed to get cold and minced. The cooked ravioli is sprinkled with the cooking liquor of the *daube*.

Mixture I. Chop finely 150 g. (5 oz., generous cup) cold braised beef. Add 150 g. (5 oz., $\frac{3}{4}$ cup) spinach which has been blanched, drained and chopped, 50 g. (2 oz., $\frac{1}{4}$ cup) brain purée, 1 tablespoon chopped shallot, 1 egg, a pinch of salt, pepper and a little grated nutmeg.

Mixture II. Chop finely 150 g. (5 oz., generous cup) cold braised or boiled beef. Add 150 g. (5 oz., $\frac{3}{4}$ cup) spinach that has been blanched, drained and chopped, 50 g. (2 oz., $\frac{1}{4}$ cup) brain purée, 2 tablespoons (3 tablespoons) chopped onion lightly cooked in butter, 50 g. (2 oz., $\frac{1}{2}$ cup) grated Parmesan, 1 egg, a pinch of salt, pepper and grated nutmeg. Mix well.

Mixture III. Chop finely 100 g. (4 oz., scant cup) cooked veal. Add 100 g. (4 oz., generous $\frac{1}{2}$ cup) spinach that has been blanched, drained and chopped, 100 g. (4 oz., $\frac{1}{2}$ cup) brain purée, 50 g. (2 oz., $\frac{1}{4}$ cup) cream cheese pressed dry, 50 g. (2 oz., $\frac{1}{2}$ cup) grated Parmesan, 1 egg, a pinch of salt, pepper and grated nutmeg. Mix well.

Mixture IV. Proceed with cold chicken meat as for the forcemeat with veal above, replacing the spinach with blanched, drained and chopped lettuce cooked lightly in butter.

Mixture V. Pound in a mortar 150 g. (5 oz.) chicken livers sautéed in butter with 1 chopped shallot; 1 chopped clove of garlic and a pinch of salt. Add 100 g. (4 oz., generous $\frac{1}{2}$ cup) spinach, blanched, drained and chopped, 1 fillet of desalted anchovy, 50 g. (2 oz., $\frac{1}{4}$ cup) butter and 1 egg. Season with salt, pepper, grated nutmeg and a little basil. Mix well and rub through a sieve.

Mixture VI. Proceed with cold braised sweetbreads as for the chicken liver forcemeat, replacing the spinach by beetroot leaves blanched, drained, chopped and cooked lightly in butter.

Mixture VII. Chop finely 300 g. (11 oz., $1\frac{1}{2}$ cups) blanched and well-drained spinach. Put into a sauté pan in which has been heated 50 g. (2 oz., $\frac{1}{4}$ cup) butter. Cook, stirring with a wooden spoon. Season with salt, pepper and a little grated nutmeg.

Sprinkle the spinach with $\frac{1}{2}$ tablespoon flour. Shake for a moment over good heat and add 1 dl. (6 tablespoons, scant $\frac{1}{2}$ cup) milk.

Bring to the boil. Take the pot from the heat; add 1 egg yolk and 50 g. (2 oz., $\frac{1}{2}$ cup) grated Parmesan. Mix well.

RAY – See SKATE.

REBLOCHON – See CHEESE.

RÉCHAUD – Small portable stove.

Also a utensil designed to keep dishes hot when they are on the table. It is heated by hot water, a flame or by electricity.

RÉCOLLET DE GÉRARDMER – See CHEESE.

RECUIRE (RECOOK) – This expression is used for different kinds of pastry preparations where the mixtures are cooked in two operations: the first time in a bowl at a low temperature, as is done in making certain biscuits (hence their name), and a second time in the oven, with the mixture (already cooked) put into a special mould.

The term is also used in sweet making to define the operation of bringing to the desired point a syrup or jelly which after the addition of some watery fruit would have become 'uncooked'.

RED MULLET – See MULLET.

RED NETTLE. ÉPIAISE DES MARAIS – The roots of this plant are edible and can be used in place of the Chinese artichoke.

REDSTART. ROUGE-QUEUE – Bird of passage, prized as game. Prepared like lark in France.

REDUCTION. RÉDUCTION – Action of reducing the volume of a liquid by evaporation, particularly a sauce, which is reduced to increase the savour and also to give it a thicker consistency. A brown sauce which has been reduced is also more brilliant in appearance. (See SAUCE.) In the U.S.A. the process of reducing is known as 'boiling down'.

REDWING. MAUVIS – Small type of thrush.

REFRIGERATION. FRIGORIFIQUE – Low temperatures can be produced by various means, the simplest being the use of freezing mixtures. These mixtures have a number of domestic uses including the preparation of ice creams and water ices.

For lower temperatures, it is necessary to use a refrigerator. Refrigerators generally work on the principle of the lowering of temperature, either through the expansion of a gas or the evaporation of a volatile liquid. There are a number of highly volatile liquids and gases which can be readily liquefied, for example, ammonia, carbonic acid gas, methyl chloride, etc. All these liquids give off a gas which is compressed to raise its temperature. It then passes through a condenser which absorbs the heat and liquefies the gas. Next, it passes through a pressure-reducing valve into an expansion chamber, thus producing the required lowering of temperature. The gas is then pumped back into the condenser, and the cycle begins again and is repeated indefinitely, as long as the motor-driven compressor is kept working.

Some refrigerators have no compressors. These work by absorption and are dependent upon the ratio of solubility to temperature in the interaction of ammonia and water. In an absorber cooled by water circulation, the greater part of the ammonia liquefies as though it had been sucked in by a pump. Next, the solution, thus enriched, passes into a distiller, heated by one of a number of methods (steam, gas or electricity). Here the ammonia is given off by the solution and collects in the enclosed chamber as though it had been compressed by piston-action. The expansion takes place at the outlet of the distiller, and causes a lowering of temperature, as with compressor refrigeration. This process is used

Réchaud with candles, and an electric réchaud
(*La Carpe. Phot. Nicolas*)

especially in certain types of domestic refrigerator. In large industrial refrigerators, an intermediate cooler is generally used. This may be a system of ventilation or a non-freezing brine which circulates through the pipes laid in the cold-cupboard or refrigeration chamber.

Finally, mention must be made of a modern method of refrigeration in which the place of ice is taken by solidified carbonic acid gas. This is much less bulky than ice and has the further advantage of producing a lower temperature without any liquid condensation whatsoever.

Refrigerator (*Philips. Phot. X*)

REFRIGERATOR. RÉFRIGÉRATEUR – Apparatus, usually made in the form of a cupboard, working by gas or electricity, used to refrigerate and conserve foodstuffs.

RÉGALADE – To drink *à la régalade* is to drink from a bottle without letting it touch the lips, in such a way that the liquid is poured directly into the mouth.

RÉGENCE – See RESTAURANTS OF BYGONE DAYS.

RÉGENCE – See GARNISHES.

REGIONAL COOKING IN FRANCE. CUISINE RÉGIONALE – The various French provinces have each their particular *cuisine*. However, it should be observed that the dishes with a regional name are not always authentically and exclusively regional.

Real culinary specialities are numerous in some regions of France. For convenience these have been treated as a separate study, giving the principal local dishes and main food products. This information will be found under ALSACE, ANJOU, ARTOIS, AUVERGNE, BRESSE, BRITTANY, CHAMPAGNE, LANGUEDOC, NORMANDY, PROVENCE, etc.

REINDEER. RENNE – The flesh of this animal provides venison, inferior, however, to that of the roebuck or deer. Prepared in the same way as these last. (See ROEBUCK.)

REINE (À LA) – See FRENCH CULINARY NAMES.

REINE (Queen) – A category of chicken whose size is intermediate between *poulet de grain* and the fat hen or *poularde*.

The name is also given to a preparation of chicken purée, or of a mixture of cut-up chicken with mushrooms and truffles bound with an *Allemande sauce* or chicken *velouté sauce*. The name is also given to a thick soup made with chicken purée.

REINETTE – See APPLE.

RÉJANE – See GARNISHES.

RELÂCHER – Culinary term meaning to add liquid to a purée or sauce to thin it to the desired consistency.

RELIEFS – French term for the remains or left-overs of a meal; food which is not used at table.

RELIGIEUSE – This gâteau, which appears to have originated in Paris, is made with éclairs filled with coffee, chocolate or vanilla-flavoured cream, iced with fondant and superimposed one on top of the other; or with *choux* similarly filled and iced, rising in a pyramid one on top of the other.

The éclairs and *choux* are set on a base of sweet pastry and decorated with piped cream.

The name *religieuse* is also used for a pastry made by spreading a strip of puff pastry with a mixture of apple jam, apricot jam and currants, and covering it with strips of pastry in a criss-cross pattern.

Religieuse

REMONDOU – See CHEESE.

REMONTER – Term meaning to add a condiment to a sauce or *ragoût* to heighten its taste, or to add alcohol to a wine to give it greater strength.

RÉMOULADE – Mayonnaise to which gherkins, capers, parsley, spring onions, chervil, chopped tarragon and anchovy essence are added.

REMOVE. RELEVÉ – Dish which, in French, 'relieves' (in the sense that one sentry relieves another) the soup or the fish. This course precedes the *entrée*.

RENAISSANCE (À LA) – Garnish of various new vegetables, arranged in little heaps around pieces of meat served as *entrées*, generally roasts.

RENNET. PRÉSURE – Ferment having the property of coagulating the casein of milk.

Animal rennet. PRÉSURE ANIMALE – This substance, which comes from the abomasum or fourth stomach of calves, lambs and kids, is used to curdle milk in the cheese industry. An extract, marketed commercially in liquid or paste form (solid rennet), is most often used for this purpose.

Vegetable rennets. PRÉSURES VÉGÉTALES – Substances contained in certain plants (thistle, yellow bedstraw, common fig, etc.) having the property of coagulating milk.

REPÈRE – Mixture of flour and egg white, used to stick together the sections of a decoration or to fix them to a dish. For this latter use it is advisable to heat the dishes (if metal) before sticking on decorations with *repère*.

The flour-and-water paste, which is used to seal casseroles and *marmites* during cooking, is sometimes erroneously referred to as *repère*.

RESTAURANT – A public establishment where food is served. The origin of restaurants, as we know them, is not very old. In the eighteenth century one could eat only in the inns, which served at fixed times an equally fixed menu, or at the shops of the *traiteurs* (eating-house keepers) who could only sell whole pieces of food.

In 1765 a man named Boulanger, a vendor of soup in the Rue Poulies, gave to his soups the name of *restaurants,* i.e. restoratives, and inscribed on his sign: 'Boulanger sells magical restoratives', a notice which he embellished with a joke in culinary Latin: *Venite ad me; vos qui stomacho laboratis et ego restaurabo vos.* (Come to me, you whose stomach labours, and I will restore you.)

Wishing to augment his menus and unable to serve sauces or *ragoûts* because he was not a member of the corporation of *traiteurs,* he had the idea of offering his clients sheep's feet in white wine sauce. The *traiteurs* did not fail to bring a lawsuit against him, which was a tremendous advertisement for the innovator and his sheep's feet. In the end, Boulanger won the case, a solemn judgement of Parliament having decreed that sheep's feet in white sauce were not a *ragoût*. This was a great triumph; all Paris rushed to Boulanger's to taste this extraordinary dish on the recommendation of Moncrif, who raved about it. Louis XV himself had it served at Versailles, but the king, who was a real gourmand, did not share the general enthusiasm.

It is nevertheless true that Boulanger created, as Brillat-Savarin says, a profession which commands a fortune for all who pursue it with good faith, orderliness and skill.

After Boulanger, the first restaurant worthy of the name was that which Beauvilliers founded in 1783 – an establishment which, because of the revolutionary activities of 1793, its founder felt himself obliged to close. Then followed the restaurant which Barthélémy, Maneille and Simon opened in 1786 at the Palais-Royal under the sign *'Aux Trois Frères Provençaux',* although they were neither brothers nor Provençal. This restaurant shut its doors in 1869, and it was in this house that Dugléré, Casimir Moisson and several other great *cuisiniers* of the nineteenth century carried out their first campaigns.

The progress in the culinary art which restaurants have brought about is immense. 'Connoisseurs', says Brillat-Savarin, 'have kept in mind the names of many artists who have shone in Paris since the introduction of the restaurants. One may cite Beauvilliers, Méot, Robert, Rose, Legacque, the brothers Véry, Henneveu and Baleine (of the *Rocher de Cancale*) . . . Some of these establishments owed their prosperity to special attractions, as: *le Veau qui tette*, to sheep's feet (doubtless cooked *à la poulette*); *les Frères Provençaux*, to salt cod and garlic; *Véry*, to *entrées* with truffles; *Robert*, to specially ordered dinners; *Baleine* to the care he took to have excellent fish; *Henneveux* to the mysterious boudoirs in the fourth floor . . .'

Under the Revolution, following the abolition of corporations and privileges, the restaurants multiplied, spreading good cheer, permitting everyone, as Brillat-Savarin says, 'to make, according to his purse or according to his appetite, copious or delicate meals, which formerly were the perquisite of the very rich.'

Among the principal restaurateurs of this far-away epoch we may cite the two Marseillaise brothers, whose name culinary history has not preserved, who founded *'le Boeuf à la mode'*, and whose sign caricatured the fashions of the day. To the Terrasse des Feuillants came Legacque, whose establishment later got into difficulties and ended up as a fixed-price restaurant in the Palais-Royale. In the same period Véfour founded the Café de Chartres, and Baleine, at the *Rocher de Cancale*, was host to Grimod de Reynière's 'Jury of Tasters', Carême declared him a second-class *traiteur*, and his neighbour Philipe supplanted him.

In the new boulevards were established the *Café Hardy*, the *Café de Foy* which later became the *Café Bignon*, and the *Café Anglais*, opened in 1802. Bonnefoy opened in the rue de l'Échelle and then moved out to the boulevard Montmartre. Bonvalet competed on the Boulevard du Temple with the *Cadran Bleu*, directed by Henneveux and La Galiote; *Père Lathuile* Avenue de Clichy, where the allies established their headquarters in 1815; the *Moulin Rouge*, Avenue d'Antin, where Escoffier began: *Paillard, Vachette-Brébant, Voisin*; the old *Café de Paris*; the *Café Riche*, the *Restaurant Marguery*, and others, too numerous to mention.

Some very old restaurants are changing and becoming 'Americanised', which seems a great pity. Some become 'cold buffet counters', others become 'automatic', others again become 'cafeterias'.

Behind the scenes in a Paris restaurant
(French Government Tourist Office)

It is regrettable to see celebrated Parisian eating-houses thus disappear – or at least become transformed. French cooking has nothing to gain by these changes.

The wine shops, the *trouquets*, as they are familiarly known, where it is possible to eat, are also very numerous in Paris. In some of these houses, frequented by workmen and people in modest employment, the cooking is excellent, because it is simple and honest. It is still possible to find in Paris some establishments of this kind where one may regale oneself with succulent boiled beef, savoury pork with cabbage or a beef *'bourguignon'* done in the old-fashioned way. (See RESTAURANTS (BRASSERIES AND CAFÉS) OF BYGONE DAYS.)

RESTAURANTS (BRASSERIES AND CAFÉS) OF BYGONE DAYS. RESTAURANTS, BRASSERIES ET CAFÉS D'AUTREFOIS –

Boeuf à la mode – So called at the time of the Directoire, not in honour of the recipe, but on account of its sign which depicted a fashionably dressed ox, its shoulders draped with a shawl. This restaurant, in rue de Valois, closed down in 1936.

Despite several ups and downs, it had an excellent culinary reputation. The banquet inaugurating rue Antonin-Carême was held there in 1894. That excellent chef, Marcel Dorin, was its last proprietor.

Bonfinger – This brasserie, founded in 1864, rue de la Bastille has remained in the same family and altered very little. Its *sauerkraut, lobster mayonnaise* and clear spirits have been the delight of a century of Parisians.

Brasserie des Martyrs – This brasserie was frequented by Baudelaire, Aurelién Scholl, Monselet, Gustave Courbet, Claude Monet, Jules Vallès and a host of untalented bohemians that hung around them. Décor included candelabra in the form of caryatids and artificial flowers.

Brébant-Vachette – The restaurant Vachette, on the corner of faubourg Montmartre, was taken over by Brébant in the days of the Second Empire. Situated on the corner of boulevard Poissonnière and faubourg Montmartre, it was famous for its night meals, excellent cellar, and the literary celebrities whom Brébant welcomed with open arms. He fed them so well during the siege of Paris that a group of them, including Renan, Edmond de Goncourt and Théophile Gautier, who called themselves the 'Spartans', had a medal engraved in his honour. It bore an inscription describing how, during their fortnightly *rendez-vous* at the restaurant 'they were totally oblivious that they were dining in a city of two million beleaguered souls'. A fine token of gratitude for Brébant, who died in 1892.

Cadran bleu – Opening in 1773 on the corner of rue Charlot and boulevard du Temple, the property suffered somewhat during the storming of the Bastille, but that only enhanced its glory. Banquets and wedding feasts followed one another in an unending stream.

However, if one revolution increased its renown, another was to quench it. In June, 1848, the restaurateur, Bonvalet, installed an artillery battery (which he commanded) near the restaurant. The violence of the cannon shots was such that the building had to be evacuated.

La Cibot, concierge of *Cousin Pons*, was the 'beautiful oyster opener' of the *Cadran bleu* (Balzac).

Café Anglais – Founded in 1802 by Chevreuil, on the corner of boulevard and rue Marivaux (*'Anglais'* because of the Peace of Amiens), it became one of the most fashionable eating places in Paris. Its luxury attracted princes, emperors, society favourites and *demi-mondaines*. Duglèré was one of its greatest chefs.

The *café Anglais* closed on 1 April, 1913 (the building was due to be demolished). Suffice to say that this restaurant was responsible for creating *potage Germiny, Anna potatoes, soufflé à l'anglaise, sole Dugléré* and *chicken d'Albuféra*.

It is interesting to note that the panelling of the *'Grand Seize'* (the private salon of Offenbach's *la Vie parisienne*) is now in the *Tour d'argent* restaurant, the father of Claude Terrail having married the daughter of the last proprietor of the *café Anglais*.

Café des Aveugles – It used to be in the Palais-Royal and derived its name from an orchestra comprising a few inmates of the Quinze-Vingts (Hospital for the blind). This used to provide rather cacophonic background music to an (more or less) enraptured clientele. It was one of the earliest but by no means the only attraction offered by the arcade cafés of the Palais-Royal (then called Palais-Egalité).

Café de Flore – near the Deux-Magots (or rather it is the Deux-Magots that is near the café de Flore). *L'Action française* was created here during the Dreyfus affair. Maurras and Jacques Bainville and their disciples used to meet here.

Table of the 'Grand Seize' at the Café Anglais (*Harlingue*)

Appollinaire and a crowd of admirers and followers (among them André Billy and André Salmon) also frequented it. On 5 August, 1914, shortly after the declaration of war, Gide dined in this café with Copeau. More recently, Simone de Beauvoir worked in it alongside Jean-Paul Sartre. Existentialism was born here.

Café de Foy – This was at the Palais-Royal. It entered into history shortly after it opened when Camille Desmoulins emerged from it, with a leaf stuck in his hat, to harangue the crowd. The following day he stormed the Bastille.

Café Lemblin – Founded by Perron a few years before the Revolution. It was a very modest café situated at the Palais-Royal. Under the Empire, its standing increased, and it was here, during the Restoration, that several half-way officers plotted for a time to reinstate 'le Petit Caporal'.

Café de Paris – The first café of this name was opened on boulevard de Gand (boulevard des Italiens) in July, 1822. It ran successfully for 20 years, until the proximity of the *Maison dorée* enticed its clientele away. It disappeared in 1858. The proprietor of the building, Lord Seymour's mother, ruled that the café had to close every night at 10 o'clock.

Twenty years later, at the time of the inauguration of the avenue de l'Opera (1878), another Café de Paris was born. It disappeared after the last war.

Boulevard de Gand was frequented by Balzac, Dumas the elder, Alfred de Musset and many others.

All the elite of the Third Republic frequented the avenue de l'Opéra, and several great dishes were created in this Café de Paris: *shoulder of lamb Louis le Grand, snipe à la Diane, aubergines Opéra,* and, most important of all, *lobster Thermidor*. This was created by Léopold Mourier on the occasion of the triumphal revival of the historical play, *Victorien Sardou.*

Café de Valois – Modest but comfortable, this was the most frequented of all the famous Palais-Royal cafés. The monarchists (with Rivarol and Ange Pitou) met there at the beginning of the Revolution. It closed down in 1841.

Café des Variétés – Its destiny was closely bound up with that of the theatre with which it was associated in 1807. The two were so closely linked that, during performances, the café was completely deserted.

Under the Second Empire, it only closed for $1\frac{1}{2}$ hours in the morning. Villiers de L'Isle and Adam and Alphonse Daudet were among the many celebrities who frequented this establishment, famous for its onion soup. The bald Murger, dressed in black, scribbled *'billets doux'* on the marble tables to one or other of his 'shrews'.

Frequented by personalities of both the literary and theatre worlds, including the young Catulle Mendès, the mature Baudelaire and the ever-old Banville, the *café des Variétés* quickly became a success.

Caveau – This restaurant, situated at the Palais-Royal, was, as its name indicates, underground. Drinking hot chocolate or coffee with cream there in the period before and during the Revolution was a very expensive pastime. Lit by argon lamps, it was a favourite evening haunt. In 1802, it became the *café du Perron.* Its proprietor turned it into a restaurant which was renamed *Pavillon de la paix,* then *la Rotonde,* but it disappeared in 1885.

It was under the Consulate and the Empire that the *Caveau* had its most illustrious clientele.

Champeaux – Classified in 1843 as a restaurant 'with a reputation for good cooking', it gained celebrity in 1862, but only because of its winter garden.

Restaurant Champeaux, place de la Bourse, was a kind of haven for itinerant provincials who cherished the memory of their visit. The chef Catelain, who created *chicken Champeaux*, ended his culinary career there in 1904.

Deux-Magots – This was originally the sign of a hosiery shop in Saint-Germain-des-Prés: *'deux magots'* or, in other words, two grotesque Chinese porcelain figures. They are still there.

A café was opened here which American writers used to frequent before the war. Later the clientele used to stare at the antics of Sartre and company in the adjoining *café de Flore.*

J. Rosny frequented it, as, later, did Jean Giraudoux. The surrealists were there for a short time but were chased away by the students of *l'École des beaux-arts.*

Dinochau – At the corner of rue de Navarin and rue de Bréda. Dinochau took over the running of the restaurant from his mother. There he received the most famous journalists of the Second Empire, as well as poets, and a number of celebrated literary figures. Goncourt often mentioned the place in his *Journal.* The food was good and cheap, but Dinochau, nicknamed the 'literary restaurateur', allowed too much credit to his illustrious clients. He went bankrupt.

Divan Lepelletier – Situated on the corner of the street of the same name, this restaurant used to create quite a stir on account of the people who frequented it. Alfred de Musset went there to drink a curious concoction of beer, *eau-de-vie* and absinth. It seems that the Goncourts, too, found the beer there inferior.

Drouant – In 1880, an Alsatian called Charles Drouant opened a modest establishment that sold wine and food. Success came swiftly and the premises were periodically extended. The restaurant prospered and moved to place Gaillon. It acquired fame for its 'Goncourt lunches' which featured the fashionable *blanc de blancs.* Léon Daudet was an eminent gastronome who gave a great deal of thought and effort to the compilation of the luncheon menus. Unfortunately, these are not what they used to be.

Foyot – Formerly *café Vachette*: an establishment founded in rue de Tournon, 1802, by a certain Lacaille. It changed hands around 1817, Brébant becoming the new proprietor. (His son then took over the management of the café). Later it passed into the hands of Foyot and became *café Foyot.* Foyot had been Louis-Philippe's chef. His speciality was *sheep's trotters à la poulette.* He sold his restaurant to M. Lesserteur in 1854 and retired to his estate in the Bièvre valley.

A clientele of senators made this restaurant famous; the same establishment in which many years before, Cadoudal and Pichegru conspired against Napoleon.

It was while lunching at Foyot's in 1894 that Laurent Tailhade was seriously wounded by an anarchist bomb.

Veal chops Foyot is a classic gourmet dish.

Frascati – Founded in 1796 by the Italian Garchi, this establishment was a gambling den-cum-restaurant-cum-lodging house. Standing on the boulevard corner of the rue de Richelieu, close to rue Vivienne, its gardens were illuminated at night. Ice-creams, suppers, women of easy virtue, fireworks and, of course, gambling saloons – all could be found at Frascati's.

The restaurant lasted for 50 years. It disappeared on 1 January 1837, with the suppression of gaming houses.

Frères provençaux – Simon, Barthélemy and Maneille, three brothers-in-law from the Durance, set themselves up in rue Helvétius facing rue de Louvois. Simon and Barthélemy were employed as chefs by the prince du Condé and remained with him until he emigrated. It was Maneille who ran the restaurant *Frères provençaux.*

Under the Directoire, it was transferred to the arcades of the Palais-Royal, 38 galerie de Beaujolais, near the Montansier theatre.

The *Frères provençaux* deserves to be remembered for two important reasons: for introducing the Parisians to *brandade of salt cod*; and for being the nursery of great chefs such as

Paella: rice, *chorizos* (Spanish sausages), chicken, vegetables, lobsters, mussels and fish (*Restaurant la Paella. Phot. Nicolas*)

Hurel, Moisson, Dugléré, etc.

By 1869 the *Frères provençaux* had disappeared.

Frites révolutionnaires – Tavern-restaurant on the boulevard de Clichy, opened by Maxime Lisbonne, former communist, in 1888.

The clientele were waited upon by Napoleon III, Louis-Philippe, Boulanger, or Floquet, depending upon how they liked their chipped potatoes.

Grand Café – The underground salons of the hotel Scribe are its home today. It was here, on 28 December, 1895, that the first moving pictures were shown in Paris, an event that won it fleeting fame. Before then it had only been known for its billiards, and afterwards was forgotten once more.

Grossetête – Under the Second Empire, *Grossetête* (on the 'boulevard') did not enjoy a very good reputation. It served black-footed chickens (the type sought after among the Bresse chickens today). But people continued to frequent the restaurant because the cooking was good.

Hardy (Café) – In 1799, a modest restaurateur of les Halles district, called Hardy, opened a café at the corner of rue Laffitte. A striking innovation of this establishment was that it contained the first grill room in Paris. The client chose his 'victual', which was then cooked in front of him on a silver grill set in the white marble fireplace.

The best kidneys and cutlets of the capital were to be found there, it was said, as well as *andouilles stuffed with truffles* and *poultry joints en papillotes*. 'One had to be extremely rich to dine *chez Hardy*, and extremely hardy to dine *chez Riche*', was a remark attributed to Cambacérès.

It was on the site of *café Hardy* that the *Maison dorée* was built.

Helder (Café du) – This was situated at 29 boulevard des Italiens and was the *'rendez-vous* of officers and *saint-cyriens'*.

One of the waiters, Felix, knew the army list by heart.

Lapérouse – Rival in its time of *Magny, Lapérouse* had soon to open a first floor to accommodate its clientele. Then the rooms were transformed into private rooms. *Gratin of crayfish Georgette, navigator's woodcock, chicken Docteur* and *duck Colette* succeeded *Cancale oysters* and *entrecôtes à la manière de la Villette*.

Larue – Restaurant founded in 1887 by Larue, place de la Madeleine, and taken over in 1904 by Edouard Nignon, one of the greatest masters of French *cuisine*. It vanished after the last war.

Laveur – This was a boarding house with an unpretentious but excellent *cuisine*. The establishment opened in the present rue du Sommerard in 1840, moved to rue Pierre-Sarrazin, then to rue de La Harpe. Finally, in 1855, it moved to rue des Poitevins where it passed through the hands of Tante Rose, sister-in-law of the founder, Laveur.

Gambetta, Poincaré, Millerand, Loubet, Clemenceau, Daudet, Paul Arène, Coppée and Courbet ate there before they became famous. They sometimes paid a return visit to revive memories.

Leda (Restaurant) – Established in 1797 on the corner of the rues Saint-Anne and des Petits-Champs. It closed in 1852. Fulton was a frequent visitor when he was experimenting with his steamship on the Seine in 1803.

Talma, Dumas, David and Gérard de Nerval also dined there regularly.

Le Doyen – Opened in its present position in 1792 by Le Doyen, this restaurant was frequented by Robespierre when it was still the small popular *café Chez Doyen*. It soon became a *rendez-vous* for lovers of good food.

It was for a long time the meeting-place of the duellists from the Champs-Elysées. Here they made up their differences over cold trout and green sauce, a speciality of the house.

Lucas – In 1732, an Englishman called Richard Lucas opened the first English tavern in Paris. He offered cold meats and plum pudding (self-service). In 1862, Augis moved the establishment to place de la Madeleine and called it *Restaurant Lucas*.

Restaurant Le Doyen at the beginning of the nineteenth century (*J. Desmur*)

In 1925, the new proprietor, Francis Carton, president of the *Societé des cuisiniers de France*, added his name to that of the establishment.

Magny – In 1842, Magny, chef of the *Restaurant Philippe*, rue Montorgueil, set up his own restaurant in the present rue Mazet.

Its small but excellent cellar; its *sheep's trotters poulette*; the invention, in 1867, of *'petites marmites'* (individual portions presented on toasted bread croûtons); a remarkable *châteaubriand*; and a clientele consisting of Gavarni, Sainte-Beuve, George Sand, Renan, Goncourt, etc., made it the most famous restaurant on the Left Bank.

Maire – Opened in 1865 on the corner of boulevard de Strasbourg and boulevard Saint-Denis, it was famous for its Mercurey wine, its *entrecôte bordelaise* and its *macaroni Périgueux*. The Goncourts and their friends frequented it.

Maison dorée – This was opened in 1841 on the site of the defunct café Hardy, boulevard des Italiens. It was to have been called *'restaurant de la Cité'* but the public christened it *Maison dorée* on account of its gilded balustrades and balconies.

It was a luxurious establishment on two floors. The brothers Verdier were proprietors and Casimir Moisson was the last of its great chefs. No one in Paris knew better than he did how to make a *bouillabaisse* and he created the *timbale Nantua* while he was employed there.

The *Maison d'or* (another name for it) closed down on the last day of the year 1902. Characters from Balzac and Zola are described having supper at the *Maison dorée*.

Marguery – In 1820, a café called the *Maison Dauphin* was opened by Joseph Dauphin on boulevard Bonne-Nouvelle. Closed, then reopened, it became a soft drinks-cum-catering establishment. Finally, on 1 August, 1877, a certain Marguery secured a lease of the premises.

Marguery became one of the shrines of bourgeois gastronomy with an 'up-to-the-minute' décor. The cellar was marvellous and the *sole Marguery* all but caused *sole Dugléré* to pale into insignificance.

But despite the fashionable décor, the organisation, the

A selection of salad ingredients: lettuce, endives, chicory, tomato, beetroot and corn salad (*Phot. Nicolas*)

Mechanised washing of plates at restaurant Marguery in 1896 (*J. Desmur*)

magnificent *cuisine* and cellar, together with the bourgeois wedding feasts which were such a feature of the restaurant, *la Maison Marguery* did not survive its founder.

Méot – The restaurant *Méot,* which opened at the Palais-Royal on 26 May 1791, speedily acquired an extraordinary reputation. It was owned and run by Méot, formerly of the household of the duc d'Orléans. Word went around of baths filled with champagne; of 22 varieties of red wines and 27 varieties of white; and of a menu that offered a choice of at least 100 dishes.

It was here in 1795 that Grimod de la Reynière founded the *'Diner des mystificateurs'.*

Mère Saguet – This suburban café opened in rue Moulin-de-Beurre near the gate of Maine in 1784. It began to become well known in 1808 and was quite famous under the Restoration. This was the period in which Thiers, Charlet, Béranger, Raffet, Gavarni, Désaugiers and the brothers Hugo frequented it.

Mother Saguet, an excellent cook, was particularly adept at *rice à la Valenciennes* and *stewed cows' udders.* In 1830, tired of working, she closed down the restaurant.

Mille Colonnes – The success of this café at the Palais-Royal was due most of all to the beauty of the proprietress, Mme. Romain, who was nicknamed *'la Belle Limonadière'* ('the beautiful barmaid').

But when M. Romain (a very ugly man) died in 1826, his wife became a nun and the *Mille Colonnes* disappeared.

Mouton blanc – There was one in rue des Gobelins; another in rue de la Verrerie. Which of the two (or was there perhaps even a third?) was the legendary *rendez-vous* of Molière, Boileau, Racine and La Fontaine? Some say it was in Auteuil, where one of the poets lived. Others claim that it was in the *Mouton blanc* of rue de la Verrerie that Racine composed *les Plaideurs.* But how many *Mouton blanc* cafés were there in Paris in the seventeenth century?

Napolitain – It was while passing in a landau in front of the *café Napolitain,* boulevard des Capucines, that Lucien Guitry slapped one of his girl friends. She immediately began to shriek for help, whereupon Guitry, taking her tenderly in his arms, soothed, 'Don't be afraid. I am here.' The anecdote is all the more evocative since the incident took place during what was called the *'Belle Époque'.* Fashionable Paris witnessed the scene from the terrace of the famous ice cream café which had only just relinquished the name of *café de la Ville de Naples.*

The high society of Paris at that time selected the terrace of the Napolitain as their *rendez-vous* and there are countless anecdotes about such 'regulars' as d'Aurevilly, Mendès and Courteline.

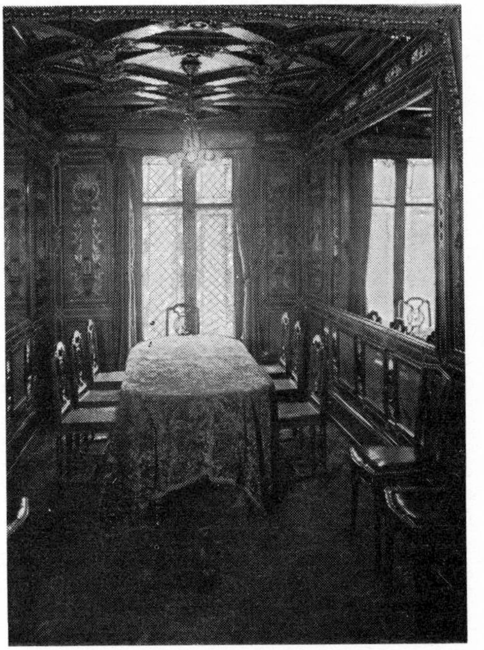

The 'Ebony salon' at restaurant Marguery

Noël Peter's – An American, Peters, founded this restaurant in 1854. It was situated in the passage des Princes and became *Noël Peters* because of his partnership with the Frenchman Noël.

At least, that is one explanation. Others maintain that it was the Frenchman, Pierre Fraysse of Sète, who, on his return to France (after working as a chef in the United States) in the second half of the nineteenth century, created this famous restaurant.

Monselet was received with honours. He gave excellent publicity to the restaurant in his chronicles.

According to Curnonsky, it was at this restaurant that Peters, alias Pierre Fraysse, created *lobster à l'américaine.*

Paillard – At the end of the nineteenth century, the elite of this period, from the future Edward VII to King Carlos of Portugal (whom the courtesans nicknamed 'His Lotion'), came here to enjoy *stuffed duck* and chicken archiduc.

Père Lathuile – Modest suburban café near the gate of Clichy, which Lathuile transformed into a restaurant in 1790.

General Moncey established his headquarters there in 1814 during the siege of Paris. Some cannon balls fired at him there made the name of Père Lathuile famous. A chicken dish with potatoes and artichoke hearts was dedicated to him.

A painting by Manet and another by Horace Vernet perpetuated the fame of this restaurant, which was frequented by artists, literary figures and carousing bourgeois.

Petit Maure – It was opened on the corner of rue de Seine and rue Visconti in the seventeenth century. They say that the poet Saint-Amant died there.

But there was also a Petit Maure at Vaugirard at about this time. There, one could enjoy the strawberries and *petits pois* that grew in the surrounding district, drink the local white wine, and eat the home-bred turkeys. It was still the countryside.

There were numerous *Petits Mores*: a sign of the times when anything exotic seemed to harbinger success.

Philippe – This began as a modest public house in rue Montorgueil. In 1820 it was serving grills.

Magny was head chef in 1842. From 1848 onwards, the ex-chef of the Jockey Club, Pascal, became proprietor, but he was struck by blindness and had to give up the restaurant.

Every Saturday at 6 p.m., the 12 members of the *Club des grands estomacs* used to meet *chez Philippe*. They spent 18 hours at the table.

Pomme de pin – This famous or at least evocative name was very popular in the eighteenth century. The well-known tavern in the rue de la Juiverie run by Robin Turgis was also called *Pomme de pin*.

François Villon frequented it (and usually received credit); Rabelais, another regular client, paid his bills on the spot.

This tavern was situated opposite the Palais de Justice. Théophile de Viau praised it in 1608 and recommended its 'class'.

Much later, Sainte-Beuve pronounced it a true 'classic tavern'. In the seventeenth century, writers were allowed to drink themselves into oblivion for nothing. This made for excellent publicity and helped the establishment to enjoy a long period of popularity.

Procope – This, they say, is the oldest café in Paris. At all events, it is the oldest of the cafés that still occupy their original sites; in this case, rue de l'Ancienne-Comédie.

It probably began as an establishment where coffee and ices were served, but it was original in that for the first time newspapers were provided for the clientele. The fashion caught on.

The *Procope* had so many famous patrons that it would be impossible to mention them all: J.-J. Rousseau, Beaumarchais, d'Alembert and Marmontel; then later, Gambetta and his friends. There were many other celebrities during the two centuries of its glory.

It closed down in 1914 and reopened after the Second World War. Medals on the walls recall its history.

Prunier – Opened in 1872 in rue Duphot by M. Alfred Prunier and his wife (an excellent cook) this restaurant swiftly won its 'stripes' because of its first-class oysters.

In 1897, Emile Prunier inherited the restaurant from his parents and introduced his own speciality, which was every variety of seafood.

Ramponneau – *The Grande Pinte* that formerly occupied the site of the Trinité church was taken over in 1760 by Jean Ramponneau, or Ramponeaux, who had previously owned the *Tambour royal*. The restaurant adopted the name of the quarter: *Aux Porcherons*. Its renown spread when it began offering white wine at half the usual price.

The restaurant expanded in 1778 when it was able to accommodate 600 people. The clientele was composed of market gardeners, waggoners, workers, and a few bourgeois and nobles who liked to frequent low company.

The tavern disappeared in 1851. Rumour has it that Jean Ramponneau abandoned the kitchen for the theatre, but no proof of this exists.

Rat-Mort – This tavern, situated in the place Pigalle, earned its name on the day a client found a dead rat under one of the benches. For a long time it was the *rendez-vous* of the Independents of politics, literature and the arts. Olivier Métra wrote his *Valse des roses* there.

Régence (La) – Founded in 1688 under the name of *'café du Palais-Royal'* it was rechristened *'café de la Régence'* in 1718. It stood on the corner of the former place du Palais-Royal and eventually fell under the pick of the 'improvers' of Paris.

It was this *café Régence* that was frequented by Diderot, Rousseau, Bonaparte (who used to play chess there) and later, Musset, advocate of the *'verte'* absinth.

Riche (Café) – Opened about 1832 on the corner of rue Le Pelletier and boulevard des Italiens and closed in 1916, by which time it had long since passed out of vogue. It reached its zenith when Bignon senior took over. Situated near the old Opéra (which was done away with in 1875) it was frequented by personalities from the theatre, literary and art worlds, the world in general, and the *demi-monde*. In some respects it was a victim of the 1870 war.

Among its specialities was *sole with shrimps and sauce Riche*, and Bouzy wine.

Café Procope. Old engraving
(*J. Desmur*)

Cabaret Ramponneau, from an old print
(*J. Desmur*)

Rocher de Cancale – Opened by Balaine at 61 rue Montorgueil, this restaurant was the centre for oyster connoisseurs at the beginning of the nineteenth century. Grimod de la Reynière chose it for the tasting sessions of his jury in 1808. The *Societé des mercredis* (with its 17 exclusive members) met there.

Borel succeeded Balaine. He, too, was an excellent chef. But the vogue of *Restaurant Philippe* was damaging to the *Rocher*. It was obliged to close down in 1860.

The characters of the *'Comédie humaine'* all met at the *Rocher de Cancale,* which Balzac himself frequented. The menu offered a selection of more than 200 dishes and 50 or so wines. The clientele was advised that 'half bottles were not served in the private rooms, and that heating was extra'.

It was here that the chef Langlais created *sole normande* in 1837.

Taverne Anglaise – Besides the English tavern *Lucas,* there was another opened in 1845 in route de la Révolte. It was moved to rue de Richelieu in 1870 and was the paradise of lovers of roast beef served with Yorkshire pudding and rhubarb tart. A butcher took over the establishment in 1876. People used to queue to eat there on feast days and Sundays.

Tortoni – Founded in 1798 by Velloni, then taken over by his head clerk, Tortoni, who called the establishment after himself. Tortoni was an ice cream maker as well as a restaurateur, and in 1830 was famous for his '*glazed meats,* his *papillotes of leveret* and his *salmon escalopes*'.

Tortoni's was *the* restaurant on the boulevard: the celebrities of the day, led by Roger de Beauvoir, appraised the pretty passers-by through their lorgnettes from the famous terrace.

Restaurant Tour d'Argent, Paris
(French Government Tourist Office)

Tour d'argent – Restaurant opened in 1582 by a certain Rourtaud and certainly the oldest in Paris.

It is said that Henri IV ate a heron pie there; that the first forks were used there; that Mme. de Sévigné praised the chocolate; that George Sand used to meet Musset there . . . And all the elite of the nineteenth century went to eat the *canard au sang* of the great Frédéric, just as one may still do today.

Véfour – Véfour was the name of the proprietor of the *café de Chartres* which enjoyed an excellent culinary reputation. In 1872, the name of the establishment was changed to the *Grand Véfour* and, according to la Reynière, its *chicken fricassée à la Marengo* was superb.

One of the brothers Véfour bought the *café de l'Europe* (also at the Palais-Royal) and made it into a restaurant.

It survived until 1920. The public nicknamed it the *'Petit Véfour'*. The great chef Raymond Olivier had made the *Grand Véfour* fashionable again.

Véry – Véry came to Paris from the Meuse valley and started his career as a kitchen boy. He turned out to be a remarkable chef and opened a restaurant at the Tuileries, the *terrasse des Feuillants*. Duroc, who was in love with Mme. Véry, lent him the support of his influence, which was enormous.

In 1808, Véry bought three arcades at the Palais-Royal and moved there. Success came rapidly. 'Impeccable décor, exquisite *cuisine*,' was the unanimous verdict of the clientele under the Empire. Fragonard died there. Balzac was reluctantly offered a Gargantuan lunch there by his publisher Werdet.

The *restaurant Véry* perished when a *prix fixé* was introduced.

A sketch of Labiche is entitled: *'Un garçon de chez Véry'*.

Voisin – A cellar famous for its Burgundy and Bordeaux wines; its clientele of Daudet, Zola, the Goncourts; its *saddle of lamb*; its *pâté de foie gras*; and a famous chef (Choron), assured the *restaurant Voison,* at the corner of rue Saint-Honoré and rue Cambon, a long and successful reputation.

Under the Commune, the English butcher, Roos, supplied *Voisin* with the finest beef and game from the Zoological Gardens. Goncourt used to dine with Arsène Houssaye on a famous *elephant pudding*.

Voltaire (Café) – This café, near the Odéon, had its hour of glory under the Restoration and the Empire. It was famous for its meat. Gambetta and Jules Vallès used to meet there when they came out of the *Procope*.

It disappeared after the Second World War.

RETICULUM or HONEYCOMB. BONNET – Second stomach of the ruminants.

RÉVEILLON – Supper eaten after midnight mass on Christmas Eve and, by extension, the supper eaten on Saint Sylvester's night (New Year's Eve) at the moment of the change of date. (See FESTIVE COOKERY.)

REVENIR (FAIRE) – French culinary term describing the action of browning various cookery ingredients in butter, fat or oil.

The object of browning meat or fish is to seal and render firm the exterior, but not to cook it. When complete cooking follows this operation, the words used are sauté for meat and *étuver* or *fondre* for vegetables.

REVERDIR – French cookery term meaning to replace green colour in vegetables which has been lost in blanching. The use of copper (which forms chlorophyl, an insoluble colouring matter) has been almost abandoned because of the metallic taste which it communicated to the food, and in the canning industry spinach green is used for this purpose.

RHINE WINES. RHIN, VINS DE – Excellent wines; most of them white. (See WINE.)

RHINOCEROS – Large, herbivorous, African and southern Asiatic pachyderm, very savage, whose flesh (mostly that of the young animals) is edible. It is preferred to that of the elephant by natives who consider hippopotamus meat to be even better, but the hippopotamus is now under protection.

RHUBARB. RHUBARBE – Plant originating in northern Asia, introduced into Europe in the fourteenth century. It was cultivated first by the monks as a medicinal plant, then as an ornamental plant.

The fleshy stems are eaten, either stewed in a compote or as jam. It can also be made into pies and tarts in the English style.

The leaves should not be eaten: they contain a large amount of oxalic acid. The root is a purgative.

Rhubarb is in season from May to July.

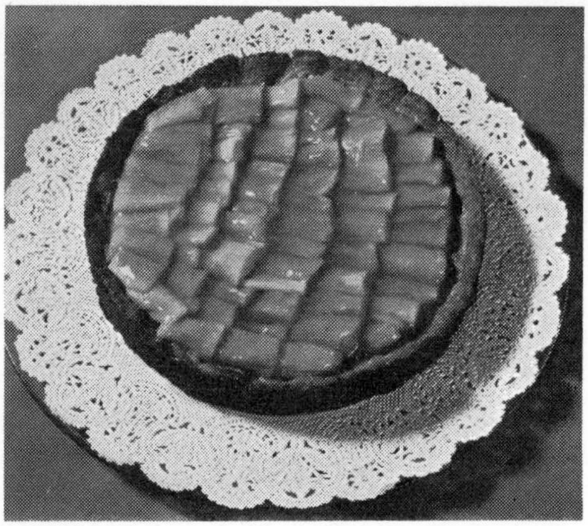

Rhubarb tart (*Claire*)

Compote of rhubarb. COMPOTE DE RHUBARBE – Divide the stems into pieces 6 to 8 cm. (2 to 3 inches) long. Peel them and remove strings. Arrange them in a copper pan and pour over very thick syrup to half cover them. Poach, covered, in the oven without stirring.

Serve in a compote dish. Pour the syrup over the rhubarb.

Rhubarb jam. CONFITURE DE RHUBARBE – Dissolve in a copper pan 800 g. ($1\frac{3}{4}$ lb.) sugar moistened with a few tablespoons water. Boil over a high flame for 8 minutes. Put in a generous 1 kg. ($2\frac{1}{4}$ lb.) rhubarb stems, carefully stripped and cut up. Poach on moderate heat with the cover on the pan.

When the rhubarb is nearly cooked remove cover, reduce heat and continue to cook, stirring all the time, until the rhubarb becomes quite tender and comes apart.

Put the jam in pots and cover them. Keep in a cool, dry place.

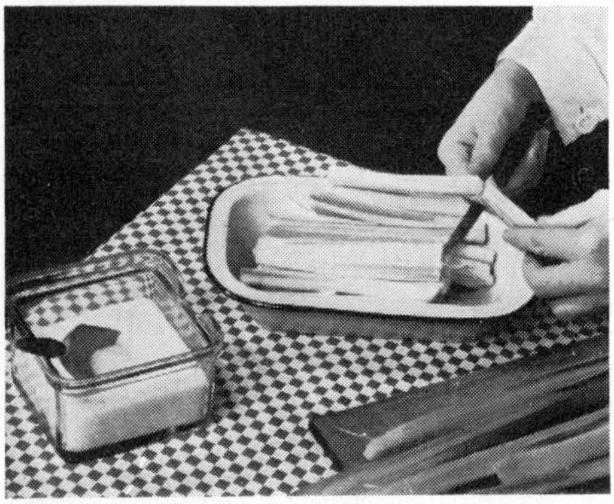

Preparing rhubarb stalks for a pie (*Claire*)

Rhubarb pie (English cookery). PÂTÉ DE RHUBARBE – Peel the tender stalks of rhubarb and cut them in pieces 3 to 4 cm. (about $1\frac{1}{2}$ inches) long. Arrange them in an English-type pie dish. Cover with sugar, add 2 or 3 tablespoons water and cover with a piece of pastry laid over a strip of pastry on the rim of the dish. Sprinkle with sugar. Cook at moderate heat in the oven for about 45 minutes.

The pie may be brushed with egg before being put in the oven. When taken out it is sprinkled with sugar and glazed with a hot iron or salamander, or under the grill.

In England, where this pie is very popular, it is served with double cream, whipped cream or custard.

RHYTON – Antique drinking vessel in the form of a ram's horn, generally decorated with a goat's head, without any flat base, so that the drinker was obliged to empty it before putting it down.

RIBBON. RUBAN – Mixture of sugar and egg yolks which, having been well beaten, forms folds rather like a ribbon that has been dropped from a height.

RICE. RIZ – Graminaceous grain, originating in India and China, introduced first of all into Egypt, then into Greece, where it was already highly prized at the time of Theophrastus. Its popularity spread to Portugal, then to Italy and America. In France Cardinal Fleury's first attempts to grow it in Auvergne were not a success. However, for the last sixty years or so, there have been rice plantations in the Camargue. Following early setbacks, these generally yield good crops (apart from years when weather conditions are particularly unfavourable). Rice requires a great deal of heat and humidity to grow well. French rice is of good quality although there is not enough of it to satisfy the demands of the home market.

Rice plant

Rice contains about half as much nitrogenous matter as wheat, but is richer in carbohydrates.

The four principal varieties of rice are: hard rice, mountain rice, glutinous rice and *fluitons*.

Rice is sold under various trade names that are not always accurately descriptive of its origin.

Carolina rice, long-grained, angular, white (or whitish with a blue tinge), bright and shiny.

Madagascar rice, large-grained, shiny.

Indo-Chinese rice, much smaller than Indian rice and an excellent variety. It cooks perfectly without disintegrating.

Java rice, more elongated grains, flat, transparent, shiny.

Japanese rice, uniform oval grains, hard, translucent, opaque at the centre, greyish white, shiny.

Patna rice, grains less hard, milky white.

Italian rice (Roman), greyish-white lustreless grains;

Piedmont, short, round-grain rice, very white and shiny, darker and opaque at the centre.

Cargo rice, unhusked, of Camargue. Rice cultivation in Camargue is less intensive than it was during the Second World War.

American rice, long-grained and usually pre-treated.

To cook rice – The peoples who depend upon rice as their staple food never stir while it is cooking and never cook it too long (average 20 minutes). In this way they ensure that the grains remain whole.

À la créole. Each separated grain is very slightly bite-resistant. This result is obtained by first rinsing the rice in cold water, then plunging it into ample boiling water.

À l'orientale or pilau-style. The rice is first browned in fat, then cooked in stock, which must be completely absorbed by the rice.

In milk. Instead of rinsing the rice in cold water, plunge it into boiling water for 2 minutes to get rid of the starch. Drain. Complete the cooking in milk (plain or spiced).

The French, it is said, do not know how to cook rice. In fact, it is frequently overcooked and instead of dry fluffy rice, there emerges a sort of pap, which is better suited to sweet than to savoury dishes. Nowadays, this dilemma can be avoided by using pre-treated, long-grain American rice, the grains of which remain separate even though overcooked.

Rice in dietetics – Rice is an excellent carbohydrate food, which contains about 79 per cent. starch. It is easily digested and nourishing: 100 g. (4 oz.) rice provides 340 calories. It is an important source of energy for those engaged in physical activities, but it is not a complete food. A diet based exclusively on rice can be damaging.

Various processes aimed at making rice whiter necessitate the removal of the outer layers of the grain (important source of minerals and vitamins) and detract considerably from its dietetic value.

Rice is given different names at the various stages of its development. *Paddy rice* is rice in its raw state complete with its *glumes* and *glumelles,* the fibrous ball to which it is attached. Once it is cleaned and husked, rice becomes *cargo rice.* This is treated in its turn to give *white rice* (the degree of whiteness depending upon how many times the rice is passed through the machines that rasp the grain). By the time the whitening process is completed, the rice has lost its pericardium and practically its entire proteic layer. *White rice* is transformed into *polished rice* by being passed through machines which remove any flour still adhering to the grain. *Shiny rice* is rice that has been specially processed to give it an attractive sheen. Unfortunately, it has been proved that husking, whitening and polishing (processes necessitating the removal of the grain casings) also take away precious nutritive elements. Proteins in the outer husk disappear when *cargo rice* becomes *white rice*; lipids become rarer the whiter rice becomes (mineral salts likewise); vitamins, especially those belonging to the B group, are present in *paddy rice,* but are considerably reduced during the whitening, polishing and shining processes.

The scarcity of vitamins in whitened or polished rice has serious effects in those regions where it constitutes the main source of nourishment. This vitamin deficiency is known as beri-beri. It is a deficiency disease unknown in Europe because of our varied diet.

The digestibility of rice is improved by the preparation it undergoes. Although the proportion of proteins in rice is only 7 to 8 per cent, they are a particularly well-balanced variety because of the amount of indispensable amino acids they contain. 75 to 100 per cent of the rice we eat is made up of glucides, which are easily assimilable. There are barely any fats. It is evident, therefore, that rice cannot satisfy our vitamin and mineral requirements.

To sum up, rice is a valuable food because of its energy-giving properties, but it must be subsidised by:

1. Animal protein (meat, fish, eggs, milk), or vegetable protein (pulses). Savoury and sweet rice containing milk, eggs and (in the case of the latter) sugar are extremely nourishing. Milk is the perfect complement to rice, adding, as it does, protein and calcium.

2. Fats. Uncooked butter (added at the last moment), uncooked oil, preferably olive oil, the type usually used for rice-based salads.

3. Mineral salts and vitamins in the form of green vegetables and fresh fruit, which ought always to be served in the course of a meal based on rice.

Boiled rice with butter. RIZ AU BLANC, AU BEURRE – Put into a saucepan with a flat, thick bottom 250 g. (9 oz., $1\frac{1}{4}$ cups) washed rice. Cover completely with cold water and season with salt. Blanch the rice for 15 minutes.

Drain, put into a sauté dish with 75 g. (3 oz., 6 tablespoons) butter cut in little pieces. Mix carefully with a fork, cover with a lid and put in the oven for 15 minutes.

Rice prepared in this way may be eaten as it is. It is mostly used as an accompaniment for eggs, poultry, fish, etc.

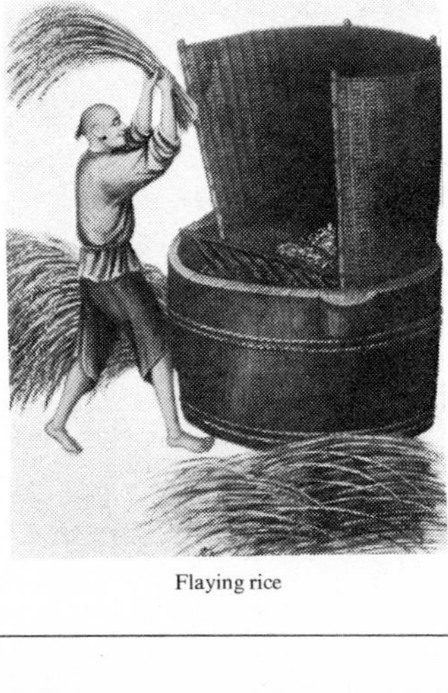

Flaying rice

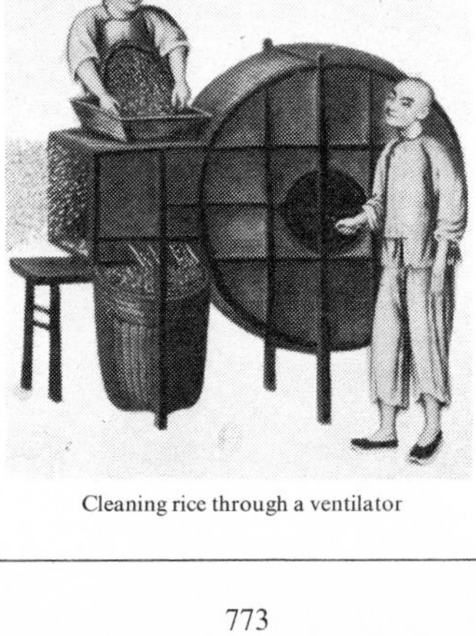

Cleaning rice through a ventilator

Sifting rice

Cooked rice (*Nicolas*)

Rice à la créole. RIZ À LA CRÉOLE – Take 1 kg. ($2\frac{1}{4}$ lb., 5 cups) Indian rice for 8 persons. Wash it in several waters. Put the rice in a thick pan with a little salt and cover with cold water. Cook on a good heat. When it is well cooked, lower the heat or set the pan, covered, at the side of the stove. It will continue to cook and will dry slowly. Allow 1 hour for cooking.

Rice croquettes – See CROQUETTES.

Rice au gras. RIZ AU GRAS – Blanch 250 g. (9 oz., $1\frac{1}{4}$ cups) rice, drain it, toss in butter and add to twice its height in the pan some *pot-au-feu* broth or rather fatty white stock. Bring to the boil. Cook, covered, in the oven, without disturbing it, for 20 minutes.

Rice à la grecque. RIZ À LA GRECQUE – Prepare the rice as for pilaf (q.v.) adding, when it is cooked, for every 500 g. (18 oz., $2\frac{1}{2}$ cups) rice measured uncooked, 1 chopped onion tossed in 2 tablespoons (3 tablespoons) butter, 50 g. (2 oz., $\frac{1}{4}$ cup) sausage meat divided into small pieces, 50 g. (2 oz., scant $\frac{1}{4}$ cup) lettuce leaves cut in thin strips and cooked in butter, 4 tablespoons (5 tablespoons) peas cooked in butter, and 50 g. (2 oz.) red pimentos cut in dice and cooked in butter.

Mix this garnish with the pilaf rice, taking care not to break the grains.

Rice à l'indienne. RIZ À L'INDIENNE – Blanch 500 g. (18 oz., $2\frac{1}{2}$ cups) rice for 15 minutes in salted water, allowing 9 g. (scant $1\frac{1}{2}$ teaspoon) salt to 1 litre ($1\frac{3}{4}$ pints, generous quart) water, stirring from time to time with a wooden spoon.

Drain the rice, wash it several times in cold water, drain again and put it on a napkin laid on a baking tin or a strainer. Fold over the edges of the napkin so as to enclose the rice. Put to dry in a warm place for 15 minutes.

Rice prepared in this way is the essential accompaniment of all curry dishes. It may also be served as accompaniment to other strongly seasoned dishes.

Rice pilaf – See PILAF.

Risotto à la milanaise – Prepare the risotto as in the following recipe. When it is cooked add a milanaise garnish and a little rich brown sauce which has been strongly flavoured with tomato.

(Milanaise garnish is composed of pickled tongue, cooked lean ham, mushrooms and truffles, cut into fairly coarse *julienne* (q.v.) strips and bound with rich brown sauce flavoured with tomato.)

Risotto à la piémontaise – Cook lightly in butter, without allowing to colour, 100 g. (4 oz., 1 cup) chopped onion. When it is cooked add 500 g. (18 oz., $2\frac{1}{2}$ cups) Piedmont rice.

Cook gently over a low heat, and stir and shake until all the grains are well impregnated with butter. Pour in, to twice the

Risotto à la piémontaise

height of the rice in the pan, some *pot-au-feu* broth or white stock. Repeat this five or six times, adding a fresh quantity of liquid only when the last lot has been absorbed by the rice. Cook this risotto, covered, for 18 to 20 minutes. Add to it, when cooked, 2 tablespoons (3 tablespoons) butter and 75 g. (3 oz., $\frac{3}{4}$ cup) grated Parmesan.

The risotto can be finished off with different ingredients, such as ham cut into dice and tossed in butter, mussels, fresh peas (which can be cooked with the rice) or black truffles, which are added to the risotto at the last moment.

DESSERT or SWEET RICE. ENTREMETS AU RIZ –

Dessert or sweet rice for croquettes and puddings. RIZ POUR BORDURES, CROQUETTES, POUDINGS – Wash 100 g. (4 oz., generous $\frac{1}{2}$ cup) rice, blanch it, drain and rinse in warm water.

Drain again and put it into a pan with 8 dl. ($1\frac{1}{3}$ pints, $1\frac{3}{4}$ pints) milk previously boiled with the chosen flavouring, 75 g. (3 oz., $\frac{1}{3}$ cup) sugar, 25 g. (1 oz., 2 tablespoons) butter and a small pinch of salt.

Begin cooking over a high flame, cover the pan and cook in the oven at a gentle heat until the rice is nearly cooked.

Take the rice from the oven and add to it 6 egg yolks, mixing them in carefully with a fork. Add more sugar, if needed. Use according to the recipe.

Dessert rice can be flavoured with vanilla, orange or lemon peel.

The proportions given in this recipe will provide the basis for a dessert for 6 to 8 people. If the rice is to be served without fruit or other accompaniment the ingredients may be augmented; and the rice should be completely cooked if it is not to be used in a dish which requires further cooking.

It is possible also to cook the rice as above, and on taking it out of the oven to bind it with 3 whole eggs. This method is less extravagant than the preceding one, but the rice is less delicate.

Creamed rice. RIZ À LA CRÈME – Cook with 6 dl. (1 pint, $2\frac{1}{2}$ cups) milk (previously boiled with the chosen flavouring), 75 g. (3 oz., $\frac{1}{3}$ cup) sugar, a small pinch of salt, and 100 g. (4 oz., generous $\frac{1}{2}$ cup) rice, blanched and drained.

When it is cooked add to it 2 dl. ($\frac{1}{3}$ pint, scant cup) thick fresh cream and 25 g. (1 oz., 2 tablespoons) butter.

Add a little more sugar if required. This preparation is used for making hot or cold sweets.

Rice flan or tart. FLAN, TARTE AU RIZ – Fill a shortcrust flan case (pie shell) with *Dessert rice* to within $\frac{1}{2}$ cm. ($\frac{1}{4}$ inch) of the edge. Sprinkle with sugar. Cook in the oven at a moderate heat for 25 to 30 minutes.

This sweet can be served hot or cold. It may be made with rice that has been mixed with chopped-up crystallised fruit soaked in kirsch or other liqueur.

Rice flan or tart with apricots. FLAN, TARTE DE RIZ AUX ABRICOTS – Proceed as in the above recipe, but fill the flan case only three-quarters full. On the rice place halves of raw apricots, soaked in kirsch and sugar. Sprinkle with sugar. Cook in the oven at a gentle heat.

Spread the top of the flan with apricot jam diluted with a little syrup and strained.

In the same way rice flans may be made with various other fruits such as sliced bananas arranged on the flan in a rosette, cherries, pears (in quarters and half-cooked in syrup), peaches (in halves, soaked in liqueur and sugar), apples, plums, etc.

Rice gâteau with caramel. GÂTEAU DE RIZ AU CARAMEL – Fill a large Charlotte mould, lined with caramelised sugar, with *Dessert rice*. Cook in the oven in a *bain-marie* for 25 to 30 minutes.

Serve hot or cold.

Gâteau or flan of rice with meringue. GÂTEAU, FLAN DE RIZ MERINGUÉ – Fill a buttered fireproof dish with *Dessert rice* mixed with crystallised fruit, cut in dice and soaked in kirsch or other liqueur. Build up the rice into a cake about 3 or 4 cm. ($1\frac{1}{4}$ to $1\frac{1}{2}$ inches) high. Cover with meringue, smoothing it all over.

Decorate the top of the flan with meringue piped through a forcing-bag. Sprinkle with sugar. Put into a very hot oven to colour the meringue lightly.

Garnish with strained apricot jam and gooseberry jelly.

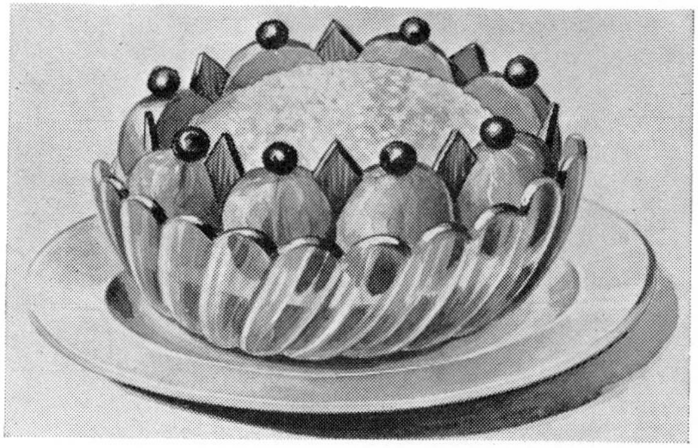

Rice à l'impératrice with a border of pears à l'impératrice

Rice à l'impératrice. RIZ À L'IMPÉRATRICE – Prepare *Dessert rice* flavouring it with vanilla. When it is almost cold, add 2 tablespoons (3 tablespoons) chopped up crystallised fruit soaked in kirsch.

Incorporate 2 dl. ($\frac{1}{3}$ pint, scant cup) thick custard (see CREAMS, *Custard cream*), mix and add at the last moment $2\frac{1}{2}$ dl. (scant $\frac{1}{2}$ pint, generous cup) whipped cream.

Pour this mixture into a Charlotte mould (or a *Bavarois* mould) the bottom of which has been spread with gooseberry jelly to a depth of a little less than 1 cm. ($\frac{1}{2}$ inch). Set on ice or in the refrigerator. Turn out into a glass bowl.

Many fruit desserts are made with a basis of *Rice à l'impératrice*. (See PEACH, *Peaches à l'impératrice*.)

Rice in milk. RIZ AU LAIT – Wash 100 g. (4 oz., generous $\frac{1}{2}$ cup) rice and blanch it. Drain, rinse it in warm water and put it back, well drained, into a pan containing 8 dl. ($1\frac{1}{3}$ pints, $1\frac{3}{4}$ pints) milk and a small pinch of salt.

Cook very slowly, with a lid on, until rice is tender. Add sugar if the rice is intended for a sweet, and if necessary lighten it with a few tablespoons boiled milk.

This rice is served hot or cold, and if served as a dessert, is flavoured with vanilla, orange peel or lemon peel.

Rice Montmorency. RIZ MONTMORENCY – Prepare *Dessert rice* flavoured with vanilla. Put into a glass bowl and decorate with banana slices alternating with cherries in syrup.

Rice pudding mould. PUDDING DE RIZ MOULÉ – Prepare *Dessert rice*. Incorporate in it, after having thickened it with egg yolks, 3 egg whites, stiffly beaten. Fill with this mixture a large Charlotte mould, buttered and sprinkled with breadcrumbs.

Cook in the oven in a *bain-marie* for 20 to 25 minutes. Leave for a few minutes before turning out of the mould. Serve with fruit sauce, custard (see CREAMS, *Custard cream*) or *zabaglione* (q.v.).

Ring of rice with fruit. BORDURE DE RIZ AUX FRUITS – Fill a buttered ring mould with *Dessert rice*. Cook in the oven in a *bain-marie* for 10 to 12 minutes. Turn out of the mould onto a dish. Fill the middle with various fruits cooked in syrup, cut in big dice and warmed in *Apricot sauce* (see SAUCE) flavoured with kirsch.

Put half apricots cooked in syrup on the rice border. Decorate with lozenges of angelica and crystallised cherries.

Pour over a few tablespoons apricot sauce flavoured with kirsch.

This sweet is also known as *Apricots Condé*.

Rijspap or saffron rice. RIZ AU SAFRAN – This pudding is very popular in the Flemish countryside.

Cook 300 g. (11 oz., generous $1\frac{1}{2}$ cups) rice in 1 litre ($1\frac{3}{4}$ pints, generous quart) milk lightly sweetened with brown sugar. Continue cooking this mixture until the grains of rice can easily be crushed. To colour the rice, add a small pinch of saffron.

Turn out the rice into flat plates, spreading it out well. Allow to cool. Sprinkle with brown or white sugar.

Subrics of rice. SUBRICS DE RIZ – Prepare the rice as for *Rice pudding mould.* Add chopped-up crystallised fruit soaked in liqueur. Spread evenly, about 3 cm. (1 inch) thick, on a buttered baking dish. Dot the surface with butter to prevent the rice from getting dry. Allow to cool.

Cut into rounds about 5 cm. (2 inches) in diameter. Put them into a pan in which clarified butter has been heated; colour them on both sides.

Arrange the subrics in a crown on a round dish and put in the middle of each 1 teaspoon gooseberry jelly or any other firm jam.

Vanilla rice à la Bourbon (Créole cookery). RIZ VANILLÉ À LA BOURBON – Cook gently in 1 litre ($1\frac{3}{4}$ pints, generous quart) milk 3 tablespoons (scant $\frac{1}{4}$ cup) rice previously blanched and drained well, until it becomes a porridge. Add sugar and vanilla to taste.

When the rice has cooled, add 3 egg yolks. Beat the whites separately into a stiff foam and fold them into the rice before turning into a deep, lightly buttered dish. Bake in the oven for 20 minutes. Sprinkle with sugar and serve in the dish in which it was cooked in the oven.

Rice water. EAU DE RIZ – Boil 25 g. (1 oz., 2 tablespoons) rice in 1 litre ($1\frac{3}{4}$ pints, generous quart) water until it is soft. Flavour with 25 g. (1 oz.) liquorice or 50 g. (2 oz.) quince syrup, replacing these with saccharine when sugar is forbidden.

RICEYS CENDRÉ – See CHEESE.

RICHE (Café) – See RESTAURANTS OF BYGONE DAYS.

RICHE (À LA) – Method of preparing fish, particularly sole. It was at the *Café Riche,* a Parisian establishment which has now disappeared, that *Riche sauce* was created (see SAUCE).

RICHEBOURG (Wine). RICHEBOURG (VIN DE) – Great *appellation controlée* vineyard of the Côte de Nuits, situated in the *commune* of Vosne-Romanée. Produces renowned, elegant, aromatic red wines. (See BURGUNDY.)

RICHELIEU (À LA) – Name given to various preparations.

In the first place the word describes a garnish composed of stuffed tomatoes and mushrooms, braised lettuce and potatoes lightly roasted in butter.

The term *à la Richelieu* also applies to a method of preparing fillets of sole or other fish. The fillets are coated in egg and breadcrumbs, cooked in butter, served with *maître-d'hôtel* butter and garnished with truffles. The name *'Richelieu'* is also given to a large sweet pastry, made as described below.

Richelieu (Pâtisserie) – *Ingredients.* 500 g. (18 oz., $2\frac{1}{4}$ cups) sugar, few drops vanilla essence, 375 g. (13 oz., 3 cups) almonds, 150 g. (5 oz., generous $\frac{1}{2}$ cup) butter, 150 g. (5 oz., $1\frac{1}{4}$ cup) flour, 16 eggs, 1 dl. (6 tablespoons, scant $\frac{1}{2}$ cup) maraschino.

Method. Pound the almonds finely, adding to them 2 egg whites and a little sugar. Rub through a sieve into a basin, add the sugar, vanilla essence, egg yolks and maraschino, and stir with a wooden spoon until the mixture becomes white.

Add the melted butter, sprinkle in the sieved flour, and finally add 10 stiffly beaten egg whites, Mix. Pour the mixture into shallow buttered moulds. Bake in a moderate oven.

Sandwich the cake layers with apricot jam and *Frangipane cream* (see FRANGIPANE). Ice with white *Fondant icing* (see ICING) flavoured with maraschino. Decorate with angelica.

RICKETS. RACHITISME – Disease affecting children, caused by digestive troubles and vitamin deficiency. Remedied by giving fruit juices (lemon, orange, grape, tomato) and certain raw foods containing vitamins (especially Vitamin D).

RIDDLE. CRIBLE – Kitchen utensil similar to a sieve, but with larger holes.

RIDGE CUCUMBER. AGOURSI – *Agoursi* is the French spelling of the Russian word *ogurtsy*. This is a species of the Cucurbitaceae family. In Russia, where cucumbers are highly appreciated, they apply to this type of cucumber all the treatments which we apply to white cucumbers: braising, *à la crème*, fried in batter, *au gratin, à la Mornay,* etc.

In France, cucumbers are most often eaten like gherkins. Formerly, it was chiefly in this guise that they were found in food shops, but they are now sold fresh in France, England and the United States.

RIGODON – Burgundian dish, very popular in some parts of Basse-Bourgogne, served as an *entrée* when it has ham or bacon in it (giving it some resmblance to the *quiche lorraine*) or as a sweet with the addition of fruit purée, making it more like a pudding. The *rigodon* is served either warm or completely cold, so that it can be made in a large enough quantity to be dished up twice. It used to be made on the day the bread was baked (in the days when each household made its own bread) and was put in the oven as soon as the bread came out.

Boil $\frac{3}{4}$ litre ($1\frac{1}{3}$ pints, $1\frac{3}{4}$ pints) milk, add to it 150 g. (5 oz., $\frac{2}{3}$ cup) sugar, a pinch of salt and $\frac{1}{2}$ vanilla pod (or few drops vanilla extract), or some lemon rind (the Burgundian housewives replace these flavours with a good pinch of cinnamon).

Cover the utensil, leave to infuse away from heat, and stir from time to time to make sure the sugar dissolves.

Cut in small dice 100 g. (4 oz., 2 cups) stale brioche; put it in a dish and sprinkle with 5 or 6 tablespoons of the sweet, flavoured milk. Chop finely 7 or 8 dried shelled walnuts. Add to these 3 crushed hazelnuts (in the season, the dried walnuts are replaced by fresh ones, doubling the quantity; but fresh or dry, walnuts must figure in rigodon).

Mix in a bowl 7 beaten eggs and 2 tablespoons rice flour. Add the sweet, flavoured milk little by little, beating well with a whisk to ensure that everything is perfectly blended. Finally, add to the mixture the diced brioche and chopped nuts and mix well together.

Pour into a deep, well-buttered dish, and dot the surface with about 25 g. (1 oz., 2 tablespoons) butter in small pieces. Cook in the oven at a good medium heat.

Its accompaniment is a purée of fruit in season: mirabelle plums, greengages, quinces, apples, etc. Whatever the fruit, it is cooked to a jam in which the quantity of sugar is in proportion to the sweetness of the fruit used.

After cooking, this jam is strained through a cloth or strainer, and boiled down over strong heat until it becomes very thick.

When the *rigodon* has been taken out of the oven, and has become no more than lukewarm, the jam is poured and spread over it very evenly.

When it is served cold, the jam can be replaced by a purée of strawberries. Purée of peaches also goes very well with *rigodon*.

Rigodon with meat. RIGODON AVEC VIANDE – 'Put into a basin 2 good tablespoons of flour (or rice flour). Add 7 eggs. Mix well. Pour in, stirring well, 1 litre ($1\frac{3}{4}$ pints, generous quart) boiled milk, lightly salted. Add 200 g. (7 oz., scant cup) cold boiled pork cut in very small dice (or an equivalent quantity of streaky bacon). Pour the mixture into a deep dish, well buttered. Put small pieces of butter here and there on the surface. Cook in a moderate oven. This flan is eaten lukewarm or cold.' (Philéas Gilbert's recipe.)

RIGOTTE DE CONDRIEU – See CHEESE.

RILLAUDS AND RILLETTES – Preparation of pork, both lean and fat, cut into very small pieces and gently cooked in lard with the usual seasoning. *Rillettes* are then pounded in a mortar. *Rillauds* or *rillons* are not.

Rillettes are made industrially almost everywhere in France. Tours and Le Mans *rillettes* are highly esteemed.

Goose and rabbit *rillettes* are made in the same way as pork *rillettes*.

Cut $2\frac{1}{2}$ kg. ($5\frac{1}{2}$ lb.) fresh belly of pork into large dice. Heat 25 g. (1 oz., 2 tablespoons) lard in a pan, add diced pork, and cook lightly. Add $\frac{1}{2}$ cup of water. Cook gently till tender, stirring frequently to make sure that the meat does not stick to the bottom. When the pieces of pork are cooked and browned, drain them.

Chop or pound the *rillettes* finely, put them in a basin, and add to them the fat from the cooking. Season with salt and pepper and mix.

Put the *rillettes* into small stone jars and allow to cool. When they are cold pour over a thin layer of lard. Cover with white paper.

Rillauds of Anjou. RILLAUDS D'ANJOU – Cut fresh belly of pork into pieces about 6 cm. ($2\frac{1}{2}$ inches) square. Season with coarse rock salt, allowing 25 g. salt per kg. ($\frac{1}{2}$ oz., per lb.), and leave for 12 hours.

The next day put the *rillauds* in a saucepan in which some lard (one third of the weight of the pork) has been heated. Cook gently for 2 hours. Put the pan over good heat, add a little caramel and cook for a few moments.

Drain the *rillauds* and serve piping hot.

Rillettes of Angers. RILLETTES D'ANGERS – Melt gently 1 kg. ($2\frac{1}{4}$ lb.) pork fat cut into very small pieces. When it is golden in colour add 4 kg. ($8\frac{3}{4}$ lb.) fresh pork, both fat and lean, cut into dice, and 100 g. (4 oz.) coarse rock salt. Cook gently for 5 to 6 hours. Beat the pieces with a wooden spoon to crush them a little. Put into pots. Allow to become cold.

Rillettes of Le Mans. RILLETTES DU MANS – Like the *Rillettes of Angers*, made of mixed pieces of goose and pork.

Rillettes of Tours. RILLETTES DE TOURS – Prepared as described in the introductory recipe using fresh collar (U.S. shoulder butt) of pork, both fat and lean. Season with salt, pepper and spices. Pound finely. Put in pots. Cover with a layer of lard.

Rillons, rillauds, rillots – Cook pieces of breast of pork as indicated in the first part of the recipe for *rillettes*.

When the pieces are cooked and well browned, drain them in a strainer, season with salt and pepper, and serve hot or cold.

RIND. ÉCORCE – The outer skin of some stalks and fruit. The rinds of cinnamon, lemon and orange are used in a great many different ways in cooking.

RING – See BORDER.

RING-BISCUIT. GIMBLETTE – Name given to various types of small biscuit made in the form of a ring.

The word *gimblette* comes from the Italian *cianbetta* which means scalded. This etymology implies that *gimblettes* should be scalded before they are put in the oven.

The best known – and their reputation is centuries old – are those of Albi.

Orange ring-biscuits (Carême's recipe). GIMBLETTES À L'ORANGE – 'Grate half an orange rind on a lump of sugar; crush the sugar to a fine powder and mix it with more fine sugar so that the whole amount measures 175 g. (6 oz., $\frac{3}{4}$ cup). Pound thoroughly 100 g. (4 oz., scant cup) fresh almonds. Place in a circle, round this mixture, 225 g. (8 oz., 2 cups) sifted cake flour. Put in the centre 1 teaspoon yeast dissolved in a quarter of a tumbler of milk. Add 50 g. (2 oz., $\frac{1}{4}$ cup) butter, 2 egg yolks, a pinch of salt, the almonds and the orange-flavoured sugar. Knead all these ingredients in the usual way and leave the dough in a warm place for 5 to 6 hours to allow the yeast to ferment.

'Now break the dough and roll it into strips, each the width of a little finger. When there are 5 or 6 strips made, cut them diagonally into pieces each 13 cm. (5 inches) in length. Make these into little rings so that the joins are invisible.

'Having prepared the dough in this way, drop the rings into a large saucepan of boiling water. Stir it gently with a spatula to prevent the rings from sticking and to bring them to the surface. Drain them and drop them into cool water.

'When they are cold, drain them in a large sieve. Now toss them to dry them. Dip each one in a little beaten egg (2 eggs should be used in all) two or three times.

'Leave them to drain for a few minutes.

'Arrange them carefully on three lightly greased baking-sheets and bake them in a slow oven until they are a good colour.

'In the same way, it is possible to make little plaited biscuits or little rolls about as long as a thumb.

'These ring-biscuits may be also flavoured with the rind of lemon, citron or Seville orange, or with aniseed, vanilla or orange-flower water.'

RISOTTO – Dishes with a rice basis. (See RICE.)

RISSOLE – Dish made with different kinds of pastry, though usually of puff pastry, filled with various sorts of forcemeat, often made in the shape of a turnover and fried in deep fat.

This dish, which may also be cooked in the oven like small patties, is served as a hot *hors-d'œuvre* or a small *entrée*. Rissoles of very small size can be used as garnish for large pieces of meat or poultry.

Rissoles, which used to be called *roinsolles*, were known in the thirteenth century. In those days they were simply a kind of pancake fried in butter or dripping. Later they came to be filled with chopped meat.

The author of the *Cris de Paris* (Cries of Paris) called rissoles '*denrées aux dés*' (dice food) because in the evenings after supper the workmen, students and other people subject to very strict rules could hazard nothing more than these pastries in their games of chance.

Method. Roll out the pastry, made according to instructions, to a thickness of $\frac{1}{2}$ cm. ($\frac{1}{4}$ inch).

Cut out the number of pieces required with a pastry-cutter. Except for rissoles made in the form of a turnover, it is necessary to cut out two pieces of pastry for each rissole.

Fill these with a piece of forcemeat the size of a walnut, as indicated in the recipe.

Moisten the edges with water. Cover with a second piece of pastry or fold over in the form of a turnover. Press the edges together to seal them. Fry at the last moment, drain, and serve. Garnish with fried parsley.

For different recipes see HORS-D'ŒUVRE, *Hot hors-d'œuvre*.

RIVESALTES (MUSCAT DE) – Very strong liqueur wine harvested at Rivesaltes, a small town in the Pyrénées-Orientales. This wine is highly flavoured.

ROACH. GARDON – Common name of a freshwater fish of the carp family, something between the carp and the bream. In U.S.A. it is called golden shiner minnow. Its fins are red, its white flesh quite delicate, but it has so many forked bones that it is difficult to eat. Roach is most commonly eaten fried.

Roach

ROAST. RÔT, RÔTI – The French word *rôt* is the most general term and the most noble, according to M. de Courchamps (author of a cookery book) to describe not only roasted meat but also the course which follows the *entrée*. The roast can be a piece of meat (though this was always the *entrée* in the *grande cuisine* of past days), poultry or game, or, in France, even fried fish or a Lenten fish *pâté*. Roasts are always served on oval dishes.

The word *rôti* describes the actual piece of meat, poultry or game, cooked on the spit or in the oven and served hot.

ROASTING. RÔTISSAGE – Method of cooking foodstuffs which must be done according to certain principles. (See CULINARY METHODS.)

ROASTING PAN. PLAQUE À RÔTIR – Kitchen utensil which must not be confused with the dripping pan used for placing under joints roasting on the spit.

The roasting pan is a tinned-copper (or some other fairly tough metal) pan, provided with a grid on which cuts of meats to be roasted in the oven are placed. It is important that the roasting joints should not lie in the fat or the gravy.

In some restaurants, which take pride in their work, roasting pans have special devices which permit the joint intended for roasting to be put on a spit.

ROB – Fruit juice thickened by evaporation to the consistency of honey.

ROBERT (Sauce) – This sauce, an accompaniment to pork chops and seasoned with vinegar, onions and mustard, is said to have been invented by a certain Robert Vinot, who, according to the legend on a print which bears his portrait, was a celebrated sauce-maker at the beginning of the seventeenth century. For the recipe, see SAUCE.

ROBIN. ROUGE-GORGE – Small passerine, sometimes eaten *en brochettes* (on skewers). Prepared in the same way as larks. The European robin is half the size of the American robin.

ROBLOT – French name given in certain regions to small mackerel.

ROCHER DE CANCALE – See RESTAURANTS OF BYGONE DAYS.

ROCK PARTRIDGE. BARTAVELLE – A variety of red-legged partridge, but bigger than the latter. It is known as the Greek partridge. The female is smaller than the male and has lighter coloured plumage. This partridge is very common in southern Europe and in the Alps, from which it comes down in the winter. Its flesh is very good.

Nostradamus, a great sixteenth-century gastronome and literary figure (1503–66) wrote that this bird originated in Greece and that it was King René of Anjou who brought it to Provence. The seventeenth-century poet, Cyrano de Bergerac, said that 'Bartavelles are to partridges as cardinals are to grey friars . . .'

Grimod de la Reynière considered that 'the bartavelles deserve such profound respect that people should go down on their knees to eat them!'

All the recipes given for partridge (q.v.) can be applied to rock partridge.

ROCKET (Cress). ROQUETTE – Strong-smelling plant with sharp and piquant flavour. Its leaves are smooth and glabrous, the flowers white or pale yellow and it grows wild in the fields. It is used as seasoning in salads.

ROE – See SOFT ROES.

ROEBUCK. CHEVREUIL – Wild European and Asiatic deer. The young of both sexes is called a *fawn* until 18 months old, *pricket* or *yearling* up to 2 years old, then *brocket*. One can establish the age of the animal in the male by the number of tines on the antlers, and in the female by the burrs. The meat of roebuck and other deer is also called venison.

The meat of the young roebuck or roedeer is delicate, especially if it has not been marinated; that of the old brockets, which is tougher, does need marinating, but not for long.

The flesh of the roebuck is, like practically all game, rather indigestible because of the poisons that accumulate, due to the excessive muscular activity of the animal when pursued.

Roebuck and hounds; painting by Oudry

Civet of roebuck (venison). CIVET DE CHEVREUIL – The parts of the roebuck used for this stew, which is made in the same way as *Civet of hare* (see HARE) are the shoulders, the neck, the breast and the upper part of the loin.

As one can seldom obtain the blood of the roebuck, it is replaced for the final liaison of the sauce with hare's blood, or that of rabbit.

Roebuck (venison) chops or cutlets. CÔTELETTES DE CHEVREUIL – These chops or cutlets are taken from the loin. Trim and beat them lightly. Season with salt and pepper and sauté in very hot oil as quickly as possible in order to keep the centre of each cutlet slightly pink.

Arrange them in the form of a crown, alternating with croûtons of bread cut into heart shapes and fried in butter.

Dress them with the sauce indicated by the particular recipe (see below) and garnish accordingly.

The meaty part of the cutlet can be larded with fine lardoons or strips of salt pork inserted in the form of a star. If the chops or cutlets are taken from an old animal they can be marinated beforehand.

Roebuck (venison) chops or cutlets with chestnuts. CÔTELETTES DE CHEVREUIL AUX MARRONS – Cook the chops or cutlets in the same way as for *Roebuck (venison) chops or cutlets poivrade* (see below). Arrange them in the form of a crown, alternating with croûtons fried in butter. Fill the centre of the dish with braised chestnuts. Pour over a *Poivrade sauce* (see SAUCE). Fix a paper frill on each cutlet.

Roebuck cutlets with chestnuts

Roebuck (venison) chops or cutlets Conti. CÔTELETTES DE CHEVREUIL CONTI – Prepare the chops or cutlets in the same way as for *Roebuck (venison) chops or cutlets poivrade* (see below). Arrange them in the form of a crown. Fill the centre of the dish with a *Lentil purée* (see PURÉE). Cover the cutlets with *Poivrade sauce* (see SAUCE).

Roebuck (venison) chops or cutlets à la crème. CÔTELETTES DE CHEVREUIL À LA CRÈME – Season the chops or cutlets with salt and paprika. Sauté them quickly in butter. Drain them. Arrange them in the form of a crown with fried croûtons. Pour over them a cream sauce prepared in the following way: for 6 cutlets pour 1 dl. (6 tablespoons, scant $\frac{1}{2}$ cup) Madeira into the pan in which the cutlets have been sautéed. Scrape the pan to blend the juices of the meat with the wine, and then boil down. Add 3 dl. ($\frac{1}{2}$ pint, $1\frac{1}{4}$ cups) thick fresh cream. Boil for a few minutes. Add a little lemon juice, strain through a sieve. Serve with *Chestnut purée* (see CHESTNUTS).

Roebuck (venison) chops or cutlets with grapes. CÔTELETTES DE CHEVREUIL AUX RAISINS – Sauté the chops or cutlets in very hot oil. Arrange them in the form of a crown, alternating with fried croûtons. Put into the pan in which the cutlets have been cooked some skinned and seeded grapes which have been soaked in a little Cognac beforehand, allowing ten grapes per cutlet. Moisten with *Poivrade sauce* (see SAUCE), not too strong, or with rich brown stock. Pour this sauce over the cutlets.

Roebuck (venison) chops or cutlets with juniper berries. CÔTELETTES DE CHEVREUIL AU GENIÈVRE – Sauté the chops or cutlets in oil or butter. Arrange them in the form of a crown, alternating them with croûtons fried in butter. Pour over them the juices released in the pan, to which 2 tablespoons of gin have been added. Moisten with 2 dl. ($\frac{1}{3}$ pint, scant cup) fresh cream and 1 dl. (6 tablespoons, scant $\frac{1}{2}$ cup) *Poivrade sauce* (see SAUCE), adding a few crushed juniper berries (1 or 2 per cutlet), and some drops of lemon juice. Boil for a few moments; sieve.

Serve with a purée of apples only very slightly sweetened.

Roebuck (venison) chops or cutlets à la minute. CÔTELETTES DE CHEVREUIL À LA MINUTE – Sauté the chops or cutlets quickly in oil or butter. Sprinkle them while they are cooking with, for 6 cutlets, 1 large tablespoon finely chopped onion. Drain the cutlets, arrange them in the form of a crown with fried croûtons. Pour over them the juices from the pan, to which 2 tablespoons (3 tablespoons) Cognac have been added, together with $1\frac{1}{2}$ dl. ($\frac{1}{4}$ pint, $\frac{2}{3}$ cup) *Poivrade sauce* (see SAUCE). Alternatively, use a rich brown stock. Season with a little lemon juice and add, away from the heat, 75 g. (3 oz., 6 tablespoons) butter. Garnish the centre of the dish with sliced mushrooms sautéed in butter.

Roebuck (venison) chops or cutlets poivrade. CÔTELETTES DE CHEVREUIL POIVRADE – Sauté the chops or cutlets in oil or butter. Add a little wine vinegar to the juices in the pan and some *Poivrade sauce* (see SAUCE). Arrange the cutlets in the form of a crown alternating them with fried croûtons. Attach a paper frill to each cutlet bone.

Roebuck (venison) chops or cutlets à la romaine. CÔTELETTES DE CHEVREUIL À LA ROMAINE – Sauté the chops or cutlets in oil. Arrange them in the form of a crown, alternating with croûtons fried in butter. Cover them with *Romaine sauce* (see SAUCE) combined with the juices in the pan, which have been de-glazed with a little white wine.

Serve with *Chestnut purée* (see CHESTNUTS).

Roebuck (venison) chops or cutlets d'Uzès. CÔTELETTES DE CHEVREUIL D'UZÈS – Sauté the chops or cutlets quickly in oil. Arrange them in the form of a crown, alternating with heart-shaped croûtons fried in butter. Fill the centre of the dish with *Dauphine potatoes* (see POTATOES). Cover the cutlets with a sauce made in the following way: scrape the bottom of the pan in which the cutlets have been cooked and to which 4 tablespoons (5 tablespoons) wine vinegar have been added. Moisten with $2\frac{1}{2}$ dl. (scant $\frac{1}{2}$ pint, generous cup) rich brown veal stock and 3 dl. ($\frac{1}{2}$ pint, $1\frac{1}{4}$ cups) cream. Boil down; add butter, away from the heat, and pass through a sieve.

To this sauce add 1 tablespoon orange rind which has been cut into tiny strips, blanched and drained, 2 tablespoons (3 tablespoons) almonds which have been peeled by dipping in hot water and dried in the oven, and 2 tablespoons (3 tablespoons) gherkins, cut into strips. Add a little orange juice, and season with freshly ground pepper.

Roebuck or venison filets mignons. FILETS MIGNONS DE CHEVREUIL – In principle the term '*filets mignons*' denotes the thin tongue of meat which is found under the bone on the animal's saddle. These can also be cut from the big fillets of the saddle.

After being trimmed and lightly beaten, the fillets are larded with thin lardoons or strips of salt pork and sautéed in butter or oil, or grilled, and served with *Poivrade sauce* (see SAUCE) and a purée of chestnuts.

The little fillets can also be prepared as for *Roebuck (venison) chops or cutlets.*

Roebuck (venison) hash. HACHIS DE CHEVREUIL – Prepared with cold roebuck or venison (see HASH, *Hash of ground game*). The hash is moistened with a thick brown game stock.

Haunch of roebuck (venison). CUISSOT, GIGUE DE CHEVREUIL – Trim the haunch, removing the thin skin which covers it. Lard it with narrow strips of larding bacon or thin strips of salt pork. Roast it in the oven or on the spit. (See CULINARY METHODS, *Average cooking times for roasts.*)

Serve separately a *Poivrade sauce* or any other sauce appropriate to furred game (see SAUCE), chestnut purée and gooseberry jelly.

Roebuck (venison) noisettes. NOISETTES DE CHEVREUIL – These little cuts are taken from the loin, but can also be taken from the upper end of the haunch or from the saddle fillets. They should be cut rather thick, in a round or oval shape.

They are cooked in the same way as for *Roebuck (venison) chops or cutlets*, and are accompanied by all the sauces and garnishes indicated for these.

Roebuck (venison) pie. PÂTÉ DE CHEVREUIL – Prepared with strips of roebuck or venison and game forcemeat in the same way as *Rabbit pie* (see PIE).

Saddle of roebuck (venison). SELLE DE CHEVREUIL – The word 'saddle' applies only to that part of the animal which is found between the loin and the haunch. However, one can leave the two loins adhering to the joint, cutting the ribs very short.

Remove the sinewy parts of the meat and lard it with strips of larding bacon or salt pork. Roast it in the oven or on the spit (see CULINARY METHODS, *Average cooking times for roasts*).

Serve with *Poivrade sauce* (see SAUCE) or any other appropriate sauce for furred game, with *Chestnut purée* (see CHESTNUTS) and gooseberry jelly.

Roebuck (venison) saddle à l'allemande. SELLE DE CHEVREUIL À L'ALLEMANDE – Trim and lard the saddle. Marinate for 12 hours in an uncooked marinade (q.v.). Dry the meat and roast it in a rather narrow roasting tin on a foundation of the vegetables from the marinade. (See CULINARY METHODS. *Average cooking times for roasts*).

When it is cooked set it on a dish and keep warm. Add a little of the liquor from the marinade to the juices and vegetables in the baking tin. Boil down almost completely. Add $3\frac{1}{2}$ dl. (generous $\frac{1}{2}$ pint, $1\frac{1}{2}$ cups) cream. Boil down by one-third. Add 1 tablespoon dissolved meat glaze or double consommé. Pass the sauce through a strainer and serve with the joint.

Roebuck (venison) saddle grand veneur. SELLE DE CHEVREUIL GRAND VENEUR – Lard the saddle with strips of larding bacon or salt pork. Roast it in the manner described above and arrange on a serving dish. Garnish with braised chestnuts and *Dauphine potatoes* (see POTATOES) arranged in clumps at each end of the dish.

Serve with *Grand veneur sauce* (see SAUCE).

Sliced roebuck (venison) with various sauces. EMINCÉS DE CHEVREUIL – Prepare with cold roebuck or venison in the same way as for sliced lamb or beef with various sauces.

Cover the slices of meat with *Poivrade sauce*, *Grand veneur sauce*, or *Chasseur sauce* (see SAUCE). Serve with *Chestnut purée* (see CHESTNUTS) and gooseberry jelly.

ROGNONNADE – Cut of veal to which the kidney has been left adhering. This piece is roasted or baked.

ROI DES CAILLES (King of quails) – Popular name for the land rail. This bird was so called because it appeared at the same time as the quails and disappeared at the same time as they did. Formerly it was believed that it directed the quails in their flight. For cooking instructions see QUAIL.

ROLL OUT. ABAISSER – To spread out pastry or any other mixture (puff pastry, short pastry, sweet pastry, almond paste, etc.) with the aid of a rolling-pin in one uniform strip of varying thinness. In the case of a biscuit or sponge, we say that it is divided in slices of the same thickness, or *abaisses*. For the method see DOUGH.

ROLLMOPS – Fillets of herrings prepared in a highly seasoned marinade, generally based on white wine, then rolled around gherkins and pinned with a wooden skewer to hold them. Rollmops are served as *hors-d'œuvre*.

ROLLOT – See CHEESE.

ROLY-POLY PUDDING – Pudding made of suet pastry spread with jam, rolled in the shape of a sausage, and cooked in water. (See PUDDING, *English suet roll pudding*.)

ROMAINE or COS LETTUCE – Variety of lettuce with firm leaves, mostly eaten in salad. Legend says that it was Rabelais who imported this variety into France. It is called *Cos* in England.

ROMALOUR – See CHEESE.

ROMANÉE – A great wine from the commune of Vosne-Romanée. There are three distinct types, the Romanée, the Romanée-Conti and the Romanée-Saint-Vivant. (See BURGUNDY.)

ROMANOV – See GARNISHES.

ROOK. FREUX – A kind of crow, which is sometimes eaten after it has been skinned.

Rook pie. PÂTÉ DE CORBEAU – Rook pie, in spite of what the sceptics and the incredulous may think, is a dish which, if properly prepared, is not to be despised. It is only prepared with fledglings straight from the nest. 'There are certain rules which it is absolutely necessary to follow to achieve a good result. First of all, the rooks are not plucked, the birds are drawn and only the breast is retained. The legs are tough and the carcase bitter.

'Having washed the breasts, they are left to soak in milk for 6 hours; they are then cut up and the pieces are arranged in a pie dish, and seasoned, sparing neither pepper nor spices. The bottom of the dish should be lined with some slices of beef. Strips of bacon are placed on top of the pieces of rook, and halved hard-boiled eggs are distributed here and there. This pie is then covered with a sheet of pastry and put in the oven for $1\frac{1}{2}$ hours.

'When the pie is taken out of the oven a little good stock to which a small quantity of half-glaze is added, is poured into the pie.' (Alfred Suzanne, *la Cuisine et la pâtisserie anglaise*.)

ROOT. RAVE – Name used for a category of vegetable plants, whose subterranean parts are swollen (see TURNIP). In cookery those mostly used are turnip, kohl-rabi, beetroot, carrot, celeriac and radish.

ROPINESS. GRAISSE DES VINS – A defection peculiar to white wines. It is encountered especially in the white wines of the Cher, Poitou, Orléans and Champagne districts.

This generally occurs as a result of pressing the grapes as soon as they are gathered. The must enclosed in the vats ferments independently of the skin, pips and stalks, which provide the tannin need to clarify the must.

At the clarification stage, the gelatinous and albuminous elements remain in suspension, which leaves the wines cloudy. At this stage, the remedy is to put tannin in the cask. This not only causes the sediment in the wine to settle, but also separates out the fish glue which has been added as a clarifying agent, and which will not be found in the next clarification.

The proportion of tannin to be used with ropy wine is 15 to 30 g. per hectolitre (100 litres).

ROQUEFORT CHEESE – See CHEESE.

ROQUILLE – French culinary term for orange peel. These skins are candied and used in confectionery.

ROSEMARY. ROMARIN – Perennial evergreen, reaching 5 ft. in height, with narrow hard leaves, green above and greyish below, with a strongly aromatic smell. The leaves, fresh and dried, are used in seasoning.

ROSETTE – Name given to a special sausage of the first quality made in the Lyons district, which is eaten uncooked. (See SAUSAGE.)

ROSSINI – See GARNISHES.

ROSSOLL or ROSOLIO – Liqueur formerly made from the sundew plant.

ROTA – Wine from the north of Spain, much used in blending.

ROTENGLE – Freshwater fish, better known in France as *gardon rouge*. Its body is a little deeper and less elongated than the common roach. It has a bright red eye and its fins are red and pink. It is cooked like roach (q.v.).

RÔTIE (Toast) – Slice of bread baked or toasted.

Rôties (pieces of toast) are buttered and served with breakfast, tea, etc. The same name is given to *canapés* spread with forcemeat which are served with game birds, roasts in general and woodcock and snipe in particular, and to small snacks made by putting an egg or some kind of spread on a slice of toasted or fried bread.

RÔTISSERIE – Part of the kitchen specially equipped for preparing roasts. It is also the word given to modern portable appliances designed to roast meat on a spit.

By extension, the word also describes the work done by the chef in this special section in the big catering establishments, a specialist in all the work of the *rôtisserie*.

The *rôtisseur*, as he is called, is employed not only in roasting but also in grilling and frying. In the most important establishments the *rôtisserie* is divided into three parts, each having a specialist in charge: the *rôtisseur* proper, the *grillardin* and the *friturier*.

Certain specialised places, where all kinds of spit-roasted poultry are cooked and sold, are also called *rôtisseries*.

ROUELLE – Cut of veal. This is a fairly thick slice across the leg.

ROUENNAIS – See CHEESE.

ROUGAIL – A form of seasoning very popular in hot countries, used in various dishes cooked in the Creóle style. Being very spicy it stimulates the appetite.

All the *rougail* recipes which are given below belong to the repertoire of Créole cookery.

Rougail of green apples. ROUGAIL DE POMMES VERTES – Cut 4 peeled green apples in tiny dice putting them into a bowl of salted water.

Drain the apple dice and put them in a napkin, squeezing to extract all the water. Put them in a dish where you will have set a layer of pimentos and ginger, pounded smoothly with a little olive oil.

If the apples are not sharp enough add a squeeze of lemon juice.

Rougail of aubergines (egg plants). ROUGAIL D'AUBERGINES – Boil 2 aubergines in salted water. Pound in a mortar 1 slice of onion, a small piece of ginger and a little pimento seasoned with salt. Put this mixture on a plate and dilute it with lemon juice and good olive oil. Take out the cooked aubergines, split them, scoop out the flesh, having removed the seeds, and add them, little by little, to the prepared sauce, mashing with a fork so that the aubergines are completely reduced to a paste. Turn into an *hors-d'œuvre* dish.

Rougail of salt cod and tomatoes. ROUGAIL DE MORUE ET DE TOMATES – De-salt a small salt cod by soaking in cool water the evening before it is wanted. Remove all skin and bones. Dry with a cloth and cut in small pieces. Flour and brown lightly in a pan with oil and fat. Push to one side of the pan. Cook 3 or 4 chopped onions over low heat so that they do not colour. Add 4 fresh peeled and deseeded tomatoes, and stew them together gently. Pound some ginger, 1 clove garlic, some thyme, some parsley and 1 small pimento. Incorporate this mixture with the gently simmering cod. Cook for about 40 minutes, then put the pan (still covered) in the oven, and leave it for 20 minutes.

Serve with rice.

Rougail of shrimps or prawns. ROUGAIL DE CREVETTES – Remove the heads and tails from some shrimps or prawns and fry them in fat. Shell them.

Crush in a mortar $\frac{1}{2}$ onion with a small piece of ginger and pimento. Season with salt.

Add the shrimps, little by little, pounding all the time. When all is reduced to a paste, add 2 small tomatoes that have been cooked in the oven, and the juice of a lemon. Mix well. Turn the mixture into an *hors-d'œuvre* dish.

This rougail is served alone or with fish curry. Often, when the rougail is made, it is reheated with olive oil in a frying pan.

Rougail of raw tomatoes. ROUGAIL DE TOMATES CRUES – Pound a little onion with a piece of ginger the size of a walnut. Add peeled and seeded tomatoes and mash all together. Incorporate some pimento and a squeeze of lemon juice. Serve in an *hors-d'œuvre* dish.

This seasoning accompanies Créole dishes served with rice.

ROUGE DE RIVIÈRE – The French common name for the *Shoveller duck*. This bird, whose flesh is succulent, is nearly always roasted. (See DUCK, *Wild duck*.)

ROUGERET – See CHEESE.

ROULADE, ROLL – Rolled piece of veal or pork.

A thin slice of meat spread with some kind of forcemeat and rolled into a sausage is also known as *roulade*.

This term is also applied to various preparations, mostly of pork or veal, made like galantines (q.v.). Thus *roulade de tête de porc* describes a pig's head, boned, stuffed with a forcemeat of chopped-up pig's tongue, streaky bacon and other ingredients, rolled like 'boar's head' and cooked in a jelly stock; *roulade de veau* describes a slice of *noix de veau* well fattened, spread with a forcemeat of some kind, mixed with meat cut in small dice, rolled into a galantine and braised or poached in white *court-bouillon* (q.v.).

ROULÉ – Rolled-out sheet of biscuit (cake) mixture, spread with thick jam, then rolled. The top is sprinkled with praline and toasted almonds.

ROULETTE (Pastry wheel) – A small toothed wheel, in wood or metal, mounted free on a handle, and used to cut pastry.

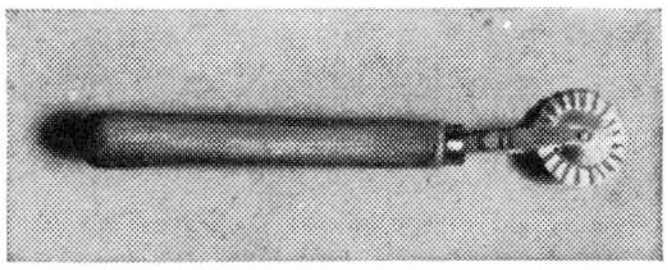

Roulette

ROUND (U.S.) or SILVERSIDE (G.B.). GÎTE À LA NOIX – Part of the leg of beef. This cut includes in particular the tendons (part tendon, part membrane) and part of the femoral biceps, the gemellus muscle, the pyramidal and the crural square.

This cut is used chiefly in hot-pots, and it may also be braised.

In Paris and other large French cities, it is sold larded, rolled and tied.

ROUSSELET. (Russet pear) – Summer pear, so named because its skin is russet colour. The flesh is sweet and well flavoured.

This pear is mostly preserved by drying.

ROUSSETTE – Name given to a kind of fritter in certain

regions of France, which in other places is known as *merveille* or *oreillette*. It is made in this way:

Make a rather thick dough of 500 g. (18 oz., $4\frac{1}{2}$ cups) sifted flour, 3 eggs, 2 tablespoons (3 tablespoons) milk, 1 tablespoon orange-blossom water, 1 small glass brandy and a pinch of salt.

Gather up the dough into a ball, wrap it in a cloth and leave it to rest in a cool place for 3 hours.

Roll out into a thin sheet, and cut out with a plain round pastry cutter. Drop into hot deep fat. Drain the *rousettes* when they are well browned and crisp. Sprinkle with sugar and arrange in a mound on a napkin.

ROUSSILLON – See LANGUEDOC AND ROUSSILLON.

ROUSSIR – To turn in smoking hot butter, or other fat, a piece of meat or poultry, in order to colour it.

The word *roussir* cannot be translated in its proper sense, because the meats so fried must be golden rather than russet.

ROUX – Mixture of butter or other fatty substance and flour, cooked together for varying periods of time depending on its final use.

The *roux* is the thickening element in sauces.

There are three kinds of roux: white *roux*, blond *roux* and brown *roux*.

Brown *roux* is used to thicken rich brown sauces like *Espagnole* and *Demi-glace* (see SAUCE). It is made by cooking flour in clarified butter in the oven, gently and for a long time, stirring frequently. The clarified fat from a *marmite* (q.v.) may also be used, but in each case the proportions are equal amounts by tablespoons of flour and butter or fat.

This *roux* should be of a good light brown colour. It can be kept for quite a long time.

Blond *roux* is made only with butter. The proportions of butter and flour are the same as for brown *roux*. It is cooked more rapidly and it is only made at the moment it is needed. Its colour should be a pale gold.

White *roux* is used for *Béchamel* and *Velouté sauce* (see SAUCE) and special thick soups. It is made by cooking flour and clarified butter for 5 minutes over the heat and stirring constantly with a wooden spoon.

ROYALE – Moulded custard, variously flavoured, which is used as garnish in clear soup. (See GARNISHES.)

ROYALE (À LA) – Name given to different preparations, for example, to consommé garnished with custard shapes, and to various dishes, particularly of poultry, poached in very little liquid, coated with *Velouté sauce* (see SAUCE) boiled down with cream and finished with truffle purée and various garnishes.

The same name is applied to sweets, hot and cold.

ROYAN – A kind of large sardine.

RUM. RHUM – The name rum or tafia is reserved for the spirit obtained from the alcoholic fermentation and distillation of either the juice of sugar cane, or the syrup (molasses) obtained from the processing of cane sugar.

Rum, like all spirits, is colourless when it emerges from the distilling apparatus. After a lengthy period in oak casks, it acquires a pale amber hue. The care (or lack of it) that goes into this ageing process makes or mars the fineness of rum. Some 'old rums' are valued just as highly as the finest spirits. The colour of ordinary rum, on the other hand, is achieved by the addition of artificial caramel colouring.

White rum is used in the preparation of tropical drinks: punch, Daiquiri, Planter's rum, etc. Full-bodied, amber-coloured rums are best suited for grogs and desserts (on account of their powerful aroma). This is why, until recently, rum was used mostly for desserts and *pâtisserie*. A few years ago, the *Comité national de gastronomie*, (which organises an annual culinary competition called the '*Poêle d'or*') dedicated the event to recipes based on rum. This encouraged the more frequent use of rum in the flavouring of fish and meat dishes, etc. Some of the recipes are given below.

Fillets of burbot à la créole. FILETS DE LOTTE CRÉOLE – Brown some chopped onion and carrots, and sprinkle with flour. Place in a pan with a little lukewarm water and bring to the boil. Add quartered tomatoes, thyme, bay leaf and garlic. Season with salt. Simmer the sauce, then sieve it. Add rum and an equal amount of fresh cream. Place the fillets in a buttered serving dish and pour the sauce over. Bake for 15 minutes.

Rabbit with prunes and rum. LAPIN AUX PRUNEAUX AU RHUM – Steep 250 g. (9 oz., $1\frac{1}{2}$ cups) prunes for 2 hours in rum blended with a little lukewarm water. Cut up the rabbit. Brown the pieces in oil with diced bacon and onions. Add the liquid in which the prunes have been steeped, a *bouquet garni*, salt and pepper, and simmer gently for 45 minutes. Add the drained prunes and simmer for 20 minutes.

Young guinea fowl à l'antillaise. PINTADEAUX À L'ANTILLAISE – Clean, singe and cut-up 2 guinea fowl into 8 pieces. Brown these quickly in a little butter, stirring all the time. When they are golden, add chopped onions, a clove of garlic, and a little flour. Moisten with 2 glasses of dry wine. Add 2 tomatoes cut in quarters. Cover and simmer gently for 20 minutes. Meanwhile, steep 4 slices of pineapple and 6 sliced bananas in white rum. Fry 6 diced, sweet potatoes in butter. Lightly brown the sliced pineapple and the bananas in a frying pan. Serve the pieces of guinea fowl on the pineapple slices. Garnish with the bananas and potatoes. Skim the fat from the cooking liquid and boil down. Coat the guinea fowl with it. (Recipe of 'Maman' Olivier, rue Médéric, Paris.)

Stuffed chicken. POULET FARCI – Make a mixture of the chicken's liver, sausage meat, breadcrumbs soaked in milk, chopped onion, salt, pepper, spices, chopped parsley and fresh cream. Stuff the chicken with this mixture. Roast in the oven. When cooked, sprinkle with rum and *flamber*. Serve with sweetcorn croquettes.

RUMP. CULOTTE – The fleshy part of the haunch of beef, used in hot-pots. This cut can also be braised and made into *ragoûts*. (See BEEF.)

Top of rump. POINTE DE CULOTTE – Piece of beef taken from the rump. (See BEEF.)

RUSCUS. PRAGON – Plant similar to asparagus. The best known variety is *butcher's broom* or knee-holly. The young shoots are eatable and are used like hop shoots.

RUSH. JONC – Most types of reed belong to the rush family. The scented Indian rush, *rattan,* is used as a spice in the East. The root of the scented Indian rush is used in infusion as a carminative and appetite-stimulant. The chopped root blended with alcohol produces a tincture that may also be used for stomach upsets.

RUSKS. BISCOTTES – Slices of special bread, cut from the loaf and re-baked in the oven.

Diet rusks. BISCOTTES DE RÉGIME – There are various types of rusks in the shops, of different degrees of hardness and friability, sweet rusks and salty rusks, etc. There are also special types of rusks with salt content completely or partially extracted, as well as rusks enriched with gluten, containing additional casein (legumen), but with reduced starch content. Others are very rich in starch but their content in gluten and nitrogenous elements is reduced to a minimum.

Paris rusks. BISCOTTES PARISIENNES – Pound 500 g. (18 oz., generous $3\frac{1}{2}$ cups) bitter almonds in a mortar, moistening with 2 egg whites and 3 tablespoons (scant $\frac{1}{4}$ cup) kirsch or other liqueur.

When the almonds have been reduced to a smooth paste, put it into a bowl and add to it 10 egg yolks, one at a time, stirring with a wooden spoon. Add 500 g. (18 oz., $2\frac{1}{4}$ cups) castor sugar, a pinch of salt, and 8 egg whites whisked to a stiff froth. Sprinkle with 200 g. (7 oz., generous cup) potato flour. Pipe this mixture through a forcing-bag onto buttered baking sheets and bake in the oven.

RUSSIA – See INTERNATIONAL COOKERY.

RUSSULA. RUSSULE – Fungus with white flesh and a pleasant flavour known in various regions of France as *russule, bordet vert, vert bonnet, palomet, berdanel, blavet* and *verdette.*

They are found in summer and autumn on the edges of woods, in fallow land and near birch trees. They are prepared like mushrooms (see MUSHROOM).

RUTABAGA, SWEET TURNIP – Turnip with yellowish flesh, edible but seldom used in France as foodstuff.

RYE. SEIGLE – The most important European cereal after wheat, originating in the region between the Austrian Alps and the Caspian Sea. Very hardy, very resistant to cold and earlier than wheat, rye grows in the worst soils.

Rye flour, rather greyish in colour, consists mainly of gluten-casein. It has little agglutinative quality and darkens quickly. It can nevertheless be made into bread, which is brown in colour, has an agreeable taste and keeps fresh for a long time, but is more difficult to digest than white bread. Rye flour is used to make spiced bread and cakes.

SABLAGE – In times past this word, which means 'sanding', was used to describe a table decoration made with sands of different colours. The sand was spread on the tablecloth so as to form different designs – flowers, landscapes, coats of arms, monograms, etc.

This type of decoration has today been completely abandoned.

SABLÉ – Biscuit or cake, originating in Normandy. Make a circle of 500 g. (18 oz., $4\frac{1}{2}$ cups) sifted flour on a large board. Place in the middle 400 g. (14 oz., $1\frac{3}{4}$ cups) butter, 6 egg yolks, 150 g. (5 oz., $\frac{2}{3}$ cup) sugar, 1 vanilla pod (or a few drops of vanilla essence) and a pinch of salt.

Mix the butter, sugar, egg yolks, vanilla and salt, and mix with the flour. Finish the operation as quickly as possible.

Blend the ingredients by breaking up the paste with the palm of the hand. Form it once more into a ball and leave it for 1 hour. Roll out the mixture 1 cm. ($\frac{1}{2}$ inch) thick. Cut into rounds about 12 cm. (5 inches) in diameter. Divide these into 4 wedges. Put on a buttered baking sheet and cook in a low oven for about 18 to 20 minutes.

SACCHARINE – Commercial name for a crystalline chemical substance, soluble in water, with a very sweet taste, having also a faint taste of bitter almonds and leaving a dryness in the throat. The sensation of sweetness that it provides is 250 to 300 times stronger than that of sugar, 5 centigrams being equivalent to a normal-sized sugar cube. But it has no chemical analogy with sugar and has none of its nutritional value.

It is chiefly used to give an illusion of sweetness for diabetics, to whom sugar is forbidden.

SACCHAROMETER. PÈSE-SIROP – Hydrometer calibrated to give the specific gravity or density of sugar solutions.

SACRISTAIN – Small puff pastry made in the shape of a paper twist.

SADDLE. SELLE, RABLE – In terms of butchery the French word *selle* describes the part of the hindquarters extending from the last ribs to the leg on both sides (mutton, lamb, roebuck).

The word *rable* describes the fleshy part extending from the base of the shoulder to the tail of small domestic or wild animals (rabbits, hares) formed by the sacro-lumbar, long dorsal and transverse spinal muscles. In English cookery, the hare is the only small animal to which the word 'saddle' is applied.

SAFFRON. SAFRAN – The dried stamens of the saffron or cultivated crocus, originating in the East and introduced into Spain by the Arabs, and cultivated in France, particularly in the Gâtinais, since the sixteenth century. Saffron contains a volatile oil and a colouring substance. It is the indispensable condiment for *bouillabaisse*.

A good saffron should be a dark orange colour all over without white streaks; it is sometime falsified with safflower (bastard saffron) which is redder in colour.

It is said that a dish is *safrané* (saffroned) when it contains saffron or when it is saffron coloured.

Saffron of the Indies – See CURCUMA.

SAGE. SAUGE – Name of various *Labiatae* of which there are some 500 species with a distinct perfume and with an aromatic, slightly bitter taste, among which are three French varieties, great sage (*grande sauge*), of ramose inflorescence, with thick, oblong, hairy leaves, ashy green in colour; the small Provençal sage (*petite sauge* de Provence), with smaller, whiter leaves and a more pronounced scent, which is the most highly esteemed species; and the Catalogne sage, which is even smaller. All these species are used in making flavoured vinegar.

Sage is used in cookery to flavour marinades and forcemeats, and is threaded into meat that is to be roasted. Small birds are wrapped in it, particularly thrushes. It is also added during the cooking of green beans, peas and broad beans to flavour them. Some sweet fritters are made with it. In certain parts of Northern Europe the young shoots are eaten as a salad.

In England there are two indigenous sages, *Salvia verbenaca* which is very common and *Salvia pratensis*, which is rare. Our culinary sage, *Salvia officinalis*, is not a native plant. The culinary sage, the common garden sage and the white sage, *Salvia officinalis alba*, are grown in the U.S.A., but not in sufficient quantity, and tons of sage are imported every year.

SAGO. SAGOU – Floury extract of the marrow of various kinds of palm tree.

This yellowish flour, tending to red or brown, is used for cooking and baking as a liaison element, and often also to prepare soups and dishes that are recommended for special diets.

Sago consommé – See SOUPS AND BROTHS, *Consommé with sago*.

Sago pudding – See PUDDING.

Sago with red wine (Russian cookery). SAGOU AU VIN ROUGE – Blanch 250 g. (9 oz., $1\frac{1}{2}$ cups) sago for 2 minutes, drain and cool.

Cook in a saucepan with 1 litre ($1\frac{3}{4}$ pints, generous quart) red Bordeaux wine, 100 g. (4 oz., $\frac{1}{2}$ cup) sugar, a small pinch of salt, the peel of $\frac{1}{2}$ lemon and a good pinch of powdered cinammon. Simmer over low heat for 25 minutes, discard the lemon rind and serve. The dish can also be made with white wine, and served cold.

SAGUET (LA MÊRE) – See RESTAURANTS OF BYGONE DAYS.

SAIGNEUX – French butchery term for the neck of veal or mutton.

SAINT-AGATHON – See CHEESE.

SAINTE-MAURE – See CHEESE.

SAINTE-MENEHOULD – District of the Marne, renowned for its excellent *charcuterie*, and particularly for its *Pigs' feet*.

SAINT-ÉMILION – Small commune of the Gironde in the Libourne district, celebrated for its wines, which, after the Bordelais, most nearly approach the wines of Burgundy. (See BORDEAUX, *Wines of Bordeaux*.)

SAINT-ESTÈPHE – Commune in the Gironde (the Médoc region) that has given its name to highly reputed *appellation controlée* red wines. (See MÉDOC, BORDEAUX.)

SAINT-FLORENTIN – See CHEESE.

ST GEORGE'S AGARIC. MOUSSERON – Small mushroom which grows in the fields in the autumn and spring. It is cooked in the same way as the cultivated mushroom, and mainly used to flavour stews.

In south-western France, this mushroom is dried, and has to be steeped in water before use. (See MUSHROOMS.)

SAINT-GERMAIN – Thick soup made with fresh peas. (See SOUPS AND BROTHS, *Purée of fresh pea soup*.)

The term also applies to a garnish whose principal ingredient is fresh peas, prepared in a variety of ways (see GARNISHES). The word is used for a preparation of grilled fillets of fish served with *béarnaise sauce*. (See SOLE, *Fillets of sole Saint-Germain*.)

A purée of dried peas is erroneously called Saint-Germain.

Saint-Honoré

SAINT-HONORÉ – Cake, a speciality of Parisian pastry-cooks, so called in memory of Saint Honoré, the patron saint of pastry-cooks and bakers.

The Saint-Honoré is made with two different kinds of pastry: *Fine lining paste* for the base and *Chou paste* for the little iced *choux*, which are arranged in a crown on the base. (See DOUGH.)

To make the Saint-Honoré. With the rolled-out lining paste make a circle 18 to 20 cm. (7 to 8 inches) in diameter. Moisten the edges with a brush, and pipe a thick ring of *chou paste* round the damp edge. Bake in the oven. On a separate baking sheet make two dozen little round *choux* the size of walnuts. Brush with egg and bake in a moderately hot oven for about 15 minutes.

To cook the sugar and icing for the choux. Put into a copper pan 250 g. (9 oz., generous cup) sugar, some glucose as big as a walnut and 2 dl. ($\frac{1}{3}$ pint, scant cup) water. Cook rapidly over a good heat to small crack degree (see SUGAR). Take the pan from the heat and dip the *choux* into the sugar, icing the tops only. Dip the bottoms into the sugar very lightly, and set them on to the ring of *chou pastry*.

Cream filling for the Saint-Honoré. Heat $\frac{3}{4}$ litre ($1\frac{1}{3}$ pints, $1\frac{3}{4}$ pints) *French pastry cream* (see CREAMS). Add to it while warm 6 leaves gelatine or 25 g. (1 oz., 4 tablespoons) powdered gelatine previously soaked in cold water and softened.

Beat 6 egg whites stiffly, sprinkling them lightly with sugar when firm. Add them rapidly to the pastry cream, and fill the inside of the Saint-Honoré with the resulting cream, using a forcing bag and a large, fluted nozzle.

SAINT-JACQUES – See SCALLOPS.

ST JOHN'S WORT (Hypericum). MILLEPERTUIS – Plant with an aromatic and resinous fragrance, bitter in taste, whose flowering tops are used in infusions. In former times, liqueurs were made from this plant.

SAINT-JULIEN – This area in the Gironde (the Médoc region) has given its name to highly reputed *appellation contrôlée* red wines.

SAINT-MARCELLIN – See CHEESE.

SAINT-MICHEL (Pâtisserie) – Cook a fine Genoese pastry mixture (see GENOESE) in a cake tin. When cool, cut it into 3 equal-sized layers. Spread each with a layer of butter which has been beaten with coffee essence. Put the cake layers one on top of the other. Cover the top and sides with vanilla-flavoured *Butter cream* (see CREAMS) and smooth it over. Sprinkle the cake with chopped roasted almonds, and decorate with coffee-flavoured butter cream, using a forcing bag.

SAKÉ – Alcoholic drink used in Japan, obtained by fermenting rice. It is usually served warm before a meal.

SALAD. SALADE – Dishes made up of herbs, plants, vegetables, eggs, meat and fish, seasoned with oil, vinegar, salt and pepper, with or without other ingredients.

Certain salads, blanched by being cultivated in cellars or by being earthed up to keep out light and air (like Belgian endives, the chicory known as *barbe du capucin*, white dandelion leaves, etc.) are almost entirely without mineral salts, chlorophyll or vitamins. Their contents are restricted to cellulose and water, which act only as bulk.

Salads are of two kinds, plain or mixed.

PLAIN SALADS. SALADES SIMPLES – These can be sub-divided into green salads, served raw, and salads of cooked vegetables, consisting of a single kind of vegetable.

These salads, whether raw or cooked, are served with the roast, hot or cold.

Dressings for plain salads. ASSAISONNEMENTS – Dressings for

Green salad (*Robert Carrier*)

plain salads are made with oil, mustard, wine vinegar, salt and pepper. These are generally known as *vinaigrette*. They may also be seasoned in the ways shown below:

Anchovy – For celery, endives or cooked vegetables.

Take 2 de-salted anchovy fillets and rub through a sieve. Put them in the salad dish and add oil, vinegar and pepper.

Cream – For cabbage and romaine (cos) lettuces.

Mix 4 tablespoons (5 tablespoons) fresh cream, not too thick, with 1 teaspoon wine vinegar (or lemon juice). Add salt and pepper.

Indian – For cooked vegetables.

Cook 1 tablespoon finely chopped onion in 1 tablespoon oil. Sprinkle with 1 teaspoon curry powder. Add oil, lemon juice, salt, pepper and a little crushed garlic.

Gasconne – For curly and other endives.

As for *Marseillaise* with the addition of crusts rubbed with garlic.

Bacon fat – For 'wild' chicory, red cabbage, corn salad, dandelion.

Render down 100 g. (4 oz., 6 slices) diced bacon. Pour the fat on the salad, which has been set in a hot salad dish and seasoned with salt and pepper. Add I tablespoon vinegar heated in the frying pan.

Marseillaise – For early endive, 'wild' chicory and other endives.

Crush a clove of garlic in the salad bowl; add oil, vinegar, salt and pepper.

Mustard cream – For raw and cooked celeriac cut in *julienne*, and endives.

Mix 2 tablespoons (3 tablespoons) mustard with 4 tablespoons (5 tablespoons) fresh cream; add a few drops lemon juice, and salt and pepper.

Rémoulade – For all salads, raw or cooked.

Rub through a sieve, or crush, 3 hard-boiled egg yolks. Put in the salad bowl and blend, as for mayonnaise, with oil, vinegar, salt and pepper.

Paprika – For celery or for cooked vegetables.

Bake an onion in the oven and chop it. Put it in the salad bowl and add oil, vinegar, salt and paprika.

Tomato juice – For cooked baby marrows (zucchini), potatoes, Jerusalem artichokes, etc.

Rub 2 raw tomatoes through a fine sieve. Boil down the juice by half and add oil, vinegar, salt and pepper.

Note on the seasoning of salads. Olive oil is the best for all salads. It can nevertheless be replaced, according to taste, by a good nut or vegetable oil.

Wine vinegar may also be replaced by lemon juice, verjuice, or cider vinegar.

Lettuce salad with hard-boiled eggs

Complementary garnishes for plain salads – For green salads or salads in season, the most usual garnishes are aromatic herbs, such as chervil, chives, tarragon, parsley and savory. These herbs are used coarsely chopped, or the leaves are picked from the stems and used whole.

The following herbs and vegetables are also used to garnish plain salads, raw or cooked:

Beetroot, baked in the oven, peeled, cut into rounds, in dice or in a *julienne*; capers, whole or chopped; crusts of bread rubbed with garlic and seasoned with vinaigrette; gherkins, whole, in dice, rounds, *julienne* or chopped; borage flowers, nasturtiums or violets; hard-boiled eggs cut in halves or quarters, or chopped; peeled tomatoes cut in thin slices or quarters; truffles, raw or cooked, cut in thin slices in *julienne* or large dice.

Raw salads. SALADES SIMPLES (À SERVIR CRUES) –

	Dressing:
'Wild' chicory (*Barbe du capucin*)	Mustard cream
Chopped celery	*Vinaigrette*
Celery in sticks	*Rémoulade*
Celeriac	Mustard cream
Curly or other endive	*Vinaigrettes* (with garlic-rubbed crust), *Rémoulade*, Bacon fat.
Kohl-rabi, coarsely grated	*Vinaigrette* or Mayonnaise
Red cabbage, cut in *julienne*	*Rémoulade*, Bacon fat, or *Vinaigrette*
Green cabbage (the tender parts, cut in *julienne*)	Mustard cream
Cucumber cut in rounds and left to stand in salt	*Vinaigrette* or Cream
Cress	*Vinaigrette*
Watercress	*Vinaigrette*
Chicory	*Rémoulade*
Fennel	Anchovy
Lettuces of all kinds	*Vinaigrette*
Romaine or cos lettuce	Cream
Corn salad	Bacon fat
Turnip tops (greens)	*Vinaigrette*
Samphire (rare in U.S.A.)	*Vinaigrette*
Salad burnet	*Vinaigrette*
Dandelion	Bacon fat
Leeks (the green parts)	*Vinaigrette*
Purslane	*Vinaigrette*
Radish (the tender leaves and the radishes chopped)	*Vinaigrette*
Rampion	*Vinaigrette*
Rocket cress	Bacon fat
Salsify (the stems or tender leaves)	Cream
Soya bean shoots	Mustard cream

Plain salads from cooked vegetables. SALADES SIMPLES (À SERVIR CUITES) –

	Dressing:
Artichokes (bottoms)	*Vinaigrette*
Aubergines (rounds blanched in salt water)	Mustard cream
Artichokes (white and green)	*Vinaigrette* or Mayonnaise
Beetroot (in rounds), served always as *hors-d'œuvre*	Mustard cream
Celeriac (cut in *julienne*)	Mustard cream
Sprouting broccoli	*Vinaigrette*
Brussels sprouts	*Vinaigrette*
Sea-kale	*Vinaigrette*
Rutabaga or Swede turnip	Mustard cream
Kohl-rabi	Mustard cream

Red cabbage (cut in *julienne*) ...	*Vinaigrette*
Green cabbage (as hors d' œuvre)	*Vinaigrette*
Courgette (zucchini)	*Vinaigrette*
Chinese artichoke	*Rémoulade*
Spinach leaves (very lightly blanched)	*Vinaigrette*
Broad beans	*Vinaigrette* (with savory)
Haricot beans (shell beans)	*Vinaigrette* (with chopped onion)
French beans	*Vinaigrette*
Kidney and other beans	*Vinaigrette*
Lettuce hearts (blanched and drained)	*Vinaigrette*
Lentils....................................	*Vinaigrette*
Sweet potatoes	*Vinaigrette*
Leeks (white parts cooked in water)	Mayonnaise
'*Mange-tout*' peas	*Vinaigrette*
Potatoes (cooked in water, cut up when hot and soaked in white wine)	*Vinaigrette* or Mayonnaise
Salsify	*Vinaigrette* or Mayonnaise
Parsnips	*Vinaigrette* or Mayonnaise

Dried vegetables as well as fresh farinaceous vegetables gain by being seasoned while still hot, even if the salad is to be served cold. Such salads are usually garnished with parsley, onion or chopped chives.

MIXED (COMBINATION) SALADS. SALADES COMPOSÉES – Mixed salads are sub-divided into several categories. The first, based on mixed cooked vegetables, is prepared in the same way as for a plain salad. Others contain a variety of ingredients, not only mixed vegetables, but also truffles, mushrooms, sliced fish, shellfish, poultry, tongue, ham, etc.

Some of these salads, by reason of their elaborate preparation, come into the realm of *grande cuisine*, and constitute cold *entrées* rather than salads in the ordinary sense. In this category are various mayonnaises, chicken salads *en bellevue*, etc.

Mixed salads with only a base of vegetables are served like plain salads with the roast, hot or cold. Salads with multiple ingredients, particularly those demanding a rather elaborate arrangement, are served by themselves or as an accompaniment to a special cold dish, such as *chaud-froids*, ham mousse, chicken mousse, etc.

Dressings for mixed salads. ASSAISONNEMENT – All salads with a vegetable basis are dressed in the same way as plain salads. They are garnished with the additional ingredients given previously, with the exception of those with too strongly marked a character, such as grated garlic or garlic-rubbed crusts.

These salads are served in glass bowls. The various vegetables of which they are composed are arranged in separate groups, the colours arranged to contrast.

If the salads are dressed in advance in the kitchen and then mixed together, *macédoine* fashion, they are garnished, after having been arranged in a dome in the salad dish, with little heaps and bunches of vegetables, decoratively arranged.

When the dressing used is *vinaigrette*, the vegetables composing the salad can be seasoned separately and arranged in 'bouquets'.

Mixed salads with a multiple basis are often dressed with mayonnaise. According to the type of salad, and according to the way in which it is to be arranged and served, the

Salad vegetables

Potato salad

mayonnaise is used in its normal creamy form, or very thick and stiff.

Some of these salads are moulded in aspic, and become cold *entrées* rather than salads.

Albignac salad. SALADE D'ALBIGNAC – The white meat of chicken finely sliced, raw white truffles in thin slices, black truffles cut in *julienne*, shelled crayfish, celeriac cut in a fine *julienne*, lettuce hearts, hard-boiled eggs, chervil and tarragon.

Put the celeriac dressed with mayonnaise in the middle of the salad bowl, arranging it in a dome. Surround alternately with the chicken meat, seasoned with oil, lemon juice, salt and pepper, the crayfish seasoned with tomato ketchup, and the white truffles sprinkled with olive oil and seasoned with salt and paprika. Insert lettuce hearts and hard-boiled eggs between the groups of garnish.

Sprinkle the *julienne* of black truffles over the celeriac. Sprinkle with oil and lemon juice just before serving.

Ali-Baba salad. SALADE ALI-BAB – Sweet potatoes, cooked, peeled and cut in slices; baby marrows (zucchini) cut in slices, cooked in salted water and drained; tomatoes, peeled, drained, seeded and chopped; quarters of hard-boiled eggs, nasturtium flowers, shrimps in mayonnaise with chopped parsley, chervil and tarragon.

Arrange the shrimps in a dome in mayonnaise. Surround with garnish as above. Just before serving sprinkle the garnish with a few tablespoons *Vinaigrette sauce* (see SAUCE).

Allemande salad. SALADE À L'ALLEMANDE – Dice 300 g. (11 oz., 2 cups) boiled potatoes and 100 g. (4 oz., 1 cup) rather tart eating apples. Season with 3 tablespoons (scant $\frac{1}{4}$ cup) mayonnaise. Arrange in a dome in a salad dish, and garnish with slices of cooked beetroot and onions.

Put trimmed salt herring fillets and gherkins, cut in strips. on top of the potatoes. Sprinkle with chopped parsley. Just before serving pour a little oil and vinegar over the garnish.

American salad I. SALADE AMÉRICAINE – Celeriac cut in *julienne*, seasoned with *Vinaigrette sauce* (see SAUCE) arranged in a dome. Surround with sliced potatoes and tomatoes. Garnish with quartered hard-boiled eggs. Put thin slices of onions on top of the celeriac and sprinkle with chopped chervil and tarragon.

American salad II. SALADE AMÉRICAINE – Thin cucumber slices, soaked in salt, rinsed, and seasoned with *Vinaigrette sauce* (see SAUCE). Surround with lettuce hearts, slices of tomato and quarters of hard-boiled eggs. Sprinkle with a few tablespoons *vinaigrette sauce*.

This salad must be served very cold, even iced.

Andalusian salad. SALADE ANDALOUSE – Cook rice in salted water, drain and season with oil, vinegar, salt and paprika. Add chopped onion, parsley, and a little grated garlic. Surround with alternate heaps of sweet pimentos, peeled, seasoned and cut in *julienne*, and quarters of tomatoes. Sprinkle with chopped chervil.

Argenteuil salad. SALADE ARGENTEUIL – Season diced potatoes with mayonnaise and chopped chervil. Put white asparagus tips, seasoned with oil and lemon, on top. Garnish with a border of shredded lettuce and quarters of hard-boiled eggs.

Arlésienne salad. SALADE ARLÉSIENNE – Sliced potatoes; sliced artichoke bottoms seasoned with oil, vinegar, salt and pepper, chopped chervil and tarragon, arranged in a salad bowl. Garnish with endives cooked in a flour-and-water *court-bouillon*, cut in small quarters, tomatoes cut in quarters and large stoned olives. Place fillets of anchovies arranged in a criss-cross pattern on top.

Bagration salad. SALADE BAGRATION – Artichoke bottoms cut in thick strips, celeriac in short strips, and chunks of macaroni. Season with mayonnaise flavoured with tomato, and surrounded with chopped hard-boiled egg, truffle and scarlet tongue. Sprinkle with chopped parsley.

Beef salad à la Parisienne. SALADE DE BOEUF À LA PARISIENNE – See BEEF, *Cold boiled beef à la parisienne*.

Beetroot salad. SALADE DE BETTERAVES – Cut cooked beetroot into *julienne* or thin round slices. Dress with *Vinaigrette sauce* (see SAUCE). Arrange in an *hors-d'œuvre* dish, and sprinkle with chopped parsley. Garnish with small raw onion rings, if liked.

Beetroot salad à la crème. SALADE DE BETTERAVES À LA CRÈME – Cut the beetroot as above. Dress with *Mustard cream sauce* (see SAUCE).

Beetroot salad à la polonaise. SALADE DE BETTERAVES À LA POLONAISE – Cut the beetroot in *julienne* and season with mustard to which has been added a few tablespoons of cream and lemon juice, salt and pepper. Sprinkle with grated horseradish and chopped hard-boiled eggs.

Bressane salad. SALADE BRESSANE – This preparation constitutes a cold *entrée* rather than a salad in the true sense.

Garnish the bottom of a salad bowl with shredded lettuce seasoned with *Vinaigrette sauce* (see SAUCE) and pressed down to line the bowl. Add thin slices of chicken, season with oil, lemon juice, salt, pepper and chopped chervil. Cover with mayonnaise mixed with tomato juice and seasoned with

American salad (*Claire*)

paprika. Garnish with sliced truffles and surround with peeled green and red peppers, sliced in *julienne* and seasoned with *vinaigrette sauce*, with asparagus tips and quartered hard-boiled eggs.

Brimont salad. SALADE BRIMONT – Mix diced potatoes and artichoke bottoms with mayonnaise seasoned with curry powder.

Surround with crayfish tails and stoned olives seasoned with oil and vinegar, separating them by quartered hard-boiled eggs. Garnish with sliced truffles.

Calves' brain salad. (Carême's recipe). SALADE DE CERVELLE DE VEAU – After the brains have been blanched in salted water to which vinegar and tarragon have been added, Carême says 'They should be braised, masked with thin slices of lemon and covered with pieces of bacon fat, some stock and seasoning.

'When cold, the brains are cut in half and arranged in the following way (these look more like the texture of a mayonnaise rather than a salad).

'Arrange them in a crown on an *entrée* dish, the bottom of which will have been lined with shredded lettuce seasoned as a salad. Garnish the brains with more lettuce, then make an elegant border of hard-boiled eggs and garnish with lettuce hearts and fillets of anchovies.

'Before serving mask the brains with a *Ravigote sauce* (see SAUCE).'

Cancalaise salad. SALADE CANCALAISE – Fill lettuce leaves with 1 tablespoon each diced potatoes mixed with mayonnaise.

Put on each lettuce leaf 3 oysters poached in their own liquor, drained, de-bearded and seasoned with oil, lemon juice and pepper, and topped with a slice of truffle. Arrange the lettuce leaves in the form of a flower on a dish.

This dish can be served as a cold *hors-d'œuvre*.

Celeriac salad with cress. SALADE DE CÉLERI-RAVE À LA CRESSONIÈRE – Cut the celeriac in *julienne*, blanch in salted water, drain and season with *Vinaigrette* or *Mayonnaise sauce* (see SAUCE). Arrange in a salad bowl alternately with bunches of cress.

Demi-deuil salad. SALADE DEMI-DEUIL – Made up of equal parts of potatoes and truffles cut in *julienne* and seasoned with mustard and cream. Garnish with slices of truffles and slices of potato set alternately in a border.

Doria salad. SALADE DORIA – Celeriac cut in *julienne* and seasoned with mayonnaise, arranged in a dome. Cover with thin slices of white truffle. Garnish with separate heaps of asparagus tips and beetroot cut in a *julienne*. Sprinkle with hard-boiled egg yolk and chopped parsley.

Dubarry salad. SALADE DUBARRY – Arrange in a shallow salad dish flowerets of cauliflower cooked in salted water and well drained. Garnish with radishes and shredded watercress. Season with a sauce made with oil, lemon juice, salt, pepper and chopped chives.

Favourite salad. SALADE FAVORITE – Arrange in a salad dish, in separate heaps, asparagus tips, shelled crayfish and sliced white truffles. Season with oil, lemon juice, salt and pepper. Sprinkle with chopped celery and herbs.

Flemish salad. SALADE FLAMANDE – Season together chicory and potatoes, cut in thick strips, with oil, vinegar, salt and pepper. Add a few sliced, cooked onions. Arrange in a dome and garnish with fillets of salt herring. Sprinkle with chopped parsley and chervil.

Francillon or Japanese salad. SALADE FRANCILLON, DITE JAPONAISE – Mix an equal part of potatoes marinated in Chablis and mussels cooked as for *Mussels à la marinière* (see MUSSEL), with celery. Arrange in the shape of a *calotte de savant* ('wise man's skull cap'). Garnish with sliced truffles.

This salad is usually served under the name of Japanese salad.

Salad Dubarry (*Claire*)

Fruit salad. SALADE DE FRUITS – Fruit salads come into the category of sweet dishes rather than that of salads. They are seasoned with sugar and a liqueur. (See ORANGE, *Orange salad*.)

Certain fruits made into a salad, but without liqueur, are served as an accompaniment to game, goose and duck.

Imperia salad. SALADE IMPÉRIA – Choose white lettuce leaves, regular in shape. Fill each with a mixture of asparagus tips and truffles. Arrange flower fashion in shallow glass bowls.

Italian salad. SALADE ITALIENNE – Made of equal parts of the following ingredients: carrots, turnips and potatoes, cut in dice or shaped with a small vegetable cutter, diced asparagus tips, peas. Mix with mayonnaise. Garnish with fillets of anchovies, tomatoes, stoned olives and capers. Surround with quartered hard-boiled eggs. Sprinkle with chopped chervil.

This salad can be set in aspic.

Japanese salad. SALADE JAPONAISE – *Francillon salad* is often known under this name. In Japan this salad is made with chrysanthemum flowers.

There is also a salad known as 'Japanese' which consists of pineapple, oranges and tomatoes cut in pieces, seasoned with lemon juice, arranged in a salad bowl and sprinkled with soured cream. Garnish with lettuce hearts.

Lobster salad. SALADE DE HOMARD – Line the bottom of a salad bowl with a layer of shredded lettuce, seasoned with oil and vinegar and arranged in a dome. On top of this set the flesh of the lobster claws, shelled and cut into large dice, seasoned with oil and vinegar. Add the rest of the lobster meat, sliced and seasoned with *vinaigrette*. Sprinkle with chopped chervil and tarragon. Garnish with quartered hard-boiled eggs and lettuce hearts.

Spiny lobster salad. SALADE DE LANGOUSTE – Like *Lobster salad*, but made with the flesh of spiny lobster.

Maharajah salad. SALADE MAHARADJAH – Season rice cooked in salted water with oil, vinegar, curry and salt. Mix with crab flesh cut in dice. Surround with diced celeriac, blanched and seasoned, diced courgettes, blanched and seasoned, and quartered tomatoes. Sprinkle with chopped egg yolk and chives.

Mikado salad. SALADE MIKADO – Mix diced potatoes with shrimps. Bind together with mayonnaise flavoured with soya sauce.

Garnish the top of the salad with small chrysanthemum petals, blanched, drained and seasoned with oil, lemon juice, salt and pepper. Surround with a border of sweet pimentos, peeled and cut in *julienne*, and diced tomatoes. Sprinkle with chopped chervil.

Niçoise salad. SALADE NIÇOISE – Mix equal parts diced potatoes and French beans. Season with oil, vinegar, salt and pepper. Mix with anchovy fillets, olives and capers. Garnish with quartered tomatoes. Sprinkle with chopped chervil and tarragon.

Oriental salad. SALADE ORIENTALE – Season rice cooked in salted water and well drained, with oil, vinegar, salt, paprika and chopped onion. Surround with peeled, diced and seasoned sweet peppers, quartered tomatoes and black olives. Sprinkle with chopped chervil.

Parisian salad. SALADE PARISIENNE – Vegetable salad with the addition of sliced spiny lobster or crayfish and truffles, seasoned with very thick mayonnaise, arranged in a domed mould (like *Russian salad*, see below) coated with jelly and lined with thin slices of spiny lobster or crayfish and truffles.

This salad can also be served in a dish, all the ingredients mixed, seasoned with mayonnaise and truffles, and garnished with quartered hard-boiled eggs and lettuce hearts.

Pernollet salad. SALADE PERNOLLET – Mix shelled crayfish and diced truffles with mayonnaise.

Fill large shell-shaped lettuce leaves with this salad. Put on each leaf a few green asparagus tips seasoned with oil and lemon juice. Arrange the leaves flower fashion on a round dish.

This dish is mostly served as an *hors-d'œuvre*.

Sweet pimento salad à la créole. SALADE DE PIMENTS DOUX À LA CRÉOLE – Arrange in separate small mounds in a salad dish, seeded and peeled sweet pimentos, well balanced in salted water and drained, and rice cooked in salted water and drained. Put on each mound of rice slices of raw tomato and on the pimentos 1 teaspoon chopped chives. Season with oil, vinegar, salt and paprika.

Port-Royal salad (*Claire*)

Port-Royal salad. SALADE PORT-ROYAL – Arrange on a shallow glass salad dish a mixture of potatoes, sliced eating apples and diced French beans, all seasoned with mayonnaise. Coat the whole salad with more mayonnaise. Surround with quarters of lettuce and quartered hard-boiled eggs. Garnish with French beans.

Raphael salad

Rachel salad. SALADE RACHEL – Equal parts of celery, artichoke bottoms, diced or *julienne* potatoes, mixed with mayonnaise. Garnish with green asparagus tips.

Raphael salad. SALADE RAPHAEL – Garnish the bottom of a salad dish that has rather high sides with shredded lettuce mixed with paprika-seasoned mayonnaise. Add thinly sliced cucumber, previously sprinkled with salt and left to stand, white asparagus tips cooked in water and well drained, peeled and seeded tomatoes divided into quarters, small lettuce hearts and unpeeled radishes cut in rounds. Season with olive oil, lemon juice, salt, pepper and chopped chervil.

Reine Pédauque salad. SALADE REINE PÉDAUQUE – Arrange quarters of lettuce hearts in a crown. Coat these with a sauce made with thick fresh cream, oil, mustard, lemon juice, salt and paprika. Fill the middle of the dish with shredded lettuce seasoned with oil and vinegar. Put stoned cherries on top. On each lettuce heart put a piece of peeled orange.

Rossini salad. SALADE ROSSINI – From a letter of Rossini: 'What is going to interest you much more than my opera is the discovery I have just made of a new salad, for which I hasten to send you the recipe.

'Take Provence oil, French vinegar, a little lemon juice, pepper and salt. Whisk and mix all together. Then throw in a few truffles, which you have taken care to cut in tiny pieces. The truffles give to this seasoning a kind of nimbus to plunge the gourmand into an ecstasy.'

Russian salad. SALADE RUSSE – Add to a mixed vegetable salad (seasoned with mayonnaise) pickled tongue, sausage, cooked mushrooms, lobster or crawfish meat and truffles, cut in dice or *julienne*.

Garnish with fillets of anchovies, truffles, scarlet tongue, capers, gherkins, etc.

In classical cookery, Russian salad, seasoned with very thick mayonnaise, is put into a domed mould lined with jelly and decorated. After having been well chilled on ice the salad is turned out on to a plate.

German sauerkraut salad. SALADE DE CHOUCROUTE À L'ALLEMANDE – Sauerkraut cooked in consommé or water, piled in a dome in a salad dish. Garnish with hard-boiled eggs and rounds of beetroot. Season with *Vinaigrette sauce* (see SAUCE).

Shellfish salad. SALADE DE CRUSTACÉS – Made with the flesh of lobster or crawfish, crab, shrimps, etc.

Slice the tail of the shellfish as well as the claws if it be lobster. Cut the rest of the flesh in big dice. Season the whole with oil, vinegar, salt, pepper, chopped parsley and chervil.

On a base of seasoned and shredded lettuce set first the diced fish, then the sliced. Garnish with fillets of anchovies, capers, olives, quartered hard-boiled egg and lettuce hearts. Sprinkle with chopped chervil and parsley.

Shrimp salad. SALADE DE CREVETTES – See SHRIMP.

Shrimp salad à la dieppoise. SALADE DE CREVETTES À LA DIEPPOISE – Made like *Cancalaise salad*, replacing the oysters by shrimps and mussels seasoned with oil, vinegar and pepper.

This dish can be served as a cold *hors-d'œuvre*.

Truffle salad. SALADE DE TRUFFES – See *Rossini salad*.

Vegetable salad. SALADE DE LÉGUMES – In general principle this is made up of all kinds of fresh vegetables.

Season with oil, vinegar, salt and pepper. Arrange in a salad dish, garnish with a floweret of cauliflower set on the summit, and sprinkle with chopped chervil and parsley.

In a restaurant the different ingredients of this salad are set in the salad dish in separate mounds. The seasoning, and thus the mixing, is done before the customer.

Watercress salad. SALADE CRESSONIÈRE – Half watercress and half potato salad, sprinkled with chopped hard-boiled egg and chopped parsley.

SALAD BURNET. PIMPRENELLE – Hardy perennial herb with slightly villous leaves which smell like cucumbers when crushed.

Salad burnet is available from June to November and in the following spring, and is mainly used as a seasoning. The tender fresh leaves of this plant can also be used in salads like watercress.

SALAMANDER. SALAMANDRE – Oven, generally gas-heated, into which dishes are put to glaze or brown the surface very rapidly.

The word also means breadcrumbs fried in butter, which are sprinkled over certain preparations.

Salambô cakes (*Maison Desmeuzes. Phot. Larousse*)

SALAMBÔ – Small cake made with *Chou paste* (see DOUGH), filled with *French pastry cream* (see CREAMS) flavoured with kirsch. The top is iced.

SALAMI – Product of Italian *charcuterie* eaten like *mortadella* (q.v.).

Salamis are commercial products sold in food shops. The most renowned is that of Bologna.

In Germany and various northern countries of Europe the name is given to a variety of similar preparations.

SALANGANE – Sea swallow of the Far East whose nests, constructed of seaweed fixed with the birds' saliva, are highly esteemed by the gourmets of China. They are sold in Europe as *Swallows' nests* (see NESTS; SOUPS AND BROTHS, *Consommé with birds' nests*).

SALÉ – Salted or pickled foodstuffs, synonymous with *salaison*.

Petit salé – Name for a piece of *charcuterie* made with the first bone of the flank end of belly of pork on which a little meat has been allowed to remain. It is left to salt for 12 hours in a light brine and cooked with other pieces of boiled *charcuterie*.

The *petit salé* is served hot or cold as an *hors-d'œuvre*.

The term is also used for pieces of collar or neck, lightly pickled in brine and used in *potées* or served by themselves, after having been poached in an aromatic stock.

SALEP – Edible substance, which comes from Persia and Asia Minor, in the form of small tubers 1 to 2 cm ($\frac{1}{2}$ to $\frac{3}{4}$ inch) in diameter, strung together in bunches. Translucent, yellowish grey in colour, horny in texture, and gelatinous in flavour, the salep comes from the tubers of various species of orchis, taken up after the stalks of the plant have faded and dried in the sun. They contain a floury substance and gelatine, and constitute an easily digested foodstuff highly esteemed in the East.

Indigenous orchis, treated in the same way, provide a salep comparable in every way with that of the East. Prepared as a jelly or soup.

Salep jelly. GELÉE AU SALEP – Mix, without allowing to curdle, 1 teaspoon salep in 2 dl. ($\frac{1}{3}$ pint 1 scant cup) water. Cook over low heat, keeping at boiling point for 4 or 5 minutes. Add a little cinnamon and 2 tablespoons (3 tablespoons) tamarind or pineapple syrup and allow to get cold.

Salep soup. POTAGE AU SALEP – Mix, without allowing to curdle, 1 teaspoon salep in 2 dl. ($\frac{1}{3}$ pint., 1 scant cup) unsalted vegetable stock. Add 1 sprig of tarragon and 1 teaspoon soya sauce.

SALMIGONDIS – *Ragoût* of several kinds of meat reheated. Reheated poultry *ragoût* is called *capilotade*.

SALMIS – The origin of *salmis* goes back as far as the fourteenth century. The *canard à la sauce dodine* of which Taillevent speaks in his *Viandier* was a kind of *salmis*. Some writers, however, say that this dish was invented at the beginning of the eighteenth century.

Duck à la rouennaise, one of the finest dishes of Normandy cooking, is a kind of *salmis* made with red wine. In the same way it is also possible to class as *salmis, caneton en chemise, canard sauvage (wild duck)* or *bécasse (woodcock) au Chambertin*, and a number of other preparations of birds which, before being finished in a special sauce, are two-thirds roasted.

Cook the bird in the oven or on the spit, for two-thirds of the necessary time. Divide into joints, remove the skin and trim the pieces. Arrange them in a buttered sauté dish with mushrooms and sliced truffles (*salmis* being a dish that is often finished off at the table before the guests, it is important to choose a decorative pan made of silver plate or some other good-looking metal). Sprinkle with a few tablespoons *Demi-glace sauce* (see SAUCE) and cook over hot water for 30 minutes.

Heat the broken-up carcases and trimmings of the bird in butter in a casserole. Add the cooking juices diluted with white wine, and a few tablespoons game-flavoured *Espagnole sauce* (see SAUCE, *Salmis sauce*). Boil for a few moments and strain, pressing all the time, first through a strainer and then through a cloth. Boil it down, add butter, and pour it over the pieces of bird and the garnish. Heat, still without boiling, 5 minutes more, and serve, either on a big croûton of bread spread with *à gratin forcemeat* (see FORCEMEATS) and put for a short time in the oven, or in a dish. In the latter case surround with heart-shaped croûtons fried in butter and spread with *à gratin forcemeat*.

This method of preparation is applicable not only to game birds (woodcock, wild duck, pheasant, partridge, etc.) but also to some poultry (duck, pigeon, guinea-fowl, etc.).

SALMON. SAUMON – Migratory fish living in the sea but spawning in fresh water. At the time of spawning it makes its way up certain rivers.

Salmon take no nourishment so long as they are in fresh water, so their flesh is at its driest and least good when they go down the rivers again to the sea.

Born in the rivers, the young salmon begins to develop there, not going far from its birthplace during the first few weeks. Then, following the flow of the river, it goes down to the depths of the sea, where its nourishment consists mainly of the post-larvae of herrings and other fish.

The salmon can live without going to the sea, as has been observed in Norway and Sweden, where it inhabits certain freshwater lakes; during the winter and in spring it goes up the river to spawn. It returns to the lakes later to build itself up again, just as the salmon of other rivers return to the sea.

The same thing happens in certain Canadian lakes where salmon hibernate. But these develop much less rapidly than the salmon which travel to the sea, and the quality of their flesh is inferior to that of their fellows who have followed the natural law of their existence.

Salmon which have attained their maximum development measure from $1\frac{1}{4}$ to $1\frac{1}{2}$ m (4 to 5 ft.) in length and their weight ranges from 5 to 7 kg. (11 to 15 lb.). They achieve this size at the age of about 6 years. In Scotland, salmon have been fished weighing up to 35 kg. (75 lb.). In the U.S.A. the Pacific coast salmon varies in weight from $2\frac{3}{4}$ to 27 kg. (6 to 60 lb.)

The flesh of salmon is preserved by drying, smoking, canning or freezing. The fish is cooked whole or cut in chunks or cutlets (steaks).

In France, salmon is often poached, whole or in pieces, in a flavoured *court-bouillon* (see below), and served hot or cold, with, in the case of the hot fish, one or other of the sauces normally served with fish cooked in *court-bouillon*, such as: *Anchovy, Butter, Caper, Shrimp, Lobster, Mousseline, Nantua, Ravigote, Vénitienne,* etc.

Cold salmon is accompanied by cold sauces such as: *Mayonnaise, Tartare, Verte, Rémoulade, Vincent*, etc. (see SAUCE).

Salmon may also be braised whole (stuffed or otherwise), and cooked very slowly in fish *fumet* (q.v.) made with red or white wine. Prepared in this way various garnishes, plain or mixed, accompany the salmon.

Whole or cut into smaller pieces, it may also be cooked on the spit.

Côtelettes of salmon are cooked in many ways: in *court-bouillon* and served with the same sauces as those prescribed for salmon cooked whole or in sections; grilled, or sautéed in butter, or braised. These have the same garnishes as for large pieces or whole salmon.

Salmon may also be prepared in fillets, which are cooked whole, braised or otherwise, or cut in slices which are sautéed in butter and accompanied by a variety of sauces and garnishes.

The flesh of the salmon, which is pinkish and becomes bright pink when cooked, is extremely delicate. It is fatty and often a little indigestible.

Court-bouillon for salmon. COURT-BOUILLON POUR CUIRE LE SAUMON – Put into a saucepan $2\frac{1}{2}$ litres ($4\frac{1}{2}$ pints, $5\frac{1}{2}$ pints) water, 1 dl. (6 tablespoons, scant $\frac{1}{2}$ cup) vinegar or lemon juice, 300 g. (11 oz., $2\frac{3}{4}$ cups) carrots and 250 g. (9 oz., $2\frac{1}{4}$ cups) onions, both finely chopped, 50 g. (2 oz., $1\frac{1}{2}$ cups) parsley stalks, a bayleaf, a sprig of thyme and 25 g. (1 oz., 1 tablespoon) rock salt. Boil very slowly for 1 hour. Ten minutes before taking it off the heat add 10g. ($1\frac{1}{2}$ teaspoons) peppercorns. Strain through a fine sieve and cool before using.

To cook a whole salmon in a court-bouillon. Place the salmon on the grid of the fish-kettle. Cover with cold *court-bouillon*. Bring the liquid up to boiling point. Skim, turn the heat very low, and let it poach without boiling.

To cook salmon côtelettes in court-bouillon. The *côtelettes* are cooked in *court-bouillon* prepared as above, but they are put into the liquid when it is already boiling. Cook over low heat without boiling.

To cook large cuts of salmon in court-bouillon. Proceed as for whole salmon.

Salmon, whether whole, in large cuts or cutlets, may equally well be cooked in a *court-bouillon* prepared with half white wine and half water. This is flavoured with the same vegetables as are indicated for ordinary *court-bouillon*, but they should first be cooked in butter before putting them in the liquor. This latter *court-bouillon* is used chiefly when the salmon is to be served cold and will be cooled in its cooking liquor.

HOT SALMON. SAUMON CHAUD –

Salmon attereaux. ATTEREAUX DE SAUMON – Marinate pieces of salmon in oil, lemon juice, chopped parsley, salt and pepper. Thread them on skewers with sliced mushrooms. Coat in *Villeroi sauce* (see SAUCE), and when this is cold, dip in egg and breadcrumbs. Fry in deep fat and garnish with fried parsley and quarters of lemon.

Boiled salmon with various sauces. DARNE DE SAUMON BOUILLIE – Cook a chunk of salmon in *court-bouillon*. Drain it and garnish with fresh parsley and boiled potatoes. Serve with one or other of the sauces that accompany fish: *Anchovy,*

Salmon

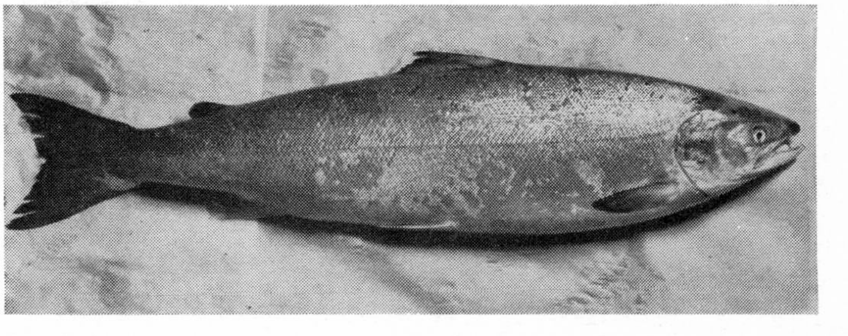

Butter, *Caper*, *Cardinal*, *Shrimp*, *Curry*, *Diplomat*, *Hollandaise*, *Lobster*, *Laguipière*, *Mousseline*, *Mustard*, *Nantua*, *Noisette*, *Ravigote*, *Riche*, *Vénitienne*, *White wine* (see SAUCE).

Boiled salmon à l'anglaise. SAUMON BOUILLI À L'ANGLAISE – Cook the salmon in salted water without herbs or condiments. Drain, and serve with *Lobster sauce* or *Parsley sauce* (see SAUCE) and cucumber salad.

Braised salmon. SAUMON BRAISÉ – Whole braised salmon may be prepared with or without stuffing. It is usually garnished with *Pike forcemeat* (see FORCEMEATS) to which truffles or a shellfish butter may be added.

The salmon is set on the well-buttered grid of the fish-kettle. The bottom of the pan is lined with chopped carrots and onions, lightly tossed in butter. Fish *fumet* made with white or red wine is poured in to come half-way up the salmon. A *bouquet garni* and seasoning are added and the salmon is poached in the usual way (see CULINARY METHODS, *Poaching*).

Once cooked, the salmon is drained, skinned, and glazed in the oven. It is set on a low dish, surrounded with the prescribed garnish, and coated with a sauce prepared with its cooking liquor.

All the ways of preparing slices and chunks of salmon given elsewhere are applicable to whole, braised salmon.

Salmon Chambord. DARNE DE SAUMON CHAMBORD – Cut a thick slice from the salmon. Braise it very slowly in *fumet* made with red or white wine.

Drain the salmon and glaze it in a slow oven for a few minutes. Set on a serving dish and surround it with *Chambord garnish* (see GARNISHES).

Coat with *Genevoise sauce* (see SAUCE) made with the braising juices.

Cutlets of salmon. CÔTELETTES DE SAUMON – Cutlets of salmon describe the following:

1. Salmon cutlets or slices which have been halved down the middle and trimmed into the shape of cutlets. These are cooked in butter, and sprinkled with a little of their cooking butter or accompanied by any of a variety of sauces and garnishes.

2. Croquette made with a croquette mixture (see HORS-D'ŒUVRE, *Hot hors-d'œuvre cutlets*) fashioned into the shape of cutlets, coated in egg and breadcrumbs and cooked in butter.

3. Light dish served as hot *hors-d'œuvre* or small *entrée*, in which a salmon quenelle mixture is put into cutlet-shaped moulds and poached.

Cutlets of salmon à l'américaine. CÔTELETTES DE SAUMON À L'AMÉRICAINE – Half slices of salmon trimmed into cutlet shape, seasoned with salt and pepper and floured. Cook in half butter and half oil.

Drain the pieces, set them on a dish, and put on top of each a slice of lobster prepared *à l'américaine* (see LOBSTER). Garnish the middle of the dish with a *salpicon* of diced lobster (made with the rest of the lobster flesh). Coat with *American sauce* (see SAUCE).

Cutlets of salmon braised with red wine. CÔTELETTES DE SAUMON BRAISÉES AU VIN ROUGE, DITE À LA BOURGUIGNONNE – Cook the *côtelettes* in a fish *fumet* made with red wine. Drain them and set on a serving dish or on heart-shaped croûtons of bread fried in butter. Garnish with little cooked mushrooms and little glazed onions.

Boil down the cooking liquor and thicken it with *Kneaded butter* (see BUTTER). Add more butter and strain. Pour over the fish.

Instead of mixing butter and flour into this sauce it may be thickened by adding 2 or 3 tablespoons *Espagnole Sauce II* (see SAUCE).

Cut raw salmon into slices across the width of the body; the tail piece is cut lengthwise

Cutting cooked salmon (*Larousse*)

First make a full length incision

Fold back the skin on both sides of the incision

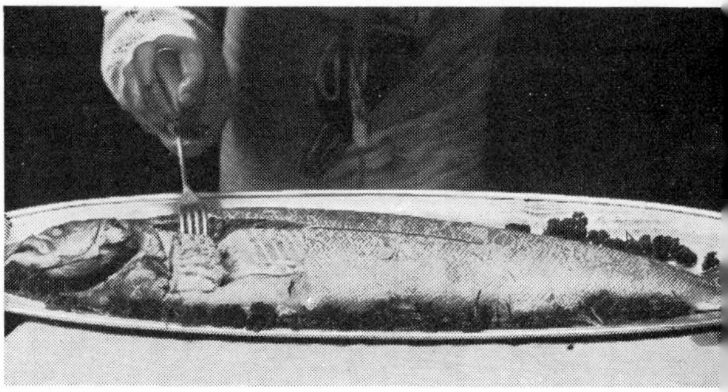

Divide the flesh into portions and remove with a fork

Cutlets of salmon braised with white wine. CÔTELETTES DE SAUMON BRAISÉES AU VIN BLANC – Cook the *côtelettes* very slowly in fish *fumet* made with white wine.

Drain and arrange them on a dish in the shape of a crown. Decorate with the required garnish. Coat with *White wine sauce* (see SAUCE) to which has been added (before straining) some of the cooking liquid, well boiled down.

Thus prepared, the *côtelettes* may be accompanied by one or other of the garnishes usually served with braised fish and coated with a sauce which will blend with the garnish.

Cutlets of salmon à la florentine. CÔTELETTES DE SAUMON À LA FLORENTINE – The *côtelettes* are cooked very slowly in concentrated fish *fumet*. Drain and arrange them in a fireproof dish on a layer of spinach which has been cooked, drained, dried, roughly chopped, simmered in butter, and seasoned with salt and pepper. Coat with *Mornay sauce* (see SAUCE).

Sprinkle with grated cheese and a little melted butter, and brown well.

Cutlets of salmon Mornay. CÔTELETTES DE SAUMON MORNAY – Prepare in the same way as *Cutlets of salmon à la florentine*, but leave out the layer of spinach.

Cutlets of salmon with mushrooms à la crème. CÔTELETTES DE SAUMON AUX CHAMPIGNONS À LA CRÈME – Season the *côtelettes*, flour them and cook in butter. When they are half-cooked put 2 or 3 mushrooms for each *côtelette* into the pan. Finish cooking together.

Drain the pieces and arrange them on a dish or on heart-shaped croûtons of bread fried in butter. Set the mushrooms on top of the *côtelettes*. Coat with the cooking juices diluted with Madeira, with fresh cream and butter added, and 1 or 2 tablespoons fish *Velouté sauce* (see SAUCE) for thickening, the whole boiled down and strained.

Cutlets of salmon with mushrooms and Madeira. CÔTELETTES DE SAUMON AUX CHAMPIGNONS AU MADÈRE – Cook the fish and mushrooms as above. Coat with a sauce made by diluting the cooking juices with Madeira and adding a few tablespoons *Espagnole sauce II* (see SAUCE), boiled down, extra butter added, and the sauce strained.

Cutlets of salmon Pojarski. CÔTELETTES DE SAUMON POJARSKI – Mash 300 g. (11 oz.) salmon flesh, adding 75 g. (3 oz., $1\frac{1}{2}$ cups) breadcrumbs which have been soaked in milk and pressed as dry as possible, and 75 g. (3 oz., 6 tablespoons) fresh butter.

Season with salt, pepper and a pinch of grated nutmeg. Divide this mixture into the shape of cutlers.

Cook in clarified butter, until they are browned on both sides. To serve, sprinkle with the cooking butter.

Salmon cutlets Pojarski are usually accompanied by sautéed potatoes or a green vegetable tossed in butter, and any of the sauces designed for fish.

Cutlets of salmon with truffles. CÔTELETTES DE SAUMON AUX TRUFFES – Sauté the cutlets in butter. When they are almost cooked put into the pan thick slices of truffles seasoned with salt and pepper. Finish cooking, with the pan covered, over slow heat.

Arrange the cutlets on a dish and set the truffle slices on top. Sprinkle with the cooking juices diluted with Madeira to which have been added 2 tablespoons (3 tablespoons) *Demi-glace sauce* (see SAUCE) based on concentrated fish stock.

Cutlets of salmon with truffles and cream. CÔTELETTES DE SAUMON AUX TRUFFES À LA CRÈME – As above, but diluting the cooking juices with Madeira and fresh cream.

Cutlets of salmon variously garnished. CÔTELETTES DE SAUMON HACHÉES, PANÉES – Prepare the cutlets as for *Cutlets of salmon Pojarski*, but coat them with egg and breadcrumbs.

Cook in clarified butter. Set in the form of a crown on a serving dish, fill the middle with the prescribed accompaniments, and pour round the sauce. Sprinkle the cutlets with *Noisette butter* (see BUTTER, *Compound butters*) and put paper frills on the ends.

Coulibiac of salmon. COULIBIAC DE SAUMON – 1 kg. ($2\frac{1}{4}$ lb.) *Brioche dough II* (see DOUGH) made without sugar and kept rather firm so that it can be easily rolled out.

Sauté 750 g. ($1\frac{1}{2}$ lb.) salmon, cut in small slices, quickly in butter. Season with salt and pepper. Allow to cool.

Cook in light consommé or salted water, for $3\frac{1}{2}$ hours, 75 g. (3 oz.) sturgeon notochord (the spinal cord of the sturgeon) which has been previously soaked in cold water for 5 hours. Drain and chop it roughly.

Prepare a *kasha* or pudding of semolina in the following way: mix 200 g. (7 oz., generous cup) large grain wheat semolina with 1 beaten egg. Spread in a baking tin and dry out in a slow oven. Put the semolina through a coarse sieve. Cook it in consommé, drain, and allow it to cool. Chop 3 hard-boiled eggs.

Cook 75 g. (3 oz., $\frac{3}{4}$ cup) chopped onion, 100 g. (4 oz., 2 cups) cultivated chopped and pressed mushrooms. Remove onion and mushrooms, and toss the chopped eggs in the cooking butter.

To make and cook coulibiac. Roll out the brioche dough into a rectangle 30 to 35 cm. (12 to 14 inches) long and 20 cm (8 inches) wide. In the middle set the various ingredients of the filling, arranging them in layers one on top of the other – cooked semolina, slices of salmon, sturgeon notochord, hard-boiled eggs and mushrooms mixture, all these ingredients being quite cold. Finish with a layer of cooked semolina.

Close up the paste by folding over the edges from each side. The edges should be lightly damped with water before pressing together. Put the *coulibiac* on a baking tin, turning it over so that the sealed side is on the bottom. Put it in a warm place for 30 minutes for the dough to rise.

Brush the surface with melted butter, sprinkle with bread-crumbs. Make an opening in the top to let the steam escape.

Cook in a moderately hot oven for 45 minutes to 1 hour, according to the size of the *coulibiac*.

When taking it from the oven pour into it, through the hole in the top, a few tablespoons melted butter.

Coulibiac is served without the accompaniment of a sauce.

Small coulibiacs of salmon. PETITS COULIBIACS DE SAUMON – Small *coulibiacs*, which are served as *hors-d'œuvre* or light *entrées*, are made by filling with the same ingredients as above pieces of *Ordinary brioche dough* (see DOUGH) cut out with a fluted-edged pastry-cutter about 12 cm. ($4\frac{1}{2}$ inches) in diameter.

Creamed salmon au gratin. BORDURE DE SAUMON CRÈME GRATIN – Made with left-over salmon like *Creamed cod au gratin* (see COD).

Croquettes and cromesquis of salmon. CROQUETTES, CROMESQUIS DE SAUMON – These are both made with a *salpicon* of cooked salmon mixed with diced truffles and mushrooms bound with *Allemand* or *Béchamel sauce* (see SAUCE, CROQUETTES, CROMESQUI).

Salmon Daumont. DARNE DE SAUMON DAUMONT – Braise a chunk of salmon in a fish *fumet* (q.v.) made with white wine.

Drain and set it on a serving dish. Surround with *Daumont garnish* (see GARNISHES). Coat with its strained cooking juices and serve with *Nantua sauce* (see SAUCE).

Escalopes of salmon. ESCALOPES DE SAUMON – These are cut from fillets of salmon, and should weigh about 100 g. (4 oz.) each.

They are lightly flattened and trimmed if necessary so that they are oval in shape. Cook in butter, or poach in concentrated fish *fumet*.

All the ways described for preparing *côtelettes* and slices of salmon are applicable to escalopes.

Salmon fillets. FILETS DE SAUMON – Thin slices of salmon cut from raw fillets. They are prepared like salmon cutlets, steaks and escalopes, and are fried, either coated in egg and breadcrumbs or dipped in batter.

Orly of fillets of salmon with tomato sauce (Plumerey's recipe). ORLY DE FILETS DE SAUMON, SAUCE TOMATE – 'Trim 14 fillets (see above) of salmon; put them in a bowl with salt, mignonette, a little grated nutmeg, 2 chopped shallots, parsley on its stalks, the juice of 2 lemons, $\frac{1}{2}$ cup olive oil and a little thyme and bay leaf. Take care to move the fillets about in this seasoning and drain off the water they will exude. An hour before serving, drain them and remove all the ingredients that have served to give them taste, including the mignonette. Put a handful of flour on top and shake them about to dry them well. Reshape them with the blade of a knife and dip them into beaten egg to coat them and ensure that they fry a good colour. At the moment of serving arrange them in the form of a crown and serve with a light *Tomato sauce* (see SAUCE).'

Salmon fritters. FRITOT DE SAUMON – Soak sliced or diced salmon for 30 minutes in oil, lemon juice, chopped parsley, salt and pepper. Dip in light batter and fry in deep fat.

Drain and dry the pieces on a cloth. Season with dry fine salt. Garnish with fried parsley and lemon. Serve with *Tomato sauce* (see SAUCE).

Kedgeree of salmon. CADGERY DE SAUMON – Made with cooked, flaked salmon, *Rice pilaf* (see PILAF), *Béchamel sauce* (see SAUCE) flavoured with curry, and diced hard-boiled eggs, in the same way as *Turbot kedgeree* (see TURBOT).

Mousse of salmon. MOUSSE ET MOUSSELINE DE SAUMON – See MOUSSES, MOUSSELINES.

Hot salmon pie à la française. PÂTÉ CHAUD DE SAUMON À LA FRANÇAISE – 'Cut a thick slice of salmon, remove the bone and skin, and stud it with truffles and de-salted anchovies. Wash the flesh of a medium-sized pike and use it to make a *Fish forcemeat* (see FORCEMEATS). Wash the scraps remaining from the 2 fish and cook them in butter with chopped carrots and onions, parsley on its stems, thyme, bay leaf, 1 clove garlic, 2 cloves and a small pinch of salt. Pour over $\frac{1}{2}$ bottle Chablis.

'Surround the salmon with light bards of bacon fat and tie it; put it like this into the saucepan. Strain the fish stock at the end of 45 minutes, during which it will have simmered gently. Pour it over the salmon and give it 20 to 30 minutes longer. Drain it and allow to cool. Strain the fish stock, remove all grease from it and boil it down, so that it can be used to make a *Financière sauce* (see SAUCE).

'Line a mould with pastry suitable for a hot *entrée*. Spread the bottom and sides with the prepared pike forcemeat, to which add 2 chopped raw truffles. Slightly trim the salmon, put it into the pie and cover with pastry. Bake in the oven for 1 hour. Take off the pastry lid and the forcemeat which are masking the top of the salmon, and carefully remove all grease. Garnish the top with a *ragoût* of soft roes, truffles and mushrooms, and coat with the prepared *financière sauce*.

'If it is desired to serve the pie cold, prepare in the same way, but do not take off pastry lid. The fish stock should be more concentrated, with $\frac{1}{2}$ glass Madeira added to it, poured into the pie through the opening left in the pastry lid. Do not serve this *pâte* until 24 hours after it has been cooked.' (Plumerey's recipe, slightly modified.)

Salmon pilaf. PILAF DE SAUMON – Prepare with pieces of salmon sautéed in butter in the same way as *Pilaf of mutton* (see PILAF).

Garnish with mushrooms or truffles sautéed in butter, and surround with a border of *Tomato sauce* (see SAUCE), tomatoes cooked till soft in butter, or any sauce for fish.

It may also be garnished with shelled shrimps or crayfish. In this case the pilaf is surrounded with a border of *White wine sauce* or *Butter sauce* (see SAUCE) finished off with a prepared butter of the shellfish used.

Salmon à la princesse. DARNE DE SAUMON PRINCESSE – Cook a chunk of salmon very slowly in fish *fumet*. Drain and garnish with green asparagus tips in butter. Coat with a sauce prepared with the cooking liquor with fish *Velouté sauce* (see SAUCE) which has been enriched with cream and butter and strained. Put slices of truffles heated in butter on top of the salmon. Make a border of light fish glaze round the fish.

Salmon quenelles. QUENELLES DE SAUMON – Salmon quenelles are prepared either with ordinary *Quenelle forcemeat* or *Mousseline forcemeat* (see FORCEMEATS). They may be large or small. The latter are shaped with a tablespoon or poached in special moulds.

Small salmon quenelles are used as an element in garnishes. Large salmon quenelles are served as a small *entrée* and are themselves accompanied by various garnishes and coated with a sauce to blend with the particular garnish. They may have some kind of *salpicon* added to them.

Salmon quenelles, various sauces and garnishes. QUENELLES DE SAUMON – Poach the quenelles. Set them on a dish or place each one on an oval croûton of bread fried in butter.

Garnish with the prescribed garnish: mushrooms, shrimps, crayfish tails, lobster, spiny lobster in a *salpicon* or vegetables in butter. Coat the quenelles with a sauce that will blend with the garnish.

Salmon risotto. RISOTTO DE SAUMON – Prepare like *Salmon pilaf*, replacing the pilaf rice by risotto.

Roast salmon. SAUMON RÔTI – Roasted whole or in large cuts. Whole salmon are most often stuffed. Season and cover with thin bards of bacon fat, holding these in place with a few pieces of string. Fix on the spit with the aid of skewers.

Cook the salmon under a hot heat. Baste often during the cooking, allowing 30 to 35 minutes per kg. (15 to 18 minutes per lb).

Before taking the salmon off the spit, remove the bards and allow it to colour. Remove from the spit. Serve with the cooking juices diluted with white wine and lemon juice.

Alternatively the salmon may be roasted in a moderately hot oven.

Salmon in scallop shells. COQUILLES DE SAUMON – Pipe a thin border of thickened potato purée round the edge of scallop shells with the aid of a forcing bag. Put into the bottom of each shell 1 tablespoon of *Mornay sauce* (see SAUCE), and the fish divided into small pieces, with the skin and bones carefully removed, on top.

Garnish, and coat with more sauce. Sprinkle with Parmesan and a little melted butter. Brush the potato border with egg.

Place the scallops in a baking tin containing a little warm water and brown in a very hot oven. Garnish with fresh parsley.

Instead of potato purée, chopped boiled potatoes may be used for the border.

Salmon in scallop shells à la florentine. COQUILLES DE SAUMON À LA FLORENTINE – Put into the bottom of scallop shells 2 tablespoons (3 tablespoons) spinach leaves simmered in butter, and pieces of salmon on top. Coat with *Mornay sauce* (see SAUCE) and cover with grated Parmesan. Sprinkle with melted butter. Brown in the oven or under the grill.

Salmon in scallop shells à la Mornay. COQUILLES DE SAUMON À LA MORNAY – Arrange pieces of salmon in scallop shells. Coat with *Mornay sauce* (see SAUCE) and cover with grated Parmesan. Sprinkle with melted butter. Brown in the oven or under the grill.

Salmon in scallop shells à la provençale. COQUILLES DE SAUMON À LA PROVENÇALE – Arrange pieces of salmon, truffles, stoned olives and mushrooms in scallop shells. Cover with *Provençale sauce* (see SAUCE). Sprinkle with pale golden breadcrumbs and a little olive oil. Brown in the oven or under the grill, then place on each scallop an anchovy fillet curved into a ring, and sprinkle with chopped parsley.

Salmon in scallop shells with shrimps. COQUILLES DE SAUMON AUX CREVETTES – Arrange pieces of salmon and shelled shrimps in scallop shells. Coat with *Mornay sauce* (see SAUCE) finished off with *Shrimp butter* (see BUTTER). Sprinkle with Parmesan and a little melted butter. Brown in the oven or under the grill.

Salmon in scallop shells à la Victoria. COQUILLES DE SAUMON À LA VICTORIA – Arrange pieces of salmon, truffles and mushrooms in scallop shells. Coat with *Nantua sauce* (see SAUCE). Sprinkle with Parmesan and melted butter. Brown in the oven, and place a slice of truffle heated in butter on each scallop.

Skewered salmon. BROCHETTES DE SAUMON – Thread pieces of salmon cut in squares on metal skewers, alternating them with mushrooms cut in thick slices and tossed in butter. Season with salt and pepper, pour over melted butter, coat with freshly made breadcrumbs and grill gently.

Set on a serving dish. Sprinkle with half-melted *Mâitre d'hotel butter* (see BUTTER) or serve this butter separately. Garnish with fresh parsley and surround with half slices of lemon cut with fluted edges.

One of the sauces recommended for grilled fish may be served separately with grilled skewered salmon.

Fried skewered salmon. BROCHETTES DE SAUMON FRITES – Sauté the pieces of salmon lightly in butter before threading them on the skewers. Coat the skewered pieces in egg and breadcrumbs.

Fry in deep fat and garnish with fried parsley and quarters of lemon. Serve with *Tomato sauce*, or any other sauce appropriate to fish (see SAUCE).

Salmon soufflé. SOUFFLÉ DE SAUMON – Rub cooked salmon through a sieve, mix with *Béchamel sauce* (see SAUCE), bind with egg yolks and stiffly beaten egg whites folded in at the last moment. (See SOUFFLÉ.)

Salmon steak à l'américaine. DARNE DE SAUMON À L'AMÉRICAINE – Cut a slice about 6 to 8 cm. ($2\frac{1}{2}$ to 3 inches) thick from the middle of the salmon. Season with salt and pepper. Cook in a buttered sauté pan on a layer of 2 tablespoons (3 tablespoons) *matignon* (q.v.) of raw root vegetables. Sprinkle with 4 tablespoons ($\frac{1}{3}$ cup) melted butter. Begin cooking over a good heat. Cover the pan and continue cooking in the oven, basting frequently with the butter, but without adding any liquid.

Prepare a spiny lobster as for *Lobster à l'américaine* (see LOBSTER). Remove the shell from the tail and slice the latter into 6 equal slices.

Split the body in half, longways, and take out all the flesh without breaking the half shells. Dice this flesh, add to it an equal quantity of cooked, diced mushrooms and bind with 1 dl. (6 tablespoons, scant $\frac{1}{2}$ cup) concentrated *Allemande sauce (*see SAUCE) to which chopped tarragon and chervil have been added.

Fill the half shells with the mixture. Smooth over the surfaces and sprinkle them with grated Parmesan and a little melted butter. Put the half shells on a baking tin and brown them in a very hot oven 10 minutes before serving.

The sauce. Add the *matignon* with which the salmon was cooked to the *American sauce* from the lobster. Add 3 dl. ($\frac{1}{2}$ pint, $1\frac{1}{4}$ cups) fish *fumet* and 1 dl. (6 tablespoons, scant $\frac{1}{2}$ cup) *Velouté sauce* (see SAUCE). Boil down by one-third over good heat, stirring with a wooden spoon.

Thicken the sauce away from the heat with the coral rubbed through a sieve and blended with 100 g. (4 oz., $\frac{1}{2}$ cup) fresh butter. Add chopped parsley, chervil and tarragon, the juice of $\frac{1}{2}$ lemon, salt and pepper if necessary, and mix well with a whisk.

Place the salmon, very hot, on a croûton of bread fried in butter, on a large dish. Put at each end the half shells of spiny lobster and the slices of spiny lobster set into tartlets of fine pastry, lightly coated with *American sauce* at the sides. Coat the salmon with the rest of the sauce and serve.

Salmon steak à l'anglaise. DARNE DE SAUMON À L'ANGLAISE – Slice of salmon coated in egg and breadcrumbs and cooked in butter. Served with *Maître d'hôtel butter* (see BUTTER).

Fried salmon steaks. DARNE DE SAUMON FRITE – Cut the salmon in thin slices, soak them in cold boiled milk, flour lightly, and fry in smoking hot oil.

Drain the slices and garnish with fried parsley and quarters of lemon.

Grilled salmon steak. DARNE DE SAUMON GRILLÉE – Season the salmon steak with salt and pepper. Brush with oil or melted butter. Cook under the grill at moderate heat.

Serve with *Maître d'hôtel butter* (see BUTTER), or any sauce recommended for grilled fish.

Grilled salmon steaks

Salmon steak à la meunière. DARNE DE SAUMON A LA MEUNIÈRE – Cut the salmon into slices. Season, sprinkle lightly with flour, and fry in smoking hot butter.

Arrange the slices on a dish, sprinkle with chopped parsley, and squeeze over a little lemon juice. When ready to serve, pour over the cooking butter, very hot. Surround with half slices of lemon.

Salmon steak à la Nantua. DARNE DE SAUMON À LA NANTUA – Cook a chunk of salmon in fish *fumet*. Drain, set it on a serving dish, and surround with shelled crayfish tails.

Coat with *Nantua sauce* (see SAUCE) to which the concentrated cooking juices of the fish have been added.

Salmon steak poached in white wine, various garnishes. DARNE DE SAUMON POCHÉE AU VIN BLANC – Poach the salmon steaks, cut rather thick, in fish *fumet* made with white wine. Drain and set them on a serving dish. Surround with the prescribed garnish. Coat with *White wine sauce* (see SAUCE) to which the concentrated cooking liquor of the fish has been added.

Tronçon of salmon Philéas Gilbert. TRONÇON DE SAUMON PHILÉAS GILBERT – Remove the bone of a large chunk of salmon, weighing $2\frac{1}{2}$ kg. ($5\frac{1}{2}$ lb.). Cook 3 carrots and half a celery heart, cut in a short *julienne* (q.v.), in butter. Add 3 tablespoons (scant $\frac{1}{4}$ cup) truffles and an equal quantity of mushrooms, also cut in *julienne*. Pour in $1\frac{1}{2}$ dl. ($\frac{1}{4}$ pint, $\frac{2}{3}$ cup) sherry and boil down. Bind with a few tablespoons very thick *Béchamel sauce* (see SAUCE) and season.

Stuff the fish with this mixture. Cover each end with a thin bard of bacon fat, and tie securely so that the stuffing cannot escape. Put the salmon in a fish kettle on a layer of chopped carrot and onion cooked in butter, mushroom and truffle skins, and a *bouquet garni.*

Season the salmon. Pour over some melted butter, and fill the pan with sherry to half-way up the fish. Start cooking over heat, then cook in the oven for 40 to 45 minutes, with the fish kettle covered.

When the salmon is cooked, skin the middle part, leaving only a thin strip of skin at either end. Keep the salmon warm in the oven, covering it with buttered paper, while preparing the sauce.

Strain the cooking liquor through a fine strainer and boil down; add 4 dl. (scant $\frac{3}{4}$ pint, $1\frac{3}{4}$ cups) thin *Espagnole sauce* (see SAUCE), well skimmed. Reduced again, adding gradually 4 dl. (scant $\frac{3}{4}$ pint, $1\frac{3}{4}$ cups) thick, fresh cream. When the sauce is ready, add 100 g. (4 oz., $\frac{1}{2}$ cup) butter and strain through muslin.

Garnish with 12 *barquettes* filled with a *ragoût* of crayfish tails *à la Nantua* (see CRAYFISH); 24 oysters fried *à la Villeroi*; 24 big mushrooms, cooked in a white *court-bouillon*; 12 truffles, cooked in sherry (the parings of these and the mushrooms are used to colour the stock), and 4 fillets of sole encrusted with half slices of truffles, lightly poached in fish *fumet*. When cooked, these fillets are placed over the skinned portion of the salmon.

Arrange the salmon with the garnishes on a long dish. Pour over it some spoonfuls of the sauce, and serve the rest separately.

COLD SALMON. SAUMON FROID –

Cold whole salmon or cuts of salmon with various sauces and garnishes. SAUMON ENTIER, EN TRONÇONS (FROID) – Poach the salmon, whole or in large cuts, in *court-bouillon*. Leave to cool in the cooking liquor.

Drain the fish and wipe it dry. Set on a large dish. Garnish with fresh parsley or with quartered hard-boiled eggs and lettuce hearts.

Accompanying sauces. Cold salmon is usually served with cold sauces made with an oil and egg yolk base, such as:

Andalouse, *Chantilly*, *Gribiche*, *Mayonnaise*, *Ravigote*, *Rémoulade*, *Russian*, *Tartare*, *Vincent*, *Vinaigrette*, etc. (see SAUCE, *Cold sauces*).

Garnishes for cold salmon. These are varied. Apart from lettuce hearts and hard-boiled eggs, they consist chiefly of vegetable salads mixed with mayonnaise (with the addition of gelatine) or *vinaigrette sauce*.

When cold salmon is served *à l'anglaise* it should be accompanied by cucumber salad.

The garnishes most often used with cold salmon are:

Small aspics of crayfish tails or shrimps, of lobster or crayfish, various *salpicons* or *macédoines* of vegetables, etc.

Tartlets or *barquettes* made of fine pastry, filled with caviar, *macédoine* of vegetables, etc., various mousses or purées, various *salpicons*, etc.

Barquettes or *cassolettes* made of beetroot or cucumber, filled as above.

Scallop shells with any of the fillings described above.

Artichoke bottoms (cooked in a flour-and-water *court-bouillon*) garnished with the same preparations used to fill *barquettes*, etc.

Stuffed hard-boiled eggs, using mousses and purées of various kinds for filling.

Small tomatoes, scooped out, marinated and filled with salad, or some kind of mousse or purée.

The garnishes enumerated above apply chiefly to salmon poached in a *court-bouillon*. Instructions will be found below for cold salmon cooked in a white wine fish stock.

Salmon poached in *court-bouillon* may also be prepared with *Montpellier butter* (see BUTTER, *Compound butters*), and salmon steaks or chunks may be served in the same way.

Cold boiled salmon, with various sauces and garnishes. SAUMON BOUILLI FROID – Cook in *court-bouillon* (whole, in large cuts or slices); cool in the cooking liquor.

Drain the fish, dry it, and garnish with fresh parsley, hard-boiled eggs or lettuce hearts. Serve with one or other of the sauces recommended for cold fish.

In England it is usual to serve cold salmon with cucumber seasoned with *Vinaigrette sauce* (see SAUCE) or plain, cut in thin slices.

Cutlets of salmon in aspic. CÔTELETTES DE SAUMON À LA GELÉE – Coat half slices of salmon that have been cooked in a *court-bouillon*, cooled and drained, with fish aspic jelly, or braise in a fish aspic jelly (see JELLY, *Fish jelly stock*) made with wine.

These cutlets, when cool, are decorated with truffles and glazed with jelly. Arrange in the form of a crown on a dish and garnish with chopped jelly.

Salmon cutlets may also be put into *barquettes* made of *Fine lining paste* (see DOUGH) cooked empty, on a layer of chopped jelly. Or they may be set on a croûton of bread cut into the same shape as the cutlet and covered with one of the compound butters (see BUTTER).

Cutlets of salmon à la moscovite. CÔTELETTES DE SAUMON À LA MOSCOVITE – Braise the cutlets in an aspic jelly stock (see JELLY, *Fish jelly stock*) made with dry champagne. Coat them, once they are cold, with white *Chaud-froid sauce* (see SAUCE) with the addition of blanched and drained chopped chives.

Set them in *barquettes* of *Fine lining paste* (see DOUGH), garnished with 1 good tablespoon of fresh caviare. Arrange the *barquettes* on a dish and garnish with fresh parsley. Serve with *Tartare sauce* (see SAUCE).

Cutlets of salmon à la Nantua. CÔTELETTES DE SAUMON À LA NANTUA – Cook the cutlets in an aspic jelly stock (see JELLY, *Fish jelly stock*) made with white wine. Allow them to cool.

Coat with *Chaud-froid sauce* (see SAUCE) that has been finished off with *Crayfish butter* (see BUTTER, *Compound butters*). Decorate them with broad thin slices of truffle topped with crayfish or shrimp tails. Glaze the cutlets with jelly.

Set in a bowl on a layer of well-set jelly. Garnish the middle with *Crayfish mousse* (see CRAYFISH) formed into a dome. Decorate with crayfish tails and slices of truffle arranged in alternate layers. Glaze with jelly and set on ice.

Cutlets of salmon à l'orientale. CÔTELETTES DE SAUMON À L'ORIENTALE – Proceed, with half-slices of salmon, as for *Red mullet à l'orientale* (see HORS-D'ŒUVRE, *Cold hors-d'œuvre*).

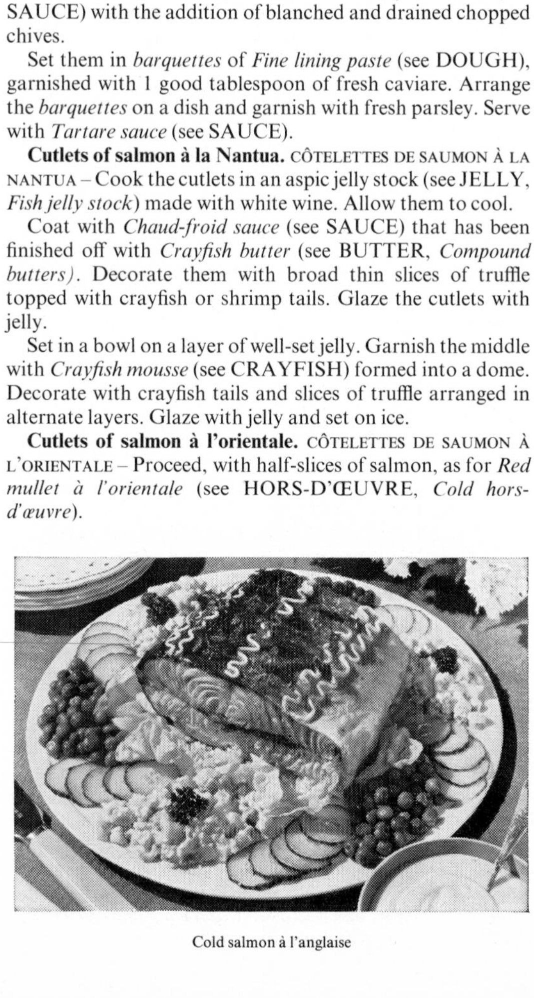

Cold salmon à l'anglaise

Cutlets of salmon à la parisienne. CÔTELETTES DE SAUMON À LA PARISIENNE – Line scallop shells with vegetable salad mixed with mayonnaise. Arrange slices of salmon on top. Coat with gelatine-strengthened mayonnaise.

Arrange round the edge of each scallop a little border of asparagus tips, pieces of carrot scooped out with a vegetable baller, and diced French beans, all previously cooked in salted water and well drained. Set a slice of truffle on top of each shell.

Cutlets of salmon à la russe. CÔTELETTES DE SAUMON À LA RUSSE – Line scallop shells with shredded lettuce seasoned with oil and vinegar. Set slices of salmon on top. Coat with gelatine-strengthened *Mayonnaise sauce* (see SAUCE).

Decorate with very small lettuce hearts, quartered hard-boiled eggs, olives, capers and anchovy fillets.

Galantine of salmon. GALANTINE DE SAUMON – This dish, known in old cookery under the name of *sous-presse de saumon*, is prepared in the same way as *Galantine* or *Ballottine of eel* (see EEL), with truffles, fillets of salmon and *Pike forcemeat* (see FORCEMEATS).

It is cooked, rolled up in a linen cloth, in a strengthened fish stock or *fumet*. When cooked, it is untied and rolled up again in a linen cloth, secured with twine, and cooled under light pressure.

Decorate with truffles or some other garnish of the same kind and glaze with jelly (see JELLY, *Fish jelly stock*). Serve on a long dish and surround with chopped jelly, the edges of the dish being decorated with jelly croûtons. It is served with mayonnaise or some other cold sauce.

Glazed salmon Bellevue in aspic. SAUMON GLACÉ BELLEVUE, EN ASPIC – Cook the salmon, whole or in large cuts, in an enriched *Fish jelly stock* (see JELLY). Cool in its cooking liquor.

Drain the fish, skin without breaking the flesh, and wipe with a cloth. Coat with half-set jelly (prepared with the liquor in which the fish was cooked, clarified in the usual way). Apply several layers of jelly until it is covered with a uniform coating.

Put the salmon on a dish covered with a layer of firmly set jelly. Decorate with cut-out jelly shapes. Keep in a cold place until ready to serve.

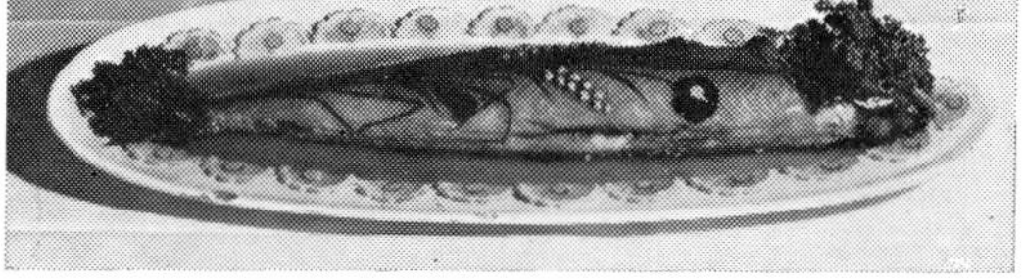

Glazed salmon au chambertin (*Larousse*)

Glazed salmon au chambertin. SAUMON GLACÉ AU CHAMBERTIN – Proceed as for *Glazed salmon Bellevue in aspic*, using a *Fish jelly stock* (see JELLY) prepared with Chambertin.

Glazed salmon cutlets au Chambertin. CÔTELETTES DE SAUMON GLACÉES AU CHAMBERTIN – Braise the salmon cutlets in Chambertin. Let them cool in the cooking liquor.

Finish off as for *Cutlets of salmon in aspic*.

The cutlets may be prepared in the same way with champagne, Bordeaux, Alsace or Rhine wine, etc.

Glazed salmon à la champenoise. SAUMON GLACÉ À LA CHAMPENOISE – Like *Glazed salmon Bellevue in aspic*, using a *Fish jelly stock* (see JELLY) made with dry champagne.

Glazed cutlets of salmon with macédoine of vegetables. CÔTELETTES DE SAUMON GLACÉES À LA MACÉDOINE DE LÉGUMES – Cut the salmon in slices 2 cm. ($\frac{3}{4}$ inch) thick and divide each one in half. Shape these halves in the form of cutlets (U.S. chops.)

Arrange them in a buttered dish; season with salt and pepper. Pour over fish *fumet* made with white wine and add a squeeze of lemon juice. Poach gently, keeping the dish covered. Cool under pressure. Drain and dry the cutlets, and decorate them with truffles or tarragon leaves. Glaze them with jelly.

Arrange in the form of a circle on a dish or on a shaped base of rice. Garnish the middle of the dish with a vegetable salad mixed with very thick mayonnaise and shaped into a dome. Decorate the top with truffles, lobster coral, anchovy fillets, etc. Surround the cutlets with jelly croûtons. Serve with mayonnaise.

Glazed salmon à l'impériale. SAUMON GLACÉ À L'IMPÉRIALE – Cook the salmon as for *Glazed salmon Bellevue in aspic*. Skin the fish and decorate it with truffles and hard-boiled egg whites cut in the form of scales. Coat with the jelly.

Set on a long dish or on a bed of rice. Surround with a garnish of little *mousselines* of crayfish, *barquettes* of fine pastry filled with soft carp roes poached in white wine and coated with *White chaud-froid sauce* (see SAUCE) based on fish *fumet* and halved hard-boiled eggs.

Serve with mayonnaise mixed with truffle purée.

Glazed salmon Monselet. SAUMON GLACÉ MONSELET – Cook the salmon in the same way as for *Glazed salmon Bellevue in aspic*. Skin the fish and decorate it with truffles and lobster coral. Glaze with jelly.

Set on a dish or on a bed of rice. Surround with a garnish of very small artichoke bottoms filled with a salad of green asparagus tips and truffles, and small *Tomato mousses* (see TOMATO) decorated with tarragon leaves. Serve with mayonnaise mixed with tomato juice.

Glazed salmon à la parisienne (*Larousse*)

Glazed salmon à la parisienne. SAUMON GLACÉ À LA PARISIENNE – Cook and cool the salmon as for *Glazed salmon Bellevue in aspic*.

Decorate it with truffles and glaze with jelly.

Surround with a garnish *à la parisienne* for cold fish (see GARNISH) arranged in clusters, separated from each other by lettuce hearts and halved hard-boiled eggs. Decorate with chopped jelly. Serve with mayonnaise.

Glazed salmon à la russe. SAUMON GLACÉ À LA RUSSE – Cook the salmon as for *Glazed salmon à la parisienne* and allow it to cool. Drain, skin it, decorate with truffles and tarragon leaves and glaze with *Fish jelly stock* (see JELLY).

Set on a long dish on a bed of rice. Surround with small Russian salads moulded in *darioles* lined with jelly, small *barquettes* made out of cucumber which has been blanched, drained and marinated with oil, lemon juice, salt and pepper, and filled with caviare and quartered hard-boiled eggs. Garnish the edges of the plate with chopped jelly.

Salmon mayonnaise. SAUMON FROID EN MAYONNAISE – Put in the bottom of a salad dish a layer of shredded lettuce seasoned with salt and pepper, oil and vinegar, piled up a little in the form of a dome. Place on this a mound of sliced or flaked cooked salmon.

Cover with mayonnaise. Smooth over so as to obtain a regular shape. Decorate with anchovies, capers, chervil or tarragon leaves, and stoned olives. Surround with quartered hard-boiled eggs and lettuce hearts.

All the garnishes suggested elsewhere for cold fish may be used as garnish for salmon mayonnaise.

Médaillons of cold salmon. MÉDAILLONS DE SAUMON FROID – Cut the salmon in slices, divide each in two and trim into rounds or *médaillons*.

Cook and finish off according to any of the recipes given for salmon cutlets.

Cold salmon with Montpellier butter. SAUMON FROID AU BEURRE DE MONTPELLIER – Cook the salmon, whole or in large cuts, in a *Fish jelly stock* (see JELLY) made with white wine, as for *Glazed salmon Bellevue in aspic*. Allow to cool in its cooking liquor.

Drain the fish; remove the skin from the central part, keeping only a narrow strip at each side. Wipe dry.

Cover the skinned part with *Montpellier butter* (see BUTTER, *Compound butters*), and smooth over. Decorate it with small pieces of truffles dipped in half-set jelly. Glaze with half-set jelly made with the liquor in which the fish was cooked.

Set the fish on a dish on a bed of rice, or a buttered croûton of bread. Surround with a garnish of hard-boiled eggs, lettuce hearts, croûtons spread with *Montpellier butter*, and jelly.

Cold salmon steak with various sauces and garnishes. DARNES DE SAUMON FROIDES – All the recipes given for cold cutlets of salmon can be applied to salmon steaks.

The steaks, cooked in *court-bouillon* and left to cool in the liquor, are garnished with quartered hard-boiled eggs and lettuce hearts, and served with a cold sauce (*Mayonnaise*, *Rémoulade*, *Tartare*, *Verte*, etc.; see SAUCE, *Cold sauces*).

SALMON TROUT. TRUITE SAUMONÉE – Trout with pink flesh (see TROUT).

SALPICON – Preparation of one or more ingredients cut in small dice and bound with a sauce.

Salpicons, with other *hors-d'œuvre* mixtures, are used to fill pastry *barquettes* and other tartlets, *canapés*, pastry cases, *croustades* or hollowed bread cases, rissoles and *timbales*. They may be made into *cromesquis*, cutlets and croquettes, and are used to stuff eggs, poultry, game, fish and some cuts of meat.

Cold *salpicons* are seasoned with *Vinaigrette* or *Mayonnaise sauce* (see SAUCE).

In pastry making and confectionery *salpicons* of fresh or candied fruit are used.

Salpicon à l'américaine (hot) – Lobster or spiny lobster flesh *à l'américaine*, bound with *American sauce* (see SAUCE).

Salpicon of anchovies (hot or cold). SALPICON D'ANCHOIS – De-salted anchovy fillets cut into dice. Use hot or cold according to the particular recipe.

Salpicon of artichokes (cold). SALPICON D'ARTICHAUTS – Artichoke bottoms cooked in flour and water *court-bouillon* drained, dried, cut in dice, and bound with mayonnaise thickened with jelly.

Used to garnish eggs, fish, cold chicken, pastry boats and tartlets.

Salpicon of artichokes with cream. SALPICON D'ARTICHAUTS À LA CRÈME – Dice artichoke bottoms half cooked in flour and water *court-bouillon*. Finish cooking in butter. Season and bind with a few tablespoons thick *Cream sauce* (see SAUCE).

This *salpicon*, like all the vegetables in the recipes which follow, may be bound with thick *Velouté sauce* (see SAUCE) instead of cream sauce.

Used as garnish with eggs, *barquettes* and tartlets, with small cuts of meat, poultry, and with fish.

Salpicon of green asparagus (cold). SALPICON D'ASPERGES VERTES – Dice green asparagus and cook in salted water. Drain, dry, and bind with thick mayonnaise.

Same uses as the *Salpicon of artichokes*.

Salpicon of aubergines in cream. SALPICON D'AUBERGINES À LA CRÈME – Cook diced aubergines in butter. Season, bind with *Cream sauce* (see SAUCE).

Same uses as the *Salpicon of artichokes*.

Salpicon of beetroot (cold). SALPICON DE BETTERAVES – Dice a cooked beetroot. Season with oil, vinegar, salt and pepper or with thick mayonnaise.

Salpicon à la bohémienne (cold) – The same mixture as in the recipe which follows (see below), bound with meat jelly.

Salpicon à la bohémienne (hot) – Mixture of *foie gras* and diced cooked truffles, bound with *Madeira sauce* (see SAUCE) made with truffle essence.

This *salpicon* sometimes has the addition of a small quantity of diced onion stewed in butter and seasoned with paprika. Used for *canapés*, tartlets, poached eggs, etc.

Salpicon of brains (hot). SALPICON DE CERVELLE – Bound with *Allemande*, *Béchamel* or *Velouté sauce* (see SAUCE).

Salpicon cancalaise (hot) – Mixture of poached oysters and cooked mushrooms, bound with *Normande sauce* or *Velouté sauce* (see SAUCE), based on concentrated fish stock.

Salpicon cardinal (hot) – Mixture of diced lobster, truffles and mushrooms bound with *Cardinal sauce* (see SAUCE).

Salpicon of carrots à la crème. SALPICON DE CAROTTES À LA CRÈME – Dice the orange part of some carrots, cover with water, add 50 g. (2 oz., $\frac{1}{4}$ cup) butter to each $\frac{1}{2}$ litre (scant pint, $2\frac{1}{4}$ cups) water, season with salt and a very little sugar and cook till all the liquid is absorbed. Bind with *Cream sauce* (see SAUCE).

Same uses as the *Salpicon of artichokes*.

Salpicon of celeriac (cold). SALPICON DE CÉLERI-RAVE – Cook diced celeriac in salted water. Drain, dry, bind with thick mayonnaise.

Same uses as the *Salpicon of artichokes*.

Salpicon of celeriac (hot). SALPICON DE CÉLERI-RAVE À LA CRÈME – Dice a celeriac root. Cook in butter in a covered pan. Season, and bind with *Cream sauce* (see SAUCE).

Same uses as the *Salpicon of artichokes*.

Salpicon of cèpes à la crème. SALPICON DE CÈPES À LA CRÈME – Dice cooked cèpes. Stew in butter. Bind with *Cream sauce* (see SAUCE).

Same uses as the *Salpicon of artichokes*.

Salpicon à la chalonnaise (hot) – Mixture of cocks' combs and truffles, bound with *Allemande sauce* (see SAUCE).

Salpicon chasseur (hot) – Dice chicken livers, sauté in butter and mix with mushrooms, bound with concentrated *Chasseur sauce* (see SAUCE).

Salpicon of chicken. SALPICON DE VOLAILLE – This is made with left-over chicken. Dice the chicken and bind with *Allemande*, *Béchamel*, *Cream* or *Velouté sauce* (see SAUCE). A brown veal stock may also be used.

This *salpicon* is used as a filling for *vol-au-vent*, *barquettes* and *croustades*, as a garnish for poached or soft-boiled eggs, or for *croquettes*.

Salpicon of chicken livers. SALPICON DE FOIES DE VOLAILLES – Like *Salpicon of foie gras*.

Salpicon of cocks' combs. SALPICON DE CRÊTES – Bound with *Allemande*, *Béchamel* or *Demi-glace sauce* (see SAUCE), or brown veal stock, concentrated and thickened. (See COCK'S COMB for other *salpicons*.)

Salpicon of crayfish. SALPICON D'ÉCREVISSES – Bound with *Béchamel, Nantua* or *Crayfish sauce* (hot); with *Vinaigrette* or *Mayonnaise sauce* (cold) (see SAUCE).

Salpicon of cucumbers (cold). SALPICON DE CONCOMBRES – Split cucumbers lengthwise, remove their seeds, and dice. Spread on a cloth, sprinkle with salt and leave till they are

AUCISSON
RO

translucent. Dry them, season with oil and vinegar or bind them with thick mayonnaise.

Same uses as *Salpicon of artichokes*.

Salpicon Cussy (hot) – Mixture of sweetbreads, truffles and mushrooms, bound with concentrated *Madeira sauce* (see SAUCE).

Salpicon cutlets. CÔTELETTES DE SALPICONS – These are made with a *salpicon* of various ingredients, to which diced mushrooms and truffles are added and combined with an *Allemande* or a *Béchamel sauce* (see SAUCE).

Make into cutlet shapes, dip in egg and breadcrumbs, and cook in clarified butter.

Salpicon à la dieppoise (hot) – Mixture of crayfish, mussels and mushrooms, bound with *Normande sauce* or *White wine sauce I* (see SAUCE).

Salpicon à l'écarlate (hot) – Pickled tongue bound with *Demi-glace sauce* (see SAUCE).

Salpicon of hard-boiled eggs. SALPICON D'OEUFS DURS – Bound with *Allemande*, *Béchamel*, *Cream* or *Velouté sauce* (hot); with *Vinaigrette* or *Mayonnaise sauce* (cold) (see SAUCE).

Salpicon à la financière (hot) – Mixture of quenelles, cocks' combs, cocks' kidneys, mushrooms and truffles, bound with concentrated *Financière sauce* (see SAUCE).

Salpicon of fish. SALPICON DE POISSON – Cooked fish bound with *Béchamel*, *Normande* or *White wine sauce I* (hot); with *Vinaigrette* or *Mayonnaise sauce* (cold) (see SAUCE).

Salpicon of foie gras – Bound with *Madeira*, *Port* or *Sherry sauce* (see SAUCE) or game stock (hot), in jelly (cold).

Salpicon of French beans (cold). SALPICON DE HARICOTS VERTS – Like *Salpicon of green asparagus*.

Salpicon of French beans à la crème (hot). SALPICON DE HARICOTS VERTS À LA CRÈME – Dice French beans and cook briskly in salted water, but keep fairly firm. Simmer in butter in covered pan. Bind with *Cream sauce* (see SAUCE).

Same uses as the *Salpicon of artichokes*.

Salpicons of fruit. SALPICONS DE FRUITS – These *salpicons*, made with fresh fruit cooked in syrup (apricots, cherries, peaches, pears, apples, plums, etc.) are used as filling or garnish for a great many pastries and sweet dishes. *Salpicons* may also be made from candied fruits, used in the same way.

Fruit *salpicons* should be soaked in liqueur.

Salpicon of game. SALPICON DE GIBIER – Bound with white or brown sauce, based on the game used (hot); bound with jelly (cold).

Salpicon of ham (hot). SALPICON DE JAMBON – Made with cooked ham.

Cut the ham into small dice and bind with *Demi-glace sauce* (see SAUCE). Various garnishes and forcemeats can be added. When cold use for *canapés* and other cold *hors-d'œuvre*.

Salpicon of Jerusalem artichokes. SALPICON DE TOPINAMBOURS – Like *Salpicon of artichokes*, made with Jerusalem artichokes cooked in salted water.

Salpicon à la Joinville (hot) – Mixture of crayfish, truffles and mushrooms bound with *Joinville sauce* (see SAUCE).

Salpicon of lobster. SALPICON DE HOMARD – Bound with *Béchamel*, *Lobster* or *Nantua sauce* (hot); with *Vinaigrette* or *Mayonnaise sauce* (cold) (see SAUCE).

Salpicon of meat. SALPICON DE VIANDES DE DESSERTE – Made with left-over meats (beef, veal, lamb, mutton, pork) cut in dice and bound with brown or white sauce.

These *salpicons* are used to make croquettes and *kromeskies* or to fill pastry cases, hollowed crusts, etc.

Salpicon à la Montglas (hot) – Mixture of *foie gras*, pickled tongue, truffles and mushrooms, bound with concentrated *Madeira sauce* (see SAUCE).

Salpicon of mushrooms (cold). SALPICON DE CHAMPIGNONS – Diced mushrooms cooked and bound with thick mayonnaise.

Same uses as *Salpicon of artichokes*.

Salpicon of mushrooms and other fungi (hot). SALPICON DE CHAMPIGNONS DE COUCHE – Dice peeled and washed mushrooms. Cook gently in butter, bind with *Cream sauce* (see SAUCE).

Same uses as *Salpicon of artichokes*.

Salpicon of mushrooms with Madeira (hot). SALPICON DE CHAMPIGNONS AU MADÈRE – Cook diced mushrooms in butter. Dilute the cooking juices with a little Madeira or other liqueur wine. Bind with concentrated *Demi-glace sauce* (see SAUCE) based on mushroom stock. Same uses as *Salpicon of artichokes*.

Salpicon of mussels (hot). SALPICON DE MOULES – Bound with *Allemande*, *Poulette*, or *White wine sauce* (hot); with *Vinaigrette* or *Mayonnaise sauce* (cold) (see SAUCE).

Salpicon of onion. SALPICON D'OIGNON – *White*. Cook the onions in butter, bind with *Cream sauce* (see SAUCE).

Brown. Bind the cooked onions with concentrated *Demi-glace sauce* (see SAUCE).

Salpicon à la périgourdine (hot) – Mixture of *foie gras* and truffles bound with concentrated *Madeira sauce* (see SAUCE).

Salpicon of potatoes (cold). SALPICON DE POMMES DE TERRE – Potatoes cooked in their jackets, peeled, cut into dice, and mixed with *Vinaigrette* or *Mayonnaise sauce* (see SAUCE).

Same use as *Salpicon of artichokes*.

Salpicon à la reine (hot) – Mixture of white chicken meat, mushrooms and truffles, bound with *Allemande sauce* (see SAUCE).

Salpicon à la royale (hot) – Mixture of truffles and mushrooms bound with chicken purée.

Salpicon à la Saint-Hubert (hot) – Game meat, bound with *Demi-glace sauce* (see SAUCE) boiled down with the pan juices left from cooking the game.

Salpicon of shrimps (hot). SALPICON DE CREVETTES – Bound with *Béchamel* or *Shrimp sauce* (hot); with *Vinaigrette* or *Mayonnaise sauce* (cold) (see SAUCE).

Salpicon of spiny lobster or crawfish. SALPICON DE LANGOUSTE – Like *Salpicon of lobster*.

Salpicon of sweetbreads (hot). SALPICON DE RIS D'AGNEAU, DE VEAU – Bound with *Allemande*, *Béchamel*, *Demi-glace*, *Madeira* or *Suprême sauce* (see SAUCE).

Salpicon of tomatoes I. SALPICON DE TOMATES – Peel the tomatoes and remove the seeds. Cut them in dice. Season with salt and lay them on a cloth to yield some of their moisture. Use as they are, or season with oil and vinegar.

Same uses as *Salpicon of artichokes*.

Salpicon of tomatoes II. SALPICON DE TOMATES – Dice the tomatoes. Put them in a wire basket, plunge them for a minute into boiling salted water.

Use as an auxiliary ingredient in soups, sauces and mixed salpicons.

Salpicon of truffles. SALPICON DE TRUFFES – Made with fresh truffles, raw or cooked in Madeira, or with tinned truffles.

Cut them in dice, season with salt and pepper, oil and lemon juice, or leave them as they are for cold preparations.

For hot dishes, simmer them in butter or bind them in a few tablespoons of *Demi-glace sauce* flavoured with Madeira, or with *Velouté* or *Cream sauce* (see SAUCE). Used cold as a garnish in *hors-d'œuvre*, with eggs, fish, made-up salads; hot in *barquettes*, tartlets, etc., and as a supplementary ingredient in sauces, forcemeats, and various mixtures.

Salpicon of veal. SALPICON DE VEAU – Bound with *Allemande*, *Béchamel* or *Demi-glace sauce* (see SAUCE) or brown veal stock (hot); bound with jelly (cold).

SALSIFY or OYSTER PLANT. SALSIFIS – The name of salsify, or oyster plant, is used not only for the root of the plant of the *Compositae* family, but also for that of another plant of the same family which botanically is called *Scorzonera.*

While one of these roots, that of the true salsify, is white outside, that of the scorzonera is blackish. The flesh of these two roots is very similar in taste, and they are prepared in the same way.

The word scorzonera comes from the Catalan *escorso*, which means viper. The plant was so called, it is said, because formerly, in Spain, it was used as a remedy for the bite of this dangerous snake.

The wild salsify, commonly known as goat's beard, grows in the fields and in damp and rich pastureland. The young shoots of this plant can be eaten in salad and can also be prepared like spinach. The roots are eaten like those of scorzonera.

The stalks or tender shoots of salsify and scorzonera may also be prepared in various ways. They are mostly eaten raw in salad.

To cook salsify. Scrape the salsify roots and divide them into chunks 7 to 8 cm (about 3 inches) long. Plunge them as they are prepared into water with a little lemon or vinegar in it, to prevent them from turning black. Cook, covered, in a boiling flour-and-water *court-bouillon* over a gentle heat, for about 2 hours. Put into a basin and keep in a cool place.

Drain and dry the salsify before preparing it in any way. It is served by itself as a vegetable or used as a garnish.

When it is not to be used immediately, it can be kept in its cooking liquor and left for several days without deteriorating.

To cook leaves or shoots of salsify or oyster plant. Pick the tender shoots, wash them in plenty of water and cook in a flour-and-water *court-bouillon* for 40 minutes. Drain, dry, and prepare according to the recipe.

Salsify in béchamel. SALSIFIS À LA BÉCHAMEL – Cook in flour-and-water *court-bouillon* and cut into chunks 4 to 5 cm ($1\frac{1}{2}$ to 2 inches) long. Put them in a sauté pan, cover with thin *Béchamel sauce* (see SAUCE) and simmer. Before serving add a few tablespoons fresh cream.

Salsify prepared in this way is often described as *à la crème.*

Salsify au beurre noisette. SALSIFIS AU BEURRE NOISETTE – Cook the salsify in a flour-and-water *court-bouillon.* Serve piping hot in a dish sprinkled with a few tablespoons of *Noisette butter* (see BUTTER).

Salsify à la crème. SALSIFIS À LA CRÈME – Prepared like *Salsify in béchamel.*

Alternatively, the salsify, after being lightly cooked in butter, may be covered with fresh cream and simmered gently.

Salsify fritters. SALSIFIS FRITS, FRITOT DE SALSIFIS – Cook salsify roots in a flour-and-water *court-bouillon*, drain, and cut in pieces. Put them in a deep dish, season with salt and pepper, sprinkle with chopped parsley, oil and lemon juice and leave them to soak for 30 minutes.

Take them out of the marinade with a perforated spoon, dip them in a light batter (see BATTERS FOR FRYING) and fry in smoking hot deep fat. Drain, garnish with fried parsley and serve.

Salsify Mornay. SALSIFIS MORNAY – Stew the salsify in butter and put them in a gratin dish lined with a layer of *Mornay sauce* (see SAUCE). Coat with more sauce and sprinkle with grated Parmesan. Pour over a little melted butter and brown in the oven.

Salsify à la polonaise. SALSIFIS À LA POLONAISE – Arrange in a shallow dish the salsify roots cooked in a white *court-bouillon*, as above, and stewed in butter. Sprinkle with chopped yolks of hard-boiled eggs, and parsley. Before serving pour over a little *Noisette butter* (see BUTTER, *Compound butters*) in which some freshly made breadcrumbs have been fried, allowing 25 g. (1 oz., $\frac{1}{2}$ cup) breadcrumbs to 100 g.(4 oz., $\frac{1}{2}$ cup) butter.

Salsify salad. SALSIFIS EN SALADE – Cook the salsify in a flour-and-water *court-bouillon.* Drain them, dry and cut into pieces. Season with oil, vinegar (or lemon juice), salt and pepper. Sprinkle with chopped parsley, chervil and tarragon.

Salsify shoots. TIGES DE SALSIFIS – These may be cooked and prepared as for salsify, or served raw in salads.

Salsify sautéed au beurre. SALSIFIS SAUTÉS AU BEURRE – Cook salsify roots in a flour-and-water *court-bouillon*, drain, dry, cut in pieces and sauté in hot butter. Season.

Salsify sautéed aux fines herbes. SALSIFIS SAUTÉS AUX FINES HERBES – As above, adding chopped parsley to the salsify.

Salsify sautéed à la provençale. SALSIFIS SAUTÉS À LA PROVENÇALE – Sauté the salsify in a mixture of butter and oil (half-and-half). Add 1 tablespoon of chopped garlic and parsley.

Salsify in veal stock. SALSIFIS AU BLOND DE VEAU, SALSIFIS AU JUS – Partly cook salsify roots in a flour-and-water *court-bouillon*, drain, dry and cut in pieces. Stew for a few moments in butter until lightly browned. Moisten with a few tablespoons veal stock.

Finish cooking the salsify in this stock.

SALT. SEL – Sodium chloride, the first salt to be discovered by man, which has given its name to all analagous chemical products.

There are two sorts of salt: sea salt, distilled from sea-water, and rock salt, found in the earth in crystalline form.

Sea salt is the only mineral condiment that we add to our food, and it may be noted that the higher the vegetable content of the diet, the greater is the need of salt. This is true among animals as well; herbivorous creatures are greedy for salt but carnivorous animals have no desire for it.

The average consumption of salt, among people who do not abuse the use of this condiment, is about 8 to 10 g. a day. Foodstuffs (before salt is added) contain 1 to $1\frac{1}{2}$ g. in an ordinary diet and the rest is added during cooking or at the table. Complete abstinence from salt has not been found possible even in the most austere monastic orders.

Some culinary practices influence the consumption of – or need for – salt. Boiling vegetables in a large quantity of water deprives them of a large part of their mineral salts, a deficiency which one instinctively corrects by adding salt at the table; potatoes cooked in hot ashes or in the oven have sufficient taste to be eaten without salt, while those cooked in a great deal of water are almost uneatable without this seasoning. Vegetables stewed in their own juices also need much less salt.

Different kinds of salt. Grey (rock) salt is less pure, but among its 'impurities' there are traces of valuable minerals such as arsenic; it is thus rational to use this for cooking and keep the white salt for the table.

Various brands of table salt are marketed; some, generally as the result of adding phosphate of lime, have the advantage that the salt keeps its powder form, whereas pure salt tends to return to its crystalline state under the action of humidity. Other products, chemically produced, contain a much weaker proportion of sodium chloride or are even made up entirely of different types of salt which have a taste more or less comparable with sea salt. These products are designed to give an illusion of salt to invalids on a salt-free diet.

Generally speaking these various products must be added to foodstuffs at the table, their taste being much weakened – or even disappearing altogether – if they are dissolved.

When making up a salt-free diet it is important to recognise that fruit, most vegetables and, with certain exceptions, cereals are the least rich in salt; meat and eggs have less than milk. A salt-free diet demands a special bread with a genuinely low salt content or the replacement of bread in the diet by potatoes.

Celery salt. SEL DE CÉLERI – Fine salt flavoured with dried and powdered celery. This condiment, which is commercially prepared and marketed, is excellent.

Spiced salt (for forcemeats). SEL ÉPICÉ – Mix 1 kg. ($2\frac{1}{4}$ lb.) fine dry salt with 200 g. (7 oz., $1\frac{3}{4}$ cups) white pepper and 200 g. (7 oz., $1\frac{3}{4}$ cups) mixed spices.

SALT GRINDER. ÉGRUGEOIR – Small mortar or mill made of wood and used for grinding rock salt to powder.

SALTING. SALAISON – Operation which consists of treating meat, fish and various other substances with salt, or of immersing them in brine, to preserve them for a long time. (See BRINE.)

Meats and other foodstuffs which have been treated in this way are called *salaisons* in French.

SALTING TUB. SALOIR – Large bucket in which pieces of meat are put to be pickled in brine.

There are different kinds of salting tubs. One kind, a simple receptacle, is used in domestic kitchens to salt pieces of meat, mostly pork; others are great vats of wood, stone or cement, of various shapes, which in different regions of France are called *baignoires*, *bagnons* or *barbantelles*.

Salting tubs in stone or cement are the best. Each is provided with a lattice-work frame, which fits inside the receptacle. On this are placed stones or other heavy objects, so that the substances put in the brine are completely immersed.

SALT MEADOW. PRÉ-SALÉ – Young sheep fattened in meadows bordering the sea. These are rich in aromatic pasture which greatly increases the delicacy of the flesh.

SALTPETRE – Potassium nitrate, nitre, a white crystalline salty substance, odourless, fresh tasting, piquant and a little bitter, easily soluble in hot water, less so in cold water. Used in the salting industries because it gives an agreeable red colour to meat, but only in small doses because it toughens. (It is also used as a constituent of gunpowder.)

SAMOS – Sweet wine harvested on the island of the same name in the Greek Archipelago.

SAMPHIRE. BACILE – Hardy plant which grows on cliffs, by the sea. It is also known under the names of Peter's cress and sea-fennel. It is grown in gardens, in dry and rocky soil, and is eaten principally as a salad.

It can also be cooked in butter or cream, like purslane, or pickled in vinegar like gherkins.

SAND EEL. ÉQUILLE – Common name for a small fish found on sandy beaches. It buries itself in the sand at low tide. It is cooked in the same way as the smelt (q.v.).

Sand eel is also called *lançon* in French.

SANDPIPER. MAUBÈCHE – Small edible water sparrow, cooked in the same way as snipe (q.v.).

SANDWICH – Foodstuff composed of two slices of buttered bread with some edible substance between.

It has long been the custom in the French countryside to give workers in the fields meat for their meal enclosed between two pieces of wholemeal or black bread. In all the south-west districts it was customary to provide people setting out on a journey with slices of meat, mostly pork or veal, sprinkled with their succulent juices, between two pieces

Samphire

of bread. Sandwiches made with sardines, tunny fish, anchovies, sliced chicken and even with flat omelettes were known in France well before the word, coming from England, had entered into French culinary terminology.

To make sandwiches. Sandwiches are made with English-type bread or French bread, with ordinary or enriched bread, black bread, or with special boat-shaped rolls made with *Brioche dough* (see DOUGH). The latter are mostly served at parties and in France are often called *petits pains fourrés*.

Sandwiches in brioche bread. SANDWICHS EN PAIN BRIOCHE – Made like ordinary sandwiches, using boat-shaped rolls made of brioche mixture (like English bridge rolls).

Sandwiches of French bread. SANDWICHS EN PAIN FLÛTE OU EN PAIN DE MÉNAGE – Sandwiches in France are usually made from *petits pains*, i.e. crusty rolls, either round or sausage-shaped, split open, buttered and filled with the same fillings as for English-type bread.

Long French loaves are split and made into sandwiches in the same way.

Sandwiches with loaf bread. SANDWICHS AU PAIN DE MIE – Spread slices of bread with butter mixed with a little mustard. Press meat between two slices. Trim the sandwiches at the sides and cut into rectangles or triangles.

Sandwiches made with English-type bread are filled with various kinds of meat, cut into thin slices: ham, tongue, *mortadella*, roast pork, pressed beef, chicken or other poultry, roast beef, roast veal, etc.

They may also be filled with the following: cucumbers pickled in the Russian style between two buttered slices of bread sprinkled with grated horseradish, anchovies and other filleted salt fish such as herrings, kilkis, sprats, etc., artichokes (artichoke bottoms cut in small dice, mixed with hard-boiled eggs, also cut in dice), cress or watercress, shrimps or prawns, crayfish, lobsters, spiny lobster (the butter mixed with a purée made from their shells), lettuce (the leaves left whole or

Sandwiches with loaf bread and cheese

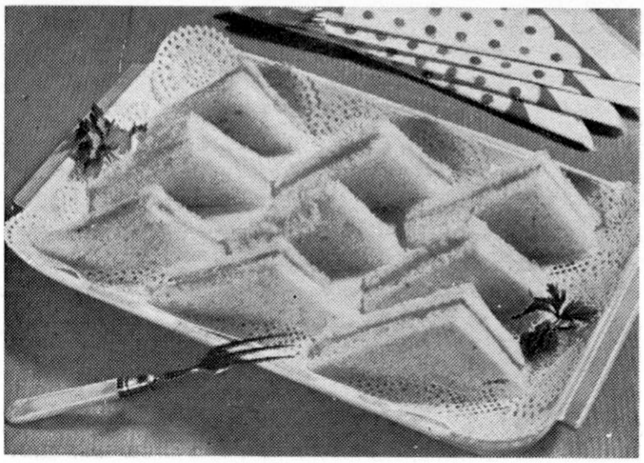

Presentation of sandwiches with loaf bread (*Claire*)

shredded), corn salad (lamb's lettuce), hard-boiled eggs (the eggs cut in slices or small dice), sweet peppers, *poutargue* (mullet roes), sardines or other fish preserved in oil or salt, salmon, tomatoes (sliced with the seeds removed and soaked in salt to remove their moisture), truffles (raw truffles cut in thin slices and seasoned).

Sweet sandwiches. SANDWICHS D'ENTREMETS – Prepared with thin slices of stale brioche or Genoa cake. They are buttered or not, according to what is used for the filling.

These sandwiches may be made with chopped up fruit, jam, thick custards, etc.

Toasted sandwiches. SANDWICHS AU PAIN GRILLÉ – Prepared with lightly toasted, sliced tin loaf, French bread or split rolls.

The filling for these sandwiches is the same as for untoasted bread.

Alsatian sandwiches. SANDWICHS ALSACIENS – Fill bread spread with butter mixed with grated horseradish with Strasbourg sausage, peeled and cut in slices.

Antibois sandwiches. SANDWICHS ANTIBOIS – Fill slices of toasted bread spread with butter mixed with chopped tarragon, with hard-boiled eggs, capers and chopped gherkins.

Basil sandwiches. SANDWICHS AU BASILIC – Fill thin slices of toasted bread spread with butter to which chopped fresh basil has been added, with chopped hard-boiled eggs.

Bookmaker's sandwiches. SANDWICHS DU BOOKMAKER – Butter slices of bread. Fill with a 1-cm. ($\frac{1}{2}$-inch) thick grilled steak, seasoned with salt and pepper, and spread, when cold, with English mustard.

Dijon sandwiches. SANDWICHS DIJONAIS – Fill slices of French bread spread with butter mixed with Dijon mustard, with diced hard-boiled egg and parsley ham (a regional speciality of Dijon).

Foie gras sandwiches. SANDWICHS DE FOIE GRAS – Spread a slice of bread with a layer of *foie gras*. Cover with another slice.

These sandwiches can also be made by filling lightly buttered slices of loaf bread, crusty rolls or brioche mixture rolls (bridge rolls) with slices of truffled *foie gras*.

Périgourdine sandwiches. SANDWICHS À LA PÉRIGOURDINE – Fill slices of toasted bread spread with truffle purée with small slices of *foie gras*.

Tartare sandwiches. SANDWICHS À LA TARTARE – Spread slices of bread with a thick layer of minced raw beef mixed with half its weight of butter, chopped chives, salt and paprika.

SANGLER – To pack ice, or ice and salt, around a mould placed in a wooden receptacle, in order to freeze water ice or ice cream mixtures.

SANGRI – Stimulating beverage obtained by mixing Madeira with water, sugar and a little grated nutmeg.

SANGRIA – Spanish drink consisting of a blend of wine, lemonade and sometimes alcohol, garnished with orange and lemon slices.

SANGUINE – A dish known under this name in some districts of France, notably Berry, is called *sanquette* in the south-west.

Cook 100 g. (4 oz., 1 cup) chopped white onions lightly in butter. When they are cooked and golden in colour, pour into the pan the blood of 2 chickens. Season, shake to mix well and cook like a pancake.

SANGUINE (Blood orange) – Variety of sweet orange with red flesh.

SANSONNET – Colloquial name for the starling, properly called *étourneau* in French, considered edible and cooked like the lark (q.v.).

The same word is used in French for a small mackerel.

SAPID. SAPIDE – That which is savoury and agreeably excites the sense of taste.

SAPODILLA or NASEBERRY PLUM. SAPOTILLE – Name of Malay origin given in Java and the East Indies to a fruit which in French is called *sapotille*. Scientifically it is the *Sapota achras*. It is about as large as a lemon. Its exterior colour is greyish; the flesh is reddish-yellow, like that of an apricot. The taste is delicious but this fruit can only be eaten where it grows.

SARACEN CORN (Buckwheat). SARRASIN – Herbaceous plant, sometimes known in France as *blé noir*, classed as a cereal. It prefers a granitic terrain and is grown more in Brittany than in any other part of France.

Unsuitable for making bread, its grain is used for porridges, *galettes* and pancakes. (See BUCKWHEAT.)

SARDINE – Migratory fish of the family *Clupeidae*, which in some provinces of the north-west of France is called *cardeau* and *harenguet*, and, at Bordeaux, *royan*.

It is fished abundantly in Sardinia, from which it takes its name.

It is also fished along the coasts of Brittany, where the preservation of sardines in oil is done on a large scale.

In the Mediterranean region, particularly between Menton

Sardine

and Marseilles, the sardines fished are extremely delicate and are eaten fresh; they cannot be sent long distances without deterioration.

Thus the fish is known slightly salted, or completely preserved in brine or, its most frequent form, tinned in oil. Conserved in oil or salt, the sardine is served as *hors-d'œuvre*.

The recipes which follow are for fresh sardines unless otherwise stated. In U.S.A. young fresh herring can be substituted for the European sardine.

Sardines à l'anglaise – Open fresh sardines and take out the bones. Coat the sardines with egg and breadcrumbs and fry them in clarified butter. Cover with half-melted *Maître d'hôtel butter* (see BUTTER, *Compound butters*).

Sardines à l'antiboise – Take off the heads of fresh sardines. Open the fish and take out the backbones. Coat with egg and breadcrumbs and fry in olive oil.

Arrange on a dish in the form of a crown. Garnish the middle of the dish with *Tomato fondue* (see FONDUE) seasoned with a little garlic.

Bouillabaisse of sardines (Provençal cookery). BOUILLABAISSE DE SARDINES – Scale, clean, wash and wipe 500 g. (18 oz.) large fresh sardines.

Cook lightly in 3 tablespoons (scant $\frac{1}{4}$ cup) oil, 2 tablespoons (3 tablespoons) chopped onion and 1 tablespoon chopped leek.

Add 2 peeled, seeded and chopped tomatoes, 2 crushed cloves of garlic, a pinch of salt, pepper, thyme, half a bay leaf, a little fennel and a small piece of bitter orange rind.

Pour in 7 dl. ($1\frac{1}{4}$ pints, $1\frac{1}{2}$ pints) water, add 300 g. (11 oz., 2 scant cups) potatoes cut in thick slices, and begin cooking on good heat.

Add a pinch of saffron, and when the potatoes are three-quarters cooked, put the sardines on top. Cover the pan and cook briskly for 8 to 10 minutes.

Drain the sardines and potatoes and set them on a dish. Sprinkle with chopped parsley.

Pour the broth into another dish lined with 1 dozen thick slices of French bread. Sprinkle this, too, with chopped parsley.

Serve both dishes together.

Sardine butter. BEURRE DE SARDINES – Pound 75 g. (3 oz.) fillets of sardines in oil. Add 100 g. (4 oz., $\frac{1}{2}$ cup) butter. Rub through a fine seive.

Use cold for *hors-d'œuvre*, hot for *canapés*, fried hollow crusts and pastry cases.

Dartois of sardines. DARTOIS AUX SARDINES – Like *Dartois of anchovies* (see HORS-D'ŒUVRE, *Hot hors-d'œuvre*).

Fried sardines. SARDINES FRITES – Cooked like *Fried smelts* (see SMELT).

Grilled sardines. SARDINES GRILLÉES – Brush fresh sardines with oil. Season them. Cook under the grill at moderate heat. Serve with *Maître d'hôtel butter* (see BUTTER, *Compound butters*).

Sardines in oil. SARDINES À L'HUILE – Sardines are found marketed commercially in this form. They are served as *hors-d'œuvre*.

Sardines in paper cases au gratin. SARDINES EN CAISSES AU GRATIN – Arrange fresh sardines, stuffed and cooked in white wine (see below, *Sardines with white wine*) in paper cases (oiled and dried in the oven). Garnish with 1 good tablespoon of thick *duxelles* (q.v.).

Add 1 or 2 tablespoons (1 to 3 tablespoons) *duxelles* and 1 tablespoon tomato sauce to the liquor in which the sardines were cooked and spoon some of this sauce over them.

Sprinkle with breadcrumbs and melted butter and brown lightly in the oven. Put chopped parsley on top and arrange the paper cases on a dish.

Sardines in paper cases à l'italienne. SARDINES EN CAISSES À L'ITALIENNE – Prepare and cook fresh sardines like *Sardines with white wine* (see below).

When they are cooked set each one in a little rectangular paper case (previously rubbed with oil and dried in the oven) garnished on the bottom with 1 good tablespoon chopped mushrooms.

Sardines in paper cases à la portugaise. SARDINES EN CAISSES À LA PORTUGAISE – Like *Sardines in paper cases au gratin*, replacing the *duxelles* with *Tomato fondue* (see FONDUE).

This preparation can be made with oil in place of butter.

Sardines en papillotes – Take off the heads and remove the bones of large fresh sardines. Brush with oil, season and grill lightly.

Wrap each in a sheet of paper prepared in the same way as for *Red mullet en papillote* (see MULLET, RED), covering the fish with very thick *duxelles*.

Put the *papillotes* for a short time in a very hot oven and serve at once.

Sardines en paupiettes – Scale, clean, wipe and fillet large fresh sardines.

Lay the fillets flat on the table, skin downwards, and using a forcing bag, pipe on to each a thin line of quenelle *Fish forcemeat* (see FORCEMEATS) or very thick *duxelles*.

Roll up the fillets *en paupiettes*, and put them in rows in a buttered sauté dish. Pour over a little white wine, mushroom juice or fish stock, and cook very gently, covered, for 8 minutes.

Serve with *White wine* or other sauce (see SAUCE).

Sardines au plat – Put the sardines, seasoned with salt, on a buttered fireproof dish which has been sprinkled with chopped shallot. Pour over, for 12 sardines, 4 tablespoons (5 tablespoons) dry white wine and a little lemon juice. Dot with

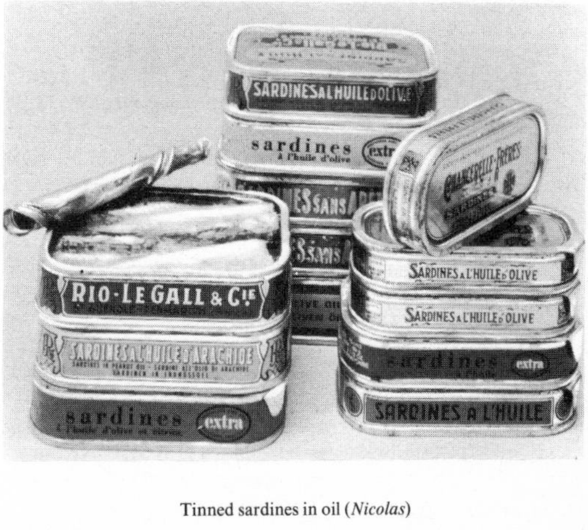

Tinned sardines in oil (*Nicolas*)

A brown sauce (*Robert Carrier*)

little pieces of butter. Cook in the oven at a good heat for 8 to 10 minutes. Sprinkle with parsley.

Salted sardines (preserved). SARDINES SALÉES – Proceed, using fresh sardines, as described in the recipe for *Preserved anchovies* (see ANCHOVY).

Sardines with spinach à la provençale. SARDINES AUX ÉPINARDS À LA PROVENÇALE – Clean and bone fresh sardines, coat with egg and breadcrumbs, and fry in butter. Arrange on leaf spinach tossed in *Noisette butter* (see BUTTER, *Compound butters*) and seasoned with grated garlic.

Sardines with white wine (stuffed). SARDINES AU VIN BLANC – Scale, clean and bone 12 large fresh sardines.

Stuff them with a small quantity of quenelle *Fish forcemeat* (see FORCEMEATS). Press lightly to stick them together and set in a buttered baking dish. Season with salt and pepper. Pour over 1 dl. (6 tablespoons, scant $\frac{1}{2}$ cup) white wine. Start cooking on top of the stove, then put in the oven for 8 to 10 minutes.

Drain the sardines and arrange them on a dish. Add the strained cooking liquor to *White wine sauce* (see SAUCE) and just before serving pour a few tablespoons of the sauce over the sardines.

SARGASSO. SARGASSE – Seaweed eaten in Spain in the form of a salad.

SASSENAGE – Principal town of the canton of Isère, famous for its grottoes in which its celebrated cheese is made. (See CHEESE, *Sassenage*.)

SATYRION – Orchid with a goat-like smell whose tubers contain an edible, floury substance analogous to salep.

SAUCE – Liquid seasoning for food.

Classed as sauces in the French *cuisine* are many preparations quite different from each other, not only in their taste and appearance but in the way they are made; the juices of roasted meats; *vinaigrette* and its derivatives, *hollandaise*, *mayonnaise*, *béarnaise*; stock thickened with flour, with *fécule* (like potato or cornflour), with blood, etc.

At the beginning of the nineteenth century, Carême included among his sauces *espagnole*, *allemande*, *suprême*, *tarragon*, *ravigote*, *vert-pré*, *béchamel*, *financière*, *Périgueux*, *tortue*, *matelote*, *Champagne*, *sauce à la régence*, *bourguignonne*, *sturgeon*, *poivrade*, *chevreuil* (roebuck), *aigre-doux* (sweet-sour), *piquante*, *salmis*, *tomato*, *leveret* thickened with blood, *parisienne*, *Robert*, *raifort* (horseradish), *magnonaise* (Carême thus designated mayonnaise), *provençale*, *crayfish butter*, *lobster*, *shrimp*, *oyster*, *anchovy butter*, *cream*, *sauce à la pluche*, *butter or bâtarde*, and *caper*.

Today the French culinary repertory includes almost 200 recipes for sauces, brown and white, hot and cold (not including variations). It is in this order that they will be described, beginning with the basic, or great sauces, brown and white, followed by compound sauces, brown and white. Cold sauces and dessert sauces will be found at the end of this section.

BASIC or GREAT SAUCES. SAUCES MÈRES, GRANDES SAUCES – These are so called because they are used in the preparation of many other sauces.

BROWN BASIC SAUCES. SAUCES BRUNES –

Demi-glace or rich brown sauce. DEMI-GLACE – Boil down by two-thirds 5 dl. (scant pint, $2\frac{1}{4}$ cups) *Espagnole sauce* (see below) to which 8 dl. (generous $1\frac{1}{3}$ pints, $1\frac{3}{4}$ pints) clear brown stock have been added. Remove from heat, add $\frac{1}{2}$ dl. (3 tablespoons, scant $\frac{1}{4}$ cup) Madeira. Strain.

A handful of mushroom skins may be added during cooking.

Espagnole sauce I (based on meat stock). SAUCE ESPAGNOLE (GRASSE) – To make $2\frac{1}{2}$ litres ($4\frac{1}{2}$ pints, $5\frac{1}{2}$ pints) sauce make a *roux* using 150 g. ($5\frac{1}{2}$ oz, scant $\frac{3}{4}$ cup) butter and 150 g. ($5\frac{1}{2}$ oz., scant $1\frac{1}{2}$ cups) flour and add 4 litres ($3\frac{1}{2}$ quarts, $4\frac{1}{2}$ quarts) warm, light brown stock. Mix and boil over a brisk heat.

Reduce the heat. Make a *mirepoix* of 100 g. (4 oz., $\frac{2}{3}$ cup) carrot and 100 g. (4 oz., 1 cup) onion cut in dice and lightly fried, with 75 g. (3 oz., generous $\frac{1}{4}$ cup) diced lean bacon.

Pour off the bacon fat, dilute the pan juices with 1 dl. (6 tablespoons, scant $\frac{1}{2}$ cup) white wine and add to the sauce, together with a sprig of thyme and half a bay leaf.

Cook the *espagnole* very gently for $2\frac{1}{2}$ hours, skimming frequently. Strain, pressing the vegetables well to extract their juice. Put back in a pan and add 6 to 8 dl. (1 pint, $2\frac{1}{2}$ cups to generous $1\frac{1}{3}$ pints, $1\frac{3}{4}$ pints) stock.

Cook for $2\frac{1}{2}$ hours, skimming frequently. Strain into a basin. Stir with a wooden spoon until it is cold.

Next day put the *espagnole* back to cook again, adding 1 litre ($1\frac{3}{4}$ pints, generous quart) stock and $\frac{1}{2}$ litre (scant pint, $2\frac{1}{4}$ cups) tomato purée.

Mix well, cook very slowly for 1 hour, skim often, so as to obtain a brilliant textured sauce. Remove all grease, strain through muslin. Use according to the instructions in the particular recipe.

Espagnole sauce II (based on fish stock). SAUCE ESPAGNOLE (MAIGRE) – For $2\frac{1}{2}$ litres ($4\frac{1}{2}$ pints, $5\frac{1}{2}$ pints) sauce:

Proceed as for the ordinary *espagnole*, replacing the meat stock with fish stock, and fry the *mirepoix* in butter instead of lard. Add 150 g. (5 oz., 5 cups) mushroom skins.

Finish off as for the ordinary *espagnole*.

Tomato sauce I (based on meat stock). SAUCE TOMATE (AU GRAS) – Apart from its use as accompaniment to a great number of dishes, tomato sauce is used as an auxiliary ingredient in numerous preparations. It adds the final touch to most brown sauces and *ragoûts*.

For $2\frac{1}{2}$ litres ($4\frac{1}{2}$ pints, $5\frac{1}{2}$ pints) sauce:

Ingredients. 2 litres ($3\frac{1}{2}$ pints, $4\frac{1}{2}$ pints) purée of tomatoes, or 3 kg. ($6\frac{1}{2}$ lb.) pressed fresh tomatoes; 100 g. (4 oz., $\frac{1}{2}$ cup) lean blanched diced bacon, 150 g. (5 oz.) blanched knuckle of ham, 100 g. (4 oz., $\frac{2}{3}$ cup) diced carrot, 100 g. (4 oz., 1 cup) diced onion, a *bouquet garni*, 1 unpeeled clove of garlic, 50 g. (2 oz., $\frac{1}{4}$ cup) butter, 75 g. (3 oz., $\frac{3}{4}$ cup) flour; 10 g. ($1\frac{1}{2}$ teaspoons) salt, 20 g. $\frac{3}{4}$ oz., $1\frac{1}{2}$ tablespoons) sugar, a pinch of pepper; 1 litre ($1\frac{3}{4}$ pints, generous quart) white stock.

Method. Cook the bacon lightly in butter in a heavy-bottomed pan. Add the vegetables and cook them until they are quite soft. Sprinkle with flour. Cook together till the flour colours, but not too much. Add the tomato purée (or the fresh tomatoes, pressed and cut in quarters). Add the clove of

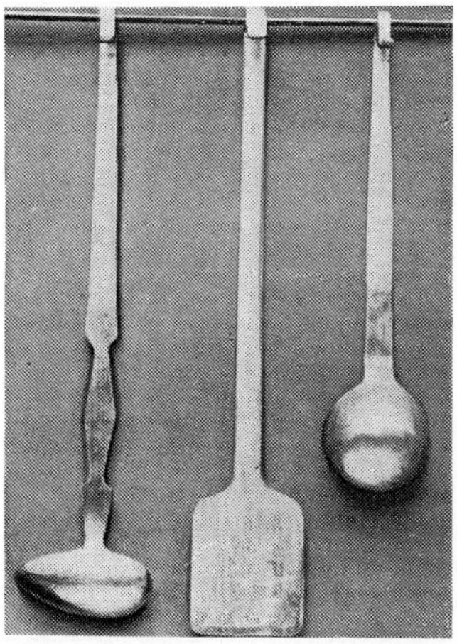

Spoon, spatula and ladle used in making sauces

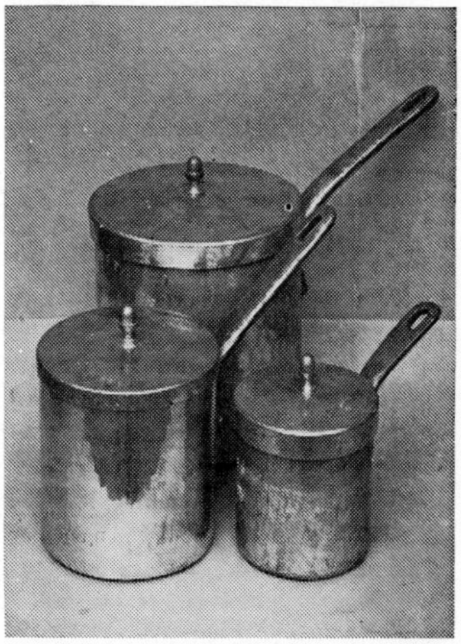

Bain-maries in which to keep sauces

garlic, the *bouquet garni*, the ham knuckle and liquid. Season.

Bring to the boil, stirring. Cover the pan and cook in the oven at low heat for 2 hours.

Take out the *bouquet garni*, the garlic and the knuckle of ham.

Strain the purée through a cloth, pressing it with a spatula, or put it through a fine strainer. Pour into a basin and whisk to make the sauce as smooth as possible. Butter the surface to prevent a skin forming.

Keep in a very cool place. Use as instructed.

Tomato sauce II (meatless). SAUCE TOMATE (AU MAIGRE) – Proceed as in the preceding recipe, leaving out the bacon and ham knuckle and using water instead of stock.

Tomato sauce III (coulis de tomate). SAUCE TOMATE AU NATUREL, COULIS DE TOMATE – Cook gently in butter a *mirepoix* composed of 50 g. (2 oz., $\frac{1}{2}$ cup) shredded carrots and 50 g. (2 oz., $\frac{1}{2}$ cup) shredded onion. Add $1\frac{1}{2}$ kg. ($3\frac{1}{4}$ lb.) fresh tomatoes, pressed and cut in quarters. Season with salt, a little sugar and a pinch of pepper. Add a small *bouquet garni* (q.v.). Stir over good heat to blend the ingredients. When the mixture comes to the boil, cover the pot and cook in a slow oven. Put through a fine strainer. Boil down over strong heat until the sauce thickens to the right consistency. Use according to instructions.

Tomato sauce, and *coulis* of tomatoes, can be made with tinned tomato purée.

WHITE BASIC SAUCES. SAUCES BLANCHES –

Allemande sauce – This sauce is often wrongly included among 'basic' sauces. *Allemande*, which in spite of its name is entirely French in origin, is a compound sauce. (See below, *compound sauces*.)

Béchamel sauce. SAUCE BÉCHAMEL – In modern practice this sauce is prepared quite differently from the way it used to be made. Formerly *béchamel* was a *velouté sauce* with cream blended into it, whereas nowadays it is made by stirring boiling milk into a *roux* of butter and flour.

Béchamel sauce I (based on meat stock). SAUCE BÉCHAMEL GRASSE – For $2\frac{1}{2}$ litres ($4\frac{1}{2}$ pints, $5\frac{1}{2}$ pints) stir $2\frac{3}{4}$ litres (scant 5 pints, 6 pints) boiling milk into a white roux made of 150 g. (5 oz., generous $\frac{1}{2}$ cup) butter and 150 g. (5 oz., $1\frac{1}{4}$ cups) flour. Mix well. Add 150 g. (5 oz.) lean veal cut into dice, cooked in butter without colouring with 50 g. (2 oz., $\frac{1}{2}$ cup) chopped onion. Season, add a sprig of thyme, a fragment of bay leaf and a little grated nutmeg. Simmer very gently for 45 minutes to 1 hour. Strain through a cloth.

Béchamel sauce II (meatless). SAUCE BÉCHAMEL MAIGRE – As above, leaving out the veal.

Suprême sauce. SAUCE SUPRÊME – The same applies here as to *Allemande sauce*. *Suprême sauce* is a combined sauce, the recipe for which will be found below, under *Compound sauces*.

Velouté sauce. VELOUTÉ, SAUCE BLANCHE GRASSE – For $2\frac{1}{2}$ litres ($4\frac{1}{2}$ pints, $5\frac{1}{2}$ pints) stir $2\frac{3}{4}$ litres (scant 5 pints, 6 pints) white stock made with veal or chicken (see STOCK) into pale blond *roux* made with 150 g. (5 oz., generous $\frac{1}{2}$ cup) butter and 150 g. (5 oz., $1\frac{1}{4}$ cups) flour.

Blend well together. Bring to the boil, stirring with a wooden spoon until the first bubbles appear. Cook the *velouté* very slowly for $1\frac{1}{2}$ hours, skimming frequently. Strain through a cloth. Stir until it is completely cold.

Velouté is a great basic sauce, and it may be prepared in advance. It may also be made just before it is required.

As the white stock used for making it is seasoned and flavoured, it is not necessary to add other flavourings. An exception is made for skins and trimmings of mushrooms, which may be added when available, this addition making the sauce yet more delicate.

Velouté sauce II (based on chicken stock). VELOUTÉ DE VOLAILLE – Made like ordinary *Velouté sauce*, using white chicken stock to stir into the blond roux.

Velouté sauce III (based on fish stock). VELOUTÉ DE POISSON, DIT VELOUTÉ MAIGRE – Made like ordinary *Velouté sauce*, replacing the veal or chicken stock with fish stock.

COMPOUND BROWN SAUCES.* SAUCES COMPOSÉES, BRUNES –

African sauce (for small cuts of meat, pot-roasted chicken). SAUCE AFRICAINE – Cook in oil till soft 100 g. (4 oz., 1 cup) diced onions, then add 2 tomatoes peeled, drained and cut in dice, and 2 green peppers, peeled and also cut in dice. Season with salt, paprika, a small clove of grated garlic, and a *bouquet garni*, composed of parsley, thyme, bay leaf and a sprig of basil. Cook for 10 minutes. Pour in 1 dl. (6 tablespoons, scant $\frac{1}{2}$ cup) white wine. Boil down. Add 2 dl. ($\frac{1}{3}$ pint, scant cup) concentrated and thickened brown veal stock. Cook for 15 minutes.

Aigre-douce sauce (for small cuts of meat, white giblets). SAUCE AIGRE-DOUCE – Caramelise lightly in a small saucepan 3 lumps of sugar moistened with 3 tablespoons (scant $\frac{1}{4}$ cup) wine vinegar. Pour in $1\frac{1}{2}$ dl. ($\frac{1}{4}$ pint, $\frac{2}{3}$ cup) white wine. Add 1 tablespoon chopped shallots. Boil down. Pour in $2\frac{1}{2}$ dl. (scant $\frac{1}{2}$ pint, generous cup) *Demi-glace sauce*. Boil for a few moments and strain through a fine sieve. Boil; add 2 tablespoons (3 tablespoons) stoned raisins which have been soaked in cold water, and 1 tablespoon capers.

Alboni sauce, for venison (English cookery). SAUCE ALBONI – Boil down by two-thirds 1 dl. (6 tablespoons, scant $\frac{1}{2}$ cup) white wine to which 1 tablespoon chopped shallot, a sprig of thyme, a piece of bay leaf, a sprig of parsley and a pinch of paprika have been added.

Pour in 2 dl. ($\frac{1}{3}$ pint, scant cup) *Demi-glace sauce* (see above) and 2 tablespoons (3 tablespoons) concentrated game stock. Add 10 crushed juniper berries. Boil for a few moments, strain, and add 1 tablespoon redcurrant jelly and 1 tablespoon pine kernels browned in the oven.

Aniseed sauce (for roast venison). SAUCE À L'ANIS – Cook 2 large lumps of sugar and 3 tablespoons (scant $\frac{1}{4}$ cup) wine vinegar to a caramel. Add 1 dl. (6 tablespoons, scant $\frac{1}{2}$ cup) white wine and 1 teaspoon green anise. Boil, strain, boil again, and boil down by two-thirds. Add 3 dl. ($\frac{1}{2}$ pint, $1\frac{1}{4}$ cups) thickened brown veal stock. Boil for a few moments and strain.

Bigarade sauce I (old recipe). SAUCE À LA BIGARADE – 'Take off in strips from top to bottom the peel of a bitter orange; take care to cut it very thin so that there will be no white pith.

How to reduce a sauce (*Larousse*)

Cut evenly in fine shreds, and throw into boiling water. After boiling for a few minutes drain and put in a saucepan with enough very smooth *Espagnole sauce* to sauce an *entrée*, a little game glaze, a pinch of mignonette and the juice of half a bitter orange. After having brought it to the boil several times, add a piece of fine butter'. (Carême, *L'Art de la cuisine française au XIXe siècle.*)

Bigarade sauce II (for duck or duckling, roasted or pot-roasted). SAUCE BIGARADE – Dilute the thick juices in the roasting pan with a stock prepared in the following way: cook to a pale caramel 25 g. (1 oz., 2 tablespoons) sugar soaked in 1 tablespoon wine vinegar. When the sugar begins to change colour, pour in 2 dl. ($\frac{1}{3}$ pint, scant cup) brown veal stock. Pour this mixture into the roasting pan and blend with the juices.

Cook for 5 minutes over strong heat. Add the juice of an orange and a squeeze of lemon juice and strain. Add 2 tablespoons (3 tablespoons) orange peel which has been blanched, cooled in cold water, drained and cut in a fine *julienne.*

Ducks and ducklings *à la bigarade* are garnished with quarters of peeled and seeded oranges. They are surrounded with a border of half slices of oranges, cut with fluted-edged cutters.

Bigarade sauce can be flavoured with a very small quantity of curaçao, added at the last moment.

One-third lemon peel cut in a fine *julienne* is sometimes added to the *julienne* of orange peel.

Bigarade sauce III. SAUCE BIGARADE – When the duck is cooked, dilute the thick juices in the roasting pan with 1 glass white wine. Boil down. Pour in $1\frac{1}{2}$ dl. ($\frac{1}{4}$ pint, $\frac{2}{3}$ cup) white stock or consommé. Boil for 5 minutes. Thicken with 1 teaspoon potato flour or arrowroot blended with cold water. Add the juice of an orange and a squeeze of lemon juice. Strain and finish with a *julienne* of orange peel.

Bigarade sauce IV. SAUCE BIGARADE – Dilute the thick pan juices with 1 dl. (6 tablespoons, scant $\frac{1}{2}$ cup) Madeira or port. Pour in 2 dl. ($\frac{1}{3}$ pint, scant cup) brown veal stock. Boil down by one-third, thicken with 1 teaspoon arrowroot or corn starch mixed with a few drops of wine vinegar, and bring to the boil. Add the juice of an orange and a squeeze of lemon juice, strain, add orange peel cut in a fine *julienne.*

Bonnefoy sauce (for meat and grilled fish). SAUCE BONNEFOY – Proceed as for *Bordelaise sauce I* but use white wine.

This sauce can also be made with finely chopped shallot and used unstrained.

Bordelaise sauce I (for grilled meat). SAUCE BORDELAISE – Boil down by two-thirds 2 dl. ($\frac{1}{3}$ pint, scant cup) red wine with 1 tablespoon chopped shallot, a sprig of thyme, a piece of bay leaf and a pinch of salt.

Pour in 2 dl. ($\frac{1}{3}$ pint, scant cup) *Demi-glace sauce* (see above). Boil down by one-third, remove from heat, add 25 g. (1 oz., 2 tablespoons) butter and strain.

Add 25 g. (1 oz.) beef marrow cut in dice, poached and drained, and 1 teaspoon chopped parsley.

Grilled meats served with *bordelaise sauce* are usually garnished with slices of poached and drained beef marrow.

Bordelaise sauce II. SAUCE BORDELAISE – Prepare some concentrated red wine as in the preceding recipe, but boil it down only by half. Thicken with 40 g. ($1\frac{1}{2}$ oz., 3 tablespoons) *Kneaded butter* (see BUTTER, *Compound butters*). Boil for a few moments. Add meat glaze or meat extract equal in bulk to a walnut. Finish as in the preceding recipe.

Bordelaise sauce III (old recipe). SAUCE À LA BORDELAISE – 'Put in a saucepan 2 cloves garlic, a pinch of tarragon leaves, the seeded flesh of a lemon, a little bay leaf and 2 cloves, 1 glass Sauternes and 2 teaspoons Provence olive oil. Simmer all together over low heat. Skim off all fat, add enough smooth *Espagnole sauce* to sauce an *entrée*, and 3 to 4 tablespoons light veal stock. Boil down, add $\frac{1}{2}$ glass Sauternes, still simmering. When the sauce reaches the right consistency, strain. Just before serving, add a little butter and the juice of $\frac{1}{2}$ lemon'. (Carême, *L'Art de la cuisine française au XIXe siècle.*)

Bourguignonne sauce – See *Burgundy sauce*, below.

Bread sauce (old recipe). SAUCE À LA MIE DE PAIN À L'ANCIENNE – 'Chop 1 clove garlic, 1 shallot and some parsley, put them in a saucepan with $\frac{1}{2}$ glass white wine, boil down, then mix in 2 tablespoons (3 tablespoons) very fine bread-crumbs, a little butter, a pinch of mignonette and grated nutmeg, 2 tablespoons (3 tablespoons) good consommé and 2 tablespoons (3 tablespoons) light veal stock. Boil down by half and add the juice of a lemon.' (Carême, *L'Art de la cuisine française au XIXe siècle*).

Fried bread sauce (English cookery) (for small roasted birds). SAUCE AU PAIN FRIT – Bring to the boil $2\frac{1}{2}$ dl. (scant $\frac{1}{2}$ pint, generous cup) consommé, 25 g. (1 oz., 2 tablespoons) lean diced ham and 1 tablespoon finely chopped shallot. Simmer for 10 minutes.

Add 50 g. (2 oz., 1 cup) breadcrumbs fried in butter, a pinch of chopped parsley and a few drops lemon juice.

Breton or bretonne sauce I. SAUCE À LA BRETONNE – 'Cut 6 large onions in rings, colour them in clarified butter. Drain them on a horsehair sieve, mix with 2 tablespoons (3 tablespoons) consommé and 2 tablespoons (3 tablespoons) well-beaten *Espagnole sauce*. Add a little sugar, a little butter and a little chicken glaze, then strain, pressing the sauce through a fine cloth'. (Carême, *L'Art de la cuisine française au XIXe siècle.*)

Breton sauce II (to bind flageolet and haricot beans). SAUCE BRETONNE – See FONDUE, *Onion fondue*.

Brown gravy, for roast veal (English cookery). SAUCE AU JUS COLORÉ – Add 2 dl. ($\frac{1}{3}$ pint, scant cup) *Butter sauce II*, to 1 dl. (6 tablespoons, scant $\frac{1}{2}$ cup) juices from the roast. Finish off with a few drops of Harvey sauce or Worcestershire sauce and ketchup.

Burgundy or bourguignonne sauce I or Red wine sauce I (for eggs, meat, poultry). SAUCE BOURGUIGNONNE, SAUCE AU VIN ROUGE – Cook 2 tablespoons (3 tablespoons) chopped onion in butter. Stir in 5 dl. (scant pint, $2\frac{1}{4}$ cups) red wine, season, add a *bouquet garni* (q.v.) and boil down by two-thirds. Add 3 dl. ($\frac{1}{2}$ pint, $1\frac{1}{4}$ cups) *Espagnole sauce*, boil down by half and strain. Before serving, add 50 g. (2 oz., $\frac{1}{4}$ cup) butter.

Bourguignonne sauce intended to accompany a piece of sautéed meat or poultry must be made in the sauté pan in which this was cooked. The onion, previously cooked in butter till soft, is put into the pan at the same time as the wine.

A handful of mushroom skins may be added.

Burgundy or bourguignonne sauce II (for poached eggs). SAUCE BOURGUIGNONNE – Boil down by a half 1 litre ($1\frac{3}{4}$ pints, generous quart) red wine to which has been added 1 tablespoon chopped shallots, a small *bouquet garni* (q.v.), a pinch of salt and a little freshly ground pepper.

Thicken with 40 g. ($1\frac{1}{2}$ oz., 3 tablespoons) *Kneaded butter* (see BUTTER, *Compound butters*). Simmer for a few moments, and add 50 g. (2 oz., $\frac{1}{4}$ cup) butter.

Burgundy or bourguignonne sauce III (for fish). SAUCE BOURGUIGNONNE – Prepare a fish *fumet* with 1 litre ($1\frac{3}{4}$ pints, generous quart) red wine, the bones and trimmings from the fish that is being prepared, a medium-sized chopped onion, a small *bouquet garni* and a handful of mushroom skins. Season.

Strain, boil down by half, and finish with *Kneaded butter* (see BUTTER, *Compound butters*) as in the preceding recipe.

If the fish is braised, keep 1 dl. (6 tablespoons, scant $\frac{1}{2}$ cup) red wine *fumet* to cook it in, and add this to the sauce.

Burgundy or bourguignotte sauce for freshwater fish (old recipe). SAUCE À LA BOURGUIGNOTTE – 'Clean a medium-sized eel, cut it in chunks and put it in a saucepan with 2 onions, 225 g. ($\frac{1}{2}$ lb., 4 cups) chopped mushrooms, 2 cloves garlic, 2 shallots, a *bouquet garni*, a pinch of powdered pepper, a pinch of *four spices*, 4 washed anchovies and $\frac{1}{2}$ bottle Volnay. Boil down a little on low heat, then strain this essence, using pressure. Add 2 tablespoons (3 tablespoons) well mixed *Espagnole sauce*, and 225 g. ($\frac{1}{2}$ lb., 4 cups) peeled mushrooms with their stalks. Cook over strong heat in the usual way, and pour in another glass of Volnay. When the sauce is the right consistency, put it into a *bain-marie*. Before serving add crayfish butter, 30 crayfish tails, and the same number of small white mushrooms.' (Carême, *L'Art de la cuisine française au XIXe siècle*.)

Chambertin sauce. SAUCE AU CHAMBERTIN – See *Burgundy sauce*. Use Chambertin to make the sauce.

Chambord sauce. SAUCE CHAMBORD – *Genevoise sauce* prepared with the cooking liquor of the fish used, blended with red wine. (See CARP, *Carp Chambord*.)

Chapelure or bread sauce (old recipe). SAUCE À LA CHAPELURE – 'Chop 2 shallots, cut up finely a little lean ham, put in a saucepan with 2 to 3 tablespoons light veal stock and a pinch of mignonette, simmer over low heat. When the sauce is boiled down, remove the ham and add 2 tablespoons (3 tablespoons) very fine breadcrumbs, a little fresh butter, 2 tablespoons (3 tablespoons) good consommé and the juice of a lemon. Boil for a few minutes and serve.' (Carême, *L'Art de la cuisine française au XIXe siècle*.)

Charcutière sauce I (for cuts of grilled or sautéed pork). SAUCE CHARCUTIÈRE – Cook 2 tablespoons (3 tablespoons) finely chopped onion until soft in 1 tablespoon of lard or butter. Stir in 2 dl. ($\frac{1}{3}$ pint, scant cup) *Demi-glace sauce*. Boil for a few moments. Strain, and add 2 tablespoons (3 tablespoons) gherkins cut in *julienne* or dice.

Charcutière sauce II. SAUCE CHARCUTIÈRE – Proceed as above, but dilute the thick pan juices with 1 tablespoon wine vinegar before adding the *Demi-glace sauce*. Finish with the gherkins.

Charcutière sauce III. SAUCE CHARCUTIÈRE – Mix the cooked onion with 1 tablespoon white wine, stir in *Demi-glace sauce* and add the gherkins and 1 teaspoon of made mustard.

Charcutière sauce IV. SAUCE CHARCUTIÈRE – Sprinkle the cooked onion with 1 tablespoon flour. Cook till golden. Dilute with a little wine or wine vinegar and stir in white stock (or water with the addition of meat glaze or meat extract). Boil for a few moments. Finish as above.

Chasseur or hunter sauce I (for small cuts of meat and sautéed fowl). SAUCE CHASSEUR – Sauté 100 g. (4 oz., 2 cups) chopped mushrooms in butter, season with salt. When they are three-quarters cooked add 1 tablespoon finely chopped shallot.

Mix with 1 dl. (6 tablespoons, scant $\frac{1}{2}$ cup) white wine, boil down by half, stir in $1\frac{1}{2}$ dl. ($\frac{1}{4}$ pint, $\frac{2}{3}$ cup) *Demi-glace sauce* and 1 dl. (6 tablespoons, scant $\frac{1}{2}$ cup) *Tomato sauce* (see above). Boil for a few moments. Add 25 g. (1 oz., 2 tablespoons) butter and 1 tablespoon chopped parsley, chervil and tarragon.

The mushrooms may also be sautéed in a mixture of butter and oil.

Chasseur or hunter sauce II. SAUCE CHASSEUR – Chop the mushrooms, toss in butter with the chopped shallots and remove from the pan.

Put into the cooking butter 1 tablespoon flour, cook gently till golden, mix with 1 dl. (6 tablespoons, scant $\frac{1}{2}$ cup) white wine, then stir in 2 dl. ($\frac{1}{3}$ pint, scant cup) consommé or white stock and 1 tablespoon tomato purée.

Boil down, put back the mushrooms in the sauce, and finish off as above.

Chateaubriand sauce I (for grilled meat). SAUCE CHATEAUBRIAND – Boil down by two-thirds 1 dl. (6 tablespoons, scant $\frac{1}{2}$ cup) white wine with 1 tablespoon chopped shallot. Add $1\frac{1}{2}$ dl. ($\frac{1}{4}$ pint, $\frac{2}{3}$ cup) *Demi-glace sauce*. Boil down by half. Remove from the heat.

Add 100 g. (4 oz., $\frac{1}{2}$ cup) fresh butter and 1 tablespoon chopped tarragon. Season with a little cayenne and a few drops of lemon juice. Mix well. Do not strain.

Chateaubriand sauce II. SAUCE CHATEAUBRIAND – Heat 1 tablespoon meat glaze or extract mixed with 2 tablespoons (3 tablespoons) white stock or water. Add 100 g. (4 oz., $\frac{1}{2}$ cup) fresh butter cut into fragments, 1 tablespoon chopped parsley and a few drops lemon juice. Season with a little cayenne. Mix well.

Chaud-froid sauce, brown (for various meats). SAUCE CHAUD-FROID BRUNE – To make 5 dl. (scant pint, $2\frac{1}{4}$ cups) sauce: put in a thick-bottomed saucepan $3\frac{1}{2}$ dl. (generous $\frac{1}{2}$ pint, $1\frac{1}{2}$ cups) *Demi-glace sauce* (see above) and 2 dl. ($\frac{1}{3}$ pint, scant cup) clear brown stock. Boil down over strong heat, stirring with a wooden spoon. Add, a little at a time, 4 dl. ($\frac{3}{4}$ pint, scant 2 cups) *Meat jelly stock* (see JELLY).

Boil down until the sauce has the right consistency. Chill a small quantity of the sauce on ice; if it is not firm enough add a few tablespoons jelly and boil down.

Remove from heat, add 2 tablespoons (3 tablespoons) Madeira or other wine indicated in the recipe, and strain. Stir the sauce until it is quite cold.

To obtain a perfect coating, the sauce must be poured over the meat when cold but not set.

Chaud-froid sauce, chicken. SAUCE CHAUD-FROID POUR VOLAILLES – Proceed as for the ordinary *Chaud-froid sauce*, replacing brown stock by chicken stock. Flavour with wine, or, according to its final use, with a few tablespoons *Truffle essence* (see ESSENCE).

Chaud-froid sauce, fish. SAUCE CHAUD-FROID POUR POISSON – Proceed as for ordinary *Chaud-froid sauce*, using *Espagnole sauce* based on fish stock, well skimmed.

Chaud-froid sauce, game flavoured. SAUCE CHAUD-FROID À L'ESSENCE DE GIBIER – Proceed as for ordinary *Chaud-froid sauce*, replacing the brown stock by 1 dl. (6 tablespoons, scant $\frac{1}{2}$ cup) game essence or *fumet* prepared with the carcases and trimmings of the game being used.

Flavour the sauce with Madeira or similar wine.

For certain game, notably for thrushes, add to this sauce a few drops of Cognac or gin.

Chaud-froid sauce with orange (for duck and duckling). SAUCE CHAUD-FROID À L'ORANGE – Proceed as for *Chaud-froid sauce I*, replacing the brown stock by $1\frac{1}{2}$ dl. ($\frac{1}{4}$ pint, $\frac{2}{3}$ cup) duck *fumet* prepared by using the carcases and trimmings of the duck.

Concentrate this sauce more than usual so that it will not be made too thin by the addition of the orange juice.

Strain, add to it the strained juice of an orange, and 2 tablespoons (3 tablespoons) orange peel blanched, cooled in cold water, drained, and cut in a fine *julienne*.

This sauce can also be used to coat various kinds of game, the duck *fumet* being replaced by that of the game being used.

Chaud-froid sauce with tomatoes. SAUCE CHAUD-FROID À LA TOMATE – Boil down by one-third 5 dl. (scant pint, $2\frac{1}{4}$ cups) tomato pulp to which $3\frac{1}{2}$ dl. (generous $\frac{1}{2}$ pint, $1\frac{1}{2}$ cups) *Meat jelly stock* (see JELLY) have been added.

Strain, and stir until completely cold.

Chaud-froid sauce with truffle essence. SAUCE CHAUD-FROID À L'ESSENCE DE TRUFFES – Prepare game-flavoured *Chaud-froid sauce* with 1 dl. (6 tablespoons, scant $\frac{1}{2}$ cup) *Truffle essence* (see ESSENCE).

Chaud-froid sauce à la niçoise. SAUCE CHAUD-FROID À LA NIÇOISE – Proceed as for *Chaud-froid sauce, fish*. Add to the finished sauce a few drops anchovy essence and 1 tablespoon chopped tarragon.

Dried cherry sauce for venison (old recipe). SAUCE AUX CERISES SÈCHES – 'Peel and wash 500 g. ($\frac{1}{2}$ lb.) dried cherries, pound them in a mortar and boil them in a saucepan with 2 tablespoons (3 tablespoons) sugar, 2 glasses good Burgundy, $\frac{1}{4}$ glass wine vinegar, a pinch of coriander and a little lemon peel. Simmer for 20 to 25 minutes and mix with it 2 tablespoons (3 tablespoons) *Espagnole sauce* and the juice of a lemon. Boil down, stirring all the time over strong heat. Strain through a cloth, using pressure.' (Carême, *L'Art de la cuisine française au XIXe siècle*.)

Colbert sauce (for grilled fish and meat and for vegetables). SAUCE COLBERT – Bring to the boil 3 to 4 tablespoons (scant $\frac{1}{4}$ to $\frac{1}{3}$ cup) meat glaze diluted with 1 tablespoon white stock or water. Remove from heat and incorporate 100 g. (4 oz., $\frac{1}{2}$ cup) softened butter.

Season, and add a little grated nutmeg and a pinch of cayenne. Add, stirring all the time, the juice of $\frac{1}{2}$ lemon, 1 tablespoon chopped parsley and 1 tablespoon Madeira.

Cranberry sauce for roast fowl, particularly turkey (Anglo-American cookery). SAUCE AUX AIRELLES – Cook 250 g. (9 oz.) cranberries with 5 dl. (scant pint, $2\frac{1}{4}$ cups) water in a covered pan for a few minutes, until the berries split. Drain and rub through a fine sieve.

Dilute with a few tablespoons of the cooking juice to make a thick sauce. Sweeten and heat through. Chill before serving.

Diable or devilled sauce I (for grilled chicken etc.) SAUCE À LA DIABLE – Boil down by two-thirds $1\frac{1}{2}$ dl. ($\frac{1}{4}$ pint, $\frac{2}{3}$ cup) white wine and 1 tablespoon vinegar with 1 tablespoon chopped shallot, a sprig of thyme, $\frac{1}{4}$ bay leaf and a good pinch of freshly ground pepper. Stir in 2 dl. ($\frac{1}{3}$ pint, scant cup) *Demi-glace sauce*. Boil for a few moments and strain. Add 1 teaspoon chopped parsley and season with cayenne pepper.

The wine can be boiled down with vinegar alone. A small quantity of fresh butter may be added, but first remove the saucepan from heat.

Diable or devilled sauce II. SAUCE À LA DIABLE – Prepare the wine and herbs as above. Pour in stock or water to which meat glaze or extract has been added. Thicken with *Kneaded butter* (see BUTTER, *Compound butters*). Finish off as above.

Diable or devilled sauce III for grilled chicken, etc. (English cookery). SAUCE À LA DIABLE – Boil down by half $1\frac{1}{2}$ dl. ($\frac{1}{4}$ pint, $\frac{2}{3}$ cup) wine vinegar to which 1 tablespoon chopped shallot has been added.

Stir in $2\frac{1}{2}$ dl. (scant $\frac{1}{2}$ pint, generous cup) *Espagnole sauce* and 2 tablespoons (3 tablespoons) tomato purée. Cook for 5 minutes. Add 1 tablespoon Worcestershire sauce, 1 table-spoon of Harvey sauce, and a little cayenne. Strain.

Duxelles sauce (for eggs, small cuts of meat, fish, chicken). SAUCE DUXELLES – Stir in 1 dl. (6 tablespoons, scant $\frac{1}{2}$ cup) white wine to 2 tablespoons (3 tablespoons) chopped mushrooms prepared as *duxelles*. Boil down, stir in $1\frac{1}{2}$ dl. ($\frac{1}{4}$ pint, $\frac{2}{3}$ cup) *Demi-glace sauce* (see above) and 1 dl. (6 tablespoons, scant $\frac{1}{2}$ cup) tomato purée. Boil for a few moments. Add 1 tablespoon chopped parsley.

In times past this was known as *sauce aux fines herbes*.

Espagnole demi-glace – This is a rich sauce, used as a basis for many lesser sauces. After adding a specified quantity of white or brown clear stock to the basic stock and boiling it down, the brown sauce becomes very thick, almost jellied. This can be used in the preparation of different brown sauces.

Espagnole demi-glace is often replaced by stock or brown veal stock, brought to the right consistency by boiling it down or by thickening it with potato flour or arrowroot. This latter method gives a very good result.

Financière sauce I (for sweetbreads, fowl, timbales, vol-au-vent, etc.). SAUCE FINANCIÈRE – Add to 2 dl. ($\frac{1}{3}$ pint, scant cup) *Madeira sauce* as it cooks, 1 dl. (6 tablespoons, scant $\frac{1}{2}$ cup) truffle essence, and strain.

This sauce is rarely used by itself. Its most important function is to bind the *Financière garnish* (see GARNISHES).

Financière sauce II (old recipe). SAUCE FINANCIÈRE – 'Put into a saucepan some shredded lean ham, a pinch of mignonette, a little thyme and bay leaf, some mushroom and truffle trimmings and 2 glasses dry Madeira. Boil down over low heat and add 2 tablespoons (3 tablespoons) consommé and 2 tablespoons (3 tablespoons) well-beaten *Espagnole sauce* (see above). Boil down by half, strain, then put it back on the heat and mix in $\frac{1}{2}$ glass Madeira. Boil down in a *bain-marie*.

When this sauce is intended for a game *entrée*, the chicken consommé is replaced by an appropriate game *fumet*. Add a little butter just before serving.' (Carême, *L'Art de la cuisine française au XIXe siècle*.)

Fines herbes sauce I (for small cuts of meat). SAUCE AUX FINES HERBES – Add 2 tablespoons (3 tablespoons) chopped parsley, chervil and tarragon to $1\frac{1}{2}$ dl. ($\frac{1}{4}$ pint, $\frac{2}{3}$ cup) strained *Demi-glace sauce* or concentrated brown stock. Add a few drops lemon juice.

Fines herbes sauce II. SAUCE AUX FINES HERBES – Boil down 1 dl. (6 tablespoons, scant $\frac{1}{2}$ cup) white wine with a handful of parsley, chervil and tarragon leaves. Add 2 dl. ($\frac{1}{3}$ pint, scant cup) *Demi-glace sauce*. Finish off as for *Tarragon sauce*.

Fines herbes sauce III. SAUCE AUX FINES HERBES – Toss in butter 1 tablespoon chopped shallot. Add 1 dl. (6 table-spoons, scant $\frac{1}{2}$ cup) white wine, boil down and add 2 dl. ($\frac{1}{3}$ pint, scant cup) stock. Thicken with 40 g. ($1\frac{1}{2}$ oz., 3 tablespoons) *Kneaded butter* (see BUTTER, *Compound butters*). Boil for a few moments, strain, and add 1 tablespoon chopped parsley, chervil and tarragon and a few drops of lemon juice.

This *Fines herbes sauce* was formerly made like the *Duxelles sauce* for which the recipe is given previously.

Genevoise sauce (for fish, chiefly trout and salmon). SAUCE GENEVOISE – Cook gently in butter a *mirepoix* of 50 g. (2 oz., $\frac{1}{2}$ cup) diced carrot, 50 g. (2 oz., $\frac{1}{2}$ cup) diced onion, a stick of celery, a sprig of thyme, a piece of bay leaf and 10 parsley sprigs.

Add 500 g. (18 oz.) salmon head cut in small pieces or an equal quantity of bones and trimmings of other fish.

Cook slowly with a lid on for 15 minutes. Strain the liquid and discard the seasonings. Add 6 dl. (1 pint, $2\frac{1}{2}$ cups) good red wine and boil down by half.

Add 3 dl. ($\frac{1}{2}$ pint, $1\frac{1}{4}$ cups) *Espagnole sauce II* based on fish stock. Bring to the boil, skim, and simmer over low heat for 1 hour, skimming frequently and adding extra fish *fumet*, if necessary.

Strain the sauce through a fine strainer, pressing the ingredients. Remove all grease, put the sauce into a saucepan, dilute with a few tablespoons fish *fumet* made with red wine, and boil down by one-third to one-half.

Strain the sauce, remove from the heat and incorporate 75 g. (3 oz., 6 tablespoons) fresh butter and 1 teaspoon anchovy essence.

The delicate flavour of this sauce will be improved by adding, in the course of the cooking, a handful of mushroom skins. When the fish it accompanies has been braised add the braising liquor to the sauce.

To obtain a brown and brilliant *genevoise sauce* mix with a wooden spoon when the butter is incorporated. This applies to all brown sauces with butter.

Genoise sauce with Bordeaux wine (old recipe). SAUCE GENOISE AU VIN DE BORDEAUX – 'Pour into a saucepan 2 glasses (cups) red Bordeaux wine, add 2 tablespoons (3 tablespoons) mushrooms, truffles, parsley and 2 shallots, all blanched and chopped, a pinch of *four-spices* and a pinch of finely ground pepper. Boil down almost completely, add 2 tablespoons (3 tablespoons) of consommé, 3 to 4 tablespoons *Espagnole sauce* and 1 glass Bordeaux wine. Boil down to the desired consistency and transfer the sauce to a *bain-marie*. Blend in a little Isigny butter.' (Carême, *L'Art de la cuisine française au XIX siècle*.)

Gooseberry sauce (English cookery). SAUCE AUX GROSEILLES – Cook $\frac{1}{2}$ litre (scant pint, $2\frac{1}{4}$ cups) green gooseberries, topped and tailed, with $\frac{1}{2}$ dl. (3 tablespoons, scant $\frac{1}{4}$ cup) water and 75 g. (3 oz., 6 tablespoons) sugar.

Rub through a fine strainer.

Grand Veneur sauce I (for venison). SAUCE GRAND VENEUR – Add 1 tablespoon gooseberry jelly to 2 dl. ($1\frac{1}{3}$ pint, scant cup) concentrated and strained *Pepper or poivrade sauce II*.

Grand Veneur sauce II. SAUCE GRAND VENEUR – Finish off *Pepper or poivrade sauce II* with gooseberry jelly and 2 to 3 tablespoons (3 tablespoons to scant $\frac{1}{4}$ cup) cream. Mix.

Grand Veneur sauce III. SAUCE GRAND VENEUR – Add to *Pepper or poivrade sauce II* a few tablespoons hare's blood diluted with a little of the marinade of the game being used.

Hachée sauce I (for minced meat and other dishes made with left-overs). SAUCE HACHÉE – Cook 1 large tablespoon chopped onion in 1 tablespoon butter. When it is three-quarters cooked, add $\frac{1}{2}$ tablespoon chopped shallot.

Stir in 1 dl. (6 tablespoons, scant $\frac{1}{2}$ cup) wine vinegar, boil down, and add $1\frac{1}{2}$ dl. ($\frac{1}{4}$ pint, $\frac{2}{3}$ cup) *Demi-glace sauce* (see above) and 1 dl. (6 tablespoons, scant $\frac{1}{2}$ cup) tomato purée. Simmer for a few moments. Add 1 tablespoon chopped lean ham, 1 tablespoon dry *duxelles*, 1 tablespoon chopped capers and gherkins, and 1 tablespoon chopped parsley.

Hachée sauce II (old recipe). SAUCE HACHÉE – 'Pour into a saucepan 2 tablespoons (3 tablespoons) vinegar, add 1 tablespoon chopped mushrooms, half this quantity parsley, 2 chopped shallots, a little garlic, a fragment of thyme and bay leaf, 2 cloves, a good pinch of white pepper and a little grated nutmeg. Cook this seasoning over low heat. Take out the bay leaf, thyme and cloves and add 2 tablespoons (3 tablespoons) consommé and 2 big tablespoons (3 tablespoons) *Espagnole sauce*. Boil down and transfer it to a *bain-marie*. Before serving mix in a little anchovy butter, 2 small gherkins chopped very finely and some capers.' (Carême, *L'Art de la cuisine française au XIXe siècle*.)

Herb sauce for boiled fish and joints (English cookery). SAUCE AUX AROMATES – Put in a saucepan 1 chopped shallot, a sprig of thyme, a pinch of chives, a pinch of savory, a pinch of marjoram, a good pinch of sage, a good pinch of basil, 4 peppercorns and a little grated nutmeg. Pour in $2\frac{1}{2}$ dl. (scant $\frac{1}{2}$ pint, generous cup) boiling consommé. Cover the pan and allow to infuse for 10 minutes. Strain. Stir into a blond *roux* prepared with 25 g. (1 oz., 2 tablespoons) butter and 25 g. (1 oz., $\frac{1}{4}$ cup) flour. Mix, simmer for a few moments, strain, and add 1 tablespoon chopped, blanched chervil and tarragon, and a squeeze of lemon juice.

Hunter sauce – See *Chasseur sauce*.

Italian sauce I (for small cuts of meat, fowl). SAUCE ITALIENNE – Prepare 2 dl. ($\frac{1}{3}$ pint, scant cup) *Duxelles sauce* and add 1 tablespoon chopped lean cooked ham and 1 tablespoon chopped parsley, chervil and tarragon.

Italian sauce II (for grilled fish). SAUCE ITALIENNE – Proceed as in the foregoing recipe, but use *Espagnole sauce* based on fish stock to add to the *duxelles*, and leave out the ham.

Lyonnaise sauce I (for small cuts of meat, chiefly for leftovers). SAUCE LYONNAISE – Cook 3 tablespoons (scant $\frac{1}{4}$ cup) finely chopped onion in 1 tablespoon butter. Moisten with $\frac{1}{2}$ dl. (3 tablespoons, scant $\frac{1}{4}$ cup) wine vinegar and an equal quantity white wine. Boil down, and add 2 dl. ($\frac{1}{3}$ pint, scant cup) *Demi-glace sauce*. Cook at boiling point for a few moments.

A small quantity of tomato purée may be added.

Lyonnaise sauce II. SAUCE LYONNAISE – Cook the onion in butter. Sprinkle with 1 tablespoon flour and colour lightly. Stir in wine vinegar, white wine, and stock. Finish off as above.

Madeira sauce I (for small cuts of meat). SAUCE AU MADÈRE – Add to 2 dl. ($\frac{1}{3}$ pint, scant cup) concentrated *Demi-glace sauce*, 3 tablespoons (scant $\frac{1}{4}$ cup) Madeira.

Madeira sauce II. SAUCE AU MADÈRE – Sauté in butter the piece of meat being used. Take it out of the pot, dilute the cooking juices with 1 tablespoon Madeira, and add 2 dl. ($\frac{1}{3}$ pint, scant cup) stock, or water to which a little meat glaze or extract has been added. Bring to the boil. Thicken with 40 g. ($1\frac{1}{2}$ oz., 3 tablespoons) *Kneaded butter* (see BUTTER, *Compound butters*). Finish with 2 tablespoons (3 tablespoons) Madeira and strain.

Marrow sauce (for grilled meat, vegetables, poached eggs). SAUCE À LA MOELLE – Like *Bordelaise sauce* but replace the red wine with white wine.

Marrow sauce II (for grilled fish). SAUCE À LA MOELLE – Boil down 1 dl. (6 tablespoons, scant $\frac{1}{2}$ cup) white wine with 1 good tablespoon chopped shallot. Season with salt and a little freshly ground pepper. Add 2 tablespoons (3 tablespoons) concentrated and thickened brown stock or 1 tablespoon meat glaze or meat extract. Mix.

Add, away from the heat, 100 g. (4 oz., $\frac{1}{2}$ cup) butter cut in tiny pieces and 50 g. (2 oz., $\frac{1}{2}$ cup) marrow, blanched, drained, and cut into small dice.

Add a few drops lemon juice and 1 tablespooon chopped parsley.

This sauce, a variant of *Bercy sauce*, is poured directly on the grilled fish.

Matelote sauce (for eel and freshwater fish). SAUCE MATELOTE – See *Red wine sauce*.

Mushroom sauce I (for small cuts of meat; sautéed poultry). SAUCE AUX CHAMPIGNONS – Sauté in butter 100 g. (4 oz., $1\frac{1}{3}$ cups) peeled mushroom caps or large sliced mushrooms. Season, pour in 2 dl. ($\frac{1}{3}$ pint, scant cup) *Demi-glace sauce* and 1 tablespoon Madeira, and simmer over gentle heat without allowing to boil'. Canned mushrooms can be used.

Mushroom sauce II. SAUCE AUX CHAMPIGNONS – Sauté the mushrooms in butter and remove from the pan. Put 1 scant tablespoon flour in the butter and cook till pale golden colour.

Stir in 3 dl. ($\frac{1}{2}$ pint, $1\frac{1}{4}$ cups) white stock or consommé and boil down by one-third. Put the mushrooms back in the sauce, heat without boiling, and add 1 tablespoon Madeira.

Mustard sauce (for grilled meat, particularly for pig's trotters St. Menehould). SAUCE MOUTARDE – Cook gently in butter 50 g. (2 oz., $\frac{1}{2}$ cup) finely chopped onion, season with salt, pepper, a pinch of thyme and powdered bay leaf.

Stir in $1\frac{1}{2}$ dl. ($\frac{1}{4}$ pint, $\frac{2}{3}$ cup) white wine, boil down, add $1\frac{1}{2}$ dl. ($\frac{1}{4}$ pint, $\frac{2}{3}$ cup) *Demi-glace sauce*. Boil down by one-third. Add 1 good tablespoon Dijon mustard, 1 tablespoon butter and a squeeze of lemon juice.

Napolitaine sauce for game and venison (old recipe). SAUCE À LA NAPOLITAINE – 'Put in a saucepan 1 tablespoon grated horseradish, a little chopped lean ham, a seasoned *bouquet garni*, a little mignonette and grated nutmeg, and 1 glass dry Madeira. Boil down over very low heat, take out the *bouquet*, add 2 tablespoons (3 tablespoons) consommé and 2 tablespoons (3 tablespoons) *Espagnole sauce*. Strain the sauce through a cloth and boil down again, mixing in, little by little, 1 glass Malaga and $\frac{1}{4}$ pot redcurrant jelly. Add a little butter and game glaze.

How to strain a sauce through muslin, using two wooden spatulas (*Larousse*)

'For *entrées* of braised fillets of beef and roasts served *à la napolitaine*, add sultanas, picked over and washed, to the sauce. A little candied citron cut in small dice and blanched may also be added.' (Carême, *L'art de la cuisine française au XIXe siècle*.)

Noisette sauce. SAUCE NOISETTE – *Hollandaise sauce* with *Noisette butter* added (see BUTTER, *Compound butters*).

Orange sauce (for duck and teal, spit or oven roasted). SAUCE À L'ORANGE – After cooking the duck, remove the grease and dilute the cooking juices in the pan with 1 glass white wine. Boil down, add 2 dl. ($\frac{1}{3}$ pint, scant cup) concentrated and thickened brown stock. Simmer for a few moments and add the juice of an orange.

Strain through muslin and add 2 tablespoons (3 tablespoons) orange peel cut in fine *julienne*, blanched and drained.

Oyster sauce or brown oyster sauce for grilled meat, meat pudding, grilled cod (English cookery). SAUCE AUX HUÎTRES – Stir 1 dl. (6 tablespoons, scant $\frac{1}{2}$ cup) of the liquor in which oysters were cooked and 2 dl. ($\frac{1}{3}$ pint, scant cup) light brown stock into a brown *roux* composed of 25 g. (1 oz., 2 tablespoons) butter and 15 g. ($\frac{1}{2}$ oz., 2 tablespoons) flour.

Season very lightly, bring to the boil, and cook for 10 minutes. Strain, add 12 poached, de-bearded and sliced oysters, and a pinch of cayenne.

Pepper or poivrade sauce I (for meat). SAUCE POIVRADE – Cook 1 dl. (6 tablespoons, scant $\frac{1}{2}$ cup) vegetable *mirepoix* gently in butter. When the vegetables are soft, moisten them with $\frac{1}{2}$ dl. (3 tablespoons, scant $\frac{1}{4}$ cup) wine vinegar and the same amount of white wine. Boil down by half.

Stir in 2 dl. ($\frac{1}{3}$ pint, scant cup) *Espagnole sauce* and 2 dl. ($\frac{1}{3}$ pint, scant cup) white stock. Cook very slowly for 1 hour. Skim the sauce from time to time and add a few tablespoons white stock if the boiling down is too rapid.

A few minutes before straining the sauce add 5 crushed peppercorns.

Strain, pressing well. Add 3 or 4 tablespoons (scant $\frac{1}{4}$ or $\frac{1}{3}$ cup) stock and put back the sauce to boil for a few minutes.

If the *poivrade sauce* is to accompany marinated meat, add to it, in the course of cooking, a few tablespoons of the marinade. If the recipe demands butter, add it just before serving.

The characteristic of this sauce is its peppery taste, blending with that of the various vegetables and aromatics and sharpened by the vinegar.

Pepper must only be added to the preparation at the last moment. Allowed to cook for a long time it develops an acrid taste. A small amount, added at the end of the preparation of a dish, produces a better result than a large quantity put in at the beginning.

Pepper or poivrade sauce II (for game). SAUCE POIVRADE AU GIBIER – Cook the *mirepoix* of vegetables in butter until they are soft, as in the preceding recipe, adding to them the trimmings of the game being used, cut in small pieces.

When everything is cooked, moisten with wine vinegar and white wine and finish off as for the ordinary *Poivrade sauce*.

The *mirepoix* may be cooked in oil instead of butter. To heighten the fine flavour of *poivrade sauces*, add to them, in the course of cooking, a handful of mushroom skins.

Pepper or poivrade sauce III (old recipe). SAUCE POIVRADE – 'Put in a saucepan 2 chopped onions and 2 chopped carrots, add a little lean ham, a few sprigs of parsley, a little thyme and bay leaf, a good pinch of mignonette, a little mace, 2 tablespoons (3 tablespoons) good vinegar, and 2 tablespoons (3 tablespoons) consommé. Simmer on very low heat.

'When the boiling down is complete, add 2 tablespoons (3 tablespoons) consommé and 2 tablespoons (3 tablespoons) well-stirred *Espagnole sauce*. Simmer for a few moments, strain the sauce, using pressure, and boil it down to the desired consistency. Add a little butter.' (Carême, *L'Art de la cuisine française au XIXe siècle*.)

Périgourdine sauce (for small cuts of meat, fowl, etc.). SAUCE PÉRIGOURDINE – A variant of *Périgueux sauce*. The only difference is that in this version the truffles are cut in thick round slices.

Périgueux sauce I (for small cuts of meat, fowl, game, timbales, vol-au-vent, etc.). SAUCE PÉRIGUEUX – Boil down by one-third 2 dl. ($\frac{1}{3}$ pint, scant cup) *Demi-glace sauce* (see above) with 2 or 3 tablespoons (3 tablespoons or scant $\frac{1}{4}$ cup) *Truffle essence* (see ESSENCE).

Strain. Add 2 tablespoons (3 tablespoons) diced cooked truffles away from the heat.

After the truffles have been added the sauce must not be boiled again.

Périgueux sauce II. SAUCE PÉRIGUEUX – Cook gently in butter 2 tablespoons (3 tablespoons) diced truffles. Season with salt and pepper and drain.

Dilute the juices in the pan with 1 tablespoon Madeira. Stir in 2 dl. ($\frac{1}{3}$ pint, scant cup) thickened brown stock. Simmer for a few moments. Strain. Put the truffles back in the sauce, add 2 tablespoons (3 tablespoons) Madeira and keep hot without allowing to boil.

Pine kernel sauce à l'italienne (old recipe). SAUCE AUX PIGNOLES À L'ITALIENNE – 'Put into a saucepan 50 g. (2 oz., $\frac{1}{4}$ cup) brown or white sugar, 2 tablespoons (3 tablespoons) good vinegar, 2 tablespoons (3 tablespoons) light veal stock, a seasoned *bouquet garni*, a pinch of grated nutmeg and a pinch of mignonette. Simmer all together over moderate heat. When the boiling down is complete, add 2 tablespoons (3 tablespoons) *Espagnole sauce* and 1 glass of red Bordeaux wine. When the sauce has boiled down, strain it through a cloth, add 1 tablespoon of the white pine kernels which the Italians call *pignoli*. The *pignoli* should boil for a second in the sauce.' (Carême, *L'Art de la cuisine française au XIXe siècle.*)

Piquante sauce (for small cuts of meat and various left-over meat dishes). SAUCE PIQUANTE – Make 2 dl. ($\frac{1}{3}$ pint, scant cup) *Diable or devilled sauce* (see above) with wine vinegar.

Add 1 tablespoon chopped gherkins and 1 tablespoon chopped parsley.

Poor man's sauce I (for dishes made with left-overs). SAUCE PAUVRE HOMME – Colour lightly in 1 tablespoon butter 1 good tablespoon flour. Moisten with $\frac{1}{2}$ dl. (3 tablespoons, scant $\frac{1}{4}$ cup) wine vinegar, boil down, and stir in 2 dl. ($\frac{1}{3}$ pint, scant cup) stock or water with a little meat glaze or extract. Season and simmer for a few seconds.

Add 1 tablespoon blanched chopped shallots, 1 tablespoon chopped parsley and 2 tablespoons (3 tablespoons) golden breadcrumbs.

The shallot may be replaced by chives, or both may be used.

Poor man's sauce II. SAUCE PAUVRE HOMME – Fry in 1 tablespoon butter 2 tablespoons (3 tablespoons) golden breadcrumbs. Moisten with $\frac{1}{2}$ dl. (3 tablespoons, scant $\frac{1}{4}$ cup) wine vinegar. Boil down and stir in stock. Simmer for a few moments and finish off with blanched, chopped shallots and onions, together with 2 tablespoons (3 tablespoons) chopped parsley.

Poor man's sauce III (English cookery). SAUCE PAUVRE HOMME – Colour lightly in butter 50 g. (2 oz., $\frac{1}{2}$ cup) chopped onion. Moisten with $\frac{1}{2}$ dl. (3 tablespoons, scant $\frac{1}{4}$ cup) white wine and $\frac{1}{2}$ dl. (3 tablespoons, scant $\frac{1}{4}$ cup) wine vinegar.

Boil down by two-thirds, stir in $1\frac{1}{2}$ dl. ($\frac{1}{4}$ pint, $\frac{2}{3}$ cup) consommé and thicken with brown *roux* made with 10 g. ($\frac{1}{2}$ oz., 1 tablespoon) butter and 10 g. ($\frac{1}{2}$ oz., 2 tablespoons) flour. Cook for 10 minutes.

Finish off with 1 dessertspoon capers, 1 dessertspoon chopped parsley and a little cayenne.

Port wine sauce I (for meat, fowl, foie gras). SAUCE AU PORTO – Proceed as for *Madeira sauce*, replacing the latter with port wine.

Port wine sauce II for game birds, particularly wild duck (English cookery). SAUCE AU PORTO – Boil down by half 1 dl. (6 tablespoons, scant $\frac{1}{2}$ cup) port to which $\frac{1}{2}$ tablespoon chopped shallot, a sprig of thyme and a piece of bay leaf have been added. Add the juice of 1 orange and $\frac{1}{2}$ lemon, and a pinch grated orange rind. Stir in 2 dl. ($\frac{1}{3}$ pint, scant cup) thickened brown veal stock. Simmer for a few moments and strain.

Portugaise sauce I (for eggs, fish, meat and poultry). SAUCE PORTUGAISE – Cook 1 good tablespoon finely chopped onion in 1 tablespoon oil. When it is golden in colour, add 4 peeled, coarsely chopped, tomatoes and a little grated garlic. Season.

Begin cooking over good heat, then cover the pan and cook very slowly, stirring from time to time, for 25 minutes. Stir in 4 tablespoons ($\frac{1}{3}$ cup) thickened brown stock. Add 1 tablespoon chopped parsley and a little freshly ground pepper.

Portugaise sauce II for braised or roasted fillet of beef, and for ham (old recipe). SAUCE À LA PORTUGAISE – 'Take off carefully 2 small pieces of lemon peel and the same amount of orange peel; put them into a saucepan, adding 1 teaspoon coriander seeds, 1 teaspoon sugar and 1 glass Malaga. Simmer over a low heat, add 2 tablespoons (3 tablespoons) consommé and strain this seasoning through a cloth. Add enough *Espagnole sauce* to accompany an *entrée*. After having boiled down the sauce to the desired point, add 1 glass Malaga. Boil down again, then pour the sauce into a *bain-marie*, and add the juice of a lemon and a little butter.' (Carême, *L'Art de la cuisine française au XIXe siècle.*)

Provençal sauce (for eggs, fish, small cuts of meat, fowl, vegetables). SAUCE PROVENÇALE – Cook 50g. (2oz., $\frac{1}{2}$ cup) chopped onion in oil until soft. Add 4 large peeled and pressed tomatoes, 1 small clove of crushed garlic, salt and pepper. Cook for a few minutes over good heat. Moisten with $1\frac{1}{2}$ dl. ($\frac{1}{4}$ pint, $\frac{2}{3}$ cup) dry white wine. Boil down. Add $2\frac{1}{2}$ dl. (scant $\frac{1}{2}$ pint, generous cup) light veal stock. Cook for 15 minutes. Add 1 good teaspoon chopped parsley.

Ravigote sauce (old recipe). SAUCE RAVIGOTE À L'ANCIENNE – 'Chop an onion and cook it lightly in a little clarified butter. Add a glass of Chablis, 1 tablespoon consommé, the juice of a lemon, a little garlic and shallot, a chopped gherkin, 1 tablespoon capers, some parsley roots, tarragon leaves, a small *bouquet garni*, a clove, a pinch of nutmeg and crushed peppercorns. Simmer for 20 minutes, strain into a saucepan containing 2 large tablespoons boiling *Espagnole sauce* and carefully remove all grease from this sauce. Boil down to the desired point, mix in 1 teaspoon fine mustard and strain through a cloth. When ready to serve, blend in a little fresh butter and 1 tablespoon chopped chervil and tarragon.' (Carême, *L'Art de la cuisine française au XIXe siècle.*)

Straining a sauce through muslin by twisting (*Larousse*)

Red wine sauce I. SAUCE AU VIN ROUGE – See *Burgundy or bourguignonne sauce.*

Red wine sauce II (for eggs and fish). SAUCE AU VIN ROUGE – Cook in butter ½ dl. (3 tablespoons, scant ¼ cup) vegetable *mirepoix*, seasoned with thyme and bay leaf till soft.

Pour in 5 dl. (scant pint, 2¼ cups) red wine, add 1 small clove garlic, crushed, and a handful of mushroom skins. Boil down by half. Add 3 dl. (½ pint, 1¼ cups) *Espagnole sauce* and a few tablespoons light stock or *fumet* from the fish being cooked. Boil down by half.

Add 50 g. (2 oz., ¼ cup) butter, and a few drops anchovy essence, away from heat. Add a pinch of cayenne. Strain.

Red wine sauce III (for fish). SAUCE AU VIN ROUGE – Cook the fish in a liquor prepared with ½ dl. (3 tablespoons, scant ¼ cup) vegetable *mirepoix* cooked in butter until soft, 5 dl. (scant pint, 2¼ cups) red wine, 1 clove garlic and some mushroom skins.

Boil down the liquid by one-third. Thicken with 40 g. (1½ oz., 3 tablespoons) *Kneaded butter* (see BUTTER, *Compound butters*).

Finish off as above with butter and anchovy essence.

Reform sauce for mutton cutlets (English cookery). SAUCE RÉFORME – Add to 2½ dl. (scant ½ pint, generous cup) *Poivrade sauce* a garnish composed of 1 gherkin, 1 hard-boiled egg white, 2 cooked mushrooms, 25 g. (1 oz.) pickled tongue and 1 small cooked truffle, all cut in short strips.

After the garnish is added to the sauce, avoid boiling.

Régence sauce for sweetbreads, oven-roast or braised chicken (old recipe). SAUCE RÉGENCE – 'Cook without colouring, with 50 g. (2 oz., ¼ cup) butter, 100 g. (4 oz., ½ cup) lean ham cut in big dice and 1 onion cut in quarters. When the onions are almost cooked, add 1 chopped shallot.

'Moisten with 1 dl. (6 tablespoons, scant ½ cup) Graves, boil down by two-thirds, and add 2 dl. (⅓ pint, scant cup) chicken stock. Cook over low heat.

'Rub the cooked onions through a fine sieve, add 4 dl. (¾ pint, scant 2 cups) *Demi-glace sauce* and 1 dl. (6 tablespoons, scant ½ cup) concentrated chicken stock. Boil down until the sauce will coat the spoon. Strain.' (Carême, *L'Art de la cuisine française au XIXe siècle.*)

Robert sauce I (for grilled meat, mostly grilled pork). SAUCE ROBERT – Cook 2 tablespoons (3 tablespoons) finely chopped onion in 1 tablespoon of butter or lard till soft.

Moisten with 1 dl. (6 tablespoons, scant ½ cup) white wine. Boil down and add 2 dl. (⅓ pint, scant cup) *Demi-glace sauce*. Simmer for a few seconds. Add 1 tablespoon mustard.

Robert sauce II. SAUCE ROBERT – Sprinkle the cooked onion with 1 tablespoon flour, allow to colour lightly, moisten with white wine and add stock. Finish off with mustard.

Robert sauce III (old recipe). SAUCE ROBERT – 'Cut 3 onions into small dice, cook till they are golden in clarified butter, drain and mix with some consommé and 2 large tablespoons (3 large tablespoons) *Espagnole sauce*. Boil down the sauce to the desired consistency, mix in a little sugar, a little pepper, a little vinegar and 1 tablespoon fine mustard.' (Carême, *L'Art de la cuisine française au XIXe siècle.*)

Roebuck sauce I (for small cuts of meat). SAUCE CHEVREUIL – Boil down by one-third 3 dl. (½ pint, 1¼ cups) ordinary *Poivrade sauce*, adding in the course of cooking ½ dl. (3 tablespoons, scant ¼ cup) red wine, poured in little by little. Season with a little cayenne and strain through a cloth.

Roebuck sauce II. SAUCE CHEVREUIL – Proceed as in the above recipe using *Pepper or Poivrade sauce II for game.*

Roebuck sauce III (English cookery). SAUCE CHEVREUIL – Cook 2 tablespoons (3 tablespoons) chopped onion and 40 g. (1½ oz., 3 tablespoons) diced ham in butter until they colour. Add a *bouquet garni*, pour in ¾ dl. (5 tablespoons, generous ¼ cup) wine vinegar and boil down almost to nothing.

Add 2 dl. (⅓ pint, scant cup) *Espagnole sauce*, boil for 25 minutes, skimming frequently.

Take out the *bouquet garni* and finish off the sauce with ½ glass port and 1 tablespoon redcurrant jelly.

Romaine sauce I (for venison). SAUCE À LA ROMAINE – Cook to a pale caramel 3 large lumps of sugar. Moisten with 1 tablespoon vinegar, add 2 dl. (⅓ pint, scant cup) *Demi-glace sauce* and 4 tablespoons (⅓ cup) game *fumet*. Simmer for a few minutes. Strain through a cloth. Add 1 tablespoon pine kernels, roasted lightly in the oven, and 1 tablespoon currants and sultanas, washed, soaked till swollen in warm water, and dried.

Romaine sauce II (old recipe). SAUCE À LA ROMAINE – 'Chop up the white part of a celery heart and put it in a saucepan with a good pinch of coriander, a pinch of sugar, a clove of garlic, a little basil, bay leaf and 2 glasses Champagne. Simmer over low heat. When the celery is cooked, add 2 large tablespoons (3 large tablespoons) consommé and 2 tablespoons (3 tablespoons) *Espagnole sauce*. Boil down, pour in ½ glass Champagne and boil down again. Strain the sauce, using pressure, and before serving add a little butter and the juice of a lemon.' (Carême, *L'Art de la cuisine française au XIXe siècle.*)

Rouennaise sauce (for duck; may also be served with poached eggs). SAUCE ROUENNAISE – Bring to the boil 2 dl. (⅓ pint, scant cup) *Bordelaise sauce* (see above). Remove from direct heat, but keep the sauce hot, and add the finely chopped liver of a Rouen duck. Stir, season with salt, freshly ground pepper and a small pinch of spice. Strain through a cloth, pressing with a wooden spoon. Keep hot in the *bain-marie*.

This sauce may also be made with chicken livers.

Sainte-Menehoulde sauce (for grilled pork, chiefly pigs' trotters). SAUCE SAINTE-MENEHOULDE – Cook 1 large tablespoon finely chopped onion in 1 tablespoon butter till soft. Season with a pinch of salt and a little thyme and powdered bay leaf.

Moisten with 1 dl. (6 tablespoons, scant ½ cup) white wine and 1 tablespoon vinegar. Boil down completely. Stir in 2 dl. (⅓ pint, scant cup) *Demi-glace sauce*. Simmer for a few seconds over good heat and add 1 tablespoon each of mustard, chopped gherkins and chopped parsley and chervil, and a pinch of cayenne.

Salmis sauce (for game birds prepared in salmis). SAUCE SALMIS – Cook till soft in butter 1 dl. (6 tablespoons, scant ½ cup) vegetable *mirepoix*, together with the chopped carcase, skin and trimmings of the game being cooked. (See WOODCOCK, *Salmis of woodcock.*)

Moisten with 1 dl. (6 tablespoons, scant ½ cup) white wine and boil down. Add 2 dl. (⅓ pint, scant cup) *Demi-glace sauce* and 2 or 3 tablespoons game *fumet* or light stock. Simmer for 25 minutes and sieve, using pressure. Put the sauce back in the pan with 2 dl. (⅓ pint, scant cup) game *fumet* or light stock. Simmer for 20 minutes, skim and strain.

Pour over the pieces of game arranged in the sauté pan. Heat without boiling. The sauce must be thick enough to coat the pieces of game.

Salmis sauce with Champagne (old recipe). SAUCE SALMIS AU VIN DE CHAMPAGNE – 'Put into a saucepan ½ bottle Champagne, add the trimmings of 6 partridges prepared for a *salmis*, a piece of bay leaf, 2 shallots and 2 tablespoons (3 tablespoons) consommé and simmer this *fumet* for an hour. Strain it through a sieve and boil it down by half. Add 2 large tablespoons (3 large tablespoons) *Espagnole sauce*.

'When the sauce is almost boiled down to the proper point, pour into it ½ glass Champagne, and boil it down again to the desired consistency. Strain through a cloth and, before serving, blend in a little fine butter.

'To make a salmis with Bordeaux use a bottle of Bordeaux wine in place of the Champagne and for ordinary salmis make the *fumet* simply with stock, a shallot and a piece of bay leaf.' (Carême, *L'Art de la cuisine française au XIX*[e] *siècle*.)

Salmis sauce with red wine. SAUCE SALMIS AU VIN ROUGE – Proceed as in the above recipe, using red wine instead of white.

Tarragon sauce I (for eggs, small cuts of meat, etc.). SAUCE À L'ESTRAGON – Boil down 1 dl. (6 tablespoons, scant $\frac{1}{2}$ cup) white wine with 10 g. (scant $\frac{1}{2}$ oz.) tarragon leaves, roughly chopped. Add 2 dl. ($\frac{1}{3}$ pint, scant cup) *Demi-glace sauce* or thickened brown stock. Boil for a few moments and strain through a cloth.

Add 1 tablespoon chopped tarragon. Garnish whatever is to be served with this sauce with tarragon leaves blanched for a moment in boiling salted water, cooled in cold water and drained.

Tarragon sauce II. SAUCE À L'ESTRAGON – Sauté the meat or poultry in butter. Drain, dilute the juices in the saucepan with 1 dl. (6 tablespoons, scant $\frac{1}{2}$ cup) white wine, add a handful of chopped tarragon, boil down, pour in stock or water with meat glaze or extract added, and bind with *Kneaded butter* (see BUTTER, *Compound butters*).

Tarragon sauce III (for poached fowl). SAUCE À L'ESTRAGON – Put a good handful of tarragon into the white stock in which the chicken was poached.

Remove all grease, strain the stock through muslin, boil it down, and thicken with arrowroot (corn starch) or potato flour.

Finish off with chopped tarragon.

Poached fowl served with this sauce is garnished with blanched tarragon leaves.

Tortue sauce for calf's head or other offal (U.S. variety meats) served 'en tortue'. SAUCE TORTUE – Bring to the boil 1 dl. (6 tablespoons, scant $\frac{1}{2}$ cup) white wine. Add a sprig of thyme, quarter of a bay leaf, a sprig of crushed parsley, 1 or 2 sage leaves, a sprig of rosemary and a sprig of basil.

Cover the pan and allow to infuse over low heat, without boiling, for 15 to 20 minutes. Strain.

Add to $2\frac{1}{2}$ dl. (scant $\frac{1}{2}$ pint, generous cup) *Demi-glace sauce* 1 dl. (6 tablespoons, scant $\frac{1}{2}$ cup) tomato sauce, 1 dl. (6 tablespoons, scant $\frac{1}{2}$ cup) light stock and a handful of mushroom skins. Boil down by half. Add the strained infusion.

Simmer for few moments, and add a pinch of cayenne, a little spice, and 3 tablespoons (scant $\frac{1}{4}$ cup) Madeira. Strain through a cloth.

Tortue sauce with Madeira (old recipe). SAUCE TORTUE AU VIN DE MADÈRE – 'Put into a saucepan 1 glass dry Madeira, a little chopped lean ham, a pinch of mignonette, a pinch of pimento, a pinch of cayenne and a chopped shallot. Simmer over low heat and add 2 tablespoons (3 tablespoons), consommé, 2 large tablespoons (3 large tablespoons) well-stirred *Espagnole sauce* and a little tomato sauce.

'When this sauce is boiled down to the desired point, add to it $\frac{1}{4}$ glass of Madeira. Bring to the boil once or twice, strain through a cloth and, before serving, add a little fresh butter.' (Carême, *L'Art de la cuisine française au XIX*[e] *siècle*.)

Venison sauce. SAUCE VENAISON – See above, *Grand Veneur sauce*.

Venison sauce (old recipe). SAUCE VENAISON – 'Pour into a saucepan 1 glass old Burgundy wine, 2 tablespoons (3 tablespoons) ordinary vinegar, 2 tablespoons (3 tablespoons) sugar, the flesh of $\frac{1}{2}$ lemon with its seeds removed, $\frac{1}{2}$ pot of redcurrants. Boil down and add 2 tablespoons (3 tablespoons) *Espagnole sauce*. Boil down again, mixing in at intervals a second glass of Burgundy. When the sauce is concentrated, strain through a cloth.' (Carême, *L'Art de la cuisine française au XIX*[e] *siècle*.)

Victoria sauce for venison (English cookery). SAUCE VICTORIA – Add $1\frac{1}{2}$ dl. ($\frac{1}{4}$ pint, $\frac{2}{3}$ cup) port and 3 tablespoons (scant $\frac{1}{4}$ cup) redcurrant jelly to $2\frac{1}{2}$ dl. (scant $\frac{1}{2}$ pint, generous cup) *Espagnole sauce*. Add 8 peppercorns, 2 cloves, a fragment of cinnamon and the peel of 1 orange.

Boil down by one-third, add the juice of an orange and a little cayenne and strain through a cloth.

Yorkshire sauce for braised ham and roast and braised duck (English cooking). SAUCE YORKSHIRE – Cook 1 large tablespoon of orange peel cut in a fine *julienne* in 2 dl. ($\frac{1}{3}$ pint, scant cup) port.

Drain the peel. Add 2 tablespoons (3 tablespoons) *Espagnole sauce* and 1 tablespoon redcurrant jelly to the port. Season with a pinch of powdered cinnamon and a pinch of cayenne and simmer for a few moments. Add the juice of an orange and strain. Finish off with the orange peel cooked in port.

Zingara sauce (for small cuts of meat and poultry). SAUCE ZINGARA – Add a *julienne* composed of 1 tablespoon each of lean cooked ham, pickled tongue and mushrooms, and 1 heaped teaspoon truffles, to 2 dl. ($\frac{1}{3}$ pint, scant cup) *Demi-glace sauce* cooked with a few tablespoons tomato sauce and a few tablespoons mushroom stock. Season with a little paprika and keep warm without allowing the sauce to boil.

COMPOUND WHITE SAUCES: SAUCES COMPOSÉES, BLANCHES –

Aigrelette sauce with verjuice (old recipe). SAUCE AIGRELETTE AU VERJUS – 'Wash 30 verjuice grapes, pound them and press out the juice through a cloth. Boil 2 tablespoons (3 tablespoons) *Allemande sauce* with a little chicken glaze, a little butter, a pinch of nutmeg and finely ground pepper, and enough verjuice to render the sauce sharp and appetising.' (Carême, *L'Art de la cuisine française au XIX*[e] *siècle*.)

Albert sauce for braised beef (English cookery). SAUCE ALBERT – Cook at boiling point for 20 minutes 75 g. (3 oz., $\frac{1}{2}$ cup) grated horseradish moistened with 1 dl. (6 tablespoons, scant $\frac{1}{2}$ cup) light consommé.

Add $1\frac{1}{2}$ dl. ($\frac{1}{4}$ pint, $\frac{2}{3}$ cup) *Butter sauce II* 1 dl. (6 tablespoons, scant $\frac{1}{2}$ cup) cream and 25 g. (1 oz., $\frac{1}{2}$ cup) fine breadcrumbs. Boil down over strong heat, stirring all the time. Strain, pressing with spoon. Put back in the saucepan, thicken with 1 egg yolk and season with salt and pepper.

Finish off with $\frac{1}{2}$ teaspoon English mustard diluted with a few drops vinegar.

Albuféra sauce (for sweetbreads and poached or braised poultry). SAUCE ALBUFÉRA – Add 2 dl. ($\frac{1}{3}$ pint, scant cup) *Suprême sauce* to 2 tablespoons (3 tablespoons) concentrated veal stock and 1 tablespoon *Pimento butter* (see BUTTER).

Allemande sauce I or thick Velouté (for offal or U.S. variety meats, poached chicken, vegetables and eggs). SAUCE ALLEMANDE, VELOUTÉ LIÉ – For 5 dl. (scant pint, $2\frac{1}{4}$ cups) of sauce put into a pan with a thick, flat bottom, 2 egg yolks (3 if they are small) and 4 dl. ($\frac{3}{4}$ pint, scant 2 cups) light veal or chicken stock. Mix together. Add 5 dl. (scant pint, $2\frac{1}{4}$ cups) *Velouté sauce*. Mix with a whisk.

Begin cooking over good heat, stirring with a wooden spoon to keep the sauce from sticking to the bottom of the pan. Boil down carefully, until the sauce coats the spoon. Add 50 g. (2 oz., $\frac{1}{4}$ cup) butter, and strain through a cloth.

Keep in the *bain-marie* until ready to use. Whisk the sauce while it is in the *bain-marie* and butter the surface to prevent skin forming.

Depending on its use this sauce can be seasoned with a pinch of grated nutmeg and a squeeze of lemon juice.

Allemande sauce II (fish). SAUCE ALLEMANDE – Proceed as in the preceding recipe, using fish stock or *fumet* in place of the stock, and fish *Velouté sauce* in place of the *Velouté sauce* made with meat or poultry stock.

Allemande sauce III (mushroom flavoured). SAUCE ALLEMANDE AU FUMET DE CHAMPIGNONS – Proceed as in first recipe; add to the *Velouté sauce* a few tablespoons of the cooking juices of mushrooms. You can also add, in course of cooking, a good handful of mushroom skins and stalks.

Allemande sauce IV (truffle flavoured). SAUCE ALLEMANDE AU FUMET DE TRUFFES – As above. Replace the mushroom juices with *fumet* of truffles.

American sauce (for fish, shellfish, eggs). SAUCE AMÉRICAINE – In principle this sauce is the product of preparing lobster or crayfish *à l'américaine*.

It is used to coat braised fish, poached eggs and boiled eggs.

Anchovy sauce I (for fish). SAUCE ANCHOIS – Add to 2 dl. ($\frac{1}{3}$ pint, scant cup) *Normande sauce* or *White wine sauce* 2 tablespoons (3 tablespoons) anchovy butter or 1 tablespoon anchovy essence or paste. Strain.

Anchovy sauce II. SAUCE ANCHOIS – As above, using *Béchamel sauce* instead of *Normande sauce*.

Anchovy sauce III. SAUCE ANCHOIS – As above, using *Butter sauce* instead of *Normande sauce*.

Andalouse sauce (for eggs, fish, poultry). SAUCE ANDALOUSE – Add to 2 dl. ($\frac{1}{3}$ pint, scant cup) thick *Velouté sauce*, $\frac{1}{2}$ dl. (3 tablespoons, scant $\frac{1}{4}$ cup) tomato essence or strongly concentrated tomato purée. Add 2 tablespoons (3 tablespoons) sweet pimentos that have been peeled, braised and cut in dice, and 1 teaspoon chopped parsley.

This sauce may be seasoned with a little grated garlic.

Aurora sauce (for eggs, poultry, sweetbreads). SAUCE AURORE – Add to 2 dl. ($\frac{1}{3}$ pint, scant cup) *Velouté sauce* $\frac{1}{2}$ dl. (3 tablespoons, scant $\frac{1}{4}$ cup) very thick tomato purée.

Finish off with 50 g. (2 oz., $\frac{1}{4}$ cup) butter and strain.

Banquière sauce (for eggs, poultry, offal or U.S. variety meats, vol-au-vent). SAUCE BANQUIÈRE – Add to 2 dl. ($\frac{1}{3}$ pint, scant cup) *Suprême sauce* $\frac{1}{4}$ dl. (3 tablespoons, scant $\frac{1}{4}$ cup) Madeira. Strain through a cloth. Finish off with 2 tablespoons (3 tablespoons) chopped truffles.

Bâtarde sauce (for boiled fish and vegetables). SAUCE BÂTARDE – See *Butter sauce*.

Béarnaise sauce (for grilled or sautéed meat, grilled fish). SAUCE BÉARNAISE – Put into a saucepan 1 tablespoon chopped shallot, 2 tablespoons (3 tablespoons) tarragon and chopped chervil, a sprig of thyme, and a fragment of bay leaf. Moisten with $\frac{1}{2}$ dl. (3 tablespoons, scant $\frac{1}{4}$ cup) each vinegar and white wine. Season with a pinch of salt and a pinch of mignonette pepper. Boil down by two-thirds. Allow to cool. Put into the pan 2 raw egg yolks mixed with 1 tablespoon water. Beat the sauce with a whisk over very low heat. As soon as the yolks begin to thicken, incorporate 100 g. (4 oz., $\frac{1}{2}$ cup) fresh butter, little by little, whisking all the time.

Season the sauce, sharpen it if necessary with a squeeze of lemon juice and a pinch of cayenne. Strain. Finish off with 1 tablespoon each of chopped tarragon and chervil. Keep warm in a *bain-marie*.

Béarnaise sauce, tomato flavoured, or Choron sauce (for grilled meat). SAUCE BÉARNAISE, SAUCE CHORON – Add 2 dl. ($\frac{1}{3}$ pint, scant cup) strained *Béarnaise sauce* to 2 good tablespoons (3 good tablespoons) concentrated tomato purée.

Beauharnais sauce (for grilled and sautéed meat and grilled fish). SAUCE BEAUHARNAIS – Add 2 dl. ($\frac{1}{3}$ pint, scant cup) strained *Béarnaise sauce* to 2 good tablespoons (3 good tablespoons) green *Tarragon butter* (see BUTTER, *Compound butters*).

Béchamel sauce with onion. BÉCHAMEL SOUBISE – Add *Onion purée (soubise)* (see PURÉE) to *Béchamel sauce*.

Bercy sauce (for fish). SAUCE BERCY – Cook 1 tablespoon chopped shallot gently in butter without letting it colour. Moisten with 1 dl. (6 tablespoons, scant $\frac{1}{2}$ cup) white wine and 1 dl. (6 tablespoons, scant $\frac{1}{2}$ cup) fish *fumet*.

Boil down by half. Add 2 dl. ($\frac{1}{3}$ pint, scant cup) *Velouté sauce* based on fish stock. Cook at boiling point for a few moments over good heat. Add, away from the heat, 50 g. (2 oz., $\frac{1}{4}$ cup) butter, and 1 tablespoon chopped parsley. Do not strain.

Bontemps sauce (for grilled meat and poultry). SAUCE BONTEMPS – Cook 1 tablespoon finely chopped onion in butter. Season with a pinch of salt and a little paprika. Pour in 2 dl. ($\frac{1}{3}$ pint, scant cup) cider. Boil down by two-thirds.

Add 2 dl. ($\frac{1}{3}$ pint, scant cup) *Velouté sauce*. Cook at boiling point for a few moments. Remove from heat and add 50 g. (2 oz., $\frac{1}{4}$ cup) butter and 1 tablespoon mustard. Strain.

Brandade à la provençale for boiled fish, principally salt cod (old recipe). SAUCE BRANDADE À LA PROVENÇALE – 'Put into a saucepan 2 tablespoons (3 tablespoons) fish *Allemande sauce*, 3 egg yolks, a pinch of grated nutmeg, a pinch of finely ground pepper, a little pounded garlic, the juice of a large lemon and a little salt. After having mixed this seasoning perfectly, set the saucepan on some hot cinders, stirring all the time to obtain a perfectly thick and velvety sauce. Take it off the heat in order to mix in, spoonful by spoonful, $1\frac{1}{2}$ glasses good oil, Provençal olive oil. Add the juice of a lemon and 1 tablespoon chopped and blanched chervil or tarragon.' (Carême, *L'Art de la cuisine française au XIX*[e] *siècle*.)

Bread sauce for poultry and roast game birds (English cookery). SAUCE AU PAIN – Put 75 g. (3 oz., $1\frac{1}{2}$ cups) freshly prepared breadcrumbs into 5 dl. (scant pint, $2\frac{1}{4}$ cups) boiling water. Add 1 small onion studded with a clove, 25 g. (1 oz., 2 tablespoons) butter and a pinch of salt. Mix, bring to the boil, and cook gently for 15 minutes. Take out the onion and add to the sauce 1 dl. (6 tablespoons, scant $\frac{1}{2}$ cup) cream. Whisk until smooth.

Breton sauce (for eggs, fish, white meat, poultry, offal or variety meats). SAUCE BRETONNE – Prepare a fine *julienne* of $\frac{1}{2}$ medium-sized onion, the white of a leek and $\frac{1}{4}$ celery heart. Season with a pinch of salt and a little sugar. Cook slowly till soft with 1 tablespoon butter. Add 2 tablespoons (3 tablespoons) uncooked mushrooms cut in *julienne*.

Moisten with $\frac{1}{2}$ dl. (3 tablespoons, scant $\frac{1}{4}$ cup) white wine. Boil down to almost nothing, add $1\frac{1}{2}$ dl. ($\frac{1}{4}$ pint, $\frac{2}{3}$ cup) *Velouté sauce* based on meat or fish stock, according to the final use. Cook at boiling point for a few moments over strong heat. Add 50 g. (2 oz., $\frac{1}{4}$ cup) fresh butter and 1 tablespoon thick fresh cream. Do not strain.

When Breton sauce is to accompany braised fish, the latter must cook in the *julienne* indicated above, moistened with a few tablespoons of fish *fumet* or white wine. After the fish is cooked finish off the sauce as shown above.

Butter sauce I or Bâtarde sauce (for vegetables, boiled fish). SAUCE AU BEURRE, SAUCE BÂTARDE – Melt in a saucepan 25 g. (1 oz., 2 tablespoons) butter, add 25 g. (1 oz., $\frac{1}{4}$ cup) flour, mix, and moisten with $2\frac{1}{2}$ dl. (scant $\frac{1}{2}$ pint, generous cup) boiling salted water.

Stir the mixture vigorously with a whisk, and add 1 egg yolk mixed with 1 tablespoon cold water.

Add, over very low heat, 100 g. (4 oz., $\frac{1}{2}$ cup) fresh butter cut into small pieces, stirring all the time. Season the sauce and strain. It may be sharpened with a few drops of lemon juice.

Butter sauce II (English cookery). SAUCE AU BEURRE À L'ANGLAISE – Proceed as above using 25 g. (1 oz., 2 tablespoons) butter and 25 g. (1 oz., $\frac{1}{4}$ cup) flour.

Do not thicken the sauce with egg yolk.

Butter sauce III (old recipe). SAUCE AU BEURRE – 'Put into a saucepan 1 small tablespoon flour and a little butter. Stir with a wooden spoon. Add ½ glass water or consommé, a little salt and grated nutmeg and the juice of ½ lemon. Stir over brisk heat, and as soon as it comes to the boil, remove the sauce. Mix in a good piece of butter. The sauce should then be velvety, very smooth and excellent to the taste.' (Carême, *L'Art de la cuisine française au XIXe siècle.*)

In his *Traité des petites sauces*, Carême gives a variety of white sauces deriving from this sauce. In modern practice all these are prepared using *Allemande sauce* or *Suprême sauce* as their base, and their recipes are given in their alphabetical order.

Butter sauce with chervil (old recipe). SAUCE AU BEURRE À LA PLUCHE DE CERFEUIL – 'Bring to the boil in a saucepan 1 large tablespoon *Butter sauce*, adding to it a little salt, pepper and grated nutmeg, the juice of ½ lemon, a good piece of butter and 1 tablespoon blanched chervil leaves.' (Carême, *L'Art de la cuisine française au XIXe siècle.*)

Caper sauce I (for boiled fish). SAUCE AUX CÂPRES – Add to 2½ dl. (scant ½ pint, generous cup) *Hollandaise sauce* 2 tablespoons (3 tablespoons) well-drained capers.

Caper sauce II. SAUCE AUX CÂPRES – Proceed as above, using *Butter sauce*.

Caper sauce III, English (for boiled fish). SAUCE AUX CÂPRES À L'ANGLAISE – Prepare *Butter sauce II*. Finish it off with well-drained capers and a little anchovy essence.

Caper sauce IV, English (for boiled leg of mutton). SAUCE AUX CÂPRES A L'ANGLAISE – Prepare a white *roux* as for English *Butter sauce*, moisten it with the cooking broth of the mutton. Cook the sauce, strain it, finish off with the capers.

Caper sauce made with water can be served with boiled leg of mutton. This sauce is also served with boiled rabbit.

Cardinal sauce I (for fish). SAUCE CARDINAL – Boil down by half 2 dl. (⅓ pint, scant cup) *Velouté sauce* based on fish stock, and 1 dl. (6 tablespoons, scant ½ cup) fish *fumet*.

Add 1 dl. (6 tablespoons, scant ½ cup) cream, simmer for a few moments, remove from heat, add 50 g. (2 oz., ¼ cup) *Lobster* or *Spiny lobster butter* (see BUTTER) a pinch of cayenne. Strain through a cloth. Add 1 tablespoon chopped truffles.

When this sauce is used for fish garnished with slices of truffle, leave out the chopped truffles.

Cardinal sauce II. SAUCE CARDINAL – Proceed as above, replacing the *Velouté sauce* by *Béchamel sauce*.

Celery sauce for boiled and braised poultry (English cookery). SAUCE AU CELERI – Put into a sauté pan the trimmed hearts of 3 heads of celery. Add a *bouquet garni* and 1 small onion stuck with a clove. Cover with light consommé. Cook slowly. Drain the celery, pound it, and sieve into a saucepan. Add to it an equal quantity of *Cream sauce*, dilute with 1 or 2 tablespoons of the concentrated celery cooking liquor and mix well. Heat without allowing to boil.

Chantilly sauce (for poultry and white offal or U.S. variety meats). SAUCE CHANTILLY – Blend 2 dl. (⅓ pint, scant cup) thick *Suprême sauce* with 1 dl. (6 tablespoons, scant ½ cup) whipped cream.

White chaud-froid sauce I (for eggs, poultry, white offal or U.S. variety meats). SAUCE CHAUD-FROID BLANCHE – Put into a thick-bottomed sauté pan 3½ dl. (generous ½ pint, 1½ cups) *Velouté sauce* and 1 dl. (6 tablespoons, scant ½ cup) mushroom *fumet*. Boil down over good heat, stirring with a wooden spoon. Add, a little at a time, 4 dl. (¾ pint, scant 2 cups) chicken or veal jelly and 1½ dl. (¼ pint, ⅔ cup) cream.

Boil down until the sauce will coat the spoon. To be certain of this consistency, chill on ice a small quantity of the sauce. If it is not firm enough add a few more tablespoons of jelly and boil down again.

Strain the sauce and whisk until it is quite cold.

Depending on its final use, *chaud-froid sauce* may be left as it is or flavoured with wine such as Madeira, sherry, etc., which is added to the sauce when it is almost cold.

Whit chaud-froid sauce II (for fish and shellfish). SAUCE CHAUD-FROID BLANCHE MAIGRE – Proceed as for *White chaud-froid sauce I* using *Veloute sauce* based on fish stock and fish aspic jelly in place of meat *Velouté sauce* and jelly. Strain.

Chaud-froid sauce à l'allemande. SAUCE CHAUD-FROID À L'ALLEMANDE – Proceed as for *White chaud-froid sauce I*, replacing the *Velouté sauce* with *Allemande sauce*.

Reduce the proportion of cream added in the course of cooking so that the sauce is less thick in consistency. Flavour with Madeira or other similar wine.

Chaud-froid sauce à l'andalouse. SAUCE CHAUD-FROID À L'ANDALOUSE – Prepare the sauce as for *Chaud-froid sauce I*. Flavour it with sherry and add 2 tablespoons (3 tablespoons) orange peel cut in a vey fine *julienne*, blanched, cooled in water and drained.

Chaud-froid sauce à l'aurore. SAUCE CHAUD-FROID À L'AURORE – Add to *White chaud-froid sauce I* 3 tablespoons (scant ¼ cup) concentrated tomato purée. Strain.

Chaud-froid sauce à la banquière. SAUCE CHAUD-FROID À LA BANQUIÈRE – Add strained *White chaud-froid sauce I* to finely chopped truffles. Add 3 tablespoons (scant ¼ cup) Madeira.

Chaud-froid sauce Beauharnais. SAUCE CHAUD-FROID BEAUHARNAIS – Colour *White chaud-froid sauce I* before straining with 2 tablespoons (3 tablespoons) purée of green herbs (tarragon and chervil) blanched, cooled in water, drained and rubbed through a fine sieve.

Chaud-froid sauce, blonde. SAUCE CHAUD-FROID BLONDE – Add to *White chaud-froid sauce I* during cooking 2 tablespoons (3 tablespoons) blond chicken glaze, and strain.

Chaud-froid sauce à l'écossaise. SAUCE CHAUD-FROID À L'ÉCOSSAISE – Add to *White chaud-froid sauce I*, finished and strained, 2 tablespoons (3 tablespoons) fine *brunoise* of carrot, the white part of leek and celery, all cooked gently in light stock, also 1 tablespoon diced pickled tongue and 1 tablespoon diced truffles. Flavour with Madeira.

Chaud-froid sauce à la hongroise. SAUCE CHAUD-FROID À LA HONGROISE – Add to *White chaud-froid sauce I*, in course of cooking, 2 tablespoons (3 tablespoons) finely chopped onion which has been blanched, drained and cooked in 1 dl. (6 tablespoons, scant ½ cup) white wine till no liquid remains. Season with a good pinch of paprika. Strain through a cloth.

Chaud-froid sauce à l'indienne. SAUCE CHAUD-FROID À L'INDIENNE – Proceed as above. Season the chopped onion with 1 teaspoon curry. Strain through a cloth.

Chaud-froid sauce à la Nantua. SAUCE CHAUD-FROID À LA NANTUA – Recommended for fish and shellfish. Add to the ordinary *White chaud-froid sauce II* before straining 2 tablespoons (3 tablespoons) crayfish purée.

Strain, and add 1 tablespoon chopped truffles.

Chaud-froid sauce à la royale. SAUCE CHAUD-FROID À LA ROYALE – Add to *White chaud-froid sauce I*, before straining, 2 tablespoons (3 tablespoons) truffle purée diluted with 1 tablespoon sherry.

Chaud-froid sauce à la sicilienne. SAUCE CHAUD-FROID À LA SICILIENNE – Add to the *White chaud-froid sauce I*, before straining, 2 tablespoons (3 tablespoons) pistachio nuts, blanched, pounded finely in a mortar, diluted with a little cream and put through a fine sieve.

Chivry sauce I (for eggs and poultry). SAUCE CHIVRY – Boil down 1 dl. (6 tablespoons, scant ½ cup) white wine by half with 1 teaspoon chopped shallot and 1 large tablespoon chopped chervil and tarragon.

Add 2 dl. (⅓ pint, scant cup) chicken *Velouté sauce* and 1 dl. (6 tablespoons, scant ½ cup) white stock. Boil down by one-third. Add 2 large tablespoons (3 large tablespoons) *Printanier butter* (see BUTTER, *Compound butters*). Strain.

Chivry sauce II (for braised fish). SAUCE CHIVRY – Proceed as above, replacing the chicken *Velouté sauce* with *Velouté sauce* based on fish stock and the white stock by fish stock or *fumet*.

Choron sauce (for grilled and sautéed meat). SAUCE CHORON – The same as *Béarnaise sauce* tomato flavoured.

Crayfish sauce I for fish (English cookery). SAUCE AUX QUEUES D'ÉCREVISSES À L'ANGLAISE – Proceed as for *Lobster sauce II*. Replace the lobster by diced crayfish tails.

Crayfish sauce II (old recipe). SAUCE AUX ÉCREVISSES – 'Wash 50 medium-sized crayfish and cook them with ½ bottle Champagne, 1 chopped onion, a *bouquet garni*, a pinch of mignonette and a little salt. When the crayfish are cold, drain them and strain the cooking liquor through a silk strainer. Boil down by half, and add 2 tablespoons (3 tablespoons) *Allemande sauce*. Boil down to the desired consistency and add ½ glass Champagne. Strain the sauce through a cloth. Add a little glaze and best butter, and the shelled crayfish tails.

'Add to the sauce crayfish butter made from the crayfish shells.' (Carême, *L'Art de la cuisine française au XIXe siècle*.)

Cream sauce (for vegetables, fish, eggs, poultry). SAUCE À LA CRÈME – Boil down by one-third 2 dl. (⅓ pint, scant cup) *Béchamel sauce* to which has been added 1 dl. (6 tablespoons, scant ½ cup) cream.

Remove from heat, add 50 g. (2 oz., ¼ cup) butter and 3 tablespoons (scant ¼ cup) cream. Strain.

(See also *English cream sauce*.)

Curry or Indian sauce I (for eggs, poultry, mutton). SAUCE AU CURRIE, SAUCE INDIENNE – Cook till pale golden 100 g. (4 oz., 1 cup) chopped onion in 25 g. (1 oz., 2 tablespoons) butter. Add 2 roots of parsley and 1 chopped stick of celery, a sprig of thyme, half a bay leaf and a fragment of mace. Sprinkle with 25 g. (1 oz., ¼ cup) flour, and 1 small teaspoon curry powder. Mix and colour lightly.

Stir in 4 dl. (¾ pint, scant 2 cups) light stock or consommé, blend, bring to the boil, and simmer very slowly for 40 minutes. Strain through a cloth, pressing with a wooden spoon. Put back in the saucepan and reheat. Add 4 tablespoons (⅓ cup) fresh cream and a squeeze of lemon juice.

The liquid for curry sauce can be ¾ white stock and ¼ coconut milk.

Curry sauce II. SAUCE AU CURRIE – Cook 100 g. (4 oz., 1 cup) chopped onion gently in butter. Sprinkle in 1 small teaspoon curry powder, add 1 seeded and chopped tomato, 1 grated clove of garlic, a sprig of parsley, a sprig of thyme and a fragment of bay leaf.

Stir in 3 dl. (½ pint, 1¼ cups) thin *Velouté sauce* based on meat stock. Cook for 35 minutes, stirring frequently. Boil down by one-third, adding, in the course of cooking, 1 dl. (6 tablespoons, scant ½ cup) cream.

Strain the sauce through a cloth, reheat it and add a squeeze of lemon juice.

Curry sauce III (for poached eggs or shelled boiled eggs). SAUCE AU CURRIE – Cook 100 g. (4 oz., 1 cup) chopped onions slowly in butter. Sprinkle in 1 small teaspoon curry powder. Stir in 3 dl. (½ pint, 1¼ cups) *Béchamel sauce* not too thick. Boil down over strong heat, and strain through a cloth. Heat, and add 50 g. (2 oz., ¼ cup) butter.

Curry sauce IV (for fish and shellfish). SAUCE AU CURRIE – Proceed as in the first recipe, replacing the consommé by fish stock or *fumet*.

Curry sauce à l'indienne (old recipe). SAUCE AU CURRIE À L'INDIENNE – 'Put into a saucepan a few slices of lean ham, 1 chopped onion, a *bouquet garni*, 2 punnets of mushrooms, chopped, 3 cloves, a good pinch of pimento, a pinch of cayenne pepper and a little mace. Add 2 tablespoons (3 tablespoons) chicken consommé. Simmer over very low heat, strain, and remove all grease. When it is somewhat boiled down mix in some *Allemande sauce*. Add a small infusion of saffron so as to colour it yellow, then strain through a cloth. Before serving, put in a little butter and 3 punnets of small mushrooms.

'Small green gherkins cut to look like olives can be added to this sauce.' (Carême, *L'Art de la cuisine française au XIXe siècle*.)

Diplomat sauce or Riche sauce (for fish). SAUCE DIPLOMATE, SAUCE RICHE – Add 2 dl. (⅓ pint, scant cup) *Normande sauce* to 2 tablespoons (3 tablespoons) *Lobster butter* (see BUTTER). Add 1 tablespoon brandy, and a pinch of cayenne. Strain through a cloth.

If this sauce is served separately, add to it 1 tablespoon diced truffles and 1 tablespoon diced lobster flesh.

Écossaise sauce I (for eggs, poultry and white offal or U.S. variety meats). SAUCE ÉCOSSAISE – Add 2 dl. (⅓ pint, scant cup) strained *Cream sauce* to ½ dl. (3 tablespoons, scant ¼ cup) vegetable *brunoise* cooked in butter until soft. Add diced French beans to the usual vegetables.

Écossaise sauce II. SAUCE ÉCOSSAISE – Proceed as above. Replace the cream sauce by *Allemande sauce*.

Écossaise sauce III. SAUCE ÉCOSSAISE – As above, with *White wine sauce*.

Egg sauce for fish, chiefly haddock and cod (English cookery). SAUCE AUX OEUFS À L'ANGLAISE – Stir 2½ dl. (scant ½ pint, generous cup) boiling milk into a white *roux* composed of 30 g. (1 oz., 2 tablespoons) butter and 15 g. (½ oz., 2 tablespoons) flour. Season with salt, white pepper and nutmeg. Bring to the boil and cook for 6 minutes. Finish the sauce with 2 hot hard-boiled eggs cut in dice.

Egg and butter sauce for large boiled fish (English cookery). SAUCE AUX OEUFS AU BEURRE – Add 100 g. (4 oz., ½ cup) melted butter seasoned with salt, pepper and a squeeze of lemon juice to 2 hot hard-boiled eggs cut in large dice, and 1 teaspoon chopped and blanched parsley.

Egg sauce à l'écossaise. SAUCE AUX OEUFS À L'ÉCOSSAISE – Prepare the sauce as above. Add the egg whites cut in small strips, and the yolks pressed into vermicelli-like threads through a strainer.

Mix very lightly so that the pieces of egg can be seen.

English sauce or Sauce à l'anglaise for poultry (old recipe). SAUCE À L'ANGLAISE – 'Chop the yolks of 4 hard-boiled eggs very finely, mix them, in a saucepan, with enough half-thickened *Velouté sauce* to sauce an *entrée*. Add a pinch of pepper and grated nutmeg, the juice of 1 lemon and a little anchovy butter'. (Carême, *L'Art de la cuisine française au XIXe siècle*.)

English bread and butter sauce for roast game birds (old recipe). SAUCE AU BEURRE ET AU PAIN À L'ANGLAISE – 'Bring to the boil 1 tablespoon breadcrumbs in 2 large tablespoons (3 large tablespoons) consommé, adding 1 small onion cut in two and a clove. Add a little salt, grated nutmeg and cayenne pepper. Simmer for 10 minutes, remove the onion and the clove, mix in 1 tablespoon *Butter sauce*. Before serving, add a little best butter.' (Carême, *L'Art de la cuisine française au XIXe siècle*.)

English cream sauce. SAUCE CRÈME À L'ANGLAISE – Stir 3½ dl. (generous ½ pint, 1½ cups) white consommé, 3 tablespoons (scant ¼ cup) *Mushroom essence* (see ESSENCE) and 1 dl. (6 tablespoons, scant ½ cup) cream into a white *roux* made of 50 g. (2 oz., ¼ cup) butter and 30 g. (1 oz., ¼ cup) flour. Mix together.

Fennel sauce I (old recipe). SAUCE AU FENOUIL – 'Pick over and wash some fennel, chop it and put 1 tablespoon into a saucepan containing 2 large tablespoons (3 large tablespoons) boiling *Allemande sauce*. Add a little chicken glaze, a little butter, a pinch of nutmeg and the juice of a lemon.' (Carême, *L'Art de la cuisine française au XIXe siècle*.)

Fennel sauce II for grilled or boiled fish, chiefly mackerel (English cookery). SAUCE AU FENOUIL – Add 1 tablespoon chopped and blanched fennel to $2\frac{1}{2}$ dl. (scant $\frac{1}{2}$ pint, generous cup) *Butter sauce II.*

Fines herbes sauce (for fish). SAUCE AUX FINES HERBES – Add $\frac{1}{2}$ dl. (3 tablespoons, scant $\frac{1}{4}$ cup) finely grated shallot to 2 dl. ($\frac{1}{3}$ pint, scant cup) *White wine sauce.* Strain through a cloth. Add 1 tablespoon chopped chervil and parsley.

Foyot sauce (for grilled meat). SAUCE FOYOT – Add 2 tablespoons (3 tablespoons) meat glaze to 2 dl. ($\frac{1}{3}$ pint, scant cup) strained *Béarnaise sauce.* Meat glaze is prepared by boiling down strong meat stock until it becomes a tacky syrup.

French sauce for fish (old recipe). SAUCE A LA FRANÇAISE – 'Put into a saucepan some *Béchamel sauce* based on fish stock. When it is almost boiling, add a little garlic, a little grated nutmeg and *Mushroom essence* (see ESSENCE). When it has boiled for a moment, and just before serving, add *Crayfish butter* (see BUTTER) to give it a pinkish colour.

'Shelled crayfish tails and small peeled mushrooms may be added to this sauce. I served this sauce for the first time in the house of Prince Paul de Wurtemberg.' (Carême, *L'Art de la cuisine française au XIXe siècle.*)

Freshwater fish sauce (English cookery) – Cut 25 g. (1 oz.) carrot and 15 g. ($\frac{1}{2}$ oz.) parsley roots into a fine *julienne*. Add 2 teaspoons shredded orange peel.

Put all together in a small saucepan, moisten with 1 dl. (6 tablespoons, scant $\frac{1}{2}$ cup) white wine and boil until the liquid is completely absorbed. Moisten again with 1 dl. (6 tablespoons, scant $\frac{1}{2}$ cup) fish *court-bouillon* made with white wine. Boil down until all liquid is absorbed. Add $2\frac{1}{2}$ dl. (scant $\frac{1}{2}$ pint, generous cup) *Hollandaise sauce* to the *julienne*.

Finish off with a few leaves of blanched parsley.

Garlic sauce – See GARLIC.

Godard sauce (for sweetbreads and poultry). SAUCE GODARD – Boil down by half 2 dl. ($\frac{1}{3}$ pint, scant cup) Champagne with 2 tablespoons (3 tablespoons) *mirepoix* of vegetables.

Add 2 dl. ($\frac{1}{3}$ pint, scant cup) *Demi-glace sauce* and 1 dl. (6 tablespoons, scant $\frac{1}{2}$ cup) *Mushroom essence* (see ESSENCE). Boil down by one-third and strain.

Greek sauce (for fish). SAUCE À LA GRECQUE – Cook together in 1 tablespoon butter 2 tablespoons (3 tablespoons) onion and $\frac{1}{4}$ celery heart, both chopped. Add a *bouquet garni* composed of a stalk of fennel, a little thyme and bay leaf.

Moisten with 1 dl. (6 tablespoons, scant $\frac{1}{2}$ cup) white wine, add 10 coriander seeds and boil down by two-thirds. Stir in 1 dl. (6 tablespoons, scant $\frac{1}{2}$ cup) *Velouté sauce* based on fish stock and 1 dl. (6 tablespoons, scant $\frac{1}{2}$ cup) cream. Boil down by one-third, finish off with 50 g. (2 oz., $\frac{1}{4}$ cup) butter and strain.

Hollandaise sauce I (for vegetables, fish and eggs). SAUCE HOLLANDAISE – Boil down by two-thirds 4 tablespoons (5 tablespoons) wine vinegar mixed with 2 tablespoons (3 tablespoons) water, a pinch of salt and a pinch of coarsely ground pepper.

Let the saucepan cool a little, then add 5 raw egg yolks beaten slightly with 1 tablespoon water.

Whisk the sauce over very gentle heat. As soon as the yolks thicken to a creamy consistency add, little by little and beating all the time, 450 g. (1 lb., 2 cups) lukewarm melted butter.

Add 2 tablespoons (3 tablespoons) water, a few drops at a time. Season and add a few drops lemon juice. Strain through a cloth. Keep warm in a *bain-marie*.

Hollandaise sauce can be made in a *bain-marie*.

Hollandaise sauce II (old recipe). SAUCE HOLLANDAISE – 'Put into a saucepan 5 egg yolks, a little fine butter, salt, pepper and grated nutmeg. Stand the pan over very low heat. Stir the sauce constantly with a wooden spoon, and as it develops mix in small quantities of butter. After having added more than 225 g. (8 oz.), mix in 1 tablespoon vinegar.' (Carême, *L'Art de la cuisine française au XIXe siècle.*)

Hollandaise sauce suprême (old recipe). SAUCE HOLLANDAISE AU SUPRÊME – 'Break 5 egg yolks into a saucepan, blend in a little best butter, salt, fine pepper, grated nutmeg, 1 tablespoon *Allemande sauce* and 1 tablespoon chicken glaze. Stir over very low heat, and as it continues to thicken, add to it a little butter three or four times, taking care to stir all the time. Before serving pour in a little vinegar and add a good piece of butter.' (Carême, *L'Art de la cuisine française au XIXe siècle.*)

Horseradish sauce, hot (English cookery). SAUCE RAIFORT CHAUDE – Proceed as for *Albert sauce.*

Hungarian sauce I (for small cuts of sautéed meat, eggs, fish, offal or U.S. variety meats, and poultry). SAUCE HONGROISE – Cook in butter, without allowing to colour, 2 large tablespoons chopped onion. Sprinkle with a good pinch of paprika, season with a pinch of salt, moisten with 1 dl. (6 tablespoons, scant $\frac{1}{2}$ cup) white wine and add a small *bouquet garni*. Boil down by two-thirds.

Stir in $2\frac{1}{2}$ dl. (scant $\frac{1}{2}$ pint, generous cup) *Velouté sauce* based on either meat or fish stock. Simmer over good heat for 5 minutes, strain through a cloth and finish off with 50 g. (2 oz., $\frac{1}{4}$ cup) butter.

Hungarian sauce II. SAUCE HONGROISE – Cook the chopped onion in butter and sprinkle it with 1 tablespoon flour and a good pinch of paprika. Moisten with 1 dl. (6 tablespoons, scant $\frac{1}{2}$ cup) white wine and add a small *bouquet garni.* Boil down by two-thirds. Stir in 3 dl. ($\frac{1}{2}$ pint, $1\frac{1}{4}$ cups) light consommé or stock, or water to which a small quantity of meat glaze or extract has been added.

Cook very slowly for 25 minutes and finish off as above.

Hungarian sauce III. SAUCE HONGROISE – Stir the cooking liquor of 8 oysters into a white *roux* composed of 1 tablespoon butter and 1 tablespoon flour. Add $1\frac{1}{2}$ dl. ($\frac{1}{4}$ pint, $\frac{2}{3}$ cup) mushroom or fish *fumet.* Cook very slowly for 20 minutes. Thicken with 2 egg yolks, strain through a cloth, finish off with 50 g. (2 oz., $\frac{1}{4}$ cup) butter and add the poached, drained and de-bearded oysters.

Indian sauce. SAUCE INDIENNE – See *Curry sauce.*

Ivoire sauce (for eggs, sweetbreads, poultry). SAUCE IVOIRE – Add 2 tablespoons (3 tablespoons) concentrated brown veal stock or 1 tablespoon meat glaze to 2 dl. ($\frac{1}{3}$ pint, scant cup) *Suprême sauce.*

Joinville sauce (for fish). SAUCE JOINVILLE – Add to 2 dl. ($\frac{1}{3}$ pint, scant cup) *Shrimp sauce* 1 tablespoon truffles cut in a fine *julienne*. This sauce is also prepared with crayfish butter, and sometimes with mixed shrimp and crayfish butter.

Laguipière sauce I (for fish). SAUCE LAGUIPIÈRE – Add 2 tablespoons (3 tablespoons) chopped truffles infused in 1 tablespoon Madeira to 2 dl. ($\frac{1}{3}$ pint, scant cup) *Normande sauce.*

Laguipière sauce II (old recipe). SAUCE LAGUIPIÈRE – 'Put into a saucepan 1 large tablespoon *Butter sauce* add 1 tablespoon good consommé or a little chicken glaze, a pinch of salt, some nutmeg and vinegar or lemon juice. Boil for a few seconds, and mix in a good piece of fine butter.

'This may be made with fish glaze instead of chicken glaze.' (Carême, *L'Art de la cuisine française au XIXe siècle.*)

Lobster sauce I (for fish). SAUCE HOMARD – Add 2 dl. ($\frac{1}{3}$ pint, scant cup) *White wine sauce* to 2 tablespoons (3 tablespoons) *Lobster butter* (see BUTTER). Add a pinch of cayenne and strain through a cloth. Add 1 tablespoon lobster flesh cut in very small dice.

Lobster sauce II, for fish (English cookery). SAUCE HOMARD À L'ANGLAISE – Add $2\frac{1}{2}$ dl. (scant $\frac{1}{2}$ pint, generous cup) *Béchamel sauce* to $\frac{1}{2}$ tablespoon anchovy essence or paste and

40 g. ($1\frac{1}{2}$ oz., $\frac{1}{4}$ cup) lobster flesh cut in dice. Add a pinch of cayenne.

Lyonnaise sauce (old recipe). SAUCE À LA LYONNAISE – 'Blanch 4 large diced onions and simmer them in clarified butter. When almost cooked, drain them on a horsehair sieve, and mix them with 2 tablespoons (3 tablespoons) game *fumet* and 2 large tablespoons (3 large tablespoons) *Allemande sauce*, stirring vigorously. When this is boiled down, add a little chopped and blanched tarragon, the juice of a lemon, a little grated nutmeg, a little butter, and a little game glaze.' (Carême, *L'Art de la cuisine française au XIXe siècle.*)

Maître d'hôtel sauce (old recipe). SAUCE À LA MAÎTRE D'HÔTEL LIÉE – 'Put into a saucepan 2 tablespoons half thickened *Velouté sauce*. Just before serving it should be boiling. Remove from heat, blend in a little glaze and some *Maître d'hôtel butter* (see BUTTER, *Compound butters*). Mix thoroughly.' (Carême, *L'Art de la cuisine française au XIXe siècle.*)

Maltaise sauce I (for boiled vegetables). SAUCE MALTAISE – Add 2 dl. ($\frac{1}{3}$ pint, scant cup) *Hollandaise sauce* to blood-orange juice and 1 small tablespoon finely grated orange peel.

Maltaise sauce II. Proceed as above, using tangerine juice and peel.

This sauce may be flavoured with a few drops of Curaçao.

Marinière sauce (for fish, mussels, timbales, vol-au-vent). SAUCE MARINIÈRE – Prepare a *Bercy sauce* with mussel cooking liquor. Thicken it with egg yolks as for *White wine sauce*.

Morel sauce (old recipe). SAUCE AROMATIQUE AUX MORILLES – 'Put into a saucepan a pinch of rosemary, the same amount of sage, thyme and basil, quarter of a bay leaf, a clove, a little mignonette and a pinch of nutmeg. Add 1 chopped onion and 1 tablespoon good consommé. Simmer for a few minutes, strain through a cloth, using pressure. Put into it 30 sound and well washed small morels. When boiling is established pour in enough *Allemande sauce* for an *entrée* and boil down to the desired point.

'Before serving, blend in a little chicken glaze, a little fine butter, the juice of 1 lemon and 1 tablespoon chopped and blanched chervil.' (Carême, *L'Art de la cuisine française au XIXe siècle.*)

Mornay sauce I (for eggs and vegetables). SAUCE MORNAY – Boil down by one-third 2 dl. ($\frac{1}{3}$ pint, scant cup) *Béchamel sauce* mixed with 1 dl. (6 tablespoons, scant $\frac{1}{2}$ cup) fresh cream. Add 40 g. ($1\frac{1}{2}$ oz., $\frac{1}{2}$ cup) grated Gruyère and Parmesan cheese, mix, incorporate 50 g. (2 oz., $\frac{1}{4}$ cup) butter, and strain.

Mornay sauce II (for chicken or eggs). SAUCE MORNAY – Proceed as in the preceding recipe, replacing the cream with light chicken stock.

Mornay sauce III (for fish). SAUCE MORNAY – Proceed as above, cooking the *Béchamel sauce* with fish stock or *fumet* in which the fish was cooked.

Mousseline sauce or Chantilly sauce (for fish and boiled vegetables). SAUCE MOUSSELINE, SAUCE CHANTILLY – Add 2 dl. ($\frac{1}{3}$ pint, scant cup) *Hollandaise sauce* to 1 dl. (6 tablespoons, scant $\frac{1}{2}$ cup) whipped cream.

Mousseuse sauce (for fish and boiled vegetables). SAUCE MOUSSEUSE – Put into a basin, rinsed with boiling water and wiped dry, 250 g. (9 oz., generous cup) very fine butter softened to a creamy consistency, and season with a pinch of salt.

Whisk while adding, little by little, 2 dl. ($\frac{1}{3}$ pint, scant cup) cold water and a squeeze of lemon juice. Add 2 or 3 tablespoons (3 tablespoons or scant $\frac{1}{4}$ cup) whipped cream. This sauce is served cold.

Mustard sauce I (for boiled or grilled fish). SAUCE MOUTARDE – Add 1 tablespoon mustard to 2 dl. ($\frac{1}{3}$ pint, scant cup) *Butter sauce*. Strain.

Mustard sauce II. SAUCE MOUTARDE – Proceed as above, replacing the butter sauce by *Hollandaise sauce*.

Nantua sauce I (for eggs, fish, shellfish). SAUCE NANTUA – Boil down by half 1 dl. (6 tablespoons, scant $\frac{1}{2}$ cup) *Béchamel sauce* to which have been added 1 dl. (6 tablespoons, scant $\frac{1}{2}$ cup) each of the cooking liquor of crayfish and of cream.

Finish off with 50 g. (2 oz., $\frac{1}{4}$ cup) *Crayfish butter* (see BUTTER, *Compound butters*), a few drops of brandy and a pinch of cayenne. Strain.

Nantua sauce II. SAUCE NANTUA – Heat 1 dl. (6 tablespoons, scant $\frac{1}{2}$ cup) crayfish purée and dilute to the desired consistency with 50 g. (2 oz., $\frac{1}{4}$ cup) butter and a few tablespoons cream. Add a pinch of cayenne. Strain.

Normande (Normandy) sauce I (for fish). SAUCE NORMANDE – Mix in a saucepan 2 dl. ($\frac{1}{3}$ pint, scant cup) *Velouté sauce* based on fish stock, 1 dl. (6 tablespoons, scant $\frac{1}{2}$ cup) each of fish *fumet* and mushroom cooking liquor. Boil down by one-third over good heat. Add 2 egg yolks mixed with 2 tablespoons (3 tablespoons) cream.

Finish off with 50 g. (2 oz., $\frac{1}{4}$ cup) butter and 3 tablespoons (scant $\frac{1}{4}$ cup) cream. Strain through a cloth.

Normande (Normandy) sauce II. SAUCE NORMANDE – Boil down by half 2 dl. ($\frac{1}{3}$ pint, scant cup) fish *fumet* to which 2 tablespoons (3 tablespoons) mushroom skins have been added.

Add 2 dl. ($\frac{1}{3}$ pint, scant cup) *Velouté sauce* based on fish stock and 1 dl. (6 tablespoons, scant $\frac{1}{2}$ cup) cream. Boil down by half. Add 50 g. (2 oz., $\frac{1}{4}$ cup) butter and 4 tablespoons (5 tablespoons) cream. Strain through a cloth.

Onion sauce for boiled mutton, poultry, braised game, rabbit, tripe (English cookery). SAUCE AUX OIGNONS – Cook 100 g. (4 oz., 1 cup) chopped onions in 3 dl. ($\frac{1}{2}$ pint, $1\frac{1}{4}$ cups) milk with salt, pepper and nutmeg. Drain as soon as they are cooked and chop again more finely.

Stir the milk in which the onions were cooked into a white *roux* composed of 25 g. (1 oz., 2 tablespoons) butter and 25 g. (1 oz., $\frac{1}{4}$ cup) flour. Bring to the boil, add the onions and cook gently for 8 minutes. Pour over the meat it accompanies.

Oyster sauce I (for fish). SAUCE AUX HUÎTRES – Add 2 dl. ($\frac{1}{3}$ pint, scant cup) *Normande* or *White wine sauce* (incorporating concentrated oyster cooking liquor) to 8 poached, drained and de-bearded oysters.

Oyster sauce II, for boiled cod (English cookery). SAUCE AUX HUITRES – Stir 1 dl. (6 tablespoons, scant $\frac{1}{2}$ cup) oyster cooking liquor, and 1 dl. (6 tablespoons, scant $\frac{1}{2}$ cup) each of milk and cream into a white *roux* of 25 g. (1 oz., 2 tablespoons) butter and 15 g. ($\frac{1}{2}$ oz., 2 tablespoons) flour. Season with a very small pinch of salt, bring to the boil and cook for 20 minutes.

Strain through a cloth, add 12 poached, de-bearded and sliced oysters, and a pinch of cayenne.

Paloise sauce (for grilled meat and poultry). SAUCE PALOISE – Proceed as for *Béarnaise sauce*, replacing the tarragon by mint.

Parsley sauce I for calves' head, boiled poultry and rabbit, and braised veal (English cookery). SAUCE PERSIL – Add 1 tablespoon chopped and blanched parsley and a few drops of lemon juice to $2\frac{1}{2}$ dl. (scant $\frac{1}{2}$ pint, generous cup) *Butter sauce*.

Parsley sauce II (for mackerel and salmon). SAUCE PERSIL – Stir $2\frac{1}{2}$ dl. (scant $\frac{1}{2}$ pint, generous cup) parsley-flavoured *court-bouillon* left from cooking the fish into a white *roux* composed of 15 g. ($\frac{1}{2}$ oz., 1 tablespoon) butter and 15 g. ($\frac{1}{2}$ oz., 2 tablespoons) flour. Simmer for 8 minutes and strain.

Finish off with 1 tablespoon chopped parsley and a squeeze of lemon juice.

Piemontaise sauce for braised and pot-roasted chicken (old recipe). SAUCE À LA PIÉMONTAISE – 'Cut 2 large onions into very small dice, and cook them to a golden colour in clarified butter. Strain, cook them in good consommé and remove all grease. Blend in enough *Béchamel sauce* to accompany an *entrée*, 225 g. ($\frac{1}{2}$ lb.) Piedmont truffles cut in large dice, and 2 tablespoons (3 tablespoons) *pignoli* (pine kernels). After the sauce has boiled for an instant, mix in a little chicken glaze, a little garlic butter and the juice of a lemon.' (Carême, *L'Art de la cuisine française au XIXe siècle.*)

Polonaise sauce (old recipe). SAUCE POLONAISE – 'Scrape a root of horseradish and grate half. Put 3 tablespoons (scant $\frac{1}{4}$ cup) into a saucepan with 1 tablespoon sugar. Dilute it little by little with half-thickened *Velouté sauce* (see above) in sufficient quantity to accompany an *entrée*. When the sauce comes to the boil, add the juice of 1 lemon, a little glaze and some fine butter.' (Carême, *L'Art de la cuisine française au XIXe siècle.*)

Poulette sauce (for vegetables and poached offal or U.S. variety meats). SAUCE POULETTE – Add 1 tablespoon chopped parsley and a few drops lemon juice to 2 dl. ($\frac{1}{3}$ pint, scant cup) *Allemande sauce*.

Princesse sauce (old recipe). SAUCE PRINCESSE – 'Add some blanched, chopped parsley, a pinch of grated nutmeg, a little chicken glaze, a little butter and the juice of a lemon to 2 tablespoons (3 tablespoons) boiling *Allemande sauce*.' (Carême, *L'Art de la cuisine française au XIXe siècle.*)

Printanière sauce (for eggs and poultry). SAUCE PRINTANIÈRE – Finish 2 dl. ($\frac{1}{3}$ pint, scant cup) *Allemande sauce* with 50 g. (2 oz., $\frac{1}{4}$ cup) green *Printanier butter* (see BUTTER, *Compound butters*). Strain.

Provençal garlic sauce (old recipe). SAUCE À L'AIL À LA PROVENÇALE – 'Simmer in a saucepan 4 cloves garlic, a lightly seasoned *bouquet garni*, a pinch of mignonette pepper and 2 tablespoons (3 tablespoons) consommé. Boil down, take out the garlic and the *bouquet*, and add 2 large tablespoons (3 large tablespoons) *Velouté sauce* and the beaten yolks of 3 eggs. Boil for a few minutes, strain through a cloth, and mix in a little butter and lemon juice.' (Carême, *L'Art de la cuisine française au XIXe siècle.*)

Ravigote sauce (for offal or U.S. variety meats and poultry). SAUCE RAVIGOTE – Boil down by two-thirds 2 tablespoons (3 tablespoons) white wine and 2 tablespoons (3 tablespoons) vinegar, to which have been added 1 chopped shallot, a sprig of thyme, a fragment of bay leaf, a sprig of parsley, a pinch of salt and a pinch of coarsely ground pepper.

Stir in 2 dl. ($\frac{1}{3}$ pint, scant cup) *Velouté sauce* and 1 dl. (6 tablespoons, scant $\frac{1}{2}$ cup) mushroom cooking liquor. Boil down by one-third, finish off with 50 g. (2 oz., $\frac{1}{4}$ cup) butter and 3 tablespoons (scant $\frac{1}{4}$ cup) cream. Add a pinch of cayenne and strain through a cloth.

Riche sauce (for fish) – See *Diplomat sauce*.

Richelieu sauce (old recipe). 'Dice 4 large onions, cook till golden in clarified butter, drain on a horsehair sieve and cook in 2 large tablespoons (3 large tablespoons) consommé, adding a little sugar, a little grated nutmeg and some coarsely ground pepper. Add 2 large tablespoons (3 large tablespoons) *Allemande sauce*, a little chicken glaze and a little fine butter. Strain the sauce through a cloth, using pressure.

'Add $\frac{1}{2}$ tablespoon chopped and blanched chervil.' (Carême, *L'Art de la cuisine française au XIXe siècle.*)

Royal sauce (for poached eggs and boiled chicken). SAUCE ROYALE – Boil down by half 2 dl. ($\frac{1}{3}$ pint, scant cup) chicken *Velouté sauce*, thinned with 1 dl. (6 tablespoons, scant $\frac{1}{2}$ cup) white chicken stock. Add, in the course of cooking, 1 dl. (6 tablespoons, scant $\frac{1}{2}$ cup) cream, and 2 tablespoons (3 tablespoons) sieved truffles. Finish off with 50 g. (2 oz., $\frac{1}{4}$ cup) butter and 1 tablespoon sherry. Strain.

Russian sauce for large cuts of beef (old recipe). SAUCE À LA RUSSE – 'Chop and blanch 1 tablespoon parsley, chervil and tarragon, drain, and mix them into some half-thickened *Velouté sauce*. Add 1 tablespoon fine mustard, $\frac{1}{2}$ tablespoon sugar, a pinch of fine pepper and the juice of a lemon.' (Carême, *L'Art de la cuisine française au XIXe siècle.*)

Sage and onion sauce for roast pork and goose (English cookery). SAUCE À LA SAUGE – Chop 2 large onions, previously cooked in salted water and drained.

Put them into a saucepan with 100 g. (4 oz., 2 cups) freshly grated breadcrumbs and 25 g. (1 oz., 2 tablespoons) butter. Season with salt and pepper and add 1 tablespoon chopped sage. Cook for 5 minutes, mixing well with a wooden spoon. Add 3 tablespoons (scant $\frac{1}{4}$ cup) of the pan juices.

St. Malo sauce I (for grilled fish). SAUCE SAINT-MALO – Moisten with 1 dl. (6 tablespoons, scant $\frac{1}{2}$ cup) white wine 2 tablespoons (3 tablespoons) chopped onion lightly cooked in butter without colouring. Garnish with a sprig of thyme, a piece of bay leaf and a sprig of parsley. Boil down by two-thirds.

Stir in $1\frac{1}{2}$ dl. ($\frac{1}{4}$ pint, $\frac{2}{3}$ cup) *Velouté sauce* based on fish stock and 1 dl. (6 tablespoons, scant $\frac{1}{2}$ cup) *Espagnole sauce* based on fish stock. Thin down with 1 dl. (6 tablespoons, scant $\frac{1}{2}$ cup) mushroom or fish *fumet* and boil down by one-third. Strain, pressing well. Finish off with 1 tablespoon mustard, a few drops Worcestershire sauce and 1 tablespoon butter.

St. Malo sauce II. SAUCE SAINT-MALO – Add to 2 dl. ($\frac{1}{3}$ pint, scant cup) *White wine sauce* $\frac{1}{2}$ tablespoon chopped shallot cooked in white wine, 1 small tablespoon mustard and a few drops anchovy essence or $\frac{1}{2}$ teaspoon anchovy paste.

Scotch egg sauce for cod (English cookery). SAUCE À L'ÉCOSSAISE – Stir 2 dl. ($\frac{1}{3}$ pint, scant cup) boiling milk into a white *roux* composed of 25 g. (1 oz., 2 tablespoons) butter and 15 g. ($\frac{1}{2}$ oz., 2 tablespoons) flour. Season with salt and pepper and a little grated nutmeg. Mix well and bring to the boil.

Add the chopped whites of 2 hard-boiled eggs, and blend in the yolks, rubbed through a coarse sieve.

Shallot sauce. SAUCE À L'ÉCHALOTE – Another name for *Bercy sauce*.

Shrimp sauce I (for fish). SAUCE AUX CREVETTES – Finish off 2 dl. ($\frac{1}{3}$ pint, scant cup) *Normande* or *White wine sauce* with 2 tablespoons (3 tablespoons) *Shrimp butter* (see BUTTER). Add a pinch of cayenne and strain through a cloth.

Shrimp sauce II (English cookery). SAUCE AUX CREVETTES À L'ANGLAISE – Add to $2\frac{1}{2}$ dl. (scant $\frac{1}{2}$ pint, generous cup) English *Butter sauce* $\frac{1}{2}$ teaspoon anchovy essence, 40 g. ($1\frac{1}{2}$ oz.) tiny shelled shrimps, and a pinch of cayenne.

Soubise sauce (old recipe). SAUCE SOUBISE – 'Cut 4 onions in half, make incisions from top to bottom down the onion, then cut them across and throw them into boiling water for a moment. Drain, and put them into a saucepan with a good piece of butter and a little consommé. Simmer over low heat. Strain again and pour into the saucepan with 2 good tablespoons (3 good tablespoons) concentrated consommé from which all grease has been removed. Add 2 large tablespoons (3 large tablespoons) *Béchamel sauce* a pinch of nutmeg, a little sugar and a little chicken glaze. Strain through a cloth, using pressure. Before serving, blend in a little butter.' (Carême, *L'Art de la cuisine française au XIXe siècle.*)

Suprême sauce I (for eggs, poultry, offal or U.S. variety meats and vegetables). SAUCE SUPRÊME, VELOUTÉ À LA CRÈME – For 5 dl. (scant pint, $2\frac{1}{4}$ cups) sauce stir 5 dl. (scant pint, $2\frac{1}{4}$ cups) chicken stock in a thick-bottomed saucepan. Boil down by half over good heat, adding, during the cooking, 3 or 4 dl. ($\frac{1}{2}$ pint, $1\frac{1}{4}$ cups or $\frac{3}{4}$ pint, scant 2 cups) fresh cream.

When the sauce coats the spoon, incorporate, away from the heat, 50 g. (2 oz., $\frac{1}{4}$ cup) fresh butter. Strain. Keep in a *bain-marie* until needed.

Suprême sauce II (old recipe). SAUCE AU SUPRÊME – 'Put into a saucepan some *Allemande sauce* in sufficient quantity to accompany an *entrée*. When it is almost boiling and just before serving, add 3 to 4 tablespoons (scant $\frac{1}{4}$ cup to 5 tablespoons) chicken consommé and 2 small pats of butter.' (Carême, *L'Art de la cuisine française au XIXe siècle*.)

Talleyrand sauce. SAUCE TALLEYRAND – Boil down by half 2 dl. ($\frac{1}{3}$ pint, scant cup) chicken *Velouté sauce* (see above) and 2 dl. ($\frac{1}{3}$ pint, scant cup) white stock. As soon as it is boiling add 4 tablespoons (5 tablespoons) fresh cream and $\frac{1}{2}$ dl. (3 tablespoons, scant $\frac{1}{4}$ cup) Madeira. Incorporate, away from the heat, 50 g. (2 oz., $\frac{1}{4}$ cup) butter. Strain.

Add 1 tablespoon vegetable *mirepoix* (q.v.) and 1 tablespoon truffles and pickled tongue cut in very small dice.

Velouté sauce with green onions (old recipe). SAUCE VELOUTÉE À LA CIVETTE – 'Put into a saucepan 1 large tablespoon *Allemande sauce* and 1 tablespoon *Tomato sauce* (see above). Add a pinch of grated nutmeg, pepper, and the juice of a lemon. Boil for a moment then blend in shrimp butter and 1 small teaspoon very finely chopped onion.' (Carême, *L'Art de la cuisine française au XIXe siècle*.)

Venetian sauce I (for eggs and poultry). SAUCE VÉNITIENNE – Boil down by two-thirds 1 dl. (6 tablespoons, scant $\frac{1}{2}$ cup) vinegar to which 1 chopped shallot and 2 tablespoons (3 tablespoons) chopped chervil and parsley have been added.

Stir in 2 dl. ($\frac{1}{3}$ pint, scant cup) *Allemande sauce*, finish off with 50 g. (2 oz., $\frac{1}{4}$ cup) *Green butter* (see BUTTER, *Compound butters*), strain, and add 1 tablespoon chopped chervil and tarragon.

Venetian sauce II (old recipe). SAUCE VÉNITIENNE – 'Boil in a saucepan 2 tablespoons (3 tablespoons) *Allemande sauce*, a good pinch of shredded tarragon leaves blanched and drained on a silk strainer, 1 tablespoon chicken glaze, a little butter, a pinch of grated nutmeg and a few drops good tarragon vinegar.' (Carême, *L'Art de la cuisine française au XIXe siècle*.)

Véron sauce (for fish). SAUCE VÉRON – Cook the wine and herbs as for *Béarnaise sauce*. Stir in 2 dl. ($\frac{1}{3}$ pint, scant cup) *Normande sauce* and 2 tablespoons (3 tablespoons) very concentrated brown veal stock or fish glaze. Add a pinch of cayenne, strain, and add 1 tablespoon chopped chervil and tarragon.

Victoria sauce (for fish). SAUCE VICTORIA – Prepare $2\frac{1}{2}$ dl. (scant $\frac{1}{2}$ pint, generous cup) *Lobster sauce*.

Add 2 tablespoons (3 tablespoons) lobster flesh and truffles cut in very small dice.

Villeroi sauce (to coat foodstuffs to be fried à la Villeroi). SAUCE VILLEROI – Boil down 2 dl. ($\frac{1}{3}$ pint, scant cup) *Allemande sauce* thinned with 4 tablespoons (5 tablespoons) light stock and mushroom *fumet* until it will coat the back of the spoon. Strain, and stir well until it is cold.

This sauce is used when almost cold to coat foodstuffs which are then dipped in a mixture of egg, oil and seasoning, and breadcrumbed before being fried in deep fat.

According to the recipe chosen, this sauce may be finished with *Truffle essence* (see ESSENCE), tomato purée or *Onion soubise* (see PURÉE). It may also have truffles, chopped mushrooms, *mirepoix* of vegetables, etc. added to it.

Villeroi sauce for fish is prepared with *Allemande sauce* based on fish stock.

White wine sauce I (for fish). SAUCE VIN BLANC – Boil down by two-thirds $1\frac{1}{2}$ dl. ($\frac{1}{4}$ pint, $\frac{2}{3}$ cup) fish *fumet* made with white wine. Allow to cool a little and add 2 egg yolks. Whisk over low heat until it thickens, as for *Hollandaise sauce*.

Add, little by little, 150 g. (5 oz., generous $\frac{1}{2}$ cup) melted butter, beating all the time. Season. Add a few drops lemon juice, and strain through a cloth.

Mushroom skins and stalks may be added to the sauce in the course of the cooking.

White wine sauce II. SAUCE VIN BLANC – Prepare 2 dl. ($\frac{1}{3}$ pint, scant cup) *Hollandaise sauce*, adding in the course of preparation $\frac{1}{2}$ dl. (3 tablespoons, scant $\frac{1}{4}$ cup) concentrated fish *fumet* made with white wine. Season and strain through a cloth.

White wine sauce III (for fish to be glazed). SAUCE VIN BLANC – Boil down by half 1 dl. (6 tablespoons, scant $\frac{1}{2}$ cup) fish *Velouté sauce* to which 1 dl. (6 tablespoons, scant $\frac{1}{2}$ cup) fish *fumet*, made with white wine, has been added.

Add 2 egg yolks, cook for a few moments over low heat, beating and incorporating, little by little, about 75 g. (3 oz., 6 tablespoons) butter divided into tiny pieces. Season and strain.

COLD SAUCES. SAUCES FROIDES – Mayonnaise is the basis of many cold sauces which are used for *hors-d'œuvre* and cold *entrées*, and may be varied in a number of ways. Some of the best known cold sauces are given below.

Aïoli or beurre de Provence – Pound finely in a small mortar 5 cloves garlic. Add 1 raw egg yolk and a pinch of salt. Mix with the pestle. Pour into the mortar, little by little, stirring all the time, $2\frac{1}{2}$ dl. (scant $\frac{1}{2}$ pint, generous cup) olive oil.

Add a few drops lemon juice and a few drops of water to thin down the consistency of the sauce.

Anchovy sauce. SAUCE ANCHOIS – Pound together hard-boiled eggs and anchovy purée or paste. Add oil, vinegar, and a little pepper.

Andalouse sauce. SAUCE ANDALOUSE – *Mayonnaise sauce* to which has been added $\frac{1}{4}$ its weight of concentrated tomato juice and sweet pimentos, peeled, cut in dice and cooked in oil.

Apple sauce for pork, duck and goose (English cookery). SAUCE AUX POMMES – Cook the apples with very little sugar till they are soft. Flavour with powdered cinnamon.

This sauce is commonly used as accompaniment to a roast in Germany, England, Belgium and Holland.

Cambridge sauce for cold meat (English cookery). SAUCE CAMBRIDGE – Pound together hard-boiled egg yolks, anchovy fillets, capers, chives, chervil and tarragon. Add English mustard. Beat in oil and vinegar as for mayonnaise. Rub through a fine sieve or a cloth. Add chopped parsley and a pinch of cayenne.

Chantilly sauce (for asparagus and other boiled vegetables served cold). SAUCE CHANTILLY – *Mayonnaise sauce I* to which stiffly whipped cream has been added.

Cingalaise sauce. SAUCE CINGALAISE – A fine *salpicon* of hard-boiled egg yolks, sweet pimentos, tomatoes, boiled courgettes (zucchini), and cucumbers, seasoned with curry and salt and mixed with oil and lemon juice. Add chopped parsley and chives.

Collioure sauce. SAUCE COLLIOURE – *Mayonnaise sauce I* to which has been added essence or *purée* of anchovies and chopped parsley, with a little grated garlic.

Cressonnière sauce. SAUCE CRESSONNIÈRE – Season with oil, vinegar, salt and pepper, finely chopped watercress and finely chopped hard-boiled egg yolks. Mix.

Cumberland sauce for cold venison (English cookery). SAUCE CUMBERLAND – Add 1 small tablespoon chopped shallot, blanched and drained, 2 tablespoons (3 tablespoons) orange and lemon peel cut in a fine *julienne* and blanched, and 1 tablespoon Dijon mustard to 2 dl. ($\frac{1}{3}$ pint, scant cup) melted red currant jelly. Add 2 dl. ($\frac{1}{3}$ pint, scant cup) port, the juice of an orange and lemon. Season with salt, ginger and cayenne.

Dijonnaise sauce. SAUCE DIJONNAISE – Pound together 4 hard-boiled egg yolks and 4 tablespoons (5 tablespoons) Dijon mustard. Season with salt and pepper. Beat with oil and lemon juice like a mayonnaise.

Gribiche sauce (for cold fish and shellfish). SAUCE GRIBICHE – Hard-boiled egg yolks reduced to a paste, beaten with oil and

Mayonnaise sauce (*Robert Carrier*)

vinegar like a mayonnaise. Season with salt and pepper. Add chopped gherkins, capers, parsley, chervil and tarragon. Add the egg whites cut in a short *julienne*.

Horseradish sauce. SAUCE RAIFORT – Mix grated horseradish with breadcrumbs soaked in milk and squeezed. Season with salt and sugar. Add thick fresh cream and a little vinegar.

Indienne sauce. SAUCE INDIENNE – *Mayonnaise sauce I* seasoned with curry and with chopped chives added.

Maltaise sauce (for asparagus). SAUCE MALTAISE – *Mayonnaise sauce I* to which the juice of a blood orange and a *julienne* of blanched, rinsed and dried orange peel have been added.

Mayonnaise sauce I. SAUCE MAYONNAISE – *Ingredients.* 3 egg yolks, 5 dl. (scant pint, $2\frac{1}{4}$ cups) olive oil, 1 tablespoon vinegar or lemon juice, 1 teaspoon salt, pinch of white pepper.

Method. Put the egg yolks into a bowl. Add the salt (very dry), white pepper and a few drops vinegar or lemon juice. Mix these ingredients with a whisk, not beating too hard.

Add the oil, drop by drop at first, then in a thin trickle, beating either with a whisk or with a wooden spoon. Absorb the whole of the oil into the mayonnaise in this way. Thin down the consistency of the sauce from time to time by adding a few drops of the vinegar or lemon juice. As soon as the sauce is finished, add, beating all the time, 2 or 3 tablespoons (3 tablespoons, or scant $\frac{1}{4}$ cup) boiling water. This is to preserve the texture of the mayonnaise and prevent it from 'curdling' if it is to be kept for some time.

To be sure of success in making this sauce, bear the following points in mind:

1. Keep to the exact proportions of egg and oil. The maximum amount of oil is 2 dl. ($\frac{1}{3}$ pint, scant cup) per egg yolk of medium size.

2. Use oil at room temperature, and if, in winter, the oil has coagulated, warm it very slightly before adding it to the yolks.

3. Add the oil drop by drop at the beginning. When the sauce begins to thicken a little, let it pour in a very thin trickle.

Mayonnaise sauce II (old recipe). SAUCE MAYONNAISE – 'Put into a medium-sized bowl 2 fresh egg yolks, a little salt and white pepper and a little tarragon vinegar. Stir quickly with a wooden spoon. As soon as it begins to thicken, blend in, little by little, 1 tablespoon olive oil and a little vinegar, taking care to beat the sauce against the sides of the bowl.

'On this continued beating depends the whiteness of the mayonnaise. As it takes on more body, add more oil, a little more vinegar and, at the beginning, a little aspic jelly. It is essential to put these ingredients in a little at a time, to prevent curdling.

'You will need for this preparation 2 glasses oil, $\frac{1}{2}$ glass aspic jelly and enough tarragon vinegar to give an appetising taste. To make it whiter, add lemon juice.' (Carême, *L'Art de la cuisine française au XIXᵉ siècle.*)

Mayonnaise sauce III (thick, to bind mixed salads, and coat various foodstuffs). SAUCE MAYONNAISE – Add to $2\frac{1}{2}$ dl. (scant $\frac{1}{2}$ pint, generous cup) mayonnaise 1 dl. (6 tablespoons, scant $\frac{1}{2}$ cup) melted *Meat jelly stock* (see JELLY). Whisk well.

As soon as the jelly has been added to the mayonnaise, the sauce must be used promptly, because it will set very quickly. (This sauce is used in the same way as *White chaud-froid sauce.*)

Thick or jelly-strengthened mayonnaise may be finished off with various flavourings or with any of the ingredients specified for the different mayonnaise sauces.

Mayonnaise sauce with anchovy. SAUCE MAYONNAISE À L'ANCHOIS – Add 1 small tablespoon anchovy essence or anchovy purée or paste to $2\frac{1}{2}$ dl. (scant $\frac{1}{2}$ pint, generous cup) mayonnaise. Mix well.

Mayonnaise sauce with caviare. SAUCE MAYONNAISE AU CAVIAR – Pound in a mortar 25 g. (1 oz., 2 tablespoons) caviare. Add, pounding constantly, 3 tablespoons (scant $\frac{1}{4}$ cup) mayonnaise. Strain through a fine sieve, add it to 2 dl. ($\frac{1}{3}$ pint, scant cup) mayonnaise and blend well.

Mayonnaise sauce with cress. SAUCE MAYONNAISE AU CRESSON – Add to the mayonnaise, kept very thick, chopped and pressed cress.

Green mayonnaise. SAUCE VERTE – Add mayonnaise to a purée of green herbs (spinach, watercress, parsley, chervil, tarragon, all blanched, cooled in water and pounded in a mortar). Strain.

Mayonnaise sauce à la russe. SAUCE MAYONNAISE À LA RUSSE – Add to 3 dl. ($\frac{1}{2}$ pint, $1\frac{1}{4}$ cups) mayonnaise 4 dl. ($\frac{3}{4}$ pint, scant 2 cups) liquid jelly and 1 tablespoon vinegar. Whisk on ice until the mixture takes on the character of a mousse. (Use for moulded vegetable salads.)

Mayonnaise sauce with shrimps. SAUCE MAYONNAISE AUX CREVETTES – Pound in a mortar 50 g. (2 oz., $\frac{1}{3}$ cup) shrimps and 3 tablespoons (scant $\frac{1}{4}$ cup) mayonnaise.

Put this mixture through a fine sieve, add it to 2 dl. ($\frac{1}{3}$ pint, scant cup) mayonnaise, colour with a drop of carmine, and mix well.

Mayonnaise sauce with tarragon. SAUCE MAYONNAISE À L'ESTRAGON – Add to the mayonnaise, kept very thick, some finely chopped, fresh tarragon.

Mint sauce (English cookery). SAUCE MENTHE – Pour over 50 g. (2 oz.), shredded or chopped fresh mint 4 dl. ($\frac{3}{4}$ pint, scant 2 cups) boiling vinegar. Season with salt, pepper and brown or white sugar.

Mousquetaire sauce. SAUCE MOUSQUETAIRE – Add to 5 dl. (scant pint, $2\frac{1}{4}$ cups) *Mayonnaise sauce I*, 2 tablespoons (3 tablespoons) chopped shallot cooked in white wine till all liquid is absorbed, and 1 tablespoon dissolved meat glaze. Add a pinch of cayenne.

Mustard and cream sauce. SAUCE MOUTARDE À LA CRÈME – Add $\frac{1}{3}$ Dijon mustard to $\frac{2}{3}$ very thick cream. Season with a little lemon juice, salt and pepper. Mix well with a whisk to render the sauce a little frothy.

Niçoise sauce. SAUCE NIÇOISE – Chop up finely 2 pimentos, add 2 tablespoons (3 tablespoons) tomato purée and a few leaves of tarragon. Pass through a coarse sieve and add to 285 ml. ($\frac{1}{2}$ pint) *Mayonnaise sauce I.*

Orientale sauce. SAUCE ORIENTALE – A mixture of three parts *Mayonnaise sauce III*, tomatoes cooked to a *fondue* in oil and seasoned with saffron, and a *salpicon* of sweet peppers.

Parisian sauce (for cold asparagus). SAUCE PARISIENNE – Pound in a bowl 2 small Gervais cheeses (*Petits suisses* or 50 g., 2 oz. Philadelphia cream cheese). Season with salt and paprika. Beat with oil and lemon juice like a mayonnaise. Add 1 tablespoon chopped chervil.

Provençal sauce. SAUCE PROVENÇALE – Season with oil, vinegar, salt and pepper, a mixture of peeled tomatoes, hard-boiled eggs, capers, gherkins and parsley, all chopped. Flavour with a little garlic.

Ravigote sauce. SAUCE RAVIGOTE – Season with oil, vinegar, salt and pepper, a mixture of capers, onions, chives, parsley, chervil and tarragon, all chopped.

Rémoulade sauce. SAUCE RÉMOULADE – *Mayonnaise sauce I* to which has been added mustard, anchovy essence, gherkins, capers, parsley and chervil, all chopped.

Rémoulade sauce is also made by seasoning with oil, vinegar, salt and pepper a mixture of hard-boiled eggs, capers, gherkins and herbs, all chopped.

Russian sauce. SAUCE RUSSE – Add to some *Mayonnaise sauce I* a quarter of its volume of a purée made with caviare and the creamy parts (coral, etc.) of a lobster, all pounded and rubbed through a fine sieve. Add mustard.

Vinaigrette sauce (*Robert Carrier*)

Sardalaise sauce. SAUCE SARDALAISE – Pound 6 hard-boiled egg yolks with 2 or 3 tablespoons (3 tablespoons or scant $\frac{1}{4}$ cup) thick fresh cream. Add to 4 large tablespoons (5 large tablespoons) fresh sieved truffles.

Beat this sauce with oil and lemon like a mayonnaise, season with salt and pepper and add 1 tablespoon Armagnac.

Shallot sauce (for raw oysters and shellfish). SAUCE ÉCHALOTE – Vinegar to which has been added finely chopped shallot seasoned with salt and freshly milled pepper.

Swedish sauce (for goose and cold pork). SAUCE SUÉDOISE – Mayonnaise to which apples cooked without sugar are added, seasoned with grated horseradish or mustard.

Tartare sauce. SAUCE TARTARE – Mayonnaise made with hard-boiled egg yolks and with chopped chives added.

La Varenne sauce. SAUCE LA VARENNE – Mayonnaise to which dry *duxelles*, made with oil and chopped parsley and chervil, have been added.

Verdurette sauce. SAUCE VERDURETTE – Put into a bowl 4 large tablespoons (5 large tablespoons) chopped chives which have been boiled, cooled in water and drained, 2 finely chopped hard-boiled egg yolks and 2 tablespoons (3 tablespoons) chopped chervil, tarragon and parsley. Add oil, vinegar, salt and pepper.

Vinaigrette sauce. SAUCE VINAIGRETTE, SAUCE À L'HUILE – Salads are usually seasoned at table. This seasoning is made in the proportion of 1 scant tablespoon vinegar to 3 tablespoons (scant $\frac{1}{4}$ cup) oil. Add salt and pepper.

Separately prepared *Vinaigrette sauce* is served with asparagus, cauliflower, boiled fish, etc. It is also served with calf's head, but with the addition of chopped parsley and onion, and sometimes thickened with pounded calf's brain.

Vincent sauce. SAUCE VINCENT – Add to some mayonnaise a purée of green herbs (sorrel, parsley, chervil, watercress, chives and burnet) and chopped hard-boiled egg yolks.

DESSERT SAUCES. SAUCES POUR LES ENTREMETS –

Apricot sauce. SAUCE À L'ABRICOT – Rub 12 ripe apricots through a fine sieve or crush in the blender. Put the pulp into a small copper pan and dilute it with 5 dl. (scant pint, $2\frac{1}{4}$ cups) light syrup. Bring to the boil, take off scum and remove from heat when the sauce coats a spoon. Pass through a muslin bag or fine strainer. Flavour with 1 tablespoon liqueur.

Apricot sauce, which is used as an accompaniment to hot or cold sweets, can be served hot or cold, depending on the nature of these dishes. If served hot, it can be made smoother in texture by adding a very small quantity of fresh butter. When stewed, fresh, canned or bottled apricots are used, the syrup should be used for diluting the sauce.

Apricot sauce can also be made by diluting apricot jam with hot water. This sauce should be strained and flavoured, as described above.

Cherry sauce. SAUCE AUX CERISES – Prepare with fresh cherry pulp or cherry jam in the same way as for *Apricot sauce*. It is used as an accompaniment for hot or cold sweets.

Chocolate sauce I. CRÈME AU CHOCOLAT – Moisten 100 g. (4 oz.) grated semi-sweet chocolate with 2 dl. ($\frac{1}{3}$ pint, scant cup) lukewarm water. Stir over low heat until it softens. Add 3 tablespoons (scant $\frac{1}{4}$ cup) thick fresh cream and 1 tablespoon butter.

This sauce is served hot or cold.

Chocolate sauce II. CRÈME AU CHOCOLATE – Add softened sweet chocolate to 1 dl. (6 tablespoons, scant $\frac{1}{2}$ cup) custard cream, prepared according to the recipe for *Custard cream* (see CREAMS.)

Custard sauces – See CREAMS, *Custard creams*.

Pineapple sauce. SAUCE À L'ANANAS – Use syrup in which pineapple has been cooked. Bring to the boil and thicken with 1 tablespoon arrowroot or cornstarch.

Sauceboat with coat of arms of Mme de Pompadour
(*Musée des Arts décoratifs*)

Pass this syrup through a fine sieve or muslin bag and flavour it according to the recipe, with kirsch, rum or any other liqueur.

This thickened syrup is used for pouring over sweet dishes, hot or cold, such as tarts, puddings, etc. It takes the place of apricot sauce, which is normally used for this purpose.

Raspberry sauce. SAUCE AUX FRAMBOISES – Made in the same way as *Strawberry sauce*, substituting raspberries for strawberries.

Strawberry sauce. SAUCE AUX FRAISES – Use either strawberry jam or fresh strawberry pulp, diluted with syrup and flavoured with liqueur.

SAUCEBOAT. SAUCIÈRE – Part of dinner service, in porcelain or metal, generally oval in form.

Silver sauceboats are often supplied with a double bottom which can be heated.

SAUCISSON – There is a great variety of *saucissons*, large sausages which are served sliced.

The saucisson
(*French Government Tourist Office*)

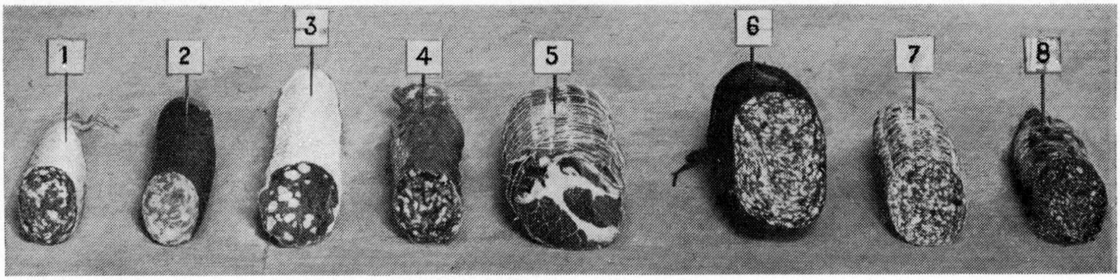

Varieties of saucisson:
1. Saucisson de ménage; 2. Saucisson de Paris; 3. Saucisson de Lyon; 4. Saucisson d'Arles; 5. Lonzo de Corse; 6. Danish salami; 7. Milan salami; 8. Hungarian salami

Among the best-known French *saucissons* which require no cooking are those of Lyon, Arles, Lorraine, Brittany, Mortagne, Strasbourg and Luchon.

Italy produces those from Milan, Bologna and Florence. The *mortadella* of Bologna is also a *saucisson*.

Salami comes from Italy, Germany, Switzerland and other countries of Europe.

The manufacture of these large sausages is strictly controlled in France. They may be made with pork meat only, lean and fat, to which there may sometimes be added, for certain specialities, beef, veal or mutton.

Any sausages containing horse, donkey or mule meat, or having a proportion of flour, must carry labels detailing these contents exactly.

Dried sausage, such as comes from Arles or Lyon, the *saucisson de ménage*, the *saucisson de montagne* and other sausage of the same type, is eaten raw, as *hors-d'œuvre*.

The *saveloy* sausage of Paris, Lyon, Nancy and other places is poached in water and eaten as *hors-d'œuvre*, hot or cold.

Household or home-made sausage. SAUCISSON DE MÉNAGE, SAUCISSON VIEUX – This sausage is made in large pig's intestines with a forcemeat composed of lean pork meat, minced or chopped, seasoned with 45 g. ($1\frac{1}{2}$ oz., 2 tablespoons) salt, 1 teaspoon pepper, $\frac{1}{2}$ teaspoon peppercorns, $\frac{1}{4}$ teaspoon saltpetre and a little chopped garlic for every 1 kg ($2\frac{1}{4}$ lb.) forcemeat.

Fill the skins, tie them lengthways and round, and hang in a drying place. After 3 or 4 weeks the skin becomes pink and small white marks appear here and there on the surface, showing that the sausages have 'ripened'.

This sausage is eaten when it has become well dried.

Lyon sausage (dry). SAUCISSON DE LYON (SEC) – Ham made from fresh pork, carefully trimmed and with all fat removed, is used to make this sausage. The meat is chopped, and seasoned with 45 g. ($1\frac{1}{2}$ oz., 2 tablespoons) salt and $\frac{1}{2}$ teaspoon pepper for each 1 kg. ($2\frac{1}{4}$ lb.) meat.

Add, for every 1 kg. ($2\frac{1}{4}$ lb.) forcemeat, 135 g. (5 oz., generous cup) diced pork fat taken from a firm piece of pork fat which has been salted dry for 10 days.

Add to this mixture $\frac{1}{2}$ teaspoon white peppercorns and a little chopped garlic. Press into a pig's intestine and tie at 45-cm. (18-inch) lengths. Hang in a drying place and leave for 48 hours. Press at each end to solidify the contents, and re-tie them. String the sausages lengthways and crossways so as to make them straight. Hang them again in the drying place, where they must be left for 3 or 4 months, until they are very dry.

Some beef, well trimmed and with all gristle, etc. removed, may be added to the pork. This addition hastens the drying of the sausages and does not harm the quality.

Lyon sausage is eaten raw as *hors-d'œuvre*.

Parisian saucisson. SAUCISSON-CERVELAS DE PARIS – Made with a forcemeat similar to that described above, seasoned, with 40 g. ($1\frac{1}{2}$ oz., 2 tablespoons) salt, $\frac{1}{2}$ teaspoon pepper, a pinch of pounded pimento and a small pinch of saltpetre for each 1 kg. ($2\frac{1}{4}$ lb.). Fill skins as described above. Divide into sections of equal length. Hang the sausages above the stove for a day or two so that they dry and redden in colour.

Prepare for the table by poaching in water.

Plain saucisson. SAUCISSON-CERVELAS ORDINAIRE – Trim carefully some lean fresh pork and remove all gristle. Chop roughly. For every 5 kg. (11 lb.) of lean meat add 1 kg. ($2\frac{1}{4}$ lb.) finely chopped, fresh pork fat.

Season with 25 g. (1 oz., $1\frac{1}{2}$ tablespoons) salt, $\frac{1}{2}$ teaspoon pepper and a pinch of saltpetre to each 1 kg. ($2\frac{1}{4}$ lb.) pork.

Blend the mixture well and press into beef gut. Divide it into lengths of 20 to 30 cm. (8 to 12 inches), tying the ends of each sausage. Smoke lightly.

To cook. Poach in water or light stock for 30 to 45 minutes according to the size of the sausages.

These are served hot or cold, usually accompanied by a potato salad.

SAUERKRAUT (Pickled cabbage). CHOUCROUTE – Finely shredded cabbage, which has been fermented in brine flavoured with juniper berries. The fermentation, which deprives the cabbage of a part of its nutritive value, makes it more digestible. The indigestibility attributed to *sauerkraut* really derives from the salted or smoked and fat meats which normally accompany it.

The fermenting of the cabbage leaves encourages the production of lactic acid in the intestine. This acid is the antidote for colibacillosis.

Preparation of the cabbage. Remove the green and torn leaves surrounding the cabbage, and the stem. With the help of a slicing device or a knife with a large blade, slice the

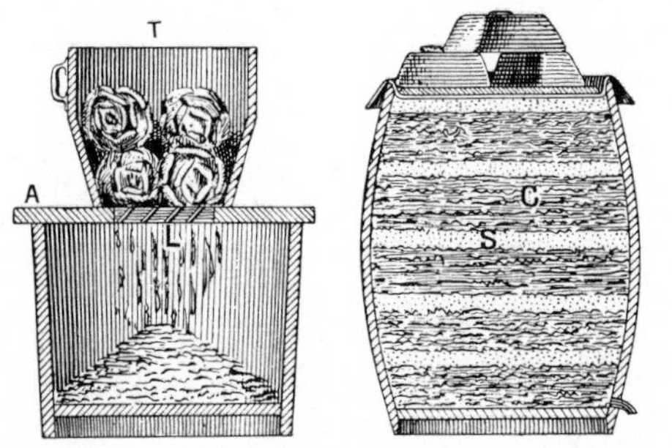

Apparatus for shredding cabbage — Barrel with sauerkraut

Manufacture of sauerkraut
T. Hopper into which the cabbages are fed; A. Lid with shredder; L. Strips of shredded cabbage; C. Layer of cabbage; S. Layer of salt

cabbage finely. Wash it well, drain, and put into an earthenware crock which has been lined with cabbage leaves or vine leaves. Arrange the cabbage in layers, pressed down, each layer sprinkled with sea salt (coarse salt) and strewn with juniper berries. Put a handful of sea salt on the last layer, allowing $1\frac{1}{2}$ kg. ($3\frac{1}{4}$ lb.) salt for every 100 kg. (220 lb.) cabbage.

Cover with a cloth and set on top of it a round wooden lid, the diameter of which is smaller than the aperture. Put a non-porous stone on top of the lid.

Next day the water will have risen above the lid under this pressure. See that this is always so. Keep the barrel or crock in an airy place. At the end of about 3 weeks, when no more froth appears on top of the cabbage, the *sauerkraut* is ready. Replace the liquid with fresh water.

Each time some cabbage is taken out, remove the liquid with a wooden bowl. After taking out the cabbage add fresh water, put back the cloth, cover, and store.

Sauerkraut as soup garnish. CHOUCROUTE POUR GARNITURE DE POTAGE – Wash, soak and press the *sauerkraut*, and put it in a white consommé to cook gently. Drain and add it to the soup.

Sauerkraut à l'alsacienne. CHOUCROUTE À L'ALSACIENNE – Soak $2\frac{1}{2}$ kg. ($5\frac{1}{2}$ lb.) *sauerkraut* for a few hours in cold water. Drain by pressing it well between the palms of the hands to extract all the water. Spread it out, so that it is not congealed into lumps. Season with salt and freshly ground pepper. Put it in a heavy pan lined with smoked bacon rinds, and add 2 or 3 onions, each stuck with a clove, 3 quartered carrots, a large *bouquet garni*, 75 g. (3 oz., $\frac{1}{2}$ cup) juniper berries tied in a muslin bag, 300 g. (11 oz.) blanched fat breast of pork, a slice of smoked pork and 150 g. (5 oz., generous $\frac{1}{2}$ cup) goose fat or lard.

Add enough white consommé to come to the top of the *sauerkraut*. Cover with bards of larding bacon. Boil on the stove, then put the pan in the oven for 4 hours. Remove the lean and smoked pork.

When the *sauerkraut* is cooked, take the vegetables, *bouquet garni* and juniper berries out of the pan. Arrange the *sauerkraut*, well drained, in a deep dish. Garnish with the smoked pork cut into slices, the lean pork cut into rectangles, thin slices of ham, poached Strasbourg sausages and smoked saveloys.

Add potatoes which have been pared into a neat shape and boiled, or serve these separately.

Sauerkraut can be prepared with other garnishes. For instance, a salted brisket (U.S. corned beef), smoked goose, a smoked loin of pork, or salt pork can be cooked in the *sauerkraut*.

All these meats, which are intended to impart their flavour to the *sauerkraut*, must be removed from the pan before the cooking is completed, or they would be overcooked.

Sauerkraut prepared in the Frankfurt manner is much the same as *à l'alsacienne*, but the Strasbourg sausages in the garnish are replaced by frankfurters.

It is customary in Alsace to accompany the *sauerkraut* with a dish of pease-pudding and boiled potatoes.

Sauerkraut à la strasbourgeoise. CHOUCROUTE À LA STRASBOURGEOISE – This name is given sometimes to *Sauerkraut à l'alsacienne* (see above).

Sauerkraut garnish I. CHOUCROUTE POUR GARNITURE – Line a casserole with lard, bacon rinds, and sliced onions and carrots. Put in 1 kg. ($2\frac{1}{4}$ lb.) soaked, rinsed and pressed *sauerkraut*. Put a *bouquet garni* and 12 juniper berries tied in muslin in the middle of the *sauerkraut*. Moisten with a white consommé from which not all the fat has been skimmed. Cover with bacon rinds. Bring to the boil on top of the stove, then cook in the oven for 3 hours.

Sauerkraut garnish II. CHOUCROUTE POUR GARNITURE – Line a buttered casserole with slices of onion and carrot. Put the *sauerkraut*, which has been first washed, soaked, and pressed, on to this base. Season, and add a *bouquet garni* and a few juniper berries tied in muslin. Moisten with water. Cover with buttered paper. Cook in the same way as above.

Sauerkraut salad à l'allemande. CHOUCROUTE EN SALADE À L'ALLEMANDE – Cook the *sauerkraut* in a white consommé or in water with whole onions. When the *sauerkraut* is cooked remove the onions and cut them into small dice. Add to the drained *sauerkraut*. Season with oil, vinegar, salt and pepper. Mix well. Arrange in a bowl in a dome. Garnish with hard-boiled eggs and slices of cooked beetroot.

SAUMUR – Town in the *département* of Maine-et-Loire, situated on the right bank of the Loire and famous for its château and cavalry school. It has given its name to a vinicultural region in Anjou where excellent dry white wines are produced. These also make attractive sparkling wines following the *méthode champenoise*. There are also rosés, Cabernet rosés and the red wines of Saumur-Champigny. (See ANJOU.)

SAUPIQUET – In the Middle Ages the *saupiquet* was a wine sauce thickened with *pain hallé* (grilled bread or toast) which was served with roast rabbit, and also with waterfowl. Here is the recipe which Taillevent gives in the *Viandier* for this sauce:

'To make *saupiquet* for coney or other roast, toast some bread and soak in some bouillon, melt bacon fat in a frying pan, put in some onion cut up very small and fry it. To serve four, take 50 g. (2 oz., $\frac{1}{2}$ cup) cinnamon, 15 g. ($\frac{1}{2}$ oz., 2 tablespoons) ginger and 7 g. ($\frac{1}{4}$ oz., 1 tablespoon) small spices, some red wine and some vinegar. Mix the bread and all the spices together and boil in a pan, then pour over the roast.'

This sauce is similar to one made today in the south-west of France which accompanies roast hare.

SAUR – Herring that has been both salted and smoked. The word was formerly *sauret* or *soret*. (See HERRING.)

SAUREL – Long fish resembling the mackerel and sometimes in England called *horse mackerel*. Less positive in colour than the proper mackerel, it also lacks its false fins near the tail and has a row of spines on either side of the back. The flesh, of good quality, is not so fine as that of the real mackerel.

In U.S.A. the horse mackerel is the name given to an Atlantic species of tuna fish. The Atlantic bluefish is also

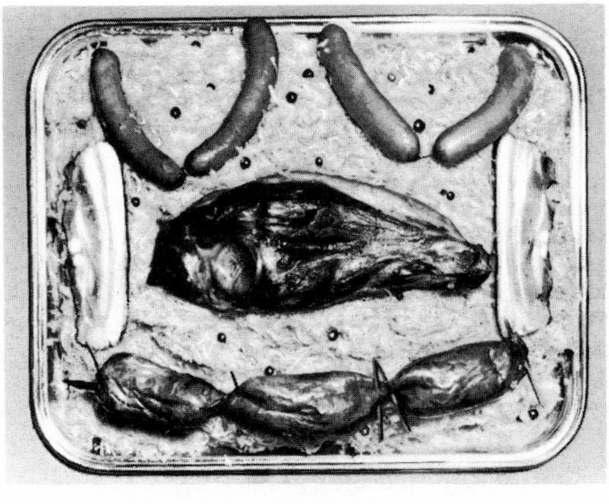

Sauerkraut garnie (*Chédeville. Phot. Nicolas*)

sometimes called horse mackerel, and more closely resembles the *saurel*.

Prepare like mackerel (q.v.).

SAUSAGE. SAUCISSE – This word comes from the Latin *salsisium*, from *salsus*, salted.

Sausages of all kinds are usually bought already prepared. In France ordinary sausages, made from fresh pork, are made both long and flat in shape. The flat sausages are called *crépinettes*. They are grilled, fried in butter or fat, or boiled. This last method is chiefly used for 'dry' sausages or smoked sausages, such as those of Frankfurt, Strasbourg, Spain (*chorizos*), Vienna, etc. See also under PORK.

Augsburgerwürste. SAUCISSES D'AUGSBOURG – Made in beef gut, with a forcemeat of coarsely chopped lean pork mixed with bacon fat cut in small dice, seasoned with salt, pepper, cloves, nutmeg and saltpetre. These sausages, after having been dried, are lightly smoked. They are poached in water.

Chorizos, red sausages. SAUCISSES ROUGES – Spanish speciality. They are made like *Country sausages* (see PORK), using pork forcemeat strongly flavoured with red pepper, and are used as an ingredient of *potées*. They are most frequently cooked with *garbanzos*, i.e. chick-peas, stewed *à la mode d'Espagne* (Spanish style).

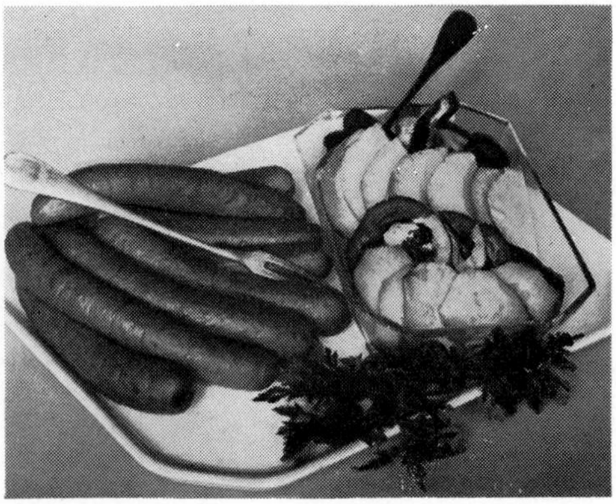

Smoked sausages served with a salad of cucumber, tomato and celeriac (*Claire*)

Frankfurt sausages or Frankfurterwürste. SAUCISSES DE FRANCFORT – German speciality, most often used to accompany *sauerkraut*, and also served hot, as *hors-d'œuvre*, with grated horseradish. They are made from a forcemeat of lean beef, trimmed of all fat and well beaten, and pork meat. Saltpetre is added to give a slightly pink colour. They are tied together in pairs and smoked.

Plunge the sausages into boiling water. Cover the pan, and poach, just boiling, for 10 minutes. Drain and serve.

Gehirnwürste. SAUCISSES DE CERVELLE – Made in pork gut with a forcemeat of equal parts of pork brains cooked in salted water to which vinegar has been added, and pork meat, half fat, half lean, seasoned with salt, pepper and mace. The sausages, tied together in pairs, are poached for 5 minutes in boiling water, then cooled and cooked in butter.

Sausages for garnish. SAUCISSES POUR GARNITURE – Small sausages, called chipolatas, are used as a garnish. They are pricked lightly with a needle and cooked under a grill or in the oven, as indicated in the recipe.

Grilled sausages. SAUCISSES GRILLÉES – Ordinary long or flat sausages are prepared in this way.

The long sausage is divided into lengths of 12 to 15 cm. (5 to 6 inches) or left whole, whatever its length, in which case it is twisted into a coil and secured with 2 skewers put in crossways.

Grilled sausages should be cooked slowly with moderate heat. They are generally served with mashed potatoes.

Grützwürste. SAUCISSES AU GRUAU – Made in pork gut in 10-cm. (4-inch) lengths with a forcemeat of wheat meal cooked in an aromatic stock, and rather fat pork skin, cooked and chopped, seasoned with salt, pepper, mace and chopped lemon peel. Submerge the sausages for 3 minutes in boiling water, drain and dry them, and toss in butter.

Knackwürste. SAUCISSES CROQUANTES – Made in pork gut with a forcemeat of 5 parts lean pork, 3 parts beef and 2 parts fresh pork fat, seasoned with salt, cumin, garlic and saltpetre.

The sausages are tied together in pairs, dried for 4 days, then smoked cold. They are poached for 10 minutes in water.

Knoblauchwürste. SAUCISSES À L'AIL – Sausage encased in pork gut made from a forcemeat of fat and lean pork, seasoned with salt, pepper, spices and pounded garlic.

Kochwürstel or Mettwürste. SAUCISSES À BOUILLIR – Made in beef gut with a forcemeat of lean pork meat and fresh pork fat, seasoned with salt, pepper and saltpetre. Poached in water.

Königswürste. SAUCISSES ROYALES – Made in pork gut with a forcemeat of equal parts of chicken and partridge meat. Add chopped truffles and mushrooms, bind with eggs, season with salt, pepper and mace and flavour with Rhine wine.

These sausages, which are rather large, are braised, then sliced when cold and served as *hors-d'œuvre*.

Sausages à la languedocienne. SAUCISSES À LA LANGUEDOCIENNE – Twist 1 kg. ($2\frac{1}{4}$ lb.) *Toulouse sausage* (see below) into a coil and secure with 2 crossed skewers. Heat 3 tablespoons (4 tablespoons) lard or goose fat in a sauté pan and put in the sausage. Add 4 chopped garlic cloves and a *bouquet garni*. Cook with a lid on for 18 minutes. Drain the sausage, put it on a dish and pour over the pan juices, diluted with 2 tablespoons (3 tablespoons) vinegar, moistened with 3 dl. ($\frac{1}{2}$ pint, $1\frac{1}{4}$ cups) *Demi-glace sauce* (see SAUCE) and 1 dl. (6 tablespoons, scant $\frac{1}{2}$ cup) tomato purée. Boil for a few moments. Add 3 tablespoons (4 tablespoons) capers pickled in vinegar, and 1 tablespoon chopped parsley to the sauce.

Long sausages. SAUCISSES LONGUES – Ordinary sausages, thus called to distinguish them from the flat sausages or *crépinettes*.

Madrilène sausages. SAUCISSES MADRILÈNES – Small sausages made in beef gut with a forcemeat of veal, fresh pork fat and sardine fillets in oil. These sausages are tied into rings, poached for 10 minutes in light veal stock, cooled, and fried in butter.

Nurnbergerwürste. SAUCISSES DE NUREMBERG – Made in pork gut with lean pork, seasoned with salt, pepper, thyme, nutmeg and marjoram, with the addition of bacon fat cut in small dice and flavoured with kirsch. They are tied into 100-g. (4-oz.) sections and fried in butter.

Polnischewürste. SAUCISSES DE POLOGNE – Made in pork gut, in 250 g. (9-oz.) sections, with a forcemeat of two-thirds lean and one-third fat pork, seasoned with salt, pepper, pimento and cloves, and bound with pig's blood, allowing 1 dl. (6 tablespoons scant $\frac{1}{2}$ cup) to 500 g. (generous 1 lb.). These sausages are dried, then smoked. To serve, poach in water.

Rindfleischkochwürste. SAUCISSES DE BOEUF À BOUILLIR – Made in beef gut with a forcemeat of 3 parts lean beef and 2 parts fresh pork fat, seasoned with salt, pepper, coriander and saltpetre. These sausages are tied in pairs and dried for 48 hours. Poach for 10 minutes in water.

Sausage meat – See PORK, *Pork sausages*.

Sausages with risotto. SAUCISSES AU RISOTTO – Cook

chipolata sausages in butter and white wine. Put them in the middle of a border of risotto, turned out onto a dish. Add 1 tablespoon meat jelly to the pan juices and pour over the sausages.

Sausages with risotto à la piémontaise. SAUCISSES AU RISOTTO, À LA PIÉMONTAISE – Cook the sausages as described above, adding to them, towards the end of cooking, white truffles cut in thin slices. Put them in the middle of a risotto border and pour the pan juices over.

In Italy, a small quantity of chopped green cabbage is added to the risotto during cooking.

Sausage roll. FRIAND – Puff pastry filled with sausage meat.

Smoked sausages. SAUCISSES FUMÉES – Prepare like *Country sausages* (see PORK) and smoke in a smokehouse for 2 days. Poach in water.

These sausages are used as an ingredient for *potées*. They are also served hot, as an *hors-d'œuvre*.

Strasbourg sausages. SAUCISSES DE STRASBOURG – Alsatian speciality, made like smoked *Frankfurt sausages*. They are mainly used for garnishing *sauerkraut*.

Toulouse sausages. SAUCISSES DE TOULOUSE – Big sausages the forcemeat for which is chopped by hand. Grill or fry as ordinary long sausages.

Vienna sausages. SAUCISSES DE VIENNE – Austrian speciality found ready-made in food shops. They are prepared like *Frankfurt sausages* and are accompanied by the same garnishes.

Sausages in white wine. SAUCISSES AU VIN BLANC – Cook long sausages in butter in the oven. Drain them and arrange on croûtons fried in butter or toasted under the grill, allowing 2 sausages per croûton. Dilute the pan juices with white wine, add *Demi-glace sauce* (see SAUCE) and butter, and pour over the sausages.

Or: Brown 12 long sausages in butter in a sauté pan. Moisten them with $1\frac{1}{2}$ dl. ($\frac{1}{4}$ pint, $\frac{2}{3}$ cup) dry white wine. Cook in the oven with a lid on.

Drain and arrange in pairs on croûtons fried in butter. Boil down the white wine by two-thirds, bind with egg yolk, add a dash of lemon juice, 1 tablespoon meat jelly and 50 g. (2 oz., $\frac{1}{4}$ cup) butter. Blend well.

Würstchen – Small sausages made in sheep's gut with a forcemeat of 2 parts lean pork, 1 part veal and 1 part throat meat of pork, seasoned with salt, pepper, pimento and cardamon and mixed with Rhine wine. The sausages are tied together in bunches. Poach for 3 minutes in salt water, then cool and grill.

Würste von Kalbsgekröse. SAUCISSES DE FRAISE DE VEAU – Made in pork gut with calf's mesentery, washed, blanched, finely chopped and cooked for a few moments in vinegar and then in an aromatic *court-bouillon*. Season with salt, pepper and nutmeg and bind, for every 1 kg. ($2\frac{1}{4}$ lb.) with 2 eggs and $1\frac{1}{2}$ dl. ($\frac{1}{4}$ pint, $\frac{2}{3}$ cup) fresh cream. Poach the sausages for 10 minutes, allow to cool, and toss in butter.

SAUTÉ. SAUTER – To cook over a strong heat in fat or oil, shaking the pan and making whatever is in it *sauter* or jump, to keep it from sticking to the bottom. (See CULINARY METHODS.)

SAUTÉ – This generic term applies to preparations made from meat, fowl, game or fish, cut up into pieces of equal size, which are cooked over good heat in butter, oil or other fat.

Sautés differ from *ragoûts* in that the former are not sprinkled with flour before liquid is added, as is the case with *ragoûts*. A thickened liquid is added to the pan juices.

Sauté of fish. SAUTÉS DE POISSONS – Fillet large fish (perch, brill, cod, salmon, tunny, etc.). Trim the fillets and use the bones and scraps to make a *fumet* for the final sauce.

Cut the fillets in pieces 3 to 4 cm. (1 to 1 inches) long. Season and sauté them briskly in butter or oil. Drain. Dilute the pan juices with white or red wine, depending on the recipe. Add the prescribed sauce. Simmer for a few moments, add butter and strain through a cloth. Put the pieces of fish into this sauce and heat without allowing to boil.

Various garnishes may be added to sauté of fish, such as: mushrooms, aubergines, courgettes, artichoke bottoms, tomatoes, truffles, etc. Sautéed fish may be browned, or cooked without allowing to colour.

Sauté of game. SAUTÉS DE GIBIERS – Prepared with game meat or game birds. Recipes given under PHEASANT, RABBIT.

Sauté of meat. SAUTÉS DE VIANDES DE BOUCHERIE – Lamb, pork and veal are chiefly prepared in this way, though the method may be used with beef and mutton, bearing in mind that the latter should remain a little pink inside, and should not be allowed to boil in the accompanying sauce which is added after the pieces have been fried.

Sauté of poultry. SAUTÉS DE VOLAILLES – Recipes will be found under CHICKEN.

Sauté pan (*Larousse*)

SAUTÉ PAN. SAUTOIR – Pan with a thick base and rather low sides used to sauté meat, vegetables, etc.

SAUTERNES – Commune of the Gironde, a district of Bazas, renowned for its sweet white wines. The communes of Barsac, Preignac, Sauternes, Bommes and Fargues together make up the territory whose right to give to its wines the name of Sauternes has been recognised. (See BORDEAUX.)

SAUVIGNON – Species of wine-producing vine cultivated in the Armagnac and the Bordelais. In the Sauternes district the Sauvignon gives some renowned wines.

SAVARIN – Cake made with a yeast mixture, soaked in flavoured syrup with rum or kirsch added.

Ingredients. 500 g. (18 oz., $4\frac{1}{2}$ cups) sifted flour, 375 g. (13 oz., generous $1\frac{1}{2}$ cups) butter, 25 g. (1 oz., 2 tablespoons)

Savarin mould (*Larousse*)

sugar, 25 g. (1 oz.) yeast, 8 eggs, scant 1 dl. (6 tablespoons, scant $\frac{1}{2}$ cup) warm milk, $1\frac{1}{2}$ teaspoons salt.

Method. Make a dough in the same way as for baba dough (see BABA).

Put the dough into a buttered ring mould of the type known as a *savarin* mould, filling it not more than three-quarters full.

Leave in a warm place until the dough has risen to the top of the mould. Cook in a hot oven for 45 minutes. Allow to cool completely before turning out.

To serve. Soak the *savarin* in a liqueur-flavoured syrup prepared in the following way:

Melt over heat 500 g. (18 oz., $2\frac{1}{4}$ cups) sugar and $\frac{1}{2}$ litre (scant pint, $2\frac{1}{4}$ cups) water. Add 10 g. ($\frac{1}{2}$ oz.) star anise, 2 teaspoons cinnamon, a few grains of coriander and a fragment of mace (the outer covering of the nutmeg).

When the syrup is boiling, flavour it with 2 dl. ($\frac{1}{3}$ pint, scant cup) rum or kirsch. Put the *savarin* on a dish and sprinkle it with the hot syrup. When the cake is well soaked, take it out of the dish, place it on a clean one and sprinkle over a few more tablespoons of the rum or kirsch before serving.

Cherry savarin à la Chantilly. SAVARIN AUX CERISES À LA CHANTILLY – Stone 1 kg. ($2\frac{1}{4}$ lb.) Morello (dark) cherries, put them in a deep dish and sprinkle with sugar. Add a dozen crushed cherry stones tied in a muslin bag.

When the juice begins to run, cook the cherries in this juice over low heat. Allow to cool.

Prepare *Chantilly cream* (see CREAMS) flavoured with cherry brandy.

Drain the cherries and dry them, set them in the middle of a *savarin* soaked in the cherry juice and flavoured with cherry brandy or kirsch.

Cover the cherries with the *chantilly cream* piled into a dome. Decorate with cherries.

Savarin à la crème – Fill the inside of a soaked and flavoured *savarin* with $\frac{1}{2}$ litre (scant pint, $2\frac{1}{4}$ cups) very thick *French pastry cream* (see CREAMS) mixed with 50 g. (2 oz., $\frac{1}{2}$ cup) crushed macaroons. Serve cold or hot. In the latter case the top of the cream is sprinkled with fine sugar and glazed with a glazing iron.

Savarins served hot should normally be accompanied by a fruit sauce (apricot, redcurrant, or strawberry) flavoured with liqueur.

Savarin Montmorency – Remove the stalks and stones from 500 g. (generous 1 lb.) pale red semi-sweet cherries and poach them in 1 litre ($1\frac{3}{4}$ pints, generous quart) light syrup. After about 4 minutes boiling, drain them and cook for a few minutes in a pan with 1 dl. (6 tablespoons, scant $\frac{1}{2}$ cup) kirsch. Use them to fill the middle of a *savarin*.

SAVORY. SARRIETTE – Aromatic garden herb with a scent recalling that of thyme, used as seasoning.

SAVOURIES – In Britain this term describes a range of light preparations. Served at the end of dinner, after dessert, these might be called 'post- œuvre' as distinct from *hors-d'œuvre*, which are served at the beginning of the meal. The following are the principal savouries: cheese straws, angels on horseback (oysters and bacon, grilled), cheese fritters, various foodstuffs cooked on skewers, *chou profiteroles* with cheese, fried Camembert, canapés, various foodstuffs on toast, devilled chicken legs and wings, cheese *condés*, fried cheese custard shapes, various croquettes and kromeskies, *diablotins*, rib bones of beef seasoned with mustard and cayenne and grilled, *paillettes* seasoned with Parmesan or paprika, cheese pancakes, tartlets and *barquettes* with various fillings, Welsh rarebit and other toasted cheese dishes, etc.

SAVOURING. DÉGUSTATION – The palatal appreciation of the flavour of a solid or liquid. The savouring or 'tasting' of wines and spirits is a highly refined art.

The preliminary operations consist of scrutinising the wine so as to judge its colour, detect any impurities and assess its limpidity and brilliance. Next, the sense of smell appreciates the aroma given off by the wine. The taste buds are dispersed throughout the mouth, some having specialised functions. Sourness is recognised with the tip of the tongue; sweetness with the flat of the tongue; under the tongue are the buds which respond especially to bitterness; tartness reacts upon the inner surface of the cheeks. Professional tasters put this specialised sensitivity to good use.

To savour a wine, for instance, a small sip is first taken. This is held in the front of the mouth against the teeth, while the tip of the tongue is gently moved back and forth to appreciate the sourness of the wine. Next, the head is tilted back a little and a deep breath is taken which is mixed with the liquid. At this point the aroma is savoured (this is given off by one of the essential oils contained in the skin of the grape and consequently depends on the variety); this aroma is present in unmatured wines. It becomes more subtle and refined with maturity. Later the bouquet develops. This is present only in old wines and is due to the slow blending of the more volatile spirits, the ethers, aldehydes and essences of the wine. Finally,

Wine tasting in a cellar (from a lithograph)

in these early stages, the taster takes note also of the special properties of the wine, the native tang, the standard flavour of the hybrid growths, the taste of cask, musk, sulphur, etc.

The wine is then spread over tongue and palate for about two seconds. At this point the taster will recognise the warmth of a full-bodied wine or its absence in a wine of less generous quality. He will experience a burning sensation if raw alcohol has been added. At the same time, the sweetness, smoothness and texture of the wine are appreciated, that is to say the relative proportions of sugar and tannin. Finally, the tartness and astringency are appreciated by rolling the wine against the cheeks.

At this point, professional tasters usually stop, spitting out the mouthful, since their vast experience enables them to judge a host of other subtle qualities in the wine.

There is something to be said, however, for swallowing the mouthful, provided that one is not obliged to taste too large a number of samples at the same session. By swallowing slowly, with the mouth closed, there are still further shades of taste to be distinguished. First of all some flavours which take about 10 seconds to develop, then the 'readiness' which arises from the fusion of aroma and bouquet, and finally the perfumed aftertaste which indicates that the wine 'ends well'.

The tasting of oil, butter, tea and other foods is carried out in the same way. It should be undertaken in the mornings on an empty stomach, or at least some considerable time after a meal. Above all, the taster *should not smoke* before tasting.

Haute Savoie (Château de Menthon)
(*French Government Tourist Office*)

SAVOY. SAVOIE – The territory of the Savoy, jagged with mountains, offers only a restricted space for the cultivation of such crops as cereals, buckwheat and potatoes, but the gentler slopes of the Alps provide fine pasture lands which nourish livestock for meat and dairy produce. The milk and cream used in the *Savoyarde* kitchen are culinary ingredients of the highest order. Vines are grown on the hillsides which face the midday sun. Fine orchards are planted with cherry, plum, pear and cider apple trees. Walnut trees and chestnuts prosper. The clearings in the woods abound with fragrant little strawberries, and the cool earth of the forests and meadows encourages the growth of mushrooms in summer.

Game, nourished by the aromatic herbs of the grasslands, is particularly good to eat; hares, partridges, quails and woodcock are plentiful. Excellent fish abounds in the cold waters of the lakes and rivers and torrents: carp, eel, perch, trout, char and burbot. Two delicious fish, the *lavaret* and the *féra*, are almost unique to the province. The crayfish are small but good. The bees provide excellent honey, that of Tarentaise in particular being renowned.

Culinary specialities – Savoyarde cooking, done with ingredients of the highest quality, is good but a little heavy. There exist some special dishes.

Under the name of *civet*, hare and pork are prepared with a very rich sauce in which spices and aromatics are combined with the blood of the animal, wine and fresh cream.

In this cheese-producing region *gratin* dishes are greatly relished: *gratins* of crayfish, cardoons and potatoes have a place of honour.

The *farçon* is a local potato dish which constitutes a sweet pudding. *Rissoles* of meat or other mixtures and preparations made with veal and lamb offal (U.S. variety meats) – ears, sweetbreads, brains and liver – are much appreciated.

Savoyarde housewives are expert in the art of making sausages and *pâtés*. The hams of Celliers and Taninges, dried and smoked in the open air, are of high repute, as are the game *pâtés* of Bonneville. Among the fish dishes are: *batter-fried perch* and *trout*; the *salmon trout*; *Trout à la meunière*; *char* cooked in *court-bouillon*. The fishermen of Lake Léman prepared a fish soup similar to the *chaudrées*, *cotriades* and *bouillabaisses* of the sea coast.

Among the vegetables, cardoons are notable. The *nouilles* (noodles) and *nouillettes aux oeufs* of Albertville and Chambéry have a high reputation. Nut oil is much used for cooking and salad dressings.

Cheeses are numerous and choice: Chevrette; Reblochon; Vacherin – which is an imitation of Gruyère – and Tome de Sixt, which is eaten very hard, several years after making.

The *matefaim* is a pancake which can be eaten with salt or sugar according to taste.

At Chamonix are made *bonbons au miel des Alpes* (Alpine honey sweets); *nougat* and good pastries; *biscuits* are made at Thonon; *chocolate* at Sallanches. At Saint-Genis-d'Aoste and at Taninges *gateaux de Savoie* are made according to the ancient tradition of the region.

Wines – Savoy produces some attractive wines. There are two *appellations contrôlées*: Crépy and Seyssel, both white; also a sparkling Seyssel.

All the other wines belong to the V.D.Q.S. category. The *appellations* are: Vins de Savoie, Roussette de Savoie, Vins de Savoie mousseaux. The best known vineyards are: Marestel, Monthoux, Chautagne on the left bank of the Rhône; Monterminod, Chignin, Charpignat on the shores of Lake Bourget; Abymes, Apremont, Montmélian, Arbin, Cruet, Saint-Jean-de-la-Porte on the right bank of the Isère.

Cider is a popular drink in many of the cantons; Chambéry, Annecy and Rumilly brew beer. Savoy also produces an excellent kirsch, a marc brandy and a special spirit called lie, which is often added to coffee. The best known dessert wine of the province is Chambéry vermouth.

SAVOYARDE (À LA) – Name given to two different preparations:

1. *Omelette à la savoyarde*; pancake omelette filled with slices of potato sautéed in butter and thin shavings of Gruyère. (see EGGS.)

2. Potatoes chopped up raw, mixed with grated Gruyère and consommé and cooked in an earthenware dish. (See POTATOES, *Potatoes à la savoyarde*.)

SAVOY BISCUIT. SAVOIE (BISCUIT DE) – See SPONGE CAKE, *Savoy sponge cake*.

Gastronomic map of Savoy

SAWO MANILA – Malaysian name given in Java and in the Indian Archipelago to a fruit we know as *American medlar* or *sapodilla.* Its botanical name is *Achras sapota.* It is roughly the size of a lemon with a greyish skin and reddish-yellow, almost apricot-coloured, flesh. This fruit has an exquisite flavour but can only be enjoyed in its native habitat.

SAXIFRAGES – Name of a number of fleshy-leaved plants, some of which can be used as vegetables or in soup.

SCABIOUS. SCABIEUSE – Name of several different plants, formerly used as depuratives. *Field scabious* has succulent leaves which may be eaten cooked or in salad. Scabious is prepared like spinach.

SCALD. ÉBOUILLANTER – To plunge any food into boiling water to harden it and facilitate peeling. This process is also known as blanching.

SCALE. ÉCAILLER – To remove the scales of a fish. This is part of the process of *dressing* a fish before cooking.

SCALLION or SPRING ONION. CIBOULE – Plant closely related to the onion, but whereas the onion, when young, has leaves of a pale green tending to white at the bottom of the stem, those of the scallion or spring onion are dark green all the way down.

Scallions are found in the market in spring. They are chopped and eaten raw in green salads.

SCALLOP. PÉTONCLE – A species of bivalve mollusc with ribbed, rounded shells, belonging to the *Pectinidae* family. It is commonly found in France on the Channel and Atlantic coasts and is variously called *olivette*, *vanette* or *vanneau.* Scallops are common on the American coasts, varying in size from very small (bay scallops) to some very large varieties. Found rarely on the Mediterranean coast.

SCALLOP SAINT-JACQUES. COQUILLE SAINT-JACQUES – Bivalve mollusc, commonly known as the pilgrim shell, and called in French *Coquille Saint-Jacques.*

Before preparing scallops wash and scrub them well and

Sawo manila

put them in the oven at a very low heat, the rounded part downwards. They will open completely.

Take out the flesh and the little coral tongue, which is a great delicacy. Do not discard the shells. Scrub them and keep for future use for various scallop shell dishes.

Poach the flesh and the coral in a *court-bouillon* made with white wine, well seasoned and flavoured with onion, thyme and bay leaf. Drain the scallops. They are now ready to be treated according to the recipe.

In U.S.A., the scallops have no coral and are rarely sold in the shells. All but the hinge is discarded.

Fried scallops. COQUILLES SAINT-JACQUES FRITES – Cook the scallops in *court-bouillon*, drain and slice. Marinate them for 30 minutes in oil, lemon juice and chopped parsley. Dip them in a light batter and fry in smoking-hot deep fat. Drain. Garnish with fried parsley and quarters of lemon.

Scallops fried in batter. FRITOT DE COQUILLES SAINT-JACQUES – Prepare like *Fried scallops*. Serve with *Tomato sauce* (see SAUCE).

Fried scallops Colbert. COQUILLES SAINT-JACQUES FRITES COLBERT – Dip the white flesh of the scallops in egg and breadcrumbs. Fry in clarified butter. Heap on a serving dish, garnish with chopped parsley and serve with *Colbert butter* (see BUTTER, *Compound butters*).

Scallop brochettes. COQUILLES SAINT-JACQUES EN BROCHETTES – Open the scallops and remove the flesh and coral. Rinse these thoroughly in several waters. Pat dry in a towel.

Cut some bacon into small squares (about 1 cm., $\frac{1}{2}$ inch). Slide a clove of garlic backwards and forwards on each skewer then discard it. Alternate scallops, bacon and coral on the skewers. Season with salt and pepper. Sprinkle with oil and grill, turning occasionally, for 12 to 15 minutes.

Scallops au gratin. COQUILLES SAINT-JACQUES AU GRATIN – Cook the scallops as described at the beginning of this entry, cut in slices and set in scallop shells on a layer of *duxelles*, with the chopped onion bound with tomato sauce. Place the coral on top of the scallop slices.

Coat with tomato-flavoured *Duxelles sauce* (see SAUCES). Sprinkle with breadcrumbs and melted butter. Brown lightly in the oven.

Scallops au gratin à la dieppoise. COQUILLES SAINT-JACQUES AU GRATIN À LA DIEPPOISE – Set the cooked scallops and coral in the shells. Finish as for *Brill à la dieppoise* (see BRILL).

Scallops in mayonnaise. COQUILLES SAINT-JACQUES EN MAYONNAISE – Set the cooked scallops, seasoned with oil and vinegar and sprinkled with chopped parsley, in the shells, lined with a little shredded and seasoned lettuce. Coat with mayonnaise. Garnish with the coral, fillets of anchovies and capers. Surround with lettuce hearts, quartered hard-boiled eggs and stoned olives.

Scallops Mornay. COQUILLES SAINT-JACQUES MORNAY – Edge the scallop shells with a border of *Duchesse potato mixture* (see POTATOES) piped through a forcing bag. Line the bottoms of the shells with a spoonful of *Mornay sauce* (see SAUCE).

Add slices of scallop flesh and the coral. Coat with *Mornay sauce*. Sprinkle with grated cheese and melted butter and brown in the oven.

Fried scallops à la tartare. COQUILLES SAINT-JACQUES FRITES

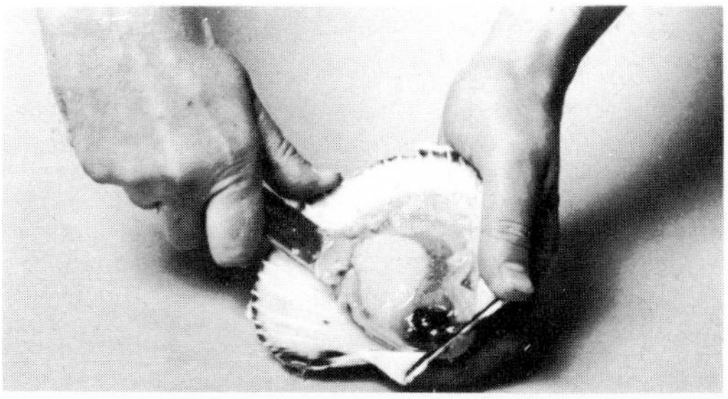

Scallops Saint-Jacques (*Prunier. Phot. Nicolas*)
Top right: how to detach them
Bottom right: scallops on skewers

Scallops Saint-Jacques (*Larousse*)

À LA TARTARE – Prepare the flesh of the scallops as for *Fried scallops Colbert*. Serve with *Tartare sauce* (see SAUCE).

Scallops fried in this way can be served with various sauces, such as *Béarnaise, Hongroise, Portugaise*, etc. (see SAUCE).

SCAMPI – See DUBLIN BAY PRAWNS.

SCARUS, PARROT-FISH. SCARE – Mediterranean fish with fine flesh which was particularly esteemed by the Romans. It is called parrot-fish because of its bright colours. Prepared in *court-bouillon, à la meunière* or fried.

SCHALETH, JEWISH. SCHALETH À LA JUIVE – Prepare *Noodle paste* (see NOODLES) as long in advance as possible, so that it is well 'rested' before using.

Roll out thinly, and line a large metal, well-buttered basin. Fill to three-quarters of its capacity with sweet apple purée prepared in this way:

Boil down 800 g. (1¾ lb., 4⅔ cups) apple jam. Add 150 g. (5 oz., 1 cup) raisins, cleaned and seeded, and 250 g. (9 oz., 1½ cups) currants and sultanas, picked over, washed, and soaked in warm water. Add ½ teaspoon each of chopped orange and lemon peel, 125 g. (4 oz., ½ cup) sugar and a little grated nutmeg. Bind with 5 whole eggs and 3 yolks. Add 1 dl. (6 tablespoons, scant ½ cup) Malaga and mix well.

Cover the basin with a layer of pastry. Make a hole in the middle to allow steam to escape. Cook in a moderately hot oven for 50 minutes to 1 hour. Allow to stand for a few minutes before turning out.

SCHNITZEL. SCHNITZEL – Escalope (thin cutlet) of veal coated with egg and breadcrumbs and cooked in butter or oil, is known by this name in Germany and Austria. (See VEAL.)

SCOLYMUS. SCOLYME – Plant of the *Compositae* family found in the south-west of France. The Spanish scolymus has an edible root which is eaten in the same way as salsify.

SCOTER-DUCK. MACREUSE – Genus of duck among which are Polar species which migrate to both the Old and New World. Their oily flesh is strong in flavour but edible if the birds are young and properly cooked.

SCUM. ÉCUME – Froth which forms on the surface of a boiling liquid, or the skin which forms on top of a protein liquid such as soup, through the coagulation of soluble proteins when the liquid is cold.

SEA ANEMONES. ANÉMONES DE MER – Name commonly given to *Actinia* or starfish, edible molluscs which abound on the coasts of France, particularly on the Mediterranean side.

SEA BASS. LOUP DE MER – Name given in some districts to the sea perch.

In U.S.A. the *sea bass* of the eastern coast and the *groupers* of the southern shores are very similar to the French *loup de mer*.

Sea bream

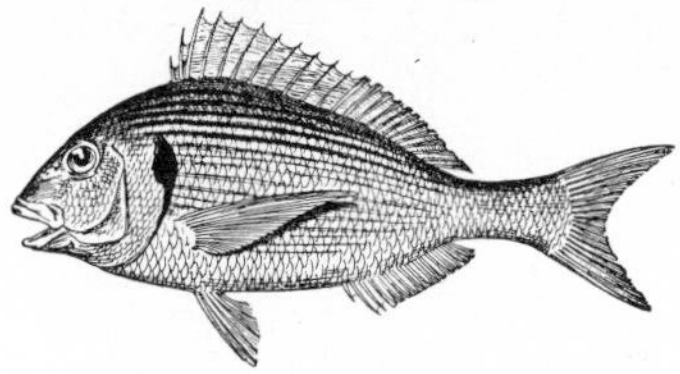

SEA BREAM. DAURADE – Very delicately flavoured fish found in the Mediterranean end of the Gulf of Gascony and very occasionally in the English Channel.

The back is bluish white or dark blue, the flanks silvery-yellow, the belly white. The ancients called it *golden eyebrow* because of the brilliant golden crescent between its eyes. The French name for this fish is *daurade*.

Sea bream is best grilled *à la meunière* or boiled and served with melted butter.

SEA COW, MANATEE. LAMANTIN – The flesh of this herbivorous sea mammal, which tastes something like pork, is much esteemed in the West Indies, as is the 'bacon' made from it.

SEA EEL – See EEL.

SEAFOODS. FRUITS DE MER – Name applied to crustaceans and shellfish of various kinds, which are served together, raw or cooked. It is used, in particular, of a dish of raw shellfish served as an *hors-d'œuvre*, such as oysters.

Seafoods, which sometimes include slices of various fish, can be cooked in many different ways. They can be made into *ragoûts*, flans (tarts), risottos, stuffings, etc.

Seafood risotto. RISOTTO AUX FRUITS DE MER – Cook 2 litres (quarts) mussels and 1 litre (quart) cockles or small clams separately in white wine, seasoned with spices and herbs. Drain the shellfish and remove from their shells. Put them in a casserole with 200 g. (7 oz., generous 1 cup) shelled shrimps and 4 shelled scallops, previously cooked in white wine. Add 4 dl. (¾ pint, scant 2 cups) fish *Velouté sauce* (see SAUCE) which has been prepared separately by using the combined

Dish of seafoods (*Larousse*)

cooking liquors and a white *roux* of butter and flour. This sauce is cooked for 25 minutes and should be very smooth. Add 5 tablespoons (6 tablespoons) cream and simmer for a few minutes. Add 40 g. ($1\frac{1}{2}$ oz., 3 tablespoons) butter and strain.

The *ragoût*, with the *velouté* added to it, should be kept hot without boiling.

Prepare the risotto. Sauté a chopped onion in butter without letting it brown. Mix in 250 g. (9 oz., $1\frac{1}{4}$ cup) rice, stirring well so that all the grains are well coated with butter. Add meat stock twice the volume of the rice a little at a time, allowing the rice to absorb the liquid before pouring on any more.

Cover, and cook for 15 to 20 minutes, stirring from time to time. Add 50 g. (2 oz., $\frac{1}{4}$ cup) butter and 50 g. (2 oz., $\frac{1}{2}$ cup) grated cheese.

Arrange the rice in a border on a large dish. Place in the centre the seafood *ragoût* and arrange the coral of the scallops on top.

SEA HOG – See PORPOISE.

SEAKALE. CHOU MARIN – This plant, which is appreciated in England, is little known in France, although it was introduced into cultivation a long time ago: M. Massey cultivated it in the royal vegetable garden at Versailles in 1820.

Seakale takes the form of a strong root out of which grow leaf rosettes consisting of long thick stalks terminating in fringed rounded crests, pale in colour.

The vegetable grows wild on the coasts of most of western Europe. The leaf stalks have a nutty flavour when cooked.

Seakale is eaten in the same way as asparagus or cardoons.

Trim and wash the seakale and tie 6 to 8 stalks at a time in bundles. Cook in boiling salted water. Drain.

SEAL. PHOQUE – Marine mammal hunted for its skin and the oil which is extracted from its fat. Seal's flesh is eaten by the Eskimos who, it is said, are particularly fond of its liver, lungs, heart and blood, which they make into sausages.

SEA PERCH. PERCHE DE MER – Name sometimes given to bass.

SEA SLUG. HOLOTHURIE – A creature rather like a worm. Some breeds are edible, among them the *tripang* found in Chinese waters, which is said to be highly prized among the gastronomes of the Far East.

SEASONING. ASSAISONNEMENT – This word defines both the act of seasoning a dish with one of the special substances (salt, for instance) and the substance itself.

Seasoning and flavouring are not the same things. Seasoning a preparation consists of adding a large or small amount of salt to it: flavouring a dish means enhancing its taste by the addition of condiments, aromatics and spices.

SEA URCHIN. OURSIN – Popular name of the marine animals of the *Echinus* species, with spines, several species of which are edible.

The best are the *green sea urchin* and the *black sea urchin*. The latter, called by various names in various regions – *sea hedgehog*, *sea egg*, etc. – is found at low tide on rocks.

There are few recipes for preparing the sea urchin. It is chiefly eaten, lightly boiled, like an egg. Cook it in salted boiling water, drain, open by cutting with scissors on the concave side (where the sea urchin's mouth is situated), drain it completely, throwing out the excremental part, then dip buttered morsels of bread into the shell.

In the region of Marseilles, where sea urchins are considered a delicacy, they are eaten out of the shell, as described, but uncooked. They are opened, washed (in sea water if possible) and buttered sippets of bread are dipped into the yellow substance clinging to the walls of the shell.

Sea urchins (*Merveilles des mers – Charlot I. Phot. Larousse*)

It is said that sea urchin has great restorative powers. Its taste, when cooked, is not unlike crayfish.

Sea urchin purée. PURÉE D'OURSINS – Open 3 dozen well washed sea urchins and remove the part resembling hard roe. Rub this substance through a sieve. Add an equal quantity of thick *Béchamel sauce* (see SAUCE). Simmer for 5 minutes, then blend in 40 g. ($1\frac{1}{2}$ oz., 3 tablespoons) butter.

This purée can be used for filling tartlets or puff pastry *vol-au-vent* cases. It can also be spread on pieces of bread, lightly fried in butter, sprinkled with grated cheese, and put in a very hot oven to brown the top.

SEA WRACK, ROCK-WEEK. FUCUS – Species of seaweed of the membranous or filament type.

It is said that the inhabitants of Iceland, the Faroe Islands, Scotland, Norway, Denmark and North America use it for food in times of scarcity. In Scotland, the young stems of the tangle or sea-lettuce are sometimes eaten as a salad.

In Japan there is a flourishing industry in the by-products of seaweed in general and sea wrack in particular. *Amanori* and *kombu* are greatly prized for their gelatinous properties, used as condiments rather than as actual food.

SÉBILLE – Saucer or small bowl, usually made of wood, used in French cookery for beating eggs.

In large kitchens, parsley and other chopped ingredients set out for a particular dish are assembled in wooden *sébilles* of various capacities.

SELTZER-WATER. SELTZ, EAU DE SELTZ – Sparkling mineral water from Selters (Duchy of Nassau), sold in bottles. Artificial seltzer-water is effervescent water charged with carbonic gas under pressure, and sold in siphons.

SEMI-SPARKLING. MOUSTILLE – Certain red and white wines, which are not quite sparkling, have traces of effervescence. These are said to be semi-sparkling.

SEMOLINA. SEMOULE – Food made with cereals, mostly wheat, reduced to granules by coarse milling.

Semolina, particularly wheat semolina, is used to make groats, soups, puddings and various other dishes.

Semolina kasha (Russian cookery). KACHE DE SEMOULE – Mix 250 g. (9 oz., $1\frac{1}{2}$ cups) coarse semolina and one beaten

Semolina pudding with stewed fruit (*Claire*)

egg. Spread this mixture over a baking tin and dry it in the oven at low heat.

Sieve and poach for 20 minutes in consommé. Drain.

This kasha is used with coulibiac and various *hors-d'œuvre* in Russian cookery.

Semolina pudding. POUDING DE SEMOULE – Shower 250 g. (9 oz., 1½ cups) semolina into 1 litre (scant quart, generous quart) boiling milk sweetened and flavoured with vanilla. Add 40 g. (1½ oz., 3 tablespoons) butter and a pinch of salt. Mix well. Cook in the oven for 30 minutes.

Thicken, away from the heat, with 4 beaten eggs.

English semolina pudding. POUDING DE SEMOULE À L'ANGLAISE – Add to semolina prepared as in the previous recipe 4 egg yolks and 1 dl. (6 tablespoons, scant ½ cup) fresh cream for each litre (scant quart, generous quart) of the mixture.

Put in a buttered pie dish and cook in the oven in a *bain-marie*.

French semolina pudding – See PUDDING.

Semolina subrics. SUBRICS DE SEMOULE – Cook 125 g. (4½ oz., ¾ cup) semolina in ½ litre (scant pint, 2¼ cups) of consommé. Add 40 g. (1½ oz., 3 tablespoons) butter. Cover and cook for 25 minutes in the oven. Bind with 2 whole eggs and one extra yolk, and 50 g. (2 oz., ½ cup) grated cheese. Spread this mixture on a buttered baking tin. Butter the surface. Allow to cool. Cut out subrics with a round pastry cutter about 5 cm. (2 inches) in diameter. Fry on both sides in clarified butter.

Set in a crown and sprinkle with melted butter.

To simplify the operation the subrics may be made in squares or rectangles.

In the same way subrics may be made of maize (polenta), rice, vermicelli, noodles and all kinds of cereals and their derivatives.

Semolina subrics (sweet). SUBRICS DE SEMOULE (ENTREMETS) – Sprinkle 125 g. (4½ oz., ¾ cup) semolina into ½ litre (scant pint, 2¼ cups) milk previously boiled with 100 g. (4 oz., ½ cup) sugar, half a pod of vanilla and a pinch of salt.

Add 40 g. (1½ oz., 3 tablespoons) butter and mix well. Cook in the oven, covered, for 25 minutes.

Remove from the heat and bind with 4 egg yolks. Turn the mixture onto a baking tin in a layer 2 cm. (¾ inch) thick. Butter the surface and allow to cool.

Cut out in rings with a pastry cutter and fry on both sides in very hot butter. Arrange in a crown. Garnish the middle of each subric with apricot or redcurrant jelly.

SEPARATOR. ÉCRÉMEUSE – Implement used in dairies for separating the cream from the milk.

SEPT-ŒIL – Name (Seven-eye) sometimes given to the lamprey. The spawn of this fish are also called *sept-œil.*

SERDEAU or SERS-D'EAU – Official of the court of the King of France who received the dishes cleared from the table by the *maître d'hôtel*. Also the place to which these left-overs were taken and from which they were re-sold. Formerly at the court of France it was the custom to keep food always ready to serve to those whose duty or business brought them in touch with the king.

To this end dishes cleared from the royal table were brought to a special room or *serre*, which came to be called the *serre d'hôte*, and, by corruption, the *serdeau* i.e. to be kept hot. A 'serre' is a hothouse.

Later, the custom of regaling the king's visitors fell into disuse and the left-overs, brought immediately to the *serdeau* as before, were sold by auction. This custom still existed at the time of Louis XIV and many Versailles households were cheaply provisioned in this way.

News-gatherers of the end of the eighteenth century were greatly amused by an adventure which happened at Versailles to an old gentleman whose state of fortune obliged him to make economies, and who was in the habit of making up his dinner from left-overs provided for him by the *serdeau* servants.

He had been called unexpectedly into a salon of the palace, when it was discovered that a very valuable snuff-box had suddenly disappeared without anybody having been seen to leave the room. To allay suspicion everybody present turned their pockets inside out, and, after a certain hesitation, the economy-minded courtier followed suit. One may imagine the burst of laughter that greeted the appearance of a piece of chicken that had been buried in his pocket, and which had been intended to constitute the poor gentleman's dinner.

The story appeared in all the papers after having acquired a number of embellishments.

SERRÉ – See CHEESE.

SERVICE – The word service used to mean a group of dishes composing part of a meal. There were at least three services. After each the table was cleared with the exception of the *dormants* or table centres and the *bouts de table*, on which were arranged the dishes for the next course.

The second sense of the word describes the manner of presenting the dishes to the guests. If the dishes are put on the table, each artistically arranged and set symmetrically, this is service *à la française*. Then there is the service *à la russe*, now widely adopted, in which the dishes are passed in a pre-determined order to each guest, the meat being cut up in advance. Some details of these two kinds of service are given below.

Table service can also be taken to mean the *ensemble* of objects which are used at table: linen, plates, glass and silver. In particular the utensils required to serve a special part of the meal are called services – e.g. coffee service, tea service, fruit service, etc.

In French the personnel of the restaurant who are responsible for serving meals are also called the *service.*

Service à la française and à la russe – The great *service à la française*, as it was practised during the First Empire and even more frequently during the Second, was only the continuation, in an already diminished form, of the ceremonial of the table observed under Louis XIV, which was called *le grand couvert*.

A meal served *à la française* was divided in three quite distinct parts, which were the *services*. The first service consisted of the series of dishes inscribed on the menu from soup to roast, including the *hors-d'œuvre*. The second comprised everything on the menu following the roast – cold second roasts and vegetables, continuing to the last item, the sweet dishes. The third service, completely independent of the kitchen, came from the pastrycook, which included decorated pieces, various pastries, *petits fours*, sweets, ices and fruit, all of which constituted the dessert.

The order of the menu was regulated by the number of *entrées*, that is to say the dishes of the second service had to be equivalent in number to those of the first service and never adding up to an odd number. But there were some deviations from the rule.

Thus in a menu in which there were 8 entrées, there had to be 2 soups, 2 large 'removes', 2 roasts, 2 cold pieces for the second roast, 2 side dishes and 2 vegetables (or 1 vegetable and a mixed salad).

Certain menus left by Carême (authentic menus for meals served principally at the table of the Prince Talleyrand) mention 32 and sometimes 48 entrées.

All the dishes for the first service were arranged on the table before the entry of the guests into the dining room, set on *réchauds* (hot plates) to keep them hot and covered with cloche lids.

This magnificence, this satisfaction in the display of riches, had its reverse side and presented various difficulties. It is easy to understand how overloaded were the tables if to these covered dishes are added the great table centres, baskets of flowers, candelabras full of candles, set places, glass, etc. But the greatest inconvenience of this service, almost inevitably, was that in spite of the *réchauds* the last dishes of the series, however great the dexterity of the carving and the speed of serving, had become somewhat chilled and no longer at their best. Moreover, it is equally evident that the guests could not try such a large number of dishes and must make a choice of one or two.

The service *à la russe*, popularized by Urbain Dubois round about 1860, is less rich, less representative and expressive of luxury, but it has the advantage of meeting in full the imperious demands of the table to 'serve hot'. The fundamental rule of this service is that everything should be organised in advance to this end. Here there is no more useless ornamentation, no more vulgar decoration; on the contrary, everything must be arranged so that the carving is done in the minimum time and the dish served to the guests before there is any change in its taste. By this method the guests help themselves – or have food served to them; but even though the carving is done in advance, the arrangement of the food on the dishes still demands correctness and an attractive appearance, especially when they are accompanied by a variety of different 'garnishes', which must always blend perfectly with the principal ingredient of the dish.

In service *à la russe* everything can be served piping hot if whoever is in charge of the kitchen can calculate from the time for which the meal is fixed the moment at which he must begin to dish up, working out for this purpose the time taken in cooking and the exact instant at which the food must be presented to the guests.

This rapid service, which proscribes all decoration or complicated arrangement of hot dishes, gives no scope to the culinary artist to exercise his talents. However, there is nothing in service *à la russe* to exclude cold dishes which are not spoilt by waiting, such as various *chauds-froids*, decorated shellfish in aspic, fancy *terrines*, glazed chickens, mousses in aspic, etc. In foodstuffs of this type the modern cuisine has made real progress in adopting a system of serving in bowls or deep dishes, so that there is no need for any supplementary preparation. Moulds have been almost completely abandoned.

In service *à la russe*, the guests at a party are divided into groups of 10 or 12 people, each group being served by one waiter, who is instructed in advance by the mistress of the house which guests to serve first and last. At a ceremonial meal it is customary to serve all the ladies first, beginning at the right of the master of the house. Dishes are offered on the left-hand side of the seated person; the plate is put down and taken away on the right. Wine is served on the right in the same order as the dishes, but the first drops are poured into the glass of the master of the house, so that small crumbs of cork do not fall into the glass of a guest.

On a less ceremonious occasion, where the master of the house carves and serves the food himself, the dishes, or the filled plates, should be passed round, beginning with the person on his right.

Service-berry

SERVICE-BERRY. ALISE – Fruit of various trees which should not be confused with sorb apple.

Wild service-tree as well as whitebeam tree, commonly called *shadbush*, grows freely in the mountainous regions of Europe.

The Fontainebleau wild service-tree is found chiefly in the wooded parts along the banks of the Seine.

The fruit of wild service-trees has a very pleasant acid taste.

SERVIETTE, TABLE NAPKIN – Piece of linen to protect the clothing and to wipe mouth and fingers at table.

Its use is much less ancient than that of tablecloth or towel. Up to the fifteenth century one wiped one's fingers on the tablecloth or on the *doublier*, a second cloth, covered in its turn with a *longière*, yet a third, intended for this use. Later came napkins or *touailles*, but they were few and generally attached to the walls. It was only in the sixteenth century that the use of the individual table napkin became general. At first it was kept over the left arm, then the fashion for starched ruffs made it necessary for them to be tied round the diners' necks.

At court, the king's napkin, wrapped up and placed in the *nef* (the golden vessel which contained his personal cruet and cutlery) was presented to him after his food had been tested, by the personage of the highest rank among those present, a prince of the blood royal or a high dignitary.

The *Maître d'hôtel* carried a rolled-up napkin over his left shoulder as an insignia of office.

SERVIETTE (À LA) – Describes a way of serving certain foodstuffs, notably truffles. Truffles *à la serviette* are not cooked in a table napkin but are served in one, folded into a kind of pocket.

These truffles are cooked in liqueur wine and set in a bowl or a silver dish which is placed in a folded napkin.

Truffles cooked in hot ashes in the old-fashioned style are

served *à la serviette*. Potatoes cooked in their jackets in the oven or in hot ashes are also served *à la serviette*.

Rice *à la serviette* is rice cooked for 15 minutes in salted water, drained, rinsed under the cold tap, and finished in a very low oven or special drying oven wrapped in a napkin. This recipe will be found under *Rice à l'indienne* in the section on RICE.

Folded napkins are used in serving certain dishes, placed under earthenware dishes and casseroles or under metal dishes, under vol-au-vents and patties, and under the glass bowls in which cold jellied foods, mixed salads, iced sweets, etc., are served.

SESAME – Annual herbaceous tropical and subtropical plant, known to the ancient Greeks and Hebrews, the Egyptians and Persians, where its fruit or seeds have been used from time immemorial as a food grain and as oil.

These seeds, chiefly used to make halva (Turkish sweet), are also used for cakes, cookies (biscuits), and confectionery.

Industrially they are used to make an oil for oleomargarine, cosmetics and soap.

SET. PRIS – Used in terms of cookery for liquids coagulated by heat (custards) or cold (ice creams and jellied preparations).

SETIER – Old French measure of capacity for grain equal to 156 litres or measure of capacity for liquids equal to 8 pints.

Demi-setier is a term used in Paris to mean a quarter of a litre.

SEYSSEL – Commune of the *département* of Ain where a well-known white wine of the same name is made.

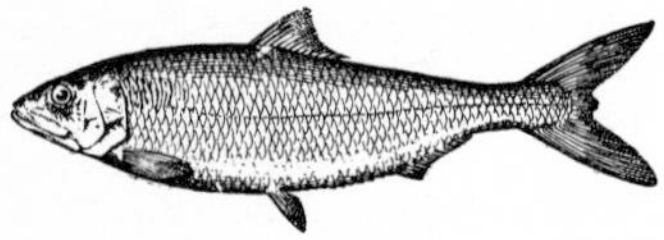

Shad

SHAD. ALOSE – Migratory fish bearing some similarity to herring, but bigger in size. In the spring, the shad go up the rivers to spawn in fresh water.

There are two distinct species of shad: the *Allis shad* which is the more valued, and the *Waite shad* which is smaller and coarser.

The flesh of the shad, although a little heavy, is very delicate. The female is to be preferred to the male, but the latter are prized for their milt (soft roe). If caught soon after spawning these fish have the tastiest of flesh but they have numerous bones.

In U.S.A. a species of shad exists which is called *Alosa menhaden*. Shad's roe is much prized in U.S.A.

Like all fish, the shad must be eaten very fresh. Its freshness can be recognized by its shiny skin and clear eye.

In addition to the recipes given below, all those given for the preparation of bass, cod, herring and mackerel can be applied to shad, whether cooked whole, sliced or in fillets.

Scrape off the scales and clean the fish. Wash it quickly and dry. Keep the soft and the hard roes to prepare them as described in special recipes.

Shad Claudine. ALOSE CLAUDINE – Cut the shad into slices of uniform thickness. Butter an ovenproof dish, line the bottom with chopped shallots cooked in white wine, uncooked mushroom and chopped parsley. Put the slices of fish on top of these.

Moisten with a few tablespoons white wine. Season, scatter a few small dabs of butter and bake in the oven, basting frequently. Pour in $1\frac{1}{2}$ dl. ($\frac{1}{4}$ pint, $\frac{2}{3}$ cup) thick fresh sour cream. Glaze in the oven.

Garnish with new potatoes tossed in butter.

Fried shad. ALOSE FRITE – Cut into slices, soak in milk, dredge with flour and deep-fry in sizzling fat.

Drain the shad and arrange on a napkin, garnish with fried parsley and quarters of lemon.

Fried shad à l'anglaise. ALOSE FRITE À L'ANGLAISE – Cut shad fillets into slices, dip them in egg and breadcrumbs and fry. Serve with *Maître d'hôtel butter* (see BUTTER, *Compound butters*).

Fried shad Orly. ALOSE FRITE ORLY – Marinate the fillets of shad in oil, lemon juice, chopped parsley, salt and pepper.

Dip in batter and fry in deep fat. Serve with *Tomato sauce* (see SAUCE).

Grilled shad (whole). ALOSE GRILLÉE (ENTIÈRE) – Clean a medium-sized shad, scrape off scales, wash and thoroughly wipe it. Make a few deep incisions in the fleshy part of the back, on both sides. Season with salt and pepper and marinate for an hour in oil, lemon juice, parsley, thyme and bay leaf.

Cook under a grill, on moderate heat, for 30 minutes.

Arrange on a long dish. Garnish the borders of the dish with half slices of lemon. Serve with *Maître d'hôtel butter* or with any other sauce suitable for grilled fish (see BUTTER, *Compound butters* or SAUCE).

Grilled shad (in slices). ALOSE GRILLÉE (EN TRANCHES) – Cut the shad into slices 2 cm ($\frac{3}{4}$ inch) thick, season, marinate in oil, lemon juice, parsley, thyme and bay leaf for 15 to 20 minutes. Grill for 12 to 15 minutes. Serve in the same way as whole shad.

Shad with mushrooms, à la bonne femme. ALOSE AUX CHAMPIGNONS, À LA BONNE FEMME – Proceed as described in the recipe for *Brill à la bonne femme*. (See BRILL).

Shad on plank (American cookery). ALOSE SUR PLANCHETTE – Fillet a medium-sized shad. Trim and marinate for an hour in oil, lemon juice, salt and pepper. Put it, skin side down, on a buttered plank. If a female shad is being cooked, place the roes in the middle of the fillets. Secure the whole with two heated, buttered skewers.

Cook in the oven or under the grill. From time to time baste the fish with melted butter.

Put the plank on a long platter. Withdraw the skewers. Garnish with quarters of lemon and little sprigs of parsley. Serve with *Maître d'hôtel butter*, and a cucumber salad.

The cooking of certain dishes on planks, both fish and meat, is very popular in U.S.A. For this purpose an oak board is used, 35 cm. (14 inches) long, 30 cm (12 inches) wide and 3 cm ($1\frac{1}{4}$ inches) thick. These boards have a ring at each corner.

Shad au plat. ALOSE AU PLAT – Choose a shad weighing about 700 to 800 g. ($1\frac{1}{2}$ to $1\frac{3}{4}$ lb.). Coat the inside with 50 g. (2 oz., $\frac{1}{4}$ cup) kneaded butter, 1 tablespoon chopped parsley, a teaspoon chopped shallots, salt and pepper.

Put in a buttered ovenproof dish. Season with salt and pepper, sprinkle with 1 dl. (6 tablespoons, scant $\frac{1}{2}$ cup) white wine or mushroom stock, scatter a few small dabs of butter on the fish, and cook in the oven at 190°C. (375°F., Gas Mark 5) from 25 to 30 minutes.

Baste frequently during cooking. If the pan juices boil down too quickly, add a few drops mushroom stock or water.

Serve in the dish in which the fish is cooked.

Stuffed shad à l'ancienne. ALOSE FARCIE À L'ANCIENNE – Proceed as described in the recipe for *Stuffed carp à l'ancienne* (see CARP).

Stuffed shad à la ménagère. ALOSE FARCIE À LA MÉNAGÈRE –

Fill the shad with a stuffing prepared with a mixture of breadcrumbs, butter, lightly fried chopped onion, chopped parsley and chervil, all well seasoned.

Cook the shad as described in the recipe for *Shad au plat*.

Stuffed shad à la mode de Cocherel. ALOSE ÉTOUFFÉE À LA MODE DE COCHEREL – Stuff a shad weighing 2 kg. (4½ lb.) with the following: Pound the flesh of whiting in a mortar, season with salt, pepper and grated nutmeg and add, whilst still pounding, (for 300 g., 11 oz., whiting) one egg white. Rub through a fine sieve. Add 3½ dl. (generous ½ pint, 1½ cups) fresh double cream, little by little. Add 2 good tablespoons (3 tablespoons) chopped, blanched and drained spring onions, and one tablespoon of chopped parsley, blending with a wooden spoon.

Wrap the shad in very thin bacon rashers, secure with string and thread on skewers. Grill under medium heat for about 30–45 minutes. A few minutes before removing the skewers, take off the rashers and brown the fish.

Arrange the shad in a large dish and surround with the following garnish, arranged in separate groups: small new potatoes cooked in butter, quarters of young artichokes, blanched, drained and stewed in butter, small glazed new onions.

Dilute the pan juices with a glass of dry white wine, add 4 dl. (¾ pint, scant 2 cups) cream, boil down, add butter, strain, and serve in a sauceboat.

Stuffed shad à la portugaise. ALOSE FARCIE À LA PORTUGAISE – Stuff the shad as described in the preceding recipe, but add chopped mushrooms, lightly fried in oil, and a crushed clove of garlic to the stuffing.

Cook in oil in a fireproof dish. When half cooked add 2½ dl. (scant ½ pint, generous cup) *Tomato fondue* (see TOMATO). Finish cooking everything together, basting frequently. A few moments before removing from the oven, sprinkle with breadcrumbs, add a dash of oil and brown lightly.

SHAD-BUSH. AMELANCHIER – Genus of service-tree covering several types of shrubs bearing edible fruit.

This fruit, which is slightly astringent and has a tart flavour, is better when slightly over-ripe. It is popular with children.

SHAGGY INK CAP. COPRIN – Edible mushroom characterized by black spores, from which its name derives. Prepared in the same way as mushrooms. It should only be eaten when very young, while the gills are still pink.

SHALLOT. ÉCHALOTE – Pot vegetable which, according to Candolle (French botanist 1806–1893) is merely a derivative of the onion, with a slight taste of garlic. Some people find the shallot more readily digestible than onion.

Shallot butter. BEURRE D'ÉCHALOTE – Pound finely in a mortar 125 g. (4½ oz.) shallot, blanched, cooled under running water, drained and squeezed. Add 125 g. (4½ oz., ½ cup) fresh butter. Mix. Rub through a cloth or hair sieve.

This composite butter is used for cold *hors-d'œuvre* preparations, especially *canapés*; also as an additional ingredient in some sauces, and is served with grills.

Essence of shallot. ESSENCE D'ÉCHALOTES – Bring 2 dl. (⅓ pint, scant cup) vinegar to the boil. Add 50 g. (2 oz., ½ cup) chopped shallot. Boil for 5 minutes. Strain through muslin. Essence of shallot can be made with white wine instead of vinegar.

SHARK. REQUIN – Name of a number of carnivorous fish whose size varies from a few cm (inches) to several metres (yards) long. The flesh of the shark, though very tough, is used as a foodstuff by the Lapps and by some negro peoples who are very partial to it.

Shark fins are much esteemed by the Chinese.

SHARPEN. AIGUISER – Term in pastry-making, used figuratively speaking, of a cream or liquid, which means sharpening up, making it acid by adding lemon juice or citric acid.

The word is also used in the sense of spicing a dish strongly.

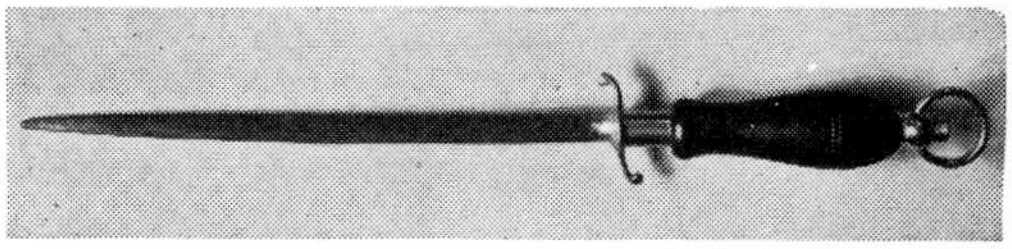

Sharpening steel
(Coutellerie André. Phot. Larousse)

SHARPENING STEEL. FUSIL – Steel instrument used by butchers and cooks to sharpen their knives.

SHCHI – Russian soup. See SOUPS AND BROTHS.

SHE-ASS. ÂNESSE – Female ass. Its milk in content comes nearer to human milk than that of any other domestic animal. (See MILK.)

Ass's milk was much valued in France for medicinal purposes since François I took it as a cure. All the courtesans hastened to imitate their king, and that began the vogue for ass's milk.

SHEATH. GAINE – Type of wooden case bound with copper, nickel or leather in which butchers and cooks used to carry their knives. Such sheaths are no longer much in use today.

SHEEP – See MUTTON, LAMB.

Sheeps' brains. CERVELLE DE MOUTON – All recipes for lambs' and calves' brains are suitable for sheeps' brains. (See OFFAL or VARIETY MEATS.)

Sheep's or lamb's kidney pilaf I. PILAF AUX ROGNONS DE MOUTON – Put the rice into a buttered border (ring) mould and turn out on to a dish. Cover the rice with halved sheep's kidneys, sautéed in butter and finished as described in the recipe for *Kidney sautéed in white wine* (see OFFAL or VARIETY MEATS).

Sheep's or lamb's kidney pilaf II. PILAF AUX ROGNONS DE MOUTON – Proceed as described in the recipe for *Shrimp pilaf II* (see SHRIMPS) garnishing the pilaf with sheep's or lamb's kidneys, sliced, fried in butter and finished as described in the recipe for *Kidneys sautéed in white wine* (see OFFAL or VARIETY MEATS).

Sheep's liver. FOIE DE MOUTON – This liver is rather inferior in flavour. It can be cooked in the same way as calves' liver (see OFFAL or VARIETY MEATS).

SHELL. ÉGRENER – To detach corn or other cereal grain from the stalk.

The French terms *écaler* and *écosser* also mean to shell. *Écaler* is applied to removing shells or husks of fruit and vegetables, shelling eggs and shellfish. *Écosser* means to remove the shell or pod from peas and beans.

SHELLFISH – See CRUSTACEANS.

SHEPHERD'S PURSE (Corn salad). BOURSE-À-PASTEUR – Common name for a plant which is also known as *bourse-à-berger* and *boursette* or *bourcette*, often found in shady places. It is sometimes used in salads. If picked at flowering time, its taste is not unlike that of watercress. It is also called *lamb's lettuce*.

SHERBETS. SORBETS – These ices, which in France are usually served between the main courses, take the place nowadays of the liqueurs which formerly used to be served in the middle of the meal and which in some parts of France were called *coup du milieu*, and in others *trou normand.*

Sherbets are made from fruit, liqueurs and heavy wines.

Here is the recipe most commonly used:

For 1 litre (quart) of sherbet. $\frac{1}{2}$ litre (scant pint, $2\frac{1}{4}$ cups) of any sweet wine, the juice of 2 lemons and 1 orange, syrup (1 cup sugar and 2 cups water boiled 5 minutes, strained and cooled).

All sherbet mixtures must be made from a light syrup. The saccharometer should never register more than 15° (see SUGAR). Sherbets are iced as follows:

Pour the mixture into a Churn freezer already embedded in ice. Set the mechanism working. Alternatively, pour the mixture into a container and place in a food freezer.. From time to time scrape the inside of the freezer to detach any sherbet sticking to the sides. This should not, however, be stirred into the rest of the mixture, as the sherbet, once it is frozen, should have a slightly gritty texture.

Stir in very gently some *Italian meringue* (a quarter of the volume of the sherbet, see MERINGUE) or, if preferred, the same amount of whipped cream, and whatever liqueur or dessert wine is desired.

Presentation of sherbets. The mixture should be removed from the freezer with a special conical scoop. Each portion should be set, point upwards, in a sherbet cup and sprinkled with the same liqueur or wine as that used in the mixture.

SHERRY. XÈRÈS, JEREZ – Name given in England to the Spanish wine Xeres.

Sherry is a fortified wine, produced principally from the Palomino grape in the countryside surrounding Jerez de la Frontiera in Spain. There is a great variety of sherries ranging, in colour, from a pale gold to dark brown and, in taste, from very dry to sweet. The dry sherries include *Fino, Vino de Pasto, Manzanilla* and a darker, older variety called *Amontillado.* Slightly sweeter varieties include those called *Oloroso* and *Amoroso* and among the dark and quite sweet varieties are *Cream, Brown* and *East India.*

Spanish sherries, unlike many of their imitators, are subject to a very special process of fermentation, ageing and blending which make their product unequalled in the world.

Sherry cobbler – Iced drink. Put into a glass, one-third filled with crushed ice, one tablespoon sugar and $1\frac{1}{2}$ tablespoons (2 tablespoons) of Curaçao. Fill up the glass with sherry. Add a slice of orange.

SHIN. JARRET – Part of the leg of an animal behind the knee-joint. It corresponds with the tibia-tarsal or radio-carpal bone in humans. The shin of veal is used in the preparation of stock. It can also be cut into sections and braised. (See VEAL, *Knuckle of veal.*)

SHIRR – To break eggs into a baking dish and cook them either in the oven or on top of the stove. (See EGGS.)

SHORTBREAD – Make pastry with 500 g. (18 oz., $4\frac{1}{2}$ cups) flour, 200 g. (7 oz., scant cup) sugar, 500 g. (18 oz., $2\frac{1}{4}$ cups) softened butter, 125 g. ($4\frac{1}{2}$ oz., 1 cup) ground almonds, 3 egg whites and powdered vanilla.

Press out on to a buttered baking sheet through a forcing bag fitted with a fluted pipe. Bake for 50 minutes in the oven at 140°C. (275°F., Gas Mark 1).

SHOULDER. ÉPAULE – The front leg of quadrupeds. Cuts from shoulder of beef are braised or used in hot-pots.

Shoulder of veal, usually boned and rolled into a long, tight bundle, is braised, pot-roasted or roasted. It is also used in sautés and *ragoûts.*

Shoulder of mutton and lamb, boned or whole, is cooked in the same way as the legs. It is also used in stews.

The shoulder of different types of venison is cooked in the same way as haunch of venison, but is more commonly used in *civets.*

SHOVELLER – See DUCK, *Wild duck.*

SHREDDER AND SLICER. MANDOLINE – A kind of plane, sometimes fluted, used for shredding or slicing vegetables, especially potatoes.

It is with an implement of this type that vegetables are shredded into matchsticks or straws or sliced very thin, as for potato crisps.

SHRIKE. PIE-GRIÈCHE – Popular name for small perching bird of the family *Laniidae.* It can be prepared in any way suitable for lark.

Sword shrimps
(*Kollar*)

SHRIMPS. CREVETTES – Little shellfish used for *hors-d'œuvre* and garnishes.

The two principal European types are 1. the *Sword shrimp* (*crevette rose*), the head of which is armed with a long-toothed beak. It becomes rosy when cooked and the flesh is white and firm; 2. the *Common shrimp (crevette grise)* which is smaller, with a smooth short beak. It takes on a pinkish-grey colour when cooked. The flesh, which is rather limp, is less appreciated than that of the sword-shrimp.

Cooking of shrimps. Put the shrimps alive into boiling salted water. Do not add seasoning. When possible cook the shrimps in sea water which has been strained through muslin or through a fine sieve.

Cooked in this way and cooled, the shrimps are served as an *hors-d'œuvre.*

Shrimps in U.S.A. vary from the large size found off the southern shores, which average a dozen to 450 g. (pound), to the tiny ones, averaging 40 to 450 g. (pound). These small ones fished off the Alaskan and northern New England shores are less popular, although of a good flavour.

Shrimp aspic. ASPIC DE CREVETTES – Arrange peeled cooked shrimps in layers in a mould lined with clear aspic jelly, leaving the centre of the mould free. Fill the centre with a shrimp mousse made with the shrimp peelings or with *Shrimp mousse* described below.

Cover completely with aspic jelly which is almost set. Chill on ice or in the refrigerator before turning out.

Shrimp butter – See BUTTER, *Compound butters.*

Shrimp canapés – See HORS-D'ŒUVRE, *Cold hors-d'œuvre.*

Shrimp coquilles. COQUILLES DE CREVETTES – Made with peeled shrimps and *Béchamel sauce* (see SAUCE), to which shrimp butter is added.

Fried shrimps. CREVETTES FRITES – Cook the shrimps in boiling oil. Drain, and season with fine salt. Garnish with fried parsley.

Cold shrimp mousse. MOUSSE FROIDE DE CREVETTES – Cook the shrimps in a *mirepoix* in the same way as crayfish. (q.v.). Peel some of the shrimps in order to have enough tails with which to decorate the mould. Pound the rest with the *mirepoix* in which they were cooked. Pass the mixture through a fine sieve.

Add to the purée a quarter of its volume of *Velouté sauce* (see SAUCE) based on fish stock which has been boiled down. For every 500 g. (18 oz., 2 cups) purée, add 2 dl. ($\frac{1}{3}$ pint, scant cup) fish aspic. Add $2\frac{1}{2}$ dl. (scant $\frac{1}{2}$ pint, generous cup) cream, which has been whipped not too stiff.

Put the mousse in a mould lined with aspic and decorated with the shrimp tails, and if desired with some truffle decoration. Cover with aspic. Allow to get thoroughly cold. Turn out and arrange in a bowl.

Shrimp pilaf I. PILAF DE CREVETTES – Cook the rice and add to it 125 g. ($4\frac{1}{2}$ oz.) peeled shrimps. Mix carefully so as not to damage the rice grains.

Shrimp pilaf II. PILAF DE CREVETTES – Cook the rice and line a buttered mould with it.

Add a *ragoût* of peeled shrimps bound with *Shrimp sauce II* (see SAUCE). Cover with the rest of the rice, pressing lightly with the back of a spoon to pack the rice properly. Put in the oven for a few moments. Turn out on to a dish and surround with a ring of shrimp sauce.

Shrimp salad. SALADE DE CREVETTES – Season peeled shrimps with *vinaigrette* or mayonnaise. Decorate with quarters of hard-boiled eggs and lettuce hearts.

Shrimp salad à la dieppoise – See SALAD.

Shrimp soup: coulis, cream or bisque. POTAGES AUX CREVETTES: COULIS, CRÈME OU BISQUE – Prepare with shrimps cooked in a *mirepoix* like the soups of a similar nature prepared with crayfish. (See SOUPS AND BROTHS, *Purée of shrimp soup.*)

SILK-COTTON TREE. FROMAGER – Tree, native to tropical Africa. Its trunk is of white wood, somewhat reminiscent of cheese in appearance. For this reason, it is called *'fromager'* in French. Oil is extracted from its fruit.

SILKWORMS (Chinese cookery). VERS À SOIE – This rather unusual foodstuff was very well thought of in the 'Celestial Empire', if we are to believe the account of a French missionary in China, Father Favaud:

'It is some centuries', he wrote, 'since our farmers in the Midi took up the production of silkworms, but I know they have never dreamed of using any of them for nourishment. In China it is not the same thing at all. During the long stay I have made in that country, I have often seen people eat silkworm chrysalids, and I have eaten them myself. I can state that they constitute an excellent stomachic, strengthening and refreshing at the same time, which delicate persons often use with successful results.

'The cocoons having been unwound, a certain quantity of the chrysalids are gilled in the pan so that the watery part runs right off. Their outer covering comes off, and they are presented in the form of small yellow objects, rather like carp roes.

'These are fried in butter, fat or oil, and sprinkled with stock (chicken stock is the best).

'When they have boiled for five minutes they are crushed with a wooden spoon, and the whole mass is carefully stirred so that nothing is left in the bottom of the vessel. Some egg yolks are beaten, in the proportion of 3 to every 100 chrysalids, and poured over, and in this way a beautiful cream, golden yellow and of an exquisite flavour, is obtained.

'Thus this foodstuff was prepared for the mandarins and the wealthy. As for the poor, after having grilled the chrysalids and removed their outer covering, they fried the rest in butter or fat and seasoned them with a little salt, pepper or vinegar; or even ate them just as they were, with rice, content simply to have removed their outer covering.'

SILLERY – Renowned Champagne wine harvested in the country around the commune of Sillery in the *département* of the Marne.

SILVER. ARGENTERIE DE TABLE – This term describes all the utensils in silver or silver-plated metal used at table.

More specifically this applies to individual pieces of silver which go in to make up what is called the 'cover', (U.S.A. 'place setting'), i.e. spoon, fork and knife, when the latter has a silver or silver-plated handle. (See FORK, SPOON.)

Table silver also includes other articles which in the olden days were called silver plate, articles of various shapes, such as round or oval dishes, large or small bowls, soup tureens, sauceboats, pie dishes, etc.

Among table silverware are also included decorative silver and silver-plate pieces, such as salvers, fruit baskets, pedestal dishes, etc.

SILVER BIRCH. BOULEAU BLANC – In the spring this tree, which grows in northern countries, contains a great deal of sour-sweet sap which, when fresh, makes a very pleasant drink.

SILVERSIDE or ATHERINE. PRÊTRE – Small regional sea fish of France about the size of a smelt, 10 to 18 cm. (4 to 7 inches) long, showing on its sides a silvery mark like a star. Its flesh is quite delicate.

SIMAROUBA – Tree, native to Guiana, whose bark is used for a bitter tonic.

SIMMER. MIJOTER – To cook gently over a very low flame.

SIMMERING. FRÉMISSEMENT – The slight quivering of a liquid just before it comes to the boil. When poaching, the liquid should be kept in this state all the time.

Some foods, such as *pot-au-feu*, are cooked entirely by simmering.

SINGEING. FLAMBAGE – Process of rotating poultry and winged game, etc. over a spirit lamp or gas flame to burn off feathers and hair.

SINGER – French culinary term of unknown origin meaning to sprinkle with flour a *ragoût* or other preparation in order to thicken the sauce.

SINK. ÉVIER – The domestic equivalent of the professional chef's small washing-up sink. It is used for washing dishes, for washing vegetables and occasionally for washing small articles of cloth. This multiplicity of purpose requires that it be thoroughly cleaned after use. Sinks are made of ceramic, stone, enamelled cast-iron, plastic, or, most commonly nowadays, of stainless steel. They are single or double, round or rectangular, of varying depths and often equipped with a draining board that doubles up as a working surface. Sinks are supplied with hot and cold water. The evacuation of the water is done by means of a plug. Some sinks are equipped with a waste disposal unit.

SIPHON – Carafe of thick glass, often encased in wicker or metal, holding water that has been made effervescent with carbonic gas under pressure. Siphons are closed with a metal top provided with a lever which allows the liquid to escape. Some siphons allow Seltzer-water to be made with the aid of capsules called sparklets.

Water jug
(early seventeenth century)

Wine jug
(early seventeenth century)

Sugar caster
(late seventeenth century)

Ewer
(early eighteenth century)

Sugar basin
(Picasso, 1740)

Sauceboat
(Depris, 1723)

Teapot
(Germain, 1750)

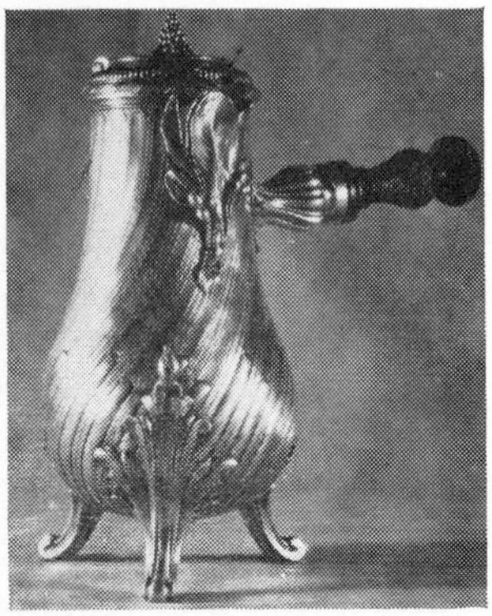
Coffee pot
(Germain, 1750)

Tray
(Germain, 1756)

Teapot
(Germain, late eighteenth century)

Tureen
(Joubert, 1761)

Cooler for glasses
(1790)

TABLE SILVER

Plate and dishes (Daurat)

Soup tureen (Daurat)

Coffee and tea service (Christofle)

Tea service in silver and ebony (Daurat)

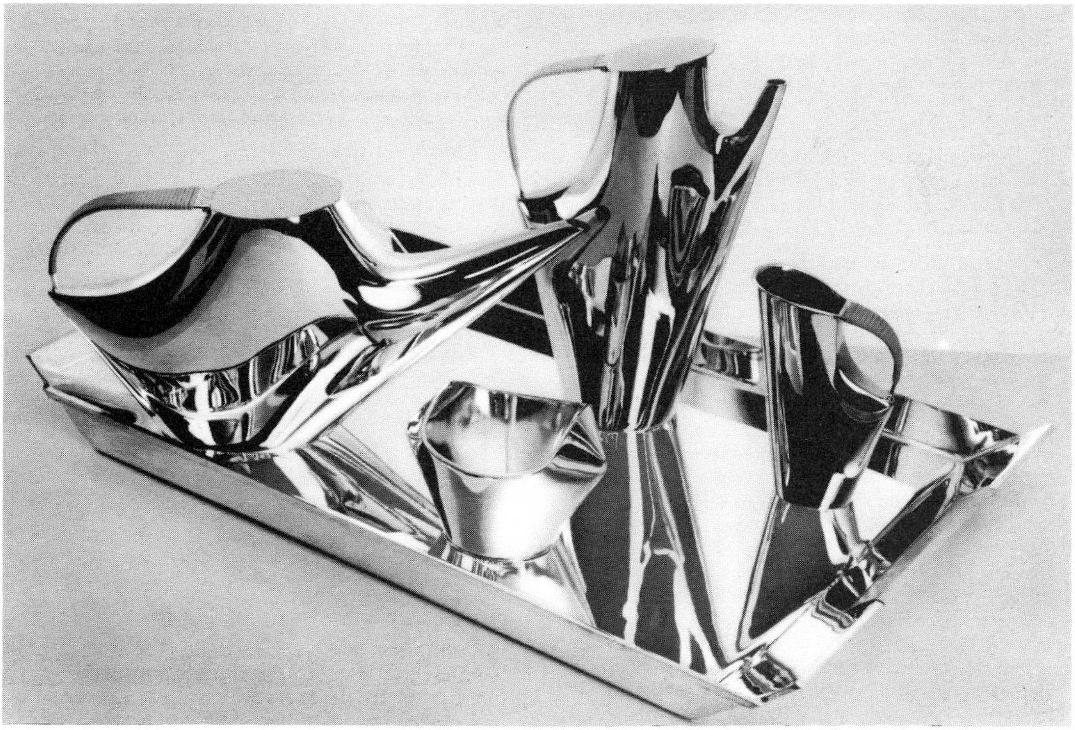

Modern silverware "Como" (Christofle) (*Kollar*)

MODERN SILVERWARE

Modern siphons (*La Carpe. Phot. Nicolas*)

SIRLOIN. ALOYAU – This joint includes the lumbar region, starting from the last rib down to and including the top part of the pelvic basin (sacrum). The different parts are: fillet, sirloin and rump steak.

Sirloin, whole or divided transversally into pieces of varying weight, is roasted or braised.

When served as a roast, it is treated as *contrefilet* or ribs of beef.

All recipes for the preparation of sirloin, whole, or cut into pieces, will be found under BEEF.

Tip of sirloin. BAVETTE – The lateral abdominal wall of the ox which gives a second grade of meat suitable for *pot-au-feu* and *ragoûts*. This cut also makes tasty steaks. (See BEEF.)

SKATE or RAY, RAIE – Name of flat scaleless fish, flattened vertically, characterised by the development of pectoral fins in the form of wings, with a long and relatively thick tail.

The skin of the skate is covered with a viscous coating which continues to re-form itself for 10 hours after death, so that it is possible by wiping the fish with a cloth and observing whether or not the coating re-forms to judge how fresh it is. The skate is the only fish which gains from being slightly 'high', though this should not be allowed to get to the point where the smell alters.

The flesh of the skate is less digestible than that of white fish; the liver is sought after by some connoisseurs.

In England, Belgium and Holland the skate is found in the shops already skinned.

To cook skate. Cut up the skate in chunks or divide it into the two wings. Put the pieces into a sauté pan and cover with water with 2 dl. ($\frac{1}{3}$ pint, scant cup) wine vinegar to each litre (quart) of water seasoned with salt. Bring to the boil, skim, reduce heat and gently poach the fish.

Drain. Remove the skin from both sides. Serve according to recipe.

Skate au beurre noir. RAIE AU BEURRE NOIR – Proceed with skate cooked in *court-bouillon*, drained and set on a serving dish the same as *Salt cod with brown butter* (see COD).

Skate au beurre noisette. RAIE AU BEURRE NOISETTE – Prepared like *Salt cod with noisette butter* (see COD), using skate cooked in *court-bouillon*.

Boiled skate with various sauces. RAIE BOUILLIE, AVEC SAUCES DIVERSES – Cook the skate in *court-bouillon*. Drain. Garnish with fresh parsley. Serve with it one of the sauces suitable for boiled fish, (*Bâtarde sauce, Cream sauce, Hollandaise sauce, etc.*, see SAUCE).

Fried skate. RAIE FRITE – Skin small skate. Cut in chunks, or, if they are very small, leave them whole. Soak in cold, boiled milk. Drain and flour them lightly. Fry in deep smoking fat. Drain, dry, season with salt, and garnish with fried parsley and lemon.

Skate au gratin. FAIE AU GRATIN – Prepared with the wings of small skates. Proceed in the same way as for *Sole au gratin* (see SOLE.)

Jellied skate. RAIE À LA GELÉE – Poach the wings of skate in fish stock with white wine. Let them cool in this liquor. Drain and set on a serving dish. Make aspic jelly from the cooking liquor, clarify it and pour over the skate. (See JELLY.)

Skate liver. FOIE DE RAIE – The liver of skate is very tasty. It is poached with the skate and served with it.

It can also be made into fritters. Poach pieces of skate liver, steep in oil, lemon juice and parsley, dip in butter, and deep-fry in boiling fat.

Skate liver can be served in shells, scooped-out breadcrust, or cooked in tarts and pâtes.

Skate liver croûtes. CROÛTE AU FOIE DE RAIE – Fill hollow crusts of fried bread with skate liver, cooked in a *court-bouillon* and sliced. Coat with *Mornay sauce* (see SAUCE), cover with grated cheese, sprinkle with melted butter and brown.

Skate liver fritters. BEIGNETS DE FOIE DE RAIE – Poach skate liver in white wine. Allow to cool. Cut into slices and marinate in oil, lemon juice, chopped parsley, salt and pepper. Dip in light batter and fry in smoking fat. Drain, season with salt, and garnish with fried parsley and lemon.

Skate à la meunière. RAIE À LA MEUNIÈRE – Use the wings of small skates in the same way as for *Sole à la meunière* (see SOLE).

SKEWER. BROCHETTE – Small spit, made of silver or other metal and sometimes of wood, on which various substances can be threaded before being grilled or fried.

Preparations cooked on skewers are called *brochettes* in French. Thus we have: *Brochette of chicken livers, Brochette of lamb's sweetbreads, Brochette of kidneys*, etc.

Whole skate and wing of skate

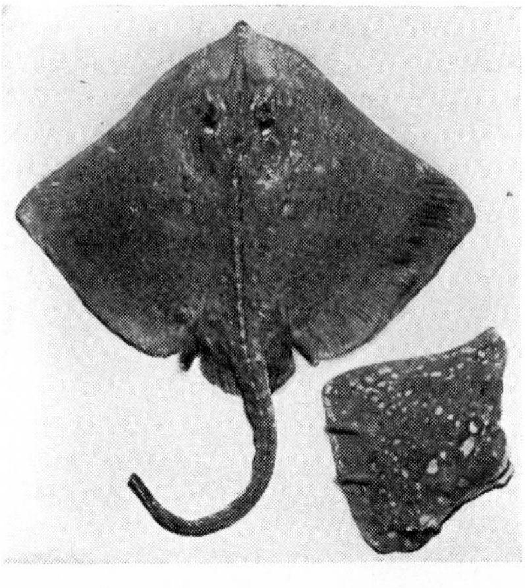

(See OFFAL or VARIETY MEATS, *Calf's kidneys on skewers*; CHICKEN, *Chicken brochettes*.)

SKIM. ÉCRÉMER, ÉCUMER, DÉPOUILLER – To skim cream from milk is expressed in French by the word *écrémer*. To remove with a spoon or skimmer the scum which rises to the surface of a stock, sauce or *ragoût* is expressed by the words *écumer* or *dépouiller*.

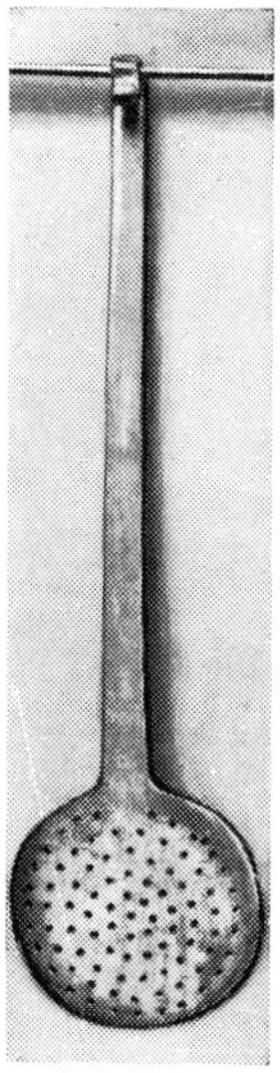

Skimmer (*Dehillerin. Phot. Larousse*)

SKIMMER. ÉCUMOIRE – Flat perforated spoon, used for skimming.

SKIN. PEAU – The skin forms one-fifth of butcher's meat and is not normally used for food (except for the oxtail and muzzle). The skin of sucking pig, of poultry and of winged game is eaten. The skin of some aquatic birds is oily and has an unpleasant taste; it should, therefore, be taken off.

The skin of fruit contains valuable ferments and vitamins, but, being exposed to impurities, it should be peeled or carefully washed.

SKINNING. DÉPOUILLER – To remove the skin from ground game, e.g. skinning a hare (or rabbit).

Eels and conger eels are also said to be skinned when they are stripped for cooking.

SKIRRET. GIROLE, GIROLLE – Popular name for the mushroom which is known also as *chanterelle*. (See MUSHROOMS.)

SLAUGHTER. ABATAGE – The methods of killing the animals have a considerable influence on the appearance and the keeping quality of meat. They vary, however, according to the type of establishment and the kind of animal slaughtered.

In France, slaughtering, which should be preceded by an ante-mortem inspection of the livestock animal on the hoof, should be carried out only after a period of rest of several days, allowing the animals to recover from fatigue and ending with a day of complete fasting. These different rules are rarely complied with. The animals which are bled before being stunned give a meat of better quality and a higher keeping quality. The cutting of the medulla will avoid the suffering of

Slaughtering an ox in Egyptian times

a prolonged agony. Immediately after slaughter, the animals must at once be viscerated and undergo (this time compulsory) post-mortem inspection by a qualified inspector, at least in the slaughter houses of large towns.

In Great Britain, the law says that slaughtering can be carried out after 48 hours of resting and 24 hours of complete fasting. Regulations demand that all animals must be stunned humanely, the only exception being made in the case of kosher or Mohammedan butchers where the severing of the medulla is not recommended. Both ante- and post-mortem inspections are compulsory.

In the U.S.A., a high percentage of the slaughtering is centralised in a few very large slaughtering and packing houses, over which rigid control is exercised by the Department of Agriculture through ante- and post-mortem inspection of all animals. Every animal is stunned before butchering. Each state is responsible by law for local slaughter houses under the Department of Health.

SLAUGHTER HOUSE. ABATTOIR – Establishment where butchers kill animals for the market.

There are model slaughter houses, like those of Chicago. In large cities, animals cannot be slaughtered except in public slaughter houses which provide for reliable ante- and post-mortem inspection, which is impossible in the privately owned slaughter houses, of which there are still too many in the country.

A modern slaughter house consists of:

A common slaughter hall, well lit, well aired, well equipped for the washing and transport of meat, in which each butcher is given sufficient floor space to perform his work.

A refrigerator, which may or may not be preceded by a cold room, used as a salesroom.

Lairages and pens for the livestock, where the animals arrive by rail and from where they have only a short walk to the main slaughter hall.

A tripe shop, with premises for washing and cleaning the viscera.

An inspection service with a well-equipped laboratory.

An industrial slaughter house consists of a building of several storeys. The animals are slaughtered on the top floor, to which they have access on foot; from there the carcase-meat on the one hand, and the by-products (blood, tallow, hide and various offals and scraps) on the other, are taken down to departments on lower floors by means of chutes on rails.

In these slaughter houses the workers each specialise in one type of work. A carcase passes through the hands of some fifty specialists. This contributes to increase of output since it

Slaughter house La Villette: de-boning the animals (*Phot. X*)

is possible to slaughter up to 60 oxen an hour, thus lowering the manufacturing cost considerably. Inspection is provided and all the work is done in hygienic conditions.

The carcases are scrubbed, washed in hot water at 18°C. (65°F.), from which they are sent to the refrigerator after having passed from 16 to 24 hours in pre-refrigeration in the hanging rooms.

These industrial slaughter houses are generally equipped with various installations which enable work to go on with processing and canning of meat.

SLEEVE-FISH. ENCORNET – Common name of the calamary. (q.v.).

SLIMNESS. MAIGREUR – Slimness, which is compatible with perfect health, should not be confused with emaciation. Some persons remain thin and do not put on weight, even if they eat a lot.

SLIVER. LÈCHE – Thin slice of bread or meat.

SLOE. PRUNELLE – Fruit of the sloe tree, also called the *blackthorn*, a tree found all over Europe.

The sloe, a tiny plum, dark blue in colour, is scarcely eatable, its flesh being very sour and sharp tasting.

In the Haute-Saône, there is a cultivated sloe which is used mainly in distilling, and for making jams. At Angers a much esteemed liqueur is made from sloes.

Sloes boiled in red wine have a very pleasant flavour and are a very effective cure for dysentery. Sloes may also be used to make vinegar and wine.

SMALLAGE. ACHE DES MARAIS – Wild plant (wild celery) which has been replaced in cookery by cultivated celery. It was used in cookery by the Romans.

This plant can be used as a salad.

SMALL FILLETS. PETITS FILETS – Term applied to little round slices of fillet of beef taken from the top or bottom end of the fillet or tenderloin.

Small fillets are cut into pieces weighing from 100 to 125 g. (4 to 4½ oz.). They are grilled or fried in butter and, like beef *Tournedos* (see BEEF), can be served with various garnishes and sauces.

SMELL. ODORAT – The sense of smell is active not only before a meal is taken, but also during the meal. The aroma released by fragrant parts of the food is inhaled and penetrates into the back-throat and nasal chambers.

It has been proved by experience that smell brings about the loosening of gastric secretion. In fact a strong secretion of gastric juices can be brought about by simply inhaling fragrant steam, provided it comes from a nourishing substance such as meat bouillon. It can therefore be said that the smell of well cooked food aids the digestion.

SMELT. ÉPERLAN – This fish, says Rondelet, is so called (*éperlan* – pearly fish) 'for its beautiful, pure whiteness, comparable with that of the pearl'. The smelt is one of the most delicate of all freshwater fish. It is classed as a freshwater fish although it lives in the sea, because, like a good many other migratory fish, it spawns in fresh water. Nevertheless, smelts seldom run up river beyond the tide-line. Thus in the Seine, where this fish is now much less common than it used to be, smelts are seldom found beyond the Martet weir near Elbeuf. The greatest abundance of smelts is to be found near Caudebec, and it is for this reason that there are three smelts on the civic arms of this French town. Smelts are also fairly plentiful around La Mailleraye and Villequier.

These tiny fish usually migrate up river between February 20th and March 15th and this is also the best season for catching them. They are, however, to be found in these waters all the year round, though less abundantly than during the spring run.

Freshly caught smelts have a strong smell, similar to that of the violet. This little fish is most delicate in flavour and fried smelts are regarded as one of the finest of all fish dishes.

Method of preparation. Gut and wash the smelts, leaving them in water for as short a time as possible. Dry them and proceed according to the recipe.

Smelts à l'anglaise. ÉPERLANS À L'ANGLAISE – Slit the smelts along the back. Open out gently. Dip in egg and breadcrumbs and fry in clarified butter.

To serve, pour over them half-melted *Maître d'hôtel butter* (see BUTTER, *Compound butters*).

Smelts en escabèche. ÉPERLANS EN ESCABÈCHE – See HORS-D'ŒUVRE, *Cold hors-d'œuvre, Escabèche of various fishes.*

Fried smelts. ÉPERLANS FRITS – Dip the smelts in salted milk and flour. Shake off excess flour and plunge into deep hot fat. Drain. Dry in a cloth. Season with very dry table salt. Arrange in a clump with fried parsley and lemon.

Fried smelts, skewered. ÉPERLANS FRITS EN BROCHETTES – Impale the smelts on metal skewers, 6 to each skewer, and deep-fry as indicated in the previous recipe.

Smelts au gratin. ÉPERLANS AU GRATIN – Arrange the smelts in a long ovenware dish, buttered and lined with chopped shallots which have been cooked in white wine till the liquid is reduced to a coating in the pan. Put a small cooked mushroom on top of each smelt. Surround with finely sliced mushrooms. Mask with *Mornay sauce* (see SAUCE). Sprinkle with breadcrumbs. Pour on melted butter. Cook in the oven and brown.

Grilled smelts. ÉPERLANS GRILLÉS – Slit the smelts along the back. Take out the bone. Season and flour. Baste with melted butter and grill.

Garnish with fresh parsley and slices of lemon. Serve with *Maître d'hôtel butter* (see BUTTER, *Compound butters*) or some other sauce suitable for grilled fish.

Grilled smelts à l'anglaise. ÉPERLANS GRILLÉS À L'ANGLAISE – Clean the smelts. Slit them lengthwise along the back and take out the bone. Open them out gently.

Pour melted butter over them. Season with salt and cayenne pepper and dust with fresh breadcrumbs. Grill fairly slowly. Turn the smelts over once during cooking, and serve with half-melted *Maître d'hôtel butter* (see BUTTER, *Compound butters*).

It may seem difficult to grill such a small fish as the smelt. It is simple enough provided that the grill pan and grid are perfectly clean and well greased with oil. Some hardware stores sell grills especially designed for smelts.

Cold marinade of smelts. ÉPERLANS MARINÉS – See HORS-D'ŒUVRE, *Cold hors-d'œuvre, Smelts in marinade.*

Smelts on skewers. BROCHETTES D'ÉPERLANS – Clean the smelts and thread them through the eyes on metal skewers, allowing 8 to 10 small smelts per skewer. Soak in milk. Dredge lightly with flour. Deep-fry in sizzling fat.

Drain, dry on a cloth and sprinkle with fine very dry salt. Garnish with fried parsley and halves of lemon.

SMOKING. FUMAGE – Preserving process used especially for meat and fish. Woodsmoke is generally used because of its drying and sterilising properties. (See PRESERVATION OF FOOD.)

Sides of beef, especially rib and brisket, hams and other cuts of pork, sausages, poultry (goose in particular) and certain fish (herrings, salmon, eels, etc.), and some shellfish, can all be smoked.

Before smoking, all meat must be soaked in pickling brine. After it has been thoroughly wiped and dried, it is hung in a large chimney, not too near the fire, so that it may be dried right through. If the heat were too great, it would seal the meat and prevent the smoke from penetrating. For the same reason, the meat is very lightly smoked to begin with.

Some fish, such as herrings, are smoked without previous soaking. To get a suitable smoke, hardwood is used (oak, hornbeam), rather than wood of a resinous type. Green wood gives out more smoke than dry wood. Aromatic wood is often added to give an extra fragrance to the smoke, such as juniper with its berries, rosemary, laurel. Sometimes, though this is less common, spices are also added (liquorice, cloves, etc.).

Change the position of the smoking meat from time to time, so that all parts may be thoroughly impregnated. The length of time needed to complete the process varies with the size of the meat or fish. Smoking can be speeded up by injecting pickling brine flavoured with spices into the meat.

Various types of smoking chambers are used in the smoking of foodstuffs. Some are smoking boxes which can be used in household kitchens. Others, used in large pork-butchers' establishments, are elaborately constructed. They consist of several chambers through which the smoke, coming from a wood fire in the basement or on the ground floor of the building, passes, escaping through an outlet in the ceiling of the last chamber.

SNAIL. ESCARGOT – Common name for a land gastropod mollusc. It was highly prized as food as far back as Roman times. The art of fattening snails is said to have been discovered by a Roman named Fulvius Lupinus.

In France, the vineyard snail is the most popular. As there are not enough of these to meet all demands another variety, the *petit-gris* of southern France is also used.

To avoid the risk of poisoning, snails must be deprived of food for some time before they are eaten, for they may have fed on plants harmless to themselves but poisonous to humans. Furthermore, it is advisable only to eat snails which have sealed themselves into their shells to hibernate.

From a nutritional point of view, snails' flesh has little food

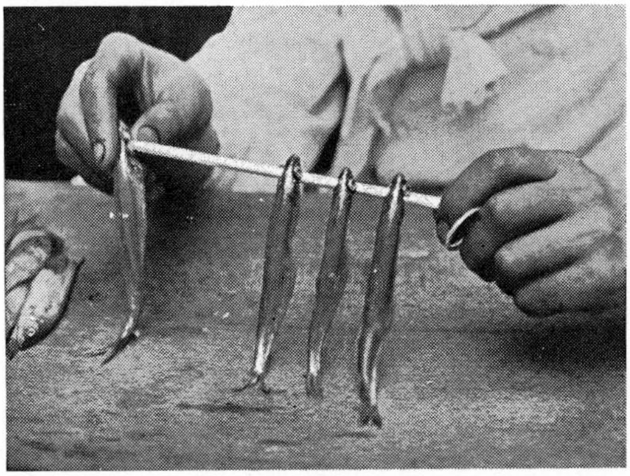

Skewering smelts (*Larousse*)

Fried smelts (*Debillot. Phot. Larousse*)

Vineyard snail

value and is rather indigestible. However, it does contain a large quantity of both Vitamin C and mineral salts (calcium, magnesium, etc.).

Snails à l'arlésienne. ESCARGOTS À L'ARLÉSIENNE – 'Warm a little diced pork in a saucepan. Sprinkle with flour and moisten with a bottle of white wine. Add the snails, prepared in advance as follows:

'Take medium-sized snails, and soak them in tepid water. Next, blanch them with a handful of salt.

'Take them out of their shells and drain. Put them in the saucepan with a few cloves of garlic and plenty of herbs. Bring to the boil and leave to simmer slowly. When they are ready, drain them and put them back in their shells. Add a glass of Madeira and a pinch of cayenne pepper. Put the snails in the sauce and stir. Sprinkle with a little chopped parsley and the juice of a lemon.' (A. Hélie's recipe.)

Snails à la bourguignonne. ESCARGOTS À LA BOURGUIGNONNE – Scrape away the chalky substance sealing the shells. Wash the snails in several waters and soak them for 2 hours with coarse salt, vinegar and a pinch of flour. Wash them again in plenty of water and blanch them for 5 minutes in boiling water. Drain and cool under running water. Take the snails out of their shells. Remove the black part at the end of the tail known as the cloaca.

Put the snails in a saucepan. Moisten with equal parts of white wine and clear broth. The liquid should just cover the snails. Add carrots, onions, shallots and a large *bouquet garni*. Season with 8 g. (1 teaspoon) salt to every litre (quart) of stock. Simmer for 3 to 4 hours. Leave to cool in the stock.

Boil the empty shells for 30 minutes in water with soda crystals added. Drain them, wash in cold water and dry. Put inside each shell a piece of butter *à la bourguignonne*, about the size of a hazelnut. Put the snails in the shells and seal with *Butter for snails, à la bourguignonne* (see BUTTER, *Compound butters*).

Put the filled shells in a dish with a little water at the bottom or in a snail dish. Sprinkle with fresh breadcrumbs. Warm in a hot oven and serve.

Snail broth. BOUILLON D'ESCARGOTS – Soak 24 snails thoroughly as indicated in the recipe for *Snails à la bourguignonne*. Break the shells and remove the snails. (Do not dip them in boiling water as this will wash away their natural gelatine.) Put them in a saucepan and moisten with 3 litres ($5\frac{1}{4}$ pints, $6\frac{1}{2}$ pints) water. Add 1 or 2 lettuces, a handful of purslane leaves and a little salt. (A piece of calf's head can also be added.) Skim. As soon as the broth is boiling steadily, lower the heat and simmer slowly for 3 hours. Add to the broth 30 g. (1 oz.) gum arabic dissolved in a glass of tepid water. Strain through muslin.

Snail dish or escargotière (*Dehillerin. Phot. Larousse*)

Snails à la chablisienne. ESCARGOTS À LA CHABLISIENNE – Proceed as indicated for *Snails à la bourguignonne*, pouring into each shell a few drops white Chablis wine cooked with chopped shallot and parsley, enriched with meat essence and seasoned.

Put the snails back in the shells and seal with *Butter for snails, à la bourguignonne* (see BUTTER, *Compound butters*).

Snails Comtesse Riguidi. ESCARGOTS COMTESSE RIGUIDI – During the season when snails are unobtainable, said Grimod de la Reynière, cooks sometimes amuse themselves by cheating our palates by a not unpleasant imitation. A very fine stuffing is made either of game or fish, with fillets of anchovy, nutmeg, fine spices, *fines herbes*, bound with egg yolks. Snail shells are thoroughly washed and warmed. Each one is filled with the stuffing and served piping hot.

Here is another recipe for *Mock snails Comtesse Riguidi*. 'Put into large well washed snail shells little balls of lambs' sweetbread tossed in butter. Fill up the shell with a chicken cream stuffing and chopped truffles mixed together. Put the mock snails in an ovenware dish or a special snail dish. Sprinkle with breadcrumbs and cook for a few minutes in the oven.'

Special snail pincers and fork (*Larousse*)

A popular variant of this delicate dish consists in filling the snail shells with cocks' kidneys cooked in white wine.

Snails à la poulette. ESCARGOTS À LA POULETTE – Soak the snails in a pan of boiling water, with a pinch of salt and some ashes. Boil for 5 minutes, take out the snails and put them in cold water. Wash them with great care. Drain. Boil in a *court-bouillon* with salt, pepper, thyme, bay leaves and parsley for $1\frac{1}{2}$ hours. Take the snails out of the *court-bouillon* and drain. Brown some chopped onions. Moisten with equal parts of white wine and water. When the liquid begins to boil, add a little *Allemande sauce* (see SAUCE). Put in the snails. Leave them for 5 to 7 minutes. Before serving, blend in a little best quality butter, egg yolks and a little lemon juice. Add more salt and pepper.

SNIPE. BÉCASSINE – Migratory bird bearing great resemblance to the woodcock, but only about half the size of the latter.

It can be prepared in any way suitable for woodcock, but the best method is roasting. In U.S.A. the *Wilson's snipe* or *American snipe* is almost identical.

Casserole of snipe. BÉCASSINES EN CASSEROLE – Truss the

Snipe

snipe, draw the heads round and run the beaks through the legs. Cover each with a rasher of fat bacon. Put them into a metal or earthenware casserole in which some butter has been heated. Season, and baste with butter. Cook in a hot oven for about 12 minutes. Put each bird on a small croûton fried in butter. Sprinkle with a tablespoon brandy and 2 or 3 tablespoons (3 or 4 tablespoons) game *fumet*.

Croustade of snipe with truffles. CROUSTADE DE BÉCASSINES AUX TRUFFES – Bone the snipe. Stuff with a piece of *à gratin forcemeat* (see FORCEMEAT) about the size of a small egg, mixed with diced truffles, well seasoned and sprinkled with a little brandy. Brown lightly in butter for a few moments. Arrange on a bed of *Quenelle forcemeat* (see FORCEMEAT) made with game. Cover with thin slices of truffles, seasoned and sprinkled with a little brandy. Cover with flaky pastry. Decorate the top of the *croustade* with pieces of rolled-out pastry cut in fancy shapes. Make a hole in the middle. Brush with egg yolk and bake in a hot oven. Pour into the croustade a few tablespoons of boiled down *Demi-glace sauce* (see SAUCE) based on a concentrated game stock.

Hot snipe pâté Lucullus. PÂTÉ CHAUD DE BÉCASSINES LUCULLUS – Bone 6 snipe. Stuff with a *Fine panada forcemeat* (see FORCEMEAT) mixed with one-third of its weight of *foie gras*, as well as the birds' trail, chopped.

Put a layer of this stuffing on the snipe, laid out flat on a table, and a piece of foie gras and a piece of truffle in the middle of each bird. Reshape the snipe in their original form and sprinkle with a few drops of brandy.

Line an oval-shaped mould for hot *pâtés* with pie pastry. Coat the inside of the mould with a layer of *Fine panada forcemeat* mixed with *à gratin forcemeat*, half and half. (See FORCEMEAT.)

Put the stuffed snipe into the *pâté*, packing them in tightly, and sealing them in with a layer of forcemeat similar to the one used for lining the *pâté*. Finish with a layer of forcemeat and cover with a rasher of fat bacon and a piece of rolled-out pastry. Seal and crimp the edges. Decorate with pastry cut in fancy shapes. Make an opening in the middle of lid to allow steam to escape. Brush with beaten egg, place on a baking sheet and bake in a moderate oven from 45 minutes to an hour.

Remove the pastry lid, cutting it carefully with a knife all around. Take off the bacon rasher covering the forcemeat. Unmould.

Pour into the *pâté* a *ragoût* of sliced truffles blended with a few tablespoons Madeira-flavoured, concentrated game stock. Replace the pastry lid on the *pâté*. Heat thoroughly in the oven.

This *pâté* can also be served cold. Pour into the *pâté*, when it is just warm, a few tablespoons cold but liquid aspic jelly based on game stock, and chill.

GREAT SNIPE. BÉCASSIN – Name commonly given to *cul-blanc*, a variety of snipe, which has distinctive white feathers on the tail.

It is prepared in any way suitable for snipe, mainly roasting.

SNOW. NEIGE – Certain cold dishes are served on a bed of ice grated with a special grater. This grated ice is known as *neige*.

SNOWBALL. BOULE DE NEIGE – Use a spherical mould. Line with chocolate ice cream. Fill with vanilla-flavoured *Mousse mixture* (see ICE CREAMS AND ICES) and diced crystallised fruit steeped in Maraschino. When the ice is turned out, cover it entirely with *Chantilly cream* (see CREAMS), put through a forcing bag with a fluted nozzle.

SNOW PARTRIDGE. ARBENNE – Variety of grouse also called *Tibetan partridge*. They are found in the Valais (Switzerland), in Savoy and in Piedmont. Snow partridge is treated like grouse (q.v.) or partridge (q.v.).

SOAKING. TREMPAGE – Immersion in water, principally of dried vegetables. Used also to describe the moistening of some gâteaux with syrup (see BABA, SAVARIN).

SOBRONADE (Soup) – Country soup, very popular in the Périgord countryside. It is made with both fresh and salt pork cut in large dice, and a variety of vegetables: haricot beans, carrots, leeks, celery and root vegetables. This is really a kind of *potée*.

SODA-WATER – Effervescent drink manufactured industrially. Soda-water, which is highly charged with carbonic gas, is added to syrups, fruit juices, whisky, etc.

SOFT ROE. LAITANCE, LAITE – The milt or sperm of the male fish, a smooth, white substance. It is a food rich in fat and phosphorus, and is easily digested.

Preparation of soft roes. Before they are cooked, soft roes must be cleansed in cold water and stripped of the little blood vessel that runs down one side. They are poached for a short time in stock made from a little water, lemon juice and butter, seasoned with salt.

For some purposes, soft roes can be lightly floured and fried in very hot butter. This method of preparation is called *à la meunière*. *Soft roes à la meunière* are served on *canapés*, toast or in tartlets, *barquettes*, etc.

Soft roes of carp and other fish. LAITANCES DE CARPES ET AUTRES POISSONS – The soft roes of carp are perhaps the most delicate of all edible soft roes. Next in order of merit are the roes of herring and mackerel.

Soft roes can be cooked in a number of ways: as fritters, in tartlets or *barquettes*, on *canapés*, in small *vol-au-vent*, as hot or cold *hors-d'œuvre* or as a light main dish. They can also be used as a garnish for braised or poached fish.

Soft roes à l'anglaise. LAITANCES À L'ANGLAISE – Clean the soft roes. Poach them for 2 minutes in stock as indicated above. Drain and leave to cool. Dip them in egg and breadcrumbs. Fry in butter, browning on both sides. Serve with half-melted *Maître d'hôtel butter* (see BUTTER, *Compound butters*) on top, surrounded by fluted half slices of lemon.

Soft roes in barquettes. LAITANCES EN BARQUETTES – Poach the soft roes in stock as indicated above. Drain and place in baked *barquettes* filled with a *salpicon* of mushrooms blended with *Velouté* or *Béchamel sauce* (see SAUCE) based on fish stock. Spoon over some *Normande sauce* or other white sauce based on fish stock. Brown in a very hot oven.

Soft roes in brown butter I. LAITANCES AU BEURRE NOIR – Poach the soft roes in stock as indicated above. Garnish with capers and chopped parsley. Pour on a little lemon juice and a few spoonfuls *Brown butter* (see BUTTER *Compound butters*).

Soft roes in brown butter II. LAITANCES AU BEURRE NOIR – Arrange the cooked soft roes on a dish, and garnish with capers. Pour over them a few drops of vinegar, and a few tablespoons brown butter in which 1 or 2 tablespoons shredded parsley have been fried.

Cold soft roes served with cold fish. LAITANCES FROIDES – Poach the soft roes in white wine and lemon juice. Leave them to cool in this stock. Drain, and dry them in a cloth.

If they are to be used as a garnish for cold fish, arrange them in *barquettes* of thin pastry baked blind. Cover them with mayonnaise or some other cold sauce.

If the roes are to be used as an ingredient of a composite salad, put them, drained and dried, on top of the salad and season with oil, vinegar or lemon juice, salt and pepper.

Soft roes on croutons. LAITANCES EN CROÛTES – See FISH, *Fish roes on toast*.

Soft roe fritters. LAITANCES EN BEIGNETS – Poach the soft roes in stock as indicated above. Leave them to cool. Put them in a marinade of oil, lemon juice and chopped parsley. Dry. Dip them in batter and deep-fry.

Serve with fried parsley.

Soft roes as a garnish. LAITANCES POUR GARNITURES – Cleanse the soft roes in cold water. Put them in a casserole with a few tablespoons water, a squeeze of lemon juice, a pinch of salt and a small knob of butter. Bring them to the boil and simmer very gently for 3 minutes.

Soft roes in mayonnaise. MAYONNAISE DE LAITANCES – Poach the soft roes in salt water. Drain and dry.

Fill a salad bowl with a mound of finely shredded lettuce seasoned with oil, vinegar, salt and pepper, and drained. Place the soft roes on top.

Cover with mayonnaise. Surround with quartered hard-boiled eggs and lettuce hearts. Decorate with fillets of anchovy and capers.

Soft roes à la meunière. LAITANCES À LA MEUNIÈRE – Season the roes, dip them in flour and fry in butter. Proceed thereafter as in recipe for *Sole à la meunière* (see SOLE).

Soft roes in noisette butter. LAITANCES AU BEURRE NOISETTE – Proceed as for *Soft roes in browned butter*, without the capers and chopped parsley, and substituting *Noisette butter* for *Brown butter* (see BUTTER, *Compound butters*).

Soft roes in scallop shells à la normande. LAITANCES EN COQUILLES À LA NORMANDE – Poach and drain the soft roes as indicated above. Put them in scallop shells surrounded by a border of *Duchess potato* (see POTATOES) previously lightly browned in the oven. Place on top an oyster, poached and drained, a cooked mushroom, a teaspoon of shrimps and mussels. Cover with *Normande sauce* (see SAUCE) and decorate each shell with a generous strip of truffle.

Soft roe tartlets. LAITANCES EN CAISSES – Proceed as for *Soft roes à la meunière*. Serve in baked tartlets. Brown a handful of breadcrumbs in the cooking butter and pour this over the roes. Add lemon juice and chopped parsley.

SOFTENING, BLETTING. BLET, BLETTE – Term used to define the state of over ripeness (i.e. 'sleepiness') in certain kinds of fruit, preceding rotting.

In the case of some species of fruit (medlars, persimmons) the fruit does not attain the right state of ripeness, i.e. become edible, until it is bletted. In the case of other fruit (apples, pears, etc.), softening or over ripeness is a sign of the beginning of decay.

SOLE – Flat fish, in shape an elongated oval, almost completely surrounded by fins and covered with very small hard scale which are firmly attached to the skin. The colour of the skin varies according to the depth in which the sole is fished and varies from a dark brown to pale grey, but it is generally an olive brown with blackish irregular markings. The blind side of the sole is whitish in colour.

The eyes of the fish, placed on the right side (the brown side) are small and rather far apart; the mouth is arched, the teeth fine and pointed, and the lower jaw has short white barbels.

The sole is considered the best of the flat fish. Its flesh is white, firm, and delicate and is easily detached from the bones. It is very digestible.

This sole, which is fished in most European waters but not American waters, should not be confused with the fish known as lemon sole, which, though quite good to eat, is not to be compared with the true sole.

Sole can be prepared in a number of ways. Whole, they are fried, boiled, poached, braised, *à la meunière* and grilled. Filleted, they may be prepared in every way.

Each of the recipes for whole soles given below is applicable to fish weighing from 350 to 400 g. (12 to 14 oz.), enough to serve two people. Soles of medium size should be used for frying, *à la meunière* or grilling, because these are usually served one to each guest.

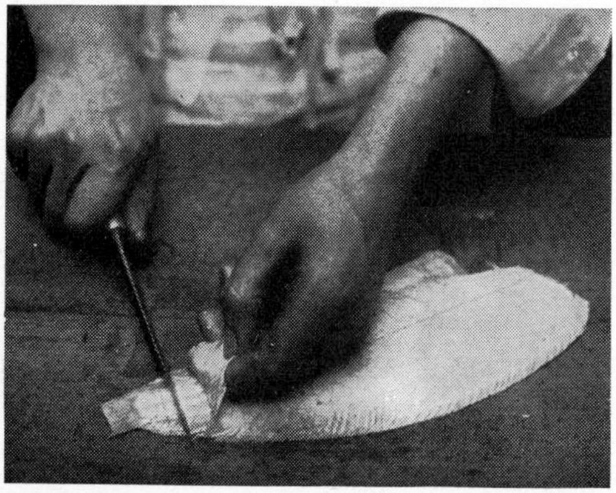

To remove the skin from sole, first make an incision near the tail

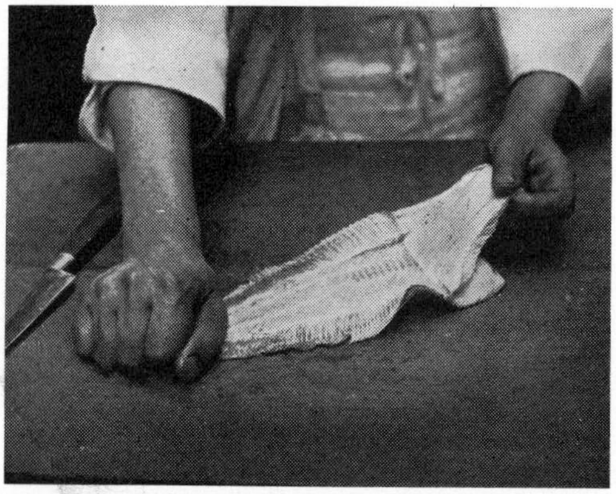

Holding the sole down with the right hand, pull off the skin with the left hand (*Larousse*)

Trim the fish to the edge of the fillets before cooking. Soles trimmed in this way appear smaller, but they are easier to serve. If the backbone is broken before cooking it can be removed before serving.

The American 'sole' is not the same family as the English Dover sole, and differs markedly in texture. Lemon sole, dab, winter flounder and grey sole can be used in the following recipes.

Sole à l'américaine – Split the sole on the side from which the skin has been removed. Raise the fillets slightly and break the backbone in two or three places. Season the inside of the fish.

Poach the sole very gently in a white wine fish *fumet*. Drain. Surround with a *Salpicon à l'américaine* of lobster or spiny lobster (see SALPICON). Put 2 slices of lobster or spiny lobster on top of the sole. Coat with *Américaine sauce* (see SAUCE) to which some concentrated *fumet* and butter have been added.

This dish is often called *Sole à l'armoricaine*, since many people think that *Lobster à l'américaine* should really be *à l'armoricaine*.

Sole à l'amiral – Only very large soles with thick fillets are prepared in this way. For the recipes see *Brill à l'amiral* under BRILL.

Sole à l'anglaise – This name generally means a grilled sole accompanied by melted butter or *Maître d'hôtel butter* (see BUTTER, *Compound butters*) and boiled potatoes. It can also be sole poached in salted water and milk, accompanied by melted butter and boiled potatoes.

The same name is applied to a sole boned when raw, coated in egg and breadcrumbs, cooked in clarified butter and served with rather soft *maître d'hôtel butter*.

Sole à l'arlésienne – Poach the sole in *fumet*. Garnish with very small tomatoes peeled and cooked in butter, and sliced artichoke bottoms cooked in butter and their own juices, and finished in a little cream.

To coat the sole, boil down the cooking liquor and add a little fish aspic jelly and concentrated tomato pulp mixed with butter and a little grated garlic.

Attereaux of sole à l'ancienne. ATTEREAUX DE SOLES À L'ANCIENNE – Cut each fillet into 3 or 4 pieces. Season and seal them in butter. Thread the pieces on a silver skewer, alternating them with sliced truffles and mushrooms. Dip the skewers into *Villeroi sauce* (see SAUCE). Coat in egg and breadcrumbs and fry in clarified butter. Garnish with fried parsley and quarters of lemon.

Attereaux of sole à la moderne. ATTEREAUX DE SOLES À LA MODERNE – Prepare as above, but without dipping in *villeroi sauce*. Serve with *Tomato sauce* (see SAUCE) or other suitable sauce.

Sole with aubergines. SOLE AUX AUBERGINES – Cook the sole in butter *à la meunière*. Surround with slices of aubergines cooked with butter or oil. Sprinkle with chopped parsley and a few drops of lemon juice and pour over the hot butter in which the fish was cooked.

Alternatively, poach the sole in a *fumet* over very low heat. Drain, wipe, and surround with slices of aubergines cooked in butter. Coat with *White wine sauce* (see SAUCE). Glaze in a hot oven.

The sole may be prepared with courgettes (Italian marrows or zucchini), cucumbers cut in oval chunks and simmered in butter, sliced artichoke bottoms sautéed in butter, celeriac quartered and simmered in butter, or sweet pimentos cut in large *julienne* cooked in butter or oil. Drain off the cooking liquor. Boil it down by one-third and thicken with a tablespoon kneaded butter. Add a good tablespoon of butter. Coat the sole with this sauce and glaze in a hot oven.

Barquettes or tartlets of sole. BARQUETTES, TARTELETTES DE SOLES – Made with *salpicon* of sole, truffles and mushrooms, bound with a brown or white sauce.

Beignets of sole. BEIGNETS DE SOLES – Make a *salpicon* of sole, as for ordinary croquettes. Bind with *Velouté* or *Béchamel sauce* (see SAUCE) and allow to cool.

Divide into small portions and roll each into a ball. Dip into a light batter and fry in deep fat. Serve in a mound, and garnish with fried parsley. Serve with *Tomato sauce* (see SAUCE) or any sauce suitable for fried fish.

Sole Bercy I – Put the sole on a fireproof dish which has been buttered and sprinkled with chopped shallot and parsley.

Moisten with 2 tablespoons (3 tablespoons) white wine and a squeeze of lemon juice. Scatter 20 g. ($\frac{3}{4}$ oz., $1\frac{1}{2}$ tablespoons) butter cut up into small pieces on top.

Cook the sole in the oven, basting often so as to glaze the fish.

Sole Bercy II – Put the sole in a fireproof dish on a layer of chopped onions lightly cooked in butter without becoming too much coloured. Surround with 4 trimmed, sliced mushrooms, sautéed in butter. Season. Moisten with $1\frac{1}{2}$ dl. ($\frac{1}{4}$ pint, $\frac{2}{3}$ cup) red Burgundy. Cook in the oven.

Drain off the cooking liquor. Boil down by one-third and thicken with 20 g. ($\frac{3}{4}$ oz., $1\frac{1}{2}$ tablespoons) butter worked together with flour. Add 20 g. ($\frac{3}{4}$ oz., $1\frac{1}{2}$ tablespoons) of butter. Coat the sole with this sauce and glaze in a hot oven.

Sole à la bonne femme – Trim a medium-sized sole, slit it longways along the side from which the skin has been removed and raise the fillets a little on each side to loosen the backbone.

Season inside and out and put into a buttered fireproof dish lined with a layer of chopped raw mushrooms and a pinch of chopped parsley.

Add 1 dl. (6 tablespoons, scant $\frac{1}{2}$ cup) white wine and a few drops lemon juice. Dot the surface with 15 g. ($\frac{1}{2}$ oz., 1 tablespoon) butter cut in tiny pieces.

Bring to the boil, then put in the oven, cover and cook for 10 minutes. Drain off the cooking liquor into a pan. Boil it down and thicken with 15 g. ($\frac{1}{2}$ oz., 1 tablespoon) butter worked together with flour.

Coat the sole with this sauce. Glaze in a hot oven.

Sole à la bourguignonne – The same as *Sole with red wine*, the recipe for which is given below.

Sole à la bretonne – Season the sole and put it on a buttered baking tin spread with 1 dl. (6 tablespoons, scant $\frac{1}{2}$ cup) *Vegetable fondue* (see FONDUE). Pour over 1 dl. (6 tablespoons, scant $\frac{1}{2}$ cup) fish *fumet* made with white wine. Cook, covered, in the oven, basting often.

Drain the fish. Coat with its cooking liquor to which 2 tablespoons (3 tablespoons) fresh cream have been added.

Brochettes of sole à la duxelles. BROCHETTES DE SOLES À LA DUXELLES – Cut the fillets into pieces of equal size. Sandwich them together two by two with a stuffing made of hard-boiled egg yolks, breadcrumbs and chopped parsley. Thread them on skewers, alternating them with slices of mushrooms dipped in butter. Season, and brush them with melted butter. Cover with white breadcrumbs and grill. Set on a dish on a layer of *duxelles* bound with *Velouté sauce* (see SAUCE).

Sole cardinal – Stuff a boned sole with *Pike forcemeat* (see FORCEMEAT) mixed with *Lobster butter* (see BUTTER, *Compound butters*). Poach it in nearly boiling white wine. Garnish with slices of lobster or spiny lobster, or surround with a *salpicon* of one or other of these shellfish. Coat with *Cardinal sauce* (see SAUCE) to which some of the concentrated cooking liquor has been added. Sprinkle with chopped lobster coral.

Fillets of sole are prepared in this way, spread with the pike forcemeat and folded in two.

Sole Colbert – Split the sole along the side from which the skin has been removed. Raise the fillets. Break the backbone in two or three places so that it may easily be removed after cooking.

Soak the sole in cold boiled milk, flour it, coat in egg and breadcrumbs. Roll back the fillets on themselves so as to leave the backbone free.

Fry the sole, drain it, remove the backbone. Fill the cavity with *Maître d'hôtel butter* (see BUTTER, *Compound butters*).

Croquettes and kromeskies of sole. CROQUETTES, CROMESQUIS DE SOLES – These small preparations are served as a hot *hors-d'œuvre* or a small entrée. They are made like ordinary croquettes, the recipe for which is given under HORS-D'ŒUVRE, *Hot hors-d'œuvre*.

Curried sole. SOLE À L'INDIENNE – Spread on a baking dish a layer of chopped onions cooked till soft in butter, mixed with 2 tablespoons (3 tablespoons) peeled, pressed, chopped tomatoes also cooked in butter. Season with a teaspoon curry. Set a trimmed sole on top, and pour over it 2 tablespoons (3 tablespoons) mushroom stock. Poach in the oven.

Add to the cooking liquor 2 tablespoons (3 tablespoons) *Velouté* or *Béchamel sauce* (see SAUCE) based on fish stock and 3 tablespoons (4 tablespoons) thick fresh cream. Boil for a few moments. Finish off with a teaspoon butter and a few drops lemon juice. Coat the fish with this sauce and serve with Indian-style rice (see RICE, *Rice à l'indienne*).

Recipes given below for *Fillets of sole à l'indienne* can also be applied to whole sole.

Sole à la diplomate – Split the sole, raise the fillets, remove the backbone, and stuff with a whiting forcemeat (see FORCEMEAT, *Fish forcemeat*) with cream and diced truffles. Poach in a *fumet* that is nearly boiling. Drain and dry. Remove the side bones. Surround by a *salpicon* of lobster. Coat with *Diplomat sauce* (see SAUCE). Put on top of the sole four thick slices of truffles glazed with fish aspic jelly (see ASPIC, *Aspic of fish*).

Sole dorée – See *Golden sole* below.

Fillets of sole. FILETS DE SOLES – Fillets of sole are removed when raw.

According to their final use, the fillets are either left as they are and flattened lightly, or rolled after being slightly flattened.

All methods of preparation given for the whole sole, as well as those given elsewhere for flat fish of various kinds, are applicable to fillets of sole. These can be served *à la meunière*, fried, boiled, poached and grilled. They are accompanied by various sauces and garnishes.

Fillets of sole can be rolled up to make *paupiettes*, recipes for which are to be found below.

Each of the recipes which follow requires 8 fillets.

Fillets of sole cooked *à la meunière* or in a white wine *fumet* may also be garnished with aubergines, cucumbers cut into 'pigeons' eggs' and cooked in butter, pimentos peeled, cut in strips and stewed in butter or oil, tomatoes halved and cooked in butter or oil, and other vegetables cooked in butter or oil, braised, boiled or stewed in their own juices.

Instead of coating the fillets with white wine sauce, they may be covered with *Mornay sauce* (see SAUCE) and browned in the oven.

Fillets of sole à l'américaine. FILETS DE SOLES À L'AMÉRICAINE – Poach the folded fillets in white wine. Drain them and finish off as described in the recipe for *Sole à l'américaine*.

This dish is often served under the name of *Fillets of sole à l'armoricaine*.

Fillets of sole à l'ancienne. FILETS DE SOLES À L'ANCIENNE – Coat 8 lightly flattened fillets of sole with a thin layer of whiting forcemeat (see FORCEMEAT, *Fish forcemeat*) to which a third of its weight of dry *duxelles* has been added. Fold the fillets, and coat with egg and breadcrumbs; cook in clarified butter. Arrange in a circle on a dish, alternating them with little cutlets of whiting forcemeat made in special moulds and poached. Garnish the middle of the dish with a *ragoût* composed of shrimps, mushrooms and truffles bound with fish *Velouté sauce* (see SAUCE), mixed with cream and flavoured with Madeira. Sprinkle the fillets with a little *Noisette butter* (see BUTTER, *Compound butters*).

Fillets of sole à l'anglaise I. FILETS DE SOLES À L'ANGLAISE – Flatten and season the fillets and coat them with egg and breadcrumbs. Cook in clarified butter. Cover with softened *Maître d'hôtel butter* (see BUTTER, *Compound butters*).

Serve with boiled or steamed potatoes.

Fillets of sole à l'anglaise II. FILETS DE SOLES À L'ANGLAISE – Fillets of sole poached in salted water and milk, served with boiled potatoes and melted butter.

Fillets of sole à l'armoricaine. FILETS DE SOLES À L'ARMORICAINE – The same as *Fillets of sole à l'américaine*.

Aspic of fillets of sole à la parisienne. ASPIC DE FILETS DE SOLES À LA PARISIENNE – Cook 8 large fillets in a concentrated *fumet*, based on fish stock and made with white wine. Drain

How to cut fillets of sole (*Larousse*)

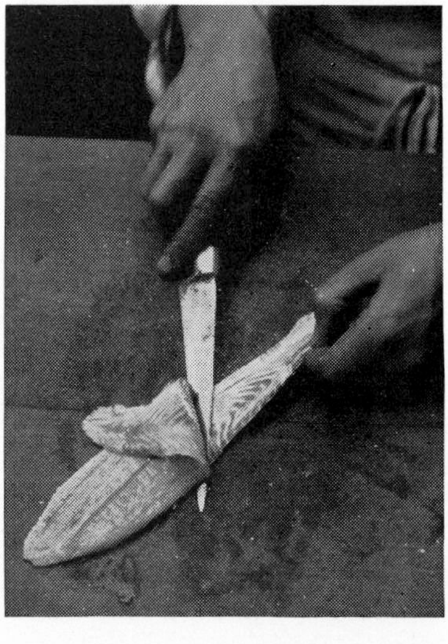

How to skin fillets of sole (*Larousse*)

and cool under pressure. Cut each into two pieces and coat with *White chaud-froid sauce* (see SAUCE). Decorate with cut-out pieces of truffle and glaze with jelly. Set in an aspic mould lined with fish jelly and decorated on the bottom and sides. The fillets should be arranged upright, one against the other. Fill the middle of the mould with a *Parisian salad* (see SALAD) dressed with thick mayonnaise. Cover with a layer of fish jelly. Set on ice.

Turn out the aspic either directly onto a dish or on a base of rice or a buttered croûton of bread. Decorate with quartered hard-boiled eggs and small lettuce hearts. Surround with chopped jelly.

Fillets of sole Bercy. FILETS DE SOLES BERCY – Proceed, using fillets, as for *Sole Bercy*.

Fillets of sole, boiled or poached. FILETS DE SOLES BOUILLIS, POCHÉS – Poach the flattened fillets in salted water and milk. Drain. Serve with melted butter or some other sauce such as *Butter*, *Hollandaise* or *Cream sauce* (see SAUCE).

Fillets of sole Boitelle. FILETS DE SOLES BOITELLE – Arrange in a circle in a buttered sauté pan the folded and seasoned fillets. For 8 fillets add 100 g. (4 oz., 2 cups) chopped mushrooms, 2 tablespoons (3 tablespoons) concentrated fish *fumet* and a squeeze of lemon juice. Poach, keeping the pan covered.

Arrange the fillets in a deep dish, put the mushrooms in the middle and pour over the pan juices to which 50 g. (2 oz., 4 tablespoons) butter have been added.

Fillets of sole à la bonne femme. FILETS DE SOLES À LA BONNE FEMME – Using flat fillets of sole, prepare like *Sole à la bonne femme*.

Fillets of sole à la bordelaise. FILETS DE SOLES À LA BORDELAISE – Season the fillets, set them in a buttered fish kettle with slices of carrot and onion and a *bouquet garni*. Moisten with a glass of red Bordeaux. Poach for 8 minutes.

Drain the fillets and set them on a dish with peeled mushrooms and small glazed onions.

Boil down the cooking liquor, adding to it 2 tablespoons (3 tablespoons) *Demi-glace sauce* (see SAUCE). Beat butter into this sauce, strain, and coat the fillets.

Border of fillets of sole à la dauphine. BORDURE DE FILETS DE SOLES À LA DAUPHINE – This dish is served under the name of *Fillets of sole à la dauphine*.

Border of fillets of sole diplomate. BORDURE DE FILETS DE SOLES DIPLOMATE – Poach the fillets in a *fumet* made with white wine. Drain, wipe, and set on a moulded border made with whiting forcemeat (see FORCEMEAT, *Fish forcemeat*), alternating the fillets with slices of round truffles. Surround the border with a few spoonfuls of *Diplomat sauce* (see SAUCE). Fill the middle of the dish with a *salpicon* of lobster. Coat the fillets and the truffles with the cooking liquor, boiled down, with butter added.

Fillets of sole cardinal

Fillets of sole à la bourguignonne. FILETS DE SOLES À LA BOURGUIGNONNE – Prepared like *Sole à la bourguignonne*.

Fillets of sole à la cancalaise. FILETS DE SOLES À LA CANCALAISE – Fold the fillets and cook them in a concentrated fish *fumet*, to which the liquor from oysters poached for the garnish has been added. Drain, dry, and set them in the form of a circle. Fill the middle of the dish with peeled shrimps. Put two poached and de-bearded oysters on top of each fillet. Coat with *White wine sauce* (see SAUCE) to which some boiled down *fumet* has been added.

Fillets of sole cardinal. FILETS DE SOLES CARDINAL – Stuff the fillets with pike or whiting forcemeat, finished with lobster or crawfish butter, and poached in fish *fumet* that is nearly boiling.

Arrange the fillets on a dish in a circle, alternating them with slices of lobster or spiny lobster. Coat with *Cardinal sauce* (see SAUCE) to which some of the concentrated *fumet* has been added. Sprinkle with chopped lobster coral.

Fillets of sole à la catalane. FILETS DE SOLES À LA CATALANE – Coat lightly flattened fillets with egg and breadcrumbs mixed with a little chopped parsley. Cook in half oil, half butter. Set on a layer of *Tomato fondue* (see FONDUE) seasoned with a little garlic. Surround with diced aubergines sautéed in oil. Put a slice of peeled lemon on top of each fillet. Sprinkle with the cooking butter.

Fillets of sole with Chambertin or other red wine. FILETS DE SOLES AU CHAMBERTIN OU AUTRE GRAND VIN ROUGE – Poach the fillets in a fish *fumet* made with red wine (Chambertin, Mâcon, Romanée, Vougeot, Corton or other fine red Burgundy) as for *Sole with red wine* (see below).

The garnish for these fillets of sole is usually composed of mushrooms and small glazed onions. The whole sole or the fillets cooked with red wine may also be garnished with soft roes, mushrooms, truffles, shrimps or crayfish, pike quenelles, etc.

Fillets of sole Chauchat

Fillets of sole Chauchat. FILETS DE SOLES CHAUCHAT – Cook rolled fillets in butter and lemon juice, without letting them brown. Cover with *Mornay sauce* (see SAUCE). Surround with a border of sliced fried potatoes. Sprinkle with grated cheese, dot with butter and brown.

Fillets of sole Chivry. FILETS DE SOLES CHIVRY – Cook rolled fillets with chopped shallot and concentrated fish *fumet*. Drain, and arrange in a circle on a dish, alternating them with heart-shaped croûtons of bread fried in butter. Coat with *Chivry sauce* (see SAUCE). Pour round the fillets a border of *Fish jelly* (see JELLY).

Fillets of sole, cold. FILETS DE SOLES FROIDS – Fillets of sole can be prepared as aspics (see ASPIC); rings (see BORDERS, *Cold rings*); glazed with Chambertin, Champagne or jelly; as a mayonnaise (like *Salmon mayonnaise*); as a salad (like *Lobster* or *Spiny lobster salad*). Cold sole can also be made into *pâtés* and *terrines*.

Fillets of sole with courgettes (zucchini) I. FILETS DE SOLES AUX COURGETTES – Cook the flattened fillets *à la meunière*. Surround with courgettes cut in thick slices, cooked in butter or oil. Sprinkle with chopped parsley and a few drops of lemon juice. Pour over the cooking butter, very hot.

Fillets of sole with courgettes (zucchini) II. FILETS DE SOLES AUX COURGETTES – Cook the folded fillets in fish *fumet* made with white wine. Surround them with slices of courgettes cooked in butter. Coat with *White wine sauce* (see SAUCE) to which some concentrated *fumet* has been added. Glaze in a hot oven.

Fillets of sole Crécy. FILETS DE SOLES CRÉCY – Poach the rolled fillets in fish *fumet*. Drain them. Coat with a sauce made by boiling down the cooking liquid and adding 2 tablespoons (3 tablespoons) *Béchamel sauce* (see SAUCE) and 2 tablespoons (3 tablespoons) carrot purée.

Garnish with small new carrots, glazed.

Fillets of sole Cubat. FILETS DE SOLES CUBAT – Cook the flattened fillets in mushroom stock and butter. Set them on a fireproof dish. Coat with thick *Mushroom purée* (see PURÉE). Put 2 slices of truffle on each fillet. Coat with *Mornay sauce* (see SAUCE) and brown in the oven.

Fillets of sole Daumont. FILETS DE SOLES DAUMONT – Spread the sole fillets with fish forcemeat (pike or whiting) finished off with *Crayfish butter* (see BUTTER, *Compound butters*.) Poach them in nearly boiling fish *fumet*. Drain and dry.

Set on a dish, each fillet placed on top of a large mushroom cap cooked in butter and filled with a *Salpicon of crayfish* (see CRAYFISH).

Coat with *Normande sauce* (see SAUCE). Garnish with soft roes coated with egg and breadcrumbs and sautéed in butter.

Fillets of sole dauphine. FILETS DE SOLES DAUPHINE – Poach the rolled fillets in Madeira which has had truffle and mushroom skins infused in it. Cool, drain, and mask with *Villeroi sauce* (see SAUCE) which has had some of the cooking liquor and *Crayfish butter* (see BUTTER, *Compound butters*) added. Coat with breadcrumbs and fry in clarified butter.

Drain and set on a moulded border of *Pike forcemeat* (see FORCEMEAT) cooked in a ring mould in a *bain marie*. Put in the middle of the dish a *ragoût* composed of cooked mushrooms, little pike quenelles, crayfish and sliced truffles, bound with thick *Velouté sauce* (see SAUCE). Serve with *Nantua sauce*.

Fillets of sole à la dieppoise. FILETS DE SOLES À LA DIEPPOISE – Cook the fillets in a nearly boiling fish *fumet*. Drain and dry. Surround with a *Dieppoise garnish* (see GARNISHES) composed of shelled mussels cooked in white wine and grey or pink shelled crayfish. Coat with *White wine sauce* (see SAUCE) to which the boiled down cooking liquor from the fillets and mussels has been added.

Fillets of sole à la diplomate. FILETS DE SOLES À LA DIPLOMATE – See *Border of fillets of sole à la diplomate*.

Fillets of sole à l'espagnole. FILETS DE SOLE À L'ESPAGNOLE – Season the fillets with salt and paprika. Flour and fry in oil. Set on a dish on a bed of tomatoes that have been peeled, drained, chopped, cooked in oil, and seasoned with salt, paprika and a little garlic.

Put at each end of the dish sweet pimentos, peeled, cut in strips and fried in oil, and place on top of the fillets slices of onion floured and fried in oil.

Fillets of sole à la fécampoise. FILETS DE SOLES A LA FÉCAMPOISE – Name sometimes given to *Fillets of sole à la trouvillaise*.

Fillets of sole à la florentine. FILETS DE SOLES À LA FLORENTINE – Cook seasoned fillets in butter and lemon juice, without the addition of *fumet*.

Set on a fireproof dish on a layer of blanched leaf spinach, drained and simmered in butter. Coat with *Mornay sauce* (see SAUCE). Sprinkle with grated Parmesan and a little melted butter. Brown in the oven.

Fillets of sole, fried. FILETS DE SOLES FRITS – Prepare like other fried fish.

Fried fillets of sole are arrange in a mound and garnished with fried parsley and lemon. They may also be cooked on metal skewers.

Fillets of sole en goujons

Fillets of sole en goujons. FILETS DE SOLES EN GOUJONS – Cut the fillets diagonally across in pieces 2 cm ($\frac{3}{4}$ inch) wide. Dip these in milk, drain, and flour them, shaking well to remove excess flour. Fry in deep fat or oil.

Drain and add salt. Garnish with fried parsley and lemon.

Sole fillets prepared in this way are often used as garnish for large braised fish.

Fillets of sole au gratin. FILETS DE SOLES AU GRATIN – Prepare, using slightly flattened fillets, as *Sole au gratin*.

Fillets of sole, grilled. FILETS DE SOLES GRILLÉS – Flatten the fillets slightly and season them. Brush with oil or melted butter and cook under the grill at a moderate heat. Surround with slices of lemon and small sprigs of fresh parsley.

Grilled fillets of sole are usually accompanied by melted butter or softened *Maître d'hôtel butter* (see BUTTER, *Compound butters*). They may also be served with one of the sauces recommended for grilled fish.

It is customary to serve boiled potatoes with grilled fillets of sole, as well as mushrooms, tomatoes, etc.

Fillets of sole à la hongroise. FILETS DE SOLES À LA HONGROISE – Put the folded fillets, seasoned with salt and paprika, into a sauté pan with 50 g. (2 oz., $\frac{1}{2}$ cup) finely chopped onion cooked until soft in butter, with a peeled, drained and crushed tomato, seasoned with paprika, added when the onion is almost cooked. Add 4 tablespoons ($\frac{1}{3}$ cup) fish *fumet* made with white wine. Cover, and cook all together. Drain the fillets and arrange in a ring, alternating them with heart-shaped croûtons.

Pour over the fillets the cooking liquor, boiled down and mixed with 4 tablespoons ($\frac{1}{3}$ cup) thick fresh cream, with butter and a squeeze of lemon juice added.

Potatoes cut to look like olives and cooked in butter and water may be added to this dish, set in the middle of the ring.

Fillets of sole à l'indienne I. FILETS DE SOLES À L'INDIENNE – Divide each fillet into two pieces and fry in clarified butter.

Set the fillets on a bed of rice *à l'indienne* and pour a *Curry sauce* based on fish stock (see SAUCE) round.

Fillets of sole à l'indienne II. FILETS DE SOLES À L'INDIENNE – Cut the fillets into narrow strips and into a little knot. Prepare separately the following *coulis*:

Cook 2 tablespoons (3 tablespoons) chopped onion in butter until soft. Add a small eating apple, peeled and cut in dice, a medium-sized tomato, peeled and pressed, a little grated garlic, a sprig of thyme, and a powdered bay leaf. Sprinkle with curry. Pour in $1\frac{1}{2}$ dl. ($\frac{1}{4}$ pint, $\frac{2}{3}$ cup) coconut milk or milk of almonds. Season. Cook for 10 minutes. Stir in $1\frac{1}{2}$ dl. ($\frac{1}{4}$ pint, $\frac{2}{3}$ cup) thick cream, bring to the boil, and add a squeeze of lemon juice.

Put the twists of sole fillets to cook in this sauce. Serve with *Rice à l'indienne* (see RICE).

Fillets of sole à la Jacques. FILETS DE SOLES À LA JACQUES – 'Put in a deep saucepan some chopped onion that has previously been cooked in butter till soft, 250 g. (9 oz., $1\frac{1}{2}$ cups) sliced potato and 250 g. (9 oz., $2\frac{1}{2}$ cups) sliced mushrooms.

'Pour in a little white wine and fish *fumet*. Season with salt and pepper and add a *bouquet garni*. Cook, boiling rapidly.

'When the potatoes are three-quarters cooked, put into the saucepan 8 fillets of sole, each cut in two. Add a small pinch of powdered saffron and cook briskly for 6 minutes. Take out the fillets. Boil down the liquid if necessary.

'To serve, arrange the potatoes and mushrooms in a deep dish, put the fillets on top, sprinkle with the cooking liquor, chopped parsley and chervil.' (Azéma.)

Fillets of sole Joinville. FILETS DE SOLES JOINVILLE – Poach the folded fillets in *fumet* that is nearly boiling. Drain, and arrange them in a circle on a dish, placing them with the points upwards instead of in the usual way. Fix a peeled pink shrimp on the tip of each fillet.

Put in the middle of the circle a *Joinville garnish* composed of shrimps, mushrooms and diced truffles, all bound with *Joinville sauce* (see SAUCE). Coat the fillets with *Joinville sauce* to which has been added some of the concentrated cooking liquor. Put on each fillet a slice of truffle glazed with fish jelly.

Fillets of sole en julienne. FILETS DE SOLES EN JULIENNE – Prepared and fried like *Fillets of sole en goujons*, but the fillets are cut more finely.

Fillets of sole Marguery. FILETS DE SOLES MARGUERY – This is the recipe given by M. Mangin, who for some thirty years was head chef of the celebrated *Restaurant Marguery*, at the time when M. Marguery directed the establishment himself.

'Fillet two fine soles. Use the bones and trimmings to make a white wine *fumet*, flavoured with a little chopped onion, a sprig of thyme, quarter of a bay leaf and a little parsley. Season with salt and pepper. Simmer for 15 minutes. Add to this *fumet*, which should be strained and concentrated, the strained cooking liquor of a litre (quart) of mussels cooked in the usual way, using white wine.

'Place the fillets of sole, floured and lightly flattened, on a buttered baking dish. Sprinkle over a few tablespoons of the *fumet*. Cover with buttered greaseproof paper and poach gently.

'Drain the fillets well. Set them in an oval dish and surround with a double row of shelled mussels and shrimps. Keep hot, while the sauce is prepared.

'*The sauce*. Add the cooking juices of the soles to the *fumet* and strain. Boil down by two-thirds. Remove from the heat, allow the sauce to cool a little, then add 6 egg yolks. Whisk the sauce over gentle heat, like a *hollandaise*, incorporating about 350 g. (12 oz., $1\frac{1}{2}$ cups) of the finest butter, slightly melted. Season the sauce and strain. Coat the fillets with it, and garnish. Brown in a hot oven.'

Fillets of sole Marivaux. FILETS DE SOLE MARIVAUX – Poach the folded fillets in *fumet* that is nearly boiling. Drain and set them on a dish in the middle of a border of *Duchess potato mixture* (see POTATOES) piped through a forcing bag on top of a layer of chopped *Mushrooms cooked in cream* (see MUSHROOMS) mixed with chopped truffles. Coat with a light *Mornay sauce* (see SAUCE). Brush the border with egg, sprinkle with grated Parmesan and brown in the oven.

Fillets of sole à la meunière. FILETS DE SOLES À LA MEUNIÈRE – Flat fillets fried in butter as for *Sole à la meunière*.

Fillets of sole Montreuil. FILETS DE SOLES MONTREUIL – Made with flat fillets in the same way as *Sole Montreuil*.

Fillets of sole Montrouge. FILETS DE SOLES MONTROUGE – Cook the folded fillets in butter, moistening them with a few drops of white wine. Drain them. Garnish with small peeled mushrooms cooked in butter and bound with cream.

Coat the whole with a sauce made by adding to the cooking juices 1 dl. (6 tablespoons, scant $\frac{1}{2}$ cup) *Mushroom purée* (see PURÉE), a few tablespoons cream and some butter.

Fillets of sole Mornay. FILETS DE SOLES MORNAY – Cook the fillets, left flat, in *fumet* that is nearly boiling. Coat with *Mornay sauce* (see SAUCE), sprinkle with grated Parmesan and brown in the oven.

Fillets of sole Murat. FILETS DE SOLES MURAT – Cut the fillets in strips, flour and sauté them in butter.

Sauté separately, for every 8 fillets, 2 medium-sized diced potatoes and two half-cooked diced artichoke bottoms. When these are cooked mix the fillets with them, and sauté together over heat for a few moments. Set in a deep dish. Put on top 8 slices of tomatoes seasoned and sautéed in oil. Sprinkle with chopped parsley, add a little meat glaze and a squeeze of lemon juice, and pour over a few tablespoons *Noisette butter* (see BUTTER, *Compound butters*).

Fillets of sole with mushrooms. FILETS DE SOLES AUX CHAMPIGNONS – Cook folded fillets of sole and 2 peeled mushrooms for each sole in a nearly boiling white wine fish *fumet*. Set the fillets on a dish with the mushrooms on top.

Boil down the cooking liquor with an equal quantity of fresh cream, add butter, strain, and pour over the fillets.

These fillets may also be coated with *White wine sauce* (see SAUCE) with concentrated *fumet* added before straining.

Fillets of sole with mussels. FILETS DE SOLES AUX MOULES – Poach the folded fillets in fish *fumet* and the cooking liquor of mussels. Set on a dish, and surround with mussels cooked in white wine. Coat with *White wine sauce* (see SAUCE) to which some concentrated cooking liquor has been added.

Fillets of sole à la Nantua. FILETS DE SOLES AUX ÉCREVISSES À LA NANTUA – Poach the folded fillets in a fish *fumet* that is nearly boiling. Drain, dry, and set them in a circle on a dish. Coat with *Nantua sauce* (see SAUCE) to which some boiled down cooking liquor has been added. Put a slice of truffle on each fillet.

Fillets of sole à la Nantua (old recipe). FILETS DE SOLES À LA NANTUA – Poach the fillets very gently in white wine. Set them, well drained, on a moulded border made with *Pike forcemeat* (see FORCEMEAT) finished off with *Crayfish butter* (see BUTTER, *Compound butters*). Garnish the middle of the dish with *Crayfish tail ragoût à la Nantua* (see CRAYFISH). Coat the fillets with *Nantua sauce* (see SAUCE) to which some *fumet* has been added. Put a large slice of truffle on top of each fillet.

Fillets of sole à la normande. FILETS DE SOLES À LA NORMANDE – Poach the fillets, left flat, gently in *fumet*. Drain, set them on a serving dish, and surround them with *Normande sauce* (see SAUCE). Finish as for *Sole à la normande*.

Fillets of sole à l'orientale. FILETS DE SOLES À L'ORIENTALE – Prepare, using flat fillets, like *Red mullet à l'orientale* (see HORS-D'ŒUVRE). This dish is served hot or cold.

Fillets of sole à la normande

Fillets of sole Orly. FILETS DE SOLES ORLY – Prepare as for *Whiting Orly* (see WHITING).

Fillets of sole with oysters. FILETS DE SOLES AUX HUÎTRES – Fold the fillets and cook them in fish *fumet*. Drain and dry. Put on top of each fillet 2 oysters de-bearded and poached in their own liquor. Coat with *Normande sauce* or *White wine sauce* (see SAUCE) to which some boiled down *fumet* and oyster liquor have been added.

Fillets of sole à la panetière. FILETS DE SOLES À LA PANETIÈRE – Flatten and trim the fillets and fold them in 2. Season with salt and pepper, flour and sauté them in butter.

Prepare separately a *ragoût* of mushrooms *à la crème*. Arrange the fillets in a crown on a thick, round slice of bread, hollowed out, buttered and crisped in the oven. Put the mushrooms in the middle. Warm for a few moments in the oven and serve.

Fillets of sole Parmentier. FILETS DE SOLES PARMENTIÈRE – Poach the fillets in *fumet* and drain them. Set each into half of a medium-sized potato baked in the oven and partly scooped out, as for *Potatoes Georgette* (see POTATOES). Coat the fillets with *Mornay sauce* (see SAUCE) to which some concentrated cooking liquor has been added. Sprinkle with grated Parmesan and melted butter. Brown in the oven.

Fillets of sole à la paysanne. FILETS DE SOLES À LA PAYSANNE – Prepare with folded fillets like *Sole à la paysanne*.

Fillets of sole à la piémontaise. FILETS DE SOLES À LA PIÉMONTAISE – Season the folded fillets, flour, and sauté in butter. Set each on a croûton cut out of a layer of polenta to the same size as the fillets, and fried in butter.

Put on top of each fillet 4 slices of white truffles seasoned with salt and pepper and lightly sautéed in olive oil. Pour round the cooking juices diluted with white wine, to which have been added a few tablespoons tomato purée and butter.

Fillets of sole en pilaf. FILETS DE SOLES EN PILAF – Cut the fillets into little squares. Season, flour, and sauté briskly in butter. Set the fillets in the middle of a border of *Pilaf rice* (see PILAF). Serve with *Tomato sauce* or *Curry sauce* (see SAUCE).

Fillets of sole sur le plat. FILETS DE SOLES SUR LE PLAT – This dish is most often prepared with a whole sole, but may be made with fillets. (See *Sole sur le plat*, below).

Fillets of sole princesse. FILETS DE SOLES PRINCESSE – Poach the folded fillets in *fumet*. Set them on a dish and coat them with *Normande sauce* (see SAUCE) to which some concentrated cooking liquor has been added.

Garnish with very small fine pastry *barquettes*, filled with green asparagus tips bound with butter, and slices of truffles dipped in fish aspic jelly.

Alternatively, the fillets may be coated with egg and breadcrumbs and sautéed in clarified butter. Garnish with alternate clusters of asparagus tips in butter and diced truffles sautéed in butter and bound with a few drops of *Madeira sauce* (see SAUCE). Sprinkle the fillets with *Noisette butter* (see BUTTER, *Compound butters*.)

Fillets of sole Riche. FILETS DE SOLES RICHE – *Riche sauce* is so called because it was a speciality of the famous Parisian restaurant *Riche*, which has now disappeared.

The sauce is made with *Normande sauce* (see SAUCE) finished off with *Lobster butter* (see BUTTER) and a few tablespoons *Truffle essence* (see ESSENCE).

Poach the folded fillets in hot *fumet*. Drain, and arrange them on a dish in a circle. Garnish the middle with a *salpicon* of lobster flesh and truffles. Coat with *Riche sauce* (see SAUCE).

Fillets of sole Richelieu

Fillets of sole Richelieu. FILETS DE SOLES RICHELIEU – Coat the fillets with egg and breadcrumbs and fry them in butter. Garnish with slices of truffles and cover with *Maître d'hôtel butter* (see BUTTER, *Compound butters*.)

Fillets of sole Saint-Germain. FILETS DE SOLES SAINT-GERMAIN – Flatten lightly 8 fillets, season them with salt and pepper, brush with melted butter and coat with freshly made breadcrumbs. Sprinkle with butter and grill on both sides at a moderate heat, letting them colour slightly.

Surround with rather thick *Béarnaise sauce* (see SAUCE) and garnish with *Noisette potatoes* (see POTATOES).

Fillets of sole with shrimps. FILETS DE SOLES AUX CREVETTES – Cook the folded fillets in fish *fumet* made with white wine. Drain, surround with peeled shrimps, and coat with *Shrimp sauce* (see SAUCE) to which has been added boiled down *fumet* left from the cooking.

Fillets of sole Sylvette. FILETS DE SOLES SYLVETTE – Put 8 fillets in a sauté pan lined with 3 tablespoons (4 tablespoons) fine *mirepoix* composed of carrot, the white of leek, onion and celery cut in very small dice, cooked until soft in butter.

Moisten with $\frac{1}{2}$ dl. (3 tablespoons, scant $\frac{1}{4}$ cup) sherry. Cook, covered. When three-quarters cooked, add 4 tablespoons ($\frac{1}{3}$ cup) mixed truffles and mushrooms cut in small dice.

Garnish with very small tomatoes stuffed with a white fish purée, topped with crumbs and browned in the oven. Boil down the cooking liquor, add to it a few tablespoons thick fresh cream and butter, and pour over the fillets.

Timbale of fillets of sole à l'ancienne. TIMBALE DE FILETS DE SOLES À L'ANCIENNE – Prepare a *Timbale pie crust* (see TIMBALE). Cook empty. Turn it out of the mould, return it to the oven and allow it to become golden brown.

Cook 12 *paupiettes* of sole, prepared with pike forcemeat finished off with lobster butter, in concentrated *fumet*.

Prepare separately a *ragoût*, made of de-bearded and poached oysters, shelled mussels cooked in white wine, slices of lobster, cooked mushrooms and slices of truffle. Bind this *ragoût* with fish *velouté sauce* mixed with fresh cream, finished off with *Lobster butter* (see BUTTER, *Compound butters*) and a few drops of brandy.

Three-quarters cook some macaroni in salted water, drain, finish with fresh cream seasoned and dressed with butter. Put a layer of macaroni in the pie while still hot. On top put half of the *ragoût* and 6 of the *paupiettes*. Cover with macaroni, add another layer of *ragoût* and the other 6 *paupiettes*. Finish with the rest of the macaroni and a row of truffle slices.

Put back the pastry 'lid' on the *timbale* and return it to the oven for a few minutes.

Timbale of fillets of sole Grimaldi. TIMBALE DE FILETS DE SOLES GRIMALDI – Prepare like *Fillets of sole à l'ancienne* with fillets of sole spread with truffled *Fish forcemeat* (see FORCEMEAT), *Crayfish tail ragoût à la Nantua* (see CRAYFISH), slices of truffles and macaroni with cream.

This *timbale* can also be made with *langoustines* (i.e. scampi or Dublin Bay prawns) and sauce finished with crayfish butter instead of crayfish and crayfish sauce.

Timbale of fillets of sole à la normande. TIMBALE DE FILETS DE SOLES À LA NORMANDE – Prepare as above with *paupiettes* of sole spread with whiting forcemeat, poached oysters, mussels cooked in white wine, peeled shrimps, truffle slices and macaroni with cream.

Instead of a pastry 'lid' place on top of the pie trussed crayfish and gudgeon coated in egg and breadcrumbs and fried.

Timbale of fillets of sole Victoria. TIMBALE DE FILETS DE SOLES VICTORIA – Prepare in a broad, shallow pastry crust that has been cooked empty.

Spread the fillets with *Pike forcemeat* (see FORCEMEAT) finished off with *Truffle purée* (see PURÉE), and cook them in concentrated fish *fumet* made with white wine.

Prepare a *ragoût* of sliced spiny lobster, oysters, mushrooms and truffles bound with *velouté sauce* mixed with cream and finished off with *Lobster butter* (see BUTTER, *Compound butters*) and brandy.

Put a few spoonfuls of *ragoût* in the bottom of the pie and arrange the *paupiettes*, well drained, in a circle on top. Fill the centre with the rest of the *ragoût*. Coat with *Normande sauce* (see SAUCE) and put on top of each *paupiette* a slice of truffle dipped in fish aspic jelly.

Fillets of sole en torsade. FILETS DE SOLES EN TORSADE – Arrange flattened and seasoned fillets of sole in a buttered savarin mould. Place the fillets crossways, overlapping each other a little and leaving their ends just outside the mould.

Using a forcing bag, fill the inside of the mould with some *Fish forcemeat* (see FORCEMEAT) (e.g., *quenelles*, *mousseline*, etc.), adding, according to the kind of forcemeat used, truffles, mushrooms, *Lobster or other shellfish butter* (see BUTTER, *Compound butters*). Tap the mould to settle the contents. Fold the ends of the fillets over the forcemeat and press them down.

Poach in a *bain-marie* in a moderately hot oven. Take out of the oven, allow to cool for a few minutes, then turn out and serve with a sauce suitable for fish (see SAUCE).

Fillets of sole à la trouvillaise. FILETS DE SOLES À LA TROUVILLAISE – Prepare like *Fillets of sole à la dieppoise*, but coat the fillets with *White wine sauce* (see SAUCE) to which *Shrimp butter* (see BUTTER, *Compound butters*) has been added.

Turban of fillets of sole. TURBAN DE FILETS DE SOLES – Prepare in the same way as *Fillets of sole en torsade*.

Fillets of sole à la vénitienne I. FILETS DE SOLES À LA VÉNITIENNE – Poach the folded fillets in *fumet*. Arrange in a ring, alternating them with heart-shaped croûtons of bread fried in butter. Coat the fillets with *Venetian sauce* (see SAUCE) to which some of the boiled down cooking liquor has been added.

Fillets of sole à la vénitienne II. FILETS DE SOLES À LA VÉNITIENNE – Plumerey, the successor of Carême, gives a different recipe for this preparation: 'The fillets of folded soles are poached in white wine, then drained, wiped and arranged in a crown. The centre is garnished with a *salpicon* of lobster and truffles bound with *Venetian sauce* (see SAUCE), without herbs but finished with *Lobster butter* (see BUTTER). The fillets are coated with green Venetian sauce and garnished with chopped and blanched parsley.'

Fillets of sole Véron. FILETS DE SOLES VÉRON – Coat the fillets with egg and breadcrumbs and cook in clarified butter. Serve on a layer of *Véron sauce* (see SAUCE).

Fillets of sole Victoria. FILETS DE SOLES VICTORIA – Poach the folded fillets in *fumet* that is nearly boiling. Drain and arrange on a serving dish in a circle. Garnish the middle of the dish with a *salpicon* of spiny lobster flesh and truffles. Coat with *White wine sauce* (see SAUCE) finished off with *Lobster or spiny lobster butter* (see BUTTER, *Compound butters*.) Brown in a hot oven.

Vol-au-vent of fillets of sole. VOL-AU-VENT DE FILETS DE SOLES – Prepare with fillets or *paupiettes* of sole and a garnish of mushrooms and truffles in the same way as for *Chicken vol-au-vent* (see VOL-AU-VENT).

Fillets of sole Walewska. FILETS DE SOLES WALEWSKA – Poach the fillets, left flat, in fish *fumet* that is nearly boiling. Put on top of each fillet a slice of lobster or spiny lobster and a slice of raw truffle. Coat with *Mornay sauce* (see SAUCE) finished off with *Lobster or spiny lobster butter* (see BUTTER, *Compound butters*). Brown in a hot oven.

Fillets of sole with red wine. FILETS DE SOLES AU VIN ROUGE – Made with red wine like *Fillets of sole with Chambertin*.

Fillets of sole with white wine. FILETS DE SOLES AU VIN BLANC – Poach folded fillets in a *fumet* made with white wine, like *Sole with white wine*.

Sole à la florentine – Poach in fish *fumet* that is nearly boiling. Drain and remove the backbone. Set on a fireproof dish on a bed of blanched, drained and pressed leaf spinach simmered in butter. Coat with *Mornay sauce* (see SAUCE). Sprinkle with butter and melted cheese. Brown in oven.

Fried sole. SOLE FRITE – Soak the sole in milk, drain and flour it. Plunge into hot fat or oil. Drain as soon as it is a golden colour, and season with very dry salt. Garnish with fried parsley and lemon.

Sole fritters. FRITOT DE SOLES – Marinate the fillets for 30 minutes in oil, lemon juice, chopped parsley, salt and pepper. Dip in a light batter and fry in deep fat. Arrange in a mound. Garnish with fried parsley and lemon. Serve with *Tomato sauce* (see SAUCE).

Golden sole. SOLE DORÉE – Cook the sole, floured, in clarified butter. Top with a row of lemon slices and sprinkle with *Noisette butter* (see BUTTER, *Compound butters*).

Sole au gratin I – Put a sole weighing about 300 g. (11 oz.) into a buttered fireproof dish lined with 1 or 2 tablespoons (2 or 3 tablespoons) of dry *duxelles*. Season with salt and pepper.

Garnish with mushrooms cut in thick slices. Place 3 or 4 cooked mushroom caps on top of the soles. Coat with *Duxelles sauce* (see SAUCE) to which some concentrated fish *fumet* has been added. Sprinkle with breadcrumbs. Cook in a moderate oven until brown. Squeeze over a few drops of lemon juice.

Sole au gratin II – Put the sole, well seasoned, into a buttered fireproof dish lined with chopped shallot and parsley moistened with 2 tablespoons (3 tablespoons) white wine and a few drops of lemon juice. Dot little pieces of butter on top. Cook in the oven for 5 minutes. Drain off the cooking liquor, boil down, and add to it 4 tablespoons (5 tablespoons) *duxelles*. Add a teaspoon *Tomato purée* (see PURÉE).

Garnish the sole with mushrooms and pour the sauce over. Sprinkle with breadcrumbs and melted butter. Brown in a hot oven.

Grilled sole. SOLE GRILLÉE – Make shallow incisions across the sole, season it, brush with oil or melted butter, and cook under the grill at a moderate heat. Surround with slices of lemon and small bunches of fresh parsley, and serve with *Maître d'hôtel butter* (see BUTTER, *Compound butters*) or any sauce suitable for grilled fish.

Gulyas of sole. GULYAS DE SOLES – Cut the fillets into square pieces. Season and put them into a sauté pan in which (for 8 fillets) 100 g. (4 oz., 1 cup) chopped onion seasoned with $1\frac{1}{2}$ teaspoons paprika have been cooked in butter. Sauté the pieces of sole quickly on each side. Take them out of the pan and put in 2 tablespoons (3 tablespoons) *Béchamel sauce* (see SAUCE), 1 tablespoon tomato purée and 2 dl. ($\frac{1}{3}$ pint, scant cup) fresh cream. Simmer for a few moments. Put the pieces of sole back in the pan and cook for another 3 minutes. Serve with boiled potatoes.

Sole marchand de vin – Insert into a sole, with the fillets cut and raised a little, a piece of butter the size of a walnut seasoned with salt and pepper. Put the fish on a buttered baking dish spinkled with a tablespoon of chopped shallot. Season, pour over $1\frac{1}{2}$ dl. ($\frac{1}{4}$ pint, $\frac{2}{3}$ cup) red wine and poach in the oven.

Set the sole on a serving dish. Coat with a sauce made by boiling down the poaching liquor and adding to it a teaspoon of fish or meat glaze, 40 g. ($1\frac{1}{2}$ oz., 3 tablespoons) butter, a pinch of chopped parsley and a few drops of lemon juice.

Sole à la marinière – Poach the sole very gently in a fish *fumet* to which chopped shallot has been added. Drain, and set it on a dish. Surround with *Mussels à la marinière* (see MUSSELS) removed from their shells and de-bearded. Coat with *Marinière sauce* (see SAUCE) to which concentrated *fumet* has been added.

This dish is sometimes garnished with peeled shrimps.

Sole en matelote à la normande. – Cut 2 large thick soles into pieces. Season with salt and pepper and arrange in a sauté pan in which a chopped onion has been cooked very gently without being allowed to colour. Pour over 3 dl. ($\frac{1}{2}$ pint, $1\frac{1}{4}$ cups) dry white wine and a squeeze of lemon juice.

Cook for 10 minutes. Drain the pieces and put them in a sauté dish, together with mushrooms cooked in a flour and water *court-bouillon*, peeled shrimps, and *Mussels à la marinière* (see MUSSEL) removed from their shells. Pour over a *Normande sauce* (see SAUCE) incorporating the cooking liquor of both the soles and the mussels. Heat without allowing to boil.

Arrange the pieces of sole on a dish and garnish with the mussels, shrimps, and the mushrooms arranged in groups. Set thin slices of truffles heated in butter on top of each piece, and garnish with smelts coated in egg and breadcrumbs and fried, and croûtons of bread fried in butter.

This dish may also be prepared using cider as the cooking liquid.

Sole à la ménagère – Put the sole in a fireproof dish on a layer of carrots, onion and celery, chopped and cooked in butter until soft. Season with salt, pepper, a pinch of thyme and powdered bay leaf. Moisten with 1 dl. (6 tablespoons, scant $\frac{1}{2}$ cup) red wine. Cover and cook in the oven. Drain off the cooking wine. Thicken this with a tablespoon *Kneaded butter* (see BUTTER, *Compound butters*), then stir in extra butter. Coat the sole with this sauce. Glaze in a hot oven.

Sole à la meunière – Season and flour the sole and cook in butter.

Set on a serving dish. Sprinkle with chopped parsley and squeeze over a few drops of lemon juice. Pour over the hot cooking butter.

Sole à la meunière, various garnishes. SOLE À LA MEUNIÈRE – Cook the sole as indicated above. Set on a dish and surround with a garnish. Finish as in the last recipe. Garnish with:

Aubergines cut in rounds and sautéed in butter, *cèpes* sliced and sautéed in butter (with the addition, if liked, of chopped shallot or a little garlic), sliced sautéed mushrooms set on top of the fish, courgettes prepared in the same way as aubergines, potatoes cut in large dice and sautéed in butter, orange, peeled and sliced, the sole having a few drops of orange juice instead of lemon juice squeezed over it with the cooking butter, grapes, peeled and sprinkled with butter, sliced tomatoes sautéed in butter or oil, truffles cut in thick strips, cooked lightly in the butter in which the sole was cooked.

Sole meunière Mont-Bry – 'Prepare in advance 200 g. ($\frac{1}{2}$ lb.) noodles cut very finely (dried noodles will not do for this purpose). Heat and peel 6 large tomatoes and press them to remove all seeds and juice. Add to these a medium-sized onion, chopped and cooked in butter until golden, a pinch of salt, a pinch of sugar and a little crushed garlic. Cover and cook gently.

'Prepare separately 3 soles weighing about 450 g. (about 1 lb.) each. Detach the fillets a little from the backbone (on the side from which the brown skin has been removed) and season with salt and pepper. Toss them in flour and cook in clarified butter until golden brown.

'In another pan heat 100 g. (4 oz., $\frac{1}{2}$ cup) clarified butter. Put in the noodles and sauté them until they are lightly fried and crisp.

'Set the soles on a heated dish, squeeze over a little lemon juice, sprinkle chopped parsley over, surround with the tomato, and arrange the noodles in a mound at each end of the dish. Sprinkle the soles generously with *Noisette butter* (see BUTTER, *Compound butters*) and serve immediately so that when the dish arrives at the table the butter is still hot and frothy.' (Philéas Gilbert.)

Sole Montreuil – Poach the sole in nearly boiling *fumet*. Surround with potato balls cooked in salted water. Coat the sole with *White wine sauce* and the potato balls with *Shrimp sauce* or any other pink sauce made with a shellfish butter (see SAUCE).

Sole Mornay – Cooked like *Brill Mornay*, see BRILL.

Sole Mousse. MOUSSE DE SOLES – Small preparations made with the same mixture as for large mousses (see FISH, *Fish mousse*), but cooked in *dariole* moulds, *cassolettes* or goffered paper cases.

Cold *mousselines* of sole are used to garnish large cold fish.

Sole with mushrooms. SOLE AUX CHAMPIGNONS – Prepare with whole sole in the same way as for *Brill with mushrooms* (see BRILL) or *Fillets of sole with mushrooms*.

Sole à la Nantua – Cooked in the same way as *Brill with crayfish à la Nantua* (see BRILL).

Sole à la niçoise – Season the sole, brush it with oil, and grill. Surround with a *niçoise garnish* composed of tomatoes cooked in butter until soft, tarragon mixed with a little anchovy butter, black olives and capers; these being arranged in separate groups. Place anchovy fillets and slices of peeled lemon on the sole.

Sole Noël – Poach the sole in the cooking liquor of mussels or in Chablis. Cook 4 peeled mushroom caps in the same baking dish.

Set the sole, well drained, in a fireproof dish, with the mushrooms on top. Surround with shelled mussels and shrimps.

Boil down the cooking liquor. Thicken it with 2 egg yolks and beat in extra butter. Coat the sole and garnish with this sauce. Brown quickly in a very hot oven. (Octave Vaudable's recipe.)

Sole à la normande – *Sole au vin blanc* accompanied by a complicated garnish, including ingredients such as truffles, which have no fundamental place in Normandy cooking. The dish came from Normandy in the guise of *stewed fish with cream*, being originally prepared with cider instead of white wine. Experts have added a rich garnish.

Trim the sole, split it, and raise the fillets a little from the skinned side. Break the backbone in two or three places. Poach in fish *fumet* made with white wine, nearly boiling, to which the cooking juices of the mussels, oysters and mushrooms have been added. Drain and wipe the fish, and remove the backbone.

Garnish, for a sole weighing about 400 g. (14 oz.): 4 poached and de-bearded oysters, 12 mussels cooked in white wine, 25 g. (1 oz.) peeled shrimps and 4 peeled mushrooms cooked in white wine, 6 slices truffles, 4 fried gudgeon, 4 trussed crayfish cooked in *court-bouillon*, and 4 croûtons of bread fried in butter.

Coat with *Normande sauce* (see SAUCE) made with the *fumet* in which the fish was cooked. Add the other garnishes: the truffles, glazed with fish aspic jelly, the oysters and the mushrooms set in a straight line down the middle of the fish, the croûtons of bread fried in butter alternating with the truffles on top of the fish, the fried gudgeon and the crayfish arranged on the sides of the dish. Coat the sole with sauce and pour a ring of light fish jelly, or meat aspic jelly around the fish.

Croûtons of fried bread are often replaced by small cut-outs of puff pastry. Frequently, too, the fried gudgeon are replaced by fried smelts.

Pâté of sole (hot and cold). PÂTÉS DE SOLES CHAUDS ET FROIDS – Prepare like other fish pies, using fillets of sole (usually spread with forcemeat and rolled in *paupiettes*), *Pike forcemeat* (see FORCEMEAT) or forcemeat made of any other fish, and truffles. (See PÂTÉ.)

When these pies are to be served hot, pour into them, before serving, a few tablespoons of *Fish fumet* (see FUMET) mixed with cream, or a few tablespoons of the accompanying sauce.

When served cold, a few tablespoons of *Fish aspic* (see ASPIC) are poured in through the hole in the top of the 'lid'. This should be done only when the pie is completely cold.

Paupiettes of sole. PAUPIETTES DE SOLES – Fillets of sole spread with a fish forcemeat or some other mixture, rolled up and cooked slowly in a fish *fumet*, or in butter.

All the garnishes and sauces used for fillets of sole are applicable to *paupiettes*. Rolled *paupiettes* of sole are also served cold.

Paupiettes of sole Mont-Bry. PAUPIETTES DE SOLES MONT-BRY – Spread fillets thinly with *Fish forcemeat* (see FORCEMEAT). Roll them in *paupiettes*. Cook very gently in fish *fumet* made with white wine.

Paupiettes of sole Mont-Bry

Drain the *paupiettes* and set each one in a tomato which has been cooked in oil and half-filled with risotto seasoned with saffron. Coat the *paupiettes* with the cooking liquor concentrated and mixed with fresh cream, to which chopped chervil and tarragon have been added.

Paupiettes of sole à la nissarde. PAUPIETTES DE SOLES À LA NISSARDE – Spread the fillets with *Pike forcemeat* (see FORCEMEAT) finished off with *Anchovy essence* (see ESSENCE) or purée and chopped parsley. Roll in *paupiettes*.

Poach these in concentrated *fumet*, drain them, and set each into half a courgette cooked in butter and slightly hollowed out. Place on a dish.

Boil down the cooking liquor, add tomato purée and butter, blend, and pour over the *paupiettes*. Sprinkle with grated Parmesan and a few drops of oil. Brown in the oven.

Paupiettes of sole Paillard. PAUPIETTES DE SOLE PAILLARD – 'Lay out on the table the flattened fillets of sole. Season and spread them thinly with *Fish forcemeat* (see FORCEMEAT) finished off with mushroom purée. Roll them into cork-shaped pieces. Put them into a sauté pan lined with chopped onions and mushrooms, add a *bouquet garni* and moisten with fish *fumet* or dry white wine. Cook, covered, in the oven for 12 minutes.

'Drain the *paupiettes*, arrange them in a deep, buttered dish, cover and keep warm.

'Strain the cooking liquor through muslin and add to it an equal quantity of mushroom purée, 2 egg yolks and 2 dl. ($\frac{1}{3}$ pint, scant cup) fresh cream. Bring just to the boil, whisking all the time, and add the seasoning.

'Coat the *paupiettes* with this sauce, glaze in a very hot oven, and serve immediately.' (A. Deland, formerly head chef at the *Restaurant Paillard*.)

At the *Restaurant Paillard*, these *paupiettes* were served on artichoke bottoms.

Sole à la paysanne – For a sole weighing 350 g. (12 oz.): Cook a carrot, an onion, a tender stick of celery and the white part of a leek gently in butter, seasoning them with salt and a pinch of sugar. When cooked, moisten them with just enough warm water to cover them. Add 1 tablespoon diced French beans and 1 tablespoon fresh green peas. Finish cooking the vegetables together, boiling down the liquid a little.

Put the sole, seasoned with salt and pepper, into a buttered earthenware dish. Cover with the vegetable mixture and its cooking liquor. Poach the sole in this liquid, and drain off as much as possible, boiling down the liquid. Add 15 g. ($\frac{1}{2}$ oz., 1 tablespoon) butter, stirring well. Pour this sauce over the sole and glaze in a hot oven.

This method of preparation is sometimes described on menus as *sole à la russe*, but it is more logical to call it *à la paysanne* because the vegetables are cooked *à la paysanne*.

Pilaf of sole. PILAF DE SOLES – Cut the fillets of sole into small square pieces and sauté them in butter. Add sliced mushrooms, also sautéed in butter. Set the fish in the middle of *Rice pilaf* (see PILAF) shaped into a border mould. Coat the fish with *Tomato sauce* or *Normande sauce* (see SAUCE.)

Sole sur le plat – Put a little butter, seasoned with salt and pepper, inside a sole whose fillets have been slightly raised, and set in a buttered fireproof dish. Season further with salt and pepper. Moisten with 1 dl. (6 tablespoons, scant $\frac{1}{2}$ cup) fish *fumet* and a few drops of lemon juice. Dot small pieces of butter over the fish.

Cook in the oven, basting frequently, until the liquor is reduced to a syrupy consistency and has given the sole a blonde glaze. Serve in the dish in which it was cooked.

Sole sur le plat may also be prepared replacing the *fumet* with wine: Alsace wine, Chablis, dry Champagne, Cassis,

Sauternes, Monbazillac, Seyssel, Jurançon, Muscadet, *vin rosé*, various red wines of Burgundy, Bordelais and other regions.

Poached sole, various sauces. SOLE BOUILLIE, POCHÉE – Cook the sole in a stock or *court-bouillon* made of milk and water seasoned with salt. Drain and set on a perforated dish. Garnish with parsley and boiled potatoes. Serve with melted butter or a sauce suitable for poached fish: *Hollandaise*, *Fines herbes*, *Lobster*, etc. (see SAUCE).

Sole à la portugaise – Put the seasoned sole into a fireproof dish lined with cooked tomatoes mixed with chopped onion cooked in oil and seasoned with a little garlic. Moisten with 2 tablespoons (3 tablespoons) fish *fumet* and 3 to 4 tablespoons (4 to 5 tablespoons) olive oil. Cook in the oven, basting often. Sprinkle the sole with breadcrumbs and brown lightly. Add chopped parsley and a few drops of lemon juice.

Sole à la provençale – Put the seasoned sole into an oiled dish. Moisten with 1 dl. (6 tablespoons, scant $\frac{1}{2}$ cup) fish *fumet* with a little garlic. Sprinkle over a tablespoon of oil and cook in the oven. When almost cooked, surround with halved tomatoes sautéed in oil. Set 4 slices of peeled lemon on the fish. Sprinkle with breadcrumbs and finish cooking in the oven. Sprinkle with chopped parsley and serve in the cooking dish.

Purée of sole. PURÉE DE SOLES – Cook fillets of sole in butter and press through a fine sieve. Bind with *Béchamel sauce* or with fish *Velouté sauce* mixed with cream (see SAUCE).

This filling is used mostly as a filling for flaky pastry, patties, tartlets, *barquettes* or similar preparations.

Quenelles of sole. QUENELLES DE SOLES – Quenelle forcemeat made with sole is prepared in the same way as *Pike forcemeat*. (See QUENELLE and FORCEMEAT.)

It is set on cut-out pieces of puff pastry or oval croûtons of bread fried in butter, and accompanied by garnish prescribed for fillets of sole, and coated with sauce to blend with the rest of the dish.

Sole Richelieu – Prepared with a whole sole in the same way as *Fillets of sole Richelieu*.

Risotto of sole. RISOTTO DE SOLES – Made of *Pilaf of sole* with *Risotto* (see RICE) instead of pilaf rice.

Shelled mussels or shrimps or any other shellfish may be added to these dishes, as well as mushrooms.

Sole à la russe – See *Sole à la paysanne*.

Sole Saint-Germain – This method is mainly applied to fillets of fish.

Coat the sole with butter and breadcrumbs, sprinkle with melted butter, and cook under the grill at a low heat. Set on a hot dish, surround with potatoes cut to look like olives and cooked in butter. Serve with *Béarnaise sauce* (see SAUCE).

Scallop shells of sole. COQUILLES DE SOLES – Prepare with fillets of sole cooked in butter, like *Brill in scallop shells* (see BRILL).

Sole with shrimps. SOLE AUX CREVETTES – Prepare with the whole sole poached in a fish *fumet* that is almost boiling. Drain the sole, set on a dish, and surround with mussels cooked in white wine, and peeled shrimps. Coat with *White wine sauce* (see SAUCE). Serve as it is, or glaze in a hot oven.

Sole with red wine. SOLE AU VIN ROUGE – Season the sole with salt and pepper. Put it in a baking dish on a layer of chopped onions and carrots which have been tossed in butter. Add a sprig of thyme, a piece of bay leaf and mushroom skins. Dot the top of the fish with tiny pieces of butter. Poach, covered, in the oven. Drain, dry, trim and remove the backbone.

Set on a dish, and coat with its cooking liquor finished off according to the instructions given elsewhere for *Red wine sauce for fish* (see SAUCE). Garnish with mushrooms and small white onions.

Red wine used to poach fish may be of any of a number of different vintages, Bordeaux, Burgundy, Côtes du Rhône, Touraine, etc. Vin ordinaire may also be used.

Sole with white wine. SOLE AU VIN BLANC – Poach the sole very gently in a *fumet* made with white wine. Drain the fish, trim it, remove the backbone. Coat with a *White wine sauce* prepared with the *fumet* in which the fish was cooked, according to one of the recipes given for this sauce (see SAUCE).

Serve as it is or glaze in a very hot oven.

SOLILEM or SOLIMEME – Cake, Alsatian in origin.

Ingredients. 500 g. (1 lb. 2 oz., $4\frac{1}{2}$ cups) sifted flour, 125 g. (4 oz., $\frac{1}{2}$ cup) butter, 15 g. ($\frac{1}{2}$ oz., 1 tablespoon) sugar, 15 g. ($\frac{1}{2}$ oz., $\frac{1}{2}$ cake) yeast, 1 dl. (6 tablespoons, scant $\frac{1}{2}$ cup) cream, 4 eggs, 10 g. ($1\frac{1}{2}$ teaspoons) salt.

Method. Make a paste with a quarter of the flour, the yeast and a little warm water. Leave in a warm place to rise.

Add 2 eggs and $\frac{1}{2}$ dl. (3 tablespoons, scant $\frac{1}{4}$ cup) of the cream. Add the rest of the flour and knead the dough. Incorporate in this paste the butter, the rest of the cream and the eggs, added little by little. Beat the dough. It should be quite soft, and may have a little more cream added to it if it is too firm.

Half-fill a round buttered mould with the dough. Leave to rise. Bake in the oven. Turn the cake out of the mould, cut in two layers, sprinkle each layer with melted, slightly salted butter. Put the two pieces together and serve very hot.

SOLOMON'S SEAL. MUGUET ANGUMEUX – Plant found in the woods. The young shoots are edible and are prepared like asparagus.

This plant is also known as *sceau de Solomon*.

SOMMELIER – Employee charged with the care of the cellars or a member of a religious order concerned with the convent plate, linen, bread and wine.

In large restaurants the *sommelier* is in charge of the wines, both in the cellar and the wine sold in the restaurant. The function of a *sommelier* in a large establishment demands extensive knowledge of wines. He must also understand how to choose wines to blend with particular foods.

A *sommellerie* is either a group of persons engaged in looking after the cellars and drinks in a royal household, or the place where the work of the *sommelier* is done, notably in monasteries and convents.

SOMMIER – Name formerly given to the servants of the kitchen, pantry and *sommellerie* in the palace of the French kings.

SORB-APPLE. SORBE – Fruit of the sorb, a tree of the *Rosaceae* family. Two varieties are known: The *rowan* or *mountain ash*, whose fruits, much relished by thrushes, are highly astringent but used in some districts for distilling; and the *sorb* or *service tree* whose fruits become edible when overripe and serve to make a kind of cider.

SORBETS – See SHERBETS.

SORGHUM. SORGHO – Cereal, native of Africa but long cultivated in southern Europe and China. It is a kind of millet. Its grain is used mostly to make porridges and flat cakes; the stalks, which serve for fodder, contain a high percentage of sugar and can be used to make a fermented drink.

SORREL. OSEILLE – Hardy perennial herb which dates back before 300 B.C. and still grows wild today in Asia, Europe and North America. It is also cultivated.

In the thirteenth century it was listed as an English herb; it has long been used in the making of soups and sauces. The

Sorb-apples on branch

young under-leaves of this plant, also called *sour grass*, are used as salad greens or as a vegetable.

Braised sorrel or sorrel purée. OSEILLE BRAISÉE, PURÉE D'OSEILLE – Put 1 kg. ($2\frac{1}{4}$ lb.) sorrel, picked over and washed in several waters, into a big saucepan. Moisten with $\frac{1}{2}$ dl. (3 tablespoons, scant $\frac{1}{4}$ cup) water and cook on slow heat until it goes down in volume. Drain in a sieve.

Prepare a blond *roux* (q.v.) made of 60 g. (2 oz., $\frac{1}{4}$ cup) butter and 30 g. (1 oz., $\frac{1}{4}$ cup) flour. Mix well, add 6 dl. (1 pint, $2\frac{1}{2}$ cups) white stock, season with salt and a little castor sugar, cover the pan and cook in the oven for 2 hours.

Rub the sorrel through a fine sieve and put it back in the pan to reheat. Bind with a liaison of 3 whole eggs (or 6 yolks), beaten, mixed with 1 dl. (6 tablespoons, scant $\frac{1}{2}$ cup) cream, strained and blended with 150 g. (5 oz., 10 tablespoons) butter. Stir well. Add to the *roux*.

Chiffonnade of sorrel. CHIFFONNADE D'OSEILLE – Pick over, wash and shred the sorrel into a fine *julienne*. Simmer gently in butter until all the water has evaporated.

Chiffonnade of sorrel in butter is used as an element of garnish for various dishes. (See SOUPS AND BROTHS; EGGS, *Sorrel omelette*.)

Chiffonnade of sorrel with cream. CHIFFONNADE D'OSEILLE À LA CRÈME – Cook the chiffonnade on slow heat until it goes down in volume, as described in the preceding recipe. When the liquid is completely evaporated, moisten with a few tablespoons fresh double cream. Simmer for a few minutes.

This is used for the same purposes as the sorrel *chiffonnade* cooked with butter.

Preserved sorrel. CONSERVE D'OSEILLE – Pick over, wash and cook the sorrel slowly as described above. Dry off thoroughly, extracting all the water. Compress it into a stone jar with a wide neck. Cool. Pour over a thick layer of clarified beef fat to seal it and keep in a cool place.

Sorrel can also be bottled by putting it, after it is cooked, into jars or cans and treating them in a steriliser in the usual manner.

SOT-L'Y-LAISSE – This term, meaning 'a fool leaves it', is used to describe the small piece of flesh situated above the parson's nose of a chicken or other fowl which is considered a delicacy. In old French cookery '*ragoûts* of sot-l'y-laisse' are often mentioned.

SOUBISE – Purée of onions and rice used as an accompaniment to various cuts of meat, large and small. (See PURÉE.)

SOU-FASSUM (Nice cookery) – Stuffed cabbage. Blanch the cabbage as for *Stuffed cabbage* (see CABBAGE), and stuff with a forcemeat made of 500 g. (generous 1 lb., 2 cups) sausage meat, 200 g. (7 oz., $1\frac{1}{2}$ cups) diced streaky bacon, blanched and fried, 100 g. (4 oz., 1 cup) chopped onion, lightly cooked in butter, 250 g. (9 oz., $3\frac{1}{2}$ cups) blanched and chopped beetroot leaves, 2 peeled and chopped tomatoes, 100 g. (4 oz., $\frac{3}{4}$ cup) fresh peas, 100 g. (4 oz., $\frac{1}{2}$ cup) blanched rice, the chopped cabbage heart, chopped parsley, crushed garlic, salt and pepper.

Reform the cabbage, wrap in muslin, and cook for 3 hours in a mutton or ordinary *pot-au-feu*.

Serve with *Tomato sauce* (see SAUCE).

SOUFFLÉS – Sweet and savoury, made of ingredients cooked to a purée, thickened with egg yolks and with stiffly beaten egg whites folded in, poured into a soufflé dish or into *cassolettes* and baked in the oven.

The same name has been extended to include quite different preparations, more like mousses or *mousselines*, served either hot or cold.

Small soufflés are made in *cassolettes* of fireproof procelain, ovenproof glass or metal or in special goffered paper cases.

Prepare the soufflé mixture according to the recipe. Turn the mixture into the buttered *cassolettes*, filling these three-quarters full. Smooth the surface.

Set the *cassolettes* on a baking sheet and cook in a cool oven for 8 to 12 minutes. Serve immediately.

True soufflés are divided into two main categories: savoury soufflés, served as *hors-d'œuvres* or small entrées or sometimes as a savoury, and sweet soufflés.

SAVOURY SOUFFLÉS. SOUFFLÉS DE CUISINE – Prepare the basic ingredient, whether purée of meat, fish, shellfish or vegetable, or a *bouillie*.

Bind this ingredient, away from the heat, with 3 egg yolks for every 250 g. (9 oz.) of the mixture. Season quite strongly so as to compensate for the weakening effect of adding egg whites. Mix.

Incorporate 3 or 4 stiffly beaten egg whites and mix quickly, but do not beat. Fill a buttered soufflé dish with this mixture to within a finger's breadth from the top. Smooth over the surface. Cook in a moderate oven for 20 to 25 minutes. Serve immediately.

The same method is used to cook small soufflés in *cassolettes*.

Brain soufflé. SOUFFLÉ DE CERVELLE – Bind 250 g. (9 oz., 1 cup) *Brain purée* (see PURÉE) with $1\frac{1}{2}$ dl. ($\frac{1}{4}$ pint, $\frac{2}{3}$ cup) thick *Béchamel sauce* (see SAUCE). Season with salt, pepper and grated nutmeg.

Add 3 egg yolks, and fold in 3 stiffly beaten egg whites. Fill a buttered soufflé dish with the mixture. Finish as above.

Brain soufflé à la chanoinesse. SOUFFLÉ DE CERVELLE À LA CHANOINESSE – Prepare the mixture as above. Add 50 g. (2 oz., $\frac{1}{2}$ cup) grated Parmesan and 2 tablespoons (3 tablespoons) truffles cut in a fine *julienne*. Finish as above.

Brain soufflés are often served as an *hors-d'œuvre* and cooked in *cassolettes* as for small soufflés.

Calf's liver or chicken liver soufflé. SOUFFLÉ DE FOIE DE VEAU, FOIES DE VOLAILLE – Pound in a mortar 250 g. (9 oz.) diced calf's liver, sautéed in butter and mixed with 35 g. ($1\frac{1}{2}$ oz., 3 tablespoons) butter and 1 dl. (6 tablespoons, scant $\frac{1}{2}$ cup) thick *béchamel sauce*. Season.

Press through a strainer. Add 2 egg yolks and 3 beaten egg whites. Finish as above.

Chicken liver soufflé is prepared in the same way.

Cheese soufflé. SOUFFLÉ AU FROMAGE – Make a white *roux* of 50 g. (2 oz., $\frac{1}{4}$ cup) butter, 60 g. ($2\frac{1}{2}$ oz., $\frac{2}{3}$ cup) flour and 2 dl. ($\frac{1}{3}$ pint, scant cup) milk. Season with salt, pepper and grated nutmeg. Stir over strong heat until boiling.

Table piece with a hunting theme (*Collection air de chasse. Phot. Nicolas*)

Cheese soufflé

Remove from heat, add 50 g. (2 oz., $\frac{1}{2}$ cup) grated Gruyère, 3 egg yolks and 3 beaten egg whites. Finish as above.

This mixture is also cooked in *cassolettes* and served as an *hors-d'œuvre*.

Soufflés are also made with Parmesan, Cheddar or Dutch cheese.

Chestnut soufflé. SOUFFLÉ DE MARRONS – Proceed with chestnut purée, as for *Potato soufflé*.

Chestnut soufflé soubise. SOUFFLÉ DE MARRONS SOUBISE – Prepare the basic mixture in the usual way, using two-thirds *Chestnut purée* and one-third *Onion soubise I* (see PURÉE).

Chicken soufflé. SOUFFLÉ DE VOLAILLE – Pound in a mortar 250 g. (9 oz.) cooked white chicken meat with 2 to 3 tablespoons (3 to 4 tablespoons) thick *béchamel sauce*. Season and press through a sieve.

Cool, add 1 tablespoon butter and mix. Incorporate 3 egg yolks and 3 beaten egg whites. Finish as above.

This recipe applies to chicken, turkey and guinea fowl. The mixture can be served in *cassolettes* as an *hors-d'œuvre*.

Chicken soufflé à la mirepoix. SOUFFLÉ DE VOLAILLE À LA MIREPOIX – Add to the mixture prepared as above, 2 tablespoons (3 tablespoons) *Vegetable mirepoix* (see MIREPOIX). Finish as above.

Chicken soufflé with truffles (soufflé à la reine). SOUFFLÉ DE VOLAILLE AUX TRUFFES – Add to the mixture, prepared as above, 2 tablespoons (3 tablespoons) chopped truffles.

Chicory soufflé. SOUFFLÉ DE CHICORÉE – Dry 250 g. (9 oz.) sieved braised chicory over heat, stirring and shaking to prevent sticking.

Chicory soufflé with Parmesan. SOUFFLÉ DE CHICORÉE AU PARMESAN – Proceed as above, finishing the mixture with 60 g. ($2\frac{1}{2}$ oz., $\frac{2}{3}$ cup) grated Parmesan.

Crayfish soufflé à la normande. SOUFFLÉ D'ÉCREVISSES À LA NORMANDE – Prepare the basic mixture in the same way as for *Shrimp soufflé* (see below). Replace the shrimps with a similar quantity of crayfish.

Turn into a buttered soufflé dish, alternating layers of the soufflé mixture with a *salpicon* of poached and drained oysters, truffles and mushrooms. Finish as in the preceding recipes.

Fish soufflé. SOUFFLÉ DE POISSON – Cook the fish in butter, and press through a sieve. For every 250 g. (9 oz.) fish add $1\frac{1}{2}$ dl. ($\frac{1}{4}$ pint, $\frac{2}{3}$ cup) thick *béchamel sauce*. Bind with 3 egg yolks and incorporate 3 or 4 beaten egg whites. Finish as in the preceding recipes.

This recipe applies to all fish. It can also be applied to left-over fish which has been cooked in butter or white wine.

Soufflé of foie gras (à la Périgueux) – See MOUSSES, *Foie gras mousse (hot)*.

Game soufflé. SOUFFLÉ DE GIBIER – Pound in a mortar 250 g. (9 oz.) cooked game with $1\frac{1}{2}$ dl. ($\frac{1}{4}$ pint, $\frac{2}{3}$ cup) *Béchamel sauce* (see SAUCE) based on game *fumet*. Season and sieve.

Add 3 egg yolks and 3 stiffly beaten egg whites. Finish as in the preceding recipes.

Chiefly served in *cassolettes* as an *hors-d'œuvre*.

Game soufflé à la Périgueux. SOUFFLÉ DE GIBIER À LA PÉRIGUEUX – Add to the above mixture 2 tablespoons (3 tablespoons) chopped truffles. Finish as above.

Ham soufflé. SOUFFLÉ DE JAMBON – Proceed, with 250 g. (9 oz.) lean cooked ham, as for *Game soufflé*.

Served chiefly in *cassolettes* as an *d'œuvre*.

Ham soufflé à la strasbourgeoise. SOUFFLÉ DE JAMBON À LA STRASBOURGEOISE – Add to *Ham purée* (see PURÉE) one third of its weight of *Pâté de foie gras* and 1 tablespoon chopped truffles. Finish as in the preceding recipes.

Soufflé à la hongroise – Prepare a mixture as for *Brain soufflé*, adding 2 tablespoons (3 tablespoons) chopped onion cooked in butter till soft and seasoned with paprika, and 2 tablespoons (3 tablespoons) diced mushrooms sautéed in butter. Finish off as in the preceding recipes.

Chiefly served in *cassolettes* as an *hors-d'œuvre*.

Jerusalem artichoke soufflé. SOUFFLÉ DE TOPINAMBOURS – Proceed in the same way as for *Potato soufflé* using a *Jerusalem artichoke purée* (see PURÉE) instead of potato purée.

Lettuce soufflé. SOUFFLÉ DE LAITUES – Proceed as for *Chicory soufflé*, replacing the chicory with braised, chopped lettuces. Grated Parmesan may be added, if liked.

Lobster soufflé. SOUFFLÉ DE HOMARD – Proceed as for *Shrimp soufflé*, replacing the shrimps with lobster purée.

Meat soufflé. SOUFFLÉ DE VIANDES – Proceed with the meat as for *Calf's liver soufflé*. Any meat may be used for this soufflé if it has been poached or braised, and according to the kind of meat, *béchamel sauce*, *velouté sauce* or any other sauce that will blend with the meat is used to bind the purée.

Parmesan soufflé. SOUFFLÉ AU PARMESAN – Blend 75 g. (3 oz., $\frac{3}{4}$ cup) sifted flour with 2 dl. ($\frac{1}{3}$ pint, scant cup) boiled milk. Season with salt, pepper and grated nutmeg.

Stir over good heat until boiling, then take off the heat and add 50 g. (2 oz., $\frac{1}{2}$ cup) grated Parmesan, 25 g. (1 oz., 2 tablespoons) butter, 3 egg yolks and 3 beaten whites. Finish as in the preceding recipes.

Also served in *cassolettes* as an *hors-d'œuvre*.

Potato soufflé. SOUFFLÉ DE POMMES DE TERRE – Bind 4 dl. ($\frac{3}{4}$ pint, scant 2 cups) *Potato purée* (see POTATOES) with 4 tablespoons ($\frac{1}{3}$ cup) cream. Season. Add 3 egg yolks and 3 beaten egg whites. Finish in the usual way.

Potato soufflé with cheese. SOUFFLÉ DE POMMES DE TERRE AU FROMAGE – As above, adding to the purée 50 g. (2 oz., $\frac{1}{2}$ cup) grated Gruyère or Parmesan.

Potato soufflé à la hongroise. SOUFFLÉ DE POMMES DE TERRE À LA HONGROISE – As above, incorporating chopped onion softened in butter and seasoned with paprika in the potato purée.

Sweet potato soufflé. SOUFFLÉ DE PATATES – Proceed with sweet potato purée in the same way as for *Potato soufflé*.

Shrimp soufflé (or other crustacean). SOUFFLÉ DE CREVETTES – Bind 200 g. (7 oz., $\frac{3}{4}$ cup) *Shrimp purée* (see PURÉE) with $1\frac{1}{2}$ dl. ($\frac{1}{4}$ pint, $\frac{2}{3}$ cup) thick *Béchamel sauce* (see SAUCE) to which the reduced cooking liquor from the shrimps has been added.

Add 3 egg yolks and fold in 3 beaten egg whites. Finish as in the preceding recipes.

Prawn, crayfish, lobster, spiny lobster and crab soufflés are prepared in the same way. A *salpicon* of shrimps or the flesh of the shellfish used may be added to the mixture.

These soufflés are chiefly served as an *hors-d'œuvre*, cooked in *cassolettes*.

Spinach soufflé

Spinach soufflé. SOUFFLÉ D'ÉPINARDS – Proceed as for *Chicory soufflé*, replacing the chicory with an equal quantity of spinach, blanched, drained, pressed and chopped or sieved, and simmered in butter. Finish as in the preceding recipes.

Spinach soufflé à la florentine. SOUFFLÉ D'ÉPINARDS À LA FLORENTINE – Prepare the basic mixture as above, adding 50 g. (2 oz., ½ cup) grated Parmesan to the cooked spinach. Finish as in the preceding recipes.

Spiny lobster soufflé. SOUFFLÉ DE LANGOUSTE – Prepare as for *Shrimp soufflé*, but using a spiny lobster purée instead of a shrimp purée.

Sweetbread soufflé. SOUFFLÉ DE RIS DE VEAU – Proceed as for *Calf's liver soufflé*, replacing the liver with an equal quantity of calf's sweetbreads.

Mostly served in *cassolettes* as an *hors-d'œuvre*.

Tomato soufflé. SOUFFLÉ DE TOMATES – Bind 3 dl. (½ pint, 1¼ cups) thick tomato purée with 1 dl. (6 tablespoons, scant ½ cup) thick *béchamel sauce*. Remove from heat and add 50 g. (2 oz., ½ cup) grated Parmesan, 3 egg yolks and 3 beaten egg whites.

Finish as in the preceding recipes.

This soufflé may be made without the addition of grated Parmesan, or chopped tarragon may be added instead.

Truffle soufflé (Soufflé à la royale). SOUFFLÉ AUX TRUFFES – Bind 150 g. (5 oz., ⅔ cup) *Truffle purée* (see PURÉE) with 1½ dl. (¼ pint, ⅔ cup) *béchamel sauce* made with *Truffle essence* (see ESSENCE). Season.

Add 3 egg yolks and 3 beaten egg whites. Finish as in the preceding recipes.

Chiefly served in *cassolettes* as an *hors-d'œuvre*.

Truffle soufflé with Parmesan. SOUFFLÉ AUX TRUFFES ET AU PARMESAN – Add to a Parmesan soufflé mixture 60 g. (2½ oz., ¾ cup) truffles cut in a fine *julienne*. Finish as in the preceding recipes.

Mostly served in *cassolettes* as an *hors-d'œuvre*.

Vegetable soufflé. SOUFFLÉ DE LÉGUMES – Any vegetable, reduced to a purée, may be used to make soufflé. Before egg yolks are added, these purées should be dried out over heat and *béchamel sauce* should be added as necessary, if they are too thin.

Proceed in the same way as for *Chicory soufflé*.

Artichokes, asparagus, aubergines, carrots, celery, mushrooms, cauliflower, courgettes, turnips, etc., may be used to make soufflés in this way.

SWEET SOUFFLÉS. SOUFFLÉS D'ENTREMETS – Several kinds of basic mixture are used for these soufflés. They can be divided into two principal types: cream-based and fruit-based.

The cream-based mixtures are used for the greater number of soufflés, the basic recipe is varied by the flavouring used and the ingredients added.

Soufflés are made in straight-sided containers of silver, fireproof porcelain or ovenproof glass. Silver soufflé dishes are sometimes provided with an inner dish in which the soufflé is cooked. These utensils are buttered and sprinkled with fine sugar.

Soufflés are cooked in a moderate oven so that the heat penetrates right to the middle of the mixture. A few moments before cooking is finished the soufflé is sprinkled with sugar and glazed in the hottest part of the oven.

The cooking time varies according to the size of the soufflé, but for the quantities given below should be 14 to 16 minutes.

Once cooked and glazed the soufflé must be served without delay.

Cream-based mixtures. APPAREILS À LA CRÈME –

Mixture A. Bring 1 dl. (6 tablespoons, scant ½ cup) milk to the boil with 40 g. (1½ oz., 3 tablespoons) sugar and a pinch of salt. Add 25 g. (1 oz., ¼ cup) sifted flour blended with a little cold milk. Flavour as required. Cook, stirring, for 2 to 3 minutes. Remove from the heat and add 2 egg yolks, 10 g. (½ oz., 1 tablespoon) butter and 3 stiffly beaten egg whites.

Mix quickly and fill a buttered and sugared soufflé dish. Smooth the surface of the soufflé. Cook in a moderate oven. Two minutes before serving sprinkle with sugar to glaze.

Mixture B. Proceed in the same way as for *Mixture A*, replacing the flour with a teaspoon of potato starch.

Mixture C. Mix 65 g. (2½ oz., ⅔ cup) flour, 65 g. (2½ oz., ⅓ cup) fine sugar, a pinch of salt, 1 whole egg and 1 egg yolk in a saucepan.

Stir in 2½ dl. (scant ½ pint, generous cup) boiling milk and cook, stirring well to keep the mixture from sticking to the bottom. Flavour as required.

Remove from the heat and add 25 g. (1 oz., 2 tablespoons) butter, 1 egg yolk, and 3 stiffly beaten egg whites. Finish as above.

Mixture D. Place 25 g. (1 oz., ¼ cup) sifted flour, 40 g. (1½ oz., 3 tablespoons) sugar and a pinch of salt in a saucepan. Mix smoothly with 1 dl. (6 tablespoons, scant ½ cup) cold milk, add flavouring and cook for a few minutes over moderate heat, stirring all the time.

Remove from the heat and add 3 egg yolks, 10 g. (½ oz., 1 tablespoon) butter, and fold in 3 stiffly beaten egg whites.

Finish as above.

Mixture E. Blend 1½ teaspoons arrowroot with 1 dl. (6 tablespoons, scant ½ cup) cold milk in a saucepan. Add 40 g. (1½ oz., 3 tablespoons) sugar and a pinch of salt. Bring to boiling point and cook for a moment, stirring all the time.

Add, away from the heat, 2 egg yolks and 2 stiffly beaten egg whites. Finish as above.

This mixture is used in invalid cookery.

Mixture F. Put 40 g. (1½ oz., 3 tablespoons) sugar, 3 egg yolks and a pinch of salt into a small saucepan. Beat well with a spatula.

Stir in 1 dl. (6 tablespoons, scant ½ cup) boiling molk. Stir over the heat until the first bubbles begin to appear. Remove from the heat and add 2 or 3 stiffly beaten egg whites. Finish as above.

This recipe is also used in invalid cookery.

Flavouring soufflés. The flavour is added to the basic mixture during or after cooking. Vanilla pods and lemon, orange and mandarin peel are added during cooking. Liqueurs are added away from the heat before incorporating egg whites.

Chopped candied fruits are also added just before folding in the egg whites.

Fruit-based mixtures. APPAREILS À PURÉE DE FRUITS – Add

250 g. (9 oz., scant $1\frac{1}{4}$ cups) sugar, cooked to small crack degree (see SUGAR) to 200 g. (7 oz., scant cup) fruit purée. Boil for a moment. Pour the mixture onto 5 or 6 stiffly beaten egg whites, and mix quickly.

Turn into a buttered soufflé dish sprinkled with sugar. Cook in the same way as described in the preceding recipes.

Although soufflés of fresh fruit are made with this mixture, they may also be made with a cream-based mixture. A very thick fruit purée is added before incorporating the egg whites.

Almond soufflé. SOUFFLÉ AUX AMANDES – Fill a soufflé dish with a cream-based mixture in which *Almond milk* (see ALMOND) has been used instead of ordinary milk, and to which 2 or 3 tablespoons chopped roasted almonds, have been added. Cook in the usual way. Sprinkle with chopped almonds.

Fresh almond soufflé. SOUFFLÉ AUX AMANDES FRAÎCHES – As above, replacing the roasted almonds with fresh, blanched almonds.

Ambassadrice soufflé. SOUFFLÉ AMBASSADRICE – Cream-based soufflé well flavoured with vanilla, with the addition of 2 crumbled macaroons and 2 to 3 tablespoons fresh, blanched almonds flavoured with rum.

Apple soufflé. SOUFFLÉ AUX POMMES – Proceed as for Apricot soufflé (see below) using stewed apples or apple jam.

Russian apple soufflé. SOUFFLÉ AUX POMMES À LA RUSSE – Add some thick apple purée to the stiffly beaten egg whites (two-thirds apple purée and one-third egg white).

Fill a soufflé dish with the mixture and cook in the usual way.

Apricot soufflé I. SOUFFLÉ AUX ABRICOTS – Fill a buttered soufflé dish, sprinkled with sugar, with a cream-based mixture flavoured with kirsch, and with the addition of pieces of apricot cooked in syrup, well drained then soaked in kirsch.

Apricot soufflé II. SOUFFLÉ AUX ABRICOTS – Proceed as above, using one of the cream-based mixtures with the addition of a very thick apricot purée flavoured with kirsch.

Apricot soufflé III. SOUFFLÉ AUX ABRICOTS – Fill the soufflé dish with apricot purée, made as described in the recipe for fruit-based mixtures and flavoured with kirsch.

In all the above recipes for apricot soufflé, a *salpicon* of candied apricots, soaked in kirsch or some other liqueur, should be added.

Alternatively, as the dish is filled, spoonfuls of very thick apricot jam may be added to the soufflé mixture.

Cherry soufflé I. SOUFFLÉ AUX CERISES – Cream-based soufflé mixture flavoured with kirsch or cherry brandy, mixed with stoned cherries cooked in their own juice with sugar.

Cherry soufflé II. SOUFFLÉ AUX CERISES – Cream-based soufflé mixture made with cherry pulp according to the recipe for fruit-based soufflé mixture.

Chestnut soufflé – See *Mont-Bry soufflé*.

Chocolate soufflé. SOUFFLÉ AU CHOCOLAT – Cream-based soufflé mixture to which 50 g. (2 oz., $\frac{2}{3}$ cup) grated chocolate, melted over a very low heat or dissolved in a little milk has been added. Powdered cocoa may be used instead of grated chocolate.

Cocoa soufflé – See *Chocolate soufflé*.

Coffee soufflé. SOUFFLÉ AU CAFÉ – Cream-based soufflé mixture with the addition of 4 or 5 tablespoons of coffee essence.

Curaçao soufflé. SOUFFLÉ AU CURAÇAO – Cream-based soufflé mixture flavoured with orange peel and a small glass of Curaçao.

Hazelnut soufflé. SOUFFLÉ AUX AVELINES – Cream-based mixture to which 2 to 4 tablespoons hazelnut praline have been added.

Soufflés made with almonds, hazelnuts, walnuts and pistachio nuts are usually made without any flavouring. A little vanilla or a liqueur, preferably rum or kirsch, may, however, be added.

Lemon soufflé. SOUFFLÉ AU CITRON – Cream-based soufflé mixture flavoured with finely chopped lemon peel.

Liqueur-flavoured soufflé. SOUFFLÉ AUX LIQUEURS – Proceed, using the required liqueur, as for *Curaçao soufflé*.

To all liqueur-flavoured soufflés, in addition to the liqueur used in the basic mixture, sponge finger biscuits, cut into small squares and soaked in the same liqueur, may be added.

Mont-Bry soufflé. SOUFFLÉ MONT-BRY – Cream-based soufflé mixture mixed with one-third of its volume of chestnuts cooked in syrup and strongly flavoured with vanilla. Garnish with *marrons glacés* soaked in kirsch.

Orange or mandarin soufflé. SOUFFLÉ À L'ORANGE, À LA MANDARINE – Cream-based soufflé mixture flavoured with the finely chopped peel of orange or mandarins.

Palmyra soufflé. SOUFFLÉ PALMYRE – Cream-based soufflé mixture well flavoured with vanilla, mixed with small pieces of sponge finger biscuits soaked in kirsch and anisette.

Peach soufflé. SOUFFLÉ AUX PÊCHES – Use one of the recipes given for *Apricot soufflé*, substituting peaches.

Pear soufflé. SOUFFLÉ AUX POIRES – Use one of the recipes for *Apricot soufflé*, replacing the apricots with pears cooked in sugar and their own juice without any added liquid.

Praline soufflé. SOUFFLÉ PRALINE – Cream-based soufflé mixture flavoured with vanilla, with 2 to 3 tablespoons of praline added.

When making this soufflé the praline may be put into the milk used to make the cream-based mixture.

Rothschild soufflé I. SOUFFLÉ ROTHSCHILD – Cream-based soufflé mixture to which 2 to 3 tablespoons of *salpicon* of candied fruits soaked in brandy have been added.

When the soufflé is almost cooked, decorate with crystallised cherries.

Rothschild soufflé II. SOUFFLÉ ROTHSCHILD – Cream-based soufflé mixture to which 2 tablespoons (3 tablespoons) of *salpicon* of candied fruits, soaked in Danziger goldwasser, have been added.

When the soufflé is almost cooked, decorate with large strawberries.

Strawberry soufflé I. SOUFFLÉ AUX FRAISES – Cream-based soufflé mixture mixed with wild strawberries or ordinary large strawberries sprinkled with sugar.

Strawberry soufflé II. SOUFFLÉ AUX FRAISES – Cream-based soufflé mixture mixed with a very thick strawberry pulp.

Strawberry soufflé III. SOUFFLÉ AUX FRAISES – Strawberry pulp prepared as a fruit-based soufflé mixture.

Tea soufflé. SOUFFLÉ AU THÉ – Cream-based soufflé mixture prepared with milk in which tea has been infused.

Vanilla soufflé. SOUFFLÉ À LA VANILLE – Cream-based soufflé mixture flavoured with vanilla.

Violet soufflé. SOUFFLÉ AUX VIOLETTES – Cream-based soufflé mixture flavoured with a few drops of essence of violets and with candied violets added.

In the same way soufflés may be made with other candied flowers such as roses and orange flower petals.

Walnut soufflé. – SOUFFLÉ AUX NOIX – Cream-based soufflé mixture mixed with lightly toasted and chopped walnuts and flavoured with walnut juice. This soufflé can be made with fresh walnuts.

SOUPE – The French word *soupe* was once used to describe various ingredients put into a *bouillon* or broth, whether made with fish or meat. Thus, for example, the croûtons of bread or the meat in the broth were *soupes*.

Nowadays in France the word *soupe*, as distinct from the more frequently used *potage*, is used to designate a peasant-

Coffee soufflé (*Robert Carrier*)

style soup, of which the principal examples are cabbage soup, *garbure* and various thick vegetable soups, usually garnished with bread.

SOUPS AND BROTHS. POTAGES, SOUPES – In the seventeenth century the word *potage* did not have the same meaning as it has today. In those days the name was given to big dishes of meat or fish boiled with vegetables:

'Cependant on apporte un potage:
Un coq y paraissait en pompeux equipage'.
'A *potage* is, however, brought in:
A cock is seen in it, in state.'

(Boileau, *Satire III*).

The old *potage à la jambe de bois* is a good example of such a dish.

The soup is now what Grimod de la Reynière described so well when he said: 'It is to a dinner what a portico or a peristyle is to a building; that is to say, it is not only the first part of it, but it must be devised in such a manner as to set the tone of the whole banquet, in the same way as the overture of an opera announces the subject of the work'.

In other words, the soup must be in harmony with the whole menu.

At a family gathering, or at an intimate dinner, soup is served in a soup tureen placed on the table, and the master or the lady of the house serves it to the guests.

At ceremonial dinners, especially of the kind where the menu includes two soups – a clear and a thick – this service is performed at a table placed not far from the dining table and the servants pass the plates to the guests. Whatever manner is adopted, soup must be served piping hot, in very hot plates.

Soups are based on meat stocks or made with water, with bread added to them, supplemented by vegetables, *quenelles*, *chiffonades*, pasta products, cereal starches and various other garnishings. (See GARNISHES.)

Depending on their consistency, soups can be classified into two big categories: clear soups and thick soups.

A clear soup is a consommé with various light garnishes added. The garnishings must be of the kind that go with the consommé: meat stock clarified and at the same time strengthened with lean chopped beef, diced aromatic vegetables and egg whites.

There are several kinds of thick soups. The liaison, or thickening, is obtained either naturally by the dissolving of the farinaceous contents of the ingredients used, or by an addition of *roux* or some other element such as cooked rice, bread boiled to pulp, purée of a starchy vegetable, etc. A number of thick soups are bound with a liaison of egg yolks and cream just before serving.

In this section thick soups are classified under three sub-headings: cream, purées and *velouté*.

Potage à la jambe de bois

Purée soups are either purées of feculent vegetables or leguminous plants, when the liaison is achieved naturally by the starch constituents of these vegetables, or purées of shellfish (*bisques*), fish, meat and vegetables, the liaison of which is obtained by the addition of a supplementary element.

In the cream soups (shellfish, fish, meat and vegetable) the liaison is obtained by the addition of a certain quantity of *Béchamel sauce* (see SAUCE).

In *velouté* (whether shellfish, fish, meat or vegetable) the liaison is obtained by the addition of *Velouté sauce* (see SAUCE) and the final binding with yolks and cream.

The following should also be mentioned:

1. Thickened consommés. Ordinary or double consommés based on meat, fish or vegetable stock, to which egg yolks and fresh cream are added at the last moment.

2. Compound or mixed thick soups. Made by mixing, in well-defined proportions, different kinds of soups which do not clash in flavour. These can be thickened with egg yolks and fresh cream.

3. Special flour of various cereals, oatmeal, corn (maize), barley, rice, etc., diluted with meat or vegetable stock, which are sometimes called *bouillies*, can also be put in the category of thick soups. These soups can also be bound with egg yolks and cream. They are mainly given to children.

Following the section on thick *velouté* soups, there is a section dealing with special and *velouté* soups, another on classical and regional soups, and one on international soups and broths.

CLEAR SOUPS. POTAGES CLAIRS –

Simple white consommé or grande marmite – Ordinary meat stock made in a big stockpot is called *simple white consommé*. We specify the big stockpot, *grande marmite*, to differentiate it from a soup called *petite marmite*, the recipe for which is given elsewhere in this book.

This simple consommé serves as a basis for all clear soups. If it is prepared with all the usual nutritive and aromatic ingredients, it should be very savoury.

The following cuts of meat are best for consommé: Round of beef and silverside, these cuts make a savoury stock, but give rather dry boiled beef if it is to be eaten separately.

Leg of beef (comprising the whole of the upper tibial part, sold in transversal sections), shin, which also makes good stock.

Shoulder of beef, shoulder blade, neck and ox-cheek furnish cuts which also produce good stock. Boned ox-cheek makes quite good stock.

Various sub-divisions of the shoulder: clod, chuck end, the gemellus muscle (situated in front of the shoulder blade) – all of which are cuts of the second category – produce good stock. To these various cuts butchers usually add, as 'make-weight', pieces of knuckle, leg, and other bony and gristly parts.

Rib of beef, which makes excellent stock, is subdivided into fore-ribs (five ribs situated in the shoulder part), and middle-rib, (four ribs from the eighth to the eleventh rib); and chuck end of the clod (three ribs).

The top of sirloin, and the flank which with the lower end of the breast (gristle, middle and thick end) constitute the *pis de boeuf*.

In addition to the basic cuts of meat mentioned above, it is a good idea to add chicken bones and giblets (previously browned in the oven) to the stockpot, as this improves the stock.

Marrow bones (broken into chunks and each wrapped in a piece of muslin) can also be added. The cooked marrow can be extracted and spread on bread or toast.

Ingredients. For 5 litres (4½ quarts, 5½ quarts) consommé:

Nourishing ingredients. 2 kg. (4½ lb.) lean beef, 1½ kg. (3¼ lb.) beef knuckle (with bone).

Aromatic ingredients. 3 or 4 big carrots, 2 or 3 turnips, 1 parsnip, 3 to 4 leeks tied in a bundle, 2 stalks of celery, one medium-sized onion with one or two cloves stuck in it, one clove of garlic, a sprig of thyme and a quarter of a bay leaf (optional).

Method I. Tie the meat with string and put it into a big stockpot. Add 7 litres (6 quarts, 7½ quarts) cold water.

Bring to the boil. When boiling is established a layer of slightly coagulated albumen forms on the surface. Remove this carefully, i.e. skim the stockpot clean. Season with 35 g. (1½ oz., 2 tablespoons) coarse salt.

Put all the vegetables into the stockpot. Simmer very slowly, so that the boiling is hardly perceptible, for 5 hours. Remove surplus fat carefully and strain the stock through a cloth, or through a very fine strainer.

Stock should not go on cooking for longer than 5 hours.

Method II. Put the bones, broken into small pieces, into the stockpot and cover with cold water. Bring to the boil, skim, add salt and simmer slowly for 2½ hours. Bring to the boil and put in the meat, boned and tied with string. Bring to the boil again, skim and season. Add the vegetables. Simmer slowly for about 4 hours.

Do not put in all the salt at the beginning; complete the seasoning at the end of the cooking, if necessary.

To serve or use stock. Skim off fat and strain the stock. Use it for making soup, add it to sliced bread, various pasta products and other garnishings, as indicated in the recipe.

Use the meat and the vegetables as described in the recipe for *Boiled beef with root vegetables* (see BEEF).

Clarified consommé or consommé riche. CONSOMMÉ CLARIFIÉ OU CONSOMMÉ RICHE – *Ingredients.* For 2 litres (3½ pints, 4½ pints) consommé:

Nourishing ingredients. 750 g. (1½ lb.) chopped lean beef, with all sinews and gristle removed.

Aromatic ingredients. 1 large carrot, 100 g. (4 oz., 1 cup) white part of leeks.

Clarifying element. 1 raw egg white.

Liquid. 3 litres (5¼ pints, 6½ pints) simple stock.

Method. Put the chopped meat, diced vegetables and egg white into a saucepan. Mix and add cold or warm stock. Bring to the boil, stirring constantly with a wooden spoon or with a whisk. When boiling is established, draw the saucepan to the edge of the burner and simmer very slowly for 1½ hours.

Remove surplus fat and strain the consommé.

Simple chicken consommé. CONSOMMÉ SIMPLE DE VOLAILLE – Proceed as described in the recipe for *Simple white consommé*, adding to the nourishing ingredients indicated a small chicken, previously browned in the oven, or an equivalent quantity of chicken giblets and carcases.

Clarified chicken consommé. CONSOMMÉ DE VOLAILLE CLARIFIÉ – Proceed, using the same ingredients, as described in the recipe for *Clarified consommé*, adding to the beef 3 sets chopped chicken giblets. It is also recommended to add a small chicken, previously browned in the oven, and the bones of a roast chicken, if available. The addition of chicken is almost essential to give the consommé the desired flavour. The chicken can later be made up into various dishes.

Simple fish consommé. CONSOMMÉ SIMPLE DE POISSON –

Ingredients. For 5 litres (4½ quarts, 5½ quarts) consommé:

Nourishing ingredients. 1½ kg. (3¼ lb.) pike or other fish, 600 g. (1 lb. 6 oz.) bones of sole or other fish, 1 kg. (2¼ lb.) turbot or other fish head.

Aromatic ingredients. 300 g. (11 oz., 2½ cups) chopped onions, 2 to 3 leeks, a handful of parsley, 25 g. (1 oz., ⅓ cup) chopped celery, a pinch of thyme, one bay leaf.

Seasoning. 40 g. (1½ oz., 2 tablespoons) coarse salt.

Liquid. 5 litres (4½ quarts, 5½ quarts) water, 6 dl. (1 pint, 2½ cups) white wine.

Method. Proceed as described in the recipe for *Simple white consommé.* Add onions cut in slices and finely sliced leeks. Boil slowly for 45 minutes. Strain the stock and use as indicated in the recipe.

Clarified fish consommé. CONSOMMÉ DE POISSON CLARIFIÉ – For 2 litres (3½ pints, 4½ pints):

Nourishing ingredients. 750 g. (1½ lb.) of the flesh of pike or whiting (net weight, without bones or skin).

Aromatic ingredients. 75 g. (3 oz., ¾ cup) chopped leeks, several sprigs parsley.

Clarifying element: 2 egg whites.

Liquid: 2½ litres (4½ pints, 5½ pints) fish stock.

Method. Proceed as described in the recipe for *Clarified beef consommé.* Simmer very slowly for 30 minutes. Strain the consommé and use as indicated in the recipe.

Simple game consommé. CONSOMMÉ SIMPLE DE GIBIER – Game which is too old to be cooked in any other way is used for this consommé.

Ingredients. For 5 litres (4½ quarts, 5½ quarts) consommé:

Nourishing ingredients. 2 kg. (4½ lb.) shoulder and neck of venison, 1 kg. (2¼ lb.) forequarter of hare, or an equivalent quantity of rabbit, one old pheasant, one old partridge.

Aromatic ingredients. 2 to 3 carrots, 300 g. (11 oz., 2½ cups) chopped onions, 3 leeks, 150 g. (5 oz., 1¼ cups) chopped celery, several sprigs parsley, 2 cloves of garlic, 2 sprigs of thyme, one bay leaf, 50 g. (2 oz., ¼ cup) juniper berries, 3 cloves.

Seasoning. 40 g. (1½ oz., 2 tablespoons) coarse salt.

Liquid: 6 litres (5½ quarts, 6½ quarts) cold water.

Method. Brown all the game in the oven and put in the stockpot. Add cold water and bring to the boil.

Skim, season, and add the vegetables, lightly browned in the fat rendered by the game. Add a *bouquet garni*, the juniper berries, and the cloves in a herb bag.

Draw the stockpot to the edge of the stove and simmer slowly for 3½ hours. Remove surplus fat and strain the stock. Use as indicated in the recipe.

The game which is served for making this consommé can be used for preparing patties, croquettes, hashes, etc., as well as for purée and *salpicon.*

Petite marmite – For 6 persons:

Nourishing ingredients. 400 g. (14 oz.) top of rump, 200 g. (7 oz.) rib of beef, 100 g. (4 oz.) marrow bone, 2 sets chicken giblets.

Aromatic ingredients. 2 to 3 small carrots, 1 small turnip, 2 to 3 leeks (white part only, cut in chunks), 2 small onions, quarter of a head of celery, quarter of a small head of cabbage.

Liquid. 2½ litres (4½ pints, 5½ pints), cold *simple consommé.*

Method. Put the meat, the marrow bone (wrapped in a piece of muslin) and the cold consommé into a pan. Bring to the boil and skim.

Add carrots and turnips, cut down to a uniform size and shape (blanching the vegetables, if they are old); leeks, cut in chunks and blanched; small onions lightly cooked on the stove; celery, blanched and cut into small pieces; cabbage, also blanched and rolled into a tight ball. Simmer very gently for 4 hours, adding a little stock from time to time to make up for the loss of liquid by evaporation.

One hour before serving, add the chicken giblets and continue cooking

Remove surplus fat, but bear in mind that *petite marmite* should have a few light circlets of fat on the surface. Remove the marrow bone, unwrap and put it back into the pan.

Serve with bread, sliced and dried in the oven, or rusks.

The chicken giblets can be browned in the oven before being put in the stock.

The cabbage, instead of being cooked in the pan, can be cooked separately in fat stock, and added to the consommé just before serving.

Petite marmite with chicken. PETITE MARMITE AVEC VOLAILLE – Proceed as described in the above recipe.

Add a small chicken, previously browned in the oven.

Serve in the same way as ordinary *Petite marmite*.

Pot-au-feu – Family soup, prepared in earthenware, cast-iron or aluminium utensils in the same way as *Petite marmite*.

This preparation provides two dishes: the soup – which should have toasted bread, pasta products, rice and, in general, all garnishings suitable for clear soups, added to it – and meat and vegetables. Gherkins, samphire pickled in vinegar, coarse salt and mustard are served with the boiled beef. tomato sauce, grated horseradish or horseradish sauce can also be served with it (see SAUCE).

The classical *pot-au-feu* is made of beef and chicken. In certain regions of France it is customary to add veal, pork and sometimes mutton. The chicken is occasionally replaced by duck or turkey.

Whatever meat is used for this dish, the method is the same. It is important only to make sure that the various meats are given long enough time to cook.

Pot-au-feu à l'albigeoise – Prepare the *pot-au-feu* as described in the recipe for *Petite marmite*, but using the following nourishing ingredients: silverside, veal knuckle, salted pork knuckle. When all the ingredients are nearly cooked, add a dry *Country sausage* (see PORK) and, a few minutes before serving the soup, a quarter of *Confit d'oie* (see GOOSE).

This *pot-au-feu* should have plenty of vegetables, particularly cabbage. Serve as described in the basic recipe for *Pot-au-feu*.

Pot-au-feu à la béarnaise, called Poule-au-pot – Prepare the *pot-au-feu* as described in the preceding recipe, adding a chicken stuffed with a forcemeat made of fresh pork and chopped Bayonne ham, mixed with chopped onion, garlic, parsley and chicken liver.

Serve as described in the basic recipe for *Pot-au-feu*.

Pot-au-feu à la languedocienne – Prepare like the basic *Pot-au-feu*, adding a piece of fat bacon previously blanched and rinsed in cold water.

Serve as indicated in the basic recipe for *Pot-au-feu*.

CONSOMMÉS WITH GARNISHES. CONSOMMÉS GARNIS – The recipes which follow have been worked out for 5 persons and are based on various kinds of consommés: beef, chicken, game, fish. The quantity of consommé required is $1\frac{1}{2}$ litres ($2\frac{3}{4}$ pints, $3\frac{1}{4}$ pints).

Directions for the supplementary ingredients of these consommés will be found under the heading GARNISHES.

In some of these recipes the consommé has to be thickened with arrowroot, starch or tapioca. This liaison should be very light, just sufficient to give the consommé a mellow texture.

Consommé à l'alsacienne – To simple consommé add *sauerkraut* cooked in stock and *Strasbourg sausages* (see SAUSAGES), poached, skinned and cut into slices.

Consommé à l'ambassadrice – Chicken consommé thickened with tapioca, garnished with 24 small, truffled chicken quenelles and 12 small *profiteroles* filled with a purée of *Foie gras* and chervil leaves.

All garnished consommés, thickened with arrowroot or tapioca, should be strained through a muslin cloth immediately after the liaison has been effected.

Consommé à l'américaine I – Proceed as described in the recipe for *Consommé à la madrilène II*. Serve cold in cups.

Consommé à l'américaine II – Chicken consommé thickened with arrowroot, garnished with gombos (okra or ladies' fingers) blanched in salted water then drained and cooked in stock, together with diced tomatoes cooked in stock, and chervil leaves.

Consommé à l'amiral – Fish consommé thickened with arrowroot. Garnish with 24 small quenelles made of *Pike forcemeat* (see FORCEMEAT) flavoured with crayfish butter, 6 oysters poached, de-bearded and cut in half, and 2 tablespoons (3 tablespoons) *julienne* of truffles cooked in Madeira. Sprinkle with chervil leaves.

Consommé à l'ancienne – See *Consommé croûte au pot à l'ancienne*.

Consommé à la basquaise – Simple consommé garnished with 2 tablespoons (3 tablespoons) *julienne* of sweet pimentos cooked in stock, 2 tablespoons (3 tablespoons) diced tomatoes cooked in stock, and 4 tablespoons ($\frac{1}{3}$ cup) rice cooked in stock. Sprinkle with chervil leaves.

Consommé Beauharnais – Chicken consommé thickened with arrowroot, garnished with *paupiettes* of lettuce, poached in stock and cut into slices, asparagus tips and a *julienne* of truffles. Sprinkle with chervil leaves.

Consommé with birds' nests. CONSOMMÉ AUX NIDS D'HIRONDELLES – Prepare a strong chicken consommé, clarify and strain through muslin.

Soak swallows' nests in cold water for 2 hours. When they swell and become transparent, clean them carefully, i.e. remove bits of egg shell and other foreign matter which they may contain, even though they have already been cleaned before being sold. Blanch these nests for 5 or 6 minutes and drain.

Put the nests into boiling consommé. Poach, keeping them on a gentle but sustained boil, for 45 minutes. Serve boiling hot. This soup is always served in cups.

Consommé Bizet – Chicken consommé thickened with tapioca, garnished with very small *Chicken quenelles* (see QUENELLES) mixed with chopped tarragon leaves. Sprinkle with chervil leaves.

Serve with very small *profiteroles* filled with a *brunoise* of vegetables.

Consommé à la bourgeoise – Simple consommé garnished with diced carrots and turnips, diced potatoes boiled in stock, and chervil leaves.

Consommé Brancas – Simple consommé garnished with 2 tablespoons (3 tablespoons) *chiffonade* of lettuce and sorrel, 2 tablespoons (3 tablespoons) vermicelli poached in stock, 2 tablespoons (3 tablespoons) *julienne* of mushrooms fried in butter, and chervil leaves.

Consommé with bread. CONSOMMÉ AU PAIN – Serve boiling consommé with a plate of long French bread, thinly sliced and dried in the oven, and grated cheese.

Consommé Brillat-Savarin – Chicken consommé, thickened with tapioca, garnished with 2 tablespoons (3 tablespoons) *julienne* of breast of chicken, 2 tablespoons (3 tablespoons) savoury pancakes (*crêpes*) cut into lozenges, 2 tablespoons (3 tablespoons) *chiffonade* of lettuce, sorrel and chervil leaves.

Consommé brunoise – Cut into small dice 3 small carrots, 1 small turnip, 2 to 3 leeks (white part only), 25 g. (1 oz., $\frac{1}{4}$ cup) chopped onion and 50 g. (2 oz., $\frac{1}{2}$ cup) of the white part of celery.

Season with salt and a pinch of sugar. Cook gently in 50 g. (2 oz., $\frac{1}{4}$ cup) butter in a covered pan for 25 minutes. Moisten with 3 dl. ($\frac{1}{2}$ pint, $1\frac{1}{4}$ cups) consommé and cook for an hour. 25 minutes before serving, add a tablespoon fresh garden peas and a tablespoon diced French beans. Add $1\frac{1}{4}$ litres ($2\frac{1}{4}$ pints, $2\frac{3}{4}$ pints) consommé. Boil for a few minutes, skim and sprinkle with chervil leaves.

Fresh garden peas and French beans can be replaced by the tinned (canned) variety, in which case they are added only at the last moment, just before serving.

Consommé brunoise with various garnishes – Prepare the soup as described above. Add garnish, such as pasta products, tapioca, pearl barley, rice, semolina, etc., which can either be cooked in the consommé itself, or separately.

Consommé brunoise can also be served with very small poached eggs, quenelles, *profiteroles*, and *plain royale* (savoury custard, cut into slices and then into fancy shapes) or a *royale* of vegetables. (See GARNISHES.)

Consommé à la cancalaise – Fish consommé thickened with arrowroot, garnished with 24 small *Pike quenelles* (see QUENELLES), 12 oysters, poached, de-bearded and cut in half, and chervil leaves.

Consommé Célestine – Chicken consommé thickened with tapioca, garnished with 2 tablespoons (3 tablespoons) small slices of rolled pancakes stuffed with *Chicken forcemeat* (see FORCEMEAT), and chervil leaves.

Consommé chasseur – Game consommé, thickened with tapioca, garnished with 2 tablespoons (3 tablespoons) *julienne* of mushrooms cooked in $\frac{1}{2}$ dl. (3 tablespoons, scant $\frac{1}{4}$ cup) Madeira wine, and chervil leaves. Serve with 20 small *profiteroles* filled with game purée.

Consommé aux cheveux d'ange – Basic consommé garnished with 4 tablespoons ($\frac{1}{3}$ cup) fine, poached vermicelli.

Consommé with chicken giblets. CONSOMMÉ AUX ABATIS DE VOLAILLE – Prepare a *pot-au-feu* and put into it 4 chicken pinions (wing tips) and 2 necks, cut into 3 or 4 pieces and tied in a piece of muslin.

Serve the consommé with the pinions and the *pot-au-feu* vegetables cut into small pieces.

Consommé with stuffed chicken giblets. CONSOMMÉ AUX ABATIS DE VOLAILLE FARCIS – Prepare chicken consommé and poach in it 4 chicken pinions, boned and stuffed with *Quenelle forcemeat* (see FORCEMEAT).

Strain the consommé and add the giblets. This consommé is prepared using a full set of giblets, consisting of 2 pinions, neck (with a part of the head left attached), the skinned gizzard and 2 feet.

Often, however, it is made only with pinions. This consommé is frequently served under the name of *Consommé with chicken pinions*.

Consommé with chicken pinions (wing tips). CONSOMMÉ AUX AILERONS – Using chicken pinions, proceed as described in the recipe for *Consommé with chicken giblets*.

The consommé can also be made of turkey and duck pinions.

Consommé with chicken pinions (wing tips) and rice. CONSOMMÉ AUX AILERONS AU RIZ – Prepare the consommé as described in the recipe for *Consommé with chicken giblets*. Add 2 tablespoons (3 tablespoons) rice, blanched and cooked in stock.

Consommé à la chilienne – Chicken consommé garnished with rice cooked in stock and a *salpicon* of green pimentos, also cooked in stock, sprinkled with chervil leaves. Serve *diablotins* at the same time.

Consommé à la Colbert – Chicken consommé garnished with a *brunoise* of spring vegetables, 4 small poached eggs, and chervil leaves.

Consommé Colnet – Chicken consommé garnished with a *brunoise* of carrots and celery, lightly cooked in butter, *oeufs filés* (beaten egg, strained into the consommé through a fine strainer, to look like threads – see GARNISHES, *Spun eggs*), and chervil leaves.

Consommé Commodore – Fish consommé thickened with arrowroot, garnished with poached, de-bearded clams cut in small pieces, and diced tomatoes cooked in stock.

Consommé à la Crécy – Chicken consommé thickened with tapioca, garnished with a *brunoise* of carrots lightly cooked in butter, and chervil leaves.

Consommé with garden cress. CONSOMMÉ AU CRESSON ALÉNOIS – Pick the leaves off the stalks of garden cress, blanch them for a minute in salted water, drain and rinse in cold water. Add to 1 litre (scant quart, generous quart) boiling consommé.

Consommé croûte au pot – *Pot-au-feu* consommé garnished with the stockpot vegetables (carrots, turnips, leeks and cabbage) cut in small pieces.

Serve with hollowed-out crusts of bread dried in the oven, or sprinkled with stockpot fat and browned lightly.

Consommé croûte au pot à l'ancienne – As above. Serve with hollowed-out crusts of bread filled with chopped stockpot vegetables and browned in the oven or under a grill.

Consommé Dalayrac – Chicken consommé thickened with tapioca, garnished with a *julienne* of breast of chicken, mushrooms and truffles.

Consommé aux diablotins – Chicken consommé thickened with tapioca. Serve with slices of bread covered with cheese and browned as described in the recipe for *diablotins*.

Consommé à l'écossaise – Pearl barley cooked in consommé, garnished with a *julienne* of carrot, celery and leek, lightly cooked in butter, and chervil leaves.

Consommé Edward VII – Chicken consommé thickened with arrowroot, garnished with a *royale* of truffles, thin slices of cold *Chicken loaf* (see CHICKEN) and asparagus tips. Add a few tablespoons of port to the consommé.

Consommé à la flip – Chicken consommé thickened with tapioca, garnished with a *julienne* of lettuce and leeks, lightly cooked in butter and dropped into the consommé. Add cooked ham cut in *julienne* strips, and chervil leaves.

Consommé Florence – Basic consommé garnished with vermicelli cooked in stock. Add to the boiling consommé à *julienne* of uncooked truffles. Cover the saucepan and simmer without allowing it to boil.

Consommé à la florentine – Chicken consommé with *œufs filés* (see GARNISHES, *Spun eggs*), 2 tablespoons (3 tablespoons) rice cooked in stock, and chervil leaves.

Consommé Florette – Chicken consommé thickened with tapioca, garnished with a *julienne* of leek, lightly cooked in butter, and rice cooked in stock. Serve with thick fresh cream and grated Parmesan cheese.

Consommé à la gauloise – Chicken consommé thickened with tapioca, garnished with very small, poached cocks' combs, small cocks' kidneys, pancakes cut in *julienne* strips, and chervil leaves.

Consommé with gombos (okra or ladies' fingers) à l'orientale. CONSOMMÉ AUX GOMBOS À L'ORIENTALE – Fennel-flavoured chicken consommé thickened with rice or potato flour, garnished with gombos (okra), blanched, drained, and cooked in stock; and with rice cooked in stock and spiced with a pinch of cayenne pepper.

Consommé Grimaldi – Chicken consommé with tomato juice, garnished with a *juleinne* of celeriac cooked in stock, tomato *royale* and chervil leaves.

Consommé à la hollandaise – Consommé seasoned with paprika, garnished with 2 tablespoons (3 tablespoons) small quenelles of calf's liver, 2 tablespoons (3 tablespoons) diced bone marrow poached in stock, and chervil leaves.

Consommé houblonnière – Consommé thickened with rice or potato flour, garnished with hop shoots cooked in stock, and chervil leaves.

Consommé Hudson – Fish consommé with tomato juice, thickened with arrowroot, garnished with crab flesh cut into small pieces, diced cucumbers cooked in stock, and chervil leaves.

Consommé à l'impériale – Proceed as described in the recipe for *Consommé à la gauloise*, replacing the savoury pancakes by rice cooked in stock and adding some fresh garden peas, cooked in water and drained.

Consommé à l'infante – Chicken consommé thickened with arrowroot. Serve with 24 small *profiteroles* filled with a purée of *foie gras* mixed with thick chicken *Velouté* (see SAUCE).

Consommé à l'irlandaise – Simple consommé with a *salpicon* of mutton cooked in the consommé, pearl barley, diced stockpot vegetables, and chervil leaves.

Consommé à l'italienne – Chicken consommé garnished with three kinds of *Royale* (see GARNISHES), cut into dice or slices: *royale* of chicken purée, *royale* of asparagus tips and *royale* of tomato purée. Sprinkle with chervil leaves.

Consommé julienne – Cut 3 small carrots, 1 small turnip, 2 leeks (white part only), 40 g. ($1\frac{1}{2}$ oz., $\frac{1}{3}$ cup) chopped onion and 40 g. ($1\frac{1}{2}$ oz., $\frac{1}{3}$ cup) tender celery into very thin sticks 2–5 cm. (1 inch) long.

Season with a pinch of salt and another of sugar. Soften in a pan in 50 g. (2 oz., $\frac{1}{4}$ cup) butter on slow heat for 25 minutes.

Add 50 g. (2 oz., $\frac{3}{4}$ cup) cabbage heart cut into *julienne* strips, blanched and drained, and a shredded lettuce.

Cook everything together, with the lid on, for 45 minutes. Moisten with 3 dl. ($\frac{1}{2}$ pint, $1\frac{1}{4}$ cups) consommé and simmer gently for 35 minutes.

25 minutes before serving, add 25 g. (1 oz., $\frac{3}{4}$ cup) sorrel shredded into a fine *chiffonnade* and a tablespoon fresh garden peas.

Add $1\frac{1}{4}$ litres ($2\frac{1}{4}$ pints, $2\frac{3}{4}$ pints) consommé, boil for a few seconds, skim, add chervil leaves.

Consommé julienne with various garnishes. CONSOMMÉ JULIENNE AVEC GARNITURES DIVERSES – This consommé, based on meat, fish or vegetable stock, can be served with the following garnishes: pasta products, pearl barley, rice, semolina or tapioca.

Quenelles, *profiteroles* or ordinary *royale* can also be added to it.

Consommé Léopold – Consommé thickened with semolina. Add 2 tablespoons (3 tablespoons) of a *julienne* of sorrel lightly cooked in butter, and chervil leaves.

Consommé Leverrier – Chicken consommé thickened with tapioca, garnished with various *royales* cut out in the shape of stars, and sprinkled with chervil leaves.

Consommé with macaroni. CONSOMMÉ AU MACARONI – Consommé garnished with macaroni cut in very small pieces and three-quarters cooked in salted water, drained, and finished off in the consommé. Serve with grated cheese.

Consommé à la madrilène I – Chicken consommé with 2 dl. ($\frac{1}{3}$ pint, scant cup) concentrated tomato pulp added to it, seasoned with a pinch of cayenne pepper.

This is mostly served very cold in cups.

Consommé a la madrilène II – Prepare the consommé, adding to it during clarification 3 dl. ($\frac{1}{2}$ pint, $1\frac{1}{4}$ cups) raw tomato pulp rubbed through a sieve.

Strain the consommé through a muslin cloth, pressing lightly, and chill before serving.

Diced sweet pimentos, cooked in stock, are often added to *consommé madrilène*.

Consommé Mercédès – Chicken consommé, with $\frac{1}{2}$ dl. (scant pint, $2\frac{1}{4}$ cups) sherry and a pinch of cayenne pepper added, garnished with 2 tablespoons (3 tablespoons) cocks' kidneys, skinned and cut in very thin slices, 2 tablespoons (3 tablespoons) cocks' combs, split in two and cut into star shapes, and chervil leaves.

Consommé à la messine – *Petite marmite* consommé, with very small chipolata sausages, poached and skinned, and small cabbage rolls.

Consommé à la neige de Florence – Serve separately as an accompaniment to boiling consommé, *Neige de Florence*, which the guests add to the soup themselves.

Neige de Florence, a pasta product which is found in shops, is a substance presented in the shape of extremely fine white flakes.

Consommé Nesselrode – Game consommé with *profiteroles* filled with *Chestnut purée soubise* (mixture of onion and chestnut purées – see PURÉE, *Vegetable purées*) and a *salpicon* of mushrooms.

Consommé Nemrod – Game consommé, thickened with arrowroot, flavoured with 2 tablespoons (3 tablespoons) port, garnished with 4 tablespoons ($\frac{1}{3}$ cup) very small *quenelles* made of game forcemeat mixed with chopped truffles.

Consommé with noodles. CONSOMMÉ AUX NOUILLES – Consommé with 70 to 90 g. ($2\frac{1}{2}$ to $3\frac{1}{2}$ oz.) fresh noodles, three-quarters cooked in water, drained and finished off in the consommé. Serve with grated cheese.

Consommé à la d'Orléans – Chicken consommé thickened with tapioca, garnished with 4 tablespoons ($\frac{1}{3}$ cup) small *quenelles* made of three kinds of *Chicken forcemeat* (see FORCEMEAT): one with cream, one with tomato and one with pistachio nuts or spinach. Add a sprinkling of chervil leaves.

Oxtail consommé or soup à la française. CONSOMMÉ OU POTAGE QUEUE DE BOEUF À LA FRANÇAISE – Put 2 kg. ($4\frac{1}{2}$ lb.) oxtail, cut into chunks, with 500 g. (generous 1 lb.) veal knuckle into a stockpot. Add 3 litres ($5\frac{1}{4}$ pints, $6\frac{1}{2}$ pints) white stock. Bring to the boil, skim, season, add the usual vegetable garnish and simmer gently, so that boiling is hardly perceptible, for 5 hours.

Strain the stock. Pour it into a pot into which you have put 400 g. (14 oz.) lean beef and veal, chopped, browned in butter, and sprinkled with a tablespoon of arrowroot (cornstarch). Clarify, strain the stock through a muslin cloth or a fine strainer. Add the pieces of oxtail and 250 g. (9 oz.) carrots and turnips, scooped out to look like small, uniform balls and cooked in stock.

This soup used to be called *grand hochepot*.

Consommé à la parisienne – Chicken consommé with a *macédoine* of vegetables, slices of plain *royale*, and chervil leaves.

Consommé with pasta products. CONSOMMÉ AUX PÂTES D'ITALIE – Pour 75 to 90 g. (3 to $3\frac{1}{2}$ oz., scant cup) pasta into $1\frac{1}{2}$ litres ($2\frac{3}{4}$ pints, $3\frac{1}{4}$ pints) boiling consommé. Cook, keeping up slow but sustained boiling from 8 to 12 minutes, depending on the nature of the pasta.

Serve with grated cheese.

Consommé with pearl barley. CONSOMMÉ À L'ORGE PERLÉ – Consommé with 75 g. (3 oz., $\frac{1}{2}$ cup) pearl barley, washed in warm water, blanched and cooked in white stock for $2\frac{1}{2}$ hours. The barley can be cooked in the consommé.

Consommé Pépita – Chicken consommé with tomato juice, seasoned with paprika, garnished with tomato *royale* (see GARNISHES, *Royale of tomato purée*) cut in dice, peeled and diced pimentos cooked in stock, and chervil leaves.

Consommé with plover or lapwing eggs. CONSOMMÉ AUX OEUFS DE PLUVIER, DE VANNEAU – Chicken consommé with poached plover or lapwing eggs.

Consommé with poached eggs. CONSOMMÉ AUX OEUFS POCHÉS – Consommé garnished with six small poached eggs.

Consommé princesse – Chicken consommé thickened with tapioca, garnished with very small chicken forcemeat quenelles, 2 tablespoons (3 tablespoons) green asparagus tips, and chervil leaves.

Consommé Princess Alice – Chicken consommé thickened with tapioca, garnished with a tablespoon of a *julienne* of artichoke hearts, a tablespoon of a *chiffonnade* of lettuce, 2 tablespoons (3 tablespoons) fine vermicelli cooked in stock, and chervil leaves.

Consommé printanier – Consommé with spring vegetables added to it, sprinkled with chervil leaves.

Consommé printanier aux perles or au riz – As above. Reduce the proportion of vegetables and add barley or rice cooked in stock, sprinkle with chervil leaves.

Poached eggs, quenelles, *profiteroles*, *royales*, etc., can also be served in *consommé printanier*.

Consommé with profiteroles. CONSOMMÉ AUX PROFITEROLES – Consommé thickened with tapioca, sprinkled with chervil leaves.

Serve with *profiteroles* filled with purée.

Consommé with quenelles. CONSOMMÉ AUX QUENELLES – Clear or thickened consommé garnished with chicken or other quenelles, and sprinkled with chervil leaves.

Consommé Rachel – Chicken consommé thickened with tapioca, garnished with very small chicken forcemeat quenelles, small lettuce rolls, filled with purée of *Chicken sauté à la crème*, and chervil leaves.

Consommé with ravioli. CONSOMMÉ AUX RAVIOLI – Thickened or clear consommé with 24 small ravioli, filled according to taste and sprinkled with chervil leaves.

Consommé à la reine – Chicken consommé thickened with tapioca, garnished with plain *royale*, a *julienne* of breast of chicken, and chervil leaves.

Consommé à la Reine-Jeanne – Chicken consommé thickened with tapioca, garnished with very small chicken quenelles and chervil leaves.

Serve with *profiteroles* filled with a chicken purée bound with almond milk.

Consommé with rice. CONSOMMÉ AU RIZ – Consommé to which 60 to 80 g. (2 or 3 oz., $\frac{1}{4}$ to $\frac{1}{2}$ cup) rice, cooked in white stock, is added. Serve with grated cheese.

Consommé à la royale – Chicken consommé, thickened with tapioca, garnished with diced *royale*, and sprinkled with chervil leaves.

Consommé with sago. CONSOMMÉ AU SAGOU – Using sago, proceed as above.

Consommé à la Saint-Hubert – Game consommé thickened with tapioca, garnished with a game purée *royale* and a *julienne* of mushrooms cooked in butter with Madeira.

Consommé with salep. CONSOMMÉ AU SALEP – Using salep, proceed as described in the recipe above.

Consommé with semolina. CONSOMMÉ À LA SEMOULE – Pour 75 to 90 g. (3 to $3\frac{1}{2}$ oz., $\frac{1}{2}$ cup) semolina into $1\frac{1}{2}$ litres ($2\frac{3}{4}$ pints, $3\frac{1}{4}$ pints) boiling consommé. Simmer 18 to 20 minutes. Serve with grated cheese.

Consommé à la strasbourgeoise – Consommé flavoured with a light infusion of juniper berries, thickened with rice or potato flour, garnished with 4 tablespoons ($\frac{1}{3}$ cup) of a *julienne* of red cabbage cooked in stock and a Strasbourg sausage, poached, skinned and cut in thin slices. Serve with grated horseradish.

Consommé with tapioca. CONSOMMÉ AU TAPIOCA – Pour 80 to 100 g. (3 to 4 oz., $\frac{1}{2}$ to $\frac{2}{3}$ cup) tapioca into $1\frac{1}{2}$ litres ($2\frac{3}{4}$ pints, $3\frac{1}{4}$ pints) boiling consommé. Stir to avoid formation of lumps and cook, keeping up sustained boiling from 15 to 20 minutes. Serve with grated Parmesan cheese.

Consommé with vermicelli. CONSOMMÉ AU VERMICELLE – Pour 75 to 90 g. (3 to $3\frac{1}{2}$ oz., $\frac{1}{2}$ cup) vermicelli into $1\frac{1}{2}$ litres ($2\frac{3}{4}$ pints, $3\frac{1}{4}$ pints) boiling consommé. Cook, keeping up sustained boiling, from 5 to 12 minutes, depending on the thickness of the vermicelli. Serve with grated Parmesan.

COLD CONSOMMÉS. CONSOMMÉS FROIDS – These consommés, intended for luncheons or suppers, are served in cups.

Their preparation is similar to that of hot consommés. They should be strongly flavoured and very clear.

Celery-flavoured consommé. CONSOMMÉ À L'ESSENCE DE CÉLERI – Prepare $1\frac{1}{2}$ litres ($2\frac{3}{4}$ pints, $3\frac{1}{4}$ pints) consommé. Clarify and add half a bunch of finely chopped celery. Strain and chill before serving.

Consommé flavoured with game fumet. CONSOMMÉ AU FUMET DE GIBIER – Prepare as described in the recipe for *Game consommé*.

Tarragon-flavoured consommé. CONSOMMÉ À L'ESSENCE D'ESTRAGON – Add 20 g. (4 tablespoons, $\frac{1}{3}$ cup) fresh tarragon leaves to consommé before straining. Leave to infuse without boiling. Strain and serve as described above.

Tomato-flavoured consommé – See *Consommé à la madrilène*.

Truffle-flavoured consommé. CONSOMMÉ À L'ESSENCE DE TRUFFES – Add to clarified consommé 60 g. (2 oz., 2 cups) parings of fresh truffles. Strain, remove surplus fat, and add 2 tablespoons (3 tablespoons) Madeira or port.

Consommé with various wines. CONSOMMÉ AUX VINS DIVERS – Clarify and strain consommé. When it is nearly cold, add various wines, such as Madeira, Marsala, Port, sherry, etc., allowing about 8 to 10 cl. (6 tablespoons, scant $\frac{1}{2}$ cup) per litre (scant quart, generous quart) consommé.

THICK SOUPS. POTAGES LIÉS – Cream, purée and *velouté* soups are classed in this category. Cream soups are composed of a purée of shellfish, vegetables, fish, or poultry, thickened with *Béchamel sauce* (see SAUCE).

Purées of starchy vegetables or leguminous plants are composed of vegetables rich in starch, such as sweet potatoes, potatoes, etc.; of leguminous plants, such as white or red dried beans, kidney beans, lentils split peas, etc. These ingredients, being sufficiently rich in starch content, require no additional element for the purpose of liaison.

Purées of fresh vegetables, less rich in starch, are thickened with additional elements: cooked rice or a purée of some other vegetable richer in starch content.

Meat, poultry or fish purées are composed of these various ingredients with the addition of supplementary liaison: rice, bread to pulp, purées of leguminous plants or cereals.

Shellfish purée soups, better known as *bisques*, which are thickened with rice or, according to the old method, with bread reduced to pulp, are also classified in this category.

Veloutés are also composed of a purée, bound with *velouté* and with a final liaison of egg yolks and cream.

CREAM SOUPS. POTAGES CRÈMES – Soups, the basic element of which includes a certain quantity of *béchamel*, finished off with fresh cream.

Like all other thickened soups, cream soups can be garnished with pasta products, rice, barley, tapioca, *julienne*, *brunoise*, *chiffonnade*, quenelles, croûtons, etc.

The recipes which follow have been worked out to serve 4 to 6 helpings.

Basic method of preparing cream soups (vegetable). Shred and blanch the vegetable indicated and cook in butter, allowing 60 to 80 g. (2 to 3 oz., 6 tablespoons) butter to 500 g. (generous 1 lb.) vegetable.

Add 8 dl. ($1\frac{1}{3}$ pints, $1\frac{3}{4}$ pints) *béchamel* prepared by diluting a white roux of 35 g. ($1\frac{1}{2}$ oz., 3 tablespoons) butter and 45 g. (2 oz., $\frac{1}{2}$ cup) flour, with $8\frac{1}{2}$ dl. ($1\frac{1}{2}$ pints, 2 pints) milk. Simmer very gently from 12 to 18 minutes, depending on the nature of the vegetables used. Rub through a sieve. Heat and blend in 2 dl. ($\frac{1}{3}$ pint, scant cup) fresh cream.

Cream of artichoke soup. POTAGE CRÈME D'ARTICHAUTS – Cook eight blanched and sliced artichoke hearts in butter. Add 8 dl. ($1\frac{1}{3}$ pints, $1\frac{3}{4}$ pints) *béchamel* and simmer gently for 12 minutes.

Rub through a sieve. Dilute with 2 dl. ($\frac{1}{3}$ pint, scant cup) white consommé and heat to boiling point. Add seasoning if necessary, and 2 dl. ($\frac{1}{3}$ pint, scant cup) fresh cream and a tablespoon chervil leaves.

Cream of asparagus soup (green). POTAGE CRÈME D'ASPERGES VERTES – As above, using green asparagus tips, blanched and cooked slowly in the *béchamel.*

Cream of white asparagus, called Argenteuil. POTAGE CRÈME D'ASPERGES BLANCHES, DIT ARGENTEUIL – Using the tips of 1 kg. ($2\frac{1}{4}$ lb.) white asparagus blanched and simmered in butter in a covered pan, proceed as described in the recipe for *Cream of artichoke soup.*

Rub through a sieve as soon as the asparagus is put into the *béchamel.*

Cream of barley soup I. POTAGE CRÈME D'ORGE – Wash 300 g. (11 oz., $1\frac{1}{2}$ cups) pearl barley in several waters and soak it for an hour in warm water. Put it into 8 dl. ($1\frac{1}{3}$ pints, $1\frac{3}{4}$ pints) white consommé, add a sliced stalk of celery, bring to the boil and simmer gently for $2\frac{1}{2}$ hours.

Rub through a sieve, dilute with a few tablespoons consommé, heat and finish off with 2 dl. ($\frac{1}{3}$ pint, scant cup) fresh cream. Add 2 tablespoons (3 tablespoons) pearl barley cooked in consommé.

The consommé can be replaced by milk.

Cream of barley soup II. POTAGE CRÈME D'ORGE – Using barley flour, proceed as described in the recipe for *Cream of oatmeal soup* (see below).

Cream of bean soup. POTAGE CRÈME DE HARICOTS VERTS – Like *Cream of artichoke soup*, replacing the artichokes by 500 g. (generous 1 lb.) French beans, three-quarters blanched.

Cream of celery soup. POTAGE CRÈME DE CÉLERI – Using 2 bunches of blanched and shredded celery, proceed as described in the recipe for *Cream of artichoke soup.*

Cream of chicken soup. POTAGE CRÈME DE VOLAILLE – Put a plump, tender chicken into a saucepan with 8 dl. ($1\frac{1}{3}$ pints, $1\frac{3}{4}$ pints) *simple white consommé.* Season, add 2 leeks and a stalk of celery, tied in a bundle. Bring to the boil, skim, cover, and simmer gently.

When the chicken is cooked, drain and bone it. Keep the breast fillets for garnishing and pound the rest of the flesh finely in a mortar. Rub this purée through a fine sieve. Mix with 8 dl. ($1\frac{1}{3}$ pints, $1\frac{3}{4}$ pints) *béchamel.* Heat to boiling point, add a few tablespoons of the consommé in which the chicken was cooked, taste for seasoning. Strain through a sieve and add 1 dl. (6 tablespoons, scant $\frac{1}{2}$ cup) fresh cream.

Dice the breast fillets and add to the soup.

Cream of chicory (U.S. endive) soup. POTAGE CRÈME D'ENDIVES – Slice the chicory and simmer it in butter in a covered pan. Finish off as described in the recipe for *Cream of endive soup* (see below).

Cream of Chinese artichoke, Occa and Jerusalem artichoke. POTAGE CRÈME DE CROSNES, OXALIS, TOPINAMBOURS – Like *Cream of artichoke soup*, replacing the latter by 400 g. (14 oz.) Chinese artichokes (or Occa, or Jerusalem artichoke), blanched and cooked in butter.

Cream of crayfish soup – See *Cream of shrimp soup* below.

Cream of endive soup. POTAGE CRÈME DE CHICORÉE – Blanch, press and chop 500 g. (generous 1 lb.) tender endives, and cook in butter.

Add 8 dl. ($1\frac{1}{3}$ pints, $1\frac{3}{4}$ pints) *béchamel sauce.* Finish off as described in the recipe for *Cream of artichoke soup.*

Cream of leek soup. POTAGE CRÈME DE POIREAUX – Shred and blanch 500 g. (generous 1 lb.) leeks and cook them in butter in a covered pan.

Finish off as described in the recipe for *Cream of artichoke soup.*

Cream of lettuce soup. POTAGE CRÈME DE LAITUES – Using lettuce, proceed as in the recipe for *Cream of endive soup.*

Cream of leek soup, garnished with duchess potatoes

Cream of lobster soup – See *Cream of shrimp soup* below.

Cream of marrow soup. POTAGE CRÈME DE COURGETTES – Like *Cream of artichoke soup*, replacing the artichokes by 400 g. (14 oz.) marrow, blanched and cooked in butter.

Cream of mushroom soup. POTAGE CRÈME DE CHAMPIGNONS – This soup is principally made from cultivated mushrooms or morels.

Slice the mushrooms, cook them in butter in a covered pan and proceed as described in the recipe for *Cream of artichoke soup.*

Cream of nettle soup. POTAGE CRÈME D'ORTIES – As *Cream of spinach soup* (see below), replacing the spinach by young nettles.

Cream of oatmeal soup. POTAGE CRÈME D'AVOINE – Pour 150 g. (5 oz., $1\frac{1}{4}$ cups) oatmeal flour, diluted with 2 dl. ($\frac{1}{3}$ pint, scant cup) cold milk, into 8 dl. ($1\frac{1}{3}$ pints, $1\frac{3}{4}$ pints) boiling milk.

Stir until smooth, bring to the boil and simmer very gently for $1\frac{1}{2}$ hours. Rub through a sieve. Re-heat. Add 1 dl. (6 tablespoons, scant $\frac{1}{2}$ cup) cream.

The milk can be replaced by consommé.

Cream of rice soup I. POTAGE CRÈME DE RIZ – Cook 200 g. (7 oz., 1 cup) blanched and drained rice very gently in a pint of white consommé, with a little butter, for 45 minutes.

Rub through a sieve and finish off as described in the recipe for *Cream of barley soup.*

Cream of rice soup II. POTAGE CRÈME DE RIZ – Using rice flour, proceed as described in the recipe for *Cream of oatmeal soup.*

Cream of shrimp (or other shellfish soup). POTAGE CRÈME DE CREVETTES ET AUTRES CRUSTACÉS – Fry 1 dl. (6 tablespoons, scant $\frac{1}{2}$ cup) *mirepoix* in butter, add 350 g. (12 oz., 2 cups) uncooked shrimps, and sauté together. Season with salt and pepper, moisten with $\frac{1}{2}$ dl. (3 tablespoons, scant $\frac{1}{4}$ cup) white wine and a tablespoon of brandy which has been set alight. Cook for 5 minutes.

Keep aside a dozen shrimps' tails for the garnish. Pound the shrimps in a mortar. Add 8 dl. ($1\frac{1}{3}$ pints, $1\frac{3}{4}$ pints) *béchamel.* Rub through a sieve.

Heat, dilute, if necessary, with a few tablespoons white consommé, taste for seasoning, and finish off with 2 dl. ($\frac{1}{3}$ pint, scant cup) fresh cream.

Cream of spinach soup. POTAGE CRÈME D'ÉPINARDS – Cook 500 g. (generous 1 lb.) blanched and pressed spinach in butter. Finish off with *béchamel* as described in the recipe for *Cream of endive soup.*

Cream of spinach soup

Cream of spiny lobster soup – See *Cream of shrimp soup*.

Cream of watercress soup. POTAGE CRÈME DE CRESSON – Using 500 g. (generous 1 lb.) watercress cooked in butter, proceed as for *Cream of endive soup*.

PURÉE SOUPS. POTAGES PURÉES – The various purée soups described below can have pasta products, rice, tapioca, *perles*, pearl barley, *brunoise*, *julienne*, *chiffonnade*, etc., added to them.

The recipes given for vegetables and leguminous plants are intended for soups to be made with meat stock. These can also be prepared as Lenten fare by replacing stock by water and using milk for the final liaison. Lean bacon, indicated as an ingredient for some of these soups, will be omitted from a Lenten soup.

The recipes have been worked out to serve 5 or 6 helpings.

Purée of bean soup. POTAGE PURÉE DE FÈVES – Cook 500 g. (generous 1 lb.) fresh shelled beans in 50 g. (2 oz., $\frac{1}{4}$ cup) butter, with a sprig of savory, a pinch of salt and 1 dl. (6 tablespoons, scant $\frac{1}{2}$ cup) water, keeping the pan covered. Rub through a fine sieve and finish off as described in the recipe for *Purée of celery soup* (see below).

Purée of red haricot bean soup, called à la Condé. POTAGE PURÉE DE HARICOTS ROUGES, DIT À LA CONDÉ – Pick over and wash 350 g. (12 oz., $1\frac{3}{4}$ cups) red haricot beans and put them into $1\frac{1}{2}$ litres ($2\frac{3}{4}$ pints, $3\frac{1}{4}$ pints) cold water. Boil, skim, add 15 g. ($\frac{1}{2}$ oz., $2\frac{1}{2}$ teaspoons) salt, a medium-sized onion studded with a clove, a quartered carrot, a *bouquet garni* and 50 g. (2 oz.) lean bacon, cut in large dice, blanched and lightly fried. Add $1\frac{1}{2}$ dl. ($\frac{1}{4}$ pint, $\frac{2}{3}$ cup) boiling red wine and leave, uncovered, to simmer very gently.

When the beans are quite done drain them, remove the garnishing, and rub through a fine sieve. Put the purée back into the pan, pour in the liquor, adding a few tablespoons of consommé if necessary. Strain, bring to the boil, and blend in 60 g. (2 oz., $\frac{1}{4}$ cup) butter.

Serve with small croûtons, fried in butter.

The bacon may be omitted. In old culinary practice this soup was made with game consommé and was sometimes garnished with rice, cooked in consommé, instead of croûtons.

Purée of white haricot bean soup, called Soissonnaise. POTAGE PURÉE DE HARICOTS BLANCS, DITE SOISSONNAISE – Using white haricot beans, proceed as described in the recipe for *Red haricot bean soup*, omitting the red wine.

Serve with small croûtons, fried in butter.

Purée of Brussels sprouts soup. POTAGE PURÉE DE CHOUX DE BRUXELLES – Proceed using Brussels sprouts, as described in the recipe for *Purée of celery soup*.

Purée of carrot soup I, called Crécy. POTAGE PURÉE DE CAROTTES, DITE CRÉCY – Cook 3 to 4 sliced carrots in 60 g. (2 oz., $\frac{1}{4}$ cup) butter in a covered pan. Add 2 tablespoons (3 tablespoons) chopped onions, a pinch of salt and a pinch of sugar. If using old vegetables, parboil them before cooking in butter.

When the carrots are quite soft add 1 litre (scant quart, generous quart) consommé and 100 g. (4 oz., 8 tablespoons) rice. Simmer gently, covered.

Rub through a sieve, dilute with a few tablespoons stock, heat, add 60 g. (2 oz., $\frac{1}{4}$ cup) butter and serve with small croûtons fried in butter.

Purée of carrot soup II, called Crécy. POTAGE CRÉCY – Cook the carrots as described in the preceding recipe, replacing the rice by an equivalent amount of stale, crustless bread, or rusks dried in the oven. Finish off as described above.

Purée of cauliflower soup, called Dubarry. POTAGE PURÉE DE CHOU-FLEUR, DIT DUBARRY – Cook together 400 g. (14 oz.) of blanched and drained cauliflower and 250 g. (9 oz., $1\frac{1}{2}$ cups) sliced potatoes, in 6 dl. (1 pint, $2\frac{1}{2}$ cups) milk with a pinch of salt.

Rub through a sieve. Dilute with 1 dl. (6 tablespoons, scant $\frac{1}{2}$ cup) milk, heat, and add 60 g. (2 oz., $\frac{1}{4}$ cup) butter and a tablespoon of chervil leaves. Serve with small croûtons, fried in butter.

The milk can be replaced by consommé.

Purée of celery soup. POTAGE PURÉE DE CÉLERI – Slice 500 g. (generous 1 lb.) of the white part of celery stalks (or the same amount of blanched celeriac) and cook in 60 g. (2 oz., $\frac{1}{4}$ cup) butter in a covered pan. Moisten with 1 litre (scant quart, generous quart) of stock, add 250 g. (9 oz., $1\frac{1}{2}$ cups) potatoes cut in quarters and simmer gently.

Rub through a sieve, dilute the purée with a few tablespoons of consommé, heat, and blend in 60 g. (2 oz., $\frac{1}{4}$ cup) butter.

Purée of chestnut soup. POTAGE PURÉE DE MARRONS – Shell and peel 500 g. (generous 1 lb.) chestnuts and cook them in 1 litre (scant quart, generous quart) white consommé. Add a quarter of a head of celery cut up and cooked in 25 g. (1 oz., 2 tablespoons) butter with a tablespoon chopped onion.

Rub through a sieve, add a few tablespoons consommé or boiled milk, and finish off with fresh butter.

Serve with small croûtons, fried in butter.

Purée of chicken soup à la reine I. POTAGE PURÉE DE VOLAILLE À LA REINE – Bring to the boil a tender chicken with 1 litre (scant quart, generous quart) white consommé and the white part of leeks and a stalk of celery tied in a bundle.

Skim, add 100 g. (4 oz., generous $\frac{1}{2}$ cup) blanched and drained rice, cover, and simmer gently.

When the chicken is cooked, drain and bone it. Pound the flesh finely in a mortar with the rice, leaving a part of the breast for garnish. Dilute this purée with a few tablespoons of the consommé in which the chicken was cooked and rub through a sieve, pressing it with a wooden spoon.

Put into a pan, heat to boiling point, and dilute with a few tablespoons white consommé. Thicken with 2 egg yolks diluted with 1 dl. (6 tablespoons, scant $\frac{1}{2}$ cup) cream. Blend and incorporate 60 to 80 g. (2 to 3 oz., 4 to 6 tablespoons) butter. Dice the breast fillets and add to the soup.

Purée of chicken soup à la reine II (old recipe). POTAGE PURÉE DE VOLAILLE À LA REINE – 'Take a *chopine* ($\frac{1}{2}$ litre, scant pint, $2\frac{1}{4}$ cups) consommé, put into it a piece of crustless bread the size of an egg and let it boil a few times. Pound finely in a mortar the breast of chicken cooked on a spit with 12 sweet almonds, 3 bitter almonds and 6 hard-boiled egg yolks. When the mixture has been well pounded, add the consommé, with the bread and a *demi-setier* (3 dl., $\frac{1}{2}$ pint, $1\frac{1}{4}$ cups) cream or good milk. Rub the sauce through a sieve, season and keep hot in a *bain-marie*.'

This recipe has been extracted from a sixteenth-century recipe book. Soup '*à la reine*' used to be served every Thursday at the Court of the Valois. Queen Marguerite de Valois, it is said, was very fond of it.

For a long time afterwards soups called '*à la reine*' were prepared from partridges or pigeons. These various soups were sometimes served poured over crusts crumbled and pulped in a plate.

Purée of chicory soup. POTAGE PURÉE D'ENDIVES – Cook a medium-size (400 g., 14 oz.) head of coarsely shredded chicory (U.S. endive) slowly in butter in a covered pan. Season with salt and a little sugar.

Add 250 g. (9 oz., $1\frac{1}{2}$ cups) sliced potatoes. Moisten with 6 dl. (1 pint, $2\frac{1}{2}$ cups) consommé. Simmer, covered, for 30 minutes.

Rub through a sieve and finish off as described in the recipe for *Purée of celery soup.*

Soup purée Condé – See *Purée of red haricot bean soup.*

Soup purée Conti – See *Purée of lentil soup* below.

Soup purée Conti à la brunoise. POTAGE PURÉE CONTI À LA BRUNOISE – Add 4 or 5 tablespoons (5 or 6 tablespoons) of an ordinary *brunoise* and chervil leaves to $1\frac{1}{2}$ litres ($2\frac{3}{4}$ pints, $3\frac{1}{4}$ pints) *Purée of lentil soup* (see below).

Soup purée Conti à la julienne. POTAGE PURÉE CONTI À LA JULIENNE – As above, replacing the *brunoise* by a *julienne.*

Purée of crab soup. POTAGE PURÉE DE CRABES – Like *Purée of crayfish soup*, replacing the crayfish by an equivalent quantity of crab.

Purée of crayfish soup or crayfish bisque. POTAGE PURÉE, BISQUE D'ÉCRIVISSES – *Ingredients.* 18 crayfish, 100 g. (4 oz., $\frac{1}{2}$ cup) butter, 2 dl. ($\frac{1}{3}$ pint, scant cup) *mirepoix*, 1 dl. (6 tablespoons, scant $\frac{1}{2}$ cup) white wine, 2 dl. ($1\frac{1}{2}$ tablespoons, 2 tablespoons) brandy, 80 g. (3 oz., $\frac{1}{2}$ cup) rice, 1 litre (scant quart, generous quart) white consommé, $1\frac{1}{2}$ dl. ($\frac{1}{4}$ pint, $\frac{2}{3}$ cup) fresh cream, salt, pepper, cayenne pepper, thyme, bay leaf, parsley.

For the garnish.

Method. Dress and wash 12 of the crayfish and add to the *mirepoix*, previously cooked in butter until soft.

Season with a pinch of salt and a little freshly ground pepper, add 2 sprigs parsley, a sprig of thyme and a fragment of a bay leaf. Sauté the crayfish on strong heat until the shell turns red.

Moisten with brandy which has been set alight, and the white wine. Boil down by two-thirds, add $1\frac{1}{2}$ dl. ($\frac{1}{4}$ pint, $\frac{2}{3}$ cup) consommé and cook for 10 minutes.

Shell the remaining crayfish, keeping the tails and shells for the garnish. Pound the shells finely in a mortar, adding the rice, cooked separately in 4 dl. ($\frac{3}{4}$ pint, scant 2 cups) consommé, and the liquor left from cooking the crayfish. Rub this purée through a sieve, pressing it with a wooden spoon into a saucepan. Dilute with the rest of the consommé, boil for a few seconds, strain, and keep hot in a *bain-marie.*

Add 80 g. (3 oz., 6 tablespoons) butter divided into tiny pieces, and the fresh cream. Blend, correct seasoning if necessary, and flavour with a small pinch of cayenne pepper. Pour into a soup tureen, garnish with the shells filled with fish forcemeat and poached, and the diced tails.

Consommé can be replaced by fish stock or *fumet.*

Soup purée Crécy – See *Purée of carrot soup.*

Soup purée Crécy aux perles. POTAGE PURÉE CRÉCY AUX PERLES – $1\frac{1}{2}$ litres ($2\frac{3}{4}$ pints, $3\frac{1}{4}$ pints) *Purée of carrots à la Crécy* with 4 tablespoons ($\frac{1}{3}$ cup) of *perles*, cooked in stock, added to it.

Soup purée Crécy with rice. POTAGE PURÉE CRÉCY AU RIZ – $1\frac{1}{2}$ litres ($2\frac{3}{4}$ pints, $3\frac{1}{4}$ pints) *Purée of carrot soup à la Crécy* with 4 tablespoons ($\frac{1}{3}$ cup) of rice, cooked in stock, added to it.

Purée of garden cress soup. POTAGE PURÉE DE CRESSON ALÉNOIS – Pick over and wash 250 g. (9 oz.) garden cress, chop it and cook in a covered pan with 50 g. (2 oz., $\frac{1}{4}$ cup) butter.

Moisten with 1 litre (scant quart, generous quart) strong stock, add 250 g. (9 oz., $1\frac{1}{2}$ cups) sliced potatoes, and simmer gently.

Rub this purée through a sieve, and add a little stock and milk, 3 tablespoons (4 tablespoons) cream and a piece of fresh butter.

Pour into a soup tureen and garnish with leaves of garden cress, blanched in salted water and drained.

Soup purée with croûtons – See *Purée of split pea soup.*

Soup purée Dubarry – See *Purée of cauliflower soup.*

Soup purée Freneuse – See *Purée of turnip soup.*

Purée of game soup. POTAGE PURÉE DE GIBIER – Roast a pheasant or 2 partridges in the oven until three-quarters done, keeping them a little on the firm side. Remove from cooking and brown $1\frac{1}{2}$ dl. ($\frac{1}{4}$ pint, $\frac{2}{3}$ cup) *mirepoix* in the fat given out by the game. Put the game and the *mirepoix* into a pan with 200 g. (7 oz., generous $\frac{3}{4}$ cup) lentils, three-quarters cooked. Add a *bouquet garni*, season, moisten with 1 litre (scant quart, generous quart) simple consommé or game consommé. Bring to the boil, cover, and simmer gently.

Drain the game and bone. Pound the flesh in a mortar, adding the drained lentils. Dilute the purée with the liquid left in the pan and rub through a sieve, pressing it with a wooden spoon. Put back in the pan. Heat, taste for seasoning and add 80 g. (3 oz., 6 tablespoons) butter.

Purée of Jerusalem artichoke soup. POTAGE PURÉE DE TOPINAMBOURS – Using Jerusalem artichokes, proceed as described in the recipe for *Purée of sweet potato soup.*

Purée of lentil soup à la Conti. POTAGE PURÉE DE LENTILLES À LA CONTI – Proceed, using lentils, as described in the recipe for *Purée of red haricot bean soup*, omitting the red wine.

Purée of lettuce soup. POTAGE PURÉE DE LAITUES – Proceed, using lettuce, as described in the recipe for *Purée of chicory soup.*

Purée of lobster soup or lobster bisque. POTAGE PURÉE, BISQUE DE HOMARD – Like *Purée of crayfish soup*, replacing the crayfish by an equivalent quantity of small lobsters, cut into pieces and sautéed with a *mirepoix.*

Garnish with diced lobster tails.

Purée of marrow soup – See *Purée of pumpkin soup* below.

Soup purée Parmentier. See *Purée of potato soup* below.

Purée of fresh pea soup, called Saint-Germain. POTAGE PURÉE DE POIS FRAIS, DIT SAINT-GERMAIN – Cook 500 g. (generous pound) fresh peas in salted water, drain, and rub through a sieve.

Dilute the purée with 8 or 10 dl. ($1\frac{1}{3}$ to $1\frac{3}{4}$ pints, $1\frac{3}{4}$ pints to a quart) white consommé. Bring to the boil and finish off with 60 g. (2 oz., $\frac{1}{4}$ cup) fresh butter. Add 2 tablespoons (3 tablespoons) fresh garden peas cooked in water and drained, and some chervil leaves.

Purée of split pea soup. POTAGE PURÉE DE POIS CASSÉS – Pick over and wash 350 g. (12 oz., $1\frac{1}{2}$ cups) split peas, soak them in cold water for 2 hours, and cook in $1\frac{1}{2}$ litres ($2\frac{3}{4}$ pints, $3\frac{1}{4}$ pints) cold water.

Bring to the boil, skim, season, add a *mirepoix* of 50 g. (2 oz., $\frac{1}{4}$ cup) diced lean bacon, blanched and fried lightly with 2 tablespoons (3 tablespoons) chopped carrots and 1 tablespoon diced onion. Put in a *bouquet garni*, adding to it the green part of 2 leeks.

After cooking, rub through a sieve, put the purée back into the pan, add a few tablespoons consommé and finish off with fresh butter and a tablespoon of chervil leaves.

Serve with small croûtons fried in butter.

This soup can also be prepared as a Lenten dish by omitting the bacon and diluting the purée with milk.

Soup purée portugaise – See *Purée of tomato soup* below.

Fresh pea soup, called Saint-Germain, with ham added (*Robert Carrier*)

Purée of potato soup Parmentier. POTAGE PURÉE DE POMMES DE TERRE, DIT PARMENTIER – Shred the white part of 2 leeks and cook lightly in 25 g. (1 oz., 2 tablespoons) butter.

Add 500 g. (1 lb.) potatoes cut in quarters. Moisten with 1 litre (scant quart, generous quart) white consommé. Season, and boil fast.

As soon as the potatoes are cooked, mash them and rub through a sieve. Add a few tablespoons consommé or cream and finish off with 60 g. (2 oz., 4 tablespoons) fresh butter and a tablespoon of chervil leaves.

Serve with small croûtons, fried in butter.

Purée of split pea soup, garnished with bacon

Purée of sweet potato soup. POTAGE PURÉE DE PATATES – Peel and quarter 600 g. (1 lb. 6 oz.) sweet potatoes and cook them in white consommé. Rub through a sieve and add $\frac{1}{2}$ litre (scant pint, $2\frac{1}{4}$ cups) consommé. Bring to the boil, stir, and finish off by incorporating 60 g. (2 oz., $\frac{1}{4}$ cup) fresh butter.

Serve with small croûtons fried in butter.

Purée of pumpkin soup I (based on meat stock). POTAGE PURÉE DE POTIRON AU GRAS – Peel and cut 500 g. (generous 1 lb.) pumpkin into pieces. Cook in (2 oz., $\frac{1}{4}$ cup) butter and 4 tablespoons ($\frac{1}{3}$ cup) water in a covered pan. Season with a good pinch of salt.

Purée of potato soup Parmentier

When the pumpkin is quite soft, rub it through a fine sieve. Put the purée back into the pan, dilute it to the desired consistency with 6 to 8 dl. (1 to $1\frac{1}{3}$ pints, $2\frac{1}{2}$ to $3\frac{1}{2}$ cups) consommé, bring to the boil, and finish off with 60 g. (2 oz., $\frac{1}{4}$ cup) fresh butter.

Serve with small croûtons, fried in butter.

Purée of pumpkin soup II (Lenten). POTAGE PURÉE DE POTIRON AU MAIGRE – Cook the pumpkin as described in the preceding recipe.

Dilute the purée with boiling milk and add 3 or 4 tablespoons (4 or 5 tablespoons) castor sugar. Finish off with butter.

Serve with small croûtons, fried in butter.

Purée of purslane soup. POTAGE PURÉE DE POURPIER – Proceed as described in the recipe for *Purée of garden cress soup*, replacing the cress by fresh purslane.

Soup purée à la reine – See *Purée of chicken soup.*

Soup purée Saint-Germain – See *Purée of fresh pea soup.*

Purée of shrimp soup or shrimp bisque. POTAGE PURÉE, BISQUE DE CREVETTES – Like *Purée of crayfish soup*, replacing the crayfish by an equivalent quantity of shrimps.

Soup purée soissonnaise – See *Purée of white haricot bean soup.*

Purée of spiny lobster soup or spiny lobster bisque. POTAGE PURÉE, BISQUE DE LANGOUSTE – Like *Purée of crayfish soup*, replacing the crayfish by an equivalent quantity of small spiny lobsters.

Purée of tomato soup

Purée of tomato soup I. POTAGE PURÉE DE TOMATES – Cook 50 g. (2 oz., $\frac{1}{2}$ cup) sliced onion in butter in a covered pan. Add 500 g. (generous 1 lb.) seeded and sliced tomatoes. Season with salt and pepper and add one crushed clove of garlic and a *bouquet garni.*

Cook gently for a few moments, stirring all the time. Add 100 g. (4 oz., generous $\frac{1}{2}$ cup) rice, moisten with 1 litre (scant quart, generous quart) consommé, stir, and simmer gently.

Rub through a sieve, put back in the pan, dilute with a few tablespoons consommé, heat, and incorporate 60 g. (2 oz., $\frac{1}{4}$ cup) butter. Add 2 tablespoons (3 tablespoons) rice cooked in consommé or water.

Purée of tomato soup II. POTAGE PURÉE DE TOMATES – Sauté the onion in butter until soft, then fry the tomatoes in the same pan for a few moments. Sprinkle with 2 tablespoons (3 tablespoons) flour. Moisten with consommé, stir, and season. Garnish and finish off as described above.

Purée of turnip soup, called à la Freneuse. POTAGE PURÉE DE NAVETS, DIT À LA FRENEUSE – Cook 500 g. (generous 1 lb.) sliced and blanched turnips gently in butter in a covered pan. Moisten with 2 dl. ($\frac{1}{3}$ pint, scant cup) consommé and cook until three-quarters done.

Add 250 g. (9 oz., $1\frac{1}{2}$ cups) sliced potatoes, moisten with 5 dl. (scant pint, $2\frac{1}{4}$ cups) consommé and finish cooking on brisk heat.

Rub through a sieve and finish off as described in the recipe for *Purée of celery soup.*

VELOUTÉ SOUPS. POTAGES VELOUTÉS – These soups are composed of a *Velouté sauce* (see SAUCE), based on vegetable, meat, fish or shellfish, cooked in *velouté*, or, in the case of shellfish, added to the *velouté* just before rubbing it through a sieve. These soups are thickened with a liaison of egg yolks, cream and butter.

Veloutés can be served with all the garnishes indicated for cream and purée soups such as pearl barley, *printanière*, asparagus tips, quenelles, *royale*, tapioca. These garnishes are added to the soup after it has been put through a sieve and thickened.

The recipes which follow have been worked out to serve from four to six persons.

For vegetable veloutés. Prepare a *velouté* using 80 g. (3 oz., $\frac{3}{4}$ cup) white *roux* and 8 dl. ($1\frac{1}{3}$ pints, $1\frac{3}{4}$ pints) simple white or chicken consommé or white stock.

Add the vegetable indicated for this *velouté*, having first blanched it, if necessary, and cooked it in butter.

Simmer gently until the vegetable is cooked. Rub through a sieve, pressing it through with a wooden spoon. Dilute the soup with a few tablespoons white consommé. Heat to boiling point. Remove from heat and thicken with a liaison of 3 egg yolks and 1 dl. (6 tablespoons, scant $\frac{1}{2}$ cup) cream. Blend in from 80 to 100 g. (3 to 4 oz., 6 to 8 tablespoons) fresh butter.

For meat, poultry or game velouté. Prepare the *velouté* as described above.

Put the meat, fowl or game into it. The meat should be boned and tied with a string, the fowl or game trussed as for an entrée. Simmer gently until the basic ingredients are cooked.

Drain, bone, if necessary, and pound in a mortar, keeping a small part as a garnish for the soup. Dilute with white consommé and finish off as described in the preceding recipe.

For fish velouté. Using boned fish, proceed as described in the recipe above for meat, poultry or game *velouté*, using Lenten or fish stock for making the *velouté*, or meat or chicken stock.

For shellfish velouté. Cook the shellfish indicated with a *mirepoix*, then pound it in a mortar with the liquor in which it was cooked. Add it to a *velouté* based on meat or fish stock. Rub through a sieve and finish off as described above.

Compound butter, flavoured with the appropriate shellfish, is usually added to shellfish *velouté* soups.

Artichoke velouté soup. POTAGE VELOUTÉ D'ARTICHAUTS – Prepare 8 dl. ($1\frac{1}{3}$ pints, $1\frac{3}{4}$ pints) *velouté* based on white consommé. Blanch and slice 8 artichoke hearts and simmer lightly in butter in a covered pan. Cook in the *velouté*.

Rub through a sieve. Dilute with white consommé. Heat, thicken with a liaison of 3 egg yolks and 1 dl. (6 tablespoons, scant $\frac{1}{2}$ cup) cream. Incorporate 80 to 100 g. (3 to 4 oz., 6 to 8 tablespoons) butter.

Garnish with artichoke hearts cooked in a *court-bouillon* and diced, and chervil leaves.

Asparagus velouté soup. POTAGE VELOUTÉ D'ASPERGES – Using the tips of 450 g. (1 lb., 3 cups) asparagus blanched and cooked in butter in a covered pan, proceed as described in the recipe for *Artichoke velouté soup.*

This soup can be made of white or green asparagus.

Celery velouté soup. POTAGE VELOUTÉ DE CÉLERI – Like *Artichoke velouté soup*, using celery cooked in butter in a covered pan.

Chicken velouté soup I. POTAGE VELOUTÉ DE VOLAILLE – Prepare 8 dl. ($1\frac{1}{3}$ pints, $1\frac{3}{4}$ pints) *velouté*. Add a medium-sized, tender young chicken. Simmer gently. Drain the chicken, bone it, keep a part of the breast fillets for garnish, and pound the rest in the mortar. Add this chicken purée to the *velouté*. Rub through a sieve and finish off as described in the recipe for *Artichoke velouté soup*. Garnish with diced breast fillets.

Chicken velouté soup II. POTAGE VELOUTÉ DE VOLAILLE – Prepare the *velouté* and cook the chicken as described in the preceding recipe.

When pounding the chicken meat, add to it 60 g. (2 oz., $\frac{1}{4}$ cup) butter and 1 dl. (6 tablespoons, scant $\frac{1}{2}$ cup) fresh double cream. Rub through a horse-hair sieve. Thicken the *velouté*, strain, and add the chicken purée. Finish off with fresh butter and cream.

Chicken velouté soup à l'écossaise. POTAGE VELOUTÉ DE VOLAILLE À L'ÉCOSSAISE – Add 4 tablespoons ($\frac{1}{3}$ cup) of a fine *brunoise* of vegetables, softened in butter, and chervil leaves, to *Chicken velouté soup*.

Chicken velouté soup à la Nantua. POTAGE VELOUTÉ DE VOLAILLE À LA NANTUA – Flavour *Chicken velouté soup* with crayfish butter. Garnish with shelled crayfish tails.

Chicken velouté soup à la portugaise. POTAGE VELOUTÉ DE VOLAILLE À LA PORTUGAISE – Add to *Chicken velouté soup* 4 tablespoons ($\frac{1}{3}$ cup) tomatoes, peeled, pressed out, cut into small pieces and cooked in butter in a covered pan.

Chicken velouté soup sultane. POTAGE VELOUTÉ DE VOLAILLE SULTANE – Flavour the soup with pistachio butter and garnish with small quenelles made of *Chicken forcemeat* (see FORCEMEAT).

Crayfish velouté soup. POTAGE VELOUTÉ D'ÉCREVISSES – Like *Shrimp velouté soup* below, replacing the shrimps by 12 crayfish, cooked with a *mirepoix* and pounded in a mortar.

Finish off with *Crayfish butter* (see BUTTER, *Compound butters*).

Endive (U.S. chicory), spinach or lettuce velouté soup. POTAGE VELOUTÉ DE CHICORÉE, D'ÉPINARDS, DE LAITUE – Like *Artichoke velouté soup*, using one or other of these vegetables.

Frog velouté soup à la sicilienne. POTAGE VELOUTÉ DE GRENOUILLES À LA SICILIENNE – Proceed as described in the recipe for *Smelt velouté soup* below, replacing the smelts with 48 frogs' legs cooked in butter.

Finish off as described in the recipe for *Artichoke velouté soup*, flavouring it with pistachio butter.

Game velouté soup – See *Partridge velouté soup* below.

Lobster velouté soup. POTAGE VELOUTÉ DE HOMARD – Like *Shrimp velouté soup*, using lobster cooked with a *mirepoix*.

Mushroom velouté soup, also called Pierre-le-grand. POTAGE VELOUTÉ DE CHAMPIGNONS, PIERRE-LE-GRAND – Like *Artichoke velouté soup*, using purée of cultivated mushrooms.

Oyster velouté soup. POTAGE VELOUTÉ AUX HUÎTRES – Prepare 8 dl. ($1\frac{1}{3}$ pints, $1\frac{3}{4}$ pints) fish *velouté*, as described in the basic recipe. Add to it the water of 24 oysters.

Thicken the soup as described in the recipe for *Artichoke velouté soup*, and garnish it with poached and de-bearded oysters.

Partridge velouté soup. POTAGE VELOUTÉ DE PERDRIX – Prepare 8 dl. ($1\frac{1}{3}$ pints, $1\frac{3}{4}$ pints) *velouté* as described in the basic recipe. Add 2 partridges, previously browned lightly in the oven. Simmer gently. Drain the partridges, bone them and pound the flesh in a mortar, except for a part of the breast fillets, kept for garnish. Add this purée to the *velouté*.

Rub through a sieve and finish off as described in the recipe for *Artichoke velouté soup*. Garnish with the breast fillets, cut in dice.

Various game *velouté* soups are prepared in the same way, using wood-grouse, pheasant, hazel-grouse, etc.

Shrimp velouté soup. POTAGE VELOUTÉ DE CREVETTES – Prepare 8 dl. ($1\frac{1}{3}$ pints, $1\frac{3}{4}$ pints) of *velouté* as described in the recipes for vegetable *veloutés*.

When sieving add 500 g. (generous 1 lb.) shrimps, cooked with a *mirepoix* and pounded in a mortar, having kept some shrimp tails for the garnish.

Finish off as described in the recipe for *Artichoke velouté soup*, but add *Shrimp butter* instead of ordinary fresh butter (see BUTTER, *Compound butters*).

Shrimp velouté soup à la normande. POTAGE VELOUTÉ DE CREVETTES À LA NORMANDE – As above. Garnish with 12 shelled shrimp tails, 8 poached and de-bearded oysters and 8 small pike quenelles.

Smelt velouté soup I. POTAGE VELOUTÉ D'ÉPERLANS – Prepare the *velouté* as described in the basic recipe, using fish consommé if desired.

Cook 250 g. (9 oz.) smelts in butter with a tablespoon chopped onion, drain, pound in a mortar, and add to the *velouté* before sieving.

Strain and finish off as described in the recipe for *Artichoke velouté soup*.

Smelt velouté soup II, à la dieppoise. POTAGE VELOUTÉ D'ÉPERLANS À LA DIEPPOISE – As above, adding to the *velouté* a few tablespoons of the liquor in which mussels were cooked and garnishing the soup with 12 poached mussels and 12 shelled shrimps' tails.

Smelt velouté soup III, à l'indienne. POTAGE VELOUTÉ D'ÉPERLANS À L'INDIENNE – As above. Sprinkle the smelt fillets with a tablespoon curry powder while cooking them in butter with chopped onion.

Spiny lobster and Dublin Bay prawn velouté soup. POTAGE VELOUTÉ DE LANGOUSTE, LANGOUSTINE – Like *Shrimp velouté soup*, using spiny lobster or Dublin Bay prawns cooked with a *mirepoix*.

SPECIAL SOUPS. POTAGES SPÉCIAUX – The recipes for these soups, based on purées or on *veloutés* with various garnishes, have been worked out to serve 4 to 6 persons.

Potage ambassadeurs – Prepare $1\frac{1}{2}$ litres ($2\frac{3}{4}$ pints, $3\frac{1}{4}$ pints) *Purée of fresh pea soup*, add to it 4 tablespoons ($\frac{1}{3}$ cup) of a *chiffonnade* of sorrel cooked in butter, 2 tablespoons (3 tablespoons) rice poached in consommé, and chervil leaves.

This soup can also be made by adding a *chiffonnade* of mixed lettuce and sorrel.

Andalusian soup. POTAGE ANDALOUSE – Add $1\frac{1}{2}$ litres ($2\frac{3}{4}$ pints, $3\frac{1}{4}$ pints) *Purée of tomato soup* to $2\frac{1}{2}$ dl. (scant $\frac{1}{2}$ pint, generous cup) tapioca cooked in consommé.

Potage Apicius (old recipe) – 'Boil down consommé by half for soup. Blanch 350 g. (12 oz.) lasagne in salted boiling water. Drain and simmer for 20 minutes in half of the boiled-down consommé, with 125 g. (4 oz., $\frac{1}{2}$ cup) best butter, a pinch coarse ground pepper and a pinch grated nutmeg. Boil down the breast of a fowl to purée, add to the lasagne and mix. Put a layer of the lasagne into a soup tureen, follow with a layer of big cocks' combs and kidneys cooked in consommé, then add a plateful of small truffles, cut to look like olives, sautéed in butter with a little chicken jelly. Sprinkle with Parmesan cheese. Continue to superimpose these various elements in successive layers. Pour over the consommé left over from cooking the lasagne and serve.'

Potage d'Artois – Prepare $1\frac{1}{2}$ litres ($2\frac{3}{4}$ pints, $3\frac{1}{4}$ pints) *Purée of white haricot bean soup*, add to it 4 tablespoons ($\frac{1}{3}$ cup) of a fine *brunoise* of vegetables cooked in butter until soft, and chervil leaves.

Potage Bagration I (based on meat) – Prepare 8 dl. ($1\frac{1}{3}$ pints, $1\frac{3}{4}$ pints) *velouté* as described in the basic recipe for these soups. Add to it 500 g. (generous 1 lb.) lean veal, cut in large dice and lightly fried in butter. Simmer gently.

Drain the veal. Pound it finely in a mortar and add to the *velouté*. Rub through a sieve and heat to boiling point. Thicken with a liaison of 3 egg yolks and 1 dl. (6 tablespoons, scant $\frac{1}{2}$ cup) cream. Add more seasoning, if necessary, and incorporate 80 to 100 g. (3 to 4 oz., 6 to 8 tablespoons) butter. Garnish with poached and diced macaroni. Serve with grated cheese.

Potage Bagration II (based on fish) – Proceed as described in the preceding recipe, using *velouté* based on fish stock and replacing the veal by 250 g. (9 oz.) fillets of sole, previously fried lightly in butter.

Potage Balvet, also called Jubilé. POTAGE BALVET, DIT AUSSI JUBILÉ – Prepare $1\frac{1}{2}$ litres ($2\frac{3}{4}$ pints, $3\frac{1}{4}$ pints) *Purée of fresh pea soup*, dilute with a little consommé and add 4 tablespoons ($\frac{1}{3}$ cup) of stockpot vegetables.

Potage bonne-femme I – Shred finely 100 g. (4 oz., 1 cup) of the white part of leeks and cook in butter in a covered pan. Moisten with $1\frac{1}{2}$ litres ($2\frac{3}{4}$ pints, $3\frac{1}{4}$ pints) white consommé. Add 250 g. (9 oz., $1\frac{1}{2}$ cups) sliced potatoes. Season and simmer gently. Add from 60 to 80 g. (2 to 3 oz., 4 to 6 tablespoons) butter and some chervil leaves. Serve with long French bread thinly sliced and dried in the oven.

The consommé can be replaced by water or milk.

Potage bonne-femme II – Cook the leeks in butter in a covered pan. Add 6 dl. (1 pint, $2\frac{1}{2}$ cups) of a very thin potato purée and $\frac{1}{2}$ l. (scant pint, $2\frac{1}{4}$ cups) consommé. Add 150 g. (5 oz., $\frac{3}{4}$ cup) sliced potatoes and simmer gently. Add 2 dl. ($\frac{1}{3}$ pint, scant cup) cream, 60 g. (2 oz., $\frac{1}{4}$ cup) butter and some chervil leaves.

Potage Camérani (old recipe) – 'Soften slowly in butter 2 dl. ($\frac{1}{3}$ pint, scant cup) of a fine *brunoise* of vegetables, with a little turnip added to it. Add 12 chicken livers, trimmed and cut in very small dice. Season and brown on brisk heat.

'Separately, and as quickly as possible, poach 125 g. (4 oz.) macaroni in salted water. Drain, dress with butter and season.

'To serve, put the macaroni into a silver dish, buttered and sprinkled with grated Parmesan cheese, alternating with layers of chopped chicken livers and sprinkling each layer with Parmesan. Heat for a few minutes on a low flame.'

Following ancient usage, this is classified as a soup.

Potage cultivateur – Cut 2 or 3 small carrots, a small turnip, 6 tablespoons ($\frac{1}{2}$ cup) of the white part of leeks and 2 tablespoons (3 tablespoons) onions, into large dice.

Season with salt and a pinch of sugar. Cook in 50 g. (2 oz., $\frac{1}{4}$ cup) butter in a covered pan. Moisten with $1\frac{1}{2}$ litres ($2\frac{3}{4}$ pints, $3\frac{1}{4}$ pints) white consommé and cook for $1\frac{1}{4}$ hours. About 25 minutes before serving, add 150 g. (5 oz., $\frac{3}{4}$ cup) sliced potatoes and 75 g. (3 oz.) well blanched diced bacon.

The potatoes can be replaced by rice.

Potage Darblay – See *Potage julienne Darblay* below.

Potage Faubonne – Add 4 tablespoons ($\frac{1}{3}$ cup) of a *julienne* of vegetables, cooked gently in butter, and some chervil leaves, to $1\frac{1}{2}$ litres ($2\frac{3}{4}$ pints, $3\frac{1}{4}$ pints) *Purée of split pea soup*.

This soup can also be made of white bean or any other vegetable purée, or a pheasant purée and a garnish composed of pheasant fillets and a *julienne* of truffles.

Potage fermière – Shred finely 2 or 3 small carrots, 1 small turnip, 6 tablespoons ($\frac{1}{2}$ cup) of the white part of leeks, chopped, 4 tablespoons ($\frac{1}{3}$ cup) onions and 75 g. (3 oz., $1\frac{1}{4}$ cups) shredded cabbage heart. Season, and simmer slowly in 50 g. (2 oz., $\frac{1}{4}$ cup) butter in a covered pan.

Moisten with 8 dl. ($1\frac{1}{3}$ pints, $1\frac{3}{4}$ pints) water in which white beans have been cooked, and 6 dl. (1 pint, $2\frac{1}{2}$ cups) white consommé. Cook for $1\frac{1}{4}$ hours. Add 1 dl. (6 tablespoons, scant $\frac{1}{2}$ cup) cream, 4 tablespoons ($\frac{1}{3}$ cup) cooked white beans and some chervil leaves.

This soup can also be prepared as a Lenten dish by omitting the consommé and using the water left over from cooking the beans.

Potage Fontanges – Prepare $1\frac{1}{2}$ litres ($2\frac{3}{4}$ pints, $3\frac{1}{4}$ pints) *Purée of fresh pea soup*, dilute with a little consommé and add

Potage Fontanges

to it 4 tablespoons ($\frac{1}{3}$ cup) of a *chiffonnade* of sorrel cooked in butter until soft, and some chervil leaves.

This soup is sometimes thickened with a liaison of egg yolks and cream and garnished with croûtons.

Potage gentilhomme – Garnish $1\frac{1}{2}$ litres ($2\frac{3}{4}$ pints, $3\frac{1}{4}$ pints) *Purée of game soup* based on lentil purée with 4 tablespoons ($\frac{1}{3}$ cup) small game quenelles.

Potage Germiny – Moisten 200 g. (7 oz.) sorrel shredded into a *chiffonnade* and softened in butter, with $1\frac{1}{2}$ litres ($2\frac{3}{4}$ pints, $3\frac{1}{4}$ pints) consommé.

Thicken with a liaison of 8 to 10 egg yolks diluted with 1 dl. (6 tablespoons, scant $\frac{1}{2}$ cup) fresh cream. Add a tablespoon of chervil leaves. Serve with long French bread, thinly sliced and dried in the oven.

Potage Jubilé – Another name for *Potage Balvet*.

Potage julienne à l'allemande – Prepare 1 litre (scant quart, generous quart) *Potage julienne*. Thicken with a liaison of 4 egg yolks diluted with 2 dl. ($\frac{1}{3}$ pint, scant cup) cream. Add 80 to 100 g. (3 to 4 oz., 6 to 8 tablespoons) butter and some chervil leaves.

Potage julienne à la cévenole – Prepare 1 litre (scant quart, generous quart) of a light *Purée of chestnut soup*. Add $\frac{1}{2}$ litre (scant pint, $2\frac{1}{4}$ cups) of a *julienne*, cooked in butter and consommé. Boil for 5 minutes. Blend in 60 g. (2 oz., $\frac{1}{4}$ cup) butter and sprinkle with a tablespoon of chervil leaves.

Potage julienne Darblay – Prepare $1\frac{1}{2}$ litres ($2\frac{3}{4}$ pints, $3\frac{1}{4}$ pints) *Purée of potato soup*, dilute with a little consommé, add 4 tablespoons ($\frac{1}{3}$ cup) of a *julienne* of vegetables lightly cooked in butter. Cook together, simmering gently for 10 minutes.

Thicken with a liaison of 3 egg yolks diluted with 1 dl. (6 tablespoons, scant $\frac{1}{2}$ cup) fresh cream. Incorporate 60 to 80 g. (2 to 3 oz., 4 to 6 tablespoons) butter and add chervil leaves.

Potage Lamballe – Add 7 dl. ($1\frac{1}{4}$ pints, $1\frac{1}{2}$ pints) rather thick consommé with tapioca to 8 dl. ($1\frac{1}{3}$ pints, $1\frac{3}{4}$ pints) *Purée of fresh pea soup*.

Potage Longchamp – Add 3 tablespoons (4 tablespoons) of a *chiffonnade* of sorrel, lightly cooked in butter, 5 dl. (scant pint, $2\frac{1}{4}$ cups) consommé with vermicelli and some chervil leaves to 1 litre (scant quart, generous quart) *Purée of fresh pea soup*.

Potage Marigny – Like *Potage Fontanges*. Decrease the proportion of the *chiffonnade* of sorrel and add 2 tablespoons (3 tablespoons) garden peas and diced French beans cooked in water.

Oyster soup I. POTAGE AUX HUÎTRES – Prepare $1\frac{1}{2}$ litres ($2\frac{3}{4}$ pints, $3\frac{1}{4}$ pints) *velouté* based on fish consommé, as described in the basic recipe for these soups. Thicken with a liaison of 3 egg yolks diluted with 1 dl. (6 tablespoons, scant $\frac{1}{2}$ cup) cream, and blend in some butter. Garnish with 12 oysters poached in their strained liquor. Add blanched and drained chervil leaves.

The liquor drained out of the oysters should be added to the *velouté*.

Spice with a pinch of cayenne pepper.

Oyster soup II. POTAGE AUX HUÎTRES – Make 80 g. (3 oz., $\frac{3}{4}$ cup) white *roux* and dilute it with 8 dl. ($1\frac{1}{3}$ pints, $1\frac{3}{4}$ pints) of the liquid in which mussels were cooked, or concentrated fish stock, mixed with the liquor of 12 oysters. Mix and simmer gently.

Thicken with a liaison of 3 egg yolks diluted with 1 dl. (6 tablespoons, scant $\frac{1}{2}$ cup) cream. Finish off as described in the preceding recipe.

Potage paysanne – Shred finely 1 medium-large carrot, 1 small turnip, 50 g. (2 oz., $\frac{1}{2}$ cup) the white part of leeks, 25 g. (1 oz., $\frac{1}{4}$ cup) chopped onion, 25 g. (1 oz.) celery and 25 g. (1 oz., $\frac{1}{3}$ cup) shredded cabbage heart.

Season with salt and a pinch of sugar. Cook slowly in 50 g. (2 oz., $\frac{1}{4}$ cup) butter in a covered pan.

Moisten with $1\frac{1}{2}$ litres ($2\frac{3}{4}$ pints, $3\frac{1}{4}$ pints) white consommé. Cook for $1\frac{1}{4}$ hours. About 25 minutes before serving, add 100 g. (4 oz., $\frac{2}{3}$ cups) thinly sliced potatoes, 2 tablespoons (3 tablespoons) fresh garden peas, 1 tablespoon chervil leaves.

Serve with long French bread, thinly sliced and dried in the oven.

This soup can be prepared as a Lenten dish by replacing the consommé with water. In that case, add 60 g. (2 oz., $\frac{1}{4}$ cup) butter before serving.

Potage Pierre-le-Grand (Peter the Great's soup) – See *Mushroom velouté soup*.

This soup can also be made by mixing mushroom and hazel-grouse purées.

Portuguese soup. POTAGE PORTUGAIS – Cook 75 g. (3 oz., $\frac{3}{4}$ cup) chopped onion and 100 g. (4 oz., $\frac{1}{2}$ cup) diced, blanched lean bacon in butter in a covered pan.

Add 500 g. (generous 1 lb.) sliced, seeded tomatoes, a small *bouquet garni*, and half a clove of garlic. Sauté for 10 minutes. Add 100 g. (4 oz., $\frac{1}{2}$ cup) rice.

Moisten with $1\frac{1}{4}$ litres ($2\frac{1}{4}$ pints, $2\frac{3}{4}$ pints) white consommé. Season and simmer gently for an hour. Rub through a sieve, pressing with a wooden spoon. Heat the purée, dilute with a few tablespoons consommé and incorporate in it 60 to 80 g. (2 to 3 oz., 4 to 6 tablespoons) butter. Add 4 tablespoons ($\frac{1}{3}$ cup) rice, cooked in consommé.

Potage Raphaël – This was classified by Carême as an Italian soup.

'Prepare a *Petite marmite* in the usual manner and cook a small chicken in it.

'Bone the chicken completely, keep one fillet of breast, pound the rest of the meat in a mortar while still hot, and rub through a fine sieve. Collect the purée in a soup tureen, pour over a few tablespoons of strained consommé, cover and keep by.

'Allowing 2 litres ($3\frac{1}{2}$ pints, $4\frac{1}{2}$ pints) of the *Petite marmite* consommé for 10 persons, skim off surplus fat and strain. Bring to the boil. Pour into it 100 g. (4 oz., $\frac{2}{3}$ cup) coarse-ground semolina and simmer gently for 25 minutes. Add the chicken purée, little by little, to the semolina, stirring with a whisk. Add 20 small cocks' combs (or 10 medium-sized ones, cut in half), cooked in a light *court-bouillon*, as well as the breast fillet and two small truffles, shredded into a fine *julienne*.' (Philéas Gilbert.)

Potage Saint-Cloud – Soup made of *Purée of fresh pea soup*, called *Saint-Germain*, served with diced croûtons, fried in butter.

Potage santé – Prepare $1\frac{1}{2}$ litres ($2\frac{3}{4}$ pints, $3\frac{1}{4}$ pints) of a light *Soup purée Parmentier* and add to it 4 tablespoons ($\frac{1}{3}$ cup) of a *chiffonnade* of sorrel, lightly cooked in butter until soft.

Thicken with a liaison of 3 yolks, diluted with 1 dl. (6 tablespoons, scant $\frac{1}{2}$ cup) cream. Incorporate 100 g. (4 oz., $\frac{1}{2}$ cup) butter and add some chervil leaves.

Serve with long French bread, thinly sliced and dried in the oven.

Potage Solférino – Cook in butter 75 g. (3 oz., $\frac{3}{4}$ cup) of the white part of leeks and 75 g. (3 oz., $\frac{2}{3}$ cup) of the red part of carrots, both shredded, until tender, in a covered pan.

Add 500 g. (generous 1 lb.) sliced and seeded tomatoes, a small *bouquet garni* and, if liked, half a clove of garlic. Cook for 10 minutes.

Moisten with 1 litre (scant quart, generous quart) white consommé, add 250 g. (9 oz., $1\frac{1}{2}$ cups) sliced potatoes. Season and simmer gently.

Remove the *bouquet garni* and the garlic. Drain the vegetables and rub them through a sieve. Add the liquor left in the pan to this purée and dilute it with a few tablespoons consommé. Bring to the boil and skim the surface. Add 80 to 100 g. (3 to 4 oz., 6 to 8 tablespoons) butter.

Garnish with 2 tablespoons (3 tablespoons) small potato balls, scooped out with a vegetable baller and cooked in white consommé, and chervil leaves.

Potage Velours – Add $\frac{1}{2}$ litre (scant pint, $2\frac{1}{4}$ cups) consommé substantially thickened with tapioca to 1 litre ($1\frac{3}{4}$ pints, generous quart) *Purée Crécy*.

Potage Xavier – Prepare $1\frac{1}{2}$ litres ($2\frac{3}{4}$ pints, $3\frac{1}{4}$ pints) *Cream of rice soup*. Thicken it with a liaison of 3 egg yolks diluted with 1 dl. (6 tablespoons, scant $\frac{1}{2}$ cup) cream. Incorporate 80 to 100 g. (3 to 4 oz., 6 to 8 tablespoons) butter.

Serve with a chicken *royale*, cut in very small dice.

CLASSICAL AND REGIONAL SOUPS. SOUPES – We have grouped here various classical and regional soups of France.

Many of these have bread added to them. The bread should be light and porous and should have innumerable small holes, so as to be easily imbued with the soup. It should be stale, cut in slices of varying thickness, depending on the nature of the soup. Toast it or dry it in the oven.

Soupe aïgo-saou (Provençal cookery) – Put into a saucepan 1 kg. ($2\frac{1}{4}$ lb.) white fish cut into pieces, a medium-sized sliced onion, 4 chopped tomatoes, 4 potatoes cut in quarters, 2 cloves of garlic and a *bouquet garni*, composed of parsley, celery, thyme and bay leaf. Season with 25 g. (4 teaspoons) salt and a good pinch of pepper. Add 2 litres ($3\frac{1}{2}$ pints, $4\frac{1}{2}$ pints) water and boil fast from 18 to 20 minutes. Strain the soup into a tureen over slices of bread spinkled with a dash of oil.

Arrange the fish and the potatoes on a dish and serve with *ailoi* or *rouille*, which is prepared as follows. Pound a big clove of garlic with a red pepper in a mortar. Add a piece of bread (crumb, i.e. soft part only) the size of a walnut, soaked and pressed out.

Over the whole, little by little and stirring constantly, pour about $2\frac{1}{2}$ dl. (scant $\frac{1}{2}$ pint, generous cup) olive oil. Add a few tablespoons fish stock.

Soupe aïgo à la ménagère (Provençal cookery) – Colour lightly a chopped onion and the white part of 3 leeks in oil. Add 2 seeded and chopped tomatoes, 4 crushed cloves of garlic, a small piece of fennel, a piece of dried orange peel, a *bouquet garni*, 4 sliced potatoes and a small pinch of saffron. Add 2 litres ($3\frac{1}{2}$ pints, $4\frac{1}{2}$ pints) water. Season with 20 g. (3 teaspoons) salt and a pinch of pepper. Boil fast for 15 minutes.

Poach eggs in this soup, allowing 1 per person. Drain the eggs, arrange them on a dish with the potatoes, which have been taken out of the saucepan and sprinkled with chopped parsley.

Strain the rest of the soup over slices of home-made bread arranged in a deep dish.

Soupe aïgo bouïdo à la ménagère (Provençal cookery) – Boil 2 litres ($3\frac{1}{2}$ pints, $4\frac{1}{2}$ pints) water into which you have put 15 crushed cloves of garlic, a *bouquet garni*, a sprig of sage, 2 dl. ($\frac{1}{3}$ pint, scant cup) olive oil, 25 g. (4 teaspoons) coarse salt and a pinch of pepper.

Pour this soup into a tureen over slices of bread sprinkled with chopped parsley.

Soupe aïgo bouïdo with poached eggs (Provençal cookery). SOUPE AÏGO BOUÏDO AUX ŒUFS POCHÉS – Prepare the soup as described in the preceding recipe and poach the eggs in it. Arrange the eggs on slices of bread in a deep dish. Pour the soup over them and add a pinch of parsley.

Soupe albigeoise – This soup is made not only in the Albi region but throughout the western part of France.

It is a *potée* with rib of beef, salt pork, sausage and *confit d'oie* (preserved goose) as basic nutritive ingredients, with the following vegetables: cabbage, carrots, turnips, leeks, onions, potatoes, and plenty of garlic.

The *potée albigeoise* differs very little from other French *potées*, the best of which is the Auvergne *potée*.

Arles soup. SOUPE ARIÉGEOISE – *Potée* prepared in the same manner as the Auvergne *potée*, with cabbage, carrots, turnips, onion, leek and potatoes, and salt pork, sometimes *confit d'oie*, and a succulent *farci*. There is always plenty of garlic.

Black pudding water soup or bougras (Périgord cookery). SOUPE À L'EAU DE BOUDIN, BOUGRAS – This soup is usually prepared during Shrovetide, when pigs are slaughtered and delicious black puddings are made.

Bring the water in which black puddings have been poached to the boil. For $2\frac{1}{2}$ litres ($4\frac{1}{2}$ pints, $5\frac{1}{2}$ pints) of this water, add a head of curly green cabbage cut into pieces and blanched, carrots, turnips, leeks, celery and quartered onions. Simmer gently for 40 minutes. Add 400 g. (14 oz.) potatoes cut in thick slices and cook for another 35 minutes.

Fifteen minutes before serving, remove some of the vegetables with a perforated spoon, slice them, fry in fat, sprinkle with flour, moisten with a few tablespoons of stock and add to the soup. (This is called '*fricassée*' in Périgord and it is added to most soups.)

Pour the boiling soup into a tureen lined with thin slices of home-made bread.

Soupe à la bonne femme – Cook gently the finely shredded white part of 4 leeks in a covered saucepan, with 40 g. ($1\frac{1}{2}$ oz., 3 tablespoons) butter, without allowing the leeks to colour. When they are quite soft, add 3 litres ($5\frac{1}{4}$ pints, $6\frac{1}{2}$ pints) ordinary consommé and bring to the boil. Add 350 g. (12 oz., 2 cups) sliced potatoes. Bring to the boil, season and simmer gently.

When the soup is ready, remove the saucepan from heat and add 60 g. (2 oz., $\frac{1}{4}$ cup) butter and 1 tablespoon of chervil leaves.

Soup with cabbage and miques (Périgord cookery). SOUPE AUX CHOUX ET AUX MIQUES – Put the cabbages into a saucepan and cover with water. Add a piece of salt unsmoked ham or a salt chine of pork, carrot, turnips, rape, onions studded with cloves, celery, garlic,a *bouquet garni* and the usual seasoning.

Using maize (U.S. corn) flour, make some *miques* (q.v.).

A few minutes before serving the soup, take some of the vegetables out with a perforated spoon, fry them in fat, sprinkle with flour, moisten with a few tablespoons stock and put back into the saucepan.

Serve with soup garnished with thin slices of bread and, on a separate dish, the ham or chine of pork placed on the cabbage and surrounded by the *miques*.

Soupe à la farine (Alsatian cookery) – Pour 3 tablespoons (4 tablespoons) flour, mixed with cold consommé or water until quite smooth, into $1\frac{1}{2}$ litres ($2\frac{3}{4}$ pints, $3\frac{1}{4}$ pints) boiling consommé. Season with salt, pepper and a pinch of grated nutmeg and mix well. Boil for 5 minutes. Add 1 dl. (6 tablespoons, scant $\frac{1}{2}$ cup) fresh cream and 2 tablespoons (3 tablespoons) butter.

Fish soup with vermicelli à la marseillaise. SOUPE DE POISSON AU VERMICELLE À LA MARSEILLAISE – Sauté 2 good tablespoons (3 tablespoons) of sliced onion in oil in a saucepan with a thick, flat bottom. When the onion is cooked, sprinkle it with a tablespoon flour and fry for a moment, stirring with a spoon.

Cover with 2 litres ($3\frac{1}{2}$ pints, $4\frac{1}{2}$ pints) water. Add 500 g. (generous 1 lb.) fish bones and trimmings cut into very small pieces. Season with salt and pepper. Add a tablespoon pounded parsley, a fragment of bay leaf, a sprig of thyme, a little crushed garlic, 4 tablespoons ($\frac{1}{3}$ cup) tomato purée and a good pinch of powdered saffron. Cook over a fairly high heat for about 20 minutes.

Strain the fish stock through a fine strainer. Bring to the boil and pour into it 4 tablespoons ($\frac{1}{3}$ cup) vermicelli. Poach for 10 minutes. Add half a tablespoon chopped parsley.

Soupe au fromage – See *Onion soup gratinée* below.

Garlic soup à la provençale. SOUPE À L'AIL À LA PROVENÇALE – Put 2 litres ($3\frac{1}{2}$ pints, $4\frac{1}{2}$ pints) water, 24 small cloves of garlic, a sprig of thyme, a clove, a branch of sage, 25 g. (4 teaspoons) salt and a pinch of pepper into a saucepan. Boil fast for 20 minutes.

Strain the soup through a fine strainer and pour it into a tureen over about 20 small slices of bread which have been sprinkled with grated cheese and placed in the oven for an instant to melt the cheese, and with 2 tablespoons (3 tablespoons) olive oil poured over them. Let the bread swell properly before serving.

Onion soup. SOUPE À L'OIGNON – Slice 250 g. (9 oz.) onions finely and fry in butter, without allowing to colour. When nearly done, sprinkle with 25 g. (1 oz., $\frac{1}{4}$ cup) flour. Stir with a wooden spoon for a few moments. Add 2 litres ($3\frac{1}{2}$ pints, $4\frac{1}{2}$ pints) white consommé, or water. Cook for 25 minutes. Pour over slices of bread dried in the oven.

Onion soup gratinée, also called cheese soup. SOUPE À L'OIGNON GRATINÉE, SOUPE AU FROMAGE – Prepare like ordinary onion soup. Pour into an ovenproof dish over slices of bread dried in the oven and arranged in layers, each being covered with grated cheese. Sprinkle with grated cheese and a little melted butter. Brown in the oven.

Périgord soup 'sobronade'. SOUPE PÉRIGOURDINE 'SOBRONADE' – This dish constitutes a solid dish rather than a soup.

Soak 750 g. ($1\frac{3}{4}$ lb., 4 cups) white beans in cold water and put them into a big saucepan. Cover with cold water. Add 500 g. (generous 1 lb.) fresh pork, fat and lean, and 250 g. (9 oz., 1 cup) ham cut into small pieces. Bring to the boil and skim.

Add one or two turnips cut in thick slices (one-third of these previously fried, *fricassée* with chopped fat bacon), 3 carrots and a quartered stalk of celery, an onion studded with 2 cloves, a *bouquet garni* and chopped garlic and parsley. Season with salt and pepper and cook, covered.

Boil for 20 minutes. Add 250 g. (9 oz., $1\frac{1}{2}$ cups) potatoes cut in thick slices. Cook on low heat for $1\frac{1}{2}$ hours. Pour this soup into a tureen over thin slices of stale bread.

Tourain périgourdin (Périgord cookery) – Make a *fricasée* by frying 150 g. (5 oz., $1\frac{1}{4}$ cups) finely sliced onions in fat, colouring them slightly but not allowing them to brown. Sprinkle with a good tablespoon flour, add 2 crushed cloves of garlic, moisten with a few tablespoons boiling water and mix until smooth.

Cook 2 big, seeded tomatoes in 2 litres ($3\frac{1}{2}$ pints, $4\frac{1}{2}$ pints) stock or water with salt and pepper. Drain the tomatoes, mash them and add to the stock. Add the *fricassée* to the stock. Simmer steadily for 45 minutes. Thicken with a liaison of 2 egg yolks diluted with a few tablespoons stock. Pour into a soup tureen over thin slices of home-made bread.

Like all onion soups, the Périgord *tourain* can be *gratinée*. Pour it into a deep dish over slices of bread, each layer of which has been sprinkled with grated Gruyère cheese. Sprinkle the surface with grated cheese and slowly brown the top in the oven.

Spelt soup (Provençal cookery). SOUPE D'ÉPEAUTRE – Put 1 kg. ($2\frac{1}{4}$ lb.) shoulder or leg of mutton into a saucepan. Cover with 3 litres ($5\frac{1}{4}$ pints, $6\frac{1}{2}$ pints) water, bring to the boil and skim. Add an onion studded with 2 cloves, 2 carrots, 1 turnip, 1 leek, 1 stalk of celery, 1 clove of garlic and season with salt.

Add 4 handfuls spelt (a kind of chaffy wheat with small brownish grain). Simmer very gently for 3 hours.

Whiting soup à la bretonne. SOUPE DE MERLAN À LA BRETONNE – This soup is a kind of *cotriade* (Breton *bouillabaisse*). It is prepared in the same manner as the latter, using whitings cut in chunks, potatoes, and all the aromatic herbs characteristic of that dish. It can, in fact, be considered as a kind of *bouillabaisse* made without tomatoes, oil, garlic or saffron. (See COTRIADE.)

INTERNATIONAL SOUPS AND BROTHS. POTAGES ET SOUPES ÉTRANGERS –

Beer soup (German cookery). SOUPE À LA BIÈRE – Stir $1\frac{1}{2}$ litres ($2\frac{3}{4}$ pints, $3\frac{1}{4}$ pints) light beer into a *roux* of 50 g. (2 oz., $\frac{1}{4}$ cup) butter and 65 g. ($2\frac{1}{2}$ oz., $\frac{2}{3}$ cup) flour. Season with salt, pepper and cinnamon. Add a teaspoon of sugar. Boil for a few minutes.

Bind with $1\frac{1}{2}$ dl. ($\frac{1}{4}$ pint, $\frac{2}{3}$ cup) thick cream and pour piping hot over slices of toast.

Beetroot (U.S.A. beet) soup à l'allemande. POTAGE DE BETTERAVE À L'ALLEMANDE – Peel a raw beetroot, cut it into chunks, and bake in the oven in a casserole with 50 g. (2 oz., $\frac{1}{4}$ cup) butter and a pinch of salt.

Rub through a fine sieve and add one-third of its volume of potato purée, prepared as described in the recipe for *Purée of potato soup*.

Dilute the soup with consommé. Place over a moderate heat, season, and add from 65 to 80 g. ($2\frac{1}{2}$ to 3 oz., 5 to 6 tablespoons) fresh butter. Serve with croûtons fried in butter.

Beetroot soup à la russe. POTAGE DE BETTERAVE À LA RUSSE – Cut a raw beetroot into *julienne*. Add one-third of its volume of onion and celery, also cut into *julienne*.

Soften the vegetables slowly in a casserole with 50 g. (2 oz., $\frac{1}{4}$ cup) butter, a pinch of salt and a teaspoon sugar. When they are cooked, add $1\frac{1}{2}$ litres ($2\frac{3}{4}$ pints, $3\frac{1}{4}$ pints) chicken consommé. Boil for 25 minutes. Skim off surplus fat and add chervil leaves to the soup, with croûtons fried in butter.

Polish borsch. POTAGE BORTSCH POLONAIS – Soften slowly in butter a *julienne* of 1 onion, the white part of 2 leeks, 200 g. (7 oz.) head of cabbage, 250 g. (9 oz.) raw beetroot (U.S.A. beet), a stalk of celery and a parsnip. Cover with 2 litres ($3\frac{1}{2}$ pints, $4\frac{1}{2}$ pints) white consommé.

Onion soup (*Robert Carrier*)

Whiting soup à la bretonne (*Claire*)

Add a small duck browned in the oven, 500 g. (generous 1 lb.) blanched brisket of beef and a small piece of blanched lean bacon. Garnish with a *bouquet garni* containing, in addition to the usual herbs, some fennel and marjoram. Bring to the boil, skim, and simmer gently until all the meats are completely cooked, removing the duck and the bacon as soon as they are done.

Fifteen minutes before serving, add 8 small chipolata sausages to poach in the soup. Remove all the meat garnish. Cut the breast of duck, beef and bacon into dice and the sausages into slices. Add a tablespoon *Mushroom essence* (see ESSENCE) to 1 dl. (6 tablespoons, scant $\frac{1}{2}$ cup) of the juice of raw, grated beetroot, and a tablespoon chopped and blanched fennel and parsley to the soup.

Serve with the meat garnish and a sauceboat of soured cream.

The sausages can be grilled instead of being poached in the soup. The soured cream is often put in the soup, instead of being served separately.

Russian borsch. POTAGE BORTSCH À LA RUSSE – $2\frac{1}{2}$ litres ($4\frac{1}{2}$ pints, $5\frac{1}{2}$ pints) stock, 3 to 4 beetroots (U.S.A. beets), 250 g. (9 oz.) fresh cabbage, 2 carrots, 1 parsnip, 2 stalks celery, 100 g. (4 oz.) boiled ham (optional), 6 Frankfurther sausages (optional), 1 large onion, 3 tablespoons (4 tablespoons) tomato purée (or 100 g., 4 oz. fresh tomatoes), 2 tablespoons (3 tablespoons) vinegar, 1 tablespoon sugar, 1 to 2 bay leaves, sprig of dill, sprig of parsley, $1\frac{1}{2}$ teaspoons salt, $\frac{1}{2}$ teaspoon pepper, $1\frac{1}{2}$ dl. ($\frac{1}{4}$ pint, $\frac{2}{3}$ cup) sour cream.

Clean and shred beetroot, carrots, parsnip, celery and the onion. Cut the root vegetables first into slices then into little 'matchsticks'. The decorative appearance of the vegetables in borsch is very important. Put into a saucepan, add tomatoes or tomato purée, sugar, and enough stock, with a little fat (if the stock has no fat, add 1 or 2 tablespoons butter), to cover the vegetables. Simmer for 15 to 20 minutes, stirring from time to time and adding stock or water to prevent sticking. Add shredded cabbage, mix well and simmer another 15 to 20 minutes. Pour in all the stock, add salt and pepper to taste, bay leaf, 1 tablespoon vinegar, and simmer until the vegetables are done. Potatoes may be put in the borsch – whole if they are small, cut into chips if large. When the borsch is ready and just before serving, a few slices of boiled ham or sausages of the Frankfurther type can be added to it.

To give the characteristic attractive colour, keep 1 beetroot for last minute use. Rub it through a fine grater, cover with a cupful of stock, bring to the boil, simmer for 2 to 3 minutes with a teaspoon of vinegar, and strain the liquid into the borsch. Sprinkle with finely chopped parsley and dill. Add the sour cream and serve. Mushroom patties or buckwheat croûtons may accompany the borsch.

Botvinya (Russian cookery). POTAGE BATWINIA – Boil 1 kg. (2 lb.) fish and leave to cool. Cook 350 g. ($\frac{3}{4}$ lb.) spinach and 225 g. ($\frac{1}{2}$ lb.) sorrel separately and rub them through a sieve. Cut fresh cucumbers into strips, grate some horseradish and chop some spring onions. Amalgamate the spinach and the sorrel purées, season with salt and pepper, add a little sugar and a teaspoonful of lemon zest and dilute with a little white wine.

Pour the botvinya into a tureen or into plates. Cut the fish into portions and put on a dish, garnish with fresh cucumbers, spring onions, horseradish and chopped dill. Surround the fish with cooked crayfish tails and lettuce hearts. Serve with ice cubes in a bowl, and a sauceboat of soured cream.

Potage Camaro à la brésilienne – Truss a chicken as for an entrée and put it into an earthenware casserole. Cover with water. Bring to the boil, skim, season and add a *bouquet* of parsley, cheryil and a medium-sized onion. Cook for 30 minutes.

Add 4 tablespoons ($\frac{1}{3}$ cup) rice and cook, simmering gently, for 2 or 3 hours, depending on the tenderness of the bird. Untruss the chicken. Put it back into the casserole and serve.

Cherry soup I (German cookery). SOUPE AUX CERISES – Put in a stewpan 500 g. (generous 1 lb.) of stoned cherries, with 2 dl. ($\frac{1}{3}$ pint, scant cup) hot water, a small piece of cinnamon bark and a small piece of lemon peel. Cook over a high heat for 8 to 10 minutes. Press the cherries through a fine sieve.

Dilute this purée with $2\frac{1}{2}$ dl. (scant $\frac{1}{2}$ pint, generous cup) Bordeaux wine, previously boiled with the crushed cherry stones and then strained through muslin. Mix, bring to the boil, and bind with a teaspoon potato flour blended with a little cold water.

Stir in a small spoonful of sugar and pour very hot into the tureen. Add some rusks broken into small pieces.

Cherry soup II. SOUPE AUX CERISES – Cook 500 g. (generous 1 lb.) stoned cherries in water, cinnamon, lemon peel and 25 g. (1 oz., 2 tablespoons) sugar. Boil for 4 minutes. Thicken with a teaspoon potato flour blended with cold water.

Dilute with 2 dl. ($\frac{1}{3}$ pint, scant cup) Bordeaux wine, previously boiled with the crushed cherry stones and strained.

Pour boiling hot into the tureen, and serve with pieces of rusk or slices of *brioche* lightly toasted.

Cherry soup III. SOUPE AUX CERISES – Melt 50 g. (2 oz., $\frac{1}{4}$

Beer soup (*Scarnati*)

cup) butter in a saucepan. Add 500 g. (generous 1 lb.) stoned cherries, 25 g. (1 oz., 2 tablespoons) sugar, a little cinnamon and some lemon peel. Moisten with 2 dl. ($\frac{1}{3}$ pint, scant cup) water. Boil for 8 minutes and pour onto slices of toast.

English chicken soup or chicken broth I. SOUPE AU POULET À L'ANGLAISE – Put into a deep stewpan or *marmite* a medium-sized chicken. Pour in $1\frac{3}{4}$ litres (3 pints, 4 pints) plain stock. Bring to the boil, skim, add salt.

Put in for flavouring an onion stuck with a clove, a bunch of herbs and a stick of celery, and add 100 g. (4 oz., $\frac{1}{2}$ cup) rice. Simmer very slowly till cooked.

Take out the chicken and cut it into small pieces. Put it back in the stewpan, having removed the onion and herbs. Add $1\frac{1}{2}$ dl. ($\frac{1}{4}$ pint, $\frac{2}{3}$ cup) chopped vegetables cooked in butter, and bring to the boil.

English chicken soup II. SOUPE AU POULET À L'ANGLAISE – Cook 2 dl. ($\frac{1}{3}$ pint, scant cup) chopped mixed vegetables in butter until they are soft. Pour in $1\frac{3}{4}$ litres (3 pints, 4 pints) plain stock. Put in a medium-sized chicken cut up while raw into small pieces. Bring to the boil, skim. Add 100 g. (4 oz., $\frac{1}{2}$ cup) rice and simmer slowly.

Chotodriec soup (Polish cookery). SOUPE CHOTODRIEC – Cut a cooked beet in thin rounds and put them in a tureen. Add 2 diced egg yolks, 2 tablespoons (3 tablespoons) peeled shrimps, and thin slices of cucumber. Sprinkle with chopped fennel and chives. Bring to the boil pickled cucumbers mixed with a little yeast and 1 litre ($1\frac{3}{4}$ pints, generous quart) sour milk. Season, mix 1 litre ($1\frac{3}{4}$ pints, generous quart) of the juice with the soup, and chill on ice.

Clam soup with vegetables or Manhattan clam chowder (American cookery). SOUPE DE CLAMS AUX LÉGUMES – Cook gently in butter 100 g. (4 oz.) salt pork cut in small dice. When almost cooked add a medium-sized diced onion. Cook without allowing it to colour. Add 2 sticks of celery and one or two peeled diced green peppers.

Sprinkle with a good tablespoon flour (optional). Cook lightly, stirring all the time. Pour in $1\frac{1}{2}$ litres ($2\frac{3}{4}$ pints, $3\frac{1}{4}$ pints) light stock or water. Bring to the boil. Add 2 medium-sized tomatoes, peeled, seeded, and cut in dice, and 300 g. (11 oz., $1\frac{3}{4}$ cups) potatoes cut in slightly bigger dice. Season and cook briskly.

Open 3 dozen hard-shelled clams, keeping their liquor. Trim them, putting aside the stomachs. Chop the trimmings and put them in a saucepan with the clam liquor and 2 dl. ($\frac{1}{3}$ pint, scant cup) water. Cook for 15 minutes. Strain through a fine strainer and add this liquid to the soup. Put into the latter the soft parts of the clams cut into large dice. Bring to the boil, cover, and leave them to poach on the lowest possible heat.

Finish the soup with a pinch of thyme, a spoonful chopped parsley and 125 g. (4 oz., $\frac{1}{2}$ cup) butter. Heat and serve with water biscuits (soda crackers) whole or broken.

New York clam chowder differs from that of New England, which is a soup made with diced salt pork, onion, potatoes, clams and rich milk.

Cock-a-leekie (Scottish cookery). SOUPE AU COQ ET POIREAUX OU COCKY-LEEKY – Add to chicken broth (made with a medium-sized fowl), strained and skimmed of its fat, 2 dl. ($\frac{1}{3}$ pint, scant cup) of the white part of leeks cut into thin strips and simmered in butter, and the flesh of the chicken cut in thin pieces.

Although this recipe seems to demand a cockerel, the soup is most often prepared with a plump, tender hen.

Gulyas soup (Hungarian cookery). POTAGE GULYAS – This soup is made of beef cut into small pieces, onion, and stock seasoned with paprika. It has either potatoes, cooked in the stock, or noodles added to it.

Gumbo or okra soup (American cookery). SOUPE AUX GOMBOS, SOUPE OKRA – Cook 2 tablespoons (3 tablespoons) chopped onions very lightly in 2 tablespoons (3 tablespoons) butter. Add 75 g. (3 oz.) bacon (or raw ham) cut in dice and cook for 3 minutes. Put in 250 g. (9 oz.) diced, raw chicken flesh. Cook lightly, shaking the pan, until the pieces of chicken are quite firm. Pour in $1\frac{1}{2}$ litres ($2\frac{3}{4}$ pints, $3\frac{1}{4}$ pints) chicken stock, bring to the boil and cook gently for 25 minutes. Add 150 g. (5 oz.) of chopped gumbos and 2 peeled, seeded, drained and crushed tomatoes. Cook for 25 minutes.

Gulyas soup (*Claire*)

Skim all fat from the soup, and before serving add 3 tablespoons (4 tablespoons) rice, boiled in salted water for 15 minutes and rinsed in cold water.

This soup should be highly seasoned. It is sometimes finished off with a few drops of Worcestershire sauce.

Hare soup (English cookery). POTAGE AU LIÈVRE – Cut the forequarters and legs of hare in pieces and cook in butter with 5 tablespoons (6 tablespoons) of a *mirepoix* consisting of carrots, onion, white part of leeks, lean ham, a sprig of parsley, thyme and a bay leaf.

When all these ingredients are well browned, sprinkle them with 30 g. (1 oz., $\frac{1}{4}$ cup) arrowroot or cornstarch. Brown the arrowroot lightly, add 2 litres ($3\frac{1}{2}$ pints, $4\frac{1}{2}$ pints) ordinary stock, season, and simmer gently for $2\frac{1}{2}$ hours.

Remove the legs with a perforated spoon, bone them, cut in small dice and keep this *salpicon* hot. Moisten with a few tablespoons of strained stock. Add the hare's liver, cut in small slices, and poach lightly.

Take out the rest of the hare with a perforated spoon and bone it. Add the liver to the boned hare meat, pound together in a mortar and rub through a sieve.

Strain the stock and skim it for 25 minutes. Flavour it with 3 tablespoons (4 tablespoons) of sweet marjoram, basil and rosemary infusion, add 60 g. (2 oz., $\frac{1}{4}$ cup) butter, and spice with a pinch of cayenne pepper.

Put the hare purée into a soup tureen and pour the stock over it. Mix well with a whisk. Add the hare *salpicon* to the soup with 4 tablespoons ($\frac{1}{3}$ cup) of port.

It is usual in England to add a tablespoon of redcurrant jelly to hare soup just before serving.

Potage Hochepot à la flamande – Put 600 g. (1 lb. 6 oz.) brisket of beef, 300 g. (11 oz.) shoulder of mutton, 300 g. (11 oz.) breast of mutton, 150 g. (5 oz.) pigs' tails, 600 g. (1 lb. 6 oz.) pigs' feet, 300 g. (11 oz.) pigs' ears and 250 g. (9 oz.) salted bacon into a big stockpot.

Cover these meats with 3 litres ($5\frac{1}{4}$ pints, $6\frac{1}{2}$ pints) water, season with 12 g. ($1\frac{1}{2}$ teaspoons) salt. Bring to the boil, skim, and simmer gently.

After 2 hours of cooking add 2 carrots, 1 onion, 4 leeks

(white part only), a head of cabbage and 3 big potatoes – slicing all these vegetables. Continue to cook, simmering gently for about 2 hours.

Serve the *bouillon* of this soup in a tureen, garnishing it with a few vegetables. Serve the meats and rest of the vegetables separately. Add 12 chipolata sausages poached in the soup.

Leberknödeln or Hungarian soup with liver dumplings. POTAGE HONGROIS – Cut 500 g. (generous 1 lb.) lean beef (taken from the top of contre-filet) into large dice and brown it in butter with 100 g. (4 oz., 1 cup) chopped onion. Season with salt, a good pinch of paprika, 3 g. (scant teaspoon) cumin and a pinch of garlic. Sprinkle with 20 g. (1 oz., $\frac{1}{4}$ cup) flour. Cook for a few moments, dilute with 2 litres ($3\frac{1}{2}$ pints, $4\frac{1}{2}$ pints) ordinary stock, bring to the boil, and simmer for 1 hour. Add 150 g. (5 oz., 1 cup) diced potatoes.

When serving, put 3 tablespoons (4 tablespoons) diced croûtons fried in butter into the soup.

Hungarian soup with liver dumplings. SOUPE AUX BOULETTES DE FOIE – Add to $1\frac{1}{2}$ litres ($2\frac{3}{4}$ pints, $3\frac{1}{4}$ pints) boiling consommé, liver dumplings prepared in this way:

Cook 150 g. (5 oz.) diced calf's or ox liver in lard or butter for a few moments. Season, and sauté over a moderately high heat.

Pound the liver in a mortar and rub it through a sieve into a basin. Stir until smooth and add 50 g. (2 oz., $\frac{1}{4}$ cup) softened butter, 50 g. (2 oz., $\frac{1}{2}$ cup) chopped onions cooked for a few moments in butter, 40 g. ($1\frac{1}{2}$ oz., $\frac{3}{4}$ cup) fresh breadcrumbs, 1 teaspoon chopped parsley, and 2 beaten eggs.

Season with salt, paprika and grated nutmeg. Mix well.

Make dumplings or long quenelles and poach them in $1\frac{1}{2}$ litres ($2\frac{3}{4}$ pints, $3\frac{1}{4}$ pints) boiling consommé for 15 minutes.

Lithuanian soup. SOUPE LITUANIENNE – Add half a celery heart, sliced into strips and cooked gently in butter, to $1\frac{1}{2}$ litres ($2\frac{3}{4}$ pints, $3\frac{1}{4}$ pints) very light potato soup (without butter). Cook for 30 minutes. Add 2 tablespoons (3 tablespoons) sorrel leaves cooked till soft in butter, 1 dl. (6 tablespoons, scant $\frac{1}{2}$ cup) sour cream and 50 g. (2 oz., $\frac{1}{4}$ cup) fresh butter.

Garnish with little squares of streaky bacon, poached and skinned chipolata sausages, and fried egg yolks.

Leber-suppe or purée of liver soup. (Hungarian cookery). SOUPE À LA PURÉE DE FOIE – Cook 50 g. (2 oz., $\frac{1}{2}$ cup) onion, 50 g. (2 oz., $\frac{1}{2}$ cup) carrot, 50 g. (2 oz.) lean salt pork and a shallot, all finely chopped, in melted butter with a sprig of thyme and half a bay leaf.

When the vegetables are cooked, add 200 g. (7 oz.) diced calf's or ox liver. Season with salt, pepper and grated nutmeg and brown quickly. Sprinkle with $1\frac{1}{2}$ tablespoons (2 tablespoons) flour. Stir in 1 dl. (6 tablespoons, scant $\frac{1}{2}$ cup) white wine and $1\frac{1}{2}$ litres ($2\frac{3}{4}$ pints, $3\frac{1}{4}$ pints) consommé. Cook for 25 minutes.

Drain the liver and vegetables and pound together in a mortar. Rub through a fine sieve. Add the cooking liquor, diluting it, if necessary, with a few tablespoons consommé. Bring to the boil and serve with small croûtons of bread fried in butter.

Livonian soup with klyotski (Russian cookery). POTAGE LIVONIEN AUX KLOSKI – Chop an onion and 50 g. (2 oz.) sorrel leaves finely and cook them in 3 tablespoons (4 tablespoons) butter in a covered pan. Add 500 g. (1 lb.) blanched, well drained spinach. Cook together for a few moments, then add 4 dl. ($\frac{3}{4}$ pint, scant 2 cups) *Béchamel sauce* (see SAUCE). Mix well and simmer gently for 15 minutes.

Rub through a sieve. Dilute with 1 litre ($1\frac{3}{4}$ pints, generous quart) ordinary stock. Put back into the saucepan for fifteen minutes, skimming frequently. Finish off with 1 dl. (6 tablespoons, scant $\frac{1}{2}$ cup) cream and 60 g. (2 oz., $\frac{1}{4}$ cup) butter, and serve with *klyotski* (quenelles) prepared as follows:

Make 200 g. (7 oz.) of unsweetened *Chou pastry* (see CHOU). Add to it a tablespoon chopped, blanched and pressed out shallots, 25 g. (1 oz., $1\frac{1}{2}$ tablespoons) chopped, lean cooked ham and 25 g. (1 oz.) very small croûtons fried in butter.

Take up a little of the mixture with a teaspoon and drop into boiling water or stock. The *klyotski* are ready when they float up to the surface.

Mille-fanti soup (Italian cookery). SOUPE MILLE-FANTI – Put into a basin 80 g. (3 oz., $1\frac{1}{2}$ cups) fresh breadcrumbs, 50 g. (2 oz., $\frac{1}{2}$ cup) grated Parmesan cheese and 2 beaten eggs. Season with salt, pepper and nutmeg and mix well. Add, little by little, to $1\frac{1}{2}$ litres ($2\frac{3}{4}$ pints, $3\frac{1}{4}$ pints) boiling consommé.

Cover the pan and cook very slowly for 8 minutes. Stir with a whisk before serving.

This soup, which is a kind of panada of cheese and egg, can be made with water in place of consommé.

Minestrone (*Claire*)

Minestrone (Italian cookery) – Melt in a sucepan 40 g. ($1\frac{1}{2}$ oz., 3 tablespoons) chopped salt pork fat and add 50 g. (2 oz., 3 slices) streaky bacon cut in small pieces, 2 tablespoons (3 tablespoons) chopped onion and the chopped white of a leek. Cook gently for 5 minutes. Pour in $1\frac{3}{4}$ litres (3 pints, 4 pints) water, season, and bring to the boil. Add a carrot, a turnip, a potato and a tender stick of celery cut in small pieces, the heart of a small cabbage similarly cut and 2 tomatoes peeled, seeded and chopped. Boil for 25 minutes. Add 50 g. (2 oz., $\frac{1}{4}$ cup) diced French beans, 1 dl. (6 tablespoons, scant $\frac{1}{2}$ cup) fresh peas and 80 g. (3 oz., $\frac{1}{2}$ cup) rice. Cook very gently for 45 minutes.

Add a tablespoon chopped salt pork fat crushed with 2 cloves of garlic, a tablespoon chopped basil and a tablespoon chopped parsley. Any vegetables in season may be put in minestrone.

Mock-turtle soup (English cookery) – Soak a calf's head in water, bone it and cook in white stock with carrots, onion, celery, a *bouquet garni*, cloves, salt and pepper. Drain the head, cut off the ears (which are not used for this soup), trim the rest of the meat and put it under a press between two plates. When it is quite cold, cut it into pieces. Keep these hot in a little of the stock, to be added to the soup later.

Prepare a clear brown gravy, made of slices of salt leg of pork, veal knuckle and a half-roasted chicken. Dilute with stock. When the meats are nearly done and gravy is boiled down, add the stock and stockpot vegetables. Simmer gently for about 2 hours.

Strain. Thicken with a little arrowroot diluted with cold

stock. Add to it an infusion of basil, spring onion, marjoram, thyme and bay leaf in Madeira or port.

Strain the soup through a muslin cloth and pour it into a soup tureen. Garnish with the pieces of calf's head kept for this purpose, and small quenelles made of forcemeat mixed with pounded, hard-boiled egg yolks.

Mulligatawny soup I – *Ingredients.* 2 litres ($3\frac{1}{2}$ pints, $4\frac{1}{2}$ pints) water, 1 kg. ($2\frac{1}{4}$ lb.) mutton, 2 onions, 2 carrots, 2 apples, 1 small turnip, a *bouquet garni*, 2 tablespoons (3 tablespoons) flour, 1 tablespoon curry powder, the juice of a $\frac{1}{2}$ lemon, salt.

Method. Remove the fat from the mutton and melt it in the saucepan. Slice the apples and vegetables and when there is sufficient liquid fat to fry them, take out the pieces of fat, put in the vegetables and cook for about 15 minutes. Sprinkle in the flour and curry powder, fry for a few minutes, add the meat cut in small pieces, a teaspoon salt, the herbs and water. Boil, remove the scum as it rises, cover, and cook gently for about 3 hours. Strain, rub the meat through a sieve, and return to the saucepan. When boiling, add the lemon juice, season, and serve with well-cooked rice.

The bones and remains of any kind of meat or poultry may be used instead of mutton.

Mulligatawny soup II (English cookery) – Cut a medium-sized chicken as for *fricassée* and cook it in 2 litres ($3\frac{1}{2}$ pints, $4\frac{1}{2}$ pints) white stock with sliced carrot and an onion, a *bouquet garni*, a sprig of parsley and 3 tablespoons (4 tablespoons) mushroom parings.

Brown a chopped onion lightly in 50 g. (2 oz., $\frac{1}{4}$ cup) butter. Sprinkle with 20 g. (1 oz., $\frac{1}{4}$ cup) cornflour and a small spoonful curry powder. Moisten with the chicken stock and cook gently for 10 minutes.

Strain through a sieve, simmer for 15 minutes, and add 2 dl. ($\frac{1}{3}$ pint, scant cup) cream.

Put the trimmed pieces of chicken into a soup tureen and strain the soup over them. Serve with *Rice à l'indienne* (see RICE).

Mutton broth (English cookery) – Cook a coarse *brunoise* composed of a carrot, a turnip, 2 leeks (white part only), a good stalk of celery and a white onion in butter. Cover with 2 litres ($3\frac{1}{2}$ pints, $4\frac{1}{2}$ pints) white stock. Add 300 g. (11 oz.) breast and neck of mutton and 100 g. (4 oz., $\frac{1}{4}$ cup) blanched barley. Simmer gently for $1\frac{1}{2}$ hours.

Drain the mutton, bone it, cut into large dice and put it back into the broth. Add a tablespoon chopped and blanched parsley.

Mutton soup à la grecque (Greek style). POTAGE DE MOUTON À LA GRECQUE – Make $1\frac{1}{2}$ litres ($2\frac{3}{4}$ pints, $3\frac{1}{4}$ pints) of light *Purée of split pea soup.*

Fry 500 g. (generous 1 lb.) boned breast of mutton, cut in large dice, in butter with 4 dl. ($\frac{3}{4}$ pint, scant 2 cups) *brunoise* of vegetables. Moisten with 3 litres ($5\frac{1}{4}$ pints, $6\frac{1}{2}$ pints) light stock or water. Season with salt and pepper. Bring to the boil, skim, and simmer gently for $1\frac{1}{2}$ hours.

Mix the *Purée of split pea soup* and the mutton stock, leaving in it the pieces of mutton and the *brunoise*. Boil for a few moments.

Clear oxtail soup (English cookery). POTAGE OXTAIL CLAIR – Put $1\frac{1}{2}$ kg. ($3\frac{1}{2}$ lb.) oxtail, cut in small chunks, into a stewpan, on a foundation of sliced carrots, leeks and onions. Sweat in the oven for 25 minutes.

Cover with $2\frac{1}{2}$ litres ($4\frac{1}{2}$ pints, $5\frac{1}{2}$ pints) stock made by cooking $1\frac{1}{2}$ kg. ($3\frac{1}{2}$ lb.) gelatinous bones for 7 or 8 hours in $3\frac{1}{4}$ litres ($5\frac{3}{4}$ pints, 7 pints) water. Season.

Simmer gently, so that the boiling is imperceptible, from $3\frac{1}{2}$ to 4 hours.

Strain the soup and skim off surplus fat. Clarify by boiling it for an hour with 500 g. (generous 1 lb.) chopped lean beef and the white part of two leeks, finely sliced, both these ingredients whisked with a raw white of egg.

Strain the stock through a cloth. Garnish with pieces of oxtail and 3 dl. ($\frac{1}{2}$ pint, $1\frac{1}{4}$ cups) of coarse *brunoise* of carrots, turnips and celery sweated in butter and dropped into the stock. Add a tablespoon of sherry.

Thick oxtail soup (English cookery). POTAGE OXTAIL LIÉ – Proceed as for *Clear oxtail.* When the broth has been strained, thicken it with 50 g. (2 oz., 4 tablespoons) brown *roux* to each litre (quart), and 3 good tablespoons (4 tablespoons) *tomato purée.* Garnish with mixed vegetables cut up and cooked in butter, as for clear oxtail soup. Flavour with sherry.

Olla-podrida soup. POTAGE OLLA-PODRIDA – See OLLA-PODRIDA.

Oyster soup with okra (American cookery) – Put 100 g. (4 oz., 1 cup) chopped pork fat into a thick-bottomed saucepan, and when the fat melts add 100 g. (4 oz., 1 cup) chopped onion and cook it gently without letting it colour. Add 3 tomatoes peeled and cut in quarters, 10 okras, 1 small green pepper finely chopped, and 1 litre (scant quart, generous quart) white stock. Season with salt and pepper (a little curry powder may be added, if liked). Cook for 15 minutes, then put in 24 de-bearded oysters with their liquor, and poach them for a few moments. Thicken the soup with a little arrowroot.

Pistou soup I (Italian cookery). SOUPE AU PISTOU – Cook, in $1\frac{1}{2}$ litres ($2\frac{3}{4}$ pints, $3\frac{1}{4}$ pints) boiling water, 250 g. (9 oz., 1 cup) diced French beans, 3 potatoes cut in small pieces, and 2 peeled tomatoes, seeded, and crushed. Season.

When the vegetables are almost cooked add 100 g. (4 oz.) spaghetti. Finish cooking very slowly.

Pound in a mortar 2 cloves of garlic with several basil leaves. Add, still pounding, 2 tablespoons (3 tablespoons) oil and 2 or 3 tablespoons (3 or 4 tablespoons) stock. Pour the soup into a tureen, adding to it the above mixture and 4 tablespoons ($\frac{1}{3}$ cup) grated Parmesan.

This soup, of Genoese origin, is popular in Provence.

Pistou soup II. SOUPE AU PISTOU – Cook gently a medium-sized onion and a leek, cut in small pieces, in a tablespoon butter. Add 2 peeled, drained and crushed tomatoes.

Pour in $1\frac{1}{2}$ litres ($2\frac{3}{4}$ pints, $3\frac{1}{4}$ pints) stock or water, bring to the boil, and add 250 g. (9 oz., 1 cup) diced French beans and 3 potatoes cut in small pieces. Season.

Finish off as in the preceding recipe.

The garlic paste prescribed for binding the pistou soup can also be prepared with chopped salt pork fat. Sometimes halved tomatoes, seeded and grilled, are also added.

Puchero soup (Spanish pot-au-feu). POTAGE PUCHERO – Prepare as for *Olla-Podrida*, but boil down the quantity of basic ingredients, especially the meats.

Potage Rahm-suppe (German cookery) – Cook 50 g. (2 oz., $\frac{1}{4}$ cup) each of butter and flour together without colouring, and stir in 1 litre (scant quart, generous quart) white stock and the same quantity boiled milk. Put in a small onion stuck with a clove, and a sprig of parsley, and season with a pinch of cumin, some grated nutmeg, 6 g. (1 teaspoon) salt and 3 peppercorns. Cook for 45 minutes. Strain the soup and thicken it with 2 dl. ($\frac{1}{3}$ pint, scant cup) sour cream, letting it boil for 1 minute. Serve with croûtons of bread fried in butter.

Rassol'nik (Russian cookery). POTAGE ROSSOLNICK – Prepare 2 litres ($3\frac{1}{2}$ pints, $4\frac{1}{2}$ pints) slightly thickened chicken broth and add 2 dl. ($\frac{1}{3}$ pint, scant cup) fresh cucumber juice. Cut celery roots and large parsley roots (Hamburg parsley) into the shape of tiny carrots, cutting a cross in the base of each. Cut pickled cucumbers into small chunks. Blanch all these vegetables well and add to the chicken broth. Cook gently for 40 minutes, keeping the soup well skimmed.

Add 2 tablespoons (3 tablespoons) cucumber juice and

bind with 2 egg yolks beaten in 1 dl. (6 tablespoons, scant $\frac{1}{2}$ cup) cream. Add very small dumplings of chicken forcemeat and poach in the soup.

Shchi (Russian cookery). POTAGE STSCHY – Cook 2 large chopped onions in 2 tablespoons (3 tablespoons) butter until they are a pale golden colour. Sprinkle with 2 tablespoons flour, cook for a few moments, and stir in $2\frac{1}{2}$ litres ($4\frac{1}{2}$ pints, $5\frac{1}{2}$ pints) white stock. Bring to the boil. Add 250 g. (9 oz.) brisket of beef cut into large dice, blanched for 10 minutes in salted water, drained and trimmed, and 250 g. (9 oz.) coarsely chopped *sauerkraut*. Add a good bunch of herbs and cook very gently for about 3 hours. Add $1\frac{1}{2}$ dl. ($\frac{1}{4}$ pint, $\frac{2}{3}$ cup) sour cream and a teaspoon chopped blanched parsley.

Solyanka (Russian cookery). POTAGE SOLIANKA – Prepare 2 litres ($3\frac{1}{2}$ pints, $4\frac{1}{2}$ pints) ham-flavoured consommé, and add 250 g. (9 oz., $1\frac{1}{2}$ cups) braised sauerkraut and a tablespoon blanched parsley leaves.

Sour cream soup I (Hungarian cookery). SOUPE À LA CRÈME AIGRE – Add to $1\frac{1}{2}$ litres ($2\frac{3}{4}$ pints, $3\frac{1}{4}$ pints) thin white sauce an onion stuck with a clove, a *bouquet garni*, a pinch of powdered cumin and grated nutmeg. Cook for 20 minutes, skimming well. Rub through a fine sieve. Add 1 dl. (6 tablespoons, scant $\frac{1}{2}$ cup) sour cream and serve with croûtons of bread fried in butter.

Sour cream soup II. SOUPE À LA CRÈME AIGRE – Make a white *roux* of 3 tablespoons (4 tablespoons) each of butter and flour. Stir in 1 litre (scant quart, generous quart) stock and $\frac{1}{2}$ litre (scant pint, $2\frac{1}{4}$ cups) boiled milk. Finish and garnish as above.

Sweet-sour soup, or Mehlsuppe, also called flour soup (German cookery). SOUPE AIGRE-DOUCE, SOUPE À LA FARINE – Cut up finely a medium-sized onion and the white parts of two leeks, and cook them for a few moments in 2 tablespoons (3 tablespoons) butter. Sprinkle with 2 tablespoons (3 tablespoons) flour. Add $1\frac{1}{2}$ litres ($2\frac{3}{4}$ pints, $3\frac{1}{4}$ pints) stock or water and cook for 25 minutes. Stir in 2 dl. ($\frac{1}{3}$ pint, scant cup) thick cream and a tablespoon fresh butter.

Milanaise tripe soup, or Butséga. SOUPE AU GRAS-DOUBLE À LA MILANAISE – Cut in thin strips 500 g. (generous 1 lb.) veal tripe, blanched, trimmed and drained. Put in a saucepan with onion and the white part of a leek, also chopped, and cooked with diced salt pork fat. Cook for a few moments, sprinkle with a tablespoon flour and stir in 2 litres ($3\frac{1}{2}$ pints, $4\frac{1}{2}$ pints) stock or water. Bring to the boil. Add 2 peeled, seeded, sliced tomatoes, a cabbage heart cut in thin strips, 5 tablespoons (6 tablespoons) peas and a few broccoli heads. Season and cook briskly.

Cutting up turtles for the preparation of turtle soup (*Wide World*)

Turtle soup (English cookery). POTAGE À LA TORTUE – This soup, made from the large sea turtle, is prepared with the bony carapace and plastron only, from which the outside or thin hard shell has been removed.

The carapace and plastron of the animal (bled for as long as possible after killing) are cut into pieces, blanched for a few minutes in boiling water, cleaned of the outer shields that cover them, put in a big stewpan with richly flavoured consommé, savoury vegetables and *Turtle herbs* (see HERBS), and cooked like an ordinary broth for 6 or 7 hours. The pieces of turtle are drained, boned, cut into pieces and kept warm in strained broth.

The liquor used to cook the turtle can be a stock made with the flesh of the interior of the animal, reinforced with some beef and chicken. The soup is strained through a cloth, reheated and enriched with 4 dl. ($\frac{3}{4}$ pint, scant 2 cups) Madeira (or sherry) to each litre (quart).

The aromatic herbs used for flavouring are basil, marjoram, sage, rosemary, savoury and thyme. Coriander and peppercorns are also added in a little muslin bag.

Just before serving, the pieces of turtle are put back in the soup.

Turtle soup (thick). POTAGE À LA TORTUE – Made in the same way as described in the previous recipe. After straining it is thickened with a *roux* of 25 g. (1 oz., 4 tablespoons) flour and 2 tablespoons butter, or with 80 g. (3 oz., $\frac{1}{2}$ cup) arrowroot to 1 litre (scant quart, generous quart) soup.

Ukha (Russian cookery). POTAGE OUKA – Prepare fish stock using sturgeon, tench or perch, well spiced with parsnip, celery, fennel and mushroom parings.

Make small *paupiettes* of lavaret or white fish and poach them. Prepare 250 g. (9 oz., $2\frac{1}{4}$ cups) *julienne* of parsnip, and the white part of leek and celery. Cook in butter, and when quite soft moisten with a few tablespoons strained fish stock.

Clarify the stock, either with caviar or chopped whiting, and strain through a cloth.

Add the *paupiettes* and *julienne* of vegetables to the soup. Serve with a timbale of cooked buckwheat and a dish of small *Rastegais* (see HORS-D'ŒUVRE, *Hot hors-d'œuvre*).

Veal soup with herbs (Dutch cookery). SOUPE DE VEAU AUX HERBES – Veal stock thickened with a white *roux*, seasoned with aromatic herbs and garnished with *quenelles* or dumplings made with veal and chopped herbs.

SOUPIR DE NONNE (Nun's sigh) – Name sometimes used for the soufflé fritter made of *chou pastry* commonly called *Pet de nonne*. (See FRITTERS, *Soufflé fritters*.)

SOUP LADLE. LOUCHE – Deep spoon used to serve soup. Soup ladles are made in different sizes.

SOUR. AIGRE – Possessing an acid and piquant taste or smell.

SOURIRE – Term meaning to simmer very gently. For example: '*Le pot-au-feu sourit*'.

SOUR-SWEET. AIGRE-DOUX – Having a sweet and sour taste.

SOUS-NAPPE (Under-tablecloth) – The custom of putting a piece of thick flannel under the tablecloth should be normal practice in the home. Utensils make no noise as they are set down.

SOUS-NOIX OF VEAL – Term used in French butchery to describe the under part of silverside of the leg of veal.

SOUTH AMERICA – See INTERNATIONAL COOKERY, *American cookery*.

SOUVAROV – *Petit-four* for which the recipe is as follows:

Make a paste with 600 g. ($1\frac{1}{4}$ lb., 5 cups) sifted cake flour, 400 g. (14 oz., $1\frac{3}{4}$ cups) butter, 200 g. (7 oz., 1 cup) sugar and a little cream. Allow to rest. Roll out thinly. Cut out with a pastry cutter with fluted edges, place on a baking sheet and cook in a fairly hot oven.

Sandwich the pieces of pastry together two by two, spread with thick apricot jam and sprinkle with icing sugar.

SOUVAROV or SOUVOROV (À LA) – Sometimes spelt *Souwaroff*. The name describes a method of preparing poultry and game birds.

A bird cooked *à la Souvarov* is done in an earthenware casserole with *foie gras* and truffles, and sealed with a strip of dough round the lid. (See CHICKEN, *Chicken Souvarov;* PHEASANT, *Pheasant à la Souvarov.*)

SOW. TRUIE – Female pig. See PORK.

SOW-THISTLE (U.S. Milkweed). LAITERON – Plant which has something of the flavour of both lettuce and chicory. It contains a milky substance.

It is somewhat leathery, but after boiling in salt water can be prepared like spinach. When the leaves are tender they can be used in salads.

In winter the roots are eaten, prepared in the same way as black and white salsify.

SOYA BEAN. SOJA – Plant of the *Leguminosae* family, a native of China, now widely cultivated. This plant has the merit of being free from attack from insect pests, and grows easily in dry country. It is the richest and cheapest source of vegetable protein, has a fairly high fat and low starch content. Soya bean in one form or another is in daily use in the East.

Soya bean curd. FROMAGE DE SOJA – Cook freshly shelled soya beans in water, without salt. When they are almost cooked pour off the greater part of the water. Continue to cook until the skins are very tender. Turn out into an earthenware dish and leave till the next day, when they will have become jellied. Reheat, drain off the liquid, and rub through a fine sieve. Add the drained-off cooking liquor.

This vegetable jelly is rich in legumin, which differs from casein only in the products of its decomposition.

Add a little milk or yeast to produce fermentation and salt to taste. Drain in a sieve. Separate into cheese and leave them to 'take' in the usual way.

Soya meat. VIANDE DE SOJA – This preparation is too complicated to be made in the home, and needs industrial equipment.

The 'vegetarian meat' has the appearance of cooked ham. It is used in sandwiches and for *hors-d'œuvre*. It may be eaten cold or reheated.

Soya milk. LAIT DE SOJA – Name for the mixture of cooking liquor and purée of soya beans before fermentation.

Soya sauce or extract. SAUCE, EXTRAIT DE SOJA – Eastern peoples use soya in the form of this condiment, which heightens the flavour of various dishes. A few drops of the extract added to a vegetable soup makes it more savoury. It is also used to strengthen sauces and stews, and as an addition to salad dressings.

Soya cheese – See CHEESE.

Sow-thistle:
a. Flower; b. Ray floret

Soya:
a. Flower; b. Pods

SPAGHETTI – One of the most popular of Italian pasta products. It is made from wheat, like macaroni, but is solid, not tubular. All methods of preparing macaroni (q.v.) are applicable to spaghetti.

Spaghetti à la napolitaine – Cook the spaghetti in plenty of boiling water, salted in the proportion of $1\frac{1}{2}$ teaspoons to 1 litre ($1\frac{3}{4}$ pints, generous quart).

As soon as the pasta is cooked (9 to 12 minutes) drain it, replace in the saucepan and hold over the heat for a moment to dry off excess moisture. Season with salt and pepper and add, shaking the spaghetti, 1 dl. (6 tablespoons, $\frac{1}{2}$ cup) thick *Tomato sauce* (see SAUCE), 25 g. (1 oz., $\frac{1}{4}$ cup) grated Parmesan and Gruyère mixed, and 50 g. (2 oz., $\frac{1}{4}$ cup) butter, for every 150 g. (5 oz., 1 cup) pasta. Shake well to mix and serve, or use to accompany meat or poultry.

SPAIN – See INTERNATIONAL COOKERY.

SPARKLET – Small ampoule containing liquid carbon dioxide, with which effervescent drinks can be made. (See SIPHON.)

SPARKLING. MOUSSEUX – This term described all wines that, after second fermentation, effervesce when poured. The French describe the various degrees of effervescence as *perlant*, *pétillant*, *crémant* and *mousseux*. Champagne is the only effervescent wine that is never described as *mousseux*.

Several methods are employed for making sparkling wines:

Méthode rurale – In this case, it is the natural sugar remaining in the wine after first fermentation which, fermenting again in the bottles, causes the effervescence (Gaillac, Blanquette de Limoux, Clairette de Die).

Méthode champenoise – So called because it was perfected in Champagne by Dom Pérignon and his successors. It is the addition to the 'still' wine of sugar-based 'liqueur' that produces the second fermentation in the bottle. This method involves a whole series of subsidiary operations: working of the deposit down towards the cork (*remuage*), extraction of the sediment-coated cork (*dégorgement*), etc. (See CHAMPAGNE, *The wine of Champagne*).

Méthode de la cuve close – Instead of the second fermentation taking place in the bottles, it is carried out in enormous vats. It is illegal in France to employ this method in the production of A.O.C. wines.

There is also *méthode de la première fermentation* used mainly in Italy for Asti. This single fermentation process is achieved by retaining part of the carbonic gas produced by the fermenting must. With the *méthode 'allemande'* second fermentation takes place in the bottles but the wine is then decanted into large vats to be processed and filtered (omitting the operations of *remuage* and *dégorgement*).

Finally, there are some very inferior commercial 'sparkling' processes involving the use of carbonic gas.

SPATULA. SPATULE – Kitchen utensil made of steel, copper or wood.

SPECULOS (Belgian pastry) – Place on the kitchen table, forming a circle, 500 g. (18 oz., 4½ cups) sifted flour. Place in the centre of the circle a small pinch of salt, 1 teaspoon bicarbonate of soda, 2 teaspoons powdered cinnamon, 3 eggs, 4 finely crushed cloves, 300 g. (11 oz., 1½ cups) brown sugar and 250 g. (9 oz., generous cup) butter. Mix these ingredients well together and, little by little, incorporate the flour. Press the dough together and leave in a cool place until the next day.

Divide the dough into several pieces. Roll out each piece and press into floured wooden moulds. Turn out on to lightly buttered baking sheets. Cook in a moderate oven.

SPETZLI (Alsatian cookery) – Mix together 500 g. (18 oz., 4½ cups) sifted flour, 4 eggs, 2 to 3 tablespoons double cream, salt, pepper and a pinch of grated nutmeg.

Using a spatula, drop pieces of this paste into a pan of salted boiling water, each piece being about the size of a small walnut. Poach. Drain the spetzli, dry them on a cloth and toss them in butter in the frying pan.

Serve in a deep dish, sprinkled with *Noisette butter* (see BUTTER, *Compound butters*).

SPICE. ÉPICE – An aromatic substance such as pepper, cloves, etc., used to season culinary preparations. A complete list of spices is given under CONDIMENTS.

It is generally agreed that most spices and condiments used in cookery have the effect of stimulating the gastric juices. However the use of spices, especially in large quantities, in diets for persons suffering from stomach disorders is generally regarded as inadvisable.

The function of tasty substances, which enhance the flavour of food, is not to act directly on the gastric juices, but to stimulate the digestive processes by reflexes following their contact with the taste buds.

In the seventeenth century, says Franklin, spices were not used in excess to quite the same extent as in previous centuries, but the passion for perfumes which poisoned the French court from the sixteenth century up to the middle of the reign of Louis XIV did not even respect stews, pastries, liqueurs, etc. Orris-root, rose water and marjoram were all mixed into them and the chef always had musk and ambergris at hand.

Green walnuts were flavoured with rose water. '*Nulles*', a type of cream, was seasoned with amber and musk. *Pâtés* and pies were flavoured with musk. Eggs were sprinkled with scented waters. Some dishes were even sprinkled with soot!

Fine spices. ÉPICES FINES – *Ingredients.* 700 g. (1½ lb., 5½ cups) white pepper. 300 g. (11 oz., 2¾ cups) allspice, 100 g. (4 oz., scant cup) mace, 50 g. (2 oz., ⅓ cup) each of nutmeg, cloves, cinnamon, bay leaves, sage, marjoram, and rosemary.

Method. Pound these ingredients in a mortar and mix them thoroughly. Rub through a fine sieve. Keep in tightly-stoppered bottles.

Mixed spices (Carême's recipe). ÉPICES COMPOSÉES – 'Dry in the oven or a hot cupboard: thyme, bay leaves, basil, sage, a little coriander and mace. When these ingredients are perfectly dry, pound in a mortar and sieve them. Add a third of fine pepper. Put them in a box with a tightly fitting lid in a dry place and use as required.'

Mixed spices (commercial). QUATRE ÉPICES, ÉPICES FINES – Most grocers sell mixed spices ready prepared.

Spiced salt. ÉPICE (SEL) – Spiced salt used for flavouring stuffings is made with 100 g. (4 oz., ⅓ cup) table salt, 2 tablespoons (3 tablespoons) pepper and 2 tablespoons (3 tablespoons) *Fine spices.*

SPICY. EXCITANT – Spicy foods are those which are strongly flavoured with condiments or which have a very pronounced flavour. Spicy foods act upon the taste buds in the mouth and stimulate the gastric juices.

Spider crab

SPIDER CRAB. ARAIGNÉE DE MER – Name given in France to various species of shellfish allied to crabs. For culinary preparation see CRAB.

The name of spider crab is also commonly given in many coastal places in France to certain fish belonging to the weever genus.

SPIGOT. FOSSET – Wooden vent-peg inserted into the hole drilled in a wine cask to enable the wine to be tasted.

SPIKENARD. NARD – A spice, very much in favour in ancient times as an ointment, and in the Middle Ages as a condiment. It is still so used in Malaysian cookery.

Indian spikenard (*Nardostachys jatamansi*) is the root of a Far-Eastern species of valerian, from which the above spice was derived. American spikenard (*Aralia racemosa*) has a powerful and pleasant fragrance, and a bitter aromatic flavour.

SPINACH. ÉPINARDS – Pot vegetable of Persian origin, cultivated for its leaves. It was unknown to the Romans and transplanted to Europe by the Moors. It has been greatly improved by cultivation. Spinach contains a viscous substance by virtue of which it has laxative properties. It also contains potassium oxalate and a fair amount of iron (though less than sorrel, leek and lettuce).

Before cooking, spinach must be stripped, carefully washed and parboiled as quickly as possible in boiling salted water. Cool under running water, drain thoroughly, squeeze to extract all moisture, and rub through a sieve or chop it. Do not cool under running water if spinach is to be served whole.

If fresh garden spinach is used, strip, wash and place in a

saucepan. For 500 g. (generous 1 lb.) spinach add 40 g. ($1\frac{1}{2}$ oz., 3 tablespoons) butter, 3 tablespoons (scant $\frac{1}{4}$ cup) water and a pinch of salt. Cover and cook rapidly. When all the moisture has evaporated, add 50 g. (2 oz., $\frac{1}{4}$ cup) butter.

Spinach à l'anglaise. ÉPINARDS À L'ANGLAISE – Parboil the spinach rapidly in boiling salted water. Drain and dry in a cloth. Serve whole in a hot dish, with fresh butter.

Spinach in butter. ÉPINARDS AU BEURRE – *Whole.* Heat a little butter in a pan. Add the spinach, parboiled, drained and dried in a cloth. Leave on the stove for a few minutes to evaporate all moisture. Season with salt, pepper and a pinch of nutmeg. When the spinach is dry, add the butter, allowing 100 g. (4 oz., $\frac{1}{2}$ cup) butter to 500 g. (generous 1 lb., 2 cups) cooked spinach.

Chopped. Parboil the spinach. Cool under running water. Drain and squeeze out as much moisture as possible. Chop coarsely and proceed as above.

Purée. Parboil the spinach. Cool under running water. Drain and dry in a cloth. Rub through a sieve and proceed as above.

Spinach in noisette butter. ÉPINARDS AU BEURRE NOISETTE – Using whole, chopped or sieved prepared spinach, heat butter in a pan until it is nut brown in colour. Add the spinach. Season with salt, pepper and a pinch of nutmeg. Mix and serve.

Spinach in cream. ÉPINARDS À LA CRÈME – Chop the spinach or rub through a sieve. Cook in butter. When all the moisture has evaporated, add fresh cream. Serve in a deep dish and surround with hot fresh cream.

Spinach can also be served in this way with *Cream sauce* (see SAUCE, *Compound white sauces*) instead of fresh cream.

Spinach croquettes. CROQUETTES AUX ÉPINARDS – Make the croquettes in the usual way using the following mixture: two-thirds chopped spinach cooked in butter and one-third *Duchess potato mixture* (see POTATOES).

Fry the croquettes just before serving. Drain them. Garnish with fried parsley.

Croûtes of spinach au gratin. CROÛTES GRATINÉES AUX ÉPINARDS – Shape sandwich bread into deep hollow cases. Fry them in butter. Fill with spinach heaped up in a dome, prepared as for *Spinach au gratin* (see below). Sprinkle with grated cheese. Pour on melted butter and brown in a hot oven.

Spinach au gratin. ÉPINARDS AU GRATIN – Parboil and dry thoroughly 500 g. (generous 1 lb.) spinach. Chop or leave whole. Simmer with 100 g. (4 oz., $\frac{1}{2}$ cup) butter. Add 75 g. (3 oz., $\frac{2}{3}$ cup) grated cheese. Season and place in a buttered ovenware dish, sprinkle generously with grated cheese, pour on melted butter, and brown in the oven.

Spinach can also be prepared in this way by adding a few tablespoons *Cream sauce* (see SAUCE, *Compound white sauces*) after cooking in butter.

Spinach in gravy. ÉPINARDS AU JUS – Blanch and drain the spinach. Chop or rub through a sieve. Cook in butter until all moisture has evaporated. Add a few tablespoons of concentrated veal stock, season, serve in a deep dish and surround with concentrated veal gravy.

Spinach pancakes. CRÊPES AUX ÉPINARDS – Blanch and drain the spinach and dry it in a cloth. Chop finely and simmer in butter. Add an equal quantity of *Savoury crêpe batter* (see CRÊPE). Season with salt, pepper and nutmeg. Mix thoroughly. Make pancakes in the usual way.

Spinach salad. SALADE D'ÉPINARDS – Plunge spinach into boiling water for a few seconds. Cool under running water, drain, dry in a cloth. Put in a salad bowl, sprinkle with chopped hard-boiled eggs, dress with oil, vinegar, salt and pepper.

Spinach soufflé – See SOUFFLÉS, *Savoury soufflés.*

Spinach subrics. SUBRICS D'ÉPINARDS – Parboil whole spinach quickly in boiling salted water. Drain and dry in a cloth. Cook in butter until all moisture has evaporated. Take the pan off the heat and add, for 500 g. (generous 1 lb.) spinach, $1\frac{1}{2}$ dl. ($\frac{1}{4}$ pint, $\frac{2}{3}$ cup) thick *Béchamel sauce* (see SAUCE), 1 whole egg, 3 yolks beaten as for an omelette, and 2 or 3 tablespoons double cream. Season with salt, pepper and nutmeg. Mix.

Heat clarified butter in a frying pan and pour the mixture into it, a spoonful at a time. Fry, taking care that the *subrics* are separated from one another in the pan to prevent them from sticking together.

Serve with cream.

Spinach with sugar. ÉPINARDS AU SUCRE – Parboil and drain the spinach. Dry in a cloth. Cook in butter until all moisture has evaporated. Sweeten lightly. Shape into a dome in a dish and cover with hot fresh cream. Garnish with fried bread cut into sponge-finger shapes.

SPINACH, GIANT MEXICAN. ÉPINARDS GÉANTS DU MEXIQUE – This vegetable derives from a shrub which is more than 2·25 m. (7 feet) tall. One plant yields from 1 to $1\frac{1}{2}$ kg. ($2\frac{1}{4}$ to $3\frac{1}{2}$ lb.) fleshy leaves, each from 18 to 23 cm. (7 to 9 inches) long.

The flavour of these leaves is between that of spinach and sorrel.

SPINACH, NEW ZEALAND. TÉTRAGONE – One of the indigenous vegetables of New Zealand, having been brought back from that country by Captain Cook. It has long, thick, whitish-green leaves with a pleasant taste, which are prepared like ordinary spinach.

SPINACH, WILD. ÉPINARD SAUVAGE – See GOOD KING HENRY.

SPINY LOBSTER. LANGOUSTE – Crustacean with a spiny shell, greenish-brown in colour, with yellow markings on the tail and with two long antennae. Its oblong body, more barrel-shaped than that of the lobster, is divided into 6 shell plates and ends in a fan-shaped tail.

Spiny lobsters have no claws, as lobsters do, and their legs are all the same size and shape. They vary in length from 30 to 50 cm.(12 to 20 inches).

Spiny lobsters are to be found in large numbers in the Atlantic and the Mediterranean. Moroccan lobsters have found their way into the continental market. They are known in France as the *Langouste royal.* This shellfish is similar in shape to the spiny lobsters caught off the French coast, except that its body is somewhat flatter. It is of excellent quality.

Another variety of spiny lobster, the Martinique lobster, is

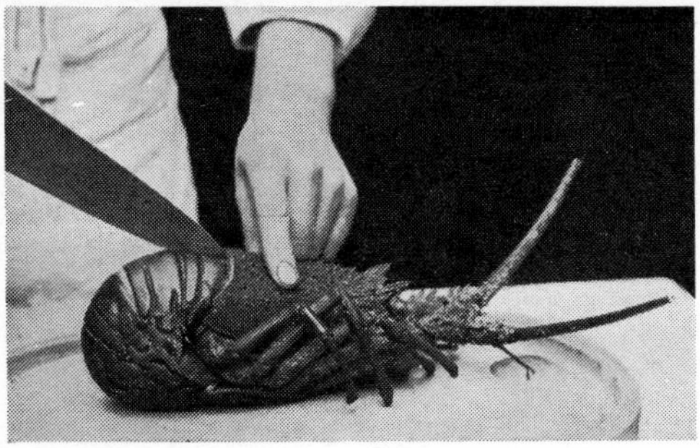
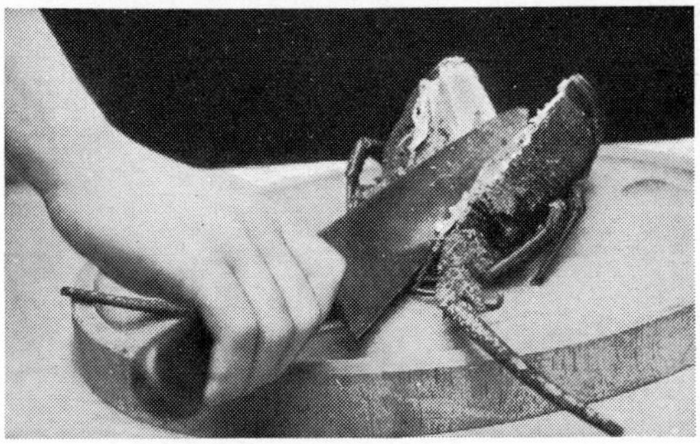

To cut open a spiny lobster, begin with the tail. Then split open the head and thorax (*Larousse*)

also sold frozen in French fish shops. These are very prolific in the West Indian Ocean and in the coastal waters of South America.

Spiny lobster à l'américaine. LANGOUSTE À L'AMÉRICAINE – Proceed as for *Lobster à l'américaine* (see LOBSTER).

Spiny lobster aspic. ASPIC DE LANGOUSTE – Proceed as for *Lobster aspic* (see LOBSTER).

Boiled spiny lobster with various sauces. LANGOUSTE BOUILLIE – Boil the spiny lobster in a *court-bouillon*, as for *Boiled lobster* (see LOBSTER).

Serve hot, with a sauce suitable for poached or boiled fish or shellfish. Serve cold, with mayonnaise or some other cold sauce.

Spiny lobster à la bordelaise. LANGOUSTE À LA BORDELAISE – Proceed as for *Lobster à la bordelaise* (see LOBSTER).

Spiny lobster à la bourgeoise (Italian cookery). LANGOUSTE À LA BOURGEOISE – Take a spiny lobster weighing approximately 700 to 800 g. ($1\frac{1}{2}$ to $1\frac{3}{4}$ lb.). Scrub it under running cold water. Cut into slices as for *Lobster à l'américaine* (see LOBSTER). Set aside the coral and the creamy parts of the lobster.

Place 500 g. (generous 1 lb.) peeled, chopped and deseeded tomatoes, 2 medium sliced onions, 1 clove garlic, $\frac{1}{2}$ a bay leaf, 1 sprig of thyme, and 1 tablespoon chopped parsley in a shallow buttered pan.

Lay the slices of spiny lobster on these vegetables. Season with salt and pepper. Pour on 2 tablespoons (3 tablespoons) olive oil, a glass of white wine, a small glass of Marsala and a small glass of brandy.

Cover, and bring to the boil. Boil for 20 minutes. Take out the lobster, and arrange it in a dish. Boil down the sauce, if necessary. Thicken it with the chopped coral, add 1 teaspoon chopped parsley and a pinch of cayenne pepper. Bring to the boil and pour over the dish.

Spiny lobster butter. BEURRE DE LANGOUSTE – Made from the shells and trimmings of the spiny lobster which have been cooked in *court-bouillon*. Pound these thoroughly. Add an equal weight of butter. Rub through a sieve.

Spiny lobster cardinal. LANGOUSTE CARDINAL – Boil the spiny lobster in a *court-bouillon*. Drain, split in two lengthwise and reserve the shell halves. Remove the flesh from the tail and cut it into 6 to 8 slices. Dice the rest of the spiny lobster flesh and place in a pan. Add diced mushrooms and truffles and bind with *Béchamel sauce* (see SAUCE) with cream added. Simmer down, blend with *Spiny lobster butter* (see butter) and strain.

Heat this *salpicon* without letting it come to the boil. Fill the halves of the shell with it. Decorate the top of each shell with lobster slices alternating with strips of truffle. Cover with *béchamel sauce* to which spiny lobster butter has been added. Sprinkle with grated cheese. Pour on melted butter.

Place the halves of spiny lobster in a baking tin. Brown in a very hot oven and garnish with parsley.

Collops of spiny lobster à l'andalouse. ESCALOPES DE LANGOUSTE À L'ANDALOUSE – Cook a spiny lobster in *court-bouillon* and leave to cool. Shell. Cut the tail into 10 thick slices. Coat these with *Chaud-froid sauce* (see SAUCE) and a purée of red peppers and truffles. Glaze with jelly. Chill on ice.

Make a salad with the rest of the lobster meat, coarsely chopped, diced truffles, peeled, cooked and diced green and red peppers, and diced potatoes. Season with paprika and stir in mayonnaise mixed with thick jelly.

Make a dome of this salad in the centre of a dish. This must be done as soon as the salad is seasoned, otherwise it will set too hard.

Surround the salad with as many *Tomato mousselines* (see TOMATO) as there are spiny lobster slices. Put a spiny lobster slice on top of each mould. Make a border of chopped jelly. Decorate the top of the salad with lettuce hearts and quartered hard-boiled eggs.

Collops of spiny lobster à la parisienne. ESCALOPES DE LANGOUSTE À LA PARISIENNE – Cook a spiny lobster in *court-bouillon*. Leave to cool. Shell. Cut the tail into slices. Cover with *Jellied mayonnaise* (see SAUCE, *Mayonnaise sauce, thick*). Decorate with truffles and carrots shaped with a small ball-scoop. Glaze with jelly. Chill thoroughly in the refrigerator.

Arrange in a circle round a *Parisian salad* (see SALAD) seasoned with jelly mayonnaise and made into a dome in the centre of a dish.

Decorate with slices of hard-boiled egg and jelly. In the centre of the dish place a lettuce heart decorated with a hard-boiled egg.

Collops of spiny lobster à l'andalouse

Collops of spiny lobster à la parisienne

Coquilles of spiny lobster (cold). COQUILLES DE LANGOUSTE – Using spiny lobster, proceed as for *Lobster in scallop shells (cold)* (see LOBSTER).

Coquilles of spiny lobster (hot). COQUILLES DE LANGOUSTE – Prepare with spiny lobsters cooked in a *court-bouillon*, shelled and diced or cut into small slices. Proceed as for *Lobster Mornay in scallop shells* (see LOBSTER).

Spiny lobster in court-bouillon. LANGOUSTE AU COURT-BOUILLON. Made with small spiny lobsters. Proceed as for *Crayfish à la nage* (see CRAYFISH).

Spiny lobsters cooked in this way are usually served hot. A suitable sauce is served separately. They can also be served cold, in which case they are usually called *Spiny lobster à la nage* (see below).

Spiny lobster in cream. LANGOUSTE À LA CRÈME – Proceed as for *Lobster in cream* (see LOBSTER).

Croquettes and kromeskies of spiny lobster. CROQUETTES, CROMESQUIS DE LANGOUSTE – Proceed as for any other croquettes or *kromeskis* (see HORS-D'ŒUVRE, *Hot hors-d'œuvre*).

Curried spiny lobster. ÉTUVÉ DE LANGOUSTE AU CURRIE – Sauté in butter 2 spiny lobsters, cut into slices as for *Spiny lobster à l'américaine*. Add 100 g. (4 oz., 1 cup) chopped onion. Season with salt, pepper and 1 to 2 teaspoons curry powder.

When the slices are a golden colour, moisten with 3 dl. ($\frac{1}{2}$ pint, $1\frac{1}{4}$ cups) white wine. Add a *bouquet garni* and 2 peeled and crushed tomatoes. Cover the pan. Simmer until almost all the stock has evaporated.

Drain the spiny lobster slices and keep warm. Remove the *bouquet garni* from the pan. Stir in 2 dl. ($\frac{1}{3}$ pint, scant cup) *Béchamel sauce* (see SAUCE) and 2 dl. ($\frac{1}{3}$ pint, scant cup) double cream. Boil for a few seconds. Replace the spiny lobster slices in the sauce. Cover and simmer for 15 minutes. Add 2 teaspoons butter and a squeeze of lemon juice to the sauce.

Serve with *Rice à l'indienne* (see RICE).

Spiny lobster demi-deuil. LANGOUSTE DEMI-DEUIL – Boil 2 spiny lobsters in a white wine *court-bouillon*. Drain and leave to cool. Split the spiny lobsters lengthwise and remove the shells. Cut the tails into slices and dice the remaining flesh.

Make a *salpicon* of truffles and mushrooms blended with a little fish-based *Suprême sauce* (see SAUCE), with fresh cream and a little Madeira added. Stir in the diced spiny lobster flesh. Put the *salpicon* in the shells and decorate with the tail slices. Cover with *suprême sauce* and brown in a very hot oven. Warm strips of truffle in white fish stock jelly, and use these to decorate the tops of the shells.

Spiny lobster au gratin. LANGOUSTE AU GRATIN – Boil the spiny lobster in a *court-bouillon*. Split it lengthwise, shell it and cut it up as for *Spiny lobster cardinal*.

Mix the diced flesh with thick *Béchamel sauce* (see SAUCE) with butter added. Add to the *salpicon* an equal quantity of diced, cooked mushrooms.

Fill the halves of the shell with the *salpicon*. Arrange the slices on top. Cover with the remainder of the sauce. Sprinkle with grated cheese, pour on melted butter and brown.

Grilled spiny lobster. LANGOUSTE GRILLÉE – Proceed as for *Grilled lobster* (see LOBSTER).

Spiny lobster Mornay. LANGOUSTE MORNAY – Another name for *Spiny lobster au gratin*.

Spiny lobster à la moscovite. LANGOUSTE À LA MOSCOVITE – Boil a large spiny lobster in a *court-bouillon*. Leave it to cool in the stock and drain. Make 2 incisions 4 cm. ($1\frac{1}{2}$ inches) apart lengthwise in the shell. Remove the part of the shell between the incisions and cut off the tail, being careful not to break it. Remove all the flesh and the creamy part from the body of the lobster.

Dice the flesh and add to it diced potatoes and diced truffles. Season with thick *Mayonnaise sauce* (see SAUCE, *Cold sauces*). Stuff the shell with this salad.

Trim a slice of buttered sandwich bread into the form of a wedge and set the spiny lobster on it. Place on a large oval dish. Garnish the dish with very clear fish aspic jelly. Chill in the refrigerator or on ice.

Slice the tail of the spiny lobster. Coat with white *Chaud-froid sauce* (see SAUCE) based on *Fish fumet* (see FUMET). When this sauce has quite set, place a strip of truffle on top of each slice and glaze with jelly. Chill.

Arrange the slices on the spiny lobster shell, starting at the head and overlapping.

Surround with the following garnish:

Very small *barquettes* of thin *Lining paste* (see DOUGH), filled with caviare, halved hard boiled eggs decorated with strips of truffle and glazed with jelly, small artichoke hearts filled with vegetable salad dressed with jelly mayonnaise, lettuce hearts.

Run a skewer between the eyes of the spiny lobster. Decorate with chopped jelly and surround the dish with rounds of jelly cut out with a pastry-cutter. Serve with mayonnaise mixed with the sieved roe of the spiny lobster.

Instead of slitting the spiny lobster along the top, it may be slit underneath, and filled with shredded lettuce salad instead of potato salad. Small *barquettes* of cucumber or beetroot should be filled with the same salad and added to the garnish.

Spiny lobster mousse and mousseline. MOUSSE, MOUSSELINE DE LANGOUSTE – Served hot or cold and prepared in the same way as *Lobster mousse* and *mousselines* (see LOBSTER).

Spiny lobster à la nage. LANGOUSTE À LA NAGE – This method of preparation is especially suitable for small spiny lobsters. Proceed as for *Lobster à la nage* (see LOBSTER).

Spiny lobster à la niçoise (cold). LANGOUSTE FROIDE À LA NIÇOISE – Boil a spiny lobster in a *court-bouillon*. Leave to cool. Split it lengthwise and shell. Cut part of the flesh into 10 slices and dice the rest.

Add cooked diced potatoes, peas, French beans and diced anchovy fillets to the diced lobster flesh. Mix with jellied mayonnaise. Fill the shells with this salad.

Arrange the shell halves on a dish. Put the slices on top. Cover with jellied mayonnaise and decorate each with rosettes of tarragon leaves.

Decorate the sides of the dish with tomatoes stuffed with the spiny lobster salad, alternating with cooked artichoke hearts filled with shredded lettuce, seasoned with French dressing and garnished with anchovy fillets and capers. At each end of the dish arrange halved hard-boiled eggs and quartered lettuce hearts.

Serve with a sauce made from mayonnaise mixed with *Tomato fondue* (see TOMATO), cooked in oil and flavoured with anchovy essence.

Spiny lobster à la parisienne. LANGOUSTE À LA PARISIENNE – Proceed as for *Spiny lobster à la moscovite*, changing the presentation and garnish as follows:

Remove the tail and empty the shell. Fill with coarsely shredded lettuce salad. Place on a buttered wedge of bread. Cut the tail flesh into slices and arrange on top of the shell. Decorate each slice with a strip of truffle and glaze with jelly.

Garnish with artichoke hearts filled with a salad of vegetables and the diced flesh of the spiny lobster dressed with jellied mayonnaise, quartered or halved hard boiled eggs glazed with jelly and quartered lettuce hearts.

Decorate the dish with chopped jelly, and arrange rounds of jelly along the edge. Run a decorated skewer between the eyes of the spiny lobster. Serve with mayonnaise.

Spiny lobster pilaf and risotto. PILAF, RISOTTO DE LANGOUSTE – Proceed as for *Lobster pilaf and risotto* (see LOBSTER).

Spiny lobster à la russe. LANGOUSTE À LA RUSSE – Proceed as for *Spiny lobster à la moscovite*, changing the presentation and garnish as follows:

Coat the spiny lobster slices with jellied mayonnaise or a white *Chaud-froid sauce* (see SAUCE). Decorate with a little of the coral and 2 chervil leaves glazed with jelly. Arrange the slices on top of the spiny lobster, which should be stuffed with a coarsely shredded lettuce salad, and set on a wedge of buttered bread.

Garnish with cylindrical moulds of Russian salad dressed with jellied mayonnaise, halves of hard boiled eggs, decorated with truffles and glazed with jelly and lettuce hearts. Skewer the lobster. Serve with *Tartare sauce* (see SAUCE, *Cold sauces*).

Spiny lobster salad. SALADE DE LANGOUSTE – Using spiny lobster, proceed as for *Lobster salad* (see SALAD).

Spiny lobster with various sauces (cold). LANGOUSTE FROIDE AUX SAUCES DIVERSES – Boil a spiny lobster in a *court-bouillon*. Leave to cool. Garnish with fresh parsley or lettuce hearts. Serve with mayonnaise or any sauce suitable for cold fish or shellfish.

Spiny lobster on the spit. LANGOUSTE À LA BROCHE – Proceed as for *Lobster on the spit* (see LOBSTER).

Spiny lobster stew (Catalan and Languedoc cookery). CIVET DE LANGOUSTE – Cut the spiny lobster into slices and proceed as for *Spiny lobster à l'américaine*, increasing the amount of tomato and flavouring it strongly with garlic.

SPIRIT. EAU-DE-VIE – Strictly, *eau-de-vie* is the product of distilled wine (brandy), but the term is extended to cover spirits distilled from fruit and even cereals.

The *eau-de-vie* of Charentes, Cognac, has a reputation equal to that of the greatest wines and is undoubtedly the prime of all spirits. Its incomparable flavour is due to a special vine, the Folle blanche, which also yields a rough, mediocre white wine. Its quality depends to a great extent on the vine growth. The first Cognacs are made from the grapes grown in chalky vineyards known as Champagnes. A distinction is made between Fines Champagnes (liqueur brandies) and Petites Champagnes, and between Fins bois and Bons bois Cognacs, according to the origin of the wine distilled. In former times distillation was carried out in a very primitive still, heated over an open fire. This process was carried out in two stages. The *brouillis* collected first was distilled afresh over greater heat to arrive at the desired strength. The products were then graded.

Immediately after distilling, Cognac, which is about 70 per cent alcohol, has scarcely any aroma. This develops by slow etherification and by changes which occur while it is stored in casks, which lower its strength and permit some evaporation of alcohol.

The manufacture and preparation of brandy casks demand particular care. After 25 years in a cask, a brandy loses about one third of its volume. It becomes slightly coloured and tart. These incomparable brandies whose aroma lingers for several hours in the glasses into which they have been poured, are not to be found in ordinary wine shops but are used to make commercial products. They are adulterated with younger spirits, after syrup and water have been added to reduce them to the commercial standard of 40 per cent alcohol. Sometimes less orthodox methods are used, the brandy being adulterated with 'sauce' mixtures, for which formulae are to be found in distillers' manuals.

Here are a few sample formulae:

1. Steep for 3 days in 1 litre ($1\frac{3}{4}$ pints, generous quart) of brandy: 60 g. (2 oz.) catechu, 10 g. ($\frac{1}{3}$ oz.) balsam of tolu, and add 85 g. (3 oz.) ammonia.

2. Steep for 3 days in 1 litre ($1\frac{3}{4}$ pints, generous quart) of brandy: 6 g. (1 teaspoon) vanilla, 80 g. (3 oz.) catechu, 8 g. ($\frac{1}{4}$ oz.) tolu, 12 g. ($\frac{1}{2}$ oz.) sassafras, 1 drop of bitter almond essence and 100 g. (4 oz.) sugar.

These ingredients are added to 100 litres (22 gallons, $27\frac{1}{2}$ gallons) unmatured brandy, and rectified spirit, heated together to blend the ingredients, and then cooled slowly.

The brandies of Armagnac are made from the vines of Gers called Picquepoul, which is merely a variety of the Folle

Storehouse for casks of maturing Cognac

Champagne glass (*Rouard. Phot. Larousse*)

Storehouse for despatch of Cognac (*Maison Remy Martin*)

blanche of Charentes. Their flavour is a little different from that of Cognac.

The wines of many other regions are distilled, but it is a notable fact that the first growths do not usually yield fine brandies.

The marc of wines is also distilled after a little water has been added to it, as are the lees which remain at the bottom of the vats and casks. Some of the products enjoy a great reputation.

Cider, to which the marc is usually added, is distilled to produce the spirits known as Calvados.

Spirits are also distilled from all fruit which is sufficiently abundant. It is first fermented, as for cider or wine. Thus, spirits are distilled from apricots, cherries, dates, figs, raspberries, mulberries, bilberries, mirabelles, pears, peaches, greengages, plums (*quetsch*, *slivovitz*) and many other kinds of fruit.

True rum is distilled from sugar cane juice, but nowadays a distillation of molasses, once known as tafia, is also called rum.

The distilled grain of cereals, especially barley, yields spirits such as Kornschnaps and whisky. Sometimes it is flavoured with juniper berries to produce gin.

The analysis of spirits is concerned with the detection of minerals which should not be present, and with the co-efficient of impurities. This co-efficient should be from 6 to 20 for rectified industrial spirits, 20 to 150 for 'medium taste' spirits. It is always more than 150 and can reach 300 in spirits of wine or fruit. This analysis is completed by the investigation of colouring matter, synthetic bouquets, saccharin and dulcin.

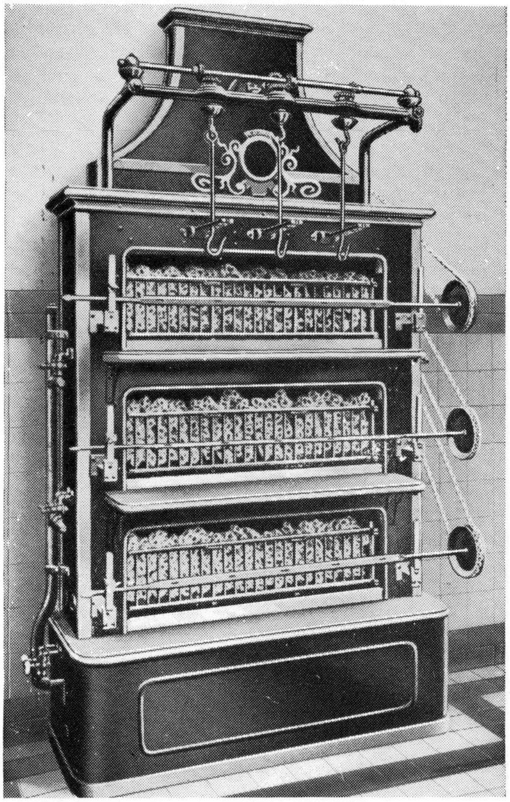

Gas roasting spit
(*Constructeurs associés de Paris*)

Modern spit. Casino d'Enghien
(*Casino d'Enghien*)

SPIT. BROCHE – Utensil on which meat, etc., can be roasted before a fire.

There are various types of spits. There is the variety on which the meat to be roasted is placed vertically, and the kind on which it is placed horizontally. Spits are hand operated or mechanically operated to make the roasts turn slowly.

Many gastronomes do not recognise any roast, as such, except one cooked on a spit before a wood fire. It was in this manner that roasts were done in the olden days. But kitchen equipment is now in line with modern needs. Gas and electric spits are excellent and enable us to produce perfect roasts.

The great Escoffier drew up some general rules for roasting:

'Of the two most usual methods of roasting, the spit is by far the superior, due to the conditions in which the operation is carried out and regardless of what type of heat is employed.

'The explanation is simple: however much care is lavished on an oven roast nothing can prevent vapours building up in the enclosed space: the roasting process takes place in this atmosphere. The effect of these fumes is all the more disastrous when the juices of the meat are rather delicate and more liable to alteration and reduction.

'Roasting on the spit, on the other hand, is done in the open air, in a dry atmosphere which detracts nothing from the quality of the juices *sui generis* of the meat. This explains why spit-roasted meat is indisputably superior to oven-roasted meat.'

From a technical point of view, spit-roasting is more akin to grilling and is quite different from oven roasting. In fact, whereas the roasting of meat in the oven is due mainly to the

Ingredients required for the preparation of sponge fingers (*Fasné Desmeuzes*)

Work the mixture to a smooth consistency as shown in the picture (*Larousse*)

Pipe the mixture through a forcing-bag on to greaseproof paper (*Fasné Desmeuzes*)

action of heat contained within it, spit-roasted meat is subjected to the radiation of glowing surfaces. There are two clearly defined stages in the process of spit-roasting:

The first is the application of intense heat upon the surface of the meat. This is intended to seal in the juices and to brown the meat. It has to be a rapid process and must on no account pass the stage of simply colouring the surface. The heat must be reduced before the second stage.

This second stage continues and completes the cooking process. The intention is to cook the inside of the meat as much or as little as individual taste dictates. In this way the chef can satisfy everybody and turn out perfectly roasted meat every time. But it is a task that requires his constant and exclusive attention.

We can see how much the spit has evolved by tracing its development from the spit used by our ancestors to the present day electric or gas ones.

SPLEEN. RATE – Ox spleen is sometimes used in *pot-au-feu*.

SPONDIAS – Indian tree whose edible fruit is known as a *hog apple*. The fruit of the spondias, which grows in many tropical regions, makes excellent preserves and a fermented drink.

SPONGE (SANDWICH) CAKES. BISCUITS – See also CAKE, GENOESE.

Almond sandwich cake. BISCUIT AUX AMANDES – Put 300 g. (11 oz., $1\frac{1}{2}$ cups) sugar, 8 egg yolks and a pinch of salt into a bowl and blend well with a wooden spoon.

When the mixture is frothy, incorporate 120 g. (4 oz., $\frac{3}{4}$ cup) sweet almonds and 4 or 5 bitter almonds, blanched and pounded in a mortar to a smooth paste with egg white. Add a few drops of orange blossom water and mix well. Add 8 egg whites, whisked to a stiff froth and 120 g. (4 oz., 1 cup) sieved flour.

Butter a sponge cake tin, sprinkle it with flour and pour in the cake mixture, filling the tin up to three quarters of its depth. Bake in a moderately hot oven.

Turn out onto a wire cake rack and allow to cool. Cut into three layers of equal thickness. Coat one layer with apricot jam, the second with raspberry jam and sandwich the layers together. Brush with apricot jam, ice with vanilla-flavoured *Fondant icing* (see ICING) and sprinkle with chopped pistachio nuts.

Sponge fingers. BISCUITS À LA CUILLER – These biscuits are prepared with dough made of flour, sugar, egg yolks and stiffly beaten egg whites.

Cream 250 g. (9 oz., generous cup) castor sugar and 8 egg yolks in a bowl until the mixture forms a ribbon. Flavour with 1 teaspoon orange blossom water, add 190 g. (7 oz., $1\frac{3}{4}$ cups) sieved flour and incorporate 8 egg whites, whisked until stiff. Blend the mixture, lifting it lightly with a spoon and folding in the egg whites gently.

Pipe through a forcing bag fitted with a wide nozzle onto sheets of greaseproof paper. Sprinkle with castor sugar, lift each sheet of paper by the two ends to shake off surplus sugar. Place on a baking tray and bake in a moderately hot oven (190°C., 375°F., Gas Mark 5) for 12 minutes.

The mixture may be flavoured with grated orange or lemon rind, or with vanilla essence.

Sponge fingers are used in the preparation of many sweet dishes, such as *Charlotte russe* (see CHARLOTTE).

Italian sandwich cake. BISCUIT À L'ITALIENNE – *Ingredients.* 500 g. (18 oz., $2\frac{1}{4}$ cups) castor sugar, 10 eggs, 125 g. ($4\frac{1}{2}$ oz., generous cup) sieved flour, 125 g. ($4\frac{1}{2}$ oz., 1 cup) sieved potato flour, 2 teaspoons vanilla-flavoured sugar or $\frac{1}{4}$ teaspoon vanilla essence.

Method. Cream the sugar and add the egg yolks one at a time. Whisk the egg whites and fold them into the mixture.

Add the flour, potato flour, and vanilla-flavoured sugar or vanilla essence, all previously mixed together on a sheet of paper. Blend well.

Pour the mixture into a charlotte mould which has been buttered and dusted with a mixture of icing sugar and potato flour in equal proportions.

Sandwich cake manqué. BISCUIT MANQUÉ – *Ingredients.* 400 g. (14 oz., $3\frac{1}{2}$ cups) sieved flour, 500 g. (18 oz., $2\frac{1}{4}$ cups) castor sugar, 18 egg yolks, 300 g. (11 oz., $1\frac{1}{3}$ cups) butter, 16 egg whites, whisked to a stiff froth, 3 tablespoons rum.

Method. Cream the sugar and the egg yolks together until the mixture is white and frothy. Add the rum and flour and mix well. Add the stiffly beaten egg whites and pour in the cooled melted butter.

Spoon the mixture into cake tins which have been buttered and dusted with flour. Bake in a moderately hot oven (190°C., 375°F., Gas Mark 5) for 40 to 45 minutes.

Punch sandwich cakes. BISCUITS PUNCH – *Ingredients.* 375 g. (13 oz., $3\frac{1}{4}$ cups) sieved flour, 500 g. (18 oz., $2\frac{1}{4}$ cups) sugar, 12 egg yolks, 3 whole eggs, 8 egg whites, whisked to a stiff froth, 300 g. (11 oz., $1\frac{1}{3}$ cups) butter, $1\frac{1}{2}$ teaspoons orange-flavoured sugar, $1\frac{1}{2}$ teaspoons lemon-flavoured sugar and 3 tablespoons (scant $\frac{1}{4}$ cup) rum. ($\frac{1}{4}$ teaspoon orange essence and $\frac{1}{4}$ teaspoon lemon essence may be used instead of the flavoured sugars).

Method. Cream together the sugar, egg yolks and whole eggs until the mixture becomes very light. Stir in the flavoured sugars, rum, flour, stiffly beaten egg whites and cooled melted butter. Mix well.

Put the mixture into buttered paper cases, buttered flan rings or sandwich tins. Bake in a moderate oven (180°C., 350°F., Gas Mark 4).

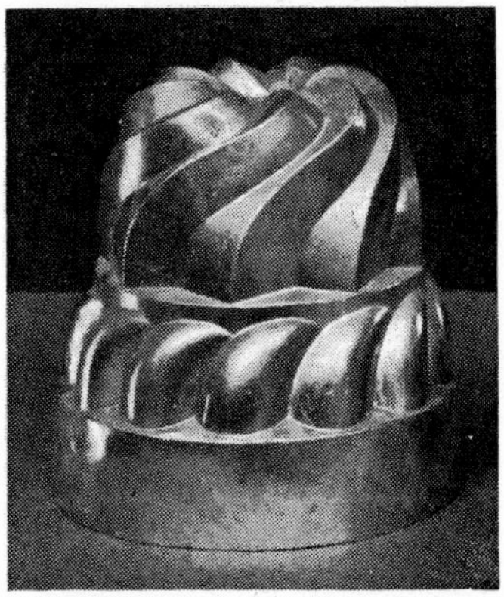

Mould for Savoy sponge cake (*Larousse*)

Savoy sandwich cake. BISCUIT DE SAVOIE – *Ingredients.* 185 g. (6 oz., $1\frac{1}{2}$ cups) sieved flour, 185 g. (6 oz., $1\frac{1}{2}$ cups) potato flour, 500 g. (18 oz.) castor sugar, 14 eggs, 1 tablespoon vanilla-flavoured sugar or $\frac{1}{4}$ teaspoon vanilla essence.

Method. Cream the sugar and the egg yolks in a bowl until the mixture forms a ribbon. Add vanilla-flavoured sugar or vanilla essence, flour and potato flour, mixed. Fold in the whisked egg whites.

Put the mixture into Savoy cake tins which have been buttered and dusted with potato flour, filling them only up to two-thirds. Bake in a moderately hot oven (180°C., 350°F., Gas Mark 4).

SPOOMS – See ICE CREAMS AND ICES.

SPOON. CUILLER – Utensil which has an oval or concave spherical form fixed to a handle (see COVER). Spoons used in cooking have various shapes and are made in different materials according to their particular uses: wooden spoons, spoons for sauces, basting spoons, soup ladles, etc.

Sprinkle the sponge fingers with castor sugar (*Larousse*)

Lift the paper to shake off surplus sugar (*Fasné Desmeuzes*)

Remove the sponge fingers from the paper when baked (*Larousse*)

SPRAT – Small sea fish 8 to 12 cm. (3 to 4½ inches) long, a little smaller than the sardine and somewhat resembling the herring. The back is blue-green and the sides silvery with a gold band at spawning time.

Gastronomically it is not held in such high esteem as the sardine. All methods of preparation for *sardine* are applicable to the sprat. It is also preserved, smoked and salted.

SPRUCE BEER. SAPINETTE – Fermented drink, obtained from branches and cones of spruce, a native of America and Russia, which is also found in the north of France. These branches are boiled and sugar, hops and yeast are added when the beer is put into casks.

'SPURS OF BACCHUS'. ÉPERONS BACHIQUES – Metaphorical expression sometimes used on menus for the ensemble of morsels making up a cold *hors-d'œuvre*. It is used especially of salty foods such as ham, sausages, saveloy and chitterlings, which, being highly seasoned, cause thirst. It is in this sense that Rabelais used the expression.

SQUAB – See PIGEON.

Varieties of squash

SQUASH. PÂTISSON – Member of the *Cucurbitaceae* family. The best-known varieties are American white, yellow and orange. These and other squashes can be prepared in any method suitable for marrow and pumpkin.

Squash, hollowed out and blanched, can be used as a container for various dishes. The scooped out pulp is cooked in butter and added to these dishes.

SQUID – See CALAMARY.

SQUILL-FISH. SQUILLE – Crustacean also known as *sauterelle de mer* (sea-grasshopper) and *mante de mer* (sea mantis), fished off the coasts of Spain and Italy and in the English Channel. They are prepared like lobsters (q.v.).

SQUIRREL. ÉCUREUIL – Wild rodent. In some countries, it is highly esteemed as game. It is cooked in the same way as rabbit.

STALK. ÉGRAPPER – To remove grapes or berries from their stalks.

STAMPPOT (Dutch cookery) – A national dish in Holland. It is prepared by serving smoked sausages on top of a hash of cabbage, potato and veal fat made into a raised bed on a dish.

STAR ANISE. ANIS ÉTOILÉ – Common name of the *badian anise*. Also known as *Chinese anise*.

Stamppot (Dutch cookery) (*Claire*)

STAR OF BETHLEHEM. ORNYTHOGALE – Plant with edible roots, which are prepared as salsify (q.v.).

STARCH. FÉCULE – In former times, all solids precipitated by juices obtained by extraction were called starches, though they differed widely from one another.

Nowadays, the term is used especially to describe pure starch powder or the white powdery starch deposit which separates out from water in which certain pounded vegetables (such as potatoes, manioc, sago, rice, etc.) have been washed.

In cookery, four main types of starch are used to thicken sauces or make *coulis* and creams. These are: local starches contained in wheat, potatoes, corn (maize) and rice; exotic starches: salep, arrowroot (manioc), sago, yam, etc.; pulse starches: haricot beans, peas, lentils, etc.; fruit starches, extracted from chestnuts, bananas and sweet nuts.

For thickening soups, stocks and sauces, potato starch and arrowroot (manioc starch) are mainly used. In the U.S.A. cornstarch is widely used.

Foods containing a high proportion of starch are said to be starchy.

STARLING. ÉTOURNEAU, SANSONNET – Bird similar to the blackbird, but smaller. The starling was much prized by the Romans. Nowadays in France it is cooked in the same way as the thrush but its flesh is tough and bitter.

STEARIN. STÉARINE – Neutral fat resulting from the combination of stearic acid with solid glycerine. It is found in varying proportions in edible fats, the quantity varying in relation to the melting point of the fat.

In former times stearin was much used in ornamental sculptures and plinths. Nowadays this usage has been almost completely abandoned, even in culinary exhibitions.

STEEPING. MACÉRATION – Process consisting of soaking various foodstuffs in an aromatic liquid preparation. During steeping, chemical changes occur both in the foodstuff and the liquid. The nature and extent of these changes depend largely on the density of the liquid used and on the soluble elements in the foodstuff.

When meat is steeped in brine, the salt penetrates the muscular tissue and the liquid absorbs a small proportion of the soluble protein in the meat. In the case of a marinade, the spices penetrate the solid in the same way.

When fruit is steeped in sweetened or diluted alcohol, the alcohol penetrates the fruit, which yields some of its juice to the alcohol.

When a solid (e.g. gentian, quassia) is steeped in pure water or water with a little alcohol added, the soluble elements in the solid dissolve in the water.

STERILISE. STÉRILISER – To render sterile, to destroy germs and arrest fermentation in foodstuffs. Heat is the most effective agent of sterilisation.

STERLET – Small sturgeon found in the Caspian Sea.

The sterlet is renowned for the delicacy of its flesh. It is eaten fresh, dried or salted. Its roe produces the finest caviare.

All methods of preparation given for salmon, salmon trout and sturgeon are applicable to the sterlet. It is, however, mostly braised in white wine. An essential condition of its preparation in Russia, and one which gourmets there once insisted should be followed, is that the sterlet shall be brought alive into the kitchen where it is to be cooked.

STICKLEBACK. ÉPINOCHE – Small river fish, mediocre in flavour. It is usually deep-fried.

STOCKFISH – Dried Norwegian cod, differing very little in appearance from the more familiar dried salt cod. It is very much liked in Germany, Belgium and Holland.

Stockfish is also eaten a great deal in the South of France, notably in Nice, where it is prepared as in the recipe below after having been soaked for at least 3 days in water.

In Belgium, Holland and Germany it is soaked in lime water and afterwards cooked like dried salt cod.

Stockfish à la niçoise – Scrape the fish well after it has been soaked in cold water; remove the bone and cut the fish into even-sized pieces.

Sauté 3 chopped large onions for every 1 kg. (2¼ lb.) stockfish, lightly in olive oil. When they are cooked, add 4 large chopped and deseeded tomatoes, 4 crushed cloves of garlic, a pinch of basil and a large *bouquet garni*. Season with salt and pepper. Cook for 20 minutes.

Add the pieces of stockfish to these cooked vegetables and sufficient boiling water to cover the fish. Cook, covered, for 50 minutes. Add 400 g. (14 oz.) potatoes, cut into thick slices, and 250 g. (9 oz., 1½ cups) black olives and cook for another 30 minutes.

STOCKS. FONDS DE CUISINE – This term refers to many culinary preparations: fat or lean stock, or meat juices used for sauces, stews or braising.

Only a limited use is made of these *fonds* in practical everyday cooking. Stocks are mainly used to make sauces, broth and a quick *roux* for thickening.

For cooking in the grand manner it is good to have on hand stocks and other basic ingredients. These will allow you to work quickly and easily and enable you to obtained sauces with much better flavour.

The necessary stocks are: broth, clear soup, veal stock, white and brown (thin and thick), juice from brasied meat, poultry and game stock, fish stock and various jellies.

These stocks, when boiled down and without any addition, are used as flavourings, essence, and glaze.

When a certain quantity of *roux* or other binding element is added, these stocks become *Basic sauces* (see SAUCE), from which many other sauces are derived.

White stock is a broth which by definition has no colour. It has white meat and aromatic vegetables as a basis.

Brown stock is made with beef, veal or poultry, which are first half cooked in butter or fat, and always with the usual aromatic vegetables, also half-cooked in butter.

Fish stock is prepared with the bones and trimmings of fish. The liquid usually consists of dry white wine and water in equal quantities, though sometimes just white wine is used. The only aromatics added are sliced onions, parsley, thyme, bay leaf and lemon juice. Stalks and parings of mushrooms could be added to this, if available.

Vegetable stock for vegetarian cooking is obtained by adding water to the following vegetables: carrots, onions and chopped celery slightly cooked in vegetable fat or butter, flavoured with parsley, thyme, bay leaf and sometimes garlic.

Use of stocks. White stock is used as the liquid in white sauces and stews and for poached poultry. Brown stock is used as a liquid in brown sauces, for braising large cuts of meat and for brown stews.

Fish stock is used in the preparation of special fish sauces, such as *Normande sauce*, *White wine sauce* or a thin *Suprême sauce* (see SAUCE) to be served with fish. It can also be used to moisten fish when it is cooked whole or in slices, before it is braised or poached.

Vegetable stock is used as a liquid for all preparations in vegetarian cooking.

Fish stock or concentrate. FONDS DE POISSON, FUMET DE POISSON – *Nourishing ingredients.* 2½ kg. (5½ lb.) bones and trimmings of fish (sole, whiting, brill, sea perch, haddock, etc.).

Aromatic ingredients. 125 g. (4 oz., ½ cup) grated onion, 150 g. (5 oz., 2½ cups) mushroom parings, 1 small bouquet of parsley, 1 sprig of thyme, ½ bay leaf, 10 drops of lemon juice.

Seasoning. 1½ teaspoons kitchen salt.

Liquid. 2½ litres (4½ pints, 5½ pints) water, ½ litre (scant pint, 2¼ cups) dry white wine.

Method. Place all the aromatics in the bottom of a stock pot. Cover these with the bones and trimmings of the fish. Moisten, season and add the lemon juice. Bring to the boil, skim, cook gently for 30 minutes. Strain through a muslin bag or fine sieve.

Fish stock or concentrate with red wine. FONDS DE POISSON AU VIN ROUGE, FUMET DE POISSON AU VIN ROUGE – Prepare as for ordinary fish stock using as liquid 1½ litres (2¾ pints, 3¼ pints) red wine and the same quantity of water. Strain through a muslin bag or fine sieve and use as directed.

Game stock. FONDES DE GIBIER – For 2½ litres (4½ pints, 5½ pints):

Nourishing ingredients. 1 kg. (2¼ lb.) shoulder, breast or other piece of venison, 1 kg. (2¼ lb.) trimmings of hare or wild rabbit, 1 old partridge, 1 old pheasant, 50 g. (2 oz.) fresh pork rind, 50 g. (2 oz., ¼ cup) dripping or butter.

Aromatic ingredients. 150 g. (5 oz.) carrots, 150 g. (5 oz.) onions, 1 *bouquet garni*, 1 sprig of sage, 10 juniper berries, 1 clove.

Seasoning. 1 tablespoon salt.

Liquid. 3 litres (5¼ pints, 6½ pints) white stock or water, ½ litre (scant pint, 2¼ cups) white wine.

Method. Tie the meat together and truss the feathered game; brush with dripping or butter and brown in the oven. Slice the vegetables and brown in the stockpot with the rind. Add the meat, moisten with stock obtained by adding white wine to the juice left in the roasting pan. Add another ½ litre (scant pint, 2¼ cups) stock. Bring to the boil, skim, season lightly, add sage, juniper berries and 1 clove. Cook gently for 3 hours. Skim off all fat and strain through a fine sieve.

This stock is used as the liquid in brown game sauces. Alternatively it can be used, without further additions, as a sauce for small pieces of game tossed in butter. Boiled down, the stock becomes game essence, and can be used to flavour different game dishes.

The nourishing ingredients used in the preparation of this stock (venison, hare, partridge, etc.) can be used afterwards for a variety of dishes, such as hash, stews and purées.

Light brown stock or estouffade. FONDS BRUN CLAIR, ESTOUFFADE – For 5 litres (4½ quarts, 5½ quarts):

Nourishing ingredients. 2½ kg. (5½ lb.) lean beef (leg or shoulder), 2½ kg. (5½ lb.) veal knuckle, 1 kg. (2¼ lb.) beef and veal bones, 300 g. (11 oz.) scalded bacon rind, 250 g. (9 oz.) blanched ham knuckle, 50 g. (2 oz., ¼ cup) meat dripping or butter.

Aromatic ingredients. 300 g. (11 oz.) carrots, 300 g. (11 oz.) onions, 1 large *bouquet garni*, 1 clove garlic.

Seasoning. 1½ tablespoons (2 tablespoons) cooking salt.

Liquid. 7 litres (6 quarts, 7½ quarts) thin white stock or water.

Bone the meat and cut it into large pieces. (After cooking the meat can be used to make a hash.)

Break the bones into small pieces. Slice the carrots and onions. Half cook all ingredients in fat. Add ½ litre (scant pint, 2¼ cups) white stock and boil down to a jelly. Add the same quantity of stock and boil down again. Add the rest of the stock. Bring to the boil and season lightly with salt. Simmer for 8 hours.

Skim off all fat from the stock and strain through a fine sieve.

Light brown stock is used in brown sauces, stews, jellies, and in different methods of braising. Chefs consider it an essential ingredient of savoury sauces.

Stock of veal or other meat. FONDS DE VEAU, DE VIANDE – With meat trimmings prepare a meat stock, which can be used as a gravy for various dishes or as a liquid to dilute the pan juices of small pieces of meat. Cut the meat into small pieces and sauté in butter, allowing 1 carrot and 1 medium onion for 250 g. (9 oz.) meat trimmings.

As soon as the ingredients begin to brown, sprinkle in 1 tablespoon flour. Stir with a wooden spoon until golden. Add 6 tablespoons (scant ½ cup) white wine. Boil down. Add 3 dl. (½ pint, 1¼ cups) meat broth. Cook slowly for 1 hour. Strain through a fine sieve.

Brown veal stock. FONDS BRUN DE VEAU, JUS BRUN DE VEAU – For 5 litres (4½ quarts, 5½ quarts):

Nourishing ingredients. 2½ kg. (5½ lb.) boned veal shoulder, 2½ kg. (5½ lb.) veal knuckle, 1 kg. (2¼ lb.) veal bones, 50 g. (2 oz., ¼ cup) dripping.

Aromatic ingredients. 300 g. (11 oz.) carrots, 300 g. (11 oz.) onions, 1 large *bouquet garni.*

Seasoning. 1½ tablespoons (2 tablespoons) salt.

Liquid. 7 litres (6 quarts, 7½ quarts) white stock.

Bone the meat, tie it up, brush with dripping, season and brown in the oven. Break the bones into as small pieces as possible. Cover the bottom of a large stock pot with the sliced vegetables. Put the bones on top of the vegetables, then the meat. Add the *bouquet garni*, cover the pot, simmer over gentle heat for 15 minutes. Moisten with ½ litre (scant pint, 2¼ cups) white stock. Boil down to a jelly. Add the same quantity of stock once more. Boil down again. Add the rest of the stock. Bring to the boil, skim, and season lightly with salt. Simmer for 6 hours. Skim off all fat and strain through a fine sieve.

Boiled down, and with a little butter added, this sauce is used for pieces of roast meat, braised vegetables and other dishes.

As this stock takes a long time to cook, one must add stock or water from time to time as the liquid boils away. This applies to all stocks which need long cooking.

Thick veal stock or thickened veal gravy. FONDS DE VEAU LIÉ, JUS DE VEAU LIÉ – Boil 2 litres (3½ pints, 4½ pints) brown veal stock until reduced by about one quarter. Thicken with 1 tablespoon arrowroot blended with 3 tablespoons clear cold veal stock. Strain through a fine sieve. Keep warm in a *bain-marie.*

This stock has many uses. It can be added to small pieces of meat or poultry previously tossed in butter, or it can be served as gravy for roasts and pot roasts.

Tomato veal stock. FONDS DE VEAU TOMATÉ – To 2 litres (3½ pints, 4½ pints) brown veal stock add 2 dl. (⅓ pint, scant cup) tomato purée. Boil down by one quarter. Strain through a fine sieve.

White stock. FONDS BLANC – *Nourishing ingredients.* 1½ kg. (3½ lb.) lean veal (shoulder), 2 kg. (4½ lb.) veal knuckle and 2 kg. (4½ lb.) poultry giblets or bones and trimmings.

Aromatic ingredients. 250 g. (9 oz.) carrots, 250 g. (9 oz.) onions, 150 g. (5 oz.) leeks, 1 *bouquet garni*, 150 g. (5 oz.) celery.

Seasoning. 1½ tablespoons (2 tablespoons) cooking salt.

Liquid. 7 litres (6 quarts, 7½ quarts) water.

These ingredients will give 5 litres (4½ quarts, 5½ quarts) stock.

Bone the meat and tie it up. Break the bones into small pieces. Place the bones, meat and giblets in a stock pot. Add liquid. Bring to the boil, skim and season. Add the vegetables and *bouquet garni*. Cook slowly for 3½ hours. Remove fat and strain the stock through a fine sieve.

White poultry stock. FONDS BLANC DE VOLAILLE – Proceed as for *White stock*, but add a chicken or a much larger quantity of giblets or bones and trimmings. After cooking, the chicken meat can be used to make croquettes.

STOLLEN (German pâtisserie) – *Ingredients.* 1 kg. (2¼ lb., 9 cups) sifted flour, 450 g. (1 lb., 2 cups) sugar, 3 eggs, 500 g. (18 oz., 2¼ cups) butter, 60 g. (2½ oz., 2½ cakes) yeast, 200 g. (7 oz., scant cup) chopped almonds, 200 g. (7 oz., 1¼ cups) currants, 200 g. (7 oz., 1¼ cups) finely chopped candied orange peel, 200 g. (7 oz., 1¼ cups) finely chopped lemon peel, grated rind of ½ lemon, few drops vanilla essence, 3 tablespoons (4 tablespoons) rum, 2½ dl. (scant ½ pint, generous cup) warm milk, 5 or 6 powdered bitter almonds.

Method. Put 750 g. (1½ lb., 6 cups) sifted flour into a bowl, make a hollow in the middle and put in the yeast. Sprinkle the yeast with sugar and pour over the warm milk. When the yeast begins to bubble mix all the ingredients into a paste. Cover this with a cloth and set near the fire. While it is rising, wash the butter in water, squeeze it to extract all moisture, and dry it with a cloth.

Add the sugar and eggs, and work the butter until it becomes frothy. Add the rest of the flour, currants, peel and other flavourings. Blend together the dough and the butter mixture, adding a little milk but not too much, because this paste should be quite firm in consistency. Beat well and set it covered, near the fire to rise.

Turn out on to a floured table and form into a thick loaf. Leave to rise for 15 minutes, then place it on a buttered baking sheet and brush with melted butter. Bake in a low oven. Brush once more with melted butter when baked and sprinkle liberally with sugar.

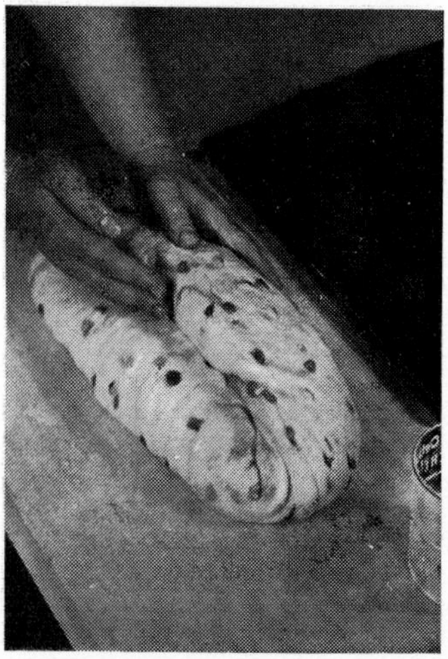

Modelling a stollen

STOMACH. ESTOMAC – The first swelling of the digestive tube and the one in which digestion begins. Ruminants have four stomachs. (See OFFAL, *Tripe*.)

Stomach hygiene. All nutritionists agree that food should be well masticated in order not to overburden the stomach. Drinking too much while eating impedes the digestion.

STONECROP. TRIQUE-MADAME – Common plant also called *orpine* has leaves somewhat resembling those of purslane, rather tasteless but edible as salad, or when cooked like purslane.

Stone-curlew

STONE-CURLEW. OEDICNÈME – Genus of European *Grallatoriae* bird comprising a dozen species. They are birds of medium size, similar to plovers. Their meat is tasty. Stone-curlews are prepared like woodcock (q.v.).

STOPPER. BOUCHON – The word 'stopper' describes all objects such as pieces of cork, glass, rubber or any other substance, usually round in shape, used to seal or cover bottles, carafes and other receptacles, made of glass, china, metal or wood.

Nowadays bottles, especially bottles of alcohol, are sealed with aluminium stoppers. These stoppers are also used for wine bottles, although gourmets still consider that cork makes the finest stoppers.

The French word *bouchon* is derived from the old French word *bousche* meaning tuft of grass or leaves, formerly used as a plug or stopper.

The advent of the cork stopper probably coincided with that of Champagne when the oil-saturated, hemp stoppers were no longer adequate.

The matter of choosing corks for wine bottles is extremely important as it can affect the taste of wine. In this respect two things can go wrong: the wine may become tainted with the foul smell of bad cork or acquire a musty smell of mildew.

This deficiency in cork very often cannot be detected before manufacture, and its effect on wine cannot be remedied. In cork-producing countries, for some years now it has been customary to cut cork boards into small cubes, and 'corky' wine becomes more rare because olfactive examination of the small pieces of cork enables specialists to sort out and eliminate those which are unfit for use. In the form of separate cubes the cork can be transported in much better ventilated conditions than in the case of boards and big pieces of bark. In the past it happened that cork, being transported in the hold of a ship in stale air, often arrived at the cork factory in a deteriorated condition.

Corks should be made of fine bark, supple to the touch and without any defects.

Before using corks, sort carefully to eliminate any which are not sound. Place in a bucket and pour on boiling water and leave to soak for some time. This operation is intended not only to render the corks more flexible, but also to rid them of any impurities.

Gas stove in school kitchen (*Keller*)

Drain and place them in a sieve or a riddle, and leave for 1 hour to dry thoroughly. Soak them for 25 minutes either in good alcohol, brandy, or wine of the same nature for which the corks are intended.

In general, when bottling good quality wines, old corks should be avoided, unless they have been washed and scalded as described above, and only used when corking bottles containing wine for immediate consumption.

STOVE, KITCHEN. FOURNEAU DE CUISINE – Apparatus made of masonry, cast iron or sheet metal, utilising the heat of a fire for the cooking of food, either in the oven or on the heated top. Most modern stoves are heated by gas or electricity instead of kerosene, wood or coal.

STRACCHINO – See CHEESE.

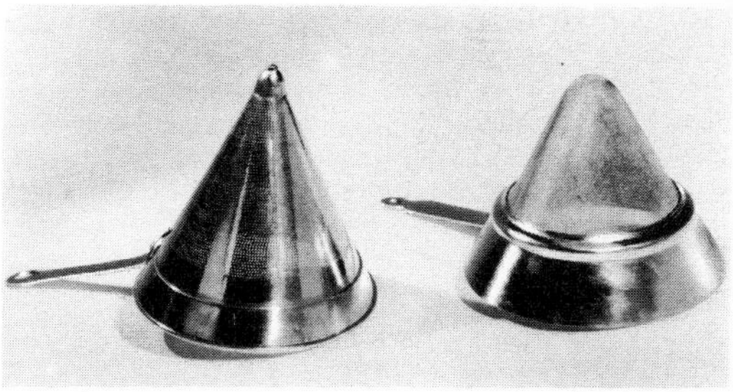

Strainers: perforated metal and wire gauze (*Larousse*)

STRAINER. PASSOIRE – Kitchen utensil used for straining sauces and other liquid preparations. The most practical strainer is the cone-shaped kind called *chinois*.

Straining of sauces and purées. PASSAGE DES SAUCES, DES PURÉES – Sauces are traditionally strained through a tammy-cloth (fine cheesecloth), by two people, each holding one end of the cloth and twisting in opposite directions.

Two people are also needed to rub purées and other comparatively thick preparations through a tammy-cloth. Each person holds one twisted end of the cloth in the left hand and rubs the purée through, using a stout wooden spatula held in the right hand.

Some thin sauces can be strained through muslin without twisting the material. In household kitchens a hair sieve is almost always used in place of a tammy-cloth, and a fine strainer in place of muslin.

STRAINING BAG. CHAUSSE – Funnel in felt or cloth used to clarify liquids, particularly syrups.

STRAW-CASE. PAILLON – Straw wrapping in which bottles are transported. This straw, after treatment in boiling water, is also used for 'dressing' the bottles.

STRAWS. ALLUMETTES – Strips of puff pastry cooked in the oven, with different garnishes. (See also ALLUMETTES.)

Anchovy straws. ALLUMETTES AUX ANCHOIS – Coat the puff pastry with *Fish forcemeat* (see FORCEMEATS) blended with *Anchovy butter* (see BUTTER, *Compound butters*). Garnish each strip with an anchovy fillet, trimmed and desalted. Bake in the oven.

Straws à la chalonnaise. ALLUMETTES À LA CHALONNAISE – Coat the puff pastry with a *Chicken forcemeat* (see FORCEMEATS) blended with cream and with a very finely chopped mixture of cocks' combs, mushrooms and truffles added to it. Bake in the oven.

Cheese straws. ALLUMETTES AU FROMAGE – Cheese straws, which are served as a cold *hors-d'œuvre* and as an accompaniment to cheeses, are made of puff pastry with the addition of finely grated cheese during the last rolling out. The straws are then cut, placed on a baking tray, and sprinkled with grated Parmesan.

Crayfish straws. ALLUMETTES AUX CREVETTES – Coat the puff pastry with finely minced *Fish forcemeat* (see FORCEMEATS) blended with *Crayfish butter* (see BUTTER, *Compound butters*) and with a finely chopped mixture of crayfish tails added to it. Bake in the oven.

STRAW POTATOES. PAILLES – Potato cut lengthways into very thin strips, then deep-fried. (See POTATOES.)

STRAW WINES. VIN DE PAILLE – Wines made from grapes which are left to dry on straw mats for some time before being pressed. The *vin de paille* of Jura (Château-Chalon) is very well known.

STRAWBERRY. FRAISE – Plant of the rose family common throughout Europe. It began to be cultivated in the thirteenth century. Five or six species of strawberries were known. From these a number of varieties have been cultivated.

Strawberries are classified into two groups: small strawberries of which the commonest variety is the ever-bearing strawberry, and large strawberries, which comprise a great many varieties. These are constantly being added to by crossings.

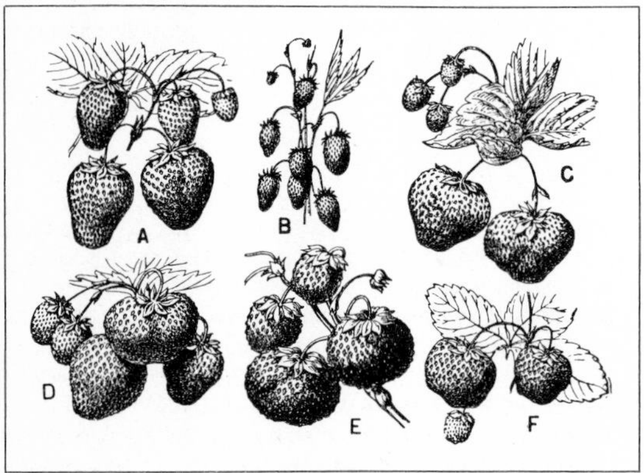

Some varieties of strawberry:
a. Marguerite; b. Reine des quatre-saison; c. Louis Gauthier; d. Doctor Morère; e. Saint Antoine; f. Viscountess Héricart de Thury

The most popular of the large French strawberries are: *Surprise des Halles, Ladette, Madame Moutot, Royal Sovereign, Gauthier, Laxton, Marie-France.* French production, which covers a wide area, usually extends from 15 April to 15 July.

The European strawberry comes from the *Haubois* strawberry: its flesh is firm and fragrant. A closely related species is the Alpine strawberry. The perpetual strawberry is a variety of this.

Large strawberries came from the United States and Canada (*Fragaria virginiana*), and from Chile (*Fragaria chiloensis*). They were imported into France by a naval officer named Fréziers, and are still cultivated today in the region of Plougastel.

Pine strawberries (also called common garden strawberries) originating from Carolina are really hybrids of that species.

The beautiful Madame Tallien bathed in strawberry water to keep her skin soft and velvety. About 10 kg. (22 lb.) were crushed for each of her baths.

Fontanelle adored strawberries and ate them daily when they were in season.

Some people are allergic to strawberries. Cooking them for a few moments in boiling water can counteract this.

Strawberries must be eaten freshly gathered because they do not keep. They are used to make a soft drink and for the extraction of spirits. They may also be eaten puréed. Strawberries are used for jam-making.

Strawberry Bavarian cream – See BAVARIAN CREAM.

Cardinal strawberries. FRAISES CARDINAL – Arrange well chilled strawberries in a fruit dish. Cover them with a sweetened purée of ripe raspberries. Sprinkle with finely chopped almonds.

Strawberries in champagne. FRAISES AU CHAMPAGNE – Sugared strawberries are arranged in individual dishes or in a fruit dish and sprinkled with Champagne. Chill thoroughly.

Strawberry compote I. COMPOTE DE FRAISES – Remove stems and clean the strawberries. Add several tablespoons boiling sugar syrup. Let the fruit soak in this syrup for some time. Serve hot or cold.

Strawberry compote II. COMPOTE DE FRAISES – Cook 250 g. (9 oz., generous cup) sugar and 1 dl. ($\frac{1}{4}$ pint, $\frac{2}{3}$ cup) water to the third degree (see SUGAR). Add to this syrup 1 kg. ($2\frac{1}{4}$ lb.) large strawberries. Soak, covered, for 10 minutes.

Strawberry Condé. FRAISES CONDÉ – Sprinkle the fruit with sugar and kirsch. Leave to soak in a cool place.

Arrange in a pyramid in a border of rice which has been cooked in milk with sugar and vanilla and bound with egg yolk. It is then moulded in a ring mould, cooked in a *bain-marie*, cooled and turned out.

Serve with a sweet purée of strawberries and raspberries.

Strawberries and cream. FRAISES À LA CRÈME – Arrange strawberries in a glass dish or individual dishes. Sprinkle with sugar and cover with thick fresh cream or sweetened whipped cream.

Strawberries Czarina. FRAISES TZARINE – Stand a dish on ice. Cover the bottom with a layer of pineapple ice cream. Arrange large strawberries, soaked in kummel and sugar and chilled, on the ice cream.

Decorate with *Chantilly cream* (see CREAMS) piped through a forcing bag with a large fluted nozzle. Sprinkle with candied violets.

Strawberry ice mixture. COMPOSITION AUX FRAISES POUR GLACES – Mix $\frac{1}{2}$ litre (scant pint, $2\frac{1}{4}$ cups) strawberry purée with ½ litre (scant pint, 2¼ cups) sugar syrup prepared cold (see SUGAR). Add the juice of 2 lemons and 1 orange. Add to this as much water as is necessary to obtain a mixture of 16° to 18° density measured by the saccharometer.

Strawberries à l'impératrice. FRAISES À L'IMPÉRATRICE – Prepare a dish of rice as for *Apricots à l'impératrice* (see APRICOT). Chill. Just before serving cover the rice with 250 g. (9 oz., 2 cups) large strawberries sweetened with vanilla-flavoured or plain sugar.

Strawberry jam – See JAMS AND JELLIES.

Strawberries with liqueurs. FRAISES AUX LIQUEURS – Remove stems, clean strawberries and sugar them in a dessert dish or in individual glasses. Sprinkle with one of the following: kirsch, maraschino, cherry brandy, raspberry brandy, kummel, Fine Champagne (best Cognac) or with some other liqueur. Serve chilled.

Strawberries à la maltaise. FRAISES À LA MALTAISE – Sugar small strawberries, add orange juice and a little Curaçao and cool on ice. Put this mixture into baskets made of the oranges from which the juice has been extracted. Arrange on a dish covered with crushed ice.

Iced strawberry mousse – See ICE CREAMS AND ICES, *Iced mousses or mousselines*.

Strawberry pulp for ices. PULPE DE FRAISES POUR GLACES – Rub very ripe strawberries through a fine sieve. To ½ litre (scant pint, 2¼ cups) of this juice add 1 litre (1¾ pints, generous quart) sugar syrup at 35° measured by the saccharometer (see SUGAR) and the juice of 1 lemon. Mix well. Place in a churn freezer.

Strawberry pulp for ices, bottled. CONSERVE DE PULPE DE FRAISES POUR GLACES – Make a purée of fresh strawberries and pass through a very fine sieve. Add 250 g. (9 oz., generous cup) sugar to each 1 kg. (2¼ lb.) fruit. Mix thoroughly and put into preserving jars. Close jars and place in a canning kettle. Cover with cold water. Boil for 5 to 6 minutes and leave to cool in the canning kettle. Take the jars out, wipe and seal them. Keep in a cool place in a slanting position.

Strawberry ratafia. RATAFIA DE FRAISES – Proceed as for *Raspberry liqueur* (see LIQUEUR) using ripe strawberries instead of raspberries.

Strawberry sauce – See SAUCE, *Dessert sauces*.

Strawberry soufflé – See SOUFFLÉS, *Sweet soufflés*.

Strawberry tarts and tartlets – See TARTS, TARTLETS.

Strawberries with various dessert wines. FRAISES AUX VINS DE LIQUEURS – Remove stems and clean strawberries. Dredge with sugar. Arrange in individual glass dishes or in a fruit dish. Sprinkle with Frontignan, muscatel, Madeira, sherry, port or Marsala. Serve chilled.

STRAWBERRY TOMATO. ALKÉKENGE – Fruit originating in Mexico where it is called Mexican tomato. It is one of several species of *physalis*. The strawberry tomato plant belongs to the same family as the tomato and the potato.

Strawberry tomato grows very well in France, in the south and around Paris. It is sometimes called husk tomato or winter cherry. The fruit is the size of a cherry, yellow in colour and has a sour-sweet taste. It is surrounded by a parchment-like calyx, yellowish-grey in colour, which does not open. Strawberry tomatoes are used in confectionery.

Strawberry tomato compote. COMPOTE D'ALKÉKENGES – *Ingredients*. 1 kg. (2¼ lb.) strawberry tomatoes, 500 g. (18 oz., 2¼ cups) sugar, 2 dl. (⅓ pint, scant cup) water, peel of 1 lemon.

Method. Make a syrup of sugar and water, bring to the boil and add the strawberry tomatoes, having removed their calyxes. Cook for 5 minutes.

Remove the fruit with a perforated spoon, transfer to an earthenware bowl and put the lemon peel in the middle. Boil down the syrup and pour it over the fruit.

It is essential not to allow the lemon peel to boil with the compote as the taste will be entirely different.

Glacé strawberry tomatoes in caramel. ALKÉKENGES GLACÉES AU CARAMEL – Open the fruit and roll in powdered gum arabic. Dip into sugar syrup cooked to crack degree (see SUGAR). Take out with a perforated spoon and place on a slab of marble or on a lightly greased metal sheet.

Glacé strawberry tomatoes in fondant icing. ALKÉKENGES GLACÉES AU FONDANT – Coat with *Fondant icing* (see ICING) white, pink or yellow, flavoured with kirsch, raspberry or pineapple essence.

Open the calyx and turn back to form a stalk. Hold the fruit by the end of the calyx and dip into hot fondant icing. Drain and place on a tray sprinkled with icing sugar. Put into paper cases.

Strawberry tomato jam. CONFITURE D'ALKÉKENGES – *Ingredients*. 1 kg. (2¼ lb.) strawberry tomatoes, 750 g. (1½ lb., 5¼ cups) loaf sugar, 6 dl. (1 pint, 2½ cups) water.

Method. Make a syrup of the sugar and water and add the strawberry tomatoes, with their calyxes removed. Bring to the boil. Remove scum as it forms. Boil for about 20 minutes. Draw the pan to the side of the stove and leave the jam to cool a little. Put into jars and seal like any other jam.

Strawberry tomato syrup. SIROP D'ALKÉKENGES – *Ingredients*. 1½ kg. (3½ lb.) strawberry tomatoes, 1½ kg. (3½ lb. 7 cups) sugar, 1½ litres (2¾ pints, 3¼ pints) water.

Method. Put the sugar and water into a large saucepan. Bring to the boil. Drop the strawberry tomatoes in and boil for 10 minutes. Drain in a fine sieve, or cheesecloth placed over an earthenware bowl. Measure with a saccharometer; it should register 28° (see SUGAR). If the degree is lower, boil down the syrup. If it is above 28°, add a little water. Whisk an egg white with 1 dl. (6 tablespoons, scant ½ cup) water in a basin using an egg whisk. Allow the syrup to clarify, leaving it for 20 minutes at the side of the stove, simmering very gently.

Strain through a muslin bag. Heat the bottles gradually and pour in the boiling syrup. Cork the bottles, securely.

STRIP. EFFEUILLER – To take the leaves or petals off the stalk of a plant. Thus globe artichoke is stripped if the heart only is to be used. Herbs, such as chervil and sorrel, are also stripped before use.

STRITZEL (Austrian cookery) – In Austria the *stritzel* is the classic Christmas cake.

Ingredients. 1 kg. (2¼ lb., 9 cups) sifted flour, 250 g. (9 oz., generous cup) butter, 6 eggs, 60 g. (2½ oz., ⅓ cup) sugar, 15 g. (½ oz., ½ cake) fresh yeast, ½ litre (scant pint, 2¼ cups) warm milk, 125 g. (4½ oz., ¾ cup) each sultanas and raisins, 2 lemons, 1½ teaspoons salt, a pinch of grated nutmeg and a pinch of powdered cumin.

Method. Make a dough with a quarter of the flour, a little milk, the yeast, salt, sugar, nutmeg and a little butter. Leave to rise.

Knock back the dough after adding to it the rest of the flour. Add the eggs, the remaining butter, the raisins and sultanas and work in the same way as for *Brioche dough* (see DOUGH), keeping the mixture fairly firm. Leave to rise again.

Knock back the dough once more. Divide it into pieces – 9 are needed to make a *stritzel*: 4 large, 3 medium and 2 small. Make all these pieces into 'tails' of the same length and plait the 4 largest. Lay this plait on a buttered baking sheet. Plait the 3 medium-sized tails and place on top of the first. Twist the 2 smallest tails and set on top of the plaits. Stick the ends together neatly. Leave to rise a little.

Brush with egg, sprinkle with a little salt and caraway seeds. Bake in a fairly hot oven.

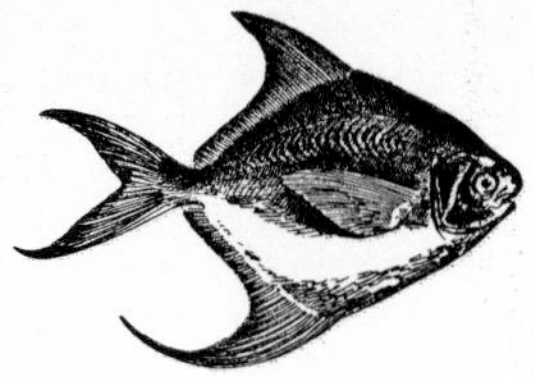

Stromateus

STROMATEUS (Rudderfish). STROMATÉE – Fish of warm and temperate seas, inhabiting the Mediterranean, where it is called *stromatée fiatole*, *lapuga*, in Nice, and *lippa*, in Sète. Its flesh is very delicate and is prepared in the same way as turbot (q.v.).

STRUDEL (Bavarian cookery) – National cake of Bavaria. It is made of noodle pastry with extra butter and is rolled out as thinly as possible.

Divide the pastry into squares and spread each with a mixture of diced apples, butter, currants and chopped almonds, flavoured with cinnamon and a little brandy.

Moisten the edges of the strudels, roll them, and put into a buttered sauté dish. Sprinkle with melted butter and brown. Pour a little milk into the dish and poach, covered, in the oven. The strudels are cooked when the milk has been absorbed. Sprinkle with sugar when they come out of the oven, and eat hot.

STUFF, TO. FARCIR – To fill with farce or other mixture (purée, *salpicon*, *ragoût*, etc.) the interior of fish, chicken, game, meat (slitting it to make a pocket), hollowed out vegetables, etc.

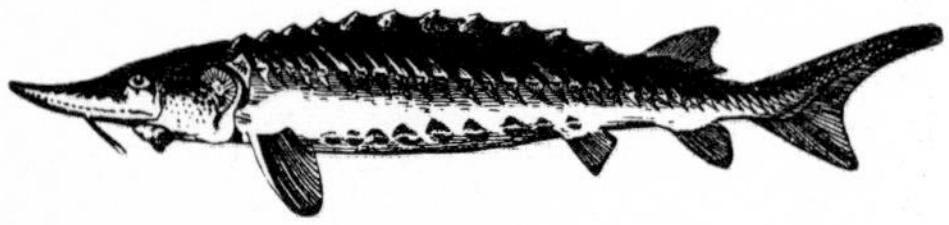

Sturgeon

STURGEON. ESTURGEON – Large migratory fish, which lives in the sea and goes up rivers to spawn.

This fish was once plentiful in certain French rivers. It is now rarely found except in the Garonne. In Germany, Russia and the Balkans, sturgeons 6 to 7 m. (20 to 23 feet) long are quite often caught.

There are two breeds to be found in European waters, the *great sturgeon* (called in England the *royal sturgeon*), and the *common sturgeon*.

The *sterlet*, a fish much prized in Russia, is a breed of sturgeon caught in the Volga.

Although rather indigestible, sturgeon is quite tasty. Those caught in fresh water in the spring are the most sought after.

Sturgeons' eggs are made into caviare, a highly prized delicacy, which has always been expensive.

Vésiga is another product of the sturgeon. It is much used in Russian cookery and is obtained by drying the spinal marrow of the sturgeon in a special manner.

In Russia, where the sturgeon is highly esteemed, it is eaten fresh or salted. In France, sturgeon is cut into steaks or thick slices or *fricandeau* which are braised like *fricandeau* of veal. It may also be smoked like salmon.

Sturgeon à la Brimont. ESTURGEON À LA BRIMONT – Fillet a medium-sized sturgeon. Trim the fillets. Thread anchovy fillets into them. Place in a baking dish lined with a *fondue* of carrots, onions and celery, finely sliced and cooked slowly in butter until very tender. Cover with 2 peeled, chopped and deseeded tomatoes mixed with 4 tablespoons coarsely diced mushrooms. Surround with potatoes cut into little balls with a ball-scoop, half cooked in salted water and drained. Moisten with 1 dl. (6 tablespoons, scant $\frac{1}{2}$ cup) dry white wine. Dot with 50 g. (2 oz., $\frac{1}{4}$ cup) butter, cut into tiny pieces. Bake in a cool oven, basting frequently. Five minutes before taking out of the oven, sprinkle with breadcrumbs and brown lightly.

Sturgeon in Champagne. ESTURGEON AU CHAMPAGNE – Skin a medium-sized sturgeon. Trim it. Stud with truffles. Steep for 1 hour in a marinade of brandy, salt, spices and pepper.

Put the fish in a pan on a buttered grid. Moisten with fish *fumet* made with dry Champagne, boiled down and enriched with 2 dl. ($\frac{1}{3}$ pint, scant cup) fine *mirepoix* made of carrots, onions and celery, cooked slowly in butter until very tender.

Bring to the boil on the stove, then cook in a moderate oven, basting frequently.

Drain the sturgeon. Glaze in the oven. Place on a large dish and surround with the garnish indicated.

Moisten the stock with $2\frac{1}{2}$ dl. (scant $\frac{1}{2}$ pint, generous cup) dry champagne. Boil down. Add $2\frac{1}{2}$ dl. (scant $\frac{1}{2}$ pint, generous cup) *Espagnole sauce* (see SAUCE) based on fish stock, carefully skimmed. Boil down. Season. Add 100 g. (4 oz., $\frac{1}{2}$ cup) butter. Strain. Pour over the fish.

Sturgeon braised in champagne can be served plain in its own juice, or with various garnishes. Among the most suitable garnishes are the following: *Chambord*, mushrooms, braised cucumbers, turtle, truffles.

Curried sturgeon. ESTURGEON AU CURRIE – Cook a fillet of sturgeon weighing about 800 g. ($1\frac{3}{4}$ lb.) in butter, with 2 large sliced onions and a *bouquet garni*. Season with salt, pepper and 2 teaspoons curry powder. Drain the sturgeon and put it on a serving dish. Keep hot.

Dilute the pan juices with 2 dl. ($\frac{1}{3}$ pint, scant cup) dry white wine. Boil down. Moisten with 3 dl. ($\frac{1}{2}$ pint, $1\frac{1}{4}$ cups) *Velouté sauce* (see SAUCE) based on fish stock. Season with 2 teaspoons curry powder mixed with 5 tablespoons (6 tablespoons) fresh cream. Boil for a few seconds. Add 3 tablespoons (scant $\frac{1}{4}$ cup) butter. Strain this sauce and pour over the sturgeon. Serve with *Rice à l'indienne* (see RICE).

Fillets of sturgeon Boris. FILETS D'ESTURGEON BORIS – Fillet a medium-sized sturgeon. Trim the fillets. Steep for 1 hour in a marinade of oil, lemon juice, salt, paprika and spices. Drain.

Put them in an ovenware dish lined with 2 dl. ($\frac{1}{3}$ pint, scant cup) dry *duxelles* mixed with chopped chives. Moisten with 2 dl. ($\frac{1}{3}$ pint, scant cup) dry white wine. Bring to the boil on the stove then cover and cook in the oven for 10 minutes. Cover the fillets with coarsely shredded truffles. Pour the marinade over them. Moisten with 3 dl. ($\frac{1}{2}$ pint, $1\frac{1}{4}$ cups) fresh cream. Dot with tiny pieces of butter. Finish cooking in a cool oven, basting frequently with cream. Serve in the ovenware dish.

Fricandeau of sturgeon à la hongroise. FRICANDEAU D'ESTURGEON À LA HONGROISE – Brown a thick slice of sturgeon in butter with finely diced onions. Season with salt, paprika and a *bouquet garni*. Moisten with 2 dl. ($\frac{1}{3}$ pint, scant cup) white wine. Boil down. Add 3 dl. ($\frac{1}{2}$ pint, $1\frac{1}{4}$ cups) *Velouté sauce* (see SAUCE) based on fish stock. Finish cooking in a slow oven. Add butter to the sauce and pour it over the fish. Serve with boiled potatoes.

Fricandeau of sturgeon au jus. FRICANDEAU D'ESTURGEON AU

JUS – Cut a slice or *fricandeau* from a rather thick sturgeon fillet weighing 800 g. to 1 kg. (1¾ to 2¼ lb.). Thread with thin lardoons. Cook as for *Veal fricandeau* (see VEAL).

Fricandeau of sturgeon with sorrel. FRICANDEAU D'ESTURGEON À L'OSEILLE – Cook as for *Veal fricandeau* (see VEAL) and serve with braised sorrel.

Sturgeon steaks in cream. DARNES D'ESTURGEON À LA CRÈME – Skin the sturgeon and cut it into slices or steaks. Season with salt and paprika. Line a baking dish with chopped onion, cooked slowly in butter until very tender. Lay the slices of sturgeon on top. Moisten with 2 dl. (⅓ pint, scant cup) white wine. Bring to the boil on the stove. Bake in the oven for 15 minutes. Pour on thick fresh cream. Dot with tiny pieces of butter. Finish cooking in the oven, basting frequently.

SUBRICS – Small preparations served as an *hors-d'œuvre*, small *entrée* or garnish.

Subrics are a variety of croquettes, but they are never coated in egg and breadcrumbs. They are cooked in butter in a sauté pan, not in deep fat.

Bind the basic ingredient, cut into dice, with a mixture of *Allemande sauce* or *Béchamel sauce* (see SAUCE) and beaten egg. Season.

Using a spoon, divide this mixture into 50 to 60 g. (2 to 2½ oz.) pieces and cook in a pan in clarified butter or oil.

Keep the subrics apart in the pan so that they can spread without running into each other. Drain the subrics, arrange them in a circle on a dish and garnish with fried parsley. Serve with sauce, or as they are.

Some subric mixtures are bound only with egg, some have flour, cream or cheese added to them.

Beef subrics à la ménagère. SUBRICS DE BOEUF À LA MÉNAGÈRE – Dice 300 g. (11 oz., 2½ cups) left-over boiled beef. Put it into a basin and add 2 eggs beaten with 1 tablespoon of flour and 50 g. (2 oz., ½ cup) grated Gruyère. Season with salt and pepper and mix well.

In a frying pan, heat equal quantities of butter and oil or cooking fat. Put the beef mixture into the pan, spoonful by spoonful. Cook on both sides.

Serve with *Tomato sauce* or *Piquante sauce* (see SAUCE).

Subrics may be also made from veal, chicken, pork, sweetbreads, brains, tongue, left-over fish, etc.

Foie gras subrics. SUBRICS DE FOIE GRAS – Dice 200 g. (7 oz., 1 cup) *foie gras*. Bind with a mixture of 75 g. (3 oz., ¾ cup) flour, 1 egg and 4 or 5 tablespoons fresh double cream. Season with salt, pepper and spices.

Cook as for *Beef subrics*.

Potato subrics. SUBRICS DE POMMES DE TERRE – Break up with a fork the flesh of 6 large potatoes baked in their skins in the oven. Bind with an egg and a little *Béchamel sauce* (see SAUCE). Some grated cheese may be added if liked. Cook and serve as for *Beef subrics*.

Semolina subrics – See SEMOLINA.

Spinach subrics – See SPINACH.

SUC – Liquid obtained by squeezing an animal or vegetable substance, or by boiling down some kind of juice.

Suc of meat. SUC DE VIANDE – Name given to much reduced consommé or to the juice which runs from roast meat; also to juice pressed from raw meat.

SUCÉES – A type of *petit four* made as follows:

Mix together in a basin 250 g. (9 oz., generous cup) sugar, 250 g. (9 oz., generous cup) butter, 150 g. (5 oz., 1¼ cups) sifted flour and 5 egg yolks. Add 150 g. (5 oz., ¾ cup) finely chopped candied fruit. Fold in 5 stiffly beaten egg whites.

Make into round shapes on a buttered and floured baking sheet. Bake in a hot oven.

SUCKER. BARBIER – Name applied to various types of fish which have either a cup-shaped sucker (*Lepadogaster de Gouan*), or a sharp spine on a fin (perch).

SUCRAGE – French term for the process of adding sugar to grape juice during wine-making. (See WINE.)

SUÉDOISE – A sweet dish made by arranging fruit, cooked in syrup, in layers in an aspic mould, which is then filled with fruit or liqueur-flavoured jelly.

SUGAR. SUCRE – Sweet substance extracted from many plants; its chief sources are sugar cane, sugar beet, sugar

Manufacture of sugar in the 17th century (*Centre d'étude pour l'utilisation du sucre*)

maple and various species of palm. There are many types of sugar with various molecular structures. The most important are sucrose (cane sugar), levulose (fruit sugar), maltose (malt sugar) and lactose (milk sugar).

History – In ancient times, honey and fruit took the place of sugar all over Europe. Sugar cane was probably first grown in India, in the Ganges basin, and then in China. The word sugar seems to have been derived from the Sanskrit word *sarkara*.

Greece and Rome imported sugar as a luxury commodity or as a medicament. In the fifth century the Persians discovered a way of refining syrup. The Arabs took sugar to Egypt, Rhodes, Cyprus, North Africa, Spain and Syria. By the tenth century the sugar trade was established in the Mediterranean, centred on Venice. In the fifteenth century Lisbon took over from Venice as the centre for sugar refining.

With the coming of coffee and cocoa, the consumption of sugar increased in Europe and refineries were set up in Germany, France, Holland and England. By the eve of the French revolution, Bordeaux had 26 refineries producing a fifth of the sugar for the European market, from raw sugar cane imported from the Antilles, Maurice, and Réunion Islands. It was not until the time of Napoleon that sugar beet plantations were developed in France.

Cane sugar – Sugar cane, originating in India, then the West Indies and America, is like a reed with a spongy marrow and grows chiefly in tropical and sub-tropical areas. It is the source of about half the sugar produced commercially. The juice is pressed from the canes and is then subjected to a series of treatments to free it from impurities. The molasses is taken from the sugar, leaving a yellow sugar, known in Great Britain as Demerara sugar. This sugar is crushed fine and is known as brown sugar. Further processes of refinement remove the colour and produce granulated, castor, icing (confectioner's) and lump sugar.

Beet sugar – In 1747 a German chemist, Margraf, discovered sugar in beet juice. One of his followers, a French refugee named Achard, set up an experimental factory but had no financial success. His business failed but was started again in France at the instigation of Napoleon at the time of the Continental blockade. Manufacture of sugar by this method developed from that time until it became a big industry.

At first, beet sugar was said to have a bad taste and to be less sweetening than cane sugar. It was alleged to have various defects and it was necessary to show, by experiment, an absolute chemical identity between the sugar from beet and sugar from cane before consumption of beet sugar became generally accepted. It is now almost as large a source of sugar as sugar cane.

Different sorts of refined sugar – Granulated sugar is obtained by purifying the sugar obtained from beet or cane. The sugar is dissolved in water and treated for impurities. The solution is then evaporated and crystallised to give crystals of the required size.

Castor sugar is produced in the same way but the process is altered to yield smaller crystals. It can also be produced by grinding down granulated sugar.

Icing sugar results from crushing granulated sugar to produce a fine powder.

Loaf or cube sugar is made by pressing damp granulated sugar into moulds and then drying it to make the crystals stick together.

Brown sugar is sugar with the molasses removed but it is otherwise unrefined. It is obtained by crystallising from the syrup remaining at the end of the refining process. There is an even less-refined type of sugar called *vergeoise* in France.

Sugar candy is manufactured by the slow crystallisation of

Sugar model of the Merchandise Mart in Chicago, made by an American cook

sugar syrup. This contains a certain proportion of invert sugar. It is used in the manufacture of Champagne wines. When heated to the crack degree, lightly coloured and acidulated, it becomes barley sugar, or apple sugar if it is left transparent. If this sugar is pulled it takes on a silky appearance. True barley sugar used to be manufactured from a concoction from barley, but this is rarely done these days.

Properties of sugar – Sugar melts at 160°C. (320°F.) and, on cooling, takes on a glossy appearance (barley sugar, candy sugar) but tends after a while to resume its crystalline structure. If it is heated further, it becomes a straw-colour, then brown, forming caramel at 180°C. (356°F.), becoming dark caramel at 190°C. (374°F.), black jack at 210°C. (410°F.): finally it decomposes.

Sugar is easily soluble in water which, when cold, can dissolve double its own weight of sugar. Solubility increases with rising temperature and saturated solutions would contain:

	C.	F.
64·18 per cent of sugar at	0°	(32°)
64·87 per cent of sugar at	5°	(41°)
65·56 per cent of sugar at	10°	(50°)
66·33 per cent of sugar at	15°	(59°)
67·09 per cent of sugar at	20°	(68°)
67·89 per cent of sugar at	25°	(77°)
68·70 per cent of sugar at	30°	(86°)
69·55 per cent of sugar at	35°	(95°)
70·42 per cent of sugar at	40°	(104°)
71·32 per cent of sugar at	45°	(113°)
72·25 per cent of sugar at	50°	(122°)
73·20 per cent of sugar at	55°	(131°)
74·18 per cent of sugar at	60°	(140°)
75·18 per cent of sugar at	65°	(149°)
76·12 per cent of sugar at	70°	(158°)
77·27 per cent of sugar at	75°	(167°)
78·38 per cent of sugar at	80°	(176°)
79·46 per cent of sugar at	85°	(185°)
80·61 per cent of sugar at	90°	(194°)
81·77 per cent of sugar at	95°	(203°)
82·97 per cent of sugar at	100°	(212°)

As the quantity of sugar dissolved in a given volume of water is increased so the density of the solution increases and the boiling point is raised. These factors provide a means of classifying sugar solutions and syrups.

Food value of sugar – Sugar is a reasonably pure carbohydrate food. It has a high calorific value: 100 g. ($3\frac{1}{2}$ oz.) of sugar yields 393 calories. It is therefore a very concentrated energy foodstuff which is readily absorbed and leaves practically no residue. Thanks to its rapid assimilation, sugar restores energy very quickly, though only for a limited time, in subjects exhausted by fatigue. This has been shown by tests carried out on different armies.

It is necessary therefore to consider sugar as a condiment, an energy food and something which is eaten frequently. For culinary purposes, sugar is used for sweet dishes, confectionery and for making sauces, *ragoûts*, etc. Sugar boiled to the caramel degree is used as a colouring agent for soups, stocks and sauces.

Sugar boiling – Only good quality sugar should be used for cooking. A heavy-based saucepan is the most suitable cooking utensil.

Before proceeding with sugar boiling it is necessary to prepare a syrup by dissolving a certain quantity of sugar in one third of its weight of water. The mixture is put over heat and the sugar should be thoroughly dissolved before the solution is brought to the boil. It is skimmed carefully to remove the impurities of the sugar which rise to the surface. The sides of the pan should be cleaned occasionally with a clean, damp pastry brush to remove any scum which has collected. Do not stir the syrup while it is boiling otherwise crystals will form in the solution and cause graining.

A further method of preventing sugar graining is to add 125 g. (4 oz., 1 cup) glucose for every 500 g. (18 oz., $2\frac{1}{4}$ cups) sugar.

When the boiling produces small bubbles close together, the sugar has begun to cook. From then on it is important to watch the syrup carefully in order to stop the cooking at the required degree.

Before arriving at the caramel degree, the sugar passes through six different stages, which are designated by the following terms: small thread, large thread, small ball, large ball, small crack, hard crack. Beyond this degree the sugar becomes caramel.

The various sugar degrees can be determined by the following indications which after careful practice can easily be recognised.

First degree: small gloss or small thread. Using a teaspoon, take a little of the sugar solution and place it in a cup of cold water. Hold the cooled sugar between the thumb and forefinger and pull gently apart. The formation of short threads indicates that the sugar is at the small thread degree.

Second degree: large gloss or large thread. Continue boiling for a short while, then carry out the preceding test again. When the sugar is pulled between the thumb and forefinger it should form longer, stronger threads. This shows that the sugar is at the large thread stage.

Third degree: small ball. Boil the syrup for a little longer before testing for this stage. Place $\frac{1}{2}$ teaspoon of the syrup in a cup of cold water. The sugar should form a small ball when rolled between the thumb and fingers. This indicates that the sugar has reached the small ball degree.

Fourth degree: large ball. Boil the syrup for a short while then repeat the previous test. The ball which is formed between the fingers should be firmer but still malleable. This indicates that the large ball degree has been reached.

Fifth degree: small crack. Continue boiling the syrup for a little longer, then dip a teaspoon into the syrup and immediately into cold water. The cooled sugar from the spoon will harden immediately to form a brittle thread. This thread will bend and then break if pressure is applied, indicating that the sugar is at the small crack stage.

Sixth degree: hard crack. Once the sugar has arrived at the previous stage it must be watched very carefully for it will pass rapidly through the last stage and turn into caramel. The above test is repeated. The sugar should form very brittle strands which break without bending if it has reached the hard crack degree.

Caramel: When the sugar has arrived at the hard crack degree it takes only a few seconds for it to become caramel. It is comparatively easy to recognise when sugar has turned into caramel. The sugar becomes light golden then the colour deepens to give a dark brown syrup. When cooled the sugar is very brittle and breaks easily.

As soon as the desired degree is obtained, the saucepan must be taken away from the heat and the sugar kept at the same temperature on the edge of the stove.

Some writers use the term *à la nappe* to designate a degree which precedes small thread. Others distinguish certain intermediate degrees between the thread degree and the ball degree, these being called small pearl, large pearl, little soufflé and large soufflé. At the small pearl degree the sugar boils, forming itself into small balls, like pearls. At the large pearl degree the pearls are better formed and more separated. At the soufflé degree small balls detach themselves from the skimmer when one blows across its holes after having dipped it in the syrup. In the large soufflé degree the bubbles are like snow-flakes.

To identify these various degrees or density one can use a saccharometer or Baumé sugar weight-scale which is graduated from 0° to 44°. The degrees usually registered on the Baumé thermometer or saccharometer, and their equivalents on Fahrenheit and Centigrade scales are as follows:

Names	*Density degrees*	°*C*	°*F*
Small thread or small gloss	30°	101°	214°
Large thread or large gloss	30°	103°	217°
Small pearl	33°	103°–105°	217°–221°
Large pearl	35°	107°	224°
Soufflé (blow)	37°	110°	230°
Large soufflé (feather)	37°	111°	232°
Small ball	38°	116°	241°
Large ball	39°	121°	250°
Crack	40°	149°–150°	300°–302°
Light caramel		150°	302°
Dark caramel			

The crack degree cannot be registered on the Baumé thermometer but various other degrees can be recognised on a special thermometer, graduated from 100°C. to 175°C. (212°F. to 347°F.) With this apparatus, which is used in the manufacture of confectionery, it is easy to distinguish one degree from another up to a point very close to caramel.

	°*C.*	°*F.*
Light crack	129°	264°
Medium crack	133°	271°
Hard crack	143°	289°
Extra hard crack	168°	334°
Caramel	180°	356°

The instructions given for the boiling of sugar must be observed carefully. The intervals between the various stages in the cooking are very short. The sugar used to obtain a perfect boiling must be first grade.

Sugar syrup prepared cold – When sugar syrup prepared in advance is used, it is necessary to check the exact quantity of sugar and water that it contains. Here are two small tables which enable one to recognise both the quantity of sugar and the quantity of water corresponding to the Baumé scale.

For 1 litre ($1\frac{3}{4}$ pints, generous quart) sugar solution:

Degrees Baumé	*Weight of sugar*
1°	20 g. ($\frac{2}{3}$ oz.)
2°	40 g. ($1\frac{1}{2}$ oz.)
3°	60 g. (2 oz.)
5°	120 g. ($4\frac{1}{2}$ oz.)
10°	250 g. (9 oz.)
15°	500 g. (18 oz.)
21°	750 g. (25 oz.)
25°	875 g. (31 oz.)
27°	1000 g. (35 oz.)
29°	1225 g. (41 oz.)
31°	1250 g. (42 oz.)

For 1 kg. ($2\frac{1}{4}$ lb., $2\frac{1}{2}$ cups) sugar:

Degrees Baumé	*Weight of water*
32°	50 g. ($1\frac{3}{4}$ oz.)
30°	70 g. (2 oz.)
25°	100 g. ($4\frac{1}{2}$ oz.)
22°	130 g. ($3\frac{1}{2}$ oz.)
20°	150 g. ($5\frac{1}{2}$ oz.)
19°	170 g. (6 oz.)
18°	200 g. (7 oz.)

There are two other methods of classifying syrups, one of which is to note the temperature at boiling point. The other is to determine the density of the syrup with a hygrometer which gives the density based on the water content. There is also a special syrup measuring instrument from which a simple reading of the strength of the sugar solution can be taken.

The following points can also prove useful: 2 kg. ($4\frac{1}{2}$ lb., 9 cups) sugar dissolved in 1 litre ($1\frac{3}{4}$ pints, generous quart) cold water measures 34°. The same quantity of sugar dissolved in hot water would only measure 32°.

FLAVOURED SUGARS USED IN CONFECTIONERY, PÂTISSERIE. SUCRES EMPLOYÉS EN PÂTISSERIE, EN CONFISERIE

Anise sugar. SUCRE D'ANIS – Dry 50 g. (2 oz.) anise, wrapped in paper, in a warm oven. Pound finely in a mortar with 500 g. (18 oz., $2\frac{1}{4}$ cups) sugar. Sift through a fine sieve. Keep in a well-stoppered jar in a dry place.

Anise sugar is used to make *petits fours*, as are all flavoured sugars.

Cinnamon sugar. SUCRE À LA CANNELLE – Proceed as for *Vanilla sugar* (see below), replacing the vanilla with 1 thin stick of cinnamon. Chop the cinnamon, mix with 1 tablespoon castor sugar then pound with another tablespoon castor sugar. Sift through a fine sieve. Pound the cinnamon remaining in the sieve with another tablespoon of sugar and sift.

Clove sugar. SUCRE DE GIROFLE – Proceed as for *Anise sugar* with 20 g. ($\frac{3}{4}$ oz.) cloves and 500 g. (18 oz., $2\frac{1}{4}$ cups) sugar.

Ginger sugar. SUCRE DE GINGEMBRE – Proceed as for *Anise sugar* with 30 g. (1 oz.) ginger and 500 g. (18 oz., $2\frac{1}{4}$ cups) sugar.

Icing sugars and pastillage – See ICING, PASTILLAGE.

Lemon peel sugar. SUCRE AU ZESTE DE CITRON – Pare enough lemons to yield 60 g. (2 oz.) lemon peel. Dry this peel in the shade and chop it. Put into a mortar with 500 g. (18 oz., 4 cups) lump sugar. Pound. Press through a fine sieve.

Orange sugar (Carême's recipe). SUCRE D'ORANGE – 'Take some sweet Maltese oranges with very fine skins. Grate the peel with a lump of sugar, but lightly, so as not to reach the white pith which is immediately under the peel, because this is very bitter and spoils the fruit flavour.

'As the surface of the sugar becomes coloured, scrape it with a knife to remove the peel which becomes stuck to it by repeated rubbing. Recommence the operation with the same care. Dry the sugar in a low oven, or at the open door of a warm oven. Crush it and press through a fine sieve.

'For Seville orange, lemon, citron or mandarine sugar, proceed in the same way.'

Orange flower sugar. SUCRE DE FLEURS D'ORANGER – Proceed as for *Anise sugar* with 250 g. (9 oz.) orange flower petals which have been dried, and 500 g. (18 oz., $2\frac{1}{4}$ cups) sugar.

Orange peel sugar. SUCRE AU ZESTE D'ORANGE – Prepare with orange peel in the same way as for *Lemon peel sugar*.

Perfumed sugar (Carême's recipe). SUCRE ODORÉS – 'The pastrycooks in the shops use distilled essences such as that of lemon, bergamot, rosewater, orange flower water and powdered orris. These are used to flavour their sweet cakes and biscuits.

'The true pastrycook in the home rejects these perfumes and flavours his sweets with the pleasant natural tastes of orange, Seville orange, lemon, orange flowers, coffee, vanilla, green anise or saffron.

Vanilla sugar. SUCRE VANILLÉ – Split 60 g. (2 oz.) vanilla pods and chop them finely. Put into a mortar with 500 g. (18 oz., 4 cups) lump sugar and pound finely. Press through a fine sieve.

SULTAN-HEN. POULE SULTAN – Web-footed aquatic bird, prepared for the table in the same way as the coot.

SULTANE – Large pastry set in the middle of a pattern of lattice-work sugar, surmounted by spun sugar plumes.

SULTANE (À LA) – Name applied to various preparations. *Velouté de volaille à la sultane* is a soup finished off with pistachio butter. All dishes called *à la sultane* are characterised by the inclusion of pistachios, generally in the form of pistachio butter.

The name *à la sultane* is also used for sweets and pastries, for example *apricots à la sultane*, and *bavarois à la sultane*.

SUMMER SNIPE or SEA-LARK. ALOUETTE DE MER – Plover of the order of waders, which hunters call sandpipers. Its flesh is quite delicate. All recipes given for woodcock are applicable to summer snipe.

SUMPTUOUS. SOMPTEUEX – That which is magnificent and which costs a great deal. In gastronomy, sumptuousness is not always synonymous with culinary perfection.

SUNDAES (ICED COUPES). COUPES GLACÉES – Composite sweet with ice cream as the main ingredient, served in glass or silver ice-cups; for this reason they are called *coupes* in France.

The glasses are usually filled with one or more kinds of ice cream and decorated with fresh or crystallised fruit, or with *Chantilly cream* (see CREAMS).

Sundaes may be presented in a great many ways. The *coupe Jaques* is regarded as the classic sundae. Recipes for this and other iced *coupes* are given in the section on ICE CREAMS AND ICES.

Sundaes à la cévenole. COUPES GLACÉES À LA CÉVENOLE – Make $\frac{1}{2}$ litre (scant pint, $2\frac{1}{4}$ cups) *Vanilla ice cream* (see ICE CREAMS AND ICES). Whisk enough cream with sugar to make 3 dl. ($\frac{1}{2}$ pint, $1\frac{1}{4}$ cups) *Chantilly cream* (see CREAMS). Break 250 g. (9 oz.) *marrons glacés* into tiny fragments and steep them for 30 minutes in a glass of kirsch.

To serve; line the bottom of the ice cream glasses with *marrons glacés*. Top with a smooth layer of vanilla ice cream.

Raspberry sundae

Decorate with *marrons glacés* and Chantilly cream piped through a forcing bag.

SUNDEW. ROSSOLIS – Aromatic plant whose leaves can be eaten as salad, or cooked.

SUNFLOWER. TOURNESOL – This plant, *Helianthus annuus*, originally from Mexico and Peru, was introduced into Europe by the Spaniards. Nowadays it is cultivated mainly in southern Russia, Poland and Italy.

From a nutritional point of view one must differentiate between certain edible species and others which are only valuable for their oil.

Sunflower oil is rich in essential fatty acids and seems to bring about the lowering of the blood cholesterol level. It is a valuable aid in the diets of sufferers from atherosclerosis.

Sunflower seeds are especially popular in Russia and Poland, where they are nibbled like almonds. They are an excellent energy food.

SUPERSTITIONS OF THE TABLE. SUPERSTITIONS DE TABLE – There have always been superstitions connected with eating. Some have an explanation; others remain a mystery. We have chosen only a few, well known and not so well known, to give a general idea of the form these superstitions took, but have not included the superstitions linked with old wives' tales concerning the care and curing of the sick, nor those connected with witchcraft. These are outside the subject dealt with here.

Unlucky thirteen – You have invited some friends to dine. There ought to have been fifteen, but two were unable to attend. You are appalled to find that you have thirteen guests. Make haste and find a fourteenth person or ask the thirteenth not to come; for, among these thirteen, one is sure to die before the year is out.

It was thirteen apostles who celebrated Easter. One of them betrayed his master and hanged himself. The number thirteen is therefore unlucky; among thirteen persons there is one who is a traitor and a potential hanged man.

The number thirteen is only dangerous at table, for it was there that the treachery of Judas was discovered. There is no need to worry if numbers total thirteen elsewhere.

Misplaced fork and spoon – Your young son having no idea of the misfortunes the misplacing of a fork and spoon may engender, places his fork and spoon crosswise on his plate. Destroy this fatal sign immediately, for it is possible that the food you serve him will poison and eventually kill him. The crossed fork and spoon, in the form of a Saint Andrew's cross, presaged no good to our forebears.

Spilt salt – Your host has served you with a slice of tender beef, thick and juicy. You decide to whet the gravy with a little salt. You grasp the salt cellar but inadvertently capsize it. The salt spills on to the table and suddenly there is disquiet all round. Quickly collect a few of the scattered grains and fling them over your shoulder to keep away evil. Salt was the symbol of friendship, each person offering it to the other at the beginning of the meal. It was essential not to capsize the salt cellar, which would have been a sign of disagreement. Likewise, one took great care not to give a knife as a present, for it would break the friendship.

Egg shell – Ought one to break the shell of an egg after eating the contents? This custom has its roots in the past. It is referred to by ancient and modern writers.

The Romans attached great importance to it. The egg was regarded as an emblem of nature, a substance that was both mysterious and sacred. People were convinced that magicians used eggs in their incantations, emptying them and drawing magic characters from inside the shell. These had the power to cause much harm. One crushed the shell to destroy the evil spell. Occasionally it was enough to pierce it with a knife, or to rap it three times.

Eggs are also used as an augury. Julia, daughter of Augustus, being pregnant by Tiberius, ardently desired a son. To make sure that her desires would be realised, she placed an egg in her bosom and warmed it carefully. When she was obliged to remove it, she gave it to a wet nurse who continued to impart the precious warmth. The omen was a fortunate one, according to Pliny, and did not disappoint the desires of the princess: she had a young cock from the egg and a male child from her husband.

Upside-down bread – If bread, the staff of life, is turned upside down it signifies death. Respect due to bread demands that it should never be in such a position on the table, otherwise misfortune will result.

The last drop of wine in the bottle – If you drink it there is the chance that you will marry within the year or, if you are already married, you will have a daughter. No one knows why. The reason has been long forgotten. Perhaps it is the symbol of poverty. Marriage, like daughters, it is said, costs man dearly.

Spilt wine – In Rome, a little wine used to be spilt on the table before a repast in honour of the gods. It is therefore a lucky gesture, an expression of gratitude which one hopes will be rewarded.

Blossoming of the vine (taken from an 1830 manual) – 'Does it cause the wines to ferment in their casks? And what about other fruit? Does it make liqueurs and jams ferment?

'You assure me, mademoiselle, that your redcurrant, blackcurrant jellies, your cherry, plum and apricot jams ferment in their jars whenever the redcurrant and blackcurrant bushes, cherry trees, etc., in your garden begin to flower. Your butler attests that the same phenomenon takes place in your casks when the vine is in blossom. You conclude from this that there is an evident connection between wine and the blossoming of the vine; between preserves and the blossoming fruit trees and bushes; that these flowers send out corpuscles which mix with the wine and jams and make them ferment.

'Allow me to amend your views. By a law of nature, a single cause reacts identically on two bodies which have the same dispositions. Thus two strings of an instrument that are in unison need only a single vibration to reverberate together. During the blossoming period of trees and vines, the air is at exactly the right temperature to ferment whatever substances are prone to fermentation; its action may extend to the wine, even though it is enclosed in casks, and to your berries although they are in pots. The phenomenon you refer to occurs in America and Asia as it does in Europe and at precisely the same moment despite the different seasons in those latitudes. Now, would you have it that the vines of France, of the Canaries, of Spain send corpuscles to Asia and America to make the wine ferment? Would you have it that these swarms of corpuscles leave our shores, cross the seas, searching in thousands of places until they find the precise cask of wine analogous to them? The famous Sir Digby supported this paradox, but he only wished to make fun of us. In the end, it is we who have made fun of him.'

Saint Stephen's cabbage – It is said that St. Stephen hid in a field of cabbages to escape martyrdom. For this reason it is inadvisable to eat this excellent vegetable on St. Stephen's day.

Does melon make one feverish? (from a book of the nineteenth century) – 'The origin of the melon is rather obscure. Was it brought to us by world conquerors like so many other fruits that enrich our gardens and decorate our tables? Was it perhaps discovered during the conquest of Africa by the Scipios and Metellus? It was not raised here in our temperate zones, under our cold and cloudy skies. Its delicate temperament, the attentive care it demands, the precautions it calls for, all proclaim it a foreigner who has not yet acquired his right of naturalisation.

'Under a thick outer skin it hides valuable and distinguished qualities; and as a man of great wit declared: "Like a rough diamond, the more rough and rugged its outward appearance, the better it is."

'Pliny acknowledged that its flesh is fine, delicate and sweet but also pointed out that it was difficult to digest, and made its effect felt next morning. However, he attests that there is nothing harmful in the melon despite the fact that at least two emperors have died as a result of eating too much of it.

'Blame must not be laid on the melon for the autumnal fevers that crop up at the end of September, but on certain atmospheric conditions that remain something of a mystery. It would be dangerous to eat it when perspiring heavily, just as it would be dangerous to drink cold water under such circumstances. If the melon were responsible for producing autumnal fevers then the rich would suffer most, since it is they who eat most melons; but such fevers are more common among those who eat very few melons and among country people who hardly ever see one.'

SUPPORT or PRESENTATION BASE. SUPPORT OU FOND DE DRESSAGE – Piece of food used in the presentation of hot or cold dishes. The base or mount for hot dishes is usually a croûton of a sandwich loaf cut to the shape and size of the piece of food that is to be placed upon it. These croûtons are fixed in position with a mixture of egg white and flour on the heated serving dish. Their rôle is to raise the principal item of food sufficiently to allow the garnishes to be arranged around it attractively.

Formerly the mounts were made of pounded, cooked rice which was moulded to the desired shape and decoratively trimmed.

Bread croûtons are also used for the presentation of cold foods that are slightly raised in order to accommodate the garnish. They are trimmed to a decorative shape and spread with half-melted butter. The recognised procedure was to pipe the croûtons supporting cold foods with coloured butter.

The above bases and mounts should only be used if the recipe specifically requires them. The simplest arrangements are the most attractive.

SUPRÊMES – See CHICKEN, *Suprêmes of chicken*. All the methods of preparation given in that section are also applicable to *suprêmes* of partridge and other game birds.

SURESNES – The vineyards of Suresnes were planted in 918 by the priests of the abbey of Saint-Germain-des-Prés, squires of Suresnes by the grace of Charles III.

The principal vineyard, called 'des Seigneurs', covers 18 arpents (59,000 square metres). Others followed, and at the census of 1789, there were 42 arpents and 11 perch planted with vines.

Between the end of the nineteenth century and the beginning of the twentieth century, this light, bitter, slightly laxative wine had lost the qualities that had made its reputation in the past.

There is constant mention of the *petit vin de Suresnes* of which Henri IV was so fond. King Henry had a delicate palate and the acid wine of the Seine at the foot of Mont Valerien could not begin to compare with the delicate wines served at Court. There seems to have been some confusion over the place of origin. It was definitely not the wine of Suresnes that the 'Vert-Galant' loved so well but that of Surène, from the name of a vineyard situated near Vendôme, which still exists today.

SWALLOW. HIRONDELLE – In spite of the fact that swallows are protected birds in France they are still sometimes eaten in the guise of spit-roasted 'small birds'.

The nests of the salangane or Far-Eastern sea-swallow, which these birds make by regurgitating a gelatinous substance contained in their crops, are highly prized as food by the Chinese. (The jelly produced by the birds comes from the seaweed on which they feed.) So-called 'swallows nests' are sold in Europe, but these are sometimes made from agar-agar.

Salangane swallows' nests ar not used in China solely for the preparation of the celebrated birds' nest soup. They are also used as garnishes for various dishes, taking the place of cocks' combs and cocks' kidneys, mushrooms and truffles in composite *ragoûts* (see NESTS, *Swallows' nests*).

Swallows' nest soup CONSOMMÉ AUX NIDS D'HIRONDELLES – Make a *Chicken consommé* (see SOUPS AND BROTHS), rich in nourishing ingredients, and very clear.

Meanwhile, soak the nests for 2 hours in cold water in order to swell the sticky substance of which they are made. After it has been soaked, this substance should be transparent. Clean the filaments of the nests very carefully, removing all debris such as feathers, shells and other impurities.

Blanch the nests in boiling water for 5 to 6 minutes. Bring the *consommé* to the boil and put in the nests. Simmer gently for 45 minutes. During cooking, the nests disintegrate into thin gelatinous filaments. The sticky substance which held them together gives the soup its characteristic viscous texture.

In China, this soup is made with duck stock. It is usually served in tiny porcelain cups.

SWAN. CYGNE – Graceful web-footed lamellirostrum, tame or wild. In the Middle Ages it ranked with the peacock in providing a sumptuous roast at state banquets. It was carefully plucked before being impaled on the spit. After cooking, it was dressed in its feathers and brought ceremoniously to the table with a piece of blazing camphor or wick in its beak.

Nowadays swan is regarded as too oily and leathery for the connoisseur.

SWEDE. CHOUX-NAVETS – A root vegetable, also known as the Swedish turnip. All methods of preparation for turnip (q.v.) are applicable to swede.

SWEETBREAD. RIS – Name of the thymus of calf and lamb. This organ, situated at the top of the chest, is in two parts, of which one, round in shape, is called in French the *noix*, and the other, more elongated and less regular, is the throat sweetbread or *gorge*. The flesh of the sweetbread is white and rather soft. Chemical analysis of this substance shows that it contains 3 times more albumen and 4 to 5 times more gelatine than beef and only half as much fibre.

Calves' and lambs' sweetbreads are considered to be the most delicate products of butchery. (See OFFAL or VARIETY MEATS.)

SWEETEN. ADOUCIR – To reduce the acridity of a dish by prolonged cooking. This term also applies to diminishing the degree of saltiness in a dish by diluting it with water, milk or light stock.

SWEET POTATO. PATATE – Hardy plant with edible tubers resembling the potato. A native of India, it has now adapted to grow in all warm countries. Its taste is sweet and resembles slightly the taste of artichoke.

There are many varieties of sweet potatoes; the best are *Virginian*, with tasty yellow flesh, *White Spanish*, *Algerian*, *West Indian*, which is very large and floury, and the *Malaga Pink*. Other species of sweet potatoes cultivated in France are also very good.

Sweet potatoes, particularly *Malaga Pink*, are made into jam. They can also be preserved in syrup, when they resemble *marrons glacés*.

In the areas where sweet potatoes are cultivated, the young leaves are eaten like spinach.

Baked sweet potatoes, or sweet potatoes in jackets. PATATES EN CHEMISE, EN ROBE DE CHAMBRE – Bake the sweet potatoes in their jackets in the oven. Serve with butter.

Boiled sweet potatoes with honey (Créole cookery). PATATES AU NATURAL AVEC MIEL – Boil the sweet potatoes in water, place in the oven just long enough to dry them, and serve with honey.

Sweet potatoes à la crème. PATATES À LA CRÈME – Proceed as described in the recipe for *Potatoes à la crème* (see POTATOES).

Sweet potato croquettes. PATATES EN CROQUETTES – Prepare like *Potato croquettes* (see POTATOES).

Fried sweet potatoes. PATATES FRITES – Prepare like *Fried potatoes* (see POTATOES).

Fried sweet potatoes (Créole recipe). PATATES FRITES – Choose round, even-sized sweet potatoes. Boil them without salt. While still warm, cut into thick slices. Fry in very hot fat and serve sprinkled with vanilla-flavoured sugar.

Sweet potatoes au gratin. PATATES AU GRATIN – Proceed as described in the recipe for *Potatoes au gratin* (see POTATOES).

Sweet potatoes à l'impériale, or Henri (American cookery). PATATES À L'IMPÉRIALE – Butter a *gratin* dish or a shallow metal *timbale* and put in sliced sweet potatoes, cooking apples and bananas, well mixed and seasoned with salt and paprika. Scatter small pieces of butter on top. Bake in a slow oven. Take out of the oven and cover with apricot or redcurrant pulp.

This dish is served as an accompaniment to meat, poultry or game.

Sweet potato purée. PURÉE DE PATATES – Prepare like *Potato purée* (see POTATOES).

Sweet potato salad. SALADE DE PATATES – Prepare as for *Potato salad* (see SALAD).

Stewed sweet potatoes. PATATES À L'ÉTUVÉE – Cut 500 g. (generous 1 lb.) sweet potatoes into slices. Put into a sauté pan with 50 g. (2 oz., $\frac{1}{4}$ cup) butter, 1 dl. (6 tablespoons, $\frac{1}{2}$ cup) water and a pinch of salt. Bring to the boil, cover, and simmer for 30 minutes. Serve piled in a vegetable dish.

SWEET POTATO DESSERTS. PATATES ENTREMETS –

Sweet potato pudding (Créole cookery). GÂTEAU DE PATATES DOUCES – Boil 5 sweet potatoes in their skins in unsalted water. When they are cooked, drain, peel, and mash them to a fine paste. Add some vanilla-flavoured sugar or vanilla essence and 1 tablespoon of flour, stirring vigorously. Stir in a little milk. Break in 4 eggs, one at a time, reserving 1 egg white. Whisk the egg white to a stiff froth, and fold into the mixture to make it smooth and light.

Add 150 g. (5 oz., 1 cup) seedless raisins which have been steeped in rum. Pour the mixture into a buttered charlotte mould. Cook for a few minutes in a *bain-marie*, then in the oven. Serve cold, plain or with custard.

Sweet potato soufflé. SOUFFLÉ AUX PATATES – Using sweet potato bound with egg yolks and mixed with stiffly beaten whites, prepare a soufflé, which can be served as a small *entrée* or as a sweet soufflé.

SWIFT. MARTINET – Type of swallow. Its flesh is edible though rather tasteless.

SWISS CHARD, WHITE BEET or STRAWBERRY SPINACH. BETTE, BLETTE, POIRÉE À CARDE – Also known under the name of *chard* or *seakale beet*, this is a vegetable of the same type as beetroot, cultivated for its spinach-like leaves with broad white petioles and midribs. It is widely cultivated in France, particularly in the Lyons district, where this vegetable is greatly appreciated. It is found in the markets from July to the first frosts.

Preparation of chard. Trim the chard (white ribs) keeping the green parts for another dish. Scrape them and remove all stringy parts. Cut into 6 to 8-cm. ($2\frac{1}{2}$ to 3-inch) pieces. Cook in a *court-bouillon* for vegetables. Drain and prepare as indicated in the recipe.

The chard can also be boiled in salted water. Drain, immerse in cold water to cool, dry in a cloth, chop and prepare like spinach.

Swiss chard à la béchamel. BETTES À LA BÉCHAMEL – Cook 500 g. (generous 1 lb.) chard in a *court-bouillon*. Drain and put into a sauté pan with 3 dl. ($\frac{1}{2}$ pint, $1\frac{1}{4}$ cups) of not too thick *Béchamel sauce* (see SAUCE). Simmer, covered, for 5 minutes. Put into a vegetable dish. Add 80 g. (3 oz., $\frac{1}{3}$ cup) butter to the sauce and pour it over the chards.

Swiss chard au blanc. BETTES AU BLANC – This is another name for *Swiss chard à la béchamel*.

Buttered Swiss chard I. BETTES AU BEURRE – Cook 500 g. (generous 1 lb.) chard in *court-bouillon*, drain, and put into a sauté pan with 100 g. (4 oz., $\frac{1}{2}$ cup) butter. Simmer, covered, over low heat for 15 to 20 minutes. Serve in a vegetable dish, sprinkled with the butter in which it was cooked.

Buttered Swiss chard II. BETTES AU BEURRE – Trim the chard and cut into chunks. Blanch slightly in salted water, drain and immerse in cold water to cool. Drain again, then simmer in a sauté pan with 2 dl. ($\frac{1}{3}$ pint, scant cup) water and 100 g. (4 oz., $\frac{1}{2}$ cup) butter for 500 g. (generous 1 lb.) vegetables. Transfer to a vegetable dish and sprinkle with butter.

Swiss chard in cream. BETTES À LA CRÈME – Cook 500 g. (generous 1 lb.) chard in *court-bouillon*; drain. Simmer for 5 minutes with 50 g. (2 oz., $\frac{1}{4}$ cup) butter. Add 4 dl. ($\frac{3}{4}$ pint, scant

2 cups) hot fresh cream and boil to reduce by half. Transfer to a vegetable dish. Add 60 g. (2 oz., $\frac{1}{4}$ cup) butter to the pan liquor then pour the sauce over the chards.

Swiss chard au gratin. BETTES AU GRATIN – Prepare *Swiss chard à la béchamel*. Put into an ovenproof dish on a layer of *béchamel sauce* and cover with the same sauce.

Sprinkle with grated cheese and melted butter and brown in a hot oven.

Swiss chard in gravy. BETTES AU JUS – Cook 500 g. (generous 1 lb.) chard in *court-bouillon*. Drain and put into a sauté pan with 3 dl. ($\frac{1}{2}$ pint, $1\frac{1}{4}$ cups) brown veal gravy. Leave to simmer, covered, for 10 minutes. Transfer to a vegetable dish. Add 50 g. (2 oz., $\frac{1}{4}$ cup) butter to the gravy and pour it over the chard.

Swiss chard à la hollandaise. BETTES À LA HOLLANDAISE – Trim and cut the chard into long strips. Tie into bundles as you would asparagus, and cook in boiling salted water. Drain, put on a serving dish for asparagus (with perforations to allow drainage) or on a napkin. Serve with *Hollandaise sauce* (see SAUCE).

Chard prepared this way can also be served with various other sauces, such as melted butter, *Cream sauce*, *Maître d'hôtel sauce*, *Mousseline*, *Vinaigrette*, (see SAUCE).

Swiss chard à l'italienne. BETTES À L'ITALIENNE – Prepare like *Swiss chard in gravy*, replacing the veal gravy with *Italian sauce* (see SAUCE).

Swiss chard à la lyonnaise. BETTES À LA LYONNAISE – Prepare like *Swiss chard in gravy*, replacing the gravy with *Lyonnaise sauce* (see SAUCE).

Swiss chard à la milanaise. BETTES À LA MILANAISE – Cook the chard in salted water. Drain, dry, and prepare like *Asparagus à la milanaise* (see ASPARAGUS).

Swiss chard à la moelle. BETTES À LA MOELLE – Drain the chards, dry them and prepare like *Cardoons with marrow* (see CARDOON).

Swiss chard Mornay. BETTES MORNAY – Another name for *Swiss chard au gratin*.

Swiss chard à la polonaise. BETTES À LA POLONAISE – Cook the chards in salted water, drain, dry, and prepare like *Asparagus à la polonaise* (see ASPARAGUS).

SWISS ROLL. BÛCHE – Thin sponge cake baked in a special tin, then covered with jam or cream and rolled up like the French *Bûche de Noël*.

Chocolate-flavoured Swiss roll

SWIZZLE STICK. MOUSSOIR – Little wooden or metal implement used to whisk chocolate and Champagne.

SWORDFISH. ESPADON – Fish which is found in the North Sea, the Baltic and off the coast of Sicily. It can reach 7 m. (23 feet). Its flesh is white, fine and quite delicate. Recipes for tunny (fresh tuna fish) can be used for swordfish.

Decorating pâtisserie with a butter syringe

SYRINGE. SERINGUE – Instrument used in *pâtisserie* instead of a forcing bag and pipe when it is necessary to make decorations with a substance that is rather firm in consistency.

SYRUP. SIROP – Solution of sugar and water or sugar and fruit juice, concentrated to a sticky consistency. It can be hot or cold.

Almond syrup. SIROP D'AMANDE, SIROP D'ORGEAT –

Ingredients. 500 g. (18 oz., $3\frac{2}{3}$ cups) sweet almonds, 150 g. (5 oz., 1 cup) bitter almonds, 3 kg. ($6\frac{1}{2}$ lb.) sugar, $1\frac{3}{4}$ litres (3 pints, 4 pints) distilled water, $2\frac{1}{2}$ dl. (scant $\frac{1}{2}$ pint, generous cup) orange flower water.

Method. Blanch the almonds, pound them to a paste in a mortar with 75 g. (3 oz., $\frac{1}{3}$ cup) sugar and $1\frac{1}{2}$ dl. ($\frac{1}{4}$ pint, $\frac{2}{3}$ cup) water. Dilute, little by little, with the rest of the water. Squeeze through a cloth, straining a little water through the residue so as to obtain $2\frac{1}{4}$ kg. (5 lb.) of liquor. Dissolve the remaining sugar in this in a *bain-marie*. Add the orange flower water when the syrup is cold.

Blackcurrant syrup. SIROP DE CASSIS – Strip the blackcurrants from their stalks, crush them and press out the juice through a muslin bag. Weigh the juice and add sugar in the ratio of 900 g. (2 lb., 4 cups) sugar to 500 g. (18 oz.) juice. Stir this in a pan over low heat, stirring all the time to encourage the sugar to dissolve and prevent it from sticking to the bottom.

Skim carefully and verify the degree of concentration, which should be 31° (at boiling point). Decant into bottles, cork, seal, and keep in a cool, dry place.

Cherry, raspberry, gooseberry or mulberry syrup. SIROP DE CERISE, DE FRAMBOISE, DE GROSEILLE, DE MÛRE – Dissolve the sugar in the filtered fruit juice, using, if possible, a copper pan (not tinned). Place over heat and strain as soon as the mixture begins to boil. The amount of sugar required depends on the sweetness of the fruit juice.

Citric acid syrup. SIROP D'ACIDE CITRIQUE, SIROP DE LIMON – Dissolve, by shaking, 10 g. ($\frac{1}{3}$ oz.) citric acid in 990 g. ($2\frac{1}{4}$ lb.) plain syrup. Add 20 g. ($\frac{2}{3}$ oz.) of alcoholic tincture of lemon.

Coffee syrup. SIROP DE CAFÉ – Make a very strong infusion with 500 g. (generous 1 lb.) fresh finely ground coffee. Strain 2 litres ($3\frac{1}{2}$ pints, $4\frac{1}{2}$ pints) boiling water twice through the ground coffee to give about $1\frac{1}{4}$ litres ($2\frac{1}{4}$ pints, $2\frac{3}{4}$ pints) well-flavoured coffee.

Put $2\frac{1}{2}$ kg. ($5\frac{1}{2}$ lb., 11 cups) sugar into a copper pan. Pour in the coffee infusion and melt over low heat. As soon as the syrup begins to boil it should be removed.

Gum syrup. SIROP DE GOMME – *Ingredients.* 100 g. (4 oz.) washed white gum, 300 g. (11 oz., $1\frac{1}{2}$ cups) white sugar, $3\frac{1}{2}$ dl. (generous $\frac{1}{2}$ pint, $1\frac{1}{2}$ cups) distilled water.

Method. Dissolve the gum, then the sugar, in the water. Heat to boiling point. Remove when the first bubbles appear, and strain.

Orange syrup I. SIROP D'ORANGE – Make a cold sugar syrup, melting $1\frac{3}{4}$ kg. (4 lb., 8 cups) sugar in 1 litre ($1\frac{3}{4}$ pints, generous quart) water. It takes 24 hours for the sugar to melt completely. Filter through wet flannel.

Dissolve 100 g. (4 oz.) citric acid in a little water and flavour it with orange extract which is obtained by soaking finely cut orange peel in alcohol. To double the strength of the extract, reinfuse with fresh orange peel after it has stood for 1 month. It is important to use only the coloured part of the skin, the white pith imparts a bitter taste.

Orange syrup can be prepared for immediate use by rubbing the outsides of the oranges with sugar lumps until there is no more juic left in the skins. For 6 oranges allow 2 kg. ($4\frac{1}{2}$ lb. 9 cups) sugar, taking from this sufficient quantity for rubbing the skins. Melt all the sugar in $1\frac{1}{2}$ litres ($2\frac{3}{4}$ pints, $3\frac{1}{4}$ pints) cold water. Add 250 g. (9 oz.) citric acid.

Orange syrup II. SIROP D'ORANGE – Choose fine ripe oranges. Pare the rind off 2 or 3 of these, very finely and keep on one side to flavour the syrup. Crush the pulp of the oranges and squeeze out the juice in a damp cloth. Weigh the juice. Allow 800 g. ($1\frac{3}{4}$ lb., $3\frac{1}{2}$ cups) sugar for every 500 g. (18 oz.) juice. Set over heat in a copper pan.

Spread a damp cloth over a wooden frame. Put the orange peel on this. As soon as the syrup boils pour it over the peel. Cool before bottling.

Lemon syrup can be made in the same way, but since lemon juice is much more acid than orange juice it is necessary to add an equal quantity of water and to use additional sugar.

Orgeat syrup. SIROP D'ORGEAT – Mix sweet and bitter almonds in the proportion of 750 g. ($1\frac{3}{4}$ lb., 5 cups) sweet almonds to 150 g. (5 oz., 1 cup) bitter almonds.

Blanch them for a few moments in boiling water. The skins are easily removed by rubbing them between thumb and forefinger.

Rinse the almonds in cold water, drain, and toss them in a cloth so as to remove all traces of moisture. Pound the almonds, little by little, in a marble mortar. Allow $1\frac{1}{4}$ litres ($2\frac{1}{4}$ pints, $2\frac{3}{4}$ pints) water and $2\frac{1}{4}$ kg. (5 lb.) loaf sugar for 900 g. (2 lb., 6 cups) almonds. Add 100 g. (4 oz., $\frac{1}{2}$ cup) sugar little by little to the almonds being pounded in the mortar, and, from time to time, a few drops of water. This prevents the almonds turning to oil.

When they are completely pounded, dilute the almonds to a paste by adding a little more than half of the total amount of water. Strain the diluted paste through a damp cloth, wringing out the cloth thoroughly to extract all the almond milk.

Put back the residue in the mortar, pound it afresh with about 50 g. (2 oz., $\frac{1}{4}$ cup) sugar, then add the rest of the water. Strain this also through the cloth, squeezing out every drop of liquid. Mix together the first and second pressings of almond milk, and dissolve the rest of the sugar in it.

Pour into a pan and heat, stirring frequently. Remove as soon as the first bubbles appear; the syrup must not be allowed to boil. Away from the heat add half a glass of orange flower water.

If the chosen flavouring is lemon, cut the lemon in slices and leave them in the syrup for 15 minutes.

Orgeat syrup can also be made by putting the almond milk in a china bowl with the lump sugar broken up into small pieces. Set in a *bain-marie* and stir from time to time. As soon as the sugar is completely dissolved and the liquid is near boiling point, remove from the heat. When the syrup is cold, flavour it with orange flower water poured on to the surface of the syrup. After a few moments, stir, then strain through a white cloth and pour into bottles.

Plain syrup. SIROP DE SUCRE – To prepare cold, dissolve (4 lb., 8 cups) sugar in 1 litre ($1\frac{3}{4}$ pints, generous quart) water. This syrup does not keep as well as syrup prepared hot, which is made by adding 1650 g. ($3\frac{1}{2}$ lb., 7 cups) sugar to 1 litre ($1\frac{3}{4}$ pints, generous quart) water heated to boiling point. Strain and filter.

TABLECLOTH. NAPPE – Piece of linen used to cover the table for meals. It has a long history and goes back to the early Middle Ages. Up to the fifteenth century the tablecloth was very wide and was folded in two so that it could be turned over. It was then known as the 'double cloth'. From this period, fashion decreed that tablecloths should be of single width instead of double. They were often damascened or embroidered.

The tablecloth played an important role in feudal ceremonial. It was acceptable for persons of different rank to dine at the same table, but the host's place alone had the distinction of being covered with a cloth, which set him apart from those present. If the table was entirely covered with a cloth, the host's place was singled out from the rest in being covered with a special napkin.

Until the end of the fourteenth century, when the individual napkin had not yet come into use, the tablecloth was covered with a 'runner', a long narrow strip of linen laid along the edge of the cloth, which was used by the guests to wipe their fingers and mouths.

Table linen came into general use in the sixteenth century, when each diner had his own napkin. At this period, luxury was carried so far that napkins were changed several times during a meal. They were tied round the neck to protect the fine muslin collars worn at that period. As the operation of knotting the two ends of the napkin was not an easy one for the diner to undertake himself, it was necessary to seek assistance from a fellow-guest, from which came the expression 'making both ends meet.'

Table napkins also began to be folded in different ways. This custom, however, was soon abandoned, but was to return three hundred years later. In the sixteenth century it was fashionable to fold napkins in the shapes of fruits and birds. It was also customary to perfume napkins and table cloths with rose water and other essences.

Table linen was now woven (by craftsmen known as *telliers* and *tisserands*) in such a way as to incorporate designs in the weave of the fabric itself.

Damascene cloths and napkins began to be woven in France at Rheims and in Normandy, especially in the Caen area. These were as beautiful as those which had hitherto been made in Flanders and Venice. A man called Graindorge had the idea of weaving chequered patterns and flowers into table linen. His son, Richard, made damascene cloth with designs of human figures, animals and other designs. Michel, Richard's son, founded several factories for the production of damask table linen and its use spread throughout the kingdom.

TABLE DECORATIONS – Table decorations should not impede the service or make it difficult for people to speak or to see one another. The fashion for complicated decorations went out long ago; nowadays one or two low baskets or bowls of flowers make an elegant and practical décor. Centrepieces, mirrors with Japanese gardens arranged on them, are suitable for formal occasions. *Chemins de fleurs* in little crystal *jardinières*, long and narrow, arranged end to end to make a border of roses, violets or nasturtiums, look charming, as do sprays of autumn flowers and leaves on the tablecloth.

Bowls or baskets of fruit can replace floral decorations. A table setting with brightly coloured linen and dishes makes an informal meal very cheerful; glazed earthenware jugs, plates and dishes lend themselves to many decorative ideas.

Place settings should be at least 30 cm. (12 inches) apart. A thick flannel padding or heat-resistant mats should be placed under the tablecloth. The fork is placed at the left-hand side of the plate, the spoon and knife at the right; the cutting edge of the latter should be turned inwards towards the plate. Glasses for water, wine, Madeira and Champagne are arranged either in a group or in a line, in order of size. Carafes of water and *vin ordinaire* are grouped along the table alternately with the salt cellars and pepper pots.

TACAUD – Name for a variety of cod, also called *officier* and *morue borgne*. The flesh is quite pleasant to eat but full of bones. All recipes given for cod (q.v.) can be applied to this fish.

TACON – Young salmon (see SALMON).

TAILLEVENT – Famous cook who was the author of one of the oldest books on cookery.

Guillaume Tirel, called *Taillevent*, was born in 1326. From 1346 to 1350 he was head cook to Philippe VI de Valois, from 1355 to 1368 head cook and master of the kitchen to the Dauphin, the Duke of Normandy, and from 1368 to 1371 head cook to Charles VI: *'premier écuyer de cuisine et maistre des garnisons de cuisine'* (first master of the kitchen and master of the art of garnishing).

Taillevent died in 1395 and probably wrote his *Viandier* between 1373 and 1380.

TAILLOIR or TRANCHOIR – Special slices of bread which in olden days took the place of plates. They were placed in turn on pieces of coloured or plain wood and on slices of bread on which the food was served. After each service the bread was gathered up in baskets and distributed among the poor.

Talleyrand (1754–1838)

Nowadays the word *tailloir* describes a wooden platter on which meat is cut up.

TALLEYRAND – Charles Maurice de Talleyrand-Périgord, celebrated statesman and diplomat, was born in Paris on 13 February 1754, and died in the same city on 17 May 1838. He was one of the greatest French gastronomes.

At the age of 21 he became Abbot of Saint-Denis and in 1788 Bishop of Autun, but high ecclesiastical office did not prevent him from leading a brilliant and dissipated worldly life. His lack of moral scruples and an aptitude for diplomacy and intrigue enabled him to retain a high position throughout the Revolution, the Directory, the Empire and the Restoration, with only short periods of reversal of fortune.

While he was an important personage at Court, the luxury of his table and the splendour of his entertaining were celebrated. At the time of the First Empire he had as his cook the illustrious Carême.

The extravagance of Talleyrand's table was not entirely for the sake of pure gastronomical satisfaction; he believed that the pleasure he offered his guests at these receptions was an important element in the success of his diplomacy and intrigues.

He never let religious or moral scruples interfere with the pursuit of his career and personal pleasures. Part of a letter written in 1791 to his friend the Duc de Lauzun demonstrates this side of his character. A bill of excommunication had been issued against several members of the clergy. Talleyrand, whose name was included, wrote ironically, 'You have heard the news; excommunicated. Come and dine to console me. Everyone refuses me fire and water, so we will eat nothing but glazed cold meats and drink only chilled wines.'

TALMOUSE – Cheese tartlet, served as *hors-d'œuvre* (see HORS-D'ŒUVRE).

TAMARIND. TAMARIN – Fruit of the tamarind tree, a leguminous plant of the West Indies. The pods are filled with an acid juicy pulp which is used to prepare a *limonade* and can replace vinegar. Medicinally it has laxative properties.

TAMMY CLOTH. ÉTAMINE – Piece of woollen material through which purées are rubbed by means of a spatula. It is also used for straining sauces and stocks.

TANGERINE. MANDARINE – Fruit of a species of orange-tree, originally from China. It is cultivated in the south-east of France, and in southern U.S.A. The tangerines of Nice and Algeria are renowned.

The tangerine is a delicious fruit. It is usually eaten raw. Like the orange, it can be treated in various ways in confectionery, in the preparation of cold sweets and in cooking.

Many recipes for oranges are suitable for tangerines. (See ORANGE.)

Tangerine tart or flan – See TART, FLAN.

Iced tangerines. MANDARINES GLACÉES – Remove the pulp from tangerines without tearing the skin. Make an ice cream mixture with the pulp (see ICE CREAMS AND ICES) and fill the skins with it.

Tangerines en surprise. MANDARINES EN SURPRISE – Empty the tangerines as indicated in the previous recipe. Fill with a heaped tablespoon of tangerine ice cream or Neapolitan ice cream flavoured with tangerine. Spread a layer of tangerine soufflé mixture on top. Sprinkle with icing sugar. Put in a very hot oven for a few seconds to brown.

Tangerines in syrup. COMPOTE DE MANDARINES – Prepare in the same way as *Orange compote* (see ORANGE).

TANKARD or BEER GLASS. BOCK – Receptacle in glass or stoneware of $\frac{1}{2}$ litre (scant pint, $2\frac{1}{4}$ cups) capacity which is used for drinking beer.

Beer glasses generally have a handle. Those made of stoneware are often ornamented with designs in relief, generally representing carousing scenes.

TAPIOCA – Farinaceous food extracted from the roots of cassava or manioc plant. It is very digestible and is used to thicken soups and broths, and make milk puddings.

Tapioca pudding. POUDING AU TAPIOCA – See PUDDING.

TAPIR – Large mammiferous South American animal, rather resembling a pig. The flesh is highly thought of, and can be prepared like that of boar (see WILD BOAR).

Branch of tarragon

TARRAGON. ESTRAGON – Pot-herb used with chervil and chives to flavour green salads. Tarragon is also used to flavour some sauces. A liqueur is made from it.

Bottled tarragon. CONSERVE D'ESTRAGON – Press down well in clean, dry small bottles some young sprigs of fresh tarragon which have been stripped, washed and dried in a cloth. Cork the bottles and cover with paper caps. Tie string round the necks of the bottles. Put them, in straw wrappers, in a large pan lined with straw, or place them on a canning rack. Cover with cold water. Boil continuously for 40 minutes. Leave the bottles to cool in the pan. Drain and dry them. Keep in a cool place.

Treated in this way, tarragon can be kept for a very long time without losing any of its aroma. It is used in the same way as fresh tarragon.

Tarragon cream. CRÈME D'ESTRAGON – Boil, until almost completely dry, 100 g. (4 oz., 1 cup) fresh crushed tarragon leaves, moistened with $1\frac{1}{2}$ dl. ($\frac{1}{4}$ pint, $\frac{2}{3}$ cup) dry white wine.

Add 3½ dl. (generous ½ pint, 1½ cups) very thick *Béchamel sauce* (see SAUCE). Season. Boil for a few seconds. Rub through muslin. Heat and add a little fresh butter.

This purée is used as a filling for small *vol-au-vent*, *barquettes* or *canapés*, and for stuffing certain vegetables such as artichoke hearts, mushrooms, etc.

Dried tarragon. ESTRAGON SÈCHÉ – Strip and wash fresh branches of tarragon, recently picked, and dry thoroughly in a cloth. Tie them into bunches of 6 to 8 with string. Hang these in a cool dry place and leave until they are completely dry.

Dried tarragon is used in the same way as fresh or bottled tarragon but as the flavour is more concentrated use slightly less.

Pickled tarragon. CONSERVE D'ESTRAGON AU VINAIGRE – Strip branches of fresh tarragon and break into little sprigs. Wash in cold water and dry thoroughly in a cloth. Put the sprigs in small bottles, fill with very strong vinegar, cork the bottles tightly, tie with string, and keep in a cool place.

Tarragon purée. PURÉE D'ESTRAGON – *Hot*. Made with tarragon and very thick *béchamel sauce* as indicated for *Tarragon cream*. It can also be made by adding a purée of tarragon leaves, blanched, cooled under running water, drained, pounded in a mortar, rubbed through muslin, to twice its volume of mashed potatoes. This purée is used as a filling for small *vol-au-vent*, *canapés* or similar preparations; and to stuff artichoke hearts, small tomatoes, etc.

Cold. Pound together in a mortar 100 g. (4 oz., 1 cup) blanched, cooled and drained tarragon leaves, with 6 hard boiled egg yolks. Add 2 tablespoons (3 tablespoons) fresh butter. Rub through a fine sieve.

This purée is used in the preparation of various cold *hors-d'œuvre* or to decorate cold fish.

Tarragon vinegar. VINAIGRE À L'ESTRAGON – Ordinary vinegar in which small tarragon shoots are steeped. It is used to moisten sauces and in salad dressing.

TARTARE – Name given chiefly to a cold sauce; mayonnaise prepared with crushed hard boiled egg yolks and oil, with chopped chives added.

À la tartare is the name given to minced beef steak seasoned with salt and pepper, reshaped into a steak and served uncooked with a raw egg on top, and, on the side, capers, chopped onion and parsley.

TART (FLAN). TARTE – The words *tarte* or 'tart' and 'flan' are often used interchangeably in England and France to designate a pastry filled with fruit, jam, custard or some other filling. The American term most often used is open or single crusted 'pie'. Almost all such dishes are cooked and served in the United States in a pie dish, whereas in England or France a metal flan or pastry ring, placed on a metal baking sheet, is used. (For tarts and flans with savoury fillings, see FLANS.)

Lining a circular tart tin with pastry
(*'A l'Alsacienne', Maison Morand. Phot. Larousse*)

Recipes for sweet fillings suitable for desserts are given below. All recipes are suitable for baking in either an American pie dish or a flan ring.

In England the tart is often a two-crusted, fruit-filled dessert baked in a dish. This would be called a pie in U.S.A., whereas a tart would designate a small single-crusted pie which the French call *tartelette*.

Tart (flan) cases baked blind (unfilled). CROÛTES À FLAN CUITES À BLANC – Made with *Short pastry* (see DOUGH). Roll out 225 g. (8 oz.) pastry to a circle 25 cm. (10 inches) in diameter. Transfer this to a circular, buttered flan ring, pressing it round the inside of the tin. Cut off the excess pastry.

Make the rim of the tart out of the band of pastry rising up the sides of the tin. Lift it away from the edge and pinch it with finger and thumb or pastry pinchers.

Prick the bottom of the tart to prevent the pastry from bubbling up during baking. Line the edge and bottom of the pastry with greaseproof paper. Fill it with dried beans or rice. Bake in a moderately hot oven for about 25 minutes.

Remove the paper and temporary filling. Brush the tart with egg. Dry it for a few moments in the oven. Fill with whatever is indicated in the recipe.

Alsatian tart. TARTE ALSACIENNE – *Ingredients*. 125 g. (4 oz., ½ cup) butter, 250 g. (9 oz., 2 cups) castor sugar, 1 egg, 250 g. (9 oz., 2 cups) sifted flour, 250 g. (9 oz., 2 cups) ground almonds.

Method. Cream together the butter, sugar and egg. Add the flour and the almonds. Mix well. Roll out three-quarters of the dough into a round piece about 1 cm. (½ inch) thick. Roll out the rest of the pastry and cut it into thin strips. Surround the round piece of pastry with one of these strips and arrange the others criss-cross on top, sealing them together with cold water.

Fill each space with a different kind of jam or marmalade. Bake in a moderately hot oven.

Apple tart

Apple tart. TARTE AUX POMMES – Sprinkle a flan case made of *Fine lining paste* or *pastry dough I*, *Short pastry I* or *Flaky pastry* (see DOUGH) with fine sugar, and fill with peeled eating apples cut into quarters or thin slices.

Bake in a hot oven. Coat the fruit with apple jelly or sieved apricot jam, flavoured with liqueur.

Apple tart à l'alsacienne. FLAN DE POMMES À L'ALSACIENNE – Fill a flan case with quartered small tart apples. Proceed as for *Apricot tart à l'alsacienne* (see below), flavouring the custard with cinnamon.

Apple tart with lattice-work decoration. FLAN AUX POMMES GRILLÉ – Line a flan ring with *Short pastry I* (see DOUGH). Fill with rather thick apple purée. Decorate the top with a latticed design made with thin strips of pastry. Press down well at the edges. Brush with egg and bake in a hot oven.

Messina apple tart. TARTE AUX POMMES À LA MESSINE – Prepare a flan case in the usual way. Fill with thin slices of sugared eating apples and seeded raisins. Sprinkle with sugar and bake in a hot oven.

Apricot tart. TARTE AUX ABRICOTS – Line a flan with *Fine lining paste I* or *Flaky pastry* (see DOUGH) 1 cm. ($\frac{1}{2}$ inch) thick. Flute the edges. Prick the paste and place on a baking dish. Sprinkle with fine sugar and fill with halves of apricots.

Bake in a moderately hot oven for about 30 minutes. Remove the flan ring and brush the tart with beaten egg. Put back in the oven for 5 minutes to finish cooking. Put the tart on a cooling rack and coat the fruit with a thin covering of sieved apricot jam or apricot purée. Place a few sweet almonds or apricot kernels on top.

The tart may be sprinkled with vanilla-flavoured sugar instead of using jam, but the latter gives a better appearance. The tart must not be left to cool on the baking sheet because the steam will escape too slowly and the pastry will lose its crispness.

Apricot tart à l'alsacienne. FLAN AUX ABRICOTS À L'ALSACIENNE – Fill a flan case with halved apricots which have been steeped in kirsch and sugar. Before putting the flan in the oven, pour in a custard mixture thickened with a teaspoon of potato flour or arrowroot.

Cherry tart

Cherry tart. TARTE AUX CERISES – Proceed as for *Apricot tart*, filling the pastry with stoned cherries.

When the tart is baked, cover with a film of redcurrant jelly flavoured with sieved raspberry or cherry jam to which a little kirsch or cherry brandy has been added.

Cherry tart à l'alsacienne. FLAN AUX CERISES À L'ALSACIENNE – Proceed as for *Apricot tart à l'alsacienne*. Preserved cherries can be used for this flan.

Tart of Demoiselles Tatin. TARTE DES DEMOISELLES TATIN – Butter a baking dish 6 cm. ($2\frac{1}{2}$ inches) deep. Put in a layer of fine sugar about 5 mm. ($\frac{1}{4}$ inch) thick. Fill with peeled and quartered apples, and put small pieces of butter and some more sugar on top.

Cherry tart à l'alsacienne

Cover with a paper-thin sheet of *Fine lining paste* (see DOUGH).

Bake in a moderately hot oven for about 20 to 25 minutes. The sugar should be well caramelised. Turn it out on to a serving dish so that the pastry is on top. Serve hot.

Fig tart. TARTE AUX FIGUES – Make with fresh figs, peeled and soaked in liqueur in the same way as *Strawberry tart* (see below). Coat the fruit with apricot jam, sieved and flavoured with liqueur.

Fruit tart l'allemande. TARTE AUX FRUITS DIVERS À L'ALLEMANDE – Under this heading comes a series of good tarts of deservedly high reputation. Each has a special name according to the fruit used.

Apfelkuchen or apple tart. Made like *Cherry tart.*

Aprikosenkuchen or apricot tart. Made like *Cherry tart.*

Erdbeerkuchen or strawberry tart. Differs from the preceding tarts in that the fruit is not cooked with the pastry. The tart shell is baked first and, when cold, filled with the strawberries, thickly sprinkled with sugar and coated with a thick layer of whipped cream, sweetened and flavoured with vanilla.

Himbeerkuchen or raspberry tart. Prepared in the same way as the above, substituting raspberries for strawberries.

Johannisbeerkuchen or redcurrant tart. Prepared like *Stachelbeerkuchen or gooseberry tart* (see below).

Kirschenkuchen or German cherry tart. Roll out and turn some *Flaky pastry* (see DOUGH) six times, and roll it into a round sheet of the desired size about $2\frac{1}{2}$ mm. ($\frac{1}{8}$ inch) thick. Set in a pie dish lightly moistened in the middle. Damp the edges of the pastry and pinch them to make a border. Prick with a fork to keep it from blistering during cooking. Sprinkle over a little fine sugar and powdered cinnamon.

Arrange the stoned cherries, either fresh or preserved, on the pastry, bake in a moderate oven. Prepare a thick cherry syrup by cooking cherries and sugar together. Strain, and when the tart is cold pour a good layer over the fruit.

To finish off, bake fine breadcrumbs a pale golden colour and sprinkle over the tart.

Pflaumenkuchen or greengage tart. Made like *Kirschenkuchen.*

Stachelbeerkuchen or gooseberry tart. Bake the pastry shell in the oven. Add the picked-over fruit to the same weight of sugar cooked to crack degree (see SUGAR). When the sugar is melted, strain out the fruit with a skimmer and boil down the juice until it begins to jell. Remove from the heat and put back the fruit. Boil together for a moment then pour all together into a basin. When this mixture is quite cold, make a thick layer in the tart, and coat with sweetened, vanilla-flavoured whipped cream.

Fruit tart à l'alsacienne. TARTE AUX FRUITS DIVERS À L'ALSACIENNE – Made with quetsch and mirabelle plums, apples or cherries, like an ordinary fruit tart. Pour custard or light *French pastry cream* (see CREAMS) over the fruit after it has been set in the pastry.

English fruit tart (pie). TARTE AUX FRUITS DIVERS À L'ANGLAIS – Fill a pie dish with cut up apples or other fruit, cover with white or brown sugar mixed with a little chopped lemon peel. Place an egg cup or a saucer upside down in the centre of the dish.

Moisten with half a glass of water. Cover the tart with *Ordinary lining paste or pastry dough II* (see DOUGH) made with an egg yolk. Put a band of pastry round the edge of the dish and press down the edges. Brush the surface of the tart with water and sprinkle over fine sugar. Bake in a moderately hot oven for 40 to 50 minutes.

These tarts can also be flavoured with cinnamon or cloves. The top may be decorated with cut-out pieces of pastry and brushed with egg.

Linzertorte (Austrian tart). TARTE À L'AUTRICHIENNE – Viennese pastry which takes its name from the town of Linz in Austria.

It is a tart of *Lining paste* (see DOUGH) strongly flavoured with cinnamon, filled with strawberry jam and covered with criss-cross strips of pastry. *Linzertorte* is generally made from a special rich pastry which includes ground almonds, cinnamon, lemon juice and egg yolks in its composition.

Me'gin tart (Messina pastry). TARTE AU ME'GIN – Made like *quiche lorraine* with a mixture of eggs, a white cheese called *Fremgin*, well drained, and fresh cream.

Nectarine tart. FLAN AUX BRUGNONS – Using halved nectarines, proceed as for *Apricot tart.*

Peach tart. FLAN AUX PÊCHES – Proceed as for *Apricot tart* using halved or quartered peaches.

Pear tart. TARTE AUX POIRES – Made with small ripe pears cut into small pieces, like *Apple tart.*

Pineapple tart I. TARTE À L'ANANAS – Prepare the crust with *Short pastry I or II* or *Flaky pastry* (see DOUGH). Bake the pastry case empty. Fill, when cooked, with half-slices of pineapple cooked in syrup. Cover with sieved apricot jam flavoured with kirsch or rum.

Pineapple tart II. TARTE À L'ANANAS – Roll out a round or square of *Flaky pastry* (see DOUGH). Incise this lightly 3 cm. ($1\frac{1}{4}$ inches) from the edge. Set in the middle thin slices of cooked or raw pineapple. Sprinkle with fine sugar. Brush the edges of the pastry with egg and bake in a hot oven. When cooked, coat the pineapple with sieved apricot jam.

Plum tart. TARTE AUX PRUNES – Made with greengages, mirabelles or quetsches like *Apricot tart.*

Plum tart à l'alsacienne. TARTE AUX PRUNES À L'ALSACIENNE – Made with quetsches in the same way as *Apple tart à l'alsacienne.*

Raspberry tart. TARTE AUX FRAMBOISES – Made with raw raspberries as described in the recipe for *Strawberry tart.*

English rhubarb tart. TARTE À LA RHUBARBE À L'ANGLAISE – Use a special English pie dish or a fireproof dish.

Cut 750 g. ($1\frac{1}{2}$ lb.) of rhubarb from the pale pink stalks in the middle of the plant. Wash, dry, peel and cut them into chunks 5 cm. (2 inches) long. Arrange these in layers in the dish, and sprinkle with a mixture of white and brown sugar, allowing 125 g. (4 oz., 1 cup) of each. Pour in 3 tablespoons (4 tablespoons) water.

Roll out *Flaky pastry* or *Ordinary lining paste or pastry dough II* (see DOUGH) into an oval shape $\frac{3}{4}$ cm. ($\frac{1}{3}$ inch) thick, a little bigger than the top of the dish. Fix a strip of pastry $3\frac{1}{2}$ cm. ($1\frac{1}{2}$ inches) wide to the edge of the pie dish with water. Moisten lightly, place the pastry sheet on top, cut off the surplus paste, and press the edges well.

Brush lightly with egg. Make a hole in the middle of the pastry lid to allow steam to escape, and bake in a moderately hot oven for about 30 to 40 minutes.

This tart is eaten cold and is usually served with sweetened whipped cream.

Strawberry tart. TARTE AUX FRAISES – Line a flan ring with *Lining paste (Pastry dough I* or *II)* or *Short pastry* (see DOUGH). Bake empty, and fill with strawberries, hulled and rolled in sugar. Coat with currant jelly flavoured with raspberry, or with sieved cherry jam flavoured with kirsch.

Tangerine flan. GÂTEAU (TARTE) À LA MANDARINE – *Ingredients.* 125 g. (4 oz., $\frac{3}{4}$ cup) blanched almonds, 125 g. (4 oz., $\frac{1}{2}$ cup) fine sugar, 4 eggs, 2 candied tangerine peels, 2 drops essence of bitter almond, 1 to 2 drops vanilla essence, 1 tablespoon thick apricot purée.

Method. Pound the almonds finely in a mortar, adding the eggs one by one. Add the tangerine peel, very finely chopped, the sugar, vanilla and almond essence and the purée. Mix well.

Line a flan ring with *Short pastry II* (see DOUGH). Spread

Linzertorte (*Claire*)

Quetsch plum tart (*'A l'Alsacienne'. Phot. Larousse*)

a layer of tangerine purée on the bottom. Fill with the mixture prepared in the mortar, and bake in a moderate oven. When the flan is cold, spread with apricot jam and sprinkle with chopped almonds. Put in the oven for a few seconds to brown the almonds.

TARTARIC ACID. TARTRIQUE – Acid found in a large number of fruits and which is extracted from the lees (dregs or sediment) of wine.

It is used to prepare mineral drinks, a syrup, and effervescent powders, and is also added to a 'must' which lacks acidity (its use is tolerated in this case, but not for wines which have to be acidulated, if necessary, with citric acid). It is also used as a raising agent.

Garnished tartlets and other little hot pastry hors-d'oeuvre

TARTLET. TARTELETTE – This small cake is of ancient origin, and was already known in the sixteenth century when it was called a *flannet*, a word which is a diminutive of *flan*.

Tartlets are made in the same way as large tarts and are filled in the same way, either with fruits of different kinds, creams, or other mixtures.

Tartlets with savoury fillings are served as *hors-d'œuvre* or small *entrées*. (See HORS-D'ŒUVRE, *Hot hors-d'œuvre*.)

Filling tartlet cases baked blind

Tartlet cases or shells. CROÛTES DE TARTELETTES – Cases or shells made in round pastry tins, either fluted or plain, and of various diameters, according to the nature of the preparation.

The tins are lined with *Short pastry*, *Semi-flaky* or *Flaky pastry* (see DOUGH).

Apricot tartlets. TARTELETTES AUX ABRICOTS – Made in various shapes, round, oval, boat-shaped (*barquettes*), in moulds and rings, which are buttered and lined with very thin *Lining paste (pastry dough I)* or *Flaky pastry* (see DOUGH). The fillings and the baking are the same as for tarts.

Cherry tartlets. TARTELETTES AUX CERISES – Line tartlet moulds with *Lining paste (pastry dough I)* or *Flaky pastry* (see DOUGH). Prick the bottoms lightly with a fork. Fill with stoned cherries. Bake in a fairly hot oven.

Turn out the tartlets and coat the fruit with melted redcurrant jelly. These tartlets may be made with cherries preserved in syrup.

Strawberry, raspberry, pear, apple, plum tartlets. TARTELETTES AUX FRAISES, FRAMBOISES, POIRES, POMMES, PRUNES – Made in the same way as the previous tartlets.

TARTINE – Slice of bread spread with butter, jam or any other substance of the right consistency. It is also another name for a small tart.

Swiss tartines. TARTINES SUISSES – Roll out *Flaky pastry* (see DOUGH), about $2\frac{1}{2}$ mm. ($\frac{1}{8}$ inch) thick after it has been turned 7 times. Cut into rectangles 10 cm. (4 inches) long and 5 cm. (2 inches) wide. Set these on a baking sheet, brush with egg, and bake in a fairly hot oven. Sprinkle with fine sugar and return to the oven to glaze. Cool on a cake rack.

Split the tartines on one side and fill with the following cream:

Mix together in a saucepan 100 g. (4 oz., 1 cup) sugar, 50 g. (2 oz., $\frac{1}{2}$ cup) sifted flour and 4 egg yolks. Add a pinch of vanilla sugar or a few drops of vanilla essence. Stir in 4 dl. ($\frac{3}{4}$ pint, scant 2 cups) milk and mix. Cool, stirring constantly. Remove from heat and add 25 g. (1 oz., 2 tablespoons) butter and 3 stiffly beaten egg whites.

TASTE, FLAVOUR. SAVEUR – Sensation excited in certain organs of the mouth by contact with various substances.

A classification of flavours has often been attempted, but as there is no standard of measurement such classifications remain vague and uncertain. It is possible to distinguish tastes that are sweet, acid, salty, sour and bitter but the difficulty lies in establishing the demarcation between one type and another. These are far from being precise; the flavour of each substance comes from the combination of a number of basic flavours.

Sweet, salty and sour tastes are generally better perceived when cold than when hot. Some flavours, apparently opposed, may actually reinforce each other if they are combined in certain proportions; a sweet solution appears sweeter if a salty or sour solution, diluted just to the point where it has no more taste of its own, is added to it. A little salt is sometimes added to sweet dishes.

TASTING – See SAVOURING.

TÂTE-VIN – Silver or silver-plated cup, often decorated, used for examining and tasting wine.

TAVEL – A very popular, full-bodied dry rosé wine from the *département* of Gard. It has an *appellation d'origine contrôlée* and is usually placed in the category of Côtes du Rhône méridionales.

TEA. THÉ – Tea, the most universally consumed of all beverages, is made from the leaves of *Camellia sinensis*, a tree that in its wild state can reach the height of 10 metres (30 feet).

Tâte-vin

It is native to Assam, China and Japan. Tea was brought to Europe by the Dutch in 1610 and to England in 1644. It arrived in the U.S.A. in the early eighteenth century.

Tea-growing in China and Japan dates back to prehistoric times, but it was not started in India and Ceylon (now called Sri Lanka) until 1865.

India and Ceylon are now the largest tea exporters in the world. The largest tea import to the United States comes from Japan and Formosa; England and Russia import enormous quantities from India and China respectively. China is the largest producer of tea but does not lead in the export trade.

Tea is grown both on open fields and on terraced hillsides. It requires a warm climate with a very heavy rainfall 225–500 cm (90 to 200 inches). For fine tea, the first one or two tiny leaves which appear at the end of each twig, during 'flushes' or growing periods, are plucked. The third and fourth leaves are used only in coarse teas. These pickings occur 10 to 25 times a year in Formosa and every 10 to 12 days in Ceylon.

The principal difference in teas lies in the treatment of the leaves. Black tea comes from leaves that, partly dried, are piled up to ferment before being toasted. Green tea comes from leaves that have been fired immediately after harvesting, and is unfermented. Oolong tea is semi-fermented.

The following are the best known grades of tea: Pekoe, orange Pekoe, Souchong, Lapsang, Congou and Oolong.

Infusions of tea contain aromatic ingredients, caffeine and tannin. It is a pleasant, stimulating drink which, taken in moderate quantities, aids the digestion and in hot countries constitutes one of the best ways to drink water, since this must necessarily be boiled before it is used.

Harvesting tea (from a Chinese painting)

To make tea. Tea is very delicate and must be kept in air-tight containers in a dry place, well away from any food whose odours might contaminate it. The teapot, for the same reason, must be kept exclusively for making tea. Only pure water must be used to make it, and that as free from lime as possible.

It is very important to rinse the teapot first by rinsing it out with boiling water. When this has been done, the tea is put in, one teaspoon for each person plus one 'for the pot'. The water must be absolutely boiling. The infusion is ready at the end of 5 or 6 minutes. After this time it becomes too strong, charged with tannin. That is why teapots which cut off contact between the tea-leaves and the infusion are to be recommended, as are tea-balls and tea-spoons. Certain brands of tea are sold in small muslin or paper sachets, each containing enough tea for one, two or more cups. These sachets are

Branch of tea with fruits

Tea caddy of Queen Marie-Antoinette, soft-paste Sèvres porcelain, enamel work by Cotteau (1784–1785)

Tea: teapots and cup (*Nicolas*)

practical because they allow the tea to be made always to the same strength and check infusion at the right moment.

The name 'tea' is sometimes given to other infusions such as Jesuit's tea, Paraguay tea (see MATÉ), *thé St.-Germain, thé de santé* (health tea), a purgative, or Swiss tea, a healing lotion. In the same way the name beef tea is given to a preparation made from minced meat.

Tea ice – See ICE CREAMS AND ICES.

TEAL. SARCELLE – Wild palmiped, bird of passage with a light brown breast marked with black, white-bellied, with grey wings, white at the tip. Its flesh is oily, and generally little regarded. Teal is cooked like wild duck (see DUCK).

TEAPOT. THÉIÈRE – Receptacle made of pottery, porcelain or metal used to infuse and serve tea.

TENCH. TANCHE – Small, scaled freshwater fish of a deep olive green colour. Its flesh is rather delicate if it is fished directly from streams and rivers, otherwise it can be rather tough and should be soaked in water before cooking.

Lémery claimed that it is capable of jumping out of the frying pan even after having been cut up and partially fried!

Tench is used mainly as an ingredient of *matelote* (q.v.). It may also be fried or prepared *à la meunière* (see MEUNIÈRE, À LA).

TENDON – Roped fibres, round or flat in form and varying in length, which finish off the muscular mass and constitute its means of attachment to the bone. Tendon fibres cannot be digested by the human intestines. In cooking they exude a certain amount of gelatine.

TERFEZIA – Large white African truffle, which is almost tasteless. It can be used like black truffle, but is most often eaten raw in salad. (See TRUFFLE.)

TERRAPIN. TERRAPÈNE – Small turtle originating in North America. It is greatly prized by some Americans, who, because of the shape of the faceted scales that cover its shell, call it *diamond-back*.

Red spotted Mongolian tench

Common tench

To cook terrapin. Put the turtle in a large bowl of fresh water and leave it there for a time, changing the water every half hour. Wash and scald it by plunging it into a saucepan of boiling water. Leave it in this water until the white skin which covers the head and feet can be taken off by rubbing with a cloth.

Cook the terrapin in boiling water without salt, or steam it. This cooking, which varies in time with the size of the animal, should not exceed 45 minutes. If the flesh on the feet 'gives' under gentle pressure of the fingers, the terrapin is ready.

Allow to cool. Remove the hard scales, and with a knife detach the flat part, or *pastron*, from under the shell. Also remove the feet; cut these into pieces about 4 cm. ($1\frac{1}{2}$ inches) in size.

Remove the liver, taking care not to puncture the gall bladder; remove this from the liver and cut off all parts of the liver adjoining it. The heart, entrails and internal white muscles must be discarded.

Remove the eggs very carefully. Put these in a heat-proof dish with the feet, the sliced liver and the shell cut into pieces the same size as the feet. Season with salt, pepper and cayenne. Barely cover with water, bring to the boil, and finish cooking in a cool oven for 25 to 30 minutes.

TERRINE – Earthenware dish in which meat, game and fish are cooked. The word *terrine* is also used to designate the food itself; for example, *terrine of foie gras, of chicken*, etc.

Terrines of meat, fish, etc. must be completely cold before they are eaten. They can be kept for some days in perfect condition if they are put in a cool place.

Terrine of duckling. TERRINE DE CANETON – Bone a duckling completely and reserve the skin. Remove all the flesh from the legs and breast. Cut the breast into large dice. Put into a bowl with 100 g. (4 oz., 1 cup) diced lean ham and 100 g. (4 oz., 1 cup) diced bacon fat. Season with salt, pepper and spices. Sprinkle with 2 tablespoons (3 tablespoons) brandy. Marinate for 2 hours.

Chop finely the flesh of the legs and add to it 150 g. (5 oz., $1\frac{1}{4}$ cups) lean pork meat, 150 g. (5 oz., $1\frac{1}{4}$ cups) veal and 250 g. (9 oz., $2\frac{1}{4}$ cups) fresh pork fat, all finely chopped. Pound together in a mortar and season with spiced salt. Bind with 2 whole eggs. Add 2 liqueur glasses brandy. Rub through a sieve.

Put this mixture into the bowl where the duckling has been marinating. Add the liver cut into small pieces and fried in very hot butter. Mix well. Re-fill the skin of the duckling with this mixture and shape into a roll. Press into an oval terrine lined with thin pieces of bacon fat.

Put the *terrine* in a baking tin half-filled with warm water. Cook, covered, in a moderately hot oven, for about $1\frac{1}{4}$ hours. (The cooking time of *terrines* of poultry and other meats can be judged by the appearance of the fat that rises to the surface; if this fat is clear, the *terrine* is cooked. It can also be tested by inserting a long trussing needle into the meat. If the needle is hot when it is withdrawn the meat is cooked.)

Cool the *terrine* under pressure (a weight set on a cover cut to the shape of the *terrine*). The next day remove the fat which has risen to the surface and replace it with a layer of jelly made from a knuckle, a calf's foot and the duckling giblets. Cool the *terrine* once more. Turn out before serving.

If the *terrine* is to be kept for several days, the jelly should be replaced by half-melted lard.

TÊTE D'ALOYAU – In French butchery, the part of beef found at the end of the rump.

TÊTE DE CUVÉE – Choice wine obtained from crushing the grape (*vin de goutte*) before the wine-press is used.

TÊTE DE MORT – See CHEESE.

TÉTON DE VÉNUS – A variety of peach.

THAO – Japanese name for the agar-agar or *gelose*. (See AGAR-AGAR.)

THICKENING. LIAISON – Process designed to give body to a liquid food, sauce or broth. Thickening with flour or starch consists of making a stable paste by heating. Thickening with egg yolk or blood, which forms emulsions, must be effected at a temperature below 80°C. (175°F.) since the proteins curdle at a higher temperature.

Thickening with arrowroot. LIAISON À L'ARROW-ROOT – Pour 3 to 4 g. (1 teaspoon) arrowroot mixed with a few tablespoons of cold stock into $\frac{1}{2}$ litre (scant pint, $2\frac{1}{4}$ cups) boiling stock or juice. Leave it on heat for a few seconds. Mix and strain.

Thickening with kneaded butter. LIAISON AU BEURRE MANIÉ – A very quick method of thickening, mainly used to give the desired consistency to the sauces of stewed fish or *matelotes*.

To thicken 1 litre ($1\frac{3}{4}$ pints, generous quart) of liquid, mix thoroughly 75 g. (3 oz., $\frac{3}{4}$ cup) flour with 100 g. (4 oz., 1 cup) butter.

Thickening à la meunière. LIAISON À LA MEUNIÈRE – A smooth mixture of flour and water. This is added to stocks and sauces to give them the desired consistency.

Thickening with a roux. LIAISON AU ROUX – A *roux* can be white, golden or brown. Usually it is made from butter and flour, but other fat may be used instead of butter. (See ROUX.)

Thickening with tapioca for soups. LIAISON AU TAPIOCA POUR POTAGE – Bring to the boil 1 litre ($1\frac{3}{4}$ pints, generous quart) clear soup (consommé). Sprinkle 3 tablespoons (scant $\frac{1}{4}$ cup) of tapioca into it. Boil for 18 minutes. Strain through muslin or fine sieve.

THIRTEEN AT TABLE. TREIZE À TABLE – See SUPERSTITIONS OF THE TABLE.

THISTLE. CHARDON – Wild plant from which artichokes and cardoons derive. Different kinds of wild thistle are eaten, some for their flower head like the artichoke, some for their stems and leaves, like the cardoon, and some for their roots.

THONINE – Species of tunny (tuna fish) found only in the Mediterranean. (See TUNNY.)

THONNE – A way of cooking veal. The meat is marinated for a long time with oil, lemon juice, thyme, bay leaf and spices before being cooked, and is cooked with tuna fish.

THORINS – Wine harvested in the *département* of Saône-et-Loire, classed among the best Burgundies.

THOURINS or TOURIN – Onion-based soup much favoured in the south of France and other parts of the country.

It should not, however, be confused with *soupe à l'oignon* also called *soupe au fromage*, eaten under the name of *gratinée*.

Cook in butter, without allowing them to brown, 300 g. (11 oz., 3 cups) finely chopped onions. Sprinkle them with 25 g. (1 oz., $\frac{1}{4}$ cup) flour, stirring all the time with a wooden spoon. Stir in 2 litres ($3\frac{1}{2}$ pints, $4\frac{1}{2}$ pints) boiled milk. Season with salt and freshly ground pepper. Cook very slowly for 25 minutes.

A few minutes before serving thicken the soup with 4 egg yolks beaten with 3 dl. ($\frac{1}{2}$ pint, $1\frac{1}{4}$ cups) fresh cream, and add 2 tablespoons (3 tablespoons) butter.

Serve with thin slices of French bread dried in the oven.

Thourins à la provençale – Prepare the soup as above. Before thickening it with egg yolks and cream, add 75 g. (3 oz., $\frac{1}{2}$ cup) coarse vermicelli and poach in the soup. Serve with grated cheese.

THRUSH. GRIVE – Bird of medium size whose plumage is speckled with black or reddish spots. There are various types of thrush. The *song thrush* makes excellent eating, it grows fat on a diet of grapes! The *missal thrush*, also called the *great thrush*, has less delicate flesh than the song thrush. The *redwing* is excellent game but the *fieldfare*, a native of Northern Europe, in insipid in flavour.

Thrushes can be cooked in various ways. They are best roasted, and should be served on a slice of bread fried in the cooking fat. Although common in England and U.S.A., thrushes are rarely, if ever, eaten in these countries. In England they are protected birds and not allowed to be killed.

Thrushes à l'ardennaise. GRIVES EN CROÛTE À L'ARDENNAISE – Bone 8 thrushes along the back. Season with *Spiced salt* (see SALT). Stuff each with a little fine stuffing the size of a walnut, enriched with chopped thrush's livers, diced *foie gras* and truffles, well seasoned, with a few crushed juniper berries added. Fold the birds back into shape. Wrap each in a piece of pig's caul or salt pork. Place them, closely packed, in a pan containing the bones and trimmings of the birds, a chopped carrot and onion, all browned in butter.

Sprinkle with melted butter. Braise in the oven for 12 minutes. Drain the thrushes and remove wrapping, and put them in a large bread crust which has been scooped out, buttered inside and browned in the oven. Line the crust with the following *gratin stuffing*: chicken livers browned in grated bacon fat, well seasoned mushrooms pounded in a mortar, and mixed with sieved egg yolks.

Put this 'pie' into the oven for a few minutes. Just before serving pour the following sauce over the thrushes. Moisten the boiled-down braising stock with 2 dl. ($\frac{1}{3}$ pint, scant cup) sherry. Boil down. Add 3 dl. ($\frac{1}{2}$ pint, $1\frac{1}{4}$ cups) *Demi-glace sauce* (see SAUCE). Boil for a moment or two, strain, and add thick slices of truffle tossed in very hot butter.

Thrush à la bonne femme. GRIVES À LA BONNE-FEMME – Truss and cook the birds in butter in a heat-proof casserole with small pieces of larding bacon and diced fried bread. Sprinkle with a little brandy and pour on some game gravy. Serve in the casserole in which the birds were cooked.

All birds cooked *à la bonne femme* should be garnished with potatoes, cut in to olive shapes, small onions and larding bacon, cooked with the poultry or game.

For small birds (quails, thrushes, larks etc.) the *bonne femme* garnish consists only of small pieces of larding bacon and diced bread fried in the butter in which the bird has been cooked.

Thrush en caisses. GRIVES EN CAISSES – Bone and season the thrushes. Fill each with a little *à gratin game stuffing* (see FORCEMEAT) the size of a walnut containing a small piece of *foie gras* and a square of truffle. Remake the birds into their original shape and wrap in pieces of buttered greaseproof paper. Put them, closely packed, in a buttered heat-proof casserole. Cover the thrushes with their carcases and trimmings, first tossed in butter with an onion and a finely sliced carrot. Pour over the dish $1\frac{1}{2}$ dl. ($\frac{1}{4}$ pint, $\frac{2}{3}$ cup) Madeira. Cover and simmer for 10 minutes. Moisten with a few tablespoons of game stock and braise in the oven for 12–15 minutes until tender.

Drain the thrushes and remove the paper wrapping. Brown the birds. Serve them in buttered paper cases on a layer of sliced mushrooms and truffles tossed in butter. Pour the braising stock, strained and boiled down, over the birds.

Casserole of thrush or thrush en cocotte. GRIVES EN CASSEROLE, OU EN COCOTTE – Proceed as for *Casserole of quail* (see QUAIL).

Chaud-froid of thrush. GRIVES EN CHAUD-FROID – Made from thrushes boned and stuffed with *foie gras* and truffles, as for *Chaud-froid of quail* (see QUAIL).

Thrushes with grapes. GRIVES AUX RAISINS – Cook in a casserole as *Casserole of quails with grapes* (see QUAIL).

Thrushes au gratin. GRIVES AU GRATIN – Put inside each bird a piece of *à gratin game stuffing* (see FORCEMEAT) the size of a walnut, with the chopped giblets of the thrushes added. Flavour with a few crushed juniper berries.

Truss the birds and brown them quickly in butter. Spread on a buttered heat-proof dish a layer of *à gratin game stuffing* (see FORCEMEAT) 1 cm ($\frac{1}{2}$ inch) thick. Press the thrushes gently into the stuffing. Coat them with thick *Duxelles sauce* (see SAUCE). Sprinkle with breadcrumbs, pour melted butter over them, and brown in a very hot oven.

Thrushes à la liégeoise. GRIVES À LA LIÉGEOISE – Put inside each bird a piece of butter the size of a walnut, with a few crushed juniper berries added. Brown them in a heat-proof casserole in which a little butter has been melted. Sprinkle the birds with crushed juniper berries, about 2 berries for each. Cover, and cook in a moderately hot oven for 30–40 minutes or until tender. Two minutes before taking the casserole out of the oven, cover each bird with a piece of bread fried in butter. Sprinkle with a few drops of gin.

Cold thrush pâté. PÂTÉ FROID DE GRIVES – Proceed as for *Cold woodcock pâté* (see WOODCOCK).

Hot thrush pâté. PÂTÉ CHAUD DE GRIVES – Bone the thrushes and stuff them with *foie gras* and truffles. Proceed as for *Hot woodcock pâté* (see WOODCOCK).

Thrush pie. TOURTE DE GRIVES À LA PÉRIGOURDINE – Bone the thrushes. Stuff each with a little *à gratin game stuffing* (see FORCEMEAT) the size of a walnut, containing a small piece of *foie gras* with a piece of truffle embedded in it. Partly braise the thrushes in Madeira-flavoured stock. Allow to cool.

Put the thrushes in a thin pie-crust lined with a little more stuffing, covered with strips of truffle. Cover the birds with a thin layer of *à gratin game stuffing*. Cover with a piece of *Short pastry I* (see DOUGH) and seal the edges.

Decorate the top of the pie with little motifs of thin pastry. Brush with beaten egg. Bake in a moderately hot oven for 40 to 45 minutes. After the pie has been taken out of the oven, pour in a few tablespoons of *Salmis sauce* (see SAUCE).

Potted thrush. TERRINE DE GRIVES – Made from boned birds stuffed with *foie gras* and truffles like other types of potted game. (See TERRINE.)

Roast thrushes. GRIVES RÔTIES – Wrap each bird in a thin strip of larding bacon. Roast them in a hot oven for 20 to 30 minutes. Serve each bird on a *canapé* of bread fried in butter. Dilute the gravy and serve separately.

THYME. THYM – Plant with small, grey-green leaves and a pleasant, pungent smell, much used as a flavouring. Wild thyme is a variety of the garden thyme.

THYMUS – A ductless gland situated in the upper part of the thorax in children and young vertebrates, which becomes atrophied in puberty.

In butchered animals it is called the *sweetbread* (calf, lamb) and constitutes a very delicate food. It should be eaten only in moderation, or not at all, by sufferers from gout. For culinary preparation see OFFAL or VARIETY MEATS.

TIERED PLINTH. GRADINS – In former times, carved wooden stands were used for the presentation of cold dishes, especially set pieces of confectionery. These stands were made in tiers. They were decorated with *pâte d'office*, almond paste, sugar motifs or icing sugar.

Nowadays, such plinths are made from sandwich bread, as, for example, for poultry *chaud-froids* (see CHAUD-FROID).

Carême tells us how tiered plinths were decorated in his day: 'Let us suppose, for example, that you wish to decorate a

Tiered plinth made from sandwich bread

plinth with laurel leaves. You first cut out a laurel wreath in paper. Next you give the base of the plinth a light coating of icing, and stick the paper wreath to it. Now you cover the rest of the plinth with a medium grade of coarse sugar. When this is done, you remove the paper, after which you sprinkle the imprint of the leaves with pistachio-green sugar. Now, you have a laurel crown surrounding the base of the plinth.

'For a large, three-tiered set piece, each tier can be individually decorated. This creates a graceful and elegant effect.

'I have also sometimes embellished my tiers with laurel crowns made from biscuit pastry shaped like laurel leaves and coloured green, or with garlands of spun sugar. This last decoration has both brilliance and elegance.

'I have also created tiered plinths out of almond paste, moulded in basket moulds.'

But although he favoured the presentation of set pieces on plinths, Carême maintained that 'young practitioners' should not forget 'that plinths of German or Italian waffles, of *nougat*, of glazed *duchesse* cakes, of puff pastry, baked without filling or in the shape of fish scales, or in round or oval rings, of Genoese cake, or of nut toffee, are immensely effective and properly belong in the realm of the great pastry-making establishments.'

TIGER. TIGRE – The flesh of the tiger is sometimes eaten in some countries.

TIMBALE – By definition this word (which comes from the Arab *thabal* meaning *drum*) means a small metal receptacle, round in shape and intended to hold a beverage.

Timbales are chiefly made of silver, sometimes of gold or silver plate, some simple, others ornamented.

The word *timbale*, which in early days was only applied to individual drinking cups, has taken on a much wider meaning, and is used to describe all kinds of bowls, of metal, earthenware, and china. The same word is still used in the phrase *dresser en timbale* to describe the serving of some preparation in a large bowl, which may be a vegetable dish or *légumier*, although used for many other foodstuffs than vegetables. Thus in these *timbales-légumiers* are served scrambled eggs, food in sauce, purées, custards and other preparations, all to some extent semi-liquid. *Dresser en timbale* also means to heap the food on a platter in a pyramid shape, usually garnished.

Timbale generally means a preparation of any kind cooked or served in a pie crust, which, instead of being made in a hinged mould is made in a plain round mould with high sides, often decorated with motifs.

Timbales are filled before cooking with forcemeat and meats of various kinds. Below will be found instructions for the various stages of preparation of a *timbale* in a mould with goffered sides. This is the true classic form of the *timbale*, of which a typical example is the *timbale de macaroni* or *timbale milanaise*.

There are many other kinds of *timbale* which are not filled until after the crust has been cooked. In this case the crust is baked empty. Among these are *timbale of sole à la Grimaldi, timbale de volaille à la royale, timbale of lamb's sweetbreads a la périgourdine, timbale of truffles à l'impériale*, and in the case of sweet *timbales, timbale of apricots à la frangipane, timbale of fruit à l'ancienne, timbale of cherries à la Chantilly*, etc.

Timbale cases are made in fireproof porcelain in the same shape and colour of the real pie-crusts. But the true gourmand is not satisfied with a *timbale* whose crust is not edible; when served with a real *timbale*, he enjoys not only the contents but the container, too.

Large timbale case or crust (mixed entrée). CROÛTE DE GRANDE TIMBALE – Butter the interior of a large charlotte mould, and decorate the sides with little shapes of noodle paste.

Roll short pastry into a round 20 cm. (8 inches) in diameter. Sprinkle lightly with flour and fold in half. Fold again and roll it out to make an even thickness of about $\frac{3}{4}$ cm. ($\frac{1}{3}$ inch). Press it in the mould, without disturbing the noodle paste decorations.

Insert a fine buttered paper and fill it up with dried raw beans as for a flan case or tart (see TART). Put a dome-shaped piece of paper on top of the dry filling, and a thin sheet of pastry on top of this, joining the edges together by gently pressing. Make the rim of the pie by pinching this border with pastry pincers. Moisten lightly with water the part forming the lid, and decorate with leaves, roses, etc., cut from a thin sheet of pastry.

Put on top of the lid 3 or 4 circles of pastry, with the middles cut out to make circles. Stick these circles together and make an opening in the pastry to allow for the escape of steam during the cooking. Brush the outside of the pie with egg and bake in the oven at a moderate heat for 30 to 35 minutes.

Remove the lid. Take out the paper and dried beans, brush the inside with egg, and let it dry in the oven for a few minutes. Fill the *timbale* as desired.

Timbale cases cooked in this way are used as containers for a variety of mixed *entrées*. They can be filled with *ragoûts*, with garnishes such as *Financière, Godard, Joinville, Milanaise, Toulouse* and others of a similar nature (see GARNISHES).

They are frequently filled with macaroni arranged in alternate layers with a *ragoût* bound with brown or white sauce. See below.

Small timbales Agnes Sorel (old recipe). PETITES TIMBALES AGNÈS SOREL – 'Butter a dozen *dariole* moulds. Sprinkle in one-half truffles and one-half scarlet tongue, both finely chopped.

'Prepare 500 g. (1 lb., 4 cups) chicken forcemeat with cream. Add a few tablespoons *Onion soubise* (see PURÉE). Fill the moulds with this forcemeat, taking care to leave a hole in the middle and to keep the forcemeat rather thick on the bottom and round the sides. Fill the hole in the middle with a *salpicon* of chicken and truffles bound with *Espagnole sauce* (see SAUCE) made with Madeira.

'Close the tops of the moulds with a layer of raw forcemeat. Set the moulds in a saucepan and pour in hot water to half way up the sides. Poach the *timbales* in a moderately hot oven for 12 to 15 minutes. Turn out of the moulds and set them on a thin layer of poached forcemeat. Spoon over a little

Making a timbale case (*'A l'Alsacienne', Maison Morand. Phot. Larousse*)

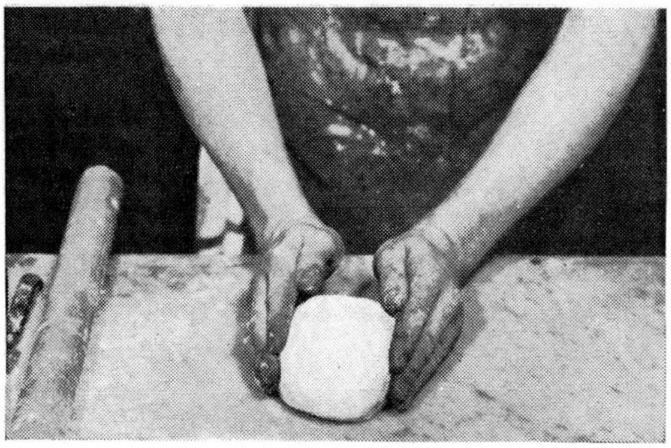

Shape the dough into a ball

Roll out to a round

Fold the rolled out round of pastry in half

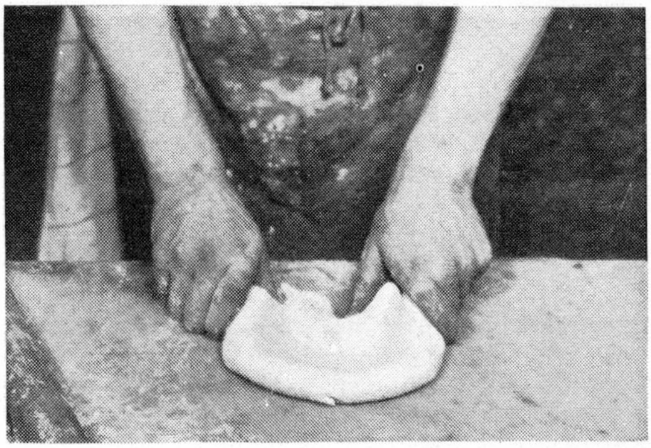

Shape to form an inverted dome

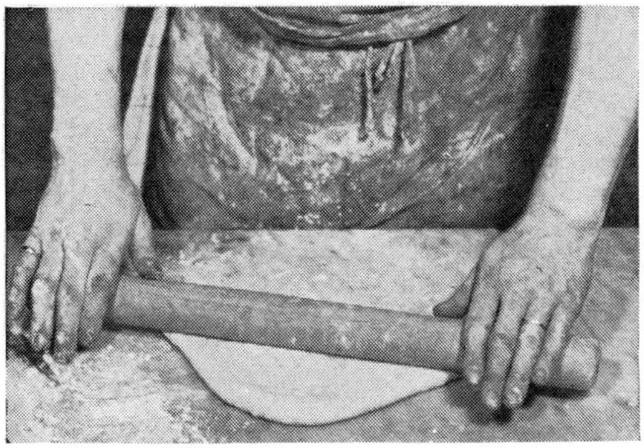

Sprinkle with flour and roll out again to an even thickness of about $\frac{3}{4}$ cm. ($\frac{1}{3}$ inch)

Press the pastry into the mould, right to the base, with the edges overlapping

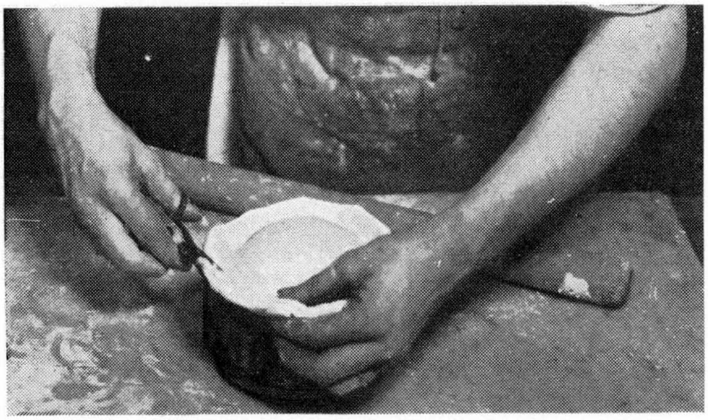

Trim the pastry edges to the rim of the mould

Cover with a decorated lid of pastry and 'chimney'

espagnole sauce cooked with the trimmings and liquor of the truffles.

'Serve with the rest of the sauce.'

Timbale Brillat-Savarin – Hollow out a *Brioche mousseline* (see BRIOCHE) cooked in a charlotte mould, to make a pie crust. Brush with apricot purée flavoured with kirsch, and heat in the oven. Fill it with alternate layers of quartered pears cooked in vanilla syrup and well drained, and *French pastry cream* (see CREAMS) mixed with finely crushed macaroons. Finish off by covering the top with pears mounted in a dome. Decorate with candied fruits. Heat again in a low oven.

Serve with apricot purée flavoured with kirsch.

Timbale Elysée – First prepare 8 pastry cups from crisp, biscuit-type pastry made by thoroughly blending 100 g. (4 oz., 1 cup) flour, 100 g. (4 oz., $\frac{1}{2}$ cup) sugar, 1 egg, 50 g. (2 oz., $\frac{1}{4}$ cup) rather soft butter. Flavour with vanilla.

Spoon this pastry (1 heaped tablespoon for each pastry cup) onto a buttered and floured baking tray. Bake in a moderately hot oven until crisp and lightly browned.

While the pastry rounds are still hot, mould each of them over some object with a flattened dome shape (e.g. bottom of an upturned bowl or ladle) to produce a cup shape.

Place a small slice of sponge soaked in a kirsch-flavoured syrup at the bottom of each pastry cup. Add a spoonful of vanilla ice cream and cover with sliced fresh fruit; strawberries, raspberries, etc.

Coat this with a spoonful of kirsch-flavoured redcurrant jelly, then pipe a ribbon of *Chantilly cream* (see CREAMS) round the inside edge of the cup.

Finally, cover each of the garnished cups with a cage of spun sugar made by cooking sugar to a hard crack using 200 g. (7 oz., 1 cup) sugar, 40 g. ($1\frac{1}{2}$ oz., 1 heaped tablespoon) glucose (for 8 spun sugar cages) then threading this sugar in as delicate a lattice as possible over the bowl of a suitably-sized ladle. (Recipe from the restaurant *Lasserre.*)

Macaroni timbale à l'américaine. TIMBALE DE MACARONI À L'AMÉRICAINE – Prepare a *timbale* crust of *Fine lining paste* (see DOUGH) and bake it empty. Fill with alternate layers of macaroni cooked in water, drained and bound with Parmesan cheese and butter, and a *salpicon* of *Lobster à l'américaine* (see LOBSTER).

Finish off by placing on top a row of sliced lobster, and coat with *Américaine sauce* (see SAUCE). Cover the *timbale*, heat for a few moments in the oven, and serve.

Macaroni timbales à la milanaise. TIMBALES DE MACARONI À LA MILANAISE – Place slices of truffle in well buttered *dariole* moulds, and fill with thick macaroni, cooked in salted water and drained well. Arrange the macaroni in spirals in the moulds. Add a thin layer of *Quenelle forcemeat* (see FORCEMEAT) and fill with macaroni cut into small dice prepared *à la milanaise* (see MACARONI). Add a garnish of scarlet tongue, cooked ham, truffles and mushrooms, all cut in *julienne*. Cover the *timbales* with a layer of quenelle forcemeat. Put into a *bain-marie* and poach in a moderately hot oven for 18 to 20 minutes. Turn out the *timbales* on to a dish. Pour in a few tablespoons of *Demi-glace sauce* flavoured with a little tomato and Madeira (see SAUCE).

Timbale of sole à l'américaine, or Timbale Monselet. TIMBALE DE SOLES À L'AMÉRICAINE – Prepare a *timbale* crust of *Fine lining paste* (see DOUGH) and bake it empty.

Fill with *Paupiettes of sole* (see SOLE) cooked in white wine, cooked macaroni bound with butter and Parmesan, and a *salpicon* of lobster prepared *à l'américaine*. Coat with *Américaine sauce* (see SAUCE).

Timbale of fillets of sole Grimaldi. TIMBALE DE SOLE GRIMALDI – see SOLE, *Fillets of sole.*

Small timbales of vegetables. PETITES TIMBALES DE LÉGUMES – To garnish cold meats, etc. Coat small *dariole* moulds with jelly based on fish or meat stock, according to the food that is to be garnished. Decorate the moulds with pieces of truffle, hard boiled egg whites, scarlet tongue and tarragon leaves. Fill with vegetable salad bound with mayonnaise thickened with jelly. Pour a layer of jelly over the salad. Chill the timbales on ice or in the refrigerator.

Timbales of vegetables to garnish cold dishes (which can also be served as *hors-d'œuvre* or small *entrée*) can be filled with a single vegetable, asparagus tips, French beans, little carrot balls, diced artichoke bottoms, etc., dressed with *vinaigrette* or mayonnaise.

Tinamou

TINAMOU – Partridge-like bird native to South America. It has been acclimatised in France.

All the recipes given for pheasant (q.v.) are applicable to *tinamou.*

TIN. ÉTAIN – A metal often used in the form of 'silver' paper or foil to wrap foods (confectionery, chocolate, cheese, *saucisson*, etc.) Tinware and tin measures were widely used in the past; pewter, in particular, is very beautiful. Both are back in fashion again but much more for their aesthetic value than for their usefulness. Wine combines very well with tin or pewter, so does English beer.

TINNING. ÉTAMAGE – The process of covering a metal with a layer of tin.

The tinning or retinning of vessels or utensils used in food preparation must be done in a bath containing a minimum of 97 per cent pure tin and a maximum of 0·50 per cent lead and $\frac{1}{10}$ ml. arsenic.

TINPLATE. FER-BLANC – Tinplate is pressed iron covered with tin. A great many utensils used in cooking and confectionery used to be made from it, but pots and pans made of aluminium, nickel, fireproof porcelain, heat-resisting glass, cast-iron, stainless steel, etc. are replacing them.

TIRETTE – French butchery term describing a broad, flat tendon.

TISANE – This word comes from the Latin *ptisana*, barley water.

The *tisane* of Hippocrates was barley water; today the name tisane is applied to drinks for invalids prepared by soaking or infusion.

Digestive tisanes. TISANES DIGESTIVES – The habit of drinking these after a meal is to be discouraged. Tisanes are virtually medicines and ought to be treated as such.

However, some of them have well-proven digestive properties and may be safely drunk after the meal by those suffering from digestive troubles.

Boldo. A bush that grows in Chile and has not been successfully grown in Europe. Its leaves are therefore only to be obtained from herbalists and chemists. They resemble those of the periwinkle and contain two active constituents, *boldine* and *boldoglucine*, which have a stimulating and tonic effect on the liver. It is used in the infusion of 10 g. ($\frac{1}{2}$ oz., 1 tablespoon) leaves per litre ($1\frac{3}{4}$ pints, generous quart) of water, one cupful to be drunk after each main meal. An elixir can also be made from it: steep 25 g. (1 oz., $\frac{1}{4}$ cup) leaves in 1 dl. (6 tablespoons, scant $\frac{1}{2}$ cup) alcohol and $\frac{1}{2}$ litre (scant pint, $2\frac{1}{4}$ cups). Madeira wine for 8 days; strain, then add 300 g. (12 oz., $1\frac{1}{2}$ cups) sugar; filter after 3 or 4 days. Take one liqueur glass daily.

Centaury (Lesser). CENTAURÉE (PETITE) – Do not confuse the lesser centaury of the gentian family with the common centaury which is related to the blueberry. The stem of the lesser centaury is 20 to 40 cm. (8 to 16 inches) high divided at the top into branches which bear small clusters of pink flowers. It is found in woods, pastures and on sandy ground. The whole plant is used and contains constituents that stimulate the salivary and gastric juices, aid digestion and allay stomach pains. It is used in infusion: 25 g. (1 oz., $\frac{1}{4}$ cup) stalk and dried flowering tops per litre ($1\frac{3}{4}$ pints, generous quart) of boiling water. Drink a cupful before or after meals.

Gentian (Yellow). GENTIANE – This plant grows in the mountains and is well anchored in the soil by a root which can be over 1 m. (approximately 3 feet) long and weigh up to 10 kg. (22 lb.). The yellow flowers rise in tiers up the stem which can be up to 1 m. (3 feet) high. The root is used in the preparation of bitter alcohol-based *apéritifs* of a beautiful golden hue. The bitter constituents of this root (gentiamarine and gentisine) increase the salivary secretions and stimulate the digestive juices making this plant the most precious of all tonics. It is used in a tisane: 100 g. (4 oz., 1 cup) finely chopped root per litre ($1\frac{3}{4}$ pints, generous quart) of water; boil for 2 to 3 minutes then allow to infuse. Take one cupful before and after each meal. It is also macerated: 3 g. (about 1 teaspoon) chopped root per cupful of boiling water; leave to steep for 4 hours; take 1 cupful before and after each meal. Finally, there is a gentian wine: steep 25 g. (4 oz., 1 cup) chopped root in 1 litre ($1\frac{3}{4}$ pints, generous quart) white wine for 1 week. Take half a wine glassful after each meal. Alternatively, the gentian root may be steeped in $\frac{1}{2}$ dl. (3 tablespoons, scant $\frac{1}{4}$ cup) alcohol and 1 litre ($1\frac{3}{4}$ pints, generous quart) red wine.

Melissa. MÉLISSE – A plant from the South with a stem about 60 cm. (2 feet) high and oval serrated leaves. The pleasantly lemon-scented flower is usually white but can have a reddish hue. Melissa is used in infusion: 10 g. ($\frac{1}{2}$ oz., 2 tablespoons) leaves per litre ($1\frac{3}{4}$ pints, generous quart) water. Take 1 cupful before main meals. There is also a melissa wine: steep 50 g. (2 oz., $\frac{1}{2}$ cup) leaves in 1 litre ($1\frac{3}{4}$ pints, generous quart) white wine for 48 hours. Take 1 or 2 tablespoons at each meal. Finally here is a recipe for *Melissa water* which is well known for its stimulative and anti-spasmodic properties. *Ingredients.* 50 g. (2 oz., $\frac{1}{2}$ cup) melissa, 5 g. ($1\frac{1}{4}$ teaspoons) cinnamon, 15 g. (2 tablespoons) fresh lemon zest, 10 g. ($\frac{1}{2}$ oz., 1 tablespoon) angelica, 15 g. ($1\frac{1}{2}$ teaspoons) coriander, 10 g. ($\frac{1}{2}$ oz., 2 teaspoons) cloves, 15 g. ($1\frac{1}{2}$ teaspoons) nutmeg.

Method. Macerate for 15 days in 1 litre ($1\frac{3}{4}$ pints, generous quart) white *eau-de-vie*. Filter, squeezing the juice out of the residue as you do so. Bottle. Take $1\frac{1}{4}$ teaspoons in sweetened water for as long as disturbances last.

TISANE DE CHAMPAGNE – Name for a Champagne that is rather lighter than some.

TOAST – Slice of bread, thick or thin, square or rectangular in shape, put under the grill or in an electric toaster and 'toasted' on both sides. It is sometimes served in a special holder called a toast-rack.

TOASTER. GRILLE-PAIN – Special small grille for toasting slices of bread. They are usually electric.

TOBACCO. TABAC – Solanaceous plant, originating on the island of Tobago, the leaves of which are prepared in various ways and either smoked, taken as snuff or chewed.

Smoking before a meal dulls the sense of taste. Professional tasters are obliged to renounce it. Smoking during a meal is simply barbaric; tobacco smoke completely prevents one from savouring the dishes and annoys other people in those restaurants where this habit is allowed. Tobacco has its rightful place after a meal, when its aroma blends agreeably with that of coffee.

TOCANE – New Champagne made from the first pressing.

TODDY PALM. ARBRE À LIQUEUR – Species of palm tree, also known as milk tree. It grows in great numbers in the Moluccas and is none other than sago palm, which produces sap during a part of the year, fermented into a very strong alcoholic beverage much appreciated by the local inhabitants.

TOKAY – White wine originally harvested in Tokaj, Hungary. The name *Tokai* is also used for a variety of wine cultivated chiefly in Alsace.

Fresh tomatoes despatched in a box

TOMATO. TOMATE – Herbaceous plant of South American origin, of which there are many varieties, with red or yellow, round or oval fruit. In olden days these fruits were called *pommes d'amour* – 'love apples'.

The tomato is rich in Vitamins A, B, C and E; it is an aperient, a diuretic and a detoxicant. The abundance of salts it contains (citrates, tartrates, oxalates) give it its acid taste. Sufferers from skin troubles, arthritis, etc., should not eat too many tomatoes.

The principal French varieties are: (among the earliest) *Marmande*, of which there are a number of varieties, *Pierrette*, *Ronde hâtive*; seasonal varieties including *Saint-Pierre*, *Casaque rouge*, *Joffre*, *Marglobe*.

French production is concentrated mostly in the south-east and in the Garonne valley. The season is at its height between June and October, but the markets are well stocked the whole year round with tomatoes from North Africa, the Canaries, Spain; hothouse tomatoes are available both in France and Holland.

Tomato fondue. FONDUE DE TOMATES – Tomatoes peeled,

pressed, chopped and cooked till soft in butter, seasoned in various ways, usually with chopped garlic included. Tomato fondue is used as a garnish with various dishes, eggs, fish, meat, poultry, etc. and to fill *bouchées*, tartlets and *croustades*.

Tomato fondue à la grecque. FONDUE DE TOMATES À LA GRECQUE – Put into a saucepan 12 g. (1 tablespoon) chopped onions and cook till soft in 2 tablespoons (3 tablespoons) oil. Add 6 peeled and roughly chopped tomatoes, and 2 sweet pimentos, peeled and cut in very small dice. Season with salt and paprika and a little chopped garlic. Cook gently until the liquid from the tomatoes is well concentrated.

Tomato fondue à la niçoise. FONDUE DE TOMATES À LA NIÇOISE – Prepare the fondue as above. Season with extra garlic and add a teaspoon chopped tarragon.

Tomato fondue à la portugaise. FONDUE DE TOMATES À LA PORTUGAISE – Like *Tomato fondue à la niçoise* but without the tarragon.

Tomato fondue à la turque. FONDUE DE TOMATES À LA TURQUE – Like *Tomato fondue à la grecque* but without the pimento.

Fried tomatoes. TOMATES FRITES – Heat and peel tomatoes of medium size. Cut them in slices 1 cm. ($\frac{1}{2}$ inch) thick. Season with salt and pepper, dip in a light batter and drop them into smoking hot fat or oil.

Drain the tomatoes and garnish with fried parsley. Serve immediately, as they will quickly become limp.

Concentrated tomato glaze. SUC DE TOMATES CONCENTRÉ, GLACE DE TOMATES – Rub through a fine sieve 1 kg. ($2\frac{1}{4}$ lb.) tomatoes without removing seeds or juice. Cook over strong heat. When the pulp is boiled down by half, strain through a very fine strainer.

Cook once more. Strain again when it is well concentrated. Cook the pulp again until it is of a syrupy consistency.

This glaze, when it has been reduced to the desired point, can be kept for a long time. It should be put in small glass or china pots. It is used to heighten the flavour of certain sauces and preparations such as stuffings, *salpicons*, salads, etc.

Gratin of tomato and aubergine. GRATIN DE TOMATES ET D'AUBERGINES – Arrange in layers in an oiled or buttered gratin dish tomatoes and aubergines previously fried in butter or oil. Sprinkle with breadcrumbs, then with oil or melted butter. Brown in a moderate oven.

Grilled tomatoes. TOMATES GRILLÉS – Cut a circle off the top of the tomatoes on the stalk side and through this opening carefully remove the seeds. Season and brush with oil or melted butter. Grill at a low heat.

The tomatoes may be halved before being grilled.

Tomato jam – See JAM.

Tomato ketchup or catsup – English condiment, very highly spiced, found ready-made in grocers' and other foodshops. It is used in English cookery to season certain sauces and it accompanies cold meats. For recipe see KETCHUP.

Tomato loaf. PAIN DE TOMATES – Boil down some *Tomato sauce* (see SAUCE), and when it is well thickened add 6 beaten eggs for every 500 g. (18 oz., 1 cup) of the sauce. Season with salt, pepper and a pinch of spice.

Fill a well-buttered mould with the mixture. Poach in a *bain-marie* in a cool oven.

Leave for a few moments before turning out of the mould. Coat with *Tomato sauce* with added butter (see SAUCE).

Tomato loaf is chiefly used as an accompaniment to meat and served in small *dariole* moulds.

Cold tomato mousse. MOUSSE FROIDE DE TOMATES – Peel, press out seeds and juice and chop 500 g. (18 oz., 1 cup) tomato flesh.

When the pulp has well dried out, add 1 dl. (6 tablespoons, $\frac{1}{2}$ cup) *Velouté sauce* (see SAUCE) to which $1\frac{1}{2}$ tablespoons (2 tablespoons) powdered gelatine, softened in cold water, have been added.

Strain the mixture through a sieve. Put into a bowl, whisk until smooth, cool, and add half its volume of whipped cream. Season, and add a little cayenne and a few drops lemon juice. Mix well.

Pour into a glass dish or, when the tomato mousse is to be used as an accompaniment to cold dishes, into small dariole moulds lined with a layer of jelly.

Chill on ice or in the refrigerator.

Cold tomato mousselines. MOUSSELINES FROIDES DE TOMATES – Prepared with the same mixture as the above, but served in *cassolettes* of metal, china, glass or goffered paper, or moulded in small moulds lined with jelly.

These *mousselines* are served as cold *hors-d'œuvre*, or used as part of the garnish for a cold dish.

Fresh tomato pulp. PULPE DE TOMATES FRAÎCHES – This pulp should not be confused with tomato sauce or tomato purée. It is an ingredient of a number of made-up dishes, and, cold, is used to dress some salads. It is also used to make tomato jam (see JAM).

Wash $2\frac{1}{2}$ kg. ($5\frac{1}{2}$ lb.) ripe, sound tomatoes, cut in slices, and rub them through a sieve. Put the pulp into a saucepan (or into a preserving pan if the pulp is to be used for jam) and boil for a few moments.

Strain through a cloth to get rid of the water completely. The thick pulp which remains in the cloth is used according to the instructions in the recipe.

Tomato purée. PURÉE DE TOMATES – See SAUCE, *Tomato sauce*.

Tomato salad. SALADE DE TOMATES – Scald the tomatoes, peel them and remove the pips. Cut in slices, not too thick. Lay on a folded cloth, season with salt and leave for 30 minutes to yield their liquid.

Arrange in an *hors-d'œuvre* or salad dish. Season with oil, vinegar, pepper and chopped parsley. This salad can also be made with the tomatoes cut in quarters.

Tomato salad (which is normally served as an *hors-d'œuvre*) may be sprinkled with various aromatic herbs, such as tarragon, fresh fennel, fresh basil, etc.

When served in *hors-d'œuvre* dishes, the tomatoes may also be covered with thin slices of new onions.

Tomato sauce. SAUCE TOMATE – See SAUCE.

Tomatoes sauté aux fines herbes. TOMATES SAUTÉES AUX FINES HERBES – Cut the tomatoes in half. Press the halves to extract the seeds, and season with salt and pepper. Fry lightly in butter. Set on a dish and sprinkle with parsley and the cooking butter, very hot, in which a small quantity of freshly made breadcrumbs have been fried.

Tomatoes sauté à la lyonnaise. TOMATES SAUTÉES À LA LYONNAISE – Fry halved tomatoes as above. Set on a dish on a layer of chopped onions cooked in butter. Sprinkle with chopped parsley. Pour over the cooking butter, to which 3 tablespoons (4 tablespoons) chopped onion, previously cooked in butter, have been added.

Tomatoes sauté à la provençale. TOMATES SAUTÉES À LA PROVENÇALE – Prepared in oil like *Tomatoes sauté aux fines herbes*, adding a little chopped garlic.

Tomato soufflé. SOUFFLÉ DE TOMATES – Prepare 6 dl. (1 pint, $2\frac{1}{2}$ cups) very thick tomato purée (see SAUCE, *Tomato sauce*). Add to this $\frac{1}{2}$ cup thick *béchamel sauce* and 6 egg yolks. Season with salt, pepper and grated nutmeg. Add 6 stiffly beaten egg whites. Mix quickly.

Turn into a buttered soufflé dish, filling only to within 1 cm. ($\frac{1}{2}$ inch) of the top. Smooth over the surface of the soufflé. Cook in the oven like an ordinary soufflé.

Soufflé tomatoes. TOMATES SOUFFLÉES – Empty some firm, regular-shaped tomatoes into a baking dish without breaking. Sprinkle them with oil or melted butter and cook in the oven for 5 minutes. Allow to cool, and fill them with tomato soufflé mixture made according to the recipe for *Tomato soufflé*.

Fill the tomatoes to the top, smooth the surface, sprinkle with grated Parmesan cheese and cook in a slow oven for about 10 minutes.

Grated Parmesan may be added to the mixture.

Stuffed tomatoes. TOMATES FARCIES – Choose medium-sized tomatoes. Cut a circle round the stalk and open them. Press lightly to remove the juice and seeds and season with salt and pepper.

Set in rows on an oiled baking tin. Pour a few drops of oil into each tomato and put into a very hot oven for 5 minutes.

Drain the tomatoes and stuff them with thickened *duxelles* seasoned with a little garlic, and with the addition of diced lean ham and freshly made breadcrumbs. Pile the stuffing in a dome. Set the tomatoes on an oiled baking tin, put breadcrumbs on top, sprinkle with oil, and cook in the oven for 12 to 15 minutes.

Cold stuffed tomatoes. TOMATES FROIDES – Served as *hors-d'œuvre* or used as garnish with various cold dishes.

Empty firm tomatoes without breaking the skin. Season with salt and pepper. Sprinkle with oil and a few drops of vinegar or lemon juice. Leave upside down to drain for 1 hour.

Mix the scooped-out insides with a little garlic, diced ham and a few white breadcrumbs. Use to fill the tomatoes. Garnish with truffles, hard boiled egg whites, tarragon or chervil leaves.

Stuffed tomatoes à la bonne femme. TOMATES FARCIES À LA BONNE FEMME – Halve large tomatoes, remove the seeds and season with salt and pepper. Fry them in very hot oil. Stuff with sausage meat to which chopped onion cooked until soft in butter, freshly made breadcrumbs and chopped parsley and garlic, have been added. Cover with breadcrumbs and sprinkle with oil. Cook in a moderately hot oven.

Stuffed tomatoes à la languedocienne. TOMATES FARCIES À LA LANGUEDOCIENNE – Sauté halves of tomatoes, seasoned with salt and pepper, in hot oil. Stuff them with a mixture of sausage meat, chopped hard boiled egg yolks, chopped onion, lightly cooked in oil, and chopped parsley and garlic.

Place in a buttered ovenproof dish. Cover with breadcrumbs and sprinkle with oil. Cook in a moderately hot oven until the breadcrumbs are golden brown.

Stuffed tomatoes à la niçoise. TOMATES FARCIES À LA NIÇOISE – Stuff halves of tomatoes prepared as in the preceding recipe with a mixture of rice cooked in a meat stock, aubergine cooked in oil and chopped, breadcrumbs, chopped parsley and chopped garlic, the whole well seasoned and mixed.

Put the tomatoes in a buttered ovenproof dish, cover them with breadcrumbs and sprinkle with oil. Cook in a moderately hot oven until the breadcrumbs are golden brown.

Stuffed tomatoes à la parisienne. TOMATES FARCIES À LA PARISIENNE – Cook whole tomatoes lightly in oil. Take out the seeds and fill them with a fine forcemeat mixed with a *salpicon* of truffles and mushrooms cooked in butter (see FORCEMEAT). Put into a buttered ovenproof dish. Cover with breadcrumbs and sprinkle with melted butter. Cook in a

Stuffed tomatoes (*Robert Carrier*)

moderately hot oven until the breadcrumbs are golden brown.

Stuffed tomatoes à la piémontaise or à l'italienne. TOMATES FARCIES À LA PIÉMONTAISE, À L'ITALIENNE – Slice off the tops of medium-sized tomatoes and press them to remove the juice and seeds, taking care not to break the skin. Season the inside. Stuff them, before cooking, with *Risotto* (see RICE) to which concentrated tomato purée has been added. Put the tomatoes on a buttered baking tin, sprinkle with melted butter and cook gently in a moderately hot oven for about 15 minutes. Set them on a dish, surround with *Tomato sauce* (not too thick – see SAUCE) and sprinkle with chopped parsley.

Stuffed tomatoes à la reine. TOMATES FARCIES AU SALPICON DE VOLAILLE, DITES À LA REINE – Fill medium-sized seeded tomatoes, lightly cooked in butter, with a *salpicon* of poultry mixed with diced truffles and mushrooms bound with thick *Velouté sauce* (see SAUCE).

Put the tomatoes on a buttered baking tin. Cover them with breadcrumbs, sprinkle with melted butter and cook in a moderately hot oven until the breadcrumbs are golden brown.

Tomatoes à la vinaigrette. TOMATES À LA VINAIGRETTE – Plunge tomatoes into boiling water, cool in cold water, and dry them.

Peel them completely and remove the seeds and juice without breaking them. Cut into thin slices or quarters.

Lay these on a napkin folded in four. Season with salt and leave them for 10 minutes.

Serve the tomatoes in an *hors-d'œuvre* dish and sprinkle with a few tablespoons of *Vinaigrette* (see SAUCE). Sprinkle with chopped parsley and, if liked, chervil and tarragon. Serve very cold.

TOMBER – This old French cookery term (literally 'to fall'), describes a way of cooking meat in a saucepan without any other liquid than that produced by the meat itself. The moisture must, after cooking is complete, be *tombé* (that is to say must fall or go down), to a syrupy consistency.

Tomber à glace – Phrase used when some substance, such as onion or shallot, is moistened during cooking with liquid which is then completely boiled down.

TONGS. PINCE – Name of various instruments of different shapes, according to the use for which they are intended. The following types of tongs are used at table: asparagus tongs, *escargot* tongs, sugar tongs, etc.

TONGUE (OX, CALF, SHEEP, PIG). LANGUES DE BŒUF, DE MOUTON, DE PORC – See OFFAL or VARIETY MEATS.

TONKA BEAN. FÈVE TONKA – Fruit of a leguminous plant rich in coumarin. The latter is used in the manufacture of certain liqueurs.

TORPEDO. TORPILLE – Large fish, somewhat resembling the skate, which is common in the Mediterranean. The flesh of the torpedo-fish is edible but mediocre. It is prepared like skate (q.v.).

TOT. BOUJARON – A small measure of 6 cl. (1 dram) which was used for distributing rum to sailors.

TÔT-FAIT (Pastry) – Mix 250 g. (9 oz., 2 cups) sifted flour, 250 g. (9 oz., 2 cups) sugar, a small pinch of salt, a little grated lemon rind and 3 whole eggs in a basin. When smooth add 250 g. (9 oz., 2 cups) melted butter. Blend. Fill a buttered *manque* mould with the mixture.

Cook in a moderately hot oven for about 45 minutes. Turn out and allow it to cool before serving.

TOUFFE – Stalks tied together in a bunch. Thus parsley arranged in a bunch is called a *touffe de persil*.

TOULOUSAINE (À LA) – Name given to various different preparations. It is mostly used for a *ragoût* bound with a white sauce, an accompaniment to poached or roast poultry; or as a filling for *croustades*, tarts and *vol-au-vent*.

TOUR D'ARGENT – See RESTAURANTS OF BYGONE DAYS.

TOUR DE FEUILLETAGE – French term for treatment (turns) given to pastry to make it flaky (see DOUGH).

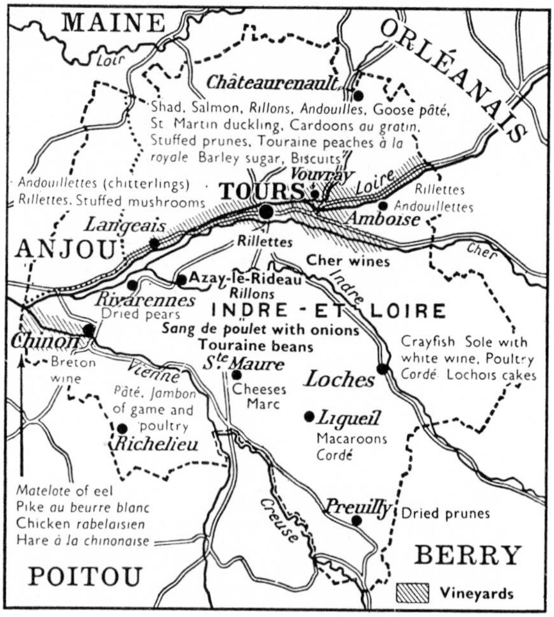

Gastronomic map of Touraine

TOURAINE – The Touraine, cradle of Gargantua, is the home of famous cooks.

Its meadows and fields, woods and its waters provide food of the highest quality: shad from the *Loire*, pike from the *Cher*, carp from the *Indre*, chicken, butter, veal, and pork. Its vegetables include delicious mushrooms, and the fruit is plentiful. *Chasselas* grapes from the slopes above the *Loire*, William pears, plums from *Sainte-Catherine* and *Rochecorbon*, eating apples from *Azay-le-Rideau*; and a whole range of delicious wines.

Culinary specialities – *Touraine* cookery is French cookery *par excellence* – wholesome, simple and admirably prepared. It contains few regional specialities, but old-fashioned dishes like *sang de poulet aux oignons* (chicken blood with onions), *rôtie au vin rouge* (roast meat with red wine) are still prepared in Touraine; and there are *fricassées* of chicken and *fritures* of fish, *cerneaux*, which are green walnuts, served as *hors-d'œuvre*. *Hare à la chinonaise* is a speciality.

The *charcuterie* is renowned, notably *rillettes* and *rillons*, *andouilles* and *andouillettes* of Tours, Vouvray and Chinon. Richelieu has its *pâtés* and its *jambons* of game and poultry.

The sweetmeats of this district are barley-sugar and biscuits from Tours, macaroons from Cormery and Ligueil, cakes called *le Lochois* and *le Tourangeau*. Worthy of praise are the stuffed prunes of Tours and dried prunes of Preuilly and Huismes, the dried pears of Rivarennes and the traditional pastries: the *cordés*, *russerolles*, *fouaces*, and *cassemuse*.

Touraine kitchen, Plessis-les-Tours
(French Government Tourist Office)

Wines – Touraine produces delightful dry wines, at once strong and smooth, which have an extremely agreeable aroma. The best among the white wines are made from the Pineau grape of Vouvray, then Mont-Louis, Saint-Avertin, Rochecorbon, Candes and Sache; among red wines the Bourgueil with its aroma of strawberries and the Breton of Chinon which smells of raspberries.

Several pleasant fruity red wines, good rosés and aromatic dry wines are produced under the general name of 'Touraine'. These wines can also be *pétillant* or *mousseux* (see SPARKLING).

Certain communes have the right to add their own name to that of Touraine. They are Touraine-Amboise (white, red and rosés), Touraine-Azay-le-Rideau (white), Touraine-Mesland (white, red and rosés).

TOURNE-BRIDE – Old word for a country inn established near a château where visitors' servants used to be lodged.

Nowadays this is the name given to certain inns where guests may retire for a siesta after the meal.

TOURNEDOS – Small slices taken from the heart of the fillet of beef. This cut is sautéed or grilled and garnished in various ways (see BEEF, *Tournedos*).

TOURNÉE – Old name for *Allemande sauce* (see SAUCE).

TOURNER – Literally *to turn*, and describing the action of rounding off, while peeling, certain vegetables. Thus potatoes are 'turned' into the shape of olives, cobnuts, etc. Carrots, turnips and other pot-herbs are 'turned', and so are cultivated mushrooms, to peel and trim them to the right shape. Olives are also 'turned' when they are used as a garnish.

TOURTE – The word *tourte*, say some culinary writers, is derived from the Latin *tortus*, which means 'making round' thus indicating in a general way that the tourte should be round in shape.

There are sweet tourtes, but these are really tarts, which also are usually round in shape (see also TART).

Tourtes as entrées. TOURTE D'ENTRÉE – 'The tourte served as an *entrée*,' said Carême in his treatise *Entrées chaudes de pâtisserie*, 'is no longer sufficiently sumptuous to appear on our opulent tables because its shape is too common; even the bourgeois classes disdain it and eat only hot *pâtés* and *vol-au-vent*, where formerly the rich merchants and their families used to regale themselves with the humble tourte.

'But then these merchants did not pride themselves on being gastronomes. How times have changed! Our great cooks in the old days used to serve tourte at the tables of princes . . . !'

Since Carême wrote these observations on the discredit suffered by the tourte in his days, this excellent hot *entrée* has come back into fashion, and now it is not only 'merchants' who regale themselves with it, but also the most fastidious gastronomes.

The recipe that Carême gave for making the tourte is as follows:

Tourte d'entrée à l'ancienne – 'Make and roll out pastry as for a *timbale*. Cut out a round about 20 cm. (8 inches) in diameter; place this on a metal baking tin. Make 36 to 40 *boulettes* (*quenelles* of *godiveau*, about the size of a pigeon's egg). Place half of these in the bottom of the tourte, keeping them $2\frac{1}{2}$ cm. (1 inch) away from the edge. Set on top some slices of lamb's or calf's sweetbreads (cooked *aux fines herbes*), some mushrooms and some artichoke bottoms cut into eighths; then put on the rest of the *boulettes*, and, on top, the shelled claws and tails of 4 good crayfish, mushrooms and artichoke bottoms, to make the top into a perfect dome.

'Next roll out some more pastry in the same way as for the bottom of the tourte and cut it into a round 22 cm. (9 inches) in diameter; it should be about 5 mm. ($\frac{1}{4}$ inch) thick. Lightly moisten the edges of the first piece of pastry; over this and its garnish with the piece of pastry and press the edges together all round almost as far as the *boulettes*. Make a small hole so that the steam can escape.

'Raise and press the edges of the lower piece of pastry over the edges of the second, so as to seal them as perfectly as possible. Moisten the upper edge lightly and set on it a strip of puff pastry not more than 5 mm. ($\frac{1}{4}$ inch) thick, then fix and press down this strip.

'Brush the upper pastry lightly with egg, place in the middle of a pretty rosette, at least 15 cm. (6 inches) in diameter, made of rolled strips of the same pastry as the tourte, or a little top of puff pastry trimmings.

'Brush with egg, surround the edges with a band of strong, buttered paper, and put into a brisk oven; allow $1\frac{1}{2}$ hours baking time.

'Cut a little lid $7\frac{1}{2}$ cm. (3 inches) wide out of the top, pour in a good *Espagnole sauce* (see SAUCE), and recover.'

Tourte of truffles à la périgourdine. TOURTE DE TRUFFES À LA PÉRIGOURDINE – See TRUFFLES.

SWEET TOURTES. TOURTES D'ENTREMETS – To make pastry use *Puff pastry* (see DOUGH) 'turned' 6 times. When the last turn has been given it should be 80 cm. (about $2\frac{1}{2}$ feet) long. Make a band by cutting 1 cm. ($\frac{1}{2}$ inch) off the edge of the pastry, then roll the band $2\frac{1}{2}$ cm. (1 inch) wide.

Give one more turn to the rest of the pastry and from it cut out a base 20 cm. (8 inches) in diameter. Set the base on a baking tin. Moisten lightly round the edges. Set the band of pastry on the moistened edge, join the two ends of the band by pressing them together, and brush with egg.

Fill the inside of the tourte with a cream or fruit (see below). Bake in a hot oven. Sprinkle with icing sugar and glaze in the oven.

Tourtes can be filled with all kinds of preparations, such as *French pastry cream*, *Frangipane* (see CREAMS), jam, raw or cooked fruit.

Apricot tourte I. TOURTE AUX ABRICOTS – Prepare a tourte crust with puff pastry rolled and turned 6 times as described above. Prepare a tourte crust. Sprinkle fine sugar over the base, avoiding the band surrounding it. Fill the tourte with halves of well-ripened apricots. Brush the band with egg and bake in a hot oven. Coat the apricots lightly with apricot jam diluted with a little syrup and strained.

Apricot tourte II (for home cooking). TOURTE AUX ABRICOTS – 'Roll out some fine pastry; set it on a *tourtière* (pie dish) lightly moistened in the middle. Cut it to the desired size, well rounded in shape. Prick the middle and moisten the edges, fixing on them a band of puff pastry 2½ cm. (1 inch) wide and 1 cm. (½ inch) thick.

'Fill the tourte like a tart, but do not let the fruit touch the band of pastry, because this would prevent it from rising evenly during cooking. Brush the upper surface of the band with egg and mark it lightly with the edge of a knife.

'Bake for 45 minutes in a moderate oven. Five minutes before it is completely cooked, powder it lightly with icing sugar so that when it is put back in the oven the sugar glazes.' (Montbry.)

Tourte à la mode béarnaise – 'Melt 500 g. (18 oz., 2 cups) butter and pour it over 100 g. (4 oz., 4 cakes compressed) yeast in a bowl. Mix together.

'Add 500 g. (18 oz., 2¼ cups) sifted sugar, 12 eggs, a small glass of rum, a little grated lemon peel, a pinch of salt, and enough flour to obtain a firm mixture. Allow to rise for 24 hours.

'Divide into small pieces and put them into buttered moulds. Bake in the oven.'

Corsican tourte. TOURTE CORSE – *Bouillie* of chestnut flour prepared like *polenta* with the addition of pine kernels and dried fruits flavoured with anise, poured into a *tourtière* and baked in the oven.

Tourte with various fruits. TOURTE AUX FRUITS DIVERS – Made like *Apricot tourte* with any kind of fruit, raw or cooked, whole or in halves, quarters or slices.

Tourtes made with strawberries or raspberries are filled with the fruit after the pastry is cooked.

TOURTEAU – Name for the large edible crab.

TOURTIÈRE – Pie dish in which to make tourtes, made of earthenware or metal. There are *tourtières* with plain sides and others with goffered edges.

TRAGACANTH (gum dragon). ADRAGANTE – Gum provided by several species of plants. Tragacanth gum is mentioned in ancient writings.

Perfume-makers, confectioners and pastry-cooks use tragacanth gum to bind their oils or to give body to their pastes.

TRAIT – Term used by barmen preparing cocktails to describe a fixed quantity of liquor, usually about a spoonful.

To pour out with precision these small quantities the bottle is usually stoppered with a special metal cork. Turned rapidly upside down a bottle fitted with this cork allows only a little liquid to pour at a time.

The bottle is turned sharply up and down once for every *trait* required.

TRAITEUR – *Traiter* means to treat, to receive or welcome one to the table.

A *traiteur* is someone who provides meals for payment.

The *traiteur* was, in fact, the predecessor of the restaurateur. During the eighteenth century people dined out at the *traiteur's*. By the middle of the nineteenth century, the term had acquired a slightly derogatory sense, and was scarcely applied except to restaurateurs of the lowest class and wine merchants who provided meals. There still exist in Paris, in some of the populous districts, establishments whose signs carry the words: *Marchand des vins – Traiteur*.

In the eighteenth century, before the institution of restaurants, not only were people obliged to buy whole joints, fowls, etc. from the *traiteurs*, but were even unable, when the latter were only food merchants, to eat on the premises. It was in this epoch, says Brillat-Savarin (about 1770), that 'strangers had as yet very few resources in the way of good cheer . . . they were forced to have recourse to the innkeepers who were generally bad. . . . It was possible to go to the *traiteurs* but they could only sell whole pieces; and he who wished to entertain some friends had to order in advance, so that those who had not the good luck to be invited to some wealthy house left the great city without knowing the resources and delights of Parisian cuisine.' (*Physiologie du goût – Meditation XXVII.*)

A certain number of the *traiteurs* did, in fact, provide meals in their establishments and were restaurateurs of an early kind, long before the first restaurant, founded in 1765 by one Boulanger, was opened in the Rue des Poulies. This was not a 'restaurant' in the accepted sense of the word. Boulanger was still only a *traiteur*, and there existed in Paris at that time a number of establishments similar to his.

TRANCHANT (Equerry) – Officer in charge of cutting meat at table in the great houses.

TRANCHE GRASSE (Top rump) – The part of the leg of beef which extends the whole length of the *tende de tranche* (topside) as far as the rump.

Tranche au petit os is the middle of the silverside.

TRANCHEUR – Waiter in a restaurant in charge of cutting meat.

TRANCHOIR, TRENCHER – Wooden dish on which meat is sliced. A slice of bread served as a plate in the Middle Ages. These were also called *tailloirs*.

TRAPPISTES – See CHEESE.

TRAVAILLER – To 'beat'. It is much used in cookery and pastry-making. To beat or *travailler* a sauce is to stir it with a spatula or wooden spoon to make it smooth, or mix it with a whisk to incorporate other substances.

A forcemeat or other similar mixture is also beaten, or *travaillé*, to render it homogenous. A paste or batter is beaten to ensure perfect blending.

Travailler is also used to indicate a change in the nature of something. Thus in speaking of wine it means to ferment. It is used also to describe a dough that rises.

TREFOIL (TRIFOLIUM). TRÈFLE – Type of leguminous plant of which one species is eaten as a vegetable in Iceland. Another, the marsh trefoil, has large smooth dark green leaves resembling those of the broad bean. These leaves are bitter and are sometimes used instead of hops. The farinaceous root is edible and it is eaten like carrot.

Trefoil tea stimulates the appetite; it is an excellent remedy for troubles of the digestive tract because its bitter constituents blend instantly with the gastric juices and activate the digestion.

TREMPER – Term used in the expressions *tremper la soupe* which means to soak slices of bread in soup, and *tremper le vin*, to mix wine with water.

TREMPETTE – A word derived from *tremper*, to soak, meaning a small slice of bread which has been dipped in a liquid.

TRÉPIED – A three-legged kitchen utensil for supporting cauldrons and soup pots over an open fire.

TRESS. TRESSE – Design in which some pastries are made, called a plait or 'braid'. It is also called *natte* in French.

TRICLINIUM – The special room in which the ancient Romans took their meals.

This is how, according to Mazois (*Palais de Scaurus*), the triclinium or dining room of the Romans was arranged:

'... As we were about to pass through the door of the anteroom which precedes the *triclinium*, a child, posted there for the purpose, warned us to enter with the right foot, so as not to bring in evil portents.

'... As soon as we had been announced slaves relieved us of our *bracae* (breeches) and our striped Gaulish *sagi* (*military coats*), and re-clothed us in fine robes to be worn only at the table.

'... We entered the *triclinium* and were scarcely seated before Egyptian slaves came and poured cold water over our hands while others, having taken off our sandals, washed our feet and cleaned our toenails, even though the same service had already been performed for us in the bath. The *triclinium* or dining room is twice as long as it is wide and is divided into two. The upper part is occupied by the table and couches; the lower is kept free for the service and for entertainment. Around the former part the walls are ornamented up to a certain height with costly paintings. The decoration of the rest of the room is noble, and, at the same time, in keeping with its character; the pillars, festooned with ivy and vines, divide the walls into sections, each of which is bordered with fanciful ornaments. In the centre of each panel there have been painted with admirable grace young fauns or *bacchantes* bearing *thyrsi*, vases, cups and all the paraphernalia of the feast. Above these columns runs a great frieze divided into twelve tableaux, each of which is surmounted by one of the signs of the Zodiac and represents the foodstuffs which are most sought after in the month to which the sign belongs; so that underneath Sagittarius have been painted shrimps, shellfish and birds of passage, under Capricorn, lobsters, sea-fish, a wild boar and game birds; under Aquarius duck, plover, pigeons and water-rails, etc.

'Bronze lamps, suspended from chains of the same metal or supported by candelabras of rare workmanship, shed a bright light; slaves detailed to look after them were careful to cut the wicks from time to time and see that they did not lack oil.

'The table, made of cedar wood brought from the heart of Mauretania and prized above gold, rested on feet of ivory. It was covered with a massive tray of silver weighing five hundred pounds, ornamented with chasing and anaglyphs. The dining couches, enough for thirty persons, were of bronze, enriched with ornament in silver, gold and tortoise-shell; the mattresses of purple-dyed wool from Gaul and the rich feather-filled cushions were covered with brilliantly coloured materials, woven and embroidered with silk mixed with gold thread. Chrysippus told us that they had been made at Babylon and that they cost four million sesterces.

'The mosaic floor represented, by a curious caprice of the artist, all sorts of scraps of food, as though they had fallen naturally to the ground, so that at first glance it seemed not to have been swept since the last meal. . . . At the end of the room there had been set up some Corinthian brass vases. This *triclinium*, the largest of four that Scaurus had in his palace, could easily hold a table with sixty couches, but it was seldom that so many guests met there, and when, on great occasions, there were five or six hundred people invited, they were received in the atrium. This dining room was reserved for autumn, winter and spring; the Romans made a study of the enjoyment of changing seasons.

'The service was regulated so that for each triclinium there were a great number of tables of different kinds, each with its own vases, dishes and servants.'

TRIGGERFISH. BALISTE – Genus of fish distinguishable by their dorsal fin armed with a spine which is projected into an erect position when the fish is threatened with any danger.

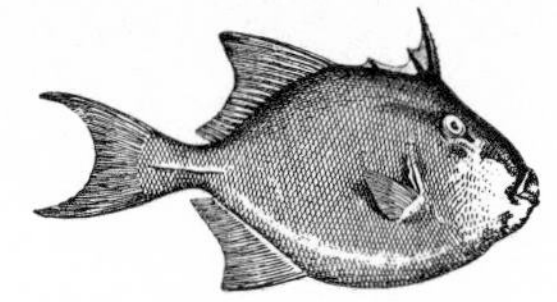

Triggerfish

This genus includes several species, all remarkable for their brilliant metallic colouring and thick granulous skin, which has the texture of armour.

Only one species of the genus is found on the French Mediterranean coast. These, when caught, are heard to make a grunting sound, resembling that of pigs. In U.S.A. the so-called pigfish is very abundant on the South Atlantic coast and averages about 225 g. (8 oz.) in weight.

The flesh is quite delicate and they are prepared like sturgeon or tunny (tuna fish).

TRIGLE. GURNARD – Species of fish, of which several varieties exist (see GURNET).

TRIM. PARER – To remove all parts which spoil the correct appearance of food.

Parer la marchandise ('to trim the goods') means to make a display of goods, featuring the best and concealing the others – those which are to be delivered to the customer.

TRIMMINGS. PARURES – This term applies to all the parts of meat, such as sinews, skin, etc., which are removed before the meat is cooked.

Fresh meat trimmings, especially veal, beef and pork trimmings, are used for making stocks, used in preparing sauces (see STOCKS).

Mutton and lamb trimmings should only be used for stocks intended for sauces to accompany these same meats.

TRIPE. TRIPES – The stomach of ruminants used as food. Only tripes from certain butchered animals, such as pigs and sheep, are considered edible. The latter are used in Provence for the preparation of *pieds-paquets à la marseillaise*, and in the southwest of France to make a dish known as *pétéram*.

Pig's intestines are used to enclose large and small sausages, *boudins* and saveloy, and to make *andouilles* and *andouillettes*.

Tripe, rich in gelatine and tasty as it may be, is nonetheless like most offal heavy and indigestible. It should therefore be eaten in moderation even by those who enjoy good health.

It is not recommended for those who suffer from dyspepsia, gout or uricaemia. For the preparation of tripe see OFFAL or VARIETY MEATS.

The first stomach of oxen (beef) is used for the famous *tripes à la mode de Caen* and *gras-double à la lyonnaise*.

'The origin of these dishes goes back far into the past. Athenaeus praised this dish. Homer noted the excellence of tripe. William the Conqueror enjoyed tripe accompanied by Neustrian apple juice, but history has neglected to mention that a question of tripe was the cause of the quarrel between William the Bastard and Phillip I, King of France, which provoked a pleasantry by the latter. William replied by a promise as historic as it is threatening: "That he would come and be churched at Notre-Dame de Paris with ten thousand lances instead of candles."

'And thus, in the eleventh century, a gastronomic quarrel led to the invasion of the Norman Vexin. However, at this time the dreary *cuisine* of the Middle Ages had not known how to prepare tripe. It was only three centuries later that the great Benoît had the intelligence to add to the tastelessness of the original dish that which is at the heart of all good cooking, to wit, well-judged seasoning. This was the cook who immortalised his district gastronomically.

'On the tables of famous restaurants tripe comes on a fixed day, steaming in brown *terrines* fixed in silver heaters. At the wine merchants' and at the door of the dairy, a placard announces that the menu of the day includes tripe. There it is eaten from thick china plates.

'It cannot be denied that the preparation is long and laborious, and that a large quantity must be made in order to achieve the greatest succulence.

'But the perfect succulence is there, so long as the squares of mesentery bathe in the golden juices, whose perfume whets the appetite, and a few bottles of the pure juice of Neustrian apples, the true Norman cider, father of golden drunkenness, make their appearance at the same time!' (Philéas Gilbert.)

The detailed recipe for *tripes à la mode de Caen* will be found under OFFAL or VARIETY MEATS.

TRIPERIE – The sale of tripe, or the place in which it is sold.

As well as tripe of the ordinary kind, the *triperie* sells other kinds of offal (variety meats): calf's and sheep's head, brains, sweetbreads, udder, feet, tongue, hearts, liver, spleen and kidneys.

Mould to make Trois Frères

TROIS FRÈRES (Pastry) – Pastry created by the three Julien brothers, celebrated pastry-cooks of the nineteenth century, for which a special mould called the *moule à trois frères* was created.

Ingredients. 500 g. (18 oz., 3 cups) rice flour, 376 g. (13 oz., $2\frac{3}{4}$ cups) sugar, 400 g. (14 oz., $1\frac{2}{3}$ cups) butter, 15 eggs, 1 liqueur glass maraschino, pinch of salt, 50 g. (2 oz., $\frac{1}{2}$ cup) candied angelica cut in small dice.

Method. Put the sugar, eggs and salt into a copper pan, placing it in a *bain-marie*, which is placed in turn in a sauté pan filled with hot water. Whisk until it becomes thick and frothy.

Add the rice flour, melted butter and maraschino. Fill buttered and floured moulds with the mixture. Bake in a fairly hot oven. Set the cakes on a base of sweet pastry. Cover with apricot syrup and sprinkle with chopped almonds and the diced angelica.

TROGNON – Edible heart of a vegetable or fruit. *Trognons* of certain vegetables, notably those of chicory and cabbage, can be prepared in various ways (see CHICORY).

TRONÇON (CHUNK) – Term for a piece of food which is cut so that it is longer than it is wide. Used to describe pieces cut from the middle of a large fish.

TROPIQUE – The hottest part of the oven.

TROU DU MILIEU or COUP DU MILIEU – Glass of *eau-de-vie* or other liqueur which used to be drunk in the middle of a large and elaborate meal.

The *coup du milieu* was replaced by *sorbets* which are served between the *entrée* and the roast.

Certain peoples of the North of Europe, notably the Swedes, drink *eau-de-vie* (aquavit) between courses.

The *trou normande* is the same as the *trou du milieu*, but the former must always be *eau-de-vie* distilled from apples.

TROUSSE – Sheath that holds the butcher's or cook's implements. The *trousse* is suspended from the apron string.

Rainbow trout (*Baufle*)

TROUT. TRUITE – Species of fish of the same group as the salmon, whose flesh, very delicate, is white, pinkish or 'salmon' coloured, according to the waters it inhabits.

In French fresh waters two kinds of trout are found: common trout (*truite commune*, *truite de rivière*, *de ruisseau* or *de torrent*) which live in running water. They correspond to the American mountain trout, dolly vardens, brook or speckled trout. The salmon trout (*truite saumonée*, *truite de mer* or *truite de Dieppe*) are fish whose flesh is pink and which, like the salmon, go up the rivers and correspond to the American brown or river trout. Another variety of trout, called the rainbow trout, also an anadromous species, is a native of California. It was imported into Europe some years ago, has now become acclimatised and is increasing rapidly. It is robust and does well in waters less fresh than those demanded by the common trout.

There are also lake trout which, living in very deep water, grow to a very large size, but their flesh is less delicate than that of river trout.

All methods of preparation given for fillets of sole or whiting (see SOLE, WHITING) are applicable to trout.

RIVER TROUT. TRUITES DE RIVIÈRE –

Blue trout. TRUITE AU BLEU – The trout must be absolutely fresh. Ten minutes before serving take the fish out of the water, kill them with a hard blow on the head, gut and clean them, sprinkle with vinegar, and plunge into a *court-bouillon* containing a high proportion of vinegar. Cook as rapidly as possible, allowing 7 to 8 minutes for fish weighing about 150 g. (5 oz.) each.

Drain the trout and garnish with fresh parsley. Serve with melted butter or *Hollandaise sauce* (see SAUCE).

Blue trout (cold). TRUITES AU BLEU FROIDES – Prepared as above. Allow to cool in the *court-bouillon*. Garnish with fresh parsley. Serve with *Ravigote sauce* (see SAUCE).

Boiled river trout with various sauces. TRUITES DE RIVIÈRE BOUILLIES – Cook the fish in *court-bouillon*, drain and serve with *Hollandaise sauce* or any other sauce suitable for boiled fish (see SAUCE).

River trout à la bourguignonne. TRUITES DE RIVIÈRE À LA BOURGUIGNONNE – Prepare like *River trout in red wine* (see below), using red Burgundy. Garnish with mushrooms and small glazed onions. Coat with sauce prepared as in the recipe for *River trout in red wine*.

River trout Colbert. TRUITES DE RIVIÈRE COLBERT – Open the fish down the back and remove the central bone. Coat the trout with egg and breadcrumbs, and fry in hot deep fat or oil. When crisp and golden-brown, drain and set on a dish. Put in the middle of each trout a tablespoon of *Colbert butter* (see BUTTER, *Compound butters*). Garnish with a bunch of fried parsley at each end of the dish.

River trout, cold. TRUITES DE RIVIÈRE FROIDES – All the methods of preparing cold salmon trout are applicable to river trout. See below.

Fillets of river trout en papillotes à l'ancienne. FILETS DE TRUITES DE RIVIÈRE EN PAPILLOTES À L'ANCIENNE – Fillet the trout, season, and half cook them in butter. Put them, two by two, on greaseproof paper or aluminium foil, cut into the shape of hearts and oiled, on a layer of *duxelles* mixed with chopped truffles and bound with concentrated *Velouté sauce* (see SAUCE) based on fish stock. Cover the fillets with the same mixture. Close the *papillotes*, folding over the edges carefully. Cook in the oven.

Fried trout

Fried trout. TRUITES DE RIVIÈRE FRITES – Small trout are prepared in this way. Proceed as for *Fried bass* (see BASS).

Grilled river trout. TRUITES DE RIVIÈRE GRILLÉES – Make shallow cuts on the back of the trout. Season, flour lightly, brush with oil or melted butter, and cook under the grill at a gentle heat. Serve with *Maître d'hôtel butter* (see BUTTER, *Compound butters*) or any other sauce suitable for grilled fish (see SAUCE).

River trout à l'hôtelière. TRUITES DE RIVIÈRE À L'HÔTELIÈRE – Coat the trout with egg and breadcrumbs and fry. Set on a dish on a mixture of *duxelles* and *Maître d'hôtel butter* (see BUTTER, *Compound butters*) in the ratio of 1 tablespoon of *duxelles* to 100 g. (4 oz., 6 tablespoons) butter. Put half slices of lemon with fluted edges along the sides of the dish.

River trout à la hussarde. TRUITES DE RIVIÈRE À LA HUSSARDE – Stuff 10 river trout with *Fish forcemeat* (see FORCEMEAT) mixed with chopped onion cooked till tender in butter, allowing 100 g. (4 oz., $\frac{1}{2}$ cup) onion, 500 g. (18 oz., generous 2 cups) forcemeat. Season.

Put the trout in a baking tin lined with 100 g. (4 oz., $\frac{1}{2}$ cup) finely chopped onions lightly cooked in butter, without colouring. Add a small *bouquet garni*. Pour over 2 dl. ($\frac{1}{3}$ pint, 1 cup) dry white wine. Dot small pieces of butter over the top. Cook in the oven, basting frequently.

Drain the trout, set on a serving dish, coat with the cooking liquor thickened with a little *Velouté sauce* (see SAUCE) based on fish stock, enriched with butter and strained. Glaze in a very hot oven.

Jellied river trout in red wine. TRUITES DE RIVIÈRE À LA GELÉE AU VIN ROUGE – Prepared like *Glazed salmon au chambertin* (see SALMON).

Jellied trout can be prepared in the same way using various wines: Barsac, Chambertin, Champagne, Chinon, Madeira and others.

Trout en matelote à la bourguignonne. TRUITES EN MATELOTE À LA BOURGUIGNONNE – Cut the trout into chunks, put them in a sauté pan lined with chopped onions and carrots lightly cooked in butter. Add a *bouquet garni*. Pour over enough red

Grilled trout garnished with duchess potatoes

Burgundy to cover the fish. Season, and cook, covered, for 10 minutes. Drain the trout and replace in the pan. Add small glazed onions and small mushrooms sautéed in butter. Pour over the cooking liquor thickened with *Kneaded butter* and strained (see BUTTER, *Compound butters*).

Simmer for 15 minutes. Serve the trout in a deep dish, garnished with croûtons fried in butter.

Trout en matelote à la normande. TRUITES EN MATELOTE À LA NORMANDE – Cook the trout as above, using white wine. Drain and put in a sauté pan with small mushrooms cooked in a flour and water *court-bouillon*, and shelled crayfish. Pour over a *Normande sauce* (see SAUCE) made with the cooking liquor. Simmer gently. Serve the trout in a deep dish garnished with fried croûtons and crayfish cooked in *court-bouillon*.

River trout en matelote à la tourangelle. TRUITES DE RIVIÈRE EN MATELOTE À LA TOURANGELLE – Cut the trout in half or in pieces, according to their size. Cook them in red wine (see MATELOTE). Set on a dish and garnish with small glazed onions, mushrooms and *lardons* cooked with the fish, crayfish cooked in *court-bouillon* and heart-shaped croûtons fried in butter.

Trout à la meunière. TRUITES À LA MEUNIÈRE – Cook the trout in butter with a pinch of salt. Arrange them on a platter. Add the juice of a lemon and a little fresh cream to the butter in the pan. Warm it slightly and pour over the trout. Serve immediately.

River trout à la vauclusienne. TRUITES DE RIVIÈRE À LA VAUCLUSIENNE – Prepared like *Trout à la meunière*, replacing the butter with olive oil.

River trout au vert. TRUITES DE RIVIÈRE AU VERT – This recipe is mainly suitable for small trout. Prepare as for *Eels au vert* (see EEL).

River trout in red wine I. TRUITES DE RIVIÈRE AU VIN ROUGE – Season the trout inside and out with salt and pepper. Put in a heat-proof dish, lined, for every 4 trout, 1 onion and 1 carrot, chopped and lightly cooked in butter. Pour over enough red wine to almost cover the trout. Start cooking on top, then cover and cook in a hot oven for 10 minutes.

Drain the trout, wipe and set on a serving dish. Coat with a red wine sauce prepared as follows:

Strain the fish cooking liquor, thicken it with 1 tablespoon of *Kneaded butter* (see BUTTER, *Compound butters*) and cook for a minute. Add 2 tablespoons (3 tablespoons) butter. Strain.

River trout in red wine II. TRUITES DE RIVIÈRE AU VIN ROUGE – Put the trout, seasoned with salt and pepper in a buttered baking dish. Pour over *fish fumet* made with red wine. Cook in the oven. Drain the trout. Set on a dish and coat with the cooking liquor thickened with 3 dl. ($\frac{1}{2}$ pint, $1\frac{1}{4}$ cups) *Espagnole sauce* based on fish stock, enriched with butter and strained (see SAUCE).

River trout in white wine. TRUITES DE RIVIÈRE AU VIN BLANC – Prepare as for *Brill in white wine* (see BRILL).

SALMON TROUT. TRUITE SAUMONÉE – This trout usually has pink flesh, like salmon, hence its name. Trout with very pale flesh, sometimes even completely white, are also found, and are no less excellent in quality.

All the methods of preparation given for salmon (q.v.) are equally applicable to salmon trout. In addition we give the following recipes, which are also applicable to salmon.

Salmon trout Beauharnais. TRUITE SAUMONÉE BEAUHARNAIS – Stuff a medium-sized salmon trout with *Fish forcemeat* (see FORCEMEAT) mixed with 4 tablespoons ($\frac{1}{3}$ cup) *mirepoix* of diced carrots, celery, onions cooked until soft in butter for every 250 g. (9 oz., 1 cup) of forcemeat.

Put the trout on the grid of a buttered fish-kettle. Pour in fish *fumet*, made with white wine, to reach half-way up the fish. Cook in the oven, basting frequently.

Set the trout on a dish and garnish each end with *Noisette potatoes* (see POTATOES) cooked in butter, and the sides with very small artichoke bottoms cooked in butter and filled with *Beauharnais sauce* (see SAUCE).

Salmon trout Berchoux. TRUITE SAUMONÉE BERCHOUX – Stuff a salmon trout weighing about 2 kg. (4 lb.) with *Pike forcemeat à la crème* (see FORCEMEAT) to which chopped truffles have been added.

Put the trout on the buttered grid of a fish kettle, the bottom of which is lined with chopped carrot and onion cooked until soft in butter, a good handful of mushroom peelings and a *bouquet garni*.

Pour in fish *fumet* made with white wine to reach half-way up the trout. Season and start cooking on top of the stove, then cover the fish kettle and cook in a slow oven for about 40 minutes, basting the fish often during cooking.

Drain the trout, set it on a dish, remove the central part of the skin so that the black parts of the flesh are seen. Sprinkle the fish with a few tablespoons of its cooking liquor, previously strained, and glaze lightly in the oven.

Surround the trout with the following garnish, the various elements of which should be grouped separately: 8 *barquettes* filled with carp roes and coated with *Normande sauce* (see SAUCE), 8 small croquettes made with *salpicon* of crayfish, mushrooms and truffles bound with *Velouté sauce* (see SAUCE) and fried, and 8 very small artichoke bottoms, half cooked in a flour-and-water *court-bouillon*, simmered in butter, filled with a large-diced *salpicon* of truffles bound with cream, sprinkled with grated Parmesan and browned under the grill.

Strain the cooking liquor. Add to this 3 dl. ($\frac{1}{2}$ pint, $1\frac{1}{4}$ cups) *velouté sauce* based on fish stock. Boil down over strong heat, adding to the sauce, little by little, 3 dl. ($\frac{1}{2}$ pint, $1\frac{1}{4}$ cups) thick fresh cream. Add butter to the sauce and strain. Pour a few tablespoons of sauce into the bottom of the dish and serve the rest in a sauceboat.

Cold salmon trout with various sauces. TRUITE SAUMONÉE FROIDE – Cook the trout in a *court-bouillon* as for salmon. Allow to cool in its cooking liquor. Drain and wipe. Garnish with sprigs of parsley. Serve with mayonnaise or any cold sauce suitable for cold fish (see SAUCE).

Salmon trout en douillette. TRUITE SAUMONÉE EN DOUILLETTE – Fillet a medium-sized trout, season with salt and pepper, and cook quickly in butter to seal them. Allow to cool.

Roll out some ordinary *Brioche dough* (see DOUGH) made without sugar and kept rather firm.

Put a thin layer of *Pike forcemeat à la crème* (see

Cold salmon trout

FORCEMEAT) in the middle of the dough. Place a fillet on this forcemeat. Cover the fillet with more forcemeat, to which some diced crayfish and truffles have been added. Put the second fillet on top of this and cover with another thin layer of forcemeat. Put a rolled-out piece of brioche dough on top of the fish. Press edges together. Make an opening in the middle to allow steam to escape. Put in a warm place to rise. Brush over the surface with melted butter and sprinkle with fine breadcrumbs. Bake in a moderate oven for about 45 minutes. Set on a dish. Pour over a few tablespoons of melted butter. Serve with *Nantua sauce* (see SAUCE).

Glazed salmon trout au chambertin. TRUITE SAUMONÉE FROIDE AU CHAMBERTIN – Prepare like *Glazed salmon au chambertin* (see SALMON).

TROYES – See CHEESE.

TRUELLE. TROWEL – Spatula with a curved handle similar to a mason's trowel, used to serve fish and pastries.

TRUFFLAGE – Term for adding pieces of truffle to chicken or game.

TRUFFLE. TRUFFE – Subterranean fungus of which a number of varieties exist. The black truffle of Périgord and that of the Lot are the most highly esteemed. Truffles are also gathered in Dauphiné, Burgundy and Normandy and in various other regions of France, but all these are inferior in quality and have a less delicate aroma.

The truffle that grows at the base of 'truffle' oaks is gathered with the assistance of pigs and (more commonly nowadays) by specially trained dogs.

The white truffle of Piédmont has a slight flavour of garlic which goes well with some dishes. It is most often eaten raw, cut in very thin slices.

To prepare truffles for use with poultry and game – Peel the truffles and cut them in quarters, or if they are small, leave them whole. Season with salt, pepper, thyme, and powdered bay leaf. Cook for 8 to 10 minutes in pork fat, which may be mixed with *foie gras*, prepared in the following way:

Pound 1 kg. ($2\frac{1}{4}$ lb.) of fresh pork fat in a mortar with the trimmings of the truffles being used. If a more delicate mixture is desired add 250 g. (9 oz.) *foie gras*, both fat and *foie gras* cut in large dice. Season with salt, pepper and a pinch of spice. Melt gently over low heat and put through a fine strainer.

The truffles, having been cooked in this truffled fat, should be cooled before being used to 'truffle' the bird.

Tinned (canned) truffles. CONSERVE DE TRUFFES – Wash the truffles, soak them in warm water, and scrub them under fresh water. Peel them, taking care to remove all earth deposited in holes and folds.

Season the truffles with very fine salt mixed with spice and pepper, and leave them in this seasoning for 2 hours.

Glazed salmon trout au chambertin

Boil some Madeira wine, and add to it the truffle peelings and a pinch of salt. Cover and leave to cool. Strain.

Put the truffles in 1 litre ($1\frac{3}{4}$ pints, generous quart) tins. Pour over 3 dl. ($\frac{1}{2}$ pint, $1\frac{1}{4}$ cups) Madeira. Seal the tins. Put them in a pot and cover completely with cold water. Set a weight on top to keep them covered with the water and bring to a high boiling point, which should continue without interruption for $2\frac{1}{4}$ to $2\frac{1}{2}$ hours. Add more boiling water when necessary.

Remove from the heat and allow to cool completely.

Any tin (can) which, after boiling, is 'blown', should be considered doubtful and put under observation.

Boiling point can be raised by adding a good handful of salt to the water. For $\frac{1}{2}$ litre (scant pint, $2\frac{1}{4}$ cups) tins, allow one and a half hours. For glass jars with special closures the cooking time is the same. Jars or bottles must not be taken from the water until quite cold.

They are then wrapped in straw and set on a thick layer of straw placed in the bottom of the pan.

Truffles preserved in goose fat are also excellent. Freezing in no way affects the flavour of truffles.

Truffles with Champagne. TRUFFES AU CHAMPAGNE – Put well-cleaned large truffles in a deep saucepan with, for every 450 g. (1 lb.) truffles, 2 tablespoons (3 tablespoons) *mirepoix* of vegetables cooked in butter until soft. Add 3 dl. ($\frac{1}{2}$ pint, $1\frac{1}{4}$ cups) Champagne. Season. Cook, covered, for 15 minutes. Put the truffles into a deep dish. Sprinkle them with the pan juices boiled down almost to nothing and mixed with a few tablespoons of thick brown veal stock. Cover the dish and keep hot, without allowing the liquid to boil, for 8 to 10 minutes.

It is customary to prepare truffles cooked in Champagne or in any other wine without peeling them, but many people prefer to peel the truffles before they are cooked.

Truffles en chaussons (in turnovers). TRUFFES EN CHAUSSONS – Peel medium-sized truffles and season with spiced salt. Wrap each in a thin rasher of fat bacon and place on a circle of puff pastry. Moisten the edges of the pastry with water and fold over. Put on a baking sheet, brush with egg, make a little opening in the centre and bake in a hot oven for 18 to 20 minutes.

Truffles à la crème. TRUFFES À LA CRÈME – Stew 450 g. (1 lb.) truffles peeled and cut into thin slices gently taking care not to let them dry out.

Season with salt and pepper. Sprinkle with a little brandy.

Truffle, whole and cut open (*J. Boyer*)

Truffles (*Fauchon. Phot. Larousse*)

Cover with boiling cream and boil for a moment. Drain and put them in a deep dish. Boil down the cream and add to it 2 or 3 tablespoons (3 tablespoons or $\frac{1}{4}$ cup) *Béchamel sauce* (see SAUCE). Add butter, season, strain through a cloth, then pour, boiling hot, over the truffles.

Truffles cooked in embers. TRUFFES SOUS LA CENDRE – Season large, cleaned truffles with salt, pepper and spices, and sprinkle with a little brandy. Wrap each in a very thin bard of fat bacon, then in greaseproof paper, sealing them into the paper by sticking the edges together with *repère* (a mixture of flour and egg white).

Put the wrapped truffles into a *tourtière* (metal pie dish or tin plate) on hot ashes mixed with glowing embers. Cover with cinders and embers.

Cook the truffles in the cinders for 40 to 45 minutes. Remove from the paper and serve as they are.

It is difficult nowadays to find houses, in towns at least, where there are wood fires and where, consequently, truffles could be cooked in this way. We have nevertheless included this rather archaic recipe because it might possibly be used in country places.

The title *truffes sous la cendre* is also given to truffles cooked in a pie.

Truffle fritters. BEIGNETS DE TRUFFES – Cut peeled truffles in thick slices. Soak them for an hour in brandy, salt, pepper, thyme and powdered bay leaf.

Dip the slices in light batter and fry in clarified butter.

Truffles for garnish. TRUFFES POUR GARNITURE – According to the type of dish to be garnished, the truffles are cut, after being peeled, into slices, dice, quarters, or oval shapes to look like olives.

Cook them gently in butter for a few minutes only, until they are just cooked and no more. Truffles, especially when cut into small pieces or slices, must not be dried out in cooking.

Moisten with a few tablespoons of wine appropriate to the dish to be garnished and keep hot without boiling.

In principle, truffles used for garnish should cook with the food they are to accompany, and should be put into the saucepan with it towards the end of the cooking time.

Instead of fresh truffles, whose season only lasts for a few months in winter, tinned truffles may be used. When using these truffles, which have usually been cooked twice already, it is not necessary to do more than heat them with the food they are to accompany.

Truffles with Madeira or other liqueur. TRUFFES AU MADÈRE – Proceed as for *Truffles with Champagne*, replacing the latter with Madeira or other wine.

Truffles à la maréchale. TRUFFES À LA MARÉCHALE – 'Remove the skins from 1 kg. ($2\frac{1}{4}$ lb.) of scrubbed truffles. Cut them in thick round slices.

'Melt in a saucepan a quarter of butter and a piece of chicken glaze the size of an egg with 2 tablespoons (3 tablespoons) of Madeira. Boil a little but without letting it catch. Sauté the truffles in it, and afterwards let them steam for 10 to 12 minutes. Sauté them in a second time and leave them again, well covered. Above all, do not let them fry, but glaze lightly. Add 4 tablespoons ($\frac{1}{3}$ cup) fresh butter, a drop of lemon juice and some small bread croûtons amounting to half the quantity of the truffles and cut to the same size, fried in butter. Mix them well with the truffles and serve.' (Plumerey's recipe.)

Truffles in pastry à la périgourdine. TRUFFES EN PÂTÉ À LA PÉRIGOURDINE – Prepare as for *Truffles en chaussons*, putting under the truffles small slices of *foie gras* seasoned with salt and pepper. Cook in the oven for 18 to 20 minutes.

Truffle purée. PURÉE DE TRUFFES – Rub 250 g. (9 oz.) raw truffles through a fine sieve and add to 3 dl. ($\frac{1}{2}$ pint, $1\frac{1}{4}$ cup) thick *Béchamel sauce* (see SAUCE) which has been diluted with a few tablespoons fresh cream. Season, strain through a cloth, heat the purée and add butter.

Truffle purée is used to fill *bouchées* (patties), tartlets and other small preparations of the same kind, or to stuff vegetables, artichoke bottoms, mushrooms, etc.

Truffle rissoles à l'ancienne. RISSOLES DE TRUFFES À L'ANCIENNE – Cut large peeled truffles in very thick slices. Season with salt, pepper and spices and sprinkle with brandy. Leave to soak for an hour.

Fold each truffle slice in a piece of ordinary *Brioche dough* (see DOUGH). Fry in deep fat or oil. Drain and serve.

Truffle rissoles à la Valromey. RISSOLES DE TRUFFES À LA VALROMEY – Sandwich together, two by two, thick slices of truffle with a slice of *foie gras* in between. Season with salt, pepper and spices and sprinkle with a little brandy.

Set on rounds of puff pastry cut out with a fluted cutter, a little larger in diameter than the truffles. Cover with rounds of pastry. Press the edges together.

Cleaning truffles
(*French Government Tourist Office*)

Fry, arrange in a mould and garnish with fried parsley. Serve with *Périgueux sauce* (see SAUCE).

Truffle salad. SALADE DE TRUFFES – Made with raw truffles, chopped or cut in a *julienne*, when truffles are in season, but usually made with preserved truffles.

They are usually mixed either with sliced boiled potatoes, or chopped artichoke bottoms (*impératrice salad*).

Truffle salad is seasoned with oil, lemon juice, salt and pepper, and should not be flavoured with the aromatic herbs often used with other salads.

Truffle sauce. SAUCE AUX TRUFFES – Simmer a very black fresh truffle in half Madeira wine, half rich beef stock for about 10 minutes. Remove the truffle and dice it. Cover the pan tightly and reduce the liquid to a few teaspoonsful. Add 2 yolks of egg and the diced truffle. Thicken with 200 g. (7 oz., generous $\frac{3}{4}$ cup) clarified butter as for a *Béarnaise sauce* (see SAUCE). Add salt and freshly ground pepper. This sauce makes an excellent accompaniment to poached fish, white meats and Lauris asparagus. (Recipe given by chef Denis of 'Chez Denis', Paris.)

Sauté of truffles Brillat-Savarin. SAUTÉ DE TRUFFES BRILLAT-SAVARIN – Peel 12 perfectly ripe, black, firm large truffles. Cut each into thick slices. Season with salt, freshly ground pepper and spice.

A few minutes before serving, sauté them in quail fat, taking care not to fry them. Drain, and set them in a low crust of puff pastry.

Dilute the cooking juices with Madeira, add a little concentrated veal stock, boil down, and pour over the truffles.

Sauté of truffles à la provençale. TRUFFES SAUTÉES À LA PROVENÇALE – Peel the truffles and cut them in thick slices. Season with salt and pepper.

Sauté for a few moments in a few tablespoons of hot olive oil with an unpeeled clove of garlic. Avoid over-cooking, which makes truffles tough.

Truffles à la serviette. TRUFFES À LA SERVIETTE – This dish is so called because it is served in a napkin folded either in the 'artichoke' or 'portfolio' style.

Cook in Madeira, set in a deep dish or in *cassolettes*, and present on or under a folded napkin.

Truffles à la serviette (*Larousse*)

Truffles à la serviette cooked in Champagne. TRUFFES À LA SERVIETTE AU VIN DE CHAMPAGNE – 'Take three pounds of truffles, the biggest you can find, round, smooth, firm and very black. Scrub them in two or three waters. When they are well drained, place them in a saucepan lined with bards of fat bacon and cover them in the same way.

'Cut in large dice a pound of ham which has been desalted and the same quantity of fillet of veal and fresh bacon fat, and heat in butter in a saucepan, adding chopped carrots and onions, sprigs of parsley and little pieces of thyme, bay leaf, basil, half a clove of garlic and two cloves. Season with very little salt, white pepper, grated nutmeg and a pinch of spice. When these ingredients begin to colour lightly, pour in two bottles of sparkling Champagne. Bring to the boil, skim and simmer gently on the stove, without boiling down; then strain, using pressure, over the truffles. Cook the truffles for an hour before serving. Allow to boil gently for three quarters of an hour, then take off the fire and keep very hot, but without boiling. At the moment of serving, drain the truffles and arrange them in a folded napkin on a silver dish, covering them in order to send them to the table very hot.' (Plumerey's recipe.)

Small truffle soufflés. PETITS SOUFFLÉS DE TRUFFES – These soufflés, served as a hot *hors-d'œuvre*, are made like ordinary soufflés (q.v.), using purée of truffles bound with egg yolks, to which stiffly beaten egg whites are added. Put into *cassolettes* and cook in the oven in the ordinary way.

Timbale of truffles. TIMBALE DE TRUFFES – Line a shallow buttered *timbale* mould with *Ordinary lining paste* (see DOUGH). Cover the bottom and sides with thin strips of bacon fat. Fill to within 10 mm. ($\frac{1}{2}$ inch) of the top with peeled raw truffles seasoned with salt, pepper and spices and sprinkled with brandy.

Moisten with a glass of Madeira and 3 tablespoons (4 tablespoons) very concentrated brown veal stock. Cover the truffles with a bard of bacon fat and the *timbale* with pastry.

Brush with egg. Cook in a hot oven 50 to 55 minutes. Turn out the timbale and serve.

Truffle tourte à la périgourdine. TOURTE DE TRUFFES À LA PÉRIGOURDINE – Spread a layer of *foie gras* cut in large dice on a round of *Lining paste* (see DOUGH) set on a baking tray, covering the pastry to within 10 mm. ($\frac{1}{2}$ inch) of the edge. Season with salt, pepper and spices, and sprinkle with brandy.

Top with scrubbed and peeled truffles. Season with salt, pepper and spices, and sprinkle with brandy. Place small slices of seasoned *foie gras* on the truffles.

Cover with a round of pastry and seal the edges. Decorate the top with cut-out shapes of pastry. Make a small opening in the middle to allow steam to escape. Brush with egg. Cook in a hot oven 40 to 45 minutes. Pour in a few tablespoons *Demi-glace sauce* (see SAUCE) boiled down with Madeira and *Truffle essence* (see ESSENCE).

Tourte aux truffes is served hot or cold.

WHITE TRUFFLES. TRUFFES BLANCHES – White truffles come from the North of Italy, principally from Piedmont, and are called Piedmont truffles. They are also found in North Africa and in some regions of France, but these are unlike those which come from Italy, either in aroma or texture.

The white truffle, which has a slight taste of garlic, is eaten raw, cut in thin slices. When it is used as a garnish for hot dishes it is added at the very end of the cooking, and is not cooked itself other than by the heat of the food it accompanies. It is used in this way with *risotto aux truffes blanches*, when cooking is completely finished.

White truffles cut in dice or thin slices are used to garnish egg dishes, notably omelettes and scrambled eggs, being added after the scrambled eggs are cooked; they are put, raw, into the beaten egg before making the omelettes.

The white truffle is most often used in salad, seasoned with olive oil, lemon juice, salt and pepper.

White truffle risotto. TRUFFES BLANCHES AU RISOTTO – Cover a Parmesan risotto, set in a deep dish with white truffles, peeled, cut into thin slivers and seasoned. Keep hot for 5 minutes on a corner of the stove, covered.

Sauté of Piedmont truffles. SAUTÉ DE TRUFFES DU PIÉMONT – 'Take a dozen Piedmont truffles, well scrubbed; remove the skin carefully and cut them into very thin rounds. Dissolve chicken glaze the size of an egg in 4 tablespoons ($\frac{1}{3}$ cup) hot oil on low heat. Put in the truffles and season with a white pepper, salt and grated nutmeg. Cover, and cook over good heat for 10 minutes, tossing them often (they need no more cooking). Add a few pieces of fresh butter, the juice of half a lemon, and serve.

'In Paris the oil is replaced by butter, but oil is the true stamp of the Italian manner.

'Some noblemen like to cook Piedmont truffles themselves. This is how they are prepared: Chop the truffles with a cucumber slicer. Put in a silver casserole a few spoonfuls olive oil or butter, according to taste, and some good glaze the size of an egg cut into small pieces. Place the truffles on top with some salt, white pepper and grated nutmeg. Sprinkle a few drops of oil over the truffles, or set a few pieces of fine butter on top.

'The casserole, its lid in place, is set on top of a spirit heater, set alight, set in front of the host, who with the aid of a spoon turns the truffles frequently, replacing the lid of the casserole each time.

'Seven to eight minutes are enough for the cooking. The *seigneur* adds the juice of a lemon and serves his guests.' (Plumerey's recipe).

TRUFFLE (To). TRUFFER – To garnish or stuff with truffles. Used also to describe the action of studding a foodstuff with small pieces of truffle.

TRUIE DE MER – A French name generally given to a fish called *rascasse*.

TRUMPET FISH. BÉCASSE DE MER – This fish is also called *voilier porte-glaive* (sword-bearer sailfish) because of its lance-like jaw.

The trumpet fish attains 2 to 3 metres (6 to 9 feet) in length. Its flesh is mediocre. Prepare as for tunny fish (see TUNNY).

TRUSS. BRIDER – To thread a string to secure the legs and wings of poultry and game, with the aid of a strong needle called a trussing needle.

The trussing of poultry and game is done in different ways, depending on the nature of the finished dish. For roasting, the legs are left outside; for braising, poaching or pot-roasting the end bones are worked under the skin.

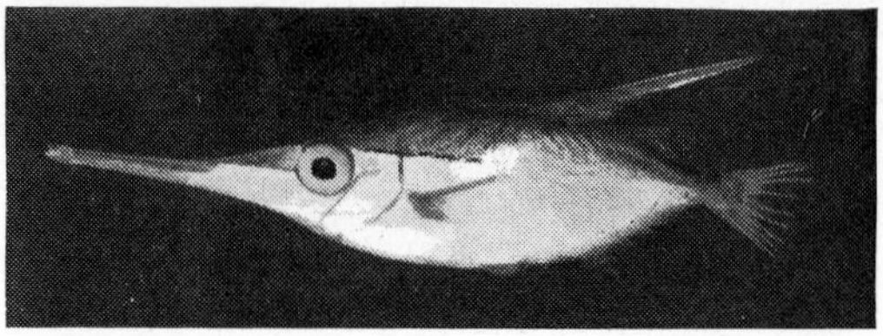

Trumpet fish

Before being trussed, poultry and game should be dressed – that is, plucked, cleaned and singed.

TUFTED LARK. HUPPE – A kind of lark whose flesh sometimes has a musky flavour. It is cooked in the same way as lark.

TUILES (PETITS FOURS) – Cream together in a bowl 250 g. (8 oz., 1 cup) butter and 250 g. (8 oz., 1 cup) fine sugar. Add 5 eggs, one by one, 250 g. (8 oz., 2 cups) sifted flour. Pipe the mixture on to a baking tin in rounds with the aid of a forcing bag. Bake in the oven.

When ready, bend each one over a rolling pin to give the shape of curved tiles (*tuiles*).

Tuiles with almonds. TUILES AUX AMANDES – Mix together in a bowl 250 g. (8 oz., 1 cup) ground almonds, 250 g. (8 oz., 1 cup) sugar and 4 egg whites. Flavour with vanilla essence or any other flavouring. Pipe on to a baking tin and bake in the oven. Finish off as above.

TULIP. TULIPE – There are a great many different kinds of tulip but only one, the 'wild tulip', a plant growing in the South of France, is edible. The root is eaten, and may be prepared like *Jerusalem artichoke* or *sweet potato*.

TUN. FÛT – Cask large enough to hold several hogs heads.

TUNNY (TUNA FISH). THON – A large, strong, spindle-shaped fish found in warm and temperate seas.

It lives in the warm parts of the Atlantic and the Mediterranean, and is scarcely ever found beyond the Bay of Biscay. Many species of tunny, all related to the mackerel family, are found off both the Atlantic and Pacific coasts of the United States. The white tunny or *germon* is found as high

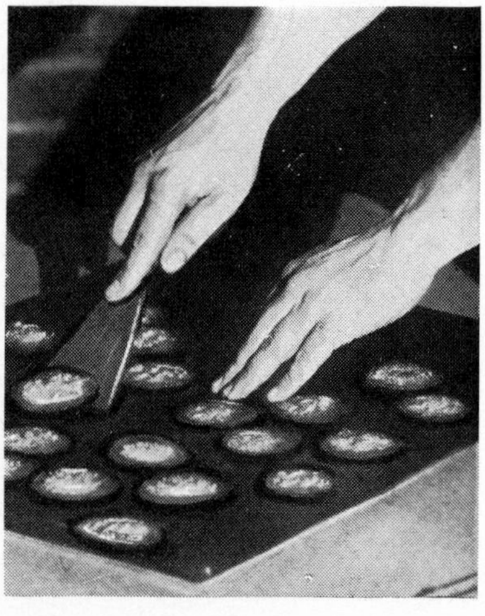

Removing *tuiles* from the baking tray (*Desmeuzes*)

Bending the *tuiles* over a rolling pin (*Larousse*)

as the coast of Brittany. This is similar to the albacore of the Pacific. The *thonine*, which is called the *thouna* at Nice and the *thounina* at Sète, is found only in the Mediterranean. It never grows to more than 1 metre (3 feet) in length and is fished in the region of Nice from May to October. Its flesh is firm, oily and savoury and has some resemblance to veal. Tunny is eaten fresh, salted, smoked or canned in oil.

Tunny (tuna) à la provençale. THON À LA PROVENÇALE – Stud a round cut of tunny with anchovy fillets. Marinate it in oil, lemon juice, salt and pepper for an hour. Colour the fish on both sides in hot oil in a sauté pan. Add a chopped onion lightly cooked in butter (or oil), 2 peeled, seeded and crushed large tomatoes, a small clove of garlic, also crushed, and a *bouquet garni*. Pour over $1\frac{1}{2}$ dl. ($\frac{1}{4}$ pint, $\frac{2}{3}$ cup) white wine. Finish cooking in the oven, basting often.

Drain the fish and set on a dish. Cover with the concentrated cooking liquor to which a little *Espagnole sauce* (see SAUCE) and some capers have been added. Instead of thickening the sauce with *espagnole*, a spoonful of *Kneaded butter* may be used (see BUTTER, *Compound butters*).

TURBAN – Word much used in French cookery to describe the way some foods are arranged on a dish in a circle.

The same word is used to describe certain preparations, mostly forcemeat, which are cooked in border moulds. Turbans of fish, various kinds of poultry, game, etc., can be made in this way.

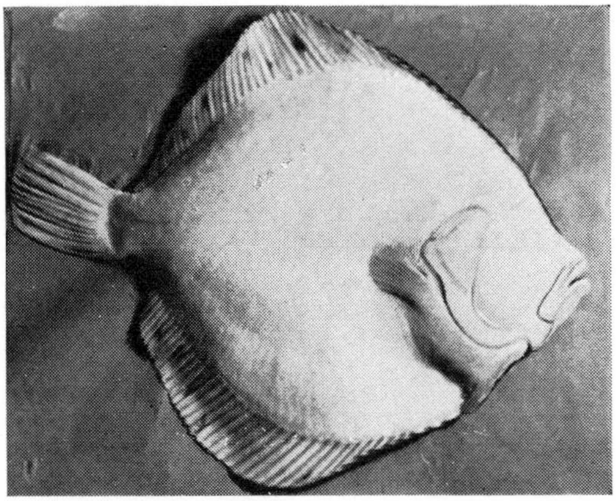

Turbot, white side

TURBOT – Large European flat fish, one of the most delicate of its kind.

The turbot has a lozenge-shaped body, and has such minute scales they need not be removed. Its eyes are on the left side of its body, which is yellowish-grey or brown, dotted with black and white marks. The other side is white. On the grey or brown side the conical tubercles which gives the turbot its name of *turbot piquant* are to be found. *Turbot double* is a species which has coloured skin on both sides. Its flesh is mediocre.

The normal size of the turbot is from 41 cm. to 1 m. (16 to 32 inches). Its flesh is white, firm, flaky and savoury.

The brill, sometimes called *turbot lisse* in French, belongs to the same family.

Small-sized turbots, known as chicken turbot in English, are *turbotins* in French. They are cooked in the same way as ordinary turbot.

Turbot à l'américaine – Prepare as for *Brill à l'américaine* (see BRILL).

Turbot à l'amiral – Prepare as for *Brill à l'amiral* (see BRILL).

Turbot à la Bercy – Prepare as for *Brill à la Bercy* (see BRILL).

Boiled turbot with various sauces. TURBOT BOUILLI – Large turbots, whole, or cut into chunks or *darnes* (like salmon) are cooked in a *court-bouillon* of salted milk and water, with slices of lemon. Allow to each litre ($1\frac{3}{4}$ pints, generous quart) of water: 1 dl. (6 tablespoons, scant $\frac{1}{2}$ cup) milk, 15 g. ($2\frac{1}{2}$ teaspoons) salt and one slice of peeled lemon.

To prevent damage during cooking, the head of the turbot can be tied. It is put into the *turbotière* (a fish kettle specially shaped to cook turbot), using the grid so that it can more easily be removed when cooked. Pour over enough cold *court-bouillon* to cover the fish. As soon as the liquid begins to boil, remove the *turbotière* to a corner of the stove and leave to poach, allowing 12 minutes per kg. (6 minutes to every lb).

Drain and wipe the fish, set on a large dish, and garnish with fresh parsley in bunches. Serve with boiled potatoes and one or other of the sauces suitable for boiled fish.

Turbot à la bonne femme – Prepare as for *Brill à la bonne femme* (see BRILL).

Braised turbot with various garnishes and sauces. TURBOT BRAISÉ – Turbot left whole, cut in pieces or filleted, is braised in white or red wine, in any of the ways given for *Braised brill* (see BRILL).

Turbot à la cancalaise – Turbot left whole, cut in pieces or filleted, cooked in white wine. Drain the fish, set it on a serving dish, garnish with poached, drained and de-bearded oysters and shelled crayfish. Coat with *Normande sauce* (see SAUCE) to which the strained oyster liquor has been added.

Cold turbot. TURBOT FROID – Whole turbot or turbot cut in chunks or *darnes* may be served cold.

It is accompanied by one of the cold sauces suitable for cold fish, such as *Mayonnaise*, *Tartare*, *Rémoulade*, *Verte*, *Gribiche*, etc. (see SAUCE).

Served garnished with fresh parsley, or surrounded with one of the garnishes recommended for cold fish (see GARNISHES).

Creamed turbot au gratin. TURBOT À LA CRÈME AU GRATIN – Prepare with sliced left-over turbot like *Creamed cod au gratin* (see COD).

Turbot Dugléré

Turbot Dugléré – Prepare as for *Bass Dugléré* (see BASS).

Fillets of turbot. FILETS DE TURBOT – Turbot is filleted raw, and medium-sized fish should be chosen.

All methods of preparation given for fillets of brill or sole are applicable to fillet of turbot.

Fried turbot. TURBOT FRIT – Only very small turbots, fillets or *darnes* are fried (see BRILL, *Fried brill*).

However, Brillat-Savarin, who in his *Twelfth Meditation* devoted a long study to frying, assures his readers that it is possible to fry very large turbots.

Turbot fried in batter. FRITOT DE TURBOT – Cut filleted turbot into 'matchsticks'. Soak these for 30 minutes in oil, lemon juice, chopped parsley, salt and pepper.

Before serving, dip them one by one, into light batter and fry them in hot deep fat or oil. Drain, wipe, and season with fine dry salt. Serve heaped on a dish and garnish with fried parsley and lemon. Serve with *Tomato sauce* (see SAUCE).

Turbot au gratin – Prepared whole if they are small fish, or cut in pieces if large. Prepare as for *Sole au gratin*.

Grilled turbot. TURBOT GRILLÉ – Chicken turbot or *turbotins* are prepared in this way. Large turbots can also be grilled, cut into thickish *darnes* or filleted.

Grilled turbot is accompanied either by *Maître d'hôtel butter*, or by one of the sauces usually served with grilled fish (see BUTTER, *Compound butters*; SAUCE).

Cook the turbot in the same way as *Grilled brill* (see BRILL).

Turbot kedgeree. CADGERY DE TURBOT – Cut 450 g. (1 lb.) cooked turbot in small slices. Heat in butter. Set in a deep dish in layers, alternating with 450 g. (1 lb.) *Rice pilaf* (see PILAF) prepared in the usual way but not too much cooked, and bound with 5 dl. (scant pint, $2\frac{1}{4}$ cups) thin *Béchamel sauce* (see SAUCE) seasoned with curry. Sprinkle diced hard boiled eggs over each layer of turbot. Coat the last layer of rice with the same sauce.

Turbot or chicken turbot en matelote – Cut the turbot into regular pieces. Prepare as *Sole en matelote à la normande* (see SOLE).

Set on a dish and garnish with crayfish, fried smelts and croûtons.

Turbot à la pèlerine – Season the turbot with salt and pepper. Put it on a baking tin lined, for a fish of 2 kg. (4 lb.) with 150 g. (5 oz., generous cup) chopped onion cooked until tender in butter without colouring.

Sprinkle with melted butter. Cook gently in the oven. Place in an ovenproof dish. Dilute the pan juices with white wine, add thick fresh cream, boil down, add butter, strain and pour over the fish. Glaze well in the oven. Garnish with fried scallops set in a mound at each end of the dish.

Turbot à la Saint Malo – This method is suitable for small fish.

Make shallow cuts on both sides, season with salt and pepper, brush with oil and grill gently. Put on a serving dish. Surround with boiled potatoes cut into thick slices and fried in butter. Garnish with fresh parsley. Serve with *Saint-Malo sauce* (see SAUCE).

Scalloped turbot. COQUILLES DE TURBOT – Prepared with left-over turbot like *Brill in scallop shells* (see BRILL).

Turbot à la venitienne – Prepare as for *Fillets of sole à la venitienne* (see SOLE).

Turbot Victoria – Prepare as for *Brill à la Victoria* (see BRILL).

Turbot in white wine. TURBOT AU VIN BLANC – Prepare with the turbot left whole, in chunks or in fillets, like *Brill in white wine* (see BRILL).

Turbotière (*Dehillerin. Phot. Larousse*)

TURBOTIÈRE – Square-shaped fish kettle, provided with a removable grid called *turbotière,* chiefly used for cooking turbot and other flat fish.

TUREEN. SOUPIÈRE – Broad, deep dish in which soup is served.

Soup tureens:
Above, left to right: 18th century silver tureens and Empire style tureen

Side, left to right: porcelain tureen of Tièntsin (*Rouard*) and Rouen faïence tureen (*Rouard*)

It was not until the eighteenth century that the tureen made its appearance on the French table. Before that soup had been poured out of the kitchen *marmite* directly into covered bowls which were carried, filled, to the guests. In the reign of Louis XV, the goldsmith Thomas Germain (see SILVERWARE) made magnificent tureens. The most beautiful were made at Sèvres, Strasbourg, Moustiers, Rouen, etc. In the nineteenth and twentieth century the tureen continued to make part of the dinner service, and to follow the evolution of fashion and style.

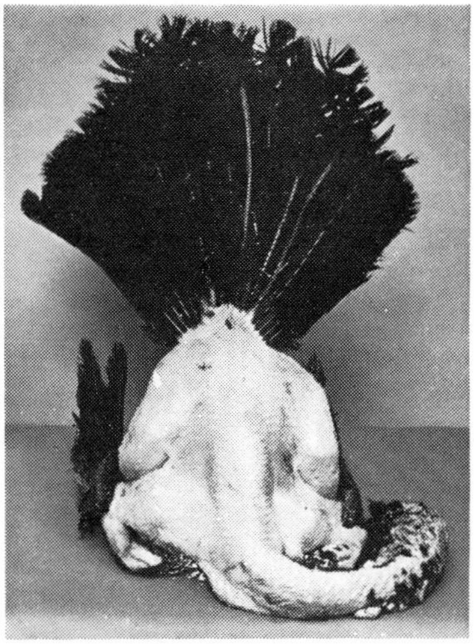

Plucked turkey (*Pietrement. Phot. Larousse*)

TURKEY. DINDE, DINDON, DINDONNEAU – There are two main varieties of turkey: the wild turkey, native of North America, and the farmyard turkey, bred in poultry runs. The origin of this bird is uncertain. Some authorities believe that it comes from Bermuda, others that its original habitat was North America.

It seems likely that the first home of the turkey was that immense tract of land which stretches from the extreme northwestern boundary of the United States to the isthmus of Panama.

In Canada and other parts of North America, wild turkeys were once very plentiful, but they are now mainly found towards the centre of the continent, which to this day is more sparsely settled.

Brillat-Savarin, who devoted a long paragraph of his *Sixth Meditation* to turkeys and turkey-lovers, says 'The turkey is one of the finest gifts made by the New World to the Old.' and adds: 'The name of the bird is in France *dinde* or *d'Inde*, meaning from India since in the past America was known as the West Indies.

'The turkey appeared in Europe towards the end of the seventeenth century. It was imported by the Jesuits, who reared these birds in large numbers, especially on a farm which they owned in the region of Bourges. From there they spread all over France, which is why in popular speech in many parts of the country people refer to a turkey as a "Jesuit". America is the only place in which wild turkeys have been found in a natural state, and on the farms of North America, where turkeys are very common, they are bred either from wild eggs hatched by a tame hen or from young poults caught in the woods and tamed, with the result that the flocks are closer to nature and retain more of their natural plumage.'

In French the word *dindon* (turkey-cock) is scarcely ever used in the language of cookery. On menus the bird is called *dindonneau* (young turkey) or sometimes, with reference to a hen bird, *dinde* (turkey hen), which implies a young, tender hen-bird of about $2\frac{1}{4}$ to 4 kg. (5 to 8 lb).

All recipes for chicken are suitable for hen turkeys and young turkey-cocks.

Turkey à l'anglaise. DINDONNEAU À L'ANGLAISE – Truss the turkey with the legs pressed tightly against the breast. Poach in a poultry stock (see CHICKEN, *Boiled chicken à l'anglaise*).

Ballottine of turkey à la toulousaine. BALLOTTINE DE DINDONNEAU À LA TOULOUSAINE – Bone a young turkey: stuff it with *Quenelle forcemeat II* (see FORCEMEAT) mixed with a *salpicon* of lambs' sweetbreads, mushrooms and truffles. Roll the bird into a long tight bundle (ballottine). Wrap in a fine cloth and poach in a very little concentrated poultry stock.

Drain the ballottine. Put it on a serving dish, either directly on the dish or on a slice of fried bread. Surround with *Toulouse garnish* (see GARNISHES). Coat with *Suprême sauce* (see SAUCE) with the concentrated cooking stock added to it.

Ballottine of turkey can be served brown instead of white by cooking it in braising stock as indicated for braised chicken (see CHICKEN). Serve with various garnishes such as *chipolata*, *financière*, *godard*, *turtle*, etc., or with braised vegetables or *pasta* prepared *à l'italienne*, *à la milanaise* or *à la napolitaine*, or with *risotto*.

Ballottine of turkey to be served cold is prepared in the same way. It is poached, like galantine of chicken, in a jelly stock. After cooling under a weight, it is served, coated with its own jelly (clarified), or served in a bowl completely covered in jelly.

Braised turkey (with various garnishes). DINDONNEAU BRAISÉ AVEC GARNITURES DIVERSES – Cook a trussed turkey in braising stock. When it is ready, drain and untruss it. Put it on a serving dish surrounded with the garnish. Skim all fat off the braising stock. Boil down, strain and pour over the turkey.

Braised turkey-hens or cocks can be garnished with different vegetables, some of which should be cooked with the bird, others separately. Among the garnishes are: *alsacienne*, braised sauerkraut, smoked belly of pork, Strasbourg sausages, *bourguignonne* (the bird being braised in red wine with mushrooms and glazed onions), belly of pork lardoons, braised celery, mushrooms, chipolatas, *fermière*, *financière*, *languedocienne*, *napolitaine*, *milanaise*, *piémontaise*, *strasbourgeoise* (see GARNISHES).

Braised stuffed turkey. DINDONNEAU FARCI BRAISÉ – Stuff the turkey with fine stuffing or some other mixture, and proceed as for *Stuffed chicken* (see CHICKEN).

All garnishes indicated for chicken may be used.

Casserole or cocotte of turkey. DINDONNEAU EN CASSEROLE, EN COCOTTE – Prepare as for *Chicken casserole* (see CHICKEN).

Turkeys cooked *en casserole* or *en cocotte* can be served with various garnishes such as artichokes, mushrooms, aubergines, small marrows (zucchini, courgettes), small onions, potatoes, truffles, etc.

Turkey à la chipolata. DINDONNEAU À LA CHIPOLATA – Truss a turkey with the legs tightly pressed against the breast. Bard it. Pot-roast in butter.

Serve it on a serving dish raised on a large piece of bread, fried in butter.

Surround with a garnish of chipolatas arranged in little clumps with spaces between (see GARNISHES). Pour on the cooking stock diluted with Madeira and thickened brown veal stock, or chicken stock boiled down and strained.

Cold turkey. DINDONNEAU FROID – All recipes for cold chicken are suitable for turkey.

Daube of turkey à la bourgeoise. DINDONNEAU EN DAUBE À LA BOURGEOISE – For this dish a tender turkey hen $2\frac{1}{4}$ to $3\frac{1}{2}$ kg. (5 to 7 lb.) must be used and not a young turkey cock. Braise the bird in a brown stock as indicated for braised chicken (see CHICKEN). When it is three parts cooked, drain. Strain the braising stock. Put the bird back in the braising pan. Surround with a *bourgeoise* garnish made of carrots cut into pear shapes, three parts cooked as for glazed carrots, small glazed onions and pieces of blanched and fried belly of pork. Pour the strained braising stock over. Cover the pan and finish cooking in a moderate oven.

Fricassée of turkey. FRICASSÉE DE DINDONNEAU – Using a young and tender turkey, prepare as for *Fricassée of chicken* (see CHICKEN).

Galantine of hen-turkey en bellevue. DINDE EN GALANTINE EN BELLEVUE – Prepare with a young hen-turkey $2\frac{1}{4}$ to $3\frac{1}{2}$ kg. (5 to 7 lb.) as indicated for *Galantine of chicken* (see CHICKEN). Cook the turkey in a jelly stock containing calves' feet, knuckle of veal, poultry carcases, fresh pork skin.

Drain the galantine. Unwrap it and cool under a weight. Mask the galantine with *White chaud-froid sauce* flavoured with Madeira and made with some of the poultry stock, the remainder of this being used to make a poultry jelly (see JELLY, SAUCE).

Garnish the galantine with truffles, pickled tongue and the white of hard boiled egg. Add the jelly, cut into pieces.

This galantine can also be served on a dish or a plinth.

Turkey giblets. ABATIS DE DINDONNEAU – Prepare as for giblets of chicken and other poultry (see GIBLETS).

Grilled turkey. DINDONNEAU GRILLÉ – Only very small turkeys are prepared in this way. Prepare as for *Grilled chicken* (see CHICKEN).

Braised turkey legs with various garnishes. CUISSES DE DINDONNEAU BRAISÉES – The legs of large turkeys, whose wings or breasts have been used in some other way, are prepared thus:

Bone the legs. Fill with a suitable forcemeat (see FORCEMEAT). Roll them into little long, tight bundles (*ballottines*). Braise in white or brown stock. Glaze in the oven. Arrange on a serving dish and garnish according to the recipe selected. Mask with the cooking sauce.

Legs of turkey prepared in this way are often called turkey hams.

Turkey liver. FOIE DE DINDONNEAU – All recipes for chicken liver are suitable for turkey liver. They can be served with *pilaf* or *risotto*, or sautéed with various garnishes, etc. (see GARNISHES). Turkey livers can be used as an ingredient of various stuffings.

They are also served sliced and sautéed and as a garnish for eggs cooked in different ways, especially omelettes and scrambled eggs.

Hot turkey pâté. PÂTÉ CHAUD DE DINDONNEAU – Using boned turkey, prepare as for *Hot chicken pâté* (see PÂTÉ).

Turkey *pâté* can also be served cold, when a few tablespoons of concentrated poultry jelly are poured into the pâté through a hole made to allow steam to escape during cooking.

Turkey pinions. AILERONS DE DINDONNEAU – These are usually stuffed and braised, and served with various garnishes (see PINIONS).

Poupeton of turkey Brillat-Savarin. POUPETON DE DINDONNEAU BRILLAT-SAVARIN – Bone a small turkey as for a galantine. Stuff with a mixture of fine veal stuffing and *à gratin stuffing* (see FORCEMEAT) enriched with lambs' sweetbreads braised in white stock, diced *foie gras* and coarsely diced truffles.

Roll the turkey into a long tight bundle. Wrap it in pigs' caul, then in muslin or cheesecloth. Tie it securely.

Put this *poupeton* in a buttered *daube* pan lined with raw ham, onion rings and carrots. Cover and cook gently for 15 minutes. Pour over it a glass of Madeira. Boil down. Moisten with poultry stock and finish cooking in the oven, covered. Strain, boil down the cooking stock, and serve as sauce with the turkey.

Turkey *poupeton* can also be served cold. After cooking, it is left to cool under a weight and served masked with poultry jelly.

Ragoût of turkey. RAGOÛT DE DINDONNEAU – Using turkey cut into pieces, prepare as for *Goose ragoût* (see GOOSE). Various garnishes can be served with turkey ragoût. Among the most suitable are the following: *Bourgeoise*, new carrots, celeriac, mushrooms, chipolata, artichoke hearts, chestnuts, potatoes (see GARNISHES).

Roast turkey. DINDONNEAU RÔTI – Truss a small turkey and bard the breast with pork fat. Roast on the spit, allowing 20 minutes per 500 g. (1 lb.), or in the oven for 25 minutes per 500 g. (1 lb.).

Before the turkey is fully cooked, remove the barding and brown the breast evenly. Serve with the diluted cooking stock and with watercress.

Roast turkey à l'anglaise (*John Cowderoy*)

Roast turkey à l'anglaise. DINDONNEAU RÔTI À L'ANGLAISE – Stuff the turkey with a sage and onion stuffing prepared as follows: Bake the onions in their skins in the oven. Peel and chop them. Toss in butter. Season with a pinch of chopped sage. Mix with an equal quantity of breadcrumbs, dipped in milk and squeezed, and half their quantity of chopped veal fat.

Roast the turkey in the usual way (see ROASTING). Put it on a serving dish surrounded with slices of bacon or grilled sausages. Serve with the cooking gravy and *Bread sauce* (see SAUCE).

Turkey with chestnut stuffing. DINDONNEAU FARCI AUX MARRONS – Stuff a medium-sized turkey $2\frac{1}{4}$ kg. (5 lb.) with best sausage meat, allowing 575 to 750 g. ($1\frac{1}{4}$ to $1\frac{1}{2}$ lb.), according to the size of the bird, mixed with chestnuts and two-thirds cooked in clear chicken or veal stock flavoured with celery.

Remove the breast bone. Truss the turkey and bard it. Roast on the spit or in the oven, basting frequently during cooking. Serve with its own gravy.

Stuffed hen-turkey grand-duc. DINDE ÉTOUFFÉE GRAND-DUC – 'Slit open a hen-turkey (about $2\frac{3}{4}$ kg., 6 lb.), along the back and stuff with the following mixture:

'500 g. (1 lb.) chicken rubbed through a fine sieve, $\frac{1}{2}$ litre (scant pint, 2¼ cups) double cream, 250 g. (½ lb.) *foie gras*, poached in port wine and rubbed through a sieve. Mix all these ingredients thoroughly and season.

'Add 12 truffles, peeled and cooked for 10 minutes in a little liqueur brandy, and 24 chicken hearts which have been soaked in water, the veins removed, steeped in white Malaga wine, drained, dried in a cloth, stuffed with a purée of York ham, and poached for 15 minutes in *Truffle essence* (see ESSENCE).

'Fold the stuffed turkey carefully into shape. Wrap in slices of raw ham or bacon. Encase it in a large layer of *Lining paste* (see DOUGH), taking care to keep the shape of the bird as far as possible. Bake in the oven for 2½ hours.

'During cooking, which must be slow, cover the turkey with greaseproof paper folded in 4, so that it will cook all through without browning too soon.

'To serve, present the turkey as it comes out of the oven, and serve with it a sauce-boat of *Demi-glace sauce* (see SAUCE) flavoured with truffle essence.' (Recipe of M. Valmy-Joyeuse, who created this dish in 1906 while he was in charge of the kitchens of the Marquise of Mazenda.)

Truffled turkey. DINDONNEAU TRUFFÉ – Discriminating gourmets believe that to achieve the best results a truffled bird should be stuffed with truffles 4 or 5 days before cooking. After the truffles have fulfilled their function of flavouring the bird, they are removed and discarded, and the bird is stuffed afresh with more truffles mixed with pork fat or raw *foie gras*, and then cooked.

The following method of preparing truffled turkey or any other poultry or winged game is more practical:

Prepare a *Forcemeat for truffled poultry* (see FORCEMEAT).

Draw the turkey, leaving the skin of the neck very long so as to be able to close the opening in the bird securely when trussing. (This can be done by your poultry dealer.)

Under the skin of the turkey, insert a dozen large slices of truffle, seasoned and sprinkled with a few drops of brandy. Stuff and truss the turkey and wrap it in a sheet of buttered greaseproof paper. Leave to stand in a cool place for 24 hours.

Bard the turkey. Wrap it in buttered paper. Roast on the spit in front of a hot fire, allowing 30 minutes per 500 g. (1 lb.) or roast in the oven uncovered, allowing 25 to 30 minutes per 500 g. (1 lb.).

Unwrap and untruss the turkey. Brown it. Put it on a serving dish and serve with its own diluted gravy, enriched, if desired, with *Périgueux sauce* (see SAUCE).

The truffled pork fat stuffing can be made without *foie gras*, but this ingredient greatly improves the flavour.

TURKEY – See INTERNATIONAL COOKERY.

TURNIP. NAVET – Pot vegetable of European origin with a fleshy and sweetish root. It was cultivated in India before the Aryan invasion.

Young, tender turnips are usually easy to digest but large turnips are somewhat indigestible. Turnips have the property of absorbing large quantities of fat (like haricot beans), and for this reason they are traditionally served with fatty meat (mutton, duck, etc.).

Turnips, which are sold in French markets all the year round, are mainly used, like carrots, parsnips, leeks and onions, as pot vegetables. In France, the best turnips for this purpose come from Meaux.

Spring turnips are used in *navarins*, and especially as a garnish for duckling. Turnips are also used in the preparation of thick and cream soups. They are less commonly eaten as a vegetable on their own.

Turnips can be put in two main classes, the long-rooted and the flat-rooted. The latter is superior for flavour and sweetness.

Boiled turnips. NAVETS À LA CRÈME – Prepare as for *Glazed carrots* (see CARROT).

Turnips to be further cooked in the sauce of the main dish are prepared in this way: Trim the turnips to look like olives (or if they are small, leave them whole). Sauté in butter. Season with salt and sprinkle with castor sugar. Sauté for a few seconds over a very high flame to brown them slightly. Finish cooking with the main dish.

Turnips au gratin or Mornay. NAVETS AU GRATIN DITS MORNAY – Cut the tunips into thick slices and parboil. Cool under running water. Drain. Cook slowly in butter. Put them in an ovenware dish lined with *Mornay sauce* (see SAUCE) and cover with more sauce. Sprinkle with grated cheese, pour on melted butter and brown slowly.

Turnip mould. PAIN DE NAVETS – Prepare, using purée of turnips, as for *Carrot timbale* (see CARROT).

Turnips with chopped parsley. NAVETS AUX FINES HERBES – Trim the turnips to look like olives or cut into slices. Parboil them in salt water until they are fairly tender. Cool under running water and drain. Sauté in butter. Season with salt and a large pinch of castor sugar. Cook slowly, tossing frequently. To serve, sprinkle with chopped parsley.

Turnip purée. PURÉE DE NAVETS – Prepare, using turnips, as indicated in the recipe for *Cardoon purée* (see CARDOON).

Purée of turnip soup – See SOUPS AND BROTHS.

Turnip soufflé. SOUFFLÉ AUX NAVETS – Proceed, using purée of turnips, as indicated for *Carrot soufflé* (see CARROT).

Stuffed turnips. NAVETS FARCIS – Peel round turnips of equal size. Cut round the base of the stalks and scoop out. Parboil the scooped-out turnips until they are fairly tender. Make a purée of the scooped-out pulp. Add to it half its weight of mashed potatoes. Mix well, season and add butter. Stuff the turnips with this mixture, smoothing it into the shape of a dome. Put the turnips in a buttered baking dish, pour on melted butter, and finish cooking in the oven, basting frequently.

Stuffed turnips (garnish). NAVETS FARCIS – Peel large turnips. Press a corer into each one, starting at the base of the stalks, but do not drive it through to the other side.

Parboil the turnips until they are fairly tender. Cool them under running water, drain, and remove the cores. Rub the cores through a sieve. Add an equal quantity of dry *duxelles*. Fill the turnips with this stuffing and smooth the surface into a dome. Put the turnips in a buttered baking dish, pour on melted butter, and bake in the oven, basting frequently.

As soon as the turnips are cooked, sprinkle with breadcrumbs and brown quickly.

Stuffed turnips à la duxelles. NAVETS FARCIS À LA DUXELLES – Prepare as for *Stuffed turnips*, filling the scooped-out turnips with a *duxelles* mixture to which the pulp of the turnips has been added after having been stewed and rubbed through a sieve.

Put the turnips in a buttered baking dish. Moisten with a few tablespoons of clear soup or clear veal stock. Sprinkle with breadcrumbs, pour on melted butter, and bake in a slow oven.

Stuffed turnips à la piémontaise. NAVETS FARCIS À LA PIÉMONTAISE – Prepare as for *Stuffed turnips*, filling the turnips with *Risotto* (see RICE) mixed with the finely diced pulp stewed in butter. Sprinkle with grated Parmesan. Pour on melted butter and brown in a slow oven.

Turnips in sugar. NAVETS AU SUCRE – Peel and quarter the turnips. Trim to look like olives. Parboil them if they are old. Sauté in butter, seasoning with salt and a little sugar. When they are browned, put them in a stew-pan. Moisten with veal stock, cover, and stew until all the moisture has evaporated.

To make an apple turnover:
Fill half the round of pastry with the apple preparation. Fold over the pastry and join the edges
(*Larousse*)

Serve in a vegetable dish, or use as a garnish.

Turnip tops. FEUILLES DE NAVET – Turnip tops are prepared like spinach or cabbage.

TURNOVER. CHAUSSON – This name applies particularly to a preparation made with a circle of flaky pastry filled with a mixture, folded over and baked in the oven.

Although included primarily in the domain of sweet pastries, the name is extended to cover small preparations served as an *hors-d'œuvre* or as a small *entrée*. These are made with a forcemeat filling or with a *salpicon* of various fishes; there are *foie gras* and truffle turnovers, turnovers filled with purée, or with a *salpicon* of various meats, of fowl, game, etc.

Apple turnover. CHAUSSON AUX POMMES – Fill the centre of a circle of *Flaky pastry* (see DOUGH) with a few tablespoons of apples prepared as for a charlotte, sliced, cooked in a sauté pan with butter and sugar, and flavoured with vanilla, cinnamon, or other flavouring (see CHARLOTTE, *Apple charlotte*). Add when cold, and fold over the pastry into a turnover. Join the edges. Set on a buttered baking tin. Mark the top with a few incisions, brush with egg and bake for about 15 minutes at 230°C. (450°F.).

Turnovers filled with various fruits can be made in the same way: apricots, pineapples, cherries, peaches, pears, plums, etc. These can be put on the pastry uncooked or cooked in syrup. When using raw fruits it is best to soak them first in sugar and liqueur.

Sweet turnovers can also be made with a preparation of fruit soaked in sugar and liqueurs and combined either with *French pastry cream* (see CREAMS), thick fresh cream, or apricot jam.

Sweet turnovers of this kind are served warm or cold.

Turnovers à la Cussy. CHAUSSONS À LA CUSSY – These turnovers and the following are served as *hors-d'œuvre* or as a small entrée.

Fill circles of *Flaky pastry* (see DOUGH) with a forcemeat of creamed whiting or other white fish to which anchovy fillets, cut into small strips, and chopped truffles are added. Fold the pastry over into turnovers. Set them on a buttered baking-tin, brush with beaten egg and bake in a 230°C. (450°F.) oven until golden brown.

Baked apple turnover (*Larousse*)

Turnovers à la lyonnaise. CHAUSSONS À LA LYONNAISE – Fill circles of *Flaky pastry* (see DOUGH) with a good spoonful of creamed pike or other white fish finished with *Crayfish butter* (see BUTTER, *Compound butters*) mixed with a preparation of crayfish tails and truffles, flavoured with a little Cognac.

Fold over the pastry in a turnover, seal the edges, put them on a buttered baking sheet, brush with egg, and bake in a hot oven (230°C., 450°F.) until golden.

Turnovers à la Nantua. CHAUSSONS À LA NANTUA – Prepare in the same way as *Turnovers à la lyonnaise*, with a *Crayfish tail ragoût à la Nantua* (see CRAYFISH) in place of the pike mixture.

Turnovers à la périgourdine. CHAUSSONS À LA PÉRIGOURDINE – Fill circles of *Flaky pastry* (see DOUGH) with a preparation of *foie gras* and truffles seasoned with salt and pepper and sprinkled with Cognac. Fold over into turnovers. Put them on a buttered baking sheet, and bake in a hot oven (230°C., 450°F.). Serve very hot.

Turnovers à la reine. CHAUSSONS À LA REINE – Prepare in the same way as *Turnovers à la périgourdine*, but replace the preparation of *foie gras* and truffles with a purée of creamed chicken mixed with chopped truffles and mushrooms.

The rissoles for which recipes will be found under HORS-D'ŒUVRE, *Hot hors-d'œuvre* are, in fact, turnovers when they are prepared with circles of pastry and folded over, but this type of turnover is deep-fried instead of being baked in the oven.

TURNSPIT. TOURNEBROCHE – Old-fashioned turnspits were of various kinds. Some worked mechanically by clockwork, others by a dog shut in a cage who turned the spit. Others were turned by a *galopin*, a young apprentice *hasteur*, who often burned his face in front of the immense brazier.

Later, spits operated by heat rising from the fire, turned a winged wheel. They still exist in great numbers today. Power-driven spits, on which a whole side of beef or several chickens at a time can be roasted, are found in some establishments. But nowadays meat and poultry are generally roasted by spit-appliances operated by electricity or gas.

TURNSTONE. TOURNE-PIERRE OU VIRE-PIERRE – Small edible bird of the wader family which is prepared like snipe (q.v).

TURRON (Confectionery). TOURON – *Turron*, which originated in Spain, is a kind of almond paste, flavoured often with pistachio nuts, hazel nuts or candied fruits.

In France the name *touron* is used for a *petit four* made in the following way:

Ingredients: 225 g. ($\frac{1}{2}$ lb., 2 cups) blanched almonds, 400 g. (14 oz., scant 2 cups) sugar, 4 egg whites, 100 g. (4 oz., 1 cup) pounded pistachio nuts, 100 g. (4 oz., 1 cup) *Royal icing* (see ICING), icing or confectioner's sugar, orange peel.

Pound the almonds with 2 egg whites. Add half the powdered sugar and knead together on marble. Sprinkle with sugar and roll out 1 cm. ($\frac{1}{2}$ inch) thick.

Chop finely blanched pistachios with the rest of the sugar, mixed with orange peel. Put in a bowl with *Royal icing* and the rest of the egg whites and mix well with a wooden spoon. Spread in a uniform layer on the rolled-out sheet of *Almond paste* (see ALMOND). Cut out with a round cutter, and with another cutter of lesser diameter cut out the middles, turning them into rings. Set these on a buttered, floured baking-tin and dry them in a very low oven.

TURTLE. TORTUE – General term for reptiles with bodies encased in a bony carapace (shell).

There are land turtles (see TERRAPIN) and water turtles.

Water turtle (green turtle)

The flesh of both kinds can be eaten, but it is the water turtle that is made into the famous turtle soup.

'Turtle soup is a soup that the English hold in high esteem, and this is fully justified, because, in the opinion of connoisseurs, it does combine the qualities of succulence and nourishment for which it is universally reputed. It is the aristocratic soup *par excellence*, often served at the great diplomatic dinners and ceremonial repasts.

'Turtles are imported from South America, Africa and Australia. The best and the most highly priced on the market come from the West Indies.' (A. Suzanne, *La Cuisine Anglaise*.)

Turtle flesh that has been dried in the sun is also imported from these countries, but does not make good soup. Connoisseurs of turtle cookery particularly prize the flippers.

Turtle flippers. NAGEOIRES DE TORTUE – Cook the flippers in the soup until two-thirds done. Then cook in one of the following ways:

Turtle flippers à l'américaine. NAGEOIRES DE TORTUE À L'AMÉRICAINE – Braise in white wine. Cover with highly seasoned *Américaine sauce* (see SAUCE). Simmer for a few minutes.

Turtle flippers à la financière. NAGEOIRES DE TORTUE À LA FINANCIÈRE – Braise in Madeira. Set on a dish and surround with a *Financière garnish* (see GARNISHES). Boil down the braising liquor and pour over the flippers.

Turtle flippers à l'indienne. NAGEOIRES DE TORTUE À L'INDIENNE – Braise in white wine. Cover with *Curry sauce* (see SAUCE). Simmer for a few moments. Serve with *Rice à l'indienne* (see RICE).

Turtle soup – See SOUPS AND BROTHS.

TURTLE HERBS. HERBES À TORTUE – Mixture of aromatic herbs used to season soups or sauces called *à la tortue*. These herbs, which are sold commercially ready-prepared, are basil, thyme, bay and marjoram.

TURTLE-DOVE. TOURTERELLE – One of the pigeon family found in all Europe, Asia and Africa. The flesh of the turtle-dove is edible. All the methods of preparing pigeon (q.v.) are applicable.

TWAROGUE (Russian cookery) – Pressed cream cheese mixed with softened butter, bound with eggs then seasoned with salt and pepper. Used to fill patties *à la russe* (see PATTIES, *Little Russian patties*).

UDDER. TETINE – Calf's and cow's udder can be braised in the same way as *noix de veau*. It can be eaten fresh, salted or smoked.

It should first be soaked in cold water, blanched, cooled in cold water and flattened under pressure. It may also be studded with small pieces of bacon fat.

Braised calf's udder is accompanied by one or other of the garnishes given for *Noix de veau* (see VEAL).

UGLI. AEGLÉ – Common tree of East Indies which generally grows to a great height. Its numerous cylindrical branches are armed with long twin thorns between the leaves. The fruit is globular, about the size of an orange, with a thick hard skin. This fruit is commonly called *bilva* or *mahura* by the Indians and is much prized, in spite of its rather strong smell and insipid taste. The English who live in the West Indies eat it baked in the cinders and sprinkled with sugar. It is exported to a certain extent to England and also in the form of jam. It is extremely nourishing although slightly laxative.

The skin of the ugli provides scent which is highly valued.

UKHA (Russian cookery) – This is Russian for a fish soup and there is an enormous variety of them. The stock can be prepared from any sea or river fish: small perch, bass, ling, pike-perch, pike, tench, cod, eel, salmon, trout and carp, as well as the traditional sturgeon and sterlet.

Boil 1 sliced onion, 1 parsnip, a sprig of parsley, bay leaf and 6 peppercorns in 2 litres ($3\frac{1}{2}$ pints, $4\frac{1}{2}$ pints) of water for $\frac{1}{2}$ hour. Cool the stock, then add the fish in large portions if it is to be served separately, whole if it is to be used for stock only. Season with salt and simmer slowly for 25 to 30 minutes. Remove the main portions. Heads, tails and bones from filleted fish can be left to simmer another 15 to 20 minutes. Strain before use.

For a really good, clear *ukha*, you need an assortment of fish to give it taste, strength, sweetness and a certain viscosity. Perch and bass can be recommended for their flavour and gelatinous qualities, ling and allied fish for sweetness and delicacy.

The best *ukha* is made of the freshest fish. The more fish used, the richer the soup. Small perch used for stock only are washed and gutted; the scales need not be scraped off, as this adds to the texture. Perch for stock is boiled until the fish disintegrates, then it is strained.

To give *ukha* a perfect translucency, Russian cooks clarify it with caviare. Pound 50 g. (2 oz.) caviare, either pressed or soft, in a mortar. Add 3 or 4 tablespoons cold water, a little at a time, and mix well. Dilute with a good cupful of very hot, strained fish stock. Pour half this mixture into the hot soup, stirring all the time, and bring to the boil. Add the second half of the caviare 'clarifier', bring to the boil once again, simmer on the lowest heat for a few minutes, remove from heat and leave to stand for 15 minutes for the caviar to settle. Strain, re-heat and serve either with a good portion of boiled fish, or with fish *coulibiac*.

The following are the most famous of traditional *ukhas*: sterlet with ling roes, burbot with pike quenelles, salmon and Champagne soup, sturgeon and pearl barley, eel and peas, whitebait and *sauerkraut*, carp and sorrel soup.

ULLUCUS or ULLUCO. ULLUCO OU ULLUQUE – There is only one species of this plant, *Ullucus tuberosus*. It is widely cultivated in Bolivia and Peru for the culinary value of its small tubers. Attempts to cultivate it in Europe as a substitute for the potato have not been very successful.

ULMARIA. ULMAIRE – Herbaceous plant more commonly known as *meadow-sweet* or *goat's beard*. The flowering heads are used in infusion as a diuretic. Added to wine, they give it a *muscat* flavour.

ULVA. ULVE – Seaweed eaten in certain countries, notably Japan, but has little nutritional value.

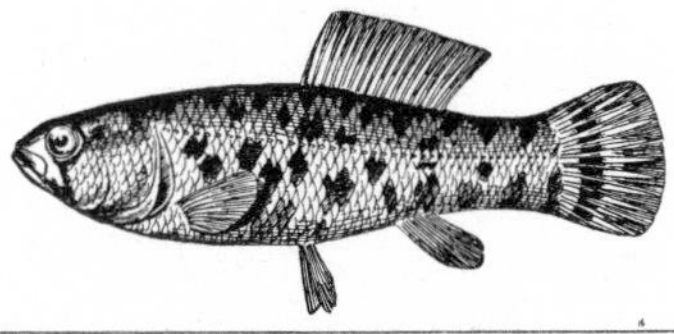

Umbra

UMBRA, MUD-MINNOW. UMBRE – European fish found in fresh water but not commonly marketed.

UMBRINE or UMBRA. OMBRINE, OMBRE DE MER – Mediterranean fish which is sometimes sold for bass. It resembles the perch and its weight reaches about 14 kg. (32 lb.). The flesh is very delicate and was greatly prized by the Romans. It is prepared like bass (q.v.).

UNCORKING. DÉBOUCHER – The uncorking of a wine bottle must be done without shaking the bottle. Wine-waiters generally use a drill for this purpose, but, unless one has the knack of operating this tool, it is wiser to use a corkscrew.

UNFERMENTED WINE. MOÛT – Grape juice which has not yet been fermented. The term is more loosely applied to all fruit juices or cereal decoctions intended for fermentation.

It is also used of certain vegetable juices from which alcoholic drinks are made.

UNITED STATES. – See INTERNATIONAL COOKERY.

UNTRUSSING. DÉBRIDER – To untie the string used to truss poultry or winged game.

UNUSUAL FOODS. METS INSOLITES – One may well ask what constitutes an unusual food. Was it Marie-Laure de Noailles who said, 'No food is unusual as long as it tastes good'? While Joseph Delteil, co-operating in an investigation carried out by Robert J. Courtine, considered nothing more delicious than a peach plucked afresh from the tree and gave Peach Melba as an example of an unusual dish!

Unusual means any type of cooking or any variety of ingredient that is not in common use; olive oil, for example, is unusual to the people of Normandy as they always use butter. But with the ever-increasing speed of transport bringing faraway places closer and closer, so the unexpected food makes a more frequent appearance on our tables. The shift of populations during and after the Second World War, added to popular tourism, has made dishes that were once rare at least shorn of their former mystique. The Parisian boy of today speaks of the *pizza* as though it were his own native dish; and since the mushrooming of Sino-Vietnamese restaurants throughout the city, birds' nest soup has become just another speciality of French *gourmandise*. Moreover, holidaymakers returning from distant places are beginning to include a recipe or two with the holiday snaps.

Every year the *Société nationale d'acclimatation de France* offers a reunion lunch to its members. None of them are astonished at the menu. Here is a list of the dishes offered on 7 June, 1958:

Vietnamese banh cuon (mushroom-stuffed rice *galettes*)
Threadfin (perch from the great lake of Tchad)
African elephant trunk
Fonio couscous (graminaceae from the Ivory Coast), served with water chestnuts
Cascaval (Bulgarian ewes' milk cheese)
Fruit from Guinea

One importer of exotic produce, M. Paul Corcellet, prepares and freezes unusual dishes to ensure a regular supply for his Parisian customers. Here is the list he offers: West Indian buffalo, antelope or venison, crocodile's tails with American sauce, hippopotamus *ragoût* with green peppers, jugged monkey, boa *matelote*, elephant's trunk, *fricassée* of sea turtle (cooked in white wine), bear *pâté*, braised reindeer's tongue, sauté of whale.

Paul Corcellet's recipes are adapted to modern methods of food preparation, but there are some much older recipes which still retain some of the mystique that befits such rare meats:

Boiled ostrich. AUTRICHE BOUILLIE – Place the following ingredients in an earthenware cooking pot: pepper, mint, toasted cumin, wild celery seeds, ordinary or caryota dates, honey, vinegar, raisin wine, garum, and a little oil. Bring this mixture to the boil then bind with cornflour or arrowroot. Arrange the pieces of boiled ostrich on a serving dish; coat with the sauce and sprinkle with pepper. Serve.

Buffalo. BUFFLE – Purge, blanch and thoroughly rinse a buffalo's muzzle, then scrape and singe it to remove all trace

Colman-Belgique grapes for a grape cure
(*Fauchon. Phot. Nicolas.*)

of hair. Simmer in a good stock for 3 hours. Check from time to time to see if it is cooked, then drain and place on a serving dish. Coat with a good, highly-seasoned *Hachée sauce* (see SAUCE). Serve.

Elephants' feet. ÉLÉPHANTS (PIEDS D') – Take the feet of one or several young elephants and purge them in warm water for 4 hours. Remove the skin and bones, then cut each foot lengthwise into four pieces; cut each of these in half. Blanch for 15 minutes, rinse in cold water, and drain.

Place the following in a tightly covered stewpan: 2 slices Bayonne ham, the portioned feet, 4 onions, 1 head of garlic, some spices, $\frac{1}{2}$ bottle Madeira wine, 3 tablespoons (4 tablespoons) concentrated stock. Cover and simmer gently over a low heat for 10 hours. Thoroughly skim the cooking liquor, strain it and add 1 glass of port and 50 small green peppers.

See that the sauce is well seasoned.

Fillets of sautéed kangaroo. KANGAROU SAUTÉS (FILETS DE) – Remove the two fillets of a kangaroo, trim, season, and arrange in a flat pan coated with melted butter. Prepare a little gravy stock using the bones and scraps of the animal. Strain it, skim off the fat, and add 4 tablespoons ($\frac{1}{3}$ cup) vinegar into a saucepan and add a *bouquet garni.* Boil down as for a *Demi-glace sauce* (see SAUCE) until a light sauce is obtained. Cook rapidly for a few minutes then reduce the heat and add 2 tablespoons (3 tablespoons) redcurrant jelly and a sliver of lemon rind. Ten minutes later add a handful of small currants previously soaked in warm water. Cook for about an hour. At the last minute add the fillets and poach gently. Drain them, and serve coated with the sauce.

This is a rare and excellent dish.

Parrot. PERROQUET – Roast the bird. Pound some peppercorns, lovage, wild celery seeds, roasted sesame seeds, parsley, mint, dried onion and caryota dates with honey, oil and cooked wine. Blend these ingredients thoroughly together. Serve with the roast parrot.

URANOSCOPUS. URANOSCOPE – Species of fish found in warm and temperate seas. The only type of uranoscopus found on the coasts of France, very rare in the Atlantic Ocean but common in the Mediterranean, is the *uranoscoperrat* or white hogfish. Its flesh, mediocre in quality, is used in making *bouillabaisse.*

URTICARIA. URTICAIRE – Skin eruption accompanied by itching, similar to that caused by a stinging nettle. It affects certain people without any apparent cause but usually after they have eaten such foods as strawberries, fish and shellfish.

Treatment consists of desensitizing the person by giving him a small portion of the offending food one hour before it is to be served at the meal. If the food that causes the ill effects is not known, consult the doctor.

UVAL – French word meaning 'pertaining to grapes'. More particularly the word is used in the phrase *cure uvale*, grape cure, a health treatment consisting of raw grapes and fresh grape juice. At the season when grapes are ripe, counters where fresh grapes and grape juice are sold may be seen in certain places, such as the big railway stations in Paris and the grape producing centres. They are called *stations uvales.*

VACHERIN – Sweet (dessert) made with meringue 'crowns' mounted one on top of the other on a sweet pastry base, decorated with meringue piped through a forcing bag and dried out in a very low oven; or with circles of almond paste similarly mounted on top of each other. These are filled either with *Chantilly cream* (see CREAMS), ice cream flavoured with vanilla, or with some other flavouring, or with a *bombe* mixture.

Vacherin with almond paste crown. VACHERIN AVEC COURONNE EN PÂTE D'AMANDES –

Almond paste. Pound finely in a mortar 500 g. (18 oz., 4 cups) sweet almonds including a few bitter almonds about 25 g. (1 oz., ¼ cup). Moisten while pounding with the juice of half a lemon. Put the almonds in a copper pan with 500 g. (18 oz., 4 cups) icing (confectioners' sugar) and an egg white. Mix well.

Dry out over heat, stirring with the spatula. Cook the almonds, stirring all the time, until the paste no longer sticks to the finger when pressed. Remove the pan from the heat, spread out the paste on marble, turn with the spatula so that it cools equally. Add to it 5 g. (1¼ teaspoons) gum tragacanth dissolved in water.

To make the vacherin. Roll out some of the paste into a circle 20 cm. (8 inches) in diameter and 5 mm. (¼ inch) thick. With the remaining paste make another circle 15 cm. (6 inches) wide and 5 cm. (2 inches) thick. Dry both in a low oven.

Vacherin with strawberries
(Nezard-Debillot. Phot. Larousse)

Place the larger circle on paper sprinkled with sugar. Fix the smaller circle on top of this with rather stiff *Royal icing* (see ICING), and put into the oven to colour. Cool completely and place on a serving plate. Fill with firm *Chantilly cream* (see CREAMS), flavoured with vanilla or other flavouring.

Vacherin with crown of meringue. VACHERIN AVEC COURONNE DE MERINGUE – With a forcing bag make circles of plain meringue (q.v.) on buttered and floured baking sheets, the diameter of the rings varying according to the size of the sweet to be prepared. Sprinkle with fine sugar and cook in the oven at low heat until the meringue is well dried.

Put on a baking sheet, one on top of the other. Coat them with meringue. Using a pipe, decorate this 'box' with more meringue, sprinkle it with sugar and dry it again in the oven. Fill the box with sugar cooked to the crack stage (see SUGAR), added to a base of *Chou pastry I* (see DOUGH). When the *vacherin* is quite cold, fill with stiffly beaten, vanilla-flavoured cream, rounded into a dome.

VACHERIN – See CHEESE.

VACHETTE (Café) – See RESTAURANTS OF BYGONE DAYS.

VAISSELLE – French collective term (literally 'vessel') for all the plates and dishes used for the table, the kitchen and the house. *Vaisselle plate* is plate, i.e. dishes, etc., of silver (cf. Spanish *plata*, silver). (See SILVERWARE, PORCELAIN, FAÏENCE.)

VALENÇAY – See CHEESE.

VALENCIA. VALENCE – Describes Spanish oranges. In Paris, by extension, it is used to describe all oranges.

VALENCIENNES (À LA) – Method of cooking, applied in particular to chicken, which includes a rice garnish.

VALESNIKI – Preparation made with cream cheese in the style of kromeskies. (See HORS-D'ŒUVRE, *Hot hors-d'œuvre.*)

VALOIS (À LA) – Name for various dishes and pastries. Jules Gouffé described a *béarnaise sauce* finished off with meat glaze as *Valois sauce*.

VALOIS (Café de) – See RESTAURANTS OF BYGONE DAYS.

VANILLA. VANILLE – Pod of a climbing plant, a native of Mexico, and cultivated in various tropical regions. The pods are gathered before they are completely ripe, plunged into

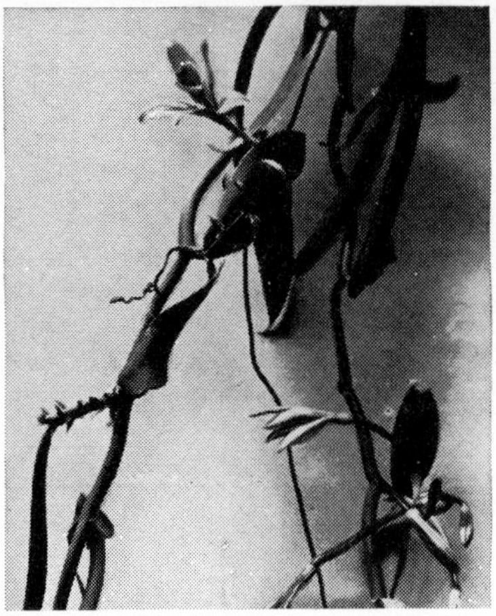

Branch of vanilla with flowers and pods

boiling water, then, before they are quite dry, shut in tins, where their aroma develops. The best quality pods, very smooth in flavour, are covered with a frost of vanilline crystals. Three kinds of vanilla are sold commercially:

1. Fine vanilla, the pod 20 to 30 cm. (8 to 12 inches) long, the surface black, smooth and frosted.

2. Woody vanilla, the pods 12 to 20 cm. (5 to 8 inches) long, reddish-brown, the surface dry and dull and not much frosted.

3. *Vanillons*, 10 to 12 cm. (4 to 5 inches) long, the pods thicker, flat and soft, almost always opened and rarely frosted; the scent stronger and a little bitter.

Yet another sort of vanilla exists which comes from the Indies, yellowish in colour and almost scentless.

The Mexican vanilla is the most highly esteemed; after it come those of Guiana, Guadaloupe and of Réunion.

Vanilla is much used as an aromatic flavouring, either in its original form, in powder form, or as an extract.

It is sometimes falsified, either by emptying the pods and filling them with a neutral paste or by brushing ordinary vanilla with Peruvian balsam to frost them artificially with benzoic acid crystals.

Always use the vanilla pod in preference to powder or essence.

VANILLA SUGAR – Sugar flavoured with vanilla.

VANNER – Culinary term for stirring a sauce with a spoon to make it smooth and keep a skin from forming.

VARENIKI – See HORS-D'ŒUVRE, *Hot hors-d'œuvre*.

VARIÉTÉS (Café des) – See RESTAURANTS OF BYGONE DAYS.

VARIETY MEATS – See OFFAL.

VASQUE – Shallow bowl, generally round in shape, made of crystal, moulded glass, china, silver, used for serving cold foods, *chaud-froids*, mousses, *foie gras en gelée*, etc.

Fresh fruit, cooked fruit, liquid custards and other cold sweets are also served in *vasques*.

VATEL – Celebrated *maître d'hôtel*, born in 1635 of Swiss parentage, who died in 1671.

'A legend, three centuries old, presents Vatel to us as the great master-cook of the Louis XIV era. Let us speak solely and briefly of Vatel, and ask ourselves whether the echo of Vatel's culinary genius would have come down to us without the witty gossip of Madame de Sévigné.

'Nothing has come down to us from him, and yet in all periods the great cooks have handed on their professional work in writing.

'But even if Vatel was only a *maître d'hôtel*, he was part of the structure.

'Oh, you who by profession preside at meals
Spare him some regrets, but do not imitate him.'

(Philéas Gilbert.)

(Vatel committed suicide.)

VATRUSHKI (Russian cookery) – Small open tarts made with *Brioche dough* (see DOUGH), filled with cream cheese or other compositions.

Vatrushki with cream cheese. VATRUSHKI AU FROMAGE BLANC – Make and roll out some ordinary unsweetened *Brioche dough* (see DOUGH). Cut with a fluted-edged pastry-cutter into pieces 10 cm. (4 inches) in diameter. Fill with cream cheese.

Crimp up the edges of the dough, put on a baking tray, brush over with egg, and bake in a slow oven for 15 to 18 minutes.

Vatrushki can also be made with *Lining paste* (see DOUGH) or with *Coulibiac dough* (see COULIBIAC).

Vatrushki with onion. VATRUSHKI À L'OIGNON – Prepare as *Vatrushki with cream cheese*, replacing the cheese with onion purée blended with a thick *Velouté sauce* (see SAUCE).

V.D.Q.S. (Vins délimités de qualité supérieure) – See WINE.

VEAL. VEAU – Flesh of calf, i.e. young of the cow. The best meat comes from animals aged $2\frac{1}{2}$ to 3 months, fed on milk and eggs. It must be white with a slight greenish tinge (reddish coloration shows that the animal has been given solid food). It is not greasy to the touch like pork: its fat is white and satiny and smells of milk. Veal killed too young is more gelatinous and of less nutritional value.

Veal is divided into three categories so far as market value is concerned. Since veal butchering differs in France, England and the U.S.A., the joints or cuts designated are the nearest approximations rather than equivalents.

1. *Cul* or *Quasi* (English, chump end of loin; U.S.A., standing rump. *Noix* (English, topside; U.S.A., rump). *Rouelle* (English, fillet end of leg; U.S.A., round roast). *Longe* (English and U.S.A., loin with or without kidney. *Carré* (English, best end of neck; U.S.A., rib roast).

2. *Épaule* (English and U.S.A., shoulder). *Basses-côtes* (English, end chops; U.S.A., shoulder chops). *Poitrine* (English and U.S.A., breast). *Ventre* (English, belly; U.S.A., flank).

3. *Collet* (English and U.S.A., neck). *Jarret* (English, knuckle; U.S.A., shank).

Amourettes of veal. AMOURETTES DE VEAU – In French cookery the spinal marrow of veal is known as *amourettes*. The substance of this marrow has a great resemblance to calf's brains, and all the methods of preparing the latter are applicable to *amourettes*. It may, like the brains, be prepared as a dish by itself; more often, however, it is used as an ingredient of a garnish. (See OFFAL or VARIETY MEATS.)

Veal blanquette. BLANQUETTE DE VEAU – Cut into pieces 750 g. ($1\frac{1}{2}$ lb.) veal taken from the shoulder, the breast, or end chops (shoulder chops). Put into a shallow saucepan with enough white stock, light broth or plain water to cover the meat. Add salt and bring to the boil, removing all scum.

Add a carrot, an onion stuck with a clove, a leek and a *bouquet garni* composed of parsley, thyme, bay leaf and celery. Cook very slowly for $1\frac{1}{2}$ hours.

Thicken three-quarters of the cooking liquor with 50 g. (2 oz., $\frac{1}{4}$ cup) each of butter and flour *roux*. Use this sauce or a *Velouté sauce* (see SAUCE), and add to it a handful of

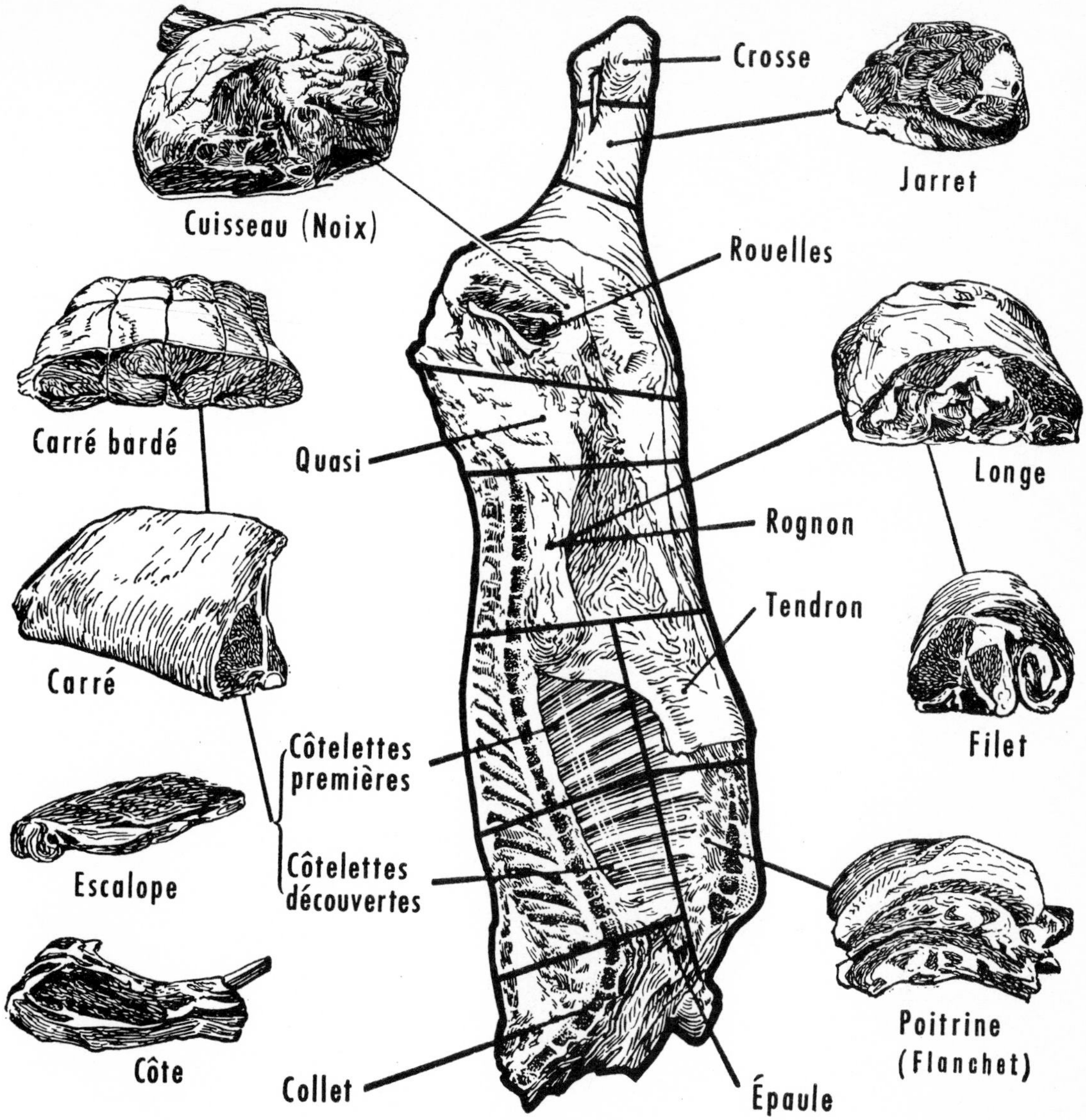

French cuts of veal

mushroom trimmings (from the mushrooms to be used in the *blanquette*). Cook for 15 minutes, stirring from time to time.

Remove the pieces of veal from the liquid. Remove any little bones which have become loose. Put the meat in a sauté pan with 12 small onions previously cooked in a flour-and-water *court-bouillon*, and 12 peeled mushrooms. Strain the sauce through a muslin bag, thicken with 3 egg yolks and $1\frac{1}{2}$ dl. ($\frac{1}{4}$ pint, $\frac{2}{3}$ cup) cream, and pour over the veal.

Season with a little grated nutmeg and a squeeze of lemon juice. Keep warm on a corner of the stove, covered, taking care that it does not boil. Serve with croûtons of bread fried in butter.

Veal blanquette with various garnishes. BLANQUETTE DE VEAU AVEC GARNITURES DIVERSES – Prepare the *blanquette* as in the preceding recipe. After the first cooking, and after the pieces of veal have been drained, put them back in the sauté pan with the prescribed vegetables. Pour over the strained sauce and finish cooking in the usual way.

Veal *blanquette* may also be prepared with celeriac cut in quarters, half-cooked in butter, or halved celery hearts; cucumbers cut into chunks and blanched for 3 minutes in boiling salted water; braised lettuce hearts cut in half; *matignon*; carrots, turnips, celery or leeks, sliced and stewed in butter.

Veal blanquette à l'ancienne. BLANQUETTE DE VEAU À L'ANCIENNE – Like *Blanquette of lamb à l'ancienne* (see LAMB).

Breast of veal. POITRINE DE VEAU – This cut is usually boned, stuffed and braised. It may also be used to make *ragoûts*. Stuff with the following forcemeat:

Add 1 kg. ($2\frac{1}{4}$ lb.) *Fine pork forcemeat* (see FORCEMEAT), 175 g. (6 oz., $1\frac{1}{2}$ cups) chopped onion cooked until tender in butter and 1 tablespoon of chopped parsley, and bind with a whole egg. Season with salt, pepper and spices and mix well.

The boned breast may also be stuffed with quenelle

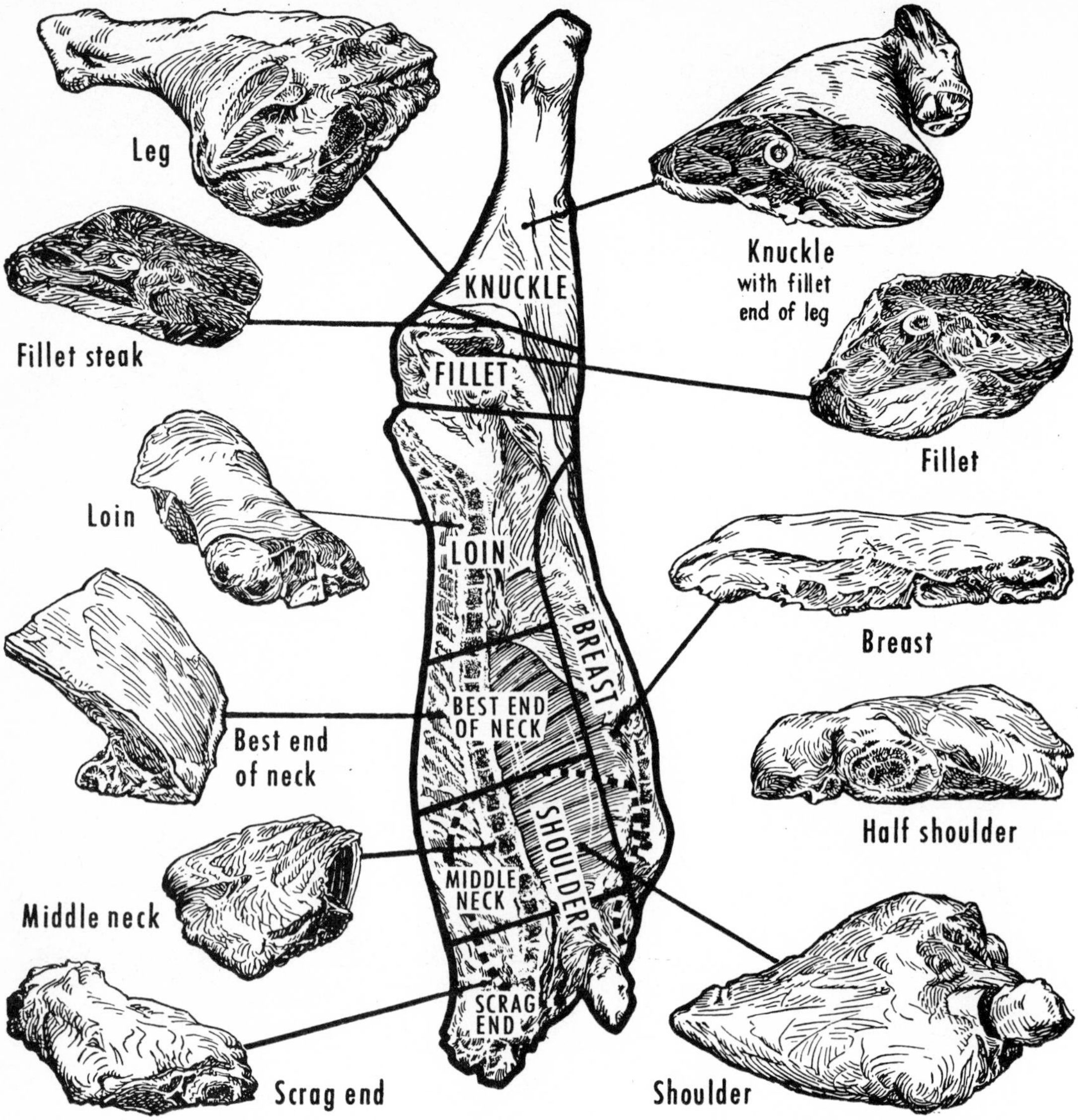

English cuts of veal

forcemeat, fine pork forcemeat mixed with chopped spinach lightly cooked in butter, sausage meat mixed with dry *duxelles*, etc.

The cooking time for a stuffed breast of veal weighing 5 kg. (11 lb.) is $3\frac{1}{2}$ to 4 hours. For the method of braising see CULINARY METHODS.

Breast of veal à l'allemande. POITRINE DE VEAU À L'ALLEMANDE – Poach in light stock a breast of veal stuffed as above. Serve surrounded by carrots, leeks, etc., that have been cooked with it; serve with hot *Horseradish sauce* (see SAUCE).

Breast of veal à l'alsacienne. POITRINE DE VEAU À L'ALSACIENNE – Braise the breast until it is half cooked, then finish off in the braising pan with blanched sauerkraut.

Breast of veal à l'anglaise. POITRINE DE VEAU À L'ANGLAISE – Stuff the breast with the forcemeat described below, and poach it gently in a light stock or salted water. Serve with boiled bacon.

Stuffing for breast of veal. Add to chopped beef or veal kidney the same quantity of chopped veal udder and breadcrumbs soaked in milk and pressed. Bind this forcemeat with 2 eggs to every 1 kg. ($2\frac{1}{4}$ lb.), and season.

Brochettes of veal. BROCHETTES DE VEAU – Cut some fillet of veal into pieces about $7\frac{1}{2}$ cm. (3 inches) thick. Put them on skewers alternately with blanched pieces of bacon. Season the meat on the skewers, dip in melted butter, cover them with breadcrumbs, sprinkle with more melted butter and cook under the grill.

Carré de veau – See *Rib of veal* below.

Veal chops. CÔTES DE VEAU – These cuts, taken from the best end of loin, must not be too thin.

Veal chops are usually sprinkled with their boiled down juices and sautéed in butter. They may be garnished in various ways, but should always be sprinkled first with their own cooking juices.

Veal chops may also be grilled. They are served with

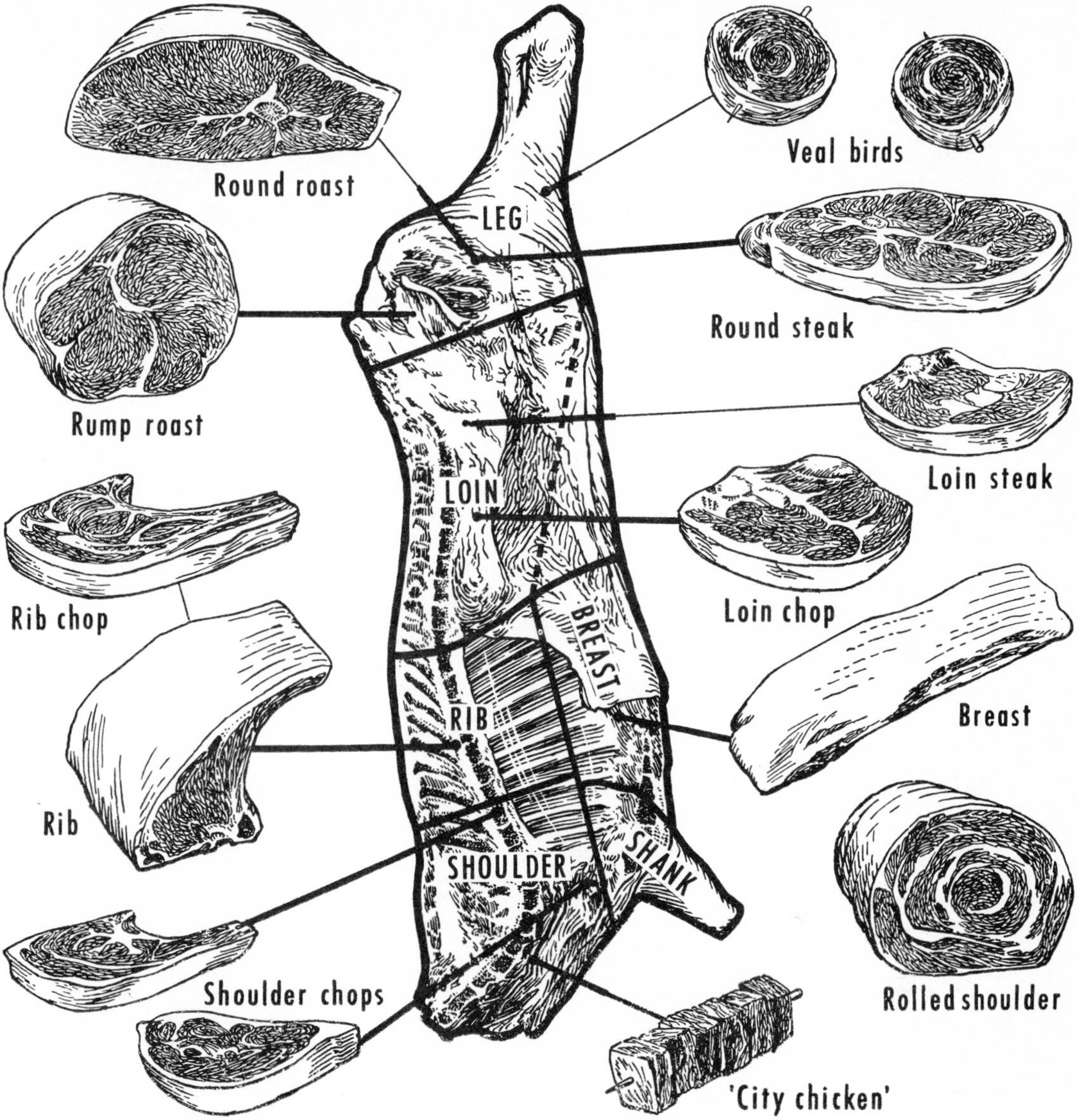

American cuts of veal

Maître d'hôtel butter (see BUTTER, *Compound butters*) or any other sauce usually served with grilled meat.

Veal chops à l'ancienne. CÔTES DE VEAU À L'ANCIENNE – Cook 6 chops in butter without browning. Surround with a garnish composed of cocks' combs and kidneys, lambs' sweetbreads, truffles and mushrooms, heated in Madeira and bound with chicken *Velouté sauce* (see SAUCE) diluted with cream.

Dilute the pan juices with Madeira, add equal quantities of concentrated and thickened brown veal stock and cream. Simmer down, add butter, strain, and pour over the chops.

Veal chops with basil. CÔTES DE VEAU AU BASILIC – Season chops with salt and pepper and sauté in butter. Drain. Sprinkle with a sauce made by diluting the pan juices with white wine and adding a few tablespoons veal stock, $\frac{1}{2}$ teaspoon chopped basil, and butter.

Veal chops Bellevue (cold). CÔTES DE VEAU BELLEVUE – Braise chops, cut rather thick; let cool in the liquor.

Put into an *hors-d'œuvre* dish or deep dish lined with jelly and decorated with mixed vegetables (carrots and turnips in little balls, peas, diced French beans, etc.). Cover the chops with their cooking liquor. Fill the dish with half melted jelly. Chill well on ice.

Turn out the chops on to a dish and garnish with chopped jelly.

Veal chops à la bonne femme. CÔTES DE VEAU À LA BONNE FEMME – Cook seasoned chops lightly in an earthenware casserole, browning them on both sides. Add, for each chop, 6 small lardoons of lean bacon, blanched and fried lightly in butter, 6 small fried onions and 12 new potatoes (or an equal quantity of old potatoes cut to look like olives), partly cooked in butter. Cook gently in the oven. Add 6 tablespoons ($\frac{1}{2}$ cup) thickened brown gravy and serve in the casserole in which they were cooked.

Veal chop bouchère. CÔTE DE VEAU BOUCHÈRE – Name for a chop taken from the collar end of the neck and not trimmed.

Veal

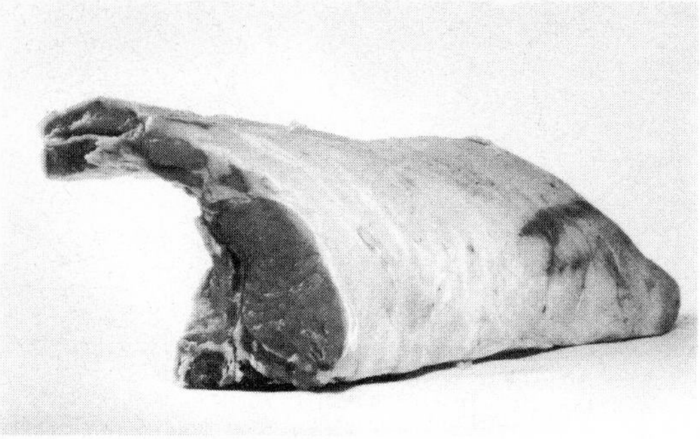

loin

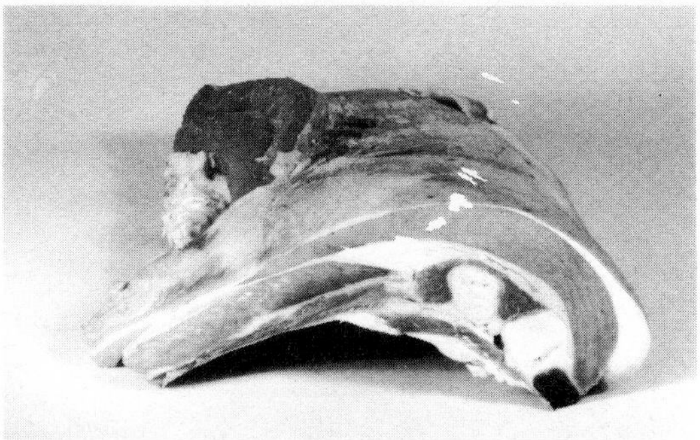

breast/ribs

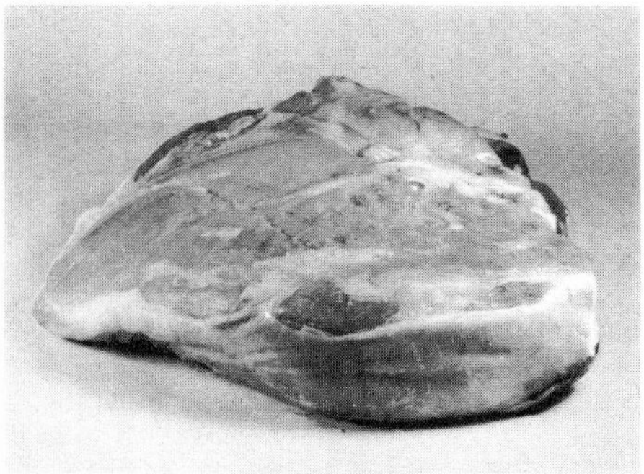

topside

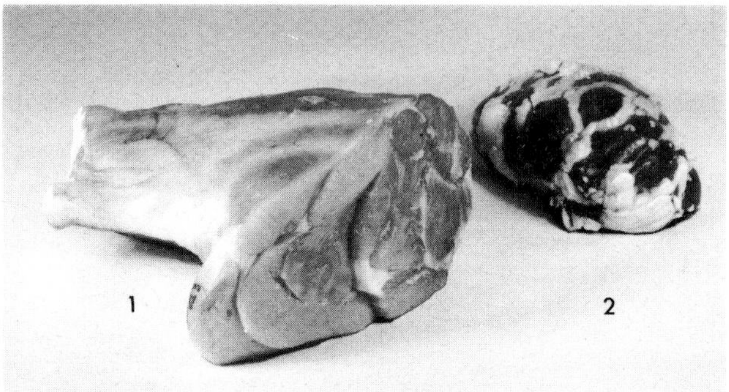

1. knuckle 2. kidneys

This cut is generally grilled, but it can also be sautéed in butter. It is served as it is, accompanied by vegetables to taste.

Veal chops bourguignonne. CÔTES DE VEAU BOURGUIGNONNE – Sauté chops in butter. When half cooked add for each chop 6 small glazed onions, 4 small mushrooms and 6 lardoons of lean, blanched bacon. Cook all together. Set the chops on a serving dish. Dilute the pan juices with red wine, thicken with a tablespoon *Kneaded butter* (see BUTTER, *Compound butters*), add a teaspoon meat jelly, boil down, add butter, and pour over the chops.

Braised veal chops. CÔTES DE VEAU BRAISÉES – Cut the chops rather thick and season with salt and pepper. Put them in a buttered sauté dish lined with strips of bacon rind, chopped onions and carrots. Cook gently in the oven, covered, for 10 minutes.

Pour in, for each chop, $\frac{1}{2}$ dl. (3 tablespoons, scant $\frac{1}{4}$ cup) white wine and boil down. Add clear brown stock to halfway up the meat. Add a small *bouquet garni*. Bring to the boil on top of the stove then cook in the oven, covered, for 45 minutes to 1 hour, according to size.

Drain the chops, set them on a dish and coat with a sauce made by straining the braising liquor, removing all grease and boiling down.

Braised veal chops can be accompanied by various garnishes. All those indicated elsewhere for sautéed veal chops are applicable.

Veal chops en casserole. CÔTES DE VEAU EN CASSEROLE – Season the chops with salt and pepper. Cook gently in butter in an earthenware casserole. Sprinkle with thickened veal gravy and serve in the same casserole.

Veal chops en casserole with various garnishes. CÔTES DE VEAU EN CASSEROLE, AVEC GARNITURES DIVERSES – Cook the chops in a casserole, remove, and replace with some of the following garnishes by cooking all together:

Aubergines cut in pieces, sautéed in butter or oil; glazed carrots (either small new carrots or large carrots cut into oval pieces); celeriac cut in oval pieces and simmered in butter; cèpes or cultivated mushrooms, sautéed in butter; cucumbers cut into large olive-shaped pieces, cooked in butter; artichoke bottoms in quarters; French beans cooked in water and tossed in butter; glazed turnips (also cut into olive-shaped pieces); salsify, cooked in a flour and water *court-bouillon* and sautéed in butter; Jerusalem artichokes cooked in butter.

The following may also be used, but should be added only when the meat is completely cooked: braised chicory; Brussels sprouts, lightly fried in butter; cauliflower flowerets sautéed in butter; braised endive; leaf spinach chopped with butter or cream; new broad beans with butter; stewed gumbos (okra or ladies' fingers) with tomato; hop shoots in butter; flageolet beans in butter; French beans in butter or cream; braised lettuce; braised chestnuts; noodles in butter; purée of sorrel; peas in butter or *à la française*; quartered tomatoes, stewed in butter.

Veal chops chasseur. CÔTES DE VEAU CHASSEUR – Prepare like *Mutton chops chasseur* (see MUTTON).

Veal chops chaud-froid. CÔTES DE VEAU EN CHAUD-FROID – *In white sauce.* Cook chops in butter without letting them colour. Allow to cool. Coat with *Chaud-froid sauce* (see SAUCE), to which the pan juices diluted with Madeira or any other wine have been added.

Garnish the top of each chop with truffles, pickled tongue, lean ham, tarragon leaves, etc. Glaze with jelly. Chill well. Set on a dish and garnish with chopped jelly.

In brown sauce. Braise the chops, browning them. Allow

them to cool in the braising liquor. Drain them and coat with *Brown chaud-froid sauce* to which the braising liquor has been added. Garnish and glaze with jelly.

Veal chops *en chaud-froid* may be accompanied by vegetable salad bound with mayonnaise, halves of hard boiled eggs or lettuce hearts.

Veal chops en cocotte. CÔTES DE VEAU EN COCOTTE – Alternative name for *Veal chops en casserole*. *Veal chops à la bonne femme* are also sometimes known by the same name.

Veal chops en cocotte with various garnishes. CÔTES DE VEAU EN COCOTTE, AVEC GARNITURES DIVERSES – Can be accompanied by any of the garnishes given for *Veal chops en casserole with various garnishes*.

Veal chops à la crème. CÔTES DE VEAU À LA CRÈME – Sauté the chops in butter. Drain and set on a dish. Coat with the cooking juices diluted with white wine or Madeira and fresh cream, boiled down and strained.

Add a tablespoon *Velouté sauce* (see SAUCE) to the cream to thicken the sauce.

Veal chops à l'indienne. CÔTES DE VEAU À L'INDIENNE – Sauté chops in butter. When browned on both sides, put them into the pan with 2 tablespoons (3 tablespoons) chopped onion. Season with 1 teaspoon curry powder. Cook gently, covered. Set the chops on a dish and coat with the following sauce. Dilute the cooking juices with $\frac{1}{2}$ dl. (3 tablespoons, scant $\frac{1}{4}$ cup) dry white wine. Add 4 tablespoons ($\frac{1}{3}$ cup) thick cream. Boil down to a good consistency. Add a squeeze of lemon juice.

Serve with *Rice à l'indienne* (see RICE).

Veal chops Cussy. CÔTES DE VEAU CUSSY – Cut a pocket in thick veal chops taken from the middle of the best end of the neck (U.S.A. rib). Fill with a *salpicon* composed of mushrooms, carrots and lean ham, bound with *Béchamel sauce* (see SAUCE) and well seasoned. Coat with egg and breadcrumbs. Cook in clarified butter, browning on both sides.

Prepare a creamy risotto (see RICE), bind with cheese and add a *salpicon* of truffles. Set the chop on a dish. Garnish with the truffle risotto. Pour around a few tablespoons tomato-flavoured brown gravy and sprinkle with 2 tablespoons (3 tablespoons) *Noisette butter* (see BUTTER, *Compound butters*).

Veal chops à la Custine. CÔTES DE VEAU À LA CUSTINE – 'Braise the veal chops, coat each one with a good tablespoon of *duxelles* (q.v.). Dip in the sauce, then in breadcrumbs, then in beaten eggs and in breadcrumbs a second time. Fry until golden in butter and serve with a light tomato sauce.' (Carême's recipe.)

Veal chops à la Dreux (old style). CÔTES DE VEAU À LA DREUX – 'Stud 12 veal chops, cut rather thick and lightly flattened, with pickled tongue and truffles. Tie them with string.

'Line a shallow casserole with the trimmings from the chops, 2 carrots, 2 onions and a *bouquet garni*, cover with thin pieces of bacon fat and place the chops on top. Pour over some consommé and a wineglass of Madeira and cook for a good three-quarters of an hour.

'Drain on a *plafond* (an old-fashioned copper baking tin) with a cover on top to keep them under pressure until they are cold. Strain the pan juices and remove all grease. Boil down to a light glaze.

'When the chops are cold, trim them carefully so that the tongue and truffles can be seen distinctly. Put them in a sauté dish with their glaze and allow to simmer for 15 minutes before serving. Garnish the middle with a *Ragoût à la*

Veal blanquette

Veal ragoût

financière (see RAGOÛT) and use the glaze as sauce.' (Plumerey's recipe.)

Veal chops à la Dreux (modern style). CÔTES DE VEAU À LA DREUX – Stud the chops, cut rather thick, with pickled tongue and truffles. Cook gently in butter. Trim the flat surfaces slightly so that the tongue and truffles show more clearly.

Set on a dish and surround with a *Financière garnish* (see GARNISHES). For sauce use the pan juices diluted with Madeira and mixed with thickened brown veal stock.

Veal chops à la duxelles. CÔTES DE VEAU À LA DUXELLES – Sauté the chops in butter. When almost cooked put into the pan 4 tablespoons ($\frac{1}{3}$ cup) dry *duxelles* (q.v.). Cook all together over a gentle heat for a few moments. Set the chops on a dish and sprinkle with the pan juices to which white wine and tomato-flavoured *Demi-glace sauce* (see SAUCE) have been added. Sprinkle with chopped parsley.

Veal chops à la fermière. CÔTES DE VEAU À LA FERMIÈRE – Cooked in a cocotte like *Veal chops à la paysanne* (see below), but without potatoes.

Veal chops aux fines herbes. CÔTES DE VEAU AUX FINES HERBES – Sauté 4 chops in butter. Drain and arrange on a dish. Dilute the pan juices with $\frac{1}{2}$ dl. (3 tablespoons, scant $\frac{1}{4}$ cup) white wine to which a teaspoon of chopped shallot has been added. Add *Demi-glace sauce* (see SAUCE). Boil for a few moments, then add 1 tablespoon chopped parsley, chervil and tarragon. Pour the sauce over the chops.

Veal chops à la gelée (Carême's recipe). CÔTES DE VEAU À LA GELÉE – 'Trim the veal chops and stud them with ham and bacon fat or pickled tongue. Put them in a pan lined with bards of bacon fat and put more bards of bacon fat on top. Over these place the trimmings of the chops, 2 carrots, 2 onions, 2 cloves and a good bouquet of thyme, bay leaf and basil. Add salt, a glass of white wine, 1 tablespoon brandy and 2 tablespoons (3 tablespoons) consommé. Cover with buttered paper and place the pan on the fire.

'When it has come right to the boil, cook over a gentle heat, in such a way that the chops boil only lightly for 2 hours. This cooking time is for thick chops weighing about 225 g. (8 oz.) each.

'Drain them. When they are almost cold, press them between 2 *plafonds* (baking tins), putting a weight on top. When they are quite cold trim them, glaze them with their braising liquor boiled down and strained, and set them on a dish garnished with chopped jelly. Garnish the top of each chop lightly with jelly, and surround with a border of jelly croûtons.'

Grilled veal chops. CÔTES DE VEAU GRILLÉES – Season the chops with salt and pepper, sprinkle with melted butter or oil and cook under a moderate grill. Set on a dish, put a paper frill on the bone and garnish with watercress.

Grilled veal chops are generally served as they are, but can be accompanied by a *Compound butter* (see BUTTER) or some kind of garnish, the most usual being potatoes.

Veal chops à la hongroise. CÔTES DE VEAU À LA HONGROISE – Season the chops with salt and paprika and sauté them in butter. When they are well browned on both sides put into the pan a good tablespoon chopped onion, cooked till tender in butter and seasoned with paprika. Cook gently, covered.

Drain the chops and set them on a dish. Coat with a sauce made by diluting the pan juices with white wine, adding cream, boiling down and adding butter.

Veal chops à la languedocienne. CÔTES DE VEAU À LA LANGUEDOCIENNE – Sauté 4 chops in goose fat. When they are browned on both sides put into the pan 1 tablespoon chopped onion and 2 tablespoons (3 tablespoons) diced raw ham. Cook gently all together. Add 12 stoned and blanched green olives and a little chopped garlic. Set the chops on a dish and surround with potatoes cut to look like olives and fried. Pour the sauce and the potatoes over the chops.

Veal chops à la lyonnaise. CÔTES DE VEAU À LA LYONNAISE – Sauté 4 chops in butter. Put into the pan 4 tablespoons ($\frac{1}{3}$ cup) chopped onions gently cooked in butter. Finish cooking together. Set the chops on a dish. Add 2 tablespoons (3 tablespoons) vinegar, 1 tablespoon chopped parsley and a little meat glaze to the onions, and pour over the chops.

Veal chops Maintenon. CÔTES DE VEAU MAINTENON – Prepare like *Mutton chops Maintenon* (see MUTTON).

Veal chops à la maraîchère. CÔTES DE VEAU À LA MARAÎCHÈRE – Sauté in butter. Garnish with chunks of salsify cooked in a flour and water *court-bouillon* and fried in butter, Brussels sprouts sautéed in butter, and potatoes cut to look like olives and cooked in butter.

For sauce use the pan juices diluted with white wine and with veal stock added.

Veal chops à la maréchale. CÔTES DE VEAU À LA MARÉCHALE – Flatten the chops lightly, season with salt and pepper, and coat with egg and breadcrumbs. Cook in clarified butter.

Garnish with asparagus tips in butter and slices of truffles, placed on top of the chops. Pour veal gravy around and sprinkle with *Noisette butter* (see BUTTER, *Compound butters*).

Veal chops à la milanaise. CÔTES DE VEAU À LA MILANAISE – Flatten the veal chops and season with salt and pepper. Coat with egg and breadcrumbs mixed with grated Parmesan. Cook in clarified butter. Set on a dish and surround with *Macaroni à la milanaise* (see MACARONI). Top each chop with a slice of peeled lemon and sprinkle with *Noisette butter* (see BUTTER, *Compound butters*).

This is how *veal chops à la milanaise* are prepared in Paris restaurants. In Italy they are generally served with sautéed potatoes but without the macaroni.

Minced veal chops Grimod de la Reynière. CÔTES DE VEAU HACHÉES GRIMOD DE LA REYNIÈRE – Chop the veal chops finely, adding to each one-third of its weight of breadcrumbs soaked in milk and pressed, and a teaspoon chopped truffles. Season with salt, pepper and a little grated nutmeg.

Put this forcemeat back on to the bone of the chop and re-form it to its original shape. Coat with egg and breadcrumbs and cook in clarified butter. Garnish with buttered asparagus tips and surround with concentrated veal stock. Sprinkle with *Noisette butter* (see BUTTER, *Compound butters*).

Minced veal chops with various vegetables. CÔTES DE VEAU HACHÉES AVEC LÉGUMES DIVERS – Chop the meat of the chops finely as for *minced veal chops Grimod de la Reynière*, but without adding truffles. Re-form the chop. Sauté in clarified butter. Garnish with vegetables. Surround with thickened brown veal stock. Sprinkle with *Noisette butter* (see BUTTER, *Compound butters*).

Veal chops à la Morland (Carême's recipe). CÔTES DE VEAU À LA MORLAND – Dip veal chops in beaten egg and coat them with finely chopped truffles. Sauté in clarified butter. Set them on a serving dish and a mushroom purée in the middle. Use *Demiglace sauce* (see SAUCE).

Veal chops with mushrooms. CÔTES DE VEAU AUX CHAMPIGNONS – Season chops with salt and pepper. Brown both sides in butter in a sauté pan.

When half cooked add peeled raw mushroom heads and finish cooking. Garnish with the mushrooms.

Sprinkle over the cooking juices diluted with Madeira and *Demi-glace sauce* (see SAUCE).

Veal chops with mushrooms à la crème. CÔTES DE VEAU AUX CHAMPIGNONS À LA CRÊME – Prepare as above. After having set the chops on a dish, dilute the cooking juices with Madeira and fresh cream and boil down. Coat the chops and mushrooms with this sauce.

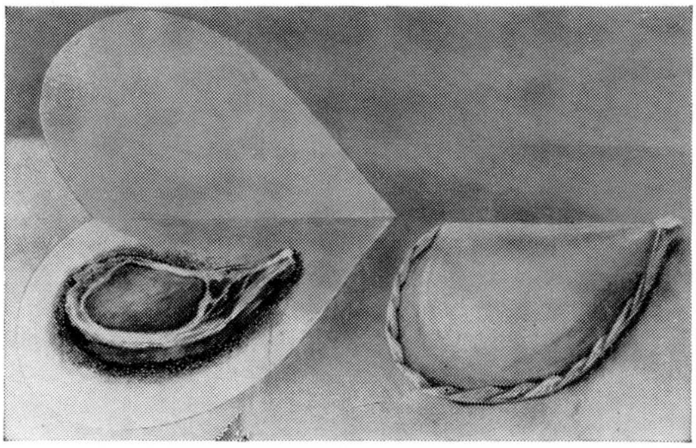

Veal chops en papillote

Veal chops en papillote. CÔTES DE VEAU EN PAPILLOTE – Sauté the chops in butter. Set on a sheet of oiled paper cut in the shape of a heart, placing the chop on one half of the heart on a slice of cooked ham covered with 1 tablespoon thick *Duxelles sauce* (see SAUCE). Put another tablespoon of the sauce on top of the chop and cover with another slice of ham.

Close the *papillote*, folding over the edges. Cook in the oven long enough to puff up the paper and colour it a little.

Veal chops Parmentier. CÔTES DE VEAU PARMENTIER – Season 4 chops with salt and pepper. Fry in butter on both sides. When they are half cooked, put in the pan 225 g. (8 oz.) potatoes cut in pieces 2 cm. ($\frac{3}{4}$-inch) square. Finish cooking together.

Set the chops on a dish and surround with the potatoes. Pour over the pan juices diluted with 2 tablespoons (3 tablespoons) veal stock. Sprinkle with chopped parsley.

Veal chops à la paysanne. CÔTES DE VEAU À LA PAYSANNE – Cook 4 chops in butter. When they are almost ready, add 1 dl. (6 tablespoons, scant $\frac{1}{2}$ cup) vegetable *fondue*, with the addition of 6 tablespoons chopped bacon, fried in butter, and 175 g. (6 oz., $1\frac{1}{2}$ cups) diced potatoes, cooked in butter. Finish cooking all together. Sprinkle over 1 dl. (6 tablespoons, scant $\frac{1}{2}$ cup) of veal stock.

Veal chops à la paysanne can be cooked and served in an earthenware casserole, as can all dishes cooked *à la paysanne*.

Veal chops à la piémontaise. CÔTES DE VEAU À LA PIÉMONTAISE – Season the chops with salt and pepper, and coat with egg and breadcrumbs mixed with grated cheese. Sauté in clarified butter. Garnish with *Risotto à la piémontaise* (see RICE). Pour round *Demi-glace sauce* (see SAUCE) flavoured with tomato.

Veal chops Pojarski. CÔTES DE VEAU POJARSKI – Chop finely the meat of the chops and mix with a quarter of its weight of butter and an equal quantity of breadcrumbs soaked in milk and pressed. Season this forcemeat with salt, pepper and a little grated nutmeg. Put it back on the bone and reshape the chops. Flour and cook in clarified butter. Garnish with the chosen vegetable, and put a slice of peeled lemon on top of each chop. Sprinkle with *Noisette butter* (see BUTTER, *Compound butters*).

Veal chops en portefeuille (grilled). CÔTES DE VEAU EN PORTEFEUILLE – Cut open the lean meat of a thick veal chop. Season inside and out with salt and pepper, and fill this pocket with a forcemeat. Wrap the chop in a piece of pig's caul or pork fat, previously soaked in cold water. Cook under the grill at a gentle heat.

Serve with a garnish of vegetables. Pour round some veal gravy with butter added.

Veal chops en portefeuille (sautéed). CÔTES DE VEAU EN PORTEFEUILLE – Prepare the chops as above. Cook in butter in a sauté pan. Garnish with the prescribed vegetables. Dilute the pan juices with white wine and thickened veal gravy.

Veal chops à la portugaise. CÔTES DE VEAU À LA PORTUGAISE – Sauté the chops in oil, set on a dish. Add to the pan juices for each chop 2 tablespoons (3 tablespoons) *Tomato fondue* (see FONDUE). Add 1 dl. (6 tablespoons, scant $\frac{1}{2}$ cup) white wine, season with a little garlic, boil down, add 2 teaspoons chopped parsley and pour over the chops.

Veal chops à la provençale. CÔTES DE VEAU À LA PROVENÇALE – Sauté the chops in a mixture of butter and oil. Garnish with tomatoes stuffed with *duxelles* (q.v.), covered with grated cheese and browned. Dilute the pan juices with white wine, add *Tomato sauce* (see SAUCE), and a little garlic for seasoning. Pour over chops. Sprinkle with chopped parsley.

Sautéed veal chops with various garnishes. CÔTES DE VEAU SAUTÉE AVEC GARNITURES DIVERSES – Sauté the chops in butter, and garnish with some of the following vegetables.

Dilute the pan juices with white wine, add brown veal gravy and pour over the chops.

Garnishes. Quartered artichokes or artichoke bottoms; asparagus tips in butter; diced aubergines, sautéed in butter or oil; carrots, *à la creme*, glazed or Vichy; celery, braised or simmered in butter; *cèpes* or other edible fungi sautéed in butter or oil; braised chicory (U.S.A. endive); Brussels sprouts, sautéed in butter; cauliflower, sautéed in butter; sliced or diced Italian marrows or courgettes sautéed in butter or oil; braised endive (U.S.A. chicory); leaf spinach stewed in butter, or chopped or sieved in butter, cream or gravy; hop shoots in butter or cream; kidney beans in butter or *à la bretonne*; sweet corn in butter or cream; braised sorrel; peas in butter or *à la française*; potatoes, prepared in various ways; pilaf rice or risotto; salsify in cream, in stock or sautéed in butter; halved tomatoes sautéed in butter, grilled, or cooked slowly in butter or oil.

Veal chops with truffles. CÔTES DE VEAU AUX TRUFFES – Season the chops with salt and pepper. Sauté in butter. When almost cooked, put into the pan for each chop, 6 rather thick slices of truffles. Set the chops on a dish and cover with the truffles. Sprinkle with the cooking juices diluted with Madeira and *Demi-glace sauce* (see SAUCE), flavoured with truffle essence.

Veal chops vert-pré. CÔTES DE VEAU VERT-PRÉ – Grill the chops and garnish as for *Entrecôte au vert-pré* (see BEEF, *Entrecôte*).

Veal chops Vichy. CÔTES DE VEAU VICHY – Sauté the chops in butter. Put into the pan for each chop, 5 tablespoons (6 tablespoons) carrots prepared as for *à la Vichy* (see CARROT). Sprinkle with the diluted pan juices.

Veal chops à la viennoise. CÔTES DE VEAU À LA VIENNOISE – Prepare as for *Escalopes of veal à la viennoise*.

Veal chops Zingara. CÔTES DE VEAU ZINGARA – Season with salt and paprika. Sauté in butter. Set the chops on a dish and put on top of each a slice of ham sautéed in butter. Coat with *Zingara sauce* (see SAUCE).

Escalopes of veal. ESCALOPES DE VEAU – Escalopes of veal are usually cut from the fillet end of the leg. They can also be taken from the topside or silverside.

These pieces, which average about 100 g. (4 oz.) should be oval, round or heart-shaped. They are lightly flattened and sautéed in butter.

All the recipes given for veal chops are applicable to escalopes. Those given below for escalopes can equally well be used for veal chops. The recipes given for *tournedos* (see BEEF) and for *noisettes* of lamb or mutton (see LAMB, MUTTON), can be applied to veal chops and escalopes.

Escalopes of veal à l'anglaise. ESCALOPES DE VEAU À L'ANGLAISE – Flatten the escalopes lightly and coat them with egg and breadcrumbs. Cook in clarified butter. Set them in a 'crown' on a serving dish and sprinkle with *Noisette butter* (see BUTTER, *Compound butters*).

Escalopes of veal à l'anversoise. ESCALOPES DE VEAU À L'ANVERSOISE – Sauté the escalopes in butter. Set them on croûtons of bread fried in butter. Garnish with hop shoots in cream and small potatoes, fried in butter. For sauce use the cooking juices diluted with white wine and thick brown gravy.

Escalopes of veal with French (string) beans or other green vegetables. ESCALOPES DE VEAU AUX HARICOTS VERTS – The escalopes can be coated in egg and breadcrumbs or left plain. Sauté them in butter. Garnish with French beans sautéed in butter and surround with veal stock. Sprinkle with the cooking butter.

Escalopes prepared in this way can be garnished with flageolet beans, broad beans, asparagus tips, peas, etc., cooked in salted water, drained and mixed with butter.

Escalopes of veal Brancas. ESCALOPES DE VEAU BRANCAS – Cover the seasoned escalopes with a thin layer of *mirepoix* of vegetables cooked in butter until very tender. Coat in egg and breadcrumbs and sauté in clarified butter.

Set on a base of *Annette potatoes* (see POTATOES). Put a *Chiffonnade of lettuce* (see LETTUCE) mixed with a rather thick cream sauce on top of each escalope.

Pour round a few tablespoons *Demi-glace sauce* (see SAUCE) with Madeira and butter.

Escalopes of veal Casimir. ESCALOPES DE VEAU CASIMIR – Season escalopes taken from the fillet with salt and paprika and sauté them in butter. Set each on an artichoke bottom cooked gently in butter. Put on top a *julienne* of carrot, cut short and thick, stewed in butter with a *julienne* of truffles, cut to the same size and added when the carrots are cooked.

Coat with the cooking juices diluted with cream and seasoned with paprika.

Escalopes of veal with courgettes or aubergines. ESCALOPES DE VEAU AUX COURGETTES, AUX AUBERGINES – Season 4 escalopes taken from the best end of the neck, trimmed and flattened, with salt and pepper. Sauté them in butter.

Fry 2 peeled, sliced courgettes or aubergines in oil.

Garnish the escalopes with the courgettes or aubergines, and sprinkle with the cooking juices from the escalopes, diluted with a little white wine and concentrated meat juice seasoned with a little grated garlic. Sprinkle with chopped parsley.

Escalopes of veal à la jardinière. ESCALOPES DE VEAU À LA JARDINIÈRE – Coat the escalopes in egg and breadcrumbs and sauté in butter. Garnish with a *jardinière* (see GARNISHES) of vegetables bound with butter or cream. Surround with veal stock and sprinkle with the cooking butter.

Escalopes of veal with rosemary (Italian cookery). ESCALOPES DE VEAU AU ROMARIN – Cut from a piece of boned loin of veal 6 slices about $2\frac{1}{2}$ cm (1 inch) thick. Season with salt and pepper and coat them with flour. Fry in hot butter in a sauté pan.

When they are a good colour on both sides, pour in a glass of white wine. Add a small sprig of fresh rosemary. Cover the pan, and cook slowly, without boiling, for 18 to 20 minutes.

Place the escalopes on a dish and sprinkle with their juice.

Escalopes of veal à la viennoise. ESCALOPES DE VEAU À LA VIENNOISE – Flatten the escalopes well, season, coat with egg and breadcrumbs, and cook them in butter. Arrange on a layer of *Anchovy butter* (see BUTTER, *Compound butters*). On top of each escalope put a slice of peeled lemon and a stoned olive surrounded by a fillet of anchovy.

Set the whites and yolks of hard boiled eggs, chopped separately, round the escalopes, together with capers and chopped parsley.

Feuilleton of veal 'l'Échelle'. FEUILLETON DE VEAU 'L'ÉCHELLE' – Seal quickly in very hot butter a boned and seasoned fillet of veal. Allow to cool. Cut it at regular intervals, lengthways, so as to make 'leaves', attached only at the base.

Fill the spaces with a mixture of dry *duxelles*, (q.v.) chopped lean ham, diced truffles and an equal quantity of a fine *mirepoix* (q.v.) of vegetables, bound with beaten egg.

Re-form the fillet, cover it with *mirepoix* and wrap it in pigs' caul or paper-thin salt pork previously soaked in cold water. Spread with a little butter, place in a casserole, cover and cook in the oven.

Garnish the fillet with braised lettuce and potatoes fried in butter. For sauce use the cooking juices diluted with Madeira and brown veal stock.

Feuilleton of cold veal in jelly. FEUILLETON DE VEAU FROID À LA GELÉE – See FEUILLETON.

Fillet of veal. FILET DE VEAU – Loin of veal, boned or unboned, a part which includes not only the fillet (U.S.A. sirloin), but also the part which corresponds to what would be called the eye of the sirloin (U.S.A. tenderloin) in beef.

The true fillet of veal is a very delicate cut and can be prepared alone. From it may be cut escalopes, *noisettes* or *médaillons*, the two last being treated in the same way as the escalopes.

Fillet of veal, cut in square pieces, may also be used to make *sautées à la minute*, skewered to make brochettes, or lightly flattened and grilled.

Veal forcemeat or godiveau – See FORCEMEATS.

Fricadelles of veal. FRICADELLES DE VEAU – Prepared with raw or cooked veal as for *Fricadelles of beef* (see BEEF).

Veal fricandeau. FRICANDEAU – This name is given mainly to a dish made of loin of veal (*noix de veau*) larded, braised or roasted (see *Noix of veal* below).

Fricassée of veal. FRICASSÉE DE VEAU – Prepare with veal cut into pieces of regular shape and size like *Fricassée of chicken* (see FRICASSÉE).

Grenadins of veal. GRENADINS DE VEAU – Name which describes pieces cut from the fillet end of leg, like escalopes, but smaller and thicker. They are studded with bacon fat and braised like *Noix of veal* below. All the garnishes given for *Noix of veal* are applicable to *grenadins*.

Knuckle of veal à l'italienne or Osso-bucco. JARRET DE VEAU À L'ITALIENNE – Rounds of knuckle of veal braised in a stock which includes tomato purée.

Saw 750 g. ($1\frac{1}{2}$ lb.) knuckle of veal into rounds 5 cm. (2 inches) thick. Season with salt and pepper, sprinkle with flour and brown in 2 to 3 tablespoons lard. Add 4 tablespoons ($\frac{1}{3}$ cup) chopped onion, cook until pale golden, add 2 dl. ($\frac{1}{3}$ pint, scant cup) white wine, boil down, add 4 large peeled, seeded and pressed tomatoes and pour in 2 dl. ($\frac{1}{3}$ pint, scant cup)

white stock or broth. Add a crushed clove of garlic and a *bouquet garni* and cook, covered, in the oven for $1\frac{1}{2}$ hours.

Set the pieces of knuckle on a dish and coat them with the concentrated cooking liquor. Sprinkle a little lemon juice and some chopped parsley over.

Knuckle of veal à la provençale. JARRET DE VEAU À LA PROVENÇALE – Saw the knuckle into rounds of the same thickness. Season with salt and pepper. Cook lightly in oil. Add (for one whole knuckle) 150 g. (5 oz. $1\frac{1}{4}$ cups) finely chopped onion. When the onion is partly cooked, add 4 large peeled, seeded and pressed tomatoes. Season with garlic, pour in $1\frac{1}{2}$ dl. ($\frac{1}{4}$ pint, $\frac{2}{3}$ cup) white wine and a few tablespoons brown veal gravy. Add a *bouquet garni* and cook covered, for $1\frac{1}{2}$ hours.

Veal loaf. PAIN DE VEAU – Prepare with *Fine panada forcemeat I* (see FORCEMEAT) using veal.

Loin of veal. LONGE DE VEAU – This is the part of the carcase which extends from the point of the haunch to the first ribs.

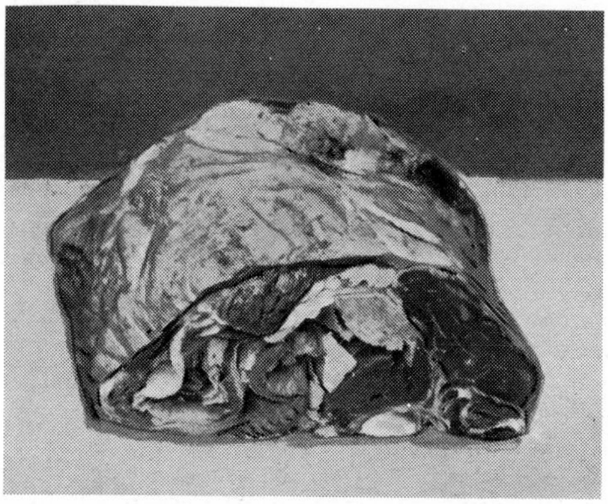

Loin of veal (*Larousse.*)

Loin of veal, which is served as an *entrée*, can be braised, cooked, covered in the oven, or roasted. When it is roasted it is usually boned first, leaving a strip of skin long enough to wrap round the fillet. The kidney is usually included in this joint, part of the fat surrounding it having been removed.

The loin thus prepared is sometimes called a *rognonnade de veau*. It can also be braised, and is usually accompanied by any of the garnishes prescribed for *Noix of veal* (see below).

Matelote of veal. MATELOTE DE VEAU – This is sautéed veal, the cooking juices diluted with red wine, small onions and mushrooms added, and the sauce thickened with *Kneaded butter* (see BUTTER, *Compound butters*).

Médaillons of veal. MÉDAILLONS DE VEAU – Small round pieces cut from the fillet end of the leg. They are prepared like *Escalopes of veal*.

Neck of veal, best end of neck – See *Rib* below.

Noisettes of veal. NOISETTES DE VEAU – Small round pieces, usually cut from the fillet. Prepare like *Escalopes of veal*.

Noisettes à la Bénévent. NOISETTES À LA BÉNÉVENT – 'The *noisette* of veal,' says Plumerey, 'is that fat part, oblong in shape, found in the shoulder of veal to the left of the blade bone. In the middle is found an extremely delicate piece of meat about the size of a walnut.

'Procure 16 of these *noisettes*, which should be soaked in water on a corner of the stove for 2 hours and then blanched. Cool in cold water and when nearly cold drain and wipe on a cloth and put them under pressure.

'The *noisettes* should then be cooked in a braising stock with a *mirepoix* and Madeira. They are served garnished with a *macédoine* of vegetables, a purée of sorrel or braised chicory.'

Noix, sous-noix and fricandeau of veal. NOIX, SOUS-NOIX, FRICANDEAU DE VEAU – The *noix* of veal is like the topside of beef, the fleshy upper part of the leg, cut lengthwise.

Below this piece is found another fleshy part which is called in French the *sous-noix* or *noix pâtissière*, also cut lengthwise.

The *noix* is always studded with fine bacon fat, but only the parts next to the bone of the chump end. This part is mostly used for braising.

The *sous-noix* is also studded with bacon fat and cooked in the same way as the *noix*.

The *fricandeau* is cut from the *noix*. This is a slice cut along the grain of the meat and should not be more than $3\frac{1}{2}$ cm. ($1\frac{1}{2}$ inches) thick. It is studded with fine bacon fat and usually braised, like *noix* and *sous-noix*.

Garnishes applicable to the *noix*, *soux-nois* and *fricandeau* of veal are *bouquetière*, *bourgeoise*, endive, mushrooms, *Clamart*, braised chicory, spinach, *jardinière*, various vegetables, braised; celery, lettuce, *macédoine*, *milanaise*, sorrel, *piémontaise*, risotto.

Noix, sous-noix and fricandeau, cold. NOIX, SOUS-NOIX, FRICANDEAU, FROIDS – These pieces may be served cold. Braise and allow to cool in the strained braising liquor. Coat with the same liquor, jellied, and garnish with chopped jelly.

Serve with any of the garnishes used to garnish cold meat and poultry.

Veal offal or variety meats. ABATS DE VEAU – Veal offal or variety meat is delicate in flavour and lends itself to a considerable number of treatments. (See OFFAL or VARIETY MEATS.)

Paupiettes of veal. PAUPIETTES DE VEAU – The *paupiettes* are made with escalopes of veal flattened well, rolled up and spread with *Quenelle forcemeat* (see FORCEMEAT) mixed with *duxelles* (q.v.) or chopped truffles.

Braise very slowly, coat with the braising liquor, and serve with one of the garnishes given for veal chops or escalopes.

Paupiettes of veal braised à blanc. PAUPIETTES DE VEAU BRAISÉES À BLANC – Proceed, using *paupiettes*, in the same way as for *Calf's sweetbreads braised in white stock* (see OFFAL or VARIETY MEATS).

Paupiettes of veal braised à brun. PAUPIETTES DE VEAU BRAISÉES À BRUN – Spread the *paupiettes* with *Pork forcemeat* (see FORCEMEAT) mixed with dry *duxelles* (q.v.) and chopped parsley and bound with egg. Roll them up, bard with bacon and tie them. Put them into a buttered sauté pan, lined with strips of pork skin or bacon rinds and chopped onions and carrots, lightly cooked in butter. Put a *bouquet garni* in the middle. Season with salt and pepper. Cover and cook gently on the stove for 10 minutes. Pour in 2 dl. ($\frac{1}{3}$ pint, scant cup) white wine or Madeira for every 10 paupiettes. Boil down this liquid to almost nothing. Pour in, to three-quarters of the depth of the *paupiettes*, thickened veal gravy. Cook, covered, in the oven, basting often, for 45 minutes to 1 hour.

Drain the *paupiettes*, untie them and remove the bards. Glaze them. Set on a serving-dish and coat with the braising liquor, boiled down and strained.

Paupiettes braised à brun are accompanied by vegetables mixed with butter or braised. These may be cooked with the veal, as in *Paupiettes of veal à la bourgeoise, à la bourguignonne, à la chipolata*, etc.

When the *paupiettes* are accompanied by buttered vegetables or puree of vegetables, the vegetables are served separately.

Paupiettes of veal à la grecque – See PAUPIETTES.

Hot fillet of veal pâté – See PÂTÉS.

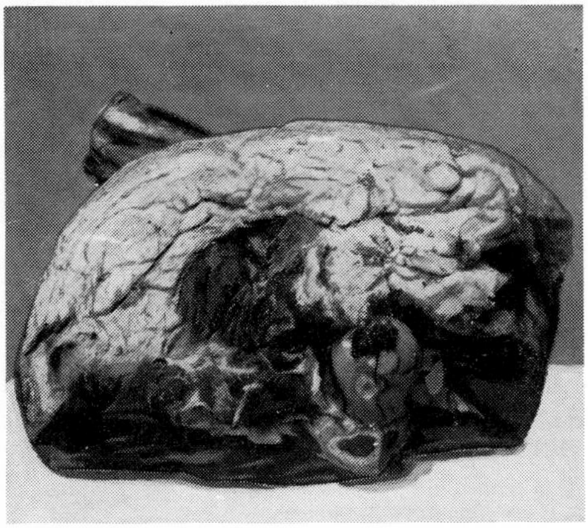

Leg of veal, from which the topside is cut

Quasi and rouelle of veal (English chump end of loin, U.S.A. standing rump and heel of round). QUASI ET ROUELLE DE VEAU – The quasi is a piece taken from the leg. It is cooked in a covered pan in butter, or braised.

Rib (carré) of veal. CARRÉ DE VEAU – Best end of neck (U.S.A. rib) is scarcely ever cooked in one piece. This joint is nevertheless excellent, baked, roasted or braised.

Cut down the top of the joint, and remove the spinal bone (this makes the joint easier to carve). Season and wrap in thin bards of bacon fat.

Roast in the oven, allowing 30 minutes to the pound at 160°C. (325°F., Gas Mark 3) or pot-roast or braise it.

Remove the bacon fat and string. Garnish with watercress and serve with its cooking juices, diluted if the meat has been roasted. If it has been braised or cooked covered, surround it with the garnish.

Any of the garnishes indicated elsewhere for loin or *noix* of veal are applicable to the *carré*, whether roasted, pot-roasted or braised.

Cold rib of veal. CARRÉ DE VEAU FROID – Roast the rib of veal, trim, coat with jelly, set on a serving dish and garnish with cress.

Cold rib of veal may be prepared as described in any of the recipes given elsewhere for loin or *noix* of veal.

How to cut ribs of veal

Saddle of veal. SELLE DE VEAU – This cut consists of the entire back of the animal. It is braised, pot-roasted or roasted, and accompanied by any of the garnishes normally served with meat, especially those given for *Noix of veal.*

Sautéed veal. SAUTÉS DE VEAU – Made from the same cuts as *ragoûts*. After the meat has been lightly fried, the juices in the pan are diluted with white wine, and stock or sauce of some kind, varying according to the recipe, is added.

Cut the veal into pieces of regular size and shape. Season and cook lightly in butter, oil or fat, according to the nature of the preparation. Drain off the fat, dilute the remaining juices with white wine and add veal gravy or *Demi-glace sauce* (see SAUCE).

Cook covered for 1 or $1\frac{1}{2}$ hours.

Drain the pieces of meat. Trim them and put into another saucepan. Add the garnish, pour over the strained sauce from which all grease has been removed, and simmer together for 15 to 20 minutes over a low heat.

Serve in a deep dish, with a border of rice.

When thick veal gravy or *demi-glace sauce* is not available, the veal may be moistened with stock or water and thickened with *Kneaded butter* (see BUTTER, *Compound butters*). It may also be treated in the way suggested for *ragoûts*, and sprinkled with flour and moistened with the prescribed liquid.

Sautéed veal with aubergines. SAUTÉ DE VEAU AUX AUBERGINES – Like *Sautéed lamb with aubergines* made with shoulder chops or end chops of veal, boned and cut into square pieces.

Sautéed veal with cèpes, morels or St. George's agarics. SAUTÉ DE VEAU AVEC CÈPES, MORILLES, MOUSSERONS – Prepare as for *Sautéed lamb with cèpes* (see LAMB).

Sautéed veal chasseur. SAUTÉ DE VEAU CHASSEUR – Cook 750 g. ($1\frac{1}{2}$ lb.) veal lightly in a mixture of butter and oil. Dilute with a little dry white wine, add 4 chopped shallots and stir in veal stock and *Tomato sauce* (see SAUCE). Add a *bouquet garni*. Cook for $1\frac{1}{2}$ hours.

Sautéed veal Clamart. SAUTÉ DE VEAU CLAMART – Prepare the sautéed veal as in the first recipe. When the pieces of veal are almost cooked, drain them and put them in the sauté pan. Cover them with peas cooked *à la française*, but not completely cooked. Pour over strained liquor from the sauté. Finish cooking, covered, in the oven.

Sautéed veal à la crème. SAUTÉ DE VEAU À LA CRÈME – Prepare like *Sautéed lamb à la crème* (see LAMB), using boned veal cut into small squares.

Sautéed veal aux fines herbes. SAUTÉ DE VEAU AUX FINES HERBES – Prepare like *Sautéed lamb aux fines herbes* (see LAMB).

Sautéed veal à la hongroise. SAUTÉ DE VEAU À LA HONGROISE – Cook 750°. ($1\frac{1}{2}$ b.) veal lightly in butter. When it is half cooked add 2 tablespoons (3 tablespoons) chopped onion and sprinkle with paprika. Dilute the pan juices with white wine, stir in 8 dl. ($1\frac{1}{3}$ pints, $1\frac{3}{4}$ pints) light *Velouté sauce* (see SAUCE) and add a *bouquet garni*. Cook for $1\frac{1}{2}$ hours.

Drain the pieces, trim and put into another sauté pan. Pour over the sauce, strained and diluted with a few tablespoons cream. Simmer for 15 minutes. Serve in a deep dish.

Sautéed veal à l'indienne. SAUTÉ DE VEAU À L'INDIENNE – Cook the veal lightly in butter. When it is half cooked add 2 tablespoons (3 tablespoons) chopped onion. Cook together for 5 minutes.

Drain off the fat, sprinkle with a teaspoon curry powder and a tablespoon flour. Cook till golden. Stir in 8 dl. ($1\frac{1}{3}$ pints, $1\frac{3}{4}$ pints) white stock and add a *bouquet garni*. Cook for $1\frac{1}{2}$ hours.

Serve with *Rice à l'indienne* (see RICE).

Sautéed veal Marengo. SAUTÉ DE VEAU MARENGO – Cook 750 g. ($1\frac{1}{2}$ lb.) veal lightly in oil. When it is half cooked add 2

How to turn out a rice border for a sauté of veal

tablespoons (3 tablespoons) chopped onion and a crushed clove of garlic.

Dilute the pan juices with white wine. Stir in 6 dl. (1 pint, $2\frac{1}{2}$ cups) thickened veal stock and 2 dl. ($\frac{1}{3}$ pint, scant cup) *Tomato sauce* (see SAUCE). Add a *bouquet garni*. Cook for $1\frac{1}{2}$ hours.

Drain the pieces, trim them and put them back in a sauté pan with 12 small glacé onions and 12 mushrooms sautéed in oil. Pour over them the sauce, strained and with all grease removed, and simmer for 15 minutes.

Set in a deep dish, sprinkle with chopped parsley and garnish with heart-shaped croûtons fried in butter or oil.

Although a preparation *à la Marengo*, a style chiefly applied to chicken (see CHICKEN, *Sautéed chicken à la Marengo*) normally includes truffles, crayfish and fried egg yolks, this veal sauté is garnished only with onions and mushrooms.

Sautéed veal à la minute. SAUTÉ DE VEAU À LA MINUTE – Cut boned shoulder chops or end chops of veal into small squares. Season them with salt and pepper and sauté quickly in hot butter. Finish cooking in the oven.

Arrange in a deep dish and pour over a sauce made by diluting the pan juices with $1\frac{1}{2}$ dl. ($\frac{1}{4}$ pint, $\frac{2}{3}$ cup) white wine, boiling down, adding a tablespoon dissolved meat glaze, 3 tablespoons (scant $\frac{1}{4}$ cup) butter and the juice of half a lemon and stir well. Sprinkle with chopped parsley.

Sautéed veal with mushrooms. SAUTÉ DE VEAU AUX CHAMPIGNONS – Fry 750 g. ($1\frac{1}{2}$ lb.) veal, cut as for a *ragoût* and seasoned with salt and pepper, lightly in butter.

Drain off all fat, dilute the pan juices with white wine and add 8 dl. ($1\frac{1}{3}$ pints, $1\frac{3}{4}$ pints) stock or thickened veal stock or a light *Demi-glace sauce* (see SAUCE).

Add a *bouquet garni*, and cook very slowly for $1\frac{1}{2}$ hours.

Drain the pieces of meat, trim and put them into another sauté pan with 250 g. (9 oz., 3 cups) mushrooms previously sautéed in butter, whole if they are small, sliced if they are large.

Pour over the strained sauce from which all grease has been removed. Boil down, if necessary. Simmer all together for 15 minutes.

Sautéed veal à la portugaise. SAUTÉ DE VEAU À LA PORTUGAISE – Cook the veal lightly in oil with 1 tablespoon chopped onion and a crushed clove of garlic.

Dilute the pan juices with white wine. Stir in 2 dl. ($\frac{1}{3}$ pint, scant cup) concentrated and thickened veal gravy and 4 dl. ($\frac{3}{4}$ pint, scant 2 cups) *Tomato sauce* (see SAUCE). Season, add a *bouquet garni* and cook for $1\frac{1}{2}$ hours.

Drain the pieces, trim them, put into another sauté pan with 6 or 8 peeled, seeded, pressed tomatoes, cooked lightly in oil. Add a tablespoon chopped parsley, pour over the sauce, strained and boiled down, and simmer together for 15 minutes.

Sautéed veal à la printanière. SAUTÉ DE VEAU À LA PRINTANIÈRE – Prepare as for *Sautéed veal with mushrooms*. Garnish with 4 or 5 small new carrots, 2 small new turnips cut to look like olives, 12 small glazed onions and 100 g. (4 oz., $\frac{3}{4}$ cup) peas.

Small new potatoes may also be added to the garnish.

Sautéed veal with red wine I, or matelote of veal. SAUTÉ DE VEAU AU VIN ROUGE, MATELOTE DE VEAU – Cook 750 g. ($1\frac{1}{2}$ lb.) veal lightly in butter with a large onion cut into quarters. Pour in 6 dl. (1 pint, $2\frac{1}{2}$ cups) red wine and 2 dl. ($\frac{1}{3}$ pint, scant cup) white stock. Add a crushed clove of garlic and a *bouquet garni*. Cook for $1\frac{1}{2}$ hours.

Drain the pieces, trim and put into another sauté pan with 12 small glazed onions and 100 g. (4 oz., 1 cup) sliced mushrooms, sautéed in butter.

Pour in the cooking liquor boiled down by one-third, thickened with 2 tablespoons (3 tablespoons) *Kneaded butter* (see BUTTER, *Compound butters*) and strained. Simmer, covered, for 15 minutes.

Sautéed veal with red wine II. SAUTÉ DE VEAU AU VIN ROUGE – Brown the pieces of veal, and sprinkle them with 1 tablespoon flour. Cook until the flour colours lightly. Stir in red wine and white stock and finish off in the same way as for *Ragoûts à brun* (see RAGOÛT, *Method of cooking brown ragoûts*).

Shoulder of veal. ÉPAULE DE VEAU – This large cut is generally boned before being cooked.

The meat must be well beaten, seasoned with salt and pepper, rolled and tied. Thus prepared, it can be pot-roasted, roasted or braised. Braised shoulder is prepared in the same way as *Noix of veal* and is served with the same garnishes.

The shoulder can also be stuffed with forcemeat. Boned, it is used to make *ragoûts*, *fricassées*, *blanquettes* and *sautés*, and different kinds of forcemeat (see FORCEMEAT).

Shoulder of veal à la boulangère. ÉPAULE DE VEAU À LA BOULANGÈRE – Proceed with a boned and rolled shoulder of veal as for *Shoulder of mutton à la boulangère* (see MUTTON).

Shoulder of veal à la bourgeoise. ÉPAULE DE VEAU À LA BOURGEOISE – Rolled, stuffing optional. Braise the shoulder in the usual way (see CULINARY METHODS, *Braising white meat*). Serve with a *Bourgeoise garnish* (see GARNISHES).

Stuffed shoulder of veal. ÉPAULE DE VEAU FARCIE – Bone a medium-sized shoulder of veal and beat the inside surface well. Season with salt, pepper and a pinch of spice. Spread with a thick layer of fine forcemeat or sausage meat mixed with chopped herbs and well seasoned. Roll up the shoulder and tie it to keep a good shape. Braise in the usual way.

Drain and remove the strings. Glaze the shoulder and set on a serving dish. Pour over a little of the braising liquor boiled down and strained, and serve either as it is or accompanied by a garnish.

Shoulder of veal stuffed à l'anglaise. ÉPAULE DE VEAU FARCIE À L'ANGLAISE – Stuff the boned shoulder with a forcemeat made of one-third calf's or ox kidney, one-third udder or veal fat (both these ingredients finely chopped), one-third bread-crumbs soaked in milk and pressed, and 2 eggs. Season and mix well.

Roll and tie the shoulder. Braise or roast as preferred. Serve accompanied by boiled bacon and sprinkled with some of the concentrated braising liquor or, if the shoulder is roasted, with its own juices.

Tendrons (breast) of veal. TENDRONS DE VEAU – These pieces are cut from the extremities of the ribs, from the point at which the chops are generally cut, to the sternum.

To qualify for the name *tendron* these pieces must include the full width of the breast. Cut across, they are not *tendrons*. Cut in square pieces they are sautéed or used to make *ragoûts*.

Tendrons are braised with very little liquid and can be accompanied by one of the garnishes given either for the *Noix of veal* or *Fricandeau*, or for the rib or loin. They may also be cooked in butter, without moisture, in a covered pan.

Tendrons à la bourgeoise. TENDRONS DE VEAU À LA BOURGEOISE – Braise 4 *tendrons*. When half-cooked add 12 small glazed onions, 12 carrots cut to look like olives and glazed, and 50 g. (2 oz.) diced streaky bacon, blanched and fried. Finish cooking together. Glaze the meat, set on a serving dish with the garnish and sprinkle with the cooking juices.

Tendrons chasseur. TENDRONS DE VEAU CHASSEUR – Cover the *tendrons* with butter and bake. In the same casserole cook lightly 150 g. (5 oz., $1\frac{1}{4}$ cups) chopped mushrooms. Dilute the cooking juices with 1 dl. (6 tablespoons, scant $\frac{1}{2}$ cup) white wine, add 1 dl. (6 tablespoons, scant $\frac{1}{2}$ cup) *Demi-glace sauce* and $\frac{1}{2}$ dl. (3 tablespoons, scant $\frac{1}{4}$ cup) *Tomato sauce* (see SAUCE).

Boil for a few moments, pour over the *tendrons* and sprinkle with chopped parsley, chervil and tarragon.

Tendrons à la jardinière. TENDRONS DE VEAU À LA JARDINIÈRE – Braise the *tendrons* or pot-roast them, covered with butter. Set them on a serving dish with a *Jardinière garnish* (see GARNISHES). Sprinkle with cooking juices.

Tendrons with mushrooms. TENDRONS DE VEAU AUX CHAMPIGNONS – Prepare as for *Tendrons à la jardinière*. Garnish with 150 g. (5 oz., $1\frac{1}{4}$ cups) peeled mushrooms.

Tendrons with noodles or risotto. TENDRONS DE VEAU AUX NOUILLES, AU RISOTTO – Braised or pot-roasted *tendrons* accompanied by noodles or a risotto. Sprinkle with their cooking juices.

Tendrons à la provençale. TENDRONS DE VEAU À LA PROVENÇALE – Prepare in the same way as *Knuckle of veal à la provençale*.

Tendrons with risotto. TENDRONS DE VEAU AU RISOTTO – Braise the *tendrons* with as little liquid as possible. Set them on a dish and garnish with a *risotto* to which diced mushrooms and truffles has been added.

Tendrons with spinach or sorrel. TENDRONS DE VEAU AUX ÉPINARDS, À L'OSEILLE – Braise the *tendrons* and serve sprinkled with their cooking juices accompanied by spinach in butter or sorrel, braised separately.

VÉFOUR – See RESTAURANTS OF BYGONE DAYS.

VEGETABLE. LÉGUME – A vegetable is any kitchen-garden plant used for food. Vegetables are very important in our diet. The great variety of dishes available to us is due to the plants, vegetables, and condiments which provide a rich range of flavours. Vegetables have been fundamental to the art of cooking since that remote time in antiquity when one of our ancestors first hit upon the idea of cooking a piece of meat and a few roots in the same pot.

All the essentials of a balanced diet are present in vegetables: protein, fats, carbohydrates, mineral salts and vitamins. Though the amount of each of these elements varies in different vegetables, in no other type of food are they more readily assimilable.

A vast number of plants, edible in their wild state, have been greatly improved by cultivation and selective breeding. In some vegetables one part is edible, in others, another. Roots, bulbs or tubers are eaten such as potatoes, sweet potatoes, yams, root chervil, various kinds of Jerusalem artichoke, carrots, various kinds of turnips, black radishes, radishes, kohlrabi, celeriac, beetroot, black and white salsify, Chinese artichoke, onions, sorrel, etc. We eat the young shoots of asparagus, hops, bramble, etc., and the stems of leeks, edible thistle, celery, beet and rhubarb, etc. We eat the leaves of spinach, orach, tetragonia, purslane, sorrel, all kinds of cabbage, lettuce, chicory, endive, watercress, dandelion, corn-salad, etc. In the case of cauliflowers and artichokes, etc., we eat the 'flowers'.

Tomatoes, cucumbers, small and large marrows (squashes), melons, ladies' fingers (okra), sweet peppers and pumpkins are all fruits. We also eat ripe seeds, such as cereals and pulses, and other seeds before they are fully ripe, such as green peas, sugar-peas and beans, green corn, etc. If we add fungi and truffles to this list, it will be obvious that strict vegetarians need not want for a varied diet.

Green vegetables have a particularly important part to play in nutritional equilibrium for they contain alkaline substances which neutralise the acids produced by protein foods. Some contain minerals, such as calcium, iron, sulphur, sodium, magnesium, potassium and iodine, also some of the vitamins A, the B group, and C, which play an active part in balancing the nerve cells. Their nutritional value is not very high (an average of 20 calories per 100 g.) so it is wise to alternate them with starchy and dried vegetables.

Most vegetables lose some of their water in cooking (this is true even of boiled vegetables) and, in consequence, suffer a loss of weight. This loss is much more substantial in the case of green vegetables than roots or tubers. Cereals and pulses generally increase in weight in cooking. This is especially true of dried vegetables. Dried vegetables are often soaked in water before cooking. It is always advisable to cook them in the water in which they have been soaking.

Modern methods of preserving vegetables, especially freezing, keep their nutritive values although they may never replace garden-fresh vegetables. However, preserved vegetables provide great variety to the menu. (See PRESERVATION OF FOOD.)

Vegetable fumet. FUMET DE LÉGUMES – This *fumet* is made by boiling down to make a very strong stock of different vegetables, such as carrots, onions, leeks and celery.

Vegetable julienne à la bretonne. JULIENNE DE LÉGUMES À LA BRETONNE – Shred finely the white part of 2 leeks, 4 sticks of white celery and 1 small onion. Cook them slowly in 3 tablespoons (scant $\frac{1}{4}$ cup) butter. Season. When the vegetables are almost cooked, add 50 g. (2 oz., 1 cup) shredded raw mushrooms.

According to the main dish with which it is to be served,

blend either with meat or vegetable *Velouté sauce* (see SAUCE) and a few tablespoons cream, or serve plain.

Vegetable loaves. PAIN DE LÉGUMES – These loaves are usually made of braised vegetables, mixed with eggs beaten as for an omelette, poured into a buttered plain mould and cooked in a *bain-marie*.

By following the recipe given for *Endive loaf* (see ENDIVE), various other vegetable loaves can be made: artichoke, aubergine, carrot, cauliflower, spinach, lettuce, turnip, etc.

This type of loaf, made in large moulds, is served as a small *entrée*. It usually has a cream sauce, poured over.

Small vegetable loaves are used as a garnish for meat and broiled, braised or poached poultry. They can also be used for garnishing fish dishes or poached or soft-boiled eggs.

Vegetable pickles (achards) (commercial product) – A mixture of different vegetables and fruit spiced with vinegar and mustard. Achards can be bought ready-made but here is a recipe to prepare it in the home. Divide into quarters, or pieces: asparagus tips, very small maize (corn), new carrots, white and red radishes, celeriac, turnips and artichoke hearts. Add flowers of cauliflower, whole almonds still green and hardly formed, a few blanched almonds, small green walnuts, cumquats, very small apricots, green apples in quarters, green and red pimentos, mushrooms and gherkins.

Blanch all these ingredients for 1 minute in boiling salt water, drain, and marinate them for 24 hours in vinegar. Drain, mix together and put them in a jar. Cover with the following marinade: To make 4 litres ($3\frac{1}{2}$ quarts, $4\frac{1}{2}$ quarts) in all; boil 3 litres ($5\frac{1}{4}$ pints, $6\frac{1}{2}$ pints) strong vinegar, remove from heat and add 25 g. (1 oz., $\frac{1}{4}$ cup) coriander, 100 g. (4 oz., 1 cup) powdered ginger, 50 g. (2 oz., $\frac{1}{2}$ cup) peppercorns, 4 tablespoons ($\frac{1}{3}$ cup) mustard, 4 teaspoons paprika pepper, 4 teaspoons saffron and 2 tablespoons (3 tablespoons) salt.

Cover the marinade and let it stand for 10 minutes. Strain through a cloth and filter. Add 1 litre ($1\frac{3}{4}$ pints, generous quart) oil and mix well. Put the vegetables and fruit in jars and cover with the marinade. Seal firmly and expose to the sun for 8 to 10 days.

Vegetable stalks and stumps. MOELLES VÉGÉTALES – The French word *moelle* derives from *molle* (soft) and is applied in cookery to certain tender vegetable stalks and the tender parts of vegetable stumps.

VEGETABLE CALENDAR. CALENDRIER DES LÉGUMES –

January – White or common garlic, Provençal artichokes (early variety usually eaten raw, often in oil), forced asparagus (early, very scarce and very expensive), asparagus, beetroot, cardoons, medium-length carrots, celery and celeriac, chervil, bulbous chervil, mushrooms (cultivated), endive (chicory) and escarole, improved wild chicory (smaller rosettes) and wild chicory (*barbe-de-capucin*), Belgian endive. Round-headed white cabbages and curly Savoy cabbages, Brussels sprouts, cauliflowers from Brittany and the Midi, swedes and flat-rooted turnips, watercress, Japanese artichokes. Shallots. Haricot beans (early, imported), dried haricot beans. Chinese yams (roots similar in taste to the potato). Lettuces (early, forced), cos lettuces from the Midi (early), dried lentils. Corn salad. Flat-rooted turnips and tankard turnips. Yellow onions, sorrel. Parsnips, round and long, common parsley and large-rooted parsley (rare), white dandelions (improved cultivated variety), Parisian long leeks, very large leeks from Rouen and Carentan, Swiss chard, green peas from Algeria (early), yellow and red pumpkins. Radishes, round and medium-length (early, forced), black winter radishes, wild horseradish (roots). White salsify and black salsify (scorzonera), Spanish *scolyme* (a kind of rare salsify). Tomatoes (early, imported), truffles.

February – White or common garlic, Provençal artichokes (early variety, usually eaten raw, often in oil, forced asparagus (early, very scarce and very expensive). Red salad beetroot (sold cooked). Celery, celeriac, chervil, bulbous chervil, mushrooms (cultivated), endive (chicory) and escarole, improved wild chicory (smaller rosettes), wild chicory (*barbe-de-capucin*) Belgian chicory, round-headed white cabbages and curly Savoy cabbages, red cabbages, Brussels sprouts, cauliflowers (from Brittany and the Midi), swedes and kohlrabi, watercress, Japanese artichokes. Shallots, spinach. String beans (imported, early). Chinese yams (roots similar in taste to the potato). Lettuces (forced), cos lettuces from the Midi (early), bay laurel. Lambs-lettuce. Flat-rooted turnips and tankard turnips. Yellow onions, sorrel (expensive). Parsnips, long and round, common parsley, dandelions (improved cultivated white variety, forced), Swiss chard, green peas (imported), split peas, long leeks from Rouen and Carentan, old potatoes, new potatoes from Algeria (early), winter gourds (U.S. winter squash). Round and medium-length radishes (early), black winter radishes, wild horseradish (roots). White salsify, scorzonera or black salsify. Tomatoes (imported, early), Jerusalem artichokes.

March – White or common garlic, Midi artichokes (for eating raw, and cooking), asparagus (branched or *petits pois* variety, expensive), forced asparagus (less expensive than the preceding month). Red salad beetroot (sold cooked). Red carrots, globural type (early), celery, celeriac, chervil, mushrooms (cultivated), endive (chicory) and escarole, wild chicory (*mignonette* variety), wild chicory, improved wild chicory (rosettes), Belgian chicory, round-headed white cabbage and savoy cabbage (late), red cabbages, Brussels sprouts, cauliflowers, swedes, cucumbers, green and white varieties. Japanese artichokes. Shallots, spinach. String beans (imported, early). dried haricot beans. Cabbage and cos lettuces (forced). Lambs-lettuce, melons (imported and forced, very expensive). Flat-rooted and long-rooted turnips. Yellow onions, sorrel. Parsnip, round and long, common parsley, green dandelions (field variety), white dandelions (forced), long leeks from Rouen and Carentan, green peas (early), old potatoes, new potatoes from Algeria (early), yellow and red gourds, squashes and pumpkins. Radishes, round and medium-length (early), black radishes. White salsify and black salsify. Thyme, imported tomatoes (early), Jerusalem artichokes, truffles.

April – White or common garlic, artichokes from Provence and Algeria, asparagus (seasonal variety). Carrots, old and new, celery, chervil, mushrooms (cultivated), mushrooms and morels (expensive), wild chicory (*mignonnette*), improved wild chicory, Belgian chicory, (more and more scarce), late round-headed white cabbage, new headed cabbage, late savoy cabbage, Brussels sprouts (the last), cauliflowers (from all quarters), sprouting broccoli, spring onions and chives, cucumbers, green and white, seakale, watercress. Shallots, (the last), spinach, tarragon. Dried haricot beans. Cabbage lettuces and cos lettuces, bay laurel, dried lentils. Lambs-lettuce (the last), melons (early, expensive). Turnips, white medium-length (early). Onions, white and yellow, (new), sorrel (new). Parsnip (the last), common parsley and curled parsley, green dandelions (field variety), forced white dandelions (the last), leeks, long and stout from Rouen, green peas (early), peas, *mange-tout* (early), potatoes, early and late. Radishes, round and medium-length (early), horseradish (roots). Scorzonera or black salsify (the last). Thyme, imported tomatoes (early), Jerusalem artichokes.

May – Artichokes (from Provence, Algeria and Brittany), Argenteuil asparagus. Basil (the whole aromatic plant, condiment). Carrots, new, mushrooms (cultivated), mush-

rooms, morels and *cèpes*, chervil, endive (chicory) and wild chicory (mignonnette), York cabbage and bullock's heart, cauliflower and broccoli, spring onions and chives, cucumbers (green and white), gherkins from the Midi, seakale, watercress. Spinach, tarragon. String beans (from the Midi and Algeria). Summer cabbage, lettuce and cos lettuce, yellow and green, bay laurel. Melons (early). Turnips, white, round and medium-length (early). Sorrel. Samphire, common and curly parsley, leeks (the last), green peas (from the Midi and Algeria), new potatoes (there are no more old ones). Round and medium length radishes (early), horseradish (roots), rhubarb (stalks for stewing and preserves). Thyme, tomatoes (imported).

June – Garlic (new), garden orach (leaves eaten like spinach), artichokes from Provence and Brittany, artichokes from Laon (last two weeks), Argenteuil asparagus (early). Basil (the whole aromatic plant, condiment). Early carrots (new hardy), chervil, mushrooms (cultivated), cèpes and chanterelles, endive, York cabbages and bullock's heart, cauliflowers, spring onions and chives, cucumbers and gherkins, watercress, shallots (new), tarragon. Broad beans. String beans from the Midi and Algeria, dried haricot beans. Cabbage and cos lettuces (any amount), bay laurel. Melons (forced and from the Midi). Turnips (hardy). White onions (seasonal), sorrel. Parsnips (new), samphire, common and curly parsley, leeks (new), green peas, potatoes (new, hardy), green purslane. Rhubarb (stalks for stewing and preserves). Thyme, tomatoes (imported).

July – Garlic (new), garden orach (leaves eaten like spinach), green artichokes from Laon and the *camus* artichokes from Brittany, late asparagus (the last), aubergines. Basil (the whole aromatic plant, condiment). Carrots (premature, outdoor), mushrooms (cultivated), *cèpes* and *chanterelles*, chervil, cucumbers, gherkins, endive (chicory), white-heart York cabbage and bullock's heart, cauliflowers, watercress, garden cress, courgettes. Tarragon. Broad beans. String beans from Bagnolet called *petits gris* and others, butter beans and *mange-tout*, fresh shelling haricot beans. Summer cabbage and cos lettuce, bay laurel, lavender and rosemary. Cantaloup melons and others. Long-rooted and flat-rooted turnips. White onions, sorrel. Parsnip (new), common and curly parsley, peppers, imported or from the Midi, leeks (new summer variety), small green peas, large sweet rugose peas, split peas, potatoes (new, outdoor), green and golden purslane (for salads). Round and medium-length radishes. New Zealand spinach, thyme, tomatoes from the Midi.

August – Garlic, garden orach, green artichokes from Laon, large *camus* artichokes from Brittany, aubergines. Carrots (red, short and medium-length), chervil, mushrooms, Bordeaux *cèpes*, endive and escarole, curly savoy cabbage (early), round-headed cabbages (second season), cauliflowers, kohlrabi, spring onions and chives, cucumbers and gherkins, watercress, garden cress. Shallots, tarragon. String beans (of all varieties), fresh podding haricot beans. Cabbage and cos lettuces, bay laurel, Cantaloup melons and others. Long-rooted and flat-rooted turnips. Yellow onions, sorrel. Parsnips (long and round), peppers, summer leeks (short leeks), Clamart peas and others, large sweet rugose peas, peas (*mange-tout*), early potatoes, purslane, green and gold, for salad. Savory, thyme, tomatoes, spinach.

September – Pink garlic, Laon artichokes, aubergines. Carrots, (red, short and medium length), celery, chervil, mushrooms (cultivated), *cèpes* and *chanterelles*, skirret (a kind of salsify), endive and escarole, round-headed cabbages and curly savoy cabbages, cauliflowers, spring onions and chives, cucumbers and gherkins, gourds (winter squash – premature), watercress, garden cress. String beans, French beans (*mange-tout*), fresh podding haricot beans (white and coloured). Cabbage and cos lettuces, bay laurel, dried lentils. Chestnuts and *marrons* (Lyons variety) water melons (*pasteques*). Long-rooted and flat-rooted turnips. Yellow onions, sorrel. Parsnips, common and curly parsley, peppers, new leeks, Swiss chard, late green peas and large sweet rugose peas (*mange-tout*), potatoes (mature), purslane, green and gold, (salad variety). Radishes, long and medium-length. Spanish scolyme (a kind of salsify). Thyme, tomatoes (outdoor). New Zealand spinach.

October – Garlic, Laon artichokes, aubergines. Red carrots, (short, medium-length and long) celery, celeriaç, mushrooms (cultivated), cèpes and chanterelles, skirret, chervil, endive and escarole, wild chicory. Belgian chicory, round-headed and curly savoy cabbages (autumn variety), cauliflowers, spring onions and chives, various gourds, watercress. Shallots, spinach. String beans, French beans (*mange-tout*), fresh podding haricot beans (white and coloured). Various varieties of cabbage lettuce, cos lettuces, yellow and green. Corn salad, chestnuts and *marrons*, Lyon variety, cantaloup melons and others. Long-rooted and flat-rooted turnips. Yellow onions, sorrel. Parsnips, common and curly parsley, peppers, dandelions (from the fields), leeks, Swiss chard, green peas, large sweet rugose peas, potatoes of all varieties, gourds and pumpkins. Radishes, long and medium-length (monthly), black winter radishes, horseradish (roots), rampion (the small white roots are eaten along with the leaves). White salsify, black salsify or scorzonera, Spanish scolyme. Thyme, tomatoes.

November – Garlic, green artichokes from Laon (scarce). Red beetroot (already cooked). Cardoons, red carrots, medium-length and long. Celery, celeriac, chervil, mushrooms (cultivated), skirret, endive and escarole, Belgian chicory, round-headed white cabbages and curly Savoy cabbages (autumn variety), Brussels sprouts, cauliflowers (late), swedes and kohlrabi, watercress, Japanese artichokes. Spinach. String beans, French beans (*mange-tout*), fresh podding haricot beans. Cabbage and cos lettuces. Lambs-lettuce. Long-rooted and flat-rooted turnips. Yellow onions, sorrel. Parsnips, round and long, common and curly parsley, leeks, Swiss chard, dandelions (from the fields), all varieties of potato, gourds and pumpkins. Radishes, round and medium-length (monthly), black winter radishes, rampion. White salsify, black salsify. Thyme, tomatoes (imported), truffles.

December – Garlic, forced asparagus (very scarce and very expensive, early). Salad beet (already cooked). Red carrots, long and medium-length, celery, celeriac, chervil, bulbous chervil, endive (chicory) and escarole, wild chicory, Belgian chicory, round-headed cabbages, curly savoy cabbages, Brussels sprouts, cauliflowers (late), swedes, spring onions and chives, watercress, Japanese artichokes. Shallots, spinach, dried haricot beans, string beans (imported, scarce, early variety). Winter lettuces (scarce and expensive). Lambs-lettuce. Long-rooted and flat-rooted turnips. Yellow onions, sorrel (grown under glass). Parsnip, common and curly parsley, white dandelions (forced), Swiss chard, potatoes (all varieties), pumpkins. Radishes (forced), horseradish (roots), rampion. White salsify, black salsify. Thyme, tomatoes (imported), truffles.

VEGETABLE PEAR – See CHAYOTE.

VELOUTÉ – This name is used more than anything else for a white sauce made with white veal or chicken stock, used as a base for a number of other sauces, notably *allemande*.

The word is also used to describe certain thickened soups (see SOUPS AND BROTHS).

There are meat and fish *veloutés*. The first is obtained by adding white stock, veal or poultry to white *roux* (a blend of

butter and flour). The second is made with fish stock or fish *fumet*.

When egg yolks are added for thickening, the *velouté* becomes *allemande sauce*. This sauce is used very frequently.

Velouté is the basis for most white sauces. Recipes for these are to be found in alphabetical order under SAUCE.

VELVET SWIMMING CRAB. ENTRILLE – Common name for the small, delicate-fleshed crab (see CRAB).

VENISON. VENAISON – The meat of any kind of deer. In French, and formerly in English, it described the meat of any kind of game animal or wild beast killed for food, and *basse venaison* is the meat of hare or wild rabbit.

For other recipes for venison, see ROEBUCK.

Haunch of venison (English cookery). HANCHE DE VENAISON – Rub the quarter of venison with a mixture of flour and pepper, and hang it in a cool, well-aired place and leave for 3 or 4 days.

To cook. Trim and cover completely with *Flour-and-water paste* (see DOUGH). Wrap in strong paper, tie with string. Roast, basting often, allowing 3 to 4 hours for a haunch of venison.

Ten minutes before removing from the oven take off the flour-and-water paste, pour melted butter over the meat and sprinkle it with salt and flour. Brown in a very hot oven.

The custom in England is to serve the haunch of venison with boiled French beans and redcurrant jelly.

VENUS – Type of mollusc usually called the cockle, found in all seas.

All types of these are edible. They are eaten raw, like oysters, or cooked like mussels.

VERJUICE. VERJUS – Acid juice extracted from large unripened grapes, used like vinegar.

Some writers say that in former times the word *verjus* meant *sauce verte*, which was sold in the streets of Paris.

VERJUICE JELLY. CLAREQUETS DE VERJUS – Here is an ancient recipe for this jelly:

'Dilute 4 tablespoons ($\frac{1}{3}$ cup) apple purée with $3\frac{1}{2}$ litres (6 pints, $7\frac{1}{2}$ pints) water; sieve until $3\frac{1}{2}$ litres (6 pints, $7\frac{1}{2}$ pints) of the mixture is obtained; pound and sieve $3\frac{1}{2}$ litres (6 pints, $7\frac{1}{2}$ pints) of under-ripe verjuice grapes.

'Clarify 750 g. ($1\frac{3}{4}$ lb., $3\frac{1}{4}$ cups) sugar and cook to a hard crack (see SUGAR). Remove from the heat and add the verjuice and the apple mixture previously blended together with a wooden spoon.

'Reheat without boiling, then pour the jelly into *clarequet* (small) moulds and put in a warm place to set.'

VERMICELLI – A pasta whose descriptive name suggests its wormlike form. It is used for soups, puddings and soufflés.

VERMOUTH – Word deriving from the German *vermut* which means absinthe. A white wine flavoured with various bitter ingredients such as absinthe, anise, cinnamon, coriander, bitter orange peel, cloves, quassia, quinine, elderberries, etc.

VÉRON (Café) – See RESTAURANTS OF BYGONE DAYS.

VERT-PRÉ – Method of preparing certain grilled meats, garnished with straw potatoes and watercress and served with *Maître d'hôtel butter* (see BUTTER, *Compound butters*), containing plenty of chopped parsley.

Certain foodstuffs, such as poultry or fish, coated with *Green mayonnaise* (see SAUCE), are also called *vert-pré*.

VERVAIN, VERBENA. VERVEINE – Plant cultivated in gardens. The dried leaves of verbena, which are highly scented, are used to make infusions.

VÉRY – See RESTAURANTS OF BYGONE DAYS.

VESPÉTRO – Old liqueur, which formerly had a high reputation, now hardly ever made in France.

It was made in the district round Metz, and its fame, which was very great in the eighteenth century, came chiefly from the fact that Louis XV drank a great deal of it to restore his failing strength. It was flavoured with the seeds of angelica, coriander, anise and fennel.

VETCH. GESSE – Name used for several different pulses, some of them used as food. The cultivated vetch, originally from the Caucasus, then cultivated in Spain, was imported into France about the middle of the seventeenth century. Its seeds are eaten green, like peas.

Chick-vetch is used in the same way as chick-peas. The tuber-vetch has a starchy root which is roasted in hot ash, and tastes rather like chestnuts.

VICHY (Carrots à la) – Carrots are thought to be good for afflictions of the liver and are much used at Vichy, whose waters are particularly favourable for hepatic conditions. For the preparation of *Carrots à la Vichy* (see CARROTS).

VICTORIA – There are a great number of dishes dedicated to Queen Victoria. Some of the best known are: *sole (or other fish) Victoria, poularde Victoria, salade Victoria* and *bombe Victoria*.

VICTORIA CAKE – Made like plum cake using 1 kg. ($2\frac{1}{4}$ lb., $4\frac{1}{2}$ cups) butter, 750 g. ($1\frac{3}{4}$ lb., $3\frac{1}{2}$ cups) sugar, 250 g. (9 oz., generous 2 cups) ground almonds mixed with 2 eggs, 22 eggs (put in one by one), $1\frac{1}{2}$ kg. ($3\frac{1}{2}$ lb., 14 cups) flour mixed with 3 teaspoons baking powder, 500 g. (18 oz., $2\frac{1}{4}$ cups) crystallised cherries, 400 g. (14 oz., $1\frac{3}{4}$ cups) chopped peel, 1 dl. (6 tablespoons, scant $\frac{1}{2}$ cup) rum, the grated rind of 2 lemons, 2 teaspoons cinnamon and 2 teaspoons powdered cloves.

VIDELLE – Small implement used in confectionery to remove the stones from fruits. Also known by this name is a kind of wheel pastry-cutter.

VIENNESE PASTRY. KNUSPER – Make a short pastry from 350 g. (12 oz., 3 cups) sieved flour, 225 g. (8 oz., 1 cup) butter, 175 g. (6 oz., scant cup) sugar, 1 teaspoon cinnamon and, if necessary, a little milk. Let the dough stand for 15 minutes. Roll it out and spread in a buttered baking tin. Brush the surface with egg and sprinkle with chopped almonds and crystallised sugar. Bake at 190°C. (375°F., Gas Mark 5). When the cake is a good colour, take it out of the oven. While it is still hot cut it into rectangles. It can be eaten fresh or kept for several days in a tin.

VIERGE – Butter mixed with salt, pepper and lemon juice, beaten well in a bowl until it becomes frothy. This whipped butter is served with asparagus and other boiled vegetables.

VILLEDIEU – See CHEESE.

VIN DU MARCHÉ or POT DE VIN – Formerly this was the wine given as a present to someone who had acted as an intermediary in a business transaction. It was later replaced by a present of any kind or a sum of money.

VIN DES NOCES (Marriage wine) – This wine was a gift offered to the priest who performed a marriage ceremony. 'In certain dioceses,' says M. Chernel (*Dictionnaire historiques des institutions, moeurs et coutumes de France*) 'the priest, in blessing the nuptial bed, mixed together red and white wine to symbolize the union of the bride and bridegroom.

'In the diocese of Amiens, the priest began by blessing the

bread and wine. He then dipped three *roties* (rusks) in the wine, one for himself, one for the bridal pair and the third for the friends and relations present at the ceremony. After taking his own, he gave the bridal pair theirs and finished with that of the other guests. Then he blessed the bed.'

VINAGE, FORTIFICATION – Addition of alcohol to a must or a wine.

VINAIGRETTE – Mixture of oil and vinegar seasoned with salt and pepper and sometimes with the addition of chopped herbs. (See SAUCE, *Cold sauces.*)

VINAIGRIER – Small barrel, of wood or earthenware, in which vinegar is made.

VINCENT – Cold sauce prepared with various herbs, blanched, pounded and sieved, and hard boiled eggs. (See SAUCE, *Cold sauces.*)

Pruning the vine in the Médoc

VINE. VIGNE – Plant growing wild in Europe and Asia Minor, whose discovery is attributed to divine intervention. It is mentioned in Genesis and in the most ancient Egyptian and Greek documents. In antiquity the Greek vine growers of Scio were particularly renowned. Among the Romans the wines of Campania, Falernia, Massicus, etc. held first place.

It appears from recent archaeological discoveries that vines had been cultivated in Gaul long before the country's occupation by the Greeks and the Romans. But although the invaders were not responsible for introducing the vine to the country, they probably gave considerable impetus to its development. And while they may not have actually taught the Gauls how to make wine from fermented grape juice, they were almost certainly responsible for introducing more elaborate processes of vinification.

The legend of the vine (from the Talmud):

Noah planted the vine.

'And what are you doing there?' the devil asked him.

'I am planting a vine.'

'What is the use of that?'

'Its fruit, freshly picked or dried, is sweet and good: the pressed juice gladdens the heart of man.'

'Let us work together,' said the devil.

Spraying vines in the Gironde

'I should like that,' said Noah.

The vine planted, the devil went in search of a lamb, a lion, a monkey and a pig. He cut their throats and poured their blood on the ground.

'That is why when man eats the fruit of the vine he is as gentle as a lamb, when he drinks wine he believes himself a lion, if by chance he drinks too much he grimaces like a monkey and when he is often drunk he is nothing more than a vile pig.'

Vine leaves. FEUILLES DE VIGNE – See LEAF.

VINEGAR. VINAIGRE– Produce of the acetic fermentation of wine under the action of a fungus, the *Mycoderma aceti*, making its first appearance in the form of a light veil, which penetrates the liquid more and more, forming a thick, folded, sticky skin, which is called the *mère de vinaigre*. This micro-organism is developed between 15° and 30°C. (59° and 86°F.).

A good vinegar must be clear and transparent, colourless if it is made from white wine, pinkish if it comes from red wine, but always lighter coloured than the latter. It must have a frankly acid taste, and an aroma recalling that of the wine from which it comes.

Vinegar is made of any kind of alcoholic liquid (alcoholised water, beer, cider, perry, milk, etc.). Alcohol vinegar is colourless if it has not been tinted with caramel. Cider vinegar is yellowish, always less acid than wine vinegar; beer vinegar is yellow, slightly bitter and its flavour recalls that of bitter beer. Glucose vinegar has a taste of fermented flour; wood vinegar has an acid taste; vinegar made from *piquettes* or from marc has a characteristic smell.

It is an everyday condiment, serving to conserve some substances in marinades or pickles, and has no disadvantages, so long as acid condiments are not forbidden in the diet. For table use, vinegar is often flavoured with tarragon, onion, shallot, herbs, etc.

The use of vinegar as seasoning for foodstuffs has a high place in the story of human diet. Greek and Roman antiquity, *oxybaphon* and *acetabulum* (vinegar vessel) were the names for bowls that were placed, filled with vinegar, on the dining table, for guests to dip their bread in.

In the thirteenth century, among the street vendors who had the right to cry their wares in Paris, some rolled a barrel in the street, announcing to the *hôteliers* and housewives:

'Vinaigres bons et biaux! vinaigre de moutarde i aïl!' ('Good and beautiful vinegars! Mustard and garlic vinegar!').

'In 1657, an edict of Charles IX accorded the bourgeois of Paris the privilege of selling vinegar made from the wine of their vineyards, in small quantities and *à pot*, and it was chiefly this that the young boys sold as they wheeled their barrows from one district to another, crying at every door, '*marchand de vinaigre! du bon vinaigre!*'

Aromatic vinegar. VINAIGRE AROMATIQUE – A mixture of 125 g. (4 oz.) spirit of aromatic herbs with 9 dl. ($1\frac{1}{2}$ pints, 2 pints) vinegar.

Raspberry vinegar. VINAIGRE FRAMBOISE – Pour into a stoneware jar 2 litres ($3\frac{1}{2}$ pints, $4\frac{1}{2}$ pints) vinegar and as many raspberries as it will hold. Leave for 8 days. Strain without pressure through a horsehair strainer.

Rose vinegar. VINAIGRE ROSAT – Add 100 g. (4 oz.) red rose petals to 1 litre ($1\frac{3}{4}$ pints, generous quart) of vinegar and leave to macerate for 10 days.

VIOLET. VIOLETTE – The sweet violet is one of the species of *fleurs pectorales*. Their petals are candied in sugar.

Candied violets are used in pastry-making, confectionery, the making of ices and iced mousses, and in the preparation of salads.

VIRGOULEUSE – Winter pear, so called because it comes from the commune of Virgoulée, near Limoges.

VISNISKI (Russian cookery) – Rissole made with *coulibiac* paste (see COULIBIAC) filled with fish forcemeat seasoned with fennel, and fried.

Fish visniski. VISNISKI AU POISSON – Make some *coulibiac* dough. Roll out and cut with a pastry-cutter into pieces about 5 cm. (2 inches) in diameter.

Garnish with chopped cooked fish to which chopped fennel has been added. Season and blend with a thick meatless *Velouté* (see SAUCE). The portions of the garnish should be the size of a walnut. Cover with a round of *coulibiac* dough of the same size as the first one.

Put the *visniski* on a baking-tray. Let them rise in a warm place for 25 minutes. Fry in very hot oil. Drain and serve.

VITAMINS. VITAMINES – Substances indispensable to nutrition, whose absence can cause serious disorders.

Vitamin A. Derived mainly from carotene, a yellow pigment that is found extensively in some vegetables, particularly green ones and carrots. The vitamin also exists in some animal foods. Its absence gives rise to eye troubles and, in young people, a stoppage of growth.

Vitamin B. This was first discovered in the husks of rice. It is nowadays seen as a compound, composed mainly of three factors:

Vitamin B_1. Nitrogen base, related to the alkaloids destroyed by high temperatures and alkalis. It is an antineurotic factor and plays its part in the equilibrium of the nervous system.

Vitamin B_2. Riboflavin, a yellow substance found in milk, eggs and in liver. It resists all but very high degrees of heat and alkalis. It has an effect on growth, and its absence causes skin troubles similar to pellagra.

Vitamin B_3. Resists heat, but is destroyed by alkalis; it is a factor in the utilisation of foodstuffs by the body.

These three elements are usually found together, but in proportions which vary from one foodstuff to another.

Absence of vitamin B from the diet gives rise to neurotic complaints and to beri-beri. There is a tendency to attribute certain digestive complaints, like constipation, diarrhoea, vomiting, loss of appetite, etc., to a slight deficiency of vitamin B.

Vitamin C. This is also known as ascorbic acid. It is found mainly in citrus fruits, blackcurrants and green vegetables. Necessary for the growth of children, and healthy skin and firm, strong muscles.

Vitamin D. Necessary for the absorption and laying down of calcium and phosphorus in bones which helps to keep them strong. It is found in dairy products and oily fish.

Vitamin E. Essential for normal metabolism and found in vegetable oils, wheat germ and eggs.

Vitamins in dietetics – The role that vitamins play in the phenomena of nutrition is still not completely clear but there is no doubt that these chemical substances so extraordinarily active in infinitesimal amounts are essential for the proper functioning of the human organism. A tolerably accurate assessment of individual vitamin requirements has been reached as a result of a multiple series of experiments on animals and humans. Such experiments took into account the geographical location, temperament, age of the individual and the muscular effort required of him.

Vitamins are divided into two categories: those soluble in fats (liposoluble vitamins), namely Vitamins A, D, E and K; and those soluble in water (hydro-soluble vitamins) – the Vitamin B groups and Vitamin C. The whole art of the dietician lies in calculating an individual's daily needs in terms of the properties of each of these vitamins. It is essential to remember that in this domain every case is different.

Lack of vitamins upsets the equilibrium of our organs, tissues and endocrine glands and consequently the whole physiological process of growth, mental and physical development, youth, vigour, resistance to disease and longevity.

Vitamins are rather unstable organic compounds which, nevertheless, are only partially destroyed by cooking. On the other hand, they are particularly sensitive to prolonged exposure to air and light; it is therefore desirable to consume vegetables and fruit as fresh as possible. A well-balanced diet including a moderate amount of raw fruit and vegetables assures a sufficiency of varied vitamins for a healthy individual. It is not necessary to eat an excessive amount of raw vegetables to obtain the proper amount of vitamins. Nor is it enough just to swallow the vitamins: the important thing is to assimilate them. Too many vitamins can sometimes be as harmful as too few, and it is advisable to be wary of pharmaceutical 'synthetic' vitamins unless prescribed by a doctor. Their action cannot be compared to that of natural vitamins, for the simple reason that the molecules of the latter are linked to those of the plant.

Foods classified (in descending order) according to their richness in specific vitamins. (M[me.] Lucie Randoin).

Vitamin A. Butter, cod liver oil, liver, egg yolk, beef fat, tomatoes, cream, milk powder, cream cheese, spinach, carrots, cabbage, lemon, orange, fish oil, herring, brains, heart, kidney, fatty meat, mushrooms, cauliflower, lettuce, cereal grain, wheat bran, wholemeal bread, fresh peas, beetroot, artichokes, lentils, almonds, walnuts, bananas, pumpkin, haricot beans.

Vitamin B. Brewer's yeast, cereal germ, lentils, egg yolk, brain, liver, cabbage, carrots, spinach, cauliflower, onions, kidneys, fresh and dried peas, apples, pears, beetroot, artichokes, potatoes, wholemeal bread, haricot beans, dried milk, milk, whey, malt extract, lemons, oranges, tomatoes, almonds, walnuts, chestnuts, mushrooms, pumpkin, plums, grapes, bananas, lettuce, lean meat.

Vitamin C. Lemons, oranges, blackcurrants, cabbage, tomatoes, oysters, onions, lettuces, dandelions, rutabaga (swede turnip), fresh peas, spinach, cauliflower, grapes, bananas, beetroot, carrots, french beans, rhubarb, turnip, apples, plums, meat juices, milk, whey.

Vitamin D. Cod liver oil, fish oils, animal fats, milk, cream.

Vitamin E. Wheatgerm oil.

VOISIN – See RESTAURANTS OF BYGONE DAYS.

VITELOTTE. KIDNEY POTATO – Type of potato which remains firm when cooked.

VIVEURS – Name given to various preparations characterised by strong seasoning with cayenne or paprika, such as *potage* or *consommé des viveurs*.

VOL-AU-VENT – 'This *entrée*,' said Carême, 'is pretty and good without a doubt. It is eaten with pleasure for its extreme delicacy and lightness, but to cook it perfectly demands the utmost care. This is the essential part of the operation, so that the flakiness of the pastry is not lost in dampness.'

To make the pastry. Take a half quantity of *Flaky pastry* (see DOUGH) and divide it into 2 pieces. Roll out each piece to a thickness of about 5 mm. ($\frac{1}{4}$ inch).

Cut the first piece in a circle 15 cm. (6 inches) in diameter and place it on a baking sheet which has been brushed with water. Cut the second piece into a circle of the same thickness and remove a round from the middle so as to leave an interior diameter of 11 cm. ($4\frac{1}{2}$ inches) and an exterior diameter of 16 cm. ($6\frac{1}{2}$ inches). Brush the first piece with water and place the pastry circle on top. Press lightly to fix and leave for 10 minutes.

Brush the top with beaten egg. Lightly cut a circle on the central part, which, after cooking, will form a 'lid'. Pink the edges at regular intervals. Cook in a hot oven for 20 to 25 minutes, according to the size of the *vol-au-vent*. After cooking detach the 'lid'.

Fill the *vol-au-vent* case with various kinds of mixtures bound with brown and white sauce. Among the most usual for this purpose are: *Financière*, *Marinière*, purée of chicken or purée of shellfish, *Toulouse*, various *salpicons*, etc. (see GARNISHES, SALPICON).

VOLAILLE – See CHICKEN.

VOLIÈRE (EN) – Style of serving game birds, much used formerly but now abandoned. This rather ostentatious presentation was done by placing on the cooked bird, each in its proper position, the head, the tail, and outspread wings. All these were fixed with little wooden pegs.

Peacocks were served in this way in the Middle Ages adorned with their plumage, and holding between their beaks, which were gilded, a little piece of burning tow.

Service *en volière*, applied chiefly to pheasants and woodcock, was in vogue up to the end of the nineteenth century. Quite often, during the same period, game was served under the title of *chasse royale*, the birds adorned with their plumage being set on a great silver dish, the largest on croûtons of fried bread and the smallest arranged in a border round the sides.

Today, roasts of game or any other meat are put on the serving dish or on a croûton of fried bread spread with forcemeat and garnished with watercress.

VOLNAY – A highly esteemed Burgundy wine which comes from Volnay in the Côte d'Or. (See BURGUNDY.)

VOSNE – Red wine from the Côte d'Or. (See BURGUNDY.)

VOUGEOT – One of the greatest Burgundies, from Vougeot, a community of the Côte d'Or, not far from Beaune.

VOUVRAY – Reputed white wine from the district of Vouvray, near Tours. This wine, which is highly flavoured and a little musky, is mildly sparkling, but is often treated like champagne to make it more so.

VOYAGE (German cookery) – Sweet pastry which keeps for a long time, an apricot biscuit with an individual flavour due to the substitution of breadcrumbs for flour.

Ingredients. 225 g. (8 oz., 1 cup) fine sugar, 7 eggs, 250 g. (9 oz., $2\frac{1}{4}$ cups) breadcrumbs, 2 teaspoons vanilla sugar, 175 g. (6 oz., $\frac{1}{2}$ cup) apricot jam.

Method. Cream the sugar and egg yolks together in a basin.

Beat the egg whites stiffly and fold them into the sugar and yolk mixture, which will become very light, frothy and whitish. Mix in the breadcrumbs and sugar. Fill a forcing-bag fitted with a plain nozzle about 1 cm. ($\frac{1}{2}$ inch) wide with the mixture. Pipe circles on to buttered, floured baking sheets. Bake them in a low oven and cool on a cake rack.

When the biscuits are quite cold, spread the first with apricot jam flavoured with kirsch. Cover with a second biscuit and spread this, too, with jam. Superimpose 5 or 6 biscuits in this way and sprinkle the top one with icing sugar mixed with powdered cinnamon.

Wrap at once in aluminium foil. Keep in a cool place.

WADERS. CHEVALIERS – Birds of passage (sandpipers, redlegs, gambets, etc.) some of which have delicate meat. They are prepared like woodcock (q.v.) or snipe (q.v.).

WAFFLE. GAUFRE – The French waffle is a very light type of sweet pastry cooked between the two buttered and heated plates of a waffle iron. The plates, decorated with embossed patterns, are fixed to the ends of two long iron stems hinged together.

Waffles are mentioned in the poems of the end of the twelfth century when they were made and sold in the streets. On great religious feast days the waffle-sellers would set up their stalls at the doors of the churches and bake their waffles, which were eaten piping hot. The best quality waffles were called *métiers*.

Filled waffles I. GAUFRES FOURRÉES – *Ingredients.* 500 g. (18 oz., $4\frac{1}{2}$ cups) sieved flour, 250 g. (9 oz., generous cup) butter, 50 g. (2 oz., $\frac{1}{4}$ cup) sugar, 3 eggs, $1\frac{1}{2}$ teaspoons bicarbonate of soda, $\frac{1}{2}$ vanilla pod or $\frac{1}{2}$ teaspoon vanilla essence.

Method. Make a circle of flour on the table, add butter, sugar, eggs, bicarbonate and vanilla. Mix everything together without working the dough too hard.

Let this dough stand for 2 hours. Roll it out to a thickness of 1 cm. ($\frac{1}{2}$ inch) and cut it into round or oval shapes with a

Waffles (*Nicolas*)

fluted pastry-cutter. Heat the waffle iron on both sides. Butter the iron and put a piece of dough between the plates. Close the iron and cook on high heat. Turn the iron once during the cooking.

Take out the waffles, and slice them across while they are still hot. Put them under a weight and allow to cool, and spread them with the cream for which a recipe is given below. Sandwich the two halves together and keep them in a tin in a dry place until they are required. They will keep for 2 or 3 days. Put in the filling as required.

Cream filling for the waffles. 250 g. (9 oz., generous cup) butter, 250 g. (9 oz., generous cup) icing sugar and 200 g. (7 oz., 1 cup) *praline* (q.v.).

Warm a basin and place the butter, sugar and *praline* in it. Work with a whisk. When the mixture is blended to a smooth paste, use it as a filling for the waffles.

Filled waffles II. GAUFRES FOURRÉES – *Ingredients.* 500 g. (18 oz., $4\frac{1}{2}$ cups) flour, 125 g. (4 oz., $\frac{1}{2}$ cup) butter, 25 g. (1 oz., 2 tablespoons) fine sugar, 15 g. ($\frac{1}{2}$ oz., $\frac{1}{2}$ cake) dry or compressed yeast, $1\frac{1}{2}$ teaspoons salt, 4 eggs, about 2 dl. ($\frac{1}{3}$ pint, scant cup) milk.

Method. Mix together as for all other batters.

This waffle dough should be made the night before and left to rise in an earthenware dish covered with a cloth, in a cool place. Next morning shape the dough into little balls the size of half an egg and put on a floured baking sheet. Allow to rise to double their size and proceed with the cooking as in the previous recipe.

Open the irons as soon as the waffles are cooked. Put them under a weight and fill them with cream.

Liége waffles. GAUFRES LIÉGEOISES – Place 500 g. (18 oz., $4\frac{1}{2}$ cups) flour on a board. Add dry or compressed yeast, about 1 teaspoon, in the centre. Mix the yeast with a little warm water, and mix in with the flour. Leave to rise.

Add a pinch of salt, 125 g. (4 oz., $\frac{1}{2}$ cup) sugar, 200 g. (7 oz., scant cup) butter, a pinch of ground cinnamon and 4 eggs. Mix well. Work the dough with the palm of the hand. Divide it into pieces the size of an egg. Roll into the shape of sausages. Put them on a floured slab and let them stand for half an hour.

Heat a waffle iron and butter it. Put a piece of dough between the plates. Cook on both sides over moderate heat.

Northern waffles or Dutch wafers. GAUFRES DU NORD, GAUFRETTES HOLLANDAISES – *Ingredients.* 250 g. (9 oz., generous cup) flour, 125 g. (4 oz., $\frac{1}{2}$ cup) sugar, 175 g. (6 oz., $\frac{3}{4}$ cup) butter, 1 egg white, a small pinch of salt, vanilla essence, ground cinnamon or grated orange or lemon peel, according to taste.

Method. Arrange the flour in a circle. Place the sugar, salt and flavouring in the centre. Dissolve the sugar in the egg white, add the butter and mix all the ingredients. Shape the dough into a ball. Cook the waffles in the usual way.

Plain waffles (old recipe). GAUFRES ORDINAIRES – *Ingredients.* 450 g. (1 lb., 4 cups) flour, 1 dl. (6 tablespoons, 1 cup) fresh cream, 450 g. (1 lb., 2 cups) sugar and 4 drops of orange flower water.

Method. Beat the flour with half the cream. When it is quite smooth, add the sugar, the rest of the cream and orange flower water, so that the mixture is as thin as milk. Heat and grease the waffle-iron with melted butter. Place one and a half spoonfuls of the mixture between the plates to make each waffle. A little pressure is exerted to make the waffles thinner.

To discover whether the waffle is ready, open up the iron a little. If the waffle is a good colour, remove it by sliding a knife under and prising it free. Put the waffles, one by one, in a warm oven to keep them crisp.

Plain waffles (modern recipe). GAUFRES ORDINAIRES – *Ingredients.* 250 g. (9 oz., generous cup) butter, 250 g. (9 oz., generous cup) lump sugar, 16 egg yolks, 200 g. (7 oz., scant cup) *praline* (q.v.), 1 dl. (6 tablespoons, scant $\frac{1}{2}$ cup) water.

Method. Put the sugar and water in a basin. Cook to ball degree, i.e. until a drop of the mixture forms a ball when plunged into cold water (see SUGAR). While the sugar is cooking, skim it until the surface is clear, strain through a fine strainer.

Put the egg yolks in a basin and pour the sugar on to them in a thin trickle. Mix with a beater, working the mixture until it is quite cold. Next add the butter, softened to the consistency of a paste. Add the *praline*, still whisking.

Drop a spoonful of mixture on the heated and buttered waffle iron. Cook on both sides.

Vanilla waffles. GAUFRES À LA VANILLE– *Ingredients.* 500 g. (18 oz., $4\frac{1}{2}$ cups) sieved flour, 250 g. (9 oz., generous cup) butter, 4 eggs, 4 tablespoons ($\frac{1}{3}$ cup) sugar, vanilla pod or $\frac{1}{2}$ teaspoon vanilla essence, $1\frac{1}{2}$ teaspoons bicarbonate of soda.

For the butter cream. 250 g. (9 oz., generous cup) butter, 250 g. (9 oz., 2 cups) icing sugar, 5 egg yolks, 1 pod of vanilla or $\frac{1}{2}$ teaspoon vanilla essence.

Mardi Gras waffles (seventeenth century)

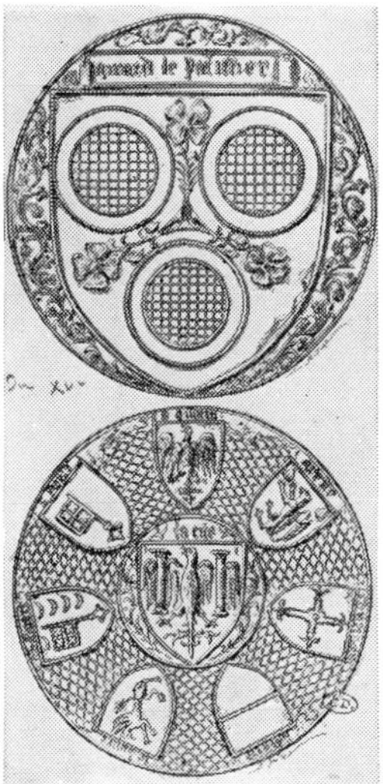

Fifteenth century waffle irons

Walnuts (*Nicolas*)

Method. Arrange the flour in a circle and place the sugar, butter, eggs, the inside of the vanilla pod (or the essence) and the bicarbonate of soda in the middle.

Mix quickly to avoid lumps. Roll the dough into a ball and let it stand for 2 hours.

Roll out the dough to a thickness of 5 mm. ($\frac{1}{4}$ inch) and cut into oval shapes with a fluted pastry cutter. Place on a floured slab. Heat and butter the waffle iron lightly. Place the pastry in the middle, close, and cook.

Turn over the iron to ensure that the waffle is cooked on both sides. As soon as the waffle is ready, remove it, slice it across, and put it under a weight to keep it in shape.

Butter cream. Put the butter in a bowl. Work it to the consistency of a paste, add the icing sugar, and the egg yolks. Mix thoroughly. Spread the halves of the waffle on the inside with this cream.

WAFFLE IRON. GAUFRIER – Special mould used in the preparation of waffles, made of two cast-iron plates which fit together and are embossed with matching designs.

WAGTAIL. HOCHEQUEUE – European bird, cooked in the same way as the lark.

WALEWSKA (À LA) – Method of preparing fish, particularly fillets of sole. Fish cooked in this way is poached in fish *fumet* (q.v.) set on a fireproof dish, garnished with slices of spiny lobster and truffles, and coated with *Mornay sauce* (see SAUCE) with *Spiny lobster butter* (see BUTTER, *Compound butters*).

WALNUT. NOIX – Fruit of the walnut tree, which grows in Europe. Walnuts and walnut oil have been known from the earliest times. The Greeks knew it four centuries before Christ and towards the end of the fourth century, the Romans extended its cultivation all over Europe.

Before they are quite ripe walnuts are known as green walnuts. The fleshy casing of the walnut is called the shuck. An excellent liqueur (*brou*) is made from walnut shucks.

When it is fresh, the walnut is very pleasant to eat and easily digestible. The dried walnut, used a great deal in cookery and confectionery, is more difficult to digest, because of its high fat content.

The best-known varieties of French walnuts are *Franquette*, *Mayette* and *Parisienne*, cultivated in Isère and Savoy; *Corne* and *Marbot* cultivated in Périgord. The 'Grenoble' walnut can apply to any of the first three varieties.

Vegetarians mix walnuts with crushed cereals to make 'vegetarian steaks' as a substitute for meat.

In winter, dried walnuts can be given the appearance of fresh by soaking them (unshelled) in hot milk overnight, then drying and draining them. This steeping produces a vapour inside the shell, which moistens the endocarp.

Pickled walnuts. NOIX AU VINAIGRE – Choose fairly large green walnuts with husks that can be easily pierced with a pin. Wipe and prick them quite deeply all over. Marinate them for 3 days in brine – 125 g. (4 oz., 1 cup) salt per litre ($1\frac{3}{4}$ pints, generous quart) water – then bring them up to the boil. Repeat this operation three times, resting the nuts for 3 days between each boiling.

Drain the walnuts and place them in jars. Cover generously with boiling spiced vinegar prepared thus: simmer 5 litres ($4\frac{1}{2}$ quarts, $5\frac{1}{2}$ quarts) vinegar seasoned with 50 g. (2 oz., $\frac{1}{2}$ cup) black peppercorns, 25 g. (1 oz., $\frac{1}{4}$ cup) allspice, 25 g. (1 oz., $\frac{1}{4}$ cup) cloves,, 25 g. (1 oz., $\frac{1}{4}$ cup) mace, 40 g. ($1\frac{1}{2}$ oz., $\frac{3}{4}$ cup) crushed root ginger. Pour this mixture, unstrained, over the walnuts.

Seal the jars. Store in a cool place.

Walnut cordial. BROU DE NOIX. See LIQUEUR, *Walnut liqueur or ratafia.*

Walnut ketchup (English condiment) – Put in a tub, with about $1\frac{1}{4}$ kg. ($2\frac{3}{4}$ lb. $3\frac{1}{2}$ cups) rock salt, about 2 kg. ($4\frac{1}{2}$ lb., $8\frac{1}{2}$ cups) green walnuts. Mix well and leave for 6 days, crushing the shells from time to time with a pestle. Leave the tub tilted to one side after each operation so that the juice which runs from the fruit can be poured off every day, until only the pulp remains. Boil this juice and skim it. Add 100 g. (4 oz., 1 cup) ginger, 100 g. (4 oz., 1 cup) powdered spice, 50 g. (2 oz., $\frac{1}{2}$ cup) cayenne pepper and an equal quantity of cloves. Simmer for half an hour. Put into small bottles, seal hermetically and keep in a very dry place. Leave for several months before using.

Walnut oil. HUILE DE NOIX – Walnut oil has a pronounced nutty flavour. It goes well with certain salads. (See OIL.)

WARBLER. FAUVETTE – This bird is protected but its flavour is considered to be as delicate as that of garden warblers. It is prepared as for lark (q.v.).

WARTHOG. PHACOCHÈRE – Type of wild boar indigenous to Africa. Prepare as for wild boar (q.v.).

WASTE MATTER. DÉCHETS – Inedible parts of foods (bone, skin, tendons of meat; husks, pods, skin of fruit or vegetables).

A water carrier (*lithograph by Joseph Felon, nineteenth century*)

WATER. EAU – Water accounts for 65 per cent of an adult's weight, 70 per cent of a child's weight. This proportion indicates how important a part it plays in the organism. An adult absorbs an average of 34 g. water daily per k. (2·2 lb.) of his weight, that is 2,200 to 2,700 daily; a child drinks (comparatively) much more. 'Solid' foods, after allowing for the proportion of these eliminated as waste matter, provide about 1 litre ($1\frac{3}{4}$ pints, generous quart), beverages have therefore to make up the difference.

Drinking water. EAU POTABLE – Water suitable for drinking must be clear, colourless, aerated, odourless even when boiled, pleasant-tasting, neutral in reaction, and fresh. From the point of view of chemical analysis, it must dissolve soap, reveal no traces of lead (sometimes present when water flows through lead pipes), leave no more than 0·50 dry residue per litre after evaporation, contain less than 66 mg. chloride per litre, less than 50 mg. sulphates, less than 3 mg. organic matter, less than 1 mg. ammonia, less than 10 mg. nitrates, contain no trace of albuminoids or nitrites, and contain at least 8–12 mg. dissolved oxygen per litre. All this explains the remark of Dr. Besançon: 'Pure water is a myth.'

After the above, water must be examined under a microscope in order to detect algae, infusoria, and (later) helminth eggs (intestinal worms), and it should be examined bacteriologically to discover the number and nature of microbes present. This final examination is extremely important, especially where the town water supply is concerned, and should be carried out at regular intervals.

Insufficiently aerated water is heavy; water rich in calcareous salts is hard; consequently it does not dissolve soap and is bad for cooking vegetables. If water contains salts of any kind it has an alkaline, earthy, bitter or briny taste, depending upon the nature of the salt.

One must stress the importance of using bacteria-free drinking water, for many contagious diseases are transmitted through water. Chemical purity is no less important; to give an example, medical statistics show that the number of cases of stones in the bladder have considerably diminished in Glasgow by supplying a purer type of drinking water than that in previous use. Water deficient in minerals is another cause of health disorders; for example, the high incidence of goitre in certain regions is attributed to the absence of iodine in the mountain springs. Natural spring or river water is a living food and not simply the liquid vehicle of inert minerals. It is possible to live for twenty, thirty or forty days without eating if ample water is available.

Water is the only natural beverage, and only man can claim to appease his thirst with any other liquid. Dieticians lay down no hard and fast rules, but recommend that only a moderate amount should be drunk with meals, so as not to over-dilute the digestive juices, and to avoid dilating the stomach. But there is no harm in drinking one or two glasses of water between meals. Constant thirst indicates the organism's need to dilute substances ingested to excess, particularly salt, spices, sugar. More frequently, it is an indication of the body's need to rid itself of toxins present in the organs and body fluids.

Distilled water is heavy and flat, but is acceptable as drinking water provided it is aerated by beating. It is used on ships.

Rainwater has been soiled by all the impurities of the roof, when it is collected there, and must not be consumed unless the first flow, which washes the gutters and roofs, is diverted before collecting the remainder in the cisterns.

Spring water is considered to be the best but much depends on the soil. Water of granitic soil is seriously lacking in mineral salts. The water of Siluria, Devonia, Triassic and Jurassic soils is the best, provided it has not been subjected to contamination through fissures in the ground, frequently found in deforested areas.

River water varies in purity according to the part of the river from which it is drawn. It is always polluted after passing through built-up areas. Aeration and insolation have a purifying effect and the water becomes naturally pure again 50 to 80 kilometres downstream.

Canal water has the same disadvantages as river water, but purifies itself less easily because of its lack of current.

Mountain water is the product of melting snows and glaciers. It is heavy because of lack of aeration, but pure at its source, and rapidly enriches itself with minerals.

Ditch and drainage canal water is usually impure.

The *water of the great lakes* is invariably pure if drawn far from the shore or from a certain depth. The organic matter and minerals of the streams and rivers that feed the lakes form a deposit before reaching their destination.

The *waters of marshes and ponds*, are almost always impure, as the absence of current gives rise rapidly to microbic pollution.

Well water varies considerably according to the installation, depth and positioning of the well. It is often polluted by infiltrations from the surrounding area.

The composition of the water of *artesian wells*, which are artificial springs, depends upon the sheet of water used.

There are various methods of purifying suspect water and making it drinkable. For town supplies filter beds are used, as well as other physical or chemical purification processes too involved to describe here. From a bacteriological point of view such water is qualified as drinkable but it is more or less devitalized, sometimes unpleasant to the taste, and often contains an excess of calcareous salts, often responsible for visceral disorders and rheumatism. This calcareous excess can be corrected by means of equipment called 'water softeners' which convert the water to something akin to distilled water, though not of a high standard. Some of the processes for purifying suspect water, based on the oxidising process of potassium permanganate or iodine have already been mentioned. Here are a few formulae (for 1 litre water):

Dissolve 1 packet of:

Powdered potassium permanganate	3 cg.
Common alum	5 cg.

Decolourise after 10 minutes with a second packet of:

Powdered hyposulphate of soda	3 cg.
Carbonate of lime	5 cg.

or pour in 5 drops of the solution:

Iodine	5 g.
Sodium iodide	2 g.
Alcohol at 60°	100 cl.

and then decolourise, using the same quantity of a 10 per cent hyposulphate of soda solution.

Simpler still, 30 minutes before using the water, pour 5 to 6 drops of tincture of iodine into a carafe. The addition of a little red wine or any liquid containing tannin will be enough to neutralize the iodine and to mask its taste.

Suspect water may also be sterilised by the addition of a few drops of bleach (sodium hypochlorite) per litre. Passing the water through a filter of activated charcoal removes the taste and smell of the bleach. The water can be used after lengthy boiling in the form of tea or other infusions.

Temperature of water –

Water is very cold below	8°C.	(46·5°F.)
Cold from	8 to 12°C.	(46·5 to 53·5°F.)
Cool up to	16°C.	(61°F.)
Tepid from	16 to 35°C.	(61° to 97°F.)
Hot from	35 to 40°C.	(97° to 110°F.)

Piping hot above this temperature.

Sea water. EAU DE MER – Contains 33 to 38 g. mineral substances per litre (depending on the latitude), four-fifths of which consist of sodium chloride. It is not drinkable but contains plankton which, under certain conditions, can serve as human food. Experiments are in progress to extract new nutritional elements (algae, etc.) from the sea. Frozen sea water is used to conserve fish at the fishing grounds.

Sea water is also used to cook certain shellfish: shrimps, for example.

Natural mineral waters. EAUX MINERALES NATURELLES – See MINERAL WATERS.

Table waters. EAUX DE TABLE – Among the best known are Volvic water (natural, not aerated) and Evian water which is also the freshest and is, with mineralisation at 0·40 per litre, one of the best. It can be alternated with the light Contrexéville or Vittel Grande Source, less frequently with an alkaline water like Badoit or Vichy Célestins, which should be drunk in moderation. Alternating table waters like this ensures that the organism absorbs a little of each of the hydrous salts, and guards against any deficiency. It is said that such waters are especially active at the mineral water spring from which they come, but that some of their quality is lost once they are bottled. It is, however, almost exclusively bottled mineral water that dieticians use. A number still contain valuable properties long after bottling, but have to be drunk in larger quantities than mineral waters taken at the spring itself. The expression *thermal waters* refers exclusively to hot mineral springs, although it is sometimes used to describe all mineral waters, hot and cold.

Albuminous water. EAU ALBUMINEUSE – Whisk together 4 whites of egg and 1 litre of ordinary water; add 10 g. orange flower water. This water is used as an antidote to poison and is especially effective if taken after eating poisonous fungi.

Melissa water. EAU DE MÉLISSE – See MELISSA.

Aromatic medicated water. EAUX DISTILIÉES OU HYDROLATS – Water charged with volatile constituents by distillation over aromatic plants; distilled water of bitter almonds, pineapple, cinnamon, orange flowers, lettuce, roses, melissa, valerian, etc. Used mainly in pharmacy and perfumery.

WATER CHESTNUT. MACRE OU CHATAÎGNE D'EAU – Herbaceous water plant with edible fruit. Water chestnuts are eaten boiled or roasted. Their pulp bears some resemblance to ordinary chestnuts but has less flavour.

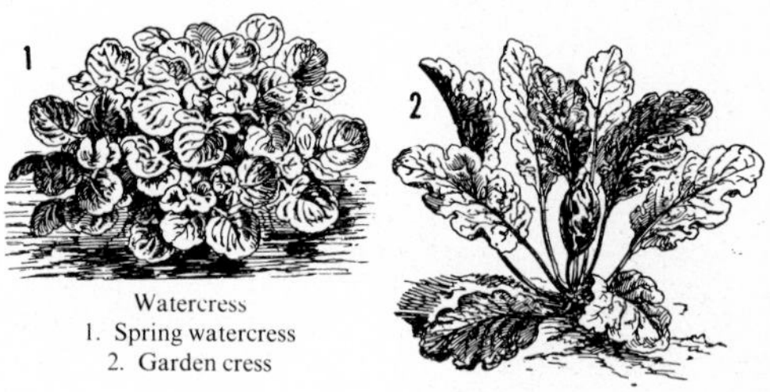

Watercress
1. Spring watercress
2. Garden cress

WATERCRESS. CRESSON – See also CRESS. Watercress is used raw to garnish grilled and roast meats, or in salads. Cooked, it provides excellent dishes.

Watercress cooked with butter. CRESSON ÉTUVÉ AU BEURRE – Blanch the cress rapidly in salt water, drain, dry, and simmer in butter in the same way as spinach.

Watercress cooked with cream. CRESSON ÉTUVÉ À LA CRÈME – Cook in the same way as above. Add a few tablespoons fresh boiling cream.

Watercress cooked au jus. CRESSON ÉTUVÉ AU JUS – The same as above. Finish with the addition of some juice from the roast.

Watercress garnish. GARNITURE DE CRESSON – Trim, wash and drain the cress. Arrange it in bunches beside grilled or roast meat.

Watercress purée. PURÉE DE CRESSON – Simmer watercress in butter and sieve. Add a third of its volume of potato purée. Finish with fresh butter or boiled cream, according to the recipe.

Watercress salad. SALADE DE CRESSON – Trim, wash, drain and dry the watercress. Season in the usual way with oil, vinegar or lemon juice, salt and pepper.

This salad must only be dressed at the last moment.

Watercress sandwiches. SANDWICHES AU CRESSON – Cover buttered slices of bread with watercress which has been dried, or with a *chiffonnade* of watercress.

Sandwiches can also be made with watercress which has been finely chopped and mixed with a rather thick mayonnaise.

Cream of watercress soup – See SOUPS AND BROTHS.

WATERFISCH – Dutch word used in France for 'freshwater fish'. The name *waterfisch* or *patervisch* is used in cookery for a kind of sauce served with freshwater fish, particularly perch.

Waterfisch sauce (cold). SAUCE WATERFISCH – Prepared with the *court-bouillon* (q.v.) of the fish being used. Add gelatine, strained and mixed with a *julienne* of vegetables (see below) cooked in a *court-bouillon* (or fish *fumet* (q.v.)). Add sweet pimentos, gherkins and capers.

This sauce (jelly) is used to coat the fish after it has been cooked in *court-bouillon*, cooled in the same liquid, skinned and wiped dry. It is then decorated with anchovy fillets cut into thin strips. Serve with *Rémoulade sauce* (see SAUCE).

Waterfisch sauce (hot). SAUCE WATERFISCH – Cook 50 g. (2 oz., $\frac{1}{2}$ cup) carrots, 25 g. (1 oz., $\frac{1}{4}$ cup) white part of leeks, 25 g. (1 oz., $\frac{1}{4}$ cup) celery and 25 g. (1 oz., $\frac{1}{4}$ cup) parsley roots, all cut in a fine *julienne* gently in butter till soft. Add 2 dl. ($\frac{1}{3}$ pint, scant cup) *court-bouillon* (q.v.) or fish *fumet* (q.v.). Boil down the liquid, and add 4 dl. ($\frac{3}{4}$ pint, scant 2 cups) *White wine sauce* (see SAUCE).

WATERMELON. PASTÈQUE – Fruit of a *cucurbitaceae* family plant. There are many varieties, with white, yellow, and red coloured flesh. They can be pleasantly musky or rather insipid. Water melons, unlike ordinary melons, have no central cavity. They are eaten raw or made into jam.

Water parsnip

WATER PARSNIP. BERLE – Aquatic plant, the leaves of which have some similarity to those of celery. It is also called *Water parsley*, *Creeping watercress* and *Water smallage*.

The leaves of the water parsnip are eaten in salads. Only the leaves should be eaten, as its roots are poisonous.

WATERZOOTJE Flemish cookery. WATERZOI – A fish dish having some analogy with the *cotriade* of the Breton fishermen, but which is solid rather than a soup.

In Holland and Belgium this preparation is equivalent to bouillabaisse but without tomato, garlic and saffron. It is

Chicken waterzootje or waterzoi
(*Robert Carrier*)

cooked not with oil, like the Provençale soup, but with butter.

Line a buttered sauté pan with 200 g. (7 oz., $1\frac{3}{4}$ cups) of the white part of celery, chopped. Put on top 2 kg. ($4\frac{1}{2}$ lb.) freshwater fish (eel, carp, pike, tench, etc.) cut in chunks. Season with salt and pepper, add a *bouquet garni* of parsley, thyme, bay leaf and 2 or 3 leaves of sage. Cover with water (or fish *fumet* (q.v.)). Dot the top with 100 g. (4 oz., $\frac{1}{2}$ cup) butter cut into small pieces.

Begin cooking on high heat. Cover the pan and continue cooking very slowly, so that the liquid is boiled down while the fish cooks.

Add stock to give the desired consistency and a little biscotte (melba toast) reduced to powder. Remove the *bouquet garni*. Serve with slices of buttered bread.

Chicken waterzootje. WATERZOI DE VOLAILLE – Although *waterzootje* is the name for a fish dish, it is sometimes prepared with jointed chicken cooked in a white stock flavoured with onions, leeks, *bouquet garni*, celery, thyme, bay leaf and cloves. Bring to the boil, then add a little white wine. Season with salt and pepper, and simmer very slowly for $1\frac{1}{2}$ hours. Cut into pieces, remove the *bouquet garni* and serve in the stock, garnished with chopped parsley.

WAXWING. JASEUR – European bird of the sparrow family. It is edible and is cooked in the same way as lark.

WEEVER. VIVE – Type of European fish found on the sandy coasts. The *greater weever*, whose firm white flesh is highly esteemed, has an elongated body, pinkish or yellowish in colour with dark bands. It has stiff spines along the dorsal fin, whose pricks are poisonous, even after the fish is dead. All the methods of cooking whiting (q.v.) are applicable to the weever.

Weever en matelote vierge (Carême's recipe). VIVE EN MATELOTTE – 'Take 6 weevers, clean them and cut each into 3 chunks, not using the head. Put into a buttered saucepan with a *bouquet garni*, chopped onions, 2 cloves garlic, 2 cloves, salt and grated nutmeg. Pour in a bottle of white Burgundy. Start cooking over strong heat, then skim and moderate the heat so that the fish simmers.

'As soon as it becomes firm to the touch, drain and put it into another saucepan. Strain the liquor. Make a white *roux* to thicken the liquid and add the trimmings of 1 kg. ($2\frac{1}{4}$ lb.) peeled and cooked mushrooms.

'Remove all grease, boil down, thicken with 3 egg yolks, strain through a cloth and keep it hot in a *bain-marie*.

'Arrange the pieces of weever in a pyramid, keeping them in place with heart-shaped croûtons of bread fried in butter. Pour over the sauce, to which the mushrooms have been added, together with a piece of the finest butter as big as an egg.'

WEIGHTS AND MEASURES. POIDS ET MESURES – We have quoted several old French recipes in which the quantities of the ingredients are given in old French units. Often we have indicated the metric equivalents, but here is all the data in a comparative table.

Measures of weight – Livre (pound): this old unit of measure of weight has had varied values, but it is generally accepted to be the equivalent of 489·5 g.

Marc. Equalled half a livre, i.e. 244·75 g.

Quarteron. Quarter of a livre, i.e. about 122 g.

Once. One-sixteenth part of a livre, i.e. 30·59 g.

Gros. One-eighth part of an once, i.e. 3·825 g.

Grain. About one-eighteenth of a gram, i.e. 0·053 g.

Measures of capacity – *Muid* represented 2 *feuillettes* or 4 *quartauts*, i.e. 268·23 litres.

Pinte. Equalled 0·93 litre (in Paris).

Quartaut. 72 French pints, i.e. about 67 litres.

Setier. 8 Paris pints, i.e. 7·45 litres.

Chopine. Used to be half a French pint.

Some of the old measures of capacity have remained in use, particularly for Champagne wines, the value differing slightly from the old values, the metric equivalents being expressed in round figures. A bottle may at times have the same capacity as the old pint, i.e. 0·93 litre, but the present-day bottle generally equals 0·80 litre.

Muid = 260 litres.
Trentain = 300 litres.
Poincon = 200 litres.
Caque = 100 litres.
Queue de Reims = 396 litres.
Queue de Champagne = 366 litres.
Sapinée = 30 pints (28 litres).
Velte = 1 setier = 7·45 litres.
Quartaut = 50 litres.
Feuillette = 114 litres.
Pièce = 200 litres.

Old linear measures – The *foot* equalled 0·3248 m., it was divided into 12 inches of 0·017 m. The inch equalled 12 lines of 0·225 cm.

WELL. PUITS – Word used for the space left empty in the middle of a circle of flour, in which are placed the ingredients necessary to make pastry or other mixtures; the central part of food arranged in the form of a crown, 'turban' or circle, where various garnishes are placed; the hollow made in the middle of a cake or pudding; the metal sleeve or chimney in the middle of certain moulds and cake tins.

WELS. SILURE – Large freshwater fish with smooth soft skin and barbelled mouth.

The European *wels*, which is not found in France except in the River Doubs, and which is also called the *glanis*, grows up to over 2 m. ($6\frac{1}{2}$ feet) in length and weighs 25 kg. (55 lb.).

The dwarf wels, or freshwater catfish, originating in America whence it has been imported and used to stock French rivers, grows to 40 to 60 cm. (16 to 24 inches) in length. Its flesh is very delicate. The pectoral and dorsal fins have spikes, whose prick is disagreeable but not dangerous.

This fish is prepared like the freshwater burbot (q.v.).

WELSH RABBIT or RAREBIT – English toasted cheese preparation, made as follows:

Put into a saucepan with a little English beer, 8 oz. (225 g., 2 cups) Gloucester cheese cut in small pieces. Add a little English mustard. Cook this mixture stirring all the time until the cheese has melted. Pour over slices of toasted and buttered bread. Brown well under the grill.

WHALE. BALEINE – In the Middle Ages whale meat, under the name of *crapois* or Lenten bacon, was sold on meatless days and formed the staple diet of the poor. The flesh of this cetacean is most indigestible and remains tough even after 24 hours cooking.

There are several kinds of whales, which differ in name, appearance and size. From the gastronomical point of view, only whale calves are of any interest. The flesh of these is of a reddish colour and somewhat similar to beef in appearance, but not in taste. Whale meat was not greatly esteemed by our grandfathers, but they set some store by the tongue of the animal, usually salted. Ambroise Paré says that 'it is tender and delicious'. They also much appreciated whale fat which they ate 'during Lent, with peas'.

As whale meat can be kept for quite a long time without going bad, sailors used to store it, to cook as required. It can be prepared like tunny (tuna fish) (q.v.).

There are not many recipes for whale meat.

Dr. Félix Brémont tells how he had an occasion to eat

whale meat in 1892 in a restaurant near the Halles: 'I will not say anything bad about whale meat, but neither can I find it in me to say anything good about it. Boil a piece of lean beef in water which has been used to wash a not-too-fresh mackerel, and you will have a dish similar to that which was served to me under the name of *Escalope of whale à la Valois*'. Whale steaks are often served in Norway.

Whale Calf. BALEINEAU – The young of the whale. Its flesh is very delicate and is prepared as for tunny (q.v.).

WHEAT. BLÉ, FROMENT – Cereal crop known and cultivated from the earliest times. Wheat appears to have originated in Chaldea. From there it found its way all over the East and to Italy. The Gauls, according to Herodotus, discovered it as a result of their overseas expeditions. In Caesar's time, it was cultivated in Gaul on a very limited scale. In the sixteenth century the poor had only barley or rye bread to eat. Wheaten bread was reserved exclusively for the rich man's table.

Wheat grain, which is a fruit in the botanical sense of the word, consists of three parts: shell (or pericarp), nut (or caryopsis) and seed (or embryo). The shell represents 14·36 per cent of the grain. The nut, consisting of *gluten*, is filled with starch cells.

According to strain and race, it contains on the average from 9 to 11 per cent of gluten and from 56 to 75 per cent of starch. It represents 84·21 per cent of the grain.

The embryo (1·43 per cent of the grain) is rich in nitrogenous matter and fats. It also contains ferment and odoriferous substances. In addition to starch and gluten, wheat grain also contains soluble sugar, dextrines and mineral salts (ash).

There is a considerable number of varieties, which can be classified in two groups: hard grain, richer in gluten, and soft grain, richer in starch.

The main uses of grain are in the making and manufacture of cereals, flours, pasta products and bread (see BREAD).

Germinated wheat. BLÉ GERMÉ – Wheat is not only eaten in the form of flour and bread; dieticians recommend eating it raw after germination of the grain. It has a remarkable amino acid content which increases by 130 per cent during the germination period. At this stage, too, an amylose appears which partly hydrolizes the reserve starch and aids its transformation in the digestive tract. Last but not least, the seeds are rich in Vitamin B. Ripe wheat can contain as much as 10 to 20 mg. per 100 g. of this precious vitamin.

Wheatgerm, therefore, constitutes a first-class energy food and strengthens resistance to disease.

How to prepare germinated wheat. Dr. Pierre Oudinot offers this simple and practical recipe: 'Select good quality seed corn, enough for three days' needs. Pick over, if necessary, and wash in cold water. Soak in plenty of cold water, preferably spring or rain water, but this is of secondary importance. A large soup plate or similar dish serves the purpose.

'The wheat must be completely immersed for twenty-four hours. At the end of this period, drain the grains, rinse them in fresh water, and replace, damp, in the dish. Repeat this operation every twenty-four hours. After forty-eight hours, the grain will have softened and the barely perceptible white speck of the germ will have emerged. The grain may be eaten at this point, but is edible for a further two days. It is essential to ensure that the grain never dries. If necessary, it should be moistened in the course of the day. In winter, keep the wheat in the kitchen; in summer, choose a cooler room. With practice, these small precautions become a matter of routine.'

Ten or so grains of germinated wheat should be taken to begin with, and thoroughly masticated to a pap. This may be gradually increased to a level teaspoon for adults and adolescents. Five or six well-crushed grains are sufficient for children.

It should be taken daily, preferably at the beginning of the meal along with the *hors-d'œuvre* or salad; alternatively, in the morning at breakfast time. There is no fixed rule as to the duration of the cure; it varies from individual to individual according to his constitutional needs and his tolerance of this unusual food. Generally speaking, wheatgerm can be taken regularly for periods of 12 to 15 days followed by rest periods of the same duration.

Wheat in dietetics. BLÉ EN DIETETIQUE – Cereals, and wheat in particular, are very important nutritionally. The flours extracted from them occupy pride of place in the normal daily diet: bread, pastries, dessert, sauces and other culinary preparations. Thirty-five per cent of the calories and 31 per cent of the proteins of the daily diet are derived from cereals.

The following constitutes a grain of wheat. There is first the exterior husk, the pericarp, which is very hard and encrusted with lignite. Then come the intermediary layers: the seed coat and the hyaline band. Attached to this triple casing is an important part of the grain, the proteic layer, containing a substance called *aleuron*, a mixture of proteins, vitamins and mineral salts. Beneath this there is the kernel containing proteins and starch; it constitutes four-fifths of the volume of the grain. Finally, in the lower part of the convex surface is the germ, very small, 1·5 per cent of the whole grain, containing all the vital force, the embryo.

Modern milling processes using metal rollers deprive the flour of the most vital and important constituents of wheat: the whole of the husk with the proteic layer, and the germ. The flour we use to make our bread is thus stripped of an essential part of its food and energy value. This is the reason for the controversy over the merits of wholemeal bread as opposed to white bread. (See BREAD, *Bread in dietetics.*)

WHIPPED CREAM. CRÈME FOUETTÉE – Cream whipped with a whisk or beater.

WHISK. FOUET – Utensil to beat eggs, cream, white sauces, *béarnaise*, *hollandaise*, *mayonnaise*, etc. For cooking, whisks made of metal are used. For baking and confectionery whisks

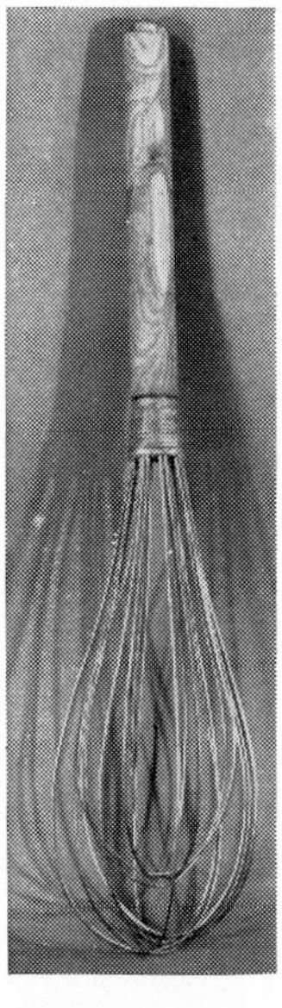

Large egg-whisk
(*Larousse*)

made of box-wood or wicker are also used. Modern rotary hand and electric beaters are often used to replace the whisk, but many professionals find these inferior to the whisk.

WHISKY or WHISKEY – Grain spirit from Scotland or Ireland distilled from barley, rye and other cereals, malted and fermented.

There were only the three lines above on this subject in the 1938 edition of *Larousse gastronomique*. Evidence enough of the rapid spread of this spirit in France, which now has a place on the shelves of the most modest provincial tavern.

The origin of whisky is obscure, but its name comes from the Celtic. *Uisgebeatha*, in the Gaelic that is still spoken in Ireland and in the Highlands of Scotland, means 'water of life'. We suppose, therefore, that whisky was first distilled in Ireland from where it spread to Western Scotland.

Originally, it was a distillation of malt, home made by the crofters. It was a robust drink suited to the hard local climate. Soon it began to be manufactured industrially but, after 1830, instead of being made from malt, it was made from grain and was lighter in character with a finer bouquet.

Nowadays, the best-known manufacturers produce skilful blends of different types of whisky, malt and grain. The grain can be malted barley, unmalted barley, maize, rye or even a mixture of these.

'Scotch' or Scottish whisky is in a class of its own because of the peaty water used in its manufacture. It is usually a 50-50 blend of malt and grain whiskies. Irish whiskey (spelt differently to distinguish it from the others) has an unusual and quite individual flavour; it is an indispensable ingredient of Irish coffee. Production is comparatively small. Rye whisky (Canadian or American whisky) is made from malted rye or barley, with the addition of a quantity of unmalted rye which provides the sugar. Bourbon (American whisky) is made from malted wheat and maize.

Not surprisingly, French 'manufacturers' have tried to produce their version of whisky: it is as undrinkable as the Cognac manufactured outside France.

Whisky, like all spirits, is clear when it comes from the still. In the course of maturation in oak barrels, its colour deepens and its quality improves. Whisky lovers drink it with 'flat' water or 'on the rocks' (on ice), but true connoisseurs know that whisky should not be refrigerated or served with ice. It should be served at the same temperature as the small amount of unaerated water that accompanies it. This is especially relevant for old whiskies such as Chivas, Legacy and the even more venerable ones over ten years old.

Unauthorised propaganda attributes a certain health value to whisky; that it is a remedy for heart troubles. This is not strictly true. All the same, besides producing the same ill effects on the body as other alcoholic beverages, whisky is both a stimulant and a vasodilator. Its absorption in moderate doses can therefore be justified for fatigue, colds, influenza, etc. Like all grain spirits, it does not release esters, and ages better than spirits made from fruit. According to some connoisseurs whisky is by far superior to other spirits used in cooking.

Whisky, then, may be substituted for Cognac or Armagnac in *flambages*, etc.

In Geneva there is a *'Confrérie du bon vieux whisky'*.

Finally, here is the genuine Shannon recipe for the 'Irish coffee' that so pleases the connoisseurs and which many consider to be the best dessert of all.

Irish coffee – Gently warm a large glass. Pour in a measure of Irish whiskey. Add several lumps of sugar, according to taste. (Some people do not add sugar at all and this is perhaps an improvement.) Fill the glass to within 3 cm. ($1\frac{1}{4}$ inches) of the brim with very strong black coffee. Stir to dissolve the sugar. Slowly add chilled thick cream. Do not stir again as the cream should float on the top.

WHITEBAIT. BLANCHAILLE – The 'fry' or young of the common herring (*Clupea harengus*) and sprat (*Clupea sprattus*), which abound in the Thames and along the coasts of the North Sea. It is also found in vast numbers in the mouth of the Garonne.

These little fishes are mostly fried in deep fat.

All the recipes given for nonats (q.v.) (the 'fry' of a small Mediterranean goby) are applicable to whitebait.

WHITE BEET. POIRÉE – Variety of chard (q.v.).

WHITE-TAIL. CUL-BLANC – Several migrant birds are known by this name, especially the wheatear, prized in France as game, and cooked in the same way as lark (q.v.).

Whiting

WHITING. MERLAN – The European whiting is a gadoid fish with a long, somewhat compact body. It has soft rounded scales and is greyish or olive green along the back, with copper or pale yellow shading. Its flanks are white, speckled with yellow, and its belly silvery. It is between 26 and 41 cm. (10 and 16 inches) long. Whiting is caught mainly in the English Channel and the Baltic. Its flesh is fine in texture, flaky and easy to digest.

Another species of whiting, the pollack, is similar in appearance but is yellowish in colour and darker. Its flesh, though of good quality, is less delicate than that of the whiting proper.

The American whiting is also known as silver hake and is fished off the New England coast. The average whiting is 31 to 36 cm. (12 to 14 inches) long but larger specimens are not uncommon.

Whiting à l'anglaise. MERLAN À L'ANGLAISE – Slit the fish along the back and remove backbone. Season, flour, dip in egg and breadcrumbs and fry in butter, browning well on both sides.

Serve on a dish covered with slightly softened *Maître d'hôtel butter* (see BUTTER, *Compound butters*).

Grilled whiting, served with melted butter and boiled potatoes, is also called *whiting à l'anglaise*.

Whiting à la Bercy. MERLAN À LA BERCY – Make a shallow incision along the back. Put the whiting in a buttered fireproof dish and sprinkle with a teaspoon of chopped shallot.

Season, moisten with 1 dl. (6 tablespoons, scant $\frac{1}{2}$ cup) white wine and dot with 2 teaspoons butter cut into tiny fragments. Bring to the boil on the stove, then bake in the oven, basting frequently.

When the fish is cooked, glaze in a very hot oven. Squeeze a a few drops of lemon juice over the fish and sprinkle with chopped parsley.

Boiled whiting with melted butter or other sauce. MERLAN

BOUILLI AVEC BEURRE FONDU – Boil the whiting in salt water. Drain, and garnish with potatoes and fresh parsley. Serve with melted butter or any sauce suitable for boiled fish.

Whiting à la bonne femme. MERLAN À LA BONNE FEMME – Prepare as for *Brill à la bonne femme* (see BRILL).

Whiting à la cancalaise. MERLAN À LA CONCALAISE – Prepare as for *Brill à la cancalaise* (see BRILL).

Whiting Colbert. MERLAN COLBERT – Slit the whiting along the back and remove backbone. Season with salt and pepper, sprinkle with flour, dip in egg and breadcrumbs and deep fry.

Put into the slit in the fish 1 tablespoon *Maître d'hôtel butter* (see BUTTER, *Compound butters*).

Whiting à la dieppoise. MERLAN À LA DIEPPOISE – Prepare as for *Brill à la dieppoise* (see BRILL).

Whiting à l'espagnole. MERLAN À L'ESPAGNOLE – Dip in egg and breadcrumbs as indicated for *Whiting à l'anglaise*. Fry in oil until well browned on both sides. Serve on a bed of *Tomato fondue* (see FONDUE) seasoned with a little crushed garlic. Garnish each end of the dish with a clump of onion rings fried in oil.

Fillets of whiting. FILETS DE MERLAN – Fillets of whiting can be prepared in all ways suitable for whole whiting.

Recipes given for fillets of sea perch, brill, sole, etc., are also suitable for fillets of whiting.

Whiting forcemeat. FARCE DE MERLAN – Made of whiting, *panade* (q.v.) cream and eggs, in the same way as *Pike forcemeat* (see FORCEMEATS).

Fried whiting. MERLAN FRIT – Slit the whiting, dip in milk and flour. Fry, drain, and season with dry table salt.

Serve with fried parsley and lemon halves.

Whiting au gratin. MERLAN AU GRATIN – Prepare as for *Sole au gratin* (see SOLE).

Grilled whiting. MERLAN GRILLÉ – Make a shallow incision in the whiting. Season, dredge with flour, brush with melted butter or oil and grill under gentle heat.

Garnish with parsley and slices of lemon and serve with melted butter, *Maître d'hôtel butter*, or any sauce suitable for grilled fish. (See BUTTER, *Compound butters*, and SAUCE.)

Whiting loaf – See LOAVES, *Fish loaves*.

Whiting en lorgnette (fried). MERLAN FRIT EN LORGNETTE – Fillet a large whiting, starting at the tail and working towards the head. Shave off the flesh very close to the bone. Remove the bone, cutting it off at the base of the head. Season the fish and dip in egg and breadcrumbs. Roll the fillets. Skewer them to keep them in shape.

Deep fry in hot fat and garnish with fried parsley and lemon.

Whiting en lorgnette (poached). MERLAN POCHÉ EN LORGNETTE – Split the whiting open as indicated above and remove the bone. Season the fillets. Spread them with a layer, not too thick, of *Fish forcemeat* (see FORCEMEATS), roll them up, and put them in a buttered baking dish moistened with concentrated fish *fumet* (q.v.). Cook in the oven, basting frequently.

Drain the fish, and serve with the garnish and sauce indicated.

Whiting à la meunière. MERLAN À LA MEUNIÈRE – Prepare as MERLAN AUX COURGETTES, AUBERGINES – Season the whiting, dredge with flour and fry in butter.

Garnish with little Italian marrows or aubergines, diced and sautéed in oil. Squeeze a little lemon juice over the fish, sprinkle with chopped parsley, and pour on 2 tablespoons (3 tablespoons) browned butter.

Whiting à la meunière. MERLAN À LA MEUNIÈRE – Prepare as for *Bass à la meunière* (see BASS).

Whiting mousse. MOUSSE DE MERLAN – Using raw whiting, prepare as indicated for *Fish mousse* (see FISH).

Fill a deep dish three-quarters full of this mixture and cook in a *bain-marie*.

Serve with garnish and sauce as indicated in the recipe.

Filleting Whiting

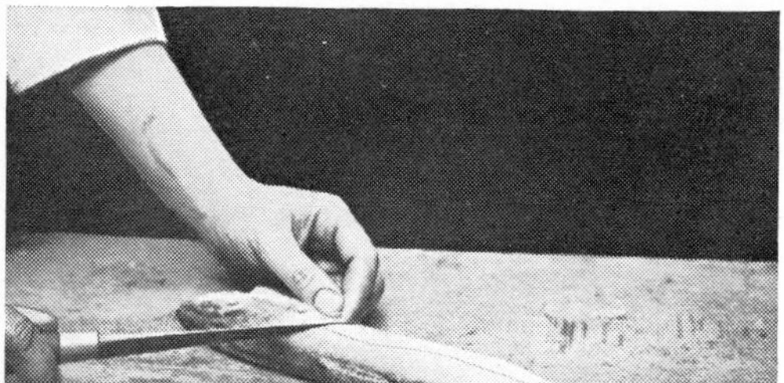

Make an incision just below the head

Cut along the length of the backbone

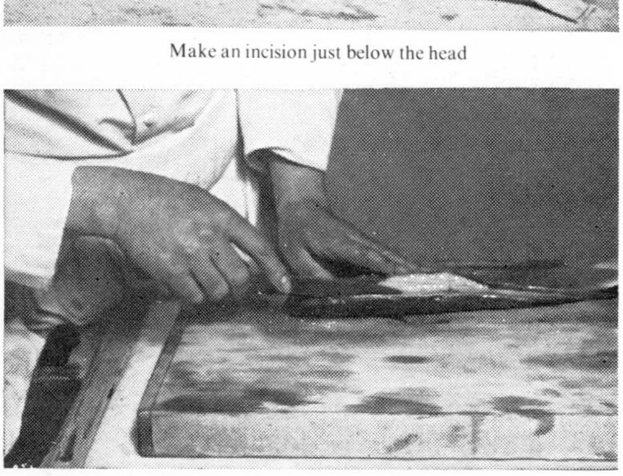

Cut the fillet away completely from the bone and remove

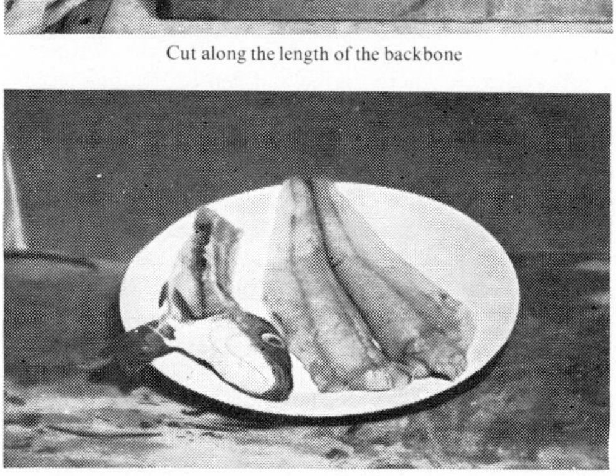

The two fillets cleaned and ready for cooking

Whiting with mushrooms. MERLAN AUX CHAMPIGNONS – Proceed as for *Brill with mushrooms* (see BRILL).

Whiting Orly. MERLAN ORLY – Fillet a large raw whiting. Dip the fillets in a lighter batter.

Deep-fry in hot fat. Drain, sprinkle with table salt, and garnish with fried parsley. Serve with *Tomato sauce* (see SAUCE).

Whiting with oysters. MERLAN AUX HUÎTRES – Prepare the whiting as indicated for *Brill with oysters* (see BRILL). Garnish with poached oysters, drained and trimmed.

Whiting sur le plat. MERLAN SUR LE PLAT – Make a shallow incision along the back of the whiting. Season. Put it in a buttered fireproof dish and pour on 2 to 3 tablespoons white wine and a few drops lemon juice. Bring to the boil on the stove and finish cooking in the oven, basting frequently. Serve in the cooking dish.

Whiting Richelieu. MERLAN RICHELIEU – Prepare as for *Whiting à l'anglaise.* Cover with *Maître d'hôtel butter* (see BUTTER, *Compound butters*) and arrange 4 strips of truffle on top.

Whiting paupiettes. MERLAN EN PAUPIETTES – Fillet the whiting. Spread the inside with a thin layer of fish forcemeat. Roll the fillets tightly and poach in concentrated fish stock. Prepare according to the recipe selected.

Paupiettes of whiting can be prepared *à la Bercy*; *à la dieppoise*; *aux fines herbes*; *au gratin*; *à la Nantua*, *à la normande*; in white wine. All garnishes and sauces indicated for sole are suitable for this dish.

Whiting with shrimps. MERLAN AUX CREVETTES – Prepare as for *Brill with shrimps* (see BRILL).

Whiting in wine. MERLAN AU VIN BLANC – Prepare as for *Brill in white wine* (see BRILL).

WHOLEMEAL (WHOLE-WHEAT). BIS – Term applied to loaves of homemade bread which contain a certain proportion of bran, or made of a mixture of wheat and rye flour. The crust of wholemeal bread is of a brown colour. (See BREAD.)

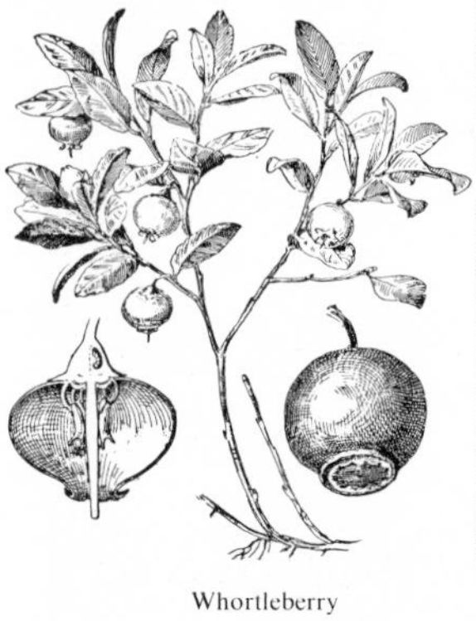

Whortleberry

Small branches of whortleberry

WHORTLEBERRY or HUCKLEBERRY. AIRELLE – The French name *airelle* is often used to define different berries; bilberry (U.S.A. huckleberry), whortleberry, etc. The real whortleberry is a small reddish berry, acid in taste, which is used mostly in compotes in Germanic countries (*preisel-beere* in German). It makes a sweet-sour accompaniment to red meats and game. Its properties resemble those of cranberries and bilberries.

Whortleberry or huckleberry accompaniment to cold meats. AIRELLES – Separate berries from the stem. Measure 2 litres ($3\frac{1}{2}$ pints, $4\frac{1}{2}$ pints) berries, wash, drain, and put them in a basin. Add 2 dl. ($\frac{1}{3}$ pint, scant cup) red wine, a pinch powdered cinnamon, 5 cloves and 500 g. (18 oz., $2\frac{1}{4}$ cups) fine sugar. Bring to the boil, skim and cook for 30 minutes.

Drain the whortleberries and boil down the juice until it reaches the consistency of a thick syrup. Put the berries back into the syrup and mix well. Cool, and put in jars. Seal firmly and keep in a cool place.

Serve with boiled beef and with cold meats.

Whortleberry or huckleberry compote. COMPOTE D'AIRELLES – Prepare a syrup of 500 g. (18 oz., $2\frac{1}{4}$ cups) sugar, 2 dl. ($\frac{1}{3}$ pint, scant cup) water, the peel of $\frac{1}{2}$ lemon and a piece of cinnamon bark. Pick over 1 kg. ($2\frac{1}{4}$ lb.) whortleberries, remove stalks and put into the syrup. Boil fast.

Remove the berries with a perforated spoon as soon as they are cooked and put into a dish. Boil down the syrup and pour over the fruit. Chill before serving.

Whortleberry or huckleberry jam. CONFITURE D'AIRELLES – For 2 kg. ($4\frac{1}{2}$ lb.) seeded whortleberries allow $1\frac{1}{2}$ kg. ($3\frac{1}{2}$ lb., $6\frac{1}{2}$ cups) sugar. Melt the sugar with $\frac{1}{2}$ litre (scant pint, $2\frac{1}{4}$ cups) water in a copper or stainless steel pan. Add the berries. Cook, stirring frequently with a wooden spoon to prevent the fruit sticking to the pan.

Finish off as described in the general rules for making jam (see JAMS AND JELLIES). Pour into jars and seal.

Whortleberry or huckleberry jelly. GELÉE D'AIRELLES – 2 kg. ($4\frac{1}{2}$ lb.) seeded whortleberries, 1 kg. ($2\frac{1}{4}$ lb.) seeded red currants and 3 kg. ($6\frac{1}{2}$ lb., 13 cups) sugar.

Press the whortleberries and the red currants to extract all juice. Put this into a pan with the sugar. Mix well and bring to the boil.

Skim carefully and cook for 5 minutes. Leave to stand until lukewarm. Pour into jars and seal.

Whortleberry or huckleberry kissel (Russian cookery). KISSEL D'AIRELLES – Pound 1 kg. ($2\frac{1}{4}$ lb.) whortleberries in a mortar, adding about $2\frac{1}{2}$ litres ($4\frac{1}{2}$ pints, $5\frac{1}{2}$ pints) water. Press through a napkin to extract all juice.

Put 6 tablespoons cornflour or potato starch into a pan, pour the juice over it and stir. Add 225 g. (8 oz., 1 cup) sugar. Boil, stirring all the time. As soon as the mixture thickens and becomes transparent, transfer it into a bowl. Serve hot. Serve very thick cream separately.

WIDERKOMM. VIDRECOME – Large glass used in Germany in the Middle Ages for ceremonial feasts.

WILD ARUM, LORDS AND LADIES. GOUET, PIED-DE-VEAU – This plant has a tuberous stem very rich in starch, which can be extracted and used in cooking. When it is fresh, it contains a bitter, corrosive substance, but this can be eliminated by washing or drying.

WILD BOAR. SANGLIER – Wild mammal, very near to the domestic pig (*bête noire*, in French hunting terms). Its flesh, which has a pronounced 'wild' taste, does not make good eating except in the young animals. The flesh of the adult animals is tough and only becomes palatable if left to marinate for a long time.

Up to the age of six months the wild boar is called a *marcassin*; from six months to a year, a *bête rousse*; between one year and two, a *bête de compagnie*; after two years, a *ragot*; at three years a wild boar *à son tiers an*; at four years he is a *quartenier*, older, a *porc entier*, and finally, when he is advanced in age, he is given the name of *solitaire* or *ermite*. He can attain the age of thirty.

Only the *marcassins* and the *bêtes rousses* are used in their entirety in the kitchen. Every part of these creatures, leg, saddle, loin, shoulder and back is excellent. In an old boar only the head is eatable, and even then it is necessary to add to it a great number of other ingredients, such as fine pork

forcemeat, chicken meat, fresh pork tongue, fat bacon, truffles and pistachios.

Before being cooked in any way the meat of the *marcassin* or *bête rousse* should be left for a time in a strong marinade.

Chine of marcassin (young wild boar) à la chipolata. ÉCHINE DE MARCASSIN À LA CHIPOLATA – The chine is the whole or part of the backbone and adhering flesh. After having marinated the chine for several hours, drain, dry and braise it in a well seasoned braising stock. (See CULINARY METHODS, *Braising*.)

When it is threee-quarters cooked, drain the chine. Put it back in the saucepan with a *Chipolata garnish* (see GARNISHES). Pour over the strained juices from the braising. Finish cooking, simmering very slowly.

Civet of marcassin (young wild boar). CIVET DE MARCASSIN – Prepared like *Civet of hare* (see HARE).

Cutlets (U.S.A. chops) of marcassin (young wild boar). CÔTELETTES DE MARCASSIN – Prepared like *Cutlets (chops) of roebuck* or of *pork*. (See ROEBUCK and PORK.)

Wild boar ham. JAMBON DE SANGLIER – This is cured and cooked in exactly the same way as pork ham (see HAM) and can be eaten cooked or raw. It is garnished with a vegetable purée, usually chestnut.

Wild boar ham, sweet-sour. JAMBON DE SANGLIER À L'AIGRE-DOUCE – Braise the ham, in the same way as pork ham (see HAM). When it is cooked drain it, pour over a few tablespoons of the strained braising juices, sprinkle with sugar and glaze in the oven.

Finish off the braising juices like a *Romaine sauce* (see SAUCE). Add to this sauce 12 prunes soaked in water and stoned, and 24 cherries pickled in vinegar. Add a little chocolate dissolved in water. Serve the ham with the sauce, accompanied by a garnish.

This way of preparing wild boar is popular in the north of Europe.

Wild boar ham, sweet-sour à l'italienne. JAMBON DE SANGLIER, À L'AIGRE-DOUCE, À L'ITALIENNE – Made like the preceding recipe, but add to the sauce pine kernels, citron peel and chopped candied orange.

Boar's head. HURE DE SANGLIER – The cooking of boar's head, which is a very large dish, involves many different ingredients. The actual boar's head is the most insignificant part of this preparation, because apart from the tongue and a few pieces of lean flesh which are taken off the skull, this cold dish uses only the cutaneous parts covering the animal's head.

For a head of about 5 kg. (11 lb.) when cooked: $4\frac{1}{2}$ kg. (10 lb.) *Fine pork forcemeat* (see FORCEMEAT), 1 kg. ($2\frac{1}{4}$ lb.) chicken meat boned and trimmed, 750 g. ($1\frac{1}{2}$ lb.) cooked lean ham, 4 fresh pork tongues heated, skinned and pickled in brine, 500 g. (1 lb.) scarlet tongue, 500 g. (1 lb.) fat bacon, 400 g. (14 oz.) peeled truffles, 125 g. (4 oz., 1 cup) blanched pistachios.

Singe and scrape the head carefully, and bone it completely, taking care not to tear the skin. Cut off the ears (which must be cooked separately), take out the tongue and remove the small fleshy pieces from next to the skin.

Trim these pieces of lean flesh and cut them into dice. Put them together with the tongue and the skin of the head to marinate for 10 hours with carrots, chopped onions, thyme, bay leaf, salt, pepper and spices.

Prepare a *salpicon* by cutting into dice the wild boar's tongue, the cooked pork tongues, the scarlet tongue, ham, chicken and bacon. Add the truffles cut into large dice, the pistachio nuts and the pieces of lean meat taken from the head of the boar. Marinate for 2 hours with brandy, salt, pepper and spices.

Add to this *salpicon* the fine pork forcemeat and 4 whole eggs. Mix all well together.

Boar's head, after Carême

Spread the skin from the boar's head, the outside downwards on a cloth that has been soaked in cold water and wrung out. Put the above mixture in the middle. Fold the skin over the mixture, and wrap it completely in the cloth, reshaping it in its original form. Tie up firmly.

Cook in a jelly stock (see JELLY), using the bones and trimmings of the boar's head as well as the carcase and trimmings of the chicken. Cook gently for $4\frac{1}{2}$ hours. One hour before it is ready, put in the ears. When cooked, drain. Leave to stand for 30 minutes, then untie it. Wash the cloth and wring it out well to remove the moisture. Roll the head in the cloth again, securing it firmly with string, taking care to keep the shape; begin tying at the snout end. Leave to cool for at least 12 hours.

Untie the head and wipe it carefully. Skewer the two ears, coated with a layer of brown *Chaud-froid sauce* (see SAUCE) or dissolved meat jelly, in their places. Coat the whole of the boar's head, placed on a grid or rack, with the same sauce or with meat jelly, and put back the tusks in their place. Using hard boiled egg white and truffles, make the eyes.

Decorate with *Montpellier butter* (see BUTTER, *Compound butters*) or with cut-out egg white, truffles and blanched pistachios. Glaze with jelly. Chill before serving.

Instead of being set on a platter the head may be put on a foundation of shaped rice, and truffles skewered to it.

In home cooking, and even in *grande cuisine*, the boar's head is most often covered, when quite cold, with a thick layer of golden breadcrumbs, the ears cut up in a *salpicon* before being cooked and added to the other ingredients. When thus served, the head is a kind of galantine or roll of boar's head.

Loin of marcassin (young wild boar). CARRÉ DE MARCASSIN – Cooked whole like the *Loin of roebuck* (see ROEBUCK), but more often divided into cutlets (chops) which are prepared like those of roebuck or pork.

Scalloped marcassin (young wild boar). ESCALOPES DE

MARCASSIN – All the recipes given for *Scalloped roebuck* or *Noisettes of roebuck* are applicable to young wild boar. (See ROEBUCK.)

WILD CHICORY. BARBE DE CAPUCIN – Variety of wild chicory blanched by being grown in a dark place. It has a slight bitterness which is not unpleasant.

Wild chicory is greatly valued as a salad, because it is always tender. It can be prepared like chicory, and can also be cut into chunks and pickled in vinegar like gherkins.

The slightly purgative tisane of wild chicory is excellent for regulating the circulation. Eaten raw in salad, it helps to prevent constipation in sufferers from hepatitis.

WILD THYME. SERPOLET – Labiate-flowered plant, scented and aromatic, used as condiment and for infusions.

WILLIAM – Variety of eating pear that is very juicy and sweet-flavoured. It ripens in September. A well known spirit is made from this variety of pear.

Old Médoc vines

WINE. VIN – According to the legal definition, wine is 'the product of the alcoholic fermentation of fresh or dried grapes or the juice of fresh grapes.'

The making of wine, which varies a little from region to region, was done differently in ancient times.

The Greeks dried the grapes in the sun on wicker trays which were brought in each evening to prevent the dew falling on them. They tried to make wine that was strong and heavy. The Romans, too, liked their wines to be very concentrated, exposing them to the heat in amphorae. This wine was always mixed with water at mealtimes.

Vinification – The various processes involved in contemporary wine-making are described below.

Vendange or harvest. The date at which the grapes are picked varies according to the region, the temperature and local custom. Where there is a *ban de vendange* the gathering must not be done before a given date.

The grape harvest takes place when the density of the must, taken from a number of bunches, is found to be stationary, so that the grape has nothing more to gain from remaining on the plant. As far as possible a spell of fine dry weather is chosen for harvesting.

Égrappage or removal from the stalks. According to the region and the growth the fruit may next be partly removed from the stalks. This is more usual in making white wine than red, and is also done when the must is acid or the grapes are over-ripe.

The skins of the grapes are then burst by crushing. Grapes used to be treaded, but nowadays crushing is a mechanical process. The grapes used in the manufacture of white wine are not burst before being pressed, nor are all the grapes used in the manufacture of red wines; sometimes they have to remain whole, e.g. in the case of carbonic maceration.

Cuvaison or fermentation. For the making of red wine, once the grape harvest has been crushed it is put into huge vats, which are made of wood (for fine wines), stone, brick, cement (sometimes coated with silicate), and in hotter countries in enamelled or japanned iron. It is also becoming increasingly common for vintage wines to be fermented in stainless steel vats. The success of the fermentation depends to a great extent on the surrounding temperature, so that in cold districts the vats must be thick and the cellars must be heated, whereas in Algeria and Tunisia, thin-walled vats, which are good heat conductors and are cooled by being wrapped in wet cloths, are used.

Fermentation. Fermentation is due to the action of fungi of the species *Saccharomyces*, very small in size (the average diameter is 5 to 6 thousandths of a mm.). These are found on the surface of the skins and persist in the soil, where they can resist the most intense cold. At −4°C. (25°F.) they become torpid and inactive, but recover their vitality with the first warmth. Yeasts are of different types, among them *Saccharomyces apiculatus, pastorianus* and *ellipsoidus*, the most active of all, which appears later on the bunches, when the fruit is ripe. Cultivated on barley must, they provide a barley wine which would have been the cervisia of the Gauls. Each growth has its individual fermenting agent.

By submitting a sterilised must to fermentation with leavens coming from Médoc, Burgundy or Champagne, it is possible to obtain wines which resemble those from which the leaven originated, without ever quite equalling their quality.

For fermentation to take place in the best conditions, the temperature of the cellars should not drop below 18°C. (64°F.) or the fermentation will be too slow, nor should it rise above 35°C. (95°F.) or it will become excessive, to the detriment of the quality of the wine, which thereby loses a large part of its volatile products. The best temperature for fine wines is 25°C. (77°F.).

Fermentation takes place spontaneously, due to the leavening agent in the grapes. Sometimes selected leavens are used. In a hot country, leavens adapted to higher temperatures obtain a better yield of alcohol. If the grape harvest has been soaked by rain, a fully active yeast is introduced into the vat which will prevent the development of harmful ferments. It is always advisable in the latter case to use a yeast from the same district as the harvest or from its immediate neighbourhood; from this a ferment is prepared which is in full activity at the time it is put into the vat.

The ferment breaks down the glucose (grape sugar), and from the beginning of fermentation the carbonic gas which is freed raises the solid parts of the grapes, *le chapeau*, to the level at which fermentation is most active. If it is allowed to float, the process is unevenly distributed, the marc evaporates less and acid ferments develop on the surface on contact with the air. These difficulties are prevented by sprinkling and pressing back the 'hat', a risky task, carrying with it some danger of asphyxia. Wine-growers sometimes prefer fermentation to be carried out *à chapeau sourmergé*, keeping it down in the must with the aid of wicker racks.

Fermentation, at first quite violent, later becomes calmer. This is generally the moment chosen for the *décuvage*, when

The making of Burgundy wine about 1470, as represented on an old tapestry

the wine is drawn off from the vats. The length of time the wine stays in the vats is variable; a short period gives finer, more delicately flavoured wines, richer in alcohol, less acid and paler in colour; a prolonged period in the vats gives wines that are more robust, stronger and darker in colour. This period lasts from 10 to 15 days in the Médoc, 4 to 8 days in Burgundy and less in Algeria.

Décuvage. This has the effect of separating the fermented wine from the marc; a tap placed at the base of the vat allows the first wine to be drawn off. This is called the *vin de goutte* or *pied du cuve*, the bottom of the vat.

Pressurage or pressing. The solid residue known as marc (if no wine of second growth is to be made) is then put under the press and submitted to moderate pressure. The *vin de presse* is always richer in tannin than the *vin de goutte*, with which it is mixed. The marc is pressed again, more strongly, giving a more astringent, acid wine, less rich in alcohol. Finally the marc is pressed once more. The wine from this third pressing always has a distinct taste of the husks.

On average the wine harvest gives 63 per cent *vin de goutte*, 25 per cent wine of the first pressing and 10 per cent wines of the second and third pressings.

Vinification (of white wine). White wine can be made of white or red grapes, with the exception of a few vines whose juice is coloured. These varieties are called *teinturiers*. The grapes are taken as quickly as possible to the press, without previous crushing and the juice alone is set to ferment. The operation of '*débourbage*' commonly used for *vins ordinaires* is strictly forbidden for fine wines. The object of this *débourbage* is to eliminate the bulk of impurities from the must; this is done either by drawing off the clear must or by adding massive doses of sulphur dioxide. This operation has the effect of arresting fermentation which must then be quickly restarted.

The fermentation of fine wines has to be carried out at a low temperature, 15° to 20°C. (59° to 68°F.), in oak vats or in glass-lined tanks. After its fermentation the wine must rest for a long time until the lees drop to the bottom. This ensures that the wine drawn off will be clear.

Subsequent operations – On removal from the vats, the wine is drawn off into casks where malo-lactic fermentation takes place. Repeated ullaging is necessary to ensure that the casks are always full.

Soutirages or drawings off. Drawing-off has the effect of

An old wine press

decanting wines from lees. The first *soutirage* takes place two to four weeks after the *décuvage*, the drawing-off from the vats. The second is in January in the South of France and in March and April in colder parts of France.

The part played by the yeasts, though they have by now become much less active, is not yet finished. After fermentation they develop the taste-producing elements, provided that air is excluded; this is why ullage is carried out in the first place and the barrels afterwards placed 'side bung' or *bonde sur le côté*.

Filtering and clarifying. Before being released for consumption the wine is filtered and clarified to give it greater limpidity. Different substances are used for this, which, by coagulating on contact with tannin, form a kind of screen which entraps and deposits the particles in suspension.

As a rule gelatine or dried albumen is used for *vins ordinaires* (10 to 15 g. per hectolitre), fresh egg whites for fine wines (2 or 3 per hectolitre), and isinglass for white wines (10 to 15 g. per hectolitre dissolved in 2 to 3 litres water along with 2 g. tartaric acid).

The technique of *collage*, which is often practised as part of the treatment given to wine after it has arrived in the cellar, is described below.

Other operations are sometimes carried out, such as pasteurisation – heating to 55°C. (131°F.) and 60°C. (140°F.), with air excluded, the presence of air giving wine a 'cooked' taste at 35°C. (95°F.), to assure that the wine will keep. This is chiefly done after blending to amalgamate the mixture. The pasteurisation which is sometimes carried out to remedy maladies of the wine will be considered later.

Wine presses
(*Remy Martin*)

Fortification, where French wines are concerned, is a matter of adding alcohol to wines which are too deficient in it to keep well, thereby raising the content by one or two degrees at the most. This addition of alcohol is legally forbidden for wines destined to be consumed in France and is strictly limited to wines for export.

Other practices have more relation to chemistry than genuine wine-making.

Chaptalisation. This practice, authorised under certain conditions, consists of enriching must deficient in saccharose, and has the effect of raising the alcoholic strength of the finished product. The process takes place during fermentation. For the amount of must contained in a 228-litre Burgundy barrel, or a 225-litre Bordeaux barrel, the addition of 4 kg. (9 lb.) sugar is equivalent to an increase of one alcoholic degree. White crystallised sugar is generally used.

Chaptalisation must be employed only to re-establish the biological balance of a weak vintage. It should never be used artificially to increase the alcoholic strength of a well-balanced wine. The taxing of wine according to its alcoholic strength has had the unfortunate effect of encouraging the vine growers to chaptalise excessively; this practice has led to a shifting of public taste to wine of high alcoholic strength.

Plâtrage or plastering. This was formerly done, chiefly in the Mediterranean region, to augment the acidity and add brilliance to the colour. The practice has fallen into disuse in France.

Phosphatage (addition of phosphate of lime). This has much the same effect as *plâtrage*, but does not improve the colour.

Tanisage or treatment with tannin. This corrects lack of astringency. Alcohol tannin is used for this purpose, usually in the proportion of 4 to 8 g. per hectolitre.

Salage. Also a very ancient practice, known to the ancient Greeks, who added sea water to their wines. Usually salt is added (up to 1 g. per litre is permitted) to augment the extract and perhaps to cloak some adulteration such as fortification or watering-down.

Shellisage or addition of glycerine. This makes the wine smooth, gives it body, improves its keeping qualities and above all, increases the proportion of extract. The addition of glycerine is forbidden by law, and can easily be detected by the expert.

The use of sulphur, in the form of sulphuric acid, obtained by burning sulphurated wicks or by adding alkaline bisulphates, is recommended by all oenologists as a preventative against the maladies of the wine. Part of the sulphuric acid is eliminated by the *soutirage* or drawing off.

These chemical processes, which remove wine somewhat from its legal definition, present many disadvantages, especially when several of them are done simultaneously, and they may be dangerous to the consumer.

Among the processes which are plainly fraudulent are the use of saccharine, dulcine, antiseptics and of mineral, vegetable and organic colouring matter.

Ageing of wine – This takes place naturally by the wine being left to rest, in cask, side bung, for one, two or more years, according to the nature of the wine, but can be induced artificially by agitation, by heating, by refrigeration, and by the use of electrical impulses. These can never replace the effect of natural ageing.

Fine wines are subsequently put into bottles, which has the effect of slowing down the processes resulting from oxidization and etherification. These develop the bouquet, and allow the wine to acquire what is called 'bottle age'.

Wines of second and third pressing – Obtained by adding

A burgundian fermenting room

Cement vats for wine storage
(*Demay frères*)

sugared water to the marc (50 kg. per hectolitre) and fermenting this anew. These wines always have less extract, cream of tartar and tannin, but they still provide a healthy drink which is worth about two-thirds as much as natural wine.

Piquettes – Made from the fermentation of marcs to which unsweetened water has been added. Very poor in alcohol and extract, they are normally used for home consumption and for blending with wines of second and third pressings.

Wine from dried fruit – Raisins are generally used after having been cooked in warm water. The resulting wines, always white, are characterised by the presence of 0·7 per cent to 1 per cent levogyrous sugar of which there is no trace in natural wine. They are mostly used for blending.

Sparkling wines – See SPARKLING.

Luxury or liqueur wines – Wines which are sweeter or richer in alcohol than those in current consumption. The following varieties are distinguished:

Vins doux mutés or *mistelles*. Obtained by adding alcohol to partly fermented must immediately after its extraction.

Vins doux semi-mutés. Obtained by the addition of alcohol to partly fermented must so as to obtain about 15°.

Vins doux passerillés. Obtained from musts with a strong sugar content and from raisins dried on the plant, in the sun or in ovens. The must is such as to give a wine of 13° to 15° alcoholic content without the addition of alcohol. Part of the sugar should remain, not decomposed.

Wines muted by the addition of alcohol. This is done immediately after fermentation while still containing much sugar (port).

Dry wines. Fortified after fermentation, like sherry.

Wines with a dry wine base. Blended to give them smoothness (Madeira, Marsala).

Cooked wines. The cooking of the must augmenting the sugar concentration and transforming it partly into caramel (Malaga).

Maladies of wines – A liquid which is essentially alive, wine is subject to various maladies.

Fleurs de vin. Small whitish efflorescences which develop on wines deficient in alcohol on contact with the air when ullage is neglected: these are due to a fungus, *Mycoderma vini*. The *fleurs du vin* are often the first stage of *acescence*, which can be checked at the outset by the addition of chalk or neutral tartrate of potassium (3 to 7 g. per g. of acetic acid). When it is marked, the only thing to do is to turn the wine into vinegar.

Amertume. Literally 'bitterness', manifests itself chiefly in Burgundies and is due to a ferment which decomposes the glycerine in wines which have been kept too long in barrels, and in wines deficient in alcohol. It can be treated, when taken in the early stages, by adding tannin, tartaric acid and alcohol. A simple means of dispersing *amertume* is to mix the affected wine with a younger wine. A wine which has contracted the taste of *amertume* in bottles can re-establish itself in a short time if the bottles are well corked, and stacked carefully on their sides in a properly arranged cellar. It is possible to decant the bottles into a perfectly clean, well-fumigated cask, add younger wine and clarify.

Acescence. When casks have not been ullaged regularly, the wine is quickly attacked by *acescence*. This is a very common malady due to an acetic ferment which turns into vinegar. This ferment develops mostly in barrels which have a *vidange*, that is to say a gap between the upper part and the wine itself, and can attack good quality wines, though it principally attacks weak wines whenever they are exposed to heat.

Development of the ferment is prevented by drawing-off the wine and by keeping the barrels full all the time, side bung, so that as little air as possible is allowed to penetrate.

A wine is *piqué*, or pricked, when it is attacked by an acetic ferment. It is very difficult to save a pricked wine. Several methods are advocated. Neutral tartrate of potassium lessens the vinegary taste a little but the wine so treated must be used immediately.

Pasteurisation. The surest way to achieve an appreciable result is to pasteurise the spoiled wine. Heated by means of a pasteuriser, the wine is freed from all the ferment-producing germs which spoil its keeping qualities. There are numerous types of pasteurisers operated by steam, hot air or gas.

The wine to be pasteurised must be clarified and drawn off and have perfect limpidity. To save time the wine can be filtered, then heated to a maximum temperature of 60° to 72°C. (140° to 161°F.). The pasteurised wine should be put into perfectly clean and strongly fumigated barrels which should then be set in a very clean place. This operation, done with care, has satisfactory results.

Pasteurisation can be done in bottles. These are placed upright in a double-bottomed heater which is filled up to the

necks of the bottles. One, used for testing, is filled with water and provided with a thermometer to show the rise in temperature and the correct moment to remove from the heat.

Pasteurisation will not restore to its normal state a wine that is badly soured, but it nevertheless has the effect of killing off the existing acetic ferments so that the liquid can be used. Pasteurised wines can remain on ullage, i.e. with an air-filled gap in the barrel, for quite a long time without being affected.

Pasteurisation has the effect of ageing the wine. Some people claim that the process benefits the wine, but opinions are divided. Certainly wines that have slight natural alcoholic content or deteriorate quickly can be helped by pasteurisation.

Goût d'évent. Wine put into barrels which have not been properly cleaned, are very old or badly corked, loses part of its bouquet and takes on a particular taste which is called *goût d'évent*.

To get rid of this taste the wine is drawn off into a clean, well fumigated barrel. If the taste is too strong, the wine should be mixed with another, which has a higher alcohol content. It must then be clarified and drawn off immediately the wine is clear and the *goût d'évent* has gone.

Vins tournés. Wine usually 'turns' as a result of a poor quality grape harvest. It is a common mistake to confuse 'turned' wine with wine that is *piqué* or soured. In cask, wine begins to turn from the bottom, whereas souring always begins on the surface.

A wine that turns completely may be recognised by its dull colour, it is clouded like muddy water and has a smell of rotting organic matter; it has no characteristic of wine.

There are several remedies for turned wine, of which the best and most used is as follows: As soon as it is seen that the wine has turned, citric acid should be added to it, without exceeding the authorized proportion (50 g. per hectolitre). The bright red colour will return in a few days. To restore the spoiled wine completely, it should be mixed with another wine of good quality and the mixture clarified. Pasteurisation is also indicated in these circumstances; the wine should be heated to a temperature of 60 to 70°C. (140 to 158°F.).

Wines which become ropey (gras), stained (taché) or yellow (jaune). It is said that a wine has become ropey or *gras* when it is oily and viscid. This malady is particularly rampant among the white wines of the centre of France, but it also attacks weak red wines.

Use alcohol tannin in a proper dosage (8 g. per hectolitre). Shake the wine from time to time for two or three days to mix well, then clarify thoroughly.

If white wine becomes *taché*, that is to say slightly reddened, a combination of sulphuric acid and animal black can be used to lighten the colour again.

White wines which become yellow are also treated in the same way, but there is a simpler method, invariably successful, which is to clarify the yellowed wine according to the instructions given below under the heading *Clarifying wine (collage)*, then to filter and draw off a fortnight later.

Wines which taste stagnant or mildewed. It often happens that the utensils used in making wine have been badly cleaned or incompletely dried. Water has been left in the casks and has become stagnant. It is therefore understandable that the wine may acquire the same taste.

Wine generally passes unharmed from the press to the vat but if it is put into mildewed casks, the bad taste is quickly communicated. To get rid of this, the wine is drawn off into a clean cask and a litre of pure olive oil is added, the barrel being vigorously shaken A few days later, when the oil has risen to the surface, the wine is drawn off. Alternatively the oil floating on the top may be expelled by introducing a certain amount of wine through a tube. This takes the place of the oil, which is expelled through the bung-hole.

When a bottled wine contracts a corked taste (*goût de bouchon*), it can be treated in the same way, but this happens rarely on important scale. The corked taste is usually found in one or two bottles only and it is better to sacrifice them.

Casse. Under the name *casse* three sorts of malady are known. *Casse brune*, which may be observed on red and white wines, is due to oxidization and insolubility of the colouring matter under the influence of an oxide. It is seen in wines whose fermentation has been slowed down by too high a temperature or made with grapes attacked by *pourriture grise* (grey rot). Exposed to the air the wine becomes cloudy, forms a considerable deposit and develops a taste first insipid then bitter. At the outset, *casse brune* can be treated with tannin (4 to 10 g. per hectolitre), followed by drawing off into a well fumigated cask, or adding bisulphate. It is then clarified and pasteurised.

Wine may develop *casse* as a result of a considerable change of temperature, or a long journey. If it is a robust wine it will right itself after a few days.

Casse bleue or casse ferrique which attacks white and red wines is due to an excess of iron salts in the wine (the grapes having been tainted with ferruginous earth or contact with iron instruments or receptacles). The iron salts combine with tannin to form ferrous tannates which, by oxidisation, are transformed into insoluble ferric tannates. The treatment is to add citric acid (20 to 40 g. per hectolitre), to clarify with egg whites and draw off into a fumigated cask.

Pousse and *tourne* are troubles caused by the presence of an anaerobic bacillus which attacks the tartaric acid and which develops in weak wines. On contact with the air the surface of the wine becomes iridescent, discoloured, loses its clarity and acidity, and forms a brownish deposit.

It liberates, at the expense of bitartrate of potassium, lactic acid, propionic acid and carbonic acid gas, which tend to dilate the cask and blow off the bottom. The taste, at first insipid, becomes bitter and nauseating. If the malady is taken at the outset it can be checked by an addition to the wine of tartaric acid (20 to 30 g. per hectolitre), followed 30 to 40 hours later by treatment with tannin (10 g. per hectolitre), then clarification with gelatine.

The causes of these troubles are dirty cellars, insufficient care of vessels and utensils used in the wine-making and imperfect cleaning of casks, failure to use only sound grapes, or too high a temperature in the cellars.

Wines unsuitable for consumption – According to the decree of 1 February 1930, wine is considered unfit for consumption if it is suffering from any malady, with or without *acescence*, which gives it an abnormal appearance and taste, and when it has either a deficiency of tartaric acid, or of bitartrates of potassium, or at least two of the following characteristics:

1. Volatile acids in excess of $1\frac{1}{2}$ g. per litre expressed as sulphuric acid;

2. Total acidity expressed as a bitartrate of potassium less than $1\frac{1}{4}$ g. per litre;

3. Ammonia content higher than 20 mg. per litre.

Care of the finished wine – The first requirement of a cellar is not that it should be extremely cold but that its temperature should be as constant as possible.

In a large town, where there is heavy traffic, it is important to see that the cellar is not shaken when heavy vehicles pass. Repeated shocks of this kind can cause lees to rise, which, mixed with the wine, can turn it sour.

A wine cellar must be kept scrupulously clean. No rubbish should be left in it, no vegetables with a strong odour (carrots, cabbage, onions, turnips), no cheese, no barnyard animals

and no liquids such as petrol, mineral oils, etc. All these easily communicate their aroma *sui generis* to the wine, as has often been observed.

The wooden stands on which the casks are set must be firmly fixed, 20 to 30 cm. (8 to 12 inches) above the ground on crossbars made of wood or stone. In this way the air circulates freely under the barrels and will prevent the hoops becoming damp.

Care should be taken to fix the casks with wedges so that one can be removed without others being shaken, since this might cause the lees to rise.

Clarifying wine (collage) – It is necessary to clarify (*coller*) wine which is going to be bottled. The purpose of the *collage* is to give the wine its limpidity; it precipitates to the bottom of the barrel the solids which the liquid holds in suspension, and which can give rise to the maladies already detailed.

A barrel of red wine containing 225 litres is clarified with 4 egg whites well beaten in a litre of wine. For white wine a tablet of special gelatine dissolved in ½ litre of hot water for each hectolitre of wine is used.

The bung having been extracted, 4 or 5 litres of wine are removed with a rubber tube, a special suction pump or a siphon. Failing any of these tools, the barrel can be pierced with a gimlet for the necessary amount of wine to be withdrawn. The clarifying agent is poured in through the bunghole, then with the aid of a stick split into four at the end the liquid is vigorously whisked to mix in the *colle*. The wine which was drawn off is now poured back, and more wine is added, if needed. The barrel is banged again and again to make the sediment fall and get rid of bubbles, and the bung is replaced. The wine is then rested for 20 days.

Age at which wine should be bottled – Wines are bottled at different 'ages' according to their colour, character, origin and vintage year. Generally speaking, wines that must be drunk young or '*en fraîcheur*' – and therefore have to preserve their fruit – e.g. the white wines of the Loire, rosé wines and the lighter red wines – should be bottled at an early stage. Red Bordeaux and Médoc wines, in particular, are not bottled until they are at least three years old. Burgundy *grands crus* are bottled after two or three years. However, in a poor vintage year, wines, even the *grands crus*, may be bottled earlier in order to emphasise the fruity character of the lighter wine.

The bottles – Bottles are of the same capacity to within a few centilitres, but their shape differs from one wine district to another. It is therefore best to put each wine into bottles which come from its district of origin.

Cleaning. The bottles are washed in hot water in which soda has been dissolved (20 kg. to 100 litres). When they are half filled with this solution a quantity of small shot is poured in and the bottles are shaken vigorously to scour the glass thoroughly.

If the bottom of the bottle is very much encrusted, a long-handled brush is used to clean it. It is then rinsed in cold water and turned upside down on a perforated shelf (*planche à égoutter*), on a draining-board of galvanized iron, or on a metal contrivance with spikes. They are often dried by hot air.

Bottling, corking, sealing, capping. Bottling should preferably be done in spring or autumn. Cool, dry weather should be chosen, a day when the wind blows from the north or the east. Stormy weather should be avoided.

It is not necessary to draw off the clarified wine before bottling but it must be absolutely clear. This is easily verified

Bottled wine stored in a cellar

by filling a glass with wine from the barrel and holding it up to the light.

The next requirement is a tap of rust-proof metal or wood. A hole is made in the base of the barrel with a brace and bit exactly in the middle, about the same size as the tap, care being taken not to come on a joint. The tap is carefully fixed so that it will not leak. A clean wooden bucket or deep dish is placed below so that none of the wine is lost. One or two bottles are drawn to 'clear', then the others are filled until the barrel is empty.

The choice of corks is very important. They must be of fine, soft, supple cork, giving to pressure from the fingers and without blemishes. Before using they should be put into a receptacle and boiling water poured over them. This is intended not only to make them more supple but also to ensure that they are freed of any impurities. They are then drained for an hour in a strainer, and finally soaked for 10 to 15 minutes in good quality alcohol, either brandy or an old marc which has lost its aroma.

It is preferable not to re-use old corks, or to use them only for *vins ordinaires* which are going to be drunk soon.

The bottles are corked immediately, with a small space left at the top, so that if strong pressure is exerted on the cork, it will not burst the neck of the bottle.

In private cellars the implement used to knock the cork down into the bottle is a kind of bat; the cork is put in and hit with the *batte* until it is well down in the neck.

In industrial premises, large restaurants, etc., apparatus is used which allows many bottles to be corked in a short time without fear of breakage.

To seal the corks, Spanish wax is dissolved in boiling water. (This wax is sold in paint shops and by grocers in France. It is essential to add a little fat to the wax so as to make it less breakable, and, at the same time, more adhesive.) When the wax has been softened the neck of the bottle is held in the left hand and the base in the right hand and the end of the cork and a very small part of the neck are dipped into it. The bottle is gently turned with the right hand for a moment so as to coat the cork and bottle neck well, then the bottle is set upright.

The purpose of the wax is to preserve the cork and to prevent it from being nibbled by insects, which are always numerous in cellars.

Sealing with wax is now generally replaced by sealing with metal caps, which cover the cork either partly or completely. These are made in many types and sizes. When a machine is not available, a strong string is attached to a large nail firmly fixed in a wall or door. The string is held in one hand and the bottle with the cap in place is held in the other. The string is wound round the cap just below the ridge which ends the neck, and thus attached is pulled to and fro, keeping the string taut, so that the cap is pressed right.

Placing the bottles. The bottles are set in two rows in this way: at the back a row of bottles with their bottoms against the wall and their necks in front. The space in front is filled with another row with bottoms facing towards and the necks fitting between two necks of the bottles in the back row. On top of these two rows others are piled in the same way. A tiny bubble of air should be visible in the middle of the bottle when it is lying on its side and will indicate whether or not it is lying level. Attention to this may prevent breaking, often caused by lack of stability.

To be certain that the bottles are exactly horizontal set laths on top of each row of bottles, both front and back.

For a stack of bottles to be perfectly steady, it is essential to use uniform-sized bottles.

Portable iron racks are often used. These can hold the equivalent of half a barrel, a barrel or more, according to size. This method of stacking bottles is much easier but less favourable to the conservation of the wine, which should be exposed to light and air as little as possible.

Appellations contrôlées (controlled names) of wines and brandies – The general principle of repressing frauds in the naming of wine dates from 1905, but it was not until 6 May 1919 that a law was introduced to control naming. Even this was still incomplete, because it made the name depend entirely on the place in which the wine was made. The result was that unscrupulous producers were able to sell under a celebrated name mediocre wines from commonplace plants grown in places unsuitable for vine-growing but situated in the region designated and therefore without any breach of the law, since these wines came from the region indicated.

The Institut national des appellations d'origine des vins et eaux-de-vie (I.N.A.O.) was created by an Order-in-Council of 30 July 1935.

The viticultural crisis (1930 to 1937) was responsible for the birth of this official and legal body. The government took measures to cut down overproduction; these included the uprooting of vines, slowing of wine sales and the compulsory distillation of wines. Only fine wines, those bearing an *appellation d'origine*, were exempt. There was an immediate increase of harvesting declarations boasting *appellations d'origine*; in 1934, 20 per cent of French home-produced wines was described thus. This infringement had serious adverse effects on the marketing of genuine vintage wines. The honest producers of such wines found themselves victims of unfair competition and the consumers were cheated. Senator Capus and the trade union leaders representing the leading vine growers had the idea of creating an organisation linking professional wine growers and State representatives in order to curb the violations, and at the same time to improve the quality of genuine fine wines.

The purpose of the I.N.A.O. is therefore a multiple one: to determine which are the wines and spirits of *appellation d'origine* that genuinely correspond to the quality upon which their reputation has been founded, to draw up regulations for their production, to supervise the application of these regulations (which explains the term '*appellations contrôlées*) not only at production level but also at the later stages of wholesale and retail marketing. In this way *appellations* were protected from being fraudulently exploited in France and abroad.

The I.N.A.O. accomplishes this with the help of administrative departments in Paris, agents based in the great wine-producing regions, and correspondents throughout the world.

The technical administrative department in Paris has, with the assistance of specialists, succeeded in marking the boundaries of wine-producing areas. It also checks the authenticity of wine-harvesting declarations in liaison with the important State departments.

Besides operating this supervisory control of the vine

Ancient coat of arms of wine sellers

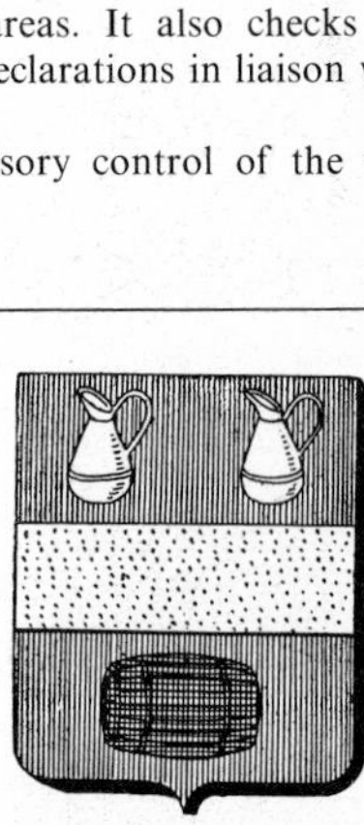

growers, the technical advisers of the I.N.A.O. are valued consultants on the best vine cultural methods and on the care and treatment of the wine. They also serve as liaison agents between the various viticultural associations with which the I.N.A.O. are anxious to preserve close relations.

A disputed claims department follows up all proceedings instituted in France for fraud of *appellations d'origine*. The I.N.A.O. intervenes in such cases in the role of a plaintiff claiming damages. From 1942 to 1963 it had 1,595 vine growers, 3,512 wholesalers and 9,049 retailers convicted.

The action of the I.N.A.O. outside France is very varied because it has to take into account the legislation of the individual countries. Some countries, such as Belgium, Italy, Switzerland and Germany give full protection to *appellations d'origine*; others, such as Anglo-Saxon and South American countries allow the French *appellations d'origine* to be usurped. This is why we find 'Australian Burgundy', 'Californian Sauternes' 'Pommard Industria Argentina', etc.

When a country's legislation prevents the possibility of instituting successful proceedings, the I.N.A.O. tries to have commercial trademarks that contain French *appellations* suppressed or, with the help of the Foreign Office and the Ministry of Economic Affairs, tries to negotiate the signing of bilateral agreements to ensure the protection of French *appellations d'origine*. The I.N.A.O. has lawyers and correspondents in almost every country who keep it informed of all violations. The I.N.A.O. knows that such defence action alone is not enough and has joined forces with the *Comité de propagande en faveur de vin* and commercial advisers abroad in a publicity campaign aimed at expanding what, to our knowledge, is one of the oldest and certainly the most prestigious of French productions.

To serve wine – This is how wine should be served at table according to Grimod de la Reynière (*Almanach des Gourmands*):

'Wines of Orléans, Auxerre, Joigny, Coulanges, Vermanton and other vintages of Basse-Bourgogne, and the common wines of Bordeaux, are generally adopted for the everyday use of the demi-gourmand, or for hosts of a demi-fortune.

'Often, after the soup, a wise gourmet offers a glass of dry Madeira or Teneriffe; *vin ordinaire* occupies the table until the second service; then with the roast it is customary to serve the Beaune, the Pommard, the Clos-Vougeot, the Chambertin or, according to the taste of the guests, the second quality Bordeaux, Saint-Emilion, Château Margaux or Graves.

'As soon as the third service has succeeded the roast, with the entremets, the vegetables, the elegant pastries, the Bordeaux-Lafite, the delicious Romanée, the Hermitage, the Côte Rôtie, or if the guests prefer, the white wine of Bordeaux, the Sauternes or the Saint-Péray, etc. should be served. But dessert soon follows the third service. Then all the special wines of Spain or Greece make their appearance, the old port, the sweet Malvoisie, the Royal-Jurançon, the Malaga and the Muscat, the Rota and the wine of Cyprus. Tokay wine is poured into very small glasses. Finally, to crown the feast, Champagne froths into crystal, and gaiety, which has already spread itself among the guests, is manifested in cheerful talk and lively repartee.

'This is, more or less, the order of service of wines. Doubtless the personal taste of each host causes variations to be made from time to time. But the order indicated is generally observed.'

Brillat-Savarin declared: 'The correct order of service of wines is to begin with the most temperate and progress to the headiest and most fragrant.' (Aphorism XII).

In fact, personal taste must be the criterion and there are no rigid rules except, perhaps, the following two:

Never serve vintage sweet white wines with game or brown meat. Never serve vintage red wines with shellfish and fish.

Serving wine is an art. Which wine to choose? And with which dish? From what type of glass ought it to be drunk? And at what temperature? When there are a number of wines, in what order ought they to be offered? It is in this domain that the skills of a good host are most apparent.

The glasses – In every wine-growing region of France there exists a special type of glass created to enhance the qualities of the wine or wines produced there. But it would be a difficult task, indeed, to build up a collection of all these glasses.

The form, transparency and fineness of a glass all contribute greatly to the savouring of a wine. The glass must be spacious and deep, so that it need never be filled; it should be *bombé* so that the wine has room to expand, and should narrow towards the lip to capture the bouquet. The sides of the glass should be as thin as possible and absolutely transparent; all barriers between the wine, the lips or the gaze being practically non-existent. Heavy or coloured glasses are not correct.

Bordeaux wine glasses tend to be elongated; Burgundy glasses rounder; but the former can quite well be used for all wines, even, if need be, for Champagne. The fluted glass is better; the 'tulip' glass, so-called because of its resemblance to a barely-opened tulip, is the best of all.

The temperature of wines –
Champagne: 5° to 7°C. (41° to 45°F.)
Dry white wines: 5° to 8°C. (41° to 46·5°F.)
Sweet white wines: 2° to 5°C. (36° to 41°F.)
Rosé wines: 8° to 10°C. (46·5° to 50°F.)
Light-bodied red wines: 10° to 12°C. (50° to 53·5°F.)
Vintage Burgundies: 15° to 17°C. (59° to 62·5°F.)
Vintage clarets: 16° to 18°C. (61° to 64·5°F.)

Decanting – A delicate operation much practised in Bordelais. It consists of transferring the contents of a bottle of wine into a carafe, taking care to leave the sediment at the bottom of the bottle. The liquid must be poured slowly from one receptacle to the other. The operation is carried out by the light of a candle placed behind the neck of the bottle, and continues until the first filaments of sediment appear.

Usually it is only old wines that are decanted. Care must be taken not to decant fragile wines too soon in case they go flat. On the other hand, robust tannic wines improve with aeration.

Wine in dietetics – Dieticians are quick to treat wine with suspicion because of its alcoholic content. Nevertheless, since wine provides the body with 500 to 800 calories, a large number of mineral salts, iron, tannin, and a considerable quantity of B vitamins, no-one can deny its anti-toxic, mineralising and nourishing action. Only a limited amount of it should be consumed because of the alcohol it contains. If a sedentary adult absorbs more than $\frac{1}{2}$ litre (scant pint, $2\frac{1}{4}$ cups) daily (1 litre for heavy workers), the body finds it impossible to assimilate the excess alcohol.

Try to drink only good wine; fine wines which have not been subjected to any chemical 'treatment' nor had any preservative added to them. Such wine is rather expensive but it is the only one that is a natural, complete and living food.

Young wines are quality foods, far superior nutritionally to mature wines; red wines are generally better tolerated than white wines mainly because of the type of manufacturing processes involved. Apart from the sulphur derivatives that are currently used to prevent certain fermentations and to hasten the blanching process, wine merchants almost always resort to potassium ferrocyanide to prevent the wine becoming cloudy or 'going flat'. Dieticians condemn the addition of such an extremely toxic substance. They maintain that it is better to resign oneself to drinking water than to drink such wines which, unfortunately, are the ones that usually appear

TABLE RELATING WINES TO FOOD

Food	White wines	Red wines	Rosé wines
HORS-D'ŒUVRE COLD MEATS	*Dry & light* Bourgogne aligoté Petit chablis Mâcon blanc Sancerre Pouilly-fumé Montlouis Crépy Edelzwicker Sylvaner	*Light* Bordeaux supérieur Passe-tous-grains Givry Mâcon rouge Beaujolais Chinon, bourgueil Gris meunier	Bordeaux clairet Bourgogne rosé Anjou, touraine Côtes de Provence Saint-pourçain Rosé de Béarn
FOIE GRAS	*Fine wines* Graves Meursault Montrachet Champagne Coulée de serrant Riesling Hermitage blanc Château-grillet *Fine sweet wines* Sauternes Barsac Quart-de-chaume Bonnezeaux Gewurztraminer Frontignan Samos	*Grands crus* Médoc, graves Saint-émilion Pomerol Musigny Romanée-conti Beaune, volnay Hermitage Banyuls grand cru Porto	
ENTRÉES	*Dry or mellow* Graves, cérons Meursault Chassagne-montrachet Beaune blanc Champagne Vouvray Saumur Anjou Riesling	*Supple* Margaux Saint-julien Beaune Savigny Mercurey Beaujolais Chinon Bourgueil	*Fruity* Sancerre rosé Rosés d'Anjou ou de Touraine Pinot rosé d'Alsace
OYSTERS AND SHELLFISH	*Dry* Graves Entre-deux-mers Chablis Pouilly-fuissé Chassagne-montrachet Chevalier-montrachet Champagne Champagne nature Riesling Sancerre Pouilly-fumé Quincy Savennières Roche-aux-moines Muscadet Gros-plant Cassis, bandol Arbois blanc		
FISH, CRUSTACEANS, GRILLED OR POACHED	*Dry* See above		*Dry* Cassis, bandol Côtes de Provence Tavel, lirac Rosé de Béarn
FISH, CRUSTACEANS, IN SAUCES	*Dry* (full-bodied for highly seasoned sauces) Graves Chablis Meursault Corton-charlemagne Les montrachet Pouilly-fuissé Hermitage blanc Condrieu Riesling Arbois blanc-vin jaune *Mellow wines* (for sweet sauces) Sauternes Monbazillac Vouvray Coteaux du Layon Gewurztraminer		
GRILLED WHITE MEATS		*Light-bodied* Médoc, graves Beaune Savigny Volnay Beaujolais Chinon, bourgueil Saumur-champigny	
WHITE MEATS WITH WHITE WINE SAUCES	Graves Sauternes Montrachet Meursault Riesling Vouvray Anjou Champagne		
WHITE MEATS WITH RED WINE SAUCES		Saint-émilion Chambertin Beaujolais Chinon Bourgueil	
GRILLED OR ROAST RED MEAT		*Well-matured* Médoc, graves Saint-émilion Pomerol Côtes de Nuits Côtes de Beaune Morgon Fleurie Moulin-à-vent Hermitage Cornas Côte-rôtie Châteauneuf-du-pape	
RAGOÛTS, HAM, PORK STEWS		Bordeaux supérieur Côtes de Fronsac Cahors Madiran Santenay Mercurey Beaujolais Sancerre rouge Touraine-amboise Côtes du Rhône	

Choosing the right wine is the prerequisite to a perfect meal
(*La tour d'argent. Phot. Nicolas*)

TABLE RELATING WINES TO FOOD

Food	White wines	Red wines	Rosé wines
FEATHERED GAME	Champagne Arbois-vin jaune	Margaux Saint-julien Graves Musigny Beaune Volnay Beaujolais de crus Arbois rouge Hermitage	
OTHER GAME	Château-chalon	Pauillac Saint-estèphe Saint-émilion Pomerol Tous les grands crus de la Côte de Nuits Corton Pommard Côte-rôtie Châteauneuf-du-pape	
COAGULATED CHEESES		Médoc, graves Saint-émilion Pomerol Vins de la Côte de Beaune Beaujolais Chinon Bourgueil	
FERMENTED CHEESES		Pomerol Canon-fronsac Vins de la Côte de Nuits Corton Morgon Hermitage Côte-rôtie Châteauneuf-du-pape	
VEINED CHEESES	Sauternes Meursault Arbois-vin jaune Gewurz-traminer Champagne	Vins de la Côte de Nuits Hermitage Châteauneuf-du-pape	
GOATS' MILK CHEESES	Sancerre Pouilly-fumé Mâcon blanc Arbois blanc	Mercurey Givry Beaujolais Chinon Bourgueil	Bordeaux clairet Bourgogne rosé Sancerre rosé
DESSERTS	Champagne Vins mousseux de méthode champenoise Sauternes Barsac Monbazillac Vouvray moelleux Coteaux du Layon Muscat d'Alsace Gewurz-traminer Muscat de: Rivesaltes, Frontignan, Lunel, Beaumes-de-Venise, Samos	Maury Rivesaltes Grand roussillon Banyuls Porto Madère Malaga	

Wine suitable for accompanying soups and egg dishes are not included here; ordinary carafe wines do very well.

on the market. The only wine allowed (on condition that it is drunk in moderation) is that produced from vine stock absolutely free of hybrids; the grapes of which have not been 'enriched' during vinification by the addition of beet sugar, have been fermented naturally without the addition of sulphur dioxide (or only in very reduced quantities, and only at this stage so as not to interfere with the action of the natural yeasts). The only nutritionally safe red wines are those that have undergone carbonic maceration only.

FRENCH WINES. VINS DE FRANCE – A list of the great and small regional wines appears under the name of each province, also the names of its *appellation contrôlée* wines.

PRINCIPAL *CÉPAGES* (VARIETIES OF VINE) IN FRANCE.

BORDELAIS

Cépages rouges. Cabernet Sauvignon, Cabernet franc, Merlot, Malbec, Petit Verdot, (The first three constitute the principal vine stock of the wines of Médoc, Graves, Saint-Emilion and Pomerol.)

Cépages blancs. Sémillon, Sauvignon, Muscadelle.

Pinot blanc

BURGUNDY

Cépages rouges. Pinot noir, almost exclusively, for the red wines of the Côte-d'Or and Chalonnais; Gamay noir, with added white grape juice, for the wines of Beaujolais and Mâconnais.

Cépages blancs. Chardonnay for all the appellation white wines; Pinot blanc, Aligoté.

ALSACE

CÉPAGES BLANCS –

A. *Cépages nobles.* Riesling, Traminer and Gewurztraminer, Clevner, Pinot gris or Tokay d'Alsace, Muscat d'Alsace, Sylvaner. (A blend of *cépages nobles* is called 'Edelzwicker'.)

B. *Cépages courants.* Knipperle, Chasselas, Goldriesling. (A blend of *cépages courants* is called 'Zwicker'.)

CÉPAGES ROUGES – Pinot noir or Burgunder. Pinot Meunier (clairet wines 'Schillerwein').

CÔTES DU RHÔNE

As in all southern vineyards there is a wide variety of vines used. Here are the principal ones, not the accessory ones. (The proportion of these is limited by law.)

APPELLATION GÉNERALE CÔTES DU RHÔNE – *Cépages rouges.* Grenache, Syrah, Mourvèdre, Picpoul, Terret noir, Picardan, Cinsault; *Cépages blancs.* Clairette, Roussette or Roussane, Marsanne, Bourboulenc, Viognier.

Birds for the table: chicken, guinea fowl, pigeon and duck
(*Leveillé-Delaunay. Phot. Nicolas*)

Clairette

NORTH REGION – *Cépages rouges.* Syrah (the *appellations* Ermitage, Cornas, etc.). *Cépages blancs.* Viognier, Roussane, Marsanne.

SOUTH REGION – *Cépages rouges.* Grenache, Cinsault, Mourvèdre, Carignan, Syrah, Picpoul, and some others for local use. *Cépages blancs.* Grenache blanc, Clairette, Ugni blanc, Bourboulenc, Roussane, Marsanne, Picpoul. (The proportions authorized of these different vines vary from one *appellation* to the other.).

LOIRE VALLEY

Cépages rouges. (red and rosé wines): Pinot noir (Sancerre), Cabernet franc or 'Breton' (Touraine, Anjou), Gamay, Groslot, Cot (Touraine, Anjou rosés) Pinot Meunier (Orléanais).

Cépages blancs: Sauvignon (Sancerre, Cher wines, Pouilly-Fumé), Chasselas (Pouilly-sur-Loire), Chénin (Touraine, Anjou), Muscadet or Melon, Gros-Plant or Folle Blanche (Nantes region).

MEDITERRANEAN COAST

Like the Côtes du Rhône méridionales, there are a large number of vines, which vary from one appellation to the other.

Cépages rouges. Grenache, Carignan, Mourvèdre, Ginsault, Terret, Picpoul noir, Cournoise, Aramon.

Cépages blancs. Ugni, Clairette, Mauzac, Carignan blanc, Picpoul blanc.

NATURAL SWEET WINES – The principal vine for natural sweet wines is the Grenache, particularly the Grenache noir (Banyuls, Maury, Rivesaltes, etc.). Also the Maccabeo, Malvoisie, Muscat, Carignan, Blanquette, Alicante; Muscat doré (golden) for the muscats (Frontignan, etc.).

EASTERN REGION

Cépages blancs. Savagnin (Jura, Château-Chalon), Roussette (Seyssel), Chasselas or Fendant (Crépy, Savoy), Clairette (Clairette de Die, with Muscat).

Cépages rouges. Poulsard, Trousseau, Pinot noir (Arbois, Jura).

SOUTH WEST

The basic vine stock of the South-West (Garonne basin) is the same as that of Bordelais with the addition of some local vines.

Cépages rouges. Cabernets. Merlot, Malbec.

Cépages blancs. Sémillon, Sauvignon, Muscadelle, Mauzac, Ondenc, Gros et Petit Manseng (Jurançon), Barroque (Tursan), Folle Blanche.

CHAMPAGNE

Cépages blancs. Sémillon, Sauvignon, Muscadelle, Mauzac, Ondenc, Gros et Petit Manseng (Jurançon),

Cépages blancs. Chardonnay for the 'Blancs de blancs' (natural or effervescent).

HOME-MADE WINES – See BEVERAGES.

INTERNATIONAL WINES. VINS ÉTRANGERS – After France, Italy has the biggest vinicultural production in Europe (around 35 million hectolitres from a wine-growing area of 2 million hectares); Spain is in third position. Other

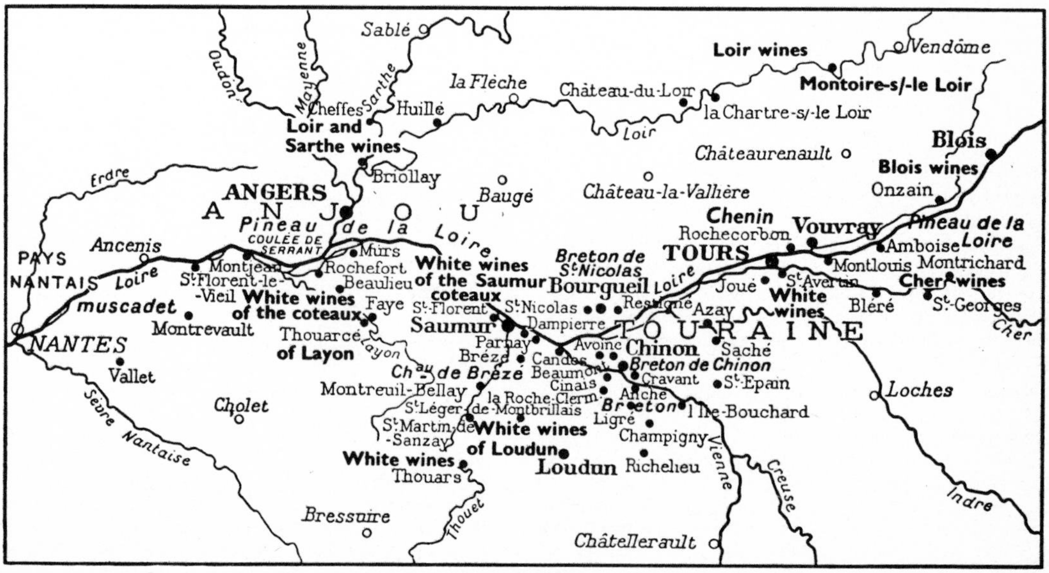

The vineyards of Anjou

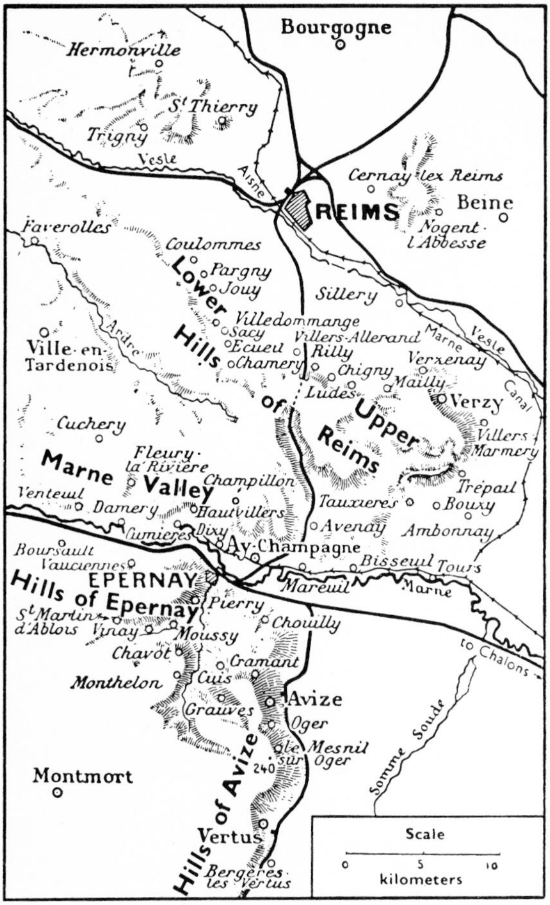

The vineyards of Champagne

continents that produce wine are America (which is the biggest wine-producing continent after Europe); Africa (South Africa as well as North Africa); Australia (50,000 hectares in New South Wales and in Victoria); and even Asia, for although Israel as a State is abstemious, there are enough vines grown to produce a *kosher* wine, which is exported to the Israeli restaurants of Europe.

EUROPE

Germany. ALLEMAGNE – The German vineyards are the most northern of Europe. They produce well known white wines, especially in the Moselle and Rhine valleys; also red wines of local repute.

Rheingau, Rhein-Hessen and Nahe. The great white wines of the Rhine (dry or sweet, made from late-gathered grapes) come from Riesling, Traminer, Gutedel, Müller-Thurgau vine stocks. Some of the best known vineyards are Johannisberg (former domain of the prince de Metternich), Rüdesheimer, Hochheimer, Sonnenberg. The famous Liebfraumilch is not a vineyard, but a type of wine of which there are several brands. There are also the red wines of Assmannshausen.

The Rhein-Hessen region follows after Rheingau on the left bank of the river. Its wines are fruity and elegant. The most important wine-growing communes are Worms, Liebfrauenstift, Mettenheim, Alsheim, Guntersblum, Oppenheim, Nierstein, Mayence, Bingen, etc.

The Nahe, which is a tributary of the Rhine, has given its name to the wines produced in its valley; these have a pronounced bouquet. Three of the communes are Bade-Kreuznach, Münster, Böchelheim. There are also red wines produced from the black Pinot grape.

Moselle, Saar and Ruwer. The elegant, highly reputed Moselle wines are not so full bodied as the Rhine wines. Piesporter, Braunberger, Zeltinger are just a few of the vineyards. Among the *communes* are Piesport, Traben, Trarbach, Bernkastel, Graach, Lieser, Wehlen, Zeltingen, Eitelsbach, Kasel in the valley of the Ruwer; Trier, Kanzen, Serrig, in the Saar valley.

Franconia. The white wines of Franconia are dry, full-bodied with a very distinctive flavour. These Steinwein are sold in flat, flagon-shaped bottles called 'Bocksbeutel'. The most important wine-producing area is Würzburg.

Baden and Württemberg. The vineyards of Baden are planted around Lake Constance and on the slopes of the Black Forest. They produce both white and red grapes (of very high quality around Kaiserstuhl). Württemberg produces highly esteemed red and rosé wines, also a clairet, Schillerwein.

Palatinate. An extension of the Alsatian vineyards, Palatinate produces heady, fruity wines and Auslese, white wines of excellent quality made from late-gathered grapes.

Austria. AUTRICHE – Austria produces good-quality dry white wines, sometimes agreeably mellow, and red wines of local interest.

South of Vienna lies the region of Sudbahn, which produces quality white wines made from the Riesling, Sylvaner and Muscat grapes. A wine made from half-dried grapes (not unlike Tokay) is produced near Lake Neusiedel.

Bulgaria. BULGARIE – Wine production is as much as 2 million hectolitres in the good years from a wine-growing area of 165,000 hectares. Two-thirds of the wines are red.

The best-known of the red wines are Gamza, Pamid, Navrovd, Takia, Karabounar, Melnik, Zartchin. The white include Dimiat, Vinenca as well as Muscat and sparkling wines.

Spain. ESPAGNE – Spain comes third in world wine production with an average yield of 15 to 20 million hectolitres. This includes quite a number of good quality table wines, reputed wines from named vineyards, and some special sweet wines known the world over, like sherry, Muscatel, Malaga, which are drunk as *apéritif* or dessert wines.

The principal wine-growing regions of Spain:

Rioja. Rioja wines are produced in a demarcated area of the province of Logroño, south of the Basque country. They are red, rosé and white. The red wines from Garnache and Tempanillo vine stocks are generous, glowing wines with a relatively high alcohol content. They are usually drunk young, but also mature well, especially in Upper Rioja. This is done by leaving the wine in casks for several years before bottling it.

White wines are produced mainly from the Malvoisie grape. They are full-bodied wines with a low acid content and are often sweet. They acquire a very fine *bouquet* when left to mature.

Galicia. Light red wines are produced here; these are somewhat '*verts*' (immature). There are also the fresh, fruity white wines of Ribeiro de Avia. Both white and red wines are produced in Amandi, Cocabelos, Ponferrada.

Valladolid. Red *vins ordinaires* and quality white wines from the Verdelho vine stock (Nava la Seca and Rueda).

La Mancha. Very large production of smooth, versatile, red and white wines of quite considerable alcohol strength. These make good ordinary table wines, most of which are exported. The most esteemed vineyards are, for the white wines, Manzanarès; for red and white wines, Valdepeñas.

Catalonia. Rosés and clairets from Panadès. The 'tintos' (reds) also have a good reputation; Cugat is known for white wines.

Tarragona. Here we find the strong red wines of Priorato and the light, fruity, white wines of Peralada and Alella.

Levant. There are the red and rosé wines of Requena and Utiel; in Murcia, we find the highly alcoholic wines of Yecla and Jumilla.

Andalusia. The red wines of Rota and the dry white wines of Manzanilla and Helva.

The Balearic Islands and the Canary Islands. Also produce splendid, generous wines with a fine bouquet.

Malaga. Its almost black colour, natural alcoholic content and distinctive flavour have earned this wine a well-deserved reputation. It comes principally from Moscatel and Pedro-Ximénez grapes. The vines grow on schistose soil which is favourable for them. There are several varieties of Malaga wine, each the result of a special manufacturing and blending process.

White Malaga, delicate and sweet, produced exclusively from the Pedro-Ximénez vine stock; dark red Malaga, produced from a blend of white Malaga and a cooked wine, *arrope*; Muscat Malaga; rancid black Malaga.

Sherry (Jerez or Xérès). This famous wine is produced in the province of Cadiz (Jerez de la Frontera). The principal vine stock is the Palomino, close relation of the Savagnin from which the yellow wines of Jura are produced. Vinification is the same: grapes gathered by successive selection and pressed when they are almost crystallised. After fermentation and maturation for several years in casks the action of the yeast causes a thin skin to form on the surface of the wine and helps to develop its characteristic nutlike flavour.

There are several varieties of sherry, the best known being: Fino, Amontillado, Manzanilla, Oloroso. The first three are dry; Oloroso is the most mellow and aromatic.

Moscatel. These wines are produced in many regions of Spain. They are based on the musts of muscat grapes muted with alcohol. The varieties differ from producer to producer.

Spain produces a number of sparkling wines, mostly in Catalonia, Perzlada, and in Villafranca del Panades; also in Navarra and in the Rioja region.

Greece. GRÈCE – The Greeks did not invent wine but viticulture in Greece goes far back into the mists of time, as mythological tales and legends show. In ancient times Greek wines had a very high reputation; and, today, in the land of Dionysus, the vine is held in high honour. Wine is produced in all the provinces of the Greek mainland, in Crete, and in the Aegean islands. A great many of these wines bear an *appellation d'origine*. They fall into two categories: wines that undergo the whole process of fermentation and wines of which the fermentation is stopped by a mutage of alcohol.

In the first category we find the dark red wines of Santa Maura, Euboea, Paros, Crete, Corfu and Nemea; then the dry white, red or rosé wines of Messenia, Olympia, Patras, Tripolis, Attica, Euboea, Crete, Thíra, Cephalonia, Zante, Ithaca, Macedonia, Samos.

In the second category, that of natural sweet wines, we find the world-renowned Muscat of Samos and the Muscat wines of Patras and of Cephalonia. Besides these, there are the sweet wines of Crete, the Pelopennese, the Ionian Islands and the *mavrodaphni*.

Production of regulation *appellation* wines was 369,000 hectolitres in 1958; while for the same year the production of *vins ordinaires* rose to 3,334,410 hectolitres.

Hungary. HONGRIE – Tokay has a worldwide reputation. It is full-bodied, sweet without being too mellow, strong and aromatic. The grapes are picked as late as possible almost at crystallisation stage from the Furmint and Muscat vine stocks. The region where they are produced is situated in the upper valley of the Tisza on the slopes of the Carpathian Mountains.

Hungary also produces dry white wines and a red wine called 'Bull's blood'.

Italy. ITALIE – Italy leads wine growing countries in the quantity it produces. Apart from the very many varieties of wine for every day consumption, the various regions have excellent quality wines to offer.

Piedmont. Here are the red wines Barolo, Barbaresco, Barbera, Freisa, Gattinara, Grinolino, Nebbiolo; the white wines, Cortese, Gavi. In the region of Asti there is a wine made from the Muscat grape, Moscato; and the famous Asti Spumante, a sparkling wine made according to a process which has much in common with the *méthode champenoise*.

Liguria. Offers the dry or sweet white wines of Cinqueterre near La Spezia, and of Coronato. Then there are the red wines of Dolceacque.

Lombardy. Has a number of highly reputed wines produced in the Valtellina: Grumello, Sassello and Inferno. There are light red and rosé wines from the banks of Lake Garda; Moscato from around Pavia.

Venetia (Veneto). Produces the white wines: Soave, Gambellara, Prosecco, Cartizze: The red wines are Valpolicella, Valpentena.

Upper Adige and Trent (Trento). Here we find dry white wines made from the Riesling (Italian), and Traminer grapes, Marzemino and Toreldego. The red wines, are made from black Pinot grapes.

Tuscany. The home of Chianti, which is the Italian wine best known outside the country, also the Brunello di Montalcino and Montepulciano.

The other regions of Italy also produce a number of well-known wines: the red Lambrusco and the white Alba or Emilia; the Frascati, Velletri and Marino of Latium; the Orvieto of Umbria; Lacrima Christi produced around Naples along with Capri (a white wine) and Ischia wine.

Sicily. Excellent red and white wines: the dessert wine of Syracuse and the famous Marsala. Excellent Muscat grapes grow in the island of Pantelleria.

Luxembourg – The Grand Duchy produces fine dry white wines noted for their pronounced bouquet; they bear a close resemblance to German Moselle. Higher standard of production of these wines in recent years has led to a marked improvement in their quality and quantity. They are Riesling, Sylvaner and Elbing.

Portugal – Portuguese wine production is fourth in world importance. They comprise *vins ordinaires*, wines bearing an *appellation d'origine* and, most important of all, port and Madeira.

Madeira. This wine is produced in the island of the same name that lies off the coast of Africa. It is made from Malvasia vine stock imported from Crete in 1418. This dessert wine is muted with *eau-de-vie* and undergoes a special ageing process induced by prolonged steaming in chambers heated to a temperature of 40° to 50°C. (104° to 122°F.).

Dry or sweet, they are easily recognisable by their engaging, velvety aroma. Madeira is used in cooking to enrich sauces with its flavour and mildness.

The Moscatel of Setubal. Also a sweet wine. Made from Muscat grapes, it is a beautiful amber-coloured wine, generous and fruity. It is produced in the Setubal region, south of the Tagus.

Green wines (vinho verde). The name does not refer to their colour (there is red and white *vinho verde*); it is their lightness and their acidulous freshness that has led to their being called thus. They are drunk young and cool. Green wines are produced in a demarcated region between Minho in the north

and Douro in the south. The productive vines are unusual in that they are trained on living supports, in trellises and espaliers, not in vineyards but on the borders of fields and roads.

Finally, there are the delicious fragrant red wines of Colares on the slopes of the Bay of Tagus, and the red and white wines of the Dão.

Rumania. ROUMANIE – In a good year wine production is in the region of 5 to 6 million hectolitres for a wine-growing area of 250,000 hectares. This comprises 30 per cent superior wines and 70 per cent *vins ordinaires*.

The most important Rumanian vineyards are (for white wines): Murfatlar, Vales Târnavelor, Drâgâsâni, Odobesti, Nicoresti, Muscel, Husi, Teremia, Diosig; white wines predominate too in Cotnar and Dealul Mare; Sarica-Niculitel produces red wines.

Switzerland. SUISSE – Vineyards cover an area of approximately 13,000 hectares. Annual production is in the region of 750,000 hectolitres. White wines predominate especially in French and Italian Switzerland. The country produces mostly *vins ordinaires*; it has few recognised *appellations*. It is the latter that we shall examine here.

The most extensively grown white grape is Chasselas or Fendant; Riesling and Sylvaner are also used. The red grapes are the black Pinot and the Gamay; also Merlot and Syrah.

The great wine-growing regions of Switzerland are the cantons of Vaud, Valais, Neuchâtel and Geneva, German Switzerland, Grisons and Ticino (Tessin).

The Canton of Vaud is the largest of the wine-growing cantons, covering an area of 3,600 hectares and producing 100,000 to 300,000 hectolitres. It is divided into four regions:

La Côte. The steep slopes between Geneva and Lausanne produce dry white wines, light and fresh and often '*moustillants*' (sparkling) from the vineyards of Beguins, Luins, Bursins, Vinzel, Mont, Malessert, Perroy, Bougy and Féchy in the Rolle and Aubonne districts. Beyond these are the more gentle slopes of Morges, Saint-Prex, Lonay and Echandens.

Lavaux. This region, situated to the east of Lausanne, produces wines made from the Chasselas grape, full-bodied, glowing, well-rounded wines of which the most esteemed is Dézaley. The most important wine-growing centres are Vilette, Grandvaux, Cully, Riez, Epesses, Rivaz, Saint-Saphorin, Chardonne, Vevey.

Chablais. Situated in the Rhône valley on the north bank, Chablais Vaudois produces dry white wines, distinguished wines with a fine *bouquet*. The principal centres are Yvorne, Aigle and Villeneuve. Wines from the black Pinot grape are produced in Aigle and Villeneuve.

Jura. Delicate white wines of Arnex, Orbe, Rances, Champvent, Montagny, Granson, Champagne, Bonvillars and Coneise.

The wine-growing area of Valais is the second largest in the country covering an area of 3,000 hectares and with an average production in the region of 200,000 hectolitres. It is situated for the most part on the right bank of the Rhône with the Bernese and Valaisan Alps protecting it from the winds.

The white wines produced from the Fendant grape are full-bodied and age well. They are produced in Sion, Sierre, Fully and Martigny, Leytron. Among the named vineyards are Mont-d'Or, Molignon, Ravaney, Uvrier, Coquemprey the *claives* and the *bans*. Besides the Fendant wines, Valais produces Malvoisie, Ermitage, Johannisberg, and dried Muscat.

Dôle produces a strong red wine with a pronounced *bouquet* made mainly from the black Pinot grape.

The wine-growing district of the Neuchâtel canton covers 850 hectares and produces an average of 70,000 hectolitres. It is situated on Lake Neuchâtel. The white wines are lively, light and '*font l'étoile*' (make stars) when they are poured. Their '*pierre à fusil*' (flinty) taste and their sparkling quality combine to make them very attractive wines. The red wines, and one of the best is Cortaillod, come from the black Pinot grape; Oeil de Perdrix (partridge's eye) is also derived from barely fermented black Pinot grapes.

The wine-growing district of the canton of Geneva covers an area of about 1,000 hectares. It is divided between the Genoese Petite Côte, the Côte du Mandement and the commune of Satigny on the right bank of the Rhône. There are also vineyards on the left bank of the Léman, between Hermance and Coligny.

The white wines come from the Fendant grape; the red from the Pinot and Gamay.

The vineyards of the German cantons, although smaller than those of French Switzerland, also produce excellent wines.

In the Bernese Oberland there are the Chasselas wines of the banks of Lake Biel, also the Schafiser and the Twanner, the black Pinot and the Riesling-Sylvaner from the shores of Lake Thun.

Aargau produces wines made from Riesling-Sylvaner. Red wines include Herrenberg, Schartenfels, Golwändler.

The canton of Thurgau produces well-known red and white wines at the Carthusian monastery of Ittingen and at Château Arenenberg.

The town of Schaffhausen offers a first class quality 'Tokay' and excellent black Pinot wines. The wines on the shores of Lake Zurich yield flavoursome fruity wines, white (Riesling-Sylvaner) and red (black Pinot) from the vineyards of Shipfgut, Sternenhalde, Lattenberg, Stammheim, Shiterberg.

A low-fermentation red wine, light-coloured and *moustillant* (sparkling) is produced in Graubünden (Grisons) at Chur, Zizers, Trimmins. It is called Schiller. There is also a famous red Pinot wine produced in Herrschaft.

In the Ticino (Tessin) Valley, the vines are planted on the shores of Lakes Maggiore and Lugano. Here we get full-flavoured white wines made from Chasselas and Sémillon grapes. The Bourdeaux Merlot vine stock produces aromatic red wines, rounded and glowing. We must not forget the local red wine which is tending to take the place of Merlot.

U.S.S.R. – The wine-growing area of the Soviet Union exceeded a million hectares in 1960 and boasted a production of 7,500,000 hectolitres of wine.

The great viticultural regions of the U.S.S.R. are: Russia, Ukraine, Uzbekistan, Kazakhstan, Georgian SSR, Azerbaijan SSR, Moldavian SSR, Kirghizia, Tadshik SSR, Armenian SSR, Turkmen SSR.

Cultivation is divided between *sovkhoz* and *kokhoz* (collective farms) grouped in large wine-producing 'combines' which are under the jurisdiction of a Ministry.

It is mostly white and sparkling wines that are produced; production of the latter reaching 32,800,000 bottles in 1958.

Yugoslavia. YOUGOSLAVIE – The average wine production in a vinicultural area of 272,000 hectares varies between 3·5 and 4·5 million hectolitres apart from exceptional years like 1958 when it reached 5,759,000 hectolitres.

The principal wine-producing regions are Croatia, which accounts for half the production, then in order of importance, Slovenia, Macedonia, Bosnia-Hercegovina, Montenegro.

The dry white wines of Slovenia are worth mentioning. They are: Traminer, Fermint, Sauvignon. The red wines of Dalmatia are much esteemed.

AMERICA

United States. ÉTATS-UNIS – The largest wine-producing

area of the United States is California; it accounts for four-fifths of vine-growing country. In 1959, Californian production rose to 5,532,410 hectolitres (total American wine production 6,303,430 hectolitres.) The other wine-producing regions are New York State, New Jersey, Illinois, Michigan and Washington State.

The United States produces *apéritif* wines, red wines, rosés and white table wines, dessert wines and sparkling wines.

There are no *appellations d'origine*. American wines often borrow their names from those of European wines which they claim to resemble (port, sherry, Chablis, Burgundy, Champagne, etc.). Occasionally they adopt the name of the vine stock from which they come (and, fortunately, this is becoming more and more the rule); these are Cabernet, Pinot Noir, Gamay, Traminer, Riesling, etc.

Argentina. ARGENTINE – The wine-growing country covers an area of 230,000 hectares, the principal region being Mendoza, covering more than 150,000 hectares. In 1958, the total vintaging of 14,041,437 hectolitres was divided as follows: *vins ordinaires*, 11,365,789 hectolitres; fine wines, 1,213,248 hectolitres; special wines, 1,462,400 hectolitres.

The Argentine has an embryonic system of wine legislation using the denomination of 'Wine from the region of . . .' followed by the province of origin. These wines must not be diluted or mixed with the wine of other regions.

Brazil. BRÉSIL – The area allotted to wine-growing was 63,000 hectares in 1960, with a production of 1,230,000 hectolitres, two-thirds of which were red wines.

In Brazil the *appellations* correspond to the denominations of the vine stock growths used (at least of the principal vine stocks, the proportion of which is laid down by the law). For the *appellations* Trebbiano, Malvazia, Riesling, Merlot, at least 60 per cent; Barbara, at least 50 per cent; Moscatel, at least 35 percent.

Chile. CHILI – Average production is in the region of 4 million hectolitres for an area of 112,000 hectares (figures of 1960), 70 per cent being red wines.

The principal productive regions are Santiago, O'Higgins and Conchagua; Curicô and Talca; Līnarēs and Maule; Nuble, Concèpcion and Bio-Bio. Apart from a few large domains, the Chilean vineyards are very broken up (average 3 hectares).

Mexico. MEXIQUE – The wine-growing area of Mexico covered an area of 12,000 hectares in 1960. The average wine production then was about 60,000 hectolitres (only 25 per cent of the grapes cultivated are made into wine). Mexican wines are divided between red and white table wines, aromatized wines (vermouth) and 'generous' types of wine such as Moscatel, sherry, port. There are also some sparkling wines produced.

AFRICA

South Africa. AFRIQUE DU SUD – The vineyards of the Republic of South Africa are situated in Cape Province. Production is in the region of 3 to 3½ million hectolitres.

The wines are mostly red and white table wines (rather full-bodied ones) and 'fortified wines'. The latter consist of wines similar to port ('Cape ports') with an alcoholic strength of 18° to 20°, sherry-type wines (South African sherries).

South Africa also produces a number of sparkling wines.

Algeria. ALGÉRIE – See ALGERIA.

Egypt. EGYPTE – The Egyptian vineyards lie in the north of the country, west of the Nile delta. Wine production is not very large (about 30,000 hectolitres). Worth mentioning are the following vineyards and their wines: 'Ptolemy' (white), the 'Clos Mariout' (white), 'Clos Matamix' (red).

Morocco. MAROC – Annual wine production is in the region of 2 to 2½ million hectolitres. Almost all of the wines are *vins ordinaires* and are mainly for exportation. Red wines predominate; there are also Muscat wines and vermouths.

The principal wine-growing regions are Oujda, Fès, Meknès, Rabat, Casabłanca, Marrakesh.

Tunisia. TUNISIE – Average production is around 1½ million hectolitres. *Vins ordinaires* account for most of the production, but there are also some excellent 'quality' wines and more particularly sweet wines, Muscats.

The *appellation contrôlée* 'Muscat de Tunisia', was accorded in 1959. The other *appellations d'origine* are held by the Muscat wines of Thibar, Rhadès, Kelibia.

ASIA

Iran – Notwithstanding the fact that Iran is supposed to be the birthplace of the vine and despite all the songs of praise Persian poets have dedicated to their wine, production is quite small, due mainly to the interdiction of the Moslems. Raisin wine is the most common of what wine is produced, but most of the 75,000 hectares of vineyards cultivate dessert grapes.

Israel. ISRAËL – In Israel, too, most of the grapes produced are destined for the table. Average wine production is 200,000 hectolitres for an area of 3,500 hectares. A large part of this consists of '*kosher*' wine much of which is exported to Jewish communities in Europe.

Lebanon. LIBAN – The wine-growing area of the Lebanon covers approximately 24,000 hectares. Most of the production is devoted to dessert or dried grapes (raisins, etc.) and grape juice. Actual wine production amounts to little more than 35,000 hectolitres.

Asian Russia. RUSSIE D'ASIE – A large part of the Russian vineyards are situated in the continent of Asia in the regions of Turkestan and the Caucasus.

Turkey. TURQUIE – Although most of the 700,000 hectares of vineyards are given over to the cultivation of dessert grapes (580,000 tons in 1960) and dried grapes (more than 100,000 tons). Turkey has an average annual wine production of 250,000 hectolitres.

Besides the *vins ordinaires* there are 'quality' wines in the following *appellations*: Izmir, Tekirgad, Mürefte, Bozcaada, Ankara, Tokat, Elazig, Antep.

AUSTRALASIA

Australia. AUSTRALIE – Average production between 1 and 1½ million hectolitres. Part of this is exported to Britain. The principal vinicultural area is South Australia. New South Wales, Victoria, Western Australia and Queensland follow.

WINKLE or PERIWINKLE. BIGORNEAU – Name applied to many small gastropod molluscs of the genus *Littorina*, which occurs on all coasts from the Arctic and Antarctic to the equator.

In various regions of France this mollusc, with a brown coloured spiral shell with a corneous operculum, is called by different names: in Brittany it is called *vignot* or *vignette*, in Normandy *brelin* and in Aunis *escargot de mer* or *guignette*.

At Croisic and in the Auray region winkle farms have been set up where winkles are cultivated.

In France there is an order of winkles called the *Compagnons du bigorneau*. Sir Winston Churchill was one of its most illustrious members.

Generally speaking winkles are eaten raw, but they can be cooked like cockles. To eat it, the mollusc is extracted from its shell with a pin.

WINTERTHUR (À LA) – Spiny lobster prepared as *Spiny lobster cardinal* (see SPINY LOBSTER), but stuffed with peeled shrimps as well as a *salpicon* (q.v.) of spiny lobster.

WITLOOF – Belgian endive blanched in cellars. (See ENDIVE, CHICORY.)

Woodcock

WOODCOCK. BÉCASSE – The woodcock is considered the best winged game. It is a migratory bird, and goes to France about the end of September and stays the whole winter, its mating season. In Great Britain it is a 'classified' game bird and can only be shot, in season, from September to January. Towards the end of February it flies back to its land of origin.

There are three varieties of woodcock; the large which is the size of a medium-sized partridge, the medium and the small.

People who like eating woodcock insist that it should be cooked undrawn. Only the gizzard has to be removed.

The woodcock, they say, being insect-eating and berry-eating, should not be drawn any more than thrushes, blackbirds, rails or the garden-warbler, for its full flavour to be appreciated.

But there are some people who hold the view that woodcock is difficult to digest, indeed harmful to health, especially when it is prepared as a *salmis* (q.v.). This opinion is erroneous, the gourmets assure us, particularly where sound woodcock is concerned, that is, birds which are not excessively high. Allowing winged or ground game to get too high is quite wrong gastronomically and is often done out of snobbery. Game which has reached the state of decomposition is difficult to digest and often even toxic.

Some decry the use of *rôtie*, which is usually prepared by spreading pieces of fried bread with the bird's trail (i.e. the intestines) chopped up finely, blended with a little chopped bacon fat or *foie gras*, strengthened with a dash of brandy, seasoned with salt and pepper and flavoured with spices. Gourmets, however, consider woodcock and the trail, which is normally served with it, one of the most succulent morsels.

Pierre Belon wrote:

'The woodcock has plenty of rich fat. It sharpens one's discernment of the wines; those who are well off, knowing this, eat it to appreciate the wine.'

Brillat-Savarin wrote in his *Physiologie du goût*:

'The woodcock is a very distinguished bird but few people know its charms. It is in its full glory when roasted before the eyes of the hunter, especially the hunter who shot it.'

Godard d'Aucour sings its praises as a purée:

'When a woodcock is reduced to a purée
Prepared by skilful art,
This dish, so rare, and not less precious,
Should only be served at the banquets of gods.'

But nothing can rival a roast woodcock cooked to a turn, or *Woodcock in brandy* (*à la fine Champagne*).

Woodcock à l'Armagnac. BÉCASSE A L'ARMAGNAC – Prepare, using Armagnac, as described in the recipe for *Woodcock in brandy (à la fine Champagne)*.

Woodcock in brandy (à la fine Champagne). BÉCASSE À LA FINE CHAMPAGNE – Cook the woodcock from 10 to 12 minutes. Cut it into pieces and put them into a buttered casserole or low-sided terrine, arranging them in a pyramid. Cover the casserole. Keep hot on a hot-plate without allowing to boil.

Dilute the juices in which the woodcock was cooked with a small glass of previously flamed fine Champagne brandy. Add the chopped intestines, blended with the blood left from pressing the carcase and the trimmings, 1 tablespoon concentrated game stock boiled down to the consistency of a *fumet* (q.v.) and a dash of lemon juice. Season with a pinch of cayenne pepper. Pour this sauce over the woodcock and reheat without allowing it to boil.

Woodcock au Calvados. BÉCASSE AU CALVADOS – Prepare, using Calvados, as described in the recipe for *Woodcock in brandy (à la fine Champagne)*.

Woodcock in casserole or cocotte. BÉCASSE EN CASSEROLE, EN COCOTTE – Truss the woodcock as for an *entrée*, cover with a thin rasher of bacon or salt pork, put into a casserole in which some butter has been heated, season, and cook in the oven from 15 to 18 minutes, basting frequently. Drain and remove trussing string. Put in the casserole a dash of brandy and a few tablespoons concentrated game stock boiled down to a consistency of a *fumet* (q.v.), or use thickened brown gravy. Put the woodcock back in the casserole.

As usual with roast woodcock, serve the trail at the same time. This can either be put underneath the bird in the casserole or served separately. For the preparation of trail, see recipe for *Roast woodcock* (see below).

Woodcock au Chambertin. BÉCASSE AU CHAMBERTIN – A kind of *salmi*, which can be garnished with truffles and mushrooms.

Truss a woodcock as for an *entrée* and cook in the oven from 8 to 10 minutes. Divide it into pieces. Remove the intestines and keep two-thirds to prepare the *rôtie*, and the rest for thickening the sauce.

Put the pieces of woodcock into a buttered serving dish, cover with sliced truffles and mushrooms, the latter lightly tossed in butter. Keep hot without allowing to boil. Chop up the carcase and all the trimmings. Put them into a chambertin wine sauce prepared in the following manner:

Brown in butter a *mirepoix*, consisting of half a carrot and half an onion cut into dice, 25 g. (1 oz.) raw lean ham, a sprig of thyme and a piece of bay leaf. Moisten with 3 dl. ($\frac{1}{2}$ pint, $1\frac{1}{4}$ cups) Chambertin wine. Boil down completely. Moisten with $2\frac{1}{2}$ dl. (scant $\frac{1}{2}$ pint, generous cup) *Demi-glace* (see SAUCE) based on a game *fumet* (q.v.). Simmer for 20 minutes. Add to this sauce the chopped carcase and trimmings of the woodcock and a small glass of previously flamed brandy. Rub through a fine sieve. Put back on the heat, bind, using one-third of the intestines rubbed through a fine sieve, as a liaison. Add a tablespoon butter and pour over the pieces of woodcock. Heat over a low heat without allowing it to boil.

Serve with the *rôtie* made with the rest of the intestines.

Chaud-froid of woodcock. BÉCASSE EN CHAUD-FROID – Cook the woodcock in the oven, leaving it slightly under-done. Cut in pieces and remove the skin. Coat them with brown *Chaud-froid sauce* (see SAUCE) based on concentrated game stock. Decorate each piece with slices of truffles, white of hard boiled eggs, salt beef tongue or cooked ham, and glaze with jelly. Allow to cool thoroughly. (See CHAUD-FROID.)

Arrange the pieces of woodcock either on a foundation of well-set jelly, or on a buttered croûton. Garnish with chopped jelly.

Woodcock à la crème. BÉCASSE À LA CRÈME – Prepare the woodcock as described in the preceding recipe. After removing the trussing string, put the bird back in the casserole, sprinkle with a dash of brandy and add a few tablespoons thick fresh cream. Simmer in the oven for a few moments.

Woodcock en daube à l'ancienne. BÉCASSE EN DAUBE À L'ANCIENNE – Dress the woodcock, removing the backbone. Season the inside with *Spiced salt* (see SALT). Stuff with a large piece of raw *foie gras* studded with pieces of truffle, seasoned with spiced salt and sprinkled with brandy.

Enclose the *foie gras* in the bird. Truss as for an *entrée*, and bard with a lean rasher of bacon. Put the woodcock in an earthenware casserole in which 2 tablespoons (3 tablespoons) butter have been heated. Baste with this butter and cook in the oven for 10 minutes.

Add 8 mushroom caps and 8 thick slices of truffles, and finish cooking together, with a lid on, for 6 minutes. Drain the bird and garnish. Dilute the juices left in the casserole with half a glass red wine (Bordeaux or Burgundy), boil down, add 2 dl. ($\frac{1}{3}$ pint, scant cup) game *fumet* (q.v.), or *Demi-glace sauce* (see SAUCE) with the chopped carcase added to it. Boil for a few moments, and add finely chopped intestines blended with 2 tablespoons (3 tablespoons) brandy and 1 tablespoon butter. Strain.

Remove trussing string and put the woodcock and the garnish into the casserole. Pour the sauce over it and heat for a few moments without allowing it to boil.

Woodcock en daube (cold) I. BÉCASSE EN DAUBE – Prepare and cook the woodcock as described in the above recipe but do not add mushrooms to the garnish.

When the bird is cooked, drain, remove trussing string and barding bacon, and put it with some truffles into an earthenware *cocotte*. Cover with the sauce prepared as described in the above recipe, adding meat jelly, strained and with all the fat carefully skimmed off. Chill.

Woodcock en daube (cold) II. BÉCASSE EN DAUBE – Bone the woodcock completely without tearing the skin. Spread the bird on a piece of muslin which has been soaked in water, wrung out and stretched on the table.

Season with *Spiced salt* (see SALT) and sprinkle with a few drops of brandy. Cover the middle with a layer of finely pounded pork forcemeat mixed with one-third of its weight of *à gratin game forcemeat* (see FORCEMEATS) together with the bird's intestines, rubbed through a sieve. On this forcemeat put a piece of *foie gras* of about 75 g. (3 oz., scant $\frac{1}{2}$ cup), studded with large pieces of uncooked truffles, seasoned with spiced salt, well pressed in and sprinkled with a dash of brandy. Cover the *foie gras* with a layer of forcemeat, enclose the whole in the woodcock and wrap the bird in the piece of muslin.

Tie with string at both ends and in the middle, tightening it to give the ballottine its correct shape. Cook for 40 minutes in concentrated game stock to which the carcase and the trimmings of the bird have been added.

Drain the ballottine, unwrap it, rinse the piece of muslin in hot water, wring it out and wrap the ballottine in it once again. Put into a *terrine*. Strain the liquor left over in the pan, skim off fat, allow it to cool thoroughly and pour over the ballottine.

Take the ballottine out and unwrap it. Put it in a dish on a foundation of well-set jelly, clarified in the usual manner (see JELLY) with the liquor left over from cooking the woodcock. Cover the ballottine completely with the half set jelly and chill on ice before serving.

Ballottine of woodcock can be served on a buttered croûton of bread, and garnished with chopped jelly. It can also be lightly coated with a brown chaud-froid sauce based on a game *fumet* (q.v.) decorated with pieces of truffles, white of hard boiled eggs and salt beef tongue, and glazed with jelly.

Woodcock à la Diane (cold). BÉCASSE À LA DIANE – The recipe which follows comes from Leopold Mourier:

'Roast the woodcock but remove from heat while still markedly underdone, and cut it into fillets.

'Pound the carcase and the intestines with a piece of *foie gras* the size of a walnut, a piece of butter the size of a hazelnut, some nutmeg and brandy. Rub through a sieve and season well.

'Arrange this forcemeat on large pieces of uncooked truffles, steeped in fine Champagne brandy.

'Reshape the woodcock, sandwiching the fillets together with slices of truffles covered with forcemeat. Cover the whole with very concentrated game jelly. Chill thoroughly before serving.'

Woodcock au fumet. BÉCASSE AU FUMET – Prepare like *Woodcock in brandy (à la fine Champagne)*. When it is cooked but quite underdone cut it into pieces, put in a casserole and finish off on a hot-plate, pouring over it the blood pressed out of the carcase, thickened a little with finely chopped intestines and a dash of previously flamed fine Champagne brandy.

Serve the rest of the trail on a piece of fried bread.

Woodcock à l'orange. BÉCASSE À L'ORANGE – Cook the woodcock on a spit or in the oven. Arrange it on a croûton spread with the trail. (See *Roast woodcock* below.)

Dilute the pan juices with 1 dl. (6 tablespoons, scant $\frac{1}{2}$ cup) dry white wine, add a few tablespoons concentrated game stock boiled down to the consistency of a *fumet* (q.v.). Simmer for 5 minutes. Add the juice of an orange, strain through a fine strainer or muslin bag, add finely shredded rind of the orange, blanched and well drained, and blend in 1 teaspoon butter. Pour this sauce over the woodcock. Garnish with slices of orange.

Woodcock with oysters à l'ancienne. BÉCASSE AUX HUÎTRES À L'ANCIENNE – Although a woodcock cannot be considered as abstinence fare, it is often served as such during Lent.

Stuff the woodcock with 8 oysters *à la crème*, i.e. poached in their own liquid, drained, de-bearded and dried, then put into very thick *Velouté sauce* (see SAUCE) based on concentrated fish stock and the liquor left over from the oysters.

Truss the woodcock and cook in the oven, until light golden. Spread with finely chopped intestines blended with 2 pounded anchovy fillets, seasoned with salt, pepper, grated nutmeg and lemon juices on a croûton, fried in oil, and brown the top. Arrange the woodcock on the croûton.

Dilute the cooking juices with a dash of brandy, blend in 2 tablespoons butter and pour over the bird. Surround it with 4 oysters dipped in egg and breadcrumbs and fried, and lemon cut in quarters.

Hot woodcock pâté à la périgourdine I. PÂTÉ CHAUD DE BÉCASSE À LA PÉRIGOURDINE – Cut off the breast fillets of 2

Woodcock pâté

woodcocks. Using the boned flesh of the rest of the birds, and adding to it the flesh of another whole woodcock and a quantity of fat bacon equal to half the total weight of the woodcocks' flesh, prepare a very finely pounded forcemeat. Season with salt, pepper and spices, and sprinkle with a small glass of brandy.

Coat a hinged pâté dish, lined with *Short pastry* (see DOUGH), with the forcemeat, on this put 2 fillets, slightly flattened with a steak-beater, and 4 small slices of *foie gras* and 8 thick slices of truffles. Cover with another layer of forcemeat, to be followed by the other 2 fillets and slices of *foie gras* and truffles. Finish off with another layer of forcemeat. Cover with a lid of pastry. Seal the edges and crimp with a pastry crimper. Make a small hole in the middle of the *pâté* to allow steam to escape. Decorate with pieces of pastry cut in fancy shapes. Brush with yolk of egg. Put on a baking tray and cook in a slow oven for about an hour.

Unhinge the mould, take out the *pâté* and arrange it on a dish. Through the hole in the top pour in a few tablespoons *Demi-glace sauce* (see SAUCE), based on concentrated game stock boiled down to the consistency of a *fumet* (q.v.), and essence of truffles.

Hot woodcock pâté à la périgourdine II. PÂTÉ CHAUD DE BÉCASSE À LA PÉRIGOURDINE – Bone 2 woodcocks completely. Lay them out on the table and spread each with a forcemeat as described in the above recipe, with *foie gras* and truffles. Roll into ballottines and wrap each in a piece of muslin. Poach for 12 minutes in Madeira-flavoured braising stock, made from the carcases and trimmings of the birds. Drain and allow to cool. When quite cold, unwrap the ballottines.

Prepare a finely pounded forcemeat, composed of two-thirds *à gratin game forcemeat* and one-third *veal forcemeat* (see FORCEMEATS). Line a hot *pâté* mould with *Short pastry* (see DOUGH), and coat with the above forcemeat. Put the ballottines on this forcemeat, laying them side by side, cover with 10 slices of *foie gras* heated in butter and 20 slivers of truffles. Cover with the rest of the forcemeat and a lid of pastry and finish off as described above.

Cook in a slow oven from 40 to 45 minutes, pour into the *pâté* through the opening in the top, several tablespoons *Périgueux sauce* (see SAUCE).

Cold woodcock pâté. PÂTÉ FROID DE BÉCASSE – This can be prepared in the same way as *Hot woodcock pâté II.*

Allow the *pâté* to cool without taking it out of the mould. Pour into it a few tablespoons liquid aspic jelly flavoured with Madeira, port or sherry. Leave to get cold for 12 hours.

Take the *pâté* out of the mould and serve.

Woodcock à la périgourdine. BÉCASSE À LA PÉRIGOURDINE – Stuff the woodcock with a forcemeat of the bird's chopped intestines, chopped or diced, *foie gras* and truffles, seasoned with salt, pepper and spices and strengthened with a dash of Armagnac. Truss the woodcock as for an *entrée.* Heat 2 tablespoons (3 tablespoons) butter in an earthenware casserole and put the woodcock in. Season, and brown on all sides. Add 6 small peeled truffles. Sprinkle with a small glass of Armagnac. Cook in the oven, uncovered, from 15 to 18 minutes. Remove trussing string. Baste with 4 tablespoons ($\frac{1}{3}$ cup) concentrated game stock boiled down to a consistency of a *fumet* (q.v.). Serve in the casserole.

This dish is a variation of *Woodcock à la Souvarov* (see below).

Woodcock pie with truffles. TOURTE DE BÉCASSE AUX TRUFFES – Fill the middle of a round piece of *Flaky pastry* (see DOUGH), with a layer of *à gratin game forcemeat* (see FORCEMEAT). On this put 2 woodcocks cut into serving pieces and briskly fried in sizzling butter to brown them lightly. Cover with slices of truffles. Season with salt and pepper and scatter a few dabs of butter over.

Cover with puff paste and seal the edges. Make a hole in the middle to allow steam to escape. Decorate the top with pastry cut in fancy shapes and brush with egg yolk. Bake in a hot oven. Pour into the pie a few tablespoons concentrated game stock.

Purée of woodcock. PURÉE DE BÉCASSE – Cook a woodcock in the oven for 10 minutes, allow to cool and bone completely. Pound the flesh in a mortar, together with the intestines. Rub this purée through a fine sieve. Heat in a *bain-marie*, casserole or *timbale.* Add a few tablespoons of very concentrated game *fumet* (q.v.) made from the carcase and the trimmings of the woodcock and with rich *Demi-glace* (see SAUCE). Add 2 tablespoons (3 tablespoons) of fine Champagne brandy and stir.

You can add to this purée diced truffles, cooked in Madeira, or a few tablespoons of truffle purée. The woodcock purée can be served by itself, pyramided on a platter and garnished with puff pastry rosettes or heart-shaped croûtons fried in butter. It can also be used as a garnish for various dishes: soft boiled or poached eggs on woodcock purée, and especially for plover eggs. It is used for filling *barquettes* and other tartlets, patties, *vol-au-vent* cases, and also dishes of similar nature which are served as small *entrées*, or *entrées volantes.*

Woodcock à la Riche. BÉCASSE À LA RICHE – This dish was the speciality of the old *Café Riche*, famous for the excellence of its cuisine, which disappeared in 1917.

This woodcock is prepared as *Woodcock in brandy (à la fine Champagne)*. It is arranged on a croûton of fried bread, spread with *à gratin game forcemeat* (see FORCEMEATS). The gravy which is poured over the woodcock is thickened with purée of *foie gras* and butter. The bird is cut into pieces at the last moment.

Roast woodcock. BÉCASSE RÔTIE – Truss the woodcock, drawing the head round and running the beak through the legs. Bard it and tie with string. Cook on a spit on a very lively fire, from 18 to 20 minutes, or in the oven from 15 to 18 minutes. Arrange the bird on a *canapé* of bread fried in butter, or fried golden in the dripping pan or in the roasting pan.

Roast woodcock must always be served with its *rôtie*, i.e. croûton of fried bread spread with the intestines of the bird taken out after cooking. It is prepared as follows.

Chop up finely the woodcock's intestines (the gizzard having been removed) with an equal quantity of *foie gras* or fresh grated bacon fat. Season with salt and pepper and add a pinch of grated nutmeg and a dash of Cognac. Spread this mixture on pieces of bread, either fried or cooked in the dripping pan. Sprinkle with freshly ground pepper straight from the pepper mill. Put in a very hot oven for a few moments.

The *rôties*, i.e. pieces of fried bread with the trail on them, can be garnished with peeled grapes. Instead of Cognac, the mixture can be flavoured with Armagnac or Calvados.

It is customary for making croûtons for serving the trail of woodcock or other winged game to use crustless bread, or what is called in France 'English bread'. These croûtons are best made from home-made bread.

Salmis of woodcock. SALMIS DE BÉCASSE – Roast a woodcock for a short time so it is slightly underdone, and cut into pieces. Skin and trim the pieces, and put them into a buttered sauté pan. Place 12 small mushrooms tossed in butter, or sliced large mushrooms, and 8 to 10 slices of truffles on them. Sprinkle with a tablespoon of previously flamed brandy. Keep hot, with a lid on, but do not allow to boil.

Chop or pound finely the carcase of the woodcock. The carcase can be chopped together with the intestines, or the trail can be kept for spreading on garnish croûtons.

Add these ingredients to 2 dl. ($\frac{1}{3}$ pint, scant cup) dry white wine boiled down in a pan with 2 small chopped shallots. Moisten with $2\frac{1}{2}$ dl. (scant $\frac{1}{2}$ pint, generous cup) thickened brown veal stock to which $1\frac{1}{2}$ dl. ($\frac{1}{4}$ pint, $\frac{2}{3}$ cup) game *fumet* (q.v.) has been added. Boil for 10 minutes. Strain through a sieve, pressing to extract all the juices from the carcase. Put the strained sauce into a sauté pan, add to it 1 or 2 tablespoons veal stock, and boil down to the right consistency. Season the sauce to taste, add 1 tablespoon previously flamed brandy, and strain through a fine strainer. Pour this sauce over the pieces of woodcock and heat without allowing to boil.

Put the pieces of woodcock into a *timbale,* pour the sauce over them and garnish with heart-shaped croûtons fried in butter.

The *salmis* of woodcock can be served on a croûton cooked in butter and spread with the trail of the bird. When it is served with heart-shaped croûtons these can be spread with *à gratin game forcemeat* (see FORCEMEATS).

All the recipes for the preparation of various *salmis* will be found under the entry SALMIS.

Sautéed woodcock à la Brillat-Savarin. BÉCASSE SAUTÉE BRILLAT-SAVARIN – Prepare the woodcock as described in the recipe for *Sautéed woodcock in Champagne* (see below) replacing Champagne by Madeira.

Arrange the pieces of woodcock in a flan case lined with *Short pastry* (see DOUGH). Garnish with a *ragoût* of cocks' combs and kidneys, sautéed lamb sweetbreads, truffles and mushrooms, bound with boiled down *Demi-glace* (see SAUCE) based on a game *fumet* (q.v.). Pour over the gravy left from cooking the woodcock.

Sautéed woodcock in Champagne. BÉCASSE SAUTÉE AU CHAMPAGNE – Cut the woodcock into pieces. Use the carcase and the trimmings to prepare a *fumet* (q.v.) and add rich *Demi-glace* (see SAUCE).

Put the pieces of woodcock in a sauté pan just big enough to hold them and brown briskly in butter. Cover the pan and simmer for 8 minutes. Drain the pieces, arrange in a *timbale* or in a shallow dish, and keep hot.

Dilute the pan juices with a glass of dry Champagne, add the strained concentrated woodcock *fumet* (q.v.) and boil for a few moments. Thicken this sauce with the chopped intestines, season with a small pinch of cayenne and add a teaspoon butter and a dash of lemon juice. Strain the sauce and pour it over the woodcock, piping hot.

Sautéed woodcock with truffles. BÉCASSE SAUTÉE AUX TRUFFES – Prepare the woodcock as described in the recipe for *Sautéed woodcock in Champagne*. Rub the woodcock's intestines through a fine sieve, mix with *à gratin game forcemeat* (see FORCEMEATS) spread on a croûton, fried in butter, and brown the top. Arrange the woodcock on this croûton.

Toss a dozen thick slices of truffles in the cooking butter, season with salt and pepper, moisten with 1 dl. (6 tablespoons, scant $\frac{1}{2}$ cup) Madeira and boil down. Add 5 tablespoons ($\frac{1}{3}$ cup) game *fumet* (q.v.) and pour over the woodcock.

Woodcock soufflé. SOUFFLÉ DE BÉCASSE – Bone an uncooked woodcock and prepare a soufflé mixture, adding a little *foie gras* and the bird's intestines rubbed through a sieve.

Fill a buttered soufflé dish three-quarters full with the mixture and poach in the oven, in a *bain-marie* from 25 to 35 minutes, according to the size of the dish. Serve with *Madeira sauce* (see SAUCE) based on game essence.

Woodcock soufflé can also be prepared using cooked flesh pounded in a mortar and rubbed through a sieve. Add to it either *Demi-glace* or *Velouté sauce* made with concentrated game stock (see SAUCE). Bind with a liaison of 2 egg yolks and fold in the stiffly beaten whites.

Cook like an ordinary soufflé.

Woodcock à la Souvarov. BÉCASSE À LA SOUVAROV – Prepare like *Partridge à la Souvarov* (see PARTRIDGE).

Suprêmes of woodcock. SUPRÊMES DE BÉCASSE – Prepare like any of the recipes for chicken suprêmes. (See CHICKEN.)

Timbale of woodcock (hot). TIMBALE DE BÉCASSE – Line a pie-dish with pie pastry and add thin rashers of fat bacon. Coat the dish with *à gratin game forcemeat* (see FORCEMEATS), mixed with diced truffles.

Bone 2 woodcocks, stuff with a piece of *foie gras* studded with pieces of truffle, roll into ballottines, brown briskly in butter and put into the dish.

Cover the woodcocks and fill in the spaces with fine forcemeat, mixed with a purée of *foie gras* and the intestines, rubbed through a sieve, well seasoned and flavoured with a dash of brandy. Over this forcemeat put a layer of *à gratin game forcemeat,* piling it slightly into a dome shape. Cover with thin rashers of fat bacon, then with pastry cut to the diameter of the dish, sealing the edges to form a ridge. Decorate with pastry cut in fancy shapes. Make a hole in the centre to allow steam to escape. Brush with beaten egg and cook in a hot oven for $1\frac{1}{4}$ hours.

Leave for a few moments before taking it out of the pie dish. Arrange on a dish and pour in a few tablespoons of *Demi-glace* (see SAUCE), based on concentrated game stock.

Usually hot *timbales*, whatever their nature, are lined with ordinary *Pastry dough* (see PASTRY) its main purpose being its strength.

The pie dish can be lined with *Short pastry* (see DOUGH) which will make the crust more edible.

Timbale of woodcock (cold). TIMBALE DE BÉCASSE – Prepare in a pie dish, lined with *Fine lining paste* (see DOUGH) and cook as described in the recipe for *Timbale of woodcock (hot)*.

Leave to cool. Pour into it liquid aspic jelly based on concentrated game stock, flavoured with Madeira or some other wine. Allow to get quite cold before taking out of the pie dish.

Truffled woodcock (in casserole). BÉCASSE TRUFFÉE – Prepare the woodcock as described in the recipe below for *Truffled roast woodcock*. Cook it in an earthenware casserole as described in the recipe for *Woodcock in casserole*. At the end of cooking, sprinkle with a dash of brandy and a few tablespoons of game *fumet* (q.v.).

Truffled roast woodcock. BÉCASSE TRUFFÉE RÔTIE – Remove the backbone and stuff the woodcock with lard mixed with truffles, prepared as described in the recipe for *Forcemeat for truffled poultry* (see FORCEMEATS) and with truffles, cut in pieces, tossed for a few moments in the heated lard, and seasoned with *Spiced salt* (see SALT).

Suprême of woodcock

Slip a dozen thin slices of truffle under the skin of the woodcock, raising it gently. Truss and bard the bird. Wrap it in a piece of buttered greaseproof paper and cook on a spit from 20 to 25 minutes, or in the oven from 18 to 20 minutes. Arrange the woodcock on a *canapé* of fried bread, which may be spread with the trail, as described in the recipe for *Roast woodcock*. Serve with its own juices or with *Périgueux sauce* (see SAUCE).

Truffled woodcock should be stuffed with truffles and forcemeat at least two days before it is cooked.

WOODEN PLINTH. MANDRIN – Formerly, these plinths were covered with such substances as modelling fat, butter, decorative sugar motifs, etc., for the presentation of cold dishes displayed on plinths. This method of presentation has now been almost completely abandoned and is merely of historical interest.

In former times, these wooden plinths were much used. Carême, in his writings, often speaks of them for, at that time, dishes were almost always presented on plinths or supports of one kind or another, all more or less elaborately decorated.

Nowadays it is usual to serve cold food either simply laid out on a dish, or covered with jelly in a bowl.

WOOD GROUSE. COQ DE BRUYÈRE – Bird belonging to the *Gallinae* order. The wood grouse is the largest type of feathered game which is to be found in Europe. In its size and weight it resembles the turkey. The bird, which has very delicate flesh, is found in considerable abundance in the countries of northern Europe, in Russia, Poland, Hungary, and in the Black Forest region of Germany.

It is rarer in France, but is still found in the Ardennes, the Vosges, the Alpes, and the Pyrenees. In these districts the great grouse or *grand coq de bruyère*, a magnificent bird, is prepared and cooked in the same way as pheasant.

In north European countries, the bird is first left to soak for 2 to 3 days in cream. For its preparation, see PHEASANT.

WOODPECKER. PIC – Edible scansorial bird which, in France, is prepared like blackbird (q.v.) or thrush (q.v.).

WOOD PIGEON. PALOMBE – Species of ring dove or wild pigeon, prepared like ordinary pigeon. This bird is called *palombe* or *ramier* in French.

WORCESTERSHIRE SAUCE – Highly spiced sauce originally manufactured in Worcester.

WORMSEED (U.S.A. Mexican tea) – A kind of tea produced by the ambroissier shrub with a sweet-smelling flower. Restorative and stomachic properties are attributed to the infusion of this plant.

WORMWOOD. GENEPI – Name applied to several species of plants, among which are the *Alpine yarrow*, used in the preparation of medicinal herb-teas, and the *musk milfoil*, which is believed to aid digestion. The musk milfoil is the main ingredient of a liqueur (*liqueur d'Ira* or *Irabitter*) made in Switzerland and Italy from a number of different Alpine herbs. Originally, the liqueur distilled at the *Grande Chartreuse* bore this name.

WRAP. EMBALLER – To envelope a joint of meat, etc. first in a slice of pork or pig's caul, then in a cloth or, in the case of certain puddings and other similar preparations, in a buttered and floured cloth.

XIMENIA. XIMÉNIE – Type of small plant found in hot countries, of which there are a number of species, among them the ximenia of Gabon which is widespread in Africa. The fruits, known as mountain plums or wild limes, are edible.

XYLOPIA. XYLOPIE – The fruit of this tropical tree is a condiment (a substitute for pepper) known as *malaguetta pepper* or *grains of paradise*.

YAK. YACK – Long-haired humped grunting wild or domesticated ox of Tibet.

The flesh of the yak is edible; the milk is abundant, rich in butter and casein. It is more like goat's milk than cow's milk.

YAM. IGNAME – Climbing plant. Its very large root is edible and is prepared in the same way as the sweet potato. A starch called Guiana arrowroot, also extracted from yams, is much used in cookery and confectionery.

YEAST. LEVURE – Microscopic organism of a fungus group, which multiplies rapidly and produces ferments which are capable of converting starch and sugars into carbon dioxide and alcohol. There are three main types of yeast – fresh, dried and brewer's. Fresh and dried yeast are used in making breads and some cakes. If an amount of fresh yeast is mentioned in a recipe, dried yeast can be used instead, but only half the amount should be used as it is more concentrated. Brewer's yeast (which is slightly liquid) is used mainly in the brewing of beer and ale. Yeast is a good source of Vitamin B and is often prescribed, medicinally, in the form of yeast tablets or concentrated extract.

YOGHOURT, YOGURT. YAOURT – Curdled milk product from the Balkans made with lactic ferments which have a much greater acidifying power than the natural fermenting agents.

The use of yoghourt is not so recent as might be thought, at least in France. History recounts that King François I, suffering from an intestinal complaint which had resisted the whole *pharmacopoeia* of the day, heard that a Jewish doctor from Constantinople had been responsible for marvellous cures in similar cases, with milk curds prepared in a certain way. He brought this practitioner to Paris. The doctor arrived on foot with a flock of sheep and cured his royal client, but refused to divulge the secret of his concoction.

The method used in Bulgaria for making yoghourt consists of reducing the partially skimmed milk by one-third over a slow heat. The milk is then divided up into bowls. When it has cooled to about 30°C. (86°F.) some leaven from a previous fermentation is introduced. It is called *Maya* and is slipped under the skin which has formed on the surface of the milk without breaking it. The bowls are left for 24 hours at a temperature of about 25°C. (77°F.), then kept for 24 hours in a cool place before being used.

In Europe, since these oriental curds have come into fashion, they have been factory-produced, evaporated whole-cream milk being treated with a purée culture of selected lactic ferments.

YORK HAM. JAMBON DE YORK – York ham, which is prepared in the town of the same name in England, has the reputation of being the best in Europe.

Yorkshire pigs are remarkable for their early maturity, but their fat is a little soft, and their meat is accompanied by a large proportion of fat.

YORKSHIRE PUDDING – A kind of thick pancake rather than a pudding in the ordinary sense. In England, it is served with roast beef.

It is made as follows:

Mix together without lumps 500 g. (18 oz., $4\frac{1}{2}$ cups) flour with 4 eggs and $1\frac{1}{4}$ litres ($2\frac{1}{4}$ pints, $2\frac{3}{4}$ pints) milk. Season with salt, pepper and grated nutmeg. Pour into a deep pan in which has been heated some of the fat from the roast. Bake in the oven.

If the piece of beef is being spit-roasted, place the Yorkshire pudding underneath it when taking it from the oven, so that the pudding is impregnated with the juice dripping from the beef.

Cut the Yorkshire pudding into squares or lozenges and set it on the edges of the dish on which the beef is served, or serve it separately.

YULE LOG – See CAKES, *Christmas Yule log*.

ZABAGLIONE. SABAYON – A cream mousse of Italian origin which is used to coat hot puddings but which can also be served in cups or glasses, as a sweet.

The word *sabayon* in French is a corruption of the Italian word *zabaglione*, and for this word the dictionary gives the following definition: Composed of the yolks of fresh eggs, sugar, wine and some flavourings, cooked while beating to make it thicken.

Beat together in a basin 250 g. (9 oz., generous cup) sugar and 6 egg yolks until the mixture forms a 'ribbon'. Flavour with 1 tablespoon vanilla sugar, orange, lemon or tangerine peel, or vanilla extract.

Add $2\frac{1}{2}$ dl. (scant $\frac{1}{2}$ pint, generous cup) sweet or dry white wine. Cook in a *bain-marie* or in a double saucepan over a very low heat, whisking vigorously until the mixture becomes frothy and stiff.

Zabaglione à l'asti. SABAYON À L'ASTI – Made as above, using Asti Spumante instead of white wine.

Zabaglione au Champagne. SABAYON AU CHAMPAGNE – Follow basic *zabaglione* recipe, using Champagne instead of white wine.

Zabaglione au frontignan (or other sweet wine). SABAYON AU FRONTIGNAN OU AUTRES – Follow basic *zabaglione* using Frontignan (or any other type of liqueur such as Madeira, Malaga, Marsala, port or sherry).

Zabaglione à la créole. SABAYON À LA CRÉOLE – Make a *zabaglione* with white wine, flavouring it with orange peel. As soon as it becomes frothy, cool it by plunging the *bain-marie*

Zabaglione

into a basin of cold water, still whisking at the same time.

Add 4 tablespoons ($\frac{1}{3}$ cup) rum and $2\frac{1}{2}$ dl. (scant $\frac{1}{2}$ pint, generous cup) of stiffly whipped cream. Mix and serve in a bowl set in crushed ice. Serve immediately.

Zabaglione à la kola. SABAYON À LA KOLA – Prepare some *zabaglione* using port wine. When the mixture begins to set, add 2 teaspoons of the following mixture: equal quantities of liquid cola extract and liquid coca extract flavoured with a little syrup made from the rind of bitter oranges.

This *zabaglione*, which should be eaten very hot, is not only a very tasty dessert, but also an excellent medicine.

Zabaglione aux liqueurs. SABAYON AUX LIQUEURS – Follow basic *zabaglione* recipe flavoured with a liqueur (Cognac, anisette, cherry brandy, Chartreuse, kirsch, rum, kummel, etc.).

ZAKUSKI – *Hors-d'œuvre* served in Russia. These *hors-d'œuvre* are usually eaten immediately after drinking a glass of vodka.

In a certain corps of the Imperial Guard it was the tradition when entertaining young officers to provoke them to drink so many toasts with the *zakuski* that they could go no further and had to be carried to beds which had usually been prepared for them in advance!

ZAMPINO – See PORK, *Stuffed pig's leg.*

ZARA (Maraschino). MARASQUIN DE ZARA – Renowned liqueur made at Zara, a Dalmatian village situated on the Adriatic, which was ceded to Italy by the Treaty of Rapallo. This liqueur is much used in pastry-making and confectionery to flavour sweets and ices.

ZEBU – Bovine mammal, widely domesticated in Africa and Asia. Its flesh can be eaten and is prepared like beef.

ZEELAND (Oysters). HUÎTRES DE ZÉLANDE – This province of the Low Countries, made up almost entirely of islands, is situated at the mouths of the rivers l'Escaut and Meuse. Zeeland oysters are famous. For various preparations see OYSTER.

ZEPHIR. ZEPHYR – Name used by some chefs to designate light and frothy preparations.

It is often, quite wrongly, applied to mousses and *mousselines* of *foie gras*, fish and chicken.

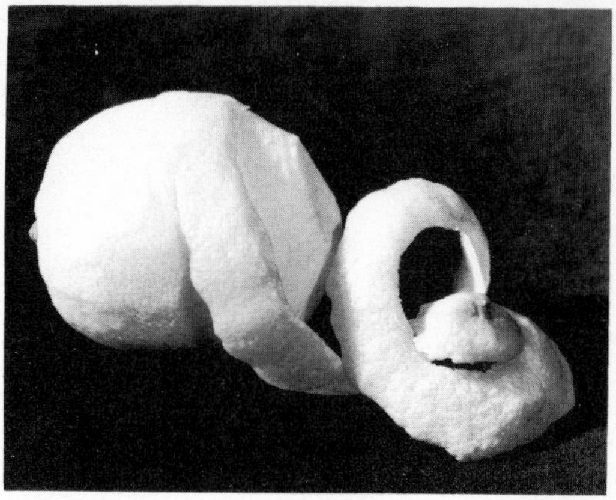

Zeste of lemon *(Larousse)*

ZESTE – French for 'peel', the exterior, coloured, flavoured part of the skin of lemon, orange, tangerine, citron, etc.

ZESTER – Term meaning to peel an orange or lemon. This operation is made easier by using a special instrument called a *zesteur*.

ZIBET. ZIBETH – Variety of chives from tropical Asia, used to season sauces, *ragoûts* and salads.

ZINGARA – Garnish which accompanies small cuts of meat and poultry. It is made up of finely chopped or shredded lean ham, tongue, mushrooms and truffles, bound with *Demi-glace sauce* (see SAUCE) flavoured with tomato and tarragon essence.

ZISTE – French word for the white pith found in oranges and lemons just underneath the outer peel. This substance has a rather bitter taste.

ZUCCHINI – Italian marrows. In U.S.A. these slender green vegetables are called Italian squash or zucchini. In England they are known as baby marrows or courgettes. For recipes see ITALIAN MARROWS.

ZWIEBACK – *Biscotte* or rusk found in French bakeries.

Index

INDEX

p = photograph or illustration

A

C

D

E

F

G

H

I

J

K

L

M

P

Q

R

S

T

U

V

W

X

Y

Z